BAKER'S
BIOGRAPHICAL DICTIONARY OF
MUSICIANS

CREDITS

Laura Kuhn
Classical Editor

Dennis McIntire
Associate Classical Editor

Lewis Porter
Jazz Editor

William Ruhlmann
Pop Editor

Key to Contributors

AB	Andrew Barlett	ETA	E. Taylor Atkins	NAL	Nancy Ann Lee
AG	Andrew Gilbert	GB	Greg Baise	NC	Norene Cashen
BH	Brock Helander	GBr	Gig Brown	NS	Nicolas Slonimsky
BJH	B. J. Huchtemann	GJ	Gregg Juke	PK	Peter Keepnews
BM	Bill Moody	GK	Gregory Kiewiet	PM	Patricia Myers
BP	Bret Primack	GM	Garaud MacTaggart	PMac	Paul MacArthur
BR	Bryan Reesman	HB	Hank Bordowitz	RB	Ralph Burnett
BW	Bill Wahl	JB	Joshua Berrett	RC	Richard Carlin
CH	Chris Hovan	JC	John Chilton,	RI	Robert Iannapolto
DB	Dan Bindert		*Who's Who of Jazz*	SC	Safford Chamberlain
DCG	David C. Gross	JC-B	John Chilton,	SH	Steve Holtje
DD	David Demsey		*Who's Who of British Jazz*	SKB	Susan K. Berlowitz
DDD	Dean D. Dauphinais	JE	James Eason	SP	Sam Prestianni
DK	Dan Keener	JM	Jeff McMillan	TP	Ted Panken
DM	Dennis McIntire	JO	Jim O'Rourke	TS	Tom Smith
DO	David Okamoto	JTB	John T. Bitter	WB	Will Bickart
DPe	Damon Percy	LK	Laura Kuhn	WF	Walter Faber
DPr	David Prince	LP	Lewis Porter	WKH	W. Kim Heron
DR	Dennis Rea	MF	Michael Fitzgerald	WR	William Ruhlmann
ED	Eric Deggans	MM	*Music Master Jazz*		
EH	Ed Hazell		*and Blues Catalogue*		
EJL	Eric J. Lawrence	MS	Matthew Snyder		

BAKER'S
BIOGRAPHICAL DICTIONARY OF
MUSICIANS

VOLUME 3
HAAR - LEVI

Centennial Edition

NICOLAS SLONIMSKY
Editor Emeritus

LAURA KUHN
Baker's Series Advisory Editor

Schirmer Books
an imprint of the Gale Group
New York • Detroit • San Francisco • London • Boston • Woodbridge, CT

Copyright © 1900, 1905, 1919, 1940, 1958, 1971 by G. Schirmer, Inc.
Copyright © 1978, 1984, 1992 by Schirmer Books
Copyright © 2001 by Schirmer Books, An Imprint of the Gale Group

Schirmer Books
1633 Broadway
New York, New York 10019

Gale Group
27500 Drake Road
Farmington Hills, Michigan 48331-3535

The title *Baker's Biographical Dictionary of Musicians* is a registered trademark.

Silhouette of Nicolas Slonimsky used with the permission of Electra Yourke.

Library of Congress Catalog Card Number: 00-046375

Printed in the United States of America

Printing number
1 2 3 4 5 6 7 8 9 10

Library of Congress Cataloging-in-Publication Data

Baker's biographical dictionary of musicians.—Centennial ed. / Nicolas Slonimsky, editor emeritus.
    p. cm.
  Includes bibliographical references and discographies.
  Enl. ed. of: Baker's biographical dictionary of musicians. 8th ed. / rev. by Nicolas Slonimsky.
  ISBN 0-02-865525-7 (set : alk. paper) — ISBN 0-02- 865526-5 (vol. 1) — ISBN 0-02-865527-3 (vol. 2) — ISBN 0-02-865528-1 (vol. 3) — ISBN 0-02-865529-X (vol. 4) — ISBN 0-02-865530-3 (vol. 5) — ISBN 0-02-865571-0 (vol. 6)
  1. Music—Bio-bibliography—Dictionaries. I. Slonimsky, Nicolas, 1894-
II. Slonimsky, Nicolas, 1894- Baker's biographical dictionary of musicians.

  ML105.B16 2000
  780'.92'2—dc21
  [B]
                                                       00-046375

ABBREVIATIONS

A.B.	Bachelor of Arts
ABC	American Broadcasting Company
A.M.	Master of Arts
ASCAP	American Society of Composers, Authors, and Publishers
assn./Assn.	association/Association
assoc.	associate
aug.	augmented
b.	born
B.A.	Bachelor of Arts
bar.	baritone
BBC	British Broadcasting Corporation
bjo.	banjo
B.M.	Bachelor of Music
brs.	brass
bs.	bass
CBC	Canadian Broadcasting Corporation
CBS	Columbia Broadcasting System
Coll.	College
cons./Cons.	conservatory/Conservatory
d.	died
dept./Dept.	department/Department
diss.	dissertation
D.M.A.	Doctor of Musical Arts
drm.	drums
ed(s).	edit(ed), editor(s), edition(s)
enl.	enlarged
f.	formed
flt.	flute
gtr.	guitar
har.	harmonica
H.S.	High School
IRCAM	Institut de Recherche et de Coordination Acoustique/Musique
ISCM	International Society for Contemporary Music
inst./Inst.	institute/Institute

kybd.	keyboards
M.A.	Master of Arts
mdln.	mandolin
M.M.	Master of Music
MS(S)	manuscript(s)
Mus.B.	Bachelor of Music
Mus.D.	Doctor of Music
Mus.M.	Master of Music
NAACP	National Association for the Advancement of Colored People
NBC	National Broadcasting Company
n.d.	no date
NEA	National Endowment for the Arts
NHK	Japan Broadcasting Company
no(s).	number(s)
N.Y.	New York
org.	organ
op(p).	opus
orch./Orch.	orchestra/Orchestra
p(p).	page(s)
PBS	Public Broadcasting Service
perc.	percussion
perf.	performance
Ph.D.	Doctor of Philosophy
phil./Phil.	philharmonic/Philharmonic
pno.	piano
posth.	posthumously
prof.	professor
publ.	publish(ed)
RAI	Radiotelevisione Italiana
rds.	reeds
rec.	recorded
rel.	released
rev.	revised
RIAS	Radio in the American Sector
S.	San, Santo, Santa
sax.	saxophone
sop.	soprano
Ss.	Santi, Sante
St(e).	Saint(e)
sym(s).	symphony (-ies)
synth.	synthesizer
tamb.	tamborine
ten.	tenor
tr.	translate(d), translation
trmb.	trombone
trpt.	trumpet
univ./Univ.	university/University
vln.	violin
voc.	vocals
vol(s).	volume(s)
WDR	Westdeutscher Rundfunk (West German Radio)
wdwnd.	woodwinds

H

Haar, James, American musicologist; b. St. Louis, July 4, 1929. He studied at Harvard Univ. (B.A., 1950) and at the Univ. of N.C. (M.A., 1954); then returned to Harvard to complete his training under John Ward and Nino Pirrotta (Ph.D., 1961, with the diss. *Musica mundana: Variations on a Pythagorean Theme*); served on its faculty (1960–67). He taught at the Univ. of Pa. (1967–69), N.Y.U. (1969–78), and the Univ. of N.C. (from 1978). Haar also was general ed. of the *Journal of the American Musicological Society* (1966–69), later serving as the society's president (1976–78). With L. Bernstein, he ed. *The Duos of Jhan Gero* (1977). He publ. *The Tugendsterne of Harsdorffer and Staden* (1965) and *Essays on Italian Poetry and Music in the Renaissance, 1350–1600* (1986). With I. Fenlon, he publ. *The Italian Madrigal in the Early Sixteenth Century: Sources and Interpretation* (1989). P. Corneilson ed. his *The Science and Art of Renaissance Music* (Princeton, 1998).—NS/LK/DM

Haarklou, Johannes, Norwegian organist and composer; b. Forde, Sunnfjord, near Bergen, May 13, 1847; d. Oslo, Nov. 26, 1925. He was a pupil of L. Lindeman in Christiania, or Reinecke, Jadassohn, Kretzschmar, and Richter at the Leipzig Cons. (1873–75), and of Haupt, Kiel, and Bungert at the Berlin Hochschule für Musik (1877). He served as organist at the Akers Church in Christiania (1880–1920). He wrote 5 operas, including *Marisagnet* (1909), 4 syms. (1883–88), *Skapelsen*, oratorio (1891; Christiania, 1924), chamber music, piano pieces, organ works, including 2 syms. (1916, 1924), and choruses.

BIBL.: F. Benestad, *J. H.: Mann og verket* (Oslo, 1961).
—NS/LK/DM

Haas, Joseph, eminent German composer and pedagogue; b. Maihingen, March 19, 1879; d. Munich, March 30, 1960. He was a pupil of Reger (composition) in Munich and Leipzig (1904–08), and also in the latter city of Straube (organ) and Ruthardt (piano). In 1911 he became a teacher and in 1916 a prof. of composition at the Stuttgart Cons. In 1921 he settled in Munich as a prof. in the Catholic church music dept. of the Akademie der Tonkunst, and later was president of the Hochschule für Musik (1946–50). In 1949 a Joseph Haas Soc. was formed to promote his music, which is written in a well-crafted and accessible style. He publ. a biography of Reger (Bonn, 1949), and a collection of his speeches and articles was ed. by K. Fellerer as *Reden und Aufsätze* (Mainz, 1964).

WORKS: DRAMATIC: *Die Bergkönigin,* theater piece (1927); *Tobias Wunderlich,* opera (1934–37; Kassel, Nov. 24, 1937); *Die Hochzeit des Jobs,* comic opera (1940–43; Dresden, July 2, 1944). **ORCH.:** *Das Grab im Busento* (1902); *Ein symphonisches Idyll* (1903); *Felice notte* (1903); *Symphonische suite* (1913); *Heitere Serenade* (1913–14); *Variationen und Rondo über ein altdeutsches Volkslied* (1916–17); *Variationen-Suite* (1924; Cologne, March 3, 1925); *Lyrisches Intermezzo* (1937); *Ouvertüre zu einem frohen Spiel* (1943; Munich, Sept. 27, 1946); *Der Tod auf dem Apfelbaum* (1945). **CHAMBER:** 2 violin sonatinas (both 1905); 2 string quartets (1905, 1919); Violin Sonata (1908); *Divertimento* for Violin, Viola, and Cello (1909); *Ein Kränzlein Bagatellen* for Oboe and Piano (1910); *2 Grotesken* for Cello and Piano (1910); Horn Sonata (1910); *Ein Sommermarchen* for Cello (1910; also for Cello and Piano, 1923); *Divertimento* for 2 Violins, Viola, and Cello (1911); Chamber Trio for 2 Violins and Piano (1912), *Grillen* for Violin and Piano (1912); *Capriccio* for Violin and Piano (1915); 2 church sonatas for Violin and Organ (1925–26). **KEYBOARD: Piano:** *Ballade* (1902); *Bagatellen* (1902–04); *5 Stücke* (1904); *Lose Blätter* (1908); *Frohe Launen* (1909); *Hausmärchen* (3 vols., 1911, 1916, 1920); *Eulenspiegeleien* (1912); *Alte unnennbare Tage* (1915); 3 sonatas (1918, 1923, 1923); *Deutsche Reigen und Romanzen* (1919); *Schwänke und Idyllen* (1921); *Märchentänze* (1927); 4 sonatinas (all 1943); many other pieces. **Organ:** 10 chorale preludes (1905); 3 preludes and fugues (1906); Sonata (1907); *8 Charakterstücke* (1907); 2 suites (1908, 1909); *Variationen über ein Originalthema* (1911); *Impromptu* (1912); *Introduktion und Fuge* (1912); 8 preludes (1936). **VOCAL:** *Rum bidi bum!* for 2 Children's Voices and Piano (1911); *Trali Trala* for Children's Chorus or Chorus and Piano (1918); *Tag und Nacht* for High Voice and Orch. (1921–22; Cologne, Oct. 22, 1922); *Zehn Marienlieder* for Women's Voices or Children's Chorus and Organ (1922); *Deut-*

sche Vesper for Chorus (1929); *Speyerer Domfest-Messe* for Chorus and Organ or Small Orch. (Speyer, July 13, 1930); *Die heilige Elisabeth,* oratorio for Soprano, Speaker, Chorus, and Orch. (Kassel, Nov. 11, 1931); *Christnacht* for Women's or Children's Chorus, Chorus, Soloists, Speaker, and Small Orch. (1932); *Das Lebensbuch Gottes,* oratorio for Chorus or Women's Chorus, Soloists, and Organ or Small Orch. (Essen, Nov. 6, 1934); *Christ-König-Messe* for Chorus and Organ or Orch. or Wind Orch. (Limburg am Lahn, Aug. 11, 1935); *Das Lied von der Mutter,* oratorio for Soprano, Baritone, Choruses, and Orch. (1938–39; Cologne, Dec. 19, 1939); *Te Deum* for Soprano, Baritone, Chorus, and Orch. (1945; Munich, Dec. 8, 1946); *Totenmesse* for Speaking Voices, Chorus, and Instruments (Bavarian Radio, Munich, Nov. 1945; also for Speaking Voices, Choruses, and Orch., 1947; Fulda, April 6, 1952); *Müncher Liebfrauen- Messe* for Chorus and Organ or Orch. or Wind Orch. (1946); *Das Jahr im Lied,* oratorio for Chorus, Soloists, Speaker, and Orch. (1951–52; Kassel, April 23, 1952); *Deutsche Weihnachtsmesse* for Chorus and Organ or Small Orch. (1954); *Die Seligen* for Chorus, Children's Chorus, Soloists, and Orch. (1956; Kassel, April 12, 1957); *Schiller-Hymne* for Chorus, Baritone, and Orch. (Mannheim, Oct. 20, 1957); *Deutsche Kindermesse* for Soprano, Mezzo-soprano, and Organ (1958; also as the *Deutsche Chormesse* for Chorus and Organ, 1965); *Marianische Kantate* for Women's Chorus, Soloists, and Organ (1960); many choruses and songs.

BIBL.: K. Laux, *J. H.* (Mainz, 1931); *Festgabe J. H.* (Mainz, 1939); K. Laux, *J. H.* (Düsseldorf, 1954); *J. H.: Verzeichnis Sämtlicher Werke* (Mainz, 1990); S. Gmeinwieser, W. Haas, H.-M. Palm-Beulich, and F. Schieri, *J. H.* (Tutzing, 1994).—**NS/LK/DM**

Haas, Karl (Wilhelm Jacob), German conductor and musicologist; b. Karlsruhe, Dec. 27, 1900; d. London, July 7, 1970. He studied at the univs. of Munich and Heidelberg, then worked for the Karlsruhe and Stuttgart radios. He was active as a collector of valuable early instruments, and made microfilms of early music. In 1939 he emigrated to England, and in 1943 organized the London Baroque Ensemble, which he led until 1966 in performances of little-known Baroque music. He also ed. works by Haydn, Boccherini, and Cherubini. —**NS/LK/DM**

Haas, Monique, French pianist; b. Paris, Oct. 20, 1906; d. there, June 9, 1987. She studied at the Paris Cons. with Lazare-Lévy (piano; premier prix, 1927), Tournemire (chamber music), Demarquez (harmony), and Emmanuel (music history), and also received private instruction from R. Casadesus, Serkin, and Enesco. Following her debut in 1927, she toured as a soloist with orchs. and as a recitalist. She also appeared in duo recitals with Enesco and Fournier. In 1968–69 she was a prof. at the Paris Cons. While her repertory included works from the Classical and Romantic eras, she became known primarily for her performances of music of the 20th century. Her interpretations of Debussy and Ravel were particularly notable. She was married to **Marcel Mihalovici.—NS/LK/DM**

Haas, Pavel, Czech composer; b. Brünn, June 21, 1899; d. in the concentration camp in Auschwitz, Oct. 17, 1944. He studied piano and composition in Brünn. He was a soldier in the Austrian army in World War I. After the Armistice, continued his study with Petrželka

at the Brno Cons. (1919–21) and at the master class there with Janáček (1920–22). He tried to leave Czechoslovakia after its occupation by the Nazi hordes, but the outbreak of World War II made this impossible. In 1941 he was deported to the Jewish ghetto camp in Theresienstadt, where he continued to compose until, in Oct. 1944, he was sent to Auschwitz and put to death. His extant MSS are preserved in the Moravian Museum in Brno.

WORKS: DRAMATIC: O p e r a : *Šarlatán* (The Charlatan), to his own libretto (1934–37; Brno, April 2, 1938). **ORCH.:** *Zesmutnělé Scherzo* (Mournful Scherzo) (1921); *Předehra pro rozhlas* (Overture for Radio) for Narrator, Men's Chorus, and Orch. (1930); Sym. (1941; unfinished); *Studie* for Strings (1943; Theresienstadt camp, Sept. 13, 1944); *Variations* for Piano and Orch. (1944). **CHAMBER:** 3 string quartets (1920, 1925, 1938); *Fata morgana,* piano quintet, with Tenor Solo (1923); Wind Quintet (1929); Suite for Piano (1935); Suite for Oboe and Piano (1939). **VOCAL:** *Introduction and Psalm XXIX,* cantata (1931); songs.

BIBL.: L. Peduzi, *P. H.:Života dilo skladatele* (Brno, 1993). —**NS/LK/DM**

Haas, Robert (Maria), distinguished Austrian musicologist; b. Prague, Aug. 15, 1886; d. Vienna, Oct. 4, 1960. He received his primary education in Prague, then studied music history at the univs. of Prague, Berlin, and Vienna, obtaining his Ph.D. in 1908 from the Univ. of Prague with his diss. *Das Wiener Singspiel.* He then was an assistant to Guido Adler at the Inst. for Music History in Vienna (1908–09). During World War I he was in the Austrian army; then joined the staff of the Nationalbibliothek in Vienna, becoming chief of the music division in 1920. He completed his Habilitation at the Univ. of Vienna in 1923 with his *Eberlins Schuldramen und Oratorien,* and then became a lecturer there. He also devoted much of his time to the music of the Baroque and Classical eras. After the founding of the International Bruckner Soc., he became ed. of the critical edition of Bruckner's works; he also edited works for Denkmäler der Tonkunst in Österreich. He retired in 1945.

WRITINGS: *Gluck und Durazzo im Burgtheater* (Vienna, 1925); *Die estensischen Musikalien: Thematisches Verzeichnis mit Einleitung* (Regensburg, 1925); *Die Wiener Oper* (Vienna, 1926); *Wiener Musiker vor und um Beethoven* (Vienna, 1927); *Die Musik des Barocks* (Potsdam, 1928); *Aufführungspraxis der Musik* (Potsdam, 1931); *W. A. Mozart* (Potsdam, 1933; 2nd ed., 1950); *Anton Bruckner* (Potsdam, 1934); *Bach und Mozart in Wien* (Vienna, 1951); *Ein unbekanntes Mozart-Bildnis* (Vienna, 1955). —**NS/LK/DM**

Haas, Werner, German pianist; b. Stuttgart, March 3, 1931; d. in an automobile accident in Nancy, Oct. 11, 1976. He studied with Lili Kroebec-Asche at the Stuttgart Hochschule für Musik (1947–54) and in Gieseking's master classes at the Saarbrücken Staatlichen Konservatoirum (1954–56). After making his public debut in Stuttgart in 1955, he toured widely in Europe. He was especially admired for his perceptive interpretations of Debussy and Ravel.—**NS/LK/DM**

Haase, Hans, German musicologist; b. Neumunster, Schleswig-Holstein, May 12, 1929. He studied with

Blume and Albrecht at the Univ. of Kiel (1950–55). From 1954 to 1958 he was an editorial contributor to *Die Musik in Geschichte und Gegenwart*; also wrote music criticism for newspapers. He publ. the monographs *Jobst vom Brandt* (Kassel, 1967) and *Heinrich Schütz* (Wolfenbüttel, 1972), and numerous valuable articles on German composers of the Reformation. He also became interested in applied psychology and lectured on this subject in Zürich and Vienna. He publ. *Die harmonikalen Wurzeln der Musik* (Vienna, 1969) and *Aufsätze zur harmonikalen Naturphilosophie* (Graz, 1974).—NS/LK/DM

Hába, Alois, notable Czech composer and pedagogue, brother of **Karel Hába**; b. Vizovice, Moravia, June 21, 1893; d. Prague, Nov. 18, 1973. He studied with Novák at the Prague Cons. (1914–15), then privately with Schreker in Berlin (1918–20), continuing as his student at the Hochschule für Musik (1920–22). He became interested in the folk music of the Orient, which led him to consider writing in smaller intervals than the semitone. His first work in the quarter tone system was the 2nd String Quartet (1920); in his 5th String Quartet (1923), he first applied sixth-tones, and in his 16th String Quartet (1967), he introduced fifth-tones. He notated these fractional intervals by signs in modified or inverted sharps and flats. The piano manufacturing firm A. Förster constructed for him 3 types of quarter tone pianos (1924–31), a quarter tone (1928) and a sixth-tone (1936) harmonium, and a quarter tone guitar (1943); other firms manufactured at his request a quarter tone clarinet (1924) and trumpet (1931). From 1924 to 1951 (World War II excepted) he led a class of composition in fractional tones at the Prague Cons., attracting a large number of students, among them his brother, Karel, the conductors Ančerl and Susskind, and the composers Dobiáš, Ježek, Kowalski, Kubín, Lucký, Ponc, Reiner (who, along with E. Schulhoff, specialized in quarter tone piano playing and premiered 10 of Hába's works), Seidel and Srnka, as well as such foreigners as Iliev, Osterc, and Akses. Hába publ. an important manual of modern harmony, *Neue Harmonielehre des diatonischen, chromatischen, Viertel-, Drittel-, Sechstel-, und Zwölfteltonsystems* (New Principles of Harmony of the Diatonic, Chromatic, Fourth-, Third-, Sixth-, and Twelfth-Tone Systems; Leipzig, 1927), detailing new usages introduced by him in his classes; he further publ. *Harmonicke základy čtvrttónove soustavy* (Harmonic Foundation of the Quarter Tone System; Prague, 1922), *Von der Psychologie der musikalischen Gestaltung, Gesetzmässigkeit der Tonbewegung und Grundlagen eines neuen Musikstils* (On the Psychology of Musical Composition; Rules of Tonal Structure and Foundation of New Musical Style; Vienna, 1925), and *Mein Weg zur Viertel- und Sechstetonmusik* (Düsseldorf, 1971). As a composer, he cultivated a "non- thematic" method of writing, without repetition of patterns and devoid of development. In 1963 he was made an Artist of Merit and in 1968 he received the Order of the Republic in recognition of his contributions to Czech music.

WORKS: DRAMATIC: O p e r a : *Matka* (Mother; 1927–29; in quarter tones, 1st perf. in German as *Die Mutter*, Munich, May 17, 1931; 1st perf. in Czech, Prague, May 27, 1947); *Nová Zeme* (The New Land; 1934–36; only overture perf.,

Prague, April 8, 1936); *Přijd královstvi Tvé* (Thy Kingdom Come; 1937–40; in fractional tones). **ORCH.:** Overture (Berlin, Dec. 9, 1920); *Symphonic Fantasy* for Piano and Orch. (1921); *Cesta života* (The Path of Life; Winterthur, March 15, 1934); *Valašská suita* (Prague, Oct. 29, 1953); Violin Concerto (1955; Prague, Feb. 17, 1963); Viola Concerto (1955–57). **CHAMBER:** Violin Sonata (1951); string quartets Nos. 1, 7, 8, 9, 13, and 15 (1919; 1951; 1951; 1952; *Astronautic*, 1961; 1964); *Fantasy* for Flute or Violin and Piano (1928; also for Bass Clarinet and Piano, 1967); 4 nonets for Wind and String Instruments (1931, based on a 12–tone row; 1932, based on a 7–tone row; 1953; 1963); Sonata for Solo Guitar (1943); Sonata for Chromatic Harp (1944); Sonata for Diatonic Harp (1944); *Intermezzo and Preludium* for Diatonic Harp (1945); Suite for Bassoon (1950; also for Bass Clarinet, 1968); Suite, quartet for Bassoons (1951); Sonata for Solo Clarinet (1952); suites for Solo Violin (1955), Cello (1955), Cymbalom (1960), Bass Clarinet (1964), and Saxophone (1968); Suite for Bass Clarinet and Piano (1969); *Observations from a Journal* for Narrator and String Quartet (1970); Suite for Violin and Piano (1972). **KEYBOARD: P i a n o :** 2 *morceaux* (1917–18; arranged for String Orch. by R. Kubin, 1930); Sonata (1918); *Fugue Suite* (1918); *Variations on a Canon by Schumann* (1918); 6 *Pieces* (1920); 4 *Modern Dances* (1927); *Toccata quasi una Fantasia* (1931); 6 *Moods* (1971). **O r g a n :** Fantasy (1951); Fugue (1951). **OTHER: W o r k s i n Q u a r t e r - t o n e s :** String quartets Nos. 2, 3, 4, 6, 12, and 14 (1920, 1922, 1922, 1950, 1960, 1963); *Fantasy* for Violin (1921); *Music* for Violin (1922); *Fantasy* for Cello (1924); *Fantasy* for Violin and Piano (1925); Suite No. 1 for Clarinet and Piano (1925); *Fantasy* for Viola and Piano (1926); Fantasy for Cello and Piano (1927); 2 suites for Guitar (1943, 1947); Suite No. 2 for Clarinet (1943–44); Suite for Trumpet and Trombone (1944); Suite for 4 Trombones (1950); Suite for Violin (1961–62); 6 suites for Piano (1922, rev. 1932; 1922, rev. 1932; 1923; 1924; 1925; 1959); 11 fantasies for Piano (Nos. 1 10, 1923 26; No. 11, 1959), Piano Sonata (1947). **W o r k s i n F i f t h - t o n e s :** String Quartet No. 16 (1967). **W o r k s i n S i x t h - t o n e s :** String quartets Nos. 5, 10, and 11 (1923, 1952, 1958); Duo for 2 Violins (1937); Suite for Violin (1955); Suite for Cello (1955); 6 *Pieces* for Harmonium (1928). **VOCAL:** Songs and choral pieces, many in the quarter-tone system.

BIBL.: J. Vysloužil, *A. H.: Život a dílo* (Prague, 1974); J. Vysloužil, *A. H., 1893–1973* (Vizovice, 1993).—NS/LK/DM

Hába, Karel, Czech composer and music educator, brother of **Alois Hába**; b. Vizovice, Moravia, May 21, 1898; d. Prague, Nov. 21, 1972. He spent his entire life in Prague, where he studied violin with Karel Hoffmann and Jan Mařák, and theory with Novák, Křička, and Foerster at the Cons.; he also attended his brother's class in quarter-tone music there (1925–27). After playing violin in the Czech Radio Orch. (1929–36), he was head of the music education dept. of the Czech Radio (1936–50). He then lectured on music education at the Charles Univ. (1951–63), and also was active as a music critic. Hába faithfully followed the athematic method of composition espoused by his brother.

WORKS: DRAMATIC: O p e r a : *Jánošík* (1929–32; Prague, Feb. 23, 1934); *Stará historia* (The Old Story; 1934–37); *Smoliček*, children's opera (Prague, Sept. 28, 1950); *Kalibův zločin* (Kaliba's Crime; 1957–61; Košice, May 16, 1968). **ORCH.:** Overture (1922); Violin Concerto (Prague, March 6, 1927); *Scherzo* (1928); Cello Concerto (Prague, Sept. 1, 1935); 2 syms. (1947–48; 1953–54); *Brigand's Suite* (1955); Suite (1963). **CHAM-**

BER: 4 string quartets (1922, 1924, 1943, 1969); Trio for Violin, Cello, and Quarter Tone Piano (1926); *3 Pieces* for Violin and Piano in quarter tones (1927); Flute Sonatina (1927); Septet for Violin, Clarinet, Viola, Horn, Cello, Bassoon, and Piano (1928–29); Duo for Violin and Cello (1935); Piano Trio (1940); Wind Quintet (1944); *3 Inventions* for Harp (1945); Nonet (1950); Trio for 2 Violins and Viola (1952); *15 Concert Études* for Violin (1956); Sonatina for 2 Violins (1960); Sonatina for 3 Clarinets (1960); *3 Instructive Duos* for 2 Violins (1968). **P i a n o :** 2 suites (1920, 1929); Suite for Quarter Tone Piano (1925); Sonata (1942). **VOCAL:** Cantata; choruses; songs.—**NS/LK/DM**

Habeneck, François-Antoine, eminent French conductor; b. Mézières, Jan. 22, 1781; d. Paris, Feb. 8, 1849. His father, a native of Mannheim and a member of a regimental band, taught him the violin. In 1800 he entered the Paris Cons., where he studied violin with Baillot. In 1804 he became a violinist in the orch. of the Opéra-Comique. Shortly thereafter he joined the orch. of the Paris Opéra, becoming principal violin in 1817. From 1806 to 1815 he conducted the student orch. at the Paris Cons., and also taught violin there (1808–16; 1825–48). From 1824 to 1831 he was *premier chef* (with Valentino) of the Paris Opéra, holding that post alone from 1831 to 1846. During his tenure there he conducted the premieres of *Guillaume Tell, La Juive, Les Huguenots,* and *Benvenuto Cellini.* In 1828 he founded the Société des Concerts du Conservatoire de Paris, which initially consisted of an orch. of 86 musicians and a chorus of 79 singers (the average complement of orch. members was 60). At his first concert on March 9, 1828, he conducted Beethoven's *Eroica* Sym. He subsequently championed Beethoven's syms. in his concerts, giving the first Paris performance of the 9th Sym. on March 27, 1831. Under his guidance the orch. became the finest in its day, gaining the praise of such musicians as Mendelssohn and Wagner. He led it for 20 years, conducting his last concert on April 16, 1848. A pioneering figure among conductors, Habeneck retained many of the characteristics of the earlier violin- leader type of conductor: for instance, he used the violin part, with other instruments cued in, instead of a full score, he directed with a violin bow, and, at the beginning of his career, he played along with his musicians. Nevertheless, he assumed a foremost place among the conductors of his era. He was also a composer, but his works are not significant. With Isouard and Benincori he wrote an opera, *Aladin ou La Lampe merveilleuse* (Paris Opéra, Feb. 6, 1822). He also composed 2 violin concertos and other violin music, and publ. a *Méthode théorique et pratique de violon* (Paris, 1835).—**NS/LK/DM**

Haberbier, Ernst, German pianist and composer; b. Königsberg, Oct. 5, 1813; d. while giving a concert in Bergen, Norway, March 12, 1869. He studied with his father, an organist. He left home in 1832, and went to Russia, where he became a court pianist in St. Petersburg in 1847. He gave concerts in London in 1850, and in 1852 appeared in Paris, where he scored a sensational success. In 1866 he settled in Bergen. He perfected what he considered a novel system of piano technique, divid-

ing difficult passages between the 2 hands, but this had been done by Scarlatti and Bach long before. He wrote a number of effective piano pieces, of which *Études-Poésies* (op.53) are the best known.—**NS/LK/DM**

Haberl, Franz Xaver, eminent German organist, music theorist, music editor, and historiographer; b. Oberellenbach, Lower Bavaria, April 12, 1840; d. Regensburg, Sept. 5, 1910. He studied in the Boys' Seminary at Passau, and took Holy Orders in 1862. He was Cathedral Kapellmeister and music director at the Seminary (1862–67), organist at S. Maria dell'Anima in Rome (1867–70), and Cathedral Kapellmeister at Regensburg (1872–82), where he founded, in 1875, a world-renowned school for church music. He was an authority on Catholic church music. In 1872 he assumed the editorship of the collection Musica Divina, and ed. the periodical *Musica Sacra* in 1888. In 1876 he began to publ. the *Cäcilienkalender,* the scope of which was greatly widened until, after 1885, it was issued under the more appropriate name of *Kirchenmusikalisches Jahrbuch;* as such it has become one of the most important publications for historical studies concerning the church music of the 15th, 16th, and 17th centuries. Haberl continued as ed. until 1907, when he resigned and was succeeded by Karl Weinmann. He founded the Palestrina Soc. in 1879, and (beginning with vol. X) was ed. in chief of Breitkopf & Härtel's complete edition of Palestrina's works (33 vols., completed on the tercentenary of Palestrina's death, 1894), which he aided not only by his experience and learning, but also by rare MSS from his private collection. In 1899 he was elected president of the Allgemeiner Cäcilienverein, and became ed. of its official organ, *Fliegende Blätter für Katholische Kirchenmusik.* In 1889 he was made Dr.Theol. *honoris causa* by the Univ. of Würzburg, and in 1908, "Monsignore." Under his general supervision, a new ed. of the *Editio Medicea* (1614) of the plainchant melodies was issued, with papal sanction, at Regensburg (1871–81). When modern scholarship proved that the original ed. had not been publ. with papal sanction and had not been revised by Palestrina—that, in fact, it contained the old melodies in badly distorted and mutilated form—the papal sanction was withdrawn, and the ed. suppressed and replaced by a new *Editio Vaticana* in 1904. The result of this was that Haberl's books dealing with plainchant (which had been held in the highest esteem, and had passed through many eds.) fell into desuetude. The books thus affected are *Praktische Anweisung zum harmonischen Kirchengesang* (1864), *Magister Choralis* (1865; 12th ed., 1899; tr. into Eng., Fr., It., Span., Pol., and Hung.), *Officium hebdomadae sanctae* (1887, in Ger.), and *Psalterium vespertinum* (1888). His other writings, the value of which remains unimpaired, are *Bertalotti's Solfeggien* (1880), *Wilhelm Dufay* (1885), *Die römische "Schola Cantorum" und die päpstlichen Kapellsänger bis zur Mitte des 16. Jahrhunderts* (1887), and *Bibliographischer und thematischer Musikkatalog des päpstlichen Kapellarchivs im Vatikan zu Rom* (1888).—**NS/LK/DM**

Habermann, Franz (actually, **František Václav**), Bohemian composer; b. Kynžvart, Sept. 20, 1706; d. Cheb, April 8, 1783. He studied in Prague, and, while traveling in Italy, Spain, and France, pursued his training. After serving as music director at the courts of the Prince of Condé and the Duke of Tuscany in Florence, he was again in Prague by 1743 and active as a choirmaster. In 1773 he became cantor in Cheb. He composed an opéra-comique for the coronation of Empress Maria Theresia as Queen of Bohemia (Prague, May 12, 1743), oratorios, church music, and instrumental pieces. Habermann was greatly esteemed for his mastery of contrapuntal writing. Handel borrowed music from five of his masses for use in his own *Philomela pia, Jephtha,* and an organ concerto. Among Habermann's students were Franz Duschek and Josef Mysliveček.—**LK/DM**

Habert, Johannes Evangelista, Bohemian organist, composer, and writer on music; b. Oberplan, Oct. 18, 1833; d. Gmunden, Sept. 1, 1896. He was organist at Gmunden from 1861. He wrote sacred music and organ pieces. A complete ed. of his works was publ. by Breitkopf & Härtel. He was founder and ed. of the *Zeitschrift für katholische Kirchenmusik* (1868–83), and also publ. *Beiträge zur Lehre von der musikalischen Komposition* (4 vols., 1889 et seq.).

BIBL.: A. Hartl, *J. E. H., Organist in Gmunden* (Vienna, 1900).—**NS/LK/DM**

Habich, Eduard, German baritone; b. Kassel, Sept. 3, 1880; d. Berlin, March 15, 1960. He studied in Frankfurt am Main with Max Fleisch. He made his operatic debut in Koblenz in 1904, then sang in Posen, Halle, and Düsseldorf, at the Berlin Royal (later State) Opera (1910–30), at the Bayreuth Festivals (1911–31), at London's Covent Garden (1924–36; 1938), and at the Chicago Civic Opera (1930–32). He made his Metropolitan Opera debut in N.Y. on Dec. 20, 1935, as Peter in *Hänsel und Gretel,* and remained on its roster until 1937. He later taught voice in Berlin. Among his admired roles were Beckmesser, Faninal, Alberich, Telramund, and Klingsor.—**NS/LK/DM**

Hacker, Alan (Ray), English clarinetist, conductor, and pedagogue; b. Dorking, Sept. 30, 1938. He studied at Dulwich Coll. and the Royal Academy of Music in London; continued his training in Paris, Vienna, and Bayreuth. He played clarinet in the London Phil. (1959–66), and in 1965 was a founding member of the Pierrot Players, which became the Fires of London in 1970. In 1971 he founded his own group, Matrix, and in 1977, the Classical Orch. As a guest conductor, he appeared in various European music centers. He taught at the Royal Academy of Music (1960–76) and the Univ. of York (1976–85). In 1988 he was made an Officer of the Order of the British Empire. His extensive repertoire ranges from early music to contemporary scores. —**NS/LK/DM**

Hackett, Charles, American tenor; b. Worcester, Mass., Nov. 4, 1889; d. N.Y., Jan. 1, 1942. He was a student of Arthur J. Hubbard at the New England Cons. of Music in Boston and of Vincenzo Lombardi in Florence. After making his operatic debut in Genoa as

Thomas's Wilhelm Meister in 1914, he sang throughout Italy, including Milan (La Scala, 1916); he also sang at the Teatro Colón in Buenos Aires. On Jan. 31, 1919, he made his Metropolitan Opera debut in N.Y. as Count Almaviva, remaining on the roster until 1921; after singing with the Chicago Civic Opera (1923–32), he was again on the roster of the Metropolitan Opera (1933–39). His other roles included the Duke of Mantua, Alfredo, Roméo, Rodolfo, Lindoro, and Pinkerton.—**NS/LK/DM**

Hacquart, Carolus, Netherlands composer and instrumentalist; b. Bruges, c. 1640; d. c. 1701. He received training in viola da gamba, lute, organ, and composition. Following a sojourn in Amsterdam, he went to The Hague in 1679. He publ. a distinguished set of 10 sonatas, a 3, 4, as *Harmonia parnassia* (Utrecht, 1686). Among his other works were 12 viola da gamba suites (1686) and sacred music.

BIBL.: P. Andriessen, *C. H.* (Brussels, 1974).—**LK/DM**

Hadley, Henry (Kimball), noted American conductor and composer; b. Somerville, Mass., Dec. 20, 1871; d. N.Y., Sept. 6, 1937. He received training in piano, violin, and conducting from his father, and then studied harmony with Emery and counterpoint and composition with Chadwick in Somerville and at the New England Cons. of Music in Boston. He then took lessons in counterpoint with Mandyczewski in Vienna (1894–95) and in composition with Thuille in Munich (1905–07). After teaching at St. Paul's School in Garden City, N.Y. (1895–1902), he devoted himself fully to conducting and composing. He was conductor of the Mainz Stadttheater (1907–09) and of the Seattle Sym. Orch. (1909–11). In 1911 he became conductor of the newly organized San Francisco Sym. Orch., which he conducted until 1915. After serving as assoc. conductor of the N.Y. Phil. (1920–27), he was founder-conductor of the Manhattan Sym. Orch. (1929–32). In 1934 he founded the Berkshire Music Festival in Stockbridge, Mass., which he conducted for 2 seasons. In 1924 he was elected a member of the American Academy of Arts and Letters. In 1933 he organized the National Assn. for American Composers and Conductors, which subsequently endowed the Henry Hadley Memorial Library at the N.Y. Public Library. In 1938 the Henry Hadley Foundation was organized in N.Y. to further Hadley's championship of American music. In his own compositions, Hadley wrote well-crafted scores in a late Romantic vein. His 2nd Sym. received the Paderewski Prize in 1901.

WORKS: DRAMATIC: *Happy Jack,* operetta (1897); *Nancy Brown,* operetta (1903); *Safie,* opera (Mainz, April 4, 1909); *The Atonement of Pan,* incidental music (1912; also an orch. suite, 1912); *The Pearl Girl,* operetta (n.d.); *Azora, Daughter of Montezuma,* opera (1914; Chicago, Dec. 26, 1917); *The Masque of Newark,* pageant (1916); *Bianca,* opera (1917; N.Y., Oct. 15, 1918); *The Fire Prince,* operetta (1917); *Cleopatra's Night,* opera (1918; N.Y., Jan. 31, 1920); *Semper virens,* music drama (1923); *A Night in Old Paris,* opera (1924); *The Legend of Hani,* incidental music (1933; also an orch. suite, 1933); *The Red Flame,* musical (n.d.). **ORCH.:** Ballet Suite (1895); *Festival March* (1897); 5 syms.: No. 1, *Youth and Life* (N.Y., Dec. 2, 1897), No. 2, *The 4 Seasons* (N.Y.,

Dec. 20, 1901), No. 3 (1906; Berlin, Dec. 27, 1907), No. 4, *North, East, South, and West* (Norfolk, Conn., Jan. 6, 1911), and No. 5, *Connecticut* (Norfolk, Conn., 1935); *Herod*, overture (1901); *In Bohemia*, overture (Boston, Dec. 16, 1901); *Oriental Suite* (1903); *Symphonic Fantasia* (1904); *Salome*, tone poem (1905–06; Boston, April 12, 1907); *Konzertstück* for Cello and Orch. (1907); *The Culprit Fay*, rhapsody (1908; Grand Rapids, Mich., May 28, 1909); *Lucifer*, tone poem (1910; Norfolk, Conn., June 2, 1914); *Silhouettes*, suite (1918; Philadelphia, July 17, 1932); *Othello*, overture (Philadelphia, Dec. 26, 1919); *The Ocean*, tone poem (1920–21; N.Y., Nov. 17, 1921); *Suite ancienne* (1924); *Streets of Pekin*, suite (Tokyo, Sept. 24, 1930); *San Francisco*, suite (1931); *Youth Triumphant*, overture for Band (1931); *Alma mater*, overture (1932); *Scherzo diabolique* (Chicago, Aug. 1934). **CHAMBER:** Violin Sonata (1895); 2 string quartets (c. 1896, 1934); 2 piano trios (c. 1896, 1933); Piano Quintet (1919); piano pieces. **VOCAL: C a n t a t a s :** *In Music's Praise* for Soloists, Chorus, and Orch. (1898); *The Princess of Ys* for Women's or Mixed Voices and Orch. (1903); *A Legend of Granada* for Soloists and Women's Chorus (1904); *The Fate of Princess Kiyo* for Soloists, Women's Chorus, and Orch. (1907); *The Nightingale and the Rose* for Soloist, Women's Chorus, and Orch. (1911); *The Golden Prince* for Soloists, Women's Chorus, and Orch. (1914); *The Fairy Thorn* for Soloists, Women's Voices, and Piano or Orch. (1917); *Prophecy and Fulfillment* for Soloists, Chorus, and Orch. (1922); *The Admiral of the Seas* for Soloist, Chorus, and Orch. (1928); *Belshazzar* for Soloists, Chorus, and Orch. (1932). **O t h e r :** *The Fairies* for Soprano, Chorus, and Orch. or Piano (1894); *Lelawala* for Chorus and Orch. (1898); *Merlin and Vivian*, lyric drama for Soloists, Chorus, and Orch. (1906); *Music: An Ode* for Soloists, Chorus, and Orch. (1915); *In Arcady*, idyll for Chorus and Orch. (c. 1918); *The New Earth*, ode for Soloists, Chorus, and Orch. (1919); *Resurgam*, oratorio for Soloists, Chorus, and Orch. (1922); *Mirtil in Arcadia*, pastoral for Soloists, Narrator, Chorus, Children's Chorus, and Orch. (1926); anthems; choruses; more than 200 songs.

BIBL.: H. Boardman, *H. H., Ambassador of Harmony* (Atlanta, 1932); P. Berthoud, ed., *The Musical Works of Dr. H. H.* (N.Y., 1942); J. Canfield, *H. K. H. (1871–1937): His Life and Works* (diss., Fla. State Univ., 1960).—**NS/LK/DM**

Hadley, Jerry, American tenor; b. Princeton, Ill., June 12, 1952. He studied music education at Bradley Univ. (B.A., 1974) and voice at the Univ. of Ill. (M.A., 1977), where he found a mentor in David Lloyd; then studied with Thomas LoMonaco in N.Y. In 1976 he made his professional operatic debut as Ferrando at the Lake George (N.Y.) Opera Festival. On Sept. 14, 1979, he made his first appearance at the N.Y.C. Opera as Lord Arturo Bucklaw in *Lucia de Lammermoor*, remaining with the company until 1985; also appeared regularly with the Washington (D.C.) Opera (from 1980). He made his debut at the Vienna State Opera in 1982 as Nemorino, and in 1983 he sang for the first time at the Bavarian State Opera in Munich, the Glyndebourne Festival, and the Netherlands Opera in Amsterdam. In 1984 he made his debut at London's Covent Garden as Fenton and his Carnegie Hall recital debut in N.Y.; his Metropolitan Opera debut in N.Y. followed on March 7, 1987, as Massenet's Des Grieux; he sang there regularly from 1990. In 1991 he sang in the premiere of McCartney's *Liverpool Oratorio*. In 1994 he was engaged as Tom Rakewell in London and at the Lyric Opera in Chicago, a role he reprised at the Metropolitan Opera in 1997. In

1997 he also created the title role in Myron Fink's *The Conquistador* in San Diego. He also toured extensively as a concert artist. In addition to his Mozart and *bel canto* roles, Hadley has found success as Berlioz's and Gounod's Faust, Offenbach's Hoffmann, Verdi's Alfredo, and Stravinsky's Tom Rakewell. His performances in works by Weill, Kern, Rodgers and Hammerstein, Bernstein, and Lerner and Lowe have added further luster to his success.—**NS/LK/DM**

Hadley, Patrick (Arthur Sheldon), English composer and teacher; b. Cambridge, March 5, 1899; d. King's Lynn, Norfolk, Dec. 17, 1973. He studied at the Royal Coll. of Music in London with Vaughan Williams and others (1922–25). He then taught there (1925–62), and from 1938 to 1946 also held a fellowship at Gonville and Caius Coll., Cambridge, where he subsequently was prof. of music from 1946 to 1962. He composed mostly vocal music, numbering among his works are the cantatas *The Trees So High* (1931), *La Belle Dame sans merci* (1935), *Travelers* (1940), *The Hills* (1944), *Fen and Flood* (1954), *Connemara* (1958), and *Cantata for Lent* (1960), as well as many songs.

BIBL.: W. Todds, *P. H.; A Memoir* (London, 1974; with catalog of works).—**NS/LK/DM**

Hadow, Sir W(illiam) H(enry), English music educator, writer on music, and composer; b. Ebrington, Gloucestershire, Dec. 27, 1859; d. London, April 8, 1937. He studied at Malvern Coll. (1871–78) and Worcester Coll., Oxford (1878–82), receiving the degrees of M.A. (1885) and Mus.B. (1890). He was a lecturer at Worcester Coll. (1885–1909). After serving as principal of Armstrong Coll. in Newcastle upon Tyne (1909–18), he was vice-chancellor of the Univ. of Sheffield (1919–30). In 1918 he was knighted. He wrote a cantata, *The Soul's Pilgrimage*, String Quartet, 2 violin sonatas, Viola Sonata, and a number of anthems. Hadow's importance, however, lies in his books, written in a lively journalistic style. His book *A Croatian Composer: Notes toward the Study of Joseph Haydn* (London, 1897), claiming that Haydn was of Slavonic origin, aroused considerable controversy; later research disproved this theory. Of more solid substance are his other writings: *Studies in Modern Music* (2 vols., 1892–95; 10th ed., 1921); *Sonata Form* (1896; 2nd ed., 1915), *The Viennese Period* (vol. 5 of the *Oxford History of Music*, 1904; 2nd ed., 1931), *William Byrd* (1923), *Music* (1924; 3rd ed., rev., 1949, by G. Dyson), *Church Music* (1926), *A Comparison of Poetry and Music* (1926), *Collected Essays* (1928), *English Music* (1931), *The Place of Music among the Arts* (1933), and *Richard Wagner* (1934). He also ed. songs of the British Isles (1903) and was ed.-in-chief of the *Oxford History of Music* (1901–05 and 1929).—**NS/LK/DM**

Hadzidakis, Manos, Greek composer; b. Xanthi, Macedonia, Oct. 23, 1925; d. Athens, June 15, 1994. He wrote piano pieces in an advanced idiom, recalling Prokofiev, then turned to film music. He became best known for his theme song composed for the film released in America under the title *Never on Sunday* (1960).—**NS/LK/DM**

Haebler, Ingrid, esteemed Austrian pianist; b. Vienna, June 20, 1929. She began her musical training with her mother, and then pursued her studies with Scholz at the Salzburg Mozarteum (1940–42; 1948–49) and with Weingarten (1943–47) and Hauser (1952–53) at the Vienna Academy of Music. She also attended the master classes of Magaloff at the Geneva Cons. (1950–51; Prix de Virtuosité, 1951) and of Long at the Paris Cons. (1953). In 1952 she was co-winner of the 2nd prize at the Geneva Competition (no 1st prize was awarded), and in 1954 she took 1st prize in both the Munich Competition and the Geneva Schubert Competition. She then appeared with many of the leading orchs. of the day and at the principal festivals. In 1959 she made her U.S. debut as soloist with the Minneapolis Sym. Orch. She also appeared as a recitalist and chamber music player. As a duo recitalist, she often performed with Szeryng. From 1969 to 1971 she was a prof. at the Salzburg Mozarteum. She was awarded the Mozart medals of Vienna in 1971 and of the Salzburg Mozarteum in 1980, and in 1986 she received the Medal of Honor of Vienna. In addition to her admired interpretations of Mozart, she has won distinction for her performances of J. C. Bach (on the fortepiano), Haydn, Beethoven, Schubert, Schumann, and Chopin.—NS/LK/DM

Haeffner, Johann Christian Friedrich, German organist, conductor, and composer; b. Oberschönau, near Suhl, March 2, 1759; d. Uppsala, May 28, 1833. He was a pupil of Vierling in Schmalkalden. He studied at the Univ. of Leipzig, and served as proofreader for Breitkopf; then became conductor of a traveling opera troupe. In 1781 he arrived in Stockholm, where he was an organist at St. Gertrud until 1793. He composed several operas in the style of Gluck which had a favorable reception: *Electra* (July 22, 1787), *Alcides inträde i Världen* (Nov. 11, 1793), and *Renaud* (Jan. 29, 1801). In 1792 he was appointed director of the Swedish Royal Orch. In 1808 he went to Uppsala, where he remained for the rest of his life, acting as organist of the Cathedral and music director of the Univ. He took great interest in Swedish national music, publishing Swedish folk songs with accompaniment and revising the melodies of the Geijer-Afzelius collection. He also ed. a *Svenska Choralbok* (2 parts, 1819–21), in which he restored the choral melodies of the 17th century, and added preludes (1822); also arranged a collection of old Swedish songs in 4 parts (1832–33; he finished only 2 books).—NS/LK/DM

Haefliger, Ernst, noted Swiss tenor; b. Davos, July 6, 1919. He studied at the Zürich Cons., with Fernando Carpi in Geneva, and with Julius Patzak in Vienna. After making his debut as the Evangelist in Bach's *St. John Passion* in 1942, he sang at the Zürich Opera (1943–52). He gained wide recognition when he created the role of Tiresias in Orff's *Antigonae* at the Salzburg Festival on Aug. 9, 1949. From 1952 to 1974 he was a member of the Berlin Städtische (later Deutsche) Oper, but he also appeared as a guest artist with many of the principal European opera houses. His roles in Mozart's operas were particularly esteemed. He pursued a distinguished career as a concert singer and lieder artist. His appearances as the Evangelist in Bach's passions and his lieder recitals were notable. In commemoration of the 250th anniversary of Bach's death in 2000, Haefliger was engaged as the Evangelist in the *St. Matthew Passion* in Winterthur. He was a prof. at the Munich Hochschule für Musik from 1971 to 1981. Haefliger publ. the book *Die Singstimme* (Bern, 1983).—NS/LK/DM

Haenchen, Hartmut, German conductor; b. Dresden, March 21, 1943. He was a student of Matschke, Neuhaus, and Förster at the Dresden Hochschule für Musik (1960–66), and of Koch and Höft in Berlin. In 1971 he won 1st prize in the Carl Maria von Weber competition in Dresden. After serving as director of the Robert-Franz-Singakadamie and the Halle orch. (1966–72), he was chief conductor of the Zwickau Theater (1972–73). From 1973 to 1976 he was permanent conductor of the Dresden Phil., and, from 1974 to 1976, of the Phil. Choir of Dresden. He then was chief conductor of the Mecklenburg State Theater (1976–79). He was a prof. of conducting at the Dresden Hochschule für Musik (1980–86), and also music director of the C.P.E. Bach Chamber Orch. in Berlin (from 1980). In 1986 he became music director of the Netherlands Opera in Amsterdam. Haenchen has appeared as a guest conductor with major opera houses throughout Europe, North America, and Japan.—NS/LK/DM

Haendel, Ida, Polish-born English violinist; b. Chelm, Dec. 15, 1923. She was a child prodigy. At 4, she began formal studies with Miecyzslaw Michalowicz at the Warsaw Cons., where she won its gold medal in 1933. She then pursued training in Paris and London with Flesch and Enesco. In 1935 she won the Polish prize offered at the 1st Wieniawski Competition in Warsaw. At 14, she attacted notice in London when she appeared as soloist in the Brahms Concerto under Sir Henry Wood's direction at a Proms concert. During World War II, she gave many concerts for Allied troops. In 1940 she became a naturalized British subject. In 1946–47 she made her first tour of the U.S. Although she lived in Montreal from 1952 to 1989, she made annual tours of Europe, and also appeared regularly in South America and Asia, including a tour of China in 1973 as soloist with John Pritchard and the London Phil. From 1991 she was also active as a teacher. In 1982 she was awarded the Sibelius Medal. Her career was the subject of the CBC-TV documentary "Ida Haendel: A Voyage of Music" in 1988. In 1991 she was made a Commander of the Order of the British Empire. She publ. the autobiographical vol. *Woman with Violin* (London, 1970). Haendel's virtuoso technique, ably complemented by a thoroughgoing musicianship, has won her admirers in both the concerto and recital repertoires. Her extensive concerto repertoire embraces scores from Bach to Walton.—NS/LK/DM

Hafez (Shabana), Abdel Halim, renowned Egyptian singer; b. Zakazik, Sharkia, 1929; d. London, March 30, 1977. He rose to prominence in Egypt, and the Arab world in general, as the foremost interpreter of romantic and nationalistic songs. He won renown for his renditions of *Safini Marra* and *Ala Kad el Shouk*. He used Western instruments in his performances, and even utilized the Moog synthesizer. So widespread was his fame at the time of his death that 100,000 Egyptians lined the streets of the funeral procession in Cairo. —**NS/LK/DM**

Hafgren, Lily (Johana Maria), Swedish soprano; b. Stockholm, Oct. 7, 1884; d. Berlin, Feb. 27, 1965. She was educated in Frankfurt am Main, then began her career as a pianist. Siegfried Wagner encouraged her to consider an operatic career, and she studied voice in Stuttgart with Max Fleisch. In 1908 she made her operatic debut as Freia at the Bayreuth Festival, where she sang again in 1911, 1912, and 1924. She also sang in Mannheim (1908–12), at the Royal (later State) Opera in Berlin (1912–21), and appeared in Paris, Rome, Milan, Dresden, Stockholm, Prague, and other operatic centers. She retired in 1934. In later years, she used her married names, Hafgren-Waag and Hafgren-Dinkela. Among her finest roles were Brünnhilde, Eva, and Isolde.—**NS/LK/DM**

Hagegård, Håkan, outstanding Swedish baritone; b. Karlstad, Nov. 25, 1945. After initial training in Karlstad, he studied at the Stockholm Musikhögskolan and with Erik Werba and Gerald Moore in Salzburg. He made his operatic debut at the Royal Theater in Stockholm as Papageno (1968); after further study with Tito Gobbi, he made his first venture outside his homeland at the Glyndebourne Festival in 1973. He gained wide recognition through his notable portrayal of Papageno in Ingmar Bergman's film version of *Die Zauberflöte* (1975); subsequently appeared throughout Europe in opera and concert. On Dec. 7, 1978, he made his Metropolitan Opera debut in N.Y. as Dr. Malatesta. He appeared as Wolfram at his debut at London's Covent Garden in 1987. On Dec. 19, 1991, he created the role of Beaumarchais in the premiere of Corigliano's *The Ghosts of Versailles* at the Metropolitan Opera in N.Y. In 1992 he portrayed Wolfram at the Deutsche Oper in Berlin. He sang at the Metropolitan Opera Gala in 1996. He is married to **Barbara Bonney**. He particularly distinguished himself in operas by Mozart, Rossini, Donizetti, and Verdi; also became highly esteemed as a concert singer, excelling as an interpreter of lieder.—**NS/LK/DM**

Hageman, Maurits (Leonard), Dutch violinist, conductor, and composer, father of **Richard Hageman;** b. Zutfen, Sept. 25, 1829; d. Nijmegen, April 16, 1906. He studied with Bériot and Fétis at the Brussels Cons., graduating in 1852. After playing violin in the Italian Opera orch. at Brussels, he became a conductor at Groningen. He then was director of the Cons. of Batavia, Java (1865–75), and conductor of the orch. there. Returning to the Netherlands, he founded a music school in Leeuwarden. He wrote an oratorio, *Daniel*, several other choral works, piano pieces, and songs.—**NS/LK/DM**

Hageman, Richard, distinguished Dutch-American pianist, conductor, and composer, son of **Maurits (Leonard) Hageman;** b. Leeuwarden, July 9, 1882; d. Beverly Hills, March 6, 1966. He studied music with his father, then took courses at the Brussels Cons. with Gevaert and Arthur de Greef. He held an auxiliary position as conductor at the Royal Opera in Amsterdam (1899–1903). After playing accompaniments for Mathilde Marchesi in Paris (1904–05), he went to the U.S. as accompanist for Yvette Guilbert in 1906. He was on the conducting roster of the Metropolitan Opera in N.Y. (1908–10; 1911–21; 1935–37), the Chicago Civic Opera (1922–23), and the Los Angeles Grand Opera (1923). In 1938 he settled in Hollywood, where he was engaged as a composer of film music. He wrote 2 operas: *Caponsacchi* (1931; 1st perf. as *Tragödie in Arezzo*, Freiburg im Breisgau, Feb. 18, 1932; received the David Bispham Memorial Medal) and *The Crucible* (Los Angeles, Feb. 4, 1943). He achieved a lasting reputation mainly through his solo songs, of which *Do Not Go My Love* (to words by Rabindranath Tagore; 1917) and *At the Well* (1919) became extremely popular.—**NS/LK/DM**

Hagen, Francis Florentine, American Moravian minister and composer; b. Salem, N.C., Oct. 30, 1815; d. Lititz, Pa., July 7, 1907. He served as a teacher and minister in various Moravian congregations. He ed. and compiled the *Church and Home Organist's Companion*. He wrote a number of anthems, in which a definite sense for distinguished popular melody is noticeable, as well as a cantata and an overture. His *Morning Star*, a Christmas carol, which in Moravian communities stood in continuous favor for almost a century, was reprinted in 1939.—**NS/LK/DM**

Hagen, Friedrich Heinrich von der, German scholar; b. in the Ukraine, Feb. 19, 1780; d. Berlin, June 11, 1856. He was a prof. of German literature at the Univ. of Berlin. He publ. the valuable collection *Minnesinger* (5 vols., 1838–56; in Vol. III are *Minnegesänge* in notation according to the Jena Codex and other sources, with a treatise on the music of the Minnesinger), as well as *Melodien zu der Sammlung deutscher, vlämischer und französicher Volkslieder* (1807; with Büsching).—**NS/LK/DM**

Hagen-Groll, Walter, German choral conductor; b. Chemnitz, April 15, 1927. He studied at the Stuttgart Hochschule für Musik (1947–52) and with J. Pembaur Jr. (piano) in Munich. After serving as a répétiteur and conductor at the Stuttgart Opera (1952–57), he was chorus master at the Heidelberg Opera (1957–61). In 1961 he became chorus master of the Berlin Deutsche Oper and conductor of the chorus of the Berlin Phil.; he also was chorus master at the Salzburg Festival (from 1965) and conductor of the New Philharmonia Orch. Chorus in London (1971–74). In 1984 he became chorus master of the Vienna State Opera. He was named choral director at the Salzburg Mozarteum in 1986. He also was director of the Vienna Singakademie from 1987. —**NS/LK/DM**

Hager, Leopold, Austrian conductor; b. Salzburg, Oct. 6, 1935. He took courses in piano, organ, harpsichord, conducting, and composition at the Salzburg Mozarteum (1949–57), his principal teachers being

Paumgartner, Wimberger, Bresgen, J. N. David, and Kornauth. He was asst. conductor at the Mainz City Theater (1957–62). After conducting the Linz Landestheater (1962–64), he held the post of 1st conductor of the Cologne Opera (1964–65). After serving as Generalmusikdirektor in Freiburg im Breisgau (1965–69), he was chief conductor of the Mozarteum Orch. and of the Landestheater in Salzburg (1969–81). On Oct. 14, 1976, he made his Metropolitan Opera debut in N.Y. conducting *Le Nozze di Figaro*, and remained on its roster until 1978. He also appeared as a guest conductor with other opera houses as well as orchs. in Europe and the U.S. In 1981 he became chief conductor of the Orchestre Symphonique de Radio-Télé Luxembourg.—**NS/LK/DM**

Hagerup Bull, Edvard, Norwegian composer; b. Bergen, June 10, 1922. He was an organ student of Sandvold at the Oslo Cons. (graduated, 1947); he also received training in piano from Erling Westher and Reimar Riefling, and in composition from Brustad and Irgens Jensen. After further studies at the Paris Cons. with Milhaud, Koechlin, and Rivier (Prix de composition, 1952), he completed his training with Blacher and Rufer at the Berlin Hochschule für Musik. His early neo-Classical style tended later toward free tonality.

WORKS: DRAMATIC: O p e r a : *Den Grimme Aelling* (1972–77); *Fyrtjet* (1973–74). **B a l l e t :** *Munchhausen* (1961). **ORCH.:** *Le Soldat de plomb*, ballet suite (1948–49); *Serenade* (1950); *Morceaux rapsodiques*, divertimento (1950); 2 trumpet concertos (1950, 1960); *Sinfonia di teatro*, symphonic prelude (1950–51); *Petite suite symphonique* for Small Orch. (1951); *Escapades*, suite (1952); *Divertimento* for Piano and Orch. (1954); 6 syms.: No. 1, *3 mouvements symphoniques* (1955), No. 2, *In modo d'una sinfonia* (1958–59), No. 3, *Sinfonia espressiva* (1964), No. 4, *Sinfonia humana* (1968), No. 5, *Sinfonia in memoriam* (1971–72), and No. 6, *Lamentazione, Sinfonia da camera pour la Pologne, Solidarité et Lech Walesa* (1981–82); *3 morceaux brefs* for Saxophone and Orch. (1955); *Cassation* for Chamber Orch. (1959); *Epilogue* for Strings (1961); *Undecim Sumus* for Chamber Orch. of Soloists (1962); *Dialogue* for Flute, Strings, and Piano (1965); *6 épigrammes* for Chamber Ensemble (1969); Concerto for Flute and Chamber Orch. (1969); *Air solennel*, symphonic movement (1972); *Chant d'Hommage à Jean Rivier*, symphonic movement (1975); Alto Saxophone Concerto (1980); *Movimenti* (1985); *Piece héroique pour le centenaire d'un géant* (1991); *Hymne joyeux pour un jubilé de fete* (1992); *Giocoso bucolico*, concertino for Tuba and Orch. (1992). **CHAMBER:** Clarinet Sonata (1950); *3 bucoliques* for Oboe, Clarinet, and Bassoon (1953); 2 duos for Violin and Piano (1956, 1973); *Ad usum amicorum* for Flute, Violin, Cello, and Piano (1957); *Marionnettes sérieuses* for Wind Quintet (1960); *Quadrige* for 4 Clarinets (1964); Sextet for Flute, Oboe, Clarinet, Horn, Bassoon, and Alto Saxophone or Clarinet (1965); *Sonata cantabile* for Flute, Violin, Cello, and Piano (1966); *Concert* for Trumpet, Horn, and Trombone (1966; also for 2 Trumpets, Horn, Trombone, and Tuba); Wind Quintet No. 2 (1973); *Posthumes* for 8 Wind Instruments and Double Bass (1978); *Profils pour un Drame Rustique* for Piano, Flute, Oboe, Clarinet, and Bassoon (1978); *Sonata con Moto* for Violin, Cello, and Piano (1982); *Sonata a Quatro* for String Quartet (1983); Sextet for Flute, Clarinet, Violin, Cello, Piano, and Percussion (1985); *Musique for 4 Strings* (1988); piano pieces. **VOCAL:** Songs. —**NS/LK/DM**

Hägg, Jakob Adolf, Swedish composer; b. Oestergarn, June 27, 1850; d. Hudiksvall, March 1, 1928. He was a remote relative of **Gustaf Wilhelm Hägg (Peterson)**. He studied at the Stockholm Cons., then received a stipend to take courses in Denmark with Gade, who exercised a decisive influence on his style of composition. He further studied piano with Anton Door in Vienna and music theory with Kiel in Berlin. Ambition to learn and relentless diligence in his studies upset his mental equilibrium so that he had to spend 15 years in a sanatorium (1880–95). He recovered but retired to the country, reducing his activity to a minimum. Despite this misadventure he was able to leave a considerable legacy of works, among them 5 syms., of which *Nordische Symphonie* (1870; rev. 1890) was the best known, 3 overtures, Cello Sonata, Piano Trio, String Quartet, and other chamber music, piano pieces, and songs.

BIBL.: G. Hetsch, *J. A. H.* (Leipzig, 1903).—**NS/LK/DM**

Haggard, Merle (M. Ronald), hard-livin' country singer; b. Bakersfield, Calif., April 6, 1937. The mythic life of Merle Haggard—born to grinding poverty, a stint in prison, followed by rehabilitation and success wrought from hard work and harder livin'—is as much responsible for his success as his songs. Like Woody Guthrie, Haggard is an Okie who took his real-life experiences and molded them into his music. Like Guthrie, too, he has been uncompromising in producing records that reflect that experience. Unlike Guthrie, though, Haggard has enjoyed great success on the country charts, nearly ruling the Top Ten from the mid-1960s through the mid-1970s.

Haggard's parents were displaced Okies from the small town of Checotah (halfway between McAlester and Muskogee); like many others, they were driven off their land by the ravaging dust storms of the mid-1930s, moving west to Calif. in search of a better way of life. They found living conditions tough there, and jobs few; the family was living in a converted boxcar when Haggard was born. They fared better after Merle's father got a job with the Santa Fe Railroad, but this brief period of prosperity ended with his premature death when Merle was nine.

Haggard attributes his troubled teenage years to his father's passing. He became difficult and unruly, constantly running away from home. He ended up serving time in reform school, and then, when he reached age 17, 90 days in prison for stealing. Merle hung with a tough crowd, and when he was released he was soon in trouble again. One night, Haggard and a drunken friend tried to break into a restaurant that they thought was closed; it turned out it was earlier than the boys thought, and the owner greeted them at the back door just after they had removed the hinges to break in! Haggard spent two and a half years in prison following his arrest. While in prison, he heard Johnny Cash perform, which renewed his interest in country music and his desire to write songs that would reflect his own experiences.

Upon his release in early 1960, he was determined to turn his life around. He began working for his brother who was an electrician, while also performing at night in local bars and clubs. In 1963, he was hired by Wynn Stewart to play in his backup band in Vegas; there, Fuzzy Owen heard him play and signed him to his Tally record label. Haggard had his first solo hit with "Sing Me a Sad Song," followed by a minor hit with a duet with Bonnie Owens on "Just Between the Two of Us" (Owens was married to Buck Owens at the time, although she would soon leave him to marry Haggard and join his road show). His first Top Ten hit came in 1964 with "(My Friends Are Gonna Be) Strangers," written by Bill Anderson, which also gave Merle the name for his backup band.

Haggard was signed to Capitol Records by producer Ken Nelson who was in charge of the label's growing country and folk rosters. His first hit for the label, "I'm a Lonesome Fugitive," written by Liz and Casey Anderson, defined the classic Haggard stance: that of a man who had been in trouble with the law, but now rued his rough-and-rowdy earlier days (and was still subject to temptation). More prison ballads followed, including Merle's own compositions "Branded Man" and his first #1 hit, "Sing Me Back Home," a true story of a man about to be executed who asked to hear, for one last time, a country song to remind him of his long-lost youth. Although this song literally drips with sentiment, Haggard's dry-as-dust delivery and unquestioned tough-guy credentials made it (and many more like it) instantly credible to his audience. His 1968 hit, "Mama Tried," told of the difficulty his mother had in raising him, expressing regret for his difficult teenage years.

Unlike many other country artists of the day who were often backed with tons of strings and smothering vocal choruses, Haggard formed a lean, tough backup band he named the Strangers, after his 1964 hit. The original band included Roy Nichols (lead gtr.), Norm Hamlet (steel gtr.), Bobby Wayne (gtr.), Dennis Hormak (bs.), and Biff Adam (drm.). The band's pared-down sound became a hallmark of Haggard's recordings, and he also wrote songs with its members, including Nichols and drummer Roy Burris (who replaced Adam in 1968).

Haggard gained his greatest notoriety for his 1969 recording of "Okie from Muskogee," a song that enraged hippies and the antiwar movement, while it cemented Haggard's position in mainstream, conservative country circles. Haggard was inspired when drummer Burris spotted a road sign for Muskogee during a tour through Okla.; the drummer commented, "I bet the citizens of Muskogee don't smoke marijuana." The song inspired many loony parodies, including Pat Sky's immortal remake (with the ending of the first verse changed to: "Love me, or I'll punch you in the mouth") and the Youngblood's "Hippie from Olema." Haggard feels his message was misinterpreted, although he followed the song with the equally jingoistic "The Fightin' Side of Me," full of old-time American bravado, and began hanging out with President Nixon.

One of Haggard's heroes from his youth was Bob Wills, who regularly performed in Southern Calif. at the time. So great was his admiration for Wills that Haggard began to rigorously practice the fiddle, seeking to emulate the swinging style of Wills's best lead fiddlers. He paid homage to the master fiddler in 1970 with an album of Wills standards, recorded with many of Wills's then-retired sidemen, including mandolinist Tiny Moore, who soon joined Haggard's traveling show. It was quite a gutsy move to record this decidedly "noncommercial" album, showing Haggard's considerable clout at the height of his career. (Six years later, he had a hit with Wills's "Cherokee Maiden," arranged by Moore.)

By the mid-1970s, Haggard's life and career were in disarray; his marriage to Bonnie Owens was on the rocks, and he broke with his long-time record label, Capitol, in 1977. He took a brief break from the music business, hinting that he would no longer perform, although he quickly reemerged as a performer and recording artist (with ex-wife Bonnie still singing in his show!) He recorded a duet, "The Bull and the Bear," in 1978 with Leona Williams (who also cowrote the song); the two were married soon after. (The marriage lasted only until 1983).

Haggard's recording career has been more sporadic in the 1980s. He had his greatest success in 1983 when he recorded a duo album with Willie Nelson, yielding the #1 hit and title track, "Pancho and Lefty" (written by Texan Townes van Zandt, and introduced to the pair by Haggard's daughter). Since then, he has had occasional chart hits, while continuing to tour with one of the tightest country revues on the road, stubbornly performing his own brand of country balladry. He has also had a few roles on TV and in films, most notably appearing in Clint Eastwood's *Bronco Billy*, yielding the 1980 hit "Bar Room Buddies" a duet with the equally grizzled actor that really made his day.

The winner of many awards, Haggard was elected to both the Songwriters Hall of Fame in 1977 and the Country Music Hall of Fame in 1994.

DISC.: *Strangers* (1965); *Just Between the Two of Us* (1966); *I'm a Lonesome Fugitive* (1967); *Branded Man/I Threw Away the Rose* (1967); *Legend of Bonnie & Clyde* (1968); *Mama Tried* (1968); *Sing Me Back Home* (1968); *Pride in What I Am* (1969); *A Portrait of Merle Haggard* (1969); *Okie from Muskogee* (1969); *Same Train, Different Time* (1969); *Introducing My Friends, the Strangers* (1970); *The Fighting Side of Me* (1970); *A Tribute to the Best Damn Fiddle Player* (1970); *Honky Tonkin'* (1971); *Hag* (1971); *Someday We'll Look Back* (1971); *Land of Many Churches* (1971); *Let Me Tell You About a Song* (1972); *It's Not Love (But It's Not Bad)* (1972); *A Christmas Present* (1973); *If We Make It Through December* (1974); *My Love Affair with Trains* (1976); *Songs I'll Always Sing* (1976); *A Working Man Can't Get Nowhere Today* (1977); *Ramblin' Fever* (1977); *Eleven Winners* (1978); *All Night Long* (1978); *Serving 190 Proof* (1979); *The Way I Am* (1980); *Big City* (1981); *A Taste of Yesterday's Wine* (1982); *That's the Way Love Goes* (1983); *Pancho & Lefty* (1983); *It's All in the Game* (1984); *Kern River* (1985); *Merle Haggard—Songwriter* (1986); *Seashores of Old Mexico* (1987); *Chill Factor* (1988); *5:01 Blues* (1989); *Blue Jungle* (1990); *The Family Bible* (1992); *The One & Only* (1996); *Live at Billy Bob's Texas* (1999).—**RC**

Haggin, B(ernard) H., American music critic; b. N.Y., Dec. 29, 1900; d. there, May 29, 1987. He was a music critic for the *Brooklyn Daily Eagle* (1934–37) and the *Nation* (1936–57), and also wrote record reviews for the *Yale Review*. Haggin pursued a polemical style of personal journalism.

WRITINGS (all publ. in N.Y. unless otherwise given): *A Book of the Symphony* (1937); *Music on Records* (1938; 4th ed., 1945); *Music for the Man Who Enjoys Hamlet* (1944; 2nd ed., rev., 1960); *Music in The Nation* (1949); *The Listener's Musical Companion* (New Brunswick, N.J., 1956; new ed., 1991, by T. Hathaway); *Conversations with Toscanini* (Garden City, N.J., 1959; 2nd ed., 1979); *Music Observed* (1964); *The New Listener's Companion and Record Guide* (1967; 5th ed., 1978); *The Toscanini Musicians Knew* (1967); *A Decade of Music* (1973); *Music and Ballet, 1973–1983* (1984).—**NS/LK/DM**

Hägg (Peterson), Gustaf Wilhelm, eminent

Swedish organist and composer; b. Visby, Nov. 28, 1867; d. Stockholm, Feb. 7, 1925. Hägg was his mother's name, which he legally adopted; his father's name was Peterson. He was a remote relative of **Jakob Adolf Hägg**. He studied organ at the Stockholm Cons., and in 1893 he was appointed organist at the Klara Church in Stockholm, retaining this position for the rest of his life. In the interim he traveled for further study in Germany and France (1897–1900). In 1904 he joined the staff of the Stockholm Cons., as a teacher of harmony and organ playing. He enjoyed a distinguished reputation in Sweden as an organist, and gave numerous recitals in which he played the works of Cesar Franck and other organ composers. He also composed 5 organ concertos and other organ pieces, several cantatas, and songs. He arranged and publ. collections of Swedish songs (Stockholm, 1908), and an album, *Songs of Sweden* (N.Y., 1909). —**NS/LK/DM**

Hahn, Reynaldo, Venezuelan-born French con-

ductor, music critic, and composer; b. Caracas, Aug. 9, 1874; d. Paris, Jan. 28, 1947. His father, a merchant from Hamburg, settled in Venezuela c. 1850; the family moved to Paris when Reynaldo was 5 years old. He studied singing and apparently had an excellent voice; a professional recording he made in 1910 testifies to that. He studied theory with Dubois and Lavignac and composition with Massenet at the Paris Cons., who exercised the most important influence on Hahn's own music. He also studied conducting, achieving a high professional standard as an opera conductor. In 1934 he became music critic of *Le Figaro*. He remained in France during the Nazi occupation at a considerable risk to his life, since he was Jewish on his father's side. In 1945 he was named a member of the Institut de France and in 1945–46 was music director of the Paris Opéra. Hahn's music is distinguished by a facile, melodious flow and a fine Romantic flair. Socially, he was known in Paris for his brilliant wit. He maintained a passionate youthful friendship with Marcel Proust, who portrayed him as a poetic genius in his novel *Jean Santeuil*; their intimate correspondence was publ. in 1946. He was a brilliant journalist; his articles were publ. as *Du Chant* (Paris, 1920; 2nd ed., 1957), *Notes. Journal d'un musicien* (Paris, 1933), *L'Oreille au guet* (Paris, 1937), and *Thèmes variés* (Paris, 1946). A series of his letters dating from 1913–14 were publ. in an Eng. tr. by L. Simoneau as *On Singers and Singing* (Portland, Ore., 1990).

WORKS: DRAMATIC: *Fin d'amour*, ballet-pantomime (1892); *L'île du reve*, opera (Paris, March 23, 1898); *La carmélite*, opéra comique (Paris, Dec. 16, 1902); *La pastorale de Noël*, Christmas mystery (1908); *Le bal de Béatrice d'Este*, ballet (1909); *La fête chez Thérèse*, ballet (1909); *Le bois sacré*, ballet-pantomime (1912); *Le dieu bleu*, ballet (Paris, May 14, 1912); *Fête triomphale*, opera (Paris, July 14, 1919); *Nausicaa*, opéra comique (Monte Carlo, April 10, 1919); *La colombe de Bouddah*, conte lyrique (Cannes, March 21, 1921); *Ciboulette*, operetta (Paris, April 7, 1923); *Mozart*, musical comedy (Paris, Dec. 2, 1925); *La reine de Sheba*, scène lyrique (1926); *Une revue* (1926); *Le temps d'aimer*, musical comedy (Paris, Nov. 6, 1926); *Brummel*, operetta (1930; Paris, Jan. 20, 1931); *O mon bel inconnu!*, musical comedy (Paris, Oct. 5, 1933); *Malvina*, operetta (Paris, March 23, 1935); *Le marchand de Venise*, opera (Paris, March 25, 1935); *Beaucoup de bruit pour rien*, musical comedy (1936); *Aux bosquets d'Idalie*, ballet (1937); *Le oui des jeunes filles*, opera (orchestrated by H. Büsser; Paris, June 21, 1949); also incidental music to Daudet's *L'obstacle* (1890), Croisset's *Les deux courtisanes* (1902), Hugo's *Angelo* (1905), Racine's *Esther* (1905), Mendès's *Scarron* (1905), Hugo's *Lucrèce Borgia* (1911), and Magre's *Méduse* (1911). **ORCH.:** *Nuit d'amour bergamasque*, symphonic poem (1897); Violin Concerto (1927; Paris, Feb. 26, 1928); Piano Concerto (1930; Paris, Feb. 4, 1931); *Concerto provençal* (n.d.); *Strasbourg reconquise* (n.d.). **CHAMBER:** Violin Sonata (1927); 2 string quartets (n.d., 1943); Piano Quintet (n.d.); piano pieces, including *Portraits de peintres* (1894). **VOCAL:** *Prométhée triomphant* for Solo Voices, Chorus, and Orch. (1908); several song cycles.

BIBL.: D. Bendahan, *R. H. Su vida y su obra* (Caracas, 1973); B. Gavoty, *R. H.: Le Musicien de la belle époque* (Paris, 1976); M. Milanca Guzmán, *R. H., caraqueño: Contribución a la biografía caraqueña de R. H. Echenagucia* (Caracas, 1989).—**NS/LK/DM**

Haibel, (Johann Petrus) Jakob, Austrian

tenor and composer; b. Graz, July 20, 1762; d. Djakovar, March 24, 1826. He was engaged in Vienna as a tenor. In 1806 settled in Djakovar, where he married Sophie Weber, sister of Mozart's widow. He produced several stage works in Vienna, among them the ballet *Le nozze disturbate* (May 18, 1795) and a Singspiel, *Der Tyroler Wastl* (May 14, 1796), which became very popular. —**NS/LK/DM**

Haieff, Alexei (Vasilievich), Russian-Ameri-

can composer; b. Blagoveshchensk, Siberia, Aug. 25, 1914; d. Rome, March 1, 1994. He received his primary education at Harbin, Manchuria. In 1931 he went to the U.S., where he studied with Goldmark and Jacobi at the Juilliard School of Music in N.Y. (1934–38). In 1938–39 he also studied with Boulanger in Paris and in Cambridge, Mass. He held a Guggenheim fellowship in 1946 and again in 1949, and was a Fellow at the American Academy in Rome (1947–48). He was a prof. at the Univ. of Buffalo (1962–68), and composer-in-residence at the Univ. of Utah (1968–70). His Piano Concerto won the N.Y. Music Critics' Circle Award and his 2nd Sym. the American International Music Fund Award. In his music, Haieff followed Stravinsky's neo-Classicism, observing an austere economy of means, but achieving modernistic effects by a display of rhythmic agitation, often with jazzy undertones.

WORKS: DRAMATIC: Ballet: *The Princess Zondilda and Her Entourage* (1946); *Beauty and the Beast* (1947). **ORCH.:** 3 syms.: No. 1 (1942), No. 2 (Boston, April 11, 1958), and No. 3

(New Haven, Conn., April 11, 1961); Divertimento (N.Y., April 5, 1946); Violin Concerto (1948); Piano Concerto (N.Y., April 27, 1952); *Éloge* for Chamber Orch. (1967). **CHAMBER:** Sonatina for String Quartet (1937); *3 Bagatelles* for Oboe and Bassoon (1939); *Serenade* for Oboe, Clarinet, Bassoon, and Piano (1942); *Eclogue* for Cello and Piano (1947); *La Nouvelle Héloïse* for Harp and String Quartet (1963); Cello Sonata (1963); *Rhapsodies* for Guitar and Harpsichord (1980); Wind Quintet (1983). **P i a n o :** Sonata for 2 Pianos (1945); Sonata (1955). **VOCAL:** *Caligula* for Baritone and Orch., after Robert Lowell (N.Y., Nov. 5, 1971); songs.—**NS/LK/DM**

Haile, Eugen, German-American composer; b. Ulm, Feb. 21, 1873; d. Woodstock, N.Y., Aug. 14, 1933. He studied at the Stuttgart Cons. He emigrated to America in 1903. He wrote about 200 songs to German texts, some of them of excellent quality (*Herbst, Der Todesengel singt, Teufelslied, Soldaten kommen*, etc.). His musical setting to a spoken drama ("gesprochene Oper"), *The Happy Ending*, produced in N.Y. on Aug. 21, 1916, is an interesting attempt to combine spoken words in the play with pitch inflections in the vocal parts, in the manner of *Sprechtstimme*. His other opera, *Harold's Dream*, was produced in Woodstock on June 30, 1933. —**NS/LK/DM**

Hailstork, Adolphus (Cunningham), black American composer and teacher; b. Rochester, N.Y., April 17, 1941. He studied composition with Mark Fax at Howard Univ. in Washington, D.C. (B.Mus., 1963), Boulanger at the American Cons. in Fontainebleau (summer, 1963), Ludmila Ulehla, Flagello, Giannini, and Diamond at the Manhattan School of Music in N.Y. (B.Mus., 1965; M.Mus., 1966), and H. Owen Reed at Mich. State Univ. in East Lansing (Ph.D., 1971). He also attended sessions on synthesizer and computer music given by John Appleton and Herbert Howe at the N.H. Electronic Music Inst. (summer, 1972), and on contemporary music at the State Univ. of N.Y. at Buffalo (summer, 1978). In 1987 he held a Fulbright fellowship for study in Guyana. He taught at Mich. State Univ. (1969–71), Youngstown (Ohio) State Univ. (1971–76), and Norfolk (Va.) State Univ. (from 1977). Several of his works reflect his Afro- American experience. He has received various commissions, and a number of his works have been performed by major U.S. orchs.

WORKS: DRAMATIC: O p e r a : *Paul Laurence Dunbar: Common Ground* (1994). **ORCH.:** *Phaedra*, tone poem (1966); *SA-1* for Jazz Ensemble (1971); *Bellevue* (1974); *Celebration* for Orch. or Concert Band (1974); Concerto for Violin, Horn, and Orch. (1975); *American Landscape No. 1* for Concert Band (1977) and *No. 3* (1982); *Epitaph: In Memoriam: Martin Luther King Jr.* (1979); *Norfolk Pride*, march for Concert Band (1980); *Sport of Strings* for Strings (1982); *American Guernica* for Piano and Concert Band (1983); *An American Port of Call* (1984); *2 Struts with Blues* for Strings, Flute, Horn, and Jazz Quartet (1985); Sym. No. 1 (1988); *My Lord What a Mourning* for Chamber Orch. (1989); *Sonata da Chiesa* for Strings (1991); *Intrada* (1991); Piano Concerto (1992); *Festival Music* (1992); *And Deliver Us From Evil* for Band (1994). **CHAMBER:** Horn Sonata (1966); *Capriccio for a Departed Brother: Scott Joplin* for Strings (1969); *From the Dark Side of the Sun* for 3 Flutes, Soprano Saxophone, Strings, and Percussion (1971); String Sextet (1971);

Violin Sonata (1971); *Spiritual* for Brass Octet (1975); *American Landscape No. 2* for Violin and Cello (1978); *Variations* for Trumpet (1981); *Music* for 10 Players (1982); Trio for Violin, Cello, and Piano (1985); *3 Preludes* for Guitar (1989); *Arabesques* for Flute and Percussion (1991); *2 Impromptus* for Harp (1993); Consort Piece for Chamber Ensemble (1993). **P i a n o :** *Ignis Fatuus* (1976); *5 Friends* (1978); 2 sonatas (1980, 1989); *Reflections* (1981); Sonata for 2 Pianos (1987); Trio Sonata (1991). **VOCAL:** *My Name Is Toil* for Chorus, Brass, and Timpani (1973); *Oracle* for Tenor, Women's Chorus, 3 Flutes, 2 Percussion, and Tape (1977); *Psalm 72* for Chorus, Brass, and Organ (1981); *Look to this Day* for Chorus and Concert Band (1982); *Songs of Isaiah* for Chorus and Orch. (1987); *Break Forth* for Chorus, Organ, Brass, and Timpani (1990); *Hodie (Christus Natus Este)* for Chorus (1994); other choruses and songs.—**NS/LK/DM**

Haimovitz, Matt, Israeli-born American cellist; b. Tel Aviv, Dec. 3, 1970. His family emigrated to Calif. when he was 5. After taking lessons with Gabor Rejto, he studied with Leonard Rose and Channing Robbins at the Juilliard School in N.Y. (1982–87); also received private lessons with Yo-Yo Ma. He pursued his education at Princeton (1989–91) and Harvard (from 1993) univs. After winning the Avery Fisher Career Grant in 1985, he was engaged as a soloist with majors orchs. and as a recitalist in the U.S., Europe, and Israel. In 1988 he made his first tour of Japan. In 1989 he made a major recital tour of Europe, then of the U.S. in 1990. In 1991 he played the solo cello repertoire in N.Y. and Paris recitals, and also made his first tour of Australia. In addition to his appearances with orchs. and as a recitalist, Haimovitz has played in many chamber music settings. His adventuresome repertoire embraces masters from Bach to Ligeti.—**NS/LK/DM**

Hainl, François, French cellist, conductor, and composer; b. Issoire, Nov. 16, 1807; d. Paris, June 2, 1873. He was a pupil of Norblin at the Paris Cons., graduating with the premier prix in cello in 1830. After conducting at the Lyons Grand Théâtre (1841–63), he returned to Paris and conducted at the Opéra (1863–72), where he led the premieres of Meyerbeer's *L'africaine* (1865), Verdi's *Don Carlos* (1867), and Thomas's *Hamlet* (1868). He also was conductor of the Société des Concerts du Conservatoire (1863–72). He composed several cello pieces and publ. the vol. *De la musique à Lyons depuis 1713 jusqu'à 1852.*—**NS/LK/DM**

Haitink, Bernard (Johann Herman), eminent Dutch conductor; b. Amsterdam, March 4, 1929. He studied violin as a child, and later at the Amsterdam Cons., where he took a conducting course with Felix Hupka. He then played in the Radio Phil. in Hilversum. In 1954–55 he attended the conducting course of Ferdinand Leitner, sponsored by the Netherlands Radio. In 1955 he was appointed to the post of 2nd conductor of the Radio Phil. in Hilversum, becoming its principal conductor in 1957. In 1956 he made his first appearance as a guest conductor with the Concertgebouw Orch. of Amsterdam. He made his U.S. debut with the Los Angeles Phil. in 1958. In 1959 he conducted the Concertgebouw Orch. in England. In 1961 he became co-principal conductor of the Concertgebouw Orch., sharing his duties with Eugen Jochum; that same year, he led it on a tour of the U.S., followed by one to Japan in 1962. In 1964 he became chief conductor of the Concertgebouw Orch., a position he held with great distinction until 1988. In 1982 he led it on an acclaimed transcontinental tour of the U.S. In 1967 he also assumed the post of principal conductor and artistic adviser of the London Phil., later serving as its artistic director from 1969 to 1978. He made his first appearance at the Glyndebourne Festival in 1972, and from 1978 to 1988 was its music director. In 1977 he made his Covent Garden debut in London conducting *Don Giovanni*. On March 29, 1982, he made his debut at the Metropolitan Opera in N.Y. conducting *Fidelio*. In 1987 he became music director of the Royal Opera House at London's Covent Garden. On Dec. 1, 1999, Haitink conducted the gala performance at the reopening of the refurbished Royal Opera House. His tenure as its music director concluded in 2002. He also was guest conductor with the Berlin Phil., Vienna Phil., N.Y. Phil., Chicago Sym., Boston Sym., and Cleveland Orch. In his interpretations, Haitink avoids personal rhetoric, allowing the music to speak for itself. Yet he achieves eloquent and colorful effect; especially fine are his performances of the syms. of Bruckner and Mahler; equally congenial are his projections of the Classical repertoire. He has received numerous international honors, including the Netherlands' Royal Order of Orange-Nassau (1969), the Medal of Honor of the Bruckner Soc. of America (1970), and the Gustav Mahler Soc. Gold Medal (1971); he was named a Chevalier de l'Ordre des Arts et des Lettres of France (1972). He received the rare distinction of being made an Honorary Knight Commander of the Order of the British Empire by Queen Elizabeth II in 1977. In 1991 he was awarded the Erasmus Prize of the Netherlands.

BIBL.: S. Mundy, *B. H.: A Working Life* (London, 1987).
—NS/LK/DM

Haizinger, Anton, esteemed Austrian tenor; b. Wilfersdorf, March 14, 1796; d. Karlsruhe, Dec. 31, 1869. He studied harmony with Wölkert and voice with Mozzati in Vienna, and later was a student of Salieri. In 1821 he made his operatic debut as Gianetto in *La gazza ladra* at the Theater an der Wien. Weber chose him to create the role of Adolar in *Euryanthe* (Vienna, Oct. 25, 1823). After engagements in Prague, Pressburg, Frankfurt am Main, Mannheim, and Stuttgart, he was a member of the Théâtre-Italien in Paris (1829–30) and of Covent Garden in London (1832–33). Following appearances in St. Petersburg (1835) and Vienna (1838), he settled in Karlsruhe and ran his own singing school. He was the author of a manual on singing. Haizinger's most distinguished roles were Mozart's Tamino, Beethoven's Florestan, and Weber's Max.—NS/LK/DM

Hajdu, André, Hungarian-born Israeli composer and teacher; b. Budapest, March 5, 1932. He studied with Kodály, Szabó, Szervánszky, and Kosá at the Budapest Academy of Music (1947–56) and with Milhaud and Messiaen at the Paris Cons. (1957–59). He taught at the Tunis Cons. (1959–61). Hajdu emigrated to Israel in 1966, and in 1967 became a teacher at the Tel Aviv Academy of Music. In 1997 he received the Israel Music Prize. His music is folkloristic in its sources of inspiration, while the harmonic idiom is fairly advanced.

WORKS: DRAMATIC: *Jonah*, children's opera (1986). **ORCH.:** *A Little Hell* (1960); *Babeliana* (1964); 2 piano concertos (1968; 1988–90); *Terouath Melech*, Jewish rhapsody for Clarinet and Strings (1973); *Stories about Mischievous Boys* (1976); *Concerto for 10 Little Pianists and Grand Orchestra* (1978; also arranged for 2 Pianos); *Of Light and Depth: Preludes and Interludes* for Chamber Orch. (1983–84); *Overture in the Form of a Kite* (1985); *Little Sym.* for Winds (1988); *Symphonie Concertante* for Soloists and String Orch. (1993; Tel Aviv, May 18, 1994). **CHAMBER:** *Military Diary (The Art of the Canon)*, 50 canons for different instrumental combinations (1976); *5 Sketches in a Sentimental Mood* for Piano Quartet (1976); *Plasmas* for 10 Players (1982); String Quartet (1985); Octet (1989); *Black Upon White* for Piano (1989); *Continuum* for Piano and 15 Instruments (1996). **P i a n o :** *Book of Challenges I-IV* (1991–99). **VOCAL:** *Gypsy Cantata* (1956); *Ludus Paschalis* for 8 Soloists, Children's Chorus, and 9 Instruments (1970); *The Prophet of Truth and the Prophet of Deceit* for Narrator and String Orch. (1977); *Psalms* for Bass, Children's Choruses, and Orch. (1982); *Sueños en España*, cantata for Mezzo-soprano, Tenor, Children's Chorus, Mixed Chorus, and Orch. (1991; Jerusalem, Jan. 13, 1992); *Jacob and His Comforters*, oratorio (1992); *Ecclesiastes* for Narrator, Solo Cello, and Cello Ensemble (1994).—NS/LK/DM

Hajdu, Mihály, Hungarian composer and teacher; b. Orosháza, Jan. 30, 1909. He settled in Budapest and studied composition with Kodály and piano with Thomán and Székely at the Academy of Music (1929–33). After teaching in a private music school (1933–40), he taught at the Upper Music School (1941–49) and the Béla Bartók Music School (1949–60); subsequently he was prof. of theory at the Academy of Music (1960–77). In 1957 he received the Erkel Prize.

WORKS: DRAMATIC: O p e r a : *Kádár Kata* (1957). **ORCH.:** 2 suites (1934, 1958); *Serenade* (1941); *A munka dícsérete* (In Praise of Work), symphonic poem (1958); Piano Concertino (1962); *Capriccio all'ongarese* for Clarinet and Orch. (1969); *8 Etudes* for Youth String Orch. (1970); *Herendi porcelánok* (Herend Porcelain), suite (1976); *Divertimento* for Chamber Orch. (1978). **CHAMBER:** 2 string quartets (1936, 1970); Clarinet Duets (1951); *Magyar pásztordalok* (Hungarian Shepherd Songs) for Flute and Piano (1953); 2 violin sonatas (1953, 1977); *Variations and Rondo* for Cello and Piano (1955); *3 Clarinet Pieces* for Clarinet and Piano (1956); Piano Trio (1957); Wind Trio (1958); Cello Sonatina (1969); *30 Little Pieces* for Cello and Piano (1973; also for 2 Cellos); *2 Concert Études* for Harp (1978); *4 Movements* for Wind Quintet (1979). **P i a n o :** *3 Scherzos* (1931); *Elegy* (1932); Sonata (1940); Sonatina (1952); *5 Piano Pieces* (1955); *3 Pieces* for 2 Pianos (1971); *6 Bagatelles* (1987). **VOCAL:** Choruses; song cycles; solo songs; folk song arrangements. —NS/LK/DM

Håkanson, Knut (Algot), Swedish composer, pianist, conductor, teacher, and music critic; b. Kinna, Nov. 4, 1887; d. Göteborg, Dec. 13, 1929. He studied composition and counterpoint with Johan Lindegren in Stockholm (1906–08) and piano with Knut Bäck (1909–10). He also took courses in languages and philosophy at the Univ. of Uppsala (1906–13) before completing his musical training with Ruben Liljefors (1913–15) and on the Continent. He settled in Borås, where he was director of the orch. soc. (1916–25). He also was founder-director of the Borås Music Inst. (1922–25) and music critic of the *Göteborgs Handels-och sjöfarts-tidning* (from 1927). His most important compositions were classically inclined and often incorporated folk tunes he had collected.

WORKS: DRAMATIC: B a l l e t : *Mylitta* (1918). **ORCH.:** *Sérénade dramatique* for Violin and Orch. (1914); *Festmarsch* (1914; arranged as *Bröllopsmarsch* [Wedding March] for Organ or Piano); *Från skogstemplet* (From the Forest Temple; 1921–22; also for Piano); *Svensk svit* No. 1 for Piano and Orch. (1923; also for Piano and String Trio) and No. 2 (1925); *Marbolåtar* (Marbo Melodies; 1923; also for Piano); *Variationer och final över ett tema av Lomjansguten* (Variations and Finale on a Theme by Lomjansguten; 1926–28); *Divertimento* (1927). **CHAMBER:** 2 string trios; 2 string quartets; *Midsommarkransen* (Midsummer Wreath) for Clarinet Quintet (1921; also for Piano); *Prelude and Fugue* for String Trio (1928; also for Piano); piano pieces, including *10 variationer och fuga över en svensk folkvisa* (10 Variations and Fugue on a Swedish Folksong; 1929). **VOCAL:** *Skåne* for Solo Voices, Chorus, and Orch. (1928); *4 madrigaler* for Chorus (1929); *3 Karlfeldtskörer* for Chorus (1929); other choral pieces; about 120 solo songs; folk song arrangements.—**NS/LK/DM**

Hakenberger, Andreas,
German composer; b. Köslin, c. 1574; d. Danzig (buried), June 5, 1627. He was a singer and lutenist to King Sigismund III at the Polish royal chapel in Warsaw from 1602 to 1607. Although opposed by some on account of his Catholic faith, his admirable gifts as a composer won him the position of Kapellmeister at the Protestant Marienkirche in Danzig in 1608, a post he held with distinction for the rest of his life. Notable among his works is a vol. of 41 motets publ. as *Harmonia sacra* for 6 to 10 and 12 Voices with basso continuo (organ) (Frankfurt an der Oder, 1617). —**LK/DM**

Hakim, Talib Rasul (real name, Stephen Alexander Chambers),
black American composer; b. Asheville, N.C., Feb. 8, 1940; d. New Haven, Conn., March 31, 1988. He studied at the Manhattan School of Music in N.Y. (1958–59), the N.Y. Coll. of Music (1959–63), and Adelphi Univ. (1978). He taught at Pace Univ. (1970–72), Nassau Community Coll. (1971–81), Adelphi Univ. (1972–79), and Morgan State Univ. (1978–79). After converting to Sufism, he took the name Talib Rasul Hakim in 1973. His output followed a dissonant path.

WORKS: ORCH.: *Shapes* (1965); *Visions of Ishwara* (1970); *Re/Currences* (1974); *Concepts* (1976); *Arkan-5* for Orch. and Tape (1980); jazz band pieces. **CHAMBER:** *Peace-Mobile* for Wind Quintet (1964); *Encounter* for Wind Quintet, Trumpet, and Trombone (1965); *Portraits* for Flute, Bass Clarinet, Piano, and 3 Percussion (1965); *Currents* for String Quartet (1967); *Placements* for Piano and 5 Percussion (1970); *On Being Still-on the 8th Wind* for 4 Winds, Cello, Double Bass, Piano, and Percussion (1978); *Fragments from Other Places—Other Times* for 5 Percussion (1978); piano pieces. **VOCAL:** *Sound-Image* for Women's Voices, Brass, Strings, and Percussion (1969); *Tone-Prayers* for Chorus and Percussion (1973); *Music for Soprano and 9 Players* (1977); *Psalm of Akhnaton: ca. 1365–1348* for Mezzo-soprano, Piccolo or Flute or Alto Flute, and Piano (1978); *Quote-unquote* for Tenor, Oboe, Trumpet, and Percussion (1983); *Spiritual and Other Fragments from Another Time and Other Places* for Chorus, Winds, Brass, Piano, and Strings (1983); solo songs. —**NS/LK/DM**

Halász, László,
Hungarian-born American conductor; b. Debrecen, June 6, 1905. He studied piano and conducting at the Budapest Cons., graduating in 1929. He toured Europe as a pianist and conductor until emigrating to the U.S. in 1936, where he became a naturalized American citizen in 1943. He was music director of the St. Louis Grand Opera (1937–42). In 1944 he was appointed music director of the N.Y.C. Opera, where he established an audacious policy of producing modern operas, but became embroiled in personal difficulties with the management, and resigned in 1951. From 1949 to 1952 he conducted opera in Chicago, and from 1955 to 1959 was conductor of the German repertoire at the Barcelona Opera. He served as artistic director of N.Y.'s Empire State Music Festival (1957–65) and the National Grand Opera (from 1983). He was head of the conducting dept. at the Eastman School of Music in Rochester, N.Y. (1965–67), then was on the faculty of the State Univ. of N.Y. Coll. at Old Westbury (1968–71) and at Stony Brook (1971–75).—**NS/LK/DM**

Hale, Philip,
eminent American music critic; b. Norwich, Vt., March 5, 1854; d. Boston, Nov. 30, 1934. He took music lessons in his early youth, and as a boy played the organ in the Unitarian Church at Northampton, Mass. He went to Yale Univ. to study law, and was admitted to the bar in 1880. He then took organ lessons with Dudley Buck; subsequently went to Europe (1882–87), where he studied organ with Haupt in Berlin, and composition with Rheinberger in Munich and with Guilmant in Paris. Returning to America, he served as a church organist in Albany and Troy, N.Y., and in Boston, but soon abandoned this employment for his true vocation, that of drama and music critic. Hale was music critic for the *Boston Home Journal* (1889–91), the *Boston Post* (1890–91), the *Boston Journal* (1891–1903), and the *Boston Herald*, of which he was also drama ed. (1904–33). He was also ed. of the *Boston Musical Record* (1897–1901). From 1901 to 1933 he compiled the program books of the Boston Sym. Orch., setting a standard of erudition and informative annotation. He was joint author, with L. Elson, of *Famous Composers and Their Works* (1900), and was ed. of the collection *Modern French Songs* (2 vols., 1904). J. Burk ed. *Philip Hale's Boston Symphony Programme Notes* (Garden City, N.Y., 1935; 2nd ed., rev., 1939). Hale was a forceful and brilliant writer; his articles were often tinged with caustic wit directed against incompetent performers and, regrettably, against many modern composers; he also disliked Brahms, and was credited with the celebrated but possibly apocryphal quip that the exits in the newly opened Sym. Hall in Boston should have been marked not "Exit in Case of Fire," but "Exit in Case of Brahms." Another verbal dart attributed to Hale was his dismissal of a singer with the concluding sentence, "Valuable time was consumed."—**NS/LK/DM**

Hale, Robert, American bass-baritone; b. Kerrville, Tex., Aug. 22, 1943. He studied with Gladys Miller at the New England Cons. of Music in Boston, with Ludwig Bergman at Boston Univ., in Okla., and with Boris Goldovsky in N.Y. In 1965 he made his operatic debut as Mozart's Figaro in Denver, and then joined the N.Y.C. Opera in 1967. He made guest appearances in Philadelphia, Pittsburgh, San Diego, San Francisco, and other U.S. opera centers. In 1978 he made his European debut in Stuttgart as the Dutchman. He sang Escamillo in Cologne in 1983. After appearing as Scarpia in Berlin in 1987, he sang for the first time at London's Covent Garden in 1988 as Jochanaan. On Jan. 17, 1990, he made his Metropolitan Opera debut in N.Y. as the Dutchman, the same year that he appeared as Pizarro at the Salzburg Festival and as Wotan at the San Francisco Opera. In 1992 he sang Barak at the Salzburg Festival. During the 1992–93 season, he appeared as Wotan in the *Ring* cycle at the Vienna State Opera, and then sang that role at the Théâtre du Châtelet in Paris in 1994 and at the Metropolitan Opera in 1996. He married **Inga Nielsen.** —NS/LK/DM

Halévy (real name, **Levy**), (**Jacques-François-**) **Fromental (-Elie),** celebrated French composer; b. Paris, May 27, 1799; d. Nice, March 17, 1862. The family changed its name to Halévy in 1807. He entered the Paris Cons. at age 9 as a student of Cazot, then studied with Lambert (piano), Berton (harmony), and Cherubini (counterpoint); he also studied with Méhul, winning the 2nd Prix de Rome in 1816 and 1817 and the Grand Prix de Rome in 1819 with his cantata *Herminie*. He became chef du chant at the Théâtre-Italien in 1826. His first stage work to be performed was the opéra-comique *L'Artisan* (Opéra-Comique, Jan. 30, 1827), which had a modicum of success. He gained further notice with his *Clari*, introduced to Paris by Malibran (Théâtre-Italien, Dec. 9, 1828). His first major success came with *Le Dilettante d'Avignon* (Opéra-Comique, Nov. 7, 1829). He then was chef du chant at the Paris Opéra (1829–45), where he scored his greatest triumph with *La Juive* (Feb. 23, 1835), which established his name and was performed throughout Europe and the U.S. His next opera, *L'Éclair* (Opéra-Comique, Dec. 16, 1835), also enjoyed a favorable reception. Among later operas of note were *La Reine de Chypre* (Dec. 22, 1841), *Charles VI* (March 15, 1843), and *La Magicienne* (March 17, 1858), all first performed at the Opéra. He was also active as a teacher at the Paris Cons., being made a prof. of harmony and accompaniment (1827), of counterpoint and fugue (1833), and of composition (1840). His students included Gounod, Bizet (who became his son-in-law), and Saint-Saëns. He was elected to membership in the Institut in 1836, and served as its secretary from 1854. Halévy was an extremely apt composer for the stage, winning the admiration of both Berlioz and Wagner. Yet he could never equal Meyerbeer in popular success; as time went by, only *La Juive* gained a permanent place in the world repertoire.

WRITINGS: *Leçons de lecture musicale ... pour les écoles de la ville de Paris* (Paris, 1857); *Souvenirs et portraits* (Paris, 1861); *Derniers souvenirs et portraits* (Paris, 1863).

WORKS: DRAMATIC: Opera (all 1st perf. in Paris unless otherwise given): *L'Artisan*, opéra-comique (Jan. 30, 1827); *Le Roi et le batelier*, opéra-comique (Nov. 8, 1827; in collaboration with L. Rifaut); *Clari*, opera semi-seria (Théâtre-Italien, Dec. 9, 1828); *Le Dilettante d'Avignon*, opéra-comique (Nov. 7, 1829); *Attendre et courir*, opéra-comique (May 28, 1830; in collaboration with H. de Ruolz); *La Langue musicale*, opéra-comique (Dec. 11, 1830); *La Tentation*, ballet-opera (Opéra, June 20, 1832; in collaboration with C. Gide); *Les Souvenirs de Lafleur*, opéra-comique (March 4, 1833); *Ludovic*, opéra-comique (May 16, 1833; completion of an opera by Herold); *La Juive* (Feb. 23, 1835); *L'Éclair*, opéra-comique (Dec. 16, 1835); *Guido et Ginevra, ou La Peste de Florence* (March 5, 1838); *Les Treize*, opéra-comique (April 15, 1839); *Le Sherif*, opéra-comique (Sept. 2, 1839); *Le Drapier* (Jan. 6, 1840); *Le Guitarrero*, opéra-comique (Jan. 21, 1841); *La Reine de Chypre* (Dec. 22, 1841); *Charles VI* (March 15, 1843); *Le Lazzarone, ou Le Bien vient en dormant* (March 23, 1844); *Les Mousquetaires de la reine*, opéra-comique (Feb. 3, 1846); *Les Premiers Pas*, prologue (Opéra-National, Nov. 15, 1847; in collaboration with Adam, Auber, and Carafa); *Le Val d'Andorre*, opéra-comique (Nov. 11, 1848); *La Fée aux roses*, opéra-comique (Oct. 1, 1849); *La Tempestà*, opera italien (Her Majesty's Theatre, London, June 8, 1850); *La Dame de pique*, opéra-comique (Dec. 28, 1850); *Le Juif errant* (Opéra, April 23, 1852); *Le Nabab*, opéra-comique (Sept. 1, 1853); *Jaguarita l'indienne*, opéra-comique (Théâtre-Lyrique, May 14, 1855); *L'Inconsolable*, opéra-comique (Théâtre-Lyrique, June 13, 1855; perf. under the nom de plume Alberti); *Valentine d'Aubigny*, opéra-comique (April 26, 1856); *La Magicienne* (March 17, 1858); *Noé* (unfinished; completed by Bizet and perf. as *Le Déluge*, Karlsruhe, April 5, 1885); *Vanina d'Ornano* (unfinished). **Ballet:** *Manon Lescaut* (Opéra, May 3, 1830). **OTHER:** *Les Derniers Moments du Tasse*, cantata (won 2nd Prix de Rome, 1816); *La Mort*, cantata (won 2nd Prix de Rome, 1817); *Herminie*, cantata (won Grand Prix de Rome, 1819); *Marche funèbre et De profundis* for 3 Voices and Orch. (1820); *Ouverture* for Orch. (1822); *Les Cendres de Napoléon* for Military Band (1840); *Les Plages du Nil* for Voice and Piano (1846); *Prométhée enchaîné* for Solo Voices, Chorus, and Orch. (1849); *Ave verum* for Solo Voices, Chorus, and Orch. (1850); *Messe de l'Orphéon* for 4 Men's Voices, Sopranos, and Organ ad libitum (1851; *Agnus Dei* and *Sanctus* by Halévy; remainder by Adam and Clapisson); *Cantata* (1856); *Italie*, cantata (1859); *La Nouvelle Alliance* for 4 Men's Voices (1860); *France et Italie* for 4 Men's Voices (1860); *Come dolce a me favelli*, cavatina for Voice and Orch.; other vocal works; piano pieces.

BIBL.: C. de Lorbac, *Fromenthal H.: Sa vie, ses oeuvres* (Paris, 1862); L. Halévy, *F. H.: Sa vie et ses oeuvres* (Paris, 1862; 2nd ed., 1863); A. Catelin, *F. H.: Notice biographique* (Paris, 1863); E. Monnais, *F. H.: Souvenirs d'un ami* (Paris, 1863); A. Pougin, *F. H.: Écrivain* (Paris, 1865); R. Jordan, *F. H.: His Life and Music, 1799–1862* (London, 1994).—NS/LK/DM

Halffter (Escriche), Ernesto, esteemed Spanish composer and conductor, brother of **Rodolfo Halffter (Escriche)** and uncle of **Cristóbal Halffter (Jiménez-Encina);** b. Madrid, Jan. 16, 1905; d. there, July 5, 1989. He was trained in composition by Manuel de Falla and Adolfo Salazar. At the outbreak of the Spanish Civil War in 1936, he went to Lisbon. In 1960 he returned to Madrid. In addition to Falla, his output reflects the influence of such French masters as Ravel and Poulenc. He completed and orchestrated Falla's scenic cantata *Atlántida* (Milan, June 18, 1962; later rev. and perf. in concert form, Lucerne, Sept. 9, 1976).

WORKS: DRAMATIC: C h a m b e r   O p e r a :
Entr'acte (1964). **B a l l e t :** *Sonatina* (1928); *Dulcinea* (1940);
Cojo enamorado (1954); *Fantasía galaica* (1955). **ORCH.:** Sinfo-
nietta (Oxford, July 23, 1931); *Fantaisie portugaise* (Paris, March
23, 1941); *Rapsodia portuguesa* for Piano and Orch. (1962); Guitar
Concerto (1968). **VOCAL:** *Canticum in memoriam P. P. Johan-
nem XXIII* for Soprano, Baritone, Chorus, and Orch. (1964);
Psalmen for Soloist, Chorus, and Orch. (1967).—**NS/LK/DM**

Halffter (Escriche), Rodolfo, eminent Spanish-
born Mexican composer and pedagogue, brother of
Ernesto Halffter (Escriche) and uncle of **Cristóbal
Halffter (Jiménez- Encina);** b. Madrid, Oct. 30, 1900; d.
Mexico City, Oct. 14, 1987. He was mainly autodidact
although he received some instruction from Falla in
Granada (1929). Halffter became a prominent figure in
the promotion of modern Spanish music, and was made
chief of the music section of the Ministry of Propaganda
(1936) and then a member of the Central Music Council
(1937) of the Spanish Republic. Following the defeat of
the regime in the Spanish Civil War, Halffter fled in 1939
to France and then to Mexico, where he became a
naturalized Mexican citizen. In 1940 he founded the
contemporary ballet ensemble La Paloma Azul. From
1941 to 1970 he taught at the Conservatorio Nacional de
México in Mexico City. In 1946 he founded the publishing firm Ediciones Mexicanas de Música and the journal
Nuestra Música, which he ed. until 1952. In 1969 he was
made a member of the Academia de Artes de Mexico
and in 1984 he was made an honorary member of the
Real Academia de Bellas Artes in Madrid. In his early
works, Halffter followed in the path of Falla but he later
explored contemporary techniques, including 12–tone
writing. His *Tres Hojas de Álbum* (1953) was the earliest
12–tone music publ. in Mexico.

WORKS: DRAMATIC: *Clavileño*, opera buffa (1934–36;
not extant); *Don Lindo de Almería*, ballet (1935; Mexico City, Jan.
9, 1940; orch. suite, 1936); *La madrugada del panadero*, ballet
(Mexico City, Sept. 20, 1940; orch. suite, 1940); *Lluvia de toros*,
ballet (1940); *Elena la traicionera*, ballet (Mexico City, Nov. 23,
1945); *Tonanzintla*, ballet (1951; also as *Tres Sonatas de Fray
Antonio* for Orch.); much film music. **ORCH.:** *Tres piezas*
(1924–25; rev. as an orch. suite, 1924–28; rev. 1930; Madrid, Nov.
5, 1930); *Diferencias sobre La Gallarda Milanesa de Félix Antonio de
Cabezón* (1930); *Obertura concertante* for Piano and Orch. (1932;
rev. version, Valencia, May 23, 1937); *Impromptu* (1932; not
extant); *Preludio atonal: Homenaje a Arbós* (1933); Violin Concerto
(1939–40; Mexico City, June 26, 1942; rev. 1952); *Tres Sonatas de
Fray Antonio Soler* (1951; also as the ballet *Tonanzintla*); *Obertura
festiva* (1952; Mexico City, May 25, 1953); *Tres piezas* for Strings
(1954; Mexico City, Aug. 10, 1955); *Tripartita* or *Tres piezas* (1959;
Mexico City, July 15, 1960); *Diferencias* (Mexico City, Sept. 13,
1970; rev. 1975 and 1985); *Alborada* (1975; Mexico City, May 9,
1976; incorporated in *Dos ambientes sonoros*, 1975–79); *Dos
ambientes sonoros* (1975–79; incorporates *Alborada*, 1975); *Elegía:
In memoriam Carlos Chávez* for Strings (1978). **CHAMBER:**
Giga for Guitar (1930); *Divertimento* for String Quartet (1930;
not extant); *Pastorale* for Violin and Piano (1940); *Tres piezas
breves* for Harp (1951); Quartet for String Instruments (1957–58);
Cello Sonata (1959–60); *Tres movimientos* for String Quartet
(1962); *Ocho tientos* for String Quartet (1973); *Capricho* for Violin
(1978); *Epinicio* for Flute (1979); *...huésped de las nieblas...Rimas sin
palabras* for Flute and Piano (1981); *Egloga* for Oboe and Piano
(1982); *Paquiliztli* for 7 Percussion (1983). **P i a n o :** *Naturaleza

muerta (1922); *Dos Sonatas de El Escorial* (1928; rev. 1929); *Preludio
y fuga* (1932); *Danza de Avila: En lo alto de aquella montaña* (1936);
Perpetuum mobile: Homenage a Francis Poulenc (1936); *Para la
tumba de Lenin: Variaciones elegíacas* (1937); *Muñieira des vellas*
(1938); *Homenaje a Antonio Machado* (1944); 3 sonatas (1947, 1951,
1967); *Once bagatelas* (1949); *Al sol puesto* (1952); *Copla* (1952);
Tonada (1952); *Tres hojas de álbum* (1953); *Música* for 2 Pianos
(1965); *Laberinto: Cuatro intentos de acertar con la salida* (1971–72);
Nocturno: Homenaje a Arturo Rubinstein (1973); *Facetas* (1976);
Secuencias (1977); *Escolio* (1980); *Una vez y otra, con coda: Cantilena variada* (1982). **VOCAL:** *Marinero en Tierra* for Voice and
Piano (1925–60); *Canciones de la Guerra Civil Española* for Solo-
ists, Chorus, and Orch. (1937–38); *Dos Sonetos* for Voice and
Piano (1940–46); *La nuez* for Children's Chorus (1944); *Tres
Epitafios* for Chorus (1947–53); *Desterro* for Voice and Piano
(1967); *Pregón para una pascua pobre* for Chorus, Trumpets,
Trombones, and Percussion (1968).

BIBL.: J. Alcaraz, *R. H.* (Madrid, 1987); X. Ruiz Ortiz, *R. H.:
Antología, Introducción y Catalogos* (Mexico City, 1990); A. Igle-
sias, *R. H.: Tema, Nueve décadas y Final* (Madrid, 1991).
—**NS/LK/DM**

Halffter (Jiménez-Encina), Cristóbal, prominent Spanish composer and conductor, nephew of
Ernesto Halffter and **Rodolfo Halffter (Escriche);** b.
Madrid, March 24, 1930. He studied composition with
Conrado del Campo at the Madrid Cons. (1947–51) and
with Tansman in Paris (1959). From 1953 he was active
as a conductor in Spain, and later conducted abroad.
After serving as a teacher of composition (1961–66) and
as director (1964–66) at the Madrid Cons., he lectured at
the Univ. of Navarra (1970–78). He was president of the
Spanish section of the ISCM (1976–78). In 1979 he was
artistic director of the electronic music studio of the
Heinrich Strobel-Stiftung in Freiburg im Breisgau. He
was made a member of the Royal Academy of Fine Arts
of San Fernando in 1983, of the Berlin Academy of Arts
in 1985, and of the Swedish Royal Academy in Stockholm in 1988. As a composer, Halffter has perfected a
highly personal style that makes use of the full range of
contemporary means of expression, from dodecaphony
to electronics.

WORKS: DRAMATIC: *Saeta*, ballet (Madrid, Oct. 28,
1955); *El pastor y la estrella*, children's television chamber opera
(Madrid, Dec. 28, 1959); *Don Quijote*, opera (Madrid, Feb. 23,
2000). **ORCH.:** *Scherzo* (1951); 2 piano concertos (1952–53, rev.
1956; 1987); Concertino for Strings (1956; also as String Quartet
No. 1, *Tres piezas*, 1955); *Dos movimientos* for Timpani and
Strings (1956); *Partita* for Cello and Orch. (1957–58; also for
Guitar and Orch., 1973); *Cinco Microformas* (1959–60); *Rapsodia
española* for Piano and Orch. (1959–60); *Sinfonía* for 3 Instrumental Groups (1961–63); *Secuencias* (1964); *Líneas y puntos* for 20
Winds and Electronics (1966); *Anillos* (1967–68; rev. 1969);
Fibonaciana for Flute and Orch. (1969); *Requiem por la libertad
imaginada* (1971); *Pinturas negras* for Orch. and Concertante
Organ (1972); 2 cello concertos (1974; *...No queda más que el
silencio...*, 1985); *Tiempo para espacios* for Harpsichord and Strings
(1974); *Elegías a la muerte de tres poetas españoles* (1975); 2 violin
concertos: No. 1 (1979) and No. 2 for Violin and Strings
(1990–91); *Tiento* (1980–81); *Fantasía über einen Klang von G. F.
Händel* for 4, 8, or 12 Cellos and String Orch. (1981); *Sinfonía
ricercata* for Organ and Orch. (1982); *Versus* (1983); Double
Concerto for Violin, Viola, and Orch. (1984); *Paráfrasis über die
Fantasía über einen Klang von G. F. Händel* (1984); *Tiento del primer

tono y batalla imperial (1986); *Dortmunder Variationen* (1986–87); *Preludio à Nemesis* (1988–89); Saxophone Quartet Concerto (1989–90; also as *Fractal* for Saxophone Quartet, 1991); *Pasacalle escurialense* for Strings (1992); *Mural Sonante* (1993–94); *Odradek: Hommage à Franz Kafka* (Prague, March 13, 1997). **CHAMBER:** 3 string quartets: No. 1, *Tres piezas* (1955; also as the Concertino for String Orch., 1956), No. 2, *Mémoires 1970* (1970; also as *Pourquoi* for 12 Strings, 1974), and No. 3 (1978); *Tres piezas* for Flute (1959; also as the Sonata for Solo Violin, 1959); *Epitafio a Ramón Gómez de la Serna* for 3 Percussion and Tape (1963; also as *Espejos* for 4 Percussion and Tape, 1963); *Codex* for Guitar (1963); *Antiphonismoi* for Flute, Oboe, Clarinet, Violin, Viola, Cello, and Piano (1967); *Oda para felicitar a un amigo* for Flute, Bass Clarinet, Viola, Cello, and Percussion (1969); *Planto por las víctimas de la violencia* for Chamber Ensemble and Electronics (1970–71); *Noche activa del espíritu* for 2 Pianos and Ring Modulators (1972–73); *Procesional* for 2 Pianos, Winds, and Percussion (1973–74); *Variation über das Thema eSACHERe* for Cello (1975); *Variaciones sobre la resonancia de un grito* for 11 Instruments, Tape, and Electronics (1976–77); *Mizar I* for 2 Flutes, 3 Percussion, and Strings (1977; also as *Mizar II* for 2 Flutes and Electronics, 1979); *Adieu* for Harpsichord (1978); *Debla* for Flute (1980); Concerto for Flute and String Sextet (1982); *Canción callada* for Violin, Cello, and Piano (1988); *Fandango* for 8 or More Cellos (1988–89); *Con bravura y sentimiento* for String Quartet (1991); *Fractal* for Saxophone Quartet (1991; also as the Saxophone Quartet Concerto, 1989–90); *Tinguely-Fanfare* for Brass Ensemble (Basel, Sept. 30, 1996); Sonata for Solo Guitar (Vienna, Nov. 11, 1998). **KEYBOARD: P i a n o :** Sonata (1951); *Introducción, fuga y final* (1957); *Formantes* for 2 Pianos (1960–61); *Cadencia* (1983); *El ser humano muere solamente cuando lo olvidan* (1987). **O r g a n :** *Ricercare* (1981). **VOCAL:** *Antífona Pascual* for Soloists, Chorus, and Orch. (1952); *Dos canciones* for Soprano and Guitar (1952; also for Soprano and Chamber Orch., 1955); *Misa Ducal* for Chorus and Organ or Orch. (1955–56); *In Exspectatione Resurrectionis Domini*, cantata for Baritone, Men's Chorus, Mixed Chorus ad libitum, and Orch. (1961; rev. 1964–65); *Drei Brechtlieder* for Medium Voice and 2 Pianos (1964–65; also for Medium Voice and Orch., 1967); *Misa da la juventud* for Chorus and Orch. (1965); *Symposion* for Baritone, Chorus, and Orch. (1965–66; rev. 1972); *In Memoriam Anaïck* for Child Speaker, Chorus, Winds, and Percussion (1966); *Yes, speak out, yes* for Soprano, Baritone, 2 Choruses, 2 Orchs., and 2 Conductors (1968; rev. 1969); *Noche pasiva del sentido* for Soprano, 2 Percussion, and Electronics (1969–70); *Faudium et Spes—Beunza* for 2 Choruses and Tape (1971–73); *Oración a Plutero* for Speaker, Children's Chorus, Mixed Chorus, and 5 Percussion (1974); *Officium Defunctorum* for Soloists, Chorus, Children's Voices, and Orch. (1977–78); *Jarchas del dolor de ausencia* for 12 Voices (1978–79); *Himno a Santa Teresa* for Soprano, Chorus, Winds, Percussion, and Organ (1981); *Leyendo a Jorge Guillén* for Speaker, Viola, and Cello (1982); *Dona nobis pacem* for Chorus and Instruments (1983–84); *Tres poemas de la lìrica española* for Baritone and Orch. (1985–86); *Canciones de Al Andalus* for Mezzo-soprano and String Quartet (1987–88); *Dos motetes* for 3 Choruses (1988; also as *Dos corales litúrgicos* for 3 Choruses and Instrumental Ensemble, 1990); *Muerte, mudanza y locura* for Voice and Electronics (1989); *Preludio para Madrid '92* for Chorus and Orch. (1991); *Siete cantos de España* for Soprano, Baritone, and Orch. (1991–92); *Veni creator spiritus* for 2 Choruses and Instrumental Ensemble (1992). **OTHER:** *Nocturno (30 de Mayo de 1972)*, tape collage (1972); *...La soledad sonora/La música callada...*, audio-visual environment (1982–83).

BIBL.: T. Marco, *C. H.* (Madrid, 1972); E. Casares Rodicio, *C. H.* (Oviedo, 1980).—NS/LK/DM

Halir, Karl (original name, **Karel Haliř**), Bohemian violinist and teacher; b. Hohenelbe, Feb. 1, 1859; d. Berlin, Dec. 21, 1909. He was a student of Bennewitz at the Prague Cons. (1867–73) and of Joachim in Berlin (1874–76). He was concertmaster of the Weimar Court Orch. (1883–93) and of the Berlin Royal Opera Orch. (1893–97). After touring the U.S. in 1896–97, he became 2nd violin in the Joachim Quartet in 1897. He also led his own quartet and was a prof. at the Berlin Hochschule für Musik. He prepared a vol. of violin exercises, *Neue Tonleiterstudien*. In 1888 he married the soprano Teresa Zerbst.—NS/LK/DM

Hall, David, American writer on music; b. New Rochelle, N.Y., Dec. 16, 1916. He was educated at Yale Univ. (B.A., 1939) and Columbia Univ. (graduate study in psychology, 1939–40). He worked for Columbia Records and NBC (1942–48); from 1948 to 1956 he was music director of the classics division of the Mercury Record Corp., where he pioneered in the development of high-fidelity recordings; then was music ed. of *Stereo Review* (1957–62); later was president of Composers Recordings, Inc. (1963–66). From 1967 to 1980 he was head of the Rodgers and Hammerstein Archives of Recorded Sound at the N.Y. Public Library, and from 1980 its curator. He publ. several annotated guides to recordings; also contributed countless articles and record reviews to leading publications.—NS/LK/DM

Hall, Frederick Douglass, black American music educator and composer; b. Atlanta, Dec. 14, 1898; d. there, Dec. 28, 1982. He studied at Morehouse Coll. in Atlanta (B.A., 1921), Chicago Musical Coll. (B.Mus., 1924), Columbia Univ. Teachers Coll. (M.A., 1929; D.Mus. Ed., 1952), Royal Academy of Music in London (licentiate), and Univ. of London (1933–35). He taught at various institutions, including Dillard Univ. in New Orleans (1936–41; 1960–74), where he led a male quartet, and Ala. State Coll. in Montgomery (1941–55). His compositions include an oratorio, *Deliverance* (1938), a song-cycle, *Afro-American Religious Work Songs* (1952), and some 20 art songs. He also prepared choral arrangements of spirituals (6 vols., 1929–55).—NS/LK/DM

Hall, Jim (actually, **James Stanley**), revered jazz guitarist, composer; b. Buffalo, N.Y., Dec. 4, 1930. He spent his early years in Cleveland; his mother was a pianist, and other relatives were also musical, including his uncle who played guitar. Hall began working in local bands from the age of 13. During his teen years, he studied with guitarist Fred Sharp, who had previously worked with Red Norvo in N.Y. and introduced Hall to the music of Django Reinhardt. Hall studied theory at the Cleveland Inst. of Music (1955). On graduation, he moved to L.A. and worked with a variety of ensembles, beginning with the Jimmy Giuffre Three and Chico Hamilton quintet. In 1958, Hall moved to N.Y. Hall popularized the rhythms of bossa nova in the U.S. with his collaborative album (with Sonny Rollins) *What's*

New, which was produced in 1962 after Hall's visit to Brazil in May of 1960. He toured and recorded with Rollins (1961–62), then Art Farmer (1963–65). During this time he also recorded a celebrated series of LPs with Paul Desmond, and experimented with classical "third-stream" music with John Lewis and Gunther Schuller. In the 1960s Hall also worked as a studio guitarist for the Merv Griffin TV show. In 1966, he formed a partnership with bassist Ron Carter, and the two often worked together through the 1970s and 1980s. From 1978–79, Hall played with experimental trombonist Bob Brookmeyer; later, in 1984, he was featured in a symphonic work by Brookmeyer written for the Stockholm Radio Sym. Hall has continued to record and tour widely in a variety of settings; besides his own trio, he has worked with artists as wide-ranging as classical violinist Itzhak Perlman and fusion-jazz musicians like Wayne Shorter. He was the subject of a tribute concert as part of the 1990 JVC festival and won the Jazzpar Award 1998. A scholarship fund at Berklee Coll. is named in his honor. Of late, Hall has focussed his attention on composing chamber music; he teaches jazz ensemble at N.Y.'s New School. Hall is admired among guitarists and jazz sophisticates for his purity of tone, imagination, and elegant taste. He has been a primary influence on a whole school of players including Pat Metheny and Bill Frisell.

DISC.: *Jazz Guitar* (1957); *Good Friday Blues* (1960); *Guitar Workshop* (1967); *Where Would I Be?* (1971); *It's Nice to Be with You* (1971); *Alone Together* (1972); *J. H. Live!* (1975); *Concierto* (1975); *Commitment* (1976); *J. H. and Red Mitchell* (1978); *Circles* (1981); *Live at Village West* (1985); *J. H.'s Three* (1986); *Subsequently* (1990); *Live at Town Hall, Vols. 1 & 2* (1990); *Youkali* (1992); *Dedications and Inspirations* (1993); *Textures* (1997; chamber music by Hall). Art Farmer: *"Live" at the Half-Note* (1963).—**LP/NS**

Hall, John, English physician and writer on medicine and religion; b. c. 1529; d. c. 1566. He publ. a collection of didactic and sacred verses as *The Court of Vertue* (London, 1565; ed. by R. Fraser, London, 1961), for which, it is assumed, he also composed the music. —**NS/LK/DM**

Hall, Marie (actually, **Mary Paulina**), English violinist; b. Newcastle upon Tyne, April 8, 1884; d. Cheltenham, Nov. 11, 1956. As a small child, she gave performances in the homes of music-lovers in Newcastle, Malvern, and Bristol with her father, an amateur harp player, her uncle (violin), her brother (violin), and her sister (harp). Elgar heard her, and was impressed by her talent; he sent her to Wilhelmj in London for regular study; she also studied with Johann Kruse. At the age of 15, she won the 1st Wessely Exhibition at the Royal Academy of Music. She was recommended by Jan Kubelik to Ševčik in Prague (1901), from whom she received a rigorous training; she made her professional debut in Prague (1902); then played in Vienna. After a highly successful London concert (Feb. 16, 1903), she made her American debut as soloist with the N.Y. Sym. Orch., Walter Damrosch conducting (Nov. 8, 1905); toured Australia (1907) and India (1913). On Jan. 27,

1911, she married her manager, Edward Baring, and settled in Cheltenham; she continued to appear in concerts in England until 1955, with her daughter, Pauline Baring, as her accompanist.—**NS/LK/DM**

Hall, Minor (Ram), jazz drummer, brother of **Tubby Hall;** b. Sellers, La., March 2, 1897; d. Los Angeles, Calif., Oct. 16, 1959. Hall's family is related to the New Orleans Humphrey family. He moved with his family to New Orleans during the early 1900s and studied at New Orleans Univ. until 1914. He did his first paid gigs for Henry Martin in Kid Ory's Band. He later worked regularly with bassist Oke Gaspard and the Superior Band. He moved with his family in 1917 to Chicago, replacing his brother Tubby in Lawrence Duhe's Band at the De Lure Cafe, and then served in U.S. Army (1918–19). He played drums with King Oliver from 1921–22 in Chicago and went with the band to San Francisco; however, he left after two months (replaced by Baby Dodds), returning to play in Chicago with Jimmie Noone's Band. In 1927 Hall moved to Calif. permanently and played with Mutt Carey's Jeffersonians until 1932 (mainly in Culver City). Hall played regularly with the Winslow Allen Band during the 1930s. He spent six months in the U.S. Army from September 1942, and then was given honorable discharge and began working in the Douglas Aircraft factory. In 1945 he returned to regular playing in Kid Ory's Band, working with Ory until being taken ill on a European tour in 1956. He suffered from cancer during the last years of his life, but played occasionally with the New Orleans Creole Jazz Band early in 1959 before entering the hospital for a final time.—**JC/LP**

Hall, Pauline (Margarete), Norwegian composer; b. Hamar, Aug. 2, 1890; d. Oslo, Jan. 24, 1969. She studied piano with Johan Backer Lunde (1908–10) and theory and composition with Catharinus Elling (1910–12) in Christiania, then completed her studies in Paris and Dresden (1912–14). She was the Berlin music and drama correspondent for the Norwegian newspaper *Dagbladet* (1926–32), and then was its music critic in Oslo (1934–42; 1945–64). In her early works, she was greatly influenced by French Impressionism. She later evolved a neo-Classical style seasoned by disturbing dissonance.

WORKS: DRAMATIC: *Markisen* (The Marquise), ballet (1950); incidental music. **ORCH.:** *Poème élégiaque* (1920); *Verlaine Suite* (1929); *Cirkusbilder* (1939). **CHAMBER:** Suite for Wind Quintet (1945); *Little Dance Suite* for Oboe, Clarinet, and Bassoon (1958); *4 tosserier* for Soprano, Clarinet, Bassoon, Horn, and Trumpet (1961); *Variations on a Classical Theme* for Flute (1961); piano pieces. **VOCAL:** Choral works; songs. —**NS/LK/DM**

Hall, Robert Browne, American cornetist, bandmaster, and composer; b. Bowdoinham, Maine, June 30, 1858; d. Portland, Maine, June 8, 1907. He began cornet studies in childhood, and after playing in bands in Maine and Boston, he was made director of the Bangor (Maine) Band (1882). He later became director of the Waterville (Maine) Military Band (c. 1890). He wrote a number of marches, which led to his being described as the "New England March King."—**NS/LK/DM**

Hall, Sir Peter (Reginald Frederick), noted English theater and opera producer; b. Bury St. Edmunds, Nov. 22, 1930. He was educated at St. Catharine's Coll., Cambridge. In 1955–56 he was director of the Arts Theatre, London. He was managing director of the Royal Shakespeare Theatre from 1960 to 1968; from 1973 to 1988 he was director of the National Theatre; worked also at the Royal Opera House, Covent Garden. In 1970 he began a long and fruitful association as an opera producer at Glyndebourne, serving as its artistic director from 1984 to 1990. He was head of his own Peter Hall Production Co. (from 1988). For several years he was married to **Maria Ewing**. He was made a Commander of the Order of the British Empire in 1963 and was knighted in 1977. He is known for his versatility, having produced operas by Cavalli, Mozart, Wagner, Tchaikovsky, Schoenberg, and Tippett. In 1983 he produced the new *Ring* cycle at Bayreuth for the 100th anniversary of Wagner's death, with Solti conducting. —NS/LK/DM

Hall, Tubby (Alfred), jazz drummer; brother of **Minor Hall;** b. Sellers, La., Oct. 12, 1895; d. Chicago, Ill., May 13, 1946. The family moved to New Orleans in the early 1900s. Hall played drums from his early teens, working with various marching bands, then worked regularly with the Crescent Orch. from 1914; he also worked with the Eagle Band and Silver Leaf. He moved to Chicago in March 1917, joining Sugar Johnny Smith's Band that May. He served in U.S. Army for two years, then played in Chicago for various bandleaders including King Oliver, Jimmie Noone, Tiny Parham, Clarence Black, Carroll Dickerson, Louis Armstrong, Earl Hines, and Boyd Atkins. During the 1930s, Hall did several stints with Johnny Dodds and Jimmie Noone. He also led his own groups on occasion (1935; 1945–46). He continued to play regularly until shortly before his death.—JC/LP

Hall and Oates, veteran Philadelphia-soul session musicians of the late 1960s, formed their singer-songwriter duo in the early 1970s. **MEMBERSHIP:** Daryl Hall (b. Philadelphia, Pa., Oct. 11, 1948); John Oates (b. N.Y., April 7, 1949).

Hall and Oates recorded several overlooked R&B-inflected albums for Atlantic Records. Breaking through with "Sara Smile" in 1976 on RCA, the duo scored a series of catchy but superficial hit songs in the 1980s, which eventually led to their surpassing the Everly Brothers as the most-charted duo of rock. Although only "I Can't Go for That (No Can Do)" and "One on One" became smash R&B hits, Hall and Oates placed more singles on the black charts than any other white act.

Daryl Hall and John Oates met in 1967 at Temple Univ. in Philadelphia. Both had early musical training, Hall in voice and classical piano, Oates on accordion and, later, guitar. Hall sang and recorded with the Temptones in 1966–67. Hall and Oates each worked sessions at Sigma Sound in Philadelphia under songwriter-producers Kenny Gamble and Leon Huff, playing with soul groups such as The Delfonics and The Stylistics. The two began writing songs together and

formed the group Gulliver, cutting one album for Elektra Records before breaking up in 1970.

Hall and Oates began performing as a duo, eventually signing with Atlantic Records in 1972. Their debut album was overlooked, but their second, *Abandoned Luncheonette,* yielded a minor hit with "She's Gone." The song became a top R&B hit for Tavares in 1974, the year Hall and Oates recorded their final Atlantic album, *War Babies.* Switching to RCA Records in April 1975, Hall and Oates scored a smash pop and major R&B hit with Hall's "Sara Smile" at the beginning of 1976. Spurred by its success, Atlantic rereleased "She's Gone," and the single became a near-smash hit. Daryl Hall recorded the controversial and esoteric *Sacred Songs* with Robert Fripp in 1977. That year the duo scored a top pop hit with "Rich Girl" and a major hit with "Back Together Again." Subsequent major hits included "It's a Laugh" in 1978 and "Wait for Me" in 1979.

Daryl Hall and John Oates established themselves with *Voices* in 1980. It stayed on the album charts for nearly two years and yielded four hit singles, including the top hit "Kiss on My List," the smash "You Make My Dreams," and a remake of the Righteous Brothers' "You've Lost That Lovin' Feeling." The follow-up, *Private Eyes,* also produced four hits, including the top hits "Private Eyes" and "I Can't Go for That (No Can Do)" (also a top R&B, easy-listening, and dance hit!) and the near-smash "Did It in a Minute." *H2O,* perhaps their best-selling album, included the top hit "Maneater" and the near-smashes "Family Man" and "One on One" (an R&B near-smash). The anthology set *Rock 'n' Soul, Part 1* included two new songs, "Say It Isn't So" and "Adult Education," which became smash hits. *Big Bam Boom* continued Hall and Oates's hit-making ways with "Out of Touch" and "Method of Love."

Following 1985's *Live at the Apollo,* recorded with former Temptations David Ruffin and Eddie Kendrick, Hall and Oates ceased working together. Oates produced the Canadian group The Parachute Club and cowrote "Electric Blue," a near-smash for the Australian group Icehouse. Hall recorded *Three Hearts in the Happy Ending Machine,* which yielded three hits, including the smash "Dreamtime" and "Somebody Like You." The duo reunited in 1988 for *Ooh Yeah!* on Arista Records. It yielded three hits: the smash "Everything Your Heart Desires" (their last R&B hit), "Missed Opportunity," and "Downtown Life." "So Close" became Daryl Hall and John Oates's final major pop hit in 1990.

DISC.: GULLIVER: *Gulliver* (1970). **DARYL HALL AND JOHN OATES:** *Past Times Behind* (rec. 1969–1972; rel. 1977); *Whole Oates* (1972); *Abandoned Luncheonette* (1973); *War Babies* (1974); *No Goodbyes* (1977); *Daryl Hall and John Oates* (1975); *Bigger than Both of Us* (1976); *Beauty on a Back Street* (1977); *Livetime* (1978); *Along the Red Ledge* (1978); *X-Static* (1979); *Voices* (1980); *Private Eyes* (1981); H_2O (1982); *Rock 'n' Soul, Part 1: Greatest Hits* (1983); *Big Bam Boom* (1984); *Live at the Apollo* (1985); *Soulful Sounds* (1992); *Best* (1995); *Ooh Yeah!* (1988); *Change of Season* (1990); *The Atlantic Collection* (1996); *Marigold Sky* (1997). **DARYL HALL:** *Sacred Songs* (1980); *Three Hearts in the Happy Ending Machine* (1986); *Soul Alone* (1993).—BH

Hallberg, Björn Wilho, Norwegian-born Swedish composer; b. Oslo, July 9, 1938. After training with Brustad and Mortensen at the Oslo Cons., he settled in Stockholm in 1962 and completed his studies at the Musikhögskolan with Blomdahl, Wallner, and Linholm. In 1968 he became a naturalized Swedish citizen.

WORKS: DRAMATIC: O p e r a : *Evakueringen* (Stockholm, Dec. 9, 1969); *Josef* (1976–79); *Förföraren* (Stockholm, Dec. 22, 1981); *Regina* (1985); *Majdagar* (Stockholm, Dec. 16, 1989); *Orfika* (1990–95). B a l l e t : Various works.—NS/LK/DM

Hallé, Sir Charles (original name, **Carl Hallé**), renowned German-born English pianist and conductor; b. Hagen, April 11, 1819; d. Manchester, Oct. 25, 1895. A child prodigy, he began to play the piano at age 4, making his formal debut in a recital when he was 9. He made his conducting debut in Hagen at 11. He subsequently studied harmony and counterpoint with Rinck in Darmstadt (1835–36) and piano with George Osborne in Paris, where he moved in the circles of Chopin, Liszt, Berlioz, and Wagner; made his debut in Paris as a pianist in a trio with Alard and Franchomme in 1840. In 1842 he made a concert tour of Germany, which was followed by his London debut in 1843. He was the first pianist to play all the Beethoven piano sonatas in Paris. After the Revolution of 1848 he went to England, where he founded a series of chamber music concerts in Manchester. He then reorganized the Gentlemen's Concerts in 1849 and formed a choral society in 1850, and in 1857 he established subscription concerts with his own orch., which developed into the famous Charles Hallé's Orch. (inaugural concert, Jan. 30, 1858). The ensemble endured after his death, eventually becoming the esteemed Hallé Orch. He conducted the Bristol Festivals (1873–93) and the Liverpool Phil. Soc. (1883–95), and also served as the 1st principal of the Royal Manchester Coll. of Music (1893–95), where he was also a prof. of piano. He was a champion of Berlioz in England, and gave several complete performances of Berlioz's *Damnation de Faust*. His first wife was Désirée Smith de Rilieu. With his second wife, the violinist **Wilma Neruda**, he made 2 Australian tours (1890, 1891). He was knighted in 1888. Halle established a very high standard of excellence in orch. performance, which greatly influenced musical life in England. He published *Pianoforte School* (1873) and edited *Musical Library* (1876). M. Kennedy edited *The Autobiography of Charles Hallé* (London, 1972).

BIBL.: L. Engel, *From Handel to H.* (London, 1890); C. and M. Halle, *Life and Letters of Sir C. H.* (London, 1896); C. Rigby, *Sir C. H.* (Manchester, 1952); C. Rees, *100 Years of the H.* (London, 1957); M. Kennedy, *H. Orchestra* (Manchester, 1968; rev. ed., 1976); idem, *The H. 1858–1983* (Manchester, 1983); A. Kersting, *C. H.: Ein europäischer Musiker* (Hagen, 1986).—NS/LK/DM

Hallén, (Johannes) Andreas, Swedish conductor and composer; b. Göteborg, Dec. 22, 1846; d. Stockholm, March 11, 1925. He studied with Reinecke in Leipzig, Rheinberger in Munich, and Rietz in Dresden. Upon his return to Sweden, he conducted in Göteborg (1872–78; 1883–84), and then was conductor of the Phil. Concerts in Stockholm (1885–95) and of the Royal Opera (1892–97). From 1908 to 1919 he was a prof. of composition at the Stockholm Cons. He composed in a Wagnerian style.

WORKS: DRAMATIC: O p e r a : *Harald der Wiking* (Leipzig, Oct. 16, 1881); *Häxfällan* (Stockholm, March 16, 1896); *The Treasure of Waldemar* (Stockholm, April 8, 1899); *Walpurgis Night* (rev. version of *Häxfällan*; Stockholm, March 15, 1902). OTHER: 2 symphonic poems: *En Sommarsaga* (1889) and *Die Toteninsel* (1898); *Sphärenklänge* (1905); cantatas; overtures.

BIBL.: P. Vretblad, *A. H.* (Stockholm, 1918).—NS/LK/DM

Hallgrímsson, Haflidi (Magnus), Icelandic cellist and composer; b. Akureyri, Sept. 18, 1941. He studied cello at the Reykjavík Coll. of Music (1958–62), and then with Mainardi at the Accademia de Santa Cecilia in Rome (1962–63). He pursued training in composition with Simpson at the Royal Academy of Music in London (1964–67), and then privately with Bush and Maxwell Davies (1968–72). After playing in the Haydn String Trio (1967–70) and the English Chamber Orch. (1968–74) in London, he was principal cellist of the Scottish Chamber Orch. in Glasgow (1977–83). He then was a member of the Mondrian Piano Trio in Edinburgh (1984–88). His *Poemi* for Violin and Strings won the Nordic Council Music Prize in 1986.

WORKS: DRAMATIC: *Mini Stories* for Narrator, Soprano, and Small Ensemble (Thurso, Scotland, Sept. 8, 1997). ORCH.: *Poemi* for Violin and Strings (1984; Reykjavík, Jan. 31, 1985); *Daydreams in Numbers* for Strings (1986); *Herma* for Cello and Strings (1994–95; Glasgow, March 15, 1995); *Still Life* (1995; Glasgow, April 25, 1996); *Crucifixion* (1997); *Ombra* for Viola and Strings (St. Andrew, Scotland, Oct. 28, 1999). CHAMBER: *Solitaire* for Cello (1970; rev. version, Listasafn Islands, Sept. 29, 1991); *Verse I* for Flute and Cello (London, May 4, 1975); *Fimma* for Cello and Piano (London, Oct. 14, 1976); *Strönd* for Harpsichord (1982; rev. version, Skalholt, July 16, 1988); *Jacob's Ladder* for Guitar (Reykjavík, June 13, 1984); *Tristia* for Guitar and Cello (Reykjavík, June 13, 1984); String Quartet No. 1, *From Memory* (Copenhagen, Feb. 14, 1989); *Four Movements for String Quartet: In Memoriam Bryn Turley* (Edinburgh, Dec. 3, 1990); *Intarsia: Six Movements for Wind Quintet* (Edinburgh, April 23, 1991; rev. 1992); *The Flight of Icarus* for Flute (Listasafn Islands, Sept. 29, 1991); *Offerto (In Memoriam Karl Kvaran)* for Violin (Listasafn Islands, Sept. 29, 1991); *Sketches in Time* for Piano (1992); *Metamorphoses* for Violin, Cello, and Piano (1993; Edinburgh, March 15, 1994); *Ears Stretch a Sensitive Sail* for Percussionist and String Quartet (Thurso, Scotland, Sept. 8, 1998). VOCAL: *Elegy* for Mezzo-soprano, Flute, 2 Cellos, Piano, and Celesta (1971); *You Will Hear Thunder* for Soprano and Cello (1982); *Triptych* for Voices (1986); *Words in Winter* for Soprano and Orch. (Reykjavík, Oct. 29, 1987); *Syrpa* for Soprano, Clarinet, Cello, and Piano (Edinburgh, March 8, 1993); *Ríma* for Soprano and String Orch. (1993–94; Lillehammer, Feb. 19, 1994).—NS/LK/DM

Hallnäs, (Johan) Hilding, distinguished Swedish composer, organist, and teacher; b. Halmstad, May 24, 1903; d. Stockholm, Sept. 11, 1984. He was a pupil of Gustaf Hägg and Otto Olsson at the Stockholm Cons. (1924–29), where he took diplomas as an organist and music teacher. He then studied organ with Cellier in Paris and composition with Grabner in Leipzig. After serving as an organist in Strömstad and Jönköping, he went to Göteborg and was organist of the Johanneberg parish from 1933 to 1968. He also taught theory at the Orchestral Assn. (until 1951) and was active in contemporary music circles, serving as chairman of the Göteborg Composers Assn. (1957–72). In 1974 he settled in Stockholm. In 1952 he was made a member of the Royal Academy of Music in Stockholm. In his early music, Hallnäs followed a neo-Classical path. After World War II, he embraced the 12–tone method of composition albeit in a manner that allowed him to develop a personal style all his own.

WORKS: DRAMATIC: B a l l e t : *Kärlekens ringdans* (1955–56); *Ifigenia* (1961–63). **ORCH.:** 9 syms., but 2 withdrawn: No. 1, *Sinfonia pastorale* (1944; Göteborg, March 22, 1945), No. 2, *Sinfonia notturna* (Göteborg, March 4, 1948), No. 3, *Little Symphony* (Göteborg, Oct. 3, 1948), No. 4, *Metamorfose sinfonische* (Göteborg, April 17, 1952; rev. 1960), No. 5, *Sinfonia aforistica* (1962; Göteborg, Jan. 24, 1963), No. 6, *Musica intima* (Malmö, Nov. 7, 1967), and No. 7, *A Quite Small Symphony*, for Chamber Orch. (Minneapolis, June 12, 1974); *Divertimento* (1937); 2 violin concertos (1945, 1965); Piano Concerto (1956); 2 concertos for Flute, Strings, and Percussion (1957, 1962); Concerto for Strings and Percussion (1959); *Epitaph* for Strings (1963); *En grekisk saga* (1967–68); *Momenti bucolichi* for Oboe and Orch. (1969); *Horisont och linjespel* for Strings (1969); Triple Concerto for Violin, Clarinet, Piano, and Orch. (1972–73); Viola Concerto (1976–78); Cello Concerto (1981). **CHAMBER:** 4 string quartets (1949; 1967; with soprano, 1976; 1980); Quintet for Flute, Oboe, Viola, Cello, and Piano (1954); 2 violin sonatas (1957, 1975); Piano Trio, *Stanze sensitive* (1959); *24 Preludes* for Guitar (1967); *3 momenti musicali* for Violin, Horn, and Piano (1971); Trio for Clarinet, Cello, and Piano, *Confessio* (1973); *Triptykon* for Violin, Clarinet, and Piano (1973); *4 Monologues* for Clarinet (1974); *Legend* for Clarinet and Organ (1974); *Trauma* for 4 Strings and Piano (1979); *Musikaliska aforismer* for String Trio (1982). **KEYBOARD: P i a n o :** 4 sonatas (1963–83). **O r g a n :** 2 sonatas (*De Profundis*, 1965; 1977); *Passionmusik*, 15 pieces (1968). **VOCAL:** Cantata for Soprano, Flute, Clarinet, Cello, and Piano (1955); *Cantica lyrica* for Tenor, Chorus, and Orch. (1957); *Rapsodie* for Soprano and Chamber Orch. (1963); *Invocatio* for Chorus and String Quartet (1971).—**NS/LK/DM**

Hallström, Ivar (Christian), Swedish composer; b. Stockholm, June 5, 1826; d. there, April 11, 1901. He studied jurisprudence at the Univ. of Uppsala, where he became a friend of Prince Gustaf, who was himself a musical amateur. On April 9, 1847, jointly with Gustaf, he produced in Stockholm an opera, *Hvita frun på Drottningholm* (The White Lady of Drottningholm). In 1853 he became librarian to Prince Oscar, and from 1861 to 1872 he was director of Lindblad's music school in Stockholm. His opera *Hertig Magnus och sjöjungfrun* (Duke Magnus and the Mermaid) was produced at the Royal Opera in Stockholm on Jan. 28, 1867, but had only 6 performances in all, purportedly because it contained more arias in minor keys (10, to be exact) than those in major (only 8). He then produced another opera, *Den förtrollade Katten* (The Enchanted Cat; Stockholm, April 20, 1869), which was more successful. With his next opera, *Den Bergtagna* (The Bewitched One), produced in Stockholm on May 24, 1874, he achieved his greatest success; it had repeated performances not only in Sweden, but also in Germany and Denmark. In this work Hallstrom made use of Swedish folk motifs, a pioneer-

ing attempt in Scandinavian operatic art. His next opera, *Vikingarna* (Stockholm, June 6, 1877), was but moderately successful; there followed *Neaga* (Stockholm, Feb. 24, 1885), to a libretto by Carmen Sylva (Queen Elisabeth of Romania). He also wrote several ballets, cantatas, and arrangements of Swedish folk songs for piano.—**NS/LK/DM**

Halm, August Otto, German writer on music and composer; b. Gross-Altdorf, Württemberg, Oct. 26, 1869; d. Saalfeld, Feb. 1, 1929. A member of a family of scholars, he received an excellent general education. He then studied theology at Tübingen. In 1892 he went to Munich, where he took courses with Rheinberger. Subsequently he devoted himself mainly to musical pedagogy. He taught in various schools in Thuringia, conducted choral societies, and wrote music criticism. He wrote 2 syms., a Piano Concerto, 8 string quartets, 2 suites for String Trio, and piano studies. He publ. *Harmonielehre* (Berlin, 1905), *Von zwei Kulturen der Musik* (Munich, 1913; 3rd ed., 1947), *Die Symphonien Anton Bruckners* (Munich, 1914; 2nd ed., 1923), *Von Grenzen und Ländern der Musik: Gesammelte Aufsätze* (Munich, 1916), *Einführung in die Musik* (Berlin, 1926), and *Beethoven* (Berlin, 1927).—**NS/LK/DM**

Halmen, Pet(re), Romanian opera designer and producer; b. Talmaciu, Nov. 14, 1943. He received training in Berlin. After working in Kiel and Düsseldorf, he collaborated as a designer on productions with Jean-Pierre Ponnelle. Their staging of a Monteverdi cycle in Zürich in 1975 won critical accolades. From 1978 he was active at the Bavarian State Opera in Munich, where he prepared designs for the premieres of Reimann's *Lear* that year and for his *Troades* in 1986, as well as for Wagner's *Das Liebesverbot* in 1983 and Berg's *Lulu* in 1985. His designs for *Aida*, in collaboration with Ponnelle, were seen in Berlin in 1982, Chicago in 1983, and at London's Covent Garden in 1984, where controversy raged over his iconoclastic leanings. In 1987 he produced *Lohengrin* in Düsseldorf. With Ponnelle, he mounted a controversial production of *Parsifal* in San Francisco in 1988. After producing Paër's *Achille* in Bologna (1988) and *La straniera* at the Spoleto Festival in Charleston, S.C. (1989), he staged *Nabucco* in Munich in 1990 and *La clemenza di Tito* in Toulouse in 1992. He produced *Don Giovanni* in Hamburg in 1996, followed by *Orfeo* in Halle in 1997, and *Idomeneo* in Salzburg in 1998.—**NS/LK/DM**

Halpern, Steven (Barry), American composer, performer, and producer; b. N.Y., April 18, 1947. He played trumpet and guitar in jazz and rock bands as a youth, and in the late 1960s began to explore the effects of music on the listener. He studied at the State Univ. of N.Y. at Buffalo (B.A., 1969), Lone Mountain Coll. in San Francisco (M.A., 1973), and Sierra Nevada Univ. in Barcelona (Ph.D., 1977). He became absorbed in musical therapy, and developed a study curriculum of healing through music. In 1976 he began distributing his music to bookshops and health food stores, creating what has become Sound Rx Productions, a distribution company, which promotes therapeutic methods in music. He is a pioneer of New Age music, particularly the variety that is intended to be therapeutic; many of his recordings include subliminal suggestions for physical and mental improvement (sleep enhancement, sexual ecstasy, safe driving, weight loss, flourishing plants, self esteem, substance abuse, etc.). Among his many solo and collaborative recordings, both audio and video, are *Spectrum Suite* (1975), *Dawn* (1981), *Radiance* (1988), *Accelerating Learning* (1991), *Higher Ground* (1992), and *Music for Sound Healing* (1999). From 1986 to 1988 he ed. *New Frontier Magazine*. He also publ. *Tuning the Human Instrument* (Belmont, Calif., 1978) and *Sound Health* (N.Y., 1985).—**NS/LK/DM**

Halstead, Anthony (George), versatile English horn player, harpsichordist, conductor, and teacher; b. Salford, Lancashire, June 18, 1945. He was a student of Sydney Coulston at the Royal Manchester Coll. of Music (1962–66), and then of Horace Fitzpatrick (1966, 1978), George Malcolm (1979), and Myron Bloom (1979–80). He played in the Bournemouth Sym. Orch. (1966), the BBC Scottish Sym. Orch. in Glasgow (1966–70), the London Sym. Orch. (1970–73), and the English Chamber Orch. in London (1972–86). In 1972 he became a prof. at the Guildhall School of Music and Drama in London. Halstead has won an international reputation as a virtuoso on the natural horn. He has appeared as a soloist and as a conductor with various early music ensembles, and has made many recordings. He has made many appearances and recordings with the Hanover Band.—**LK/DM**

Halvorsen, Johan, notable Norwegian conductor and composer; b. Drammen, March 15, 1864; d. Oslo, Dec. 4, 1935. He began violin lessons at 7 and, while still a youth, played several instruments in the local civil defense band. He pursued his musical training with Lindberg and Nordquist at the Stockholm Cons. In 1885 he made his debut as a soloist in the Beethoven Violin Concerto in Bergen, where he served as concertmaster of the Harmonien Music Soc. He then was a violinist in the Gewandhaus Orch. in Leipzig, where he studied violin with Brodsky. After serving as concertmaster of the Aberdeen Musical Soc., he taught at the Helsinki Cons. (1889–92). He also completed his studies in St. Petersburg, Berlin (composition with Becker), and Liège (violin with Thomson). Upon returning to Bergen in 1893, he became conductor of the orch. of the theater and of the Harmonien Music Soc. In 1899 he was called to Christiania (Oslo) as conductor of the orch. of the newly opened National Theater, where he led symphonic as well as theater scores until his retirement in 1929. He was married to a niece of Grieg. Halvorsen's compositions were influenced by Grieg, Svendsen, and the folk melodies of his native land. Outside of Norway he is best known for his celebrated orch. march *Entry of the Boyars* (1893), as well as the Passacaglia for Violin and Viola, after a Handel keyboard suite (1897), the *Andante religioso* for Violin and Orch. (1903), and *Bergensiana, Rococo Variations on an Old Melody from Bergen* for Orch. (1913). Among his other works were 3 syms.: No. 1 (Christiania, 1923), No. 2, *Fatum* (1923; Christiania,

March 15, 1924; rev. 1928), and No. 3 (1928; Oslo, March 15, 1929), Violin Concerto; *Norwegian Festival Overture* (1899), several orch. suites, including *Nordraakiana*, after 5 works of R. Nordraak, 2 Norwegian rhapsodies (1919–20), incidental music to more than 30 plays, and *Reisen til Julestjernen* (Journey to the Christmas Star), a popular children's Christmas play (1924).—**NS/LK/DM**

Halvorsen, Leif, Norwegian violinist, conductor, and composer; b. Christiania, July 26, 1887; d. there (Oslo), Dec. 28, 1959. He studied violin with local teachers, then went to St. Petersburg, where he became a pupil of Auer. Upon his return to Norway, he served as concertmaster in the National Theater Orch., Christiania (1915–17). He then was an opera conductor (1918–21), and also led the Fredrikstad Singing Soc. (1925–47). He wrote much incidental music, an orch. suite, *Peasant's Legend*, piano pieces, and songs. —**NS/LK/DM**

Hamal, Henri-Guillaume, Belgian organist and composer; b. Liège, Dec. 3, 1685; d. there, Dec. 3, 1752. He studied with Lambert Pietkin, maître de chapelle of St. Lambert. As a youth, he excelled as a harpsichordist, cellist, and singer. He wrote songs to texts in many languages, all of which are lost. His son, Jean-Noël Hamal (b. Liège, Dec. 23, 1709; d. there, Nov. 26, 1778), studied with his father, becoming a chorister at St. Lambert (1716), where he studied with Canon Henri Dupont; he also studied with Giuseppe Amadori at the Liège Coll. of Rome (1728–31). He then became a Cathedral musician in Liège, where he was made director of music in 1738. His *6 ouvertures de camera, a 4*, op.1 (Paris, 1743), presage the Classical school; he also wrote 4 operas, 3 oratorios, 33 masses, 32 grands motets, 51 petits motets, etc. His nephew, Henri Hamal (b. Liège, July 20, 1744; d. there, Sept. 17, 1820), studied with his uncle, then at the Liège Coll. of Rome (1763–69). He was deputy director of music to his uncle at the Liège Cathedral (1770–78), and then director (1778–93). He wrote much sacred choral music.

BIBL.: L. de Lavalleye, *Les H. de Liège* (Liège, 1860); M. de Smet, *Jean-Noël H. (1709–1778), chanoine impérial et Directeur de la Musique de la Cathédrale Saint-Lambert de Liège: Vie et oeuvre* (Brussels, 1959).—**NS/LK/DM**

Hamari, Julia, Hungarian mezzo-soprano; b. Budapest, Nov. 21, 1942. She studied with Fatime Martin. After further training at the Budapest Academy of Music, she won the Erkel competition in 1964, and then completed her studies at the Stuttgart Hochschule für Musik. In 1966 she made her debut as a soloist in the *St. Matthew Passion* in Vienna, and subsequently was notably successful as a concert and lieder artist in Europe. In 1967 she made her stage debut in Salzburg. In 1972 she made her U.S. debut as a soloist with the Chicago Sym. Orch. As an opera singer, she appeared with the opera houses in Düsseldorf and Stuttgart. On April 24, 1982, she made her Metropolitan Opera debut in N.Y. as Rossini's Rosina. Her concert and lieder repertoire extends from Monteverdi to Verdi. Among her other operatic roles are Cherubino, Dorabella, Cenerentola, Carmen, and Octavian.—**NS/LK/DM**

Hambourg, noted family of Russian-born musicians:

(1) Michael (Mikhail) Hambourg, pianist and teacher; b. Yaroslavl, July 12, 1855; d. Toronto, June 18, 1916. He studied with N. Rubinstein and Taneyev in St. Petersburg and at the Moscow Cons., and was prof. at the latter (1880–90) and at the Guildhall School of Music in London (1890–1910). He went to Toronto in 1911 and founded the Hambourg Cons. of Music with his son Boris. All of his sons were musicians:

(2) Mark Hambourg, pianist; b. Bogutchar, June 12, 1879; d. Cambridge, Aug. 26, 1960. He studied with his father, making his debut in Moscow at age 9. He then studied with Leschetizky in Vienna. After international tours, he settled in England and became a naturalized British subject. He publ. *How to Play the Piano* (Philadelphia, 1922), *From Piano to Forte: A Thousand and One Notes* (London, 1931), and *The Eighth Octave* (London, 1951).

(3) Jan Hambourg, violinist; b. Voronezh, Aug. 27, 1882; d. Tours, Sept. 29, 1947. He studied with Sauret and Wilhelmj in London, Sevčik in Prague, and Ysaÿe in Brussels, and played in a trio with his brothers. He died during a concert tour in France.

(4) Boris Hambourg, cellist; b. Voronezh, Jan. 8, 1885; d. Toronto, Nov. 24, 1954. He studied with his father and with H. Walenn in London, H. Becker at the Frankfurt am Main Cons. (1898–1903), and Ysaÿe (1904), and played in a trio with his brothers. He went to Toronto in 1911 and founded the Hambourg Cons. of Music with his father, serving as its director until 1951. He also played in the Hart House Quartet (1924–46). —NS/LK/DM

Hamboys, John
See **Hanboys, John**

Hambraeus, Bengt, prominent Swedish composer, organist, musicologist, and pedagogue; b. Stockholm, Jan. 29, 1928. He studied organ with Alf Linder (1944–48), and also pursued training in musicology at the Univ. of Uppsala (1947–56; M.A., 1950; Fil.Lic., 1956) and attended the summer courses in new music in Darmstadt (1951–55). After service with the Inst. of Musicology at the Univ. of Uppsala (1948–56), he joined the music dept. of the Swedish Broadcasting Corp. in Stockholm in 1957, where he later was head of its chamber music section (1965–68) and production manager (1968–72). He subsequently was a prof. at McGill Univ. in Montreal from 1972. In 1967 he was made a member of the Swedish Royal Academy of Music in Stockholm. In addition to his numerous articles and essays, he publ. *Codex Carminum Gallicorum* (Uppsala, 1961), *Portrait av Bach* (with others; Stockholm, 1968), and *Om Notskrifter* (Stockholm, 1970). Hambraeus is one of the pioneering figures of the Swedish avant-garde. His *Doppelrohr* for Tape (1955) was one of the earliest electronic pieces by a Scandinavian composer. While he has found inspiration in both the Western and non-Western musical traditions, he has pursued an adventuresome course in his oeuvre.

WORKS: DRAMATIC: O p e r a : *Experiment X*, church opera (1968–69; Stockholm, March 9, 1971); *Se människen*, church opera (1970; Stockholm, May 15, 1972); *Sagan*, radio opera (1978–79; Swedish Radio, Aug. 31, 1980); *L'Oui-dire* (1984–86). **ORCH.:** Concerto for Organ and Strings (1948); *Kleine Musik* for Oboe, Strings and Timpani (1949); *Rota* for 3 Orchestral Groups, Percussion, and Tape (1956–62; Stockholm, May 27, 1964); *Transfiguration* (1962–63; Swedish Radio, Feb. 20, 1965); *Rencontres* (1968–71; Swedish Radio, Sept. 8, 1971); *Pianissimo in due tempe* for 20 Strings (1970–72; Uppsala, April 16, 1972); *Invocation* (Ames, Iowa, Nov. 11, 1971); *Continuo a partire de Pachelbel* for Organ and Orch. (1974–75; Nuremberg, June 15, 1976); *Ricordanza* (1975–76; Norrköping, April 29, 1977); *Parade* for Wind Orch. (1977); *That Harmony* for Brass Band (1983); *Quodlibet re BACH* (1984; Toronto, March 15, 1985); *Litanies* (1988–89; Stockholm, May 13, 1990); Piano Concerto (1992); Horn Concerto (1995–96; Swedish TV, March 27, 1999); *Quatre tableaux*, chamber concerto for Oboe, Strings, and Percussion (1998). **CHAMBER:** Concerto for Organ and Harpsichord (1947–51); *Music for Ancient Strings* for String Ensemble and Harpsichord (1948); 3 string quartets (1948–67); *Musique* for Trumpet (1949); *Kammarmusik* for Flute, Oboe, Clarinet, Alto Saxophone, Viola, and Harpsichord (1950); *Recitativ och Koral* for Violin and Piano (1950); *Giuco del Cambio* for Flute, English Horn, Bass Clarinet, Vibraphone, Harpsichord, Piano, and 3 Percussion (1952–54; Stockholm, Jan. 29, 1955); *Komposition for Studio II* for Vibraphone, Chimes, 3 Percussion, Piano, Harpsichord, and Organ (1955); *Introduzione—Sequenze—Coda* for 3 Flutes and 6 Percussion (1958–59; Stockholm, Dec. 11, 1959); *Segnali* for Electric Guitar, Harp, Violin, Viola, Cello, and Double Bass (1959–60; Swedish Radio, April 8, 1962); *Mikrogram: 7 Aphorisms* for Alto Flute, Viola, Vibraphone, and Harp (Stockholm, Dec. 4, 1961); *Notazioni* for Harpsichord, 3 Flutes, English Horn, Bass Clarinet, 3 Trumpets, 3 Trombones, Celesta, and 6 Percussion (1961; Stockholm, March 17, 1965); *Notturno de vecchi strumenti* for Soprano Recorder, Crumhorn, Alto Bassoon, Viola d'amore, Bass Gamba, Clavichord, 2 Glockenspiels, and Tambourine (1961; Stockholm, Nov. 17, 1963); *Transit II* for Horn, Trombone, Electric Guitar, and Piano (Malmö, Nov. 30, 1963); *Advent: Veni redemptor gentium* for Organ, 4 Trumpets, 4 Trombones, and Percussion (1975); *Jeu de cinq* for Wind Quintet (1976; Toronto, Feb. 24, 1977); *Relief—haut et bas* for 2 Flutes, 3 Horns, Trombone, 2 Percussion, and 2 Double Basses (1979; Montreal, April 10, 1980); *Strata* for 2 Oboes, 2 Clarinets, 2 Basset Horns, 2 Bassoons, 2 Horns, and Double Bass (1979–80; Stockholm, Sept. 20, 1980); *Sheng* for Oboe and Organ (1983; Toronto, Sept. 12, 1984); *Monologo* for Flute (1984); Trio Sonata for Free Bass Accordion, Trombone, and Prepared Piano (1985); *Mirrors* for Oboe and Tape (1986–87); *Night Music* for Guitar and Percussion (1988); *Dos recercadas* for Guitar and Cello (1988); *Cinque studi canonici* for 2 Flutes (1988); *Nazdar M J* for 3 Trumpets, 4 Horns, 3 Trombones, Tuba, Timpani, and Chimes (1989); *Archipel* for 15 Instruments (1997); Clarinet Quintet (1997–98). **KEYBOARD: P i a n o :** *Toccata* (1947–49); *Cercles* (1948); *Klockspel* (1968); *Carillon: Le Recital oublié* for 2 Pianos (1972–74); *Tre intermezzi* (1984); *Vortex* for 2 Pianos (1986). **O r g a n :** *Koralforspel* (1948); *Toccata pro tempore pentecostes* (1948); *Introitus et Triptychon* (1949–50); *Musik* (1950); *Liturgia* (1951–52); *Permutations and Hymn: Nocte surgentes* (1953); *Constellations I* (1958), *II* with Tape (1959), *III* with Tape (1961), and *IV* with Percussion (1978); *Interferenzen* (1961–62); *Tre pezzi* (1966–67); *Nebulosa* (1969); *Toccata pro organo: Monumentum per Max Reger* (1973); *Ricercare* (1974); *Icons* (1974–75); *Extempore* (1975); *Antiphonie* (1977); *Livre d'orgue* (4 vols., 1981); *Voluntary* *on a Swedish Hymn Tune from Dalecarlia* (1981); *Variations sur un thème de Gilles Vigneault* (1984); *La Passacaille errante—autour Haendel 1985* (1984); *Pedalexercitium* (1985); *Après-Sheng* (1988); *Cadenza* (1988); *Riflessioni* (1999). VOCAL: *Cantigas de Santa Maria* for Soprano, Alto, Baritone, and 3 Instrumental Groups (Stockholm, Dec. 17, 1949; also for Chorus and Organ, 1950); *Triptychon* for Chorus (1950); *Spectrogram* for Soprano, Flute, Vibraphone, and Percussion (1953); *Antiphonies en rondes* for Soprano and Orch. (1953); *Psalmus CXXI* and *CXXII* for Soprano and Organ (1953); *Gacelas y casidas de Federico García Lorça* for Tenor, Flute, English Horn, Bass Clarinet, Vibraphone, Bells, and Percussion (Stockholm, Jan. 23, 1953); *Crystal Sequence* for Soprano Chorus, 2 Trumpets, Vibraphone, Bells, Percussion, and 12 Violins (1954); *Responsorier* for Tenor, Chorus, Congregation, and 2 Organs (1964; Uppsala, June 16, 1966); *Praeludium, Kyrie, Sanctus* for 2 Choruses, Soloist, 2 Organs, and Congregation (Stockholm, Aug. 13, 1966); *Motectum archangeli Michaelis* for Chorus and Organ (Stockholm, Oct. 15, 1967); *Nonsens* for Chorus (1970); *Inductio* for Soprano, Alto Mixed Chorus, 3 Trumpets, and 3 Trombones (1979; Montreal, Feb. 8, 1980); *Alpha—Omega* for Chorus and Organ (1982); *Constellations V* for 2 Amplified Sopranos, Chorus, and Organ (1982–83; Nuremberg, Sept. 16, 1983); *Symphonia sacra in tempore passionis* for Soloists, Chorus, Winds, and Percussion (1986; Montreal, March 6, 1987); *Apocalipsis cum figuris secundum Duerer 1498* for Bass, Chorus, and Organ (1987; Nuremberg, Oct. 7, 1988); *5 Psalms* for Chorus (1987); *Echoes of Loneliness* for 4 Choruses (1988). ELECTRONIC: *Doppelrohr* (1955; Cologne, May 30, 1956); *Fresque sonore* (1956–57); *Visioner over en svensk folkvisa* (Swedish Radio, Nov. 13, 1959); *Intrada* (1976).

BIBL.: P. Broman, N. Engebretsen, and B. Alphonce, eds., *Crosscurrents and Counterpoints: Offerings in Honor of B. H. at 70* (Göteborg, 1998).—NS/LK/DM

Hameenniemi, Eero (Olavi), Finnish composer; b. Valkeakoski, April 29, 1951. He studied with Heininen at the Sibelius Academy in Helsinki (1973–78), Schaeffer in Kraków, Donatoni in Italy (1979), and Schwantner and Warren Benson at the Eastman School of Music in Rochester, N.Y. (1980–81). In 1975 he became active with Korvat Auki, the Finnish society for the promotion of contemporary music, serving as its chairman (until 1979; 1981–82). He also taught at the Sibelius Academy (from 1977).

WORKS: DRAMATIC: B a l l e t : *Loviisa* (1985–86; Helsinki, March 19, 1987). ORCH.: *...Only the Earth and Mountains* (1981); 2 syms.: No. 1 (1982–83) and No. 2 (Helsinki, Aug. 31, 1988); *Soitto* (1984); *Dialogi* for Piano and Orch. (1985). CHAMBER: *Duo I* for Flute and Cello (1976); *Dedicato...* for 12 Instruments (1978); *Aria* for Horn (1978); Piano Sonata (1979); Clarinet Sonata (1983); *Efisaes* for Piano and 12 Solo Strings (1983); *Canterai...* for Flute (1983); String Quartet (1989). —NS/LK/DM

Hamelin, Marc-André, Canadian pianist; b. Montreal, Sept. 5, 1961. He began piano lessons at the age of 5, and at 9 became a pupil of Yvonne Hubert and Sister Rita-de-la-Croix at the École Vincent-d'Indy in Montreal. He completed his training with Harvey Wedeen and Russell Sherman at Temple Univ. in Philadelphia (B.Mus., 1983; M.Mus., 1985). After placing 1st in both the International Stepping Stones of the Canadian Music Competition and the Pretoria, South Africa

competition (1982), he won 1st prize at the International Competition of American Music at N.Y.'s Carnegie Hall in 1985. Thereafter he appeared as soloist with various North American orchs., as a recitalist, and as a chamber music player. In 1987 he was a soloist with the Montreal Sym. Orch. on its tour of Europe. From 1989 he toured in a duo with the cellist Sophie Rolland. Hamelin's repertoire includes not only standard works but rarely performed pieces from all eras, including many by contemporary Canadian and American composers. —NS/LK/DM

Hamerik (real name, **Hammerich**), **Ebbe,** Danish conductor and composer, son of **Asger Hamerik** and nephew of **Angul Hammerich;** b. Copenhagen, Sept. 5, 1898; d. there (drowned in the Kattegat), Aug. 11, 1951. He studied with his father and with Frank van der Stucken. He was active mainly as a conductor. He held the post of 2nd conductor at the Royal Danish Theater in Copenhagen (1919–22) and conductor of the Copenhagen music society (1927–31) and the State Radio Sym. Orch.

WORKS: DRAMATIC: O p e r a : *Stepan* (Mainz, Nov. 30, 1924); *Leonardo da Vinci* (Antwerp, March 28, 1939); *Marie Grubbe* (Copenhagen, May 17, 1940); *Rejsekammeraten*, after Andersen (Copenhagen, Jan. 5, 1946); *Drmmerne* (posthumous; Århus, Sept. 9, 1974). ORCH.: 5 syms., *Ur cantus firmus I-V* (1937; 1947; 1947–48; 1949; 1949). CHAMBER: Wind Quintet (1942); 2 string quartets (1917, 1917); piano pieces. VOCAL: Songs.—NS/LK/DM

Hamilton, Chico (Foreststorn), jazz drummer, leader; b. Los Angeles, Calif., Sept. 21, 1921. A former clarinet player, Hamilton played drums in high school in L.A., along with fellow students Dexter Gordon, Charles Mingus, Ernie Royal, and Buddy Collette. He subsequently worked with Floyd Ray, Lionel Hampton, and Slim Gaillard, then spent four years in the army, where he studied (among other things) drums with Jo Jones. Brief encounters with Lester Young, Jimmy Mundy, and Count Basie led to his first long gig, a seven-year stint with Lena Horne, during which he toured often. He also worked in the early 1950s with Gerry Mulligan before forming his own quintet in 1955. The self- styled chamber-jazz unit used flute, clarinet, and cello. It had an intimate sound and elements of "cool" and symphonic music. The group achieved great popularity through their recordings and appearances in festival films, including the famous movie *Jazz on a Summer Day*. Hamilton has been among the best at spotting and debuting new talent. The list of major names who started with him includes Buddy Collette, Jim Hall, Paul Horn, Eric Dolphy, Ron Carter, Charles Lloyd, Gabor Szabo, John Abercrombie, and Arthur Blythe. In 1960 he was a boxing sparring partner for Miles Davis. In the mid-1960s, he formed a production company to write advertising jingles and soundtracks, but continued to work in jazz. He has taught at the New School since 1987. In 1989, he reunited his 1950s-era quintet for a European tour and recording. Through the 1990s, he continues to lead his own groups on record and on the road.

DISC.: *Spectacular* (1955); *C.H. Quintet* (1955); *Music of Fred Katz* (1956); *C.H. Quintet in Hi Fi* (1956); *C.H. Quintet* (1956); *Sweet Smell of Success* (soundtrack; 1957); *C.H. Trio* (1957); *Gongs East* (1958); *Three Faces of C.* (1959); *May 18th and 20th, 1959* (1959); *Ellington Suite* (1959); *C.H. Special* (1960); *Transfusion* (1962); *Passin' Thru* (1962); *Man from Two Worlds* (1962); *Drumfusion* (1962); *Different Journey* (1963); *Chic Chic C.* (1965); *El C.* (1965); *Further Adventures of El Chico* (1966); *Dealer* (1966); *Gamut* (1967); *Head Hunters* (1969); *El Exigente* (1970); *Montreux Festival* (1973); *C. the Master* (1974); *Peregrinations* (1975); *C.H. and the Players* (1976); *Nomad* (1979); *Reunion* (1989); *Euphoria* (1989); *Trio!* (1992); *My Panamanian Friend* (1992); *Arroyo* (1990); *Dancing to a Different Drummer* (solo percussion; 1993).—**LP**

Hamilton, David (Peter), American music critic; b. N.Y., Jan. 18, 1935. He was educated at Princeton Univ. (1952–56; A.B., 1956; M.F.A., music history, 1960). He was music and record librarian there (1961–65). In 1965 he became asst. music ed. of W.W. Norton & Co. in N.Y., and was music ed. from 1968 to 1974. In 1967 he became a contributing ed. of *High Fidelity*, and in 1968, music critic of the *Nation*. He also served as N.Y. music correspondent for the *Financial Times* of London (1969–74) and assoc. ed. of the *Musical Newsletter* (1971–77). He wrote *The Listener's Guide to Great Instrumentalists* (N.Y., 1981) and *The Metropolitan Opera Encyclopedia: A Comprehensive Guide to the World of Opera* (N.Y., 1987), and also publ. *The Music Game: An Autobiography* (London, 1986).—**NS/LK/DM**

Hamilton, Iain (Ellis), remarkable Scottish composer; b. Glasgow, June 6, 1922; d. London, July 21, 2000. He was taken to London at the age of 7, and attended Mill Hill School; after graduation, he became an apprentice engineer, but studied music in his leisure time. He was 25 years old when he decidedly turned to music; won a scholarship to the Royal Academy of Music, where he studied piano with Harold Craxton and composition with William Alwyn; concurrently studied at the Univ. of London (B.Mus., 1950). He made astonishing progress as a composer, and upon graduation from the Royal Academy of Music received the prestigious Dove Prize (1950); other awards included the Royal Phil. Soc. Prize for his Clarinet Concerto (1951), the Koussevitzky Foundation Award for his 2nd Sym. (1951), the Edwin Evans Prize (1951), the Arnold Bax Gold Medal (1957), and the Vaughan Williams Award (1974). From 1951 to 1960 he was a lecturer at Morley Coll. in London; he also lectured at the Univ. of London (1952–60). He served as Mary Duke Biddle Prof. of Music at Duke Univ. in Durham, N.C. (1961–78), where he was chairman of its music dept. (1966–67); also was composer-in-residence at the Berkshire Music Center at Tanglewood, Mass. (summer, 1962). In 1970 he received an honorary D.Mus. from the Univ. of Glasgow. His style of composition is marked by terse melodic lines animated by a vibrant rhythmic pulse, creating the impression of kinetic lyricism; his harmonies are built on a set of peculiarly euphonious dissonances, which repose on emphatic tonal centers. For several years he pursued a sui generis serial method, but soon abandoned it in favor of a free modern manner; in his operas,

he makes use of thematic chords depicting specific dramatic situations.

WORKS: DRAMATIC: *Clerk Saunders*, ballet (1951); *The Royal Hunt of the Sun*, opera (1966–68; 1975; London, Feb. 2, 1977); *Agamemnon*, dramatic narrative (1967–69); *Pharsalia*, dramatic commentary (1968); *The Cataline Conspiracy*, opera (1972–73; Stirling, Scotland, March 16, 1974); *Tamburlaine*, lyric drama (1976; BBC, London, Feb. 14, 1977); *Anna Karenina*, opera (1977–78; London, May 7, 1981); *Dick Whittington*, lyric comedy (1980–81); *Lancelot*, opera (1982–83; Arundel, England, Aug. 24, 1985); *Raleigh's Dream*, opera (1983; Durham, N.C., June 3, 1984); *The Tragedy of Macbeth*, opera (1990); *London's Fair*, opera (1992). **ORCH.:** 4 syms.: No. 1 (1948), No. 2 (1951), No. 3, *Spring* (1981; London, July 24, 1982), and No. 4 (1981; Edinburgh, Jan. 21, 1983); *Variations on an Original Theme* for Strings (1948); 2 piano concertos: No. 1 (1949) and No. 2 (1960; rev. 1967, 1987; BBC, Glasgow, May 1989); Clarinet Concerto (1950); Sinfonia Concertante for Violin, Viola, and Chamber Orch. (1950); 2 violin concertos: No. 1 (1952) and No. 2, *Amphion* (1971); *Scottish Dances* (1956); *Sonata per orchestra da camera* (1956); *Overture: 1812* (1957); Concerto for Jazz Trumpet and Orch. (1957); *Sinfonia* for 2 Orchestras (1958); *Ecossaise* (1959); *Arias* for Small Orch. (1962); *The Chaining of Prometheus* for Wind Instruments and Percussion (1963); *Cantos* (1964); Concerto for Organ and Small Orch. (1964); *Circus* for 2 Trumpets and Orch. (1969); *Alastor* (1970); *Voyage* for Horn and Chamber Orch. (1970); *Commedia*, concerto (London, May 4, 1973); *Aurora* (N.Y., Nov. 21, 1975); *The Alexandrian Sequence* for Chamber Orch. (1976). **CHAMBER:** 2 quintets for Clarinet and String Quartet: No. 1 (1948) and No. 2, *Sea Music* (1974); 4 string quartets (1949, 1965, 1984, 1984); Quartet for Flute and String Trio (1951); *3 Nocturnes* for Clarinet and Piano (1951); Viola Sonata (1951); *Capriccio* for Trumpet and Piano (1951); Clarinet Sonata (1954); Piano Trio (1954); 2 octets: No. 1 for Strings (1954) and No. 2 for Winds (1983); *Serenata* for Violin and Clarinet (1955); 2 cello sonatas (1958, 1974); Sextet for Flute, 2 Clarinets, Violin, Cello, and Piano (1962); *Sonatas and Variants* for 10 Wind Instruments (1963); Brass Quintet (1964); *Sonata notturna* for Horn and Piano (1965); Flute Sonata (1966); Violin Sonata (1974); *Hyperion* for Clarinet, Horn, Violin, Cello, and Piano (1977); *Spirits of the Air* for Bass Trombone (1977). **KEYBOARD: Piano:** 3 sonatas (1951, rev. 1971; 1973; 1978); *3 Pieces* (1955); *Nocturnes with Cadenzas* (1963); *Palinodes* (1972); *Le Jardin de Monet* (1986). **Organ:** *Fanfares and Variants* (1960); *Aubade* (1965); *Threnos—In Time of War* (1966); *Paraphrase of the Music for Organs in Epitaph for this World and Time* (1970); *Roman Music* (1973); *A Vision of Canopus* (1975); *Le Tombeau de Bach* (1986). **VOCAL:** *The Bermudas* for Baritone, Chorus, and Orch. (1956); *Cinque canzone d'amore* for Tenor and Orch. (1957); *Nocturnal* for 11 Solo Voices (1959); *A Testament of War* for Baritone and Small Instrumental Ensemble (1961); *Dialogues* for Coloratura Soprano and Small Instrumental Ensemble (1965); *Epitaph for This World and Time* for 3 Choruses and 3 Organs (1970); *The Golden Sequence* for Chorus, Congregation, and Organ (1973); *Te Deum* for Chorus, Winds, Brass, and Percussion (1973–74); *Cleopatra*, dramatic scene for Soprano and Orch. (1977); *Requiem* for Chorus (1979; BBC, Glasgow, May 1980); *Mass* for Chorus (1980; London, April 4, 1981); *Vespers* for Chorus, 2 Pianos, Harp, and Percussion (1980); *The Morning Watch* for Chorus and 10 Wind Instruments (1981); *The Passion of Our Lord According to St. Mark* for Soprano, Alto, Tenor, Bass, Chorus, and Orch. (1982; London, May 6, 1983); *The Bright Heavens Sounding* for Soprano, Alto, Tenor, Bass, Chorus, and Instrumental Ensemble (1985;

London, June 27, 1986); *Prometheus* for Soprano, Mezzo-soprano, Tenor, Baritone, Chorus, and Orch. (1986); *Paris de Crépuscule à l'aube* for Voice and Orch. or Piano (1986); *La Mort de Phèdre* for Voice and Orch. (1987).—**NS/LK/DM**

Hamilton, Jeff, versatile and musical drummer; b. Richmond, Ind., Aug. 4, 1953. He is probably best known for his collaborations with the Ray Brown Trio (1988–95) and for following Shelly Manne in 1978 as drummer for The L.A.4, a group co-led by Laurindo Almeida and Bud Shank with Ray Brown. Hamilton studied percussion for two years at Ind. Univ., where his fellow students included Peter Erskine and John Clayton, and he also learned jazz drumming from John Van Ohlen in Indianapolis. He played with The Tommy Dorsey Orch. under the leadership of Murray McEachern, and worked briefly with the Lionel Hampton band in 1975, Monty Alexander's trio (1975–77), and Woody Herman's Thundering Herd (1977–78), recording three albums with the latter. After making a series of recordings for the Concord label with The L.A.4, he became part of the Concord stable, regularly recording as sideman on many albums. From 1983–87 Hamilton performed with Ella Fitzgerald, the Count Basie Orch., Rosemary Clooney, and Monty Alexander. During the 1990s he toured internationally with the Ray Brown Trio and Oscar Peterson, worked with the Clayton Brothers' Quartet, and, from 1989, co-led the Clayton-Hamilton Orch. In addition to recording albums for Capri and Lake Street Records with the Clayton-Hamilton Orch., he has made over 100 recordings with artists such as Natalie Cole, Barbra Streisand, Mel Tormé, George Shearing, Milt Jackson, Herb Ellis, Barney Kessel, Scott Hamilton, Mark Murphy, and Toshiko Akiyoshi. Adept with both sticks and brush work, he is every bit as comfortable driving a big band or small groups, and has recorded with his own trio, formed in 1994.

DISC.: *Watch What Happens* (1978); *Live at Montreux* (1979); *Zaca* (1980); *Groove Shop* (1990); *Heart and Soul* (1991); *Absolutely!* (1994); *It's Hamilton Time* (1994); *Jeff Hamilton Trio: Live!* (1996); *Dynavibes* (1997).—**NAL**

Hamilton, Jimmy (actually, **James**), jazz clarinetist, tenor saxophonist, arranger, best known for his tenure with Duke Ellington 1943–68; b. Dillon, S.C., May 25, 1917; d. St. Croix., Virgin Islands, Sept. 20, 1994. His father played clarinet in a brass band. Raised in Philadelphia, Hamilton started on baritone horn at seven, and later studied piano, trumpet, and trombone. He worked on trombone and trumpet with several bandleaders in Philadelphia, then concentrated on sax and clarinet, inspired by Benny Goodman. He spent brief spells with Lucky Millinder and Jimmy Mundy, then was with Teddy Wilson from 1940 until 1942. He worked with a couple of other N.Y. bands before joining Duke Ellington, replacing Barney Bigard, in May 1943; he remained with Ellington until the summer of 1968. He led his own group in the U.S., then moved to St. Croix, Virgin Islands. He continued to play, and teach (1971). In the 1980s, he joined John Carter and The Clarinet Summit. He also worked during this period with Mercer Ellington and various Ellington reunion bands. His wife, pianist Vivian Hamilton (born Jones),

recorded under the name of Vivian Smith.

DISC.: *Benny Morton and J. H.* (1945); *Swing Low Sweet Clarinet* (1960); *Can't Help Swinging* (1961); *It's About Time* (1961).—**JC/LP**

Hamilton, Scott, jazz tenor saxophonist; b. Providence, R.I., Sept. 12, 1954. He is a traditionalist who recalls Ben Webster, Flip Phillips, and others, but plays with such authenticity that one forgets the comparisons. He was influenced by his father's record collection. He played harmonica, then took up the tenor sax at 16 and formed a quartet at 18 with which he still plays: Chuck Riggs (drums), Chris Flory (guitar) and Phil Flanigan (bass); sometimes John Bunch played piano. He became famous in New England circles in the 1970s, then moved to N.Y. in 1976. That year he met a frequent collaborator, cornetist Warren Vache, in a club. He was also recommended to Benny Goodman by Bunch, and worked with Goodman until 1978; he worked again briefly with Goodman in 1982. His tenure with Goodman led to a contract with Concord Records and a stint with the Concord All-Stars (1978–82), and widespread publicity that touted him as leader of a swing revival. From 1982–88 he worked with Ruby Braff, while also leading his own quintet. In the 1990s he has had a much lower profile.

DISC.: *Good Wind Who Is Blowing Us No Ill* (1977); *Back to Back* (1978); *With S.'s Band in N.Y.* (1978); *S.H.* (1978); *S.H. 2* (1978); *Grand Appearance* (1978); *Skyscrapers* (1979); *Tenorshoes* (1979); *S.'s Buddy* (1980); *Apples & Oranges* (1981); *Close Up* (1982); *Second Set* (1983); *S.H. Quintet in Concert* (1983); *A First* (1985); *Major League* (1986); *Right Time* (1986); *S.H. Plays Ballads* (1989); *Radio City* (1990); *At Last* (1991); *With Strings* (1992); *Groovin' High* (1992); *East of the Sun* (1993); *Organic Duke* (1994); *Live at the Beacon Jazz Festival* (1995), *My Romance* (1995); *After Hours* (1997); *Christmas Love Song* (1997); *Red Door: Remember Zoot Sims* (1998); *Blues Bop & Ballads* (1999); *Late Night Christmas Eve* (2000).—**MM/LP**

Hamm, Charles (Edward), American musicologist; b. Charlottesville, Va., April 21, 1925. He studied at the Univ. of Va. (B.A., 1947) and Princeton Univ. (M.F.A., 1950; Ph.D., 1960, with the diss. *A Chronology of the Works of Guillaume Dufay*; publ. in Princeton, 1964). He taught at Princeton Univ. (1948–50; 1958), at the Cincinnati Cons. of Music (1950–57), and at Tulane Univ. (1959–63). In 1963 he was appointed prof. of musicology at the Univ. of Ill. In 1976 he joined the faculty of Dartmouth Coll. He served as president of the American Musicological Soc. from 1973 to 1974, and in 1993 he was made an honorary member. A versatile scholar, Hamm publ. books on a variety of subjects, including *Opera* (Boston, 1966), *Yesterdays: Popular Song in America* (N.Y., 1979), *Music in the New World* (N.Y., 1983), *Afro-American Music, South Africa, and Apartheid* (N.Y., 1988), *Putting Popular Music in Its Place* (Cambridge, 1995), and *Irving Berlin: Songs From the Melting Pot: The Formative Years, 1907–1914* (N.Y., 1997).—**NS/LK/DM**

Hammerich, Angul, Danish musicologist, brother of **Asger Hamerik** and uncle of **Ebbe Hamerik;** b. Copenhagen, Nov. 25, 1848; d. Frederiksberg, April

26, 1931. He studied cello with Rudinger and Neruda, and piano and theory with C. F. E. Horneman. He received the first Ph.D. awarded by a Danish univ., from the Univ. of Copenhagen (1892; with the diss. *Musikken ved Christian den Fjerdes hof*; publ. in Copenhagen, 1892), and subsequently was its first reader in music history (1896–1922). He also was founder-director of the Museum of the History of Music in Copenhagen (1899–1931).

WRITINGS: *Musikforeningens historie 1836–1886* (Copenhagen, 1886); *Kjøbenhavns Musikkonservatorium 1867–1892* (Copenhagen, 1892); *Kammermusikforeningen 1868–1893* (Copenhagen, 1893); *Musikmindesmaerker fra middelalderen i Danmark* (Leipzig, 1912; Eng. tr., 1912, as *Mediaeval Musical Relics of Denmark*); *J. P. E. Hartmann: Biografiske essays* (Copenhagen, 1916); *Kammermusikforeningen 1868–1918* (Copenhagen, 1918); *Dansk musikhistoire indtil ca. 1700* (Copenhagen, 1921).
—NS/LK/DM

Hammerschlag, János, organist, conductor, writer on music, and composer; b. Prague, Dec. 10, 1885; d. Budapest, May 21, 1954. He studied composition with Kodály and organ at the Budapest Academy of Music. He taught at the Budapest Cons. from 1919, where he also conducted choral concert. In 1920 he founded a chamber music group for the performance of early music. It developed into the Motet and Madrigal Soc. in 1923. He publ. a book on Bach (Budapest, 1926).
—NS/LK/DM

Hammerschmidt, Andreas, important Bohemian-born organist and composer; b. Brüx, 1611 or 1612; d. Zittau, Nov. 8, 1675. He received his musical training in Freiberg im Breisgau, Saxony. He was organist to Count Rudolf von Bünau at his castle in Weesenstein, Saxony (1633–34), and at St. Petri in Freiberg im Breisgau (1634–39), then organist at St. Johannis in Zittau from 1639 until his death. During his tenure in Zittau, he became one of the most celebrated musicians of the day. He wrote a large body of sacred vocal music, some 400 works publ. in 14 collections. His compositions for the Lutheran liturgy are of great significance. He was one of the earliest composers to adopt the new Italian style of writing elaborate instrumental accompaniments to polyphonic vocal works. H. Leichtentritt, ed., *Andreas Hammerschmidt: Ausgewählte Werke* in Denkmäler Deutscher Tonkunst, XL (1910).

WORKS: VOCAL: S a c r e d : *Musicalischer Andacht, erster Theil, das ist, Geistlische Concerten* for 1 to 4 Voices and Basso Continuo (Freiberg im Breisgau, 1639); *Musicalischer Andachten, ander Theil, das ist, Geistliche Madrigalien* for 4 to 6 Voices, Chorus for 5 Voices ad libitum, and Basso Continuo (Freiberg im Breisgau, 1641); *Musicalischer Andachten, dritter Theil, das ist, Geistliche Symphonien* for 1 and 2 Voices, 2 Violins, Cello, and Basso Continuo (Freiberg im Breisgau, 1642); *Dialogi, oder Gespräche zwischen Gott und einer gläubigen Seelen, erster Theil* for 2 to 4 Voices and Basso Continuo (Dresden, 1645; ed. in Denkmäler der Tonkunst in Österreich, XVI, Jg. VIII/1, 1901); *Geistlicher Dialogen ander Theil, darinnen Herrn Opitzens Hohes Lied Salomonis* for 1 and 2 Voices, 2 Violins, Cello, and Basso Continuo (Dresden, 1645); *Vierter Theil, Musicalischer Andachten, geistlicher Moteten und Concerten* for 5 to 10, 12, and more Voices, and Basso Continuo (Freiberg im Breisgau, 1646); *Motettae* for 1

and 2 Voices and Basso Continuo (Dresden, 1649); *Chormusic auff Madrigal Manier: Fünffter Theil Musicalischer Andachten* for 5 to 6 Voices and Basso Continuo (Freiberg im Breisgau and Leipzig, 1652–53); *Musicalische Gespräche über die Evangelia* for 4 to 7 Voices and Basso Continuo (Dresden, 1655); *Ander Theil geistlicher Gesprache uber die Evangelia* for 5 to 8 Voices and Basso Continuo (Dresden, 1656); *Fest-, Buss- und Danklieder* for Voices and 5 Instruments ad libitum (Zittau and Dresden, 1658–59); *Kirchen- und Tafel-Music* for 1 to 3 Voices, 4 to 6 Instruments, and Basso Continuo (Zittau, 1662); *Missae, tam vivae voci, quam instrumentis variis accommodatae* for 5 to 12 and more Voices (Dresden, 1663); *Fest- und Zeit-Andachten* for 6 Voices and Basso Continuo (Dresden, 1671). **S e c u l a r :** *Erster Theil weltlicher Oden oder Liebesgesänge* for 1 and 2 Voices, Violin Obbligato, and Viola da Gamba or Theorbo (Freiberg im Breisgau, 1642; ed. in Das Erbe Deutscher Musik, 1st series, XLIII, 1962); *Ander Theil weltlicher Oden oder Liebesgesänge* for 1 to 3 Voices, Violin Obbligato, and Viola da Gamba or Theorbo (Freiberg im Breisgau, 1643; ed. in Das Erbe Deutscher Musik, 1st series, XLIII, 1962); *Dritter Theil geist- und weltlicher Oden und Madrigalien* for 1 to 5 Voices and Basso Continuo (Leipzig, 1649; ed. in Das Erbe Deutscher Musik, 1st series, XLIII, 1962). **O c c a - s i o n a l w o r k s :** *Hertzliche Aufmerkung und heiligen Weihnachtsgruss zu Ehren Matthia Albert und Jacob Rüdiger* for 4 Voices (Freiberg im Breisgau, 1639; not extant); *Stölichen Schiessen bei der Hochzeit Herrn Rothens zu Zittau und Christine Stoll, 29 Oct. 1640* (Görlitz, 1640; not extant); *Der auff den...seligen Hintritt des...Herrn M. Michaelis Theophili Lehmanns...erwehlte Leichen-Text: Ich bin gewiss, dass weder Tod noch Leben* for 5 Voices (Freiberg im Breisgau, 1650); *Lob- und Danck Lied aus dem 84. Psalm...auff die rümliche Einweihung der wider erbauten Kirche S. Elisabeth in Breslau* for 9 Voices, 5 Trumpets, 3 Trombones, 5 Violas, and Basso Continuo (Freiberg im Breisgau, 1652); *Bussfertiges Friedens- Seufftzerlein...Ihr Jungen und ihr Alten hört* (M. Francke) for 3 Voices (Coburg, 1658); also hymn melodies publ. in various collections. **INSTRUMENTAL:** *Erster Fleiss allerhand neuer Paduanen, Galliarden, Balletten, Mascharaden, françoischen Arien, Courenten und Sarabanden* for 5 Viols and Basso Continuo (Freiberg im Breisgau, 1636; ed. in Das Erbe Deutscher Musik, 1st series, XLIX, 1957); *Ander Theil neuer Paduanen, Canzonen, Galliarden, Balletten, Mascharaden* for 3 and 5 Viols and Basso Continuo (Freiberg im Breisgau, 1639; ed. in Das Erbe Deutscher Musik, 1st series, XLIX, 1957); *Dritter Theil neuer Paduanen* for 3 to 5 Instruments and Basso Continuo (Leipzig and Freiberg im Breisgau, 1650).—NS/LK/DM

Hammerstein, Oscar II (Greeley Clendenning), homespun American lyricist and librettist; b. N.Y., July 12, 1895; d. Doylestown, Pa., Aug. 23, 1960. Unlike such peers as Irving Berlin, Cole Porter, and Lorenz Hart, Hammerstein was known more for the musicals he wrote than for the individual songs featured in those shows. When collaborating with operetta composers such as Rudolf Friml (*Rose-Marie*) and Sigmund Romberg (*The Desert Song*), Hammerstein's work represented a throwback to the comic opera style of Victor Herbert, but his forward-looking shows with Jerome Kern (notably *Show Boat*) and Richard Rodgers (*Oklahoma!* and its successors) established the style of the integrated musical that became the dominant trend of the second half of the 20th century. His work largely rejected the sophistication of his peers in favor of a direct, emotional expression of romantic and family themes. Despite his focus on Broadway shows, he also wrote many popular songs, among them "Indian Love Call," "Who?," "Ol' Man River," "When I Grow Too Old to Dream," "All the Things You Are," "Some Enchanted Evening," and "No Other Love."

Hammerstein was born into a theatrical family. His grandfather, Oscar Hammerstein I, was an opera impresario; his father, William Hammerstein, managed the Victoria Theatre; his uncle, Arthur Hammerstein, was a theatrical producer. Nevertheless, Hammerstein was not encouraged to enter the profession himself. His first contact with the theater came in 1915, during his junior year at Columbia Coll., when he appeared in the varsity show *On Your Way*. He combined his senior year with his first year at Columbia Univ. Law School, earning his undergraduate degree in the spring of 1916, after appearing in the next varsity show, *The Peace Pirates*. During his second year at law school he collaborated with Rodgers on the songs "Can It," "There's Always Room for One More," and "Weaknesses," used in the amateur production *Up Stage and Down* (N.Y., March 8, 1917), a benefit for the Infants Relief Society, and he cowrote the lyrics and libretto and appeared in the Columbia varsity show *Home, James* (N.Y., March 28, 1917). (Rodgers went on to a long-term songwriting partnership with Lorenz Hart.)

Hammerstein quit law school after his second year and took a job in his uncle's theatrical production company in June 1917, initially working as assistant stage manager on *You're in Love*, a show composed by Friml. On Aug. 22, 1917, he married Myra Finn; they had two children. He had his first song performed in a Broadway show with "Make Yourselves at Home" (music by Silvio Hein), used in *Furs and Frills* (N.Y., Oct. 9, 1917).

Hammerstein wrote *The Light*, a play without music, which closed out of town in May 1919. His first Broadway musical, for which he wrote the book and lyrics, with music by Herbert Stothart, was *Always You*, which ran for 66 performances. For *Tickle Me* he cowrote the lyrics with Otto Harbach and the libretto with Harbach and Frank Mandel; the show ran 207 performances, making it Hammerstein's first real professional success. His first real hit came in 1923 with *Wildflower*, another collaboration on libretto and lyrics with Harbach and with music by Vincent Youmans. It ran 477 performances and generated two hit songs: "Bambalina," which became a best-seller for Paul Whiteman and His Orch. in June 1923, and the title song, a hit for Ben Bernie and His Orch. in July. Both recordings, however, were instrumentals. Hammerstein was joined by William Cary Duncan for book and lyrics; Youmans was joined by Stothart for music, on *Mary Jane McKane*, a modest success at the end of the year.

Hammerstein's biggest hit yet came with the 581–performance run of the Friml operetta *Rose-Marie*, on which he again collaborated for the book and lyrics with Harbach. Whiteman scored hits with instrumental versions of the title song and "Indian Love Call" (a sheet-music million-seller) in the winter of 1925. That year Hammerstein had two more Broadway successes, both in collaboration with Harbach though with different composers. *Sunny* marked his first work with Kern;

it had a 517–performance run and brought hits to George Olsen and His Orch. (who appeared in the show) with instrumental treatments of the title song and "Who?," a best-seller in February 1926 that reportedly went on to sell a million copies. *Song of the Flame* had music by Stothart and George Gershwin. It ran for more than 200 performances; the title song was a hit for Vincent Lopez and His Orch., and "Cossack Love Song" scored for The Ipana Troubadors in June 1926. Again, both were instrumental recordings.

In 1926, Hammerstein and Harbach (with Mandel contributing to the book) next teamed up with Romberg for *The Desert Song*, which ran 471 performances and produced two hits for Nat Shilkret and His Orch. in the winter of 1927: "One Alone" (an instrumental) and "The Riff Song" (with vocals by The Revelers). *Golden Dawn*, on which Hammerstein and Harbach worked with composers Stothart and Emmerich Kalman, was a moderate success with a run of 184 performances and included the hit song "Dawn" (music by Stothart and Robert Stolz), recorded by Shilkret.

But the most important work of Hammerstein's early career was *Show Boat*, based on the sprawling Edna Ferber novel, for which he wrote the book and lyrics alone, and which he codirected. With a run of 575 performances, it was a smash hit. It also included four hit songs with lyrics by Hammerstein. "Ol' Man River" was recorded by several artists but became a bestseller in April 1928 for Whiteman, with Bing Crosby on vocals. Whiteman quickly rerecorded the song with Paul Robeson for another hit version; the song was associated with Robeson for the rest of his career. "Make Believe" also became a hit for Whiteman with Crosby singing. "Can't Help Lovin' Dat Man" was a hit for Helen Morgan, who sang it in the show. And Shilkret scored a hit with "Why Do I Love You?" The score also featured "Life upon the Wicked Stage," "You Are Love" (finally made into a record hit in November 1932 by opera singer and movie actor James Melton), and "Bill," a hit interpolation with lyrics by P. G. Wodehouse. Even more significant than its initial success, however, *Show Boat* marked a coming-of-age for the Broadway musical, a move toward seriousness and stronger plots that Hammerstein would pursue further with Rodgers in the 1940s and 1950s.

Hammerstein returned to Romberg and to operetta with *The New Moon* in 1928, collaborating on the libretto with Mandel and Laurence Schwab. The result was another enormous success, as the show ran 519 performances and four of its songs became hits: "Softly, as in a Morning Sunrise" and "One Kiss" for Shilkret, "Marianne" for the Arden-Ohman Orch., and "Lover, Come Back to Me" for Whiteman among others. The show also included the stirring march song "Stouthearted Men."

Hammerstein and his wife divorced in 1929; he married Dorothy Blanchard Jacobson on May 14. They had one son, and the marriage lasted until Hammerstein's death 31 years later. His next show was *Sweet Adeline*, composed by Kern. A moderate success at 233 performances, it produced the hit "Why Was I Born?" recorded by Helen Morgan, for whom the show had been written. Hammerstein then signed a contract with

Warner Bros. to write songs and screenplays for films and went to Hollywood.

The Desert Song and *Show Boat* had been made into movies in 1929, and film versions of *Song of the Flame*, *Golden Dawn*, *Sunny*, and (minus the definite article) *New Moon* followed in 1930. (The perennially popular *New Moon* also generated a hit recording in 1930 for Perry Askam pairing "Lover, Come Back to Me" and "Stouthearted Men.") Hammerstein's first effort for Warner, for which he wrote the screenplay and the lyrics to songs by Romberg, was *Viennese Nights*, released in November 1930. It was not a success. Back in N.Y., his presence was felt with several interpolations into *Ballyhoo* (N.Y., Dec. 22, 1930), among them "I'm One of God's Children (Who Hasn't Got Wings)" (music by Louis Alter, lyrics also by Harry Ruskin), which became a hit for Libby Holman in February 1931.

When *Children of Dreams*, Hammerstein's second screenplay for Warner, again with songs by him and Romberg, became a box office failure upon release in July 1931, the studio bought him out of his contract. Unfortunately, his next Broadway efforts, *Free for All* (with composer Richard A. Whiting) and *East Wind* (with Romberg), were no more successful.

Music in the Air, for which Hammerstein wrote book and lyrics (to Kern's music), and which he directed, was a substantial hit, running 342 performances in the depth of the Depression and featuring two hits that became standards: "I've Told Ev'ry Little Star" and "The Song Is You," both recorded by Jack Denny and His Orch.

Music in the Air was Hammerstein's last successful musical for more than 10 years, though several songs he wrote became popular hits. *Three Sisters*, a British musical he wrote and directed with Kern, was a flop, running only 45 performances, but it included "I Won't Dance," which became a hit after its lyric was revised by Dorothy Fields and it was used in the film *Roberta* (1935). *The Night Is Young*, an MGM film for which Hammerstein and Romberg wrote the songs, included "When I Grow Too Old to Dream," which was on the newly established hit parade for Glen Gray and the Casa Loma Orch. in the spring of 1935.

The release of a film version of *Rose Marie* (Hollywood having eliminated the hyphen in the title) in 1936 led to a recording of "Indian Love Call" by its stars, Jeanette MacDonald and Nelson Eddy, that reportedly sold a million copies. "A Mist over the Moon," one of the songs Hammerstein wrote with composer Ben Oakland for *The Lady Objects*, earned a 1938 Academy Award nomination. Hammerstein wrote the book and lyrics for and codirected *Very Warm for May*, which marked Kern's return to Broadway and his final stage musical. It was another flop, running only 59 performances, but "All the Things You Are" from the score became a big hit for Tommy Dorsey and His Orch., topping the hit parade in January and February 1940.

Following the Nazi occupation of Paris in June 1940, Hammerstein wrote the lyric "The Last Time I Saw Paris" and sent it to Kern, who set it to music. The song was introduced on radio by Kate Smith and interpolated into the film version of *Lady Be Good* (1941). On Feb. 26, 1942, it won the 1941 Academy Award for Best Song.

During 1942, Hammerstein worked on *Carmen Jones*, an English adaptation of Georges Bizet's opera *Carmen*, to be set in contemporary times with an African-American cast. He was also approached by the Theatre Guild to write a musical version of Lynn Riggs's play *Green Grow the Lilacs*. He agreed to work with Richard Rodgers, because Lorenz Hart was not interested in the project. The result was *Oklahoma!*, for which Hammerstein wrote both lyrics and libretto. Its plot and characters integrated with its music and dance, the show fulfilled the promise of *Show Boat* and influenced everything that came after it in the musical theater. (It won a special Pulitzer citation in 1944.) With a run of 2,212 performances, it was the most successful musical ever up to that time.

Though it opened during a musicians' strike that prevented recordings for nearly six months, *Oklahoma!* revolutionized the recording industry. Two of its songs, "People Will Say We're in Love" and "Oh, What a Beautiful Mornin'," became Top Ten hits for Bing Crosby and Trudy Erwin, but more significant was the success of Decca's original cast album, the first such recording to become broadly popular. (After the introduction of the LP at the end of the 1940s, the reissued album reportedly sold several million copies.) Before *Oklahoma!*, record companies rarely recorded cast albums from Broadway shows; after it (at least for the next 25 years), they rarely failed to do so. The *Oklahoma!* album also spawned a hit single in Alfred Drake's performance of "The Surrey with the Fringe on Top." Hammerstein's return to success on Broadway in 1943 was capped by the opening of *Carmen Jones*, which ran 502 performances.

The success of *Oklahoma!* and the death of Lorenz Hart on Nov. 22, 1943, made the team of Rodgers and Hammerstein permanent. They next adapted the Ferenc Molnár play *Liliom* into the musical *Carousel*. Despite its dark tone, the show was another success, running 890 performances. The lengthy "Soliloquy" became a standard, and the other hits included "If I Loved You," a million-seller recorded by Perry Como among others, "June Is Bustin' Out All Over," recorded by Hildegarde, and "You'll Never Walk Alone," recorded by Frank Sinatra. As with *Oklahoma!*, however, the most popular recording was the cast album, which topped the charts in August 1945.

That same month Rodgers and Hammerstein's next work, the movie musical *State Fair*, was released. The biggest hits from the film were "That's for Me," recorded by Jo Stafford, and "It Might as Well Be Spring," by Sammy Kaye and His Orch., the latter capturing the 1945 Academy Award. Original soundtrack albums were virtually unknown at the time, but Dick Haymes, the film's star, recorded a *State Fair* album that topped the charts in February 1946.

Jerome Kern's final film project before his death on Nov. 11, 1945, was *Centennial Summer*, which included his last collaboration with Hammerstein, "All Through the Day." Upon the film's release in the spring of 1946, several artists recorded the song, the most successful being Sinatra, who scored a Top Ten hit. The song also earned an Academy Award nomination.

Eschewing adaptation, Hammerstein wrote a new, original libretto for his and Rodgers's next show, the experimental *Allegro*. Though the show was a failure, it is remembered for "The Gentleman Is a Dope" and "So Far," which Sinatra recorded for a Top Ten hit.

South Pacific, based on a book of short stories by James Michener, was Rodgers and Hammerstein's biggest hit since *Oklahoma!*, running 1,925 performances and winning the Pulitzer Prize for Best Play and the Tony Award for Best Musical. Perry Como had a #1 hit with "Some Enchanted Evening" and a Top Ten hit with "Bali Ha'i"; Margaret Whiting had a hit with "A Wonderful Guy"; the score also included "A Cockeyed Optimist," "Happy Talk," "Honey Bun," "I'm Gonna Wash That Man Right Outa My Hair," "There Is Nothin' Like a Dame," "This Nearly Was Mine," the socially conscious "You've Got to Be Carefully Taught," and "Younger than Springtime"; and the biggest record hit was the original cast album, featuring stars Mary Martin and Ezio Pinza, which became the longest running #1 recording in the history of the *Billboard* magazine album chart—a remarkable 69 weeks. Belatedly certified gold in 1966, the album reportedly sold about three million copies.

Originally intended as a star vehicle for stage veteran Gertrude Lawrence but subsequently more identified with Yul Brynner, *The King and I* was another enormous hit, running 1,246 performances and winning the Tony Award for Best Musical. From its score, only "We Kiss in a Shadow" became a minor hit for Sinatra, but the cast album—which also featured "I Whistle a Happy Tune," "Hello, Young Lovers," "Getting to Know You," "Something Wonderful," "I Have Dreamed," and "Shall We Dance?"—reached the Top Ten and stayed in the charts for over a year.

The year 1951 also saw the third film version of *Show Boat*, starring Kathryn Grayson, Ava Gardner (whose singing voice was dubbed by Annette Warren), and Howard Keel. The film became one of the year's top moneymakers, and the soundtrack album topped the charts during the summer and fall.

Hammerstein had rewritten the lyrics to a Harry Ruby Bert Kalmar song, "Moonlight on the Meadow," in the mid-1930s to create "A Kiss to Build a Dream On." Intended for the 1935 Marx Brothers film *A Night at the Opera*, the song was not used and had to wait until 1951 to turn up in the motion picture *The Strip*, where it was performed by Louis Armstrong. Armstrong recorded a hit version of the song, but the most popular recording was by Hugo Winterhalter and His Orch. and Chorus, which made the Top Ten in February 1952. In September country singer Slim Whitman reached the Top Ten with a revival of "Indian Love Call" that earned a gold record.

Me and Juliet, Rodgers and Hammerstein's next musical, was only a modest success, though it featured "No Other Love," which became a #1 hit for Perry Como in August 1953; the cast album reached the Top Ten. Hammerstein was also represented in the charts by a revival of "Lover, Come Back to Me" by Nat "King" Cole in the fall.

Released Oct. 11, 1955, the film version of *Oklahoma!*, which benefited from a heavy involvement by Rodgers and Hammerstein, was a box office smash, becoming one of the most popular movies of the year and generating a soundtrack album that topped the charts and sold over two million copies. *Pipe Dream*, their next show, was a flop, however, with the shortest run of any Rodgers and Hammerstein musical. Nevertheless, four of its songs reached the charts, the last not until 1962: "All at Once" (Perry Como) and "Everybody's Got a Home but Me" (Eddie Fisher), both of which made the Top 40, "The Next Time It Happens" (Carmen McRae), and "Sweet Thursday" (Johnny Mathis).

The success of *Oklahoma!* on film led to movie versions of *Carousel* and *The King and I* in 1956, resulting in hit soundtracks. *The King and I* went to #1 and earned a gold record; *Carousel* missed the top of the charts but sold a million copies.

Rodgers and Hammerstein's next effort was a musical version of *Cinderella* for television. The program starred Julie Andrews and produced a chart record in Vic Damone's version of "Do I Love You Because You're Beautiful?" (A second television production in 1965 starred Leslie Ann Warren.)

The year 1958 brought the film version of *South Pacific*, which became the biggest box office success of the year, while the gold-selling soundtrack album became the best-selling LP of the year. *Flower Drum Song*, the next new Rodgers and Hammerstein musical, was solid if not a spectacular success. Only "You Are Beautiful" from the score generated a chart record, by Johnny Mathis, but the cast album reached #1 in February 1959 and went gold.

The last of the gigantic Rodgers and Hammerstein hits was *The Sound of Music*, which ran 1,443 performances and won the Tony Award. The score generated chart records for Mitch Miller and His Orch. and Chorus ("Do-Re-Mi," Rodgers and Hammerstein's biggest sheet-music-seller), Tony Bennett ("Climb Every Mountain"), and Patti Page (the title song), while the cast album, which also featured such songs as "My Favorite Things," topped the charts, went gold, and became the best-selling album of 1960. It also won the Grammy Award for Best Show Album.

Doubtless, Rodgers and Hammerstein would have continued to produce successful work had Hammerstein not succumbed to stomach cancer in 1960 at age 65. During the 1960s his songs were revived frequently: Paul Anka had a Top 40 hit with "Hello, Young Lovers" in 1960; Linda Scott reached the Top Ten with "I've Told Ev'ry Little Star" in 1961; in 1965, "If I Loved You" was in the Top 40 for Chad and Jeremy, and Jay and the Americans had a Top 40 hit with "Some Enchanted Evening"; and Herb Alpert and the Tijuana Brass had an instrumental chart record with "My Favorite Things" (which had become a Christmas standard) in 1969. "You'll Never Walk Alone" enjoyed four chart revivals during the decade, by Patti LaBelle and Her Blue Belles in 1964, Gerry and the Pacemakers in 1965, Elvis Presley in 1968, and the Brooklyn Bridge in 1969. *Flower Drum Song* was made into a film in 1961, resulting in a successful soundtrack album. *State Fair* was given a second film treatment in 1962, also accompanied by a charting soundtrack LP. In 1965 the film version of *The Sound of Music*, starring Julie Andrews, became the biggest box office success ever up to that time, while the soundtrack record topped the charts and went gold.

But Hammerstein's work is best remembered in the numerous and ongoing performances of his shows around the world. There have also been frequent Broadway revivals. In August 1995 a stage version of *State Fair*, co-directed by Hammerstein's son James and featuring interpolations of songs from some of Rodgers and Hammerstein's less-successful shows, began a national tour, appropriately in Des Moines, Iowa. The production enjoyed a successful run on Broadway in 1996.

WORKS (only works for which Hammerstein was one of the primary, credited lyricists are listed): **MUSICALS/ REVUES** (dates are for N.Y. openings unless otherwise indicated): *Always You* (Jan. 5, 1920); *Tickle Me* (Aug. 17, 1920); *Jimmie* (Nov. 17, 1920); *Daffy Dill* (Aug. 22, 1922); *Queen o' Hearts* (Oct. 10, 1922); *Wildflower* (Feb. 7, 1923); *Mary Jane McKane* (Dec. 25, 1923); *Rose-Marie* (Sept. 2, 1924); *Sunny* (Sept. 22, 1925); *Song of the Flame* (Dec. 30, 1925); *The Wild Rose* (Oct. 20, 1926); *The Desert Song* (Nov. 30, 1926); *Golden Dawn* (Nov. 30, 1927); *Show Boat* (Dec. 27, 1927); *The New Moon* (Sept. 19, 1928); *Rainbow* (Nov. 21, 1928); *Sweet Adeline* (Sept. 3, 1929); *Free for All* (Sept. 8, 1931); *East Wind* (Oct. 27, 1931); *Music in the Air* (Nov. 8, 1932); *Ball at the Savoy* (London, Sept. 8, 1933); *Three Sisters* (London, April 9, 1934); *May Wine* (Dec. 5, 1935); *Very Warm for May* (Nov. 17, 1939); *American Jubilee* (May 12, 1940); *Sunny River* (Dec. 4, 1941); *Oklahoma!* (March 31, 1943); *Carmen Jones* (Dec. 2, 1943); *Carousel* (April 19, 1945); *Allegro* (Oct. 10, 1947); *South Pacific* (April 7, 1949); *The King and I* (March 29, 1951); *Me and Juliet* (May 28, 1953); *Pipe Dream* (Nov. 30, 1955); *Flower Drum Song* (Dec. 1, 1958); *The Sound of Music* (Nov. 16, 1959); *State Fair* (March 27, 1996). **FILMS:** *The Desert Song* (1929); *Song of the West* (1930); *Viennese Nights* (1930); *Sunny* (1930); *New Moon* (1930); *Children of Dreams* (1931); *Music in the Air* (1934); *Sweet Adeline* (1935); *The Night Is Young* (1935); *Rose Marie* (1936); *Give Us This Night* (1936); *Show Boat* (1936); *High, Wide and Handsome* (1937); *The Lady Objects* (1938); *The Great Waltz* (1938); *New Moon* (1940); *Sunny* (1941); *State Fair* (1945); *Show Boat* (1951); *The Desert Song* (1953); *Rose Marie* (1954); *Carmen Jones* (1954); *Oklahoma!* (1955); *Carousel* (1956); *The King and I* (1956); *South Pacific* (1958); *Flower Drum Song* (1961); *State Fair* (1962); *The Sound of Music* (1965).

WRITINGS: *Lyrics* (N.Y., 1949); with R. Rodgers, eds., *The Rodgers and Hart Songbook* (1951); *Jerome Kern Song Book* (1955); *The Rodgers and H. Song Book* (N.Y., 1958).

BIBL.: D. Taylor, *Some Enchanted Evenings* (N.Y., 1952); S. Green, *The Rodgers and H. Story* (N.Y., 1963); H. Fordin, *Getting to Know Him: A Biography of O. H.* (N.Y., 1977); F. Nolan, *The Sound of Their Music* (N.Y., 1978); S. Green, ed., *Rodgers and H. Fact Book* (N.Y., 1980); *Berlin, Kern, Rodgers, Hart, and H.: A Complete Song Catalogue* (Jefferson, N.C., 1990); E. Morden, *Rodgers and H.* (N.Y., 1992); S. Citron, *The Wordsmiths: O. H. 2nd and Alan Jay Lerner* (N.Y., 1995).—**WR**

Hammerstein, Oscar, celebrated German-American impresario, grandfather of **Oscar (Greeley Clendenning) Hammerstein II**; b. Stettin, May 8, 1846; d. N.Y., Aug. 1, 1919. At the age of 16 he ran away from home. He spent some time in England, then went to America, where he worked in a N.Y. cigar factory. Possessing an inventive mind, he patented a machine for shaping tobacco leaves by suction; later ed. a tobacco trade journal. At the same time, he practiced the violin, learned to write music, and dabbled in playwriting. In 1868 he produced in N.Y. a comedy in German and also wrote the libretto and music of an operetta, *The Kohinoor* (N.Y., Oct. 24, 1893). His main activity, however, was in management. He built the Harlem Opera House (1888), the Olympia Music Hall (1895), and the Republic Theater (1900), and presented brief seasons of plays and operas in all three. In 1906 he announced plans for the Manhattan Opera House in N.Y., his crowning achievement. The enterprise was originally planned as a theater for opera in English, but it opened with an Italian company in Bellini's *I Puritani* (Dec. 3, 1906). Hammerstein entered into bold competition with the Metropolitan Opera, and engaged celebrated singers, among them Melba, Nordica, Tetrazzini, and Garden; among the spectacular events presented by him were the first U.S. performances of 5 operas by Massenet, Charpentier's *Louise*, and Debussy's *Pelléas et Mélisande*. The new venture held its own for 4 seasons, but in the end Hammerstein was compelled to yield; in April 1910, he sold the Manhattan Opera House to the management of the Metropolitan for $1.2 million, and agreed not to produce grand opera in N.Y. for 10 years. He also sold to the Metropolitan (for $100,000) his interests in the Philadelphia Opera House, built by him in 1908. Defeated in his main ambition in the U.S., he transferred his activities to England. There he built the London Opera House, which opened with a lavish production of *Quo Vadis* by Nougues (Nov. 17, 1911). However, he failed to establish himself in London, and after a season there, returned to N.Y. In contravention of his agreement with the Metropolitan, he announced a season at the newly organized American Opera House in N.Y., but the Metropolitan secured an injunction against him, and he was forced to give up his operatic venture.

BIBL.: V. Sheean, *O. H., I: The Life and Exploits of an Impresario* (N.Y., 1956); J. Cone, *O. H.'s Manhattan Opera Company* (Norman, Okla., 1966).—**NS/LK/DM**

Hammond, Dame Joan (Hood), prominent New Zealand soprano; b. Christchurch, May 24, 1912; d. Bowral, Australia, Nov. 26, 1996. She studied at the Sydney Cons., in Vienna, and with Borgioli in London. In 1929 she made her operatic debut in Sydney as Siebel. In 1938 she made her London debut in a recital, and then sang in Vienna. From 1942 to 1945 she appeared with the Carl Rosa Opera Co. in London. On Oct. 6, 1948, she made her debut at London's Covent Garden as Verdi's Leonora, and continued to sing there until 1951; she appeared there again in 1953. She made her N.Y.C. Opera debut as Cio-Cio-San on Oct. 16, 1949, and remained on its roster for the season. She also pursued an active concert career. After her retirement in 1965, she taught voice in Wellington at Victoria Univ. Her autobiography was publ. as *A Voice, a Life* (London, 1970). She was made an Officer (1953), a Commander (1963), and a

Dame Commander (1974) of the Order of the British Empire. Among her finest operatic roles were Beethoven's Leonore, Violetta, Marguerite, Tatiana, Rusalka, Salome, and Tosca.—NS/LK/DM

Hammond, Frederick (Fisher), American musicologist and keyboardist; b. Binghamton, N.Y., Aug. 7, 1937. He was educated at Yale Univ. (B.A., 1958; Ph.D., 1965, with the diss. *The Summa de Speculatione Musicae of Walter Odington: A Critical Edition and Commentary*), where he received training in harpsichord from Kirkpatrick. He taught at the Univ. of Chicago (1962–65) and at Queens Coll. of the City Univ. of N.Y. (1966–68). In 1969 he made his N.Y. recital debut. His engagements took him throughout the U.S., Canada, and Europe. From 1968 to 1992 he taught at the Univ. of Calif. at Los Angeles. He was asst. music director of the Castelfranco Veneto Festival from 1975 to 1980. In 1986 he founded the E. Nakamichi Festival of Baroque Music, serving as its director until 1990. In 1989 he became the Irma Brandeis Prof. of Romance Studies at Bard Coll. and in 1995 music director of the Clarion Music Soc. His honors include a Rome Prize Fellowship (1965–66), a Harvard Renaissance Center Fellowship (1971), and the Cavaliere al merito della Repubblica of Italy (1986). His research has focused on 17th century Rome. His biography of Frescobaldi (1983) is a standard source.

WRITINGS: *Girolamo Frescobaldi* (Cambridge, Mass., 1983); *Girolamo Frescobaldi: A Guide to Research* (N.Y., 1988); *Music and Spectacle in Baroque Rome* (New Haven, 1994); ed. *Ambiente Barocco: Life and the Arts in the Baroque Palaces of Rome* (New Haven, 1999).—NS/LK/DM

Hammond, John Hays, Jr., American organist and manufacturer of organs; b. San Francisco, April 13, 1888; d. N.Y., Feb. 12, 1965. He studied at Yale Univ. (B.S., 1910), then devoted himself to improving pipe-organ mechanisms.—NS/LK/DM

Hammond, Laurens, American manufacturer of keyboard instruments; b. Evanston, Ill., Jan. 11, 1895; d. Cornwall, Conn., July 1, 1973. He studied engineering at Cornell Univ., then went to Detroit to work on the synchronization of electrical motor impulses, a principle he later applied to the Hammond Organ (1933), an electronic keyboard instrument, resembling a spinet piano, which suggests the sound of the pipe organ. Still later, he developed a newfangled electrical device which he called the Novachord that was designed to simulate the sound of any known or hypothetical musical instrument; he gave the first demonstration of the Novachord in the Commerce Dept. auditorium in Washington, D.C., on Feb. 2, 1939. In 1940 he introduced the Solovox, an attachment to the piano keyboard that enables an amateur player to project the melody in organlike tones. A further invention was the "chord organ," which he introduced in 1950, and which is capable of supplying basic harmonies when a special button is pressed by the performer.—NS/LK/DM

Hammond-Stroud, Derek, English baritone; b. London, Jan. 10, 1929. He was a student of Elena Gerhardt in London and of Gerhard Hüsch in Vienna and Munich. In 1954 he made his London recital debut, followed by his operatic debut there in 1955 as Creon in Haydn's *L'anima del filosofo ossia Orfeo ed Euridice* at St. Pancras Town Hall. From 1961 to 1971 he was a principal member of the Sadler's Wells Opera in London, and then sang at London's Covent Garden from 1971. In 1973 he made his first appearance at the Glyndebourne Festival. He made his U.S. debut with the Houston Grand Opera in 1975. On Dec. 5, 1977, he made his first appearance at the Metropolitan Opera in N.Y. as Faninal. In addition to his operatic appearances, he also pursued an active concert career. In 1987 he was made an Officer of the Order of the British Empire. His successful operatic roles included Papageno, Bartolo, Don Magnifico, Melitone, Alberich, and Beckmesser.—NS/LK/DM

Hampe, Michael (Hermann), German opera and theater director and Intendant; b. Heidelberg, June 3, 1936. He studied cello at Syracuse Univ. in N.Y. and pursued training in literature, musicology, and philosophy at the Univ. of Munich and the Univ. of Vienna (Ph.D.). After working as a theater producer in Bern (1961–64) and Zürich (1965–70), he was director of the Mannheim National Theater from 1972 to 1975. From 1975 to 1995 he served as Intendant of the Cologne Opera. In 1993 he became Intendant of the Dresden Music Festival. Hampe has worked in many principal opera houses and theaters, including those of Germany, Austria, England, France, the U.S., and Australia.

BIBL.: F.-P. Kothes, ed., *Oper in Köln: M. H.* (Cologne, 1995).—NS/LK/DM

Hampel, Anton Joseph, Bohemian horn player, teacher, and inventor; b. Prague, c. 1710; d. Dresden, March 30, 1771. He became a member of the Dresden royal orch. about 1731. He was the first horn player to learn to negotiate the low register of his instrument with aplomb and perfected the technique of performing the chromatic scale by hand-stopping. He also worked on perfecting the non-transposing mute. With the instrument maker Johann Werner, he brought out the Inventionshorn, which made it possible for crooks to be placed into the body of the horn. Among his students was Punto.—LK/DM

Hampel, Gunter, free-jazz inspired vibraphonist, clarinetist, flutist, saxophonist, pianist, composer; b. Gottingen, Germany, Aug. 31, 1937. He has promoted his music, an outgrowth of free jazz though usually quite tuneful, through his own Birth label since 1969.

His father was a pianist, and Hampel heard both local folk music and American jazz at an early age. He began playing and composing on piano from an early age, and took up clarinet at age 13. He began learning other reeds, and at age 17 was focusing on vibraphone and by 1958 was leading groups. He spent a year in the army, then attended the univ. at Brunswick. By the early 1960s he was playing around Europe with his own groups, mostly playing vibes. A personal milestone of sorts happened in 1964 during the Charles Mingus Jazz

Workshop's tour. Hampel put up Eric Dolphy in a house in Paris for a few days. They jammed together for long periods of time. At Dolphy's suggestion they switched instruments for a while, Dolphy on vibraphone and Hampel on bass clarinet, and Dolphy encouraged him to pursue the bass clarinet. Hampel turned to free music almost exclusively, and toured in Africa, Asia and South America. He was also influenced by Willem Breuker and by Marion Brown, with whom he toured in 1968–69. Perhaps most importantly, in 1966 he met singer/poet/future spouse Jeanne Lee, who plays a vital role in Hampel's music to this day. These connections fell together in Hampel's first major musical statement, *July 8, 1969*, a recording featuring Breuker, Lee, Anthony Braxton, drummer Steve McCall, and bassist Arjen Gorter, which marked the debut of Hampel's Birth Records. He performed solo concerts at the 1972 Munich Olympic Games and at that year's Berlin Jazz Festival. In 1971 he began a long-term association with Perry Robinson, who became a member of The Galaxie Dream Band which Hampel founded in 1973. Hampel and his players were also employed by the composers Hanz Werner Henze and Krysztof Penderecki to play their music. He has continued to compose and work with his Galaxie Dream Band through the 1990s. He has also written music for films.

Disc.: *Heartplants* (1965); *Music from Europe* (1966); *July 8, 1969* (1969); *People Symphony* (1970); *Out of New York* (1971; w. Perry Robinson); *Familie* (1972); *Unity Dance: European Concert* (1973); *Journey to the Song Within* (1974); *Enfant Terrible* (1975); *Cosmic Dancer* (1975); *Transformation* (1976); *All Is Real* (1978); *Live at the Berlin Jazz Festival* (1978); *Wellen-Waves: Berlin Soloflight* (1980); *Celestial Harmony* (1981); *Life on This Planet* (1981); *Companions* (1982); *Jubilation* (1983); *Fresh Heat: Live at Sweet Basil* (1985).—**LP/MS**

Hampel, Hans, Bohemian pianist and composer; b. Prague, Oct. 5, 1822; d. there, March 30, 1884. He was a piano pupil of Tomaschek. He composed a large output of piano music in an accomplished Romantic vein. —**LK/DM**

Hampson, Thomas, admired American baritone; b. Elkhart, Ind., June 28, 1955. He studied at Eastern Washington Univ. (B.A., 1977), Fort Wright Coll. (B.F.A., 1979), the Univ. of Southern Calif., and the Music Academy of the West at Santa Barbara, where he won the Lotte Lehmann award (1978). In 1980 he took 2nd prize at the 's-Hertogenbosch International Vocal Competition, and in 1981 1st place in the Metropolitan Opera Auditions. In 1981 he appeared with the Deutsche Oper am Rhein in Düsseldorf, and in 1982 attracted wide notice as Guglielmo in *Così fan tutte* with the Opera Theatre of St. Louis. In subsequent seasons, he appeared with opera companies in Santa Fe, Cologne, Lyons, and Zürich. In 1985 he made his N.Y. recital debut. On Oct. 9, 1986, he made his Metropolitan Opera debut in N.Y. as Count Almaviva. During the 1986–87 season, he sang for the first time with the Bavarian State Opera in Munich and the Vienna State Opera. In 1988 he appeared at the Salzburg Festival as Mozart's Count Almaviva. In 1989 he made his debut at the Berlin Deutsche Oper as Don Giovanni. He appeared for the first time at the San Francisco Opera as Ulisse in *Il Ritorno d'Ulisse* in 1990. In 1992 he made his Carnegie Hall recital debut in N.Y. In 1993 he made his debut at London's Covent Garden as Rossini's Figaro. He created the role of Vicomte de Valmont in Susa's *Dangerous Liaisons* in San Francisco in 1994. In 1997 he was engaged as Riccardo in *I Puritani* at the Metropolitan Opera, portrayed Eugene Onegin at the Vienna State Opera, and sang in Schubert's *Alfonso und Estrella* at the Vienna Festival. After singing Guillaume Tell at the Vienna State Opera in 1998, he returned to the Metropolitan Opera as Werther in 1999. He has won particular success for roles in operas by Mozart, Rossini, Donizetti, Verdi, and Puccini. As a concert artist, Hampson has appeared as a soloist with orchs. and as a recitalist in principal music centers of the world. His concert repertoire embraces works from Bach to Cole Porter and beyond.—**NS/LK/DM**

Hampton, Calvin, esteemed American organist, choirmaster, and composer; b. Kittanning, Pa., Dec. 31, 1938; d. Port Charlotte, Fla., Aug. 5, 1984. He studied organ and composition at the Oberlin (Ohio) Coll. Cons. of Music (B.M., 1960), and then at Syracuse Univ. (M.M., 1962). He was organist-choirmaster at N.Y.'s Calvary Episcopal Church (later combined with Holy Communion and St. George's; 1963–83). Hampton was a brilliant recitalist who played his own notable transcriptions of works by Chopin and Mussorgsky. On March 2, 1980, at St. George's, he conducted what is thought to be the first complete U.S. performance, in French, of Franck's oratorio *Les Béatitudes*. His compositions fuse popular and classical influences with striking effect, producing a lyrical and romantic underpinning that belies the modernity of their instrumentation. Some of his anthems are found in supplements to the Episcopal hymnal.

Works: *Prisms* for Piano (1963); *Catch-Up* for Tape and 2 Quarter Tone Pianos (1967); *Triple Play* for Ondes Martenot and 2 Quarter Tone Pianos (1967); *Prelude and Variations on Old 100th* for Organ (1970); *Transformation and Despair* for Organ (1971); *God Plays Hide and Seek* for Synthesizer and Organ (1971); *The Road to Leprachaunia* for Soprano, Synthesizer, and Organ (1973); Concerto for Saxophone Quartet, Strings, and Percussion (1973); *Labyrinth* for Soprano and Saxophone Quartet (1973); *O Lord, Support Us* for Chorus and Prerecorded Synthesizer (1974); *Pentecost Cantata* for Soli, Chorus, and Percussion (1977); *Candlelight Carol Service* for Soli, Chorus, Dancers, Pantomime, Organ, and Orch. (1978); Concerto for Organ and Strings (St. Paul, June 18, 1980); Concerto for Solo Organ (1981); *Cantata for Palm Sunday* for Tenor, Chorus, and Organ (1981); *In Praise of Humanity* for Organ (1981); *Dances* for Organ (1982); *It Happened in Jerusalem*, music drama for Soli, Speakers, Actors, Dancers, Chorus, Organ, Percussion, and Tape (1982); *Variations on "Amazing Grace"* for English Horn and Organ (1983); songs and anthems.—**NS/LK/DM**

Hampton, Lionel (Leo), exuberant American bandleader, vibraphonist, and drummer; b. Louisville, Ky., April 20, 1908. Hampton was the first notable vibraphone soloist in jazz and a successful bandleader for over 50 years. His biggest hits include "Flying Home," "Hey! Ba-Ba-Re- Bop," and "Rag Mop."

Hampton was the son of Charles Edward and Gertrude Morgan Hampton. His father was a railroad worker who went missing in action in World War I; Hampton rediscovered him in a veteran's hospital more than 20 years later, blind and near death. Hampton was raised by his mother's family, primarily his maternal grandmother, in Birmingham, Ala., and, as of about 1919, in Chicago. He displayed an early interest in drums and was given his first formal instruction in them by Sister Petra at the Holy Rosary Academy in Collins, Wisc. Back in Chicago, he learned harmony from Major N(athaniel) Clark Smith, former bandmaster for Theodore Roosevelt's Rough Riders, who was director of the *Chicago Defender* Youth Band, organized by the newspaper and made up of its newsboys. Hampton played in Chicago bands, then moved to Calif. to work with Les Hite. He made his recording debut in November 1924 with the Reb Spikes band, Reb's Legion Club Forty-Fives. In the late 1920s he became a member of the band at Frank Sebastian's New Cotton Club, then led by Hite. Louis Armstrong fronted the band in 1930–31, and Hampton recorded with him, notably playing the vibraphone at a session on Oct. 16, 1930, that marked the first serious use of the instrument for jazz.

In the early 1930s, Hampton organized his own band and toured the West Coast, establishing a residency at the Red Car Club (later the Paradise) in L.A. in 1933. In 1934 he studied harmony and music theory at the Univ. of Southern Calif. In August 1936, Benny Goodman invited him to join the trio that played separate from his big band, and Hampton disbanded and moved to N.Y. to do so. On the way east he married his longtime companion, seamstress Gladys Riddle, who had become his personal manager, on Nov. 11, 1936.

Hampton's four-year tenure with Goodman, plus the all-star recordings he made under his own name for RCA Victor starting in 1937, brought him enough exposure that he was able to launch his own band when Goodman temporarily disbanded in 1940. Lionel Hampton and His Orch. debuted on Nov. 6, 1940, in L.A. Over the next decade he scored a series of R&B and pop hits: "Flying Home" (music by Goodman and Hampton), which reached the R&B Top Ten in two different versions in 1943; "On the Sunny Side of the Street" (music by Jimmy McHugh, lyrics by Dorothy Fields), a 1937 recording that made the R&B Top Ten when reissued during the recording ban, in January 1944; "Hamp's Boogie Woogie" (music by Milt Buckner and Hampton), which topped the R&B chart in September 1944; "Beulah's Boogie," which made the R&B Top Ten in December 1945; "Hey! Ba- Ba-Re-Bop" (music and lyrics by Hampton and Curley Hamner), which topped the R&B charts in March 1946 and made the pop Top Ten; "Blow-Top Blues," featuring Dinah Washington, an R&B Top Ten in May 1947; "I Want to Be Loved (But Only by You)" (music and lyrics by Savannah Churchill), an R&B Top Ten in June 1947; "Rag Mop" (music and lyrics by Johnnie Lee Wills and Deacon Anderson), which made both the R&B and pop Top Ten in February 1950; and "Everybody's Somebody's Fool," an R&B Top Ten in October 1950.

Hampton appeared in several films, notably *A Song Is Born* (1948), *The Benny Goodman Story* (1955), and *Mister Rock and Roll* (1957). He began to tour internationally in 1953. Despite the downturn in popularity of big bands and swing music after the 1940s, he was able to maintain his orch. until 1965, when he disbanded and formed a smaller unit called the Jazz Inner Circle. But he occasionally fronted larger units for special performances and tours. He continued to perform into the 1990s and recorded on his own Glad Hamp Records and other labels. He earned three Grammy Award nominations: in 1984 for Best Rock Instrumental Performance, for the track "Vibramatic"; in 1986 for Best Jazz Instrumental Performance, Big Band, for the album *Sentimental Journey*; in 1990 for Best Jazz Instrumental Performance, Big Band, for the album *Cookin' in the Kitchen*; and in 1991 for Best Jazz Instrumental Performance, Group, for the album *Lionel Hampton & the Golden Men of Jazz Live at the Blue Note*.

DISC.: *Stompology* (1937); *Tempo and Swing* (1939); *Hamp* (1942); *Mess Is Here* (1944); *Jazz Heritage: Sweatin' with Hamp* (1945); *Midnight Sun* (1946); *The Original Stardust* (1947); *Lionel Hampton with the Just Jazz All Stars* (1947); *Hot House* (1948); *Moonglow* (1950); *The Blues Ain't News to Me* (1951); *The King of the Vibes* (1953); *The Lionel Hampton Quartet* (1953); *Air Mail Special* (1953); *Lionel Hampton in Paris* (1953); *Lionel Hampton Plays Love Songs* (1954); *Swingin' with Hamp* (1954); *Hamp's Big Four* (1954); *Hallelujah Hamp* (1954); *Hot Mallets* (1954); *Lionel Hampton and His New French Sound* (1955); *The Hampton-Tatum-Rich Trio* (1955); *Hamp and Getz* (1955); *Hamp Roars Again* (1955); *Hamp in Hi Fi* (1956); *Golden Vibes* (1958); *Hamp's Big Band* (1959); *Silver Vibes* (1960); *Soft Vibes, Soaring Strings* (1961); *Many Splendored Vibes* (1962); *Lionel Hampton in Japan* (1963); *You Better Know It* (1964); *Newport Uproar* (1967); *Where Could I Be?* (1971); *Transition* (1974); *Blues in Toulouse* (1977); *As Time Goes By* (1978); *Hamp in Harlem* (1979); *Sentimental Journey* (1985); *Mostly Blues* (1988); *Live at the Metropole Café, New York City* (1989); *Just Jazz: Live at the Blue Note, Vol. 1, 2* (1991); *I'm in the Mood for Swing* (1992); *For the Love of Music* (1994); *Jivin' the Vibe* (1996); *Triple Play: Live at the Blue Note* (1999); *Live at Carnegie Hall* (1999); *Just One of Those Things* (1999).

WRITINGS: With D. Gornston, *The L. H. Vibraphone Method* (1941); with J. Haskins, *Hamp: An Autobiography* (N.Y., 1989).

BIBL.: O. Flückiger, *L. H.: Selected Discography, 1966–78* (Reinach, Switzerland, 1978; rev. ed., *L. H.: Porträt Mit Discography, 1966–79*, 1980).—**WR**

Hampton, Slide (Locksley Wellington),

trombonist, composer, arranger; b. Jeannette, Pa., April. 21, 1932. He played in the 1950s with Lionel Hampton and Maynard Ferguson (writing as well as playing), and also with Buddy Johnson (with whom he made his recording debut on June 24, 1957), before forming his own octet in 1959. He worked for R&B and blues singer Lloyd Price as musical director and did freelance arranging in the 1960s. He toured Europe in November 1962 with George Coleman, then played in N.Y. with Art Blakey and the Thad Jones–Mel Lewis Orch. He joined Woody Herman in 1968, with whom he toured Europe. Hampton settled there following the tour, doing radio work in Germany. He returned to N.Y. in 1977 and began heading his 12–piece band, the World of Trombones. Around 1982 he also formed Continuum, which recorded a tribute LP to Tadd Dameron. Since the 1980s he has been one of the most in- demand jazz composers, receiving numerous commissions including a version of Coltrane's "A Love Supreme" (the first three movements) for the Carnegie Hall Jazz Band, which premiered in February 1998. He has also done many workshops with college bands.

DISC.: *And His Horn of Plenty* (1959); *Sister Salvation* (1960); *Somethin' Sanctified* (1960); *Jazz with a Twist* (1961); *Two Sides of Slide* (ca. 1961); *Explosion!* (1962); *Drum Suite* (1962); *Fabulous S.H. Quartet* (1969); *World of Trombones* (1979); *Roots* (1985); *Dedicated to Diz* (1993). **CONTINUUM:** *Mad About Tadd* (1982).—**MF/LP**

Han (Hahn), Ulrich (known as Udalricus Gallus),
German music printer; b. Ingolstadt, c. 1425; d. Rome, after 1478. He is believed to be the first to print music with movable type, in his *Missale secundum consuetudinem curie romane* (Rome, 1476). In this work the double- process method was employed, i.e., 2 impressions were made; first, the lines of the staff were printed, then the note forms (mostly square black heads with a stem at the right side) were superimposed over them.—**NS/LK/DM**

Hanboys (or Hamboys), John,
English music theorist who flourished in the 15th century. He held an ecclesiastic rank. His Latin treatise *Summa super musicam continuam et discretam*, which describes the musical notation of his time, was printed by Coussemaker in his *Scriptorum de musica medii aevi* (Vol. I, Paris, 1864). —**NS/LK/DM**

Hancock, Herbie (actually, Herbert Jeffrey),
highly influential jazz and fusion-funk pianist, keyboardist, composer, leader; b. Chicago, Ill., April 12, 1940. Classically trained, he won a competition to play with the Chicago Sym. Orch. at 11; the Mozart concerto he preferred to play wasn't available so he had to learn another one quickly. In high school, he became interested in jazz through classmates, initially influenced by George Shearing, Oscar Peterson, Dave Brubeck, Horace Silver, and Erroll Garner. He began leading his own band, and also gigged with Coleman Hawkins, Donald Byrd, and others while he studied music and electrical engineering at Grinnell Coll. (1956–60). He worked for a time for the post office in Chicago while gigging at night. By February 1961 he had replaced Duke Pearson in the Donald Byrd- Pepper Adams Quintet. He moved to N.Y. (at the urging of Byrd) on June 18, 1961, and continued in the Quintet through at least the end of 1962. He also worked with Phil Woods around September 1962. He took courses at the Manhattan School of Music and the New School for Social Research. While recording with Byrd for Blue Note he was invited to make his 1962 debut album *Takin Off*, which featured the now-classic "Watermelon Man." In the summer of 1963 he was contacted by Miles Davis to come to a rehearsal, and was later casually asked by Davis to join the quintet. He stayed until mid-1968, earning international fame for his brilliant soloing, accompanying and writing. Davis also introduced him to the electric Fender Rhodes piano. In 1966 Hancock wrote some music for the film *Blow Up*, which made the pop charts. Three

years later, he composed the music for Bill Cosby's TV special, *Hey, Hey, Hey, It's Fat Albert*. In 1968 he organized a sextet, and soon he began using synthesizers as well as the Fender Rhodes in long, dreamy and freely improvised compositions. In 1972 he settled in L.A., and in 1973 he took up a form of Buddhism. In a pattern typical of his generation (see Chick Corea, Sonny Rollins), at the same time he began playing electric music with a decidedly danceable beat, scoring a big hit with "Chameleon," a group-written piece from the album *Headhunters*, released early in 1974. Also typically, he began to divide his time between acoustic-piano work and electric playing. His acoustic jazz dates included touring and recordings with V.S.O.P. (which was the old Davis quintet with Freddie Hubbard and later Wynton Marsalis substituting for Davis) and in duet with Chick Corea. In all, he had 11 albums on the charts during the 1970s and early 1980s. His 1983 piece "Rockit," a collaboration with Material from the gold-selling *Future Shock* album, won him a Grammy (Best R&B; Instrumental), and the video (including some stop-motion animation) won five MTV Awards. The title song from his next album *Sound System* also won a Grammy. He said he was even more moved when he won an Oscar in 1986 for his acoustic jazz soundtrack for Bertrand Tavernier's film *'Round Midnight*. (He acted in the film as well). Hancock went on to compose soundtracks for *Colors* and *A Soldier's Story*. From 1989 to 1991 he hosted a music series for Showtime called *Coast to Coast* and in the mid-1990s performed on the Rock School instructional "how to play" series. Since the early 1990s, he's been a partner in a video production company that develops interactive educational products (e.g., Rock School; CD-ROM history of jazz). In 1996 he toured Japan with Dave Holland and Gene Jackson and played a week at the Blue Note in N.Y. In 1997–98 he toured with a reunion of the Headhunters band.

Hancock is clearly one of the great jazz pianists, a brilliant and inventive musician with an amazingly flexible sense of time. At times surprisingly modest, for example, in his repeated denial that he can play unaccompanied piano successfully, he has found himself increasingly in the "pop star" category since 1973. Yet, he continually returns to playing acoustic jazz, and has been able to find an audience in both pop and jazz worlds.

DISC.: *Takin' Off* (1962); *My Point of View* (1963); *Inventions and Dimensions* (1963); *Empyrean Isles* (1964); *Maiden Voyage* (1965); *Blow Up* (music from the film; 1966); *Speak Like a Child* (1968); *Prisoner* (1969); *Mwandishi* (1969); *Fat Albert Rotunda* (1969); *Crossings* (1971); *Sextant* (1972); *Headhunters* (1973); *Thrust* (1974); *Death Wish* (music from the film; 1974); *V.S.O.P. Quintet* (1977); *Tempest in the Colosseum* (V.S.O.P.; 1977); *Sunlight* (1977); *H. H. Trio* (1977); *Flood* (live album issued in Japan; 1977); *Live in Japan* (1977); *Evening with Chick Corea and H. H.* (1978); *Live under the Sky* (V.S.O.P.; 1979); *In Concert* (duets with Corea; 1979); *Quartet* (with W. Marsalis; 1981); *Mr. Hands* (1982); *Future Shock* (1983); *Hurricane* (acoustic trio concert video; 1984); *H. H. and the Rockit Band* (1984); *The Best of H. H.: The Blue Note Years* (1988); *Jazz Africa* (1990); *Secrets* (1991); *Monster* (1991); *Man-Child* (1991); *Dis Is Da Drum* (1995); *Cantelope Island* (1995); *1+1* (duets with Wayne Shorter; 1996); *Headhunters* (1997); *Gershwin's World* (1998); *The Best of H. H.: The Hits!* (2000).—**LP**

Handel, George Frideric (the Anglicized form of the name, adopted by Handel in England; the original German spelling was **Georg Friedrich Händel**; other forms used in various branches of the family were Hendel, Hendeler, Händler, and Hendtler; the early spelling in England was Hendel; in France it is spelled Haendler; the Russian transliteration of the name from the Cyrillic alphabet, which lacks the aspirate, is Gendel), great German-born English composer; b. Halle, Feb. 23, 1685; d. London, April 14, 1759. His father was a barber-surgeon and valet to the Prince of Saxe-Magdeburg; at the age of 61 he took a second wife, Dorothea Taust, daughter of the pastor of Giebichenstein, near Halle; Handel was their second son. As a child, he was taken by his father on a visit to Saxe-Weissenfels, where he had a chance to try out the organ of the court chapel. The Duke, Johann Adolf, noticing his interest in music, advised that he be sent to Halle for organ lessons with Friedrich Wilhelm Zachau, the organist of the Liebfrauenkirche there. Zachau gave him instruction in harpsichord and organ playing and also introduced him to the rudiments of composition. Handel proved to be an apt student, and substituted for Zachau as organist whenever necessary; he also composed trio sonatas and motets for Sunday church services. After the death of his father in 1697, he entered the Univ. of Halle in 1702, and was named probationary organist at the Domkirche there. In 1703 he went to Hamburg, where he was engaged as "violino di ripieno" by Reinhard Keiser, the famous composer and director of the Hamburg Opera. There he met Johann Mattheson, and in 1703 the two undertook a journey to Lübeck together, with the intention of applying for the post of organist in succession to Buxtehude, who was chief organist there. There was apparently a quarrel between Mattheson and Handel at a performance of Mattheson's opera *Cleopatra*, in which he sang the leading male role of Antonio, while Handel conducted from the keyboard as maestro al cembalo. When Mattheson completed his stage role, he asked Handel to yield his place at the keyboard to him; Handel declined, and an altercation ensued, resulting in a duel with swords, which was called off when Mattheson broke his sword on a metal button of Handel's coat. There is no independent confirmation of this episode, however, and the two apparently reconciled.

Handel's first opera, *Almira*, was premiered at the Hamburg Opera on Jan. 8, 1705; his next opera, *Nero*, was staged there on Feb. 25, 1705. He was then commissioned to write 2 other operas, *Florindo* and *Daphne*, originally planned as a single opera combining both subjects. In 1706 he undertook a long voyage to Italy, where he visited Florence, Rome, Naples, and Venice. The first opera he wrote in Italy was *Rodrigo*, presented in Florence in 1707. Then followed *Agrippina*, premiered in Venice on Dec. 26, 1709; it obtained an excellent success, being given 27 performances. In Rome, he composed the serenata *Il trionfo del Tempo e del Disinganno*, performed there in the spring of 1707. Handel's oratorio *La Resurrezione* was given in Rome on April 8, 1708. On July 19, 1708, he brought out in Naples his serenata *Aci, Galatea, e Polifemo*; its score was remarkable for a bass solo that required a compass of 2 octaves and

a fifth. During his Italian sojourns, he met Alessandro and Domenico Scarlatti. In 1710 he returned to Germany and was named Kapellmeister to the Elector of Hannover, as successor to Agostino Steffani. Later that year he visited England, where his opera *Rinaldo* was first performed at the Queen's Theatre in London on Feb. 24, 1711; it received 15 performances. After a brief return to Hannover in June 1711, he made another visit to London, where his operas *Il Pastor fido* (Nov. 22, 1712) and *Teseo* (Jan. 10, 1713) were premiered. He also wrote an ode for Queen Anne's birthday, which was presented at Windsor Palace on Feb. 6, 1713; it was followed by 2 sacred works, performed on July 7, 1713, to celebrate the Peace of Utrecht; these performances won him royal favor and an annuity of 200 pounds sterling.

An extraordinary concurrence of events persuaded Handel to remain in London, when Queen Anne died in 1714 and Handel's protector, the Elector of Hannover, became King George I of England. The King bestowed many favors upon the composer and augmented his annuity to 400 pounds sterling. Handel became a British subject in 1727, and Anglicized his name to George Frideric Handel, dropping the original German umlaut. He continued to compose operas, invariably to Italian librettos, for the London stage. His opera *Silla* was premiered in London on June 2, 1713; it was followed by *Amadigi di Gaula* on May 25, 1715. In 1716 Handel wrote *Der für die Sünden der Welt gemarterte und sterbende Jesus*, to the text of the poet Heinrich Brockes. In 1717 he wrote one of his most famous works, written expressly for King George I, his *Water Music*. On July 17, 1717, an aquatic fête on the Thames River was held by royal order; the King's boat was followed by a barge on which an orch. of 50 musicians played Handel's score, or at least a major portion of it. The final version of the *Water Music* combines 2 instrumental suites composed at different times: one was written for the barge party; the other is of an earlier provenance. In 1717 Handel became resident composer to the Duke of Chandos, for whom he wrote the so-called *Chandos Anthems* (1717–18), the secular oratorio *Acis and Galatea* (1718), and the oratorio *Esther* (1718). He also served as music master to the daughters of the Prince of Wales; for Princess Anne he composed his first collection of *Suites de pièces pour le clavecin* (1720), also known as *The Lessons*, which includes the famous air with variations nicknamed *The Harmonious Blacksmith*. In 1719 he was made Master of Musick of a new business venture under the name of the Royal Academy of Music, established for the purpose of presenting opera at the King's Theatre. The first opera he composed for it was *Radamisto* (April 27, 1720). In the fall of 1720 the Italian composer Giovanni Bononcini joined the company. A rivalry soon developed between him and Handel that was made famous by a piece of doggerel by the poet John Byrom ("Some say, compar'd to Bononcini, that Mynheer Handel's but a ninny. Others aver that he to Handel is scarcely fit to hold a candle. Strange all this difference should be twixt tweedledum and tweedledee"). Handel won a Pyrrhic victory when Bononcini had the unfortunate idea of submitting to the London Academy of Music a madrigal which he had appropriated *in extenso* from a choral piece by the Italian composer Antonio Lotti; Lotti discovered it, and an embarrassing controversy ensued, resulting in Bononcini's disgrace and expulsion from London (he died in obscurity in Vienna, where he sought refuge). The irony of the whole episode is that Handel was no less guilty of plagiarism. An article on Handel in the 1880 ed. of the *Encyclopaedia Britannica* spares no words condemning Handel's conduct:"The system of wholesale plagiarism carried on by Handel is perhaps unprecedented in the history of music. He pilfered not only single melodies but frequently entire movements from the works of other masters, with few or no alterations, and without a word of acknowledgment." Between 1721 and 1728 he composed the following operas for the King's Theatre: *Florindante, Ottone, Flavio, Giulio Cesare, Tamerlano, Rodelinda Scipione, Alessandro, Admeto, Riccardo Primo, Siroe,* and *Tolomeo;* of these, *Giulio Cesare* and *Rodelinda* became firmly established in the operatic repertoire. In 1727 he composed 4 grand anthems for the coronation of King George II and Queen Caroline. In the spring of 1728 the Royal Academy of Music ceased operations, and Handel became associated with the management of the King's Theatre. The following year, he went to Italy to recruit singers for a new Royal Academy of Music. Returning to London, he brought out the operas *Lotario, Partenope, Poro, Ezio, Sosarme,* and *Orlando;* only *Orlando* proved a lasting success. On May 2, 1732, Handel gave a special performance of a revised version of his oratorio *Esther* at the King's Theatre; it was followed by the revised version of *Acis and Galatea* (June 10, 1732) and the oratorio *Deborah* (March 17, 1733). On July 10, 1733, his oratorio *Athalia* was first performed at Oxford, where he also appeared as an organist; he was offered, but declined, the degree of Mus.Doc. (*honoris causa*).

Discouraged by the poor reception of his operas at the King's Theatre, Handel decided to open a new season under a different management. But he quarreled with the principal singer, the famous castrato Senesino, who was popular with audiences, and thus lost the support of a substantial number of his subscribers, who then formed a rival opera company called Opera of the Nobility. It engaged the famous Italian composer Porpora as director, and opened its first season at Lincoln's Inn Fields on Dec. 29, 1733. Handel's opera *Arianna in Creta* had its premiere at the King's Theatre on Jan. 26, 1734, but in July of that year both Handel's company and the rival enterprise were forced to suspend operations. Handel set up his own opera company at Covent Garden, inaugurating his new season with a revised version of *Il Pastor fido* (Nov. 9, 1734); this was followed by *Ariodante, Alcina, Atalanta, Arminio, Giustino,* and *Berenice,* all staged between 1735 and 1737; only *Alcina* sustained a success; Handel's other operas met with indifferent reception. On Feb. 19, 1736, he presented his ode *Alexander's Feast* at Covent Garden, and on March 23, 1737, he brought out a revised version of his oratorio *Il trionfo del Tempo e della Verità.* His fortunes improved when he was confirmed by the Queen as music master to Princesses Amelia and Caroline. He continued to maintain connections with Germany, and traveled to Aachen in 1737. Upon his return to London, he suffered from attacks of gout, an endemic illness of British

society at the time, but he managed to resume his work. On Jan. 3, 1738, he brought out his opera *Faramondo,* and on April 15, 1738, presented his opera *Serse* (a famous aria from this opera, *Ombra mai fù,* became even more famous in an instrumental arrangement made by parties unknown, under the title "Handel's Celebrated Largo"). There followed a pasticcio, *Giove in Argo* (May 1, 1739), and *Imeneo* (Nov. 22, 1740). On Jan. 10, 1741, his last opera, *Deidamia,* was premiered there, which marked the end of his operatic enterprise.

In historical perspective, Handel's failure as an operatic entrepreneur was a happy turn of events, for he then directed his energy toward the composition of oratorios, in which he achieved greatness. For inspiration, he turned to biblical themes, using English texts. On Jan. 16, 1739, he presented the oratorio *Saul;* on April 4, 1739, there followed *Israel in Egypt.* He also wrote an *Ode for St. Cecilia's Day,* after Dryden (Nov. 22, 1739), and his great set of 12 Concerti grossi, op.6. Milton's *L'Allegro* and *Il Penseroso* inspired him to write *L'Allegro, il Penseroso, ed il Moderato* (Feb. 27, 1740). In 1741 he was invited to visit Ireland, where he composed his greatest masterpiece, *Messiah;* working with tremendous concentration of willpower and imagination, he completed Part I in 6 days, Part II in 9 days, and Part III in 6 days. The work on orchestration took him only a few more days; he signed the score on Sept. 14, 1741. The first performance of *Messiah* was given in Dublin on April 13, 1742, and its London premiere was presented on March 23, 1743. If contemporary reports can be trusted, King George II rose to his feet at the closing chords of the "Hallelujah" chorus, and the entire audience followed suit. This established a tradition, at least in England. Handel's oratorio *Samson,* first performed in London on Feb. 18, 1743, was also successful, but his next oratorio, *Semele* (Feb. 10, 1744), failed to arouse public admiration. Continuing to work, and alternating between mythological subjects and religious themes, he composed *Joseph and His Brethren* (March 2, 1744), *Hercules* (Jan. 5, 1745), and *Belshazzar* (March 27, 1745). His subsequent works, composed between 1746 and 1752, were the *Occasional Oratorio, Judas Maccabaeus, Joshua, Alexander Balus, Susanna, Solomon, Theodora, The Choice of Hercules,* and *Jephtha.* Of these, *Judas Maccabaeus, Solomon,* and *Jephtha* became public favorites. Besides oratorios, mundane events also occupied his attention. To celebrate the Peace of Aachen, he composed the remarkable *Music for the Royal Fireworks,* heard for the first time in Green Park in London on April 27, 1749. In 1750 he revisited Germany. But soon he had to limit his activities on account of failing eyesight, which required the removal of cataracts; the operation proved unsuccessful, but he still continued to appear in performances of his music, with the assistance of his pupil John Christopher Smith. Handel's last appearance in public was at the London performance of *Messiah* on April 6, 1759; 8 days later, on April 14, the Saturday between Good Friday and Easter, he died. He was buried at Westminster Abbey; a monument by Roubiliac marks his grave. (It should be noted that the year of birth on Handel's gravestone is marked as 1684 rather than 1685; this discrepancy is explained by the fact that at that time the calendar year in England and other European countries began in March, not in January.)

A parallel between the two great German contemporaries, Bach and Handel, is often drawn. Born a few months apart, Bach in Eisenach, Handel in Halle, at a distance of about 130 kilometers, they never met. Bach visited Halle at least twice, but Handel was then away, in London. The difference between their life's destinies was profound. Bach was a master of the Baroque organ who produced religious works for church use, a schoolmaster who regarded his instrumental music as a textbook for study; he never composed for the stage, and traveled little. By contrast, Handel was a man of the world who dedicated himself mainly to public spectacles, and who became a British subject. Bach's life was that of a German burgher; his genius was inconspicuous; Handel shone in the light of public admiration. Bach was married twice; survivors among his 20 children became important musicians in their own right. Handel remained celibate, but he was not a recluse. Physically, he tended toward healthy corpulence; he enjoyed the company of friends, but had a choleric temperament, and could not brook adverse argument. Like Bach, he was deeply religious, and there was no ostentation in his service to his God. Handel's music possessed grandeur of design, majestic eloquence, and lusciousness of harmony. Music-lovers did not have to study Handel's style to discover its beauty, while the sublime art of Bach could be fully understood only after knowledgeable penetration into the contrapuntal and fugal complexities of its structure.

Handel bequeathed the bulk of his MSS to his amanuensis, John Christopher Smith, whose son presented them in turn to King George III. They eventually became a part of the King's Music Library; they comprise 32 vols. of operas, 21 vols. of oratorios, 7 vols. of odes and serenatas, 12 vols. of sacred music, 11 vols. of cantatas, and 5 vols. of instrumental music. Seven vols. containing sketches for various works are in the Fitzwilliam Collection at Cambridge. In 1991 the Neue Deutsche Händel-Gesellschaft was founded in Bonn.

WORKS: DRAMATIC: O p e r a : *Almira* (Theater am Gänsemarkt, Hamburg, Jan. 8, 1705; part of music not extant); *Nero* (Theater am Gänsemarkt, Feb. 25, 1705; music not extant); *Rodrigo* (Accademia degli Infuocata, Florence, 1706 or 1707; part of music not extant); *Florindo* and *Daphne* (presented as 2 separate operas, Theater am Gänsemarkt, Jan. 1708; only a small part of music extant); *Agrippina* (Teatro San Giovanni Grisostomo, Venice, Dec. 26, 1709); *Rinaldo* (Queen's Theatre, London, Feb. 24, 1711; major rev., King's Theatre, London, April 6, 1731); *Il Pastor fido* (Queen's Theatre, Nov. 22, 1712; rev. versions, King's Theatre, May 18, 1734, and Nov. 9, 1734 [the latter with ballet *Terpsicore*]); *Teseo* (Queen's Theatre, Jan. 10, 1713); *Silla* (Queen's Theatre, or Burlington House, June 2, 1713); *Amadigi di Gaula* (King's Theatre, May 25, 1715); *Radamisto* (King's Theatre, April 27, 1720; rev. versions there, Dec. 28, 1720, and Jan.-Feb. 1728); *Floridante* (King's Theatre, Dec. 9, 1721; rev. version there, March 3, 1733); *Ottone, rè di Germania* (King's Theatre, Jan. 12, 1723; rev. versions there, Feb. 8, 1726, and Nov. 13, 1733); *Flavio, rè di Longobardi* (King's Theatre, May 14, 1723; major rev. there, April 18, 1732); *Giulio Cesare in Egitto* (King's Theatre, Feb. 20, 1724; rev. versions there, Jan. 2, 1725,

and Jan. 17, 1730); *Tamerlano* (King's Theatre, Oct. 31, 1724); *Rodelinda, regina de' Longobardi* (King's Theatre, Feb. 13, 1725); *Scipione* (King's Theatre, March 12, 1726; rev. version there, Nov. 3, 1730); *Alessandro* (King's Theatre, May 5, 1726); *Admeto, rè di Tessaglia* (King's Theatre, Jan. 31, 1727; rev. version there, Dec. 7, 1731); *Riccardo Primo, rè d'Inghilterra* (King's Theatre, Nov. 11, 1727); *Siroe, rè di Persia* (King's Theatre, Feb. 17, 1728); *Tolomeo, rè di Egitto* (King's Theatre, April 30, 1728; major rev. there, May 19, 1730); *Lotario* (King's Theatre, Dec. 2, 1729); *Partenope* (King's Theatre, Feb. 24, 1730; rev. version there, Dec. 12, 1730; later rev. for Covent Garden, London, Jan. 29, 1737); *Poro, rè dell'Indie* (King's Theatre, Feb. 2, 1731; rev. versions there, Nov. 23, 1731, and Dec. 8, 1736); *Ezio* (King's Theatre, Jan. 15, 1732); *Sosarme, rè di Media* (King's Theatre, Feb. 15, 1732); *Orlando* (King's Theatre, Jan. 27, 1733); *Arianna in Creta* (King's Theatre, Jan. 26, 1734; rev. for Covent Garden, Nov. 27, 1734); *Oreste*, a pasticcio with music by Handel (Covent Garden, Dec. 18, 1734); *Ariodante* (Covent Garden, Jan. 8, 1735); *Alcina* (Covent Garden, April 16, 1735); *Atalanta* (Covent Garden, May 12, 1736); *Arminio* (Covent Garden, Jan. 12, 1737); *Giustino* (Covent Garden, Feb. 16, 1737); *Berenice* (Covent Garden, May 18, 1737); *Faramondo* (King's Theatre, Jan. 3, 1738); *Alessandro Severo*, pasticcio with music by Handel (King's Theatre, Feb. 25, 1738); *Serse* (King's Theatre, April 15, 1738); *Giove in Argo*, pasticcio (King's Theatre, May 1, 1739); *Imeneo* (Lincoln's Inn Fields, London, Nov. 22, 1740); *Deidamia* (Lincoln's Inn Fields, Jan. 10, 1741). Also *Muzio Scevola* (Act 3 by Handel; Act 1 by F. Amadei and Act 2 by G. Bononcini; King's Theatre, April 15, 1721); *Genserico* (only part of Act 1 drafted); *Tito* (only scenes 1–3 of Act 1 composed); *Alceste* (greater part of music used in the oratorio *The Choice of Hercules*; see below). **ORCH.:** Six Concerti Grossi, op.3: No. 1, in B-flat major; No. 2, in B-flat major; No. 3, in G major; No. 4, in F major; No. 5, in D minor; No. 6, in D major/D minor (publ. as a set in London, 1734); 12 Concerti Grossi, op.6: No. 1, in G major; No. 2, in F major; No. 3, in C minor; No. 4, in A minor; No. 5, in D major; No. 6, in G minor; No. 7, in B-flat major; No. 8, in C minor; No. 9, in F major; No. 10, in D minor; No. 11, in A major; No. 12, in B minor (publ. as a set in London, 1740). Also 19 organ concertos; 3 *Concerti a due cori* (mostly arranged from other works); *Water Music* (greater part of music perf. during the royal barge excursion on the Thames River, July 17, 1717); *Music for the Royal Fireworks* (Green Park, London, April 27, 1749); overtures; sinfonie; many marches. **CHAMBER:** Twenty trio sonatas: op.2, no. 1, in B minor, for Flute or Violin, Violin, and Basso Continuo; op.2, no. 2, in G minor, for 2 Violins and Basso Continuo; op.2, no. 3, in E-flat major, for 2 Violins and Basso Continuo; op.2, no. 4, in F major, for Flute or Recorder or Violin, Violin, and Basso Continuo; op.2, no. 5, in G minor, for 2 Violins and Basso Continuo; op.2, no. 6, in G minor, for 2 Violins and Basso Continuo; op.5, no. 1, in A major, for 2 Violins and Basso Continuo; op.5, no. 2, in D major, for 2 Violins and Basso Continuo; op.5, no. 3, in E minor, for 2 Violins and Basso Continuo; op.5, no. 4, in G major, for 2 Violins and Basso Continuo; op.5, no. 5, in G minor, for 2 Violins and Basso Continuo; op.5, no. 6, in F major, for 2 Violins and Basso Continuo; op.5, no. 7, in B-flat major, for 2 Violins and Basso Continuo; in C minor, for Recorder or Flute, Violin, and Basso Continuo; in F major, for 2 Violins and Basso Continuo; in E major, for 2 Violins and Basso Continuo; in E minor, for 2 Flutes and Basso Continuo; in F major, for 2 Violins and Basso Continuo; in C major, for 2 Violins and Basso Continuo; 17 solo sonatas with Basso Continuo: No. 1, in A minor, for Recorder; No. 2, in B-flat major, for Recorder; No. 3, in C major, for

Recorder; No. 4, in D minor, for Recorder; No. 5, in F major, for Recorder; No. 6, in G minor, for Recorder; No. 7, in E minor, for Flute; No. 8, in B-flat major, for Oboe; No. 9, in C minor, for Oboe; No. 10, in F major, most likely for Oboe; No. 11, in A major, for Violin; No. 12, in D major, for Violin; No. 13, in D minor, for Violin; No. 14, in G minor, for Violin; No. 15, in G minor, for Violin; No. 16, in G minor, for Viola da Gamba; No. 17, in A major, for Violin. Also *Suites de pièces pour le clavecin* (2 books, London, 1720 and 1733) and additional works for keyboard. **VOCAL: O r a t o r i o s :** *Oratorio per la Resurrezione di Nostro Signor Gesù Cristo* (Palazzo Ruspoli, Rome, April 8, 1708); *Acis and Galatea* (Cannons, 1718; major rev., King's Theatre, June 10, 1732; also subsequent revs.); *Esther* (Cannons, 1718; major rev., King's Theatre, May 2, 1732; also subsequent additions); *Deborah* (King's Theatre, March 17, 1733; also subsequent revs.); *Athalia* (Sheldonian Theatre, Oxford, July 10, 1733; major rev., Covent Garden, April 1, 1735); *Il Parnasso in festa* (greater part of music from *Athalia*; King's Theatre, March 13, 1734); *Saul* (King's Theatre, Jan. 16, 1739; also subsequent revs.); *Israel in Egypt* (King's Theatre, April 4, 1739; also subsequent extensive changes); *Messiah* (New Music Hall, Dublin, April 13, 1742; also numerous revs. made for many subsequent perfs.); *Samson* (Covent Garden, Feb. 18, 1743; also subsequent revs.); *Semele* (Covent Garden, Feb. 10, 1744); *Joseph and His Brethren* (Covent Garden, March 2, 1744; also subsequent revs.); *Hercules* (King's Theatre, Jan. 5, 1745); *Belshazzar* (King's Theatre, March 27, 1745; rev. version, Covent Garden, Feb. 22, 1751); *Occasional Oratorio*, pasticcio (Covent Garden, Feb. 14, 1746); *Judas Maccabaeus* (Covent Garden, April 1, 1747; also many subsequent revs.); *Alexander Balus* (Covent Garden, March 23, 1748; rev. version, March 1, 1754); *Susanna* (Covent Garden, Feb. 10, 1749); *Solomon* (Covent Garden, March 17, 1749); *Theodora* (Covent Garden, March 16, 1750); *The Choice of Hercules* (greater part of music from *Alceste*; Covent Garden, March 1, 1751); *Jephtha* (Covent Garden, Feb. 26, 1752); *The Triumph of Time and Truth* (greater part of music from *Il trionfo del Tempo e della Verità*; Covent Garden, March 11, 1757). **P a s s i o n s :** *Passion According to St. John* (most likely spurious; Hamburg, Feb. 17, 1704); *Der für die Sünden der Welt gemarterte und sterbende Jesus*, the so-called *Brockes Passion* (Hamburg?, 1716). **S e r e n a t a s :** *Il trionfo del Tempo e del Disinganno* (Rome, 1707?; major rev. as *Il trionfo del Tempo e della Verità*, Covent Garden, March 23, 1737); *Aci, Galatea, e Polifemo* (Naples, July 19, 1708). **O d e s :** *Ode for the Birthday of Queen Anne* (Windsor, Feb. 6, 1713); *Ode for St. Cecilia's Day* or *Alexander's Feast* (Covent Garden, Feb. 19, 1736). **E n g l i s h C h u r c h M u s i c :** *Te Deum* and *Jubilate* in D major, "Utrecht" (for the Peace of Utrecht; St. Paul's, London, July 7, 1713); *Te Deum* in D major, "Caroline" (Chapel Royal, London, Sept. 26, 1714); *11 Chandos Anthems: As pants the hart; Have mercy upon me, O God; In the Lord put I my trust; I will magnify thee, O God; Let God arise; My song shall be alway; O be joyful; O come let us sing unto the Lord; O praise the Lord with one consent; O sing unto the Lord; The Lord is my light* (1717–18); *Te Deum* in B-flat major, "Chandos" (c. 1718); *Te Deum* in A major (based upon the "Chandos" *Te Deum*; 1721–26); *4 Coronation Anthems: Let thy hand be strengthened; My heart is inditing; The king shall rejoice; Zadok the priest* (for the coronation of King George II; Westminster Abbey, London, Oct. 11, 1727); *Funeral Anthem: The ways of Zion do mourn* (for the funeral of Queen Caroline; Westminster Abbey, Dec. 17, 1737); *Te Deum* and *Anthem* in D major, "Dettingen" (for the victory at Dettingen; Chapel Royal, Nov. 27, 1743); *Anthem on the Peace: How beautiful are the feet* (for the Peace of Aix-la-Chapelle; Chapel Royal, April 25, 1749); *Found-ling Hospital Anthem: Blessed are they that considereth the poor* (Foundling Hospital, London, May 27, 1749). **L a t i n C h u r c h M u s i c :** *Laudate pueri Dominum* in F major (c. 1706); *O qualis de caelo sonus* in G major, motet (Vignanello, June 12, 1707); *Coelestis dum spirat aura* in D/G major, motet (Vignanello, June 13, 1707); *Laudate pueri Dominum* in D major (1707); *Dixit Dominus* in G minor (1707); *Nisi Dominus* in G major (1707); *Silete venti* in B-flat major, motet (c. 1729). **S e c u l a r C a n t a t a s , D r a m a t i c** (unless otherwise indicated, date is unknown): *Aminta e Fillide* (1708); *Clori, Tirsi e Fileno* (1707); *Il duello amoroso* (1708); *Apollo e Dafne* (c. 1708); *Olinto, Il Tebro, Gloria* (1708); etc. **S o l o a n d D u o C a n t a t a s w i t h I n s t r u m e n t s :** *Agrippina condotta a morire* (c. 1708); *Ah! crudel nel pianto mio* (c. 1707); *Alpestre monto; Armida abbandonata* (1707); *Cantata spagnuola* (1707); *Carco sempre di gloria* (1737); *Cecilia, volgi un sguardo* (1736); *Clori, mia bella Clori; Crudel tiranno amor* (1721); *Cuopre tal volta; Il delirio amoroso* (1707); *Diana cacciatrice* (1707); *Figlio d'alte speranze; Languia di bocca lusinghiera; Mi palpita il cor; Pensieri notturni di Filli; Notte placida e cheta* (1708); *Qual ti riveggio, oh Dio; Spande ancor; Splende l'alba in oriente; Tra le fiamme; Tu fedel? tu costante?* (1707); *Un alma innamorata* (1707); *Venus and Adonis* (c. 1711). **S o l o C a n t a t a s w i t h B a s s o C o n t i n u o :** *Ah, che pur troppo e vero; Allor ch'io dissi; Aure soavi e liete* (1707); *Bella ma ritrosetta; Care selve; Chi rapi la pace* (1709); *Clori, degli occhi miei; Clori, ove sei; Clori, si ch'io t'adoro* (may not be by Handel); *Clori, vezzosa Clori* (1708); *Dal fatale momento; Dalla guerra amorosa* (1709); *Da sete ardente afflitto* (1709); *Deh! lasciate e vita e volo; Del bel idolo mio* (1709); *Dimmi, o mio cor; Dite, mie piante* (1708); *Dolce pur d'amor l'affanno; E partirai, mia vita?; Figli del mesto cor; Filli adorata e cara* (1709); *Fra pensieri quel pensiero; Fra tante pene* (1709); *Hendel, non puo mia musa* (1708); *Ho fuggito amore; Irene, idolo mio; L'aure grate, il fresco rio; Lungi dal mio bel nume* (1708); *Lungi da me pensier tiranno* (1709); *Lungi da voi, che siete poli* (1708); *Lungi n'ando Fileno* (1708); *Manca pur quanto sai* (1708); *Mentre il tutto è in furore* (1708); *Menzognere speranze* (1707); *Mi, palpita il cor; Nel dolce tempo; Nell-africane selve; Nella stagion, che di viole* (1707); *Ne' tuoi lumi, o bella Clori* (1707); *Nice che fa? che pensa?; Ninfe e pastori* (1709); *Non sospirar, non piangere; Occhi miei, che faceste?; O lucenti, o sereni occhi; O numi eterni* (1709); *Parti, l'idolo mio; Poichè giuraro amore* (1707); *Qual fior che all'alba ride* (c. 1739); *Qualor crudele si mia vaga Dori; Qualor l'egre pupille* (1707); *Qual sento io non conosciuto* (may not be by Handel); *Quando sperasti, o core* (1708); *Sans y penser; Sarai contenta un di; Sarei troppo felice* (1707); *Sei pur bella, pur vezzosa* (1707); *Sento là che ristretto* (1709); *Se pari è la tua fe* (1708); *Se per fatal destino* (1707); *Siete rose rugiadose; S'il ne falloit; Solitudini care, amata libertà; Son gelsomino; Stanco di più soffrire* (1708); *Stelle, perfide stelle; Torna il core al suo diletto; Udite il meo consiglio* (1707); *Un sospir a chi si muove; Vedendo amor; Venne voglia ad amore; Zeffiretto, arresta il volo* (1709). Also 22 duets and trios with Continuo; more than 30 English songs; 9 German arias; Italian songs; French songs.

BIBL.: COLLECTED EDITIONS, SOURCE MATERIAL: The first ed. of Handel's collected works was edited by S. Arnold in 180 installments in 54 vols. (1787–97). It was superseded by the monumental ed. prepared by F. Chrysander under the title *G. F. H.s Werke: Ausgabe der deutschen Händelgesellschaft* (100 vols., Leipzig and Bergedorf bei Hamburg, 1858–94; 6 suppl. vols., 1888–1902). In 1955 the Hallische H.-Ausgabe was begun as a suppl. to the Chrysander ed.; however, it soon became a new critical ed. in its own right, being edited by M. Schneider and R. Steglich as the *Hallische H.-Ausgabe im Auftrage der Georg Friedrich H.-Gesellschaft*, and publ. in Kassel. A. Bell ed. a *Chronological Catalogue of H.'s Work* (Greenock, Scotland, 1969). Other sources include the following: N. Flower, *Catalogue of a H. Collection Formed by Newman Flower* (Sevenoaks, 1920); W. Squire, *Catalogue of the King's Music Library, I: The H. Manuscripts* (London, 1927); H. Shaw, *A First List of Word-books of H.'s "Messiah," 1742–83* (Worcester, 1959); W. Smith and C. Humphries, *H.: A Descriptive Catalogue of the Early Editions* (London, 1960; 2nd ed., rev., 1970); H. Federhofer, *Unbekannte Kopien von Werken G. F. H.s* (Kassel, 1963); K. Sasse, *H.-Bibliographie* (Leipzig, 1963; new ed., 1967; with suppl., 1969); W. Smith, *A H.ian's Notebook* (London, 1965); P. Krause, *Handschriften und altere Drucke der Werke G. F. H.'s in der Musikbibliothek der Stadt Leipzig* (Leipzig, 1966); A. Hyatt King, *H. and His Autographs* (London, 1967); W. Meyerhoff, ed., *50 Jahre Göttinger H.-Festspiele. Festschrift* (Kassel, 1970); H. Clausen, *H.s Direktionspartituren ("Handexemplare")* (Hamburg, 1972); A. Walker, *G. F. H.: The Newman Flower Collection in the Henry Watson Music Library* (Manchester, 1972); H. Marx, *Göttinger H.-Beitrage I* (Kassel, 1984); B. Baselt, *Verzeichnis der Werke G. F. H.s (HWV)* (Leipzig, 1986); M. Parker-Hale, *G. F. H.: A Guide to Research* (N.Y., 1988); D. Burrows and M. Ronish, *A Catalogue of H.'s Musical Autographs* (Oxford, 1993); D. Burrows, ed., *The Cambridge Companion to H.* (Cambridge, 1997). **BIOGRAPHICAL:** J. Mainwaring, *Memoirs of the Late G. F. H.* (London, 1760; reprint, 1967); J. Mattheson, *G. F. H.s Lebensbeschreibung* (based almost entirely on Mainwaring's biography; Hamburg, 1761; reprint, 1976); C. Burney, *An Account of the Musical Performances in Westminster Abbey and the Pantheon May 26th, 27th, 29th; and June 3rd and 5th, 1784: In Commemoration of H.* (London, 1785; reprint, 1965); W. Coxe, *Anecdotes of G. F. H. and John Christopher Smith* (London, 1799; reprint, 1980); R. Clark, *Reminiscences of H.* (London, 1836); K. Förstemann, *G. F. H.s Stammbaum* (Leipzig, 1844); W. Callcott, *A Few Facts in the Life of H.* (London, 1850); H. Townsend, *An Account of H.'s Visit to Dublin: With Incidental Notices of His Life and Character* (Dublin, 1852); V. Schoelcher, *The Life of H.* (London, 1857); A. Stothard, *H.: His Life, Personal and Professional* (London, 1857); F. Chrysander, *G. F. H.* (3 vols., Leipzig, 1858–67; reprint, 1966); J. Marshall, *H.* (London, 1881; 3rd ed., 1912); W. Rockstro, *The Life of G. F. H.* (London, 1883); J. Opel, *Mitteilungen zur Geschichte der Familie des Tonkünstlers H.* (Leipzig, 1885); A. Ademollo, *G. F. H. in Italia* (Milan, 1889); F. Volbach, *G. F. H.* (Berlin, 1897; 3rd ed., 1914); W. Cummings, *H.* (London, 1904); F. Williams, *H.* (London, 1904); J. Hadden, *Life of H.* (London, 1905); R. Streatfeild, *H.* (London, 1909; reprint, 1964); R. Rolland, *H.* (Paris, 1910; 2nd ed., 1974; Eng. tr., 1916; reprint, 1975); M. Brenet, *H.* (Paris, 1912); H. Davey, *H.* (London, 1912); G. Thormälius, *G. F. H.* (Stuttgart, 1912); R. Streatfeild, *H., Canons and the Duke of Chandos* (London, 1916); N. Flower, *G. F. H.: His Personality and His Times* (London, 1923; 3rd ed., rev., 1959); H. Leichtentritt, *H.* (Stuttgart, 1924); H. Moser, *Der junge H. und seine Vorgänger in Halle* (Halle, 1929); J. Müller-Blattau, *G. F. H.* (Potsdam, 1933); E. Dent, *H.* (London, 1934); L. Liebeman, *G. F. H. und Halle* (Halle, 1935); E. Müller, ed., *The Letters and Writings of G. F. H.* (London, 1935); C. Williams, *H.* (London, 1935); H. Weinstock, *H.* (N.Y., 1946; 2nd ed., rev., 1959); P. Young, *H.* (London, 1946; 3rd ed., rev., 1975); W. Smith, *Concerning H., His Life and Works* (London, 1948); A.-E. Cherbuliez, *G. F. H.: Leben und Werk* (Olten, 1949); H. and E.H. Müller von Asow, *G. F. H.: Briefe und Schriften* (Lindau, 1949); O. Deutsch, *H.: A Documentary Biography* (N.Y., 1954, and London, 1955); W. Siegmund-Schultze, *G. F. H.: Leben und Werke* (Leipzig, 1954; 3rd ed., rev., 1962); W. Serauky, *G. F. H.: Sein Leben, sein Werk* (only vols. III-V publ.; Kassel, 1956–58); P. Nettl, *G. F. H.* (Berlin, 1958); R. Friedenthal, *G. F. H. in*

Selbstzeugnissen und Bilddokumenten (Hamburg, 1959; 3rd ed., Reinbeck, 1967); J. Müller-Blattau, *G. F. H.: Der Wille zur Volldendung* (Mainz, 1959); W. Rackwitz and H. Steffens, *G. F. H.: Persönlichkeit, Umwelt, Vermächtnis* (Leipzig, 1962); S. Sadie, *H.* (London, 1962); P. Lang, *G. F. H.* (N.Y., 1966); K. Sasse, *Bildsammlung; Hogarth-Grafik; Darstellung zur Geschichte, H.-pfege und Musikkunde* (Halle, 1967); M. Szentkuthy, *H.* (Budapest, 1967); W. Siegmund-Schultze, ed., *G. F. H.: Beiträge zu seiner Biographie aus dem 18. Jahrhundert* (Leipzig, 1977); C. Hogwood, *H.* (London, 1984); H. C. Robbins Landon, *H. and His World* (Boston, 1984); J. Keates, *H.: The Man and His Music* (London, 1985); W. Rackwitz, *G. F. H.: Lebensbeschreibung in Bildern* (Wiesbaden, 1986); C. Ludwig, *G. F. H.: Composer of Messiah* (Milford, Mich., 1987); D. Burrows, *H.* (N.Y., 1994); S. Pettitt, *H.* (N.Y., 1994); K. Hortschansky and K. Musketa, eds., *G. F. H.: Ein Lebensinhalt: Gedenkschrift für Bernd Baselt (1934–1993)* (Halle an der Saale, 1995); J.-J. Schmelzer, *Siehe, dein König kommt: Leben und Musik des G. F. H.: Eine Biographie* (Düsseldorf, 1995). **CRITICAL, ANALYTICAL** (in addition to the writings listed below, important articles may be found in the *H.-Jahrbuch* [1928–33; 1955 et seq.]): G. Gervinus, *H. und Shakespeare: Zur Ästhetik der Tonkunst* (Leipzig, 1868); R. Franz, *Über Bearbeitungen älterer Tonwerke, namenlich Bachscher und H.scher Vokalmusik* (Leipzig, 1871; reprinted by R. Bethge as *Gesammelte Schriften über die Wiederbelebung Bachscher und H.scher Werke*, Leipzig, 1910); E. Frommel, *H. und Bach* (Berlin, 1878); F. Chrysander, *H.s biblische Oratorien in geschichtlicher Betrachtung* (Hamburg, 1897); F. Volbach, *Die Praxis der H.-Aufführung* (Charlottenburg, 1900); G. Vernier, *L'Oratorio biblique de H.* (Cahors, 1901); J. Garat, *La Sonate de H.* (Paris, 1905); E. Bernoulli, *Quellen zum Studium Handelscher Chorwerke* (Leipzig, 1906); S. Taylor, *The Indebtedness of H. to Works by Other Composers* (Cambridge, 1906); P. Robinson, *H. and His Orbit* (London, 1908); A. Schering, *Geschichte des Oratoriums* (Leipzig, 1911); H. Abert, *H. als Dramatiker* (Göttingen, 1921); E. Bairstow, *The Messiah* (London, 1928); F. Kahle, *H.s Cembalo-Suiten* (Berlin, 1928); E. Bredenfoerder, *Die Texte der H.-Oratorien* (Leipzig, 1934); F. Ehrlinger, *H.s Orgelkonzerte* (Erlangen, 1934); E. Völsing, *G. F. H.s englische Kirchenmusik* (Leipzig, 1940); J. Eisenschmidt, *Die szenische Darstellung der Opern H.s auf der Londoner Bühne seiner Zeit* (Wolfenbüttel, 1940–41); J. Herbage, *Messiah* (London, 1948); R. Myers, *H.'s Messiah, A Touchstone of Taste* (N.Y., 1948); P. Young, *The Oratorios of H.* (London, 1949); G. Abraham, ed., *H.: A Symposium* (London, 1954); R. Myers, *H., Dryden and Milton* (London, 1956); J. Larsen, *H.'s Messiah: Origins, Composition, Sources* (London, 1957; 2nd ed., rev., 1972); H. Wolff, *Die H.-Oper auf der modernen Bühne* (Leipzig, 1957); W. Dean, *H.'s Dramatic Oratorios and Masques* (London, 1959); H. Dietz, *Die Chorfuge bei G. F. H.* (Tutzing, 1961); H. Shaw, *The Story of H.'s Messiah* (London, 1963); J. Tobin, *H. at Work* (London, 1964); H. Shaw, *A Textual and Historical Companion to H.'s Messiah* (London, 1965); D. Kimbell, *A Critical Study of H.'s Early Operas* (diss., Univ. of Oxford, 1968); W. Dean, *H. and the Opera Seria* (Berkeley, Calif., 1969); J. Tobin, *H.'s Messiah* (London, 1969); S. Sadie, *H. Concertos* (London, 1972); H. Friedrichs, *Das Verhältnis von Text und Musik in den Brockespassionen Keisers, H.s, Telemanns und Matthesons* (Munich and Salzburg, 1975); G. Beeks, *The Chandos Anthems and Te Deum of G. F. H.* (diss., Univ. of Calif., Berkeley, 1977); E. Harris, *H. and the Pastoral Tradition* (London, 1980); H. Hoffmann, *G. F. H.: Vom Opernkomponisten zum Meister des Oratoriums* (Marburg an der Lahn, 1983); D. Burrows, *H. and the Chapel Royal* (London, 1984); R. Strohm, *Essays on H. and Italian Opera* (Cambridge, 1985); P. Williams, ed., *Bach, H. and Scarlatti: Tercentenary Essays* (Cambridge, 1985); H. Meynell, *The Art of*

H.'s Operas (Lewiston, N.Y., 1986); W. Dean and J. Knapp, *H.'s Operas 1704–1726* (Oxford, 1987); N. Pirrotta and A. Zino, eds., *H. e gli Scarlatti a Roma: Atti del convegno internazionale di studi (Roma, 12–14 giugno 1985)* (Florence, 1987); J. Larsen, *Essays on H., Haydn, and the Viennese Classical Style* (tr. by U. Krämer; Ann Arbor, 1988); P. Rogers, *Continuo Realization in H.'s Music* (Ann Arbor, 1988); S. Sadie and A. Hicks, eds., *H. Tercentenary Collection* (Ann Arbor, 1988); D. Burrows, *H.: Messiah* (Cambridge, 1991); C. LaRue, *H. and His Singers: The Creation of the Royal Academy Operas, 1720–1728* (Oxford, 1995); R. Smith, *H.'s Oratorios and Eighteenth-Century Thought* (Cambridge, 1995); A. Mann, *H., the Orchestral Music: Orchestral Concertos, Organ Concertos, Water Music, Music for the Royal Fireworks* (N.Y., 1996); U. Etscheit, *H.s "Rodelinda"* (Kassel, 1998); H. Marx, *H.s Oratorien, Oden und Serenaten: Ein Kompendium* (Göttingen, 1998). **—NS/LK/DM**

Handford, Maurice, English conductor; b. Salisbury, April 29, 1929; d. Warminster, Dec. 16, 1986. He studied horn at the Royal Academy of Music in London. He was principal horn in the Hallé Orch. in Manchester (1949–61). In 1960 he made his conducting debut with it, and then served as its asst. (1964–66) and assoc. (1966–71) conductor. In 1961 he became conductor of the Royal Academy of Music First Orch. He also was conductor with the City of Birmingham Sym. Orch. (1970–74) and music director of the Calgary (Alberta) Phil. (1971–75).**—NS/LK/DM**

Handl (also **Händl, Handelius, Hähnel**), **Jacob,** important Slovenian composer, also known as **Jacobus Gallus**; b. probably in Ribniča, between April 15 and July 31, 1550; d. Prague, July 18, 1591. He went to Austria about 1565. After a stay at the Benedictine abbey in Melk, he went to Vienna about 1568, where he was a singer in the imperial chapel of Maximilian II in 1574–75. Following extensive travels, he served as choirmaster to Stanislaus Pavlovský, Bishop of Olmütz (1579?–85). By 1586 he was Kantor at St. Jan na Brzehu in Prague, a post he retained until his death. His large output included 445 motets, about 20 masses, 3 Passions, and many secular songs. Handl was particularly influenced by the Netherlands and Italian schools. His polychoral writing is outstanding.

WORKS: VOCAL: S a c r e d : M a s s e s : (16) *Selectiores quaedam missae* for 4 to 8 Voices (4 vols., Prague, 1580; ed. by P. Pisk in Denkmäler der Tonkunst in Österreich, LXXVIII, Jg.XLII/1, 1935, and ibid., XCIV-XCV, 1959, CXVII, 1967, and CXIX, 1969). **M o t e t s :** *Opus musicum* for 4 to 6 and 8 Voices (4 vols., Prague, 1586–91; ed. by E. Bezecný and J. Mantuani in Denkmäler der Tonkunst in Österreich, XII, Jg.VI/1[1899], XXIV Jg.XII/1 [1905], XXX, Jg.XV/1 [1908], XL, Jg.XX/1 [1913], XLVIII, Jg.XXIV [1917], and LI-LII, Jg.XXVI [1919]); *Undique flammatis Olomucum sedibus arsit* for 7 Voices (Prague, 1579); *Epicedion...Caspari Abbatis Zabrdovicensis ac Syloensis* (Prague, 1589). **S e c u l a r :** *Harmoniae morales* for 4 Voices (3 vols., Prague, 1589–90; ed. by D. Cvetko, Ljubljana, 1966); *Moralia* for 5, 6, and 8 Voices (Prague, 1596; ed. by D. Cvetko, Ljubljana, 1968, and by A. Skei in Recent Researches in the Music of the Renaissance, VII-VIII, 1970).

BIBL.: D. Cvetko, *Jacobus Gallus: Sein Leben und Werk* (Munich, 1972); S. Pontz, *Die Motetten von J. G.: Untersuchungen zu den Tonarten der klassischen Vokalpolyphonie* (Munich, 1996). **—NS/LK/DM**

Handley, Vernon (George), admirable English conductor; b. London, Nov. 11, 1930. He was educated at Balliol Coll., Oxford, and the Guildhall School of Music and Drama in London. He made his debut with the Bournemouth Sym. Orch. in 1961. From 1962 to 1983 he was principal conductor of the Guildford Phil. He was also a prof. at the Royal Coll. of Music in London (1966–72). In 1982 he was appointed assoc. conductor of the London Phil. In 1983 he became principal guest conductor of the BBC Scottish Sym. Orch. in Glasgow. He was principal conductor of the Ulster Orch. in Belfast (1985–89) and the Malmö Sym. Orch. (1985–91). From 1989 to 1994 he was principal guest conductor of the Royal Liverpool Phil., and also of the Melbourne Sym. Orch. from 1993 to 1995. He was chief conductor of the West Australian Sym. Orch. in Perth from 1994 to 1996. Handley has won particular distinction for his championship of British music.**—NS/LK/DM**

Handschin, Jacques (Samuel), eminent Swiss organist and musicologist; b. Moscow, April 5, 1886; d. Basel, Nov. 25, 1955. He studied organ in Moscow, and in 1905 mathematics and history at the Univ. of Basel. He then went to Munich to pursue his academic studies, and also studied organ and theory with Reger. He later attended some of the lectures in musicology given in Leipzig by Riemann and in Berlin by Hornbostel, and took additional courses in organ with Straube in Leipzig and with Widor in Paris. Returning to Russia, he taught organ at the St. Petersburg Cons. (1909–20). He gave numerous organ recitals in Russia, and promoted contemporary organ works by Russian composers, among them Glazunov and Taneyev. Included these works in his anthology *Les Maîtres contemporains de l'orgue* (Paris, 1913–14). In 1920 he returned to Switzerland, and in 1921 he received his Ph.D. from the Univ. of Basel with the diss. *Choralbearbeitungen und Kompositionen mit rhythmischem Text in der mehrstimmigen Musik des 13. Jahrhunderts*; completed his Habilitation there in 1924 with his *Über die mehrstimmige Musik der St. Martial-Epoche sowie die Zusammenhänge zwischen Notre Dame und St. Martial und die Zusammenhänge zwischen einem dritten Stil und Notre Dame und St. Martial*. In 1924 he became Privatdozent at the Univ. of Basel, and later he was a prof. of musicology there (1935–55). He also served as a church organist in Zürich and Basel. He was greatly esteemed for his erudition and the soundness of his analytical theories; he evolved philosophical principles of musical aesthetics seeking the rational foundations of the art. His most important work is *Der Toncharakter: Eine Einführung in die Tonpsychologie* (Zürich, 1948), which sets down his principles of musical aesthetics. Other works include *La Musique de l'antiquité* (Paris, 1946) and *Musikgeschichte im Überblick* (Lucerne, 1948).

BIBL.: H. Oesch, *Gedenkschrift J. H.: Aufsätze und Bibliographie* (Bern and Stuttgart, 1957); H. Anglés et al., eds., *In memoriam J. H.* (Strasbourg, 1962); M. Maier, *J. H.s "Toncharakter": Zu den Bedingungen seiner Entstehung* (Stuttgart, 1991). **—NS/LK/DM**

Handt, Herbert, American tenor and conductor; b. Philadelphia, May 26, 1926. He studied at the Juilliard

School of Music in N.Y. and the Vienna Academy of Music, making his operatic debut at the Vienna State Opera (1949). After making his conducting debut in Rome (1960), he prepared performing eds. of rarely heard Italian scores; he later settled in Lucca, where he was founder-director of the Associazione Musicale Lucchese, the Lucca Chamber Orch., and the Marlia International Festival.—NS/LK/DM

Handy, Craig (Mitchell), jazz saxophonist; b. Oakland, Calif., Sept. 25, 1962.

Handy has established himself as a forceful and original player based in the N.Y. area. His mother was a pianist, his father, John Handy, was a famed jazz saxophonist. He began on guitar at age nine, then progressed through piano, trombone, and finally alto sax. He won a Charlie Parker Scholarship to attend North Tex. State Univ., but ended up studying psychology rather than saxophone. He played with Galen Jeter's Dallas Jazz Orch. from 1983–86, and then Abdullah Ibrahim (1987–90). He has worked regularly with the Mingus Big Band since 1987. From 1988–90, he led his own quintet, and from 1990–92 toured Europe as a solo act. He toured Italy in 1995 with Lovano, Bunky Green, Steve Coleman, Kenny Davis and Ralph Peterson. He has been featured in Herbie Hancock's acoustic quartet since 1996. He scored the television program *The Cosby Mysteries* (1994) and appeared and played in the film *Kansas City* (1996).

Disc.: *Split Second Timing* (1991); *Introducing Three for All & One* (1993).—LP

Handy, W(illiam) C(hristopher), foresighted American composer of early blues and jazz, bandleader, and brass player; b. Florence, Ala., Nov. 16, 1873; d. N.Y., March 28, 1958.

Though he may not have lived up to his billing as the Father of the Blues, Handy was the first important musician to popularize the form. Steeped in classical music traditions and a veteran of decades of leading bands in the South, he nevertheless recognized the appeal of rural blues and nascent jazz music and began to compose in these idioms relatively late in life. His best-known songs, particularly "The St. Louis Blues" but also "The Memphis Blues" and "The Beale Street Blues," touched off the first boom in blues music in the 1920s.

The son and grandson of ministers, Handy encountered family resistance to his early ambition to make a career of music. Nevertheless, he was able to learn to play the guitar, take organ lessons in sacred music, and study music in school. He also learned the cornet and played in the Florence Brass Band. At 15 he joined Bill Felton's minstrel show as first tenor in a vocal quartet, but the group broke up after a brief tour. He also sang in the church choir. He taught school locally for a year after graduating in 1891. In September 1892 he went to Birmingham, Ala., to take a teaching examination; he passed it but became a manual laborer in Bessemer because the pay was better. There he organized a brass band and led a small string orch.

Moving back to Birmingham, Handy organized the Lauzetta Quartet, which traveled to Chicago for the 1893 World's Fair, though it did not appear there. The group then went to St. Louis, where it disbanded. Handy endured a period of destitution in St. Louis and Evansville, Ind. (later reflected in "The St. Louis Blues"), then joined the Hampton Cornet Band and moved to Henderson, Ky. There he met Elizabeth Virginia Price, whom he married on July 19, 1898. The couple had six children: Lucile, Katherine (who became a singer), William, Florence (who died in infancy), Elizabeth, and Wyer. After his wife's death, Handy married his former secretary, Irma Louise Logan, on Jan. 1, 1954.

Handy's major career break came in August 1896, when he joined W. A. Mahara's Minstrels, eventually becoming the troupe's bandmaster. He stayed with Mahara until 1900, then joined the faculty of the Agricultural and Mechanical Coll. in Normal, Ala., as musical director. He stayed there for two years, then returned to Mahara for a year. In 1903 he took over the Knights of Pythias Band in Clarksdale, Miss. There he became acquainted with the blues music of the Miss. Delta and began to adapt his own music to the style. He moved on to Thornton's Knights of Pythias Band in Memphis and also organized a dance orchestra in that city.

In 1909, Handy wrote "Mr. Crump," a campaign tune in support of Edward H. Crump's successful run for mayor of Memphis. In 1912 it was published as "The Memphis Blues," the first published commercial blues song and the first published song incorporating an improvisational jazz break. Handy sold the rights to the song, and lyrics were added by George A. Norton for its 1913 re-publication. Nevertheless, the first successful recording, by Prince's Orch. in 1914, was an instrumental. That same year the dance team of Vernon and Irene Castle, introduced to the song by their bandleader, James Reese Europe, were inspired by it to invent the fox-trot, their most popular dance. Other successful early recordings were made by the Victor Military Band (also an instrumental) and by Arthur Collins and Byron Harlan. Ted Lewis revived the song on record in 1927; it was used in the film *Birth of the Blues* in 1941, where it was sung by Bing Crosby; and Harry James's 1942 recording became a hit during the recording ban in 1944.

Though Handy did not benefit financially from the song's success until he renewed its copyright in 1940, he was identified as its author, and his career as a bandleader blossomed to the extent that he employed three touring bands. He also was inspired to do more composing, and in September 1914 he wrote "The St. Louis Blues," an even greater success than "The Memphis Blues," which was published by Pace and Handy Music Co., his own firm. Again, Prince's Orch. made the first successful recording, in 1916. Other hit recordings of the song were achieved by Al Bernard (1919), Marion Harris (1920), the Original Dixieland Jazz Band (with Bernard on vocals; 1921), Handy himself (1923), Bessie Smith (with Louis Armstrong on cornet; 1925), Armstrong (1930), Rudy Vallée (1930), Cab Calloway (1930 and again in 1943), the Mills Brothers (1932), the Boswell Sisters (1935), the Benny Goodman Quartet (1936), Guy Lombardo (1939), Earl Hines (under the title "Boogie Woogie on the St. Louis Blues"; 1940), and Billy Eckstine (1953). The song also was used in half a dozen Broadway shows and in nearly a dozen motion pictures. Reportedly the most recorded song of the first half of the century, "The St. Louis Blues" had been recorded more than 400 times by 1950, when it was still earning Handy $25,000 a year in royalties.

Handy's other major songs include "Yellow Dog Blues" (successfully recorded by Joseph C. Smith's Orch., Ben Pollack, Lewis, Joe Darensbourg, and Johnny Maddox), "Joe Turner Blues" (a hit for Prince's Orch.), "Hesitating Blues" (a hit for Prince's Orch. and for Art Hickman), and "Loveless Love" (recorded by Ray Charles as "Careless Love" and by Smith as "Careless Love Blues"). His most successful song after "The St. Louis Blues" was "The Beale Street Blues" (1917), which produced hits for Prince's Orch., Earl Fuller, Harris, Alberta Hunter, Joe Venuti, and Lombardo between 1917 and 1942.

Handy contracted to make recordings for a variety of labels, including Banner, Black Swan, Columbia, Lyratone, Okeh, Paramount, Puritan, and Varsity, and he frequently traveled to N.Y. to record. He recorded a total of about 50 sides between 1917 and 1939, most of the sessions taking place in the late 1910s and early 1920s. In 1918 he gave up full-time bandleading and moved his family and his publishing company to N.Y. Initially this venture was a success, as compositions such as "Aunt Hagar's Blues" (1920) and "John Henry Blues" (1922) became hits. But the business declined as his partner, Harry H. Pace, withdrew; he also suffered from eyesight problems, eventually becoming blind. Still, he managed to reestablish his company as Handy Brothers Music, and he remained active as a publisher and musician until shortly before his death.

Just after he died, Handy was the subject of the biographical film *St. Louis Blues*, starring Nat "King" Cole. This renewed the popularity of the title song, which was recorded on more than a dozen chart albums over the next 10 years, including renditions by Cole, Pat Boone, Perry Como, Duane Eddy, and Lou Rawls. In the 1970s and 1980s the song was recorded by a diverse collection of artists, ranging from Deodato to Hank Williams Jr.

WRITINGS: ed., *Blues: An Anthology* (N.Y., 1926; rev. ed. *A Treasury of the Blues*, 1950; rev. by J. Silverman, 1972); *Negro Authors and Composers of the United States* (N.Y., 1935); *W. C. H.s Collection of Negro Spirituals* (N.Y., 1938); *Father of the Blues: An Autobiography* (N.Y., 1941); *Unsung Americans Sung* (N.Y., 1944). —**WR**

Hanff, Johann Nikolaus, German organist and composer; b. Wechmar, near Mühlhausen, 1665; d. Schleswig, 1711 or 1712. He was organist in Eupin and later in Hamburg (1706–11). A few months before his death, he was appointed organist at the Cathedral of Schleswig. He was a master of the chorale prelude, and his works considerably influenced J. S. Bach's style in this form. Only 6 of his chorale preludes are extant (publ. 1907 by K. Straube in his *45 Choralvorspiele alter Meister*; reprinted by E. White in *Masterpieces of Organ Music*, N.Y., 1949); also extant are 3 cantatas.

BIBL.: H. Schillings, *Tobias Eniccelius, Friedrich Meister, N. H.: Ein Beitrag zur Geschichte der evangelischen Frühkantate in Schleswig- Holstein* (Kiel, 1934).—**NS/LK/DM**

Hanfstängel, Marie (née **Schröder**), German soprano; b. Breslau, April 30, 1846; d. Munich, Sept. 5, 1917. She studied at Baden-Baden with Viardot-García, making her debut as Agathe in *Der Freischütz* at the Théâtre-Lyrique in Paris (Feb. 27, 1867). On the declaration of the Franco-Prussian War, she returned to Germany, and was engaged at the Stuttgart Opera (1870). She publ. *Meine Lehrweise der Gesangskunst* (1902).—**NS/LK/DM**

Hanisch, Joseph, German organist and composer; b. Regensburg, March 24, 1812; d. there, Oct. 9, 1892. He studied with his father, and with Proske, with whom he went to Italy as an assistant (1834). In 1839 he became organist at the Regensburg Cathedral. He wrote *Missa auxilium Christianorum, Quatuor hymni pro festo corporis Christi* and also composed pieces for organ solo. He was a master of improvisation, and was regarded as one of the greatest in this field in his time.—**NS/LK/DM**

Hanke, Karl, German composer; b. Rosswald, Silesia, c. 1750; d. Flensburg, June 10, 1803. As a young man he was sent to Vienna to pursue his music studies, where he briefly associated himself with Gluck, and profited by the master's advice. He then held the post of music director in Brünn (1778–81), Warsaw (1781–83), and Hamburg (1783–86). He was in Schleswig from 1786 to 1792. In 1792 he settled in Flensburg, where he remained until the end of his life. He composed several pieces for the stage, including the Singspiel *Der Wunsch mancher Mädchen* (1781), dedicated to Gluck, which was performed on various occasions with some success. Two albums of his songs were publ. in 1796–97.—**NS/LK/DM**

Hann, Georg, Austrian bass-baritone; b. Vienna, Jan. 30, 1897; d. Munich, Dec. 9, 1950. He was a student of Lierhammer at the Vienna Academy of Music. From 1927 until his death he was a member of the Bavarian State Opera in Munich; he also made guest appearances in Vienna, Berlin, Salzburg, London, Milan, and Paris. He was noted for such buffo portrayals as Leporello, Nicolai's Falstaff, Kecal, Baron Ochs, and La Roche, which he created (Munich, Oct. 28, 1942); his admired dramatic roles included Sarastro, Pizarro, Amfortas, Gunther, and Rigoletto.—**NS/LK/DM**

Hannan, Michael (Francis), Australian composer, pianist, teacher, and writer on music; b. Newcastle, New South Wales, Nov. 19, 1949. He was educated at the Univ. of Sydney (B.A., 1972; Ph.D., 1979; Graduate Diploma in Musical Composition, 1982). In 1983–84 he was a postdoctoral scholar at the Univ. of Calif. at Los Angeles. He taught at the univs. of New South Wales (1975–76) and Sydney (1977–83). In 1985–86 he was a lecturer in composition at the Queensland State Conservatorium in Brisbane. In 1986 he joined the faculty of the School of Arts at the Northern Rivers Coll. of Advanced Education in Lismore, New South Wales, where he became head of the Performing Arts and Music Divisions in 1987. Exceptionally gifted for the exploration of tonal, polytonal, and atonal techniques of composition, Hannan also possesses a saving grace of humor, as revealed in such works, recorded on electronic tape, as *Alphabeat* [sic] and *Slonimsky Variations*. In his purely scholarly pursuits, he compiled the section on musical terms to the *Macquarie Dictionary* (1981). He also contributed essays on Australian music to various publications and compiled the critical biography *Peter Sculthorpe: His Music and Ideas, 1929–79* (1982).

WORKS: CHAMBER: *Eliza Survivor* for Speaker, Piano, Flute, and Live Electronics (1978); *Garland Piece* for Large Ensemble (1979); *Occasional Medley* for String Quartet (1981); *Island Song* for Large Recorder Ensemble, Percussion, and Organ (1983); *Interaction I* for Ensemble (1987). **Piano:** *Piano Collage I* (1978) and *II* (1979) for Piano and Tapes; *7 Studies for Single Hands* (1981); *Riff Madness* for Jazz Pianist (1981); *3 Improvisatory Mobiles* (1981); *Zen Variations* (1982); *3 Meditations for Dane Rudhyar* (1983–84); *Resonances I* (1986–87), *II* (1989), *III* (1992), and *IV* (1994–95); *Beethoven Deranged* (1987); *Mysterious Flowers* (1990); *Minimal Study I* (1990); *Homage to Chopin* (1990–91); *Mood Variations* (1991); *Terrains* for Piano Interior (1999). **OTHER:** *Bracefell's Story* for Voice and Piano (1990); *Haka I* for Vocal Ensemble (1992); numerous works with dancers.—NS/LK/DM

Hannay, Roger D(urham), esteemed American composer and teacher; b. Plattsburg, N.Y., Sept. 22, 1930. He studied composition with Ernst Bacon and Franklin Morris at Syracuse Univ. (1948–52), Gardner Read and Hugo Norden at Boston Univ. (1952–53), Bernard Rogers and Howard Hanson at the Eastman School of Music in Rochester, N.Y. (1954–56; Ph.D., 1956), and Lukas Foss and Aaron Copland at the Berkshire Music Center at Tanglewood (summer, 1959). He then worked with Roger Sessions, Milton Babbitt, and Elliott Carter at the Princeton Seminar for Advanced Studies (summer, 1960). In 1966 he joined the music faculty of the Univ. of N.C., where he taught composition, lectured in theory and contemporary music, formed and directed the UNC New Music Ensemble, the Electronic Music Studio, and the Composer-Concerts Series, and was chairman of the Division of Fine Arts (1979–82), subsequently serving as prof. emeritus from 1995. He received grants from the NEA (1976) and the Kenan (1976) and Pogue (1992) foundations. In 1982 he held a residency at the MacDowell Colony and, successively, at the Va. Center for the Creative Arts, the Centrum Arts Center, and Yaddo (1992). In 1993 he was nominated for candidacy to the American Academy of Arts and Letters. He is the author of an unpublished monograph of autobiographical essays, *My Book of Life* (1997).

WORKS: DRAMATIC: Opera: *Two Tickets to Omaha*, comic opera (1960); *The Fortune of St. Macabre* (1964); *The Journey of Edith Wharton* (1982); *Scenes from a Literary Life* (1990); *Dates and Names*, after *Baker's Biographical Dictionary of Musicians* (1991). **Theater and Multimedia:** *Marshall's Medium Message* for Improvisational Percussion Quartet and Mod-Girl Announcer (1967); *Live and in Color1* for Improvisational Percussion Quartet, Female Reader, Action Painter, Films, and Slide Projections (1967); *The Nightingale and the Rose* for Soprano, Flute, Guitar, and Double Bass, after Oscar Wilde (1986). **ORCH.:** 7 syms.: No. 1 (1953; rev. 1973), No. 2 (1956), No. 3, *The Great American Novel*, for Chorus and Orch. (1976–77), No. 4, *American Classic*, for Vocal Soloists and Orch.

(1977), No. 5 (1987–88), No. 6 for Strings (1992), and No. 7 (1994–95); *Music for Strings* (1954; rev. 1994); *Dramatic Overture* (1955; rev. 1981); *Summer Festival Overture* (1958); *Prelude and Dance* (1959; rev. 1974); *Sonorous Image* (1968); *Listen* (1974); *Celebration*, overture (1975; rev. 1993); *The Age of Innocence* (1983); *Rhapsody (Serenade)* for Piano and Orch. (1991); *Arriba!* (1992); *Vikingrwest* (1993); *Consortium* (1994). **Band:** Sym. (1961). **CHAMBER:** *Rhapsody* for Flute and Piano (1952); *2 Sketches* for Clarinet and Piano (1956); *Sinfoniette* for Piano and Strings (1958; rev. 1995); *Divertimento* for Woodwind Quintet (1958); 4 string quartets (1962; *Lyric*, 1963; *Designs*, 1963; *Quartet of Solos*, 1974); *Fantôme* for Clarinet, Viola, and Piano (1967); *The Fruit of Love* for Chamber Ensemble, after Millay (1969); *O Solo Viola* (1974); *Suite* for Flute, Clarinet, Cello, and Piano (1981); *Trio-Rhapsody* for Flute, Cello, and Piano (1984); *Pavane* for Flute, Oboe, and Guitar (1986); *A Farewell to Leonard Bernstein* for Chamber Ensemble (1990). **Piano:** *Abstractions* (1962); Sonata (1964); *Sonorities* (1966; rev. 1991); *Piano Episodes* (1971; rev. 1991); *Luminere* (1988). **VOCAL:** *Doth Not Wisdom Cry*, cantata for Chorus and Orch. (1952; rev. 1994); *Carol* for Men's Chorus and Piano (1956; also for Chorus, 1964); *Christmas Tide* for Men's Chorus (1956); *Requiem* for Chorus and Orch., after Walt Whitman (1961); *Sayings for Our Time* for Chorus and Orch., after texts adapted from the popular media (1968); *Choral Fantasias I* and *II* (1970; rev. 1984); *Hold the Fort* for Chorus and Piano (1989); *Prologue to the Tales of Canterbury* for Chorus and Piano, after Chaucer (1989); *Songs from Walden* for Soprano and Piano, after Thoreau (1990); *Make We Joy* for Chorus and Organ (1991).—NS/LK/DM

Hannikainen, distinguished family of Finnish musicians:

(1) Pekka (or Pietari) (Juhani) Hannikainen, conductor and composer; b. Nurmes, Dec. 9, 1854; d. Helsinki, Sept. 13, 1924. He was self-taught. He was active as a choral conductor and teacher of choral singing in Helsinki. He wrote a number of choral works and songs that became popular in his native country. His wife, Alli (née Laura Alfhild; b. Helsinki, June 21, 1867; d. there, April 12, 1949), was a teacher of singing and conductor of a women's choir. Their sons also became prominent musicians:

(2) (Toivo) Ilmari Hannikainen, pianist and composer; b. Jyväskylä, Oct. 19, 1892; d. Kuhmoinen, July 25, 1955. He studied piano and composition at the Helsinki music school (1911–13), then with Schreker in Vienna (1913–14) and Siloti and Steinberg in Petrograd (1916–17). He made his debut in Helsinki in 1914 and later toured with his brothers Tauno (Heikki) and Arvo (Sakari) in a trio. He also taught piano at his alma mater and then at the Sibelius Academy (1939–55). He wrote a folk play, *Talkoottanssit* (1930), a Piano Concerto, a Piano Quartet, and many pieces for solo piano.

(3) Tauno (Heikki) Hannikainen, cellist and conductor; b. Jyväskylä, Feb. 26, 1896; d. Helsinki, Oct. 12, 1968. He studied cello with O. Forström in Helsinki, making his debut there as a soloist in 1920. He then took lessons with Casals in Paris (1921). After making his conducting debut in 1921, he served as conductor of the Finnish Opera in Helsinki until 1927. He also played in a trio with his brothers (Toivo) Ilmari and Arvo (Sakari). He was conductor of the Turku Sym. Orch. (1929–39), then went to the U.S., where he was music director of the Duluth (Minn.) Sym. Orch. (1942–46). Subsequently he was conductor of the Chicago Civic Orch. (1947–50), as well as asst. conductor (1947–49) and assoc. conductor (1949–50) of the Chicago Sym. Orch. From 1950 to 1963 he was conductor of the Helsinki Phil.

(4) Arvo (Sakari) Hannikainen, violinist and conductor; b. Jyväskylä, Oct. 11, 1897; d. Helsinki, Jan. 8, 1942. He studied violin in Helsinki (1915–17), in Berlin and Weimar (1920–23), with Thibaud and Ysaÿe in Paris, and with Jacobsen in Berlin (1931). In 1917 he became a member of the Helsinki orch., then 1st violinist in 1923. He also played in a trio with his brothers (Toivo) Ilmari and Tauno (Heikki). He taught at the Sibelius Academy, and was conductor of its student orch.

(5) Väinö (Aatos) Hannikainen, harpist and composer; b. Jyväskylä, Jan. 12, 1900; d. Kuhmoinen, Aug. 7, 1960. He studied in Helsinki and Berlin. He was 1st harpist in the Helsinki orch. (1923–57). He wrote several symphonic poems, a Harp Concerto, a Harp Sonata, and songs.—NS/LK/DM

Hanon, Charles-Louis, French pianist and pedagogue; b. Renescure, near Dunkerque, July 2, 1819; d. Boulogne-sur-Mer, March 19, 1900. Next to Czerny, Hanon was the most illustrious composer of piano exercises, embodied in his chef d'oeuvre, *Le Pianiste-virtuose,* which for over a century has been the vade-mecum for many millions of diligent piano students all over the face of the musical globe. He further wrote a collection of 50 instructive piano pieces under the title *Méthode élémentaire de piano,* a useful compilation, *Extraits des chefs-d'oeuvres des grands maîtres,* and a selection of 50 ecclesiastical chants, *50 cantiques choisis parmi les plus populaires.* He also attempted to instruct uneducated musicians in the art of accompanying plainchant in a curious didactic publication, *Système nouveau pour apprendre à accompagner tout plainchant sans savoir la musique.*—NS/LK/DM

Hansen, (Emil) Robert, Danish cellist, conductor, and composer; b. Copenhagen, Feb. 25, 1860; d. Århus, July 18, 1926. He received his first instruction from his father, then studied with F. Neruda at the Copenhagen Cons., and with Friedrich Grutzmacher in Dresden. He was a member of the Court Orch. in Copenhagen (1877–89). After a stay in London, he settled in 1891 in Leipzig, where he joined the Gewandhaus Orch. and became a prof. at the Cons. From 1918 he was conductor of the Århus Orch. His works include the opera *Frauenlist* (Sondershausen, 1911) and the operetta, *Die wilde Komtesse* (Eisenach, 1913), as well as Sym., Symphonic Suite for Strings and 2 Horns, Piano Concerto, Cello Concerto, Piano Quintet, and String Quartet.—NS/LK/DM

Hansen, Wilhelm, Danish music publishing firm founded in Copenhagen in 1857 by Jens Wilhelm Hansen (1821–1904). His sons, Jonas Wilhelm (1850–1919) and Alfred Wilhelm Hansen (1854–1922), were also active in the business. Alfred's sons, Asger Wilhelm (1889–1965) and Svend Wilhelm Hansen (1890–1959), and, later, Svend's daughters, Hanne Wilhelm (b. 1927) and Lone Wilhelm Hansen (b. 1930), carried on the business. The firm publ. many works by Scandinavian composers, as well as many by Europeans. It has branches in Frankfurt am Main, London, N.Y., Oslo, Stockholm, Århus, and Odense.—NS/LK/DM

Hanslick, Eduard, greatly renowned Austrian music critic of Czech descent; b. Prague, Sept. 11, 1825; d. Baden, near Vienna, Aug. 6, 1904. He studied law in Prague and Vienna, taking the degree of Dr.Jur. in 1849 and qualifying himself for an official position. But having already studied music Tomaschek at Prague, in 1848–49 he served as music critic for the *Wiener Zeitung,* and soon adopted a literary career. His first work, *Vom Musikalisch-Schön: Ein Beitrag zur Revision der Aesthetik der Tonkunst* (Leipzig, 1854; Fr. tr., 1877; Span., 1879; Ital., 1884; Eng., 1891; Russ., 1895), brought him worldwide fame. Its leading idea is that the beauty of a musical composition lies wholly and specifically in the music itself; i.e., it is immanent in the relations of the tones, without any reference whatever to extraneous (non-musical) ideas, and can express no others. Such being his point of view through life, it follows logically that he could not entertain sympathy for Wagner's art; his violent opposition to the music-drama was a matter of profound conviction, not personal spite; he in fact wrote a moving tribute after Wagner's death. On the other hand, he was one of the very first and most influential champions of Brahms. From 1855 to 1864 Hanslick was music ed. of the *Presse,* and then of the *Neue Freie Press* from 1864 to 1895 in Vienna. He also was a lecturer in music history and aesthetics (1856–61), prof. extraordinary (1861–70), and a full prof. (1870–95) at the Univ. of Vienna. What gives his writings permanent value is the sound musicianship underlying their brilliant, masterly style. Yet in music history he is chiefly known as a captious and intemperate reviler of genius; Wagner caricatured him in the part of Beckmesser (in any early version of *Die Meistersinger von Nürnberg* the name was to have been Veit Hanslich). A collection of Hanslick's articles in the *Neue Freie Presse* was publ. in Eng. tr. as *Vienna's Golden Years of Music, 1850–1900* (N.Y., 1950)

WRITINGS: *Geschichte des Concertwesens in Wien* (1869); *Aus dem concertsaal* (1870); a series begun with *Die moderne Oper* (1875) and followed by 8 more vols.: II, *Musikalische Stationen* (188), III, *Aus dem Opernleben der Gegenwart* (1884), IV, *Musikalisches Skizzenbuch* (1888), V, *Musikalisches und Litterarisches* (1889), VI, *Aus dem Tagebuch eines Jahrhunderts* (1899), and IX, *Aus neuer und neuester Zeit* (1900); *Suite, Aufsätze über Musik und Musiker* (1885); *Konzerte, Komponisten und Virtuosen der letzten fünfzehn Jahre* (1886); *Aus menem Leben* (2 vols., 1894).

BIBL.: R. Schafke, *E. H. und die Musikästhetik* (1922); S. Deas, *In Defence of H.* (London, 1940); A. Wilhemer, *Der junge H.* (Klagenfurt, 1959); D. Glatt, *Zur geschichtichlen Bedeutung der Musikästhetik E. H.s* (Munich, 1972); W. Abegg, *Musikästhetik und Musikkritik bei E. H.* (Regensburg, 1974); D. Strauss, *E. H.: Von Musikalisch-Schönen: Ein Beitrag zur Revision der Ästhetik in der Tonkunst* (Mainz, 1990 et seq.); G. Payzant, *E. H. and Ritter Berlioz in Prague: A Documentary Narrative* (Calgary, 1991).—NS/LK/DM

Hanson, three Okla. brothers who ruled teen pop in the late 1990s; formed 1992. **MEMBERSHIP:** Isaac Hanson, gtr., pno, voc. (b. Tulsa, Okla., 1981); Taylor Hanson, kybd, voc. (b. Tulsa, Okla.,1983); Zach Hanson, drm, voc. (b. Tulsa, Okla., 1986). Coming out of an evangelical Christian family from Tulsa, the Hanson Brothers—three charismatic, handsome, squeaky clean all-American young men—became the darling of pop fans everywhere in the summer of 1997 with their infectious hit "MMMBop." They had several advantages over most groups of their ilk, however. They were not pre-fab; as a family they performed together organically. They were not the creation of a musical Svengali; they wrote most of their own songs (including the big hit) and played their instruments. They not only appealed to the teen audience; they also topped the singles portion of the 1997 *Village Voice* "Pazz and Jop" critics poll and earned good reviews from the critical curmudgeons at *Spin*, *The New York Times*, and *Rolling Stone*.

The Hansons' father worked for an oil company and their mother home- schooled them and their three younger siblings. During the late 1980s, their father spent a year in Venezuela and took the family with him. On returning to America, the brothers would entertain themselves by singing a cappella. They became good enough to entertain at barbecues and company picnics, and within two years they were ready for bigger audiences. They started playing local amusement parks and did regular Friday afternoon "happy hour" concerts in the parking lot of a local café. They performed to accompaniment tapes that the eldest brother, Isaac, made. In 1994, they went to the annual South by Southwest music business confab in Austin, Tex., performing a cappella for anyone who'd listen. Chris Sabec listened and was so impressed he became their manager. The group cut a self-distributed album, *Boomerang*, which they sold at shows. They started eschewing the tracks in favor of playing their own instruments. They cut a second album, *MMMBop* on which they played all the instruments. In 1996, after getting a passel of rejection notices, Sabec got the group a contract with Mercury. They recorded sessions with noted producers the Dust Brothers and Steve Lironi, and cowrote tunes with such luminaries as Barry Mann and Cynthia Weil and Desmond Child.

The album came out in the spring of 1997. The first single, a revamped version of "MMMBop," entered the charts at #13 in April. By May, it topped the chart. The new version, rife with hip-hop beats and tricky samples, was propelled by the brother's harmonies, very reminiscent of the Jackson 5. Their album *Middle of Nowhere* was selling 100,000 copies a week and lodged in the Top Ten. For Christmas that year, they put out *Snowed In*, which did very well among the hordes of holiday albums. They reissued tracks from their self-released albums as *3 Car Garage* the next year, as well as a live record/video, keeping the pumps primed for their second major label studio release. That record got held up when their record company decided they didn't like the direction producer Ric Ocasek was taking the group and replaced him with Lironi. Whether their momentum has slowed down remains to be seen, but as David Fricke noted in *Rolling Stone*: "Wanna pick on Hanson for writing immature lyrics and singing formulaic ballads? Wait until they're old enough to know better."

DISC.: *Boomerang* (1995); *MMMBop* (1996); *Middle of Nowhere* (1997); *Snowed In* (1997); *3 Car Garage* (1998); *Live from Albertane* (1998); *This Time Around* (2000).—**HB**

Hanson, Howard (Harold), eminent American composer, music educator, and conductor; b. Wahoo, Nebr., Oct. 28, 1896; d. Rochester, N.Y., Feb. 26, 1981. After obtaining a diploma from Luther Coll. in Wahoo (1911), he studied with Goetschius at the Inst. of Musical Art in N.Y. (1914) and with Oldberg and Lutkin at Northwestern Univ. in Evanston, Ill. (B.A., 1916). In 1915–16 he was an asst. teacher at Northwestern Univ. In 1916 he became a teacher of theory and composition at the Coll. of the Pacific in San Jose, Calif., where he was made dean of its Cons. of Fine Arts in 1919. In 1921 he received the Rome Prize for his *California Forest Play of 1920*. During his stay at the American Academy in Rome, he received training in orchestration from Respighi and composed his first major work, the Sym. No. 1, *Nordic*, which he conducted in its premiere on May 17, 1923. Returning to the U.S., he conducted the premiere of his "symbolic" poem *North and West* with the N.Y. Sym. Orch. in January 1924. In subsequent years, Hanson appeared often as a guest conductor throughout the U.S. and Europe championing not only his own music but numerous scores by other American composers. In 1924 he was appointed director of the Eastman School of Music in Rochester, N.Y., which he molded into one of the outstanding music schools of the U.S. As both a music educator and conductor, he proved profoundly influential. He promoted the cause of music education through his energetic work with many national organizations, among them the Music Teachers National Assn., of which he was president (1930–31), the Music Educators National Conference, the National Assn. of Schools of Music, and the National Music Council, of which he was founder- president. From 1925 to 1935 he conducted a series of American Composers' Concerts, and from 1935 to 1971 he was director of the Festivals of American Music. For the 50th anniversary of the Boston Sym. Orch., Hanson was commissioned to compose his Sym. No. 2, *Romantic*. Koussevitzky conducted its premiere on Nov. 28, 1930, and the score remains Hanson's most famous orch. work. His opera *Merry Mount* was first heard in a concert performance under the composer's direction in Ann Arbor on May 20, 1933. It received its stage premiere at the Metropolitan Opera in N.Y. on Feb. 10, 1934. While it failed to find a place in the operatic repertoire, an orch. suite (1936) won favor. Hanson's Sym. No. 4, *The Requiem*, was composed in memory of his father. The composer conducted its first performance with the Boston Sym. Orch. on Dec. 3, 1943. In 1944 it was awarded the Pulitzer Prize in Music. Hanson remained as director of the Eastman School of Music until 1964, the year he founded the Inst. of American Music. In 1935 he was elected a member of the National Inst. of Arts and Letters. In 1979 he was elected a member of the Academy of the American Academy and Inst. of Arts and Letters. He also received many other notable honors, including various awards and numerous honorary doctorates. As a composer, Hanson eschewed serialism and other modern techniques to pursue a neo-Romantic course. While much has been made of the influence of Grieg and especially of Sibelius on his works, his compositions remain basically true to the American spirit. At his most inspired, Hanson's oeuvre displays an array of sonorous harmonies, bold asymmetrical rhythms, and an overall mastery of orchestration one would expect of a remarkable compositional craftsman.

WORKS: DRAMATIC: *California Forest Play of 1920* (1919; Calif. State Redwood Park, July 1920, composer conducting); *Merry Mount*, opera (1933; concert perf., Ann Arbor, May 20, 1933, composer conducting; stage perf., N.Y., Feb. 10, 1934, Serafin conducting; suite, N.Y., March 23, 1936, Iturbi conducting); *Nymphs and Satyr*, ballet (Chautauqua, N.Y., Aug. 9, 1979). **ORCH.:** *Symphonic Prelude* (1916); *Concerto da camera* for Piano and Strings (1916–17; Rome, April 1922; also for Piano and String Quartet); *Symphonic Legend* (1917; incorporated with *Symphonic Rhapsody* to form *Legend and Rhapsody*); *Symphonic Rhapsody* (1919; Los Angeles, May 26, 1921, composer conducting; incorporated with *Symphonic Legend* to form *Legend and Rhapsody*); *Before the Dawn* (1919–20); *March Carillon* (1920; arranged from *2 Yuletide Pieces* for Piano); *Exaltation* (1920; also for 2 Pianos and Small Ensemble); 7 syms.: No. 1, *Nordic* (1922; Rome, May 17, 1923, composer conducting), No. 2, *Romantic* (1928–30; Boston, Nov. 28, 1930, Koussevitzky conducting), No. 3 (1937–38; NBC, N.Y., March 15, 1938, composer conducting; rev. with wordless choral finale, 1957), No. 4, *The Requiem* (1940–43; Boston, Dec. 3, 1943, composer conducting), No. 5, *Sinfonia Sacra* (1954; Philadelphia, Feb. 18, 1955, Ormandy conducting), No. 6 (N.Y., Feb. 28, 1968, composer conducting), and No. 7, *A Sea Symphony* for Chorus and Orch., after Whitman (Interlochen, Mich., Aug. 7, 1977, composer conducting); *North and West*, "symbolic" poem with chorus obbligato (1923; N.Y., Jan. 1924, composer conducting); *Concerto for Organ, Strings, and Harp* (1923; CBS, Aug. 29, 1943; based on *North and West*); *Lux Aeterna*, symphonic poem with viola obbligato (1923; also for Viola and String Quartet); *Pan and Priest*, symphonic poem with piano obbligato (1925–26; London, Oct. 26, 1926); *Organ Concerto* (1926; Rochester, N.Y., Gleason organist, composer conducting; based on the *Concerto for Organ, Strings, and Harp*); *Fantasy* for Strings (1939–43; also as *Quartet in 1 Movement*); *Variations on a Theme by Eugene Goossens* (1944; Cincinnati, March 23, 1945, Goossens conducting; with 9 other composers); *Serenade* for Flute, Harp, and Strings (Boston, Oct. 25, 1945, Koussevitzky conducting); Piano Concerto (Boston, Dec. 31, 1948, Firkušný pianist, Koussevitzky conducting); *Pastorale* for Oboe, Strings, and Harp (1948–49; Philadelphia, Oct. 20, 1950, Ormandy conducting; also for Oboe and Piano); *Symphony of Freedom* (Cleveland, April 1, 1949, composer conducting); *Fantasy Variations on a Theme of Youth* for Piano and Strings (Evanston, Ill., Feb. 18, 1951); *Elegy* or *Elegy in Memory of Serge Koussevitzky* (1955; Boston, Jan. 20, 1956, Munch conducting); *Mosaics* (Cleveland, Jan. 23, 1958, Szell conducting); *Summer Seascape* (1958–59; New Orleans, March 10, 1959, composer conducting; incorporated in *Bold Island Suite*); *Bold Island Suite* (1961; Cleveland, Jan. 25, 1962, Szell conducting; incorporates *Summer Seascape*); *For the First Time* (1962; Rochester, N.Y., May 16, 1963, composer conducting; also for Piano); *Summer Seascape II* for Viola and Strings (1965; Raleigh, N.C., April 20, 1966; also for Viola and String Quartet); *Dies Natalis* (1967; Omaha, May 1968); *Fanfare and Chorale* (Cincinnati, Feb. 20, 1976; also for Concert Band); *Rhythmic Variations on 2 Ancient Hymn Tunes* for Strings (Interlochen, Mich., Aug. 7, 1977). **Concert Band:** *Chorale and Alleluia* (West Point, N.Y., Feb. 26, 1954); *Centennial March* (Columbus, Ohio, Jan. 6, 1967);

Dies Natalis II (Rochester, N.Y., April 7, 1972, Hunsberger conducting); *Young People's Guide to the 6–tone Scale* for Piano and Concert Band (Rochester, N.Y., Nov. 17, 1972, Hunsberger conducting); *4 French Songs* (c. 1972); *Laude* (San Francisco, Feb. 7, 1975); *Fanfare and Chorale* (1976; also for Orch.); *Variations on an Ancient Hymn* (1977; also known as *Chorale Variations* for Wind Ensemble). **CHAMBER:** Piano Quintet (1916); *Concerto da camera* for Piano and String Quartet (1916–17; Pacific May Festival, May 1917; also for Piano and String Orch.); *Exaltation* for 2 Pianos and Small Ensemble (1920; also for Orch. with piano obbligato); Quartet in 1 Movement (1923; Washington, D.C., Oct. 30, 1925; also for *Fantasy* for String Orch.); *Lux Aeterna* for Viola and String Quartet (1923; also for Viola and Orch.); *Festival Fanfare* for 4 Horns, 3 Trumpets, 3 Trombones, Tuba, and Timpani (1937–38; Rochester, N.Y., April 28, 1938, composer conducting); *Fanfare for the Signal Corps* for 4 Horns, 3 Trumpets, 3 Trombones, Tuba, Timpani, and Percussion (1942); *Pastorale* for Oboe and Piano (1948–49; also for Oboe, Strings, and Harp); *Summer Seascape II* for Viola and String Quartet (1965; Washington, D.C., April 7, 1966; also for Viola and String Orch.); *Elegy* for Viola and String Quartet (1966). **Piano:** *Prelude and Double Fugue* for 2 Pianos (1915); *4 Poems* (1917); Sonata (1917; San Jose, Calif., April 7, 1919); *Scandinavian Suite* (1918–19); *Clog Dance* (1919); *3 Miniatures* (1918–19); *3 Etudes* (1919); *2 Yuletide Pieces* (1919); *Enchantment* (1935); *Dance of the Warriors* (1935); *The Bell* (1942); *For the First Time* (1962; also for Orch.); *The Big Bell and the Little Bell* (1964); *Horn Calls in the Forest* (1964); *Tricks or Treats* (1964). **VOCAL:** *The Lament for Beowulf* for Chorus and Orch. (1925; Ann Arbor, 1926); *Heroic Elegy* for Chorus and Orch. (1927); (3) *Songs from "Drum Taps,"* after Whitman, for Baritone, Chorus, and Orch. (Ann Arbor, May 15, 1935, composer conducting); *Hymn for the Pioneers (Banbrytarhymn)* for Men's Chorus (Wilmington, Del., June 10, 1938); *The Cherubic Hymn* for Chorus and Orch. (1949; Rochester, N.Y., May 11, 1950, composer conducting); *Centennial Ode* for Baritone, Speaker, Chorus, and Orch. (Rochester, N.Y., June 10, 1950, composer conducting); *How Excellent Thy Name* for Women's Chorus and Piano (1952); *The Song of Democracy* for Chorus and Orch. (Washington, D.C., April 9, 1957, composer conducting); *Creator of Infinities Beyond Our Earth* for Chorus (Rochester, N.Y., Oct. 23, 1960); *Song of Human Rights* for Chorus and Orch. (Washington, D.C., Dec. 10, 1963); *4 Psalms* for Baritone, Cello, and String Quartet (Washington, D.C., Oct. 31, 1964); *One Hundred Fiftieth Psalm* for Men's Chorus (1965; also for Mixed Chorus and Piano or Organ; incorporated in *2 Psalms*); *One Hundred Twenty-first Psalm* for Alto or Baritone and Chorus (1968; incorporated in *2 Psalms*); *2 Psalms* for Alto or Baritone, Chorus, and Orch. (1968); *Streams in the Desert* for Chorus and Orch. (Lubbock, Tex., May 18, 1969, composer conducting); *The Mystic Trumpeter* for Chorus, Narrator, and Orch. (Kansas City, Mo., April 22, 1970); *Lumen in Christo* for Chorus and Orch. (Rochester, N.Y., Oct. 15, 1974; also for Women's Chorus and Orch.); *A Prayer of the Middle Ages* for Chorus (1976; also as *Hymn of the Middle Ages*); *New Land, New Covenant* for Soprano, Baritone, Narrator, Chorus, Optional Children's Chorus, Organ, and Small Orch. (Bryn Mawr, Pa., May 2, 1976); songs.

WRITINGS: *Harmonic Materials of Modern Music: Resources of the Tempered Scale* (N.Y., 1960).

BIBL.: R. Watanabe, *Music of H. H.* (Rochester, N.Y., 1966); R. Monroe, *H. H.: American Music Educator* (diss., Fla. State

Univ., 1970); A. Caruine, *The Choral Music of H. H.* (diss., Univ. of Tex., 1977); J. Perone, *H. H.: A Bio-Bibliography* (Westport, Conn., 1993); M. Plain, *H. H.: A Comprehensive Catalog of the Manuscripts* (Rochester, N.Y., 1997).—**NS/LK/DM**

Hanssens, Charles-Louis, Belgian cellist, conductor, and composer; b. Ghent, July 12, 1802; d. Brussels, April 8, 1871. As a child of 10 he played in the orch. of the National Theater in Amsterdam. After serving as 1st cellist of the orch. in the Brussels theater (1824–27), he taught harmony at the Brussels Cons. He subsequently conducted opera at The Hague and in Ghent. From 1848 to 1869 he was conductor at the Théâtre de la Monnaie in Brussels. Among his works were 8 operas, 15 ballets, 9 syms., overtures, orch. fantasies, a Violin Concerto, a Cello Concerto, a Clarinet Concerto, several piano concertos, string quartets, masses, cantatas, and a cappella choruses.

BIBL.: L. de Burbure, *Notice sur C.-L. H.* (Antwerp, 1872); L. Bäwolf, *C.-L. H.* (Brussels, 1895).—**NS/LK/DM**

Hanuš, Jan, Czech composer; b. Prague, May 2, 1915. He became a composition student of Jeremiáš in 1934, and he also studied conducting at the Prague Cons. with Dědeček (1935–37; 1939–41). He worked as an ed. in music publishing houses and was active in Czech music organizations. His music is marked by a lyrical Romanticism tinged by stringent dissonant textures. Hanuš completed the instrumentations of the unfinished operas *Tkalci* by Nejedlý and *Balada o lásce* by Doubrava.

WORKS: DRAMATIC: O p e r a : *Plameny* (Flames; 1942–44); *Sluha dvou pánů* (Servant of 2 Masters; 1958); *Pochodeň Prométheova* (Torch of Prometheus; 1961–63); *Pohádka jedné noci* (Story of 1 Night; 1961–68). **B a l l e t :** *Sůl nad zlato* (Salt is Worth More than Gold; 1953); *Othello* (1955–56); *Labyrint* (1981). **ORCH.:** 7 syms. (1942, 1951, 1957, 1960, 1965, 1978, 1990); *The Eulogy,* sinfonietta for Soprano and Orch. (1945); Concertante Symphony for Organ, Harp, Timpani, and Strings (1953–54); *Petr a Lucie,* fantasy (1955); Overture after Whitman's *The Bugler's Secret* (1961); Double Concerto for Oboe, Harp, and Orch. (1965); *Relay Race* (1968); *Musica Concertante* for Cello, Piano, Winds, and Percussion (1969–70); Concerto Grosso for Large Wind Orch. (1971); *Pražská nokturna* for Chamber Orch. (1972–73); *3 Essays* (1975–76); *Variations and Collage* (1982–83); *Concerto-fantasia* for Cello and Orch. (1990–91). **CHAMBER:** *Fantasy* for String Quartet (1939); Sonata-Rhapsody for Cello and Piano (1941); Suite to Paintings by Manes for Violin and Piano (1948); *Serenata semplice* for Nonet (1953; rev. 1970); *Suita dramatica* for String Quartet (1959); Piano Trio, *Frescoes* (1961); *Suita domestica* for Wind Quintet (1964); Concertino for 2 Percussionists and Tape (1972); *Sonata Seria* for Violin and Percussion (1974); *Sonata Variata* for Clarinet (1976); *Tower Music* for Brass Quintet (1976); *In Praise of Chamber Music,* sextet for Flute, Oboe, Violin, Viola, Cello, and Harpsichord (1979); *Lyric Triptych* for String Quartet (1987–88); *Sonata variata a tre* for Clarinet, Percussion, and Piano (1996); piano pieces; organ music. **VOCAL:** 7 masses (1943; 1950; 1954; 1959; 1966; 1972–73; 1985); *The Message* for Baritone, Chorus, 2 Prepared Pianos, Electric Guitar, Percussion, and Tape (1969); *The Swallows,* concerto piccolo for Chorus, Flute, and Cello (1973); *The Passion According to Matthew* for Solo Voices and Chorus

(1977–78); *Ecce Homo,* oratorio (1980); *The Passion According to John* for Solo Voices and Chorus (1982); *Litanie k Panně* (Litany to the Virgin) for Soloist, Chorus, and Orch. (1997); cantatas; choruses; songs.—**NS/LK/DM**

Hanuszewska-Schaeffer, Mieczyslawa Janina, Polish writer on music; b. Borszów, Oct. 1, 1929. She studied musicology with Jachimecki at the Jagiello Univ. in Kraków (1948–52). In 1963 she joined the staff of Kraków's *Zycie Literackie,* producing a weekly chronicle on the world's music. She has written extensively on modern music, including detailed studies on Ives, Messiaen, and the early works of Boulez. She was a contributor to *Wielka Encyklopedia Muzyczna* and *The New Grove Dictionary of Music and Musicians* (1980). With her husband, **Bogusław Schaeffer,** she ed. *Almanach wspólszesnych kompozytorów polskich* (Almanac of Modern Polish Composers; Kraków, 1966; new ed., 1989). She also ed. *1000 kompozytorów* (1,000 Composers; 5th ed., Kraków, 1986).—**NS/LK/DM**

Haquinius, (Johan) Algot, Swedish pianist, teacher, and composer; b. Stockholm, July 30, 1886; d. there, Feb. 6, 1966. He studied piano with Hilda Thegerstrom and Lennart Lundberg and composition with Ernst Ellberg at the Stockholm Cons. (1898–1906), then pursued training in composition with Johan Lindegren and piano with Moszkowski in Paris and Friedman in Berlin. He had a distinguished career as a pianist in Sweden and also taught. In 1941 he became a member of the Swedish Royal Academy of Music. His works, which include orch. pieces, chamber music, piano pieces, and songs, effectively combine Romantic and expressionist elements.—**NS/LK/DM**

Harasiewicz, Adam, Polish pianist; b. Chodziez, July 1, 1932. He studied with Kazimierz Mirski until 1950, then at the Kraków State Coll. of Music. He entered the Chopin Contest in 1949, but failed to win a prize. In 1955 he competed again and won 1st prize. —**NS/LK/DM**

Harasowski, Adam, Polish pianist and writer on music; b. Delatyn, Sept. 16, 1904. He was brought up in a musical family. He studied at the Lwow Cons. with Adam Soltys (1923–29), and also took private lessons in composition with Szymanowski during his frequent visits at Lwow. Concurrently he studied mechanical engineering, graduating from the Lwow Polytechnic in 1931, and subsequently earned his living mainly as an engineering draftsman. At the outbreak of World War II, he went to England with the Polish Air Force, and remained with the Royal Air Force of Great Britain as a flight lieutenant (1943–58). He then devoted himself to journalism, both in Polish and in English. He publ. *The Skein of Legends around Chopin* (Glasgow, 1967) and also compiled collections of Polish songs.—**NS/LK/DM**

Harašta, Milan, Czech composer; b. Brno, Sept. 16, 1919; d. there, Aug. 29, 1946. He studied musicology at the Univ. of Brno before taking a course in composition with Kaprál at the Brno Cons. (1938–42). His music, written in a forward-looking, post- Janáček style, included the opera *Nikola Šuhaj* (1941–44), 3 syms. (the last unfinished), vocal music, and piano pieces.

BIBL.: M. Barík, *M. H.* (Prague, 1956).—**NS/LK/DM**

Harászti, Emil, Hungarian musicologist; b. Nagyvárad, Nov. 1, 1885; d. Paris, Dec. 27, 1958. He was a pupil of Albert Geiger (piano) and Edmund Farkas (composition), and also pursued his academic education at the Univ. of Budapest (Ph.D., 1907; Habilitation, 1917), where he taught musicology from 1917; he also was director of the Budapest Cons. (1918–27). In 1945 he settled in Paris.

WRITINGS: *Hubay Jenő élete és munkái* (Jenő Hubay: His Life and Works; Budapest, 1913); *Wagner Rikárd és Magyarország* (Richard Wagner and Hungary; Budapest, 1916); *Schallnachahmung und Bedeutungswandel in der Instrumentenkunde mit Rücksicht auf die ungarische Organographie* (Budapest, 1928); *A zenei formák története* (The History of Musical Structure; Budapest, 1930); *Bartók Béla* (Béla Bartók; Budapest, 1930); *La musique hongroise* (Paris, 1933); *Béla Bartók: His Life and Works* (Paris, 1938); *Un Centenaire romantique: Berlioz et la Marche Hongroise d'après des documents inédits* (Paris, 1946); *Franz Liszt* (Paris, 1967).—**NS/LK/DM**

Hara (Tsukahara), Nobuo, jazz tenor saxophonist, leader; b. Toyama, Japan, Nov. 19, 1926. His popular big band the Sharps and Flats is the longest-running band in Japan (from 1951). His performance at Newport in 1967 was well received because it consisted entirely of Japanese folk material arranged for big band. The band also recorded two albums with Hozan Yamamoto, a bamboo flute (shakuhachi) performer who has recorded several jazz records. The band still performs and records, with a handful of original members. They are said to have recorded over 100 albums and received numerous awards; special concerts were held on the group's 30th and 40th anniversaries.

DISC.: *Sharps and Flats in Newport* (1969).—**ETA**

Harbach (real name, Hauerbach), Otto (Abels), American lyricist and librettist; b. Salt Lake City, Aug. 18, 1873; d. N.Y., Jan. 24, 1963. He studied at Knox Coll. and Columbia Univ. In 1908 he collaborated with the composer Karl Hoschna on the successful musical *Three Twins*. He subsequently wrote more than 40 works for Broadway, with such composers as Oscar Hammerstein II, Rudolf Friml, Vincent Youmans, Jerome Kern, and Sigmund Romberg; he also wrote for films. His most popular lyrics included "Rose-Marie" and "Indian Love Call" from Friml's *Rose-Marie* (with Hammerstein; 1924), "The Night Was Made for Love" from Kern's *The Cat and the Fiddle* (1931), and "Smoke Gets in Your Eyes" from Kern's *Roberta* (1932). —**NS/LK/DM**

Harbison, John (Harris), esteemed American composer, conductor, and teacher; b. Orange, N.J., Dec. 20, 1938. He studied violin, viola, piano, tuba, and voice while attending Princeton (N.J.) H.S. During this time, he also profited from advice from Sessions and developed a facility as a jazz pianist. At 16, he won an award in a BMI composition contest. He pursued his education with Piston at Harvard Univ. (B.A., 1960), Blacher at the Berlin Hochschule für Musik (1961), and Sessions and Kim at Princeton Univ. (M.F.A., 1963). He also attended the conducting courses of Carvalho at the Berkshire Music Center in Tanglewood and of Dean Dixon in Salzburg. In 1968–69 he was composer-in-residence at Reed Coll. in Portland, Ore. In 1969 he joined the faculty of the Mass. Inst. of Technology. He also conducted the Cantata Singers and Ensemble (1969–73; 1980–82), and then the new music group Collage (from 1984). He was composer-in-residence of the Pittsburgh Sym. Orch. (1982–84) and of the Berkshire Music Center in Tanglewood (summer, 1984). After serving as new music advisor of the Los Angeles Phil. (1985–86), he was its composer-in-residence (1986–88). In 1992 he returned to Tanglewood as composer-in-residence, and also served as director of its contemporary music festival. In 1978 he received a Guggenheim fellowship. In 1980 he won the Kennedy Center Friedheim Award for his Piano Concerto. He was awarded the Pulitzer Prize in Music in 1986 for his sacred ricercar *The Flight Into Egypt*. In 1989 he received a MacArthur fellowship. In 1992 he was elected to membership in the American Academy and Inst. of Arts and Letters. Harbison's works are distinguished by their outstanding craftsmanship, rhythmic intensity, and lyricism. His experience as a conductor has made him a master of orchestral resources. He has also demonstrated a rare sensitivity in setting vocal texts.

WORKS: DRAMATIC: *The Merchant of Venice*, incidental music to Shakespeare's play (1971; Francestown, N.H., Aug. 12, 1973); *Winter's Tale*, opera (1974; San Francisco, Aug. 20, 1979; rev. 1991); *Full Moon in March*, opera (1977; Cambridge, Mass., April 30, 1979); *Ulysses*, ballet (1983); *The Great Gatsby*, opera after F. Scott Fitzgerald (N.Y., Dec. 20, 1999). **ORCH.:** Sinfonia for Violin and Double Orch. (1963; Cambridge, Mass., March 10, 1964); *Diotima* (1976; Boston, March 10, 1977); *Descant-Nocturne* (1976; N.H. Festival, July 14, 1980); Piano Concerto (1978; N.Y., May 12, 1980); Violin Concerto (1980; Boston, Jan. 24, 1981; rev. 1987); 3 syms.: No. 1 (1981; Boston, March 22, 1984), No. 2 (San Francisco, May 13, 1987), and No. 3 (1990; Baltimore, Feb. 28, 1991); *Ulysses' Bow* (1983; Pittsburgh, May 11, 1984); *Ulysses' Raft* (1983; New Haven, March 6, 1984); Concerto for Oboe, Clarinet, and Strings (Sarasota, Fla., June 14, 1985); *Remembering Gatsby: Foxtrot* (1985; Atlanta, Sept. 11, 1986); *Music for 18 Winds* (Cambridge, Mass., April 18, 1986, composer conducting); *Fanfare for Foley's* (Houston, Oct. 11, 1986); Concerto for Double Brass Choir and Orch. (1988; Los Angeles, April 26, 1990); Viola Concerto (1989; Bridgewater, N.J., May 18, 1990); *David's Fascinating Rhythm Method* (1990; Baltimore, Feb. 14, 1991); Oboe Concerto (1991; San Francisco, Dec. 3, 1992); *3 City Blocks* (1992; Fort Smith, Ark., Aug. 2, 1993); *The Most Often Used Chords: Gli accordi più usati* for Chamber Orch. (Los Angeles, Oct. 22, 1993); Cello Concerto (1993; Boston, April 7, 1994); *I, II, III, IV, V: Fantasia on a Ground* (Weston, Mass., April 3, 1993); Flute Concerto (1994; N.Y., Oct. 29, 1995). **CHAMBER:** Duo for Flute and Piano (N.Y., Aug. 20, 1961); Sonata for Solo Viola (1961); *Confinement* for Chamber Ensemble (1965; N.Y., Feb. 1967); *4 Preludes* for 3 Oboes or for Flute, Clarinet, Violin or Flute, Oboe, and Clarinet (1967; Cambridge, Mass., April 1969); *Serenade* for Flute, Clarinet, Bass Clarinet, Violin, Viola, and Cello (1968; Portland, Ore., May 1969); Piano Trio (Cambridge,

Mass., April 1969); *Bermuda Triangle* for Amplified Cello, Tenor Saxophone, and Electric Organ (1970; N.Y., April 1973); *Die Kürze* for Flute, Clarinet, Piano, Violin, and Cello (N.Y., Feb. 1970); *Amazing Grace* for Oboe (1972; N.Y., Jan. 1973); *Snow Country* for Oboe and String Quintet (1979; Boston, March 1981); Wind Quintet (Boston, April 15, 1979); *Organum for Paul Fromm* for Glockenspiel, Marimba, Vibraphone, Harp, and Piano (1981; Chicago, Jan. 1982); Piano Quintet (Santa Fe, Aug. 7, 1981); *Variations* for Clarinet, Violin, and Piano (Sante Fe, July 23, 1982); *Exequiem for Calvin Simmons* for Alto Flute, Bass Clarinet, Vibraphone, Piano, 2 Violas, and Cello (1982; Williamstown, Mass., Feb. 15, 1983); *Overture: Michael Kohlhaas* for Brass Ensemble (Madison, Wisc., Nov. 1982); 3 string quartets: No. 1 (Washington, D.C., Oct. 11, 1985), No. 2 (Boston, Nov. 20, 1987), and No. 3 (1993; Waltham, Mass., April 30, 1994); *Twilight Music* for Horn, Violin, and Piano (N.Y., March 22, 1985); *4 Songs of Solitude* for Violin (Cambridge, Mass., Dec. 11, 1985); *Magnum Mysterium* for Brass Quintet (Rochester, N.Y., Dec. 21, 1987); *2 Chorale Preludes for Advent* for Brass Quintet (1987; Rochester, N.Y., Dec. 24, 1989); *Fantasy Duo* for Violin and Piano (Washington, D.C., Dec. 2, 1988); *November 19, 1828* for Piano Quartet (1988; Atlanta, Nov. 30, 1989); *Little Fantasy on the 12 Days of Christmas* for Brass Quintet (1988; Rochester, N.Y., Dec. 24, 1989); *Nocturne* for Brass Quintet (N.Y., Dec. 1, 1989); *Fanfares and Reflection* for 2 Violins (1990; N.Y., March 26, 1992); *Variations (in first position)* for String Quartet (1992; Weston, Mass., April 3, 1993); *14 Fabled Folksongs* for Violin and Marimba (1992); *Inventions for a Young Percussionist* (1992; Weston, Mass., April 3, 1993); Suite for Cello (1993). P i a n o : *Parody Fantasia* (1968; N.Y., Jan. 1973); Sonata: *In Memoriam Roger Sessions* (1987; Amherst, Mass., July 15, 1988); *3 Occasional Pieces* (1978; Cambridge, Mass., Oct. 3, 1987, composer pianist); *4 More Occasional Pieces* (1987–90; Boston, Nov. 17, 1991); *Inventions for a Young Pianist* (1992; Weston, Mass., April 3, 1993). V O C A L : *He Shall Not Cry* for Women's Chorus and Organ (1959; Princeton, N.J., Dec. 18, 1962); *Ave Maria* for Women's Chorus (1959; Boston, May 1960); *Autumnal* for Mezzo-soprano and Piano (1965); *Shakespeare Series*, sonnets for Mezzo-soprano and Piano (1965); *Music When Soft Voices Die* for Chorus and Harpsichord or Organ (1966); *5 Songs of Experience on Poems of William Blake* for Chorus, 2 Percussion, 2 Violins, Viola, and Cello (1971; Cambridge, Mass., Feb. 28, 1973, composer conducting); *Elegiac Songs* for Mezzo-soprano and Chamber Orch. (1974; N.Y., Jan. 12, 1975); *Book of Hours and Seasons* for Mezzo-soprano or Tenor, Flute, Cello, and Piano (1975; Cambridge, Mass., March 1976); *Moments of Vision* for Soprano, Tenor, and Renaissance Consort (1975; Amherst, Mass., Feb. 12, 1988); *3 Harp Songs* for Tenor and Harp (1975; Cambridge, Mass., Nov. 18, 1976); *Nunc Dimittis* for Men's Chorus (1975; Cambridge, Mass., Dec. 12, 1981); *The Flower-Fed Buffaloes* for Baritone, Chorus, and 7 Instrumentalists (1976; Boston, Feb. 27, 1978); *Samuel Chapter* for Soprano or Tenor and 6 Instrumentalists (Cambridge, Mass., Nov. 7, 1978, composer conducting); *Motetti di Montale* for Soprano and Piano (1980; Sante Fe, Aug. 4, 1981); *Mirabai Songs* for Soprano and Piano (1982; Boston, Nov. 15, 1983; also for Soprano and Chamber Ensemble, Cambridge, Mass., Feb. 1, 1984); *The Flight into Egypt*, sacred ricercar for Soprano, Baritone, Chorus, and Orch. (Boston, Nov. 21, 1986); *The Natural World* for Soprano or Mezzo-soprano and 5 Instrumentalists (1987; Los Angeles, Nov. 13, 1989, composer conducting); *Rot und Weiss* for Voice and 4 Instrumentalists (1987; Los Angeles, Feb. 1, 1988); *Christmas Vespers* for Reader and Brass Quintet (1988; Rochester, N.Y., Dec. 24, 1989); *The 3 Wise Men* for Reader and Brass Quintet (1988; Rochester, N.Y., Dec. 24, 1989); *Im*

Spiegel for Voice, Violin, and Piano (Los Angeles, Nov. 7, 1988); *Simple Daylight* for Soprano and Piano (1988; San Francisco, May 22, 1990); *Words from Paterson* for Baritone and Chamber Ensemble (1989; Washington, D.C., May 9, 1990); *2 Emmanuel Motets* for Chorus (Boston, Dec. 17, 1990); *Ave Verum Corpus* for Chorus (1990; Boston, Jan. 3, 1991; also for Chorus and String Orch., Ojai, Calif., June 2, 1991, composer conducting); *O Magnum Mysterium* for Chorus (1991; Weston, Mass., April 3, 1993; expanded setting, Boston, Dec. 13, 1992); *Between 2 Worlds* for Soprano, 2 Pianos, and 2 Cellos (Chicago, July 27, 1991); *The Flute of Interior Time* for Baritone and Piano (1991; Berlin, Jan. 11, 1992); *The Rewaking* for Soprano and String Quartet (Pittsburgh, Oct. 14, 1991); *Communion Words* for Chorus (1993; Boston, Jan. 16, 1994); *Concerning Them Which Are Asleep* for Chorus (Boston, April 17, 1994); *4 Psalms* for Soloists, Chorus, and Orch. (Chicago, April 22, 1999).—**NS/LK/DM**

Harburg (Hochberg), E(dgar) Y(ipsel) "Yip",

politically oriented American lyricist and librettist; b. N.Y., April 8, 1896; d. Los Angeles, Calif., March 5, 1981. Harburg's socially conscious lyrics and librettos of the 1930s, 1940s, and 1950s made him a major influence on the politically charged popular music of the 1960s, when many of his peers were in eclipse. He also wrote lasting song standards that did not have explicitly political themes. Working with his primary collaborators, Harold Arlen and Burton Lane, as well as such others as Ira Gershwin, Vernon Duke, and Jerome Kern, he wrote the Depression-era anthem "Brother, Can You Spare a Dime?," "April in Paris," "It's Only a Paper Moon," and "Over the Rainbow," the last from his best- remembered movie musical, *The Wizard of Oz*. Dividing his time between Broadway and Hollywood, he also wrote such successful stage works as *Finian's Rainbow*, which typically combined his interest in political issues with an affection for hopeful fantasy.

Harburg was the child of poor Russian immigrant parents on N.Y.'s Lower East Side. By grade school he was writing parodies of popular songs and light verse. At Townsend Harris H.S. he coedited the literary column of the school newspaper with fellow student Ira Gershwin. He and Gershwin also attended the City Coll. of N.Y. together.

During his college years, Harburg began to publish his poetry in periodicals. After earning a B.S. degree in 1917, he took a job with an American firm in Uruguay, staying until 1920, when he returned to the U.S. and founded an electrical appliance company. In 1923 he married Alice Richmond. They had two children but separated in 1929 and later divorced.

In 1929, Ira Gershwin introduced Harburg to composer Jay Gorney, musical supervisor at the Paramount film studio in Astoria, Queens, N.Y. With Gorney, Harburg wrote several songs used in the Broadway revue *Earl Carroll's Sketch Book* (N.Y., July 1, 1929), which, with a 392–performance run, was the biggest musical hit of the 1929–30 season. Harburg and Gorney also wrote "What Wouldn't I Do for That Man?"; it was sung by Helen Morgan in two Paramount releases, *Applause* (Oct. 9, 1929) and *Glorifying the American Girl* (Dec. 7, 1929), and became a record hit for Ruth Etting in November. These successes, combined with the failure of Harburg's business in the wake of the stock market crash, determined him on a career as a lyricist.

In 1930, Harburg had songs in four Paramount features and two shorts as well as in four stage musicals. His most successful songs of the year were "I Am Only Human After All" (music by Vernon Duke, lyrics also by Ira Gershwin), which was featured in the revue *The Garrick Gaieties* (N.Y., June 4, 1930) and became a hit for the Colonial Club Orch. in July, and "I'm Yours" (music by Johnny Green), used in the short *Leave It to Lester* (June 11, 1930), interpolated into the touring version of the Richard Rodgers and Lorenz Hart show *Simple Simon*, and a hit for Bert Lown and His Orch. in November. (Significantly, "I'm Yours" is the only one of Harburg's published songs to use the phrase "I love you.")

Harburg's film work dried up in 1931, as the movie studios temporarily lost interest in musicals, but he continued to write extensively for the theater, contributing to three more musicals, though *Accidentally Yours*, his and Gorney's first attempt to write a show themselves, was not a success. *Ballyhoo of 1932*, written with composer Lewis E. Gensler, did only slightly better, running for 94 performances. *Americana* had only 77 performances, the play *The Great Magoo*, to which Harburg contributed a song, was performed only 11 times, and *Walk a Little Faster* ran for a barely respectable 119 showings. But among the songs Harburg wrote for these stage works were three that became standards. *Americana* featured "Brother, Can You Spare a Dime?" (music by Gorney), Harburg's first-person account of the effect of the Depression on working men; it became a best-seller for both Bing Crosby and Rudy Vallée and is remembered as the defining song of the era—a rare instance of a popular song with an overt political viewpoint prior to the 1960s.

Harburg's song for *The Great Magoo* was originally entitled "If You Believed in Me" (music by Arlen, lyric also credited to producer Billy Rose). Renamed "It's Only a Paper Moon," the song was used in the Paramount film *Take a Chance* (Nov. 26, 1933) and recorded for a hit by Paul Whiteman and His Orch., and by Cliff Edwards, who appeared in the movie. *Walk a Little Faster* featured "April in Paris" (music by Duke), a song Harburg wrote without ever visiting the city. It took recording artists a year to find the song, but in December 1933, Freddy Martin scored a hit with it. Thus Harburg had written three of his most memorable songs during 1932.

Harburg's only other hit of 1933 was "Isn't It Heavenly" (music by Joseph Myer), one of his few songs not related to a show or a film, which had a popular recording by Eddy Duchin and His Orch. in June. In August he earned his first major film credit, writing lyrics to Gorney's songs in Universal's *Moonlight and Pretzels*.

Harburg had two Broadway shows in 1934. *Ziegfeld Follies of 1934* had only a legal right to the name, since impresario Florenz Ziegfeld had died and his widow had sold the rights to the *Follies* to his rivals, the Shuberts. But the revue was a success, running 182 performances, and it featured a hit in "What Is There to Say?" recorded by Emil Coleman and His Orch. *Life Begins at 8:40*, for which Harburg and Ira Gershwin shared lyric duties for Harold Arlen's music, was an even more successful revue, running 238 performances and generating two hits: "Fun to Be Fooled," recorded by Henry King and His Orch., and "You're a Builder Upper," recorded by Leo Reisman and His Orch. with the composer providing the vocal. Harburg had another independent hit in September when Fats Waller recorded "Then I'll Be Tired of You" (music by Arthur Schwartz).

Harburg relocated to Hollywood in late 1934, initially contracting himself unproductively to Universal, then signing up with Warner Bros., where Arlen was working. The two scored three films in 1936: *The Singing Kid*, an Al Jolson vehicle; *Stage Struck*; and *Gold Diggers of 1937*. They then returned to N.Y., where Harburg conceived the story and wrote the lyrics for his first book musical, *Hooray for What?* Intended as both an antiwar political satire and as a vehicle for comedian Ed Wynn, the show ended up being more of the latter than the former, which helped it to a successful run of 200 performances. Its most memorable song was "God's Country," which was interpolated into the film version of *Babes in Arms* (Oct. 19, 1939) and revived as a hit recording by Frank Sinatra and by Vic Damone in 1950.

Harburg and Arlen returned to Hollywood in 1938, signing to MGM, where their first assignment was a film adaptation of L. Frank Baum's children's book *The Wizard of Oz*. The result was a timeless classic that made a star of Judy Garland and featured her signature song, the Academy Award-winning "Over the Rainbow," which topped the hit parade in September and October 1939 in recordings by Garland and by Glenn Miller and His Orch. Harburg and Arlen's delightful score also featured "Ding-Dong! The Witch Is Dead," "We're Off to See the Wizard," and "If I Only Had a Brain." Before the end of the year, the team had contributed four songs to the Marx Brothers film *At the Circus*, including the patter song "Lydia, the Tattooed Lady," written in the style of Gilbert and Sullivan and a signature song for Groucho Marx.

Harburg teamed with Burton Lane in 1940 to write the songs for *Hold On to Your Hats*, a stage vehicle for Al Jolson that had a 158–performance run on Broadway, curtailed only by the star's decision to abandon it. Back at MGM, Harburg contributed to many movie musicals during the war years, notably working with Lane on *Ship Ahoy*, a vehicle for Tommy Dorsey and His Orch. that led to hit recordings of "The Last Call for Love" (music and lyrics by Harburg, Lane, and Margery Cummings) and "I'll Take Tallulah," the latter with a vocal by Frank Sinatra. He added songs to the film version of *Cabin in the Sky*, among them "Happiness Is a Thing Called Joe" (music by Arlen) sung by Lena Horne and nominated for an Academy Award. Harburg married Edelaine Gorney, the ex-wife of his former writing partner, in 1943.

Harburg wrote the lyrics for and produced MGM's *Meet the People* in 1944, then went back to Broadway with Arlen for *Bloomer Girl*, which presciently touched on issues of civil and women's rights. It was his biggest stage success yet, running 657 performances. In a score that included such notable songs as "The Eagle and Me," the hit was "Evelina," taken into the Top Ten by Bing Crosby in Jan. 1945. By that time Harburg had returned to Hollywood and collaborated with Jerome Kern at Universal on the Deanna Durbin vehicle *Can't Help Singing.* "More and More" from the film earned an Academy Award nomination and became a Top Ten hit for Tommy Dorsey in March 1945. Later in the year, Ella Fitzgerald and Benny Goodman each recorded revivals of "It's Only a Paper Moon" that made the Top Ten.

Harburg cowrote the libretto as well as codirecting and contributing the lyrics to Burton Lane's songs for his biggest stage success, *Finian's Rainbow,* in 1947. The show, which conflated the story of a leprechaun with an examination of Southern racism, boasted a strong score, including "Look to the Rainbow" and "When I'm Not Near the Girl I Love," as well as two songs that became hits: "Old Devil Moon," recorded by Margaret Whiting, and "How Are Things in Glocca Morra?" which gave Top Ten records to Buddy Clark, Martha Tilton, Tommy Dorsey, and Dick Haymes. The show ran 725 performances.

Harburg's outspoken political views made him a target of the anti- Communist witch hunts of the late 1940s and early 1950s. As a victim of the blacklist, he had trouble finding work, especially in Hollywood. He collaborated with composer Sammy Fain on the songs for the stage musical *Flahooley* in 1951, also cowriting the libretto and codirecting, but it was a flop, running only 48 performances.

Harburg's last major success came in 1957 with *Jamaica,* a stage vehicle for Lena Horne for which he cowrote the libretto and contributed lyrics to the songs by Arlen. The show ran 555 performances. In 1961, Harburg adapted the music of 19th century opera composer Jacques Offenbach into songs for *The Happiest Girl in the World,* based on Aristophanes's antiwar play *Lysistrata*; it ran 97 performances. After being blacklisted in Hollywood for more than a decade, Harburg had two film projects released in the early 1960s, both with music by Arlen: *Gay Purr-ee* was an animated movie featuring eight songs sung by Judy Garland, Robert Goulet, and others; and *I Could Go On Singing* (May 15, 1963), to which the songwriters contributed the title song, marking Garland's final film appearance.

Harburg had a surprise hit in 1967 when the Fifth Estate took a recording of "Ding Dong! The Witch Is Dead" into the Top 40. In 1968 he had his last new Broadway production with *Darling of the Day,* which had music by Jule Styne; it ran 32 performances. The film version of *Finian's Rainbow,* released more than 20 years after the Broadway musical, proved timely, and the soundtrack album, featuring Fred Astaire and Petulia Clark, was in the charts for six months. Harburg's last attempt at a Broadway musical came with *What a Day for a Miracle,* based on the novel *Our Lives Have Just Begun* by Henry Myers, who wrote the libretto and some of the music. The show had a one-week tryout at the Univ. of Vt. in Burlington, starting on April 29, 1971. Though it seems to have been written earlier, Harburg's last musical work to be produced was *The Great Man's*

Whiskus, based on the play *The Great Man's Whiskers* by Adrian Scott, with music by Earl Robinson, which was broadcast on NBC-TV.

In 1981, a month before what would have been his 85th birthday, Harburg died of a heart attack while driving to a meeting to discuss a movie musical version of Robert Louis Stevenson's *Treasure Island.*

WORKS (only works for which Harburg was a primary, credited lyricist are listed): **MUSICALS/REVUES** (dates refer to N.Y. openings): *Accidentally Yours* (1931); *Ballyhoo of 1932* (Sept. 6, 1932); *Americana* (Oct. 5, 1932); *Walk a Little Faster* (Dec. 7, 1932); *Ziegfeld Follies* (Jan. 4, 1934); *Life Begins at 8:40* (Aug. 27, 1934); *Hooray for What?* (Dec. 1, 1937); *Hold On to Your Hats* (Sept. 11, 1940); *Bloomer Girl* (Oct. 5, 1944); *Finian's Rainbow* (Jan. 10, 1947); *Flahooley* (May 14, 1951); *Jamaica* (Oct. 31, 1957); *The Happiest Girl in the World* (April 3, 1961); *Darling of the Day* (Jan 27, 1968). **FILMS:** *Moonlight and Pretzels* (Aug. 22, 1933); *The Singing Kid* (April 3, 1936); *Stage Struck* (Sept. 27, 1936); *Gold Diggers of 1937* (Dec. 24, 1936); *The Wizard of Oz* (Aug. 17, 1939); *At the Circus* (Nov. 16, 1939); *Rio Rita* (May 7, 1942); *Ship Ahoy* (June 25, 1942); *Cairo* (Nov. 5, 1942); *Cabin in the Sky* (May 27, 1943); *Kismet* (Aug. 22, 1944); *Meet the People* (Sept. 7, 1944); *Can't Help Singing* (Dec. 25, 1944); *California* (Jan. 14, 1947); *Gay Purr-ee* (Dec. 5, 1962); *Finian's Rainbow* (Oct. 9, 1968). **TELEVISION:** *The Great Man's Whiskus* (Feb. 13, 1973).

WRITINGS: *Rhymes for the Irreverent* (N.Y., 1965); *At This Point in Rhyme* (N.Y., 1976).

BIBL.: H. Meyerson and E. Harburg (his son), *Who Put the Rainbow in the Wizard of Oz? Y. H., Lyricist* (Ann Arbor, Mich., 1993).—**WR**

d'Harcourt, Eugène, French conductor and composer; b. Paris, May 2, 1859; d. Locarno, March 4, 1918. He studied at the Paris Cons. with Massenet, Durand, and Savard (1882–86), then took courses in Berlin with Bargiel. In 1892 he built the Salle d'Harcourt in Paris, where he presented 3 seasons of Concerts Éclectiques Populaires. He wrote an unsuccessful opera, *Le Tasse* (Monte Carlo, 1903), in addition to 3 unnecessary syms. and some passable chamber music.—**NS/LK/DM**

d'Harcourt, Marguerite (née **Béclard**), French folk-song collector and composer; b. Paris, Feb. 24, 1884; d. there, Aug. 2, 1964. She studied composition with d'Indy and Emmanuel. She composed 2 syms., *Rapsodie péruvienne* for Oboe, Clarinet, and Bassoon, and many songs. With her husband, Raoul d'Harcourt, she publ. a valuable treatise, *Musique des Incas et ses survivances* (2 vols., Paris, 1925), based on materials gathered during their journeys in Peru. Another valuable publication was her compilation of 240 songs, *Chansons folkloriques françaises au Canada* (Quebec, 1956). —**NS/LK/DM**

Hardee, John, hard-driving Tex. tenor saxophonist; b. Corsicana, Tex., Dec. 20, 1918; d. Dallas, Tex., May 18, 1984. Both parents were musical. An uncle, Ashford Hardee, was a professional trombonist. Hardee played piano at local dances, then saxophone with the Blue Moon Syncopators, Florenz O'Harris and Rick Calhoun. He played in the Bishop Coll. Band, then spent six months in Don Albert's Band (1937–38). He returned to coll. until 1941. During Army service he performed in the Signal Corps Band and was stationed near N.Y. After leaving the Army he worked with Tiny Grimes then led his own band. He is best-known for his late 1940s R&B–styled recordings with Grimes ("Tiny's Boogie Woogie") and his own small groups ("Hardee's Partee," "River Edge Rock"). He played club dates in N.Y. before moving to Dallas in 1949 to become a school band director, while still playing local club dates. However, he quit playing from the early 1960s until late 1974. He made a triumphant appearance at the Nice Jazz Festival in 1974. However, he was mostly inactive in the remaining decade of his life.—JC/LP

d'Hardelot, Guy (actually, **Mrs. W. I. Rhodes**, née **Helen Guy**), French composer; b. Boulogne-sur-Mer, 1858; d. London, Jan. 7, 1936. She studied at the Paris Cons. and then was active as a song composer.—NS/LK/DM

Hardenberger, Håkan, Swedish trumpeter; b. Malmö, Oct. 27, 1961. He began trumpet lessons at the age of 8 with Bo Nilsson in Malmö, and later pursued more extensive training with Pierre Thibaud at the Paris Cons. and with Thomas Stevens in Los Angeles. He also received instruction from Dokshitscher in Moscow, Herseth in Chicago, and Tarr in Basel. He began performing while still a youth, making his solo debut with orch. when he was 15. After winning prizes in competitions in Paris, Munich, Toulon, and Geneva, he toured extensively in Europe and North and South America. His repertoire includes both standard and contemporary works.—NS/LK/DM

Harding, A(lbert) A(ustin), American bandmaster; b. Georgetown, Ill., Feb. 10, 1880; d. Champaign, Ill., Dec. 3, 1958. At 14 he began to play cornet, then trombone and other wind instruments. After graduation from high school in Paris, Ill., he conducted the local concert band. In 1902 he enrolled as an engineering student at the Univ. of Ill. (B.A., 1906). At the same time, he developed many campus music contacts, and in 1905 was made acting leader of the Univ. Band; in 1907 he was appointed director, a post he held until 1948. Harding was the first to succeed in raising college bands to a "symphonic" level in which oboes, saxophones, and other reed instruments supplied variety to the common brass-heavy contingent; thanks to this sonic enhancement, he was able to arrange orch. works of the general repertoire and perform them in a satisfactory musical manner; he was credited with 147 such transcriptions. John Philip Sousa, who greatly admired Harding, bequeathed to him and his band his own entire music library. Harding was a charter founder of the American Bandmasters' Assn. in 1929 and was its president in 1937–38; was honorary life president from 1956 until his death. He also was active in founding the Coll. Band Directors' Assn., of which he was honorary life president from its founding in 1941.—NS/LK/DM

Harding, Buster (Lavere), jazz arranger, pianist; b. Buxtom, Ontario, Canada, March 19, 1917; d. N.Y.,

Nov. 14, 1965. He was raised in Cleveland. He led his own band there during the early 1930s, then worked in Buffalo with Marion Sear's band. He led his own trio at Boston's Savarin Cafe (1938), then settled in N.Y. He played second piano and arranged for Teddy Wilson's Big Band (late 1939 to spring 1940), and also arranged for Coleman Hawkins's Big Band (late 1939). He led his own quartet at Nick's, N.Y. (May 1940) and was a staff arranger for Cab Calloway (1941–42), then did prolific freelance arranging for Artie Shaw, Count Basie, Dizzie Gillespie, and Benny Goodman, among many others. He was musical director (and occasional accompanist) for Billie Holiday (ca. 1954). He was seriously ill for the last few years of his life, but continued to arrange, and worked occasionally in various small groups including a brief spell with Jonah Jones in the 1960s.—JC/LP

Hardwick(e), Otto (Toby), jazz alto (and bass and baritone) saxophonist long associated with Duke Ellington; b. Washington, D.C., May 31, 1904; d. there, Aug. 5, 1970. He started on string bass at the age of 14, worked with Carroll's Columbia Orch. (ca. 1920), then switched to "C" melody sax. He began gigging with Duke Ellington in and around Washington, and also worked for Elmer Snowden at Murray's Casino, Washington (ca. 1922). He went to N.Y. with Duke Ellington in 1923 and shared many of that leader's early experiences, including a week with Wilbur Sweatman (March 1923) and residencies with Elmer Snowden. He occasionally doubled on violin and string bass in the mid-1920s, but specialized on alto sax. He worked regularly with Ellington until the spring of 1928. He went to Paris, worked in a band led by bassist John Ricks, led his own band and played briefly with Noble Sissle and Nekka Shaw's Orch. before returning to N.Y. He had a brief stint with Chick Webb (1929), then led his own band at the Hot Feet Club in N.Y. (1930), subsequently led at Small's, then worked with Snowden before rejoining Ellington in spring 1932. Except for brief absences he remained with Ellington until May 1946. He retired from music, worked in hotel management, and also ran his own farm in Md.—JC/LP

Hardy, Emmett (Louis), early jazz cornetist; b. New Orleans, June 12, 1903; d. there, June 16, 1925. He never recorded, but his name lives on due to word-of-mouth and his supposed influence on the young Bix Beiderbecke. Both parents were musicians. He began on piano and guitar, then played cornet from age of 12. At 14 he began playing in Jack "Papa" Laine's Band. Later he worked with Norman Brownlee's Orch. He left New Orleans in a band accompanying variety artiste Bea Palmer. He left this band in Davenport, Iowa, and joined Carlisle Evans's Band on the S.S. Capitol for eight months (1919). He returned to New Orleans and led his own band, then joined Tony Catalino's Band on S.S. Sydney. He moved to Chicago to augment the New Orleans Rhythm Kings at Friars' Inn, but after a dispute with the local musicians' union he returned to New Orleans. He later played briefly with Norman Brownlee's Orch., and was then inactive for the last year of his life. He suffered from tuberculosis, which led to his early death.—JC/LP

Harewood, Sir George (Henry Hubert Lascelles), 7th Earl of, distinguished English arts administrator, music critic, and music editor; b. London, Feb. 7, 1923. He was educated at Eton and King's Coll., Cambridge. In 1950 he founded the journal *Opera*, of which he was ed. until 1953. He was on the board of directors of the Royal Opera at Covent Garden (1951–53; 1969–72), serving as its administrative executive (1953–60). He was general-director of the Leeds Festival (1958–74), later serving as its chairman (1988–90), and also director of the Edinburgh Festivals (1961–65) and chancellor of the Univ. of York (1962–67). In 1972 he was appointed managing director of the Sadler's Wells Opera (known after 1974 as the English National Opera) in London. He retained this position until 1985, and then was its chairman from 1986. In 1988 he was artistic director of the Adelaide Festival. He was knighted in 1987. He ed. *Kobbé's Complete Opera Book* in 1954, 1963, and 1972; it was publ. as *The New Kobbé's Complete Opera Book* in 1976, then as *The Definitive Kobbé's Opera Book* (1987). His autobiography was publ. as *The Tongs and the Bones* (1982).—NS/LK/DM

Hargrove, Roy (Anthony Jr.), jazz-revival trumpeter; b. Waco, Tex., Oct 16, 1969. He began on clarinet, then started studying cornet at age nine. He became more excited at 13 upon witnessing Fathead Newman perform at his junior high school. While in high school he played a duet with Larry Willis at a local club. He won an IAJE Young Talent Award in 1986 in Atlanta along with Stephen Scott. His first big break was sitting in with Wynton Marsalis at a Fort Worth club. A few months later he was touring Europe with Frank Morgan in a band that included Ronnie Mathews and Walter Booker. He earned a scholarship to Berklee Coll. in the fall of 1987. John Hicks began championing Hargrove, inviting him to sit in at his N.Y. club dates in 1988. Scott and Christian McBride were members of Hargrove's first organized quintet in 1990. Hargrove studied under Jimmy Cobb in 1990 after transferring from Berklee to the New School for Social Research (N.Y.). In the summer of 1991, Hargove and McBride were members of the Jazz Futures band. *The Love Suite: In Mahogany*, a composition in five-movements, was commissioned in 1993 by the jazz department at Lincoln Center; Hargrove played the solo at the work's premiere that September. From the mid-1990s, he led his own small groups and, on occasion, a big band. After performing at the Havana, Cuba, jazz festival in 1996, he formed a Cuban-influenced quintet called Crisol along with pianist Chucho Valdes and Cuban percussionists; the group toured and recorded through 1997.

DISC.: *Diamond in the Rough* (1990); *Public Eye* (1990); *Tokyo Sessions* (1991); *Vibe* (1992); *Of Kindred Souls* (1993); *With the Tenors of Our Time* (1994); *Approaching Standards* (1994); *Parker's Mood* (1995); *Family* (1995; w. W. Marsalis).—LP

Harich-Schneider, Eta (Margarete), German musicologist and harpsichordist; b. Oranienburg, Nov. 16, 1897; d. Vienna, Oct. 16, 1986. She studied piano and musicology in Berlin, making her debut in 1924 with the first performance of Hindemith's *1922 Suite*. She then studied harpsichord with Landowska (1929–35), subsequently forming an early music ensemble; then became a prof. at the Berlin Hochschule für Musik, but was dismissed in 1940 when she refused to join the Nazi party. She then fled to Tokyo, where she directed the music dept. of the U.S. Army Coll. and also taught Western music at the imperial court (1947–49). After her move to N.Y. in 1949, she pursued Japanese studies at Columbia Univ.; she also took courses in sociology at the New School for Social Research (M.A., 1955). From 1955 to 1961 she taught harpsichord at the Vienna Academy of Music. She wrote important books on harpsichord technique and repertoire and on Japanese art music; also made notable recordings of works by the Baroque masters and of collections of Japanese music. She received a Guggenheim fellowship in 1955.

WRITINGS: *Die Kunst des Cembalospiels* (Kassel, 1939; 3rd ed., 1970); *Gendai ongaku to Nippon no sakkyokusha* (Contemporary Music and Japanese Composers; Tokyo, 1950); *The Harpsichord: An Introduction to Technique, Style and the Historical Sources* (Kassel, 1954; 3rd ed., 1973); *A History of Japanese Music* (London, 1973).—NS/LK/DM

Harline, Leigh, American composer; b. Salt Lake City, March 26, 1907; d. Long Beach, Calif., Dec. 10, 1969. He studied music at the Univ. of Utah. He went to Los Angeles in 1928 and became arranger for Walt Disney (1931–42). He then worked as a film-music composer in Hollywood. His song "When You Wish upon a Star" received an Academy Award in 1940.—NS/LK/DM

Harling, William Franke, English-American composer; b. London, Jan. 18, 1887; d. Sierra Madre, Calif., Nov. 22, 1958. He was taken to the U.S. in his infancy. He filled various jobs as a church organist. Eventually he settled in Hollywood. He wrote an opera, *A Light from St. Agnes* (Chicago, Dec. 26, 1925), *Deep River*, a "native opera with jazz" (Lancaster, Pa., Sept. 18, 1926), instrumental music, and more than 100 songs. He was also the composer of the march *West Point Forever*.—NS/LK/DM

Harman, Carter, American music critic, recording-firm executive, and composer; b. N.Y., June 14, 1918. He studied with Sessions at Princeton Univ. (B.A., 1940) and continued his studies at Columbia Univ. (M.A., 1949). He was a music critic for the *N.Y. Times* (1947–52) and later music ed. of *Time* magazine (1952–57); from 1958 to 1967 he lived in Puerto Rico, where he became president of the West Indies Recording Corp. In 1967 Harman became producer and executive vice-president of Composers Recordings, Inc., in N.Y., devoted mainly to recording contemporary American music; was its executive director from 1976 to 1984. He publ. *A Popular History of Music from Gregorian Chant to Jazz* (N.Y., 1956; rev. 1968). Among his compositions are the ballet *Blackface* (N.Y., May 18, 1947), 2 children's operas: *Circus at the Opera* (1951) and *Castles in the Sand* (1952), children's songs, and *Alex and the Singing Synthesizer*, an entertainment of electronically synthesized nursery rhymes (1974–77).—NS/LK/DM

Harmat, Artur, Hungarian composer; b. Nyitrabajna, June 27, 1885; d. Budapest, April 20, 1962. He studied at the Budapest Academy of Music and later took courses in Prague and Berlin. From 1920 to 1946 he was an inspector of singing in the Budapest schools, and from 1924 to 1959 he was a prof. of religious music at the Budapest Academy of Music. He wrote 2 valuable manuals on counterpoint (1947, 1956) and composed a great quantity of church music, based on the lines of Palestrina's polyphony.

WORKS: *Te Deum* for Chorus and Organ (1912–29); *Tu es Petrus* for Chorus and Orch. (1929); *Psalm 150* for Chorus and Instruments (1929); *De Profundis* for Chorus (1932); *Szep Ilonka* (Fair Helen), cantata (1954); Organ Sonata (1956).—**NS/LK/DM**

Harmati, Sándor, Hungarian-born American violinist, conductor, and composer; b. Budapest, July 9, 1892; d. Flemington, N.J., April 4, 1936. He studied at the Royal Academy of Music in Budapest. After serving as concertmaster of the Budapest Sym. Orch., he emigrated to the U.S. in 1914 and became a naturalized American citizen in 1920. He was a violinist in the Letz (1917–21) and Lenox (1922–25) string quartets, conductor of the Omaha Sym. Orch. (1925–30) and the Musicians' Sym. Orch. for the Unemployed in N.Y., and prof. of music at Bard Coll. in Annandale-on-Hudson, N.Y. (1934–36). He wrote the opera *Prelude to a Melodrama* (1928), incidental music to *The Jeweled Tree* (1926), symphonic poem *Folio* (1922), String Quartet (1925), solo violin pieces, and many songs, including *The Bluebird of Happiness* (1934), his best-known piece.—**NS/LK/DM**

Harnisch, Otto Siegfried, German composer; b. Reckershausen, near Göttingen, c. 1568; d. Göttingen (buried), Aug. 18, 1623. He was educated at the Univ. of Helmstedt (1585–93), during which time he served as cantor at St. Blasius in Braunschweig (1588–89), and then in Helmstedt (1593–94) and at the gymnasium and at the Marienkirche in Wolfenbüttel (1594–1600). After serving as Kapellmeister at the ducal court in Iburg, near Osnabrück, he was cantor at the Academy and at the Johanniskirche in Göttingen from 1603 until his death. Harnisch was a notable composer of sacred music. In his *Passio dominica* (1621), he was the first composer to set the turbae to 5 voices. His other works include 3 vols. of German secular songs for 3 Voices in the Italian villanella manner (1587, 1588, 1591) and 2 vols. of motets (1592, 1621). He also publ. the theoretical treatise *Artis musicae delineatio* (Frankfurt am Main, 1608).

BIBL.: H.-O. Hiekel, *O. S. H.: Leben und Werk* (diss., Univ. of Hamburg, 1956).—**LK/DM**

Harnoncourt, Nikolaus (in full, **Johann Nikolaus de la Fontaine und d'Harnoncourt-Unverzagt**), eminent Austrian cellist, conductor, and musicologist; b. Berlin, Dec. 6, 1929. His father, an engineer, also played the piano and composed; the family settled in Graz. He began to study the cello at the age of 9, later training with Paul Grümmer and at the Vienna Academy of Music with Emanuel Brabec. He was a cellist in the Vienna Sym. Orch. (1952–69). He founded the Vienna Concentus Musicus (1953), which began giving concerts in 1957, playing on period instruments or modern copies. The group made its first tour of England, the U.S., and Canada in 1966. From the mid-1970s he also appeared internationally as a guest conductor, expanding his repertoire to include music of later eras. His writings include *Musik als Klangrede: Wege zu einem neuen Musikverständnis* (Salzburg and Vienna, 1982; Eng. tr., 1988, as *Baroque Music Today: Music as Speech; Ways to a New Understanding of Music*), *Der musikalische Dialog: Gedanken zu Monteverdi, Bach und Mozart* (Salzburg, 1984; Eng. tr., 1989, as *The Musical Dialogue: Thoughts on Monteverdi, Bach, and Mozart*), and *Die Macht der Musik: Zwei Reden* (Salzburg, 1993). His wife, Alice Harnoncourt (b. Vienna, Sept. 26, 1930), studied violin with Feist and Moraves in Vienna and with Thibaud in Paris. She became concertmistress of the Vienna Concentus Musicus at its founding.—**NS/LK/DM**

Harnoy, Ofra, Israeli-born Canadian cellist; b. Hadera, Jan. 31, 1965. She began cello lessons at age 6 under her parents' guidance. After the family emigrated to Canada in 1972, she studied with Vladimir Orloff in Toronto. She also received instruction from William Pleeth in London and attended the master classes of Rostropovich, Fournier, and Du Pré. At age 10, she made her professional debut as soloist in a C. Stamitz concerto with Boyd Neel and his orch. in Toronto. In 1978 she won 1st prize in the Montreal Sym. Orch. competition, in 1979 the Canadian Music Competition, and in 1982 the Concert Artists Guild Award of N.Y. In 1981 she made her European debut in a London recital; her U.S. debut followed in 1982 as soloist in the Tchaikovsky *Rococo Variations* with the Shreveport (La.) Sym. Orch. That same year, she also made her Carnegie Recital Hall debut in N.Y. In 1983 she was soloist in the world premiere of a long-lost Cello Concerto by Offenbach in N.Y. Thereafter she appeared as a soloist with various orchs., as a recitalist, and as a chamber music artist.—**NS/LK/DM**

Harper, Billy (R.), tenor saxophonist, flutist; b. Houston, Tex., Jan. 17, 1943. At age five he was singing at sacred and secular functions and participating in choral and solo singing events. By age 14, he formed his first Billy Harper Quintet. He performed as saxophonist and singer, played with R&B bands, and with saxophonists James Clay and Fred Smith. Graduating cum laude, he went on to study saxophone and music theory at North Tex. State Univ. and received his bachelor's degree in music. He continued graduate studies at NTSU and became a member of their big band. That year, 1965, the band won first prize at the Kans. Jazz Festival. After moving to N.Y. in 1966, Harper toured Calif. with Gil Evans, played in Art Blakey's Jazz Messengers for two years, and worked with Elvin Jones in 1970. Later came periods with Max Roach, The Thad Jones–Mel Lewis Orch., and Lee Morgan. He performed, recorded and toured Europe, Japan, Africa and throughout the U.S. from 1966–79 with these groups, as well as his own Billy Harper Quintet. He has primarily led his own groups since 1973, but worked on occasion with Roach until 1978, and Evans into the 1980s. He has taught at Livingston Coll. of Rutgers Univ. since 1975.

He has received a grant from the N.J. State Council for the Arts to teach improvisation at 15 high schools. Awards and honors included three music composition grants; two from the National Endowment of the Arts, and one from the Creative Arts Program. He received the *Down Beat* International Critics Award for Tenor Saxophone for two years consecutively. During the 1990s, he toured for the U.S. Information Service.

Disc.: *Capra Black* (1973); *Black Saint* (1975); *In Europe* (1979); *Trying to Make Heaven My Home* (1979); *Destiny Is Yours* (1989); *Somalia* (1995).—LP

Harper, Edward (James), English composer, pianist, and teacher; b. Taunton, March 17, 1941. After studies at Christ Church, Oxford (1959–63), he received instruction in composition from Gordon Jacob at the Royal Coll. of Music in London (1963–64) and with Donatoni in Milan (1968). From 1964 he lectured on music at the Univ. of Edinburgh. He also was director of the New Music Group of Scotland (1973–91).

Works: DRAMATIC: O p e r a : *Fanny Robin* (1974; Edinburgh, Feb. 5, 1975); *Hedda Gabler* (1984–85; Glasgow, June 5, 1985); *The Mellstock Quire* (1987–88; Edinburgh, Feb. 10, 1988). **ORCH.:** Piano Concerto (1969; Edinburgh, Jan. 29, 1970); Sonata for Chamber Orch. (1971; Edinburgh, Feb. 25, 1973); *Bartók Games* (Edinburgh, Nov. 26, 1972); *Fantasia I* for Chamber Orch. (Edinburgh, March 27, 1976), *IV* for Violin, Piano, and Small Orch. (1980; St. Andrews, Feb. 26, 1981), and *V*, passacaglia for Chamber Orch. (St. Magnus Festival, June 24, 1985); *Fern Hill* for Chamber Orch. (1976; St. Andrews, Feb. 23, 1977); Sym. (1978–79; Edinburgh, March 1979); Clarinet Concerto (1981–82; Llandaff, June 3, 1982); *Intrada after Monteverdi* for Chamber Orch. (1982; Edinburgh, Oct. 6, 1983); Double Variations for Oboe, Bassoon, and Winds (Manchester, Aug. 12, 1989). **CHAMBER:** Quintet for Flute, Clarinet, Violin, Cello, and Piano (Glasgow, May 1974); *Ricercari in Memoriam Luigi Dallapiccola* for Chamber Group (Edinburgh, Aug. 30, 1975); *Fantasia II* for 11 Solo Strings (Dundee, April 21, 1976) and *III* for Brass Quintet (Edinburgh, Nov. 3, 1977); String Quartet No. 2 (London, Dec. 17, 1986); *In memoriam (Kenneth Leighton)* for Cello and Piano (Edinburgh, May 8, 1990); Trio for Clarinet, Cello, and Piano (Glasgow, Oct. 19, 1997); *Souvenir* for 2 Pianos, Vibraphone, and Marimba (Edinburgh, Nov. 8, 1998). **VOCAL:** *7 Poems by e.e. cummings* for Soprano and Orch. (Glasgow, Nov. 1, 1977); *Chester Mass* for Mixed Voices and Orch. (Chester Cathedral, Oct. 20, 1979); *The Universe* for Chorus (1979); *Mass: Qui creavit coelum* for Double Chorus (1986; Oxford, May 28, 1987); *Homage to Thomas Hardy* for Baritone and Chamber Orch. (1989); *The Lamb* for Soprano, Chorus, and Orch. (Glasgow, Dec. 9, 1990).—NS/LK/DM

Harper, Heather (Mary), distinguished Irish soprano; b. Belfast, May 8, 1930. She studied at Trinity Coll. of Music in London and also took voice lessons with Helene Isepp and Frederic Husler. She made her debut as Lady Macbeth with the Oxford Univ. Opera in 1954. She was a member of the English Opera Group (1956–75); first sang at the Glyndebourne Festival in 1957, at Covent Garden as Helena in *A Midsummer Night's Dream* in 1962, and at the Bayreuth Festival as Elsa in 1967; also sang in the U.S. and South America. Although she formally retired as a singer in 1990, she sang with Rattle and the City of Birmingham Sym.

Orch. at the London Proms in 1994. From 1985 she was a prof. at the Royal Coll. of Music in London; she also was director of singing studies at the Britten-Pears School in Snape (from 1986) and the first visiting lecturer-in-residence at the Royal Scottish Academy of Music in Glasgow (from 1987). Her notable roles included Arabella, Marguerite, Antonia, Gutrune, Hecuba, Anne Trulove in *The Rake's Progress*, The Woman in *Erwartung*, and Ellen Orford in *Peter Grimes*; she also created the role of Nadia in Tippett's *The Ice Break* (1977). An esteemed concert artist, she sang in the premieres of Britten's *War Requiem* (1962) and Tippett's 3rd Sym. (1972). In 1965 she was made a Commander of the Order of the British Empire.—NS/LK/DM

Harrell, Lynn (Morris), outstanding American cellist, conductor, and teacher, son of **Mack Harrell;** b. N.Y., Jan. 30, 1944. He studied at the Juilliard School of Music in N.Y. with Leonard Rose and at the Curtis Inst. of Music in Philadelphia with Orlando Cole. He also attended master classes given by Gregor Piatigorsky in Dallas (1962) and Pablo Casals in Marlboro, Vt. (1963). In 1961 he made his debut as a soloist at a N.Y. Phil. young peoples' concert. From 1964 to 1971 he was 1st cellist of the Cleveland Orch. In 1971 he made his N.Y. recital debut, followed by his European debut in 1974. From 1971 to 1976 he taught at the Univ. of Cincinnati Coll.-Cons. of Music. With Murray Perahia, he shared the first Avery Fisher Prize in 1975. In succeeding years, he toured throughout the world as a soloist with orchs., as a recitalist, and as a chamber music artist. In 1986 he held the International Chair of Cello Studies at the Royal Academy of Music in London. From 1987 to 1993 he served as the Gregor Piatigorsky Prof. of Cello at the Univ. of Southern Calif. in Los Angeles, and he also was artistic director of the Los Angeles Phil. Inst. from 1988 to 1991. He was principal of the Royal Academy of Music from 1993 to 1995. As a cellist, Harrell's playing is marked by ingratiating tonal mellowness and a facile, unforced technical display. His artistry won him Grammy Awards in 1981, 1987, and 1988. He has also made appearances as a conductor.—NS/LK/DM

Harrell, Mack, distinguished American baritone, father of **Lynn (Morris) Harrell;** b. Celeste, Tex., Oct. 8,1909; d. Dallas, Jan. 29, 1960. He studied violin and voice at the Juilliard School of Music in N.Y. In 1938 he made his concert debut at N.Y.'s Town Hall. After winning the Metropolitan Opera Auditions in 1938, he made his debut with the company in N.Y. on Dec. 16, 1939, as Biterolf; he remained on the roster until 1948, and returned there for the 1949–50, 1952–54, and 1957–58 seasons. On May 18, 1944, he made his first appearance at the N.Y.C. Opera as Germont, and returned there in 1948, 1951–52, and 1959. He also pursued a notably successful concert career. From 1945 to 1956 he taught voice at the Juilliard School of Music. He publ. *The Sacred Hour of Song* (N.Y., 1938). Harrell's voice was one of remarkable lyrical beauty. Among his operatic roles were Papageno, Kothner, Amfortas, Jochanaan, Wozzeck, and Nick Shadow in *The Rake's Progress*, which role he created in its U.S. premiere at the Metropolitan Opera on Feb. 14, 1953.—NS/LK/DM

Harrell, Tom, jazz trumpeter, flugelhornist; b. Urbana, Ill., June 16, 1946. His family moved to L.A. when he was six years old. He began studying trumpet at age eight, and was working with local bands by age 13. He attended Stanford, where he earned a degree in composition in 1969. Upon graduation, he was hired by Stan Kenton, and toured with him through the end of 1969. He then worked with Woody Herman in 1970 and 1971, and spent four years with Horace Silver. He also performed and recorded with Chuck Israel's National Jazz Ensemble (1976), and played with Arnie Lawrence, Cecil Payne, Bill Evans and Lee Konitz's nonet. Harrell worked with George Russell in 1982, then joined Phil Woods in 1983, with whom he worked through 1989. He has often worked and recorded with Joe Lovano. During the 1990s, he has primarily led his own groups, although he has played as a member of Charlie Haden's Liberation Orch. (beginning in 1988) as well as in the N.Y. Jazz Giants (1992). He was voted Trumpeter of the Year in *Down Beat*'s Readers and Critics Polls for 1996. He is one of the top soloists despite a serious schizophrenic condition which requires constant treatment.

DISC.: *Aurora/Total* (1976); *Play of Light* (1982); *Moon Alley* (1985); *Open Air* (1986); *Visions* (1987); *Stories* (1988); *Sail Away* (1989); *Form* (1990); *Passages* (1991); *Upswing* (1993); *Labyrinth* (1996); *Art of Rhythm* (1997); *Time's Mirror* (1999).—**LP**

Harrer, (Johann) Gottlob, German composer; b. Görlitz, May 8, 1703; d. Carlsbad, July 9, 1755. He studied law at the Univ. of Leipzig (1722–25), and then was sent to Italy to study music by Count Heinrich von Brühl. In 1731 he entered the count's service in Dresden. In 1750 he was made Bach's successor as the Leipzig Thomaskantor. Among his extensive output were Passions, oratorios, church music, many syms., and chamber music.—**LK/DM**

Harrhy, Eiddwen (Mair), Welsh soprano; b. Trowbridge, England, April 14, 1949. She studied at the Royal Manchester Coll. of Music, where she sang Mozart's Despina in 1970. After further training in London and Paris, she made her formal operatic debut as Mozart's Ilia in Oxford in 1974. That same year she appeared at London's Covent Garden as Wellgunde. In 1977 she made her first appearance at the English National Opera in London as Adele in *Le Comte Ory*. She sang for the first time at the Glyndebourne Festival in 1979 as Diana in *La Fedeltà premiata*. In 1986 she sang Berg's Marie at the Welsh National Opera in Cardiff and made her U.S. debut in Los Angeles as Morgana in Handel's *Alcina*. She returned to the English National Opera in 1989 to create the role of Marian Singleton in Blake's *The Plumber's Gift*, and also appeared at the London Promenade Concerts. In 1991 she sang Hecuba in *King Priam* with Opera North in Leeds. She appeared in *Owen Wingrave* at the Glyndebourne Festival in 1997. —**NS/LK/DM**

Harries, Kathryn, English soprano; b. Hampton Court, Feb. 15, 1951. She was a student of Constance Shacklock at the Royal Academy of Music in London. In 1977 she made her concert debut at London's Royal Festival Hall. Her operatic debut followed in 1982 as Leonore with the Welsh National Opera in Cardiff, where she returned as Sieglinde in 1984 and as Gutrune in 1985. In 1983 she made her first appearance at the English National Opera in London as Irene in *Rienzi*, and returned there in such roles as Eva, Kát'a Kabanová and Donna Anna. She created the title role in Edward Harper's *Hedda Gabler* at the Scottish Opera in Glasgow in 1985. Her debut at the Metropolitan Opera in N.Y. followed on April 10, 1986, as Kundry, where she returned as Gutrune in 1989. In 1987 she sang Berlioz's Dido in Lyons and Senta at the Paris Opéra. She made her first appearance at London's Covent Garden in 1989 in the British premiere of Berio's *Un re in ascolto*, and returned there in 1991 as Gutrune. Following engagements as Dido in Brussels and as Carmen in Orange in 1992, she appeared as Brangäne at the Scottish Opera in 1994. In 1997 she sang Kundry at the Opéra de la Bastille in Paris, a role she sang again at the English National Opera in 1999.—**NS/LK/DM**

Harris, (William) Victor, American pianist, organist, conductor, teacher, and composer; b. N.Y., April 27, 1869; d. there, Feb. 15, 1943. He was a student of Charles Blum (piano), William Courtney (voice), Frederick Schilling (composition), and Anton Seidl (conducting). He was first active as a church organist in N.Y.; later he was conductor of the Utica Choral Union (1893–94) and the St. Cecilia Club in N.Y. (1902–36); he also was active as an accompanist and teacher. He wrote some orch. music, piano pieces, a cantata, and quartets for Men's and Women's Voices, but became best known for his numerous solo songs.—**NS/LK/DM**

Harris, Barry (Doyle), jazz pianist, educator, theorist; b. Detroit, Mich., Dec. 15, 1929. His mother was a church pianist, and began teaching him to play at age four. By 1946, he was playing jazz locally. He was known as a master teacher in Detroit in the late 1950s. His national reputation began in Cannonball Adderley's group in 1960, and he moved to N.Y., working frequently with Coleman Hawkins, Yusef Lateef, and Charles McPherson, as well as his own groups. He made many sideman appearances in the 1960s and 1970s, with the first recordings of his own for Riverside and Prestige during the 1960s. As an educator (sometimes known as "professor"), he is especially known for his brilliant ability to distill from the works of Bud Powell and Charlie Parker a series of melodic principles which he calls "bebop scales." (They are perhaps more accurately described as licks since they are built from existing scales rather than new ones.) For example, he has noted that beboppers tended to fill in certain steps chromatically when descending but not when ascending. John Coltrane was among many musicians who was said to have consulted with him. In 1982, Harris founded the Jazz Cultural Center, where he taught group classes and led a big band; after five years, he could no longer afford to keep the center open, and moved on to teaching at other venues. Among his protégés are Dan Faulk and Sue Terry. He was the recipient of NEA's Jazz Masters award in 1989 and the Mid Atlantic Arts Foundation's 1996 Living Legacy Jazz

Award. He was honored with Gregory Hines at Tap Extravaganza 98, held at N.Y.'s Town Hall.

Disc.: *Breakin' It Up* (1958); *Barry Harris at the Jazz Workshop* (1960); *Listen to B. H.* (1961); *Chasin' the Bird* (1962); *Luminescence* (1967); *Magnificent* (1969); *B. H. Plays Tadd Dameron* (1975); *Live in Tokyo* (1976); *B. H. Plays B. H.* (1978); *Beautiful Africa* (1979); *Stay Right with It* (1979); *Bird of Red and Gold* (1989); *Live at Maybeck Recital Hall, V* (1990); *Confirmation* (1991). —**LP**

Harris, Beaver (William Godvin), free-jazz drummer, leader; b. Pittsburgh, Pa., April 20, 1936; d. N.Y., Dec. 22, 1991. He played clarinet and alto sax as teenager. He played professional baseball in the Negro Leagues. He took up drums in the service, encouraged by Max Roach, then moved to N.Y. in 1963. He played with Sonny Rollins, became especially interested in free jazz and worked most regularly with Archie Shepp from 1966 on. He also went to Europe with Albert Ayler, played drum clinics with Roach and Kenny Clarke, and did gigs with Sonny Stitt, Dexter Gordon, Clifford Jordan, Clark Terry, Joe Henderson, and Freddie Hubbard. In 1969, he formed a co-op group with Grachan Moncur III, the 360 Degree Experience. The band continued to perform through the mid-1980s when Don Pullen was the band's co-leader. In 1970 he played with Shepp for LeRoi Jones's play *Slave Ship*, and 1973 for Aishah Rahman's *Lady Day: A Musical Tragedy*. He continued to work with Shepp in the 1970s, also Thelonious Monk, Chet Baker and, on occasion, Dixieland groups. He toured Japan with a Newport Jazz Festival tour in the mid-1970s, and also recorded in the 1970s with Steve Lacy, Pharoah Sanders, Gato Barbieri, and Ayler. The 1980s were spent mostly playing in the N.Y. area with the 360 Degree Experience.

Disc. *From Ragtime to No Time* (1974); *In: Sanity* (1976); *Beautiful Africa* (1979); *Live at Nyon* (1979); *Negcaumongus* (1979); *Beaver Is My Name* (1983); *Well Kept Secret with Don Pullen* (1984).—**LP**

Harris, Bill (Willard Palmer), jazz trombonist; b. Philadelphia, Pa., Oct. 28, 1916; d. Hallandale, Fla., Aug. 21, 1973. One of the most admired of all jazz trombonists, he is well known for his work with Woody Herman. His influence was limited by the rise of J. J. Johnson and by his own choice to settle outside the jazz mainstream in the 1960s. His half-brother, Bob Harris, was a professional bass player. Bill played piano as a child, then played tenor sax and trumpet before concentrating on trombone. He played locally in the later 1930s, then spent two years in the merchant marine during World War II. Around 1943, he moved to N.Y. with Bob Chester, then played with Benny Goodman from August 1943 until March 1944, including soundtrack work for the film *Sweet and Lowdown*. That August he joined Woody Herman for the first time, remaining with him through 1946. Harris was the featured soloist on several of Herman's recordings of this period. He combined a warm, bluesy sound on ballads with the ability to blow all out on uptempo work. During 1947 he was back in N.Y. leading his own band for club work and also playing with Charlie

Ventura. He returned to Woody Herman (1948–50, early 1956–58, and finally for a 1959 tour of Europe). From 1950 he began regular touring with J.A.T.P, shows, also led his own small groups and worked with Oscar Pettiford (1952) and with Sauter-Finegan Orch. (1953). He first went to Fla. in 1958, and except for a brief stint with Benny Goodman from August until November 1959 (including European tour), he remained there in semi-retirement, working as a DJ although he continued to play. Besides leading his own groups, he worked with Red Norvo (early 1960s and again 1965–66) and Charlie Teagarden's Band (spring of 1962 until 1964, including stint in Las Vegas). Through the later 1960s he worked as a deejay in Miami and also in a house band at a local hotel.

Disc.: *Collates* (1952); *B. H. Herd* (1956); *B. H.* (1956); *H. Touch* (1957); *Fabulous B. H.* (1957); *Ex- Hermanites* (1957); *B. H. and Friends* (1957); *B. H. Rhythm* (1973).—**JC/LP**

Harris, Donald, American composer and music educator; b. St. Paul, Minn., April 7, 1931. He was a student of Paul Wilkinson in St. Paul, of Ross Lee Finney at the Univ. of Mich. at Ann Arbor (B.Mus., 1952; M.Mus., 1952), and of Max Deutsch in Paris. He also had studies with Boulanger in Paris, Blacher and Foss at the Berkshire Music Center in Tanglewood (summers, 1954–55), and Jolivet at the Centre Français d'Humanisme Musical in Aix-en-Provence (1960). From 1968 to 1977 he held administrative posts at the New England Cons. of Music in Boston. In 1977 he became prof. of music at the Hartt School of Music at the Univ. of Hartford, where he was chairman of the composition and theory dept. (1977–80) and then dean of the school (1980–88). In 1988 he became dean of the Coll. of the Arts at Ohio State Univ. in Columbus, where he also was a prof. (from 1988) and acting director (1989–91) of the School of Music. After concluding his tenure as dean in 1997, he served as a prof. of composition and theory there. From 1994 to 1996 he also served as president of the International Council of Fine Arts Deans. With C. Hailey and J. Brand, he ed. *The Berg-Schoenberg Correspondence* (N.Y., 1987), which won the ASCAP/Deems Taylor Award in 1989. In 1956 he received a Fulbright scholarship. In 1962 he won the Prince Rainier III of Monaco Composition Award. He held a Gugggenheim fellowship in 1966. From 1973 he received annual AS-CAP awards. In 1974 he received an NEA fellowship grant. He received an award from the American Academy and Inst. of Arts and Letters in 1991. As a composer, he follows the trends of the cosmopolitan avant-garde.

Works: DRAMATIC: *The Legend of John Henry*, ballet (1954; rev. 1979); *The Golden Deer*, ballet (1955); *Intervals*, dance piece (1959); *The Little Mermaid*, opera (1985–95); *Twelfth Night*, incidental music to Shakespeare's play (1989). **ORCH.:** *Symphony in 2 Movements* (1958–61); *On Variations* for Chamber Orch. (1976); *Prelude to a Concert in Connecticut* (1981); *Mermaid Variations* for Chamber Orch. (1992). **B a n d :** *A Fanfare for the Seventies*, march (1978). **CHAMBER:** *Fantasy* for Violin and Piano (1957); *String Quartet* (1965); *Ludus I* for 10 Instruments (1966) and *II* for 5 Instruments (1973); *3 Fanfares* for 4 Horns (1984); *A Birthday Card for Gunther* [Schuller] for Violin (1985); *Canzona and Carol* for Double Brass Quintet and Timpani (1986).

KEYBOARD: P i a n o : Sonata (1957); *Balladen* (1979). O r - g a n : Improvisation themes for Marie-Claire Alain (1980); *Meditations* (1984). VOCAL: *Charmes* for Soprano and Orch. (1971–80); *For the Night to Wear* for Mezzo-soprano and Chamber Ensemble (1978); *Of Hartford in a Purple Light* (1979); *Les Mains* (1983); *Pierrot Lieder* for Soprano and Chamber Ensemble (1988).—NS/LK/DM

Harris, Emmylou,

Harris, Emmylou, emerging from the remnants of the East Coast folk scene in the late 1960s, was introduced to traditional country music by Gram Parsons, with whom she toured and recorded as a backup vocalist; b. Birmingham, Ala., April 2, 1947.

Virtually a full collaborator on Parsons's final album, *Grievous Angel,* Harris established herself as a prime purveyor of country music with a rock sound during the 1970s. Essentially a song interpreter, her success was based largely on her astute selection of material and the excellence of her bands, which have included James Burton, Rodney Crowell, Ricky Skaggs, and Sam Bush. Introducing Crowell and Skaggs to a wider audience, Emmylou Harris bolstered the late-1980s movement toward simple production and uncluttered instrumentation among country performers such as Dwight Yoakam, Lyle Lovett, and k. d. lang.

Emmylou Harris moved with her family to the Washington, D.C., area from her native Ala., and obtained her first guitar at age 16. She initiated her musical career in 1967, performing around Washington and N.Y. in folk clubs. Signed to Jubilee Records in 1969, her debut album was virtually ignored upon release in 1970. Retiring for a time and unsuccessfully attempting a breakthrough in Nashville during the latter half of 1970, Harris was "discovered" at the Cellar Door in Washington by members of the Flying Burrito Brothers. She was asked to join the group before its second incarnation dissolved. Introduced to Gram Parsons in late 1971, Harris was summoned to Los Angeles to sing backup on his debut solo album, *GP.* She toured with Parsons in spring 1973 as a member of his Fallen Angels band, and worked on his landmark *Grievous Angel* album, which included their collaboration "In My Hour of Darkness." However, Gram Parsons died unexpectedly on Sept. 19, 1973.

Emmylou Harris signed with Warner Bros. in mid-1974, recording two albums for the label's subsidiary Reprise. Her debut for the label, *Pieces of the Sky,* contained standard country-and-western material, such as the country smash (and minor pop hit) "If I Could Only Win Your Love" (by the Louvin Brothers), Merle Haggard's "The Bottle Let Me Down," and "Queen of the Silver Dollar," as well as Lennon and McCartney's "For No One" and the original "Boulder to Birmingham," cowritten with Bill Danoff. In 1975 Harris formed her Hot Band with songwriter Rodney Crowell (rhythm gtr.), James Burton (lead gtr.), Glen D. Hardin (kybd.), Hank DeVito (pedal steel), Emory Gordy (bs.), and John Ware (drm.). *Elite Hotel* included three Gram Parsons's songs ("Wheels," "Sin City," and "Ooh, Las Vegas") and yielded three country smashes with Buck Owens's "Together Again," Don Gibson's "Sweet Dreams," and "One of These Days." Other inclusions were "Ama-rillo," cowritten by Harris and Crowell; the minor pop hit "Here, There and Everywhere"; and "Feelin' Single—Seein' Double."

After a triumphant tour of Europe and Britain in 1976, Emmylou Harris recorded *Luxury Liner,* replacing guitarist James Burton with Briton Albert Lee. The album contained Gram Parsons's title song as well as Townes Van Zandt's "Pancho and Lefty" and two near-smash country hits with Kitty Wells's "Making Believe" and Chuck Berry's "C'est la Vie." *Quarter Moon in a Ten-Cent Town,* recorded with the Hot Band, included three country hits—Dolly Parton's "To Daddy," Delbert McClinton's "Two More Bottles of Wine," and "Easy from Now On"—plus two Jesse Winchester songs and Rodney Crowell's "Ain't Living Long Like This" and "Leaving Louisiana in the Broad Daylight."

In February 1978 Emmylou Harris began work on an album with Dolly Parton and Linda Ronstadt, but the project, with its promise of the first female country supergroup, was later abandoned. Harris next recorded the bluegrass-flavored *Blue Kentucky Girl* with the Hot Band and multi-instrumentalist Ricky Skaggs. The album contained the country smashes "Save the Last Dance for Me," the title cut, and "Beneath Still Waters," as well as Gram Parsons's "Hickory Wind," Rodney Crowell's "Even Cowgirls Get the Blues," and Willie Nelson's "Sister's Coming Home." The follow-up bluegrass-style *Roses in the Snow,* again recorded with Skaggs, yielded near-smash country hits with "Wayfaring Stranger" and Paul Simon's "The Boxer." Harris subsequently scored a smash country (and minor pop) hit with "That Lovin' You Feelin' Again" in duet with Roy Orbison; recorded the Christmas album *Light of the Stable;* and registered another pop and country hit with a remake of the Chordettes's 1954 hit "Mister Sandman," recorded with Parton and Ronstadt. Other early 1980s country smashes were "Tennessee Rose" with vocal backing by the Whites, and "Born to Run" from *Cimarron.* Harris's last major solo album success came with the live set *Last Date* (now deleted), which included the smash country hits "(Lost His Love) On Our Last Date" and "I'm Movin' On."

Emmylou Harris's subsequent 1980s albums fared less well than previous releases. These included the rock-and-roll set *White Shoes* and the song cycle *The Ballad of Sally Rose,* cowritten with new husband Paul Kennerley. Moving to Nashville in 1984, Harris assembled a new edition of the Hot Band with lead guitarist Frank Reckard, pedal steel guitarist Steve Fishell, and rhythm guitarist–vocalist Barry Tashian for touring.

In 1986 Linda Ronstadt, Dolly Parton, and Emmylou Harris finally recorded their album, *Trio,* with a stellar backup cast that included Albert Lee, David Lindley, and Mark O'Connor. A best-seller, the album stayed on the charts for nearly a year, yielding smash country hits with "To Know Him Is to Love Him," "Those Memories of You," Linda Thompson's "Telling Me Lies," and Parton's "Wildflowers." Harris subsequently scored smash country hits with "We Believe in Happy Endings," in duet with Earl Thomas Conley, and "Heartbreak Hill," from the album *Bluebird. Duets* assembled her recorded duets with the likes of Gram Parsons, Roy Orbison, Neil Young, Ricky Skaggs, and Willie Nelson.

In 1990 Emmylou Harris debuted her new backing band, the Nash Ramblers, on tour. Members included former New Grass Revival leader Sam Bush (mdln., fdl.), Al Perkins (dobro.), Jon Randall Stewart (gtr.), and Roy Huskey Jr. (bs.). On April 30, 1991, Harris and the group recorded at Nashville's Ryman Auditorium, the original home of the Grand Ole Opry. The resulting album and cable television show (on the Nashville Network) included songs by Bill Monroe, plus Steve Earle's "Guitar Town," Bruce Springsteen's "Mansion on the Hill," and John Fogerty's "Lodi."

Emmylou Harris was inducted into the Grand Ole Opry in 1992 and recorded *Cowgirl's Prayer* for Asylum in 1993. The following year she recorded *Songs of the West* with Linda Ronstadt, Dolly Parton, Rodney Crowell, Willie Nelson, and others for Warner Bros. A major change in direction came in 1995, when she joined with producer Daniel Lanois, famous for his atmospheric production work with the Neville Brothers, Bob Dylan, and U2. They produced the album *Wreckin' Ball*, featuring a more hard-edged accompaniment, including Lanois on guitar, and Harris taking on a rougher vocal style; the title cut by Neil Young attracted some radio play. Harris and Lanois subsequently toured as a duo.

DISC.: GRAM PARSONS (WITH EMMYLOU HARRIS): *GP* (1973); *Grievous Angel* (1974); *GP/Grievous Angel* (1990). GRAM PARSONS AND THE FALLEN ANGELS (WITH EMMYLOU HARRIS): *Live 1973* (1982). EMMYLOU HARRIS: *Gliding Bird* (1970); *Pieces of the Sky* (1975); *Elite Hotel* (1976); *Luxury Liner* (1977); *Quarter Moon in a Ten-Cent Town* (1978); *Profile: The Best of E. H.* (1978); *Blue Kentucky Girl* (1979); *Roses in the Snow* (1980); *Light of the Stable—The Christmas Album* (1980); *Evangeline* (1981); *Cimarron* (1981); *Last Date* (1982); *White Shoes* (1983); *Profile II: The Best of E. H.* (1984); *The Ballad of Sally Rose* (1985); *Thirteen* (1986); *Angel Band* (1987); *Bluebird* (1989); *Duets* (1990); *Brand New Dance* (1990); *Cowgirl's Prayer* (1993); *Songs of the West* (1994); *Wrecking Ball* (1995); *Spyboy* (1998); *Red Dirt Girl* (2000). EMMYLOU HARRIS, DOLLY PARTON, AND LINDA RONSTADT: *Trio* (1987); *Trio II* (1999). EMMYLOU HARRIS AND LINDA RONSTADT: *Western Wall: The Tucson Sessions* (1999). EMMYLOU HARRIS AND THE NASH RAMBLERS: *At the Ryman* (1992).—BH

Harris, Jerome (Estese), jazz electric bassist, guitarist; b. Flushing, Queens, N.Y., April 5, 1953. His formative musical experiences included singing and playing rural and urban blues, folk and gospel music, in addition to the full range of American popular music genres. After studying psychology and social relations at Harvard Univ. (A.B. 1973), Harris attended the New England Cons. of Music as a scholarship student in jazz guitar, studying with George Russell, William Thomas McKinley, Jaki Byard, Phil Wilson, Barry Galbraith, and Sal Salvador, and graduating with honors (B.M.) in 1977. His first major professional performing experience came as bassist with Sonny Rollins in 1978. More recently he has played guitar for Rollins, and has also recorded and/or performed live with Jack DeJohnette, Bobby Previte, Bill Frisell, Oliver Lake, Ray Anderson,

Bob Stewart, George Russell, Julius Hemphill, Amina Claudine Myers, Ned Rothenberg, Bob Moses, and many others. Harris's extensive international touring has included several stints in Japan with Sonny Rollins, as well as U.S. State Department tours of India and the Middle East with Jay Hoggard and of five African nations with Oliver Lake and Jump Up.—LP

Harris, Joe, jazz trombonist, singer; b. Sedalia, Mo., 1908; d. Fresno, Calif., summer 1952. He took up trombone at 16, played with local bands in Okla., then moved to Seminole, Tex. (where he met Jack Teagarden in1927). He played for a while in Canada, then temporarily gave up full-time music, but continued to gig in Sedalia. He played in riverboat band on the SS *Idlewild*, then joined Joe Haymes's Band in Springfield, Mo. In late 1932 he joined Frankie Trumbauer for a residency in Chicago, then a tour of Tex. He left to take Jack Teagarden's place in Ben Pollack's Band (Chicago, May 1933). He freelanced in N.Y., then became a member of Bob Crosby's first band (1935), recorded with Benny Goodman (April 1935), then joined Benny Goodman from August 1935 until May 1936. He left to join the MGM studio staff in Hollywood, and played for various leaders including George Stoll and Victor Young until February 1937, when he suffered a fractured skull in a car accident. He was out of music until joining a big band led by sax-arranger Lyle "Spud" Murphy (February 1938). He did studio work and a spell in Carl Hoff's Orch., then rejoined Ben Pollack from March until July 1940. In 1942 played for seven months in Pee Wee Erwin's Band, then three months with Bob Chester before returning to studio work. He rejoined Benny Goodman from spring 1943 until August 1943, then played in Eddie Miller's Big Band. He returned to studio work, and during the late 1940s was gigging in Calif. with various bands including Ted Jefferson's Mel-o-tones. He lost his life in a second car crash.—JC/LP

Harris, Roy (actually, **Leroy Ellsworth**), significant American composer; b. Chandler, Okla., Feb. 12, 1898; d. Santa Monica, Calif., Oct. 1, 1979. His parents, of Irish and Scottish descent, settled in Okla.; in 1903 the family moved to Calif., where Harris had private music lessons with Henry Schoenfeld and Arthur Farwell. In 1926 he went to Paris, where he studied composition with Boulanger; continued his stay in Paris thanks to two consecutive Guggenheim fellowships (1927, 1928). Upon his return to the U.S., he lived in Calif. and in N.Y.; several of his works were performed and attracted favorable attention; Farwell publ. an article in the *Musical Quarterly* (Jan. 1932) in which he enthusiastically welcomed Harris as an American genius. In his compositions, Harris showed a talent of great originality, with a strong melodic and rhythmic speech that was indigenously American. He developed a type of modal symbolism akin to Greek ethos, with each particular mode related to a certain emotional state. Instrumental music is the genre in which he particularly excelled. His Sym. No. 3 (Boston, Feb. 24, 1939) became his best-known and most frequently perf. work; it was the first American sym. to be played in

China, during the 1973 tour of the Philadelphia Orch. under the direction of Eugene Ormandy. Harris never wrote an opera or an oratorio, but made astute use of choral masses in some of his works. He held the following teaching positions: Westminster Choir School, Princeton (1934–35); Cornell Univ. (1941–43); Colo. Coll. (1943–48); Utah State Agricultural Coll. in Logan (1948–49); Peabody Coll. for Teachers at Nashville (1949–51); Sewanee, Tenn. (1951); Pa. Coll. for Women (1951–56); Univ. of Southern Ill. (1956–57); Ind. Univ. (1957–60); Inter-American Univ., San Germán, Puerto Rico (1960–61); Univ. of Calif., Los Angeles (1961–73). In 1973 he was appointed composer-in-residence at Calif. State Univ., Los Angeles, a post he held until his death. He received honorary D.Mus. degrees from Rutgers Univ. and the Univ. of Rochester in N.Y.; in 1942 he was awarded the Elizabeth Sprague Coolidge Medal "for eminent services to chamber music." In 1936 he married the pianist and teacher Johana Harris (née Beula Duffey; b. Ottawa, Ontario, Jan. 1, 1913; d. Los Angeles, June 5, 1995); she assumed her professional name Johana in honor of J. S. Bach; the single 'n' was used owing to some esoteric numerologic considerations to which Harris was partial. After his death, she married, on Dec. 18, 1982, her 21–year-old piano student **Jake Heggie**.

WORKS: DRAMATIC: B a l l e t : *From This Earth* (Colorado Springs, Aug. 7, 1941); *Namesake* (Colorado Springs, Aug. 8, 1942); *What So Proudly We Hail* (Colorado Springs, Aug. 8, 1942). **ORCH.:** *Andante* (1925); *American Portrait 1929*, sym. (1929; withdrawn); 13 other syms.: No. 1, *Symphony 1933* (1933; Boston, Jan. 26, 1934), No. 2 (1934; Boston, Feb. 28, 1936), No. 3 (Boston, Feb. 24, 1939), No. 4, *Folksong Symphony*, for Chorus and Orch. (Cleveland, Dec. 26, 1940; rev. version, N.Y., Dec. 31, 1942), No. 5 (1942; Boston, Feb. 26, 1943), No. 6, *Gettysburg* (Boston, April 14, 1944), No. 7 (Chicago, Nov. 20, 1952; rev. 1955), No. 8, *San Francisco* (1961; San Francisco, Jan. 17, 1962), No. 9 (1962; Philadelphia, Jan. 18, 1963), No. 10, *Abraham Lincoln*, for Speaker, Chorus, Brass, 2 Pianos, and Percussion (Long Beach, Calif., April 14, 1965), No. 11 (1967; N.Y., Feb. 8, 1968), No. 12, *Pere Marquette*, for Tenor/Speaker and Orch. (1968–69; Milwaukee, Nov. 8, 1969), and No. 13, *Bicentennial Symphony*, for Chorus and Orch. (1975–76; 1st perf. as Sym. No. 14, Washington, D.C., Feb. 10, 1976); *Concert Piece* (1930); *Andantino* (1931; rev. 1932); *Toccata* (1931); *From the Gayety and Sadness of the American Scene*, overture (Los Angeles, Dec. 29, 1932); *When Johnny Comes Marching Home: An American Overture* (1934; Minneapolis, Jan. 13, 1935); *Farewell to Pioneers: A Symphonic Elegy* (1935; Philadelphia, Feb. 28, 1936); *Prelude and Fugue* for Strings (1935; Philadelphia, March 27, 1936); Concerto for Piano and Strings (1936; arranged from the Piano Quintet); *Time Suite* (ABC, N.Y., Aug. 8, 1937); 2 violin concertos: No. 1 (1938; withdrawn) and No. 2 (1949; Wilmington, N.C., March 21, 1984); *Prelude and Fugue* for Strings and 4 Trumpets (1939; arranged from the String Quartet No. 3); *American Creed* (Chicago, Oct. 30, 1940); *Acceleration* (Washington, D.C., Nov. 2, 1941; rev. 1942); *Evening Piece* (1941; 2nd movement of *3 Pieces*); *Mirage* (c. 1941); *Ode to Truth* (San Francisco, March 9, 1941); *3 Pieces* (N.Y., April 9, 1941; nos. 1 and 3 from the *Folksong Symphony*); *Fanfare for the Forces* (c. 1942); *Folk Rhythms of Today* (1942; Minneapolis, Jan. 29, 1943); Concerto for Piano and Band (Ann Arbor, April 7, 1942); *March in Time of War* (N.Y., Dec. 30, 1942; rev. 1943); Chorale for Organ and Brass (Cambridge, Mass., Sept. 26, 1943); *Fantasia* for Piano and Band (1943);

Children's Hour (1943–44); *Chorale* (London, July 22, 1944); 2 piano concertos: No. 1 (Colorado Springs, Aug. 1944) and No. 2 (Louisville, Dec. 9, 1953); *Toccata* for Organ and Brass (Cambridge, Mass., Sept. 24, 1944); *Ode to Friendship* (N.Y., Nov. 16, 1944); *Memories of a Child's Sunday* (1945; N.Y., Feb. 21, 1946); *Variation* [No. 7] *on a Theme by Goossens* (Cincinnati, March 23, 1945; with 9 other composers); *Celebration Variations on a Timpani Theme from Howard Hanson's Third Symphony* (Boston, Oct. 25, 1946); *Melody* (N.Y., May 12, 1946); *Radio Piece* for Piano and Orch. (Rochester, N.Y., May 18, 1946); Concerto for 2 Pianos and Orch. (1946; Denver, Jan. 21, 1947); *The Quest* (1947; Indianapolis, Jan. 29, 1948); *Theme and Variations* for Accordion and Orch. (Chicago, June 1, 1947); *Elegy and Paean* for Violin and Orch. (Houston, Dec. 14, 1948); *Kentucky Spring* (Louisville, April 5, 1949); *Cumberland Concerto for Orchestra* (Cincinnati, Oct. 19, 1951); *Fantasy* for Piano and Pops Orch. (1951); *Symphonic Fantasy* (1953; Pittsburgh, Jan. 30, 1954); *Symphonic Epigram* (N.Y., Nov. 14, 1954); *Fantasy* for Piano and Orch. (Hartford, Conn., Nov. 17, 1954); *Ode to Consonance* (1956); *Elegy and Dance* (Portland, Ore., April 19, 1958); *These Times* for Piano and Small Orch. (La Jolla, Calif., Aug. 14, 1963); *Epilogue to Profiles in Courage JFK* (Los Angeles, May 10, 1964); *Horn of Plenty* (Beverly Hills, June 14, 1964); *Salute to Youth* (1964; Santa Barbara, Calif., Feb. 28, 1965); *Fantasy* for Organ, Brass, and Timpani (1964); *Rhythms and Spaces* (N.Y., April 7, 1965; arranged from the String Quartet No. 2); Concerto for Amplified Piano, Brass, String Basses, and Percussion (Los Angeles, Dec. 9, 1968); *Folksong Suite* for Harp and Orch. (1973). **B a n d :** *Sad Song* for Jazz Band (1938); *Cimarron*, overture (Enid, Okla., April 18, 1941); *When Johnny Comes Marching Home* (1941; Ann Arbor, Jan. 24, 1942); *Rhythms of Today* (1943); *Conflict* (1944); *Sun and Stars* (1944); *The Sun from Dawn to Dusk* (1944); *Take the Sun and Keep the Stars* (1944); *Fruit of Gold* (Westwood, Calif., May 10, 1949); *Dark Devotion* (1950); *Kentucky Jazz Piece* (1950); Sym., *West Point* (West Point, N.Y., May 30, 1952); *Ad majorem gloriam Universitatis Illinorum*, tone poem (1958); *Bicentennial Aspirations* (San Diego, July 4, 1976). **CHAMBER:** *Impressions on a Rainy Day* for String Quartet (1925); Concerto for Piano, Clarinet, and String Quartet (1926; Paris, May 8, 1928); 3 string quartets: No. 1 (1929), No. 2, *Variations on a Theme* (1933), and No. 3, *4 Preludes and Fugues* (1937); Concerto for String Sextet (1932); *Fantasy* for Winds, Horn, and Piano (Pasadena, Calif., April 10, 1932); *4 Minutes—20 Seconds* for Flute and String Quartet (1934); Piano Trio (1934); *Poem* for Violin and Piano (1935); Piano Quintet (1936); *Soliloquy and Dance* for Viola and Piano (1938); String Quintet (1940); Violin Sonata (1942); *Lyric Studies* for Woodwind and Piano (1950); Cello Sonata (1964; rev. 1968); *Childhood Memories of Ocean Moods* for Piano, String Quartet, and Double Bass (1966). **KEYBOARD: P i a n o :** Sonata (1928); *Little Suite* (1939); *Toccata* (1939); *Suite in 3 Movements* (1939–43); *American Ballads* (2 vols., 1942–45). **O r g a n :** *Études for Pedals* (1964; rev. 1972). **VOCAL:** *Challenge 1940* for Bass, Chorus, and Orch. (N.Y., June 25, 1940); *Railroad Man's Ballad* for Chorus and Orch. (1940; N.Y., Feb. 22, 1941); *Freedom's Land* for Baritone, Chorus, and Orch. (Pittsburgh, Nov. 11, 1941); *Rock of Ages* for Chorus and Orch. (N.Y., Sept. 19, 1944); *Blow the Man Down* for Countertenor, Baritone, Chorus, and Orch. (Cleveland, May 12, 1946); *The Brotherhood of Man* for Chorus and Orch. (1966); numerous other choral works.

BIBL.: D. Stehman, *R. H.: An American Musical Pioneer* (Boston, 1984); idem, *R. H.: A Bio-Bibliography* (N.Y., 1991).—NS/LK/DM

Harris, Sir Augustus (Henry Glossop),

celebrated English operatic impresario; b. Paris, 1852; d. Folkestone, June 22, 1896. He was an asst. manager to Mapleson before becoming a prominent figure in London operatic circles. In 1879 he became lessee of the Drury Lane Theatre. In 1883 he brought the Carl Rosa Opera Co. to London and managed its seasons until 1887. In 1887–88 he oversaw his own Italian opera season before becoming manager of Covent Garden in 1888. He presented brilliant seasons of opera at Covent Garden, whose audiences were exposed to operas in the original language. Among the famous artists he engaged were Melba, the de Reszkes, Maurel, and Mahler. He did much to promote the cause of Wagner's music. In 1891 he was knighted.—NS/LK/DM

Harris, Wynonie ("Mr. Blues"),

singer, composer; b. Omaha, Nebr., Aug. 24, 1915; d. Oakland, Calif., June 14, 1969. He started his professional life as a buck-and-wing dancer, doubling on drums. He worked under various names: "Peppermint Cane," "Mississippi Mockingbird," etc. He settled in L.A. during the early 1940s, and worked with Lucky Millinder and Lionel Hampton. During the mid-1940s he began making a series of highly successful R&B singles, which gained him international fame. Among his hits were "Bloodshot Eyes" and "Good Rockin' Tonight." Despite this he worked mostly in Calif., occasionally visiting the East Coast. On his last tour, in 1967, he appeared at the Apollo in Harlem. He died of lung cancer in 1969. His son, Wesley Devereaux, is also a blues vocalist.—JC/LP

Harrison, Beatrice,

English cellist, sister of **May Harrison**; b. Roorkee, India, Dec. 9, 1892; d. Smallfield, Surrey, March 10, 1965. She was taken to England in infancy. She entered the Royal Coll. of Music in London, winning a prize at the age of 10. She was 14 when she made her first public appearance as a soloist with an orch. (London, May 29, 1907). She then went to Berlin, where she took lessons with Hugo Becker. She was the winner of the prestigious Mendelssohn Prize. She made several European tours, most of them in company with her sister, and also toured the U.S. in 1913 and 1932. Delius wrote his Double Concerto for her and her sister. —NS/LK/DM

Harrison, Donald ("Duck"),

jazz-revivalist alto and soprano saxophonist; b. New Orleans, La., June 23, 1960. He is the son of a "long time Mardi Gras Indian," and his nephew Christian Scott plays trumpet. He studied under Alvin Batiste and Ellis Marsalis. He attended Berklee in 1979. He played with Roy Haynes from 1980–81 and Jack McDuff in 1981, and then spent four years with Art Blakey from 1982–86. Harrison co-led a quintet with fellow New Orleans musician trumpeter Terence Blanchard from 1987–88, then returned to Haynes. From 1989–90, he taught at N.Y.'s New School, and also played on the Soundtrack of Spike Lee's *Do the Right Thing*. In 1991, he formed the group Guardians of the Flame Mardi Gras Band, combining modern jazz elements with traditional Mardi Gras music, which continues to perform. In the mid-

1990s he began touring with a quartet and calling his music "Nouveau Bop."

DISC.: *Eric Dolphy & Booker Little Remembered* (1986); *Crystal Stair* (1987); *Black Pearl* (1988); *For Art's Sake* (1990); *Power of Cool* (1991); *Indian Blues* (1991).—LP

Harrison, Frank (Francis) L(lewellyn),

Irish musicologist; b. Dublin, Sept. 29, 1905; d. Tunbridge Wells, Dec. 31, 1987. He studied in Dublin at the Royal Irish Academy of Music and at Trinity Coll. (Mus.B., 1926; Mus.D., 1929), and later was a postdoctoral fellow under Schrade and Hindemith at Yale Univ. (1946). He taught at Queen's Univ., Kingston, Ontario (1935–46), Colgate Univ. (1946–47), Washington Univ. in St. Louis (1947–52), the Univ. of Oxford (1952–70), and the Univ. of Amsterdam (1970–76). He helped launch the Early English Church Music series, serving as its general ed. from 1961 to 1972; held a similar position with the Polyphonic Music of the Fourteenth Century series from 1962 to 1974. In 1981 he was made a corresponding member of the American Musicological Soc.

WRITINGS: *Music in Medieval Britain* (1958; 2nd ed., 1963); with J. Westrup, ed. *Collins Music Encyclopedia* (1959; U.S. edition, 1960, as *The New Coll. Encyclopedia of Music*); with M. Hood and C. Palisca, *Musicology* (1963); with J. Rimmer, *European Musical Instruments* (1964); *Time, Place and Music: An Anthology of Ethnomusicological Observations c. 1550–c. 1800* (1973); with E. Dobson, *Medieval English Songs* (1979). —NS/LK/DM

Harrison, George,

neither the most prolific nor the most successful of the former Beatles, the group member most involved in Eastern music and mysticism; b. Wavertree, Liverpool, England, Feb. 25, 1943. One of the first rock artists to express spiritual and humanitarian concerns in his music, Harrison's first post-Beatles album, *All Things Must Pass*, was hailed as one of the rock masterpieces of the 1970s despite its occasional lapses into didacticism and pedantry. His humanitarian impulses produced the benefit show Concert for Bangladesh, the forerunner of mid-1980s benefits such as Live Aid. In 1974 he formed his own record company, Dark Horse, and became the first former Beatle to tour America. In 1978 Harrison and his personal manager formed Hand Made Film Productions, which became a respected force in the British film industry. A return to performing in 1987 with a new solo album, and the formation of the mock supergroup the Traveling Wilburys, brought Harrison renewed attention at the decade's end.

George Harrison took up guitar and formed his first group, the Rebels, at age 13. In 1958 he joined Paul McCartney and John Lennon in the skiffle group the Quarrymen, but they disbanded around the end of 1959. Harrison, McCartney, and Lennon then formed the Moondogs, later changing their name to the Silver Beatles. Regularly performing at the Cavern Club in Liverpool after January 1961 and making occasional forays into Hamburg, Germany, the Beatles' lineup was completed with the August 1962 addition of drummer Ringo Starr. Harrison, overshadowed by songwriters Lennon and McCartney, made his songwriting debut with "Don't Bother Me" from *Meet the Beatles* (1964; issued as *With the Beatles* in the United Kingdom and on CD in the U.S./U.K.). Later Beatles songs written by Harrison included "If I Needed Someone," "Taxman," "Within You, Without You," the classic "While My Guitar Gently Weeps," "Something" (his first #1 hit with the Beatles), and "Here Comes the Sun." During his tenure with the Beatles, Harrison recorded *Wonderwall Music*, an Eastern- sounding instrumental album, and the experimental *Electronic Sound* album, one of the few releases on the short-lived Zapple label.

Although Paul McCartney did not sue for dissolution of the Beatles until December 1970, George Harrison was essentially independent of the group by the May 1970 release of *Let It Be*. His debut solo album, *All Things Must Pass*, was coproduced by Phil Spector and recorded with Eric Clapton and Billy Preston. An instant best-seller, the album yielded the top hit "My Sweet Lord" (backed with "Isn't It a Pity") and the near-smash "What Is Life," as well as "Wah-Wah," "If Not for You," "Beware of Darkness," and "Apple Scruffs."

Concerned with the famine overwhelming Bangladesh, Harrison organized two benefit performances staged in N.Y.'s Madison Square Garden on Aug. 1, 1971. Enlisting the services of Ringo Starr, Billy Preston, and Leon Russell (among others), Harrison was able to coax both Bob Dylan and Eric Clapton (both in semiretirement) into performing at the charity show. The resulting multirecord set, *Concert for Bangladesh*, accrued hundreds of thousands of dollars for relief of the heinous situation in Bangladesh (although it took years of legal haggling for the money to be finally released).

In the meantime, George Harrison took nearly two years to complete his second solo album, *Living in the Material World*. Finally released in mid-1973, the album was critically lambasted despite yielding the top hit "Give Me Love (Give Me Peace on Earth)." Also included were the title song as well as "Try Some Buy Some" and the satiric "Sue Me, Sue You Blues," inspired by the bickering among the former Beatles. Meanwhile, Harrison himself faced a lawsuit because of the remarkable similarities between his "My Sweet Lord" and the Chiffons' 1963 top hit "He's So Fine" (the melody is clearly the same).

In June 1974 Harrison announced the formation of Dark Horse Records. The label's first signing was longtime friend Ravi Shankar, the sitar player. During November 1974 Harrison became the first former Beatle to tour the United States, with Shankar. However, the tour was met by scathing reviews, due in large part to voice problems and a muddled sound mix. The soon-released *Dark Horse* took another critical drubbing, although it contained two hits, "Dark Horse" and "Ding Dong, Ding Dong," and a rewritten version of the Everly Brothers' "Bye Bye, Love," an apparent indictment of Eric Clapton's cuckolding of Harrison. (Clapton had become involved with Harrison's then-wife, Patti Boyd, inspiring the song "Layla"; the Harrisons were divorced, and Clapton married Boyd.)

Following *Extra Texture* and its hit "You," George Harrison released *Thirty-Three & 1/3*, which produced the major hits "This Song," which refers to the plagia-rism suit regarding "He's So Fine," and "Crackerbox Palace." Also in 1976, Capitol issued *The Best of George Harrison*, which included seven of his hits recorded by the Beatles. In March 1978 he appeared in a small part in the television special *The Rutles: All You Need Is Cash*, Monty Python alumnus Eric Idle's Beatles parody. During that year Harrison formed Hand Made Film Productions with his personal manager, Denis O'Brien. The company produced the irreverent and controversial Monty Python film *Life of Brian*, released in 1979. Subsequent film projects included 1981's *Time Bandits*, with Pythons Terry Gilliam and Michael Palin, and 1982's *The Missionary*, with Palin.

In 1981 George Harrison scored a smash hit with the tribute to the slain John Lennon, "All These Years Ago," recorded with Ringo Starr and Paul and Linda McCartney. Following 1982's uninspired *Gone Troppo*, Harrison remained largely out of sight. Hand Made Films produced the wry 1985 film *A Private Function*, the 1986 flop *Shanghai Surprise* (with Madonna and then-husband Sean Penn), and the critically acclaimed *Mona Lisa* (1986) and *Withnail and I* (1987). Harrison reemerged musically in 1987 with *Cloud Nine*, coproduced by Jeff Lynne; it had a top hit with "Got My Mind Set on You," originally recorded by R&B singer James Ray in 1962, and a major hit, "When We Was Fab," which was reminiscent (in its lyrics and in its arrangement, complete with sitar) of the Beatles. In 1988 and again in 1990, Harrison recorded as one of the Traveling Wilburys with Bob Dylan, Jeff Lynne, and Tom Petty (and Roy Orbison in 1988); the group had a hit with Harrison's "Handle with Care." In late 1991 George Harrison toured Japan with Eric Clapton and his band, resulting in *Live in Japan*. In 1995 the three living former Beatles reunited to promote their *Anthology* TV/CD/video package, and recorded two new songs based on demo tapes by John Lennon that prominently featured George Harrison's guitar work and harmony vocals.

DISC.: GEORGE HARRISON: *Wonderwall Music* (1968); *Electronic Sound* (1969); *All Things Must Pass* (1970); *Living in the Material World* (1973); *Dark Horse* (1974); *Extra Texture* (1975); *The Best of G. H.* (1976); *33 & 1/3* (1976); *G. H.* (1979); *Somewhere in England* (1981); *Gone Troppo* (1982); *Cloud Nine* (1987); *The Best of Dark Horse, 1976–1989* (1989); *Live in Japan* (1992). **GEORGE HARRISON AND FRIENDS:** *The Concert for Bangladesh* (1972). **THE TRAVELING WILBURYS:** *Volume One* (1988); *Volume 3* (1990).

BIBL.: Ross Michael, *G. H.: Yesterday and Today* (N.Y., 1977); Alan, Clayson, *The Quiet One: A Life of G. H.* (London, 1990). —BH

Harrison, Guy Fraser, English-American conductor; b. Guildford, Surrey, Nov. 6, 1894; d. San Miguel de Allende, Mexico, Feb. 20, 1986. He studied at the Royal Coll. of Music, where he won an organ scholarship. He served as an organist of the Episcopal Cathedral in Manila (1914–20), then was organist of St. Paul's Cathedral in Rochester, N.Y. (1920–24) and then conductor of the Eastman Theater Orch. in Rochester (1924–29) and the Rochester Civic Orch. (1930–51). He was also assoc. conductor of the Rochester Phil. (1930–51). From 1951 to 1973 he was conductor of the Okla. City Sym. Orch.—NS/LK/DM

Harrison, Julius (Allan Greenway), English

conductor, composer, and teacher; b. Stourport, Worcestershire, March 26, 1885; d. Harpenden, Hertfordshire, April 5, 1963. He studied with Bantock in Birmingham and at the Midland Inst. In 1913 he conducted for the first time at London's Covent Garden. After serving as conductor of the Scottish Orch. in Glasgow (1920–23), he was a conductor with the Beecham Opera Co. and the British National Opera Co. in London (1922–27). He subsequently was conductor of the Hastings Municipal Orch. (1930–40) and a prof. of composition at the Royal Academy of Music in London. His music was principally influenced by Elgar.

WORKS: *The Canterbury Pilgrims*, opera; *Worcestershire Pieces*, orch. suite; *Bredon Hill* for Violin and Orch.; *Cornish Sketches* for Strings; *Troubadour Suite* for Strings, Harp, and 2 Horns; String Quartet; sonatas; piano pieces; Mass; Requiem; *Cleopatra*, cantata; songs.

BIBL.: G. Self, *J. H. and the Importunate Muse* (Brookfield, 1993).—NS/LK/DM

Harrison, Lou (Silver), inventive American

composer and performer; b. Portland, Ore., May 14, 1917. He studied with Cowell in San Francisco (1934–35) and with Schoenberg at the Univ. of Calif. at Los Angeles (1941). From 1945 to 1948 he was a music critic for the *N.Y. Herald-Tribune*. He was also an active promoter of contemporary music, including the works of Ives, Ruggles, Varèse, and Cowell. He prepared for publication Ives' 3rd Sym., and conducted its premiere (N.Y., April 5, 1946). He taught at Reed Coll. in Portland, Ore. (1949–50) and at Black Mountain Coll. in N.C. (1951–52). In 1952 and 1954 he held Guggenheim fellowships. In 1961 he visited the Far East. In 1963 he served as the senior scholar at the East-West Center of the Univ. of Hawaii. From 1967 to 1980 he taught at San Jose State Univ., and from 1980 to 1985 at Mills Coll. in Oakland, Calif. In 1983 he was a senior Fulbright scholar in New Zealand. Harrison's extensive output reflects his belief that the entire sound world is open to the creative musician. He has made use of both Western and non-Western musical traditions. He has demonstrated a preoccupation with pitch relations, most notably just intonation. In some of his works, he has utilized non-Western instruments or folk instruments, and he has also constructed various instruments of his own invention. He has even been bold enough to explore the use of unconventional "instruments," such as flowerpots, washtubs, and packing cases. Whatever the resources used, Harrison molds them into his own eclectic style in which melody and rhythm predominate.

WORKS: DRAMATIC: Opera: *Rapunzel* (Rome, 1954); *Young Caesar*, puppet opera (Aptos, Calif., Aug. 21, 1971). Theater Piece: *Jeptha's Daughter* (1940–63; Aptos, Calif., March 9, 1963). Dance Scores: *Changing World* (1936); *Green Mansions* (1939); *Something to Please Everybody* (1939); *Johnny Appleseed* (1940); *Omnipotent Chair* (1940); *Orpheus* (1941–69); *Perilous Chapel* (1948); *Western Dance* (1948); *The Marriage at the Eiffel Tower* (1949); *The Only Jealousy of Emer* (1949); *Solstice* (1949); *Almanac of the Seasons* (1950); *Io and Prometheus* (1951); *Praises for Hummingbirds and Hawks* (1951). OTHER: Incidental music to plays and film scores. ORCH.: Suite for Symphonic Strings (1936–60); Sym. No. 3 (1937–82);

Concerto for Violin and Percussion Orch. (1940–59); *Elegiac Symphony* (1941–75); *Alleluia* (1944); 2 suites for Strings (1947, 1948); *Symphony on G* (1948–54; rev. 1966); Suite for Violin, Piano, and Small Orch. (1951); *Moogunkwha, se tang ak* for Korean Court Orch. (1961); *Pacifika rondo* for Chamber Orch. (1963); Concerto for Organ, Percussion, and Orch. (1972–73); *Simfony in Free Style* (1980); Double Concerto for Violin, Cello, and Large Javanese Gamelan (1981–82); Piano Concerto (N.Y., Oct. 20, 1985); *Last Symphony* (N.Y., Nov. 2, 1990); *A Parade for M.T.T.* (San Francisco, Sept. 6, 1995). CHAMBER: Concerto No. 1 for Flute and Percussion (1939); *Canticle No. 1* for 5 Percussion (1940) and *No. 3* for Flute or Ocarina, Guitar, and Percussion (1941; rev. 1989); *Song of Queztecoatl* for Percussion Quartet (1940); *Double Music* for Percussion Quartet (1941; in collaboration with J. Cage); *Fugue* for Percussion Quartet (1941); *Labyrinth* for 11 Players of 91 Percussion Instruments (1941); *Schoenbergiana* for 6 Woodwinds (1945); *Siciliana* for Wind Quintet (1945); *Motet for the Day of Ascension* for 7 Strings (1946); String Trio (1946); Suite for Cello and Harp (1949); Suite No. 2 for String Quartet (1949–50); *7 Pastorales* for 4 Woodwinds, Harp, and Strings (1952); *Koncherto* for Violin and 5 Percussion (1959); *Concerto in slendro* for Violin, Celesta, 2 Tack Pianos, and Strings (1961); *Quintal taryung* for 2 Flutes and Changgo (1961); *Prelude* for P'iri and Harmonium (1962); *Majestic Fanfare* for Trumpets and Percussion (1963); *At the Tomb of Charles Ives* for Chamber Group (1964); *Avalokiteshvara* for Harp and Jaltarang (1965); *Music for Violin and Other Instruments* (1967–69); *Beverly's Troubadour Piece* for Harp and 2 Percussion (1968); *In Memory of Victor Jowers* for Clarinet and Piano (1968); Suite for Violin and American Gamelan (1972–73; in collaboration with R. Dee); *Arion's Leap* for Justly Tuned Instruments and Percussion (1974); *Main bersama-sama* for Horn and Sundanese Gamelan Degung (1978); *Serenade for Betty Freeman and Franco Asseto* for Sundanese Gamelan Degung and Suling (1978); *String Quartet Set* (1978–79); Suite for Guitar and Percussion (1978–79); *Threnody for Carlos Chávez* for Sundanese Gamelan Degung and Violin (1979); *Ariadne* for Flute and Percussion (1987); *Varied Trio* for Violin, Piano, and Percussion (1987); many Javanese gamelan pieces; piano music. VOCAL: Mass for Chorus, Trumpet, Harp, and Strings (1939–54); *Easter Cantata* for Soloists, Chorus, and Orch. (1943–46); *Alma redemptoris mater* for Baritone, Violin, Trombone, and Tack Piano (1949); *A Political Primer* for Soloists, Chorus, and Orch. (1951); *Holly and Ivy* for Voice, Harp, and Strings (1951); *Peace Piece 3* for Voice, Violin, Harp, and Strings (1953); *4 Strict Songs* for 8 Baritones and Orch. (1955); *A Joyous Procession and a Solemn Procession* for Chorus, Trombones, and Percussion (1962); *Nova odo* for Chorus and Orch. (1962); *Haiku* for Unison Voices, Xiao, Harp, and Percussion (1968); *Peace Piece 2* for Tenor, 3 Percussion, 2 Harps, and String Quintet (1968); *Peace Piece 1* for Unison Voices, Trombone, 3 Percussion, 2 Harps, Organ, and String Quintet (1968); *La koro sutro* for Chorus, American Gamelan, and Percussion Orch. (1972); *Scenes from Cavafy* for Baritone, Men's Voices, and Large Javanese Gamelan (1979–80); *The Foreman's Song Tune* for Chorus and Gamelan (1983).

WRITINGS: *About Carl Ruggles* (N.Y., 1946); *Music Primer: Various Items About Music to 1970* (N.Y., 1971); with others, *Soundings: Ives, Ruggles, Varèse* (Santa Fe, N.Mex., 1974); P. Garland, ed., *A Lou Harrison Reader* (Santa Fe, N.Mex., 1987).

BIBL.: V. Rathbun, *L. H. and his Music* (thesis, San Jose State Univ., 1976); C. Rutman, *The Solo Piano Works of L. H.* (diss., Peabody Cons. of Music, 1983); L. Miller and F. Lieberman, *L. H.: Composing a World* (N.Y., 1998).—NS/LK/DM

Harrison, May, English violinist, sister of **Beatrice Harrison;** b. Roorkee, India, March 1891; d. South Nutfield, Surrey, June 8, 1959. She was a pupil of Arbos and Rivarde at the Royal Coll. of Music in London, winning its gold medal at age 10. In 1904 she made her debut in London. After completing her training with Auer in St. Petersburg, she pursued her career mainly in England, often appearing in concerts with her sister. Delius composed his Double Concerto for the Harrison sisters, and also dedicated his 3rd Violin Sonata to May. —NS/LK/DM

Harrison, William, English tenor and operatic impresario; b. London, June 15, 1813; d. there, Nov. 9, 1868. He was trained at the Royal Academy of Music in London. On May 2, 1839, he made his operatic debut at London's Covent Garden in Rooke's *Henrique.* He then sang at London's Drury Lane, where he created roles in works by Balfe (*The Bohemian Girl,* 1844), Benedict (*The Brides of Venice,* 1844, and *The Crusaders,* 1846), and Wallace (*Maritana,* 1845). In 1854 he made a concert tour of the U.S. With the soprano Louisa Pyne, he organized the Pyne-Harrison English Opera Co. in 1856. It presented performances at Covent Garden (1858–64), premiering works by Balfe, Benedict, Wallace, and other British composers.—NS/LK/DM

Harriss, Charles A(lbert) E(dwin), English-Canadian organist, conductor, impresario, and composer; b. London, Dec. 16–17 (midnight), 1862; d. Ottawa, July 31, 1929. He was the son of the English musician Edwin Harriss. After studies with Sir Frederick Ouseley at St. Michael's Coll., Tenbury (1873–75), he was organist and choirmaster in Reading and Welshpool. In 1882 he went to Ottawa as organist at St. Alban the Martyr. In 1883 he went to Montreal as organist and choirmaster at Christ Church Cathedral, and then was his father's successor in those capacities at St. James the Apostle (1886–94). Having married into wealth in 1897, he subsequently was able to pursue his interests as an impresario and traveler. He organized various concerts, festivals, and performing groups in Canada and England, and also served as the first director of the McGill Cons. in Montreal (1904–07). His works include the operas *Torquil* (1894) and *The Admiral* (1902), *Canadian Fantasie* for Orch. (1904), *Festival Mass* (1901), *Coronation Mass for Edward VII* (1903), cantatas, the ode *The Crowning of the King* (1911), anthems, songs, and keyboard pieces.—NS/LK/DM

Harsanyi, Janice (née **Morris**), American soprano and teacher; b. Arlington, Mass., July 15, 1929. She studied at Westminster Choir Coll. in Princeton, N.J. (B.Mus., 1951) and at the Philadelphia Academy of Vocal Arts (1952–54). In 1954 she launched her career, concentrating on appearances as a soloist with orchs. and as a recitalist. She also sang in opera, becoming especially well known for her championship of contemporary music. She taught voice (1951–63) and was chairman of the voice dept. (1963–65) at Westminster Choir Coll.; also lectured on music at the Princeton Theological Seminary (1956–63). After serving as artist-in-residence at the Interlochen (Mich.) Arts Academy (1967–70), she taught voice at the N.C. School of the Arts in Winston-Salem (1971–78) and at Salem Coll. (1973–76). She was prof. of voice at Fla. State Univ. in Tallahassee from 1979. In 1952 she married **Nicholas Harsanyi.**—NS/LK/DM

Harsanyi, Nicholas, Hungarian-born American conductor and teacher; b. Budapest, Dec. 17, 1913; d. Tallahassee, July 19, 1987. He was a pupil of Hubay, Bartók, Dohnányi, Kodály, and Weiner at the Budapest Academy of Music (M.M., 1936). In 1938 he emigrated to the U.S. and in 1943 became a naturalized American citizen. He played in the Lener (1945–47) and Roth (1948–50) string quartets, and also taught at Westminster Choir Coll. in Princeton, N.J. (1948–69) and at Princeton Univ. (1953–68). He was conductor of the Princeton (N.J.) Sym. Orch. (1950–65), the Philadelphia Chamber Orch. (1955–58), the Colonial Sym. Orch. in Madison, N.J. (1955–65), the Trenton (N.J.) Sym. Orch. (1958–65), the Princeton (N.J.) Chamber Orch. (1964–70), and the Interlochen (Mich.) Arts Academy Orch. (1968–70). From 1970 to 1979 he was dean of the N.C. School of the Arts in Winston-Salem, where he conducted its orch. as well as the Piedmont Chamber Orch. In 1980 he founded the Tallahassee Sym. Orch., which he served as music director until his death. In 1952 he married **Janice** (née **Morris**) **Harsanyi.**—NS/LK/DM

Harsányi, Tibor, Hungarian composer; b. Magyarkanizsa, June 27, 1898; d. Paris, Sept. 19, 1954. He studied at the Budapest Academy of Music with Kodály; in 1923 he settled in Paris, where he devoted himself to composition. The melodic material of his music stems from Hungarian folk melos; his harmonic idiom is largely polytonal; the rhythms are sharp, often with jazzlike syncopation; the form remains classical.

WORKS: DRAMATIC: O p e r a : *Les Invités,* chamber opera (Gera, Germany, 1930); *Illusion,* radio opera (Paris, June 28, 1949). B a l l e t : *Le Dernier Songe* (Budapest, Jan. 27, 1920); *Pantins* (Paris, 1938); *Chota Roustaveli* (Monte Carlo, 1945; in collaboration with A. Honegger and A. Tcherepnin); *L'Amour et la vie* (1951). O t h e r : *L'Histoire du petit tailleur,* puppet show for 7 Instruments and Percussion (1939). ORCH.: *La Joie de vivre* (Paris, March 11, 1934, composer conducting); 2 divertissements (1940–41; 1943); Violin Concerto (Paris Radio, Jan. 16, 1947); *Figures et rythmes* (Geneva, Nov. 19, 1947, composer conducting); *Danses variées* (Basel, Feb. 14, 1950, composer conducting); Sym. (Salzburg Festival, June 26, 1952). CHAMBER: Violin Sonatina (1918); 2 string quartets (1918, 1935); Cello Sonata (1928); *3 Pieces* for Flute and Piano (1924); Nonet for String and Wind Instruments (Vienna, June 21, 1932); *Rhapsody* for Cello and Piano (1939); *Picnic* for 2 Violins, Cello, Double Bass, and Percussion (1951); many piano pieces, among them *5 études rythmiques* (1934), *3 pièces lyriques,* and albums for children. VOCAL: Choral works, including *Cantate de Noël* for Voices, Flute, and Strings (Paris, Dec. 24, 1945).—NS/LK/DM

Harshaw, Margaret, outstanding American mezzo-soprano, later soprano; b. Narberth, Pa., May 12, 1909; d. Libertyville, Ill., Nov. 7, 1997. She studied in Philadelphia and then was a scholarship student at the

Juilliard Graduate School of Music in N.Y., where she studied voice with Anna Schoen-René, graduating in 1942. Shortly after graduation, she won the Metropolitan Opera Auditions of the Air and made her debut with the company in N.Y. as a mezzo-soprano in the role of the 2nd Norn in *Gotterdämmerung* on Nov. 25, 1942; subsequently sang contralto and mezzo-soprano roles in German, Italian, and French operas; she also acquitted herself brilliantly as a dramatic soprano in her debut appearance in that capacity as Senta at the Metropolitan Opera on Nov. 22, 1950; was particularly successful in Wagnerian roles; she sang Isolde, Sieglinde, Kundry, Elisabeth, and all 3 parts of Brünnhilde. She also excelled as Donna Anna in *Don Giovanni* and Leonore in Beethoven's *Fidelio*. She was a guest soloist with the opera companies of Philadelphia, Cincinnati, San Francisco, and Covent Garden in London, and at the Glyndebourne Festivals. On March 10, 1964, she made her farewell appearance at the Metropolitan Opera as Ortrud. In 1962 she joined the faculty of the Ind. Univ. School of Music in Bloomington, where she taught voice until retiring in 1993.—NS/LK/DM

Hart, Antonio, American alto saxophonist; b. Baltimore, Md., 1969. He is one of the most exciting young alto saxophonists working in the post-bop tradition. He draws heavily from Gary Bartz and Cannonball Adderley, though he has also listened closely to Johnny Hodges, and is increasingly coming into his own sound. He studied classical saxophone for four years at the Baltimore School of the Arts yet did not begin playing jazz until his late teens, just before moving to Boston to study at Berklee. After graduating, he moved to N.Y. in 1990 and hooked up with his Berklee classmate trumpeter Roy Hargrove, with whom he toured extensively and recorded a number of fine albums. He has recorded four albums on Novus and appeared as a sideman on sessions with a wide array of musicians, including Phil Woods, Vincent Herring, Freddie Cole, Nat Adderley, Cecil Bridgewater, Monty Alexander, and Robin Eubanks.

DISC.: *For the First Time* (1991); *Don't You Know I Care* (1992); *The Vibe* (1992); *For Cannonball & Woody* (1993); *Mental Images* (1994); *It's All Good* (1995).—AG

Hart, Frederic Patton, American composer; b. Aberdeen, Wash., Sept. 5, 1894. He studied at the American Cons. in Chicago and at the Art Inst. there, and later took courses with Rubin Goldmark, with Ernest Hutcheson, and at the Diller-Quaile School in N.Y. He taught at Sarah Lawrence Coll. (1929–47) and at the Juilliard School of Music (1947–60), and then settled in Los Angeles. His works include the operas *The Wheel of Fortune* (1943) and *The Farewell Supper* (posthumous; N.Y., Feb. 3, 1984), the opera-ballet, *The Romance of Robot* (1937), chamber music, piano pieces, and songs. —NS/LK/DM

Hart, Fritz (Bennicke), English conductor and composer; b. Brockley, Kent, Feb. 11, 1874; d. Honolulu, July 9, 1949. He studied at the Royal Coll. of Music in London (1893–96). In 1908 he went to Australia and in

1915 became director of the Melbourne Cons. In 1927 he was appointed joint artistic director of the Melbourne Sym. Orch. He conducted the Honolulu Sym. Orch. (1932 until his death). He settled in Honolulu in 1936 when appointed prof. of music at the Univ. of Hawaii; retired in 1942. He wrote operas, operettas, orch. works, chamber music, choruses, and over 500 songs. —NS/LK/DM

Hart, James, English bass and composer; b. York, 1647; d. London, May 8, 1718. He was a singer in York Minster until 1670. He was then appointed Gentleman of the Chapel Royal and lay-vicar of Westminster Abbey. He settled in London and composed songs, publ. in *Choice Ayres and Songs* (1673–84), *The Theater of Music* (1685–87), *Banquet of Musick* (1688–90), and *Comes amoris* (1687–94). He wrote *Adieu to the pleasures and follies of love* for Shadwell's operatic adaptation of *The Tempest* (1674), publ. as one of 6 "Ariel's Songs."—NS/LK/DM

Hart, Lorenz (Milton), urbane American lyricist and librettist; b. N.Y., May 2, 1895; d. there, Nov. 22, 1943. Working almost exclusively with composer Richard Rodgers, Hart was the primary lyricist for songs in 29 Broadway and West End musicals and 9 original movie musicals between 1920 and 1942. His frequently bittersweet sentiments were expressed with remarkable wit in inventive rhymes in such popular songs as "Manhattan," "Blue Moon," "There's a Small Hotel," "My Funny Valentine," "The Lady Is a Tramp," and "Where or When." Along with Cole Porter and Ira Gershwin, he helped set the standard for sophisticated songwriting in the interwar period.

Hart was the son of German immigrants Max Meyer Hart (formerly Hertz), a private businessman, and Frieda Eisenberg Hart. He was writing verse by the age of six or seven. In 1915 he entered the Columbia Univ. School of Journalism and wrote a skit for the Columbia Varsity Show *On Your Way*. His first lyrics to be heard on the professional stage came with German translations he did for *Die Tolle Dolly* (N.Y., Oct. 23, 1916). In 1917 he quit Columbia and took a job for United Plays translating German plays into English.

Hart met the 16-year-old Rodgers in the spring of 1919, and the two immediately formed a songwriting partnership. Their first published song was "Any Old Place with You," interpolated into comic Lew Fields's musical *A Lonely Romeo* (N.Y., June 10, 1919) in August 1919. After writing two amateur musicals, *You'd Be Surprised* (N.Y., March 6, 1920) for the Akron Club, and *Fly with Me* (N.Y., March 24, 1920), the 1920 Columbia Varsity Show, the team was hired by Fields to write the songs for his next Broadway production, *Poor Little Ritz Girl*. But Fields replaced half of the score with interpolations by Sigmund Romberg and Alex Gerber by opening night; the show ran 93 performances.

Hart and Rodgers struggled for the next five years, writing material for a variety of amateur productions while Hart continued to do translations and Rodgers attended school. Their professional work was sparse: Hart produced the play *The First Fifty Years* (N.Y., March 13, 1922), which ran 46 performances, and they combined with Lew Fields's son Herbert Fields under the pseudonym Herbert Richard Lorenz as authors, composers, and lyricists of the play *The Melody Man*, which contained two songs and ran 61 performances. Rodgers was preparing to take a job selling babies' underwear when they took on yet another amateur production, writing songs for what was intended to be a two-performance benefit revue for the Theatre Guild at the Garrick Theatre called *The Garrick Gaieties*. The show ended up running 161 performances and generated two hits, "Manhattan" and "Sentimental Me," both of which were given their most successful recordings in instrumental versions by Ben Selvin and His Orch. in the fall of 1926. By then, their first book musical, *Dearest Enemy*, had opened for its 286–performance run, including the hit song "Here in My Arms," which was given its most popular recording, also as an instrumental, by Leo Reisman and His Orch. in May 1926.

Perhaps making up for their long apprenticeship, Rodgers and Hart staged five musicals in 1926, four of which were hits. *The Girl Friend* ran 409 performances and featured hits in the title song, recorded by George Olsen and His Orch. in August, and "The Blue Room," given its most popular recording by the Revelers in October. The second edition of *The Garrick Gaieties* ran 174 performances and featured "Mountain Greenery," a rural counterpart to "Manhattan," which became a hit for Roger Wolfe Kahn and His Orch. in September in an instrumental recording. *Lido Lady*, a British show that used "Here in My Arms" and a few interpolations by other songwriters as well as some new Rodgers-and-Hart songs, had a healthy run of 259 performances. *Peggy Ann* ran an even better 333 performances on Broadway, and two of its songs became hits: "Where's That Rainbow?" for Olsen in May 1927, and "A Tree in the Park" for Helen Morgan in September.

Rodgers and Hart also had hits in London and N.Y. in 1927, as the revue *One Dam Thing After Another* ran for 237 performances in the West End and the musical *A Connecticut Yankee* gave 418 performances on Broadway. Both shows featured "My Heart Stood Still," a hit for several recording artists in early 1928, especially George Olsen, while "Thou Swell," a clever combination of Medieval diction and contemporary slang that set the tone for *A Connecticut Yankee*, was a hit for Ben Selvin.

A Connecticut Yankee was Rodgers and Hart's last big success on Broadway for more than eight years, though they continued to work regularly and to enjoy individual hit songs from their shows. *Present Arms* ran a modest 155 performances but produced "You Took Advantage of Me," a hit for Paul Whiteman and His Orch. in August 1928. *Spring Is Here* ran only 104 performances, but its score featured "With a Song in My Heart," a hit for Leo Reisman in May 1929 and later the signature song of Jane Froman, whose 1952 film biography bore that title. *Simple Simon* ran 135 performances and remains memorable for "Ten Cents a Dance," performed onstage by Ruth Etting, who made a hit of it in May 1930. "Dancing on the Ceiling" was cut from *Simple Simon* before it opened, then was used in *Ever Green*; it became a hit for Jack Hylton and His Orch. in February 1932.

Rodgers and Hart began working in film shortly after the dawn of the sound era in 1928; in the spring of 1929 they were featured as themselves in a Paramount short, *Makers of Melody*, performing several of their songs and explaining how they wrote. In September the film adaptation of the De Sylva, Brown, and Henderson musical *Follow Thru* used one of the four songs Rodgers and Hart wrote for it. Hollywood was also filming Rodgers and Hart's own shows, retaining only two or three songs from the stage versions of *Spring Is Here*, *Present Arms* (retitled *Leathernecking* by RKO), and *Heads Up!*, all of which were released in 1930. That year, the team signed their first contract to write an original musical for the movies, earning $50,000 in five weeks while working on *The Hot Heiress* for Warner Bros.–First National. Their initial experiences in Hollywood helped form the basis for the musical satire *America's Sweetheart*, which ran 135 performances and featured "I've Got Five Dollars," a hit for Emil Coleman and His Orch. in February 1931. But those experiences did not prevent them from returning to Calif.; indeed, it was nearly five years before they wrote another show for Broadway.

In 1931, Rodgers and Hart signed a deal with Paramount resulting in *Love Me Tonight*, starring Maurice Chevalier and Jeanette MacDonald. Of the eight Rodgers-and-Hart songs used in the film, four became popular: "Lover," recorded in advance of the movie's release by Whiteman and a hit in April 1932; "Isn't It Romantic?," a hit for Harold Stern and His Orch.; the title song, recorded by George Olsen; and "Mimi," recorded by Chevalier. Rodgers and Hart moved to United Artists in 1932 for *Hallelujah, I'm a Bum*, starring Al Jolson. The film was not a success, but Jolson's recording of the title song became a minor hit in March 1933, and "You Are Too Beautiful," though not a hit on records at the time, became a standard. Rodgers and Hart joined MGM in 1933, writing incidental songs for several of the company's films in release in 1934.

Their biggest hit of the period was a song that was bounced from one film to another, acquiring three different sets of lyrics in the process. As "Prayer," it was intended for Jean Harlow in what became *Hollywood Party*, but it was not used. As "The Bad in Every Man" it was used in *Manhattan Melodrama*. But it was under the title "Blue Moon" that it was published independently and became a best-seller for Glen Gray and the Casa Loma Orch. in January 1935. Rodgers and Hart's most unusual project at MGM was a film adaptation of the operetta *The Merry Widow*, released in October 1934, for which they collaborated with lyricist Gus Kahn and composer Herbert Stothart, though in its finished form the film contained only Franz Lehár's original music, with the original German lyrics of Victor Leon and Leo Stein translated and adapted by Hart. Rodgers and Hart ended their sojourn in Hollywood back at Paramount for *Mississippi*, starring Bing Crosby and W. C. Fields, for which they wrote "Soon," the first song to top the newly established hit parade in April 1935, and another hit parade entry, "It's Easy to Remember," both recorded by Crosby.

Rodgers and Hart returned to Broadway in the fall of 1935 with Billy Rose's circus extravaganza *Jumbo*, which ran 233 performances but failed to make money because of its expense. The score featured such later Rodgers-and-Hart favorites as "Little Girl Blue" and "My Romance." The team's real return to prominence came with *On Your Toes*. They cowrote the libretto for the show with George Abbott and contributed a score that included "There's a Small Hotel," which reached the hit parade for Hal Kemp and His Orch., and "Glad to Be Unhappy," which was not a hit at the time but become one of Rodgers and Hart's best-remembered songs. The show ran 315 performances, making it the biggest box office success of the 1935–36 season.

Rodgers and Hart had their most memorable score with *Babes in Arms*, which ran 289 performances and featured "I Wish I Were in Love Again," "Johnny One Note," "The Lady Is a Tramp," "My Funny Valentine," and "Where or When." Though each of these songs earned its share of recordings, none were substantial hits upon publication, yet all became standards. Rodgers and Hart's other show of 1937 was the political satire *I'd Rather Be Right*, which ran 290 performances and included another song that became a standard without ever being a hit, "Have You Met Miss Jones?"

In 1938 came *I Married an Angel*, for which Rodgers and Hart wrote the book as well as the songs, the most successful of which was the title song, on the hit parade in the summer for Larry Clinton and His Orch. The score also included "I'll Tell the Man on the Street" and "Spring Is Here"; the show ran 338 performances. Before the year was out, Rodgers and Hart were back with a musical adaptation of Shakespeare's *The Comedy of Errors*, *The Boys from Syracuse*, which ran 235 performances and featured "This Can't Be Love," a hit parade entry for Benny Goodman and His Orch. in the winter of 1938–39, as well as "Falling in Love with Love."

By 1939, Hart's bohemian lifestyle, which included alcoholism and, apparently, homosexuality, began to make him an unreliable songwriting partner for Rodgers, who was sometimes forced to complete song lyrics himself. Nevertheless, the duo continued to produce musicals at the rate of two per season. In the 1939–40 season those shows were *Too Many Girls*, which ran 249 performances and featured the Benny Goodman hit "I Didn't Know What Time It Was," and *Higher and Higher*, which had a short 109–performance run but featured the standard "It Never Entered My Mind." And the duo's show for the 1940–41 season, the hard-edged *Pal Joey*, had one of their longest runs at 374 performances and was arguably their most influential work. Because of the ASCAP radio ban that began in early 1941, the songs were prevented from becoming hits initially, but they included "Bewitched, Bothered, and Bewildered" and "I Could Write a Book," both of which achieved success over time.

Rodgers and Hart did some film work in the early 1940s, contributing new songs to the film versions of *The Boys from Syracuse* and *Too Many Girls* in 1940 and writing the score for RKO's *They Met in Argentina* in 1941. They were back on Broadway in 1942 with the longest running show of their career, *By Jupiter*, which had 427 performances. It was also their last new show together, however. Rodgers turned to Oscar Hammer-

stein II when Hart declined to work on the show that became *Oklahoma!* in the spring of 1943. Rodgers then produced a revised version of *A Connecticut Yankee* (N.Y., Nov. 17, 1943), for which he and Hart wrote several new songs, notably the caustic "To Keep My Love Alive," but this was Hart's final work. Taken ill at the show's premiere, he contracted pneumonia and died within days.

A revival of interest in the songs of Rodgers and Hart began with the December 1948 release of MGM's film biography *Words and Music*, with the unlikely casting of Mickey Rooney as Hart. Perry Como, who sang "The Blue Room" in the film, had a hit with it in February 1949, and Mel Tormé, who sang "Blue Moon" also had a hit recording. "Bewitched, Bothered, and Bewildered," its title abbreviated to "Bewitched," became an enormous hit in the spring of 1950, with chart versions by several performers, Bill Snyder and His Orch.'s Top Ten recording the most successful. This led to Columbia Records' decision to record a studio cast LP of *Pal Joey* featuring Vivienne Segal from the original cast. That, in turn, led to a stage revival of *Pal Joey* (N.Y., Jan. 3, 1952), which, at 542 performances, became the longest running Rodgers- and-Hart show ever and the longest running revival up to that time. (When a film version starring Frank Sinatra was released in 1957, the soundtrack album became a Top Ten hit.)

Rodgers-and-Hart songs enjoyed periodic revivals in the 1950s and 1960s: Peggy Lee's revamped arrangement of "Lover" was a Top Ten hit in 1952; Elvis Presley scored one of his earliest chart records with "Blue Moon" in 1956; Dion and the Belmonts took "Where or When" into the Top Ten in early 1960; The Marcels' doo-wop version of "Blue Moon" was a #1 hit in the spring of 1961; and the Mamas and the Papas had a Top 40 hit with "Glad to Be Unhappy" in the fall of 1967. In addition to these pop renditions, Hart's sophisticated lyrics and Rodgers's intricate melodies have made their songs perennial favorites for jazz and nightclub performers since their heyday.

WORKS (only works for which Hart was the primary, credited lyricist are listed): **MUSICALS/REVUES** (all dates refer to N.Y. openings unless otherwise noted): *Poor Little Ritz Girl* (July 28, 1920); *The Melody Man* (May 13, 1924); *The Garrick Gaieties* (May 17, 1925); *Dearest Enemy* (Sept. 18, 1925); *The Girl Friend* (March 17, 1926); *The Garrick Gaieties* (May 10, 1926); *Lido Lady* (London, Dec. 1, 1926); *Peggy-Ann* (Dec. 27, 1926); *Betsy* (Dec. 28, 1926); *One Dam Thing After Another* (London, May 20, 1927); *A Connecticut Yankee* (Nov. 3, 1927); *She's My Baby* (Jan. 3, 1928); *Present Arms* (April 26, 1928); *Chee-Chee* (Sept. 15, 1928); *Spring Is Here* (March 11, 1929); *Heads Up!* (Nov. 11, 1929); *Simple Simon* (Feb. 18, 1930); *Ever Green* (London, Dec. 3, 1930); *America's Sweetheart* (Feb. 10, 1931); *Jumbo* (Nov. 16, 1935); *On Your Toes* (April 11, 1936); *Babes in Arms* (April 14, 1937); *I'd Rather Be Right* (Nov. 2, 1937); *I Married an Angel* (May 11, 1938); *The Boys from Syracuse* (Nov. 23, 1938); *Too Many Girls* (Oct. 18, 1939); *Higher and Higher* (April 4, 1940); *Pal Joey* (Dec. 25, 1940); *By Jupiter* (June 2, 1942). **FILMS:** *Spring Is Here* (1930); *Heads Up!* (1930); *The Hot Heiress* (1931); *Love Me Tonight* (1932); *The Phantom President* (1932); *Hallelujah, I'm a Bum* (1933); *Hollywood Party* (1934); *The Merry Widow* (1934); *Mississippi* (1935); *Dancing Pirate* (1936); *Fools for Scandal* (1938); *Babes in Arms* (1939); *The Boys from Syracuse* (1940); *Too Many Girls* (1940); *They Met in*

Argentina (1941); *Pal Joey* (1957); *Billy Rose's Jumbo* (1963).

BIBL.: R. Rodgers and O. Hammerstein II, eds., *The Rodgers and H. Song Book* (N.Y., 1951); S. Marx and J. Clayton, *Rodgers and H.: Bewitched, Bothered and Bedevilled* (N.Y., 1976); D. Hart (his sister-in- law), *Thou Swell, Thou Witty: The Life and Lyrics of L. H.* (N.Y., 1976); R. Kimball and D. Hart, eds., *The Complete Lyrics of L. H.* (N.Y., 1987); F. Nolan, *L. H.: A Poet on Broadway* (N.Y., 1994).—**WR**

Hart, Philip, English organist and composer; b. London, c. 1674; d. there, July 17, 1749. He was asst. organist (1696–97) and organist (1697–1749) at St. Andrew, Undershaft, and also organist at St. Michael, Cornhill (1704–23) and St. Dionis, Backchurch (1724–49). He wrote a number of keyboard pieces and vocal works, his finest work being the *Ode in Praise of Musick or Ode to Harmony* (1702). He also wrote *The Morning Hymn* for 2 Voices, Cello, and Harpsichord, after Milton's *Paradise Lost*, Book V (London, c. 1729).—**NS/LK/DM**

Hart, Weldon, American composer; b. Place-Bear Spring, Tenn., Sept. 19, 1911; d. (suicide) East Lansing, Mich., Nov. 20, 1957. He studied in Nashville, at the Univ. of Mich., and at the Eastman School of Music in Rochester, N.Y., with Hanson and Rogers, receiving his Ph.D. in 1946. He was head of the music dept. of Western Ky. State Coll. (1946–49) and director of the School of Music of the Univ. of W.Va. (1949–57). In 1957 he was engaged as head of the music dept. of Mich, State Univ. in East Lansing; upon arrival there, he became despondent over his inability to produce an impression with a concert of his works, and killed himself with carbon monoxide exhaust in his car. Yet his music, although not innovative, was well crafted. He wrote *The Dark Hills*, symphonic poem (1939), *Sinfonietta* (1944), Sym. (1945), Violin Concerto (1951), *3 West Virginia Folk Songs* for Chorus and Orch. (1954), several violin pieces, and choruses.—**NS/LK/DM**

Hart & Sons, a firm of London violin makers, founded in 1825 by John Hart. His son, John Thomas Hart (b. Dec. 17, 1805; d. London, Jan. 1, 1874), a pupil of Gilkes, made a complete study of Cremonese and other violins of Italian make, establishing a reputation as an expert in his field. His son, George Hart (b. London, March 23, 1839; d. near Newhaven, April 25, 1891), succeeded him and publ. *The Violin: Its Famous Makers and Their Imitators* (London, 1875; French ed., Paris, 1886) and *The Violin and Its Music* (London, 1881). His sons, George and Herbert Hart, inherited the business.—**NS/LK/DM**

Harth, Sidney, American violinist, conductor, and pedagogue; b. Cleveland, Oct. 5, 1925. He studied at the Cleveland Inst. of Music (Mus.B., 1947), and then took lessons with Joseph Fuchs and Georges Enesco. He was a recipient of the Naumburg prize in 1948 and made his debut at Carnegie Hall in N.Y. in 1949. He served as concertmaster and asst. conductor of the Louisville Orch. (1953–58), then was concertmaster of the Chicago Sym. Orch. (1959–62) and of the Casals Festival Orch. in San Juan (1959–65; 1972). From 1963 to 1973 he was a

prof. of music and chairman of the music dept. at Carnegie-Mellon Univ. in Pittsburgh. He served as concertmaster and assoc. conductor of the Los Angeles Phil. (1973–79), was interim concertmaster of the N.Y. Phil. in 1980, and also served as music director of the Puerto Rico Sym. Orch. (1977–79). He was director of orch. studies at the Mannes Coll. of Music in N.Y. (1981–84), prof. of violin at the State Univ. of N.Y. at Stony Brook (1981–82) and at the Yale Univ. School of Music (from 1982), and director of orch. studies at Carnegie-Mellon Univ. (1989–90). From 1990 to 1993 he was music director of the Northwest Chamber Orch. He also was director of orch. activities at the Hartt School of Music in Hartford, Conn. (1991–93). With his wife, Teresa Testa Harth, he gave duo-violin concerts.—**NS/LK/DM**

Hartig, Heinz (Friedrich), German composer; b. Kassel, Sept. 10, 1907; d. Berlin, Sept. 16, 1969. He studied piano at the Kassel Cons., and musicology at the Univ. of Vienna. Unable to hold a teaching post under the Nazi regime, he occupied himself with performances as a harpsichord player; in 1948 he joined the Hochschule für Musik in Berlin. In his compositions, he applied varied techniques of modern music, from neo-Classicism to serialism, with formal unity achieved by the principle of free variations. He wrote a ballet, *Schwarze Sonne* (1958), chamber opera, *Escorial* (1961), Violin Concerto (1952), *Concertante Suite* for Guitar and Orch. (1954), Piano Concerto (1959), *Mass after a Holocaust*, after Dylan Thomas, for Baritone, Chorus, and Orch. (1960), *Wohin*, oratorio (1965), *Immediate* for Flute, Clarinet, Piano, and 2 Cellos (1966), *Concerto strumentale* for Violin and Orch. (1969), and *Komposition in 5 Phasen* for Cello, Orch., Chorus, and Tape (1969).

BIBL.: W. Burde, *H. H.* (Berlin, 1967).—**NS/LK/DM**

Hartke, Stephen (Paul), American composer and teacher; b. Orange, N.J., July 6, 1952. He studied with Drew at Yale Univ. (B.A., 1973), Rochberg at the Univ. of Pa. (M.A., 1976), and Applebaum at the Univ. of Calif. at Santa Barbara (Ph.D., 1982), where he also lectured (1981–83; 1985–87); was also a Fulbright prof. of composition at the Univ. of São Paulo in Brazil (1984–85). In 1987 he joined the faculty of the Univ. of Southern Calif. in Los Angeles. From 1988 to 1992 he also was composer-in-residence of the Los Angeles Chamber Orch. In addition to several commissions, his honors include a Kennedy Center Friedheim Award (1985), several NEA grants (1988; 1989–90; 1991–92), the American Academy in Rome Prize Fellowship (1991–92), an American Academy of Arts and Letters Award (1993), the Stoeger Prize (1998), a Guggenheim fellowship (1998), and a Commission Award from the Inst. for American Music (1998).

WORKS: ORCH.: *Alvorada*, madrigals for Strings (Pasadena, Calif., March 8, 1983); *Maltese Cat Blues* (1986); *Pacific Rim* (Los Angeles, Sept. 16, 1988); Sym. No. 2 (1990; Los Angeles, Feb. 8, 1991); Violin Concerto (1992; Troy, N.Y., March 12, 1993); *The Ascent of the Equestrian in a Balloon* (Washington, D.C., Nov. 2, 1995). **CHAMBER:** *Caoine* for Violin (1980; Santa Barbara, Calif., May 5, 1981); *Sonata- Variations* for Violin and Piano

(1984; Los Angeles, Feb. 26, 1985); *Oh Them Rats Is Mean in My Kitchen* for 2 Violins (1985; Ojai, Calif., May 1986); *Precession* for 13 Instruments (1986; Los Angeles, March 10, 1987); *The King of the Sun* for Violin, Viola, Cello, and Piano (Los Angeles, Nov. 15, 1988); *Night Rubrics* for Cello (1990; Lausanne, June 1991); *Wir küssen Ihnen tausendmal die Hände*, homage to Mozart for Clarinet, Horn, Violin, Viola, Cello, and Fortepiano (Los Angeles, Oct. 31, 1991); *Un tout petit trompe-l'oreille* for Guitar (1992); *Wulfstan at the Millennium* for 10 Instruments (Cambridge, Mass., April 13, 1995); *The Horse with the Lavender Eye* for Violin, Clarinet, and Piano (1997); *The Rose of the Winds* for String Octet (1998). P i a n o : *Post-Modern Homages*, 2 sets (1984–92; first complete perf., Los Angeles, Feb. 25, 1993); *The Piano Dreams of Empire* (Los Angeles, July 4, 1994); Sonata (1999). VOCAL: 2 *Songs for an Uncertain Age* for Soprano and Orch. (1981; São Paulo, Aug. 24, 1987); 4 *Madrigals on Old Portuguese Texts* for Soloists and Chorus or Chamber Chorus (1981; Santa Fe, N.Mex., Oct. 15, 1988); *Canções modernistas* for High Voice, Clarinet, Bass Clarinet, and Viola (1982); *Iglesia abandonada* for Soprano and Violin (Santa Barbara, Calif., May 10, 1982); *Sons of Noah* for Soprano, 4 Flutes, 4 Guitars, and 4 Bassoons (1996); *Tituli* for 5 Solo Men's Voices, Violin, and 2 Percussionists (1999).—NS/LK/DM

Hartley, Walter S(inclair),

American composer, pianist, and teacher; b. Washington, D.C., Feb. 21, 1927. He studied with Phillips, Rogers, and Hanson at the Eastman School of Music in Rochester, N.Y. (B.M., 1950; M.M., 1951; Ph.D., 1953). He taught at the National Music Camp in Interlochen, Mich. (1956–64), and at Davis and Elkins Coll. in W.Va. (1958–69). He then was prof. of music at the State Univ. of N.Y. Coll. at Fredonia (1969–91), and was also active as a pianist, especially in chamber music settings. His works for brass and saxophones and for band or wind ensemble have been widely performed.

WORKS: ORCH.: *Sinfonietta* (1950); 3 *Patterns* for Small Orch. (1951); *Triptych* (1951); *Elegy* for Strings (1952); Sonatina for Trumpet and Small Orch. (1952); Piano Concerto (1952); *Concert Overture* (1954); Chamber Sym. (1954); *Scenes from Lorca's Blood Wedding* (1956); *Elizabethan Dances* (1962); *Festive Music* (1963); *Psalm* for Strings (1964); *Partita* for Chamber Orch. (1964); *Variations* (1973); Sym. No. 3 (1983); Sinfonia No. 7 (1986); Concerto No. 2 for Alto Saxophone and Small Orch. (1989); *Fantasia* for Tuba and Chamber Orch. (1989); *Bagatelles* (1992); Concerto for Saxophone Quartet and Orch. or Wind Ensemble (1992); *Concerto breve* for Bass Trombone and Small Orch. (1995); Sinfonia No. 11 (1996). BAND OR WIND ENSEMBLE: Concerto for 23 Winds (1957); several sinfonias (1961–98); Alto Saxophone Concerto (1966); 2 syms. for Winds (1970, 1978); *Southern Tier Suite* (1972); *Bacchanalia* (1975); Concertino for Tenor Saxophone and Band (1977–78); *Coast Guard Overture* (1981); *Catskill Suite* (1982); Concerto No. 2 for Piano and Wind Ensemble (1992); *Lyric Symphony* (1993); *Centennial Symphony* (1995); Triple Quartet for Trombone, Euphoniums, and Tubas (1995); *Music for 12 Saxophones* (1997); Trio Concerto for Saxophones and Band (1999); 2 *Studies* for Band (1999). CHAMBER: 2 string quartets (1950, 1962); Woodwind Quartet (1950); Violin Sonata (1951); Viola Sonata (1952); Trio for Violin, Viola, and Cello (1953); Divertimento for Cello and Woodwind Quintet (1956); *Sonata concertante* for Trombone and Piano (1958); Trio for Piano, Violin, and Cello (1960); *Serenade* for Woodwind Quintet and String Bass (1963); Tuba Sonata (1967); Suite for Saxophone Quartet (1972); Concerto for Tuba

and 6 Percussion Players (1974); Baritone Saxophone Sonata (1976); 3 brass quintets (n.d., 1977, 1997); Quintet for Saxophones (1981); Trio for Saxophones (1984); *Sonata Elegiaca* for Alto Saxophone and Piano (1987); Sinfonia No. 8 for 5 Percussion Players (1987); Quartet for 4 Guitars (1987); Trio for Reeds and Piano (1987); Chamber Concerto for Baritone Saxophone and Wind Octet (1988); Sextet for Euphonium and Woodwind Quintet (1993); Double Quartet for Saxophones and Brass (1994); Concertino for Piano and Saxophone Quartet (1994); *Concertino da camera* for Soprano Saxophone and Brass Quintet (1994); Sonata for Oboe or Soprano Saxophone and Piano (1994); Alto Saxophone Quartet (1996); *Andante and Scherzo* for 4 Bassoons (1998); Clarinet Quartet (1998); *Prelude, Cadenza, and Rondo* for Cello and Piano (1999). P i a n o : 2 sonatas (1955, 1968); 3 *Preludes* (1977); Suite for 2 Pianos (1995; orch. 1999). VOCAL: *A Psalm Cycle* for Voice, Flute, and Piano (1967); *Canticles* for Soloists, Chorus, and Wind Ensemble (1970–71). —NS/LK/DM

Hartmann,

family of eminent Danish musicians of German descent:

(1) Johann Ernst (Joseph) Hartmann, violinist and composer; b. Gross Clogau, Silesia, Dec. 24, 1726; d. Copenhagen, Oct. 21, 1793. He was a member of the orch. of the Prince-Bishop of Breslau (1754–57). In 1761 he was at the Rudolstadt court and at the ducal court in Plön Holstein, where he became Konzertmeister. He then was a member of Sarti's Italian opera orch. in Copenhagen (1762–64), where he settled as a member of the Royal Chapel (1766), becoming 1st violinist (1767) and music director (1768). He is recognized as the founder of the Danish national school of Romantic opera. His most notable singspiels, among the many composed for the Royal Theater, are *Balders død* (The Death of Balder; Copenhagen, Jan. 30, 1779) and *Fiskene* (The Fishermen; Copenhagen, Jan. 31, 1780); the latter includes the final stanza of the Danish national anthem, *Kong Christian stod ved højen mast*; however, the present melody was not in the original score, so Hartmann may not have composed it. Most of his other MSS were destroyed in the Christiansborg Palace fire of 1794. The MSS of his Violin Concerto (composed in collaboration with his pupil Claus Schall; 1780), 3 cantatas, and *VI sonates à deux violons et basse*, op.1, are extant; also his publ. works, *Simphonie périodique* (No. 7; Amsterdam, 1770) and *Air favori varié pour le clavecin ou harpe avec un violon obligé* (Copenhagen, 1792). He prepared a *Violin-Schule* (MS, 1777).

(2) August Wilhelm Hartmann, violinist, organist, and composer, son of the preceding; b. Copenhagen, Nov. 6, 1775; d. there, Nov. 15, 1850. He studied with his father. He was 1st violinist in the Royal Chapel (1796–1817) and then organist and choirmaster at Copenhagen's Garnisonskirke (1817–24).

(3) Johann Peter Emilius Hartmann, celebrated organist and composer, son of the preceding; b. Copenhagen, May 14, 1805; d. there, March 10, 1900. He studied piano, organ, violin, and theory with his father, and began to compose when still a child; he succeeded his father as organist at Copenhagen's Garnisonskirke (1824), and then studied law at the Univ. of Copenhagen (graduated, 1828). While retaining a government post (1828–70), he pursued an active career as a musician. He joined the faculty of Siboni's cons. in 1827. Hartmann helped to organize the Musikforening in 1836, and also was active with the Studentersanforening from 1839, serving as its president from 1868. He visited Germany, Switzerland, Austria, and France in 1836, meeting such famous musicians as Marschner, Cherubini, Chopin, Rossini, Paër, Spohr, and Spontini. Hartmann met Franz Berwald and Clara Wieck in Berlin and Mendelssohn and Schumann in Leipzig in 1839. He won the critical admiration of Schumann, who wrote about him in the pages of the *Neue Zeitschrift für Musik*. He subsequently met Liszt in Hamburg in 1841. Hartmann was a guest conductor with the Leipzig Gewandhaus Orch. in 1844. He was appointed organist of Vor Frue Kirke, Copenhagen's cathedral, in 1843, and continued in that capacity until his death. He was also a founder of the Copenhagen Cons. (1866), serving as joint director with Gade (his son-in-law) and Paulli. As the leading representative of the Danish Romantic movement in music, he was held in the greatest esteem by his countrymen. He received an honorary Ph.D. from the Univ. of Copenhagen in 1874.

WORKS: DRAMATIC: O p e r a : *Ravnen, eller Broderprøven* (The Raven, or The Brother Test; Copenhagen, Oct. 29, 1832; rev. version, Copenhagen, April 23, 1865); *Korsarerne* (The Corsairs; Copenhagen, April 23, 1835); *Liden Kirsten* (Little Christina; Copenhagen, May 12, 1846; rev. version, Copenhagen, Oct. 29, 1858). **B a l l e t :** *Et folkesagn* (A Folk Tale; Copenhagen, March 20, 1854; in collaboration with Gade); *Valkyrien* (Copenhagen, Sept. 13, 1861); *Thrymskviden* (The Legend of Thrym; Copenhagen, Feb. 21, 1868); *Arcona* (Copenhagen, May 7, 1875). **O t h e r :** A melodrama, *Guldhornene* (The Golden Horns; 1834), incidental music to more than 15 plays. **ORCH.:** 2 syms.: No. 1, in G minor, op.17 (Copenhagen, April 17, 1836; rev. version, Copenhagen, May 17, 1851) and No. 2, in E major, op.48b (1848; Copenhagen, March 14, 1849). **O v e r t u r e s :** D minor (1825); *Gejstlig Ouverture* in C minor (1827); C major (1852); *En efteraarsjagt* (An Autumn Hunt; 1863); also overtures to Oehlenschlaeger's *Axel og Valborg* (1856) and *Correggio* (1858). **CHAMBER:** Sonata for Flute or Clarinet (1825); 3 violin sonatas (1826, 1846, 1886); Suite for Violin or Clarinet (1864); *Fantasi-Allegro* for Violin or Clarinet (1889); works for organ; piano pieces. **VOCAL:** Many cantatas; choruses; songs.

BIBL.: W. Behrend, *J.P.E. H.* (Copenhagen, 1895); A. Hammerich, *J.P.E. H.: Biografiske essays* (Copenhagen, 1916); W. Behrend, *J.P.E. H.* (Copenhagen, 1918); R. Hove, *J.P.E. H.* (Copenhagen, 1934); V. Bitsch, *J.P.E. H.* (Hellerup, 1955); L. Brix, *Die Klaviermusik von J.P.E. H.* (diss., Univ. of Gottingen, 1971); I. Sørensen, *J.P.E. H. og hans kreds: En komponistfamilies breve 1780–1900* (Copenhagen, 1999).

(4) Emil (Wilhelm Emilius Zinn) Hartmann, organist and composer, son of the preceding; b. Copenhagen, Feb. 21, 1836; d. there, July 18, 1898. He studied organ and theory with his father and piano with Anton Ree, and later studied in Leipzig. He began composing songs as a child; his first mature work was the *Passionssalme* (1858), followed by the ballet *Fjeldstuen* (The Mountain Cottage; Copenhagen, May 13, 1859), written in collaboration with his brother-in-law August Winding. Although he continued to write for the stage, he became best known as a composer of instrumental music. He was organist of St. John's (1861–71) and of the Chris-

tiansborg Palace Church (1871–98).

WORKS (all 1st perf. in Copenhagen): **DRAMATIC: O p e r a :** *En nat mellem fjeldene* (A Night in the Mountains; April 11, 1863); *Elverpigen* (The Elf Girl; Nov. 5, 1867); *Korsikaneren* (The Corsican; April 7, 1873); *Ragnhild* (Runic Spell; 1896); *Det store lod* (The Big Prize; 1897; probably not perf.). **B a l l e t :** *Fjeldstuen* (The Mountain Cottage; May 13, 1859; in collaboration with A. Winding); *En bryllupsfest i Hardanger* (A Wedding Feast in Hardanger; 1897; not perf.). **ORCH.:** 7 syms.; *Hakon Jarl*, symphonic poem; Piano Concerto; Violin Concerto; Cello Concerto; etc. **VOCAL:** *Passionssalme* for Soprano, Chorus, and Orch. (Maundy Thursday, 1858); choruses; songs.—**NS/LK/DM**

Hartmann, Arthur (Martinus), American violinist, teacher, and composer; b. Philadelphia, July 22, 1881; d. N.Y., March 30, 1956. He studied violin with Martinus Van Gelder in Philadelphia, making his debut there at 6. He then studied violin with Loeffler and composition with Homer Norris in Boston. From the age of 12 he made concert tours. After garnering critical accolades as a soloist with the Philadelphia Orch. (1906) and the N.Y. Phil. (1908), he went to Paris and gave recitals with Debussy, who became his close friend. At the outbreak of World War I in 1914, he returned to the U.S. and made a transcontinental tour in 1916–17. In subsequent years he was active in N.Y. as a performer, teacher, and composer until 1954. He prepared numerous transcriptions and arrangements.—**NS/LK/DM**

Hartmann, Carl, German tenor; b. Solingen, May 2, 1895; d. Munich, May 30, 1969. He was a student in Düsseldorf of Scnff. In 1928 he made his operatic debut as Tannhäuser in Elberfeld, and then toured the U.S. as a member of Gadski's opera company in 1930. After appearing with the Cologne Opera (1933–35), he sang in Berlin and Vienna, and also made guest appearances in Italy, France, and Switzerland. On Dec. 3, 1937, he made his Metropolitan Opera debut in N.Y. as Siegfried, and remained on its roster until 1940; in 1938 he sang Tristan at the Bayreuth Festival. He was principally known as a Wagnerian.—**NS/LK/DM**

Hartmann, Karl Amadeus, outstanding German composer; b. Munich, Aug. 2, 1905; d. there, Dec. 5, 1963. He enrolled in the teachers training college in Pasing, near Munich, in 1919. From 1924 to 1929 he studied at the Munich Academy of Music. After the Nazis came to power in 1933, Hartmann withdrew from public life and forbade the performance of his music in Germany. However, he composed a number of major works during the Nazi era, and his 1st String Quartet, *Carillon*, won 1st prize in the Geneva Chamber Music Competition in 1936. His defiance of the Nazi regime was manifested in his *Concerto funebre* for Violin and String Orch. (1939), composed in tribute to Czechoslovakia in the wake of its dismemberment; the score is notable for its metamorphosis, in the minor, of the famous Hussite chorale *Ye Who are God's Warriors*. In 1942 Hartmann pursued advanced training with Webern in Maria Enzersdorf, near Vienna. After the defeat of the Third Reich in 1945, he became dramaturg at the

Bavarian State Opera in Munich. He also co-founded that city's Musica Viva concerts, which he oversaw for the rest of his life. In 1949 he was awarded the music prize of the City of Munich, and in 1950 he received the arts prize of the Bavarian Academy of Fine Arts there, to which he was elected to membership in 1953. He was awarded the Grand Arts Prize of Nordrhein-Westfalen in 1957, the arts prize of the City of Berlin in 1961, and an honorary doctorate from the Spokane (Wash.) Cons. in 1962. Despite his acceptance of a highly chromatic, atonal idiom and his experimentation in the domain of rhythm (patterned after Blacher's "variable meters"), he retained the orthodox form and structural cohesion of basic Classicism. He was excessively critical of his early works, and discarded many of them, some of which were retrieved and performed after his death.

WORKS: DRAMATIC: Opera: *Wachsfigurenkabinett*, collective title for 5 small operas (1929–30; 1, *Leben und Sterben des heiligen Teufels*; 2, *Der Mann, der vom Tode auferstand*, completed by G. Bialas and H. W. Henze; 3, *Chaplin-Ford- Trott*, completed by W. Hiller; 4, *Fürwahr...?!*, completed by H. W. Henze; 5, *Die Witwe von Ephesus*; all 1st perf. in Munich, May 29, 1988); *Simplicius Simplicissimus* (1934–35; concert perf., Munich, April 2, 1948; stage perf., Cologne, Oct. 20, 1949; new version, 1956–57; Mannheim, July 9, 1957). **ORCH.:** Chamber Concerto for Clarinet, String Quartet, and String Orch. (1930–35; Zürich, June 17, 1969); *Kleines Konzert* for Strings and Percussion (1931–32; Brausnchweig, Nov. 29, 1974; also for String Quartet and Percussion, Munich, Sept. 1932); Trumpet Concerto (1933); *Miserae*, symphonic poem (1934; Prague, Sept. 2, 1935); 9 syms.: No. 1 for Alto and Orch., after Whitman (1935–36; new version, 1954–55; Vienna, June 22, 1957), *Sinfonia tragica* (1940–43; Munich, May 20, 1989), No. 2, *Adagio* (1941–46; Donaueschingen, Sept. 10, 1950), No. 3 (1948–49; Munich, Feb. 10, 1950), No. 4 for Strings (1946–47; Munich, April 2, 1948), No. 5, Symphonie concertante (1950; Stuttgart, April 21, 1951), No. 6 (1951–53; Munich, April 24, 1953), No. 7 (1958; Hamburg, March 15, 1959), and No. 8 (1960–62; Cologne, Jan. 25, 1963); *Concerto funebre* for Violin and Strings (1939; new version, Braunschweig, Nov. 12, 1959); *Symphonische Hymnen* (1941–43; Munich, Oct. 9, 1975); *Symphonische Ouvertüre* (1942; Darmstadt, July 26, 1947; rev. 1962; Nuremberg, Nov. 28, 1975); *Klagegesang* (1944–45; Pittsburgh, May 11, 1990); Concerto for Piano, Winds, and Percussion (Donaueschingen, Oct. 10, 1953); Concerto for Viola, Piano, Winds, and Percussion (1954–56; Frankfurt am Main, May 25, 1956). **CHAMBER:** 2 sonatas for Solo Violin: No. 1 (1927; Munich, June 28, 1987) and No. 2 (1927; Munich, June 28, 1987); 2 suites for Solo Violin: No. 1 (1927; Spokane, April 6, 1986) and No. 2 (1927; Spokane, Feb. 5, 1984); *Tanzsuite* for Clarinet, Bassoon, Trumpet, Horn, and Trombone (1931); *Burleske Musik* for Winds, Percussion, and Piano (1931); *Kleines Konzert* for String Quartet and Percussion (1931–32; Munich, Sept. 1932; also for String Orch. and Percussion, Braunschweig, Nov. 29, 1974); 2 string quartets: No. 1, *Carillon* (1933) and No. 2 (1945–46); *Scherzo* for Percussion Ensemble (1956; Munich, May 30, 1992). **Piano:** 2 suites (n.d.); *Jazz-Toccata und -Fugue* (1928); Sonatine (1931; Munich, Jan. 4, 1932); Sonata, *27 April 1945* (1945; Munich, June 13, 1982). **VOCAL:** *Friede Anno 48* for Soprano, Chorus, and Piano, after Gryphius (1936; Cologne, Oct. 22, 1968); *Lamento*, cantata for Soprano and Piano, after Gryphius (1936–37; rev. version, Konstanz, May 26, 1955); *Ghetto* for Alto, Baritone, and Small Orch. (1960–61; Cologne, Jan. 14, 1966; part of the collaborative piece *Jüdische Chronik* with B. Blacher, P. Dessau, H.W. Henze, and R. Wagner-

Régeny); *Gesangsszene* for Baritone and Orch., after Giraudoux (1962–63; unfinished; completed by H. Moldenhauer; Frankfurt am Main, Nov. 12, 1964).

BIBL.: J. Distefano, *The Symphonies of K. A. H.* (diss., Fla. State Univ., 1972); A. McCredie, *K. A. H.* (Wilhelmshaven, 1980); R. Wagner, ed., *K. A. H. und die Musica Viva* (Mainz, 1980); A. Jaschinski, *K. A. H.: Symphonische Tradition und ihre Auflösung* (Munich, 1982); A. McCredie, ed., *K. A. H.: Thematic Catalogue of His Works* (Wilhelmshaven, 1982); U. Dibelius et al., *K. A. H.* (Tutzing, 1995); R. Behschnitt, *"Die Zeiten sein so wunderlich...":* *K. A. H.s Oper Simplicus Simplicissimus* (Hamburg, 1998). **—NS/LK/DM**

Hartmann, Pater (real name, **Paul Eugen Josef von An der Lan-Hochbrunn**), German organist and composer; b. Salurn, near Bozen, Dec. 21, 1863; d. Munich, Dec. 5, 1914. He entered the Franciscan order at the age of 16, and studied theology and music in various monasteries. He then completed his musical studies with Josef Pembaur in Innsbruck. He was ordained a priest in 1886, and then appointed organist at the Church of the Redeemer in Jerusalem (1893) and at the Church of the Holy Sepulchre (1894). In 1895 he was transferred to Rome as organist of the monastery Ara Coeli and director of the Scuola Musicale Cooperativa. From 1906 until his death he lived in the Franciscan monastery of St. Anna at Munich.

WORKS: ORATORIOS: *Petrus* (1900); *Franziskus* (1902); *Das letzte Abendmahl* (1904); *Der Tod des Herrn* (1905); *Septem ultima verba Christi in Cruce* (1908). **OTHER:** *Te Deum* (1913); masses; organ works.**—NS/LK/DM**

Hartmann, Rudolf, German opera director and administrator; b. Ingolstadt, Oct. 11, 1900; d. Munich, Aug. 26, 1988. He was trained in stage design in Munich and was a student of Berg-Ehlert in Bamberg. He was an opera director in Altenburg (1924–27), Nuremberg (1928–34; 1946–52), the Berlin State Opera (1934–37), and the Bavarian State Opera in Munich (1937–44); from 1952 to 1967 he was the Bavarian Staatsintendant. He was especially known for his staging of works by Richard Strauss, and was chosen to stage the premieres of Strauss's *Friedenstag* (Munich, 1938) and *Capriccio* (Munich, 1942); he also directed the official premiere of Strauss's *Der Liebe der Danae* (Salzburg, 1952). In his stagings, he fused the best of traditional elements with contemporary stage practices. He publ. an autobiography as *Das geliebte Haus: Mein Leben mit der Oper* (Munich, 1975). His other writings included *Oper: Regie und Bühnenbild heute* (Stuttgart, 1977) and *Richard Strauss: Die Bühnenwerke von der Uraufführung bis heute* (Munich and Fribourg, 1980; Eng. tr., 1982, as *Richard Strauss: The Staging of His Operas and Ballets*). His correspondence with Strauss was ed. by R. Schlötterer as *Richard Strauss—Rudolf Hartmann: Ein Briefwechsel* (Tutzing, 1984).**—NS/LK/DM**

Hartmann, Thomas (Alexandrovich de), Russian composer; b. Khoruzhevka, Ukraine, Sept. 21, 1885; d. Princeton, N.J., March 26, 1956. He studied piano with Essipova and composition with Taneyev and Arensky at the St. Petersburg Cons. His first important work, the ballet *The Little Crimson Flower*, was premiered at the Imperial Theater in St. Petersburg in 1907 with Pavlova, Karsavina, Nijinsky, and Fokine. After the Revolution, he went to the Caucasus; taught at the Tiflis Cons. (1919); then went to Paris, where he remained until 1951, when he settled in N.Y. His early music is in the Russian national style, influenced particularly by Mussorgsky; from about 1925, he made a radical change in his style of composition, adopting many devices of outspoken modernism.

WORKS: DRAMATIC: O p e r a : *Esther* (not perf.). **B a l l e t :** *The Little Crimson Flower* (St. Petersburg, Dec. 16, 1907); *Babette* (Nice, March 10, 1935). **ORCH.:** 4 syms. (1915; 1944; 1953; 1955, unfinished); Cello Concerto (1935; Boston, April 14, 1938); Piano Concerto (1940; Paris, Nov. 8, 1942); Double Bass Concerto (1943; Paris, Jan. 26, 1945); Harp Concerto (1944); Violin Concerto (Paris, March 16, 1947); Flute Concerto (Paris, Sept. 27, 1950); *12 Russian Fairy Tales* (Houston, April 4, 1955). **CHAMBER:** Violin Sonata (1937); Cello Sonata (1942); Trio for Flute, Violin, and Piano (1946); piano pieces. **VOCAL:** 3 song cycles to words by Verlaine, Proust, and James Joyce; other songs. **OTHER:** Music to Kandinsky's *The Yellow Sound* (arranged by G. Schuller; N.Y., Feb. 9, 1982). **—NS/LK/DM**

Hartog, Eduard de, Dutch pianist, pedagogue, and composer; b. Amsterdam, Aug. 15, 1829; d. The Hague, Nov. 8, 1909. He studied piano with Bertelman and Litolff and composition with Heinze in Amsterdam. Later he studied with Hoch and Dulcken in Germany, and with Dameke, K.A.F. Eckert, and Elwart in Paris, where he was active as a pianist and a pedagogue (1852–1900). He composed the operas *Le Mariage de Don Lope* (Paris, 1865) and *L'Amour et son Hôte* (Brussels, 1873), 3 symphonic poems, a set of orch. sketches, chamber music, and piano pieces.**—NS/LK/DM**

Härtwig, Dieter, distinguished German musicologist; b. Dresden, July 18, 1934. He was a student of Besseler, Serauky, Wolff, and Eller at the Univ. of Leipzig (Ph.D., 1963, with the diss. *Der Opernkomponist Rudolf Wagner-Régeny: Leben und Werk*; publ. in Berlin, enl. ed., 1965 as *Rudolf Wagner-Régeny: Der Opernkomponist*; Habilitation, 1970, with his *Fidelio F. Finke: Leben und Werk*). He was a dramaturg at the theaters in Schwerin (1959–60) and Dresden-Radebeul (1960–65), and then was chief dramaturg of the Dresden Phil. (from 1965). He also was a lecturer (1960–62; 1973–80), Dozent (1980–84), and prof. (1984–91) of music history at the Dresden Hochschule für Musik.

WRITINGS: *Die Dresdner Philharmonie: Eine Chronik des Orchesters 1870 bis 1970* (Leipzig, 1970); *Kurt Masur* (Leipzig, 1975); *Die Dresdner Philharmonie* (Leipzig, 1985; 2nd ed., 1989; new ed., Berlin, 1992); *Carl Maria von Weber* (Leipzig, 1986; 2nd ed., 1989); *125 Jahre Dresdner Philharmonie: 1870–1995* (Altenburg, 1995).**—NS/LK/DM**

Harty, Sir (Herbert) Hamilton, eminent Irish conductor, pianist, and composer; b. Hillsborough, County Down, Dec. 4, 1879; d. Brighton, Feb. 19, 1941. He received most of his musical training from his father, William Harty, the parish organist and a music teacher.

He learned to play the piano, organ, and viola, and began composing while still a youth. In 1894 he was made organist at Magheragall Church in County Antrim, and then was a church organist in Belfast (1895–96) and Bray in County Wicklow (1896–1901). During the latter period, he profited from the guidance of Michele Esposito and established himself as a piano accompanist in Dublin. In 1901 he went to London. For the Feis Ceoil, Dublin's competitive music festival, he composed *An Irish Symphony* and won a special prize. On May 18, 1904, he made his conducting debut in Dublin leading its first performance. From 1904 he also appeared as a conductor in London, the year he married **Agnes Nicholls.** He composed several works for his wife and appeared as her accompanist. In 1913 he made his debut at London's Covent Garden, and subsequently devoted most of his time to conducting. From 1920 to 1933 he was conductor of the Hallé Orch. in Manchester, which he brought to a high level of performance. In 1931 he made his first conducting tour of the U.S. From 1932 to 1934 he was artistic adviser and conductor-in-chief of the London Sym. Orch. Although stricken with a brain tumor in 1936 which cost him his right eye, he continued to make occasional appearances as a conductor until Dec. 1940. In 1925 he was knighted and in 1934 he was awarded the Gold Medal of the Royal Phil. Soc. of London. Harty's well-crafted compositions follow along traditional lines with an infusion of Irish inflections. While none of his compositions entered the standard repertoire, his effective suites for large orch. arranged from Handel's *Water Music* (1920) and *Music for the Royal Fireworks* (1923) were popular concert staples for many years. As a conductor, he was highly esteemed as a consummate podium figure.

WORKS: ORCH.: *The Exile*, overture (c. 1900); *An Irish Symphony* (Dublin, May 18, 1904; rev. 1915 and 1924); *A Comedy Overture* (1906; rev. 1908); Violin Concerto (1908); *With the Wild Geese*, poem (1910); *Variations on a Dublin Air* or *Irish Variations* for Violin and Orch. (1912); *Fantasy Scenes* (1919); Piano Concerto (1922); *À la campagne* for Oboe and Orch. (c. 1931; also for Oboe and Piano, 1911); *Orientale* for Oboe and Orch. (c. 1931; also for Oboe and Piano, 1911); *In Ireland*, fantasy for Flute, Harp, and Orch. (1935; also for Flute and Piano, 1915); *The Children of Lir*, poem (1938; London, March 1, 1939). **CHAMBER:** 3 string quartets (1898, c. 1900, c. 1902); 2 *Fantasiestücke* for Piano, Violin, and Cello (c. 1901); *Romance and Scherzo* for Cello and Piano (1903); Quintet for Piano, 2 Violins, Viola, and Cello (c. 1904); 2 *Pieces* for Cello and Piano; *Waldesstille* and *Der Schmetterling* (1907); *Chansonette* for Oboe and Piano (1911); *Irish Fantasy* for Violin and Piano (1912); *Spring Fancies*, 2 preludes for Harp (1915); *Fanfare* for 4 Trumpets and Side Drum (1921); Suite for Cello and Piano (1928); *A Little Fantasy and Fugue* for Carillon (1934); piano pieces. **VOCAL:** *Ode to a Nightingale* for Soprano or Tenor and Orch. (1907); *The Mystic Trumpeter* for Baritone, Chorus, and Orch. (1913); choruses; many songs.

BIBL.: D. Greer, ed., *H. H.: His Life and Music* (Belfast, 1978). **—NS/LK/DM**

Hartzell, Eugene, American-born Austrian composer; b. Cincinnati, May 21, 1932. He studied at Kent State Univ. (B.S., 1953) and Yale Univ. (B.M., 1954; M.M., 1955), and with H.E. Apostel in Vienna (1956–58). He then lived in Vienna, working in various positions only peripherally connected with music. He adopted the 12–tone method of composition; his works in this idiom include *14 Monologues* for Assorted Instruments (1957–84) and *10 Workpoints* (1977–82), inspired by the English writer Lawrence Durrell, for every binary combination, from the Woodwind Quintet.

WORKS: ORCH.: *2 Pieces* (1962); 2 syms.: No. 1 for Strings (1965) and No. 2 for Wind Quintet and Strings (1968); *Synopsis for Symphony* (1970); Sinfonietta for Strings (1980). **CHAMBER:** *14 Monologues* (1957–84); Trio for Flute, Bass Clarinet or Bassoon, and Piano (1969); *Projections* for Wind Quintet (1970); *Companion Pieces to a Wind Quintet* (1973); *Outgrowths of a Wind Quintet* (1973); *10 Workpoints* (1977–82); String Quartet (1979); Clarinet Sonata (1981). **P i a n o :** *Suite for a Young Pianist* (1963); *9 Uncritical Pieces* (1968). **VOCAL:** *Psalm 130* for Chorus and Organ (1973); *3 Latin Lyrics* for Chorus (1976); *A Keats Songbook* for Tenor and Guitar (1978); *9 Haikus* for Baritone and Clarinet (1978); *3 American Folksongs* for Voice and Piano (1979); *Grounds for John Donne* for Tenor and Harp (1979); *4 Latin Lyrics* for Tenor and Orch. (1981). —NS/LK/DM

Harvey, Jonathan (Dean),

significant English composer; b. Sutton Coldfield, Warwickshire, May 3, 1939. He was a scholarship student at St. John's Coll., Cambridge, and also received private instruction from Erwin Stein and Hans Keller; after obtaining his Ph.D. from the Univ. of Glasgow (1964), he attended the Darmstadt summer courses in new music (1966) and studied with Babbitt at Princeton Univ. He taught at the Univ. of Southampton (1964–77) and at the Univ. of Sussex (from 1977). In 1985 he received the Koussevitzky Foundation Award. He received honorary doctorates from the univs. of Southampton (1991) and Bristol (1994). In 1993 he received the Britten Award for composition. He was made a fellow of the Royal Coll. of Music in 1994. In his ultimate style of composition, Harvey astutely synthesized a number of quaquaversal idioms and techniques ranging from medieval modalities to ultramodern procedures, occasionally making use of electronic resources.

WORKS: DRAMATIC: O p e r a : *Passion and Resurrection,* church opera (Winchester Cathedral, March 21, 1981); *Inquest of Love* (1991–92). **ORCH.:** *Little Concerto for Strings* (1961; rev. version, 1997; London, March 14, 1998); Sym. (1966); *Chaconne on Iam dulcis amaica* (1967); *Benedictus* (1970); *Persephone's Dream* (1972; London, Jan. 18, 1973); *Smiling Immortal* for Chamber Ensemble and Tape (London, July 11, 1977); *Whom Ye Adore* (Glasgow, Sept. 19, 1981); *Bhakti* for Chamber Orch. and Tape (Paris, Dec. 3, 1982); *Easter Orisons* for Chamber Orch. (1983; Newcastle upon Tyne, Jan. 15, 1984); *Gong-Ring* for Chamber Ensemble and Electronics (Edinburgh, Sept. 1, 1984); *Madonna of Winter and Spring* Orch., Synthesizers, and Electronics (London, Aug. 27, 1986); *Lightness and Weight* for Tuba and Orch. (Poole, Feb. 18, 1987); *Timepieces* (1987; Saarbrücken, Sept. 23, 1988); Cello Concerto (1990); *Fanfare for Utopia* for 2 Horns, Trumpet, and Strings (Bath, April 6, 1995); Percussion Concerto (London, July 26, 1997); *Calling Across Time* for Chamber Orch. (London, June 13, 1998); *Tranquil Abiding* for Small Orch. (1998; N.Y., June 10, 1999). **CHAMBER:** *Dialogue* for Cello and Piano (1965); *Variations* for Violin and Piano (1965); *Transformation of "Love Bade Me Welcome"* for Clarinet and Piano (1968); *Studies* for 2 Clarinets (1970); Trio for Violin, Cello, and Piano (1971); *Quantumplation* for Flute, Clarinet, Violin, Cello, Percussion,

and Piano (1973); *Inner Light I* for Flute or Piccolo, Clarinet, Violin, Viola, Cello, Percussion, Piano, and Tape (1973); *Smiling Immortal* for Chamber Group and Tape (1977); 3 string quartets: No. 1 (1977; Southampton, March 6, 1979), No. 2 (1988; Brussels, March 17, 1989), and No. 3 (1995; Birmingham, Jan. 23, 1996); *Concelebration* for Flute, Clarinet, Cello, Piano, and Percussion (1979; rev. 1981); *Be(coming)* for Clarinet and Piano (1981); *Modernsky Music* for 2 Oboes, Bassoon, and Harpsichord (1981); *Curve with Plateaux* for Cello (1982); *Nataraja* for Flute and Piano (1983); *Flight-Elegy* for Violin and Piano (1984); *Ricercare una melodie* for Trumpet or Flute or Oboe and Tape Delay (1985); *Tendril* for Chamber Group (1987); *The Valley of Aosta* for Chamber Group (1988); *Serenade in Homage to Mozart* for 10 Winds (1991); *Lotuses* for Flute Quartet (1992); *Scena* for Violin and Chamber Group (1992); *Chant* for Viola (1992; rev. version, Brussels, March 24, 1994); *The Riot* for 3 Players (1993; Bristol, March 28, 1994); *Soleil Noir/Chitra* for 9 Players, 1 Technician, and Live Electronics (1993–94; Brussels, March 3, 1995); *Adavaya* for Cello, Electronic Keyboard, and Electronics (Paris, June 27, 1994); *Pastorale* for Cello and Harp (1994); *Hidden Voice 1* for Chamber Orch. (1995; London, Feb. 8, 1996) and *2* for Chamber Ensemble and CD (London, May 15, 1999); *Still* for Tuba and Electronics (1997); *Sufi Dance* for Guitar (Nottingham, Nov. 9, 1997); *Wheel of Emptiness* for Chamber Ensemble (1997; Brussels, Jan. 22, 1998); *Death of Light/Light of Death* for Chamber Ensemble (1997–98; Paris, April 10, 1998). **KEYBOARD: P i a n o :** *Tombeau de Messiaen* for Piano and DAT [Digital Audio Tape] (Cambridge, Nov. 2, 1994); *ff* (London, June 22, 1996); *Haiku* (1997). **O r g a n :** *Toccata* for Organ and Tape (1980). **VOCAL:** Cantatas: *I* for Soprano, Baritone, Chorus, Organ, and Strings (1965), *II: 3 Lovescapes* for Soprano and Piano (1967), *III* for Soprano and 7 Instruments (1968), *IV: Ludus amoris* for Soprano, Tenor, Speaker, Chorus, and Orch. (1969), *V: Black Sonnet* for Soprano, Mezzo-soprano, Baritone, Bass, and Wind Quintet (1970), *VI: On Faith* for Small Chorus and Small String Orch. (1970), and *VII: On Vision* for Soprano, Tenor, Chorus, and Chamber Group (1972); *Iam dulcis amica* for 2 Soprano, 2 Tenors, and 2 Basses (1967; also for Chorus); *In memoriam* for Soprano, Flute, Clarinet, Violin, and Cello (1969); *Angel Eros* for High Voice and String Quartet (1973); *Spirit Music* for Soprano, 3 Clarinets, and Piano (1975); *Inner Light II* for 2 Sopranos, Alto, Tenor, Bass, Chamber Group, and Tape (1977); *Magnificat and Nunc Dimittis* for Chorus and Organ (1978); *Hymn* for Chorus and Orch. for the 900th anniversary of Winchester Cathedral (Winchester Cathedral, July 12, 1979); *Resurrection* for Double Chorus and Organ (1981); *The Path of Devotion* for Chorus and Small Orch. (1983); *Come, Holy Ghost* for Double Chorus (1984); *Nachtlied* for Soprano, Piano, and Tape (1984); *Song Offerings* for Soprano and 8 Instruments (1985); *God Is Our Refuge* for Chorus and Organ (1986); *Lauds* for Chorus and Cello (1987); *From Silence* for Soprano, Violin, Viola, Percussion, 3 Synthesizers, and Tape (1988); *You* for Soprano, Clarinet, Viola, Cello, and Double Bass (1992); *One Evening...* for Soprano, Mezzo-soprano, Chamber Ensemble, 2 Technicians, and Electronics (1993–94; Cologne, June 14, 1994); *The Angels* for Chorus (Cambridge, Dec. 24, 1994); *Dum transisset sabbatum* for Chorus (London, July 2, 1995); *Missa Brevis* for Chorus (London, July 9, 1995); *How could the soul not take flight* for Chorus (Suva, Fiji, July 23, 1996); *Ashes Dance Back* for Chorus and Electronics (London, Sept. 27, 1997); *Marahi* for Chorus (Stuttgart, June 17, 1999). **OTHER:** *Time-points* for Tape (1970); *Mortuos plango, vivos voco* for Computer-manipulated Concrete Sounds on Tape (1980); *Ritual Melodies* for Tape (1990).—NS/LK/DM

Harwood, Basil, English organist and composer; b. Woodhouse, Gloucestershire, April 11, 1859; d. London, April 3, 1949. He studied piano with J. L. Roeckel and organ with George Risely, then studied with Reinecke and Jadassohn at the Leipzig Cons. He also studied theology with Corfe at Trinity Coll., Oxford. He was organist at St. Barnabas Church, Pimlico (1883–87), Ely Cathedral (1887–92), and Christ Church, Oxford (1892–1909); also was the 1st conductor of Oxford's Bach Choir (1896–1900). He ed. the *Oxford Hymn Book* (1908); wrote a number of sacred works for chorus, organ pieces (2 sonatas, Organ Concerto, *Christmastide, Dithyramb,* etc.), and a cantata, *Ode on May Morning,* after Milton (Leeds Festival, 1913).—NS/LK/DM

Harwood, Elizabeth (Jean), English soprano; b. Barton Seagrave, May 27, 1938; d. Ingatestone, June 21, 1990. She studied at the Royal Manchester Coll. of Music (1955–60). In 1960 she won the Kathleen Ferrier Memorial Prize and in 1963 the Verdi Prize of Busseto. She made her operatic debut in 1960 as the 2nd boy in *Die Zauberflöte* at the Glyndebourne Festival, and returned there to sing Fiordiligi, Countess Almaviva, and the Marschallin. In 1961 she became a member of the Sadler's Wells Opera in London, where she appeared as Susanna, Zerbinetta, and Massenet's Manon. In 1967 she made her first appearance at London's Covent Garden as Fiakermilli, and returned there to sing such roles as Marzelline, Gilda, Norina, and Donna Elvira; she also sang at Glasgow's Scottish Opera (1967–74). In 1970 she sang for the first time at the Salzburg Festival and in 1972 at Milan's La Scala. On Oct. 15, 1975, she made her Metropolitan Opera debut in N.Y. as Fiordiligi, remaining on the roster for that season; she returned for the 1977–78 season. In 1986 she made a tour of Australia. Among her other roles were Constanze, Lucia, Musetta, Sophie, and Hanna Glawari. —NS/LK/DM

Haselböck, Hans, Austrian organist, pedagogue, and composer, father of **Martin Haselböck;** b. Nesselstauden, July 26, 1928. He received training in literature and musicology at the Univ. of Vienna (1947–52) and in organ with Walter Pach at the Vienna Academy of Music (1948–53). From 1953 he served as titular organist at the Dominikanerkirche in Vienna. He took 1st prize in the Haarlem organ competitions in 1958, 1959, and 1960. In 1961 he became prof. of organ and improvisation at the Vienna Hochschule für Musik, where he was head of its department of sacred music from 1964. He publ. the study *Barocker Orgelschatz in Niederösterreich* (Vienna, 1972). Among his compositions are sacred vocal pieces and various organ works.

BIBL.: H. Kronsteiner, ed., *De arte organistica: Festschrift H. H. zum 70. Geburtstag* (Vienna, 1998).—NS/LK/DM

Haselböck, Martin, Austrian organist, harpsichordist, conductor, and teacher, son of **Hans Haselböck;** b. Vienna, Nov. 23, 1954. He received training in organ, harpsichord, composition, and church music, his principal mentors being his father, Michael Radulescu, and Anton Heiller at the Vienna Hochschule für Musik

and Jean Langlais at the Paris Schola Cantorum. In 1972 he won 1st prize in the Vienna-Melk International Improvisation Competition. He commenced his career as a keyboard player in 1970, and subsequently toured all over the world as a recitalist and as a soloist with leading orchs. He also held titular positions as director of music at the Augustinerkirche and as organist at the former Court Chapel in Vienna. In 1979 he became a prof. at the Vienna Hochschule für Musik, and in 1986 at the Lübeck Hochschule für Musik. He also gave master classes in keyboard playing in various locales. In 1985 he founded the Wiener Akademie, a period-instrument ensemble which he conducted at home and abroad. He also appeared as a guest conductor with many European orchs. In 1993 he became principal guest conductor of the Estonian State Sym. Orch. in Tallinn, a position he also assumed with the Hamburg Sym. Orch. in 1997. As both a keyboard player and conductor, Haselböck maintains a catholic repertoire extending from the early to modern masters.—NS/LK/DM

Häser, August Ferdinand, German composer, brother of **Charlotte (Henriette) Häser;** b. Leipzig, Oct. 15, 1779; d. Weimar, Nov. 1, 1844. He was educated at the Thomasschule in Leipzig, and studied theology at Leipzig Univ. In 1817 he was engaged in Weimar as music teacher to Princess Augusta (the future German empress). He also conducted the chorus at the Court Opera there, and was a church organist and a teacher of Italian. He publ. *Versuch einer systematischen Übersicht der Gesanglehre* (Leipzig, 1822) and *Chorgesangschule für Schul- und Theaterchore* (Mainz, 1831). He composed 3 operas, an oratorio, *Die Kraft des Glaubens,* many sacred choruses, 4 overtures, and several instrumental works in salon style.—NS/LK/DM

Häser, Charlotte (Henriette), German soprano, sister of **August Ferdinand Häser;** b. Leipzig, June 24, 1784; d. Rome, May 1, 1871. She studied with her father, the composer Johann Georg Haser (1729–1809), then sang in Dresden. In 1806 she went to Italy, where she enjoyed tremendous success. She was also one of the first women to sing male roles. After she left the stage, she settled in Rome.—NS/LK/DM

Haskil, Clara, eminent Romanian-born Swiss pianist; b. Bucharest, Jan. 7, 1895; d. Brussels, Dec. 7, 1960. A precocious child, she entered the Bucharest Cons. when she was 6. At 7, she was sent to Vienna and profited from the tutelage of Richard Robert. She was only 7 when she made her public debut there. At 10, she was sent to Paris to continue her training with Morpain, and, at 12, entered the Cons. as a pupil of Cortot. In 1909 she took 1st prize in the Concours de l'Union Française de la Jeunesse of Paris, and also 2nd prix at the Cons.; in 1910 she won the premier prix at the Cons. From 1920 she toured in Europe, and also made some appearances in the U.S. However, she became best known in France and Switzerland. In 1942 she sought refuge in the latter country and in 1949 she became a naturalized Swiss citizen. From 1950 she pursued an international career as a soloist with the foremost orchs. and as a recitalist.

She also appeared in duo recitals with Arthur Grumiaux. In spite of the fact that illness hampered her throughout her career, she succeeded in becoming a keyboard artist of consummate musicianship. Her interpretations of the Classical and Romantic masters, especially Mozart, Beethoven, Schubert, Schumann, and Chopin, were greatly admired.

BIBL.: R. Wolfensberger, *C. H.* (Bern, 1961); J. Spycket, *C. H.* (Paris, 1975).—**NS/LK/DM**

Haslinger, Tobias, Austrian music publisher; b. Zell, March 1, 1787; d. Vienna, June 18, 1842. He went to Vienna in 1810 after studying music in Linz. He was a bookkeeper in Steiner's music establishment. He later became a partner and, after Steiner's retirement in 1826, sole proprietor. A gregarious and affable person, he made friends with many musicians, and was on excellent terms with Beethoven, who seemed to enjoy Haslinger's company; many letters to him from Beethoven are extant, among them the humorous canon *O Tobias Dominus Haslinger.* He was succeeded by his son Carl Haslinger (b. Vienna, June 11, 1816; d. there, Dec. 26, 1868). The latter studied with Czerny and became a brilliant pianist as well as an industrious composer. He publ. more than 100 works of various kinds. Continuing the tradition of his father, he publ. several syms., piano concertos, overtures, and other works by Beethoven, and later Liszt's Piano Concerto in E-flat. He was also the publisher of many Strauss waltzes. In 1875 the firm was bought from his widow by Schlesinger of Berlin (subsequently, R. & W. Lienau). —**NS/LK/DM**

Hass, Sabine, German soprano; b. Braunschweig, April 8, 1949; d. Klagenfurt, Feb. 17, 1999. She received vocal training in Berlin and Munich. In 1970 she made her operatic debut in Stuttgart as Pamina, where she continued to sing regularly. In 1976 she appeared for the first time at the Bavarian State Opera in Munich and at the Vienna State Opera. Following an engagement as Reiza in *Oberon* at the Bregenz Festival in 1977, she sang in various European festivals and opera houses. In 1983 she made her debut at Milan's La Scala as Isabella in *Das Liebesverbot.* She made her Metropolitan Opera debut in N.Y. on Jan. 4, 1986, as Elsa. In 1988 she appeared in the title role in *Die Liebe der Danae* at the Munich Festival, and also portrayed Sieglinde at the Berlin Deutsche Oper. Following engagements in Seattle and Paris as Leonore in 1989, she sang Senta at the Bayreuth Festival in 1991. In 1992 she portrayed Wagner's Elisabeth in Berlin and his Brünnhilde in *Götterdammerung* in Bologna. She appeared as Strauss's Empress in Florence in 1993, the same year she sang his Dyer's Wife at the Théâtre du Châtelet and Wagner's Senta at the Opéra de la Bastille in Paris. In 1997 she was engaged as Elektra in Rome.—**NS/LK/DM**

Hasse, Faustina (née **Bordoni**), famous Italian mezzo-soprano; b. Venice, c. 1700; d. there, Nov. 4, 1781. She found patrons in Alessandro and Benedetto Marcello, who entrusted her vocal training to M. Gasparini. She made her debut in Pollarolo's *Ariodante* in Venice in 1716, and then entered the service of the Elector Palatine. In addition to appearances in Venice until 1725, she also sang in Reggio (1719), Modena (1720), Bologna (1721–22), Naples (1721–23), and Rome (1722). She made her first appearance in Germany in P. Torri's *Griselda* in Munich in 1723 with notable success, returning in 1724, 1728, and 1729. She created a number of roles in operas by Handel, including Rossane in *Alessandro* (London debut, May 5, 1726), Alcestis in *Ameto* (Jan. 31, 1727), Pulcheria in *Riccardo Primo* (Nov. 11, 1727), Emira in *Siroe* (Feb. 17, 1728), and Elisa in *Tolomeo* (April 30, 1728). Her rivalry with Cuzzoni became a public scandal, culminating in a physical altercation during a performance of *Astianatte* on June 6, 1727. Her other performances were in Florence (1728–29), Parma (1729–30), Turin (1729, 1731), Venice (1729–32), Milan (1730), and Rome (1731). She sang in the premieres of **Johann Adolf Hasse**'s *Dalisa* and *Arminio* in Venice in 1730, and married the composer that same year. Her career thereafter was closely related to her husband's, and she frequently appeared in his operatic and concert works. In 1731 they were called to the Saxon court in Dresden, where she became prima donna assoluta and her husband Kapellmeister; she also made frequent visits to Italy to sing in the principal music centers. She made her farewell stage appearance in the premiere performance of her husband's *Ciro riconosciuto* in Dresden on Jan. 20, 1751. She continued to receive her salary of 3,000 thaler and retained her title of virtuosa da camera until 1763, when she and her husband were dismissed by the new elector. They lived in Vienna until 1773, and then retired to Venice. According to contemporary accounts, she possessed one of the finest voices of the day. She also possessed great physical beauty, which greatly enhanced her dramatic gifts.

BIBL.: A. Niggli, *F. B.-H.* (Leipzig, 1880); M. Hogg, *Die Gesangskunst der F. H. und das Sängerinnenwesen ihrer Zeit in Deutschland* (Berlin, 1931).—**NS/LK/DM**

Hasse, Johann Adolf, celebrated German composer; b. Bergedorf, near Hamburg (baptized), March 25, 1699; d. Venice, Dec. 16, 1783. He studied in Hamburg (1714–17), and then was engaged as a tenor at the Opera there (1718); he was a member of the Braunschweig Opera (1719–21), where he sang in the premiere of his opera *Antioco* (Aug. 11, 1721). He then went to Naples, where he studied with A. Scarlatti. The success of his serenata *Antonio e Cleopatra* (Naples, Sept. 1725), sung by the famous castrato Farinelli and Vittoria Tesi, brought him a commission from the Teatro San Bartolomeo. There he produced his opera *Il Sesostrate* (Naples, May 13, 1726), which launched his career as a major dramatic composer. His *Artaserse* (Venice, Feb. 1730) was a particular favorite of Farinelli, who was later called upon to sing the arias *Per questo dolce amplesso* and *Pallido il sole* while in the service of the ailing King Philip V of Spain (1737–46). Hasse married **Faustina Hasse** (née **Bordoni**) in 1730, the same year in which she sang in the premieres of his *Dalisa* and *Arminio* in Venice. He went to the Saxon court in Dresden in 1731 as Kapellmeister; his wife joined him there as prima donna. His first opera for Dresden was *Cleofide* (Sept. 13, 1731). As his fame increased, the court allowed him frequent leaves of absence to produce his operas in other major music centers, often with his wife singing leading roles. He scored a major success with *Seroe, rè de Persia* (Bologna, May 2, 1733). His admiration for the renowned librettist Metastasio led to their remarkable personal and professional relationship from 1743. During this period, Hasse was acknowledged as the preeminent composer of opera seria in Germany, Austria, and Italy. Although Porpora served the Dresden court as Kapellmeister from 1748 to 1751, Hasse succeeded in maintaining his own position and was elevated to the post of Oberkapellmeister in 1750. His wife made her farewell appearance in opera in the premiere of his *Ciro riconosciuto* (Jan. 20, 1751). His *Solimano* (Feb. 5, 1753), with its huge cast of singers, actors, and even animals, proved a major court event. His last opera written for Dresden was *L'Olimpiade* (Feb. 16, 1756); he remained in the court's service until the advent of the new elector in 1763. In the meantime, he found an appreciative court in Vienna, where he produced the operas *Alcide al bivio* (Oct. 8, 1760), *Zenobia* (Carnival 1761), and *Il trionfo di Clelia* (April 27, 1762). Following the success of these works, he settled in Vienna; after bringing out his opera *Egeria* there (April 24, 1764), he wrote *Romolo ed Erisilia* for the Innsbruck court (Aug. 6, 1765). His success in Vienna continued with the productions of his *Partenope* (Sept. 9, 1767) and *Piramo e Tisbe* (Nov. 1768). But his *Il Ruggiero ovvero L'eroica gratitudine* (Milan, Oct. 16, 1771) failed to please the Italian public, and he decided to cease composing for the stage. In 1773 he retired to Venice. Hasse was a master of bel canto writing; his extraordinary craftsmanship is revealed in his command of harmony and orchestration; in addition to his dramatic works, he also distinguished himself as a composer of sacred music.

WORKS: DRAMATIC: O p e r a : *Antioco* (Braunschweig, Aug. 11, 1721); *Antonio e Cleopatra*, serenata (Naples, Sept. 1725); *Il Sesostrate* (Naples, May 13, 1726); *La Semele o sia La richiesta fatale*, serenata (Naples, 1726); *L'Astarto* (Naples, Dec. 1726); *Enea in Caonia*, serenata (Naples, 1727); *Gerone tiranno di Siracusa* (Naples, Nov. 19, 1727); *Attalo, rè di Bitinia* (Naples, May 1728); *L'Ulderica* (Naples, Jan. 29, 1729); *La Sorella amante*, commedia per musica (Naples, 1729); *Tigrane* (Naples, Nov. 4, 1729; rev. version, Naples, Nov. 4, 1745); *Artaserse* (Venice, Feb. 1730; rev. version, Dresden, Sept. 9, 1740); *Dalisa* (Venice, May 1730); *Arminio* (Milan, Aug. 28, 1730); *Ezio* (Naples, 1730; rev. version, Dresden, Jan. 20, 1755); *Cleofide* (Dresden, Sept. 13, 1731; rev. version, Venice, Carnival 1736; subsequent revs. 1738 and 1743); *Catone in Utica* (Turin, Dec. 26, 1731); *Cajo Fabricio* (Rome, Jan. 12, 1732; subsequent revs. for Naples, 1733; Dresden, July 8, 1734; Berlin, Sept. 1766); *Demetrio* (Venice, Jan. 1732; subsequent revs. for Vienna [as *Cleonice*], Feb. 1734; Venice, Carnival 1737; Dresden [as *Cleonice*], Feb. 8, 1740; Venice, Carnival 1747); *Euristeo* (Venice, May 1732); *Issipile* (Naples, Oct. 1, 1732; rev. version by Leo, Naples, Dec. 19, 1742; 2nd rev. version by P. Cafaro, Naples, Dec. 26, 1763); *Siroe rè di Persia* (Bologna, May 2, 1733; subsequent revs. for Naples, Nov. 4, 1747; Warsaw, Carnival 1763); *Sei tu, Lidippe, ò il sole*, serenata (Dresden, Aug. 4, 1734); *Senz'attender che di maggio*, cantata (Dresden, 1734); *Tito Vespasiano* (Pesaro, Sept. 24, 1735; subsequent revs. for Dresden, Jan. 17, 1738; Naples, Jan. 20, 1759); *Senocrita* (Dresden, Feb. 27, 1737); *Atalanta* (Dresden, July 26, 1737); *Asteria*, favola pastorale (Dresden, Aug. 3, 1737); *Irene*

(Dresden, Feb. 8, 1738); *Alfonso* (Dresden, May 11, 1738); *Viriate* (Venice, Carnival 1739); *Numa Pompilio* (Hubertusburg, Oct. 7, 1741); *Lucio Papirio* (Dresden, Jan. 18, 1742; rev. version by G. de Majo, Naples, Nov. 4, 1746; 2nd rev. version by Hasse or Graun, Berlin, Jan. 24, 1766); *Asilio d'amore*, festa teatrale (Naples, July 1742); *Didone abbandonata* (Hubertusburg, Oct. 7, 1742; rev. version by N. Logroscino, Naples, Jan. 20, 1744; subsequent revs. for Berlin, Dec. 29, 1752; Versailles, Aug. 28, 1753); *Endimione*, festa teatrale (Naples, July 1743); *Antigono* (Hubertusburg, Oct. 10, 1743?; rev. version by A. Palella, Naples, Dec. 19, 1744); *Ipermestra* (Venice, Jan. 8, 1744; rev. version by A. Palella, Naples, Jan. 20, 1746; 2nd rev. version, Hubertusburg, Oct. 7, 1751); *Semiramide riconosciuta* (Naples, Nov. 4, 1744; subsequent revs. for Dresden, Jan. 11, 1747; Warsaw, Oct. 7, 1760); *Arminio* (Dresden, Oct. 7, 1745; rev. version, Dresden, Jan. 8, 1753); *La Spartana generosa, ovvero Archidamia* (Dresden, June 14, 1747); *Leucippo*, favola pastorale (Hubertusburg, Oct. 7, 1747; subsequent revs. for Venice, May 1749; Dresden, Jan. 7, 1751; Berlin, Jan. 7, 1765); *Demofoonte* (Dresden, Feb. 9, 1748; subsequent revs. for Venice, Carnival 1749; Naples, Nov. 4, 1758); *Il natal di Giove*, serenata (Hubertusburg, Oct. 7, 1749); *Attilio Regolo* (Dresden, Jan. 12, 1750); *Ciro riconosciuto* (Dresden, Jan. 20, 1751); *Adriano in Siria* (Dresden, Jan. 17, 1752); *Solimano* (Dresden, Feb. 5, 1753; rev. version, Dresden, Jan. 7, 1754); *L'Eroe cinese* (Hubertusburg, Oct. 7, 1753; rev. version, Potsdam, July 18, 1773); *Artemisia* (Dresden, Feb. 6, 1754); *Il Rè pastore* (Hubertusburg, Oct. 7, 1755); *L'Olimpiade* (Dresden, Feb. 16, 1756; subsequent revs. for Warsaw, Carnival 1761; Turin, Dec. 26, 1764); *Nitteti* (Venice, Jan. 1758; rev. version, Vienna, 1762); *Il sogno di Scipione*, azione teatrale (Warsaw, Oct. 7, 1758); *Achille in Sciro* (Naples, Nov. 4, 1759); *Alcide al bivio*, festa teatrale (Vienna, Oct. 8, 1760); *Zenobia* (Vienna, Carnival 1761); *Il trionfo di Clelia* (Vienna, April 27, 1762; rev. version by G. de Majo, Naples, Jan. 20, 1763); *Egeria*, festa teatrale (Vienna, April 24, 1764); *Romolo ed Ersilia* (Innsbruck, Aug. 6, 1765); *Partenope*, festa teatrale (Vienna, Sept. 9, 1767; rev. version, Berlin, July 18, 1775); *Piramo e Tisbe*, intermezzo tragico (Vienna, Nov. 1768; rev. version, Vienna, Sept. 1770); *Il Ruggiero ovvero L'eroica gratitudine* (Milan, Oct. 16, 1771). **I n t e r m e z z o s :** *Miride e Damari* (Naples, May 13, 1726); *Larinda e Vanesio* (Naples, Dec. 1726; subsequent revs. for Dresden, July 8, 1734; Venice, Carnival 1739); *Grilletta e Porsugnacco* (Venice, May 1727; subsequent revs. for Naples, Nov. 19, 1727; Dresden, Aug. 4, 1747); *Carlotta e Pantaleone* (Naples, May 1728; subsequent revs. for Naples, Carnival 1734; Potsdam, 1749); *Scintilla e Don Tabarano* (Naples, 1728; subsequent revs. for Venice, 1731; Dresden, July 26, 1737); *Merlina e Galoppo* (Naples, Jan. 29, 1729; subsequent revs. for Venice, 1741; Dresden, 1749); *Dorilla e Balanzone* (Naples, Nov. 4, 1729; rev. version, Venice, 1732); *Lucilla e Pandolfo* (Naples, 1730; subsequent revs. for Dresden, 1738; Venice, 1739; Dresden, 1755); *Arrighetta e Cespuglio* (Naples, c. 1730); *Pimpinella e Marcantonio* (Hubertusburg, Oct. 7, 1741; subsequent revs. for Dresden, Jan. 14, 1743; Versailles, Aug. 28, 1753); *Rimario e Grilantea* (Nov. 3, 1741). **O r a t o r i o s :** *Daniello* (Vienna, Feb. 15, 1731); *Serpentes ignei in deserto* (Venice, c. 1731); *S. Petrus et S. Maria Magdalena* (Venice, c. 1731); *Il cantico de'tre fanciulli* (Dresden, April 23, 1734); *Le virtù appiè della croce* (Dresden, April 19, 1737); *Giuseppe riconosciuto* (Dresden, March 31, 1741); *I Pellegrini al sepolcro de Nostro Signore* (Dresden, March 23, 1742); *La caduta di Gerico* (Dresden, April 12, 1743); *La deposizione dalla croce di Gesu Cristo, salvatore nostro* (Dresden, April 4, 1744); *S. Elena al Calvario* (Dresden, April 9, 1746); *La conversione di S. Agostino* (Dresden, March 28, 1750).

INSTRUMENTAL: Twelve Concertos in 6 parts for Flute, 2 Violins, Viola, and Harpsichord or Cello, op.3 (London, 1741); 6 Concertos for Harpsichord or Organ (London, 1743; keyboard reduction of pieces from op.3); 6 Concertos in 6 parts for Flute, 2 Violins, Viola, and Harpsichord or Cello, op.6 (London, c. 1745); various other concertos; 3 quartets; many trio sonatas; numerous keyboard sonatas; etc.

BIBL.: F. Kandler, *Cenni storico-critici intorno alla vita ed alle opere del cel. Gio. Adolfo H. detto il Sassone* (Venice, 1820); U. de Gheltof, *La "nuova Sirena" e il "caro Sassone"* (Venice, 1890); B. Zeller, *Das Recitativo accompagnato in den Opern J. A. H.s* (Halle, 1911); W. Müller, *J. A. H. als Kirchenkomponist* (Leipzig, 1911; with thematic catalog); L. Kamienski, *Die Oratorio von J. A. H.* (Leipzig, 1912); R. Gerber, *Der Operntypus J. A. H. und seine textlichen Grundlagen* (Leipzig, 1925); S. Hansell, *The Solo Cantatas, Motets and Antiphons of J. A. H.* (diss., Univ. of Ill., 1966); idem, *Works for Solo Voice of J. A. H.* (Detroit, 1968; a catalog); F. Millner, *The Operas of J. A. H.* (Ann Arbor, 1979).—NS/LK/DM

Hasse, Karl, German musicologist and composer; b. Dohna, near Dresden, March 20, 1883; d. Cologne, July 31, 1960. He studied with Kretzschmar and Riemann at the Univ., and with Straube, Nikisch, and Ruthhardt at the Cons. in Leipzig, and then with Reger and Mottl in Munich. In 1907 he became Wolfran's assistant at the Univ. of Heidelberg. In 1909 he became organist and Kantor at the Chemnitz Johanneskirche, and in 1910 he was made music director in Osnabrück, where he also founded a cons. In 1919 he became music director and prof. extraordinary at the Univ. of Tübingen, where he took his Ph.D. in 1923 and was responsible for founding its music inst. and music dept. From 1935 to 1945 he was director of the Cologne Staatliche Hochschule für Musik. His compositions include a Sym., Piano Concerto, Violin Concerto, Cello Concerto, orch. suites, chamber music, piano pieces, organ music, and choral works.

WRITINGS: *Max Reger* (Leipzig, 1921; 2nd ed., 1930); *Johann Sebastian Bach* (Leipzig, 1925); *Musikstil und Musikkultur* (Kassel, 1927); *Von deutscher Kirchenmusik* (Regensburg, 1935); *Max Reger: Mensch und Werk* (Berlin, 1936); *Johann Sebastian Bach* (Cologne and Krefeld, 1938; 2nd ed., 1941); *Johann Sebastian Bach* (Leipzig, 1949); *Max Reger* (Leipzig, 1949); *Max Reger* (Dortmund, 1951).—NS/LK/DM

Hassell, Jon, American composer; b. Memphis, Tenn., March 22, 1937. He was trained as a trumpet player; then studied composition with Bernard Rogers at the Eastman School of Music in Rochester, N.Y. (B.M., 1969; M.M., 1970). Progressing away from traditional arts, he also took courses in advanced electronic techniques with Stockhausen and Pousseur in Cologne (1965–67). He was composer-in-residence and a performer at the Center for Creative and Performing Arts in Buffalo (1967–69). In 1969 he moved to N.Y., where he pursued independent activities in music and in sculpture. Among his compositions from this period are *Goodbye Music* for Mixed Media (Buffalo, May 4, 1969), *Superball* for 4 Players with Hand-held Magnetic Tape Heads (Ithaca, Oct. 29, 1969), and *Map 1* and *2* for Hand-held Magnetic Playback Heads (exhibited in Buffalo as sculptures, 1969). In the 1970s he studied Indian music with Pandit Pran Nath, and developed a vocal style of trumpet playing; he combined this with avant-garde and jazz backgrounds to create a series of works marked by their remarkable syntheses of African, Asian, and Western music. His popular works in this style appear on the recordings *Earthquake Island* (1978), the synthetically sampled *Aka/Darbari/Java- Magic Realism* (1983), *Power Spot* (1986), and *The Surgeon of the Nightsky Restores Dead Things by the Power of Sound* (1987). On the recording *Flash of the Spirit* (1989), he performs with the West African group Farafina.—NS/LK/DM

Hasselmans, family of Belgian-French musicians:

(1) Josef H. Hasselmans, Belgian harpist, violinist, and conductor; b. Antwerp, 1814; d. 1902. He studied harp with Antoine Prumier, and also learned to play the violin. He was 1st violinist in the Antwerp theater orch., and subsequently its conductor. He then was conductor of the Strasbourg theater orch. and director of the Cons. (from 1854).

(2) Alphonse (Jean) Hasselmans, Belgian-born French harpist and composer, son of the preceding; b. Liège, March 5, 1845; d. Paris, May 19, 1912. He began harp studies with his father, then continued his training with Gottlieb Krüger in Stuttgart, Xavier Désargus *fils* in Brussels, and Ange-Conrad Prumier in Paris. He began his career as a harpist in the orch. of Brussels's Théâtre de la Monnaie, then settled in Paris, where he attracted notice with a series of solo concerts in 1877. He subsequently was principal harpist in the orchs. of the Opéra, the Opéra-Comique, and the Cons. He was prof. of harp at the Cons. from 1884. He became a French citizen in 1903. Many composers wrote works for him. His own compositions include some 50 works and numerous transcriptions.

(3) Louis Hasselmans, French cellist and conductor, son of the preceding; b. Paris, July 15, 1878; d. San Juan, Puerto Rico, Dec. 27, 1957. He studied with Godard, Lavignac, and Massenet; also studied cello with Jules Delsart at the Paris Cons., winning the premier prix in 1893. He was a member of the Capet Quartet (1904–09). After making his conducting debut with the Lamoureux Orch. in 1905, he conducted at the Opéra-Comique (1909–11; 1919–22), the Montreal Opera and Marseilles Concerts Classiques (1911–13), and the Chicago Civic Opera (1918–19). Later he was a conductor at the Metropolitan Opera in N.Y. (1922–36). From 1936 to 1948 he taught at the La. State Univ. School of Music. —NS/LK/DM

Hassler, eminent family of German musicians:

(1) Isaak Hassler, organist; b. Joachimsthal, c. 1530; d. Nuremberg (buried), July 14, 1591. He studied in Joachimsthal with Johann Matthesius, the local headmaster, and with Nicolaus Herman, the Kantor. In 1554 he settled in Nuremberg, where he was active as both a lapidary and a musician. He was highly esteemed as a musician, as were his 3 sons:

(2) Caspar Hassler, organist, editor, and composer; b. Nuremberg (baptized), Aug. 17, 1562; d. there, Aug. 19, 1618. He studied with his father. In 1586 he became organist of the Egidienkirche and then of St. Lorenz, where he remained until 1616, when he became organist of St. Sebald. He was renowned as an organist and as an authority on organ design; restored the organ at St. Sebald in 1617. He was ennobled by Emperor Rudolf II in 1595. He ed. valuable collections of works by the leading Italian masters, which included some works by his brother Hans Leo Hassler and other German composers (1598, 1600, 1600, 1613). His only extant work is a 4-part *Fantasia* in German organ tablature (ed. in Denkmäler der Tonkunst in Bayern, VII, Jg. IV/2, 1903).

(3) Hans (Johann) Leo Hassler, celebrated organist and composer; b. Nuremberg (baptized), Oct. 26, 1564; d. Frankfurt am Main, June 8, 1612. He began his musical training with his father, then in 1584 continued his education in Venice, where he was a pupil of Andrea Gabrieli. He was named chamber organist to Octavian II Fugger in Augsburg in Jan. 1586, and quickly established himself as one of the leading musicians in Germany. In 1591 the emperor granted him the privilege of copyrighting his compositions. He was ennobled by the emperor in 1595, and was given a coat of arms and the title of Hassler von Roseneck in 1604. While in Augsburg, he also became active as a manufacturer of mechanical musical instruments, an enterprise that led to numerous litigations with business rivals. After Octavian's death in 1600, he was made director of the town music in Augsburg. He also served as Kaiserlicher Hofdiener to the court of Emperor Rudolf II, a position which may have been purely honorary. He obtained a year's leave of absence from Augsburg for a stay in Ulm in 1604, and then decided to remain there the following year; became a citizen of Ulm in 1607 and a member of its merchants' guild in 1608. He was appointed the Saxon electoral chamber organist in Dresden in 1608, and later assumed the duties of Kapellmeister. Following his move to Dresden, he was stricken with tuberculosis. He died during the visit of the court chapel to Frankfurt am Main for the election and coronation of Emperor Matthias. Hassler excelled as a composer of both sacred and secular vocal works. His sacred compositions reflect the influence of Lassus and others of the Venetian school, while his secular compositions display a pronounced individuality. His organ music follows the precepts of Andrea and Giovanni Gabrieli. The *Sämtliche Werke*, ed. by C. Crosby, commenced publication in Wiesbaden in 1961.

WORKS: *Canzonette* for 4 Voices, *libro I* (Nuremberg, 1590); *Cantiones sacrae de festis praecipuis totius anni* for 4 to 8 *et plurium vocum* (Augsburg, 1591); *Madrigali* for 5 to 8 Voices (Augsburg, 1596); *Neue teutsche Gesang nach Art der welschen Madrigalien und Canzonetten* for 4 to 8 Voices (Augsburg, 1596); *Missae* for 4 to 8 Voices (Nuremberg, 1599); *Lustgarten neuer teutscher Gesang, Balletti, Gaillarden und Intraden* for 4 to 8 Voices (Nuremberg, 1601); *Sacri concentus* for 4 to 12 Voices (Augsburg, 1601; 2nd ed., aug., 1612); *Psalmer und christliche Gesänge* for 4 Voices, *auff die Melodeyen fugweiss componiert* (Nuremberg, 1607); *Kirchengesänge: Psalmen und geistlicher Lieder, auff die gemeinen Melodeyen* for 4 Voices, *simpliciter gesetzet* (Nuremberg, 1608); *Venusgarten: oder neue lustige liebliche Tantz* for 4 to 6 Voices (Nuremberg, 1615); *Litaney teutsch* for 7 Voices (Nuremberg, 1619); also vocal works in various contemporary collections.

BIBL.: J. Neyses, *Studien zur Geschichte der deutschen Motette des XVI. Jahrhunderts: I. Die Form der H.schen Motette* (diss., Univ. of Bonn, 1926); M. Jarvis, *The Latin Motets of H. L. H.* (diss., Univ.

of Rochester, 1959); F. Hartmann, *H. L. H.: Gedenkschrift* (Frankfurt am Main, 1969).

(4) Jakob Hassler, organist and composer; b. Nuremberg (baptized), Dec. 18, 1569; d. probably in Eger, between April and Sept. 1622. He studied with his father, and was apprenticed as a town wait in Augsburg in 1585; then received a stipend from his patron, Christoph Fugger. He was ennobled by Emperor Rudolf II in 1595. In 1595–96 he became entangled in legal problems, culminating in his incarceration; he was released through the efforts of his brother Hans Leo Hassler. He was organist at the Hohenzollern court in Hechingen (1597–1601), and later imperial court organist to Emperor Rudolf II in Prague. Following the emperor's death in 1612, he pursued mining in Eger.

WORKS: *Madrigali* for 6 Voices (Nuremberg, 1600); *Magnificat 8 tonorum* for 4 Voices, *cum missa* for 6 Voices, *et psalmo li* for 8 Voices (Nuremberg, 1601); also keyboard works, some of which were ed. by E. von Werra in Denkmäler Tonkunst in Bayern, VII, Jg. IV/2 (1903).—**NS/LK/DM**

Hassler, Johann Wilhelm, German organist, composer, and pianist; b. Erfurt, March 29, 1747; d. Moscow, March 29, 1822. His father was a maker of men's headwear. He followed his father's trade while studying organ with his uncle, Johann Christian Kittel. At the age of 14, he was able to earn his living as organist at an Erfurt church. After his father's death, in 1769, he maintained for some years a manufactory of fur muffs. A meeting in Hamburg with C. P. E. Bach gave him a fresh impetus toward continuing his musical activities. He gave concerts as a pianist, and publ. several piano sonatas. On Feb. 8, 1779, he married his pupil Sophie Kiel. In 1780 he opened public winter concerts in Erfurt; his wife appeared there as a singer and choral director. In 1789 he played in Berlin and Potsdam; in Dresden he took part in a contest with Mozart, as organist and pianist, without producing much impression either on Mozart himself or on the listeners. In 1790 he went to London, where he performed piano concertos under the direction of Haydn. In 1792 he went to Russia, where he remained until his death. In Moscow he became greatly renowned as a pianist, as a composer, and particularly as a teacher. Most of his works were publ. in Russia; these included sonatas, preludes, variations, fantasies, etc., and also pieces for piano, 4–hands. His style represents a transition between Bach and Beethoven, without attaining a degree of the imagination or craftsmanship of either. However, his piano pieces in the lighter vein have undeniable charm. His *Grande gigue* was well known. His autobiography is included in W. Kahl, *Selbstbiographien deutscher Musiker* (Cologne, 1948).

BIBL.: H. Strobel, *J.W. H.s Leben und Werke* (diss., Univ. of Munich, 1922).—**NS/LK/DM**

Hastings, Thomas, notable American composer, tunebook compiler, teacher, choirmaster, and writer on music; b. Washington, Litchfield County, Conn., Oct. 15, 1784; d. N.Y., May 15, 1872. When he was 12, his family moved to Clinton, N.Y., where he led a village choir in his teens. During the winter of 1806–07, he opened a singing school in Bridgewater, N.Y., and later had singing-schools in Utica, Troy, and Albany. He became well known via his editorship of the Utica religious weekly *The Western Recorder* (1823–32). In 1832 he settled in N.Y., where he was busily engaged as a teacher, choirmaster, tunebook compiler, and writer on music. He was founder-ed. of the monthly *Musical Magazine* (1835–37). In 1858 he received an honorary D.Mus. degree from N.Y.U. Hastings was an influential figure in the promotion of American sacred music. He composed the celebrated *Rock of Ages*. He set the hymn to words by Augustus Toplady, paying tribute to the author by naming his tune *Toplady*. His first tunebook, *Musica sacra* (Utica, 1815; 2nd ed., 1816), was combined with S. Warriner's *Springfield Collection* (Boston, 1813), and subsequently was publ. as *Musica sacra: or, Springfield and Utica Collection* (10 eds., Utica, 1818–38). Among his subsequent tunebooks were *The Manhattan Collection* (1836), *The Sacred Lyre* (1840), *Sacred Songs for Family and Social Worship* (1842; 2nd ed., rev. and enl., 1855), *Songs of Zion* (1851), *The Presbyterian Psalmodist* (1852), and *Selah* (1856). He also collaborated on tunebooks with other compilers. Hastings's *Dissertation on Musical Taste* (Albany, 1822; 2nd ed., 1853) was the earliest detailed musical treatise publ. by a native American musician.

BIBL.: J. Dooley, *T. H.: American Church Musician* (diss., Fla. State Univ., 1963).—**NS/LK/DM**

Hatrík, Juraj, Slovak composer and teacher; b. Orkucany, May 1, 1941. He went to Bratislava and studied with A. Moyzes at the Academy of Music and Drama (1958–63). After teaching at the Košice Cons. (1963–65), he returned to Bratislava and pursued postgraduate studies at the Academy of Music and Drama (1965–68), and subsequently worked in its music theory dept. (1968–71). From 1972 to 1990 he was a consultant to the Slovak Music Fund. In 1991 he became senior lecturer in composition and music theory at the Academy of Music and Drama.

WORKS: DRAMATIC: *Janko Polienko* (1976); *Šťastný princ* (The Happy Prince; 1977–78); *Mechúrik Koščúrik*, musical fairy tale (1980); *Turčan Poničan* (1985); *Adamove deti* (Adam's Children), tragifarce (1990); *The Little Brave Tin Soldier*, musical (1994). **ORCH.:** *Sinfonietta* (1962); *Monumento malinconico* for Organ and Orch. (1964); *Concerto grosso facile* for Violin, Cello, Piano, and String Orch. (1966); *Concertino in modo classico* for Piano and Orch. (1967); *Double Portrait: Sancho Panza and Don Quixote* (1970); *De capo al fine: Song of a Human Life*, poem (1972); *Choral Fantasia* for Accordion and Chamber Orch. (1975); 2 syms.: No. 1, *Sans Souci* (1979) and No. 2, *VICTOR*, for Tenor, Chorus, and Orch. (1986–87); *Still Life with Violin* for Violin and String Orch. (1987). **CHAMBER:** *Contrasts* for Violin and Piano (1963); *Monologues* for Accordion (1965–67); *Dreams for My Son* for 2 Violins and Piano (1966); *Dispute Over a Plastered Dwarf*, anti-duet for 2 Accordions (1969); *Metamorpheses after Gogol* for Guitar (1972–80); Sonatina for Violin and Cello (1979–80); Sonatina for Solo Guitar (1981); *Vox memoriae* for Oboe, Bassoon, Harpsichord, Cello, and Easily mastered Instruments (1983); *Looking for a Song* for Violin and Piano (1985); Sonata for Solo Accordion (1987); *Diptych* for Violin, Cello, and Piano (1988); *Partita giocosa* for Accordion (1992); *An die Musik (A Message to Schubert)*, sonata for Violin, Clarinet, Cello, and Piano (1995). **P i a n o :** Sonata (1961); *Sonata ciaccona* (1971).

VOCAL: *Expectation* for Reciter, Flute, Harp, Percussion, and String Quartet (1966); *Home Are the Hands You May Weep On*, cantata for Reciter, Tenor, Chorus, and Orch. (1967); *Introspection to Latin Texts* for Soprano and Chamber Orch. (1967); *3 Nocturnes* for Soprano, Viola, and 2 Pianists (1971); *A Bird Flew Up*, cantata profana for Soloists, Chorus, and Chamber Orch. (1976); *The Diary of Tanya Savichevova*, monodrama for Soprano and Wind Quintet (1976); *Organ Music* for Bass, 2 Organists, and Chorus (1982); *Submerged Music*, sonata for Soprano, Violin, and 12 Strings (1982); *Canzona in memoriam A. Moyzes* for Alto, Viola, and Organ (1984); *Moment musical avec J. S. Bach*, chamber cantata for Soprano, Flute, Horn, Violin, Double Bass, and Piano (1985); *Schola ridicula*, cantata for Children's Chorus and Small Orch. (1989); *The Lost Children* for Bass and String Quartet (1993); *The Light*, sonata-cantata for Alto, Viola da Gamba, and Harpsichord (1996).—**NS/LK/DM**

Hatton, John Liptrot, English composer; b. Liverpool, Oct. 12, 1808; d. Margate, Sept. 20, 1886. He acquired facility as a pianist and singer, and appeared on the vaudeville stage as a musical comedian. He publ. a great number of songs, among which "Anthea" and "Good-bye, sweetheart, good-bye" became extremely popular. In 1832 he went to London, where he composed the operetta, *The Queen of the Thames, or The Anglers* (Feb. 25, 1842). He then went to Vienna, where his opera *Pascal Bruno* was staged (March 2, 1844). For some of his numbers he used the punning pseudonym Czapek (genitive plural of the Hungarian word for "hat"). From 1848 to 1850 he made an extensive American tour. Returning to England, he was music director at the Princess's Theatre (1853–59). He wrote music for several Shakespeare plays there, as well as a cantata, *Robin Hood* (Bradford Festival, Aug. 26, 1856), a grand opera, *Rose, or Love's Ransom* (London, Nov. 26, 1864), and a sacred drama, *Hezekiah* (Dec. 15, 1877). He also ed. collections of old English songs.—**NS/LK/DM**

Hatze, Josip, Croatian composer; b. Split, March 21, 1879; d. there, Jan. 30, 1959. He studied with Mascagni in Italy, and belongs to a generation of Croatian composers entirely influenced by Italian music. He wrote the operas *Povratak* (The Return; Zagreb, March 21, 1911) and *Adel i Mara* (Zagreb, March 1, 1933) as well as many songs.—**NS/LK/DM**

Haubenstock-Ramati, Roman, Polish composer; b. Kraków, Feb. 27, 1919; d. Vienna, March 3, 1994. He studied with J. Koffler at the Lwów Academy of Music (1939–41) and also took courses in philosophy at the univs. of Kraków and Lwów. From 1947 to 1950 he was music director of Radio Kraków, and then director of the State Music Library in Tel Aviv (1950–56). In 1957 he settled in Vienna, where he worked for Universal Edition until 1968. He then was a prof. of composition at the Vienna Academy of Music (from 1973). In 1981 he was awarded the Austrian State Prize. In 1959 he organized in Donaueschingen the first exhibition of musical scores in graphic notation. He evolved an imaginative type of modern particella in which the right-hand page gives the outline of musical action for the conductor while the left-hand page is devoted to instrumental and vocal details. This type of notation combined the most advanced type of visual guidance with an aide-memoire of traditional theater arrangements. Several of his works bear the subtitle "Mobile" to indicate the flexibility of their architectonics.

WORKS: *Ricercari* for String Trio (1950); *Blessings* for Voice and 9 Players (1952); *Recitativo ed Aria* for Harpsichord and Orch. (1954); *Papageno's Pocket-Size Concerto* for Glockenspiel and Orch. (1955); *Les Symphonies des timbres* for Orch. (1957); *Chants et Prismes* for Orch. (1957; rev. 1967); *Séquences* for Violin and Orch. in 4 groups (1957–58); *Interpolation*, "mobile" for Flute (1958); *Liaisons*, "mobile" for Vibraphone and Marimbaphone (1958); *Petite musique de nuit*, "mobile" for Orch. (1958); *Mobile for Shakespeare* for Voice and 6 Players (1960); *Credentials or "Think, Think Lucky"* for Speech-voice and 8 Players, after Beckett (1960); *Jeux 6*, "mobile" for 6 Percussionists (1960); *Decisions*, 10 pieces of musical graphics for Variable Instrumentation (1960–68); *Amerika*, opera after Kafka's novel (1962–64; Berlin, Oct. 8, 1966); *Vermutungen über ein dunkles Haus*, 3 pieces for 3 Orchs., 2 of which are on tape (1963); *Klavierstücke I* for Piano (1963–65); *Jeux 2 and 4*, "mobiles" for 2 and 4 Percussionists (1965, 1966); *Hotel Occidental* for Speech-chorus, after Kafka (in 3 versions, 1967); *Tableau I, II, and III* for Orch. (1967, 1968, 1970); *Symphonie "K"* (1967; material from the opera *Amerika*); *Psalm* for Orch. (1967); *Divertimento*, text collage for Actors, Dancer, and/or Mime, and 2 Percussionists (1968; after *Jeux 2*); *La Comédie*, "anti-opera," after Beckett, for 1 Male and 2 Female Speech-singers and 3 Percussionists (St. Paul-de-Vence, Alpes-Maritimes, France, July 21, 1969; German version as *Spiel*, Munich, 1970; Eng. version as *Play*); *Catch I* for Harpsichord (1969), *II* for 1 or 2 Pianos (1970), and *III* for Organ (1971); *Multiple I-VI* for Various Instrumental Combinations (1969); *Alone* for Trombone and Mime (1969); *Describe* for Voice and Piano (1969); *Hexachord I and II* for 2 Guitars (1972); *Concerto a tre* for Piano, Trombone, and Percussion (1973); 2 string quartets (1973, 1978); *Shapes (in Memory of Stravinsky) I* for Organ and Tape, and *II* for Organ, Piano, Harpsichord, and Celesta (both 1973); *Endless, endless* "mobile" for 7 Players and Conductor (1974); Sonata for Solo Cello (1975); *Musik* for 12 Instruments (1976); *Ulysses*, ballet (1977); *Concerto per archi* (Graz, Oct. 11, 1977); *Symphonien* (1977; Baden-Baden, May 10, 1978); *Song* for Percussion (1978); *Self I* for Bass Clarinet or Clarinet (1978) and *II* for Saxophone (1978); *3 Nocturnes* for Orch. (1981, 1982, 1985); *Mirrors/Miroirs I*, "mobile" for 16 Pianos (1984), *II*, "mobile" for 8 Pianos (1984), and *III*, "mobile" for 6 Pianos (1984); *Cantando* for 6 Players (1984); Piano Sonata (1984); String Trio No. 2 (1985); *Enchaîné* for Saxophone Quartet (1985); *Sotto voce* for Chamber Orch. (1986).—NS/LK/DM

Haubiel (real name, **Pratt**), **Charles Trowbridge**, American composer; b. Delta, Ohio, Jan. 30, 1892; d. Los Angeles, Aug. 26, 1978. His father's last name was Pratt, but he adopted his mother's maiden name, Haubiel, as his own. He had piano lessons with his sister Florence Pratt, an accomplished pianist. In 1911 he went to Europe, where he studied piano with Rudolph Ganz in Berlin; also took composition lessons with Alexander von Fielitz in Leipzig. Returning to the U.S. in 1913, he taught music at various schools in Okla. When the U.S. entered World War I in 1917, he enlisted in the field artillery and served in France. After the Armistice, he resumed serious study of composition with Rosario Scalero at the David Mannes Music School in N.Y. (1919–24), while continuing piano lessons with

Rosina and Josef Lhévinne (1920–26). In 1928 he won 1st prize in the Schubert Centennial Contest with his symphonic variations *Karma*. Intermittently he taught musical subjects at the Inst. of Musical Art in N.Y. (1921–31) and at N.Y.U. (1923–47). In 1935 he organized the Composers Press, Inc., with the purpose of promoting the publication of American music, and served as its president until 1966. His compositions reveal an excellent theoretical and practical grasp of harmony, counterpoint, instrumentation, and formal design. In his idiom, he followed the models of the Romantic school of composition, but he embroidered the basic patterns of traditional music with winsome coloristic touches, approaching the usage of French Impressionism. He was extremely prolific; many of his works underwent multiple transformations from a modest original, usually for solo piano or a chamber group, to a piece for full orch.; in all these forms, his compositions remain eminently playable.

WORKS: DRAMATIC: *Brigands Preferred*, comic opera (1929–46); *Passionate Pilgrim*, incidental music (c. 1937); *The Witch's Curse*, fairy tale opera (1940); *The Birthday Cake*, operetta (c. 1942); *Sunday Costs 5 Pesos*, folk opera (1947; Charlotte, N.C., Nov. 6, 1950); *The Enchanted Princess* (c. 1955); *Adventures on Sunbonnet Hill*, children's operetta (c. 1971). **ORCH.:** *Mars Ascending* (1923); *Karma*, symphonic variations (1928; rev. 1968 as *Of Human Destiny*); *Vox Cathedralis* (1934; N.Y., May 6, 1938); *Portraits: 3 ritratti caratteristici* (Chicago, Dec. 12, 1935); *Solari* (1935–36); *Suite Passacaille* (Los Angeles, Jan. 31, 1936); *Symphony in Variation Form* (1937); *Miniatures* for Strings (1938–39; N.Y., April 23, 1939); *Passacaglia Triptych* (1939–40); *1865 A.D.* (1945; rev. 1958 as *Mississippi Story*; Los Angeles, April 21, 1959); *Pioneers: A Symphonic Saga of Ohio* (1946; rev. 1956; Los Angeles, Feb. 19, 1960); *American Rhapsody* (1948); *A Kennedy Memorial* (1965); *Heroic Elegy* (1970); also many transcriptions of chamber and instrumental pieces. **CHAMBER:** *Ecchi classici* for String Quartet (1924); *Duoforms* for Piano Trio (1929–33); *Lodando la danza* for Oboe, Violin, Cello, and Piano (1932); *Romanza* for Piano Trio (1932); Piano Trio (1932); *Cryptics* for Bassoon and Piano (1932); *Nuances* for Flute and Piano (1938); *En saga* for Violin and Piano (1938); *In the French Manner* for Flute, Cello, and Piano (1942); Trio for Flute, Cello, and Piano (1942); String Trio (1943); *Shadows* for Violin or Cello and Piano (1947); *Pastoral Trio* for Flute, Cello, and Piano (1949); *Epochs* for Violin and Piano (1954–55); Trio for Clarinet, Cello, and Piano (1969); *Cryptics* for Cello and Piano (1973); many piano pieces. **VOCAL:** *Portals*, symphonic song cycle for High Voice and Orch. (1963); *Threnody for Love* for Alto, Flute, Clarinet, Violin, Cello, and Piano (1965); 3 cantatas; choral pieces with orch.; solo songs.—NS/LK/DM

Haudebert, Lucien, French composer; b. Fougères, April 10, 1877; d. Paris, Feb. 24, 1963. He studied organ, then went to Paris, where he took lessons in composition with Fauré. He followed in his music the traditions of César Franck, preferring large sonorities and clear tonal harmonies. He stood aloof from modern developments in France and had little recognition even among traditional musicians, despite praise from Romain Rolland. His most effective work is the oratorio *Dieu Vainqueur* (1916–22). Other significant works are the oratorio *Moïse* (1928), *Symphonie bretonne* (1936),

Symphonie française (1941), *Voyage en Bretagne* for Orch. (1953), and *Chants de la mer* for Voices and Orch. (1950). He also wrote chamber music, including a Quartet for Saxophones.—**NS/LK/DM**

Hauer, Josef Matthias, significant Austrian composer and music theorist; b. Wiener-Neustadt, near Vienna, March 19, 1883; d. Vienna, Sept. 22, 1959. After attending a college for teachers, he became a public school instructor; at the same time, he studied music. An experimenter by nature, with a penchant for mathematical constructions, he developed a system of composition based on "tropes," or patterns, which aggregated to thematic formations of 12 different notes. As early as 1912, he publ. a piano piece, entitled *Nomos* (Law), which contained the germinal principles of 12–tone music; in his theoretical publications, he elaborated his system in greater detail. These were *Über die Klangfarbe*, op.13 (Vienna, 1918; aug. as *Vom Wesen des Musikalischen*, Leipzig and Vienna, 1920; 3rd ed., rev. and aug., 1966); *Deutung des Melos: Eine Frage an die Künstler und Denker unserer Zeit* (Leipzig, Vienna, and Zürich, 1923); *Vom Melos zur Pauke: Eine Einführung in die Zwölftonmusik* (Vienna, 1925; 2nd ed., 1967); *Zwölftontechnik: Die Lehre von den Tropen* (Vienna, 1926; 2nd ed., 1953); *Zwölftonspiel-Neujahr 1947* (Vienna, 1962). Hauer vehemently asserted his priority in 12–tone composition; he even used a rubber stamp on his personal stationery proclaiming himself the true founder of the 12–tone method. This claim was countered, with equal vehemence, but with more justification, by Schoenberg; indeed, the functional basis of 12–tone composition in which the contrapuntal and harmonic structures are derived from the unifying tone row did not appear until Schoenberg formulated it and put it into practice in 1924. Hauer lived his entire life in Vienna, working as a composer, conductor, and teacher. Despite its forbidding character, his music attracted much attention.

WORKS: DRAMATIC: O p e r a : *Salambo* (1930; Austrian Radio, Vienna, March 19, 1983); *Die schwarze Spinne* (1932; Vienna, May 23, 1966). **VOCAL:** *Lateinische Messe* for Chorus, Chamber Orch., and Organ (1926; unfinished; Vienna, June 18, 1972); *Wandlungen*, oratorio for 6 Soloists, Chorus, and Chamber Orch. (1927; Baden-Baden, April 16, 1928); 2 cantatas: *Emilie vor ihrem Brauttag* for Alto and Orch. (1928) and *Der Menschen Weg* for 4 Soloists, Chorus, and Orch., after Hölderlin (1934; Vienna, June 1953); *Vom Leben*, after Holderlin, for Narrator, Small Chorus, and Small Orch. (1928). **OTHER WORKS:** *Nomos* (Sym. No. 1) for 1 or 2 Pianos or Orch. (1912–13; version for 2 Pianos, Sankt Pölten, June 7, 1913); *Nomos* (Sym. No. 2) for Piano or Small Orch. (1913); *Nomos*, 7 little piano pieces (1913); *Apokalyptische Phantasie* (Sym. No. 3) for 2 Pianos or Orch. (1913; version for 2 Pianos, Wiener-Neustadt, May 9, 1914; version for Orch., Graz, Oct. 21, 1969); *Oriental Tale* for Piano (1916); *Nomos* for Piano and String Ensemble (1919); Quintet for Clarinet, Violin, Viola, Cello, and Piano (1924); 6 string quartets (1924–26); 8 suites for Orch. (1924; 1924; 1925, with Baritone; 1926; 1926; 1926, also for String Quartet; 1926; 1927); *Romantische Fantasie* for Small Orch. (1925); *7 Variations* for Flute, Clarinet, Violin, Viola, Cello, and Double Bass (1925); *Symphonische Stücke (Kammerstücke)* for Strings, Piano, and Harmonium (1926); Sinfonietta (1927; Berlin, Dec. 13, 1928); Violin Concerto (1928; Berlin, Nov. 12, 1929); Piano Concerto (1928); *Diverti-*

mento for Small Orch. (1930); *Konzertstücke* for Orch. (1932; from the opera *Die schwarze Spinne*); *Tanzphantasien Nos. 1* and *2* for 4 Soloists and Orch. (1933) and *Nos. 3–7* for Chamber Orch. (1934); *2 Tanzsuiten* for 9 Solo Instruments (1936); *Labyrinthischer Tanz* for Piano, 4–Hands (1952); *Langsamer Walzer* for Orch. (1953); *Chinesisches Streichquartet* (1953); *Hausmusik* for Piano, 4–Hands (1958). Also a series of pieces begun in 1940, each ostentatiously bearing the subtitle *Zwölftonspiel*, for orch. and chamber combinations of all descriptions—their total number exceeding 100—with each one designated by the month and year composed.

BIBL.: H. Picht, *J. M. H., Ein Vorkämpfer geistiger Musikauffassung* (Stuttgart, 1934); M. Lichtenfeld, *Untersuchungen zur Theorie der Zwölftontechnik bei J. M. H.* (Regensburg, 1964); W. Szmolyan, *J. M. H.* (Vienna, 1965); M. Keyton, *A Mathematical Construction of the "Tropen" Occurring in H.'s Musical System* (thesis, La. State Univ., 1976); H. Götte, *Die Kompositionstechniken J. M. H.s: Unter besonderer Berücksichtigung deterministischer Verfahren* (Kassel, 1989).—**NS/LK/DM**

Haufrecht, Herbert, American composer; b. N.Y., Nov. 3, 1909; d. Albany, N.Y., June 23, 1998. He studied piano with Severin Eisenberger at the Cleveland Music School Settlement and composition with Herbert Elwell and Quincy Porter at the Cleveland Inst. of Music, then completed his training in composition with Rubin Goldmark at the Juilliard Graduate School in N.Y (1930–34). He was a composer and arranger for the WPA Federal Theater in N.Y. (1937–39), national music director of Young Audiences, Inc. (1961–68), and an ed. and arranger for several N.Y. music publishers (1968–77). He also was active as a collector of folk music and publ. such vols. as *Folk Sing* (1960), *'Round the World Folk Sing* (1964), *Travelin' on with the Weavers* (1966), *The Judy Collins Songbook* (1969), *Folk Songs in Settings by Master Composers* (1970), and, with N. Cazden and N. Studer, *Folk Songs of the Catskills* (1982). Among his own works are the folk operas *Boney Quillen* (1951) and *A Pot of Broth* (1961–63).—**NS/LK/DM**

Haug, Gustav, Swiss organist, teacher, and composer; b. Strasbourg, Nov. 30, 1871; d. St. Gallen, April 22, 1956. He studied at the Strasbourg Cons., then settled in St. Gallen, where he was active as a church organist and voice teacher. As a composer, he produced a number of singable choral anthems, several works for solo voice with orch. accompaniment, and many songs to German texts.—**NS/LK/DM**

Haug, Hans, Swiss conductor, teacher, and composer; b. Basel, July 27, 1900; d. Lausanne, Sept. 15, 1967. He studied with Petri and Levy at the Basel Cons., with Busoni, and with Courvoisier and J. Pembaur Jr. at the Munich Academy of Music. He served as music director in Grandson and Solothurn; after working as choirmaster and asst. conductor at the Basel City Theater (1928–34), he conducted at the Interlaken Kursaal and at the Swiss Radio in Lausanne (1935–38) and in Zürich (1938–43). He subsequently devoted himself mainly to teaching and composing. His works were in an eminently appealing style.

WORKS: DRAMATIC: O p e r a : *Don Juan in der Fremde* (1929; Basel, Jan. 15, 1930); *Madrisa* (1933; Basel, Jan. 15,

1934); *Tartuffe* (Basel, May 24, 1937); *Der unsterbliche* (1946; Zürich, Feb. 8, 1947); *La colombe égarée* (Basel Radio, 1951); *Le miroir d'Agrippine* (1953–54); *Les fous* (1957; Geneva Radio, Nov. 1959); *Le souper de Venise* (1966); *Le gardien vigilant* (1966). **O p e r a - b a l l e t :** *Orfée* (RTF, Paris, Sept. 24, 1954; 1st stage perf., Lausanne, June 12, 1955). **O p e r e t t a :** *Liederlig Kleeblatt* (1938); *Gilberte de Courgenay* (1940); *Annely us der Linde* (1940); *Barbara* (1942); *Leute von der Strasse* (1944); *La mère Michel* (1945). **O t h e r :** Stage pieces and incidental music. **ORCH.:** *Charlie Chaplin,* symphonic poem (1930); 2 piano concertos (1938, 1962); Sym. (1948); Guitar Concerto (1952); Double Concerto for Oboe, Viola, and Orch. (1953). **CHAMBER:** 3 string quartets; Wind Quartet; Wind Quintet. **VOCAL:** *Michelangelo,* oratorio (1942; Solothurn, Feb. 28, 1943); many cantatas.

BIBL.: J.-L. Matthey, eds., *H. H. Werkverzeichnis* (Lausanne, 1971).—**NS/LK/DM**

Haughton, Chauncey, jazz clarinetist, saxophonist, pianist; b. Chestertown, Md., Feb. 26, 1909; d. July 1, 1989. He was the brother of trombonist John E. "Shorty" Haughton (b. 1904) and trumpeter Clifton Haughton. Their father was also a musician. He began on piano at eight, and took up clarinet while at high school in Baltimore. He later played clarinet and sax in the Morgan Coll. Band. His first professional work in 1927 was with Ike Dixon's Band. He then worked with Elmer Calloway (brother of Cab) and the White Brothers' Band. He came to N.Y. (1932) with Gene Kennedy's Band, worked with Blanche Calloway until 1935, then with Claude Hopkins, Noble Sissle, and Fletcher Henderson before joining Chick Webb. He left Webb in November 1937 to join Cab Calloway, but left him in January 1940 to join a band led by Ella Fitzgerald. He remained with her until 1942 (apart from a brief period with Benny Carter's big band in 1940). He was with Duke Ellington from the summer of 1942 until being drafted in April 1943. After leaving the Army, he did a long U.S.O. tour (winter 1945 to summer 1946) with vocalist Frances Brock, then went to Europe in Don Redman's Band (September 1946). After that unit disbanded in Europe, he played briefly in Scandinavia during 1947, then returned to the U.S. Besides brief work with Cab Calloway in the late 1940s (and a recording session in 1958), he left full-time music making after that.—**JC/LP**

Haugland, Aage, Danish bass-baritone; b. Copenhagen, Feb. 1, 1944. He studied with Mogens Wöldike and Kristian Riis in Copenhagen, making his operatic debut as the Brewer in Martinů's *Veselohra na mostě* at the Norwegian Opera in Oslo in 1968. He then sang with the Royal Opera in Copenhagen (from 1973), and also made guest appearances with other major European opera houses, including London's Covent Garden as Hunding (1975), Milan's La Scala as the King in *Lohengrin* (1981), in Salzburg as Rocco (1982), and in Bayreuth as Hagen (1983). In 1979 he made his U.S. debut as Boris Godunov in St. Louis, as well as his Metropolitan Opera debut in N.Y. (Dec. 13, 1979) as Baron Ochs. He continued to sing at the Metropolitan Opera with success in operas by Wagner, Mussorgsky, Tchaikovsky, Strauss, and Janáček. In 1990 he appeared as King Marke at the Edinburgh Festival. After singing Boris in *Lady Macbeth of the District of Mtsensk* at La Scala in 1992, he was engaged as Varlaam at the Salzburg Easter Festival in 1994. During the 1996–97 season, he appeared as Schoenberg's Moses at the Royal Festival Hall in London. His other roles include Leporello, Sarastro, Gounod's Méphistophélès, and the Grand Inquisitor.—**NS/LK/DM**

Hauk, Minnie (real name, **Amalia Mignon Hauck**), celebrated American soprano; b. N.Y., Nov. 16, 1851; d. Triebschen, near Lucerne, Switzerland, Feb. 6, 1929. Her father was a German carpenter who became involved in the political events of 1848, emigrated to America, and married an American woman; he named his daughter Mignon after the character in Goethe's *Wilhelm Meister.* The family moved to Atchison, Kans., when Minnie was very young; her mother maintained a boarding house at a steamboat landing on the Mo. In 1860 they moved to New Orleans, where Minnie began to sing popular ballads for entertainment. She made her operatic debut at the age of 14 in Brooklyn, in *La Sonnambula* (Oct. 13, 1866), then took lessons with Achille Errani in N.Y. On Nov. 15, 1867, she sang Juliette at the American premiere of Gounod's opera in N.Y. She attracted the attention of the rich industrialist Leonard Jerome and the music publisher Gustave Schirmer, who financed her trip to Europe. She sang in opera in Paris during the summer of 1868; made her London debut at Covent Garden on Oct. 26, 1868; in 1870 she sang in Vienna. She sang the title roles in the first American performances of *Carmen* (N.Y., Oct. 23, 1878) and Massenet's *Manon* (N.Y., Dec. 23, 1885); made her debut at the Metropolitan Opera in N.Y. as Selika in *L'Africaine* on Feb. 10, 1891. She continued to appear there for that season, but following a disagreement with the management, decided to organize her own opera group; with it, she gave the first Chicago performance of *Cavalleria rusticana* (Sept. 28, 1891). She then settled in Switzerland with her husband, Baron Ernst von Hesse-Wartegg, whom she had married in 1881; after his death she lived mostly in Berlin; lost her fortune in the depreciation of her holdings in Germany. In 1919 Geraldine Farrar launched an appeal to raise funds for her in America. Hauk's autobiography, collated by E. Hitchcock, was publ. as *Memories of a Singer* (London, 1925). —**NS/LK/DM**

Haupt, Karl August, German organist, pedagogue, and composer; b. Kuhnau, Silesia, Aug. 25, 1810; d. Berlin, July 4, 1891. He studied with Dehn in Berlin. He played in various churches and became famous for his masterly improvisations in the style of Bach. He was one of the experts consulted for the specifications in building the grand organ at the Crystal Palace in London. He had many distinguished pupils, including about 40 American organists. He publ. a valuable *Choralbuch* (1869). Many of his compositions for organ remain in MS.—**NS/LK/DM**

Hauptmann, Cornelius, German bass; b. Stuttgart, 1951. He studied at the Stuttgart Hochschule für

Musik (graduated, 1982), and with Jakob Stampfli at the Bern Cons., Fischer-Dieskau in Berlin, and Tappy and Schwarzkopf in Salzburg. In 1981 he joined the Stuttgart Opera, where he first attracted notice as Masetto. From 1985 to 1987 he sang with the Heidelberg Opera, where he portrayed King Philip and Osmin. In 1987 he joined the Karlsruhe State Theater and appeared in such roles as Monteverdi's Plutone, Mozart's Sarastro and Figaro, and Verdi's Sparafucile. His appearance as a soloist in the *St. Matthew Passion* under Gardiner's direction in Stuttgart in 1988 led to frequent appearances with leading conductors of the day. In 1991 he sang Osmin at the Royal Festival Hall in London and Sarastro at the Deutsche Oper in Berlin. He portrayed the Speaker in *Die Zauberflöte* at the Opéra de la Bastille in Paris in 1993. In 1995 he was engaged as Sarastro at the Lyons Opera, where he returned in 1996 as Rocco. He also pursued an active career as a lieder artist.—NS/LK/DM

Hauptmann, Moritz, eminent German music theorist, pedagogue, and composer; b. Dresden, Oct. 13, 1792; d. Leipzig, Jan. 3, 1868. His father was an architect and hoped to bring up his son in that profession; however, there was no parental opposition to music studies. Hauptmann took lessons with Scholz (violin), Grosse (piano and harmony), and Morlacchi (composition) in Dresden. He later studied with Weinlig, and in 1811 went to Gotha to study violin and composition with Spohr, becoming his lifelong friend. He went to Vienna in 1813 as a violinist in Spohr's orch. at the Theater an der Wien. In 1812 he joined the Dresden Court Orch. as violinist, and in 1815 he became music teacher in the family of the Russian military governor of Dresden, Prince Repnin, and went with them to Russia, where he remained for 5 years. In 1820 he returned to Dresden, and in 1822 Spohr engaged him as violinist in the Court Orch. at Kassel. In 1842, at Mendelssohn's recommendation, he was appointed cantor at the Thomasschule and prof. of composition at the Leipzig Cons., retaining these posts until his death. He became greatly renowned as a teacher of violin and composition. Among his pupils were Ferdinand David, Joachim, Hans von Bülow, Jadassohn, and Arthur Sullivan. A master of classical form, he was a polished composer, in the tradition of Spohr and Mendelssohn; the architectonic symmetry of his instrumental works and the purity of part-writing in his vocal music aroused admiration among his contemporaries; yet his music failed to endure, and rapidly went into decline after his death. He publ. about 60 works, among them 3 violin sonatas, 4 violin sonatinas, 2 string quartets, piano pieces, sacred works, and a number of lieder, a genre in which he excelled. His theoretical work *Die Natur der Harmonik und Metrik* (Leipzig, 1853; 2nd ed., 1873; Eng. tr., London, 1888) is an attempt to apply Hegel's dialectical philosophy to the realm of music. It exercised considerable influence on the later development of German theory of harmony; among other German scholars, Riemann was influenced by it. Hauptmann's other writings are *Erläuterungen zu J. S. Bachs Kunst der Fuge* (Leipzig, 1841; 2nd ed., 1861), *Die Lehre von der Harmonik* (ed. by O. Paul; Leipzig, 1868; 2nd ed., 1873), and *Opuscula* (misc. writings, ed. by E. Hauptmann; Leipzig, 1874). His letters to Spohr and others were ed. by F. Hiller (Leipzig, 1876). A. Coleridge publ. a selection, in Eng., of Hauptmann's correspondence as *Letters of a Leipzig Cantor* (1892).

BIBL.: O. Paul, *M. H., Eine Denkschrift zur Feier seines Siebzigjährigen Geburtstages am 13. Oktober 1862* (Leipzig, 1862); S. Krehl, *M. H.: Ein Dank- und Gedenkwort* (Leipzig, 1918); P. Rummenhöller, *M. H. als Theoretiker* (Wiesbaden, 1963); D. Jorgenson, *M. H. of Leipzig* (Lewiston, N.Y., 1986).—NS/LK/DM

Hauschild, Wolf-Dieter, German conductor; b. Greiz, Sept. 6, 1937. He was a student of Gerster, Abendroth, and Pflüger at the Weimar Hochschule für Musik before completing his training with Scherchen and Celibidache. After conducting at the Weimar National Theater and at the Kleist Theater in Frankfurt an der Oder, he was conductor of the Radio Choir (1971–74) and the Radio Sym. Orch. (1974–78) in East Berlin. From 1978 to 1985 he was chief conductor of the Leipzig Radio Sym. Orch. and Choir, during which time, in 1981, he became a prof. of conducting at the Berlin Hochschule für Musik. He was music director of the Stuttgart Phil. from 1985 to 1991, and also chief guest conductor of the Berlin Sym. Orch. In 1988 he became a prof. of conducting at the Stuttgart Hochschule für Musik. From 1991 to 1997 he was Generalmusikdirektor in Essen, where his tenure culminated in a mounting of the *Ring* cycle. He also appeared as a guest conductor with various opera houses and orchs. in Germany and abroad.—NS/LK/DM

Hauschka, Vincenz, gifted Bohemian cellist and composer; b. Mies, Jan. 21, 1766; d. Vienna, Sept. 13, 1840. He was a pupil of his father, a schoolteacher, and became chorister in the Prague Cathedral. He also studied composition with Zöger and cello with Christ. He was appointed cellist to Count Joseph von Thun in Prague (1782). He made successful concert tours through Germany performing not only on the cello, but also on the baryton (a popular instrument at the time). He publ. 9 sonatas for cello and a book of vocal canons. In MS are several pieces for the baryton.—NS/LK/DM

Hausegger, Friedrich von, Austrian musicologist, father of **Siegmund von Hausegger;** b. St. Andra, Carinthia, April 26, 1837; d. Graz, Feb. 23, 1899. He was a pupil of Salzmann and Dessoff, and also studied law and became a barrister at Graz. In 1872 he became a teacher of history and theory of music at the Univ. of Graz. He contributed to music periodicals.

WRITINGS: *Musik als Ausdruck* (Vienna, 1885); *Richard Wagner und Schopenhauer* (1890); *Vom Jenseits des Künstlers* (1893); *Die künstlerische Persönlichkeit* (1897); *Unsere deutschen Meister* (ed. by R. Louis; 1901); his *Gesammelte Schriften* was brought out by his son in 1939.—NS/LK/DM

Hausegger, Siegmund von, esteemed Austrian conductor and composer, son of **Friedrich von Hausegger;** b. Graz, Aug. 16, 1872; d. Munich, Oct. 10, 1948. He studied with his father and with Karl Pohlig. At the age of 16, he composed a grand Mass, which he himself conducted; at 18 he brought out in Graz an opera,

Helfrid. Richard Strauss thought well enough of Hausegger as a composer to accept for performance his comic opera *Zinnober*, which he conducted in Munich on June 19, 1898. In 1895–96 Hausegger conducted at the Graz City Theater; in 1897 he was an asst. conductor in Bayreuth. He was the conductor of the Volk-Symphonie-Konzerte in Munich (1899–1902), the Museum Concerts in Frankfurt am Main (1903–06), and the Phil. Concerts in Hamburg (1910–20). From 1918 to 1934 he was director of the Academy of Musical Art in Munich; in 1920 he was named Generalmusikdirektor of the Munich Konzertverein, which became the Munich Phil. in 1928; remained there until his retirement in 1938. He acquired a fine reputation as a conductor in Germany, becoming a champion of Bruckner's syms. in their original versions. As a composer, he wrote in a late German Romantic style. He publ. a monograph, *Alexander Ritter, Ein Bild seines Charakters und Schaffens* (Berlin, 1907), and his father's correspondence with Peter Rosegger (Leipzig, 1924). His collected articles appeared under the title *Betrachtungen zur Kunst* (Leipzig, 1921).

WORKS: DRAMATIC: O p e r a : *Helfrid* (Graz, 1890); *Zinnober* (Munich, June 19, 1898, R. Strauss conducting). **ORCH.:** *Dionysische Fantasie* (1899); 2 symphonic poems: *Barbarossa* (1900) and *Wieland der Schmied* (1904); *Natursymphonie* for Chorus and Orch. (1911); *Aufklänge*, symphonic variations on a children's song (1919). **VOCAL:** Pieces for Men's Chorus and Orch.—NS/LK/DM

Hauser, Franz (actually, František), Bohemian baritone; b. Krasowitz, near Prague, Jan. 12, 1794; d. Freiburg im Breisgau, Aug. 14, 1870. He was a student of Tomaschek in Prague. In 1817 he made his operatic debut there as Sarastro, and continued to sing there until 1821. He then appeared in Kassel (1821–35), Dresden (1825–26), Frankfurt am Main (1826–29), Vienna (1829), London (1832), and Berlin (1835). In 1837 he went to Vienna as a voice teacher, and later served as director of the Munich Cons. (1846–64). In 1866 he brought out a singing manual. Among his finest roles were Figaro, William Tell, and Spohr's Faust.—LK/DM

Hauser, Miska, Austrian violinist and composer; b. Pressburg, 1822; d. Vienna, Dec. 8, 1887. He studied with Kreutzer in Vienna, and traveled as a child prodigy in Europe; from 1853 to 1858 made a grand tour of America and Australia. He wrote an operetta, *Der blinde Leiermann*, numerous violin pieces, of which his meretricious *Rapsodie hongroise* and *Lieder ohne Worte* enjoyed undeserved popularity, and *American Rhapsody* for Violin and Piano (1855). During his American tour he sent correspondence to the *Ostdeutsche Post* which was collected and publ. in 2 vols., *Aus dem Wanderbuch eines österreichischen Virtuosen* (Leipzig, 1858–59). *History of Music in San Francisco* (San Francisco, 1939) contains Eng. trs. of some of these reports, which are not devoid of interest.—NS/LK/DM

Hausmann, Robert, notable German cellist and pedagogue; b. Rottleberode, Harz, Aug. 13, 1852; d. Vienna, Jan. 18, 1909. He was a student of Theodor

Müller in Braunschweig before pursuing training at the Berlin Hochschule für Musik; later he studied with Piatti in London and with Cadenabbia. After playing in Count Hochberg's quartet in Dresden (1872–76), he was a member of the Joachim Quartet in Berlin (1879–1907). He also was a prof. at the Berlin Hochschule für Musik (from 1879). Brahms wrote his 2nd Cello Sonata for Hausmann, who also was soloist (with Joachim) in the premiere of the Brahms Double Concerto (Cologne, Oct. 18, 1887).—NS/LK/DM

Haussermann, John (William Jr.), American composer; b. Manila, Philippines, Aug. 21, 1909; d. Denver, May 5, 1986. He was taken to New Richmond, Ohio, as a child and studied piano with local teachers. In 1924 he enrolled in the Cincinnati Cons. of Music, studying organ with Parvin Titus and theory with George Leighton. In 1930 he went to Paris, where he studied organ with Dupré and composition with Le Flem. Upon returning to the U.S., he was mainly active as a composer. His music is marked by a pragmatic sense of formal cohesion, which does not exclude a flair for innovation, as exemplified by his Concerto for Voice and Orch.

WORKS: ORCH.: 3 syms.: No. 1 (1938; partial perf., N.Y., May 28, 1939), No. 2 (1941; Cincinnati, March 31, 1944), and No. 3 (1947; Cincinnati, April 1, 1949); *The After Christmas Suite* (Cincinnati, March 22, 1938); Concerto for Voice and Orch. (Cincinnati, April 24, 1942); *Ronde carnavalesque* (N.Y., Feb. 6, 1949); *Stanza* for Violin and Orch. (Mallorca, Spain, Feb. 22, 1956); Concerto for Organ and Strings (1985). **CHAMBER:** Quintet for Flute, Oboe, Clarinet, Bassoon, and Harpsichord (1935); String Quartet (1937); *Suite rustique* for Flute, Cello, and Piano (1937); *Divertissements* for String Quartet (1940); *Poème et Clair de lune* for Violin and Piano (1940); Violin Sonata (1941); *Serenade* for Theremin and Strings (1945). **KEYBOARD: P i a n o :** *24 préludes symphoniques* (1932–33); *Sonatine fantastique* (1932); *Pastoral fantasie* for 2 Pianos, 4–Hands (1933); *Ballade, Burlesque, et Légende* (1936); *7 Bagatelles* (1948); *9 Impromptus* (1958); *5 Harmonic Études* (1968). **O r g a n :** Numerous pieces. **VOCAL:** *Sacred Cantata* for Baritone and Orch. (Cincinnati, Jan. 31, 1965); many songs.—NS/LK/DM

Haussmann, Valentin, significant German composer; b. Gerbstedt, near Eisleben, c. 1565; d. c. 1614. He studied at the Regensburg Gymnasium Poeticum, receiving instruction in music from the Kantor, Andreas Raselius. He then traveled extensively throughout Germany, serving various courts, municipalities, and private patrons. He was also active in collecting and editing music. He tr. Italian texts for several anthologies, which helped to spread Italian music in Germany. His most important contribution to German music was his instrumental music, which included intradas, pavanes, galliards, and the *Fuga prima*. A musician named Valentin Haussman and 2 others named Valentin Bartholomaeus Haussmann were apparently related to him. See F. Boelsche, ed., *Valentin Haussmann: Ausgewahlte Instrumentalwerke* in Denkmäler Deutscher Tonkunst, XVI (1904).

WORKS (all publ. in Nuremberg unless otherwise given): **VOCAL: S e c u l a r :** *Neue teutsche weltliche Lieder...lieblich zu singen, und auff Instrumenten wol zu gebrauchen* for 5 and 6

Voices (1592); *Eine fast liebliche art derer noch mehr teutschen weltlichen Lieder* for 4 and 5 Voices (1594); *Neue teutsche weltliche Canzonette, lieblich zu singen, und auff Instrumenten zugebrauchen* for 4 Voices (1596); *Neue teutsche weltliche Lieder, mit höfelichen kurtzweiligen Texten, lieblich zu singen, und auff Instrumenten zugebrauchen* for 5 Voices (1597); *Andere noch mehr neue teutsche weltliche Lieder, nach art der Canzonetten, auff schöne lustige Text gesetzt* (1597); *Neue liebliche Melodien unter neue teutsche weltliche Texte, deter jeder einen besonden Namen anzeiget, dess mehrern theils zum Täntze zugebrauchen* for 4 Voices (1598; not extant; 2nd ed., 1600); *Neue artige und liebliche Tantze, zum theil mit Texten, dass man kan mit Menschlicher Stimme zu Instrumenten singen, zum Theil ohne Text gesetzt* for 5 Voices (1598; not extant; 2nd ed., 1599); *Fragmenta, oder, 35 noch übrige neue weltliche teutsche Lieder* for 4 and 5 Voices (1602); *Venusgarten, darinnen 100 ausserlesene gantz liebliche mehrerntheils polnische Täntze, unter welche ersten 50 feine höfliche amorosische Texte, von ihme Haussmann gemacht und untergelegt seind* (1602); *Fasciculus neuer Hochzeit und Braut Lieder* for 4 to 6 Voices (1602); *Extract auss...fünff Theilen der teutschen weltlichen Lieder...mit lustigen kurtzen lateinischen lemmatibus gezieret: Der erste Theil* for 5 Voices (1603); *Der ander Theil dess Extracts auss...fünff Theilen der teutschen weltliche Lieder...diser Theil* for 4 Voices (1603); *Rest von polnischen und andern Täntzen, nach art, wie im Venusgarten zu finden, colligirt, und zume Theil gemacht, auch mit weltlichen amorosischen Texten unterlegt* for 5 Voices (1603); *Ausszug auss...zweyen unterschiedlichen Wercken...mit und ohne Text* for 5 Voices (1608); *Melodien unter weltliche Texte, da jeder einen besonden Namen anzeiget, umb ein guten Theil vermehret und von neuem auffgelegt* for 5 Voices (1608); *Musicalische teutsche weltliche Gesänge, nach art der italianischen Canzonen und Madrigalien* for 4 to 8 Voices (1608). **S a c r e d :** *Manipulus sacrarum cantionum* for 5 and 6 Voices (1602); *Ad imitationem cantionis italicae Fuggi pur se sai &c. missam* for 8 Voices *...cum duabus motectis* for 10 and 14 Voices (1604); also a Magnificat for 8 Voices; a Mass for 8 Voices; motets. **OCCASIONAL WORKS:** *Psalmus XLVI, Magnifico, nobilibus, amplissimis...viris, Dn. Burgrabio regio, coss: & reliquis senatorij ordinis viris inclytae Reipub: Elbingensis* for 5 Voices (Königsberg, 1588); *Threnodia (Justorum animae) in obitum reverendi et clarissimi viri D. Ludovict Rabus* for 6 Voices (Tübingen, 1592); *Ode sapphica adv. Turcae immanitatem* for 6 Voices (Magdeburg, 1597; not extant); *Epithalamium nuptiis Keckii* for 6 Voices (Magdeburg, 1597; not extant); *Harmonia melica (Tempus adest) nuptiis Georgii Reimanni...et Catharinae...Ketneri* for 5 Voices (Königsberg, 1598); *Hochzeit Lied zu Ehren dem D. Schitzing* for 5 Voices (Königsberg, 1598; not extant); *Teutsche Villanel aus dem 10: capitel der Sprüche Salomonis, auff den Nahmen des Herrn Zacharias Kreelen in Elbing* for 5 Voices (Königsberg, 1598; not extant); *2 Brautlieder zu Ehren dem L. Levit* for 5 Voices (Königsberg, 1598; not extant; in collaboration with Emmelius); *Harmonia melica pro felicissimi novi anni viris* (Königsberg, 1599); *Urbs Mariaeburgum fortissima* for 5 Voices (Königsberg, 1599; not extant); *Villanellae nuptiales duae* for 4 Voices (Frankfurt an der Oder, n.d.). **I n s t r u m e n t a l :** *Neue Intrade...fürnemlich auff Fiolen lieblich zugebrauchen: nach disen sind etliche englische Paduan und Galliarde anderer Composition zu finden, a 5 and 6* (1604); *Neue paduane und Galliarde...fürnemlich auff Fiolen lieblich zugebrauchen, a 5* (1604). **EDITIONS:** *Ausszugauss L. Marentii 4 Theilen seiner italienischen Villanellen und Neapolitanen, mit teutschen Texten gezierest* for 3 Voices (1606); *Canzonette Horatii Vecchi und Gemignani Capi Lupi...mit teutschen Texten beleget* for 3 Voices (1606); *Johann Jacobi Gastoldi und anderer Autorn Tricinia...mit teutschen weltlichen Texten* for 3 Voices (1607; including 5 works by Haussmann); *Liebliche frölichce Ballette welche zuvor von T. Morlei unter*

italienische Texte gesetzt...mit unterlegung teutscher Texte for 5 Voices (1609); *Die erste Class der Canzonetten Horatii Vecchi...mit Unterlegung teutscher Texte* for 4 Voices (1610; including 1 work by Haussmann); *Die ander Class der Canzonetten Horatii Vecchi...mit Unterlegung teutscher Texte* for 4 Voices (1610); *Die dritte Class der Canzonetten Horatii Vecchi...mit Unterlegung teutscher Texte* for 4 Voices (1610).

BIBL.: R. Lynn, *V. H. (1565–70–ca. 1614): A Thematic-Documentary Catalogue of His Works* (includes documentary biography of K.-P. Koch; Stuyvesant, N.Y., 1997).—NS/LK/DM

Hausswald, Günter, distinguished German musicologist; b. Rochlitz an der Mülde, March 11, 1908; d. Stuttgart, April 23, 1974. He studied piano with Max Pauer and composition with Karg-Elert in Leipzig, theory with Grabner at the Leipzig Hochschule für Musik, and musicology with Kroyer and others at the Univ. of Leipzig, where he took his Ph.D. in 1937 with the diss. *Johann David Heinichens Instrumentalwerke* (publ. in Wolfenbüttel and Berlin, 1937); he completed his Habilitation in 1949 at the Dresden Technical Coll. with his *Mozarts Serenaden* (publ. in Leipzig, 1951). From 1933 to 1945 he taught school in Dresden; then was dramaturge at the Dresden State Opera (1947–53); he also lectured at the Dresden Hochschule für Musik and at the Univ. of Jena from 1950 to 1953. He then settled in West Germany, where he ed. the monthly *Musica* (1958–70); was also program director for the South German Radio at Stuttgart (1960–68). His important monographs include *Heinrich Marschner* (Dresden, 1938), *Die deutsche Oper* (Cologne, 1941), *Die Bauten des Staatstheater Dresden* (Dresden, 1948), *Das neue Opernbuch* (Dresden, 1951; 5th ed., 1956), *Richard Strauss* (Dresden, 1953), and *Dirigenten: Bild und Schrift* (Berlin, 1966). He also contributed exemplary eds. to the complete works of Telemann, Gluck, Bach, and Mozart.—NS/LK/DM

Hautzig, Walter, Austrian-born American pianist and teacher; b. Vienna, Sept. 28, 1921. He studied at the Vienna Academy of Music, then left Austria after the rise of the Nazis to power, and went to Jerusalem and studied at the Cons. there. He continued his musical education at the Curtis Inst. of Music in Philadelphia with Harry Kaufmann and Mieczyslaw Munz; also in N.Y. with Artur Schnabel. On Oct. 31, 1943, he made his debut at N.Y.'s Town Hall. He became a naturalized American citizen in 1945. After World War II, he made tours all over the world. In 1979 he represented the U.S. in the first visit of an American pianist to the People's Republic of China since the Cultural Revolution. He taught at the Peabody Cons. in Baltimore from 1960 to 1987; also gave master classes at the Hartt School of Music in Hartford, Conn. (from 1969).—NS/LK/DM

Havelka, Svatopluk, Czech composer; b. Vrbice, May 2, 1925. He studied in Prague with Jirák (1945–47) and at the Charles Univ. there with Hutter, Sychra, and Leibich (graduated, 1949). He worked in the music dept. of the Czech Radio in Ostrava (1949–50), and concurrently was founder–artistic director of the NOTA Ensemble. After working as an instructor and composer with the Army Art Ensemble (1950–54), he devoted himself fully to composition. He was a prof. of composition at the Prague Academy of Performing Arts from 1990. In 1961 and 1989 he was awarded the State Prize, and in 1987 he was made a Merited Artist of his nation. After composing in the nationalist tradition with infusions of Moravian modalities, he turned to a progressive style that embraced various modern techniques.

WORKS: DRAMATIC: Music for over 70 full-length and 150 short films; incidental music to plays; *Pyrrhos*, ballet (1970). **ORCH.:** *Night Music* (1944); Suite for Small Orch. (1947); *Pastorale* Nos. 1 (1948) and 2 (1951); Sym. (Prague, Nov. 5, 1956); *Foam*, symphonic poem (1965; Olomouc, Feb. 9, 1966); *Ernesto Ché Guevara*, symphonic poem (1969); *Hommage à Hieronymus Bosch*, symphonic fantasy (1974); *Children's Suite* (1982); *Sign of the Times* (1996). **CHAMBER:** Nonet (1976); *Percussionata*, suite for Percussion (1978); *Quiet Joy* for Viola (1985); *Disegno* for Flute (1986); *Hommage to Fra Angelica* for Guitar (1987); *Soliloquia animae ad Deum* for Clarinet and Piano (1991); *The Hidden Manna and a White Stone* for 2 Percussionists (1992). **VOCAL:** *4 Baroque Songs* for Medium Voice and Piano (1944; rev. as *Rose of Wounds* for Medium Voice and Orch., 1974); *4 Musical-Dramatic Suites* for Solo Voice, Narrator, Chorus, and Chamber Orch., after Moravian folk poetry (1948, 1949, 1949, 1951); *Spring*, vocal rhapsody for 3 Solo Voices, Chorus, Children's Chorus, and Orch. (1949); *In Praise of Light*, cantata for Soprano, Alto, Bass, Chorus, and Orch. (1959); *Heptameron: Poem on Nature and Love* for Soprano, Alto, Tenor, Bass, Narrator, and Orch. (1964); *Epistle of Poggio Bracciolini to Leonardo Bruni of Arrezo on the Condemnation of Master Jeroným of Prague*, oratorio for Soprano, Alto, Tenor, Bass, 3 Choruses, Orch., and Organ (1984); *Profeteia* for Children's Chorus, Orch., and Organ (1988); *Agapé je Láska* (Agape is Love) for Soprano, 3 Strings, and Piano (1998).—NS/LK/DM

Havemann, Gustav, German violinist and teacher; b. Güstrow, March 15, 1882; d. Schöneiche, near Berlin, Jan. 2, 1960. He was a pupil of Joachim at the Berlin Hochschule für Musik and, while still a youth, played in the Schwerin Court Orch. He was concertmaster in Lübeck, Darmstadt (1903–09), and of the Hamburg Phil. (from 1909). In 1911 he became a teacher at the Leipzig Cons. After serving as concertmaster of the Dresden Court (later State) Opera Orch. (1915–20), he was a prof. at the Berlin Hochschule für Musik (1920–45). He also was founder–1st violinist of the Havemann Quartet, which played much modern music. He publ. *Die Violintechnik bis zur Vollendung* (2 vols., Cologne, 1928).—NS/LK/DM

Havens, Richie, long-careered folk-protest singer; b. Brooklyn, N.Y., Jan. 21, 1941. Richie Havens's father was a "by ear" piano player who worked with several bands around N.Y. while raising his family in the notorious Brownsville section of Brooklyn (shortly before it started to earn its notoriety). There, young Richard sang gospel and doo-wop. He escaped to Greenwich Village in his late teens, first as a beat style poet, then as a painter. He finally picked up a guitar in the early 1960s, figured out how to tune it to an open D chord and started playing chords with his thumb, dulcimer style. Before long, his singular, intensely rhythmic style and unique gruff voice earned him a

good sized following at local clubs. He recorded demos for noted producer Alan Douglas. Havens hooked up with Bob Dylan's manager, Albert Grossman, in the mid-1960s. Grossman helped sign him to Verve's new folk label. Haven's first album, *Mixed Bag* contained the song "Handsome Johnny," co-written by aspiring actor Louis Gossett Jr. His next album, *Somethin' Else Again* hit the charts, drawing with it both *Mixed Bag* and the set of electric demos he recorded with Alan Douglas that Douglas finally saw fit to release.

While he enjoyed a mildly successful recording career, live performance was his mainstay. A fixture at festivals since the 1966 Newport Folk festival, Havens appeared at England's Isle of Wight and was the opening act at the original Woodstock festival. He had originally been slated to go on third and play for 20 minutes, but he was the first artist to arrive due to the traffic. He went on stage with his guitar and a conga player and commanded the stage for nearly three hours, improvising his last (of six) encores, a variation on the old hymn "Sometimes I Feel Like a Motherless Child" that he called "Freedom." This track was immortalized in both the film of the event and on the soundtrack. Haven's first album after the film was released, *Alarm Clock*, featured a version of the Beatles' "Here Comes the Sun." It became Havens's only pop hit, charting at #16 in 1971. The album rose as high as #29. It represented the peak of his recording career.

Havens has recorded steadily since then, turning out several dozen albums that sell modestly. He continues to play more than 200 shows a year. He has also acted in several films, including *Catch My Soul* (1974) and the Richard Pryor film *Greased Lightning* (1977). He has done voiceover work for McDonalds, Budweiser and even won one of advertising's cherished Clio awards for his work on a Kodak commercial. His book, *They Can't Hide Us Anymore* came out during the summer of 1999.

DISC.: *The Richie Havens Record* (1965); *Electric Havens* (1966); *Mixed Bag* (1967); *Somethin' Else Again* (1968); *Stonehenge* (1970); *A State of Mind* (1971); *Alarm Clock* (1971); *The Great Blind Degree* (1971); *Richie Havens on Stage* (live; 1973); *Portfolio* (1973); *Mixed Bag 2* (1974); *Richie Havens* (1975); *The End of the Beginning* (1976); *Mirage* (1977); *Connections* (1980), *Richard P Havens* (1983); *Common Ground* (1984); *Simple Things* (1987); *Live at the Cellar Door* (1990); *Sings Beatles & Dylan* (1990); *Now* (1991); *Cuts to the Chase* (1994); *Yes* (1994).

WRITINGS: Richie Havens and Steve Davidowitz, *They Can't Hide Us Anymore* (N.Y., 1999).—HB

Havingha, Gerhardus, Dutch organist and music theorist; b. Groningen, Nov. 15, 1696; d. Alkmaar, March 6, 1753. He studied with his father, a church organist at Groningen, and then became an organist at various churches in the Netherlands. He publ. *Oorspronk en Voortgang der orgelen* (Alkmaar, 1727; reprinted 1973), an apologia defending his reconstruction of the Alkmaar organ utilizing equal temperament. He publ. a vol. of Suites for Harpsichord (Amsterdam, 1724; ed. by J. Watelet in Monumenta Musicae Byzantinae, VII, 1951).—NS/LK/DM

Hawel, Jan Wincenty, Polish composer, conductor, and pedagogue; b. Pszów, July 10, 1936. He studied music education (degree, 1960), composition with Bolesław Szabelski (degree, 1964), and conducting with Karol Stryja (degree, 1967) at the State Higher School of Music in Katowice. He then joined its faculty as a teacher of composition and conducting, and from 1981 to 1987 and again from 1990 served as rector. In 1981 he founded the Silesian Chamber Orch., which he subsequently served as artistic director and conductor. His compositions have won various prizes, including 1st prize in the Artur Malawski Competition in 1970, 1st prize in the Grzegorz Fitelberg Competition and in the Opole Spring Competition in 1972, and 1st prize in the National Competition in Warsaw in 1981.

WORKS: ORCH.: 7 syms.: No. 1 (1962), No. 2 (n.d.), No. 3 (1974; Rzeszów, June 16, 1979), No. 4 (1976–77), No. 5 (1978; Katowice, March 14, 1979), No. 6 (n.d.), and No. 7, *Musica sacra* for Voice, Chorus, and Orch. (1990–91); *Kontrasty* (Contrasts; 1964; Wrocław, Nov. 14, 1965); *Konstrukcje* (Constructions; 1965); *Sinfonia concertante No. 2* for Organ and Orch. (1972) and *No. 6* for Piano and Orch. (1979; Katowice, April 29, 1983); *Pieśń o radości* (Song About Joy) for 2 Wind Orchs. and Percussion (Warsaw, July 6, 1980); *Medytacje wielkanocne* (Eastern Meditations) for Strings (1983); *Odgłosy lata* for Oboe and/or English Horn and Strings (1985–86); Concertino for Harpsichord or Piano and Strings (1985); Violin Concerto (1986–87); *Moments musicaux* for Strings (1988); *Tatra's Landscape* for Strings (1993). CHAMBER: 6 string quartets: No. 1 (1959), No. 2 (1971–72), No. 3 (1980; Kraków, April 4, 1981), No. 4 (1982; Kraków, Dec. 15, 1983), No. 5 (1985), and No. 6, *Requiem* (1991; Wrocław, Feb. 26, 1992); 2 Pieces for Chamber Ensemble (1959–60); Wind Septet (1960); *Radosne pieśni* (Joyful Songs) for 14 Instruments (1963); *Divertimento* for Trombone, Piano, and Percussion (1968); *Capriccio-Fantasia No. 1* for Double Bass (1970) and *No. 3, Kyrie eleison* for Violin (1996); *Preludium* for Double Bass (1975; Katowice, May 23, 1979); *Interludium* for Double Bass (1976; Katowice, May 23, 1979); Sonata for Solo Violin (1976; Katowice, April 5, 1978); *Musica concertante* for 6 Players (1976; Kraków, Dec. 15, 1977); Concertino for Harpsichord and 2 String Quartets (1978); Concerto for Solo Guitar (1978; Katowice, Feb. 27, 1980); *Sonata morska* (Sea Sonata) for Cello (1979; Katowice, May 20, 1980); *Tryptyk* for Amplified Harpsichord and Piano (1980); *Canto "Gaudeamus omnes"* for String Quartet (1998). KEYBOARD: P i a n o : *Variazioni* (1968); *Witrae* (Stained Glass Windows; 1972); *Capriccio-Fantasia No. 2* for 2 Pianos (1975; Słupsk, Sept. 8, 1976); *Rapsodia "Gloria"* (1997). O r g a n : *Studium* (1967); *Passacaglia* (1968; Katowice, March 24, 1977). H a r p s i c h o r d : *Partita* (1979; Kraków, Aug. 30, 1981). VOCAL: *Profile* for Men's Chorus and Orch. (1962); *Impresje leśne* (Woodland Impression), oratorio for Reciter, Chorus, and Orch. (1969); *Magnificat* for Vocal Ensemble and Orch. (1974; Poznań, March 30, 1989); *Barwy dnia—Trzy zdarzenia muzyczne* (Colors of the Day—Three Musical Happenings) for 2 Soloists, Flute, Cello, Harpsichord, and Tape (1978); *Hymnus* for Chorus and Winds (Katowice, Dec. 18, 1980); Vocal Concerto (1981; Katowice, March 27, 1984); 3 Poems for Voice and Instrumental Ensemble, after Miłosz (1981); *Oratorium polski* (Polish Oratorio) for Soloists, Reciter, 2 Choruses, and Orch. (1981; Katowice, April 29, 1983); *Missa pro pace* for Chorus (1982–83); *Threnody* for Chorus (1986–87); *Cztery pierwsze pieśni* (Four First Songs) for Voice and Orch. (1991); 3 Poems for Voice and Chamber Orch. (1992); *Vesper Psalms* for Soloist, Chorus, and Orch. (1994); *Psalm—Laudate Dominum* for Voice, Chorus, and Orch. (1995); various choruses.—NS/LK/DM

Hawes, William, English violinist, conductor, and composer; b. London, June 21, 1785; d. there, Feb. 18, 1846. He was a chorister in the Chapel Royal (1795–1801). From 1802 to 1805 he played violin in the orch. at London's Covent Garden; he also became a deputy lay vicar at Westminster Abbey in 1803. In 1805 he was made a Gentleman of the Chapel Royal, serving as its master of the children from 1817; he also was master of the choristers at St. Paul's Cathedral from 1812. From 1824 to 1836 he served as music director of the English Opera House (Lyceum) in London, where he introduced Weber's *Der Freischütz* to the English public in 1824, to which he added some airs of his own. He adapted many operas for the English stage. His own works included light operas, glees, madrigals, and sacred pieces.—NS/LK/DM

Hawkins, Coleman (Randolph), famed and influential jazz tenor saxophonist; b. St. Joseph, Mo., Nov. 21, 1904; d. N.Y., May 19, 1969. At the age of four Hawkins began to study the piano, at seven the cello, and at nine the saxophone. He studied music at Washburn Coll. in Topeka, Kans. (where he's not found in the records but may have gone part-time), and in Chicago. At 16 he was playing professionally in and around Kansas City. In the summer of 1921, he was signed by Mamie Smith to join her Jazz Hounds and began recording with her that year. He toured extensively with Smith until early in 1923, when he left her to remain in N.Y. Hawkins gigged with various bands and also did freelance recordings with Fletcher Henderson. He was part of a group of freelance musicians who chose Henderson to front them for an audition in 1923, and landed a gig. Hawkins was a regular member of Henderson's Orch. from 1924 until early 1934, occasionally doubling on bass sax and very occasionally soloing on clarinet. His early solos were rugged and sometimes used slap- tonguing; in later years, he disowned these early attempts. However, by 1929, he had a smoother sound and a flowing use of double-time as on the medium-slow "One Hour." In 1932 he was experimenting with free rhythms in a string of solos with Henderson such as on "Honeysuckle Rose" and "New King Porter Stomp." Though Hawkins was not generally known as a composer, in 1933 Henderson recorded his whole-tone essay "Queer Notions." By the end of that year he had developed a rhythmically more straightforward, harmonically complex style and had met Lester Young and other tenor challengers at a legendary Kansas City jam session in December. At an invitation from Jack Hylton of England, he left Henderson to tour Europe as a soloist. He arrived in England in March 1934 and remained abroad until July 1939, working all across Europe accompanied by various local bands and also other expatriates including Benny Carter. Hawkins returned to N.Y. in July 1939 and formed his own big band for club work by November. Hawkins recorded "Body and Soul" that month (the band only provides the closing chord), a Top 20 hit at the time and an enduring jazz classic. The big band was active until February 1941, then reverted to a small band that worked through 1943. Unlike many of his generation, he had no problem with bop; he led what is often called the first bop session, a medium-sized band with Dizzy Gillespie and Max Roach, in February 1944. He recorded and toured in 1944 with Thelonious Monk, whom he would continue to champion. Hawkins led his own sextet in Calif. with Howard McGhee for most of 1945, including an appearance in the film *The Crimson Canary*. Perhaps during that year, or a few years later (many sources says 1949), he recorded the first unaccompanied saxophone solos: "Hawk Variation" and the astonishing "Picasso," which appears to be very loosely based on an out of tempo treatment of the chords to a standard ("Body and Soul" or "Prisoner of Love") but more importantly retains the feeling of free improvisation. It was said to have required 11 takes but the others appear to be lost. (He did other solo saxophone pieces in the 1950s, inspiring Sonny Rollins to do the same.)

In 1946, Hawkins took part in first national Jazz at the Philharmonic tour. He used as sidepersons young musicians Miles Davis, Fats Navarro, J. J. Johnson, and Hank Jones; this group made the first recordings of Monk's tunes "Well You Needn't" and "I Mean You." Hawkins returned to Europe in May 1948 for appearances at Paris Jazz Festival, and again visited Europe in late 1949–50. During the 1950s he did extensive touring with Norman Granz's J.A.T.P, including several trips to Europe. He also co- led a successful quintet with Roy Eldridge and toured American Service Bases in Europe with Illinois Jacquet's Band (autumn 1954). Through the 1950s, Hawkins made prolific freelance recordings; he was featured at all major jazz festivals in the U.S. and appeared on major television shows and films devoted to jazz. During the early- to mid-1960s, Hawkins continued to work N.Y. clubs leading his own small groups. In 1962, he recorded with Duke Ellington. During the last years of his life he toured Britain as a soloist in November 1967. Hawkins continued to work regularly until a few weeks before his death, and appeared with Roy Eldridge on a Chicago television show early in 1969.

Hawkins's harmonic detail, full tone, and wide vibrato became the standard for tenor saxophone. Some credited him with being the first great jazz performer on the instrument, although Hawkins himself granted this honor to earlier musicians. Nonetheless, he was considered the unchallenged leader on the instrument until the advent of Lester Young in the late 1930s. (Hawkins pointedly omitted Young when discussing saxophonists, perhaps his way of dealing with the perceived competition.) During the late 1940s, Hawkins initiated a second career, championing younger musicians and adapting to the changing musical landscape from swing to bop. He remained a vibrant player into his later years, outliving his rival.

DISC.: *H. in Holland* (1935); *Body and Soul* (1939); *At the Savoy Gardens* (1940); *Thanks for the Memory* (1944); *Rainbow Mist* (1944); *Bean's Talking Again* (1944); *Hollywood Stampede* (1945); *H. Variation* (1945; solo saxophone); *Bean and the Boys* (1946); *C. H. Set* (1949); *Disorder at the Border* (1952); *Think Deep* (1957); *H. Flies High* (1957); *C. H. Encounters Ben Webster* (1957); *C. H. and His Friends* (1958; Art Ford soundtracks); *H. Eyes* (1959); *Dali* (1959); *Centerpiece* (1959); *Blowin' up a Breeze* (1959); *At the Bayou Club, Vol. 1, 2* (1959); *Essen Jazz Festival All Stars* (1959; w. Bud Powell); *C. H.* (1960; with Thad Jones); *Bean Stalkin'* (1960); *H.!*

Eldridge! Hodges! Alive (1962); *H.! Alive! at the Village Gate* (1962); *Duke Ellington Meets C. H.* (1962); *Desafinado* (1962); *Today and Now* (1963); *Wrapped Tight* (1965); *Rifftide* (1965); *Meditations* (1965); *Sirius* (1966).

BIBL.: J. Chilton, *The Song of the Hawk: The Life and Recordings of C. H.* (Ann Arbor, Mich., 1990).—**JC/LP**

Hawkins, Erskine (Ramsey), jazz trumpeter, band leader; b. Birmingham, Ala., July 26, 1914; d. Willingboro, N.J., Nov. 11, 1993. He was one of the most popular bandleaders in black America, recording for RCA Victor from 1938–50. When the black newspapers in the 1940s had headlines about "Hawkins" or "Hawk," it was almost always Erskine who was meant. His father was killed in action during World War I. He started playing drums at the age of seven, switched to trombone, then specialized on trumpet from the age of 13 and was an immediate Louis Armstrong devotee. He spent several years at the State Teachers Coll. in Montgomery, Ala., and was appointed leader of the school band, The Bama State Collegians. The band originally came to N.Y. in 1934, fronted by J. B. Sims, but subsequently worked under Hawkins's name. Their big hits included "Tuxedo Junction" (1939; later covered by Glenn Miller), "Tippin' In" (1945), "Somebody's Rocking My Dreamboat," and "After Hours" (1940), written by Avery Parrish, the band's pianist. Hawkins was a high-note specialist on trumpet, billed as, with some PR hyperbole, "The 20th Century Gabriel." Other band soloists included Dud Bascomb and Julian Dash (who co-wrote "Tuxedo Junction" with Hawkins). Throughout the 1940s and 1950s the band retained its big following, particularly at the Savoy Ballroom (N.Y.). During the 1940s, they traveled all over the South from their N.Y. base. In the 1960s, Hawkins occasionally led big band for specific bookings (and a May 1971 recording), but worked mainly with his own quartet, including a long residency at the Concord Hotel (N.Y.) (1971) and other gigs through the late 1970s. In 1947 received an Honorary Doctorate of Music from Ala. State Coll.

DISC. *Tuxedo Junction* (1938); *At the Blue Room* (1945); *Tippin' In* (1945); *Live at Club Soul Sound* (1971).—**JC/LP**

Hawkins, John, Canadian composer, pianist, and teacher; b. Montreal, July 26, 1944. He studied piano with Lubka Kolessa at the Montreal Cons. (premier prix, 1967); he also studied piano and composition (with Anhalt) at McGill Univ. in Montreal (B.Mus., 1967; Concert Diploma, 1968; M.M.A., 1970), and attended Boulez's conducting class in Basel (1969). In 1970 he became a teacher at the Univ. of Toronto. In 1983 he won the Jules Léger Prize for his *Breaking Through* for Voice, Piano, and Percussion. His works primarily reflect the examples set by Stravinsky and Webern, with an individualistic streak notable for their lyrical qualities.

WORKS: *8 Movements* for Flute and Clarinet (1966); *5 Pieces for Piano* (1967); *3 Cavatinas* for Soprano and Chamber Ensemble (1967); *Remembrances* for Chamber Ensemble (1969); *2 Pieces* for Orch. (1970); *Waves* for Soprano and Piano (1971); *Spring Song* for Chorus (1974); *Études* for 2 Pianos (1974); Trio for Flute, Cello, and Xylophone (1975); Wind Quintet (1977); *Prelude and Prayer* for Tenor and Orch. (1980); *Dance, Improvisa-*

tion and Song for Clarinet and Piano (1981; rev. 1982); *Breaking Through* for Voice, Piano, and Percussion (1982); *Dance Variations* for Percussion Quartet (1983; rev. 1986); *3 Archetypes* for String Quartet (1984; rev. 1986); *substance-of-we- feeling* for 2 Percussion (1985); *2 Popular Pieces* for 2 Guitars (1986); *The Cicada's Song to the Sun* for Soprano, Oboe, and Guitar (1987); *Light to Dark* for Soprano, Clarinet, and Piano (1987); *The 1st Fable*, children's entertainment for Mezzo-soprano, Soprano, Dancers/Mimes, Narrator, Oboe, Cello, Percussion, and Piano (1988).—**NS/LK/DM**

Hawkins, Micah, American composer; b. Head of the Harbor, near Stony Brook, N.Y., Jan. 1, 1777; d. N.Y., July 29, 1825. In 1798 he settled in N.Y.C., where he worked as a carriage builder, grocer, and innkeeper. He was also a member of amateur music groups, such as the Euterpian and Apollo societies. He wrote the dialect song "Backside Albany" (1815), which became notably successful, and "Massa Georgee Washington and General LaFayette," to celebrate Lafayette's visit to the U.S. in 1824. His opera, *The Saw-Mill, or A Yankee Trick* (1824), is the earliest work of its kind by an American on an American subject.

    BIBL.: O. Wegelin, *M. H. and The Saw-Mill* (N.Y., 1917). —**NS/LK/DM**

Hawkins, Sir John, eminent English music historian; b. London, March 29, 1719; d. there, May 21, 1789. He studied law while serving as a clerk, and soon was able to act as an attorney. An ardent devotee of music, he entered the musical society of the time and was on friendly terms with Handel; he also participated in literary clubs, and knew Samuel Johnson, Goldsmith, and others. A wealthy marriage (1753) enabled him to devote his leisure to literature and music. In 1761 he became a magistrate, and in 1763 chairman of the Quarter Sessions. He was knighted in 1772. His first publication dealing with music was *Memoirs of the Life of Sig. Agostino Steffani* (1758). He then brought out *An Account of the Institution and Progress of the Academy of Ancient Music* (1770). The culmination of 16 years of labor was his monumental *A General History of the Science and Practice of Music* (5 vols., 1776). The first vol. of Burney's *General History of Music* appeared at the same time; thus, Hawkins undoubtedly held priority for the first general history of music publ. in England. However, its reception was rather hostile; Burney himself derided Hawkins in an unpubl. poem. Yet the Hawkins work contained reliable information, particularly dealing with musical life in London in the 18th century. Hawkins died of a paralytic stroke and was buried in Westminster Abbey.

    BIBL.: P. Scholes, *The Life and Activities of Sir J. H.* (London, 1953); B. Davis, *A Proof of Eminence: The Life of Sir J. H.* (Bloomington, Ind., and London, 1973).—**NS/LK/DM**

Hawley, C(harles) B(each), American bass, organist, choirmaster, teacher, and composer; b. Brookfield, Mass., Feb. 14, 1858; d. Eatontown, N.J., Dec. 29, 1915. He studied organ at the Cheshire Military Academy. In 1875 he settled in N.Y. and studied composition with Dudley Buck. In 1876 he became solo bass at

Calvary Episcopal Church. After serving as asst. organist at St. Thomas Church, he was bass soloist and choirmaster at the Broadway Tabernacle (1883–1900) and organist and choirmaster at the Madison Ave. Methodist Church (from 1912). He taught voice for many years, and also was co-founder–director of the Metropolitan Cons. of Music. Hawley was remarkably successful as a composer of solo songs, of which he wrote hundreds. Among his other works were some sacred choral pieces, men's and women's part songs, and comic glees.—**LK/DM**

Hay, Edward Norman, Irish composer and organist; b. Faversham, April 19, 1889; d. Belfast, Sept. 10, 1943. He studied organ with Koeller and Eaglefield-Hull, and was organist of various churches in Ireland. He won the Feis Ceoil Prize in 1916 with his Cello Sonata on Irish folk tunes, the Cobbett Prize (1917) with his *Folksong Phantasy* for String Quartet, and the Carnegie Award (1918) with his String Quartet in A. He also wrote the orch. compositions *The Gilly of Christ, Dunluce* (1921), etc., organ works, and songs.—**NS/LK/DM**

Hayasaka, Fumio, Japanese composer, b. Sendai-City, Aug. 19, 1914; d. Tokyo, Oct. 15, 1955. He studied in Tokyo with A. Tcherepnin, winning the Weingartner Prize (1938). He was particularly successful in writing for Japanese films. He wrote the score for the film *Rashomon*, which received 1st prize at the International Festival in Venice (1952). Among his other works were *The Ancient Dance* (Tokyo, May 15, 1939), Overture (Tokyo, March 17, 1940), Piano Concerto (Tokyo, June 22, 1948), and *Yukara*, suite (Tokyo, June 9, 1955). —**NS/LK/DM**

Hayasaka, Sachi, avant-garde jazz alto and soprano saxophonist, b. Tokyo, Japan, Feb. 26, 1960. Leader of the eclectic group Stir Up!, Hayasaka is a protégé of leading avant-gardists such as Yosuke Yamashita and Leo Wadada Smith. After graduating from Tamagawa Univ., she performed in her own groups and toured Western Europe with the Hans Reichel Trio in 1987. She plays in Germany and N.Y. nearly every year, either as a member of other groups or with Stir Up! (which includes her husband Nagata Toshiki on bass). Stir Up! performs one of Japan's most popular annual jazz events, the "2.26" concert, which is the mutual birthday of Hayasaka, drummer Tsunoda Ken, and guest pianist Yamashita.

    DISC.: *Straight to the Core* (1990); *2.26* (1994).—**ETA**

Hayashi (Nagaya), Kenzō, Japanese musicologist; b. Osaka, May 1, 1899; d. Nara, June 9, 1976. He graduated from the Tokyo Arts School in 1924, and became a moderately successful sculptor. He also wrote some music for brass instruments. In 1928 he met the Chinese scholar Kuo Mo-jo, who encouraged him to write about his findings in the field of ancient Asian music. His first book, on music of the Sui and T'ang dynasties, was tr. into Chinese by Kuo (Shanghai, 1936). In 1948 he was commissioned to begin what became his life's work, research on early Chinese instruments kept in the imperial storehouse in Hara dating as far back as the 8th century. He publ. some theoretical findings, among them *Ming yüen pa-tiao yen- chiu* (8 Musical Modes of the Ming Dynasty; Shanghai, 1957), *T'un-huang p'i-pa pu ti chieh-tu yen-chiu* (An Attempt to Interpret the T'un-huang Pipa Notation; Shanghai, 1957), and *Higashi Ajia gakki kō* (Musical Instruments of East Asia; Tokyo, 1973).—NS/LK/DM

Hayashi, Hikaru, Japanese composer; b. Tokyo, Oct. 22, 1931. He was a student of Otaka and Ikenouchi at the Tokyo Academy of Music.

WORKS: DRAMATIC: O p e r a : *The Naked King*, radio opera (1955); *Amanjaku and Urikohime*, television opera (1958); *The Wife in the Picture* (1961); *The Chalk Circle* (1978; orch. suite, 1982); *Legend of White Beasts* (1979); *Gorsh, the Cellist* (1986); *Joan of Arc Wearing a Skirt* (1987); *12th Night* (1989); *Hamlet's Hour* (1990); *12 Months and a Girl* (1992); *3 Clever Students* (1994); *Salesman K's Melancholy* (1996); *Midsummer Night's Dream* (1996); *I Am a Cat* (1998). OTHER: Ballet music. ORCH.: *Movement* (1953); 2 syms.: No. 1 (1953) and No. 2, *Canciones* (Tokyo, May 18, 1985); *Allegro* for Strings (1954); *Variations* (1955); *The Humid Area* (1960); *Music* (1965); *Carnival: A Windborn Premonition* (1985); *Awakening* (1991); *North/South*, chamber concerto for Strings (1993); *Northern Sail*, guitar concerto (1993); *Elegia*, viola concerto (1995). CHAMBER: *Rhapsody I* (1965) and *II: Winter on 72nd Street* (1968) for Violin and Piano; *Contrasts* for 2 Marimbas (1965); *Flute Sonata* (1967); *AYA I* for Flute and Harp (1970) and *II* for Harp (1972); *Play I* for 10 Players (1971) and *II* for Voice, Violin, and Piano (1971–72); *Shirabe* for 3 Flutes (1974); *America Suite* for Flute, Clarinet, Cello, Piano, and Percussion (1983); *Legende for String Quartet* (1989–90); piano pieces. VOCAL: *Beggar's Song*, oratorio (1962); *Children of War* for Soloists, Narrator, Chorus, and Chamber Orch. (1984); *At Noon, the August Sun* for Soprano and Orch. (1990); *3 Images* for Chorus and Orch. (1998); choruses; solo songs.—NS/LK/DM

Haydn, (Franz) Joseph, great Austrian composer who was a master of the Classical style; b. Rohrau, Lower Austria, probably March 31, 1732 (baptized, April 1, 1732); d. Vienna, May 31, 1809. He was the 2nd of 12 children born to Mathias Haydn, a wheelwright, who served as village sexton, and Anna Maria Koller, daughter of the market inspector and a former cook in the household of Count Harrach, lord of the village. Their 2nd son, Michael, also became a musician. On Sundays and holidays music was performed at home, the father accompanying the voices on the harp, which he had learned to play by ear. When Haydn was a small child his paternal cousin Johann Mathias Franck, a choral director, took him to Hainburg, where he gave him instruction in reading, writing, arithmetic, and instrumental playing. When Haydn was 8 years old, Karl Georg Reutter, Kapellmeister at St. Stephen's Cathedral in Vienna, engaged him as a soprano in the chorus. After his voice began to break, he moved to the household of Johann Michael Spangler, a music teacher. He obtained a loan of 150 florins from Anton Buchholz, a friend of his father's, and was able to rent an attic room where he could use a harpsichord. In the same house lived the famous Italian poet and opera librettist

Pietro Metastasio, who recommended Haydn to a resident Spanish family as a music tutor. He was also engaged as accompanist to students of Nicolò Porpora, for whom he performed various menial tasks in exchange for composition lessons. He made a diligent study of *Gradus ad Parnassum* by Fux and *Der vollkommen Capellmeister* by Mattheson. Soon he began to compose keyboard music. In 1751 he wrote the Singspiel *Der krumme Teufel*. A noblewoman, Countess Thun, engaged him as harpsichordist and singing teacher; he met Karl Joseph von Fürnburg, for whom he wrote his first string quartets. In 1759 Haydn was engaged by Count Ferdinand Maximilian von Morzin as Kapellmeister at his estate in Lukaveč. On Nov. 26, 1760, he married Maria Anna Keller, the eldest daughter of his early benefactor, a Viennese wigmaker.

A decided turn in Haydn's life was his meeting with Prince Paul Anton Esterházy. Esterházy had heard one of Haydn's syms. during a visit to Lukaveč, and engaged him to enter his service as 2nd Kapellmeister at his estate in Eisenstadt; Haydn signed his contract with Esterházy on May 1, 1761. Prince Paul Anton died in 1762, and his brother, Prince Nikolaus Esterházy, known as the "Magnificent," succeeded him. He took Haydn to his new palace at Esterháza, where Haydn was to provide 2 weekly operatic performances and 2 formal concerts. Haydn's service at Esterháza was long-lasting, secure, and fruitful; there he composed music of all descriptions, including most of his known string quartets, about 80 of his 104 syms., a number of keyboard works, and nearly all his operas; in 1766 he was elevated to the rank of 1st Kapellmeister. Prince Nikolaus Esterházy was a cultural patron of the arts, but he was also a stern taskmaster in his relationship with his employees. His contract with Haydn stipulated that each commissioned work had to be performed without delay, and that such a work should not be copied for use by others. Haydn was to present himself in the "antichambre" of the palace each morning and afternoon to receive the Prince's orders, and he was obliged to wear formal clothes, with white hose and a powdered wig with a pigtail or a hairbag; he was to have his meals with the other musicians and house servants. In particular, Haydn was obligated to write pieces that could be performed on the baryton, an instrument which the Prince could play; in consequence, Haydn wrote numerous pieces for the baryton. He also wrote 3 sets of 6 string quartets each (opp. 9, 17, and 20), which were brought out in 1771–72. His noteworthy syms. included No. 49, in F minor, *La passione*; No. 44, in E minor, known as the *Trauersinfonie*; No. 45, in F-sharp minor; and the famous *Abschiedsinfonie* (the *Farewell* Sym.), performed by Haydn at Esterháza in 1772. The last movement of the *Farewell* Sym. ends in a long slow section during which one musician after another ceases to play and leaves the stage, until only the conductor and a single violinist remain to complete the work. The traditional explanation is that Haydn used the charade to suggest to the Prince that his musicians deserved a vacation after their arduous labors, but another and much more plausible version, found in *Anedotti piacevoli ed interessanti*, publ. in 1830 by G. G. Ferrari, who personally knew Haydn, is that the Prince had decided to disband the orch. and that Haydn wished to impress on him the sadness of such a decision; the known result was that the orch. was retained. In 1780 Haydn was elected a member of the Modena Phil. Soc.; in 1784 Prince Henry of Prussia sent him a gold medal; in 1785 he was commissioned to write a "passione istrumentale," *The 7 Last Words*, for the Cathedral of Cadiz; in 1787 King Friedrich Wilhelm II gave him a diamond ring; many other distinctions were conferred upon him. During his visits to Vienna he formed a close friendship with Mozart, who was nearly a quarter of a century younger, and for whose genius Haydn had great admiration. If the words of Mozart's father can be taken literally, Haydn told him that Mozart was "the greatest composer known to me either in person or by name." Mozart reciprocated Haydn's regard for him by dedicating to him a set of 6 string quartets. Prince Nikolaus Esterházy died in 1790, and his son Paul Anton (named after his uncle) inherited the estate. After he disbanded the orch., Haydn was granted an annuity of 1,000 florins; nominally he remained in the service of the new Prince as Kapellmeister, but he took up permanent residence in Vienna.

In 1790 Johann Peter Salomon, the enterprising London impresario, visited Haydn and persuaded him to travel to London for a series of concerts. Haydn accepted the offer, arriving in London on Jan. 1, 1791. On March 11 of that year he appeared in his first London concert in the Hanover Square Rooms, presiding at the keyboard. Haydn was greatly feted in London by the nobility; the King himself expressed his admiration for Haydn's art. In July 1791 he went to Oxford to receive the honorary degree of Mus.D. For this occasion, he submitted his Sym. No. 92, in G major, which became known as the *Oxford* Sym.; he composed a 3–part canon, *Thy Voice, O Harmony, Is Divine*, as his exercise piece. It was also in England that he wrote his Sym. No. 94, in G major, the *Surprise* Sym. The surprise of the title was provided by the loud drum strokes at the end of the main theme in the slow movement; the story went that Haydn introduced the drum strokes with the sly intention of awakening the London dowagers, who were apt to doze off at a concert. On his journey back to Vienna in the summer of 1792 Haydn stopped in Bonn, where young Beethoven showed him some of his works, and Haydn agreed to accept him later as his student in Vienna. In 1794 Haydn went to London once more. His first concert, on Feb. 10, 1794, met with great success. His London syms., also known as the *Salomon* syms., because Haydn wrote them at Salomon's request, were 12 in number, and they included No. 99, in E-flat major; No. 100, in G major, known as the *Military* Sym.; No. 101, in D major, nicknamed *The Clock* because of its pendulum-like rhythmic accompanying figure; No. 102, in B-flat major; No. 103, in E-flat major, known as the *Drum Roll* Sym.; and No. 104, in D major. A philatelic note: Haydn sent the MS of his oratorio *The Creation* to Salomon in London for its first performance there. The package was delivered on March 23, 1800, by stagecoach and sailboat from Vienna, and the postage was £30 16s. 0d., a sum equal to £650 today, c.$1,000. In 1800 this sum was enough to buy a horse, or to pay the living expenses for a family of 4 for a year.

Returning to Vienna, Haydn resumed his contact with the Esterházy family. In 1794 Prince Paul Anton died and was succeeded by his son Nikolaus; the new Prince revived the orch. at Eisenstadt, with Haydn again as Kapellmeister. Conforming to the new requirements of Prince Nikolaus, Haydn turned to works for the church, including 6 masses. His Mass in C major was entitled *Missa in tempore belli* (1796), for it was composed during Napoleon's drive toward Vienna. The 2nd Mass, in B-flat major, the *Heiligmesse*, also dates from 1796. In 1798 he composed the 3rd Mass, in D minor, which is often called the *Nelsonmesse*, with reference to Lord Nelson's defeat of Napoleon's army at the Battle of the Nile. The 4th Mass, in B-flat major (1799), is called the *Theresienmesse*, in honor of the Austrian Empress Maria Theresa. The 5th Mass, in B-flat major, written in 1801, is known as the *Schöpfungsmesse*, for it contains a theme from the oratorio *Die Schöpfung* (The Creation). The 6th Mass, in B-flat major (1802), is referred to as the *Harmoniemesse*, for its extensive use of wind instruments; the word "harmonie" is here used in the French meaning, as the wind instrument section. Between 1796 and 1798 Haydn composed his great oratorio *Die Schöpfung*, which was first performed at a private concert for the nobility at the Schwarzenburg Palace in Vienna on April 29, 1798. In 1796 he wrote the Concerto in E-flat major for Trumpet, which became a standard piece for trumpet players. In 1797 Haydn was instructed by the Court to compose a hymn-tune of a solemn nature that could be used as the national Austrian anthem. He succeeded triumphantly in this task; he made use of this tune as a theme of a set of variations in his String Quartet in C major, op.76, no. 3, which itself became known as the *Emperor* Quartet. The original text for the hymn, written by Lorenz Leopold Haschka, began "Gott erhalte Franz den Kaiser." This hymn had a curious history: a new set of words was written by August Heinrich Hoffmann during a period of revolutionary disturbances in Germany preceding the general European revolution of 1848; its first line, "Deutschland, Deutschland uber alles," later assumed the significance of German imperialism; in its original it meant merely, "Germany above all (in our hearts)." Between 1799 and 1801 Haydn completed the oratorio *Die Jahreszeiten*; its text was tr. into German from James Thomson's poem *The Seasons*. It was first performed at the Schwarzenburg Palace in Vienna on April 24, 1801. In 1802, beset by illness, Haydn resigned as Kapellmeister to Prince Nikolaus.

Despite his gradually increasing debility, Haydn preserved the saving grace of his natural humor; in response to the many salutations of his friends, he sent around a quotation from his old song *Der Alte*, confessing his bodily weakness. Another amusing musical jest was Haydn's reply to a society lady who identified herself at a Vienna party as a person to whom Haydn had dedicated a lively tune ascending on the major scale; she sang it for him, and he replied wistfully that the tune was now more appropriate in an inversion. Haydn made his last public appearance at a concert given in his honor in the Great Hall of the Univ. of Vienna on March 27, 1808, with Salieri conducting *Die Schöpfung*. When Vienna capitulated to Napoleon, he ordered a guard of honor to be placed at Haydn's residence. Haydn died on May 31, 1809, and was buried at the Hundsturm Cemetery. In consequence of some fantastic events, his skull became separated from his body before his reinterment at Eisenstadt in 1820; it was actually exhibited under glass in the hall of the Gesellschaft der Musikfreunde in Vienna for a number of years, before being reunited with his body in the Bergkirche in Eisenstadt on June 5, 1954, in a solemn official ceremony.

Haydn was often called "Papa Haydn" by his intimates in appreciation of his invariable good humor and amiable disposition. Ironically, he never became a papa in the actual sense of the word. His marriage was unsuccessful; his wife was a veritable termagant; indeed, Haydn was separated from her for most of his life. Still, he corresponded with her and sent her money, even though, according to a contemporary report, he never opened her letters.

In schoolbooks Haydn is usually described as "father of the symphony," the creator of the classical form of the sym. and string quartet. Historically, this absolute formulation cannot be sustained; the symphonic form was established by Stamitz and his associates at the Mannheim School; the string quartet was of an even earlier provenance. But Haydn's music was not limited to formal novelty; its greatness was revealed in the variety of moods, the excellence of variations, and the contrast among the constituent movements of a sym.; string quartets, as conceived by Haydn, were diminutions of the sym.; both were set in sonata form, consisting of 3 contrasting movements, *Allegro, Andante, Allegro*, with a *Minuet* interpolated between the last 2 movements. It is the quality of invention that places Haydn above his contemporaries and makes his music a model of classical composition. A theory has been put forward that Haydn's themes were derived from the folk melodies of Croatian origin that he had heard in the rural environment of his childhood, but no such adumbrations or similarities can be convincingly proved.

The intimate *Volkstümlichkeit*, a popular impressiveness of Haydn's music, naturally lent itself to imaginative nicknames of individual compositions. There are among his syms. such appellations as *Der Philosoph* and *Der Schulmeister*; some were titled after animals: *L'Ours* and *La Poule*; others derived their names from the character of the main theme, as in *The Clock*, the *Surprise*, and the *Drum Roll*. Among Haydn's string quartets are *La Chasse*, so named because of the hunting horn fanfares; the *Vogelquartett*, in which one hears an imitation of birdcalls; the *Froschquartett*, which seems to invoke a similarity with frog calls in the finale; and the *Lerchenquartett*, containing a suggestion of a lark call. The famous *Toy* Sym., scored for an ensemble which includes the rattle, the triangle, and instruments imitating the quail, cuckoo, and nightingale, was long attributed to Haydn but is actually a movement of a work by Leopold Mozart.

Haydn played a historic role in the evolution of functional harmony by adopting 4–part writing as a fundamental principle of composition, particularly in his string quartets. This practice has also exercised a profound influence on the teaching of music theory.

The precise extent of Haydn's vast output will probably never be known. Many works are lost; others, listed in various catalogs, may never have existed or were duplications of extant works; some are of doubtful authenticity, and some are definitely spurious. The following list of his works attempts to be comprehensive in scope, but it is not an exhaustive compilation.

WORKS: DRAMATIC: *Der krumme Teufel*, Singspiel (1751?; 1st confirmed perf., Vienna, May 29, 1753; not extant); *Der neue krumme Teufel (Asmodeus, der krumme Teufel)*, Singspiel (1758?; music not extant); *Acide*, festa teatrale (1762; Eisenstadt, Jan. 11, 1763; only fragment and libretto extant; rev. version, 1773; only fragment extant); *Marchese (La Marchesa Nespola)*, comedia (1762?; only fragment extant; dialogues not extant); *Il Dottore*, comedia (1765?; not extant); *La Vedova*, comedia (1765?; not extant); *Il scanarello*, comedia (1765?; not extant); *La Canterina*, intermezzo in musica (Bratislava, Sept. 11?, 1766); *Lo speziale (Der Apotheker)*, dramma giocoso (Esterháza, Autumn 1768); *Le Pescatrici (Die Fischerinnen)*, dramma giocoso (1769; Esterháza, Sept. 16?, 1770); *L'infedeltà delusa (Liebe macht erfinderisch; Untreue lohnt sich nicht; Deceit Outwitted)*, burletta per musica (Esterháza, July 26, 1773); *Philemon und Baucis oder Jupiters Reise auf die Erde*, Singspiel/marionette opera (Esterháza, Sept. 2, 1773); *Hexenschabbas*, marionette opera (1773?; not extant); *L'incontro improvviso (Die unverhoffte Zusammenkunft; Unverhofftes Begegnen)*, dramma giocoso (Esterháza, Aug. 29, 1775); *Dido*, Singspiel/marionette opera (Esterháza, March ?, 1776; music not extant); *Opéra comique vom abgebrannten Haus* (not extant; may be identical with the following work); *Die Feuerbrunst*, Singspiel/marionette opera (1775?-78?; may be by Haydn; dialogues not extant); *Il mondo della luna (Die Welt auf dem Monde)*, dramma giocoso (Esterháza, Aug. 3, 1777); *Die bestrafte Rachbegierde*, Singspiel/marionette opera (Esterháza, 1779; music not extant); *La vera costanza*, dramma giocoso (1778?; Esterháza, April 25, 1779; only music extant appears in the rev. version of 1785); *L'isola disabitata (Die wüste Insel)*, azione teatrale (Esterháza, Dec. 6, 1779; rev. 1802); *La fedeltà premiata (Die belohnte Treue)*, dramma pastorale giocoso (1780; Esterháza, Feb. 25, 1781); *Orlando paladino (Der Ritter Roland)*, dramma eroicomico (Esterháza, Dec. 6, 1782); *Armida*, dramma eroico (1783; Esterháza, Feb. 26, 1784); *L'anima del filosofo ossia Orfeo ed Euridice*, dramma per musica (1791; composed for London but not perf.; 1st confirmed perf., Florence, June 10, 1951); *Alfred, König der Angelsachsen, oder Der patriotische König* (perf. as the incidental music to *Haldane, König der Dänen*, Eisenstadt, Sept. 1796). **ORCH.: S y m s**: The generally accepted list of Haydn's authentic syms. numbers 104. For detailed information, consult the monumental study by H. C. Robbins Landon, *The Symphonies of J. H.* (London, 1955; suppl., 1961); see also his exhaustive biography *H.: Chronicle and Works* (5 vols., Bloomington, Ind., and London, 1976–80). The numbering follows the thematic catalog prepared by Anthony van Hoboken. Also included are the descriptive titles, whether authorized by Haydn or not. No. 1, in D major (1759); No. 2, in C major (1761); No. 3, in G major (1762); No. 4, in D major (1760); No. 5, in A major (1760); No. 6, in D major, *Le Matin* (1761); No. 7, in C major, *Le Midi* (1761); No. 8, in G major, *Le Soir* (1761); No. 9, in C major (1762); No. 10, in D major (1761); No. 11, in E-flat major (1760); No. 12, in E major (1763); No. 13, in D major (1763); No. 14, in A major (1764); No. 15, in D major (1761); No. 16, in B-flat major (1763); No. 17, in F major (1762); No. 18, in G major (1764); No. 19, in D major (1760); No. 20, in C major (1763); No. 21, in A major (1764); No. 22, in E-flat major, *The Philosopher* (1764); No. 23, in G major (1764); No. 24, in D major (1764); No. 25, in C major (1761); No. 26, in D minor, *Lamentatione* (1770); No. 27, in G major (1761); No. 28, in A major (1765); No. 29, in E major (1765); No. 30, in C major, *Alleluja* (1765); No. 31, in D major, *Hornsignal* (1765); No. 32, in C major (1760); No. 33, in C major (1760); No. 34, in D minor/D major (1767); No. 35, in B-flat major (1767); No. 36, in E-flat major (1765); No. 37, in C major (1758); No. 38, in C major (1769); No. 39, in G minor (1765); No. 40, in F major (1763); No. 41, in C major (1770); No. 42, in D major (1771); No. 43, in E-flat major, *Mercury* (1772); No. 44, in E minor, *Trauersinfonie* (1772); No. 45, in F-sharp minor, *Abschiedsinfonie* (1772); No. 46, in B major (1772); No. 47, in G major (1772); No. 48, in C major, *Maria Theresia* (1769); No. 49, in F minor, *La passione* (1768); No. 50, in C major (1773); No. 51, in B-flat major (1774); No. 52, in C minor (1774); No. 53, in D major, *Imperial* or *Festino* (1778); No. 54, in G major (1774); No. 55, in E-flat major, *The Schoolmaster* (1774); No. 56, in C major (1774); No. 57, in D major (1774); No. 58, in F major (1768); No. 59, in A major, *Fire* (1769); No. 60, in C major, *Il Distratto* (1774); No. 61, in D major (1776); No. 62, in D major (1780); No. 63, in C major, *La Roxelane* or *Roxolana* (1779); No. 64, in A major, *Tempora mutantur* (1773); No. 65, in A major (1773); No. 66, in B-flat major (1776); No. 67, in F major (1776); No. 68, in B-flat major (1774); No. 69, in C major, *Laudon* or *Loudon* (1776); No. 70, in D major (1779); No. 71, in B-flat major (1779); No. 72, in D major (1765); No. 73, in D major, *La Chasse* (1782); No. 74, in E-flat major (1781); No. 75, in D major (1781); No. 76, in E-flat major (1782); No. 77, in B-flat major (1782); No. 78, in C minor (1782); No. 79, in F major (1784); No. 80, in D minor (1784); No. 81, in G major (1784); Paris syms.: No. 82, in C major, *L'Ours* or *The Bear* (1786), No. 83, in G minor, *La Poule* or *The Hen* (1785), No. 84, in E-flat major (1786), No. 85, in B-flat major, *La Reine* or *The Queen* (1785), No. 86, in D major (1786), and No. 87, in A major (1785); No. 88, in G major (1787); No. 89, in F major (1787); No. 90, in C major (1788); No. 91, in E-flat major (1788); No. 92, in G major, *Oxford* (1789); *London* or *Salomon* syms.: No. 93, in D major (1791; London, Feb. 17, 1792), No. 94, in G major, *Mit dem Paukenschlag* or *The Surprise* (1791; London, March 23, 1792), No. 95, in C minor (London, 1791), No. 96, in D major, *The Miracle* (London, 1791), No. 97, in C major (London, May 3 or 4, 1792), No. 98, in B-flat major (London, March 2, 1792), No. 99, in E-flat major (1793; London, Feb. 10, 1794), No. 100, in G major, *Militar* or *Military* (1793–94; London, March 31, 1794), No. 101, in D major, *Die Uhr* or *The Clock* (1793–94; London, March 3, 1794), No. 102, in B-flat major (1794; London, Feb. 2, 1795), No. 103, in E-flat major, *Paukenwirbel* or *Drum Roll* (London, March 2, 1795), and No. 104, in D major, *London* or *Salomon* (London, May 4, 1795); also the Concertante (now called Sinfonia Concertante) in B-flat major, listed in the Hoboken catalog as No. 105 (London, March 9, 1792). Hoboken also lists No. 106, in D major (1769; only 1st movement extant; may have been composed as the overture to *Le Pescatrici*); No. 107, in B-flat major (1761; may be by Wagenseil); and No. 108, in B-flat major (1761). **C o n c e r t o s :** 4 for Violin: No. 1, in C major (1765); No. 2, in D major (1765; not extant); No. 3, in A major (1770); No. 4, in G major (1769); 2 for Cello: No. 1, in C major (1765), and No. 2, in D major (1783); another cello concerto may be lost or has been confused with No. 1; 2 for Organ or Harpsichord: C major (1756) and D major (1767); also most likely by Haydn are 3 others for Organ or Harpsichord, all in C major (1763, 1766, 1771); 1 for Violin, and Harpsichord or Organ, in F major (1766); 3 for Harpsichord: in F major (1771), G major (1770; also for Piano), and D major (1784; also for Piano); 1 for Trumpet, in E-flat major (1796); 5 for 2 Lire Organizzate: in C major (1787),

F major (1786), G major (1787), F major (1787), and G major (1787); also divertimenti, notturni, etc. Several other concertos for oboe, flute, horn, and bassoon are either lost or spurious. **OTHER:** Various works, including overtures to dramatic pieces: G minor (to *L'isola disabitata*); D major (to *L'incontro improvviso*); G major (to *Lo speziale*); B-flat major (to *La vera costanza*); C major (to *L'infedeltà delusa*); C minor/C major (to *Il ritorno di Tobia*); also the *Musica instrumentale sopra le 7 ultime parole del nostro Redentore in croce ossiano 7 sonate con un'introduzione ed al fine un terremoto* (1786; for Cadiz). **C H A M - B E R : S t r i n g Q u a r t e t s :** Op.1 (c. 1757–59): No. 1, in B- flat major, *La Chasse*; No. 2, in E-flat major; No. 3, in D major; No. 4, in G major; No. 5, in E-flat major; No. 6, in C major; op.2 (c. 1760–62): No. 1, in A major; No. 2, in E major; No. 4, in F major; No. 6, in B-flat major; op.9 (1771): No. 1, in C major; No. 2, in E-flat major; No. 3, in G major; No. 4, in D minor; No. 5, in B-flat major; No. 6, in A major; op.17 (1771): No. 1, in E major; No. 2, in F major; No. 3, in E-flat major; No. 4, in C minor; No. 5, in G major, *Recitative*; No. 6, in D major; *Sun Quartets*, op.20 (1772): No. 1, in E-flat major; No. 2, in C major; No. 3, in G minor; No. 4, in D major; No. 5, in F minor; No. 6, in A major; *Russian Quartets; Jungfernquartette*, op.33 (1781): No. 1, in B minor; No. 2, in E-flat major, *The Joke*; No. 3, in C major, *The Bird*; No. 4, in B-flat major; No. 5, in G major, *How do you do?*; No. 6, in D major, *The Frog*; op.42, in D minor (1785); *Prussian Quartets*, op.50 (1787): No. 1, in B-flat major; No. 2, in C major; No. 3, in E-flat major; No. 4, in F-sharp minor; No. 5, in F major, *Ein Traum*; No. 6, in D major, *The Frog; Tost Quartets*, op.54 (1788): No. 1, in G major; No. 2, in C major; No. 3, in E major; *Tost Quartets*, op.55 (1788): No. 1, in A major; No. 2, in F minor, *The Razor*; No. 3, in B-flat major; *Tost Quartets*, op.64 (1790): No. 1, in C major; No. 2, in B minor; No. 3, in B-flat major; No. 4, in G major; No. 5, in D major, *The Lark*; No. 6, in E-flat major; *Apponyi Quartets*, op.71 (1793): No. 1, in B-flat major; No. 2, in D major; No. 3, in E-flat major; *Apponyi Quartets*, op.74 (1793): No. 1, in C major; No. 2, in F major; No. 3, in G minor, *The Rider; Erdödy Quartets*, op.76 (1797): No. 1, in G major; No. 2, in D minor, *Fifths*; No. 3, in C major, *Emperor*; No. 4, in B-flat major, *Sunrise*; No. 5, in D major; No. 6, in E-flat major; *Lobkowitz Quartets*, op.77 (1799): No. 1, in G major; No. 2, in F major; op.103, in D minor (1803?; unfinished; only movements 2 and 3 finished). **OTHER:** 21 string trios (3 not extant); a great number of works for baryton, written for Prince Esterházy, who was an avid baryton player: about 125 baryton trios (divertimentos), various works for 1 or 2 barytons, etc.; 29 keyboard sonatas (3 listed as trios), most of them for harpsichord or piano, with violin and cello; 47 solo keyboard sonatas (7 not extant, 1 not complete), almost all of them for harpsichord; etc. **A r r a n g e m e n t s :** Of the orch. version of the *Musica instrumentale sopra le 7 ultime parole del nostro Redentore in croce...* for String Quartet (1787), as well as pieces from the operas *La vera costanza* and *Armida* **VOCAL: M a s s e s :** *Missa Rorate coeli desuper*, in G major (date unknown; not extant, or identical with the following); Mass in G major (date unknown; composed by G. Reutter Jr., Arbesser, and Haydn; publ. in London, 1957); *Missa brevis* in F major (1749?); *Missa Cellensis in honorem Beata Maria Virgine*, in C major, *Cäcilienmesse* (1766); *Missa Sunt bona mixta malis*, in D minor (1769?); *Missa in honorem Beata Maria Virgine*, in E-flat major, *Missa Sancti Josephi; Grosse Orgelmesse* (1769?); *Missa Sancti Nicolai*, in G major, *Nicolaimesse*; *6/4–Takt- Messe* (1772); *Missa brevis Sancti Joannis de Deo*, in B-flat major, *Kleine Orgelmesse* (1775?); *Missa Cellensis*, in C major, *Mariazeller Messe* (1782); *Missa Sancti Bernardi von Offida*, in B- flat major, *Heiligmesse* (1796); *Missa in tempore belli*, in C major, *Kriegsmesse; Pauken-*

messe (Vienna, Dec. 26, 1796?); Missa in D minor, *Nelsonmesse; Imperial Mass; Coronation Mass* (Eisenstadt, Sept. 23, 1798?); Missa in B-flat major, *Theresienmesse* (1799); Missa in B-flat major, *Schöpfungsmesse* (Eisenstadt, Sept. 13, 1801); Missa in B-flat major, *Harmoniemesse* (Eisenstadt, Sept. 8, 1802). **O r a - t o r i o s :** *Stabat Mater* (1767); *Applausus (Jubilaeum virtutis Palatium),* allegorical oratorio/cantata (Zwettl, April 17, 1768); *Il ritorno di Tobia* (1774–75; Vienna, April 2 and 4, 1775, in 2 parts; rev. 1784); *Die sieben letzten Worte unseres Erlösers am Kreuze* (1795–96; Vienna, 1796); *Die Schöpfung* (1796–98; 1ˢᵗ private perf., Schwarzenburg Palace, Vienna, April 29, 1798; 1ˢᵗ public perf., Kärnthnertortheater, Vienna, March 19, 1799); *Die Jahreszeiten* (1799–1801; Schwarzenburg Palace, Vienna, April 24, 1801). **O T H E R :** 2 Te Deums (both in C major); offertories; secular cantatas; secular vocal works for orch.; more than 50 songs with keyboard accompaniment; vocal duets, trios, and quartets with keyboard accompaniment; more than 50 canons; arrangements of Scottish and other songs; and *Gott erhalte Franz den Kaiser* (God Save the Emperor Franz; 1797; was the Austrian national anthem until 1918).

BIBL.: COLLECTED EDITIONS, SOURCE MATE-RIAL: The first attempt to publ. a complete edition was made by Breitkopf & Härtel; *J. H.s Werke,* ed. by G. Adler, H. Kretzschmar, E. Mandyczewski, M. Seiffert, and others, reached only 10 vols. in its coverage (Leipzig, 1907–33). An attempt to continue it after World War II as *J. H.: Kritische Gesamtausgabe,* under the editorship of Jens Peter Larsen and the sponsorship of the Haydn Soc. of Boston, also failed; only 4 vols. were issued (Boston, Leipzig, and Vienna, 1950–51). Finally, in 1955, through the efforts of Friedrich Blume and the publisher Günter Henle, the Joseph Haydn-Institut of Cologne was founded to sponsor a monumental critical ed. The new ed., *J. H.: Werke,* also includes accompanying Kritische Berichte. Jens Peter Larsen ed. the first series of vols. (Munich, 1958–61); he was succeeded as editor by Georg Feder. H. C. Robbins Landon has ed. all of the syms. in a separate series, issued in miniature score as *J. H.: Kritische Ausgabe sämtlicher Symphonien* (I-XII, Vienna, 1965–68). A. van Hoboken prepared a thematic catalog, *J. H.: Thematisch-bibliographisches Werkverzeichnis* (2 vols., Mainz, 1957, 1971). Invaluable articles may be found in the *H. Yearbook* (1962 et seq.) and *H. Studien* (Joseph Haydn-Institut, Cologne, 1965 et seq.). Other sources include the following: A. Csatkai, *J. H.: Katalog der Gedächtnisausstellung in Eisenstadt 1932* (Eisenstadt, 1932); A. Orel, *Katalog der H.-Gedächtnisausstellung Wien 1932* (Vienna, 1932); J. Larsen, *Die H.-Überlieferung* (Copenhagen, 1939); J. Larsen, ed., *Drei H. Kataloge in Faksimile: Mit Einleitung und ergänzenden Themenverzeichnissen* (Copenhagen, 1941; 2ⁿᵈ ed., rev., 1979); R. Feuchtmuller, F. Hadamowsky, and L. Nowak, *J. H. und seine Zeit: Ausstellung Schloss Petronell (N. Ö.) Mai bis Oktober 1959* (Vienna, 1959); L. Nowak, ed., *J. H.: Ausstellung zum 150. Todestag: Vom 29. Mai bis 30. September 1959* (Vienna, 1959); S. Bryant and G. Chapman, *A Melodic Index to H.'s Instrumental Music* (N.Y., 1982); E. Badura-Skoda, ed., *Congress Report: International F. J. H. Congress: Vienna 1982* (Munich, 1987); F. and M. Grave, *F. J. H.: A Guide to Research* (N.Y., 1990); W. Sutcliffe, ed., *H. Studies* (Cambridge, 1998). **CORRESPON-DENCE:** H. C. Robbins Landon, ed., *The Collected Correspondence and London Notebooks of J. H.* (London, 1959); D. Bartha, ed., *J. H.: Gesammelte Briefe und Aufzeichnungen: Unter Benützung der Quellensammlung von H. C. Robbins Landon* (Kassel, 1965). **BIOGRAPHICAL:** S. Mayr, *Brevi notizie istoriche della vita e delle opere di H.* (Bergamo, 1809); A. Dies, *Biographische Nachrichten von J. H.: Nach mündlichen Erzählungen desselben entworfen und herausgegeben von Albert Christoph Dies, Landschaftmahler*

(Vienna, 1810; modern ed. by H. Seeger, Berlin, 1959; 4ᵗʰ ed., 1976; Eng. tr. in V. Gotwals, ed., *J. H.: Eighteenth- century Gentleman and Genius,* Madison, 1963; 2ⁿᵈ ed., 1968, as *H.: Two Contemporary Portraits*); G. Carpani, *Le Haydine, ovvero Lettere su la vita e le opere del celebre maestro Giuseppe H.* (Milan, 1812; 2ⁿᵈ ed., 1823; Eng. tr. as *The Life of H. in Letters,* 1839); T. von Karajan, *J. H. in London, 1791 und 1792* (Vienna, 1861); C. von Wurzbach, *J. H. und sein Bruder Michael: Zwei bio-bibliographische Künstler-Skizzen* (Vienna, 1861); C. Pohl, *Mozart und H. in London:* Vol. II, *H. in London* (Vienna, 1867); idem, *J. H.* (incomplete; 2 vols.; Vol. I, Berlin, 1875; 2ⁿᵈ ed., 1878; Vol. II, Leipzig, 1882; Vol. III, completed by H. Botstiber, Leipzig, 1927); J. Hadden, *H.* (London and N.Y., 1902; 2ⁿᵈ ed., rev., 1934); F. Artaria and H. Botstiber, *J. H. und das Verlagshaus Artaria: Nach den Briefen des Meisters an das Haus Artaria & Compagnie dargestellt* (Vienna, 1909); M. Brenet, *H.* (Paris, 1909; 2ⁿᵈ ed., 1910; Eng. tr., 1926); H. von Hase, *J. H. und Breitkopf & Härtel* (Leipzig, 1909); A. Schnerich, *J. H. und seine Sendung* (Zürich, 1922; 2ⁿᵈ ed., 1926, with suppl. by W. Fischer); K. Geiringer, *J. H.* (Potsdam, 1932); E. Schmid, *J. H.: Ein Buch von Vorfahren und Heimat des Meisters* (Kassel, 1934); K. Geiringer, *H.: A Creative Life in Music* (N.Y., 1946; 3ʳᵈ ed., rev., 1983); R. Hughes, *H.* (London, 1950; 6ᵗʰ ed., rev., 1989); L. Nowak, *J. H.: Leben, Bedeutung und Werk* (Zürich, 1951; 3ʳᵈ ed., rev., 1966); R. Sondheimer, *H., A Historical and Psychological Study Based on His Quartets* (London, 1951); D. Bartha and L. Somfai, *H. als Opernkapellmeister: Die H.-Dokumente der Esterházy-Opernsammlung* (Budapest, 1960; rev. ed. in *New Looks at Italian Opera: Essays in Honor of Donald J. Grout,* Ithaca, N.Y., 1968); H. Seeger, *J. H.* (Leipzig, 1961); A. van Hoboken, *Discrepancies in H. Biographies* (Washington, D.C., 1962); L. Somfai, *J. H.: Sein Leben in zeitgenössischen Bildern* (Budapest and Kassel, 1966; Eng. tr., 1969); H. C. Robbins Landon, *H.* (London, 1972); B. Redfern, *H.: A Biography, with a Survey of Books, Editions and Recordings* (London, 1972); H. C. Robbins Landon, *H.: Chronicle and Works* (5 vols., Bloomington, Ind., and London; Vol. I, *H.: The Early Years, 1732–1765* [1980]; Vol. II, *H. at Esterháza, 1766–1790* [1978]; Vol. III, *H. in England, 1791–1795* [1976]; Vol. IV, *H.: The Years of "The Creation," 1796–1800* [1977]; Vol. V, *H.: The Late Years, 1801–1809* [1977]); idem, *H.: A Documentary Study* (London, 1981); N. Butterworth, *H.* (Sydney, 1983); H. C. Robbins Landon and D. Jones, *H.: His Life and Music* (London, 1988); M. Vignal, *J. H.* (Paris, 1988); W. Marggraf, *J. H.: Versuch einer Annäherung* (Leipzig, 1990); P. Autexier, *La lyre maçonne: H., Mozart, Spohr, Liszt* (Paris, 1997); E. Sisman, ed., *H. and His World* (Princeton, 1997). **CRITICAL, ANALYTICAL:** L. Wendschuh, *Über J. H.'s Opern* (Halle, 1896); B. Rywosch, *Beiträge zur Entwicklung in J. H.'s Symphonik, 1759–1780* (Turbenthal, 1934); H. Wirth, *J. H. als Dramatiker: Sein Bühnenschaffen als Beitrag zur Geschichte der deutschen Oper* (Wolfenbüttel and Berlin, 1940); C. Brand, *Die Messen von J. H.* (Würzburg, 1941); H. Therstappen, *J. H.s sinfonisches Vermächtnis* (Wolfenbüttel, 1941); H. Wirth, *J. H.: Orfeo ed Euridice; Analytical Notes* (Boston, 1951); H. C. Robbins Landon, *The Symphonies of J. H.* (London, 1955; suppl., 1961; for additional information, consult his *H.: Chronicle and Works,* Bloomington, Ind., and London, 5 vols., 1976–80); R. Hughes, *H. String Quartets* (London, 1966); H. C. Robbins Landon, *H. Symphonies* (London, 1966); I. Saslav, *Tempos in the String Quartets of J. H.* (diss., Ind. Univ., 1969); A. Brown, *The Solo and Ensemble Keyboard Sonatas of J. H.: A Study of Structure and Style* (diss., Northwestern Univ., 1970); D. Cushman, *J. H.'s Melodic Materials: An Exploratory Introduction to the Primary and Secondary Sources Together with an Analytical Catalogue and Tables of Proposed Melodic Correspondence and/or Variance* (diss., Boston

Univ., 1972); W. Steinbeck, *Das Menuett in der Instrumentalmusik J. H.s* (Munich, 1973); J. Webster, *The Bass Part in H.'s Early String Quartets and in Austrian Chamber Music, 1756–1780* (diss., Princeton Univ., 1973); R. Barrett-Ayres, *J. H. and the String Quartet* (London and N.Y., 1974); L. Finscher, *Studien zur Geschichte des Streichquartetts, Vol. I: Die Entstehung des klassischen Streichquartetts: Von den Vorformen zur Grundlegung durch J. H.* (Kassel, 1974); J. Drury, *H.'s Seven Last Words: An Historical and Critical Study* (diss., Univ. of Ill., 1975); W. Koller, *Aus der Werkstatt der Wiener Klassiker: Bearbeitung H.s* (Tutzing, 1975); B. Wackernagel, *J. H.s frühe Klaviersonaten: Ihre Beziehungen zur Klaviermusik um die Mitte des 18. Jahrhunderts* (Tutzing, 1975); I. Lowens, *H. in America* (Detroit, 1979); C. Wolff, ed., *The String Quartets of H., Mozart, and Beethoven: Studies of the Autograph Manuscripts* (Cambridge, Mass., 1980); M. Huss, *J. H.: Klassiker zwischen Barock und Biedermeier* (Eisenstadt, 1984); S. Fisher, *H.'s Overtures and Their Adaptations as Concert Orchestral Works* (diss., Univ. of Pa., 1985); A. Peter Brown, *Performing H.'s Creation* (Bloomington, Ind., 1986); H. Keller, *The Great H. Quartets: Their Interpretation* (London, 1986); M. Bandur, *Form und Gehalt in den Streichquartetten J. H.s: Studien zur Theorie der Sonatenform* (Pfaffenweiler, 1988); S. Fruehwald, *Authenticity Problems in J. H.'s Early Instrumental Works: A Stylistic Investigation* (N.Y., 1988); J. Larsen, *Essays on Handel, H., and the Viennese Classical Style* (tr. by U. Krämer; Ann Arbor, 1988); J. Taggart, *F. J. H.'s Keyboard Sonatas: An Untapped Gold Mine* (Lewiston, N.Y., 1988); D. Schroder, *H. and the Enlightenment: The Late Symphonies and Their Audience* (Oxford, 1990); N. Temperley, *H.: The Creation* (Cambridge, 1991); G. Wheelock, *H.'s Ingenious Jesting with Art: Contexts of Musical Wit and Humor* (N.Y., 1992); E. Sisman, *H. and the Classical Variation* (Cambridge, Mass., 1993); R. Wochnik, *Die Musiksprache in den opere semiserie J. H.s* (Eisenach, 1993); U. Leisinger, *J. H. und die Entwicklung des klassischen Klavierstils bis ca. 1785* (Laaber, 1994); H. Haimo, *H.'s Symphonic Form: Essays in Compositional Logic* (Oxford, 1995); L. Somfai, *The Keyboard Sonatas of J. H.: Instruments and Performance Practice, Genres and Styles* (Chicago, 1995); L. Schenbeck, *J. H. and the Classical Choral Tradition* (Chapel Hill, 1996); D. Schroeder, *H. and the Enlightenment: The Late Symphonies and Their Audience* (Oxford, 1997); W. Caplin, *Classical Form: A Theory of Formal Functions for the Instrumental Music of H., Mozart, and Beethoven* (N.Y., 1998); G. Feder, *H.s Streichquartette* (Munich, 1998); B. Harrison, *H.: The "Paris" Symphonies* (Cambridge, 1998); B. MacIntyre, *H.: The Creation* (N.Y., 1998); B. Moosbauer, *Tonart und Form in den Finali der Sinfonien von J. H. zwischen 1766 und 1774* (Tutzing, 1998); G. Feder, *J. H., Die Schöpfung: Werkeinführung* (Kassel, 1999).
—NS/LK/DM

Haydn, (Johann) Michael, distinguished Austrian composer, brother of **(Franz) Joseph Haydn;** b. Rohrau, Lower Austria (baptized), Sept. 14, 1737; d. Salzburg, Aug. 10, 1806. He went to Vienna about 1745 and became a chorister at St. Stephen's Cathedral; his voice was remarkable for its wide range, extending 3 octaves. In addition to the academic and musical training he received as a chorister, he also studied composition on his own by absorbing the theories of Fux as propounded in his treatise on counterpoint, *Gradus ad Parnassum.* He then obtained the post of Kapellmeister to the Bishop of Grosswardein in 1757, and subsequently was named a court musician and Konzertmeister to Archbishop Sigismund Schrattenbach of Salzburg in 1762. In 1768 he married Maria Magdalen Lipp (1745–1827), daughter of the court organist Franz Ignaz Lipp and a soprano in the archbishop's service. Haydn also became principal organist of the Dreifatigkeitskirche in 1777, and was Mozart's successor as cathedral organist in 1781. Part of his time he devoted to teaching; Carl Maria von Weber and Anton Diabelli were among his students. When Archbishop Hieronymus Colloredo abdicated in 1800 and the French took control of Salzburg, Haydn lost his positions. Although his last years were made difficult by this change in his fortunes, he turned down the post of Vice-Kapellmeister to Prince Nikolaus Esterházy, his famous brother's patron. He was a prolific composer of both sacred and secular music, and particularly esteemed for his mastery of church music. His outstanding Requiem in C minor, *Pro defuncto Archiepiscopo Sigismundo*, was composed in memory of his patron in 1771; it was also performed at Joseph Haydn's funeral. He also wrote a fine Mass, the *Sotto il titulo di S. Teresia*, for the Empress Maria Theresia, who sang the soprano solos under his direction in Vienna in 1801. His secular output included dramatic works, syms., serenades, divertimentos, chamber music, etc. His Sym. in G major (1783) was long attributed to Mozart (who composed an introduction to its 1st movement) as K.444/425a.

WORKS: VOCAL: S a c r e d : Over 400 works, including 38 masses; among the most notable are Requiem in C minor, the *Pro defuncto Archiepiscopo Sigismundo* (Salzburg, Dec. 31, 1771; ed. in Accademia Musicale, VIII [Vienna, 1970]), *S. Hieronymi* (Salzburg, Sept. 14, 1777; ed. in Accademia Musicale, VII [Vienna, 1970]), *S. Aloysii* (Salzburg, Dec. 21, 1779; publ. in Zürich, 1942); *A due cori or Missa hispanica* (Salzburg, Aug. 4, 1786; ed. by C. Sherman, Vienna, 1966), *Sotto il titulo di S. Teresia* (Vienna, Aug. 3, 1801), and *S. Leopoldi* (Salzburg, Dec. 22, 1805; ed. by W. Reinhart, Zürich, 1952); 6 settings of the Te Deum, 4 of the *Litaniae lauretanae*, 4 vespers, 6 responsories, 130 gradual motets, 65 offertory motets, 20 settings of the *Tantum ergo*, 13 settings of the *Salve Regina*, etc.; also 8 German masses, 9 German offertory motets, etc. **DRAMATIC: S i n g - s p i e l s :** *Rebekka als Braut* (Salzburg, April 10, 1766); *Die Hochzeit auf der Alm* (Salzburg, May 6, 1768); *Die Wahrheit der Natur* (Salzburg, July 7, 1769); *Der Bassgeiger zu Wörgl* (c. 1773–75); *Abels Tod* (c. 1778; only fragment extant); *Der englische Patriot* (c. 1779); *Die Ährenleserin* (Salzburg, July 2, 1788). **O p e r a S e r i a :** *Andromeda e Perseo* (Salzburg, March 14, 1787). **O r a t o r i o s :** *Die Schuldigkeit des ersten Gebots* (1767; part 2 by Haydn; remainder in collaboration with Mozart and Adlgasser; not extant); *Der Kampf der Busse und Bekehrung* (Salzburg, Feb. 21, 1768); *Kaiser Constantin I. Feldzug und Sieg* (Salzburg, Feb. 20, 1769; part 3 by Haydn, part 1 by Adlgasser, and part 2 by Scheicher); *Der reumütige Petrus* (Salzburg, March 11, 1770); *Der büssende Sünder* (Salzburg, Feb. 15, 1771); *Oratorium de Passione Domini nostri Jesu Christi* (c. 1775); *Figura: In emigratione nostra* (Salzburg, Aug. 24, 1782). **O t h e r :** Incidental music to Voltaire's *Zaïre* (Salzburg, Sept. 29, 1777; ed. by K. Geiringer, Vienna, 1934), cantatas, songs, canons, part-songs, etc. **INSTRUMENTAL:** About 40 syms. composed between 1759 and 1789; 3 violin concertos (1759–61; 1760; 1775–76); 2 flute concertos (1766, 1771); Trumpet Concerto (1764); Horn Concerto (1775–76); etc. He also wrote about 30 divertimentos, 2 serenatas, 3 notturnos, dances, marches, and other pieces. **CHAMBER:** 12 string quartets (1776–1802); sonatas; etc. Much of his instrumental music is available in modern eds.

BIBL.: [J.]G. Schinn and [F.]J. Otter, *Biographische Skizze von M. H.* (Salzburg, 1808); C. von Wurzbach, *Joseph Haydn und sein Bruder M.* (Vienna, 1861); A. Schnerich, *Der Messentypus von H. bis Schubert* (Vienna, 1892); J. Engl, *Zum Gedenken J. M. H.s* (Salzburg, 1906); O. Schmid, *J. M. H....Sein Leben und Wirken* (Langensalza, 1906); H. Jancik, *M. H.: Ein vergessener Meister* (Vienna, 1952); R. Pauly, *M. H.'s Latin "Proprium Missae" Compositions* (diss., Yale Univ., 1956); R. Hess, *Serenade, Cassation, Notturno und Divertimento bei M. H.* (Mainz, 1963); C. Sherman, *The Masses of M. H.: A Critical Survey of Sources* (diss., Univ. of Mich., 1967); G. Croll and K. Vössing, *J. M. H.: Sein Leben—sein Schaffen—seine Zeit: Eine Bildbiographie* (Vienna, 1987).—**NS/LK/DM**

Haydn (Hayden) Quartet, The,

one of the most successful vocal quartets of the early 20th century. Original members were John Bieling, Harry Macdonough, S. H. Dudley, and William F. Hooley. The top American recording group of the 1900s, the Haydn Quartet was formed as the Edison Male Quartet and scored a major hit under that name with Stephen Foster's "My Old Kentucky Home" (1898). As the Haydn Quartet, their hits included "Because" (1900), "In the Good Old Summer Time" (1903), "Bedalia" (1904), "Blue Bell" (1904), "Sweet Adeline (You're the Flower of My Heart)" (1904), "Sunbonnet Sue" (1908), and "Put on Your Old Gray Bonnet" (1909).

On the hits "Toyland" (1904), "Dearie" (1905), and "How'd You Like to Spoon with Me?" (1906), they were accompanied by Connie Morgan; Billy Murray joined them on the hits "Take Me Out to the Ball Game" (1908) and "By the Light of the Silv'ry Moon" (1910).

Reginald Werrenrath frequently replaced Dudley in later years, when they were known as the Hayden Quartet. The group disbanded in 1914, with Macdonough, Hooley, and Werrenrath going on to form the Orpheus Quartet with Lambert Murphy. This group scored a major hit with "Turn Back the Universe and Give Me Yester Day" (1916) but did not match the original quartet's success.—**WR**

Haydon, Glen,

eminent American musicologist; b. Inman, Kans., Dec. 9, 1896; d. Chapel Hill, N.C., May 8, 1966. He studied at the Univ. of Calif., Berkeley (B.A., 1918; M.A., 1921), then went to Paris, where he studied clarinet and composition. He then enrolled at the Univ. of Vienna, where he obtained his Ph.D. in 1932 with the diss. *Zur Entwicklungsgeschichte des Quartsextakkordes; The Evolution of the Six-Four Chord: A Chapter in the History of Dissonance Treatment* (publ. in Berkeley, 1933). Returning to America, he became head of the dept. of music at the Univ. of N.C. at Chapel Hill (1934), and held this post until his death. He was the author of the valuable textbook *Introduction to Musicology* (N.Y., 1941).

BIBL.: J. Pruett, ed., *Studies in Musicology: Essays in the History, Style and Bibliography of Music in Memory of G. H.* (Chapel Hill, 1969).—**NS/LK/DM**

Hayes, Catherine,

Irish soprano; b. Limerick, Oct. 25, 1825; d. London, Aug. 11, 1861. She studied with Antonio Sapio in Dublin, where she began her career as a concert artist in 1840. She later pursued training with Manuel García in Paris and Domenico Ronconi in Milan. On May 10, 1845, she made her operatic debut as Bellini's Elvira in Marseilles, and then sang with fine success at Milan's La Scala and in Vienna. From 1849 she appeared in London. She also made tours of the U.S., Australia, and India. She was especially admired for her roles in operas by Rossini, Mercadante, Donizetti, and Verdi.—**NS/LK/DM**

Hayes, Edgar (Junius),

jazz pianist, arranger, leader; b. Lexington, Ky., May 23, 1904; d. Riverside, Calif., June 28, 1979. Hayes earned a bachelor of music degree at Wilberforce Univ. in 1922. After graduating, he toured the South with Fess Williams. He spent most of 1924–25 working out of Cleveland, leading his own groups, and working as a sideman. By 1926, he had moved on to play with Madison's Commodore Orch. in Buffalo. In the spring of 1927, Hayes led the group The Eight Black Pirates for the touring show *Rarin to Go*. That August, he settled in N.Y., where he led his own Symphonic Harmonists until 1930. In 1931, he joined The Mills Blue Rhythm Band, remaining with the group through various leaders (including "Baron Lee" [Jimmy Ferguson] and Lucky Millinder) until 1936. In 1937, Hayes formed his own big band (with several ex-members of Millinder's Band), which he continued to lead until 1941, including a tour of Belgium and Scandinavia in March and April 1938. His fine version of "Stardust" in 1938 had on the B-side Joe Garland's "In the Mood," which was covered with enormous success by Glenn Miller the next year. Hayes moved to Calif. in the summer of 1942 and began long residency at Somerset House, Riverside, until early 1946. He then led his own quartet, The Stardusters, until the early 1950s. From the mid-1950s, he played as a solo act in various Calif. clubs, remaining active until a few years before his death.—**JC/LP**

Hayes, Isaac,

session musician to Otis Redding and other Stax/Volt artists, and coauthor (with David Porter) of 1960s soul classics such as "Hold On! I'm Comin'" and "Soul Man,"; b. Covington, Tenn., Aug. 20, 1942. Isaac Hayes established himself as a recording artist with 1969's *Hot Buttered Soul*. The album established the "rap" introduction format to songs later exploited by Barry White, and popularized the sensual, romantic side of soul later plied by White and Marvin Gaye; it broke soul music's preoccupation with the three-minute song and infused it with an unprecedented level of musical sophistication and complexity. Hayes's 1971 album *Shaft* established both the scratch guitar rhythm and wah-wah bass in soul music, and was the first of a spate of massively successful soundtrack albums to 1970s black-oriented movies.

Isaac "Ike" Hayes began singing with the Morning Stars vocal group after moving to Memphis with his family. He later took up piano and saxophone, and worked as a session musician, songwriter, and producer at Stax/Volt Records after meeting Floyd Newman of the Mar-Keys. Otis Redding's longtime keyboard accompanist, Hayes played organ on Redding's first major pop hit, "I've Been Loving You Too Long (To Stop

Now)." In collaboration with David Porter, Hayes wrote "I Got to Love Somebody's Baby" for Johnnie Taylor and "B-A-B- Y" for Carla Thomas. The team also wrote three smash soul and major pop hits for Sam and Dave: "Hold On! I'm Comin'," "Soul Man," and "I Thank You."

Initiating his own recording career in 1967 on Enterprise Records, Isaac Hayes scored a smash success with 1969's *Hot Buttered Soul*. The album featured "rap" song introductions, elaborately orchestrated arrangements, and lengthy song renditions that became standard soul music practices (and eventually clichés) while yielding the two-sided pop and soul hit "Walk on By"/"By the Time I Get to Phoenix." The best-selling follow-up, *The Isaac Hayes Movement*, included the major soul and moderate pop hit "I Stand Accused." In 1971 he achieved a smash soul and major pop hit with "Never Can Say Goodbye."

Isaac Hayes arranged, performed, and wrote, in part, the soundtrack to the immensely popular 1971 movie *Shaft*. Released a year before Curtis Mayfield's *Super Fly*, *Shaft* was the first of a series of best- selling soundtracks to black-oriented movies. Of the 15 tracks, only three featured vocals; "Theme from Shaft" became a smash soul and pop hit, and "Do Your Thing" became a smash soul and major pop hit.

Assuming the persona of Black Moses, replete with shaven head, gold chains, and an entourage of beautiful women, Isaac Hayes was soon established on the supper-club circuit, as evidenced by *Live at the Sahara Tahoe*. He scored a smash soul and major pop hit with "Joy—Pt. 1" in 1974, the year he composed the score for the movies *Tough Guys* and *Truck Turner*; he starred in both films. Forming Hot Buttered Soul (HBS) Records under the affiliation of ABC Records in 1975 for five albums, including a live duet set with Dionne Warwick, Hayes later switched to Polydor for his last major pop hit, a remake of Roy Hamilton's "Don't Let Go," and five albums, including *Royal Rappin's*, recorded with Millie Jackson. Moving to Columbia Records in the mid-1980s, Isaac Hayes scored a near-smash soul hit with "Ike's Rap" in 1986. Isaac Hayes eventually returned to the studio for two 1995 albums for Pointblank Records, *Branded* and the instrumental *Raw and Refined*.

DISC.: ISAAC HAYES: *Presenting I. H.* (1968); *Hot Buttered Soul* (1969); *The I. H. Movement* (1970); *To Be Continued ...* (1970); *Shaft* (soundtrack; 1971); *Black Moses* (1971); *In the Beginning* (1972); *Live at the Sahara Tahoe* (1973); *Joy* (1973); *Tough Guys* (soundtrack; 1974); *Truck Turner* (soundtrack; 1974); *The Best of I. H.* (1975); *Chocolate Chip* (1975); *Groove-a-Thon* (1976); *Juicy Fruit (Disco Freak)* (1976); *New Horizon* (1977); *Hotbed* (1978); *For the Sake of Love* (1978); *Don't Let Go* (1979); *Enterprise: His Greatest Hits* (1980); *And Once Again* (1980); *Lifetime Thing* (1981); *Greatest Hit Singles* (1982); *U-Turn* (1986); *Love Attack* (1988); *Tough Guys/Truck Turner* (soundtracks; 1993); *Branded* (1995); *Raw and Refined* (1995); *Ultimate Collection* (2000). **ISAAC HAYES AND DIONNE WARWICK:** *A Man and a Woman* (1977). **ISAAC HAYES AND MILLIE JACKSON:** *Royal Rappin's* (1979).—BH

Hayes, Philip, English organist and composer, son of **William Hayes;** b. Oxford (baptized), April 17, 1738;

1502

d. London, March 19, 1797. He studied mainly with his father, and also received a Mus.B. from Oxford (May 18, 1763). He became a Gentleman of the Chapel Royal in 1767, organist of New Coll., Oxford in 1776, and succeeded his father as organist of Magdalen Coll. and prof. of music at the univ. in 1777, the same year he received his Mus.D. He also became organist of St. John's Coll. (1790). He ed. *Harmonia Wiccamica* (London, 1780).

WORKS: Oratorio, *Prophecy* (Oxford, 1781); masque, *Telemachus*; odes; anthems; services; Psalms; glees; 6 concertos for Organ, Harpsichord, or Piano (1769); also some numbers in Dibdin's *The 2 Misers* and Arnold's *2 to 1*.

BIBL.: S. Heighes, *The Lives and Works of William and P. H.* (N.Y., 1995).—NS/LK/DM

Hayes, Roland, outstanding black American tenor; b. Curryville, Ga., June 3, 1887; d. Boston, Jan. 1, 1977. He was born to former slaves. After vocal studies with A. Calhoun in Chattanooga, he attended Fisk Univ. He then pursued his vocal training with Arthur J. Hubbard in Boston. On Nov. 15, 1917, he made his recital debut there, and then made a successful concert tour of the U.S. In 1920 he went to Europe to complete his studies, finding mentors in Ira Aldridge, Victor Beigel, Sir George Henschel, and Theodor Lierhammer. After singing with leading orchs. in London, Paris, Berlin, Vienna, and Amsterdam, and giving recitals, he returned to the U.S. and made his first appearance at N.Y.'s Carnegie Hall in recital in 1923. In subsequent years, he made numerous appearances in the U.S. until retiring from the concert stage in 1973. Hayes was greatly esteemed for his compelling interpretations of German lieder and French songs, as well as for his unforgettable and poignant performances of black spirituals. He publ. expert arrangements of 30 black spirituals as *My Songs* (1948).

BIBL.: M. Helm, *Angel Mo' and her Son, R. H.* (Boston, 1942). —NS/LK/DM

Hayes, Tubby (Edward Brian), jazz tenor saxophonist, vibraphonist, composer; b. Raynes Park, London, England, Jan. 30, 1935; d. Hammersmith, London, England, June 8, 1973. He was the best-known and best-loved British jazzman of his generation. His father was a violinist who played with the BBC Revue Orch. Hayes began on violin at age eight, then two years later took up piano, and the following year, sax. He was a professional at 15, working in various big bands led by Kenny Baker (1951), Vic Lewis (1953), and Jack Parnell (1954), among others. Hayes led his own octet in the mid-1950s, with which he toured England. He started playing vibes a year later and co-led the Jazz Couriers with Ronnie Scott from 1957–59. In the fall of 1961 he was in N.Y. During the early and mid-1960s, he became a featured soloist at several clubs in America, while also having a regular television show in England from 1961–63. He played with Duke Ellington at Royal Festival Hall in 1964. From the mid-1960s, he suffered from ongoing heart trouble, which led him to concentrate on composing rather than performing, although during the early 1970s he made one last run as a performer/leader.

He died during heart surgery in mid- 1973.

DISC.: *Little Giant of Jazz* (1955); *T.'s Groove* (1959); *T. the Tenor* (1961); *N.Y. Sessions* (1961); *Introducing T.* (1961); *Couriers of Jazz* (1961); *T.'s Back in Town* (1962); *Return Visit* (1962); *Late Spot at Scott's* (1962); *Tribute: T.* (1963); *100% Proof* (1966); *Mexican Green* (1967); *For Members Only* (1967).— JC-B/LP

Hayes, William, English organist and composer, father of **Philip Hayes;** b. Gloucester, Dec. 1707 (baptized, Jan. 26, 1708); d. Oxford, July 27, 1777. He was a chorister at Gloucester Cathedral. He was organist of St. Mary's, Shrewsbury (1729–31), then of Worcester Cathedral (1731–34). In 1734 he became organist and master of the choristers of Magdalen Coll., Oxford. He received a Mus.Bac. (Oxford, 1735), then was univ. prof. of music (1742). In 1749 he received a Mus.D. He conducted the Gloucester music festival in 1757, 1760, and 1763. His canons *Allelujah* and *Miserere nobis* and his glee *Melting airs soft joys inspire* won prizes offered by the Catch Club in 1763. He also wrote a masque, *Circe,* Psalms, odes, glees, canons, ballads, and cantatas. He wrote *Remarks on Mr. Avison's Essay on Musical Expression* (1762) and *Anecdotes of the Five Music-Meetings* (1768), and was co-ed. of Boyce's *Cathedral Music.*

BIBL.: S. Heighes, *The Lives and Works of W. and Philip H.* (N.Y., 1995).—**NS/LK/DM**

Haym (Haim), Nicola Francesco, Italian cellist, composer, and librettist of German descent; b. Rome, July 6, 1678; d. London, Aug. 11, 1729. He was a violone player in the private orch. of Cardinal Ottoboni in Rome under Corelli (1694–1700), then went to London, where he was composer and cellist to the 2nd Duke of Bedford (1701–11). He later was a bass player in the employ of the Duke of Chandos. He was a major figure in organizing performances of Italian opera in London. In 1722 he became the official librettist and Italian secretary of the Royal Academy of Music, the business venture responsible for presenting Italian opera in London. His works include 2 oratorios, *David sponsae restitutus* (1699) and *Santa Costanza* (1700), a serenata, *Il reciproco amore di Tirsi e Clori* (1699), a secular cantata, *Lontan del idol mio* (1704), and instrumental pieces, including *12 Sonate a tre* (1703) and *12 Sonate a tre* (1704). His historical importance, however, rests upon his adaptations for Handel's scores, including *Teseo* (1713), *Radamisto* (1720), *Ottone* (1723), *Flavio* (1723), *Giulio Cesare* (1724), *Tamerlano* (1724), *Rodelinda* (1725), *Siroe* (1728), and *Tolomeo* (1728).—**NS/LK/DM**

Hayman, Richard (Warren Joseph), American conductor, harmonica player, arranger, and composer; b. Cambridge, Mass., March 27, 1920. He received training in composition from Alfred Newman and Max Steiner, and in conducting from Arthur Fiedler. In 1938 he launched his career as a harmonica player, and soon began working as a composer and arranger for Hollywood film studios. After serving as arranger and director of the Vaughan Monroe Orch. (1945–50), he was director of music and of artists and repertoire of Mercury Records (1950–65) and music director of Time-Mainstream Records (1960–70); from 1950 to 1990 he also was chief arranger for the Boston Pops. As a guest conductor, he found his niche as a purveyor of light musical fare with various North American orchs. —**NS/LK/DM**

Hayman, Richard, American composer; b. Sandia, N. Mex., July 29, 1951. He studied humanities and philosophy at Columbia Univ., where he attended Ussachevsky's classes in electronic music; he also studied flute with Eleanor Laurence at the Manhattan School of Music, Indian vocal music with Ravi Shankar, and conducting with Boulez at the Juilliard School of Music. He then descended into the avant-garde maelstrom and produced a series of "works" ranging from graffiti exhibitions to *Dali* for Orch. (1974), notated on a toothpick, with instructions to "ascend chromatically in slow pulse."—**NS/LK/DM**

Haymes, Joe, pianist, arranger; b. Marshfield, Mo., 1908; d. 1964. While in his teens he worked with a traveling circus as a trapeze artist, and also played bass drum in the circus band. He later worked as a self-taught pianist and arranger. He joined Ted Weems as staff arranger before forming his own band, which came to N.Y. in the early 1930s for residencies at leading dance halls, including Roseland. The band did many recordings; some were issued under Haymes's name, many were issued using nom-de-discs. In 1934 Haymes turned the band over to Buddy Rogers, but later reformed a band, 12 members of which became the original Tommy Dorsey Band (1935). Haymes again reformed and continued recording. He continued leading in the 1930s, but occasionally fronted other bands (includine a tour with Les Brown in 1938). During the 1940s he lived for a while in Okla., then worked in Hollywood Studios before joining the CBS studio band in N.Y.—JC/LP

Haymon, Cynthia, black American soprano; b. Jacksonville, Fla., Sept. 6, 1958. She was educated at Northwestern Univ. In 1984 she made her operatic debut at the Santa Fe Opera in the U.S. premiere of Henze's *We Come to the River,* returning there to sing Xanthe in the U.S. premiere of Strauss's *Die Liebe de Danae* in 1985. That same year, she created the title role in Musgrave's *Harriet, the Woman Called Moses* at the Norfolk (Va.) Opera. In 1986 she made her European debut as Gershwin's Bess at the Glyndebourne Festival. In subsequent years, she was engaged with opera companies on both sides of the Atlantic, including London's Covent Garden, the Hamburg State Opera, the Bavarian State Opera in Munich, the Deutsche Oper in Berlin, the Canadian Opera, the Baltimore Opera, the San Francisco Opera, and the Opéra de la Bastille in Paris. She also appeared as a soloist with notable orchs. Among her other roles are Gluck's Amor, Mozart's Pamina and Susanna, Bizet's Micaëla, and Puccini's Liù and Mimi.—**NS/LK/DM**

Haynes, Cyril, jazz pianist, arranger; b. Panama Canal Zone, May 8, 1918. He is the brother of saxophonist Ronald Haynes, who died in March 1938. He was raised in N.Y. and started on piano before he was 10. He gigged with local teenagers George Foster and Charlie Shavers and worked with local bands while majoring in music at Columbia Univ. He did a brief road tour with the *Dixie on Parade* revue before joining Billy Hick's Sizzling Six until September 1937. He joined A. Cooper's Savoy Sultans in late November 1937 and worked regularly with the band until 1943. During the 1940s, Haynes played residencies as house pianist at Cafe Society, Onyx, and other N.Y. clubs, and also recorded as a leader and sideman. In 1947 he worked for a while as accompanist for vocalist Lena Horne. He had solo residencies in Calif. (1948–50), played with Noble Sissle in 1950, then played solo piano at the Reuben Bleu in N.Y. He played with various bands in the 1950s including Andy Kirk, Cab Calloway, and Reuben Phillips's Big Band. During the 1960s, he did several annual tours (accompanying Calloway) with the *Harlem Globetrotters* shows. During the 1970s he worked as a club pianist in N.Y.—JC/LP

Hayne van Ghizeghem, Franco-Burgundian composer; b. c. 1445; d. between 1472 and 1497. He was in the service of Charles, Count of Charolais (later Charles the Bold). He was a fine composer of chansons. B. Hudson ed. his works in Corpus Mensurabilis Musicae, LXXIV (1977).—LK/DM

Hays, Sorrel (actually, **Doris Ernestine**), American composer, pianist, and mixed-media artist; b. Memphis, Tenn., Aug. 6, 1941. She was educated at the Univ. of Chattanooga (B.M., 1963), the Munich Hochschule für Musik (piano and harpsichord diploma, 1966), the Univ. of Wisc. (M.M., 1968), and the Univ. of Iowa (composition and electronic music, 1969). In 1971 she won 1st prize in the International Competition for Interpreters of New Music in Rotterdam, and subsequently toured as a performer of contemporary music. Hays has become well known for her championship of cluster piano music, especially the works of Henry Cowell. She was prof. of theory at Queens Coll. of the City Univ. of N.Y. (1974–75), and a guest lecturer and performer at various institutions. In 1984 she adopted Sorrel as her first name.

WORKS: DRAMATIC: *Love in Space*, radio opera/music theater (1986); *The Glass Woman*, opera (1989–95); *Touch of Touch*, video opera (1989); *Dream in Her Mind*, opera (1994–95; WDR, Cologne, April 14, 1995); *Mapping Venus*, opera (1999); film scores; various works for radio. **INSTRUMENTAL:** *Scheveningen Beach* for Flute Quintet (1972); *After Glass* for 10 Percussionists (1974; rev. 1998); *Pieces from Last Year* for 16 Instruments (1976); *SensEvents* for 6 Instruments and Tape (1970–77); *Characters*, concerto for Harpsichord, String Quartet, and 3 Woodwinds (1978); *Segment/Junctures* for Viola, Clarinet, and Piano (1978); *Tunings* for Double Bass (1978), for Flute, Clarinet, and Bassoon (1979), for Flute, Clarinet, Violin, and Soprano (1979), for Clarinet, Piano, and Soprano (1979), for String Quartet (1980), for Viola (1980), for 2 Violins (1980), and for Violin, Cello, Piano, and Soprano (1981); *UNI*, dance suite for String Quartet, Flute, Chorus, and Tape (1978); *Lullabye* for Flute, Violin, and Piano (1979); *Tommy's Trumpet* for 2 Trumpets (1979); *Fanfare Study* for Horn, Trumpet, and Trombone (1980); *Southern Voices* for Orch. and Soprano (1982); *Harmony* for

Strings (1983); *Rocking* for Flute, Violin, and Viola (1983); *Juncture Dance III* for 7 Percussionists (1989); *It All Sounds Like Music to Me* for Percussionist (1994); *Split Tree Festival March* for Symphonic Band (1996); *Traveling* for Didjeridu, Casio Saxophone, Ultraproteus, Oboe, and Tibetan Singing Bowl (1997); *Traveling to Istanbul* for Electronic Saxophone, Ultraproteus, Electronic Keyboard, Gongs, and Electronic Processors (1998); *Wake Up and Dream* for Trombone and Tape (1998); other chamber works; piano pieces. **VOCAL:** *Star Music* for Chorus, Tape, and Bells (1974); *Hands Full* for 2–part Chorus, Drums, and Tape (1977); *In-de-pen-dance* for Chanter and Nylon String (1979); *Hush* for Voice, Reco-reco, and Sand Block (1981); *Rest Song* for Chorus and Optional Flute (1981); *Something (to Do) Doing* for Scat Singer, 15 Chanters, and 2 Actors (1984); *Hei-Ber-Ny-Pa-To-Sy-Bei-Mos* for Soprano, Flute, and Percussion (1989); *The Clearing Way: A Chant for the Nineties* for Contralto, Chorus, and Orch. (1991); *A Birthday Book* for Baritone, Oboe, and Tuba (1997); *Ain't I a Woman* for Treble Voices, Trumpet, 3 Percussionists, and Keyboard (1998); *Quilt for a New Century* for Baritone, Soprano, Piano, Orch., and Video (2000); other vocal works. **ELECTRONIC AND MIXED MEDIA:** *Hands and Lights* for Piano and Lights (1971); *Duet* for Pianist and Audience (1971); *Certain: Change* for Piccolo, Bass Flute, and Tape (1978); *Reading Richie's Paintings* for Synthesizer, Flute, and Slides (1979); *Exploitation* for Soprano or Chanter and Tape (1981); *The Gorilla and the Girl* for Tape (1981); *Only* for Piano, 2 Tapes, Slides, and Film (1981); *Water Music* for Soprano, Tape, Water Pump, Slides, Optional Violin, and Optional Baby Pool (1981); *Celebration of No* for Tape, Film, and Optional Violin or Soprano or Piano Trio (1983); *The Needy Sound* for Tape (1983); *M.O.M. 'n P.O.P.* for 3 Pianos, Tape, Film, Slides, and Mime (1984); *Weaving (Interviews)* for Optional Soprano, Piano, Film, and Slides (1984); *Sound Shadows* for Oboe, Didjeridu, Saxophone, Synthesizer, Percussion, Dancer, Video, and Tape (1990); *Take a Back Country Road* for Oboe, Didjeridu with Digital Delay, Keyboard, Drum Machine, and Saxophone (1990–91); *The Hub-Metropolis Atlanta* (1990–97); *Structure 123* for Electronic Orch. (1995); *Traveling to Copenhagen* for Electronic Saxophone, Ultraproteus Tone Generator, and DX-7 Keyboard (1996); other tape pieces; sound structures.—NS/LK/DM

Hays, W(illiam) S(hakespeare), American composer; b. Louisville, Ky., July 19, 1837; d. there, July 22, 1907. He worked on Ohio and Mississippi riverboats, and later wrote the "River" column for the *Louisville Courier-Journal*. He became successful as a writer of verse and a composer of songs, in spite of the fact that he had no formal training. Some 20 million copies of his songs were publ., including such popular numbers as "Evangeline" (1857), "The Drummer Boy of Shiloh" (1862), and "Mollie Darling" (1873).

BIBL.: F. Stoll, *W. S. H.: Kentucky Composer, Marine Editor, Poet* (thesis, Univ. of Ky., 1943); G. Grise, *W. S. H.: His Life and Works* (thesis, Western Ky. State Teachers Coll., 1947); M. Chrisman, *W. S. H.: A Biography* (thesis, Univ. of Minn., 1980). —NS/LK/DM

Haywood, Cedric, jazz pianist; b. Houston, Tex., 1914; d. there, Sept. 9, 1969. He played in the high school band alongside Amett Cobb. He joined Chester Boone's Band in 1934, then was with Milton Larkin's Band from 1935–40, and again briefly in 1942. After working briefly in other bands, he moved to San Francisco in 1943 shortly before enlisting in the Army. On his release, he worked with various bands including three years mainly with Illinois Jacquet (1949–51). In 1952, he returned to San Francisco, where he worked with the Cal Tjader Quartet. For the next few years, he worked as a freelance player and arranger, and then joined Kid Ory in 1955, worked mainly with Ory for several years including two tours of Europe. In the early 1960s, he was working regularly with tenorist Brew Moore then, moved back to Houston in the summer of 1963, where he did club work leading his own big band. He died after suffering a stroke in 1969.—JC/LP

Hazel, Monk (Arthur),

jazz drummer, cornetist, mellophonist; b. Harvey, La., Aug. 15, 1903; d. New Orleans, La., March 5, 1968. He originally specialized on drums (his father was a drummer). While still in his teens he gigged with Emmett Hardy, who gave him a cornet. He worked mainly on drums, but doubled on cornet throughout his career. During the 1920s he worked with many bandleaders in and around New Orleans. During the late 1920s and early 1930s, he led his own Bienville Roof Orch. in New Orleans; they recorded in 1928. After a stint in the early 1930s in N.Y., he toured as cornetist in vocalist Gene Austin's band, ending up in Hollywood. During the later 1930s, he spent several years in Lloyd Danton's Quintet until spending a year in the Army (1942–43). After service, he returned to New Orleans, where he supported himself as a truck driver. He worked with Sharkey Bonano in the late 1940s and then was inactive for a period in the 1950s due to illness; he returned to performing in the late 1950s with Bonano and other local leaders.

DISC.: *Monk Hazel* (1954).—JC/LP

Hazeltine, David,

jazz pianist, organist; b. Milwaukee, Wisc., Oct. 27, 1958. He made his professional debut at age 13 in clubs in Milwaukee, Chicago, and Minneapolis. He was an immediate convert to Buddy Montgomery when he first heard him at the Bombay Bicycle Room around 1976. He was Co-founder/Director of the Jazz School in Milwaukee (1984–85) and the head of Jazz Studies at Wisc. Cons. of Music (1985–92). Meanwhile he served as house pianist at the Milwaukee Jazz Gallery working with Charles McPherson, Eddie Harris, Sonny Stitt, Pepper Adams, and Chet Baker. Baker encouraged him to make the move in 1992 to N.Y., where he is in constant demand. A member of the Louis Hayes Quintet, he also holds the piano chair in Slide Hampton's Jazz Masters Big Band as well as touring with the Carnegie Hall Jazz Band under the leadership of Jon Faddis. He also serves as Music Director for singer Marlena Shaw and often accompanies Allan Harris.

DISC.: *Four Flights Up* (1995); *Classic Trio* (1997); *How It Is* (1998); *A World for Her* (1999).—LP

Headington, Christopher (John Magenis),

English pianist, writer on music, and composer; b. London, April 28, 1930. He studied piano with Percy Waller and composition with Lennox Berkeley at the Royal Academy of Music in London, and also received private instruction in composition from Britten (1947–54) and studied piano with Lefebure and composition with Lutoslawski at the Dartington International Summer School (1963). He then devoted much time to teaching, and was active with the BBC in London (1964–65). He toured as a pianist in Europe, the Middle East, and the Far East, and also was active as a broadcaster.

WRITINGS: *The Orchestra and Its Instruments* (1965); *The Bodley Head History of Western Music* (1974; 2nd ed., rev., 1980); *Illustrated Dictionary of Musical Terms* (1980); *The Performing World of the Musician* (1981); *Britten* (1981); *Listener's Guide to Chamber Music* (1982); *Opera: A History* (1987); *Sweet Sleep* (lullaby anthology; 1990); *Peter Pears: A Biography* (1993).

WORKS: DRAMATIC: Ballet: *Chanson de l'eternelle tristesse* (1957). **ORCH.:** *Variations* for Piano and Orch. (1950); *Introduction and Allegro* for Chamber Orch. (1951); Violin Concerto (1959); *Sinfonietta* for Chamber Orch. (1985); Piano Concerto (1990). **CHAMBER:** Cello Sonata (1953); 3 string quartets (1953, 1972, 1982); Piano Quartet (1978); Bassoon Sonata (1988). **Piano:** 3 sonatas (1955, 1974, 1985). **VOCAL:** *Towards a Pindaric Ode* for Soprano, Mezzo-soprano, and Piano (1965); *A Bradfield Mass* for Chorus, Congregation, and Organ (1977); *The Healing Fountain: In memoriam Benjamin Britten* for Medium Voice and Orch. (1978).—NS/LK/DM

Healey, Derek,

English composer and pedagogue; b. Wargrave, May 2, 1936. He was a student of Darke (organ) and Howells (composition) at the Univ. of Durham (B.Mus., 1961), and received training in piano, organ, and flute at the Royal Coll. of Music in London; he then continued his composition studies with Petrassi and Berio in Italy, principally with Porena in Rome (1962–66). He also studied conducting with Celibidache at the Accademia Musical Chigiana in Siena (summers, 1961–63 and 1966). He taught at the Univ. of Victoria, British Columbia (1969–71) and at the Univ. of Toronto (1971–72); he concurrently taught at the Univ. of Waterloo. After teaching at the Univ. of Guelph (1972–78), he was prof. of theory and composition at the Univ. of Ore. in Eugene from 1979 to 1988. In 1980 he was awarded the International Composition Prize of the Univ. of Louisville.

WORKS: DRAMATIC: *Il Carcerato,* ballet (1965); *The 3 Thieves,* ballet (1967); *Mr. Punch,* children's opera (1969); *Seabird Island,* opera (Guelph, May 7, 1977). **ORCH.:** *The Willow Pattern Plate* (1957); Concerto for Organ, Strings, and Timpani (1960); *Ruba'i* (1968); *Arctic Images* (1971); *Noh,* triple concerto for Flute, Piano, Synthesizer, and Orch. (1974); *Primrose in Paradise* for Chamber Orch. (1975); *Tribulation* (1977); Sym. No. 3, *Music for a Small Planet* (1984); Sym. No. 2, *Mountain Music,* for Large Wind Ensemble and Percussion (1985). **CHAMBER:** String Quartet (1961); Cello Sonata (1961); *Partita bizzara* for Oboe and Piano (1962); *Divisions* for Brass Quintet (1963); *Mobile* for Flute, Vibraphone, Celesta, Harp, 2 Percussionists, and Cello (1963); *Movement* for Flute, Oboe, Clarinet, and String Trio (1965); *Laudes* for Flute, Horn, Percussion, Harp, 2 Violins, and Cello (1966); *Stinging* for Alto Recorder, Cello, Harpsichord, and Tape (1971); *Solana Grove* for Wind Quintet (1982); piano pieces; organ music. **VOCAL:** *Butterflies* for Mezzo-soprano and Small Orch. (1970); *Wood II* for Soprano and String Quartet (1978; rev. 1981); songs.—NS/LK/DM

Heap, Charles Swinnerton, English pianist, organist, conductor, and composer; b. Birmingham, April 10, 1847; d. there, June 11, 1900. He studied with Hauptmann, Moscheles, Reinecke, and Richter at the Leipzig Cons. (1865–67) before completing his training at the Univ. of Cambridge (Mus.D., 1872). He conducted choral societies in Birmingham, where he also led the Phil. Union (1870–86). Among his works were overtures, chamber music, organ pieces, *The Captivity*, oratorio, cantatas, and songs.—NS/LK/DM

Heard, J(ames) C(harles), jazz drummer, singer; b. Dayton, Ohio, Oct. 8, 1917; d. Southfield, Mich., Sept. 27, 1988. His family moved to Detroit when Heard was two years old. He worked as a dancer as a child, and then learned drums when he was a teenager. From his teen years, he worked with local bands and also played in Detroit with Sam Price's Trio. He moved to N.Y. in the late 1930s to join Teddy Wilson's Big Band in April 1939; the band was soon reduced to a sextet. Heard worked with Wilson through the summer of 1942, except for a brief period during 1940 when he was sidelined by illness. From autumn 1942 until September 1945, he was mainly with Cab Calloway, but also did dates with other leaders. From early 1946 until 1953, he led his own band at Cafe Society and other N.Y. clubs, while continuing to actively freelance. He also worked regularly with Norman Grant's "Jazz at the Philharmonic" shows, including several European and U.S. tours through the 1950s. From 1953–57, Heard lived in Japan, led his own group there, and toured the Pacific area including Australia. On his return to the U.S., he continued to lead his own groups in N.Y., while freelancing and gigging with many others, including Coleman Hawkins (1959), the Teddy Wilson Trio (1961), pianist Dorothy Donegan (1963), and Red Norvo (in Las Vegas, 1964). Heard returned to Detroit in 1966, and led a trio at the Playboy Club and other local venues. During the 1970s, he made several European tours with his own groups. He was less active in the final decade of his life.

DISC.: *This Is Me, J. C.* (1958); *Cafe Society* (1974); *Some of This, Some of That* (1986).—JC/LP

Heart, enduring female-fronted rock band with three decades of hits; formed 1973 in Seattle, Wash. **MEMBERSHIP:** Anne Wilson, voc. (b. San Diego, June 19, 1951); Nancy Wilson, gtr. voc. (b. San Francisco, March 16, 1954); Howard Leese, kybd., gtr. (b. Canada, June 13, 1952). Two daughters of a Marine captain, Anne and Nancy Wilson both took a serious interest in music. Nancy learned to play guitar and flute and ventured out as a folk musician. Anne became the vocalist of an all-male rock band from Vancouver, British Columbia. The group started as the Army and became White Heart. The band featured Steve Frossen on bass, Roger and Mike Fisher on guitars and Michael DeRosier on drums. They gigged around the Pacific Northwest. Nancy joined the band in 1974. Almost immediately, the Wilson sisters became involved with the Fisher Brothers. Mike gave over the guitar role to Nancy and became the band's manager/soundman. In 1975, the group signed to the Canadian label Mushroom Records. While making their debut album, *Dreamboat Annie*, they added

multi-instrumentalist Howard Leese to help out in the studio with keyboards and guitar parts. The group's first single, the melodic hard rocker "Crazy on You" started the ball rolling, garnering heavy album rock play and reaching #35 on the pop charts. The follow-up, the somewhat slower "Magic Man" stormed to #9, pulling the group's debut to #7 and platinum sales.

The group had already started to make a follow-up album for Mushroom, but on the strength of *Dreamboat Annie*'s performance, they entered protracted legal proceedings to extricate themselves from the deal with Mushroom and sign to Epic/Portrait records. Their Epic debut, *Little Queen*, produced "Barracuda," a hard rocker in the vein of "Crazy on You," giving Anne a chance to explore the wailing edge of her high register. The tune took album rock by storm before hitting #11 on the pop charts. The album sold triple platinum and hit #9. Early in 1978, Mushroom released the record Heart had been working on before they left, *Magazine*; it produced the hit "Heartless" (#24 pop) and sold platinum, hitting #17 on the charts.

A more sedate and acoustic album, *Dog and Butterfly* did feature a rocker, "Straight On," which climbed to #15 on the pop charts and the sedate title track, which peaked at #34. The album went double platinum, hitting #17 on the charts. But all was not well with Heart. The Wilson sisters and Fisher brothers broke up and Roger left the band to be permanently replaced by Leese. Their next album, *Bebe Le Strange* offered up the album rock hit "Even It Up" which reached #33 on the pop charts. The album peaked at #5 on the charts, but only went gold.

After touring *Bebe Le Strange*, the rest of the band's original male contingent left, replaced by the new rhythm section of bassist Marc Andes, formerly of Spirit and Firefall (making him uniquely qualified to handle both the folk and rock leanings of the band) and drummer Denny Carmassi. While breaking in this line up, the band released a combined greatest hits and live record. From the live side, Anne virtually shrieked a version of Aaron Neville's hit "Tell It Like It Is." The tune rode up to #8, and the album hit #13 and went double platinum.

Over the next couple of years, the band's fortunes started to fade. Their 1982 album *Private Audition* produced the forgettable #33 hit "This Man Is Mine." The album only hit #25 on the charts and for the first time in their recording career didn't even go gold. *Passionworks* did even more poorly, the first Heart album to not produce a hit single. The album went to #39 and quickly fell from sight. Many in the music business wrote Heart off. However *Passionworks*' producer, Keith Olson, enjoyed working with Heart to the extent that he asked Anne to do a duet with Mike Reno from the band Loverboy for a soundtrack project. The soundtrack was *Footloose* and the tune they did, the power ballad "Almost Paradise," topped the adult contemporary charts and hit #7 pop in 1984.

In the meantime, after the dismal performance of Heart's previous two albums, they negotiated their exit from Epic and signed to Capitol. Primed by Anne's success, they cut an eponymous album rife with the kind of power ballads Loverboy had turned into a de rigeur part of the pop sound. Breaking with tradition, the band took a hiatus from the songwriting chores for the most part using the work of outside writers. The formula seemed to work like a magic reviving potion. *Heart* spawned four Top Ten hits: "What About Love" hitting #10, "Never" rising to #4, the band's first ever chart topper "These Dreams," and the #10 "Nothing at All." The album topped the charts and sold over five million copies. Heart had reached heights they only dreamed about with their previous success. It took two years for *Heart* to run its course—the album spent over a year in the Top 40 alone. The follow-up record, *Bad Animals*, was nearly as successful. The power ballad "Alone" also topped the charts. "Who Will You Run To" rose to #7 and "There's the Girl" fell just shy of the Top Ten at #12. The album went to #2 and sold over three million copies.

Brigade began the 1990s as if the 1980s had never ended for the band. While the album was slightly more experimental and acoustic than its two predecessors, it still had the hit formula. The tune "All I Want to Do Is Make Love to You" (not the Willie Dixon tune) rose to #2 and became the band's first gold single. While "I Didn't Want to Need You" at #23 and the #13 "Stranded" were lesser successes, the album still hit #3 and sold double platinum.

After nearly a steady decade of arena rock, the Wilson sisters decided to take a break from Heart and formed a group that took them back to the acoustic sound that informed some of the early Heart records. They called their new group the Lovemongers. The band played out quite a bit and recorded an EP that included a version of Led Zeppelin's "The Battle of Evermore." They continued the band as a parallel project to Heart through the 1990s.

When they decided to record another Heart record, Leese was still with them, but they had to replace their rhythm section. Bassist Fernando Saunders joined the band as did drummer Denny Fongheiser. The album *Desire Walks On* produced the #39 hit "Will You Be There in the Morning." When they hit the road, they took the Lovemongers as their opening act.

In 1985, the band celebrated their 20th anniversary by booking the Back Stage club for a week and enlisted former Led Zeppelin bassist John Paul Jones to produce. *The Road Home* merged The Lovemongers' gestalt with the Heart repertoire in a live acoustic set. Both bands continue to play, but not as much with all three of the core members involved in raising families. The Lovemongers released a full indie album in 1997 and a Christmas record in 1998.

DISC. HEART: *Dreamboat Annie* (1976); *Little Queen* (1977); *Dog & Butterfly* (1978); *Magazine* (1978); *Bebe Le Strange* (1980); *Private Audition* (1982); *Passionworks* (1983); *Heart* (1985); *Bad Animals* (1987); *With Love From* (1988); *Brigade* (1990); *Rock the House Live!* (1991); *Brigade* (1991); *Desire Walks On* (1993); *The Road Home* (1995); *Greatest Hits* (Capitol; 1997); *Greatest Hits* (Legacy/Epic; 1998); *Greatest Hits: 1985–1995* (2000). **LOVE- MONGERS:** *Battle of Evermore* (1993); *Whirlygig* (1997); *Here Is Christmas* (1998).—**HB**

Heartz, Daniel (Leonard), American musicologist; b. Exeter, N.H., Oct. 5, 1928. He studied at the Univ. of N.H. in Durham (A.B., 1950) and at Harvard Univ. (A.M., 1951; Ph.D., 1957, with the diss. *Sources and Forms of the French Instrumental Dance in the Sixteenth Century*). From 1957 to 1960 he was on the faculty of the Univ. of Chicago; in 1960 he was appointed to the music faculty of the Univ. of Calif., Berkeley. In 1967–68 and 1978–79 he held Guggenheim fellowships. He publ. *Pierre Attaingnant, Royal Printer of Music: A Historical Study and Bibliographical Catalogue* (Berkeley, 1969), *Mozart's Operas* (Berkeley, 1990), and *Haydn, Mozart, and the Viennese School, 1740–1780* (N.Y., 1995); ed. *Preludes, Chansons, and Dances for Lute, Published by P. Attaingnant, Paris (1529–1530)* (Neuilly-sur-Seine, 1964) and *Keyboard Dances of the Earlier Sixteenth Century*, in Corpus of Early Keyboard Music, VIII (1965); also contributed numerous articles on Renaissance music to various music journals. —**NS/LK/DM**

Heath, Albert "Tootie", bebop drummer; brother of **Jimmy Heath** and **Percy Heath;** b. Philadelphia, Pa., May 31, 1935. He began working locally in the 1950s with Bill Carney, a singer, percussionist, and impresario active in Philadelphia since the late 1940s. In 1954, "Mister C," as he is known, put together a trio called the Hi- Tones with Shirley Scott (later it was Trudy Pitts, who became Carney's wife), Heath, and John Coltrane. Coltrane felt that this was a real serious jazz group, telling Gitler, "We were too musical for certain rooms." They played in and around Philadelphia on and off for at least a year, including N.J., and to Buffalo a couple of times. They played bebop (including "Half Nelson" and "Groovin' High"); they rehearsed Coltrane's arrangements of standards. In the late 1950s, Heath moved to N.Y. where he worked with J. J. Johnson from 1958–60; he also freelanced and recorded prolifically through the mid-1960s. In 1965, he moved to Stockholm, and worked in Europe for the next three years. In 1968, he was back in the U.S. He joined Herbie Hancock's sextet a year later, and then played with Yusef Lateef from 1970–74. From 1975–78, he played in the Heath Brothers band; during this period, he settled in L.A. Heath turned his attention to education, but also continued to work on and off with his brothers through the 1980s and 1990s. Heath also worked with the Modern Jazz Quartet in the 1995 after Connie Kay's death.

DISC.: *Kawaida* (1969); *Kwanza (The First)* (1973).—**LP**

Heath, Percy (Jr.), jazz bassist; brother of **Jimmy Heath** and **Al (Tootie) Heath;** b. Wilmington, N.C., April 30, 1923. He is famous for having spent most of his career (1952–74 and then on occasion during the 1980s and 1990s) with the Modern Jazz Quartet, but he is stylistically important for other reasons. For example, his distinctive walking bass lines behind Miles Davis and Monk in 1954 are among the first to use double stops as part of the line.

Heath began violin at age eight, and also sang on local radio, but did not become serious about music until the mid-1940s. He attended Philadelphia's Granoff

School of Music in 1946 while working as house bassist at the local Down Beat Club. In 1947, he moved to N.Y. where he was active playing with various bop musicians. From 1950–52, he worked with Dizzy Gillespie while also freelancing; in 1951, he joined the Milt Jackson Quartet which would evolve, within a year, into the Modern Jazz Quartet. After MJQ disbanded in 1974, he formed the Heath Brothers group with his brothers Tootie and Jimmy. He continued to work with his brothers and the revived MJQ through the 1980s and 1990s. The French Government made him an Officer of Arts and Letters in 1988, and the Thelonious Monk Inst. gave him their Founders' Award in 1995.—**LP**

Hebenstreit, Pantaleon, German musician; b. Eisleben, 1667; d. Dresden, Nov. 15, 1750. In his early years, he was engaged variously as a violinist and a dancing master in Leipzig, but fled from his creditors to Merseburg. There the idea of improving the dulcimer was suggested to him, and he invented the instrument with which he made long and brilliant concert tours, and which Louis XIV named the Pantaleon, after its originator's Christian name. As a precursor of the piano, it has disappeared in the process of evolution. In 1706 Hebenstreit was appointed Kapellmeister and dancing master to the court at Eisenach, and in 1714, "pantaleon chamber musician" at the Dresden court.—**NS/LK/DM**

Heckel, Johann Adam, German manufacturer of musical instruments; b. Adorf, July 14, 1812; d. Biebrich, April 13, 1877. From 1824 to 1835 he worked with the bassoonist Carl Almenräder on experiments for improving the clarinet and the bassoon. His son and successor, Wilhelm (b. Biebrich, Jan. 25, 1856; d. there, Jan. 13, 1909), continued his experiments with success and constructed the "Heckelphone" (a baritone oboe; used by Strauss in the score of *Salome*) in 1904; also made various changes in the construction of other woodwind instruments. He wrote *Der Fagott. Kurzgefasste Abhandlung über seine historische Entwicklung, seinen Bau und seine Spielweise* (1899; new ed., 1931).—**NS/LK/DM**

Heckscher, Céleste de Longpré (née **Massey**), American composer; b. Philadelphia, Feb. 23, 1860; d. there, Feb. 18, 1928. Of an artistic family (her grandfather was the artist Louis de Longpré), she studied piano and participated in the musical affairs of her native city. She wrote the operas *The Flight of Time* and *Rose of Destiny* (Philadelphia, May 2, 1918), *Dances of the Pyrenees*, orch. suite (Philadelphia, Feb. 17, 1911), a fantasy, *To the Forest*, for Violin and Piano (1902), songs, and piano pieces. Her style, melodious and without pretensions, is akin to Chaminade's.—**NS/LK/DM**

Hedges, Anthony (John), English composer and teacher; b. Bicester, March 5, 1931. He studied at Keble Coll., Oxford (M.A., B.Mus.) and at the Royal Academy of Music in London. After teaching at the Royal Scottish Academy of Music in Glasgow (1957–63), he was on the faculty of the Univ. of Hull from 1963, where he was made senior lecturer in 1968 and then

reader in composition in 1978. He publ. the book *Basic Tonal Harmony* (1987).

Works: Dramatic: *The Birth of Freedom*, ballet (1961); *Shadows in the Sun*, opera (1976); *Minotaur*, musical (1978); music for films and television. **Orch.:** *Sinfonietta* (1955); *Comedy Overture* (1962; rev. 1967); *Sinfonia Semplice* (1963); *Expressions* (1964); *Prelude, Romance, and Rondo* for Strings (1965); *Concertante Music* for Piano and Orch. (1965); *Variations on a Theme of Rameau* (1969); *An Ayrshire Serenade* (1969); *4 Diversions* for Strings (1971); Sym. (1972–73); *Celebrations* (1973); *Festival Dances* (1976); *Heigham Sound*, overture (1978); *4 Breton Sketches* (1980); *Scenes from the Humber* (1980); Sinfonia Concertante (1981); *A Cleveland Overture* (1984); Concertino for Horn and Strings (1987). **Chamber:** *Rondo Concertante* for Clarinet, Horn, Violin, and Cello (1967); Sonata for Violin and Harpsichord (1967); String Quartet (1970); Piano Trio (1977); *Fantasy* for Violin and Cello (1981); Cello Sonata (1983); *Variations on a Tyneside Air* for Wind Quintet (1984); Trio for Flute, Clarinet, and Piano (1985); Clarinet Quintet (1987). **Vocal:** *A Manchester Mass* for Chorus, Brass Band, and Orch. (1974); many pieces for Chorus and Orch., including *Cantiones Festivals* (1960), *Epithalamium* (1969), *To Music* (1972), *Songs of David* (1977), *The Jackdaw of Rheims* (1980), *I Sing the Birth* (1985), *I'll Make Me a World* (1990), etc.; anthems; part songs.—**NS/LK/DM**

Hedley, Arthur, English musicologist; b. Dudley, Northumberland, Nov. 12, 1905; d. Birmingham, Nov. 8, 1969. He studied French literature at the Federal Univ. of Durham (1923–27), and music with W. G. Whittaker at Newcastle. An ardent Chopinist, he learned the Polish language to be able to study Chopin documentation in the original. He publ. a biography, *Chopin* (London, 1947; 3rd ed., rev., 1974, by M. J. E. Brown), and edited and tr. *Selected Correspondence of Fryderyk Chopin* (London, 1962).—**NS/LK/DM**

Hédouin, Pierre, French government official, writer, and composer; b. Boulogne, July 28, 1789; d. Paris, Dec. 20, 1868. He studied law in Paris, and, after practicing in Boulogne, he was called to Paris in 1842 as head of the Ministry of Public Works. Among his writings were *Éloge de Monsigny* (Paris, 1820), *Gossec: Sa vie et ses ouvrages* (Paris, 1852), *Mosaïque* (Paris, 1856; a collection of articles), novels, and opera librettos. He also composed nocturnes, romances, and songs. —**NS/LK/DM**

Hedwall, Lennart, Swedish pianist, organist, conductor, teacher, writer on music, and composer; b. Göteborg, Sept. 16, 1932. He received training in organ and piano. He was a composition student of Bäck and Blomdahl at the Stockholm Musikhögskolan (1951–59), and also studied conducting with Mann and in Vienna with Swarowsky. He also pursued composition studies abroad with Fortner, Krenek, and Jelinek. He conducted at the Riksteatern (1958–60), the Stora Teatern in Göteborg (1962–65), the Drottningholmteatern (1966–70) and the Royal Theater (1967–68) in Stockholm, and with the Örebro Orchestral Foundation (1968–74). After teaching at the Göteborg Coll. of Speech and Drama (1963–67), he taught at the school of the Royal Theater in Stockholm (1968–70; 1974–80; 1985–97). He also served as director of the Swedish National Music Museum in Stockholm (1981–83). As a performing musician, he was very active as an accompanist. His writings include 2 books on Alfvén (monograph, 1973; pictorial biography, 1990), a study of the Swedish symphony (1983), and a pictorial biography of Peterson-Berger (1983). The idiom of his music ranges from the traditional to the audaciously modern.

WORKS: DRAMATIC: O p e r a : *Herr Sleeman kommer* (1976–78; Örebro, March 16, 1979); *Amerika, Amerika* (1980–81). ORCH.: 4 pieces for Strings (1950–69); Oboe Concerto (1956; Swedish Radio, Dec. 21, 1961); *Variazioni piccoli* (1958); *Canzona* for Strings (1965); Concerto for Cello and String Orch. (1970); *Fantasia on Veni redemptor gentium* for Strings (1972); *Uvetyr till Fortunios visa* (1980); *Sagan*, symphonic fantasy (Örebro, Sept. 13, 1986); *Jul igen en liten tid: En lätt säsongsbetonad rapsodi* (1992); Concerto for Flute and Strings (1996); Sym. No. 1, *Sinfonia retrospettiva* (1996–97). CHAMBER: 2 string trios (1952, 1960); 2 sonatas for Solo Flute (1954; 1989–90); Trio for Flute, Viola, and Cello (1955); Sonata for Solo Violin (1957); *Partita* for 13 Winds (1961); Trio for Flute, Clarinet, and Bassoon (1962); Wind Quintet (1965); String Quartet (1965); 2 sonatas for Solo Bassoon (1977, 1992); *Circuli II* for Cello (1980); *Arioso* for Flute and Organ (1982); *Une petite musique de soir*, wind sextet (1984); Sonata for Solo Oboe (1990); Sonata for Solo Clarinet (1991); *Vårvinter*, alto saxophone sonata (1994–95). KEYBOARD: P i a n o : Sonata (1960). O r g a n : 2 suites (1958–59; 1970); Sonata (1971); *Triptyk* (1984). VOCAL: *Lyric Music* for Soprano and Orch. (1959); cantatas; choral pieces; songs.—NS/LK/DM

Heermann, Hugo, distinguished German violinist and teacher; b. Heilbronn, Wurttemberg, March 3, 1844; d. Merano, Italy, Nov. 6, 1935. As a boy, he was taken to Rossini in Paris for advice. He then studied with Bériot and Meerts at the Brussels Cons., graduating in 1861; subsequently took lessons with Joachim. In 1865 he became 1st violinist of the Frankfurt String Quartet; also taught at the Hoch Cons. In 1904 he founded his own violin school. He made extended tours as a concert violinist in Europe, the U.S., and Australia. From 1906 to 1909 he taught violin at the Chicago Musical Coll., and then at the Stern Cons. in Berlin and the Geneva Cons. (1911–22). He had the distinction of having been the first to play the Violin Concerto of Brahms in Paris, N.Y., and Australia. He publ. a book of memoirs, *Meine Lebenserinnerungen* (Leipzig, 1935).—NS/LK/DM

Hegar, Friedrich, Swiss conductor, pedagogue, and composer; b. Basel, Oct. 11, 1841; d. Zürich, June 2, 1927. He studied in Basel and then with Hauptmann, Richter, David, Rietz, and Plaidy at the Leipzig Cons. (1857–59). After playing violin in the Gewandhaus Orch. in Leipzig, he joined the Bilse orch. in Warsaw in 1860. In 1861 he became conductor of the choir and orch. in Gebweiler, Alsace. In 1862 he settled in Zürich, where he was concertmaster (until 1865) and conductor (1865–1906) of the Tonhalle Orch. From 1864 to 1901 he conducted the Choral Soc., and also led other choral groups. In 1876 he helped to found the Music School (later Cons.), and served as its director until 1914. Hegar was best known as a composer of choral music, his most successful score being the oratorio *Manasse* for Men's Voices (Zürich, Oct. 25, 1885; rev. version for Soloists,

Chorus, and Orch., Zürich, Jan. 10, 1888). Among his other works were a *Festival Overture* (1895), Cello Concerto (1919), *Ballade* for Violin and Orch. (1922), chamber music, and songs.

BIBL.: A. Steiner, *F. H.: Sein Leben und Wirken* (Zürich, 1928); W. Jerg, *H.: Ein Meister des Männerchorliedes* (Lachen, 1946); F. Müller, *F. H.: Sein Leben und Wirken in Briefen* (Zürich, 1987).—NS/LK/DM

Hegedüs, Ferenc, Hungarian violinist; b. Fünfkirchen, Feb. 26, 1881; d. London, Dec. 12, 1944. His precocious talent was carefully fostered by his father, a professional cellist (his mother was also a musician); he then studied at the Budapest Cons. with Hubay. His style of playing had the manner of the Hungarian school, but his performances of Beethoven and other classics were entirely traditional. He lived in Switzerland after 1930, then went to London.—NS/LK/DM

Heger, Robert, German conductor and composer; b. Strasbourg, Aug. 19, 1886; d. Munich, Jan. 14, 1978. He studied in Strasbourg, with Kempter in Zürich, and with Schillings in Berlin. After conducting opera in Strasbourg (1907–08), Ulm/Donau (1908–11), and Barmen (1911), he conducted at the Vienna Volksoper (1911–13). From 1913 to 1921 he was conductor of the Nuremberg Opera, and then conducted at the Bavarian State Opera in Munich. He conducted at the Vienna State Opera from 1925 to 1933; concurrently he conducted the concerts of Vienna's Gesellschaft der Musikfreunde and conducted opera at London's Covent Garden. From 1933 to 1945 he conducted at the Berlin State Opera; he also was music director of the Kassel State Theater (1935–41) and of the Zoppot Waldoper. After conducting at the Berlin Städtische Oper (1945–50), he settled in Munich as a regular conductor at the Bavarian State Opera. He also served as president of the Munich Hochschule für Musik (1950–54). Heger acquired a respectable position among opera conductors in Germany. While his compositions failed to maintain themselves in the repertoire, his orchestrations of several of Richard Strauss' songs have become well known.

WORKS: DRAMATIC: O p e r a : *Ein Fest auf Haderslev* (Nuremberg, Nov. 12, 1919; rev. 1943); *Der Bettler Namenlos* (1931; Munich, April 8, 1932); *Der verlorene Sohn* (1935; Dresden, March 11, 1936; rev. 1942); *Lady Hamilton* (1941; Nuremberg, Feb. 11, 1951); *Das ewige Reich* (n.d.; rev. 1972 as *Trägodie der Zweitracht*). ORCH.: 3 syms.; *Hero und Leander*, symphonic poem; Violin Concerto; Cello Concerto. OTHER: Chamber music; *Te Deum* for 2 Soloists, Chorus, and Orch. (1971); choral pieces; songs.—NS/LK/DM

Heggie, Jake (actually **John Stephen**), promising American pianist and composer; b. West Palm Beach, Fla., March 31, 1961. He was reared in primarily in Ohio and Calif. His father was a jazz pianist, and Jake began piano lessons at an early age. He began composing at the age of 11, shortly after his father's suicide in 1972. His first serious composition teacher was Ernst Bacon, with whom he studied privately in Orinda, Calif. from 1977 to 1979, and his first serious compositional efforts were settings of the poetry of Emily Dickinson.

He traveled to Paris in 1979 for studies at the American Coll. (A.A., 1981) and also privately with Helene Mouzalas. In 1981 he returned to Calif. and studied with Johana Harris at the Univ. of Calif. at Los Angeles (B.A., 1984); he also studied there with Paul Des Marais, Roger Bourland, David Raksin, and Paul Reale (1987–89). Heggie and Harris were married on Dec. 18, 1982, when he was 21 and she was 69. They toured together for several years and Heggie began developing a compositional style, mostly writing chamber music and songs. However, in 1989 he developed a repetitive stress problem in his right hand and was forced to stop performing. He found work running a private performing arts series in Los Angeles and eventually became a writer in the public relations dept. at the Univ. of Calif. at Los Angeles's Performing Arts. Having separated from Harris, in 1993 Heggie moved to San Francisco, working first at Cal Performances at the Univ. of Calif. at Berkeley and then at the San Francisco Opera, as the company's staff writer (1994–97). He met many important singers of the day, including Frederica von Stade, who began to champion his work. Having regained the use of his right hand, he also began performing once again. Von Stade engaged him as her accompanist, as did many younger singers, and Heggie began to write songs which were included in their international recitals. In 1995 he was one of 8 winners of the G. Schirmer American Art Song competition, and in 1996 Jennifer Larmore recorded 5 of his songs on her American song CD, "My Native Land." In 1998 Heggie became the first composer-in-residence of the San Francisco Opera and received a commission for his first opera, *Dead Man Walking*, to a libretto by Terrence McNally, based on the book by Sister Helen Prejean. In 1999 11 singers gathered to make a recording of 26 of Heggie's songs; at the same time, G. Schirmer published 50 of Heggie's songs. In May 2000, von Stade and others performed full evenings of Heggie's songs at N.Y.'s Alice Tully Hall and San Francisco's Herbst Theatre. Heggie has been commissioned by the Houston Grand Opera to compose his second opera, based on *The Ghost and Mrs. Muir*, for a 2003 premiere. He also wrote a 10–minute operatic scene for N.Y.'s EOS Orchestra, *Again*, a satirical spoof on the relationship between Lucille Ball and Desi Arnez as depicted on the popular television program, "I Love Lucy." Current works in progress include a song cycle for baritone and orchestra for Thomas Hampson as well as a full evening program of songs and text for 3 opera singers based on a new play by Terrence McNally.

WORKS: DRAMATIC: O p e r a : *Dead Man Walking*, after Terrence McNally (1998–2000); *Again*, operatic scene in 10 minutes, after Kevin Gregory (2000). CHAMBER: "Lugalla," string quartet (1984); "Glengariff," trio for Violin, Cello, and Piano (1985); *Variations from "Martha and Mary"* for Violin and Piano (1986); *Lullabye* for Violin and Piano (1987); *One Day at the Duck Pond* for Strings, Winds, Guitar, Piano, and Percussion (1987); *Echo* for Strings and Winds with Piano, score for a short animated film by S. Silver (1989); *Prelude and Aria* for Clarinet and Piano (1990); *Iris* for Strings and Flute, score for a short film by B. Starkie with dancer Iris Pell (1991); *Coward/Cabaret* for Cello and Piano, after songs by Noel Coward (1996). P i a n o : *Indiana Bound* (1982); *Inishfallen* (1983); *Shrovetide* (1984); *Innisfree* for 2 Pianos (1985); *Skellig Variations* for 2 Pianos (1986);

Isadora's Dress, score for a short film by B. Starkie, in tribute to Isadora Duncan (1988); *Divertimento* for 2 Pianos (1990); *Christmas Nocturnes* (1991); *Homage a Poulenc* (1992). VOCAL: *Fates of Flesh and Stone* for Tenor, Clarinet, String Quartet, and Piano (1984); *Before the Storm* for Mezzo-soprano, Cello, and Piano (1986; rev. 1998); *Three Shropshire Songs of A. E. Housman* for Tenor, Bassoon or Cello, and Piano (1986); *Three Songs of Foreboding* for Soprano, Bassoon, and Piano (1986); *Faith Disquiet* for Chorus, after Dickinson (1987); *In Love and Despair* for Baritone, String Quartet, and Piano, after Dickinson and Housman (1987); *To Say Before Going to Sleep* for Mezzo-soprano and Piano, after Rilke (1988); *Trois Poemes Intérieurs de Rainer Maria Rilke* for Baritone and Piano (1988); *White in the Moon* for Mezzo-soprano and Piano, after Housman (1990); *A Wreath of Carols* for Men's Chorus and Piano (1992); *Three Folk Songs* for Mezzo-soprano and Piano (1994; also for Mezzo-soprano, Violin, Viola, Cello, and Piano, and for Orch.); *As well as Jesus? At last, to be identified!* for Soprano and Piano, after Dickinson (1995); *Encountertenor* for Countertenor and Piano or Fortepiano (1995); *I shall not live in vain* for Soprano and Piano, after Dickinson (1995; also for Mezzo-soprano, Girl's Chorus, Handbells, and Piano, 1998); *Eve- Song* for Soprano and Piano (1996); *My True Love Hath My Heart* for Soprano, Cello, and Piano (1996; also for Soprano and Piano, and for Soprano, Mezzo-soprano, Cello, and Piano); *On the Road to Christmas* for Mezzo- soprano and String Orch. (1996); *Thoughts Unspoken* for Baritone and Piano (1996); *"Why do I love" You, Sir?* for Mezzo-soprano and Piano, afer Dickinson (1996); *Natural Selection* for Soprano and Piano (1997); *Paper Wings* for Mezzo-soprano and Piano (1997; also for Mezzo- soprano and Orch., 1999); *So Many Notes!* for 11 Singers and Orch. (1997); *Everyone Sang* for Baritone and Piano (1998); *From Emily's Garden* for Soprano and Piano or with Flute, Violin Cello, and Piano (1998); *Of Gods and Cats* for Mezzo-soprano and Piano (1998); *Patterns* for Mezzo-soprano, Women's Chorus, and Piano (1998); *Songs to the Moon, Part 1:"Fairy-Tales for the Children"* for Mezzo-soprano and Piano (1998); *Sophie's Song* for Mezzo-soprano and Piano (1998); *Anna Madrigal Remembers* for Mezzo-soprano and 12 Men's Voices, after A. Maupin (1999); *Ample make this bed* and *The sun kept setting* for Soprano and Piano, after Dickinson (1999); *Songs and Sonnets to Ophelia* for Soprano and Piano (1999). OTHER: Various arrangements.—LK/DM

Hegner, Otto, Swiss pianist; b. Basel, Nov. 18, 1876; d. Hamburg, Feb. 22, 1907. He studied piano with Eugene d'Albert. At the age of 12, he made an American tour and was hailed as one of the most phenomenal young pianists. His early death, at the age of 30, cut short his brilliant career. His sister Anna Hegner (b. Basel, March 1, 1881; d. there, Feb. 3, 1963) was a violinist.—NS/LK/DM

Hegyesi (real name, Spitzer), Louis, noted Hungarian cellist; b. Arpad, Nov. 3, 1853; d. Cologne, Feb. 27, 1894. He studied with Demis in Vienna and with Franchomme in Paris. In 1888 he was appointed to the faculty of the Cologne Cons. He publ. several brilliant cello pieces and a valuable theoretical manual, *Neue rhythmische Tonleiter- und Akkordstudien.* —NS/LK/DM

Heiden, Bernhard, German-born American composer and pedagogue; b. Frankfurt am Main, Aug. 24,

1910; d. Bloomington, Ind., May 1, 2000. He studied piano, clarinet, violin, theory, and harmony. From 1929 to 1933 he studied at the Hochschule für Musik in Berlin, where his principal teacher was Hindemith. In 1935 he emigrated to the U.S. and became a naturalized American citizen in 1941. He taught at the Art Center Music School in Detroit, and was also conductor of the Detroit Chamber Orch., as well as pianist, harpsichordist, and chamber music artist. He served in the U.S. Army (1943–45); then studied musicology with Grout at Cornell Univ. (A.M., 1946). In 1946 he joined the faculty of the Ind. Univ. School of Music in Bloomington, retiring in 1981. His music was neo-Classical in its formal structure, and strongly polyphonic in texture; it was distinguished also by its impeccable sonorous balance and effective instrumentation.

WORKS: DRAMATIC: Incidental music to *Henry IV* (1940) and *The Tempest* (1942); *Dreamers on a Slack Wire*, dance drama for 2 Pianos and Percussion (1953); *The Darkened City*, opera (1962; Bloomington, Ind., Feb. 23, 1963). ORCH.: 2 syms. (1933, 1954); *Euphorion: Scene for Orchestra* (1949); Concerto for Small Orch. (1949); *Memorial* (1955); Concerto for Piano, Violin, Cello, and Orch. (1956); *Philharmonic Fanfare* (1958); *Variations* (1960); *Envoy* (1963); Cello Concerto (1967); Concerto for Strings (1967); Horn Concerto (1969); *Partita* (1970); Tuba Concerto (1976); Concerto for Trumpet and Wind Orch. (1981); *Recitative and Aria* for Cello and Orch. (1985; Pittsburgh, May 8, 1986); *Fantasia concertante* for Alto Saxophone, Winds, and Percussion (1987); Concerto for Recorder and Chamber Orch. (1987); *Salute* (1989); Concerto for Bassoon and Chamber Orch. (1990); *Voyage* for Symphonic Band (1991; Bloomington, Ind., Feb. 25, 1992); *Symfonietta Concertante* for Flute, Cello, and Chamber Orch. (1995; Ernen, Switzerland, Aug. 6, 1996). CHAMBER: Alto Saxophone Sonata (1937); Horn Sonata (1939); 2 string quartets (1947, 1951); Sinfonia for Woodwind Quintet (1949); Quintet for Horn and String Quartet (1952); Violin Sonata (1954); Quintet for Clarinet and Strings (1955); Serenade for Bassoon, Violin, Viola, and Cello (1955); Trio for Violin, Cello, and Piano (1956); Cello Sonata (1958); Viola Sonata (1959); Quintet for Oboe and Strings (1962); *Intrada* for String Quartet (1962); 7 Pieces for String Quartet (1964); Woodwind Quintet (1965); 4 Dances for Brass Quintet (1967); *Intrada* for Woodwind Quintet and Saxophone (1970); 5 Canons for 2 Horns (1971); Variations for Tuba and 9 Horns (1974); Quintet for Flute, Violin, Viola, Bassoon, and Contrabass (1975); 4 Movements for Saxophone Quartet and Timpani (1976); Variations on *Lilliburlero* for Cello (1976); Terzetto for 2 Flutes and Cello (1979); Quartet for Horns (1981); Sextet for Brass Quintet and Piano (1983); Quartet for Piano, Violin, Cello, and Horn (1985); Trio Serenade for Violin, Clarinet, and Piano (1987); *Préludes* for Flute, Bass, and Harp (1988); Trio for Oboe, Bassoon, and Piano (1992); *Divertimento* for Tuba and 8 Solo Instruments (1992); *Serenata* for 4 Cellos (1993); *Prelude, Theme, and Variations* for Alto Recorder (1994); *Encounters* for Brass Quintet (1994); Clarinet Trio (1996); 5 *Inventions* for Flute and Cello (1998); 4 *Canons* for 2 Clarinets (1998). KEYBOARD: Piano: 2 sonatas (1941, 1952); Sonata for Piano, 4–Hands (1946); *Variations* (1959); *Fantasia* for 2 Pianos (1971); *Hommage à Scarlatti* (1971); 3 *Preludes and Fugues* for Piano, Right Hand (1994). Organ: Variations on *The Cruel Ship's Carpenter* (1950). VOCAL: 2 *Songs of Spring* for Women's Chorus (1947); 4 *Songs from the Song of Songs* for Soprano and Orch. or Piano (1948); *Divine Poems* for Chorus, after John Donne (1949); *In Memoriam* for Chorus (1964); *Advent Song* for Chorus (1965);

Riddles of Jonathan Swift for Women's Chorus (1975); *Sonnets of Louise Labe* for Soprano and String Quartet (1977); *Triptych* for Baritone and Orch. (1983); *A Bestiary* for Soprano, Tenor, and Chamber Orch. (1986); *Dona Nobis Pacem* for 3 Voices (1995).
—NS/LK/DM

Heifetz, Daniel (Alan), American violinist and teacher; b. Kansas City, Mo., Nov. 20, 1948. He studied with several teachers in Los Angeles, then went to Philadelphia, where he had advanced training with Zimbalist, Galamian, and Jascha Brodsky at the Curtis Inst. of Music (1966–71). In 1969 he won 1st prize in the Merriweather Post Competition in Washington, D.C. On Jan. 20, 1970, he made his debut in Tchaikovsky's Violin Concerto with the National Sym. Orch. of Washington, D.C., on tour in N.Y. He then entered the Tchaikovsky Competition in Moscow, winning 4th prize (1978). He concertized in Europe and throughout the Americas; from 1980 he taught at the Peabody Cons. of Music in Baltimore.—NS/LK/DM

Heifetz, Jascha (Iossif Robertovich), great Russian-born American violinist; b. Vilnius, Feb. 2, 1899; d. Los Angeles, Dec. 10, 1987. His father, Ruben Heifetz, an able musician, taught him the rudiments of violin playing at a very early age; he then studied with Ilya Malkin at the Vilnius Music School, and played in public before he was 5 years old; at the age of 6, he played Mendelssohn's Concerto in Kovno. In 1910 he was taken by his father to St. Petersburg, and entered the Cons. there in the class of Nalbandian; after a few months, he was accepted as a pupil by Leopold Auer. He gave his first public concert in St. Petersburg on April 30, 1911. The following year, with a letter of recommendation from Auer, he went to Berlin; his first concert there (May 24, 1912), in the large hall of the Hochschule für Musik, attracted great attention: Artur Nikisch engaged him to play the Tchaikovsky Concerto with the Berlin Phil. (Oct. 28, 1912), but his appearance proved uneventful. He then decided to continue his studies with Auer in St. Petersburg and in Germany. While visiting Auer in Norway in 1916, he played in a joint concert with Toscha Seidel before the king and queen of Norway. After the Russian Revolution of 1917, he went to America, by way of Siberia and the Orient. His debut at Carnegie Hall in N.Y. (Oct. 27, 1917) won for him the highest expression of enthusiasm from the public and in the press. Mischa Elman, the prime violinist of an older generation, attended the concert in the company of the pianist Leopold Godowsky. When Elman complained that it was too hot in the hall, Godowsky retorted, "Not for pianists." Veritable triumphs followed during Heifetz's tour of the U.S., and soon his fame spread all over the world. He made his first London appearance on May 5, 1920; toured Australia (1921), the Orient (1923), Palestine (1926), and South America. He revisited Russia in 1934, and was welcomed enthusiastically. He became a naturalized American citizen in 1925, and made his home in Beverly Hills, Calif. Heifetz made regular tours throughout the world, appearing not only with the foremost orchs. but as a recitalist. As a chamber music artist, he played in trios with Rubinstein and Feuermann, and later with

Pennario and Piatigorsky. He taught classes of exceptionally talented pupils at the Univ. of Southern Calif. in Los Angeles (1962–72). In 1974 he made his last public appearance and thereby brought to a close one of the most extraordinary violin careers in history.

The Olympian quality of Heifetz's playing was unique in luminous transparency of texture, tonal perfection, and formal equilibrium of phrasing; he never allowed his artistic temperament to superimpose extraneous elements on the music; this inspired tranquillity led some critics to characterize his interpretations as impersonal and detached. Heifetz made numerous arrangements for violin of works by Bach, Vivaldi, and contemporary composers; his most famous transcription is *Hora Staccato* by Grigoraş Dinicu, made into a virtuoso piece by adroit ornamentation and rhythmic elaboration. In his desire to promote modern music, he commissioned a number of composers (Walton, Gruenberg, Castelnuovo-Tedesco, and others) to write violin concertos for him, and performed several of them.

BIBL.: H. Axelrod, ed., *H.* (Neptune City, N.J., 1976; 2nd ed., aug., 1981); A. Weschler-Vered, *J. H.* (London, 1986). **—NS/LK/DM**

Heiller, Anton, esteemed Austrian organist, conductor, pedagogue, and composer; b. Vienna, Sept. 15, 1923; d. there, March 25, 1979. He received training in piano, organ, harpsichord, and composition at the Vienna Academy of Music (1941–42). After winning the Haarlem competition for organ improvisation in 1952, he was notably successful as an organ virtuoso, excelling especially in the music of Bach. In 1945 he joined the faculty of the Vienna Academy of Music; after it became the Vienna Hochschule für Musik, he was made a prof. there in 1971. In 1969 he was awarded the Austrian State Prize for Music. In his compositions, he displayed an adept handling of polyphonic writing; in some of his music, he utilized the 12–tone method.

WORKS: *Toccata* for 2 Pianos (1945); 2 organ sonatas (1946, 1953); *Tentatio Jesu*, chamber oratorio for Tenor, Bass, Chorus, and 2 Pianos (1952); *In festo corporis Christi* for Organ (1957); *Missa super modos duodecimales* for Chorus and 7 Instruments (1960); Organ Concerto (1963); *In principio eret verbum* for Tenor, Chorus, Orch., and Organ (1965); *Stabat mater* for Chorus and Orch. (1968); *Adventsmusik* for Chorus and Organ (1971); *Passionsmusik* for Children's Chorus and Organ (1975); other masses; cantatas.**—NS/LK/DM**

Heilman, William Clifford, American composer; b. Williamsport, Pa., Sept. 27, 1877; d. there, Dec. 20, 1946. He studied at Harvard Univ. (B.A., 1900) and in Europe with Rheinberger and Widor. He was a member of the music dept. of Harvard Univ. from 1905 until 1930. Among his works are a symphonic poem, *By the Porta Catania* (1916), Piano Trio, *Romance* for Cello and Piano, a number of character pieces for piano, and choruses. He also made arrangements of Negro spirituals.**—NS/LK/DM**

Heinefetter, family of German opera singers, all sisters:

(1) Sabine Heinefetter, soprano; b. Mainz, Aug. 19, 1809; d. Illemau, Nov. 18, 1872. She made her operatic debut in Ritter's *Der Mandarin* in Frankfurt am Main in 1822. Spohr then engaged her for Kassel, but she broke her contract to continue vocal study with Banderali and Tadolini in Paris. After appearances at the Théâtre-Italien there, she sang with brilliant success all over Europe. She created the role of Adina in *L'elisir d'amore* (Milan, 1832). She made her farewell appearances in Marseilles in 1846. She died insane.

(2) Clara Heinefetter, soprano; b. Mainz, Sept. 7, 1813; d. Vienna, Feb. 23, 1857. She studied with her sister Sabine and with Ciccimarra in Vienna, making her debut there in 1831. She subsequently sang under the name of Mme. Stöckl-Heinefetter. From 1840 to 1842 she appeared in London. Like her sister, she died insane.

(3) Kathinka Heinefetter, soprano; b. Mainz, Sept. 12, 1819; d. Freiburg im Breisgau, Dec. 20, 1858. She studied with her sister Sabine and with Ponchard in Vienna, making her debut in Frankfurt am Main in 1836. She retired from the stage in 1853. Three other Heinefetter sisters, Fatima, Eva, and Nanetta, also appeared professionally on the operatic stage.**—NS/LK/DM**

Heinemann, Alfred, German composer; b. Buckeburg, April 10, 1908. He played piano as a child, and began to compose at the age of 10. In 1936 he went to Johannesburg, South Africa. In 1944 he moved to Cape Town, where he was active mainly as a teacher. In 1949 he settled in the U.S., and in 1967 joined the staff of Broadcast Music Inc. His music follows the tenets of enlightened functionalism, without transgressing the natural capacities of the instruments.

WORKS: DRAMATIC: O p e r a : *Torso* (1958). **B a l l e t :** *Galaxy* (1941); *Roulette* (1946); *La Manie des titres et des abbréviations* (1953); *Kobold* (1963). **ORCH.:** Piano Concerto (1941); Violin Concerto (1942); *March of the Neanderthal Men* (Cape Town, April 7, 1946); Sym. (1959–64).**—NS/LK/DM**

Heinemeyer, Ernst Wilhelm, outstanding German flutist; b. Hannover, Feb. 25, 1827; d. Vienna, Feb. 12, 1869. He studied with his father, Christian Heinemeyer (1796–1872), who was the chamber flutist at Hannover. In 1847 he went to Russia, where he played the flute in the Imperial Orch. at St. Petersburg. In 1859 he returned to Hannover, and in 1866 he went to Vienna. He wrote several concertos for the flute.**—NS/LK/DM**

Heinichen, Johann David, notable German music theorist and composer; b. Krössuln, near Weissenfels, April 17, 1683; d. Dresden, July 16, 1729. He received training in organ and harpsichord from Kuhnau at the Leipzig Thomasschule (1695–1702). After studying law at the Univ. of Leipzig (1702–06), he worked as an advocate in Weissenfels. His first opera, *Der Karneval von venedig, oder Der angenehme Betrug,* may have been performed in Weissenfels as early as 1705. In 1709 he went to Leipzig as an opera composer, where he was director of the Collegium Musicum; he also was court composer in Zeitz and opera composer to the court in Naumburg. He accompanied Councillor Buchta of Zeitz to Italy (1710–16), during which sojourn he brought out several operas. In 1717 he was named court

Kapellmeister to the Prince-Elector of Saxony, Frederick Augustus, in Dresden, sharing his duties with J. C. Schmidt. After a violent quarrel between Heinichen and the singer Berselli, the Dresden Opera was dissolved. However, Heinichen remained at the court as director of church and chamber music until his death. In addition to operas, he also composed 4 syms., 2 overtures, 30 concertos, much chamber music, 2 oratorios, 16 masses, 63 cantatas, and over 100 other sacred works. Many of his MSS housed in the Dresden Court (later State) Library perished in the Allied fire-bombing of the city in 1945. Few of his works have been published, although the championship of his music by Reinhard Goebel via recordings has proved noteworthy. Heinichen's importance rests principally upon his valuable theoretical work, *Neu erfundene und grundliche Answeisung zu vollkommener Erlernung des General-Basses* (Hamburg, 1711; 2nd ed., rev. and greatly aug., Dresden, 1728, as *Der General-Bass in der Composition, oder: Neue und gründliche Anweisung*).

BIBL.: G. Seibel, *Das Leben des Königliche Polnischen und Kürfurstlich Sächsischen Hofkapellmeisters J. D. H.* (Leipzig, 1913); R. Tanner, *J. D. H. als dramatischer Komponist* (Leipzig, 1916); G. Hausswald, *J. D. H.s Instrumentalwerke* (Wolfenbüttel and Berlin, 1937); G. Buelow, *Thorough-Bass Accompaniment According to J. D. H.* (Berkeley, Calif., 1966; 3rd ed., rev., 1992); M. Unger, *The German Chorale Compositions of J. D. H. (1683–1729)* (Lang, N.Y., 1990).—NS/LK/DM

Heininen, Paavo (Johannes), significant Finnish composer and teacher; b. Helsinki, Jan. 13, 1938. After studying privately with Merilainen, he took courses with Merikanto, Rautavaara, Englund, and Kokkonen at the Sibelius Academy in Helsinki (composition diploma, 1960). He later took courses with Zimmermann in Cologne (1960–61), and with Persichetti and Steuermann at the Juilliard School of Music in N.Y. (1961–62), worked with Lutosławski in Poland, and attended theory classes at the Univ. of Helsinki. In 1962–63 he was on the faculty of the Sibelius Academy. He then taught in Turku (1963–66) before resuming his position at the Sibelius Academy, where he was mentor to a generation of Finnish composers. He was also active as a pianist, conductor, and program annotator. He developed a highly complex compositional style, employing styles and techniques ranging from neo- Classicism to dodecaphonic and serial procedures culminating in a stream-of- consciousness modality.

WORKS: DRAMATIC: *Silkkirumpu* (The Silken Drum), concerto for Singers, Players, Words, Images, and Movements (1981–83; Helsinki, April 5, 1984); *Veitsi* (The Knife), opera (1985–88; Helsinki, July 3, 1989). **ORCH.:** 4 syms.: No. 1 (1958; rev. 1960; Helsinki, March 24, 1964), No. 2, *Petite symphonie joyeuse* (Helsinki, Dec. 7, 1962), No. 3 (1969; rev. 1977; Helsinki, Jan. 24, 1978), and No. 4 (1971; Oslo, Sept. 4, 1972); *Preambolo* (1959); *Tripartita* (1959; Helsinki, Nov. 11, 1960); Concerto for Strings (1959; Helsinki, April 19, 1960; rev. 1963; Turku, May 30, 1963); *Soggetto* (1963; Helsinki, Jan. 12, 1965); *Adagio...concerto per orchestra in forma di variazioni...* (1963; Helsinki, Jan. 24, 1964; rev. 1966; Camden Festival, Feb. 19, 1967); 3 piano concertos: No. 1 (1964; Turku, Jan. 23, 1965), No. 2 (Turku, Dec. 1, 1966), and No. 3 (1981; Helsinki, March 13, 1982); *Arioso* for Strings (Helsinki, May 21, 1967); *Deux chansons* for Cello and Orch.

(1976; Tampere, Feb. 25, 1977); *Tritopos* (1977; Helsinki, March 7, 1978); *Dia* (Helsinki, Sept. 12, 1979); *Attitude* (Helsinki, Dec. 10, 1980); *...floral view with maidens singing...* for Chamber Orch. (1982; Kokkola, April 8, 1983); *Dicta, "Nonette avec milieu"* for 9 plus 14 Players in the Audience (Helsinki, March 25, 1983); Saxophone Concerto (Helsinki, Aug. 29, 1983); *KauToKei* for Double String Orch. (1985; Helsinki, Feb. 12, 1986); Cello Concerto (1985; Helsinki, Feb. 26, 1986); *Lamentation and Praise* (1995); *5 Lightnings* (1997; Turku, Aug. 9, 1998). **CHAMBER:** Quintet for Flute, Saxophone, Piano, Vibraphone, and Percussion (1961); *Musique d'été* for Flute, Clarinet, Violin, Cello, Harpsichord, Vibraphone, and Percussion (1963; rev. version, Tampere, Oct. 11, 1967); *Discantus I* for Alto Flute (1965), *II* for Clarinet (1969), and *III* for Alto Saxophone (1976); *Poesie des pensées* for Cello (1970); *Cantilena I* for Viola or Violin or Cello (1970), *II* for Cello (1970), and *III* for Violin (1976); Violin Sonata (1970; Helsinki, Feb. 18, 1973); *Deux chansons* for Cello and Piano (1974); String Quartet (1974; Helsinki, Jan. 21, 1976); *Gymel* for Bassoon and Tape (1978); *Touching* for Guitar (1978); *Jeu I* for Flute and Piano (1980) and *II* for Violin and Piano (1980); *Beateth* for Percussion (1982). **KEYBOARD: Piano:** *Toccata* (1956); Sonatine (1957); *Libretto della primavera* (1971); Sonata, *Poesia squillante ed incandescente* (1974); *Préludes-études-poèmes* (1974); *Poesies-periphrases* (1975); *Triple apercu d'une amie qui fut* (1984); *Cinq moments de jour* (1984). **Organ:** *Oculus aquilae-trittico* (1968); *...irdisch gewesen zu sein...* (1972); *...des Säglichen Zeit...* (1972). **VOCAL:** *Canto di Natale* for Soprano and Piano (1961); *Cantico delle creature* for Baritone and Orch. (1968); *Love's Philosophy* for Tenor and Piano (1968–73); *The Autumn* for Chorus (1970); *Schatten der Erde* for Mezzo-soprano and Piano (1973); *...cor meum...* for Chorus (1976–79); *Reality* for Soprano and 10 Instruments (1978); *Virsi-81* (Hymn-81) for Chorus and Organ (1981); *4 Lullabies* for Men's Voices (1986). **Electroacoustic:** *Maiandros* (1977).—NS/LK/DM

Heiniö, Mikko, Finnish composer and musicologist; b. Tampere, May 5, 1948. He was a student in piano of Liisa Pohjola and in composition of Kokkonen at the Sibelius Academy in Helsinki (1971–75; composition diploma, 1977). He also studied composition with Szalonek on a Deutscher Akademischer Austauschdienst scholarship in Berlin (1975–77). From 1977 to 1985 he taught at the Univ. of Helsinki, where he took his Ph.D. in musicology in 1984 with a diss. on the idea of innovation and tradition in the musical philosophy of contemporary Finnish composers. In 1986 he became prof. of musicology at the Univ. of Turku. He publ. several monographs and journal articles on various aspects of contemporary Finnish music. In his compositions, he is a modernist who draws upon the varied resources offered by serialism, aleatory, minimalism, and the popular genres.

WORKS: DRAMATIC: *Hermes*, dance pictures for Piano, Soprano, and Strings (1994; Turku, Aug. 11, 1995). **ORCH.:** 5 piano concertos: No. 1 (1972), No. 2 (1973; Helsinki, Feb. 26, 1975), No. 3 (1981; Tampere, Feb. 23, 1984), No. 4, *Genom kvällen* (Through the Evening), for Piano, Chorus, and Strings (1986; Espoo, May 21, 1989), and No. 5 (1989; Turku, April 5, 1990); Concerto grosso for Strings and Harpsichord (1975; Oslo, April 22, 1977); *Tredica* (1976; Helsinki, Dec. 13, 1978); Bassoon Concerto (1977; Bergen, March 2, 1978); Horn Concerto (1978; Pori, March 5, 1980); *Concerto for Orchestra* (Turku, Nov. 11, 1982); *Possible Worlds*, sym. (Turku, Dec. 10, 1987); *Dall'ombra all'ombra* for Orch. and Synthesizer (Turku, Nov. 28, 1992); *Trias*

1513

(Turku, May 26, 1995). CHAMBER: Suite for Flute and 2 Guitars (Helsinki, May 10, 1974); *Lindgreniana* for Oboe (1975; Helsinki, March 10, 1980); Trio for Oboe, Bassoon, and Harpsichord (Helsinki, July 29, 1976); Suite for Bassoon (1976); *Diberlimento* for 4 Flutes, 4 Trombones, and 3 Percussionists (1976; Berlin, Feb. 2, 1977); *Canto caotico* for 4 Cellos (1976; Berlin, Feb. 16, 1977); *Ākāśa* for 6 Trombones (Jyväskylä, July 7, 1977); *Notturno di fiordo* for Flute or Piccolo and Harp (1978); *Brass Mass* for 4 Trumpets, 4 Trombones, and Tuba ad libitum (1979; Helsinki, April 15, 1980); Duo for Violin and Piano (1979; Finnish Radio, May 5, 1980); *Champignons à l'herméneutique* for Flute and Guitar (1979; Helsinki, Dec. 16, 1980); *Minimba 1* for 4 or 3 Guitars (1982; Espoo, May 3, 1984); *...in spe* for Saxophone and Marimba or Vibraphone (1984); Trio for Violin, Cello, and Piano (1988); *In G* for Cello and Piano (1988); *Aurora*, fanfare for 11 Brass Instruments (1989; Turku, May 9, 1990); *Wintertime* for Vibraphone or Marimba and Harp (1990; Stockholm, Nov. 8, 1991); Piano Quintet (1993; Kuhmo, July 20, 1994). P i a n o : *Deductions 1* (Helsinki, Nov. 23, 1979); *3 Repetitive Dreams* (1982; Jyväskylä, July 4, 1983); *Into Sleep* (1986); *Ritornelli* (1991; Helsinki, April 28, 1992). VOCAL: *4 Night Songs* for Baritone or Contralto and Piano or Orch. (1972); *Agnus Dei* for Children's Chorus, Flute, Guitar, and String Orch. (1974; Helsinki, Oct. 30, 1979; also for Children's Chorus and Organ); *Kinerva* for Tenor and Men's Chorus (1978; Helsinki, May 14, 1980); *The Land That Is Not* for Children's or Women's Chorus and Piano (1980; Helsinki, May 12, 1981); *The Shadow of the Future* for Soprano, 4 Trumpets, 4 Trombones, and Tuba (1980; Helsinki, March 14, 1981); *Vuelo de alambre* for Soprano and Orch. (1983; Helsinki, April 3, 1985); *Continent Cantata* for Soprano, Baritone, Chorus, and Orch. (1985); *La* for Soprano, Mezzo- soprano or Contralto, Tenor, Bass, and Piano (1985; Helsinki, March 9, 1986); *Minimba 2* for Men's Chorus (1988); *Wind Pictures* for Chorus and Orch. (1991; Turku, Nov. 26, 1992); *Leceat* for Chorus (Helsinki, Dec. 6, 1992).—NS/LK/DM

Heinitz, Wilhelm, German musicologist; b. Hamburg-Altona, Dec. 9, 1883; d. Hamburg, March 31, 1963. He studied the bassoon, and played in various orchs. He then became interested in phonetics and studied primitive music and the languages of Africa and Polynesia. He took a Ph.D. in psychology at the Univ. of Kiel (1920), and completed his Habilitation at the Univ. of Hamburg (1931) with his *Strukturprobleme in primitiver Musik* (publ. in Hamburg, 1931). In 1915 he became an assistant in the phonetics laboratory at the Univ. of Hamburg; was founder-director of its dept. of research for comparative musicology (1931–49). He wrote a number of valuable papers on the structural problems of speech, which he publ. in specialized journals; also the books *Klangprobleme im Rundfunk* (Berlin, 1926), *Instrumentenkunde* (Potsdam, 1929), *Neue Wege der Volksmusikforschung* (Hamburg, 1937), *Erforschung rassischer Merkmale aus der Volksmusik* (Hamburg, 1938), and *Physiologische Reaktion und Pulsationsmessung* (Hamburg, 1958).—NS/LK/DM

Heinrich, Anthony Philip (actually, **Anton Philipp**), prominent American composer of German-Bohemian descent; b. Schönbüchel, March 11, 1781; d. N.Y., May 3, 1861. He was adopted by a wealthy uncle and given lessons in violin and piano; all the same, he was mainly autodidact as a musician. At his uncle's

death, he came into a rich inheritance, including property and a flourishing business. In 1805 he visited the U.S., and returned there in 1810 to pursue his business interests but without success. In the wake of the Austrian financial debacle of 1811, he lost his wealth and returned to the U.S. in a vain attempt to restore his fortunes. After he failed again in business in 1817, he set out on a trek through the American wilderness, which took him from Philadelphia to Pittsburgh, and then down the Ohio River to Bardstown, Ky. He managed to find enough musicians to conduct one of Beethoven's syms. in Lexington, Ky., on Nov. 12, 1817, the first known performance of a Beethoven sym. in America. In 1818 he began to compose in earnest, which resulted in the publication of his op.1, *The Dawning of Music in Kentucky, or The Pleasures of Harmony in the Solitudes of Nature* (Philadelphia, 1820; rev. 1820–23), a collection of piano music, pieces for violin and piano, and songs. It was followed by the collections *The Western Minstrel*, op.2 (Philadelphia, 1820; rev. 1820–23) and *The Sylviad, or Minstrelsy of Nature in the Wilds of N. America*, op.3 (Boston, 1823, and 1825–26). From 1826 to 1831 he pursued his career in Europe, returning there in 1833. In 1836 he received critical accolades as a composer in Graz. In 1837 he settled in N.Y. and acquired a notable reputation. His works were heard at festivals there in 1842, 1846, and 1853, and critics hailed him as "the Beethoven of America." He became affectionately known as "Father Heinrich." In 1856 he returned once more to Europe. By the time he returned to N.Y. in 1859, interest in his career had plummeted and he ended his days in poverty. While Heinrich wrote some fine piano pieces and songs, he was a composer dedicated to scores on a grand scale. His often amusingly titled symphonic works may be the product of a composer of an eccentric bent, but they are not without redeeming qualities. He was much taken by descriptive writing, and remains historically important as the first major composer in America to consider the American Indian as a subject worthy of serious compositional effort.

WORKS: ORCH.: *Pushmataha, a Venerable Chief of a Western Tribe of Indians* (1831); *A Concerto for the Kent Bugle* (1834); *Complaint of Logan, the Mingo Chief* (1834); *The Indian War Council* (1834); *The Mocking Bird to the Nightingale* (1834); *The Tower of Babel* (1834); *The Treaty of William Penn with the Indians*, concerto grosso (1834; rev. 1847); *The Wildwood Troubadour*, overture (1834–53); *The Jäger's Adieu* (1835); *Gran sinfonia eroica* (c. 1835); *Pocahontas* (1837); *The Columbiad*, sym. (1837); *The Hunters of Kentucky*, sym. (1837); *Schiller*, grande sinfonia dramatica (1830s; rev. 1847); *The Wild Wood Spirits' Chant* (c. 1842); *Musica sacra no. 1: The Tower of Babel* (1843; rev. 1852); *National Memories*, overture (1844–52); *Johannis Berg* (c. 1844); *Manitou Mysteries*, sym. (c. 1844); *The Indian Carnival*, sinfonia erotica fantachia (c. 1844); *The War of the Elements* (c. 1844); *Boadicèa*, overture (c. 1845); *Shenandoah* (c. 1845); *The Empress Queen and the Magyars*, sinfonia patriotica-dramatica (c. 1845); *The Mastodon*, sym. (c. 1845); *To the Spirit of Beethoven*, sym. (c. 1845); *The Ornithological Combat of Kings*, sym. (1847; rev. 1856); *The Tomb of Genius: To the Memory of Mendelssohn-Bartholdy*, sinfonia sacra (c. 1847); *The Castle in the Moon* (1850); *Austria: The Flight of the Double Eagle*, overture (c. 1853); *Bohemia*, sinfonia romantica (c. 1853); *Homage à la Bohème*, sym. (1855); *Austria: Heil dir ritterlicher Kaiser*, march (c. 1858); *Die Allianz beider Hemispheren* (c.

1858); *The Harper of Kentucky*, overture (n.d.). **BRASS BAND AND PERCUSSION:** *Marcia funerale* (c. 1851); *Marcia funebre for the Heroes* (c. 1852). **CHAMBER:** *Ode to the Memory of Commodore O. H. Perry* for Piano and Violin or Flute (1820); *Tema di Mozart and an Original Air* for 2 Violins, Double Bass or Cello, and Piano ad libitum (1820); *The Yankee Doodleiad* for 3 Violins, Double Bass or Cello, and Piano (1820); *Storia d'un violino* for Violin (1831); *Souvenir of the Hudson Highlands* for Piano and Violin (1851); *Trip to the "Catskill Mountain House"* for Violin and Piano (1851); *Otetto* for 3 Violins, 2 Violas, 2 Cellos, Double Bass, and Triangle (c. 1858); numerous solo piano pieces. **VOCAL:** *O santa Maria* for Soprano, Tenor, and Chamber Orch. (1834); *Musica sacra, No. 2: Adoramus te Christe* for 3 Voices and Orch. (1835) and *No. 3: O Santa Maria* for Chorus and Chamber Orch. (c. 1835); *The Jubilee* for 5 Soloists, Chorus, and Orch. (1841); *The Warriors' March* for 4 Soloists, Chorus, and Orch. (1845); *Coro funerale* for 5 Soloists, Chorus, Semichorus, Orch., and Organ (c. 1847); *Amor patriae—Our Native Land* for 5 Soloists, Chorus, and Orch. or Piano (c. 1853); *Noble Emperor* for 5 Soloists, Chorus, and Orch. (c. 1854); choruses; many solo songs.

BIBL.: F. Mussik, *Skizzen aus dem Leben des sich in Amerika befindenden deutschen Tondichters A.P. H., nach authentischen Quellen bearbeitet* (Prague, 1843); *A.P. H. ("Vater Heinrich"): Zur Lebensgeschichte des Veteran Kompositeurs, unsers aus der neuen Welt beimgekehrten Landsmannes* (Prague, 1857); W. Upton, *A.P. H.: A Nineteenth-century Composer in America* (N.Y., 1939); F. Bruce, *The Piano Pieces of A.P. H. Contained in "The Dawning of Music in Kentucky" and "The Western Minstrel"* (diss., Univ. of Ill., 1971); D. Barron, *The Early Vocal Works of A.P. H.* (diss., Univ. of Ill., 1972); W. Maust, *The Symphonies of A.P. H. Based on American Themes* (diss., Ind. Univ., 1973).—**NS/LK/DM**

Heinroth, Johann August Gunther, German composer and writer on music; b. Nordhausen, June 19, 1780; d. Göttingen, June 2, 1846. He studied with his father, an able organist. He then attended the Univs. of Leipzig and Halle. In 1804 he became attached to the School of Jewish Studies organized by Israel Jacobson. This was the beginning of a lifelong study of the Jewish liturgy, which he reorganized, adding numerous original melodies that became part of the Jewish service. He also attempted to introduce a simplified musical notation by figures. From 1818 he served as music director of the Univ. of Göttingen, in succession to Forkel.

WRITINGS (all publ. in Göttingen): *Gesangunterrichts-Methode für höhere und niedere Schulen* (3 parts; 1821–23); *Volksnoten oder vereinfachte Tonschrift* (1828); *Kurze Anleitung, das Klavier oder Forte-Piano spielen zu lehren* (1828); *Musikalisches Hilfsbuch für Prediger, Kantoren und Organisten* (1833).

BIBL.: W. Boetticher, *Die Musik an der Georgia Augusta-Universität zu Göttingen* (1958).—**NS/LK/DM**

Heinsheimer, Hans (Walter), German-born American publishing executive and writer on music; b. Karlsruhe, Sept. 25, 1900; d. N.Y., Oct. 12, 1993. He studied law in Heidelberg, Munich, and Freiburg im Breisgau (Juris Dr., 1923), and then joined Universal Edition in Vienna, where he was in charge of its opera dept. (1924–38), and supervised the publication of such important stage works as Berg's *Wozzeck*, Krenek's *Jonny spielt auf*, Weinberger's *Schwanda*, Weill's *Aufstieg und Fall der Stadt Mahagonny*, and Antheil's *Transatlantic*.

He went to the U.S. in 1938 and was associated with the N.Y. branch of Boosey & Hawkes. In 1947 he was appointed director of the symphonic and operatic repertoire of G. Schirmer, Inc., and in 1957 he became director of publications and in 1972 vice-president of the firm. In these capacities, he promoted the works of Barber, Menotti, Bernstein, and Carter. He retired in 1974 and devoted himself mainly to writing. A brilliant stylist in both German and English, he contributed numerous informative articles to *Melos, Musical Quarterly, Holiday, Reader's Digest*, etc. He publ. the entertaining books *Menagerie in F-sharp* (N.Y., 1947) and *Fanfare for Two Pigeons* (1952); the 2 works were publ. in German in a single vol. entitled *Menagerie in Fis-dur* (Zürich, 1953); he also wrote *Best Regards to Aida* (publ. in Ger. as *Schönste Grüsse an Aida*; Munich, 1968).—**NS/LK/DM**

Heintze, Gustaf (Hjalmar), Swedish pianist, organist, pedagogue, and composer; b. Jönköping, July 22, 1879; d. Saltsjöbaden, March 4, 1946. His grandfather, Gustav Wilhelm Heintze (1825–1909), and father, Georg Wilhelm Heintze (1849–95), were well-known organists. He studied organ in Lund and Stockholm, and studied composition and instrumentation with Joseph Dente (1897–1900) and piano with Richard Andersson (1901) in Stockholm; then taught piano at Andersson's school (1901–18). He subsequently founded his own piano school, and was also organist at the Maria Magdalena Church. He wrote 2 piano concertos (1917, 1926), 2 violin concertos (1921, 1932), a Concerto for 2 Pianos and Orch. (1933), 3 cantatas (1923, 1934, 1940), and piano pieces.—**NS/LK/DM**

Heinze, Gustav Adolf, German conductor and composer; b. Leipzig, Oct. 1, 1820; d. Muiderberg, near Amsterdam, Feb. 20, 1904. He received his early musical education from his father, a clarinetist in the Gewandhaus Orch. in Leipzig, and joined that orch. as clarinetist at the age of 16. He then conducted at the Breslau City Theater (1844–49), where he successfully produced 2 operas: *Loreley* (1846) and *Die Ruinen von Tharandt* (1847). In 1850 he went to Amsterdam, where he founded a singing school (1862–69); he later founded a music school in Bussum (1885). He composed, besides his operas, several oratorios and other choral works. He publ. an autobiography (Amsterdam, 1905).—**NS/LK/DM**

Heinze, Sir Bernard (Thomas), eminent Australian conductor; b. Shepparton, near Melbourne, July 1, 1894; d. Sydney, June 9, 1982. He studied at the Univ. of Melbourne, the Royal Coll. of Music in London, with d'Indy at the Schola Cantorum in Paris, and with Willy Hess (violin) in Berlin. In 1924 he joined the faculty of the Melbourne Conservatorium, where he was a prof. from 1925 to 1956. In 1924 he also became conductor of the Univ. of Melbourne Orch. After it merged with the Melbourne Sym. Orch. in 1932, Heinze served as conductor of the latter until 1949. He also was conductor of the Royal Phil. Soc. in Melbourne (1927–53) and with the Australian Broadcasting Co. (1929–32), and its successor, the Australian Broadcasting Commission (from

1932), as well as adviser to the Sydney Sym. Orch. (1934–43). From 1956 to 1966 he was director of the New South Wales State Conservatorium in Sydney. He was knighted in 1949 and was made a Companion of the Order of Australia in 1976 for his manifold contributions to Australian music.

BIBL.: T. Radic, *B. H.: A Biography* (South Melbourne, 1986). —NS/LK/DM

Heise, Peter (Arnold), esteemed Danish composer; b. Copenhagen, Feb. 11, 1830; d. Stockkerup, Sept. 12, 1879. He studied music with Berggreen in Copenhagen and with Hauptmann at the Leipzig Cons. Returning to Denmark, he became a music teacher and organist at Sorö, where he remained until 1865. He then settled in Copenhagen. He composed 2 successful operas, *Paschaens datter* (The Pasha's Daughter; Sept. 30, 1869) and *Drot og marsk* (King and Marshal; Sept. 25, 1878), as well as a Sym., chamber music, but it was in his many lieder to Danish texts that Heise achieved enduring fame.

BIBL.: G. Hetsch, *P. H.* (Copenhagen, 1926).—NS/LK/DM

Heiss, Hermann, German composer and teacher; b. Darmstadt, Dec. 29, 1897; d. there, Dec. 6, 1966. He studied with Bernhard Sekles in Frankfurt am Main (1921), then took a course in 12–tone music with Hauer (1925). He was active as a teacher in Frankfurt am Main and Vienna; from 1946 he taught at the Darmstadt summer courses for new music. In his compositions, he adopted ultra-modern techniques.

WORKS: DRAMATIC: B a l l e t : *Herz auf bürgerliche Art* (1953); *Der Manager* (1954). **ORCH.:** *Sinfonia atematica* (1950); *Sinfonia giocosa* (1954); *Configurationen I-II* (1956–59); *Polychromatica* (1959); *Bewegungsspiele* (1959). **OTHER:** Chamber music; electronic pieces.

BIBL.: B. Reichenbach, *H. H.* (Mainz, 1975).—NS/LK/DM

Heiss, John, American flutist, conductor, teacher, and composer; b. N.Y., Oct. 23, 1938. He studied mathematics at Lehigh Univ. (B.A., 1960) before pursuing graduate studies in music with Leuning at Columbia Univ. (1960–65). He also took courses in composition (with Milhaud) and in flute at the Aspen (Colo.) Music School (summers, 1962–63). His training in composition was completed under Babbitt and Kim at Princeton Univ. (M.F.A., 1967). From 1969 to 1974 he was principal flute with Boston Musica Viva. He also played flute with other ensembles and made occasional appearances as a conductor. After teaching at Columbia Univ. (1963–65) and Barnard Coll. (1964–65), he taught at the New England Cons. of Music in Boston (from 1967), where he was director of its Contemporary Ensemble. Among his honors were a Guggenheim fellowship, 4 NEA grants, and annual ASCAP awards.

WORKS: ORCH.: *4 Short Pieces* (1962); *Music* (1968); *Inventions, Contours, and Colors* for Chamber Orch. (1973); Concerto for Flute and Chamber Orch. (1977; recomposed as the Chamber Concerto for Flute, Clarinet, Piano, and Percussion); *Festival Prelude* (1983); *Mosaics I* for Flute Orch. (1986), *II* for Cello Choir (1987), *III* for Trombone Choir (1989), and *IV* for Clarinet Choir (1991). **CHAMBER:** *4 Lyric Pieces* for Flute (1962); Flute Sonatina (1962); *5 Pieces* for Flute and Cello (1963); *4 Movements* for 3 Flutes (1969); Quartet for Flute, Clarinet, Cello, and Piano (1971); *Capriccio* for Flute, Clarinet, and Percussion (1976); Chamber Concerto for Flute, Clarinet, Piano, and Percussion (1977; recomposition of the Concerto for Flute and Chamber Orch.); *Eloquy* for Flute, Oboe, Clarinet, and Bassoon (1978); *Études* for Flute (1979–80); *Episode I* for Violin (1980), *II: Elegia* for Double Bass (1992), and *III: Arietta* for Viola (1993); *So-nar-ity* for Piano, 4–Hands, Harp, Percussion, Flute, and Clarinet (1982); *A Place in New England* for Brass Quartet or Choir and Organ (1982); *Epigrams* for Flute and Percussion (1985); Fanfare for 4 Trombones (1992); *Fantasia Appassionata* for Flute (1994). **VOCAL:** *3 Songs from Sandburg* for Treble Chorus, Piano, and Bassoon (1963); *Rejoice in the Lord* for Treble or Mixed Chorus and Keyboard (1964); *Songs of Nature* for Mezzo-soprano, Flute, Clarinet, Violin, Cello, and Piano (1975); *From Infinity Full Circle,* chamber cantata for Treble Chorus and Piano (1979); *Duple Play* for Soprano Vocalise, String Quartet, and Woodwind Quartet (1984); *Songs from James Joyce* for Mezzo-soprano, Flute, Clarinet, Violin, Cello, and Piano (1986). —NS/LK/DM

Heitmann, Fritz, German organist and pedagogue; b. Ochsenwerder, near Hamburg, May 9, 1891; d. Berlin, Sept. 7, 1953. He studied organ with Straube and Pembaur and composition with Reger. In 1912 he became organist at Schleswig Cathedral. Upon settling in Berlin, he was organist at the Kaiser Wilhelm Gedächtniskirche (from 1918) and of the Singakademie (from 1920). In 1925 he became prof. at the Staatlichen Akademie für Kirchen- und Schulmusik, from 1930 was organist at the Cathedral, and from 1945 prof. at the Hochschule für Musik. Heitmann won distinction as both a virtuoso organist and as a teacher.

BIBL.: R. Voge, *F. H.: Das Leben eines deutschen Organisten* (Berlin, 1963).—NS/LK/DM

Hekking, André, French cellist of Dutch descent, brother of **Anton** and cousin of **Gérard Hekking;** b. Bordeaux, July 30, 1866; d. Paris, Dec. 14, 1925. He was the son of the Dutch- born French cellist Robert Gérard Hekking (1820–75), who settled in France and from whom he received his training. From 1909 he lived in Paris, and in 1919 he was appointed prof. at the Paris Cons. He also taught at the American Cons. in Fontainebleau. He publ. *Violoncelle, Exercices quotidiens* (Paris, 1927).—NS/LK/DM

Hekking, Anton, Dutch cellist and teacher, brother of **André Hekking;** b. The Hague, Sept. 7, 1856; d. Berlin, Nov. 18, 1935. He was the son of the Dutch-born French cellist Robert Gérard Hekking (1820–75). He studied with Joseph Giese at the Paris Cons. After touring the U.S. with Essipova, he was 1st cellist in the Berlin Phil. (1884–88; 1898–1902), the Boston Sym. Orch. (1889–91), and the N.Y. Sym. Orch. (1895–98). He also taught at the Stern Cons. in Berlin.—NS/LK/DM

Hekking, Gérard, French cellist and teacher, cousin of **André Hekking** and **Anton Hekking;** b. Nancy, Aug. 22, 1879; d. Paris, June 5, 1942. He studied at the Paris Cons., winning 1st prize (1899). He was 1st cellist of the Concertgebouw Orch. in Amsterdam (1903–14) and taught at the Amsterdam Cons.; also made tours in Russia, Spain, Germany, and France. In 1927 he became a prof. at the Paris Cons. He wrote several cello pieces, and also revised *Principes de la technique du violoncelle* of François Gervais (Paris, 1930). —NS/LK/DM

Hekster, Walter, Dutch clarinetist, teacher, and composer; b. Amsterdam, March 29, 1937. He studied clarinet and composition at the Amsterdam Cons. (graduated, 1961). After playing clarinet in the Conn. Sym. Orch. (1962–65), he studied with Sessions at the Berkshire Music Center in Tanglewood (summer, 1966). He taught clarinet and composition at Brandon Univ. in Canada (1965–71), and then at the conservatories in Utrecht and Arnhem.

WORKS: DRAMATIC: Opera: *The Fog* (1987). ORCH.: *Mobiles* (1973); *The Auroras of Autumn* for Oboes and Orch. (1975); *Parts of a World* for Viola and Orch. (1976); *Sunday* (1976); *Transport to Summer* for Clarinet and Orch. (1977); *Between 2 Worlds* for Saxophone and Orch. (1977); *Sea Surface Full of Clouds* for Strings (1978); *Primavera*, "Spring Concerto" for Piano and Orch. (1979); Guitar Concerto (1981); Clarinet Concerto (1982); Oboe Concerto (1984); Cello Concerto (1985); *Sonant* (1986); *Toward the Edge of Night* for Flute and Orch. (1989). CHAMBER: *Epitaphium (In Memoriam Eduard van Beinum)* for Strings (1959); *Pentagram* for Wind Quintet (1961); *Reflections* for Clarinet, Horn, Cello, Vibraphone, Celesta, and Percussion (1964); Sonata for Solo Cello (1967); *Foci* for Violin and Chamber Ensemble (1965–66); *Facets* (1967–68); *Branches* for 15 Strings (1969; rev. 1979); *Fresco* for Clarinet and String Trio (1970); *Ambage* for String Quartet (1970); *Nocturnal Conversation* (1970–71); *Early One Morning* for 15 Winds (1972); *Tropos* for Flute, Oboe, Violin, Viola, Cello, and Piano (1974–75); *Graffiti* for Ondes Martenot, Percussion, and Piano (1975); *Pulsations* for Wind Quintet (1976); *Ideas of Order* for Wind Quintet (1980); Quintet (1982); *Setting No. 1* for Flute and Harp (1982), *No. 2* for Flute (1982), *No. 4* for Guitar (1984), *No. 5* for English Horn, Clarinet, Saxophone, and Bassoon (1985), *No. 6* for Clarinet, Cello, and Piano (1985), *No. 7* for Baritone Saxophone and Percussion (1985), and *No. 8* for 4 Saxophones (1986); *Shadows in a Landscape* for Wind Quintet (1987); *Nara* for Clarinet, Violin, Cello, and Piano (1993); piano pieces. VOCAL: Various works.—NS/LK/DM

Helder, Bartholomäus, German composer; b. Gotha, 1585; d. Remstedt, near Gotha, Oct. 28, 1635. He studied theology in Leipzig. After serving as a schoolteacher at a village near Gotha (1607–16), he was for 20 years a pastor at Remstedt. He died of the plague. He publ. a collection of Christmas and New Year's songs, *Cymbalum genethliacum* (1614), and a book of Psalm tunes, *Cymbalum Davidicum*. Many of his secular songs are included in contemporary anthologies. His New Year's song *Das alte Jahr vergangen ist* became very popular.—NS/LK/DM

Heldy, Fanny (real name, **Marguerite Virginia Emma Clémentine Deceuninck**), Belgian-born French soprano; b. Ath, near Liège, Feb. 29, 1888; d. Paris, Dec. 13, 1973. She studied in Liège and Brussels. She made her operatic debut as Elena in Gunsbourg's *Ivan le Terrible* at the Théâtre Royal de la Monnaie in Brussels, where she sang regularly while accepting guest engagements in Monte Carlo, Warsaw, and St. Petersburg. In 1917 she made her Paris debut as Violetta at the Opéra-Comique, and sang there until 1920; then was a member of the Paris Opéra (1920–39). In 1926 and 1928 she sang at London's Covent Garden. Among her admired portrayals were Marguerite, Nedda, Mélisande, Louise, Manon, Concepción, and Thaïs.—NS/LK/DM

Hèle, George de la, Flemish composer; b. Antwerp, 1547; d. Madrid, Aug. 27, 1586. He studied with Antoine Barbé at Notre Dame Cathedral in Antwerp before serving as a choirboy in the chapel of Philip II in Madrid; he also studied at the univs. of Alcalá and Louvain. In 1572 he became choirmaster at St. Rombaut, and then at Tournai Cathedral about 1574. In 1580 he was made master of the royal chapel in Madrid by Philip II. His most important collection was *Octo missae quinqkue, sex et septem vocum* (Antwerp, 1578). L. Wagner ed. it, along with his other extant works, in Corpus Mensurabilis Musicae, LVI (1972).

BIBL.: L. Wagner, *The Octo Missae of G. d.L.H.* (diss., Univ. of Wisc., 1957).—LK/DM

Helfer, Walter, American composer; b. Lawrence, Mass., Sept. 30, 1896; d. New Rochelle, N.Y., April 16, 1959. He studied at Harvard Univ., then took courses in composition with Caussade in Paris and with Respighi in Rome. Returning to the U.S., he joined the staff of Hunter Coll. in N.Y. He wrote an orch. *Fantasy on Children's Tunes* (1935), *Symphony on Canadian Airs* (1937), Concertino for Piano and Chamber Orch. (1947), *Soliloquy* for Cello and Piano, String Quartet, String Trio, *Elegiac Sonata* for Piano, minor piano pieces, and songs. —NS/LK/DM

Helfert, Vladimír, distinguished Czech musicologist; b. Plánice, near Klatovy, March 24, 1886; d. Prague, May 18, 1945. He took courses in history and geography at the Univ. of Prague, and then studied musicology with Kretzschmar, Stumpf, and Wolf at the Univ. of Berlin (1906–07); completed his studies with Hostinský at the Univ. of Prague (Ph.D., 1908, with the diss. *Jiří Benda a Jean Rousseau*). He was active as a history and geography teacher in Prague until 1919. He then moved to Brno, where he became a lecturer (1921), docent (1926), and prof. of musicology (1931) at the Univ. He was founder-ed. of the Musica Antiqua Bohemica series, as well as ed. of several journals. He founded the Baroque, Classical, and Janáček collections at the Moravian Museum, and also conducted the amateur Brno Orchestrálni Sdružení. He was arrested by the Nazis in 1940 and held in Breslau until 1943; then was rearrested in 1945 and taken to the Terezín concentration camp, where he contracted typhus; he died a few days after his liberation.

WRITINGS (all publ. in Prague unless otherwise given): *Smetanismus a wagnerismus* (1911); *Hudební barok na českých zámcích* (The Musical Baroque in Czech Castles; 1916); *Smet-*

anovské kapitoly (Chapters on Smetana; 1917; 2nd ed., 1954); *Naše hudba a český stát* (Our Music and the Czech State; 1918; 2nd ed., 1970); *Hudba na Jaroměřickém zámku: František Míča 1696–1745* (Music in the Jaromerice Castle: František Míča 1696–1745; 1924); *Tvůrčí rozvoj Bedřicha Smetany, I* (Bedrich Smetana's Creative Development; 1924; 2nd ed., 1953; Ger. tr., 1956); *Jiří Benda* (Brno, 1929–34); ed. with G. černušák, *Pazdírkův hudební slovník naučný* (Pazdírek's Scientific Music Dictionary; Brno, 1929; 1933–41); *Základy hudební výchovy na nehudebnich školách* (Principles of Musical Education in Secondary Schools; 1930); *česka moderní hudba* (Czech Modern Music; Olomouc, 1936; Fr. and Ger. trs.,1938); with E. Steinhard, *Histoire de la musique dans la république Tchecoslovaque* (1936; Ger. tr., 1936; 2nd ed., rev., 1938, as *Die Musik in der tschechoslovakischen Republik*); *Útok na českou moderní hudbu* (The Attack on *česká moderní hudba*; Olomouc, 1937); *Leoš Janáček, I* (Brno, 1939); *Státní hudebně historický ústav* (The State Inst. of Music History; ed. by G. černušák; 1945); *O Janáčkovi* (ed. by B. Štědroň; 1949); *O Smetanovi* (ed. by B. Štědroň; 1950); *O české hudbě* (On Czech Music; ed. by B. Štědroň and I. Poledňák; 1957); *Vybrané studie, I: O hudební tvořivosti* (Selected Studies, I: On Musical Creativity; ed. by F. Hrabal; 1970).

BIBL.: B. Štědroň, *Dr. V. H.* (Prague, 1940); R. Pečman and J. Vysloužil, eds., *V. H.: Pokrokový vedec a člověk* (V. H.: Progressive Scholar and Man; Brno, 1975).—**NS/LK/DM**

Helffer, Claude, French pianist; b. Paris, June 18, 1922. He studied piano with Robert Casadesus; following classical studies at the École Polytechnique (1939–42), he studied harmony, counterpoint, and composition with Leibowitz. In 1948 he made his debut in Paris and subsequently made tours of Europe. In 1966 he made his first tour of the U.S.; also appeared in South America, Australia, and Japan. While a master of the standard repertory, he became best known for his championship of 20th century music. In addition to Debussy, Ravel, Bartók, and Schoenberg, he was a convincing interpreter of Boulez, Barraqué, Xenakis, Amy, and others. With B. Albèra, he wrote *Entretiens avec Claude Helffer* (Geneva, 1995).—**NS/LK/DM**

Helfman, Max, Polish-born American choral conductor and composer; b. Radzin, May 25, 1901; d. Dallas, Aug. 9, 1963. He was taken to the U.S. in 1909. He studied at the David Mannes School of Music in N.Y. and at the Curtis Inst. of Music in Philadelphia, where his teachers were Scalero in composition and Reiner in conducting. He subsequently was active mainly as a conductor of Jewish choral groups; was in charge of choral singing at Temple Emanuel in Paterson, N.J. (1926–39), Temple B'nai Abraham in Newark (1940–53), and Temple Sinai in Los Angeles (1954–57); was music director at the Brandeis Inst. in Santa Susanna, Calif., and dean of the arts at the Univ. of Judaism in Los Angeles (1958–62). He wrote a dramatic cantata, *New Hagadah* (1949), and several pieces of Jewish liturgical music; ed. a series of choral works for the Jewish Music Alliance.

BIBL.: P. Moddel, *M. H.* (Berkeley, 1974).—**NS/LK/DM**

Helfritz, Hans, German ethnomusicologist and composer; b. Hilbersdorf, July 25, 1902. He studied with Hindemith at the Hochschule für Musik in Berlin, and with Wellesz in Vienna. In 1936 he went to South America and lived mostly in Chile, where he worked on problems of musical folklore. In 1956 he undertook a journey along the west coast of Africa and made recordings of native songs. In 1962 he settled in Ibiza in the Balearic Islands. He composed orch. works and chamber music; in some of them, he makes use of South American and African motifs.

WRITINGS: *Amerika, Land der Inka, Maya und Azteken* (Vienna, 1965); *Die Götterburgen Mexikos* (Cologne, 1968); *Mexiko, Land der drei Kulturen* (Berlin, 1968).—**NS/LK/DM**

Helias, Mark, jazz bassist, composer, pianist; b. New Brunswick, N.J., Oct. 1, 1950. He was in the first graduating class of the music department at Livingston Coll., Rutgers Univ., in 1974 (B.M.) and finished a Masters Degree at the Yale School of Music in 1976. He has enjoyed long musical associations with Edward Blackwell, Anthony Davis, Dewey Redman, Ray Anderson, Don Cherry, and Gerry Hemingway, and has worked with Barry Altschul, Oliver Lake, the Slickaphonics, Abbey Lincoln, Don Cherry, Cecil Taylor, and Ray Anderson. He did two Japanese tours and some gigs in N.Y. (including Central Park) with the JB Horns in the early 1990s, as well as some with Maceo Parker as leader. He performed in the Anthony Davis operas *X, The Life and Times of Malcolm X* (1986) and *Under the Double Moon*, as well as performance, dance, film, and video collaborations with Mary Perillo and John Sanborn. He has composed numerous pieces ranging from solo bass to sym. orch. Since 1981 he has been awarded 13 composition and performance grants, mostly from the NEA. In 1992 his piece "Upside the Downside" was premiered in St. Louis, Mo., by the String Trio of N.Y. The piece was commissioned by Meet the Composer/Readers Digest. In 1996 he collaborated with director Jay Anania in scoring the feature film *The Pagan Life of Arthur Rimbaud*. He taught privately from 1973–95. He has conducted workshops at the Creative Music Studio (1979–80), Berklee Coll. (1988), and in Amsterdam, Vancouver, and Switzerland. He has taught classes at Sarah Lawrence Coll. since 1997. He has toured regularly as a leader, primarily in Europe, since 1987. His ongoing projects are The Marks Brothers with Mark Dresser in bass duets, The Grid with Erik Friedlander and Chris Speed, Attack the Future featuring Ellery Eskelin and Tom Rainey, and Open/Loose, an improvising trio with rotating personnel.

DISC.: *Split Image* (1984); *Current Set* (1987); *Desert Blue* (1989); *Attack the Future* (1992); *The Current Set* (1992); *Loopin the Cool* (1995); *Come Ahead Back* (1998).—**LP**

Hellendaal, Pieter, Dutch-born English organist, violinist, and composer; b. Rotterdam (baptized), April 1, 1721; d. Cambridge, April 19, 1799. He was taken as a child to Utrecht, where he became organist at St. Nicolas Church. When the family went to Amsterdam in 1737, he found a patron in the city secretary Mattheus Lestevenon, who helped him to study with Tartini in Italy. In 1751 he went to London, where he was organist at St. Margaret's Church, King's Lynn (1760); Pembroke

Hall Chapel, Cambridge (1762); and Peterhouse Chapel, Cambridge (1777). He was also active as a violinist and a composer. His concerti grossi and violin sonatas are skillfully written.

WORKS: (6) *Sonate* for Violin and Basso Continuo, op.1 (Amsterdam, c. 1745); *VI Sonate* for Violin and Basso Continuo, op.2 (Amsterdam, c. 1750); *6 Grand Concertos* for Strings and Basso Continuo, op.3 (London, c. 1758; ed. in Monumenta Musicae Neerlandicae, I, 1959); *6 Solos* for Violin and Basso Continuo, op.4 (London, c. 1777); *8 Solos* for Cello and Basso Continuo, op.5 (Cambridge, c. 1780); *3 Grand Lessons* for Harpsichord or Piano, Violin, and Cello, op.6 (London, c. 1790); *Hellendaal's Celebrated Rondo* for Violin and Basso Continuo (Cambridge, c. 1790); also 11 sonatas for Violin and Basso Continuo in MS. His other works include the cantata *Strephon and Myrtilla* for Voice, Violin or Flute, and Basso Continuo (Cambridge, c. 1785); *A Collection of Psalms and Hymns...* for 3 to 4 Voices and Basso Continuo (Cambridge, 1790); glees; catches; etc.—**NS/LK/DM**

Heller, Hans Ewald, German-American composer; b. Vienna, April 17, 1894; d. N.Y., Oct. 1, 1966. He studied with J. B. Foerster and Camillo Horn. He was engaged in Vienna as a music critic and teacher. In 1938 he settled in the U.S. Among his compositions were the light operas *Satan* (Vienna, 1927), *Messalina* (Prague, 1928), and *Der Liebling von London* (Vienna, 1930), an overture, *Carnival in New Orleans* (1940), a cantata, *Ode to Our Women* (1942), 2 string quartets, Suite for Clarinet and Piano, and about 150 songs.—**NS/LK/DM**

Heller, James G., American composer; b. New Orleans, Jan. 4, 1892; d. Cincinnati, Dec. 19, 1971. He studied at Tulane Univ. in New Orleans (B.A., 1912), the Univ. of Cincinnati (M.A., 1914), the Hebrew Union Coll. (Rabbi, 1916), and the Cincinnati Cons. (Mus.D., 1934). For 12 years, he wrote the program notes for the Cincinnati Sym. Orch.; then taught musicology at the Cincinnati Cons. of Music. Among his works were *Elegy and Pastorale* for Voice and String Orch. (Cincinnati, Dec. 30, 1934); String Quartet; Violin Sonata; Jewish services (New Union Hymnal, 1930–32).—**NS/LK/DM**

Heller, Stephen, celebrated Hungarian pianist and composer; b. Pest, May 15, 1813; d. Paris, Jan. 14, 1888. He was of a Jewish family, but was converted to Christianity as a youth. He studied piano with Franz Brauer and showed such extraordinary ability that he was sent to Vienna to continue his studies; he studied briefly with Czerny before taking lessons with Anton Halm. In 1828 he began a tour through Hungary, Transylvania, Poland, and Germany. However, the exertion of travel proved too much for him; while in Augsburg in 1830, he became ill, and decided to remain there for a time; financial means were provided by a wealthy family. In 1838 he went to Paris, where he became friendly with Berlioz, Chopin, and Liszt. Soon he became very successful as a pianist; some critics even judged him as superior to Chopin. He began to compose piano pieces somewhat akin to Schumann's: brilliant salon dances, studies, and character pieces that became exceedingly popular. In 1849 he visited London, where

his concerts charmed a large circle of music-lovers. A nervous ailment forced him to curtail his appearances; in 1862 he revisited England and played with Hallé at London's Crystal Palace. He then returned to Paris, where he remained for the rest of his life. He wrote in all several hundred piano pieces, arranged in groups in 158 opus numbers. Among the most notable were 4 sonatas (1829, 1844, 1856, 1878), *Spaziergänge eines Einsamen* (1851), *Blumen-, Frucht- und Dornenstücke* (1853), *Präludien* (1853), *Im Walde* (3 vols., 1854, 1871, 1873), *Ein Heft Walzer* (1878), and 3 sonatinas (1878, 1878, 1879). He also wrote various mazurkas, caprices, nocturnes, variations, and other pieces.

BIBL.: H. Barbedette, *S. H.* (Paris, 1876; Eng. tr., 1877); R. Schutz, *S. H.* (Leipzig, 1911); R. Booth, *The Life and Music of S. H.* (diss., Univ. of Iowa, 1969); J.-J. Eigeldinger, ed., *S. H.: Lettres d'un musicien romantique à Paris* (Paris, 1981).—**NS/LK/DM**

Hellermann, William (David), American composer and guitarist; b. Milwaukee, July 15, 1939. He studied mechanical engineering at the Univ. of Wisc. (B.S., 1962) and composition at Columbia Univ. (M.A., 1969; D.M.A., 1976), his principal mentors being Wolpe, Chou Wen-chung, Luening, and Ussachevsky. From 1966 to 1972 he was on the music faculty at Columbia Univ. He also held a composer's fellowship to the Berkshire Music Center at Tanglewood (summer, 1967) and the Prix de Rome fellowship to the American Academy in Rome (1972). In 1977 he was composer-in-residence at the Center for the Creative and Performing Arts at the State Univ. of N.Y. at Buffalo. As a guitarist, he has been especially active as a proponent of contemporary music. His compositions are thoroughly modern in range and utilization of resources. He has become particularly well known for his creations in the realm of music sculpture.

WORKS: DRAMATIC: *Parts Sequences 1 for an Open Space* for 4 Musicians, 4 Actors, 4 Dancers, and 4 Sets (N.Y., March 24, 1972); *Extraordinary Histories*, experimental opera (N.Y., April 28, 1982); *3 Sisters Who Are Not Sisters*, theater piece (1984; Barcelona, Oct. 23, 1985); *Blood on the Dining Room Floor*, theater piece (N.Y., Nov. 21, 1991). **ORCH.:** *Time and Again* (1969; Utrecht, Sept. 14, 1970); *"anyway..."* (Greenwich, Conn., March 22, 1977). **CHAMBER:** *Formata* for Trombone and 4 Instruments (1967); *Ek-stasis II* for Timpani, Piano, and Tape (1970); *Round and About* for 2 or More Instruments (1970); *Circle Music 1* for 4 Instruments, *2* for 2 or More Instruments, and *3* for 6 Performers (all 1971); *Passages 13: The Fire* for Trumpet and Tape (1971); *Distances/Embraces* for Guitar (1972); *On the Vanishing Point* for Piano and Tape Delay (1973); *Stop/Start* for 2 Soloists and 6 Players (1973); *Long Island Sound* for 4 Instruments (1974); *To the Last Drop* for 6 Vibraphones (1974); *"But, the moon..."* for Guitar and 13 Instruments (Paris, March 13, 1975); *Still and All* for Guitar (1975); *Experimental Music* for Variable Instruments (1975); *To Brush Up On* for 6 Cellos (1976); *2 Vibraphones* for 2 Vibraphones (1976); *Squeek* for Soloist (1977); *Tremble* for Guitar (1978); *3 Weeks in Cincinnati in December* for Flute (1979); *The Violin Between Us* for Violin (1981); *Tremble II* for Double Bass (1981); *On the Vanishing Point* for 4 Instruments (1989); *Post/Pone* for Guitar, Clarinet, Viola, Trombine, and Piano (1990). **P i a n o :** *Row Music (Tip of the Iceberg)* (1973); *For Otto (A Line in Return)* (1974); *At Sea* (1976). **VOCAL:** *Entrances* for Chorus (1976); *Local Exits* for Soprano and Chamber

Ensemble (1976); *Nests* for Soloist and Chorus (1976); *City Games* for 3 Vocalists, Tape, and Sculpture (1978); *Sheet Music* for Soloist and Synthesizer (1984). **OTHER**: *Ariel* for Tape (1967); *Juicy Music* for Tape and Sculpture (1982); *El Ropo* for Keyboard, Tape, and Sculpture (1984); *1 Bar Blues* for Tape and Sculpture (1984).—**NS/LK/DM**

Hellinck, Lupus (Wulfaert),

important Flemish composer; b. c. 1496; d. Bruges, Jan. 14?, 1541. He was a choirboy at St. Donatian in Bruges (1506–11), then verger there (1513–15). After studying for the priesthood, he returned there as an installed cleric (1519). He then was maître de chapelle at Notre Dame there (1521–23), and subsequently at St. Donatian from 1523. His output was widely dispersed in his day. Among his finest works are 13 parody masses. He also composed motets, chorales, chansons, and Flemish songs. See J. Wolf, ed., *Newe deudsche geistliche Gesenge, 1544* in Denkmäler Deutscher Tonkunst, XXXIV (1908).

BIBL.: B. Blackburn, *The L. Problem* (diss., Univ. of Chicago, 1970).—**NS/LK/DM**

Hellmesberger,

family of famous Austrian musicians:

(1) Georg Hellmesberger Sr., violinist, conductor, and composer; b. Vienna, April 24, 1800; d. Neuwaldegg, near Vienna, Aug. 16, 1873. His father, a country schoolmaster, gave him his first instruction in music. He succeeded Schubert as a chorister in the Hofkapelle. After making his concert debut on Dec. 9, 1819, he studied violin with Bohm and composition with E. Forster at the Vienna Cons. He then was made assistant to Bohm in 1821, and subsequently was titular prof. (1826–33) and prof. (1833–67). He became concertmaster of the Hofoper in 1830, and also a member of the Hofkapelle. He served as conductor of the Vienna Phil. with Nicolai (1845–47), and then was its sole conductor (1847–48). He made appearances as a violinist in London in 1847, and was also active as a teacher. In addition to his sons, he taught Ernst, Auer, and Joachim. He composed 2 violin concertos, some chamber music, and some pieces for solo violin. His 2 sons became musicians of distinction:

(2) Joseph Hellmesberger Sr., violinist and conductor; b. Vienna, Nov. 3, 1828; d. there, Oct. 24, 1893. He studied violin with his father at the Vienna Cons. He was named soloist in the orch. of the Hofoper when he was 17. He was artistic director and conductor of the Gesellschaft der Musikfreunde concerts (1851–59), and concurrently taught violin at the Vienna Cons. (1851–77), where he then was director until 1893. He was also concertmaster of the Vienna Phil. (1855–77) and the Hofoper (1860–77), and was named Hofkapellmeister in 1877. In 1849 he founded the renowned Helmesberger Quartet, in which he played 1st violin, retiring in 1891.

BIBL.: A. Barthlme, *Vom alten H.* (Vienna, 1908); R. Prosl, *Die H.: Hundert Jahre aus dem Leben einer Wiener Musikerfamilie* (Vienna, 1947).

(3) Georg Hellmesberger Jr., violinist and composer; b. Vienna, Jan. 27, 1830; d. Hannover, Nov. 12, 1852. He studied violin and music theory with his father and

composition with Rotter, then toured Germany, and subsequently accompanied his father to London in 1847. He was named Hofkonzertmeister in Hannover in 1850. Among his 9 operas were *Die Burgschaft* and *Die beiden Koniginnen*. He also wrote syms., chamber music, violin pieces, and songs. His promising career was tragically cut short by tuberculosis.

(4) Joseph Hellmesberger Jr., violinist, conductor, and composer, son of **Joseph Hellmesberger Sr.**; b. Vienna, April 9, 1855; d. there, April 26, 1907. He studied with his father, making his debut at a Vienna Cons. concert when he was 8 and becoming 2nd violinist in his father's quartet when he was 15. He was concertmaster of the Vienna Phil. (1870–84); was also made solo violinist of the Hofkapelle and the Hofoper in 1878, and prof. of violin at the Cons. He became conductor of the new Ringtheater in 1881, but his tenure was cut short by a disastrous fire (Dec. 8, 1881), which destroyed the building. He then became conductor of the Carltheater in 1882, and subsequently (1884) was made concertmaster and music director of the ballet at the Hofoper. He was named Vizehofkapellmeister in 1889, and then Hofkapellmeister in succession to Richter in 1890. He also succeeded his father as 1st violin in the Hellmesberger Quartet in 1891, and later served as conductor of the Vienna Phil. (1901–03) and of the Stuttgart Opera (1904–05). He wrote 10 operettas, the most celebrated being *Das Veilchenmadel* (Vienna, Feb. 27, 1904).

(5) Ferdinand Hellmesberger, cellist and conductor, son of **Joseph Hellmesberger Sr.**; b. Vienna, Jan. 24, 1863; d. there, March 15, 1940. He studied at the Vienna Cons. He became a member of the Hofkapelle in 1879, and also played in his father's quartet (from 1883). He taught cello at the Vienna Cons. (1884–1902), and was solo cellist in the orch. of the Hofoper (1886–1902). He then was conductor of the Volksoper (1902–5), and subsequently ballet conductor at the Berlin Hofoper (1905–10). He later conducted various spa orchs. —**NS/LK/DM**

Hellwig, Karl (Friedrich) Ludwig,

German organist and composer; b. Wriezen, July 23, 1773; d. Berlin, Nov. 24, 1838. He learned to play all the string instruments and piano, then studied theory with Zelter and others. At the same time, he was engaged in the manufacture of paint, which enabled him to pursue his musical studies as an avocation. He became a member of the Singakademie in 1793. He was a conductor with it from 1803, serving as joint deputy conductor (1815–33). In 1813 he became organist of the Berlin Cathedral, and was its director of music from 1815. He wrote 2 operas, *Die Bergknappen* (Dresden, April 27, 1820) and *Don Sylvio di Rosalbo* (unperf.), much church music, and a number of German lieder, which show a certain poetic sensitivity and a ballad-like quality in the manner of Zelter and other early German Romanticists. —**NS/LK/DM**

Helm, Anny,

Austrian soprano; b. Vienna, July 20, 1903. She was a student of Gutheil-Schoder and Gertrude Förstel in Vienna, and of Grenzebach in Berlin. In 1924 she made her operatic debut in Magdeburg, and then appeared at the Berlin State Opera (1926–33) and at the Bayreuth Festivals (1927–31). In 1933 she settled in Italy, where she sang under the name Anny Helm-Sbisa (her husband, Giuseppe Sbisa, was director of the Teatro Giuseppe Verdi in Trieste). In 1939 she appeared at London's Covent Garden. She devoted herself mainly to teaching from 1941. Her finest roles included Donna Anna, Brangäne, Isolde, Brünnhilde, Turandot, and Elektra.—NS/LK/DM

Helm, E(rnest) Eugene, American musicologist; b. New Orleans, Jan. 23, 1928. He was educated at Southeastern La. Coll. (B.M.E., 1950), La. State Univ. (M.M.E., 1955), and North Tex. State Univ. (Ph.D., 1958, with the diss. *The Musical Patronage of Frederick the Great*). He taught at La. Coll. (1953–55), Wayne (Nebr.) State Coll. (1958–59), the Univ. of Iowa (1960–68), and the Univ. of Md. (from 1968), where he was also chairman of the musicology division (1971–87). He served as coordinating ed. of the Carl Philipp Emanuel Bach Edition (from 1982).

WRITINGS: *Music at the Court of Frederick the Great* (1960); with A. Luper, *Words and Music* (1971; 2nd ed., 1982); *Thematic Catalogue of the Works of Carl Philipp Emanuel Bach* (1989); *The Canon and the Curricula: A Study of Musicology and Ethnomusicology Programs in America* (1994).—NS/LK/DM

Helm, Everett (Burton), American composer and musicologist; b. Minneapolis, July 17, 1913; d. Berlin, June 25, 1999. He studied at Harvard Univ. (M.A., 1936; Ph.D., 1939), and also in Europe (1936–38) with Malipiero, Vaughan Williams, and Alfred Einstein. Returning to the U.S., he taught at Western Coll. in Oxford, Ohio (1943–44). From 1948 to 1950 he was a music officer under the U.S. military government in Germany. Except for a stint as ed. in N.Y. for *Musical America* (1961–63), Helm lived in Europe from 1948, mostly in Germany. A linguist, he contributed articles to various music magazines in several languages; he made a specialty of the music of Yugoslavia and was a guest lecturer at the Univ. of Ljubljana (1966–68).

WRITINGS: *Béla Bartók in Selbstzeugnissen und Biddokumenten* (Reinbek-bei-Hamburg, 1965; reduction and Eng. tr., N.Y., 1972); *Composer, Performer, Public: A Study in Communication* (Florence, 1970); *Franz Liszt* (Hamburg, 1972); *Music and Tomorrow's Public* (Wilhelmshaven, 1981).

WORKS: *Adam and Eve*, adaptation of a medieval mystery play (Wiesbaden, Oct. 28, 1951); Concerto for 5 Instruments, Percussion, and Strings (Donaueschingen, Oct. 10, 1953); 2 piano concertos: No. 1 (N.Y., April 24, 1954) and No. 2 (Louisville, Feb. 25, 1956); *The Siege of Tottenburg*, radio opera (1956); *Le Roy fait battre tambour*, ballet (1956); *500 Dragon- Thalers*, Singspiel (1956); *Divertimento* for Flutes (1957); *Sinfonia da camera* (1961); Concerto for Double Bass and String Orch. (1968); 2 string quartets; Woodwind Quintet (1967); numerous piano pieces and songs.—NS/LK/DM

Helm, Theodor (Otto), Austrian music critic; b. Vienna, April 9, 1843; d. there, Dec. 23, 1920. He studied jurisprudence in Vienna and became a government employee, and in 1867 he began writing music criticism for various Viennese publications. In 1874 became a

music teacher at Horák's music school. From 1875 to 1901 he was ed. of Fromme's *Kalender für die Musikalische Welt*. He publ. *Beethovens Streichquartette: Versuch einer technischen Analyse im Zusammenhang mit ihrem geistigen Gehalt* (Leipzig, 1885; 2nd ed., 1910). —NS/LK/DM

Helmholtz, Hermann (Ludwig Ferdinand) von, celebrated German scientist and acoustician; b. Potsdam, Aug. 31, 1821; d. Berlin, Sept. 8, 1894. He studied medicine at the Friedrich Wilhelm Medical Inst. in Berlin (M.D., 1843) and also learned to play the piano. He was an assistant at Berlin's Anatomical Museum and prof. extraordinary at the Academy of Fine Arts (1848–49), asst. prof. and director of Königsberg's Physiological Inst. (1849–55), and prof. of anatomy and physiology at the Univ. of Bonn (1855–58) and the Univ. of Heidelberg (1858–71). He became prof. of physics at the Univ. of Berlin in 1871, and from 1888 served as the 1st director of the Physico-Technical Inst. in Berlin. He was ennobled in 1882. His most important work for those interested in music was his *Lehre von den Tonempfindungen als physiologische Grundlage für die Theorie der Musik* (Braunschweig, 1863; Eng. tr. by A. Ellis as *On the Sensations of Tone as a Physiological Basis for the Theory of Music*, London, 1875; new ed., N.Y., 1948), in which he established a sure physical foundation for the phenomena manifested by musical tones, either single or combined. He supplemented and amplified the theories of Rameau, Tartini, Wheatstone, Corti, and others, furnishing impregnable formulae for all classes of consonant and dissonant tone effects, and proving with scientific precision what Hauptmann and his school sought to establish by laborious dialectic processes. His labors resulted primarily in instituting the laws governing the differences in quality of tone (tone color) in different instruments and voices, covering the whole field of harmonic, differential, and summational tones, and those governing the nature and limits of music perception by the human ear.

BIBL.: S. Epstein, *H. v.H. als Mensch und Gelehrter* (Stuttgart, 1896); L. Konigsberger, *H. v.H.* (3 vols., Braunschweig, 1902–03; 1 vol., 1911); E. Waetzman, *Zur H.schen Resonanztheorie* (Breslau, 1907); H. Ebert, *H. v.H.* (Stuttgart, 1949).—NS/LK/DM

Helmont, Charles-Joseph van, South Netherlands organist and composer; b. Brussels, March 19, 1715; d. there, June 8, 1790. He was a pupil of Pierre Bréhy at the collegiate church of Ste. Gudule in Brussels, where he was made titular organist in 1733. After serving as choirmaster at the parish church of Notre Dame de la Chapelle (1737–41), he returned to Ste. Gudule in that capacity (1741–77). He wrote much sacred music, including masses, motets, Magnificats, and litanies. Among his secular works were an opera, a divertissement, *Pieces de clavecin* (Brussels, 1737), and 6 organ fugues. His son, Adrien-Joseph van Helmont (b. Brussels, Aug. 13, 1747; d. there, Dec. 28, 1830), a composer and teacher, was choirmaster at Ste. Gudule (1777–94; 1802–18). He composed sacred music and an opéra-comique.—LK/DM

Helps, Robert (Eugene), American composer, pianist, and teacher; b. Passaic, N.J., Sept. 23, 1928. He attended the preparatory dept. of the Juilliard School of Music in N.Y. (1936–43), and then studied piano with Abby Whiteside and composition with Roger Sessions; he also took courses at Columbia Univ. (1947–49) and at the Univ. of Calif. at Berkeley (1949–51). After teaching piano at Stanford Univ. (1968–69), the San Francisco Cons. of Music (1968–70), the Univ. of Calif. at Berkeley (1969–70), the New England Cons. of Music in Boston (1970–72), the Manhattan School of Music (1972–78), and at Princeton Univ. (1972–78), he served as prof. of music at the Univ. of South Fla. in Tampa (from 1980). As a pianist, he acquired a fine reputation as an interpreter of modern music. He received various awards and commissions, and in 1966 held a Guggenheim fellowship. He developed a personal style of expression while utilizing 12–tone procedures.

WORKS: ORCH.: Sym. (1955); *Cortège* (1963); 2 piano concertos (1969, 1976). **CHAMBER:** String Quartet (1951); Piano Trio (1957); *Serenade* in 3 parts: 1, *Fantasy* for Violin and Piano (1963), 2, *Nocturne* for String Quartet (1966), and 3, *Postlude* for Horn, Violin, and Piano (1965); Quintet for Flute, Clarinet, Violin, Cello, and Piano (1976); *Second Thoughts* for Flute (1978). **Piano:** *Fantasy* (1952); 3 études (1956); *Images* (1957); *Starscape* (1958); *Recollections* (1959); *Portrait* (1960); *Solo* (1960); *Saccade* for 4–Hands (1967); *Quartet* (1971); 3 *Homages* (1973); *Nocturne* (1973); *Music for the Left Hand* (1974); *Valse mirage* (1977). **VOCAL:** 2 songs for Soprano and Piano (1950); *The Running Sun* for Soprano and Piano (1972); *Gossamer Noons* for Soprano and Orch. (1977).—**NS/LK/DM**

Helsted, Gustaf, Danish organist, teacher, and composer; b. Copenhagen, Jan. 30, 1857; d. there, March 1, 1924. He was a pupil of Hartmann and Gade. From 1892 he was a prof. of theory, and from 1904 also a prof. of organ, at the Copenhagen Cons. From 1915 he was organist of the Frauenkirche. He wrote 2 syms., a Decimet for Woodwinds and Strings, a String Sextet, 3 string quartets, a Piano Trio, 2 violin sonatas, and 2 cantatas: *Gurresänge* (Copenhagen, April 18, 1904) and *Vort Land* (Copenhagen, April 19, 1909).—**NS/LK/DM**

Hely-Hutchinson, (Christian) Victor, South African-born English pianist, conductor, administrator, and composer; b. Cape Town, Dec. 26, 1901; d. London, March 11, 1947. He studied at Balliol Coll., Oxford, at the Royal Coll. of Music, London, and with Tovey before returning to Oxford to take his D.Mus. in 1940. In 1922 he became a lecturer in music at the South African Coll. of Music in Cape Town; in 1926 he joined the staff of the BBC in London, and later was head of its Midlands Region in Birmingham (1933–44); also was a prof. of music at the Univ. of Birmingham (1934–44) before serving as director of music of the BBC in London (1944–47). Among his compositions are *A Carol Symphony*, a Piano Quintet, a String Quintet, a Viola Sonata, choral pieces, songs, and film scores. —**NS/LK/DM**

Hemberg, (Bengt Sven) Eskil, Swedish composer, administrator, and conductor; b. Stockholm, Jan. 19, 1938. He studied organ and was a student of Blomstedt (conducting) at the Stockholm Musikhög-

skolan (1957–64). From 1959 to 1964 he conducted the Stockholm Academic Choir, and then was its artistic director from 1964 to 1984. He was executive producer for the Swedish Broadcasting Corp., serving as head of its choral section (1963–70), and then was head of planning of the Inst. for National Concerts (1970–83) and president of the Swedish Soc. of Composers (1971–83). After serving as artistic director of the Stora Teatern in Göteborg (1984–87), he held that title with the Royal Theater in Stockholm from 1987 to 1996. In 1974 he was elected a member of the Royal Academy of Music in Stockholm. He has written much vocal music, ranging from operas to sacred scores, in which traditional procedures are enhanced by ventures into contemporary harmony.

WORKS: DRAMATIC: Opera: *Love, love, love* (1973–80); *The Pirates in the Deep Green Sea* (1975–77); *St. Erik's Crown*, church opera (1979); *Herr Apfelstädt wird Kunstler*, chamber opera (1989); *Utopia* (1997). **Other:** Film music. **ORCH.:** *Migraine* (1973); *Thulegräs* for Strings (1987). **CHAMBER:** *Zona rosa* for String Quartet (1973); *Les Adieu* for String Quartet (1982); Trio for Violin, Viola, and Cello (1984; also for Flute, Violin, and Cello, 1986); *Rondo festivo* for Violin and Piano (1993); piano pieces; organ music, including *Tocata e fuga* (1999). **VOCAL:** *18 Movements* for Chorus (1967); *Messa d'oggi* for 5 Soloists and Chorus (1968–70); Passion after St. Mark for Soloists, Chorus, and Orch. (1972–84); *Cantica* for Soloists, Chorus, and Orch. (1973); *Songbook from Österbotten* for Men's Voices, English Horn, Clarinet, Small Drum, and Double Bass (1975); *With God and his Friendship*, "a Mass about belief and politics" for Priest, Congregation, Chorus, Trumpet, and Organ (1976); *Women*, scenic cantata for Soloists, Women's Chorus, and Orch. (1978–79); *Concerning My Negotiations With Myself and With God* for Solo Quartet, Double Chorus, and Organ (1980); *Love Fancies* for Baritone, Bassoon, and String Orch. (1980); *Canticles I-III* for Soloists and Instruments (1981); *Lützener Te Deum* for Double Chorus and 3 Trombones (1982); *Canti di luce e di stelle* for Soprano and 7 Instruments (1982–91); *Magnificat* for Double Chorus (1982); *To the Light*, cantata for Soloists, Men's Chorus, and Chamber Orch. (1984); *Psalm 150* for Chorus, Viola d'Amore, and Cello (1985); *Requiem Aeternam* for Chorus (1987); *San Francisco Peace Cantata* for Soloists, Chorus, Trumpet, and Crotales (1989); *Psalm 96* for Chorus (1992); Suite for Soprano, Wind Quintet, and String Quartet (1992); *Requiem* for Chorus (1994); *Värmländska låtar* for Baritone and Chamber Orch. (1995–96).—**NS/LK/DM**

Hemel, Oscar van, Dutch composer; b. Antwerp, Aug. 3, 1892; d. Hilversum, July 9, 1981. He was a student of L. Mortelmans and de Boeck at the Royal Flemish Cons. in Antwerp. In 1914 he settled in the Netherlands, and later pursued his training with Pijper in Rotterdam (1931–33). The style of his works oscillated between Austro-German Romantic trends and the more complex technical structures of the Dutch modernists.

WORKS: DRAMATIC: Radio Opera: *Viviane* (Hilversum Radio, 1950). **ORCH.:** 5 syms.: No. 1 (1935), No. 2 (1948), No. 3, Sinfonietta for Small Orch. (1952), No. 4 (1962), and No. 5 (1963–64; rev. 1980); Suite for Chamber Orch. (1936); Suite for Flute and Chamber Orch. (1937; also for Flute and Piano); Piano Concerto (1941–42); *Ballade* (1942); 3 violin concertos (1945, 1968, 1977); *De stad*, symphonic poem (1949); Viola Concerto (1951); *Feestelijke ouverture* (1952); *Olof Suite* (1953); *Entrada festante* (1953); *Tema con variazioni* (1953); Oboe Concerto

(1955); Concerto for Wind Orch. (1960); *Concerto da camera* for Flute and Strings (1962); Cello Concerto (1963); *Divertimento* for Strings (1964); *Entrada* (1964); *Serenade* for 3 Solo Winds and Strings (1965); *Polonaise* (1966); Concerto for 2 Violins and String Orch. (1970–71); *Divertimento* for Piano and Orch. (1974). **CHAMBER:** 6 string quartets (1931, 1936, 1947, 1953, 1956, 1961); 2 violin sonatas (1933, 1945); Piano Trio (1937); Piano Quartet (1938); Viola Sonata (1942); String Trio (1951); Clarinet Quintet (1958); Trio for Flute, Oboe, and Bassoon (1959); Sextet for Piano and Winds (1962); *Donquichotterie* for 4 Trombones (1962); *About Commedia dell'arte* for Oboe Quartet (1967); Wind Quintet (1972). **VOCAL:** *Maria Magdalena*, sacred cantata for Contralto, Tenor, and Orch. (1941); *Ballade van Kapitein Joos de Decker* for Contralto, Bass, Chorus, and Orch. (1943; rev. 1959); *De bruid* for Soprano, Men's Chorus, and Orch. (1946); *Da liet van Alianora* for Soprano, Men's Chorus, and Orch. (1946); *Ballade van Brabant* for Baritone/Reciter, Boy's Chorus, Men's Chorus, and Orch. (1952); *Krans der middeleeuwen* for Baritone, Chorus, and 7 Instruments (1952); *Canticum psalmorum* for Contralto, Men's Chorus, 2 Pianos, and Timpani (1954); *Le Tombeau de Kathleen Ferrier* for Contralto and Orch. (1954); *Herdenkingshymne 1940–1945* for Chorus, Children's Chorus, Brass, and Percussion (1955; with full Orch., 1970); *Les Mystères du Christ*, symphonic hymn for Contralto, Baritone, Men's Chorus, and Orch. (1958); *Te Deum* for Soprano, Contralto, Tenor, Bass, Chorus, and Orch. (1958); *Tuin van Holland* for Soprano, Baritone, Chorus, and Orch. (1958); *Trittico liturgico* for Soprano and Organ or Strings (1959); *Huwellijkscantate Beatrix* for Soprano, Tenor, Chorus, and Orch. (1966); *Song of Freedom* for Chorus and Orch. (1968–69; rev. 1981).—**NS/LK/DM**

Heming, Percy, English baritone; b. Bristol, Sept. 6, 1883; d. London, Jan. 11, 1956. He studied in London at the Royal Academy of Music and with Henschel and Thomas Blackburn; also with Grose in Dresden. In 1915 he made his operatic debut as Paris in *Roméo et Juliette* with the Beecham Opera Co. in London, with which he appeared until 1919. In 1920 he made a tour of the U.S. in *The Beggar's Opera*. In 1922 he joined the British National Opera Co. in London, and also appeared there at Sadler's Wells (1933–35; 1940–42); also served as artistic director of London's Covent Garden English Co. (1937–39) and as artistic advisor at Covent Garden (1946–48). He was greatly admired as one of England's finest baritones. His repertory was extensive, but he excelled particularly as Mozart's Dr. Bartolo, Ford, Amfortas, Macheath, and Scarpia.—**NS/LK/DM**

Hemingway, Gerry, jazz percussionist, composer; b. New Haven, Conn., March 23, 1955. Between 1972–79 he made a living primarily as a jazz drummer and percussionist, but also worked in electronic music, chamber ensembles, theater, experimental film, and world music. In New Haven he became associated with George Lewis, Robert Dick, David Mott, and in particular Anthony Davis and Leo Smith, who inspired his development as a composer and improvisor. In 1976 he founded the Creative Musicians Improvisors Forum with Smith and Bobby Naughton, a non-profit organization that produced numerous large ensemble performances and recordings. In the fall of 1979 he moved to N.Y. and began performing as a solo artist. During the 1980s he began working with digital sampling, comput-

ers, and MIDI triggering. During the later 1980s and 1990s, he toured the U.S. and Europe with a quintet of baritone saxophone, trombone, cello, bass, drums/steel drums. He was a member of The Anthony Braxton Quartet (1983–95), and is an ongoing member of the Reggie Workman Ensemble, Anthony Davis's Episteme, BassDrumBone, a collective trio (with Georg Grawe and Ernst Reijseger), Tambastics (with Robert Dick, Denman Maroney, and Mark Dresser), and The Iliad Quartet. He also performs in duo with Marilyn Crispell and saxophonist/live electronics player Earl Howard. As a composer, Hemingway has received numerous commissions for works for tape and live performance. In January 1995 he presented works from 1988–94 at Merkin Hall in N.Y. His multimedia work includes *Waterways*, for multiple slide projectors, tape and percussion, as well as an ongoing collaboration with video artist/animator Beth Warshafsky.

DISC.: *Kwambe* (1978); *Solo Works* (1981); *Tubworks* (1983); *Outerbridge Crossing* (1985); *Special Detail* (1989); *Down to the Wire* (1991); *Demon Chaser* (1993); *The Marmalade King* (1994); *Acoustic Solo Works* (1983–94); *Electro-Acoustic Solo Works* (1984–95); *Perfect World* (1996); *Waltzes, Two Steps and other Matters of the Heart* (1996) *Terrains* (1997); *Slamadam* (live recordings from three different tours; 1999).—**LP**

Hemke, Frederick (LeRoy), American saxophonist and teacher; b. Milwaukee, July 11, 1935. He studied at the Univ. of Wisc. (1953–55), then with Marcel Mule at the Paris Cons., becoming the first American to win a premier prix for saxophone (1956). He then continued his studies with Joseph Mariano and Robert Sprenkle at the Eastman School of Music in Rochester, N.Y., and at the Univ. of Wisc. (D.M.A., 1975). He taught at Northwestern Univ. (from 1962), serving as chairman of the dept. of wind and percussion instruments (from 1964); was also a member of the Chicago Sym. Orch. (1962–82). He publ. *The Early History of the Saxophone* (1975) and *The Teacher's Guide to the Saxophone* (1977). He commissioned Pettersson's Sym. No. 16 for Alto Saxophone and Orch., and played in its premiere (Stockholm, Feb. 24, 1983).—**NS/LK/DM**

Hemmel, Sigmund, German composer; b. place and date unknown; d. probably in Tübingen, 1564. He was a tenor in the Stuttgart Hofkapelle by 1544, being named Hofkapellmeister in 1549. He continued in the service of the court when it was in Tübingen (1551–53), but after it returned to Stuttgart he gave up his post as Hofkapellmeister in 1554–55 while remaining a singer in the Kofkapelle. In 1564 he was again with the court of Tübingen, where he most likely died of the plague. Hemmel was one of the leading composers of Protestant church music of his day. His *Der gantz Psalter Davids, wie derselbig in teutsche Gesänge verfasset* for 4 Voices was publ. posthumously in Tübingen in 1569.—**LK/DM**

Hempel, Frieda, brilliant German soprano; b. Leipzig, June 26, 1885; d. Berlin, Oct. 7, 1955. She studied piano at the Leipzig Cons. (1900–1902) before pursuing vocal training with Selma Nicklass-Kempner at the Stern Cons. in Berlin (1902–05). After making her operatic debut in Breslau in 1905, she appeared with the Berlin Royal Opera for the first time on Aug. 22, 1905, as Frau Fluth in Nicolai's *Die lustigen Weiber von Windsor.* Following appearances with the Schwerin Court Opera (1905–07), she returned to Berlin and was a leading member of the Royal Opera until 1912. On May 2, 1907, she made her debut at London's Covent Garden as Bastienne in Mozart's opera and as Gretel in Humperdinck's opera in a double bill. She made her first appearance at the Metropolitan Opera in N.Y. on Dec. 27, 1912, as the Queen in *Les Huguenots.* She remained on its roster until 1919, gaining renown for her portrayals of such roles as the Queen of the Night, Susanna, Rosina, Lucia, Offenbach's Olympia, Eva, and Violetta. In 1914 and again in 1920–21 she sang with the Chicago Grand Opera. Thereafter she devoted herself to concert appearances in which she impersonated Jenny Lind in period costume. Her memoirs were publ. as *Mein Leben dem Gesang* (Berlin, 1955). Hempel possessed a remarkable coloratura voice. Her repertoire extended from Mozart to Richard Strauss, including the latter's Marschallin.—NS/LK/DM

Hemphill (Jr.), Julius (Arthur), alto saxophonist, composer; b. Fort Worth, Tex., Jan. 24, 1938; d. N.Y., April 2, 1995. His mother was a pianist. Hemphill studied clarinet with John Carter during the early 1950s. After serving in the Army in the early 1960s (and playing in the band), he worked with The Ike and Tina Turner Revue in the middle of the decade. In 1968, he moved to St. Louis, joined BAG (the Black Artists Group collective) with Oliver Lake and Lester Bowie. In 1971, he played in a group with pianist John Hicks. He formed his own record company, Mbari, 1972. In 1973, he moved to Chicago and began performing with Anthony Braxton; later that year, he performed in Paris and Sweden before settling in N.Y. During the 1970s, he played and recorded with Bowie, Kool and the Gang, and other popular acts. He was a cofounder of the World Saxophone Quartet in 1977 with Oliver Lake, Hamiet Bluiett, and David Murray; Hemphill continued to play with them until 1991. During the 1980s, Hemphill led his own small groups and on occasion a big band, in addition to working with Murray's octet and The Yah band. Due to complications from diabetes, he had to have both legs amputated in 1990. In 1997 the Jazz Composers Alliance Annual Jazz Composition Contest was renamed the Julius Hemphill Composition Awards in his honor. A re-formed big band played a tribute to him in N.Y. in 1998. In addition to performing, Hemphill composed a number of extended compositions.

DISC.: *Dogon A.D.* (1972); *Coon Bid'ness* (1975); *Roi Boye and the Gotham Minstrels* (1977); *Raw Materials and Residuals* (1977); *Blue Boye* (1977); *Buster Bee* (1978); *Flat Out Jump Suite* (1980); *Georgia Blues* (1984); *Julius Hemphill Big Band* (1988); *Big Band* (1988); *Live from the New Music Café* (1991); *Fat Man and the Hard Blues* (1991); *Oakland Duets* (1992); *Five Chord Stud* (1993).—**LP**

Hemsi (Chicurel), Alberto, Italian conductor, ethnomusicologist, and composer of Jewish descent; b. Cassaba, Turkey, Dec. 23, 1896; d. Aubervilliers, near Paris, Oct. 7, 1975. He studied music in Izmir, and later took courses in piano, theory, and composition at the Milan Cons. He was music director of the Grand Synagogue in Alexandria, Egypt (1927–57), and founder-conductor of the Alexandria Phil. (1928–40); also founded the Édition Orientale de Musique (1929) and was active as a teacher. In 1957 he settled in Paris as prof. at the Jewish Seminary. He was particularly interested in Sephardic Jewry. His compositions were of an oriental flavor, the most characteristic being the symphonic suite *Croquis égyptiens* (1930); other works include *Poème biblique* for Voice and Orch., *Suite Séfardie* for Violin and Piano, *6 danses turques* for Piano, and a number of songs.—NS/LK/DM

Hemsley, Thomas (Jeffery), English baritone; b. Coalville, April 12, 1927. He studied at Brasenose Coll., Oxford, and received private vocal training from Lucie Manén. In 1951 he made his operatic debut as Purcell's Aeneas at London's Mermaid Theatre; he then sang regularly at the Glyndebourne Festivals (1953–71). He also sang at the Aachen City Theater (1953–56), the Deutsche Oper am Rhein in Düsseldorf (1957–63), the Zürich Opera (1963–67), the Bayreuth Festivals (1968–70), and at London's Covent Garden (from 1970). He likewise pursued a career as a concert singer. In later years, he was active as an opera director and as a teacher. Prominent among his roles were such portrayals as Don Fernando, Count Almaviva, Dr. Malatesta, Beckmesser, and Massetto. Hemsley publ. the study *Singing and Imagination: A Human Approach to a Great Musical Tradition* (Oxford, 1998).—NS/LK/DM

Henderson, Alva, American composer; b. San Luis Obispo, Calif., April 8, 1940. He studied voice and theory at San Francisco State Coll. He wrote mainly vocal works, including the operas *Medea* (San Diego, Nov. 29, 1972), *The Tempest* (n.d.), and *The Last of the Mohicans* (Wilmington, Del., June 12, 1976).—NS/LK/DM

Henderson, Fletcher (Hamilton Jr.; aka Smack), highly influential jazz bandleader, arranger, pianist; b. Cuthbert, Ga., Dec. 18, 1897; d. Harlem Hospital, N.Y., Dec. 29, 1952. Several respectable sources give his birth year as 1898, and his first name as James, or perhaps James Fletcher; brother of **Horace Henderson.** His mother was a classical pianist, and started him on the keyboards at age six. He studied at Atlanta Univ. Coll. from 1916–, majoring in chemistry and math. He moved to N.Y. in 1920 intending to do post-graduate research there, but there were few jobs for blacks, so instead became a song demonstrator for the Pace-(W.C.) Handy Music Company (sheet music). He later left the company and became recording manager for the Black Swan Recording Company (the first African-American-owned record label), and organized his first band to tour accompanying Ethel Waters's Black Swan Troubadours (autumn 1921 to summer 1922). He returned to N.Y., became house pianist for recording companies, and played gigs with violinist Shrimp Jones's Band at Broadway Jones's Club in N.Y. In early 1924, he was elected leader of the band newly formed for a residency at the Club Alabam (N.Y.). Late that summer, Coleman

Hawkins joined the group and the band took up residency at the Roseland Ballroom, N.Y., working there for the next 10 years. The band played pop tunes, novelties and blues, but transformed when Louis Armstrong joined for a year in late 1924. Armstrong's solos with the band made recordings like "Copenhagen," "Sugar Foot Stomp," and "Go Long Mule" instant classics. Don Redman wrote virtually all the arrangements for the band until 1927; thereafter Benny Carter and Henderson wrote some, and by 1930 Henderson was beginning to write most of them. Henderson's Band appeared regularly at Roseland, but also played at many other N.Y. ballrooms and theatres, did regular touring and played dates in other cities. Despite many personnel changes and at least two complete reshuffles (in 1934 his men deserted him, and he was without a regular band for six months) Henderson continued to lead regularly until 1939. Early in the 1930s he supplemented his income by selling arrangements to other bandleaders including Benny Goodman, Teddy Hill, Will Bradley, Isham Jones, Jack Hylton, The Casa Loma Orch., and many others. Count Basie used his "Honeysuckle Rose" and others in late 1936 and for his first recordings in 1937.

Beginning in 1936, the Henderson band undertook a long residency at Grand Terrace (Chicago); at this time, the lineup was augmented by such new stars as Roy Eldridge, Chu Berry, and Sid Catlett. Henderson continued to lead various bands through June 1939, when he joined Benny Goodman as arranger (and sextet pianist). From late 1939, he ceased playing piano for Goodman and worked solely as staff arranger. Goodman in his autobiography *The Kingdom of Swing* credited his success to Henderson's arrangements such as "King Porter Stomp" and "Sometimes I'm Happy," but the public tends to remember the performer that they saw, not the composer offstage.

Through the 1940s, Henderson led various bands in N.Y. and on the road, none lasting longer than a few months. He also returned briefly to working for Goodman in the later 1940s, and worked as an accompanist for Ethel Waters toward the end of the decade (summer 1948–December 1949). He was back leading his own small group in N.Y. in 1950 when he suffered a stroke on Dec. 21. He was never able to resume playing, and his recovery was slow. About a year and a half later, he suffered a heart attack, and six months later died.

DISC.: *The Stampede; Sometimes I'm Happy; King Porter Stomp; Study in Frustration* (1923); *Complete F. H.* (rec. 1927–31); *Under the Harlem Moon* (1932); *Hocus Pocus* (1934); *F. H.'s Sextet* (1950); *Big Reunion* (1957; Henderson's sidepersons reunite). **BIBL.:** W. C. Allen, *H.: The Music of F. H. and His Musicians* (Highland Park, N.J., 1973).—JC/LP

Henderson, Horace (W.), jazz arranger, pianist, leader; b. Cuthbert, Ga., Nov. 22, 1904; d. Denver, Aug. 29, 1988; brother of **Fletcher Henderson**. He began piano studies at 14, spent a year at Atlanta Univ., then studied at Wilberforce Coll. for three years (A.B. degree). He formed his own student band, The Collegians, and began to work at composing at least as early as did his brother. During summer vacation of 1924 the band worked at the Bamville Club in N.Y. During the follow-

ing year they played a residency at Lawrence, Mass., then began regular touring (using the Wilberforce campus as a base until summer of 1926), with Rex Stewart and Benny Carter in the lineup. The group changed its name to The Dixie Stompers in 1928. In late 1928, Henderson temporarily disbanded and worked with Sammy Stewart, but regrouped for touring in 1929, and then played further residencies in N.Y. (1929–31). In 1931 he relinquished leadership to Don Redman, although he continued to work with Redman until early 1933. He played in Fletcher Henderson's Band from early 1933 until July 1937, except for a brief period in spring 1935; he also provided many arrangements for the group. In July 1937, he relocated to Chicago, where he led a band at various clubs through the early 1940s. From November 1942–August 1943, he served in the U.S. Army and then rejoined Fletcher in Chicago until May 1944. Horace then moved to N.Y. to become the accompanist for vocalist Lena Horne, but by summer 1945 had reformed his big band in L.A., working there through mid-1949. He spent the 1950s touring with his own bands, working in Chicago, Minneapolis, Las Vegas, Calif., and elsewhere. He worked with The Billy Williams Revue in the early 1960s, and also toured with own big band. From the late 1960s through the 1980s, he worked mainly in Denver, leading a hotel combo.

Henderson was a fine writer and pianist. More than 30 of his arrangements were incorporated into his brother's band, among them "Hot and Anxious" and "Comin' and Goin'," and the popular "Christopher Columbus." He also led a small splinter group in the early 1930s for recordings. "Hot and Anxious" briefly included the traditional riff that would eventually be recorded by the Glenn Miller Orch. on "In the Mood." —JC/LP

Henderson, Joe, prolific American jazz musician; b. Lima, Ohio, April 24, 1937. With the release of 1992's *Lush Life* he arrived. For 30 years he had been an outstanding leader and sideman but had remained relatively unknown. Recent acclaim has not made him complacent, however. He continues to play with the same intensity and fire that has been the hallmark of his career. His burnished tone and penchant for melodic ornamentation are instantly identifiable. One of 15 children, Henderson was encouraged by his parents and an older brother to study music. Early musical interests included drums, piano, saxophone, and composition. He was particularly enamored of his brother's record collection and listened to Lester Young, Flip Phillips, Stan Getz, Lee Konitz, Charlie Parker, and the popular Jazz at the Philharmonic recordings. At age 18 Henderson became active on the Detroit jazz scene, playing in jam sessions with visiting N.Y. stars of the mid-1950s. The diverse musical opportunities allowed him to learn flute and bass, as well as further developing his saxophone and compositional skills. By the time he arrived at Detroit's Wayne State Univ., he had transcribed and memorized so many Lester Young solos that his professors believed he had perfect pitch. Classmates Yusef Lateef, Barry Harris, and Donald Byrd undoubtedly provided additional inspiration.

After a two-year hitch in the U.S. Army (1960–62), he arrived in N.Y., where trumpeter Kenny Dorham provided valuable guidance. Although his earliest recordings were marked by a strong hard-bop influence, his playing encompassed not only the bebop tradition, but R&B, Latin, and avant garde as well. After leaving Silver's band in 1964, he resumed freelancing and also co-led a big band with Kenny Dorham. His arrangements for the band went unrecorded until his Verve album, *Big Band*, in 1996. From 1963 to 1968 Henderson appeared on nearly 30 albums for Blue Note that ranged from relatively conservative hard-bop sessions to more avant-garde explorations. This experience was invaluable to his continuing development. He played a prominent role in many seminal recordings: Horace Silver's swinging and soulful *Song for My Father*, Herbie Hancock's dark and densely orchestrated *Prisoner*, and Eric Dolphy's landmark avant-garde album *Out to Lunch*. This adaptability and eclecticism became even more apparent during his tenure with Milestone during the 1970s.

In 1967 there was a notable, but brief, association with Miles Davis's great quintet featuring Herbie Hancock, Wayne Shorter, Ron Carter, and Tony Williams. Although the band was unrecorded, Henderson is reputed to have occasionally stolen the show. Signing with Orrin Keepnews's fledgling Milestone label in 1967 marked a new phase in his career. He co-led the Jazz Communicators with Freddie Hubbard from 1967–68, then joined Herbie Hancock's fusion-ish sextet from 1969–70 and was featured on *Fat Albert Rotunda*. It was here that Henderson began to experiment with increasingly avant-garde structures, jazz-funk fusion, studio overdubbing, and other electronic effects. Songs and albums titled *Power to the People*, *In Search of Blackness*, and *Black Narcissus* reflected his growing political awareness and social consciousness. After a brief stint with Blood, Sweat and Tears in 1971, Henderson moved to San Francisco and added teaching to his résumé. He continued to record and perform as always, but seemed to be taken for granted. Though he occasionally worked with Echoes of an Era, The Griffith Park Band, and Chick Corea, Henderson remained primarily a leader throughout the 1980s. An accomplished and prolific composer, he began to focus more on reinterpreting standards and his own earlier compositions. Blue Note attempted to position him at the forefront of a resurgent jazz scene in 1986 with *State of the Tenor*. And although the album featured the most notable tenor trio since Sonny Rollins's in 1957, insufficient support from Blue Note prevented wider renown. The recording did, however, establish Henderson's basic repertoire for the next seven or eight years, with "Ask Me Now" becoming his signature tune. Verve's recent "songbook" approach to recording Henderson, coupled with a considerable marketing and publicity campaign, has successfully positioned him at the forefront of the current jazz scene. Henderson's sound can float prettily like that of Stan Getz or Lester "Prez" Young, and yet also dig in with the bluesy fervor of T-Bone Walker. The increasing complexity and ornamental nature of his current output suggests Henderson has successfully created his own unique vocabulary of phrases, licks, and saxophone effects.

DISC.: *Page One* (1963); *In 'n' Out* (1964); *Inner Urge* (1964); *Mode for Joe* (1966); *The Kicker* (1967); *Tetragon* (1968); *Straight, No Chaser* (1968); *Four!* (1968); *Multiple* (1973); *The Elements* (1973); *Canyon Lady* (1973); *Barcelona* (1978); *Mirror, Mirror* (1980); *Relaxin' at Camarillo* (1981); *Live in Montreux* (1981); *State of the Tenor* (1986); *An Evening with Joe Henderson* (1987); *Lush Life: The Music of Billy Strayhorn* (1992); *The Standard Joe* (1993); *So Near, So Far (Musings for Miles)* (1993); *Milestone Years* (1994); *Double Rainbow: The Music of Antonio Carlos Jobim* (1995); *Big Band* (1996); *Porgy & Bess* (1997).—JE

Henderson, Ray (actually, **Raymond Brost**), popular composer; b. Buffalo, N.Y., Dec. 1, 1896; d. Greenwich, Conn., Dec. 31, 1970. Henderson was best known as the composing member of the songwriting team of De Sylva, Brown, and Henderson, which wrote songs for nine Broadway shows and four Hollywood movies between 1925 and 1931, making them the most successful partnership of the period. The trio specialized in timely, upbeat songs, such as their major hits "The Best Things in Life Are Free," "You're the Cream in My Coffee," and "Button Up Your Overcoat," which caught the frothy spirit of the 1920s. In addition to his association with De Sylva and Brown, Henderson wrote similarly cheery songs such as "I'm Sitting on Top of the World," "Five Foot Two, Eyes of Blue (Has Anybody Seen My Girl?)," and "Bye, Bye, Blackbird" for Tin Pin Alley. After the trio's breakup, such Henderson songs as "Animal Crackers in My Soup" and "Life Is Just a Bowl of Cherries" helped to counter the dire effects of the Depression.

Both of Henderson's parents were musicians, and he was encouraged to pursue music as a child. His mother gave him piano lessons, and he played organ at church. After years of private study in Buffalo, he apparently studied academically (accounts vary), perhaps at the Chicago Cons. of Music. (He is said to have studied later with composers Vittorio Giannini and Benjamin Britten.) He moved to N.Y. around 1918 and became a song plugger, staff pianist, and arranger at a succession of music-publishing companies, establishing the contacts that allowed him to become a songwriter.

"Humming" (lyrics by Louis Breau) was Henderson's first songwriting success; it was interpolated into the musical *Tip Top* (N.Y., Oct. 5, 1920) and recorded by Paul Whiteman and His Orch. for a hit in July 1921. Henderson was working for publishers Shapiro-Bernstein in 1922 when Louis Bernstein introduced him to lyricist Lew Brown. Their first success together was "Georgette," which was performed in the *Greenwich Village Follies* (N.Y., Sept. 12, 1922) by Ted Lewis and His Band and recorded by them for a hit in November 1922.

Henderson also succeeded on Tin Pan Alley, scoring his biggest hit yet in 1923 with "That Old Gang of Mine" (lyrics by Billy Rose and Mort Dixon), which drew a number of hit recordings, the most successful of which was the duet by Billy Murray and Ed Smalle that became a best-seller in November. The team of Henderson, Rose, and Dixon followed with two hits in 1924: "Follow the Swallow," which was featured in the *Zieg-*

feld Follies of 1924 (N.Y., June 24, 1924) and recorded by Al Jolson, and "I Wonder Who's Dancing with You Tonight," recorded by Benny Krueger and His Orch. in July. Henderson also scored a hit with Brown, "Why Did I Kiss That Girl?" (music also by Robert A. King), recorded by Whiteman with the American Quartet on vocals, in June.

Henderson first teamed with B. G. De Sylva for "Alabamy Bound" (lyrics also by Bud Green), which became a hit for Blossom Seely in May 1925 and sold a million copies of sheet music. De Sylva had been writing songs with George Gershwin for the revue series *George White's Scandals*, and when Gershwin moved on to book musicals, White brought in Henderson to replace him; Henderson brought in Brown to collaborate on lyrics, and the team of De Sylva, Brown, and Henderson first worked together on the 1925 edition of *Scandals*. Though it did not produce any song hits, the show had a healthy run, encouraging White to bring the trio back for the 1926 edition.

Meanwhile, Henderson continued to work on independent material for Tin Pan Alley. The comic song "Don't Bring Lulu" (lyrics by Rose and Brown) provided equally popular record hits to both Billy Murray and the team of Ernest Hare and Billy Jones in August 1925; "If I Had a Girl Like You" (lyrics by Rose and Dixon) was a hit for Benny Krueger in November; Murray and Aileen Stanley had a hit with the comic song "Keep Your Skirts Down, Mary Ann" (lyrics by Andrew Sterling, music also by Robert A. King) in January 1926; Ted Lewis scored with "Bam, Bam, Bammy Shore" (lyrics by Dixon) in February; and Henderson wrote two best-sellers with the team of Sam L. Lewis and Joe Young: "I'm Sitting on Top of the World" for Jolson in April, and "Five Foot Two, Eyes of Blue (Has Anybody Seen My Girl?)" for Gene Austin in May.

The 1926 edition of *George White's Scandals* was the breakthrough success for De Sylva, Brown, and Henderson, running 432 performances and generating three hits: "Lucky Day," recorded by George Olsen and His Orch.; "The Birth of the Blues," a best-seller for Paul Whiteman; and the dance sensation "Black Bottom," recorded by Johnny Hamp and His Orch. With a fourth best-seller in 1926, "Bye, Bye, Blackbird" (lyrics by Dixon), recorded by Gene Austin among others, Henderson was clearly established as the top pop composer of the year.

Henderson's success continued into 1927, a year when he scored eight hits, all with De Sylva and Brown. The first was "It All Depends on You," which Al Jolson interpolated into the road tour of his show *Big Boy*, and which was recorded most successfully by Paul Whiteman. Whiteman also had hits in 1927 with the independent De Sylva/Brown/Henderson songs "So Blue" and "Just a Memory," and with "Broken Hearted," which was used in the revue *Artists and Models* (N.Y., Nov. 15, 1927). But the biggest beneficiary of Henderson's melodies in 1927 was bandleader George Olsen, who appeared onstage in De Sylva/Brown/Henderson's longest running musical, *Good News!* (it played 551 performances), and recorded the most popular versions

of all four of its hit songs, "The Best Things in Life Are Free," "Lucky in Love," "The Varsity Drag," and "Good News." Due to the success of the 1926 edition of *George White's Scandals*, White did not mount an edition in 1927, but the musical *Manhattan Mary*—which he produced and directed and which featured the songs of De Sylva, Brown, and Henderson—was the next best thing; it ran for 264 performances.

The next De Sylva, Brown, and Henderson hit was the independent song "Together," which became a bestseller for Whiteman in April 1928. In July the team saw the opening of their third *George White's Scandals*. It ran 230 performances and produced a hit in "I'm on the Crest of a Wave," recorded by Whiteman, among others.

De Sylva, Brown, and Henderson were in Atlantic City working on their next show when they received a call from Al Jolson in Hollywood wanting a song for his film *The Singing Fool*. De Sylva and Brown's maudlin lyric for "Sonny Boy" reportedly was written facetiously, but that didn't keep the song from becoming the biggest hit of 1928, and the biggest recording of Jolson's career, a million-seller in sheet music and on records, while *The Singing Fool* became the biggest box office success in movie history up to that time.

De Sylva, Brown, and Henderson completed their show, *Hold Everything!*, which ran 413 performances and contained the hit "You're the Cream in My Coffee," recorded by Ben Selvin and His Orch. Within days, the team also had the musical *Three Cheers*, which ran 210 performances and featured "Pompanola," also a hit recording for Selvin. Meanwhile, "For Old Times' Sake," which had been interpolated into Jack McGowan's long-running play *Excess Baggage* (N.Y., Dec. 26, 1927), finally became a record hit in November 1928 for Annette Hanshaw.

De Sylva, Brown, and Henderson's next show, *Follow Thru*, debuting at the start of 1929, was another hit, running 401 performances. Helen Kane successfully recorded two of its songs, "Button Up Your Overcoat" and "I Want to Be Bad," while Paul Whiteman scored with a third, "My Lucky Star." Later in January, the Fox feature *In Old Arizona* used the team's "My Tonia"; it became a hit for Nick Lucas in March. "The Song I Love," an independent song, was a hit for Fred Waring's Pennsylvanians in February. In June, "My Sin," another independent song, was a hit for Ben Selvin among others.

Following the success of "Sonny Boy" and *The Singing Fool*, De Sylva, Brown, and Henderson were a natural choice to write the songs for Al Jolson's next film, *Say It with Songs*. Following its release in Aug. 1929, Jolson made hits out of four of the songs he sang in the movie: "Little Pal," a similarly themed follow-up to "Sonny Boy," which became a best-seller; "I'm in Seventh Heaven"; "Why Can't You?"; and "Used to You."

The songwriters' next project was also a movie musical, *Sunny Side Up*, released in October 1929. It produced another four hits: Johnny Hamp recorded "If I Had a Talking Picture of You" and Paul Whiteman cut "I'm a Dreamer, Aren't We All?" while Earl Burtnett and

His L.A. Biltmore Orch. had the most popular versions of the title song and "Turn on the Heat."

De Sylva, Brown, and Henderson returned to Broadway for the last time in March 1930 with *Flying High*, which was the biggest musical comedy hit of the 1929–30 season and featured "Thank Your Father," recorded by Al Goodman and His Orch. The songwriters then moved permanently to Hollywood under contract to Fox. While they prepared their next film, "If I Had a Girl Like You" was revived by Rudy Vallée in June and became an even bigger hit than it had been five years before. In September, film versions of *Good News* and *Follow Thru* were released. In October, Ruth Etting had a hit with the independent song "Don't Tell Her What Happened to Me."

In addition to writing the songs for the ambitious science-fiction musical *Just Imagine*, released in November, De Sylva, Brown, and Henderson wrote the screenplay and produced the film. It was not a success. In early 1931 the songwriters contributed a song to Gus Arnheim and His Orch., "One More Time," which was a hit in a recording featuring Bing Crosby, and they collaborated on the screenplay for the Gloria Swanson vehicle *Indiscreet* with director Leo McCary in addition to writing the songs, which included "Come to Me," a hit for The High Hatters. But in March 1931 the team split up, with De Sylva remaining in Hollywood to pursue a career as a producer while Brown and Henderson returned to N.Y.

Brown and Henderson's first project as a duo was a new edition of *George White's Scandals* that proved nearly as successful as previous ones. Featuring Ethel Merman and Rudy Vallée, it ran 204 performances and four of its songs became hits: Vallée scored with "Life Is Just a Bowl of Cherries," "The Thrill Is Gone," and "My Song," and Kate Smith recorded "That's Why Darkies Are Born." There was also a 12-inch disc featuring a medley of songs from the show as performed by Crosby, the Mills Brothers, and the Boswell Sisters. Kate Smith scored a hit at the end of 1931 backed by Guy Lombardo and His Royal Canadians on the ironically titled De Sylva, Brown, and Henderson composition "You Try Somebody Else."

Brown and Henderson's next musical, *Hot-Cha!*, was produced by impresario Florenz Ziegfeld; it ran 118 performances. The songwriters then collaborated on the libretto, production, and direction of *Strike Me Pink*, which ran 122 performances. The Hotel Commodore Orch. had a hit in May 1933 with "Let's Call It a Day" from the score, a title that gained resonance when Brown and Henderson split up the same month.

In 1934, Henderson wrote songs with lyricists Jack Yellen and Irving Caesar for the film *George White's Scandals of 1934*, and Rudy Vallée, who appeared onscreen, made hits out of "Hold My Hand" and "Nasty Man" in April. Henderson teamed with playwright Jack McGowan to produce the musical *Say When*, for which McGowan wrote the libretto and Henderson collaborated on the songs with Ted Koehler. It ran only 76 performances. In 1935, Henderson wrote the songs for the Shirley Temple film *Curly Top*, released in August, including "Animal Crackers in My Soup" (lyrics by

Koehler and Caesar), which became one of Temple's signature songs. At the end of the year, Henderson wrote one more edition of *George White's Scandals* for the stage, this one with lyrics by Yellen and starring Rudy Vallée; it ran 110 performances.

Henderson reunited with Brown and continued to write songs, but without notable success after the mid-1930s. Henderson became a director of ASCAP in 1942, a position he held until 1951. With Yellen, Henderson wrote the songs for a new *Ziegfeld Follies* in 1943 starring Milton Berle. It became a wartime hit, running 553 performances.

The July 1944 release of the home-front melodrama *Since You Went Away* gave new life to "Together," which was prominently used in the film. The most successful of a series of new recordings was the one by Dick Haymes and Helen Forrest that made the Top Ten. In December 1947, MGM released a lavish remake of *Good News* starring Peter Lawford and June Allyson that spawned a Top Ten soundtrack album in 1948.

As Henderson retired to Conn., where he died of a heart attack in 1970, there were periodic revivals of his work: "Five Foot Two, Eyes of Blue (Has Anybody Seen My Girl?)" charted for Benny Strong and His Orch. in 1949; Johnny Ray hit the Top Ten in 1952 with "Broken Hearted"; Frank Sinatra charted with "The Birth of the Blues" the same year; Les Paul and Mary Ford had a Top Ten version of "I'm Sitting on Top of the World" in 1953; and Connie Francis revived "Together" for a Top Ten hit in 1961.

In September 1956, 20th Century–Fox released a film biography of De Sylva, Brown, and Henderson called *The Best Things in Life Are Free*.

WORKS (only works for which Henderson was the primary, credited composer are listed): **MUSICALS/REVUES** (dates refer to N.Y. openings): *George White's Scandals* (June 22, 1925); *George White's Scandals* (June 14, 1926); *Good News!* (Sept. 6, 1927); *Manhattan Mary* (Sept. 26, 1927); *George White's Scandals* (July 2, 1928); *Hold Everything!* (Oct. 10, 1928); *Three Cheers* (Oct. 15, 1928); *Follow Thru* (Jan. 9, 1929); *Flying High* (March 3, 1930); *George White's Scandals* (Sept. 14, 1931); *Hot-Cha!* (March 8, 1932); *Strike Me Pink* (March 4, 1933); *Say When* (Nov. 8, 1934); *George White's Scandals* (Dec. 25, 1935); *Ziegfeld Follies* (April 1, 1943). Films: *The Singing Fool* (1928); *Say It with Songs* (1929); *Sunny Side Up* (1929); *Good News* (1930); *Follow Thru* (1930); *Just Imagine* (1930); *Indiscreet* (1931); *A Holy Terror* (1931); *George White's Scandals of 1934* (1934); *Curly Top* (1935); *Good News* (1947).—**WR**

Henderson, Roy (Galbraith),

Scottish baritone, conductor, and pedagogue; b. Edinburgh, July 4, 1899; d. London, March 16, 2000. He studied at the Royal Academy of Music in London (1920–25). He made his London debut as Zarathustra in *A Mass of Life* by Delius in 1925; his operatic debut followed in 1928 as Donner in Wagner's *Das Rheingold* at Covent Garden; he also sang at the Glyndebourne Festivals (1934–39). He was founder and conductor of the Nottingham Oriana Choir (1936–52); was a prof. of singing at the Royal Academy of Music (1940–74). He was made a Commander of the Order of the British Empire in 1970.

Henderson was especially esteemed as a concert singer, becoming well known for his championship of music by English composers. As a teacher, he numbered Kathleen Ferrier among his gifted students.—**NS/LK/DM**

Henderson, Skitch (actually, **Lyle Russell Cedric**), English-born American pianist, conductor, composer, and arranger; b. Birmingham, Jan. 27, 1918. He settled in the U.S. as a youth and pursued his training at the Univ. of Calif. at Los Angeles and at the Juilliard School of Music in N.Y.; among his mentors were Schoenberg (theory and harmony) and Reiner (conducting). He worked in film studios and on the radio. While in military service during World War II, he became a naturalized American citizen. In 1949 he joined the staff of NBC. He became well known as a conductor, composer, and arranger for various television programs, particularly Steve Allen's show (1954–56) and Johnny Carson's "Tonight Show" (1962–66). In subsequent years, he toured as a conductor in the U.S. and Europe, leading concerts of both classical and popular scores. After serving as music director of the Tulsa Phil. (1971–74), he founded the N.Y. Pops Orch. which gave its inaugural concert at Carnegie Hall in 1983.—**NS/LK/DM**

Henderson, W(illiam) J(ames), noted American music critic; b. Newark, N.J., Dec. 4, 1855; d. (suicide) N.Y., June 5, 1937. He was a graduate of Princeton Univ. (B.A., 1876; M.A., 1886); also studied piano with Carl Langlotz (1868–73) and voice with Torriani (1876–77); was chiefly self-taught in theory. He was first a reporter (1883–87), then music critic of the *N.Y. Times* (1887–1902) and the *N.Y. Sun* (1902–37); lectured on music history at the N.Y. Coll. of Music (1889–95; 1899–1902); from 1904, lectured on the development of vocal art at the Inst. of Musical Art in N.Y. A brilliant writer, Henderson was an irreconcilable and often venomous critic of modern music; he loved Wagner, but savagely attacked Debussy and Richard Strauss. Henderson, in turn, was the butt of some of Charles Ives's caustic wit.

WRITINGS (all publ. in N.Y.): *The Story of Music* (1889; 2nd ed., enl., 1912); *Preludes and Studies* (1891); *How Music Developed* (1898); *What Is Good Music?* (1898; 6th ed., 1935); *The Orchestra and Orchestral Music* (1899); *Richard Wagner, His Life and His Dramas* (1901; 2nd ed., 1923); *Modern Musical Drift* (1904); *The Art of the Singer* (1906; 2nd ed., aug., 1938, as *The Art of Singing*); *Some Forerunners of Italian Opera* (1911); *Early History of Singing* (1921). —**NS/LK/DM**

Hendl, Walter, American conductor; b. West New York, N.J., Jan. 12, 1917. He began piano lessons in childhood; after further piano training with Clarence Adler (1934–37), he was a scholarship student of Saperton (piano, 1938) and Reiner (conducting, 1939) at the Curtis Inst. of Music in Philadelphia; during the summers of 1941–42, he attended Koussevitzky's conducting courses at the Berkshire Music Center in Tanglewood. He was asst. conductor of the N.Y. Phil. (1945–49) and a faculty member of the Juilliard School of Music in N.Y. (1947–50). From 1949 to 1958 he was music director

of the Dallas Sym. Orch., and also of the Chautauqua (N.Y.) Sym. Orch. (1953–72). He was assoc. conductor of the Chicago Sym. Orch. (1958–64) and music director of its Ravinia Festival (1959–63). From 1964 to 1972 he was director of the Eastman School of Music in Rochester, N.Y. He was music director of the Erie (Pa.) Phil. from 1976 to 1990.—**NS/LK/DM**

Hendricks, Barbara, greatly admired black American soprano; b. Stephens, Ark., Nov. 20, 1948. She sang in church and school choirs before majoring in chemistry and mathematics at the Univ. of Neb. (graduated, 1969). During the summer of 1968 she began vocal training with Tourel at the Aspen (Colo.) Music School, continuing under her guidance at the Juilliard School in N.Y. (1969–71); she also attended Callas's master class there. In 1971 she won the Geneva International Competition, and in 1972 both the International Concours de Paris and the Kosciuszko Foundation Vocal Competition. On Feb. 20, 1973, she made her debut in Thomson's *4 Saints in 3 Acts* in the Mini-Metropolitan Opera production presented at the Lincoln Center Forum Theatre in N.Y.; later that year, she made her first concert tour of Europe. In 1974 she appeared as Erisbe in Cavalli's *Ormindo* at the San Francisco Spring Opera, and in the title role of Cavalli's *La Calisto* at the Glyndebourne Festival. On Feb. 26, 1975, she made her formal N.Y. debut as Inez in a concert performance of *La Favorite* at Carnegie Hall. In 1976 she sang Amor in Gluck's *Orfeo ed Euridice* with the Netherlands Opera at the Holland Festival, and on Nov. 14 of that year made her N.Y. recital debut at Town Hall. At the Berlin Deutsche Oper in 1978 she appeared as Mozart's Susanna, a role she quickly made her own. In 1980 she sang Gilda and in 1981 Pamina at the Orange Festival in France; in 1982 she appeared as Gounod's Juliet at both the Paris Opéra and London's Covent Garden. On Oct. 30, 1986, she made her Metropolitan Opera debut in N.Y. as Strauss's Sophie. In 1988 she sang at the 70th-birthday celebration for Leonard Bernstein at the Tanglewood Festival, and also starred as Mimi in Luigi Comencini's film version of *La Bohème*. In 1989 she appeared at the Bolshoi Theater in Moscow. In addition to her operatic career, she has won notable distinction as a recitalist. In 1991 she sang Manon in Parma and in 1992 she sang Micaëla in Orange. Her interpretations of the German and French lieder repertoire, as well as of Negro spirituals, have won accolades. In 1986 she was made a Commandeur des Arts et des Lettres of France. Her unswerving commitment to social justice led the High Commissioner for Refugees at the United Nations to name her a goodwill ambassador of the world body in 1987.—**NS/LK/DM**

Hendrix, Jimi (actually, **James Marshall**), superstar guitar player of the 1960s, one of the master virtuosos of the electric guitar; b. Seattle, Wash., Nov. 27, 1942; d. London, England, Sept. 18, 1970. THE JIMI HENDRIX EXPERIENCE: Jimi Hendrix, lead gtr., lead voc.; Noel Redding, bs., background voc. (b. Folkstone, Kent, England, Dec. 25, 1945); John "Mitch" Mitchell, drm. (b. London, England, July 9, 1946).

James Hendrix obtained his first acoustic guitar at the age of 11, graduating to electric guitar at 12. He was playing in a number of Seattle-area bands by 14; he dropped out of high school at 16 and eventually joined the U.S. Army in 1961. While serving, he became a paratrooper and met and jammed with bassist Billy Cox. Discharged after slightly more than a year because of a back injury sustained in a parachute jump, Hendrix subsequently toured the South's "chitlin" circuit, backing artists such as B. B. King, Sam Cooke, and Jackie Wilson. He moved to N.Y. in 1964 to record with The Isley Brothers and King Curtis. The following year, he was a member of Little Richard's backup band and Curtis Knight's group. In June 1966, Hendrix formed his own group, Jimmy James and The Blue Flames, for engagements in Greenwich Village coffeehouses. "Discovered" there in July by former Animals bassist Bryan "Chas" Chandler, Hendrix went to England at Chandler's behest in September, forming The Jimi Hendrix Experience with two English musicians, Noel Redding and Mitch Mitchell.

The Jimi Hendrix Experience became an immediate success in Great Britain, scoring major hits with "Hey Joe," "Purple Haze," and "The Wind Cries Mary" in the first half of 1967. Commencing their first British tour in March and their first European tour in May, the group's debut album, *Are You Experienced?*, performance included Dylan's "Like a Rolling Stone" and the awe-inspiring finale "Wild Thing," which culminated in the torching of Hendrix' lighter fluid-drenched guitar. Word of Hendrix's spectacular, flamboyant Monterey performance spread rapidly. *Are You Experienced?*, upon American release on Reprise Records in August, became an instant best-seller, remaining on the album charts for over two years. Yielding only minor hit singles with the classics "Purple Haze" and "Foxey Lady," the album also included "Hey Joe," "Are You Experienced?," and the poignantly lyrical "The Wind Cries Mary." Following an abortive tour with The Monkees (a mismatch if ever there was one), Hendrix returned to England.

The Jimi Hendrix Experience's *Axis: Bold as Love*, released stateside in early 1968, became another immediate best-seller, producing the minor hit "Up from the Skies" and containing the masterful "Little Wing," the gentle "One Rainy Wish," and the ominous "If 6 Was 9," later used in the breakthrough Peter Fonda–Dennis Hopper movie *Easy Rider*. *Electric Ladyland*, The Experience's final album and the crowning achievement of their brief recording career, yielded the group's only major hit with Dylan's "All Along the Watchtower" in its definitive version. Included on the double-record set were the vituperative "Crosstown Traffic," the lilting "Rainy Day, Dream Away," the challenging "1983," and the extended jam "Voodoo Chile," featuring Stevie Winwood on organ.

Tours by The Experience in 1968 saw Hendrix retreating from his role as psychedelic, flash guitarist-showman, much to the chagrin of inflexible fans. Chandler stopped managing the group in September and, in November, The Jimi Hendrix Experience announced their intention to disband, although contractual obligations kept the group together through June 1969. Noel

Redding formed Fat Mattress in 1969, Road in 1971, and The Noel Redding Band in 1975. Mitch Mitchell continued to play with Hendrix on and off until his death, briefly becoming a member of Ramatam with former Iron Butterfly guitarist Mike Pinera in 1972.

During 1969, Jimi Hendrix began building his own studio, Electric Ladyland, in N.Y., while seldom performing publicly. He eventually logged over 600 hours of studio tapes with various participants, including jazz musicians such as John McLaughlin. In August, Hendrix, backed by Mitch Mitchell and Army buddy Billy Cox, played the Woodstock Festival. The performance closed with a stunning version of "The Star Spangled Banner," which appropriately segued into "Purple Haze" (later included on the first *Woodstock* album).

On New Year's Eve 1969, the all-black Band of Gypsys (Hendrix, Cox, and drummer Buddy Miles) debuted at Bill Graham's Fillmore East. The performance, recorded and later released in album form, included Miles's "(Them) Changes" and Hendrix' 12–minute-plus "Machine Gun." However, the group never really worked out, perhaps due to Buddy Miles's overbearing drum style.

Jimi Hendrix was soon recording his next album, a double-record set tentatively entitled *First Rays of the New Rising Sun*, with Mitch Mitchell and Billy Cox. During the spring and summer of 1970, Hendrix toured with them, opening his Electric Ladyland studio shortly before their August appearance at the Isle of Wight. On Sept. 18, 1970, Jimi Hendrix died of "inhalation of vomit due to barbiturate intoxication" in London at the age of 27.

Much of the material from *First Rays of the New Rising Sun* was ultimately released on *The Cry of Love* and *Rainbow Bridge*, and reissued on *Voodoo Soup* in 1995. *The Cry of Love* featured Buddy Miles on "Ezy Rider" and Noel Redding on "My Friend" and included two excellent but overlooked slow blues songs, "Drifting" and "Angel." *Rainbow Bridge* contained "Dolly Dagger," "Pali Gap," and the live "Hear My Train a Comin'." *Hendrix in the West* assembled live recordings such as Chuck Berry's "Johnny B. Goode" and the Hendrix originals "Red House," "Little Wing," and "Voodoo Chile." *War Heroes* contained nearly completed recordings by Hendrix, including "Izabella" and "Stepping Stone." *Soundtrack Recordings from the Film "Jimi Hendrix"* compiled live performances and interviews.

In 1974, the estate of Jimi Hendrix hired producer Alan Douglas to sort through the tape archives left by Jimi Hendrix. For *Crash Landing* and *Midnight Lightning*, Douglas erased the original sidemen and grafted on L.A. sessions players, while *Nine to the Universe* was taken from the jam sessions recorded in 1969 and 1970. Subsequent album releases included the live compilation *The Jimi Hendrix Concerts*, the complete *Jimi Plays Monterey*, *Radio One* (live recordings made for the BBC in 1967), and the four-CD anthology of alternate takes, demonstration records, live performances and interviews, *Lifelines*. The Jimi Hendrix Experience was inducted into the Rock and Roll Hall of Fame in 1992 and, the following year, Reprise issued the tribute album *Stone Free*, on which various contemporary artists from

Ice-T to Eric Clapton, The Pretenders to Nigel Kennedy, recorded versions of Jimi Hendrix's songs. In July 1995, after years of court battles, Jimi Hendrix's father, Al, was awarded the rights to his son's music.

Undoubtedly, the most adventurous and daring electric guitarist of the 1960s, Hendrix is regarded by some as rock's single most important instrumentalist and perhaps the most influential guitarist ever. He enormously expanded the possibilities of the electric guitar, masterfully manipulating devices such as the wah-wah pedal, fuzz-box, and tape-delay mechanism to produce sounds alternately gentle and melodic, loud and psychedelic, even extraterrestrial and aquatic. His masterful and imaginative use of studio techniques with equipment that would be regarded as primitive by today's standards vastly extended the potential of recorded electric music. His carefully controlled use of distortion and feedback laid the foundation for *all* the heavy metal guitarists that followed, while inspiring jazz musicians such as Miles Davis to adopt certain elements of rock music, leading to the development of fusion music.

DISC.: JIMI HENDRIX AND LITTLE RICHARD: *Roots of Rock* (1974); *Jimi Hendrix and Little Richard Together* (1975). JIMI HENDRIX WITH THE ISLEY BROTHERS: *In the Beginning* (1971). JIMI HENDRIX AND CURTIS KNIGHT: *Get That Feeling* (1967); *Flashing* (1968). JIMI HENDRIX AND LONNIE YOUNGBLOOD: *Together* (1971). THE JIMI HENDRIX EXPERIENCE/OTIS REDDING: *At Monterey* (1970). THE JIMI HENDRIX EXPERIENCE: *Are You Experienced?* (1967); *Axis: Bold as Love* (1968); *Electric Ladyland* (1968); *Smash Hits* (1969); *The Ultimate Experience* (1993); *Radio One* (rec. 1967; rel. 1989); *The Experience Collection* (1993); *BBC Sessions* (rec. 1967–69; rel. 1998); *The Jimi Hendrix Experience* (box set; 2000). FAT MATTRESS: *Fat Mattress* (1969); *Fat Mattress II* (1971). THE NOEL REDDING BAND: *Clonkakilty Cowboys* (1975); *Blowin'* (1976), *The Missing Album* (1995). RAMATAM: *Ramatam* (1972); *In April Came the Dawning of the Red Suns* (1973). THE BAND OF GYPSYS: *The Band of Gypsys* (1970); *The Band of Gypsys 2* (1986). LIVE RECORDINGS BY JIMI HENDRIX: *Hendrix in the West* (1972); *In Concert* (1972); *The Jimi Hendrix Concerts* (1982); *Jimi Plays Monterey (June 18, 1967)* (1986); *Live at Winterland (October 1968)* (1987); *The Last Experience Concert* (1990); *Woodstock (Aug. 18, 1969)* (1994). POSTHUMOUS JIMI HENDRIX RELEASES: *The Cry of Love* (1971); *Rainbow Bridge* (1971); *War Heroes* (1972); *Soundtrack Recordings from the Film "Jimi Hendrix"* (1973); *Crash Landing* (1975); *Midnight Lightning* (1975); *The Essential Jimi Hendrix* (1978); *The Essential Jimi Hendrix, Vol. II* (1979); *Nine to the Universe* (1980); *Kiss the Sky* (1984/1985); *Lifelines: The Jimi Hendrix Story* (1991); *Stages* (1991); *Blues* (1994); *Voodoo Soup* (1995); *First Rays of the New Rising Sun* (1997); *Experience Hendrix: The Best of Jimi Hendrix* (1997); *South Saturn Delta* (1997).

BIBL.: C. Welch, *Hendrix: A Biography* (N.Y., 1973); C. Knight, *Jimi* (N.Y., 1974); G. Carey, *Lenny, Janis and Jimi* (N.Y., 1975); D. Henderson, *J. H.: Voodoo Child of the Aquarian Age* (Garden City, N.Y., 1978); D. Henderson, *'Scuse Me While I Kiss the Sky: The Life of J. H.* (N.Y., 1981, 1996); J. Hopkins, *Hit and Run: The J. H. Story* (N.Y., 1983); J. Benson, *Uncle Joe's Record Guide: Eric Clapton, J. H., The Who* (Glendale, Calif., 1987); C. S. Murray, *Crosstown Traffic: J. H. and the Post-War Rock 'n' Roll Revolution* (N.Y., 1989, 1991); M. Mitchell, with J. Platt, *J. H.:*

Inside The Experience (N.Y., 1990); H. Shapiro and C. Glebbeek, *Electric Gypsy: J. H.* (N.Y., 1991, 1995); J. Hopkins, *J. H.: Starchild* (Wilmington, Del., 1992); J. McDermott, with E. Kramer, *Hendrix: Setting the Record Straight* (N.Y., 1992); J. Hendrix, *Cherokee Mist: The Lost Writings* (N.Y., 1993); A. Boot and C. Salewicz (compilers), *J. H.: The Ultimate Experience* (N.Y., 1995); J. McDermott, with B. Cox and E. Kramer, *Jimi Hendrix Sessions: The Complete Studio Recording Sessions, 1963–70* (Boston, 1995); M. Mitchell, *The Hendrix Experience* (N.Y., 1998).—**BH**

Hengeveld, Gerard, Dutch pianist and composer; b. Kampen, Dec. 7, 1910. He studied piano with Carl Friedberg. He appeared as a soloist with European orchs. and in recitals; also was on the piano faculty at the Royal Cons. of Music at The Hague. He composed a Violin Sonata (1944), Concertino for Piano and Orch. (1946), Piano Concerto (1947), Cello Sonata (1965), *Musica concertante* for Oboe and Chamber Orch. (1968), and numerous teaching pieces for piano.—**NS/LK/DM**

Henkel, Heinrich, German pianist, son of **(Johann) Michael Henkel;** b. Fulda, Feb. 17, 1822; d. Frankfurt am Main, April 10, 1899. He was a pupil of his father, and also studied with Aloys Schmitt. He settled in Frankfurt am Main in 1849, as a teacher. He publ. a piano method, *Vorschule des Klavierspiels*, an abridged ed. of A. André's *Lehrbuch der Tonsetzkunst* (1875), and *Mitteilungen aus der musikalischen Vergangenheit Fuldas* (1882). His compositions include piano pieces and songs.—**NS/LK/DM**

Henkel, (Johann) Michael, German organist, pedagogue, and composer, father of **Heinrich Henkel;** b. Fulda, June 18, 1780; d. there, March 4, 1851. He began his music training in Fulda, and then studied organ and thoroughbass with J. G. Vierling in Schmalkalden. After returning to Fulda, he was Episcopal court violinist (1800–03), and then served as cantor at the Cathedral and at the town parish church from 1804; he also was active as a teacher (1805–48). He publ. a chorale book for the Fulda diocese (1804) and songs for school use. His other works included organ pieces, chamber music, and songs.—**NS/LK/DM**

Henkemans, Hans, Dutch pianist, composer, physician, and psychiatrist; b. The Hague, Dec. 23, 1913. He studied piano and composition with Sigtenhorst-Meyer (1926–31), and then composition with Pijper (1933–38). He also took courses in medicine at the Univ. of Utrecht (from 1931) and later took his doctorate at the Univ. of Amsterdam (1981). After making his debut as a pianist in his own Piano Concerto at 19, he pursued a successful concert career until 1969 when he decided to practice medicine and psychiatry. In his compositions, he succeeded in developing an original voice while utilizing traditional forms.

WORKS: DRAMATIC: Opera: *Winter Cruise* (1977). **ORCH.:** 3 piano concertos (1932, 1936, 1992); Sym. (1934); *Voorspel* (1935–36); *Passacaglia and Gigue* for Piano and Orch. (1941–42); Flute Concerto (1945–46); Violin Concerto (1948–50); Viola Concerto (1954); Harp Concerto (1955); *Partita* (1960); *Barcarola fantastica* (1962); *Dona montana* (1964); *Elégies* for 4

Flutes and Orch. (1967); Horn Concerto (1981); *Villanelle* for Horn and Orch., after Dukas (1984); *Riflessioni* for Strings (1985–86); Cello Concerto (1988). **CHAMBER:** 2 wind quintets (1934, 1962); 3 string quartets; Cello Sonata (1936); *Primavera* for 12 Instruments (1944; rev. 1959); Violin Sonata (1944); *Epilogue* for Flute and Piano (1947); *4 Pieces* for Harp and Flute (1963); *Aere festivo* for 3 Trumpets and 2 Trombones (1965). **Piano:** 2 études (1937); Sonata for 2 Pianos (1943); Sonata (1958). **VOCAL:** *Driehonderd waren wij* for Chorus and Orch. (1933; rev. 1941); *Ballade* for Contralto and Chamber Orch. (1936); *Bericht aan de levenden* for Chorus, Reciter, and Orch. (1964); *Villonnerie* for Baritone and Orch. (1965); *Tre aspetti d'amore* for Chorus and Orch. (1967–68); *Canzoni amorose del duecento* for Soprano, Baritone, and Orch. (1972–73).—NS/LK/DM

Henley, Don, the most successful of the former members of The Eagles, both artistically and financially; b. Gilmer, Tex., July 22, 1947. Henley's father, a farmer who also owned an auto parts store, instilled a love of the land and nature. His mother, a teacher, taught him to take in everything, making him one of the few college dropouts to drop bits of Thoreau and Emerson into conversation. Henley worked with a variety of bands in East Tex. One of them, Shiloh, came to the attention of Kenny Rogers. Rogers urged them to L.A., and Henley dropped out of North Tex. State, where he was studying English with thoughts of following in his mother's footsteps. Rogers produced an album for the band. While the album didn't make much noise, Henley met labelmate Glenn Frey, and the two of them joined Linda Rondstadt's touring band. While on the road with Rondstadt, they hatched the plans for their own band, which would become The Eagles. For their debut album, Henley co-wrote the hit "Witchy Woman," the band's first Top Ten hit. He also co-wrote the group's first chart topper, "Best of My Love." He co-wrote two more chart toppers for the band's watershed album *Hotel California*, "New Kid in Town" and the title track. He co-wrote the band's final #1 tune, "Heartache Tonight," as well.

When The Eagles broke up in 1980, fans eagerly anticipated the band's solo output, but most of the albums lacked The Eagles' flair. Henley's first foray was a duet with Stevie Nicks on a 1981 cover of "Leather and Lace" that eschewed the more country elements for a heavier blues orientation. Henley's solo debut, the biting *I Can't Stand Still*, carried on his penchant for social commentary. The blisteringly funny "Dirty Laundry" rose to #3 on the pop charts, going gold. The album also went gold, rising to #24. It took a little over two years to follow it up, but *Building the Perfect Beast* expanded on both the polished rock and lyrical eloquence of its predecessor. The affectionate "Boys of Summer" rose to #5; the funkier "All She Wants to Do Is Dance" hit #8; "Not Enough Love in the World" went to #34; and the melancholy "Sunset Grill" charted at #22. The album hit #13 and went triple platinum.

In 1989, Henley launched one of the most impressive and successful pop records of the year, *The End of the Innocence*. The slick, downbeat title track, co-written with Bruce Hornsby (who played piano), hit #8. Reminiscent of The Eagles, "Last Worthless Evening" rose to

#21, as did "Heart of the Matter." Other tunes, like "New York Minute," became favorites on rock radio. The album rose to #8, spending nearly three years on the charts and going quintuple platinum.

However, with the exception of a #2 gold duet with Patty Smythe, culled from her eponymous album in 1992, Henley's solo career has taken a back seat to his environmental activism and a bit over a year spent with the revived Eagles in the mid-1990s. Rumors abound of a new solo album, but they remain rumors.

DISC.: *I Can't Stand Still* (1982); *Building the Perfect Beast* (1984); *The End of the Innocence* (1989); *Actual Miles: Henley's Greatest Hits* (1995); *Inside Job* (2000).

BIBL.: D. Henley, ed., *Heaven Is Under Our Feet* (1991).—HB

Henneberg, (Carl) Albert (Theodor), Swedish composer, son of **Richard Henneberg;** b. Stockholm, March 27, 1901; d. Sollentuna, April 14, 1991. He studied composition with Ellberg at the Stockholm Cons. (1920–24) and later in Vienna and Paris (1926–30). Returning to Stockholm in 1931, he became active as a conductor; later he served as secretary (1945–49) and treasurer (1947–63) of the Soc. of Swedish Composers. His compositions were conceived in a late Romantic style.

WORKS: DRAMATIC: Opera: *Inka* (1935–36); *Det jäser i Småland* (1937–38); *Den lyckliga staden* (1940–41); *Bolla och Badin* (1942–44); *I madonnans skugga* (1946). **ORCH.:** 6 syms.: No. 1, *På ledungsfärd* (1925), No. 2 for Baritone and Orch. (1927), No. 3, *Vårvindar* (1927), No. 4, *Pathétique* (1930–31), No. 5 (1935), and No. 6, *Vinterskärgård* (1953–54); Piano Concerto (1925); Chamber Sym. (1927); *Valborgsmässonatt*, symphonic poem (1928); *Serenade* for Strings (1931; also for String Quartet); *Sommar*, suite (1932); *Det ljusa landet* for Soloists, Chorus, and Orch. (1933); Trumpet Concerto (1934); Trombone Concerto (1935); *I brytningstider*, symphonic suite (1943); *Gustavianska kapriser* (1943); Concertino for Flute and Strings (1944); Cello Concerto (1948); Concertino for Bassoon and Strings (1956); Concertino for Clarinet, Strings, Piano, and Percussion (1960). **CHAMBER:** 2 string quartets (1931); *Little Quartet* for Flute, Oboe, Bassoon, and Horn; Violin Sonata.—NS/LK/DM

Henneberg, Johann Baptist, Austrian organist, conductor, and composer; b. Vienna, Dec. 6, 1768; d. there, Nov. 26, 1822. He succeeded his father as organist at Vienna's Schottenstift. In 1790 he became a conductor and composer at Schikaneder's Freihaus Theater in Vienna, and later at his Theater an der Wien. In 1803 he was made organist to Count Esterházy in Eisenstadt, and subsequently was named his Kapellmeister in 1811. After returning to Vienna, he served as choirmaster at the Am Hof church before being made court organist in 1818. He composed many Singspiels, of which the most successful was *Die Waldmänner* (Vienna, Oct. 14, 1793). Among his other works were orch. music and sacred scores.—NS/LK/DM

Henneberg, Richard, German conductor and composer, father of **(Carl) Albert (Theodor) Henneberg;** b. Berlin, Aug. 5, 1853; d. Malmöo, Oct. 19, 1925. He studied piano with Liszt, then traveled as accompanist with various artists, including Wieniawski. He held posts as operatic coach at the Italian Opera in London, and at various theaters in Berlin and Stockholm. From 1885 to 1907 he conducted at the Stockholm Opera, and from 1914 to 1920 he was conductor of the Malmö Orch. Henneberg gave the first performance of *Tannhäuser* in Stockholm (1876) and the first complete production of the *Ring of the Nibelung* in Sweden (1907), and was an ardent propagandist of Wagner's music. He wrote a comic opera, *Drottningens Vallfart* (Stockholm, 1882), incidental music to Ibsen's *Brand*, various Shakespearean pieces, a ballet, *Undine,* and some choral works and songs.—NS/LK/DM

Hennerberg, Carl Fredrik, Swedish organist and musicologist; b. Algaras, Jan. 24, 1871; d. Stockholm, Sept. 17, 1932. As a young man, he was an organist at Varola. He then went to Stockholm, where he studied at the Cons. (1899–1903) and remained on the faculty as a harmony teacher. In 1909 he was appointed organist at the Royal Chapel. He specialized in the study of organ manufacture, and traveled in European countries to collect information. He publ. *Die schwedischen Orgeln des Mittelalters* (Vienna, 1909) and *Orgelns byggnad och vard* (Uppsala, 1912; 2nd ed., 1928). —NS/LK/DM

Hennessy, Swan, American composer; b. Rockford, Ill., Nov. 24, 1866; d. Paris, Oct. 26, 1929. He was the son of an Irish-American settler. After studying general subjects at Oxford, and music in Germany, he traveled in Italy, France, and Ireland, eventually settling in Paris. He wrote about 70 compositions, several of which are derived from Irish folk melos; his technical equipment was thorough, and his idiom impressionistic. Among his Irish-inspired works are *Petit trio celtique* for Violin, Viola, and Cello, *Rapsodie celtique* for Violin and Piano, *Rapsodie gaelique* for Cello and Piano, *Sonata in Irish Style* for Violin and Piano, several piano albums *"à la manière de..."*, characteristic piano pieces in a humorous vein, such as *Epigrammes d'un solitaire, Impressions humoristiques,* etc., and 4 string quartets. —NS/LK/DM

Hennig, Carl, German organist, choral conductor, and composer, father of **Carl Rafael Hennig;** b. Berlin, April 23, 1819; d. there, April 18, 1873. He began to conduct choral groups at an early age, then became a church organist at the Sophienkirche in Berlin. He also was conductor of the Lyra Choral Soc. He wrote a great number of miscellaneous pieces, sacred works, and cantatas, as well as popular dances for piano. —NS/LK/DM

Hennig, Carl Rafael, German organist, choral conductor, music theorist, and composer, son of **Carl Hennig;** b. Berlin, Jan. 4, 1845; d. Posen, Feb. 6, 1914. He studied music with his father, then with Richter in Leipzig and Kiel in Berlin; at the same time, studied law. After a brief period of teaching in Berlin, he went to Posen, where he founded the Hennig Vocal Soc. He also served as a church organist. He composed several cantatas, choruses, songs, and instrumental pieces, but

it is as a writer on theoretical subjects that he is mainly remembered.

WRITINGS: *Die Methodik des Schulgesang-Unterrichts* (Leipzig, 1885); *Die Unterscheidung der Gesangregister auf physiologischer Grundlage* (Leipzig, 1892); *Beitrag zur Wagner-Sache* (Leipzig, 1893); *Ästhetik der Tonkunst* (Leipzig, 1896); *Über die Entstehung der "hohen Resonanz"* (Leipzig, 1902); *Musiktheoretisches Hilfsbuch* (Leipzig, 1903; 2nd ed., 1906); *Einführung in das Wesen der Musik* (Leipzig, 1906); excellent analyses of Beethoven's 9th Sym. and *Missa Solemnis.*—NS/LK/DM

Henning, Carl Wilhelm, German conductor and composer; b. Öls, Jan. 31, 1784; d. Berlin, March 1867. He was a student of Seidler and Gürrlich. He spent his entire career in Berlin, where he became a violinist in the orch. of the Hofoper (1807) and in the Hofkapelle (1811). After serving as Konzertmeister (1822–24) and conductor (1824–26) of the Königstädter-Theater, he was conductor of the Phil. Soc. concerts (1832–36). In 1836 he was named Royal Musikdirektor, and in 1840 Royal Kapellmeister. In 1848 he was pensioned. He composed the opera *Die Rosenmädchen* (Berlin, 1825), ballets, incidental music, and chamber pieces. —LK/DM

Henning, Ervin Arthur, American composer; b. Marion, S.Dak., Nov. 22, 1910; d. Boston, July 27, 1982. He studied music in Chicago with Roslyn Brogue, whom he subsequently married. In 1944 he entered the New England Cons. of Music in Boston, graduating in 1946. He wrote mostly for chamber music combinations; in his later works, he adopted the 12–tone method of composition.

WORKS: Quintet for Flute, Horn, Violin, Viola, and Cello (1946); Partita for String Quartet (1948); Suite for Viola Concertante, 2 Violins, and Cello (1950); *Divertimento* for Bassoon (1950); Trio for Clarinet, Viola, and Piano (1959); Piano Sonata (1959); pieces for recorders; arrangements of Bach for various woodwind ensembles.—NS/LK/DM

Henriot-Schweitzer, Nicole, French pianist; b. Paris, Nov. 25, 1925. She was a student at the Paris Cons. of Marguerite Long, taking the premier prix when she was 14. Following the close of World War II, she began to tour extensively; in 1948 she made her first visit to the U.S. In later years, she was active as a teacher and served as a prof. at the Liège Cons. (1970–73). Her interpretations of the French repertory were highly regarded.—NS/LK/DM

Henriques, Fini (Valdemar), Danish violinist, conductor, and composer; b. Copenhagen, Dec. 20, 1867; d. there, Oct. 27, 1940. He studied violin with Valdemar Tofte in Copenhagen, and with Joachim at the Hochschule für Musik in Berlin; studied composition with Svendsen. Returning to Copenhagen, he was a violinist in the Court Orch. (1892–96); also appeared as a soloist. He organized his own string quartet, and traveled with it in Europe; also conducted orchs. As a composer, he followed the Romantic school; he possessed a facile gift of melody; his *Danish Lullaby* became a celebrated song in Denmark. He also wrote an opera, *Staerstikkeren*

(Copenhagen, May 20, 1922), several ballets (*The Little Mermaid*, after Hans Andersen; *Tata*; etc.), *Hans Andersen Overture*, 2 syms., String Quartet, Quartet for Flute, Violin, Cello, and Piano, Violin Sonata, and piano pieces.

BIBL.: S. Berg, *F.V. H.* (Copenhagen, 1943).—**NS/LK/DM**

Henry, (Frank) Haywood, jazz saxophonist; b. Birmingham, Ala., Jan. 10, 1913; d. Bronx, N.Y., Sept. 15, 1994. Originally a clarinetist, he played in the 'Bama State Collegians from 1931–32. He left the band to go to N.Y., played in the 131st Street Church Band, then worked with Leon Englund's Band at the Arcadia Ballroom before rejoining the 'Bama State Collegians, which subsequently became Erskine Hawkins's Band. He remained with that band from 1935 until the early 1950s. He worked with Tiny Grimes in the early 1950s, then did active freelance work on all saxes, played baritone in Henderson Re-union Band in 1957 and 1958, and worked occasionally on clarinet with Wilbur de Paris in the early 1960s. He worked regularly with Earl Hines from late 1969 until early 1971 (including a tour of Europe). He worked with various leaders during the 1970s, toured Europe with Sy Oliver, and with the N.Y. Jazz Repertory Company. In the 1980s and early 1990s he performed as a member of The Duke's Men and The Harlem Jazz and Blues Band. During the 1990s, he led his own quartet in N.Y., as well as recording with Clark Terry, Bill Doggett, and Charles Brown, and making occasional trips to Denmark.—**JC/LP**

Henry, Jehan, Le Jeune, France violinist and composer; b. Paris, Aug. 1560; d. there, Jan. 1635. He was the son of Jehan Henry l'aîné, "maître joueur d'instruments," and served as a violon de la chambre du roi and as a member of the 24 violons du roi. M. Mersenne publ. several of his instrumental works in his *Harmonie universelle* (Paris, 1636–37; *Traité des instruments*, books 4–5). His brother, **Michel Henry** (1554–1635), also served as a violon de la chambre du roi and as a member of the 24 violons du roi, but is principally known for his MS listing of ballets he performed at the court (1580–1620).—**LK/DM**

Henry, Leigh Vaughan, English conductor, writer on music, and composer; b. Liverpool, Sept. 23, 1889; d. London, March 8, 1958. He received his earliest training from his father, John Henry, a singer and composer, then studied with Bantock in London, Viñes in France, and Buonamici in Italy. He taught music at Gordon Craig's Theatrical School in Florence (1912), then was in Germany, where he was interned during World War I. Returning to England, he ed. a modern-music journal, *Fanfare* (1921–22). He also was active in various organizations promoting modern music. He was music director of the Shakespeare Festival Week in London in 1938, 1945, and 1946, and organized and conducted orch. concerts of British music, and the National Welsh Festival Concerts. He also conducted at the BBC. Among his compositions were *The Moon Robber*, opera, *Llyn-y-Fan*, symphonic poem, and various pieces on Welsh themes.

WRITINGS: *Music: What It Means and How to Understand It* (1920); *The Growth of Music in Form and Significance* (1921); *The Story of Music* (1935); *Dr. John Bull* (largely fictional; London, 1937); with R. Hale, *My Surging World*, autobiography (1937). —**NS/LK/DM**

Henry, Michel, a member of the 24 "violons du roi" under Henry IV and Louis XIII; b. Paris, Feb. 1555; d. date and place unknown. He wrote ballets for the court. His younger brother, **Jehan Henry,** known as Le Jeune, also in the "violons du roi," composed some very interesting instrumental music: a *Fantaisie* for 5 Violins, another *Fantaisie,* for 5 *cornetti,* and Pavane for 6 Oboes, some of which this is reproduced by P. Mersenne in his *Harmonie universelle* (Vol. 3, pp. 186–277). Dolmetsch made a modern arrangement of the *Fantaisie* for 5 Violins.—**NS/LK/DM**

Henry, Pierre, influential French composer and acoustician; b. Paris, Dec. 9, 1927. He was a student of Nadia Boulanger (piano), Félix Passeronne (percussion), and Olivier Messiaen (harmony) at the Paris Cons. In 1949 he joined Pierre Schaeffer in experiments in musique concrète on the French Radio. From 1950 to 1958 he was conductor of Schaeffer's Groupe de musique concrète, and then experimented on his own projects in electroacoustic music and the electronic synthesis of sounds. With Schaeffer, he wrote *Symphonie pour un homme seul* (1949–50), *Orphée 51* (1951), and *Orphée 53* (1953). Henry's own varied and vast output includes such works as *Microphone bien tempéré* (1950–52), *Musique sans titre* (1951), *Concerto des ambiguités* (1951), *Le Voile d'Orphée I* and *II* (1953), *Coexistence* (1958), *Investigations* (1959), *La Noire à 60* (1961), *Le Voyage* (1962), *Variations pour une forte et un soupir* (1963), *Le reine verte* (1963), *La Messe de Liverpool* (1967), *Messe pour la temps present* (1967), *Apocalypse de Jean* (1968), *Fragments pour Artaud* (1970), *Movement-Rhythme-Étude* (1970), *Deuxième symphonie* (1972), *Kyldex* (1973), *Enivrez-vous* (1974), *Futuristie* (1975), *Parcours cosmogonie* (1976), *Dieu* (1977), *Dixième symphonie* (1979), *Noces chymiques* (1980), *Pierres réfléchies* (1982), *Paradis Perdu I* (1982), *Hugosymphonie* (1985), *Le livre des morts Egyptien* (1988), *Crital/Mémoire* (1988), *Autoportraits* (1988), *Une Maison de Sons* (1989), *Maldoro/Feuilleton* (1991–92), *Intérieur/Extérieur* (1996), *Antagonismes* (1996), *Histoire Naturelle ou les roues de la terre* (1997), *Une Tour de Babel* (1999), and *Apparitions concertées* (1999). Henry won the Grand Prix National de la Musique in 1985, the Grand Prix de la SACEM in 1987, and the Grand Prix de la Ville de Paris and the Grand Prix de la SACD in 1996. He is an Officier de la Légion d'honneur, a Commandeur des Arts et Lettres, and an Officier de l'ordre National du Mérite. —**NS/LK/DM**

Henry V, English king; b. Monmouth, Sept. 1387; d. Bois de Vincennes, Aug. 31, 1422. During his reign (1413–22), he established a flourishing musical service at the Chapel Royal. He was a musician himself, and probably the author of a Gloria and a Sanctus for 3 Voices in the Old Hall MS (transcribed into modern notation, and publ. by the Plainsong and Medieval Music Soc., Vols. I and III, 1933–38, where they are ascribed to Henry VI).—**NS/LK/DM**

Henry VI, English king; b. Windsor, Dec. 6, 1421; d. London, May 21, 1471. He reigned from 1422 to 1471. For a long time, he was regarded as the "Roy Henry" who was the author of a Gloria and a Sanctus in the Old Hall MS; however, research by M. Bukofzer tends to indicate that the works may actually be by Henry V. —NS/LK/DM

Henry VIII, English king; b. Greenwich, June 28, 1491; d. Windsor, Jan. 28, 1547. He reigned from 1509 to 1547. He received regular instruction in music. Of his 34 extant works, 33 are found in Henry VIII's MS, which also includes works by other composers of England and the Continent. Actually, of the 20 vocal works given as his, some are merely arrangements. The MS also includes 13 instrumental works. His only extant sacred work is the motet *Quam pulchra es* for 3 Voices (Baldwin MS). All of his vocal music was ed. by Lady Mary Trefusis in *Songs, Ballads and Instrumental Pieces Composed by King Henry the Eighth* (Oxford, 1912); all of his secular vocal and instrumental music was ed. by J. Stevens in Musica Britannica, XVIII (London, 1962). —NS/LK/DM

Henschel, Lillian June (née **Bailey**), American soprano; b. Columbus, Ohio, Jan. 17, 1860; d. London, Nov. 4, 1901. She made her professional debut in Boston at 16, then went to Paris to study with Viardot-García. On April 30, 1879, she appeared in London, at a Phil. concert, when she sang, besides her solo number, a duet with **George Henschel**. She then studied with him and on March 9, 1881, married him. When Henschel was appointed first conductor of the Boston Sym. Orch., she appeared as a soloist with him accompanying her at the piano, also in duets at Boston Sym. concerts. Until her untimely death, the Henschels were constantly associated in American artistic life. Her well-trained voice and fine musical feeling won her many admirers.

BIBL.: H. Henschel, *When Soft Voices Die: A Musical Biography* (London, 1944).—NS/LK/DM

Henschel, Sir (Isidor) George (actually, **Georg**), esteemed German-born English baritone, pianist, conductor, teacher, and composer; b. Breslau, Feb. 18, 1850; d. Aviemore, Scotland, Sept. 10, 1934. His parents were of Polish-Jewish descent but he converted to Christianity when young. He was a student of Julius Shäffer in Breslau, of Moscheles (piano), Götze (voice), Papperitz (organ), and Reinecke (theory) at the Leipzig Cons. (1867–70), and of Kiel (composition) and Adolf Schulze (voice) at the Berlin Cons. He gave concerts as a tenor before making his debut as a pianist in Berlin in 1862. In 1866 he first appeared as a bass in Hirschberg, and then as a baritone as Hans Sachs in a concert performance in Leipzig in 1868. He subsequently sang throughout Europe. In 1881 he was selected as the first conductor of the Boston Sym. Orch., which post he held until 1884; he also appeared as a concert singer in Boston and N.Y. He then settled in England, where he was founder-conductor of the London Sym. Concerts (1886–97). He taught voice at the Royal Coll. of Music in

London (1886–88) and was conductor of the Scottish Orch. in Glasgow (1891–95); later he taught voice at the Inst. of Musical Art in N.Y. (1905–08). In 1928, at the age of 78, he sang Schubert lieder in London in commemoration of the 100th anniversary of the composer's death. In 1931 he was invited to conduct the 50th anniversary concert of the Boston Sym. Orch. In 1881 he married **Lillian June Henschel** (née **Bailey**). In 1890 he became a naturalized British subject and in 1914 he was knighted. He publ. *Personal Recollections of Johannes Brahms* (1907), *Musings and Memories of a Musician* (1918), and *Articulation in Singing* (1926). His compositions were in the German Romantic tradition. They included the opera *Nubia* (Dresden, Dec. 9, 1899), *Stabat Mater* (Birmingham, Oct. 4, 1894), *Requiem* (Boston, Dec. 2, 1902), Mass (London, June 1, 1916), String Quartet, and about 200 songs.—NS/LK/DM

Hensel, Fanny (Cäcilie) (née **Mendessohn-Bartholdy**), German pianist and composer, sister of **(Jacob Ludwig) Felix Mendelssohn (-Bartholdy);** b. Hamburg, Nov. 14, 1805; d. Berlin, May 14, 1847. She began her musical training with her mother, then studied piano with Berger and composition with Zelter, and subsequently studied with Marie Bigot in Paris (1816). She later attended Humboldt's lectures on physical geography and Holtei's lectures on experimental physics in Berlin (1825), but music remained her great love. She married the painter W. Hensel on Oct. 3, 1829. From 1843 she oversaw the Sunday morning concerts at Berlin's Elternhaus. Her untimely death was a great shock to Mendelssohn, who died a few months afterward. She was a talented composer; 6 of her songs were publ. under her brother's name in his opp. 8 and 9 (*Heimweh, Italien, Suleika und Hatem, Sehnsucht, Verlust,* and *Die Nonne*). Other works publ. under her own name, including some posthumously, include 4 books of songs, a collection of part-songs entitled *Gartenlieder,* and *Lieder ohne Worte* for Piano.

BIBL.: S. Hensel, *Die Familie M. 1729–1847, nach Briefen und Tagebüchern* (Berlin, 1879; 18th ed., 1924; 19th ed., rev. and abr., 1959; Eng. tr., 1882); *F. H.: Dokumente ihres Lebens,* Ausstellungskatalog der Staatsbibliothek Preussicher Kulturbesitz, II (Berlin, 1972); M. Citron, ed., *The Letters of F. H. to Felix Mendelssohn* (Stuyvesant, N.Y., 1987); F. Tillard, *F. M.* (Paris, 1992); P.-A. Koch, *F. H. geb. M. (1805–1847): Kompositionen* (Hofheim, 1993); H.-G. Klein, *Die Kompositionen F. H.s in Autographen und Abschriften aus dem Besitz der Staatsbibliothek zu Berlin, Preussicher Kulturbesitz: Katalog* (Tutzing, 1995); M. Helmig, ed., *F. H., geb. M. B.* (Munich, 1997); A. Maurer, *Thematisches Verzeichnis der klavierbegleiteten Sololieder F. H.s* (Kassel, 1997); A. Olivier, *Mendelssohns Schwester F. H.: Musikerin, Komponistin, Dirigentin* (Düsseldorf, 1997); E. Weissweiler, ed., *"Die Musik will gar nicht rutschen ohne Dich:" Briefwechsel 1821 bis 1846 F. und Felix Mendelssohn* (Berlin, 1997); B. Borchard and M. Schwarz-Danuser, eds., *F. H., geb. M. B.: Komponieren zwischen Gesellikeitsideal und romantischer Musikästhetik* (Stuttgart, 1999). —NS/LK/DM

Hensel, Heinrich, German tenor; b. Neustadt, Oct. 29, 1874; d. Hamburg, Feb. 23, 1935. He studied with Gustav Walter in Vienna and with Eduard Bellwidt in Frankfurt am Main. He sang in Freiburg im Breisgau (1897–1900), Frankfurt am Main (1900–06), and then at Wiesbaden (1906–11), where Siegfried Wagner heard him and engaged him to create the chief tenor part in his opera *Banadietrich* (Karlsruhe, 1910) and also to sing Parsifal at the Bayreuth Festival. He obtained excellent success; subsequently sang at Covent Garden, London (1911–14). He made his American debut at the Metropolitan Opera in N.Y. as Lohengrin (Dec. 22, 1911) and was hailed by the press as one of the finest Wagnerian tenors; he also appeared with the Chicago Opera (1911–12); he then was a leading Heldentenor at the Hamburg Opera (1912–29). He was married to the soprano Elsa Hensel-Schweitzer (1878–1937), who sang in Dessau (1898–1901) and then in Frankfurt am Main (from 1901).—NS/LK/DM

Hensel, Walther (real name, **Julius Janiczek**), Bohemian-born music educator; b. Moravska Trebova, Sept. 8, 1887; d. Munich, Sept. 5, 1956. He studied in Vienna, Prague, and Freibourg, where he obtained his Ph.D. (1911). He taught languages in Prague (1912–18). He traveled in Europe (1918–25) as an organizer of folk-song activities, with the aim of raising the standards of choral music for the young. From 1925 to 1929 he was head of the Jugendmusik School at the Dortmund Cons. In 1930 he went to Stuttgart, where he organized an educational program for the promotion of folk music. In 1938 he returned to Prague and taught at the German Univ. there. After 1945 he went to Munich. He ed. a number of folk-song collections, and publ. *Lied und Volk, Eine Streitschrift wider das falsche deutsche Lied* (1921), *Im Zeichen des Volksliedes* (1922; 2nd ed., 1936), *Musikalische Grundlehre* (1937), and *Auf den Spuren des Volksliedes* (1944).—NS/LK/DM

Henselt, (Georg Marin) Adolf von, notable German pianist, pedagogue, and composer; b. Schwabach, May 9, 1814; d. Warmbrunn, Silesia, Oct. 10, 1889. He was taken to Munich by his family when he was 3, and began piano studies at 5. When he was 15, he made his public debut as a pianist. In 1831 he received a stipend from King Ludwig I of Bavaria, which enabled him to study piano with Hummel in Weimar and theory with Sechter in Vienna. After making a highly successful concert tour of Germany in 1836, he went to Russia and scored further success in St. Petersburg in 1838. He soon was named court pianist and teacher of the children of the imperial family. He later gained great influence as a pedagogue via his appointment as inspector of music in all of the imperially endowed girls' schools. Henselt won extraordinary praise from his contemporaries as a piano virtuoso, although stage fright led him to curtail his public appearances. Nevertheless, he became well known for his artful execution, in legato, of widely extended chords and arpeggios, which he achieved via diligent practice of extremely difficult extension studies of his own composition. He publ. 2 vols. of lyrical studies for piano as *Douze études caractéristiques de concert,* op.2 (1837) and *Douze études de salon,* op.5 (1838). His virtuoso Piano Concerto in F minor (1844) was premiered by Clara Schuman, and

subsequently taken up by many eminent pianists, including Liszt, Bülow, Friedheim, Sauer, Busoni, and Petri. In the late 20th century it was revived, at least via recordings, by Ponti and Hamelin. Among his other works were some chamber scores and various small salon pieces for piano.

BIBL.: W. von Lenz, *Die grossen Pianoforte-Virtuosen unserer Zeit aus persönlicher Bekanntschaft: Liszt, Chopin, Tausig, H.* (Berlin, 1872).—NS/LK/DM

Hentschel, Franz, German conductor and composer; b. Berlin, Nov. 6, 1814; d. there, May 11, 1889. He studied with A. W. Bach. After conducting theater orchs. in provincial towns, he settled in Berlin as a music teacher. He wrote an opera, *Die Hexenreise,* and numerous marches for military band.—NS/LK/DM

Hentschel, Theodor, German conductor and composer; b. Schirgiswalde, March 28, 1830; d. Hamburg, Dec. 19, 1892. He studied with Reissiger and Ciccarelli in Dresden, then was active as a theater conductor in Bremen (1860–90), and then at Hamburg. He wrote the operas *Matrose und Sänger* (Leipzig, 1857), *Der Königspage* (Bremen, 1874), *Die Braut von Lusignan, oder Die schöne Melusine* (Bremen, 1875), *Lancelot* (Bremen, 1878), and *Des Königs Schwerdt* (Hamburg, 1891), as well as overtures and symphonic marches for orch., piano music, and songs.—NS/LK/DM

Henze, Hans Werner, outstanding German composer; b. Gütersloh, July 1, 1926. He entered the Braunschweig State Music School in 1942, where he studied until being called to military service in World War II in 1944. After the German collapse in 1945, he worked as a répétiteur at the Bielefeld City Theater. In 1946 he entered the Inst. for Church Music in Heidelberg, and also became a private student of Wolfgang Fortner. After working at the Deutsches Theater in Konstanz in 1948, he became artistic director and conductor of the ballet of the Hessisches State Theater in Wiesbaden in 1950. In 1951 he was awarded the Robert Schumann Prize of the City of Düsseldorf. After winning the Premio RAI of Italy in 1953, Henze settled there. His commitment to the Left eventually led him to join the Italian Communist Party. In 1960 he was made a member of the Akademie der Künste in West Berlin, but his radical political stance prompted him to resign his membership in 1968. From 1962 to 1967 he led master classes at the Salzburg Mozarteum, and in 1967 he was a visiting prof. at Dartmouth (N.H.) Coll. In 1968 Henze accepted an assoc. membership in the Akademie der Künste in East Berlin. He further consolidated his Leftist credentials with an extended stay in Cuba in 1969–70. All the same, he found an audience among the culturally inclined bourgeoisie. In 1976 Henze founded the Cantiere Internazionale d'Art in Montepulciano, where a number of his works were subsequently premiered. From 1980 to 1991 he was prof. of composition at the Cologne Staatliche Hochschule für Musik. In 1983 and 1988 he was composer-in-residence at the Berkshire Music Center in Tanglewood, and in 1987 he held the International Chair for Composition at the Royal Academy of Music in London. In 1988 Henze founded and became artistic director of the Munich Biennale, which became a showcase for contemporary music theater scores. He was composer-in-residence of the Berlin Phil. in 1991, the same year that he was honored with the Grand Cross for Distinguished Service of the Order of Merit of the Federal Republic of Germany. In 1991–92 he was a fellow of the Berlin Wissenschaftskolleg. He was awarded the Hans von Bülow Medal of the Berlin Phil. in 1997. Henze's autobiography was publ. as *Reiselieder mit böhmischen Quinten: Autobiographische Mitteilungen 1926–1995* (Frankfurt am Main, 1996; Eng. tr., 1998, as *Bohemian Fifths: An Autobiography*).

In a remarkable compositional career spanning more than 50 years, including all of the second half of the 20th century, Henze has managed to eschew the predictable by embracing various means of expression. He has displayed a genius for sustaining and invigorating the traditional genres of dramatic, orchestral, chamber, and vocal music. As the new millennium beckoned, he had attained a place of world eminence accorded only a very few of his contemporaries in Western art music.

WORKS: DRAMATIC: *Das Wundertheater*, opera for Actors, after Cervantes (1948; Heidelberg, May 7, 1949; version for Singers, 1964; Frankfurt am Main, Nov. 30, 1965); *Ballett-Variationen*, ballet (concert perf., Düsseldorf, Sept. 26, 1949; stage perf., Wuppertal, Dec. 21, 1958; rev. 1992; Berlin, Nov. 15, 1998); *Le disperazioni del Signor Pulcinella/Die Verzeiflung des Herrn Pulcinella*, dance comedy (1949; Wiesbaden, Dec. 30, 1950, composer conducting; rev. 1995; Schwetzingen, May 25, 1997); *Das Vokaltuch der Kammersänger Rosa Silber*, ballet (1950; concert perf., May 8, 1951; stage perf., Cologne, Oct. 15, 1958; rev. 1990; London, Jan. 14, 1991, composer conducting); *Labyrinth*, ballet (1951; concert perf., Darmstadt, May 29, 1952, composer conducting; rev. 1996; Schwetzingen, May 25, 1997); *Ein Landarzt*, radio opera, after Kafka (NDR, Hamburg, Nov. 19, 1951, for broadcast, Nov. 29, 1951; new version, 1964; Frankfurt am Main, Nov. 30, 1965; rev. 1994; WDR, Cologne, Sept. 27, 1996; also as a monodrama for Baritone and Small Orch., 1964; Berlin, Oct. 13, 1965; Fischer-Dieskau soloist, composer conducting); *Boulevard Solitude*, lyric drama (1951; Hannover, Feb. 17, 1952); *Der Idiot*, scenic mimodrama (Berlin, Sept. 1, 1952; rev. 1990; Basel, March 26, 1996); *Pas d'action*, ballet (1952; suite, Hamburg, Jan. 15, 1953; rev. as the ballet *Tancredi*, 1964; Vienna, May 14, 1966); *Das Ende einer Welt*, radio opera (NDR, Hamburg, Dec. 4, 1953; rev. 1993; WDR, Cologne, Sept. 27, 1996; also as an opera buffa, 1964; Frankfurt am Main, Nov. 30, 1965); *König Hirsch*, opera (1953–56; partial perf., Berlin, Sept. 23, 1956; complete perf., Stuttgart, May 5, 1985; shortened version as *Il Re Cervo oder Die Irrfahrten der Wahrheit*, 1962; Kassel, March 10, 1963, composer conducting); *Maratona*, dance drama (1956; Berlin, Sept. 24, 1957); *Ondine/Undine*, ballet (1956–57; London, Oct. 27, 1958, composer conducting; *Der Prinz von Homburg*, opera, after Kleist (1958–59; Hamburg, May 22, 1960; rev. 1991; Munich, July 24, 1992); *L'usignolo dell'imperatore/Des Kaisers Nachtigall*, ballet-pantomime (Venice, Sept. 16, 1959); *Elegie für junge Liebende/Elegy for Young Lovers*, opera, after Auden and Kallman (1959–61; Schwetzingen, May 20, 1961; rev. 1987; Venice, Oct. 28, 1988; *Der junge Lord*, comic opera (1964; Berlin, April 7, 1965); *The Judgement of Calliope/Das Urteil der Kalliope*, satyr play, after Auden and Kallman (1964; Giessen, Oct. 29, 1997); *The Bassarids/Die Bassariden*, music drama, after Auden and Kallman (1964–65; Salzburg, Aug. 6, 1966; rev. 1992);

Moralities/Moralitäten, 3 scenic plays, after Aesop and Auden (1967; Cincinnati, May 18, 1968; shorter version, Saarbrücken, April 1, 1970); *Der langwierige Weg in die Wohnung der Natascha Ungeheuer*, show (Rome, May 17, 1971, composer conducting); *La Cubana, oder Ein Leben für die Kunst*, television opera (1973; WNET, N.Y., March 4, 1974, composer conducting; stage perf., Munich, May 28, 1975); *We Come to the River/Wir erreichen den Fluss*, actions for music (1974–76; London, July 12, 1976); *Don Chisciotte*, comic opera, arranged from Lorenzi and Paisiello (Montepulciano, Aug. 1, 1976); *Orpheus*, ballet (1978; Stuttgart, March 17, 1979; new version, Vienna, June 20, 1986); *Pollicino*, fairy tale for music (1979–80; Montepulciano, Aug. 2, 1980); *The English Cat/Die englische Katze*, opera (1980–83; Schwetzingen, June 2, 1983); *Il ritorno d'Ulisse in patria*, free reconstruction of Monteverdi's opera (1981; Salzburg, Aug. 18, 1985); *Das verratene Meer*, music drama (1986–89; Berlin, May 5, 1990); *Il re Teodoro in Venezia*, new version of Paisiello's opera (1991–92; Montepulciano, July 16, 1992); *Venus und Adonis*, opera (1993–95; Munich, Jan. 11, 1997); *Le fils de l'air/Der Sohn der Luft* or *L'enfant changé en jeune homme*, ballet (1995–96; Schwetzingen, May 25, 1997). **ORCH.:** Chamber Concerto for Piano, Flute, and Strings (Darmstadt, Sept. 27, 1946); Concertino for Piano, Winds, and Percussion (Baden-Baden, Oct. 5, 1947); 10 syms.: No. 1 (Bad Pyrmont, Aug. 25, 1948; version for Chamber Orch., 1963; Berlin, April 9, 1964, composer conducting; rev. version, Berlin, Oct. 2, 1991, composer conducting), No. 2 (Stuttgart, Dec. 1, 1949), No. 3 (1949–50; Donaueschingen, Oct. 7, 1951), No. 4 (1955; Berlin, Oct. 9, 1963, composer conducting), No. 5 (1962; N.Y., May 16, 1963), No. 6 (Havana, Nov. 26, 1969, composer conducting; new version, Munich, Dec. 8, 1994), No. 7 (1983–84; Berlin, Dec. 1, 1984), No. 8 (1992–93; Boston, Oct. 1, 1993), No. 9 for Chorus and Orch. (1995–97; Berlin, Sept. 11, 1997), and No. 10 (2000); 3 violin concertos: No. 1 (1947; Baden-Baden, Dec. 12, 1948), No. 2 (1971; Basel, Nov. 2, 1972), and No. 3 (Berlin, Sept. 12, 1997); 2 piano concertos: No. 1 (1950; Düsseldorf, Sept. 14, 1952, Mewton-Wood soloist, composer conducting) and No. 2 (1967; Bielefeld, Sept. 29, 1968); *Ode an den Westwind* for Cello and Orch. (Bielefeld, April 30, 1954); *Quattro Poemi* (Frankfurt am Main, May 31, 1955); 3 *Symphonische Etüden* (Hamburg, Feb. 14, 1956; new version, 1964); *Maratona*, suite for 2 Jazz Bands and Orch., after the ballet (1956; WDR, Feb. 8, 1957); *Jeux des Tritons*, divertissement for Piano and Orch. after the ballet *Ondine* (1956–57; Zürich, March 28, 1960; new version, Berlin, April 1, 1967); 2 sonatas for Strings: No. 1 (1957–58; Zürich, March 21, 1958) and No. 2 (1995; Leipzig, Nov. 7, 1996); 3 *Dithyramen* for Chamber Orch. (Cologne, Nov. 27, 1958); *Ondine*, 2 suites from the ballet (both 1958); *Trois Pas de Tritons*, after the ballet *Ondine* (1958; Rome, Jan. 10, 1959); *Antifone* (1960; Berlin, Jan. 10, 1962); *Los Caprichos*, fantasia (1963; Duisburg, April 6, 1967); *Zwischenspiele*, after the opera *Der junge Lord* (1964; Berlin, Oct. 12, 1965, composer conducting); *In memoriam: Die Weisse Rose* for Chamber Orch. (Bologna, March 16, 1965); *Fantasia* for Strings (Berlin, April 1, 1967); Double Bass Concerto (Chicago, Nov. 2, 1967); *Musik* for Viola and 22 Players, *Compases para preguntas ensimismadas* (1969–70; Basel, Feb. 11, 1971); *Heliogabalus Imperator*, allegoria per musica (Chicago, Nov. 16, 1972; rev. 1986; Rome, June 28, 1989); *Tristan* for Piano, Orch., and Tape (1973; London, Oct. 20, 1974); *Ragtimes und Habaneras* for Brass Ensemble (London, Sept. 23, 1975); *Katharina Blum*, concert suite for Small Orch. (1975; Brighton, May 6, 1976, composer conducting); *Aria de la folía española* for Chamber Orch. (St. Paul, Minn., Sept. 17, 1977; also for Orch., Bournemouth, April 23, 1979, composer conducting); *Il Vitalino raddoppiato*, chaconne for Violin and Chamber

Orch. (Salzburg, Aug. 2, 1978); *Barcarola* (1979; Zürich, April 22, 1980); *Apollo trionfante,* after the dance drama *Orpheus* (1979; Gelsenkirchen, Sept. 1, 1980); *Arien des Orpheus* for Guitar, Harp, Harpsichord, and Strings (1979; Gelsenkirchen, Nov. 16, 1980; also for Large String Orch., Chicago, Nov. 25, 1981, composer conducting); *Dramatische Szenen aus Orpheus I* (1979; Frankfurt am Main, Sept. 12, 1982) and *II* (1979; Zürich, Jan. 6, 1981, composer conducting); *I sentimenti di Carl Philipp Emmanuel Bach* for Flute, Harp, and Strings, transcription of Bach's *Clavier- Fantasie* (1787) (Rome, April 14, 1982); *Le Miracle de la Rose* for Clarinet and 13 Players (1981; London, May 26, 1982, composer conducting); *Liebeslieder* for Cello and Orch. (1984–85; WDR, Cologne, Dec. 12, 1986); *Kleine Elegien* for Early Instrument Chamber Orch. (1984–85; WDR, Cologne, Dec. 13, 1986); *Fandango,* after Soler (1985; Paris, Feb. 5, 1986; new version, 1992; Prague, Nov. 30, 1995); *Cinque piccoli concerti e ritornelli* (1987; London, Jan. 24, 1988); *Tanz- und Salonmusik* for Chamber Orch., after the scenic mimodrama *Der Idiot* (Bristol, June 5, 1989); *Requiem,* 9 sacred concertos for Piano, Trumpet, and Orch. (1990–92; Cologne, Feb. 24, 1993); *La selva incantata/Der verwunschene Wald* (Frankfurt am Main, April 6, 1991); *Introduktion, Thema und Variationen* for Cello, Harp, and Strings (1992; Salzburg, Aug. 25, 1994); *Appassionatamente,* fantasy, after the music drama *Das verratene Meer* (1993–94; Vienna, March 25, 1995); *3 Orchesterstücke,* after piano music of Karl Amadeus Hartmann (1995; Munich, July 5, 1996); *Voie lactée ô soeur lumineuse* for Chamber Orch. (Basel, May 7, 1996); *Pulcinellas Erzählungen* for Chamber Orch., after the ballet *Le disperazioni del Signor Pulcinella* (1996; Cologne, Jan. 16, 1998); *Zigeunerweisen und Sarabanden,* after the ballet *Le fils de l'air* (1996; Cologne, Jan. 16, 1998); *Erlkönig,* fantasy after Schubert (1996; Paris, Jan. 31, 1997); *7 Boleros* (1998; Las Palmas, Feb. 2, 2000); *Fraternité* (N.Y., Nov. 11, 1999). **CHAMBER:** Violin Sonata (1946); Flute Sonata (1947); 5 string quartets: No. 1 (1947), No. 2 (Südwestfunk, Baden-Baden, Dec. 16, 1952), No. 3 (1975–76; Berlin, Sept. 12, 1976), No. 4 (1976; Schwetzingen, May 25, 1977), and No. 5 (1976; Schwetzingen, May 25, 1977); Chamber Sonata for Piano, Violin, and Cello (1948; Cologne, March 16, 1950; rev. 1963); *Apollo et Hyazinthus* for Harpsichord, Alto, and 8 Instruments (1948–49; Frankfurt am Main, June 26, 1949); *Serenade* for Cello (1949); Wind Quintet (1952; Radio Bremen, Feb. 15, 1953); *3 Tentos* for Guitar (NDR, Hamburg, Nov. 26, 1958); *Prison Song* for Percussion and Other Instruments (1971); *Carillon, Récitatif, Masque,* trio for Mandolin, Guitar, and Harp (1974; London, Feb. 2, 1977); Trumpet Sonatina (1974); *Royal Winter Music,* 2 sonatas on Shakespearean characters for Guitar: No. 1 (1975–76; Berlin, Sept. 20, 1976) and No. 2 (1975–76; Brussels, Nov. 25, 1980); *Amicizia!,* quintet for Clarinet, Trombone, Cello, Percussion, and Piano (Montepulciano, Aug. 6, 1976); Sonata for Solo Violin (1976–77; Montepulciano, Aug. 10, 1977; rev. 1992); *L'autunno* for 5 Wind Instruments (1977; London, Feb. 28, 1979); *S. Biagio 9 agosto ore 12.07* for Double Bass (1977); *5 Scenes from the Snow Country* for Marimba (1978; Süddeutscher Rundfunk, Stuttgart, Oct. 12, 1982); Viola Sonata (1979; Witten, April 20, 1980); Violin Sonatina (1979; London, Dec. 2, 1980); *Capriccio* for Violin (1981; Linz, Sept. 24, 1983); *Canzona* for 7 Instruments (Stuttgart, June 6, 1982); Sonata for 8 Wind Instruments (Berlin, Sept. 17, 1983); Sonata for 6 Players (London, Sept. 26, 1984); *Selbst- und Zwiegespräche,* trio for Viola, Guitar, and Small Organ (1984–85; Brühl, Sept. 29, 1985); *Serenade* for Violin (Bad Goesberg, June 1, 1986); *5 Nachstücke* for Violin and Piano (London, May 16, 1990); Piano Quintet (1990–91; Berkeley, Calif., March 25, 1993); *Adagio adagio,* serenade for Violin, Cello, and Piano (Darmstadt, March 18, 1993);

Minotauros Blues for 6 Percussionists (1996; Cologne, Jan. 16, 1998); *Trauer-Ode für Margaret Geddes,* sextet for Cellos (Kronberg, Oct. 19, 1997); *Trio in 3 Sätzen* for Violin, Viola, and Cello (1998; Schwetzingen, May 12, 1999). **KEYBOARD: P i a n o :** *Variationen* (Hessischer Rundfunk, Frankfurt am Main, June 17, 1949); Sonata (Berlin, Sept. 26, 1959); *Lucy Escott Variations* (1963; Berlin, March 21, 1965; also for Harpsichord); *Divertimenti* for 2 Pianos (N.Y., Nov. 30, 1964); *6 Stücke für junge Pianisten* (1980; Stuttgart, Oct. 13, 1982); *Cherubino* (1980–81; Berlin, Aug. 23, 1981); *Une petite phrase* (1984); *La mano sinistra* (1988); *Pulcinella disperato* (1992; Munich, May 8, 1994); *Toccata mistica* (Cologne, Nov. 13, 1994). **H a r p s i c h o r d :** *6 Absences* (1961; Mainz, Nov. 7, 1963); *Euridice* (1981; N.Y., Oct. 2, 1986; rev. 1992). **VOCAL:** *5 Madrigale* for Chorus and 2 Instruments, after Villon (1947; Frankfurt am Main, April 25, 1950); *Chor gefangener Trojer* for Chorus and Orch., after Goethe (1948; Bielefeld, Feb. 6, 1949; rev. 1964); *Whispers from Heavenly Death,* cantata for High Voice and 8 Instruments, after Whitman (1948; Stuttgart, June 14, 1950); *Vokalsinfonie* for Soloists and Orch., after the opera *König Hirsch* (1955); *Szenen und Arien* for Soprano, Tenor, Chorus, and Orch., after the opera *König Hirsch* (1956); *Cinque canzoni napoletane/Fünf neapolitanische Lieder* for Baritone and Chamber Orch. (Hessischer Rundfunk, Frankfurt am Main, May 26, 1956); *Nachstücke und Arien* for Soprano and Orch. (Donaueschingen, Oct. 20, 1957); *Kammermusik 1958* for Tenor, Guitar, and 8 Instruments (NDR, Hamburg, Nov. 26, 1958; also for Tenor and Guitar); *Novae de infinito laudes,* cantata for Soprano, Alto, Tenor, Bass, Chorus, and Instruments, after Giordano Bruno (1962; Venice, April 24, 1963, composer conducting); *Being Beauteous,* cantata for Soprano, Harp, and 4 Cellos, after Rimbaud (1963; Berlin, April 12, 1964); *Ariosi* for Soprano, Violin, and Orch., after Tasso (1963; Edinburgh, Aug. 23, 1964; also for Soprano, Violin, and Piano, Mannheim, Nov. 19, 1965); *Cantata della fiaba estrema* for Soprano, Chamber Chorus, and 13 Instruments (1963; Zürich, Feb. 26, 1965); *Lieder von einer Insel* for Chamber Chorus and Chamber Ensemble (1964; Selb, Jan. 23, 1967); *Musen Siziliens* for Chorus, 2 Pianos, Winds, and Timpani, after Virgil (Berlin, Sept. 20, 1966); *Das Floss der Medusa,* oratorio for Soprano, Baritone, Speaker, Chorus, and Orch., in memoriam Ché Guevara (NDR, Hamburg, Dec. 9, 1968, composer conducting; concert perf., Vienna, Jan. 29, 1971; stage perf., Nuremberg, April 15, 1972; rev. 1990); *Versuch über Schweine* for Speaker and Orch. (1968; London, Feb. 14, 1969, composer conducting); *El Cimarrón* for Baritone, Flute, Guitar, and Percussion, after Estéban Montejo (Aldeburgh, June 22, 1970); *Voices/Stimmen* for Mezzo-soprano, Tenor, and Instrumental Group (1973; London, Jan. 4, 1974, composer conducting); *Jephtha,* realization of Carissimi's oratorio, for Soloists, Chorus, and Orch. (London, July 14, 1976, composer conducting); *Orpheus* for Speaker and Orch. (1978; Cologne, March 4, 1983, composer conducting); *El Rey de Harlem* for Mezzo-soprano and Small Ensemble, after García Lorca (1979; Witten, April 20, 1980); *Szenen und Arien* for 4 Soloists and Orch., after Monteverdi's opera *Il ritorno di Ulisse in patria* (1981; London, Sept. 4, 1988, composer conducting); *Orpheus Behind the Wire/Orpheus hinter dem Stacheldraht* for Chorus (1981–83; Southampton, Sept. 10, 1985); *3 Auden Songs* for Tenor and Piano (Aldeburgh, June 15, 1983); *3 Lieder über den Schnee* for Soprano, Baritone, and 8 Instruments (Frankfurt am Main, Sept. 8, 1989); *Paraphrasen über Dostojewsky* for Speaker and Instruments (1990; London, Jan. 12, 1991); *2 Konzertarien* for Tenor and Small Orch. (Montepulciano, July 28, 1991); *Lieder und Tanze* for Mezzo-soprano and Chamber Ensemble, after the television opera *La Cubana oder Ein Leben für die Kunst* (1992–93; Zürich,

Sept. 12, 1993); *6 Gesänge aus der Arabischen* for Tenor and Piano (1997–98; Cologne, Nov. 23, 1999); *Richard Wagnersche Klavierlieder* for Mezzo-soprano, Baritone, Chorus, and Orch. (1998–99; Berlin, Aug. 28, 1999).

WRITINGS: *Musik und Politik: Schriften und Gespräche, 1955–1975* (Munich, 1976; in Eng. as *Music and Politics: Collected Writings, 1953–81*, London and Ithaca, N.Y., 1982).

BIBL.: K. Geitel, *H.W. H.* (Berlin, 1968); E. Restagno, ed., *H.* (Turin, 1986); D. Rexroth, ed., *Der Komponist H.W. H.: Ein Buch der Alten Oper Frankfurt, Frankfurt Feste '86* (Mainz and N.Y., 1986); P. Petersen, *H.W. H., ein politischer Musiker: Zwölf Vorlesungen* (Hamburg, 1988); W. Schottler, *"Die Bassariden" von H.W. H.: Der Weg eines Mythos von der antiken Tragödie zur modernen Oper: Eine Analyse von Stoff, Libretto und Musik* (Trier, 1992).
—NS/LK/DM

Heppener, Robert, Dutch composer and teacher; b. Amsterdam, Aug. 9, 1925. He studied piano with Jan Öde and Johan van den Boogert at the Amsterdam Cons., and composition with Bertus van Lier. He taught theory at the Rotterdam Cons., and then went to Amsterdam to teach theory at the Muzieklyceum and composition and instrumentation at the Sweelinck Cons. In later years, he taught composition at the Maastricht Cons. He received the Fontein- Tuynhout Prize in 1969, the Willem Pijper Prize in 1974, and the Matthijs Vermeulen Prize in 1992. In 1995 he was awarded the Johan Wagenaar Prize for his complete creative output.

WORKS: DRAMATIC: O p e r a : *Een ziel van hout* (1996). **ORCH.:** Sym. (1957); *Derivazioni* for Strings (1958; rev. 1980); *Sinfonietta* (1961); *Cavalcade* (1963); *Eglogues* (1963); *Scherzi* for Strings (1965); *Air et sonneries* (1969); *Hymns and Conversations* for 28 Harps (1969); *Music for Streets and Squares* (1970); *Sweelinck Fanfare* (1978) Viola Concerto (1979); *Boog* (1988). **CHAMBER:** Septet (1958); *Arcadian Sonatina* for 2 Recorders and Violin (1959); *A fond de fleurettes* for String Quartet (1961); Quartet for Alto Flute, Violin, Viola, and Cello (1967); *Canzona* for Saxophone Quartet (1969); *Trail* for 11 Instruments (1993). **P i a n o :** *Nocturne* (1953); *Pas de quatremains* for Piano, 4–Hands (1975); *Spinsel* (1986). **VOCAL:** *Cantico delle creture di S. Francesco d'Assisi* for Soprano, Harp, and Strings (1952; rev. 1954); *The 3rd Country* for Chorus and Chamber Orch. (1962); *Carnival Songs* for Chorus (1966); *Fanfare trionfale* for Chorus, Winds, Timpani, and Piano (1967); *Del iubilo del core che esce in voce* for Chorus (1974); *Nachklänge* for Chamber Chorus (1977); *Memento* for Soprano and 8 Instruments (1984); *Im Gestein* for Chorus and Ensemble (1992).
—NS/LK/DM

Heppner, Ben, outstanding Canadian tenor; b. Murrayville, British Columbia, Jan. 14, 1956. He studied at the Univ. of British Columbia and the Univ. of Toronto. In 1979 he took 1st prize in the CBC Talent Festival, and then sang in concert and oratorio settings in Canada. In 1987 he appeared as Strauss's Bacchus at the Victoria State Opera in Sydney. He made his European operatic debut as Lohengrin at the Royal Opera in Stockholm in 1988. That same year, he won the Metropolitan Opera Auditions and the Birgit Nilsson Prize, which led to his U.S. debut at a state concert for the King and Queen of Sweden at N.Y.'s Carnegie Hall. Following an engagement as Lohengrin at the San Francisco

Opera in 1989, he sang Bacchus at the Vienna State Opera and Walther von Stolzing at Milan's La Scala and London's Covent Garden in 1990. He made his debut at the Metropolitan Opera in N.Y. on Dec. 11, 1991, as Idomeneo. In 1992 he sang Dvořák's Dimitrij in Munich and Mozart's Tito in Salzburg, and also created the title role in Bolcom's *McTeague* in Chicago. In 1994 he was engaged as Lohengrin at the Seattle Opera. He appeared as Peter Grimes in Vancouver and as Tchaikovsky's Hermann at the Metropolitan Opera in 1995. After singing Andrea Chénier in Seattle in 1996, he appeared as Calaf in Chicago in 1997. In 1998 he returned to Seattle as Tristan and to the Metropolitan Opera as Lohengrin and Walther von Stolzing. He made his N.Y. recital debut at Carnegie Hall on Jan. 30, 1999. Heppner's engagements as a soloist with orchs. and as a recitalist have taken him to the world's leading music centers.—NS/LK/DM

Herbage, Julian (Livingston), English musicologist; b. Woking, Sept. 4, 1904; d. London, Jan. 15, 1976. He studied harmony and counterpoint with Charles Wood at St. John's Coll., Cambridge. In 1927 he became a member of the music staff of the BBC; from 1940 to 1946 he was asst. director of music there. With his wife, Anna Instone, he ed. the BBC "Music Magazine" radio program from 1944 to 1973. He also made appearances as a conductor of music by Baroque composers. He wrote the book *Handel's Messiah* (London, 1948).—NS/LK/DM

Herbart, Johann Friedrich, German philosopher, educator, writer on music, and composer; b. Oldenburg, May 4, 1776; d. Göttingen, Aug. 14, 1841. He studied in Jena with Fichte. In 1805 he was appointed prof. of philosophy at Göttingen. From 1809 to 1835 he was at Königsberg, then from 1835 to his death again at Göttingen. Of importance to music theory is his *Psychologische Bemerkungen zur Tonlehre* (1811). He composed a Piano Sonata (Leipzig, 1808) and other works.

BIBL.: W. Kahl, *H. als Musiker* (Langensalza, 1926).
—NS/LK/DM

Herbeck, Johann (Franz), Ritter von, prominent Austrian conductor, pedagogue, and composer; b. Vienna, Dec. 25, 1831; d. there, Oct. 28, 1877. He was a choirboy at the Heiligenkreuz Cistercian monastery, where he had piano lessons with Borschitzky. After training in composition from Rotter in Vienna (1845–46), he attended lectures in philosophy and law at the Univ. there (1847). He pursued his career in Vienna, receiving his first post as choirmaster of the Piaristenkirche in 1852. From 1856 to 1866 he was conductor of the Männergesangverein. In 1857 he joined the faculty of the Cons. of the Gesellschaft der Musikfreunde, and also served as director of the latter's choral soc. from 1858 to 1870, and again from 1875 to 1877. In 1863 he was made Vice-Kapellmeister and in 1866 Kapellmeister of the Hofkapelle. After serving as co-director of the Court Opera in 1869–70, he was its director from 1870 to 1875. Herbeck was especially admired as a conductor of choral music. He also did much to promote the music of his contemporaries. Among his own works were many choral pieces of considerable merit.

BIBL.: L. Herbeck, *J. H.: Ein Lebensbild* (Vienna, 1885); J. Braun, *J.R. v. H. und das Wiener Hofoperntheater* (diss., Univ. of Vienna, 1949).—NS/LK/DM

Herberigs, Robert,

Belgian composer and novelist; b. Ghent, June 19, 1886; d. Oudenaarde, Sept. 20, 1974. He studied voice at the Ghent Cons. In 1908 he made his operatic debut as a baritone at the Flemish Opera in Antwerp, but then abandoned his operatic aspirations to study composition. In 1909 he won the Belgian Grand Prix with his cantata *La Legénde de St. Hubert*, and subsequently composed prolifically. He also publ. several novels. His compositions followed along Romantic lines.

WORKS: DRAMATIC: *Le Mariage de Rosine*, comic opera (1919; Ghent, Feb. 13, 1925); *L'Amour médecin*, comic opera (1920); *Lam Godsspel* or *Jeu de l'Agneau Mystique*, open-air play (1948); *Antoine et Cleopatra*, radio play (1949); *Le Château des comtes de Gand*, light and sound play (1960). **ORCH.:** 2 piano concertos (1932, 1952); *Sinfonia breve* (1947); Organ Concerto (1957); numerous symphonic poems and suites, including *Cyrano de Bergerac* (1912), *Le Chant d'Hiawatha* (1921), *Vlaanderen, O Welig Huis* (1949), *Rapsodia alla Zingara* (1952), *La Petite Sirène* (1955), *4 saisons* (1956), *4 odes a Botticelli* (1958), *Hamlet* (1962), *Roméo et Juliette* (1963), and *Reinaut et Armida* (1967). **CHAMBER:** String Quartet (1921); *Poème* for Piano Trio (1923); Violin Sonata (1932); *Concert champêtre* for Wind Quintet (1938); Piano Quartet (1939); *Suite Miniature* and Sonatine for Flute and String Trio (both 1954). **Piano:** 21 sonatas and sonatinas (1941–45); other pieces. **VOCAL:** *La Legénde de St. Hubert* (1909) and other cantatas; *Te Deum laudamus* (1912); masses; song cycles and solo songs.—NS/LK/DM

Herbert, Victor (August),

famous Irish-born American composer, cellist, and conductor; b. Dublin, Feb. 1, 1859; d. N.Y., May 26, 1924. He was a grandson of Samuel Lover, the Irish novelist; his father died when he was an infant; his mother married a German physician and the family moved to Stuttgart in 1867. He entered the Stuttgart high school, but did not graduate; his musical ability was definitely pronounced by then, and he selected the cello as his instrument, taking lessons from Bernhard Cossmann in Baden-Baden (1874–76). He soon acquired a degree of technical proficiency that enabled him to take a position as cellist in various orchs. in Germany, France, Italy, and Switzerland; in 1880 he became a cellist of the Eduard Strauss waltz band in Vienna; in 1881, he returned to Stuttgart, where he joined the Court Orch., and studied composition with Max Seifritz at the Cons. His earliest works were for cello with orch.; he performed his Suite with the Stuttgart orch. on Oct. 23, 1883, and his 1st Cello Concerto on Dec. 8, 1885. On Aug. 14, 1886, he married the Viennese opera singer Therese Förster (1861–1927); in the same year, she received an offer to join the Metropolitan Opera in N.Y., and Herbert was engaged as an orch. cellist there, appearing in N.Y. also as a soloist (played his own Cello Concerto with the N.Y. Phil., Dec. 10, 1887). In his early years in N.Y., Herbert was overshadowed by the celebrity of his wife, but soon he developed energetic activities on his own, forming an entertainment orch. which he conducted in a repertoire of light music; he also participated in chamber music concerts; was a soloist with the Theodore Thomas and Seidl orchs. He was the conductor of the Boston Festival Orch. in 1891; Tchaikovsky conducted this orch. in Philadelphia in a miscellaneous program, and Herbert played a solo. He was assoc. conductor of the Worcester Festival (1889–91), for which he wrote a dramatic cantata, *The Captive* (Sept. 24, 1891). In 1893 he became bandmaster of the 22nd Regiment Band, succeeding P. S. Gilmore. On March 10, 1894, he was soloist with the N.Y. Phil. in his 2nd Cello Concerto. In the same year, at the suggestion of William MacDonald, the manager of the Boston Ideal Opera Co., Herbert wrote his first operetta, *Prince Ananias*, which was premiered with encouraging success in N.Y. (Nov. 20, 1894). He quickly established himself as a leading composer in the genre, winning enduring success with such scores as *The Serenade* (1897), *Babes in Toyland* (1903), *Mlle. Modiste* (1905), *Naughty Marietta* (1910), *Sweethearts* (1913), and *The Only Girl* (1914). In 1900 he directed at Madison Square Garden, N.Y., an orch. of 420 performers for the benefit of the sufferers in the Galveston flood. On April 29, 1906, he led a similar monster concert at the Hippodrome for the victims of the San Francisco earthquake. In 1904 he organized the Victor Herbert Orch. in N.Y. In 1908 he was elected to the National Inst. of Arts and Letters.

In his finest operettas, Herbert united spontaneous melody, sparkling rhythm, and simple but tasteful harmony; his experience as a symphonic composer and conductor imparted a solidity of texture to his writing that placed him far above the many gifted amateurs in this field. Furthermore, he possessed a natural communicative power in his music, which made his operettas spectacularly successful with the public. In the domain of grand opera, he was not so fortunate. When the premiere of his first grand opera, *Natoma*, took place in Philadelphia on Feb. 25, 1911, it aroused great expectations; but the opera failed to sustain lasting interest. Still less effective was his second opera, *Madeleine*, staged by the Metropolitan Opera in N.Y. on Jan. 24, 1914. Herbert was one of the founders of ASCAP in 1914, and was vice-president from that date until his death. In 1916 he wrote a special score for the film *The Fall of a Nation*, in synchronization with the screenplay. He also wrote a film score for *Indian Summer* (1919).

WORKS: DRAMATIC: Operettas: *Prince Ananias* (N.Y., Nov. 20, 1894); *The Wizard of the Nile* (Wilkes Barre, Pa., Sept. 26, 1895); *The Gold Bug* (N.Y., Sept. 21, 1896); *The Serenade* (Cleveland, Feb. 17, 1897); *The Idol's Eye* (Troy, N.Y., Sept. 20, 1897); *The Fortune Teller* (Toronto, Sept. 14, 1898); *Cyrano de Bergerac* (Montreal, Sept. 11, 1899); *The Singing Girl* (Montreal, Oct. 2, 1899); *The Ameer* (Scranton, Pa., Oct. 9, 1899); *The Viceroy* (San Francisco, Feb. 12, 1900); *Babes in Toyland* (Chicago, June 17, 1903); *Babette* (Washington, D.C., Nov. 9, 1903); *It Happened in Nordland* (Harrisburg, Pa., Nov. 21, 1904); *Miss Dolly Dollars* (Rochester, N.Y., Aug. 30, 1905); *Wonderland* (Buffalo, Sept. 14, 1905); *Mlle. Modiste* (Trenton, Oct. 7, 1905); *The Red Mill* (Buffalo, Sept. 3, 1906); *Dream City* (N.Y., Dec. 25, 1906); *The Magic Knight* (N.Y., Dec. 25, 1906); *The Tattooed Man* (Baltimore, Feb. 11, 1907); *Algeria* (Atlantic City, Aug. 24, 1908; rev. as *The Rose of Algeria*, Wilkes Barre, Pa., Sept. 11, 1909); *Little Nemo* (Philadelphia,

Sept. 28, 1908); *The Prima Donna* (Chicago, Oct. 5, 1908); *Old Dutch* (Wilkes Barre, Pa., Nov. 6, 1909); *Naughty Marietta* (Syracuse, Oct. 24, 1910); *When Sweet 16* (Springfield, Mass., Dec. 5, 1910); *Mlle. Rosita* (later called *The Duchess*; Boston, March 27, 1911); *The Enchantress* (Washington, D.C., Oct. 9, 1911); *The Lady of the Slipper* (Philadelphia, Oct. 8, 1912); *Sweethearts* (Baltimore, March 24, 1913); *The Madcap Duchess* (Rochester, N.Y., Oct. 13, 1913); *The Débutante* (Atlantic City, Sept. 21, 1914); *The Only Girl* (Atlantic City, Oct. 1, 1914); *The Princess Pat* (Atlantic City, Aug. 23, 1915); *Eileen* (Cleveland, Jan. 1, 1917, as *Hearts of Erin*); *Her Regiment* (Springfield, Mass., Oct. 22, 1917); *The Velvet Lady* (Philadelphia, Dec. 23, 1918); *Angel Face* (Chicago, June 8, 1919); *My Golden Girl* (Stamford, Conn., Dec. 19, 1919); *Oui Madame* (Philadelphia, March 22, 1920); *The Girl in the Spotlight* (Stamford, Conn., July 7, 1920); *Orange Blossoms* (Philadelphia, Sept. 4, 1922); *The Dream Girl* (New Haven, April 22, 1924). **O p e r a :** *Natoma* (Philadelphia, Feb. 25, 1911); *Madeleine* (1913; N.Y., Jan. 24, 1914). **OTHER:** *Miss Camille*, burlesque (1907); *The Song Birds*, musical skit (1907); *The Century Girl*, revue (N.Y., Nov. 6, 1916; in collaboration with I. Berlin); music for the films *The Fall of a Nation* (1916) and *Indian Summer* (1919), and for Ziegfeld's Follies. **ORCH.:** Suite for Cello and Orch. (Stuttgart, Oct. 23, 1883); 2 cello concertos: No. 1 (1884; Stuttgart, Dec. 8, 1885) and No. 2 (N.Y. March 10, 1894); *Serenade* for Strings (1888); *Irish Rhapsody* (1892); *American Fantasia* (1898); *Hero and Leander*, symphonic poem (1900; Pittsburgh, Jan. 18, 1901); *Suite romantique* (1901); *Soixante-neuf* for Strings (1902); *Columbus*, suite (1902; Pittsburgh, Jan. 2, 1903); *L'encore* for Flute, Clarinet, and Orch. (1910); *Whispering Willows* (1915); *Little Old N.Y.*, overture (1923); *Under the Red Robe*, overture (1923). **B a n d :** *The Gold Bug*, march (1896); *The Serenade*, march (1897); *McKinley Inauguration March* (1897); *March of the 22nd Regiment* (1898). **OTHER:** Over 20 chamber pieces; about 25 piano works; several choral works, including the dramatic cantata *The Captive* (Worcester Festival, Sept. 24, 1891); about 80 songs; around 70 arrangements of scores by other composers.

BIBL.: J. Kaye, *V. H.* (N.Y., 1931); C. Purdy, *V. H.—American Music Master* (N.Y., 1944); E. Waters, *V. H.: A Life in Music* (N.Y., 1955).—**NS/LK/DM**

Herbig, Günther, German conductor; b. Ústí-nad-Labem, Czechoslovakia, Nov. 30, 1931. He studied conducting with Abendroth at the Weimar Hochschule für Musik, and received further training from Scherchen, Yansons, and Karajan. He was conductor of the German National Theater in Weimar (1957–62), music director of the Hans Otto Theater in Potsdam (1962–66), and conductor of the (East) Berlin Sym. Orch. (1966–72). He was Generalmusikdirektor (1970–72) and chief conductor (1972–77) of the Dresden Phil., and then was chief conductor of the (East) Berlin Sym. Orch. (1977–83), and principal guest conductor of the Dallas Sym. Orch. (1979–81) and BBC Northern Sym. Orch. in Manchester (1981–83). From 1984 to 1990 he was music director of the Detroit Sym. Orch., and from 1990 to 1994 of the Toronto Sym.—**NS/LK/DM**

Herbst, Johann Andreas, German violinist, music theorist, and composer; b. Nuremberg (baptized), June 9, 1588; d. Frankfurt am Main, Jan. 24, 1666. He received training in Nuremberg. He was Kapellmeister at the courts of Butzbach (1614–18) and Darmstadt (1618–23), and then in Frankfurt am Main (1623–36). After serving in that capacity in Nuremberg (1636–44), he again held that post in Frankfurt am Main from 1644 until his death. His extant theoretical works comprise *Musica practica* (Nuremberg, 1642; 2nd ed., 1653 and 3rd ed., 1658 as *Musica moderna prattica*) and *Musica poetica* (Nuremberg, 1643), the latter being the first book in the German language on the composer's art. Herbst was one of the earliest German composers to adopt the use of the basso continuo and the concertato style. His works were ed. by J. Muller-Blattau in Das Erbe Deutscher Musik, 2nd series, I (1937).

BIBL.: A. Allerup, *Die "Musica Practica" des J.A. H.* (Kassel, 1931).—**LK/DM**

Herbst, Johannes, German-American Moravian minister and composer; b. Kempten, Swabia, July 23, 1735; d. Salem, N.C., Jan. 15, 1812. He went to the U.S. in 1786 to serve as minister at Lancaster, Pa., and later at Lititz. In 1811 he was elevated to the episcopate and transferred to the Southern Province of the Moravian Church at Salem. When he emigrated to the U.S. he brought with him a large number of musical MSS, this being the practice of those traveling to the American Moravian settlements. During the following years, in which he was a performing musician, composer, and teacher, he added to his collection, copying MSS brought from Europe by other Moravians, and music composed by American Moravians; altogether there are almost 12,000 pages in his hand, constituting the most extensive individual collection of 18th- and 19th-century Moravian (and non-Moravian) music in the U.S. The Herbst Collection is in the Archives of the Moravian Music Foundation in Winston-Salem, N.C., and is available on either microfiche or roll microfilm: A. 493 MS scores of about 1,000 vocal-instrumental pieces (Congregation Music); B. 45 MS scores or parts of larger vocal works by C. P. E. Bach, Mozart, Haydn, and others, including Herbst and other Moravians; C. 6 miscellaneous vols. of keyboard works, texts, etc.; the entire collection totals 11,676 pages. An itemized *Catalog of the Johannes Herbst Collection*, prepared by M. Gombosi, was publ. in Chapel Hill, N.C., in 1970 and includes a biographical sketch of Herbst and a short history of the collection. Herbst was the most prolific of all the American Moravian composers, having to his credit some 127 choral anthems and songs. Many of his works show him to have been a highly skilled musical craftsman.

BIBL.: J. Falconer, *Bishop J. H. (1735–1812), An American Moravian Musician, Collector and Composer* (2 vols., diss., Columbia Univ., 1969).—**NS/LK/DM**

Hercigonja, Nikola, Croatian composer; b. Vinkovcim, Feb. 19, 1911. He studied in Zagreb, and in 1950 became a prof. of the Music Academy in Belgrade. In his music he follows a general trend of realistic composition, inspired by national folk songs.

WORKS: *Vječni Žid u Zagrebu* (The Wandering Jew in Zagreb), musical burlesque (1942); *Gorski vijenac* (Mountain Wreath), opera-oratorio (Belgrade, Oct. 19, 1957); *Planetarium*, scenic action for Voices, Speaking Chorus, and Orch. (1960); numerous choruses.—**NS/LK/DM**

Herford (real name, **Goldstein**), **Julius,** German-American pianist, choral conductor, and pedagogue; b. Anklam, Feb. 22, 1901; d. Bloomington, Ind., Sept. 17, 1981. He studied piano with Kwast and composition with Klatte and Willner at the Stern Cons. in Berlin (1917–23). After touring Europe as a pianist (1923–25), he returned to Berlin as a teacher. In 1939 he emigrated to the U.S. He taught at Teachers Coll. of Columbia Univ. (1939–41), the Juilliard School of Music in N.Y. (from 1946), the Berkshire Music Center in Tanglewood (from 1946), the Union Theological Seminary in N.Y. (from 1949), the Manhattan School of Music in N.Y. (1949), and Westminster Choir Coll. in Princeton, N.J.; he also was director of graduate studies in choral conducting at the Ind. Univ. School of Music in Bloomington (1964–80). With H. Decker, he ed. the vol. *Choral Conducting* (1973; 2nd ed., rev., 1988 as *Choral Conducting Symposium*).—NS/LK/DM

Herincx, Raimund (Fridrik), English bass-baritone of Belgian descent; b. London, Aug. 23, 1927. He received his training from Van Dyck in Belgium and from Valli in Italy. In 1950 he made his operatic debut as Mozart's Figaro with the Welsh National Opera. In 1956 he joined the Sadler's Wells Opera in London, where his roles included Count Almaviva, Pizzaro, Germont, Rigoletto, and Stravinsky's Nick Shadow and Creon. In 1966 he was a soloist in Delius's *A Mass of Life* in N.Y., and in 1967 he sang in opera in Boston. From 1968 he appeared at London's Covent Garden, winning success as the King Fisher in the *Midsummer Marriage*, Macbeth, and Escamillo, and creating roles in the premieres of *The Knot Garden* (1970) and *Taverner* (1972). In 1973–74 he sang at the Salzburg East Festivals, and then in the *Ring* cycles at the English National Opera in London (1974–76). On Jan. 18, 1977, he made his debut as Mathiesen in *Le Prophète* at the Metropolitan Opera in N.Y., and then sang with the Seattle (1977–81) and San Francisco (1983) operas. In 1986 he returned to Boston to sing in the U.S. premiere of *Taverner.*—NS/LK/DM

Hering, Karl Gottlieb, German music pedagogue and composer; b. Bad Schandau, Oct. 25, 1765; d. Zittau, Jan. 4, 1853. He studied academic subjects at Leipzig Univ. and music with J. G. Schicht. In 1811 he was appointed music teacher at the Zittau seminary, and remained there until 1836, when he retired. He publ. *Praktisches Handbuch zur leichten Erlernung des Klavier-Spielens* (Halberstadt, 1796) and *Praktische Violin-Schule* (Leipzig, 1810), and also compiled *Zittauer Choralbuch* (Leipzig, 1822) and other collections, including original compositions. Some of his pieces for children became celebrated in Germany and elsewhere, particularly *Steckenpferd* ("Hopp, hopp, hopp, Pferdchen lauf Galopp"), *Weihnachtsfreude* ("Morgen, Kinder, wird's was geben"), and (most famous of all) *Grossvaterlied,* which was used by Schumann in his *Carnaval.* —NS/LK/DM

Héritte-Viardot, Louise-Pauline-Marie, French voice teacher and composer, daughter of **Pauline Viardot-Garcia**; b. Paris, Dec. 14, 1841; d.

Heidelberg, Jan. 17, 1918. She was for many years a singing teacher at the St. Petersburg Cons. She then taught in Frankfurt am Main, Berlin, and Heidelberg. She was also a composer. Her opera *Lindoro* was performed in Weimar (1879). She further wrote the cantatas *Das Bacchusfest* (Stockholm, 1880) and *Le Feu de ciel,* some chamber music, and vocal exercises. Her memoirs (tr. from the original German) were publ. in Eng. as *Memories and Adventures* (London, 1913).—NS/LK/DM

Herman, Nicolaus, German composer; b. Altdorf, near Nuremberg, 1500; d. Joachimsthal, West Bohemia, May 15, 1561. He was an organist, schoolmaster, and cantor in Joachimsthal from 1518 to 1560. As a composer, he was known for his Lutheran hymns, for which he wrote both texts and music.—LK/DM

Herman, Vasile, Romanian composer; b. Satu-Mare, June 10, 1929. He studied piano in his hometown, and composition with Demian, Toduţă, and Comes at the Cluj Cons. (1949–57), where he subsequently was appointed to its staff. His music is cautiously modernistic, with occasional overflow into aleatoric indeterminacy.

WORKS: ORCH.: *Variante* for 2 Clarinets, Piano, and Percussion (1963–64); *4 Ritornele* (1964); *Cantilaşii* (1967); *Polifonie* for 7 Instrumental Groups (1968); *Episoade* (1968); *Postludiu* (1971); *Syntagma I* for 14 Instruments and Piano (1971); Double Concerto for Flute, Oboe, and Orch. (1973); *Simfonii şi fantezzi* (1974–75); 5 syms., including No. 1 (1976), No. 2, *Memorandum* (1980), and No. 3, *Metamorfoze* (1982); *Unison* (1977–78); Concerto for Strings (1979); Concertino for Trombone, Double Bass, and Orch. (1981). **CHAMBER:** *Sonata-Baladă* for Oboe and Piano (1961); *Triptic* for Violin (1964); *Melopee* for Flute (1965); Flute Sonata (1965–66); *Aforisme* for Oboe and Piano (1970); 2 string quartets: No. 1, *Omagiu lui Enescu* (1971) and No. 2, *Refrene* (1977); *3 Pieces* for Violin and Piano (1974); *Syntagma II* for Chamber Ensemble (1975); *Monofonii* for Oboe (1975); Trio for Violin, Cello, and Piano (1979); *Neanes* for Chamber Ensemble (1979); *Sonata de camera* for Flute, Oboe, Cello, and Harpsichord (1981); *Panrhytmicon* for 5 Percussion Groups (1982). **Piano:** 2 sonatas: No. 1, *Sonata da ricercar* (1958) and No. 2 (1967); *Partita* (1961); *Microforme* (1965); *Grafică* for 1 or 2 Pianos (1969); other works. **VOCAL:** 6 cantatas (1969, 1970, 1974, 1977, 1980, 1983); songs.—NS/LK/DM

Herman, Woody (actually, **Woodrow Charles**), renowned jazz leader, clarinetist, alto and soprano saxophonist, singer; b. Milwaukee, May 16, 1913; d. Los Angeles, Oct. 29, 1987. He sang and danced in vaudeville theatres from early childhood. He took up sax at age 11, clarinet at 14 and incorporated them in his variety act. He worked with Myron Stewart's Band and toured Tex. with Joe Lichter's Band (ca. 1928), then briefly became a student at Marquette Univ. He played with Tom Gerun (Gerunovitch) from 1929–34. He formed his own band in 1933 but it was not successful. He spent eight months in the Harry Sosnick Band (1934), two months with Gus Arnheim, and gigged with Joe Moss until joining Isham Jones's Juniors. He joined the band in Denver (ca. late 1934), and remained with it until Jones disbanded in late summer of 1936. Herman and five other ex-members formed the nucleus of a co-operative band, with Herman as leader. This unit played first at the Schroeder Hotel in Milwaukee, but made its official debut at the Roseland in Brooklyn. The orch. (billed as "The Band That Plays the Blues") gradually achieved popularity, its box-office appeal greatly enhanced by the success of "The Woodchoppers Ball" recording (1939). Herman also recorded with the King's Jesters in 1938.

In the early 1940s the band underwent extensive personnel changes, and became involved in the new music. For example, Gillespie wrote for them "Down Under" (recorded in 1943) and "Woody 'N' You" (not recorded by them). Herman began buying shares as the original members left, but the musical evolution was mostly undocumented because it occurred during the musicians' union strike against record companies, so that the Herd burst upon an astonished audience in 1945. Chubby Jackson and Ralph Burns joined in 1943, both from the Charlie Barnet band; Jackson helped to recruit Neal Hefti, Dave Tough, Flip Phillips, Bill Harris and others until Billy Bauer replaced the last remaining member of the old band. Both Candoli brothers played trumpet mid- 1944 (16–year-old Conte played on summer holiday from high school). The band, later known as the First Herd, performed Stravinsky's "Ebony Concerto" at Carnegie Hall in March 1946 (reportedly Goodman, who had a classical background, helped Herman to prepare the piece). They disbanded in December of that year. He enjoyed several Top pop hits in the 1940s. He re- formed a "Second Herd" in 1947, also known as the "Four Brothers" band, after a composition by Jimmy Giuffre, because the unusual saxophone section of Herman, three tenors (Zoot Sims, Stan Getz, Herbie Steward) and a baritone (Serge Chaloff) were all inspired by Lester Young. Due to financial troubles and rampant drug addiction among the new generation, Herman cut down to a small band in late 1949. He formed the Third Herd in 1950.

During the 1950s Herman continued leading various Herds; in spring 1954 his band did their first European tour. During the late 1950s and 1960s, for several months each year, he led his own big bands, usually specially assembled for specific tours. In spring of 1959 he brought a few star sidemen to Europe and toured with an Anglo-American band; during the 1960s he toured Europe several times. In the later 1960s and early 1970s, he made waves by recording big-band arrangements of rock hits, including a rousing "Light My Fire." He appeared in many films, and won a Grammy in 1973. He did extensive touring throughout the 1970s, and recovered from serious auto crash in 1977. In the mid- 1970s, Frank Tiberi brought Coltrane pieces into the band; as Herman aged Tiberi took over direction of the band. The group also worked with Chick Corea. Herman's last years were plagued with tax problems (his manager had failed to file payroll taxes, instead using the monies to finance a gambling habit). The IRS seized his home while his health was failing, an unusually cruel gesture. Since Herman's death the band has toured under the musical directorship of Tiberi.

DISC.: Bijou; Four Brothers; Blues in the Night (1936); Woodchopper's Ball (1941); Northwest Passage (1945); One Night Stand with W. H. (1945); At Carnegie Hall (1946); Sequence in Jazz (1946); Early Autumn (1948); Hollywood Palladium 1948 (1948); Live 1948, Vol. 1, 2 (1948); Keeper of the Flame: Complete Capitol Recordings (1948); Live in New Orleans (1951); Third Herd, Vol. 1, 2 (1952); Men from Mars (1952); Jazz, the Utmost! (1952); Hey! Heard the Herd? (1952); Omaha, Nebraska 1954 (1954); Jackpot! (1955); Blues Groove (1956); Live in Stereo (1957); Live at Peacock Lane Hollywood (1958); W. H. Sextet at the Roundtable (1959); Live at Monterey (1959); W.'s Big Band Goodies (1963); Encore: W. H. (1963); W.'s Winners (1965); Live in Antibes (1965); W. Live: East and West (1967); Live in Seattle (1967); Concerto for Herd (1967); Heavy Exposure (1969); Brand New (1971); Raven Speaks (1972); Giant Steps (1973); Feelin' So Blue (1973); Thundering Herd (1974); Children of Lima (1974); King Cobra (1975); Herd at Montreux (1975); 40th Anniversary Carnegie Hall (1976); W. H. and Flip Phillips (1978); Plays Chick, Donald, Walter and Woodrow (1978); La Fiesta (1978); World Class (1982); Fiftieth Anniversary Tour (1986).—**JC/MM/LP**

Hermann, Hans, German composer; b. Leipzig, Aug. 17, 1870; d. Berlin, May 18, 1931. He studied with W. Rust in Leipzig, E. Kretschmer in Dresden, and H. von Herzogenberg in Berlin. From the age of 18, he played the double bass in various European orchs. He then taught at the Klindworth- Scharwenka Cons. in Berlin (1901–07). He publ. some 100 songs, of which several became fairly well known (Drei Wanderer, Alte Landsknechte, etc.); he had a flair for imitating the simple style of the folk ballad. He further wrote a Sym., Lebensepisoden, a stage work, Der rote Pimpernell, pieces for clarinet with piano; etc.—**NS/LK/DM**

Hermann, Roland, German baritone; b. Bochum, Sept. 17, 1936. He attended the Univs. of Freiburg im Bresgau, Mainz, and Frankfurt am Main, and received his vocal training from Margarete von Winterfeldt, Paul Lohmann, and Flaminio Contini. In 1961 he took 1st prize in the competition of the German radio stations. In 1967 he made his operatic debut as Mozart's Figaro in Trier, then joined the Zürich Opera in 1968. He also sang opera in Munich, Cologne, Buenos Aires, Paris, Berlin, and other cities. His engagements as a soloist with orchs. and as a recitalist took him to many of the major music centers of Europe, the U.S. (debut with the N.Y. Phil., 1983), and the Far East. In addition to such operatic roles as Don Giovanni, Wolfram, Germont, and Amfortas, he sang in such rarely performed works as Schumann's Genoveva, Marschner's Der Vampyr, Busoni's Doktor Faust, and Schoenberg's Moses und Aron. He also sang in several premieres, among them Keltenborn's Der Kirschgarten (Zürich, 1984) and Höller's Der Meister und Margarita (Paris, 1989).—**NS/LK/DM**

Hermannus (surnamed Contractus on account of his paralyzed limbs), Swabian theoretician and composer; b. Saulgau, July 18, 1013; d. Altshausen, near Biberach, Sept. 24, 1054. He was the son of Hermann, Count of Vehringen. He was a student in the Reichenau monastery, and, under the guidance of his tutor, Abbot Berno, he acquired wide learning. In 1043 he entered the

Benedictine order. His best-known work (containing valuable historical notices on music) is a chronology from the time of Christ to 1054. It has been republ. several times, and is to be found in Peres's (Pertz's) *Monumenta* (Vol. V). Hermannus was the author of *Opuscula musica*, in which he gives a thorough discussion of the church modes and criticizes the Daseian notation used in the 10th-century tract *Musica enchiriadis*. He proposed his own notation by Greek and Latin letters. In the indication of a change in pitch, it had an advantage over neume notation. His notation is written above the neume notation in some MSS of the 11th and 12th centuries in the Munich Library. The sequence *Grates, honis, hierarchia* and an office for St. Afra, *Glorioso et beatissima*, are the only compositions which have been definitely established as being by Hermannus. L. Ellinwood ed. *Musica Hermanni Contracti* (Rochester, N.Y., 1936), which gives the Latin text (prepared from the Vienna MS and an 11th- century MS at the Eastman School of Music in Rochester, N.Y.), an Eng. tr., and commentary.

BIBL.: W. Brambach, *Hermanni Contracti Musica* (Leipzig, 1884); H. Oesch, *Berno und Hermann von Reichenau als Musiktheoretiker* (Bern, 1961).—**NS/LK/DM**

Herman's Hermits,

one of the few bands to give The Beatles a run for their money in the mid 1960s; formed 1963, Manchester, England; **MEMBERSHIP:** Peter Noone, voc. (b. Manchester, England, Nov. 5, 1947); Karl Green, bs. (b. Manchester, England, July 31, 1947); Keith Hopwood, gtr. (b. Manchester, England, Oct. 26, 1946); Derek "Lek" Leckenby, gtr. (b. Leeds, England, May 14, 1946; d. Manchester, England, June 4, 1994); Barry Whitwam, drm. (b. Manchester, England, July 21, 1946). Peter Noone's father was a sometimes musician. Noone attended the Manchester School of Music and Drama. Initially, he took to acting, regularly appearing as a child in the long-running British soap opera *Coronation Street* as well as other English TV shows and plays. As a preteen, he turned down a role in a Hollywood film, which curtailed his acting career. By the time he was 16, he hooked up with a local band called The Heartbeats. They came to the attention of local managers Harvey Lisberg and Charlie Silverman who suggested they change their name. One of the band members remarked how similar Noone looked to the character of Sherman in the Mr. Peabody segment of the *Rocky and Bullwinkle* show. He misheard it as "Herman," however. The band became known as Herman and his Hermits and finally just Herman's Hermits.

With Noone's youthful good looks and track record, it wasn't long before they were signed to EMI/Columbia in England by producer Mickey Most. In addition to the band, studio musicians like future Led Zeppelin members John Paul Jones and Jimmy Page were used. They went into the studio to record a Carole King/Gerry Goffin tune, "I'm into Something Good," which former Cookie's lead singer Earl Jean took to #38 earlier that year. The tune went up the charts to #1 in England, topping out at #13 in the U.S. Their next U.S. single, "Can't You Hear My Heartbeat," went to #2 in the U.S., their first in a raft of Top Ten singles for the year 1965. They released their first U.S. album, *Introduc-*

ing Herman's Hermits. A deejay heard the tune "Mrs. Brown You've Got a Lovely Daughter," on the album. An antidote to Beatlemania, the song had come from a BBC television production of a few years previous, but sounded like something that might have been performed in the pre-war British music halls. This deejay started playing it, and got fantastic response. MGM released it as a single and it topped the charts for three weeks less than two months after their previous hit, and went gold.

The Hermits followed this in the U.S. with their second British single, a cover of The Rays' "Silhouettes." During a brief tour of the U.S., they performed in the Connie Francis movie *When the Boys Meet the Girls* and the movie *Hold On*. In the U.K., on a brief wave of Hermits mania, the film's title tune rose to #3; in the U.S. it hit #5. On a similar note, they covered Sam Cooke's "Wonderful World," which hit #7 in the U.K. and #4 in the U.S. But none of these matched "Mrs. Brown." Seeking the music hall sound of that single, Most and the band dug into the real music hall repertoire and pulled out a tune that had been a hit on the circuit in 1911 for Harry Champion called "I'm Henry VIII, I Am." While the single cut too close to the bone for the U.K., the U.S. audiences ate it up. It went to #1 and went gold. The band finished off 1965 with the #7 "Just a Little Bit," their sixth Top Ten hit of the year.

The Hermits kicked off 1966 with the #8 "Must to Avoid," a jangly return to their quasi-Merseybeat roots, featured in *Hold On*. Less than two months later, they were at #3 with "Listen People," the tune they performed in *When the Boys Meet the Girls*. They took anther music hallesque tune, "Leaning on a Lamp Post" (also from *Hold On*), to #9 in April, bringing them to a run of nine straight Top Ten songs. The streak ended, however, with "This Door Swings Both Ways," which only managed to reach #12. This was the first sign that the band's popularity was beginning to wane. They managed to score one final Top Ten U.S. single, 1967's "There's a Kind of Hush," which rose to #4. The group placed three more singles in the Top 40 that year, including "No Milk Today" a track that featured a full orchestra, written by future 10cc member Graham Goulding, which hit #35 in the U.S., but went Top Ten in the U.K. All in all, by the time they had run their course in 1968, they had placed 18 hits in the Top 40 in a little under three and a half years.

The band continued playing together for another couple of years, eventually becoming "Peter Noone and Herman's Hermits." Noone, in the meantime, started to flex his acting muscles some more. He starred in a film version of *Mrs. Brown You've Got a Lovely Daughter* and made cameo appearances in several other movies. The band moved to the Milwaukee and started playing around 200 gigs a year. By 1970, Noone had left, though they agreed to play together again for a sold-out British Invasion nostalgia concert at N.Y.'s Madison Square Garden in 1973. Noone took another role in *Coronation Street* for a while, hosted a show for VH-1 called *My Generation* early in the 1990s, and played venues ranging from oldies shows to cruise ships. Leckenby died of cancer in 1994.

DISC.: *Introducing Herman's Hermits* (1965); *Mrs. Brown, You've Got a Lovely Daughter* (1965); *Herman's Hermits* (1965); *British Go Go* (1965); *On Tour: Their Second Album* (1965); *When the Boys Meet the Girls* (1965); *Both Sides of Herman's Hermits* (1966); *Again* (1966); *Lucky13* (1966); *Hold On!* (1966); *There's a Kind of Hush All Over the World* (1967); *X15* (1967); *Blaze* (1967); *Most of Herman's Hermits* (1972); *A Whale of a Tale (Hermits) Not Issued* (1972); *Golden Album Odeon* (1973); *Something Good* (1982); *Remember the...* (1986); *No Milk Today* (1996). **PETER NOONE:** *One of the Glory Boys* (1982); *Pirates of Penzance (Original Cast)* (1986); *I'm into Something Good* (1989).—**HB**

Hermanson, Åke (Oscar Werner), Swedish composer; b. Mollosund, June 16, 1923; d. Stockholm, Aug. 8, 1996. After training from Knut Bäck and Herman Asplöf in Göteborg, he went to Stockholm and studied organ with Alf Linder and Henry Lindroth, and composition with Rosenberg (1949–52). From 1969 to 1971 he was chairman of the Soc. of Swedish Composers. In 1973 he was elected a member of the Royal Academy of Music in Stockholm. In 1982 he received the Nordic Council Prize and in 1986 the Rosenberg Prize. In his music, he pursued a concentrated brevity marked by an alternation of short contrasting motifs, a usage he defined as "pendulum dynamics."

WORKS: ORCH.: *Invoco* for String (1958–60; Norrköping, May 24, 1961); *In nuce* (In a Nutshell; 1962–63; Stockholm, Oct. 9, 1964); 4 syms.: No. 1 (1964–67; Stockholm, Oct. 29, 1967), No. 2 (1973–75; Stockholm, Sept. 26, 1976), No. 3 (1980), and No. 4, *Oceanus* (1981–84; Stockholm, Dec. 19, 1984); *Appel I-IV* (1968–69; Swedish Radio, Dec. 12, 1970); *Ultima* (1971–72; Swedish Radio, Nov. 18, 1972); *Utopia* (1977–78). **CHAMBER:** *Lyrical Metamorphoses* for String Quartet (1954–57); *A due voci* for Flute and Viola (1957–58); *Suoni d'un flauto* for Alto Flute (1961); *Alarme* for Horn (1969); *In sono* for Flute, Oboe or English Horn, Viola, and Cello (1970); *Flauto d'inverno* for Bass Flute (1976); *Ars lineae* for 6 Winds (1976); *Thrice* for Oboe, Clarinet, and Trombone (1976–79); *La Strada* for Horn and Organ (1979–80); String Quartet (1982–83). **VOCAL:** *Stadier* for Soprano, Flute, Bass Clarinet, Viola, and Percussion (1960–61); *Bild* for Tenor and Trombone (1978–79); *Äggjakten* for Narrator, Tenor Saxophone, Guitar, and Percussion (1979); choruses.—**NS/LK/DM**

Hermesdorff, Michael, German organist, musicologist, and composer; b. Trier, March 4, 1833; d. there, Jan. 1885. He entered the priesthood, and was appointed organist of Trier Cathedral. He founded the Choral Soc., chiefly for the exposition of Gregorian plainchant, on which he was an authority by virtue of his study of original sources. He ed. the *Graduale ad usum Romanum cantus S. Gregorii* (Leipzig, 1876–82, 10 nos.) in the monthly supplements of the *Cäcilia* journal, but died before its completion. He publ. a *Kyriale*, *Harmonica cantus choralis a 4*, a *Graduale*, several anthems and *Praefatio* (prayers used in the Trier diocese), and 3 masses of his own.—**NS/LK/DM**

Hermstedt, (Johann) Simon, famous German clarinetist; b. Langensalza, Dec. 29, 1778; d. Sondershausen, Aug. 10, 1846. He was educated at the Annaberg school for soldiers' children, and studied with Knoblauch and Baer. He was a court musician in Sondershausen. He made improvements in his instrument, and also composed concertos, variations, and other pieces for clarinet. Spohr wrote a Clarinet Concerto for him.—**NS/LK/DM**

Hernández, Hermilio, Mexican composer; b. Autlán, Jalisco, Feb. 2, 1931. He studied music with José Valadez and Domingo Lobato at the Escuela Superior Diocesana de Música Sagrada in Guadalajara, graduating in 1956. He then studied in Italy and Paris.

WORKS: ORCH.: *5 Pieces* (1955); Violin Concerto (1960); Sonata for Chamber Orch. (1964). **CHAMBER:** Suite for Violin and Piano (1952); String Quartet (1954); Piano Trio (1955); Cello Sonata (1962); Wind Quintet (1965); *Poliédros* for Oboe, Bassoon, and Piano (1969); *Music for 4 Instruments* for Flute, Violin, Cello, and Piano (1970). **KEYBOARD: Piano:** 2 sonatinas (1955, 1971); *Tema transfigurado* (1962); *6 Inventions* (1968); Sonata (1970); *Diálogos* for 2 Pianos (1970). **Organ:** *Fantasia* (1970). **VOCAL:** *Cantata Adviento* (1953); songs. —**NS/LK/DM**

Hernández Sales, Pablo, Spanish composer; b. Saragossa, Jan. 25, 1834; d. Madrid, Dec. 10, 1910. He was first a church chorister, and at 14 played organ at the San Gil church in Saragossa. At 22 he went to Madrid to study with Eslava at the Madrid Cons. He graduated with a gold medal (1861), and joined the faculty in 1863 as a singing teacher. He wrote 2 zarzuelas: *Gimnasio higienico* and *Un Sevillano en la Habana*; also many sacred works.—**NS/LK/DM**

Hernándo (y Palomar), Rafael (José María), Spanish composer; b. Madrid, May 31, 1822; d. there, July 10, 1888. He studied with Carnicer, Saldoni, and P. Albeniz at the Madrid Cons. (1837–43), then went to Paris, where he took lessons with Auber. His *Stabat Mater* was performed there, and a grand opera, *Romilda*, was accepted for performance at the Théâtre des Italiens, but the revolutionary upheaval of 1848 prevented its production. Hernándo returned to Madrid, where he produced a number of zarzuelas, of which the most successful was *El duende* (June 6, 1849); others included *Palo de ciego* (Feb. 15, 1849), *Colegialas y soldados* (March 21, 1849), *Bertoldo y Comparsa* (May 23, 1850), *Cosas de Juan* (Sept. 9, 1854), *El tambor* (April 28, 1860), and *Aurora*. He also collaborated with Barbieri, Oudrid, and Gaztambide in *Escenas de Chamberi* (Nov. 19, 1850) and *Don Simplicio Bobadilla* (May 7, 1853). In 1852 he became secretary of the Madrid Cons. where he also taught harmony.—**NS/LK/DM**

Hernried, Robert (Franz Richard), Austrian-American musicologist and composer; b. Vienna, Sept. 22, 1883; d. Detroit, Sept. 3, 1951. He was trained in Vienna at the Cons. and the Univ. He taught theory at the Mannheim Academy of Music (1919–22), the Heidelberg Cons. (1923), in Erfurt (1924–26), and in Berlin at the Stern Cons. (1926–28) and the Staatliche Akademie für Kirchen- und Schulmusik (1927–34). In 1939 he went to the U.S. and taught at St. Ambrose Coll. in Davenport, Iowa (1940–42), the State Teachers Coll. in Dickinson, N. Dak. (1942–43), and St. Francis Coll. in Fort Wayne, Ind. (1943–46); he then was prof. of theory and composition at the Detroit Inst. of Musical Art (1946–51). He publ. studies on Jaques-Dalcroze (Geneva, 1929) and Brahms (Leipzig, 1934), as well as *Allgemeine Musiklehre* (Berlin, 1932) and *Systematische Modulationslehre* (Berlin, 1935; 2nd ed., 1948). Among his compositions were the operas *Francesca da Rimini* and *Die Bäuerin*, orch. works, and much choral music. —NS/LK/DM

Hérold, (Louis-Joseph) Ferdinand, celebrated French composer; b. Paris, Jan. 28, 1791; d. Thernes, near Paris, Jan. 19, 1833. His father, François-Joseph Hérold (b. Seltz, Bas-Rhin, March 18, 1755; d. Paris, Oct. 1, 1802), a piano teacher and composer, did not desire his son to become a musician, and sent him to the Hix school, where his aptitude for music was noticed by Fétis, then asst. teacher there. After his father's death, Hérold began to study music seriously; in 1806 he entered the Paris Cons., taking piano lessons with Louis Adam, and winning 1st prize for piano playing in 1810. He studied harmony under Catel, and (from 1811) composition under Méhul; in 1812 his cantata *Mlle. de la Vallière* won the Prix de Rome. From Rome he went to Naples, where he became pianist to Queen Caroline; he produced his first opera, *La gioventù di Enrico Quinto* (Jan. 5, 1815), which was well received. From Naples he went to Vienna, and after a few months' stay returned to Paris, where he finished the score of Boieldieu's *Charles de France*, an "opéra d'occasion" (Opéra-Comique, June 18, 1816), and where all the rest of his operas were produced. The flattering reception of *Charles de France* led to the successful production of *Les Rosières* (Jan. 27, 1817), *La Clochette* (Oct. 18, 1817), *Le Premier Venu* (Sept. 28, 1818), *Les Troqueurs* (Feb. 18, 1819), and *L'Auteur mort et vivant* (Dec. 18, 1820); the failure of the last-named opera caused him to distrust his natural talent, and to imitate, in several succeeding stage works, the style then in vogue—that of Rossini. With the comic opera *Marie* (Aug. 12, 1826) Hérold returned, however, to his true element, and won instant and brilliant success. Meantime he had obtained the post of chorus master at the Italian Opera (1824); during this period he brought out *Le Muletier* (May 12, 1823), *Lasthénie* (Sept. 8, 1823), *Vendôme en Espagne* (Dec. 5, 1823), *Le Roi René* (Aug. 24, 1824), and *Le Lapin blanc* (May 21, 1825). In 1826 he was appointed to the staff of the Grand Opéra, for which he wrote several melodious and elegant ballets: *Astolphe et Jaconde* (Jan. 29, 1827), *La Somnambule* (Sept. 19, 1827), *Lydie* (July 2, 1828), *La Fille mal gardée* (Nov. 17, 1828), *La Belle au bois dormant* (April 27, 1829), and *La Noce de village* (Feb. 11, 1830). *La Somnambule* furnished Bellini with the subject of his popular opera. On July 18, 1829, Hérold produced *L'Illusion*, a 1-act opera full of charming numbers. *Emmeline*, a grand opera (Nov. 28, 1829), was a failure, but his next opera, *Zampa* (May 3, 1831), was sensationally successful and placed him in the first rank of French composers. He then wrote *L'Auberge d'Aurey* (May 11, 1830) jointly with Carafa, and *La Marquise de Brinvilliers* (Oct. 31, 1831), in collaboration with Auber, Batton, Berton, Blangini, Boieldieu, Carafa, Cherubini, and

Paër; he also produced *La Médecine sans médecin* (Oct. 15, 1832). His last completed work, *Le Pré aux clercs* (Dec. 15, 1832), had a remarkable vogue. He died of tuberculosis shortly before his 42nd birthday. His unfinished opera *Ludovic* was completed by Halévy and produced posthumously at the Opéra-Comique on May 16, 1833. Hérold's piano music (55 opus numbers) consists of sonatas, caprices, rondos, divertissements, fantasies, variations, and potpourris.

BIBL.: B. Jouvin, *H.: Sa vie et ses oeuvres* (Paris, 1868); A. Pougin, *H.* (Paris, 1906).—NS/LK/DM

Herold, Johannes, German composer; b. Jena, c. 1550; d. Weimar (buried), Sept. 8, 1603. He was active in Klagenfurt by 1593, where he served as cantor of the evangelical collegiate school and as director of plainchant and polyphony at the church of St. Egydi. In 1601 he was made Kapellmeister of the Weimar court chapel. Herold distinguished himself as a composer of Protestant church music, most notably in his German Passion *Historia des Leidens und Sterbens unsers Herrn und Heilands Jesu Christi aus dem Heiligen Evangelisten Mattheo mit 6 Stimmen componiert* (Graz, 1594; ed. in Musik alter Meister, IV, 1955).—LK/DM

Herold, Vilhelm (Kristoffer), Danish tenor; b. Hasle, March 19, 1865; d. Copenhagen, Dec. 15, 1937. He studied in Copenhagen, and then with Devillier and Sbriglia in Paris. He made his debut at the Royal Danish Theater in Copenhagen in 1893 as Faust; was a member of the Royal Theater in Stockholm (1901–03; 1907–09); also made guest appearances in London, Berlin, Dresden, and Hamburg. In 1915 he retired from the operatic stage. He served as director of Copenhagen's Royal Theater (1922–24). Herold was best known for his Wagnerian roles.—NS/LK/DM

Herpol, Homer (Latinized as **Homerus Herpolitanus**), South Netherlands composer; b. St. Omer, c. 1520; d. Konstanz, between Dec. 12, 1573 and Jan. 8, 1574. He was active as a cleric. In 1554 he became cantor at the collegiate church of St. Nikolaus in Fribourg. He then went to Germany and studied with Heinrich Glarean in Freiburg im Breigau (1555–57). In 1569 he became Informator choralium at Kostanz Cathedral. His most significant achievement was a vol. of 54 motets on the Gospel texts of the ecclesiastical year publ. as *Novum et insigne opus musicum* (Nuremberg, 1565). Among his other works were 7 Magnificats, motets, a *Salve regina*, and a *Regina coeli*.—LK/DM

Herrera de la Fuente, Luis, Mexican conductor and composer; b. Mexico City, April 26, 1916. He took lessons in piano and violin before pursuing training in composition with Rodolfo Halffter. He composed some stage works but devoted himself principally to conducting. After establishing himself as a conductor in Mexico City with the Fine Arts Chamber Orch., he was music director of that city's Orquesta Sinfónica Nacional (1955–72); he also served in that capacity with the Orquesta Sinfónica Nacional of Peru in Lima (1965–71). As a guest conductor, he appeared with orchs. in North

America and Europe. After serving as music director of the Okla. City Sym. Orch. (1978–88), he returned to Mexico City and was music director of the Filarmónica de la Ciudad de México from 1990.—NS/LK/DM

Herreweghe, Philippe, esteemed Belgian conductor; b. Ghent, May 2, 1947. He studied piano with Marcel Gazelle at the Ghent Cons. He also pursued training in medicine and psychiatry at the Univ. of Ghent, graduating in 1975. His musical training continued at the Ghent Cons. with Gabriel Verschraegen (organ) and Johan Huys (harpsichord), where he took a prize in 1975. In 1969 he founded the Collegium Vocale in Ghent, which soon acquired distinction as one of Europe's finest early music groups. He organized the Ensemble Vocal La Chapelle Royale in Paris in 1977, which won acclaim for its performances of a vast repertoire ranging from the Renaissance to the contemporary era. From 1982 he also served as artistic director of the Saintes early music festival. In 1989 he founded the Ensemble Vocal Européen, which also won distinction. He organized the Orchestre des Champs-Elysées in Paris in 1991, which he conducted in performances of Classical and Romantic scores on original instruments. From 1998 he was chief conductor of the Royal Phil. in Flanders.—NS/LK/DM

Herrmann, Bernard, American conductor and composer; b. N.Y., June 29, 1911; d. Los Angeles, Dec. 24, 1975. He studied violin and began to compose as a child. At 16, he commenced formal training in composition with Gustav Heine, and then attended N.Y.U. (1929–30) where he studied with James (composition) and Stoessel (conducting). He subsequently continued his studies with the latter as a fellowship student at the Juilliard School of Music in N.Y. (1930–32), where he also studied with Wagenaar (composition and harmony). In 1932–33 he attended Grainger's lectures at N.Y.U. In 1933 he organized the New Chamber Orch. in N.Y., and then in 1934 joined the staff of CBS in N.Y. working as an arranger, composer, and rehearsal conductor. In 1935 he became a staff conductor at CBS. As a composer, he found success with the various scores he wrote for such CBS programs as the "Columbia Workshop" (1937) and the "Mercury Theatre on the Air" (1938–39), where he was closely associated with Orson Welles. It was Welles who chose Herrmann to compose the score for his film *Citizen Kane* (1941), and thereafter Herrmann devoted much of his creative efforts in writing for films, with outstanding success. His score for the film *All That Money Can Buy* (1941) won him an Academy Award. From 1943 to 1951 Herrmann was chief conductor of the CBS Sym. Orch., with which he pursued a bold approach to programming. In addition to conducting broadcasts of early and rarely heard works, he also led programs of much contemporary music, ranging from Ives and Schoenberg to Elgar and Vaughan Williams. After leaving CBS, he made occasional guest conducting appearances but devoted most of his time to composing film scores and for television. Particularly outstanding were his film scores for Hitchcock's *Vertigo* (1958) and *Psycho* (1960), and Truffaut's *Fahrenheit 451* (1966). Throughout his career, Herrmann

also composed serious works, generally along neo-Romantic lines.

WORKS: DRAMATIC: Film: *Citizen Kane* (1941); *All That Money Can Buy* (1941; also known as *The Devil and Daniel Webster*); *The Magnificent Ambersons* (1942); *Jane Eyre* (1943); *Hangover Square* (1945); *Anna and the King of Siam* (1946); *The Ghost and Mrs. Muir* (1947); *Portrait of Jennie* (1948; theme music only); *The Day the Earth Stood Still* (1951); *On Dangerous Ground* (1951); *5 Fingers* (1952); *The Snows of Kilimanjaro* (1952); *White Witch Doctor* (1953); *Beneath the 12–Mile Reef* (1953); *King of the Khyber Rifles* (1953); *Garden of Evil* (1954); *The Egyptian* (1954; in collaboration with A. Newman); *Prince of Players* (1954); *The Trouble with Harry* (1955); *The Kentuckian* (1955); *The Man Who Knew Too Much* (1956); *The Man in the Gray Flannel Suit* (1956); *The Wrong Man* (1956); *Williamsburg: The Story of a Patriot* (1956); *A Hatful of Rain* (1957); *Vertigo* (1958); *The Naked and the Dead* (1958); *The 7th Voyage of Sinbad* (1958); *North by Northwest* (1959); *Blue Denim* (1959); *Journey to the Center of the Earth* (1959); *Psycho* (1960); *The 3 Worlds of Gulliver* (1960); *Mysterious Island* (1961); *Tender Is the Night* (1962); *Cape Fear* (1962); *Jason and the Argonauts* (1963); *The Birds* (1963); *Marnie* (1964); *Joy in the Morning* (1965); *Torn Curtain* (1966); *Fahrenheit 451* (1966); *The Bride Wore Black* (1968); *Twisted Nerve* (1968); *The Night Digger* (1971); *The Battle of Neretva* (1971); *Endless Night* (1971); *Sisters* (1972); *It's Alive* (1974); *Obsession* (1976); *Taxi Driver* (1976). **OTHER:** Ballet music for *Americana Revue* (1932); *The Skating Rink*, ballet (1934); ballet music for the play *The Body Beautiful* (1935); *Wuthering Heights*, opera (1943–51; recorded 1966; stage premiere in a drastically cut version, Portland, Ore., Nov. 6, 1982); *The King of Schnorrers*, musical comedy (1968; East Haddam, Conn., April 17, 1970). Also many radio scores; television music, including the operas *A Christmas Carol* (CBS-TV, Dec. 23, 1954) and *A Child Is Born* (CBS-TV, Dec. 23, 1955). **ORCH.:** *The Forest*, tone poem (1929); *November Dusk*, tone poem (1929; also known as *Late Autumn*); *Marche Militaire* for Chamber Orch. (1932); *Orchestral Variations on "Deep River" and "Water Boy"* (1933); *Prelude to "Anathema"* for Chamber Orch. (1933); *Aubade* for Chamber Orch. (1933; also known as *Silent Noon*); *The City of Brass*, symphonic poem (1934); *Nocturne and Scherzo* (1935); *Sinfonietta for Strings* (1935); *Currier and Ives*, suite (1935); *Violin Concerto* (1937; unfinished); *Sym.* (1939–41; CBS, July 27, 1941); *The Devil and Daniel Webster*, suite after the film *All That Money Can Buy* (1942); *For the Fallen* (N.Y., Dec. 16, 1943); *Welles Raises Kane*, suite (1943). **CHAMBER:** *Twilight*, pastoral for Violin and Piano (1929); *Aria* for Flute and Harp (1932); *String Quartet* (1932); *Echoes* for String Quartet (1965; also as the ballet *Ante Room*, 1971); *Souvenirs de Voyage*, clarinet quintet (1967). **VOCAL:** *Moby Dick*, cantata for Soloists, Men's Chorus, and Orch. (1937–38; N.Y., April 11, 1940); *Johnny Appleseed*, cantata for Soloists, Chorus, and Orch. (1940; unfinished); *The Fantasticks*, song cycle for Soprano, Alto, Tenor, Bass, Chorus, and Orch. (1942); songs.

BIBL.: E. Johnson, *B. H.: Hollywood's Music Dramatist* (London, 1977); G. Bruce, *B. H.: Film Music and Narrative* (Ann Arbor, 1985); S. Smith, *A Heart at Fire's Center: The Life and Music of B. H.* (Berkeley, 1991).—NS/LK/DM

Herrmann, Gottfried, German pianist, organist, violinist, conductor, and composer; b. Sondershausen, May 15, 1808; d. Lübeck, June 6, 1878. He first studied violin with his father, and then was a pupil of Seebach (piano) and Mühling (piano and organ); he later studied with Spohr (violin), Hauptmann (theory and composition), and Aloys Schmitt. In 1827 he became 1st violinist in the Hannover Hofkapelle, and then a violinist in the Frankfurt am Main city orch. in 1829. In 1832 he went to Lübeck as deputy organist of the Marienkirche. In 1833 he was promoted to organist and also was made music director of the city. In 1844 he went to Sondershausen as Royal Kapellmeister. In 1852 he returned to Lübeck as conductor. As an instrumentalist and conductor, Herrmann championed the music of many of his contemporaries. Among his own works were operas, syms., concertos, and chamber pieces.—LK/DM

Herrmann, Hugo, German composer, teacher, and organist; b. Ravensburg, April 19, 1896; d. Stuttgart, Sept. 7, 1967. He studied at the Stuttgart Cons., and then with Gmeindl and Schreker at the Berlin Hochschule für Musik. He was organist and choirmaster in Balingen and Ludwigsburg (1919–23), and then at the Church of the Holy Redeemer in Detroit (1923–25). After working in Reutlingen (1925–29; 1932–35) and Wiesbaden (1929–32), he served as director of the Trossingen Städtische Musikschule (1935–62), where he was a prof. (from 1950). Herrmann was an advocate of Gebrauchsmusik, of which he left many examples. He wrote significant pieces for the accordion and also composed for the harmonica.

WORKS: DRAMATIC: O p e r a : *Gazellenhorn* (1929); *Vasantasena* (1930); *Das Wunder* (1937); *Paracelsus* (1943); etc. ORCH.: *Vorspiel zu einer hohen Feier* (1925); Chamber Sym. (1926); 2 organ concertos (both 1928); *Symphonik Musik* (1928); 5 syms. (1928, 1929, 1950, 1951, 1955); Violin Concerto (1930); Harpsichord Concerto (1931); Viola da Gamba Concerto (1931); 2 accordion concertos (1941, 1944); Concerto for Accordion, Harp, and Orch. (1951); *Symphonik Metamorphosen* (1953). CHAMBER: 4 string quartets; Violin Sonata; Piano Trio; 7 *neue Spielmusiken* for Accordion. VOCAL: *Galgenlieder*, chamber cantata for Chorus (1928); *Jesus und seine Jünger*, oratorio for Chorus (1931); *Apokalypse 1945* for 2 Solo Voices and Strings (1945); *Cantata primavera* for Chorus (1956); masses; choruses.

BIBL.: A. Fett, *H. H. sum 60. Geburtstag* (Trossingen, 1956). —NS/LK/DM

Hersch, Fred(erick S.), jazz pianist; b. Cincinnati, Ohio, Oct. 21, 1955. His maternal grandfather is a violinist, and his paternal grandmother was mostly an amateur pianist. When he was three or four he started playing by ear, and at age five he began to study classical piano. He became interested in jazz during his coll. years when he went to a jazz club in Cincinnati. He left coll. (where he had begun to study art history) and started to play around town at jam sessions for about two years. From 1975–77, he attended the New England Cons., in the same class as Jerome Harris and Marty Ehrlich. He graduated and moved to N.Y. in 1977, where he began to work with Jane Ira Bloom, Charlie Haden, Eddie Daniels, Toots Thielemans, and a number of singers. In the early 1980s, he worked with Art Farmer; Farmer and Hersch did a record with Joe Henderson, and he started playing with Henderson as well as subbing in Stan Getz's band during this time. From 1984–89, he ran a recording studio, Classic Sound, in his loft apartment. Since the mid-1980s, he has primarily worked as leader; his first trio with Joey Baron and Marc Johnson didn't perform much, while his

second with Michael Formanek and Jeff Hirschfield, toured a bit in the U.S. In fall 1997 he toured the U.S. and played in London with the BBC Symphony and in solo recital. He taught at the New England Cons. from 1980–86, then privately in N.Y.

When he was about 29, he found out that he was HIV-positive. He has since participated in a number of AIDS fundraising projects. A sensitive soloist and accompanist, he has a unique and brilliant concept of solo piano involving a true counterpoint with the left hand and constant offbeat punctuations.

DISC.: *Horizons* (1984); *Sarabande* (1986); *E.T.C.* (1988); *French Collection* (1989); *Heartsongs* (1989); *Forward Motion* (1991); *Red Square Blue: Jazz Impressions* (1992); *Dancing in the Dark* (1992); *F. H. at Maybeck* (1993); *F. H. Trio Plays...* (1994); *Last Night When We Were Young* (1994); *Point in Time* (1995); *Passion Flower* (1995).—LP

Herschel, Sir (Frederick) William (Friedrich Wilhelm), eminent German-born English astronomer, violinist, organist, and composer; b. Hannover, Nov. 15, 1738; d. Slough, near Windsor, Aug. 25, 1822. The son of a military musician, he was brought up to be a musician. He became an oboist and violinist in the regimental Hannoverian band at age 14 and was sent with it to Durham in 1755. He became director of the Leeds subscription concerts in 1762. He was organist at Halifax Parish Church (1766) and at Octagon Chapel, Bath (1766–82). Long interested in astronomy, he constructed the great "Herschel" telescope, which led to his discovery of the planet Uranus in 1781. He subsequently abandoned music and was made "Astronomer Royal" to King George III in 1781. He became a British citizen in 1802, and was knighted in 1816. Among his compositions are 24 syms., a number of concertos, chamber music, organ pieces, and sacred works, including many anthems.—NS/LK/DM

Herseth, Adolph, outstanding American trumpeter; b. Lake Park, Minn., July 25, 1921. He studied with Marcel LaFosse and Georges Mager at the New England Cons. of Music in Boston (1946–48). In 1948 he was appointed 1st trumpeter of the Chicago Sym. Orch., a position he held with distinction for more than 45 years. He also made many appearances as a soloist, as in the premiere of Husa's Trumpet Concerto (Chicago, Feb. 11, 1988), and was active as a teacher.—NS/LK/DM

Hertel, Johann Wilhelm, distinguished German violinist, harpsichordist, and composer; b. Eisenach, Oct. 9, 1727; d. Schwerin, June 14, 1789. His father, Johann Christian Hertel (b. Oettingen, 1699; d. Strelitz, Oct. 1754), was an accomplished violist and composer. Johann Wilhelm studied with J. H. Heil, and began touring as harpsichord accompanist to his father when he was 12. After violin studies with Carl Hockh in Zerbst, he served as violinist and harpsichordist at the Strelitz court (1744–53). He also studied with Franz Benda in Berlin, and then was court composer in Schwerin from 1754. He wrote much vocal music, including masses, Passions, sacred and secular cantatas, and lieder. He also composed syms. and keyboard concertos. Between 1752 and 1784 he wrote 2 autobiographical accounts of his life, which were ed. and publ. by E. Schenk (Graz and Cologne, 1957).—NS/LK/DM

Hertog, Johannes den, Dutch conductor and composer; b. Amsterdam, Jan. 20, 1904; d. there, Oct. 18, 1982. He studied with his father, Herman Johannes den Hertog, then with Cornelis Dopper. He was director and conductor of the Wagner Soc. in Amsterdam, where, from 1938 to 1941, he was asst. conductor of the Concertgebouw Orch. In 1948 he was appointed conductor of the Flemish Opera in Antwerp, and from 1960 to 1965 was artistic director of the Netherlands Opera in Amsterdam. He wrote an opera, *Pygmalion* (1957), a musical play, *Pandora* (1968), orch. music, chamber pieces, choral works, and songs.—NS/LK/DM

Hertz, Alfred, eminent German-born American conductor; b. Frankfurt am Main, July 15, 1872; d. San Francisco, April 17, 1942. After completing his academic studies, he entered the Hoch Cons. in Frankfurt am Main, where he studied with Anton Urspruch. He then held positions as an opera conductor in Halle (1891–92), Altenburg (1892–95), Barmen-Elberfeld (1895–99), and Breslau (1899–1902). On Nov. 28, 1902, he made his first appearance at the Metropolitan Opera in N.Y. conducting *Lohengrin.* He conducted the first American performance of *Parsifal* there (Dec. 24, 1903), which took place against the wishes of the Wagner family. Consequently, Hertz could no longer obtain permission to conduct Wagner in Germany. He made his Covent Garden debut in London in 1910. From 1915 to 1930 he led the San Francisco Sym. Orch. He also founded the summer series of concerts at the Hollywood Bowl (1922), and conducted more than 100 concerts there; he was affectionately known as the "Father of the Hollywood Bowl." From 1930 he was director of the Federal Music Project for Northern Calif., and conductor of the San Francisco Federal Sym. Orch. His autobiography was publ. in the *San Francisco Chronicle* (May 3–14, 1942). —NS/LK/DM

Hertzka, Emil, Austrian music publisher; b. Budapest, Aug. 3, 1869; d. Vienna, May 9, 1932. He studied chemistry at the Univ. of Vienna and received training in music. In 1893 he joined the firm of the music publisher Weinberger and then in 1901 of Universal Edition, of which he served as director from 1907. He purchased the catalogs of the Wiener Philharmonischer Verlag and the Albert J. Gutmann Co. (which publ. Bruckner and Mahler), and acquired the publication rights to works by many celebrated modern composers (Bartók, Schoenberg, Berg, Weill, and Krenek); also represented Soviet composers. An impassioned believer in the eventual worth of experimental music, he encouraged young composers, and took active part in the organization of concerts of modern music. An Emil Hertzka Foundation was established by his family after his death, for the purpose of helping unknown composers secure performances and publication of their works. —NS/LK/DM

Hertzmann, Erich, German-American musicologist; b. Krefeld, Dec. 14, 1902; d. Berkeley, Calif., March 3, 1963. He studied at the Hoch Cons. in Frankfurt am Main and with Abert, Blume, Hornbostel, Sachs, Schering, and Wolf at the Univ. of Berlin (Ph.D., 1931, with the diss. *Adrian Willaert in der weltlichen Vokalmusik seiner Zeit;* publ in Leipzig, 1931). In 1938 he emigrated to the U.S. and taught at Columbia Univ. until his death; he also lectured at Princeton Univ. (1946–49) and in 1949 held a Guggenheim fellowship. His major field of research was in Renaissance music and the creative process in the music of Mozart and Beethoven, subjects he treated in many articles in German and American music journals.—NS/LK/DM

Hervé (real name, **Florimond Ronger**), French organist, singer, and composer; b. Houdain, near Arras, June 30, 1825; d. Paris, Nov. 3, 1892. He was a chorister at St.-Roch, where he received instruction in singing, organ, and harmony. After studying harmony with Elwart at the Paris Cons., he had lessons in composition with Auber. He served as organist at the Bicêtre asylum (1839–45) and at St. Eustache (1845–53). In 1848 he sang in *Don Quichotte et Sancho Pansa,* an interlude of his own composition, at the Opéra National. In 1851 he conducted at the Palais Royal; in 1854 he opened the Folies-Concertantes, a small theater for the production of pantomimes, *saynètes* (musical comediettas for 2 persons), etc., and, with phenomenal activity, he developed the light French operetta from these diminutive and frivolous pieces, writing both librettos and music, conducting the orch., and often appearing as an actor on the stage. From 1856 to 1869 he led this feverish life in Paris, producing his works at various theaters, and responding to failures by doubling his efforts. In 1870–71, when the Franco-Prussian War and the Commune stopped theatrical activities in Paris, he went to London, where he produced several of his light operas; he revisited London many times afterward; was music director of the Empire Theater there from 1886. He wrote about 50 operettas, of which the most celebrated Parisian scores were *L'Oeil crevé* (Oct. 12, 1867), *Chilpéric* (Oct. 24, 1868), *Le Petit Faust* (April 28, 1869), *La Femme à papa* (Dec. 3, 1879), *Lili* (Jan. 10, 1882), and *Mam'zelle Nitouche* (Jan. 26, 1883). He also wrote a grand opera, *Les Chevaliers de la table ronde* (Paris, Nov. 17, 1866), the ballets *Sport* and *La Rose d'Amour,* and *Les Bagatelles.*

BIBL.: L. Schneider, *Les Maîtres de l'operette française, H. et Charles Lecocq* (Paris, 1924); R. Cariven and D. Ghesquiere, *H., un musicien paradoxale* (Paris, 1992); J. Rouchouse, *H., ou l'Opérette, une histoire* (Paris, 1992).—NS/LK/DM

Hervey, Arthur, Irish writer on music and composer; b. Paris, Jan. 26, 1855; d. London, March 10, 1922. At first intended for the diplomatic service, he embraced a musical career in 1880. He was a critic for *Vanity Fair* (1889–92), and then was on the staff of the London *Morning Post* (1892–1908).

WRITINGS (all publ. in London): *Masters of French Music* (1894); *French Music in the XIXth Century* (1904); *Alfred Bruneau* (1907); *Franz Liszt and His Music* (1911); *Meyerbeer* (1913); *Rubinstein* (1913); *Saint-Saëns* (1921).—NS/LK/DM

Hervig, Richard (Bilderback), American composer and teacher; b. Story City, Iowa, Nov. 24, 1917. He studied English at Augustana Coll. in Sioux Falls (B.A., 1939) and composition with Clapp at the Univ. of Iowa in Iowa City (M.A., 1941; Ph.D., 1947), where he then was on its faculty (1947–52). After serving as assoc. prof. of composition and theory at Long Beach (Calif.) State Coll. (1952–55), he returned to the Univ. of Iowa as a prof. in 1955; he also headed its composition dept., and later was co-director of its Center for New Music (1966–84).

WORKS: ORCH.: 2 syms. (1947, 1950); *Music for a Concert* (1959); *A Diversion* (1962); *President's Fanfare* for Band (1964). CHAMBER: 2 clarinet sonatas (1953, 1971); String Quartet (1955); *Music* for Wind and Percussion (1960); *Diversion* for Trombone and Percussion (1969); *Chamber Music for 6 Players* for Flute, Clarinet, Violin, Double Bass, Piano, and Percussion (1976); *An Entertainment* for Clarinet and Vibraphone or Marimba (1978); *Violin Sonata* (1979); *Lyric Piece* for Trumpet and Harp (1981); Suite for Vibraphone or Marimba (1981); *Airs and Roulades* for Clarinet and Winds (1983); "*As I drew near...*" for Viola and Piano (1984); *The Tree* for 9 Instruments (1984). VOCAL: *Ubi sunt?* for Chorus and Brass Quartet (1964); *Quid est musica?* for Chamber Chorus and 12 Instruments (1972); *5 Romantic Songs* for Medium Voice and Piano (1982); *3 Modern Parables* for Chorus (1983); *Epitaph* for Chorus (1985). —NS/LK/DM

Herz, Henri (actually, **Heinrich**), famous Austrian pianist, teacher, and composer; b. Vienna, Jan. 6, 1803; d. Paris, Jan. 5, 1888. He began piano studies with his father, and after further training with Hünten in Coblenz, he entered the Paris Cons. in 1816, and pursued studies with Pradher, Reicha, and Dourlen, winning the premier prix. He improved himself in Moscheles's style after that virtuoso's visit in 1821. Herz was in high repute as a fashionable teacher and composer, his compositions realizing 3 and 4 times the price of those of his superior contemporaries. In 1831 he made a tour of Germany with the violinist Lafont; visited London in 1834, where at his first concert Moscheles and Cramer played duets with him. From 1842 to 1874 he was a piano prof. at the Paris Cons. He suffered financial losses through partnership with a piano manufacturer, Klepfer, and thereupon undertook a concert tour through the U.S., Mexico, and the West Indies (1845–51). He then established a successful piano factory, his instruments receiving 1st prize at the Paris Exhibition of 1855. As a composer, he acknowledged that he courted the popular taste; his numerous works (over 200) include piano concertos, variations, sonatas, rondos, nocturnes, dances, marches, fantasias, etc. He publ. an interesting and vivid book, *Mes voyages en Amérique* (1866), a reprint of his letters to the *Moniteur Universel*.

BIBL.: R. Lott, *The American Concert Tours of Leopold de Myer, H. H., and Sigismond Thalberg* (diss., City Univ. of N.Y., 1986).—NS/LK/DM

Herz, Joachim, German opera director; b. Dresden, June 15, 1924. After training in piano, clarinet, and theory, he studied at the Dresden Hochschule für Musik (1945–49) and took courses in musicology at the Hum-

boldt Univ. in Berlin (1949–51). In 1950 he began his career as an opera director at the Dresden State Opera, and worked with its touring company (1951–53). After serving as an assistant to Felsenstein at the Berlin Komische Oper (1953–56), he worked at the Cologne Opera (1956–57). In 1957 he became principal stage director of the Leipzig Opera, and later served as its opera director (1959–76). During his Leipzig years, he staged *Die Meistersinger von Nürnberg* for the inauguration of the new opera house in 1960, and later staged a *Ring* cycle replete with social significance (1973–76). From 1976 to 1980 he was Intendant of the Berlin Komische Oper. He was principal opera director at the Dresden State Opera from 1981 to 1991. In 1985 he staged *Der Freischütz* at the inauguration of the restored Semper Oper in Dresden. His productions have been staged in various European and North American opera centers. Herz has lectured widely at home and abroad.

WRITINGS: With W. Felsenstein, *Musiktheater: Beiträge zur Methodik und su Inszenierungskonzeptionen* (Leipzig, 1970; 2nd ed., 1976); *Joachim Herz über Musiktheater* (Berlin, 1974); *Und Figaro lässt sich scheiden: Oper als Idee und Interpretation* (Munich, 1985); *Joachim Herz: Theater, Kunst des erfüllten Augenblicks: Briefe, Vorträge, Notate, Gespräche, Essays* (Berlin, 1989).

BIBL.: H.-J. Irmer and W. Stein, *J. H.: Regisseur im Musiktheater* (Berlin, 1977); U. and U. Müller, eds., *Opern und Opernfiguren: Festschrift für J. H.* (Anif, 1989); I. Kobán, ed., *J. H.: Interviews* (Berlin, 1990).—NS/LK/DM

Herzog, Emilie, Swiss soprano; b. Ermatingen, Dec. 17, 1859; d. Aarburg, Sept. 16, 1923. She studied in Zürich and Munich. She made her debut in a minor role at the Munich Court Opera in 1880, and afterward sang in other German opera houses, including Bayreuth. In 1889 she was engaged at the Berlin Royal Opera, where she became one of the best interpreters of soubrette roles; also gave recitals in Germany as a lieder artist. She made guest appearances in the opera houses of London, Paris, Vienna, and Brussels, and in 1896 sang at the Bolshoi Theater in Moscow; she made her Metropolitan Opera debut in N.Y. as a Flower Maiden in *Parsifal* on Nov. 24, 1904. Returning to Europe, she continued to sing at the Berlin Royal Opera (until 1910). She then taught at the Zürich Cons. (1910–22).—NS/LK/DM

Herzog, George (actually, **György**), Hungarian-born American ethnomusicologist; b. Budapest, Dec. 11, 1901; d. Indianapolis, Nov. 4, 1983. He studied musicology and anthropology in Budapest and Berlin. In 1925 he went to America and became a research assoc. in anthropology at the Univ. of Chicago in 1929. He was a member (1930–31) of its expedition to Liberia, where he made a thorough study of West African music, and then was on the faculty of Yale Univ. (1932–35). He was a visiting lecturer at Columbia Univ. in 1936–37, and took his Ph.D. there in 1937 with the diss. *A Comparison of Pueblo and Pima Musical Styles*, which was publ. in the *Journal of American Folklore*, XLIX, 1936. He subsequently was a visiting asst. prof. there (1937–38), and then an asst. prof. of anthropology (1939–48). In 1948 he was appointed prof. of anthropology and folk music at Ind. Univ. in Bloomington; was made prof.

emeritus in 1962. In 1962 he was made an honorary member of the American Musicological Soc. He publ. *Jabo Proverbs from Liberia: Maxims in the Life of a Native Tribe* (with C. Blooah; Oxford, 1936) and *Research in Primitive and Folk Music in the United States: A Survey* (Washington, D.C., 1936).—**NS/LK/DM**

Herzog, Johann Georg, German organist, pedagogue, and composer; b. Hummendorf, near Kronach, Aug. 5, 1822; d. Munich, Feb. 3, 1909. He was trained at the music school in Schmölz, and began his career as an organist when he was 11. He then went to Munich, where he was made organist (1843) and cantor (1848) of the Evangelical Church. From 1850 he also was prof. of organ at the Cons. In 1854 he went to Erlangen as director of the Univ.'s church music inst. He also was organist of the Univ. church and a singing teacher at the Gymnasium (1859–79). From 1861 he attracted notice with a series of historical organ concerts. In 1866 he was awarded an honorary Ph.D. After his retirement in 1888, he settled in Munich. Herzog was a prolific composer of organ music and sacred vocal works. He publ. a number of pedagogical works, several of which were widely used in Europe.

BIBL.: M. Herzog, *Erinnerungen an Dr. J.G. H.* (Munich, 1915).—**NS/LK/DM**

Herzogenberg, (Leopold) Heinrich (Picot de Peccaduc), Freiherr von, Austrian composer; b. Graz, June 10, 1843; d. Wiesbaden, Oct. 9, 1900. He entered the Univ. of Vienna as a student of philosophy and law in 1861, then studied composition at the Cons. with Dessoff (1862–64), through whom he met and became a close friend of Brahms. He went to Leipzig in 1872. He was one of the founders of the Bach-Verein (1874) and served as its director (1875–85). He then became prof. of composition at the Berlin Hochschule für Musik (1885), taking charge of its master class (1889). His activities were halted by ill health for a time, but he resumed teaching in 1892, retiring in 1900. As a composer, he was greatly influenced by Schumann, Wagner, and Brahms. His wife, Elisabeth (née von Stockhausen; b. Paris, April 13, 1847; d. San Remo, Jan. 7, 1892), was a fine pianist and, like her husband, a close friend of Brahms. See M. Kalbeck, ed., *Johannes Brahms im Briefwechsel mit Heinrich und Elisabeth von Herzogenberg* (Berlin, 1907).

WORKS: ORCH.: 3 syms.: No. 1, *Odysseus* (1876), No. 2 (1885), and No. 3 (1890); Concerto for Flute, Oboe, Clarinet, 2 Bassoons, 2 Horns, and String Orch. (1879). **CHAMBER:** Piano Quintet (1876); Quintet for Piano, Oboe, Clarinet, Horn, and Bassoon (1888); Quintet for 2 Violins, 2 Violas, and Cello (1892); 2 piano quartets (1892, 1897); 5 string quartets (1876, 1884, 1884, 1884, 1890); 2 piano trios (1877, 1884); Trio for Piano, Oboe, and Horn (1889); 2 string trios (1879); piano pieces; organ music. **VOCAL: Sacred Choral:** Requiem for Chorus and Orch. (1891); *Totenfeier,* cantata for Soloists, Chorus, and Orch. (1894); Mass for Soloists, Chorus, and Orch. (1895); *Die Geburt Christi,* oratorio for Soloists, Chorus, Children's Chorus, Oboe, Harmonium, Organ, and Strings (1895); *Die Passion,* oratorio for Soloists, Chorus, Harmonium, Organ, and Strings (1896); *Erntefeier,* oratorio for Soloists, Chorus, Organ, and Orch. (1899); *Gott ist gegenwärtig,* cantata for Chorus and Orch. (1901); 2 biblical scenes: *Der Seesturm* for Baritone, Chorus, Organ, and Strings (1903) and *Das kananäische Weib* for Soprano, Baritone, Men's Voices, and Organ (1903); also motets, Psalms, liturgical songs, etc. **Secular Choral:** *Columbus,* dramatic cantata for Soloists, Men's Voices, and Orch. (c. 1870); *Der Stern des Lieds,* ode for Chorus and Orch. (1887); *Die Weihe der Nacht* for Alto, Chorus, and Orch. (1887); *Nannas Klage* for Soprano, Alto, Chorus, and Orch. (1888). **OTHER:** Various works with piano accompaniment or unaccompanied; songs.

BIBL.: B. Wiechert, *H. v. H., 1843–1900: Studien zu Leben und Werk* (Göttingen, 1997).—**NS/LK/DM**

Hesch, Wilhelm (real name, **Vilém Heš**), Bohemian bass; b. Týnec nad Labem, July 3, 1860; d. Vienna, Jan. 3, 1908. He studied with Jan Ludvík Lukes and František Pivoda. On Dec. 5, 1880, he made his operatic debut as Kečal in *The Bartered Bride* in Brünn. He then sang with the Pištěk Theater Co. before becoming a principal member of the Prague National Theater in 1882. After singing at the Hamburg Opera (1893–96), he was a leading member of the Vienna Court Opera (from 1896). He was especially notable in buffo roles, particularly in Smetana's operas and as Papageno, Leporello, Dr. Bartolo, and Beckmesser.—**NS/LK/DM**

Hesdin, Nicolle des Celliers de, French composer; b. place and date unknown; d. Beauvais, Aug. 21, 1538. He was master of the choirboys at Beauvais Cathedral from 1536. Among his esteemed works were masses, mass sections, 2 Magnificats, motets, and chansons.—**LK/DM**

Heseltine, Philip (Arnold), brilliant English composer and writer on music who used the pen name Peter Warlock; b. London, Oct. 30, 1894; d. (suicide) there, Dec. 17, 1930. He studied at Eton with Colin Taylor (1908–10), in Germany, and at Oxford. A meeting with Delius in France in 1910 influenced him profoundly in the direction of composition, and he adopted a style that was intimately connected with English traditions of the Elizabethan period and yet revealed impressionistic undertones in harmonic writing. Another influence was that of Bernard van Dieren, from whom he absorbed an austerely contrapuntal technique. He publ. all his musical works under his pen name. He was a conscientious objector during World War I. In 1917–18 he was in Ireland, and after the Armistice he returned to London. In 1920 he founded the progressive journal of musical opinion the *Sackbut.* He wrote criticism and made transcriptions of early English music. Suffering from depression, he committed suicide by gas in his London flat. He ed. (with P. Wilson) 300 early songs, and was co-editor of Oxford Choral Songs and the Oxford Orchestral Series, a collection of early English and Italian dances.

WRITINGS (all publ. in London): *Frederick Delius* (1923); *Songs of the Garden* (1925); *The English Ayre* (1926); with C. Gray, *Carlo Gesualdo, Prince of Venosa: Musician and Murderer* (1926); ed. with J. Lindsay, *J. Harrington: The Metamorphosis of Ajax* (1927); *Thomas Whythorne* (1929); *Merry-go-down* (1929); *English*

Ayres, Elisabethan and Jacobean: A Discourse (1932); *Giles Earle his Books* (1932).

WORKS: ORCH.: *An Old Song* (1917); *Serenade for Delius on his 60th Birthday* for Strings (1921–22); *Capriol,* suite for Strings (1926; for Orch., 1928). **OTHER:** *Corpus Christi* for Soprano, Baritone, and String Quartet (1919–23); *The Curlew,* song cycle for Tenor, Flute, English Horn, and String Quartet (1920–21; rev. 1922); *3 Carols* for Chorus and Orch. (1923); *Sorrow's Lullaby* for Soprano, Baritone, and String Quartet (1927); other choral works and solo songs.

BIBL.: C. Gray, *Peter Warlock: A Memoir of P. H.* (London, 1934); F. Tomlinson, *A Peter Warlock Handbook* (2 vols., Rickmansworth, 1974, 1977); I. Copley, *The Music of Peter Warlock: A Critical Survey* (London, 1979); M. Pilkington, *Gurney, Ireland, Quilter, and Warlock* (London, 1989); D. Cox and J. Bishops, eds., *Peter Warlock: A Centenary Celebration: The Man-his Music-his World* (London, 1994); I. Parrott, *The Crying Curlew: Peter Warlock: Family & Influences: Centenary 1994* (Llandysul, Dyfed, 1994); B. Smith, *Peter Warlock, The Life of P. H.* (Oxford, 1994); B. Collins, *Peter Warlock: The Composer* (Aldershot, 1996). —NS/LK/DM

Hess, Dame Myra, eminent English pianist; b. London, Feb. 25, 1890; d. there, Nov. 25, 1965. She was a student of Julian Pascal and Orlando Morgan at the Guildhall School of Music in London; when she was 12, she won a scholarship to the Royal Academy of Music in London, where she completed her studies with Tobias Matthay. On Nov. 14, 1907, she made her debut as soloist in Beethoven's 4th Piano Concerto under Beecham's direction in London, and then performed throughout England. In 1922 she made her U.S. debut in N.Y. Thereafter she toured widely in Europe and the U.S. In 1936 she was made a Commander of the Order of the British Empire. In 1939 she organized the National Gallery Concerts in London, and performed there regularly throughout the course of World War II. Her perseverance in the face of the blitz did much to bolster morale during England's "finest hour," and in 1941 a grateful King George VI made her a Dame Commander of the Order of the British Empire. After the War, Hess commenced touring again and continued her notable career until her farewell concert in 1962. In addition to her solo engagements, she also played in duo concerts with her cousin Irene Scharrer. Hess was greatly admired for her interpretations of Mozart, Beethoven, and Schumann. In 1926 she publ. her own piano transcription of Bach's *Jesu, Joy of Man's Desiring* (from the Cantata No. 147), which became a great favorite with her audiences.

BIBL.: D. Lassimonne and H. Ferguson, eds., *M. H., By Her Friends* (London, 1966); M. McKenna, *M. H.: A Portrait* (London, 1976).—NS/LK/DM

Hess, Joachim, Dutch organist, harpsichordist, and music scholar of German descent; b. Leeuwarden, Sept. 24, 1732; d. Zeist, Dec. 27, 1819. While still a youth, he served as organist at the Lutheran church in Leeuwarden. After serving as organist at the Lutheran church in Gouda (1749–53) and at the Grote Kerk in Maasluis (1753–54), he returned to Gouda as organist at the Grote Kerk (1754–1813). Hess was an authority on the organ. His *Dispositien der merkwaardigste Kerk-Orgelen, welken in de zeven vereenigde provincien als mede in Duytsland en elders aagetroffen worden* (Gouda, 1774), continued in MS (c. 1815), and in *Korte schets van de allereerste uitvinding en verdere voortgang der orgelen tot op dezen tijd* (Gouda, 1810), are primary sources on the history of organ building. He also wrote two guides to performing practice, *Luister van het orgel* and *Over de vereischten in eenen organist* (Gouda, 1807).—LK/DM

Hess, Ludwig, German tenor and composer; b. Marburg, March 23, 1877; d. Berlin, Feb. 5, 1944. He studied singing with Vidal in Milan. He gave concerts of German lieder throughout Europe, specializing in the modern repertoire. He made a successful tour of the U.S. and Canada in 1911, and conducted a choral society in Königsberg (1917–20). He then settled in Berlin. He wrote the operas *Abu und Nu* (Danzig, 1919), *Vor Edens Pforte,* after Byron (n.d.), and *Kranion* (Erfurt, 1933), as well as a Sym., *Himmelskonig mit musizierenden Engeln,* symphonic poem, *Ariadne,* cantata, many choral works, and numerous songs. He publ. *Die Behandlung der Stimme vor, während und nach der Mutation* (Marburg, 1927).—NS/LK/DM

Hess, Willy, noted Swiss musicologist; b. Winterthur, Oct. 12, 1906; d. there, May 9, 1997. He studied piano and theory at the Zürich Cons. and musicology at the Univ. of Zürich. He played bassoon in the Winterthur Stadtorchester (1942–71). As a musicologist, he devoted most of his effort to the compilation of a Beethoven catalog. He ed. a valuable *Verzeichnis der nicht in der Gesamtausgabe veröffentlichten Werke Ludwig van Beethovens* (Wiesbaden, 1957); also ed. the extensive supplement *Ludwig van Beethoven: Sämtliche Werke: Supplement zur Gesamtausgabe* (14 vols., Wiesbaden, 1959–71). His other important writings include *Ludwig van Beethoven* (Geneva, 1946); *Beethovens Oper Fidelio und ihre drei Fassungen* (Zürich, 1953); *Beethoven* (Zürich, 1956; 2nd ed., rev., 1976); *Die Harmonie der Künste* (Vienna, 1960); *Die Dynamik der musikalischen Formbildung* (2 vols., Vienna, 1960; 1964); *Vom Doppelantlitz des Bösen in der Künst, dargestellt am Beispiel der Musik* (Munich, 1963); *Vom Metaphysischen im Künstlerischen* (Winterthur, 1963); *Parteilose Künst, parteilose Wissenschaft* (Tutzing, 1967); *Beethoven-Studien* (Munich, 1972); also an autobiography, *Aus meinem Leben: Erlebnisse, Bekenntnisse, Betrachtungen* (Zürich, 1976). He was also a prolific composer, including in his works several fairy-tale operas, a Sym., a Sonata for Bassoon and Small Orch., a Horn Concerto, and numerous pieces of chamber music, including a curious work for double bassoon and string quartet.—NS/LK/DM

Hesse, Adolph (Friedrich), German organist, conductor, and composer; b. Breslau, Aug. 30, 1808; d. there, Aug. 5, 1863. His father was an organ builder, and Hesse received his first instruction from him; he further profited by the advice of Hummel and Spohr. He was church organist at Breslau and also active as a conductor. He wrote 6 syms., 5 overtures, the oratorio *Tobias,* and much organ music.—NS/LK/DM

Hesse, Ernst Christian, German viola da gambist and composer, father of **Ludwig Christian Hesse;** b.

Grossgottern, April 14, 1676; d. Darmstadt, May 16, 1762. He learned to play the viola da gamba in his youth. In 1692 he entered the service of the Giessen court, and also studied law at the Univ. of Giessen. In 1694 he went to the Darmstadt court, where he pursued music training with W. C. Briegel. After further studies wiht A. Forqueray and M. Marais in Paris (1698–1701), he returned to Darmstadt as a court musician and as secretary for war; he also toured widely as a virtuoso in Europe. From 1707 to 1714 he was Kapelldirektor in Darmstadt, and continued to serve the court thereafter in non-musical capacities; he also continued making concert tours. In 1713 he married **Johanna Döbricht**. His extant works comprise the Italian opera, *La fedeltà coronata* (c. 1712), a divertimento, *Apollo in tempe*, a Flute Sonata, and a duo for Viola da Gamba.—**NS/LK/DM**

Hesse, Ludwig Christian, German viola da gambist and composer, son of **Ernst Christian Hesse;** b. Darmstadt, Nov. 8, 1716; d. there, Sept. 15, 1772. After music training with his father, he went to Halle as a law student. He served as a lawyer and chamber musician at the Darmstadt court (1738–41), and then was in the service of the Royal Chapel in Berlin. In 1766 he was made a chamber musician and legal advisor to the Prince of Prussia. His compositions were lost during World War II.—**LK/DM**

Hesse, Max, German music publisher; b. Sondershausen, Feb. 18, 1858; d. Leipzig, Nov. 24, 1907. In 1880 he founded a publishing house, with headquarters in Leipzig, and in 1915 the firm moved to Berlin. Among its most important publications were the 3rd through 11th eds. of Riemann's *Musik Lexikon* (1887–1929) and H. J. Moser's *Musik-Lexikon*. Great devastation was wreaked on the physical materials of the firm by air bombardment during World War II. After the war the firm was re- established in Berlin.

BIBL.: *80 Jahre M. H.s Verlag* (Berlin, 1960).—**NS/LK/DM**

Hesse-Bukowska, Barbara, Polish pianist; b. Łódź, June 1, 1930. She studied piano with Margerita Trombini- Kazuro, then continued her musical education at the Warsaw Academy of Music. In 1949 she won 2nd prize in the Chopin Competition in Warsaw, and in 1953 she was awarded the Chopin Prize at the Long-Thibaud Competition in Paris. From that time she made regular appearances in London, Paris, Moscow, Vienna, and Rome, and also made extensive tours of India, Egypt, and Japan. In 1963 she became a member of the faculty of the Academy of Music in Wroclaw, and in 1973 she joined the Academy of Music in Warsaw. She is regarded as a fine interpreter of Chopin and also a leading champion of contemporary Polish music. —**NS/LK/DM**

Hesselberg, Edouard Gregory, Latvian-American pianist, teacher, and composer; b. Riga, May 3, 1870; d. Los Angeles, June 12, 1935. He studied at the Cons. of the Moscow Phil. Soc. (1888–92), and later was a private pupil of Anton Rubinstein. In 1892 he went to the U.S., where he taught at the Ithaca Cons. (1895–96), the Music Academy in Denver (1896–1900), the Cons. of Music at Wesleyan Coll. (1900–05), Belmont Coll. in Nashville (1905–12), and the Toronto Cons. (1912–18). He wrote *Russian Suite* and *Russian Rhapsody* for Orch. and piano pieces. He also made arrangements for 2 pianos of works by Bach, Chopin, and Schubert. —**NS/LK/DM**

Hessenberg, Kurt, German composer; b. Frankfurt am Main, Aug. 17, 1908; d. there, June 17, 1994. He studied in Leipzig with Raphael (composition) and Teichmüller (piano). In 1933 he was appointed to the faculty of the Hoch Cons. in Frankfurt am Main. Possessing great facility in composition, Hessenberg evolved an effective idiom, fundamentally Classical, but containing Wagnerian elements in dramatic passages, with occasional infusion of prudential modernistic devices. His most successful work was *Struwwelpeter* (1933), a suite for Small Orch. based on a well-known German children's tale. He further wrote 3 syms. (1936, 1943, 1954), Piano Concerto (1940), Concerto for 2 Pianos and Orch. (1950), *Concerto for Orchestra* (1958), 2 flute sonatas (1932), 5 string quartets (1934–67), Cello Sonata (1941), Violin Sonata (1942), String Trio (1949), Piano Trio (1950), numerous piano pieces, a number of cantatas, and a multitude of lieder.

BIBL.: K. Laux, *K. H.* (Essen, 1949).—**NS/LK/DM**

Hetsch, (Karl) Ludwig Friedrich, German conductor; b. Stuttgart, April 26, 1806; d. Mannheim, June 28, 1872. He studied with Abeille. He was attached to the court of the King of Württemberg, and then conducted in Heidelberg (1846–56) and in Mannheim (from 1856 until his death). He wrote an opera, *Ryno* (Stuttgart, 1833), orch. works, and chamber music. —**NS/LK/DM**

Hétu, Jacques (Joseph Robert), Canadian composer and teacher; b. Trois-Rivières, Quebec, Aug. 8, 1938. He studied piano, harmony, and Gregorian chant at the Univ. of Ottawa (1955–56), then took courses in composition and counterpoint with Clermont Pépin, in harmony with Isabelle Delorme, and in fugue with Jean Papineau-Couture at the Montreal Cons. (1956–61; premier prix in composition, 1961). He also received instruction in composition from Foss at the Berkshire Music Center in Tanglewood, Mass. (summer, 1959), and completed his training in Paris with Dutilleux (composition diploma, 1963) at the École Normale de Musique and with Messiaen (analysis) at the Cons. (1962–63). He taught at Laval Univ. in Quebec (1963–77) and at the Univ. of Montreal (1972–73; 1978–79), then was a prof. at the Univ. of Quebec in Montreal (from 1979). In his music, he makes use of permissible modern devices, while hewing to Classical formal conventions.

WORKS: ORCH.: 3 syms.: No. 1 for Strings (1959), No. 2 (1961), and No. 3 (1971); *Adagio et Rondo* for String Orch. or String Quartet (1960); *Rondo* for Cello and String Orch. (1965); Double Concerto for Violin, Piano, and Chamber Orch. (1967); *L'Apocalypse* (1967); Piano Concerto (1969); *Passacaille* (1970); *Fantaisie* for Piano and Orch. (1973); *Antinomie* (1977); Bassoon

Concerto (1979); *Mirages* (1981); *Symphonie concertante* for Flute, Oboe, Clarinet, Bassoon, Horn, and Strings (1986); Clarinet Concerto (1987); Trumpet Concerto (1987); *Images de la Révolution* for the bicentennial of the French Revolution (1988); *Poème* for Strings (1989); Flute Concerto (1991; Ottawa, Feb. 26, 1992). CHAMBER: Trio for Flute, Oboe, and Harpsichord (1960); 4 Pieces for Flute and Piano (1965); Wind Quintet (1967); *Variations* for Violin or Viola or Cello (1967); String Quartet (1972); *Aria* for Flute and Piano (1977); *Incantation* for Oboe and Piano (1978); Suite for Guitar (1986); *Sérénade* for Flute and String Quartet (1988); piano pieces; organ music. VOCAL: *Les Clartés de la Nuit* for Soprano and Piano (1972; also for Soprano and Orch., 1987); *Les Djinns* for Chorus, 6 Percussion, and Piano (1975); *Les Abîmes du Rêve* for Bass and Orch. (1982); *Missa pro trecentesimo anno* for Chorus and Orch. (1985); *Les Illusions fanées* for Chorus (1988).—NS/LK/DM

Heuberger, Richard (Franz Joseph), Austrian conductor, music critic, and composer; b. Graz, June 18, 1850; d. Vienna, Oct. 27, 1914. He received musical training from W. Mayer in Graz. He settled in Vienna, where he became conductor of the Singakademie in 1878. He was music critic of the *Wiener Tageblatt* (1881–96), the *Neue Freie Presse* (1896–1901), and the *Neue Musikalische Presse* (1904–14). In 1902 he became a prof. at the Cons. As a composer, Heuberger scored his greatest success with the operetta *Der Opernball* (Vienna, Jan. 5, 1898).

WRITINGS: *Im Foyer: Gesammelte Essays über das Opernrepertoire der Gegenwart* (Lepizig, 1901); *Musikalische Skizzen* (Leipzig, 1901); *Franz Schubert* (Berlin, 1902; 3rd ed., rev., 1920, by H. von der Pfordten); *Anleitung zum Modulieren* (Vienna, 1910).

WORKS: DRAMATIC (all 1st perf. in Vienna unless otherwise given): Opera: *Abenteuer einer Neujahrsnacht* (Leipzig, 1886); *Manuel Venegas* (Leipzig, March 27, 1889; rev. as *Mirjam, oder Das Maifest*, Jan. 20, 1894); *Barfüssele* (Dresden, 1905). Operetta: *Der Opernball* (Jan. 5, 1898); *Ihre Excellenz* (Jan. 28, 1899; rev. as *Eine entzückende Frau*); *Der Sechsuhrzug* (Berlin, Jan. 17, 1900); *Das Baby* (Oct. 3, 1902); *Der Fürst von Düsterstein* (March 3, 1909); *Don Quixote* (Dec. 1, 1910). Ballet: *Struwwelpeter* (Dresden, 1897). OTHER: Choral music and songs.

BIBL.: H. Hughes, *R. H.'s Erinnerungen an Johannes Brahms: The Life, Work, and Times of Johannes Brahms as Revealed by a Contemporary* (diss., Ball State Univ., 1987).—NS/LK/DM

Heugel, Henry, Swiss-French music theorist, father of **Jacques-Léopold Heugel;** b. Neuchâtel, Switzerland, Sept. 26, 1789; d. Nantes, France, May 2, 1841. He studied in Paris with Galin and Reicha. He developed a "méthode de méloplaste" along the lines of Galin's system. He publ. *Nouvelle méthode pour l'enseignement de la musique inventée par H. Heugel et developpée par lui de manière a permettre d'apprendre sans maître* (1832). —NS/LK/DM

Heugel, Jacques Léopold, French music publisher, son of **Henry Heugel;** b. La Rochelle, March 1, 1811; d. Paris, Nov. 12, 1883. In 1839 he became a partner of the publisher Jean Antoine Meissonier (b. Marseilles, Dec. 8, 1783; d. Saint Germain-en-Laye, 1857), who had commenced business in Paris in 1812. They took over the important weekly *Le ménestrel* in 1839, which had been founded by Jules Lovy in 1833; the firm continued its publication until 1940, except for a break during the Franco- Prussian War and World War I. After Meissonier retired in 1842, Heugel became sole owner of the firm. His son, Henri Georges Heugel (b. Paris, May 3, 1844; d. there, May 11, 1916), became a partner in 1876 and his successor at his death. His nephew, Paul Chevalier Heugel (1861–1931), provided the funds for the purchase of the Hartmann catalog in 1891 and entered the firm as partner, later serving as its director (1916–19). His son, Jacques Paul Heugel (1890–1979), then headed the firm until 1944, when it became a société anonyme and he was made president and general director. His sons, François Henri and Philippe Gérard Heugel, joined the firm in 1947 and eventually took control of its affairs. In 1980 it merged with Leduc. The Heugel catalog is impressive, especially notable for its scores of major French composers of the 19th and 20th centuries. It also publishes the comprehensive practical eds. of early music known as Le pupitre, which was established in 1967.—NS/LK/DM

Heugel, Johannes, German composer; b. c. 1505; d. Kassel, by Jan. 31, 1585. He entered the service of the Hesse court in Kassel about 1533 as a trumpeter and singer. From 1547 he fulfilled the duties of a Kapellmeister, and also was active as a court composer. His music reflects the influence of the post-Josquin Flemish school. Among his almost 500 compositions are 20 Magnificat settings, over 150 motets, 16 Psalm motets, many German Psalms, and sacred German songs.

BIBL.: S. Cramer, *J. H. (ca. 1510–1584/85): Studien zu seinen lateinischen Motetten* (Kassel, 1994).—LK/DM

Heuss, Alfred (Valentin), Swiss-born German musicologist, music critic, and composer; b. Chur, Jan. 27, 1877; d. Gaschwitz, July 9, 1934. He studied at the Stuttgart Cons. (1896–98), then at the Akademie der Tonkunst in Munich, attending the Univ. of Munich simultaneously (1898–99); from 1899 to 1902 he studied musicology with Kretzschmar at the Univ. of Leipzig (Ph.D., 1903, with the diss. *Die Instrumentalstücke des "Orfeo" und die venezianischen Opernsinfonien*; publ. in the *Sammelbände der Internationalen Musik-Gesellschaft*, IV, 1902–03). He was music critic of the *Signale* (1902–05), *Leipziger Volkszeitung* (1905–12), and *Leipziger Zeitung* (1912–18), and ed. of the *Zeitschrift der Internationalen Musik- Gesellschaft* (1904–14), to which he contributed valuable articles. He was also ed.-in-chief of the *Zeitschrift für Musik* (1921–29). As a composer, he wrote mainly songs.

WRITINGS (all publ. in Leipzig): *Anton Bruckner: Te Deum* (1908); *Johann Sebastian Bachs Matthäuspassion* (1909); *Franz Liszt: Missa solemnis* (c. 1910); *Erläuterungen zu Franz Liszts Sinfonien und sinfonischen Dichtungen* (1912); *Kammermusikabende: Erläuterungen von Werken der Kammermusik-Literatur* (1919); *Beethoven* (1921).—NS/LK/DM

Heward, Leslie (Hays), esteemed English conductor; b. Littletown, Liversedge, Yorkshire, Dec. 8,

1897; d. Birmingham, May 3, 1943. He studied with his father, an organist; then continued his training at the Manchester Cathedral Choir School, where he served as asst. cathedral organist. He was made organist of St. Andrew's, Ancoats (1914), and then won a scholarship in composition to the Royal Coll. of Music in London (1917), where he studied with Stanford and Vaughan Williams. After appearing as a conductor with the British National Opera Co., he was music director of the South African Broadcasting Corp. and conductor of the Cape Town Orch. (1924–27). He then was conductor of the City of Birmingham Orch. (from 1930). He was acknowledged as one of England's finest conductors. He was also a composer, but he destroyed many of his MSS; his works included 2 unfinished operas, a symphonic poem, several orch. suites, choral works, chamber music, and songs.

BIBL.: E. Blom, ed., *L. H.: A Memorial Volume* (London, 1944).—NS/LK/DM

Hewitt, Harry Donald, unimaginably fecund American composer; b. Detroit, March 4, 1921. His paternal grandmother was a Winnebago Indian. He was completely autodidact in music, and achieved such mastery of composition in quaquaversal directions without stylistic prejudice, that in some 40 years of writing music he produced 3,300 works in every conceivable manner, using every speculative idiom, from jazz to pop, couched in every available tonal, atonal, polytonal, and incommensurate oriental scale. Entirely free from supercilious elitism, he was not ashamed to admit the authorship of a *Hymn to Mickey Mouse* or an *Homage to Bugs Bunny*. None of his 30 syms. were ever performed. The brute weight of his collected MSS is 1 1/2 tons.

WORKS: DRAMATIC: O p e r a : *The Shadowy Waters; Moby Dick; The Song of Kawas; The Happy Hymadrayad; Doctor Too-Big; Clara's Friend; Remember George; Pierre.* **OTHER:** 30 syms., 2 of which, *Amerindian Symphony* and *War Symphony*, are unnumbered; over 300 works for Orch., including 19 symphonic poems: *Kabir, The Manchild, The Night, Fairyland, The Mysterious Sea, The Seasons, In the Shade of the Upas Tree, New Year's Eclogue, The House of Sleep, Raggedy Ann, Wa-Kon-Da, The Happy Garden, In a Green Shade, 7, Selene, The Wheel, Aldebaran, Angkor,* and *Anglesley Abbey*; 2 piano concertos; Trombone Concerto; Guitar Concerto; 18 piano sonatas; 23 string quartets; and more than 100 other works for diverse chamber ensembles, e.g., *Preludes* for Flute and Marimba, *Fantasia* for Flute and Horn, *Leaf in the Stream* for Oboe and Tuba, etc.; uncountable songs and choruses.—NS/LK/DM

Hewitt, Helen (Margaret), American musicologist; b. Granville, N.Y., May 2, 1900; d. Denton, Tex., March 19, 1977. She studied at Vassar Coll. (B.A., 1921) and the Eastman School of Music in Rochester, N.Y. (B.M., 1925), and then took lessons in organ with Widor and in harmony with Boulanger at the American Cons. in Fontainebleau (1926), and in organ with Farnam at the Curtis Inst. of Music in Philadelphia (1928–30). After taking her Master of Sacred Music degree at Union Theological Seminary (1932), she pursued training in musicology with Lang at Columbia Univ. (M.A., 1933) and Besseler at the Univ. of Heidelberg; she then com-

pleted her education at Radcliffe Coll. (Ph.D., 1938, with the diss. *O Petrucci: Harmonice Musices Odhecaton A*; publ. in Cambridge, Mass., 1942; 2nd ed., 1946). In 1947 she received a Guggenheim fellowship. She taught at the State Normal School in Potsdam, N.Y. (1925–28), Fla. State Coll. for Women (1938–39), Hunter Coll. (1942), and North Tex. State Univ. in Denton (1942–69). She ed. the valuable compilation *Doctoral Dissertations in Musicology* (Denton, 1952; 4th ed., rev., 1965) and contributed important articles on Renaissance music to various journals.—NS/LK/DM

Hewitt, James, English-born American composer, publisher, organist, and violinist; b. Dartmoor, June 4, 1770; d. Boston, Aug. 1, 1827. He played in London as a youth. In 1792 he went to America and settled in N.Y., where he was described as one of the "professors of music from the Opera House, Hanover Square, and Professional Concerts under the direction of Haydn, Pleyel, etc., London." On Sept. 21, 1792, he gave a benefit concert with the violinists J. Gehot and B. Bergmann, the flutist W. Young, and a cellist named Phillips, which included Hewitt's Overture in 9 Movements, expressive of a battle. Subsequently, Young and Gehot went to Philadelphia, and in 1793 Hewitt, Bergmann, and Phillips gave a series of 6 subscription concerts; at their 5th concert (March 25, 1793) they presented for the first time in America Haydn's *Passion of Our Saviour* (i.e., *The 7 Last Words*); in 1794 Henri Capron joined Hewitt in promoting his "City Concerts"; meanwhile, Hewitt became the leader of the Old American Co. Orch., and in 1795 gave up his activities in connection with the subscription concerts. In 1798 he bought out the N.Y. branch of Carr's "Musical Repository" and established a publishing business of his own. In 1811 he went to Boston, where he played organ at Trinity Church and was in charge of the music presented at the Federal St. Theatre. In 1816 he returned to N.Y.; also traveled in the South. In N.Y. he was director of the Park Theatre. Among his works are the ballad operas *Tammany* (N.Y., 1794, under the auspices of the Tammany Soc.; only 1 song, *The Death Song of the Cherokee Indians*, survives), *The Patriot or Liberty Asserted* (1794), *The Mysterious Marriage* (1799), *Columbus* (1799), *Pizarro, or The Spaniards in Peru* (1800), *Robin Hood* (1800), *The Spanish Castle* (N.Y., Dec. 5, 1800), and *The Wild Goose Chase* (1800). Other works include an overture, *Demophon*, a set of 3 piano sonatas, *Battle of Trenton* for Piano, *The 4th of July—A Grand Military Sonata for the Pianoforte*, etc. His eldest son, John Hill Hewitt (b. N.Y., July 12, 1801; d. Baltimore, Oct. 7, 1890), studied at West Point Academy; was a theatrical manager, newspaperman, and drillmaster of Confederate recruits in the Civil War. He wrote poems and plays, about 300 songs (*The Minstrel's Return from the War, All Quiet along the Potomac, Our Native Land, The Mountain Bugle*, etc.), cantatas (*Flora's Festival, The Fairy Bridal, The Revelers,* and *The Musical Enthusiast*), and ballad operas (*Rip Van Winkle, The Vivandiere, The Prisoner of Monterey,* and *The Artist's Wife*). His admirers dubbed him the "father of the American ballad," but the ballad form existed in America long before him. He wrote a book of memoirs, *Shadows on the Wall* (1877; reprinted 1971). Another son,

James Lang Hewitt (b. N.Y., Sept. 28, 1803; d. there, March 24, 1853), was associated with the publishing firm of J. A. Dickson in Boston (1825); after his father's death he returned to N.Y. and continued his father's publishing business.

BIBL.: C. Huggins, *John Hill H.: Bard of the Confederacy* (diss., Fla. State Univ., 1964); J. Wagner, *James H.: His Life and Works* (diss., Ind. Univ., 1969); W. Winden, *The Life and Music Theater Works of John Hill H.* (diss., Univ. of Ill., 1972); F. Hoogerwerf, *John Hill H.: Sources and Bibliography* (Atlanta, 1982).—NS/LK/DM

Hewitt, Maurice, French violinist, conductor, and teacher; b. Asnières, Oct. 6, 1884; d. Paris, Nov. 7, 1971. He was trained at the Paris Cons. In 1904 he began his career as a violinist as a chamber music player; after serving as 2nd violinist in the Capet Quartet (1909–14; 1919–28), he was founder–1st violinist of his own quartet in Paris (1928–30). After teaching and playing in a quartet at the Cleveland Inst. of Music (1930–34), he became a prof. at the American Cons. in Fontainebleau in 1934. He also was founder–1st violinist of his own Quatuor Hewitt (1935–39; 1946–48) and founder-conductor of the Orchestre de Chambre Hewitt (from 1939). From 1942 to 1955 he was a prof. of chamber music at the Paris Cons.—NS/LK/DM

Hey, Julius, German singing teacher; b. Irmelshausen, April 29, 1832; d. Munich, April 22, 1909. He first studied painting, but turned to music, taking courses in harmony and counterpoint with Franz Lachner and Friedrich Schmitt. He became an ardent Wagnerian after his introduction to the master by King Ludwig II, and worked under the direction of Hans von Bülow at the Munich School of Music (established by the King in accordance with Wagner's plans). After Bülow's departure (1869), Hey vainly tried to effect a reform from a German national standpoint in the cultivation of singing, but met with so many obstacles that he resigned when Wagner died (1883), and devoted himself to finishing his method of singing, *Deutscher Gesangsunterricht* (4 vols., Mainz, 1885; ed. by F. Volbach and H. Hey as *Der kleine Hey*, Mainz, 1912; 2nd ed., rev., 1956, by F. Reusch). It contains a complete and logical exposition of Wagner's views on vocal training. His book *Richard Wagner als Vortragsmeister* (Leipzig, 1911) was publ. posthumously by his son Hans.—NS/LK/DM

Heyden (Heiden, Haiden), Hans, German organist, son of **Sebald Heyden;** b. Nuremberg (baptized), Jan. 15, 1536; d. there (buried), Oct. 22, 1613. He was his father's successor as organist at St. Sebald Church (1567–71), and the inventor of the "Geigen-Clavicymbel" ("Nurnbergisch Geigenwerk") in 1575, which he described in *Musicale instrumentum reformatum* (Nuremberg, 1605; 2nd ed., 1610; Latin tr., 1605, as *Commentatio de musicale instrumento*).—NS/LK/DM

Heyden (Heiden, Haiden), Sebald, important German music theorist, father of **Hans Heyden;** b. Bruck, near Erlangen, Dec. 8, 1499; d. Nuremberg, July 9, 1561. He was educated at the Univ. of Ingolstadt

(M.A., 1519). In 1521 he was appointed cantor at the Spitalkirche and rector of its school in Nuremberg, and in 1525 he became rector of the school at St. Sebald. He was the author of the important theoretical work *Musicae, id est, Artis canendi, libri duo* (Nuremberg, 1537; 2nd ed., 1540, as *De arte canendi, ac vero signorum in cantibus usu, libri duo;* Eng. tr. by C. Miller in Musicological Studies and Documents, XXVI, 1972). He also wrote *Rudienta [Institutiones musicae]* (Nuremberg, 1529; not extant; 2nd ed., 1532, as *Musicae stoicheiōsis*).

BIBL.: A. Kosel, *S. H. (1499–1561): Ein Beitrag zur Geschichte der Nürnberger Schulmusik in der Reformationszeit* (Würzburg, 1940).—NS/LK/DM

Heyer, Wilhelm (Ferdinand), German patron of music; b. Cologne, March 30, 1849; d. there, March 20, 1913. A wealthy co-owner of the wholesale paper manufacturing firm Poensgen & Heyer, he was an enthusiastic amateur and was active in the musical affairs of Cologne in advisory capacities. In 1906 he established a historical musical museum in Cologne, in which he assembled more than 2,600 instruments with accessories, about 20,000 autographs of musicians, 3,700 portraits, and a library of books about music, containing many rare eds. Georg Kinsky, curator of the museum from 1909, publ. an illustrated catalog of the Heyer collections. The museum was dissolved in 1927, and the instruments were acquired by the Univ. of Leipzig but sustained heavy damage during World War II.

BIBL.: G. Kinsky, *Musikhistorisches Museum von W. H. in Cöln: Katalog* (Cologne, Vol. I, 1910; Vol. II, 1912; Vol. IV, 1916). —NS/LK/DM

Heyman, Katherine Ruth Willoughby, American pianist and composer; b. Sacramento, Calif., 1877; d. Sharon, Conn., Sept. 28, 1944. She made her debut as soloist with the Boston Sym. Orch. in 1899, and from 1905 to 1915 she toured the U.S. and Europe with Schumann-Heink, Marcella Sembrich, and others. She became greatly interested in the works of Scriabin, and played recitals of his works in Europe and America. She also publ. many articles on Scriabin's theosophic ideas. In 1928 she founded in Paris the Groupe Estival pour la Musique Moderne. She publ. *The Relation of Ultra-Modern to Archaic Music* (Boston, 1921). Among her compositions were *Studies in Modern Idiom* for Piano and songs.—NS/LK/DM

Heywood, Eddie (actually, **Edward Jr.**), jazz pianist, composer, leader; b. Atlanta, Dec. 4, 1915; d. North Miami, Jan. 2, 1989. His father, Eddie Sr., a graduate of the Boston Cons. of Music, was a famous bandleader-pianist in the 1920s and 1930s. Eddie Jr., was the nephew of bandleader LeRoy Smith. He received his first lessons from his father at the age of eight; at 14 he was playing piano in a local theatre orch. He remained in Atlanta until ca. 1932, then toured with various bands until arriving in N.Y. in 1937. He gigged in N.Y., then joined the Benny Carter Orch. from January 1939 until July 1940. He worked in the Zutty Singleton Trio from July 1940, was briefly with Leonard Ware and Don Redman before leading his own band at Village Vanguard, N.Y., in 1941. This band made a series of land-mark recordings in 1943 with Bing Crosby, Billie Holi-day, Ella Fitzgerald, and the Andrews Sisters, as well as a popular instrumental version of "Begin the Beguine." His sextet played several residencies in N.Y. before working in Calif. (late 1944–45). During their stay in Hollywood they appeared in the films *The Dark Corner* and *High School Kids*. He led a sextet in N.Y. for most of 1946, returned to the West Coast early in 1947, and soon afterwards was forced by partial paralysis to quit play-ing for almost three years. He resumed regular playing in the spring of 1950 and then led his own trio. He achieved considerable success with his composition "Canadian Sunset." He also wrote "Soft Summer Breeze," "Land of Dreams," and a tone poem, "Portrait of Martha's Vineyard." He suffered a recurrence of hand paralysis in the late 1960s. He recovered by 1972 and played many concerts, also club dates in N.Y. and New England (Martha's Vineyard). He returned to promi-nence in the mid-1980s with a long stint at N.Y.'s Cookery and a Carnegie Hall concert.

Heywood was a vibrant and original soloist whose work is not well enough known in jazz circles, partly because he did many commercial numbers that did not demonstrate his jazz talents and partly because a stroke in 1947 diminished his technical ability.

DISC.: *Jazz at Cafe Society* (1944); *Swing Low Sweet H.* (1944); *Lightly and Politely* (1944); *Eight Selections* (1944); *Touch of E. H.* (1957); *Featuring E. H.* (1957); *Canadian Sunset* (1958). —JC/LP

Hiatt, John,

along with Graham Parker, was one of the most overlooked and underappreciated singer-songwriters to begin recording in the 1970s; b. India-napolis, Ind., 1952. His often acerbic songs fall into both country and R&B stylings; and although his 1987 *Bring the Family* album finally brought him critical acclaim, he has yet to find a wide audience as a performer.

John Hiatt picked up guitar at age 11, and as a teenager played in Indianapolis-area R&B bands such as the White Ducks in the late 1960s. In 1970 he moved to Nashville, where he worked as a songwriter for Tree Publishing beginning in 1971. His compositions in-cluded 1974's major pop hit "Sure As I'm Sittin' Here" for Three Dog Night and "Heavy Tears," recorded by Conway Twitty. He signed with Epic Records and recorded two albums for the label before touring solo, moving to Los Angeles, and switching to MCA for *Slug Line* and *Two-Bit Monsters*, his first albums to garner any attention. The Neville Brothers recorded his "Washable Ink" in 1978, and Dave Edmunds recorded his "Some-thing Happens" in 1981.

In the early 1980s John Hiatt recorded with Ry Cooder, contributing "The Way We Make a Broken Heart" to *Borderline* and adding guitar and vocals to *The Slide Area*. He also recorded three albums for Geffen Records, including *Riding with the King*, before suffering the suicide of his estranged wife. He subsequently cleaned up after years of alcohol and drug abuse and retreated to Nashville. During this time Rosanne Cash recorded his "Pink Bedroom," Nick Lowe his "She

Don't Love Nobody," and Rodney Crowell his "She Loves the Jerk."

John Hiatt finally made his breakthrough with 1987's *Bring the Family*, recorded with Ry Cooder, Nick Lowe on bass, and session drummer Jim Keltner. The album included "Memphis in the Meantime," "Have a Little Faith in Me," "Learning How to Love You," and "Thing Called Love"; the last song was Bonnie Raitt's first comeback hit in 1988. The follow-up, *Slow Turning*, was recorded with Hiatt's then-touring band, the Goners, and featured "Icy Blue Heart" (recorded by Emmylou Harris in 1989), "Is Anybody Out There?," the rocker "Tennessee Plates," and the oft-covered "Drive South." In 1987 Rosanne Cash scored a top country hit with his "The Way We Make a Broken Heart," and the Jeff Healey Band had a smash pop hit with his "Angel Eyes" in 1989. That year Geffen issued a compilation of his recordings made between 1979 and 1985.

Despite critical acclaim for his compelling, highly personal songwriting and distinctive, expressive voice, 1990's *Stolen Moments* also failed to produce any hit singles for John Hiatt. The album contained "Real Fine Love," "Bring Back Your Love to Me," "Rest of the Dream," and "Through Your Hands." In 1991 Hiatt joined Ry Cooder, Nick Lowe, and Jim Keltner in the collective band Little Village. The group's sole album, with Hiatt on lead vocals for 6 of the 11 songs, sold respectably, but did not really establish any of the participants as major stars.

In 1993 Rhino Records issued an album of other artists performing Hiatt's songs, while Hiatt recorded *Perfectly Good Guitar*. Rocking more than his previous three albums, it included the title cut, "Something Wild," the romantic "Straight Outta Time," and the controversial "Wreck of the Barbie Ferrari." Hiatt com-pleted his years at A&M with a live album recorded with the same band that accompanied him on *Perfectly Good Guitar*, featuring many of his better recent songs.

Hiatt moved to Capitol Records in 1995 to issue *Walk On*. This collection of songs about a failed marriage included the title track, "Cry Love" (issued as a single), and "Dust on a Country Road."

DISC.: JOHN HIATT: *Hanging Around the Observatory* (1974); *Overcoats* (1975); *Slug Line* (1979); *Two-Bit Monster* (1980); *All of a Sudden* (1982); *Riding with the King* (1983); *Warming Up the Ice Age* (1985); *Y'all Caught?: The Ones that Got Away, 1979–1985* (1989); *Bring the Family* (1987); *Slow Turning* (1988); *Stolen Moments* (1990); *Perfectly Good Guitar* (1993); *Hiatt Comes Alive at Budokan* (1994); *Walk On* (1995); *Little Head* (1997); *The Best of J. H.* (1998); *Greatest Hits: The A&M Years, '87–'94* (1999); *Crossing Muddy Waters* (2000). **LITTLE VILLAGE:** *Little Village* (1992). **TRIBUTE ALBUM:** *Love Gets Strange: The Songs of J. H.* (1993).—BH

Hickmann, Hans (Robert Hermann),

German musicologist; b. Rosslau bei Dessau, May 19, 1908; d. Blandford Forum, Dorset, England, Sept. 4, 1968. He studied musicology in Halle and with Blume, Hornbos-tel, Sachs, Schering, Schünemann, and Wolf at the Univ. of Berlin (Ph.D., 1934, with the diss. *Das Portativ*; publ. in Kassel, 1936). He then was active in Cairo, where he pursued research in Egyptian music and worked as an organist, conductor, teacher, and broadcaster. In 1957 he became director of the German Cultural Inst. in Cairo, but that same year he was made prof. of ethnomusicology at the Univ. of Hamburg; he also was director of the Archiv Produktion division of the Deutsche Grammophon Gesellschaft (from 1958) and first president of the Deutsche Gesellschaft für Musik des Orients (from 1959). Hickmann wrote many articles on ancient Egyptian music for various learned journals.

WRITINGS: Catalogue général des antiquités égyptiennes du Musée du Caire: Instruments de musique (Cairo, 1949); 45 siècles de musique dans l'Egypte ancienne à travers la sculpture, la peinture, l'instrument (Paris, 1956); Ägypten in Musikgeschichte in Bildern, ii/1 (Leipzig, 1961).—NS/LK/DM

Hickox, Richard (Sidney), esteemed English conductor; b. Stokenchurch, Buckinghamshire, March 5, 1948. He studied organ, piano, and composition at the Royal Academy of Music in London (1966–67) and was an organ scholar at Queens' Coll., Cambridge (M.A., 1970). In 1971 he made his professional debut as a conductor at St. John's Smith Square in London. He founded the City of London Sinfonia in 1971, and subsequently served as its music director. That same year he also organized the Richard Hickox Singers, which later became the City of London Sinfonia Singers. From 1972 to 1982 he was organist and master of music at St. Margaret's, Westminster. He made his debut at the London Promenade Concerts in 1973. From 1976 he was music director of the London Sym. Chorus, and from 1978 of the Bradford Festival Choral Soc. In 1979 he made his debut as an opera conductor at the English National Opera in London. From 1980 to 1984 he was principal guest conductor of the Netherlands Radio Orch. in Hilversum. After serving as artistic director of the Northern Sinfonia in Newcastle upon Tyne from 1982 to 1990, he was its principal guest conductor from 1990. In 1983–84 he was assoc. conductor of the San Diego Sym. Orch., and from 1985 of the London Sym. Orch. In 1985 he conducted for the first time at London's Covent Garden, and in 1986 at the Los Angeles Opera. With Simon Standage, he founded the Collegium Musicum 90 of London in 1990. From 1998 he was principal conductor of the Spoleto Festival in Italy, and from 2000 of the BBC National Orch. of Wales in Cardiff. As a guest conductor, he was engaged by leading orchs. in Europe and North America. Hickox's vast repertoire embraces works from the 14th century to the present era. He reveals a rare capacity for surmounting the various interpretative challenges posed by both standard and seldom performed scores of the orch., choral, and operatic repertoires.—NS/LK/DM

Hicks, Dan, San Francisco singer/songwriter who blended hippie psychedelica with jug band music and vocal jazz; b. Little Rock, Ark., Dec. 9, 1941. THE CHARLATANS: George Hunter, voc.; Mike Wilhelm, gtr.; Michael Ferguson, pno.; Richard Olson, bs.; and Dan Hicks, drm., gtr.

Dan Hicks grew up in Santa Rosa, Calif., taking up drums at the age of 11 and guitar at 20. He played locally and eventually joined The Charlatans as drummer in 1965. They debuted at a three-month engagement at the Red Dog Saloon in Virginia City, Nev., that summer before returning to Haight-Ashbury. Recording one album eventually released by Philips, The Charlatans disbanded in 1969. Before the group's breakup, however, Hicks had formed Dan Hicks and His Hot Licks with violinist David LaFlamme, who soon left to form It's a Beautiful Day.

Reconstituted with Hicks, lead guitarist John Weber, violinist Sid Page, bassist Jaime Leopold, vocalist-keyboardist Christina Gaucher, and vocalist Sherry Snow, Dan Hicks and His Hot Licks signed with Epic Records in September 1968. Their debut album, Original Recordings, included Hicks's "Canned Music," "I Scare Myself," and the classic "How Can I Miss You When You Won't Go Away." However, the album sold poorly and the group was dropped by Epic in the summer of 1970. Dan Hicks and His Hot Licks subsequently realigned, retaining Hicks, Page, and Leopold while adding Nicole Dukes (voc.), Maryann Price (voc., perc.), and Naomi Ruth Eisenberg (voc., vln.) as The Lickettes. Signed to Blue Thumb Records, their live album Where's the Money failed to sell despite favorable reviews and the first of a series of national tours. Dukes was dismissed and guitarist John Girton added for Striking It Rich!, which contained "Moody Richard," "Walkin' One and Only," and Johnny Mercer's "Old Cow Hand." As Last Train to Hicksville was becoming their best-selling album, Dan Hicks disbanded the group.

In 1978, Warner Brothers released Dan Hicks's It Happened One Bite, recorded in 1975 with Page, Girton, and Price as the soundtrack to an unreleased film. By 1979, Hicks had formed a musical partnership with guitarist Kenneth "Turtle" Van Demarr, with whom he toured for more than a decade, primarily on the West Coast. Former Charlatan Richard Olsen has led the San Francisco society dance band The Richard Olsen Orch. since the early 1980s. Sid Page resurfaced in 1984 with the jazz album Odyssey, recorded with Dave Shelander. Dan Hicks and His Acoustic Warriors eventually recorded Shootin' Straight for the On the Spot subsidiary of Private Music. The surviving members of The Charlatans (Mike Wilhelm died in 1979) ultimately reunited briefly in 1997.

DISC.: THE CHARLATANS: The Charlatans (1969); One Way (1995); First Album and Alabama Bound (1996). **DAN HICKS AND HIS HOT LICKS:** Original Recordings (1969); Where's the Money (1971); Striking It Rich! (1972); Last Train to Hicksville (1973). **DAN HICKS:** It Happened One Bite (1978). **SID PAGE AND DAVID SHELANDER:** Odyssey (1984). **DAN HICKS AND HIS ACOUSTIC WARRIORS:** Shootin' Straight (1994).—BH

Hicks, John (Josephus Jr.), jazz pianist, bandleader; b. Atlanta, Ga, Dec. 21, 1941. Hicks played road gigs with Little Milton, Albert King, Al Grey, Johnny Griffin, and Pharoah Sanders. Terry, Davis, and Oliver Nelson encouraged him to come to N.Y. in 1963. He then worked with Kenny Dorham, Lou Donaldson, and Joe Henderson before becoming a full-time member of Art Blakey's Jazz Messengers. After two years with the Messengers, he joined the Betty Carter Trio (1966–68 and 1975–80). In between, ca. 1971, he appeared on St. Louis TV with a group including Julius Hemphill and drummer Philip Wilson. He also spent 20 months with the Woody Herman Big Band. He has led his own big band on various occasions since 1984, while continuing to play with various other leaders. During the 1990s, he also played with Mingus Dynasty. He has done workshops at schools and colleges throughout the country, and tours regularly, both nationally and internationally, including in Asia and Europe.

DISC.: *Hell's Bells* (1978); *After the Morning* (1979); *Some Other Time* (1981); *John Hicks* (1984); *In Concert* (1984); *Luminous* (1985); *Two of a Kind* (1988); *Naima's Love Song* (1988); *Eastside Blues* (1988); *Power Trio* (1990); *Live at Maybeck Recital Hall* (1990); *Is That So?* (1990); *Friends Old and New* (1992); *Crazy for You* (1992); *Lover Man: Tribute to Billie Holiday* (1993); *Beyond Expectations* (1993); *Single Petal of a Rose* (1994); *In the Mix* (1994); *Gentle Rain* (1995); *A Piece for My Peace* (1996). **KEYSTONE TRIO:** *Heart Beats* (1996); *Newklear Music* (1997).—**LP**

Hidalgo, Elvira de, Spanish soprano and teacher; b. Aragón, Dec. 27, 1892; d. Milan, Jan. 21, 1980. She studied with Bordalba in Barcelona and Vidal in Milan. In 1908 she made her operatic debut as Rossini's Rosina in Naples. On March 7, 1910, she sang that role in her Metropolitan Opera debut in N.Y., returning there for the 1924–26 seasons. She also appeared at Milan's La Scala (1916), in Rome (1919), at Buenos Aires's Teatro Colón (1922), and at London's Covent Garden (1924). From 1932 she devoted herself to teaching, being the mentor of Maria Callas in Athens. She later taught in Ankara (1949–59) and then in Milan. In addition to Rosina, she was greatly admired for her portrayals of Gilda, Linda, Philine, Elvira, Musetta, and Lakmé. —**NS/LK/DM**

Hidalgo, Juan, important Spanish composer; b. Madrid, c. 1612; d. there, March 30, 1685. He became a harpist and harpsichordist at the Royal Chapel in Madrid about 1631, and from 1645 he served as maestro of chamber music; he remained in the service of the court until his death. For the semi- opera *Fortunas de Andromeda y Perseo* (1653), Hidalgo prepared the recitative, the earliest surviving example of its use in Spain. About 1658 he began to compose his own works for the stage, and soon became closely associated with the dramatist and poet Pedro Calderón de la Barca. While their opera *La púrpura de la rosa* (c. 1660) is lost, their opera *Celos aun del aire matan* (Madrid, Dec. 5, 1660) survives as one of the earliest scores in the genre in Spain. His music for Juan Vélez de Guevara's zarzuela *Los celos hacen estrellas* (1672) is the earliest zarzuela to survive with both music and text. Among his other works were some 9 autos sacramentales, incidental music to about 15 court plays, many villancicos, and some liturgical pieces. Hidalgo's significance rests upon the role he played in establishing the Italian operatic styles in Spain.

BIBL.: J. Subirá, *"Celos aun del aire matan," ópera del siglo XVII* (Barcelona, 1933); R. Pitts, *Don J. H., Seventeenth-century Spanish Composer* (diss., George Peabody Coll. for Teachers, Nashville, Tenn., 1968).—**NS/LK/DM**

Hidas, Frigyes, Hungarian composer; b. Budapest, May 25, 1928. He was a student of Viski at the Budapest Academy of Music. He served as music director of the National Theater in Budapest (1951–66), and then at the Municipal Operetta Theater in Budapest (1974–79). In subsequent years, he devoted himself solely to composition. In 1959 and 1980 he was awarded the Erkel Prize. In 1986 the Hungarian government made him a Merited Artist.

WORKS: DRAMATIC: *Színek* (Colors), ballet (1960); *Riviera*, operetta (1963); *Az Asszony és az igazság* (The Woman and the Truth), chamber opera (1965); *Tökelétes alattvaló* (The Perfect Subject), opera (1973); *Cédrus* (Cedar), ballet (1975); *Bösendorfer*, opera (1977); *Dunakanyar* (Danube Bend), opera (1984); *Álmodj Bachot* (Dream Bach), musical play (1991; Budapest, May 25, 1993). **ORCH.:** Oboe Concerto (1951); Violin Concertino (1957); 2 clarinet concertos (1958, 1977); Viola Concerto (1959); Sym. (1960); Flute Concerto (1967); 2 horn concertos (1968, 1989); Concertino for 4 Flutes, 4 Clarinets, and Strings (1969); Piano Concerto (1972); Trombone Concerto (1979); Harp Concerto (1979); Bassoon Concerto (1980); *Ballad* for Cello and Orch. (1982); *Cymbog* for Cimbalom, Oboe, and Strings (1982); *Baroque Concerto* for Alto Trombone and Strings (1983); Trumpet Concerto No. 2 (1983); *Széchenyi Concerto* (1984); *Preludium, Passacaglia, and Fugue* for 2 Cimbaloms and Strings (1984); *Quintetto Concertante* for Brass Quintet and Orch. (1986); *3 Movements* (1987); Double Concerto for Tenor and Bass Trombones and Orch. (1988); *The Undanced Ballet* (1989); *Brussels Concerto* for Violin and Orch. (1992); *String Fantasy* (1992); Suite for Small String Orch. (1993). **Concert Band:** Trumpet Concerto No. 1 (1956); *Ballet Music* (1980); Suite (1981); *Rhapsody* for Bass Trombone and Concert Band (1982); Concerto No. 2 for Flute and Wind Ensemble (1983); *Circus Suite* (1985); 2 folksong suites (1985, 1985); *4 Movements* (1991); *Almost B A C H* (1993); *Musica Solenne* (1993). **CHAMBER:** 3 string quartets (1954, 1963, 1978); Oboe Sonata (1955); 3 wind quintets (1961, 1969, 1979); *Chamber Music* for 4 Horns (1974); *5 Movements* for 3 Trumpets, 2 Trombones, and Tuba (1978); Brass Quintet (1978); *7 Bagatelles* for 12 Trombones (1979); Sextet for 3 Trumpets, Horn, 2 Trombones, and Tuba (1982); *Music for Brass* for 5 Trumpets and 5 Trombones (1983); *Divertimento* for Wind Octet (1985); *Music for 6* for String Quartet, Double Bass, and Piano (1985); *Alteba Trio* for Alto, Tenor, and Bass Trombones (1986); *1 + 5*, sextet for Bass Trombone and Wind Quintet (1989); Saxophone Quartet (1990); Tuba Quartet (1990); *Domine, Dona Nobis Pacem* for Trombone and Organ (1991); Suite for 4 Trombones (1991); *Tale* for Violin and Harp (1991); *Music for Harp and Violin* (1992); *Triga* for Trumpet, Horn, and Trombone (1992). **VOCAL:** *Missa Brevis* for Chorus and Organ (1956); *Cantate de Minoribus* for Narrator, Men's Chorus, and Orch. (1959); *From Dawn to Evening* for Children's Chorus and Chamber Orch. (1967); *Requiem for an Army* for Tenor, Baritone, Bass, Chorus, and Orch. (1973); *Missa in Honorem Reginae Pacis* for Soprano, Alto, Tenor, Bass, Chorus, and Organ (1991). —**NS/LK/DM**

Hier, Ethel Glenn, American composer, teacher, and pianist; b. Cincinnati, June 25, 1889; d. Winter Park, Fla., Jan. 14, 1971. She studied piano at the Cincinnati Cons. of Music (diploma, 1908); in 1911 she resumed piano studies there and also received instruction in composition from Kelley. During the summer of 1912, she pursued training in composition from Kaun in Germany. In 1917 she went to N.Y. and studied composition with Goetschius and Bloch at the Inst. of Musical Art; after further training with Berg, Wellesz, and Malipiero in Europe, she completed her piano studies with Friedberg (1923). In subsequent years, she was mainly active as a teacher, composer, and promoter of women in American musical life. In 1926 she helped to found the Assn. of American Women Composers. In 1948 she founded the Composers Concerts in N.Y. In her music, she leavened impressionistic elements with infusions of popular and jazz styles. Among her works were *Asolo Bells* for orch. (Rochester, N.Y., Oct. 25, 1939), *Mountain Preacher*, cantata (N.Y., Dec. 5, 1941), 2 string quartets, 3 quintets, piano pieces, and songs. —NS/LK/DM

Higginbotham, J. C. (aka **Jack; Jay C.;** and **"Higgy"**), influential early jazz trombonist; b. Social Circle, Ga., May 11, 1906; d. N.Y., May 26, 1973. A flamboyant, surprising, and expressive soloist in his early years; even when his chops were down in the late 1950s he managed to play with tremendous expressiveness and bluesiness. Two of his brothers were also brass players; "Higgy's" niece is songwriter Irene Higginbotham. He first played bugle, then his sister bought him his first trombone. Around 1922, he moved to Cincinnati to learn tailoring at a training school, but left to work as mechanic at the General Motors factory. He joined Wesley Helvey's Band (ca. 1924), led his own band, and also gigged with Wingie Carpenter. In late 1925 he toured with pianist Eugene Landrum's Jazz Band in the *Ragtime Steppers* show. In 1926 he was sent for by Wingie Carpenter and joined drummer Eugene Primus's Band in Buffalo, N.Y.; after seven months he joined another band in Buffalo led by a pianist named Jimmy Harrison. While on a visit to N.Y. in September 1928 he sat in at the Savoy Ballroom with Chick Webb and with drummer Willie Lynch's Band. He was subsequently signed by Luis Russell and remained with Russell until 1931. During this period, he also played for two brief spells with Chick Webb. He was with Fletcher Henderson from spring 1932, then with Benny Carter in autumn of 1933. He had a brief absence from music scene until summer 1934, then joined The Mills Blue Rhythm Band (directed by Lucky Millinder). He left in late 1936. He was briefly with Fletcher Henderson early in 1937, then with Louis Armstrong Big Band until November 1940. He and Red Allen had played together in most of these bands and they became fast friends, so he joined the Henry "Red" Allen Sextet (as co-leader) in December 1940 and worked regularly until February 1947. During the late 1940s and early 1950s worked mainly in Boston; from 1956 he began regular appearances at Central Plaza, N.Y., and soon moved into the Metropole and worked there on and off throughout the late 1950s (including several stints with Henry Allen). He took part in the Fletcher Henderson reunion in 1957, did extensive freelance recordings, and went to Europe with Sam Price in October 1958. During the 1960s has regularly led his own band in N.Y and also played many gigs with trumpeter Joe Thomas. He was featured at the Newport Jazz Festival in 1963; he also played in Scandinavia. In December 1966 he briefly returned to his home town in Atlanta to record an LP. He spent several months in the hospital during 1971, but then returned to performing until his death.

DISC. *Higgy Comes Home* (1966).
BIBL.: C. Jones, *J. C. H.* (London, 1944).—**JC/LP**

Higgins, Billy, jazz drummer; b. L.A., Oct. 11, 1936. He recorded with Cal Tjader and Stan Getz (1957), then Paul Bley live at the Hillcrest (1958) with Ornette Coleman and Don Cherry. He first came to prominence in Coleman's quartet of 1959 but it soon became evident that his swing and close listening were an asset to any kind of group. He played for about a month on John Coltrane's first tour of Calif. as a leader in September 1960, and recorded a session with him. From 1962–63 he worked with Sonny Rollins, and then with Coleman on and off through the early 1970s. During this period, he actively freelanced on record. In the summer of 1972, with Lee Morgan, he was using sticks with beads or rice inside so they could also serve as rattles during solos. In the mid-1980s he was a member of Charlie Haden's first Quartet West, and then worked with Cedar Walton's trio through the mid-1990s. In late 1995–early 1996 he had two kidney transplants but by 1997–98 he was back in action. However he was not well enough to tour Europe with Jackie McLean as planned for July 1999.

DISC.: *Soweto* (1979); *Soldier* (1979); *Bridgework* (1980); *Mr. B. H.* (1984); *Essence* (1985). Ornette Coleman: *Shape of Jazz to Come* (1959). Thelonious Monk: *Monk at the Blackhawk* (1960). Dexter Gordon: *Go* (1962). Art Farmer: *Art Farmer Quintet Live at Boomer's* (1976).—**LP**

Higgins, Dick (actually, **Richard Carter**), English-born American composer, performer, music publisher, and writer; b. Cambridge, March 15, 1938; d. Quebec City, Canada, Oct. 26, 1998. He was taken to the U.S. as a child. He studied piano in Worcester, Mass. After training in composition and orchestration with Harry Levenson (1953), he studied with Cowell at Columbia Univ., where he took a B.S. in English (1960), and with Cage at the New School for Social Research (1958–59). Caught up in the avant-garde movement, he became a proponent of the intermedia group who advocated the union of music with other allied arts. In 1958 he became active in the first "happenings," and from 1961 he worked in the Fluxus movement. He was founder-director of the Something Else Press (1964–73). In 1972 he founded Unpublished Editions, which became Printed Editions in 1978. He taught at the Calif. Inst. of the Arts (1970–71) and was a research assoc. in the visual arts dept. of the State Univ. of N.Y. at Purchase (from 1983). He wrote widely on music and the arts. In his compositions, he pursued the objective of total involvement, in which music is verbalized in conceptual designs without reification or expressed in physical action. He also utilized graphic notation. Among his works are *Graphis*, a series of pieces for Varying Groups (from 1958), *Danger Music*, a series of pieces for Varying Groups (1961–64), *Hrušalk*, opera (1965), *The 1000 Symphonies*, a series for Orch. (from 1968), *Piano Album, 1962–84* (1980), *26 Mountains for Viewing the Sunset From* for Singers, Dancers, and Chamber Orch. (1980), *Trinity* for Piano and Percussion (1981),

Variations on a Natural Theme for Orch. (1981), and *St. Columbia* for String Quartet, Orch. or 4 Voices, Chorus, and Tubular Chimes (1983), as well as numerous vocal works, tape pieces, many performance works with music, and film scores. Among his many books are *Foew & Ombuhnw* (N.Y., 1969), *Computers for the Arts* (Somerville, Mass., 1970), *A Dialectic of Centuries: Notes Towards a Theory of the New Arts* (N.Y., 1978; 2nd ed., rev., 1979), and *Horizons: The Poetics and Theory of the Intermedia* (Carbondale, Ill., 1983).—NS/LK/DM

Higginson, Henry Lee, American music patron; b. N.Y., Nov. 18, 1834; d. Boston, Nov. 14, 1919. He attended Harvard Univ. (1851) and studied music in Vienna (1856–60). In 1868 he became a partner in his father's Boston brokerage firm of Lee, Higginson & Co. His great love for music prompted him to found the Boston Sym. Orch. in 1881, which he subsequently nurtured as its munificent patron. In 1885 he founded the Boston Music Hall Promenade Concerts, a summer series of lighter fare which became celebrated as the Boston Pops.

BIBL.: B. Perry, *Life and Letters of H. L. H.* (Boston, 1921). —NS/LK/DM

Hignard, (Jean-Louis) Aristide, French composer; b. Nantes, May 20, 1822; d. Vernon, March 20, 1898. He studied with Halévy at the Paris Cons., taking the 2nd Grand Prix de Rome. He was an earnest composer of lofty aims, but brought out operas and other works of secondary importance. His best opera, *Hamlet* (1868), was to be performed in Paris, but, unluckily for him, *Hamlet* by Ambroise Thomas was produced that same year, with such spectacular success that Hignard could not compete with it. Accordingly, he had to be content with a provincial production in his native city (Nantes, April 21, 1888). His other operas included *Le Visionnaire* (Nantes, 1851), *Le Colin-Maillard* (Paris, 1853), *Les Compagnons de la Marjolaine* (Paris, 1855), *M. de Chimpanzé* (Paris, 1858), *Le Nouveau Pourceaugnac* (Paris, 1860), *L'Auberge des Ardennes* (Paris, 1860), and *Les Musiciens de l'orchestre* (Paris, 1861).—NS/LK/DM

Hijman, Julius, Dutch-American pianist, teacher, and composer; b. Almelo, Jan. 25, 1901; d. N.Y., Jan. 6, 1969. He studied piano privately with Dirk Schaefer, then with Paul Weingartner in Vienna; subsequently theory and composition with Sem Dresden in the Netherlands. He went to the U.S. in 1940. He was an instructor at the Houston Cons. (1940–42) and at the Kansas City Cons. (1945–49), and then taught composition at the Philadelphia Musical Academy and the N.Y. Coll. of Music. He composed mostly chamber music, including sonatas for violin, cello, saxophone, oboe, and flute, with piano, 4 string quartets, and Sonata for 2 Violins and Piano.—NS/LK/DM

Hildegard von Bingen, famous German composer, poetess, and mystic; b. Bemersheim, near Alzey, 1098; d. Rupertsberg, near Bingen, Sept. 17, 1179. Her noble parents, Hildebert and Mechtild, promised to consecrate her to the Church since she was their 10th child. Accordingly, she began her novitiate as a child, and joined with the reclusive mystic Jutta of Spanheim, who with her followers occupied a cell of the Benedictine monastery of Disibodenberg. At 15 Hildegard took the veil, and succeeded Jutta as Mother Superior in 1136. Between 1147 and 1150 she founded a monastery on the Rupertsberg (near Bingen) with 18 sisters; around 1165 she founded another house at Eibingen (near Rüdesheim). She is called "abbess" in letters drawn up by Frederick Barbarossa in 1163. She was known as the "Sybil of the Rhine," and conducted extensive correspondence with popes, emperors, kings, and archbishops. She was thus greatly involved in politics and diplomacy. Several fruitless attempts were made to canonize her, but her name is included in the Roman Martyrology, and her feast is celebrated on Sept. 17. Hildegard is musically important through her monophonic chants, several of which were settings of her lyric and dramatic poetry. She collected her poems in the early 1150s under the title *Symphonia armonie celestium revelationum*. This vol. survives in 2 sources, both in early German neumes; it comprises 70–odd liturgical poems (the exact number varies, depending on classification), all with melismatic music. The poetry is rich with imagery, and it shares the apocalyptic language of her visionary writings. The music is not typical of plainchant, but involves a technique unique to Hildegard; it is made of a number of melodic patterns recurring in different modal positions, which operate as open structures allowing for internal variation in different contexts. She also wrote a morality play in dramatic verse, *Ordo virtutum*, which includes 82 melodies that are similarly structured but distinctly more syllabic in style. She pointed out that her music is written in a range congenial to women's voices, contrasting with the formal Gregorian modes. Hildegard was also known for her literary works, which include prophecy, medical and scientific treatises, and hagiographies, as well as letters.

BIBL.: J. Gmelch, *Die Kompositionen der heiligen H.* (Düsseldorf, 1913); L. Bronarski, *Die Lieder der heiligen H.: Ein Beitrag zur Geschichte der geistlichen Musik des Mittelalters* (Zürich, 1922); M. Davic-Windstosser, *Carmina sanctae H.s: Die Lieder der heiligen H. v.B.* (Munich, 1928); B. Widmer, *Heilsordnung und Zeitgeschehen in der Mystik H.s v.B.* (Basel, 1955); M. Schrader and A. Führkotter, *Die Echtheit des Schriftums der heiligen H. v.B.* (Cologne, 1956); *H. v.B.: Briefwechsel* (Salzburg, 1965); S. Flanagan, *H. of B., 1098–1179: A Visionary Life* (London and N.Y., 1989; 2nd ed., 1998); A. Davidson, ed., *The "Ordo virtutum" of H. of B.: Critical Studies* (Kalamazoo, 1992); J. Bobko, B. Newman, and M. Fox, *Vision: The Life and Music of H. v.B.* (N.Y., 1995).—NS/LK/DM

Hiles, Henry, English organist, pedagogue, and composer; b. Shrewsbury, Dec. 31, 1826; d. Worthing, near London, Oct. 20, 1904. He was trained by his brother, John Hiles (1810–82), an organist and composer. After serving as organist in the provinces and in London, he went to Manchester in 1859. He was made a lecturer in music at Owen's Coll. (1876) and Victoria Coll. (1879) before becoming prof. of harmony at the Royal Manchester Coll. of Music (1893). He also was ed.

of the *Quarterly Musical Review* (1885–88). Among his works were an opera, an operetta, cantatas, oratorios, services, glees, and art songs. He also publ. a number of manuals.—NS/LK/DM

Hill, Alfred (Francis), noted Australian composer; b. Melbourne, Nov. 16, 1870; d. Sydney, Oct. 30, 1960. He played violin in traveling theater orchs., and then studied with Paul, Schreck, and Sitt at the Leipzig Cons. (1887–91). He subsequently was active in New Zealand and Australia as a conductor, and later as a prof. at the New South Wales State Conservatorium (1916–34). He was made an Officer of the Order of the British Empire in 1953 and a Companion of the Order of St. Michael and St. George in 1960. He wrote over 500 works, some of which employ Maori and Australian aboriginal materials. He publ. *Harmony and Melody* (London, 1927).

WORKS: DRAMATIC: O p e r a : *Whipping Boy* (1893); *Lady Dolly* (1898; Sydney, 1900); *Tapu* (1902–03); *A Moorish Maid or Queen of the Riffs* (Auckland, 1905); *Teora—The Weird Flute* (1913; Sydney, 1928); *Giovanni, the Sculptor* (1913–14; Melbourne, 1914); *Rajah of Shivapore* (Sydney, 1914); *Auster* (1919; Sydney, 1922); *The Ship of Heaven* (1923; 1st complete perf., Sydney, 1933). **ORCH.:** 13 syms., including No. 1, *Maori* (1896–1900), No. 2, *Joy of Life* (1941), No. 3, *Australia* (1951), No. 4, *Pursuit of Happiness* (1955), No. 5, *Carnival* (1955), No. 6, *Celtic* (1956), No. 7 (1956), No. 8, *The Mind of Man* (1957), No. 9, *Melodious* (1958), and No. 10 (1958), all transcribed from chamber pieces except No. 1. **CHAMBER:** 17 string quartets; 6 violin sonatas; Wind Septet (1950); piano pieces. **VOCAL: C h o r a l :** *The New Jerusalem* (1892); *Hinemoa, a Maori Legend* (1895); *Tawhaki* (1897); Mass (1931). **OTHER:** *Life* for 8 Solo Voices and Piano Quintet (1912); part songs; songs.

BIBL.: J. Thomson, *A Distant Music: The Life and Times of A. H., 1870–1960* (Oxford, 1982).—NS/LK/DM

Hill, Andrew, avant-garde jazz pianist, composer; b. Chicago, June 30, 1937. Early biographies gave his birthplace as Port Au Prince, Haiti, as a publicity stunt. He was discovered playing accordion and tap dancing on a South Side street by Earl "Fatha" Hines. Hill jammed with teen-age clarinetist John Gilmore, studied with Stan Kenton's trombonist-arranger Bill Russo, had composition lessons with Paul Hindemith, and also studied the saxophone. His first professional job was performing with Charlie Parker at the Greystone Ballroom in Detroit. During the mid-1950s, he worked with everyone from Dinah Washington to Von Freeman and Gene Ammons, to R&B bands, before moving first to L.A., then to N.Y. in the 1960s. He worked with Roland Kirk in 1962.

Hill established himself with a series of moody and unique LPs for the Blue Note Label in the 1960s. As Composer in Residence at Colgate Univ. (1970–71), where he received his doctorate, he performed and conducted workshops; he has also been a visiting artist at Harvard Univ. and Artist in Residence at Bennington Coll. An associate professor at Portland State Univ. from 1988 to 1990, he directed P.S.U.'s highly successful Summer Jazz Intensive. He was known in univs. and international cultural circles for his "Story Teller," solo

piano concerts and performances of the late 1980s and early 1990s. He has actively toured the U.S. and Europe since the early 1990s, and returned to living in the N.Y. area in 1996.

DISC.: *So in Love* (1955); *Smoke Stack* (1963); *Black Fire* (1963); *The Complete Blue Note A. H. Sessions* (1963); *Point of Departure* (1964); *Judgment!* (1964); *A.!* (1964); *Cosmos* (1965); *Compulsion* (1965); *Involution* (1966); *Grass Roots* (1968); *Dance with Death* (1968); *One for One* (1969); *Lift Every Voice* (1969); *Spiral* (1974); *Invitation* (1974); *Live at Montreux* (1975); *Divine Revelation* (1975); *Nefertiti* (1976); *From California with Love* (1978); *Strange Serenade* (1980); *Faces of Hope* (1980); *Verona Rag* (1986); *Shades* (1986); *Eternal Spirit* (1989); *But Not Farewell* (1990).—LP

Hill, Chippie (Bertha), blues/jazz singer; b. Charleston, S.C., March 15, 1905; d. May 7, 1950. She was one of 16 children. She began her professional career as a dancer at LeRoy's in Harlem (1916) and later toured as a singer and dancer with Ma Rainey's troupe. She worked as a solo act on T.O.B.A., circuit before settling in Chicago (ca. 1925). She made many recordings, accompanied by Louis Armstrong, Richard M. Jones, Lonnie Johnson, etc. She worked regularly in Chicago clubs and theatres until 1930, then left full-time music to raise her seven children. During the 1930s and early 1940s she occasionally sang in Chicago theatres, and also did long residency at the Club DeLisa. She was working in a bakery when she was rediscovered by writer Rudi Blesh in 1946. She then became a club favorite in Chicago and N.Y., as well as touring Europe. She was knocked down and killed by a car in Harlem. —JC/LP

Hill, Edward Burlingame, eminent American composer and teacher; b. Cambridge, Mass., Sept. 9, 1872; d. Francestown, N.H., July 9, 1960. A member of a distinguished family of educators (his father was a prof. of chemistry at Harvard, and his grandfather, president of Harvard), he pursued regular courses at Harvard Univ., studying music with J. K. Paine and graduating in 1894 summa cum laude. He took lessons in piano with B. J. Lang and A. Whiting, in composition with Chadwick and Bullard, and (for 1 summer) studied with Widor in Paris. He became greatly interested in the new tonal resources of the impressionist school of composers and wrote articles in the *Boston Evening Transcript* and other publications dealing with French music. He also publ. a book, *Modern French Music* (Boston, 1924). In 1908 he joined the faculty of Harvard Univ. as an instructor in music, becoming assoc. prof. in 1918, prof. in 1928, and then was the James E. Ditson Prof. (1937–40). He was a member of the National Inst. of Arts and Letters and of the American Academy of Arts and Sciences and was a Chevalier of the Legion d'Honneur. In his music, Hill reveals himself as a follower of the French school, with clarity of design and elegance of expression his chief characteristics. His best works are for orch., but he also composed some fine chamber and choral music.

WORKS: DRAMATIC: B a l l e t - p a n t o m i m e : *Jack Frost in Midsummer* (1908). **ORCH.:** *The Parting of Lancelot and Guinevere,* tone poem (St. Louis, Dec. 31, 1915); *Stevensoni-*

ana Suite No. 1 (1916–17; N.Y., Jan. 27, 1918) and *No. 2* (1921–22; N.Y., March 25, 1923); *The Fall of the House of Usher*, tone poem (Boston, Oct. 29, 1920); *Prelude to the Trojan Women* (1920); *Waltzes* (Boston, Feb. 24, 1922); *Scherzo* for 2 Pianos and Orch. (Boston, Dec. 19, 1924); *Lilacs*, tone poem (Cambridge, Mass., March 31, 1927); 3 syms.: No. 1 (1927; Boston, March 30, 1928), No. 2 (1929; Boston, Feb. 27, 1931), and No. 3 (1936; Boston, Dec. 3, 1937); *Ode for the 50th Anniversary of the Boston Symphony Orchestra* for Chorus and Orch. (Boston, Oct. 17, 1930); Piano Concertino (1931; Boston, April 25, 1932); Sinfonietta for Strings (1932; N.Y., April 3, 1936); Violin Concerto (1933–34; rev. 1937; Boston, Nov. 11, 1938); Concertino for Strings (Boston, April 19, 1940); *Music* for English Horn and Orch. (1943; Boston, March 2, 1945); Concerto for 2 Flutes and Small Orch. (1947); *4 Pieces* for Small Orch. (1948); *Prelude* (N.Y., March 29, 1953). **CHAMBER:** Flute Sonata (1926); Clarinet Sonata (1927); Sextet for Flute, Oboe, Clarinet, Bassoon, Horn, and Piano (1934); String Quartet (1935); Piano Quartet (1937); Sonata for 2 Clarinets (1938); Quintet for Clarinet and String Quartet (1945); *Diversion* for Chamber Ensemble (1946); Bassoon Sonata (1948); Cello Sonatina (1949); Violin Sonatina (1951). **Piano:** *Poetical Sketches* (1902); *Country Idyls*, 6 pieces; *Jazz Study* for 2 Pianos (1924). **VOCAL:** *Nuns of the Perpetual Adoration*, cantata for Women's Voices and Orch. or Piano (1908); *Autumn Twilight* for Soprano and Orch.; *The Wilderness Shall Rejoice*, anthem for Chorus (1915).

BIBL.: L. Tyler, *E.B. H.: A Bio-Bibliography* (N.Y., 1989). —NS/LK/DM

Hill, Ernest ("Bass"), jazz bassist; b. Pittsburgh, Pa., March 14, 1900; d. N.Y., Sept. 16, 1964. He worked with Claude Hopkins in the summer of 1924, and sailed to Europe with him in 1925 accompanying the Josephine Baker Revue. He went back to the U.S. in 1926, then again worked with Hopkins from 1926 until 1928. He was bassist in a series of bands through the 1930s, including Benny Carter (1931, 1933–34). From June 1937–39, he performed in Europe as a member of Bobby Martin's band; he remained with the group on its return to the U.S. when it was renamed the Cotton Club Serenaders. During the 1940s, he worked with various bands, including Claude Hopkins (1941–42; late 1943–44) and Zutty Singleton (with whom he traveled to L.A. in mid-1943). He returned to Europe in November 1949, where he worked with various bands before returning to the U.S. in January 1952. He gigged in the N.Y. area through the 1950s and early 1960s, and also worked at the local AFM office.—JC/LP

Hill, Faith, one of the biggest country crossover artists of the 1990s; b. Jackson, Miss., Sept. 21, 1967. Raised in the small town of Star, Miss., Hill formed her first band at 17 to play local rodeos. By 22, she had moved to Nashville, where she made ends meet selling T-shirts while trying to make connections as a performer. Eventually she took a job as a secretary with a music publishing company. In this position, she made some connections, most notably with songwriter Gary Burr, who helped her with a demo that led to a contract with Warner Bros. She became the first woman in 30 years to top the country charts for four consecutive weeks with her 1994 debut single, a rocking honky-tonk tune, "Wild One." She followed this with a version of Janis Joplin's "Piece of My Heart." Her debut went double platinum. With that success under her belt, the phones started ringing. She recorded "Where You Lead" for the 1995 tribute to Carole King's *Tapestry* and a tune for the Disney film *Mr. Wrong. People* proclaimed her one of 1995's "50 Most Beautiful People."

Hill played over 250 shows during 1994 and 1995, opening for her musical hero, Reba McEntire among others. Her sophomore album, *It Matters to Me*, sold twice as fast as her debut. The title track spent three weeks atop the country charts, her fourth single to do that. The album went double platinum. Hill was invited to perform in the closing ceremonies of the 1996 Olympics in Atlanta. She played 140 shows with Tim McGraw, a tour auspiciously billed the "Spontaneous Combustion Tour." The show lived up to its name for Hill and McGraw. On a stop in McGraw's hometown, they got married. In 1997, they had a child and a #1 country hit with the duet "It's Your Love." The song spent six weeks atop the country chart.

Hill took three years between the release of *It Matters to Me* and her third album, *Faith*, to have another child. In anticipation of the record's release, Hill went on the road with McGraw as part of the George Strait Chevy Truck Country Music Festival. By the summer of 1998, they had played for over a million people. Going into the making of *Faith*, Hill set out to record songs that were less slight than her previous hits, that reflected the maturity married life and motherhood had wrought on her. However, she didn't want to lose her energy, either. The album balanced both to the extent that the single "This Kiss" not only was the most played song of the year but crossed over pop after Hill performed the song on the *Tonight Show* and the tune was featured in the film *Practical Magic*. The song rose to #26 pop in addition hitting the #1 country spot. The album went to #7.

Hill's newfound mainstream acceptance opened new doors. She became a spokesperson for Cover Girl cosmetics. At one shoot, she met fellow modeling musician Brandy. Brandy asked Hill to be her special guest on the 1999 edition of *Divas*. After taking off on her first headlining tour, Hill recorded *Breathe*. The album featured material by Bruce Springsteen and yet another duet with McGraw, a passionate ballad called "Let's Make Love." The album debuted at #1 on both the pop and country charts. The title track reached #1 on the country charts late in 1999.

Hill has long supported pro-literacy projects including her own foundation. She supports the cause because her father, one of 13 children, had to quit school early to work on the family farm and never learned to read well. At most of her concerts, fans are urged to bring books to donate.

DISC.: *Take Me As I Am* (1994); *It Matters to Me* (1995); *Faith* (1998); *Breathe* (1999).—HB

Hill, Lauryn, innovative hip-hop rapper and singer; b. South Orange, N.J., May 26, 1975. Hill's mother taught English and her father worked as a computer consultant. Both parents enjoyed R&B records. By the time she was 13, Hill had already performed on *Showtime at the Apollo*, singing Smokey Robinson's "Who's Loving You?" At school she started a gospel choir, played basketball, ran track, was a cheerleader and homecoming queen. She hooked up with two of her schoolmates, Wyclef Jean and Prakazrel Michel, forming a rap group they called the Fugees, short for refugees, denoting the Haitian émigré status of the two young men. As if all this wasn't enough, during her junior year Hill started to work on an acting career. She landed a steady role on "As the World Turns" and acted in the films *Sister Act 2*, *Plenty*, and *Restaurant*. She also appeared in the TV specials "Daddy's Girl" and "Here and Now." Rather than taking these credentials to Hollywood, however, Hill enrolled at Columbia Univ.

However, she also kept working on her various extracurricular projects, including the Fugees. During her freshman year, they signed with Ruffhouse Records. The group's first album, *Blunted on Reality*, concentrated heavily on rap, and though it mixed elements of Caribbean music with the urban beats, the album didn't do very well. Their second album, 1996's *The Score*, however, became one of the biggest selling hip-hop records of all time—indeed one of the best-selling records in any genre—selling 17 million copies, largely owing to Hill's singing on the covers of "Killing Me Softly" and "No Woman No Cry." The group took home two Grammies that year, for Best Rap Album and Best R&B Performance by a Duo or Group with Vocal. The success of this album finally motivated Hill to leave Columbia a few semesters short of her degree in history.

After the Fugee's 1997 tour, Hill found out she was pregnant by Rohan Marley, one of the sons of reggae legend Bob Marley. She spent most of that year caring for her new son, Zion, though she found time to write "A Rose Is a Rose" for Aretha Franklin and direct the video for the song. Michel and Jean went into the studio to work on solo albums, and after a while, Hill decided to follow suit, working in N.Y. and at the Bob Marley Museum studio in Jamaica. She invited guest artists including Carlos Santana, Mary J. Blige, D'Angelo, Francis Dunnery, Earl "Chinna" Smith, and many other pop and reggae stars, to play. What finally came out of these sessions, *The Miseducation of Lauryn Hill*, might well be considered one of the masterpieces of pop music. With songs that lyrically addressed issues from sexism to motherhood, materialism to spirituality, the album earned comparisons to Marvin Gaye's *What's Goin' on* and Joni Mitchell's *Blue*. Deeper still, on a musical level, Hill blended hip-hop with old- school R&B, Caribbean rhythms, and flat-out soul. The album spawned two hits, the ubiquitous gold single "Doo Wop (That Thing)" and "Everything Is Everything," which also went gold. At the Grammy Awards, she went in with 10 nominations and came home with the statuettes for Album of the Year, Best New Artist, Best R&B Song, Best R&B Album, and Best R&B Vocal Performance. *Spin* and *Details* proclaimed her Artist of the Year, and *Time* and *The New York Times* hailed *The Miseducation* as the #1 album of the year. The album had sold seven million copies and was still in the charts at the time of this writing.

DISC.: *The Miseducation of Lauryn Hill* (1998).—**HB**

Hill, Ralph, English writer on music; b. Watford, Oct. 8, 1900; d. London, Oct. 19, 1950. He studied cello with his father at the Guildhall School of Music in London. He was active in music publishing (1920–29). He was music ed. of the *Radio Times* (1933–45) and also asst. music critic (1933–39) and later chief music critic (1945–50) of the *Daily Mail*. He publ. the following works, all in London: *An Outline of Musical History* (1929), *Brahms: A Study in Musical Biography* (1933), *Liszt* (1936; 2nd ed., 1949), *Challenges: A Series of Controversial Essays on Music* (1943), *Music without Fears* (1945), and *Prelude to Music* (1951). He also ed. *The Symphony* (1949) and *The Concerto* (1952).—**NS/LK/DM**

Hill, Richard S(ynyer), American music librarian; b. Chicago, Sept. 25, 1901; d. Naples, Fla., Feb. 7, 1961. He was educated at Phillips Exeter Academy, then studied at Cornell Univ. (B.A., 1924) and did postgraduate work at the Univ. of Oxford (1924–26). He held a research fellowship in psychology with Kurt Koffka at Smith Coll. (1927–29). He returned to Cornell Univ. for further study in psychology and musicology, the latter under Otto Kinkeldey. He joined the staff of the Music Division of the Library of Congress in Washington, D.C., in 1939, serving as ed. of *Notes*, the quarterly journal of the Music Library Assn., from 1943 to the time of his death. He also was president of the International Assn. of Music Libraries (1951–55). He contributed articles and reviews to various journals, one of the most notable being his "Schoenberg's Tone Rows and the Tonal System of the Future," *Musical Quarterly* (Jan. 1936).

BIBL.: C. Bradley and J. Coover, eds., *R.S. H.: Tributes from Friends* (Detroit, 1987).—**NS/LK/DM**

Hill, Teddy (actually, **Theodore**), jazz tenor saxophonist, other reeds, leader, b. Birmingham, Ala., Dec. 7, 1909; d. Ohio, May 19, 1978. He played drums in his school band, then switched to trumpet. While studying at the industrial high school in Birmingham, he received tuition from "Fess" Whatley, gave up trumpet and specialized on saxes and clarinet. He toured with the Whitman Sisters' show (1926–27), then joined drummer George Howe's Band (1927) at the Nest Club (N.Y.). He subsequently worked in Luis Russell's Band (1928–29), and also assisted in management of Russell's Band. He regularly led his own big band from 1932, first at N.Y.'s Lafayette Theater. At various times, his band featured many distinguished sidemen, including Roy Eldridge, Chu Berry, Dizzy Gillespie, and Dicky Wells, among many others. He toured England and France in 1937, played at Moulin Rouge in Paris before touring Britain (including bookings at the London Palladium, July 1937). He returned to the U.S., continued to lead the band until 1940, and was then active as manager of the famous early bop club at Minton's in Harlem. He managed Minton's through the late 1960s and then ran the Club Baron into the 1970s.—**JC/LP**

Hill, Tiny (actually, **Thomas**), pop-jazz drummer, vocalist and bandleader; b. Sullivan, Ill., July 19, 1906; d. Roanoke, Va., March 1972. He weighed more than 350 pounds and led a band described as "swinging cornball," and was especially popular in the midwestern U.S. His best-known record was "Angry" which was used as a theme. He also had one of several hit versions of "Slowpoke" in 1952. He carried on working well into the 1960s, making dancers happy and offending no one.

DISC.: *Uncollected Tiny Hill and His Orch.* (1944).—MM/LP

Hill, Ureli Corelli, American violinist and conductor; b. Hartford, Conn.?, c. 1802; d. (suicide) Paterson, N.J., Sept. 2, 1875. His father, Uri K. Hill, was a teacher of music in Boston and N.Y., and author of a manual, *Solfeggio Americano, A System of Singing* (N.Y., 1820). An admirer of Corelli, he named his son after him; the first name (Ureli) is a combination of the father's name, Uri, and a friend's name, Eli. Ureli played violin in various theaters in N.Y. as a boy. He was a violinist in the orch. of Garcia's opera company in 1825, then joined the N.Y. Sacred Musical Soc., and conducted it in the first American performance, with orch. accompaniment, of Handel's *Messiah* (1831). From 1835 to 1837 he was in Germany, where he studied for a year with Spohr. Returning to N.Y., he became a founder and first president of the N.Y. Phil. (1842–47). He then went West in quest of fortune, which failed to materialize. In N.Y. he exhibited a pianoforte of his own invention, in which he used small bell tuning forks in place of strings, so as to secure perfect intonation; the attempt to promote this instrument met with failure. He played the violin in the N.Y. Phil. from 1850 until 1873, when he retired because of age, although he continued to play engagements in various theater orchs. throughout his life. He then moved to Paterson, N.J., where he engaged (unsuccessfully) in real-estate schemes. Depressed on account of constant setbacks in his ventures of promotion in music and in business, he committed suicide by swallowing morphine.—NS/LK/DM

Hill, W.E. & Sons, firm of violin makers and music dealers in London. The founder of the firm was **Joseph Hill** (1715–84). He was an apprentice to Peter Wamsley, and established his business in 1750. He had 5 sons, who were violinists. **William Ebsworth Hill,** a great-grandson of the founder (b. London, Oct. 20, 1817; d. Hanley, April 2, 1895), adopted the present name of the firm; his instruments took 1st prize at the expositions in London (1851) and Paris (1867). His sons, **William Henry Hill** (b. London, June 3, 1857; d. there, Jan. 20, 1927), **Arthur Frederick Hill** (b. London, Jan. 24, 1860; d. there, Feb. 5, 1939), and **Alfred Ebsworth Hill** (b. London, Feb. 11, 1862; d. there, April 21, 1940), collaborated in the writing of *Antonio Stradivari, His Life and Work* (London, 1902). William H., Arthur F., and Alfred E. Hill also wrote *The Violin-Makers of the Guarneri Family* (London, 1931). The Ashmolean Museum at Oxford contains a valuable collection of stringed instruments, including a 1716 Stradivari violin with a bow dated 1694, presented by Arthur F. Hill. The firm continued under the direction of the descendants of the founder, **Andrew Hill** (b. London, July 3, 1942) and **David Hill** (b. London, Feb. 28, 1952).—NS/LK/DM

Hillborg, Anders, Swedish composer and teacher; b. Stockholm, May 31, 1954. He received training in counterpoint (1976–78) and in composition (from Bucht, 1978–82) at the Stockholm Musikhögskolan; also had lessons from Feldman in Buffalo (1980). He was a prof. of composition at the Malmö Musikhögskolan (from 1989). He has pursued an inventive road as a composer, utilizing both traditional and non-traditional styles.

WORKS: ORCH.: *Worlds* (1979); *Lamento* for Clarinet and Strings (Stockholm, May 13, 1982); *Himmelsmekanik* (Celestial Mechanic) for Strings (1983–85; Stockholm, Oct. 31, 1986); *Clang and Fury* (1985–89); Violin Concerto (1990–92); *Strange Singing* for Trombone and Orch. (1993–94). CHAMBER: *Hyacintrummet* for Harp (1982); *Musik* for 10 Cellos (Stockholm, Dec. 18, 1987); *Hauptosaune* for Trombone and Drum Machine or Tape (London, Oct. 6, 1990); *Fanfare* for Brass Quintet (1991); *Tampare raw* for Clarinet and Piano (1991); *Un-Tangia-Na* for Trombone and Organ (1991); *Close Ups* for Flute (1991). VOCAL: *Lilla Sus Grav* for Chorus (1978); *Stella Maris* for Chorus (1983); *Hosianna I-II* for Chorus (1989); *Variations* for Soprano, Mezzo-soprano, Flute, Saxophone, Percussion, Viola, and Double Bass (1991); *Psaltarpsalm* for Chorus, Brass Quintet, and Organ (1993). ELECTRONIC: *Mental Hygien III* (1979); *Rite of Passage* (1981); *Spöksonaten* (1982; Stockholm, Jan. 8, 1983); *Living-room* (1983); *Kamaloka* (Berlin, Feb. 14, 1984); *Musik till Friends* (1987); *Hudbason* (1990); *Strange Dances and Singing Water* (1994).—NS/LK/DM

Hillebrecht, Hildegard, German soprano; b. Hannover, Nov. 26, 1927. She made her operatic debut as Leonora in *Il Trovatore* in Freiburg im Breisgau (1951); then sang in Zürich (1952–54), Düsseldorf (1954–59), Cologne (1956–61), Munich (from 1961), and again in Zürich (from 1972). She also made guest appearances in Vienna, Hamburg, Berlin, Salzburg, Paris, and Rome. In 1967 she made her Covent Garden debut in London as the Empress in *Die Frau ohne Schatten*; on Nov. 8, 1968, she made her Metropolitan Opera debut in N.Y. as Sieglinde in *Die Walküre*. She was best known for her roles in operas by Mozart, Wagner, Puccini, Strauss, and Verdi. She also sang in the premiere of Dallapiccola's *Ulisse* in Berlin (1968).—NS/LK/DM

Hillemacher, famous French composers, brothers: **Paul Joseph Guillaume** (b. Paris, Nov. 29, 1852; d. Versailles, Aug. 13, 1933) and **Lucien Joseph Édouard** (b. Paris, June 10, 1860; d. there, June 2, 1909). They studied at the Paris Cons. Paul won the 2nd Prix de Rome in 1875, and the 1st in 1876, with the cantata *Judith*; Lucien obtained the 2nd Prix de Rome in 1879, and the 1st in 1880, with the lyric scene *Fingal*. After graduation, they decided to write music in collaboration, and adopted a common signature—P. L. Hillemacher. They also wrote a biography of Gounod (Paris, 1905; 2nd ed., 1925). Together they produced the following stage works: *Saint- Mégrin*, opéra-comique (Brussels, March 2, 1886), *Une Aventure d'Arlequin*, opéra-comique (Brussels, March 22, 1888), *Le Régiment qui passe*, opéra-comique (Royan, Sept. 11, 1894), *Le Drac*, lyric drama (in Ger. as *Der Flutgeist*, Karlsruhe, Nov. 14, 1896), *Orsola*, lyric drama (Paris, May 21, 1902), and *Circé*, lyric drama (Paris, April 17, 1907). Paul, who survived his brother by 24 years, also wrote a "tableau

musical," *Fra Angelico*, which was produced at the Paris Opéra-Comique on June 10, 1924. In addition to their operas, the brothers wrote a symphonic legend, *Loreley*, which won the prize of the City of Paris (1882), 2 orch. suites, *La Cinquantaine* and *Les Solitudes*, an oratorio, *La Légende de Sainte Geneviève* (1886), and songs.
—NS/LK/DM

Hiller, Ferdinand (von), noted German conductor, composer, and writer on music; b. Frankfurt am Main, Oct. 24, 1811; d. Cologne, May 10, 1885. He studied piano with A. Schmitt, making his public debut at age 10, then went to Weimar to study with Hummel (1825), whom he accompanied to Vienna for a visit with Beethoven (1827). He subsequently was in Paris (1828–35), where he was befriended by Chopin, Liszt, Berlioz, and other famous musicians. He became conductor of Frankfurt am Main's Cäcilien- Verein (1836). After studies in Italy (1841), he devoted himself mainly to conducting, composing, and writing on music. He was a conductor with the Leipzig Gewandhaus Orch. (1843–44), then in Dresden, where he brought out 2 of his operas (1845–47), and subsequently in Düsseldorf (1847–50). He settled in Cologne as a conductor (1850), gaining distinction in particular with the Lower Rhine Festival. He also reorganized the municipal music school, serving as its director until his death. He appeared as a guest conductor in Paris (1851–52), London (1852–72), and St. Petersburg (1870). A musical conservative, he violently attacked Wagner. His own compositions met with indifferent success, although his career as a conductor and writer on music won him many admirers.

WORKS: DRAMATIC: O p e r a : *Romilda* (Milan, 1839); *Der Traum in der Christnacht* (Dresden, 1845); *Konradin* (Dresden, Oct. 13, 1847); *Der Advokat* (Cologne, 1854); *Die Katakomben* (Wiesbaden, Feb. 15, 1862); *Der Deserteur* (Cologne, Feb. 17, 1865). **ORCH.:** 3 syms.; 3 overtures; 3 piano concertos. **CHAMBER:** 5 string quartets; 5 piano quartets; 5 piano trios; also many piano pieces. **VOCAL: O r a t o r i o s :** *Die Zerstörung Jerusalems* (Leipzig, April 2, 1840); *Saul*. **O t h e r V o c a l :** Cantatas and various other choral works; more than 100 songs.

WRITINGS: *Die Musik und das Publikum* (Cologne, 1864); *Aus dem Tonleben unserer Zeit* (2 vols., Leipzig, 1868 and 1871); *Ludwig van Beethoven: Gelegentliche Aufsätze* (Leipzig, 1871); *Felix Mendelssohn Bartholdy: Briefe und Erinnerungen* (Cologne, 1874); *Musikalisches und Persönliches* (Leipzig, 1876); *Briefe an eine Ungenannte* (Cologne, 1877); *Künstlerleben* (Cologne, 1880); *Wie hören wir Musik?* (Leipzig, 1881); *Goethes musikalisches Leben* (Cologne, 1883); *Erinnerungsblätter* (Cologne, 1884).

BIBL.: H. Hering, *Die Klavierwerke F. v.H.s* (diss., Univ. of Cologne, 1928); R. Sietz, ed., *Aus F. H.s Briefwechsel* (7 vols., Cologne, 1958–70); idem, *Der Nachlass F. H.s* (Cologne, 1970).
—NS/LK/DM

Hiller, Friedrich, Adam, German violinist, singer, conductor, and composer, son of **Johann Adam Hiller;** b. Leipzig, c. 1767; d. Königsberg, Nov. 23, 1812. He received training from his father. He began his career as a violinist in Leipzig, and then made his operatic debut as Romeo in *Romeo und Julie* in Rostock in 1789. In 1790 he became director of a music soc. in Schwerin. In 1796 he was named music director of the National Theater orch. in Altona and in 1799 of the Königsberg Theater. He composed a number of stage works and other vocal pieces, most of which are not extant. He also wrote several string quartets.
—NS/LK/DM

Hiller, Johann Adam, important German conductor, composer, and writer on music, father of **Friedrich Adam Hiller;** b. Wendisch-Ossig, near Görlitz, Dec. 25, 1728; d. Leipzig, June 16, 1804. He began his musical training as a child. After attending the Görlitz Gymnasium (1740–45), he won a scholarship to the Dresden Kreuzschule, where he studied keyboard playing and thoroughbass with Homilius (1746–51); then studied law at the Univ. of Leipzig (1751). He was active as a bass singer and flutist in Leipzig's Grosses Concert prior to serving as steward to Count Brühl in Dresden (1754–58?), and also later in Leipzig (1758–60). Thereafter he assumed a major role in the musical life of Leipzig. He organized his own subscription concert series (1762), and was director of the revived Grosses Concert (1763–71); also founded a singing school, which evolved into a music school. He was the erudite ed. of the *Wöchentliche Nachrichten* (1766–70), the first major specialized journal on music. During this same period, he helped to establish the German Singspiel in collaboration with the poet Christian Felix Weisse. He mastered the genre in his *Lottchen am Hofe* (Leipzig, April 24, 1767), in which he created effective characterizations by writing simple songs for the country people and arias in the opera seria tradition for the people of means. His finest Singspiels were *Die Liebe auf dem Lande* (Leipzig, May 18, 1768) and *Die Jagd* (Weimar, Jan. 29, 1770). He founded the Musikabende Gesellschaft (1775), with which he gave many concerts; then became conductor of the Gewandhaus concerts in 1781, leading them until 1785. This famous series of concerts has continued without interruption for more than 200 years. He also was music director of the Univ.'s Paulinerkirche (1778–85) and of the Neukirche (1783–85); then was Kapellmeister to the Duke of Courland in Mitau (1785–86) and civic music director in Breslau (1787–89). He returned to Leipzig as Kantor of the Thomaskirche in 1789, remaining there until his retirement in 1800.

WORKS: SINGSPIELS (all 1st perf. in Leipzig unless otherwise given): *Die verwandelten Weiber oder Der Teufel ist los, erster Teil* (May 28, 1766; 12 pieces by J. Standfuss); *Der lustige Schuster oder Der Teufel ist los, zweiter Teil* (1766; 7 pieces by Hiller, remainder by Standfuss); *Lisuart und Dariolette oder Die Frage und die Antwort* (Nov. 25, 1766); *Lottchen am Hofe* (April 24, 1767); *Die Muse* (Oct. 3, 1767); *Die Liebe auf dem Lande* (May 18, 1768); *Die Jagd* (Weimar, Jan. 29, 1770); *Der Dorfbalbier* (1771; with pieces by C. Neefe); *Der Aerndtekranz* (1771); *Der Krieg* (1772); *Die Jubelhochzeit* (April 5, 1773); *Die kleine Aehrenleserin*, children's operetta (publ. in Leipzig, 1778); *Das Grab des Mufti oder Die beiden Geitzigen* (Jan. 17, 1779); *Poltis oder Das gerettete Troja* (1777?). **VOCAL: S a c r e d :** (22) *Choralmelodien zu Gellerts geistlichen Oden und Liedern* for Voice and Basso Continuo (1761; 2nd ed., rev., 1792, as *25 neue Choralmelodien* for 4 Voices and Basso Continuo); *50 geistliche Lieder für Kinder* for Voice and Keyboard (1774); *Geistliche Lieder einer vornehmen curländischen Dame* for Voice and Keyboard (1780); *Religiöse Oden und Lieder* for Voice and Keyboard (1790); *3 Melodien zu Wir glauben all an einen Gott* for 4 Voices (1790); *Herr Gott, dich loben wir* for 4 Voices, Trumpets, Trombones, and Timpani (1790); *Gesang zum Charfreytage* for 4 Voices (1793); *Vierstimmige Chor-Arien zum neuen Jahre...nebst 4 lateinischen Sanctus* (1794); etc. **S e c u l a r :** *Lieder mit Melodien* (1759); *Melodien zu 6 Romanzen von Löwen* (1760); *Cantate auf die Ankunft der hohen Landesherrschaft* for Soloists, Chorus, and Orch. (1765); *Lieder für Kinder* (1769); *Lieder mit Melodien* (1772); *Der Greis, Mann und Jüngling,* cantata (1778); *Horatii Carmen ad Aelium Lamium* for Soloists, Chorus, and Keyboard (1778); *Die Friedensfeyer oder Die unvermuthete Wiederkunft* (1779); *Cantaten und Arien verschiedener Dichter* for Voice and Keyboard (1781); *Sammlung der Lieder aus dem Kinderfreunde* (1782); *Letztes Opfer in einigen Liedermelodien der comischen Muse* (1790); *Aerntelied* (1797). **O T H E R :** Instrumental music, including chamber music and pieces for keyboard. **C o l l e c t i o n s** (a number include works by Hiller): *Wöchentlicher musikalischer Zeitvertreib* (1759–60); *Sammlung kleine Klavier- und Singstücke* (4 vols., 1774); *Vierstimmige Motetten und Arien...von verschiedenen Komponisten* (6 vols., 1776–91); *Sammlung der vorzüglichsten noch ungedruckten Arien und Duetten des deutschen Theaters* (6 vols., 1777–80); *6 italienische Arien verschiedener Componisten* (1778); (49) *Lieder und Arien aus Sophiens Reise* (1779); *Italienische Duetten* for 2 Sopranos (1781); *Arien und Duetten des deutschen Theaters* (Vol. I, 1781); *Duetten zur Beförderung des Studiums des Gesanges* (1781); *Elisens geistliche Lieder* (1783); *Deutsche Arien und Duetten von verschiedenen Componisten* (Vol. I, 1785); *Meisterstücke des italienischen Gesanges...mit deutschen geistlichen Texten* (1791); *Allgemeines Choral-Melodien-Buch* for 4 Voices and Basso Continuo (1793); *Nachtrag* for 4 Voices (1797).

WRITINGS: *Anekdoten zur Lebensgeschichte grosser Regenten und berühmter Staatsmänner* (Leipzig, 1766–72); ed. *Wöchentliche Nachrichten und Anmerkungen die Musik betreffend* (Leipzig, 1766–70; suppl. publ. as *Musikalische Nachrichten und Anmerkungen,* Leipzig, 1770); *Anweisung zur Singekunst in der deutschen und italienischen Sprache* (Frankfurt am Main and Leipzig, 1773); *Musikalisches Handbuch für die Liebhaber des Gesanges und Claviers* (Leipzig, 1773); *Anweisung zum musikalisch-richtigen Gesange* (Leipzig, 1774; 2nd ed., aug., 1798); *Exempelbuch der Anweisung zum Singen* (Leipzig, 1774); *Anweisung zum musikalisch-zierlichen Gesange* (Leipzig, 1780); *Lebensbeschreibungen berühmter Musikgelehrten und Tonkünstler neuerer Zeit* (vol. I, Leipzig, 1784); *Über Metastasio und seine Werke* (Leipzig, 1786); *Nachricht von der Aufführung des Händelschen Messias in ... Berlin den 19. May 1786* (Berlin, 1786); *Fragmente aus Händels Messias, nebst Betrachtungen über die Aufführung Händelscher Singcompositionen* (Leipzig, 1787); *Über Alt und Neu in der Musik* (Leipzig, 1787); *Was ist wahre Kirchenmusik?* (Leipzig, 1789); *Beyträge zu wahrer Kirchenmusik von J.A. Hasse und J.A. Hiller* (Leipzig, 1791); *Kurze und erleichterte Anweisung zum Singen* (Leipzig, 1792); *Anweisung zum Violinspielen für Schulen und zum Selbstunterrichte* (Leipzig, 1792); *Erinnerungen gegen das Melodien- Register in Freyes kleiner Lieder-Konkordanz* (Leipzig, 1798).

BIBL.: C. Naumann, *J.A. H.: Eine bescheidene Würdigung seiner Verdienste als Mensch, Künstler und Schulmann* (Leipzig, 1804); K. Peiser, *J.A. H.* (Leipzig, 1894); G. Calmus, *Die ersten deutschen Singspiele von Standfuss und H.* (Leipzig, 1908); A. Schering, *Das Zeitalter J.S. Bachs und J.A. H.s* (Leipzig, 1940); G. Sander, *Das Deutschtum im Singspiel J.A. H.s* (diss., Univ. of Berlin, 1943); K. Kawada, *Studien zu den Singspiel von J.A. H. (1728–1804)* (Marburg, 1969).—**NS/LK/DM**

Hiller, Lejaren (Arthur Jr.), American composer and teacher; b. N.Y., Feb. 23, 1924; d. Buffalo, Jan. 26, 1994. He studied chemistry at Princeton Univ. (B.A., 1944; M.A., 1946; Ph.D., 1947), where he also took courses in composition with Babbitt and Sessions; later he studied at the Univ. of Ill. (M.Mus., 1958). After working as a research chemist (1947–52), he taught chemistry at the Univ. of Ill. (1952–58), where he subsequently was prof. of music and director of its experimental music studio (1958–68). In 1968 he became the Frederick B. Slee Prof. of Composition at the State Univ. of N.Y. at Buffalo, where he also was co-director of its Center of the Creative and Performing Arts (1968–74); from 1980 to 1989 he was the Birge-Cary Prof. of Music there. Hiller's scientific bent led him to explore the application of electronics and computers to composition. With Leonard Isaacson, he collaborated on the *Illiac Suite,* his 4th string quartet (1955–56), which was the first composition composed with the aid of a computer. With Isaacson, he publ. *Experimental Music: Composition with an Electronic Computer* (N.Y., 1959).

WORKS: D R A M A T I C : M e l o d r a m a : *John Italus* (unfinished). **O R C H . :** Piano Concerto (1949); Suite for Small Orch. (1951); 3 syms. (1953, 1960, unfinished); *Time of the Heathen,* suite for Chamber Orch. (1961); *A Preview of Coming Attractions* (1975); *The Fox Trots Again* for Chamber Ensemble (1985). **C H A M B E R :** 7 string quartets (1949; 1951; 1953; 1957, *Illiac Suite,* in collaboration with L. Isaacson; 1962; 1972; 1979); 3 violin sonatas (1949, 1955, 1970); *Persiflage* for Flute, Oboe, and Percussion (1977); *Minuet and Trio* for 6 Performers (1980); *Fast and Slow* for Saxophone Quartet (1984); *Metaphors* for Guitar Quartet (1986). **P i a n o :** 6 sonatas (1946, rev. 1968; 1947; 1950; 1950; 1961; 1972). **V O C A L :** *Computer Cantata* for Soprano, Chamber Ensemble, and Tape (1963; in collaboration with R. Baker); songs. **O T H E R :** *Nightmare Music* for Tape (1961); 7 *Electronic Studies* for Tape (1963; in collaboration with R. Baker); *Machine Music* for Piano, Percussion, and Tape (1964); *A Triptych for Hieronymus* for Actors, Dancers, Projections, Tape, and Orch. (1966); *An Avalanche* for Pitchman, Prima Donna, Player Piano, Percussionist, and Pre- recorded Playback (1968); *HPSCHD* for 1 to 7 Harpsichords and 1 to 51 Tapes (1968; in collaboration with J. Cage); *Algorithms I* for 9 Instruments and Tape (1968), *II* for 9 Instruments and Tape (1972; in collaboration with R. Kumra), and *III* for 9 Instruments and Tape (1984); *A Portfolio* for Diverse Performers and Tape (1974); *Electronic Sonata* for Tape (1976); *Midnight Carnival* for a Principal Tape, an Indeterminate Number of Subsidiary Tapes, and other events in an urban environment (1976); *Expo '85* for Multiple Synthesizers (1985; in collaboration with C. Ames and J. Myhill). —**NS/LK/DM**

Hiller, Paul (Douglas), distinguished English baritone, conductor, and teacher; b. Dorchester, Feb. 9, 1949. He trained at the Guildhall School of Music in London, and then served as vicar-choral at St. Paul's Cathedral (1973–74). In 1974 he made his formal concert debut at London's Purcell Room and also founded the Hilliard Ensemble, which he directed in performances of early music until 1990. In 1989 he founded the Theatre of Voices. He also was a prof. of music at the Univ. of Calif. at Davis from 1990. In 1996 he became a prof. and director of the Early Music Inst. at the Ind. Univ. School of Music. He publ. *300 Years of English Partsongs* (1983), *Romantic English Partsongs* (1986), and *The Catch Book* (1987).—NS/LK/DM

Hillis, Margaret (Eleanor), esteemed American conductor and teacher; b. Kokomo, Ind., Oct 1, 1921; d. Evanston, Ill., Feb. 4, 1998. She studied piano as a child and played the tuba and double bass in school bands. After taking her B.A. at Ind. Univ. (1947), she studied choral conducting at the Juilliard School of Music in N.Y. (1947–49) and with Robert Shaw, who engaged her as his assistant (1952–53). In 1950 she became music director of the American Concert Choir and Orch. in N.Y. From 1952 to 1968 she was conductor of the chorus of the American Opera Soc. there, and also was choral director of the N.Y.C. Opera (1955–56). From 1956 to 1960 she was music director of the N.Y. Chamber Soloists. In 1957 Fritz Reiner, music director of the Chicago Sym. Orch., asked Hillis to organize its chorus. She conducted it with great distinction until her retirement in 1994. She also was choral director of the Santa Fe (N.Mex.) Opera (1958–59), music director of the Kenosha (Wisc.) Sym. Orch. (1961–68), resident conductor of the Chicago Civic Orch. (1967–90), conductor of the Cleveland Orch. Chorus (1969–71), music director of the Elgin (Ill.) Sym. Orch. (1971–85), and conductor of the San Francisco Sym. Chorus (1982–83). From 1950 to 1960 she taught at the Union Theological Seminary in N.Y., and also at the Juilliard School of Music (1951–53). After serving as director of choral activities at Northwestern Univ. (1970–77), she was a visiting prof. at the Ind. Univ. School of Music in Bloomington (from 1978). She also led various master classes in choral conducting. In 1954 she founded and became director of the American Choral Union. In 1994 she was honored with the Theodore Thomas Award in recognition of her long and distinguished career.—NS/LK/DM

Hilsberg (real name, Hillersberg), Alexander, Polish-born American violinist, conductor, and teacher; b. Warsaw, April 24, 1897; d. Camden, Maine, Aug. 10, 1961. He studied violin with Auer at the St. Petersburg Cons. In 1923 he emigrated to the U.S. and became a naturalized citizen. He was made a violinist (1926), concertmaster (1931), and assoc. conductor (1945) of the Philadelphia Orch.; he also taught at the Curtis Inst. of Music (1927–53). From 1952 to 1960 he was conductor of the New Orleans Phil., and then was head of the orch. dept. at the New School of Music in Philadelphia.—NS/LK/DM

Hilton, John (the Elder), English organist and composer, father of **John Hilton (the Younger);** b. place and date unknown; d. Cambridge, before March 20, 1608. He was a countertenor at Lincoln Cathedral (1584–94), then organist at Trinity Coll., Cambridge (from 1594). It is not possible to determine which sacred works ascribed to John Hilton are by the Elder or the Younger. The anthem *Call to Remembrance* is ascribed to the Elder in one source. His only known secular work is the madrigal *Fair Oriana, Beauty's Queen,* publ. in Morley's *The Triumphes of Oriana* (London, 1601). —NS/LK/DM

Hilton, John (the Younger), English organist and composer, son of **John Hilton (the Elder);** b. probably in Cambridge, 1599; d. Westminster (buried), March 21, 1657. He studied at Trinity Coll., Cambridge (Mus.B., 1626), then became organist and clerk of St. Margaret's, Westminster (1628). He ed. a popular collection under the title *Catch that Catch Can* for 3 to 4 Voices (London, 1652; 3ʳᵈ ed., 1667, as *The Musical Companion*), which contains 42 pieces by him. Other secular works include *Ayres* or *Fa La's* for 3 Voices (London, 1627; ed. by J. Warren, Musical Antiquarian Soc., XIII, London, 1844), 14 fantasias *a* 3, several dance movements, and various songs and dialogues in MS collections (7 ed. in Musica Britannica, XXXIII, 1971). His sacred works, which include 4 Services, a Te Deum, 5 anthems, and 12 verse anthems, are open to much speculation; some may be by his father.—NS/LK/DM

Himmel, Friedrich Heinrich, German composer and pianist; b. Treuenbrietzen, Nov. 20, 1765; d. Berlin, June 8, 1814. He began his musical training with Klaus, the local organist, then, following theological studies at the Univ. of Halle (1785–86), he studied with Naumann in Dresden. In 1792 he was made chamber composer to the Prussian court in Berlin, which position made it possible for him to complete his musical training in Italy (1793–95). In 1795 he returned to the Prussian court as Kapellmeister, but he also made tours as a concert artist. In spite of his bouts with alcohol, he remained a favorite at the Prussian court. His most successful score was the Singspiel *Fanchon das Leiermädchen* (Berlin, May 15, 1804).

WORKS: DRAMATIC: Opera: *La morte di Semiramide* (Naples, Jan. 12, 1795); *Alessandro* (St. Petersburg, Jan. 1799); *Vasco da Gama* (Berlin, Jan. 12, 1801); *Frohsinn und Schwärmerei* (Berlin, March 9, 1801); *Fanchon das Leiermädchen* (Berlin, May 15, 1804); *Die Sylphen* (Berlin, April 14, 1806); *Der Kobold* (Vienna, May 22, 1813). Oratorio: *Isacco figura del redentore* (Berlin, March 14, 1792). VOCAL: Cantata: *Il primo navigatore* (Venice, March 1, 1794). Other Vocal: Songs. OTHER: Piano Concerto; chamber music; piano pieces.

BIBL.: L. Odendahl, *F.H. H.: Bemerkungen zur Geschichte der Berliner Oper um die Wende des 18. und 19. Jahrhunderts* (diss., Univ. of Bonn, 1914).—NS/LK/DM

Hindemith, Paul, eminent German-born American composer and teacher; b. Hanau, near Frankfurt am Main, Nov. 16, 1895; d. Frankfurt am Main, Dec. 28, 1963. He began studying violin at the age of 9; at 14, he entered the Hoch Cons. in Frankfurt am Main, where he studied violin with A. Rebner, and composition with Arnold Mendelssohn and Sekles. His father was killed in World War I, and Hindemith was compelled to rely on his own resources to make a living. He was concertmaster of the orch. of the Frankfurt am Main Opera (1915–23), and later played the viola in the string quartet of his teacher Rebner; from 1922 to 1929 he was violist in the Amar String Quartet; also appeared as a soloist on the viola and viola d'amore; later was engaged as a conductor, mainly in his own works. As a composer, he joined the modern movement and was an active participant in the contemporary music concerts at Donaueschingen, and later in Baden-Baden. In 1927 he was appointed instructor in composition at the Berlin Hochschule für Musik. With the advent of the Hitler regime in 1933, Hindemith began to experience increasing difficulties, both artistically and politically. Although his own ethnic purity was never questioned, he was married to Gertrud Rottenberg, daughter of the Jewish conductor Ludwig Rottenberg, and he stubbornly refused to cease ensemble playing with undeniable Jews. Hitler's propaganda minister, Goebbels, accused Hindemith of cultural Bolshevism, and his music fell into an official desuetude. Unwilling to compromise with the barbarous regime, Hindemith accepted engagements abroad. Beginning in 1934, he made 3 visits to Ankara at the invitation of the Turkish government, and helped to organize the music curriculum at the Ankara Cons. He made his first American appearance at the Coolidge Festival at the Library of Congress in Washington, D.C., in a performance of his Unaccompanied Viola Sonata (April 10, 1937). Hindemith was an instructor at the Berkshire Music Center at Tanglewood in the summer of 1940; from 1940 to 1953 he was a prof. at Yale Univ.; during the academic year 1950–51, he was the Charles Eliot Norton Lecturer at Harvard Univ. He became a naturalized American citizen in 1946. In 1953 he went to Switzerland and gave courses at the Univ. of Zürich. He also was active as a guest conductor in Europe and the U.S.

Hindemith's early music reflects rebellious opposition to all tradition; this is noted in such works as the opera *Mörder, Hoffnung der Frauen* (1919) and *Suite 1922* for Piano (1922); at the same time, he cultivated the techniques of constructivism, evident in his theatrical sketch *Hin und Zurück* (1927), in which *Krebsgang* (retrograde movement) is applied to the action on the stage, so that events are reversed; in a work of a much later period, *Ludus Tonalis* (1943), the postlude is the upside-down version of the prelude. Along constructive lines is Hindemith's cultivation of *Gebrauchsmusik*, that is, music for use; he was also an ardent champion of *Hausmusik*, to be played or sung by amateurs at home; the score of his *Frau Musica* (as revised in 1944) has an obbligato part for the audience to sing. A neo-Classical trend is shown in a series of works, entitled *Kammermusik*, for various instrumental combinations, polyphonically conceived, and Baroque in style. Although he made free use of atonal melodies, he was never tempted to adopt an integral 12–tone method, which he opposed on aesthetic grounds. Having made a thorough study of early music, he artfully assimilated its polyphony in his works; his masterpiece of this genre was the opera *Mathis der Maler*. A prolific composer, Hindemith wrote music of all types for all instrumental combinations, including a series of sonatas for each orch. instrument with piano. His style may be described as a synthesis of modern, Romantic, Classical, Baroque, and other styles, a combination saved from the stigma of eclecticism only by Hindemith's superlative mastery of technical means. As a theorist and pedagogue, he developed a self-consistent method of presentation derived from the acoustical nature of harmonies. The Auftrag der Hindemith-Stiftung began issuing a collected ed. in 1975. Thematic indexes have been compiled by K. Stone (N.Y., 1954; verified by the composer) and H. Rösner, *Paul Hindemith—Katalog seiner Werke, Diskographie, Bibliographie, Einführung in das Schaffen* (Frankfurt am Main, 1970).

WORKS: DRAMATIC: O p e r a : *Mörder, Hoffnung der Frauen*, op.12 (1919; Stuttgart, June 4, 1921); *Das Nusch- Nuschi*, op.20, marionette opera (1920; Stuttgart, June 4, 1921; rev. version, Königsberg, Jan. 22, 1931); *Sancta Susanna*, op.21 (1921; Frankfurt am Main, March 26, 1922); *Cardillac*, op.39 (Dresden, Nov. 9, 1926; rev. version, Zürich, June 20, 1952); *Hin und Zurück*, op.45a, 1–act sketch (Baden-Baden, July 17, 1927); *Neues vom Tage* (1928–29; Berlin, June 8, 1929; rev. 1953; Naples, April 7, 1954, composer conducting); *Mathis der Maler* (1934–35; Zürich, May 28, 1938); *Orfeo*, realization of Monteverdi's opera (1943); *Die Harmonie der Welt* (1950–57; Munich, Aug. 11, 1957, composer conducting); *Das lange Weihnachtsmahl* (1960; Mannheim, Dec. 17, 1961). **I n c i d e n t a l M u s i c :** *Tuttifantchen* (Darmstadt, Dec. 13, 1922). **B a l l e t :** *Der Dämon*, op.28, pantomime (1922; Darmstadt, Dec. 1, 1923); *Nobilissima visione*, dance legend in 6 scenes (perf. as *St. Francis* by the Ballets Russes de Monte Carlo, London, July 21, 1938, composer conducting); *Theme and Variations: The 4 Temperaments* for String Orch. and Piano (1940; N.Y., Nov. 20, 1946); *Hérodiade*, after Mallarmé (perf. as *Mirror before Me* by the Martha Graham Dance Co., Washington, D.C., Oct. 30, 1944). **ORCH.:** Cello Concerto, op.3 (1916); *Lustige Sinfonietta*, op.4 (1916); Piano Concerto, op.29 (1924); Concerto for Oboe, Bassoon, Violin, and Orch., op.38 (Duisburg, July 25, 1925); *Konzertmusik* for Wind Orch., op.41 (Donaueschingen, July 1926); *Konzertmusik* for Viola and Orch., op.48 (Hamburg, March 28, 1930, composer soloist); *Konzertmusik* for Piano, Brass, and 2 Harps, op.49 (Chicago, Oct. 12, 1930), *Konzertmusik* for Strings and Brass, op.50 (for 50th anniversary of the Boston Sym. Orch.; Boston, April 3, 1931); *Konzertstück* for Trautonium and Strings (1931); *Philharmonisches Konzert*, variations (Berlin, April 15, 1932); *Mathis der Maler*, sym. from the opera (Berlin, March 11, 1934, Furtwängler conducting); *Der Schwanendreher*, concerto for Viola and Small Orch. (Amsterdam, Nov. 14, 1935, composer soloist); *Trauermusik* for Solo Viola or Violin or Cello and String Orch. (written for a memorial broadcast for King George V, who died on Jan. 20, 1936; London, Jan. 22, 1936, composer soloist); *Symphonic Dances* (London, Dec. 5, 1937); *Nobilissima visione*, suite from the ballet (Venice, Sept. 13, 1938); Violin Concerto (1939; Amsterdam, March 14, 1940); Cello Concerto (1940; Boston, Feb. 7, 1941; Piatigorsky soloist); Sym. in E-flat (1940; Minneapolis, Nov. 21, 1941); *Cupid and Psyche*, overture for a ballet (Philadelphia, Oct. 29, 1943); *Symphonic Metamorphosis on Themes of Carl Maria von Weber* (1943; N.Y., Jan. 20, 1944); *Theme and Variations: The 4 Temperaments* for String Orch. and Piano (Boston, Sept. 3, 1944, Foss soloist); Piano Concerto (1945; Cleveland, Feb. 27, 1947, Sanroma soloist); *Symphonia Serena* (1946; Dallas, Feb. 2, 1947); Clarinet Concerto (1947; Philadelphia, Dec. 11, 1950, Benny Goodman soloist); Concerto for 4 Winds, Harp, and Small Orch. (N.Y., May 15, 1949); Concerto for Trumpet, Bassoon, and Strings (New Haven, Conn., Nov. 4, 1949; 3rd movement added in 1952); Sinfonietta (1949; Louisville, March 1, 1950, composer conducting); Horn Concerto (1949; Baden-Baden, June 8, 1950, Dennis Brain soloist); Sym. in B-flat for Concert Band (Washington, D.C., April 5, 1951, composer conducting); *Die Harmonie der Welt*, sym. from the opera (1951; Basel, Jan. 24, 1952); *Pittsburgh Symphony* (1958; Pittsburgh, Jan. 30, 1959, composer conducting); Organ Concerto (1962–63; N.Y., April 25, 1963, Heiller soloist, composer conducting). **CHAMBER:** *Andante and Scherzo*, op.1, trio for Clarinet, Horn, and Piano (1914); unnumbered String Quartet in C, op.2 (1915); Piano Quintet, op.7 (1917); *3 Stücke* for Cello and Piano, op.8 (1917); 6 numbered string quartets: No. 1, op.10 (Frankfurt am Main, June 2, 1919), No. 2, op.16 (Donaueschingen, Aug. 1, 1922), No. 3, op.22 (Donaueschingen, Nov. 4, 1922), No. 4, op.32 (Vienna, Nov. 5, 1923), No. 5 (Washington, D.C., Nov. 7, 1943), and No. 6 (Washington, D.C., March 21, 1946); set of 6 sonatas, opp. 11/1–6: 2 for Violin and Piano (1918), 1 for Cello and Piano (1919), 1 for Viola and Piano (1919), 1 for Solo Viola (1919), and 1 for Solo Violin (1919); *Kleine Kammermusik*, op.24/2, for Wind Quintet (1922); set of 4 sonatas, opp. 25/1–4: 1 for Solo Viola (1922), 1 for Viola d'Amore and Piano (1923), 1 for Solo Cello (1923), and 1 for Viola and Piano (1924); *"Minimax"—Reportorium für Militärmusik*, parody for String Quartet (1923); Quintet for Clarinet and String Quartet, op.30 (Salzburg Festival, Aug. 7, 1923); set of 4 sonatas, opp. 31/1–4: 2 for Solo Violin (1924), 1, *Canonic Sonatina*, for 2 Flutes (1924), and 1 for Solo Viola (1924); 2 trios for Violin, Viola, and Cello (op.34, Salzburg, Aug. 6, 1924; Antwerp, March 17, 1933); *Rondo* for 3 Guitars (1925); *3 Stücke* for 5 Instruments (1925); 7 numbered pieces titled *Kammermusik*: No. 1, op.24/1 (Donaueschingen Festival, July 31, 1922), No. 2, op.36/1, for Piano and 12 Instruments (Frankfurt am Main, Oct. 31, 1924), No. 3, op.36/2, for Cello and 10 Instruments (Bochum, April 30, 1925; composer's brother, Rudolf, soloist), No. 4, op.36/3, for Violin and Large Chamber Orch. (Dessau, Sept. 25, 1925), No. 5, op.36/4, for Viola and Large Chamber Orch. (Berlin, Nov. 3, 1927), No. 6, op.46/1, for Viola d'Amore and Chamber Orch. (1927; Cologne, March 29, 1928), and No. 7, op.46/2, for Organ and Chamber Ensemble (1927; Frankfurt am Main, Jan. 8, 1928); *8 Pieces* for Flute (1927); Trio for Viola, Heckelphone or Saxophone, and Piano, op.47 (1928); *2 Canonic Duets* for 2 Violins (1929); *14 Easy Duets* for 2 Violins (1931); *Konzertstück* for 2 Saxophones (1933); *Duet* for Viola and Cello (1934); 2 violin sonatas (1935, 1939); Flute Sonata (1936); Sonata for Solo Viola (1937); *Meditation* for Violin or Viola or Cello and Piano (1938); Quartet for Clarinet, Violin, Cello, and Piano (1938); Oboe Sonata (1938); Bassoon Sonata (1938; transcribed for Bass Clarinet in 1959 for Josef Horák); Clarinet Sonata (1939); Horn Sonata (1939); Trumpet Sonata (1939); Sonata for Solo Harp (1939); Viola Sonata (1939); English Horn Sonata (1941); Trombone Sonata (1941); *A Frog He Went a-Courting*, variations for Cello and Piano (1941); *Echo* for Flute and Piano (1942); Sonata for Saxophone or Alto Horn or Horn and Piano (1943); Septet for Winds (1948); Double Bass Sonata (1949); Sonata for 4 Horns (1952); Tuba Sonata (1955); Octet for Clarinet, Bassoon, Horn, and String Quintet (Berlin, Sept. 23, 1958). **P i a n o :** *7 Waltzes*, op.6, for 4 Hands (1916); *In einer Nacht*, op.15, a set of 14 pieces (1920); Sonata, op.17 (1917); *Tanzstücke*, op.19 (1922); *Suite "1922,"* op.26 (1922); *Klaviermusik*, op.37, incorporating *Übung in drei Stücken*, op.37/1 (1925) and *Reihe kleiner Stücke*, op.37/2 (1927); 3 numbered sonatas (1936); Sonata for 4 Hands (1938); Sonata for 2 Pianos (1942); *Ludus Tonalis*, studies (Chicago, Feb. 15, 1943). **VOCAL:** *3 Songs* for Soprano and Orch., op.9 (1917); *Melancholie* for Contralto and String Quartet, op.13 (1918); *Des Todes Tod*, op.23/1, 3 songs for Woman's Voice, 2 Violas, and 2 Cellos (1922); *Die junge Magd*, op.23/2, 6 poems for Contralto, Flute, Clarinet, and String Quartet (1922); *Lieder nach alten Texten*, op.33, for Chorus (1923); *Die Serenaden*, op.35, little cantata for Soprano, Oboe, Viola, and Cello (1925); *Der Lindenbergflug* for Soloists and Orch. (1929); *Das Unaufhörliche*, oratorio (Berlin, Nov. 21, 1931); *5 Songs on Old Texts* for Chorus (c. 1938); *6 Chansons* for Chorus, after Rilke (1939); *3 Choruses* for Men's

Chorus (1939); *The Demon of the Gibbet* for Men's Chorus (1939); *When Lilacs Last in the Dooryard Bloom'd*, an American Requiem after Whitman, for Mezzo-soprano, Baritone, Chorus, and Orch. (N.Y., May 14, 1946); *Apparebit Repentina Dies* for Chorus and Brass (Cambridge, Mass., May 2, 1947); *Das Marienleben* for Soprano and Orch., after Rilke (1938–48; rev., shortened, and orchestrated version of songs orig. for Voice and Piano, 1923); *Ite, angeli veloces*, cantata trilogy: *Chant de triomphe du roi David, Custos quid de nocte*, and *Cantique de l'espérance* (1953–55; 1st complete perf., Wuppertal, June 4, 1955); *12 Madrigals* for 5–part Chorus (1958); *Der Mainzer Umzug* for Soprano, Tenor, Baritone, Chorus, and Orch. (Mainz, June 23, 1962); Mass for Chorus (Vienna, Nov. 12, 1963). **V o i c e a n d P i a n o :** *3 Hymnen*, op.14, after Whitman (1919); *8 Songs* for Soprano, op.18 (1920); *Das Marienleben*, op.27, after Rilke (Donaueschingen, June 17, 1923; rev. radically and perf. in Hannover, Nov. 3, 1948); *6 Lieder* for Tenor and Piano (1933–35); *13 Motets* (1941–60); *9 English Songs* (1942–44).

GEBRAUCHSMUSIK: Music for Mechanical Instruments, op.40: Toccata for Player Piano, and Music for Mechanical Organ (both 1926–27); music for the film *Felix the Cat* for Mechanical Organ, op.42 (1927); *Spielmusik* for Strings, Flutes, and Oboes, op.43/1 (1927); *Lieder für Singkreise* for Voices, op.43/2 (1927); *Schulwerk für Instrumental- Zusammenspiel*, op.44 (1927); *Sing- und Spielmusiken für Liebhaber und Musikfreunde*, including: *Frau Musica* for Soli, Chorus, and Strings, op.45/1 (1928; rev. as *In Praise of Music*, 1943), *8 Canons* for 2 Voices and Instruments, op.45/2 (1928), *Ein Jäger aus Kurpfalz* for Strings and Winds, op.45/3 (1928), *Kleine Klaviermusik*, op.45/4 (1929), and *Martinslied* for Unison Chorus and 3 Instruments, op.45/5 (1929); *Lehrstück* for Male Soloists, Narrator, Chorus, Orch., Dance Group, Clowns, and Community Singing, after Brecht (Baden-Baden, July 28, 1929); *Wir bauen eine Stadt*, play for Children's Soli and Chorus, and Instruments (Berlin, June 21, 1930); *Ploner Musiktag*, in 4 sections: *Morgenmusik* for Brass Quintet, *Tafelmusik* for Strings and Brass, *Kantate* for Soli, Children's Chorus, Narrator, Strings, Winds, and Percussion, and *Abendkonzert*, 6 individual pieces for Chamber and Orch. Grouping (all 1932; Plon, June 1932); *Wer sich die Musik erkiest* for Voices and Instruments (1952).

WRITINGS: *Unterweisung im Tonsatz* (2 vols., 1937, 1939; Eng. ed. as *The Craft of Musical Composition*, N.Y., 1941; rev., 1945); *A Concentrated Course in Traditional Harmony* (2 vols., N.Y., 1943, 1953); *Elementary Training for Musicians* (N.Y., 1946); *J.S. Bach: Heritage and Obligation* (New Haven, Conn., 1952; Ger. ed., *J.S. Bach: Ein verpflichtendes Erbe*, Wiesbaden, 1953); *A Composer's World: Horizons and Limitations* (Cambridge, Mass., 1952).

BIBL.: The *H.-Jahrbuch* began publication in 1971. See also the following: H. Strobel, *P. H.* (Mainz, 1928; 3rd ed., aug., 1948); H. Schilling, *P. H.'s Cardillac* (Würzburg, 1962); A. Briner, *P. H.* (Zürich, 1970; Eng. tr., 1987); I. Kemp, *H.* (London, 1970); E. Zwink, *P. H.s Unterweisung im Tonsatz* (Göppingen, 1974); G. Skelton, *P. H.: The Man behind the Music* (London, 1975); G. Metz, *Melodische Polyphonie in der Zwölftonordnung: Studien zum Kontrapunkt P. H.s* (Baden-Baden, 1976); D. Rexroth, *Erprobungen und Erfahrungen: Zu P. H.s Schaffen in den Zwanziger Jahren* (Frankfurt am Main, 1978); G. Schubert, *H.* (Hamburg, 1981); D. Rexroth, *P. H. Briefe* (Frankfurt am Main, 1982); E. Preussner, *P. H.: Ein Lebensbild* (Innsbruck, 1984); D. Neumeyer, *The Music of P. H.* (New Haven, 1986); S. Cook, *Opera During the Weimar Republic: The Zeitopern of Ernst Krenek, Kurt Weill, and P. H.* (Ann Arbor, 1987); A. Briner, D. Rexroth, and G. Schubert, *P. H.: Leben und Werk in Bild und Text* (Zürich, 1988); S. Hinton, *The Idea of Gebrauchsmusik: A Study of Musical Aesthetics in the Weimar*

Republic (1919–1933) with Particular Reference to the Works of P. H. (N.Y. and London, 1989); L. Noss, *P. H. in the United States* (Urbana, 1989); G. Breimann, *"Mathis der Maler" und der "Fall H.:" Studien zu H.s Opernlibretto im Kontext der kulturgeschichtlichen und politischen Begingungen der 30er. Jahre* (Frankfurt am Main, 1997); M. Kube, *H.s frühe Streichquartette (1915–1923): Studien zu Form, Faktur und Harmonik* (Kassel, 1997); S. Bruhn, *The Temptation of P H.: Mathis der Maler as Spiritual Testimony* (Stuyvesant, N.Y., 1998); K. Kim, *Studien zum musikpädagogischen Werk P. H.s* (Frankfurt am Main, 1998).—NS/LK/DM

Hinderas (real name, **Henderson**), **Natalie**, black American pianist; b. Oberlin, Ohio, June 15, 1927; d. Elkins Park, Pa., July 22, 1987. Her father was a jazz musician, and her mother was a music teacher. She was a child prodigy and was accepted at the Oberlin School of Music at the age of 8; graduated at 18 (B.Mus., 1945). She subsequently took lessons with Olga Samaroff at the Juilliard School of Music in N.Y., and then studied piano with Eduard Steuermann and composition with Vincent Persichetti. She made her N.Y. debut in 1954, and later toured in Europe and the Far East. In addition to the standard piano repertoire, she included in her concert programs pieces by black composers.—NS/LK/DM

Hines, Earl (**Kenneth**; aka **Fatha**), talented and intensely creative jazz pianist, leader, singer, composer; b. Dusquene, Pa., Dec. 28, 1903; d. Oakland, April 22, 1983. His sister, Nancy, a pianist, led her own band in Pittsburgh during the 1930s; their father, Joseph, played cornet in local brass bands; their mother, Mary, was an organist (and pianist). He began playing cornet at an early age, taking piano lesssons from the age of nine. He was interested in a classical music career, but that was closed to most blacks, and he soon gravitated to jazz. He was spotted by vocalist Lois B. Deppe who secured him a place in Arthur Rideout's Orch. Later, Deppe organized The Pittsburgh Serenaders (which Hines directed) for residency at the Lieder House (Pittsburgh). He toured with Deppe (1923). He worked with Harry Collins's Orch. in Pittsburgh then moved to Chicago, played a residency at the Entertainers' Club with violinist Vernie Robinson, and later led at the same venue. He toured for almost a year with Carroll Dickerson, returned to Chicago and worked with Dickerson, Erskine Tate, and other leaders. He was musical director for Louis Armstrong's Stompers at the Sunset Cafe (1927). Later that year, Armstrong, Hines, and Zutty Singleton ran their own short-lived club. In late 1927, Hines began working with Jimmie Noone at the Apex Club. He went to N.Y. in December 1928 to record a solo session for the Q.R.S, Company, returned to Chicago, took his own band into the Grand Terrace on Dec. 28, 1928. He continued recording with Armstrong in 1929.

Throughout the 1930s Hines and His Orch. played many residencies at the Grand Terrace. They also did regular touring including the Southern states, and occasionally played dates in N.Y. While at the Grand Terrace, radio announcer Ted Pearson used to introduce him as "Fatha Hines coming through deep forest (his theme song) with his children," and the nickname "Fatha" stuck. Among the band's alumni were Omer Simeon, Budd Johnson, Trummy Young, and Ray Nance. Hines temporarily disbanded early in 1940, opened his own Studio Club in Chicago, then re-formed his big band for residencies in Calif. (late 1940). Billy Eckstine sang with him, as did Sarah Vaughan. He continued to lead his own successful big bands until 1947. Many of his young sidemen went on to gain considerable fame; one temporary innovation was the introduction of an all-girl string section in September 1943. This legendary band also included Charlie Parker on tenor and Dizzy Gillespie. It is known to have made at least one radio broadcast but no recording of the band was ever found. In March 1944 Hines briefly fronted the Ellington Band while Duke was absent with tonsillitis.

Hines disbanded in 1947 and again ran his own club in Chicago. He joined the Louis Armstrong All Stars from January 1948 until autumn 1951. Late in 1948 Hines fronted his own big band, which for a time traveled with the Armstrong All Stars. He led his own sextet from late 1951, and did residencies and touring. He visited Europe with an all-star group (headed by Jack Teagarden and Earl Hines) in autumn 1957. He worked mainly in Calif. with his own band throughout the late 1950s, primarily in a Dixieland vein. He moved with his family to Oakland in 1960, did regular tours and club residencies. He played highly successful N.Y. dates in 1964 at the Little Theatre (issued on LP and often credited with revitalizing his career) and at Birdland. From that point on he made numerous solo recordings featuring extended and freewheeling improvisations at the peak of his powers. He toured Europe in spring 1965 including Berlin, and subsequently made several visits to Europe. He toured Russia with a sextet in the summer of 1966. He did extensive engagements throughout the late 1960s and 1970s, toured Europe, Japan, and Australia. He played his last engagement in San Francisco just a week before his death.

One of the most truly improvisational artists of any generation, in unaccompanied solos he not only did not repeat himself: It takes some doing for the listener to recognize two takes of the same piece! Though raised on stride, and clearly in that tradition on his 1923 recordings, by his next sessions of 1928 (unfortunately there are none in-between), he was bursting with new and unique ideas. It was common for him to modulate into a different key, something never done, and his left hand might do anything: a bit of stride, a walking line, a chromatic scale, comping on or off the beat. He used wild dissonances, and his voice leading was often rough but attractive. He had an impact on virtually all 1930s pianists, including Teddy Wilson and, though less acknowledged, Art Tatum. His much touted "trumpet style," consisting of little more than the time-honored technique of playing in octaves, is surely the least significant and least distinctive of his many innovations. Often said to be an imitation of Armstrong, Hines himself said he developed it earlier, simply to be heard in a band. In every way his style is truly pianistic and not in the least "trumpet-like."

Disc.: *57 Varieties* (1928); *Deep Forest* (1932); *Harlem Lament* (1933); *Piano Man* (1939); *E. "Fatha" H.* (1947); *E. H. and the All Stars* (1950); *Varieties* (1952); *E. H. Trio* (1952); *E. H. Plays Fats*

Waller (1953); *E.'s Pearls* (1960); *Spontaneous Explorations* (1964); *Linger Awhile* (1964); *Legendary Little Theater Concert* (1964); *Grand Reunion, Vol. 1, 2* (1965); *At the Village Vanguard* (1965). Elvin Jones: *Once Upon a Time* (1966). *Blues and Things* (1967); *E. H. at Home* (1969); *Quintessential Recording Session* (1970); *My Tribute to Louis* (1971); *H. Does Hoagy* (1971); *E. H. Plays Duke Ellington* (1971); *Comes in Handy* (1971); *Tour De Force* (1972); *Solo Walk in Tokyo* (1972); *Quintessential Continued* (1973); *E. H. Plays George Gershwin* (1973); *E. H. and Budd Johnson* (1974); *Father of Modern Jazz Piano* (1977); *Fatha Plays Hits He Missed* (1978); *Live and in Living Jazz* (1979); *Linger Awhile* (1979).—**LP/JC**

Hines (real name, **Heinz**), **Jerome (Albert Link),** distinguished American bass; b. Los Angeles, Nov. 8, 1921. He received training in mathematics, chemistry, and physics at the Univ. of Calif. at Los Angeles (B.A., 1943), and concurrently took vocal lessons with Gennaro Curci in Los Angeles; he later studied voice with Samuel Margolis in N.Y. In 1940 he made his stage debut as Bill Bobstay in *H.M.S. Pinafore* with the Los Angeles Civic Light Opera. On Oct. 19, 1941, he made his San Francisco Opera debut as Monterone. He then made appearances as a soloist with American orchs., and also sang with the New Orleans Opera (1944–46). After winning the Caruso Award in 1946, he made his debut at the Metropolitan Opera in N.Y. as the Sergeant in *Boris Godunov* on Nov. 21, 1946; he first sang its title role there on Feb. 18, 1954, making a memorable impression. In the meantime, he sang in South America and Europe. He appeared at the Glyndebourne and Edinburgh Festivals in 1953, at the Bavarian State Opera in Munich in 1954, and at La Scala in Milan and the Bayreuth Festival in 1958. On Sept. 23, 1962, he made a dramatic debut at the Bolshoi Theater in Moscow when he sang Boris Godunov in Russian. He continued to sing regularly at the Metropolitan Opera, where he remained on the roster for over 45 years. In addition to his commanding portrayal of Boris Godunov, he also won distinction for such roles as Don Giovanni, Sarastro, Wotan, Philip II, Don Basilio, and King Marke. His deep religious faith was revealed in his choice of Christ as the subject of his opera *I Am the Way,* and in the title of his autobiography *This is My Story, This is My Song* (1968). He also publ. a book of interviews as *Great Singers on Great Singing* (1982) and the volume *The Four Voices of Man* (1997).—**NS/LK/DM**

Hingston (also **Hingeston, Hinkstone,** and **Hinkson**), **John,** English organist, viol player, and composer; b. c. 1610; d. London (buried), Dec. 17, 1683. He sang in the choir at York Minster and may have studied with Orlando Gibbons. He then was in the service of Charles I, and subsequently state organist and private musician to Oliver Cromwell (1654–58). After the Restoration, he became viol player and overseer of the court musical instruments (1660). Purcell became his apprentice in 1673. Among his works are fantasias and dances utilizing viols and violins with organ, as well as some for cornetts and sackbut. He also wrote dances for 2 and 3 bass viols.

BIBL.: E. Bock, *The String Fantasies of J. Hingeston c. 1610–1683* (diss., Univ. of Iowa, 1956).—**NS/LK/DM**

Hinrichs, Gustav, German-American conductor, teacher, and composer; b. Ludwigslust, Dec. 10, 1850; d. Mountain Lake, N.J., March 26, 1942. He studied violin and piano with his father, and received training in composition in Hamburg from Marxsen. He began conducting at 15, and at 20 went to San Francisco, where he conducted the Fabbri Opera. In 1885 he went to N.Y. as asst. conductor to Theodore Thomas and the American Opera Co. In 1888 he founded his own opera company in Philadelphia, where he conducted the U.S. premieres of *Cavalleria rusticana* (Sept. 9, 1891) and *Manon Lescaut* (Aug. 29, 1894); he also conducted the U.S. premiere of *Pagliacci* in N.Y. (June 15, 1893). On Oct. 14, 1899, he conducted *Il Barbiere di Siviglia* with the Metropolitan Opera Co. during its visit to Syracuse, N.Y. On Oct. 19, 1899, he conducted *Faust* at the Metropolitan Opera in N.Y., remaining on its roster for the season and returning there for the 1903–04 season. He taught at the National Cons. and at Columbia Univ. (1895–1906). Among his works were the opera *Onti-Ora* (Philadelphia, July 28, 1890, composer conducting), a symphonic suite, and some vocal pieces.—**NS/LK/DM**

Hinshaw, William Wade, American baritone, pedagogue, and operatic impresario; b. near Union, Iowa, Nov. 3, 1867; d. Washington, D.C., Nov. 27, 1947. He studied civil engineering (B.S., 1888), music (Mus.B., 1890), and law (LL.B., 1897) at Valparaiso (Ind.) Univ., and also pursued vocal training with Arturo Marescalchi and Alfred Hertz. In 1893 he made his debut at a concert at the World's Columbian Exposition in Chicago. From 1895 to 1899 he was head of the music dept. at Valparaiso Univ. On Nov. 6, 1899, he made his operatic debut as Gounod's Méphistophélès with Henry Savage's opera company in St. Louis. Returning to Chicago, he became secretary of the Hinshaw School of Opera and Drama; when it merged with the Chicago Cons. in 1903, he became president of the new institution; subsequently he was director of the Hinshaw Cons. (1907–10). With the tenor James Sheehan, he organized the Metropolitan Grand Opera Co. to stage operas in English at the International Theatre; Hinshaw sang Telramund in the company's first production in 1908. On Nov. 16, 1910, he made his debut at the Metropolitan Opera in N.Y. at Biterolf, and subsequently remained on its roster as a distinguished Wagnerian until 1913; he also appeared at the Wagner Festivals in Graz (1912) and Berlin (1914). In 1916 he offered a prize of $1,000 for the best 1–act opera by an American composer, which was won by Hadley with his opera *Bianca*. After serving as president of the Soc. of American Singers in N.Y. (1918–20), he toured the U.S., Canada, and Cuba with his own opera company (1920–26). He spent his remaining years compiling the *Encyclopedia of American Quaker Genealogy* (6 vols., 1936–47).—**NS/LK/DM**

Hinton, Arthur, English composer; b. Beckenham, Nov. 20, 1869; d. Rottingdean, Aug. 11, 1941. He studied at the Royal Academy of Music in London, where he subsequently taught violin. He then went to Munich for further study with Rheinberger. He composed a Sym., which he conducted at one of the concerts of the Munich

Cons. He traveled in Italy, returning to London in 1896, where his 2nd Sym. was performed in 1903. He married the pianist Katharine Goodson, who gave many performances of his piano works, including a concerto. He wrote the children's operettas *The Disagreeable Princess* and *St. Elizabeth's Rose* as well as a number of songs. —NS/LK/DM

Hinton, Milt(on John; aka **the Judge),** revered jazz bassist; b. Vicksburg, Miss., June 23, 1910. He received his first music lessons from his mother. He learned brass and string bass while at high school in Chicago. His first professional work was with the Boyd Atkins Band, and he later worked with Tiny Parham before playing at the Show Boat Cabaret in Chicago with bands led by Jabbo Smith and Cassino Simpson. He worked with Eddie South in late 1931, was briefly with Erskine Tate, then rejoined Eddie South for a long spell including a tour of Calif. (late 1932). He worked with Zutty Singleton and Fate Marable, then in late 1936 joined Cab Calloway. He remained with Calloway until 1951. (He threw the spitball that got Gillespie fired but did not admit it until years later.) He then did extensive freelance work in N.Y. He worked for two months with Count Basie, later with the Louis Armstrong All Stars (summer 1953 and again in 1954). From then until the present time he has been one of the busiest session men in N.Y. He visited Paris in November 1966, and continues to play jazz dates. He appeared at the New Orleans Jazz Fest in 1969, and at the House of Sounds Festival (Washington, D.C., September 1971). He maintained a very busy schedule since the 1970s, including overseas tours with Pearl Bailey, Bing Crosby, etc. He has also worked with Lionel Hampton, Terry Gibbs, Jimmy Rushing, Branford Marsalis, Buddy DeFranco, and many others. He also worked and recorded with Branford Marsalis in the late 1980s.

His wife Mona usually accompanies him. An accomplished photographer, he has had several exhibitions of his work presented. In addition, two books of his jazz photos, *Bass Lines* (reminiscences) and *Over Time*, were published in 1991. He also conducted several interviews with Danny Barker, Teddy Wilson, Quentin Jackson and Jo Jones for the JOHP/IJS. A talented bassist who plays expertly in many styles, Hinton is impressive not only for his longevity but his continued inventiveness. Seemingly ageless, he continues to perform and record prolifically.

DISC.: *M. H. Quartet* (1955); *M. H.* (1955); *Basses Loaded* (1955); *Rhythm Section* (1956); *Modern Art of Jazz* (1956); *Trio* (1977); *Judge's Decision* (1986); *Old Man Time* (1989); *Laughing at Life* (1994).—JC/LP

Hirai, Kozaburo, Japanese composer; b. Kochi, Sept. 10, 1910. He studied violin with Robert Pollak and composition and conducting with Klaus Pringsheim at the Tokyo Imperial Academy of Music (1929–34). He taught at the Academy (1937–47), and in 1966 he organized the Assn. of Composers and Authors (ACA).

WORKS: DRAMATIC: O p e r e t t a : *Taketori-Monogatari* (1949). B a l l e t : *Spirit of the Snow* (1942; rev. 1968). ORCH.: *Festival of Insects*, suite (Tokyo, Sept. 15, 1941); *Pastoral* for Clarinet and Strings (1943); *On the Grass*, suite (1947);

Koto Concerto (Tokyo, Nov. 12, 1950); *Festival*, concerto grosso for 3 Koto Soli and Koto Orch. (1962); *Symphonic Ballad* (1963); *Seaside Sketch* for Chamber Orch. (1967); *Marriage of the Whale*, symphonic chorus for 3 Voices, Chorus, and Orch. (Tokyo, Nov. 27, 1969); *Hakusan* for Shakuhachi, Solo Koto, Chorus, Percussion, and Koto Ensemble (1970); *Tosa Fudoki*, symphonic poem (1981); *Echoes from the Ancient Capital of Mars* (1983); *Divertimento* for Strings (1985). CHAMBER: Trio for Flute, Viola, and Guitar (1942); String Quartet No. 1, *Japanese Suite* (1943); String Trio (1946); *Fantasy* for Strings (1954); Cello Sonata (1956; rev. 1989); Sonata for Koto and Oboe (1956); *Duet* for Violin and Trombone (1966); 3 *Capriccios* for Violin (1971); *Sakura Sakura*, fantasy for Piano (1971); *Variations on "Sakura, Sakura"* for Viola and Cello (1987); *Andante* for Viola and Piano (1988); *Concert Études* for Koto (1990); *Music for Kanagawa Athletic Sports* for Brass (1998).—NS/LK/DM

Hirao, Kishio, Japanese composer; b. Tokyo, July 8, 1907; d. there, Dec. 15, 1953. He graduated from Keio Univ. in 1930, and also studied composition with Guy de Lioncourt at the Schola Cantorum in Paris (1931–34). He became a prof. at the Tokyo Music Academy.

WORKS: CHOREOGRAPHIC DRAMA: *Histoire de Wanasa—Otome* (1943). ORCH.: *Cantilène antique* (1937); *Variations on a Japanese Theme* (1938); *Suite* for Flute and Orch. (1940); *Kinuta*, symphonic poem (1942); *La Paix*, overture (1951). CHAMBER: String Quartet (1940); Flute Sonatina (1941); Octet (1944); Piano Quintet (1945); Violin Sonata (1947); Piano Sonata (1948); Trio for Flute, Violin, and Piano (1949); Wind Quintet (1950); Oboe Sonata (1951).—NS/LK/DM

Hirayoshi, Takekuni, Japanese composer; b. Kobe, July 10, 1936; d. 1998. He studied with Yoshio Hasegawa at the Tokyo Univ. of Arts (1955–61), and later attended the graduate school there (1963–67). His *Symphonic Variations* was awarded the 1969 Odaka Prize.

WORKS: ORCH.: *Composition* (1962); *Ballade* (1966); *Symphonic Variations* (Tokyo, Oct. 23, 1969); *Ballade* for Organ and Orch. (1974); *Requiem* for Violin and Orch. (1975); Guitar Concerto (1980); *A Landscape of the Sea* for Timpani and Orch. (1981); *Poem of Kobe* for Orch. (1989). CHAMBER: String Quartet (1960); *Dialog* for Marimba, Flute, Clarinet, and Cello (1968); Prelude and Fantasia for Guitar (1970); *Monodrama* for Piano (1970); *Impromptu* for Flute, Violin, and Piano (1970); *Epitaph* for Cello (1971); Octet for 4 Japanese Instruments and String Quartet (1972); *Epitaph* for 2 Flutes (1973); *Song of the Wind* for 2 Marimbas (1973); *The Carnival Has Come* for Piano, 4–Hands (1985); *Elegia* for Viola (1990); *El vent de Catalyuna* for Guitar and String Quartet (1991); *Rhapsody* for Brass Octet (1992); *Stars Party* for 5 Players (1992).—NS/LK/DM

Hirsch, Paul (Adolf), German-English music collector and bibliographer; b. Frankfurt am Main, Feb. 24, 1881; d. Cambridge, Nov. 23, 1951. He began collecting rare musical eds. in 1896, and publ. successive catalogs of his rapidly growing library. In 1936 he left Germany and was able to transport his entire collection to England. It was purchased by the British Museum in 1946, the total number of items being about 20,000. In 1922 he began the publication of new eds. (several in facsimile, and with commentaries) of rare works. See the *Music Review*, XII (1951).—NS/LK/DM

Hirst, Grayson, American tenor; b. Ojai, Calif., Dec. 27, 1939. He studied at the Music Academy of the West in Santa Barbara, Calif., with Singher at the Univ. of Calif. at Los Angeles, and with Tourel at the Juilliard School of Music in N.Y. (1963–72), making his professional debut as Cavalli's Ormindo with the Opera Soc. of Washington, D.C. (1969). His first appearance in N.Y. was as Tonio in a concert performance of *La Fille du régiment* at Carnegie Hall (1970); after singing Quint in *The Turn of the Screw* at the N.Y.C. Opera (1972), he appeared in opera throughout the U.S. and Europe while also pursuing an extensive concert career. In 1986 he joined the faculty at the Univ. of Ariz. His operatic repertoire includes over 70 roles, ranging from Mozart to contemporary roles.—NS/LK/DM

Hirt, Al(ois Maxwell), pop-jazz trumpeter and bandleader; b. New Orleans, Nov. 7, 1922; d. April 27, 1999. Hirt's exuberant Dixieland- style trumpet playing was showcased on a series of pop-oriented recordings that found commercial success during the first half of the 1960s, including the singles "Java" and "Cotton Candy" and the albums *Honey in the Horn, Cotton Candy,* and *Sugar Lips.*

Hirt's father was a policeman, and after taking up the trumpet at the age of six, Al Hirt Jr. played in the Sons of the Police Department Junior Police Band. In 1940 he entered the Cincinnati Cons. of Music, where he studied with Frank Simon. He graduated in 1941 and got married; he and his wife eventually had eight children. Following the U.S. entry into World War II, he joined the army, where he played in the Army Air Force Band. Upon his discharge in 1946, he worked in several big bands, including those of Tommy Dorsey and Jimmy Dorsey. He returned to New Orleans in the late 1940s and played at a local radio station while also working outside music.

In 1955, Hirt formed his own Dixieland band and began playing at the Pier 600 Club. He recorded for local labels, then for Verve Records, but it was not until 1960, when he signed to RCA Victor, that he began to gain a national following. His first album for the label, recorded in December 1960, was *Al (He's the King) Hirt and His Band,* but it did not reach the charts until after his second RCA album, *The Greatest Horn in the World,* did so in March 1961. That record earned him two Grammy nominations, for Best Jazz Performance, Soloist or Small Group (Instrumental), and for Best Performance by an Orch., for Other than Dancing.

Hirt had another two albums in the charts in 1962 and three in 1963, the last of which was *Honey in the Horn,* released in August. In December, RCA released "Java" (music by Allen Toussaint, Alvin Tyler, Murray Sporn, and Marilyn Schack) from the album as a single; it reached the pop Top Ten and the top of the easy-listening charts in February, and *Honey in the Horn* hit #1 and went gold in April. In May, Hirt won a Grammy for Best Performance by an Orch. or Instrumentalist with Orch.—Not Jazz or Dancing, for "Java." He had also earned three other nominations: Album of the Year for *Honey in the Horn,* and both Best Instrumental Jazz Performance, Soloist or Small Group, and Best Instru-

mental Jazz Performance, Large Group, for another of his 1963 LPs, *Our Man in New Orleans.*

Hirt's follow-up to "Java," "Cotton Candy" (music by Russ Damon), reached the Top 40 in May 1964, and that month RCA released a *Cotton Candy* LP that hit the Top Ten in June and went gold. The single brought the trumpeter a Grammy nomination for Best Instrumental Performance, Non-Jazz; the LP was nominated for Album of the Year. Hirt's next single, "Sugar Lips" (music and lyrics by William D. Killen and Billy Sherrill), reached the Top 40 in July, and the *Sugar Lips* album, released in August, hit the Top Ten in September and went gold. During this busy year, Hirt also released the chart albums *Beauty and the Beard,* recorded with actress/singer Ann-Margret, and *"Pops" Goes the Trumpet,* on which he was accompanied by the Boston Pops Orch. conducted by Arthur Fiedler.

In January 1965, RCA released the compilation *The Best of Al Hirt;* it hit the Top Ten in March and went gold. Hirt's next single, "Fancy Pants" (music by Floyd Cramer), reached the Top 40 in February and was included in his album released the same month, *That Honey in the Horn Sound,* which spent six months in the charts. In April he appeared at Carnegie Hall, and the resulting *Live at Carnegie Hall* album, released in June, also remained in the charts half a year. From June to September he hosted the musical variety series *Fanfare* on network television.

Though his commercial success declined, Hirt continued to place records in the charts through 1969, when he left RCA and began recording for small independent labels. During the summer of 1971 he returned to network television as a regular on the musical variety series *Make Your Own Kind of Music.* He opened his own club in New Orleans and returned to playing in more of a jazz style. He was still active in the late 1990s.—WR

Hirt, Franz Josef, Swiss pianist and teacher; b. Lucerne, Feb. 7, 1899; d. Bern, May 20, 1985. He studied with Hans Huber and Ernst Lévy at the Basel Cons., and later took lessons with Petri and Cortot. In 1919 he became a teacher at the Bern Cons., and also gave numerous piano recitals in Europe. He publ. *Meisterwerke des Klavierbaues* (1955; Eng. tr., 1968, as *Stringed Keyboard Instruments, 1440–1880*).—NS/LK/DM

Hirt, Fritz, Swiss violinist; b. Lucerne, Aug. 9, 1888; d. Chigny-sur-Morges, Jan. 5, 1970. He studied in Zürich and had an extended career as a violinist in Europe. He was also a member of the Basel String Quartet.—NS/LK/DM

Hislop, Joseph, Scottish tenor; b. Edinburgh, April 5, 1884; d. Upper Largo, Fife, May 6, 1977. He studied in Stockholm with Gillis Bratt. On Sept. 12, 1914, he made his operatic debut at the Royal Opera in Stockholm as Faust, and subsequently was active in Scandinavia before singing at the Teatro San Carlo in Naples (1919–20). On May 14, 1920, he made his first appearance at London's Covent Garden as Rodolfo; that same year, he made his U.S. debut in Chicago, then appeared in N.Y. in 1921 before touring the country with Scotti's company. In 1923 he sang in Venice and Turin, and was the first British tenor to sing a leading role at Milan's La Scala when he appeared as Edgardo. In 1925 he appeared at the Teatro Colón in Buenos Aires. After retiring in 1937, he taught voice in Stockholm, where his most gifted students were Jussi Björling and Birgit Nilsson. In 1947 he went to London, where he was artistic advisor at Covent Garden and subsequently at the Sadler's Wells Opera. In later years, he was active as a teacher at the Guildhall School of Music. He was admired for his roles in operas by Verdi and Puccini, the latter praising him as the ideal Rodolfo. His French roles were also noteworthy.

BIBL.: M. Turnbull, *J. H.: Gran Tenore* (Aldershot, 1992). —NS/LK/DM

Hitchcock, H(ugh) Wiley,

eminent American musicologist and editor; b. Detroit, Sept. 28, 1923. He was educated at Dartmouth Coll. (A.B., 1943) and the Univ. of Mich. (M.Mus., 1948; Ph.D., 1954, with the diss. *The Latin Oratorios of Marc-Antoine Charpentier*). He taught music at the Univ. of Mich. (1947–61), and then was prof. of music at Hunter Coll. (1961–71). In 1971 he became prof. of music at Brooklyn Coll. (named Distinguished Prof. of Music in 1980), where he also served as director of the Inst. for Studies in American Music. A recipient of numerous grants, including Fulbright senior research fellowships in 1954–55 (Italy) and 1968–69 (France), and a Guggenheim fellowship in 1968–69, Hitchcock also served on the boards of numerous organizations; in 1991–92 he was president of the American Musicological Soc., and in 1994 was made an honorary member. He was also ed. of The Prentice-Hall History of Music Series (Englewood Cliffs, N.J., 1965–), *Earlier American Music* (reprints of music; N.Y., 1972–), and *Recent Researches in American Music* (Madison, Wisc., 1976–). He was co-ed. of *The New Grove Dictionary of American Music* (4 vols., N.Y., 1986). His research interests are wide and meritorious, covering French Baroque and American music, and his editorial contributions include the works of Caccini, Leonardo Leo, Charpentier, and Lully.

WRITINGS: *Music in the United States: A Historical Introduction* (Englewood Cliffs, N.J., 1969; 2nd ed., rev. and enl., 1974; 3rd ed., 1988); *Charles Ives Centennial Festival- Conference 1974* (program book; N.Y., 1974); *Ives* (London, 1977; rev. 1983); co-ed., with V. Perlis, *An Ives Celebration: Papers and Panels of the Charles Ives Centennial Festival-Conference* (Urbana, Ill., 1977); *The Phonograph and Our Musical Life* (Brooklyn, 1980); with L. Inserra, *The Music of Ainsworth's Psalter (1612)* (Brooklyn, 1981); *The Works of Marc-Antoine Charpentier: A Catalogue Raisonné* (Paris, 1982); *Ives: A Survey of the Music* (N.Y., 1983); *Marc-Antoine Charpentier* (Oxford, 1990).

BIBL.: R. Crawford, R. Lott, and C. Oja, eds., *A Celebration of American Music: Words and Music in Honor of H.W. H.* (Ann Arbor, 1989).—NS/LK/DM

Hite, Les,

alto saxophonist, pianist, xylophonist, leader; b. DuQuoin, Ill., Feb. 13, 1903; d. Santa Monica, Calif., Feb. 6, 1962. He attended school in Urbana, then studied at the Univ. of Ill. He played sax in his family's band, then worked with Detroit Shannon's Band before touring with the Heler Dewey Show. After the show folded in L.A., he joined the Spikes Brothers Orch. (1925) and worked for various leaders: Mutt Carey, Paul Howard, Curtis Mosby, Vernon Elkins, and drummer Henry "Tin Can" Allen. He led his own band at Solomon Penny's Dance Palace, September 1930; Hite began leading at Sebastian's Cotton Club (deposing trumpeter Vernon Elkins). He led the band at the Cotton Club for many years, accompanying many guest stars including Louis Armstrong and Fats Waller. The band also did a considerable amount of film-studio work, both soundtrack and visual. Hite continued to lead in L.A. from 1942 until 1945 when he quit full-time playing to organize his own business. For the last five years of his life he managed a booking agency.—JC/LP

Hitzler, Daniel,

German theologian, music theorist, and editor of hymnbooks; b. Heidenheim an der Brenz, Württemberg, Sept. 26, 1576; d. Strasbourg, Sept. 6, 1635. He received training in theology, music, and other subjects at the Univ. of Tübingen (1595–97). After teaching at the ducal "Stipendium" in Tübingen (1600–03), he became deacon in Waiblingen in 1603, and later was the first Protestant pastor there. In 1609 he became pastor in Güglingen. In 1612 he went to Linz as superintendent, preacher, and teacher of theology at the Protestant school for the nobility. His theological dispute with Kepler led to his opponent's excommunication from the Protestant faith in 1619. After Bavaria took control of Upper Austria, Hitzler was imprisoned for his advocacy of the Bohemian Confederation (1621–22). Deprived of his positions, he went to Peuerbach, Upper Austria, in 1624 as Kantor of the Protestant church. In 1625 he was made special superintendent and pastor in Kirchheim unter Tech. From 1625 to 1630 he was also general superintendent and abbot of the Bebenhausen monastery. In 1634 he became general superintent in Stuttgart, but was compelled to flee later that year with the approach of the imperial army. Hitzler did valuable labor as a music theorist and editor of hymnbooks. He also wrote theological tomes and poems. His publs. on music include *Neue Musica* (c. 1615), *Extract aus der Neuen Musica oder Singkunst* (Nuremberg, 1623), *Neue Musica oder Singkunst...editio secunda et auctior* (Tübingen, 1628), *Christliche Kirchen-Gesang, Psalmen und geistliche Lieder* (Strasbourg, 1634), *Musicalisch figurierte Melodien aller und jeder gebräuchigen Kirchen- Gesäng, Psalmen und geistlichen Lieder, a 4, von beruhmbten autoribus musicis* (Strasbourg, 1634).—LK/DM

Hlobil, Emil,

Czech composer and teacher; b. Veselí nad Lužnici, Oct. 11, 1901; d. Prague, Jan. 25, 1987. He studied with Křička at the Prague Cons. (1920–23) and in the master classes of Suk there (1924–25; 1927–30). After teaching at the Prague Women Teachers' Inst. (1930–41), he taught at the Cons. (1941–58) and afterward at the Academy of Music and Dramatic Arts in Prague. He was made an Artist of Merit (1972) and a National Artist (1981) for his services to Czech music. He followed the national tradition of the modern Czech school, and also cautiously experimented with serial methods of composition.

WORKS: DRAMATIC: O p e r a : *Anna Karenina* (1962; české Budějovice, April 16, 1972); *Le Bourgeois gentilhomme* (1965); *Král Václav IV* (1981). **ORCH.:** 7 syms.: No. 1 (1949), No. 2, *The Day of Victory* (1951), No. 3 (1957), No. 4 (1959), No. 5 (1969), No. 6 for Strings (1972), and No. 7 (1973); 4 symphonic suites: *Summer in the Giant Mountains* (1950), *Folk Merry-Making* (1950), *Spring in the Gardens of Prague* (1951–53), and *In the Valachian Village* (1952); Violin Concerto (1955); Accordion Concerto (1956); *Labor Holiday* (1960); Organ Concerto (1963); *Concerto filharmonico* (1965); *Invocazioni* (1967); Double Bass Concerto (1968); *The Path of the Living* (1974); *Jubilace* (1977); Marimba Concerto (1979); Cello Concerto (1983). **CHAMBER:** String Quintet (1925); 4 string quartets (1931, 1936, 1955, 1969); Piano Trio (1938); Wind Quintet (1940); Horn Sonata (1942; rev. 1948); Quartet for Harpsichord, Violin, Viola, and Cello (1943); Nonet (1946); Wind Octet (1956); Violin Sonata (1959); Quartet for Flute, Oboe, Clarinet, and Bassoon (1964); Flute Sonata (1966); Trumpet Sonata (1967); Bass Clarinet Sonata (1970); Trombone Sonata (1973); Sonata for 2 Cellos (1973); Trio for Violin, Guitar, and Accordion (1976); Clarinet Sonata (1978); *Canto pensieroso* for Saxophone (1983); piano pieces, including Sonata for 2 Pianos (1958) and 2 sonatas (both 1968); organ music. **VOCAL:** Choral works; songs.

BIBL.: J. Bajer, *E. H.: Hudební putování stoletím* (Prague, 1984).—NS/LK/DM

Hoboken, Anthony van, eminent Dutch music collector and bibliographer; b. Rotterdam, March 23, 1887; d. Zürich, Nov. 1, 1983. He studied with Anton Verhey in Delft. After studies with Knorr (composition) and Sekles (harmony) at the Hoch Cons. in Frankfurt am Main, he completed his training with Schenker in Vienna (1925–34). In 1919 he began to build a private collection of first and early eds. of music and literature associated with music. His collection on Haydn proved invaluable, and amassed to more than 1,000 items. In 1927 he founded the Archiv für Photogramme musikalischer Meister-Handschriften in the music section of the Austrian National Library in Vienna. He publ. *Joseph Haydn: Thematisch-bibliographisches Werkverzeichnis* (2 vols., Mainz, 1957, 1971), designating Haydn's works by H. or Hob. numbers. In 1974 the Austrian government purchased his private collection, which was officially opened at the Austrian National Library on Hoboken's 90th birthday (March 23, 1977). J. Schmidt-Görg ed. a Festschrift for his 75th birthday (Mainz, 1962).—NS/LK/DM

Hobson, Ian, English pianist, conductor, and teacher; b. Wolverhampton, Aug. 7, 1952. He studied piano and organ at the Royal Academy of Music in London, then pursued academic studies at Magdalene Coll., Cambridge (B.A., 1972). He subsequently studied piano with Claude Frank and harpsichord with Ralph Kirkpatrick at Yale Univ. (D.M.A., 1978). He made his London debut in 1979. In 1981 he won 1st prize in the Leeds International Pianoforte Competition. He made his U.S. debut in N.Y. in 1983. He has appeared as soloist with major orchs. of Europe and North America. In 1975 he joined the faculty of the Univ. of Ill.—NS/LK/DM

Hoch, Beverly, American soprano; b. Marion, Kans., Aug. 26, 1951. She studied at Friends Univ. in Wichita (1969–73), Okla. City Univ. (B.M., 1975), and Wichita State Univ. (M.M., 1978), and in N.Y. with Michael Trimble (1977–82) and Ellen Faull (1982–86). In 1980 she won the Young Concert Artists International Auditions, made her recital debut at the 92nd Street Y in N.Y., and sang for the first time in opera at the Opera Theatre in St. Louis. From 1980 to 1988 she was a soloist with the Chamber Music Soc. of Lincoln Center in N.Y. In 1981 she made her debut as a soloist with orch. when she appeared at N.Y.'s Carnegie Hall with the St. Paul Chamber Orch. under Zukerman's direction. After singing Filene in *Mignon* at the Wexford Festival in 1986, she was engaged to sing Offenbach's Olympia at the Théâtre des Champs Elysées in Paris in 1987. She portrayed the Queen of the Night with the London Classical Players under Norrington's direction in 1990, a role she reprised in 1991 at the Glyndebourne Festival, the San Antonio Opera, and the London Promenade Concerts. She appeared as Adele at the Opéra du Rhin in Strasbourg in 1993. From 1994 she was the soprano of the Bach Aria Group in N.Y. In 1997 she sang Vespina in Haydn's *L'infedeltà delusa* at the Bard Festival in N.Y. As a soloist, Hoch has appeared with major orchs. around the world. —NS/LK/DM

Hochberg, Hans Heinrich, XIV, Bolko Graf von, German theater Intendant and composer; b. Fürstenstein Castle, Silesia, Jan. 23, 1843; d. near Salzbrunn, Dec. 1, 1926. He established and for several years maintained the Hochberg Quartet, founded the Silesian music festivals (1878), and was general Intendant of the Berlin Royal Theater (1886–1902). His works include the operas *Claudine von Villabella* (Schwerin, 1864) and *Die Falkensteiner* (Hannover, 1876; rewritten as *Der Wärwolf*, Dresden, 1881), 3 syms., 3 string quartets, 2 piano trios, a Concerto for Piano, songs, and choruses. —NS/LK/DM

Hockh, Carl, outstanding German violinist, composer, and pedagogue; b. Ebersdorf, Jan. 22, 1707; d. Zerbst, Nov. 25, 1773. He studied violin with his father, voice with the local schoolmaster, and then with Michael Schade in Pruck. After playing oboe in a military regiment, he was in the service of the governor of Warsaw as 2nd violinist and horn player. He subsequently was music director in Zerbst from 1734. He was one of the founders of the German school of violin playing, and was influential as a virtuoso, composer for the violin, and teacher.—NS/LK/DM

Hoddinott, Alun, prominent Welsh composer and teacher; b. Bargoed, Aug. 11, 1929. He studied at Univ. Coll. in Cardiff (B.A., 1949; Ph.D., 1960), and also had private instruction from Arthur Benjamin. After teaching at the Cardiff Coll. of Music and Drama (1951–59), he was a lecturer (1959–65), reader (1965–67), and prof. (1967–87) of music at Univ. Coll. From 1966 to 1989 he served as artistic director of the Cardiff Festival of Twentieth Century Music. In 1957 he was awarded the Arnold Bax Medal and in 1983 he was made a Commander of the Order of the British Empire. Hoddinott's extensive output displays a notable command of various styles, ranging from the traditional to serial and aleatoric techniques.

WORKS: DRAMATIC: O p e r a : *The Beach of Falesá* (1973; Cardiff, March 26, 1974); *Murder, the Magician* (1975; Welsh TV, Feb. 11, 1976; stage version as *The Magician*, Cardiff, April 1976); *What the Old Man Does Is Always Right* (1975; Fishguard, July 27, 1977); *The Rajah's Diamond* (television premiere, Nov. 24, 1979); *The Trumpet Major* (Manchester, April 1, 1981); *Tower* (Swansea, Oct. 23, 1999). **ORCH.:** 2 clarinet concertos: No. 1 for Clarinet and Strings (1950; BBC, March 15, 1951) and No. 2 for Clarinet and Orch. (Manchester, Feb. 20, 1987); *Fugal Overture* (1952; BBC, April 20, 1953); *Nocturne* (1952; BBC, Sept. 22, 1953); 8 syms.: No. 1 (1954–55; Pwillheli, Aug. 5, 1955), No. 2 (Cheltenham, July 11, 1962), No. 3 (Manchester, Dec. 5, 1968), No. 4 (Manchester, Dec. 4, 1969), No. 5 (1972; London, March 6, 1973), No. 6 (Cardiff, June 15, 1984), No. 7 for Organ and Orch. (Swansea, Oct. 17, 1989), and No. 8 for Brass and Percussion (1992); Concerto for Oboe and Strings (1955; Sheffield, Oct. 13, 1957); Harp Concerto (1957; Cheltenham, July 16, 1958); Concertino for Viola and Small Orch. (Llandaff, June 25, 1958); *4 Welsh Dances* (London, June 28, 1958), *Welsh Dances: 2nd Suite* (Merthyr, April 16, 1969), and *Welsh Dances: 3rd Suite* (1985); *2 Welsh Nursery Tunes* (1959; BBC, Jan. 22, 1961); *Nocturne and Dance* for Harp and Orch. (1959); 3 piano concertos: No. 1 for Piano, Winds, and Percussion (London, Feb. 22, 1960), No. 2 for Piano and Orch. (Cardiff, Aug. 5, 1960), and No. 3 for Piano and Orch. (Cheltenham, July 12, 1966); *Entry* (London, Nov. 22, 1960); Violin Concerto (Birmingham, March 30, 1961); *Folksong Suite* (1962); *Variations* (Newtown, Aug. 4, 1963; rev. 1964); *Sinfonia* for Strings (Birmingham, April 19, 1964); *Jack Straw*, overture (Aberystwyth, May 1, 1964); 2 concerti grossi: No. 1 (Caerphilly, June 11, 1965) and No. 2 (Ammanford, July 28, 1966); *Aubade and Scherzo* for Horn and Strings (1965; Cardiff, Oct. 24, 1966); *Pantomime*, overture (Croydon, July 16, 1966); *Variants* (London, Nov. 2, 1966); *Night Music* (1966; Aberystwyth, Jan. 30, 1967); Organ Concerto (Llandaff, June 19, 1967); 4 sinfoniettas: No. 1 (Cardiff, April 29, 1968), No. 2 (Cheltenham, July 4, 1969), No. 3 (Swansea, March 10, 1970), and No. 4 (Rhos, July 30, 1971); *Fioriture* (Aberdeen, Nov. 24, 1968); *Nocturnes and Cadenzas* for Cello and Orch. (Cardiff, Feb. 27, 1969); Horn Concerto (Llandaff, June 3, 1969); *Investiture Dances*& (London, June 22, 1969); *Divertimento* for Small Orch. (Llandaff, Nov. 14, 1969); Suite (Southampton, April 16, 1970); *The Sun, the Great Luminary of the Universe* (Swansea, Oct. 8, 1970); Concertino for Trumpet, Horn, and Orch. (Llangefni, April 8, 1971); *The Hawk Is Set Free* (Abergavenny, Sept. 21, 1972); *The Floore of Heav'n* (London, April 30, 1973); *Landscapes* (Criccieth, Aug. 8, 1975; rev. version, Cardiff, March 9, 1976); *Welsh Airs and Dances* for Symphonic Wind Band (Cardiff, Aug. 21, 1975); *French Suite* for Small Orch. (Cardiff, March 13, 1977); *Passagio* (Cheltenham, July 6, 1977); *The Heaventree of Stars* for Violin and Orch. (Cardiff, March 3, 1980); *Lanterne des Morts* (Cardiff, Sept. 21, 1981); *Quodlibet on Welsh Nursery Tunes* (1982; Cardiff, Jan. 9, 1983); *Doubles*, concertante for Oboe, Harpsichord, and Strings (St. David's Cathedral, June 3, 1982); *Hommage à Chopin* (1984); *Scenes and Interludes*, concertante for Trumpet, Harpsichord, and Strings (St. David's Cathedral, June 2, 1984); Concerto for Violin, Cello, Piano, and Orch. (Cheltenham, July 5, 1986); *Divisions*, concertante for Horn, Harpsichord, and Strings (Cardiff, July 2, 1986); *Concerto for Orchestra* (Cardiff, July 22, 1986); *Star Children* (London, Sept. 7, 1989); *Noctis Equi* for Cello and Orch. (London, Oct. 27, 1989). **CHAMBER:** String Trio (1949); Quartet for Clarinet, Violin, Viola, and Cello (1953–54); Septet for Clarinet, Horn, Bassoon, Piano, Violin, Viola, and Cello (BBC, Dec. 8, 1956; rev. 1973); *Rondo scherzoso* for Trumpet or Trombone and Piano (1957); Sextet for Flute, Clarinet, Bassoon, Violin, Viola, and Cello (Llandaff, April 28, 1960); *Variations* for Flute, Harp, Clarinet, and String Quartet (1962); Fanfare for 3 Trumpets, 3 Trombones, and Drums (1963); *Divertimento* for Oboe, Clarinet, Horn, and Bassoon (1963); Harp Sonata (1964); 3 string quartets (1965, 1984, 1988); *Arabesque* for Violin and Piano (1966); Clarinet Sonata (1967); Suite for Harp (1967); 5 violin sonatas (1969, 1970, 1971, 1976, 1991); 2 cello sonatas (1970, 1977); 2 piano trios (1970, 1983); Horn Sonata (1971); Piano Quintet (1972); *Ritornelli* for Trombone, Winds, and Percussion (1974); *Indian Suite* for Recorder and Guitar (1977); *Scena* for String Quartet (1979); *Masks* for Oboe, Bassoon, and Piano (1983); *Bagatelles* for Oboe and Harp (1984); Sonata for 4 Clarinets (1985); *Chorales, Variants, and Fanfares* for Organ and Brass Quintet (1992); Quintet for Flute, Oboe, Clarinet, Horn, and Bassoon (1992). **KEYBOARD: P i a n o :** 2 nocturnes (1956, 1959); 7 sonatas (1959, 1962, 1965, 1966, 1968, 1972, 1984). **O r g a n :** *Toccata alla giga* (1964); *Intrada* (1966); *Sarum Fanfare* (1970); *Passacaglia and Fugue* (1985). **VOCAL:** *The Race of Adam*, masque for Soloists, Chorus, Boy's Voices, Orch., and Organ (Llandaff, June 23, 1961); *Job* for Bass, Chorus, and Orch. (Swansea, May 18, 1962; rev. 1977); *Dives and Lazarus*, cantata for Soloists, Chorus, and Orch. or Organ (Farnham, May 20, 1965); *Eryi* for Soloists, Chorus, and Orch. (Caernarvon, July 1, 1969); *Voyagers* for Baritone, Men's Voices, and Orch. (1970); *The Tree of Life*, oratorio for Soprano, Tenor, Chorus, and Orch. (Gloucester, Aug. 25, 1971); *St. Paul at Malta*, cantata for Tenor, Chorus, and Orch. (Stroud, Oct. 14, 1971); *Sinfonia fidei* for Soprano, Tenor, Chorus, and Orch. (Llandaff, June 18, 1977); *Te Deum* for Mixed Voices and Organ (Fishguard, July 29, 1981); *Bells of Paradise*, Christmas cantata for Baritone, Chorus, and Orch. (1984); *The Legend of St Julian* for Narrator, Chorus, and Orch. (1987); *Emynau Pantycelyn* for Baritone, Chorus, and Orch. (1989); *Lines from Marlowe's Dr. Faustus* for Chorus and Brass (1989); *Songs of Exile* for Tenor and Orch. (1989); *May Song* for Children's Chorus and Orch. (1992); *Paradwys Mai* for Soprano, Piano, and String Quintet (1992); choruses; other songs.

BIBL.: B. Deane, *A. H.* (Cardiff, 1977); S. Craggs, *A. H.: A Bio-Bibliography* (Westport, Conn., 1993).—**NS/LK/DM**

Hodeir, André, jazz composer, arranger, author; b. Paris, France, Jan. 22, 1921. He studied at the Paris Cons. with Messiaen and others; in 1954 founded the Jazz Group of Paris, which he led until 1960. He writes skillful jazz-oriented chamber works. His *Jazz, Its Evolution and Essence* had a more profound impact on the American jazz scene than has generally been realized. As one of the first books to analyze the music with notation, it served as a role model for Williams and Schuller. For example, the fame of Koko begins with this book (not earlier!) and many of the contents of the Smithsonian Collection are straight from Hodeir.

DISC.: *Paris Scene* (1956); *Essais* (1956); *American Jazzmen Play* (1957); *Paris Scene* (1958); *Jazz Et Jazz* (1963).—**LP/NS**

Hodemont, Leonard (Collet) de, important South Netherlands composer; b. Liège, c. 1575; d. there, Aug. 1636. He received his musical training at Liège Cathedral, where he was senior duodenus (1589–93); then continued his education at the Pedagogie du Lys at the Univ. of Louvain. After being ordained a priest, he became succentor of the collegiate church of St. Pierre in Liège in 1610. He was made canon at Liège Cathedral in 1612, and then at St. Materne there in 1616; subsequently was maître de chant at Liege Cathedral from 1619 to 1633. He was a leading composer of sacred music. He publ. *Armonica recreatione: Villanelli* for 3 Voices and Basso Continuo (Antwerp, 1625) and *Sacri concentus* for 1 to 5 Voices, Violin, and Basso Continuo (Organ) (Liège, 1630).—NS/LK/DM

Hodes, Art(hur W.), jazz pianist, broadcaster, writer; b. Nikoliev (now Nikolayev), Ukraine (now Ukrainian SSR), Nov. 14, 1904; d. Harvey, Ill., March 4, 1993. His family moved to the U.S. when he was six months old. He went to school in Chicago. He began gigging in late teens, then toured with Dick Voynow's Wolverines (for part of the tour the band worked under the nominal leadership of Smith Ballew). He joined Wingy Manone at Eldorado (Chicago, 1928); while with Manone made his record debut (1928). He worked mainly in Chicago through the early 1930s, played with many bands including Floyd Town's and Frank Snyder's, and also led his own small groups and played solo piano at various venues. He moved to N.Y. in April 1938, gigged with Joe Marsala and Mezz Mezzrow while also leading his own bands through the 1940s. From February 1943 until November 1947, Hodes edited the fine magazine *Jazz Record*. He moved back to Chicago (early 1950). He continued to work as a soloist and bandleader over the coming decades, as well as undertaking tours of the U.S. and Europe. He remained in Chicago through the 1980s, and his strongly blues-influenced style ensured him much coverage and a healthy following right up to his death.

DISC.: *Sittin' In* (1944); *Complete Blue Note A. H. Sessions* (1944); *Chicago Rhythm Kings* (1953); *Jazz Chicago Style* (1954); *Albert Nicholas* (1959); *Plain Old Blues* (1962); *Mama Yancey Sings, A. H. Plays* (1965); *Selections from the Gutter* (1970); *Someone to Watch Over Me* (1981); *Just the Two of Us* (1981); *South Side Memories* (1983); *Apex Blues* (1983); *Pagin' Mr. Jelly* (1988); *Something Personal* (1988); *Final Sessions* (1990).—JC/LP

Hodges, Edward, English organist and composer; b. Bristol, July 20, 1796; d. Clifton, Sept. 1, 1867. He was an organist at Bristol, and received his Mus.Doc. at Cambridge (1825). In 1838 he went to North America, where he became an organist in Toronto and then in N.Y. (1839). He returned to England in 1863. His daughter, Faustina Hasse Hodges (b. near Malmesbury, Aug. 7, 1823; d. Philadelphia, Feb. 4, 1895), was also an organist in the U.S. She composed songs and instrumental pieces and publ. a biography of her father (N.Y., 1896). His son, Rev. J(ohn) Sebastian B(ach) Hodges (b. Bristol, 1830; d. Baltimore, May 1, 1915), an accomplished organist, composed many anthems and services.—NS/LK/DM

Hodges, Johnny influential alto and soprano saxophonist, famed for his long association with Duke Ellington; b. Cambridge, Mass., July 25, 1906; d. N.Y., May 11, 1970. He was the mainstay of the Ellington orch. from 1928 on, and saxophonists still marvel at Hodges's dramatic sweeping portamentos and broad, sensuous tone. He had great power on a blues or a ballad; before about 1940 he also demonstrated a great technical facility and speed that was not as evident later. He grew up on Hammond Street in Boston with such neighbors as Harry Carney, Toots Mondello, and Charlie Holmes. He played drums and piano, then sax at the age of 14; Sidney Bechet was courting his sister and gave him lessons. He followed Bechet in Willie "the Lion" Smith's Quartet at the Rhythm Club (c. 1924), then played with Bechet at the Club Basha (1925). He continued to live in Boston during the mid-1920s, traveling to N.Y. for weekend gigs. He played with Bobby Sawyer (c. 1925) and Lloyd Scott (c. 1926), then from late 1926 worked regularly with Chick Webb. He was briefly with Luckey Roberts's Orch., then joined Duke Ellington in May 1928 to replace Otto Hardwicke as lead alto, doubling on soprano. He regularly led his own recording bands from 1937, and also did freelance recordings. He was with Ellington until March 1951, after which he formed his own small band. (In summer 1948, while Ellington was on solo tour of Britain, Hodges led a quartet at the Apollo Club, N.Y.) He had a hit with "Castle Rock." John Coltrane played in the band from about March (possibly earlier) through August 1954. In March 1954 Hodges expanded his group to 12 pieces, adding Benny Golson and others, for a touring show. He continued to lead his own septet until spring 1955. After a spell of TV-studio work on the *Ted Steele Show* he rejoined Ellington in August 1955, and except for brief absences, remained with him. He took a few weeks' leave in spring 1958 to work in Fla. with Billy Strayhorn. In spring 1961, together with several band colleagues, he toured Europe in the Ellington Giants. He took engagements outside the band from time to time, making small group records and also playing with organist Wild Bill Davis and the bands of Oliver Nelson and Lawrence Welk. He was set to play the soprano sax on a recording again for the first time since 1940, when he died, shortly after being featured on the "Blues for New Orleans" from Ellington's *New Orleans Suite*.

DISC.: *Rarities and Private Recordings* (1936); *Hodge Podge* (1938); *On Keynote with Rex Stewart* (1946); *Rabbit in Paris* (1950); *Jeep Is Jumpin'* (1951); *Complete J. H. Sessions* (1951); *Castle Rock* (1951); *Used to Be Duke* (1954); *At a Dance* (1954); *Duke's in Bed* (1956); *Big Sound* (1957); *Side by Side* (1958); *Not So Dukish* (1958); *Back to Back* (1959); *J. H. with Billy Strayhorn* (1961); *Blue H.* (1961); *At the Berlin Sportpalast* (1961); *Previously Unreleased* (1963); *Blue Rabbit* (1963); *Everybody Knows* (1964); *Joe's Blues* (1965); *Blue Pyramid* (1965). Earl Hines: *Stride Right* (1966). *Swing's Our Thing* (1968); *Rippin' and Runnin'* (1969); *Three Shades of Blue* (1970).—JC/LP

Hodgson, Alfreda (Rose), English contralto; b. Morecombe, June 7, 1940; d. there, April 16, 1992. She received training at the Northern School of Music in Manchester. In 1961 she made her concert debut in Liverpool, followed by her first appearance in London (in 1963). In subsequent years, she appeared as a soloist with all of the principal British orchs.; her concert engagements abroad took her to Israel, the U.S., and

Canada. She also appeared in opera, singing for the first time in London at the English National Opera in 1974 and at Covent Garden in 1983. Her concert repertoire ranged from Bach to Britten.—NS/LK/DM

Hodkinson, Sydney P(hillip), Canadian-born American conductor, teacher, and composer; b. Winnipeg, Jan. 17, 1934. He studied composition with Louis Mennini and Bernard Rogers, and conducting with Paul White and Frederick Fennell at the Eastman School of Music in Rochester, N.Y. (M.Mus., 1958). After attending the Seminar in Advanced Musical Studies given by Carter, Sessions, and Babbitt at Princeton Univ. (1960), he studied conducting with Max Rudolf and then completed his training in composition with Bassett, Castiglioni, Finney, and George B. Wilson at the Univ. of Mich. (D.M.A., 1968). From 1970 to 1972 he was music director of the St. Paul (Minn.) Chamber Orch., concurrently serving as artist-in-residence in Minneapolis-St. Paul. He taught at the Univ. of Va. (1958–63), Ohio Univ. (1963–66), and the Univ. of Mich. (1968–73), where he conducted its Contemporary Directions Ensemble. In 1973 he joined the faculty of the Eastman School of Music, where he was also conductor of its Musica Nova Ensemble. From 1984 to 1986 he was a visiting prof. at Southern Methodist Univ. in Dallas. In 1971 he received an award from the American Academy and National Inst. of Arts and Letters. He was granted 4 awards from the NEA (1976, 1978, 1980, 1984), and in 1978–79 he held a Guggenheim fellowship. In his compositions, he explores modern techniques with pragmatic coherence.

WORKS: DRAMATIC: Opera: *The Swinish Cult* (1969 75); *The Wall* (1980); *In the Gallery* (1981), *Cutsmun* (1985). OTHER: *Lament*, fable with music for Guitar and 2 Lovers (1962); *Taiwa*, myth for Actors, Dancers, and Musicians (1965); *Vox Populous*, active oratorio for 2 Actors, Electronics Technician, 4 Vocal Soloists, and Chorus (1971–72). ORCH.: *Diversions* for Strings (1964); 6 syms., including: No. 1, *Fresco*, mural in 5 panels (1965–68; Buffalo, April 26, 1974), No. 3, *The Celestial Omnibus* (1975), No. 4, *Horae Canonica* for Soprano, Baritone, Narrator, 2 Choruses, and Orch. (1977–83), No. 5, *Sinfonia Concertante*, for Chamber Orch. (1980), and No. 6, *Sonata quasi una fantasia* (1982–83); *Caricatures* (1966; Dallas, April 5, 1969); *Stabile* (1970; Milwaukee, Feb. 6, 1972); *Valence* for Chamber Orch. (1970); *Epigrams* (1971); *Celestial Calendar* for Strings (1976); *The Edge of the Olde One*, chamber concerto (N.Y., May 13, 1977); *Bumberboom*, scherzo diabolique (Montreal, Nov. 9, 1982); *Burning Bell*, symphonic poem for Youth Orch. (1985). WIND ENSEMBLE OR BAND: *Litigo* for Winds and Percussion (1959); *Blocks* for Concert Band (1972); *Monolith: Megalith VI* for Wind Ensemble (1974); *Tower* for Concert Band (1974; Buffalo, N.Y., Dec. 12, 1976); *Cortège: Dirge- Canons* for Wind, Brass, and Percussion (1975); *Palisade: Megalith VIII* for Brass Ensemble and Percussion (1975); *Bach Variations* for Winds and Percussion (1977; Ann Arbor, Feb. 16, 1979); *Echo Preludes* for Brass Choir and Cello Obbligato (1983). CHAMBER: *Drawings: Set No. 1* for 4 Percussion (1960), *Set No. 3* for Clarinet and Drums (1961), *Set No. 4* for 3 Percussion (1961), *Set No. 6* for Violin, 2 Clarinets, and Bass Clarinet (1965), *Set No. 9* for 3 Percussion (1977), and *Set No. 10, Cerberus,* for 4 Tubas (1977); *Mosaic* for Brass Quintet (1964); *Armistice*, truce for Dancers and Musicians (1966); *Interplay*, histrionic controversy for 4 Musicians (1966; Montreal, July 17, 1967); String Quartet No. 1 for 5 Players (1967); *Dissolution of the Serial* for Piano and

1 Instrument, with Tape Excerpt (1967); *1 Man's Meat* for Double Bass and Electronic Tape (1970; Los Angeles, Feb. 9, 1972); Double Bass Sonata (1980); Sym. No. 2, *Symphonie fantastique*, for Organ, Brass, and Percussion (1974–82); String Trio, *Alla marcia* (1983); Sonata, *Das Lebewohl*, for Piano Trio (1984); *The Steps of Time*, elegy for Cello or Trombone, String Quartet, and Percussion (1984); *Trauermusik* for Trombone or Cello, Piano, and Percussion (1984); keyboard music. VOCAL: *Lengeren: Megalith V* for Medium Voice and Double Quintet (1973); *Daydream* for Chorus, Speaker, and Orch. (1974); *November Voices* for Voice, Speaker, and Small Instrumental Ensemble (1975); *Chansons de jadis: 6 Songs of Loneliness* for Voice and Orch. (1978–79); choruses; song cycles.—NS/LK/DM

Höeberg, Georg, Danish violinist, conductor, and composer; b. Copenhagen, Dec. 27, 1872; d. Vedboek, Aug. 3, 1950. He studied at the Copenhagen Cons. and in Berlin. He taught at the Copenhagen Cons. (1900–14), then was conductor at the Royal Danish Theater (1914–30). He wrote the opera *Bryllup i Katakomberne* (The Wedding in the Catacombs; Copenhagen, March 6, 1909), the ballet *The Paris Cathedral* (Copenhagen, Oct. 25, 1912), several pieces for violin and orch., a Sym., choral works, and songs.—NS/LK/DM

Hoelscher, Ludwig, noted German cellist; b. Solingen, Aug. 23, 1907. He studied cello in Leipzig with Julius Klengel and in Berlin with Hugo Becker. In 1930 he won the Mendelssohn Prize. In 1936 he became a prof. at the Berlin Hochschule für Musik; later gave master classes at the Mozarteum in Salzburg; subsequently was a prof. at the Stuttgart Hochschule für Musik from 1954. From 1931 he engaged in far-flung tours in Europe and in the Far East; gave duo-recitals with the pianist Elly Ney. A musician of great culture, Hoelscher arranged his programs covering both the classical and the modern literature, ranging from Bach to the works of Pfitzner, Krenek, Fortner, and Henze.

BIBL.: E. Valentin, *Cello, Das Instrument und sein Meister L. H.* (Pfullingen, 1955); M. Kaindl-Hönig, *L. H.* (Geneva, 1962); W.-E. von Lewinski, *L. H.* (Tutzing, 1967).—NS/LK/DM

Hoelscher, Ulf, talented German violinist; b. Kitzingen, Jan. 17, 1942. After study with Bruno Masurat at the Heidelberg Cons., he received a grant that enabled him to go to America and enroll in the classes of Galamian at the Curtis Inst. of Music in Philadelphia and of Gingold at the Ind. Univ. School of Music in Bloomington. He then developed an international career, touring Europe, Australia, and the Far East, as well as the U.S. In 1981 he became a prof. at the Karlsruhe Hochschule für Musik. In 1987 he was appointed a prof. at the Berlin Hochschule der Künste. His repertoire is commendably large, encompassing works of the Baroque era, the Romantic school, and the contemporary avant-garde.—NS/LK/DM

Hoerburger, Felix, German musicologist; b. Munich, Dec. 9, 1916. He studied composition at the Munich Academy of Music and musicology at the Univ. of Munich (Ph.D., 1941, with a diss. on the music of the Ungoni in East Africa), completing his Habilitation at the Univ. of Erlangen (1963, with a study of dance among Albanian Yugoslavs). He was organist and research assistant at the Music Research Inst. in Regensburg (1947–68) and at the Musicology Research Inst. of the Univ. of Erlangen (1968), where he later became lecturer (1970). He then was a prof. at the Univ. of Regensburg (from 1971). His extensive publications on folk music include studies of the music and dance of Bavaria, Turkey, the Balkans, Nepal, and Afghanistan.

WRITINGS: *Volkstanzkunde* (Kassel, 1961–64); *Musica vulgaris: Legengesetze der instrumentalen Volksmusik* (Erlangen, 1966); *Studien zur Musik in Nepal* (Regensburg, 1975). —NS/LK/DM

Hoérée, Arthur (Charles Ernest), Belgian-French music critic, musicologist, and composer; b. St. Gilles, near Brussels, April 16, 1897; d. Paris, June 3, 1986. He received training in organ and theory at the Brussels Cons. (1908–12) and the Institut Musical in Anderlecht (1914–16). He then pursued his education at the École Polytechnique in Brussels (1916–19), and concurrently studied with Henner (piano), De Bondt (organ), Moulaert (harmony and counterpoint), and Closson (music history). He subsequently completed his training in Paris with Gigout (organ), d'Indy (conducting), and Vidal (fugue and composition). He settled in Paris as a music critic; in 1950 he became a prof. at the École Normale Supérieure de Musique, in 1958 a prof. at the Centre de Formation Professionelle of the French Radio and Television, and in 1972 a prof. of musicology at the Sorbonne. He publ. the monograph *Albert Roussel* (Paris, 1938), the major biography *Roussel* (Paris, 1969), and *La Musique française au XX^{e}siècle* (Paris, 1974). Among his works were ballets, various film and radio scores, *Pastorale et danse* for String Quartet (1923), Septet (1923), piano music, and *Crève-Coeur, le Magicien* for Soloists, Chorus, and Orch. (1961).—NS/LK/DM

Hoesick, Ferdinand, Polish musicologist; b. Warsaw, Oct. 16, 1867; d. there, April 13, 1941. He studied at the Univs. of Heidelberg, Kraków, and Paris, returning to Warsaw in 1891. He was ed. and writer on literature, his writings on music dealing exclusively with Chopin and including the biography *Chopin* (Warsaw, 1904; rev. and enl. ed. as *Chopin: Life and Letters*, 3 vols., 1910–11; later revision, 4 vols., Kraków, 1962–68).—NS/LK/DM

Hoesslin, Franz von, German conductor and composer; b. Munich, Dec. 31, 1885; d. in an airplane crash in southern France, Sept. 28, 1946. He studied at the Univ. of Munich and with Mottl (conducting) and Reger (composition). He conducted in St. Gallen (1908–11), Riga (1912–14), Lübeck (1919–20), Mannheim (1920–22), and at the Berlin Volksoper (1922–23). After serving as Generalmusikdirektor in Dessau (1923–26), he conducted in Barmen-Elberfeld (1926–27), Bayreuth (1927–28), and Breslau (1932–35). After his wife, the singer Erna Liebenthal, was forced out of Nazi Germany, they settled in Switzerland. He composed orch. works, a Clarinet Quintet, and choral pieces. —NS/LK/DM

Hofer, Andreas, Austrian organist and composer; b. Reichenhall, 1629; d. Salzburg, Feb. 25, 1684. He was educated at the Benedictine Univ. in Salzburg. After serving as organist of the St. Lambrecht monastery in Styria (1651–53), he settled in Salzburg as vice-Kapellmeister at the court of the Prince-Archbishop in 1654, becoming Kapellmeister in 1679. He also was Kapellmeister at the Cathedral from 1666. Among his compositions were 4 masses, 2 Magnificat settings, 2 Te Deum settings, 12 offertories, 5 Psalms, and 3 litanies.

BIBL.: M. Barndt-Webb, *A. H.: His Life and Music* (diss., Univ. of Ill., 1972).—LK/DM

Høffding, (Niels) Finn, Danish composer and pedagogue; b. Copenhagen, March 10, 1899; d. Frederiksberg, March 29, 1997. He studied violin with K. Sandby (1911–21), composition and harmony with Jeppesen (1918–21), organ with R. Rung-Keller (1919–21), and music history with Laub (1920–23) in Copenhagen; he also studied with Marx in Vienna (1921–22). He taught at the Royal Danish Cons. of Music in Copenhagen (1931–69), where he was its director (1954–69). His large output followed along post-Nielsen lines.

WORKS: DRAMATIC: O p e r a : *Kejserens nye Klaeder* (The Emperor's New Clothes; 1926; Copenhagen, Dec. 29, 1928); *Kilderejsen* (The Healing Spring; 1931; Copenhagen, Jan. 13, 1942); *Pasteur*, school opera (1935; Copenhagen, March 9, 1938). **ORCH.:** 4 syms.: No. 1, *Sinfonia impetuosa* (1923; Copenhagen, Aug. 22, 1925), No. 2, *Il Canto de Liberato*, for Soprano, Chorus, and Orch. (1924), No. 3 for 2 Pianos and Orch. (1928), and No. 4, *Sinfonia concertante*, for Chamber Orch. (1934); *Overture for Small Orch.* (1930); Concerto for Oboe and Strings (1933); *Fanfare* (1939); 4 symphonic fantasies: No. 1, *Evolution* (1939; Copenhagen, Sept. 4, 1940), No. 2, *Det er ganske vist* (It Is Perfectly True; 1940; Copenhagen, March 6, 1944; as a pantomime, Copenhagen, July 1, 1948), No. 3, *Vår-Höst* (Spring-Autumn) for Baritone and Orch. (1944; Danish Radio, Jan. 24, 1946), and No. 4, *The Arsenal at Springfield*, for 3 Soloists, Chorus, and Orch. (1953; Danish Radio, Sept. 22, 1955); *Fire Minespil*, suite (1944); *Majfest* (1945); *Fantasia concertante* (Danish Radio, Copenhagen, April 1, 1965). **CHAMBER:** 2 string quartets (1920, 1925); 2 wind quintets (1940, 1954); Oboe Sonata (1943); piano pieces. **OTHER:** Various choral works, songs, and pieces for school performance.

BIBL.: S. Bruhns and D. Fog, *F. H.s Kompositionen* (Copenhagen, 1969).—NS/LK/DM

Höffer, Paul, German composer and teacher; b. Barmen, Dec. 21, 1895; d. Berlin, Aug. 31, 1949. He studied with Georgii, Bölsche, and Abendroth at the Cologne Cons., and with Schreker at the Berlin Hochschule für Musik, where he joined the faculty as a piano instructor in 1923. From 1930 he taught composition and theory, in 1933 was made a prof., and in 1948 he became its director. He made use of polytonality and atonality in his compositions.

WORKS: DRAMATIC: O p e r a : *Borgia* (1931); *Der falsche Waldemar* (1934). **B a l l e t :** *Tanz um Liebe und Tod* (1939). **ORCH.:** *Sinfonische Ouvertüre* (1922); *Sinfonische Musik* (1922); Sym. (1926–27); *Sinfonie der grossen Stadt* (1937); *Symphonische Variationen über einen Bass von Bach* (1940); *Serenade* for Strings (1944); 2 piano concertos; Violin Concerto; Cello Concerto; Concerto for Oboe and Strings. **CHAMBER:** Wind Sextet; Piano Quintet; Wind Quintet; 3 strings quartets; 2 piano trios; String Trio; Trio Sonata for Flute, Viola, and Piano; 2 sonatas for Solo Violin; much piano music. **VOCAL:** 4 oratorios: *Der reiche Tag* (1938), *Vom edlen Leben* (1942), *Mysterium Liebe* (1943), and *Die letzte Stunde* (1945–47); cantatas; choruses; songs.—**NS/LK/DM**

Höffgen, Marga, German contralto; b. Mülheim an der Ruhr, April 26, 1921; d. Müllheim, Baden, July 7, 1995. She studied at the Berlin Hochschule für Musik and with Hermann Weissenborn. She made her concert debut in Berlin in 1952; in 1953 she made a highly successful appearance in Vienna as a soloist in the *St. Matthew Passion* conducted by Karajan; she then was active as a concert singer in Europe; also appeared in opera at Covent Garden in London, at the Vienna State Opera, and at the Bayreuth Festival.—**NS/LK/DM**

Hoffman, Grace (actually, **Goldie**), American mezzo-soprano; b. Cleveland, Jan. 14, 1925. She was educated at Western Reserve Univ. in Cleveland; then studied voice with Schorr in N.Y. and Basiola in Milan. After appearances in the U.S., she sang in Florence and Zürich; in 1955 she became a member of the Württemberg State Theater in Stuttgart. On March 27, 1958, she made her Metropolitan Opera debut in N.Y. as Brangäne in *Tristan und Isolde*. She made many appearances at La Scala in Milan, Covent Garden in London, Bayreuth, and the Vienna State Opera. In 1978 she became a prof. of voice at the Hochschüle für Musik in Stuttgart. She was noted for her performances of the music of Wagner and Verdi, particularly for her roles of Brangäne, Kundry, and Eboli; also sang widely in concerts.—**NS/LK/DM**

Hoffman, Irwin, American conductor; b. N.Y., Nov. 26, 1924. He studied violin at the Juilliard School of Music in N.Y. From 1952 to 1964 he was music director of the Vancouver (B.C.) Sym. Orch. He was assoc. conductor of the Chicago Sym. Orch. (1964–70), serving as its acting music director (1968–69). In 1968 he was made music director of the Fla. Gulf Coast Sym. Orch., which post he retained when it became the Fla. Orch. in 1984; after stepping down in 1987, he was made its music director laureate. From 1972 to 1976 he was also chief conductor of the Orchestre Symphonique de la RTBF (Belgian Radio and Television) in Brussels. In 1987 he was appointed music director of the Orquesta Sinfónica Nacional of Costa Rica in San José.—**NS/LK/DM**

Hoffman, Richard, English pianist and composer; b. Manchester, May 24, 1831; d. Mt. Kisco, N.Y., Aug. 17, 1909. He studied with his father and with L. de Meyer, Moscheles, and A. Rubinstein. In 1847 he settled in N.Y., where he made his debut on Nov. 27 in Mendelssohn's 1st Piano Concerto and Hummel's Septet. He toured the U.S. with Jenny Lind (1850–52), made many appearances as a soloist with the N.Y. Phil., and performed frequently in duo-concerts with Gottschalk. Hoffman composed some 100 piano pieces, many songs, and some anthems and services. He wrote *Some Musical Recollections of Fifty Years* (N.Y., 1910; includes a biographical sketch by his widow).—**NS/LK/DM**

Hoffmann, Bruno, German glass harmonica player and composer; b. Stuttgart, Sept. 15, 1913; d. there, April 11, 1991. He studied piano, organ, and voice. In 1929 he became interested in building a modern "glass harp" and eventually expanded its range to 4 octaves, covering a full chromatic scale. With this instrument, he gave concert tours in Europe (from 1949), Asia (from 1962), the U.S. and Canada (from 1964), and South America (from 1969). He also composed a number of works for the glass harp.—**NS/LK/DM**

Hoffmann, E(rnst) T(heodor) A(madeus) (his 3rd Christian name was Wilhelm, but he replaced it with Amadeus, from love of Mozart), famous German writer, who was also a composer; b. Königsberg, Jan. 24, 1776; d. Berlin, June 25, 1822. He studied law at the Univ. of Königsberg; also studied violin with Christian Gladau, piano with Carl Gottlieb Richter, and thoroughbass and counterpoint with Christian Podbielski; after further studies with Gladau, he completed his training by taking a course in composition with J. F. Reichardt in Berlin. He served as music director at the theater in Bamberg, then conducted opera performances in Leipzig and Dresden (1813–14). In 1814 he settled in Berlin. He used the pen name of Kapellmeister Johannes Kreisler (subsequently made famous in Schumann's *Kreisleriana*); his series of articles in the *Allgemeine Musikalische Zeitung* under that name were reprinted as *Phantasiestucke* in Callot's *Manier* (1814). As a writer of fantastic tales, he made a profound impression on his period, and influenced the entire Romantic school of literature; indirectly, he was also a formative factor in the evolution of the German school of composition. His own compositions are passable from the technical viewpoint, but strangely enough, for a man of his imaginative power, they lack the inventiveness that characterizes his literary productions. His writings on music were ed. by H. von Ende (Cologne, 1896); see also D. Charlton, ed., *E.T.A. Hoffmann's Musical Writings: Kreisleriana, The Poet and the Composer, Music Criticism* (Cambridge, 1989).

WORKS: DRAMATIC: O p e r a : *Die Maske* (1799); *Scherz, List und Rache* (Posen, 1801); *Der Renegat* (Plozk, 1803); *Faustine* (Plozk, 1804); *Die ungeladenen Gäste, oder Der Canonicus von Mailand* (Warsaw, 1805); *Lustige Musikanten* (Warsaw, 1805); *Liebe aus Eifersucht* (Warsaw, 1807); *Der Trank der Unsterblichkeit* (Bamberg, 1808); *Das Gespenst* (Warsaw, 1809); *Aurora* (1811; rev. version by L. Böttcher, Bamberg, Nov. 5, 1933); *Undine* (Berlin, Aug. 3, 1816; his best work; vocal score ed. by Pfitzner, 1907); *Julius Sabinus* (unfinished). **B a l l e t :** *Harlekin.* **OTHER:** Some sacred works; Sym.; Piano Trio; 4 piano sonatas.

BIBL.: H. von Wolzogen, *E.T.A. H. und R. Wagner* (Berlin, 1906); E. Kroll, *E.T.A. H.s musikalische Anschauungen* (Königsberg, 1909); H. Ehinger, *E.T.A. H. als Musiker und Musik-Schriftsteller* (Cologne, 1954); H. Dechant, *E.T.A. H.s Oper Aurora* (Regensburg, 1975); R. Murray Schafer, *E.T.A. H. and Music* (Toronto, 1975); W. Keil, *E.T.A. H. als Komponist: Studien zur Kompositionstechnik an ausgewählten Werken* (Wiesbaden, 1986). —**NS/LK/DM**

Hoffmann, Hans, German conductor and musicologist; b. Neustadt, Silesia, Jan. 26, 1902; d. Bielefeld,

Aug. 8, 1949. He studied musicology at the Univ. of Breslau, and later in Leipzig, Berlin, and Kiel. Concurrently he took instruction in singing and for several years sang in oratorio performances in Germany. In 1933 he became a choral conductor in Hamburg, and taught theory at the Univ. of Hamburg. He was also active as a sym. and opera conductor, and in 1940 was appointed music director of the Bielefeld Opera. Among his publications were *Heinrich Schütz und Johann Sebastian Bach: Zwei Tonsprachen und ihre Bedeutung für die Aufführungspraxis* (Kassel, 1940) and *Vom Wesen der zeitgenössischen Kirchenmusik* (Kassel, 1949).—NS/LK/DM

Hoffmann, Heinrich August, German poet, philologist, literary historian, and composer who was also known as Hoffmann von Fallersleben; b. Fallersleben, near Braunschweig, April 2, 1798; d. Schloss Korvei, near Höxter, Jan. 19, 1874. He was educated at the univs. of Göttingen and Bonn. From 1823 to 1838 he was custodian of the library of the Univ. of Breslau, where he also was made extraordinary prof. of German language and literature in 1830 and ordinary prof. in 1835. His *Unpolitische Lieder* (1840–41) was viewed as a political statement by the Prussian authorities (in spite of its title), and he was removed from his Univ. position in 1842. After the revolutionary events of 1848, he returned to Prussia, and in 1860 he was made librarian to Prince Lippe in Korvei. Hoffmann was a talented composer who wrote melodies for many of his texts. Mendelssohn, Schumann, Brahms, Wolf, and other composers also set his texts. He publ. the important study *Geschichte des deutschen Kirchenliedes bis auf Luthers Zeit* (Breslau, 1832; 3rd ed., 1861); with E. Richter, he ed. the standard folk song collection *Schlesische Volkslieder mit Melodien* (Leipzig, 1842). He also publ. an autobiography (Hannover, 1868). His *Das Lied der Deutschen* (1841) includes the text of his *Deutschland, Deutschland, über alles*, which he wrote to Haydn's hymn *Gott herhalte Franz den Kaiser*. It served as the German national anthem from 1922 until the end of World War II. Its third verse, *Einigkeit und Recht und Freiheit*, was later sung as the national anthem of the Federal Republic of Germany.—NS/LK/DM

Hoffmann, Richard, Austrian-born American composer and teacher; b. Vienna, April 20, 1925. He studied at the Univ. of New Zealand (B.Mus.) before emigrating to the U.S. in 1947 and becoming a naturalized American citizen in 1964. He studied musicology at the Univ. of Calif. at Los Angeles (1949–51) and composition with Schoenberg, serving as his assistant and secretary (1948–51). In 1951–52 he taught at the Univ. of Calif. at Los Angeles, and then at Oberlin (Ohio) Coll. (from 1954). He was an ed. of the complete works of Schoenberg. In 1970 and 1977 he held Guggenheim fellowships. He developed a sui generis serial technique, in which intervals, meters, rhythms, timbres, and dynamics are systematically organized, while the tone row is not necessarily dodecaphonic; he also utilized computer-generated sounds in some of his works.

WORKS: ORCH.: *Prelude and Double Fugue* for Strings (1944); Violin Concerto (1948); 2 pieces (1952, 1961); Piano Concerto (1953–54); Cello Concerto (1956–59); *Music* for Strings (1970–71); *Souffler* (1975–76); *Intravolatura* for Strings and Percussion (1980). **CHAMBER:** 4 string quartets (1947; 1950; 1972–74; 1977, with computer-generated sounds); Trio for Piano, Violin, and Bass Clarinet (1948); Duo for Piano and Violin (1949; rev. 1965); Duo for Violin and Cello (1949); Tripartita for Violin (1950); Piano Quartet (1950); String Trio (1963); *Decadanse* for 10 Players (1972); *Changes* for 2 Chimes (1974). **KEYBOARD: P i a n o :** Sonata (1945–46); *3 Small Pieces* (1947); 2 sets of variations (1951, 1957); Sonatina (1952). **O r g a n :** *Fantasy and Fugue* (1951). **COMPUTER-GENERATED TA P E :** *In memorium patris* (1976).—NS/LK/DM

Hoffmeister, Franz Anton, German composer and music publisher; b. Rothenburg am Neckar, May 12, 1754; d. Vienna, Feb. 9, 1812. He went to Vienna as a law student, but became greatly interested in music, and in 1785 established his publishing firm, of historic significance owing to its publications of Mozart and Beethoven. In 1800 he went to Leipzig, where he organized (with Kuhnel) a "Bureau de Musique," which eventually became incorporated into the celebrated firm of C. F. Peters. In 1805 he returned to Vienna, where he devoted himself mostly to composition. Amazingly prolific, he composed 9 operas, more than 65 syms., 14 keyboard concertos, 25 flute concertos, various other orch. works, pieces for wind ensemble, over 150 string quartets, many trios, innumerable flute duets, numerous sonatas, songs, etc.

BIBL.: A. Weinmann, *Die Wiener Verlagswerke von F.A. H.* (Vienna, 1964).—NS/LK/DM

Hoffmeister, Karel, Czech pianist, pedagogue, and writer on music; b. Liblice, Sept. 26, 1868; d. Hluboká, Sept. 23, 1952. He studied piano with Jindřich Kàan, and later attended Hostinský's lectures at the Univ. of Prague and graduated from the Prague Organ School. After teaching piano in Laibach (1891–98), he was made asst. lecturer (1898) and then prof. (1902) at the Prague Cons.; from 1919, gave master classes there. With K. Stecker, he was co-ed. of *Hudební revue* (1908–18). As a pianist, Hoffmeister was a fine chamber music player, being the founder of the Czech Trio.

WRITINGS (all publ. in Prague): *Bedrich Smetana* (1915; 2nd ed., abr., 1917); *Klavir* (1923; 2nd ed., 1939); *Antonín Dvořák* (1924; Eng. tr., 1928); *Josef Klička* (1944); *Tvorba Vitĕzslava Nováka z let 1941–8* (The Works of Vitĕzslav Novák Between 1941–8; 1949); *50 let s Vitĕzslavem Novákem* (50 Years with Vitĕzslav Novák; 1949); *Vývoj klavirní virtuosity* (The Development of Piano Virtuosity; n.d.).

BIBL.: O. Kredba, *K. H.: Obraz života a dila* (K. H.: A Picture of Life and Works; Prague, 1948).—NS/LK/DM

Hoffstetter, Roman, German composer; b. Laudenbach, near Bad Mergentheim, April 24, 1742; d. Miltenberg, May 21, 1815. He was a member of the Benedictine monastery of Amorbach. After being ordained a priest in 1766, he was active as regens chori there. He settled in Miltenberg in 1803. He greatly admired the music of Haydn, and his chamber music so closely resembled Haydn's that it was long attributed to him. The works in question are the 2 string quartets written c. 1765, as well as the publ. 6 String Quartets, op.1 (Amsterdam, c. 1770), and 6 String Quartets, op.3 (Paris, 1777). He also wrote 3 cello concertos and a number of masses.

BIBL.: H. Unverricht, *Die beiden H.* (Mainz, 1968; includes thematic catalog).—**NS/LK/DM**

Hofhaimer (also **Hoffhaimer, Hoffheimer, Hofhaymer,** etc.), **Paul,** greatly celebrated Austrian organist, composer, and pedagogue; b. Radstadt, Jan. 25, 1459; d. Salzburg, 1537. Although he is believed to have been self-taught as a musician, he may have received organ instruction at the court of Emperor Frederick III. He entered the service of the court of Duke Sigmund of Tyrol in Innsbruck in 1478, and was made organist for life in 1480. He was also in the service of Emperor Maximilian I from 1489, settling in Augsburg in 1507. He was knighted and ennobled by Maximilian and the Polish king in 1515, and was granted the title of Obrister [principal] Organist by the former. Following Maximilian's death in 1519, he was made organist of the cathedral and to the archbishop of Salzburg. In addition to his fame as a virtuoso, he was renowned as a teacher. He also distinguished himself as a composer of lieder and organ works. Among his few extant works are the *Harmoniae poeticae* (Nuremberg, 1539; ed. by I. Achtleithner, Salzburg, 1868; 35 settings of Horatian odes) and 2 liturgical organ pieces, *Recordare* and *Salve Regina*. See H. J. Moser, ed., "Gesammelte Tonwerke," *Paul Hofhaimer* (Stuttgart and Berlin, 1929), K. Gudewill, ed., *G. Forster: Frische teutsche Liedlein* (1539–1556), Das Erbe Deutscher Musik, 1st series, XX (1942), H. Marx, ed., *Tabulaturen des XVI. Jahrhunderts, I: Die Tabulaturen aus dem Besitz des Basler Humanisten Bonifacius Amerbach,* Schweizerische Musikdenkmaler, VI (1967), and idem, ed., *Tabulaturen des XVI. Jahrhunderts, II: Die Orgeltabulatur des Clemens Hor,* ibid., VII (1970).

BIBL.: H. J. Moser, *P. H.* (Stuttgart and Berlin, 1929). —**NS/LK/DM**

Hofman, Shlomo, Polish-Israeli composer and musicologist; b. Warsaw, April 24, 1909. He studied at the Warsaw Cons., graduating in 1934. He then went to Paris, where he studied composition with Roger-Ducasse, Koechlin, and Milhaud (1937–38). He subsequently settled in Palestine, and in 1954 he became a lecturer in musicology at the Academy of Music in Tel Aviv. Among his works were an Oboe Concerto (1950), Hebrew cantata, *Tawashih* (1960), and Quintet for Clarinet and Strings (1945). He publ. a valuable thesis, *L'Oeuvre de clavecin de François Couperin le Grand* (Paris, 1961); also a polyglot *Dictionary of Musical Terms* (Jerusalem, 1955), *The Music of Israel* (1959), and *La Musique arabe en Israel* (1963).—**NS/LK/DM**

Hofmann, Casimir (actually, **Kazimierz**), Polish pianist, conductor, and composer, father of **Josef (Casimir) (Józef Kazimierz) Hofmann;** b. Kraków, 1842; d. Berlin, July 6, 1911. He was a pupil of R. Fischof (piano) and Gachlechner (harmony) at the Vienna Cons. (1851–56), and later studied at the Univ. of Kraków. After conducting at the Kraków Theater (1868–78), he

was prof. of harmony and counterpoint at the Warsaw Inst. of Music (1878–86); also conducted at Warsaw's Wielki Theater. He composed mainly music for the stage.—**NS/LK/DM**

Hofmann, Heinrich (Karl Johann), German composer; b. Berlin, Jan. 13, 1842; d. Gross-Tabarz, July 16, 1902. He studied at Kullak's Neue Akademie der Tonkunst in Berlin, where his mentors were Kullak, Grell, Dehn, and Wüerst. He was active as a pianist and teacher until the enormous success of his comic opera *Cartouche* (Berlin, July 22, 1869) decided his course as a composer. Several of his orch., chamber, and choral pieces were also popular for a time

WORKS: DRAMATIC: O p e r a : *Cartouche,* comic opera (Berlin, July 22, 1869); *Armin* (Dresden, Oct. 14, 1877); *Ännchen von Tharau* (Hamburg, Nov. 6, 1878); *Wilhelm von Oranien* (Hamburg, Feb. 5, 1882); *Donna Diana* (Berlin, Nov. 15, 1886). **ORCH.:** *Ungarische Suite* (1873); *Frithjof-Symphonie* (1874); Cello Concerto (1880); *Konzertstück* for Flute and Orch. (1888). **CHAMBER:** Piano Trio (1874); String Sextet (1875); Piano Quartet (1880); Violin Sonata (1883); Octet for 2 Violins, Viola, Cello, Flute, Clarinet, Horn, and Bassoon (1883); many keyboard pieces. **VOCAL:** Numerous works for Soloists, Chorus, and Orch. and over 100 songs.—**NS/LK/DM**

Hofmann, Josef (Casimir) (actually, **Józef Kazimierz**), celebrated Polish-born American pianist, son of **Casimir (Kazimierz) Hofmann;** b. Podgorze, near Kraków, Jan. 20, 1876; d. Los Angeles, Feb. 16, 1957. At the age of 4, he began to play the piano, tutored by an older sister and an aunt; at 5, he began taking regular lessons from his father. He was barely 6 when he first appeared in public in Ciechocinek, and at the age of 10, he played Beethoven's Concerto No. 1 with the Berlin Phil. under Hans von Bülow. He also made a tour of Scandinavia and played in France and England, his concerts as a child prodigy becoming a European sensation. Soon an American offer of a concert tour came from the impresarios Abbey, Schoeffel & Grau. On Nov. 29, 1887, Hofmann appeared at the Metropolitan Opera House as soloist in Beethoven's Concerto No. 1; he also played works by Chopin and some of his own little pieces. He electrified the audience, and hardheaded critics hailed his performance as a marvel. He appeared throughout the U.S., giving 42 concerts in all; then agitation was started by the Soc. for the Prevention of Cruelty to Children against the exploitation of his talent. Alfred Corning Clark of N.Y. offered $50,000 to the family for his continued education. The offer was accepted, and he began serious study with Moszkowski (piano) and Urban (composition) in Berlin. Then Anton Rubinstein accepted him as a pupil in Dresden, where Hofmann traveled twice a week for piano lessons. At the age of 18, he resumed his career, giving recitals in Dresden and elsewhere in Germany with enormous success; made his first tour of Russia in 1896, attaining huge popularity there; he reappeared in Russia frequently. In 1898 he again played in the U.S.; from then on, he appeared in American cities almost every year. At the peak of his career, he came to be regarded as one of the greatest pianists of the century.

He possessed the secret of the singing tone, which enabled him to interpret Chopin with extraordinary delicacy and intimacy. He was also capable of summoning tremendous power playing Liszt and other works of the virtuoso school. His technique knew no difficulties; but in his interpretations, he subordinated technical effects to the larger design of the work. When the Curtis Inst. of Music was founded in Philadelphia (1924), Hofmann was engaged to head the piano dept.; he was director from 1926 to 1938. He became a naturalized American citizen in 1926. On Nov. 28, 1937, his golden jubilee in the U.S. was celebrated with a concert at the Metropolitan Opera in N.Y. He performed the D-minor Concerto of Anton Rubinstein, and his own *Chromaticon* for Piano and Orch. From 1938 to his death he lived mostly in Calif., his concert career coming sadly to a close in 1945 owing to alcoholism. Hofmann was also a composer, under the pen name Michel Dvorsky (a transliteration of the literal translation into Polish of his German name, meaning "courtyard man"). Among his works are several piano concertos; some symphonic works; *Chromaticon* for Piano and Orch. (Cincinnati, Nov. 24, 1916, composer soloist); numerous piano pieces. He also publ. a practical manual, *Piano-Playing with Piano—Questions Answered* (1915).—**NS/LK/DM**

Hofmann, Leopold, notable Austrian organist, violinist, teacher, and composer; b. Vienna, Aug. 14, 1738; d. there, March 17, 1793. Following training in keyboard playing from Wagenseil, he pursued his career as an esteemed performing musician and composer in his native city. In 1766 he was made Kapellmeister at St. Peter's. In 1769 he was appointed Hofklaviermeister and in 1772 2nd court organist. He also served as Essential- und Gnadenbildkapellmeister at St. Stephen's Cathedral from 1772. His extensive output of sacred works represents an effective fusion of Austrian Baroque and Neapolitan styles. He also composed some 55 syms. in a galant style, concertos, chamber music, and lieder.

BIBL.: V. Kreiner, *L. H. als Sinfoniker* (diss., Univ. of Vienna, 1958); A. Badley, *The Concertos of L. H. (1738–1793)* (diss., Univ. of Auckland, 1976).—**NS/LK/DM**

Hofmann, Peter, outstanding German tenor; b. Marienbad, Aug. 12, 1944. He studied at the Hochschule für Musik in Karlsruhe. He made his operatic debut in 1972 in Lübeck as Tamino; in 1973 he joined the Württemberg State Theater in Stuttgart. He came to prominence in his performance of the role of Siegmund in the centennial Bayreuth productions of *Der Ring des Nibelungen* (1976); that same year, he made his first appearance at London's Covent Garden in the same role. He made his U.S. debut as Siegmund with the San Francisco Opera in 1977; sang Lohengrin on Jan. 24, 1980, at his Metropolitan Opera debut in N.Y. In 1986 he sang Tristan at the Bayreuth Festival. His other roles included Max, Florestan, Alfred in *Die Fledermaus*, Loge, and Bacchus.

BIBL.: M. Müller, *P. H.: Singen ist wie Fliegen* (Bonn, 1983). —**NS/LK/DM**

Hogarth, George, Scottish writer on music; b. Carfrae Mill, near Oxton, Berwickshire, 1783; d. London, Feb. 12, 1870. He was a practicing lawyer in Edinburgh, and an amateur musician. He settled in London in 1830. He contributed articles to the *Harmonicon*, and also wrote reviews for the *Morning Chronicle*. His daughter married Charles Dickens in 1836. When Dickens became ed. of the *Daily News* (1846), Hogarth began writing music criticism for it; also wrote for other newspapers. From 1850 to 1864 he was secretary to the Phil. Soc. of London.

WRITINGS: *Musical History, Biography, and Criticism* (1835); *Memoirs of the Musical Drama* (1838; 2nd ed., 1851, as *Memoirs of the Opera*); *The Birmingham Festival* (1855); *The Philharmonic Society of London* (1862).—**NS/LK/DM**

Hogwood, Christopher (Jarvis Haley), prominent English harpsichordist, conductor, musicologist, and broadcaster; b. Nottingham, Sept. 10, 1941. He studied classics and music at Pembroke Coll., Cambridge (B.A., 1964), received training in harpsichord from Puyana and Leonhardt, and took courses at the Charles Univ. in Prague. In 1967 he joined David Munrow in organizing the Early Music Consort, an ensemble devoted to the performance of medieval music. In 1973 Hogwood founded and became director of the Academy of Ancient Music, which he developed into one of the most outstanding early music ensembles devoted to performances on original instruments. He toured widely with it and made numerous recordings. Hogwood also appeared as a guest conductor at home and abroad, and held various other positions while retaining his position with the Academy of Ancient Music. From 1976 to 1980 he was artistic director of the King's Lynn Festival. He was honorary prof. of music at the Univ. of Keele from 1986 to 1990, which awarded him an honorary D.Mus. degree in 1991. From 1986 to 2000 he was artistic director of the Handel and Haydn Soc. of Boston, and thereafter held the title of conductor laureate. He was music director of the St. Paul (Minn.) Chamber Orch. from 1987 to 1992, and subsequently its principal guest conductor. From 1992 to 1996 he was a visiting prof. at King's Coll., London. In 1992 he became the International Prof. of Early Music Performance at the Royal Academy of Music in London, in 1993 artistic director of the Summer Mozart Festival of the National Sym. Orch. in Washington, D.C., and in 1998 assoc. director of the Beethoven Academie in Antwerp. In 1986 he received the Walter Willson Cobbett Medal and in 1989 was made a Freeman of the Company of Musicians in London. He was made a Commander of the Order of the British Empire and an honorary fellow of Jesus Coll., Cambridge, in 1989. In 1992 he was made an honorary fellow of Pembroke Coll., Cambridge. Hogwood has ed. various works and has contributed to many publications. He publ. *Music at Court* (1977), *The Trio Sonata* (1979), *Haydn's Visits to England* (1980), and *Handel* (1984). With R. Luckett, he ed. *Music in Eighteenth-Century England* (1983). He also ed. *Holmes' Life of Mozart* (1991).—**NS/LK/DM**

Hoiby, Lee, talented American composer and pianist; b. Madison, Wisc., Feb. 17, 1926. He began piano study at age 5, and while attending high school received instruction from Gunnar Johansen. He then studied at the Univ. of Wisc. (B.A., 1947), and attended Petri's master class in Ithaca, N.Y. (1944) and at Mills Coll. in Oakland, Calif. (M.A., 1952), where he also studied composition with Milhaud. He also received instruction in composition from Menotti at the Curtis Inst. of Music in Philadelphia. He received a Fulbright fellowship (1953), an award from the National Inst. of Arts and Letters (1957), and a Guggenheim fellowship (1958). In addition to his career as a composer, he appeared as a concert pianist; made his N.Y. recital debut on Jan. 17, 1978. He has composed a number of highly successful vocal and instrumental works, being particularly adept in writing operas in a manner reminiscent of Menotti—concise, dramatic, and aurally pleasing, and sometimes stimulating.

WORKS: DRAMATIC: O p e r a : *The Scarf*, after Chekhov (Spoleto, June 20, 1958); *Beatrice*, after Maeterlinck (Louisville, Oct. 23, 1959; withdrawn); *Natalia Petrovna*, after Turgenev (N.Y., Oct. 8, 1964; rev. version as *A Month in the Country*, Boston, Jan. 1981); *Summer and Smoke*, after Tennessee Williams (1970; St. Paul, Minn., June 19, 1971); *Something New for the Zoo* (1979; Cheverly, Md., May 17, 1982); *The Tempest*, after Shakespeare (1982–86; Indianola, Iowa, June 21, 1986); *This is the Rill Speaking* (1993); also *The Italian Lesson*, monodrama for Mezzosoprano and Chamber Orch. (1980; Newport, R.I., 1982); incidental music to various plays. B a l l e t : *Hearts, Meadows, and Flags* (1950); *After Eden* (1966); *Landscape* (1968). ORCH.: *Pastoral Dances* for Flute and Small Orch. (New Orleans, Nov. 6, 1956); 2nd *Suite* (1953); 2 piano concertos (1958, 1979); *Design for Strings* (1965); *Music for a Celebration*, overture (1975). CHAMBER: Violin Sonata (1951; rev. 1980); *Diversions* for Woodwind Quartet (1953); Piano Quintet (1974); *Serenade* for Violin and Piano (Washington, D.C., Nov. 4, 1988); piano pieces. VOCAL: *A Hymn of the Nativity* for Soprano, Baritone, Chorus, and Orch. (1960); *The Tides of Sleep*, symphonic song for Low Voice and Orch., after Thomas Wolfe (1961); *Galileo Galilei*, oratorio for Soloists, Chorus, and Orch. (1975); *Psalm 93* for Large Chorus, Organ, Brass, and Percussion (Cathedral of St. John the Divine, N.Y., May 17, 1985); *I Was There*, 5 songs for Baritone and Orch., after Whitman (1995).—NS/LK/DM

Hokanson, Leonard (Ray),

American pianist and teacher; b. Vinalhaven, Maine, Aug. 13, 1931. He received training in piano from Hedwig Rosenthal (1947–48), Artur Schnabel (1948–51), Karl Ulrich Schnabel (1951–53), and Claude Frank (1952–55). He pursued his academic studies at Clark Coll. (B.A., 1952) and Bennington Coll. (M.A., 1954). In 1949 he made his debut as soloist with the Philadelphia Orch., and subsequently toured internationally as a soloist with orchs., as a recitalist, as a chamber music player, and as an accompanist. He was a prof. at the Frankfurt am Main Hochschule für Musik (1976–78) and at the Ind. Univ. School of Music in Bloomington (from 1986). —NS/LK/DM

Hol, Richard,

Danish organist, conductor, and composer; b. Amsterdam, July 23, 1825; d. Utrecht, May 14, 1904. He was a student of Martens (organ) and Bertelmann (theory). In 1862 he went to Utrecht as municipal music director, after which he was Cathedral organist (1869–87) and director of the Stedelijke Musiek-school (1875–1904). He also was active in The Hague as conductor of the Cecilia men's chorus (1875–1901) and the Diligentia orch. (1886–1901), and served as co-conductor (with J. Coenen) of the Amsterdam paleis voor Volksvlijt Orch. (from 1891). He was ed. of *Het Orgel* (1886–90) and publ. a monograph on Sweelinck (1859). His autobiography appeared in 1903.

WORKS: DRAMATIC: O p e r a : *Floris V* (Amsterdam, April 9, 1892); *Uit de branding* (Amsterdam, 1894); *De schoone schaapster* (n.d.). OTHER: 4 syms. and other orch. music; *David*, oratorio (1879); choral pieces; songs; chamber music.

BIBL.: H. Nolthenius, *R. H., Levensschets* (Haarlem, 1904). —NS/LK/DM

Holborne, Antony or Anthony,

English composer; b. place and date unknown; d. Nov. 29?, 1602. He publ. *The Cittharn Schoole* (58 pieces; London, 1597) and *Pavans, Galliards, Almains...in 5 Parts* (65 pieces; London, 1599), which were popular in their day. Other works were publ. in contemporary collections. See *The Complete Works of Anthony Holborne*, Harvard Publications in Music, i, V (1967–73).

BIBL.: B. Jeffery, *The Life and Music of Antony H.* (diss., Oxford Univ., 1964; with thematic index).—NS/LK/DM

Holbrooke, Joseph (actually, Josef Charles),

English composer; b. Croydon, July 5, 1878; d. London, Aug. 5, 1958. He was a student of Corder (composition) and Westlake (piano) at the Royal Academy of Music in London. He then worked as a conductor and pianist. The success of his symphonic poem *The Raven* (1900) encouraged him to write a large body of music along Romantic lines. His most ambitious work was the operatic trilogy *The Cauldron of Annwn* (1909–29). Holbrooke's initial success as a composer was not sustained. Especially in his early years he was a trenchant critic of the musical establishment. He was the author of *Contemporary British Composers* (London, 1925).

WORKS: DRAMATIC: *Pierrot and Pierrette*, lyric drama (London, Nov. 11, 1909; rev. version as *The Stranger*, Liverpool, Oct. 1924); *The Cauldron of Annwn*, operatic trilogy: 1, *The Children of Don* (London, June 15, 1912); 2, *Dylan: Son of the Wave* (1909; London, July 4, 1914); and 3, *Bronwen* (Huddersfield, Feb. 1, 1929); *The Red Mask*, ballet; *The Moth and the Flame*, ballet; *The Enchanter*, opera-ballet (Chicago, 1915); *Coromanthe*, ballet; *The Sailor's Arms*, comic opera; *The Snob*, comic opera; *Aucassin et Nicolette*, ballet. ORCH.: 4 symphonic poems: *The Raven* (1900), *Ulalume* (1901–03), *The Viking* (1904), and *The Birds of Rhiannon* (1925); 1 unnumbered Piano Concerto (1896–1900); 2 numbered piano concertos: No. 1, *The Song of Gwynn ap Nudd* (1907) and No. 2, *L'orient* (1928); *The New Renaissance*, overture (1903); *Apollo and the Seaman* (1907); Violin Concerto, *The Grasshopper* (1917); 8 syms., including No. 3, *Ships* (1925), and No. 4, *Homage to Schubert* (1929); Cello Concerto, *Cambrian* (1936); *Tamerlaine*, concerto for Clarinet or Saxophone, Bassoon, and Orch. (1939); Sinfonietta for Chamber Orch.; military band music. CHAMBER: 6 string quartets (1896; *Belgium-Russia*, 1915; *The Pickwick Club*, 1916; nos. 4–6, 1918–19); Piano Quartet, *Byron* (1902); String Sextet, *Al Aaraaf* (1902); 2 clarinet quintets (c. 1903; *Fate, or Ligeia*, 1910); Fantasie Sonata for Cello and Piano (1904); Piano Quintet (1904); Quartet for Violin, Viola,

Clarinet, and Piano (1905); 2 sextets for Piano and Strings (*In memoriam*, 1905; 1906); Fantasie String Quartet (1906); Sextet, *Israfel*, for Piano and Winds (1906); 3 violin sonatas; Woodwind Quartet; Saxophone Sonata; Quartet for Flute, Viola, Cello, and Harp; Quintet for Winds and Piano; Quintet for Flute, Oboe, Violin, Cello, and Harp; piano pieces, including 2 sonatas. **VOCAL:** Chorus and Orch.: *Ode to Victory* (1901); *Queen Mab* (1902); *The Bells* (1903); *Byron* (1906); also *Homage to E. A. Poe*, dramatic choral sym. (1908), and numerous songs.

BIBL.: G. Lowe, *J. H. and his Work* (London, 1920); *J. H.: Various Appreciations by Many Authors* (London, 1937). —NS/LK/DM

Holde, Artur, German-American choral conductor and music critic; b. Rendsburg, Oct. 16, 1885; d. N.Y., June 23, 1962. He studied musicology at the Univ. of Berlin. From 1910 to 1936 he was music director of the Frankfurt am Main Synagogue; also was active as a music critic. In 1937 he emigrated to the U.S. He was choirmaster at the Hebrew Tabernacle in N.Y. (1937–43) and music critic of the German periodical *Aufbau* in N.Y. He publ. *Jews in Music* (N.Y., 1959) and *A Treasury of Great Operas* (N.Y., 1965) and also contributed articles to the *Musical Quarterly* and other American publications. —NS/LK/DM

Holden, Oliver, American composer and tune-book compiler; b. Shirley, Mass., Sept. 18, 1765; d. Charlestown, Mass., Sept. 4, 1844. His formal education consisted of a brief period of study in Groton, Mass., after which he was apprenticed to a Grafton cabinet-maker. He was active as a farmer in Groton and Pepperell before serving in the Revolutionary War. He then settled in Charlestown, where he was a town official for over 50 years. In 1783 he attended a singing-school, and that same year he began his own singing-schools. He also founded a church and acted as its minister. From 1818 to 1833 he was a member of the Mass. House of Representatives. Holden composed some 235 works, including 25 anthems. His best known piece is the hymn tune *Coronation* (1793), which was set to the text *All Hail the Power of Jesus' Name*. He wrote works for various special occasions, including the memorial service for George Washington on Feb. 22, 1800 (*Sacred Dirges*, Boston, 1800). He ed. over a dozen anthologies, among them the last three editions of *The Worcester Collection* (Worcester, Mass., 1797–1803), which were widely known. With H. Gram and S. Holyoke, he wrote the influential *Massachusetts Compiler of Theoretical Principles* (Boston, 1795).

BIBL.: D. McCormick, *O. H., Composer and Anthologist* (diss., Union Theological Seminary, 1963); R. Patterson, *Three American "Primitives": A Study of the Musical Styles of Samuel Holyoke, O. H., and Hans Gram* (diss., Washington Univ., 1963). —NS/LK/DM

Holewa, Hans, Austrian-born Swedish composer; b. Vienna, May 26, 1905; d. Bromma, April 24, 1991. He studied conducting at the New Cons. of Music in Vienna, and piano and theory with J. Heinz. In 1937 he settled in Stockholm as a pianist and pedagogue; there he introduced Schoenberg's 12–tone technique. From

1949 to 1970 he worked in the music library of the Swedish Broadcasting Corp.

WORKS: DRAMATIC: O p e r a : *Apollos förvandling* (1967–71). **ORCH.:** *Vier kleine Märsche* (1940); *Variations* for Piano and Orch. (1943); 6 syms.: No. 1 (1948), No. 2 (1976; Stockholm, April 28, 1978), No. 3 for Textless Soprano and Orch. (1977; Stockholm, Oct. 17, 1979), No. 4 (1980; Stockholm, June 7, 1984), No. 5 (1983; Västerås, Nov. 15, 1984), and No. 6 (1985–86; Stockholm, April 8, 1988); Violin Concerto (1963; Swedish Radio, Feb. 7, 1965); *Komposition* (1965–66; Swedish Radio, Oct. 8, 1966); *Quattro cadenze* for Cello and Orch. (1968; Swedish Radio, April 12, 1970); *Movimento espressivo* (Stockholm, April 17, 1971); 3 piano concertos: No. 1 (1972; Swedish Radio, April 28, 1973), No. 2 (1980–81; Swedish Radio, Feb. 11, 1983), and No. 3 (1984–85; Swedish Radio, Jan. 30, 1987); Concerto for 2 Pianos and Strings (1975; Uppsala, April 8, 1976). **CHAMBER:** 2 string quartets (1939, 1965); Sonata for Solo Cello (1952); Trio for Violin, Viola, and Cello (1959); 9 concertinos (1960–87); Sonata for Solo Violin (1960); Quintet for Clarinet, Trombone, Cello, Percussion, and Piano (1962); *Chamber Music* No. 1 (1964), No. 2 (1973), and No. 3 (1981) for Cello and Piano; Chamber Concerto for Viola and 11 Strings (1966); *Lamenti*, 3 pieces for Horn, Alto Saxophone, and Bassoon (1976); Quartet for Oboe, Violin, Viola, and Cello (1979); Octet for Clarinet, Horn, Bassoon, 2 Violins, Viola, Cello, and Double Bass (1982); Wind Quintet (1982); *Sonata Movement* for String Quartet (1984); Trio for Clarinet, Cello, and Piano (1984); Violin Sonata (1985); Trio for Violin, Viola, and Cello (1986); Quartet for Flute, Oboe, Cello, and Piano (1988); also numerous piano pieces. **VOCAL:** Choral works; songs.—NS/LK/DM

Holiday, Billie (Elinore Harris), definitive jazz singer; b. Philadelphia, Pa., April 7, 1915; d. N.Y., July 17, 1959. Holiday was lauded as a vocalist who brought a jazz instrumentalist's sensibility to singing; like a jazz musician, she engaged in sophisticated melodic improvisation, varying her timing and phrasing to create unique interpretations of songs. Her voice had a limited range but a distinctive, light timbre that, combined with her improvisational skills and her tendency—especially in the second half of her career—to focus on torch songs and ballads, gave her work a tremendous emotional appeal. She had a profound influence on a generation of singers that included Frank Sinatra and Peggy Lee. Her most memorable recordings include "Strange Fruit," "God Bless the Child," and "Lover Man (Oh, Where Can You Be?)."

Holiday was the illegitimate child of Sarah Julia Harris, a 19–year-old domestic, and, probably, 16–year-old Clarence Earnest Holiday (actually, Holliday), who became a professional banjo player and guitarist. She had a poor, difficult childhood in Baltimore; her mother frequently traveled north to work and she was left with relatives and friends. She was twice committed to a reformatory, once at age nine for truancy and a second time after she was raped at age 11. By 1928 she had begun to sing in public. In 1929 she joined her mother in N.Y., where she engaged in prostitution and as a result spent several months incarcerated. By the early 1930s she had begun to make her living as a singer. In the spring of 1933 she was seen in a Harlem speakeasy by record producer John Hammond, who arranged her first recording session as featured vocalist in a studio band led by Benny Goodman. On Nov. 27, 1933, they recorded "Your Mother's Son-In-Law" (music by Alberta Nichols, lyrics by Mann Holiner), released by Columbia Records. Their second recording, "Riffin' the Scotch" (music by Dick McDonough, Goodman, and Ford Lee "Buck" Washington, lyrics by Johnny Mercer), made on Dec. 18, 1933, became a hit in January 1934.

Holiday continued to appear in Harlem nightclubs during the mid-1930s. She made her theater debut at the Apollo on Nov. 23, 1934. On July 2, 1935, she began a five-year series of recordings as the vocalist in a studio orchestra led by pianist Teddy Wilson for the Brunswick label of the American Record Company (ARC), which had acquired Columbia. In September she appeared in the short film *Symphony in Black* with Duke Ellington and His Orch. and performed at the Famous Door, her first N.Y. club appearance outside Harlem, and in Montreal, her first out-of-town engagement. She was then a part of the nightclub revue *Stars over Broadway* (N.Y., Oct. 29, 1935) at Connie's Inn Downtown. Her recording with Wilson of "Twenty-Four Hours a Day" (music by James F. Hanley, lyrics by Arthur Swanstrom) entered the hit parade in November and remained in the chart for six weeks.

Holiday performed briefly as a featured vocalist for the orchestras of Jimmie Lunceford, in March, and Fletcher Henderson, in June 1936. Her success on records caused ARC to sign her to a contract, and she made her first recordings under her own name on July 10 for ARC's Vocalion label while continuing to record with Wilson on Brunswick. The Wilson-Holiday recording of "Who Loves You?" (music by J. Fred Coots, lyrics by Benny Davis) spent five weeks in the hit parade starting in October. Holiday joined the Count Basie band in March 1937, though she continued to make recordings on her own and with Wilson. "Carelessly" (music by Norman Ellis, lyrics by Charles and Nick Kenny), recorded with Wilson, entered the hit parade in April and rose to #1 in May; also in May, the Wilson-Holiday recording of "There's a Lull in My Life" (music by Harry Warren, lyrics by Mack Gordon) entered the chart for a nine-week run.

Holiday left Basie in February 1938; the following month she joined Artie Shaw's orchestra. In July, "I'm Gonna Lock My Heart" (music by Terry Shand, lyrics by Jimmy Eaton) by Billie Holiday and Her Orch. entered the hit parade for a run of eight weeks. Holiday left Shaw in November and began a celebrated seven-month engagement at the Greenwich Village nightclub Café Society on Dec. 30. During this run, she introduced "Strange Fruit" (music and lyrics by Lewis Allan, a pseudonym for Abel Meeropol), a song describing the lynchings of African-Americans in the South. Vocalion declined to record the song but allowed her to cut it for the independent Commodore label, which she did on April 20, 1939; it became a signature song for her and the recording was selected for the Grammy Hall of Fame in 1978.

Holiday's residency at Café Society established her as a popular nightclub performer, and she continued to appear regularly, primarily in clubs in N.Y., with occasional theater engagements and appearances in such major cities as Chicago and L.A., until 1947. On May 9, 1941, she recorded "God Bless the Child" (music and lyrics by Arthur Herzog Jr. and Holiday), which became a standard; the recording was selected for the Grammy Hall of Fame in 1976. She married James Norman Monroe Jr. on Aug. 25, 1941. They separated in 1942 when Monroe was imprisoned on a drug charge but remained married until 1957.

In the fall of 1942, Capitol Records released "Trav'lin' Light" (music by Jimmy Mundy and Trummy Young, lyrics by Johnny Mercer) by Paul Whiteman and His Orch., with vocals credited to "Lady Day," Holiday's nickname, for contractual reasons. The record topped the R&B charts in November. Holiday again recorded for Commodore in 1943 and 1944 and was signed to Decca Records in August 1944. Her first session for the label produced "Lover Man (Oh, Where Can You Be?)" (music and lyrics by Jimmy Davis, Roger "Ram" Ramirez, and Jimmy Sherman), which made the Top Ten of the R&B chart in May 1945 and was selected for the Grammy Hall of Fame in 1989.

In the spring of 1945, Holiday claimed to have divorced her husband and married trumpeter Joseph Luke Guy. Though this was not true, she was living with Guy as his common-law wife, and the couple organized a big band that toured during the second half of the year. Holiday had a featured role in the motion picture *New Orleans*, which opened in April 1947; it was her only feature film appearance. On May 27, 1947, she was convicted of possession of heroin and imprisoned until March 16, 1948. She never overcame her addiction and was arrested on drug charges several more times. Her 1947 conviction meant that she was effectively barred from performing in N.Y. nightclubs, and she turned to concert and theater appearances in the city—notably at Carnegie Hall on March 27, 1948, and in the short-lived revue *Holiday on Broadway* (N.Y., April 27, 1948)—and to club dates around the country.

In 1948, Holiday became involved with club owner John R. Levy, who became her manager and common-law husband. They split up in late 1950, and Holiday took up with automotive worker Louis McKay in 1951. He also lived with her and managed her, and they finally married on March 28, 1957, but then separated later that year. Holiday left Decca in 1950, briefly recorded for the small independent Aladdin label in 1951, and in 1952 signed with record executive Norman Granz, who licensed her first album with him, *Billie Holiday Sings*, to Mercury Records, then issued her recordings through 1957 on his own Clef and Verve labels.

Holiday toured Europe in 1954 and again in 1958; she appeared at the Newport Jazz Festival in 1954 and again in 1957; and she performed at the first Monterey Jazz Festival in 1958. In August 1956 her sensationalized, ghost-written autobiography, *Lady Sings the Blues*, was published. Portions of it were read during her Nov. 10, 1956, concert at Carnegie Hall. In December 1957 she re-signed to Columbia Records, making one album, *Lady in Satin*, then moved to MGM Records for her final album, *Billie Holiday*, in 1959. She made her final appearance at the Phoenix Theatre in N.Y. on May 25, 1959.

Days later she collapsed, suffering from cirrhosis of the liver, and was hospitalized. She died at 44 of congestion of the lungs complicated by heart failure.

Holiday was nominated for a 1961 Grammy Award for Best Solo Vocal Performance, Female, for the album *The Essential Billie Holiday (Carnegie Hall Concert),* drawn from her 1956 performance. The film biography *Lady Sings the Blues* opened in the fall of 1972; it became a box office hit, and the soundtrack album, featuring Holiday's songs sung by Diana Ross, hit #1 in the spring of 1973. Several Holiday reissue albums also reached the charts at this time: Decca's *The Billie Holiday Story;* Atlantic's *Strange Fruit,* containing Commodore recordings; and Columbia's *The Original Recordings.* Holiday was nominated for a 1973 Grammy Award for Best Spoken Word Recording for the Paramount album *Songs & Conversations,* drawn from an August 1955 rehearsal, and the Time-Life album *Billie Holiday (Giants of Jazz)* won the 1979 Grammy Award for Best Historical Reissue. In 1991 the 75th anniversary of Holiday's birth was marked by three multi-CD reissues: Columbia/Legacy's *The Legacy, 1933–59;* MCA/GRP's *The Complete Decca Recordings, 1944–50;* and Verve's *Lady in Autumn: The Best of the Verve Years.* Forty years after her death, most of Holiday's recordings remained in print.

DISC.: *Lady Sings the Blues* (1956); *Songs for Distingue Lovers* (1957); *Embraceable You* (1957); *Lady in Satin* (1958); *Masters of Jazz, Vol. III* (1987); *The Quintessential B. H.* (nine volumes; 1987–91); *At Storyville* (1988); *Billie's Blues* (1988); *Last Recordings* (1988); *Fine and Mellow* (1990); *The Complete Decca Recordings: 1944–50* (1991); *Lady in Autumn: The Best of the Verve Years* (1991); *Billie's Best* (1992); *16 Most Requested Songs* (1993); *Verve Jazz Masters 12* (1994); *First Issue: The Great American Songbook* (1994); *The Complete B. H. on Verve: 1945–49* (1995); *Love Songs* (1996); *Ultimate B. H.* (1997); *The Complete Commodore Recordings* (1997); *Greatest Hits* (1998); *Cocktail Hour: B. H.* (1999).

WRITINGS: With W. Dufty, *Lady Sings the Blues* (Garden City, N.J., 1956).

BIBL.: D. Bakker, *B. and Teddy on Microgroove, 1932–44* (Alphen aan de Rijn, Netherlands, 1975); J. Chilton, *B.'s Blues: The B. H. Story, 1933–59* (N.Y., 1975); J. Millar, *Born to Sing: A Discography of B. H.* (Copenhagen, 1979); A. De Veaux, *Don't Explain: A Song of B. H.* (N.Y., 1980); J. Burnett, *B. H.* (N.Y., 1984); B. James, *B. H.* (Tunbridge Wells, England, 1984); M.-E. Nabe, *L'Âme De B. H.* (Paris, 1986); J. White, *B. H.: Her Life and Times* (N.Y., 1987); B. Kliment, *B. H.* (N.Y., 1990); R. O'Meally, *Lady Day: The Many Faces of B. H.* (N.Y., 1991); D. Clarke, *Wishing on the Moon: The Life and Times of B. H.* (London, 1994); S. Nicholson, *B. H.* (London, 1995); L. Gourse, ed., *The B. H. Companion: Seven Decades of Commentary* (N.Y., 1997).—**WR**

Höll, Hartmut, distinguished German pianist and pedagogue; b. Heilbronn, Nov. 24, 1952. He was a student of Paul Buck and Konrad Richter in Stuttgart (1971–74), and also studied with Leonard Hokanson. With his wife **Mitsuko Shirai,** he began to tour extensively in lieder recitals in 1973. Their engagements took them throughout Europe, North and South America, Japan, Israel, and Africa. He also was accompanist to Fischer-Dieskau from 1982 until 1992. Among the other artists he has worked with are Sabine Meyer, Heinrich Schiff, Tabea Zimmermann, Peter Schreier, Jochen Kowalski, Andreas Schmidt, and Thomas Hampson. He

became a prof. at the Frankfurt am Main Hochschule für Musik in 1975, at the Cologne Hochschule für Musik in 1982, at the Karlsruhe Hochschule für Musik in 1990, and at the Salzburg Mozarteum in 1993. He also served as artistic director of the Internationale Hugo-Wolf-Akademie für Gesang-Dichtung-Liedkunst in Stuttgart. In 1990 Höll was awarded the Robert Schumann Prize of Zwickau. He and his wife were honored with the ABC International Music Award in 1997.—**LK/DM**

Holl, Robert, Dutch bass-baritone; b. Rotterdam, March 10, 1947. He studied with Jan Veth and David Hollestelle. After winning 1st prize in the 's-Hertogenbosch Competition in 1971, he pursued training with Hans Hotter in Munich. In 1972 he captured 1st prize in the Munich International Competition. After appearing with the Bavarian State Opera in Munich (1973–75), he pursued a concert career. From 1981 to 1983 he was engaged in opera at the Mozartwochen in Salzburg. In 1988 he sang in Schubert's *Fierabras* at the Theater an der Wien in Vienna. He appeared as Assur in *Semiramide* and as La Roche in *Capriccio* in Zürich in 1992. Following an engagement as Hans Sachs at the Bayreuth Festival and as Amfortas in Zürich in 1996, he sang in Schubert's *Des Teufels Lustschloss* at the Vienna Festival in 1997. In 1990 he was made an Austrian Kammersänger. Holl's engagements as a soloist with orchs., as an oratorio singer, and as a lieder artist have taken him all over the world.—**NS/LK/DM**

Hollaender, Alexis, German pianist, choral conductor, teacher, and composer; b. Ratibor, Silesia, Feb. 25, 1840; d. Berlin, Feb. 5, 1924. He was a pupil of Carl Schnabel (piano) and Adolf Hesse (organ) in Breslau. He then studied at the Univ. of Berlin, and also took courses in theory and composition with Eduard Greel and A.W. Bach at the Berlin Royal Academy and privately with Karl Böhmer. From 1861 he taught piano and choral singing at the Kullak Academy in Berlin, and also was active as a choral conductor. Among his works were choruses, songs, and piano pieces.—**NS/LK/DM**

Hollaender, Gustav, German violinist, pedagogue, and composer, brother of **Viktor Hollaender;** b. Leobschütz, Silesia, Feb. 15, 1855; d. Berlin, Dec. 4, 1915. He studied violin with his father, and then with David at the Leipzig Cons. Later he was a student of Joachim (violin) and Kiel (composition) at the Berlin Hochschule für Musik. He began his concert career at age 20, and after serving as concertmaster of the Gürzenich Orch. and as a teacher at the Cons. in Cologne (1881–84), he settled in Berlin as a royal chamber musician of the court opera orch. in 1884. He was head of the violin dept. at the Kullak Academy (from 1885), and then was director of the Stern Cons. (from 1894). He wrote principally solo violin pieces, in an effective virtuoso style. Among his other works were 3 violin concertos, cello pieces, and vocal duets.—**NS/LK/DM**

Hollaender, Viktor, German conductor and composer, brother of **Gustav Hollaender;** b. Leobschütz, Silesia, April 20, 1866; d. Los Angeles, Oct. 24, 1940.

After training in Berlin with Kullak, he was a theater conductor in Hamburg, Milwaukee (1890), Berlin, Chicago, and London (1894–1901). Returning to Berlin, he was musical director at the Metropoltheater (1901–08) and the Thalia-Theater (1908–09), where he brought out various revues. His more ambitious light theater scores included *San Lin* (Breslau, Jan 28, 1898), *Der rote Kosak* (Berlin, Dec. 21, 1901), *Der Sonnenvogel* or *Der Phönix* (St. Petersburg, Aug. 22, 1903), *Die schöne vom Strand* (Berlin, Feb. 5, 1915), and *Die Prinzessin vom Nil* (Berlin, Sept. 18, 1915). He had his finest success with the incidental music he composed for the pantomime *Sumurun* (Berlin, 1910). In 1934 he emigrated to the U.S. His son, Friedrich Hollaender (b. London, Oct. 18, 1896; d. Munich, Jan. 18, 1976), was a composer. He was a student at the Berlin Hochschule für Musik and of Humperdinck. After composing revues, operettas, and other light theater scores, he became best known as a composer of film scores. Among his finest film scores were *Der blaue Engel* (1930), *Die grosse Sehnsucht* (1930), *One Hundred Men and a Girl* (1937), *Destry Rides Again* (1939), *The Man Who Came to Dinner* (1942), and *Das Spukschloss im Spessart* (1962). His autobiography appeared as *Von Kopf bis Fuss, mein Leben mit Text und Musik* (Munich, 1965).—**NS/LK/DM**

Holland, Charles, black American tenor; b. Norfolk, Va., Dec. 27, 1909; d. Amsterdam, Nov. 7, 1987. He studied with May Hamaker Henley, Georges Le Pyre in Los Angeles, and Clyde Burrows in N.Y. He sang with the bands of Benny Carter and Fletcher Henderson, appeared in the film *Hullabaloo* (1941), and had his own concert program on NBC radio. In 1949 he settled in France, where he appeared on radio and television; made his European operatic debut in *Die Zauberflöte* at the Paris Opéra in 1954, and in 1955 he became the first black artist to sing at the Paris Opéra-Comique. He later sang throughout Europe, Australia, New Zealand, and Canada, making his N.Y. debut in a recital at Carnegie Hall in 1982.—**NS/LK/DM**

Holland, Dave (actually, **David**), influential jazz bassist, cello/piano/composer; b Wolverhampton, Warwickshire, England, Oct. 1, 1946. He started with the ukulele at age four, moving to the guitar at 10 and then to electric bass guitar at 13. He began playing professionally two years later. It was around this time that he began listening to jazz and began playing the acoustic bass. In fall 1963, he moved to London; soon after, he began studying classical bass while also working with a wide variety of people in the jazz community. He became a regular accompanist at London's famed jazz club, Ronnie Scott's, in 1967; it was during an engagement there in July of 1968 that Miles Davis first heard him and asked him to join his band. Holland moved to N.Y. a few weeks later and for the next two years toured and appeared on a number of recordings with Davis including *In a Silent Way* and *Bitches Brew*. In late 1970 Holland left Davis and together with Chick Corea, Anthony Braxton and Barry Altschul founded the group Circle. It was at this time that he started performing on cello as well as bass. After working together for a year Circle disbanded, and early in 1972 Holland joined Stan

Getz's group, with whom he remained through early 1973. He then began concentrating on working separately with Anthony Braxton and Sam Rivers. In 1975 he took part in the formation of Gateway, a trio with John Abercrombie and Jack DeJohnette, fellow band members from the Davis band; Gateway continued to tour and record through the 1990s. After working with Betty Carter for a few months in 1976, he spent the remainder of the decade touring and recording with Sam Rivers. In 1981 he left Rivers's band to put together his own quintet that recorded and toured extensively until 1987. In the 1990s, Holland has recorded and toured as a member of Herbie Hancock's groups, as well as continuing to work with Gateway. He has also led his own small groups. Holland has also worked as a jazz educator. In 1983 he was appointed artistic director of the summer jazz workshop at the Banff School in Banff, Canada, a position he held until 1990, and from 1987 to 1990 he was a full time faculty member of the New England Cons. of Music in Boston.

DISC.: *Music for Two Basses* (1971); *Conference of the Birds* (1972); *D. H., Vols. 1, 2* (1976); *D. H., Sam Rivers* (1976); *Emerald Tears* (1977; bass); *Life Cycle* (1982; cello); *Jumpin' In* (1983); *Seeds of Time* (1984); *Razor's Edge* (1987); *Triplicate* (1988); *Extensions* (1989); *Ones All* (1993; bass); *Dream of the Elders* (1995); *Points of View* (1997). Gateway: *Homecoming* (1994).—**LP**

Holland, Dulcie (Sybil), Australian pianist and composer; b. Sydney, Jan. 5, 1913. She studied at the Sydney Cons. with Alfred Hill, Frank Hutchens, and Roy Agnew. She then went to London, where she took courses with John Ireland at the Royal Coll. of Music. Returning to Australia, she was active as a pianist and composer. Among her works were a *Symphony for Pleasure* (1974), some theater music, and songs for children. She also publ. several school manuals. —**NS/LK/DM**

Holland, Justin, black American guitarist, teacher, and composer; b. Norfolk County, Va., 1819; d. Cleveland, March 24, 1887. He made his way to Boston when he was 14 and studied piano, guitar, and flute, and then attended Oberlin (Ohio) Coll. (1841). In 1845 he settled in Cleveland, where, in spite of racial prejudice, he carved out a successful career as a guitarist, guitar teacher, and composer. He publ. *Holland's Comprehensive Method for the Guitar* (1874) and *Holland's Modern Method for the Guitar* (1876), both of which were used throughout the U.S. and Europe. His compositions included many pieces involving the guitar, including solos, duets, music for guitar and piano, songs with guitar accompaniment, and arrangements for operatic airs for guitar and violin or flute.—**LK/DM**

Holland, Theodore (Samuel), English composer and teacher; b. London, April 25, 1878; d. there, Oct. 29, 1947. He studied with F. Corder at the Royal Academy of Music in London and with Joachim at the Hochschule für Musik in Berlin. In 1927 he became prof. of composition at the Royal Academy of Music. He was an estimable composer, particularly proficient in writing for the theater. Among his works were a children's operetta, *King Goldemar*, a musical play, *Santa Claus*, *Evening on a Lake* for Chamber Orch. (1924), *Cortège* for an Ensemble of Cellos (1939), *Spring Sinfonietta* (1943), 2 string quartets, 2 piano trios, Suite for Viola and Piano, and several song cycles.—NS/LK/DM

Holland-Dozier-Holland, Motown Records' premier songwriting-production team: Eddie Holland (b. Detroit, Oct. 30, 1939); Lamont Dozier (b. Detroit, June 16, 1941); Brian Holland (b. Detroit, Feb. 15, 1941).

Lamont Dozier began singing as a child in his grandmother's church choir, writing his first song at the age of ten. Making his recording debut with The Romeos at 15, he met Berry Gordy Jr., in 1958 and recorded as Lamont Anthony for Anna Records in 1961. Eddie Holland also met Gordy in 1958, dropping out of college to work for him and later scoring one of Motown's first hits with "Jamie" in 1962. Brother Brian Holland collaborated on two early hits for The Marvelettes, "Please Mr. Postman" and "Playboy."

In 1963, Brian and Eddie Holland and Lamont Dozier teamed up as a songwriting-production unit. Between 1963 and the end of 1967, H-D-H wrote and produced the majority of Motown's hit singles, with Brian providing the music, Eddie contributing lyrics, and Lamont supplying both music and lyrics. Their hit compositions included "Heat Wave," "Quicksand," and "Nowhere to Run" for Martha and The Vandellas; "Mickey's Monkey" for The Miracles; and "Can I Get a Witness," "You're a Wonderful One," and "How Sweet It Is (To Be Loved by You)" for Marvin Gaye. Other hit compositions included "Take Me in Your Arms" for Kim Weston and "This Old Heart of Mine" for The Isley Brothers. Eddie Holland later collaborated with Norman Whitfield on several major hits for The Temptations, including "Ain't Too Proud to Beg," "Beauty Is Only Skin Deep," and "(I Know) I'm Losing You."

Much of H-D-H's finest material was reserved for The Four Tops and The Supremes. Their song hits for The Four Tops included "Baby I Need Your Loving," "I Can't Help Myself," "It's the Same Old Song," "Reach Out, I'll Be There," "Standing in the Shadows of Love," and "Bernadette." H-D-H's biggest success came with The Supremes, for whom they wrote and produced at least ten top pop and smash soul hits as well as numerous major hits. These included ""Where Did Our Love Go," "Baby Love," "Come See about Me," "Stop! in the Name of Love," "Back in My Arms Again," "I Hear a Symphony," "My World Is Empty without You," "Love Is Like an Itching in My Heart," "You Can't Hurry Love," "You Keep Me Hangin' on," and "Love Is Here and Now You're Gone." H-D-H extended their string of hits for the group as Diana Ross and The Supremes in 1967 with "Reflections" and "In and Out of Love."

However, in late 1967, Brian Holland, Lamont Dozier, and Eddie Holland bitterly quit Motown to form their own record labels, Invictus and Hot Wax. A series of lawsuits ensued between Motown and H-D-H, and the team was enjoined from writing songs after May 1969. Nonetheless, they produced a number of hits in the early 1970s. Invictus crossover hits included ""Give

Me Just a Little More Time," "Pay to the Piper," "Chairman of the Board," and "Finder's Keepers" by Chairmen of the Board, and "Band of Gold," "Deeper and Deeper," and the controversial "Bring the Boys Home" by Freda Payne. Pop and rhythm- and-blues hits on Hot Wax included "Somebody's Been Sleeping" by 100 Proof Aged in Soul, and "Girls It Ain't Easy," "Want Ads," "Stick-Up," "One Monkey Don't Stop No Show," and "The Day I Found Myself" by Honey Cone.

Following the out-of-court settlement of the Motown–H-D-H lawsuits in early 1972, Brian Holland and Lamont Dozier returned to active recording, scoring major soul and minor pop hits on Invictus with "Don't Leave Me Starvin' for Your Love" and "Why Can't We Be Lovers," respectively. Holland and Dozier recorded as a duo in 1973, the year the overall partnership ended, and Dozier subsequently pursued a solo recording career, achieving smash soul and major pop hits with "Trying to Hold on to My Woman" and "Fish Ain't Biting," and a soul smash with "Let Me Start Tonight" on ABC Records in 1974. Dozier later switched to Warner Brothers Records, then Columbia. He produced Aretha Franklin's 1977 album *Sweet Passion* and wrote songs for Simply Red, Boz Scaggs, Eric Clapton, and Phil Collins during the 1980s. In 1991, he recorded *Inside Seduction* for Atlantic Records. Holland-Dozier-Holland were inducted into the Rock and Roll Hall of Fame in 1990.

DISC.: EDDIE HOLLAND: *Eddie Holland* (1963). **LAMONT DOZIER:** *Out Here on My Own* (1974); *Black Bach* (1974); *Love and Beauty* (1974); *Right There* (1976); *Peddlin' Music on the Side* (1977); *Bittersweet* (1978); *Working on You* (1981); *Inside Seduction* (1991).—BH

Hollander, Lorin, talented American pianist; b. N.Y., July 19, 1944. He began his training with his father, a violinist, and then was a student of Steuermann (piano) and Giannini (composition) at the Juilliard School of Music in N.Y. He also had instruction from Max Rudolf, Leon Fleisher, and Olga Stroumillo. He was only 11 when he made his Carnegie Hall debut in N.Y., and soon began appearing throughout the U.S. After his first tour of Europe in 1965, he performed with many of the leading orchs. around the world. As an advocate of musical outreach, he also played in such non-traditional settings as hospitals, nursing homes, and prisons. Hollander's extraordinary technique has been displayed in a virtuoso repertoire ranging from the masters of the past to the contemporary era. —NS/LK/DM

Hölle, Matthias, German bass; b. Rottweil am Nekkar, July 8, 1951. He was a student of Georg Jelden in Stuttgart and of Josef Metternich in Cologne. In 1976 he joined the Cologne Opera, where he made frequent appearances until 1987. From 1981 he sang at the Bayreuth Festival, where he became best known for such roles as Hunding, Fasolt, Titurel, and King Marke. He appeared in the premiere of Stockhausen's *Donnerstag aus Licht* in Milan in 1981, and returned there in 1984 to create the role of Lucifer in that composer's *Samstag aus Licht*. On Dec. 10, 1986, he made his debut at the Metropolitan Opera in N.Y. as Rocco. He portrayed Don Fernando in Brussels in 1989, and Hunding in Bonn in 1992. Following his first appearance at London's Covent Garden in 1994 as Hunding, he returned there in 1996 as Fafner.—**NS/LK/DM**

Höller, Karl, German composer and teacher; b. Bamberg, July 25, 1907; d. Hausham, April 14, 1987. He received training in piano, organ, and cello in Bamberg, and then was a student of Zilcher (composition) at the Würzburg Cons. and of Haas and Waltershausen (composition), Gatscher (organ), and Hausegger (conducting) at the Munich Academy of Music. He also took courses with Sandberger at the Univ. of Munich. After teaching at the Munich Academy of Music (1933–37) and the Frankfurt am Main Hochschule für Musik (1937–46), he taught a master class in composition at the Munich Hochschule für Musik (1949–72), where he also served as its president (1954–72). His compositional style owed much to late Romanticism.

WORKS: ORCH.: Organ Concerto (1930; rev. 1966); *Hymnen über gregorianische Choral-melodien* (1932–34); Chamber Concerto for Harpsichord and Small Orch. (1934; rev. 1958); *Symphonische Phantasie über Thema von Frescobaldi* (1935; rev. 1965); 2 violin concertos (1938, rev. 1964; 1947–48); *Passacaglia und Fuge* (1939); *Heroische Musik* (1940); 2 cello concertos (1940–41; 1949); 2 syms. (1942–46; 1973); *Sweelinck-Variationen "Mein junges Lebe hat ein End"* (1950–51); Piano Concerto (1973). **CHAMBER:** 8 violin sonatas (1929, rev. 1968; 1942; 1943; 1944; 1945; 1946; 1947; 1949); Piano Quartet (1930; rev. 1955); 6 string quartets (1938, rev. 1966; 1945; 1947; 1947; 1948; 1949); Cello Sonata (1943; also for Viola and Clarinet, 1967); Piano Trio (1944; also for Harp, Violin, and Cello, 1966); Trio Sonata (1946; also as Concerto Grosso for 2 Violins and Piano, 1965); 2 flute sonatas (1947; 1948); Viola Sonata, *"in memoriam Paul Hindemith"* (1967). **Piano:** *Zwei leine Sonaten* for Piano, 4-Hands (1943); 3 small sonatas (1946); *Tessiner Klavierbuch* (1961). **VOCAL:** *Missa brevis* (1929); *Weihnachts- und Passionmusik* (1932); *Requiem* (1932); *Tenebrae factae*, Good Friday motet (1937).—**NS/LK/DM**

Höller, York (Georg), German composer; b. Leverkusen, Jan. 11, 1944. He studied composition with Zimmermann and Eimert, piano with Alfons Kontarsky, conducting, and music education (diploma, 1967) at the Cologne Hochschule für Musik. He also took courses in musicology and philosophy at the Univ. of Cologne, and attended Boulez's analysis sessions at the summer course in new music in Darmstadt (1965). In 1971–72 he was active at the WDR Electronic Music Studio in Cologne. In 1974–75 he was in residence at the Cite Internationale des Arts in Paris. From 1976 to 1989 he taught analysis and theory at the Cologne Hochschule für Musik. His *Antiphon* for String Quartet was commissioned for the opening of the Centre Pompidou in Paris in 1977. In 1978 he realized his *Arcus* at IRCAM in Paris, which was commissioned for the opening of its Espace de Projection. The score was subsequently performed on both sides of the Atlantic by the Ensemble Inter-Contemporain. In 1979 he received the Bernd Alois Zimmermann Prize of Cologne. In 1984–85 he was in residence at the Villa Massimo in Rome. He was named Chevalier dans l'Ordre des Arts et des Lettres of France in 1986. The International Composer's Forum of UNESCO awarded him its prize for his 2nd Piano Concerto in 1987. In 1990 he became director of the WDR Electronic Music Studio. In his oeuvre, Höller has effectively utilized both traditional and electronic modes of expression.

WORKS: DRAMATIC: Opera: *Der Meister und Margarita* (1984–89; Paris, May 20, 1989); *Caligula* (1992). **ORCH.:** *Topic* (1967); 2 piano concertos: No. 1 (1970; rev. 1983–84; London, Dec. 3, 1985) and No. 2, *Pensées*, with live electronics (1992–93; Cologne, June 11, 1993); *Chroma* for Orch., Organ, and Live Electronics (1972–74); *Arcus* for Chamber Orch. and Tape (1978); *Mythos* for Chamber Orch. and Electronic Tape (1979); *Umbra* for Orch. and Tape (1979–80); *Résonance* for Orch. and Computer Sounds on Tape (1981); *Schwarze Halbinseln* for Orch. and Electronic Tape (1982); *Magische Klanggestalt* (1984; Hamburg, March 16, 1986); *Improvisation sur le nom de Pierre Boulez* für 16 Instruments (1984–85; Baden-Baden, March 31, 1985); *Fanal* for Trumpet and Orch. (1989–90; Paris, June 17, 1991); *Pensées*, Requiem for Piano, Orch., and Electronics (1990–91; Cologne, June 11, 1993); *Aura* (1991–92; Chicago, Oct. 12, 1995); *Gegenklänge* (1996); *Widerspiel* for 2 Pianos and Orch. (1997–98). **CHAMBER:** *Drei Stücke* for String Quartet (1966); Sonata for Solo Cello (1968–69); *Epitaph (for Jan Palach)* for Violin and Piano (1969); *Tangens* for Cello, Electric Guitar, Electric Organ or Piano, and 2 Synthesizers (1973); *Klanggitter* for Cello, Piano, Synthesizer, and Tape (1975–76); 2 string quartets: No. 1, *Antiphon*, with tape (1976–77) and No. 2 (1997); *Moments musicaux* for Flute and Piano (1979); *Pas de trois* for Violin, Cello, and Double Bass (1982); *Pas de deux* for Cello and Piano (Cologne, June 19, 1993); *Tagträume* for Piano Trio (1994). **Piano:** *Fünf Klavierstücke* (1964); *Diaphonie: Hommage à Béla Bartók* for 2 Pianos (1965; rev. 1974; Cologne, Feb. 26, 1984); 2 sonatas: No. 1, *Sonate informelle* (1968), and No. 2, *Hommage à Franz Liszt* (1987); *Partita* for 2 Pianos (1995–96). **VOCAL:** *Herr, es ist Zeit* for Soprano and 8 Instruments (1966); *Traumspiel* for Soprano, Orch., and Electronic Tape (Metz, Nov. 18, 1983). **ELECTRONIC:** *Horizont* (1972).—**NS/LK/DM**

Hollies, The, popular British band of the 1960s who spawned singer/songwriter Graham Nash. **MEMBERSHIP:** Allan Clarke, lead voc. (b. Salford, Lancashire, England, April 5, 1942); Graham Nash, harmony voc., gtr. (b. Blackpool, Lancashire, Feb. 2, 1942); Tony Hicks, lead gtr., voc., bjo. (b. Nelson, Lancashire, Dec. 16, 1943); Eric Haydock, bs. (b. Lancashire, Feb. 3, 1943); and Bobby Elliott, drm. (b. Burnley, Lancashire, England, Dec. 8, 1942). Later members included Bernie Calvert (b. Brierfield, Lancashire, Sept. 16, 1942) and Terry Sylvester (b. Liverpool, Lancashire, Jan. 8, 1945). Allan Clarke and Graham Nash became friends in elementary school in Manchester and later sang together as The Two Teens, Ricky and Dane, and The Guytones. They added other members and became The Fourtones and then The Deltas. In 1962, the two teamed with Tony Hicks and two others. By 1963, with one replacement, the group had become The Hollies, with Clarke, Nash, Hicks, Eric Haydock, and Bobby Elliott. Signed to Parlophone Records (Imperial in the U.S.) in early 1963, The Hollies scored British hits with "Searchin'" and "Stay" before achieving their first (minor) American hit with "Just One Look" in 1964. Although "I'm Alive" became a top British hit in 1965, the group did not have even a moderate American hit until "Look through Any Window," written by Graham Gouldman. The group toured the U.S. for the first time in the spring of 1965, replacing Haydock with Bernie Calvert in the spring of 1966. Years earlier, Calvert had been a member of The Dolphins with Tony Hicks and Bobby Elliott.

The Hollies' most successful years were 1966 and 1967. After scoring a smash British and American hit with Graham Gouldman's "Bus Stop," they achieved hits in both countries with "Stop! Stop! Stop!," "On a Carousel," "Pay You Back with Interest," and "Carrie Anne," all Clarke-Hicks-Nash collaborations, the last on Epic Records. An attempt to make inroads in the album market with *Dear Eloise/King Midas in Reverse* failed and Nash, unhappy with the prospect of recording an album of Bob Dylan songs, left the group in late 1968 to join David Crosby and Steve Stills. Nash was replaced by vocalist-rhythm guitarist Terry Sylvester, a former member of The Swinging Blue Jeans (1964's "Hippy Hippy Shake").

During 1969 and 1970, the maudlin ballad "He Ain't Heavy, He's My Brother" became a near-smash hit for The Hollies. In October 1971, the group fired Allan Clarke, who pursued a neglected solo career. Nonetheless, he was the lead vocalist on the smash hit "Long Cool Woman (In a Black Dress)" from *Distant Light*, which also produced a major hit with "Long Dark Road." *Greatest Hits*, released in 1973, included the group's hits on both the Imperial and Epic labels. Clarke returned in mid-1973 and helped record *The Hollies*, which contained the smash hit "The Air that I Breathe." The group continued to record for Epic through 1978. In 1983, Hollies mainstays Tony Hicks and Bobby Elliott reunited briefly with Allan Clarke and Graham Nash for *What Goes Around*, a major hit with a remake of The Supremes' "Stop in the Name of Love," and one round of touring. With stalwarts Clarke, Hicks, and Elliott, The Hollies continued to tour into the 1990s.

DISC.: THE HOLLIES: *Here I Go Again* (1965); *Hear! Here!* (1966); *Beat Group* (1966); *Bus Stop* (1966); *Stop! Stop! Stop!* (1967); *Evolution* (1967); *Dear Eloise/King Midas in Reverse* (1968); *Words and Music by Bob Dylan* (1969); *He Ain't Heavy, He's My Brother* (1970); *Moving Finger* (1971); *Distant Light* (1972); *Romany* (1973); *The Hollies* (1974); *Another Night* (1975); *Clarke, Hicks, Sylvester, Elliott, Calvert* (1977); *Crazy Steal* (1978); *What Goes Around* (1983). **ALLAN CLARKE:** *My Real Name Is 'Arold* (1972); *I've Got Time* (1976); *I Wasn't Born Yesterday* (1978); *Legendary Heroes* (1980). **TERRY SYLVESTER:** *Terry Sylvester* (1974).—**BH**

Holliger, Heinz, outstanding Swiss oboist, conductor, pedagogue, and composer; b. Langenthal, May 21, 1939. He commenced playing the recorder at 4 and the piano at 6. He studied oboe with Cassagnaud and composition with Veress at the Bern Cons., then oboe with Pierlot and piano with Lefébure at the Paris Cons. In 1959 he won 1st prize in the Geneva competition, and then played in the Basel Sym. Orch., and also attended Boulez's master classes in composition in Basel (1961–63). After winning 1st prize in the Munich competition in 1961, he embarked upon a brilliant international career; toured in Europe and the U.S. as soloist with the Lucerne Festival Strings in 1962. He also gave concerts with his wife, the harpist Ursula Hanggi, and his own Holliger Ensemble. In addition to giving master classes, he was a prof. at the Freiburg im Breisgau Hochschule für Musik (from 1965). He is generally recognized as the foremost oboist of his era, his mastery extending from early music to the commissioned works of such modern composers as Penderecki, Henze, Stockhausen, Krenek, Berio, Jolivet, and Lutosławski. In his own works, he is an uncompromising avant- gardist.

WORKS: DRAMATIC: *Der magische Tänzer* for 2 Singers, 2 Dancers, 2 Actors, Chorus, Orch., and Tape (1963–65; Basel, April 26, 1970); *Come and Go/Va et vient/Kommen und Gehen*, chamber opera, after Samuel Beckett (1976–77; Hamburg, Feb. 16, 1978); *Not I*, monodrama for Soprano and Tape, after Beckett (1978–80; Avignon, July 15, 1980); *What Where*, chamber opera, after Beckett (1988; Frankfurt am Main, May 19, 1989); *Schnee-wittchen*, opera (Zürich, Oct. 17, 1998). **ORCH.:** *Elis—Drei Nachtstücke* (1963; rev. 1973; Basel, May 3, 1973); *Siebengesang* for Oboe, Orch., Voices, and Loudspeakers (1966–67; Rotterdam, June 17, 1968); *Pneuma* for Winds, Percussion, Organ, and Radios (Donaueschingen, Oct. 18, 1970); *Atembogen* (1974–75; Basel, June 6, 1975); *Scardanelli-Zyklus III: Übungen zu Scardanelli* for Small Orch. and Tape (1978–85) and *IV: Ostinato funèbre* for Small Orch. (1991); *Ad marginem* for Chamber Orch. and Tape (1983; Baden- Baden, March 8, 1985); *Engführung* for Chamber Orch. (1983–84; Donaueschingen, Oct. 19, 1985); *Der ferne Klang* for Chamber Orch. and Tape (1983–84; Donaueschingen, Oct. 19, 1985); *Schaufelrad* for Chamber Orch. and 4 to 5 Women's Voices ad libitum (1983–84; Donaueschingen, Oct. 19, 1985); *Turm-Musik* for Flute, Small Orch., and Tape (1984; Basel, Jan. 17, 1985); *Tonscherben*, "Orchester-Fragmente in memoriam David Rokeah" (Geneva, Sept. 26, 1985); *Zwei Liszt-Transkriptionen* (1986; Basel, Feb. 12, 1987); *Ostinato funèbre* for Small Orch. (1991); *(S)irat'ó': Monodie* (1993); Violin Concerto (1993–95; Lausanne, Nov. 16, 1995). **CHAMBER:** *Mobile* for Oboe and Harp (1962); Trio for Oboe or English Horn, Viola, and Harp (1966); *h* for Wind Quintet (1968); *Cardiophonie* for Oboe and 3 Magnetophones (1971); String Quartet (1973); *Chaconne* for Cello (1975); *(t)air(e)* for Flute (1980–83); *Studie II* for Oboe (1981); *Trema* for Viola or Cello (1981; also for Violin, 1983); Duo I (1982; Baden-Baden, May 10, 1983) and II (1988–94) for Violin and Cello; *Vier Lieder ohne Worte* I (1982–83; Saar-brücken, May 17, 1985) and II (1985–94) for Violin and Piano; *Praeludium, Arioso und Passacaglia* for Harp (1987); *Felicity's Shake-Wag* for Violin and Cello (1988); Quintet for Piano and Winds (1989); *Sonate (in) solit(air)e* for Flute (1995–96; Tokyo, July 28, 1997); piano pieces; organ music. **VOCAL:** *Glühende Rätsel* for Alto and 10 Instrumentalists (1964); *Dona Nobis Pacem* for 12 Voices (1968–69); *Psalm* for Chorus (1971); *Scardanelli-Zyklus I: Die Jahreszeiten* for Chorus (1975); *Gesänge der Frühe* for Chorus, Orch., and Tape (1987; Cologne, March 4, 1988); *Dunkle Spiegel* for Vocal Quintet, Baritone, and 5 Instrumental Groups (Frieburg im Breisgau, Nov. 20, 1996).

BIBL.: A. Landau, ed., *H. H.: Komponist, Oboist, Dirigent* (Zürich, 1996).—**NS/LK/DM**

Hollingsworth, Stanley, American composer and teacher; b. Berkeley, Calif., Aug. 27, 1924. He studied at San Jose State Coll., with Milhaud at Mills Coll. in Oakland, Calif., and with Menotti at the Curtis Inst. of Music in Philadelphia. He held a fellowship at the American Academy in Rome (1955–57), received a Guggenheim fellowship (1958), and was awarded several NEA grants. After teaching at San Jose State Coll. (1961–63), he taught at Oakland Univ. in Rochester, Mich. (1976–95). His music follows the principles of practical modernism. He has used the pseudonym Stanley Hollier in some of his works.

WORKS: DRAMATIC: Opera: *The Mother*, after Andersen (1949; Philadelphia, March 29, 1954); *La Grande Bretèche*, after Balzac (1954; NBC-TV, Feb. 10, 1957); *The Selfish Giant* (1981); *Harrison Loved His Umbrella* (1981). **ORCH.:** Piano Concerto (1980); *Divertimento* (1982); *3 Ladies beside the Sea* for Narrator and Orch. (1983); Violin Concerto (1991). **CHAMBER:** Oboe Sonata; *3 impromptus* for Flute and Piano (1975); *Ricordanza* for Oboe and String Trio (in memory of Samuel Barber; 1981); *Reflections and Diversions* for Clarinet and Piano (1984). **VOCAL:** *Dumbarton Oaks Mass* for Chorus and String Orch.; *Stabat Mater* for Chorus and Orch. (San Jose, May 1, 1957); *Death be Not Proud* for Chorus and Orch.—**NS/LK/DM**

Holloway, Robin (Greville),

English composer, teacher, and writer on music; b. Leamington Spa, Oct. 19, 1943. He studied privately with Goehr (1959–63) and attended King's Coll., Cambridge (1961–64) before completing his education at New Coll., Oxford (Ph.D., 1971, with a diss. on Debussy and Wagner; publ. in London, 1979). In 1975 he became a lecturer in music at the Univ. of Cambridge. He has contributed various articles to periodicals and anthologies. His compositions are notable for their remarkable command of various styles and genres. While he has tended along tonal paths, he has not been averse to non-tonal and constructivist techniques. He has also made much use of "objets trouvés."

WORKS: DRAMATIC: *Clarissa*, opera after Samuel Richardson (1976; London, May 18, 1990; also *Clarissa Symphony* for Soprano, Tenor, and Orch., 1976–82; Birmingham, Dec. 9, 1982, and *Clarissa Sequence*, 1998); *Boys and Girls Time Out to Play*, opera buffa (1991–95). **ORCH.:** 2 concertinos for Small Orch.: No. 1 (1964; rev. 1968–69; London, March 14, 1969) and No. 2 (1967, 1974; London, Jan. 8, 1975); Concerto for Organ and Wind Orch. (1965–66; St. Albans, July 1, 1967); 3 concertos for Orch.: No. 1 (1966–69; Glasgow, April 25, 1973), No. 2 (1978–79; Glasgow, Sept. 22, 1979), and No. 3 (1981–94; London, April 16, 1996); *Divertimento No. 1* for Amateur or Youth Orch. and Piano (Cambridge, June 9, 1968); *Scenes from Schumann*, 7 paraphrases (Cheltenham, July 10, 1970; rev. 1986); *Domination of Black*, symphonic poem (1973–74; London, Aug. 8, 1974); *Romanza* for Violin and Small Orch. (1976; London, Aug. 8, 1978); *3 Idylls* for Small Orch.: No. 1 (1979–80; Cheltenham, July 17, 1981), No. 2 (1982–83; London, Oct. 10, 1983), and No. 3 (1993; Poole, March 23, 1994); Horn Concerto (1979–80; London, June 16, 1988); *Ode for 4 Winds and Strings* (London, June 4, 1980); *War Memorials* for Brass Band (1981–82); *Serenata notturna* for 4 Horns, 2 Trumpets, and Strings (1982; London, Dec. 9, 1984); *Seascape and Harvest*, 2 pictures (1983–84; Birmingham, April 29, 1986); Viola Concerto (1983–84; London, Sept. 7, 1985); *Romanza* for Oboe and Strings (1984; Peterborough, N.H., Aug. 30, 1986); *Ballad for Harp and Small Orch.* (1984–85; Cheltenham, July 28, 1985); Bassoon Concerto (1984–85; Newcastle upon Tyne, Jan. 8, 1986); *Inquietus* for Small Orch. (1986; London, April 3, 1987); Double Concerto for Clarinet, Saxophone, and 2 Chamber Orchs. (1987–88; London, May 20, 1988); *Panorama* (1988; London, March 28, 1989); *Wagner Nights* (1989; Bristol, April 23, 1990); Violin Concerto (1990; Manchester, March 27, 1992); *Entrance: Carousing: Embarkation* for Symphonic Band (1990; Manchester, March 27, 1992); *Serenade for Strings* (1990; Worcester, Aug. 26, 1993); *Overture on Nursery Rhymes* for Chamber Orch. (Arundel Festival, Sept. 3, 1995); Clarinet Concerto (1996); *Scenes from*

Antwerp (1998); Sym. (2000). **CHAMBER:** *Garden Music* for 9 Players (1962; rev. 1967, 1982); *Fantasy-Pieces* on Schumann's *Liederkreis* for Piano and 12 Instruments (Oxford, Dec. 11, 1971); *Evening with Angels* for 16 Players (1972; London, Jan. 1, 1973; rev. 1983); *Divertimento No. 2* for Wind Nonet (1972; London, May 31, 1975) and No. 5 for Brass Quintet (1986–87; Warwick, July 5, 1988); Concertino No. 3: *Homage to Weill* for 11 Players (1975; Aldeburgh, Jan. 23, 1977), No. 4: *Showpiece* for 14 Players (1982–83; London, May 23, 1983), No. 5: *Summer Music* for Mixed Sextet (London, Sept. 19, 1991), and No. 6: *Winter Music* for Mixed Sextet (Leamington Spa, July 6, 1993); *The Rivers of Hell*, concertante for 7 Players (London, Nov. 1, 1977); *Serenade* for Octet (1978–79; London, March 18, 1979); Sonata for Solo Violin (Linz, Sept. 29, 1981); Suite for Saxophone (1982; Cambridge, July 4, 1993); *Serenade* for Wind Quintet and String Quintet (1983; London, June 26, 1985); 2 partitas for Horn: No. 1 (1985; Bath, May 23, 1993) and No. 2 (1985; London, Nov. 25, 1989); *Serenade* for String Sextet and Double Bass (1986; Keele, May 14, 1987; also for String Orch.); Clarinet Trio (Malvern Festival, May 27, 1994); piano pieces. **VOCAL:** *Three Poems of William Empson* for Mezzo-soprano and Ensemble (1964–65; London, April 25, 1973); *The Wind Shifts* for High Voice and Strings, after Wallace Stevens (1970; Tenbury Wells, May 22, 1971); *Cantata on the Death of God* for Soloists, Speaker, Chorus, Organ, and Orch. (1972–73); *Sea-Surface Full of Clouds*, cantata for Soloists, Chamber Chorus, and Chamber Orch. (1974–75; London, May 16, 1975); *Nursery Rhymes* for Soprano and Wind Quintet (1977; BBC, London, May 5, 1979); *Hymn for Voices* for Chorus (1977; Bath, May 28, 1978); *Brand*, dramatic ballad for Soloists, Chorus, Organ, and Orch., after Ibsen (1981); *Moments of Vision* for Speaker and 4 Players (Aldeburgh, June 22, 1984); *On Hope*, cantata for Soprano, Mezzo-soprano, and String Quartet (1984), *The Spacious Firmament* for Chorus and Orch., after Dryden, Blake, and Tennyson (1990; Birmingham, Jan. 21, 1992); *Hymn to the Senses* for Chorus (1990; Cambridge, March 11, 1992); *The Blackbird and the Snail* for Narrator and Piano, after Walter de la Mare (1993; N.Y., Jan. 30, 1994); other choral pieces and many song cycles.—**NS/LK/DM**

Hollreiser, Heinrich,

German conductor; b. Munich, June 24, 1913. He studied at the Munich Academy of Music; took lessons in conducting with Elmendorff. He subsequently was engaged as an opera conductor in Wiesbaden (1932), Darmstadt (1935–38), Mannheim (1938–39), Duisburg (1939–42), and Munich (1942–45). From 1945 to 1952 he was Generalmusikdirektor in Düsseldorf. He then was a conductor at the Vienna State Opera (1952–61) and chief conductor of the Deutsche Oper in West Berlin (1961–64); also served as a regular conductor at Bayreuth for several seasons. In 1978 he made his U.S. debut with the Cleveland Orch. In subsequent years, he appeared as a guest conductor with various European orchs. and opera houses. In 1993 he became permanent guest conductor of the Deutsche Oper in Berlin.—**NS/LK/DM**

Hollweg, Ilse,

German soprano; b. Solingen, Feb. 23, 1922; d. there, Feb. 9, 1990. She studied with Gertrude Förstel at the Cologne Hochschule für Musik. In 1942 she made her operatic debut as Blondchen in Saarbrücken. From 1946 to 1951 she sang in Düsseldorf, and also appeared as Constanze at the Glyndebourne Festival (1950) and then as Zerbinetta at the Edinburgh

Festival. In 1951 she made her debut at London's Covent Garden as Gilda. Her guest engagements also took her to Berlin, Hamburg, Vienna, Salzburg, and Bayreuth. From 1955 to 1970 she was a member of the Deutsche Oper am Rhein in Düsseldorf. She also sang in works by Schoenberg, Krenek, Karl Amadeus Hartmann, Boulez, and Nono to great effect.

BIBL.: K. Ruhrberg, *I. H.* (Duisburg, 1971).—NS/LK/DM

Hollweg, Werner (Friedrich),

German tenor; b. Solingen, Sept. 13, 1936. He received his training in Detmold, Lugano, and Munich. After making his debut with the Vienna Chamber Opera in 1962, he sang in Bonn (1963–67) and Gelsenkirchen (1967–68). His success as Belmonte in Florence in 1969 and as a soloist in Beethoven's 9th Sym. under Karajan in Osaka in 1970 led to engagements with the Hamburg State Opera, the Bavarian State Opera in Munich, the Deutsche Oper in Berlin, the Deutsche Oper am Rhein in Düsseldorf, and the Vienna State Opera. He also appeared in Rome, Paris, N.Y., Los Angeles, and at London's Covent Garden (debut as Titus, 1976). He won particular distinction in such Mozart portrayals as Don Ottavio, Idomeneo, Tamino, Basilio, and Ferrando. He also sang in contemporary operas, creating the role of Matthew Levi in Höller's *Der Meister und Margarita* (Paris, 1989). His concert repertoire ranged from Haydn to Kodály. His interpretations of the songs of Schubert, Schumann, and Loewe were especially esteemed.—NS/LK/DM

Holly, Buddy (actually, Charles Hardin),

pioneering rock and roll songwriter and performer who was a prime inspiration to The Beatles and the British Invasion; b. Lubbock, Tex., Sept. 7, 1936; d. near Mason City, Iowa, Feb. 2, 1959. **THE CRICKETS:** Buddy Holly, lead gtr., voc.; Niki Sullivan, rhythm gtr.; Joe Mauldin, standup bs.; and Jerry Allison, drm. (b. Hillsboro, Tex., Aug. 31, 1939). Other members included guitarists Sonny Curtis (b. Meadow, Tex., April 9, 1937), Tommy Allsup, and Glen D. Hardin; vocalists Earl Sinks and Jerry Naylor; and bassist Waylon Jennings. Buddy Holly took up violin and piano at the age of 11, soon switching to acoustic guitar. In the seventh grade, he met guitarist Bob Montgomery, with whom he created a popular local performing duo. The two played "western and bop" music on radio station KDAV in Lubbock between 1953 and 1955, recording a number of songs later issued as *Holly in the Hills*. Adding bassist Larry Welborn and guitarist Sonny Curtis, the group opened shows for Bill Haley and Elvis Presley in Lubbock. Holly was soon signed to Decca Records, and, three times during 1956, he traveled to Nashville to record under veteran producer Owen Bradley, the second time accompanied by The Three Tunes: Curtis, bassist Don Guess, and drummer Jerry Allison. These recordings, issued in 1958 as *That'll Be the Day*, included an early version of "That'll Be the Day," as well as "Rock Around with Ollie Vee" and "Midnight Shift." However, none of Decca's 1956 singles releases became hits.

Subsequently released by Decca, Buddy Holly started recording at producer Norman Petty's studio in Clovis, N.Mex., in February 1957 with rhythm guitarist Niki Sullivan, bassist Larry Welborn, and Three Tunes drummer Jerry Allison. The session yielded another version of the Holly-Allison collaboration "That'll Be

the Day," that found its way to executive Bob Thiele after being rejected by Roulette Records. Thiele released the song on Brunswick Records under the name The Crickets and quickly signed the group. By September, the song had become a smash pop, R&B and British hit.

In April 1957 The Crickets came together with Sullivan, Allison, and standup bassist Joe B. Mauldin. Norman Petty took over the career of Buddy Holly and The Crickets as manager, producer, sessions leader and occasional keyboardist, negotiating separate contracts for The Crickets with Brunswick and for Holly with Coral Records. Holly soon scored a smash pop and R&B hit with the classic "Peggy Sue" (backed with "Everyday"), while The Crickets had major crossover hits with "Oh, Boy!" (backed with "Not Fade Away") and "Maybe Baby." The Crickets played black theaters such as N.Y.'s Apollo and Washington, D.C.'s Howard Theater and their debut album, *The "Chirping" Crickets*, was released at the end of 1957. Buddy Holly and The Crickets soon appeared on television's Ed Sullivan Show, but Niki Sullivan left the group in December. Reduced to a trio, Holly was obliged to play both lead and rhythm guitar on tours of the U.S., Australia and England.

1958's pop-only hits included "Think It Over" for The Crickets, and "Rave on" and Bobby Darin's "Early in the Morning" for Buddy Holly. Holly had recorded "Early in the Morning" in N.Y. without The Crickets, but with vocal choir and saxophonist Sam "The Man" Taylor. However, "It's So Easy," "Heartbeat" and "Love's Made a Fool of You," recorded with new guitarist Tommy Allsup, fared poorly. In the fall of 1958, Jerry Allison achieved a minor hit with the frantic "Real Wild Child" as Ivan, backed by Buddy Holly on lead guitar. In September, Holly produced Waylon Jennings's first single, "Jole Blon," with backing by saxophonist King Curtis, who also played on Holly's "Reminiscing." By October, The Crickets had split from Holly, and Holly had left Norman Petty.

Buddy Holly married Maria Elena Santiago in August and moved to N.Y., where he recorded "True Love Ways," "Raining in My Heart" and Paul Anka's "It Doesn't Matter Anymore" under producer Dick Jacobs, utilizing Jacobs's orchestra. Holly then embarked on a tour of the Midwest with guitarist Allsup, drummer Charlie Bunch, and guitarist-turned- bassist Waylon Jennings. Following a concert at Clear Lake, Iowa, on Feb. 2, 1959, Buddy Holly, then 22, Ritchie Valens ("Donna," "La Bamba"), and J. P. "Big Bopper" Richardson ("Chantilly Lace") died when their chartered plane crashed shortly after takeoff. Jennings had been bumped from the plane, and Dion and The Belmonts, also on the tour, had made other travel arrangements.

"It Doesn't Matter Anymore" (backed with "Raining in My Heart") soon became a major pop hit for Buddy Holly. With Holly's death, Sonny Curtis, Joe Mauldin, Jerry Allison and vocalist Earl Sinks continued as The Crickets, recording for Brunswick and Coral. Curtis, Sullivan and Allison recruited vocalist Jerry Naylor and switched to Liberty in 1961, staying until 1965. Subsequently reuniting in the early 1970s, The Crickets centered around Curtis, Allison and guitarist Glen D.

Hardin, who left in 1973 to join Elvis Presley's band.

Sonny Curtis wrote "Walk Right Back," a near-smash pop hit for The Everly Brothers in 1961, and "I Fought the Law," a near-smash pop hit for The Bobby Fuller Four in 1966. He also wrote the theme song of CBS-TV's *Mary Tyler Moore Show* and co-wrote, with Jerry Allison, "More than I Can Say," a minor hit for Bobby Vee in 1961 and a smash hit for Leo Sayer in 1980. Curtis recorded into the 1980s, scoring major country hits with "Love Is All Around" in 1980 and "Good Ol' Girls" in 1981. Bob Montgomery proved successful as a songwriter ("Misty Blue") and independent producer for Johnny Darrell and Bobby Goldsboro. Waylon Jennings struggled as a country-and-western artist through the 1970s, finally achieving recognition as an "outlaw" country musician in 1976. Norman Petty died on Aug. 15, 1984, in Lubbock after a long illness. In 1987 Allison, Mauldin and guitarist-vocalist Gordon Payne recorded *Three Piece*, released on Allison's Rollercoaster label. The album became *T-Shirt* on Epic Records with the addition of the title track, produced by Paul McCartney.

During the 1960s Buddy Holly's legacy was kept alive as The Rolling Stones debuted in the American charts with "Not Fade Away," Peter and Gordon hit with "True Love Ways," and The Bobby Fuller Four scored a major hit with Holly's "Love's Made a Fool of You." In the latter half of the 1970s, Linda Ronstadt recorded a number of Holly's songs, hitting with "That'll Be the Day" and "It's So Easy." In 1976 Paul McCartney bought the Holly song catalog and initiated the annual Buddy Holly Week (in September) celebration in London. In May 1978, *The Buddy Holly Story*, starring Gary Busey, was released, becoming a surprise film hit and sparking revitalized interest in Holly. Buddy Holly was inducted into the Rock and Roll Hall of Fame in its inaugural year, 1986, and the movie *Peggy Sue Got Married* featured his title song. *Buddy*, a stage musical based on the life and songs of Buddy Holly, debuted in London in October 1989 and toured the U.S. the following year. In 1996 Decca issued *Not Fade Away (Remembering Buddy Holly)*, which contained cover versions of Holly's songs by the likes of Marty Stuart and Steve Earle, Nanci Griffith, Los Lobos, Joe Ely and The Tractors.

DISC.: BUDDY HOLLY AND BOB MONTGOMERY: *Holly in the Hills* (1965); *The Hills* (1965). **BUDDY HOLLY AND THE CRICKETS:** *The "Chirping" Crickets* (1957). **BUDDY HOLLY:** *That'll Be the Day* (1958); *Buddy Holly* (1958); *The Buddy Holly Story* (1959); *The Buddy Holly Story, Vol. 2* (1960); *Reminiscing* (1963); *For the First Time Anywhere* (1983); *The Nashville Sessions* (1986). **THE CRICKETS:** *In the Style with The Crickets* (1961); *Bobby Vee Meets The Crickets* (1962); *Something Old, Something New, Something Blue, Something Else* (1963); *California Sun* (1964); *Rockin' 50s Rock and Roll* (1971); *Remnants* (1974); *T-Shirt* (1988).

BIBL.: D. Laing, *B. H.* (N.Y., 1971); E. Peer and R. Peer II, *B. H.: A Biography in Words, Pictures and Music* (N.Y., 1972); J. Goldrosen, *B. H.: His Life and Music* (Bowling Green, Ohio, 1975); C. Flippo, "The B. H. Story: Friends Say Movie's Not Cricket," *Rolling Stone* 274 (Sept. 21, 1978); J. Goldrosen, *The B. H. Story* (N.Y., 1979); J. Goldrosen and J. Beecher, *Remembering Buddy: The Definitive Biography* (N.Y., 1987); E. Amburn. *B. H.: A Biography* (N.Y., 1995); L. Lehmer, *The Day the Music Died: The Last Tour of B. H., the Big Bopper, and Richie Valens* (N.Y., 1997); P. Norman, *Rave on: The Biography of B. H.* (N.Y., 1996).—BH

Holm, Mogens Winkel, Danish composer; b. Copenhagen, Oct. 1, 1936. He was a student of Jørgen Jersild (theory and composition) and Mogens Andreassen (oboe) at the Royal Danish Cons. of Music in Copenhagen (1955–61). He then was an oboist in several Copenhagen orchs. He was a music critic for the Copenhagen newspapers *Ekstra Bladet* and *Politiken* (1965–71), and subsequently served as chairman of the Danish Composers' Soc. (1971–75; from 1982).

WORKS: DRAMATIC: Opera: *Aslak*, chamber opera (1962; Copenhagen, Jan. 27, 1963); *Sonata for 4 Opera Singers*, textless chamber opera (Copenhagen, April 19, 1968). **Ballet:** *Tropismer II* (Copenhagen, May 24, 1964); *Kontradans* (Danish Radio, July 16, 1965); *Bikt* (Swedish Radio, May 5, 1969; rev. as *Krønike* [Chronicle]); *Galgarien* (Malmö, Nov. 27, 1970); *Rapport* (Report; Danish Radio, March 19, 1972); *Tarantel* (1975); *Eurydike tøver* (Eurydice Hesitates; 1977); *Gaerdesanger under kunstig stjerneheimmel* (Whitethroat Under an Artificial Firmament; 1979–80); *Til Blåskaeg* (To Bluebeard; 1982). **ORCH.:** *Chamber Concertante* for Bassoon, String Quartet, and String Orch. (1959); *Concerto piccolo* (1961); *Cumulus* (1965); *Aiolos*, sym. (Danish Radio, March 24, 1972; symphonic version of the ballet *Rapport*); *Glasskoven* (The Glass Forest) for Glass Players and Strings (1974); *Cries* (1983–84). **CHAMBER:** Trio for Oboe, Clarinet, and Bassoon (1956); Wind Quintet (1957); *Little Chamber Concerto* for 5 Winds, Violin, and Cello (1958); String Quartet (1959); *ABRACADABRA* for Flute, Trumpet, Cello, and 4 Timpani (1960); *Tropismer I* for Oboe, Bassoon, Horn, and Piano (1961); Sonata for Woodwind Quintet (1965); *Overtoninger II* for Flute, Piano, and Cello (1972); *Syv breve til stilheden* (7 Letters to Silence) for Flute, Oboe, Guitar, Piano, Vibraphone, and Viola (1976); *Adieu* for Flute, Violin, Cello, Harp, and Percussion (1982); *Note-book* for Oboe, Clarinet, and Bassoon (1983). **VOCAL:** *A Ghost Story* for Soloists, Chorus, and Orch. (1964); *Annonce* for Soprano and Chamber Group (1965); *Overtoninger I* for Soprano, Cimbalom, and Cello (1971); *Konungens sorg* for 3 Sopranos, Harp, and 3 Oboes (1989); choruses; songs. —NS/LK/DM

Holm, Peder, Danish composer; b. Copenhagen, Sept. 30, 1926. He studied violin with Thorval Nielsen and counterpoint with Jeppesen at the Royal Danish Cons. of Music in Copenhagen (1945–47). He became a lecturer at the Esbjerg Cons. in 1949 and in 1964 was named its director.

WORKS: DRAMATIC: Opera: *Ingen mad i dag, men i morgen* (No Food Today but Tomorrow; 1962). **ORCH.:** Violin Concerto (1952); Piano Concerto (1953); *Fantasy* for Viola and Orch. (1954); *Concerto for Orchestra* (1955); Sym. No. 1 (1955); *Preludio, Scherzo, and Fantasia* (1956); *Symphonic Dance* (1957); *Capriccio* (1959); 2 concertos for Piano and Strings (1963, 1967); *Pezzo concertante* (1964); 2 Sketches for Trumpet, Trombone, and Orch. (1966); 3 Pieces (1966); *VYL* (1967; Esbjerg, May 2, 1968); *KHEBEB* for 2 Pianos and Orch. (1968); Trumpet Concertino (1970); Clarinet Concertino (1970). **CHAMBER:** String Quartet (1967); 2 Pieces for Wind Quintet (1968). **VOCAL:** *Moerlille* for Chorus and Ensemble (1987).—NS/LK/DM

Holm, Renate, German soprano; b. Berlin, Aug. 10, 1931. After winning 1st prize in a vocal competition sponsored at the RIAS in Berlin in 1952, she embarked upon a career as a pop singer; she also pursued vocal training with Maria Ivogün in Vienna. In 1958 she made her debut in Oscar Straus's *Ein Walzertraum* at the Vienna Volksoper, where she subsequently sang with fine success. In 1961 she joined the Vienna State Opera. Her guest engagements took her to the Salzburg Festival, Covent Garden in London, the Bolshoi Theater in Moscow, and the Teatro Colón in Buenos Aires. She was notably successful as Blondchen, Papagena, Rosina in *Il Barbiere di Siviglia*, Marie in *Zar und Zimmermann*, and Musetta, as well as in Viennese operettas. She was the author of *Ein Leben nach Spielplan: Stationen einer ungewöhnlichen Karriere* (Berlin, 1991).—NS/LK/DM

Holm, Richard, German tenor; b. Stuttgart, Aug. 3, 1912; d. Munich, July 20, 1988. He studied in Stuttgart with Rudolf Ritter. In 1937 he made his operatic debut in Kiel; became a member of the Kiel Opera; also made guest appearances at other German opera houses; in 1948 he joined the Bavarian State Opera in Munich. On March 15, 1952, he made his Metropolitan Opera debut in N.Y. as David in *Die Meistersinger von Nürnberg*; was on its roster until 1953. He also made successful appearances in London, Vienna, Salzburg, and Bayreuth. In 1967 he became a prof. of voice at the Hochschule für Musik in Munich. Among his roles were Xerxes, Titus, Belmonte, Tamino, Loge, Flamand, Novagerio in *Palestrina*, Robespierre in *Dantons Tod*, and Aschenbach in *Death in Venice*.—NS/LK/DM

Holmboe, Vagn, eminent Danish composer and pedagogue; b. Horsens, Jutland, Dec. 20, 1909. He was a student of Høffding and Jeppesen at the Copenhagen Cons. (1925–29), and then of Toch at the Berlin Hochschule für Musik (1930). After pursuing ethnomusicological research in Romania (1933–34), he returned to Copenhagen as a private teacher. He taught at the Royal Danish Inst. for the Blind (1940–49), and also was a music critic for the newspaper *Politiken* (1947–55). In 1950 he became a teacher at the Royal Danish Cons. of Music in Copenhagen, where he subsequently was a prof. of theory and composition from 1955 to 1965. He held a lifetime government grant to pursue composition. He publ. *Mellemspil* (Interlude; Copenhagen, 1961) and *Det Uforklarlige* (Copenhagen, 1981; Eng. tr., 1991, as *Experiencing Music: A Composer's Notes*). As the leading Danish composer in the post-Nielsen era, Holmboe pursued a neo-Classical style in which he displayed a thorough command of counterpoint and instrumentation. His symphonic compositions are notable for their development of "germ themes" which grow metamorphically. In addition to his important contribution to the symphony, he also composed an outstanding series of string quartets.

WORKS: DRAMATIC: *Fanden og borgemesteren* (The Devil and the Mayor), symphonic fairy play (1940); *Den galsindede tyrk*, ballet (1942–44); *Lave og Jon*, opera (1946–48); *Kniven* (The Knife), chamber opera (1959–60; Copenhagen, Dec. 2, 1963); music for plays, films, and radio. **ORCH.:** *Concerto for Orchestra* (1929); Concerto for Chamber Orch. (1931; Copen-hagen, April 3, 1933); *Chamber Music No. 1* for Small Orch. (1931) and *No. 2* for Strings (1932); *Divertimento No. 1* (Copenhagen, March 29, 1933) and *No. 2* for Strings (1933; Copenhagen, Jan. 31, 1944); Concerto for Strings (1933); 3 suites for Chamber Orch.: No. 1 (1935; Copenhagen, March 30, 1936), No. 2 (1935–36; Copenhagen, April 20, 1939), and No. 3 (1936; Copenhagen, Nov. 23, 1938); Chamber Sonata No. 1 (1935); 13 numbered syms.: No. 1 (1935; Århus, Feb. 21, 1938), No. 2 (1938–39; Copenhagen, Dec. 5, 1939), No. 3, *Sinfonia Rustica* (1941; Copenhagen, June 12, 1948), No. 4, *Sinfonia Sacra* (1941; rev. version, Copenhagen, Sept. 11, 1945), No. 5 (1944; Copenhagen, June 16, 1945), No. 6 (1947; Copenhagen, Jan. 8, 1948), No. 7 (1950; Copenhagen, Oct. 18, 1951), No. 8, *Sinfonia Boreale* (1951–52; Copenhagen, March 5, 1953), No. 9 (Copenhagen, Dec. 19, 1968), No. 10 (1970–71; Detroit, Jan. 27, 1972), No. 11 (1980; Copenhagen, Feb. 17, 1983), No. 12 (1988; Cardiff, Oct. 21, 1989), and No. 13 (1994); *Romanian Suite* for Piano and Chamber Orch. (1935) and *Romanian Suite* for Chamber Orch. (1938); *Rhapsody* for Flute and Chamber Orch. (1935); *Little Overture* (1936; Copenhagen, March 16, 1938); *Serenade* (1936; Copenhagen, Oct. 21, 1939); Concerto Sym. for Violin and Orch. (1937); 2 violin concertos (1938, 1979); 2 unnumbered concertinos (1938, Copenhagen, June 6, 1941; 1957, Copenhagen, Sept. 28, 1958); 13 chamber concertos: No. 1 for Piano, Strings, and Percussion (1939; Copenhagen, March 5, 1941), No. 2 for Flute, Violin, Celesta, Percussion, and Strings (1940; Copenhagen, April 21, 1942), No. 3 for Clarinet, 2 Trumpets, 2 Horns, and Strings (1940), No. 4, *Triple Concerto*, for Violin, Cello, Piano, and Chamber Orch. (1942; Copenhagen, March 22, 1943), No. 5 for Viola and Chamber Orch. (1943; Copenhagen, Feb. 14, 1946), No. 6 for Violin and Chamber Orch. (1943; Copenhagen, Dec. 12, 1944), No. 7 for Oboe and Chamber Orch. (1944–45; Copenhagen, Jan. 29, 1948), No. 8, *Sinfonia Concertante*, for Chamber Orch. (1945; Copenhagen, July 26, 1947), No. 9 for Violin, Viola, and Chamber Orch. (1945–46; Copenhagen, Oct. 26, 1954), No. 10, *Trae-messing-tarm*, for Chamber Orch. (1945–46; Randers, April 26, 1946), No. 11 for Trumpet, 2 Horns, and Strings (1948; Copenhagen, April 8, 1949), No. 12 for Trombone and Chamber Orch. (1951; Copenhagen, May 23, 1952), and No. 13, *Collegium musicum concerto No. 2*, for Oboe, Viola, and Chamber Orch. (1955–56; Randers, Nov. 6, 1958); 2 numbered concertinos: No. 1 for Violin, Viola, and Strings (1940; Copenhagen, Sept. 16, 1963) and No. 2 for Violin and Strings (1940; Copenhagen, June 12, 1948); Symphonic Overture (1941; Copenhagen, April 13, 1943); 3 chamber syms: No. 1 (Copenhagen, March 9, 1951), No. 2 (1968; Copenhagen, Jan. 20, 1969), and No. 3 (1969–70; Ålborg, Oct. 14, 1970); 2 unnumbered sinfonias: *Sinfonia in memoriam* (1954–55; Copenhagen, May 5, 1955) and *Sinfonia Sielariana* (1964); 4 symphonic metamorphoses: *Epitaph* (London, Dec. 28, 1956); *Monolith* (Århus, Sept. 9, 1960); *Epilogue* (1961–62; Göteborg, Nov. 23, 1962); and *Tempo Variable* (1971–72; Bergen, May 24, 1972); 4 sinfonias for Strings: No. 1 (1957; Copenhagen, July 3, 1958), No. 2 (1957; Århus, Nov. 20, 1958), No. 3 (1958–59; Århus, Jan. 22, 1962), and No. 4 (1962; Århus, Jan. 27, 1964); *Skoven* (1960; Randers, May 2, 1961); Cello Concerto (1974); Recorder Concerto (1974); 2 flute concertos (1975, 1981); Tuba Concerto (1976); Concerto for Brass (1984); *Intermezzo Concertante* for Tuba and Strings (1987); *Prelude: To the Victoria Embankment* for Chamber Orch. (1990). **CHAMBER:** Trio for Flute and 2 Violins (1926; also for 3 Violins); String Quintet (1928); Quartet for Flute, Oboe, Viola, and Cello (1930); *Allegro sostenuto* for Piano and Violin (1931); *5 Duets* for Flute and Viola (1932); *7 Duos* for Flute and Horn (1932); *4 Duos* for Flute and Trombone (1932); Trio for Oboe, Bassoon, and Horn (1932–39);

Quintet for Flute, Oboe, Clarinet, Bassoon, and Horn (Copenhagen, Oct. 30, 1933); 3 violin sonatas: No. 1 (Lund, Nov. 13, 1935), No. 2 (1939; Copenhagen, Jan. 16, 1942), and No. 3 (Brussels, May 4, 1965); *Serenade* for Flute, Clarinet, and Bassoon (1935); *Rhapsody* for Clarinet and Violin (1936); Quartet for Flute, Violin, Cello, and Piano (1936; Paris, July 1937); Quintet for Flute, Oboe, Clarinet, Violin, and Viola (1936; Copenhagen, July 24, 1939); *Rhapsodic Interlude* for Clarinet, Piano, and Violin (1938); *Serenade* for Flute, Piano, Violin, and Cello (1940; Vienna, March 25, 1949); *Notturno* for Flute, Oboe, Clarinet, Bassoon, and Horn (Copenhagen, Nov. 2, 1940); 20 string quartets: No. 1 (1941–44; rev. 1949), No. 2 (1948–49; Copenhagen, Jan. 31, 1950), No. 3 (1949–50; Copenhagen, Nov. 18, 1950), No. 4 (1953–54; Copenhagen, Jan. 8, 1955; rev. 1956), No. 5 (1955; Kolding, Feb. 20, 1956), No. 6 (1961; Hindsgavl, Aug. 1962), No. 7 (1964–65; Birkerod, Sept. 27, 1965), No. 8 (Frederiksberg, Dec. 14, 1965), No. 9 (1965–66; Horsens, Aug. 23, 1967; rev. 1969), No. 10 (1969; Göteborg, April 7, 1970), No. 11, *Quartetto rustico* (Soro, March 8, 1972), No. 12 (Hillerod, Nov. 19, 1973), No. 13 (1975), No. 14 (1975), No. 15 (1976–77), No. 16 (1981), No. 17, *Mattinata* (1982), No. 18, *Giornata* (1982), No. 19, *Serata* (1985), and No. 20, *Notturno* (1985); *Isomeric duo concertante* for 2 Violins and Piano (Copenhagen, July 20, 1950); *Primavera* for Flute, Piano, Violin, and Cello (1951; Copenhagen, Oct. 24, 1952); Sonata for Solo Violin (1953); Trio for Piano, Violin, and Cello (1954; Copenhagen, Oct. 24, 1956); *Quartetto medico* for Flute, Oboe, Clarinet, and Piano (1956); Sonata for Solo Flute (1957); *Aspekter* for Flute, Oboe, Clarinet, Bassoon, and Horn (1957; Copenhagen, April 9, 1958); *Tropos* for 2 Violins, 2 Violas, and Cello (Kongens Lyngby, Oct. 9, 1960); Quintet for Horn, 2 Trumpets, Trombone, and Tuba (1961); Sonata for Solo Double Bass (1962); Sonata for Violin and Viola (1963); Quartet for Flute, Violin, Viola, and Cello (Hindsgavl, July 15, 1966); Oboe Sonatina (1966); Trio for Flute, Cello, and Percussion (Kongens Lyngby, Oct. 8, 1968); Sonata for Solo Cello (1968–69); *Musik til Morten* for Oboe and String Quartet (Humlebaek, Nov. 17, 1970); *Fanden los i vildmosen* for Clarinet, 2 Violins, and Double Bass (Vra, July 30, 1971); *Ondata* for Tuned Gongs (1972); Sextet for Flute, Clarinet, Bassoon, Violin, Viola, and Cello (1972–73; Odense, Nov. 13, 1973); *Diafora* for 4 Strings (1973); *Nuigen* for Piano, Violin, and Cello (1976); *Firefir* for 4 Flutes (1976–77); Trio for Clarinet, Cello, and Piano (1978); *Notes* for 3 Trombones and Tuba (1979); 2 guitar sonatas (1979, 1979); Sonata for Recorder and Harpsichord (1980); *Gioco* for Violin, Viola, and Cello (1983); *Ballata* for Violin, Viola, Cello, and Piano (1984); Tuba Sonata (1986); *Prelude: To a Pine Tree* for Chamber Ensemble (1986); Quintet for 2 Violins, Viola, Cello, and Double Bass (1986); *Prelude: To a Dolphin* for Chamber Ensemble (1986); Duo concertante for Violin and Guitar (1986); *Prelude: To a Maple Tree* for Chamber Ensemble (1986); *Prelude: To a Willow Tree* for Chamber Ensemble (1987); Trombone Sonata (1987); *Translation* for Violin, Viola, Cello, Double Bass, and Piano (1987; rev. 1989); *Capriccio* for Clarinet and Piano (1988); Sonata for Solo Viola (1988); *Prelude: To the Pollution of Nature* for Chamber Ensemble (1989); *Epos* for 2 Pianos and Percussion (1990); *Eco* for Clarinet, Cello, and Piano (1991); *Prelude: To the Unsettled Weather* for Chamber Ensemble (1993). KEYBOARD: Piano: *Scherzo* (1928); *12 Little Pieces* (1928–29); *Chorale Fantasy* (1929); Sonata (1929); *4 Pieces* (1930); *Symphony for Piano* (1930); *5 Pieces* (1930); *5 1–and 2–part Pieces* (1930); *Allegro affetuoso* (1931); *Little Pieces* (1931; also for Recorders); *Pieces* (1931); *1–, 2–, and 3–part Pieces* (1931); *Julen* (1931); Concerto for Piano (1931); *Suites and Dances* (1931); *7 Preludes* (1932); *Capriccio* (1932); *6 Pieces* (1933); *6 Sketches* (1934); *10 Romanian Dances* (1934); *Suite* (1937); *New Pieces* (1937);

Danish Suite (1937; also for Orch.); *6 Pieces* (1939); *Étude* (1939); *Sonatina briosa* (1941); *5 Epigrams* (1942); *Suona da bardo*, suite (1949–50); *Moto austero* (1965); *Moto austero* (1972); *I venti* (1972). Organ: *Fabula I* (1972) and *II* (1973); *Contrasti* (1972). VOCAL: *Requiem* for Soloists, Chorus, and Orch. (1931); *Provinsen* for Soloists, Chorus, Flute, Oboe, Violin, and Cello (1931); 12 cantatas, including: No. 2 for Chorus and Orch. (Horsens, Dec. 19, 1941), No. 3 for Voices and Strings (Horsens, June 28, 1942), No. 4 for Voices and Orch. (1942–45; Copenhagen, Nov. 26, 1945), No. 6 for Chorus and Orch. (1947), No. 7 for Sopranos, Women's Voices, and Orch. or 2 Pianos (Copenhagen, Oct. 27, 1949), No. 8 for Baritones, Bass, Reciter, and Strings (1951; Falster, May 1, 1952), No. 9 for Women's Voices, Violin, Cello, Flute, and 2 Pianos (Randers, April 28, 1955), No. 10 for Mixed Voices (1957; Copenhagen, July 2, 1958), No. 11 for Baritone, Mezzo-soprano, Chorus, and Orch. (1958), and No. 12 for Mezzo-soprano, Contralto, Baritone, Chorus, and Orch. (1958–59; Århus, Sept. 11, 1959); *Arhundredstjernen* for Baritone, Chorus, and Orch. (1946; Copenhagen, March 18, 1947); *Liber canticorum I-IV* for Mixed Voices (1951–53); *Traeet* for Chorus and Chamber Orch. (1953); *Requiem for Nietzsche* for Alto, Tenor, Baritone, Chorus, and Orch. (1963; Copenhagen, Nov. 26, 1964); *Zeit* for Alto and String Quartet (1966); *Beatus Vir: Liber canticorum V* for Mixed Voices (1968); *Cantata profana Frise* for Mixed Voices (1970); *Edward* for Baritone and Orch. (1971); *The Wee, Wee Man* for Tenor and Orch. or Mixed Voices (1971–72); *Beatus parvo* for Mixed Voices and Orch. (1973); *Biblical Cantata* for Soloists, Chorus, and Orch. (1982); *Ode to the Soul* for Chorus and Brass (1985); *Winter* for Soprano and Chorus (1989); *Die Erfullung* for Soprano, Baritone, 2 Choruses, and 9 Winds (1990); many choruses and solo songs.

BIBL.: P. Rapoport, *V. H.: A Catalogue of His Music, Discography, Bibliography, Essays* (London, 1974; 2nd. ed., rev. and enl., Copenhagen, 1979); idem, *V. H.'s Symphonic Metamorphoses* (diss., Univ. of Ill., 1975).—NS/LK/DM

Holmès (real name, **Holmes**), **Augusta (Mary Anne),** French composer; b. Paris (of Irish parents), Dec. 16, 1847; d. there, Jan. 28, 1903. She progressed very rapidly as a child pianist, and gave public concerts. She also composed songs, under the pen name Hermann Zenta. She studied harmony with H. Lambert, an organist, and later became a pupil of César Franck. She then began to compose works in large forms, arousing considerable attention, mixed with curiosity, for she was one of the very few professional women composers of the time. Her music lacks individuality or strength. At best, it represents a conventional by-product of French Romanticism, with an admixture of fashionable exotic elements.

WORKS: DRAMATIC: Opera: *La Montagne noire* (Paris Opéra, Feb. 8, 1895); *Héro et Léandre*; *Astarte*; *Lancelot du lac*. **ORCH.:** *Andante pastoral* (Paris, Jan. 14, 1877); *Lutèce* (Angers, Nov. 30, 1884); *Les Argonautes* (Paris, April 24, 1881); *Irlande* (Paris, March 2, 1882); *Ode triomphale* (Paris, March 4, 1888); *Pologne*; *Andromède*; *Hymne à Apollon*. **VOCAL: Cantatas:** *La Vision de la Reine*; *La Chanson de la caravane*; *La Fleur de Neflier*. **Other Vocal:** 117 songs. **OTHER:** Piano pieces.

BIBL.: P. Barillon-Bauché, *A. H. et la femme compositeur* (Paris, 1912); R. Pichard du Page, *A. H.: Une Musicienne versaillaise* (Paris, 1921).—NS/LK/DM

Holmes, Alfred, English violinist and composer; b. London, Nov. 9, 1837; d. Paris, March 4, 1876. His only teacher was his father, an amateur violinist. He sang at the Oratory in London as a soprano chorister, and appeared as a violinist at the age of 9, playing a duet with his brother, Henry, with whom he went on a European tour, playing in Belgium, Germany, Sweden, Denmark, and the Netherlands (1855–61). He then lived in Paris (1861–64). He visited Russia in 1867, and then returned to Paris, making occasional visits to London. He composed 4 programmatic syms., entitled *Robinhood, The Siege of Paris, Charles XII,* and *Romeo and Juliet,* and 2 overtures, *The Cid* and *The Muses.* His brother, Henry Holmes (b. London, Nov. 7, 1839; d. San Francisco, Dec. 9, 1905), was also a precocious violinist and composer. After 1865 he settled in London, where he taught at the Royal Coll. of Music. In 1894 he went to San Francisco, where he remained until his death. He wrote 4 syms., 2 cantatas, a Violin Concerto (London, Dec. 11, 1875), and chamber music.—NS/LK/DM

Holmes, Edward, English music critic; b. London, 1797; d. there, Aug. 28, 1859. He studied music with Vincent Novello. In 1826 he became a contributor to a literary journal, *Atlas.* He also wrote for *Fraser's Magazine* and the *Spectator* (from 1830) and for the *Musical Times* (1845–49; 1850–59). He publ. *A Ramble among the Musicians of Germany* (1828; reprint, ed. by C. Cudworth, N.Y., 1969) and *The Life of Mozart* (1845; 2nd ed., rev., 1878, by E. Prout; 3rd ed., rev., 1912, by E. Newman).—NS/LK/DM

Holmes, Ralph, English violinist; b. Penge, April 1, 1937; d. Beckenham, Sept. 4, 1984. He studied with David Martin at the Royal Academy of Music in London, and later with Enesco in Paris and Galamian in N.Y. He made his London debut at a children's concert of the Royal Phil. (1951), then won prizes at international competitions in Paris (1957) and Bucharest (1958). He pursued a successful career in England before making his U.S. debut with Barbirolli and the Houston Sym. Orch. at N.Y.'s Carnegie Hall in 1966. In subsequent years, he toured widely. With Anthony Goldstone and Moray Welsh, he formed his own piano trio in 1972. He was a prof. at the Royal Academy of Music from 1964. His repertoire included all the major 20th-century concertos written for his instrument.—NS/LK/DM

Holmes, Reed K., American composer; b. Oak Ridge, Tenn., Aug. 20, 1952. He studied at the Univ. of Tenn. (B.M., 1974; M.M., 1976) and the Univ. of Tex. at Austin (Ph.D., 1981, with the diss. *Relational Systems and Process in Recent Works of Luciano Berio*), where he taught (from 1985) and was director of its Electronic Music Studio. He was a founding member of the Tex. Composers Forum (1985). He received an ASCAP Award in Composition (1989) and an NEA grant (1990–91). His spirited compositions are often minimalist in design, motivated by rhythmic and timbral processes.

WORKS: MULTIMEDIA: *Moiré* for Dancers and Computer-generated Sound (1981); *Nova* for Dissolve Slide Projections and Quadraphonic Sound (1982–83); *Around the Waves* for Dissolve Slide Projections and Quadraphonic Sound (1983); *Drumfire* for Dancers and Computer (1986); *Electric Symphonies* for Dancers and Computer (1988). **CHAMBER:** *Sound Streams* for Flute Choir (1979); *Patterns* for Any Group of Homogeneous Wind Instruments (1982); *Kaleidoscope* for 23 Musicians (1984); *Pocket Hocket* for 4 Synthesizers (or for Any 4 Parts) (1985); *Circle Sonata* for 5 Percussionists and Tape (1986); *Variations* for 6 Parts Performed by Any Homogeneous Group of Instruments (1988); *Nonet* for Soprano, English Horn or Oboe, Saxophone, Trumpet, Violin, Viola, Cello, Piano, and Mallet Percussion (1991). **SOLO, WITH TAPE:** *Dream Quest* for Percussion (1975); *Chalumeau Rain* for Clarinet (1980); *Song and Fantasy* for Trombone (1982); *With Wings They Came* for Saxophone (1983); *Cat's Cradle 4* for Cello (1990).—NS/LK/DM

Holoman, D(allas) Kern, American musicologist and conductor; b. Raleigh, N.C., Sept. 8, 1947. He pursued his academic training at Duke Univ. (B.A., 1969) and Princeton Univ. (M.F.A., 1971; Ph.D., 1974, with the diss. *Autograph Musical Documents of Hector Berlioz, c. 1818–1840*; publ. in a rev. and corrected ed. as *The Creative Process in the Autograph Musical Documents of Hector Berlioz, c. 1818–1840,* Ann Arbor, 1980), receiving a Fulbright fellowship (1972–73). In 1973 he joined the faculty of the Univ. of Calif. at Davis, where he was founder-director of its Early Music Ensemble (1973–77; 1979), conductor of its sym. orch. (from 1978), and chairman of the music dept. (1980–88). During a period of financial crisis in Calif., he was chairman of its dramatic art dept. and founder-dean of its division of humanities, arts, and cultural studies (1994–96). With J. Kerman and R. Winter, he was founding ed. of the distinguished journal *19th-Century Music* (1977), subsequently serving as its managing ed. His writings are notable for their accessible prose style and engaging, dry wit. An authority on Berlioz, he publ. the first thematic catalog of that composer's output and ed. his *Roméo et Juliette* for the New Berlioz Edition. An interest in technological advances led to his *Masterworks* (1998), the first fully integrated multimedia textbook in music appreciation.

WRITINGS: Ed. with C. Palisca, *Musicology in the 1980s* (N.Y., 1982); *Catalogue of the Works of Hector Berlioz* (Kassel, 1987); *Writing about Music: A Style-Sheet from the Editors of 19th-Century Music* (Berkeley and Los Angeles, 1988); *Berlioz* (Cambridge, Mass., 1989); *Evenings with the Orchestra: A Norton Companion for Concertgoers* (N.Y., 1992); ed. *The Nineteenth-Century Symphony* (N.Y., 1997); *Masterworks: A Musical Discovery* (Upper Saddle River, N.J., 1998).—NS/LK/DM

Holoubek, Ladislav, Slovak conductor and composer; b. Prague, Aug. 13, 1913. He studied composition with Moyzes at the Bratislava Academy of Music (1926–33) and with Novák at the Prague Cons. (1934–36). He conducted at the Slovak National Theater in Bratislava (1933–52; 1959–66) and at the State Theater in Košice (1955–58; from 1966). His operas have contributed significantly to the advancement of modern Slovak opera.

WORKS: DRAMATIC: O p e r a (all 1st perf. in Bratislava unless otherwise given): *Stella* (March 18, 1939; rev. 1948–49 and 1954–55); *Svitanie* (Dawn; March 12, 1941); *Tužba* (Yearning; Feb. 12, 1944; rev. 1963 and 1969); *Rodina* (The

Family; Nov. 12, 1960); *Professor Mamlock* (May 21, 1966); *Bačovské žarty* (Shepherds' Games; 1975; Košice, Jan. 16, 1981). **ORCH.:** Sym. (1946); *Sinfonietta* (1950); *10 Variations on an Original Theme* (1950); *Defiances and Hopes*, symphonic poem (1973). **CHAMBER:** Violin Sonata (1933); 3 string quartets (1936, 1948, 1962); Wind Quintet (1938); Trio for Flute, Violin, and Harp (1939); 2 piano sonatas (1931, 1937). **VOCAL:** Cantatas and songs.—NS/LK/DM

Holst, Gustav(us Theodore von), significant English composer, father of **Imogen (Clare) Holst;** b. Cheltenham, Sept. 21, 1874; d. London, May 25, 1934. He was of Swedish descent. He received his primary musical training from his parents. In 1892 he became organist and choirmaster in Wyck Rissington, Gloucestershire; in 1893 he entered the Royal Coll. of Music in London, where he studied composition with Stanford and Rockstro, organ with Hoyte, and piano with Sharpe; also learned to play the trombone. After graduating in 1898, he was a trombonist in the orch. of the Carl Rosa Opera Co. (until 1900) and the Scottish Orch. in Glasgow (1900–1903). His interest in Hindu philosophy, religion, and music during this period led to the composition of his settings from the Sanskrit of *Hymns from the Rig Veda* (1907–08). He worked as a music teacher in a Dulwich girls' school (1903–20); was director of music at St. Paul's Girls' School, Hammersmith (1905–34), and of London's Morley Coll. (1907–24). He became a teacher of composition at the Royal Coll. of Music (1919); was also prof. of music at Univ. Coll., Reading (1919–23). Plagued by suspicions of his German sympathies at the outbreak of World War I in 1914, he removed the Germanic-looking (actually Swedish) nobiliary particle "von" from his surname; his early works had been publ. under the name Gustav von Holst. He was deemed unfit for military service, but served as YMCA musical organizer among the British troops in the Near East in 1918. After the war, he visited the U.S. as a lecturer and conductor in 1923 and 1932. However, his deteriorating health limited his activities; his daughter described his mind in the last years of his life as "closed in gray isolation." Holst's most celebrated work, the large-scale orch. suite *The Planets*, was inspired by the astrological significance of the planets. It consists of 7 movements, each bearing a mythological subtitle: *Mars, the Bringer of War; Venus, the Bringer of Peace; Mercury, the Winged Messenger; Jupiter, the Bringer of Jollity; Saturn, the Bringer of Old Age; Uranus, the Magician; Neptune, the Mystic,* with an epilogue of female voices singing wordless syllables. It was first performed privately in London (Sept. 29, 1918); 5 movements were played in public (Feb. 15, 1920); the first complete performance followed (Nov. 15, 1920). The melodic and harmonic style of the work epitomizes Holst's musical convictions, in which lyrical, dramatic, and triumphant motifs are alternately presented in coruscatingly effective orch. dress. His music in general reflects the influence of English folk songs and the madrigal. He was a master of choral writing; one of his notable works utilizing choral forces was *The Hymn of Jesus* (1917). His writings were ed. by S. Lloyd and E. Rubbra as *Gustav Holst: Collected Essays* (London, 1974). See also I. Holst and C. Matthews, eds., *Gustav Holst:*

Collected Facsimile Edition of Autograph Manuscripts of the Published Works (4 vols., London, 1974–83).

WORKS: DRAMATIC: O p e r a : *The Revoke,* op.1 (1895); *The Youth's Choice,* op.11 (1902); *Sita,* op.23 (1899–1906); *Savitri,* chamber opera, op.25 (1908; London, Dec. 5, 1916); *The Perfect Fool,* op.39 (1918–22; London, May 14, 1923); *At the Boar's Head,* op.42 (1924; Manchester, April 3, 1925); *The Wandering Scholar,* chamber opera, op.50 (1929–30; Liverpool, Jan. 31, 1934). **O t h e r :** *Lansdown Castle,* operetta (Cheltenham, Feb. 7, 1893); *The Idea,* children's operetta (c. 1898); *The Vision of Dame Christian,* masque, op.27a (London, July 22, 1909). **B a l l e t :** *The Lure* (1921); *The Golden Goose,* choral ballet, op.45/1 (BBC, London, Sept. 21, 1926); *The Morning of the Year,* choral ballet, op.45/2 (1926–27; London, March 17, 1927). **I n c i d e n t a l M u s i c :** *The Sneezing Charm* (1918); 7 choruses from *Alcestis* (1920); *The Coming of Christ* (1927; Canterbury, May 28, 1928). **ORCH.:** *A Winter Idyll* (1897); *Walt Whitman,* overture, op.7 (1899); Sym. in F major, op.8, *The Cotswolds* (1899–1900; Bournemouth, April 24, 1902); *Suite de ballet* in E-flat major, op.10 (1899; London, May 20, 1904; rev. 1912); *Indra,* symphonic poem, op.13 (1903); *A Song of the Night* for Violin and Orch., op.19/1 (1905); *Invocation* for Cello and Orch., op.19/2 (1911); *Songs of the West,* op.21/1 (1906–07); *A Somerset Rhapsody,* op.21/2 (1906–07; London, April 6, 1910); *2 Songs without Words: Country Song* and *Marching Song* for Chamber Orch., op.22 (1906); 2 suites for Military Band: No. 1, in E-flat major, op.28/1 (1909) and No. 2, in F major, op.28/2 (1911); *Beni Mora,* oriental suite, op.29/1 (1909–10; London, May 1, 1912); *Phantastes,* suite in F major (1911); *St. Paul's Suite* for Strings, op.29/2 (1912–13); *The Planets,* op.32 (1914–16; private perf., London, Sept. 29, 1918; 1st complete public perf., London, Nov. 15, 1920); *Japanese Suite,* op.33 (1915); *A Fugal Overture,* op.40/1 (1922; as the overture to *The Perfect Fool,* London, May 14, 1923); *A Fugal Concerto* for Flute, Oboe, and Strings, op.40/2 (London, Oct. 11, 1923); *Egdon Heath: Homage to Hardy,* op.47 (1927; N.Y., Feb. 12, 1928); *A Moorside Suite* for Brass Band (London, Sept. 29, 1928); Double Concerto for 2 Violins and Orch., op.49 (1929; London, April 3, 1930); *Hammersmith: Prelude and Scherzo* for Military Band, op.52 (1930; 2nd version for Orch., 1931; London, Nov. 25, 1931); Jazz-band Piece (1932; ed. by I. Holst as *Capriccio,* 1967; London, Jan. 10, 1968); *Brook Green Suite* for Strings (1933); *Lyric Movement* for Viola and Chamber Orch. (1933; BBC, London, March 18, 1934); *Scherzo* (1933–34; London, Feb. 6, 1935). **CHAMBER:** *Fantasiestücke* for Oboe and String Quartet, op.2 (1896; rev. 1910); Quintet in A minor for Piano, Oboe, Clarinet, Horn, and Bassoon, op.3 (1896); Wind Quintet in A-flat major, op.14 (1903; London, Sept. 15, 1982); *Terzetto* for Flute, Oboe, and Viola (1925). **P i a n o :** *Toccata* (1924); *Chrissemas Day in the Morning,* op.46/1 (1926); 2 folk-song fragments: *O I hae seen the roses blaw* and *The Shoemaker,* op.46/2 (1927); *Nocturne* (1930); *Jig* (1932). **VOCAL:** *Light Leaves Whisper* for Chorus (c. 1896); *Clear and Cool* for Chorus and Orch., op.5 (1897); *Clouds o'er the Summer Sky* for Women's Chorus and Piano (c. 1898); *Ornulf's Drapa* for Baritone and Orch., op.6 (1898); 5 Part Songs, op.9a (1897–1900); *Ave Maria* for 8–part Women's Chorus, op.9b (1900); *I Love Thee* for Chorus (n.d.); 5 Part Songs, op.12 (1902–03); *King Estmere* for Chorus and Orch., op.17 (1903; London, April 4, 1908); *Thou Didst Delight My Eyes* for Chorus (c. 1903); *In Youth Is Pleasure* for Chorus (n.d.); *The Mystic Trumpeter* for Soprano and Orch., op.18 (1904; London, June 29, 1905; rev. 1912); *Songs from the Princess* for Women's Chorus, op.20a (1905); *4 Old English Carols* for Chorus or Women's Chorus and Piano, op.20b (1907); 2 carols for Chorus, Oboe, and Cello (1908, 1916); *Pastoral* for Women's Chorus (c. 1908); *Choral*

Hymns from the Rig Veda for Chorus and Orch. or Ensemble, op.26 (1908–10); *O England My Country* for Chorus and Orch. (1909); *The Cloud Messenger* for Chorus and Orch., op.30 (1909–10); *Christmas Day* for Chorus and Orch. (1910); 4 Part Songs for Women's Chorus and Piano (1910); *2 Eastern Pictures* for Women's Chorus and Harp (1911); *Hecuba's Lament* for Alto, Women's Chorus, and Orch., op.31/1 (1911); 2 Psalms for Tenor, Chorus, Strings, and Organ (1912); *The Swallow Leaves Her Nest* for Women's Chorus (c. 1912); *The Homecoming* for Men's Chorus (1913); *Hymn to Dionysus* for Women's Chorus and Orch., op.31/2 (1913); *A Dirge for 2 Veterans* for Men's Chorus, Brass, and Percussion (1914); *Nunc dimittis* (1915); *This I Have Done for My True Love*, op.34/1 (1916); *Lullay My Liking* for Soprano and Chorus, op.34/2 (1916); *Of One That Is So Fair* for Soprano, Alto, Tenor, Bass, and Chorus, op.34/3 (1916); *Bring Us in Good Ale*, op.34/4 (1916); 3 carols for Chorus and Orch. (1916–17); 3 Festival Choruses with Orch., op.36a (1916); 6 Choral Folk Songs, op.36b (1916); *Diverus and Lazarus* for Chorus (1917); 2 Part Songs for Women's Chorus and Piano (1917); *A Dream of Christmas* for Women's Chorus, and Strings or Piano (1917); *The Hymn of Jesus* for 2 Choruses, Women's Semi-chorus, and Orch., op.37 (1917; London, March 25, 1920); *Ode to Death* for Chorus and Orch., op.38 (1919; Leeds Festival, Oct. 6, 1922); *Short Festival Te Deum* for Chorus and Orch. (1919); *I Vow to Thee, My Country* for Chorus and Orch. (1921; arranged from *The Planets*, no. 4); *1ˢᵗ Choral Symphony* for Soprano, Chorus, and Orch., op.41 (1923–24; Leeds Festival, Oct. 7, 1925); *The Evening-watch* for Chorus, op.43/1 (1924); *Sing Me the Men* for Chorus, op.43/2 (1925); 7 Part Songs for Soprano, Women's Chorus, and Strings, op.44 (1925–26); 2 anthems (1927); *Wassail Song* for Chorus (1928–30); *A Choral Fantasia* for Soprano, Chorus, Organ, Strings, Brass, and Percussion, op.51 (1930; Gloucester Festival, Sept. 8, 1931); 12 Welsh Folk Songs for Chorus (1930–31); 6 choruses, some with accompaniment, op.53 (1931–32); 8 canons (1932). **S o n g s :** 4 Songs, op.4 (1896–98); 6 Songs, op.15 (1902–03); 6 Songs for Soprano and Piano, op.16 (1903–04); *Hymns from the Rig Veda*, op.24 (1907–08); *The Heart Worships* (1907); 4 Songs for Soprano or Tenor, and Violin, op.35 (1916–17); 12 Songs, op.48 (1929).

BIBL.: L. Dyer, *G. H.* (London, 1931); I. Holst, *G. H.: A Biography* (London, 1938; 2ⁿᵈ ed., 1969); E. Rubbra, *G. H.* (Monaco, 1947); I. Holst, *The Music of G. H.* (London, 1951; 3ʳᵈ ed., rev., 1986, including *H.'s Music Reconsidered*); U. Vaughan Williams and I. Holst, eds., *Heirs and Rebels* (London, 1959); I. Holst, *H.* (London, 1974; 2ⁿᵈ ed., 1981); idem, *A Thematic Catalogue of G. H.'s Music* (London, 1974); M. Short, ed., *G. H. (1874–1934): A Centenary Documentation* (London, 1974); I. Holst, ed., *A Scrapbook for the H. Birthplace Museum* (Cheltenham, 1978); J. Mitchell, *From Kneller Hall to Hammersmith: The Band Works of G. H.* (Tutzing, 1990); M. Short, *G. H.: The Man and His Music* (Oxford, 1990); R. Greene, *G. H. and a Rhetoric of Musical Character: Language and Method in Selected Orchestral Works* (N.Y., 1994); idem, *H.: The Planets* (Cambridge, 1995).—NS/LK/DM

Holst, Henry, Danish violinist of English descent; b. Copenhagen, July 25, 1899; d. there, Oct. 15, 1991. He was a pupil of Telmanyi at Copenhagen Cons. and of Hess in Berlin. In 1919 he made his debut in Copenhagen. After serving as concertmaster of the Berlin Phil. (1923–31), he was active as a soloist and chamber music player. He also taught at the Royal Manchester Coll. of Music (1931–46; 1950–53), the Royal Coll. of Music in London (1946–54), the Royal Danish Cons. of Music in Copenhagen (from 1953), and the Tokyo Univ. of the Arts (1961–63).—NS/LK/DM

Holst, Imogen (Clare), English conductor and writer on music, daughter of **Gustav(us Theodore von) Holst;** b. Richmond, Surrey, April 12, 1907; d. Aldeburgh, March 9, 1984. She studied at the St. Paul's Girls' School and the Royal Coll. of Music in London. From 1943 to 1951 she was music director of the Dartington Hall arts center. From 1952 to 1964 she was musical assistant to Britten; she also conducted the Purcell Singers (1953–67) and served as artistic director of the Aldeburgh Festival (from 1956). In 1975 she was made a Commander of the Order of the British Empire. Her most important writings include *Gustav Holst: A Biography* (London, 1938; 2ⁿᵈ ed., 1969), *The Music of Gustav Holst* (London, 1951; 3ʳᵈ ed., rev., 1986, including *Holst's Music Reconsidered*), and *A Thematic Catalogue of Gustav Holst's Music* (London, 1974). With C. Matthews, she ed. *Gustav Holst: Collected Facsimile Edition of Autograph Manuscripts of the Published Works* (London, 1974–83).

BIBL.: P. Cox and J. Dobbs, eds., *I. H. at Dartington* (Dartington, 1988).—NS/LK/DM

Holstein, Franz (Friedrich) von, German composer; b. Braunschweig, Feb. 16, 1826; d. Leipzig, May 22, 1878. His father was an army officer and at his behest, Holstein entered the Cadet School, concurrently studying music theory with Griepenkerl. While a lieutenant, he privately produced his operetta, *Zwei Nächte in Venedig* (1845). He fought in the Schleswig-Holstein campaign, then wrote a grand opera, *Waverley*, after Walter Scott. He sent the score to Hauptmann at the Leipzig Cons. who expressed willingness to accept Holstein as a student. Accordingly, he resigned from the army (1853) and studied with Hauptmann, H. Richter, and Moscheles at the Leipzig Cons. He then devoted himself to composition. He was also a poet, and wrote his own librettos. The style of his operas was close to the French type, popularized by Auber. He was a man of means, and left a valuable legacy for the benefit of indigent music students.

WORKS: DRAMATIC: O p e r a : *Der Haideschacht* (Dresden, Oct. 22, 1868); *Der Erbe von Morley* (Leipzig, Jan. 23, 1872); *Die Hochländer* (Mannheim, Jan. 16, 1876); *Marino Faliero* (unfinished). **ORCH.:** *Frau Aventiure*, overture (sketches only; orchestrated by A. Dietrich; Leipzig, Nov. 13, 1879). **CHAMBER:** Various works, including a Piano Trio. **VOCAL:** *Beatrice*, scene for Soprano, with Orch.; part-songs for Mixed and Men's Voices; etc.

Bibl.: G. Glaser, *F. v.H.: Ein Dichterkomponist des 19. Jahrhunderts* (Leipzig, 1930).—NS/LK/DM

Holt, Henry, Austrian-born American conductor and opera administrator; b. Vienna, April 11, 1934; d. Charlottesville, Va., Oct. 4, 1997. He studied with Strelitzer at Los Angeles City Coll. and with Dahl at the Univ. of Southern Calif. in Los Angeles. In 1961 he made his conducting debut with *Rigoletto* with the American Opera Co. in Los Angeles. He was general director of the Portland (Ore.) Opera from 1964 to 1966. From 1966 to 1984 he was general director of the Seattle Opera, where he conducted its acclaimed Wagner Festivals. —NS/LK/DM

Holt, Simeon ten, Dutch composer; b. Bergen, North Holland, Jan. 24, 1923. He studied with Honegger in Paris. After working at the Inst. for Sonology at the Univ. of Utrecht (1960–70), he was active with his own electronic music studio.

WORKS: ORCH.: *Diagonal Music* for Strings (1956); *Epigenese* (1964); *Centrifuga* (1979); *Une musique blanche* (1982). CHAMBER: Suite for String Quartet (1954); *Divertimento* for 3 Flutes (1957); *Triptichon* for 6 Percussionists (1965); String Quartet (1965); *Differenties* for 3 Clarinets, Piano, and Vibraphone (1969); *Scenario X* for Brass Quintet (1970); *Canto ostinato* for Instruments (1979); *Horizon* for Keyboard Instruments (1983–85); *Incantatie IV* for 5 Instruments (1990). Piano: *Compositions I-IV* (1942–45); Suite (1953); 2 sonatas (1953, 1959); *20 Bagatelles* (1954); *Allegro ex machina* (1955); *Diagonal Suite* (1957); *20 Epigrams* (1959); *Soloduiveldans I* (1959), *II* (1986), and *III* (1990); *5 Etudes* (1961); *Natalon in E* (1980); *Neither Shadow Nor Prey* for 2 Pianos (1995); *Meandres* for 4 Pianos (1997). VOCAL: *Atalon* for Mezzo-soprano and 36 Playing and Talking Instrumentalists (1967–68). ELECTRONIC: *Sevenplay* (1970); *Inferno I* (1970) and *II* (1971); *Modules I-VI* (1971); *I Am Sylvia* (1973); *Recital I* and *II* (1972–74).—LK/DM

Holt, Simon, English composer; b. Bolton, Feb. 21, 1958. He attended the Bolton Art Coll. (1977–78) before studying at the Royal Northern Coll. of Music in Manchester (1978–82), where his composition mentor was Anthony Gilbert. He first attracted notice as the featured composer at the Bath Festival in 1985. He served as a lecturer in composition at Royal Holloway, Univ. of London. Holt has received several grants and awards, and in 1993 was made a fellow of the Royal Northern Coll. of Music.

WORKS: DRAMATIC: Opera: *The Nightingale's to Blame* (1996–98; Huddersfield, Nov. 19, 1998). ORCH.: *Syrensong* (1987); *Walking With the River's Roar* for Viola and Orch. (1990–91); *Daedalus Remembers* for Cello and Orch. (Cheltenham, July 5, 1995). ENSEMBLE/CHAMBER: *Palace at 4 a.m.* for Flute, Oboe, Clarinet, and Cello (1980); *Mirrormaze* for 3 Flutes, 2 Oboes, 2 Clarinets, 2 Horns, Percussion, and Double Bass (1981); *Kites* for Flute, Oboe, Clarinet, Bassoon, Horn, and String Quintet (1983); *Shadow Realm* for Clarinet, Cello, and Harp (1983); *...era madrugada* for Piccolo, Clarinet, Horn, Piano, Viola, Cello, and Double Bass (1984); *Burlesca oscura* for Clarinet Quintet (1985); *Capriccio spettrale* for Flute, Clarinet, Horn, Trumpet, 2 Violins, 2 Violas, Cello, and Double Bass (1988); *Danger of the Disappearance of Things* for String Quartet (1989); *Sparrow Night* for Flute, Oboe, Clarinet, Horn, Harp, Piano, Violin, Viola, Cello, and Double Bass (1989); *Lilith* for Flute, Clarinet, Horn, Harp, Violin, Viola, Cello, and Double Bass (1990); *Icarus Lamentations* for 2 Clarinets, Cimbalon, Harp, and Strings (1992); *Eco- pavan* for Piano, Bass Flute, Hecklephone, Mandolin, Viola, Double Bass, Percussion, Harp, and Cimbalon (1998). VOCAL: *Wyrdchanging* for Mezzo-soprano and Chamber Ensemble (1980); *Canciones* for Mezzo-soprano, Flute, Oboe, Horn, Harp, and String Quintet (1986); *Ballad of the Black Sparrow* for 2 Sopranos, Mezzo-soprano, Tenor, Baritone, Bass, and Orch. (1988); *A Song of Crocuses and Lightning* for Soprano,

Horn, Harp, Viola, and Double Bass (1989); *Tanagra* for Soprano and Chamber Ensemble (1991); *A Knot of Time* for Soprano, Clarinet, Viola, and Double Bass (1992); *6 Caprices* for Countertenor (1998); *Sunrise's Yellow Noise* for Soprano and Orch. (1999). —NS/LK/DM

Holten, Bo, Danish conductor and composer; b. Copenhagen, Oct. 22, 1948. He studied at the Univ. of Copenhagen but was principally autodidact. He acquired a fine reputation as a conductor with his own vocal ensemble, Ars Nova, in Copenhagen. In 1990 he became a guest conductor of the BBC Singers in London. He has frequently led challenging concerts in which works from various eras and nations have appeared on the same program. As a composer, Holton has been particularly noted for his inventive counterpoint and melodic writing.

WORKS: DRAMATIC: *The Bond*, opera (1978–79); *Maria Paradis*, opera (Odense, March 6, 1999); film scores. ORCH.: *Mahler-Impromptu* (1972–73); *Venetian Rhapsody* for Chamber Orch. (1974); *Caccia* (1979); 2 syms.: No. 1 for Chorus and Orch. (1981–82) and No. 2, *Snderjysk Sommer Symfoni* for Soprano, Baritone, Chorus, and Orch. (1993); *Sinfonia Concertante* for Cello and Orch. (1985–86); Clarinet Concerto (1987); *Plainsongs* for Trumpet and Orch. (1989); *Le jardin magique de Ravel* (1991); Oboe Concerto (1992–93). CHAMBER: *Cut* for 6 Percussion (1980); *Pillows and Fragments* for 2 Trumpets, Horn, Trombone, and Tuba (1981); *Czerny Goes Mad* for 6 Percussion (1983); *Ancher Erectum* for 2 Percussion (1984); *Sarabande à trois* for Oboe, Cello, and Harpsichord (1984); *Waltz Ache I* for Vibraphone (1984); *Chaconne* for String Quartet (1987); *La marcia alla follia* for Flute, Violin, Viola, Cello, and Piano (1990). VOCAL: *Little Kirstin at the Stake* for Soprano and Chorus (1972); *Pavane Fantasia* for Soloists and Chorus (1974); Sonata for Soprano, Violin, and Cello (1976); *Tallis Variations* for Chorus and 9 Solo Strings (1976); *La douce nuit* for Chorus and Bells (1976); *The Garden of Love* for Tenor, Oboe, Clarinet, and String Quartet (1979); *Wave and Cut* for Chorus and 6 Percussion (1979); *Lumbago* for Chorus, Chamber Ensemble, and Synthesizer (1981); *The Clod and the Pebble* for 2 Choruses, 3 Clarinets, and Percussion (1982); *The Flame and the Coal* for Mezzo-soprano, Flute, Violin, Viola, Cello, and Piano (1983); *5 Motets* for Chorus and Organ (1983); *Imperia* for Chorus and Orch. (1983); *The Hours of Folly* for Medium or High Voice, Flute, Clarinet, and String Quartet (1984); *Tertia Die* for Chorus and Orch. (1985); *Waltz Ache II* for Chorus and Vibraphone (1985); *Pastell-Bilder* for Medium Voice, Flute, Clarinet, Guitar, and Percussion (1985–86); *Songs of Dusk* for Soprano, Bassoon, and Orch. (1987); *A Time for Everything* for Chorus (1990); *Rain and Rush and Rosy Bush* for Chorus (1991); *Night* for Chorus (1992).—NS/LK/DM

Holter, Iver (Paul Fredrik), Norwegian conductor and composer; b. Gausdal, Dec. 13, 1850; d. Oslo, Jan. 25, 1941. He entered the Univ. of Christiania as a student of medicine, but devoted much more time to music, which he studied under Svendsen. He then was a pupil of Jadassohn, Richter, and Reinecke at the Leipzig Cons. (1876–78). He became Grieg's successor as conductor of the Harmonien in Bergen (1882). From 1886 to 1911 he was conductor of the Musikföreningen in Christiania, and from 1890 to 1905, of the Handvaerkersångföreningen. In 1907 he founded and until 1921 conducted Holters Korförening. In 1919 the Norwegian government granted him an artist's stipend. He was ed. of the *Nordisk Musik Revue* (1900–06). His compositions include a Sym. (1885), a Violin Concerto, chamber music, several cantatas, as for the 300–year jubilee of Christiania (1924) and for the 900–year Olavs-jubilee (1930), choruses, and songs.—**NS/LK/DM**

Holtzner, Anton, German organist and composer; d. 1635. He was educated in Italy. His keyboard canzonas make use of free rhythmic transformation of themes in the manner of Frescobaldi's "variation canzonas." One of them is reprinted in A. Ritter's *Geschichte des Orgelspiels im 14.-18. Jahrhundert* (1884).—**NS/LK/DM**

Holý, Alfred, Portuguese harpist; b. Oporto, Aug. 5, 1866; d. Vienna, May 8, 1948. He studied violin and piano, then took harp lessons with Stank at the Prague Cons. (1882–85). He subsequently was 1st harpist in the orchs. of the German Opera in Prague (1885–96), the Berlin Royal Opera (1896–1903), and the Vienna Court Opera (1903–13). In 1913 he became 1st harpist of the Boston Sym. Orch., retiring in 1928. He publ. various harp transcriptions.—**NS/LK/DM**

Holyoke, Samuel (Adams), American composer; b. Boxford, Mass., Oct. 15, 1762; d. East Concord, N.H., Feb. 7, 1820. His father was a clergyman, and Holyoke was naturally drawn to composing hymns. Although he received no formal training in music, he began to compose early, following his innate musical instinct. He wrote his most popular hymn tune, *Arnheim*, when he was only 16. He attended Harvard Coll., graduating in 1789. In 1793 he organized a school of higher education, known as the Groton Academy (later Lawrence Academy). In 1800 he went to Salem, where he was active as a teacher; and also a member of the Essex Musical Assn. Holyoke was among those who did not favor the application of "fuging" tunes in sacred music, as advocated by Billings, and generally omitted that style of composition from his collections; in the preface to his *Harmonia Americana* he states his reason for this as being because of "the trifling effect produced by that sort of music; for the parts...confound the sense and render the performance a mere jargon of words." His first collection was the *Harmonia Americana* (Boston, 1791), followed by *The Massachusetts Compiler* (co- ed. with Hans Gram and Oliver Holden; Boston, 1795), *The Columbian Repository of Sacred Harmony* (Exeter, N.H., 1802; contains 734 tunes, many of his own composition), *The Christian Harmonist* (Salem, 1804), and *The Instrumental Assistant* (2 vols., Exeter, 1800–07; includes instructions for violin, German flute, clarinet, bass viol, and hautboy). He also publ. the song *Washington* (1790), and *Hark from the Tombs* (music for the funeral of Washington; 1800).

BIBL.: J. Willhide, *S. H., American Music-Educator* (diss., Univ. of Southern Calif., 1954); R. Patterson, *Three American "Primitives." A Study of the Musical Styles of S. H., Oliver Holden, and Hans Gram* (diss., Washington Univ., 1963).—**NS/LK/DM**

Holzbauer, Ignaz (Jakob), noted Austrian composer; b. Vienna, Sept. 17, 1711; d. Mannheim, April 7, 1783. He studied law and at the same time received instruction in music from members of the choir at St. Stephen's in Vienna. He also perused Gradus ad Parnassum by Fux, whom he met later and who advised him to go to Italy for further studies. He then proceeded to Venice, but soon returned home. For a brief period he served as Kapellmeister to Count Rottal of Holesov in Moravia. In 1737 he married Rosalie Andreides, a singer, and shortly thereafter they moved to Vienna, where he became a conductor and she a singer at the Court Theater; they also spent several years in Italy. In 1751 he was named Oberkapellmeister in Stuttgart. In 1753 he became Kapellmeister at the court of the elector Karl Theodor in Mannheim, a post he held until the court moved to Munich in 1778. He visited Rome in 1756, Turin in 1758, and Milan in 1759, during which visits he produced several operas. Holzbauer was greatly respected as a composer, especially for his church music; Mozart heard one of his masses in Mannheim in 1777 and found it excellent. He was an important figure among symphonic composers of the Mannheim school, writing some 65 works for orch. Of his operas, *Günther von Schwarzburg* (Mannheim, Jan. 5, 1777) is historically significant for its departure from Italian convention; it is thoroughly German in subject and treatment, and is noteworthy for the inclusion of accompanied recitative in place of the dialogue of the Singspiel. It was publ. in Mannheim in 1776, and reprinted in Denkmäler Deutscher Tonkunst, VIII-IX (1902). His other operas include *Il Figlio delle selve* (Schwetzingen, 1753), *L'isola disabitata* (Schwetzingen, 1754), *L'issipile* (Mannheim, Nov. 4, 1754), *Don Chisciotte* (Schwetzingen, 1755), *I Cinesi* (Mannheim, 1756), *Le nozze d'Arianna* (Mannheim, 1756), *Il Filosofo di campagna* (Mannheim, 1756), *La clemenza di Tito* (Mannheim, Nov. 4, 1757), *La Nitteti* (Turin, 1758), *Alessandro nell'Indie* (Milan, 1759), *Ippolito ed Aricia* (Mannheim, Nov. 4, 1759), *Adriano in Siria* (Mannheim, Nov. 4, 1768), and *Tancredi* (Munich, Jan. 1783). He also wrote ballet music for operas by J. A. Hasse: *L'Ipermestra* (Vienna, Jan. 8, 1744) and *Arminio* (Vienna, May 13, 1747). In addition, he composed 4 oratorios, 21 masses (also a *Deutsche Messe*), 37 motets, a Miserere, and other church music. His instrumental works, in addition to the syms., include concertos, divertimentos, string quartets, string quintets, etc. See U. Lehmann, ed., *Ignaz Holzbauer: Instrumentale Kammermusik*, in Das Erbe Deutscher Musik, 1st series, XXIV (1953).

BIBL.: H. Werner, *Die Sinfonien von I. H.* (diss., Univ. of Munich, 1942).—**NS/LK/DM**

Holzmair, Wolfgang (Friedrich), esteemed Austrian baritone; b. Vöcklabruck, April 24, 1952. He graduated from the Vienna Univ. of Economics but pursued training in voice with Rössl-Madjan and in lieder interpretation with Werba at the Vienna Academy of Music. After taking a prize at the 1982 International Song Competition of the Vienna Musikverein, he appeared in opera in Bern and Gelsenkirchen; also sang at the Bavarian State Opera in Munich, the Zürich Opera, and the Vienna State Opera. In 1989 he made his London debut in a recital at the Wigmore Hall. His U.S. debut followed in 1992 as soloist in Mahler's *Rückert-*

Lieder with Dohnányi and the Cleveland Orch. He made his N.Y. debut in 1993 in a recital at the Frick Museum, and that same year made his debut at London's Covent Garden as Papageno; also appeared at the Salzburg Festival. Holzmair's operatic repertoire includes Gluck's Orfeo, Don Giovanni, Rossini's Figaro, Eugene Onegin, Wolfram, Pélleas, and Wozzeck. His concert and oratorio repertoire is notably expansive, including works from all periods since the Baroque era, but he has become especially well known for his interpretations of Schubert and Mahler.—NS/LK/DM

Homer, Louise (Dilworth née Beatty), esteemed American contralto; b. Shadyside, near Pittsburgh, April 30, 1871; d. Winter Park, Fla., May 6, 1947. She studied in Philadelphia and at the New England Cons. of Music in Boston, where she received instruction in harmony from the noted American song composer **Sidney Homer** (1864–1953), who later became her husband (1895). She then went to Paris to study voice with Fidèle Koenig and dramatic acting with Paul Lhérie, making her operatic debut as Leonora in *La Favorite* in Vichy (June 5, 1898). She made her first appearance at London's Covent Garden as Lola in *Cavalleria rusticana* on May 9, 1899, and appeared there again in 1900; was also on the roster of the Théâtre Royal de la Monnaie in Brussels (1899–1900). On Nov. 14, 1900, she made her U.S. debut as Amneris with the touring Metropolitan Opera in San Francisco, which role she sang at her formal debut on Dec. 22, 1900, with the company in N.Y. She remained on its roster until 1919, the 1914–15 season excepted. She was acclaimed for her interpretation of Gluck's Orfeo in Paris in 1909, a role she repeated later that year at the Metropolitan Opera under Toscanini; she also created the roles of the Witch in Humperdinck's *Königskinder* (Dec. 28, 1910) and of Mona in Parker's opera (March 14, 1912) there. After singing with opera companies in Chicago (1920–25) and in San Francisco and Los Angeles (1926), she returned to the Metropolitan (1927), continuing on its roster until her farewell performance as Azucena on Nov. 28, 1929. She subsequently appeared in recitals with her daughter, the soprano Louise Homer Stires. In addition to Italian and French roles, she sang with great success such Wagnerian roles as Brangäne, Erda, Fricka, Ortrud, and Waltraute. Her nephew was **Samuel Barber**.

BIBL.: S. Homer, *My Wife and I* (N.Y., 1939); A. Homer, *L. H. and the Golden Age of Opera* (N.Y., 1973).—NS/LK/DM

Homer, Sidney, American composer; b. Boston, Dec. 9, 1864; d. Winter Park, Fla., July 10, 1953. He studied in Boston with Chadwick, then in Leipzig and Munich. In 1895 he married **Louise (Dilworth** née **Beatty),** his pupil, and went with her to Paris. He publ. a book of memoirs, *My Wife and I* (N.Y., 1939). He publ. about 100 songs, many of which won great favor, particularly *A Banjo Song*. Others include *Dearest, Requiem, Prospice, Bandanna Ballads, It was the time of roses, General William Booth Enters into Heaven, The Song of the Shirt, Sheep and Lambs, Sing me a song of a lad that is gone,*

and *The Pauper's Drive*. He also composed a Sonata for Organ (1922), Quintet for Piano and Strings (1932), Violin Sonata (1936), String Quartet (1937), and Piano Trio (1937).—NS/LK/DM

Homilius, Gottfried August, eminent German composer and organist; b. Rosenthal, Feb. 2, 1714; d. Dresden, June 5, 1785. He went to Leipzig to study composition and keyboard playing with Bach, where he also studied law at the Univ. In 1742 he settled in Dresden as organist of the Frauenkirche. In 1755 he was made cantor of the Kreuzkirche and teacher at the Kreuzschule, as well as music director of the Kreuzkirche, Frauenkirche, and Sophienkirche. After the Kreuzkirche was destroyed in 1760 in the wake of the Thirty Years's War, he concentrated his activities at the Frauenkirche. Homilius was a notable composer of German Protestant church music, producing more than 200 cantatas, some 60 motets, Magnificat settings, oratorios, and passion music. He also distinguished himself as a composer of organ music, especially in his esteemed chorale preludes.

BIBL.: R. Snyder, *The Choral Music of G.A. H. (1714–1785)* (diss., Univ. of Iowa, 1970); H. John, *G.A. H. und die evangelische Kirchenmusik Dresdens im 18. Jahrhundert* (diss., Univ. of Halle, 1973).—NS/LK/DM

Homs (Oller), Joaquín, Catalan composer; b. Barcelona, Aug. 22, 1906. He studied cello and later took lessons in theory with Roberto Gerhard (1931–37). He formed a constructivist style with thematic contents derived from Catalan melos.

WORKS: 7 string quartets (1938–68); Duo for Flute and Clarinet (1936); Wind Quintet (1940); Concertino for Piano and Strings (1946); Sextet (1959); String Trio (1968); *Impromptu for 10* (1970).

BIBL.: J. Casanova and A. Llanas, *J. H.* (Barcelona, 1996).—NS/LK/DM

Honauer, Leontzi, Alsatian harpsichordist and composer; b. probably in Strasbourg, c. 1730; d. c. 1790. He spent most of his career in the service of Prince Louis de Rohan in Paris. His chamber works with keyboard and his keyboard sonatas proved highly popular. He publ. 2 vols. of harpsichord sonatas (Paris, 1761, 1763), from which Mozart adapted four movements for his own early keyboard concertos. He also publ. a vol. of keyboard sonatas with violin accompaniment (Paris, 1764) and a vol. of quartets for Keyboard, 2 Violins, and Bass with horns ad libitum (Paris, 1770).—LK/DM

Honegger, Arthur (Oscar), remarkable French composer; b. Le Havre (of Swiss parents), March 10, 1892; d. Paris, Nov. 27, 1955. He studied violin in Paris with Capet, then took courses with Kempter and Hegar at the Zürich Cons. (1909–11). Returning to France in 1912, he entered the Paris Cons., in the classes of Gédalge and Widor; also took lessons with d'Indy. His name first attracted attention when he took part in a concert of Les Nouveaux Jeunes in Paris on Jan. 15, 1918. In 1920 Henri Collet publ. an article in *Comoedia* in which he drew a fortuitous parallel between the Russian Five and a group of young French composers whom he designated as Les Six. These Six were Honegger, Milhaud, Poulenc, Auric, Durey, and Tailleferre. The label persisted, even though the 6 composers went their separate ways and rarely gave concerts together. In the early years of his career, Honegger embraced the fashionable type of urban music, with an emphasis on machine-like rhythms and curt, pert melodies. In 1921 he wrote a sport ballet, *Skating Rink*, and a mock-militaristic ballet, *Sousmarine*. In 1923 he composed the most famous of such machine pieces, *Mouvement symphonique No. 1*, subtitled *Pacific 231*. The score was intended to be a realistic tonal portrayal of a powerful American locomotive, bearing the serial number 231. The music progressed in accelerating rhythmic pulses toward a powerful climax, then gradually slackened its pace until the final abrupt stop; there was a simulacrum of a lyrical song in the middle section of the piece. *Pacific 231* enjoyed great popularity and became in the minds of modern-minded listeners a perfect symbol of the machine age. Honegger's 2nd *Mouvement symphonique*, composed in 1928, was a musical rendering of the popular British sport rugby. His *Mouvement symphonique No. 3*, however, bore no identifying subtitle. This abandonment of allusion to urban life coincided chronologically with a general trend away from literal representation and toward absolute music in classical forms, often of historical or religious character. Among his most important works in that genre were *Le Roi David*, to a biblical subject, and *Jeanne d'Arc au bûcher*, glorifying the French patriot saint on the semimillennium of her martyrdom. Honegger's syms. were equally free from contemporary allusions; the first 2 lacked descriptive titles; his 3rd was entitled Liturgique, with a clear reference to an ecclesiastical ritual; the 4th was named Deliciae Basilienses, because it was written to honor the city of Basel; the somewhat mysterious title of the 5th, *Di tre re*, signified nothing more arcane than the fact that each of its movements ended on the thrice-repeated note D. Honegger spent almost all of his life in France, but he retained his dual Swiss citizenship, a fact that caused some biographers to refer to him as a Swiss composer. In 1926 he married the pianist-composer Andrée Vaurabourg (1894–1980), who often played piano parts in his works. In 1929 he paid a visit to the U.S.; he returned in 1947 to teach summer classes at the Berkshire Music Center at Tanglewood, but soon after his arrival was stricken with a heart ailment and was unable to complete his term; he returned to Paris and remained there until his death. He publ. a book, *Je suis compositeur* (Paris, 1951; Eng. tr., London, 1966).

WORKS: DRAMATIC: *Le Roi David*, dramatic Psalm for Narrator, Soloists, Chorus, and 15 Instruments (Mézières, June 11, 1921; rev. as an oratorio with Full Orch., 1923; Winterthur, Dec. 2, 1923); *Antigone*, opera (1924–27; Brussels, Dec. 28, 1927); *Judith*, biblical drama (Mézières, June 11, 1925; expanded as an opera, Monte Carlo, Feb. 13, 1926); *Amphion*, melodrama (1929; Paris, June 23, 1931); *Les Aventures du Roi Pausole*, operetta (1929–30; Paris, Dec. 12, 1930); *Cris du Monde*, stage oratorio for Soprano, Contralto, Baritone, Chorus, and Orch. (1930; Solothurn, May 3, 1931); *La Belle de Moudon*, operetta (Mézières, May 30, 1931); *Jeanne d'Arc au bûcher*, dramatic oratorio

(1934–35; concert version, without Prologue, Basel, May 12, 1938; stage premiere, in German, Zürich, June 13, 1942); *L'Aiglon*, opera (1935; Monte Carlo, March 11, 1937; in collaboration with J. Ibert); *Les Mille et Une Nuits*, spectacle for Soprano, Tenor, Chorus, and Orch. (Paris Exhibition, 1937); *Les Petites Cardinal*, operetta (1937; Paris, Feb. 20, 1938; in collaboration with J. Ibert); *Nicolas de Flue*, dramatic legend for Narrator, Chorus, Children's Chorus, and Orch. (1939; concert premiere, Solothurn, Oct. 26, 1940; stage premiere, Neuchâtel, May 31, 1941). **Ballet:** *Vérité-Mensonge*, marionette ballet (Paris, Nov. 1920); *Skating Rink* (1921; Paris, Jan. 20, 1922); *Sousmarine* (1924; Paris, June 27, 1925); *Roses de métal* (Paris, 1928); *Semiramis*, ballet-melodrama (1931; Paris, May 11, 1934); *Un Oiseau blanc s'est envolé* (Paris, June 1937); *Le Cantique des cantiques* (1937; Paris, Feb. 2, 1938); *La Naissance des couleurs* (1940; Paris, 1949); *Le Mangeur de rêves* (Paris, 1941); *L'Appel de la montagne* (1943; Paris, July 9, 1945); *Chota Roustaveli* or *L'Homme à la peau de léopard* (1945; Monte Carlo, May 5, 1946; scenes 2 and 3 by Harsányi and A. Tcherepnin); *De la musique* (1950). **Incidental Music:** *Les Dit des jeux du monde* for Flute, Trumpet, Percussion, and Strings (1918; as a ballet, Paris, Dec. 2, 1918); *La Mort de Sainte Alméenne* (1918); *La Danse macabre* (1919); *Saül* (Paris, June 16, 1922); *Fantasio* (1922); *Antigone* (1922); *La Tempête* (1923); *Liluli* (1923); *Le Miracle de Notre-Dame* (1925); *L'Impératrice aux rochers* (1925; Paris, Feb. 17, 1927); *Phèdre* (1926); *800 mètres* (1941); *Le Soulier de satin* for Soprano, Baritone, and Orch. (Paris, Nov. 17, 1943); *Charles le Téméraire* for Chorus, 2 Trumpets, 2 Trombones, and Percussion (1943–44; Mézières, May 27, 1944); *Hamlet* for Narrator, Chorus, and Orch. (Paris, Oct. 17, 1946); *Prométhée* (1946); *L'État de siège* (Paris, Oct. 27, 1948); *Tête d'or* (1948); *Oedipe-Roi* (1948). **Radio Music:** *Les Douze Coups de minuit*, "radio-mystère" for Chorus and Chamber Orch. (Paris Radio, Dec. 27, 1933); *Radio panoramique* for Tenor, Soprano, Organ, String Quintet, Wind Instruments, and Percussion (Geneva Radio, March 4, 1935; concert premiere, Paris, Oct. 19, 1935); *Christophe Colomb*, radio oratorio for 2 Tenors, Chorus, and Orch. (Lausanne Radio, April 17, 1940); *Les Battements du monde* for Woman's Voice, Child's Voice, Chorus, and Orch. (Lausanne Radio, May 18, 1944); *Saint François d'Assise* for Narrator, Baritone, Chorus, and Orch. (Lausanne Radio, Dec. 3, 1949). **Film:** *Les Misérables* (1934); *Mayerling* (1935); *Regain* (1937); *Mlle. Doctor* (1937); *Pygmalion*, after G.B. Shaw's play (1938); *Mermoz* (1943); *Bourdelle* (1950); 36 others. **ORCH.:** *Prélude pour "Aglavaine et Sélysette,"* after Maeterlinck (1916–17; Paris Cons. orch. class, April 3, 1917, composer conducting); *Le Chant de Nigamon* (1917; Paris, Jan. 3, 1920); *Entrée, Nocturne et Berceuse* for Piano and Chamber Orch. (Paris, 1919); *Pastorale d'été* (1920; Paris, Feb. 12, 1921); *Horace Victorieux*, "mimed sym." (1920–21; concert premiere, Lausanne, Oct. 30, 1921; mimed premiere, Essen, Dec. 28, 1927); *Marche funèbre* (1 section of *Les Mariés de la Tour Eiffel*, with other individual sections by Auric, Milhaud, Poulenc, and Tailleferre; Paris, June 18, 1921); *Chant de joie* (Paris, April 7, 1923); *Prélude pour "La Tempête,"* after Shakespeare (Paris, May 1, 1923); *Pacific 231* (*Mouvement symphonique No. 1*; 1923; Paris, May 8, 1924); *Piano Concertino* (1924; Paris, May 23, 1925; A. Vaurabourg soloist); Suite from incidental music to *L'Impératrice aux rochers* (1925); Suite from incidental music to *Phèdre* (1926); *Rugby* (*Mouvement symphonique No. 2*; Paris, Oct. 19, 1928, Ansermet conducting); *Prélude, Fugue et Postlude*, from the melodrama *Amphion* (1929; Geneva, Nov. 3, 1948); Cello Concerto (1929; Boston, Feb. 17, 1930); 5 syms.: No. 1 (1929–30; Boston, Feb. 13, 1931), No. 2 for Strings and optional Trumpet (1941; Zürich, May 18, 1942), No. 3, *Liturgique* (1945–46; Zürich,

Aug. 17, 1946), No. 4, *Deliciae Basilienses* (1946; Basel, Jan. 21, 1947), and No. 5, *Di tre re* (1950; Boston, March, 9, 1951); *Mouvement symphonique No. 3* (1932–33; Berlin, March 26, 1933); Suite from the film *Les Misérables* (1934; Paris, Jan. 19, 1935); *Prélude, Arioso et Fughetta sur le nom de BACH* for Strings (arranged by A. Hoérée from the piano version, 1936; Paris, Dec. 5, 1936); *Nocturne* (Brussels, April 30, 1936); *La Marche sur la Bastille* for Band, from incidental music for Romain Rolland's pageant *Le Quatorze Juillet* (Paris, July 14, 1936); *La Grande Barrage*, "image musicale" (1942); *Jour de fête suisse*, suite from the ballet *L'Appel de la montagne* (1943; Winterthur, Nov. 14, 1945); 2 extracts from the film *Mermoz* (1943); *Sérénade à Angélique* for Small Orch. (Zürich Radio, Nov. 19, 1945); *Concerto da camera* for Flute, English Horn, and Strings (Zürich, May 6, 1949); *Toccata* (1 section of *La Guirlande de Campra*, with other individual sections by Lesur, Manuel, Tailleferre, Poulenc, Sauguet, and Auric, 1950; complete work, Aix-en-Provence Festival, July 31, 1952); *Suite archaïque* (1950–51; Louisville, Feb. 28, 1951); *Monopartita* (Zürich, June 12, 1951). **CHAMBER:** 2 violin sonatas (1916–18; 1919); 3 string quartets (1916–17; 1934–36; 1936–37); *Rapsodie* for 2 Flutes, Clarinet (or 2 Violins, Viola), and Piano (1917); *Danse de la chèvre* for Flute (1919); Sonatina for 2 Violins (1920); Viola Sonata (1920); Cello Sonata (1920); *Hymn* for 10 String Instruments (1920); Sonatina for Clarinet or Cello and Piano (1921–22); 3 *contrepoints* for Flute, English Horn, Violin, and Cello (1923); *Prélude et Blues* for Quartet of Chromatic Harps (1925); Sonatina for Violin and Cello (1932); *Petite suite* for any 2 Treble Instruments and Piano (1934); Sonata for Solo Violin (1940); *Sortilèges* for Ondes Martenot (1946); *Intrada* for Trumpet and Piano (1947); *Romance* for Flute and Piano (1953). **P i a n o :** 3 *pièces* (Scherzo, Humoresque, and *Adagio espressivo*; 1910); 3 *pièces: Hommage à Ravel* (1915); *Prélude et Danse* (1919); *Toccata et Variations* (1916); 7 *pièces brèves* (1919–20); *Sarabande* (1920); *Le Cahier Romand*, 5 pieces (1921–23); *Hommage à Albert Roussel* (1928); Suite for 2 Pianos (1928); *Prélude, Arioso et Fughetta sur le nom de BACH* (1932; arranged for Strings by A. Hoérée in 1936); *Scenic-Railway* (1937); *Partita* for 2 Pianos (1940; arranged from 3 *contrepoints*); 2 *esquisses*, in Obouhov's simplified notation (1943–44); *Souvenir de Chopin* (1947). **VOCAL:** *Cantique de Pâques* for 3 Women's Voices, Women's Chorus, and Orch. (1918; Toulouse, March 27, 1923); *Pâques à New York* for Voice and String Quartet (1920); *Chanson de Ronsard* for Voice, Flute, and String Quartet (1924); 3 *chansons de la petite sirène* for Voice, Flute, and Strings or String Quartet (1926); *La Danse des morts*, oratorio for Narrator, Soloists, Chorus, Organ, and Orch. (1938; Basel, March 1, 1940); *Chant de libération* for Baritone, Unison Chorus, and Orch. (1942; Paris, Oct. 22, 1944); *Une Cantate de Noël* for Baritone, Chorus, Children's Chorus, Organ, and Orch. (sketched 1941, completed 1953; Basel, Dec. 18, 1953). **S o n g s :** 4 *poèmes* (1914–16); 6 *poèmes de Apollinaire* (1915–17; Nos. 1 and 3–6 orchestrated as 5 *poèmes de Apollinaire*, 1916–17); 3 *poèmes de Paul Fort* (1916); 6 *poésies de Jean Cocteau* (1920–23); 2 *chants d'Ariel* (1923; also arranged for Orch.); 3 *poèmes de Claudel* (1939–40); 3 *Psalms* (1940–41); 5 *mélodies- minute* (1941); 4 *Songs* for Low Voice and Piano (1944–45).

BIBL.: Roland-Manuel, *A. H.* (Paris, 1925); A. George, *A. H.* (Paris, 1926); W. Tappolet, *A. H.* (in Ger., Zürich, 1933; 2nd Ger. ed., Zürich, 1954; Fr. ed., Neuchâtel, 1938; 2nd Fr. ed., Neuchâtel, 1957); C. Gérard, *A. H.: Catalogue succinct des oeuvres* (Brussels, 1945); J. Bruyr, *H. et son oeuvre* (Paris, 1947); J. Matter, *H. ou La Quête de joie* (Lausanne, 1956); A. Gauthier, *A. H.* (London, 1957); M. Landowski, *H.* (Paris, 1957); W. Reich, ed., *A. H., Nachklang: Schriften, Photos, Dokumente* (Zürich, 1957); J. Fes-chotte, *A. H.: L'Homme et son oeuvre* (Paris, 1966); P. Meylan, *A. H., Humanitäre Botschaft der Musik* (Frauenfeld, 1970); J. Mailliard and J. Nahoum, *Les Symphonies d'A. H.* (Paris, 1974); G. Spratt, *The Music of A. H.* (Cork, 1987); H. Halbreich, *A. H.: Un musicien dans la cité des hommes* (Paris, 1992; Eng. tr., 1999); M. Kelkel, ed., *Colloque international A. H.- Darius Milhaud* (Paris, 1994); J. Roy, *Le groupe des six: Poulenc, Milhaud, H., Auric, Tailleferre, Durey* (Paris, 1994).—**NS/LK/DM**

Honegger, Henri (Charles), Swiss cellist; b. Geneva, June 10, 1904; d. Conches, Aug. 4, 1992. He studied with Ami Briquet in Geneva, Klengel at the Leipzig Cons., and Casals and Alexanian in Paris. He was 1st cellist in the Orchestre de la Suisse Romande in Geneva until 1964; he appeared as a soloist with orchs. throughout Europe, North and South America, and Japan, and also appeared as a recitalist.—**NS/LK/DM**

Honegger, Marc, French musicologist and lexicographer; b. Paris, June 17, 1926. He was educated in Paris, where he studied with Chailley and Masson (music history and theory) at the Sorbonne (1947–50), Santiago Riera (piano), Ion Constantinesco and Bigot (conducting), and Migot (composition) at the École Supérieure de Musique, and at the Univ. (docteur-ès-lettres, 1970, with 2 diss., *Les chansons spirituelle de Didier Lupi Second et les débuts de la musique protestante en France au XVIe siècle*, publ. in Lille, 1971, and *Les messes de Josquin des Pres dans la tablature de Diego Pisador (Salamanque 1552): Contribution a l'étude des alterations au XVIe siècle*). After working at the Inst. of Musicology at the Univ. of Paris (1954–58), he taught at the Univ. of Strasbourg (1958–91). He was secretary general (1973–77) and president (1977–80) of the Société française de musicologie, and vice-president of the International Musicological Soc. (1982–92).

WRITINGS: *La musique française de 1830 à 1914* (1962); *Dictionnaire de la musique* (2 vols., Strasbourg, 1970; 4th ed., rev., 1993); *Science de la musique* (4 vols., Paris, 1976); *Georges Migot humaniste* (Strasbourg, 1977); *Catalogue des oeuvres musicale de Georges Migot* (Strasbourg, 1977); *Dictionnaire des oeuvres de la musique vocale* (3 vols., Paris, 1991–92); *Dictionnaire usuel de la musique* (Paris, 1995); *Connaissance de la musique* (Paris, 1996); with P. Prévost, *Dictionnaire de la musique vocale: Lyrique, Religieuse et profane* (Paris, 1998).—**NS/LK/DM**

Höngen, Elisabeth, esteemed German mezzo-soprano; b. Gevelsberg, Dec. 7, 1906; d. Vienna, Aug. 7, 1997. She studied voice with Hermann Weissenborn and Ludwig Horth in Berlin. In 1933 she made her operatic debut as Lady Macbeth at the Wuppertal Opera, where she was a member until 1935. She then sang with the Düsseldorf Opera (1935–40) and the Dresden State Opera (1940–43). In 1943 she joined the Vienna State Opera, where she remained one of its principal artists during the next 2 decades. In 1947 she was honored as an Austrian Kammersängerin. She first sang at London's Covent Garden in 1947 as a member of the visiting Vienna State Opera, returning there in 1959–60. From 1948 to 1950, and again in 1959, she appeared at the Salzburg Festivals. In 1951 she was a soloist in Beethoven's 9th Sym. under Furtwängler at the reopening of the Bayreuth Festival. On Jan. 10, 1952, she made her Metropolitan Opera debut in N.Y. as Hérodias, returning there that season as Waltraute and Klytemnestra. She also was a guest artist in Berlin, Munich, Paris, Milan, Buenos Aires, and other operatic centers. From 1957 to 1960 she was a prof. at the Vienna Academy of Music. Among her other notable portrayals were Dorabella, Marcellina, Ortrud, Eboli, and Fricka.—NS/LK/DM

Hood, George, American minister, writer on music, and composer; b. Topsfield, Mass., Feb. 10, 1807; d. Minneapolis, Sept. 24, 1882. He studied in local singing-schools and with Lowell Mason in Boston. After being ordained in Lawrenceville, N.J. (1848), he held pastorates in Bath, N.Y. (1849–50) and Southport, N.Y. (1851–53), and then was a teacher or agent in Chester, Pa., and Princeton, N.J. He was supply minister in Bethel, N.Y. (1874–78) and Minneapolis (1880), and then superintendent of Shakopee Mission, Minn. Hood's most important book was *A History of Music in New England with Biographical Sketches of Reformers and Psalmists* (Boston, 1846). He also publ. *Can All Learn to Sing?* (Boston, c. 1840) and *Musical Manual Designed as a Text-book for Classes or Private Pupils in Vocal or Instrumental Music* (Philadelphia, 1864). He also composed congregational hymn tunes.—LK/DM

Hood, Mantle, American ethnomusicologist and composer; b. Springfield, Ill., June 24, 1918. He studied composition privately with Toch (1945–50), and was enrolled at the Univ. of Calif., Los Angeles (B.A., 1951; M.A. in composition, 1951). He then continued his studies at the Univ. of Amsterdam (Ph.D., 1954, with the diss. *The Nuclear Theme as a Determinant of Patet in Javanese Music*; publ. in Groningen, 1954). In 1954 he joined the faculty at the Univ. of Calif., Los Angeles, becoming a full prof. there in 1962 and in 1961 was appointed director of its Inst. of Ethnomusicology. In 1956–57 he traveled to Indonesia on a Ford Foundation fellowship, and in 1976 received a Fulbright fellowship for study in India. In 1976 he became an adjunct prof. at the Univ. of Md.; in 1977 was a visiting prof. at Yale Univ. and at Wesleyan Univ. He publ. *The Ethnomusicologist* (N.Y., 1971; 2nd ed., rev., 1982) and *The Paragon of the Roaring Sea* (Wilhelmshaven and N.Y., 1988), and also contributed valuable articles on oriental music to learned journals and musical encyclopedias. His compositions include a symphonic poem, *Vernal Equinox* (1955), Woodwind Trio (1950), 6 duets for Soprano and Alto Recorder (1954), and piano pieces.—NS/LK/DM

Hoof, Jef van, Belgian composer; b. Antwerp, May 8, 1886; d. there, April 24, 1959. He studied composition at the Antwerp Cons. with Gilson, Mortelmas, and Huybrechts. He composed 3 operas: *Tycho-Brahe* (1911), *Meivuur* (1916), and *Jonker Lichthart* (1928). Other works included 5 syms. (1938, 1941, 1945, 1951, 1956), choruses, lieder, and piano pieces. His style of composition was neo-Romantic, with a penchant for expansive sonorities.—NS/LK/DM

Hoogstraten, Willem van, Dutch conductor; b. Utrecht, March 18, 1884; d. Tutzing, Sept. 11, 1965. He

studied violin with Alexander Schmuller; then with Bram Eldering at the Cologne Cons. and with Ševčik in Prague. He played concerts with **Elly Ney,** whom he married in 1911 (divorced in 1927). From 1914 to 1918 he conducted the Krefeld orch., and in 1922 he was engaged as conductor of the summer concerts of the N.Y. Phil. (until 1938); was its assoc. conductor (1923–25). He was conductor of the Portland (Ore.) Sym. Orch. from 1925 to 1938. After conducting the Salzburg Mozarteum Orch. (1939–45), he was a guest conductor in Europe.—NS/LK/DM

Hook, James, English organist and composer; b. Norwich, June 3, 1746; d. Boulogne, 1827. He exhibited a precocious talent as a boy, and took lessons with Garland, organist of the Norwich Cathedral. In 1764 he went to London, where he played organ at various entertainment places. In 1765 he won a prize for his Parting Catch. He was subsequently organist and music director at Marylebone Gardens (1769–73) and at Vauxhall Gardens (1774–1820). His last position was at St. John's, Horsleydown. He publ. a manual, *Guida di musica,* in 2 parts (1785, 1794).

WORKS: DRAMATIC: Theater (all 1st perf. in London): *Cupid's Revenge* (June 12, 1772); *The Lady of the Manor* (Nov. 23, 1778); *The Fair Peruvian* (March 8, 1786); *Jack of Newbury* (May 6, 1795); *Wilmore Castle* (Oct. 21, 1800); *The Soldier's Return* (April 23, 1805); *The Invisible Girl* (April 28, 1806); *The Fortress* (July 16, 1807); *Safe and Sound* (August 28, 1809); etc. **OTHER:** Many oratorios and odes; concertos for harpsichord; sonatas, sonatinas, and divertimentos for piano; songs.—NS/LK/DM

Hooker, John Lee, American blues singer, guitarist, and songwriter; b. near Clarksdale, Miss., Aug. 22, 1917. A Mississippi Delta blues musician who made his mark long after relocating to a northern city, Hooker preserved a basic, direct style employing minimal, droning guitar work and idiosyncratic timing that was dubbed "boogie." It was a style that proved remarkably popular, adaptable, and influential in a career lasting more than 50 years and including early hits like "Boogie Chillen'" and "I'm in the Mood" in the late 1940s and 1950s and award-winning collections such as *The Healer* in the late 1980s and 1990s.

Hooker was the son of William Hooker, a minister, and Minnie Ramsey Hooker. His parents divorced when he was a child and his mother remarried William Moore, a sharecropper and blues performer who taught his stepson to play and appeared with him locally. Hooker left home as a teenager and lived primarily in Memphis and Cincinnati in the 1930s and early 1940s, working at menial jobs while moonlighting as a musician. In 1943 he settled in Detroit, marrying a woman named Martella with whom he had four sons, two of whom, Robert and John Jr., later became musicians and worked with him. He and his wife divorced in 1970.

Hooker performed in clubs in Detroit and eventually was spotted by record distributor Bernard Besman, for whom he made his first recordings on Nov. 3, 1948. These included "Boogie Chillen'," which, like nearly all of his songs, he was credited with having written, though in this case Besman claimed a cowriting credit. Besman leased Hooker's recordings to L.A.–based Modern Records, which released "Boogie Chillen'" in December. In February 1949 it topped the R&B charts. By then Hooker had also begun to record for producer Joe Von Battle, who leased his recordings to other labels under pseudonyms. In this manner, though Hooker was nominally under exclusive contract to Modern, he in fact released scores of records for others over the next five years. Nevertheless, his next hit recording was on Modern, as both sides of the single "Hoogie Boogie"/"Hobo Blues" entered the R&B charts in the spring of 1949 and reached the Top Ten.

In December 1949, Hooker again entered the R&B Top Ten with "Crawlin' King Snake" on Modern, but his next R&B chart single, "Huckle Up Baby," in February 1950 was on Besman's Sensation Records. In the fall of 1951, back on Modern, he scored the biggest hit single of his career with "I'm in the Mood" (music and lyrics by Hooker and Besman), which topped the R&B charts in November.

Hooker signed an exclusive contract in October 1955 with Chicago-based independent label Vee-Jay Records, after which he curtailed but did not cease his recording for other companies. He had recorded primarily alone with his electric guitar previously; on Vee-Jay he began to use a rhythm section and sometimes other instruments. By the end of the 1950s he sometimes reverted to performing with only an acoustic guitar, as he began to find work at colleges and music festivals during the folk music boom and recorded such albums as Riverside's *The Country Blues of John Lee Hooker* (1959) and Vee-Jay's *The Folk Lore of John Lee Hooker* (1961). His appearance at the Newport Folk Festival on June 24, 1960, was recorded and released as an album by Vee-Jay. Among his other 1960 recordings was the single "Travelin'," which earned him his first Grammy nomination for Best Rhythm & Blues Performance.

Hooker's next significant hit came in the spring of 1962 with "Boom Boom," which made the Top 40 of the R&B charts and even entered the pop charts. That year, he first toured Great Britain, as part of the American Folk Blues Festival, and his records began to be released there, influencing many emerging blues bands. He returned for a month-long tour in June 1964, at which time his 1956 recording "Dimples" made the U.K. Top 40. Evidence of his impact on the British rock scene was provided by The Animals' recording of "Boom Boom," which became a U.S. Top 40 pop hit in January 1965.

With the demise of Vee-Jay Records, Hooker again turned to extensive freelancing, notably recording the albums *John Lee Hooker and Seven Nights* for Verve/Folkways (1965) and *The Real Folk Blues* for Chess (1966). He then signed to ABC Records, which released his albums on its Impulse! and BluesWay subsidiaries and later on ABC itself during his eight-year tenure. As usual, he made recordings for other labels as well.

Hooker moved to Oakland, Calif., in 1970 and began to associate more with younger, white rock musicians. As a result, he released two double-LPs in early 1971 that vastly expanded his following. The first was *Hooker 'n Heat* (Liberty Records), recorded with the blues-rock group Canned Heat, with whom he toured. The second was *Endless Boogie* (ABC Records), on which he was accompanied by such popular rock musicians as Steve Miller. Both albums spent several months in the charts.

Hooker's next ABC album, *Never Get Out of These Blues Alive* (1972) featured guest appearances by Van Morrison and Elvin Bishop, among others, and was another pop chart entry. He followed it later in the year with *Live at Soledad Prison* (ABC), which earned him a second Grammy nomination for Best Ethnic or Traditional Recording. His third Grammy nomination, in the same category, came for the July 1973 United Artists album *John Lee Hooker's Detroit (1948–52)*, a triple-LP set of his vintage recordings. Meanwhile, his musical influence on blues-based rock performers was highlighted by the Top 40 success of ZZ Top's Hookerlike boogie song "La Grange" (music and lyrics by Billy Gibbons, Frank Beard, and Joe Hill) in June 1974.

Hooker concluded his ABC Records contract with the September 1974 release of *Free Beer and Chicken*, on which listeners noted uncredited guest appearances by Joe Cocker and others. After leaving ABC, he was less active as a recording artist, although a 1978 double album, *The Cream* (Tomato Records), recorded at the Keynote club in Palo Alto, Calif., is notable. In June 1980 his profile was heightened by a guest appearance in the film *The Blues Brothers*, and he contributed to the 1986 film *The Color Purple*. His next album release also came in 1986 with *Jealous* on Pausa Records, which earned his fourth Grammy nomination for Best Traditional Blues Recording.

Hooker enjoyed a major comeback and the biggest record sales of his career when the Chameleon label released his album *The Healer* in September 1989. The disc featured guest appearances by several performers who acknowledged his influence, including Canned Heat, Carlos Santana, Bonnie Raitt, Robert Cray, Los Lobos, and George Thorogood. It spent eight months in the U.S. charts while going gold in six other countries. Both the album and a track from it, Hooker's duet with Raitt on a remake of "I'm in the Mood," earned Grammy nominations for Best Traditional Blues Recording, with the latter winning the award. Hooker earned his seventh Grammy nomination for Best Traditional Blues Recording in 1990 for his participation in an all-star group assembled to play music for the film *The Hot Spot*. Released by Antilles Records in September 1990, the movie's soundtrack album also featured Miles Davis, and the Grammy-nominated track was "Coming to Town" (music and lyrics by Jack Nitzsche).

Released in September 1991 on the Virgin Records subsidiary Charisma, Hooker's follow-up to *The Healer* was *Mr. Lucky*, on which he was joined by Booker T. Jones, Van Morrison, Keith Richards of The Rolling Stones, Carlos Santana, and Johnny Winter, among others. The album spent three months in the U.S. charts and hit the Top Ten in the U.K. It brought Hooker his eighth Grammy nomination for Best Traditional Blues Album. *Boom Boom*, released in November 1992, was less successful, though it reached the U.K. charts and spawned a U.K. Top 40 hit in the title song.

Hooker returned to the U.K. Top 40 in May 1993, cobilled with Van Morrison on a remake of Morrison's hit with the rock group Them, "Gloria" (music and lyrics by Van Morrison). Upon the release of *Chill Out* in February 1995, Hooker announced that he would no longer tour. The album spent several weeks in the U.S. charts and won a Grammy for Best Traditional Blues Album. Van Morrison produced Hooker's next album, *Don't Look Back*, released in March 1997. It reached the U.S. charts and won two Grammys, for Best Traditional Blues Album and for Best Pop Collaboration with Vocals, for the track "The Healing Game" (music and lyrics by Van Morrison), a duet between Hooker and Morrison. Hooker was presented a Lifetime Achievement Award at the 2000 Grammy Award ceremonies.

DISC.: *The Country Blues of John Lee Hooker* (1959); *House of the Blues* (1959); *That's My Story* (1960); *John Lee Hooker Plays and Sings the Blues* (1961); *Burnin'* (1962); *Boogie Chillun* (1962); *The Big Soul of John Lee Hooker* (1963); *It Serves You Right to Suffer* (1965); *The Real Folk Blues* (1966); *Hooker 'N' Heat* (with Canned Heat; 1970); *Endless Boogie* (1971); *Free Beer and Chicken* (1974); *The Cream* (1977); *Never Get out of These Blues Alive* (1978); *This Is Hip* (1980); *Chess Masters* (1982); *Solid Sender* (1984); *Jealous* (1986); *Simply the Truth* (1988); *The Healer* (1989); *Mr. Lucky* (1991); *The Ultimate Collection, 1948–1990* (1991); *The Best of John Lee Hooker, 1963 to 1974* (1992); *John Lee Hooker: The Legendary Modern Recordings 1948–1954* (1993); *I Feel Good* (1995); *Chill Out* (1995); *Boom Boom* (1995); *The Very Best of John Lee Hooker* (1995); *Alone* (1996); *Don't Look Back* (1997); *His Best Chess Sides* (1997); *Best of Friends* (1998); *The Complete '50s Chess Recordings* (1998); *20th Century Masters: The Best of John Lee Hooker—The Millennium Collection* (1999).—**WR**

Hooper, Edmund, English organist and composer; b. North Halberton, Devon, c. 1553; d. London, July 14, 1621. He first sang at Exeter Cathedral, and then became a member of the Westminster Abbey Choir in 1582. In 1588 he was made Master of the Choristers and in 1606 organist there. In 1604 he became a Gentleman of the Chapel Royal, where he served as co-organist with Orlando Gibbons from 1615. He was esteemed as a composer of sacred music, much of which was publ. in contemporary collections. A few of his keyboard works were included in the *Fitzwilliam Virginal Book.*—**LK/DM**

Hooters, The, popular band of the 1980s; f. 1980, Philadelphia, Pa. **MEMBERSHIP:** Eric Bazilian, voc., kybd. (b. Philadelphia); Robert Hyman, voc., gtr. (b. Meriden, Conn.); David Uosikkinen, drm. (b. Cherltenham, Pa.); John Lilley, gtr. (b. West Chester, Pa.); Francis Smith, bs. (b. Mt. Laurel, N.J.). Hyman, Bazilian and Rick Chertoff met while attending the Univ. of Pa. They formed a band called Wax and played around the Philly area. By the time they were singed to Arista records in 1977, the band was called Baby Grand and had taken on overtones of progressive rock. However, it was the wrong sound at the wrong time in the era of the burgeoning new wave. They put out two albums that bombed badly.

Deep in debt, Chertoff set of to seek his fortune as a record producer. Hyman and Bazilian set out in a different musical direction. They started incorporating mandolins and other instruments as well as Caribbean rhythms into their music. They took the name for their new group, The Hooters, from what an engineer at a demo session called one of their odd instruments, the Melodica (a cross between a harmonica and a keyboard). The duo put together a new band, with a couple of former members of Robert Hazard's band (he wrote "Girls Just Wanna Have Fun"). They began playing in the Philadelphia area, developing a good sized following. At one point, the band played four sets a night, six nights a week. They kept up at this pace for two and a half years, but did not attract any interest from the record companies. Burned out after two and a half years, the band called it quits toward the end of 1982.

In the meantime, Epic had tapped Chertoff to produce an album by vocalist Cyndi Lauper. He called in his old buddies, and they played nearly every instrument on the album, with the exception of the drums and bass. That album, *She's So Unusual*, propelled Lauper to stardom, and Hazard's "Girls Just Wanna Have Fun" was the first hit off the album. Her collaboration with Hyman, "Time After Time," was the second.

Re-energized by their success with Lauper, the Hooters reformed during the summer of 1983 and went into the studio with Chertoff to cut an indie record. That disc, *Amore*, sold over 100,000 copies. That and the growing success of Lauper's record led to the group signing with Columbia. Their major label debut, *Nervous Night*, produced four singles, the album rock hit "All You Zombies" (which hit #58 pop), the #21 hit "And We Danced," the #18 "Day by Day," and "Where Do the Children Go" (#38). While the album went on to sell over a million copies and hit #12, it was not really indicative of what the Hooters did; it was a more straight ahead pop rock album, eschewing a lot of the Caribbeanisms and odd instrumental flourishes that were their live forte. Millions of people around the world heard them play live when they performed as the opening act on the Philadelphia stage for Live Aid in 1985.

The group spent the next year on the road, opening for Squeeze, Bryan Adams, and a host of others. When they went into the studio to follow up *Nervous Night*, they made a more Hooters-like album, using the acoustic instruments and some new ideas they picked up on the road. 1987's *One Way Home* went gold, but generated no real hits. Similarly, *Zig-Zag* caught Bazilian and Hyman at a strange and vulnerable time. Everything was changing, including the prevalent medium for recordings. A friend of theirs had died while they were on the road. They were closing in on 40. They recorded a version of "500 Miles" with special guest vocalists Peter Paul and Mary. The album did well overseas but stiffed in America.

Still a popular live attraction (and a huge one in Europe, Asia and Australia), the band continued touring. They played at Roger Water's "Wall" extravaganza in 1990, but it took them three years to come out with *Out of Body* and by then, their fan base in the U.S. had dwindled to a few diehards. They have made a couple of records in Europe, where they still remain popular. Bazilian wrote the hit song "One of Us," a #4 single in

1996. They keep busy doing sessions, having worked with Patti Smith on a cover of Bruce Springsteen's "Atlantic City," Mick Jagger, Sophie B. Hawkins, and Willie Nelson, to name a few. In the late 1990s, they signed to Chertoff's Blue Gorilla label.

DISC.: *Amore* (1983); *Nervous Night* (1985); *One Way Home* (1987); *Zig Zag* (1989); *Out of Body* (1993); *Johnny B.* (1997); *Live in Germany* (1998).—**HB**

Hope-Jones, Robert, English organ manufacturer; b. Hooton Grange, Cheshire, Feb. 9, 1859; d. (suicide) Rochester, N.Y., Sept. 13, 1914. As a boy, he entered the employ of Laird Bros., engineers at Birkenhead, then became chief electrician of the National Telephone Co. At the same time, was engaged as a church organist. In 1889 he set up his own business as an organ builder. In 1903 he settled in America, where he was connected with the E.M. Skinner Co. of Boston. In 1907 he founded the Hope-Jones Organ Co. at Tonawanda, N.Y., but sold the plant and his patents in 1910 to the Rudolph Wurlitzer Co. of N.Y. He introduced many innovations into the building of electrical organs, and the development of the modern organ in the U.S. owes much to his inventive genius. One of the finest of his organs is in the Auditorium at Ocean Grove, N.J.—**NS/LK/DM**

Hopekirk, Helen, Scottish-born American pianist, teacher, and composer; b. Edinburgh, May 20, 1856; d. Cambridge, Mass., Nov. 19, 1945. Following training with A. C. Mackenzie, she attended the Leipzig Cons. (1876–78). On Nov. 28, 1878, she made her debut as soloist with the Gewandhaus Orch. in Leipzig, and then toured the Continent and Great Britain. In 1882 she married the businessman, music critic, and landscape painter William A. Wilson, who subsequently served as her manager. On Dec. 7, 1883, she made her U.S. debut as soloist with the Boston Sym. Orch., and then toured the country until 1887. After piano lessons with Leschetizky in Vienna (1887–89), she pursued training in composition in Paris (1892–94). From 1897 to 1901 she taught at the New England Cons. of Music in Boston, and thereafter privately. She continued to pursue her career as a pianist, making her farewell appearance in 1939 in a concert devoted entirely to her own compositions. In 1918 she became a naturalized American citizen. As a performer, she gave the first U.S. performances of several works by Debussy and other French composers. In her own works, she gave primary concern to producing scores notable for their modal melodies and harmonies. She arranged and ed. *Seventy Scottish Songs* (Boston, 1905).

WORKS: Concertstück for Piano and Orch. (1894); Piano Concerto (Boston, Dec. 27, 1900, composer soloist); 2 violin sonatas (n.d., 1891); many piano pieces; choral works; 91 songs.

BIBL.: C. Hall and H. Tetlow, *H. H. 1856–1945* (Cambridge, Mass., 1954).—**NS/LK/DM**

Hopf, Hans, German tenor; b. Nuremberg, Aug. 2, 1916; d. Munich, June 25, 1993. He studied in Munich with Paul Bender and in Oslo with Ragnvald Bjärne. In 1936 he made his operatic debut as Pinkerton at the Bavarian Landesbühnen in Munich, and then sang with the Augsburg Opera (1939–42), the Dresden State Opera (1942–43), the Oslo Opera (1943–44), and the Berlin State Opera (1946–49). In 1949 he joined the Bavarian State Opera in Munich, and sang there regularly until his retirement in 1988. In 1951 he was a soloist in Beethoven's 9th Sym. under Furtwängler at the reopening of the Bayreuth Festival, where he later sang from 1961 to 1966. From 1951 to 1953 he appeared at London's Covent Garden, returning there in 1963. On March 15, 1952, he made his Metropolitan Opera debut in N.Y. as Walther von Stolzing, remaining on the roster until 1953; he was again on its roster for the 1954–55, 1960–62, and 1963–64 seasons. He also sang at the Salzburg Festivals from 1954, and was a guest artist in Milan, Moscow, Zürich, San Francisco, Chicago, and Buenos Aires. Among his prominent roles were Florestan, Max in *Der Freischütz*, Siegfried, Parsifal, Tristan, Tannhäuser, Otello, and the Kaiser in *Die Frau ohne Schatten*.—**NS/LK/DM**

Hopkins (real name, **Reynolds**), **Antony,** English pianist, conductor, broadcaster, writer on music, and composer; b. London, March 21, 1921. He was a pupil of Cyril Scott and Gordon Jacob at the Royal Coll. of Music in London (1939–42). He then served as music director of the Intimate Opera Co. (1952–64), for which he composed several scores. He also wrote music for films, radio, and the theater, and was active as a radio broadcaster, hosting the series "Talking about Music" (1954–92). His books include *Understanding Music* (1979), *The Nine Symphonies of Beethoven* (1980), *The Concertgoer's Companion* (2 vols., 1984, 1986), *Sounds of the Orchestra* (1993), and *The Seven Concertos of Beethoven* (1996). In 1976 he was made a Commander of the Order of the British Empire.—**NS/LK/DM**

Hopkins, (Charles) Jerome, American pianist, organist, music educator, and composer; b. Burlington, Vt., April 4, 1836; d. Athenia, N.J., Nov. 4, 1898. He was almost totally self-taught as a musician. About 1853 he settled in N.Y., where he began performing and lecturing. From 1856 he actively promoted the music of American composers. He organized the Orpheon Free Schools in 1861 to give instruction in sight-singing and basic music training to working-class children. In all, he claimed to have taught more than 30,000 pupils. From 1864 he gave annual concerts in order to raise funds for his schools, and also ed. the *Orpheonist and Philharmonic Journal*, which served to promote his schools and concerts, and which also provided him a forum for his musical and social criticism. In 1871 he launched a series of "Piano-Lecture Concerts," and made tours of the Eastern and Midwestern regions of the U.S. In 1889–90 he toured England. Hopkins became well known for his sensational methods and eccentric professional conduct, and was frequently involved in law suits. He ed. *A Collection of Sacred Song* (1859), *Canticles of the Church* (1861), and *Jerome Hopkins' Second Collection of Church Music* (1870). His niece was **Amy Fay.**

WORKS: DRAMATIC: O p e r a : *Dumb Love* (1878); *Taffy and Old Munch* (1882). **ORCH.:** *Serenade* (1870); Piano

Concerto (1872); Sym. (n.d.). **CHAMBER**: Piano Trio (1857–58); piano pieces. **VOCAL**: *Victory Te Deum* (1862); *Vespers Service* (1875); *Samuel*, oratorio (1877); songs. —**NS/LK/DM**

Hopkins, Claude (Driskett), influential early jazz pianist, leader (composer); b. Alexandria, Va., Aug. 24, 1903; d. Riverdale, Bronx, N.Y., Feb. 19, 1984. He was raised in Washington, D.C., where both parents were on the staff of Howard Univ. He began playing piano at the age of seven, and later spent two years studying medicine and music at Howard Univ. (B.A., 1923), and did a further year's study at the Washington Cons. He played in college orchs., then led his own band in Atlantic City (summer 1924), played briefly in N.Y. with Wilbur Sweatman, then again organized his own band. He sailed to Europe in September 1925, leading his own band (including Bechet) for the Josephine Baker revue. He toured throughout Europe with the show, then led his own band (comprised of Joe Hayman and several European musicians) in Italy and Spain (early 1926). He returned to N.Y. in spring of 1926 and led his own band through 1930. He then took over the leadership of Charlie Skeets's band, which performed together through 1941, including long residencies at the Roseland Ballroom (1931–34) and the Cotton Club (late 1934–36). Members included at times Jabbo Smith, Vic Dickenson, and Edmond Hall. Orlando Robersons's vocal on "Trees" turned the song into a huge hit. Hopkins was on the West Coast with a new band from 1941–42, then worked briefly in an Aircraft Plant Band during the war. From the mid-1940s through mid-1950s, he led his own groups, which decreased in size from full bands to mostly five or six piece units. From 1954, Hopkins began making regular appearances with Henry "Red" Allen. He also played in Herman Autrey's Trio in late 1950s and with clarinetist Sol Yaged in 1960. From 1960–66, he regularly led his own small group in small clubs. From late 1967–69 he played with Wild Bill Davison in The Jazz Giants. He worked briefly with Roy Eldridge in N.Y. in 1970. He played many jazz festivals during the 1970s and toured Europe with Earle Warren and Dicky Wells. Hopkins fell sick in his later years and died in a nursing home.

DISC.: *Singin' in the Rain* (1935); *Yes Indeed* (1960); *Let's Jam* (1961); *Swing Time* (1963); *Soliloquy* (1972); *Crazy Fingers* (1972). —**JC/LP**

Hopkins, Edward (John), English organist, choirmaster, writer on music, and composer; b. London, June 30, 1818; d. there, Feb. 4, 1901. He was a pupil of T. F. Walmisley. After serving as organist at Mitcham Church (1834–38), St. Peter's, Islington (1838–41), and St. Luke's (1841–43), he won distinction as organist and choirmaster at the Temple Church (1843–98). His output included many anthems and services. With E. Rimbault, he publ. the important vol. *The Organ: Its History and Construction* (London, 1855; 3rd ed., aug., 1877).

BIBL.: C. Pearce, *The Life and Works of E. J. H.* (London, 1910).—**NS/LK/DM**

Hopkins, John Henry, American clergyman and writer of hymn tunes; b. Pittsburgh, Oct. 28, 1820; d.

Hudson, N.Y., Aug. 13, 1891. He studied at schools of divinity and served as a deacon in several churches. His Christmas carol *We Three Kings of Orient Are* is a perennial favorite. He publ. a collection, *Carols, Hymns and Songs* (1862).—**NS/LK/DM**

Hopkinson, Francis, American statesman, writer, and composer; b. Philadelphia, Sept. 21, 1737; d. there, May 9, 1791. By profession a lawyer, he was deeply interested in music. He learned to play the harpsichord, and also studied theory with James Bremner. Hopkinson was a member of an amateur group in Philadelphia who met regularly in their homes to play music, and also gave public concerts by subscription. He was the composer of the first piece of music written by a native American, *Ode to Music*, which he wrote in 1754, and of the first original American song, *My days have been so wondrous free* (1759). At least, this is the claim he makes in the preface to his *7 Songs* [actually 8, the last having been added after the title page was engraved] for the harpsichord or forte piano, dated Philadelphia, Nov. 20, 1788, and dedicated to George Washington: "I cannot, I believe, be refused the Credit of being the first Native of the United States who has produced a Musical Composition." Hopkinson wrote an *Ode in Memory of James Bremner* (1780) and some songs. He also wrote the text for and arranged the music of the "oratorical entertainment" *America Independent, or The Temple of Minerva* (1781), the music by Handel et al. Hopkinson's music was couched in the conventional English style, modeled after pieces by T. A. Arne, but he possessed a genuine melodic gift. He also provided Benjamin Franklin's glass harmonica with a keyboard, introduced improvements in the quilling of the harpsichord, and invented the Bellarmonic, an instrument consisting of a set of steel bells. He was probably the compiler of *A Collection of Psalm Tunes with a Few Anthems*, etc. A MS book of songs in his handwriting is in the possession of the Library of Congress in Washington, D.C. Hopkinson's son, Joseph Hopkinson, wrote the words to *Hail Columbia*.

BIBL.: O. Sonneck, *F. H., The First American Poet-composer (1737–1791) and James Lyon, Patriot, Preacher, Psalmodist (1735–1794): Two Studies in American Music* (Washington, D.C., 1905); H. Milligan, *The First American Composer: 6 Songs by F. H.* (Boston, 1918); G. Hastings, *The Life and Works of F. H.* (Chicago, 1926).—**NS/LK/DM**

Hoppin, Richard H(allowell), American musicologist; b. Northfield, Minn., Feb. 22, 1913; d. Columbus, Ohio, Nov. 1, 1991. He studied piano at the École Normale de Musique in Paris (1933–35), and musicology at Harvard Univ. (M.A., 1938; Ph.D., 1952). He was on the music faculty of the Univ. of Tex., Austin (1949–61); in 1961 he was appointed prof. of music at Ohio State Univ. In 1959–60 he was the recipient of a Guggenheim fellowship. He ed. the important collection *The Cypriot-French Repertory of the Manuscript Torino, Biblioteca Nazionale, J. II. 9.*, Corpus Mensurabilis Musicae, XXI (1960–63), and also publ. the invaluable *An Introduction to Medieval Music* (N.Y., 1978).—**NS/LK/DM**

Horák, Adolph, Bohemian pianist and teacher, brother of **Eduard Horák;** b. Jankovic, Feb. 15, 1850; d.

Vienna, Jan. 14, 1921. With his brother he established the Horák Pianoforte School in Vienna. In collaboration, they publ. a valuable *Klavierschule*. Adolph alone wrote *Die technische Grundlage des Klavierspiels*.—NS/LK/DM

Horák, Antonin, Czech conductor and composer; b. Prague, July 2, 1875; d. Belgrade, March 12, 1910. He was an opera conductor in Prague and Belgrade. His own opera, *Babička* (Grandmother), was fairly successful at its first performance, in Prague (March 3, 1900). He also wrote cantatas and other choral works.—NS/LK/DM

Horák, Eduard, Bohemian pianist and teacher, brother of **Adolph Horák**; b. Holitz, April 22, 1838; d. Riva, Lake of Garda, Dec. 16, 1892. With his brother he founded in Vienna the Horák Pianoforte School, which soon acquired a European reputation. In collaboration with F. Spigl, he publ. *Der Klavier unterricht in neue, natürliche Bahnen gelenkt* (2 vols., Vienna, 1892), and with his brother, a practical manual, *Klavierschule*. —NS/LK/DM

Horák, Josef, Czech bass clarinetist; b. Znojmo, March 24, 1931. He attended the Brno Cons. (1945–51). He was a clarinetist in the Brno State Phil. and Prague Radio Sym. Orch. On Oct. 20, 1955, he made his debut as a performer on the bass clarinet, and began a career as a virtuoso on that instrument; along with the Dutch bass clarinetist Harry Sparnaay, Horák is responsible for the revival of interest in the bass clarinet. In 1963 he and the pianist Emma Kovárnová formed the chamber duo Due Boemi di Praga, and performed numerous specially commissioned works by Alois Hába, Jolivet, Martin, Messiaen, Stockhausen, and many, many others. In 1972 he was appointed to the faculty of the Prague Cons. —NS/LK/DM

Horak, Wenzel (Vaclav) Emanuel, Bohemian organist and composer; b. Mscheno-Lobes, Jan. 1, 1800; d. Prague, Sept. 3, 1871. He studied briefly with Josef Schubert, then received instruction in composition from B. D. Weber, Jan Kuchar, Vitasek, and Tomaschek. He taught voice (1831–32) and theory (1837–38) at the Prague Organ School; taught voice at the Prague teacher-training college (1837–53); was director of the Zofin Academy (1851–53) and was also active as a church organist. He wrote 11 masses, 3 Requiems, 2 Te Deums, and other works. He also publ. several theoretical treatises. NS/LK/DM

Horenstein, Jascha, distinguished Russian-born American conductor; b. Kiev, May 6, 1898; d. London, April 2, 1973. He began his musical training in Königsberg as a piano student of his mother, and he also studied with Max Brode. In 1911 he went to Vienna, where he studied philosophy at the Univ. and was a pupil of A. Busch (violin), Marx (theory), and Schreker (composition) at the Academy of Music; he then continued his training with Schreker at the Berlin Hochschule für Musik (1920). He served as an assistant to Furtwängler and began his career conducting the Schubert Choir

in Berlin. In 1923 he was a guest conductor with the Vienna Sym. Orch. Returning to Berlin, he conducted the Blüthner Concerts (1924) and was conductor of the Berlin Sym. Orch. (1925–28); he also appeared as a guest conductor with the Berlin Phil. In 1929 he became music director of the Düsseldorf Opera, but was removed from that position in 1933 by the Nazi regime because he was a Jew. After conducting in Europe, Australia, New Zealand, and Palestine, he went to the U.S. in 1940 and became a naturalized American citizen. Following the end of World War II, he resumed his career in Europe. He became especially admired in England, where he appeared as a guest conductor with the London Sym. Orch. In 1961 he made his debut at London's Covent Garden conducting *Fidelio*. While Horenstein's repertoire ranged widely from the Baroque era to the 20th century, he acquired his greatest renown as an interpreter of Bruckner and Mahler.

BIBL.: *Le Grand Baton* (June 1976).—NS/LK/DM

Horký, Karel, Czech composer; b. Štěmechy, near Třebíč, Sept. 4, 1909; d. Brno, Nov. 27, 1988. He played in a military band as a boy and also studied bassoon. He took lessons in composition with V. Polivka and Pavel Haas, then entered the Prague Cons. as a student of Křička, graduating in 1944. He taught harmony (1945–52) and was director (1964–71) at the Brno Cons.

WORKS: DRAMATIC: O p e r a : *Jan Hus* (Brno, May 27, 1950); *Hejtman Šarovec* (Brno, 1953); *Jed z Elsinoru* (The Poison from Elsinor), freely after Shakespeare's *Hamlet* (Brno, Nov. 11, 1969); *Dawn* (Brno, July 4, 1975); *Atlantida* (1980). **B a l l e t :** *Lastura* (The Shell; Brno, Oct. 23, 1945); *Král Ječmínek* (King Ječmínek; Brno, Sept. 21, 1951). **ORCH.:** *Klythia*, symphonic poem (1941); *Romantic Sinfonietta* (1944); Cello Concerto (1953); Violin Concerto (1955); 5 syms. (1959, 1964, 1971, 1974, 1977); *Serenade* for Strings (1963); Bassoon Concerto (1966); Horn Concerto (1971); *Fateful Preludes* for Piano and Orch. (1972); *Dimitrov*, symphonic poem, in memory of the chairman of the Bulgarian Communist Party (1972). **CHAMBER:** 4 string quartets (1938, 1954, 1955, 1963); Violin Sonata (1943); Suite for Wind Quintet (1943); Nonet (1958); Clarinet Quintet (1960); piano pieces. **VOCAL:** Choruses; songs.—NS/LK/DM

Horn, Charles Edward, English singer, conductor, and composer, son of **Karl Friedrich Horn**; b. London, June 21, 1786; d. Boston, Oct. 21, 1849. He studied with his father, and also received vocal guidance from Rauzzini. On June 26, 1809, he made his debut as a singer in M. P. King's *Up All Night* at London's Lyceum Theatre. After further vocal training with Thomas Welsh, he returned to the stage in 1814. He also was active as a conductor and composer for the theater. In 1827 he went to N.Y. and staged several of his operas. After serving as music director of London's Olympic Theatre (1831–32), he was music director of N.Y.'s Park Theatre (1832–47) and conductor of Boston's Handel and Haydn Soc. (from 1847). In addition to his stage works, he wrote the oratorio *The Remission of Sin* (N.Y., May 7, 1835; perf. in London as *Satan*, March 18, 1845).

BIBL.: R. Montague, *C.E. H.: His Life and Works* (diss., Fla. State Univ., 1959).—NS/LK/DM

Horn, Karl Friedrich, German organist and composer, father of **Charles Edward Horn;** b. Nordhausen, April 13, 1762; d. Windsor, Aug. 5, 1830. He settled in England at the age of 20, and with the patronage of Count Bruhl, Saxon ambassador in London, became a fashionable teacher. In 1823 he became organist of St. George's Chapel at Windsor. With Wesley, he prepared an English ed. of Bach's *Wohltemperierte Clavier* (1810–13). He also wrote *A Treatise on Harmony with Practical Examples* (London, 1821). He composed 12 sets of piano variations, with flute obbligato, 6 piano sonatas, and *Military Divertimentos.*—**NS/LK/DM**

Horn, Shirley, American jazz singer; b. Washington, D.C., May 1, 1934. She is also a fine pianist who is among the very best self-accompanying vocalists. She can swing powerfully as both a singer and a player, but it is her understated gift for interpreting the emotional implications of a lyric that makes her so effective on slow numbers. Though her languid ballad approach and lithe, harmonically rich piano style remain essentially unchanged since she began recording in the early 1960s, her popular breakthrough did not take place until the late 1980s, when she signed with Verve, her current label.

She began playing piano at age four, and quickly proved to be a gifted and single-mindedly devoted student. She studied composition at Howard Univ. at age 12 and later attended the school as an undergraduate, and began working in Washington, D.C., nightspots. Her first album, *Embers and Ashes,* in 1960, caught the attention of Miles Davis, who recruited her to open for him at the Village Vanguard. During the early 1960s she worked major jazz clubs, recorded albums with Quincy Jones and Jimmy Jones for Mercury and ABC/Paramount and sang on the soundtracks of the movies *For the Love of Ivy* and *A Dandy in Aspic.* By the mid-1960s, she dropped out of the national jazz scene and moved back to Washington to raise her daughter, playing enough around the city to sustain her reputation as a local legend. Her comeback started with an appearance at the 1981 North Sea Jazz Festival, which resulted in the best of her four SteepleChase albums. By the late 1980s, she was well on her way to her present jazz-star status. Her skill as an accompanist has been utilized by Carmen McRae on her Novus album *Sarah—ated to You* and Toots Thielemans on his EmArcy album *For My Lady.* She also appears in the 1990 movie *Tune in Tomorrow* and sings two songs on Wynton Marsalis's excellent soundtrack.

Disc.: *Loads of Love/Shirley Horn with Horns* (1963); *Travelin' Light* (1965); *Violets for Your Furs* (1981); *I Thought About You* (1987); *Softly* (1988); *Close Enough for Love* (1989); *You Won't Forget Me* (1991); *Here's to Life* (1992); *Light Out of Darkness* (1993); *I Love You, Paris* (1994); *The Main Ingredient* (1996); *Loving You* (1997); *I Remember Miles* (1998); *Ultimate S. H.* (1999).—**AG**

Hornbostel, Erich Moritz von, eminent Austrian musicologist; b. Vienna, Feb. 25, 1877; d. Cambridge, England, Nov. 28, 1935. He studied philosophy in Vienna and Heidelberg; received a Ph.D. in chemistry from the Univ. of Vienna (1900). In 1905–06 he was the assistant of Stumpf in Berlin; in 1906 he went to the U.S. to record and study Indian music (Pawnee); from 1906 to 1933, was director of the Phonogramm-Archiv in Berlin, and concurrently a prof. at the Univ. of Berlin (1917–33); then went again to the U.S. In 1934 he went to England. He was a specialist in Asian, African, and other non-European music; also investigated the problems of tone psychology; contributed hundreds of articles to scholarly publications on these subjects. He ed. a collection of records, *Musik des Orients* (Lindstrom, 1932); from 1922 until his death, was co-ed., with C. Stumpf, of the *Sammelbände für vergleichende Musikwissenschaft.* Hornbostel's writings were prepared for reissue, ed. by K. Wachsmann et al. (The Hague, 1975 et seq.).—**NS/LK/DM**

Horne, Lena (Mary Calhoun), attractive American singer and actress; b. N.Y., June 30, 1917. Horne was primarily a nightclub entertainer, though her career, lasting 65 years, also encompassed stints with several big bands during the Swing Era, four Broadway shows, 16 motion pictures, and numerous recordings and radio and television performances. Starting out as a dancer, she drew attention because of her photogenic appearance, then developed into an accomplished singer best known for her clearly enunciated readings of classic pop songs, many of them composed by Harold Arlen. His "Stormy Weather" became a signature song for her, and she enjoyed her greatest theatrical success with his musical *Jamaica.* But her own experience as an African-American star during a period of racial turmoil in the U.S. gradually became the dominant subject of her art, which she confirmed in her 60s with her award-winning, autobiographical Broadway show *Lena Horne: The Lady and Her Music.*

Horne's parents were Edwin F. Horne, a gambler, and Edna Scottron Horne. They divorced when she was three, but she and her mother continued to live in the home of her paternal grandparents in N.Y. When she was about five her mother embarked on a career as a traveling actress, and she remained with her grandparents until the age of six or seven, when her mother took her on the road, periodically depositing her with relatives or other caretakers, primarily in the South. When she was 11 or 12 she was returned to the care of her grandparents, but they died within months of each other when she was 13 or 14, after which she was cared for by a family friend. When she was 14 her mother, now remarried, returned to claim her.

In the fall of 1933, Horne successfully auditioned as a dancer at the Cotton Club in Harlem. With the start of the club's spring season on March 23, 1934, she was given a featured part in its revue, the *Cotton Club Parade,* singing "As Long as I Live" (music by Harold Arlen, lyrics by Ted Koehler). At this time she began to take voice lessons. During the fall 1934 season, while continuing to perform at the Cotton Club, she made her Broadway debut in *Dance with Your Gods* (N.Y., Oct. 6, 1934); it ran only nine performances.

Horne left the Cotton Club in 1935 to sing with Noble Sissle and His Orch. She made her recording debut with Sissle on March 16, 1936, singing "That's

What Love Did to Me" and "I Take to You," released on Decca Records. Later in the year, she left Sissle, and in January 1937 in Pittsburgh married Louis J. Jones, a Democratic Party political operative who had a patronage job registering and filing papers at the city coroner's office. She gave birth to a daughter in December 1937. Though she had intended to retire from show business, she accepted an offer to appear in *The Duke Is Tops*, a low-budget, all-black movie musical. It was released in July 1938. She returned to performing in the Broadway revue *Blackbirds of 1939* (N.Y., Feb. 11, 1939), but it closed after nine performances. In February 1940 she gave birth to a son, but in the fall she separated from her husband (they divorced in June 1944) and moved to N.Y. to revive her career.

Horne found work on local and network radio shows and made several film shorts. In December 1940 she became the singer in Charlie Barnet's orchestra. She left Barnet to accept a solo engagement at the prestigious Café Society Downtown nightclub in N.Y. in March 1941. She remained at the club until September, when she moved to L.A. In December she made her first solo recordings for RCA Victor Records, the label with which she was primarily associated for the next 35 years. In February 1942 she began to appear at the Little Troc club, moving to the Mocambo in July. In between these engagements, she was scouted by the movie studios, and she signed a seven-year contract with MGM, becoming the first African American contracted to a Hollywood studio. Unfortunately, except for two all-black musicals, she was restricted to performing in one or two production numbers in each of her films. The first of these was *Panama Hattie*, released in October. While at MGM, she worked with vocal coach Kay Thompson.

Horne's limited movie schedule allowed her to continue her career as a nightclub performer, and in October 1942 she returned to N.Y. and appeared at the Café Lounge of the Savoy-Plaza Hotel into early 1943 before returning to Hollywood. Her first film to be released in 1943 was the all-black musical *Cabin in the Sky*, in which she costarred with Ethel Waters, singing two songs by Harold Arlen (music) and E. Y. Harburg (lyrics); it came out in May, and Horne toured to promote it. Two months later she had another costarring role in an all-black musical, having been loaned to 20th Century–Fox for *Stormy Weather*, in which she revived the Arlen-Koehler title song and made it her own. Before the end of the year, she was also seen singing in *Thousands Cheer* (September) and *I Dood It* (November), and in 1944 she was in *Swing Fever* (January), *Broadway Rhythm* (April), and *Two Girls and a Sailor* (June). After this, her film appearances became less frequent.

During World War II, Horne undertook many tours of military bases for the USO, and after the war she established herself as a live performer at major nightclubs and hotels in the U.S. and Europe. Meanwhile, she made a few more appearances in MGM films: *Ziegfeld Follies* (March 1946); *Till the Clouds Roll by* (December 1946); *Words and Music* (December 1948); and *Duchess of Idaho* (July 1950). In December 1947 she married Leonard George "Lennie" Hayton, a staff composer, arranger, and conductor at MGM, who left the studio in 1953 to become her musical director.

Horne performed extensively throughout the first half of the 1950s. She scored her first record hit with a revival of the 1928 song "Love Me or Leave Me" (music by Walter Donaldson, lyrics by Gus Kahn), which enjoyed renewed popularity as the title song of a film biography of Ruth Etting, who introduced it. Horne's RCA Victor recording reached the Top 40 in July 1955. In March 1956 she appeared in a final MGM movie musical, *Meet Me in Las Vegas*. On Dec. 31 her performance at the Waldorf-Astoria Hotel in N.Y. was recorded; released as the LP *Lena Horne at the Waldorf Astoria*, it became a Top Ten hit in August 1957. By then she had given up nightclub work temporarily to prepare for her starring role in *Jamaica* (N.Y., Oct. 31, 1957), with songs by Harold Arlen and E. Y. Harburg. The musical was perceived as little more than a star vehicle, but her performance was enough to keep it running 555 performances. During its run, her album *Give the Lady What She Wants* reached the charts in November 1958.

Horne's next chart appearance came with her album of songs from George Gershwin's *Porgy and Bess* recorded with Harry Belafonte; it reached the Top Ten in May 1959 and earned her a Grammy nomination for Best Vocal Performance, Female. Her second Grammy nomination, in the same category, came for her 1961 album *Lena at the Sands*, which chronicled one of her regular appearances at the Sands Hotel in Las Vegas. Also in 1961, her theatrical production *Lena Horne in Her Nine O'Clock Revue* tried out in Toronto and New Haven but closed before reaching Broadway. Both of her 1962 albums, *Lena on the Blue Side* and *Lena ... Lovely and Alive*, reached the charts, and the latter earned her a third Grammy nomination for Best Solo Vocal Performance, Female.

Starting in 1963, Horne became increasingly involved in the Civil Rights Movement. Her political concerns were expressed in the single "Now!" (music by June Styne, adapted from the Israeli melody "Hava Nagila," lyrics by Betty Comden and Adolf Green), recorded for 20th Century–Fox Records, which reached the pop charts and the R&B Top 40 in November. For the balance of the 1960s she devoted more time to political activity and benefits and reduced her schedule of recordings and paid live performances.

Horne began to become more visible as an entertainer again at the end of the decade, taking a dramatic role in the film *Death of a Gunfighter*, her first movie appearance in 13 years, in April 1969, and starring in her first U.S. network television special, *Monsanto Night Presents Lena Horne* in September. That month she appeared at Caesar's Palace with Harry Belafonte, her first engagement in Las Vegas in three years. She and Belafonte then did a television special together. *Harry and Lena* was broadcast March 22, 1970, and was nominated for an Emmy for Outstanding Single Program—Variety or Musical. In May her duet album with guitarist Gabor Szabo, *Lena and Gabor*, on Skye Records, became her first chart record in seven years. It featured "Watch What Happens" (music by Michel Legrand, English lyrics by Norman Gimbel), which reached the R&B Top 40.

Lennie Hayton's death on April 24, 1971, following the recent deaths of Horne's father and son, caused her to be less active in the early 1970s. But in 1973 she launched a lengthy international tour cobilled with Tony Bennett; they performed together on Broadway in the fall of 1974 and finished in March 1975 in L.A. In addition to her usual performances, in the late 1970s, Horne spent six months of 1978 starring in a West Coast production of the Richard Rodgers–Lorenz Hart musical *Pal Joey*, and she was featured in the film version of the Broadway musical *The Wiz* (October 1978), directed by Sidney Lumet, who at the time was married to her daughter.

Horne undertook a "farewell" tour from June to August 1980, then decided not to retire. Instead she mounted an autobiographical Broadway revue, *Lena Horne: The Lady and Her Music* (N.Y., May 12, 1981), which earned excellent reviews and ran 333 performances, concluding on Broadway on her 65th birthday, June 30, 1982. She was given a special Tony Award for the show, and a double-LP cast album reached the charts and won Grammys for Best Cast Show Album and Best Pop Vocal Performance, Female. After the show closed in N.Y., she toured with it around the U.S.; she took it to London in the summer of 1984.

Horne was semi-retired by the mid-1980s. In September 1988 she released a new album, *The Men in My Life*, on the Three Cherries label, and it earned her a Grammy nomination for Best Jazz Vocal Performance, Female. After making selected live appearances in 1993, notably a tribute to her friend Billy Strayhorn at the JVC Jazz Festival in N.Y., she signed to Blue Note Records and on May 17, 1994, released *We'll Be Together Again*, which featured compositions by Strayhorn and Duke Ellington. It earned her another Grammy nomination for Best Jazz Vocal Performance. On Sept. 19, 1994, she appeared at the Supper Club in N.Y. and the show was recorded for the album *An Evening with Lena Horne*, released on March 21, 1995. She won a Grammy for Best Jazz Vocal Performance for the album.

Horne celebrated her 80th birthday, June 30, 1997, with a performance at Avery Fisher Hall at N.Y.'s Lincoln Center. On June 2, 1998, Blue Note released her album *Being Myself*.

DISC.: *It's Love* (1955); *Lena Horne at the Waldorf Astoria* (1957); *Give the Lady What She Wants* (1958); *The Songs of Burke and Van Heusen* (1959); *Porgy and Bess* (1959); *Lena Horne at the Sands* (1961); *Lena Horne Sings Your Requests* (1963); *A Lena Horne Christmas* (1966); *Watch What Happens!* (with Gabor Szabo; 1969); *Lena, a New Album* (1976); *Live on Broadway—Lena Horne: The Lady and Her Music* (1981); *Stormy Weather: The Legendary Lena (1941–58)* (1990); *We'll Be Together Again* (1994); *Love Is the Thing* (1994); *An Evening with Lena Horne: Live at the Supper Club* (1995); *Lena Horne at Metro-Goldwyn-Mayer: Ain't It the Truth—Motion Picture Anthology* (1996); *Some of the Best* (1997); *More of the Best* (1997); *Being Myself* (1998); *A&E Biography: Lena Horne, A (Musical)*; *Anthology* (1998); *The Best of the RCA Years* (1998); *Greatest Hits* (2000); *Love Songs* (2000); *Cocktail Hour: Lena Horne* (2000).

WRITINGS: With R. Schickel, *L.* (Garden City, N.Y., 1965).

BIBL.: H. Greenberg and C. Moss, *In Person: L. H.* (N.Y., 1950); A. Dobrin, *Voices of Joy, Voices of Freedom: Ethel Waters,*

Sammy Davis Jr., Marian Anderson, Paul Robeson, L. H. (1972); J. Haskins, *L. H.* (N.Y., 1983); J. Haskins with K. Benson, *L.: A Personal and Professional Biography of L. H.* (N.Y., 1984; updated ed., Chelsea, Mich., 1991); G. Buckley (her daughter), *The Hornes: An American Family* (N.Y., 1986); L. Palmer, *L. H. Entertainer* (N.Y., 1989); B. Howard, *L. H.* (Los Angeles, Melrose Square, 1991).—**WR**

Horne, Marilyn (Bernice), outstanding American mezzo-soprano; b. Bradford, Pa., Jan. 16, 1934. She studied with William Vennard at the Univ. of Southern Calif. in Los Angeles, and also attended Lotte Lehmann's master classes. She then went to Europe, where she made her professional operatic debut as Giulietta at the Gelsenkirchen Opera in 1957; remained on its roster until 1960, appearing in such roles as Mimi, Tatiana, Minnie, Fulvia in *Ezio*, and Marie in *Wozzeck*, the role she repeated in her U.S. debut at the San Francisco Opera on Oct. 4, 1960. She married **Henry Lewis** in 1960, and subsequently made a number of appearances under his direction; they were separated in 1976. In 1965 she made her debut at London's Covent Garden, again as Marie. She appeared at Milan's La Scala in 1969, and on March 3, 1970, made her Metropolitan Opera debut in N.Y. as Adalgisa; subsequently became one of the Metropolitan's principal singers. Her notable performances there included Rosina in *Il Barbiere di Siviglia* (Jan. 23, 1971), Carmen (Sept. 19, 1972), Fides in *Le Prophète* (Jan. 18, 1977), Rinaldo (the first Handel opera to be staged there, Jan. 19, 1984), Isabella in *L'Italiana in Algeri* (telecast live by PBS, Jan. 11, 1986), and Samira in the premiere of Corigliano's *The Ghosts of Versailles* (Dec. 19, 1991). In 1992 President Bush awarded her the National Medal of Arts. On Jan. 20, 1993, she sang at the inauguration of President Clinton in Washington, D.C. That same year, she founded the Marilyn Horne Foundation with the goal of encouraging young singers as art song recitalists. In 1994 she began teaching at the Music Academy of the West in Santa Barbara, where she was artist-in-residence and director of the voice program. In 1995 she received a Kennedy Center Honor. In 1996 she retired from the operatic stage, and in 1999 gave her last classical recital. Acclaimed for her brilliant portrayals in roles by Handel, Rossini, and Meyerbeer, she won equal praise as an outstanding concert artist. She publ. an autobiography (with J. Scovell; N.Y., 1983).—**NS/LK/DM**

Horneman, Christian Frederik Emil, Danish choral conductor, teacher, and composer, son of **Johan Ole Emil Horneman;** b. Copenhagen, Dec. 17, 1840; d. there, June 8, 1906. He studied at the Leipzig Cons. (1858–60), where he became a friend of Grieg. He composed light music under various pseudonyms. Returning to Copenhagen, he organized a concert society, then was founder-director of the Koncertforeningen (1874–79) and of his own Cons. (1880–1906). He wrote an opera, *Aladdin* (Copenhagen, Nov. 18, 1888), 2 string quartets, and numerous songs.—**NS/LK/DM**

Horneman, Johan Ole Emil, Danish publisher and composer, father of **Christian Frederik Emil Horneman;** b. Copenhagen, May 13, 1809; d. there, May

29, 1870. He composed music in a popular vein, and in 1846 established a publishing firm with Emil Erslev. His collection of piano pieces, *Nordiske sange uden tekst* (Nordic Songs without Text), enjoyed some popularity. He further publ. a piano manual, *Ny praktisk Piano-forteskole.*—**NS/LK/DM**

Hornsby, Bruce, one of the most challenging musical storytellers of the 1980s and 1990s; b. Williamsburg, Va., Nov. 23, 1954. Music was a family affair for Bruce Hornsby. His maternal grandfather was a theater organist and supervised music in schools. His father played sax in his uncle's band. Through high school, Hornsby played piano in the hotel lounges of Williamsburg and elsewhere throughout the southern states with his brother Bobby's band. After a stint at the Univ. of Miami (attending with such heavyweights as Pat Metheny and Jaco Pastorius), he returned to music-making with fellow alum, drummer John Molo, a fixture in Hornsby's bands since. When he went to try his skills in L.A., he worked for three years writing songs for 20th Century–Fox with his younger brother John.

In the early 1980s, Hornsby worked with other musicians and recorded countless demos. He played keyboards in Sheena Easton's band and befriended artists including Huey Lewis. All that hard work and determination worked out, as he and his band The Range signed to RCA in 1985.

Their debut album, *The Way It Is,* went triple platinum, reaching #3 in the charts. A balladeer, Hornsby sang of homelessness and social responsibility in his cool baritone, weaving little duplet fillegrees into the title track. Despite its flying in the face of the feel-good, love song pop of the time, the tune topped the pop and AC charts and won ASCAP's "Song of the Year" in 1987 as the most played song on American radio. They followed with the #4 "Mandolin Rain," which also topped the AC chart, and "Every Little Kiss," which hit #14 in a remixed version. The band won 1996's Best New Artist Grammy.

After spending close to a year on the road, Hornsby and The Range put out *Scenes from the Southside.* The album went platinum, climbing to #5. It featured the hits "The Valley Road" (#4 pop, #1 AC) and "Look Out Any Window" (#35 pop). Hornsby's compositions and collaborations were also getting notice. Huey Lewis topped the charts with his version of a tune from *Scenes,* "Jacob's Ladder." Hornsby cowrote, coproduced, and played piano on Don Henley's hit single "The End of the Innocence."

The Range's 1990 swan song, *A Night on the Town,* found the band fairly bursting to try something new. Hornsby's piano work was becoming jazzier as John Molo's drumming became more aggressive. The album went gold and spawned the #18 single "Across the River." Ironically, Hornsby won a Grammy in 1990, but as a songwriter, for a bluegrass version of "The Valley Road" on the Nitty Gritty Dirt Band's *Will the Circle Be Unbroken II.*

For the next couple of years, Hornsby worked with the spectrum of stars in contemporary pop music, including Bob Dylan; Crosby, Stills Nash and Young; Bob Seger; Willie Nelson; Bonnie Raitt; Squeeze; jazz sax player Bill Evans; and Shawn Colvin. He became an honorary member of The Grateful Dead, filling in on the road after keyboard player Brent Mydland died. Hornsby cut a track with Branford Marsalis called "Barcelona Mona" for the 1992 Olympics that wound up winning a Best Pop Instrumental Performance Grammy in 1993. He worked with Robbie Robertson, who encouraged him to show a little more "bad Bruce" on some of his albums. He also built a studio on his property.

When he finally got busy on his first post-Range record in 1993, he put together a bunch of his friends, including Branford Marsalis, Jerry Garcia, Pat Metheny, Fishbone, and drummer John Bigham. *Harbor Lights* is a looser, funkier, jazzier album than anything he had done before, and pointed a new direction for Hornsby. Without benefit of a hit single or much radio play, the album still went gold.

In 1995, Hornsby put together the star-studded *Hothouse.* The album had almost as many music juxtapositions as it did lyrical ones: On "Cruise Control" the soul band Black Street and Jerry Garcia played together. Soul singer Chaka Khan and nouveau banjo picker Bela Fleck both got paired with jazz stringbender Pat Metheny. Songs quoted Sam Cooke, John Coltrane, and Thelonious Monk.

In 1998, Hornsby released a double CD, *Spirit Trail,* an album that built on the funkiness of his previous two releases. Hornsby started exploring new technology and expanded his piano skills, and wrote one of his best crop of songs. The album, however, didn't produce any hits. He continues to tour, play and explore, and if he doesn't sell as well as he once did, he continues to grow as an artist.

DISC.: THE RANGE: *The Way It Is* (1986); *Scenes from the Southside* (1988); *A Night on the Town* (1990). **SOLO:** *Harbor Lights* (1993); *Hot House* (1995); *Spirit Trail* (1998).—**HB**

Hornstein, Robert von, German composer; b. Donaueschingen, Dec. 6, 1833; d. Munich, July 19, 1890. He studied at the Leipzig Cons., then went to Munich, where he became a teacher at the municipal school of music. He was a close friend of Wagner. He composed operas in a Romantic vein, one of which *Adam und Eva,* was produced in Munich in 1870. Other works include a ballet, *Der Blumen Rache,* incidental music to Shakespeare's *As You Like It,* and many songs.—**NS/LK/DM**

Horovitz, Joseph, Austrian-born English composer, conductor, and teacher; b. Vienna, May 26, 1926. He went to England in 1938 and studied music (with Westrup) and literature at New Coll., Oxford (M.A. and B.Mus., 1948), with Jacob at the Royal Coll. of Music in London, and with Boulanger in Paris. In 1950–51 he was music director of the Bristol Old Vic Co. From 1952 to 1963 he was assoc. director of the Intimate Opera Co. He was prof. of composition at the Royal Coll. of Music from 1961. From 1981 to 1989 he served as president of the International Council of Composers and Lyricists. In 1959 he received the Commonwealth Medal for Composition and in 1961 the Leverhulme Music Research

Award. His facility as a composer is evident in both his handling of serious and light scores.

WORKS: DRAMATIC: *Gentleman's Island*, opera (Cheltenham, July 9, 1959); *The Dumb Wife*, opera (Antwerp, Jan. 10, 1972); 16 ballets, including *Alice in Wonderland* (1953), *Les Femmes d'Alger*, *Miss Carter Wore Pink*, and *Concerto for Dancers*; theater, radio, and television scores. **ORCH.:** *Fantasia on a Theme of Couperin* for Strings (London, July 29, 1962); Trumpet Concerto (1963); Jazz Harpsichord Concerto (1965); *Horizon Overture* (1972); *Toy Symphony* for 17 Toy Instruments, Piano, and Strings (1977). **BRASS BAND:** *Ballet for Band; Sinfonietta; Concertino Classico*, double trumpet concerto; *Theme and Co-Operation* (1994). **WIND ORCH.:** *Bacchus on Blue Ridge; Wind-Harp; Ad Astra; Dance Suite; Fête Galante; Commedia dell'Arte*. **CHAMBER:** 5 string quartets; Oboe Quartet (1956); *Music Hall Suite* for Brass Quintet (1964); *Adam-Blues* for Trombone and Piano (1968); Clarinet Sonatina (1981). **VOCAL:** *Horrortorio*, nuptial cantata for Soli, Chorus, and Orch. (1959); *Captain Noah and his Floating Zoo* for Chorus (1970); *Samson*, oratorio for Chorus and Brass Band (London, Oct. 8, 1977); choruses; songs.—NS/LK/DM

Horowitz, Richard, American composer and instrumentalist; b. Buffalo, Jan. 6, 1949. In 1968 he became a pianist with Alan Sylvia's Orch., playing at European festivals. He returned to America in 1969 to study at Antioch Coll., but difficulties with the selective service led to a decade-long exodus to Europe and North Africa. From 1970 to 1980 he studied electronic music in Paris, and microtonal modulation and the ney (reed flute) in Morocco with Kasmi Nacquisabundi. He composed for the Mabou Mines and choreographer Alice Farley; he performed with Anthony Braxton, Jon Hassell, and David Byrne. His recordings include *Oblique Sequences/Solo Ney Improvisations No. 1* (1979) and *Solo Ney Improvisations No. 3*; he also collaborated with Daniel Kobialka on the album *Memoire* (1982). His film scores include Bertolucci's *The Sheltering Sky* (1990; screenplay by Paul Bowles). In 1981 he began a remarkable collaboration with the Iranian-born American vocalist, dancer, and composer Sussan Deiheim (b. Teheran, Dec. 14, 1956); their works are based on a dense tangle of Middle Eastern, jazz, and avant-garde styles, and involve improvisation, electronics, and computer processing. The works themselves are hypnotically intense but highly formal, with structures and titles based on complex puns and paradoxes; among their stage works are *Desert Equations* (1984), *Azax/Attra* (1985), *Ibn Sabbah, Ghost of the Assassin* (N.Y., 1988), and *X-Isle Isle X* (1989). They also collaborated on a recording, *Abstract Quotients* (1984).—NS/LK/DM

Horowitz, Vladimir (Samoliovich), legendary Russian-born American pianist; b. Berdichev, Oct. 1, 1903; d. N.Y., Nov. 5, 1989. Reared in a musically inclined Jewish family, he began playing piano in his early childhood under the direction of his mother, a professional pianist. His other teachers were Vladimir Puchalsky, Sergei Tarnowsky, and Felix Blumenfeld. He made his first public appearance in a recital in Kiev on May 30, 1920, that marked the opening of a fantastically successful career. The revolutionary events in Russia did not prevent him from giving concerts in and around Kiev until he decided to leave Russia; his first official concert abroad took place in Berlin on Jan. 2, 1926. Arriving in Paris in 1928, he took brief instruction with Alfred Cortot, and on Jan. 12 of that same year, he made his American debut in Tchaikovsky's 1st Piano Concerto with the N.Y. Phil. under the direction of Sir Thomas Beecham; he subsequently appeared as soloist with several other American orchs., earning the reputation of a piano virtuoso of the highest caliber, so that his very name became synonymous with pianistic excellence. In 1933 he married Wanda Toscanini, daughter of Arturo Toscanini. In 1942 he became a naturalized American citizen.

Horowitz seemed to possess every gift of public success; he was universally admired, and his concerts sold out whenever and wherever he chose to appear. His natural affinity was with the Russian repertoire; he formed a sincere friendship with Rachmaninoff, despite the disparity in their ages; Rachmaninoff himself regarded Horowitz as the greatest pianist of the century; Horowitz's performance of Rachmaninoff's 3rd Piano Concerto, which he played numerous times, was his proudest accomplishment. His performances of works by Chopin, Liszt, Schumann, and Tchaikovsky were equally incomparable. During World War II, he appeared with Toscanini in numerous patriotic concerts; it was for such a celebration in N.Y.'s Central Park that he made a vertiginous transcription for piano of Sousa's *Stars and Stripes Forever*, a veritable tour de force of pianistic pyrotechnics, which he performed for years as an encore, to the delight of his audiences. On Dec. 9, 1949, he gave the premiere of Samuel Barber's Piano Sonata in Havana. On Feb. 25, 1953, the 25th anniversary of his American debut, he gave a recital in Carnegie Hall in N.Y. After this recital, he withdrew from the stage, not to return for nearly 12 years. However, he enjoyed making recordings when he was free to change his successive versions in the sanctuary of a studio. He also accepted a few private pupils. He then announced a definite date for a concert in Carnegie Hall: May 9, 1965. Tickets went on sale 2 weeks in advance, and a line formed whose excitement and agitation would equal and surpass that of a queue of fans for a baseball game. Horowitz himself was so touched by this testimony of devotion that he sent hundreds of cups of coffee to the crowd to make the waiting more endurable on a rainy day.

On Feb. 26, 1978, he played at the White House at the invitation of President Carter, a performance that coincided with the 50th anniversary of Horowitz's American debut. On May 22, 1982, at the behest of the Prince of Wales, he gave a recital in the Royal Festival Hall in London, marking his first appearance in Europe in 31 years. Through his recordings, he formed a large following in Japan; to respond to his popularity there, he gave a series of concerts in Tokyo and other Japanese cities (June 1983). The climax of his career, which became a political event as well, was his decision to accept an invitation to revisit Russia in 1986, where he played for the first time after an absence of 61 years to enormous acclaim. His Steinway grand piano was shipped to Moscow. Horowitz himself was accompanied by his wife, a piano tuner, and his cook (to prepare the special foods consisting of fresh sole and other delicacies that were airmailed to Moscow each day). Horowitz made a short introductory speech in Russian before he played his program of works by Rachmaninoff, Tchaikovsky, and Scriabin, and also pieces by Scarlatti and Chopin.

Returning to N.Y., Horowitz resumed his concert and recording career. He was awarded the U.S. Medal of Freedom by President Reagan in 1986, and the National Medal of Arts in 1989. He made his last recording on Nov. 1 of that year; 4 days later, in the afternoon, he suddenly collapsed and died of a heart attack. His passing created a universal feeling of loss the world over. His body lay in state in N.Y. and was then flown by his wife to Italy, where it was interred in the Toscanini family plot in Milan.

BIBL.: G. Plaskin, *H.: A Biography* (N.Y., 1983); D. Dubal, *Evenings with H.: A Personal Portrait* (Secaucus, N.J., 1991); H. Schonberg, *H.: His Life and Music* (N.Y., 1992); P. Brunel, *V. H.: Le méphisto du piano* (Paris, 1997).—**NS/LK/DM**

Horsley, Charles Edward, English organist and composer, son of **William Horsley;** b. London, Dec. 16, 1822; d. N.Y., Feb. 28, 1876. He studied with his father and with Moscheles, and then in Kassel with Hauptmann (1839); later he was in Leipzig (1841–43), where he profited from the counsel of Mendelssohn. From 1853 to 1857 he was organist at St. John's in London. About 1866 he went to Melbourne as an organist. In 1872 he settled in N.Y. as organist at St. John's Chapel. His *Text Book of Harmony* (1876) was a rewritten version of his father's manual of 1847. He composed the oratorios *David* (1850), *Joseph* (1853), and *Gideon* (1860), a Sym. (1842–44), a Piano Concerto (1848), overtures, chamber music, piano pieces, and *Euterpe*, ode for the opening of N.Y.'s Town Hall (1870).—**NS/LK/DM**

Horsley, William, English organist and composer, father of **Charles Edward Horsley;** b. London, Nov. 15, 1774; d. there, June 12, 1858. At 16 he was articled to Theodore Smith, a pianist and organist, and later was influenced by John Callcott, whose daughter he married in 1813. He was organist at Ely Chapel, Holborn (1793–1802), the Asylum for Female Orphans (1802–54), Belgrave Chapel (1812–37), and the Charterhouse (1838–58). He helped to found the choral society Concentores Sodales (1798–1847), for which he wrote many works. In 1813 he also helped to found the Phil. Soc. Horsley won fame as a glee composer; 124 of his works were publ. separately and also in 5 vols. (1801, 1804, 1806, 1811, 1827). He was also a successful song and ballad composer. Among his other works were *A Collection of Canons* (1817) and many piano pieces. He publ. *An Explanation of the Musical Intervals* (London, 1825) and *An Introduction to the Study of Practical Harmony and Modulation* (London, 1847; rewritten by his son, 1876). —**NS/LK/DM**

Horst, Anthon van der, Dutch organist, conductor, pedagogue, and composer; b. Amsterdam, June 20, 1899; d. Hilversum, March 7, 1965. He studied with de Pauw (piano; Prix d'Excellence for Organ, 1919) and Zweers (composition) at the Amsterdam Cons. He was organist of Amsterdam's Grande Eglise Wallonne (1915–18) and English Reformed Church (1918–41), Hilversum's Netherland's Protestant League (1944–55), and Naarden's Grote Kerk (1955–64). Horst taught at the Amsterdam Muzieklyceum (1922–27) and Cons. (1935–65). He conducted various choral groups and was conductor of the Netherlands Bach Soc. of Amsterdam from 1931. In some of his organ and piano pieces, he adopted Pijper's scales, which he called "modus conjunctus."

WORKS: ORCH.: 3 syms. (1935–37; *Divertimento pittorale,* 1954; 1959); *Nocturne funèbre* (1950–51); Organ Concerto, *Concerto per organo romantico* (1952); Violin Concerto, *Concerto Spagnuolo* (1953); *3 études symphoniques* (1954); *Concerto in Baroque Style* for Organ and Strings (1960); *Reflexions sonores* (1962); *Ricercar svelato* for Brass, Organ, and Strings (1963); *Salutatio joyeuse* (1964). **CHAMBER:** Cello Suite (1941); *Theme, Variations, and Fugue* for Flute, Violin, and Viola (1957). **KEYBOARD: Piano:** *Tema con variazioni in modo conjunco* (1950); *Sonata in modo conjunco* for 2 Pianos (1951). **Organ:** *Suite in modo conjunco* (1943); *Partita diverse sopra Psalm 8* (1947); Suite for 31–tone Organ (1953). **VOCAL:** *Choros I-VIII* for Soloists, Chorus, and Orch. (1931–58); *Rembrandt Cantata* (1956); choruses; songs.

BIBL.: G. Oost, *A.v.d. H., 1899–1965: Leven en Werken* (Alphen aan den Rijn, 1992).—**NS/LK/DM**

Horst, Louis, American composer; b. Kansas City, Mo., Jan. 12, 1884; d. N.Y., Jan. 23, 1964. He studied violin and piano in San Francisco, and composition with Richard Stöhr in Vienna, as well as with Max Persin and Riegger in N.Y. (1925). From 1915 to 1925 he was music director of the Denishawn Dance Co., and from 1926 to 1948, of Martha Graham's dance company, for which he wrote a number of works that played a crucial role in the development of modern dance. He wrote extensively on the subject of music and dance; founded and ed. the journal *Dance Observer* (1934), and publ. the books *Pre-classic Dance Forms* (1940) and *Modern Dance Forms* (with C. Russell; 1961). He was also active as a teacher at Bennington (Vt.) Coll. (1934–45), Columbia Univ. Teachers Coll. (1938–41), and the Juilliard School of Music in N.Y. (1958–63).

BIBL.: E. Pease, *L. H.: His Theories on Modern Dance Composition* (diss., Univ. of Mich., 1953); J. Soares, *L. H.: Musician in a Dancer's World* (Durham, N.C., 1992).—**NS/LK/DM**

Horszowski, Mieczyslaw, remarkable Polish-born American pianist and pedagogue; b. Lemberg, June 23, 1892; d. Philadelphia, May 22, 1993. A child prodigy, he began to study the piano at a very early age with his mother. At age 5, he played and transposed Bach inventions. After further training with Melcér and Soltys in Lemberg, he went to Vienna in 1899, where his own *Marche Solennelle* was performed for Emperor Franz Josef II. He had lessons with Kistler (1899) and pursued his studies with Leschetizky (until 1904); later he was a pupil of Heuberger and Mouquet (harmony and counterpoint). Following his Warsaw debut as soloist in Beethoven's 1st Piano Concerto in 1902, debuts followed in Vienna and Berlin in 1903, and then in Paris in 1905. In 1906 he played in London before Queen Alexandra, at the Vatican before Pope Pius X, and in N.Y. at Carnegie Hall. After tours of Europe and the Americas (1907–11), he took courses in philosophy, literature, and art at the Sorbonne in Paris (1911–13). He then resumed his career and distinguished himself as an interpreter not only of Bach, Mozart, Beethoven, and Chopin, but also of contemporary composers. From 1914 to 1939 he lived in Milan. In 1942 he settled in the U.S. and in 1948 became a naturalized American citizen. He joined the faculty of the Curtis Inst. of Music in Philadelphia in 1942, where he remained an eminent member of the faculty for the rest of his life. In 1954–55 he played all of Beethoven's solo piano music in a series of N.Y. recitals, and in 1960 all of Mozart's sonatas. In 1961 he appeared at the White House in Washington, D.C., with Pablo Casals and Alexander Schneider, and in 1978 he played there again. In 1981 he married the Italian pianist Beatrice Costa. About this time his eyesight began to fail rapidly, which precluded him from playing concertos and appearing in chamber- music settings. All the same, he continued to give critically acclaimed recitals from memory. In 1987 he performed at the opening of the Casals Hall in Tokyo. On Oct. 31, 1991, at the astounding age of 99, he gave his last recital in Philadelphia, thus bringing to a close one of the most outstanding performing and teaching careers of the 20th century.—NS/LK/DM

Horton, Austin Asadata Dafora, Nigerian composer; b. Freetown, Sierra Leone, West Africa, Aug. 4, 1890; d. N.Y., March 4, 1965. As a youth, he became deeply interested in African folk dance festivals and studied the culture of many African tribes. He then organized a dance group in Germany. He settled in the U.S. in 1921, devoting himself to the propagation of African art, coaching singers, dancers, and drummers for performance of African dances. He utilized authentic African melorhythms in several of his stage spectacles, for which he also arranged the musical scores. Of these, *Kykunkor, the Witch,* produced at the Unity Theater Studio in N.Y. on May 7, 1934, attracted considerable attention. He also produced a dance drama, *Tunguru.*—NS/LK/DM

Horvat, Milan, Yugoslav conductor; b. Pakrac, July 28, 1919. He was educated in Zagreb, studying law at the Univ. and taking courses with Svetislav Stančič (piano), Fritz Zaun (conducting), and Zlatko Grgošević (composition) at the Academy of Music (1939–46). In 1945 he became conductor of the Zagreb Radio Chorus, and from 1946 he conducted the Zagreb Radio Orch. From 1953 to 1958 he conducted the Radio Telefís Eireann Sym. Orch. in Dublin. He was music director of the Phil. (1956–70) and Opera (1958–65) in Zagreb. After serving as chief conductor of the Austrian Radio Sym. Orch. in Vienna (1969–75), he held that title with the Zagreb Radio Orch. (from 1975). As a guest conductor, he appeared widely in Europe.—NS/LK/DM

Horvat, Stanko, Croatian composer; b. Zagreb, March 12, 1930. He studied composition with Šulek at the Zagreb Academy of Music, graduating in 1956, and then took a course with Aubin at the Paris Cons. and private composition lessons with Leibowitz (1958–59). Returning to Yugoslavia, he was appointed to the music faculty of the Zagreb Academy of Music in 1961. In his style of composition, he traversed successively a period of neo-Classical mannerisms, serialism in its dodecaphonic aspect, aleatory expressionism, and sonorism; eventually he returned to a median technique of pragmatic modernism.

WORKS: DRAMATIC: *Izabranik* (The Chosen One), ballet (1961); *3 Legends,* television opera (1971). **ORCH.:** *Sinfonietta* (1954); Sym. (1956); *Concerto rustico* for Strings (1958); Piano Concerto (1966; Zagreb, April 3, 1967); *Choral* for Strings (1967); *Taches* for Piano and Chamber Orch. (Graz, Sept. 26, 1968); *Hymnus* (1969); *Perpetuum mobile* for Strings (Zagreb, May 9, 1971); *Krik* (The Cry) for Mezzo-soprano and Orch., after García Lorca (1968; Zagreb, March 19, 1969). **CHAMBER:** *Choral Variations* for String Quartet (1953); *Contrasts* for String Quartet (1963); *Rondo* for String Quartet (1967); *Frénésie* for 2 Double Basses (1997). **Piano:** *Variants* (1965); *Sonnant* (1970); *Accords* (1979); *Ostinati* (1983); *Manual* (1984); *Paysage sombre* (1988); *De diebus furoris* (1992). **VOCAL:** *Jama* (The Pit), cantata (Zagreb, Dec. 18, 1971); *The Murmur of Winds, the Murmur of Water,* cantata for Soprano and Orch. (1992). —NS/LK/DM

Horvath, Josef Maria, Austrian composer of Hungarian descent; b. Pécs, Dec. 20, 1931. He studied piano and composition at the Franz Liszt Academy of Music in Budapest. In 1956 he went to Salzburg, where he studied composition and took instruction in electronic music. Subsequently he became a composition teacher at the Salzburg Mozarteum. Among his compositions were *Entropia,* sym. (1961), Trio for Violin, Horn, and Piano (1963), a group of works under the generic title *Redundance* for Wind Octet and/or String Quartet (1970), and *Origines* for Chamber Group (1975). —NS/LK/DM

Horvitz, Wayne, eclectic American musician; b. N.Y., 1955. Merging jazz with rock, gospel, country, blues, avant-garde, and more, he had been recording for nearly a decade when, in 1986, he relocated from N.Y. to Seattle with his wife, composer Robin Holcomb, and children. They cofounded the N.Y. Composers Orch., an ensemble formed in 1986 to perform commissioned works by himself and other innovators including Bobby Previte, Lawrence "Butch" Morris, and Anthony Braxton. Since Horvitz's relocation, the NYCO repertoire continues to be performed by the original NYCO ensemble, as well as by a Pacific West group of musicians led by Horvitz, and by other ensembles with Horvitz directing. He also leads the bands Pigpen, Zony Mash, The President, and his trio with Butch Morris and Bobby Previte.

He has performed and/or recorded as sideman or collaborator with such cutting-edge musicians as Marty Ehrlich, John Zorn, Naked City, Philip Wilson, David Moss, Curlew, Bobby Previte, Robin Holcomb, Bill Frisell, Billy Bang, Kazutoki Umezu, Fred Frith, Carla Bley, Elliott Sharp, and Michael Shrieve. He has composed music for film, television, video, and multimedia educational projects as well as theater and dance productions.

DISC.: *Some Order, Long Understood* (1983); *This New Generation* (1987); *The New York Composers Orch.* (1990); *First Program in Standard Time* (1992); *Miracle Mile* (1992); *V as in Victim* (1994); *Halfrack* (1994); *Live in Poland* (1994); *Miss Ann* (1995); *Monologue: Twenty Compositions for Dance* (1997); *Cold Spell* (1997).—**DCG/NAL/SH**

Horwood, William, English composer; b. place and date unknown; d. c. 1484. He was first listed as a member of the Fraternity of St. Nicolas, a guild of parish clerks in London, in 1459, and in 1474 he was made its master. In 1476 he was listed among the vicars-choral at Lincoln Cathedral, where he was made Informator in 1477. Horwood composed some of the earliest works of the full-choral style as represented in the Eton Choirbook. His Magnificat secundi toni à 5 is a noteworthy example.—**LK/DM**

Hoschna (Hoschner), Karl, Czech-American composer; b. Kuschwarda, Aug. 16, 1876; d. N.Y., Dec. 23, 1911. He studied piano, harmony, and composition at the Vienna Cons., then played oboe in an Austrian army band before going to the U.S. (1896), where he was an oboist in Victor Herbert's orch. After working as a music copyist and arranger, he turned to composing, turning out a number of successful operettas, mostly in collaboration with the lyricist Otto Harbach.

WORKS: DRAMATIC: O p e r e t t a : *The Belle of the West* (Chicago, Oct. 29, 1905); *The Girl from Broadway* (Philadelphia, Dec. 3, 1906); *3 Twins* (N.Y., June 15, 1908); *Prince Humbug* (Boston, Sept. 3, 1908); *The Photo Shop* (1910); *Bright Eyes* (N.Y., Feb. 28, 1910); *Madame Sherry* (N.Y., Aug. 30, 1910); *Katie Did* (Chicago, Feb. 18, 1911); *Jumping Jupiter* (N.Y., March 6, 1911); *Dr. Deluxe* (N.Y., April 17, 1911); *The Girl of My Dreams* (N.Y., Aug. 7, 1911); *The Fascinating Widow* (N.Y., Sept. 11, 1911); *The Wall Street Girl* (N.Y., April 15, 1912).—**NS/LK/DM**

Hostetler, Randy (actually, **James Randolph**), imaginative American composer, pianist, and performance artist; b. Washington, D.C., July 28, 1963; d. Los Angeles, Feb. 1, 1996. He studied at Yale Univ., receiving the Friends of Music Prize at his graduation in 1985, and at the Calif. Inst. of the Arts, graduating in 1989. He was the composer of over 50 experimental, improvisational, and multimedia works, some incorporating ambient sounds and unusual found objects. He established and coordinated The Living Room Series, a bi-monthly concert of new music in Los Angeles (1990–93). Hostetler was not only a promising young musician, but also much loved. His sudden death at the age of 32 of undiagnosed Addison's Disease was greatly lamented.

WORKS: *Cuckoo Song* for Small Chorus, on a 13th century text (1978); *Tell Me Where Is Fancy Bred?* for Small Chorus, after Shakespeare (1979); *Island Girls* for Small Chorus, after T.S. Eliot (1981); *Three Leaves* for Small Chorus, Flute, and Violin, after Walt Whitman (1982); *Randy's New Four-Track Piece* for Tape, Instruments, Toys, Sound Effects, Voice, and Digital Delay (1983); *Ingredients* for Small Chorus (1984); *There* for Tape, Piano, and Voice (1984); *Nine Minutes of Laughter* for Tape and Voices (1985); *Late Night Joint* for Tape, Electric Bass, Electric Guitar, Tenor Saxophone, Drum Machine, Conversation, Pool Balls, Ping Pong, Ice Machine, and Percussion (1985; in collaboration with Julian Saenz); *Zooming Home* for Tape and Voices (1985); *25 Years* for Saxophone Quartet (1985); Big Mac for Flute, Bass, Clarinet, Horn, Soprano, Baritone, Violin, Viola, Cello, and Contrabass (1985); *Great Big Slice of Ham* for Tape and Concrete Music (1986); *Emotional Study No. 1*, short film animating various household objects (1986); *8* for Pianist (1986); *Happily Ever After*, 45-minute storytelling collage (1987; also a 17-minute version); *I(EYE)/FRE/IOI*, sound and video installation (1988; in collaboration with Eric Forte and Francesca Talenti); *Palm Quartet* for String Quartet and Video Score (of Los Angeles palm trees) (1988; in collaboration with F. Talenti); *Floater* for String Quartet and Video Score (of white shapes moving against a black background) (1989); *P(L)ACEs*, electric groove collage for 11 Players and House Lamps (1989); *Surprise Party*, a musical postcard (1989); *Landscapes*, sound design for a film by F. Talenti (1989); *Yo...Bowling?* for Multiple Tape Decks, Record Players, Super-8 Projectors, and Video (1990; in collaboration with M. Lightcap; also a studio version); *Shower Piece* for Voice (1990); *Piece for New Year's Eve*, theatrical multimedia piece/party for Any Number of Players (1990); *Nervous System* for Black and White Slide Score and 8 Players of Office Gadgets (1990); *Francesca and Randy's Trip to Europe* for Tape (1990); *Cyclebones and Ghost Cologne* for Tape (1991); *Piece for Randy and Dave*, theatrical multimedia piece for 3 Performers (1991); *Musical Interludes*, visual tableau and improvisation structure for Drum Exterior and Interior, Big Tube, Triangle, Clarinet, and Califone (1992); *Deep* for 2 Reed Players (Saxophones and Clarinets) (1992); *Someone's Apartment* for 2 Reed Players (Saxophones and Clarinets) (1992); *Lone Pine* for 11 Players of Percussion and Sound Effects and Animated Film (4 times with different speeds with multiple non-sync soundtracks) (1992); *There It Is* for 2 Performers and Assistants (flexible instrumentation) (1992); *Indecipherable Conversation* for 6 Players (flexible instrumentation) (1993); *Song*, amplified vocal improvisation for 1 Performer (1993); *For Eric* (Hands), movement piece for 1 Performer (1993); *Circle and Triangle (aka as Two Faces)*, movement piece for 1 Performer (1993); *Off the Corner*, movement piece for 1 Performer (1995); *The Preacher*, performance piece for 1 Performer (1995); *Salvation Army*, guerrilla performance piece for a Large Number of Bell-Ringers (1995); also arrangements, including *Summertime* (Gershwin) for Small Chorus (1982), *Prelude to a Kiss* (Ellington) for Small Chorus (1982), *Round Midnight* (Monk) for Small Chorus (1983), *Theme from Tannhäuser* (Wagner) for Men's Chorus (1992).—**LK/DM**

Hostinský, Otakar, eminent Czech aesthetician; b. Martiněves, Jan. 2, 1847; d. Prague, Jan. 19, 1910. He studied law at the Univ. of Prague (1865–66) and philosophy and aesthetics at the Univ. of Munich (Ph.D., 1868), then studied composition with Smetana (1871). He was a music critic and an ed. of literary journals before becoming an instructor of aesthetics at the Univ. of Prague (1877), where he was made a prof. in 1892. He also taught music history at the Prague Cons. (1882–86). He developed what he termed concrete formalism (in opposition to Herbart's abstract formalism) in the study of aesthetics, and also made important contributions to analytical methods of ethnomusicological research and to the study of harmony.

WRITINGS: *Das Musikalisch-schöne und das Gesamth-*

kunstwerk vom Standpunkte der formalen Aesthetik (Leipzig, 1877); *Die Lehre von den musikalischen Klängen* (Prague, 1879); *O významu praktických idejí Herbartových pro všeobecnou aesthetiku* (The Importance of Herbart's Practical Ideas for General Aesthetics; Prague, 1881); *O české deklamaci hudebni* (Czech Musical Declamation; Prague, 1886); *Herbarts Aesthetik* (Hamburg, 1892); *36 nápěvů světských pisni českého lidu z XVI. stoleti* (36 Melodies from Secular Czech Folk Song of the 16th Century; Prague, 1892; 2nd ed., 1957); *Jan Blahoslav a Jan Josquin* (Prague, 1896); *Hudba v čechách* (Music in Bohemia; Prague, 1900); *B. Smetana a jeho boj o moderni českou hudbu* (Smetana and His Struggle for Modern Czech Music; Prague, 1901; 2nd ed., 1941); *O socialisaci uměni* (The Socialization of Art; Prague, 1903); *česká světska piseň lidová* (Czech Secular Folk Song; Prague, 1906); *Uměni a společnost* (Art and Society; Prague, 1907); *česká hudba 1864–1904* (Czech Music 1864–1904; Prague, 1909).

BIBL.: Z. Strejc, *Uměni a společnost v teoretickém dile O. Hostinského* (Art and Society in O. H.'s Theoretical Work; diss., Univ. of Brno, 1969); L. Juřica, *Hostinského nauka o harmonii* (H.'s Theory of Harmony; diss., Univ. of Brno, 1972).—**NS/LK/DM**

Hothby, John, English music theorist and composer; b. c. 1415; d. 1487. He was a student at Oxford. He was a member of the Carmelite order. He lived in Florence, Italy, about 1450, and was known there under the Italianized name Ottobi. Hothby was then in Lucca (1467–86), where he taught in canonic schools. In 1486 he was recalled to England by Henry VII. A. Seay ed. *The Musical Works of John Hothby* in Corpus Mensurabilis Musicae, XXXIII (1964).

WRITINGS: *Ars plane musice; Calliope legale; De canto figurato; De musica intervallosa; Dialogus; Epistola; Excitato; Quid est proportio?; Regule cantus mensurati; Regule contrapuncti; Regule de monocordo; Regule super proportionem; Regule supra contrapunctum; Tractatus quarundam regularum.*

BIBL.: A. Schmidt, *Die Calliopea legale des J. H.* (Leipzig, 1897).—**NS/LK/DM**

Hotman, Nicolas, French viol player, theorbist, and composer of German descent; b. place and date unknown; d. April 1663. He may have studied with André Maugars and Sainte-Colombe. He was in the service of the Duke of Orléans from 1656 until entering the service of the court in 1661. Hotman composed solo pieces for lute, theorbo, and viol. Ballard publ. a posthumous vol. of his *Airs à boire* (Paris, 1664).—**LK/DM**

Hotter, Hans, greatly esteemed German bass-baritone; b. Of fenbach am Main, Jan. 19, 1909. He studied voice with Matthäus Roemer, making his debut as the Speaker in *Die Zauberflöte* in Opava in 1929. He was a member of the opera there from 1930, and also sang at the German Theater in Prague (1932–34). He then sang at the Hamburg State Opera (1934–45), Bavarian State Opera in Munich (1937–72), Berlin State Opera (1939–42), and Vienna State Opera (1939–72). He made his first appearance at London's Covent Garden with the visiting Vienna State Opera in 1947. Hotter made appearances regularly at Covent Garden until 1967 and was a principal singer at the Bayreuth Festivals (1952–64), where he became renowned for his portrayal of Wotan. He also distinguished himself in such roles as Kurwenal, Hans Sachs, Amfortas, Gurnemanz, King Marke, and Pogner. He made his Metropolitan Opera debut in N.Y. as the Dutchman in *Der fliegende Holländer* on Nov. 9, 1950, remaining on its roster until 1954. He also sang at La Scala in Milan, the Paris Opéra, the Salzburg Festival, the Chicago Opera, and the Teatro Colón in Buenos Aires. He became a member of the faculty of the Vienna Hochschule für Musik in 1977. In addition to his Wagnerian roles, Hotter also created the roles of the Kommandant in *Friedenstag* (Munich, July 24, 1938), of Olivier in *Capriccio* (Munich, Oct. 28, 1942), and of Jupiter in *Die Liebe der Danae* (public dress rehearsal, Salzburg, Aug. 16, 1944) in Strauss's operas. His autobiography was publ. as *"Der Mai war mir gewogen—:" Erinnerungen* (Munich, 1996).

BIBL.: B. Wessling, *H. H.* (Bremen, 1966); P. Turing, *H. H.: Man and Artist* (London, 1983).—**NS/LK/DM**

Hotteterre, family of French musicians: **(1) Nicolas Hotteterre** (b. 1637; d. Paris, May 10, 1694), a hurdy-gurdy player; his brother **(2) Martin Hotteterre** (d. 1712), also a hurdy- gurdy player and a performer at the court ballets; **(3) Louis Hotteterre** (d. 1719), son of Nicolas, who played flute at the French court (1664–1714); his brother **(4) Nicolas Hotteterre (II)** (d. Paris, Dec. 4, 1727), who played flute and oboe in Lully's orch. at the court of Louis XIV; their cousin **(5) Jacques Hotteterre** (b. Sept. 29, 1674; d. Paris, July 16, 1762), surnamed "le Romain," evidently owing to his long sojourns in Rome, popularized the transverse (German) flute at the French court and publ. several manuals on that instrument and others: *Principes de la flûte traversière ou flûte d'Allemagne, de la flûte à bec ou flûte douce et du hautbois* (Paris, 1707; sometimes attributed to Louis; the 1728 ed. was reprinted in facsimile, Kassel, 1941; Eng. tr. by P. Douglas, N.Y., 1968; 2nd ed., 1983); *L'Art de préluder sur la flûte traversière, sur la flûte à bec*, etc. (Paris, 1712; 2nd ed. under the title *Méthode pour apprendre...*, c. 1765); *Méthode pour la musette* (1738). He also wrote sonatas, duos, trios, suites, rondes (*chansons à danser*), and minuets for flute.

BIBL.: J. Carlez, *Les H.* (Caen, 1877); E. Thoinan, *Les H. et les Chédeville* (Paris, 1894); N. Mauger, *Les H., Nouvelles recherches* (Paris, 1912).—**NS/LK/DM**

Hough, Stephen (Andrew Gill), English pianist; b. Heswall, Cheshire, Nov. 22, 1961. He began piano lessons at age 6, later becoming a pupil of Gordon Green and Derrick Wyndham at the Royal Northern Coll. of Music in Manchester and of Adele Marcus at the Juilliard School in N.Y. In 1982 he won the 1st Terence Judd Award and made his London debut; in 1983 he won the Naumburg International Piano Competition in N.Y. He made his N.Y. debut in 1984; in subsequent seasons, he appeared as a soloist with many of the world's leading orchs. and toured widely as a recitalist. His vast repertoire ranges from early keyboard works to contemporary scores.—**NS/LK/DM**

Houseley, Henry, English-American organist, conductor, and composer; b. Sutton in Ashfield, Nottinghamshire, Sept. 20, 1852; d. Denver, March 13, 1925.

He studied with Michael Costa and E. H. Turpin, then was an organist in Derby and Nottingham and on the faculty at the Univ. of Nottingham. He settled in Denver (1888), becoming organist at the Episcopal Cathedral of St. John in the Wilderness (1888–92) and director of the Denver Choral Soc. (1894); he also founded a sym. orch. (1900). His best-known work was the cantata *Omar Khayyam* (Denver, June 1, 1916). He also wrote 7 operas, some orch. pieces, anthems, ballads, and keyboard music.—NS/LK/DM

Houston, Whitney,

one of the most celebrated vocalists of the 20th century (b. Newark, N.J., Aug. 9, 1963). Whitney Houston came from a strong musical heritage—her mother, Emily "Cissy" Drinkard Houston, was one of the Drinkard Sisters, among the greatest family acts in gospel. Cissy went on to a mildly successful solo career both in gospel (she won a Best Gospel Album Grammy in 1997) and pop (her "Young Hearts" is one of the great also-rans of the disco decade). She also was an enormously in-demand backing vocalist, working with Elvis Presley, Aretha Franklin, and dozens of others as a member of the Sweet Inspirations. Whitney's cousin is Dionne Warwick. Her father managed both her mother's career and hers.

Whitney began singing in the choir of the New Hope Baptist Church, where her mother served as Minister of Music. By her early teens, she had joined her mother's nightclub act as well. Her stunning looks led to a contract as a Wilhelmina model. She also started working on recording sessions as a backing vocalist for Lou Rawls, The Neville Brothers, Chaka Khan, and others. She made her lead vocal debut working with Archie Shepp on Material's "Memories."

Clive Davis of Arista signed her to a recording contract, but did not immediately release an album by her. Instead, he carefully groomed her by having her work on several projects. She performed duets with Teddy Pendergrass and Jermaine Jackson. She recorded the song "Shock Me" for the soundtrack to the movie *Perfect*. These projects led to her eponymous debut album. The album made it clear that Houston had one of the most outstanding voices of her generation, but it was put in service of generic, middle-of-the-road material. Nonetheless, the public ate it up. Her debut single, "You Give Good Love," went gold, topping the R&B charts and hitting #3 pop. The bouncy "Saving All My Love for You" also went gold, topping both the pop, adult contemporary, and R&B charts. It earned Houston her first Grammy Award for Best Pop Vocal Performance as well as an Emmy for Outstanding Individual Performance in a Variety or Music Program for singing the tune on the Grammys. The more upbeat, almost funky "How Will I Know" featured her mother on backing vocals. The record went gold, also topping the adult contemporary, R&B, and pop charts. She scored yet another gold pop and adult contemporary chart topper with her version of "The Greatest Love of All." The album spent 14 weeks on the top of the charts and sold 11 million copies.

Houston preceded her highly anticipated sophomore effort, *Whitney*, with the platinum chart topper "I Wanna Dance with Somebody (Who Loves Me)." The song earned Houston her second Best Pop Vocal Performance Grammy. The album, chock full of material reminiscent of her first album, debuted at #1 on the charts, making her the first woman to perform that feat. It remained atop the charts for 11 weeks. While the dramatic ballad "Didn't We Almost Have It All" also topped both the pop and adult contemporary charts, it became Houston's first single not to at least score gold. The chart-topping "So Emotional" did achieve gold status. "Where Do Broken Hearts Go" topped both the pop and adult contemporary charts without going gold, but giving her a record-breaking string of seven consecutive #1 singles. "Love Will Save the Day" stopped that streak, stalling at #9. The album sold over eight million copies. She capped off 1988 with the adult contemporary chart topping, #5 pop non-LP single "One Moment in Time," the theme from that summer's Olympics.

Houston picked up her string of #1 gold singles with the release of her third album, *I'm Your Baby Tonight*, a far more upbeat and aggressive recording than her previous two albums. The title track topped R&B and pop charts, and her cover of Sister Sledge's "All the Man That I Need," featuring a sax solo by labelmate Kenny G., topped those charts and the adult contemporary chart as well. She performed "The Star Spangled Banner" at the 1991 Super Bowl, and the demand was so great, Arista released it as a single; it topped out at #20 on the charts, but went gold. "Miracle" only reached #9 and "My Name Is Not Susan" rose to #20. Though the album sold over three million copies, it was considered something of a disappointment. During the summer of 1992, Houston married singer Bobby Brown. She had met him backstage at the 1989 Soul Train Awards, and they dated for two years before marrying at Houston's N.J. estate. This marriage would prove controversial at times, serving as tabloid fodder as the couple dealt with their personal problems.

Expanding her professional horizons a little, Houston took the role of the beleaguered pop diva in the movie *The Bodyguard* in 1992, starring opposite Kevin Costner. In addition to acting, she performed six of the 12 songs on the soundtrack album. Her cover of Dolly Parton's dramatic ballad "I Will Always Love You" went quadruple platinum, staying atop the pop charts for 14 weeks, 11 weeks on top of the R&B charts, and five weeks on the adult contemporary charts. It earned Houston her third Best Pop Vocal Performance, Female, Grammy, as well as the coveted Record of the Year statuette. At the time, it was the best-selling single ever. Her version of the Ashford & Simpson/Chaka Khan hit "I'm Every Woman" went gold, hitting #4, as did "I Have Nothing," which also topped the adult contemporary chart. "Run to You" stalled out at #31, but the album sold over 13 million copies and won the Album of the Year Grammy.

Pregnant at the time the film came out, Houston took some time off to be a mother. She returned to acting in the film *Waiting to Exhale*. She sang the title song for the film, "Exhale (Shoop Shoop)," which topped the pop and R&B charts in 1995 on its way to platinum sales. A year later, she starred along with Denzel Washington and Courtney Vance in *The Preacher's Wife*, a film that gave her the opportunity to sing several blow-the-roof-off-the-church gospel numbers. However, the film was less successful at the box office than her previous two efforts.

In 1997, Houston co-executive produced and co-starred in a television remake of Rodgers and Hammerstein's *Cinderella*. A year later, she put out *My Love Is Your Love*, her first studio album in eight years. It took an even more aggressively funky approach than *I'll Be Your Baby Tonight*. Fueled with hip-hop rhythms, and guest artists including Missy Elliot, Wyclef Jean, and Lauren Hill, the album generated a bunch of hits. "Heartbreak Hotel" peaked at #2, "It's Not Right but It's Okay" hit #3, and the title track went Top Ten.

Houston manages to combine an underlying sweetness even with her more funk-oriented material, allowing her to appeal to both mainstream and R&B markets. She has truly achieved "diva" status, able to blow the roof off even the largest halls with her powerful set of lungs and her emotionally charged presence.

DISC.: *Whitney Houston* (1985); *Whitney* (1987); *I'm Your Baby Tonight* (1990); *The Bodyguard* (soundtrack; 1992); *The Preacher's Wife* (soundtrack; 1996); *My Love Is Your Love* (1998); *The Greatest Hits* (2000).

BIBL.: K. Ammons, *Good Girl, Bad Girl* (Secaucus, N.J., 1996).—HB

Houtmann, Jacques, French conductor; b. Mirecourt, March 27, 1935. He studied at the Nancy Cons. and at the École Normale de Musique in Paris with Jean Fournet and Henri Dutilleux, and then took courses in conducting with Franco Ferrara in Rome. He won 1st prize in the conductors' competition in Besancon (1961) and the Mitropoulos Competition in N.Y. (1964). He was an asst. conductor of the N.Y. Phil. (1965–66). He served as conductor with the Rhône-Alpes Phil. in Lyons (1967–71). In 1971 he went again to the U.S., and was music director of the Richmond (Va.) Sym. Orch. (until 1986); then was music director of the Lorraine Phil. in Metz (from 1986).—NS/LK/DM

Hove, Joachim van den, South Netherlands lutenist, composer, and intabulator; b. Antwerp, 1567; d. The Hague, 1620. He went to Leiden in 1594, where he acquired a notable reputation as a lutenist and lute teacher. After extensive travels, he settled in The Hague in 1615–16, where he died in poverty. Hove was a distinguished composer of lute music. In addition to his own works represented in the 22 *Praeludia testudinis* (Leiden, 1616), he also prepared collections of works by Italian composers in *Florida* (Utrecht, 1601) and *Delitcae musicae* (Utrecht, 1612; ed. by H. Monkmeyer, Hofheim an Taunus, 1967).—LK/DM

Hovhaness (real name, **Chakmakjian**), **Alan (Vaness Scott),** prolific American composer of Armenian-Scottish descent; b. Somerville, Mass., March 8, 1911; d. Seattle, June 21, 2000. He took piano lessons with Adelaide Proctor and Heinrich Gebhard in Boston, and undertook academic studies at Tufts Univ. In 1932 he enrolled in the New England Cons. of Music in Boston as a student of Frederick Converse, and then was a scholarship student of Martinů at the Berkshire Music Center at Tanglewood in the summer of 1942. He served on the faculty of the New England Cons. of Music (1948–51), then moved to N.Y. He was awarded 2 Guggenheim fellowships (1954 and 1958). In 1959 he received a Fulbright fellowship and traveled to India and Japan, where he collected native folk songs for future use and presented his own works, as pianist and conductor, receiving acclaim. In 1962 he was engaged as composer-in-residence at the Univ. of Hawaii; then traveled to Korea. In 1967 he was composer-in-residence of the Seattle Sym. Orch. From his earliest attempts at composition, he took great interest in the musical roots of his paternal ancestry, studying the folk songs assembled by Komitas. He gradually came to believe that music must reflect the natural monody embodied in national songs and ancient church hymns. In his music, he adopted modal melodies and triadic harmonies. This *parti pris* had the dual effect of alienating him from the milieu of modern composers while exercising great attraction for the music consumer at large. By dint of ceaseless repetition of melodic patterns and relentless dynamic tension, he succeeded in creating a sui generis type of impressionistic monody, flowing on the shimmering surfaces of euphony, free from the upsetting intrusion of heterogeneous dissonance; an air of mysticism pervaded his music, aided by the programmatic titles which he often assigned to his compositions. A composer of relentless fecundity, he produced over 60 syms.; several operas, quasi-operas, and pseudo-operas; and an enormous amount of choral music. The totality of his output is in excess of 370 opus numbers. In a laudable spirit of self-criticism, he destroyed 7 of his early syms. and began numbering them anew so that his first numbered sym. (subtitled *Exile*) was chronologically his 8th. He performed a similar auto-da-fé on other dispensable pieces. Among his more original compositions is a symphonic score *And God Created Great Whales*, in which the voices of humpback whales recorded on tape were used as a solo with the orch.; the work was performed to great effect in the campaign to save the whale from destruction by human (and inhuman) predators.

WORKS: DRAMATIC: Opera: *Etchmiadzin* (1946); *The Blue Flame* (San Antonio, Dec. 13, 1959); *Spirit of the Avalanche* (Tokyo, Feb. 15, 1963); *Wind Drum* and *The Burning House* (both at Gatlinburg, Tenn., Aug. 23, 1964); *Pilate* (Los Angeles, June 26, 1966); *The Travelers* (Los Altos Hills, Calif., April 22, 1967); *Pericles* (1975); *Tale of the Sun Goddess Going into the Stone House* (1979). **Operetta:** *Afton Water*, after William Saroyan (1951). **Ballet:** *Killer of Enemies* (1983); *God the Revenger* (1986).

ORCH.: Syms. (the numbering does not always coincide with the chronological order of composition): No. 1, *Exile* (BBC, London, May 26, 1939), No. 2, *Mysterious Mountain* (Houston, Oct. 31, 1955, Stokowski conducting), No. 3 (N.Y., Oct. 14, 1956), No. 4 for Concert Band (Pittsburgh, June 28, 1959), No. 5, *Short Symphony* (1959), No. 6, *Celestial Gate* (1959), No. 7, *Nanga Parvat*, for Band (1959), No. 8, *Arjuna* (1947; Madras, India, Feb. 1, 1960), No. 9, *St. Vartan* (N.Y., March 11,

1951), No. 10 (1959), No. 11, *All Men Are Brothers* (1960; New Orleans, March 21, 1961; rev. version, New Orleans, March 31, 1970), No. 12 for Chorus and Orch. (1960), No. 13 (1953), No. 14, *Ararat* (1960); No. 15, *Silver Pilgrimage* (N.Y., March 28, 1963), No. 16, *Korean Kayageum,* for Strings and Korean Percussion Instruments (Seoul, Jan. 26, 1963), No. 17 for Metal Orch., commissioned by the American Metallurgical Congress (Cleveland, Oct. 23, 1963), No. 18, *Circe* (1964), No. 19, *Vishnu* (N.Y., June 2, 1967), No. 20, *3 Journeys to a Holy Mountain,* for Concert Band (1968), No. 21, *Etchmiadzin* (1968), No. 22, *City of Light* (1970), No. 23, *Ani,* for Band (1972), No. 24, *Majnun,* for Chorus and Orch. (1973; Lubbock, Tex., Jan. 25, 1974), No. 25, *Odysseus,* for Chamber Orch. (1973; London, April 10, 1974), No. 26, *Consolation* (San Jose, Calif., Oct. 24, 1975), No. 27 (1975), No. 28 (1976), No. 29 for Horn and Orch. (Minneapolis, May 4, 1977), No. 30 (1976), No. 31 for Strings (Seattle, Dec. 7, 1977), No. 32 for Chamber Orch. (1977), No. 33 for Chamber Orch. (1978), No. 34 (1977), No. 35 for Korean Instruments and Orch. (Seoul, June 9, 1978), No. 36 for Flute and Orch. (Washington, D.C., Jan. 16, 1979; Rampal soloist; Rostropovich conducting), No. 37 (1978), No. 38 for Soprano and Orch. (1978), No. 39 for Guitar and Orch. (1978), No. 40 for Brass, Timpani, and Orch. (1979; Interlochen, April 9, 1982), No. 41, *Mountain Sunset* (1979), No. 42 (1979), No. 43 (1979; Aptos, Calif., Aug. 20, 1981), No. 44 (1980), No. 45 (1979), No. 46, *To the Green Mountains* (Burlington, Vt., May 2, 1981), No. 47, *Walla Walla, Land of Many Waters,* for Soprano and Orch. (Walla Walla, Wash., Nov. 24, 1981), No. 48, *Vision of Andromeda* (Miami, Fla., June 21, 1982), No. 49, *Christmas,* for Strings (1981), No. 50, *Mount St. Helens* (1982), No. 51 for Trumpet and Strings (1982), No. 52, *Journey to Vega* (1983), No. 53, *Star Dawn,* for Band (1983), No. 54 (1983), No. 55 (1983), No. 56 (1983), No. 57, *Cold Mountain,* for Tenor, Soprano, Clarinet, and Strings (1983), No. 58, *Sacra,* for Soprano, Baritone, Chorus, and Orch. (Valparaiso, Ind., Nov. 10, 1985), No. 59 (Bellevue, Wash., Jan. 28, 1985), No. 60, *To the Appalachian Mountains* (Knoxville, Tenn., April 24, 1985), No. 61 (Boise, Idaho, Oct. 4, 1986). No. 62, *Let Not Man Forget,* for Baritone and Strings (1987), No. 63, *Loon Lake* (1988), No. 64 (1989), and No. 65, *Artsakh* (N.Y., Oct. 6, 1991). **C o n c e r t o s :** Cello Concerto (1936); *Lousadzak* (Coming of Light) for Piano and Strings (1944; Boston, Feb. 4, 1945); *Return and Rebuild the Desolate Places,* concerto for Trumpet and Strings (N.Y., June 17, 1945); *Asori,* concerto for Flute, Cornet, Bassoon, Trumpet, Timpani, and Strings (1946); *Sosi,* concerto for Violin, Piano, Percussion, and Strings (1948; N.Y., March 6, 1949); *Artik,* horn concerto (1948; Rochester, N.Y., May 7, 1954); *Zertik Parkim,* concerto for Piano and Chamber Orch. (1948); *Elibris* (God of Dawn), concerto for Flute and Strings (1949; San Francisco, Jan. 26, 1950); *Khaldis,* concerto for 4 Trumpets, Piano, and Percussion (1951); *Talin,* concerto for Viola and String Orch. (1952); Accordion Concerto (1959); Concerto for Harp and Strings (1973); Euphonium Concerto (1977); 2 guitar concertos (1977, 1985); Soprano Saxophone Concerto (1980). Also 8 numbered concertos: No. 1, *Arevakal* (Season of the Sun), for Orch. (1951; N.Y., Feb. 18, 1952), No. 2 for Violin and Strings (1951–57), No. 3, *Diran,* for Baritone Horn or Trombone and Strings (1948), No. 4 for Orch. (1952; Louisville, Ky., Feb. 20, 1954), No. 5 for Piano and Strings (1952), No. 6 for Harmonica and Strings (1953), No. 7 for Orch. (1953), and No. 8 for Orch. (1953). **O T H E R :** *Storm on Mt. Wildcat* (1931); *Celestial Fantasy* (1944); *3 Armenian Rhapsodies* (1944); *Khiriam Hairis* for Trumpet and Strings (1944); *Tzaikerk* (Evening Song; 1945); *Kohar* (1946); *Forest of Prophetic Sounds* (1948); Overture for Trombone and Strings (1948); *Janabar,* 5 hymns for Violin, Trumpet, Piano, and Strings (1949;

N.Y., March 11, 1951); *Prelude and Quadruple Fugue* (1955); *Meditation on Orpheus* (1957–58); *Copernicus,* tone poem (1960); *Mountain of Prophecy* (1960); *Meditation on Zeami,* symphonic poem (1963; N.Y., Oct. 5, 1964); *Ukiyo, Floating World,* tone poem (1964; Salt Lake City, Jan. 30, 1965); *Fantasy on Japanese Wood Prints* for Xylophone and Orch. (Chicago, July 4, 1964); *The Holy City* (Portland, Ore., April 11, 1967); *Fra Angelico,* symphonic poem (Detroit, March 21, 1968); *Mountain and Rivers Without End* for 10 Instruments (1968); *And God Created Great Whales* for Orch., with Voices of Humpback Whales recorded on Tape (1969; N.Y., June 11, 1970); *A Rose for Emily,* ballet (1970); *Dawn on Mt. Tahoma* (1973); *Fanfare to the New Atlantis* (1975); *Ode to Freedom* for Violin and Orch. (Vienna, Va., July 3, 1976, Yehudi Menuhin soloist); *Rubaiyat* for Narrator, Accordion, and Orch. (1975; N.Y., May 20, 1977). **C H A M B E R :** 2 piano quintets (1926, rev. 1962; 1964); Piano Trio (1935); 5 string quartets (1936, 1950, 1968, 1970, 1976); Violin Sonata (1937); Suite for English Horn and Bassoon (1938); *Varak* for Violin and Piano (1944); *Anahid* for Flute, English Horn, Trumpet, Timpani, Percussion, and Strings (1944); *Saris* for Violin and Piano (1946); *Haroutiun* (Resurrection), aria and fugue for Trumpet and Strings (1948); *Sosi* (Forest of Prophetic Sounds) for Violin, Piano, Horn, Timpani, Giant Tam-tam, and Strings (1948); *Khirgiz Suite* for Violin and Piano (1951); *Orbit No. 1* for Flute, Harp, Celesta, and Tam-tam (1952) and *No. 2* for Alto Recorder and Piano (1952); *koke no kiwa* (Moss Garden) for English Horn, Clarinet, Harp, and Percussion (1954); Wind Quintet (1960); *Nagooran* for Ensemble of South Indian Instruments (1962); String Trio (1962); Sextet for Violin and 5 Percussionists (1966); *6 Dances* for Brass Quintet (1967); *Spirit of Ink,* 9 pieces for 3 Flutes (1968); *Vibration Painting* for 13 String Instruments (1969); *The Garden of Adonis* for Flute and Harp (1971); Sonata for 2 Bassoons (1973); Clarinet Quartet (1973); *Night of a White Cat* for Clarinet and Piano (1973); *Fantasy* for Double Bass and Piano (1974); Suite for 4 Trumpets and Trombone (1976); Suite for Alto Saxophone and Guitar (1976); Septet for Flute, Clarinet, Bass Clarinet, Trumpet, Trombone, Double Bass, and Percussion (1976); Sonata for 2 Clarinets (1977); *Sunset on Mt. Tahoma* for 2 Trumpets, Trombone, and Organ (1978); Sonata for Clarinet and Harpsichord (1978); Saxophone Trio (1979); 2 sonatas for 3 Trumpets and 2 Trombones (1979); *Lake Winnipesaukee,* sextet (1982); *Capuan Sonata* for Viola and Piano (1982); *Prelude and Fugue* for Brass Quartet (1983); *Spirit of Trees,* sonata for Harp and Guitar (1983); Clarinet Sonata (1983); *Starry Night* for Flute, Xylophone, and Harp (1984); Sonata for Alto Recorder and Harpsichord (1984); *Mountain under the Sea* for Alto Saxophone, Timpani, Vibraphone, Tam-tam, and Harp (1984). **K E Y B O A R D** (for Piano Solo unless otherwise given): *Mountain Lullaby* (1931); *3 Preludes and Fugues* (1935); *Sonata Ricercare* (1935); *Macedonian Mountain Dance* (1937); *Do you remember the last silence?* (1957); *Poseidon Sonata* (1957); *Child of the Garden* for Piano, 4–Hands (1958); *Madras Sonata* (1947; final rev., 1959); *Bardo Sonata* (1959); *Love Song Vanishing into Sounds of Crickets* (1979); *Sonata Catamount* (1980); *Sonata, Journey to Arcturus* (1981); *Hiroshige's Cat* (1982); Sonata No. 5 for Harpsichord (1982); *Sonata on the Long Total Eclipse of the Moon, July 6, 1982* (1982); *Tsugouharu Fujita's Cat* (1982); *Lake Sammamish* (1983); Organ Sonata No. 2, *Invisible Sun* (1984); *Lilydale* (1986); *Cougar Mountain,* sonata (1985); Sonata (1986). **V O C A L :** *Ad Lyram* for Solo Voices, Double Chorus, and Chamber Orch. (Houston, March 12, 1957); *To the God Who Is in the Fire,* cantata (Urbana, Ill., April 13, 1957); *Magnificat* for Solo Voices, Chorus, and Chamber Orch. (1957); *Fuji,* cantata for Women's Voices, Flute, Harp, and String Orch. (1960); *In the Beginning Was the Word* for Vocal Soloists, Chorus, and Orch.

(1963); *Lady of Light* for Solo Voices, Chorus, and Chamber Orch. (1969); *Saturn*, 12 pieces for Soprano, Clarinet, and Piano (1971); *The Way of Jesus*, folk oratorio (N.Y., Feb. 23, 1975); *Revelations of St. Paul*, cantata (1980; N.Y., Jan. 28, 1981); *The Waves Unbuild the Wasting Shore*, cantata for Tenor, Chorus, and Organ (1983); *Cantata Domino* for Chorus and Organ (1984); innumerable hymns, anthems, sacred and secular choruses; songs. —NS/LK/DM

Hovland, Egil, Norwegian organist, music critic, and composer; b. Mysen, Oct. 18, 1924. He studied organ and composition at the Oslo Cons. (1946–49), later studying privately with Brustad (1951–52, in Oslo), Holmboe (1954, in Copenhagen), Copland (1957, at Tanglewood), and Dallapiccola (1959, in Florence). He then was active as an organist, music critic, and composer. In 1983 he was made a Knight of the Royal Order of St. Olav for his services to Norwegian music. He cultivates a peculiarly Scandinavian type of neo-Classical polyphony, but is apt to use serial techniques.

WORKS: DRAMATIC: O p e r a : *Brunnen*, church opera (1971–72; Oslo, March 17, 1982); *Fange og fri* (1990). **B a l - l e t :** *Dona Nobis Pacem* (1982); *Den Heliga Dansen* (1982); *Veni Creator Spiritus* (1984); *Danses de la Mort* (Bergen, June 8, 1983). **ORCH.:** *Passacaglia and Fugue* for Strings (1949); *Festival Overture* (1951); 3 syms.: No. 1, *Symphonia Veris* (Sym. of Spring; 1952–53; Oslo, Dec. 10, 1954), No. 2 (1954–55; Bergen, Nov. 8, 1956), and No. 3 for Narrator, Chorus, and Orch. (1969–70; Oslo, April 9, 1970); Suite (1954); Concertino for 3 Trumpets and Strings (1954–55); *Music* for 10 Instruments (1957); Suite for Flute and Strings (1959); *Festival Overture* for Wind Orch. (1962); *Lamenti* (Oslo, April 24, 1964); *Rorate* for 5 Sopranos, Organ, Chamber Orch., and Tape (1966–67); *Rapsodi 69* (1969); Trombone Concerto (1972); Violin Concerto (1974); *Noël-Variations* (1975); Piano Concerto (1976–77; Oslo, Dec. 1, 1977); *Tombeau de Bach* (1977–78); Concerto for Piccolo, Flute, and Strings (1986; Oslo, April 20, 1989). **CHAMBER:** Suite for Flute and Piano (1950); *Motus* for Flute (1961); *Varianti* for 2 Pianos (1964); Piano Trio (1965); 2 wind quintets (1965, 1980); *Elemento* for Organist and 2 Assistants (1965; rev. 1966); Variations for Oboe and Piano (1968–69); String Quartet (1981); organ pieces. **VOCAL:** *Song of Songs* for Soprano, Violin, Percussion, and Piano (1962–63); *Magnificat* for Alto, Flute, and Harp (1964); *Missa vigilate* for Soprano, Baritone, Chorus, 2 Female Dancers, Organ, and Tape (1967); *Mass to the Risen Christ* for Chorus and Instruments (1968); *All Saints' Mass* for Soprano, Chorus, Organ, and Instruments (1970); *Den vakreste rosen* (The Most Beautiful Rose) for Narrator, 4 Sopranos, Organ, and Orch., after Hans Christian Andersen (1970); *Missa verbi* for Chorus, Organ, and Instruments (1972–73); *Pilgrim's Mass* for Chorus, Organ, 9 Brasses, and Congregation (1982).—NS/LK/DM

Howard, Ann (real name, **Pauline Swadling**), English mezzo-soprano; b. London, July 22, 1936. She was a student of Topliss Green and Rodolfa Lhombino. After singing in musical theater, she joined the chorus of the Royal Opera House, Covent Garden, London, and was awarded a grant to pursue her training with Modesti in Paris. In 1964 she made her operatic debut as Azucena with the Welsh National Opera in Cardiff; that same year, she made her first appearance at the Sadler's Wells Opera in London as Czipra in *Der Zigeunerbaron*, and subsequently appeared there regularly, and later with its successor, the English National Opera. In 1973 she made her Covent Garden debut as Amneris. As a guest artist, she sang in Europe, the U.S. (debut as Carmen in New Orleans, 1971), Canada, Mexico, and South Africa. Among her many roles were Fricka, Brangäne, Ortrud, Eboli, Clytemnestra, Dalila, Carmen, Offenbach's Hélène, Herodiade, and Jocasta. She also sang in operetta and in contemporary operas. —NS/LK/DM

Howard, Darnell, early jazz clarinetist, saxophonist violinist; b. Chicago, July 25, 1895; d. San Francisco, Sept. 2, 1966. His father, Sam, played violin, cornet, and piano; his mother played piano. Howard took up violin at the age of seven, and was already working in local theater orchs. as a teenager. His first professional work was with John H. Wickcliffe's Ginger Orch. (1913–16) in Chicago and Milwaukee. In September 1917, he traveled to N.Y. with W. C. Handy's Orch. for his first recordings (on violin). He returned to Chicago, led his own band at local clubs, then toured the Middle West with Charlie Elgar (1921). With several other Elgar sidemen, he joined the band accompanying the touring company of *Plantation Days* (led by James P. Johnson) for a brief stay in London (March–May 1923). He returned to the U.S., then revisited Europe with the five-piece Singing Syncopators (1924). On his return to Chicago, he played with Carroll Dickerson, Dave Peyton, and finally King Oliver (on alto/soprano sax, clarinet, and violin) for seven months in 1925. Howard then left the country again, this time with the N.Y. Singing Syncopators (led by pianist William Hegamin). The N.Y.S.S. were based in Shanghai, but also toured the Philippines and Japan. On his return in July 1926, he rejoined King Oliver. Through the later 1920s he worked with various leaders, sometimes playing with two different bands simultaneously, including stints with Erskine Tate (1926–October 1927), Carroll Dickerson (1927), and Dave Peyton (1928–29). He also led his own groups during these years. He spent much of the 1930s as a member of Earl Hines's Big Band (from 1931–37). He then reverted to working as a sideman for various leaders, while continuing to lead small groups for club work in Chicago. He also operated a small electronics repair business in the mid-1940s. He spent two periods working in Calif. (with Kid Ory from August–October 1945 and then Muggsy Spanier from late 1948–spring 1953). From 1955–62, he reunited with Hines, who was then leading a smaller band, but then quit due to a serious illness. He recovered enough to return to playing. He made a final European tour in early 1966, but returned home seriously ill; he suffered a stroke in June 1966, which ended his playing days. He died that September of a brain tumor.—JC/LP

Howard, Eddy, engaging popular singer, bandleader, and songwriter; b. Woodland, Calif., Sept. 12, 1914; d. Palm Springs, Calif., May 23, 1963. A crooner in the style of Rudy Vallée, Howard was one of the most popular male solo singers of the late 1940s and early 1950s. He led a band that existed mostly to support his warm, well-articulated singing of ballads and novelty songs. Including his hits as vocalist with Dick Jurgens's

Orch., he reached the charts 44 times between 1939 and 1955, his most successful recordings being "To Each His Own," "Sin," and "I Wonder, I Wonder, I Wonder." He also wrote songs, among them his theme, the chart-topping "Careless."

Howard grew up in southern Calif. and attended San Jose State Coll. and Stanford Univ. Medical School. He got a job singing on the radio in L.A., then worked with several bands. He also played guitar, but he got into the Dick Jurgens band in San Francisco in 1934 by auditioning on the trombone. He stayed with the band as its singer and guitarist until 1940. In October 1939, Jurgens's recording of "It's a Hundred to One You're in Love" (music and lyrics by Jurgens and Ronnie Kemper) with Howard on vocals made the hit parade.

Howard, Jurgens, and the band's arranger, Lew Quadling, wrote the music and lyrics for "Careless," which they submitted to Irving Berlin's publishing company. Berlin wrote a new set of lyrics without taking credit and published the song, which was given its most successful recording by Glenn Miller and His Orch.—a #1 hit in February 1940. The same month, Howard enjoyed his biggest hit with the Jurgens band, "In an Old Dutch Garden (By an Old Dutch Mill)" (music by Will Grosz, lyrics by Mack Gordon), which spent 11 weeks in the hit parade. That was enough to convince him to leave Jurgens and go it alone. Meanwhile, two of his compositions became hits, "A Million Dreams Ago" (music and lyrics by Howard, Lew Quadling, and Dick Jurgens) for Jurgens in August and "Now I Lay Me Down to Dream" (music and lyrics by Howard and Ted Fiorito) for Andy Kirk and His Clouds of Joy in November.

Howard signed to Columbia Records as a solo act and from January to May 1941 sang on Edgar A. Guest's network radio series. But he soon formed his own band. He struggled during the early 1940s but managed to land spots on the radio series *Carton of Cheer* in 1944 and 1945 and *The Gay Mrs. Featherstone* from April to October 1945. Then, having switched to the Majestic record label, he finally scored a major hit with "To Each His Own" (music by Jay Livingston, lyrics by Ray Evans), which hit #1 in August 1946 and became a million-seller. He enjoyed a second Top Ten hit in 1946 with "The Rickety Rickshaw Man" (music and lyrics by Ervin Drake) in December, then scored five Top Ten hits in 1947, including "My Adobe Hacienda" (music and lyrics by Louise Massey and Lee Penny) and "I Wonder, I Wonder, I Wonder" (music and lyrics by Daryl Hutchins). He also made the Top Ten with his album *Romance* and was the top recording artist of the year.

Howard's success brought him his own network radio series, *Sheaffer Parade*, which ran from September 1947 to September 1948. He scored two more Top Ten hits in 1948, including "(I'd Love to Get You) On a Slow Boat to China" (music and lyrics by Frank Loesser), which marked his switch to Mercury Records. There were six more Top Ten hits between 1949 and 1952, notably "Sin" (music by George Hoven, lyrics by Chester R. Shull), which hit #1 in November 1951 and sold a million copies.

Howard continued to reach the charts through 1955 while performing on radio and in live appearances. He was living in Palm Springs, Calif., in 1963 and preparing for the summer season on Catalina Island when he choked to death on food particles at 48. After his death, an Eddy Howard Orch. was organized and led by Chris Powers.—**WR**

Howard, John Tasker, eminent American writer on music; b. Brooklyn, Nov. 30, 1890; d. West Orange, N.Y., Nov. 20, 1964. He attended Williams Coll. in Williamstown, Mass., then studied composition with Howard Brockway and Mortimer Wilson. He was managing editor of the *Musician* (1919–22), and served as educational director of the Ampico Corp. (1922–28). He ed. the music section of *McCall's Magazine* (1928–30) and *Cue* (1936–38), and then taught at Columbia Univ. (1950–54). From 1940 to 1956 he was the curator of the Americana Music Collection at the N.Y. Public Library, which he enriched to a great extent. His major achievement was the publication of several books and monographs on American music and musicians. He was also a composer of modest, but respectable, attainments. He wrote a piece for Piano and Orch., *Fantasy on a Choral Theme* (Orange, N.J., Feb. 20, 1929), *Foster Sonatina* for Violin and Piano, piano pieces, and some songs.

WRITINGS (all publ. in N.Y.): *Our American Music* (1931; 4th ed., rev., 1965); *Stephen Foster, America's Troubadour* (1934; 2nd ed., rev., 1953); *Ethelbert Nevin* (1935); *Our Contemporary Composers, American Music in the 20th Century* (1941); *This Modern Music* (1942; new ed. by J. Lyons, 1957, as *Modern Music*); *The World's Great Operas* (1948); with G. Bellows, *A Short History of Music in America* (1957).—**NS/LK/DM**

Howard, Kathleen, Canadian-American contralto; b. Niagara Falls, Ontario, July 17, 1884; d. Los Angeles, Aug. 15, 1956. She studied in N.Y. with Bouhy and in Paris with Jean de Reszke. She appeared at the Metz Opera (1907–09), at Darmstadt (1909–12), at Covent Garden in London (1913), and with the Century Opera in N.Y. (1914–15). After appearing as the nurse in *Boris Godunov* with the Metropolitan Opera in Brooklyn on Nov. 14, 1916, she made her formal debut with the company in N.Y. as the 3rd Lady in *Die Zauberflöte* on Nov. 20, 1916, remaining on its roster until 1928. After her retirement from the stage, she was engaged in magazine work and was fashion ed. of *Harper's Bazaar* (1928–33). She publ. an autobiography, *Confessions of an Opera Singer* (N.Y., 1918).—**NS/LK/DM**

Howard, Kid (Avery), early jazz trumpeter; b. New Orleans, April 22, 1908; d. there, March 28, 1966. He started on drums at 14, played with Andrew Morgan and Chris Kelly, then switched to cornet. He did parade work for many years with the Eureka, Allen's Brass Band, and the Tuxedo. He organized his own band in the late 1920s, which toured as far away as Chicago. During the 1930s he played in local pit bands for shows. After recording with George Lewis in 1943, he gigged in New Orleans for several years. Howard worked regularly with Lewis from 1952 (including a tour of Europe 1959). He recovered from serious illness in 1961 and played frequently at Preservation Hall and Dixieland Hall in New Orleans during last years of his life. He died of a cerebral hemorrhage.

DISC.: *K. H.'s New Orleans Band* (1962); *K. H.'s Band* (1962); *Heart and Bowels of New Orleans* (1963); *K. H. at the San Jacinto Hall* (1965).—JC/LP

Howard, Leslie (John), Australian pianist, organist, conductor, musicologist, and composer; b. Melbourne, April 29, 1948. He was educated at Monash Univ., Victoria (B.A., 1969; M.A., 1972), the Univ. of Melbourne (1966–71), and the Accademia Musicale Chigiana in Siena (1972–75), and also received private instruction from Guido Agosti (piano), Donald Britton (organ and harpsichord), Fritz Rieger (conducting), and Franco Donatoni (composition). After making his formal debut as a pianist in Melbourne in 1967, he appeared as a soloist with orchs., as a recitalist, and as a chamber music artist in Australia, Europe, North and South America, and Asia. He also taught at Monash Univ. (1970–72) and was a prof. of piano at the Guildhall School of Music and Drama in London (1987–92). While Howard's keyboard repertoire extends from classical masterpieces to contemporary scores, he has become particularly associated with the music of Liszt, both as a performer and a researcher. In 1988 he became president of the Liszt Soc. in England. Among his honors are the Liszt Medal of Honor of the Hungarian government (1986) and the Medal of Honor of the Liszt Soc. of America (1993). His writings have appeared in various publications.

WORKS: DRAMATIC: *Fruits of the Earth*, ballet (1971); *Hreidar the Fool*, opera (1973–74). ORCH.: *Canzona Sinfonica* for Symphonic Wind Band (1977–78). CHAMBER: String Quartet (1966); Trio for Piano, Violin, and Cello (1968); Violin Sonata (1968); Sonata for Percussion and Piano (1968); *Quattro Riflessioni* for Violin, Clarinet, and Piano (1969); *Pavane* for Clarinet, 2 Violins, and Piano (1970); Horn Sonata (1970); *Ramble on a Russian Theme* for Domra or Mandolin or Violin and Piano (1972); *Romance* for Flute and Piano (1980); Cello Sonata (1983); Trio for Piano, Violin, and Viola or Clarinet (1987); *Grand Galop drolatique* for Organ and Piano (1993). KEYBOARD: Piano: *Capriccio* for 2 Pianos (1967); Sonata (1970); 2 *Album-Leaves* (1972); *Variations on a Theme by Bartók* for Piano Duet (1973); 24 *Classical Preludes* (1989). Organ: *Moto di gioia—Postludium* (1993); *Mr. Haydn's Clock—Ein Orgelstück für einer Uhr?* (1993). VOCAL: *Choral Song* for Solo Treble Voices, Chorus, and Orch. (1970); *Recitation* for Speaker, Guitar, Cello, and Double Bass (1972); *A Festival Mass* for Chorus and Organ (1973); *Missa Sancti Petri* for Double Chorus and Organ (1992–93); songs.—NS/LK/DM

Howard, Noah, free-jazz alto saxophonist; b. New Orleans, April 6, 1943. He sang in a choir as child. In 1960 he began two years in military service, then moved to Calif. and met alto saxophonist Byron Allen. This experience stimulated his interest in free jazz and led him to study alto saxophone and trumpet. In 1965 he moved to N.Y., where he played with avant-gardists including Archie Shepp, Pharoah Sanders, Sun Ra, and Sonny Sharrock. He formed a quartet and recorded two albums for ESP (1965, 1966). In 1969 he joined Frank Wright's group with pianist Bobby Few and drummer

Muhammad Ali and toured Europe with them in 1970 before leaving. During the 1970s, he mostly led his own groups, dividing his time between N.Y. and Europe. He was involved with the N.Y. Musicians Festival 1972–74. Since the early 1980s, he has been less active.

DISC.: *N. H. Quartet* (1966); *At Judson Hall* (1966); *The Black Ark* (1969); *Schizophrenic Blues: The N. H. Quartet Live in Berlin* (1977). A. Shepp: *Black Gypsy* (1969). F. Wright: *One for John* (1969).—LP

Howard, Paul (Leroy), jazz tenor saxophonist, clarinetist; b. Steubenville, Ohio, Sept. 20, 1895; d. L.A., Feb. 18, 1980. His father played cornet, his mother piano and organ. He started on cornet, then began doubling on alto sax (and also learned clarinet, oboe, bassoon, flute, and piano). He moved to L.A. in 1911. His first professional work was in 1916 with Wood Wilson's Syncopators (on tenor sax), then with Satchel McVea's Howdy Band. He continued doubling on cornet until 1917, worked for a while in San Diego, then spent a long spell with Harry Southard's Black and Tan Band, starting in 1918. During the early 1920s he also played with King Oliver and Jelly Roll Morton on the West Coast. He was with the Quality Four (Harvey Brooks on piano) from 1923, then led his own Quality Serenaders from 1924, which played long residencies at L.A.-based clubs through the early 1930s. Thereafter, he worked with various other leaders through the decade's end, until reforming his own band, which played a regular gig for the next 14 years until 1953. He continued to gig thereafter until the end of the 1950s, and then was more or less retired for the remainder of his life.—JC/LP

Howarth, Elgar, English conductor and composer; b. Cannock, Staffordshire, Nov. 4, 1935. He studied at the Univ. of Manchester (Mus.B.) and at the Royal Manchester Coll. of Music. After playing trumpet in the orch. of the Royal Opera, Covent Garden, London (1958–63), he was principal trumpeter of the Royal Phil. of London (1963–69). He was a trumpeter with the Philip Jones Brass Ensemble (1965–76) and the London Sinfonietta (1968–71). From 1970 he pursued a career as a conductor. In 1978 he conducted the premiere of Ligeti's *Le Grand Macabre* in Stockholm, and in 1982 its first British performance at the English National Opera in London. In 1985 he made his debut at Covent Garden with Tippett's *King Priam*. From 1985 to 1988 he was principal guest conductor of Opera North in Leeds. He conducted the premieres of Birtwistle's *The Mask of Orpheus* at the English National Opera in 1986, *Gawain* at Covent Garden in 1991, and *The Second Mrs. Kong* at the Glyndebourne Festival in 1994. In 1997 he conducted the British premiere of Strauss's *Die ägyptische Helena* in Garsington. With Patrick Howarth, he publ. *What a Performance! The Brass Band Plays...* (London, 1988). He composed mainly for brass instruments. —NS/LK/DM

Howarth, Judith, English soprano; b. Ipswich, Sept. 11, 1962. She was trained at the Royal Scottish Academy of Music and Drama in Glasgow and at the National Opera School, and received vocal instruction from Patricia Macmahon. In 1984 she made her debut as a soloist with the English Chamber Orch. In 1985 she was awarded the Kathleen Ferrier Prize and made her first appearance at London's Covent Garden as the First Maid in Zemlinsky's *Der Zwerg*. Her U.S. debut followed in 1989 when she appeared in concert in Seattle. In 1991 she was engaged at the London Promenade Concerts, in Salzburg, and in Aix-en-Provence. She portrayed Morgana in *Alcina* at Covent Garden in 1992, and returned there as Gilda in 1993 and as Walton's Cressida in 1995. In 1998 she sang Donizetti's Marie in Geneva.—NS/LK/DM

Howe, Mary (Carlisle), American pianist and composer; b. Richmond, Va., April 4, 1882; d. Washington, D.C., Sept. 14, 1964. She received training in piano from Richard Burmeister in Germany and with Ernest Hutcheson and Harold Randolph at the Peabody Cons. of Music in Baltimore, where she also studied composition with Gustav Strube; she also had lessons with Boulanger. She toured as a duo-pianist with Anne Hull from 1920 to 1935; with her 3 children, she appeared with the "4 Howes" singing madrigals and early music. In 1926 she helped to organize the Assn. of American Women Composers. She was an accomplished composer of works in a tonal idiom.

WORKS: DRAMATIC: B a l l e t : *Cards* (1936); *Le jongleur de Notre Dame* (1959). ORCH.: *Fugue* for Strings (1922); *Poèma* (1924); *Sand* (1926); *Castellana* for 2 Pianos and Orch. (1930); *Dirge* (1931); *Free Passacaglia with Fugue* for Chamber Orch. (1932); *American Piece: What Price Glory* (1935); *Coulennes* (1936; also for Chamber Orch.); *Stars* (1937); *Paean* (1940); *Potomac* (1940); *Polka, Waltz, and Finale* (1946); *Agreeable Overture* for Chamber Orch. (1949); *Rock* (1955); *Stars and Sand* (1963). OTHER : 3 string quartets; piano pieces; choral works; numerous songs.—NS/LK/DM

Howell, Dorothy, English pianist and composer; b. Handsworth, Feb. 25, 1898; d. London, Jan. 12, 1982. She studied composition with McEwen and piano with Matthay at the Royal Academy of Music in London, where from 1924 to 1970 she taught music theory. Among her works are a ballet, *Koong Shee*, a symphonic poem, *Lamia*, a Piano Concerto (1923), and chamber music.—NS/LK/DM

Howell, Gwynne (Richard), Welsh bass; b. Gorseinon, June 13, 1938. He was educated at the Univ. of Wales in Swansea (B.Sc.) and pursued training in town planning at the Univ. of Manchester. He also studied voice with Redvers Llewellyn, at the Royal Manchester Coll. of Music with Gwilym Jones, and in London with Otakar Kraus (1968–72). While in Manchester, he gained experience singing Hunding, Fasolt, and Pogner. In 1968 he made his first appearance at the Sadler's Wells Opera in London as Monterone, where he became a principal artist, and with its successor, the English National Opera. In 1970 he made his debut at Covent Garden in London as the 1st Nazarene in *Salome*, where he later created the title role in Maxwell Davies' *Taverner* (July 12, 1972) and sang various Italian, German, and French roles. On Jan. 21, 1985, he

made his Metropolitan Opera debut in N.Y. as Lodovico. Among his finest roles were the Commendatore, Sarastro, Pimen, Timur, Gurnemanz, the Landgrave, Philip II, and Hans Sachs. He also sang widely in concert. In 1998 he was made a Commander of the Order of the British Empire.—NS/LK/DM

Howells, Anne (Elizabeth), English mezzo-soprano; b. Southport, Jan. 12, 1941. She was a student of Frederick Cox at the Royal Manchester Coll. of Music, where she sang Eros in the first English production of Gluck's *Paride ed Elena* (1963). Following further training with Vera Rosza, she made her professional operatic debut as Flora in *La Traviata* with the Welsh National Opera in Cardiff in 1966. From 1966 she appeared regularly at the Glyndebourne Festivals. In 1967 she made her first appearance at London's Covent Garden as Flora, returning there in subsequent years as Rosina, Cherubino, Siébel, Ascanio, Mélisande, Meg Page, Despina, and Giulietta. In 1972 she made her U.S. debut as Dorabella with the Chicago Lyric Opera, which role she also sang at her debuts at the Metropolitan Opera in N.Y. (Oct. 15, 1975), and the San Francisco Opera (1979). She also had guest engagements in Geneva, Salzburg, Berlin, and Paris. Howells created the role of Régine in Rolf Liebermann's *La Forêt* (Geneva, April 11, 1987). In 1966 she married **Ryland Davies.** After their divorce in 1981, she married **Stafford Dean.**—NS/LK/DM

Howells, Herbert (Norman), eminent English composer and teacher; b. Lydney, Gloucestershire, Oct. 17, 1892; d. Oxford, Feb. 23, 1983. He received training in composition from Herbert Brewer, the organist at Gloucester Cathedral. In 1912 he was awarded a scholarship to the Royal Coll. of Music in London, where he was a student of Stanford, Parratt, Charles Wood, and Parry. In 1917 he became sub-organist at Salisbury Cathedral. In 1920 he became a teacher of composition at the Royal Coll. of Music. He also taught at St. Paul's Girls' School (1932–62), was acting organist of St. John's Coll., Cambridge (1941–45), and the King Edward VII Prof. of Music at the Univ. of London (1950–64). In 1953 he was made a Commander of the Order of the British Empire and in 1972 a Companion of Honour. While the influence of Vaughan Williams may be found in Howells's oeuvre, he developed his own voice in which church modes and the pentatonic scale predominate. Several of his orch. and chamber works display an extraordinary craftsmanship, and his organ music has acquired repertoire status. Particularly notable among his orch. works are the *Fantasia* for Cello and Orch. (1936) and the Concerto for Strings (1938). However, it is as a composer of vocal music, and most notably of choral music, that Howells has made his most significant contribution to the music of the 20th century. The death of his young son Michael in 1935 was a defining event of Howells's life. His *Requiem* (1936), which he did not allow to be published until 1980, served as an expression of his heartfelt loss. A major portion of it was utilized in Howells's greatest work, the *Hymnus Paradisi* for Soloists, Chorus, and Orch. (1938), at once personal and universal in its coming to terms with the transitory nature of life. It was first performed under the composer's direction at the Three Choirs Festival in Gloucester on Sept. 7, 1950. This masterwork was followed by two more choral works of major stature, the expansive and challenging *Missa Sabrinensis—The Severn Mass* (1954) and the finely wrought *Stabat Mater* (1963). In 1987 the Herbert Howells Soc. was founded.

WORKS: ORCH.: 2 piano concertos: No. 1 (1913; London, July 10, 1914) and No. 2 (1924); *The B's*, suite (1914; Bournemouth, Feb. 13, 1919); *3 Dances* for Violin and Orch. (1914–15); *Puck's Minuet* (1917); *Merry Eye* (London, Sept. 30, 1920); *Procession* (1922; orch. of a piano piece, 1920); *Pastoral Rhapsody* (Eastbourne Festival, Nov. 1923, composer conducting; rev. version, Bournemouth, March 1924, composer conducting); *Paradise Rondel* (Gloucester, July 25, 1925); *Pageantry*, suite for Brass Band (1934); untitled piece for Cello and Orch. (1935; orch. by C. Palmer as *Threnody* for Cello and Orch. and 1st perf. in London, Nov. 1992); *Fantasia* for Cello and Orch. (1937; London, Jan. 16, 1982); Concerto for Strings (BBC, Dec. 16, 1938); Suite for Strings (1942); *Music for a Prince* (1948; London, Jan. 23, 1949; based on 2 pieces from *The B's*, suite, 1914); *Triptych* for Brass Band (1960). **CHAMBER:** Piano Quartet (1916); *Rhapsodic Quintet* for Clarinet and Strings (1917); 3 string quartets (c. 1916–35); 3 violin sonatas (1918, 1918, 1923); Oboe Sonata (1942; Cheltenham, July 9, 1984); Clarinet Sonata (1946). **KEYBOARD: Piano:** *Polka* for 2 Pianos (1951); Sonatina (1971). **Organ:** 2 sonatas (1911, 1933); 3 *Psalm Preludes* (2 sets, 1915, 1938–39); 4 *Rhapsodies* (Nos. 1–3, 1915–18, No. 4, 1958); 6 *Pieces* (1940–45); *Siciliano for a High Ceremony* (1952; Edinburgh, Jan. 10, 1953); *Prelude De Profundis* (1958); 2 *Pieces* (1959); *Partita* (1971; London, Feb. 23, 1972). **Clavichord:** *Lambert's Clavichord*, 12 pieces (1926–27); *Howells' Clavichord*, 20 pieces (1941–61). **VOCAL:** *Mass in the Dorian Mode* for Chorus (1912); *Sine Nomine: A Phantasy* for Soprano, Tenor, Chorus, and Orch. (1922); *A Kent Yeoman's Wooing Song* for Soprano, Baritone, Chorus, and Orch. (1933; London, Sept. 10, 1953); *Requiem* for Chorus (1936); *Hymnus Paradisi* for Soprano, Tenor, Chorus, and Orch. (1938; Gloucester, Sept. 7, 1950, composer conducting); several *Te Deum* settings for Chorus (1944 et seq.); *King of Glory*, motet for Chorus and Organ (Holborn, Nov. 22, 1949); *God Is Gone Up*, motet for Chorus and Organ (Cornhill, June 14, 1950); *A Maid Peerless* for Women's Chorus and Orch. (1951); *Behold, O God, Our Defender* for Chorus and Orch. for the coronation of Queen Elizabeth II (1952; London, June 2, 1953); *The House of the Mind*, motet for Chorus and Organ (1954; Holborn, Jan. 2, 1955); *Missa Sabrinensis—The Severn Mass* for Soprano, Tenor, Alto, Baritone, Chorus, and Orch. (Worcester, Sept. 7, 1954); *An English Mass* for Chorus and Orch. (1955; Cornhill, June 4, 1956); *A Sequence for St. Michael* for Chorus and Organ (1961; Cambridge, March 1962); *Stabat Mater* for Tenor, Chorus, and Orch. (1963; London, Nov. 22, 1965); *Take Him, Earth, for Cherishing*, motet on the death of President John F. Kennedy for Chorus (1964); *The Coventry Mass* for Chorus and Organ (1968; Coventry, Oct. 5, 1969); various other sacred and secular choral works; 3 carol-anthems (1918–20), including the famous *A Spotless Rose* (1919); numerous songs, including *King David* (1921). **BIBL.:** R. Spearing, *H. H.: A Tribute to H. H. on His Eightieth Birthday* (London, 1972); C. Palmer, *H. H.: A Study* (London, 1978); idem, *H. H.: A Centenary Celebration* (London, 1993); P. Spicer, *H. H.* (Brigend, Wales, 1998).—**NS/LK/DM**

Howes, Frank (Stewart), English music critic, writer, and editor; b. Oxford, April 2, 1891; d. Standlake, Oxfordshire, Sept. 28, 1974. He studied at St. John's Coll., Oxford. In 1925 he joined the staff of the *Times* of London as music critic, and from 1943 to 1960 was its chief music critic. He was also ed. of the *Folk Song Journal* (later known as the *Journal of the English Folk Dance and Song Society*) from 1927 to 1945. He taught music history and appreciation at the Royal Coll. of Music in London (1938–70), and was Cramb Lecturer at the Univ. of Glasgow (1947 and 1952). In 1954 he was made a Commander of the Order of the British Empire.

WRITINGS (all publ. in London unless otherwise given): *The Borderland of Music and Psychology* (1926); *The Appreciation of Music* (1928); *William Byrd* (1928); *A Key to the Art of Music* (1935); with P. Hope-Wallace, *A Key to Opera* (1939); *Full Orchestra* (1942; 2nd ed., rev. and enl., 1976); *The Music of William Walton* (2 vols., 1942–43; new ed., 1965); *Man, Mind and Music* (1948); *Music: 1945–50* (1951); *The Music of Ralph Vaughan Williams* (1954); *Music and Its Meanings* (1958); *The Cheltenham Festival* (1965); *The English Musical Renaissance* (1966); *Oxford Concerts: A Jubilee Record* (Oxford, 1969); *Folk Music of Britain—and Beyond* (1970).—**NS/LK/DM**

Howlin' Wolf (originally, **Burnett, Chester Arthur**),
American blues singer, guitarist, and harmonica player; b. West Point, Miss., June 10, 1910; d. Hines, Ill., Jan. 10, 1976. Along with Muddy Waters, Howlin' Wolf was one of the most important performers of electric blues to emerge after World War II and go on to influence a generation of British and American rock musicians. His compositions and performances were re-created by The Rolling Stones, The Yardbirds, and Cream, among many others, starting in the 1960s, leading to a revival of interest in the blues and affecting the development of rock 'n' roll. As a performer, his biggest hits were "How Many More Years," "Smokestack Lightnin'," and "I Asked for Water."

Howlin' Wolf was the son of Dock Burnett, a farmer, and his wife, Gertrude. Raised on a plantation, he worked as a farmer through the 1930s while learning guitar from Charlie Patton and harmonica from Sonny Boy Williamson II (Alex "Rice" Miller), who was married to his stepsister. He himself was married to the sister of singer Willie Brown, later marrying Lillie Handley, with whom he had four children. He went into the army in 1941 and was discharged in 1945. After World War II he gradually made the transition from a farmer to a full-time entertainer, moving to West Memphis, Ark., and forming a band, then landing a show on a local radio station. He came to the attention of Sam Phillips of the Memphis Recording Service (later the studios of Phillips's Sun Records) and talent scout Ike Turner, resulting in recording sessions in 1951 and releases on Chicago-based Chess Records and L.A.-based RPM Records. He was credited with writing both sides of the Chess single "How Many More Years"/"Moanin' at Midnight" (his compositions usually were adaptations of existing traditional songs), each of which made the Top Ten of the R&B charts. With that, Chess signed him to a contract and he moved to Chicago.

Howlin' Wolf spent the 1950s recording for Chess and playing primarily in Chicago clubs. "Who Will Be Next" (music and lyrics by Melvin London) made the

R&B charts in June 1955; "Smokestack Lightnin'" (music and lyrics by Howlin' Wolf) hit the R&B Top Ten in March 1956; and "I Asked for Water" (music and lyrics by Howlin' Wolf) was in the R&B Top Ten in November 1956. In 1959, Chess released his first LP, a compilation of singles, *Moanin' at Midnight*.

In the early 1960s, Howlin' Wolf began to tour more extensively, both nationally and internationally, and as his recordings became available he attracted a larger audience. In June 1964 his recording of "Smokestack Lightnin'" entered the British charts; later in the year it was recorded by The Yardbirds, while The Rolling Stones recorded a version of his 1961 record "The Red Rooster" (music and lyrics by Willie Dixon) under the title "Little Red Rooster" and enjoyed a #1 hit with it in the U.K. in December 1964. In May 1965 the group insisted on having him as a guest star as a condition of their appearance on the U.S. television show *Shindig*.

In the summer of 1966 he appeared at the Newport Folk Festival, his performance captured on film for the motion picture *Festival* (October 1967). Meanwhile, his records continued to be covered by rock groups: The Doors, whose lead singer Jim Morrison was heavily influenced by his raucous vocal style, put a version of the 1960 disc "Back Door Man" (music and lyrics by Willie Dixon) on their self-titled debut album, released in January 1967; Cream covered "Sittin' on Top of the World" (music and lyrics by Howlin' Wolf) and "Spoonful" (music and lyrics by Willie Dixon) on its album *Wheels of Fire* (June 1968); and the Jeff Beck Group with Rod Stewart did "I Ain't Superstitious" (music and lyrics by Willie Dixon) on their debut album, *Truth* (August 1968).

Chess Records attempted to take advantage of Howlin' Wolf's increased exposure, releasing *The Howlin' Wolf Album*, his first LP to be recorded as such, in January 1969. It consisted of rock-oriented rerecordings of his earlier songs and was not well received, though "Evil" (music and lyrics by Willie Dixon) made the R&B charts in April.

Howlin' Wolf was in declining health in the 1970s, suffering two heart attacks and sustaining serious injuries in two car accidents. His next album of newly recorded material, *Message to the Young* (March 1971), earned a Grammy Award nomination for Best Ethnic or Traditional Recording (Including Traditional Blues). *The London Howlin' Wolf Sessions* (August 1971) found him fronting a band consisting of some of the British musicians most influenced by him, including Eric Clapton (of The Yardbirds and Cream) and members of The Rolling Stones. It spent more than three months in the charts. His last album was *The Back Door Wolf* (November 1973), which earned him another Grammy Award nomination for Best Ethnic or Traditional Recording (Including Traditional Blues and Pure Folk). He made his final stage appearance in November 1975 and died in January 1976 at 65 due to complications from kidney disease.

Disc.: *Howlin' Wolf Sings the Blues* (1962); *The Real Folk Blues* (1966); *More Real Folk Blues* (1967); *His Greatest Sides, Vol 1* (1967); *Evil* (1969); *The London Howlin' Wolf Sessions* (1971); *The Back Door Wolf* (1973); *London Revisited* (1974); *Howlin' Wolf* (1977); *Heart Like a Railroad Steel* (1979); *Ridin' in the Moonlight* (1982); *Cadillac Daddy: Memphis Recordings 1952* (1989); *Moaning at Midnight* (1989); *Memphis Days: Definitive Edition* (1989); *Change My Way* (1990); *Howlin' Wolf Rides Again* (1991); *Super Super Blues* (1991); *Howlin' Wolf: The Chess Box* (1991); *Ain't Gonna Be Your Dog* (1994); *Genuine Article: The Best of Howlin' Wolf* (1995); *His Best* (1997); *His Best, Vol. 2* (1999).—**WR**

Hoyland, Vic(tor), English composer; b. Wombwell, Yorkshire, Dec. 11, 1945. He studied at the Univ. of Hull and with Robert Sherlaw Johnson and Bernard Rands at the Univ. of York, where he served as a visiting lecturer in 1984. He then was a lecturer at the Univ. of Birmingham (from 1985).

Works: *Em* for 24 Voices (1970); *Es* for Voices and Ensemble (1971); *Jeux-Theme* for Mezzo-soprano and Ensemble (1972); *Ariel* for Voice and Ensemble (1975); *Esem* for Double Bass and Ensemble (1975); Serenade for 14 Players (1979); *Xingu*, music theater piece (1979); *Reed* for Double Reed Instruments (1980); *Fox* for Chamber Ensemble (1983); *Quintet of Brass* (1985); String Quartet (1985); *In Transit* for Orch. (1987); *Of Fantasy, Of Dreams, and Ceremonies* for 13 Strings (1989); Trio for Piano, Violin, and Cello (1989); Quintet for Piano and String Quartet (1990); *Le Madre*, opera (1990).—**NS/LK/DM**

Hoyoul, Balduin, South Netherlands composer; b. Liège, 1547 or 1548; d. Stuttgart, Nov. 26, 1594. He was a choirboy at the Württemberg Hofkapelle in Stuttgart. After training under Lassus in Munich (1564–65), he returned to the Württemberg Hofkapelle as a singer and composer; from 1589 he was its Kapellmeister. His Latin motets were publ. as *Sucrae cantiones* for 5 to 10 Voices (Nuremberg, 1587) and his German motets were publ. as *Geistliche Lieder und Psalmen* for 3 Voices (Nuremberg, 1589). He also wrote 8 parody Magnificat settings based on works by Lassus.

Bibl.: D. Politoske, *B. H.: A Netherlander at a German Court Chapel* (diss., Univ. of Mich., 1967).—**LK/DM**

Hřimalý, Adalbert (Vojtěch), Czech violinist, conductor, and composer, brother of **Johann (Jan)** and father of **Otakar Hřimalý**; b. Pilsen, July 30, 1842; d. Vienna, June 15, 1908. A member of an exceptionally musical family, he received an early training at home. He then studied with Mildner at the Prague Cons. (1855–61), and was subsequently active as a conductor, composer, and teacher in various towns in the Netherlands, Sweden, and Rumania. He wrote a great number of works, including an opera, *Zaklety princ* (The Enchanted Prince; Prague, May 13, 1872).—**NS/LK/DM**

Hřimalý, Johann (Jan), celebrated Czech violinist and teacher, brother of **Adalbert (Vojtěch)** and uncle of **Otakar Hřimalý**; b. Pilsen, April 13, 1844; d. Moscow, Jan. 24, 1915. He studied at the Prague Cons. At the age of 24 he went to Moscow, where he became a prof. of violin at the Cons. (1874). He remained in Moscow for 40 years until his death, and was regarded there as a great teacher; 2 generations of Russian violinists studied under him. He also organized a string quartet in Moscow. He publ. *Tonleiterstudien und Übungen in Doppelgriffen für die Violine* (Prague, 1895).—**NS/LK/DM**

Hřimalý, Otakar, Czech violinist, conductor, and composer, nephew of **Johann (Jan)** and son of **Adalbert (Vojtěch) Hřimalý;** b. Czernowitz, Bukovina, Dec. 20, 1883; d. Prague, July 10, 1945. He was trained in Vienna at the Cons. and the Univ. He went to Moscow, where he was conductor of the Cons. opera dept. (1910–16) and at the Opera (1919–22). He then lived in Czernowitz until the Russian occupation forced him to flee to Prague, where he joined the Cons. in 1940. He wrote an opera, 2 ballets, 7 syms., Piano Concerto, Violin Concerto, chamber music, and piano pieces.—**NS/LK/DM**

Hrisanide, Alexandru, Romanian composer; b. Petrila, June 15, 1936. He studied with P. Constantinescu, Ciortea, Vancea, Jora, and Mendelsohn at the Bucharest Cons. (1953–64), with Boulanger at the American Cons. in Fontainebleau (1965), and in Darmstadt (1966–67). After teaching at the Academy of Music (1959–62) and Cons. (1962–72) in Bucharest, he was a visiting prof. at the Univ. of Ore. (1972–73); he then went to the Netherlands. His output followed along constructivist lines with the application of modified serial techniques.

WORKS: ORCH.: *Poem* (1958); *Passacaglia* (1959); "*Vers-Antiqua*": *Hommage à Euripide* for Chamber Orch. (1960); *Concerto for Orchestra* (1964); *Ad perpetuam rei memoriam* (1966); *RO* (1968); *Sonnets,* harpsichord concerto (1973). **CHAMBER:** 3 flute sonatas (1956; 1956; 1960–62); Violin Sonata (1957); Trio for Violin, Viola, and Bassoon (1958); String Quartet (1958); Clarinet Sonata (1960–62); *Volumes-Inventions* for Cello and Piano (1963); *M. P. 5 (Musique pour 5)* for Violin, Viola, Cello, Saxophone or Clarinet, and Piano (1966); *Directions* for Wind Quintet (1967–69); *Première musique pour RA* for Piano and Tape (1968–69); *Seconde musique pour RA* for Piano and Tape (1969); *Troisième musique pour RA* for Piano, Percussion, and Tape (1970); *Quatrième musique pour RA* for Piano and Tape (1970); *Sixième musique pour RA* for Piano, Varying Instruments, and Tape (1970); *Soliloquium x 11* for String Quartet (1970); *Cinquième musique pour RA* for Piano, Celesta, Harpsichord, and Tape (1973); piano pieces, including 3 sonatas (1955–56; *Sonata piccola,* 1959; *Picasso Sonata,* 1956–64). **VOCAL:** *I-RO-LA-HAI* for Voice and Orch. (1971); cantatas; songs.—**NS/LK/DM**

Hristič, Stevan, Serbian conductor, teacher, and composer; b. Belgrade, June 19, 1885; d. there, Aug. 21, 1958. He studied with Nikisch (conducting) and Krehl and Hofmann at the Leipzig Cons., and then pursued studies in Moscow, Rome, and Paris. Returning to Belgrade, he was conductor of the National Opera Theater (1912–14); then was chief conductor of the Belgrade Phil. (1923–34) and Opera (1924–34); then was a prof. of composition at the Academy of Music (1937–50). He composed a music drama, *Suton* (Sunset, 1925; rev. 1954), a ballet, *Legend of Okhrid* (1933; rev. 1958), and many choral works.—**NS/LK/DM**

Hrušovský, Ivan, Slovak composer and musicologist; b. Bratislava, Feb. 23, 1927. After training at the Žilina Music School, he studied composition with A. Moyzes at the Bratislava Cons. (1947–52), continuing under his tutelage at the Bratislava Academy of Music

and Drama (graduated, 1957); he also pursued training in musicology, philosophy, and aesthetics at the Comenius Univ. in Bratislava (1947–52). He later completed postgraduate studies with his thesis on the genesis of Cikker's musical thinking (1965–66), and his Habilitation with his thesis on the development of Slovak music, 1939–48 (1967). After working at the Inst. of Musicology at the Slovak Academy of Sciences in Bratislava (1952–53), he taught at the Bratislava Academy of Music and Drama from 1953, becoming assoc. prof. of musicology in 1968 and prof. of composition in 1984. In 1990 he joined the faculty of the Matej Bel Univ. in Banská Bystrica as a teacher of music theory. In 1976 and 1986 he won the Union of Slovak Composers Prize, and in 1988 was made a Meritorious Artist of Slovakia. Among his writings are *Úvod do štúdia teórie harmónie* (Introduction to the Study of Harmony; Bratislava, 1960; 2nd ed., 1972), *Slovenská hudba v profiloch a rozboroch* (Slovak Music in Portraits and Analyses; Bratislava, 1964), and *Antonín Dvořák* (Bratislava, 1964). In his compositions, he makes effective utilization of the entire gamut of contemporary musical expression.

WORKS: ORCH.: *Pastoral Suite* for Small Orch. (1955); Piano Concerto (1957); *Tatra Poem* (1960); *Concertante Overture* for Strings (1963); *Passacaglia* (1966); *Musica nocturna per archi* (1970); *Confrontations* (1979); *Suita quasi una fantasia* for Chamber String Orch. (1980); *Little Romance* for Chamber String Orch. (1986); *Music for V. Hložník,* symphonic fresco (1986); *Noble Dances of Levoca,* suite for Chamber String Orch. (1987); 2 syms: No. 1 for Strings (1988) and No. 2, *Remembrance,* for Chamber Orch. and Piano (1995–96). **CHAMBER:** *Suita piccola* for Cello and Piano (1963); *Combinazioni sonoriche per 9,* nonet for Flute, Oboe, Bass Clarinet, Trumpet, Vibraphone, Piano, Violin, Viola, and Cello (1963); Sonata for Solo Violin (1969); *3 Canons* for Violin and Harpsichord (1980); *Dialoghi in ritmo* for Organ and Percussion (1982); 3 string quartets (1983, 1990, 1995); *Musica rustica* for Flute (1984); Septetino for Flute, Clarinet, Bassoon, Horn, Violin, Viola, and Cello (1987). **KEYBOARD: Piano:** 2 sonatas (1965, 1968); *Toccata chromatica* (1970); *Fantasia, Introduction, and Fugue in the Old Style* for Piano, 4-Hands (1986); Suite for 2 Pianos (1986; also for Piano, 4-Hands). **Harpsichord:** *Sonata in modo classico* (1977); *Suite of Old Dances from the Levoča Collection* (1978). **VOCAL:** *Against Death,* cantata trilogy: 1, *Hiroshima* for Reciter, Soprano, Baritone, Chorus, and Orch. (1961–65); 2, *White Birch, Sister of Mine...* for Mezzo-soprano and Women's Chorus (1961); and 3, *Dream about a Man* for Reciter, Soprano, Chorus, and Orch. (1964); *Madrigal Sonata* for Chorus (1974); *Odes* for 3 Choruses (1975); *Canti* for Chamber Choruses (1978); *That Love,* cantata for Mezzo-soprano and Chorus (1984); *Canticum pro pace,* oratorio for Reciter, Mezzo-soprano, Bass, Chorus, and Orch. (1985); *Cantus de caritate* for Chorus and Piano or Organ (1990); *Psalm 120* for Chorus (1996); other choral works; many song cycles. **ELECTROACOUSTIC:** *Invocation* (1973); *Idée fixe* (1976).—**NS/LK/DM**

Hsu, John (Tseng-Hsin), Chinese-born American cellist, viola da gambist, baryton player, and teacher; b. Shantou, April 21, 1931. He emigrated to the U.S. (1949) and became a naturalized American citizen (1961). He studied at Carroll Coll., the Berkshire Music Center in Tanglewood, and the New England Cons. of Music in Boston (B.Mus., 1953; M.Mus., 1955), his teachers including Josef Schroetter, Alfred Zinghera, and Samuel Mayes for cello, and Eugene Lehner and

William Kroll for chamber music performance. From 1955 he taught at Cornell Univ., and toured widely as a recitalist. He was a founding member of the Amadé Trio (1972), dedicated to performing early music on original instruments; also in 1972 he joined the Aston Magna Foundation for Music, serving as its artistic director from 1987 to 1990. He was music director of the Apollo Ensemble from 1991. In 1981 he organized the Haydn Baryton Trio for the purpose of playing Haydn's rarely heard baryton trios. He also ed. the collected works of Marais (1980) and wrote *A Handbook of French Baroque Viol Technique* (1981).—**NS/LK/DM**

Hsu, Tsang-houei, Chinese composer, musicologist, and teacher; b. Changhau, Taiwan, Sept. 6, 1929. He studied violin in Tokyo from the age of 11, remaining in Japan until 1945, when he returned to Taiwan. He studied violin and composition at the National Univ. (1949–53), and in 1954 he went to Paris to study violin at the École César Franck and music history and analysis at the Sorbonne (1956–58). He also studied with Jolivet and Messiaen at the Paris Cons. In 1959 he returned to Taiwan, where his first concert (1960), which introduced avant-garde ideas to Taiwan audiences, met with both censure and enthusiasm. He taught advanced composition techniques and founded several organizations to promote contemporary music, including the Chinese Composers' Forum (1961) and the Chinese Soc. for Contemporary Music (1969); he also was active in the League of Asian Composers. Hsu made extensive study of Taiwanese folk music, elements of which are integrated into his compositions. He co-founded the Centre for Chinese Folk Music Research (1967), and was appointed examiner in charge of folk-music research by the Taiwanese provincial government (1976). He held professorships at the National Academy of Arts, Soochow Univ., and the Coll. of Chinese Culture, and lectured throughout East Asia and the U.S. His early compositions show a variety of influences, including aspects of impressionism, atonality, and serialism, along with traditional Chinese and Taiwanese elements; his later works are less aggressively modern, but have a distinctive identity and unified style. His writings reflect his interest in folk music research.

WORKS: DRAMATIC: Opera: *The Legend of White Horse* (1979–87). **Ballet:** *Chang-o Flies to the Moon* (1968); *The Peach Blossom* (1977); *Peach Blossom Girl* (1983); *Chen San and the 5th Madame* (1985). **ORCH.:** *Chinese Festival Overture* (1965–80); *2 Movements* for Strings (1970); *White Sand Bay*, sym. (1974); *Spring for All* for Piano and Traditional Chinese Orch. (1981). **CHAMBER:** Violin Sonata (1958–59); Quintet for Flute, Clarinet, Violin, Cello, and Piano (1960–87); *5 Preludes* for Violin (1965–66); *The Blind* for Flute (1966–76); *The Reminiscence of Childhood* for Chinese Ocarina (1967); Clarinet Sonata (1973–83); *Taiwan* for Violin, Clarinet, and Piano (1973); *3 Pieces* for Hugin (1977); *Dou-o's Lament* for Cello or Viola and Piano (1988); piano pieces. **VOCAL:** Choral pieces; songs. —**NS/LK/DM**

Huang, Cham-Ber, Chinese-American harmonica player and manufacturer; b. Shanghai, Oct. 17, 1925. He commenced playing the harmonica when he was 6, and later studied violin, theory, and composition at the

Shanghai School of Music (1945–49) and St. John's Univ. in Shanghai (B.A., 1949). He went to the U.S., where he taught at N.Y.'s Turtle Bay Music School (1958–76) and at the Grand Teton Music Festival in Teton Village, Wyo. (1975–79). He also toured widely as a harmonica virtuoso, from 1979 making regular tours of China, where he helped to make his instrument popular. In 1983 he formed Huang Harmonics, a manufacturing firm in Farmingdale, N.Y.—**NS/LK/DM**

Hubay, Jenő, celebrated Hungarian violinist, pedagogue, and composer; b. Budapest, Sept. 15, 1858; d. Vienna, March 12, 1937. He received his initial training from his father, Karl Hubay, prof. of violin at the Budapest Cons. He gave his first public concert at the age of 11, and then studied with Joachim in Berlin (1873–76). His appearance in Paris, at a Pasdeloup concert, attracted the attention of Vieuxtemps, of whom he became a favorite pupil; in 1882 he succeeded Vieuxtemps as prof. at the Brussels Cons. In 1886 he became a prof. at the Budapest Cons. (succeeding his father), and from 1919 to 1934 was its director. In Budapest he formed the celebrated Hubay String Quartet. In 1894 he married the Countess Rosa Cebrain. Among his pupils were Vecsey, Szigeti, Telmanyi, Eddy Brown, and other renowned violinists. He ed. the violin études of Kreutzer (1908), Rode, Mayseder, and Saint Lubin (1910).

WORKS: DRAMATIC: Opera (all 1st perf. in Budapest): *Alienor* (Dec. 5, 1891); *Le Luthier de Crémone* (Nov. 10, 1894); *A Falu Rossza* (The Village Vagabond; March 20, 1896); *Moosröschen* (Feb. 21, 1903); *Anna Karenina* (Nov. 10, 1923); *Az álarc* (The Mask; Feb. 26, 1931). **ORCH.:** 4 syms.: No. 1 (1885), No. 2, *1914–15* (1915), No. 3, *Vita nuova*, for Soli, Chorus, and Organ (1921), and No. 4, *Petöfi-Sinfonie*, for Soli, Chorus, and Orch. (1925); *Biedermeyer Suite* (1913); 4 violin concertos; *Scènes de la Csárda*, 14 pieces for Violin and Orch. **CHAMBER:** *Sonate romantique* for Violin and Piano.—**NS/LK/DM**

Hubbard, Freddie (actually, **Frederick Dewayne**), important jazz trumpeter, flugelhornist; b. Indianapolis, April 7, 1938. His flamboyant, swaggering solos are filled with brilliant ideas and he is clearly one of the greats of jazz trumpet. He first studied mellophone in junior high school, and then switched to trumpet in high school. He studied classical trumpet privately, while also beginning to play jazz gigs with the Montgomery Brothers in the late 1950s. He moved to N.Y. in 1958 and roomed with Eric Dolphy for 18 months. He recorded with Coltrane in December 1958. He gigged with various musicians, including Phil Jo Jones (1958–59, 1961), Sonny Rollins (1959), Slide Hampton (1959–60), and Quincy Jones (1960–61, including European tour), before joining Art Blakey's Jazz Messengers in 1961, which established him as a trumpet star. Through the 1960s, he sessioned with various leaders, appearing on Eric Dolphy's *Out to Lunch*, Coltrane's *Olé and Ascension,*, and Ornette Coleman's *Free Jazz*, among many others. He led his first group from 1964–65, then disbanded to work with Max Roach. In Berlin (1965) he famously said, "Kiss my black ass" onstage due to perceived racism. From 1966 on, he worked mostly with his own quartets and quintets, including most consistently, pianist Kenny Barron. As early as 1966 he had recorded tunes with pop-oriented beats such as "Backlash" and the album *A Soul Experiment* (1969). Unlike some other artists, he publicly stated that he preferred acoustic jazz and that he hoped his success in fusion would bring him enough success to return to acoustic jazz. Nonetheless, Hubbard's work in the 1970s continued with a fusion direction; his albums *Red Clay* and *Straight Life* sold well and he scored a hit with *Sky Dive* in 1972. He took Miles Davis's role in the reconstituted Davis quintet (known as VSOP, with Herbie Hancock, Ron Carter, Tony Williams, and Wayne Shorter) from 1976–79 for recordings and tours. He continued to tour during the 1980s and 1990s, recording with Woody Shaw and Art Blakey. However, in the mid-1990s serious lip problems have reduced him to playing with a mute and there is some doubt as to his future. He is not related to saxophonist Dave Hubbard.

DISC.: *Open Sesame* (1960); *Goin' Up* (1960); *Ready for F.* (1961); *Minor Mishap* (1961); *Hub Cap* (1961); *Here to Stay* (1961); *Hub-Tones* (1962); *Caravan* (1962); *Artistry of F. H.* (1962); *Body and Soul* (1963); *Breaking Point* (1964); Lee Morgan: *Night of the Cookers* (1965). *Blue Spirits* (1965); *Backlash* (1966); *High Blues Pressure* (1967); *Soul Experiment* (1969); *Hub of H.* (1969); *Black Angel* (1969); *Straight Life* (1970); *Red Clay* (1970); *Sing Me a Song of Songmy* (1971); *First Light* (1971); *Sky Dive* (1972); *Keep Your Soul Together* (1973); *Live at the North Sea Jazz Festival* (1980); *Live at the Hague* (1980); *Back to Birdland* (1980); *Rollin'* (1981); *Outpost* (1981); *Little Night Music* (1981); *Keystone Bop* (1981); *Ride Like the Wind* (1982); *Sweet Return* (1983); *Double Take* (1985); *Salute to Pops, Vol. 2* (1987); *Eternal Triangle with Woody Shaw* (1987); *Temptation* (1991); *Live at Fat Tuesday* (1991); *Double Exposure* (1992); *Monk, Miles, Trane & Cannon* (1995).—JC/LP

Hubbell, Frank Allen, American conductor, arranger, and composer; b. Denver, May 9, 1907; d. Kirkland, Wash., April 21, 1971. He was taken to Calif. as a child and was reared on an orange grove. He learned to play the cornet and also began to compose music. In 1936 he arranged a native Hawaiian tune and launched it as "The Hawaiian War Chant," which became his most popular creation. His reputation was further enhanced by his arrangement of old Calif. songs for band, under the title *California El Dorado Suite*. His later band pieces, all in the "landscape music" genre, included *The San Diego Story* (1957), *The Oregon Story* (1959), and *The Kansas Story* (1961). He was also active on the pageant stage, and was music director of the International Beauty Congress, for which he wrote 2 theme songs, "World of Beauty" and "Sound the Trumpets."—NS/LK/DM

Hubeau, Jean, French pianist and composer; b. Paris, June 22, 1917; d. there, Aug. 19, 1992. He entered the Paris Cons. at the age of 9, and studied piano with Lévy, and composition with J. and N. Gallon and Dukas. He won the premier prix for piano at age 13, and for composition at 16. In 1934, at the age of 17, he received the 2nd Grand Prix de Rome with his cantata *La Légende de Roukmani*. He made several European tours as a pianist. From 1942 to 1957 he was director of the Versailles Cons. He then joined the staff of the Paris Cons.

WORKS: DRAMATIC: B a l l e t : *Trois fables de La Fontaine* (Paris, March 2, 1945); *La Fiancée du diable* (Paris, Dec. 8, 1945); *Un Coeur de diamant ou L'Infante* (Monte Carlo, April 7, 1949). **ORCH.:** *Tableaux hindous* (Paris, Oct. 18, 1936); Violin Concerto (Paris, March 30, 1941); Cello Concerto (Paris, Nov. 28, 1942); *Concerto heroïque* for Piano and Orch. (Paris, Dec. 22, 1946). **CHAMBER:** Violin Sonata (1941); *Sonatine-Humoresque* for Horn, Flute, Clarinet, and Piano (1942); Trumpet Sonata (1943); *Sonate-Caprice* for 2 Violins (1944); *Air varié* for Clarinet and Piano (1961); *Idylle* for Flute and Piano (1966); piano pieces. **VOCAL:** Choruses; songs.—NS/LK/DM

Huber, Hans, Swiss composer and pedagogue; b. Eppenberg, near Olten, June 28, 1852; d. Locarno, Dec. 25, 1921. He studied at the Leipzig Cons. with Richter, Reinecke, and Wenzel (1870–74), then taught music in Wesserling, Thann (Alsace), at the Basel music school (from 1889), where he was its director (1886–1917). His style combined the rhapsodic form typical of Lisztian technique with simple ballad-like writing. He often used Swiss songs for thematic material.

WORKS: DRAMATIC: O p e r a : *Weltfrühling* (Basel, March 28, 1894); *Kudrun* (Basel, Jan. 29, 1896); *Der Simplicius* (Basel, Feb. 22, 1912); *Die schöne Bellinda* (Bern, April 2, 1916); *Frutta di mare* (Basel, Nov. 24, 1918). **ORCH.:** 8 syms. (all 1st perf. in Basel except No. 2): No. 1, *William Tell* (April 26, 1881), No. 2, *Böcklinsinfonie* (Zürich, July 2, 1900), No. 3, *Heroische* (Nov. 9, 1917), No. 4, *Akademische* (May 23, 1909), No. 5, *Romantische* (Feb. 11, 1906), No. 6 (Nov. 19, 1911), No. 7, *Swiss* (June 9, 1917), and No. 8 (Oct. 29, 1921); 4 piano concertos (1878, 1891, 1899, 1910); Violin Concerto (1878). **CHAMBER:** Sextet for Piano and Wind Instruments (1900); Quintet for Piano and Wind Instruments (1914); 2 string quintets (1890, 1907); String Quartet; 2 piano quartets; 5 piano trios; 10 violin sonatas; 5 cello sonatas; piano works, among them 48 preludes and fugues for piano, 4–Hands.

BIBL.: E. Refardt, *H. H.* (Leipzig, 1906); idem, *H. H., Beiträge zu einer Biographie* (Leipzig, 1922); C. Bundi, *H. H., Die Persönlichkeit nach Briefen und Erinnerungen* (Basel, 1925); E. Refardt, *H. H.* (Zürich, 1944).—NS/LK/DM

Huber, Klaus, Swiss composer and pedagogue; b. Bern, Nov. 30, 1924. He studied violin with Geyer (1947–49) and theory and composition with his godfather Burkhard (1947–55) at the Zürich Cons., and then completed his training with Blacher at the Berlin Hochschule für Musik (1955–56). He taught violin at the Zürich Cons. (1950–60) and music history at the Lucerne Cons. (1960–63). From 1961 to 1972 he taught at the Basel Academy of Music, where he was director of the composition and instrumentation classes (1964–68) and then of the master composition class (1968–72). In 1969 he founded the international composers' seminar in Boswil, with which he was active until 1980. In 1973 he held the Deutscher Akademischer Austauschienest scholarship in Berlin. From 1973 to 1990 he taught composition and was head of the inst. for contemporary music at the Freiburg im Breisgau Hochschule für Musik. He served as president of the Swiss Composers' Assn. from 1979 to 1982. In 1975 he won the Composers' Prize of the Swiss Composers' Assn. and in 1978 was awarded the arts prize of the City of Basel. He was a member of the Bayerische Akademie der Schönen Künste of Munich and the Akademie der Künste of Berlin. He publ. *Klaus Huber: Gesammelte Schriften* (Cologne, 1995). In his music, Huber has written a large body of works notable for their exquisite craftsmanship in a highly personal style evocative of contemporary means of expression.

WORKS: DRAMATIC: O p e r a : *Jot, oder wann kommt der Herr zuruck* (1972–73; Berlin, Sept. 27, 1973); *Im Paradies oder Der Alte vom Berge* (1973–75). ORCH.: *Inventionen und Choral* (1956); *Litania instrumentalis* (1957); *Terzen-Studie* (1958); *Cantio-Moteti-Inventione* for Strings (1963; also for String Quartet, 1962–63); *Tenebrae* (1966–67); *James Joyce Chamber Music* for Harp, Horn, and Chamber Orch. (1966–67); *Alveare vernat* for Flute and Strings (1967; also for Flute and 12 Solo Strings, 1965); *Tempora,* violin concerto (1969–70); *Erinnere dich an G...* for Double Bass and Chamber Orch. (1976–77); *...ohne Grenze und Rand...* for Viola and Small Orch. (1976–77); *Zwei Sätze für Ensemble* (1978–79; 1983); *Beati Pauperes II* for Small Orch. (1979; also for 7 Solo Voices and Small Orch.); *Protuberanzen* (1985–86); *Plainte-die umgepflügte Zeit I* for Viola d'Amore and Chamber Orch. (1990; *II* for Mezzo-soprano, Tenor, Viola d'amore, and Chamber Orch.); *Intarsi,* chamber concerto for Piano and Ensemble (1993–94; Lucerne, Aug. 22, 1994); *Lamentationes de fine vicesimi saeculi* for 4 Orch. Groups and Sufi Singer ad libitum (1992–94; Frankfurt am Main, Dec. 11, 1994). CHAMBER: *Sonata da chiesa* for Violin and Organ (1953); *Partita* for Cello and Harpsichord (1954); *Concerto per la Camerata* for 6 Instruments (1954–55; rev. 1965); *2 Movements* for 2 Winds (1957–58); *3 Movements in 2 Parts* for Wind Quintet (1958–59); *Noctes intelligibilis lucis* for Oboe and Harpsichord (1961); 2 string quartets: No. 1, *Moteti-Cantiones* (1962–63; also for String Orch., 1963) and No. 2, *...von Zeit zu Zeit...* (1984–85); *Sabeth* for Flute, English Horn or Viola, and Harp (1966–67); *Ascensus* for Flute, Cello, and Piano (1969); *Ein Hauch von Unzeit III* for 2 to 7 Players (1972); *Schattenblätter* for Bass Clarinet, Cello, and Piano (1975); *Lazarus I-II* for Cello and Piano (1978); *Beati Pauperes I* for Flute, Viola, Piano, and Percussion (1979); *2 Movements* for Chamber Ensemble (1983); *Des Dichters Pflug,* trio for Violin, Viola, and Cello (1989); *Agnus Dei in umgepflügter Zeit* for 8 Instruments (1990–91); *Plainte-lieber spaltet mein Herz...* for Viola d'amore or Viola, Guitar, and Percussion (1990–92); String Quintet (1993–94); piano pieces; organ music. VOCAL: *Das Te Deum laudamus deutsch* for Soloists and Chorus (1955–56); *Antiphonische Kantate* for Chorus and Orch. (1956); *Oratio Mechtildis,* chamber sym. for Alto and Chamber Orch. (1956–57); *Des Engels Anredung an die Seele,* chamber cantata for Tenor, Flute, Clarinet, Horn, and Harp (1957); *Auf die ruhige Nacht-Zeit* for Soprano, Flute, Viola, and Cello (1958); *Soliloquia,* oratorio for Soloists, 2 Choruses, and Orch. (1959–64); *Psalm of Christ* for Baritone and 8 Instruments (1967); *Kleine deutsche Messe* for Chorus, Congregation, Organ, String Trio, and Harp (1969); *... inwendig voller Figur...* for Chorus, Orch., Loudspeaker, and Tape (1970–71); *...ausgespannt...* for Baritone, 5 Instrumental Groups, Loudspeaker, Tape, and Organ (1972); *Erniedrigt-Geknechtet-Verlassen-Verachtet* for 4 Soloists, 2 Choruses, and Orch. (1975–78; 1981–82); *Beati Pauperes II* for 7 Voices and Small Orch. (1979); *Ñudo que ansí juntáis* for 16 Solo Voices (1984); *Cantiones de circulo gyrante* for Soloists, Chorus, and Chamber Orch. (1985; reworked as *Kleines Requiem für Heinrich Böll* for Chorus and Bass Baritone ad libitum, 1994); *Spes contra Spem* for Soloists and Orch. (1986; 1988–89); *La terre des hommes* for Mezzo-soprano, Countertenor/Speaker, and Chamber Orch.

(1987–89); *Die umgepflügte Zeit* for Soloists, Speaker, Choruses, and Orch. (1990); *Agnus Dei cum recordatione,* "Hommage à Jehan Okeghem" for Countertenor, 2 Tenors, Bass Baritone, Renaissance Lute, and 2 Fiddles or Guitar and 2 Violas (1990–91); *Die Erde bewegt sich auf den Hörnern eines Ochsen* for Sufi Singer and Arab and European Instruments (1992–93). —NS/LK/DM

Huber, Kurt, eminent German musicologist of Swiss descent; b. Chur, Oct. 24, 1893; d. (executed by the Gestapo) Munich, July 13, 1943. He studied philosophy and psychology with Becher and Külpe and musicology with Kroyer and Sandberger at the Univ. of Munich (Ph.D., 1917, with the diss. *Ivo de Vento: Ein Beitrag zur Musikgeschichte des 16. Jahrhunderts,* 1; publ. in Lindenberg, 1918); then completed his Habilitation in psychology (1920). He became asst. lecturer at the Univ. of Munich's Inst. of Psychology in 1920; was made a Dozent there in 1926. From 1925 he devoted himself to collecting and recording early Bavarian folk songs, which he publ. with Paul Kiem. He actively opposed the Nazi regime, and was imprisoned and executed for his participation in student protests. In addition to his book *Die Doppelmeister des 16. Jahrhunderts* (Munich, 1920), the following vols. have been publ.: O. Ursprung ed. his *Ästhetik* (Ettal, 1954) and *Musikästhetik* (Ettal, 1954), J. Hanslmeier his *Grundbegriffe der Seelenkunde: Einführung in die allgemeine Psychologie* (Ettal, 1955), and C. Huber and O. von Müller his *Volkslied und Volkstanz: Aufsätze zur Volksliedkunde des bajuwarischen Raumes* (Ettal, 1960).

BIBL.: C. Huber, ed., *K. H. zum Gedächtnis: Bildnis eines Menschen, Denkers und Forchers* (Regensburg, 1947); E. Grave, *Die ästhetischen Kategorien in K. H.s Ästhetik* (diss., Univ. of Munich, 1957).—NS/LK/DM

Huberman, Bronislaw, famous Polish violinist; b. Częstochowa, Dec. 19, 1882; d. Corsier-sur-Vevey, Switzerland, June 15, 1947. He began to study violin with Michalowicz at age 6, making his debut when he was 7 as soloist in Spohr's 2nd Violin Concerto; then studied with Izydor Lotto. When he was 9 he was taken to Berlin, where he studied with Joachim's assistant Markees; he then studied privately with Carl Grigorovich, his most influential mentor; later took some lessons with Heermann in Frankfurt am Main and Marsick in Paris. He played in the Netherlands and Belgium in 1893, then in Paris and London in 1894. Adelina Patti heard him in London and engaged him for her farewell appearance in Vienna (Jan. 12, 1895), where he scored a brilliant success. He then played the Brahms Violin Concerto there in the presence of the composer (Jan. 29, 1896), who commended him warmly. He made his first tour of the U.S. in 1896–97; subsequently made world tours and was active as a teacher in Vienna. He went to Palestine in 1936 and founded the Palestine Sym. Orch., an ensemble composed mainly of Jewish musicians who had lost their positions in the wake of Nazism in Europe. The orch. prospered and became the Israel Phil. Orch. in 1948. He went to the U.S. in 1940, but returned to Europe at the end of World War II (1945). He publ. *Aus der Werkstatt des Virtuosen* (1912) and *Mein Weg zu Paneuropa* (1925).

BIBL.: H. Goetz, *B. H. and the Unity of Europe* (Rome, 1967); I. Ibbeken and T. Avni, eds., *An Orchestra Is Born: The Founding of the Palestine Orchestra as Reflected in B. H.'s Letters, Speeches, and Articles* (Tel Aviv, 1969).—**NS/LK/DM**

Hubert, Nikolai, Russian conductor and pedagogue; b. St. Petersburg, March 19, 1840; d. Moscow, Oct. 8, 1888. He studied with his father, then at the St. Petersburg Cons. (1863–68) with Zaremba and A. Rubinstein. In 1869 he was in Odessa as an opera conductor. In 1870 he was engaged as a prof. of music theory at the Moscow Cons. He succeeded N. Rubinstein as its director in 1881, resigning in 1883, and retiring from teaching in 1888. He also wrote music criticism in Moscow newspapers.—**NS/LK/DM**

Huberti, Gustave (-Léon), Belgian conductor and composer; b. Brussels, April 14, 1843; d. Schaerbeek, June 28, 1910. He studied at the Brussels Cons., where he won the Prix de Rome in 1865 for his cantata *La Fille de Jephté*. He was director of the Mons Cons. (1874–78), then a conductor in Antwerp and Brussels. In 1889 he was appointed a prof. at the Brussels Cons., and he was also director of the Music School of St.-Joost-ten-Noode from 1893. In 1891 he was elected a member of the Belgian Academy. He publ. a book, *Aperçu sur l'histoire de la musique religieuse des Italiens et des Néerlandais* (Brussels, 1873).

WORKS: 3 oratorios: *Een Laatste Zonnestraal* (1874), *Bloemardinne,* and *Willem van Oranjes dood;* dramatic poem, *Verlichting (Fiat lux),* for Soli, Chorus, Organ, and Orch.; symphonic poem, *Kinderlust en Leed,* for Chorus and Orch.; *Symphonie funèbre; Suite romantique; In den Garade; Triomffeest,* with Organ; Piano Concerto; marches; many French, Flemish, and German songs; piano pieces.—**NS/LK/DM**

Hübler, Klaus K(arl), German composer; b. Munich, July 12, 1956. He studied composition with Peter Kiesewetter (1975–76) and Brian Ferneyhough (1980–82), and also studied musicology at the Univ. of Munich. He received several fellowships and prizes; visited the U.S. as a participant in the Pittsburgh International Music Festival (1986). After being stricken with a serious illness in 1989, he ceased to compose. His compositions are extremely complex, demanding an intricate system of notation.

WORKS: ORCH.: *Wer die Schönheit Angeschaut mit Augen* for Cello and Chamber Orch. (1979); *Arie dissolute* for Viola and Chamber Ensemble (1986–87); *Epiphyt* for Flute and Chamber Orch. (1987–88). **CHAMBER:** *MUSICA MENSURABILIS* for 2 Violins and Viola (1975–76); 3 string quartets: No. 1, *Hommage à Alban Berg* (1977), No. 2, *sur le premier prélude* (1979–80), and No. 3, *Dialektische Fantasie* (1982–84); *Chanson sans paroles, Kafkastudie I* for Clarinet, Cello, and Piano (1978); Sonata for Solo Violin (1978); *Riflessi* for Flute, Violin, Viola, Cello, and Harp (1979); *Notturno* for 10 Instruments (1980); String Trio No. 1, *Konzertparaphrase* (1980–81); *"Feuerzauber" auch Augenmusik: Studie in/über Phantasmagorie* for 3 Flutes, Cello, and Harp (1981); *Am Ende des Kanons: Musica con(tro)versa* for Trumpet and Organ (1983); *CERCAR* for Trumpet (1983); *Grave e sfrenato* for Oboe (1985); *sklEros* for Flute, Oboe d'Amore, Clarinet,

Bassoon, and Horn Obbligato (1985–86); *Sonetto LXXXIII del Michelangelo* for Piano (1986); *Opus breve* for Cello (1987); *Reisswerck* for Guitar (1987); *Kryptogramm* for 9 Musicians (1989).—**NS/LK/DM**

Hucbald (Hugbaldus, Ubaldus, Uchubaldus), Flemish monk, music theorist, and composer; b. in or near Tournai, c.840; d. Saint-Amand, near Tournai, June 20, 930. He was a pupil of his uncle Milo, director of the singing school at Saint-Amand, and then was himself director of a similar school at Nevers. He subsequently returned to Saint-Amand and succeeded his uncle. His only extant treatise is *De Harmonica Institutione,* a guide to chant singing in which he developed a systematic approach to music. Several of his compositions are also extant.

BIBL.: C. de Coussemaker, *Mémoire sur H. et sur ses traités de musique* (1814); C. Palisca, ed., and W. Babb, tr., *H., Guido, and John on Music: Three Medieval Treatises* (New Haven, 1979). —**NS/LK/DM**

Hudson, Frederick, English organist and musicologist; b. Gateshead, Durham, Jan. 16, 1913. He studied with Edward Bairstow (1939–46) and with Gordon Slater at Lincoln Cathedral; received the degree of B.Mus. at the Univ. of Durham in 1941, and of D.Mus. in 1950. He served as organist and choirmaster at Alnwick (1941–48). He was a lecturer in music at King's Coll., Univ. of Durham (1949–70), and then a reader in music at the Univ. of Newcastle upon Tyne (from 1970). He ed. works by Bach, Handel, Giovanni Gabrieli, William Byrd, and others for the new editions of their works; contributed important papers dealing with watermarks of undated MSS and prints, making use of beta-radiography with carbon-14 sources; also compiled a catalog of the works of Charles Villiers Stanford (*Music Review,* XXXVII, 1976).—**NS/LK/DM**

Hudson, George, English composer; b. c. 1617; d. Greenwich, Dec. 1672. He was made a "musician to his Majesty for the lutes and voices extraordinary" in 1641, but lost his employment at the outbreak of the Civil War. After the Restoration, he served as a violinist and composer in the King's Private Musick from 1660. Along with others, he contributed music to Davenant's *Siege of Rhodes* (1656). Among his extant works are pieces for the lyra viol and suites for 1 or 2 violins and bass.—**LK/DM**

Hüe, Georges (Adolphe), French composer and teacher; b. Versailles, May 6, 1858; d. Paris, June 7, 1948. After piano lessons with his mother, he studied counterpoint and fugue with Paladilhe and organ and composition with Franck and Reber at the Paris Cons. In 1879 he won the Prix de Rome with his cantata *Médée* and in 1881 he received the Prix Crescent with his comic opera *Les pantins.* He devoted himself to composing and teaching in Paris. In 1922 he succeeded to Saint-Saëns' seat in the Académie des Beaux-Arts.

WORKS: DRAMATIC (all 1st perf. in Paris): *Les pantins,* opéra comique (Dec. 18, 1881); *Le roi de Paris,* opera (April 26, 1901); *Titania,* opera (1902; Jan. 20, 1903); *Le miracle,* opera (Dec.

14, 1910); *Dans l'ombre de la cathédrale*, opera (Dec. 7, 1921); *Siang-Sin*, ballet-pantomime (March 12, 1924); *Riquet à la houppe*, comédie-musicale (Dec. 17, 1928). O R C H .: *Rübezahl*, symphonic legend (1886); *Le Berger* for Violin and Orch. (1893); Sym. (n.d.); etc. V O C A L : *Médée*, cantata (1879); choral pieces; songs.—NS/LK/DM

Hueffer, Francis (real name, Franz Hüffer),
German-born English writer on music; b. Münster, May 22, 1843; d. London, Jan. 19, 1889. He studied philology and music in London, Paris, Berlin, and Leipzig. He received a Dr.Phil. degree from Göttingen Univ. for his first publication (1869), a critical ed. of the works of Guillem de Cabestant, troubadour of the 12th century. In 1869 he settled in London as a writer on music, and from 1878 was music critic of the *Times*.

WRITINGS (all publ. in London, unless otherwise given): *Richard Wagner and the Music of the Future* (1874); *The Troubadours: A History of Provencal Life and Literature in the Middle Ages* (1878); *Musical Studies* (Edinburgh, 1880; reprints of his articles from the *Times* and *Fortnightly Review*); *Richard Wagner* (1881); *Italian and Other Studies* (1883); *Half a Century of Music in England* (1889; 2nd ed., 1898).—NS/LK/DM

Huehn, Julius, American baritone; b. Revere,
Mass., Jan. 12, 1904; d. Rochester, N.Y., June 8, 1971. He studied engineering at the Carnegie Inst. of Technology, and later took voice lessons with Anna Schoen- René at the Juilliard School of Music in N.Y. He made his operatic debut with the Metropolitan Opera in N.Y. as the Herald in *Lohengrin* on Dec. 21, 1935, singing there until 1944; then served in the U.S. Air Force and carried out missions in Europe as a bombardier. He sang again at the Metropolitan after the war (1945–46). He was particularly noted for his performances of heroic baritone parts in Wagner's operas.—NS/LK/DM

Huey Lewis and the News, enormously popu-
lar band of the 1980s; formed. 1979. MEMBERSHIP: Huey Lewis, voc., har. (b. Hugh Cregg III, N.Y., July 5, 1950); Chris Hayes, gtr. (b. Sacramento, Calif., Nov. 24, 1957); Mario Cipollina, bs. (b. San Rafael, Calif., Nov. 10, 1954); Bill Gibson, drm. (b. Sacramento, Nov. 13, 1951); Sean Hopper, kybd. (b. San Francisco, March 31, 1953); Johnny Colla, sax., gtr. (b. Sacramento, July 2, 1952).

Hugh Cregg went to prep school in N.J., though his family had moved to the Bay Area years before. He hitchhiked around Europe for a year between graduation and going to Cornell. While in Europe, he became a proficient harmonica player, occasionally landing a paying gig. He attended Cornell, befriending many musicians, including future members of King Harvest ("Dancing in the Moonlight" was their one hit). Cregg joined a band and his studies fell by the wayside. He moved back to the Bay Area in 1969, aiming to make music, which he did while supporting himself as a landscaper and carpenter, among other jobs.

In 1971, Cregg hooked up with one of the Bay Area's better-known bands, Clover. He took on the stage name, Huey Louie (after two of Donald Duck's nephews), which eventually became Huey Lewis. He played harmonica for the band, occasionally singing. In 1976, Nick

Lowe—then of pub-rock heroes Brinsley Schwartz—heard them playing in L.A., and told them they'd fit perfectly into the scene in England. The band went with Lowe, but almost as soon as they arrived in England, the Sex Pistols hit and the climate changed radically. They recorded two albums that stiffed. Lewis played harmonica on Lowe's *Labor of Lust* album and fellow ex-Brinsley Dave Edmunds's *Repeat When Necessary*. Edmunds recorded Lewis's song "Bad Is Bad." Several members of the band backed Elvis Costello on his debut album, then the group headed back home. On their return, guitarist John McFee joined the Doobie Brothers, effectively disbanding the group.

Lewis kept busy, putting together a new band, mostly consisting of Van Morrison's old band, Soundhole: Mario Cipollina, brother of Quicksilver Messenger Service guitarist John Cipollina, on bass; Johnny Colla on sax and guitar; and Bill Gibson on drums. Lewis recruited guitarist Chris Hayes, brother of noted Bay Area vocalist Bonnie Hayes, and the band started playing regular gigs; they even recorded a dance version of the theme from the movie *Exodus*, called "Exo-disco." In 1980, the group signed to Chrysalis. Their eponymous debut captured their bar-band exuberance with studio slickness, a formula they would use throughout their career. The debut went nowhere, but their sophomore effort, 1982's *Picture This*, brought the group to national prominence with the #7 single "Do You Believe in Love," helped by a video that captured Lewis's cleft-chinned, frat- boy good looks. The follow-up single, "Hope You Love Me Like You Say You Do," went to #36. The album hit #13 and went gold. The band went on tour and was featured on several music television shows.

However, no one could have predicted the enormous success of their next album, 1983's *Sports*. The album built slowly, starting with the #8 blue-eyed R&B tune "Heart and Soul." The second single, "I Want a New Drug," rose to #6 and went gold. With the third single, the anthemic "The Heart of Rock & Roll," the album hit #1 and the single topped off at #6. "If This Is It," a more mid-tempo tune, also peaked at #6. The group eked one more single out of the album, "Walking on a Thin Line," which peaked at #18. By the time the dust had cleared, *Sports* had gone quintuple platinum, and has sold another million each subsequent year rising to septuple platinum. It became a major international hit, and the band spent the better part of the year on the road. At the same time they cut "The Power of Love," the theme from the film *Back to the Future*. The song became the group's first chart topper, went gold, and was nominated for an Oscar. Lewis also made a cameo appearance in the film as a teacher chaperoning a dance.

The group released *Fore!* during the summer of 1986. Following the massive hit "The Power of Love," the first single from the new album "Stuck with You" topped both the pop and adult contemporary charts. Backed by members of the San Francisco 49ers football team, "Hip to Be Square," neatly summarized the band's musical philosophy and went to #3. Capitalizing on the success of Bruce Hornsby and the Range's "The Way It Is," The News' version of Hornsby's "Jacob's Ladder" topped the charts. Another song with the 49ers, "I Know What I Like," rose to #9, and "Doing It All for My Baby" became the fifth Top Ten single from the album, rising to #6. Ironically, although the singles did better and the album topped the charts again, it sold about half as much as *Sports*, going triple platinum. Their 1988 opus, *Small World*, took a different tack, featuring overtones of jazz and reggae. The single "Perfect World" went to #3, but the title track only hit #25. The album topped out at #11 and went platinum.

The group changed record companies before releasing their next album, 1991's *Hard at Play*. While the single "Couple Days Off" rose to #11, "It Hit Me Like a Hammer" only got to #21. The album got to #27 and went gold. Their 1994 release, an album of covers called *Four Chords and Several Years Ago*, didn't even do that well, though it contained a sterling a cappella version of "But It's Alright." The "a cappella set" became an integral part of the band's act as they continued to play the hits live.

DISC.: *Huey Lewis & The News* (1980); *Picture This* (1982); *Sports* (1983); *Fore!* (1986); *Small World* (1988); *Hard at Play* (1991); *Four Chords & Several Years Ago* (1994); *Time Flies: The Best of Huey Lewis & The News* (1996).—**HB**

Huggett, Monica, English violinist; b. London, May 16, 1953. She was a student of Manoug Parikian at the Royal Academy of Music in London, and also received training in early performance practice from Sigiswald Kuijken, Gustav Leonhardt, and Ton Koopman. With Koopman, she helped to found the Amsterdam Baroque Orch. in 1980, serving as its concertmaster until 1987. She also appeared as a soloist with various early music ensembles, as a recitalist, and as a chamber music player. She likewise served as director of the Greate Consort, Trio Sonnerie, and Hausmusik. In 1992 she made her first appearance with the Portland (Ore.) Baroque Orch., and in 1996 she became its artistic director. Huggett is an advocate of the use of original instruments. Her repertoire extends from the late Renaissance to the Romantic eras.—**LK/DM**

Huggler, John, American composer; b. Rochester, N.Y., Aug. 30, 1928. He studied at the Eastman School of Music in his hometown (graduated, 1950), and with Charles Warren Fox (musicology) and Dante Fiorillo (composition). He received 2 Guggenheim fellowships (1962, 1969), and also served as composer-in-residence of the Boston Sym. Orch. (1964–65).

WORKS: ORCH.: *Elegy to the Memory of Federico García Lorca* (1952); Horn Concerto (1957); *Ecce Homo* (1959); *Divertimento* for Viola and Orch. (1961); *Music in 2 Parts* (1966); Flute Concerto (1967); Trumpet Concerto (1968); Sym. in 3 Movements (1980); *Continuum* (1985). **CHAMBER:** 9 string quartets (1951–67); 4 brass quintets (1957, 1962, 1973, 1982); 3 string quintets (1958); *Outdoor Piece for Tanglewood* for Brass and Percussion (1966); *Sinfonia* for 13 Players (1974); *Poem* for Violin and Piano (1985); *Capriccio Sregolato* for Flute, Clarinet, Violin, Viola, and Cello (1986). **Piano:** 7 Bagatelles (1953); Sonata (1957). **VOCAL:** *Sculptures* for Soprano and Orch. (1964); 7 *Songs on Poems of E. J. Leavenworth* for Soprano and Orch. (1974). —**NS/LK/DM**

Hughes, Arwel, Welsh conductor and composer; father of **Owain Arwel Hughes;** b. Rhosllanerchrugog, Aug. 25, 1909; d. Cardiff, Sept. 23, 1988. He studied with Kitson and Vaughan Williams at the Royal Coll. of Music in London, then returned to Wales, where he became a member of the music dept. of the BBC in 1935;. from 1965 to 1971 he was head of music there. He was made an Officer of the Order of the British Empire in 1969. He wrote the operas *Menna* (1950–51) and *Serch yw'r doctor* (Love's the Doctor), after Molière (1959), a Sym. (1971), choral works, and chamber music. —**NS/LK/DM**

Hughes, Dom Anselm, eminent English musicologist; b. London, April 15, 1889; d. Nashdom Abbey, Burnham, Buckinghamshire, Oct. 8, 1974. He studied at Keble Coll., Oxford (B.A., 1911; M.A., 1915), and at Ely Theological Coll. (1911–12). He was ordained a priest (1913). He was a curate and choirmaster in several London churches (1912–22) before joining the Anglican Benedictine community at Pershore Abbey. He was professed there (1923) and served as its director of music (1922–45) and prior (1936–45), continuing after its 1926 move to Nashdom Abbey. He was a leading authority on medieval and Renaissance music. He contributed articles to the 3rd, 4th, and 5th eds. of *Grove's Dictionary of Music and Musicians* and to the 2nd ed. of *The Oxford History of Music*, edited the 2nd and 3rd (with G. Abraham) vols. of *The New Oxford History of Music*, and also edited the *Old Hall Manuscript* (with H. Collins). He composed *Missa Sancti Benedicti* (1918) and other sacred pieces.

WRITINGS: *Latin Hymnody: An Enquiry into the Underlying Principles of the Hymnarium* (London, 1922); *The House of My Pilgrimage* (London, 1929); *Index to the Facsimile Edition of MS Wolfenbüttel 677* (Oxford, 1939); *Liturgical Terms for Music Students* (Boston, 1940); *Medieval Polyphony in the Bodleian Library* (Oxford, 1951); *Catalogue of the Musical Manuscripts at Peterhouse, Cambridge* (Cambridge, 1953); *Septuagesima: Reminiscences of the Plainsong and Mediaeval Music Society* (London, 1959); *Plainsong for English Choirs* (Leighton Buzzard, 1966).—**NS/LK/DM**

Hughes, Edwin, American pianist and teacher; b. Washington, D.C., Aug. 15, 1884; d. N.Y., July 17, 1965. He studied with S. M. Fabian in Washington, D.C., with Joseffy in N.Y. (1906–07), and with Leschetizky in Vienna (1907–10). He taught at the Ganapol School of Musical Art in Detroit (1910–12), the Volpe Inst. of Music in N.Y. (1916–17), and the Inst. of Musical Art in N.Y. (1918–23); lectured at various schools. From 1920 to 1926 he was special ed. of piano music for G. Schirmer, Inc. He toured widely in the U.S. and Europe after the close of World War I. He performed duo- recitals with his wife, the pianist Jewel Bethany Hughes, and also gave master classes.—**NS/LK/DM**

Hughes, Herbert, Irish music critic and composer; b. Belfast, March 16, 1882; d. Bristol, May 1, 1937. He studied at the Royal Coll. of Music in London. From 1911 to 1932 he was music critic of the *Daily Telegraph*. He collected and arranged numerous folk songs. His own works include incidental music, chamber pieces, piano music, and vocal works.—**NS/LK/DM**

Hughes, Owain Arwel, Welsh conductor, son of **Arwel Hughes;** b. Cardiff, March 21, 1942. He first studied at Univ. Coll. in Cardiff; then (1964–66) at the Royal Coll. of Music in London, where his teachers included Boult and Harvey Philips; subsequently studied with Kempe in London and Haitink in Amsterdam. He made his London debut in 1968, then appeared as a guest conductor with leading English orchs. He also conducted at the Welsh National Opera and the English National Opera. In 1977 he became music director of the Royal National Eisteddfod of Wales. He also was assoc. conductor of the BBC Welsh Sym. Orch. (from 1980) and music director of the Huddersfield Choral Soc. (1980–86). He then was assoc. conductor of the Philharmonia Orch. of London (from 1987).—NS/LK/DM

Hughes, Robert Watson, Scottish-born Australian composer; b. Leven, Fyfeshire, March 27, 1912. He emigrated to Australia in 1930 and studied with A. E. H. Nickson at the Univ. of Melbourne Conservatorium of Music (1938–40). He worked as a music librarian at the Australian Broadcasting Commission in Melbourne; was chairman of the Australian Performing Right Assn. (1977–85). In 1978 he was made a Member of the Order of the British Empire. He withdrew most of his early compositions.

WORKS: DRAMATIC: O p e r a : *The Intriguers* (1975). B a l l e t : *Xanadu* (1954); *The Forbidden Rite* (1962). ORCH.: *Festival Overture* (1948); *Farrago,* suite (1949); *Serenade* for Small Orch. (1952); Sym. (1952); *Essay I* (1953) and *II* (1982); *Masquerade Overture* (1956); Sinfonietta (1957) *Synthesis* (1969); *Sea Spell* (1973). VOCAL: *5 Indian Poems* for Chorus, Woodwinds, and Percussion (1971); *2 Indian Poems* for Soprano and Chamber Orch. (1979).—NS/LK/DM

Hughes, Rupert, American novelist, writer on music, and composer; b. Lancaster, Mo., Jan. 31, 1872; d. Los Angeles, Sept. 9, 1956. He studied with W. G. Smith in Cleveland (1890–92), E. S. Kelley in N.Y. (1899), and C. Pearce in London (1900–1901). His publications include *American Composers* (Boston, 1900; rev. 1914); *The Musical Guide* (2 vols., N.Y., 1903; republ. as *Music Lovers' Encyclopedia,* in 1 vol., 1912; rev. and newly ed. by D. Taylor and R. Kerr as *Music Lover's Encyclopedia,* 1939; rev. 1954); ed. *Thirty Songs by American Composers* (1904). He also composed a dramatic monologue for Baritone and Piano, *Cain* (1919), piano pieces, and songs. He was principally known, however, as a novelist.—NS/LK/DM

Hugon, Georges, French composer and teacher; b. Paris, July 23, 1904; d. Blauvac, Vaucluse, July 19, 1980. He studied at the Paris Cons., receiving the Prix Bizet (1926). He was director of the Boulogne-sur-Mer Cons. (1934–41), and in 1941 he became a prof. at the Paris Cons. His compositions include an oratorio, *Chants de deuil et d'espérance* (1947), 2 syms. (1941, 1949), 2 symphonic poems: *Au nord* (1930) and *La Reine de Saba* (1933), Piano Concerto (1962), Flute Sonata (1965), Piano Trio, String Quartet, piano pieces, and songs. —NS/LK/DM

Huízar (García de la Cadena), Candelario, Mexican composer; b. Jerez, Feb. 2, 1883; d. Mexico City, May 3, 1970. He studied violin and composition before training with Gustavo Campa at the Mexico City Cons. He played horn (1929–37) and was librarian (1929–48) with the Orquesta Sinfónica de Mexico. His output reflected Mexican folk modalities with an infusion of authentic Mexican themes.

WORKS: ORCH (all 1st perf. in Mexico City): 3 symphonic poems: *Imágenes* (Dec. 13, 1929), *Pueblerinas* (Nov. 6, 1931), and *Surco* (Oct. 25, 1935); 4 syms. (Nov. 14, 1930; Sept. 4, 1936; July 29, 1938; Aug. 7, 1942). CHAMBER: Sonata for Clarinet and Bassoon (1931); String Quartet (1938). VOCAL: Choral pieces; songs.—NS/LK/DM

Hull, Arthur Eaglefield, English writer on music; b. Market Harborough, March 10, 1876; d. (suicide) London, Nov. 4, 1928. He was a student of Matthay and C. Pearce. In 1912 he became ed. of the *Monthly Musical Record.* In 1918 he organized the British Music Soc. He publ. the pioneering *Dictionary of Modern Music and Musicians* (1924), a vol. flawed by many egregious errors and misconceptions; A. Einstein publ. a corrected German tr. (1926). Hull's *Music: Classical, Romantic and Modern* (1927) proved to be a pasticcio of borrowings from various English and American writers. When he was exposed, the book was withdrawn by the publisher in 1928 and Hull threw himself under a train at the Huddersfield Railway Station, dying a few weeks later. He also publ. *Organ Playing, Its Technique and Expression* (1911); *Modern Harmony: Its Explanation and Application* (1914; 3rd ed., 1923); *The Sonata in Music* (1916); *Scriabin* (1916); *Modern Musical Styles* (1916); *Design or Construction in Music* (1917); *Cyril Scott* (1918).—NS/LK/DM

Hullah, John (Pyke), English organist, writer on music, teacher, and composer; b. Worcester, June 27, 1812; d. London, Feb. 21, 1884. He was a pupil of William Horsley, and in 1833 he studied singing with Crivelli at the Royal Academy of Music in London. As a composer, he was entirely self- taught. At the age of 24 he produced an opera to a story by Charles Dickens, *The Village Coquette* (London, Dec. 6, 1836). Two other operas followed: *The Barber of Bassora* (London, Nov. 11, 1837) and *The Outpost* (May 17, 1838). In the meantime, he obtained the post of church organist at Croydon. He made several trips to Paris, where he became interested in the new system of vocal teaching established by Wilhem. He modified it to suit English requirements, and, with the sanction of the National Education Committee, he opened his Singing School for Schoolmasters at Exeter Hall (1841). The school became the target of bitter criticism; nonetheless, it prospered, and thousands of students enrolled. His wealthy supporters helped him build St. Martin's Hall for performances of vocal music by his students. The hall was inaugurated in 1850, and it was destroyed by fire in 1860. From 1844 to 1874 Hullah taught singing at King's Coll., and later at Queen's Coll. and Bedford Coll. in London. He conducted the student concerts of the Royal Academy of Music (1870–73). In 1872 he became an inspector of training schools. He held the honorary degree of LL.D. from Edinburgh Univ. (1876), and was also a member of the Cecilia Soc. in Rome and of the Academy of Music in Florence. He ed. *Wilhem's Method of Teaching Singing*

Adapted to English Use (1841). He publ. *A Grammar of Vocal Music* (1843), *A Grammar of Harmony* (1852), *A Grammar of Counterpoint* (1864), *The History of Modern Music* (1862), *The Third or Transition Period of Musical History* (1865), *The Cultivation of the Speaking Voice* (1870), and *Music in the House* (1877). He also brought out 3 useful collections of vocal music: *The Psalter, The Book of Praise Hymnal,* and *Whole Book of Psalms with Chants.* He was the composer of the celebrated song "O that we two were Maying." Other popular songs are "The Storm" and "3 Fishers." *A Life of John Hullah* was publ. by his wife (London, 1886).—NS/LK/DM

Hüllmandel, Nicolas-Joseph,

Alsatian composer; b. Strasbourg, May 23, 1756; d. London, Dec. 19, 1823. He was an illegitimate son of Michel Hüllmandel, organist at the Strasbourg Cathedral and nephew of the composer Jean-Joseph Rodolphe. Around 1776 he went to Paris, where he taught piano and the glass harmonica; among his pupils in composition were Onslow and Aubert. After the French Revolution he went to London, where he remained until his death. There he publ. a manual, *Principles of Music, Chiefly Calculated for the Pianoforte* (1795). He composed in a typical manner of his time; Mozart, in one of his letters to his father, expressed appreciation of Hüllmandel's sonatas. He publ. 25 keyboard sonatas between 1773 and 1790, some with violin accompaniment; also other works for piano or harpsichord.

BIBL.: R. Benton, *N.-J. H. and French Instrumental Music in the Second Half of the 18th Century* (diss., Univ. of Toronto, 1961). —NS/LK/DM

Human League, The,

harbingers of electropop, "allying technology with humanity and humour;" formed 1977, Sheffield, England. **MEMBERSHIP:** Phil Oakey, voc., synth. (b. Sheffield, England, Oct. 2, 1955); Martyn Ware, synth. (b. Sheffield, England, May 19, 1956); Ian Craig Marsh, synth. (b. Sheffield, England, Nov. 11, 1956); Ian Burden, bs., synth. (b. Sheffield, England, Dec. 24, 1957); Suzanne Sulley, voc. (b. Sheffield, England, March 22, 1963); Joanne Catherall, voc. (b. Sheffield, England, Sept. 18, 1962). Ian Marsh and Martyn Ware were computer operators who played synthesizers in their spare time. They started putting together all- electric bands like The Dead Daughters and The Future. In 1977, Ware brought in an old school chum, Philip Oakey, a hospital orderly with a deadpan, Bowiesque voice. They dubbed this new band The Human League, which came from a board game called "Star Force." By 1978, the group was cutting mono demos of early songs like "Being Boiled" and "Circus of Death." They also started to perform live. The band recruited Adrian Wright, a student at Sheffield Art Coll. who happened to live in the same building in which the band practiced. Wright joined the band as the visual director, preparing slide shows that accompanied the music.

The group's demos attracted the attention of Fast Records, which released a single of "Being Boiled" in June to passing interest, enough to set them on the road with Siouxsie and the Banshees. In 1979, Virgin signed the band and they put out *Reproduction,* to little notice. In 1980, Virgin helped them open their own electronic music studio in an old veterinary clinic. They recorded the single "Holiday 80" backed with a totally electronic version of Gary Glitter's "Rock 'n' Roll" that actually charted in the 1950s in England. Their sophomore album, *Travelogue,* did even better, peaking in the album charts at #16. The group went on tour.

When the group played live, a lot of the material was prerecorded. Oakey saw this as cheating; Ware and Marsh saw it as a necessity, because they weren't musicians so much as technicians. The debate came to a head during the tour supporting *Travelogue.* Ware and Marsh left the group to form the British Electric Foundation and its subgroup Heaven 17. Oakey, however, wanted to honor tour obligations (and didn't want to go back to pushing gurneys). He encouraged Wright to learn the synthesizer and brought in bassist Ian Burden and former Rezillos guitarist Jo Callis to play synthesizers as well. In a final bit of inspiration, he hired two schoolgirls he found dancing at a local disco to perform on stage and discovered to his pleasure that they could also sing.

The revamped Human League went into the studio with producer Martin Rushent. They started actually landing hits with "The Sound of the Crowd" (#12 U.K.) and "Love Action" (#3 U.K.). With the release of the group's third album, *Dare,*and the single "Don't You Want Me?" they landed the #1 slot in both the album and single charts in England. The album came out in the U.S., their first release on this side of the Atlantic, and the sprightly, electro-Motown of "Don't You Want Me?" topped the U.S. charts as well, while the album went to #3. Both were awarded gold records. *Rolling Stone* called *Dare* one of the Top 100 albums of the 1980s.

By the time the group released 1985's *Fascination,* their sound had been copied by a mix of groups like Soft Cell and even Oakey's previous cronies in Heaven 17. Still, the *Fascination* EP made it to #22 on the album charts, the title track hit #8, and "Mirror Man" hit #30 on the singles charts. It took another year, however before they released another full album. *Hysteria* did not fare as well commercially as its two immediate predecessors. Technically, it was a more complex album and more meaty. It also dared to dabble in tradition, with Burden and Callis actually playing guitar and bass. Singles like "The Lebanon" and "Life on Your Own" failed to make a significant dent in the pop market, however.

Steve Barron, who had directed several of the group's videos, asked Oakey to record a song for the soundtrack to his feature film *Electric Dreams.* It gave Oakey the opportunity to work with another electric pop pioneer Giorgio Moroder, the kingpin behind Donna Summer's greatest records. The song, "Together in Electric Dreams" went into the Top Five in England, so the duo recorded an entire album together. In 1987, the group got back together to record with producers Jimmy Jam and Terry Lewis. While they seemed an unlikely combination, their work on singles by groups like the SOS Band had impressed Oakey. While the album was by all accounts a trying project, *Crash* did land the group their first #1 single, the ballad "Human." The album rose as high as #24.

The next Human League project, 1990's *Romantic?*, sounded somewhat depressed, although still eminently danceable. The group started to feel a lack of support from their record company, even though the single "Heart Like a Wheel" eked it's way into the Top 40, peaking at #32. After that, the band all but disappeared for five years. Everyone thought they had heard the last of the Human League when the group signed with East West records and released *Octopus* in 1995. Again, the pop audience barely paid attention, although it might be the group's most thematically coherent record since the days of Marsh and Ware. The single "Tell Me When" scraped the Top 40, going to #31. The group toured with Culture Club and Howard Jones in a package called The Rewind Tour in 1998, and continued to play live.

DISC.: *Reproduction* (1979); *Travelogue* (1982); *Dare* (1983); *Love and Dancing* (1984); *Fascination!* (1985); *Hysteria* (1986); *Crash* (1987); *Greatest Hits* (1988); *Romantic?* (1990); *Octopus* (1995). **PHILIP OAKEY WITH GIORGIO MORODER:** *Philip Oakey and Giorgio Moroder* (1985).—**BH**

Humble, (Leslie) Keith, Australian pianist, conductor, teacher, and composer; b. Geelong, Victoria, Sept. 6, 1927. After obtaining his diploma at the Melbourne Cons. (1949), he studied with Vivian Langrish (piano) and Howard Ferguson (composition) at the Royal Academy of Music in London (1950–51). He then went to Paris and studied with Cortot (piano) at the École Normale de Musique (1951–52), and then privately with Leibowitz (composition and conducting, 1952–54). In 1959 he founded Le Centre de Musique in Paris, which he led as musical director until 1968. In 1966 he became senior lecturer in composition at the Melbourne Cons., and also founded its electronic music studio. From 1971 to 1974 he was a prof. at the Univ. of Calif. at San Diego. In 1974 he became the Foundation Prof. in the music dept. of La Trobe Univ. in Victoria, Australia, which position he held until 1989 when he became prof. emeritus. From 1975 to 1978 he was music director of the Australia Contemporary Music Ensemble. He was a visiting prof. at the Univ. of Calif. at San Diego from 1982 to 1990, where he made appearances as a soloist and conductor with the Ensemble Sonor. In 1982 he was made a Member of the Order of Australia. A confirmed avant-gardist, Humble early on developed a personal 12–tone method. He later experimented with improvisation in a series of works he called *Nuniques*. Still later he explored the realm of temporal composition.

WORKS: String Trio (1953); 4 piano sonatas (1959; 1977, rev. 1980; 1985; 1990); *Ainsi s'acheve* for Chamber Ensemble (1967); *Music for Monuments* for Instruments and/or Voices and Prepared Tape (1967); *Materials for Larountala* for 22 Solo Strings (1968); *Solfege I* for Diverse Instruments and Electronics ad libitum (1968) and *II* for Performer and Electronics (1969); *Nunique I-IX*, improvisation pieces (1968–84); *Arcade I-V* for Solo Instrument, Chamber Ensemble, Orch., or Tape (all 1969); *Apres La Legende* for Piano and Orch. (1969); *La Legende*, cantata for Voice, Chorus, Electronics, and Instruments (1970); *Statico I* for Organ and 2 Synthesizers (1971) and *III* for Orch. (1972–73);

A Music for Baroque Ensemble for Harpsichord, Flute, Oboe, and Double Bass (1971); *Now V*, opera (1971); *Prime Riff* for Percussion Ensemble and Tape (1974); *A.C.F.* for Chamber Ensemble (1980); Trio No. 2 for Violin, Clarinet, and Piano (1982); *Ways, By-Ways* for Chamber Ensemble (1983); Trio No. 3 for Flute, Percussion, and Piano (1985); Percussion Sonata (1986); *Soundscapes* for Chorus and Instrumental Ensemble (1987; also for Instrumental Ensemble and Pre-recorded Tape); *Etchings* for Percussion Quartet (1988); *4 All Seasons* for Strings (1989); Flute Sonata (1990); *Concert No. 1* for Flute and Strings (1991) and *No. 2* for Trombone and String Sextet or String Orch. or Chamber Music Ensemble (1992); *A Symphony (of Sorrows)* for Orch. (1994); Trio No. 5 for Organ, Trumpet, and Trombone (1995).—**NS/LK/DM**

Hume, Paul (Chandler), American music critic; b. Chicago, Dec. 13, 1915. He studied at the Univ. of Chicago, and also took private lessons in piano, organ, and voice. He was organist, choirmaster, and baritone soloist at various churches in Chicago and Washington, D.C., and also gave song recitals. From 1946 to 1982 he was music ed. and critic of the *Washington Post*. He was an instructor in music history at Georgetown Univ. (1950–77), and also active as a lecturer and radio commentator on music. He publ. *Catholic Church Music* (1956), *Our Music, Our Schools, and Our Culture* (1957), *The Lion of Poland* (1962), *King of Song* (1964), and *Verdi* (1977). Hume leaped to national fame in 1950, when President Truman, outraged by his unenthusiastic review of Margaret Truman's song recital, wrote him a personal letter threatening him with bodily injury. Hume sold the letter to a Conn. industrialist for an undisclosed sum of money.—**NS/LK/DM**

Humel, Gerald, American composer; b. Cleveland, Nov. 7, 1931. He studied at Hofstra Univ. in N.Y. (B.A., 1954), the Royal Coll. of Music in London (A.R.C.M., 1956), the Oberlin (Ohio) Coll. Cons. of Music (M.M., 1958), and the Univ. of Mich. in Ann Arbor (1958–60); in 1960 he went to Berlin, where he took private lessons with Blacher and Rufer. His music at first maintained a median line of cosmopolitan modernism, in a neo-Classical direction, but gradually he became oriented toward dodecaphonic techniques.

WORKS: DRAMATIC: O p e r a : *The Proposal* (1949); *The Triangle* (Oberlin, Nov. 14, 1958). **B a l l e t :** *Devil's Dice* (1957); *1ˢᵗ Love* (1965); *Herodias* (1967). **ORCH.:** Flute Concerto (1964); Chamber Concerto for Horn, Piano, and Strings (1966); Concerto for Wind Orch. (1968); *Flashes* for Chamber Ensemble (1968); *Fantasie* for 2 Flutes, Cello, and Piano (1968); *Lepini* (1977). **CHAMBER:** *Duo* for Viola and Cello (1964); Cello Sonata (1967); 2 sonatas for Solo Viola (1967, 1968); Clarinet Sonata (1968).—**NS/LK/DM**

Humes, Helen, pop-jazz singer; b. Louisville, Ky., June 23, 1913; d. Santa Monica, Calif., Sept. 13, 1981. Humes played both piano and trumpet as a child as well as singing in her local church band (which also featured Dickie Wells and Jonah Jones, the latter of whom she frequently worked with later in her career). She moved to N.Y. in her early teens and made her recording debut in Chicago (1927). In the early 1930s she did theater work and spent a long period with Vernon Andrade's Orch., then a residency at the Cotton Club (Cincinnati), and recording for Harry James and working with Stuff Smith and Jonah Jones. She joined Count Basie to replace Billie Holiday in July 1938 (she had previously declined an offer to join). Among her most popular recordings with Basie were "If Papa Has Outside Lovin'," "Do What You Did Last Night," "Everybody Does It Now," "Sub-Deb Blues," and "He May Be Your Man But He Comes to See Me Sometimes." She left Basie in the spring of 1941, did a residency at the Village Vanguard, then (accompanied by Clarence Love's Orch.), extensive touring. After further residencies in N.Y. she moved to Calif. in 1944. She scored with an R&B-oriented record of "Be Baba Leba" with Bill Doggett in 1945, worked mainly on the West Coast, with regular concert and television appearances, and also worked in the play *Simply Heavenly*. By 1947 she was recording and performing in a more mainstream jazz direction once more, most notably with Buck Clayton and Teddy Wilson in N.Y. and Norman Granz in Calif. By the mid-1950s, despite scoring a big hit with "Million Dollar Secret," her career was fading. In the later 1950s, she worked with Red Norvo (including an Australian tour in 1956). She retired and moved to Australia in June 1964, then returned to the U.S. when her mother fell ill in 1967. She started singing again after being persuaded to appear at the 1973 Newport Jazz Festival with Basie; this appearance was a phenomenal success and led to a deserved upswing in her fortunes. As a result of this, Humes enjoyed several successful headlining tours, an appearance at the Nice Jazz Festival, a near legendary appearance at Ronnie Scotts in 1973 and many recordings. She did U.S. residencies and overseas tours during the 1970s.

DISC. *E-Baba-Le-Ba* (1944); *H. H.* (1959); *Songs I Like to Sing* (1960); *Swingin' with H.* (1961); *H. Comes Back* (1973); *Sneakin' Around* (1974); *On the Sunny Side of the Street* (1974); *The Talk of the Town* (1975); *H. H. and the Muse All Stars* (1979); *New Year's Eve* (1980); *H.* (1980); *Let the Good Times Roll* (1981). —JC/MM/NS

Humfrey, Pelham, English composer; b. 1647; d. Windsor, July 14, 1674. He was among the first children appointed to the restored Chapel Royal in 1660, and (together with fellow-choristers John Blow and William Turner) he wrote the famous *Club Anthem.* In 1664 King Charles II sent him to study in France and Italy under the Secret Service Funds; that he worked under Lully remains unverified, nor can it be proved that he got to Italy. He returned to England in 1666 as lutenist of the Chapel Royal, and was appointed Gentleman of the Chapel Royal on Jan. 24, 1667. An entry in Pepys's diary for Nov. 15, 1667, described him as being "full of form, and confidence, and vanity" and disparaging "everything, and everybody's skill but his own." Humfrey's justification of his self-confidence lay in his undoubted mastery of the Italian declamatory style, greater than anyone had yet achieved in England. On July 14, 1672, he was appointed Master of the Children of the Chapel Royal. Two years later he died, at the early age of 27. One of his wards was the young Henry Purcell, whose style clearly shows Humfrey's influence. A number of

his secular songs were publ. in collections of his era. A complete ed. of his sacred music has been prepared by P. Dennison in Musica Britannica, XXXIV-XXXV (London, 1972).

WORKS: 22 secular songs; 5 sacred songs; a dialogue, composed with John Blow; songs and vocal ensembles for Shadwell's version of Shakespeare's *The Tempest;* 3 odes, all to Charles II; 26 anthems, of which 19 are extant (1 composed with John Blow and William Turner).

BIBL.: P. Dennison, *The Life and Works of P. H.* (diss., Oxford Univ., 1970); idem, *P. H.* (London, 1986).—NS/LK/DM

Hummel, Ferdinand, German composer and teacher; b. Berlin, Sept. 6, 1855; d. there, April 24, 1928. He began making appearances as a harpist when he was only 7. Following studies with Zamara in Vienna, he toured Germany, Scandinavia, and Russia (1864–67), accompanied by his father, a flutist in the Prussian Royal Chapel. He then completed his training in Berlin at Kullak's Academy (1868–75), the Hochschule für Musik, and the Akademie der Künst. He devoted himself primarily to teaching and composing in Berlin. In 1892 he was made music director of the Royal Theater, and in 1897 he was named Royal Kapellmeister. Several of his operas were composed in the verismo manner.

WORKS: DRAMATIC: O p e r a : *Mara* (Berlin, Oct. 11, 1893); *Angla* (Berlin, June 9, 1894); *Ein treuer Schelm* (Prague, Oct. 25, 1894); *Assarpai* (Gotha, April 6, 1898); *Sophie von Brabant* (Darmstadt, Feb. 14, 1899); *Die Beichte* (Berlin, April 10, 1900); *Die Gefilde der Seligen* (Altenburg, Jan. 19, 1917). **OTHER:** Sym.; Piano Concerto; chamber music; choral works. —NS/LK/DM

Hummel, Johann Nepomuk, celebrated Austrian pianist, composer, and pedagogue; b. Pressburg, Nov. 14, 1778; d. Weimar, Oct. 17, 1837. A child prodigy, he began to study the violin and the piano under his father's tutelage; when he was 8 the family moved to Vienna, where his father became music director of the Theater auf der Wieden. Mozart interested himself in the young musician, took him into his house, and for 2 years instructed him. Hummel made his Vienna debut in 1787, then toured under his father's guidance, visiting Bohemia, Germany, Denmark, Scotland, the Netherlands, and England, where he presented his String Quartet in Oxford. He returned to Vienna in 1793 and studied counterpoint with Albrechtsberger, composition with Salieri, and organ with Haydn. He served as Konzertmeister to Prince Nikolaus Esterházy (1804–11), carrying out the duties of Kapellmeister, although Haydn retained the title. His opera *Mathilde von Guise* was produced in Vienna on March 26, 1810. He returned there in 1811 as a teacher; then resumed his appearances as a pianist in 1814, being particularly successful at the Congress of Vienna; subsequently toured Germany in 1816. He served as court Kapellmeister in Stuttgart (1816–18); then in 1819 became Grand Ducal Kapellmeister in Weimar, a position he held until his death. His years in Weimar were marked by his friendship with Goethe. He traveled widely as a pianist; visited St. Petersburg (1822); Paris (1825), where he was made a Chevalier of the Légion d'honneur; and Belgium and the Netherlands (1826). In 1827 he was in Vienna, where he visited Beethoven on the composer's deathbed; he traveled to Warsaw in 1828 and to Paris and London in 1830. He revisited London in 1831 and 1833; during the latter visit, he conducted German opera at the King's Theater. The last years of his life were marred by ill health and much suffering. At the peak of his career as a pianist, he was regarded as one of the greatest virtuosos of his time; both as a pianist and as a composer, he was often declared to be the equal of Beethoven. His compositions were marked by excellent craftsmanship; his writing for instruments, particularly for piano, was impeccable; his melodic invention was rich, and his harmonic and contrapuntal skill was of the highest caliber. Yet with his death, his music went into an immediate eclipse; performances of his works became increasingly rare, until the name of Hummel all but vanished from active musical programs. However, some of his compositions were revived by various musical societies in Europe and America, and as a result, at least his Trumpet Concerto (1803) and chamber music were saved from oblivion. He wrote works in all genres except the sym. He also publ. *Anweisung zum Pianofortespiel* (1828), an elaborate instruction book and one of the first to give a sensible method of fingering. His wife, Elisabeth Hummel-Rockl (1793–1883), was an opera singer; they had 2 sons, a pianist and a painter.

WORKS: DRAMATIC: *Il Viaggiator ridicolo*, opera (1797; unfinished); *Dankgefühl einer Geretteten*, monodrama (March 21, 1799); *Demagorgon*, comic opera (c. 1800; only fragment extant; used in the following opera); *Don Anchise Campione*, opera buffa (c. 1800; unfinished); *Le vicende d'amore*, opera buffa (1804; rev. as *Die vereitelten Ränke*, Eisenstadt, Sept. 1806); *Die beyden Genies*, Lustspiel (1805; not extant); *Die Messenier*, grosse heroische Oper (c. 1805–10); *Pimmalione*, azione teatrale (c. 1805–15); *Mathilde von Guise*, opera (Vienna, March 26, 1810; rev. version, Weimar, Feb. 17, 1821); *Stadt und Land*, Singspiel (c. 1810; unfinished); *Dies Haus ist zu verkaufen*, Singspiel (Vienna, May 5, 1812, based on *Die vereitelten Ränke*); Aria in Castelli's pasticcio *Fünf sind Zwey* (Vienna, March 21, 1813); *Der Junker in der Mühle*, Singspiel (Nov. 1813); *Die Eselshaut, oder Die blaue Insel*, Feenspiel (Vienna, March 10, 1814); *Die Rückfahrt des Kaisers*, Singspiel (Vienna, June 15, 1814); *Attila*, opera (c. 1825–27; not extant). Also music to operas by others, incidental music to plays, ballets, and pantomimes. **OTHER:** 12 cantatas; sacred music; at least 8 piano concertos; Trumpet Concerto (1803); Bassoon Concerto; numerous works for piano solo; much chamber music.

BIBL.: K. Benyovszky, *J.N. H.: Der Mensch und Künstler* (Bratislava, 1934); D. Zimmerschied, *Thematisches Verzeichnis der Werke von J.N. H.* (Hofheim am Taunus, 1971); J. Sachs, *Kapellmeister H. in England and France* (Detroit, 1977).—NS/LK/DM

Humperdinck, Engelbert,

famous German composer and pedagogue; b. Siegburg, near Bonn, Sept. 1, 1854; d. Neustrelitz, Sept. 27, 1921. He began to study piano at 7. He commenced composing at 14, then studied at the Cologne Cons. (1872–76), where his teachers were Hiller, Gernsheim, and Jensen (harmony and composition), Hompesch, Mertke, and Seiss (piano), F. Weber (organ), and Ehlert and Rensburg (cello). After winning the Mozart Prize (1876), he studied counterpoint and fugue with Rheinberger at Munich's

Royal Music School (1877); also studied composition privately there with F. Lachner. In 1879 he won the Mendelssohn Prize of Berlin for his choral work *Die Wallfahrt nach Kevelaar* (1878); then went to Italy, where he met Wagner in Naples (1880); at Wagner's invitation, he worked in Bayreuth (1881–82). In 1881 he won the Meyerbeer Prize of Berlin, which enabled him to visit Paris in 1882. He taught at the Barcelona Cons. (1885–86) and the Cologne Cons. (1887–88); subsequently worked for the Schott publishing firm in Mainz (1888–89). After serving as private teacher to Siegfried Wagner (1889–90), he joined the faculty of the Hoch Cons. in Frankfurt am Main in 1890; was made prof. there in 1896, but resigned in 1897. During this period he also was music critic of the *Frankfurter Zeitung*. His fame as a composer was assured with the extraordinary success of his opera *Hänsel und Gretel* (Weimar, Dec. 23, 1893), written to a libretto by his sister Adelheid Wette. This fairy-tale score, with its melodies of ingenuous felicity in a Wagnerian idiom, retains its place in the repertoire. Although he continued to write for the stage, his succeeding works left little impression. He was director of a master class in composition at Berlin's Akademische Meisterschule (1900–20); was also a member of the senate of the Berlin Academy of Arts.

WORKS: DRAMATIC: Opera: *Hänsel und Gretel* (Weimar, Dec. 23, 1893, R. Strauss conducting); *Dornröschen* (Frankfurt am Main, Nov. 12, 1902); *Die Heirat wider Willen* (Berlin, April 14, 1905); *Königskinder* (N.Y., Dec. 28, 1910; based on his incidental music to Rosmer's *Königskinder*); *Die Marketenderin* (Cologne, May 10, 1914); *Gaudeamus* (Darmstadt, March 18, 1919). Also *Die sieben Geislein*, children's fairy play for Voice and Piano (Berlin, Dec. 19, 1895). **Incidental Music:** To Rosmer's *Königskinder* (Munich, Jan. 23, 1897; later expanded into an opera); for the Berlin productions of Shakespeare's *The Merchant of Venice* (Nov. 5, 1905), *The Winter's Tale* (Sept. 15, 1906), *The Tempest* (Oct. 26, 1906), *Romeo and Juliet* (Jan. 29, 1907), and *Twelfth Night* (Oct. 17, 1907); also to Aristophanes's *Lysistrata* (Berlin, Feb. 27, 1908) and Maeterlinck's *The Blue Bird* (Berlin, Dec. 23, 1912), as well as for Reinhardt's production of *The Miracle* (London, Dec. 23, 1911). **OTHER:** *Die Wallfahrt nach Kevelaar* for Chorus (1878); *Humoreske* for Orch. (1879); *Das Glück von Edenhall* for Chorus (Munich, July 15, 1879; 2nd version, 1882–83); *Die maurische Rhapsodie* for Orch. (1898); 4 *Kinderlieder* (1901).

BIBL.: O. Besch, *E. H.* (Leipzig, 1914); H. Kuhlmann, *Stil und Form in der Musik von H.s Oper "Hänsel und Gretel"* (Borna and Leipzig, 1930); L. Kirsten, *Motivik und Form in der Musik zu E. H.s Oper "Königskinder"* (diss., Univ. of Jena, 1942); K. Pullen, *Die Schauspielmusiken H.s* (diss., Univ. of Cologne, 1951); E. Thamm, *Der Bestand der lyrischen Werke E. H.s* (diss., Univ. of Mainz, 1951); W. Humperdinck, *E. H.* (Frankfurt am Main, 1965); H. Irmen, *Die Odyssee des E. H.: Eine biographische Dokumentation* (Siegburg, 1975); idem, ed., *E. H.: Briefe und Tägebucher* (Cologne, 1976); E. Humperdinck and J. Nickel, *E. H. zum 70. Todestag* (Siegburg, 1992); W. Humperdinck, *E. H.: Das Leben meines Vaters* (Koblenz, 1993); E. Humperdinck, *E. H. Werkverzeichnis: Zum 140 Geburtstag: Seinem Andenken gewidmet* (Koblenz, 1994).—NS/LK/DM

Humpert, Hans,

German composer; b. Paderborn, April 19, 1901; d. in battle in Salerno, Sept. 15, 1943. He studied at the Frankfurt am Main Cons. and in Berlin, then taught at Paderborn until he was called into the army. His music is marked by a neo-Romantic quality, with a strong contrapuntal structure. His works include 2 syms. (1937, 1942), 3 string quartets, String Trio, Violin Sonata, Viola Sonata, Sonata for Solo Flute, 5 cantatas, 4 masses, 3 motets, 7 Psalms, and choral and organ works. —NS/LK/DM

Humphrey, Percy, early jazz trumpeter, b. New Orleans, Jan. 13, 1905; d. New Orleans, July 22, 1995. His grandfather, Professor Jim Humphrey, was a cornet player and bandleader, who taught him trumpet. His father, Willie Humphrey Sr. (b. New Orleans, May 24, 1879; d. New Orleans, January 1964), played clarinet. Percy led his own band in the 1920s. He more or less retired from music during the 1930s. His comeback began in the mid-1940s, when he led The Eureka Brass Band, the premier marching band for parades and funerals. He also worked in The Humphrey Brothers Band and his own Crescent City Joymakers. He was an original member of The Preservation Hall Jazz Band, from 1961 and continued to record and perform with them until the early 1990s. His brother Willie (William James Humphrey Jr., b. New Orleans, Dec. 29, 1900; d. New Orleans, June 7, 1994) played clarinet and also worked at Preservation Hall, dying of a heart attack after playing at the club in 1994. Another brother, Earl Humphrey (b. New Orleans, Sept. 9, 1902; d. New Orleans, June 1971), was a trombonist.

DISC.: *Sounds of New Orleans, Vol. 1* (1951); *Crescent City Joymakers* (1961); *Climax Rag* (1965); *A Portrait of P. H.* (1972); *New Orleans to Scandinavia* (1972); *Living New Orleans Jazz* (1974); *P. H. at Manny's Tavern* (1990).—JC/LP

Huneker, James Gibbons, brilliant American writer on music; b. Philadelphia, Jan. 31, 1857; d. N.Y., Feb. 9, 1921. He studied piano with Michael Cross in Philadelphia, and in 1878 in Paris with Theodore Ritter; later with Joseffy at the National Cons. in N.Y., where he then taught piano (1888–98). He was music and drama critic of the *N.Y. Recorder* (1891–95) and the *Morning Advertiser* (1895–97), and music, drama, and art critic for the *N.Y. Sun* (1900–1912). In 1917–18 he was music critic of the *Philadelphia Press*. After a single season (1918–19) with the *N.Y. Times* he became music critic for the *N.Y. World*, a position he held until his death; also wrote for various journals in N.Y., London, Paris, Berlin, and Vienna. He publ. a novel dealing with artistic life in N.Y., *Painted Veils* (1921), but devoted most of his uncommon gifts to musical journalism. He was capable of rising to true poetic style when writing about Chopin and other composers whom he loved, but he also possessed a talent for caustic invective; his attacks on Debussy were particularly sharp. In addition to his literary publications, Huneker furnished introductory essays for Joseffy's ed. of Chopin's works.

WRITINGS: *Mezzotints in Modern Music* (1899); *Chopin: The Man and His Music* (1900; Ger. tr., 1914); *Melomaniacs* (1902); *Overtones, A Book of Temperaments* (1904); *Iconoclasts: A Book for Dramatists* (1905); *Visionaries: Fantasies and Fiction* (1905); *Egoists: A Book of Supermen* (1909); *Promenades of an Impressionist: Studies in Art* (1910); *Franz Liszt: A Study* (1911; Ger. tr., 1922); *The Pathos of Distance* (1913); *Old Fogy, His Musical Opinions and Grotesques* (1913); *New Cosmopolis* (1915); *Ivory Apes and Peacocks* (1915); *Unicorns* (1917); *The Philharmonic Society of New York and Its 75th Anniversary* (1917); *Bedouins* (1920); *Steeplejack* (his memoirs; 1920); *Variations* (1921).

BIBL.: B. De Casseres, *J.G. H.* (N.Y., 1925); A. Schwab, *J.G. H.: Critic of the Seven Arts* (Stanford, Calif., 1963); idem, ed., *Americans in the Arts, 1890–1920: Critiques by J.G. H.* (N.Y., 1985). —NS/LK/DM

Hungerford, Bruce, Australian pianist; b. Korumburra, Victoria, Nov. 24, 1922; d. in an automobile accident in N.Y., Jan. 26, 1977. He received his initial education in Melbourne. He studied piano with Ignaz Friedman in Sydney (1944), and later with Ernest Hutcheson at the Juilliard School of Music in N.Y. (1945–47); took private lessons with Myra Hess in N.Y. (1948–58) and also with Carl Friedberg (1948–55). He gave his first piano recital in N.Y. in 1951, after which until 1965 he appeared under the name Leonard Hungerford. Apart from his virtuoso technique, he possessed an extraordinary mastery of dynamic gradations and self-consistent musical phraseology. He also gained recognition as a color photographer and archeologist, specializing in Egyptology; he recorded a 17–part audiovisual lecture entitled "The Heritage of Ancient Egypt" (1971).—NS/LK/DM

Hüni-Mihacsek, Felice, Hungarian soprano; b. Pécs, April 3, 1891; d. Munich, March 26, 1976. She studied in Vienna with Rosa Papier. She made her operatic debut as the 1st Lady in *Die Zauberflöte* with the Vienna State Opera in 1919, remaining there until 1926; was then a member of the Bavarian State Opera in Munich (1926–44); she retired from the stage in 1953. She particularly excelled in Mozart's operas, winning distinction as the Queen of the Night, Constanze, Fiordiligi, and Donna Anna. Among her other admired roles were Elsa and Eva.—NS/LK/DM

Hunt, Jerry (Edward), American pianist and composer; b. Waco, Tex., Nov. 30, 1943; d. Canton, Tex., Nov. 27, 1993. He studied piano and composition at North Tex. State Univ. in Denton (1960–61). As a pianist, he championed the cause of contemporary music. After teaching at Southern Methodist Univ. (1967–73), he was artist-in-residence at the Video Research Center in Dallas (1974–77). Hunt was enamored of multimedia works in which he could utilize the most varied elements, ranging from live performers and performance spaces to video and microwave detection systems.

WORKS: *Helix* for Instrument(s) (1963); *Sur Dr. John Dee* for 0 to 11 Performers (1963); *Infrasolo* for Instrument(s) (1970); *Haramand Plane: Parallel/Regenerative* for Audio and Video (1973); *Cantegral Segment(s)* for Various Instruments and Electronics (1973–78); *Volta* for Voice and Electronics (1977); *Phalba (Working): Kernel* for Electronics (1980); *Volta (Stream)* for Voice(s) and Electronics (1980); *Ground: Field (Still-core-Set)* and *Ground: Field (Transform de Chelly)* for Performers and Electronics (both 1981); tape pieces.—NS/LK/DM

Hunt, Joe (actually, Joseph Gayle), drummer; b. Richmond, Ind., July 31, 1938. He studied in

Indianapolis with Willis Kirk (author of "Brush Fire"), and at Ind. Univ. with Richard Johnson. He played with the Dave Baker band 1956–59 while attending Ind. Univ. He was a member of the George Russell sextet 1960–62 (performer in residence at the Lenox School of Jazz 1960), also with John Handy. He served in the army (1962–64), and played with the Stan Getz quartet (1964–65), the Jim Hall trio (1965), the Gary Burton quartet (1966), and the Bill Evans trio (1966–67). He freelanced in N.Y. till 1971 and also attended Mannes Coll. He moved to Boston and joined the Berklee Coll. faculty in 1971 and remained there as a Professor of Percussion. He has since toured with the National Jazz Ensemble and Barry Harris. While in Boston, he has led groups including John Scofield, Jimmy Mosher, Mick Goodrick, and Mike Stern. In the mid-1990s his group included Paul Fontaine and Ray Santisi. He is a member of the Smithsonian Jazz Masterworks Orch.

Disc.: George Russell: *At the Five Spot* (1960); *Stratusphunk* (1960); *George Russell Sextet in Kansas City* (1961) *Ezzthetics* (1961); *The Stratus Seekers* (1962). Stan Getz: *Getz Au Go Go* (1964); *Getz/Gilberto #2* (1964); *Nobody Else But Me* (1964); *The Canadian Concert of Stan Getz* (1964). Don Friedman: *A Day in the City* (1961).—**LP**

Hunt, Pee Wee (Walter), trombonist, singer, leader; b. Mount Healthy, Ohio, May 10, 1907; d. Plymouth, Mass., June 22, 1979. Both of his parents were musicians; his father was a violinist, his mother a guitarist. After leaving high school in Columbus, Ohio, he studied at Ohio State Univ. He began playing banjo at 17, later graduated from the Cincinnati Cons. He played with local bands on banjo and trombone, then joined Jean Goldkette for a residency at the Pla-Mor Ballroom in Kansas City (late 1927 to early 1928). He later worked in the Hollywood Theatre Orch. in Detroit, then in 1929 became a founder-member of the Casa Loma Band (directed by Glen Gray), and was heavily featured on vocals (including a recorded duet with Louis Armstrong in 1939). He left Glen Gray in May 1943 and became a disc-jockey in Hollywood. He did regular freelancing playing, and after a spell with Freddie Fisher's Band, he joined the U.S. Merchant Marine in early 1945. He formed his own small band in L.A. (1946) and achieved great success with his tongue-in-cheek record of "Twelfth Street Rag" (1948). He led his own quartet until the mid-1950s, making similar ragtime-novelty recordings. Hunt was less active in the 1960s and 1970s.

Disc.: *Straight from Dixie* (1950); *Dixieland Detour* (1952); *Swingin' Around* (1954); *Dixieland Classics* (1955); *Pee Wee and Fingers* (1956).—**JC/LP**

Hünten, Franz, German pianist, pedagogue, and composer; b. Koblenz, Dec. 26, 1793; d. there, Feb. 22, 1878. He studied with his father, an organist, and at the age of 26 went to Paris and took courses at the Cons. with Pradher (piano) and Cherubini (composition). He composed salon music for piano (fantasies, variations on opera themes, waltzes, etc.), some 250 opus numbers in all, most of which he succeeded in publishing. He also brought out a *Méthode nouvelle pour le piano* and

other didactic compilations that became popular among teachers and students. Hünten was very much in demand as a piano teacher in Paris. Having accumulated considerable capital from his enterprises, he returned to Koblenz in 1848, and remained there until his death.

Bibl.: G. Zöllner, *F. H.: Sein Leben und sein Werk* (Cologne, 1959).—**NS/LK/DM**

Hunter, Alberta (aka Beatty, Josephine), jazz-blues singer; b. Memphis, April 1, 1895; d. Oct. 17, 1984. She ran away to Chicago at the age of 11, where she performed in various clubs as a teenager. Around 1920, she moved to N.Y. and throughout the 1920s did regular recordings (occasionally using her sister's name, Josephine Beatty, as a pseudonym) and club dates. She began recording in 1923 on Black Swan in N.Y. with Fletcher Henderson and recorded with Louis Armstrong's Jazz Babies (as Josephine Beatty) in 1924. She recorded again with Armstrong in 1926, and a year later was accompanied by Fats Waller's pipe organ. In 1928, she traveled to London where she worked in clubs and concert halls, and appeared with Paul Robeson in *Showboat* at the Drury Lane Theatre in 1928–29. Except for a brief period in 1934, she remained primarily in London (although she also visited Paris), performing in clubs and revues. In 1936, she returned to N.Y. and was featured at Connie's Inn. Towards year's end, she briefly returned to Europe, but was back in the U.S. in 1937. During the late 1930s she played long residencies in N.Y., and was also featured on an NBC radio series. During World War II she did extensive touring for the USO, including the Pacific and Europe. In the early 1950s, she toured Britain and Canada, but mostly worked out of Chicago. In 1954–55 she was an understudy for the Broadway Show *Mrs. Patterson*. In 1956, she retired from music and began working as a professional nurse. Hunter made a few recordings in the early 1960s, but made a major comeback in 1977 when she began appearing in N.Y. clubs and on the road. She made several recordings late in life and also toured South America and Europe.—**JC/LP**

Hunter, Rita (Nellie), distinguished English soprano; b. Wallasey, Aug. 15, 1933. She studied with Edwin Francis in Liverpool and with Clive Carey and Redvers Llewellyn in London, then sang in the Sadler's Wells chorus (1954–56) before touring with the Carl Rosa Opera Co. (1956–58). After further studies with Dame Eva Turner, she joined the Sadler's Wells Opera (1959), singing leading roles there from 1965, including Brünnhilde in the English-language version of *Die Walküre* (June 29, 1970). She later sang Brünnhilde in the first complete English-language version of the *Ring* cycle (July–Aug. 1973). On Dec. 19, 1972, she made her Metropolitan Opera debut in N.Y. as Brünnhilde; appeared as Norma at the San Francisco Opera in 1975. Her other notable roles included Donna Anna, Aida, Senta, and Santuzza. In 1980 she was made a Commander of the Order of the British Empire. She publ. an autobiography, *Wait Till the Sun Shines, Nellie* (London, 1986).—**NS/LK/DM**

Huntington, Jonathan, American tenor, singing teacher, and composer; b. Windham, Conn., Nov. 17,

1771; d. St. Louis, July 29, 1838. He was active as a singing teacher in Windham, in Troy, N.Y. (1806), in Northampton, Mass. (1807–11), and Boston (1812–29). While in Northampton, he became active as a singer as well. He was founder of Boston's Handel and Haydn Soc., and at its first public concert on Dec. 25, 1815, he sang *I Know That My Reedemer Liveth* from Handel's *Messiah*. In later years, he taught singing in St. Louis. He publ. the tunebooks *The Albany Collection* (1800), *The Apollo Harmony* (Northampton, Mass., 1807), *The English Extracts* (Northampton, Mass., 1809), and *Classical Church Musick* (Boston, 1812).

BIBL.: *The H. Family in America* (Hartford, Conn., 1915). **—LK/DM**

Hupperts, Paul (Henri Franciscus Marie), Dutch conductor; b. Gulpen, Jan. 1, 1919. He studied music in Utrecht; then appeared as a guest conductor in the Netherlands. In 1947 he was appointed conductor of the Limburg Orch. From 1949 to 1977 he was chief conductor of the Utrecht Sym. Orch. In his programs, he often included works by modern Dutch composers. **—NS/LK/DM**

Hurd, Michael (John), English composer, conductor, broadcaster, and writer on music; b. Gloucester, Dec. 19, 1928. He was a pupil of Thomas Armstrong and Bernard Rose at Pembroke Coll., Oxford (1950–53), and of Lennox Berkeley (1954–56). He taught at the Royal Marines School of Music (1953–59), and from 1956 was a broadcaster with the BBC. His compositions are written in an accessible style; among his lighter scores, the "pop" cantatas have been particularly successful.

WORKS: DRAMATIC: *Little Billy*, children's opera (1964); *Mr. Punch*, operatic entertainment for young people (1970); *The Widow of Ephesus*, chamber opera (Stroud, Oct. 23, 1971); *The Aspern Papers*, opera (1993). **ORCH.:** *Concerto to an Unwritten Comedy* (1970); *Dance Diversions* (1972); *Sinfonia Concertante* for Violin and String Orch. (1973); *Concerto da Camera* for Oboe and Small Orch. (1979); *A Little Suite* for Strings (1985); *Overture to an Unwritten Comedy* (1987). **CHAMBER:** Flute Sonatina (1964); Violin Sonata (1970; rev. 1986); *Harlequin Suite* for Brass (1971; rev. 1982). **VOCAL:** 12 "pop" cantatas: *Jonahman Jazz* (1966; rev. 1967), *Swingin' Samson* (1972), *Hip-Hip Horatio* (1974), *Rooster Rag* (1975), *Pilgrim* (1978), *Adam-in-Eden* (1981), *Mrs. Beeton's Book* (1982), *A New Nowell* (1986), *Captain Coram's Kids* (1988), *Prodigal* (1989), *The Liberty Tree* (1989), and *King and Conscience* (1990); also *Shepherd's Calender*, sym. for Baritone, Chorus, and Orch. (1975); choral works; songs.

WRITINGS: *Immortal Hour: The Life and Period of Rutland Boughton* (1962; rev. and enl. ed, 1993, as *Rutland Boughton and the Glastonbury Festivals*); *The Composer* (1968); *An Outline of European Music* (1968; 2nd ed., rev., 1988); *Elgar* (1969); *Vaughan Williams* (1970); *Mendelssohn* (1970); *The Ordeal of Ivor Gurney* (1978); *The Oxford Junior Companion to Music* (1979); *Vincent Novello and Company* (1981); *The Orchestra* (1981). **—NS/LK/DM**

Huré, Jean, French pianist, organist, composer, and writer on music; b. Gien, Loiret, Sept. 17, 1877; d. Paris, Jan. 27, 1930. He received his musical education at a monastery in Angers. He went to Paris in 1895, where he founded the École Normale de Musique (1910), the École Normale pour Pianistes (1912), and the monthly magazine *L'Orgue et les Organistes* (1923). In 1925 he became church organist at St. Augustin; in 1926 he won the Prix Chartier for composition. His ballet, *Le Bois sacré*, was produced at the Opéra-Comique in Paris on June 28, 1921; he further wrote incidental music to Musset's *Fantasio*; 3 syms.; Violin Concerto; *Andante* for Saxophone and Orch.; 2 string quartets; Piano Quintet; Violin Sonata; 3 cello sonatas; etc. He publ. the manuals *La Technique du piano* (1908); *La Technique de l'orgue* (1918); also *L'Esthétique de l'orgue* (1923) and *Saint Augustin, musicien* (1924).

BIBL.: G. Migot, *J. H.* (Paris, 1926).**—NS/LK/DM**

Hurford, Peter (John), noted English organist; b. Minehead, Somerset, Nov. 22, 1930. He studied law and music at Jesus Coll., Cambridge; later took organ lessons with Marchal in Paris. In 1958 he was named Master of the Music at St. Albans Abbey; in 1963 he founded the International Organ Festival there. He left St. Albans in 1979 to pursue his international career as a leading interpreter of the music of the Baroque period. He publ. the study *Making Music on the Organ* (Oxford, 1988; rev. ed., 1990). In 1984 he was made an Officer of the Order of the British Empire.**—NS/LK/DM**

Hurlebusch, Conrad Friedrich, German harpsichordist, organist, and composer; b. Braunschweig, c. 1691; d. Amsterdam, Dec. 17, 1765. He studied with his father, a scholar who played the harpsichord and organ. After sojourns in Hamburg and Vienna, and travels in Italy, he returned to Braunschweig and wrote his first opera, *L'innocenza difesa* (1721), for the court. From 1722 to 1725 he was Kapellmeister to the Swedish court. Following extensive travels in Germany, he returned to Braunschweig once again and wrote the opera *Flavio Cuniberto* (1727). In 1743 he settled in Amsterdam as organist of the Oude Kerk. In addition to his operas, Hurlebusch composed concertos, keyboard sonatas, cantatas, Psalms, and odes.

BIBL.: R. Kahleyss, *C.F. H., 1691–1765: Sein Leben und Wirken* (Frankfurt am Main, 1984).**—LK/DM**

Hurley, Laurel, American soprano; b. Allentown, Pa., Feb. 14, 1927. Of a musical family, she studied with her mother, a church organist, and at 16 appeared on Broadway (Aug. 21, 1943) as Kathie in Romberg's operetta *The Student Prince*; then toured with the company that produced it. In 1952 she made her N.Y.C. Opera debut as Zerlina. She was the winner of the Walter W. Naumburg Foundation Award, which enabled her to give a song recital in N.Y. (Nov. 6, 1952). She made her debut at the Metropolitan Opera in N.Y. on Feb. 8, 1955, as Oscar; she remained at the Metropolitan until 1967, singing such roles as Musetta, Susanna, Périchole, Adele, Mimi, and Despina.**—NS/LK/DM**

Hurlstone, William (Yeates), English pianist and composer; b. London, Jan. 7, 1876; d. there, May 30, 1906. A precocious musician, he composed waltzes as a young child. He studied at the Royal Coll. of Music in

London with Stanford (composition) and Edward Dannreuther (piano), performing his own Piano Concerto in 1896. In 1905 he was appointed a prof. at the Royal Coll. of Music, but died in the following year; his early death was much regretted.

WORKS: ORCH.: *The Magic Mirror*, fairy suite; *Variations on a Hungarian Air* and *Fantasie-Variations on a Swedish Air.* **CHAMBER:** Quartet for Flute, Oboe, Horn, and Bassoon; Quintet for Flute, Oboe, Horn, Bassoon, and Piano; Piano Trio; Trio for Clarinet, Bassoon, and Piano; Clarinet Sonata; Bassoon Sonata. **VOCAL:** Several song cycles.

BIBL.: H. Newell, *W.Y. H.: Musician and Man* (London, 1936); K. Hurlstone, ed., *W. H., Musician: Memories and Records by His Friends* (London, 1949).—NS/LK/DM

Hurník, Ilja, Czech pianist and composer; b. Poruba, near Svinov, Nov. 25, 1922. He moved to Prague in 1938 and had piano lessons with Kurz (1939–45). He studied composition with řídký and was the last pupil of Novák (1941–44); later studied piano with Štěpánová at the Cons. (1945–48) before completing his training at the Academy of Music (1948–52). He taught at the Prague Cons. and at the Bratislava Academy of Music.

WORKS: DRAMATIC: Opera: *Dámá a lupiči* (The Lady and the Gangster), after the film *The Ladykillers* (1966); *Mudrci a bloudi* (The Wise and the Foolish; 1968); *Diogenes* (1974); *Oldřich a Boženka* (1985); *Stažená hrdla* (Tightened Throat), mini-opera (1997). **Ballet:** *Ondráš* (1950). **ORCH.:** Flute Concerto (1953); *Serenade* for Strings (1954); Concerto for Winds and Percussion (1956); Concerto for Oboe, Strings, and Piano (1959); *Musikanti* (The Musicians) for 20 Instruments (1962); *Chamber Music* for Strings (1962); *Kyklopes* (Prague, June 4, 1965); Concerto for Piano and Small Orch. (1972); *Věci*, divertimento for Chamber Orch. (1977); *Overture to a Comedy* (1985); Concertino for Organ and Chamber Ensemble (1990); Concerto for Viola and Strings (1994); *Symfonietta* (1996). **CHAMBER:** 2 wind quintets (1944, 1985); 2 string quartets (1949; 2nd, with Baritone, to Old Testament texts, 1961); Viola Sonata (1952); *Die vier Jahreszeiten* for 12 Solo Instruments (1952); *Sonata da camera* for Flute, Oboe, Cello, and Harpsichord (1953); Piano Quintet (1953); *Ballet* for 9 Instruments (1954); *Esercizi* for Flute, Oboe, Clarinet, and Bassoon (1958); *Moments musicaux* for 11 Winds (1962); *Gloria di flauti* for 2 Flutes (1973); *Concerto capricioso* for Organ, 2 Violins, and Cello (1998). **KEYBOARD: Piano:** *Preludes* (1943); Sonatina (1952); *Étude* (1972); *Variations on a Theme of Pergolesi* for Piano, 4–Hands (1983; also for Chamber Ensemble); *Innocenza* for Piano, 4–Hands (1992). **Organ:** 3 sonatas (1956). **VOCAL:** *Maryka*, cantata (1948; rev. 1955); *Noe* (Noah), oratorio (1959); *Ezop* (Aesop), cantata (1964); *Sulamit*, song cycle for Woman's Voice and Orch., after the Old Testament (1963); *Ozěvna*, chamber cantata (1981); *Madrigal* for Voices (1982); *Ancient Portrait* for Children's Chorus and Orch. (1988); *Missa Vinea Crucis* for Children's Chorus and Orch. or Organ (1991).—NS/LK/DM

Hurok, Sol(omon Israelovich), famous Russian-born American impresario; b. Pogar, April 9, 1888; d. N.Y., March 5, 1974. He emigrated to the U.S. in 1906 and became a naturalized American citizen in 1914. After organizing concerts for labor groups, he attracted notice with his star performers at N.Y.'s Hippodrome in 1913. He subsequently became one of the most colorful and successful impresarios of his era, managing such celebrated artists as Chaliapin, Rubinstein, Segovia, Elman, Stern, Piatigorsky, and Marian Anderson. After World War II, he played a significant role in bringing Soviet artists and organizations to the U.S. His extraordinary career inspired the film *Tonight We Sing*. In 1973 he received the Diamond Jubilee Medal at the Metropolitan Opera in N.Y. for his services to music. He likewise was honored in death by a public funeral at Carnegie Hall in N.Y.

BIBL.: H. Robinson, *The Last Impresario: The Life, Times, and Legacy of S. H.* (N.Y., 1994).—NS/LK/DM

Hurst, George, English conductor; b. Edinburgh, May 20, 1926. He first studied piano with Isserlis, then took courses in conducting and composition at the Royal Cons. of Music of Toronto; also studied conducting with Monteux. He was a teacher and conductor at the Peabody Cons. of Music in Baltimore (1947–55), and also was conductor of the York (Pa.) Sym. Orch. (1950–55). He then was asst. conductor of the London Phil. (1955–57) and of the BBC Northern Sym. Orch. at Manchester (1958–68). Subsequently he conducted the Bournemouth Sym. Orch. (1969–71), and also was artistic advisor of the Bournemouth Sinfonietta until 1978. From 1986 to 1989 he was principal guest conductor of the BBC Scottish Sym. Orch. in Glasgow. In 1990–91 he was principal conductor of the National Sym. Orch. of Ireland in Dublin.—NS/LK/DM

Hurum, Alf (Thorvald), Norwegian pianist, conductor, composer, and painter; b. Christiania, Sept. 21, 1882; d. Honolulu, Aug. 15, 1972. He studied with Max Bruch and Robert Kahn at the Hochschule für Musik in Berlin (1905–09); later took additional courses in Paris and in Russia. He was a co-founder of the Soc. of Norwegian Composers in 1917. After touring as a concert pianist, he settled in Hawaii, where he established the Honolulu Sym. Orch. and was its conductor (1924–26). His 2nd career was that of a silk painter in the Japanese manner, which preoccupied him during his later years. In his music, he cultivated coloristic harmonies, somewhat in an impressionist mode.

WORKS: 2 violin sonatas (1911, 1916); 3 *Aquarelles* for Piano (1912); String Quartet (1913); *Exotic Suite* for Violin and Piano (1916); *Pastels*, 4 pieces for Piano (1916); *Eventyrland* (Fairy Land), suite for Orch. or Piano (1920); *Gotiske bilder*, 6 pieces for Piano (1920); *Norse Suite* for Orch. (1920); *Bendikt and Aarolilja*, symphonic poem (1923); Sym. (1927); songs; motets. —NS/LK/DM

Hurwitz, Emanuel (Henry), English violinist and conductor; b. London, May 7, 1919. He received a scholarship from Bronislaw Huberman that allowed him to study at the Royal Academy of Music in London. In 1948 he became concertmaster of the Goldsborough (later English) Chamber Orch., a position he held until 1968. He was then concertmaster of the New Philharmonia Orch. (1969–71). He was also active as a chamber music artist; was 1st violinist of the Hurwitz String Quartet (1946–51), the Melos Ensemble (1956–72), and the Aeolian Quartet (from 1970). In 1968 he founded the

Hurwitz Chamber Orch. (from 1972 known as the Serenata of London), a conductorless ensemble. He was made a Commander of the Order of the British Empire in 1978.—NS/LK/DM

Husa, Karel, distinguished Czech-born American composer, conductor, and pedagogue; b. Prague, Aug. 7, 1921. He studied violin and piano in his youth, and concurrently took courses in engineering. In 1941 he entered the Prague Cons., studying composition with řidký. In 1945–46 he attended the Academy of Music; in 1946 he was awarded a French government grant to continue his studies in Paris at the École Normale de Musique and the Cons., where his teachers included Honegger and Boulanger. He also studied conducting with Fournet and Cluytens. In 1954 he emigrated to the U.S., and joined the music dept. of Cornell Univ. as teacher of composition and conductor of the student orch., remaining there until his retirement in 1992. He also taught at Ithaca Coll. (1967–86). He became a naturalized American citizen in 1959. He appeared widely as a guest conductor, frequently including his own music in his programs. In his early works, he followed the modern Czech school of composition, making thematic use of folk tunes; later he enlarged his musical resources to include atonal, polytonal, microtonal, and even occasional aleatory procedures, without following doctrinaire prescriptions to the letter. His music is oxygenated by humanistic Romanticism; as a result, it gains numerous performances. In 1969 Husa received the Pulitzer Prize in Music for his 3rd String Quartet. In 1974 he was elected to membership in the Royal Belgian Academy of the Arts and Sciences. He received honorary doctor of music degrees from Coe Coll. (1976), the Cleveland Inst. of Music (1985), Ithaca Coll. (1986), Baldwin-Wallace Coll. (1991), St. Vincent Coll. (1995), Hartwick Coll. (1997), and the New England Cons. of Music (1998). In 1983 he received the Friedheim Award for his *Recollections* for Woodwind Quintet and Piano. He received the Sudley International Award in 1984 for his Concerto for Wind Ensemble. In 1993 he received the Grawemeyer Award of the Univ. of Louisville for his Cello Concerto. He became a member of the American Academy of Arts and Letters in 1994. In 1995 President Havel of the Czech Republic bestowed upon him the State Medal Award of Merit, 1st Class, and in 1998 he was awarded the Medal of the City of Prague.

WORKS: DRAMATIC: B a l l e t : *The Steadfast Tin Soldier* (1974); *Monodrama* (Indianapolis, March 26, 1976); *The Trojan Women* (Louisville, March 28, 1981). **ORCH.:** Overture (1st public perf., Prague, June 18, 1946); Sinfonietta (Prague, April 25, 1947); *3 fresques* (Prague, April 27, 1949; rev. as *Fresque*, Syracuse, N.Y., May 5, 1963); *Divertimento* for Strings (Paris, Oct. 30, 1949); Piano Concertino (Brussels, June 6, 1952); *Musique d'amateurs,* 4 Easy Pieces for Oboe, Trumpet, Percussion, and Strings (1953); *Portrait* for Strings (Donaueschingen, Oct. 10, 1953); 2 syms.: No. 1 (Brussels, March 4, 1954) and No. 2, *Reflections* (Greensboro, N.C., July 16, 1983); *4 Little Pieces* for Strings (Fürsteneck, March 17, 1957); *Fantasies* (Ithaca, N.Y., April 28, 1957); *Divertimento* for Brass and Percussion (Ithaca, N.Y., Feb. 17, 1960); *Poem* for Viola and Chamber Orch. (Cologne, June 12, 1960); *Mosaïques* (Hamburg, Nov. 7, 1961); *Elégie et Rondeau* for Alto Saxophone and Orch. (Ithaca, N.Y., May 6,

1962); *Serenade* for Woodwind Quintet Solo with Strings, Xylophone, and Harp (Baltimore, Jan. 7, 1964); Concerto for Alto Saxophone and Concert Band (Ithaca, N.Y., March 17, 1968); *Music for Prague 1968* (2 versions; for Band: Washington, D.C., Jan. 31, 1969; for Orch., Munich, Jan. 31, 1970; 1st Czech perf. of orch. version, Prague, Feb. 13, 1990, composer conducting); Concerto for Brass Quintet and Strings (Buffalo, Feb. 15, 1970); Concerto for Percussion and Wind Instruments (1971; Waco, Tex., Feb. 7, 1972); *Apotheosis of This Earth* for Wind Instruments (Ann Arbor, April 1, 1971; 2nd version for Chorus and Orch.: Ithaca, N.Y., April 12, 1973); *2 Sonnets from Michelangelo* (Evanston, Ill., April 28, 1972); Trumpet Concerto (Storrs, Conn., Aug. 9, 1974); *Pastoral* for Strings (Miami Beach, April 12, 1980); *Fanfare* for Brass (1981); Concerto for Wind Ensemble (Lansing, Mich., Dec. 3, 1982); *Smetana Fanfare* for Wind Ensemble (San Diego, April 3, 1984); *Symphonic Suite* (Athens, Ga., Oct. 1, 1984); *Concerto for Orchestra* (N.Y., Sept. 25, 1986); Organ Concerto, *The Sunlights* (Cleveland, Oct. 28, 1987); Trumpet Concerto (Chicago, Feb. 11, 1988); Cello Concerto (1988; Los Angeles, March 2, 1989); *Overture: Youth* (Seattle, Dec. 1, 1991); *Cayuga Lake: Memories* for Chamber Orch. (1992); Violin Concerto (N.Y., May 27, 1993); *Celebration Fanfare* (Oneonta, N.Y., July 7, 1996); *Les couleurs fauves* for Wind Ensemble (Evanston, Ill., Nov. 16, 1996); *Midwest Celebration* (Chicago, Dec. 17, 1996); *Celebración* (1997). **CHAMBER:** String Quartet (1942–43); Sonatina for Violin and Piano (Prague, Sept. 27, 1945); Suite for Viola and Piano (1945); 4 numbered string quartets: No. 1 (Prague, May 23, 1948), No. 2 (Paris, Oct. 23, 1954), No. 3 (Chicago, Oct. 14, 1968), and No. 4 (1989–90); *Evocations of Slovakia* for Clarinet, Viola, and Cello (Paris, May 4, 1952); 2 *Preludes* for Flute, Clarinet, and Bassoon (Ithaca, N.Y., April 21, 1966); *Divertimento* for Brass Quintet (Ithaca, N.Y., Nov. 20, 1968); *Studies* for Percussion (1968); Violin Sonata (N.Y., March 31, 1974); *Landscapes* for Brass Quintet (Kalamazoo, Mich., Oct. 17, 1977); *3 Dance Sketches* for Percussion (Miami Beach, April 12, 1980); *Intradas and Interludes* for 7 Trumpets and Timpani (Columbus, Ohio, June 20, 1980); *Sonata a tre* for Violin, Clarinet, and Piano (Hong Kong, March 23, 1982); *Recollections* for Woodwind Quintet and Piano (Washington, D.C., Oct. 28, 1982); *Variations* for Violin, Viola, Cello, and Piano (Atlanta, May 20, 1984); *Intrada* for Brass Quintet (Baltimore, Nov. 15, 1984); *5 Poems* for Woodwind Quintet (1994; N.Y., Feb. 10, 1995). **P i a n o :** Sonatina (1943); 2 sonatas (1950, 1975); *Elegie* (1957). **VOCAL:** *12 Moravian Songs* for Voice and Piano (1956); *Festive Ode* for Chorus and Orch. or Band (1965); *The Steadfast Tin Soldier* for Narrator and Orch. (Boulder, Colo., May 10, 1975); *An American Te Deum* for Baritone, Chorus, and Wind Ensemble (Cedar Rapids, Iowa, Dec. 4, 1976; 2nd version for Baritone, Chorus, and Orch., Washington, D.C., May 10, 1978); *3 Moravian Songs* for Chorus (1981); *Every Day* for Chorus (1981); *There are from time to time mornings* for Chorus (1981); Cantata for Men's Chorus and Brass Quintet (Crawfordsville, Ind., April 20, 1983). **EDITIONS:** W. Herschel's Sym. in D (1962); Lully's *Carnaval Mascarade* for Orch. (1964) and *Le Ballet des Muses* for Orch. (1965); Dalalande's *Cantemus Domino* for Soli, Chorus, and Orch.

BIBL.: S. Hitchens, *K. H.: A Bio-Bibliography* (N.Y., 1991). —NS/LK/DM

Hüsch, Gerhard (Heinrich Wilhelm Fritz), esteemed German baritone and pedagogue; b. Hannover, Feb. 2, 1901; d. Munich, Nov. 23, 1984. He received his training from Hans Emge in Hannover. In 1923 he made his operatic debut as Lieberau in Lortzing's *Der Waffenschmied* in Osnabrück. After singing in Bremen, he was a member of the Cologne Opera (1927–30). He then went to Berlin and sang with the City and State Operas (1930–42); he also appeared in Dresden, Hamburg, Munich, Vienna, Milan, Bayreuth (1930–31), and London (Covent Garden debut as Falke, 1930; returned there, 1931 and 1938). In later years, Hüsch became well known as an exponent of lieder. He also taught voice in Munich.—NS/LK/DM

Hus-Desforges, Pierre Louis, French cellist, conductor, and composer; b. Toulon, March 14, 1773; d. Pont-le-Voy, near Blois, Jan. 20, 1838. He was a cellist in the Lyons Grand Théâtre orch. before pursuing studies with J.-B. Janson at the Paris Cons. From 1800 to about 1810 he was director of the orch. of the Théâtre-Français in St. Petersburg, and then settled in Paris as a cellist and conductor in various theater orchs. Under the name Citoyen Desforges, he publ. the song "L'Autel de sa patrie" (Paris, 1798); he also wrote a Sinfonia Concertante with Violin and Cello obbligato and a String Quartet. He publ. *A Méthode de violoncelle à l'usage des commençants* (Paris, 1828).—NS/LK/DM

Hüsker Dü, one of the most influential punk bands of the 1980s. **MEMBERSHIP:** Bob Mould, voc., gtr. (b. Malone, N.Y., Oct. 16, 1960); Grant Hart, voc., drm. (b. St. Paul, Minn., March 18, 1961); Greg Norton, bs. (b. Rock Island, Ill., March 13, 1959). Bob Mould had pretty much given up on music when The Beatles broke up. The tawdry hard rock his peers listened to in school left him cold. It wasn't until he heard the Ramones that he became interested in music again. By the time he got to Macalester Coll. in Minn., he had played the guitar for a couple of years. While matriculating, he worked part-time at a local record store where he met Greg Norton, a local bassist, and drummer Grant Hart. They started practicing in Norton's basement, calling themselves Hüsker Dü (Hoos-ker Doo) after a Swedish board game. The name translates to "do you remember." By the early 1980s, playing a unique blend of hardcore blare with pop melody, the group built a good-sized local following. In 1981, they put out a live, independent recording, *Land Speed Record*. With 17 songs performed in somewhat less than half an hour, the album espoused the hard core punk ethos of groups like The Minutemen. Mould would later describe it affectionately as "pure noise." Their next record, the self released *Everything Falls Apart*, caught the ears of critics who heard the band as they toured all across the country, selling records as they went. The similarities between the Huskers and such Calif. bands as Black Flag and The Minutemen got them signed to their label, SST. They put out the *Metal Circus* EP.

Mould and Hart developed into a complimentary songwriting team. Their collaboration reached its pinnacle with their next album, 1984's *Zen Arcade*. This album broke nearly all of the unwritten rules of hard core punk. A double album (unheard of in punk), it had a concept that ran through the entire project (a boy leaves home only to discover it's worse on the streets), and the finale ran over 13 minutes, about ten minutes

longer than nearly anything else in the genre.

With 1985's *New Day Rising*, the group sharpened both edges of their double sided attack, the vein of pop-craft coupled with their renewed sonic assault. Robert Palmer often performed the title track of the record in concert. *Flip Your Wig* accentuated this dichotomy, couching it in crystal clear sonics. It impressed several of the major record companies, with Warner Bros. finally signing the band. With fans braced for a sell-out, Hüsker Dü beat the odds with their major label debut, 1986's *Candy Apple Grey*. While the album had some acoustic guitars and a cleaner sound, it still straddled the pop melodies played at the adrenaline edge. If anything, the lyrics became even more pointed. Later that year, Mould took some time away from the band, producing records with Minneapolis brethren Soul Asylum and the speed metal band Impaler. However, tensions had built between Hart and Mould, exacerbated by Mould overcoming his amphetamine and alcohol abuse while Hart went deeper into it and added heroin to the mix. After the band put out the double album *Warehouse: Songs and Stories* in 1987, their manager committed suicide. This put the band over the edge. When they finished a relatively uninspired tour for *Warehouse*, the band went their separate ways.

Norton left the music business, variously reported to be working as a chef and a realtor in the Twin Cities. Hart went back to SST Records and hit the stands as a solo artist with the EP *2541*, largely a chronicle of the last days of Hüsker Dü. His next album, *Intolerance*, continued this theme, with the added angst of drug and alcohol rehab. Mould signed with Virgin records. Recording with a rhythm section of former Pere Ubu members Anton Fier and Tony Maimone, in 1989 he released the surprisingly quiet and introspective *Workbook*, with only a few tracks capturing the sonic whirlwind of Hüsker Dü. Indeed, the album featured a preponderance of acoustic guitars and a prominent cellist. However, his reputation and that of Hüsker Dü put him in solid with a brace of "alternative" modern rock stations. "See the Light" became a Top Ten track on the format, and the album actually hit the charts, topping out at #127. The next year, with the same rhythm section, Mould released *Black Sheets of Rain*. This album recalled the puissance of Hüsker Dü, but also accentuated Mould's pop edge. The tune "It's Too Late" also hit the modern rock Top Ten.

Ironically, early in the 1990s both Hart and Mould felt the urge to form new bands. Hart put together The Nova Mob (after William Burroughs). After an EP, the group tackled an actual rock opera called *The Last Days of Pompeii*. They followed this with an eponymous record in 1994. Mould formed Sugar, geared toward the same melodic hard core that was coming to be known in the Pacific Northwest as "grunge," with bands like Nirvana following in Hüsker Dü's footsteps. *Copper Blue*, the group's 1992 debut, picked up essentially where *Warehouse* had left him off, featuring clean, crisp, melodic rock with a decidedly punk sonic edge. The record actually received some commercial airplay on the burgeoning "alternative" record stations. "Helpless" and "If I Can't Change Your Mind" fell into rotation on

MTV. The album went gold. *Beaster,* an EP with some of the more abrasive outtakes from the *Copper Blue* sessions was released almost as a reaction to the pop success. After a false start (all the tapes were erased), Sugar recorded *File Under: Easy Listening* in 1994. Cut in the mold of *Copper Blue,* it didn't have the power or the momentum. It sold modestly. Mould put the band on a back burner in 1995, at which time *Besides,* an album of B-sides and rarities, was put out. Mould returned to his solo career, playing all the instruments on an eponymous solo album in 1996. He resurfaced in 1998 with *The Last Dog and Pony Show.* Each displayed a growing inclination to follow his more melodic muse. Additionally, he recorded the theme for the Comedy Central Television program *The Daily Show.*

DISC.: *Land Speed Record* (live; 1981); *Everything Falls Apart* (1982); *Metal Circus* (1983); *Zen Arcade* (1984); *New Day Rising* (1985); *Flip Your Wig* (1985); *Candy Apple Grey* (1986); *Warehouse: Songs and Stories* (1987); *The Living End* (live; 1994); *Zen Arcade.* **BOB MOULD:** *Workbook* (1989); *Black Sheets of Rain* (1990); *Bob Mould* (1996); *The Last Dog and Pony Show* (1998). **SUGAR:** *Copper Blue* (1992); *File Under: Easy Listening* (1994); *Besides* (1995). **GRANT HART:** *2541* (1988); *Intolerance* (1989). **NOVA MOB:** *Admiral of the Sea* (1991); *Last Days of Pompeii* (1991); *Nova Mob* (1994).—**HB**

Husky, Ferlin, American country-music singer, guitarist, and comedian; b. near Flat River, Mo., Dec. 3, 1925. Husky reached the country singles charts with 51 recordings between 1953 and 1975, both under his own name and as his comic alter-ego, "Simon Crum," the most popular of which were "A Dear John Letter," "Gone," and "Wings of a Dove."

Husky grew up on a farm, learning to play the guitar as a child. He served in the Merchant Marine during World War II, then worked as a disc jockey and backup musician in St. Louis and in Bakersfield, Calif., performing under the name Terry Preston. He recorded for the small Four Star Records label in 1951, then moved up to Capitol Records. By 1953 he had reverted to his real name, though for several years he spelled it "Huskey." In August 1953 "A Dear John Letter" (music and lyrics by Fuzzy Owens and Lewis Tally), a duet with Jean Shepard, hit #1 on the country charts, later reaching the Top Ten on the pop charts. Shepard and Husky followed it with "Forgive Me John" (music and lyrics by Billy Barton and Jean Shepard), a country Top Ten. Husky got to the country Top Ten on his own in early 1955 with both sides of his single "I Feel Better All Over (More Than Anywhere's Else)"/"Little Tom." Within months, he was back in the country Top Ten as Simon Crum with the novelty "Cuzz Yore So Sweet" (music and lyrics by John Kane).

Husky scored the biggest country hit of 1957 with his rerecording of "Gone" (music and lyrics by Smokey Rogers), a song he had previously cut as Terry Preston. It crossed over to the Top Ten of the pop charts. As a result of this success he joined the *Grand Ole Opry,* and made his first film appearance, in *Mr. Rock & Roll* (1957), following it with *Country Music Holiday* (1958). He also reached the country Top Ten in 1957 with "A Fallen Star." His next major hit was another novelty as Simon

Crum, "Country Music Is Here to Stay" (music and lyrics by Ferlin Husky), at the end of 1958. He returned to the top of the country charts and the pop Top 40 in late 1960 with "Wings of a Dove" (music and lyrics by Bob Ferguson).

Husky reached the country charts consistently through 1975, though he only had one more Top Ten hit, "Just for You" (music and lyrics by Larry Butler and Curly Putman) in February 1968. He switched from Capitol to ABC Records in 1972 and later recorded for smaller labels. He underwent open-heart surgery in 1977 but continued to perform regularly, by the 1990s turning up in the nostalgic-music center of Branson, Mo.

Husky was married six times and had seven children.—**WR**

Husmann, Heinrich, distinguished German musicologist; b. Cologne, Dec. 16, 1908; d. Brussels, Nov. 8, 1983. He studied musicology with Ludwig at the Univ. of Göttingen, and with Hornbostel, Schering, Wolf, and Blume at the Humboldt Univ. in Berlin, receiving his Ph.D. there in 1932. In 1933 he was appointed asst. lecturer at the musicological inst. at the Univ. of Leipzig; completed his Habilitation there in 1941, and then was made its acting director in 1944. He completed a 2nd Habilitation at the Univ. of Hamburg in 1948, and organized its musicological inst. in 1949; was a reader there from 1956 and a prof. from 1958. In 1960 he became a prof. of musicology at the Univ. of Göttingen. His books include *Fünf- und siebenstellige Centstafeln zur Berechnung musikalischer Intervalle* (Leiden, 1951), *Vom Wesen der Konsonanz* (Heidelberg, 1953), *Einführung in die Musikwissenschaft* (Heidelberg, 1958), and *Grundlagen der antiken und orientalischen Musikkultur* (Berlin, 1961).

BIBL.: H. Becker and R. Gerlach, eds., *Speculum musicae artis: Festgabe für H. H.* (Munich, 1970).—**NS/LK/DM**

Huss, Henry Holden, American pianist and composer; b. Newark, N.J., June 21, 1862; d. N.Y., Sept. 17, 1953. He was a descendant of Jan Huss, the Bohemian martyr. His mother, Sophia Ruckle Holden Huss, was a granddaughter of Levi Holden, a member of George Washington's staff. Huss studied piano and theory with his father and with O. Boise. In 1882 he went to Germany, and studied organ and composition with Rheinberger at the Munich Cons.; graduated with a *Rhapsody* for Piano and Orch. (1885), which he subsequently performed with several American orchs., as well as his Piano Concerto (1894). In 1904 he married Hildegard Hoffmann, a concert singer, with whom he appeared frequently in joint recitals.

WORKS: *Rhapsody* for Piano and Orch. (1885); *Romance and Polonaise* for Orch. (1889); Piano Concerto (1894); Violin Concerto (1906); 2 symphonic poems: *Life's Conflicts* (1921) and *La Nuit* (orig. for Piano Solo, 1902; orchestrated 1939; Washington, D.C., March 12, 1942); 4 string quartets; Violin Sonata; Cello Sonata; Viola Sonata; choral works.

BIBL.: G. Greene, *H.H. H.: An American Composer's Life* (Metruchen, 1995).—**NS/LK/DM**

Huston, (Thomas) Scott (Jr.), American composer and pedagogue; b. Tacoma, Wash., Oct. 10, 1916;

d. Cincinnati, March 1, 1991. After attending the Univ. of Puget Sound (1934–35), he studied with Phillips, Rogers, and Hanson at the Eastman School of Music in Rochester, N.Y. (B.M., 1941; M.M., 1942; Ph.D., 1952). He taught at several schools of higher learning before joining the Cincinnati Cons. of Music in 1952; after it merged with the Coll. of Music in 1955, he was dean until 1956; he then taught there until 1988. His output was marked by a fine command of tonal and atonal writing.

WORKS: DRAMATIC: O p e r a : *Blind Girl* (1981; concert perf., Lake George, N.Y., May 1984). ORCH.: *Toccata* for Piano and Orch. (1951); *Abstract* (1955); Concerto for Trumpet, Harp, and Orch. (1963); 6 syms., including No. 3, *Phantasms* (1967; Cincinnati, Feb. 2, 1968), No. 4 for Strings (Cincinnati, Aug. 10, 1972), No. 5 (1975), and No. 6, *The Human Condition* (1981); *2 Images* for Strings (1964); *Fanfare for the 200th* (1975); *Impressions from Life* for Small Chamber Orch. (1977). CHAM-BER: Flute Sonata (1959); Viola Sonata (1960); *Intensity I* (1962) and *II* (1975) for Winds; Timpani Suite (1963); *Pro vita* for Piano and Brass Quintet (1965); *Phenomena* for Flute, Oboe, Harpsichord, and Double Bass (1966); Violin Sonata, *Mercury and Venus* (1967); *Life-Styles I-IV* for Piano Trio or Clarinet, Cello, and Piano (1972); *Cool to Hot* for Jazz Quartet (1973); *For Our Times*, suite for 6 Brass (1974); *Eleatron* for Viola and Piano (1975); *Fragments, Disputes, Mirrors* for 2 Oboes (1977); *Shadowy Waters* for Clarinet, Cello, and Piano (1977); *Variables* for 4 Saxophones (1979); *In Memoriam Norman Dinerstein* for Piano and Chamber Group (1983); *Optimism: A Way of Life* for Brass Quintet (1986); *The Glass Children* for Violin (1988). KEY-BOARD: P i a n o : *Penta-Tholoi* (1966); *5 Notes for Ada* for 2 Pianos (1984). O r g a n : Sonata (1960). VOCAL: *Ante mortem* for Men's Chorus, Brass, and Organ (1965); *The Oratorio of Understanding* (1969); *Divinely Superfluous Beauty and Natural Music* for Soprano and Chamber Ensemble (1971); *Tamar*, monodrama for Soprano and Prepared Piano (1974); *Ecstasies of Janus* for Countertenor and Chamber Ensemble (1978); *Time/Reflections* for Chorus and Chamber Orch. (1978); *Songs of the Courtesans* for Voice and Chamber Ensemble (1985); *An Ecumenical Mosaic of Cincinnati* for Chorus, Organ, and Double String Quartet (1987); choruses; songs.—NS/LK/DM

Huszka, Jenő, Hungarian composer; b. Szeged, April 24, 1875; d. Budapest, Feb. 2, 1960. He was a student of Hubay (violin) and Koessler (composition) at the Royal Academy of Music in Budapest. At age 24, he launched a career as a composer for the theater in Budapest. His first operetta, *Bob herceg* (Dec. 12, 1902), was followed by such successful scores as *Aranyvirág* (Nov. 6, 1903), *Gül Baba* (Dec. 9, 1905), *Rébusz báró* (Nov. 20, 1909), *Nemtudomka* (Jan. 14, 1914), *Lili bárónő* (March 7, 1919), *Mária főhadnagy* (Sept. 23, 1942), and *Szabadság, szerelem* (April 1, 1955).—NS/LK/DM

Hutchenrider, Clarence (Behrens), jazz clarinetist, saxophonist, flutist; b. Waco, Tex., June 13, 1908; d. N.Y., Aug. 18, 1991. He took up sax at the age of 14, and led his own band at high school, then played at the Adolphus Hotel (Dallas), in a band led by Jack Gardner, and was subsequently with Dick Richardson and the Claiborne Bryson Bands in Shreveport, La., before joining Ross German in 1928. He was with Tommy Tucker (1929), then with Merle Jacobs in Cleve-

land (ca. 1930). After a spell with Austin Wylie, he joined the Casa Loma Orch. (directed by Glen Gray) in autumn of 1931. He was featured mainly on clarinet with Casa Loma (occasionally on tenor: "No Name Jive," etc.) until 1943. He suffered an illness in the spring of 1943, but returned to the band until December of that year. He did radio shows and tours with Jimmy Lytell's Band for three years, then illness enforced temporary retirement from full-time music. He returned to regular playing, worked with the Glen Moore Band and Walter Davidson, then formed a highly successful trio which, through the late 1950s to the early 1970s, played long residencies in N.Y. In the later 1970s, he played with Vince Girodano's New Calif. Ramblers and also the New Orleans Nighthawks, but was then inactive for the last decade of his life.—JC/LP

Hutchens, Frank, New Zealand pianist, teacher, and composer; b. Christchurch, Jan. 15, 1892; d. Sydney, Australia, Oct. 18, 1965. He studied at the Royal Academy of Music in London with Matthay (piano) and Corder (composition); taught there from 1908 to 1914; in 1915 he was appointed a prof. at the New South Wales State Conservatorium in Sydney. In 1962 he was made an Officer of the Order of the British Empire. His compositions include *Ballade* for Orch. (1938), Concerto for 2 Pianos and Orch. (1940), *Air Mail Palestine* for Voice and Orch. (1942), and piano pieces.—NS/LK/DM

Hutcherson, Bobby (actually, **Robert**), brilliant jazz vibraphone and marimba player and composer; b. L.A., Jan. 27, 1941. He started on piano. Inspired by a recording of Milt Jackson at age 15, he took up vibraphone and studied briefly with Dave Pike. In the later 1950s, he worked with Curtis Amy and Charles Lloyd in his hometown, and then relocated to San Francisco to join the Al Grey-Billy Mitchell combo. In 1962 he went to N.Y., where he worked with Eric Dolphy, Jackie McLean, Archie Shepp (including Newport Jazz Fest. 1965), Hank Mobley, Herbie Hancock, and Andrew Hill. He moved to the San Francisco area by 1967 and played with John Handy. There he co-led an influential and popular band with Harold Land from 1965–71. Since then, he has primarily led his own small groups and also worked with the Timeless All- Stars. Although in his earlier recordings Hutcherson showed the influence of free jazz, by the late 1970s he had completely remade himself in a more traditional mold. In 1985 he began a series of recordings which incorporated strong Afro-Cuban rhythmic elements.

Hutcherson is a brilliant soloist whose relative lack of fame is probably due to the fact that he is not a saxophonist or trumpeter. His spinning lines would be stunning on any instrument.

DISC. *Components* (1965); *Spiral* (1965); *Dialogue* (1965); *Stick Up!* (1966). Herbie Hancock: *Happenings* (1966). *Total Eclipse* (1967); *Oblique* (1967); *Patterns* (1968); *Blow Up* (1969); *Natural Illusions* (1972); *Live at Montreux* (1973); *Cirrus* (1974); *Montara* (1975); *Waiting* (1976); *View from the Inside* (1976); *Knucklebean* (1977); *Dance of the Sun* (1977); *Highway One* (1978);

Un Poco Loco (1979); *Conception: The Gift of Love* (1979); *Solo/Quartet* (1981); *Good Bait* (1984); *It Ain't Easy* (1985); *Color Schemes* (1985); *In the Vanguard* (1986); *Cruisin' the Bird* (1988); *Ambos Mundos* (1989); *Mirage* (1991); *Landmarks* (1992).—**LP/NS**

Hutcheson, Ernest, Australian pianist, writer on music, teacher, and composer; b. Melbourne, July 20, 1871; d. N.Y., Feb. 9, 1951. He studied piano in Australia with Max Vogrich, and played concerts as a very young child. He then was sent to the Leipzig Cons. to study with Reinecke and Jadassohn, graduating in 1890. In 1898 he performed his own Piano Concerto with the Berlin Phil. He was head of the piano dept. at the Peabody Cons. of Music in Baltimore (1900–1912). In 1915 he created a sensation in N.Y. by playing 3 concertos (Tchaikovsky, Liszt, and MacDowell) in a single evening; in 1919 he repeated his feat, playing 3 Beethoven concertos in one evening. From 1924 to 1945 he was variously associated with the Juilliard School in N.Y., including serving as its dean (1927–37) and its president (1937–45). Among his compositions are several symphonic works and numerous piano pieces. He publ. *The Elements of Piano Technique* (N.Y., 1907), *Elektra by Richard Strauss: A Guide to the Opera* (N.Y., 1910), *A Musical Guide to the Richard Wagner Ring of the Nibelung* (N.Y., 1940), and *The Literature of the Piano* (N.Y., 1948; 2nd ed., rev., 1964).—**NS/LK/DM**

Hutchings, Arthur (James Bramwell), English musicologist; b. Sunbury-on-Thames, July 14, 1906; d. Colyton, Devon, Nov. 13, 1989. He studied violin and piano; later received his Ph.D. from the Univ. of Durham (1953), where he was prof. of music (1947–68) and then at the Univ. of Exeter (1968–71). His books, all publ. in London, include *Schubert* (1945; 4th ed., 1973), *Delius* (1948), *A Companion to Mozart's Piano Concertos* (1948; 3rd ed., 1980), *The Invention and Composition of Music* (1958), *The Baroque Concerto* (1961; 3rd ed., rev., 1973), *Church Music in the Nineteenth Century* (1967), *Mozart: The Man, the Musician* (1976), and *Purcell* (1982). —**NS/LK/DM**

Hutschenruyter (Hutschenruijter), noted family of Dutch musicians:

(1) **Wouter Hutschenruyter,** conductor and composer; b. Rotterdam, Dec. 28, 1796; d. there, Nov. 18, 1878. He studied violin, horn, and theory. He was founder-director of the band of the Rotterdam civic guard (1821) and of the music society Eruditio Musica (1826). He was a teacher at the music school of the Maatschappij tot Bevordering der Toonkunst. Among his compositions are the opera *Le Roi de Bohème* (Rotterdam, 1833), several syms., overtures, a Concertino for 8 Timpani and Orch., much band music, masses, cantatas, chamber music, and songs.

(2) **Willem Jacob Hutschenruyter,** horn player and conductor, son of the preceding; b. Rotterdam, March 22, 1828; d. there, Jan. 19, 1889. He played the horn in the orchs. of the Rotterdam Opera and his father's Eruditio Musica. He was conductor of the municipal band (1865–85).

(3) **Wouter Hutschenruyter,** noted Dutch conductor, musicologist, and composer, son of the preceding; b. Rotterdam, Aug. 15, 1859; d. The Hague, Nov. 14, 1943. He studied in Rotterdam, where he began his career as a choral conductor and teacher. He then was 2nd conductor of the Concertgebouw Orch. in Amsterdam (1890–92), and subsequently conductor of the Utrecht municipal orch. (1892–1917), which he developed into a respected Dutch ensemble. He later was director of the music school of Rotterdam's Maatschappij tot Bevordering der Toonkunst (1917–25). He composed a Piano Concerto, a *Nocturne* for Horn and Orch., various other orch. pieces, chamber music, piano pieces, and songs.

WRITINGS: *Richard Strauss* (Haarlem, 1898); *Orkest en orkestspel na 1600* (Utrecht, 1903); *Felix Weingartner* (Haarlem, 1906); *Het muziekleven in de 17e eeuw* (Baarn, 1909); *Wolfgang Amadeus Mozart* (Rotterdam, 1909; abridged ed., 1927, as *Mozart*; 2nd ed., 1943); *De geschiedenis der toonkunst* (Amsterdam, 1920); *De programma muziek* (Bussum, 1922); *De geschiedenis van het orkest en van zijn instrumenten* (Amsterdam, 1926); *Mahler* (The Hague, 1927); *De symphonieën van Beethoven en toegelicht* (The Hague, 1928; 2nd ed., 1943); *Wagner* (The Hague, 1928); *Brahms* (The Hague, 1929); with J. Kruseman, *Richard Strauss* (The Hague, 1929); *Een en ander uit de geschiedenis der militaire muziek* (Hilversum, 1930); *Grepen uit geschiedenis van de piano en vat het pianospel* (Hilversum, 1930); *De sonates van Beethoven geanalyseerd en toegelicht* (The Hague, 1930); *De dirigent* (Hilversum, 1931; 3rd ed., 1955); *De ontwikkeling der symphonie door Haydn, Mozart en Beethoven* (Hilversum, 1935); with J. Kruseman, *Musiciana* (The Hague, 1938); *Frédéric Chopin* (The Hague, 1939; 3rd ed., 1949); *Bijdrage tot de bibliographie der muziekliteratur* (Leiden, 1941–43); *Grepen uit de geschiedenis van de snaarinstrumenten en van het snarenspel* (Hilversum, 1942); *Franz Schubert* (The Hague, 1944).—**NS/LK/DM**

Hüttel, Josef, Czech conductor and composer; b. Mělník, July 18, 1893; d. Plzeň, July 6, 1951. He studied with černý (piano), Štěpán Suchý (violin), and Novák (composition) at the Prague Cons. (1908–12). After further instruction with Taneyev (composition) in Moscow (1912–13), he was active as a choirmaster there; then conducted opera in Voronezh (1918–20). In 1921 he went to Egypt, where he was conductor of the Alexandria Phil. (1929–34) and head of European music for Cairo Radio (1934–44). In 1946 he returned to Czechoslovakia and was an ed. and archivist for the Czech Radio music dept. (until 1950). Among his compositions were a *Sinfonietta* (1923), *Images égyptiennes* for Orch. (1928), *Amon Raa*, symphonic poem (1931), Sym. (1935; won the Smetana jubilee prize), String Quartet (1927), *Divertissement grotesque* for Wind Quintet and Piano (1929; won the Coolidge prize), and *Ragtime* for Violin and Piano (1929).—**NS/LK/DM**

Hüttenbrenner, Anselm, Austrian composer; b. Graz, Oct. 13, 1794; d. Ober-Andritz, near Graz, June 5, 1868. At the age of 7, he studied with the organist Gell. After law studies at the Univ. of Graz, he went to Vienna in 1815 to study with Salieri, whose pupil he remained until 1818. Schubert was his fellow student, and they became close friends. Hüttenbrenner also knew Beethoven, and was present at his death. After serving as director of the Steiermarkischer Musikverein (1825–39), he retired to his estate near Graz. He was an excellent pianist and a prolific composer; Schubert praised his works. He wrote 6 operas, an operetta, 8 syms., many overtures, 10 masses, 4 Requiems, 3 funeral marches, 2 string quartets, a String Quintet, piano sonatas, 24 fugues, and other piano pieces, some 300 male quartets and 200 songs. His unreliable reminiscences of Schubert (1854) were publ. by Otto Deutsch in 1906. Hüttenbrenner came into the possession of many Schubert MSS after Schubert's death, among them the *Unfinished Symphony*, which he gave to Herbeck in 1865 so that its premiere could finally be given in Vienna.

BIBL.: K. Kurth, *A. H. als Liederkomponist* (diss., Univ. of Cologne, 1932).—**NS/LK/DM**

Huttenlocher, Philippe, Swiss baritone; b. Neuchâtel, Nov. 29, 1942. He received vocal training in Fribourg, and then began his career with the Ensemble Vocal de Lausanne and the Choeurs de la Foundation Gulbenkian in Lisbon. In 1975 he made his first appearance at the Zürich Opera as Monteverdi's Orfeo, and thereafter sang various Baroque roles there. His guest engagements took him to such leading European music centers as London, Vienna, Berlin, Hamburg, Edinburgh, Montreux, Milan, and Strasbourg. He was especially admired for his interpretations of works by Gabrieli, Monteverdi, Charpentier, Carissimi, Bach, Handel, Rameau, Haydn, and Mozart.—**NS/LK/DM**

Hutton, Ina Ray, jazz singer, leader; b. Chicago, Ill., March 13, 1916; d. Ventura, Calif., Feb. 19, 1984. Of Jewish extraction, she was the daughter of pianist Marvel Ray and the half-sister of singer June Hutton (b. ca. 1918–21; d. 1973) During the early 1930s she sang and danced in several Broadway productions including Lew Leslie's *Clowns in Clover*, George White's *Melody Revue*, and the *Ziegfeld Follies*. In late 1934 agent Irving Mills signed her to front a big all-girl orch. (the outfit's first musical director and arranger was Alex Hill). She continued with an all-girl band through the 1930s, then during the 1940s led her own male band which disbanded in 1944, then re-formed using the alumni of Bob Alexander's Band. During the 1950s she occasionally fronted her own all-girl bands, but also did solo vocal work. She was inactive as a musician for the remainder of her life.—**JC/LP**

Huybrechts, Albert, Belgian composer; b. Dinant, Feb. 12, 1899; d. Woluwe-St.-Pierre, near Brussels, Feb. 21, 1938. He studied at the Brussels Cons. with Martin Lunssens, Paulin Marchand, Léon Dubois, and Joseph Jongen. In 1926 he gained international recognition by winning 2 U.S. prizes, the Elizabeth Sprague Coolidge Prize of the Library of Congress in Washington, D.C., for his Violin Sonata, and the Ojai Valley Prize in Calif. for his String Quartet. In 1937 he was appointed a prof. at the Brussels Cons., but a severe attack of uremia led to his premature death. He wrote in a judiciously modern idiom, seasoned with prudential dissonance.

WORKS: ORCH.: 2 symphonic poems: *David* (1923) and *Poème féerique* (1923); *Chant funèbre* for Cello and Orch. (1926); *Sérénade* (1929); *Chant d'angoisse* (1930); *Nocturne* (1931); *Divertissement* for Brass and Percussion (1931); Cello Concertino

(1932). **CHAMBER:** 2 string quartets (1924, 1927); Violin Sonata (1925); Trio for Flute, Viola, and Piano (1926); Sextet for Wind Quintet, with 2nd Flute (1927); Suite for Flute, Oboe, Clarinet, Bassoon, and Piano (1929); *Choral* for Organ (1930); *Sicilienne* for Piano (1934); *Pastourelle* for Cello and Piano (1934); Sonatine for Flute and Viola (1934); String Trio (1935); Wind Quintet (1936). **VOCAL:** Songs, including *Horoscopes* (1926). —**NS/LK/DM**

Hvorostovsky, Dmitri, prominent Russian baritone; b. Krasnoyarsk, Oct. 16, 1962. He was a student of Ekaterina Yofel at the Krasnoyarsk School of the Arts (1982–86). In 1986 he joined the Krasnoyarsk Opera. In 1987 he won the Glinka Prize, and in 1989 the BBC Cardiff Singer of the World Competition, which resulted in an appearance on BBC-TV; that same year, he made his London recital debut at the Wigmore Hall, and sang Tchaikovsky's Yeletsky in Nice. On March 4, 1990, he made an acclaimed U.S. debut in recital at N.Y.'s Alice Tully Hall. In 1991 he appeared in *War and Peace* at the San Francisco Opera. In 1992 he was engaged to sing in *I Puritani* at London's Covent Garden and appeared as Posa at Milan's La Scala. In 1993 he made his U.S. operatic debut as Germont at the Lyric Opera of Chicago and his first appearance at the London Promenade Concerts. On Oct. 26, 1995, he made his Metropolitan Opera debut in N.Y. as Yeletsky in *The Queen of Spades*. After singing in recital at the Barbican Hall in London in 1997, he was engaged as Francesco in *I masnadieri* in Baden-Baden in 1998. He sang that role with the Opera Orch. of N.Y. in 1999, the same year he portrayed Don Giovanni in Geneva. In addition to the Russian operatic and song repertoires, he has won distinction for his roles in Verdi's operas.—**NS/LK/DM**

Hvoslef (real name, **Saeverud**), **Ketil,** Norwegian composer, son of **Harald Saeverud**; b. Fana, near Bergen, July 19, 1939. He took his mother's maiden name in 1980. He studied piano with Thomas Rayna in London (1961) and took an organ diploma at the Bergen Cons. (1962); he then studied composition with Blomdahl and Lidholm in Stockholm, Jersild in Copenhagen, and Lazaroff in London. From 1963 to 1979 he was on the faculty of the Bergen Cons. After a period of hesitant serialism, he evolved a "motivic assimilation technique," wherein a central motif influences all the other thematic material in the manner of a theme with variations.

WORKS: DRAMATIC: O p e r a : *The Ballad of Narcissus and Echo* (1981); *Dode Sardiner* (1986–87); *Trio for Tretten*; *Acotral* (1987). **O t h e r :** Much incidental music. **ORCH.:** *Sinfonietta* (1963); Piano Concertino (1964); Trumpet Concerto (1968–69; Bergen, April 22, 1972); *Mi-Fi-Li*, symphonic poem (Oslo, Sept. 4, 1972); Double Bass Concerto (1973); 2 cello concertos (1976–87; 1990–91); *Variations* for Chamber Orch. (1976); Double Concerto for Flute, Guitar, and Strings (1977); Concertino (Trondheim, Sept. 20, 1979); Concerto for Bassoon and Strings (1979); Suite for School Orch. (1980); *Antigone*, symphonic variations (1981–82); *Air* (1983); *Il Compleanno* (Bergen, Oct. 8, 1985); Violin Concerto (1988–89). **CHAMBER:** Clarinet Quartet (1962); Wind Quintet (1964); *Suite* for Guitar (1966); *Ariseturo*, concerto for Percussion and 8 Wind Instruments (1966); *Duets* for Bassoons (1966); 2 string quartets (1969,

1973); *Flauto Solo* (1970); *Tromba Solo* (1971); *Kim* for 4 Crumhorns, 4 Recorders, Bass Gamba, and Percussion (1975); Trio for Oboe, Violin, and Percussion (1978); Octet for Flutes (1978); *Brass* for 13 Brass Instruments (1978); *Violino Solo* (1980); *Post*, sextet (1980); *Duodu* for Violin and Viola (1982); *Erkejubel* for 2 Trumpets, 2 Trombones, Synthesizer, and Percussion (1982); Quintet for Clarinet and String Quartet (1983); *Rikstrio* for Flute, Violin, and Synthesizer (1984); *Scheherazade Carries on With Her Story* for Violin and Harp (1986); Sextet for Flute and 5 Percussion (1988); *Framenti di Roma* for Oboe, Clarinet, and Bassoon (1988); *Kirkeduo* for Guitar and Organ (1988). **KEYBOARD: Piano:** *Rondo con variazioni* (1970); *Beethoven Fantasy* (1982). **Organ:** *Variations* (1972); *Organo Solo* (1974); *Easter Variations* (1986); *Toccata: Fontana dell'Organo, Villa d'Este* (1988). **VOCAL:** *So einsam ist der Mensch* for Chorus or Vocal Quartet, after Nelly Sachs (1970); *Or "Havamal"* (Sayings of the High One), cantata for Chorus and Orch. (1971; rev. 1974); *Kvartoni* for Voice, Recorder, Guitar, and Piano (1974); Trio for Soprano, Alto, and Piano (1974); *Collage in Black/White with Red* for Baritone Narration, Violin, Guitar, Clarinet, and Percussion (1975); Concerto for Chorus and Orch. (1977); *Spillemaend* (Fiddlers) for Chorus, Hardanger Fiddle, and Organ (1980); *Dano Tiore*, quintet for Soprano, Violin, Viola, Cello, and Harpsichord (1985); *Entrata Bergensis* for Chorus, Tape, and Orch. (1989).—**NS/LK/DM**

Hwang, Byung-Ki, Korean composer, virtuoso kayagum performer, and pedagogue; b. Seoul, May 31, 1936. He studied traditional Korean music and the kayagum (a 12–stringed Korean zither with movable bridges, dating from the turn of the 7th century) at the National Classical Music Inst. in Seoul (1951–58), his principal teachers being Yong-yun Kim, Yun-dok Kim, and Sang-gon Sim. He received 1st prize at the National Competition of Traditional Music (1954, 1956), a National Music Prize (1965), and the Korean Cinema Music Award (1973). From 1974 he was prof. of Korean traditional music at the Coll. of Music, Ewha Women's Univ., in Seoul; in 1985–86 he was a visiting scholar at Harvard Univ. Hwang is noted as the first Korean composer to write modern works for the kayagum; he is also a distinguished kayagum player, and has appeared in recital in the U.S., West Germany, France, and Austria. His U.S. debut took place in N.Y.'s Carnegie Hall on April 20, 1986, in a program which included a number of his own compositions. His works are translucent and elegant in their structures, and impressionistic in harmonic and melodic design.

WORKS: KAYAGUM: *The Forest* (1963); *The Pomegranate House* (1965); *Kara Town* (1967); *Chimhyangmu* (1974); *The Silk Road* (1977); *Sounds of the Night* (1985); *Southern Fantasy* (1989). **OTHER INSTRUMENTS:** *Pungyo* for Piri (Korean oboe; 1972); *Mandaeyop-haetan* for Korean Orch. (1976); *Chasi* for Taegum (Korean bamboo flute; 1978); *Unbak* for Korean Orch. (1979); *Harim Castle* for Taegum (1982); *Soyopsanbang* for Komungo (Korean 6–stringed plucked zither with 16 frets; 1989). **VOCAL:** *Beside a Chrysanthemum* for Voice, Komungo, and Changgu (Korean hour-glass drum with 2 heads; 1962); *Chongsando and Kanggangsullae* for Chorus (1974); *The Labyrinth* for Voice and Kayagum (1975); *Nolbujon*, narrative song (1976); *The Evening Chant* for Chorus and Percussion (1983); also dance music; film scores.—**NS/LK/DM**

Hyde, Walter, English tenor; b. Birmingham, Feb. 6, 1875; d. London, Nov. 11, 1951. He studied with Gustave Garcia at the Royal Coll. of Music in London, where he sang in student performances. He then sang in light opera before he undertook Wagnerian roles, which became his specialty. He sang Siegmund in the English-language production of the *Ring* cycle at Covent Garden in London in 1908; his other roles included Walther von Stolzing and Parsifal. He made his Metropolitan Opera debut in N.Y. on March 28, 1910, as Siegmund in *Die Walküre*; then returned to England and made regular appearances at Covent Garden until 1924; later sang with the Beecham Opera Co. and the British National Opera Co., serving as a director of the latter. He was a frequent participant at many musical festivals in England.—**NS/LK/DM**

Hye-Knudsen, Johan, Danish conductor and composer; b. Nyborg, May 24, 1896; d. Copenhagen, Sept. 28, 1975. He studied cello at the Copenhagen Cons. with Rudinger; also in Paris with André Hekking; studied conducting in Dresden with Fritz Busch. In 1925 he was named a conductor of the Royal Danish Theater in Copenhagen; concurrently led concerts of the Royal Danish Orch. He wrote a number of orch. works and 2 operas: *Orfeus i underverdenen* (Copenhagen, Jan. 1, 1934) and *Kirke og orgel* (Copenhagen, Nov. 8, 1947). —**NS/LK/DM**

Hykes, David (Bond), distinctive American composer and vocalist; b. Taos, N.Mex., March 2, 1953. He studied filmmaking at Antioch Coll. in Ohio (1970–74), and arts administration at Columbia Univ. (M.F.A., 1984). He also studied classical Azerbaijani and Armenian music with Zevulon Avshalomov (1975–77) and north Indian rāga singing with S. Dahr (1982). In 1975 he founded the Harmonic Choir, whose members employ vocal techniques borrowed from Tibetan and Mongolian music in which strongly resonated upper partials are produced in addition to the fundamental tone. From 1979 the ensemble was in residence at the ideal location of the Cathedral of St. John the Divine in N.Y., and from 1980 made tours of the U.S. and Europe. In 1981 Hykes traveled to Mongolia under the auspices of the Asian Cultural Council. In 1987 he settled in Paris, where he founded the Choeur Harmonique, which, in 1999, made a major U.S. tour. Hykes's compositions for voice use harmonics to produce rich waves of slowly changing sounds over diatonic melodies; the result resembles a sort of modernized chant with an ethereal haze of overtones. Among such compositions are *Hearing Solar Winds* (1977–83), *Current Circulation* (1983–84), and *Harmonic Meetings* (1986). Particularly noteworthy CD recordings are *Let the Lover Be* (1996), with Chemirani, zarb, and *True to the Times (How to Be?)* (1993), with Peter Biffin, dobro, Bruno Caillat, darf and zarb, and Tony Lewis, tabla. Hykes has also written several film and television scores and a number of instrumental works.—**NS/LK/DM**

Hyman, Dick (actually, **Richard Roven**), versatile jazz keyboardist, clarinetist, composer; b. N.Y., March 8, 1927. One of the most versatile studio musicians, as a jazz player he is known for his ability to play in every style, but his natural talent seems to fall into historical styles such as ragtime, stride and swing. He was active on the N.Y. scene as early as 1947. He worked with Tony Scott and Lester Young, appeared on the famous television clip with Parker and Gillespie in early 1952, and toured with Benny Goodman. He spent the first half of the 1950s as an in-house music maker for a couple of N.Y. radio stations. He recorded ragtime in the 1950s as Knuckles O'Toole. In 1956 Hyman's Trio had the greatest instrumental hit version of "Mack the Knife/Moritat." This group lasted from the mid-1950s into the 1960s. In 1969 he made another brief appearance on the U.S. Top 40 with "The Minotaur" under the billing Dick Hyman & His Electric Eclectics. He was an early exponent of the synthesizer. His career also included stints with Johnny Desmond, Percy Faith, Mitch Miller, and with Arthur Godfrey's talent show. He also played sessions on albums by Janis Ian and Don McLean. He collaborated with critic/journalist Leonard Feather on a series of "History of Jazz" concerts and did a series of major historical concerts with the N.Y. Jazz Repertory Company, re-creating the music of Louis Armstrong, James P. Johnson, Jelly Roll Morton, and Scott Joplin in the 1970s. From 1985, he has been the director of the Jazz in July series held at N.Y.'s 92nd Street Y. He has scored most of Woody Allen's recent films, as well as films by other directors, and written music in a classical style.

DISC.: *Moog: the Electric Eclectics of D. H.* (1969); *Scott Joplin*; *Sensuous Piano of "D."* (1971); *Solo Piano* (1973); *Jelly and James* (1973); *Satchmo Remembered* (1974); *Themes and Variations on "A Child Is Born"* (1977); *Music of Jelly Roll Morton* (1978); *Live at Michael's Pub* (1981); *Kitten on the Keys* (1983); *Runnin' Ragged* (1985); *Manhattan Jazz* (1987); *Plays Fats Waller* (1988); *14 Jazz Piano Favorites* (1988); *Live at Maybeck Recital Hall* (1989); *Plays Duke Ellington* (1992); *Gulf Coast Blues* (1992); *Gershwin Songbook: Jazz Variations* (1992); *From the Age of Swing* (1994).—**LP/MM**

Hynninen, Jorma, distinguished Finnish baritone and opera administrator; b. Leppävirta, April 3, 1941. He studied at the Sibelius Academy in Helsinki (1966–70); also took courses in Rome with Luigi Ricci and in Salzburg with Kurt Overhoff. He won 1st prize at the singing competition in Lappeenranta in 1969, and in the Finnish division of the Scandinavian singing competition in Helsinki in 1971. In 1970 he made his concert debut in Helsinki, as well as his operatic debut as Silvio in *Pagliacci* with the Finnish National Opera there, and subsequently sang leading roles with the company. He also made first appearances at La Scala in Milan (1977), the Vienna State Opera (1977), the Hamburg State Opera (1977), the Bavarian State Opera in Munich (1979), and the Paris Opéra (1980); gave recitals throughout Europe and the U.S. He made his N.Y. debut in a recital in 1980; his operatic debut followed in 1983, when he sang with the Finnish National Opera during its visit to America; made his Metropolitan Opera debut in N.Y. as Rodrigo in *Don Carlo* on March 30, 1984. He was artistic director of the Finnish National Opera from 1984 to 1990, and then of the Savonlinna Festival from 1992. In addition to such traditional operatic roles as Pelléas, Wolfram, Orpheus, Valentin in *Faust*, and Macbeth, he has sung parts in contemporary Finnish operas; he created the King in Sallinen's *The King Goes Forth to France* (Savonlinna, July 7, 1984), Thomas in Rautavaara's opera (Joensuu, June 21, 1985), Kullervo in Sallinen's opera (Los Angeles, Feb. 25, 1992), and Aleksis Kivi in Rautavaara's opera (Savonlinna, July 10, 1997).—**NS/LK/DM**

Hytner, Nicholas, English theater and opera producer; b. Manchester, May 7, 1956. He was educated at Trinity Coll., Cambridge (graduated, 1977), where he produced Weill's *The Threepenny Opera* while still a student. In 1979 he launched his professional career when he oversaw the production of *The Turn of the Screw* at the Kent Opera. In 1983 he brought out *Rienzi* at the English National Opera in London. He was the producer for the British premiere of Sallinen's *The King Goes Forth to War* at London's Covent Garden in 1987. Following productions of Handel's *Giulio Cesare* in Paris in 1987 and Mozart's *Le nozze di Figaro* in Geneva in 1989, he brought out the latter composer's *La clemenza di Tito* at the Glyndebourne Festival in 1991. In 1992 he staged *La forza del destino* at the English National Opera. In 1996 he oversaw the production of *The Cunning Little Vixen* in Paris. His film version of *The Crucible* appeared in 1997. In addition to his work in opera, he has also pursued an active career as a producer of stage plays. His work in the legitimate theater is reflected in his approach to opera, most notably in his ability to harmonize the dramatic and musical elements into a satisfying theater experience.—**NS/LK/DM**

Iannaccone, Anthony (Joseph), American composer, teacher, and conductor; b. N.Y., Oct. 14, 1943. He studied with Copland in N.Y. (1959–64), with Giannini and Diamond at the Manhattan School of Music (M.M., 1968), and with Adler at the Eastman School of Music in Rochester, N.Y. (Ph.D., 1971). After teaching at the Manhattan School of Music (1967–68), he became prof. of composition at Eastern Mich. Univ. in 1971, where he founded its electronic music studio and where he conducted the Collegium Musicum. Iannaccone has received several awards and commissions, and was the winner of the S.A.I./C.F. Peters Competition in 1990 and of the Ostwald Composition Competition in 1995. In his works, he applies serial methods with a certain liberality towards occurrences of tonal, and even explicitly triadic, elements. In his band music, he openly exploits tonal devices.

WORKS: ORCH.: *Suite* (1962); 3 syms. (1965; 1966; *Night Rivers*, 1990–92); *Violin Concertino* (1967); *Lysistrata: A Concert Overture* (1968); *Variations* for Violin and Orch. (1969); *Divertimento* (1983); *Sinfonia Concertante* for Flute, Violin, Viola, Cello, Piano, and Orch. (1989); *Whispers of Heavenly Death* (1989); *Concertante* for Clarinet and Orch. (1994); *Al Chiaro di Luna* (1994); *Crossings* (1996); *West End Express* (1997); *Waiting for Sunrise on the Sound* (1998); *From Time to Time* (2000). **W i n d E n s e m b l e a n d S y m p h o n i c B a n d :** *Interlude* (1970); *Antiphonies* (1972); *Scherzo* (1976); *Of Fire and Ice* (1977); *Images of Songs & Dance*: No. 1, *Orpheus* (1979) and No. 2, *Terpsichore* (1981); *After a Gentle Rain* (1979); *Plymouth Trilogy* (1981); *Apparitions* (1986); *Sea Drift* (1993). **CHAMBER:** *Parodies* for Woodwind Quintet (1958); *Piano Trio* (1959); *Viola Sonata* (1961); 3 violin sonatas (1964, 1971, 1985); 3 string quartets (1965, 1965, 1999); *Hades* for Brass Quartet (1968); *Remembrance* for Viola and Piano (1968); *3 Mythical Sketches* for Brass Quartet (1971); *Anamorphoses* for 2 Trumpets, Trombone, and Percussion (1972); *Rituals* for Violin and Piano (1973); *Bicinia* for Flute and Alto Saxophone (1974); *Night Song* for Bassoon and Piano (1975); *Sonatina* for Trumpet and Tuba (1975); *Aria concertante* for Cello and Piano (1976); *Invention* for 2 Alto Saxophones (1978); *Trio* for Flute, Clarinet, and Piano (1979); *Octet* for Flute, Oboe, Clarinet, and String Quintet (1985); *Mobiles* for 8 Brass and 2 Percussion Players (1986); *Toccata Fanfares* for 6 Brass (1986); *Piano Quintet* (1996). **KEYBOARD: P i a n o :** *Retail Rags* (1959); *Partita* (1967); *Keyboard Essays* (1972); *2-Piano Inventions* (1985). **O r g a n :** *Toccata Variations* (1983). **VOCAL:** Many folk songs for Voice and Piano (1958–89); *5 Songs on Immortality* for Soprano and Orch. (1959); *Magnificat* for Chorus and Orch. (1963); *Solomon's Canticle* for Chorus (1968); *The Prince of Peace* for Soloists, Chorus, and Orch. (1970); *With Music Strong I Come* for Chorus, 2 Pianos, and Chamber Ensemble (1974); *The Sky is Low, the Clouds are Mean* for Chorus (1976); *Song of Thanks* for Chorus (1980); *Walt Whitman Song* for Soloists, Chorus, and Wind Ensemble (1980); *A Whitman Madrigal* for Chorus and Piano (1984); *Autumn Rivulets* for Chorus and Chamber Orch. (1984); *My Comfort by Day, My Song in the Night* for High Voice and Piano (1985); *Chautauqua Psalms* for Chorus and Piano (1987). **ELECTROACOUSTIC:** *Prelude* (1968); *Times Square and Forty-Second Street* (1969); *Fission* (1971).—**NS/LK/DM**

Ibach, Johannes Adolf, German piano maker; b. Barmen, Oct. 17, 1766; d. there, Sept. 14, 1848. In 1794 he founded a piano factory at Barmen, where he also manufactured organs from 1834 with his son C. Rudolf Ibach. He then traded under the name of Adolf Ibach & Sohn. From 1839, the firm was known as Rudolf & Söhne, when his son Richard joined the firm. From 1862 the firm was known as C. Rudolf & Richard Ibach, to distinguish it from another business founded by a third son, Gustav J. The same year C. Rudolf died, and in 1869 his son Rudolf (d. Herrenalb, Black Forest, July 31, 1892) continued the piano factory alone as Rudolf Ibach Sohn. He established a branch at Cologne, gaining medals for the excellence of his pianos, and became purveyor to the Prussian court. Richard Ibach continued the organ factory.

BIBL.: *Das Haus I. 1794–1894* (1895).—**NS/LK/DM**

Ibarra (Groth), Federico, Mexican composer; b. Mexico City, July 25, 1946. He studied at the Univ.

Nacional Autónoma in Mexico City in the 1960s and then attended courses of Pierre Henry in Paris (1971) and of Rodolfo Halffter in Spain (1975). Ibarra taught at the Univ. Nacional Autónoma (1971–77) and directed its compositions workshops (from 1985). He received the Silvestre Revueltas Prize in 1975 and 1976, the Mozart Medal of Mexico in 1991, and the Prize of the Universidad Nacional in 1993. The colorful dissonance of his music produces a situation analogous to "magic realism."

WORKS: DRAMATIC: O p e r a : *Leoncio y Lena* (1980–81; Mexico City, Sept. 1981); *Orestes Parte* (1981; first stage perf., Mexico City, July 5, 1987); *Madre Juana* (1986; Mexico City, Sept. 13, 1993); *Alicia*, after Lewis Carroll (1989–90; Mexico City, July 9, 1995); *Despertar al sueño* (Mexico City, Oct. 24, 1994). **B a l - l e t :** *Imágenes del Quinto Sol* (1980; Mexico City, May 6, 1984). **ORCH.:** *Tre preludios monocromáticos* (1972; also for Piano, 4-Hands, 1964); *Cinco misterios eléusicos* (1979); Concerto for Amplified Piano and Orch. (1979–80); Cello Concerto (1988–89); 2 syms.: No. 1 (1991) and No. 2, *Las Antesalas del Sueño* (1993); *3 Pieces* (1991); *Obertura para un Nuevo Milenio* (1993); *Obertura para un Cento fantástico* (1993); *Balada* for Strings (1995); Violin Concerto (1995–97). **CHAMBER:** *Invierno* for String Quartet (1963); 2 string quartets (*Del Trasmundo*, 1975; *Orfico*, 1992); *Cinco estudios premonitorios* for Instrumental Ensemble and Piano (1976); *Música para Teatro I* for Flute, Oboe, Cello, and Piano (1982), *II* for Harpsichord (1986), and *III* for Cello and Piano (1987); Sextet for Flute, Oboe, Clarinet, and Piano Trio (1985); *Sonata Breve* for Solo Violin (1991); Cello Sonata (1992); *El viaje imaginario* for Clarinet, Violin, Cello, and Piano (1994); *Juegos Nocturnos* for Wind Quintet (1995). **P i a n o :** *Tres preludios monocromáticos* for Piano, 4-Hands (1964; also for Orch., 1972); 5 sonatas (1976; 1982; *Madre Juana*, 1988; 1990; 1995–96). **VOCAL:** 7 chamber cantatas (1967–73); *El proceso de la metamorfosis* for Narrator and Orch., after Bretón and Kafka (1970); *Rito del reencuentro* for Narrator, Strings, and 2 Pianos (1974); *Loa para ola ciudad que espera*, cycle of 3 cantatas (1986–87); *El pequeño principe* for Soloists and Chamber Orch. (1988). **—LK/DM**

Ibert, Jacques (François Antoine),

distinguished French composer; b. Paris, Aug. 15, 1890; d. there, Feb. 5, 1962. He studied at the Paris Cons. with Gédalge and Fauré (1911–14). During World War I, he served in the French navy. He then returned to the Paris Cons. after the Armistice and studied with Vidal. He received the Prix de Rome in 1919 for his cantata *Le Poète et la fée*. While in Rome, he wrote his most successful work, the symphonic suite *Escales* (Ports of Call), inspired by a Mediterranean cruise while serving in the navy. In 1937 he was appointed director of the Académie de France of Rome, holding this post until 1960; was also administrator of the Réunion des Théâtres Lyriques Nationaux in Paris (1955–56). He was elected a member of the Institut de France (1956). In his music, Ibert combined the most felicitous moods and techniques of Impressionism and neo-Classicism. His harmonies were opulent, and his instrumentation was coloristic. There was an element of humor in lighter works, such as his popular orch. *Divertissement* and an even more popular piece, *Le Petit Ane blanc*, from the piano suite *Histoires*. His craftsmanship was excellent. An experimenter in tested values, he never failed to produce the intended effect.

WORKS: DRAMATIC: O p e r a : *Angélique* (Paris, Jan. 28, 1927); *Persée et Andromède, ou Le Plus Heureux des trois* (1921; Paris, May 15, 1929); *Le Roi d'Yvetot* (Paris, Jan. 15, 1930); *Gonzague* (Monte Carlo, Dec. 7, 1931); *L'Aiglon* (Monte Carlo, March 11, 1937; in collaboration with A. Honegger); *Les Petites Cardinal* (Paris, 1938; in collaboration with A. Honegger); *Barbebleue*, radio opera (Lausanne Radio, Oct. 10, 1943). **B a l l e t** (all first perf. in Paris): *Les Rencontres* (Nov. 21, 1925); *Diane de Poitiers* (April 30, 1934); *Les Amours de Jupiter* (March 9, 1946); *Le Chevalier errant* (May 5, 1950); *Tropismes pour des Amours Imaginaires* (1957). **ORCH.:** *Noël en Picardie*, symphonic poem (1914); *Ballade de la geôle de Reading*, after Oscar Wilde (Paris, Oct. 22, 1922); *Escales*, 3 symphonic pictures (Paris, Jan. 6, 1924); *Féerique*, symphonic scherzo (Paris, Dec. 12, 1925); Concerto for Cello and Wind Instruments (Paris, Feb. 28, 1926); *Divertissement*, suite (Paris, Nov. 30, 1930; from incidental music to *Le Chapeau de paille d'Italie*); *Paris*, suite for Chamber Orch. (Venice, Sept. 15, 1932; from incidental music to *Donogoo*); Flute Concerto (Paris, Feb. 25, 1934); *Concertino da camera* for Saxophone and Chamber Orch. (Paris, May 2, 1935); *Capriccio* (1938); *Ouverture de fête* (Paris, Jan. 18, 1942); *Suite élisabéthaine* (1944); *Symphonie concertante* for Oboe and Strings (Basel, Feb. 11, 1949); *Louisville Concerto* (Louisville, Ky., Feb. 17, 1954); *Bostoniana* (1956–61); *Hommage à Mozart* (1957); *Bacchanale* (1958). **CHAMBER:** 6 pieces for Harp (1917); *2 mouvements* for 2 Flutes, Clarinet, and Bassoon (1923); *Jeux*, flute sonatina (1924); *3 pièces brèves* for Flute, Oboe, Clarinet, Horn, and Bassoon (1930); *Pastoral* for 4 Fifes (in *Pipeaux*, by various composers, 1934); *Entr'acte* for Flute and Guitar (1935); piece for Flute (1936); String Quartet (1944); Trio for Violin, Cello, and Harp (1944); *2 Interludes* for Violin and Harpsichord (1949). **P i a n o :** *Histoires* (10 pieces); *Les Rencontres*, arranged from the ballet (5 pieces); *Petite suite en 15 images* (1943). **VOCAL:** *Le Poète et la fée*, cantata (1919); *3 chansons de C. Vidrac* for Voice and Orch. or Piano (1923); *Chant de folie* for Solo Voices, Chorus, and Orch. (1923–24; Boston, April 23, 1926); *La Verdure dorée* for Voice and Piano (1924); *4 chansons de Don Quichotte* for Bass and Orch. or Piano (1932); *Chanson du rien* for Voice and Piano; *Quintette de la peur* for Chorus and Piano (1946).

BIBL.: J. Feschotte, *J. I.* (Paris, 1959); G. Michel, *J. I., L'Homme et son oeuvre* (Paris, 1968).—NS/LK/DM

Ichiyanagi, Toshi,

notable Japanese composer; b. Kobe, Feb. 4, 1933. He studied composition with Kishio Hirao and piano with Chieko Hara. At 16, he took first prize in the Mainichi/NHK composition competition, which he won again in 1951. He pursued training in N.Y. at the Juilliard School of Music (1954–58), receiving instruction in composition from John Cage and in piano from Beveridge Webster. He also was awarded the Koussevitzky Prize at the Berkshire Music Center at Tanglewood (summer, 1956). In 1967 he received a Rockefeller Foundation grant and was active in N.Y. as composer-in-residence. In 1976 he was the Deutscher Akademischer Austauschdienst composer-in-residence in Berlin. In 1989 he founded and became artistic director of the Tokyo International Music Ensemble, a traditional Japanese orch. with Buddhist chanting shomyo. He led the ensemble on many tours abroad, including visits to Europe and the U.S. His writings include *Oto o Kiku Ongaku no Asu o Kangaeru* (Listening to the Sound: Notion of Music; Tokyo, 1984) and *Ongaku to io Itonami* (Music and the Contemporary Age; Tokyo, 1998). In 1981, 1984, 1989, and 1990 he won the Otaka

Prize, in 1985 he was made a member of the Ordre des Arts et des Lettres of France, and in 1989 he won the Kyoto Music Grand Prize. Ichiyanagi's compositions reflect his penchant for exploring both Western and non-Western musical traditions, as well as for a willingness to pursue experimental paths in both traditions.

WORKS: DRAMATIC: *Momo*, opera (Tokyo, Oct. 13, 1995); *The Last Will of Fire*, opera (Tokyo, Nov. 16, 1995); film scores. **ORCH.:** *Life Music* (1964); *The Field* (1966); *Up to Date Applause* for Orch., Rock Band, and Tape (Tokyo, June 4, 1968); *In the Reflection of Lighting Image* for Percussion and Orch. (Osaka, July 25, 1980); 3 piano concertos: No. 1, *Reminiscence of Spaces* (NHK, Tokyo, Oct. 18, 1981), No. 2, *Winter Portrait* (1987; Tokyo, May 23, 1988), and No. 3, *Cross Water Roads* (Tokyo, Sept. 15, 1991); *Engen* for Koto and Orch. (Tokyo, March 26, 1982); Violin Concerto, *Circulating Scenery* (Tokyo, May 21, 1983); *Paganini Personal* for Marimba and Orch. (Sapporo, July 2, 1983); *Time Surrounding* for Percussion and Orch. (Tokyo, March 1984); 2 syms. for Chamber Orch.: No. 1, *Time Current* (1986; Paris, Feb. 20, 1987) and No. 2, *Undercurrent* (Nagoya, Sept. 19, 1993; also for Orch., Oslo, Oct. 3, 1997); *Interspace* for Strings (Sapporo, March 19, 1987); *Berlin Renshi*, sym. for Soprano, Tenor, and Orch. (Tokyo, Nov. 18, 1988); *Existence* for Organ and Orch. (Tokyo, June 9, 1989); *Voices from the Environment* (Tokyo, Sept. 24, 1989); *The Origin*, concerto for Koto and Chamber Orch. (Brussels, Oct. 3, 1989); *Kyoto* (Kyoto, Dec. 26, 1989); *Luminous Space* for Sho, Ondes Martenot, and Orch. (Tokyo, Nov. 12, 1991); *Interplay* for Flute and Strings (Mito, Nov. 7, 1992); *Cosmos Ceremony* for Ryuteki, Sho, and Orch. (Osaka, Oct. 22, 1993); *Recollection of Reminiscence Beyond*, Sym. No. 4 (Osaka, Sept. 17, 1994); *Coexistence* for Shakuhachi and Strings (Osaka, Oct. 26, 1994; also for Ondes Martenot and Orch., Osaka, Oct. 31, 1996, and for Orch., Osaka, Nov. 3, 1997); *Inner Communications*, Sym. No. 3 (1994; Yokohama, Jan. 16, 1995); *Time Perspective*, Sym. No. 5 (NHK, Tokyo, Aug. 17, 1997). **CHAMBER:** Violin Sonata (N.Y., Dec. 1954); Trio for 2 Flutes and Harp (1956); 1 unnumbered string quartet (1956; N.Y., Feb. 1957), 3 numbered string quartets: No. 1 (1964), No. 2, *Interspace* (Vancouver, Dec. 1986), and No. 3, *Inner Landscape* (Tokyo, Nov. 14, 1994); *Vein of Sounds* for Harp (Tokyo, Oct. 25, 1972); *Scenes I* for Violin and Piano (1978), *II* for Violin and Piano (1979), *III* for Violin (1980), *IV* for Violin and Piano (Tokyo, Jan. 23, 1981), and *V* for Violin and Piano (Tokyo, Oct. 27, 1982); *Distance* for Noh Performer and Instrumental Ensemble (Cologne, Oct. 1978); *Perspectives* for Noh Dance, Flute, Violin, Viola, Cello, Percussion, and Electronics (Berlin, Oct. 1978); *Recurrence* for Flute, Clarinet, Percussion, Harp, Piano, Violin, and Cello (Middelburg, Netherlands, July 1979); *Kaze no Iroai* for Flute (Tokyo, July 1980); *Time in Tree, Time in Water* for Percussion and Piano (Cologne, Sept. 19, 1981); *Before Darkness Appears* for Accordion and Piano (Tokyo, Dec. 1981); *Flowers Blooming in Summer* for Harp and Piano (Tokyo, Oct. 15, 1982); *Portrait of Forest* for Marimba (Tokyo, Sept. 28, 1983); *Wind Trace* for Keyboard and Percussion (Tokyo, June 1, 1984); *Cloud Figures* for Oboe (Tokyo, Nov. 7, 1984); *Generation of Space* for Contrabass (Tokyo, June 1, 1985); *Yami o Irodoru Mono* for 2 Violins and Piano (Kusatsu, Aug. 28, 1985); *Prāna*, quintet for Flute, Clarinet, Violin, Cello, and Piano (Paris, Sept. 1, 1985); *Présage* for 6 Ondes Martenot (1986; Marseilles, Feb. 18, 1987); *Still Time III* for Harp (Lerchenborg, Aug. 1987) and *IV* for Flute (Yokohama, April 10, 1996); *Wind Stream* for Flute (Sapporo, June 30, 1989); *The Source* for Marimba (1989; Tokyo, June 21, 1990); *Troposphere* for Ondes Martenot and Marimba (Yokohama, Sept. 14, 1990); *Trio Interlink* for Violin, Piano, and Percussion (Tokyo, Nov. 26, 1990); *Friends* for Violin (Tokyo, Dec. 17, 1990); *Intoxicant Moon* for Ondes Martenot (Yokohama, Sept. 6, 1991); *Aki o Utsu Oto* for Marimba (Tokyo, Oct. 28, 1991); *Interrelation* for Cello and Piano (Tokyo, Dec. 12, 1991); *Aquascape* for Marimba, Flute, Piano, and 2 Percussion (Tokyo, Jan. 11, 1992); *Cosmos for Coexistence* for Marimba and Piano (Osaka, Jan. 18, 1992); *Reflection* for 9 Players (Osaka, Oct. 28, 1992); *Intercross* for Violin and Piano (Paris, Jan. 30, 1993); *Rhythm Gradation* for Timpani (Tokyo, April 22, 1993); *Omniscape* for Violin (Tokyo, Sept. 7, 1993); Trio Fantasy for Piano, Violin, and Cello (Yono, Oct. 15, 1994); *Cosmic Harmony* for Cello and Piano (Kronberg, Oct. 22, 1995); *Existence* for Clarinet and Piano (Yokohama, Aug. 17, 1997); *"Mirage"* for English Horn and Double Bass (Tokyo, Sept. 1, 1998). **KEYBOARD: P i a n o :** *Two Existence* for 2 Pianos (Tokyo, June 14, 1980); *Cloud Atlas* (1984 et seq.); *Inter Konzert* (Tokyo, April 30, 1987); *Piano Nature* (Tokyo, May 31, 1989); *Inexhaustible Fountain* (Osaka, Jan. 29, 1990); *Farewell to...* (Tokyo, Feb. 6, 1992); *In Memory of John Cage* (1992–93; Tokyo, April 8, 1993); *Imaginary Scenes* (Tokyo, Nov. 17, 1995). **O r g a n :** *Multiple Spaces* (Bremen, May 25, 1976); *Dimensions* (Yokohama, Oct. 12, 1990); *Fantasy* (Tokyo, Sept. 1992). **VOCAL:** *Extended Voices* for Voices and Synthesizer (1967); *Syntax* for Chorus (Tokyo, Sept. 30, 1977); *Aru Toki* for Soprano and Piano (Tokyo, Nov. 1981); *Heso no Uta* for Children's Chorus (Tokyo, Nov. 11, 1984); *Nadare no Toki* for Chorus, Marimba, and Piano (Tokyo, March 22, 1985); *Requiem* for Men's Chorus (Tokyo, Dec. 1985); *Genshiryoku Sensuikan "Onagazame" no Seitekina Kokai to Jisatsu no Uta* for Chorus (Tokyo, Feb. 24, 1989); *Music for Art Kites* for Soprano and Flute (Shizuoka, Aug. 13, 1989); *Desire* for Chorus (Tokyo, Jan. 20, 1992); *Hikari no Toride, Kaze no Shiro* for Chorus (Nakaniida, Aug. 2, 1992); *White Horse* for Men's Chorus (Tokyo, Nov. 25, 1993); *My Song* for Mezzo-soprano and Marimba (Tokyo, Sept. 14, 1994); *Scenes of Poems I* for Chorus and Cello (Osaka, Sept. 18, 1994) and *II* for Chorus (Nakaniida, Aug. 9, 1998); *Sora ni Kotori ga Inakunatta Hi* for Chorus (Tokyo, March 20, 1995); *Voice Perspectives* for Voice and Sho (Cologne, Dec. 6, 1996); *Oral Poetry of the Native American* for Chorus and Flute (Tokyo, March 24, 1997). **ELECTRONIC:** *Tokyo 1969* (NHK, Tokyo, Jan. 1969); *Theater Music* (1969); *Mandalama* (1969); *Environmental Music 1, 2,* and *3* (1970); *Music for Living Space* (1970); *The World* (1975). **OTHER:** *Ōgenraku* for Gagaku Ensemble and Shomyo (Tokyo, Oct. 30, 1980; also for Gagaku Ensemble, Tokyo, April 9, 1996); *Wa* for 2 Kotos, Piano, and Percussion (Berlin, Sept. 12, 1981); *Enenraku* for Gagaku Ensemble (Tokyo, Oct. 30, 1982); *Rinkaiiki* for Sangen (Tokyo, Feb. 9, 1983); *Galaxy* for Sho (Tokyo, Feb. 23, 1983); *Hikari-nagi* for Ryuteki and Percussion (Tokyo, May 14, 1983); *Density* for Shakuhachi, 2 Kotos, and Sangen (Tokyo, March 1984); *Cloud Shore, Wind Roots* for Reigaku and Gagaku Ensemble (Tokyo, Sept. 28, 1984); *Yochô* for Ryuteki and Piano (Tokyo, May 7, 1985); *"Interspace"* for Sho and Harp (Tokyo, April 12, 1986); *Still Time I* for Sho (1986), *II* for Kugo (Tokyo, March 7, 1986), and *III* for Hokyo (Hong Kong, March 4, 1998); *"The Shadows Appearing Through Darkness"*, sym. for Reigaku, Gagaku, and Shomyo (Tokyo, Sept. 29, 1987); *Katachi naki Mugen no Yoka* for Koto (Sapporo, Oct. 15, 1987); *Voices of Water* for Hitsu (Tokyo, March 11, 1988); *Sensing the Color in the Wind* for Shakuhachi and 2 Kotos (Tokyo, March 16, 1988); *Ten, Zui, Ho, Gyaku* for Shakuhachi and Ondes Martenot (Tokyo, March 16, 1988); *Prāna* for Ryuteki, Hichiriki, Sho, Kugo, Hensho, and Dancer (Tokyo, Nov. 25, 1988); *Transfiguration of the Moon* for Violin and Show (Tokyo, Dec. 4, 1988); *Transfiguration of the Flower* for Koto, Sange, and Shakuhachi (Tokyo, Dec. 16, 1988); *Water Relativity* for Hitsu and Kin (Tokyo, Feb. 23, 1989); *Wind Gradation* for

Ryuteki and Piano (Los Angeles, April 22, 1989); *Jitsugetsu Byobu Isso-Kokai*, sym. for Gagaku, Reigaku, and Shomyo (Tokyo, Sept. 29, 1989); *The Way I* for 2 Ryutekis, 2 Hichirikis, 2 Shos, Shakuhachi, Biwa, 2 Kotos, 2 Percussion, and Dancer (N.Y., Feb. 21, 1990) and *II* for 4 Hichirikis, 4 Ryutekis, 5 Shos, Biwa, 2 Kotos, Shakuhachi, 3 Percussion, 10 Shomyos, and Dance (Frankfurt am Main, Oct. 2, 1990); *Projection* for Koto (Tokyo, May 27, 1991); *Compound Time–Resonance, Luster, and Color* for Shakuhachi and 2 Kotos (Tokyo, March 4, 1992); *Brightening Wind* for Sho and Piano (Tokyo, April 3, 1992); *Tenryuji* for Ryuteki, Shakuhachi, Sho, Koto, Ondes Martenot, and Percussion (Kyoto, Sept. 19, 1992); *Toki Sayuru* for Koto and Piano (Tokyo, Dec. 10, 1993); *Uchu Kuyo Bosatsu* for Gagaku, Reigaku, and Shomyo (Tokyo, July 18, 1994); *Music for Violin, Sho, and Piano* (N.Y., Feb. 24, 1995); *Spiritual Light* for Gagaku, Reigaku, Shomyo, and Cello (Yokohama, Nov. 17, 1996); *Land Mystery* for Shakuhachi and Koto (Tokyo, April 11, 1997); *"Mirage"* for Shakuhachi and Piano (London, Oct. 22, 1998).
—NS/LK/DM

Idelsohn, Abraham Zevi, eminent Latvian musicologist; b. Pfilsburg, near Libau, July 13, 1882; d. Johannesburg, Aug. 14, 1938. He began his training as a Jewish cantor in Libau. After attending the Stern Cons. in Berlin, he studied at the Leipzig Cons. with Jadassohn (harmony), Krehl (counterpoint), Zoellner (composition), and Kretzschmar (music history). He was a cantor of the Regensburg Synagogue (1903–05), and then was active in Jerusalem (1906–21), where he founded the Inst. for Jewish Music (1910) and a Jewish music school (1919). From 1924 until suffering a paralytic stroke in 1934 he was a lecturer at the Hebrew Union Coll. in Cincinnati. Idelsohn was leading authority on Jewish music. His most important work was the monumental *Hebräisch-Orientalischer Melodienschatz* (10 vols., Leipzig, 1914–32; Eng. tr. as *Thesaurus of Hebrew-Oriental Melodies*, and Hebrew tr. as *Otzar Negionoth Ysrael*). He also ed. *Sefer ha-Shirim* (A New Collection of Hebrew Songs; Berlin, 1922), *Tzelilé ha-Aretz* (Love and Folk-Songs; Berlin, 1922), and a *Jewish Song Book for the Synagogue, Home and School* (Cincinnati, 1928). Among his own compositions were the music drama *Jephtah* (1922), syngogue services, and Hebrew songs.

WRITINGS: *Phonographierte Gesänge und Aussprachsproben des Hebräischen der jemenitischen, persischen und syrischen Juden* (Vienna, 1917); *Manual of Musical Illustrations...on Jewish Music* (Cincinnati, 1926); *The Ceremonies of Judaism* (Cincinnati, 1929); *Jewish Music in its Historical Development* (N.Y., 1929); *Jewish Liturgy and Its Development* (N.Y., 1932).—NS/LK/DM

Idol, Billy (originally, **Broad, William Michael Albert**), one of the performers who made punk safe for a pop audience; b. Stanmore, Middlesex, England, Nov. 30, 1955. Although born in England, from the ages of three to seven William Broad lived in the N.Y.C. area, after which his father returned the family to England. Bored in school, one of his teachers accused him of being "Aidle," a word that would come back to haunt him. By 1975, he became part of the growing wave of British punk as a member of the group Bromley Contingent. One of the other members of the group was a woman named Susan Dallion, who like Broad would earn notoriety under another name, Siouxsie Sioux with her band The Banshees. Broad then played with Mick Jones and Brian James in a group called Chelsea. Jones went on to The Clash, James to The Damned, and Broad, now known as Billy Idol, took bassist Tony James and drummer John Towe and formed the group Generation X, named after a novel of 1960s youth culture. Riding the crest of the punk wave, Generation X put out three albums, the final one as GenX. That album had the worldwide hit "Dancing with Myself." As so frequently happens, just as the band had a hit, it developed problems with management and broke up. James went on to form Sigue Sigue Sputnik.

Idol left England and went back to N.Y. There he hooked up with former Kiss manager Bill Aucoin, producer Keith Forsey, and guitarist Steve Stevens. He kicked off his solo career with an EP that featured a remix of "Dancing with Myself" and a cover of the Tommy James and the Shondells hit "Mony Mony." Both became popular dance hits and set the stage for his eponymous solo debut album in 1982. Featuring the #23 hit "Hot in the City" and the #36 "White Wedding," with a snazzy video that became a staple on MTV, Idol started to establish himself as more than a British punk. He was becoming a pop artist to reckon with. Idol's popularity increased a year later with the release of *Rebel Yell*. While the title track became popular at both album rock and modern rock stations, it was the moody ballad "Eyes without a Face" that zoomed to #4, taking the album to #6 and double platinum. The #29 hit "Flesh for Fantasy" added to the pop power of the former punk. He launched his next album, 1986's *Whiplash Smile* with a cover of William Bell's "I Forgot to be Your Lover" whichrecorded as "To Be a Lover." He took that song to #6 propelling the album to platinum and #6. Two minor hits, the #37 "Don't Need a Gun" and the #20 "Sweet Sixteen" followed. However, after the album, Stevens split to form his own band, The Atomic Playboys.

While regrouping, Idol released a greatest hits/remix album, *Vital Idol*. The album went to #10 and sold platinum, largely due to the chart topping remix of "Mony Mony." Anxious to go into the studio, Idol began recording *Charmed Life*, but ironically fell victim to a motorcycle accident that nearly cost him a leg. His injury prevented him from taking a major role in Oliver Stone's movie *The Doors*. *Charmed Life* was finally released in 1990. Fueled by the #2 single "Cradle of Love," which was featured in the film *The Adventures of Ford Fairlane*, the album hit #11 and went platinum. Idol attempted to jump into electronic music with 1993's *Cyberpunk*. While the album made use of the CD's innate computer friendly nature with graphics and video, it nonetheless did not sell well. Since this first professional disappointment, Idol sightings became fewer and further between. He toured with the Who when they staged their all-star version of *Quadrophenia*, and contributed a song to the soundtrack to the film *Speed*. He made a cameo appearance as himself in the 1997 movie *The Wedding Singer* and voiced the villain in the animated movie *Heavy Metal FAKK 2*. He signed a new recording contract late in 1999, and future recordings are likely to follow.

DISC.: *Don't Stop* (1981); *Billy Idol* (1982); *Rebel Yell* (1983); *Whiplash Smile* (1986); *Vital Idol* (1987); *Charmed Life* (1990); *Cyberpunk* (1993).—**HB**

Ifukube, Akira, Japanese composer; b. Kushiro, March 7, 1914. As a young man, he was trained in forestry. He then took lessons from Alexander Tcherepnin. His music is rooted in Japanese modalities, but he adorns them with impressionistic harmonies.

WORKS: DRAMATIC: Ballet: *Salome* (1948); *Enchanted Citadel* (Tokyo, Dec. 20, 1949); *Fire of Prometheus* (1950); *Drums of Japan* (Tokyo, Dec. 29, 1951); *The Martyrs of Japan* (Tokyo, March 30, 1972). **ORCH.:** *Japanese Rhapsody* (1935; Boston, April 5, 1936); *Triptyque aborigène* (1937); Piano Concerto (1941; Tokyo, March 3, 1942; MS destroyed in an air raid); *Ballade symphonique* (Tokyo, Nov. 20, 1943); *Arctic Forest* (Changchun, Manchuria, April 26, 1944); 2 violin concertos: No. 1 (Tokyo, June 22, 1948) and No. 2 (1978); *Bascana* (1949); *Rapsodia concertante* for Violin and Orch. (1951); *Buddha* (1953); *Sinfonia Tapkaara* (1954; Indianapolis, Jan. 21, 1955; rev. 1979; Tokyo, April 6, 1980); *Ritmica ostinata* for Piano and Orch. (1961); *Rondo in Burlesque* for Concert Band (1972); *Lauda concertata* for Marimba and Orch. (1976; rev. 1979); *Eglogue symphonique* for Orch. and Japanese Instruments (1982); *Gotama, the Buddha,* symphonic ode for Chorus and Orch. (1989); *Tomo no Oto,* orch. paraphrase (1990); *Japanese Suite* (1991); Kushiro Marshland, symphonic tableaux (1993). **OTHER:** *Okhotsk,* choral ode for Chorus and Orch. (1958); guitar pieces.—**NS/LK/DM**

Iglesias, Julio, the leading Latin lover in the music world for nearly three decades; b. Madrid, Spain, Sept. 23, 1943. While studying law, a young Julio Iglesias was an idol in Spain as the goalie for the Real Madrid soccer team. A car accident cut short his soccer career and very nearly killed him, putting him in the hospital for three years. As part of his therapy, he was given a guitar. He learned how to play and started to explore another innate talent, writing songs. He finished his studies at Cambridge Univ. and entered his song "La Vida Sigue Igual" in the Spanish Song Festival in 1968. His performance of the tune won first prize, and he was quickly signed by Discos Columbia. Two years later, he entered the Eurovision Song Contest with the song "Gwendolyne," which he would record in French, Italian and English as well as Spanish. In the mid-1970s, Igleias became a major star in Europe and Latin America, touring incessantly. He landed international hits with his 1975 recording "Manuela" and "Hey" in 1979. In 1981 "Begin the Beguine" topped the charts in England, and he started his foray into English speaking markets in earnest. His 1983 album *Julio* introduced him to American audiences, rising to #32 in the charts and selling a million copies that year. It would go double platinum 11 years later.

His major splash into the Anglo-American market came in 1984. He and his regular producer, Ramon Arcusa, teamed with hit-making American producer Richard Petty. They paired Iglesias with icons of American pop like Willie Nelson and Diana Ross. The resulting album, *1100 Bel Air Place,* produced the #5 platinum single "To All the Girls I've Loved Before," a duet with Nelson and "All of You," which sent him and Ross to #19. The album also went to #5 and initially sold two millions copies, eventually going quadruple platinum. By the end of the 1980s, Iglesias had reportedly sold over 100 million albums worldwide. He was cited in the *Guinness Book of World Records* for Athe most record sales in more languages than any other artist." His 1987 album *Un Hombre Solo* won him a Best Latin Performance Grammy. His 1991 album *Starry Night* went gold and hit #37 on the charts. His next English Language recording, *Crazy,* included duets with Dolly Parton, Art Garfunkel, and Sting. Ironically, he thought the title track—a 1959 hit by Nelson for Patsy Cline—was a recent song written especially for political candidate Ross Perot, who used it as his theme in the 1992 presidential campaign. The album went to #30 and sold gold. Iglesias continued to record multi-language albums and play to huge, sell-out audiences. His 1997 album, *Tango,* went gold, and his 1999 *My Life: The Greatest Hits* was released in several customized versions, including Asian, Spanish, French, Italian, Portuguese, and an English/worldwide edition.

His son, Enrique (b. Madrid, Spain, May 8, 1975), became a pop phenomenon in the late 1990s. Like his father, he initially recorded in Spanish, and then expanded into Italian and Portuguese. By late 1999, he had sold over 10 million albums and toured widely through the world. In late 1999, he released his first English-language album, and immediately hit it big with the Latin-flavored single, "Bailamos."

DISC.: *Soy Discos* (1970); *A Flor de Piel* (1974); *America* (1976); *Emociones* (1979); *Hey!* (1980); *From a Child to a Woman* (1981); *Momentos* (1981); *De Niña a Mujer* (1982); *Moments* (1982); *In Concert* (live; 1983); *Julio* (1983); *Bel Air Place* (1984); *Libra* (1985); *Sentimental* (1986); *Non Stop* (1986); *A Mis 33 Años* (1986); *El Amor* (1987); *Et L'Amour Crea la Femme* (1987); *Raíces* (1987); *Un Hombre Solo* (1987); *Por una Mujer Discos* (1989); *Aimer la Vie...* (1990); *Innamorarsi alla Mia Età* (1990); *Starry Night* (1990); *Begin the Beguine Discos* (1990); *En Concierto* (live; 1991); *Calor* (1992); *Crazy* (1994); *La Carretera* (1995); *Tango* (1996); *Piano Instrumentals* (1997); *24 Grandes Éxitos Latinos* (1998); *Corazón Latino* (1998).—**HB**

Igumnov, Konstantin (Nikolaievich), distinguished Russian pianist and pedagogue; b. Lebedyan, near Tambov, May 1, 1873; d. Moscow, March 24, 1948. He studied piano with Zverev and Siloti, and theory with Taneyev, Arensky, and Ippolitov-Ivanov at the Moscow Cons., graduating as a pianist in the class of Pabst (1894). He gave numerous concerts, specializing in Romantic music, and was regarded as an artist of impeccable taste who worked out every detail of the music to the utmost perfection. But great as his artistic reputation was in Russia (he rarely, if ever, played abroad), his main accomplishment was as a piano pedagogue. He was appointed a prof. of the Moscow Cons. in 1899, and remained on its staff until his death. Among his students were Nikolai Orlov, Dobrowen, and Oborin. In 1946 he was made a People's Artist of the U.S.S.R.

BIBL.: Y. Milstein, *K.N. I.* (Moscow, 1975).—**NS/LK/DM**

Ikebe, Shin-Ichiro, Japanese composer and teacher; b. Mito City, Sept. 15, 1943. He studied with

Ikenouchi, Yashiro, and Miyoshi at the Tokyo Univ. of Fine Arts and Music (graduated, 1967), where he later was an assistant (1971–77). Subsequently he served as a prof. at the Tokyo Coll. of Music. He won the Prix Italia in 1976, the music prize of the Japanese Academy in 1980, 1984, and 1992, and the Otaka Prize in 1991.

WORKS: DRAMATIC: *The Death Goddess*, opera (NHK-TV, July 25, 1971); *The Whistling of the Wind*, television musical fantasy (1976); *The Silence*, radiophonic music drama (1977); *The Adventures of Pinocchio*, musical comedy (1981); *Hoichi, the Earless*, opera (1982); *Cleopatra, Her Love and Death*, ballet (1983); *Mobile et Immobile*, ballet (1984); *The Window*, musical drama (1986); *Chichibu-Bansho*, opera (1988); *Taro's Tree*, choral opera (1991–92); *Oshichi*, opera (1995); *Dugong's Lullaby*, opera (1996). ORCH.: *Movement* (1965); *Construction* (1966); 2 piano concertos: No. 1 (1966–67) and No. 2, *Tu M'* (1987); 6 numbered syms.: No. 1 (1967; Tokyo, March 30, 1968), No. 2, *Trias* (1979), No. 3, *Ego Phano* (1984), No. 4 (1990), No. 5, *Simplex* (1990), and No. 6, *On the Individual Coordinates* (1993); 2 unnumbered syms.: *Petite symphonie pour enfants* for Small Orch. (1969) and *Symphony for Green and Friendship* (1987); *Lion* for Brass Ensemble (1969); *Energia* for 60 Players (1970); *Dimorphism* for Organ and Orch. (1974); *Quadrants* for Japanese Instruments and Orch. (1974); *"Haru-no-umi"* (1980); Violin Concerto (1981); *Imagine* (1983); *Overture for the Time of Flying Star* (1984); *Overture for the Coming of the New Spring* (1986); *Overture for the Nile* (1988); *Spontaneous Ignition* (1989); *Hokkai Swells*, symphonic study (1992); *Fantasy of Ryukyo* (1993); *Almost a Tree*, cello concerto (1996); *Les Bois Tristes* (1998). CHAMBER: Violin Sonata (1965); *Crepa in sette capitoli* for Violin, 3 Violas, Cello, and Double Bass (1966); Trio for Oboe, Clarinet, and Bassoon (1966); *Raccontino* for Violin and Piano (1967); *Un-en* for 2 Kotos, Ju-shichi-gen, Violin, Viola, Cello, and Double Bass (1970); *Clipper by 9* for Nonet (1971); *Trivalence I* for Flute, Violin, and Piano or Organ (1971) and *II* for Harpsichord, Clarinet, and Cello (1973); *Flash!* for Flute Ensemble (1972); *Monovalence I* for Marimba (1972); *Spirals* for 9 Horns (1979); *Black Blank Blaze* for 9 Clarinets (1982); *Strata I* for String Quartet (1988), *II* for Flute (1988), *III* for Clarinet and Cello (1989), *IV* for Oboe and Double Bass (1994), and *V* for String Quartet (1995); *Safari I* and *II* for Percussion (1990); *Quinquévalence* for Violin, Viola, Cello, Double Bass, and Piano (1991); *Thermal Conductivity* for Ondes Martenot (1995); *Quatrevalence II* for Clarinet, Violin, Cello, and Piano (1997); *Bivalence I* for 2 Cellos (1997) and *II* for 2 Violins (1997). PIANO: *Hitches in the Stories* (1988). VOCAL: *Kusabi* for Women's Chorus, 11 Players, and Dancers (1972); *Mizu Kuguru Monogatari* for Soprano, Baritone, Women's Chorus, and Chamber Orch. (1984); *Oedipus's Pilgrimage* for Joruri, Men's Chorus, and 10 Players (1984); *Himeji*, symphonic poem for Chorus and Orch. (1989); *For a Beautiful Star*, cantata (1990); *The Freezing Fields, Brilliantly*, cantata (1998); choruses; songs.—NS/LK/DM

Ikenouchi, Tomojirô, Japanese composer and pedagogue; b. Tokyo, Oct. 21, 1906; d. there, March 9, 1991. He was the first Japanese student at the Paris Cons. (1926–36), where he studied with Fauchet (harmony), Caussade (fugue), and Büsser (composition) and took the premier prix in harmony. In 1936 he joined the faculty of Nihon Univ. in Tokyo, and then was prof. of composition at the Tokyo National Univ. of Fine Arts and Music from 1947. Ikenouchi was highly esteemed as a teacher. His small but well-crafted output reflects the influence of his Western training.

WORKS: DRAMATIC: *Yuya* (1942; Tokyo, Feb. 1, 1943).

ORCH.: *3 Pieces* (1937); *4 Seasons* (1938); *Umaki-Uta* (1938); Sym. (Tokyo, Nov. 4, 1951). CHAMBER: 3 string quartets (1937, 1945, 1946); *Fantasy* for Cello and Piano (1940); Flute Sonata (1946); Violin Sonata (1946); Cello Sonatina (1946). Piano: Sonatina (1946); *Ceremonial Music*, duet (1958). VOCAL: *Koi no omoni* (Burden of Love) for Baritone, Chorus, and Timpani (1974).—NS/LK/DM

Ikonen, Lauri, Finnish musicologist and composer; b. Mikkeli, Aug. 10, 1888; d. Helsinki, March 21, 1966. He studied at the Univ. of Helsinki and with Paul Juon in Berlin (1910–13). He was ed. of the Finnish music magazine *Suomen Musikkilehti* (1923–29). His music followed the Romantic tradition of Sibelius.

WORKS: ORCH.: 6 syms.: No 1, *Sinfonia inornata* (1922), No. 2 (1937), No. 3, *Lemmin poika* (Son of Lemmi; 1941; rev. 1959), No. 4, *Sinfonia concentrata* (1942), No. 5, *Sinfonia aperta* (1943), and No. 6 (1956); Violin Concerto (1939); *Concerto meditativo* for Cello and Orch. (1942). CHAMBER: Piano Trio (1941); 2 violin sonatas. Piano: *Concerto intimo* (1956); Piano Sonata. VOCAL: *Koulemaantuomitun mielialoja* (Thoughts of a Condemned Man) for Baritone and Orch. (1936); *Elaman lahja* (The Gift of Life) for Soloists, Chorus, and Orch. (1956); choral works; songs.—NS/LK/DM

Ikonomov, Boyan Georgiev, Bulgarian composer; b. Nikopol, Dec. 14, 1900; d. Sofia, March 27, 1973. He studied in Sofia (1920–26); then went to Paris, where he attended classes of d'Indy and Lioncourt at the Schola Cantorum (1928–32); also had lessons with Boulanger and Roussel, and then took a course in conducting with Weingartner in Basel (1934). Returning to Bulgaria, he was music director of Sofia Radio (1937–48) and of the Bulgarian film center (1948–56); then was head of the music dept. of Sofia Radio (1957–60). His music was rooted in Bulgarian folk songs, with an emphasis on modal melodic progressions and asymmetric rhythms.

WORKS: DRAMATIC: Opera: *Indje Voivoda* (1960). Ballet: *The 7 Mortal Sins* (1933); *The Tragedy of Othello* (1946); *The Light Floods Everything* (1967). ORCH.: *Haidouk Rhapsody* (1932); Sinfonietta (1934); *Kaliakra*, symphonic poem (1935); *Pastorale* for Chamber Orch. (1937); 4 syms. (1937, 1947, 1955, 1971); *Pastorale and Dance* (1939); *Shar Planina*, symphonic poem (1942); Violin Concerto (1951); *Divertimento* for String Quartet and Orch. (1956); Piano Concertino (1958). CHAMBER: 6 string quartets (1933, 1937, 1941, 1944, 1945, 1949); 2 trios for Oboe, Clarinet, and Bassoon (1935, 1968); Cello Sonata. VOCAL: 2 cantatas: *George Dimitrov* (1954) and *Poem about Lenin* (1969); 2 oratorios: *The Legend of Shipka* (1968) and *Vassil Levsky* (1972); choruses; songs.—NS/LK/DM

Ilerici, Kemal, Turkish composer; b. Kastamonu, Oct. 15, 1910. He studied composition with Ferit Alnar. Among his works are a symphonic suite, *In My Village* (1945), *Pastoral Fantasy* for Orch. (1951), String Quartet, Suite for Oboe and Piano, and choral works. He wrote a book on Turkish music, *Turk musikisi tonal sistemi ve armonisi* (1948).—NS/LK/DM

Iliev, Konstantin, Bulgarian conductor, teacher, and composer; b. Sofia, March 9, 1924; d. there, March 6,

1988. He studied composition with Khadzhiev and Vladigerov, and conducting with Goleminov, at the Bulgarian State Cons. in Sofia (1942–46); later took courses in composition with Řídký and A. Hába, and in conducting with Talich, at the Prague Cons. (1946–47). He conducted at the Sofia Opera (1948–49); after serving as chief conductor of the Ruse Opera and Sym. Orch. (1949–52), and then of the Varna Sym. Orch. (1952–56), he was principal conductor of the Sofia Phil. (1956–85). From 1964 to 1985 he was on the faculty of the Bulgarian State Cons. in Sofia. As a composer, he evolved a rather stimulating idiom, adroitly exploring the asymmetric Balkan rhythms and oriental melismas to create an aura of folkloric authenticity; in non-ethnic pieces he often applied serial principles of melodic formations.

WORKS: DRAMATIC: Opera: *The Master of Boyana* (Sofia, Oct. 3, 1962); *The Kingdom of the Deer* (1975). **ORCH.:** 5 syms. (1947, 1951, 1954, 1958, 1959); *Concerto grosso* for Strings, Piano, and Percussion (1949); *Symphonic Variations* (1951); *Tempi concertanti I* for Strings (1967) and *II* for Flute, Harpsichord, and 12 Instruments (1969); Violin Concerto (1971). **CHAMBER:** 4 string quartets (1949, 1952, 1953, 1956); Piano Trio (1976); *7 Bagatelles* for Clarinet and Cello (1987). **VOCAL:** *Eulogy to Constantin the Philosopher*, oratorio (1971); choruses. **—NS/LK/DM**

Ilitsch, Daniza, Serbian soprano; b. Belgrade, Feb. 21, 1914; d. Vienna, Jan. 15, 1965. She studied at the Stankovic Cons. in Belgrade, then in Berlin. She made her operatic debut as Nedda in *Pagliacci* with the Berlin State Opera (Nov. 6, 1936); was on its roster for 2 seasons, then was a member of the Vienna State Opera (1938–41). The German army of occupation put her in a concentration camp in 1944, and she spent 4 months there until the liberation of Vienna. She made her debut with the Metropolitan Opera in N.Y. as Desdemona (March 12, 1947), remaining on its roster until 1948. Thereafter she pursued her career in Europe and South America. In 1959 she settled in Vienna. She was principally known for her roles in Italian opera, including Aida, Desdemona, Gioconda, Amelia, and Cio-Cio-San. **—NS/LK/DM**

Il Verso, Antonio, Italian composer; b. Piazza Armerina, Sicily, c. 1560; d. Palermo, c. Aug. 23, 1621. Following studies with Pietro Vinci (1582–84), he lived most of his life in Palermo, where he was active as a teacher and composer. His extant works include madrigals (10 vols.), motets (3 vols.), and a vol. of instrumental pieces. A complete ed. of his works was prepared by P. Carapezza et al. in Musiche Rinascimentali Siciliane, II-III and VI-VIII (1971–78).**—LK/DM**

Ilyinsky, Alexander Alexandrovich, Russian composer; b. Tsarskoye Selo, Jan. 24, 1859; d. Moscow, Feb. 23, 1920. He graduated from the St. Petersburg Cons. (1885), and also studied in Berlin with Kullak (piano) and Bargiel (composition). Upon returning to Moscow, he was a teacher at the Phil. Inst. (1885–1905). He wrote an opera, *The Fountain of Bakhchisaray* (1911), *3 valses brillantes* for Piano, and several orch. works.**—NS/LK/DM**

Imai, Nobuko, Japanese violist; b. Tokyo, March 18, 1943. She was a student of Toshiya Eto and Hideo Saito at the Toho School of Music in Tokyo (B.A., 1965), of David Schwartz and Broadus Erle at Yale Univ. Graduate School (1965–66), and of Walter Trampler at the Juilliard School of Music in N.Y. (1966–68). She took first prize at both the Munich (1967) and Geneva (1968) international viola competitions. In 1967 she made her U.S. debut in N.Y., and in 1969 she made her British debut. From 1974 to 1979 she was a member of the Vermeer Quartet. She also appeared as a soloist with leading European and American orchs., and performed at various festivals. She was a member of the Casals Hall Quartet in Tokyo from 1990. Imai was a prof. at the Detmold Hochschule für Musik from 1985. Her repertoire encompasses scores from Haydn to Schnittke. She was a soloist in the premieres of Tippett's Triple Concerto (1980) and Takemitsu's Viola Concerto (1989). **—NS/LK/DM**

Imbrie, Andrew (Welsh), distinguished American composer and pedagogue; b. N.Y., April 6, 1921. He studied piano and composition with Ornstein (until 1942), and also received instruction in composition from Boulanger (1937) and in piano with R. Casadesus (1941). From 1937 he pursued composition studies with Sessions, graduating from Princeton Univ. with a B.A. in 1942. After serving in the U.S. Army during World War II, he completed his studies with Sessions at the Univ. of Calif. at Berkeley, where he took his M.A. in 1947. In the latter year he joined its faculty as an instructor in music, becoming an asst. prof. in 1951, assoc. prof. in 1957, and prof. in 1960, a position he held until 1991. He also taught at the San Francisco Cons. of Music, serving as chairman of its composition dept. from 1970. In 1991 he was the composer-in-residence at the Tanglewood Festival of Contemporary Music. In 1982 he was the Jacob Ziskind Visiting Professor at Brandeis Univ. He was a fellow at the American Academy in Rome (1947–49), returning there on a Guggenheim fellowship (1953–54) and as its composer-in-residence (1967–68). In 1960–61 he was in Tokyo on a second Guggenheim fellowship. In addition to various commissions, he won the N.Y. Music Critics's Circle Award for his first String Quartet (1944), the Alice M. Ditson Award (1947), and the Naumburg Award for his Violin Concerto (1954). His *Requiem* was nominated for a Grammy Award in 2000. In 1969 he was elected a member of the National Inst. of Arts and Letters, and in 1980 of the American Academy of Arts and Sciences. Imbrie's style of composition is marked by an expressive melodic line, while the polyphony is vigorously motile; harmonic confluence is dissonant but euphonious.

WORKS: DRAMATIC: Opera: *3 Against Christmas or Christmas in Peebles Town* (1960; Berkeley, Dec. 3, 1964); *Angle of Repose* (San Francisco, Nov. 6, 1976). **ORCH.:** *Ballad* (1947; Rome, June 20, 1949); Violin Concerto (1954; Berkeley, April 22, 1958); *Little Concerto* for Piano, 4-Hands, and Orch. (1956; Oakland, Nov. 14, 1961); *Legend* (San Francisco, Dec. 9, 1959); 3 syms.: No. 1 (1965; San Francisco, May 11, 1966), No. 2 (San Francisco, May 20, 1970), and No. 3 (Manchester, England, Dec. 4, 1970); Chamber Sym. (Hanover, N.H., Aug. 11, 1968); Cello Concerto (1972; Oakland, April 30, 1973); 3 piano concertos: No.

1 (Saratoga, Calif., Aug. 4, 1973), No. 2 (1974; Terre Haute, Ind., Jan. 2, 1976), and No. 3 (1992; N.Y., April 21, 1993); Flute Concerto (N.Y., Oct. 13, 1977). **CHAMBER:** 5 string quartets (1942, 1953, 1957, 1969, 1987); 2 trios for Violin, Cello, and Piano (1946, 1989); *Divertimento* for Flute, Bassoon, Trumpet, Violin, Cello, and Piano (1948); *Serenade* for Flute, Viola, and Piano (1952); *Impromptu* for Violin and Piano (1960); Cello Sonata (1966); *3 Sketches* for Trombone and Piano (1967); *Dandelion Wine* for Oboe, Clarinet, String Quartet, and Piano (1967); *To A Traveler* for Clarinet, Violin, and Piano (1971); *Pilgrimage* for Flute, Clarinet, Violin, Cello, Piano, and Percussion (1983); *Dream Sequence* for Flute, Oboe, Clarinet, Violin, Viola, Cello, Piano, and Percussion (1986); *3 Piece Suite* for Harp and Piano (1987); *Earplay Fantasy* for Flute, Clarinet, Violin, Cello, Piano, and Percussion (1996); *Spring Fever* for Flute, Oboe, Clarinet, Piano, Percussion, 2 Violins, Viola, Cello, and Contrabass (1997); *Chicago Bells* for Violin and Piano (1997); *Soliloquy* for Violin (1998); Piano Quartet (1998). **KEYBOARD: Piano:** Sonata (1947); *Short Story* (1982); *Daedalus* (1986); *Mukashi mukashi* (Once Upon a Time) for 2 Pianos (1997). **Organ:** *Prelude* (1987). **VOCAL:** *On the Beach at Night* for Chorus and String Orch., after Walt Whitman (1949); *Drum-Taps* for Chorus and Orch., after Walt Whitman (1960); *Prometheus Bound* for 3 Soloists, Double Chorus, Orch., and Dance (1979); *5 Roethke Songs* for Soprano and Piano (1980); *3 Campion Songs* for Soprano, Alto, Tenor, Bass, and Piano (1981); *Song for St. Cecilia's Day* for Chorus, Brass, Percussion, 2 Pianos, Flute, and 2 Violins (1981); *Requiem: In memoriam John Imbrie* for Soprano, Chorus, and Orch. (1984); *Adam* for Soprano, Chorus, and Small Orch., after late medieval and American Civil War era texts (1994); *Songs of Then and Now* for Girl's Chorus, Flute, Clarinet, Violin, Cello, Piano, and Percussion, after R.L. Stevenson, e.e. cummings, and Shakespeare (1998).—NS/LK/DM

Impressions, The, vocal group that combined a gospel-soul sound with socially conscious lyrics (f. 1958, disbanded 1983). **MEMBERSHIP:** Jerry Butler, voc. (b. Sunflower, Miss., Dec. 8, 1939); Curtis Mayfield, voc., gtr. (b. Chicago, June 3, 1942, d. Atlanta, Dec. 26, 1999); Fred Cash, voc. (b. Chattanooga, Tenn., Oct. 8, 1940); Sam Gooden, voc. (b. Chattanooga, Tenn., Sept. 2, 1939). Going against the prevailing doo-wop sound of the late 1950s, The Impressions came by their gospel-without-God soul sound honestly. The group came together as The Impressions with the merger of the secular group The Roosters, which featured Sam Gooden and Richard and Arthur Brooks, and two members from the Northern Jubilee Gospel Singers, Curtis Mayfield and Jerry Butler. Butler sang lead on their groundbreaking debut, "For Your Precious Love," which was released as "The Impressions featuring Jerry Butler" and went to #11 pop. This generated some inter-group jealousy, and Butler left the group to begin one of the great solo careers in soul music. Mayfield split his time between working as Butler's music director and fixing the foundering Impressions. For Butler, he wrote and played on "He Will Break Your Heart," which topped the R&B charts for seven weeks, rising to #7 pop.

The Impressions recruited Fred Cash to replace Butler, and the Brooks brothers left the group, leaving them to seek their fortunes as a trio. Mayfield started writing in earnest, becoming the group's chief songwriter. They returned to the pop charts in 1961 with his

Brazilian-flavored "Gypsy Woman," which introduced the world to Mayfield's trademark falsetto and his remarkable guitar playing. The song rose to #20. After two years away from the Top 40, they returned with their biggest hit, "It's All Right." A light-hearted bluesy shuffle with big three part harmonies, it topped the R&B charts and rose to #4 pop during the fall of 1963. This started a string of ten big hits in a little over two years. All but the traditional "Amen," which went to #7 in 1964, were written by Mayfield. These include soul standards like "Talking about My Baby" (#12, 1964) and "I'm So Proud" (#14, 1964). "Keep on Pushing" (#10, 1964) and "Amen" sent the *Keep on Pushing* album to #8. "You Must Believe" (#15, 1964) and the epochal "People Get Ready" (#14, 1965). The *People Get Ready* album rose to #23. Mayfield proved a versatile creator, writing songs of love, songs of devotion and songs that began to reflect the conditions in African-American urban America. Even those often had an element of inspiration, as the R&B chart toppers "We're a Winner" (1968, #14 pop) and "Choice of Colors" (1969, #21 pop). The *We're a Winner* album went to #35.

By 1968, the band was releasing their records on Mayfield's own Curtom label. Mayfield also continued to work outside of the band, producing hits like "The Monkey Time" for Major Lance (#8, 1963), and "Just Be True" (#19, 1964) for Gene Chandler. In 1970, he left the band, pursuing a decidedly funkier sound starting with the #29 hit "(Don't Worry) If There's a Hell Below We're All Going to Go" in 1971, from the *Curtis* album, which went gold and hit #19. The apex of his solo career came a year later with the soundtrack to the film *Superfly*. This produced two gold singles. The title track, with its funky beat and swirling strings (a precursor to the sound that would inform disco several years later), went to #8 pop. The jazzier "Freddie's Dead," with it's gritty themes of drug abuse and men dying young, went to #4. The album topped the charts for four weeks, going gold.

The group had one more pop hit without Mayfield, "Finally Got Myself Together (I'm a Changed Man)." In 1974, the song rose to #1 on the R&B charts, hitting #17 pop. They went through several singers over the years. In 1983, Butler, Mayfield, Gooden and Cash got back together for a 25th anniversary tour, after which The Impressions disbanded. Butler and Mayfield continued to record and perform as solo artists. Additionally, Butler became the Cook County Commissioner and a Chicago City Alderman. In 1990, while setting up for a show in Brooklyn's Prospect Park, a lighting rig fell and severely injured Mayfield, paralyzing him from the neck down. The band was inducted into the Rock and Roll Hall of Fame in 1991, and Mayfield was inducted as a solo artist in 1999, but was too sick to attend either ceremony. He did manage to record his 25 solo album, *New World Order* in 1996, no mean feat for a 54-year-old quadriplegic. He died the day after Christmas, 1999.

DISC.: *The Impressions* (1963); *Keep on Pushing* (1964); *Never Ending Impressions* (1964); *For Your Precious Love* (1964); *One by One* (1965); *Big16* (1965); *People Get Ready* (1965); *Ridin' High* (1966); *The Fabulous Impressions* (1967); *We're a Winner* (1968); *This Is My Country* (1968); *Versatile* (1969); *The Young Mods'*

Forgotten Story (1969); *Check Out Your Mind* (1970); *Times Have Changed* (1972); *Preacher Man* (1973); *Finally Got Myself Together* (1974); *Three the Hard Way* (1974); *First Impressions* (1975); *Sooner or Later* (1975); *It's About Time* (1976); *Originals* (1976); *Loving Power* (1976); *Come to My Party* (1979); *Fan the Fire* (1981); *Right on Time* (1983); *It's All Alright* (1995); *Impressions/Never Ending Impressions* (1995).—**HB**

Inbal, Eliahu, prominent Israeli-English conductor; b. Jerusalem, Feb. 16, 1936. He received training in violin and theory at the Jerusalem Academy of Music (diploma, 1956). In 1956 he made his debut conducting the Youth Sym. Orch. of Israel. During military service, he was active with a combined army and youth orch. A recommendation from Bernstein in 1958 resulted in his receiving a scholarship from the Israel-America Foundation to pursue conducting studies with Fourestier at the Paris Cons. (1960–62). He also studied with Ferrara and Celibidache. After winning first prize in the Cantelli Competition in 1963, he appeared as a guest conductor with leading orchs. in Europe and the U.S. He also was active as an opera conductor from 1969. From 1974 to 1990 he was chief conductor of the Frankfurt am Main Radio Sym. Orch., which he led on its first tour of the U.S. in 1980. He also was artistic director of the Teatro La Fenice in Venice from 1983 to 1986. In 1996 he became principal conductor of the Orch. Nazionale d'Italia in Turin. He became chief conductor of the Berlin Sym. Orch. in 2000. Inbal has distinguished himself as an interpreter of both standard and modern scores. He has been especially admired for his cycles of works by Schumann, Bruckner, Mahler, and Scriabin.—**NS/LK/DM**

Inch, Herbert Reynolds, American composer and teacher; b. Missoula, Mont., Nov. 25, 1904; d. La Jolla, Calif., April 14, 1988. He was a student of Josephine Swenson and A.H. Weisberg at the Univ. of Mont. in Missoula, and then of Hanson and Edward Royce at the Eastman School of Music in Rochester, N.Y. (B.M., 1925; M.M., 1928); later took his Ph.D. at the Univ. of Rochester (1941). In 1931 he received a fellowship to the American Academy in Rome. After teaching at the Eastman School of Music (1925–28; 1930–31), he taught at Hunter Coll. in N.Y. (1937–65). Inch's works display a fine feel for lyrical and contrapuntal writing.

WORKS: ORCH.: *Variations on a Modal Theme* (Rochester, N.Y., April 29, 1927); *3 Pieces* for Small Orch. (Rochester, N.Y., Oct. 24, 1930); Sym. (Rochester, N.Y., May 5, 1932); *Serenade* for Small Orch. (Rochester, N.Y., Oct. 24, 1939); Piano Concerto (1940); *Answers to a Questionnaire* (1942); *Northwest Overture* (1943); Violin Concerto (1946–47; Rochester, N.Y., May 1, 1947); 3 symphoniettas (1948, 1950, 1955). **CHAMBER:** Piano Quintet (1930); 2 string quartets (1933, 1936); *Divertimento* for Brass (1934); 3 piano sonatas (1935, 1946, 1966); Cello Sonata (1941); Piano Trio (1963). **VOCAL:** *Return to Zion* for Women's Chorus and Piano (1945); choruses.—**NS/LK/DM**

Incledon, Charles, English tenor; b. St. Keverne, Cornwall (baptized), Feb. 5, 1763; d. London, Feb. 18, 1826. He was a chorister at Exeter Cathedral, and then began his career at the Southampton theater in 1784. Following training from Rauzzini, he made his London debut at Vauxhall Gardens in 1786. He subsequently was a leading singer at various London theaters. He also appeared widely as a concert artist, and was a soloist in the London premiere of Haydn's *Creation* in 1800. Incledon was notably successful with his appearances as "The Wandering Melodist," in which he presented popular sea and patriotic ballads. In 1817–18 he made a highly successful tour of the U.S. His farewell appearance took place in 1822.—**LK/DM**

d'India, Sigismondo, outstanding Italian composer; b. Palermo, c. 1582; d. probably in Modena, before April 19, 1629. He most likely traveled throughout Italy visiting various courts (1600–10), then was director of chamber music at the court of Carlo Emanuele I, Duke of Savoy, in Turin (1611–23). After working at the Este court in Modena (1623–24), he was in the service of Cardinal Maurizio of Savoy in Rome (1624–25); subsequently was in the service of the Este court in Modena. D'India was a master of secular vocal music, excelled only by the great Monteverdi. His output included 84 chamber monodies, polyphonic madrigals, motets, and villanellas, as well as works for the stage and some sacred music. At its finest, his music represents an assured command of the styles of Marenzio, Wert, Gesualdo, and Monteverdi, with a personal style marked by bold harmonic progressions. J. Joyce and G. Watkins ed. his works in Musiche Rinascimentali Siciliane (1980 et seq.).

WORKS: DRAMATIC: *Zalizura*, pastoral; *Sant'Eustacho*, sacred drama (Rome, 1625; not extant). **VOCAL: Secular Songs and Duets:** *Le musiche* for 1 to 2 Voices and Basso Continuo (Milan, 1609); *Le musiche* for 2 Voices and Basso Continuo (Venice, 1615); *Le musiche...libro III* for 1 to 2 Voices and Basso Continuo (Milan, 1618); *Le musiche* for 1 to 2 Voices and Basso Continuo, *con alcune arie, gue...libro IV* (Venice, 1621); *Le musiche* for 1 to 2 Voices and Basso Continuo, *con alcune arie, gui...libro V* (Venice, 1623). **Madrigals and Other Pieces:** *Il primo libro de madrigali* for 5 Voices (Milan, 1606); *Villanelle alla napolitana* for 3 to 5 Voices, *libro I* (Naples, 1608; not extant; 2nd ed., 1610); *Libro secondo de madrigali* for 5 Voices (Venice, 1611); *Libro secondo delle villanelle alla napolitana* for 3 to 5 Voices (Venice, 1612); *Il terzo libro de madrigali* for 5 Voices, Basso Continuo, and Other Instruments ad libitum, *ma necessariamente per gli 8 ultima* (Venice, 1615); *Il quarto libro de madrigali* for 5 Voices (Venice, 1616); *Il quinto libro de madrigali* for 5 Voices (Venice, 1616); *Le musiche e balli* for 4 Voices and Basso Continuo (Venice, 1621); *Settimo libro de madrigali* for 5 Voices (Rome, 1624); *Ottavo libro de madrigali* for 5 Voices and Basso Continuo (Rome, 1624). **Sacred:** *Novi concentus ecclesiastici* for 2 to 3 Voices and Basso Continuo (Venice, 1610); *Liber secundus sacrorum concentuum* for 3 to 6 Voices (Venice, 1610); *Liber primus motectorum* for 4 to 5 Voices and Basso Continuo (Venice, 1627).

BIBL.: F. Mompellio, *S. d'I., musicista palermitano* (Milan, 1956); J. Joyce, *The Monodies of S. d'I.* (Ann Arbor, 1981); G. Collisani, *S. d'I.* (Palermo, 1998).—**NS/LK/DM**

Indigo Girls, The, latter-day folk rock stars (f. ca. 1989, Atlanta) **MEMBERSHIP:** Amy Ray, gtr., voc. (b. Atlanta, April 12, 1964); Emily Saliers, gtr., voc. (b. New Haven, Conn., July 22, 1963). Although they had known each other since grade school, Amy Ray and Emily

Saliers first started singing together in the choir at their high school, before forming a folk rock duo. Starting as Saliers and Ray, then the B-Band, they started playing coffee houses and bar open mike nights. By 1981, they were playing often enough that they recorded a tape (as the B-Band) called *Tuesday's Children*. Upon graduation from high school, they went their separate ways, only to find that they missed Atlanta and each other. They both enrolled at Emory and started playing together again. They started calling themselves the Indigo Girls, Amy having picked the word out of the dictionary. They put out several independent recordings, sold at shows, including a single of "Crazy Came" and "Everybody's Waiting," a cassette called *Blue Food*, a six-track EP featuring local musicians like Michelle Malone, and finally a full length album, *Strange Fire*. From the start, the two formed a yin and yang symbiosis, with Ray creating more direct and rocking tunes countered by Saliers more considered, folk-oriented compositions. They also created some of the most stunning two part harmonies to grace pop music.

With the success of artists like Tracy Chapman and 10,000 Maniacs, The Indigo Girls were signed to Epic records in 1988. Their self-titled debut album cast them as part of the burgeoning Athens, Goergia, scene as well, with Michael Stipe singing on the tune "Kid Fears." Their first single, "Closer to Fine," peaked at #52 and the album climbed to #22. Epic next re-released a somewhat edited version of *Strange Fire*, which eventually went gold. At the 1989 Grammy Awards, the duo took home the statuette for Best Contemporary Folk Recording. Eventually, the record went double platinum.

The Girls put out their sophomore effort *Nomads*Indians*Saints* in the fall of 1990. This album featured such notable performers as Mary Chapin Carpenter and Gang of Four bassist Sara Lee. The album went gold without the benefit of much airplay but with frequent touring. About seven months later, they put out the live EP *Back on the Bus, Y'all*. Their next studio album, 1992's *Rites of Passage*, featured such stellar guests as Jackson Browne, David Crosby, Budgie (from Siouxsie and the Banshees) and The Roches. It debuted at its chart peak of #22, and sold gold. Once again, they followed this with vigorous touring. They took time out, however, to appear in the film *Boys on the Side* and put a tune on the soundtrack of *Philadelphia*. With all that behind them, their spring of 1994 release, *Swamp Ophelia*, entered the charts at #9, going gold less than two months later. It eventually went platinum.

In the mid 1990s, Ray and Saliers took some time off from the unrelenting pace they set for themselves for much of the previous decade. They took part in an Atlanta stage run of the show *Jesus Christ Superstar* with Saliers playing Mary Magdalene and Ray taking the role of Jesus. The cast album came out on Ray's label, Daemon Records, which she had started several years earlier as a not-for-profit place to release local bands and other favorites. In the meantime, a greatest hits record called *4.5* was released everywhere but the U.S., bringing other territories up to speed with the duo. They followed that with a full length live album, *1200 Curfews*. It included performances from their entire career, including a track from their B-Band days. The album went gold.

The Indigo Girls went back into the studio during the fall of 1996 and put out their rockingest record to date, *Shaming the Sun*, in the spring of 1997. In addition to Lee, the album featured two local Daemon bands, Smoke and The Rock-a-Teens. The album debuted at #7. They took the album on the road, playing the Lilith Fair and headlining dates. Before the release of their 1999 record *Come on Now Social*, they duo released the song "Peace Tonight" on the World Wide Web, making it available on the Internet music site Launch.com. The album featured guest appearances by such notable women performers as Joan Osbourne, Sheryl Crow, Kate Schellenbach from the band Luscious Jackson, and Me'Shell N'degeocello, along with members of Sinead O'Connor's touring band and Garth Hudson and Rick Danko of The Band.

Disc.: *Strange Fire* (1987); *Indigo Girls* (1989); *Nomads Indians Saints* (1990); *Live: Back on the Bus Y'all* (1991); *Rites of Passage* (1992); *Swamp Ophelia* (1994); *1200 Curfews* (live; 1995); *Touch Me Fall* (1995); *Shaming of the Sun* (1997); *Come on Now Social* (1999).—**HB**

d'Indy, (Paul-Marie-Théodore-) Vincent, eminent French composer and pedagogue; b. Paris, March 27, 1851; d. there, Dec. 2, 1931. Owing to the death of his mother at his birth, his education was directed entirely by his grandmother, Countess Rézia d'Indy, a woman of culture and refinement who had known Grétry and Monsigny, and who had shown a remarkable appreciation of the works of Beethoven when that master was still living. From 1862 to 1865 he studied piano with Diémer and Marmontel; in 1865 he studied harmony with Lavignac. In 1869 he made the acquaintance of Duparc, and with him spent much time studying the masterpieces of Bach, Beethoven, Berlioz, and Wagner; at that time, he wrote his opp. 1 and 2, and contemplated an opera on Hugo's *Les Burgraves* (1869–72; unfinished). During the Franco-Prussian War, he served in the Garde Mobile, and wrote of his experiences in *Histoire du 105ᵉ bataillon de la Garde nationale de Paris en l'année 1870–71* (1872). He then began to study composition with Franck (1872); when the latter was appointed prof. of organ at the Paris Cons. (1873), d'Indy joined the class, winning a second *accessit* in 1874 and the first the following year. On his first visit to Germany in 1873, he met Liszt and Wagner, and was introduced to Brahms; in 1876 he heard the first performances of the *Ring* dramas at Bayreuth, and for several years thereafter made regular trips to Munich to hear all the works of Wagner; he also attended the premiere of *Parsifal* in 1882. From 1872 to 1876 he was organist at St. Leu-la-Foret; from 1873 to 1878, chorus master and timpanist with the Colonne Orch.; for the Paris premiere of *Lohengrin* in 1887, he drilled the chorus and was Lamoureux's assistant. In 1871 he joined the Société Nationale de Musique as a junior member, and was its secretary from 1876 to 1890, when, after Franck's death, he became president. In 1894 he founded, with Bordes and Guilmant, the famous Schola Cantorum (opened 1896), primarily as a school for plainchant and the

Palestrina style. Gradually the scope of instruction was enlarged to include all musical disciplines, and the inst. became one of the world's foremost music schools. D'Indy's fame as a composer began with the performance of his *Le Chant de la cloche* at a Lamoureux concert in 1886; the work itself had won the City of Paris Prize in the competition of the preceding year. As early as 1874, Pasdeloup had played the overture *Les Piccolomini* (later embodied as the second part in the Wallenstein trilogy), and in 1882 the one-act opera *Attendez-moi sous l'orme* had been produced at the Paris Opéra-Comique; but the prize work attracted general attention, and d'Indy was recognized as one of the most important French composers of his day. Although he never held an official position as a conductor, he frequently, and with marked success, appeared in that capacity (chiefly upon invitation to direct his own works); thus, he visited Spain in 1897, Russia in 1903 and 1907, and the U.S. in 1905, when he conducted the Boston Sym. Orch. In 1892 he was a member of the commission appointed to revise the curriculum of the Cons., and refused a proffered professorship of composition; but in 1912 he accepted an appointment as prof. of the ensemble class. Besides his other duties, he was, from 1899, inspector of musical instruction in Paris. He was made a Chevalier of the Legion of Honor in 1892, an Officer in 1912. Both as teacher and creative artist, d'Indy continued the traditions of Franck. Although he cultivated almost every form of composition, his special talent was in the field of the larger instrumental forms. Some French critics assign to him a position in French music analogous to that of Brahms in German music. His style rests on Bach and Beethoven; however, his deep study of Gregorian chant and the early contrapuntal style added an element of severity, and not rarely of complexity, that renders his approach somewhat difficult, and has prompted the charge that his music is lacking in emotional force. He wrote numerous articles for various journals, which are remarkable for their critical acumen and literary finish.

WRITINGS: *Cours de Composition musicale* (Book I, 1903; Book II: Part 1, 1909, Part 2, 1933); *César Franck* (1906; Eng. tr., 1910); *Beethoven: Biographie critique* (1911; Eng. tr., 1913); *La Schola Cantorum en 1925* (1927); *Wagner et son influence sur l'art musical français* (1930); *Introduction à l'étude de Parsifal* (1937).

WORKS: DRAMATIC: *Les Burgraves*, opera (1869–72; unfinished); *Attendez-moi sous l'orme*, comic opera (Paris, Feb. 11, 1882); *Karadec*, incidental music (Paris, May 2, 1891); *Le Chant de la cloche*, dramatic legend (Brussels, Nov. 21, 1912); *Fervaal*, lyric drama (Brussels, March 12, 1897); *Medée*, incidental music (1898); *L'Étranger*, lyric drama (Brussels, Jan. 7, 1903); *La Légende de Saint-Christophe*, lyric drama (Paris, June 9, 1920); *Le Rêve de Cynias*, lyric comedy (Paris, June 10, 1927). **ORCH.:** 3 syms.: No. 1, *Jean Hunyade* (Paris, May 15, 1875), No. 2 (Paris, Feb. 28, 1904), and No. 3, *Sinfonia brevis de bello Gallico* (1916–18; Paris, Dec. 14, 1919); 2 other syms.: *Symphonie Cévenole sur un chant montagnard français* (1886; Paris, March 20, 1887) and *La Queste de Dieu*, after *La Légende de Saint- Christophe* (1917); *Antoine et Cléopâtre*, overture (Paris, Feb. 4, 1877); *La Forêt enchantée*, symphonic legend (Paris, March 24, 1878); *Wallenstein*, symphonic trilogy: *Le Camp de Wallenstein* (April 12, 1880), *Max et Thécla* (Jan. 25, 1874; orig. *Les Piccolomini*), and *La Mort de Wallenstein* (April 11, 1884); *Lied* for Cello and Orch. (Paris, April 18, 1885); *Saugefleurie*, legend (Paris, Jan. 25, 1885); Suite

for Trumpet, 2 Flutes, and Strings (Paris, March 5, 1887); *Sérénade et Valse* for Small Orch. (1887); *Fantaisie* for Oboe and Orch. (Paris, Dec. 23, 1888); *Tableaux de voyage* (Le Havre, Jan. 17, 1892); *Istar*, symphonic variations (Brussels, Jan. 10, 1897); *Choral varié* for Saxophone and Orch. (Paris, May 17, 1904); *Jour d'été à la montagne* (Paris, Feb. 18, 1906); *Souvenirs*, tone poem (Paris, April 20, 1907); *Le Poème des rivages* (N.Y., Dec. 1, 1921); *Diptyque mediterraneen* (Paris, Dec. 5, 1926); Concerto for Piano, Flute, Cello, and Strings (Paris, April 2, 1927). **CHAMBER:** Piano Quartet (1878); Trio for Piano, Clarinet, and Cello (1888); 3 string quartets (1891, 1898, 1929); *Chansons et Danses*, divertissement for 7 Wind Instruments (Paris, March 7, 1899); Violin Sonata (1905); Piano Quintet (1925); Cello Sonata (1926); *Suite en 4 parties* for Flute, Strings, and Harp (Paris, May 17, 1930); String Sextet (1928); Trio for Piano, Violin, and Cello (1929). **KEYBOARD: P i a n o :** *3 romances sans paroles* (1870); *Petite sonate* (1880); *Poème des montagnes: Le Chant des bruyères, Danses rythmiques*, and *Plein-air* (1881); *4 pièces* (1882); *Helvetia*, 3 waltzes (1882); *Saugefleurie* (1884; also arranged for Orch.); Nocturne (1886); *Promenade* (1887); *Schumanniana*, 3 pieces (1887); *Tableaux de voyage*, 13 pieces (1889); *Petite chanson grégorienne* for Piano, 4-Hands (1904); Sonata (1907); *Menuet sur le nom de Haydn* (1909); *13 Short Pieces; 12 petites pièces faciles; 7 chants de terroir* for Piano, 4-Hands; *Pour les enfants de tous les âges*, 24 pieces; *Thème varié, fugue et chanson; Conte de fées*, suite (1926); *6 paraphrases on French children's songs; Fantaisie sur un vieil air de ronde française* (1931). **O r g a n :** *Prélude et Petit Canon* (1893); *Vêpres du Commun d'un Martyr* (1889); *Prélude* (1913). **VOCAL:** *Chanson des aventuriers de la mer* for Baritone and Men's Chorus (1870); *La Chevauchée du Cid* for Baritone, Chorus, and Orch. (1879); *Cantate Domino* (1885); *Ste. Marie-Magdeleine*, cantata (1885); *Sur la mer* for Women's Voices and Piano (1888); *Pour l'inauguration d'une statue*, cantata (1893); *L'Art et le peuple* for Men's Chorus (1894); *Deus Israël*, motet (1896); *Ode à Valence* for Soprano and Chorus (1897); *Les Noces d'or du sacerdoce* (1898); *Sancta Maria*, motet (1898); *6 Chants populaires français* for Chorus (1928, 1931); *Le Bouquet de printemps* Women's Chorus (1929); *La Vengeance du mari* for 3 Soloists, Chorus, and Orch. (1931); songs.

BIBL.: E. Deniau, *V. d'I.* (Toulouse, 1903); F. Starczewski, *La Schola Cantorum de Paris, ou V. d'I.: considéré comme professeur* (Warsaw, 1905); L. Borgex, *V. d'I.: Sa vie et son oeuvre* (Paris, 1913); A. Sérieyx, *V. d'I.* (Paris, 1913); M. de Fraguier, *V. d'I.* (Paris, 1933); L. Vallas, *V. d'I.: I. La Jeunesse, II. La Maturité, La Vieillesse* (Paris, I, 1946; II, 1950); J. Canteloube, *V. d'I.* (Paris, 1949); N. Demuth, *V. d'I.* (London, 1951); J. Guy-Ropartz, ed., *Le Centenaire de V. d'I., 1851–1951* (Paris, 1952); L. Davies, *César Franck and His Circle* (Boston, 1970).—**NS/LK/DM**

Infantas, Fernando de las, Spanish composer and theologian; b. Córdoba, 1534; d. c. 1610. He belonged to a noble family and received a thorough classical and musical education. He also enjoyed the protection of the Emperor Charles V and later of Emperor Philip II, who employed him on diplomatic missions in Italy. He went to Venice, and then lived in Rome from about 1571 to 1597. In 1584 he was ordained and subsequently served as a church chaplain. He exerted a decisive influence upon the course of Catholic church music by opposing the plan for the reform of the Roman Gradual undertaken by Palestrina in 1578 at the request of Pope Gregory XIII. Backed by the authority of Emperor Philip II of Spain, he succeeded in having the project abandoned. He publ. *Sacrarum varii styli can-*

tionum tituli Spiritus Sancti, a collection of motets in 3 books: I for 4 Voices, II for 5 Voices (both publ. in Venice, 1578), and III for 6–8 Voices (Venice, 1579), and *Plura modulationum genera quae vulgo contrapuncta appellantur super excelso gregoriano cantu* (Venice, 1579; contains 100 contrapuntal exercises for 2–8 Voices based on 1 plainsong theme; it pointed the way to a new freedom and elasticity in polyphonic writing); separate compositions were also publ. in various collections of the time.

BIBL.: R. Mitjana y Gordón, *Don F. d.l.I., teologo y músico* (Madrid, 1918).—NS/LK/DM

Infante, Manuel, Spanish pianist and composer; b. Osuna, near Seville, July 29, 1883; d. Paris, April 21, 1958. He studied piano and composition with Enrique Morera. In 1909 he settled in Paris, and gave concerts of Spanish music. He wrote numerous pieces for piano, mostly on Spanish themes: *Gitanerias, Pochades andalouses, Sevillana,* fantasy (1922), and *El Vito* (variations on a popular theme). He also composed an opera, *Almanza.* —NS/LK/DM

Ingalls, Jeremiah, American tunebook compiler and composer; b. Andover, Mass., March 1, 1764; d. Hancock, Vt., April 6, 1838. He settled in Vt., where he was active as a singing-school master, bass viol player, and choral conductor. He publ. the tunebook *The Christian Harmony, or Songster's Companion* (Exeter, N.H., 1805), which includes the first publ. spiritual folk songs, a sacred text set to a secular or folk melody.

BIBL.: D. Klocko, *J. I.'s "The Christian Harmony: or, Songster's Companion (1805)"* (diss., Univ. of Mich., 1978).—LK/DM

Ingarden, Roman (Witold), Polish music theorist and aesthetician; b. Kraków, Feb. 5, 1893; d. there, June 14, 1970. He studied philosophy with Husserl and mathematics with Hilbert at the univs. of Göttingen and Freiburg im Breisgau (Ph.D., 1918). After completing his Habilitation (1921), he joined the faculty at the Univ. of Lwów. In 1945 he became chairman of the philosophy dept. at the Jagellonian Univ. in Kraków, only to be barred from teaching in 1950 by the Communist government because of his adherence to "idealism"; during his forced sabbatical, he translated Kant's *Critique of Pure Reason*. He regained his academic post in 1956, retiring in 1963. Ingarden is regarded as the ablest of Husserl's students, preserving the cognitive core of Husserl's phenomenology that was lost in Heidegger's and Sartre's emotional reduction of it to existentialism. His *The Work of Music and the Problem of Its Identity* (Berkeley, 1986), an excerpt from his *Studia z estetyki* (Studies in Aesthetics; Warsaw, 1957–70), is an important consideration of ontology and epistemology in musical aesthetics. His other publications include *Spór o istnienie świata* (Controversy over the Existence of the World; Kraków, 1947–48), *Untersuchungen zur Ontologie der Kunst: Musikwerk, Bild, Architektur, Film* (Tübingen, 1962), *The Literary Work of Art: An Investigation on the Borderlines of Ontology, Logic, and Theory of Literature, with an Appendix on the Functions of Language in the Theater* (Evanston, Ill., 1973), and *Selected Papers in Aesthetics* (Washington, D.C., 1985).—NS/LK/DM

Inge, Edward (Frederick), jazz clarinetist, saxophonist, arranger; b. Kansas City, Mo., May 7, 1906; d. Buffalo, N.Y., Oct. 8, 1988. Inge began playing clarinet at the age of 12, and later studied in conservatories in St. Louis and Madison, Wisc. His professional debut was with the George Reynolds Orch. (1924). He played with Dewey Jackson before joining Art Simms in Milwaukee. After Simms's death, he worked with Oscar "Bernie" Young until late 1926. He was with McKinney's Cotton Pickers (late 1930–31), and with Don Redman until 1939. In early 1940, he joined Andy Kirk (replacing Don Byas), but left in 1943. He did regular arranging for Kirk, and also scored for many bandleaders including Don Redman, Jimmie Lunceford, and Louis Armstrong. Inge led his own band in Cleveland (1945), then settled in Buffalo and founded his own business. He led own band in Buffalo in the 1950s and 1960s, and also worked in Cecil Johnson's Band in the 1960s. He was with C.Q. Price's Band in Buffalo in the early 1970s.—JC/LP

Ingegneri, Marc'Antonio, important Italian composer; b. Verona, c. 1547; d. Cremona, July 1, 1592. He was a choirboy at Verona Cathedral, where he most likely studied with its maestro di cappella, Vincenzo Ruffo. Around 1568 he settled in Cremona, where he was prefect of music at the Cathedral from 1578. He acted as maestro di cappella from 1579, and was officially named to that position in 1581. Monteverdi was his pupil. Ingegneri distinguished himself as a composer of both secular and sacred music. See G. Cesari, ed., *La musica in Cremona nella seconda metà del secolo XVI e i primordi dell'arte monteverdiana,* Istituzioni e Monumenti dell'Arte Musicale Italiana, VI (1939) and B. Hudson, ed., *M.A. Ingegneri: 7 Madrigale,* Das Chorwerk, CXV (1974).

WORKS (all publ. in Venice): **VOCAL: S a c r e d :** *Liber primus missarum* for 5 and 8 Voices (1573); *Sacrarum cantionum...liber primus* for 5 Voices (1576; ed. by M. Duggan in *Marc Antonio Ingegneri: Motets for Four and Five Voices,* diss., Univ. of Rochester, 1968); *Sacrarum cantionum...liber primus* for 4 Voices (1586; ed. in the preceding diss.); *Liber secundus missarum* for 5 Voices (1587); *Responsoria hebdomadae sanctae, Benedictus, & improperia... & Miserere* for 4 and 6 Voices (1588); *Lamentationes Hieremiae* for 4 Voices (1588); *Liber sacrarum cantionum* for 7 to 10, 12, and 16 Voices and Instruments ad libitum (1589); *Sacrae cantiones...liber primus* for 6 Voices (1591); *Liber secundus hymnorum* for 4 Voices (1606). **S e c u l a r :** *Il primo libro de madrigali* for 5 and 8 Voices (not extant); *Il secondo libro de madrigali* for 5 Voices (1572); *Il primo libro de madrigali* for 4 Voices (1st ed. not extant; 2nd ed., 1578); *Il secondo libro de madrigali...con due arie di canzon francese per sonare* for 4 Voices (1579); *Il terzo libro de madrigali...con due canzoni francese* for 5 Voices (1580); *Il quarto libro de madrigali* for 5 Voices (1584); *Il primo libro de madrigali* for 6 Voices (1586); *Il quinto libro de madrigali* for 5 Voices (1587); *Il sesto libro de madrigali* for 5 Voices (1606); other madrigals in collections of the day.

BIBL.: E. Dohrn, *M.'A. I. als Madrigalkomponist* (Hannover, 1936); M. Duggan, *Marc Antonio I.: Motets for Four and Five Voices* (diss., Univ. of Rochester, 1968); A. Delfino and M. Barezzani, eds., *M.'A. I. e la musica a Cremona nel secondo Cinquecento* (Lucca, 1995).—NS/LK/DM

Ingenhoven, Jan, Dutch composer; b. Breda, May 29, 1876; d. Hoenderlo, May 20, 1951. He studied with L.

Brandts-Buys in Rotterdam and Mottl in Munich, where he conducted the noted Madrigal Soc. (1909–12); then devoted himself mainly to composition. His works are influenced by Debussy, but he preserved an element of peculiarly native melos. Among his works are *Symphonische Fantasie über Zarathustras* for Orch. (1906), *Brabant and Holland*, symphonic fantasy, 3 symphonic poems (*Lyric*; *Dramatic*; *Romantic*), 3 string quartets (1907–08; 1911; 1912), Woodwind Quintet (1911), Clarinet Sonata (1916–17), 2 violin sonatas (1919–20; 1921), 2 cello sonatas (1919, 1922), choral works, and songs.

BIBL.: D. Ruyneman, *De componist J. I.* (Amsterdam, 1938). **—NS/LK/DM**

Ingham, Keith, English pianist; b. London, England, Feb. 5, 1942. A fine, swinging pianist with an encyclopedic knowledge of songwriters, overlooked songs, and jazz piano history. He has an excellent reputation as an accomplished vocal accompanist and arranger. His many musical associations and collaborations include singers Susannah McCorkle, Peggy Lee, Barbara Lea, and the late Maxine Sullivan, guitarist Marty Grosz, clarinetists Bobby Gordon and Bob Reitmeier, and tenor saxophonist Harry Allen. His keyboard approach and sound are often reminiscent of Gene Schroeder or Jess Stacy, but he acknowledges Al Haig and Ellis Larkins as primary influences on his harmonically rich piano style.

Growing up in war-ravaged Britain, he began piano studies at age eight and showed an interest in jazz by his teens. As a prerequisite to an Oxford Univ. scholarship, he worked for the British Government in Hong Kong. It was there where he first played jazz piano, sitting in with a Filipino quartet. He left the Far East in 1962 and majored in classical Chinese language at Oxford, graduating in 1966. He returned to London and started playing in British bands with Humphrey Lyttelton, Sandy Brown, Wally Falkes, Bruce Turner, and others. By 1968, he was accompanying visiting Americans, most notably Red Allen, Pee Wee Russell, Benny Carter, and Ben Webster. In the 1970s, he recorded with Bud Freeman, Bob Wilber, and as leader with vocalist Susannah McCorkle with whom he shared a mutual love of 1920s and 1930s songs. In 1978, McCorkle and visiting musicians Billy Butterfield and Ruby Braff encouraged Ingham to move to the United States. Ingham settled in N.Y. where he freelanced and played occasional dates with Benny Goodman, the World's Greatest Jazz Band, and with McCorkle as her musical director and pianist. He plays the festival scene and selective U.S. club dates, and is a favorite at the annual Allegheny Jazz Society sessions in Western Pa. and environs. He has recorded as sideman and leader, including dates featuring singer Maxine Sullivan, guitarist Marty Grosz, clarinetist Bob Reitmeier, and others. He still finds time, however, to play his special brand of thoughtful, complex jazz piano in various N.Y. venues.

DISC.: *The Keith Ingham–Bob Reitmeier Quartet Plays the Music of Victor Young* (1989); *Keith Ingham: Out of the Past* (1990); *Marty Grosz & Keith Ingham and Their Paswonky Serenaders: Unsaturated Fats* (1990); *The Harry Allen–Keith Ingham Quintet: Are You Having Any Fun?* (1991); *Music from the Mauve Decades* (1993); *Bobby Gordon/Keith Ingham/Hal Smith Trio* (1993); *The Keith Ingham New York 9, Vol. 1* (1994); *Just Imagine: The Music of DeSylva, Brown & Henderson* (1994); *My Little Brown Book: A Celebration of Billy Strayhorn's Music, Vol. 1* (1994); *The Intimacy of the Blues: A Celebration of Billy Strayhorn's Music, Vol. 2* (1994); *Keith Ingham–Harry Allen: Back Room Romp* (1995).**—JTB**

Inghelbrecht, D(ésiré)-É(mile), noted French conductor and composer; b. Paris, Sept. 17, 1880; d. there, Feb. 14, 1965. He began violin lessons as a child, and later studied solfège and harmony with Taudou at the Paris Cons. only to be expelled as musically unpromising. After working as an orch. player, he became conductor of the Théâtre des Arts in Paris in 1908. In 1912 he organized l'Association Chorale Professionnelle. After serving as music director at the Théâtre des Champs-Elysées in Paris, he founded the Concerts Ignace Pleyel in 1919 to promote the music of the 17th and 18th centuries. From 1920 to 1923 he toured Europe as conductor of the Ballets Suédois, and then returned to Paris as music director of the Opéra-Comique in 1924–25; then held the post of second conductor of the Concerts Pasdeloup (1928–32). After serving as director of the Algiers Opera (1929–30), he was again music director of the Opéra-Comique (1932–33). In 1934 he founded l'Orchestre National de la Radio Française, serving as its director until 1944. From 1945 to 1950 he was chief conductor of the Paris Opéra, and subsequently appeared as a conductor with Radio Française. Inghelbrecht was greatly admired for his interpretations of French music, particularly the works of Debussy, Ravel, and Roussel. He was also an accomplished composer in his own right. He was the author of *Comment on ne doit pas interpréter Carmen, Faust et Pelléas* (1933); *Diabolus in musica* (1933); *Mouvement contraire: Souvenirs d'un musicien* (1947); *Le Chef d'orchestre et son équipe* (1948; Eng. tr., 1953, as *The Conductor's World*); *Claude Debussy* (1953); *Le Chef d'orchestre parle au public* (1957).

WORKS: DRAMATIC: Opera: *La nuit vénitienne* (1908). **Operetta:** *Virage sur l'aile* (1947). **Opera-ballet:** *Le chêne et le tilleul* (1960). **Ballet:** *El Greco* (Paris, Nov. 18, 1920); *Le diable dans le beffroi* (1921; Paris, June 1, 1927); *La métamorphose d'Eve* (1928); *Jeux de Couleurs* (Paris, Feb. 21, 1933). **ORCH.:** *Marine* (1903); *La serre aux nénuphars* (1903); *Automne* (1905); *Pour le jour de la première neige au vieux Japon* (1908); *Rapsodie de printemps* (1910); *3 poèmes dansés* (1923), *6 danses suédoises* (1929); *Sinfonia breve da camera* (1930); *La valse retrouvée* (1937); *Ballade dans le goût irlandais* for Harp and Orch. (1939); *Pastourelles sur des noëls anciens* (1943); *Ibériana* for Violin and Orch. (1948); *Vézelay* (1952). **CHAMBER:** *2 esquisses antiques* for Flute and Harp (1903); *Poème sylvestre* for Winds (1905); *Prélude et saltarelle* for Viola and Piano (1905); *Nocturne* for Cello and Piano (1905); *Quintet for Harp and Strings* (1918); *Sonatine for Flute and Harp* (1919); *Impromptu* for Viola and Piano (1922); *4 Fanfares* for Winds (1932); *String Quartet* (1956). **Piano:** *2 esquisses* (1903); *La nursery* (5 vols., 1905–11; also orchestrated); *Suite Petite russienne* (1908); *Paysages* (1918); *Dernières nurseries* (1932); *Pastourelles* (1949). **VOCAL:** *Cantique des créatures* for Voice and Piano (1910); *4 chansons populaires françaises* for Chorus (1915); *Vocalise- étude* for Voice and Piano (1929); *La légende du grand St. Nicolas* for Voice and Piano (1932); *Requiem* for Soprano, Tenor, Baritone, Chorus, and Orch. (1941); *Tant que noël durera* for Voice and Orch. (1943); *Chantons jeunesse* for Chorus (1946).**—NS/LK/DM**

Inghilleri, Giovanni, Italian baritone and composer; b. Porto Empedocle, March 9, 1894; d. Milan, Dec. 10, 1959. He made his operatic debut as Valentine at the Teatro Carcano in Milan in 1919, and then sang throughout Italy; was a member of La Scala in Milan from 1945. He also sang at London's Covent Garden (1928–30; 1935) and at the Chicago Civic Opera (1929–30). After his retirement in 1953, he taught voice in Pesaro and Milan. Among his best known roles were Amonasro, Amfortas, Gérard, and Scarpia. He composed an opera, *La burla,* a ballet, and songs.—NS/LK/DM

Ingólfsdóttir, Thorgerdur, Icelandic choral conductor and teacher; b. Reykjavík, Nov. 5, 1943. She was a student at the Reykjavík Coll. of Music (teacher's diploma, 1965), and also studied theology at the Univ. of Iceland and choral conducting and musicology with Robert Ottósson (1963–65). In 1966–67 she held a graduate fellowship at the Univ. of Ill., and then continued her studies with Ottósson in her homeland (1968–74). She also studied choral conducting in England, N.Y., Switzerland, Israel, Norway, and Vienna. In 1967 she founded the Hamrahlíd Choir in Reykjavík, which she molded into one of Iceland's most important performing groups. She conducted it throughout Europe and in Israel and Japan. As a teacher, she served on the faculties of the Reykjavík Coll. of Music (from 1967) and of Hamrahlíd Coll. (from 1967). In 1985 the president of Iceland made her a Knight of the Order of the Falcon for her services to Icelandic music, and in 1992 the king of Norway named her a Commander of the Royal Order of Merit.—NS/LK/DM

Ingram, James, the king of the collaborators; b. Akron, Ohio, Feb. 16, 1956. By the time James Ingram released his solo debut in 1983, people thought he'd been recording as a solo artist for years. This is not surprising, considering he had already had three major hits, including a chart topper. It just happened they were all on other people's records. Nor did he ever expect to become a hit singer. He concentrated far more on his other musical skills, playing keyboards and writing.

He began his musical career in Ohio with the band Revelation Funk. The band decided to seek their fortune in L.A., but less than a year later the band was in the van on the way back to Ohio, except for Ingram. He found work as a touring musician with Ray Charles and The Coasters, as well as working with artists like Donna Summer, Shalamar, Grover Washington Jr., and The Pointer Sisters. He also recorded demos for himself and other songwriters, often singing as well as playing the keyboards. One of these demos, for the Barry Mann/Cynthia Weil song "Just Once," came to producer Quincy Jones. He liked the songs but he loved the singer and tracked Ingram down to sing on his 1980 album, *Superdisc.* Three years later, he called on Ingram to sing lead on a couple of songs for his 1981 album, *The Dude.* Those songs included "Just Once," which went to #17, and "One Hundred Ways," which went to #14. The latter won Ingram a Best R&B Male Vocal Grammy. Jones then called him in on another production, an

album by singer Patti Austin. Their duet, "Baby, Come to Me," became the love theme on the soap opera *General Hospital,* which helped catapult the single to the top of the adult contemporary charts for three weeks and the pop charts for two. The record went gold.

Ingram didn't make his solo debut until 1983's *It's Your Night.* His duet "Yah Mo B There" with Michael McDonald went to #19, and won the two a Grammy for Best R&B Duo/Group with Vocal. Surprisingly, the album didn't make any pop chart impact, despite going gold in 1984. Ingram also joined Kim Carnes and Kenny Rogers on the #15 hit "What About Me?" He helped Mann and Weil win Song of the Year and Best Song for Motion Picture/TV Grammys in 1987 with his duet with Linda Ronstadt on their "Somewhere Out There," the theme from the animated film "An American Tale." The single went to #2 and sold gold. In 1988, Ingram released another solo album, *Never Felt So Good,* which went virtually unnoticed. Ingram finally scored a hit on his own with the chart- topping "I Don't Have the Heart" in 1990. Ironically, this didn't help his album sales, which never achieved the level of his single success. In 1998, he collaborated with John Tesh on the popular wedding song "Give Me Forever (I Do)."

DISC.: *It's Your Night* (1983); *Never Felt So Good* (1988); *It's Real* (1989); *Always You* (1993); *Forever More* (1999).—HB

Ink Spots, The, American vocal group. The Ink Spots' sound, characterized by a high tenor lead (usually Bill Kenny [b. 1915; d. March 23, 1978]) contrasted with a spoken bass voice (usually Orville ["Hoppy"] Jones [b. Chicago, Feb. 17, 1905; d. there, Oct. 18, 1944]) and accompanied by close harmonies (usually Ivory Deacon ["Deek"] Watson [b. Mounds, Ill.; d. November 1969] and Charlie Fuqua [b. ca. 1911; d. 1971]), gave them 17 Top Ten hits between 1939 and 1949, including the #1 million-sellers "The Gypsy" and "To Each His Own," as well as "Into Each Life Some Rain Must Fall" and "I'm Making Believe," on which they were accompanied by Ella Fitzgerald. The most popular male vocal group of the 1940s, they were an important influence on doo-wop and on harmony singing in popular music in general.

Based in Indianapolis, Fuqua was in a vaudeville duo with Jerry Daniels (b. ca. 1916; d. Nov. 7, 1995); as Charlie and Jerry they sang and played string instruments. They were joined in 1931 by Watson, a former member of The Four Riffs, to form the Swingin' Gate Brothers, later renamed King, Jack and Jester, and had a program on radio station WHK in Cleveland. After they moved to WLW in Cincinnati, Jones, another former member of The Four Riffs, joined. They moved to N.Y.C. and appeared on WJZ. The group name was changed to The Ink Spots due to a conflict with Paul Whiteman's vocal group, the King's Jesters.

Signed to RCA Victor, The Ink Spots first recorded on Jan. 4, 1935, cutting the single "Swingin' on the Strings"/"Your Feet's Too Big" (music and lyrics by Ada Benson and Fred Fisher). Kenny replaced Daniels in early 1936. The group moved to Decca Records and held its first recording session for the new label on May 12, 1936. But it was not until Jan. 12, 1939, that they recorded their first hit, "If I Didn't Care" (music and lyrics by Jack Lawrence), a ballad in the spare style that became their trademark. Released in February, the song reached the hit parade in June and spent seven weeks there. In the fall the group opened shows for Glenn Miller at the prestigious Paramount Theatre in N.Y.; after Miller left they were engaged as the headline attraction.

The Ink Spots returned to the Top Ten in 1940 with "When the Swallows Come Back to Capistrano" (music and lyrics by Leon René) in August, "Maybe" (music and lyrics by Allan Flynn and Frank Madden) and "Whispering Grass (Don't Tell the Trees)" (music by Doris Fisher, lyrics by Fred Fisher) in October, and "We Three (My Echo, My Shadow and Me)" (music and lyrics by Nelson Cogane, Sammy Mysels, and Dick Robertson) in December, making them one of the most popular recording acts of the year. In May 1941 the group appeared in the film *The Great American Broadcast*. "I Don't Want to Set the World on Fire" (music and lyrics by Eddie Seiler, Sol Marcus, Bennie Benjamin, and Eddie Durham) was a Top Ten hit for them in October.

The Ink Spots appeared in a second film, *Pardon My Sarong*, August 1942. They next reached the Top Ten with "Don't Get Around Much Anymore" (music by Duke Ellington, lyrics by Bob Russell) in May 1943. The record had topped the R&B charts in March, and the group had scored a second R&B #1 with "I Can't Stand Losing You" in April. Fuqua joined the service in mid-1943. He was replaced first by Bernard Mackey (b. 1909; d. 1980), then by Huey Long; he returned to the group in late 1945. "Cow-Cow Boogie (Cuma-Ti-Yi-Yi Ay)" (music and lyrics by Don Raye, Gene DePaul, and Benny Carter), on which The Ink Spots were accompanied by Ella Fitzgerald, topped the R&B charts in March 1944 and reached the pop Top Ten in April; "I'll Get By (as Long as I Have You)" (music by Fred E. Ahlert, lyrics by Roy Turk) was in the Top Ten in May; and "Into Each Life Some Rain Must Fall" (music by Doris Fisher, lyrics by Allan Roberts) and "I'm Making Believe" (music by James V. Monaco, lyrics by Mack Gordon), both with Fitzgerald, topped the pop charts in December and sold a million copies. They were some of the last recordings to feature Jones, who died of an epileptic seizure.

Jones's initial replacement was Cliff Givens, who was superseded by Kenny's brother, Herb(ert Cornelius) Kenny (b. 1914; d. Columbia, Md., July 11, 1992). Also late in 1944, Watson left the Ink Spots and attempted to form his own version of the group, though he was forced to name it the Brown Dots. He was replaced by Bill Bowen (b. 1909; d. 1982).

The team of Fuqua, Bowen, and the Kenny brothers reached the Top Ten with "I'm Beginning to See the Light" (music and lyrics by Duke Ellington, Don George, and Johnny Hodges), again with Ella Fitzgerald, in May 1945. "The Gypsy" (music and lyrics by Billy Reid), which topped the charts in May 1946, sold a million copies and became the biggest hit of the year. In 1946 The Ink Spots also reached the Top Ten with "Prisoner of Love" (music by Russ Columbo and Clarence Gaskill, lyrics by Leo Robin) in June and topped the charts with the million-selling "To Each His Own"

(music by Jay Livingson, lyrics by Ray Evans) in September, and their album *The Ink Spots Album* was one of the longest running #1 hits of the year.

The Ink Spots were less successful in the late 1940s, though they returned to the Top Ten with "You Were Only Fooling (While I Was Falling in Love)" (music by Larry Fotine, lyrics by William E. Faber and Fred Meadows) in January 1949, and "You're Breaking My Heart" (music and lyrics by Pat Genaro and Sunny Skylar) in October 1949. They last reached the charts in March 1951. By 1952 they had broken up and launched what turned out to be many competing groups using The Ink Spots name, groups that continued to exist into the 1990s.

BIBL.: I. Watson (group member), *The Story of the I. S.* (N.Y., 1967).—WR

Innes (real name, **Iniss**), **Frederick Neil,** English-American trombonist, bandmaster, and composer; b. London, Oct. 29, 1854; d. Chicago, Dec. 31, 1926. He received training in harmony from Carl Richter. He was a member of the first Life Guards before deserting to the U.S., where he played in Gilmore's Band and the Boston Cadet Band. After making tours of Europe as a trombone virtuoso, he rejoined Gilmore's band in 1880. In 1887 he founded his own Innes Band in N.Y., with which he subsequently toured the U.S. during the following two decades. After serving as director of the Denver Municipal Band (1914–16), he organized the Innes School of Music. He conducted all of his programs from memory, and presented entire concerts of Wagner's music and complete syms. by the great masters. Among his own works were 2 comic operas, orch. suites, overtures, marches, waltzes, cantatas, and numerous solo cornet and trombone pieces.—LK/DM

Insanguine, Giacomo (Antonio Francesco Paolo Michele), Italian composer, known as Monopoli; b. Monopoli, near Bari, March 22, 1728; d. Naples, Feb. 1, 1795. He studied with Abos and Feo at the Naples's Poveri di Gesù cons. in 1743, and later that year entered the San Onofrio cons. to continue his training with Abos and Durante, becoming a mastricello upon the latter's death in 1755. He became a teacher there (1767) and later secondo maestro (1774). From 1785 until his death he was primo maestro. He concurrently was made second organist at the Cappella del Tesoro di San Gennaro (1774), first organist (1776), and maestro di cappella there (1781). He wrote some 20 operas, about half of which are lost, as well as masses, cantatas, and other sacred works.

BIBL.: P. Lanizolotta, *Non oro, non gemme: G. I. detto Monopoli* (Fasano di Brindisi, 1995).—NS/LK/DM

INXS, hard rocking, funky, hit-making Australian sextet that stayed together for 20 years without a change in personnel; f. Aug. 16, 1977 in Sydney, Australia. **MEMBERSHIP:** Michael Hutchence, voc. (b. Jan. 22, 1960, d. Sydney, Australia, Aug. 16, 1997); Andrew Farriss, kybd., gtr., voc. (b. Cottesloe, Western Australia, March 29, 1959); Tim Farriss, gtr., voc. (b. Perth, Australia, Aug. 16, 1957); Jon Farriss, drm. (b. Perth, Australia,

Aug. 10, 1961); Garry Gary Beers, bs. (b. Manly, Australia, June 22, 1957); Kirk Pengilly, gtr., sax., voc. (b. Kew, Victoria, Australia, July 4, 1958). Forming out of several high school bands populated by members of the Farriss family, this sextet originally came together as The Farriss Brothers Band on Andrew Farriss's 20th birthday (which also happened to be the day that Elvis Presley died). Propelled by Hutchence's sexual insouciance and an insistent, driving beat, they spent several years traveling the length of Australia, playing bars in Perth and pubs in Sydney, honing their chops. They initially hooked up with the manager of fellow Australian stars Midnight Oil, and became their frequent opening act. Not satisfied with this situation, the band changed managers and their name, becoming INXS. In 1980, they signed with Deluxe records and put out their eponymous debut in Australia and various European countries. Through the year, they played some 300 shows across the continent to support the record. Several singles earned middling chart positions. They put out their sophomore effort *Underneath the Colours* in the fall of 1981. The album hit #15 on the Australian charts. Both albums went gold "down under."

The group felt they'd outgrown Deluxe and went to seek a new record company and producer. They signed with WEA and in the fall of 1982 put out *Shabooh Shoobah*. The single "The One Thing" reached #14 in Australia and the album went gold. All this success didn't escape WEA, and their subsidiary, Atlantic, signed the group for North America, releasing *Shabooh Shoobah*. "The One Thing" hit #30 on the U.S. charts, earning significant play on MTV. *Musician* magazine proclaimed them "The World's Best Live Band." The band toured the U.S., opening for Adam Ant. While on tour, the group met with producer Nile Rogers, and he agreed to produce their next album. Released during the winter of 1984 in Australia, *The Swing* quickly topped the Australian charts, as did the single "Original Sin," a song about an interracial love affair. The album produced three Top Five Australian singles, but only moderate response in the U.S., largely because several radio stations banned the single. In the winter of 1986, the band released *Listen Like Thieves*. By spring, the record achieved triple-platinum status in Australia and the song "What You Need" hit #5 in the U.S. With keening guitars and a catchy hook, it helped the album reach #11 and platinum.

After a short respite, the band hit the road again and then went into the studio. The album *Kick* came out in the fall of 1987. Following on the trail of "What You Need," the album spun off a spate of Top Ten singles in the U.S., beginning with the chart-topping "Need You Tonight," "Devil Inside" (#2), "New Sensation" (#3), and "Never Tear Us Apart" (#7) followed at roughly three month intervals, sending the album to #3. Hutchence was being called the Mick Jagger of the 1980s, and pundits declared he would be a bigger star than U2's Bono. The hits were all over MTV. The album would eventually sell sextuple platinum. However, the band didn't follow up the successful *Kick* for two years. In the fall of 1990, they heralded the arrival of the album *X* with the single "Suicide Blonde." The song continued their streak of U.S. Top Ten singles, hitting #9 and going

platinum. The follow-up, "Disappear," hit #8, helping propel the album to #5 and double-platinum sales, which was not bad, but something of a comedown after the success of *Kick*. They put out a live record, *Live Baby Live*, which furthered their sliding fortunes with limited sales.

In the summer of 1992, INXS released of their most challenging albums, *Welcome to Wherever You Are*. With world music flavors, samples and a full orchestra, the album was a critical success but a challenge to pop ears. The song "Beautiful Girl" was used for a U.S. campaign against the effects of anorexia and bulimia. The single "Not Enough Time" went to #28 on the charts. The album hit #16 and went gold. Returning to their rock and roll roots, the band released *Full Moon, Dirty Hearts* in 1994. However, the album did not do well despite guest appearances by Chrissy Hynde and Ray Charles. The band still managed to pack venues around the world as a live act, however, and spent close to a year on the road. They put out a greatest hits album to complete their commitment to WEA. The album included a bonus disc of remixes.

After a three year break, the group returned with 1997's *Elegantly Wasted*. The track "Don't Lose Your Head" turns up in the film *Face Off*. Although the album marked a return to INXS's creative chops, the album was a commercial disappointment. As the band prepared for its 20th anniversary tour, on Aug. 16, 1997, Hutchence was discovered hung by a belt in a Sydney hotel room. Hutchence had been at work on a solo album for two years before he died, featuring the band Gang of Four, which was finally released in Australia in fall 1999 and scheduled for U.S. release in early 2000. The other band members were said to be at work on a documentary film on the band.

DISC.: *INXS* (1980); *Underneath the Colours* (1981); *Inxsive* (1982); *Shabooh Shoobah* (1982); *Dekadance* (1983); *Innocent* (1984); *The Swing* (1984); *Listen like Thieves* (1985); *Kick* (1987); *New Sensation* (1988); *X* (1990); *Live Baby Live* (1991); *Welcome to Wherever You Are* (1992); *Full Moon, Dirty Hearts* (1993); *Kick* (Special Edition; 1995); *Elegantly Wasted* (1997). **MICHAEL HUTCHENCE:** *Michael Hutchence* (2000).—**HB**

Inzenga (y Castellanos), José, Spanish composer and teacher; b. Madrid, June 3, 1828; d. there, June 28, 1891. After studying solfège with his father, he received training in piano from Pedro Albéniz at the Madrid Cons. He later was a student in composition of Carafa at the Paris Cons. (1842–48). His first zarzuela, *El campamento* (Madrid, May 8, 1851), proved to be his greatest success in that genre. He also collaborated on the successful zarzuela *Para seguir a una mujer* (Madrid, Dec. 24, 1851). From 1860 until his death he taught voice at the Madrid Cons. In 1857 the Spanish government commissioned him to collect regional songs and dances, which he publ. as *Cantos y bailes populares de España* (3 vols., 1874–88). He also publ. a treatise on accompaniment (Madrid, 1876) and *La música en el templo católico* (Madrid, 1878).—**NS/LK/DM**

Ioannidis, Yannis, Greek composer; b. Athens, June 8, 1930. He studied piano at the Athens Cons.

(1946–55), then organ, composition, and harpsichord at the Vienna Academy of Music (1955–63). He taught at Pierce Coll. in Athens (1963–68). In 1968 went to Caracas (his family was from Venezuela), where he served as artistic director of the chamber orch. of the National Inst. of Culture and Fine Arts; he was a prof. there from 1969, and at the Caracas Cons. and Univ. from 1971. He returned to Athens in 1976. As a composer, he followed the precepts of the second Vienna School, with a firm foundation of classical forms.

WORKS: ORCH.: *Triptych* (1962); *Tropic* (1968); *Metaplassis A* and *B* (1969, 1970); *Transiciones* (1971); *Orbis* for Piano and Orch. (1975–76). **CHAMBER:** *Arioso* for String Nonet (1960); 2 string quartets (1961, 1971); Duo for Violin and Piano (1962); *Peristrophe* for String Octet (1964); *Versi* for Clarinet (1967); *Schemata (Figures)* for String Ensemble (1968); *Projections for Strings, Winds, and Piano* (1968); *Fragments I* for Cello and Piano (1969) and *II* for Flute (1970); *Actinia* for Wind Quintet (1969); *Estudio I, II,* and *III* for Piano (1971–73); *Fancy for 6* for 4 Winds, Cello, and Percussion (1972); *Nocturno* for Piano Quartet (1972); *Dance Vision* for Trombone, Clarinet, Cello, and Piano (1980). **VOCAL:** Transcriptions of Greek folk songs for chorus. —NS/LK/DM

Iokeles, Alexander, Russian pianist and teacher; b. Moscow, March 11, 1912; d. there, June 14, 1978. He was a student of Igumnov at the Moscow Cons. In 1934 he made his first appearance as a soloist with the Moscow Phil., and later played in a trio with Tsomik and Zatulovsky (1943–58). He taught at the Moscow Cons. (1931–42), the Tbilisi Cons. (1946–52), and the Gnesin Inst. in Moscow (from 1952), where he was head of its piano dept. (from 1964). Iokeles gave premiere performances of many works, including concertos by Dolukhanian, Gordeli, Makarov-Rakitin, and Taktakishvili, and also first Russian performances of many works by non-Russian composers.—NS/LK/DM

Iparraguirre y Balerdí, José María de, Spanish-Basque composer and poet; b. Villarreal de Urrechu, Aug. 12, 1820; d. Zozobastro de Isacho, April 6, 1881. He led a wandering life, improvising songs and accompanying himself on the guitar. One of his songs, *Guernikako arbola,* a hymn to the sacred tree of Guernica, became the national anthem of the Basques. As a result of the unrest in the Basque country, and his own participation in it, he was compelled to leave Spain. He spent many years in South America, and was enabled to return to Spain in 1877, where he obtained an official pension.—NS/LK/DM

Ipavec, Benjamin, Slovenian composer; b. St. Jurij, Dec. 24, 1829; d. Graz, Dec. 20, 1909. He studied medicine in Vienna and became a professional physician, with music as an avocation. He was the first to cultivate national Slovenian motifs systematically. He wrote a national Slovenian opera, *Teharski plemiči* (The Nobles of Teharje; Ljubljana, 1892), an operetta, *Tičnik* (The Aviary; 1862), and numerous songs in a Romantic vein. He also brought out collections of Slovenian folk songs.—NS/LK/DM

Ippolitov-Ivanov (real name, **Ivanov**), **Mikhail (Mikhailovich),** important Russian composer and pedagogue; b. Gatchina, Nov. 19, 1859; d.

Moscow, Jan. 28, 1935. He assumed his mother's name to distinguish himself from Michael Ivanov, the music critic. He studied composition with Rimsky-Korsakov at the St. Petersburg Cons., graduating in 1882. He then received the post of teacher and director of the Music School in Tiflis, where he remained until 1893; he became deeply interested in Caucasian folk music; many of his works were colored by the semi-oriental melodic and rhythmic inflections of that region. Upon Tchaikovsky's recommendation, he was appointed prof. of composition at the Moscow Cons. in 1893; in 1906 he became its director, retiring in 1922; then taught at the Tiflis Cons. (1924–25). Among his pupils were Glière and Vasilenko. He was also active as a conductor in Moscow, where he led the Russian Choral Soc. (1895–1901), the Mamontov Opera (1898–1906), and the Bolshoi Theater (from 1925). Outside Russia, he is known mainly for his effective symphonic suite *Caucasian Sketches* (1895). He publ. his memoirs (Moscow, 1934; Eng. tr. in the *Musical Mercury*, N.Y., 1937).

WORKS: DRAMATIC: Opera: *Ruf* (Ruth; 1883–86; Tiflis, Feb. 4, 1887); *Azra* (Tiflis, Dec. 4, 1890); *Asya* (Moscow, Oct. 11, 1900); *Izmena* (Treason; 1908–09; Moscow, Dec. 17, 1910); *Ole iz Nordlands* (Ole from the Northland; Moscow, Nov. 21, 1916); *Poslednyaya barrikada* (The Last Barricade; 1933); also completed Mussorgsky's unfinished opera *Zhenitba* (Marriage; Moscow, Oct. 18, 1931). **ORCH.:** *Symphonic Scherzo* (St. Petersburg, May 20, 1882); *Yar-Khmel,* spring overture (1882; St. Petersburg, Jan. 23, 1883); *Caucasian Sketches* (1894; Moscow, Feb. 5, 1895); *Armenian Rhapsody* (1895); *Iveria* (1896); Sym. (1908); *Mtzyri,* symphonic poem (1922); *From the Songs of Ossian* (1925); *In the Steppes of Turkmenistan* (1935); *Musical Scenes of Uzbekistan* (c. 1935); *Karelia,* suite (1935); marches. **CHAMBER:** Violin Sonata; Piano Quintet; 2 string quartets (1894, c. 1934); piano pieces. **VOCAL:** *Hymn of the Pythagoreans to the Rsing Sun* for Chorus, 10 Flutes, Tuba, 2 Harps, and Organ ad libitum (1904); *Hymn to Labor* for Chorus and Orch. (1934); mass songs; choruses.

BIBL.: S. Chemodanov, *M.M. I.-I.* (Moscow, 1933); S. Boguslavsky, *I.-I.* (Moscow, 1936); L. Podzemskaya, *M.M. I.-I. i gruzinskaya muzikalnaya kultura* (Tbilisi, 1963); N. Sokolov, ed., *M.M. I.-I.: Pisma, stati, vospominaniya* (M.M. I.-I.: Letters, Articles, Reminiscences; Moscow, 1986).—NS/LK/DM

Iradier, Sebastián de
See **Yradier, Sebastián de**

Ireland, John (Nicholson), eminent English composer and teacher; b. Inglewood, Bowdon, Cheshire, Aug. 13, 1879; d. Rock Mill, Washington, Sussex, June 12, 1962. A member of a literary family (both his parents were writers), he received a fine general education. As his musical inclinations became evident, he entered the Royal Coll. of Music in London in 1893, studying piano with Frederick Cliffe (until 1897) and composition with Stanford (1897–1901). He obtained positions as organist in various churches; the longest of these was at St. Luke's, Chelsea (1904–26). In 1905 he received the degree of Bac.Mus. at the Univ. of Durham; was awarded an honorary Mus.Doc. there in 1932. He taught at the Royal Coll. of Music (1923–39); Benjamin Britten, Alan Bush, E. J. Moeran, and other British composers were his pupils. He began to compose early in life; during his student years, he wrote a number of works for orch., chamber groups, and voices, but destroyed most of them; 2 string quartets (1895, 1897) came to light after his death. His early compositions were influenced by the German Romantic school; soon he adopted many devices of the French impressionist school; his rhythmic concepts were enlivened by the new Russian music presented by the Diaghilev Ballet. At the same time, he never wavered in his dedication to the English spirit of simple melody; his music re-creates the plainsong and the usages of Tudor music in terms of plagal modalities and freely modulating triadic harmonies.

WORKS: DRAMATIC: *Julius Ceasar*, incidental music to Shakespeare's play (BBC, London, Sept. 28, 1942); *The Vagabonds*, ballet (London, Oct. 29, 1946; based on *Mai-Dun* and the *Concertino pastorale*); *The Overlanders*, film music (1946–47). **ORCH.:** *Tritons*, symphonic prelude (1899; London, March 21, 1901); *Orchestral Poem* (1903–04); *The Forgotten Rite*, prelude (1913; London, Sept. 13, 1917); *Mai-Dun* (1920–21; London, Dec. 12, 1921); Piano Concerto (London, Oct. 2, 1930); *Legend* for Piano and Orch. (1933; London, Jan. 12, 1934); *Concertino pastorale* for Strings (Canterbury, June 14, 1939); *Epic March* (1941–42; London, June 27, 1942); *Satyricon*, overture (1944–46; London, Sept. 11, 1946). **Brass Band:** *A Downland Suite* (London, Oct. 1, 1932); *Comedy Overture* (London, Sept. 29, 1934; reworked version as *A London Overture* for Orch., London, Sept. 23, 1936). **CHAMBER:** 2 string quartets (1897, 1897); Sextet for Clarinet, Horn, 2 Violins, Viola, and Cello (1898; London, March 25, 1960); *Berceuse* for Violin and Piano (1902); 3 trios for Violin, Cello, and Piano: No. 1, *Phantasie-Trio* (1906; London, Jan. 26, 1909), No. 2 (London, June 12, 1917), and No. 3 (BBC, London, April 4, 1938); 2 violin sonatas: No. 1 (1908–09; London, March 7, 1913; rev. 1917 and 1944) and No. 2 (1915–17; London, March 6, 1917); *Bagatelle* for Violin and Piano (1911); Trio for Clarinet, Cello, and Piano (1912–14; London, June 9, 1914); Cello Sonata (1923; London, April 4, 1924; arranged as a Viola Sonata by L. Tertis, 1941; BBC, Bedford, Dec. 14, 1942); *Fantasy Sonata* for Clarinet and Piano (1943; London, Feb. 5, 1944). **Piano:** *In Those Days* (1895); *Sea Idyll* (1899–1900); *Rhapsody* No. 1 (1905–06) and No. 2 (1915); *Decorations* (1912–13); *The Almond Trees* (1913); *3 Dances* (1913); [4] *Preludes* (1913–15; No. 3, *The Holy Boy*, arranged for String Orch., 1941); [3] *London Pieces* (1917–20); *Leaves from a Child's Sketchbook* (1918); *Merry Andrew* (1918); *The Towing Path* (1918); Sonata (1918–20; London, June 12, 1920); *Summer Evening* (1919); *The Darkened Valley* (1920); *2 Pieces* (1921); *On a Birthday Morning* (1922); *Soliloquy* (1922); *Equinox* (1922); *Prelude* (1924); *2 Pieces* (1925); Sonatina (1926–27; BBC, London, April 19, 1928); *Ballade* (1929); *2 Pieces* (1929–30); *Ballade of London Nights* (1930); *Indian Summer* (1932); *Month's Mind* (1932); *Green Ways: 3 Lyric Pieces* (1937); *Sarnia: An Island Sequence* (1940–41; London, Nov. 29, 1941); *3 Pastels* (1941; BBC, Bedford, March 8, 1942); *Columbine* (1949; rev. 1951). **VOCAL:** *Vexilla Regis*, hymn for Passion Sunday for Soloists, Chorus, Brass, and Organ (1898); [5] *Songs of a Wayfarer* for Voice and Piano (1903–11); *Te Deum* for Chorus and Organ (1907); *Psalm 42* for Soloists, Chorus, and String Orch. (1908); *Greater love hath no man*, motet for Treble and Baritone Soli, Chorus, and Organ (1911; also with Orch., 1922); *Communion Service* for Chorus and Organ (1913); *Sea Fever* for Voice and Piano (1913); *The Land of Lost Content*, 6 songs for Voice and Piano (1920–21); *3 Songs to Poems by Thomas Hardy* for Voice and Piano (1925); *5 Poems by Thomas Hardy* for Baritone and Piano (1926); [6] *Songs Sacred and Profane* for Voice and Piano (1929–31); *These things shall be*, cantata for Baritone or Tenor, Chorus, and Orch. (1936–37; BBC, London, May 13, 1937); many other sacred works, choral pieces, and songs.

BIBL.: J. Longmire, *J. I.: Portrait of a Friend* (London, 1969); M. Searle, *J. I.: The Man and His Music* (Tunbridge Wells, 1979); M. Pilkington, *Gurney, I., Quilter and Warlock* (London, 1989); S. Craggs, *J. I.: A Catalogue, Discography, and Bibliography* (Oxford, 1993).—NS/LK/DM

Irgens-Jensen, Ludvig (Paul), Norwegian composer; b. Christiania, April 13, 1894; d. Piazza Armerina, Sicily, April 11, 1969. He received training in philosophy, music theory, and piano in Christiania, but was mainly self-taught in composition. In 1946 he received the Norwegian guaranteed income for art. His works were mainly influenced by late German Romanticism.

WORKS: ORCH.: *Tema con variazioni* (1925); Passacaglia (1926); *Partita sinfonica* (1937); Sym. (1942); *Canto d'omaggio*, festival overture (1950). **CHAMBER:** Violin Sonata (1924); Piano Quintet (1927). **VOCAL:** *Japanischer Frühling* for Voice and Piano (1918–19); *Der Gott und die Bajadere*, cantata (1921–32); *Heimferd* (The Journey Home), oratorio for Soloists, Chorus, and Orch. for the 900th anniversary of the death of St. Olav (1929; Oslo, 1930; also as an opera, Oslo, Aug. 27, 1947); choruses; songs.

BIBL.: H. Irgens, *L. I.-J.: His Life and His Songs* (thesis, Univ. of Iowa, 1994).—NS/LK/DM

Irino, Yoshirō, Japanese composer and pedagogue; b. Vladivostok, Nov. 13, 1921; d. Tokyo, June 28, 1980. Although of pure Japanese ancestry, he was baptized in the Greek Orthodox faith, which he retained throughout his life. His family took him to Tokyo when he was 6. He studied economics at the Univ. of Tokyo; at the same time, he took composition lessons with Saburo Moroi. He became a teacher at the Tōhō Gakuen School of Music in 1952, serving as its direction from 1960 to 1970. He then was prof. at the Tokyo Music Coll. (from 1973). A prolific composer, he wrote music of all categories, adopting a style decidedly modern in character, marked by fine instrumental coloration, with a complete mastery of contemporary techniques. Most of his vocal and stage music is imbued with a pronounced Japanese sensibility, with touches that are almost calligraphic in their rhythmic precision.

WORKS: DRAMATIC: *Kamisama ni shikarareta otoko* (The Man in Fear of God), radio operetta (NHK, May 25, 1954); *Fuefuki to Ryuo no musumetachi* (The Piper and the Dragon King's Daughters), radio opera (1959); *Sarudon no mukoiri* (The Marriage of Mr. Monkey), radio opera (NHK, Nov. 26, 1961; first stage perf., Tokyo, March 15, 1962; in collaboration with Moroi and Shimizu); *Aya no tsuzumi* (The Damask Drum), television opera (NHK, Aug. 9, 1962; first stage perf., Tokyo, March 26, 1975); *Sonezaki shinju* (The Lover's Suicide at Sonezaki), chamber opera (Osaka, April 10, 1980). **ORCH.:** *Adagietto and Allegro vivace* (1949); Sinfonietta for Chamber Orch. (1953); Ricercari for Chamber Orch. (1954); Double Concerto for Violin, Piano, and Orch. (1955); *Concerto grosso* (1957); Sinfonia (1959); Concerto for Strings (1960); Suite for Jazz Ensemble (1960); *Music* for Harpsichord, Percussion, and 19 Strings (1963); Sym. No. 2 (1964); *2 Fantasies* for 17 and 20 Kotos (1969); *Sai-un* (Colorful Clouds) for 15 Strings (1972); *Wandlungen* for 2

Shakuhachi and Orch. (1973). **CHAMBER:** 2 string quartets (1945, 1957); Piano Trio (1948); String Sextet (1950); *Chamber Concerto* for 7 Instruments (1951); Quintet for Clarinet, Saxophone, Trumpet, Cello, and Piano (1958); *Divertimento* for 7 Winds (1958); *Music* for Violin and Cello (1959); *Music* for Vibraphone and Piano (1961); *Partita* for Wind Quintet (1962); String Trio (1965); *3 Movements* for 2 Kotos and Jushichi-gen (1966); *7 Inventions* for Guitar and 6 Players (1967); Violin Sonata (1967); *3 Movements* for Cello (1969); Sonata for Piano, Violin, Clarinet, and Percussion (1970); Trio for Flute, Violin, and Piano (1970); *Globus I* for Horn and Percussion (1970), *II* for Marimba, Double Bass, and Percussion (1971), and *III* for Violin, Cello, Piano, Harp, Shō, and 2 Dancers (1975); Suite for Viola (1971); *Cloudscape* for String Ensemble (1972); *3 Scenes* for 3 Kotos (1972); *Strömung* for Flute, Harp, and Percussion (1973); *Shō-yo* for Japanese Instruments (1973); *Gafu* for Flute, Shō, and Double Bass (1976); *Movements* for Marimba (1977); Cosmos for Shakuhachi, Violin, Piano, 2 Kotos, and Percussion (1978); *Shi-dai* for Shakuhachi, 20-gen, 17-gen, and Shamisen (1979); *Duo Concertante* for Alto Saxophone and Koto (1979). **VOCAL:** Various works, including *A Demon's Bride* for Chorus, Oboe, Horn, Piano, and Percussion (1970).—**NS/LK/DM**

Iron Butterfly, pioneers in progressive and hard rock; f. 1966, San Diego, Calif. **MEMBERSHIP:** Doug Ingle, voc., org. (b. Omaha, Nebr., Sept. 9, 1946); Ron Bushy, drm. (b. Washington, D.C., Sept. 23, 1941); Eric Brann, gtr. (b. Boston, Aug. 10, 1950); Lee Dorman, bs., voc. (b. St. Louis, Mo., Sept. 19, 1945). While they are mostly remembered for their monumental 17-minute song "In-A-Gadda-Da-Vida," Iron Butterfly made important inroads for future heavy metal bands and progressive rock bands. They also received the first platinum record awarded by the RIAA. Formed in 1966 by Doug Ingle, the son of a church organist, they moved to L.A. Ingle initially saw the band as a sidelight—he wanted to take his classical training and write movie scores. The band played frequently and was signed to Atco records. Their first album, *Heavy*, did fairly well and put them on the road with a Who's Who of late 1960s rock: The Doors, Cream, The Jefferson Airplane, The Grateful Dead and The Who, among others. The Dead were busy introducing lengthy improvisations into a rock format, while The Who was experimenting with long-form songs like "Rael" and music that would eventually form the nucleus of *Tommy*. In that atmosphere, they started playing a song that Ingle had written before the tour. Originally a country-rock ballad, he introduced the tune to the band after a sleepless day and a half and a bottle of wine. Where he wrote the song as "In the Garden of Eden," drummer Ron Bushy jotted down the lyrics as he heard them, phonetically. The song remained as he heard it: "In-A-Gadda-Da-Vida." The song started taking on a life of its own as the band continued to play it live until 1969 when the band broke up. Ingle created some semi-classical organ solos; Brann added searing, feedback guitar solos; and Bushy was even allowed to clock in with a two-minute drum solo. By the time they came to record it, it ran over 17 minutes long. Recorded in one take, it was a tough sell, but eventually Atlantic released it. The side-long song became a favorite at the burgeoning "underground" FM stations—its length allowed deejays the opportunity to use the bathroom or bolt a meal. The song caught on, and the album rose to #4 on the charts, selling over four million copies and earning the RIAA's first platinum record. A Detroit AM deejay wanted to play the song and created a single-length edit, which Atco released. That version of the song went to #30. The album would spend over a year and a half in the Top Ten.

The follow-up, *Ball*, actually fared better in the charts, going to #3, but only went gold. A live album in 1970 went to #20, featuring another side-long version of "In-A-Gadda-Da-Vida," this one live. After putting out the #16 *Metamorphosis* in 1970, the band burned out and called it a day. They reformed in 1975, and again in the mid-1990s, touring with other bands from the 1960s and 1970s as part of nostalgia package tours. In 1995, Rhino released an extended version of the *In-A-Gadda-Da-Vida* album with outtakes and other previously unreleased material.

DISC.: *Heavy* (1968); *In A Gadda Da Vida* (1968); *Ball* (1969); *Iron Butterfly Live* (1970); *Metamorphosis* (1970); *Ball/Metamorphosis* (1975); *Scorching Beauty* (1975); *Sun and Steel* (1976); *In-A-Gadda-Da-Vida* (1995); *Rare Flight* (1984).—**HB**

Iron Maiden, one of the leading bands in the new wave of British Metal, ca. 1980; f. 1976, London, England. **MEMBERSHIP:** Steven Harris, bs. (b. London, England, March 12, 1957); David Murray, gtr. (b. London, England, Dec. 23, 1958); Adrian Smith, gtr. (b. Feb. 27, 1957); Bruce (real name, Paul Bruce) Dickinson, voc. (b. Nottinghamshire, England, Aug. 7, 1958); Nicko McBrain, drm. (b June 4, 1954). Formed by former pub rock bassist Steve Harris, with singer Paul Di'Anno, guitarist Dave Murray and drummer Doug Sampson, the band played around London, earning a devoted following. However, record companies couldn't get their ears and minds around the group's too-radical-for-heavy-metal yet too-heavy-for-punk sound. Harris never took to the punk comparisons, however, once claiming, "We used to frighten the life out of the punks." They cut a three-song demo, which they sent to a deejay at the hard rock club The Kingsbury Bandwagon Soundhouse. When the tape started getting heavy play at the club, the band's fortunes started looking up. They self-released the EP as the Soundhouse Tapes.

The band went through a few more personnel changes, most notably replacing Sampson with former Samson drummer Clive Burr. They signed with Harvest records and their first Harvest single, "Running Free," charted, earning them a slot on the English TV show *Top of the Pops*. They refused to lip-synch their song, making them the first live band to play the show since The Who trashed the sound stage playing the single "5:15" from *Quadrophenia* nearly a decade earlier. The band's eponymous debut album rose to #4 on the English charts. What would become the Iron Maiden formula started to gel on their next album, *Killers*. The first ingredient was their logo cum mascot, Eddie, a seven-foot tall zombie. The second ingredient was Adrian Smith joining the band, firing up the group's dual guitar attack. The weak link proved to be Di'Anno, who had a drinking problem.

The group took care of that with their third album, bringing in Burr's old mate from his Samson days, singer Bruce Dickinson. His debut, *The Number of the Beast*, proved to be the band's breakthrough album. The band started enjoying massive success with songs like "Run to the Hills" and the title track. Without the benefit of airplay, the album hit #33 and went platinum in the U.S., partly because the band toured for eight or nine months in support of the record. While other new wave British metal bands started to find their level, Iron Maiden continued to gain ground with their next release, *Piece of Mind*. Nicko McBrain replaced Burr on drums. McBrain had worked with the band Trust, which supported Iron Maiden on tour in Europe. The album went platinum in the U.S. again, hitting #14 on the charts, once more with a minimal amount of airplay.

The band's 1984 effort, *Powerslave*, covered no new ground, but in many ways that seemed to be what the band's fans wanted. They still turned out in force for concerts the world over and with tunes like "Two Minutes to Midnight," the album once again sold platinum in the U.S. and charted at #21. Their tours became increasingly more elaborate, with sets that included different permutations of Eddie. For example, the Slavery Tour featured their mascot as a 20-foot tall mechanical monster. That tour ran fully 11 months. While on the road, they recorded *Live after Death*, the de rigeur double live album. However, unlike so many live albums, this one sold platinum and went to #19 on the charts.

When they came out with their next studio album, 1986's *Somewhere in Time*, the band had taken some liberties with their sound, adding guitar synthesizers to the regular twin attack. The song "Stranger in a Strange Land" even earned the group some rock radio airplay. The album sold over a million copies in the U.S. on its way to #11. On the accompanying tour, Eddie took the form of a giant understage inflatable that lifted most of the band off the stage in his hands while McBrain took the ride on the monster's head. Elaborating on the more progressive sound even more, *Seventh Son of a Seventh Son* was actually a concept album, with another rock single, "I Can Play with Madness." The album topped the English charts and hit #12 in the U.S., going gold.

After a decade together, the band took 1987 off. Dickinson released a solo record, *Tattooed Millionaire*, and a book, *The Adventures of Lord Iffy Boatrace*. When they got back together, Harris decided that the band should get back to basics rather than getting bogged down in the technology that informed their previous albums. Smith disagreed and left the band. Janick Gers replaced him. They recorded *No Prayer for the Dying*, something of a throwback to the sound of *Powerslave*. The song "Bring Your Daughter to the Slaughter" was featured in the film *Nightmare on Elm St. 5* and awarded a Golden Raspberry as the worst song in 1989, but it topped the British charts anyway. In addition to stripping down the sound, they stripped down their show, taking it to smaller venues. The album went gold and rose to #17 on the charts.

Their 1992 album *Fear of the Dark* climbed to #12 on the charts, but failed to go gold. As the band took it on tour Dickinson announced that he was leaving the band to devote more time to his side project, Skunkworks. He

invited people to send demos. The band recorded two albums while on the road. *A Real Live One* featured their more recent material. *A Real Dead One* sported some of the band's classic tracks. The band replaced him with Blaze Bayley, formerly from the band Wolfsbane. He joined the band on the album *X-Factor*. When this failed to live up to expectations, the band put out a greatest hits package, *The Best of the Beast*, which sported on new tune, "Virus."

They put out *Virtual XI*, their 11th studio album, in 1997. The album's twin themes of soccer and video games reflected the interests of the band. They were in the process of starring in the video game *Ed Hunter* as they made the record, which was reflected in the video for the song "The Angel and the Gambler," which placed the band in a completely computer-generated environment. An album of the same name, featuring the fans' favorites as determined by an internet poll, also accompanied the game. By 1999, Bayley had left the band and both Dickinson and Smith had returned to the fold, spurring a three-guitar attack. The band floated a bond issue based on future royalties to the tune of $30,000,000 in the spring of 1999; apparently, savvy investors are counting on this group to continue to rake in the bucks through touring and records.

DISC.: *Soundhouse Tapes* (1979); *Iron Maiden* (1980); *Killers* (1981); *Maiden Japan* (1981); *The Number of the Beast* (1982); *Brain Damage Tour of Europe* (1983); *Piece of Mind* (1983); *Powerslave* (1984); *Live after Death (The World Slavery Tour)* (1985); *Somewhere in Time* (1986); *Maidenmania* (1987); *Seventh Son of a Seventh Son* (1988); *Aces High* (1988); *No Prayer for the Dying* (1990); *Running Free Run to the Hills* (1990); *The Clairvoyant* (1990); *Trooper* (1990); *Stranger in a Strange Land* (1990); *Fear of the Dark* (1992); *A Real Live One* (1993); *A Real Dead One* (1993); *Live at Donnington '92 Virgin/1* (1994); *The X Factor* (1995); *Virtual XI* (1998); *Brave New World* (2000).—**BH**

Irving, Robert (Augustine), English conductor; b. Winchester, Aug. 28, 1913; d. there, Sept. 13, 1991. He studied at Winchester Coll. (1926–32), at New Coll., Oxford (B.A., 1935), and with Sargent and Lambert at the Royal Coll. of Music in London (1934–36). He was assoc. conductor of the BBC Scottish Orch. in Glasgow (1945–48); after serving as principal conductor of the Sadler's Wells (later Royal) Ballet in London (1948–58), he was music director of the N.Y.C. Ballet (1958–89); he also conducted for the Martha Graham Dance Co. in N.Y. (1960–65; 1974–77). Although he appeared as a guest conductor with various orchs. in England the U.S., it was as an exemplary conductor of ballet that he secured his reputation. He also wrote music for the theater and for films.—**NS/LK/DM**

Irvis, Charlie (actually, Charles), jazz trombonist; b. N.Y., c. 1899; d. there, c. 1939. The brother of pianist Gibbie Irvis, Charlie began playing in a boys' band with Earle Howard, Bubber Miley, etc. He was with Lucille Hegamin's Blue Flame Syncopators (1920–21), then with Willie "The Lion" Smith at Capitol Palace. He joined the Washingtonians (Duke Ellington, Elmer Snowden) in early 1924 (replacing John Anderson), with Duke Ellington and Elmer Snowden

(1925–26). (During the 1920s, he also took part in many Clarence Williams recording sessions.) He was with Charlie Johnson (1927–28), then toured with Jelly Roll Morton (1929–30), and was a member of Bubber Miley's Band (1931). He spent most of the 1930s working with either Charlie Johnson or Elmer Snowden. Irvis is credited with creating the plunger-mute style of trombone playing that became a hallmark of Ellington's sound.—JC/LP

Irwin, Cecil, jazz saxophonist, clarinetist, arranger; b. Evanston, Ill., Dec. 7, 1902; d. near Des Moines, Iowa, May 3, 1935. Irwin was with the Carroll Dickerson Orch. (c. 1924–25), then with Erskine Tate, the Cafe de Paris Orch. (Chicago, 1927), and Junie Cobb before joining Earl Hines in December 1928 as tenor saxophonist/ arranger. He freelanced on numerous recordings in the 1920s. Other than brief absences, he remained with Earl Hines until the time of his death in an accident. He was killed instantly when the Hines's band coach was involved in a crash near Des Moines. Hines attempted, unsuccessfully, to recruit Lester Young as a replacement. —JC/LP

Irwin, Dennis (Wayne), jazz bassist; b. Birmingham, Ala., Nov. 28, 1951. His family is very musical, with one brother, David, a professional clarinetist. Irwin also played clarinet through his teens, but switched to bass at age 19 while attending North Tex. State Univ. (1969–74). After working with Red Garland from 1973–74, he relocated to N.Y., where he worked with various leaders through the mid-1970s. From 1977–80, he was a member of Art Blakey's Jazz Messengers; while a member of the group, he supplied them with several compositions, including "Kamal." He has since worked with various leaders, often at the same time, including a long stay with Mel Lewis (1981–90) and John Scofield (from 1991).—LP

Isaac, Adèle, French soprano; b. Calais, Jan. 8, 1854; d. Paris, Oct. 22, 1915. She studied with Duprez in Paris, making her debut at the Théâtre Montmartre in Paris in 1870 in *Noces de Jeannette*. She then sang at the Paris Opéra-Comique (1873; 1878–88) and the Paris Opéra (1883–85), retiring from the stage in 1894. She was noted for her performances of French operatic roles. —NS/LK/DM

Isaac (also **Isaak, Izak, Yzac, Ysack**), **Heinrich** or **Henricus,** important Flemish composer; b. Flanders, c. 1450; d. Florence, March 26, 1517. He was in the service of Lorenzo de'Medici in Florence (1485–92), and a singer at Ss. Annunziata and a member of the Cantori di S. Giovanni (until 1493). In 1496 he went to Vienna, where he was named court composer (1497). He then traveled widely before settling in Florence in 1514. He became known as Arrigo Tedesco (Henry the German; Low Latin, Arrighus), the Italian term "Tedesco" being used at the time for Flemish people as well as Germans. Isaac was a master of cantus firmus technique in both masses and motets; he also wrote French chansons, Italian frottole, and German lieder. His profound influence on German music was continued through his student Senfl, who ed. a voluminous collection of his motets as *Choralis Constantinus* (3 parts, 1550). His other works include about 40 masses and mass movements, 99 cycles of proper settings of the Mass, and various secular vocal works. A complete ed. of his works was publ. in the Corpus Mensurabilis Musicae series (1974 et seq.).

BIBL.: M. Staehelm, *Die Messen H. I.s* (3 vols., Bern and Stuttgart, 1977); M. Picker, *H. I.: A Guide to Research* (N.Y., 1991). —NS/LK/DM

Isabella Leonarda (real name, **Isabella Calegari**), Italian composer; b. Novara, 1620; d. there, c. 1700. In 1636 she became a nun and entered the convent of S. Ursula in Novara. She was made its mother superior in 1686 and in 1693 she became provincial mother superior. Her solo motets are particularly well crafted. In all, she publ. over 200 works in some 20 collections (1665–1700).—LK/DM

Isamitt, Carlos, Chilean composer; b. Rengo, Colchagua, March 13, 1887; d. Santiago, July 2, 1974. He studied both music and painting in Chile, then in Italy, Spain, France, and the Netherlands. As a composer, he became interested in the folk music of the Araucanian Indians, and made use of these authentic materials in several of his works: *4 movimientos sinfónicos* (1960), *Te kuduam mapuche* for Voice, Bassoon, and the Araucanian Drum Kultrún (1958), Harp Concerto (1957), and Sonata for Flute Solo (1954).—NS/LK/DM

Isbin, Sharon, American guitarist and teacher; b. Minneapolis, Aug. 7, 1956. She studied with Jeffrey Van in Minneapolis, then took courses at Yale Univ. (B.A., 1978; M.A., 1979); she also received instruction from Rosalyn Tureck, from Oscar Ghiglia at the Aspen (Colo.) Music School (1971–75), and from Alirio Diaz at the Banff Music Festival (1972). She won first prizes in the Toronto International Guitar Competition (1975), the Munich International Guitar Competition (1976), and the Queen Sofia Competition in Madrid (1979), subsequently appearing throughout the world as a soloist with orchs. and as a recitalist. She taught at N.Y.'s Manhattan School of Music (from 1979) and Mannes Coll. of Music (from 1984). In 1989 she became head of the guitar dept. at N.Y.'s Juilliard School. Her repertoire ranges from the Classical period to jazz, folk, and beyond. She has commissioned works from a variety of composers, including Leo Brouwer, Joan Tower, and Joseph Schwanter.—NS/LK/DM

Iseler, Elmer (Walter), Canadian choral conductor, teacher, and editor; b. Port Colborne, near Niagara Falls, Ontario, Oct. 14, 1927; d. Toronto, April 3, 1998. He began training in piano and organ in his youth. After studying organ and church music with Ulrich Leupold at Waterloo Lutheran Univ., he completed his education at the Univ. of Toronto (B.M., 1950) and the Ontario Coll. of Education. In 1951–52 he was an asst. rehearsal conductor with the Toronto Mendelssohn Choir, and then taught orchestral and choral music in Toronto high schools from 1952 to 1964. In 1954 he helped to organize the Toronto Festival Singers, which he conducted until 1978. From 1964 he was conductor of the Toronto Mendelssohn Choir and from 1965 to 1968 he taught choral music at the Univ. of Toronto. In 1978 he founded the Elmer Iseler Singers, which he conducted throughout Canada and abroad. He served as ed. of the Festival Singers of Canada Choral Series, which later became the Elmer Iseler Choral Series. In 1975 he was named an Officer of the Order of Canada. In 1990 the Assn. of Canadian Choral Conductors presented him with the National Choral Award for Distinguished Service. Iseler's repertoire was vast, but he was especially known for his interpretations of masterworks from the Tudor and 20th century eras. He was a champion of the music of Healey Willan.—NS/LK/DM

Isepp, Martin (Johannes Sebastian), Austrian pianist and harpsichordist; b. Vienna, Sept. 30, 1930. He studied at Lincoln Coll., Oxford, and at the Royal Academy of Music in London. In 1957 he joined the music staff of the Glyndebourne Festival, serving as head of its music staff from 1978 to 1993. From 1973 to 1976 he was on the faculty of the Juilliard School in N.Y. He became best known as an accompanist to many of the foremost singers of the day, including Dame Janet Baker, Hans Hotter, Elisabeth Schwarzkopf, and John Shirley-Quirk.—NS/LK/DM

Isham, Mark, American composer, instrumentalist, and synthesizer programmer; b. N.Y., Sept. 7, 1951. His mother was a violinist, and his father taught music and art. Mark studied piano, violin, and trumpet from an early age. After his family moved to Calif., he played trumpet in the Oakland and San Francisco Syms. and in the San Francisco Opera Orch. He also played in various jazz and rock bands, including the Beach Boys. He became a synthesizer programmer in the early 1970s, and in 1979 he formed (with Peter Maunu, Patrick O'Hearn, and Terry Bozzio) the groundbreaking art-rock Group 87, which produced two albums before its demise in 1986. His first solo album (1983) was the first electronic release by the New Age label Windham Hill. Named one of the top three composers of the 1980s by the American Film Inst., Isham's numerous film scores include the important documentary *The Times of Harvey Milk* (1985), as well as *A River Runs Through It* (1992), which garnered him both Academy Award and Grammy Award nominations, *Short Cuts* (1993), *Nell* (1994), which garnered a Golden Globe nomination, and *Quiz Show* (1994). From 1996 he was also active composing for television, receiving an Emmy Award for his work for the critically acclaimed *EZ Streets*. Isham's music is slow and delicate, with overlapping harmonies and rhythms in a haze of electronics. It is distinct from other New Age music in its nobility, a hieratic effect created by his special use of brass instruments. Among his early compositions are *Vapor Drawings* (1983), *Castalia* (1988), and *Tibet* (1989).—NS/LK/DM

Ishii, Kan, Japanese composer, brother of **Maki Ishii**; b. Tokyo, March 30, 1921. He is one of two sons of Baku Ishii, a renowned scholar of modern dance. He studied in Tokyo at the Musashino Music School with Goh, Ikenouchi, and Odaka (1939–43), and in 1952 he took lessons with Orff at the Hochschule für Musik in Munich. Returning to Japan, he taught at the Tōhō Gakuen School of Music in Tokyo (1954–66), the Aichi-Prefectural Arts Univ. in Nagoya (1966–86), and the Showa Music Coll. (from 1986).

WORKS: DRAMATIC: O p e r a : *Mermaid and Red Candle* (1961); *Kaguyahime* (Prince Kaguya; 1963); *En-no-Gyojia* (Tokyo, 1964); *Lady Kesa and Morito* (Tokyo, Nov. 24, 1968); *Women are Wonderful* (1978); *Kantomi* (1981). **O p e r e t t a :** *Blue Lion* (1989). **B a l l e t :** *God and the Bayadere* (Tokyo, Nov. 6, 1950); *Birth of a Human* (Tokyo, Nov. 27, 1954); *Frökln Julie* (1955); *Shakuntara* (1961); *Marimo* (Tokyo, 1963); *Biruma no tategoto* (Harp of Burma; 1963); *Haniwa* (1963); *Hakai* (1965); *Ichiyo Higuchi* (1966). **O R C H .:** *Yama* (Mountain), symphonic poem (Tokyo, Oct. 7, 1954); *Kappa's Penny* for Youth Orch. (1956). **CHAMBER:** *Music for 8 Percussionists* (1970); *Viola Sonata* (1960); *Music for Flute* (1972). **VOCAL:** *Sinfonia Ainu* for Soprano, Chorus, and Orch. (1958–59); *The Reef*, cantata for Baritone, Chorus, 4 Pianos, and Percussion (1967); *Akita the Great* for Chorus and Brass (1968); *Foot steps to Tomorrow*, cantata for Solo Soprano (1972); folk songs; choruses. —NS/LK/DM

Ishii, Maki, Japanese composer and conductor, brother of **Kan Ishii**; b. Tokyo, May 28, 1936. His father, Baku Ishii, was a celebrated scholar of modern dance. As a child, he was introduced to traditional Japanese instruments. Later he studied piano, violin, and theory. After receiving instruction in conducting from Watanabe (1952–54), he studied theory and composition with Ifukube and Ikenouchi (from 1956) in Tokyo. In 1958 he went to Berlin to study composition with Blacher, counterpoint with Pepping, and 12-tone technique with Rufer. Upon returning to Tokyo in 1961, he was active with the electronic music studio at the NHK. In 1969 he was again in Berlin on a scholarship from the Deutscher Akademischer Austauschdienst. He subsequently was active as a composer and conductor in contemporary music circles in Europe, the U.S., and Asia. From 1978 to 1984 he was host and conductor of the TBS-TV program "Here Comes the Orchestra" in Japan. After serving as artistic director of the Tokyo Summer Festival from 1985 to 1989, he founded the Asian Music Festival there in 1990. In his works, Ishii attempts to combine the coloristic effects of Japanese instruments with European techniques of serial music and electronic sounds.

WORKS: *Prelude and Variations* for 9 Players (1959–60); *7 Stücke* for Small Orch. (1960–61); *Transitions* for Small Orch. (1962); *Aphorismen I* for String Trio, Percussion, and Piano (1963) and *II* for Piano (1972); *Galgenlieder* for Baritone, Men's Chorus, and 13 Players (1964); *Characters* for Flute, Oboe, Piano, and Guitar (1965); *Hamon* for Violin, Chamber Ensemble, and Tape (1965); *Expressions* for Strings (1967); *5 Elements* for Guitar and 6 Players (1967); *Piano Piece* for Pianist and Percussionist (1968); *Kyō-ō* for Piano, Orch., and Tape (1968); *Kyō- sō* for Percussion and Orch. (1969); *La-sen I* for 7 Players and Tape (1969) and *II* for Cello (1970); *Sō-gū I* for Shakuhachi and Piano (1970) and *II* for Gagaku and Orch. (1971; work resulting from simultaneous perf. of *Music for Gagaku* and *Dipol*); *Music for*

Gagaku (1970); *Dipol* for Orch. (1971); *Sen-ten* for Percussion Player and Tape (1971); *Chō-etsu* for Chamber Group and Tape (1973); *Polaritäten* for Soloists and Orch. (1973; work exists in 3 versions, each having different soloists: *I* for Biwa and Harp, *II* for Shakuhachi and Flute, and *III* for Biwa, Harp, Shakuhachi, and Flute); *Synkretismen* for Marimba, 7 Soloists, Strings, and 3 Percussionists (1973); *Anime Amare* for Harp and Tape (1974); *Jō* for Orch. (1975); *Lost Sounds III*, violin concerto (1978); *Translucent Vision* for Orch. (1981–82); *Afro-Concerto* for Percussion and Orch. (1982); *Kaguya-Hime*, symphonic suite for Percussion Group (1984); *Gioh*, symphonic poem for Yokobue (Japanese Flute) and Orch. (1984); *Gedatsu*, concerto for Yokobue and Orch. (1985); *Herbst Variante* for Orch. (1986); *Intrada* for Orch. (1986); *Concertante* for Marimba and 6 Percussionists (1988); *Fū Shi I* for Orch. (1989) and *II* for Nō-kan and Small Orch. (1989); *Suien Densetsu/Legend of the Water Flame* for Yokobue, Percussion, Reciter, and Dance (1990); *Weisser Nachtklang*, ode to Tchaikovsky for Strings (1990); *Strange Tales: Urashima Tarō/A Fiction: Relativity Theory*, "iconological performance" for Gagaku, Syōmyō, Percussion, Bugaku, and Modern Dance (1991); *South—Fire—Summer*, percussion concerto (1992); *Floating Wind*, symphonic triptych (1992); *West—Gold—Autumn* for String Quartet (1992); *Towards Time Dragon Deep*, symphonic ballad (1994); *Episode I* for Percussion (1994; rev. 1996); *Fagotte Rhapsodie* for 3 Bassoons and Contrabassoon (1996); *Beyond a Distance* for Cello (1997); *Die Stimme der Tempelglocken*, ballet (1997).—NS/LK/DM

Isidore of Seville, Spanish cleric; b. probably in Cartagena, c.560; d. Seville, April 4, 636. He was taken to Seville as a child, and in 599 he became archbishop there. Between 622 and 633 he compiled a treatise on the arts, *Etymologiarum sive originum libri XX.* He expressed the conviction that music can only be preserved through memory, for musical sounds could never be notated (*scribi non possunt*). The text was publ. in Oxford (1911); an Eng. tr. of the pertinent parts is included in Strunk's *Source Readings in Music History* (N.Y., 1950).

BIBL.: K. Schmidt, *Quaestiones de musicis scriptoribus romanis imprimis Cassiodoro et Isidoro* (Leipzig, 1898); J. Pérez de Urbel, *San Isidoro de Sevilla* (Barcelona, 1945); J. Fontaine, *Isidore de Séville et la culture classique dans l'Espagne wisigothique* (Paris, 1959); J. Madoz, *San Isidoro de Sevilla* (Madrid, 1960). —NS/LK/DM

Isler, Ernst, Swiss organist and music critic; b. Zürich, Sept. 30, 1879; d. there, Sept. 26, 1944. He studied at the Zürich Music School (1895–99) and with Rudorff at the Berlin Hochschule für Musik (1899–1901). He was organist at Zürich's Reformed Church (1901–19) and of the Fraumünster (1919–42), and also taught at the Cons. He became music critic of the influential daily newspaper *Neue Zürcher Zeitung* in 1902, and held this position until his death; from 1910 to 1927 he was also ed. of the *Schweizerische Musikzeitung*. He publ. *Das Züricherische Musikleben seit der Eröffnung der neuen Tonhalle (1895)* (2 vols., Zürich, 1935–36).

BIBL.: H. Grossmann et al., eds., *E. I. zum Gedächtnis* (Zürich, 1944).—NS/LK/DM

Isley Brothers, The, hitmakers who endured for over five decades, producing classics like "Twist and Shout" and "The Heat Is On"; **MEMBERSHIP:** Ronald Isley (b. Cincinnati, Ohio, May 21, 1941); O'Kelly Isley (b. Cincinnati, Ohio, Dec. 25, 1937, d. Alpine, N.J., March 31, 1986); Rudolph Isley (b. Cincinnati, Ohio, April 1, 1939). In September 1969, they were joined by Ernie Isley, lead gtr., drm. (b. March 7, 1952); Marvin Isley, bs., perc. (b. Aug. 18, 1953); and Chris Jasper, kybd. Isley Brothers Ronald and O'Kelly were performing as gospel singers backed by mother Sallye Isley by the early 1950s. Joined by brothers Vernon and Rudolph, the quartet sang at churches in Cincinnati and later toured churches throughout the Midwest. Reduced to a trio by the accidental death of Vernon in 1955 at the age of 11, The Isley Brothers moved to N.Y. in April 1956, recording unsuccessful singles for Teenage, Cindy, Gone, and Mark X Records. Debuting at the Howard Theater in Washington, D.C., the brothers were later showcased at N.Y.'s Apollo Theater and signed to RCA Victor Records. In 1959, they scored a moderate hit with their own composition "Shout," a smash pop hit for Joey Dee and The Starlighters in 1962, and recorded their own "Respectable," later recorded by The Yardbirds and a major hit for The Outsiders in 1966. Later in 1959, the entire Isley family relocated to Teaneck, N.J.

Following a single album for RCA, The Isley Brothers recorded for Atlantic Records under producers Jerry Leiber and Mike Stoller with little success. They subsequently joined the Wand subsidiary of Florence Greenberg's Scepter Records, where they scored a smash rhythm-and-blues and major pop hit with the classic "Twist and Shout" (a smash pop hit for The Beatles in 1964) and recorded "Nobody but Me," a near-smash pop hit for The Human Beinz in 1968. In 1963, The Isley Brothers moved to United Artists Records, where they recorded the original version of "Who's That Lady."

In 1964, The Isley Brothers toured the "chitlin'" circuit with then-unknown guitarist Jimi Hendrix and formed their own production company, T-Neck (named after Teaneck, N.J.). Their solitary release for the company, "Testify" (with Jimi Hendrix on guitar), distributed by Atlantic, fared poorly. By late 1965, the brothers had moved to Motown Records, where they achieved a smash rhythm-and-blues and major pop hit on Tamla with "This Old Heart of Mine (Is Weak for You)" in 1966. However, subsequent success eluded The Isley Brothers at Tamla.

By 1969, The Isley Brothers had revived T-Neck, working out a distribution deal with Buddah Records. Their first release on T-Neck, "It's Your Thing," became a smash rhythm-and-blues and pop hit and "Behind a Painted Smile" became a smash British-only hit. The three vocalizing Isley Brothers were joined by younger brothers Ernie and Marvin and Chris Jasper in September 1969 to form a self-contained band. Hits through the early 1970s included the R&B smashes "I Turned You On" and Stephen Stills's "Love the One You're With" (both major pop hits), "Lay-Away," and "Pop That Thang."

The Isley Brothers switched distributorship of T-Neck to Columbia in 1973, firmly establishing themselves as album artists with *3 + 3*, which yielded the pop and R&B smash "That Lady," featuring Ernie's Hendrix-influenced lead guitar work, and the R&B smashes "What It Comes Down to" and "Summer Breeze." Following the R&B smashes "Live It Up" and "Midnight Sky," The Isley Brothers scored their biggest album success with *The Heat Is On*, which produced the top R&B and smash pop hit "Fight the Power" and major hit "For the Love of You."

Adopting a sound with elements of both rock and disco, The Isley Brothers did not score any more major pop hits, yet they continued to achieve rhythm-and-blues smashes through 1983 with "Who Loves You Better," "The Pride," "Livin' in the Life," "Take Me to Your Next Phase," "I Wanna Be with You," "Don't Say Goodnight (It's Time for Love)," "Between the Sheets," and "Choosey Lover." In 1984, Ernie and Marvin Isley and Chris Jasper left The Isley Brothers and began recording as Isley, Jasper, Isley, scoring a top R&B hit with "Caravan of Love" in 1985. Chris Jasper and Ernie Isley each recorded solo later, with Jasper managing a smash rhythm-and-blues hit with "Superbad" in late 1987.

Reduced to a duo with the death of O'Kelly Isley from a heart attack on March 31, 1986, Ronald and Rudolph Isley achieved a smash R&B hit with "Smooth Sailin' Tonight" on Warner Bros. Records in 1987. Ronald scored a major pop and top easy-listening hit in conjunction with Rod Stewart on "This Old Heart of Mine" in 1990. Late that year, Ernie, Marvin, and Ronald Isley reunited as The Isley Brothers, recording for Warner Brothers, Elektra, and Island Records, where they scored a hit with "Let's Lay Together," written and produced by R. Kelly. The Isley Brothers were inducted into the Rock and Roll Hall of Fame in 1992.

DISC.: THE ISLEY BROTHERS: *Shout* (1959); *Twist and Shout* (1962); *Twisting and Shouting* (1964); *Take Some Time Out* (1964); *This Old Heart of Mine* (1966); *Soul on the Rocks* (1967); *In the Beginning (with Jimi Hendrix)* (1971); *It's Our Thing* (1969); *Brothers Isley* (1969); *Live at Yankee Stadium* (1969); *Get into Something* (1971); *Givin' It Back* (1971); *Brother, Brother, Brother* (1972); *Live* (1973); *3 + 3* (1973); *Live It Up* (1974); *The Heat Is On* (1975); *Harvest for the World* (1976/1987); *Go for Your Guns* (1977); *Showdown* (1978); *Winner Takes All* (1979); *Go All the Way* (1980); *Grand Slam* (1981); *Inside You* (1981); *The Real Deal* (1982); *Between the Sheets* (1983/1985); *Masterpiece* (1985); *Smooth Sailin'* (1987); *Spend the Night* (1989); *Tracks of Life* (1992); *The Isley Brothers Live* (1993); *Mission to Please* (1996); *Make Your Body Sing* (1996). **ERNIE AND MARVIN ISLEY AND CHRIS JASPER:** *Broadway's Closer to Sunset Boulevard* (1984); *Caravan of Love* (1985); *Different Drummer* (1987). **CHRIS JASPER:** *Superbad* (1988); *Time Bomb* (1989). **ERNIE ISLEY:** *High Wire* (1990).—BH

Isoir, André, French organist; b. St.-Dizier, July 20, 1935. He studied in Paris at the École Cesar Franck with Souberbielle and at the Cons. with Falcinelli, where he received the premier prix in 1960. In 1965 he took first prize in the St. Alban's Competition in England, then won three consecutive annual prizes in the Haarlem Competition in the Netherlands (1966–68). He served as organist at St.-Médard (1952–67), St.-Séverin (1967–73), and St.-Germain-des-Prés (from 1973). As a recitalist, he became particularly well known for his performances of the works of J.S. Bach.—NS/LK/DM

Ísólfsson, Páll, distinguished Icelandic organist, administrator, and composer; b. Stokkseyri, Oct. 12, 1893; d. Reykjavík, Nov. 23, 1974. He was an organ student of Straube in Leipzig (1913–18), where he was an asst. organist at the Thomaskirche (1917–19). Following further training with Bonnet in Paris (1925), he settled in Reykjavík. He was founding director of the Coll. of Music (1930–57), head of the music dept. of the Icelandic State Broadcasting Service (1930–59), and organist at the Cathedral (1939–68). He also made tours as a recitalist. In 1945 the Univ. of Oslo awarded him an honorary doctorate and in 1956 he was elected a member of the Royal Swedish Academy in Stockholm. He publ. an autobiography (2 vols., 1963–64). Among his compositions were a few orch. works; much vocal music, including a cantata for the 1,000th anniversary of the Icelandic Althing (Parliament; 1930), a university cantata, and a cantata for the 900th anniversary of the bishopric of Skálholt (1956), as well mixed and men's choruses and numerous songs for voice and piano, several organ works, including preludes, chorale preludes, *Introduction and Passacaglia*, and a chaconne, and piano pieces.

BIBL.: J. Thorarinsson, *P. I.* (Reykjavík, 1963). —NS/LK/DM

Isouard, Nicolò, important Maltese-born French composer; b. Malta, Dec 6, 1775; d. Paris, March 23, 1818. He was sent to Paris to study at the Pensionnat Berthaud, a preparatory school for engineers and artillerymen, and also studied piano there with Pin. With the outbreak of the French Revolution (1789), he returned to Malta, where he worked in a merchant's office and took courses in composition with Michel-Ange Vella and counterpoint with Azzopardi. His father then sent him to Italy to act as his assistant, but he found time to study harmony with Nicolas of Amendola in Palermo. He later studied composition with Sala in Naples, where he also received counsel from Guglielmi. His first opera, *L'avviso ai maritati* (Florence, 1794), proved so successful that he decided to devote himself fully to composition. In order not to embarrass his family, he used the name Nicolò de Malte, or simply Nicolò, professionally. The singer Senesino commissioned his second opera, *Artaserse* (Livorno, 1794), which also was a success. After serving as organist of the church of St. John of Jerusalem in Malta (1795–98), he went to Paris, gaining his first major success with the opera *Michel-Ange* (Opéra-Comique, Dec. 11, 1802) and quickly establishing himself as the leading composer at the Opéra-Comique. His *Cendrillon* (Feb. 22, 1810), *Joconde ou Les Coureurs d'aventures* (Feb. 28, 1814), and *Jeannot et Colin* (Oct. 17, 1814) were popular favorites. In spite of the competition from his friend and rival Boieldieu, he remained a protean figure in the musical life of Paris until his death.

WORKS (all first perf. in Paris unless otherwise given): **DRAMATIC: Opéras-comiques:** *Le Petit Page ou La Prison d'état* (Feb. 14, 1800; in collaboration with R. Kreutzer); *Le Tonnelier* (May 17, 1801); *La Statue ou La Femme avare* (April 26, 1802); *Les Confidences* (March 31, 1803); *Le Baiser et la quittance ou Une Aventure de garnison* (June 18, 1803; in collaboration with Boieldieu, Kreutzer, and Méhul); *Le Médecin turc*

(Nov. 19, 1803); *L'Intrigue aux fenêtres* (Feb. 25, 1805); *La Ruse inutile ou Les Rivaux par convention* (May 30, 1805); *Léonce ou Le Fils adoptif* (Nov. 18, 1805); *La Prise de Passaw* (Feb. 8, 1806); *Idala ou La Sultane* (July 30, 1806); *Les Rendez-vous bourgeois* (May 9, 1807); *Les Créanciers ou Le Remède à la goutte* (Dec. 10, 1807); *Un Jour à Paris ou La Leçon singulière* (May 24, 1808); *Cimarosa* (June 28, 1808); *La Victime des arts* (Feb. 27, 1811; in collaboration with Solie and Berton Fils); *La Fête au village* (March 31, 1811); *Le Billet de loterie* (Sept. 14, 1811); *Le Magicien sans magic* (Nov. 4, 1811); *Lully et Quinault* (Nov. 27, 1812); *Les Français à Venise* (June 14, 1813); *Bayard à Mézières ou Le Siège de Mézières* (Feb. 12, 1814; in collaboration with Boieldieu, Catel, and Cherubini); *Joconde ou Les Coureurs d'aventures* (Feb. 28, 1814); *Jeannot et Colin* (Oct. 17, 1814); *Les Deux Maris* (March 18, 1816); *L'Une pour l'autre ou L'Enlèvement* (May 11, 1816). O t h e r : *L'avviso ai maritati*, opera (Florence, 1794); *Artaserse*, opera (Livorno, 1794); *Rinaldo d'Asti*, opera (Malta, *c.*1796); *Il Barbiere di Siviglia*, opera buffa (Malta, *c.*1796); *L'improvisata in campagna*, opera buffa (Malta, 1797; rev. as *L'impromptu de campagne*, June 30, 1801); *I due avari*, opera buffa (Malta, *c.*1797); *Ginevra di Scozia*, opera (Malta, *c.*1798); *Il Barone d'Alba chiara*, opera (Malta, *c.*1798); *Flaminius à Corinthe*, opera (Feb. 27, 1801; in collaboration with Kreutzer); *Michel-Ange*, opera (Dec. 11, 1802); *Cendrillon*, opéra-féerie (Feb. 22, 1810); *Le Prince de Catane*, opera (March 4, 1813); *Aladin ou La Lampe merveilleuse*, opera (Feb. 6, 1822; completed by A. Benincori). O T H E R : Sacred music, cantatas, airs, and romances.

BIBL.: E. Wahl, *N. I.: Sein Leben und sein Schaffen auf dem Gebiet der Opéra Comique* (Munich, 1906).—NS/LK/DM

Isoz, Kálmán, Hungarian musicologist; b. Budapest, Dec. 7, 1878; d. there, June 6, 1956. He studied piano and theory at the Budapest Cons. (1895–99), and later completed his training at the Univ. of Budapest (Ph.D., 1921, with the diss. *Latin zenei paleográfia és a Pray-kódex zenei hangjelzései* [Latin Musical Paleography and the Musical Notation of the Pray Manuscript]; publ. in Budapest, 1922). In 1897 he joined the staff of the Hungarian National Museum in Budapest, where he was its general secretary (from 1920); from 1908 he also taught at the Univ. of Budapest. From 1924 to 1934 he was chief librarian of the Széchényi Library in Budapest, and then served as secretary of the Hungarian Royal Academy of Music from 1934 to 1943. With D. Bartha, he ed. Musicologica Hungaria. His writings on Hungarian music and musicians remain valuable sources.

WRITINGS (all publ. in Budapest): With I. Mészáros, *A filharmóniai társaság multja és jelene, 1853–1903* (Past and Present of the Philharmonic Society, 1853–1903; 1903); *Arnold György* (1908); *Erkel és a szimfónikus zene; Erkel emlékek és levelezés* (Erkel and Symphonic Music; Erkel Documents and Correspondence; 1910); *Erkel Ferenc* (1910); *Doppler Ferenc levelei Erkelhez* (Ferenc Doppler's Letters to Erkel; 1911); *Buda és Pest zenei müvelődése, I: 1686–1873* (The Musical Culture of Buda and Pest, I: 1686–1873; 1926); *Magyar zenemüvek könyvészete: Petőfi dalok* (Hungarian Bibliography of Music: Petőfi Songs; 1931); *A Pest-Budai Hangászegyesület es nyilvános hangversenyei, 1836–1851* (The Musical Society of Pest-Buda and its Public Concerts, 1836–1851; 1934); *Erkel Ferenc "Bátori Máriá"-ja* (1944).—NS/LK/DM

Israel, Brian M., American composer, pianist, and teacher; b. N.Y., Feb. 5, 1951; d. Syracuse, N.Y., May 8, 1986. He wrote an opera before he was eight, and received BMI student composer awards in 1966 and 1968. He pursued training in composition with Kay at Lehman Coll. in N.Y. (B.A., 1971) and with Palmer, Phillips, and Husa at Cornell Univ. (M.F.A., 1974; D.M.A., 1975), where he was on the faculty (1972–75). In 1975 he began teaching at Syracuse Univ., and in 1984 was made a prof. there. As a pianist, he performed much contemporary music. At the time of his death from leukemia, he was at the height of his compositional creativity. His works form an eclectic traversal from Baroque contrapuntal devices to serialism, juxtaposing humor and grotesqueries. He wrote extensively for concert band and frequently featured lesser-used instruments in solos.

WORKS: DRAMATIC: O p e r a : *Ladies' Voices*, mini-opera (1970); *The Obtaining of Portia*, chamber opera (Bloomington, Ind., April 13, 1976); *Love and Other Important Nonsense* (1977); *Winnie the Pooh*, children's opera (Syracuse, June 1, 1979). O R C H . : *Contrasts* for Cello and Orch. (1967); Sym. No. 2 (1974), No. 4 for Women's Chorus and Orch. (1984), and No. 6 for Soprano, Bass, and Orch. (Syracuse, N.Y., May 4, 1986); Viola Concerto (1974); *Dorian Variations* for Strings (1981); 2 sinfoniettas (1983, 1985); Mandolin Concerto (1985). B a n d : Sym. No. 1 (1972–74), No. 3 (1981), and No. 5 for Men's Chorus, Organ, and Band (1983–84); *Concerto Sacra* (1974); Piano Concerto (1979; Ithaca, N.Y., March 2, 1980); *Concerto Buffo* for 9 Soloists and Band (1980); Baritone Saxophone Concerto (1982); Trumpet Concerto (1982); *Rhapsody* for Baritone Horn and Band (1983); *Winter Evening Song* (1983); Clarinet Concerto (1984); Double Concerto for Sopranino and Bass Saxophones and Band (1984). C H A M B E R : Sonata for Cello and Percussion (1969); Clarinet Sonata (1969); 3 string quartets: No. 1, *Canonic Variations* (1971), No. 2, *Musik für den nachsten toten* (1976; rev. 1983), and No. 3 (1978); *Pastoral* for Oboe, Strings, and Piano (1971); Oboe Sonata (1972); Wind Quartet (1973); Piano Quintet (1973); *Dance Variations* for Trumpet and Tape (1974); 2 sonatas for 2 Tubas (1976, 1977); Sonata for 2 Trombones (1977); *Characteristic Variations* for Trumpet (1978); Concertino for Clarinet and String Quartet (1978); *Serenade* for 3 Trumpets (1978); Piano Trio, "in memoriam Ernest Bloch" (1980); Sonata for 2 Horns (1980); Concerto for Tuba Ensemble (1980); Alto Saxophone Sonata (1980); *Sonata di Chiesa* for 4 Trumpets (1983); *Serenata* for Flute, Cello, and Harpsichord (1983); Concertino for Saxophone Ensemble (1985); *Sonatinetta* for Mandolin and Guitar (1984); *Arioso and Canzona* for Saxophone Ensemble (1985); *Surrealistic Serenade* for Mandolin and Euphonium (1985); Piano Quartet, *Variations on a Hymn Tune* (1985); *Trois Grotesques* for Clarinet or Soprano Saxophone and Piano (1985). P i a n o : *Night Variations* (1973); *6 Miniatures* (1982); *12 Bagatelles* (1985). VOCAL: *Madrigal on Nudity* for Chorus (1971); ...*Where Night Gathers* for Tenor and 2 Pianos (1974); *M'bevrashua*, after Burma Shave road signs, for Chorus and Percussion (1974); *Lovesongs, Lions, and Lullabyes (Barcarolles)* for Soprano, Clarinet, and Piano (1979); *In Praise of Practically Nothing* for Tenor and 9 Instruments (1980); *Psalm 117* for Chorus, Organ, and Trumpet (1981); *The Song of Moses*, canticle for Chorus, Organ, and Brass Quartet (1985). —NS/LK/DM

Isserlis, Julius, Russian pianist; b. Kishinev, Nov. 7, 1888; d. London, July 23, 1968. He studied with Puchalsky at the Kiev Cons.; then with Safonov and Taneyev at the Moscow Cons. He taught at the Moscow Phil. Inst. of Music (1913–23), then in Vienna (1923–28);

in 1928 he settled in London. In addition to Russian composers, he was known for his performances of Chopin. He wrote a number of character pieces for piano.—NS/LK/DM

Isserlis, Steven, English cellist; b. London, Dec. 19, 1958. He received his training at the International Cello Centre in London (1969–76) and at the Oberlin (Ohio) Coll.-Cons. of Music (1976–78). In 1977 he made his London debut at Wigmore Hall, and then performed throughout England. His tours abroad have taken him all over Europe, North America, and Israel; in addition to his solo engagements with orchs., was also active as a recitalist and chamber music performer. In 1993 he received the Gregor Piatigorsky Artist Award. His repertoire embraces the traditional cello repertoire, including early music played on original instruments, and also includes much contemporary music. In 1989 he was soloist in the premiere of Tavener's *The Protecting Veil* at the London Promenade Concerts.—NS/LK/DM

Istel, Edgar, eminent German musicologist; b. Mainz, Feb. 23, 1880; d. Miami, Fla., Dec. 17, 1948. He studied composition with Volbach in Mainz, and then took courses with Thuille at the Munich Hochschule für Musik and Sandberger at the Univ. of Munich (Ph.D., 1900, with the diss. *J.J. Rousseau als Komponist seiner lyrischen Scene "Pygmalion"*; publ. in *Publikationen der International Musikgesellschaft*, I/i, Leipzig, 1901). He was active as a lecturer, critic, and writer on music in Munich (1900–13), and then taught at Berlin's Humboldt Academy (1913–19) and Lessing Hochschule (1919–20). In 1920 he moved to Madrid, where he remained until the outbreak of the civil war in 1936; then went to England, and eventually to the U.S. (1938). He was also a composer; wrote five operas, oratorios, and smaller pieces.

WRITINGS: *Das deutsche Weihnachtsspiel und seine Wiedergeburt aus dem Geiste der Musik* (1901); *Richard Wagner im Lichte eines zeitgenössischen Briefwechsels* (1902); *Peter Cornelius* (1906); *Die Entstehung des deutschen Melodramas* (1906); *Die komische Oper* (1906); *Die Blütezeit der musikalischen Romantik in Deutschland* (1909); *Das Kunstwerk Richard Wagners* (1910); *Das Libretto* (1914; Eng. tr., 1922, as *The Art of Writing Opera Librettos*); *Die moderne Oper vom Tode Wagners bis zum Weltkrieg* (1915); *Niccolo Paganini* (1919); *Revolution und Oper* (1919); *Das Buch der Oper* (1919); *Die deutschen Meister von Gluck bis Wagner* (1919); *Bizet und Carmen* (1927).—NS/LK/DM

Istomin, Eugene (George), distinguished American pianist; b. N.Y., Nov. 26, 1925. He began piano lessons as a child with Kiriena Siloti, and then studied at the Mannes Coll. of Music in N.Y.; at 12, he entered the Curtis Inst. of Music in Philadelphia, where he was a student of Serkin and Horszowski. After winning the Philadelphia Orch. youth competition, he appeared with that orch. under Ormandy's direction as soloist in Chopin's second Piano Concerto on Nov. 17, 1943. He also won the Leventritt Award, which led to his first appearance as soloist with the N.Y. Phil. under Rodzinski's direction in Brahms's second Piano Concerto on Nov. 21, 1943. In succeeding years, he was engaged as a

soloist with principal American orchs. and was active as a recitalist. From 1956 he made regular tours abroad. He also played in the renowned Stern-Rose-Istomin Trio from 1961 until Rose's death in 1984. In 1975 he married Casals's widow Martita. Istomin was one of the leading pianists of his generation.—NS/LK/DM

Istrate, Mircea, Romanian pianist and composer; b. Cluj, Sept. 27, 1929. He studied piano and composition at the Cluj Cons. (1945–53) and in Bucharest (1954–57), where he subsequently taught piano.

WORKS: ORCH.: *Muzică stereofonică* for 2 String Orchs. (1955–57); *Algoritm* (1964); *Interferente* (Interferences) for Orch. and Electronics (1965); *Pulsations* (1973). **CHAMBER:** Flute Sonata (1954); *Burlesca* for Violin, Oboe, Clarinet, Bassoon, and Double Bass (1955); Oboe Sonata (1962); *Evenimente I- II-III*, etc., for Prepared Piano, Percussion within a Piano, Electric Guitar, Double Bass, Vibraphone, Horn, Marimba, and Tape (1966). **VOCAL:** *Evocare* for Mezzo-soprano, Women's Chorus, and Orch. (1960); *Pe o plajă japoneză* (On a Japanese Beach), sequences for Women's Chorus, Orch., and Tape (1961); songs.—NS/LK/DM

Ištvan, Miloslav, Czech composer and teacher; b. Olomouc, Sept. 2, 1928; d. Brno, Jan. 20, 1990. He was a student of Kvapil at the Brno Academy of Music and Dramatic Arts (1948–52), and then completed his postgraduate studies there (1953–56). In 1956 he joined its faculty as an asst. lecturer, becoming a lecturer there in 1966. He was also active with the avant-garde Group A and Group B, and worked in the electronic music studios of Brno Radio. In 1961 he won the Janáček Prize, and in 1982 and 1988 he was awarded prizes of the Union of Czech Composers. After following nationalist trends in his works, he adopted contemporary techniques, including serialism and electronics.

WORKS: ORCH.: Concerto for Horn, Strings, and Piano (1949); Sym. (1952); *Winter Suite* for Strings, Piano, and Percussion (1956); Concerto-Sym. for Piano and Orch. (1957); *Ballad of the South*, 3 symphonic frescoes after Lewis Allan's satirical view of the American South (1960); Concertino for Violin and Chamber Orch. (1961); *6 Studies* for Chamber Orch. (1964); Sonata for Violin and Chamber Orch. (1970); *In Memoriam Josef Berg* (1971); *Shakespearean Variations* (1975); *The Games* (1977); *Partita* for 16 Strings (1980); *Tempus Ire* (1983); *Solitude* for Strings (1988). **CHAMBER:** Trio for Clarinet, Cello, and Piano (1950); Clarinet Sonata (1954); Piano Trio (1958); *Dodekameron* for 12 Players (1962–64); 2 string quartets (1963, 1986); *Ritmi ed antiritmi* for 2 Pianos and 2 Percussionists (1966); Cello Sonata (1970); *Omaggio à J.S. Bach* for Wind Quintet (1971); *Psalmus niger* for 6 Percussionists (1971); *Blacked-out Landscape*, in memory of those fallen in World War II, for String Quartet (1975); *The Micro-Worlds Diptych: Summer Micro-Worlds* for Flute, Harp, and Harpsichord, and *Micro-Worlds of My Town* for 2 Violas, Oboe, and Clarinet (1977); *Capriccio* for Vibraphone, Marimba, and Percussion (1978); *Canto I* for Viola (1979), *II* for Prepared Violas and Woman's Voice (1980), and *III* for Flute (1983); Trio for Clarinet, Piano, and Percussion (1987); *Rotations and Returns* for Horn, Viola, and Cello (1988). **Piano:** 3 sonatas (1954, 1959, 1978); *Odyssey of a Child from Lidice* (1963); *Variations* for 2 Pianos (1972). **VOCAL:** *Conjuration of Time* for 2 Narrators and Orch. (1967); *I, Jacob* for Soprano, Pop Tenor,

Speaker, Instrumental Ensemble, and Tape (1968); *Love, Defiance, and Death* for Mezzo-soprano and Chamber Ensemble (1984); Vocal Sym. (1986); *Variations on a Renaissance Theme* for Chorus and Chamber Orch. (1988).—NS/LK/DM

Ito, Ryûta, Japanese composer; b. Kure, March 4, 1922. He graduated from the faculty of medicine of the Univ. of Tokyo in 1946 (Doctor of Medical Science, 1955). He then studied composition with Takata, Moroi, Ikenouchi, and Fukai, subsequently dividing his interests between music and medicine. He became a prof. of pharmacy at the school of medicine of Toho Univ., and also served as secretary and a member of the committee of the Japanese Soc. for Contemporary Music (1952–61).

Works: DRAMATIC: Chamber Opera: *The Court of Judgment* (1954). ORCH.: *Allemand and Aria* (1945; Tokyo, May 19, 1950); *2 Moments* (Tokyo, Oct. 29, 1947); *Divertissement* (1950); *Festival* (1953); *Suite for Strings* (1954); *Ostinato concertanto* for Piano and Orch. (Tokyo, Oct. 18, 1957); *Temariuta* (Handball Song; 1958); Concerto for Japanese Flute and Orch. (Tokyo, Nov. 28, 1958); *Suzuka*, suite (1959); *Suite* for Chamber Orch. (1959); *Suite* (1961); *Les Cloches*, symphonic suite for Japanese Instruments, Celesta, Percussion, Men's Chorus, Viola, Cello, and Double Bass (Tokyo, Nov. 9, 1971); *Movement for String Ensemble* (1983); Concerto for Shakuhachi, Jūshichi-gen, and Orch. (1989); *Fantasia alla Yoshizawa* (1990). OTHER: *Abrasion of a Life*, suite for Chorus (1984); several works for Japanese instruments, including 3 duets for Shakuhachi and Jūshichi-gen (1987–90).—NS/LK/DM

Iturbi, José, celebrated Spanish pianist and conductor; b. Valencia, Nov. 28, 1895; d. Los Angeles, June 28, 1980. He began playing the piano at the incredible age of three, and by the time he was seven he was earning a living by appearing in street cafes. Following training at the Valencia Cons. (first prize, 1908), he studied with Maláts, at the Paris Cons. with Staub (premier prix, 1912), and in Barcelona. After serving as head of the piano dept. at the Geneva Cons. (1919–23), he embarked on a brilliant career as a virtuoso. In 1923 he made a highly successful London debut, and then toured Europe and South America. On Oct. 10, 1929, he made his U.S. debut in Philadelphia, and subsequently appeared widely in America. In 1933 he made his debut as a conductor in Mexico City, and therefter pursued a dual career as a pianist and conductor, sometimes conducting from the keyboard. From 1936 to 1944 he was conductor of the Rochester (N.Y.) Phil. Iturbi was one of the most popular classical artists of his day, a popularity enhanced by his film appearances and recordings. While he had his detractors as an interpreter of the classics, there was no denying his idiomatic mastery of Spanish music. He also composed a number of piano pieces in the Spanish vein. His sister, Amparo Iturbi (b. Valencia, March 12, 1898; d. Beverly Hills, April 21, 1969), was also a talented pianist. She frequently appeared in duo concerts with her brother in the U.S. and Europe.—NS/LK/DM

Iturriberry, Juan José, Uruguayan composer; b. Pando, Oct. 24, 1936. He studied in Montevideo with Carlos Estrada and Héctor Tosar, and also took a course

in electro-acoustical techniques. His works are quaquaversal, with some requiring electronic applications. His *Meditation in F* (1975) is concentrated on the single note F, which is repeated ad nauseam.—NS/LK/DM

Ivanov, Georgi
See **Tutev, Georgi**

Ivanov, Konstantin, Russian conductor and composer; b. Efremov, May 21, 1907; d. Moscow, April 15, 1984. He played trumpet in Soviet cavalry orchs., then enrolled in the conducting class at the Moscow Cons. After graduation in 1937, he served as asst. conductor at various operatic and sym. posts. From 1941 to 1946 he was conductor of the Bolshoi Radio Orch., and from 1946 to 1975 conductor of the State Sym. Orch. of the U.S.S.R. He made world tours with the latter organization, which included the U.S. and Japan, as well as countries of Western Europe. He wrote several symphonic poems and a Double Bass Concerto.—NS/LK/DM

Ivanov, Mikhail Mikhailovich, Russian music critic and composer; b. Moscow, Sept. 23, 1849; d. Rome, Oct. 20, 1927. He studied mechanical sciences at the Technological Inst. in St. Petersburg, graduating in 1869, then went to Moscow, where he took private harmony lessons with Tchaikovsky. From 1870 to 1875 he lived in Italy, where he took music lessons with Sgambati. In 1875 he returned to St. Petersburg, where he obtained the position of music critic of the influential newspaper *Novoye Vremya*, which he held from 1880 to 1917. After the Revolution he emigrated to Italy, where he remained until his death. A critic of reactionary tendencies, Ivanov assailed the composers of the Russian national school. Endowed with a lively literary style, he made use of irony against any new musical developments; this in turn earned him the enmity of liberal musicians. He was also a composer of sorts, numbering a ballet, *Vestal Virgin* (St. Petersburg, Feb. 29, 1888), the operas *Zabava Putiatishna* (Moscow, Jan. 15, 1899) and *Potemkin Holiday* (St. Petersburg, Dec. 16, 1902), and a number of songs among his works. He publ. *Pushkin in Music* (St. Petersburg, 1899) and *The Historical Development of Music in Russia* (2 vols., St. Petersburg, 1910–12).—NS/LK/DM

Ivanov, Nikolai (Kuzmich), Russian tenor; b. Voronezh, Oct. 22, 1810; d. Bologna, July 19, 1880. He sang as a child in the Imperial Court Chapel in St. Petersburg. In 1830 Glinka took him to Italy, where he studied with Bianchi in Milan and with Fodor-Mainvielle and Nozzari in Naples. In 1832 he made his operatic debut as Percy in *Anna Bolena* at the Teatro San Carlo in Naples, and then sang in Paris at the Théâtre-Italien from 1833 to 1837. On April 15, 1834, he made his London debut at the King's Theatre, again as Percy. He sang for the first time at Milan's La Scala in 1843 as Riccardo in Pacini's *Maria, regina d'Inghilterra*. Following engagements in Vienna (1844), Rome (1845; 1847–48), Paris (1850), and Palermo (1852), he retired from the operatic stage. Ivanov was especially known for his elegant portrayals of roles in operas by Rossini, Bellini, and Donizetti.

BIBL.: S. Smolensky, *O tenore I.: Soputstvovavshem Glinka v Italiiu* (The Tenor I.: Companion to Glinka in Italy; St. Petersburg, 1904).—NS/LK/DM

Ivanov-Boretzky, Mikhail Vladimirovich,

Russian musicologist and composer; b. Moscow, June 16, 1874; d. there, April 1, 1936. He studied jurisprudence at the Univ. of Moscow, graduating in 1896, and at the same time took music lessons. In 1898 he went to St. Petersburg and became a student of composition of Rimsky-Korsakov. From 1921 to 1936 he taught at the Moscow Cons. His music was mainly imitative of Rimsky-Korsakov's works. He wrote the operas *Adolfina* (Moscow, Dec. 10, 1908) and *The Witch* (Moscow, Aug. 14, 1918), Sym., piano music, choruses, and songs. His importance to Russian music, however, lies in his writings. He publ. monographs on Palestrina, Handel, Schumann, Mendelssohn, and Beethoven; also a useful anthology of music history, with a synoptic table of 18th-century music (Moscow, 1934). A collection of his articles was publ. in Moscow in 1972.—NS/LK/DM

Ivanovici, Ion,

Romanian bandmaster and composer; b. Banat, 1845; d. Bucharest, Sept. 28, 1902. He played flute and clarinet in a Galaţi military band, and then organized his own band there in 1880. In 1889 he conducted at the Paris Exposition. In 1900 he was made inspector of military bands in Romania. He wrote the popular waltz *Valurile Dunării* (The Waves of the Danube; 1880), as well as dances for band and piano music.

BIBL.: V. Cosma, *I.* (Bucharest, 1958).—NS/LK/DM

Ivanov-Radkevitch, Nikolai,

Russian composer and teacher; b. Krasnoyarsk, Siberia, Feb. 10, 1904; d. Moscow, Feb. 4, 1962. He studied composition with Glière and orchestration with Vasilenko at the Moscow Cons., graduating in 1928, and subsequently was on its faculty (1929–48). In 1952 he was appointed instructor in orchestration at the Inst. of Military Bandleaders of the Soviet Army. He was particularly successful in writing popular marches for band, of which *Our Own Moscow* and *Victory March* received the State Prize. He also composed 4 syms. (1928, 1932, 1937, 1945), 12 symphonic suites on folk motifs, Violin Sonata, various pieces for other instruments, and film music. —NS/LK/DM

Ivanovs, Janis,

Latvian composer and teacher; b. Preili, Oct. 9, 1906; d. Riga, March 27, 1983. He studied composition with Wihtol, piano with Dauge, and conducting with Schneevoigt at the Riga Cons., graduating in 1931. He then worked at the Latvian Radio. In 1944 he was appointed to the composition faculty at the Riga Cons. An exceptionally fecund composer, he wrote 20 syms., several of a programmatic nature descriptive of the Latvian countryside, including No. 1, *Symphonie-Poème* (1933), No. 2, *Atlantida* (1941), No. 6, *Latgales* (Latvian; 1949), No. 12, *Sinfonia energica* (1967), and No. 13, *Symphonia humana* (1969). His symphonic poems also reflect nature scenes; e.g., *Varaviksne* (Rainbow; 1938) and *Padebešu Kalns* (Mountain under the Sky; 1939). He further wrote 3 string quartets (1933, 1946, 1961), Cello Concerto (1938), Violin Concerto (1951), Piano Concerto (1959), choruses, songs, piano pieces, and film music.

BIBL.: N. Grünfeld, *J. I.* (Moscow, 1959); V. Berzina, *Dzives simfonija Jana I.* (Riga, 1964).—NS/LK/DM

Ives, Burl (Icle Ivanhoe),

American singer, guitarist, and actor; b. Hunt Township, Jasper County, Ill., June 14, 1909; d. Anacortes, Wash., April 14, 1995. A folksinger, Ives also succeeded as an actor on Broadway, in films, and on television; he appeared on radio and made numerous recordings, some of which became hits on the pop, country, and easy-listening charts. The most popular of these were "On Top of Old Smoky," "A Little Bitty Tear," and the Grammy-winning "Funny Way of Laughin'."

Ives was the seventh child of tenant farmers Frank and Cordella White Ives. He learned folk songs from his parents and from his maternal grandmother. He first earned money for his singing at a picnic when he was four years old. Taking up the guitar and banjo, he earned money performing while in high school. Upon graduation he enrolled at Eastern Ill. State Teachers Coll., where he spent two years. He dropped out to travel around the country collecting songs. Settling in Terre Haute, Ind., he attended Ind. State Teachers Coll., sang over the local radio, and studied voice with Madame Clara Lyon. In August 1933 he moved to N.Y. He attended N.Y.U. and the Juilliard School of Music, studying voice with Ella Toedt and acting with Benno Schneider. He performed folk music with such associates as Woody Guthrie and Pete Seeger, sometimes singing for left-wing causes such as benefits for the Loyalist forces in the Spanish Civil War.

In the summer of 1938, Ives made his first professional stage appearances at the Rockridge Theater in Carmel, N.Y. He made his Broadway debut in the Richard Rodgers–Lorenz Hart musical *The Boys from Syracuse* (N.Y., Nov. 23, 1938), which ran 235 performances. In June 1940 he made his network radio debut as a singer, and by 1941 had his own 15-minute show, *The Wayfaring Stranger*. He also began to make nightclub appearances.

With the U.S. entry into World War II, Ives joined the army in 1942. He appeared in Irving Berlin's service musical *This Is the Army* (N.Y., July 4, 1942) and made broadcasts for the Office of War Information until he received a medical discharge in 1944. He returned to Broadway in the folk- oriented musical *Sing Out, Sweet Land!* (N.Y., Dec. 27, 1944), which ran 102 performances, and for which he won a Donaldson Award (precursor to the Tony Award) for Best Supporting Actor. When Decca Records recorded the cast album to the show, it also signed Ives to a recording contract, his first with a major label.

Ives made his concert debut at Town Hall in N.Y. on Dec. 1, 1945. Five days later he married his former radio scriptwriter, Helen Erlich. They had a son. He made his feature-film debut as a singing cowboy in *Smoky*, released in June 1946. From 1946 to 1948 he again had a

15-minute network radio series, *The Burl Ives Show*. He sang again on film in *Green Grass of Wyoming*, released in June 1948, and also appeared in *Station West*, released in September. But his breakthrough film appearance came in the Disney children's musical *So Dear to My Heart*, released in January 1949, in which he sang "Lavender Blue (Dilly Dilly)" (music by Eliot Daniel, lyrics by Larry Morey), which became his first hit on both the pop and country charts. He followed it with "Riders in the Sky (Cowboy Legend)" (music and lyrics by Stan Jones), which hit the country Top Ten and reached the pop charts in the spring of 1949.

Ives again sang in the film *Sierra*, released in September 1950, and he made further appearances on Broadway, but his career ran into trouble in the early 1950s due to the anti-Communist witchhunts that targeted his left-wing associations of the 1930s. In 1951 he testified as a friendly witness before the House Committee on Un-American Activities, which earned him the enmity of his old friends in the folk music community but allowed him gradually to revive his career.

The folk song "On Top of Old Smoky," credited to Percy Faith with Burl Ives, became a Top Ten pop hit in May 1951. In the summer of 1952, Ives and Grady Martin reached the country Top Ten and the pop charts with "Wild Side of Life" (music and lyrics by William Warren and A. A. Carter). But Ives spent the rest of the decade establishing himself as a straight actor, beginning with an appearance in a Broadway revival of *Show Boat* in May 1954. He returned to film-making in the drama *East of Eden*, released in March 1955, then memorably created the role of Big Daddy in Tennessee Williams's play *Cat on a Hot Tin Roof* (N.Y., March 24, 1955), which ran 694 performances. He turned to television with the original drama *The Miracle Worker* (Feb. 7, 1957), next appearing as a panelist on the quiz show *High-Low*, which ran during the summer of 1957. He continued to appear on television frequently for the rest of his career.

Ives focused on Hollywood in the late 1950s, and among his notable film appearances were a recreation of his stage role in *Cat on a Hot Tin Roof*, released in September 1958, and a performance in the drama *The Big Country*, released in October 1958, that won him an Academy Award for Best Supporting Actor. In the early 1960s he established himself as a country music star, beginning with "A Little Bitty Tear" (music and lyrics by Hank Cochran), which made the Top Ten of the pop and country charts and went to #1 on the easy-listening charts in the winter of 1962; it earned him Grammy Award nominations for Best Solo Vocal Performance, Male, and Best Country and Western Recording. The album *The Versatile Burl Ives!*, which contained the song, spent more than seven months in the charts. He followed it with "Funny Way of Laughin'" (music and lyrics by Hank Cochran), which reached the Top Ten of the pop, country, and easy-listening charts in the spring of 1962 and won the Grammy Award for Best Country and Western Recording. The LP *It's Just My Funny Way of Laughin'* spent eight months in the charts.

Ives continued to record country music successfully for the next couple of years, but increasingly he turned his attention to children's projects in the 1960s, notably appearing in the Disney comedy *Summer Magic*, released in August 1963, and narrating the animated television special *Rudolph the Red-Nosed Reindeer* in December 1964. He earned his next Grammy Award nomination in 1964 for Best Recording for Children for the LP *Burl Ives Chim Chim Chereee and Other Children's Choices*.

For the rest of the 1960s and through the 1970s, Ives primarily spent his time recording music and acting in film and on television. He starred in the situation comedy *O.K. Crackerby!* in the fall of 1965 and returned to Broadway in the play *Dr. Cook's Garden* in 1967. He starred in the dramatic series *The Lawyers* for three years, starting in September 1969. In 1971 he married his second wife, Dorothy. He earned another Grammy Award nomination for Best Recording for Children in 1974 for *America Sings*. He appeared in the successful television miniseries *Captains and the Kings* (1976) and *Roots* (1977). He was less active in the 1980s; he made his final film appearance in *Two-Moon Junction* (1988) and in the fall of 1988 launched a one-man touring show, *The Mystic Trumpeter: Walt Whitman at 70*, which he had written with his wife. He released his last album, *The Magic Balladeer*, in 1993. In 1995 he died of mouth cancer and congestive heart failure at the age of 85.

WRITINGS: *The Wayfaring Stranger* (N.Y., 1948); *The B. I. Song Book* (N.Y., 1953); *B. I.' Sea Songs of Sailing, Whaling and Fishing* (N.Y., 1953); *More B. I. Songs; Tales of America* (1954); *B. I. Book of Irish Songs* (1958); *The Wayfaring Stranger's Notebook* (1962); *Sailing on a Very Fine Day* (Chicago, 1954); *Song in America. Our Musical Heritage* (N.Y., 1962).—**WR**

Ives, Charles (Edward), one of the most remarkable American composers, whose individual genius created music so original, so universal, and yet so deeply national in its sources of inspiration that it profoundly changed the direction of American music; b. Danbury, Conn., Oct. 20, 1874; d. N.Y., May 19, 1954. His father, George Ives, was a bandmaster of the 1st Conn. Heavy Artillery during the Civil War, and the early development of Ives was, according to his own testimony, deeply influenced by his father. At the age of 12, he played the drums in the band and also received from his father rudimentary musical training in piano and cornet playing. At the age of 13, he played organ at the Danbury Church; soon he began to improvise freely at the piano, without any dependence on school rules; as a result of his experimentation in melody and harmony, encouraged by his father, he began to combine several keys, partly as a spoof, but eventually as a legitimate alternative to traditional music; at 13, he also wrote the *Holiday Quick Step*, which was first performed in Danbury on Jan. 16, 1888; at 17, he composed his *Variations on America* for organ in a polytonal setting. In 1894 he entered Yale Univ., where he took regular academic courses and studied organ with Buck and composition with Parker; from Parker he received a fine classical training; while still in college, he composed 2 full-fledged syms., written in an entirely traditional manner demonstrating great skill in formal structure, fluent melodic development, and smooth harmonic modulations. After his graduation in 1898, Ives joined an insurance company; he also played organ at the Central Presbyterian Church in N.Y. (1899–1902). In 1907 he formed an insurance partnership with Julian Myrick of N.Y.; he proved himself to be an exceptionally able businessman; the firm of Ives & Myrick prospered, and Ives continued to compose music as an avocation. In 1908 he married Harmony Twichell. In 1918 he suffered a massive heart attack, complicated by a diabetic condition, and was compelled to curtail his work both in business and in music to a minimum because his illness made it difficult to handle a pen. He retired from business in 1930, and by that time had virtually stopped composing. In 1919 Ives publ. at his own expense his great masterpiece, the *Concord Sonata*, for piano, inspired by the writings of Emerson, Hawthorne, the Alcotts, and Thoreau. Although written early in the century, its idiom is so extraordinary, and its technical difficulties so formidable, that the work did not receive a performance in its entirety until John Kirkpatrick played it in N.Y. in 1939. In 1922 Ives brought out, also at his expense, a vol. of *114 Songs*, written between 1888 and 1921 and marked by great diversity of style, ranging from lyrical Romanticism to powerful and dissonant modern invocations. Both the *Concord Sonata* and the *114 Songs* were distributed gratis by Ives to anyone wishing to receive copies. His orch. masterpiece, *3 Places in New England*, also had to wait nearly two decades before its first performance; of the monumental 4th Sym., only the second movement was performed in 1927, and its complete performance was given posthumously in 1965. In 1947 Ives received the Pulitzer Prize in Music for his 3rd Sym., written in 1911.

The slow realization of the greatness of Ives and the belated triumphant recognition of his music were phenomena with little precedence in music history. Because of his chronic ailment, and also on account of his personal disposition, Ives lived as a recluse, away from the mainstream of American musical life; he never went to concerts and did not own a record player or a radio; while he was well versed in the musical classics, and studied the scores of Beethoven, Schumann, and Brahms, he took little interest in sanctioned works of modern composers; yet he anticipated many technical innovations, such as polytonality, atonality, and even 12-tone formations, as well as polymetric and polyrhythmic configurations, which were prophetic for his time. In the second movement of the *Concord Sonata*, he specified the application of a strip of wood on the white and the black keys of the piano to produce an echo-like sonority; in his unfinished *Universe Symphony* he planned an antiphonal representation of the heavens in chordal counterpoint and the earth in contrasting orch. groups. He also composed pieces of quarter-tone piano music. A unique quality of his music was the combination of simple motifs, often derived from American church hymns and popular ballads, with an extremely complex dissonant counterpoint which formed the supporting network for the melodic lines. A curious idiosyncrasy is the frequent quotation of the "fate motive" of Beethoven's 5th Sym. in many of his works. Materials of his instrumental and vocal works often overlap, and the titles are often changed during the process of composition. In his orchestrations, he often indicated

interchangeable and optional parts, as in the last movement of the *Concord Sonata*, which has a part for flute obbligato; thus he reworked the original score for large orch. of his *3 Places in New England* for a smaller ensemble to fit the requirements of Slonimsky's Chamber Orch. of Boston, which gave its first performance, and it was in this version that the work was first publ. and widely performed until the restoration of the large score was made in 1974.

Ives also possessed an uncommon gift for literary expression; his annotations to his works are both trenchant and humorous; he publ. in 1920 *Essays before a Sonata* as a literary companion vol. to the *Concord Sonata*; his *Memos* in the form of a diary, publ. after his death, reveal an extraordinary power of aphoristic utterance. He was acutely conscious of his civic duties as an American, and once circulated a proposal to have federal laws enacted by popular referendum. His centennial in 1974 was celebrated by a series of conferences at his alma mater, Yale Univ.; in N.Y., Miami, and many other American cities; and in Europe, including Russia. While during his lifetime he and a small group of devoted friends and admirers had great difficulties in having his works performed, recorded, or publ., a veritable Ives cult emerged after his death; eminent conductors gave repeated performances of his orch. works, and modern pianists were willing to cope with the forbidding difficulties of his works. The influence of his music on the new generation of composers reached a high mark, so that the adjective "Ivesian" became common in music criticism to describe certain acoustical and coloristic effects characteristic of his music. All of the Ives MSS and his correspondence were deposited by his widow at Yale Univ., forming a basic Ives archive. The Charles Ives Soc., in N.Y., promotes research and publications. Letters from Ives to N. Slonimsky are reproduced in the latter's book *Music Since 1900* (5th ed., N.Y., 1993). The film *A Good Dissonance Like a Man* (1977) depicts the life of Ives with fine dramatic impact.

From 1974 to 1993 Larry Austin reworked Ives's incomplete *Universe Symphony* (1911–28, with occasional additions to 1951), in which Ives's "universe of tones" ranges from fully scored to fragmentary measures on 36 manuscript pages, and "completed" the work with a scoring that includes tape and digital synthesizer in 3 sections requiring 7 orchs. of varying sizes led by 5 conductors. Dubbed Sym. No. 5, *Universe Symphony*, it was premiered at the Univ. of Cincinnati Coll.- Cons. of Music on Jan. 28, 1994. In 1986 microtonal composer Johnny Reinhard (b. 1956) had independently come across score fragments to the *Universe Symphony*. He assembled his own "completion" using only music composed by Ives. His version is nearly twice as long as Austin's, and was premiered by 71 musicians at the American Festival of Microtonal Music at N.Y.'s Lincoln Center on June 4, 1996. The Ives editor and scholar, David Port, took Ives's uncompleted sketches for an "overture-concerto" meant as an Emerson portrait, of which some of the material found its way into Ives's *Concord Sonata*, and produced a "practical" reconstruction he dubbed the *Emerson Concerto* for Piano and Orch. (1996–98). It was premiered by the Cleveland Orch. on Oct. 1, 1998, with Alan Feinstein as soloist.

WORKS: ORCH.: March No. 2 (1892); March No. 3 (1892); Postlude (1895); Overture (1895?); 4 numbered syms.: No. 1 (1896–98; Washington, D.C., April 26, 1953, R. Bales conducting), No. 2 (1900–02; N.Y., Feb. 22, 1951, Bernstein conducting), No. 3, *The Camp Meeting* (1904; N.Y., April 5, 1946, L. Harrison conducting), and No. 4 (1909–16; first complete perf., N.Y., April 26, 1965, Stokowski conducting); *Universe Symphony* (1911–28; unfinished; Los Angeles, Dec. 13, 1984); *Fugue in 4 Keys, on The Shining Shore* for Flute, Cornet, and Strings (1897); *Yale- Princeton Football Game* (1898?); *Cartoons (Take-offs)* for Small Orch. (1898?–1916); *Ragtime Dances* Nos. 1–4 for Small Orch. (1902–04; unfinished); *Overture and March "1776"* for Small Orch. (1903); *Country Band March* for Small Orch. (1903); *The General Slocum* (1904; unfinished); *Thanksgiving and/or Forefathers' Day* (1904; N.Y., April 9, 1954, Dorati conducting); *Autumn Landscapes from Pine Mountains* for Small Orch. (1904; not extant); *The Pond* for Small Orch. (1906); *[2 Contemplations]: The Unanswered Question* and *Central Park in the Dark* for Small Orch. (1906); *Set* for Theatre or Chamber Orch. (1906–11; Danbury, Conn., Feb. 1932); *Over the Pavements* for Small Orch. (1906–13); *Emerson Overture* (1907; unfinished; also as a Piano Concerto); *Set No. 1* (1907–11), *No. 2* (1911–12), and *No. 3* (1912?–18; N.Y., Dec. 6, 1962, Schuller conducting) for Small Orch.; *Robert Browning Overture* (1908–12; N.Y., Oct. 1963, Stokowski conducting); *First Orchestral Set (A New England Symphony* or *3 Places in New England)* (1908–14?; N.Y., Jan. 10, 1931, Slonimsky conducting); *Second Orchestral Set* (1909–15); *Third Orchestral Set* for Small Orch. (1919–26); *Washington's Birthday* for Small Orch. (1909; San Francisco, Sept. 3, 1931, Slonimsky conducting); *The Gong on the Hook and Ladder* or *Firemen's Parade on Main Street* for Small Orch. (1911?; N.Y., Jan. 21, 1967, Bernstein conducting); *The Fourth of July* (1911–13; Paris, Feb. 21, 1932, Slonimsky conducting); *Tone Roads* (1911–15); *Decoration Day* (1912; Havana, Dec. 27, 1931, A. Roldán conducting); *Matthew Arnold Overture* (1912; unfinished); *Holidays* (1912?; Minneapolis, April 9, 1954, Dorati conducting); Quarter-tone Chorale for Strings (1913–14; not extant); *The Rainbow* or *So May It Be!* for Small Orch. (1914); *Chrômatimelôdtune* for Small Orch. (1919?; arranged by Schuller; N.Y., Dec. 6, 1962, Schuller conducting). **Band :** *Intercollegiate March* (1892); March (1896); *Runaway Horse on Main Street* (1905?; unfinished). **CHAMBER:** *Holiday Quickstep* for Piccolo, 2 Cornets, 2 Violins, and Piano (1887); 2 string quartets: No. 1, *From the Salvation Army* (1896; N.Y., April 24, 1957) and No. 2 (1907–13; Saratoga Springs, N.Y., Sept. 15, 1946); Pre-First Violin Sonata (1899–1903?); *From the Steeples and the Mountains* for Trumpet, Trombone, and 4 Sets of Bells (1901–02?); 4 violin sonatas: No. 1 (1902–08; N.Y., March 31, 1946), No. 2 (1907–10; N.Y., March 18, 1924), No. 3 (1913–14?; Los Angeles, March 16, 1942), and No. 4, *Children's Day at the Camp Meeting* (1906–16?; N.Y., Jan. 14, 1940); *Largo* for Violin, Clarinet, and Piano (1902?); Trio for Violin, Clarinet, and Piano (1902–03?; Berea, Ohio, May 24, 1948); *An Old Song Deranged* for Clarinet or English Horn, Harp, and String Quartet (1903?); *A Set of 3 Short Pieces*: 1, *Hymn* for String Quartet and Double Bass (1904), 2, *Holding Your Own* for String Quartet (1903–14), and 3, *The Innate* for String Quartet, Double Bass, and Piano (1908); Pre-Second String Quartet (1904–05; not extant); Trio for Violin, Cello, and Piano (1904–11); *Take-off No. 3, "Rube Trying to Walk 2 to 3!!"* for Clarinet, Bassoon, Trumpet, and Piano (1906); *Hallowe'en* for String Quartet and Piano (1906; San Francisco, May 28, 1934); *Largo risoluto* No. 1, *"as to the Law of Diminishing Returns"* (1906; N.Y., Feb. 19, 1965) and No. 2, *"a shadow made—a silhouette"* (1906) for String Quartet and Piano; *All the Way Around and Back* for Clarinet, Bugle, Violin, Bells, and Piano (1906); *Decoration Day* for Violin and Piano (1912); *In re con moto et al* for String Quartet and Piano (1913). **P i a n o :** 7 marches (c. 1890–97); 2 sonatas: No. 1 (1901–09; N.Y., Feb. 17, 1949, Masselos pianist) and No. 2, *Concord, Mass., 1840–60* (1910–15; N.Y., Jan. 20, 1939, J. Kirkpatrick pianist); *Ragtime Dances* (1902–04); *3-page Sonata* (1905); *5 Take-offs* (1906–07); *Studies* (1907–08); *Waltz-Rondo* (1911); *4 Transcriptions from Emerson* (c. 1917–22); *Varied Air and Variations* (1923?); *3 Quarter-tone Pieces* for 2 Pianos (1923–24); *The Celestial Railroad* (c. 1924); *3 Improvisations* (n.d.). **VOCAL :** Choral pieces; part songs; numerous solo songs.

BIBL.: H. and S. Cowell, *C. I. and His Music* (N.Y., 1955; reprinted with additional material, 1969); J. Kirkpatrick, *A Temporary Mimeographed Catalogue of the Music Manuscripts and Related Materials of C.E. I.* (New Haven, 1960); J. Bernlef and R. de Leeuw, *C. I.* (Amsterdam, 1969); D.-R. de Lerma, *C.E. I., 1874–1954: A Bibliography of His Music* (Kent, Ohio, 1970); V. Perlis, *C. I. Remembered: An Oral History* (New Haven, 1974); R. Perry, *C. I. and the American Mind* (Kent, Ohio, 1974); D. Wooldridge, *From the Steeples and Mountains: A Study of C. I.* (N.Y., 1974); F. Rossiter, *C. I. and His America* (N.Y., 1975); H. Wiley Hitchcock, *C. I.* (London, 1977); H. Wiley Hitchcock and V. Perlis, *An I. Celebration: Papers and Panels of the C. I. Centennial Festival- Conference* (Urbana, Ill., 1977); H. Sive, *Music's Connecticut Yankee* (N.Y., 1977); B. Chmaj, *Sonata for American Studies: Perspectives on C. I.* (Sacramento, 1978); H. Wiley Hitchcock, *I.: A Survey of the Music* (N.Y., 1983); J. Burkholder, *C. I.: The Ideas behind the Music* (New Haven, 1985); G. Block, *C. I.: A Bio-Bibliography* (Westport, Conn., 1988); M. Alexander, *The Evolving Keyboard Style of C. I.* (N.Y., 1989); W. Rathert, *C. I.* (Darmstadt, 1989); C. Henderson, *The C. I. Tunebook* (Warren, Mich., 1990); K. Niemöller, ed., *Internationale Symposion "C. I. und die amerikanische Musiktradition bis zur Gegenwart" (1988: Cologne, Germany)* (Regensburg, 1990); W. Rathert, *The Seen and the Unseen: Studien zum Werk von C. I.* (Munich, 1991); S. Feder, *C. I., "My Father's Song: " A Psychoanalytic Biography* (New Haven, Conn., 1992); L. Starr, *A Union of Diversities: Style in the Music of C. I.* (N.Y., 1992); J. Burkholder, *All Made of Tunes: C. I. and the Uses of Musical Borrowing* (New Haven, 1995); G. Block, *I., Concord Sonata: Piano Sonata No. 2 ("Concord, Mass., 1840–1860")* (Cambridge, 1996); J. Burkholder, ed., *C. I. and His World* (Princeton, 1996); J. Swafford, *C. I.: A Life With Music* (N.Y., 1996); P. Lambert, ed., *I. Studies* (Cambridge, 1997); idem, *The Music of C. I.* (New Haven, 1997).—NS/LK/DM

Ives, Elam, Jr., American music educator; b. Hamden, Conn., Jan. 7, 1802; d. there, Feb. 10, 1864. He taught piano, violin, and singing, and was active as a choirmaster. After serving as head of the Philadelphia Musical Seminary (1830–36), he ran his own music school in N.Y. He publ. numerous school songbooks, sacred music collections, and art songs. Ives was an influential figure in the development of public school music in the U.S. through his championship of Pestalozzi's theories as applied to music education.—LK/DM

Ives, Simon, English organist and composer; b. Ware (baptized), July 20, 1600; d. London, July 1, 1662. He became organist at Christ Church and a vicar-choral at St. Paul's Cathedral in London about 1630. He wrote music for masques at the court. With W. Lawes, he collaborated on music for Shirley's masque *The Triumph*

of Peace (1633–34). More than 100 of his works are extant, among them instrumental pieces, songs, catches, and rounds. Many of them were publ. in contemporary collections.—NS/LK/DM

Ivogün, Maria (real name, **Ilse Kempner**), esteemed Hungarian soprano; b. Budapest, Nov. 18, 1891; d. Beatenberg, Switzerland, Oct. 2, 1987. Her mother was the singer Ida von Günther. She studied voice with Schlemmer-Ambros in Vienna, then with Schöner in Munich, where she made her debut as Mimi at the Bavarian Court Opera (1913). She became renowned there for her portrayal of Zerbinetta, and also created the role of Ighino in Pfitzner's *Palestrina* (1917). In 1925 she joined the Berlin Städtische Oper; also made guest appearances with the touring German Opera Co. in the U.S. (1923), at the Chicago Opera (1923), at London's Covent Garden (1924, 1927), and at the Salzburg Festivals (1925, 1930). She gave her farewell performance as Zerbinetta at the Berlin Städtische Oper (1934). She was subsequently active as a teacher, later serving on the faculties of the Vienna Academy of Music (1948–50) and the Berlin Hochschule für Musik (1950–58); her most celebrated pupil was Elisabeth Schwarzkopf. She was married to **Karl Erb** (1921–32), then to her accompanist Michael Raucheisen (from 1933). Among her other notable roles were Constanze, the Queen of the Night, Norina, Gilda, and Oscar. —NS/LK/DM

Ivry, Paul Xavier Désiré, Marquis d', French composer; b. Beaune, Feb. 4, 1829; d. Hyeres, Dec. 18, 1903. He was autodidact as a composer. Ivry used the nom de plume Richard Yrvid. Among his works were the operas *Fatma* (c. 1850), *Quentin Metsys* (1854), *La*

maison du docteur (Dijon, 1855), *Omphale et Pénélope* (c. 1860), and *Les amants de Vérone* (private preview, Paris, May 12, 1867; stage premiere, Paris, Oct. 12, 1878). —NS/LK/DM

Iwaki, Hiroyuki, Japanese conductor; b. Tokyo, Sept. 6, 1932. He received training in percussion at the Academy of Music and in conducting from Saito and Watanabe (1951–54) at the Univ. of Arts in Tokyo. In 1954 he became asst. conductor of the NHK (Japanese Broadcasting Corp.) Sym. Orch. in Tokyo, serving as its principal resident conductor from 1969. From 1965 to 1967 he was also music director of the Fujiwara Opera Co., and from 1974 chief conductor of the Melbourne Sym. Orch. In 1988 he was named music director of the new Orchestra-Ensemble Kanazawa, but continued to hold his post with the NHK Sym. Orch. As a guest conductor, he appeared throughout the Far East, Europe, and North America.—NS/LK/DM

Izenzon, David, bassist; b. Pittsburgh, Pa., May 17, 1932; d. N.Y., Oct. 8, 1979. Izenzon got his start by singing in a local synagogue. He studied double bass from 1956 and soon began playing with jazz musicians in Pittsburgh, including the pianist Dodo Marmarosa (1958). In 1961 he moved to N.Y. He played with Bill Dixon, Archie Shepp, Paul Bley, and Sonny Rollins. He was a member of Ornette Coleman's trio 1962–66, doing much work in England and Europe, later sharing bass role with Charlie Haden. In the 1970s he was working in the psychiatry field, playing occasionally with Karl Berger. His opera, *How Music Can Save the World*, was premiered in 1975. He died in 1979 after suffering a heart attack.—LP

J

Jacchia, Agide, Italian conductor; b. Lugo, Jan. 5, 1875; d. Siena, Nov. 29, 1932. He studied at the Parma Cons. and at the Pesaro Liceo Musicale; won prizes as a flutist (1896), apprentice conductor (1897), and composer (1898). He made his conducting debut in Brescia on Dec. 26, 1898, and then was a theater conductor in Italy. In 1902 he accompanied Mascagni on his American tour, and also conducted the Milan Opera Co. on its American tour in 1907–09. He was conductor of the Montreal Opera Co. (1910–13), the Boston National Opera (1915–16), and the Boston Pops (1918–26), after which he returned to Italy.—**NS/LK/DM**

Jacchini, Giuseppe Maria, Italian cellist and composer; b. Bologna, c. 1663; d. there, May 2, 1727. He received training in cello from Domenico Gabrielli and in composition from Perti. He was a cellist at S. Petronio in Bologna (1689–96; 1701–27), and also served as maestro di cappella in the Collegio dei Nobili and at S. Luigi. In 1688 he was elected a member of Bologna's Accademia Filarmonica. He became well known as an instrumentalist. As a composer, he was admired for his trumpet and string sonatas.—**LK/DM**

Jachet di Mantua (Jacques Colebault), important French-born Italian composer; b. Vitre, 1483; d. Mantua, Oct. 2, 1559. He was in the service of the Rangoni family in Modena as a singer by 1519, then was at the Este court in Ferrara in 1525. Around 1526 he went to Mantua, where he became a citizen in 1534. He was titular maestro di cappella at the Cathedral of Ss. Peter and Paul (1534–59). He was one of the leading composers of sacred music of his era. A complete edition of his works, ed. by P. Jackson and G. Nugent, was publ. in the Corpus Mensurabilis Musicae series from 1970 to 1982.

Works: MASSES: *Messe del fiore...libro primo* for 5 Voices (Venice, 1561). **MOTETS:** *Celeberrimi maximeque delectabilis musici Jachet...motecta quatuor vocum* (Venice, 1539); *Jacheti musici...motecta quinque vocum* (Venice, 1539); *Primo libro di motetti di Jachet a cinque voci* (Venice, 1540); *Celeberrimi...Jachet-...motecta quatuor vocum...liber primus* (Venice, 1544); *Jachet...motecta quatuor vocum...liber primus* (Venice, 1545).

BIBL.: P. Jackson, *The Vesper Hymns of J. d.M.* (diss., Univ. of N.C., 1965); idem, *The Masses of J. d.M.* (diss., Univ. of N.C., 1968); G. Nugent, *The J. Motets and Their Authors* (diss., Princeton Univ., 1973).—**NS/LK/DM**

Jachimecki, Zdzislaw, eminent Polish musicologist; b. Lemberg, July 7, 1882; d. Kraków, Oct. 27, 1953. He studied music with Niewiadomski and Jarecki in Lemberg, then musicology with Adler at the Univ. of Vienna (Ph.D., 1906, with the diss. *Psalmy Mikołaju Gomólki*; publ. in an abr. ed., Kraków, 1907). He also studied composition with Grädener and Schoenberg in Vienna and completed his Habilitation at the Univ. of Kraków in 1911 with his *Wplywy wloskie w muzyce polskiej cześč I. 1540–1560* (Italian Influence on Polish Music, Part 1, 1540–1560; publ. in Kraków, 1911). He then was a lecturer in music history there, later being made a reader (1917) and a prof. (1921), and was also a guest lecturer at many European univs. He conducted sym. concerts in Kraków (1908–24), and composed a number of orch. pieces and songs.

WRITINGS: *Ryszard Wagner: Zycie i twórczość* (Richard Wagner: Life and Works; Lemberg, 1911; 2nd ed., aug., 1922; 4th ed., 1973); *Tabulatura organowa z biblioteki klasztoru Św. Ducha w Krakówie z roku 1548* (Organ Tablature from the Library of the Monastery of the Holy Spirit in Kraków, 1548; Kraków, 1913); *Muzyka na dworze krota Wladyslawa Jagielly 1424–1430* (Music at the Court of Wladyslaw Jagiello 1424–1430; Kraków, 1916); *Pieśń rokoszan z roku 1606* (A Rebel Song from 1606; Kraków, 1916); *Historia muzyki polskiej w zarysie* (The History of Polish Music in Outline; Warsaw, 1920); *Fryderyk Chopin: Zarys ?ycia i twórczości* (Frédéric Chopin: An Outline of His Life and Work; Kraków, 1927; 4th ed., aug., 1957); *Mikolaj Gomólka i jego poprzednicy we historii muzyki polskiej* (Mikolaj Gomolka and His Predecessors in the History of Polish Music; Warsaw, 1946); *Bartlomiej Pekiel* (Warsaw, 1948); *Muzyka polska w rozwoju historycznym od czasów najdawniejszych do doby obecnej* (The Historical

Evolution of Polish Music from the Earliest Times to the Present Day; Kraków, 1948–51); *Muzykologia i piśmiennictwo muzyczne w Polsce* (Musicology and Writing on Music in Poland; Kraków, 1948).—NS/LK/DM

Jachino, Carlo, Italian composer; b. San Remo, Feb. 3, 1887; d. Rome, Dec. 23, 1971. He studied with Luporini in Lucca and then with Riemann in Leipzig (1909–10). He taught in Parma (1928–33), Naples (1933–38), and Rome (1938–51). After serving as director of the conservatories in Naples (1951–53) and Bogotá, Colombia (1953–56), he was artistic director of the Teatro San Carlo in Naples (1961–69). He publ. *Tecnica dodecafonica* (Milan, 1948) and *Gli strumenti d'orchestra* (Milan, 1950). In his early compositions, he followed the Romantic Italian style; after adopting a modified 12-tone method, he returned to tonality in his last years.

WORKS: DRAMATIC: Opera: *Giocondo e il suo re* (1915–21; Milan, June 24, 1924). Other: Film scores. ORCH.: *Sonata drammatica* for Violin and Orch. (1930); *Pastorale di Natale* (1932); *Fantasia del rosso e nero* (1935); *Pagine di Ramon* (1937); 2 piano concertos (1952, 1957); *L'ora inquieta* for Strings (1953); Cello Concerto (1960); *Variazioni su un tema car a Napoleone I* (1966). CHAMBER: Sonata for 9 Instruments (1922); 3 string quartets (1925, 1927, 1930); Trio for Flute, Cello, and Piano (1954); *Quintetto dell'alba* for Clarinet, Horn, and String Trio (1956); keyboard music. VOCAL: Choral pieces; songs.—NS/LK/DM

Jackson, "Bull Moose" Benjamin Clarence, R&B/jazz tenor saxophonist, vocalist; b. Cleveland, Ohio, April 22, 1920; d. there, July 31, 1989. He began on violin, switched to tenor sax in high school, and worked in a local band led by trumpeter Freddy Webster before joining Lucky Millinder (1944). He began to lead his own groups after his vocal on "I Love You, Yes I Do" became a big hit in 1948. His band was called the Buffalo Bearcats. He made a number of successful R&B singles during the late 1940s and early 1950s, and also worked with Tiny Bradshaw's Band. Benny Golson toured with Jackson frequently between July 1951 and March 1953, along with, at various times, Johnny Coles, Jymie Merritt, and Philly Joe Jones; Tadd Dameron played piano and arranged the music during Golson's tenure. John Coltrane may have played an odd gig with Jackson in Philadelphia before or after this period, but probably did not tour with him. He retired from full-time music in the late 1950s, but emerged to play tour of Middle East and Africa with Buck Clayton in 1977.—JC/LP

Jackson, Chubby (Greig Stewart), jazz bassist, composer; b. N.Y., Oct. 25, 1918. Both of his parents were in show business. He was raised in Freeport, Long Island. He played clarinet in the school band at 16, then bought a bass from Arnold Fishkind. He studied at Ohio State Univ. He returned to N.Y. (1937), joined Mike Riley's Band, and was subsequently with Johnny Messner, Raymond Scott, Jan Savitt, Terry Shand, and Henry Busse before working with Charlie Barnet (1941–43). He worked regularly with Woody Herman from September 1943–46, and returned to the band several times in the late 1940s and 1950s. He worked with Charlie Ventura in 1947, and late that year toured Scandinavia with his own band. He returned to Herman in mid-l948, then again led his own big band in N.Y. He disbanded and freelanced in all-star units (including Charlie Ventura's Big Four), then moved to Chicago in 1953. He did five years' studio work and was resident compere on a children's TV program, and worked briefly in Louis Armstrong All Stars early in 1954. He moved back to N.Y. in 1958, did extensive studio work, compered television shows, and was active as a successful songwriter. In the early 1960s, he organized his own bands for specific engagements, but also worked with various small groups including the Harold Baker Quartet (1963) and Joe Coleman's Big 4 (1965). In the late 1960s, he worked mainly in Fla. with his own band. He moved to L.A. in the summer of 1971, and did prolific freelance work there and in Las Vegas. His son Duffy Jackson (b. Freeport, N.Y., July 3, 1953), is a drummer who has recorded as leader and sideman.

DISC.: *Jazz Journey* (1945); *C. J. Sextet and Big Band* (1950); *C. J.* (1951); *C.'s Back* (1957); *I'm Entitled to You* (1957); *Big Three* (1958); *C. Takes Over* (1958); *Jazz Then Till Now* (1958); *Twist Calling* (1962).—JC/LP

Jackson, Cliff (actually, **Clifton Luther**), jazz pianist; b. Culpeper, Va., July 19, 1902; d. N.Y., May 24, 1970. He played professionally in Washington and Atlantic City before moving to N.Y. in 1923. He worked in Happy Rhone's Club Orch. (1925), Lionel Howard's Musical Aces (1926), and with Elmer Snowden before forming his own Krazy Kats in January 1927. The band played several residencies in N.Y.: Capitol Palace, Murray's Roseland, Lenox Club, etc. He worked mainly as a soloist or vocal accompanist through the 1930s. He was with Sidney Bechet at Nick's in early 1940, then formed his own trio for N.Y.'s Cinderella Club. From autumn of 1944 until 1951 he was the house pianist at Cafe Society Downtown except for a 1946 tour with Eddie Condon. During the 1950s he was the featured pianist at several other N.Y. venues, and also worked in the Garvin Bushell Trio (1959), the J. C. Higginbotham Band (1960), and the Joe Thomas Band (1962). From 1963 he worked regularly in Tony Parenti's Trio at Ryan's, and also took part in filming of *The Night They Raided Minsky's*. His widow is Maxine Sullivan. He made solo recordings in 1969 and played at the RX Room (Manhattan), until the night before he died.

DISC.: *Carolina Shout* (1961).—JC/LP

Jackson, Dewey, jazz trumpeter, leader; b. St. Louis, June 21, 1900; d. 1994. He played in an Odd Fellows Boys' Band during his early teens. His first professional work was with Tommy Evans's Band in St. Louis (1916–17), then played for a year with George Reynolds's Keystone Band before joining Charlie Creath on the riverboat *J.S.* (May 1919). From 1920 until 1923 he led his own Golden Melody Band, and in spring 1924 joined Fate Marable on the S.S. *Capitol*. During the following year he led the St. Louis Peacock Charleston Orch. on the Capitol. After working on the *J.S.* steamer, he moved to N.Y. in August 1926 and spent four months with violinist Andrew Freer's Orch. at the Cotton Club, then traveled to New Orleans. to rejoin Fate Marable on the S.S. *St. Paul*. He was again with Charlie Creath (summer 1927), led his own band (1927–29), played occasional dates with Marable, then led his own band at the Castle Ballroom (St. Louis), from September 1930 until May 1932. He rejoined Creath (1934), worked in a band jointly led by Marable and Creath (1936), then from 1937 he led his own Musical Ambassadors on riverboats during the summers and in St. Louis ballrooms during the winters. He continued on riverboats until 1941, then led at various local ballrooms and clubs during the 1940s. He left full-time music to work as a hotel commissionaire, but began playing regularly again in 1950. He worked in Singleton Palmer's Band, then with pianist Don Ewell's Trio in 1951, led his own band again during the 1950s, and played occasional dates in the 1960s.—**JC/LP**

Jackson, Francis (Alan), English organist, conductor, and composer; b. Malton, Yorkshire, Oct. 2, 1917. He studied with Bairstow in York, then was made a Fellow of the Royal Coll. of Organists (1937) and later studied at Durham Univ. (D.Mus., 1957). He was organist of Malton Parish Church (1933–40), Master of the Music at York Minster (1946–82), and also conductor of the York Sym. Orch. (1947–80); made numerous tours of Europe and North America as an organist. He was made an Officer of the Order of the British Empire (1978). He wrote a Sym., choral works, and much music for the organ.—**NS/LK/DM**

Jackson, Franz (R.), jazz tenor saxophonist, clarinetist, arranger; b. Rock Island, Ill., Nov. 1, 1912. He studied at Chicago Musical Coll. He gigged with various bands before working with Cassino Simpson (1931), Carroll Dickerson (1932), Frankie Jaxon (1932), and drummer Fred Avendorph (late 1932). He toured with Reuben Reeves (spring 1933), with Eddie King and the Jesters (1933), Carroll Dickerson (1934), then joined bassist William Lyles (August 1934). He worked for Jimmie Noone for a year, was briefly with Fletcher Henderson. He then joined Roy Eldridge in Chicago, worked with him in N.Y. (1939–40). He went to Calif. with Earl Hines in October 1940, and the following year worked with Fats Waller. He was with Cootie Williams in N.Y. (early 1942), briefly with Pete Brown, and then worked in Boston with Frankie Newton. He toured with the Roy Eldridge Big Band in 1944, then (from late 1944) spent a long spell with the Wilbur de Paris Band. He was with Jesse Stone on a U.S.O. tour of the Pacific (1946), and continued touring with U.S.O. shows in late 1940s and early 1950s. He returned to Chicago where he formed his own Original Jass All Stars in 1956. The band played long successful residencies at the Red Arrow (Stickney, Ill.), played in N.Y. (December 1968), and undertook several overseas U.S.O. tours including a tour of Vietnam in autumn 1969. In 1974, he recorded with Art Hodes, and from 1980 on has worked out of Chicago.

DISC.: *No Saints* (1957); *Jass, Jass, Jass* (1959); *F.J.'s Original Jass Band* (1961); *Night at Red Arrow* (1961); *Good Old Days* (1965); *Let's Have a Party* (1981); *Snag It* (1990); *Original Jass All-Stars* (1993); *Live at Windsor Jazz Festival I* (1994).—**JC/LP**

Jackson, George K(nowil), English-American organist, editor, and composer; b. Oxford (baptized), April 15, 1757; d. Boston, Mass., Nov. 18, 1822. He was a pupil of James Nares at the Chapel Royal, and then completed his studies at the Univ. of St. Andrews (D.Mus., 1791). He went to the U.S. (1796), where he was first active in N.Y. (1801–12). He then settled in Boston (1812), where he played a leading role in the musical life of the city. He publ. *First Principles, or a Treatise on Practical Thorough Bass* (London, 1795). His works include *Dr. Watts's Divine Songs set to Music* (London, c. 1791), *David's Psalms* (Boston, 1804), 53 secular songs, 11 Masonic songs, and 13 instrumental pieces. He ed. *The Choral Companion* (Boston, 1814), *A Choice Collection of Chants in Four Voices* (Boston, 1816), *The Boston Handel and Haydn Society Collection of Church Music* (Boston, 1820), and seven instrumental collections.—**NS/LK/DM**

Jackson, George Pullen, American folklorist; b. Monson, Maine, Aug. 20, 1874; d. Nashville, Tenn., Jan. 19, 1953. He studied philology in Dresden and at the Univ. of Chicago (Ph.B., 1904; Ph.D., 1911). He was a teacher of German at Vanderbilt Univ. (1918–43), founder of the Tenn. State Sacred Harp Singing Assn., and president of the Tenn. Folklore Soc. (1942).

WRITINGS: *The Rhythmic Form of the German Folk Songs* (1917); *White Spirituals in the Southern Uplands* (1933); *Spiritual Folksongs of Early America* (1937; 3rd ed., 1965); *Down-East Spirituals* (1943; 2nd ed., 1953); *White and Negro Spirituals* (1943); *Story of the Sacred Harp* (1944); *Another Sheaf of White Spirituals* (1952).—**NS/LK/DM**

Jackson, Isaiah (Allen), black American conductor; b. Richmond, Va., Jan. 22, 1945. He majored in Russian studies at Harvard Univ. (B.A., 1966), then studied conducting at Stanford Univ. (M.A., 1967), and composition with Boulanger at the American Cons. in Fontainebleau; completed his training at the Juilliard School in N.Y. (M.S., 1969; D.M.A., 1973). He was founder-conductor of the Juilliard String Ensemble (1970–71), and also asst. conductor of the American Sym. Orch. in N.Y. (1970–71). After serving as asst. conductor of the Baltimore Sym. Orch. (1971–73), he was assoc. conductor of the Rochester (N.Y.) Phil. (1973–87) and music director of the Flint (Mich.) Sym. Orch. (1982–87). He was music director of the Royal Ballet at London's Covent Garden (from 1987) and of the Dayton (Ohio) Phil. (1987–90), and principal guest conductor of the Queensland Sym. Orch. in Brisbane (from 1993).—**NS/LK/DM**

Jackson, Janet, youngest hit-makin', hip-shakin' member of the popular music clan; b. Gary, Ind., May 16, 1966. As a member of one of the great show business families of the latter half of the 20th century, Janet Jackson was on stage by the time she was seven. While her brothers Jermaine, Tito, Jackie, Marlon, Steven and

Michael were The Jackson Five (Steven replaced Jermaine), Janet first displayed her talent as an actress, earning a recurring role on the TV show *Good Times* before her tenth birthday. While she appeared on the family's briefly broadcast Variety show, she earned kudos for her roles in *A New Kind of Family*, *Fame* and *Diff'rent Strokes*. In 1982, she cut her eponymous debut album, which presented her singing wholesome teen pop. This image, befitting a 16-year-old young woman, was furthered by a tour of high schools. While appearing in *Fame* she married James Debarge of the Debarge family, another Motown dynasty. Her family and her career advisors did not approve of the union at all. Add to that Debarge's alleged abuse of cocaine, and the marriage was annulled in a matter of months. In the midst of all this, she cut a lackluster follow-up album with dance-rock maven Georgio Moroder: *Dream Street* peaked at #147.

At 20 years old, Jackson teamed up with producers Jimmy "Jam" Harris and Terry Lewis to make *Control*. An entirely different album from her previous two, it presented her as a mature, sexual being, and an artist in charge of her own destiny. This image was reinforced by videos choreographed by Paula Abdul. Although her family disapproved of the "mature" Janet, the album was a tremendous success, launching her career. It spun off six singles, accounting for a chart presence of well over a year. Four of them—"What Have You Done for Me Lately" (#4 pop), "Nasty" (#3 pop), the chart-topping "When I Think of You," and the title track (#5 pop)—went gold. The #2 "Let's Wait a While" and the #14 "Pleasure Principle" also helped propel the album to the top of the charts and quintuple platinum sales.

Janet released another landmark album in 1989, *Rhythm Nation 1814*. An extension of the funky formula musically, it extended the message of emancipation thematically. Where *Control* was her personal declaration of independence, *Rhythm Nation* was her constitution, her foray into awareness of the world beyond her bedroom. Not that the album lacked heat, with steamy tunes like "Miss You Much" and "Love Will Never Do (Without You)." It also went sextuple platinum and topped the chart. Beyond that, the album became the first to generate seven top five hit singles, four of which—the platinum "Miss You Much" and the gold records "Escapade," "Black Cat" (with a stunning guitar solo by Living Colour guitarist Vernon Reid), and "Love Will Never Do (Without You)"—topped the charts. The title track only got to #2, but also went gold. *Rhythm Nation* was the top pop album of 1990. To support this record, Jackson embarked on her first live concert tour. While her first forays on stage were a little tentative, a month into the tour she was setting the stage on fire. Jackson was also showcased on the soundtrack to the film *Mo Money*. Her performance with Luther Vandross, BBD and Ralph Tresvant on "The Best Things in Life Are Free" reached the top of the R&B charts, topping out at #10 pop.

In 1993, Jackson returned to acting, but this time on the "big screen," appearing in the film *Poetic Justice*, opposite Tupac Shakur. Although the film was not terribly popular, Jackson's next album, *janet*, for a new

label, Virgin, also released that year, continued her success. More sexually frank than either of the previous two albums, the English music monthly *Vox* commented that "musically, she touches all the bases; lyrically, she hardly gets out of the sack." To accentuate this, she appeared on the cover of *Rolling Stone* topless, with boyfriend Rene Elizondo covering her bare breasts from behind. The first single, "That's the Way Love Goes," went platinum and spent eight weeks on top of the pop charts. It also won a Best R&B song of the Year Grammy for her, Terry Lewis, and Jimmy Jam. "Again" also went platinum, topping the charts for two weeks. The #4 single "If," based on a sample from the Motown standard "Someday, We'll Be Together," went gold as did the ten-week R&B chart topper "Any Time, Any Place" (#2 pop). With the #10 single "Because of Love" and the #8 "You Want This," the album spent six weeks atop the chart and sold sextuple platinum.

By 1995, Janet was confident enough in her own career to work with her brother Michael. Together, they recorded the song "Scream" which went to #5 and sold platinum. She also appeared in the sci-fi styled video clip for the song. In 1996, A&M released a retrospective album called *Design of a Decade*. In addition to her greatest hits on that label, it included the single "Runaway." When the single debuted at #6, it marked the highest debut ever by a female artist. "Runaway" went gold, rising to #3. That same year, Jackson renegotiated her contract with Virgin Records. Figures for the deal varied from $60–80 million, but it was generally acknowledged as the biggest deal any artist had ever signed.

Jackson's first album of new material in close to five years, 1998's *Velvet Rope*, debuted at #1 on the charts and sold platinum out of the box. The album featured the grooves people had come to expect from Jackson, including rapping by Q-Tip from A Tribe Called Quest. It sampled from diverse sources, including Joni Mitchell's "Big Yellow Taxi." An expansion on *Rhythm Nation's* social awareness, *Velvet Rope* songs addressed ongoing racial prejudice; the gold, chart-topping hit "Together Again" dealt with AIDS. However, Jackson had not abandoned discussing her own sexuality, in such songs as the #3 gold single "I Get Lonely." However, radio had become fragmented to the point that cross genre hits had become rarer and rarer. While *The Velvet Rope* did well, it was considered disappointing at triple platinum, especially in light of the deal she had signed just before its release. She toured in support of the album, donating 25 cents per ticket to America's Promise—The Alliance for Youth.

Disc.: *Janet Jackson* (1982); *Dream Street* (1984); *Control* (1986); *Control: The Remixes* (1987); *Rhythm Nation1814* (1989); *Janet* (1993); *Janet Remixed* (1995); *The Velvet Rope* (1998).—**HB**

Jackson, Javon, American saxophonist; b. Carthage, Mich., June 16, 1965. A facile and gutsy saxophonist with a muscular sound and a penchant for the stylistic nuances of fellow tenor man Joe Henderson, he is clearly entrenched in the classic hard bop approach of the 1950s and 1960s. Raised in Cleveland and Denver, he spent two years at the Berklee Coll. of Music before joining the last edition of Art Blakey's Jazz Messengers in 1987. With his reputation soon established, he promptly became a regular on the N.Y. scene, working with Freddie Hubbard, Elvin Jones, the Harper Brothers, James Williams, Charlie Haden, Benny Green, Mickey Tucker, and Billy Pierce. In recent years, he has recorded as a leader for the Blue Note label.

DISC.: *Me and Mr. Jones* (1992); *When the Time Is Right* (1993); *For One Who Knows* (1995); *A Look Within* (1996).—**CH**

Jackson, Joe,

music's great chameleon, able to go from reggae to jive to new-wave to classical, with authority; b. Burton-upon-Trent, England, Aug, 11, 1955. By the age of 11, Joe Jackson was playing the violin and convinced his parents to invest in a piano. He started writing songs in his teens while continuing his classical studies on oboe and percussion. Jackson attended the Royal Academy of Music on a scholarship, studying both jazz and classical music. In 1974, he earned a degree in composition. This led to work with cover bands and as the piano player at the Portsmouth Playboy Club. In the mid-1970s, however, he got caught up in the energy that was welling up in the London punk scene. He started writing songs in a punk/new wave style, and got a publishing contract from Albion Music in 1976. His demos attracted the attention of A&M records, recently flush with the success of the Police and Supertramp.

Jackson signed on with A&M and recorded his debut album, 1979's *Look Sharp*, in just a week and a half. He called his brand of new wave "spiv-rock" (spiv basically translates as lazy), although his vocals got him lumped in with predecessors Graham Parker and Elvis Costello. His songs had the lean sound of the new wave, but with an underpinning of humor. The song "Is She Really Going Out with Him" became a surprise hit in the summer of 1979, peaking at #20. The album also peaked at #20 and went gold.

Six months later, Jackson followed that same year with *I'm the Man*, though the record could have been called *Look Sharp II*. The songs were nearly as inspired. The songs "On the Radio" and "It's Different for Girls" became hits on rock radio. The album hit #22 on the charts.

Tired of the comparisons with Costello and Parker, Jackson started to work with reggae artists. He produced three tracks with Lincoln Thompson working with Jackson's band. He cut a three-song single with an A-side cover of Jimmy Cliff's "The Harder They Come." Then he made 1980's *Beat Crazy*, infused with ska and reggae. The album sold disappointingly. At the end of the world tour for *Beat Crazy*, Jackson disbanded his group, although bassist Graham Maby would remain with him for many more years.

Still working to assert his own identity, Jackson cut the audacious *Jumpin' Jive* album in 1981, a tribute to the music that his father loved. Recorded with a septet that included three horns, the record brought the music of Louis Jordan, Lester Young and Cab Calloway to an audience that thought pop music started with The Beatles (or perhaps Chuck Berry). He toured, playing nothing but swing. The album got virtually no airplay,

and certainly had no hits, although it forecast the swing music revival of the mid-1990s by over a decade.

In 1982, Jackson moved to N.Y. and settled in the Lower East Side of Manhattan. Rather than just picking a stylistic discipline for his next project, he set himself several paradigms: he wouldn't use guitars, he would use some of the jazz flavors he'd picked up in school, and he'd write songs that would make Cole Porter proud. With that in mind, he released *Night and Day*, a slick sophisticated pop album 180 degrees from *Look Sharp*. The song "Stepping Out" rose to #6 on the charts, followed by the ballad "Breaking Us in Two," which rose to #18. The album hit #4 and went gold.

Jackson's next challenge was scoring and writing songs for the 1983 Debra Winger film *Mike's Murder*. Neither the film nor the album did especially well, though it had some interesting songs, including the Spencer Davis flavored "Memphis." His next project, rather than a radical departure, took ideas from his previous records and expanded on them, combining the *Jumping Jive* horns, the rawness of his early work, and the slick popcraft of *Night and Day*. With cover art modeled after a Sonny Rollins album, the music for *Body and Soul* was recorded predominantly live in the studio. The propulsive "You Can't Get What You Want (Till You Know What You Want)" became a #15 pop hit. The album rose to #20.

Jackson took this live-in-the-studio approach one step further for his next album, 1986's *Big World*. Before a select audience on three consecutive nights, the album was recorded live directly to two-track tape. While the experiment was a sonic success, the album failed to generate a hit and stalled at #34.

Reaching back to his college experiences, Jackson tried his most daring experiment yet in 1987 by recording a classical album. The piece, *Will Power*, featured a 50-piece orchestra. The record predominantly mystified Joe Jackson fans. Classical fans generally rejected it out of hand. The record sold dozens. Still, it led people to take him more seriously as a composer. Francis Ford Coppola hired him to score his 1988 film *Tucker*.

Back on the rock track, A&M released the double-live album, *1979–86*. Each side captured a different tour. Finally back into the studio for a rock record, Jackson cut a semi-autobiographical concept record, 1989's *Blaze of Glory*. It sold moderately well, and "Down to London" became a minor hit on rock radio.

Jackson changed record companies and in 1991 released *Laughter and Lust*, one of the most snide pop recordings ever made. A vociferous detractor of MTV and how image had taken over the music business, he made a tongue-in-cheek video for the record, but even the catchy "Hit Single" failed to become one. After three years, he put out an album that fused pop, classical, and show tunes. Called *Night Music*, the album sold poorly, but paved the way for Jackson's next project.

After nearly a decade of poor sales, Jackson renounced pop music and went back to what he had studied in college, classical composition. In 1997, he released the daring, edgy oratorio, *Heaven and Hell* that put everything he'd done previously into a musical osterizer and blended it well. The album was arranged as a series of "songs," but played by a combined small chamber orchestra and rock band. It featured artists ranging from pop singers Jane Siberry to violinist Nadja Salerno-Sonnenberg. Opera diva Dawn Upshaw does a brilliant duet with folk-pop singer Suzanne Vega! Needless to say, there were no "hits."

Jackson's decision to renounce "pop" music is not surprising. It's likely that future projects will continue to mix elements of jazz, classical, and rock music in unexpected ways.

DISC.: *Look Sharp!* (1979); *I'm the Man* (1979); *Beat Crazy* (1980); *Jumpin' Jive* (1981); *Night and Day* (1982); *Mike's Murder Soundtrack* (1983); *Body and Soul* (1984); *Big World* (1986); *Will Power* (1987); *Live...1980–1986* (1988); *Tucker* (1988); *Blaze of Glory* (1989); *Laughter and Lust* (1991); *Night Music* (1994); *Heaven and Hell* (1997).—**HB**

Jackson, Judge, black American composer and tunebook compiler; b. Ozark, Ala., March 12, 1883; d. there, April 7, 1958. He learned shape-note hymn singing from the blacks of southeastern Ala. He was active as a singing- school teacher. He wrote shape-note religious songs and also compiled *The Colored Sacred Harp* (1934), which proved influential as a tunebook among blacks.—**NS/LK/DM**

Jackson, Mahalia, fervent American gospel singer; b. New Orleans, Oct. 26, 1911; d. Evergreen Park, Ill., Jan. 27, 1972. Widely considered the best gospel singer of her generation, Jackson was certainly the best known, with a career that embraced radio, television, and film as well as a major-label record contract. Such incursions into the secular realm made her a controversial figure among gospel fans, but with her impassioned contralto she spread the influence of gospel far beyond its previously narrow boundaries.

Jackson was the illegitimate daughter of Johnny Jackson Jr., a stevedore who also preached at a church in New Orleans, and Charity Clark. She sang first at her father's church. Following the death of her mother when she was five, she was raised by an aunt. In November 1927 she moved to Chicago to live with another aunt and began to sing with the choir at the Greater Salem Baptist Church while supporting herself as a domestic. She became a member of the Johnson Gospel Singers, a professional group, and eventually performed solo while working as a hairdresser; later she ran a beauty salon and a flower shop.

Jackson became a song demonstrator for gospel songwriter Thomas A. Dorsey in 1937. That same year she was signed to Decca Records and made her recording debut in May. She married Isaac Hockenhull, a mail carrier, in 1938; the marriage ended in divorce. She returned to recording in October 1946 for Apollo Records. An Apollo session in September 1947 produced a recording of "Move on Up a Little Higher," which was released in January 1948 and sold a reported two million copies. She made her Carnegie Hall debut in October 1950 and toured Europe in 1952.

Jackson signed to the Columbia label of CBS Records in 1954; she also had her own weekly series on the CBS radio network, *The Mahalia Jackson Show*, from September 1954 to February 1955; and she made frequent appearances on the television program *In Town Tonight* on the local CBS affiliate in Chicago in the fall of 1954. With these activities she moved beyond the religious community even while continuing to sing gospel music. She began to make appearances on national television, notably *The Ed Sullivan Show* in 1956, and performed at the Newport Jazz Festival in 1957. Her recording of "He's Got the Whole World in His Hand" (music and lyrics by Geoff Love, adapted from a traditional song) reached the singles chart in April 1958, and the same month she appeared in the film *St. Louis Blues*, a biography of W. C. Handy starring Nat "King" Cole. She returned to the Newport Jazz Festival that summer, performing with Duke Ellington, and in October she was a guest on the television special *The Bing Crosby Show*. She appeared in the film *Imitation of Life*, released in April 1959.

In March 1960 the film *Jazz on a Summer's Day*, a documentary of the 1958 Newport Jazz Festival featuring Jackson, was released. She won the first Grammy Award to be given out for Best Gospel or Other Religious Recording in 1961 for her album *Everytime I Feel the Spirit*. Her album *Sweet Little Jesus Boy*, a Christmas recording, reached the pop charts in January 1962, and in the Christmas season of 1962, Apollo Records reissued her 1950 recording of "Silent Night, Holy Night" (music by Franz Gruber, lyrics by Joseph Mohr) for a chart entry; it made the Christmas charts in 1964, 1967, 1968, 1969, and 1973. Jackson won her second consecutive Best Gospel or Other Religious Recording Grammy in 1962 for the album *Great Songs of Love and Faith*. She was nominated again in 1963 for the album *Make a Joyful Noise unto the Lord*.

Jackson married Sigmund Galloway, a musician, in 1964; they divorced in 1967. In 1969 she was nominated for a Grammy Award for Best Soul Gospel Performance for the LP *Guide Me, O Thou Great Jehovah*. She toured Europe in the fall of 1971 but was hospitalized in Munich, West Germany, in October for coronary heart disease. She died of a heart seizure at 60 in 1972.

Jackson's continuing popularity led to a series of posthumous record releases and awards. The album *How I Got Over*, which contained recordings from her radio broadcasts of 1954 and television appearances of 1963, won the Grammy Award in 1976 for Best Soul Gospel Performance; *I Sing Because I'm Happy* was nominated for the 1980 Grammy Award for Best Spoken Word, Documentary, or Drama Recording.

WRITINGS: With E. Wylie, *Movin' on Up* (N.Y., 1966).

BIBL.: J. Cornell and V. Mays, *M. J.: Queen of Gospel Song* (Champaign, Ill., 1974); K. McDearmon, *M., Gospel Singer* (N.Y., 1976); J. Jackson, *Make a Joyful Noise unto the Lord! The Life of M. J., Queen of Gospel Singers* (N.Y., 1974); L. Goreau, *Just M., Baby* (Gretna, La., 1975); E. Witter, *M. J.* (Milford, Mich., 1985); C. Wolfe, *M. J.* (N.Y., 1990); D. Donloe, *M. J.* (Los Angeles, 1992); J. Schwerin, *Got to Tell It: M. J., Queen of Gospel* (N.Y., 1992).—**WR**

Jackson, Michael, enormously successful pop /R&B singer, songwriter, and dancer; b. Gary, Ind., Aug, 29, 1958. Michael Jackson was a child prodigy who carried his brothers along with him to initial success in the pop group The Jackson Five. His father had played guitar in a local group before his marriage, and passed his dreams of pop success onto his children. The older sons (Sigmund Esco "Jackie," b. May 4, 1951; Toriano Adaryll "Tito," b. Oct. 15, 1953; Jermaine La Jaune, b. Dec. 11, 1954; all Gary, Ind.) formed a trio in the early 1960s and were quickly joined by Michael and Marlon (b. Gary, Ind., March 12, 1957) to form the original Jackson Five. The group played locally and even began to undertake limited tours as an opening act for other R&B groups. They were invited to try out for Motown Records in 1969, and their filmed audition, showing a very young Michael performing James Brown-esque dance moves, clinched the deal with Motown label chief Berry Gordy. He relocated the group to L.A. (where the label was then headquartered), and in classic Motown fashion began reshaping their image, dressing them in the latest "mod" fashions (large floppy hats, flowered shirts, exaggerated bell-bottoms, and botts). They hit it big almost immediately in January 1970 with "I Want You Back," followed quickly by the top pop and R&B hits "ABC," "The Love You Save," and "I'll Be There"; "Mama's Pearl" and "Never Can Say Goodbye" were smash hits in both fields, and "Maybe Tomorrow" and "Sugar Daddy" became smash R&B and major pop hits. The group was so popular that a cartoon series was launched in 1971 featuring animated Jacksons to appeal to the kiddie market.

Motown also tried to market the individual Jacksons as pop stars in their own right. In late 1971 Michael Jackson's solo career was launched with the crossover smash "Got to Be There" followed in 1972 by a remake of Bobby Day's "Rockin' Robin," "I Wanna Be Where You Are," and "Ben," the title song to a movie about a trained rat. Jermaine's solo career started in 1972, but his success was largely limited to a smash remake of Shep and The Limelites' "Daddy's Home" in early 1973. Jackie Jackson's solo debut on Motown from 1973 failed to produce any hits.

The Jackson Five continued to score major pop and smash R&B hits for Motown through 1973 with a remake of "Little Bitty Pretty One," "Lookin' through the Windows," "Corner of the Sky," "Hallelujah Day," and "Get It Together." "Dancing Machine" became a top R&B and smash pop hit in 1974, followed by the R&B smashes "Whatever You Got, I Want:" "I Am Love (Parts I and II)" (a major pop hit), and "Forever Caine Today." In 1975 Michael scored the R&B smashes "We're Almost There" and "Just a Little Bit of You" (a major pop hit), yet he would not achieve another hit until leaving Motown.

In 1976 The Jackson Five switched to Epic Records. Jermaine, who had married Berry Gordy's daughter Hazel in 1973, left the group and continued to record for Motown through 1982, scoring his biggest successes with 1980's "Let's Get Serious" and 1982's "Let Me Tickle Your Fancy." Adding brother Randy (real name, Steven Randall) (b. Oct. 29, 1961), the group was legally forced to abandon the name Jackson Five, becoming simply the Jacksons, after Motown sued for breach of contract. Their enormous success continued through 1980, highlighted by the pop and R&B smashes "Enjoy Yourself" and "Shake Your Body (Down to the Ground)" and the major pop and R&B smashes "Show You the Way to Go," "Lovely One," and "Heartbreak Hotel." In 1978 Michael Jackson co-starred with long-time friend Diana Ross in the movie remake of The Wizard of Oz, The Wiz, which yielded his last Motown hit, "Ease on Down the Road," in duet with Ross.

In 1979 Michael Jackson also moved to Epic Records, where his debut, Off the Wall, became a phenomenal success, staying on the album charts for more than three years and selling more than six million copies. The album yielded two top pop and R&B hits, "Don't Stop 'Til You Get Enough" and "Rock with You," and two major pop hits, "Off the Wall" (an R&B smash) and "She's Out of My Life." LaToya Jackson (b. May 29, 1956), who had sung backup with The Jackson Five, started her solo career on Polydor Records in 1980, switching to Private I Records in 1984, where she scored her only significant success with "Heart Don't Lie" a major R&B hit. She is estranged from the rest of the family, and has been the most vocally critical of her parents and siblings. LaToya has provoked scandal by posing nude for Playboy, as well as through her well-publicized brawls with her husband, who manages her career.

Thanks to the production of Quincy Jones and a carefully orchestrated and sequenced promotional campaign, Michael Jackson's 1982 release, Thriller, became the best-selling album of all time, eventually moving nearly 50 million copies worldwide. The first single, "The Girl Is Mine," a duet with Paul McCartney, became a top R&B and easy-listening and smash pop hit. The second, "Billie Jean," became a top pop and R&B hit, in large part due to frequent airplay of its promotional video on MTV, the first by a black artist to receive such extensive exposure. Jackson's incredible dance moves, a highlight of all his videos, were highlighted on the Motown 25th Anniversary TV special, helping also to launch this song. The third, "Beat It," was heavily promoted as a video by MTV and featured the dynamic lead-guitar playing of heavy-metal icon Eddie Van Halen. Subsequently, "Wanna Be Startin' Somethin'" and "Thriller" became smash pop and R&B hits, "Human Nature" became a smash pop and major R&B hit, and "P.Y.T. (Pretty Young Thing)" became a major pop hit. The elaborate video for "Thriller" was itself the subject of a documentary, the first "behind-the-scenes/making of" film which became a huge-selling home video success. In the meantime, a second duet with McCartney, "Say Say Say" from McCartney's Pipes of Peace album, became a top pop and smash R&B hit.

The year 1984 was the most successful year in the career of many of the other members of the Jackson family. Jermaine scored major pop and R&B hits with "Dynamite" and "Do What You Do " on Arista Records. Rebbie (real name, Maureen) (b. May 19, 1950), who had worked with the Jacksons from into 1977, achieved a major pop and smash R&B hit with "Centipede" on Columbia Records. Jermaine rejoined his other brothers in the Jacksons for their hugely successful Victory album and tour. The album yielded a pop and R&B smash,

"State of Shock," with lead vocals by Michael and Mick Jagger, and a major pop and R&B hit, "Torture," with lead vocals by Michael and Jermaine. However, by 1986 Michael had left The Jacksons, and the group endured into the 1990s with little success. Marlon's 1987 debut solo album on Capitol yielded the R&B smash "Don't Go."

After co-writing with Lionel Richie and performing on the "We Are the World" single in 1995 and starring in the 15-minute movie *Captain Eo* shown exclusively at Disneyland and Disney World, Michael Jackson recorded another album under producer Quincy Jones. *Bad* was released in August 1987. The album sold nearly 20 million copies worldwide in its first year and yielded an astonishing seven hits, including four top pop and R&B hits: "I Just Can't Stop Loving You " (also a top easy-listening hit) with Siedah Garrett on backing vocals, "Bad," "The Way You Make Me Feel" and "Man in the Mirror." " Dirty Diana," recorded with Billy Idol's guitarist Steve Stevens, became a top pop and smash R&B hit, and "Another Part of Me" and "Smooth Criminal" were smash R&B and major pop hits through 1988. Again, Michael produced a series of memorable videos to promote the songs, working with distinguished directors such as Martin Scorsese on "Bad." Between September 1987 and January 1989, Michael Jackson conducted his first solo tour, playing venues around the world.

In March 1991 Michael Jackson re-signed with the parent company of Epic Records, Sony Corporation. The 15-year contract was reportedly worth in the neighborhood of $1 billion. However, his next album, *Dangerous*, was met with mixed reviews, but nonetheless, produced seven hit singles. "Black or White," recorded with Guns N' Roses guitarist Slash, became a top pop hit, while "Remember the Time" and "In the Closet" became smash pop and top R&B hits. "Jam," recorded with rapper Heavy D, "Heal the World," and "Who Is It" proved major crossover hits. "Will You Be There," also featured in the movie *Free Willy*, became a smash crossover hit. In early 1993 Michael Jackson made a technologically stunning appearance during the half-time show at Super Bowl XXVII and took part in a rare television interview with Oprah Winfrey reportedly watched by 90 million viewers. However, in July, a 13-year-old boy alleged that he had been molested by Jackson. As the news dominated the front pages of newspapers worldwide, Jackson launched his next tour in August, only to cancel it in November and slip into seclusion as the press speculated about his whereabouts. He eventually surfaced in southern Calif., on Dec. 22, 1993 to tell an international television audience that the accusations were "totally false." The next month he settled out of court with the boy and his family for an estimated $20 million, although the case remained open. In the meantime, Jackson secretly married Elvis Presley's daughter, Lisa Marie, on May 26, 1994.

In 1995 Michael Jackson attempted to resume his musical career with the release of the double-CD set *HIStory—Past, Present and Future, Book 1*. Comprised of 15 remastered greatest hits and 15 new songs, the album was promoted by a $30 million campaign by Epic Records. Although his duet with sister Janet on "Scream" became an instant hit, the promotional film for *HIStory* was compared to Leni Riefenstahl's Nazi propaganda film *Triumph of the Will*. Allegations of anti-Semitism were made about the lyrics to "They Don't Care about Us," and some took exception with Jackson's use of four-letter words on an album directed at youngsters. In June, Jackson and wife Lisa Marie were interviewed live on ABC's *Prime Time Live* by Diane Sawyer. Despite the fact that the interview was seen by an audience estimated at 60 million, the appearance failed to slow the collapse of Jackson's career. Soon after, the couple separated. *HIStory* sold only around 2 million copies (not 20 million, as predicted), and by October the album was already being discounted by major record stores. Jackson further faltered when a planned concert at N.Y.'s Beacon Theater to be presented live on HBO, was canceled after the star collapsed; follow-up medical tests revealed that he was suffering from dehydration and perhaps heart and kidney disease.

Jackson has been off the charts and the pop-music scene ever since, although his name still appears in the gossip columns on occasion. He remarried, but this wedding also did not last long, although it did produce two children. Meanwhile, in late 1999 it was rumored that Jackson was back in the studios working on a new album, but no further information was available.

DISC.: JACKSON FIVE: *Diana Ross Presents The Jackson Five* (1970); *ABC* (1970); *Jackson Five Christmas Album* (1970); *Third Album* (1970); *Maybe Tomorrow* (1971); *Goin' Back to Indiana* (1971); *Lookin' through the Windows* (1972); *Skywriter* (1973); *Get It Together* (1973); *Dancing Machine* (1974); *Moving Violation* (1975); *Joyful Jukebox Music* (1976). **THE JACKSONS:** *The Jacksons* (1976); *Goin' Places* (1977); *Destiny* (1978); *Triumph* (1980); *Live* (1981); *Victory* (1984); *2300 Jackson St.* (1989). **MICHAEL JACKSON SOLO:** *Got to Be There* (1972); *Ben* (1972); *Music and Me* (1973); *Farewell My Summer Love 1984* (1984); *Forever, Michael* (1975); *One Day in Your Life* (1981); *Off the Wall* (1979); *Thriller* (1982); *Bad* (1987); *Dangerous* (1991); *HIStory—Past, Present and Future, Book 1* (1995).—HB

Jackson, Milt(on; aka **Bags),** famed jazz vibraphonist, pianist, and guitarist, best-known for his long association with the Modern Jazz Quartet; b. Detroit, Jan. 1, 1923; d. N.Y., Oct. 9, 1999. He articulated with remarkable sensitivity, bringing out certain notes within a line just as pianists and saxophonists do. This developed in his playing by the early 1950s. He began his career in 1945 with Dizzy Gillespie; after working with several other musicians, he organized the Milt Jackson Quartet in 1951, with John Lewis, Ray Brown, and Kenny Clarke. In 1952 it was renamed the Modern Jazz Quartet, a group that was crucial in the synthesis of "cool jazz" with "classical" music, which eventually came to be known as Third Stream. The Quartet disbanded in 1974, but reunited on several occasions, including a 1981 Japanese tour that led to annual reunions since. He co-led a group with Ray Brown during the 1960s. From 1992, he worked with his own quintet, with Mike LeDonne, Bob Cranshaw, and

Mickey Roker. In 1996 he was inducted into the Percussive Arts Society (PAS) Hall of Fame.

DISC.: *M. J.* (1948); *In the Beginning* (1948); *Howard McGhee and M. J.* (1948); *Bluesology* (1949); *Quartet* (1951); *M. J.* (1951); *First Q* (1951); *Wizard of the Vibes* (1952); *Quartet, Quintet* (1952); *All Star Bags* (1952); *With the Henri Renaud All Stars* (1954); *Opus De Jazz* (1955); *Second Nature* (1956); *Soul Brothers* (with Ray Charles; 1957); *Plenty, Plenty Soul* (1957); *Bean Bags* (with Coleman Hawkins; 1958); *Bags and Trane* (John Coltrane; 1959); *That's the Way It Is* (1960); *Soul Meeting* (1961); *Bags Meets Wes* (with Wes Montgomery; 1961); *Live at the Village Gate* (1963); *Jazz 'n' Samba* (1964); *At the Museum of Modern Art* (1965); *Montreux '75* (1975); *M. J. Big Four* (1975); *At the Kosei Nenkin* (1976); *Montreux '77* (1977); *M. J., Count Basie* (1978); *M. J. Sings and Plays* (1978); *Ain't But a Few of Us Left* (1981); *Mostly Duke* (1982); *In London: Memories of Thelonious Sphere Monk* (1982); *J., Johnson, Brown & Company* (with J. J. Johnson, Ray Brown; 1983); *Bebop* (1988); *Prophet Speaks* (1994); *Burnin' in the Woodhouse* (1995).

BIBL.: Roy J. Wilbraham, *M. J.: A Discography* (London). —NS/LP

Jackson, Oliver (Jr.; aka Bops; Junior), jazz drummer; b. Detroit, April 28, 1933; d. N.Y., May 29, 1994. His brother was a bass player, and other family members also were musicians. He studied music at Wayne State Coll. in his hometown with Merle Auley; at the same time, he worked with other local players, including Thad Jones, Paul Chambers, and Tommy Flanagan. From 1948–53, he worked as a duo with Eddie Locke as Bop and Locke. In 1954, he moved to N.Y. and joined Yusef Lateef's band (1954–56); he subsequently freelanced with various leaders, including stints with Teddy Wilson (1957–58), Charlie Shavers (1959–61), Lionel Hampton (1962–64), and a long period in a quartet (as well as larger bands) led by Earl Hines (1964–70). In 1969, he formed the JPJ Quartet with Budd Johnson, Bill Pemberton, and Dill Jones, which performed widely in schools thanks to corporate sponsorship. In the mid-1970s, he worked with Sy Oliver's nine-piece outfit (1975–80). From the early 1980s, he freelanced and led his own small groups.

DISC.: *Billie's Bounce* (1984). Y. Lateef: *The Sounds of Yusef* (1957); *Other Sounds* (1957); *Cry Tender* (1959). K. Burrell: *The Tender Gender* (1966). E. Hines: *Blues and Things* (1967). Newport Jazz Festival All-Stars: *The Newport Jazz Festival All Stars* (1984). Gene Ammons: *Bad Bossa Nova* (1962). Dexter Gordon: *At Montreux with Jr. Mance* (1981).—JC/LP

Jackson, Preston (originally, **McDonald, James Preston**), early jazz trombonist; b. New Orleans, Jan. 3, 1902; d. Blytheville, Ark., Nov. 12, 1983. He took the surname of his stepfather. The family moved to Chicago in 1917. His mother bought him his first trombone in August 1920. He took lessons from Chicago trombonist William Robertson; nine months later he played in local chapel band. He worked in Chicago and Milwaukee during the 1920s, including a long stint with Art Simms's Band at Wisconsin Rook (Milwaukee) (ca. 1925–spring 1930). The band was subsequently led by Oscar "Bernie" Young. He returned to Chicago in the spring of 1930, and worked with Dave

Peyton and Erskine Tate before joining Louis Armstrong in January 1931, touring with him in early 1932. He spent the balance of the 1930s working with various local leaders out of Chicago. He also wrote a regular column for *Jazz Hot* and *Hot News*. By the late 1930s, Jackson had left full-time music but continued gigging, served on the board of directors of local musicians union from 1934–57. In the 1940s, he led his own band which recorded in 1946. Occasionally he led his own band during the 1950s, and was also active with several small bands including a spell with Lil Armstrong in 1959. He continued playing and recording during the 1960s, and worked in Little Brother Montgomery's Band in late 1969. He moved to New Orleans during the 1970s, and continued to play regularly in the 1970s, including tours of Europe.—JC/LP

Jackson, Quentin (Leonard; aka Butter), jazz trombonist, singer; b. Springfield, Ohio, Jan. 13, 1909; d. N.Y., Oct. 2, 1976. He was the brother-in-law of Claude Jones. At six he received piano lessons from his mother. At 12, he played violin in the school orch. He played trombone from age 18, worked with the Gerald Hobson Band and with Lloyd Byrd's Buckeye Melodians, then with the Wesley Helvey Band from August 1929 until January 1930. he played in Zack Whyte's Chocolate Beau Brummels, then joined McKinney's Cotton Pickers as trombonist/vocalist from December 1930 until May 1932. He left to play in Don Redman's Orch., and remained with him until December 1939. He was with Cab Calloway from January 1940 until August 1946, then toured Europe with Don Redman. He returned to the U.S. in December 1946 and rejoined Calloway until 1948. he was briefly with Lucky Millinder, then in Duke Ellington's Orch. from Oct. 21, 1948 until Oct. 20, 1959. He toured Europe in Quincy Jones's Band (1960), then joined Count Basie until autumn 1962. Later that year he played with Charles Mingus, and rejoined Ellington briefly in spring of 1963. He did some studio work and played in the house band at the Copacabana (N.Y.), late 1964. From the mid-1960s, he played in several big bands specially formed in N.Y. including Louis Bellson's (1964) and Gerald Wilson's (1966). He toured with Sammy Davis (1970), and with Al Cohn Band and Jones-Lewis (1971). He suffered a fatal heart attack while playing for Broadway show *Guys and Dolls* in the mid-1970s.—JC/LP

Jackson, Ronald Shannon, American drummer; b. Ft. Worth, Tex., Jan.12, 1940. He is a polyrhythmatist of power and imagination who has developed Ornette Coleman's harmolodic music in his own highly personal direction with his group the Decoding Society. Jackson came up in Tex. playing with such esteemed locals as James Clay. Eventually moving to N.Y., he became part of the free-jazz scene, recording with Albert Ayler and Charles Tyler. Quite technically adept, he was also working with more mainstream musicians, including Betty Carter and Charles Mingus. In the 1970s he worked extensively in the bands of Coleman and Cecil Taylor. He worked throughout the 1980s as a leader, racking up an impressive discography, while also playing on the first two albums by ex- Coleman bandmate James Blood Ulmer's group Music Revelation Ensemble, the only release by the collective trio Power Tools, and a number of Bill Laswell projects.

Since returning to Tex. in the 1990s, he has become less prolific, though his Decoding Society still convenes in the studio about once a year and has made some fine albums for the Japanese DIW label.

Compositionally, he combines the collective voicing/improvisation principles of harmolodics with his complex polyrhythms, a knowledge of African music gained in travel there, and a feeling for the blues inherent in his Tex. upbringing. He prefers higher-pitched instruments, saying that's where he naturally hears musical lines, which explains his flute playing, his distinctive use of guitars, and his preference for alto and soprano saxophonists. His music is full of interlocking lines and rhythms.

DISC.: *Eye on You* (1980); *Nasty* (1981); *Street Priest* (1981); *Mandance* (1982); *Barbeque Dog* (1983); *Pulse* (1984); *Decode Yourself* (1985); *Live at the Caravan of Dreams* (1986); *When Colors Play* (1987); *Texas* (1988); *Taboo* (1990); *Red Warrior* (1990); *Raven Roc* (1992); *What Spirit Say* (1995).—**SH**

Jackson, Rudy (actually, **Rudolph**), early jazz clarinetist, alto & tenor saxophonist; b. Fort Wayne, Ind., Oct. 30, 1901; d. Winnebago, Ill., October 1969. He was raised in Chicago. Both of his parents were musicians. He worked in local bands from 1918, regularly with Carroll Dickerson in the early 1920s, then with King Oliver (late 1923 to summer 1924), then long spell of touring with traveling shows. He was with Billy Butler in N.Y. (1925), and with Vaughn's Lucky Sambo Orch. on tour (from June 1926). He was briefly with King Oliver in February 1927, then recommenced touring with the Lucky Sambo show. He joined Duke Ellington in June 1927, and was replaced by Barney Bigard in December 1927. He sailed to Europe with Noble Sissle (May 1929), returned to N.Y. with Sissle, in 1931 again went with Sissle to Europe, and spent long spells with Leon Abbey. He worked with Leddy Weatherford and Leon Abbey in India during the mid-1930s. He returned to Europe, then rejoined Teddy Weatherford in Colombo, Ceylon. He played regularly in India and Ceylon until after World War II, then returned to live in Chicago. He retired from music and worked for Western Union until his death.—**JC/LP**

Jackson, Samuel P., English-American organist, teacher, and composer; b. Manchester, Feb. 5, 1818; d. Brooklyn, July 27, 1885. He settled in N.Y. at the age of seven, serving as a church organist there from 1830 to 1875. He also engaged in teaching. He wrote four vols. of organ voluntaries (1865–74) and other sacred organ pieces.—**NS/LK/DM**

Jackson, Tony (actually, **Anthony**), jazz pianist, singer; b. New Orleans, La., June 5, 1876; d. Chicago, April 20, 1921. Jackson played in New Orleans brothels before the turn of the century, and occasionally in Adam Olivier's Band. He worked in Louisville, Ky.

(1904), and for a time partnered Glover Compton. Jackson previously worked as accompanist to the Whitman Sisters. Living briefly in New Orleans during fall 1904 and again from 1910–12, Jackson moved to Chicago permanently; he returned to New Orleans in February 1914 to attend his mother's funeral. Played in a duo with Glover Compton at Elite No. 1 and as a solo entertainer in many Chicago clubs; he also worked again as accompanist for the Whitman Sisters. Worked for several years at the De Lure Cafe, then moved to the Pekin Cafe, continued working there until shortly before his death. A prolific composer, his most famous tune is "Pretty Baby."—**JC/LP**

Jackson, Wanda, rockabilly legend; b. Maud, Okla., Oct. 20, 1937. Wanda Jackson moved to Bakersfield, Calif., with her family in 1941, returning to Oklahoma City in 1949. She took up piano and guitar in elementary school and had her own radio show on KLPR by the age of 13. Heard by honky-tonk artist Hank Thompson in 1954, she was invited to tour with Thompson and signed to Decca Records. She scored a near-smash country hit with "You Can't Have My Love," recorded with Billy Gray, that summer. She toured with Red Foley and appeared on his ABC television show *Ozark Jubilee* (later known as *Country Music Jubilee* and *Jubilee U.S.A.*) from 1955 to 1960. She toured with Elvis Presley in 1955 and 1956, and he ostensibly convinced her that she could record in the rockabilly style.

Wanda Jackson switched to Capitol Records in 1956 and began recording in L.A. with guitarists Buck Owens and Joe Maphis and pianist Merrill Moore under producer Ken Nelson. Her first Capitol single, "I Gotta Know," became a major country hit, but subsequent recordings failed to chart. These included dynamic songs such as "Hot Dog! That Made Him Mad," "Fujiyama Mama," and "Honey Bop"; and her own "Cool Love," "Mean Mean Man" and "Rock Your Baby," as well as excellent covers of "Hardheaded Woman" and "Riot in Cell Block Number Nine" through 1961. She toured with Jerry Lee Lewis and Carl Perkins in 1957 and Capitol issued her debut album for the label in 1958. Her classic rockabilly album *Rockin' with Wanda* was released in 1960, the year she achieved her first moderate pop hit with "Let's Have a Party," recorded in 1957 and previously sung by Elvis Presley in his 1956 movie *Loving You*.

Having managed little commercial success in rock 'n' roll, Wanda Jackson returned to country music in 1961 with her own "Right or Wrong," a near-smash country/major pop hit. She followed up with the country smash/major pop hit "In the Middle of a Heartache" and continued to record country material during the 1960s. Jackson also wrote "(Let's Stop) Kickin' Our Hearts Around," a near-smash country hit for Buck Owens in 1962. She achieved major country hits on her own throughout the 1960s with "The Box It Came in," "Tears Will Be the Chaser for the Wine," "You Don't Have to Drink to Have Fun," "A Woman Lives for Love," and "Fancy Satin Pillows."

Weary from years of touring and suffering from alcohol abuse, Wanda Jackson embraced Christianity in

June 1971; she recorded gospel music until the 1980s, when she returned to performing rockabilly in Europe. In 1984 she recorded *Rock 'n' Roll Your Blues Away* in Sweden and the album was reissued on Varrick in the U.S. in 1987. She toured Great Britain and Scandinavia in 1989, and her version of "Let's Have a Party" was featured in the film *Dead Poets Society*. In 1990 she dueted with new country artist Jann Brown on "I Forgot More Than You'll Ever Know." She later recorded two duets with country-rockabilly artist Rosie Flores for Flores's 1995 *Rockabilly Filly* album. Later that year Wanda Jackson resumed touring.

DISC.: *Wanda Jackson* (1958); *Rockin' with Wanda!* (1960); *There's a Party Goin' On* (1961); *Right or Wrong* (1961); *Lovin' Country Style* (1962); *Wonderful Wanda* (1962); *Love Me Forever* (1963); *Two Sides of Wanda Jackson* (1964); *Blues in My Heart* (1964); *Sings Country Songs* (1966); *Salues the Country Music Hall of Fame* (1967); *Reckless Love Affair* (1967); *You'll Always Have My Love* (1967); *Best* (1967); *Cream of the Crop* (1969); *Country!* (1970); *A Woman Lives to Love* (1970); *I've Gotta Sing* (1971); *Praise the Lord* (1972); *I Wouldn't Want You Any Other Way* (1972); *Country Keepsakes* (1973); *Now I Have Everything* (1974); *Country Gospel* (1974); *Closer to Jesus* (1978); *My Testament* (1982); *Rock 'n' Roll Your Blues Away* (1984).—**BH**

Jackson, William,

English organist and composer; b. Masham, Yorkshire, Jan. 9, 1815; d. Bradford, April 15, 1866. He left school when he was 13 to work in a mill and bakery. He was a self-taught musician, becoming an organist in Masham in 1832. In 1852 he founded a music business and became organist of St. John's Church at Bradford, and later he was conductor of the Festival Choral Soc. (from 1856). He wrote the oratorio *The Deliverance of Israel from Babylon* (Leeds, 1847).

BIBL.: J. Smith, *The Life of W. J., the Miller Musician* (Leeds, 1926).—**NS/LK/DM**

Jacob, Benjamin,

English organist and composer; b. London, May 15, 1778; d. there, Aug. 24, 1829. He was a pupil of Willoughby, Shrubsole, and Arnold (1796). He served as organist at various churches, finally at Surrey Chapel (1794–1825). With Wesley and Crotch, he gave organ recitals (1808–14), which were attended by large crowds. He conducted a series of oratorios in 1800, and the Lenten Oratorios at Covent Garden in 1818. Jacob was very active in spreading the Bach cult in London (see O. Mansfield, "J.S. Bach's First English Apostles," *Musical Quarterly*, April 1935). He publ. *National Psalmody* (London, 1819) and other collections, as well as glees and catches.—**NS/LK/DM**

Jacob, Gordon (Percival Septimus),

distinguished English composer and pedagogue; b. London, July 5, 1895; d. Saffron Walden, June 8, 1984. He studied at Dulwich Coll. and took courses in composition with Stanford, Howells, and Wood at the Royal Coll. of Music in London (D.Mus., 1935). He taught at the Royal Coll. of Music from 1926 to 1966; among his notable students were Malcolm Arnold, Imogen Holst, Elizabeth Maconchy, and Bernard Stevens. In 1968 he was made a Commander of the Order of the British Empire. Jacob produced a significant output of instrumental music, and also publ. several important books.

WRITINGS (all publ. in London): *Orchestral Technique: A Manual for Students* (1931; 3rd ed., 1983); *How to Read a Score* (1944); *The Composer and His Art* (1954); *The Elements of Orchestration* (1962).

WORKS: ORCH.: 2 viola concertos (1925, 1979); 2 piano concertos (1927, 1957); 2 syms. (1928–29; 1943–44); *Denbigh Suite* for Strings (1929); *Variations on an Air by Purcell* for Strings (1930); *Passacaglia on a Well-known Theme* (1931); 2 oboe concertos (1933, 1956); *Variations on an Original Theme* (1936); *Divertimento* (1938); 3 suites (1941; 1948–49; 1949); 3 sinfoniettas (1942, 1951, 1953); Sym. for Strings (1943); Concerto for Bassoon, Strings, and Percussion (1947); *Rhapsody* for English Horn and Strings (1948); Concerto for Horn and Strings (1951); Flute Concerto (1951); Trombone Concerto (1952); Concerto for Violin and Strings (1953); Violin Concerto (1954); *Divertimento* for Harmonica and Strings (1954); Cello Concerto (1955); *Prelude and Toccata* (1955); Sym. for Small Orch. (1958); 2 overtures (1965); Concerto for Piano Duet, 3-Hands, and Orch. (1969); Concerto for Band (1970); *A York Symphony* for Woodwinds (1971); Suite for Tuba and Strings (1972). **CHAMBER:** String Quartet (1928); Quartet for Oboe and Strings (1938); Quintet for Clarinet and Strings (1942); *Serenade* for 8 Woodwind Instruments (1950); Piano Trio (1955); Cello Sonata (1957); Sextet for Wind Quintet and Piano (1962); Suite for 4 Trombones (1968); *Divertimento* for 8 Wind Instruments (1969); Suite for Bassoon and String Quartet (1969); Trio for Clarinet, Viola, and Piano (1969); *Introduction and Rondo* for Clarinet Choir (1972); Piano Quartet (1971); Suite for 8 Violas (1976); Viola Sonata (1978); piano pieces. **VOCAL:** Sacred and secular choral works; songs.—**NS/LK/DM**

Jacob, Gunther (Wenceslaus),

Bohemian organist, choirmaster, and composer; b. Kačeřov, near Loket (baptized), Sept. 30, 1685; d. March 21, 1734. He was a singer at the Benedictine monasteries in Kladruby (1696) and St. Nicolas in the Old Town of Prague (from 1698), where he was a student of Prokop Smrkovský (music) and Isidor Vavak (organ). He also was trained in the law and theology. In 1707 he was asst. organist at St. Nicolas, and later was its choirmaster. In 1710 he received the name of Guntherus on taking his monastic vows in the Benedictine order. He distinguished himself as a composer of sacred music, including four oratorios and more than 30 masses.—**LK/DM**

Jacob, Maxime,

French composer; b. Bordeaux, Jan. 13, 1906; d. in the Benedictine Abbey in En-Calcat, Tarn, Feb. 26, 1977. He studied with Gédalge, Koechlin, Milhaud, and Nat in Paris. Pursuing a whimsical mode, he became associated with the École d'Arcueil, named after a modest Paris suburb where Satie presided over his group of disciples. He then made a 180 turn toward established religion, and in 1929 took holy orders. He adopted the name Clément as a Benedictine novice, and served mainly as an organist; also served as a soldier (1939–40) and army chaplain (1944–45) during World War II. He wrote a Piano Concerto (1961), eight string quartets (1961–69), three violin sonatas, two cello sonatas, fifteen piano sonatas, a curious *Messe syncopée* (1968), and over 500 songs. He wrote the books *L'Art et la grâce* (Paris, 1939) and *Souvenirs a deux voix* (Toulouse, 1969).

BIBL.: R. Chalupt, *M. J.* (Paris, 1927).—**NS/LK/DM**

Jacobi (real name, **Jakabfi**), **Viktor,** Hungarian- born American composer; b. Budapest, Oct. 22, 1883; d. N.Y., Dec. 10, 1921. He studied in Budapest. While still a student, he attracted attention with his first light stage piece there, *A rátartós királykisasszony* (The Proud Princess; Dec. 17, 1904). Respectable hearings were then given to such Budapest scores as *A legvitézebó huszár* (The Bravest Hussar; Dec. 30, 1905), *A tengerszem tűndére* (The Sea Fairy; Nov. 7, 1906), *Tűskerozsa* (Prickly Rose; March 23, 1907), *Van de nincs* (There Is, But There Isn't; Oct. 30, 1908), and *Jánoska* (May 7, 1909). His first major success came with *Leányvásár* (The Marriage Market; Nov. 14, 1911). Following the extraordinary success of *Szibill* (Feb. 27, 1914), Jacobi settled in the U.S. and became a naturalized American citizen. His first score for Broadway was *Rambler Rose* (Sept. 10, 1917), which failed to attract much notice. He then collaborated with Fritz Kreisler on the successful *Apple Blossoms* (Oct. 7, 1919). His subsequent works, *The Half Moon* (Nov. 1, 1920) and *The Love Letter* (Oct. 4, 1921), were failures.—**LK/DM**

Jacobi, Erwin R(euben), Swiss musicologist; b. Strasbourg, Sept. 21, 1909; d. Zürich, Feb. 27, 1979. He studied economics in Berlin, obtaining a diploma of engineering in 1933. From 1934 to 1952 he lived in Israel, where he studied harpsichord with Pelleg and composition with Ben-Haim; in 1952 he went to the U.S. to study with Landowska (harpsichord), Hindemith (composition), and Sachs (music history); completed his studies at the Univ. of Zürich (Ph.D., 1957, with the diss. *Die Entwicklung der Musiktheorie in England nach der Zeit von Jean-Philippe Rameau;* publ. in Strasbourg, 1957–60; 2nd ed., rev. and aug., Baden-Baden, 1971). He was an asst. lecturer there (from 1961), and also a visiting prof. at the Univ. of Iowa (1970) and at Ind. Univ. (1971–72). He wrote a number of valuable articles on Baroque composers for various music journals, and ed. *J.-P. Rameau: Complete Theoretical Writings* (Rome, 1967–72). He also publ. *Albert Schweitzer und die Musik* (Wiesbaden, 1975) and served as ed. of his writings. —**NS/LK/DM**

Jacobi, Frederick, American composer, conductor, and teacher; b. San Francisco, May 4, 1891; d. N.Y., Oct. 24, 1952. He was a student of Gallico, Joseffy, Goldmark, and Bloch in N.Y., and of Juon at the Berlin Hochschule für Musik. After studying the music of the Pueblo Indians in N.Mex. and Ariz., he returned to N.Y. and taught harmony at the Master School of the United Arts (1924–36) and composition at the Juilliard Graduate School (1936–50). He also served as director of the American section of the ISCM, and actively promoted the cause of contemporary American music. In 1945 he received the David Bispham Award for his opera *The Prodigal Son*. In some of his works, he made use of native American Indian themes. However, his music as a whole was characterized by an assured usage of Classical and Romantic idioms in a contemporary style.

WORKS: DRAMATIC: O p e r a : *The Prodigal Son* (1943–44). **ORCH.:** *The Pied Piper,* symphonic poem (1915); *A California Suite* (San Francisco, Dec. 6, 1917); *The Eve of St. Agnes,*

symphonic poem (1919); 2 syms.: No. 1, *Assyrian* (1922; San Francisco, Nov. 14, 1924) and No. 2 (1947; San Francisco, April 1, 1948); *Indian Dances* (1927–28); 3 *Psalms* for Cello and Orch. (1932); Piano Concerto (1934–35); Violin Concerto (1936–37); *Ave Rota: 3 Pieces in Multiple Style* for Piano and Orch. (1939); *Rhapsody* for Harp and Strings (1940); *Night Piece* for Flute and Small Orch. (1940); *Ode* (1941); Concertino for Piano and Strings (Saratoga Springs, N.Y., Sept. 3, 1946); *2 Pieces in Sabbath Mood* (1946); *Music Hall,* overture (1948). **CHAMBER:** *Nocturne* for String Quartet (n.d.); 3 *Preludes* for Violin and Piano (1921); 3 string quartets ("on Indian Themes," 1924; 1933; 1945); *Scherzo* for Flute, Oboe, Clarinet, Bassoon, and Horn (1936); *Swing Boy* for Violin and Piano (1937); *Hagiographia: 3 Biblical Narratives* for String Quartet and Piano (1938); *Fantasy* for Viola and Piano (1941); *Ballade* for Violin and Piano (1942); *Impressions from the Odyssey* for Violin and Piano (1945); *Music for Monticello* for Flute, Cello, and Piano (1945); *Meditation* for Trombone and Piano (1947); Cello Sonata (1950); *Night Piece and Dance* for Flute and Piano (1952). **KEYBOARD: P i a n o :** 6 *Pieces* (1921); *Pieces for Children* (1935); *Fantasy Sonata* (1945); *Moods* (1946); *Prelude* (1946); *Toccata* (1946); *Introduction and Toccata* (1946); *Suite fantasque* (1948). **O r g a n :** 6 *Pieces for Use in the Synagogue* (1933); 3 *Quiet Preludes* (1950). **VOCAL:** *The Poet in the Desert* for Baritone, Chorus, and Orch. (1925); *Sabbath Evening Service* for Baritone and Chorus (1930–31); *Sadia,* hymn for Men's Voices (1942); *Ahavas Olom* for Tenor, Chorus, and Organ (1945); *Contemplation* for Chorus and Piano (1947); *Ode to Zion* for Chorus and 2 Harps (1948); *Arvit I'shabbat: Friday Evening Service No. 2* for Cantor, Chorus, and Organ (1952); songs. —**NS/LK/DM**

Jacobi, Georg, German violinist, conductor, and composer; b. Berlin, Feb. 13, 1840; d. London, Sept. 13, 1906. He studied violin with Eduard and Leopold Ganz in Berlin, Bériot in Brussels (1849–52), and Massart at the Paris Cons. (1852); also composition there with Réber, Gevaert, and Chéri. After graduating with a premier prix in violin (1861), he played in the orchs. of the Opéra-Comique (1861–63) and the Opéra (1863–69). He then was conductor of the Bouffes-Parisiens (1869–71). He subsequently settled in London as conductor of the Alhambra Theatre (1871–98), and then conducted at the Crystal Palace and also taught at the Royal Coll. of Music (from 1896). He wrote a comic opera, *The Black Crook,* which attained temporary popularity, as well as 103 ballets and divertissements, two violin concertos, a Viola Concerto, violin pieces, and songs.—**NS/LK/DM**

Jacobs, Arthur (David), English music critic, editor, writer on music, and translator; b. Manchester, June 14, 1922. He studied at Merton Coll., Oxford. He was music critic for the *Daily Express* (1947–52) and deputy ed. of the journal *Opera* (1960–71). He was a prof. at the Royal Academy of Music in London (1964–79) and head of the music dept. at Huddersfield Polytechnic (1979–84); also ed. the British Music Year-book (1971–80). An accomplished linguist, Jacobs prepared admirable trs. of some 20 operas into English; he also wrote the libretto for Maw's opera *One Man Show* (1964).

WRITINGS: *Gilbert and Sullivan* (London, 1951); *A New Dictionary of Music* (Harmondsworth, 1958; 4th ed., rev., 1978);

with S. Sadie, *The Pan Book of Opera* (London, 1964; rev. ed., 1972, as *Opera: A Modern Guide*; new ed., 1984); *A Short History of Western Music* (Harmondsworth, 1972); *Arthur Sullivan: A Victorian Musician* (Oxford, 1984; 2nd ed., rev. and enl., 1992); *The Pan Book of Orchestral Music* (London, 1988); *The Penguin Dictionary of Musical Performers* (Harmondsworth, 1990); *Henry J. Wood: Maker of the Proms* (London, 1994).—NS/LK/DM

Jacobs, Paul, American pianist, harpsichordist, and teacher; b. N.Y., June 22, 1930; d. there, Sept. 25, 1983. He was a student of Hutcheson and a graduate student at the Juilliard School of Music in N.Y. (1951). He began his career performing with the Composers Forum and Robert Craft's Chamber Arts Soc. in N.Y. After making his formal debut in N.Y. in 1951, he was active in Europe in avant-garde circles. In 1956 he gave an unprecedented recital in Paris of the complete piano works of Schoenberg. Returning to the U.S. in 1960, he taught at the Mannes School of Music, the Manhattan School of Music, the Berkshire Music Center at Tanglewood, and Brooklyn Coll. In 1962 he was named the official pianist of the N.Y. Phil., and also was its official harpsichordist from 1974. While he played much Baroque music, Jacobs acquired a fine reputation as a champion of contemporary music, most notably of scores by Stravinsky, Schoenberg, Copland, Messiaen, Cage, Boulez, and Stockhausen. Jacobs was one of the first musicians of prominence to succumb to the plague of AIDS. —NS/LK/DM

Jacobs, René, noted Belgian countertenor and conductor; b. Ghent, Oct. 30, 1946. He pursued training in philology at the Univ. of Ghent, then studied voice with Louis Devos in Brussels and Lucie Frateur in The Hague; subsequently pursued an international career as a performer with various early- music groups, as an opera singer, and as a recitalist; also taught at the Schola Cantorum Basiliensis in Basel. He has been particularly successful in works by Cavalli, Monteverdi, Charpentier, Gluck, and Handel. As a conductor, he was active with his own Collegium Vocale. He conducted his own eds. of Cavalli's *Giasone* at the Innsbruck Festival in 1988 and of Monteverdi's *L'Orfeo* at the Salzburg Festival in 1993. He is the author of *La Controverse sur le timbre de contre-ténor* (1985).—NS/LK/DM

Jacobson, Maurice, English composer and music publisher; b. London, Jan. 1, 1896; d. Brighton, Feb. 1, 1976. He studied piano at the Modern School of Music (1913–16) and composition with Stanford and Holst at the Royal Coll. of Music in London. In 1923 he joined the music publ. firm of J. Curwen & Sons as a music reader; in 1933, was made its director and later its chairman (1950–72). In 1971 he was made an Officer of the Order of the British Empire. He composed a ballet, *David* (1935), the cantatas *The Lady of Shalott* (1940) and *The Hound of Heaven* (1953), many short instrumental pieces, chamber music, and songs.—NS/LK/DM

Jacobsthal, Gustav, German musicologist; b. Pyritz, Pomerania, March 14, 1845; d. Berlin, Nov. 9, 1912. He studied at the Univ. of Strasbourg (1863–70), then at the Univ. of Berlin (Ph.D., 1870, with the diss. *Die Mensuralnotenschrift des 12. und 13. Jahrhunderts*; publ. in Berlin, 1871). He subsequently completed his Habilitation at the Univ. of Strasbourg (1872), where he was a reader (1875–97) and prof. of musicology (1897–1905). He publ. *Die chromatische Alteration im liturgischen Gesange der abendländischen Kirche* (1897).—NS/LK/DM

Jacoby, Hanoch (actually **Heinrich**), German-born Israeli violist and composer; b. Königsberg, March 2, 1909. He studied composition with Hindemith, Bihnke, Mahlke, and Wolfsthal at the Berlin Hochschule für Musik (1927–30). He played in Fischer's chamber orch. (1929–30) and the Frankfurt am Main Radio Orch. (1930–33). He emigrated to Jerusalem in 1934, where he taught at the Academy of Music until 1958; also played in the Palestine (later Israel) Broadcasting Sym. Orch. (1936–58) and then in the Israel Phil.

WORKS: ORCH.: Viola Concerto (1939); 3 syms. (1940, 1951, 1960); Violin Concerto (1942); *7 Miniatures* for Small Orch. (1945); *King David's Lyre* for Small Orch. (1948); *Capriccio israélien* (1951); Sinfonietta (1960); *Serio giocoso* (1964); *Partita concertata* (1970–71); *Mutatio* (1975); *Variations* (1976); *Jewish Oriental Folklore*, suite for Strings (1977). **CHAMBER:** Concertino for String Trio (1932); 2 string quartets (1937, 1938); *Theme, Variations, and Finale* for Piano Trio (1940); Wind Quintet (1946); *Canzona* for Harp (1960); *2 Suites of Jewish Oriental Folklore* for Brass Quintet (1975); *Mutatio II* for Oboe, Bassoon, 2 Trumpets, 2 Trombones, 2 Violas, and Double Bass (1976).—NS/LK/DM

Jacopo da Bologna (Jacobus de Bononia; Magister Jachobus de Bononia), Italian composer and music theorist who flourished in the 14th century. He was one of the earliest representatives of the Florentine Ars nova. He wrote madrigals, ballate, and other works. W. Marrocco ed. his complete works (Berkeley and Los Angeles, 1954).—NS/LK/DM

Jacotin, a name applied to several musicians who flourished in the first half of the 16th century. It is now believed that **Jacotin Le Bel** (b. c. 1490; d. c. 1555), a singer in the Papal Chapel and the church of S. Luigi dei Francesi in Rome (1516–21), was the composer of the esteemed chansons publ. mainly by Attaingnant. A Jacotin Le Bel is also listed as a singer and canon at the French royal chapel (1532–55); he may be identical to the preceding. Some 30 chansons by Jacotin were publ. in contemporary collections, but only a few motets and Magnificat settings are extant.—NS/LK/DM

Jacques, (Thomas) Reginald, respected English organist and conductor; b. Ashby de la Zouch, Jan. 13, 1894; d. Stowmarket, June 2, 1969. He was educated at Queen's Coll., Oxford, where he became organist and director of music in 1926; was also conductor of the Oxford Orchestral Soc. (1930–36). From 1931 to 1960 he was conductor of the Bach Choir in London. In 1936 he founded his own Jacques Orch., which he conducted until 1960. In 1954 he was made a Commander of the Order of the British Empire.—NS/LK/DM

Jacques de Liège (Iacobus Leodiensis), Belgian music theorist; b. Liège, c. 1260; d. there, after 1330. He studied in Paris, then was a cleric in Liège.

About 1325, already at an advanced age, he wrote the important compendium *Speculum musicae*, in seven parts and 293 folios (586 pages; approximating some 2,000 pages in modern typography). It was long attributed to Johannes de Muris, but the authorship of Jacques de Liège is proved by the specific indication in the MS in the Bibliothèque Nationale in Paris that the initial letters of the seven chapters form the name of the author (I-A-C-O-B-U-S). W. Grossmann overlooked this indication in his *Die einleitenden Kapitel des Speculum Musicae von Johannes de Muris* (Leipzig, 1924). The treatise has been ed. by R. Bragard in Corpus Scriptorum de Musica, III (parts 1–5, 1955–68), and by C. de Coussemaker in Scriptorum de musica medii aevi nova series, II (parts 6–7, 1864–76; incorrectly attributed to Johannes de Muris); selections in Eng. tr. are given in O. Strunk's *Source Readings in Music History* (N.Y., 1950). —NS/LK/DM

Jacquet de la Guerre, Elisabeth-Claude, French harpsichordist and composer; b. 1666 or 1667; d. Paris, June 27, 1729. She was the daughter of Claude Jacquet, a descendant of the prominent family of organists and harpsichord makers. She was a gifted child and appeared in a Paris concert at the age of 6 as a singer accompanying herself on the harpsichord. Louis XIV and Madame de Montespan became her patrons. She sang at and composed music for the Théâtre de la Foire, and also presented concerts in her home until 1717. Among her works were the opera *Cephale et Procris* (Académie Royale de Musique, Paris, March 15, 1694), a ballet, three vols. of cantatas (1708–15?), solo and trio sonatas with violin and bass viol, and two vols. of *Pièces de clavecin* (1687, 1707). She was one of the earliest French composers to write cantatas and sonatas, and the only woman to compose a tragédie lyrique.

BIBL.: E. Borroff, *An Introduction to E.-C. J.d.a.G.* (N.Y., 1966).—LK/DM

Jacquillat, Jean-Pierre, French conductor; b. Versailles, July 13, 1935; d. in an automobile accident in Chambo-sur-Lignon, Aug. 6, 1986. He was educated at the Paris Cons., winning premiers prix in harmony, percussion, and piano, and also studied conducting with Munch, Cluytens, and Dervaux. He was asst. conductor (1967) and assoc. conductor (1968) of the Orch. de Paris; toured with it in the Soviet Union, North America, and Mexico. In 1970 he was named resident conductor and music director of the Angers Phil., and in 1971 he became permanent conductor of the Lyons Opera and the Rhône-Alpes Phil. He then was resident conductor and music adviser to the Lamoureux Orch. in Paris (1975–78), and subsequently chief conductor of the Iceland Sym. Orch. in Reykjavík (1980–86).—NS/LK/DM

Jadassohn, Salomon, German pedagogue, conductor, and composer; b. Breslau, Aug. 13, 1831; d. Leipzig, Feb. 1, 1902. He studied with Brosig, Hesse, and Lüstner in Breslau, at the Leipzig Cons. (1848–49), and with Liszt in Weimar. He then studied with Hauptmann in Leipzig, where he settled. He founded a choral society, Psalterion (1866), and conducted the concerts of the Euterpe Soc. (1867–69). In 1871 he was appointed instructor at the Leipzig Cons., being made Ph.D. (honoris causa, 1887) and Royal Prof. (1893). A scholar of the highest integrity and of great industry, he codified the traditional views of harmony, counterpoint, and form in his celebrated manuals. He was a firm believer in the immutability of harmonic laws, and became the Rock of Gibraltar of conservatism in musical teaching. Through his many students, who in turn became influential teachers in Germany and other European countries, the cause of orthodox music theory was propagated far and wide. He composed four syms., two piano concertos, chamber music, choral works, piano pieces, and songs. Although he was a master of contrapuntal forms, his music is totally forgotten.

WRITINGS: *Harmonielehre* (Leipzig, 1883; 7th ed., 1903; Eng. tr. by T. Baker, 1893, as *A Manual of Harmony*); *Kontrapunkt* (1884; 5th ed., 1909); *Kanon und Fuge* (1884; 3rd ed., 1909); *Die Formen in den Werken der Tonkunst* (1889; 4th ed., 1910); *Lehrbuch der Instrumentation* (1889; 2nd ed., 1907); *Die Kunst zu Modulieren und Präludieren* (1890); *Allgemeine Musiklehre* (1892); *Elementar-Harmonielehre* (1895); *Methodik des musiktheoretischen Unterrichts* (1898); *Das Wesen der Melodie in der Tonkunst* (1899); *Das Tonbewusstsein; die Lehre vom musikalischen Hören* (1899); *Erläuterung der in Bachs "Kunst der Fuge" enthaltenen Fugen und Kanons* (1899); *Der Generalbass* (1901).

BIBL.: B. Hiltner, S. J.: *Komponist, Musiktheoretiker, Pianist, Pädagoge: Eine Dokumentation über einen vergessenen Leipziger Musiker des 19. Jahrhunderts* (Leipzig, 1995).—NS/LK/DM

Jadin, Hyacinthe, French pianist and composer, brother of **Louis Emmanuel Jadin;** b. Versailles, 1769; d. Paris, Sept. 1802. He was a student of his father and of Hüllmandel. After appearing as a soloist in one of his own piano concertos at a Concert Spirituel in Paris in 1789, he was second keyboard accompanist at the Théâtre de Monsieur there. From 1795 he was prof. of piano at the Paris Cons. Jadin was the composer of a large output of piano music, including several fine sonatas.—LK/DM

Jadin, Louis Emmanuel, French pianist, composer, and pedagogue, brother of **Hyacinthe Jadin;** b. Versailles, Sept. 21, 1768; d. Montfort-l'Amraury, Yvelines, April 11, 1853. He studied music and violin with his father, then was a page in the household of Louis XVI. After the Revolution, he became 2nd keyboard player at the Théâtre de Monsieur (later the Théâtre Feydeau) in 1789, and then chief accompanist in 1791. He joined the music corps of the National Guard about 1792, and was busily engaged in writing festive works for special occasions during the revolutionary period. During the Napoleonic wars, he continued to write patriotic pieces. His orch. overture *La Bataille d'Austerlitz* (1806) enjoyed great popularity for a time. He also composed numerous opéras comiques. He taught solfège (1796–98), singing (1802–04), and piano (1804–16) at the newly established Paris Cons., and was gouverneur des pages of the royal chapel (1814–30). He was made a Chevalier of the Légion d'honneur (1824). He also wrote pieces for piano.—NS/LK/DM

Jadlowker, Hermann, distinguished Latvian tenor; b. Riga, July 17, 1877; d. Tel Aviv, May 13, 1953. He studied with J. Gänsbacher at the Vienna Cons. He made his operatic debut as Gomez in *Nachtlager von Granada* in Cologne (1897). After appearances in Königsberg, Stettin, Rostock, and Riga, he sang in Karlsruhe (1906–10) and at Berlin's Kroll Opera (from 1907). He made his Metropolitan Opera debut in N.Y. as Gounod's Faust (Jan. 22, 1910), and sang there until 1912; also sang in Boston (1910–12), and at the Berlin Royal Opera (1911–12). He created the role of Bacchus in Richard Strauss's *Ariadne auf Naxos* (Stuttgart, Oct. 25, 1912). After guest appearances in Europe and a period with the Berlin State Opera (1922–23), he served as chief cantor of the Riga synagogue (1929–38) and taught at the Riga Cons. (1936–38). He then settled in Tel Aviv as a teacher. Among his notable roles were Florestan, Don Carlos, Parsifal, and Lohengrin.—NS/LK/DM

Jaëll, Alfred, Austrian pianist and composer; b. Trieste, March 5, 1832; d. Paris, Feb. 27, 1882. He studied with his father, Eduard Jaëll, and appeared as a child prodigy in Venice in 1843. He then continued his studies with Moscheles (1844). His subsequent concert tours earned him the nickname "le pianiste voyageur." After touring in the U.S. (1852–54), he was court pianist in Hannover (1856–66). He married **Marie Jaëll** (née **Trautmann**) in 1866. He wrote a number of effective virtuoso pieces for piano and also made piano transcriptions of the works of Wagner, Schumann, and Mendelssohn. —NS/LK/DM

Jaëll, Marie (née **Trautmann**), French pianist and teacher; b. Steinseltz, Alsace, Aug. 17, 1846; d. Paris, Feb. 4, 1925. She studied with Hamm in Stuttgart, then with Herz at the Paris Cons., winning the premier prix; also studied composition with Franck and Saint-Saëns. She married **Alfred Jaëll** in 1866. In later years she devoted herself to teaching, her most celebrated pupil being Albert Schweitzer. She wrote characteristic pieces for piano, and publ. pedagogical works: *La Musique et la psycho-physiologie* (1895), *Le Mécanisme du toucher* (1896), *Le Toucher* (1899), *L'Intelligence et le rythme dans les mouvements artistiques* (1905), *Le Rythme du regard et la dissociation des doigts* (1906), *La Coloration des sensations tactiles* (1910), *La Résonance du toucher et la topographie des pulpes* (1912), and *La Main et la pensée musicale* (posthumous, 1925).

BIBL.: H. Kiener, *M. J.: Problèmes d'esthétique et de pédagogie musicales* (Paris, 1952).—NS/LK/DM

Jaffee, Michael, American early-music performer and instrument builder; b. N.Y., April 21, 1938. He studied music at N.Y.U. (B.A., 1959; M.A., 1963), and learned to play the guitar. While still a student, he married Kay Cross (b. Lansing, Mich., Dec. 31, 1937), a keyboard player, in 1961. Their interest in early music led Michael to master the lute and Kay the recorder; they subsequently organized the Waverly Consort, a group dedicated to performances of music from the medieval and Renaissance eras using period instruments and costumes; the group made its formal debut at N.Y.'s Carnegie Hall in 1966. The two founders became

highly proficient on a variety of instruments or copies, many of which they built themselves. The Waverly Consort toured extensively, becoming one of the most successful early-music groups in the U.S.—NS/LK/DM

Jagel, Frederick, American tenor and teacher; b. Brooklyn, June 10, 1897; d. San Francisco, July 5, 1982. He sang in local choirs as a youth and later appeared as a tenor soloist. After training from William Brady in N.Y., he completed his studies in Milan. In 1924 he made his operatic debut under the name Federico Jeghelli in Livorno as Rodolfo, and then appeared throughout Italy and with an Italian opera company in the Netherlands. On Nov. 8, 1927, he made his Metropolitan Opera debut in N.Y. as Radamès, and remained on its roster until 1950. Among his prominent roles there were Alfredo, the Duke of Mantua, Cavaradossi, Turiddu, Pinkerton, Pollione, and Peter Grimes. He also appeared in Buenos Aires (1928; 1939–41), San Francisco (debut as Jack Rance, 1930), Chicago (debut as Lohengrin, 1934), and at the N.Y.C. Opera (debut as Herod, 1947). From 1949 to 1970 he taught voice at the New England Cons. of Music in Boston.—NS/LK/DM

Jahn, Otto, learned German philologist, archeologist, and music scholar; b. Kiel, June 16, 1813; d. Göttingen, Sept. 9, 1869. He studied languages and antiquities at the Univs. of Kiel, Leipzig, and Berlin. He became a lecturer on philology in Kiel (1839), then was made prof. of archeology in Greifswald (1842). He later was director of the Leipzig Archeological Museum (1847–48), but lost this position in the wake of the political upheaval of 1848. In 1855 he was appointed prof. of archeology at the Univ. of Bonn. His magnum opus in the field of music was the biography *Wolfgang Amadeus Mozart* (4 vols., Leipzig, 1856–59; 2nd ed., 1867; Eng. tr. by P. Townsend, London, 1882; Ger. revs. by H. Deiters, 3rd ed., 1891–93 and 4th ed., 1905–07; exhaustively rewritten and rev. by H. Abert as *Wolfgang Amadeus Mozart: Neu bearbeitete und erweiterte Ausgabe von Otto Jahns "Mozart,"* 2 vols., Leipzig, 1919–21, rendering it the standard biography; further rev. by A.A. Abert, 2 vols., Leipzig, 1955–56). Jahn's biography was the first musical life written according to the comparative critical method. It reviews the state of music during the period immediately preceding Mozart, and as a comprehensive exposition has become a model for subsequent musical biographies. He intended to write a biography of Beethoven according to a similar plan, but could not complete the task; Thayer utilized the data accumulated by him in his own work on Beethoven; Pohl used his notes in his biography of Haydn. Numerous essays by Jahn were publ. in his *Gesammelte Aufsätze über Musik* (1866).

BIBL.: J. Vahlen, *O. J.* (Vienna, 1870); E. Petersen, ed., *O. J. in seinen Briefen* (Leipzig, 1912); M. Schramm, *O. J.s Musikästhetik und Musikkritik* (Essen, 1998).—NS/LK/DM

Jahn, Wilhelm, Austrian conductor and opera adminstrator; b. Hof, Moravia, Nov. 24, 1834; d. Vienna, April 21, 1900. At the age of 20 he became a theater conductor in Budapest, and then occupied similar posts in Agram, Amsterdam, and Prague. He was in Wiesbaden (1864–80), then became music director of the Vienna Court Opera (1880) and conductor of the Vienna Phil. (1882–83). He retired in 1897, and was succeeded by Mahler.—NS/LK/DM

Jähns, Friedrich Wilhelm, German vocal pedagogue, writer on music, and composer; b. Berlin, Jan. 2, 1809; d. there, Aug. 8, 1888. He studied singing with Grell and Detroit, and was a boy soprano in the chorus of the Berlin Royal Opera. He then studied voice with Stümer and Lemm, and later composition with Gorzizky. He was founder-conductor of the Jähnssche Gesangverein (1845–70). He was made royal music director (1849). From 1881 he taught declamation at the Scharwenka Cons. He was very successful as a vocal teacher, numbering some 1,000 pupils. His admiration for Weber impelled him to collect all the available materials pertaining to Weber's life and works. His collection, containing 300 autograph letters, documents, pamphlets, essays, and first editions, was acquired in 1883 by the Berlin Royal Library. He publ. a treatise on Weber, with a thematic catalog, *Carl Maria von Weber in seinen Werken* (Berlin, 1871). Apart from exhaustive biographical data, this book is historically interesting because in the preface he introduced, for the first time in print, the Wagnerian term "Leitmotiv"; this was later popularized by Wolzogen and others. He composed a Piano Trio, a Grand Sonata for Violin and Piano, a book of *Schottische Lieder*, and many other vocal pieces. —NS/LK/DM

Jairazbhoy, Nazir (Ali), English ethnomusicologist and instrumentalist of Indian descent; b. Clifton, Oct. 31, 1927. After schooling in England and India, he studied at the Univ. of Wash. (B.A., 1951) and at the School of Oriental and African Studies in London (Ph.D., 1971, with the diss. *The Rāgas of North Indian Music: Their Structure and Evolution*; publ. in London, 1971), where he lectured on Indian music (1962–69). He was assoc. prof. of Asian studies at the Univ. of Windsor, Ontario (1969–75), and prof. of ethnomusicology at the Univ. of Calif., Los Angeles (from 1975), where he later became the chairman of its Department of Ethnomusicology and Systematic Musicology (1988). His study of the evolution of different ragas and scales contributed greatly to knowledge about North Indian music. —NS/LK/DM

Jalas (real name, **Blomstedt**), **Jussi,** Finnish conductor; b. Jyväskylä, June 23, 1908. He studied at the Helsinki Cons. and with Ilmari Krohn at the Univ. of Helsinki, and later in Paris with Rhené-Baton and Monteux. He was active as a theater conductor in Helsinki (1930–45), and subsequently conducted at the Finnish National Opera there, serving as its music director until 1973. He also made guest conducting appearances throughout Europe, the U.S., and Japan. Jalas was highly regarded as an interpreter of the music of Sibelius, his father-in-law, and also excelled in performances of 20th-century works, ranging from Puccini to Shostakovich.—NS/LK/DM

Jam, The, one of the biggest bands in England during the late 1970s, who couldn't parlay their homegrown success into American stardom (f. 1973). MEMBERSHIP: Paul Weller, gtr., voc. (b. May 25, 1958); Bruce Foxton, bs. (b. Sept. 1 1955); Rick Buckler, drm., perc. (b. Dec. 6, 1955). Paul Weller, Bruce Foxton and Rick Buckler met in school in the London suburb of Woking. More mod revivalists than punks, their repertoire included songs like "Theme from Batman" and "In the Midnight Hour." However, when the Sex Pistols hit they were in the right place at the right time playing the right kind of music. From their initial release, "In the City" they charted hits in England. Their first album, recorded quickly and named after the hit single, sounding like a crisper, punchier version of the early Who, went to #20 in England. They toured Britain and America. The English tour was successful, but in the U.S. they suffered from their lack of exposure. The Jam next recorded *This Is the Modern World*, released less than ten months after their debut. They toured America, inexplicably as the opening act for Blue Oyster Cult. While the tour exposed them to large crowds, they were crowds that couldn't care less about a neo- mod band. The tour did nothing to raise the band's profile in the U.S., so when *All Mod Cons* was released in 1978, it went to #6 in the U.K. but failed to chart in the U.S. The following year, they fared slightly better with the more political *Setting Sons*, which earned some play on the growing number of new wave stations and sent the album to #137 in the U.S., while it hit #4 in the U.K. This continued with the song "Start" with its blatant cop from The Beatles' "Taxman." *Sound Affects* became their most successful album in the U.S., hitting #72. With their 1982 album, *The Gift*, the songs had become considerably more sophisticated, representing an enormous amount of growth over a period of less than five years.

While the band was at the top of their game, Weller became frustrated with the musical limitations of the power trio. He was leaning more toward a jazzier, funkier sound and informed Foxton and Buckler that he didn't think they could cut it. In 1981, they went on a farewell tour and went their separate ways. As a farewell, all 13 of their singles were re-released in England and all of them charted again. Their cover of "War" again earned some minor airplay on modern rock stations, but didn't raise their profile in the U.S. Foxton recorded a solo album for Arista that sold dozens. Weller formed the Style Council with keyboard player Mick Talbot. Loosely framed in the image of Steely Dan, the duo added studio hands for recording according to the demands of the song. Lyrically, Weller wrote from a leftist agenda, which created a somewhat surreal effect couched in slick, R&B-oriented rock. Yet the less scabrous sound (as opposed to The Jam) reached the mid-1980s, post-punk audiences. Their 1984 debut album, called *Café Bleu* in Europe and *My Ever Changing Moods* in the U.S., peaked at #5 in England and rose to #56 in the U.S. on the strength of Weller's first ever U.S. pop hit, the title track, which peaked at #29. It was his first and last Top 40 U.S. hit.

The duo did continue to have success in the U.K., however. 1985's *The Internationalist* (known as *Our Fa-*

vorite Shops in the U.K.) spawned the British hit "The Walls Come Tumbling Down," and covered Curtis Mayfield and the Stylistics. The album topped the English charts. A live album, *Home and Abroad*, peaked at #8. With *The High Cost of Loving*, the Style Council's sound became pronouncedly jazzier, and hit #2 on the U.K. charts, with the single "It Didn't Matter" hitting the Top 10. However their next (and last) album, *Confessions of a Pop Group*, didn't move fans or critics. Weller gave in to all his excessive instincts. Where he had launched his career based on short bursts of loud pop, this album contained a ten-minute orchestral suite called "The Gardener of Eden." None of the singles hit. The group produced one more album, reflecting their growing interest in contemporary dance music. The record company shelved it, effectively putting an end to the band. Both Weller and the Style Council were dropped from the label. The band called it a day officially in 1990.

Weller returned to his roots for his solo recordings, starting with his DIY project, the Paul Weller Movement, a return to the raw R&B edge of the Jam with a neo-psychedelic bent. This followed through on his eponymous solo debut album. Littered with guest stars from the early 1990s British scene, the album rose to #8 in the U.K. His next album, *Wild Wood*, was even more diverse, entering the U.K. charts at #2 and winning several awards in Europe. The tour was captured on the next album, *Live Wood*. His 1995 effort, *Stanley Road*, sold almost a million copies in the U.K. alone, and Weller decided to concentrate on where his fans were, pretty much spurning America. He has released a couple of more records in the U.K.

Early in 2000, a tribute record featuring Oasis, Everything but the Girl, and The Beastie Boys, called *Fire and Skill*, demonstrated that, even nearly 20 years after their break-up, The Jam are still influential. Weller even contributed a tune to the record, but continues to stay mostly in England, where he enjoys the status of musical elder statesman extraordinaire, something like that bestowed on his own inspiration Peter Townshend.

DISC.: *In the City* (1977); *This Is the Modern World* (1977); *All Mod Cons* (1978); *Setting Sons* (1979); *Sound Affects* (1980); *The Gift* (1982); *Dig the New Breed* (live; 1982); *Peel Sessions* (live; 1990). **BRUCE FOXTON SOLO:** *Touch Sensitive* (1984). **STYLE COUNCIL:** *Introducing the Style Council* (1983); *My Ever Changing Moods* (1984); *Cafe Bleu* (1984); *Internationalists* (1985); *Our Favourite Shop* (1985); *Home and Abroad* (live; 1986); *Cost of Loving* (1987); *Confessions of a Pop Group* (1988). **PAUL WELLER SOLO:** *Paul Weller* (1992); *Wild Wood* (1993); *More Wood* (1994); *Paul Weller Live Wood* (1994); *Stanley Road* (1995); *Heavy Soul* (1997).—**HB**

Jambe de Fer, Philibert, French composer and writer on music; b. Champlitte, c. 1515; d. probably in Lyons, c. 1566. He spent most of his life in Lyons. In addition to his numerous polyphonic settings of French Psalms trs., he wrote the significant treatise *Epitome musical des tons, sons et accordz, es voix humains, fleustes d'Alleman, fleustes à neuf trous, violes, & violons* (Lyons, 1556).—**LK/DM**

James, Bob (actually, **Robert**), the de facto inventor of pop-jazz and one of its most innovative purveyors; b. Marshal, Mo., Dec. 25, 1939. Robert James started playing piano at four years old. His early teachers discovered he had perfect pitch. By the time he was eight, he was earning extra money by playing for tap dance classes. In his high school band he played trumpet and percussion, but he competed at state fairs on the piano, earning his share of blue ribbons. He also played with local dance bands. He studied music at the Univ. of Mich., with a term at the Berklee School of Music in Boston, and eventually earned his master's degree in music composition. While in school, he wrote the music for two plays, winning the BMI Award for Best Collegiate Musical for one of them. He also put together a jazz trio, which swept the Notre Dame Jazz Festival, catching the eye of Quincy Jones. He recorded his debut, *Bold Conceptions*, with that trio for Mercury in 1962.

James moved to N.Y. in 1964, where he began doing studio work and jingles as well as performing with his trio. The group recorded *Explosion*, a decidedly ambitious and experimental album for ESP in 1965, using early synthesizers and unusual tape techniques. He wrote arrangements and played piano for sessions and live performances, serving as Sarah Vaughan's music director for four years from 1965–68. In 1973, he joined CTI records as an arranger, writing charts and playing keyboards on scads of the label's sessions for artists ranging from Ron Carter and Hank Crawford to Eric Gale and Grover Washington. He also recorded four albums of his own, the last of which, *Bob James 4*, went to #38 on the pop charts. These albums relied more on electric piano than acoustic, setting a tone for the next decade of his career and for the direction of "palatable" pop jazz. Three years later, he became director of progressive A&R at CBS, working with Paul Simon and Neil Diamond, among others. Settling in suburban Westchester, he formed his own label in 1977, Tappan Zee, after the bridge that spanned the Hudson River not far from his home. In addition to his own recordings, he signed artists including jazz virtuoso JoAnne Brackeen, Latin percussion all-star Mongo Santamaria, and funk pianist Richard Tee.

In 1979, James again reached the pop album charts with his seventh solo album, *Touchdown*, largely thanks to the song "Angela" which was the theme song to the hit TV show *Taxi*. The album went gold. Columbia president Bruce Lundvall suggested performing with guitarist Earl Klugh. The result was the 1979 album *One on One*, which won them a Grammy for Best Pop Instrumental Performance, went gold and reached #23 on the charts. He would collaborate with Klugh again a couple of years later on *Two of a Kind*, and again on *Cool* in 1993. On a whim, James recorded works of the impressionist composer Jean Phillipe Rameau, initially just as something to give to friends. The tapes came into the hands of CBS Masterworks (their classical label), who pleaded to release it. He followed these with a program of Scarlatti in 1988 and a program of Bach a year later.

In 1986 he collaborated with saxophonist David Sanborn. This duo project resulted in his second Grammy, for Best Jazz Fusion Performance, Vocal or Instrumental. By 1991, he was beginning to break out again, this time working on the solo acoustic *Grand Piano Canyon*. Conversely, he also set to work with the lite jazz super group Fourplay with Harvey Mason, Lee Ritenour (later replaced by Larry Carlton) and Nathan East. The album topped *Billboard*'s jazz charts for 34 weeks and went gold. Their 1993 release, *Between the Sheets*, followed suit. Their 1995 album *Elixir* won Jazz Album of the Year at the Soul Train awards.

James featured his daughter Hilary on one track of his 1994 *Restless* album. The next year, they decided to do a project together. They collaborated a year later on the album *Flesh and Blood*, which was followed by a father- daughter tour. Following that, he went back to his roots on *Straight Up*, an acoustic trio date with bassist Christian McBride and drummer Brian Blade. Then he went back for a fusion project with saxophonist Kirk Whalum. Ever the musical chimera, James also has spent time as VP of A&R in the jazz division at Warner Bros. Into his 60s, he continues to create a lighter than air music for piano that falls just to the jazz side of pop.

DISC.: *Bold Conceptions* (1962); *Explosions* (1965); *One* (1974); *Two* (1975); *Three* (1976); *BJ 4* (1977); *Heads* (1977); *Touchdown* (1978); *Genie* (1978); *One on One* (1979); *Lucky Seven* (1980); *H* (1980); *Sign of the Times* (1981); *All Around the Town* (live; 1981); *Flashback Follow Bob James* (1981); *Two of a Kind* (1981); *Hands Down* (1982); *The Foxie* (1983); *11* (1984); *Rameau* (1984); *Double Vision* (1986); *Obsession* (1986); *Ivory Coast* (1988); *Scarlatti Dialogues* (1988); *J. S. Bach* (1989); *Grand Piano Canyon* (1990); *Cool* (1992); *Restless* (1994); *Hapgood* (1994); *The Swan* (1995); *Flesh and Blood* (1995); *Straight Up* (1996); *Joined at the Hip* (1996); *Playin' Hooky* (1997); *Joy Ride* (1999). **FOURPLAY:** *Fourplay* (1991); *Between the Sheets* (1993); *Elixir* (1995); *4* (1998).
—HB

James, Dorothy, American composer and teacher; b. Chicago, Dec. 1, 1898; d. St. Petersburg, Fla., Dec. 1, 1982. She was a student of Gruenberg and Weidig at the Chicago Musical Coll. and the American Cons. of Music in Chicago (M.M., 1927), of Hanson at the Eastman School of Music in Rochester, N.Y., of Willan in Toronto, and of Krenek at the Univ. of Mich. In 1927 she joined the faculty of Eastern Mich. Univ. in Ypsilanti, where she was later a prof. (1962–68); she also was music critic of the *Ypsilanti Press*. She was the author of *Music of Living Women Composers* (1976). Her compositions display fine craftsmanship, particularly her choral works.

WORKS: DRAMATIC: O p e r a : *Paola and Francesca* (partial concert perf., Rochester, N.Y., April 2, 1931). ORCH.: *3 Symphonic Fragments* (Rochester, N.Y., April 2, 1931); *Elegy for the Lately Dead* (1938); *Suite for Small Orch.* (1940). CHAMBER: *3 Pastorales* for Clarinet, Strings, and Celesta (1933); *Recitative and Aria* for Viola, 2 Violins, and 2 Cellos (1944); *Morning Music* for Flute and Piano (1967); *Motif* for Oboe and Organ (1970); *Patterns* for Harp (1977). KEYBOARD: P i - a n o : *2 Satirical Dances* (1934); *Dirge* (1962); *Impressionistic Study* (1962); *Tone Row Suite* (1962); *2 in 1* (1962). O r g a n : *Autumnal* (1934); *Dedication* (1958). VOCAL: *Tears* for Chorus and Orch. (1930); *4 Preludes from the Chinese* for Alto or Bass and Piano Quintet (1930); *The Jumblies* for Women's Voices and

Orch. (1935); *Paul Bunyan* for Baritone, Women's Voices, and Orch. (1937); *Niobe* for Women's Voices and Chamber Orch. (1941); *The Golden Years* for Chorus and Orch. (1953); *The Nativity Hymn* for Chorus (1957); *Mutability* for Women's Voices and Ensemble (1967); songs.—NS/LK/DM

James, Elmer (Taylor), jazz bassist, tuba; b. Yonkers, N.Y., 1910; d. N.Y., July 25, 1954. Played tuba in Gene Rodgers's Revellers in 1928, then with the June Clark Band for a year before joining Chick Webb until December 1932. James switched to string bass, and worked briefly with Benny Carter. He returned to work with Chick Webb, then with Fletcher Henderson in spring 1934. From 1934–36 James played with Lucky Millinder, and Edgar Hayes during 1937–39; he also played in Mezz Mezzrow's Disciples of Swing in late 1937. In 1940 he worked with Claude Hopkins then left music to become a bread salesman; although, he did gig with the Zutty Singleton Trio in 1942, but he never returned to full-time playing.—JC/LP

James, Elmore (originally, **Brooks, Elmore**), one of the most influential post war blues guitarists; b. Richland, Miss., Jan. 27, 1918; d. Chicago, May 24, 1963. Elmore James's first guitar had a broom handle for a neck and a lard can for a resonator, one string played with a bottleneck slide. It was a sound he sought to emulate when he started hooking his electric guitar to amplifiers in the 1930s.

He was born with his mother's name of Brooks, but took his stepfather's name as a boy. By his early teens, he would play suppers, fish fries and juke joints, sometimes as Cleanhead James, and sometimes under his stepfather's name, Joe Willie James. While he continued to stay close to his home base, he got the opportunity to play with Robert Johnson, Howlin' Wolf and Sonny Boy Williamson through his youth. Like so many others of his contemporaries, he also plied a trade. James was a radio repairman and thus had a good sense of how amplifiers worked. By the mid-1930s, he had joined Williamson on the road, touring the South and perfecting his slide style and scabrous sound. Then World War II broke out and he was called up in the draft.

After a three-year hitch in the Navy, he moved to Memphis and worked the clubs with his cousin "Homesick" James and others. He became a regular on local radio, but was unsure of his skills in the recording studio as a leader, though he did accompany several other musicians on recording dates. It was during one such date with Williamson that he was encouraged to play Robert Johnson's "Dust My Broom." The session was recorded and became a Top Ten R&B hit in 1951 on a small indie called Trumpet records. He was quickly signed by the larger L.A. company Modern, and moved to Chicago. There, he assembled a remarkable band featuring Johnny Jones on piano, J. T. Brown on sax, and Homesick James Williamson on rhythm guitar, though he recorded "Hand in Hand" with Ike Turner on piano. Between 1953 and 1955, he also recorded such notable tunes as "Hawaiian Boogie," "Early in the Morning" and "Wild about You Baby." Other well known James tunes include "The Sky Is Crying."

Through his forties, James had a bad heart, and he would take frequent breaks from work to recover in Miss. He died while visiting his cousin Homesick James in 1963, but left behind a musical legacy that would inspire artists from Duane Allman to George Thorogood and beyond. Jimi Hendrix recorded his song "Bleeding Heart," and Fleetwood Mac did a version of "Shake Your Moneymaker."

DISC.: Blues after Blues (1960); *Blues after Hours* (1961); *Original Folk Blues* (1964); *I Need You* (1965); *Something inside of Me* (1968); *Tough Blue* (1968); *The Late Fantastically Great* (1968); *Blues in My Heart, Rhythm in My Soul* (1969); *To Know a Man Blue* (1969); *Whose Muddy Shoes* (1969); *The Resurrection of Elmore James Blues* (1969); *The Sky Is Crying* (1965); *Elmore James* (1970); *Cotton Patch* (1 Side; 1974); *Street Talkin'* (1975); *All Them Blues* (1976); *Blues Screaming* (1977); *Got to Move* (1981); *Red Hot Blues* (1983); *King of the Bottleneck Blues* (1986); *Let's Cut It* (1986); *Pickin' the Blues* (1986); *Shake Your Money Maker* (1986); *Come Go with Me* (1989); *Dust My Broom* (1990); *The Last Session* (1990); *Rolling and Tumbling* (1992); *King of the Slide* (1996).—HB

James, Etta (originally, Hawkins, Jamesetta), one of the greats of 1950s R&B who made one of the great comebacks of the 1980s; b. Los Angeles, Jan. 25, 1938. Her mother was 15 when Jamesetta Hawkins was born. Their landlord agreed to raise the young girl, giving her singing and piano lessons. They brought her to church, where she joined the choir at five. Soon the greater L.A. area heard young Jamesetta and the choir on the radio. In her teens, she and two other girls formed a vocal group and wrote an answer song to Hank Ballard's "Work with Me Annie." Called "Roll with Me Henry," they performed it for Johnny Otis one night. He took a shine to 15-year-old Jamesetta. He and his wife took her in and started mentoring her. First he took her first name and inverted it, dubbing her Etta James. Then he recorded "Roll with Me Henry," though for commercial reasons they retitled it "The Wallflower." It topped the R&B charts for four weeks in 1955, but a "white" cover of it by Georgia Gibb prevented James's record from crossing over. Ironically, she saw more songwriter royalties for the Gibb version than she did from her recording.

She continued touring and recording with Otis for another three years, landing one more hit with "Good Rockin' Daddy." In 1958, she was literally cut adrift in St. Louis, managed to get bus fare to Chicago and wound up in the office of Leonard Chess. At Chess she worked with The Moonglows' Harvey Fuqua and others, producing a spate of crossover, jazz-tinged, soulful ballads, including "All I Could Do Was Cry" (#33, 1960), "My Dearest Darling" (#34, 1960), "Trust in Me" (#30, 1961), "Don't Cry Baby" (#39, 1961), "Something's Got a Hold on Me" (#37, 1962), "Stop the Wedding" (#34, 1962) and "Pushover" (#25, 1963).

The hits stopped coming in the mid-1960s. For one thing, James had developed a serious heroin habit. For another, she found little challenge in the material she had been recording. Only "Something's Got a Hold on Me" hinted at the power and grit she could generate. In

1967, she went down to Muscle Shoals Alabama, and with their legendary rhythm section cut the barnburning "Tell Mama," which hit #23 in 1967, and the legendary ballad "I'd Rather Go Blind." Her run of Top 40 hits stopped with 1968's #35 cover of Otis Redding's "Security." By the early 1970s, she was more notorious for her addiction than her performing. A run-in with the law left her with the choice of jail or rehab, and by the mid-1970s she had quit heroin. She signed with Warner Bros., who put her back into Muscle Shoals with Jerry Wexler for "Deep in the Night." However, a stint on the road opening for The Rolling Stones left her with a taste for cognac and cocaine. She finally retreated back to L.A. and got completely clean and sober in the early 1980s.

A letter to L.A. mayor Tom Bradley landed James a slot performing for millions worldwide at the 1984 Los Angeles Olympics. She cut two live albums with Eddie "Cleanhead" Vinson, *The Late Show* and *The Early Show*, which allowed her to explore her blues and jazz chops in front of an audience. She followed this with a searing performance in Taylor Hackford's 1987 Chuck Berry tribute film *Hail Hail Rock and Roll*. Her 1988 album *Seven Year Itch* brought her back to Muscle Shoals, earning her critical plaudits. Her subsequent *Sticking to My Guns*, a more technologically informed album with a rap by Def Jeff, was less successful. She worked with Wexler again on her 1993 *The Right Time* album. That same year, James was inducted into the Rock and Roll Hall of Fame. The following year, she won Best Jazz Vocalist for her tribute to Billie Holiday, *Mystery Lady*. In 1996, James went into the British Top 10 with a reissue of her version of Willie Dixon's "I Just Want to Make Love to You," used in an English television ad. She continued recording and performing with renewed vigor through the 1990s.

DISC.: *Miss Etta James* (1961); *Second Time Around* (1961); *At Last* (1961); *Etta James* (1962); *Sings for Lovers* (1962); *Twist with* (1962); *Top Ten* (1963); *Rocks the House* (live; 1964); *The Queen of Soul* (1965); *Call My Name* (1966); *Tell Mama* (1968); *Funk* (1970); *Losers Weepers* (1971); *Etta James* (1973); *Peaches* (1973); *Come a Little Closer* (1974); *Etta Is Betta Than Evah* (1978); *Deep in the Night* (1980); *Changes* (1978); *Chess Masters* (1981); *Good Rockin' Mama* (1981); *Etta: Red Hot 'n' Live* (1982); *Tuff Lover* (1983); *Good Rockin' Mama/Tuff Lover* (1985); *R&B Queen* (1986); *Early Show, Vol.1: Blues in the Night* (1986); *Late Show, Vol. 2: Live at Maria's Memory...* (1986); *Etta James on Chess* (1988); *The Sweetest Peaches, Pt. 2* (1988); *The Gospel Soul of Etta James* (1989); *Seven Year Itch* (1989); *Stickin' to My Guns* (1990); *Tell Mama, Vol.1* (1991); *The Right Time* (1992); *Back in Blues* (1992); *I'd Rather Go Blind* (1992); *Mystery Lady: Songs of Billie Holiday* (1994); *Live from San Francisco* (1994); *Live* (1994); *Time after Time* (1995); *Respect Yourself* (1997); *Love's Been Rough on Me* (1997); *Hickory Dickory Dock* (1998); *Life, Love and the Blues* (1998); *12 Songs of Christmas* (1998); *The Heart of a Woman* (1999).

BIBL.: E. Jones and D. Ritz, *Rage to Survive* (1995).—HB

James, Harry (Haag), vibrant American trumpeter and bandleader; b. Albany, Ga., March 15, 1916; d. Las Vegas, Nev., July 5, 1983. With his bravura playing style, James was one of the most outstanding instrumentalists of the Swing Era. He also led one of the most popular big bands of the first half of the 1940s, when he

recorded such hits as "Sleepy Lagoon," "I've Heard That Song Before," and "I'll Get By (As Long as I Have You)." In a professional performing career that lasted more than 50 years, James maintained his orchestra successfully for decades after the heyday of the big bands.

At the time of his birth, James's parents were working for the Mighty Haag Circus: his father, Everett Robert James, led the band and played trumpet, and his mother, Maybelle Stewart James, was an aerialist. James himself became a circus performer as early as the age of four, appearing as a contortionist billed as the Human Eel. By about six he was playing snare drum in the band and learning the trumpet from his father. By the time he was 12, the family was working for the Christy Brothers Circus, and he was leading the second band. The circus wintered in Beaumont, Tex., where he attended school, and at 14 he won a statewide school music contest as a trumpet soloist. With that, he went professional and began playing with territory bands around the Southwest.

In 1935, James got his first job with a national touring band when he was hired by Ben Pollack. On May 4, 1935, he married singer Louise Tobin. They had two children but divorced in June 1943. James made his recording debut with Pollack in September 1936; by the end of the year he had moved to Benny Goodman's orchestra. There he was heavily featured, becoming a star player. He recorded his first session on Dec. 1, 1937, as a leader for Brunswick Records, using a pick-up band, and a year later he left Goodman and organized his own orchestra, the Music Makers, which debuted in Philadelphia in February 1939. That June he heard an unknown Frank Sinatra on a radio broadcast and hired him as the band's male singer. The Music Makers earned excellent notices from jazz critics, but they had trouble making headway in the highly competitive big band scene of 1939–40. Sinatra was hired away by the more successful Tommy Dorsey at the start of 1940, and around that time James was dropped by Columbia Records (which had absorbed Brunswick) and was forced to record for the small Varsity label.

James changed his approach in 1941, adding strings and de-emphasizing hot jazz solos in favor of a sweet, melodic style; he also returned to Columbia Records. In April he scored his first Top Ten hit, the self-composed instrumental "Music Makers." It was one of five chart singles he released during the year, the most successful of which was a million-selling instrumental revival of the 1913 song "You Made Me Love You (I Didn't Want to Do It)" (music by James V. Monaco, lyrics by Joseph McCarthy). In 1942 he had 12 recordings in the charts, six of which hit the Top Ten, among them "I Don't Want to Walk without You" (music by Jule Styne, lyrics by Frank Loesser), which featured the voice of Helen Forrest, a million- selling instrumental treatment of Irving Berlin's "Easter Parade," and the #1 instrumental "Sleepy Lagoon" (music by Eric Coates, adapted from his symphonic composition *By a Sleepy Lagoon*, lyrics by Jack Lawrence). That was enough to rank him second only to Glenn Miller as the most successful recording artist of the year, and when Miller went into

the service and James took over his radio spot on *Chesterfield Time* in September (James himself was 4-F because of a back injury), he became the top bandleader in the country.

James also found time to launch a movie career. Like other swing stars, he was given supporting roles in films, usually playing himself, with generous screen time allotted to his band's performances. In 1942 he appeared in *Syncopation* in May, *Private Buckaroo* in June, and *Swingtime in the Rockies* in November. The last is notable for featuring a performance of his next hit, "I Had the Craziest Dream" (music by Harry Warren, lyrics by Mack Gordon), sung by Helen Forrest, which topped the charts in February 1943 and sold a million copies, and for starring Betty (Elizabeth Ruth) Grable, one of the biggest movie stars of the day, whom James married on July 5, 1943. They had two children and divorced Oct. 8, 1965.

James scored his second straight #1 hit—the biggest hit of his career and the biggest hit of the year—with "I've Heard That Song Before" (music by Jule Styne, lyrics by Sammy Cahn), again featuring Helen Forrest on vocals, which topped the charts in March and sold a million copies. Its B-side, "Moonlight Becomes You" (music by James Van Heusen, lyrics by Johnny Burke) also was a reported million-seller. Although he was unable to record because of the musicians union recording ban that had taken effect on Aug. 1, 1942, James had four more chart entries in 1943, the most successful of which was a reissue of "All or Nothing at All" (music and lyrics by Jack Lawrence and Arthur Altman), which he had recorded in September 1939 with Frank Sinatra on vocals. Sinatra's emergence as a solo star in 1943 turned the record into a million-seller. Meanwhile, James was staying in N.Y. doing the Chesterfield radio show three times a week and playing such prestigious engagements as the Paramount Theatre in April 1943 and the roof of the Astor Hotel in May. In June he appeared in the film *Best Foot Forward*.

The recording ban extended into 1944, but James reached the charts ten times, all with recordings made before the start of the ban. His biggest hit of the year was a revival of the 1928 song "I'll Get By (As Long as I Have You)" (music by Fred E. Ahlert, lyrics by Roy Turk), which had been recorded in April 1941 with Dick Haymes on vocals. The reissue topped the charts in June 1944. Having completed his radio commitment in March, James appeared in two films released in June, *Two Girls and a Sailor* and *Bathing Beauty*.

With the end of the recording ban in November 1944, James went back into the studio, resulting in 11 chart records in 1945, the most successful of which were the chart-toppers "I'm Beginning to See the Light" (music and lyrics by Harry James, Duke Ellington, Johnny Hodges, and Don George) and "It's Been a Long, Long Time" (music by Jule Styne, lyrics by Sammy Cahn), both of which were sung by Kitty Kallen. In January 1945, James became a regular on the radio series *The Danny Kaye Show*, and he hosted the show as Kaye's summer replacement from June to September. In 1946 he was signed to a movie contract by 20th Century–Fox, which gave him more prominent roles in the films *Do*

You Love Me?, released in May, and *If I'm Lucky*, released in September. He still found time to enter the recording studio during the year, however, resulting in another five chart entries, the most successful of which was a Top Ten revival of the 1917 song "I'm Always Chasing Rainbows" (music by Harry Carroll, lyrics by Joseph McCarthy) with a vocal by Kitty Kallen, as well as a #1 album, *All Time Favorites*. He also went on the road for the first time in two years.

Faced with the overall decline of popularity for big-band music, James disbanded in December 1946. A few months later he returned to action with a more jazz-oriented band that reduced the number of strings; soon he eliminated strings entirely. He reached the charts with three singles in 1947, including a Top Ten revival of the 1931 song "Heartaches" (music by Al Hoffman, lyrics by John Klenner), and appeared in the film *Carnegie Hall* in May. In February 1948 he was in the film *A Miracle Can Happen* (aka *On Our Merry Way*) and the same month became a regular on the radio series *Call for Music*, which ran through the end of June. In 1950 he had two films in release. He served as musical director of *Young Man with a Horn*, for which he also dubbed the trumpet playing of Kirk Douglas, resulting in a soundtrack that became the most successful album of the year, on which he was co-billed with Doris Day. And he appeared in *I'll Get By*. He also returned to the singles charts for the first time in three years with "Mona Lisa" (music and lyrics by Jay Livingston and Ray Evans).

James was active on only a part-time basis during the early 1950s. Columbia Records A&R director Mitch Miller paired him with other label artists, resulting in the Top Ten hits "Would I Love You (Love You, Love You)" (music by Harold Spina, lyrics by Bob Russell) with Doris Day in April 1951 and "Castle Rock" (music by Al Sears, lyrics by Ervin Drake and Jimmy Shirl) with Frank Sinatra in September 1951 and the chart entry "You'll Never Know" (music by Harry Warren, lyrics by Mack Gordon) with Rosemary Clooney in January 1953. But James was unhappy with Miller, and after scoring a final chart single, "Ruby" (music by Heinz Roemheld, lyrics by Mitchell Parish), in July 1953, he left Columbia.

In 1955, James portrayed himself in the film biography *The Benny Goodman Story*, then returned to full-time work. He reorganized his band and signed to Capitol Records, re-recording his old hits for the album *Harry James in Hi-Fi*, which reached the Top Ten. In November 1956 he appeared in the film *The Opposite Sex*. In October 1957 he toured Europe, and thereafter he alternated national and international tours with long engagements at Las Vegas hotels. In June 1958 he appeared in *The Big Beat*, and he made his final film appearance in *The Ladies Man* in July 1961.

James continued to perform regularly throughout the 1960s and 1970s. In 1983 he was diagnosed with lymphatic cancer, but he continued to tour, giving his last concert on June 26, only nine days before his death at 67. A ghost band, led by trumpeter Art Depew, continued to perform into the 1990s.

WRITINGS: *H. J. Trumpet Method* (N.Y., 1969); *H. J. Studies and Improvisations for Trumpet* (N.Y., 1939).

BIBL.: F. Stacy, *H. J.'s Pin-Up Life Story* (N.Y., 1944); G. Hall, *H. J. and His Orchestra* (Laurel, Md., 1971); C. Garrod and P. Johnston, *H. J. and His Orchestra, 1937–1946* (Zephyrhills, Fla., 1975); Garrod and Johnston, *H. J. and His Orchestra, 1947–1954* (Zephyrhills, Fla., 1975); Garrod and Johnston, *H. J. and His Orchestra, 1955–1982* (Zephyrhills, Fla., 1985).—**WR**

James, (Mary) Frances, Canadian soprano and teacher; b. Saint John, New Brunswick, Feb. 3, 1903; d. Victoria, British Columbia, Aug. 22, 1988. She studied with Walter Clapperton at the McGill Cons. in Montreal, and with Emmy Hein at the Toronto Cons. of Music (1934), then was a student of Jeanne Dusseau (1936), had lessons with Enrico Rosati and Maria Kurenko in N.Y., and worked with Roland Hayes in Boston. She became well known to Canadian audiences via radio, and as a soloist and recitalist; in 1940 she made her first appearance in the U.S. From 1952 to 1973 she taught at the Univ. of Saskatchewan, and then in Victoria at the Cons. of Music and at the Univ. In 1931 she married **Murray Adaskin**. She was especially admired for her championship of the 20th-century vocal repertoire.

BIBL.: G. Lazarevich, *The Musical World of F. J. and Murray Adaskin* (Toronto, 1987).—**NS/LK/DM**

James, Philip (Frederick Wright), American organist, conductor, composer, and teacher; b. Jersey City, N.J., May 17, 1890; d. Southampton, N.Y., Nov. 1, 1975. He received rudimentary instruction in music from his sister, and later studied composition with Rubin Goldmark, Homer Norris, Elliot Schenck, and Rosario Scalero. He also studied organ with J. Warren Andrews, and later with Joseph Bonnet and Alexandre Guilmant in Paris. He served in the U.S. Army during World War I, and in 1918–19 served as bandmaster of the American Expeditionary Force General Headquarters Band. Returning to the U.S., he held various posts as organist and choirmaster in several churches in N.Y., and also conducted the Victor Herbert Opera Co. (1919–22). He then was founder-conductor of the N.J. Sym. Orch. (1922–29), and also conducted the Brooklyn Orch. Soc. (1927–30) and the Bamberger Little Sym. (WOR Radio, N.Y., 1929–36). In 1923 he joined the faculty of N.Y.U., becoming chairman of its music dept. in 1933 and retiring in 1955. In 1933 he was elected a member of the National Inst. of Arts and Letters. His compositions generally followed along late Romantic lines.

WORKS: ORCH.: 3 *Bret Harte* overtures (n.d.; 1924; 1934, rev. 1938); Kammersymphonie (1926), *Overture in Olden Style on French Noëls* for Small Orch. (1926; rev. for Large Orch., 1929; N.Y., Feb. 23, 1930); *Judith* for Reciter and Chamber Orch. (1927; N.Y., Feb. 18, 1930; also for Reciter and Piano); *Sea Symphony* for Baritone and Orch. (1928; Frankfurt am Main, July 14, 1960); *Station WGZBX*, suite (1931; N.Y., May 1, 1932); *Song of the Night*, symphonic poem (1931; N.Y., March 15, 1938); Suite for Strings (1933; N.Y., April 28, 1934); *Gwalia, Welsh Rhapsody* for Small Orch. (N.Y., Nov. 14, 1935; rev. for Large Orch., 1937); Sinfonietta for Chamber Orch. (1938; N.Y., Nov. 10, 1941; rev. 1943); *Brennan on the Moor* for Small Orch. (N.Y., Nov. 28, 1939; also for Large Orch., 1940); 2 syms.: No. 1 (1943; rev. 1961) and No. 2 (1946; Rochester, N.Y., May 7, 1966); *Miniver Cheevy and Richard Cory* for Reciter and Orch. (Saratoga Springs, N.Y., Sept.

9, 1947); *Chaumont*, symphonic poem for Small Orch. (1948; N.Y., May 2, 1951). **B a n d :** *Perstare et Praestare* (N.Y., June 10, 1942; also for Orch., 1946); *E.F.G.*, overture (1944; N.Y., June 13, 1945); *Fanfare and Ceremonial* (1955; N.Y., June 20, 1956; rev. 1962). **CHAMBER:** String Quartet (1924; rev. 1939); Suite for Woodwind Quintet (1936); Piano Quartet (1938; rev. 1948). **KEYBOARD: P i a n o :** *Our Town*, suite (1945); *12 Preludes* (1946–51). **O r g a n :** *Méditation à Ste. Clotilde* (1915); *Dithyramb* (1921); *Fête* (1921); Sonata (1929); *Pantomime* (1941); *Galarnad* (1946); *Novelette* (1946); *Solemn Prelude* (1948); *Alleluia-Toccata* (1949); *Pastorale* (1949); *Requiescat in pace* (1949; rev. 1955); *Passacaglia on an Old Cambrian Bass* (1951; also for Orch., 1956, and for Band, 1957); *Sortie* (1973). **VOCAL:** *Magnificat* for Soloists, Chorus, and Organ (1910); *Te Deum* for Chorus and Organ (1910); *The Victory Riders* for Baritone and Orch. (1919–25); *Stabat mater speciosa* for Chorus and Orch. (1921; rev. 1930); *Missa imaginum* for Chorus and Orch. (1929); *Chorus of Shepherds and Angels* for Women's Voices and Strings (1959); *Missa brevis* for Chorus (1963; rev. as *Mass in Honor of St. Mark*, 1966); about 13 cantatas (1916–66); motets; anthems; Psalms; part songs; songs.

BIBL.: H. James, *A Catalog of the Musical Works of P. J. (1890–1975)* (N.Y., 1980; suppl., 1984).—**NS/LK/DM**

James, Rick (originally, Johnson, James Jr.),

a punk funk pioneer; b., Buffalo, N.Y., Feb. 1, 1948. James and his seven brothers and sisters were brought up by their mother, who made her living primarily as a numbers runner. At 15, James joined the Navy. He went AWOL soon after, landing in Toronto. There, he formed The Mynah Birds, a band of future all-stars including Neil Young and Bill Palmer, who would shortly thereafter join Buffalo Springfield, and Goldie McJohn who would join Steppenwolf. To keep a low profile in a high profile position, he changed his name to Rick James. His uncle, Melvin Franklin of The Temptations, helped get the band signed to Motown in the mid- 1960s, though nothing ever was released. When the rest of The Mynah Birds went to L.A., James—still in trouble with the Navy—went to London where he formed a blues band. He also remained on the Motown payroll as a songwriter. He stayed there for seven years, at which point military amnesty allowed him to return to the States. He formed The Stone City Band, using a mixture of Parliament and Kiss as a blueprint, creating a funk rock hybrid. They recorded an entire album, which he brought to Berry Gordy. Gordy was impressed with the effort and signed James once again. The record, *Come and Get It*, came out during the summer of 1978, and the first single, "You and I," topped the R&B chart, rising to #13 pop. His ode to pot, "Mary Jane," followed it to #3 on the R&B charts. The album went gold and hit #13 as well.

Bustin' Out of L Seven came out the next year, spawning the R&B hits "Bustin' Out" (#8) and "High on Your Love" (#12). He went out on tour with The Mary Jane Girls (his answer to Parlet and the Brides of Funkenstein) and Prince. The tour generated a great deal of excitement on the two newcomers' often decadent stage shows and new funk and roll sound. They frequently played to sell-out houses. The album hit #16 on the pop charts. Less then ten months later, he followed that with *Fire It Up*, which produced the R&B

hit "Love Gun" (#13) and hit #34 on the pop album chart. He changed direction, recording *Garden of Love*, an album primarily of ballads including the R&B hit "Big Time" (#17).

In 1981, James released *Street Songs*, a hard core funk record that generated the chart topping R&B hit "Give It to Me Baby," (#40 pop). His follow-up, "Super Freak," went to #3 R&B and #16 pop. Both songs were sexy, funky, and slightly sleazy, in keeping with the sex-and-drugs attitude that James was projecting and actually living. When the album went platinum, he moved into a Calif. mansion previously owned by William Randolph Hearst. Tales of his excess became legend. One thing that kept him from crossing over more completely was MTV's concentration on rock, largely ignoring bands like P-Funk and James at this time. Yet James retained his musical prowess, producing hits for The Mary Jane Girls ("In My House," #7 pop 1995); Eddie Murphy ("Party All the Time" #2 & platinum, 1985); Teena Marie; Carl Carlton; and Uncle Melvin's band, The Temptations ("Standing on the Top"). His 1982 album *Throwin' Down* hit #13 on the charts and went gold on the strength of his past performances, his live show, and the minor R&B hit "Dance wit' Me." Similarly, 1983's *Cold Blooded* went gold, rising to #16 pop as the title track topped the R&B album chart, but like "Give It to Me Baby," could get no higher than #40 pop. The song "17" reached #36 on the pop charts in 1984.

With the release of *The Flag* in 1985, James's contract with Motown ended—and none too happily. He took some time away from his own career to produce Eddie Murphy's debut album, finally signing to Reprise in 1988. The label debut, *Wonderful*, didn't even crack the Top 100 albums, though the single "Loosey's Rap" with Roxanne Shante topped the R&B charts. His decadence started to catch up with him, and by his own admission he spent a great deal of the next three years smoking crack, surfacing only when his debauchery got wild enough to make the papers. However, his music went on. MC Hammer heavily sampled "Super Freak" for his hit "U Can't Touch This," without clearing the sample. James sued, and in a settlement he became a co-writer of the song. Ironically, it was his only song to get MTV exposure and his only Grammy winner (he shared R&B Song of the Year with Hammer and Alonzo Miller).

In 1991, James and his girlfriend Tanya Hijazi were named in two instances of physically abusing women and drug possession. Both found themselves in jail. During his incarceration, James finally cleaned up his act. Out of prison, he went back into the recording studio and released *Urban Rapsody* [sic] in 1997, an album with guest appearances by Snoop Dogg, Bobby Womack, and even members of the Mary Jane Girls. He married Hijazi and settled down in L.A. While on tour supporting the album, James suffered a small stroke, but was soon on the road again.

DISC.: *This Magic Moment/Dance with Me* (1971); *Come Get It!* (1978); *Bustin' Out of L Seven* (1979); *Fire It Up* (1979); *Garden of Love* (1980); *3 Times in Love* (1980); *Street Songs* (1981); *Throwin' Down* (1982); *Cold Blooded* (1983); *Reflections of Rick* (1984); *You* (1985); *Glow* (1985); *The Flag* (1986); *Wonderful* (1988); *Kickin'* (1989); *Rick and Friends* (1992); *Urban Rapsody* (1997).—**HB**

James, Sonny (originally, **Loden, James Hugh**), American country singer, guitarist, and songwriter; b. Hackleburg, Ala., May 1, 1929. James was an eclectic country singer who scored 72 country chart entries between 1953 and 1983 with a variety of songs, many of them borrowed from pop, R&B, and folk music. His biggest hits included "Young Love," "It's the Little Things," and "You're the Only World I Know."

James grew up in the musical Loden Family, which performed around the South and included his parents and four sisters. He first performed publicly at the age of four. By seven he was playing fiddle, and he then took up guitar. In his teens he was employed as a musician on a radio station in Birmingham, Ala. He served in the Army in Korea during the Korean War, 1950–52. After his discharge he returned to performing and was signed to Capitol Records, which assigned his stage name by combining his nickname and his first name.

James reached the country charts with his debut single, "That's Me without You" (music and lyrics by J. D. Miller and Bennett Wyatt), in February 1953, but he did not achieve major success until four years later, when "Young Love" (music and lyrics by Rick Cartey and Carole Joyner) topped both the country and pop charts and sold a million copies. He continued to chart with pop-styled material over the next several years, but his success with such recordings declined to the point that he left Capitol for the smaller NRC label in 1960, then moved briefly to RCA Victor. By 1962 he was off the charts.

James returned to Capitol in 1963 with a distinctly country approach and enjoyed his second country #1 after eight years in January 1965 with "You're the Only World I Know" (music and lyrics by Sonny James and Robert Tubert). The song earned him Grammy nominations for Best Country and Western Song and Best Country & Western Single, and his *You're the Only World I Know* LP earned him a nomination for Best Country & Western Vocal Performance, Male. From this point through 1972 his records regularly occupied the top of the country charts. "Behind the Tear" (music and lyrics by Ned Miller and Sue Miller) hit #1 in October 1965, as did a revival of the 1961 pop song "Take Good Care of Her" (music and lyrics by Arthur Kent and Ed Warren) in June 1966. *The Best of Sonny James* was a #1 country album in December 1966.

James began an amazing string of 16 consecutive country chart-topping singles in April 1967 with a revival of the 1949 pop song "Need You" (music and lyrics by Johnny Blackburn, Teepee Mitchell, and Lew Porter); a *Need You* LP topped the country album charts in July. "Need You" was followed at the top of the country singles charts by a revival of the 1965 pop song "I'll Never Find Another You" (music and lyrics by Tom Springfield; August 1967); "It's the Little Things" (music and lyrics by Arlie Duff; November 1967); a revival of the 1965 pop song "A World of Our Own" (music and lyrics by Tom Springfield; March 1968); "Heaven Says Hello" (music and lyrics by Cindy Walker; August 1968); a revival of the 1956 pop song "Born to Be with You" (music and lyrics by Don Robertson; December 1968); a revival of the 1960 pop song "Only the Lonely" (music and lyrics by Joe Melson and Roy Orbison; March 1969); a revival of the 1960 pop song "Running Bear" (music and lyrics by J. P. Richardson, aka The Big Bopper; June 1969); a revival of the 1956 pop song "Since I Met You, Baby" (music and lyrics by Ivory Joe Hunter; October 1969); a revival of the 1959 pop song "It's Just a Matter of Time" (music and lyrics by Brook Benton, Belford Hendricks, and Clyde Otis; February 1970); a revival of the 1966 pop song "My Love" (music and lyrics by Tony Hatch; May 1970); "Don't Keep Me Hangin' On" (music and lyrics by Sonny James and Carole Smith; August 1970); a revival of the 1959 pop song "Endlessly" (music and lyrics by Brook Benton and Clyde Otis; November 1970); a revival of the 1957 pop song "Empty Arms" (music and lyrics by Ivory Joe Hunter); a revival of the 1961 pop song "Bright Lights, Big City" (music and lyrics by Jimmy Reed; July 1971); and "Here Comes Honey Again" (music and lyrics by Sonny James and Carole Smith; November 1971).

After one single that missed the #1 spot, James scored two more in 1972, "That's Why I Love You Like I Do" (music and lyrics by Kelso Herston and Jack Morrow) in June, and his first release under a new contract with Columbia Records, "When the Snow Is on the Roses" (music and lyrics by Ernest Bader, Larry Kusick, Hans Last, and Eddie Snyder) in September. In 1973 his singles performed less well as Capitol continued to release material from its vault to compete with new Columbia recordings, thus glutting the market. But he returned to #1 with "Is It Wrong (For Loving You)" (music and lyrics by Warner Mack) in May 1974.

James's record sales declined after the mid-1970s as he moved to Monument Records in 1977 and Dimension Records in 1981. His last recording was done for Dot Records in 1986, when he re-recorded some of his hits for an album called *Sonny James*, after which he retired from performing.—**WR**

James, Tommy (actually, **Thomas Gregory Jackson**), with The Shondells had one of the few bands of the 1960s to actually surpass The Beatles; b. Dayton, Ohio, April 29, 1947. Tommy James was a child model at five. By the time he got into junior high, shortly after moving to Mich., he had formed a band called The Shondells. At 14 years old, they became recording artists, cutting a song called "Long Pony Tail." This song attracted the attention of a local deejay, who approached James about making another record. James said, "Sure," even though the band really didn't have anything to record. He recalled a song he had heard another band record, a B-side from Jeff Barry and Ellie Greenwich's band (which they had written in the hallway when they realized they needed that B-side to finish the session). Since James had only heard it once, he more or less invented his own lyrics as he went. The song, "Hanky Panky," became a regional hit in 1963.

By the time he graduated high school, James was at loose ends. A deejay from Pittsburgh tracked him down to let him know that "Hanky Panky" had reignited and that someone had sold thousands of bootleg copies because originals couldn't be had. James went to Pittsburgh, but The Shondells didn't want to leave the Midwest. James fielded requests for live appearances and realized he needed a band. A local group, The Raconteurs, filled the bill and they became The Shondells. Roulette picked up the single for national distribution in 1966. It went to the top of the charts, selling a million copies. Roulette signed James and The Shondells, and they move to N.Y. They followed this with the blue-eyed soul tune "Say I Am (What I Am)," which went to #21. Roulette hooked the group up with producers and co-writers Bo Gentry and Richie Cordell. Together, they started cranking out hit singles that crossed frat-house-rowdy with bubblegum-sweet, sometimes leaning more one way than the other, but usually with craftmanlike innovation. Their first effort, "It's Only Love," did nothing to staunch their slide down the Top 40, hitting only #31. However, their next effort, "I Think We're Alone Now," with its risqué (for the Top 40 in 1967) theme and percolating arrangement, hit #4. It was followed at two-month intervals by "Mirage" (#10) and "Getting Together" (#18). One of the windows of James midtown apartment looked out at the Mutual of N.Y. building, with its neon spire proclaiming MONY. This inspired an idea for the band's next hit, "Mony Mony," an infectious dance rock record that would prove remarkably durable (as would many James hits). The song rose to #3.

At this point, James decided that he'd learned enough from Cordell and Gentry. He took the band under his wing as writer and producer. This had as much to do with the need for a change as it did with the change popular music underwent during 1967 with the "Summer of Love." In that context, even the timeless "Mony Mony" was an anachronism. He took the band in a direction more befitting 1968. Their first effort, "Do Something to Me," a cover of a ? and the Mysterians song, barely scraped into the Top 40. In addition to the change in music was a change in the way it was consumed and promoted. Where singles ruled the day through much of the 1960s, and albums often just collected a band's singles output, with *Rubber Soul* and *Sgt. Peppers*, The Beatles had changed all that. James, always clever at spotting a trend, followed this one and put together the album *Crimson and Clover*, which featured the five-and-a-half minute title track, an extended version of the single, which topped the charts in 1968. With it's wah-wah guitars and treated vocals (achieved by running the mic through a guitar amp with the tremolo on), the song was safe as milk psychedelia. Ironically, the follow-up, "Sweet Cherry Wine," came from *Cellophane Symphony*, an album the band was working on simultaneously with *Crimson and Clover*. However, FM radio had started playing the *Crimson and Clover* track "Crystal Blue Persuasion," so both ran up to the Top Ten within months of each other. The liner notes from the *Crimson and Clover* album were written by former Vice President Hubert Humphrey. The album hit #8. Around holiday time, Roulette released a best of album that climbed to #21. Over the course of 1968 and 1969, they had sold more singles world-wide than any other artist.

After a couple more minor hits, James collapsed on stage in Ala. in 1970. He went to his farm in upstate N.Y.

and spent several months recovering. The Shondells, cut loose again, once more became a separate band called Hogs Heaven that drifted off to obscurity. After a few months of "retirement," James got bored and started cutting a few songs. He still hadn't gotten his voice back, so he invited the group Alive and Kicking to sing on the track. "Tighter and Tighter" became a #7 hit during the late summer of 1970. James started recording his own material again, to little success until the summer of 1971, when his country-ish "Draggin' the Line" hit #4 and went gold. That fall his tune "I'm Comin' Home" barely scratched the Top 40. For the next eight years, he had minor successes with several labels and still could attract crowds to see him live, but he had no bona fide hits. After leaving Roulette in 1974, James did two albums for Fantasy Records. In 1980, he signed with Millennium records, which had developed a penchant for taking previous hit makers and reviving their careers on the adult contemporary charts. They did this for James, landing "Three Times in Love" at the top of the adult charts and at #19 on the pop charts in 1980.

While he wasn't having hits on his own through the 1980s, James continued to be a force on the charts. Joan Jett took a version of "Crimson and Clover" (co-produced by Cordell) to #7 in 1982. Five years later, Billy Idol's cover of "Mony Mony" and Tiffany's version "I Think We're Alone Now" vied for the top of the pop charts, with the former following the latter into the #1 slot. James continues to be a force on the oldies circuit, and still releases the occasional album of new material.

DISC.: *Hanky Panky* (1966); *It's Only Love* (1967); *Come Softly to Me* (1967); *I Think We're Alone Now* (1967); *Gettin' Together* (1968); *Something Special* (1968); *Crimson and Clover* (1968); *Mony Mony* (1968); *Cellophane Symphony* (1969); *Travelin'* (1970); *Tommy James* (1970); *Christian of the World* (1971); *My Head, My Bed and My Red Guitar* (1971); *In Touch* (1976); *Midnight Rider* (1977); *3 Times in Love* (1980); *Easy to Love* (1980); *Short Sharp Shots* (1983); *Night in Big City* (1995). **TOMMY JAMES, SOLO:** *Tommy James* (1970); *Christian of the World* (1971); *My Head, My Bed and My Red Guitar* (1971); *In Touch* (1976); *3 Times in Love* (1980); *Easy to Love* (1980).—**HB**

Janáček, Leoš, greatly significant Czech composer; b. Hukvaldy, Moravia, July 3, 1854; d. Moravská Ostrava, Aug. 12, 1928. At the age of 11, he was sent to Brno to serve as a chorister at the Augustinian Queen's Monastery, where he was schooled under its choirmaster, Křížkovský. After studies at the German Coll., he was a scholarship student at the teacher's training college (1869–72). He then began his teaching career while serving as choirmaster at the monastery; he also served as choirmaster of the men's chorus, Svatopluk (1873–77), taking an opportunity to study organ with Skuherský at the Prague Organ School (1874–75). He conducted the Beseda Choral Soc. in Brno (1876–88), and also pursued studies at the Leipzig Cons., where he took music history courses with Oskar Paul and composition courses with Leo Grill (1879–80). He continued his composition studies with Franz Krenn at the Vienna Cons. (1880). Returning to Brno, he was appointed the first director of the new organ school (1881). His social position in Brno was enhanced by his marriage to Zdenka Schulzová, the daughter of the director of the teachers' training college. He also engaged in scholarly activities; from 1884 to 1886 he was ed. of the music journal *Hudební Listy* (Music Bulletins); he further became associated with František Bartoš in collecting Moravian folk songs. From 1886 to 1902 he taught music at the Brno Gymnasium. In 1919 he retired from his directorship of the Brno Organ School, and then taught master classes in Brno (1920–25). Throughout all these busy years, he worked diligently on his compositions, showing particular preference for operas.

Janáček's style of composition underwent numerous transformations, from Romantic techniques of established formulas to bold dissonant combinations. He was greatly influenced by the Russian musical nationalism exemplified by the "realistic" speech inflections in vocal writing. He visited St. Petersburg and Moscow in 1896 and 1902, and publ. his impressions of the tour in the Brno press. From 1894 to 1903 he worked assiduously on his most important opera, *Její pastorkyňa* (Her Foster Daughter), to a highly dramatic libretto set in Moravia in the mid- 19th century, involving a jealous contest between two brothers for the hand of Jenůfa (the innocent heroine), and infanticide at the hands of a foster mother, with an amazing outcome absolving Jenůfa and her suitors. The opera encountered great difficulty in securing production in Prague because of its grisly subject, but was eventually produced on various European stages, mostly in the German text, and under the title *Jenůfa*. Another opera by Janáček that attracted attention was *Výlet pana Broučka do XV stoleti* (Mr. Brouček's Excursion to the 15th Century), depicting the imaginary travel of a Czech patriot to the time of the religious struggle mounted by the followers of the nationalist leader Hus against the established church. There followed an operatic fairy tale, *Příhody Lišky Bystroušky* (The Adventures of the Vixen Bystrouška, or The Cunning Little Vixen), and a mystery play, *Věc Makropulos* (The Makropulos Affair). Janáček's great interest in Russian literature was reflected in his opera *Kát'a Kabanová*, after the drama *The Storm* by the Russian playwright Ostrovsky, and one after Dostoyevsky, *Z mrtvého domu* (From the House of the Dead). He further composed a symphonic poem, *Taras Bulba* (the fictional name of a Ukrainian patriot, after a story by Gogol). In 1917 Janáček became enamored of Kamila Stösslová, the 26 year-old wife of an antique dealer. His unconsummated love for her proved an inspiration and led to the composition of several major works by an aging composer. Like most artists, writers, and composers of Slavic origin in the old Austro-Hungarian Empire, Janáček had a natural interest in the Pan-Slavic movement, with an emphasis on the common origins of Russian, Czech, Slovak, and other kindred cultures; his *Glagolitic Mass*, to a Latin text tr. into the Czech language, is an example. Janáček lived to witness the fall of the old Austrian regime and the national rise of the Slavic populations. He also showed great interest in the emerging Soviet school of composition, even though he refrained from any attempt to join that movement. Inevitably, he followed the striking innovations of the modern school of composition as set forth in the works of Stravinsky and Schoenberg, but he was never tempted to experiment along those revolutionary lines.

He remained faithful to his own well-defined style, and it was as the foremost composer of modern Czech music that he secured for himself his unique place in history.

WORKS: DRAMATIC: O p e r a : *Šárka* (1887–88; rev. 1918–19, with Act 3 orchestrated by O. Chlubna; rev. 1924–25; Brno, Nov. 11, 1925); *Počátek romanu* (The Beginning of a Romance; 1891; Brno, Feb. 10, 1894); *Její pastorkyňa* (Her Foster Daughter; generally known by its German title, *Jenůfa*; 1894–1903; Brno, Jan. 21, 1904; several subsequent revisions, including final version by K. Kovařovic, 1916; Prague, May 26, 1916); *Osud* (Fate; 1903–05; rev. 1906–07; 1st complete perf., Brno Radio, Sept. 18, 1934; 1st stage perf., National Theater, Brno, Oct. 25, 1958); *Výlet pana Broučka do měsíce* (Mr. Brouček's Excursion to the Moon; 1908–17; National Theater, Prague, April 23, 1920); a sequel to the preceding, *Výlet pana Broučka do XV stoleti* (Mr. Brouček's Excursion to the 15th Century; 1917; National Theater, Prague, April 23, 1920); *Kát'a Kabanová* (1919–21; Brno, Nov. 23, 1921); *Příhody Lišky Bystroušky* (The Adventures of the Vixen Bystrouška; The Cunning Little Vixen; 1921–23; Brno, Nov. 6, 1924); *Věc Makropulos* (The Makropulos Affair; 1923–25; Brno, Dec. 18, 1926); *Z mrtvého domu* (From the House of the Dead; 1927–28; rev. and reorchestrated by O. Chlubna and B. Bakala, 1930; Brno, April 12, 1930). **F o l k   B a l l e t :** *Rákos Rákoczy* (National Theater, Prague, July 24, 1891). **ORCH.:** *Suite* for Strings (Brno, Dec. 2, 1877); *Idyll* for Strings (Brno, Dec. 15, 1878); *Suite (Serenade)*, op. 3 (1891; Brno, Sept. 23, 1928); *Adagio* (1891); *Žárlivost* (Jealousy), overture (1894; 1st concert perf., Prague, Nov. 10, 1906); *Šumařovo dítě* (The Fiddler's Child), ballad (1912; Prague, Nov. 14, 1917); *Taras Bulba*, rhapsody after Gogol (1915–18; Brno, Oct. 9, 1921); *Balada blanická* (The Ballad of Blanik), symphonic poem (Brno, March 21, 1920); *Sinfonietta* (Prague, June 29, 1926); *Dunaj* (The Danube), symphonic poem (1923–28; unfinished; completed by O. Chlubna, 1948); Violin Concerto: *Putování dušičky* (Pilgrimage of the Soul; 1926; Brno, Sept. 29, 1988). **C H A M B E R :** *Znělka* (Fanfare) for 4 Violins (1875); *Zvuky ku památce Förchgotta-Tovačovského* (Sounds in Memory of Forchgotta- Tovacovskeho) for 3 Violins, Viola, Cello, and Double Bass (c. 1875); *Romance* for Violin and Piano (1879); *Dumka* for Violin and Piano (1880); *Prohádka* (Fairy Tale) for Cello and Piano (1910; rev. 1923); *Presto* for Cello and Piano (c. 1910); Violin Sonata (1914–21; Balada only); 2 string quartets: No. 1 (1923–24; Prague, Sept. 17, 1924; based on the lost Piano Trio of 1908–9) and No. 2, *Listy důvěrné* (Intimate Letters; Brno, Sept. 11, 1928; rev. 1947 by O. Šourek); *Mládí* (Youth), suite for Wind Sextet (Brno, Oct. 21, 1924); *Pochod Modráčků* (March of the Blue Boys) for Piccolo and Piano (1924); Concertino for Piano, 2 Violins, Viola, Clarinet, Horn, and Bassoon (1925; Brno, Feb. 16, 1926); *Capriccio Vzdor* (Defiance) for Piano, Left-hand, and Chamber Ensemble (1926; Prague, March 2, 1928). **P i a n o :** *Thema con variazioni* (Zdenciny variace: Zdenka Variations; 1880); *Na památku* (In Memoriam; c. 1886); *Po zarostlém chodníčku* (On the Overgrown Path), 15 pieces (1901–8; 7 originally for Harmonium); Sonata *1.X.1905 Z ulice* (From the Street; 1905; only 2 movements extant; inspired by the abortive but sanguine Russian revolt); *V mlhách* (In the Mists; 1912; rev. 1949, by B. Štědroň); *Vzpomínka* (Reminiscence; 1928). **VOCAL: C h o r a l : S a c r e d :** *Fidelis servus* for Mixed Voices (c. 1870); *Graduale in festo purificationis B.V.M.* for Mixed Voices (c. 1870; rev. 1887); Mass (c. 1870; not extant); *Graduale (Speciosus forma)* for Mixed Voices and Organ (1874); *Introitus (in festo Ss. Nominis Jesu)* for Mixed Voices and Organ (c. 1874); *Benedictus* for Soprano, Mixed Voices, and Organ (1875); *Communio* for Mixed Voices (1875); *Exaudi Deus* for Mixed Voices and Organ (1875); *Exaudi Deus* for Mixed Voices (1875); *Odpočin si* (Take

Your Rest) for Men's Voices (c. 1875); *Regnum mundi* for Mixed Voices (c. 1878); *Sanctus* for Mixed Voices (1879); *Deset českých církevních zpěvo z Lehnerova mešního kancinonálu* (10 Czech Hymns from the Lehner Hymnbook for Mass) with Organ (1881); *Ave Maria* (1883); *Hospodine!* (Lord Have Mercy) for Soprano, Alto, Tenor, Bass, Double Chorus, Organ, Harp, 4 Trombones, and Tuba (1896); *Slavnostní sbor* (Festival Chorus) for Men's Voices (1897); *Svatý Václave!* (St. Wenceslas; 1902); *Constitues* for Men's Voices and Organ (c. 1902); *Zdrávas Maria* for Tenor, Mixed Voices, and Organ (1904); (7) *Církevni zpěvy české vicehlasné z příborského kancionálu* (Czech Hymns for Several Voices from the Pribor Hymnbook; c. 1904); Mass in E- flat major for Voices and Organ (1907–08; left incomplete; finished and orchestrated by V. Petrželka; Brno, March 7, 1943); *Veni sancte spiritus* for Men's Voices (1910). S e c u l a r (all for Men's Voices unless otherwise given): *Srbská lidová piseň* (Serbian Folk Song) for Mixed Voices (1873); *Oráni* (Ploughing; 1873); *Válečná* (War Song; 1873); *Nestálost lásky* (The Fickleness of Love; 1873); *Osámělá bez techy* (Alone without Comfort; 1874; rev. 1898 and 1925); *Divim se milému* (I Wonder at My Beloved; c. 1875); *Vínek stonulý* (A Drowned Wreath; c. 1875); *Láska opradivá* (True Love; 1876); *Když mne nechceš coz je víc* (If You Don't Want Me, What Else Is There?; 1876); *Zpěvná duma* (Choral Elegy; 1876); *Slavnostní sbor* (Festival Chorus) for Soloists and Voices (1877); *Osudu neujdeš* (You Cannot Escape Your Fate; 1878); *Na košatej jedli dva holubi sed'á* (On the Bushy Fir Tree 2 Pigeons Are Perched; c. 1878); *Píseň v jeseni* (Autumn Song) for Mixed Voices (1880); *Na prievoze* (c. 1883); *Mužské sbory* (Men's Voice Choruses; 1885); *Kačena divoká* (The Wild Duck) for Mixed Voices (c. 1885); *Tři mužské sbory* (3 Men's Voice Choruses; 1888); *Naše píseň* (Our Song) for Mixed Voices and Orch. (1890); *Zelené sem sela* (I Have Sown Green) for Mixed Voices and Orch. (1892); *Což ta naše bříza* (Our Birch Tree; 1893); *Vinek* (The Garland; 1893); *Už je slúnko z tej hory ven* (The Sun Has Risen above That Hill) for Baritone, Mixed Voices, and Piano (1894); *Čtvero mužských sborů moravských* (4 Moravian Men's Voice Choruses; 1904); *Kantor Halfar* (1906); *Maryčka Magdónova* (1906–07); *Sedmdesát tisíc* (The 70,000; 1909); *Perina* (The Eiderdown; c. 1914); *Vlčí stopa* (The Wolf's Trail) for Soprano, Women's Voices, and Piano (1916); *Hradčanské pisničky* (Songs of Hradcany) for Women's Voices (1916); *Kaspar Rucký* for Soprano and Women's Voices (1916); *Česká legie* (The Czech Legion; 1918); *Potulný šílenec* (The Wandering Madman) for Soprano and Men's Voices (1922); *Naše vlajka* (Our Flag) for 2 Sopranos and Men's Voices (1925–26); *Sbor při kladenízakladního kamene Masarykovy university v Brne* (Chorus for Laying the Foundation Stone of Masaryk Univ. in Brno; 1928). C a n t a - t a s : *Amarus* for Soprano, Tenor, Baritone, Chorus, and Orch. (1897; Kroměříž, Dec. 2, 1900; rev. 1901 and 1906); *Otče náš* (Our Father) for Tenor, Chorus, and Piano or Harmonium (Brno, June 15, 1901; rev. 1906); *Elegie na smrt dcery Olgy* (Elegy on the Death of My Daughter Olga) for Tenor, Chorus, and Piano (1903; rev. 1904; Brno Radio, Dec. 20, 1930); *Na Soláni Čarták* (Cartak on the Solan) for Tenor, Men's Voices, and Orch. (1911; Brno, March 13, 1912); *Věčné evangelium* (The Eternal Gospel) for Soprano, Tenor, Chorus, and Orch. (1914; Prague, Feb. 5, 1917; rev. 1924); *Glagolská mše* (Glagolitic Mass) for Soprano, Alto, Tenor, Bass, Chorus, Orch., and Organ (1926; Brno, Dec. 5, 1927). C h a m b e r V o c a l : *Zapisnik zmizeleho* (The Diary of One Who Disappeared), song cycle for Tenor, Alto, 3 Women's Voices, and Piano (1917–19; Brno, April 18, 1921); *Říkadla* (Nursery Rhymes), 8 pieces for 3 Women's Voices, Clarinet, and Piano (Brno, Oct. 26, 1925; rev. version, 1927, as 18 pieces and an introduction for 2 Sopranos, 2 Altos, 3 Tenors, 2

Basses, 9 Instruments, and Children's Drum). Janáček made many arrangements of folk music and prepared the following eds. of folk songs: with F. Bartoš, *Kytice z národních pisní moravských* (A Bouquet of Moravian Folk Songs; Telč, 1890; 3rd ed., rev., 1901; 4th ed., 1953, edited by A. Gregor and B. Štědroň); 53 songs (Telč, 1892–1901; 2nd ed., 1908, as *Moravaská lidová poesie v pisnich*; Moravian Folk Poetry in Songs; 4th ed., 1947, edited by B. Štědroň); with F. Bartoš, *Národní pisne moravské v nově nasbírané* (Moravian Folk Songs Newly Collected; 1899); with P. Váša, *Moravské písně milostné* (Moravian Love Songs; 1928). A complete critical ed. of the works of Janáček began publication in Prague in 1978.

WRITINGS: J. Vysloužil, ed., *O lidové písni a lidové hudbě* (Folk Song and Folk Music; Prague, 1955); Z. Blažek, ed., *Hudebně teoretické dilo* (Music Theory Works; 2 vols., Prague, 1968, 1974); M. Boyars, ed., *J.'s Uncollected Essays on Music* (London and N.Y., 1989).

BIBL.: SOURCE MATERIAL: His correspondence was ed. by A. Rektorys and J. Racek (9 vols., Prague, 1934–53); J. Racek, ed., *L. J.: Obraz života a dila* (L. J.: A Picture of His Life and Works; Brno, 1948); B. Štědroň, *L. J. v obrazech* (L. J. in Pictures; Prague, 1958); idem, *Dilo Leoše Janáčka: Abecedni seznam Janáčkových skladeb a úprav* (L. J.'s Works: An Alphabetical Catalog of J.'s Compositions and Arrangements; Prague, 1959; Eng. tr., 1959, as *The Work of L. J.*); T. Strakova, ed., *Iconographia janáčkiana* (Brno, 1975); N. Simeone, *The First Editions of L. J.: A Bibliographical Catalogue, with Reproductions of Title Pages* (Tutzing, 1991); J. Tyrrell, ed. and tr., *Intimate Letters: L. J. to Kamila Stösslová* (Princeton, 1994); M. Beckerman and G. Bauer, eds., *J. and Czech Music* (Stuyvesant, N.Y., 1995); N. Simeone, J. Tyrrell, A. Němcová, and T. Straková, *J. Works: A Catalogue of the Music and Writings* (Oxford, 1997). **BIOGRAPHICAL:** M. Brod, *L. J.: Život a dilo* (L. J.: Life and Works; Prague, 1924; Ger. ed., 1925; 2nd ed., rev., 1956); D. Muller, *L. J.* (Paris, 1930); A. Vašek, *Po stopách dra Leoše Janáčka* (On the Track of Dr. L. J.; Brno, 1930); H. Kašlik, *L. J. dirigent* (Prague, 1936); O. Jeremiáš, *L. J.* (Prague, 1938); V. Helfert, *L. J.* (Brno, 1939); idem, *O Janáčkovi* (About J.; ed. by B. Štědroň, Prague, 1949); H. Richter, *L. J.* (Leipzig, 1958); J. Vogel, *L. J.: Leben und Werk* (Kassel, 1958; Eng. tr., 1962; 2nd ed., rev., 1980); J. Šeda, *L. J.* (Prague, 1961); J. Racek, *L. J.: Mensch und Künstler* (Leipzig, 1962; 2nd ed., 1971; Czech ed., 1963); H. Hollander, *L. J.* (London, 1963; Ger. ed., 1964); M. Černohorská, *L. J.* (in Eng.; Prague, 1966); B. Štědroň, *L. J.: K jeho lidskému a uměleckému profilu* (L. J.'s Image as Man and Artist; Brno, 1976); J. Vysloužil, *L. J.* (Brno, 1978); I. Horsbrugh, *L. J.* (Newton Abbot, 1981); K. Honolka, *L. J.: Sein Leben, sein Werk, seine Zeit* (Stuttgart, 1982); S. Přibáňová, *L. J.* (Prague, 1984); C. Susskind, *J. and Brod* (London, 1986); F. Pulcini, *J.: Vita, opere, scritti* (Florence, 1993). **CRITICAL, ANALYTICAL:** L. Firkušný, *Odkaz Leoše Janáčka české opeře* (L. J.'s Legacy to Czech Opera; Brno, 1939); L. Kundera, *Janáčkova varhanická škola* (J.'s Organ School; Olomouc, 1948); B. Štědroň, *Zur Genesis von L. J.s Oper Jenůfa* (Brno, 1968; 2nd ed., 1971); A. Tučapský, *Mužské sbory Leoše Janáčka a jejich interpretační tradice* (L. J.'s Male Voice Choruses and Their Performance Tradition; Ostrava, 1968); E. Chisholm, *The Operas of L. J.* (Oxford, 1971); T. Kneif, *Die Bühnenwerke von L. J.* (Vienna, 1974); A. Geck, *Das Volksliedmaterial L. J.s: Analysen der Strukturen unter Einbeziehung von J.s Randbemerkungen und Volkstudien* (Regensburg, 1975); D. Ströbel, *Motiv und Figur in den Kompositionen der Jenufa-Werkgruppe* (Freiburg, 1975); M. Ewans, *J.'s Tragic Operas* (London, 1977); Z. Skoumal, *Structure in the Late Instrumental Music of L. J.* (diss., City Univ. of N.Y., 1992); J. Tyrrell, ed., *J.'s Operas: A Documen-*

tary Account (Princeton, N.J., 1992); P. Wingfield, *J.: Glagolithic Mass* (Cambridge, 1992); M. Beckerman, *J. as Theorist* (Stuyvesant, N.Y., 1993); W. Bernhart, ed., *L. J. Konzeption und Rezeption seines musikdramatischen Schaffens* (Anif, 1997).—**NS/LK/DM**

Jan and Dean, surf-harmony group who hit it big in the 1960s; Jan Berry (b. Los Angeles, April 3, 1941; Dean Torrance (b. Los Angeles, March 10, 1940). Jan Berry and Dean Torrance met at Emerson J.H.S. in L.A. Fascinated with the "doo-wop" sound of the 1950s, the two formed The Barons in 1957 with Arnie Ginsburg and, for a time, future Beach Boy Bruce Johnston and drummer Sandy Nelson. Reduced to a trio of Berry, Torrance, and Ginsburg, they recorded "Jennie Lee" in Jan's garage. While Dean was serving in the Army Reserve, Jan signed with the Arwin label, owned by Doris Day's husband Marty Melcher. Arwin released "Jennie Lee" under the name Jan and Arnie and the song became a near-smash hit in 1958. When Ginsburg dropped out to join the Navy in late 1958, Jan and Dean signed with the Dore label, managed by Lou Adler and Herb Alpert. They scored a near-smash on Dore with the novelty song "Baby Talk" in 1959, but the duo's next major hit didn't come until 1961, when "Heart and Soul" was released on Challenge Records.

Later in 1961, Jan and Dean signed with Liberty Records. In the summer of 1962, the duo met The Beach Boys, whose Brian Wilson provided them with their first major hit on Liberty, "Linda." Recording with sessions musicians such as Glen Campbell, Leon Russell, Steve Douglas, and Hal Blaine, Jan and Dean scored a top pop hit with Berry and Wilson's "Surf City" in the summer of 1963. Subsequent major hits included "Honolulu Lulu," "Drag City," "Dead Man's Curve," the smash "The Little Old Lady (From Pasadena)," "Ride the Wild Surf," and Wilson's "Sidewalk Surfin'," a precursor of the skateboard rage. In October 1964, Jan and Dean hosted a concert at the Santa Monica Civic Auditorium that became the 1965 film *The T.A.M.I. (Teenage Awards Music International) SHOW*, with performances by The Rolling Stones, The Beach Boys, The Supremes, The Miracles, and others. Later hits for Jan and Dean included "You Really Know How to Hurt a Guy" and "Popsicle," but, by late 1965, they were recording the songs of Bob Dylan and The Beatles.

On April 12, 1966, Jan Berry was nearly killed when his Corvette Stingray, traveling at a high rate of speed, struck a parked truck. In a coma for nearly a year, Jan spent much of the next ten years undergoing intensive physical therapy for a condition that included paralysis of his right side and impaired speech, hearing, vision, and memory. In the meantime, Dean opened Kittyhawk Graphics, where he designed album covers. Jan and Dean recorded for Columbia and Warner Bros. between 1967 and 1968 and Jan recorded solo for Ode Records from 1972 to 1974. The two reunited to perform at Hollywood's 1973 "Surfer's Stomp Reunion." After the airing of the biographical *Dead Man's Curve* special on network television in February 1978, Jan and Dean reunited for performances with The Beach Boys. Jan and Dean continued to tour as an oldies act into the 1990s.

DISC.: *Jan and Dean* (1960); *The Heart and Soul of Jan and Dean* (1961); *Jan and Dean Take Linda Surfin'* (1963); *Surf City (and Other Swingin' Cities)* (1963); *Drag City* (1963); *Ride the Wild Surf* (1964); *The Little Old Lady from Pasadena* (1964); *Command Performance—"Live" in Person* (1965); *Jan & Dean's Pop Symphony No. 1* (1965); *Folk 'n' Roll* (1965); *Filet of Soul* (1966); *Jan and Dean Meet Batman* (1966); *Popsicle* (1966); *Save for a Rainy Day* (1967). —**HB**

Jancourt, (Louis Marie) Eugène, notable French bassoonist and pedagogue; b. Château-Thierry, Aisne, Dec. 15, 1815; d. Boulogne-sur-Seine, Jan. 29, 1901. He was a student of François René Gebauer at the Paris Cons., graduating in 1836. He then was active as an orchestral player and as a soloist until 1869. From 1875 to 1891 he taught at the Paris Cons. He made various improvements to the bassoon, and also composed and made arrangements for it. His *Grande méthode* (Paris, 1847; includes studies and duet sonatas) remains an important work.—**LK/DM**

Jander, Owen (Hughes), American musicologist; b. Mount Kisco, N.Y., June 4, 1930. He was educated at the Univ. of Va. (B.A., 1951) and Harvard Univ. (M.A., 1952; Ph.D., 1962, with the diss. *The Works of Alessandro Stradella Related to the Cantata and the Opera*). In 1960 he joined the dept. of music at Wellesley Coll., where he later became the Catherine Mills Davis Prof. in Music History. He was founder of its Collegium Musicum for the performance of early music and also initiated the project to construct the outstanding Fisk Organ there for the performance of the pre-Bach repertoire. He also served as ed. of The Wellesley Edition and The Wellesley Edition Cantata Index Series (1962–74). In 1966–67 he held a Guggenheim fellowship, and in 1985 he received a National Endowment for the Humanities Fellowship for Senior Scholars. He initially devoted himself to 17th-century Italian music, but later turned to Beethoven. He contributed numerous articles to *The New Grove Dictionary of Music and Musicians* (1980), and also served as co-ed. of *Charles Benton Fisk: Organ Builder* (2 vols., 1986).—**NS/LK/DM**

Jandó, Jenő, outstanding Hungarian pianist and teacher; b. Pécs, Feb. 1, 1952. He was born into a musical family, and began formal piano instruction at an early age in Pécs with Margit Weininger. While still young, he pursued studies at the Pécs Cons. with András Ligeti and István Gyermán. At 16, he entered the Franz Liszt Academy of Music in Budapest, where his principal mentors were Pál Kadosa, Andras Mihály, and Katalin Nemes. He graduated in 1974, and then joined its faculty in 1975. In 1972 he won second prize in the György Cziffra Competition in Versailles, in 1973 first prize in the National Piano Competition of the Hungarian Radio in Budapest, and in 1975 second prize in the Dino Ciani Competition in Milan. He subsequently pursued a global career as a soloist with orchs., recitalist, and chamber music artist. He was honored with the Franz Liszt Prize in 1980, was made an Artist of Merit in 1987, and was awarded the prestigious Kossuth Prize of Hungary in 1997. Jandó's interpretations of the Classical and Romantic masters are exemplary for their combination of insightful artistry and virtuoso execution. His

vast repertoire, much of which he has recorded, includes all the Mozart piano concerti and sonatas, as well as the piano sonatas of Haydn, Beethoven, and Schubert. He has also performed works by Liszt and Bartók.
—NS/LK/DM

Janeček, Karel, Czech composer and music theorist; b. Czestochowa, Poland, Feb. 20, 1903; d. Prague, Jan. 4, 1974. He spent his boyhood in Kiev. After completing his secondary education at an industrial school, he went to Prague, where he took courses in composition with Křička (1921–24) and Novák (1924–27). From 1929 to 1941 he taught at the Plzeň Music School; then was prof. of composition at the Prague Cons. (1941–46). He subsequently helped to found the Prague Academy of Music (1947), where he taught; was a prof. there (from 1961). In his early works, Janeček adopted a traditional national style; later he occasionally employed a personalized dodecaphonic scheme.

WORKS: ORCH.: *Overture* (1926–27); 2 syms. (1935–40; 1954–55); *Lenin*, symphonic triptych (1953); *Legend of Prague*, overture for Strings (1956); *Fantasy* (1962–63); Sinfonietta (1967); *Large Symposium* for 15 Soloists (1967). CHAMBER: 3 string quartets (1924, 1927, 1934); *Divertimento* for 8 Instruments (1925–26); String Trio (1930); Trio for Flute, Clarinet, and Bassoon (1931); Duo for Violin and Viola (1938); Violin Sonata (1939); *Divertimento* for Oboe, Clarinet, and Bassoon (1949); Cello Sonata (1958); *Little Symposium*, suite for Flute, Clarinet, Bassoon, and Piano (1959); Duo for Violin and Cello (1960); *Chamber Overture* for Nonet (1960); Quartet for Flute, Oboe, Clarinet, and Bassoon (1966). P i a n o : *Trifles and Abbreviations* (1926); *Tema con variazioni*, inspired by the Nazi destruction of the village of Lidice (1942). VOCAL: Choral works, including *To the Fallen* (1950–51), *To the Living* (1951), and *My Dream* (1972); songs.

WRITINGS (all publ. in Prague): *Otakar Šin* (1944); *Hudební formy* (Musical Forms; 1955); *Melodika* (1956); *Vyjádření souzvukv* (The Writing of Chords; 1958); *Harmonie rozborem* (Harmony Through Analysis; 1963); *Základy moderní harmonie* (The Basis of Modern Harmony; 1965); *Tektonika* (Structure; 1968); *Tvorba a tvůrci* (Creativity and Creations; 1968); *Skladatelská práce v oblasti klasické harmonie* (Composition Based on Classical Harmony; 1973).—NS/LK/DM

Janequin (Jannequin), Clément, important French composer; b. Châtellerault, c. 1485; d. Paris, 1558. He is first mentioned as a clerc in the service of Lancelot du Fau, a man of the court and church, in 1505. His patron became Bishop of Luçon in 1515, and he appears to have remained in the bishop's service until 1523, at which time he entered the service of Jean de Foix, bishop of Bordeaux. Having become a priest, he received several minor prebends there. He became canon of St. Emilion in 1525, then procureur des âmes there in 1526. He was named curé of St. Michel de Rieufret in 1526, then of St. Jean de Mezos in 1530, and also doyen of Garosse that same year. With the death of his patron in 1529, he lost his prebends. However, he had become known as a composer through Pierre Attaingnant's publication of some of his chansons. Janequin served as master of the choirboys at Auch Cathedral in 1531, then was made curé of Avrille in 1533; he was also maître de

chapelle of Angers Cathedral (1534–37), and subsequently curé of Unverre. In 1549 he settled in Paris, being listed as a student at the Univ. He wrote a chanson on the siege of Metz, which brought him the honorary title of chapelain to the Duc de Guise. He later was made chantre ordinaire du roi and then compositeur ordinaire du roi. Janequin was an outstanding composer of chansons and chansons spirituelles, of which more than 400 are extant. His mastery is evidenced both in his brief and witty settings and in those more lengthy and programmatic. Among his finest are *Le Chant des oiseaux, La Chasse, Les Cris de Paris*, and his most celebrated work, *La Bataille*, most likely written to commemorate the battle of Marignano. Pierre Attaingnant publ. several of his chansons between the 1520s and the 1530s; others appeared in various collections of the time. A. Merritt and F. Lesure ed. *Clément Janequin (c. 1485–1558): Chansons polyphoniques* (Monaco, 1965–71).

WORKS: MASSES: *Missa super "L'Aveuglé Dieu," Missae duodecim* (Paris, 1554); *Missa super "La Bataille"* (1532). MOTETS: Attaingnant is believed to have publ. a vol. of his motets in Paris in 1533; however, no copy of the vol. has been found. The motet *Congregati sunt* (1538) is extant. PSALMS AND CHANSONS SPIRITUELLES: *Premier livre contenant XXVIII pseaulmes de David...* for 4 Voices (Paris, 1549); *Premier livre contenant plusieurs chansons spirituelles, avec les lamentations de Jeremie* (Paris, 1556); *Proverbes de Salomon...* for 4 Voices (Paris, 1558); *Octante deux pseaumes de David...* for 4 Voices (Paris, 1559).

BIBL.: J. Levron, *C. J., musicien de la renaissance: Essai sur sa vie et ses amis* (Grenoble and Paris, 1948).—NS/LK/DM

Jane's Addiction, the band that defined "alternative rock" before it became a genre and a buzzword (f. 1986). MEMBERSHIP: Perry Farrell (real name, Bernstein), voc. (b. Queens, N.Y., March 29, 1959); Eric Avery, bs. (b. Los Angeles, April 25, 1965); David Navarro, gtr. (b. Santa Monica, Calif., June 6, 1967); Steven Perkins, drm. (b. Los Angeles, Sept. 13, 1967). Led by rock eccentric Perry Farrell (changed from Bernstein to become a living pun on the word "peripheral"), Jane's Addiction fused art rock with a Led-Zeppelin directness, punk with a sense of beauty and added a liberal does of Morrison-esque decadence. They channeled this into one of the most original sounds to come out of L.A. since The Doors.

Farrell's father worked in N.Y.C.'s diamond district, raising his children in Long Island after Farrell's mother committed suicide. Farrell went to Calif. to attend school, but had a nervous breakdown and quit. He stayed in Calif., however, and started entertaining as a dancer. In 1981, he started fronting the goth band Psi-Con. When their bassist left in 1985, he was introduced to Eric Avery and Dave Navarro. The band morphed into something different, with Farrell's heavy make-up, Day-Glo hair, and provocative clothes still working the goth side of the street, but his high tenor fused with the fiery guitar and bass sounded more like a sleazy, punkoid Led Zeppelin. The early, raw elements of this sound are captured on their 1987 Triple X Records debut. The album sold well, and a fierce bidding war ensued for their services on a major label. Warner Bros. won, and released "Nothing's Shocking" in 1988, a sculpture of naked Siamese twins with their hair on fire on the cover. The album sold modestly, and the band toured incessantly, opening for Iggy Pop, among others. With another controversial sculpture on the cover, this time Farrell as part of a menage à trois, the band's second album, *Ritual de lo Habitual*, came out in 1990. The album caused controversy before the shrink-wrap came off: some retailers objected to Farrell's cover art. Fueled by heavy MTV rotation and alternative radio play for the song "Been Caught Stealing," the album rose to #19 in the charts and sold platinum.

Rather than take the more conventional route of a summer shed tour, Farrell came up with the idea of a traveling rock and roll circus, complete with a midway. With piercing booths, links to the World Wide Web (a new concept for most in 1991) and Jim Rose's modern freak show, in addition to two stages of music, the Lollapalooza tour turned into one of the most successful shows of the summer. That fall, Farrell got busted at a Santa Monica Holiday Inn for possession of heroin and cocaine. Farrell broke up the band, which made a farewell tour. At their last American show in Hawaii, Farrell performed the entire second half of the show completely naked.

Jane's Addiction split in half. Navarro and Avery formed a hard rock noise band called Deconstruction while Farrell and Perkins formed the more artsy Porno for Pyros. Farrell continued the Lollapalooza tours as well. For seven years, they were fixtures of the summer touring circuit, spawning "answer" festivals like H.O.R.D.E and Lilith. Porno for Pyros played several dates on the 1992 tour as a surprise guest. Their eponymous first album came out to lukewarm reviews. With a quieter, more sophisticated sound than Jane's (though distinctive with Farrell's vocals), the group often teetered on the brink of pretentiousness, and occasionally fell over it. Nonetheless, their debut album went to #3 and gold.

The second Porno for Pyros album, *Good Gods Urge*, didn't do as well, and by late 1997 Farrell was talking with Navarro and Perkins about reviving Jane's. Since Avery didn't want to be involved, they called it Jane's Relapse. Navarro had joined the Red Hot Chili Peppers, and brought Peppers' bassist Flea along for the ride. In addition to a tour, they recorded a new version of "Kettle Whistle" a tune they had performed live but never released. That tune gave a title to a collection of miscellaneous unreleased tracks that came out in the wake of the tour.

Since the dissolution of the Relapse, Perkins has worked with a band called Banyon, Navarro continues with the Chili Peppers and Farrell has struck out on his own. His album *Rev*, like *Kettle Whistle*, had two new cuts (including a cover of "Whole Lotta Love") along with various Jane's and Porno for Pyros tunes. It makes a good starting point for appreciating his musical gestalt. He signed with Virgin Records and promised *The Diamond Jubilee* for early in the year 2000, a record inspired by "global dance culture."

DISC.: *Jane's Addiction* (1987); *Nothing's Shocking* (1988); *Ritual de lo Habitual* (1990); *Live and Rare* (1991); *Kettle Whistle* (1997). **PORNO FOR PYROS:** *Porno for Pyros* (1993); *Good God's Urge* (1996). **PERRY FARRELL SOLO:** *Rev* (1999). —HB

Janiewicz, Feliks, Polish violinist and composer; b. Vilnius, 1762; d. Edinburgh, May 21, 1848. He joined the Polish royal chapel as a violinist in 1777. In 1785 he went to Vienna, where he met Haydn and Mozart. Following a sojourn in Italy, he went to Paris and played at the Concert Spirituel in 1787; later he was a member of the chapel of the Duke of Orléans. In 1792 he made his London debut. In 1794 he played in Haydn's London concerts, and then toured England. In 1803 he founded his own music business in Liverpool. About 1815 he settled in Edinburgh, but he continued to give concerts until 1829. Among his works were five violin concertos, a Piano Concerto, chamber music, piano pieces, and songs.—LK/DM

Janigro, Antonio, esteemed Italian cellist, conductor, and pedagogue; b. Milan, Jan. 21, 1918; d. there, May 1, 1989. He enrolled at the Milan Cons. at 11, where he studied cello with Gilberto Crepax. He also received advice from Casals and was a student of Alexanian at the École Normale de Musique in Paris. In 1934 he made his formal recital debut in Pavia, and then pursued an active career as a cello virtuoso. From 1939 to 1953 he was prof. of cello at the Zagreb Cons. In 1948 he launched a 2nd career as a conductor in Zagreb, where he later conducted the Radio and Television Sym. Orch from 1954 to 1964. In 1954 he founded the chamber ensemble I Solisti di Zagreb, which he conducted on extensive tours until 1967. He also was conductor of the Angelicum Orch. in Milan from 1965 to 1967. From 1968 to 1971 he was conductor of the Saarland Radio Chamber Orch. in Saarbrücken. As a guest conductor, Janigro appeared widely in Europe and North America. He also continued throughout the years to tour as a cellist. From 1965 to 1974 he was prof. of the master class in cello at the Düsseldorf Cons. His repertoire as both a cellist and conductor was remarkably comprehensive, ranging from early music to contemporary scores.

BIBL.: B. Gavoty and R. Hauert, *A. J.* (Geneva, 1962). —NS/LK/DM

Janis (real name, **Yanks**, abbreviated from **Yankelevitch**), **Byron,** outstanding American pianist; b. McKeesport, Pa., March 24, 1928. He began to study piano with a local teacher, and at the age of seven, he was taken to N.Y., where he became a pupil of Adele Marcus. Progressing rapidly, he made his professional debut in 1943, playing Rachmaninoff's second Piano Concerto with the NBC Sym. Orch. He played it again with the Pittsburgh Sym. Orch. on Feb. 20, 1944, with the 13-year-old Lorin Maazel on the podium. Vladimir Horowitz happened to be present at the concert and told Janis that he would be willing to take him as a private pupil; these private lessons continued for several years. In 1948 he toured South America, the same year that he played in Carnegie Hall, N.Y., to critical acclaim. In 1952 he made a tour of Europe. In 1960 he made his first tour of Russia, under the auspices of the

U.S. State Dept.; played there again in 1962. During a visit to France in 1967, he discovered the autograph manuscript of two waltzes by Chopin, the G-flat major, op. 70, no. 1, and the E-flat major, op. 18; in 1973 he located two variants of these waltzes in the library of Yale Univ. In 1975 he made the film *Frédéric Chopin: A Voyage with Byron Janis*, which was produced by the Public Broadcasting Service. In 1953 he married June Dickinson Wright; they were divorced in 1965; in 1966 he married Maria Veronica Cooper, the daughter of the movie star Gary Cooper. At the climax of his career, Janis was stricken with crippling psoriatic arthritis in his hands and wrists. In spite of the attendant physical and emotional distress, he persevered in his international career. On Feb. 25, 1985, he gave a special concert at the White House in Washington, D.C., at which time his illness was publicly disclosed. He was named Ambassador for the Arts of the National Arthritis Foundation, and subsequently gave concerts on its behalf. —NS/LK/DM

Janitsch, Johann Gottlieb, Silesian composer and bass viol player; b. Schweidnitz, June 19, 1708; d. Berlin, c. 1763. He studied music in Breslau and law at the Univ. of Frankfurt an der Oder (1729–33). In 1733 he became secretary to Franz Wilhelm von Happe, a minister of state. In 1736 Crown Prince Friedrich (later Frederick the Great) made him a member of his personal orch. in Ruppin. He followed Friedrich to Rheinsberg, where he organized a series of famous concerts known as the "Friday Academies." In 1740 he was named "contraviolinist" in Frederick the Great's orch. in Berlin, and continued his "Friday Academies" there. His *Sonata da camera* for Flute, Oboe, Violin, Viola, Cello, and Harpsichord, entitled *Echo*, composed in 1757, is reprinted in *Collegium musicum*, LXVIII (Leipzig, 1938); another work in this genre was publ. in 1970. A collection of his compositions has been assembled from the available manuscript by Josef Marx of the McGinnis & Marx firm of music publishers in N.Y.—NS/LK/DM

Jankélévitch, Vladimir, French philosopher and writer on music; b. Bourges, Aug. 31, 1903; d. Paris, June 6, 1985. He was educated in Paris at the School of Oriental Languages and at the École Normale Supérieure; received a degree in philosophy in 1925 and the doctorat es lettres in 1933. He was a prof. of philosophy at the Institut de Prague (1927–33), then at the univs. of Lille (1933–39; 1945–52) and Toulouse (1939–45). He was a prof. of ethics and moral philosophy at the Sorbonne in Paris (1952–78). His writings on music reflect his philosophical bent and include *Gabriel Fauré et ses mélodies* (Paris, 1938; 2nd ed., aug., 1951, as *Gabriel Fauré, Ses mélodies, son esthétique*), *Maurice Ravel* (Paris, 1939; 2nd ed., aug., 1956, as *Ravel*; new ed., rev. and aug., 1995), *Debussy et le mystère* (Neuchâtel, 1949), *La Rhapsodie, verve et improvisation musicale* (Paris, 1955), *Le Nocturne: Fauré: Chopin et la nuit: Satie et le matin* (Paris, 1957), *La Musique et l'ineffable* (Paris, 1961; 2nd ed., 1983), *La Vie et la mort dans la musique de Debussy* (Neuchâtel, 1968), *Fauré et l'inexprimable* (Paris, 1974), *Debussy et le mystère de l'instant* (Paris, 1976), with B. Berlowitz, *Quelque part dans l'inachevé, Moussorgsky,*

Liszt, Bartók, Chopin... (Paris, 1978), *Liszt et la rhapsodie: Essai sur la virtuosité* (Paris, 1979), and *La Présence lointaine, Albéniz, Severac, Mompou* (Paris, 1983).

BIBL.: L. Jerphagnon, *J.* (Paris, 1969).—NS/LK/DM

Jankó, Paul von, Hungarian pianist and inventor; b. Totis, June 2, 1856; d. Constantinople, March 17, 1919. He studied at the Vienna Polytechnic and at the Vienna Cons. with Bruckner, Krenn, and H. Schmitt. He then studied mathematics as well as piano with Ehrlich at the Univ. of Berlin (1881–82), and then settled in Constantinople. His keyboard, invented in 1882, is a new departure in piano mechanics, though standing in distant relationship to the older "chromatic" keyboard advocated by the Chroma society. It has six rows of keys; each pair of rows consists of two mutually exclusive whole-tone scales; the fingering of all diatonic scales is alike; chromatic scales are played by striking alternative keys in any two adjoining rows. A full description of the keyboard was publ. in pamphlet form by its inventor (1886). The "Jankó keyboard" was espoused by quite a few enthusiastic souls, but like many similar "inventions" it soon lapsed into innocuous desuetude.

BIBL.: F. Boyes, *Das J.-Klavier* (Vienna, 1904); H. Munnich, *Materialen für die J.-Klaviatur* (1905).—NS/LK/DM

Janků, Hana, Czech soprano; b. Brno, Oct. 25, 1940; d. Vienna, April 28, 1995. She studied with Jaroslav Kvapil in Brno, making her operatic debut there as the Countess in Novák's *Lucerna* in 1959; later sang with the Prague National Theater Opera. She made her first appearance at Milan's La Scala in 1967 as Turandot; appeared regularly at the Deutsche Oper am Rhein in Düsseldorf and the Deutsche Oper in West Berlin (from 1970). In 1973 she sang Tosca at her Covent Garden debut in London. She also made guest appearances at the Vienna State Opera, the Bavarian State Opera in Munich, the Hamburg State Opera, the San Francisco Opera, and the Teatro Colón in Buenos Aires. In addition to the Czech repertory, she was also known for such roles as Gioconda, Elsa, Kundry, Desdemona, and Ariadne.—NS/LK/DM

Jannaconi, Giuseppe, Italian composer; b. Rome, 1741; d. there, March 16, 1816. A pupil of S. Rinaldini and G. Carpani, he succeeded Zingarelli in 1811 as maestro di cappella at St. Peter's. He scored many of Palestrina's works, aided by his friend Pisari. His pupils included Baini and Abbe Santini. Some of his music is in MS in the Santini Coll. in Munster; the collection once held 32 masses, 52 psalms, 70 motets, 57 offertories, antiphons, numerous canons for 4 to 64 Voices, 2 string quintets with Double Bass, etc. Other works are held in libraries and churches.—NS/LK/DM

Janowitz, Gundula, esteemed German soprano; b. Berlin, Aug. 2, 1937. She studied with Herbert Thöny at the Graz Cons. She made her formal operatic debut as Barbarina at the Vienna State Opera (1959), and later became one of its leading members; also sang at the

Bayreuth Festivals (1960–63) and the Salzburg Festivals (from 1963); was a member of the Frankfurt am Main Opera (1963–66); then joined the Deutsche Oper in West Berlin. She appeared at the Glyndebourne Festival (1964); sang at Karajan's Salzburg Easter Festivals (1967–68). She made her Metropolitan Opera debut in N.Y. as Sieglinde on Nov. 21, 1967. She was chosen to sing the role of Mozart's Countess at the reopening of the Paris Opéra in 1973; subsequently made her debut at London's Covent Garden as Donna Anna (1976). She was made an Austrian Kammersängerin in 1970. In 1990–91 she was director of the Graz- Steiermark Theater. Her other notable roles included Fiordiligi, Agathe, Eva, Aida, Elisabeth, Desdemona, and Ariadne. She was also well known as a concert and lieder artist. —NS/LK/DM

Janowka (Janovka), Thomas Balthasar (Tomáš Baltazar), Bohemian organist and musical lexicographer; b. Kuttenberg (baptized), Jan. 6, 1669; d. Prague (buried), June 13, 1741. He received a Jesuit education at the St. Wenceslas seminary in Prague, and continued his studies at the Charles Univ. there (M.Phil., 1689). He then was organist at Týn Church there from 1691 until his death. He compiled the *Clavis ad thesaurum magnae artis musicae* (Prague, 1701; 2nd ed., 1715, as *Clavis ad musicam*), which was the 2nd (after Tinctoris) dictionary of music ever publ. Only a few copies of the original ed. are extant, but it was reprinted in 1973. —NS/LK/DM

Janowski, Marek, Polish-born German conductor; b. Warsaw, Feb. 18, 1939. He was taken to Germany while young, where he studied mathematics and music at the Univ. of Cologne. He continued his musical studies in Vienna and at the Accademia Musicale Chigiana in Siena. He conducted sym. concerts in Italy, and then opera in Aachen and Cologne. Janowski subsequently held the post of first conductor at the Deutsche Oper am Rhein in Düsseldorf (1964–69) and at the Hamburg State Opera (1969–74), and also made guest appearances in Stuttgart, Cologne, and Munich. In 1969 he made his English debut conducting the visiting Cologne Opera in the British premiere of Henze's *Der junge Lord*. From 1973 to 1975 he was chief conductor in Freiburg im Breisgau, and from 1975 to 1979 Generalmusikdirektor in Dortmund. He made his U.S. debut conducting *Lohengrin* at the Chicago Lyric Opera in 1980. He was principal guest conductor (1980–83) and artistic advisor (1983–86) of the Royal Liverpool Phil., and was also chief conductor of the Nouvel Orch. Philharmonique de Radio France in Paris (from 1984) and of the Gürzenich Orch. in Cologne (1986–91). In 1999 he became artistic director of the Orchestre Philharmonique de Monte Carlo.—NS/LK/DM

Jansa, Leopold, Bohemian violinist and composer; b. Wildenschwert, March 23, 1795; d. Vienna, Jan. 24, 1875. He studied with Jan Jahoda and Jan Zizius in Wildenschwert, then studied law in Vienna, where Vorisek encouraged him to resume his musical training. He subsequently studied composition with Emanuel

Alois Förster. He was in the service of the Count of Braunschweig (1823–24), then was a violinist at the Vienna court chapel (1824). He was made music director and prof. of violin at the Univ. of Vienna (1834), and also played first violin in Schuppanzigh's quartet after its founder's death. He lost his Viennese positions in 1851 after he took part in a concert in London for the benefit of the Hungarian revolutionists. He remained in England until the amnesty of 1868, when he returned to Vienna and received a pension. He was greatly esteemed as a violinist, numbering among his works 4 violin concertos, 36 violin duets, 8 string quartets, 3 string trios, and some sacred music.—NS/LK/DM

Janson, Alfred, Norwegian composer and pianist; b. Oslo, March 10, 1937. His mother, a piano teacher, oversaw his early music instruction. He later received some instruction in composition from Finn Mortensen. In 1962 he made his debut as a pianist in Oslo, and subsequently was frequently engaged in jazz settings. After composing in a decidedly contemporary idiom, his works took on more tonal leanings. His interest in jazz and electronics also played a role in his path as a composer.

WORKS: DRAMATIC: *Mot solen* (Towards the Sun), ballet (1969); *Et Fjelleventyret* (A Mountain Adventure), opera (1970–73; Oslo, April 9, 1973); music for theater, films, and television. **ORCH.:** *Construction and Hymn* (1963); *Canon* for Chamber Orch. and 2 Tape Recorders (1965); *Prelude* for Violin and Orch. (1973–75); *Mellomspill* (1985); *National Anthem* (1988); *Fragment* for Cello and Orch. (1991); *Norwegian Dance With Thanks to Rikard Nordraak* for Cornet and Strings (1996). **CHAMBER:** String Quartet (1978); *Tarantella* for Chamber Ensemble (1989). **Piano:** *November 1962* (1962); *Senza pedales* (1992). **VOCAL:** *Lullaby* for Soprano and String Orch. (1963); *Theme* for Chorus, Organ, Percussion, and Piano (1966); *Nocturne* for Chorus, 2 Cellos, 2 Percussionists, and Harp, after Nietzsche (1967); *Valse triste* for Voice, Jazz Quintet, and Tape (1970); *3 Poems by Ebba Lindqvist* for Chorus (1975–80); *Hymn to Josef* for Voice and Piano (1977); *Errotikk og Pollitikk* for Chorus, Organ, and Rhythmbox (1983); *Wings* for Chorus and Jazz Ensemble (1983); *Sarabande* for 2 Choruses and Instruments (1995). **OTHER:** *Diaphony* for 4 Wind Band Groups, Bugle Corps, 4 Percussionists, Dancers/Actors/Musicians, and Tape (1990; in collaboration with K. Kolberg and R. Wallin); *Frieze of Life* for Cello, Chorus, and Orch. (1998).—NS/LK/DM

Janson, Jean-Baptiste-Aimé Joseph ("l'aîné"), French cellist, teacher, and composer; b. Valenciennes, c. 1742; d. Paris, Sept. 2, 1803. He first appeared at the Paris Concert Spirituel when he was 13. Following studies with Berteau, he continued to appear at the Concert Spirituel until 1767, often performing his own works. He also was in the service of the Prince of Conti and the Duke of Braunschweig, and made concert tours throughout Europe. In 1788 he was named surintendant de musique de Monsieur (i.e., to the brother of the King, later Louis XVIII). In 1795 he became a prof. of cello at the new Paris Cons. His output included three syms., nine cello concertos, and chamber pieces. His brother, Louis-Auguste-Joseph Janson ("le jeune") (b.

Valenciennes, July 8, 1749; d. Paris, c. 1815), was also a cellist and composer. He was active in Paris, where he appeared at the Concert Spirituel (1773–80) and later was a cellist in the Opéra orch. (1789–1815).—LK/DM

Jansons, Arvid
See **Yansons, Arvid**

Jansons, Mariss, prominent Latvian conductor, son of **Arvid Yansons**; b. Riga, Jan. 14, 1943. He studied at the Leningrad Cons., where he took courses in violin, viola, piano, and conducting. He profited from initial conducting studies with his father; then studied with Swarowsky in Vienna, Karajan in Salzburg, and Mravinsky in Leningrad. In 1971 he won second prize in the Karajan Competition in West Berlin; then made appearances with major orchs. and opera houses in the Soviet Union and Eastern Europe; also conducted in Western Europe and America. In 1979 he was named chief conductor of the Oslo Phil., with which he toured Europe; also toured the U.S. with it in 1987. He likewise was closely associated with the St. Petersburg Phil., and from 1992 he was principal guest conductor of the London Phil. In 1994 he took the Oslo Phil. on a major tour of Europe and North America in celebration of its 75th anniversary. In 1996–97 he was music director designate and from 1997 music director of the Pittsburgh Sym. Orch.—NS/LK/DM

Janssen, Herbert, noted German-born American baritone; b. Cologne, Sept. 22, 1892; d. N.Y., June 3, 1965. He studied in Cologne, and then with Oskar Daniel in Berlin, making his operatic debut in Schreker's *Der Schatzgräber* at the State Opera there (May 5, 1922), and remaining on its roster until 1938. He also made regular appearances at London's Covent Garden (1926–39) and at the Bayreuth Festivals (1930–37), where he excelled in such roles as Amfortas, the Dutchman, Gunther, Kurwenal, and Wolfram. He made his Metropolitan Opera debut as Wotan during the company's visit to Philadelphia (Jan. 24, 1939); his formal debut with the company followed in N.Y. as Wolfram (Jan. 28, 1939); he continued as a prominent member on its roster until 1952. He became a naturalized American citizen in 1946. In later years, he was active as a voice teacher. He was also well known for his portrayal of Kothner.—NS/LK/DM

Janssen, Werner, American conductor and composer; b. N.Y., June 1, 1899; d. Stony Brook, N.Y., Sept. 19, 1990. He studied with Clapp at Dartmouth Coll. (B.Mus., 1921) and with Converse, Friedheim, and Chadwick at the New England Cons. of Music in Boston. He then studied conducting with Weingartner in Basel (1920–21) and Scherchen in Strasbourg (1921–25). He won the Prix de Rome of the American Academy (1930) and studied orchestration with Respighi at the Accademia di Santa Cecilia in Rome (1930–33). In 1930 he made his debut as a conductor in Rome; he gave a concert of music by Sibelius in Helsinki in 1934 and was praised by Sibelius himself; received the Finnish Order of the White Rose. He made his

American debut with the N.Y. Phil. on Nov. 8, 1934, and served as conductor of the Baltimore Sym. Orch. (1937–39). He then went to Los Angeles, where he organized the Janssen Sym. Orch. (1940–52) and commissioned American composers to write special works. He was conductor of the Utah Sym. Orch. in Salt Lake City (1946–47), of the Portland (Ore.) Sym. Orch. (1947–49), and of the San Diego Phil. (1952–54). In 1937 he married the famous film actress Ann Harding; they were divorced in 1963. As a composer, Janssen cultivated the art of literal pictorialism. His most successful work of this nature was *New Year's Eve in New York* (Rochester, N.Y., May 9, 1929), a symphonic poem for Large Orch. and Jazz Instruments; the orch. players were instructed to shout at the end "Happy New Year!" Other works were *Obsequies of a Saxophone* for 6 Wind Instruments and a Snare Drum (Washington, D.C., Oct. 17, 1929), *Louisiana Suite* for Orch. (1930), *Dixie Fugue* (extracted from the *Louisiana Suite*; Rome, Nov. 27, 1932), *Foster Suite* for Orch., on Stephen Foster's tunes (1937), 2 string quartets (1934, 1935), Quintet for 10 Instruments (1968), piano music, many film scores, and popular songs.—NS/LK/DM

Janssens, Jean-François-Joseph, Belgian composer; b. Antwerp, Jan. 29, 1801; d. there, Feb. 3, 1835. He studied with his father and later with Le Sueur in Paris. Returning to Antwerp, he practiced law until the siege of 1832 and composed in his leisure hours. Going to Cologne, he lost his manuscript and other possessions in a fire on the night of his arrival; this misfortune so affected him that he became insane. He wrote four operas, two cantatas, two syms., five masses, a number of motets, anthems, and hymns, and songs.

BIBL.: Hendricks, *Simple histoire. Boutades biographiques à l'occasion du 25ᵉ anniversaire de la mort de J.-F.-J. J.* (Antwerp, 1860); E. van der Straeten, *J.-F.-J. J., Compositeur de musique* (Brussels, 1866; contains a list of his works).—NS/LK/DM

Jaques-Dalcroze, Emile, Swiss music educator and composer, creator of "Eurhythmics"; b. Vienna (of French parents), July 6, 1865; d. Geneva, July 1, 1950. In 1873 his parents moved to Geneva. Having completed his courses at the Univ. and at the Cons. there, he went to Vienna for further study under Fuchs and Bruckner. He then went to Paris, where he studied with Delibes and Fauré. He returned to Geneva as instructor of theory at the Cons. (1892). Since he laid special stress on rhythm, he insisted that all his pupils beat time with their hands, and this led him, step by step, to devise a series of movements affecting the entire body. Together with the French psychologist Edouard Claparide, he worked out a special terminology and reduced his practice to a regular system, which he called "Eurhythmics." When his application to have his method introduced as a regular course at the Cons. was refused, he resigned, and in 1910 established his own school at Hellerau, near Dresden. As a result of World War I, the school was closed in 1914; he then returned to Geneva and founded the Institut Jaques-Dalcroze. Interest in his system led to the opening of similar schools in London, Berlin, Vienna, Paris, N.Y., Chicago, and other cities.

Aside from his rhythmical innovations, he also commanded respect as a composer of marked originality and fecundity of invention. Many of his works show how thoroughly he was imbued with the spirit of Swiss folk music.

WRITINGS: *Le coeur chante: Impressions d'un musicien* (Geneva, 1900); *Vorschläge zur Reform des musikalischen Schulunterrichts* (Zürich, 1905); *La respiration et l'innervation musculaire* (Paris, 1906); *Méthode Jaques- Dalcroze* (Paris, 1906–17); *La rythmique* (Lausanne, 1916–17); *La portée musicale* (Lausanne, n.d.); *Introduction à l'étude de l'harmonie* (Geneva, n.d.); *Le rhythme, la musique et l'education* (Paris, 1919; 2nd ed., 1965; Eng. tr., 1921; 2nd ed., 1967); C. Cox, ed., *Eurhythmics, Art and Education* (London, 1930); *Rhythmics Movement* (London, 1931); *Métrique et rythmique* (Paris, 1937–38); *Souvenirs, notes et critiques* (Neuchâtel, 1942); *La musique et nous: Notes de notre double vie* (Geneva, 1945); *Notes bariolées* (Geneva, 1948).

WORKS: DRAMATIC: O p e r e t t a : *Riquet à la houppe* (1883). **O p é r a s C o m i q u e s :** *Onkel Dazumal* (Cologne, 1905; as *Le Bonhomme Jadis*, Paris, 1906); *Les jumeaux de Bergame* (Brussels, 1908). **C o m é d i e L y r i q u e :** *Sancho Pança* (Geneva, 1897). **OTHER:** Numerous orch. works, including 2 violin concertos (1902, 1911); chamber music; piano pieces; choruses; songs.

BIBL.: P. Boepple, *Der Rhythmus als Erziehungsmittle für das Leben und die Kunst: Sechs Vorträge von E. J.-D. zur Begründung seiner Methode der rhythmischen Gymnastik* (Basel, 1907); W. Dohrn, *Die Bildungsanstalt E. J.-D.* (Dresden, 1912); M. Sadler, *The Eurhythmics of J.-D.* (London, 1912; 3rd ed., rev., 1920); K. Storck, *E. J.- D.: Seine Stellung und Aufgabe in unserer Zeit* (Stuttgart, 1912); H. Brunet- Lecomte, *J.-D., sa vie, son oeuvre* (Geneva, 1950); F. Martin et al., *E. J.-D.: L'Homme, le compositeur, le créateur de la rhythmique* (Neuchâtel, 1965); M.-L. Bachmann, *Le Rhythmique J.-D.: Une éducation par la musique et pour la musique* (Neuchâtel, 1984; Eng. tr., 1991, as *D. Today: An Education Through and Into Music*); I. Spector, *Rhythm and Life: The Work of E. J.-D.* (Stuyvesant, N.Y., 1990).—NS/LK/DM

Járdányi, Pál, Hungarian composer, ethnomusicologist, and music critic; b. Budapest, Jan. 30, 1920; d. there, July 27, 1966. He studied piano and violin as a child. In 1938 he became a composition student of Kodály and Siklós at the Budapest Academy of Music (until 1942), and concurrently studied at the Univ. of Budapest (Ph.D., 1943, with the diss. *A kidei magyarság világi zenéje;* [The Secular Music of the Kide Magyars]; publ. in Kolozsvar, 1943). He was active as a music critic (1943–49) and as a teacher at the Budapest Academy of Music (1946–59); then was a member of the folk music research commission of the Hungarian Academy. He was awarded the Erkel Prize in 1952 and in 1954 received the Kossuth Prize for his *Vörösmarty Symphony.* His works follow the style of modern Hungarian music, based on national folk songs. He publ. the vol. *Magyar népdaltípusok* (Budapest, 1961).

WORKS: ORCH.: Sinfonietta (1940); *Divertimento concertante* (1942–49); *Dance Music* (1950); *Tisza mentén* (Along the Tisza), symphonic poem (1951); *Vörösmarty Symphony* (1953); *Rhapsody from Borsod* (1953); *Symphonic March* (1953); Harp Concerto (1959); *Vivente e moriente* (1963); Concertino for Violin and String Orch. (1964); *Székely rapszódia* (1965). **CHAMBER:** Violin duets (1934–37); 2 string quartets (1947; 1953–54); Flute Sonata (1952); *Fantasy and Variations on a Hungarian Folk Song*

for Wind Quintet (1955); Quartet for 3 Violins and Cello (1958); String Trio (1959). **P i a n o :** Rondo (1939); Sonata (1940); Sonata for 2 Pianos (1942); *Bulgarian Rhythm* for Piano Duet (1956).—NS/LK/DM

Jarecki, Henryk, Polish conductor and composer, father of **Tadeusz Jarecki;** b. Warsaw, Dec. 6, 1846; d. Lwow, Dec. 18, 1918. He studied composition with Moniuszko at the Warsaw Music Inst. After playing double bass in the orch. of the Wielki Theater there (1864–72), he served as conductor of the Polish Theater in Posen (1872–73). He then was deputy conductor (1873–74) and chief conductor and director (1874–1900) of the Lemberg Opera. He wrote nine operas, a Sym., masses, chamber music, and songs.—NS/LK/DM

Jarecki, Tadeusz, Polish conductor and composer, son of **Henryk Jarecki;** b. Lemberg, Dec. 31, 1888; d. N.Y., April 29, 1955. He studied with his father, and then with Niewiadomski in Lemberg. He subsequently went to Moscow, where he studied with Taneyev at the Cons., graduating in 1913; also studied with Jaques-Dalcroze in Geneva (1912–13). In 1917–18 he lived in the U.S., then returned to Poland and conducted opera in Stanislawow (1932–37). After a sojourn in Paris and London, he returned to the U.S. in 1946. In 1921 he married the American soprano Louise Llewellyn (b. N.Y., Dec. 10, 1889; d. there, March 6, 1954). He publ. the book *The Most Polish of Polish Composers: Frédéric Chopin 1810–1849* (N.Y., 1949). Among his compositions are five syms., *Chimère,* symphonic suite (1926), *Sinfonia breve* (Lwów, Jan. 15, 1932), three string quartets, and numerous songs.—NS/LK/DM

Jarnach, Philipp, French-born German composer and pedagogue of Catalonia-Flemish descent; b. Noisy, July 26, 1892; d. Bornsen, near Bergedorf, Dec. 17, 1982. He was a son of a Catalonian sculptor and a Flemish mother. He studied with Risler (piano) and Lavignac (theory) at the Paris Cons. (1912–14). At the outbreak of World War I, he went to Zürich, where he met Busoni and taught at the Cons. (1915–21); this meeting was a decisive influence on his musical development; he became an ardent disciple of Busoni, and after his death completed Busoni's last opera, *Doktor Faust,* which was produced in Jarnach's version in Dresden on May 21, 1925. During the years 1922–27, Jarnach wrote music criticism for Berlin's *Börsen-Kurier.* In 1931 he became a naturalized German citizen. From 1927 to 1949 he was prof. of composition at the Cologne Hochschule für Musik, and from 1949 to 1970 at the Hamburg Cons. Jarnach's music is determined by his devotion to Busoni's ideals; it is distinguished by impeccable craftsmanship, but it lacks individuality. He participated in the modern movement in Germany between the two world wars, and many of his works were performed at music festivals during that period. He wrote *Prolog zu einem Ritterspiel* for Orch. (1917), *Sinfonia brevis* (1923), *Musik mit Mozart* for Orch. (1935), String Quintet (1920), String Quartet (1924), *Musik zum Gedächtnis des Einsamen* for String Quartet (1952; also for Orch.), piano pieces, and songs.

BIBL.: E. Klussmann, *Der Künstler P. J. und das Gesetz* (Hamburg, 1952); S. Weiss, *Die Musik P. J.s* (Cologne, 1996). —NS/LK/DM

Järnefelt, (Edvard) Armas, distinguished Finnish-born Swedish conductor and composer; b. Vyborg, Aug. 14, 1869; d. Stockholm, June 23, 1958. He studied with Wegelius and Busoni at the Helsinki Cons. (1887–90), with Becker in Berlin (1890), and with Massenet in Paris (1893–94). He then was conductor of the Vyborg Municipal Orch. (1898–1903) and director of the Helsinki Music Inst. (1906–07). He became a conductor at the Royal Opera in Stockholm in 1907. He was named court conductor in 1910, the same year he became a naturalized Swedish citizen; later was chief conductor of the Royal Opera (1923–32). He subsequently was chief conductor of the Finnish National Opera (1932–36) and the Helsinki Phil. (1942–43). He married the soprano Maikki Pakarinen (b. Joensuu, Aug. 26, 1871; d. Turku, July 4, 1929) in 1893; they were divorced in 1908; in 1910 he married the soprano Liva Edström (b. Vänersborg, March 18, 1876; d. Stockholm, June 24, 1971). Jarnefelt was the brother-in-law of Sibelius. His compositions, which included the symphonic poem *Korsholma* (1894), a Symphonic Fantasy for Orch. (1895), and *Berceuse* for Small Orch. (1904), were written in the Finnish national style.—NS/LK/DM

Jaroch, Jiří, Czech composer; b. Smilkov, Sept. 23, 1920; d. Prague, Dec. 30, 1986. He studied composition with Řídký at the Prague Cons. (1940–46). He was a manager and producer for Prague's Czech Radio (from 1947). As a composer, he took a median line in Central European music, within the pragmatic limits of modernistic permissiveness.

WORKS: ORCH.: *Scherzo* (1947); *Burlesque* (1951); *Symphonic Dance* (1953); *Smuteční fantasie* (Mourning Fantasy; 1954); 4 syms.: No. 1 (1954–56), No. 2 (1958–60), No. 3, *Concertante*, for Violin and Orch. (1968–69), and No. 4 (1975); *Shakuntala*, suite (1957); *Stařec a moře* (The Old Man and the Sea), symphonic poem, after Ernest Hemingway (1961); *Summer Festival*, tarantella (1964); *Fantasy* for Viola and Orch. (1966). **CHAMBER:** 2 string quartets (1949–50; 1970); *Children's Suite* for Nonet (1952); Nonet No. 2 (1963); *Metamorphosis* for 12 Winds (1967–68); Sonata for Solo Violin (1973).—NS/LK/DM

Jaroff, Sergei, Russian choral conductor; b. Moscow, March 20, 1896; d. Lakewood, N.J., Oct. 5, 1985. He studied at the Academy for Church Singing at the Imperial Synod, and then became a Cossack officer. After the Revolution and the defeat of the White Army, he left Russia and established the Don Cossack Chorus, with which he made successful tours in Europe. He eventually settled in America. The repertoire of his chorus included popular Russian songs in artful arrangements, emphasizing dynamic contrasts, and also sacred works by Russian composers.—NS/LK/DM

Jarre, Maurice (Alexis), French composer; b. Lyons, Sept. 13, 1924. He studied electrical engineering before entering the Paris Cons. in 1943, where he was a student of La Presle (harmony) and Aubert (orchestra-tion). He also profited from advice from Honegger. After working with Radiodiffusion Française (1946–50), he served as director of music at the Théâtre National Populaire in Paris (1951–63). In 1955 and 1962 he won the Prix Italia. He became especially successful as a film composer, winning Academy Awards for *Lawrence of Arabia* (1963), *Dr. Zhivago* (1965), and *A Passage to India* (1985). Among his other film scores were *The Longest Day* (1962), *Ryan's Daughter* (1970), *Shogun* (1980), and *Dead Poets Society* (1990). His other compositions include *Armida*, opéra-ballet (1954), *Fâcheuse rencontre*, ballet (1958), *Loin de Rueil*, musical comedy (1961), *Notre-Dame de Paris*, ballet (1966), *Mouvements en relief* for Orch. (1953), *Winter War*, ballet (1987; new version, 1998), *Passacaille* in memory of Honegger for Orch. (Strasbourg, June 15, 1956), *Polyphonies concertantes* for Piano, Trumpet, Percussion, and Orch. (1959), and *Mobiles* for Violin and Orch. (Strasbourg, June 20, 1961). —NS/LK/DM

Jarreau, Al(vin), pop-jazz singer; b. Milwaukee, Wisc., March 12, 1940. His voice is somewhat reminiscent of Johnny Mathis or Al Green. In 1965 while working on his Masters degree in psychology at the Univ. of Iowa, he was singing at parties and performing with the Joe Abodeely Trio at the Tender Trap in Cedar Rapids. He sat in at Jim and Tony Sotos's Celebrity Club in nearby Moline, Ill., which led to a recording session with the Abodeely Trio in June at the Sotos's studio in Rock Island, Ill. (The session was later issued without Jarreau's permission and he had it withdrawn.) Even on this early session he is distinctive, fresh and vibrant. After graduation he went to San Francisco, where he worked as a rehabilitation counselor. Jarreau began singing in local clubs, quickly garnering a following with his vocalese technique, ability to imitate instruments, and warm, sometimes even ecstatic performance style. He gained particular attention with his album *We Got By* (1975). While touring Europe, he recorded in January and February 1977, becoming one of the most popular jazz singers of the day. Other successful albums of this period, include *Look to the Rainbow* (1977) and *All Fly Home* (1978).

Jarreau established a larger following by dabbling in soul, MoR and pop; he peaked in 1981 with the U.S. Top 20 single "We're in this Love Together" and the LP *Breakin' Away*. *Trouble in Paradise*, Jarreau's follow-up album, yielded "Mornin'," his biggest U.K. hit until his theme from television's *Moonlighting* made the Top Ten in 1987. His audience changed substantially in the mid-1980s when his songs and vocal style became less adventurous. His 1994 album, *Tenderness*, boasted an all-star line-up, including saxophonists Michael Brecker and David Sanborn, but unfortunately set them to work on distinctly un-swinging songs by The Beatles and Elton John. Jarreau sang jazz again on Jon Hendricks's version of Freddie the Freeloader" (1993).

DISC.: *1965* (1965); *We Got By* (1975); *Glow* (1976); *Look to the Rainbow* (1977); *All Fly Home* (1978); *This Time* (1980); *Breakin' Away* (1981); *Jarreau* (1983); *High Crime* (1984); *Live in London* (1985); *L Is for Lover* (1986); *Heart's Horizon* (1988); *Heaven and Earth* (1992); *Tenderness* (1994); *Best of Al Jarreau* (1996); *Tomorrow*

Today (2000). **JON HENDRICKS**: *Freddie Freeloader* (1990). —NS/MM/LP

Jarrett, Keith (Daniel),

highly original jazz pianist, composer; b. Allentown, Pa., May 8, 1945. Jarrett, a descendent of Hungarian and Scottish parents, was a child prodigy who studied piano from age three and presented a full recital and was composing and improvising at seven years-old. He wrote and copyrighted three pieces, "Snap Dragon" (July 1959), "Barbara" (July 1959, under the pseudonym Danny Jay), and "Jungle Suite" (July 1961). Ornette Coleman and Paul Bley were major early influences. Jarrett briefly attended Berklee Coll. of Music and led his own trio around Boston in the early 1960s. He moved to N.Y. in 1965 where he played and recorded with Art Blakey. He gained international acclaim with the influential Charles Lloyd Quartet (1966–69). In July 1970 he appeared with Gary Burton in a stunning set at Newport; it was never captured on record. He agreed to play electric instruments in order to tour with Miles Davis (1970–71) but has always steered away from them otherwise.

In 1975 he made a sensationally popular recording of solo improvisations, *The Koln Concert*, which established his reputation as a jazz virtuoso. By the mid-1980s he was playing short pieces and even standards in his solo concerts. A concert in Tokyo was billed as the *Last Concert*, but in the early 1990s he returned to playing live performances.

His debt to Ornette Coleman became explicit when he led a quartet with Coleman's former bandmates Dewey Redman and Charlie Haden, and Bley and Bill Evans's drummer Paul Motian (1974–78). (He had been recording and occasionally performing with Haden and Motian since the early 1970s.) In 1977 he made a recording with Jan Garbarek and a Scandinavian rhythm section; they toured and recorded live in N.Y. two years later. Since then he has usually performed jazz in solo or trio. Jarrett also composed pieces for classical ensembles, drawing on a rich variety of musical traditions. From the early 1980s he made appearances as a classical pianist, specializing in modern works and especially those of Bela Bartok; in 1987 he gave a particularly spirited performance in N.Y. of Lou Harrison's Piano Concerto, a performance he repeated in Tokyo which served as the basis for the critically acclaimed 1988 recording. He canceled concerts during 1997 and 1998 due to chronic fatigue syndrome. He is an unmistakably passionate, brilliant, virtuoso, open to all kinds of music making. He has recorded everything from standards with a trio to free improvisations to over-dubbing himself playing various wind and folk instruments to written classical pieces. Within the field he is highly controversial, largely because of his outspoken and often arrogant published statements on the true nature of music, which are usually critical of others.

DISC.: *Life Between the Exit Signs* (1967); *Restoration Ruin* (1968); *Somewhere Before* (1968); *With Gary Burton* (1968); *The Mourning of a Star* (1971); *Birth* (1971); *Expectations* (1971); *Facing You* (1971); *ECM Works* (1971); *Rutya and Daitya* (1972); *In the Light* (1973); *Fort Yawuh* (1973); *Solo Concerts: Bremen and Lausanne* (live; 1973); *Treasure Island* (1974); *Belonging* (1974); *Lumi-* *nessence* (1974); *Backhand* (1974); *Personal Mountains* (1974); *The Köln Concert* (live; 1975); *Death and the Flower* (1975); *Arbour Zena* (1975); *Mysteries* (1975); *Shades* (1975); *El Juicio* (1976); *The Survivor's Suite* (1976); *Eyes of the Heart* (1976); *Spheres* (1976); *Staircase* (1976); *Hymns / Spheres* (1976); *Ritual* (1977); *Silence* (1977); *Byablue* (1977); *Bop-Be* (1977); *My Song* (1977); *Nude Ants* (1979); *Invocations* (1979); *Sacred Hymns* (1980); *The Celestial Hawk* (1980); *Concerts* (live; 1981); *Changes* (1983); *Standards, Vol. 1* (1983); *Standards, Vol. 2* (1983); *Spirits 1 & 2* (1985); *Standards Live* (1985); *Still Live* (1986); *Keith Jarrett Concerts* (live; 1986); *Changeless* (1987); *Dark Intervals* (1988); *The Well Tempered Clavier: Book 1 (Bach)* (1988); *Works by Lou Harrison* (1989); *Standards in Norway* (1989); *The Cure* (live; 1990); *Paris Concert* (live; 1990); *Book of Ways* (1991); *Vienna Concert* (live; 1991); *Bye Bye Blackbird* (1991); *The Well Tempered Clavier: Book 2 (Bach)* (1991); *At the Deer Head Inn* (1992); *Bridge of Light* (1993); *La Scala* (live; 1995); *Keith Jarrett at the Blue Note* (live; 1995); *Tokyo '96* (live; 1998); *The Melody at Night, with You* (1999).—LP

Järvi, Neeme,

prominent Estonian conductor, father of **Paavo Järvi**; b. Tallinn, June 7, 1937. He graduated with degrees in percussion and choral conducting from the Tallinn Music School, then studied conducting with Mravinsky and Rabinovich at the Leningrad Cons. (1955–60). He pursued postgraduate studies in 1968, and in 1971 captured first prize in the Accademia di Santa Cecilia conducting competition in Rome. He was active in Tallinn as music director of the Estonian State Sym. Orch. (1960–80) and of the Estonian Opera Theater (1964–77). He subsequently served as principal guest conductor of the City of Birmingham Sym. Orch. in England (1981–84). In 1982 he became music director of the Göteborg Sym. Orch. in Sweden; also was principal conductor of the Scottish National Orch. in Glasgow (1984–88). In 1990 he became music director of the Detroit Sym. Orch. His guest conducting engagements have taken him to most of the principal music centers of the world. He has won particular notice in concert settings and on recordings for his efforts in championing such rarely performed composers as Berwald, Gade, Svendsen, Stenhammar, and Tubin.

BIBL.: U. Ott, ed., *Maestro: Intervjund N. J.ga* (Tallinn, 1997). —NS/LK/DM

Järvi, Paavo,

Estonian-born American conductor, son of **Neeme Järvi**; b. Tallinn, Dec. 30, 1962. He received training in percussion and conducting at the Tallinn School of Music. After his family emigrated to the U.S. in 1980, he studied conducting with Max Rudolf at the Curtis Inst. of Music in Philadelphia and with Leonard Bernstein at the Los Angeles Phil. Inst. He appeared as a guest conductor with major orchs. in Europe, North America, and the Far East. In 1994 he became chief conductor of the Malmö Sym. Orch. and in 1995 principal guest conductor of the Stockholm Phil., a position he also held with the City of Birmingham Sym. Orch. He became music director of the Cincinnati Sym. Orch. in 2001.—LK/DM

Jarzębski, Adam,

Polish violinist and composer; b. Warka, near Warsaw, date unknown; d. Warsaw, Dec. 1648. He became a violinist in the chapel of the Elector of Brandenburg in Berlin in 1612. After studying in Italy (1615–16), he went to Warsaw as a musician in the royal chapel. In his *Canzoni e concerti* (1627), a collection of 12 works for 2 instruments, 10 works for 3 instruments, and 5 works for 4 instruments, all with continuo, he made a valuable contribution to the enhancement of chamber music writing in central Europe.—LK/DM

Jaubert, Maurice, French composer; b. Nice, Jan. 3, 1900; d. in battle in Azerailles, Meurthe-et-Moselle, June 19, 1940. He studied piano and composition at the Nice Cons., receiving first prize for piano in 1916, and then studied harmony and counterpoint with Albert Groz in Paris (1923). He wrote the successful score for the film *Carnet de bal* (1937). His other works included *Suite française* for Orch. (St. Louis, Nov. 10, 1933), *Jeanne d'Arc*, symphonic poem (1937), and *Sonata a due* for Violin, Cello, and String Orch. (Boston, Dec. 27, 1946). —NS/LK/DM

Jausions, Dom Paul, French writer on church music; b. Rennes, Nov. 15, 1834; d. Vincennes, Ind., Sept. 9, 1870. He entered the order of St. Benedict at Solesmes in 1856, and under the direction of Dom Guéranger began to study Gregorian chant; continued his investigations with Dom Pothier, whose *Mélodies grégoriennes* are the result of their joint labors. In 1869 he was sent to the U.S. to collect data for a biography of Bruté de Rémut, bishop of Vincennes (an uncle of Dom Guéranger). His interpretation of the Gregorian melodies according to the tonic accent has become one of the guiding principles in the publications of the Benedictines of Solesmes. A complete list of his writings is found in the *Bibliographie des Bénédictins de la congrégation de France* (1907).—NS/LK/DM

Jay and the Americans, a group that crossed theatrical pomp, an operatic tenor, doo-wop and Leiber and Stoller rock and roll (f. 1961). **MEMBERSHIP:** John "Jay" Traynor, voc.; Kenny Vance (real name, Kenneth Rosenberg), voc. (b. Queens, N.Y., Dec. 9, 1943); Sandy Dean (real name, Yaguda), voc. (b. Jan. 31, 1940); Marty Sanders, voc. (b. Feb. 28, 1941); Howard Kane (real name, Kirchenbaum), voc. (b. June 6, 1942); Jay Black (real name, David Blatt), voc. (b. Nov. 2, 1938). Starting as a doo-wop group called the Harbor Lites at N.Y.U. in the late 1950s, they auditioned for Jerry Lieber and Mike Stoller, who signed them to United Artists. With Traynor as the lead vocalist, they first charted with "She Cried" which went to #5 in the spring of 1962. Traynor got into an argument with one of the other band members and left. David Blatt, a friend of Sanders, replaced him, taking on the mantle of Jay and becoming Jay Black. He started off with another Lieber and Stoller composition called "Only in America." Originally a track for The Drifters, they never released their version and Jay and the Americans recorded their vocals over The Drifters' track. It earned them a #25 hit in the fall of 1963. Their next hit was with Boyce and Hart's "Come a Little Bit Closer," given a semi-mariachi arrangement, which went to #3 in the fall of 1964. The show tunish "Let's Lock the Door (And Throw Away the Key)"

started off 1965 with a #11 hit. Five months later, they took on the semi-operatic "Cara Mia," a European hit for Montavani and vocalist David Whitfield 11 years earlier. They gave the old *South Pacific* chestnut "Some Enchanted Evening" a slightly beat upgrade, taking it to #13 that fall, and gave Neil Diamond his first hit as a songwriter with "Sunday and Me," which they took to #18 just around the holiday season in 1965. They had a minor hit in 1966 with "Crying" (#25) and then dropped off the charts for three years before resurfacing with a cover of The Drifters' "This Magic Moment," which they took to #6 and gold. Their final Top 40 hit came in early 1970 with a #19 cover of The Ronettes' "Walkin' in the Rain."

David Blatt continues to perform as Jay at oldies shows. Kenny Vance became a producer, and cut several albums including *32*, which featured an astounding version of "Looking for an Echo" that became a minor local hit in N.Y. Traynor became a road manager (one of his clients was Mountain) and publisher. He occasionally sings with a big band, mostly doing Sinatra. Two of the backing musicians from the later version of The Americans, known to the band by the nicknames of Speck and Manson, were Walter Becker and Donald Fagen, who became Steely Dan. They worked on a post-Americans soundtrack with Vance.

DISC.: *She Cried* (1962); *At the Cafe Wha?* (1963); *Livin' above Your Head* (1966); *Sunday and Me* (1966); *Try Some of This* (1967); *Sand of Time* (1969); *Wax Museum, Vol. 2* (1970); *Wax Museum, Vol.1* (1970); *N.Y. City Rock & Roll* (1971); *Capture the Moment* (1975); *Sands of Time/Wax Museum* (1993); *Live & Unreleased* (1995).—HB

Jeanneret, Albert, Swiss violinist, educator, and composer; b. La Chaux-de-Fonds, Feb. 7, 1886; d. Montreux, April 25, 1973. He studied violin with Andreas Moser at the Berlin Hochschule für Musik and with Henri Marteau at the Geneva Cons., graduating with the Premier Prix de Virtuosité (1909). He then joined the staff of the Jaques-Dalcroze Inst. of Eurhythmics in Hellerau. He went to Paris in 1919, where he founded a school of rhythmic gymnastics and a children's orch. In 1939 he returned to Switzerland and settled in Vevey, where he also led a children's orch. About the same time, he became a follower of the Moral Rearmament Movement. On July 21, 1968, he purportedly received (and subsequently publ.) a telepathic message from his brother, the architect Le Corbusier (Charles Édouard Jeanneret), who had died three years before, urging him to continue his pursuits of functional art. In accordance with these ideas, which he shared with his brother, Jeanneret wrote some 25 "symphonies enfantines" for children's orch., employing "bruits humanisés" produced by graduated bottles partially filled with water at different levels, metal pipes, wooden boxes, etc. He also composed a *Suite pittoresque* for three Violins and a number of choruses for Moral Rearmament meetings. —NS/LK/DM

Jeannin, Dom Jules Cécilien, French musicologist; b. Marseilles, Feb. 6, 1866; d. Hautecombe, Feb. 15, 1933. He studied in Marseilles, and later traveled extensively in Syria and Mesopotamia, gathering material for his collection *Mélodies liturgiques syriennes et chaldéennes* (Paris: Vol. I, 1925; Vol. II, 1928; III, not publ.). He also publ. *Études sur le rythme grégorien* (Lyons, 1926), *Sur l'importance de la tierce dans l'accompagnement grégorien* (Paris, 1926), *Rythme grégorien: Réponse à Dom Mocquereau* (Lyons, 1927), *Accent bref ou accent long en chant grégorien?* (Paris, 1929), *Nuove osservazioni sulla ritmica gregoriana* (Turin, 1930), and *Rapport de l'accent latin et du rythme musical au moyen âge* (Paris, 1931).—NS/LK/DM

Jebe, Halfdan, Norwegian violinist and composer; b. Trondheim, 1868?; d. Mexico City, Dec. 17, 1937. After training in Christiania and Leipzig, he studied with Joachim (violin) in Berlin and with Massenet (composition) in Paris. He played in the Colonne Orch. in Paris (1894–97), and then was conductor of the Central Theater in Christiania (1897–98). He became a close friend of Delius, and was the first to conduct his music in England (London, May 30, 1899). Following travels in Europe and the Far East (1901–03), he went to the Americas in 1906 and eventually settled in Mexico as a teacher at the Mérida Cons. His works reflect both his Norwegian heritage and his adopted country of Mexico. He wrote several operas, including *Vesle Kari Rud* (1904–05) and *Dignidad Maya* (1932–33), ballets, orch. pieces, much chamber music, piano pieces, and songs. —LK/DM

Jedlička, Dalibor, Czech bass-baritone; b. Svojanov, May 23, 1929. He received his training from Rudolf Vašek in Ostráva. In 1953 he made his operatic debut as Mumalal in Smetana's *The 2 Widows* in Opava. In 1957 he became a member of the National Theater in Prague, where his extensive repertoire included not only standard German, Italian, and French roles but various Czech roles. He toured with the company abroad, including its visit to Edinburgh in 1970 when he sang in the first British performance of Janáček's *The Excursions of Mr. Brouček*; also appeared as a guest artist in Amsterdam, Zürich, Warsaw, Venice, Bologna, and other cities. In 1993 he made his U.S. debut at the San Francisco Opera as Kolenaty in Janáček's *The Makropulos Affair.*—NS/LK/DM

Jeep (Jepp), Johannes (Johann), German organist and composer; b. Dransfeld, near Göttingen, 1581 or 1582; d. Hanau, Nov. 19, 1644. In his youth he sang in the Celle Hofkapelle, then studied in Nuremberg and Altdorf and later traveled in France and Italy. He became Kapellmeister and organist of the court of the Count of Hohenlohe in Weikersheim (1613), deputy organist at the Frankfurt am Main Cathedral (1635–36), and then municipal Kapellmeister of Frankfurt am Main (1637–40). After working in Hanau schools, he served as Kapellmeister of the chapel of Count Ernst of Hanau-Münzenberg and organist of the St. Marien Church (1642–44). He was best known for his collection of 34 songs publ. in his *Studentengärtlein*. He also composed over 100 hymns and Psalm settings.

WORKS (all publ. in Nuremberg unless otherwise given): **SACRED:** [62] *Geistliche Psalmen und Kirchengesäng...D. Martini Lutheri und anderer frommen Christen, wie sie in christlichen Kirchen...zu singen gebräuchlich* for 4 Voices (1607; not extant; 2nd ed., 1609); [114] *Geistliche Psalmen und Kirchengesänge wie sie...auff alle Fest-, Sonn- und Feyertäge bevorab zu Weikersheim-b...zu singen gebräuchlich* for 4 Voices (1629; 26th ed. in L. Schöberlein, *Schatz des Liturgischen Chor- und Gemeindegesang*, Göttingen, 1865–72); *Hymnus-hymenaeus, das ist Lieblich- und zierliches Hochzeit-Gesang ... auss dem 2. Capitel dess Hohenlieds Salomonis...auff italiänischen Madrigalen arth* for 5 Voices and Basso Continuo (Hanau, 1640); 6 lieder for 4 Voices publ. in L. Erhard's *Harmonisches Chor- und Figural Gesangbuch* (Frankfurt am Main, 1659). **SECULAR:** *Studentengärtleins erster Theil* [17] *neuer...weltlicher Liedlein* for 3 to 5 Voices (1605; 7th ed., 1626); *Ander Theil* [17] *...Liedlein* for 4 and 5 Voices (1614; 3rd ed., 1622); both vols. ed. by R. Gerber in *Das Erbe Deutscher Musik*, 1st series, XXIX (1958); [24] *Schöne ausserlesene...Tricinia* (1610; 8th ed. in D. Kuchemann, *Zeitschrift für Spielmusik*, XLVI, Celle, 1936). **BIBL.:** P. Bohm, *Christliche Leich-Predigt...dess...kunstreichen Herrn Johann Jeppen* (Hanua, 1645); W. Jeep, *Die Familie J., 1540–1940* (Bremen, 1940).—NS/LK/DM

Jefferson, Hilton (W.), jazz alto saxophonist; b. Danbury, Conn., July 30, 1903; d. N.Y., Nov. 14, 1968. He was a marvelous soloist whose fine work is unknown to most modern listeners, although it was showcased on well- recorded LPs around 1960. He first played banjo, joining Julian Arthur's Orch. at the Hay's Theatre, Philadelphia (summer 1925); he took a brief sabbatical to learn sax and then went with the band to N.Y. in early 1926. From May 1926–28, Jefferson worked primarily with Claude Hopkins. From the late 1920s he worked for brief periods with many bands in N.Y. He had a long on-and- off relationship with Chick Webb, working for him in periods from 1929–30, late 1934, fall 1936, and 1938. Jefferson also worked with King Oliver (1930), McKinney's Cotton Pickers (1931), Fletcher Henderson (October 1932–September 1934; December 1936–early 1938), and Claude Hopkins (1935–fall 1936; 1939), among others. He spent most of the 1940s working with Cab Calloway, staying with him until 1952 (except for two years beginning in 1949 when he worked as a house musician at a N.Y. club). He then spent eight months with Duke Ellington (summer 1952–February 1953), and did a tour with vocalist Pearl Bailey in fall 1953. Although he ostensibly left full-time music to work as a guard at a N.Y. bank following this tour, he continued to do regular gigs including several recording sessions, through the late 1950s. He was a regular member of Wally Edwards's Uptown Concert Band in the late 1950s, and also worked in Mercer Ellington's Big Band during this period.

DISC.: Henry "Red" Allen: *1929–1933* (1929); *1933–1935* (1933); *The Henry Allen Collection, Vol. 2: 1932–1935* (1992); *Swing Out* (1996); *Dynamic Trumpet* (2000). Louis Armstrong: *Highlights from His Decca Years* (1924); *The Best of the Decca Years, Vol. 2: The Composer* (1935); *Best of Decca Years, Vol. 2* (1935); *New & Revised Musical Autobiography, Vol. 2* (1947); *New & Revised Musical Autobiography, Vol. 3* (1947); *American Icon* (1947); *All Time Greatest Hits* (1949). Buster Bailey: *1924–1942* (1996); *Buster*

Bailey Story, 1926–1945 (1997). Cab Calloway: *Cab Calloway and Company* (1931); *On Film (1934–1950)* (1934). Count Basie and Chick Webb: *Count Basie & His Orchestra 1937/Chick Webb & His Orchestra 1936* (1995). Chuck Berry: *Blowing up a Breeze* (1995). Nappy Brown: *Night Time Is the Right Time* (2000).—JC/LP

Jefferson, Maceo B., jazz guitarist, banjo; b. Beaufort, S.C., c. 1898; d. Bridgeport, Conn., June 15, 1974. Jefferson did his first professional work with pianist Frank Clarke in Norfolk, Va. When he moved to N.Y., he played with Wilbur Sweatman (1923) and various other bands before sailing to Europe with the Plantation Orch. in 1926. Jefferson remained in Europe through the early 1930s, working with Arthur Briggs, including a period accompanying Louis Armstrong (1934). He returned to the U.S. briefly, then back to Europe (1937). While there, he was imprisoned by the Nazis and held at the Compiegne concentration camp until late 1944. Jefferson visited N.Y. in the 1960s, then moved to Bridgeport, Conn., where he devoted considerable time to composing.—JC/LP

Jefferson Airplane, 1960s San Francisco psychedelic/social-protest band that spawned Jefferson Starship, Hot Tuna, and other permutations. **MEMBERSHIP:** Marty Balin (real name, Martyn Jerel Buchwald), voc. (b. Cincinnati, Ohio, Jan. 30, 1943); Signe Tole, voc. (b. Seattle, Wash., Sept. 15, 1941); Paul Kantner, rhythm gtr., voc. (b. San Francisco, March 12, 1942); Jorma Kaukonen, lead gtr. (b. Washington, D.C., Dec. 23, 1940); John "Jack" Casady, bs. (b.Washington, D.C., April 13, 1944); and Alexander "Skip" Spence, drm. (b. Windsor, Ontario, Canada, April 18, 1946). Tole and Spence left in 1966, to be replaced by Grace Slick (real name, Wing) (b. Chicago, Oct. 30, 1939) and Spencer Dryden (b. N.Y., April 7, 1943). Later members included drummers Joe E. Covington and John Barbata, and electric violinist "Papa" John Creach (b. Beaver Falls, Penn., May 28, 1917; d. Los Angeles, Feb. 22, 1994). HOT TUNA: **MEMBERSHIP:** Jorma Kaukonen, gtr., and Jack Casady, bs. JEFFERSON STARSHIP: **MEMBERSHIP:** Paul Kantner, gtr., voc.; Grace Slick, voc.; "Papa" John Creach, vln.; David Freiberg, kybd., bs., voc. (b. Boston, Aug. 24, 1938); Craig Chaquico, gtr. (b. Sacramento, Calif., Sept. 26, 1954); Pete Sears, kybd., voc.; and John Barbata, drm. Marty Balin, voc., joined in 1975. By 1979, The Jefferson Starship comprised Mickey Thomas, voc. (b. Cairo, Ga., Dec. 3, 1949); Paul Kantner, David Freiberg, Craig Chaquico, Pete Sears, and drummer Aynsley Dunbar. STARSHIP: **MEMBERSHIP:** Grace Slick, Mickey Thomas, Craig Chaquico, Pete Sears, and drummer Donny Baldwin.

Marty Balin recorded for Challenge Records in 1962 and performed with the folk group The Town Criers in L.A. in 1964. In San Francisco in 1965, intent on reopening a closed club, Balin assembled a group of musicians, including guitarists Paul Kantner and Jorma Kaukonen and vocalist Signe Tole, to perform at the club. Paul Kantner had been living in L.A. with David Crosby and David Freiberg before returning to the Bay Area. Kaukonen, who had accompanied Janis Joplin locally around 1963, met Kantner in Santa Cruz. Kantner later

met Balin while performing on 12-string guitar and banjo at The Drinking Gourd. Named The Jefferson Airplane, the group debuted at The Matrix on Aug. 13, 1965, performing a blend of rock and folk music. The group's original rhythm section was soon replaced by Alexander "Skip" Spence, a rhythm guitarist converted to drummer, and bassist Jack Casady, a childhood friend of Kaukonen's. On Dec. 10, 1965, The Jefferson Airplane performed at the inaugural concert at the Fillmore Auditorium, run by Bill Graham.

Signed to RCA Records, thus becoming the first of many Bay Area bands to secure a major label recording contract, The Jefferson Airplane recorded their debut album in Hollywood. Dominated by Marty Balin's songwriting and smooth rich voice, *Jefferson Airplane Takes Off* featured the distinctive vocal harmonies of Balin, Kantner, and Signe Anderson. The modest-selling album contained an early version of the "hippie" anthem "Let's Get Together," and Balin's dynamic love song "It's No Secret." Spence left the group in May 1966 to form Moby Grape and Anderson (now married) left in October to have a baby. Drummer Spencer Dryden and vocalist Grace Slick were recruited as replacements. Grace Slick, a former model, had been a member of the recently dissolved Great Society, which had been performing locally since 1964. The Great Society also included Slick's drummer-husband Jerry Slick and his brother Darby Slick. Recordings made by The Great Society for Columbia were eventually issued in 1968, following the success of The Jefferson Airplane.

Surrealistic Pillow, Grace Slick's first album with The Jefferson Airplane, contained two songs she had performed with The Great Society, Darby Slick's "Somebody to Love" and her own "White Rabbit." Both became smash pop hits for The Jefferson Airplane in 1967 and the album effectively launched the "San Francisco sound." It also included two beautiful romantic ballads by Balin, "Comin' Back to Me" and "Today" (coauthored with Kantner), as well as Balin's frenetic "3/5 of a Mile in 10 Seconds" and surreal "Plastic Fantastic Lover." Slick's piercing soprano voice, more rough and powerful than Anderson's, complemented Balin's high sensual tenor, and her flamboyant stage demeanor soon made her the visual and musical focus of The Jefferson Airplane. The group performed at the Monterey International Pop Festival in June and Slick's presence soon began to overwhelm Balin, as evidenced by *After Bathing at Baxter's*. The album contained only one Balin song, "Young Girl Sunday Blues," coauthored with Kantner. Other inclusions were Kantner's "The Ballad of You and Me and Pooneil" (a moderate hit) and the mellow "Won't You Try"/"Saturday Afternoon," Slick's "Two Heads," and psychedelic ruminations by Casady and Kaukonen such as "Spare Chaynge."

Marty Balin contributed more to *Crown of Creation*, but most attention was directed at Kantner's title song, Slick's surreal "Lather" and vitriolic "Greasy Heart," and David Crosby's previously unrecorded "Triad." In the late summer of 1968, The Jefferson Airplane toured Europe for the first time, issuing the live set *Bless Its Pointed Little Head* in early 1969. They performed at the Woodstock Music and Art Fair in August and their next album, *Volunteers*, was again dominated by Slick and Kantner. Although the standout cut was Balin and Kantner's radical political title song, the album featured Kantner's anthemic "We Can Be Together" and David Crosby, Stephen Stills, and Paul Kantner's mystical "Wooden Ships," a forerunner of the science fiction fantasies that Kantner would soon explore.

A chaotic period of solo and joint projects and personnel changes soon engulfed The Jefferson Airplane. Jorma Kaukonen and Jack Casady had been performing together as the blues-oriented Hot Tuna since 1969, often opening shows for The Jefferson Airplane. The first of many Hot Tuna albums appeared in mid-1970. Spencer Dryden quit the parent group in early 1970 to help form The New Riders of the Purple Sage, to be replaced by surf drummer Joe E. Covington. In October, at the urging of Covington, black electric violinist "Papa" John Creach joined The Jefferson Airplane, subsequently performing and recording with both The Airplane and Hot Tuna. In December, *Blows Against the Empire* was released under the name of Paul Kantner and The Jefferson Starship. The first album nominated for the science fiction writers' Hugo award, the album was recorded by Kantner, Slick, Casady, and Covington, with the assistance of Jerry Garcia, David Crosby, Graham Nash, David Freiberg, and Jorma's brother Peter Kaukonen. It featured a number of Kantner science fiction songs, the most accessible of which, "Have You Seen the Stars Tonite," was cowritten by Crosby. Conspicuously absent was Marty Balin, although he was listed as coauthor of two songs.

By the spring of 1971, Marty Balin had left The Jefferson Airplane. By that August, the group had formed their own independent label, Grunt Records, with manufacturing and distribution handled by RCA. The label's first album release, *Bark*, credited to The Jefferson Airplane, yielded a minor hit with Covington's ditty "Pretty as You Feel." Other Grunt releases included "Papa" John Creach's first solo album and *Sunfighter*, credited to Paul Kantner and Grace Slick. The latter album was recorded with members of The Airplane plus Garcia, Nash, and Crosby, and two members of Grunt Records' Steelwind, leader Jack Traylor and 16-year-old guitarist Craig Chaquico. By the spring of 1972, Covington had left The Airplane, to be replaced by sessions veteran John Barbata. That summer, The Jefferson Airplane conducted a major American tour with Barbata and bassist-keyboardist-vocalist David Freiberg, a former member of Quicksilver Messenger Service. They played their last engagement at San Francisco's Winterland in September, and Jack Casady and Jorma Kaukonen subsequently left the group to pursue Hot Tuna full-time. Subsequent Jefferson Airplane releases included the live set *Thirty Seconds over Winterland* and *Early Flight*, recordings from 1965 to 1970 that included Signe Anderson's vocal on "High Flying Bird."

During 1973, Marty Balin performed and recorded with the Marin County bar band Bodacious D.F. Their overlooked RCA album featured Balin's fine lead vocal on leader Vic Smith's "Drivin' Me Crazy." By mid-1974, the parent group had added keyboardist-vocalist Peter

Sears and lead guitarist Craig Chaquico for *Dragonfly*, credited to The Jefferson Starship. The album contained Slick and Sears's "Hyperdrive" and yielded a minor hit with Slick and Kantner's "Ride the Tiger." However, the feature cut was Marty Balin and Paul Kantner's "Caroline," with lead vocals by Balin. Balin rejoined The Jefferson Starship for their spring 1975 tour and stayed with the group for more than three years. The group's best-selling album ever, *Red Octopus*, yielded a smash hit with "Miracles," composed and sung by Balin, and exposed the group to a new wide audience. The album also included the minor hit "Play on Love" and "Tumblin'," written by Balin, Freiberg, and Grateful Dead lyricist Robert Hunter. "Papa" John Creach left the group in August 1975, forming his own band in L.A. for an inauspicious recording career. He died there of natural causes on Feb. 22, 1994, at the age of 76.

The Jefferson Starship next recorded *Spitfire*, which contained "Cruisin'" (written by Charlie Hickox of Bodacious D.F.) and the major hit "With Your Love," co-written by Balin. The follow-up, *Earth*, produced four hit singles, including the near smashes "Count on Me" (written by Jesse Barish) and "Runaway."

During the summer of 1978, The Jefferson Starship toured Europe for the first time in ten years. However, Grace Slick suddenly became ill before a scheduled appearance in Frankfurt, Germany, in June, and the subsequent cancellation of the concert led to a riot in which virtually all of the group's equipment was destroyed. Following a poor performance two nights later in Hamburg, Slick returned to the U.S., not to perform with the group again until January 1981. In October 1978, drummer John Barbata was critically injured in a northern Calif. automobile accident. He was replaced by well-traveled English drummer Aynsley Dunbar.

The Jefferson Starship was reconstituted in 1979 with former Elvin Bishop vocalist Mickey Thomas ("Fooled Around and Fell in Love"), Kantner, Freiberg, Chaquico, Sears, and Dunbar. The hard-rock *Freedom at Point Zero* produced a major hit with "Jane" and the minor hit "Girl with the Hungry Eyes." After recording two solo albums, Grace Slick returned to The Jefferson Starship in 1981 for the major hits "Find Your Way Back," "Be My Lady," and "No Way Out" through 1984. In late 1979, Marty Balin directed the rock musical *Rock Justice* at the Old Waldorf in San Francisco, later issued as an album on EMI-America. Two years later, he scored a smash hit with "Hearts" and a major hit with "Atlanta Lady" from *Balin* on EMI-America. He recorded another solo album for the label in 1983.

In 1984, Paul Kantner departed The Jefferson Starship acrimoniously. Through lawsuits, he forced the group to rename itself simply Starship. Soliciting songs from outside writers and pursuing a blatantly commercial direction, The Starship regrouped with Slick, Thomas, Chaquico, Sears, and drummer Donny Baldwin, a member since replacing Aynsley Dunbar in October 1982. The new lineup's debut album *Knee Deep in the Hoopla*, yielded four hits, including the top hits "We Built This City," cowritten by Elton John associate Bernie Taupin, and "Sara." The group scored another top hit in 1987 with "Nothing's Gonna Stop Us Now," from the movie *Mannequin*, followed by the near-smash "It's Not Over ('Til It's Over)." Pete Sears left Starship in 1987, followed by Grace Slick in 1988, and Donny Baldwin in late 1989. Their last major hit came in 1989 with "It's Not Enough." Eventually reduced to Craig Chaquico and Mickey Thomas, the group finally disbanded in 1990. Since 1992, Thomas has been performing around the Lake Tahoe region with a set of musicians as Mickey Thomas's Starship. In the 1990s, Craig Chaquico recorded three instrumental acoustic albums for Higher Octave Music.

Jorma Kaukonen and Jack Casady persevered as Hot Tuna until 1978. Casady then performed and recorded with the San Francisco heavy-metal band SVT until 1982. He and Kaukonen reunited for a tour as Hot Tuna in 1983, ultimately regrouping in 1986 as an acoustic duo, recording *Pair a Dice Found* for Epic Records in 1990.

In 1985, Paul Kantner, Marty Balin, and Jack Casady formed a new group with guitarist Slick Aguilar and keyboardist Tim Gorman, among others. Debuting at the reopening of the Fillmore Auditorium in December, the Kantner-Balin-Casady Band recorded a sole album for Arista Records in 1986, scoring a minor hit with "It's Not You, It's Not Me." They completed a national tour in 1987, but disbanded in 1988. The following year, Kantner, Balin, and Casady regrouped with Grace Slick and Jorma Kaukonen as The Jefferson Airplane, recording one abysmal album and conducting one ill-received tour. Kantner and Gorman began performing as Paul Kantner's Wooden Ships in 1991 and later performed in Paul Kantner's Jefferson Starship with Jack Casady, "Papa" John Creach, drummer Prairie Prince, and female vocalist Darby Gould. Marty Balin joined the aggregation in 1993. In 1995, Intersound Records issued *Deep Space/Virgin Sky* for The Jefferson Starship, featuring Kantner, Casady, Balin, and Slick, while Monster-Sounds released Kantner's spoken word recollection of his years with The Jefferson Airplane, *A Guide through the Chaos (A Road to the Passion)*.

BIBL.: R. J. Gleason, *The J. A. and the San Francisco Sound* (N.Y., 1969); B. Rowes, *Grace Slick: The Biography* (Garden City, N.Y., 1980); G. Slick, with A. Cagan, *Somebody to Love? A Rock-and-Roll Memoir* (N.Y., 1998).

DISC.: GRACE SLICK AND THE GREAT SOCIETY: *Conspicuous Only in Its Absence* (1968); *How It Was—Collector's Item, Vol. 2* (1968); *Collector's Item* (1971); *Born to Be Burned* (1995). **THE JEFFERSON AIRPLANE:** *Jefferson Airplane Takes Off* (1966/1989); *Surrealistic Pillow* (1967); *After Bathing at Baxter's* (1967); *Crown of Creation* (1968); *Bless Its Pointed Little Head* (1969/1989); *Volunteers* (1969); *The Worst of The Jefferson Airplane* (1970); *Bark* (1971); *Long John Silver* (1972); *Thirty Seconds over Winterland* (1973); *Early Flight* (1974); *Flight Log (1966–1976)* (1977); *Time Machine* (1986); *2400 Fulton Street—An Anthology* (1987); *Jefferson Airplane* (1989); *The Jefferson Airplane Loves You* (1992); *The Best of The Jefferson Airplane* (1993); *Live at the Fillmore East* (1998). **PAUL KANTNER AND THE JEFFERSON STARSHIP:** *Blows Against the Empire* (1970). **PAUL KANTNER AND GRACE SLICK:** *Sunfighter* (1971). **PAUL KANTNER, GRACE SLICK AND DAVID FREIBERG:** *Baron von Tollbooth and the Chrome Nun* (1973). **"PAPA" JOHN CREACH:** *Papa John Creach* (1971); *Filthy* (1972); *Playing My Fiddle for You* (1974); *I'm*

the *Fiddle Man* (1975); *Rock Father* (1976); *The Cat and the Fiddle* (1977); *Inphasion* (1978). **JOE E. COVINGTON'S FAT FANDANGO:** *Your Heart Is My Heart* (1973). **HOT TUNA:** *Hot Tuna* (1970); *Electric Hot Tuna—Recorded Live ("First Pull Up, Then Pull Down")* (1971); *Burgers* (1972); *Phosphorescent Rat* (1974); *America's Choice* (1975); *Yellow Fever* (1975); *Hoppkorv* (1976); *Double Dose* (1978); *Final Vinyl* (1979); *Splashdown* (1986); *Historic Hot Tuna* (1985); *Keep on Truckin' and Other Hits* (1990); *Pair a Dice Found* (1990); *Live at Sweetwater* (1992); *In a Can* (boxed set; 1996); *Classic Hot Tuna Acoustic* (1996); *Classic Electric Hot Tuna* (1996); *Best* (1998); *Live at Sweetwater Two* (1992). **JORMA KAUKONEN WITH TOM HOBSON:** *Quah* (1974). **JORMA KAUKONEN:** *Jorma* (1979); *Too Hot to Handle* (1986); *Magic* (1985); *Magic Two* (1986); *Land of Heroes* (1995); *Too Many Years...* (1998). **JORMA KAUKONEN AND VITAL PARTS:** *Barbeque King* (1981). **SVT:** *No Regrets* (1981). **BODACIOUS D.F.:** *Bodacious D.F.* (1973). **MARTY BALIN:** *Rock Justice* (original cast; 1980); *Balin* (1981); *Lucky* (1983); *Balince—A Collection* (1990); *Freedom Flight* (1997). **THE KBC BAND (KANTNER, BALIN, CASADY):** *The KBC Band* (1986). **GRACE SLICK:** *Manhole* (1974); *Dreams* (1980); *Welcome to the Wrecking Ball* (1981); *Software* (1984). **THE JEFFERSON STARSHIP:** *Dragonfly* (1974); *Red Octopus* (1975); *Spitfire* (1976); *Earth* (1978); *Gold* (1979); *Freedom at Point Zero* (1979); *Modern Times* (1981); *Winds of Change* (1982); *Nuclear Furniture* (1984); *The Jefferson Starship at Their Best* (1993); *The Collection* (1992). **PAUL KANTNER:** *The Planet Earth Rock and Roll Orchestra* (1983); *A Guide Through the Chaos (A Road to the Passion)* (1996). **THE KBC BAND (KANTNER, BALIN, CASADY):** *The KBC Band* (1986). **JEFFERSON STARSHIP:** *Deep Space/Virgin Sky* (1995). **STARSHIP:** *Knee Deep in the Hoopla* (1985); *No Protection* (1987); *Love among the Cannibals* (1989); *Greatest Hits (Ten Years and Change)* (1991). **CRAIG CHAQUICO:** *Acoustic Highway* (1993); *Acoustic Planet* (1994); *A Thousand Pictures* (1996).—**BH**

Jeffreys, George, English organist and composer; b. c. 1610; d. Weldon, Northamptonshire, July 1, 1685. He was a member of the Chapel Royal, and was made joint organist (with John Wilson) to King Charles I in Oxford (1643). From 1646 he was steward to Sir Christopher (later Lord) Hatton at Kirkby, Northamptonshire. He composed both Latin and English sacred music, including about 70 Latin works and about 35 English anthems and devotional songs. He also wrote six string fantasias for three parts (1629), music for plays and masques (1631), dialogues, Italian songs, etc.

BIBL.: P. Aston, *G. J. and the English Baroque* (diss., Univ. of York, 1970; includes performing eds. of all of his instrumental pieces, theater music, and secular songs, as well as 30 sacred works).—**NS/LK/DM**

Jehannot de l'Escurel or **Jehan de Lescurel,** French composer; b. place and date unknown; d. (hanged) Paris, May 23, 1304. He was still a young cleric at Notre Dame when he was charged by the authorities for debauchery and hanged. His works number 34 pieces, including ballades, rondeaux, virelais, and diz-entés. They were ed. by N. Wilkins in Corpus Mensurabilis Musicae, XXX (1966).—**LK/DM**

Jehin, Léon, Belgian conductor; b. Spa, July 17, 1853; d. Monte Carlo, Feb. 14, 1928. He was trained in

Liège and Brussels. He conducted at the Théâtre de la Monnaie in Brussels (1882–93), the Paris Opéra (1889–93), at Covent Garden in London (1891–92), and in Monte Carlo. His wife was **(Marie-) Blanche Deschamps- Jehin.—NS/LK/DM**

Jehin-Prume (originally **Jehin**), **Frantz (Françcois),** celebrated Belgian-born Canadian violinist and composer; b. Spa, April 18, 1839; d. Montreal, May 29, 1899. As a child he studied with Servais and with his uncle, François Prume, whose name he added to his own. He then took lessons with Bériot and Fétis at the Brussels Cons., winning first prizes in violin and theory. At the age of 16, after completing advanced studies with Vieuxtemps and Wieniawski, he undertook a European tour, appearing with Anton and Nikolai Rubinstein, Jenny Lind, and other celebrities. He also formed a famous trio with Kontski and Monsigny. In 1863 he traveled through Mexico, then in the U.S. and Canada (1865). He married the singer Rosita del Vecchio (1848–81) in 1866, and then divided his time between Europe and America; eventually settled in Montreal. His most famous pupil was Eugène Ysaÿe. He wrote two violin concertos and many effective pieces for solo violin. He also oversaw the publ. of his memoirs as *Une Vie d'artiste* (Montreal, 1899).—**NS/LK/DM**

Jelich (Jeličić), Vincenz, Croatian composer; b. Fiume, 1596; d. Zabern, Alsace, c. 1636. He was a choirboy in Graz (1606–09), where he studied music with Matthia Ferrabosco, then was at the Jesuit Univ. (1610–15). In 1618 he went to Zabern, where he took holy orders. He then was active as vicar and then canon at Ste. Marie, as well as serving as a court musician. He publ. *Parnassia militia concertuum* for 1 to 4 Voices and Basso Continuo (organ) (Strasbourg, 1622), *Arion primus, sacrorum concertum* for 1, 2, and 4 Voices and Basso Continuo (organ) (Strasbourg, 1628), and *Arion secundus, psalmorum vespertinorum* for 4 Voices (Strasbourg, 1628), as well as a number of motets.—**NS/LK/DM**

Jelinek, Hanns, Austrian composer; b. Vienna, Dec. 5, 1901; d. there, Jan. 27, 1969. He studied harmony and counterpoint with Schoenberg (1918–19) and piano, harmony, and counterpoint with F. Schmidt (1920–22) at the Vienna Academy of Music. Jelinek's output ranged from light music to works utilizing serial techniques. He made a living by playing piano in bars, leading his own band, and composing for films under the name Hanns Elin. He became a lecturer (1955) and a prof. (1965) at the Vienna Academy of Music. He publ. the manual *Anleitung zur Zwölftonkomposition* (2 vols., Vienna, 1952 and 1958; 2nd ed., 1967).

WORKS: DRAMATIC: Operetta: *Bubi Caligula* (1947). ORCH.: *Praeludium, Passacaglia und Fuge* for Flute, Clarinet, Bassoon, Horn, and Strings (1922; Wuppertal, March 12, 1954); 6 syms.: No. 1 (1926–30; Breslau, June 13, 1932; rev., 1940 and 1945–46), No. 2, *Sinfonia ritmica*, for Jazz Band and Orch. (1929; Vienna, March 14, 1931; rev. 1949), No. 3, *Heitere Symphonie*, for Brass and Percussion (1930–31; Vienna, June 20, 1932), No. 4, *Sinfonia concertante*, for String Quartet and Orch. (1931; rev. 1953; Vienna, May 2, 1958), No. 5, *Symphonie brevis*

(1948–50; Vienna, Dec. 19, 1950), and No. 6, *Sinfonia concertante* (Venice, Sept. 15, 1953; rev. 1957); *Sonata ritmica* for Jazz Band and Orch. (1928; rev. 1960; Vienna, Nov. 26, 1960); *Rather Fast*, rondo for Jazz Band and Orch. (1929); Suite for Strings (1931); Concertino for String Quartet and String Orch. (1951); *Phantasie* for Clarinet, Piano, and Orch. (1951; Salzburg, June 21, 1952); *Preludio solenne* (1956); *Rai buba*, étude for Piano and Orch. (1956–61); *Perergon* for Small Orch. (1957). CHAMBER: *6 Aphorismen* for 2 Clarinets and Bassoon (1923–30); Suite for Cello (1930); 2 string quartets (1931, 1935); *Das Zwölftonwerk*, a collection of 9 individually titled chamber pieces in 2 series: *Series 1* of 6 works for Piano (1947–49) and *Series 2* of 3 works for Various Instruments (1950–52); *3 Blue Sketches* for 9 Jazz Soloists (1956); Sonata for Solo Violin (1956); *Ollapotrida*, suite for Flute and Guitar (1957); *2 Blue O's* for 7 Jazz Performers (1959); *10 Zahme Xenien* for Violin and Piano (1960). Piano: *4 Structuren* (1952); *Zwölftonfibel* (1953–54). VOCAL: *Prometheus* for Baritone and Orch., after Goethe (1936); *Die Heimkehr*, radio cantata for Soloists, Chorus, Orch., and Tape (1954); *Unterwegs*, chamber cantata for Soprano, Vibraphone, and Double Bass (1957); *Begegnung*, dance scene for Chorus and Orch. (1965); songs.—**NS/LK/DM**

Jellinek, George, Hungarian-born American broadcaster, writer on music, and teacher; b. Budapest, Dec. 22, 1919. After violin studies in Hungary (1925–37), he settled in the U.S. in 1941 and became a naturalized American citizen in 1943. He was active in N.Y., where he was director of program services for SESAC, Inc. (1955–64) and recording director for Muzak, Inc. (1964–68). From 1968 to 1984 he was music director of WQXR radio, where he was host of the popular nationally syndicated program "The Vocal Scene." He was an adjunct asst. prof. of music at Long Island Univ. from 1976 to 1991. His articles appeared in various periodicals, and he also was a contributing ed. of *Stereo Review* (1958–74) and *Ovation* (1974–88) magazines. He publ. the books *Callas: Portrait of a Prima Donna* (N.Y., 1960; 2nd ed., 1986) and *History Through the Opera Glass: From the Rise of Caesar to the Fall of Napoleon* (White Plains, N.Y., 1994). He was the librettist for Zador's operas *The Magic Chair* (1966) and *The Scarlet Mill* (1968). Among his many honors were an honorary doctorate in music from Long Island Univ. in 1984 and a Grammy Award for his literary contribution to *The Heifetz Collection* CD recordings (1995).—**NS/LK/DM**

Jélyotte, Pierre de, French tenor and composer; b. Lasseube, April 13, 1713; d. Oloron, Oct. 12, 1797. He received training in harpsichord, cello, guitar, voice, and composition in Toulouse. In 1733 he made his operatic debut in Collin de Blamont's *Les fêtes grecques et romaines* at the Paris Opéra, where he was a leading singer from 1738 until his retirement in 1765. He was widely admired for his leading haute-contre roles in Rameau's operas, which displayed his brilliant vocal range (up to d"). He also appeared at the court, and in 1745 was named maître de guitare to the King. He likewise served as a cellist to Madame de Pompadour. Among his compositions was the comédie-ballet *Zéliska* (1746), as well as several vocal pieces.—**NS/LK/DM**

Jemnitz, Sándor (Alexander), Hungarian conductor, composer, and music critic; b. Budapest, Aug. 9,

1890; d. Balatonföldvár, Aug. 8, 1963. He studied with Koessler at the Budapest Royal Academy of Music (1906–08), and then briefly with Nikisch (conducting), Reger (composition), Straube (organ), and Sitt (violin) at the Leipzig Cons. After conducting in various German opera houses (1911–13), he studied with Schoenberg in Berlin. He returned to Budapest (1916) and was music critic of *Népszava* (1924–50); subsequently taught at the Budapest Cons. (from 1951). He publ. monographs on Mendelssohn (1958), Schumann (1958), Beethoven (1960), Chopin (1960), and Mozart (1961). As a composer, he followed the median line of Middle European modernism of the period between the two world wars, representing a curious compromise between the intricate contrapuntal idiom of Reger and the radical language of atonality modeled after Schoenberg's early works. He wrote mostly instrumental music.

WORKS: DRAMATIC: Ballet: *Divertimento* (1921; Budapest, April 23, 1947). **ORCH.:** Concerto for Chamber Orch. (1931); *Prelude and Fugue* (1933); *7 Miniatures* (1948); *Overture for a Peace Festival* (1951); Concerto for Strings (1954); *Fantasy* (1956). **CHAMBER:** 3 violin sonatas (1921, 1923, 1925); Cello Sonata (1922); 3 Sonatas for Solo Violin (1922, 1932, 1938); Flute Trio (1924); 2 wind trios (1925); Trumpet Quartet (1925); 2 string trios (1925, 1929); Flute Sonata (1931); *Partita* for 2 Violins (1932); Guitar Trio (1932); Sonata for Solo Cello (1933); Sonata for Solo Harp (1933); Duet Sonata for Saxophone and Banjo (1934); Sonata for Solo Double Bass (1935); Sonata for Solo Trumpet (1938); Sonata for Solo Flute (1941); Sonata for Solo Viola (1941); String Quartet (1950); 2 suites for Violin and Piano (1952, 1953); Trio for Flute, Oboe, and Clarinet (1958). **KEYBOARD: Piano:** 5 sonatas (1914, 1927, 1929, 1933, 1954); *3 Pieces* (1915); 2 sonatinas (1919); *17 Bagatelles* (1919); *Recueil* (1938–45); *8 Pieces* (1951). **Organ:** 3 sonatas (1941, 1959, 1959). **VOCAL:** Songs.—NS/LK/DM

Jencks, Gardner, American pianist and composer; b. N.Y., Jan. 7, 1907; d. Cambridge, Mass., Aug. 6, 1989. He studied piano with Heinrich Gebhard in Boston (1923) and with Josef and Rosina Lhévinne in N.Y. (from 1927); later took courses at the Diller-Quaile School (1930–34); concurrently took private lessons in composition with Franklin Robinson, and then with Gustav Strube at the Peabody Cons. of Music in Baltimore (artist's diploma, 1940). On Feb. 24, 1941, he made his debut in N.Y. as a pianist; while pursuing his career, he also studied composition with Goeb and Cowell at Columbia Univ. (1956). He wrote numerous works for piano. His idiom of composition was derived from the considerations of relative sonorous masses in chordal structures and interactive rhythmic patterns; the general effect may be likened to neo-Classical concepts; tonality and atonality are applied without prejudice in his melodic lines, as are concords and discords in contrapuntal combinations.—NS/LK/DM

Jeney, Zoltán, Hungarian composer; b. Szolnok, March 4, 1943. He was a student of Pongrácz in Debrecen, Farkas at the Budapest Academy of Music (1961–66), and Petrassi at the Accademia di Santa Cecilia in Rome (1967–68). In 1970 he helped to organize the Budapest New Music Studio, where he was active as a composer, keyboard player, and percussionist. In 1986

he joined the faculty of the Academy of Music. In 1988–89 he was in Berlin under the sponsorship of the Deutscher Akademischer Austauschdienst. Among his honors are the Erkel Prize (1982) and the Bartók-Pásztory Award (1988).

WORKS: ORCH.: *Laude* (1967–77); *Rimembranze* (1968); *Alef—Hommage à Schoenberg* (1971–72); *Quemadmodum* for Strings (1975); *Something Round* for 25 Strings (1975); *Sostenuto* (1979); *Something Like* for 25 Strings (1980). **CHAMBER:** *Soliloquium No. 1* for Flute (1967) and *No. 2* for Violin (1974–78); *Wei wu wei* for Chamber Ensemble (1968); *Round* for Piano, Harp, and Harpsichord (1972); *Movements of the Eye IV* for 1 or 3 Chamber Ensembles (1973); *4 Quartet* for 1 or More String Quartets (1973); *Orpheus's Garden* for 8 Instruments (1974); *A Leaf Falls—Brackets to e.e. cummings* for Violin or Viola, Contact Microphone, and Prepared Piano (1975); *Tropi* for 2 Trumpets (1975); *Arthur Rimbaud in the Desert* for Optional Keyboard Instruments (1976); *Complements* for Cimbalom (1976); *2 Mushrooms* for Chamber Ensemble (1977); *Impho 102/6* for 6 Antique Cymbals (1978); *Pontpoint* for 6 Percussionists (1978); *Being-Time I* (1979), *II* (1979), *V* (1985), *VI* (1985), and *IV* (1991) for 4 Optional Players; *Interlude with Sounds* for 1 Player (1979); *The End of a Game* for 6 Instruments (1980); *Arupa* for 6 to 8 Chimes and Drum (1981); *Something Found* for Piano, Harmonium or Organ, and Optional Chamber Ensemble (1981); *Etwas getragen* for String Quartet (1988); *Ouverture Étrusque* for Oboe, Synthesizer or Tape, and Antique Cymbals (1989); *Self-Quotations* for 5 Instruments (1991); *Fungi-Epitaphium John Cage* for Alto Flute (1992). **KEYBOARD: Piano:** *5 Pieces* (1962); *Soliloquium No. 3* (1980); *Endgame* (1973); *Movements of the Eye I* (1973), *II* for 2 Pianos (1973), and *III* for 3 Pianos (1973); *Desert Plants* for 2 Prepared or Unprepared Pianos or 2 Pianos and Tape (1975); *Something Lost* for Prepared Piano (1975); *Transcriptions Automatiques* (1975); *Kalah* (1983); *Meditazione su una tema di Goffredo Petrassi* (1984); *Ricercare* (1992); *A Mounderin Tongue in a Pounderin Jowl* (1993). **Organ:** *Soliloquium No. 4* (1980); *OM* for 2 Electric Organs or Electric Organ and Tape (1979); *Ricercare in variazioni sopra il motto dal Rito Funebre* (1988). **VOCAL:** *Omaggio* for Soprano and Orch. (1966); *12 Songs* for Soprano, Violin, and Piano (1975–83); *Monody (in memoriam Igor Stravinsky)* for Soprano and Piano (1977); *To Apollon*, cantata for Chamber Chorus, English Horn, Organ, and 12 Antique Cymbals (1978); *The Eternal Corridor* for Chorus and Optional Chamber Ensemble (1983); *Spaziosa calma...* for Woman's Voice and Chamber Ensemble (1984; rev. 1987); *El Silencio* for Woman's Voice and String Quartet (1986); *Movements from the Funeral Rite* for Soloists, Chorus, and Chamber Orch. (1987); *Psalmus 5* for Woman's Voice and Chamber Ensemble (1989), *102* for Chorus and 5 Instruments (1989), and *50* for Woman's Voice and String Quartet (1991); *Funeral Rite* for Soloists, Chorus, and Orch. (1994). **OTHER:** Electronic, live electronic, and tape pieces; film music; collaborative scores.—NS/LK/DM

Jenkins, David, Welsh choral conductor, composer, and editor; b. Trecastell, Breconshire, Dec. 30, 1848; d. Aberystwyth, Dec. 10, 1915. He studied with Joseph Parry at Univ. Coll. of Wales, Aberystwyth (1874–78), and was awarded the Mus.B. externally by the Univ. of Cambridge (1878). He was made instructor (1882), lecturer (1899), and prof. (1910) at Univ. Coll. of Wales, and was ed. of the music periodical *Y Cerddor*

(1889–1915). He was widely known as a choral conductor in Welsh communities in his homeland and in the U.S. He composed many choral works and hymn tunes.—NS/LK/DM

Jenkins, Freddie, jazz trumpeter; b. N.Y., Oct. 10, 1906; d. Tex., 1978. Freddie Jenkins switched to playing left-handed while in his early teens. He was taught by Lt. Eugene Mikell and played regularly in the 369th Regiment Cadet Band. He went to Wilberforce Univ. in the early 1920s, played briefly with Edgar Hayes's Blue Grass Buddies, then regularly with Horace Henderson's Collegians from 1924–28. Jenkins joined Duke Ellington in 1928 and remained with him until he came down with a severe illness in late 1934 (he occasionally doubled on E-flat cornet during 1934). He began playing again in 1935 at Adrian's Tap Room. Beginning in January 1936, Jenkins spent a brief time conducting the Luis Russell Band at Connie's Inn (in between Louis Armstrong's featured numbers), then became part-owner of the Brittwood Club, N.Y. By March 1937 he had recovered sufficiently to play in The Cotton Club Floor Show with Duke Ellington.

Late in 1938 he suffered a recurrence of severe lung ailment and spent many months in hospital, never returning to professional playing, although he was active as a songwriter, press agent, and musical adviser in Wash., N.Y., and Calif. throughout the 1940s. During the 1960s he worked in Tex. as a disc jockey and press correspondent.—JC/LP

Jenkins, George, drummer; b. Norfolk, Va., July 25, 1917; d. San Francisco, May 10, 1967; brother of vocalist Bea Foote. He played with Lionel Hampton from late 1941 until 1943, briefly touring with Lucky Millinder, then Buddy Johnson (1944–45). Jenkins rejoined Lionel Hampton from late 1945–summer 1946, then worked with Charlie Barnet until leading his own band in Detroit. In the late 1940s, he worked regularly at The Metropole, N.Y. (briefly with the Louis Armstrong All-Stars in spring 1949). He moved to Calif. and played with Benny Carter in 1951. Jenkins led his own small bands and gigged with many others. During the early 1960s he mainly led trios in Calif. and Las Vegas, returning briefly to The Metropole.—JC/LP

Jenkins, Gordon (Hill), American arranger, conductor, and songwriter; b. Webster Groves, Mo., May 12, 1910; d. Malibu, Calif., May 1, 1984. Jenkins achieved success as a songwriter, penning such hits as "P.S. I Love You" and "San Fernando Valley," and as a recording artist with "Maybe You'll Be There" and "My Foolish Heart." But he was best known for his work as an arranger and conductor for singers, including the Weavers, with whom he scored the hit "Goodnight Irene," and, from the 1950s to the 1980s, with Frank Sinatra.

The son of an organist, Jenkins occasionally substituted for his father at a movie theater in Chicago. At 15 he won a banjo-playing contest in St. Louis and became a protégé of Cliff Edwards. After playing piano in jazz bands in speakeasies, he was hired as a staff musician

and arranger by a St. Louis radio station. In the early 1930s he joined the orchestra of Isham Jones as a pianist and arranger. His first notable composition was "Blue Prelude" (music and lyrics by Jenkins and Joe Bishop), which was recorded by Bing Crosby, who scored a hit with it in July 1933. Then came two hits in 1934 for which Jenkins wrote music to lyrics by Johnny Mercer, "You Have Taken My Heart," by Glen Gray and the Casa Loma Orch. in February, and "P.S. I Love You," by Rudy Vallée in November. In 1935, Benny Goodman adopted Jenkins's mournful "Goodbye" as his closing theme.

Isham Jones disbanded in 1936 and his orchestra was reorganized by Woody Herman, who adopted "Blue Prelude" as his theme; Jenkins wrote arrangements for the new band. He wrote the orchestrations and served as the musical director of the Broadway revue *The Show Is On* (N.Y., Dec. 25, 1936). In 1938 he moved to Calif. and took a job with Paramount Pictures. Woody Herman reached the hit parade with "Blue Evening" (music and lyrics by Jenkins and Joe Bishop) in July 1939. The same year, Jenkins became musical director for NBC in Hollywood, conducting radio orchestras for a variety of shows through 1948.

Jenkins joined Capitol Records upon its formation in 1942 as musical director and as a recording artist, scoring one of the label's first chart hits with "He Wears a Pair of Silver Wings" (music by Michael Carr, lyrics by Eric Maschwitz) in August. In April 1944, Bing Crosby hit #1 with Jenkins's composition "San Fernando Valley." In 1945, Jenkins moved to Decca Records as staff conductor, and the label released the first version of his "musical narrative" *Manhattan Tower* as an album of 78s. His recording of "Maybe You'll Be There" (music by Rube Bloom, lyrics by Sammy Gallop) peaked in the Top Ten in October 1948 and sold a million copies. At the same time he was conducting the orchestras backing such Decca stars as Dick Haymes and the Andrews Sisters on their hits.

Jenkins wrote his only Broadway score for the revue *Along Fifth Avenue* (N.Y., Jan. 13, 1949), which ran 180 performances. But he enjoyed greater success during the year as a recording artist, reaching the Top Ten with "Again" (music by Lionel Newman, lyrics by Dorcas Cochrane) in May and "Don't Cry Joe (Let Her Go, Let Her Go, Let Her Go)" (music and lyrics by Joe Marsala) in November, and making personal appearances at such venues as the Capitol Theatre in N.Y. He topped the charts with "My Foolish Heart" (music by Victor Young, lyrics by Ned Washington) in June 1950 and reached the Top Ten with "Bewitched" (music by Richard Rodgers, lyrics by Lorenz Hart) in July.

Jenkins had seen The Weavers performing at the Village Vanguard in N.Y. earlier in 1950 and persuaded Decca to sign them. The folk group's debut single, "Goodnight Irene" (music and lyrics by Lead Belly, adapted by John Lomax)/"Tzena, Tzena, Tzena" (an Israeli folk song composed by Issachar Miron [Michrovsky], rewritten by Julius Grossman, arranged by Spencer Ross, and with English lyrics by Jenkins), was credited to "Gordon Jenkins and His Orch. and The Weavers" upon its release in the summer of 1950; both songs were hits, with "Goodnight Irene" spending months at #1, and the disc sold more than two million copies. In a duet with Artie Shaw, Jenkins again reached the Top Ten with "I'm Forever Blowing Bubbles" (music by John W. Kellette, lyrics by Jean Kenbrovin) in October 1950. "So Long (It's Been Good to Know Yuh)" (music and lyrics by Woody Guthrie) peaked in the Top Ten for Jenkins and the Weavers in February 1951.

Jenkins had a series of minor chart records in 1951 and 1952, many in tandem with singers; he returned to the Top Ten co-billed with Peggy Lee on "Lover" (music by Richard Rodgers, lyrics by Lorenz Hart) in July 1952. December saw the release of the only film for which he wrote a complete score, *Bwana Devil*. In August 1953 the Hilltoppers peaked in the Top Ten with a million-selling revival of "P.S. I Love You." As a recording artist, Jenkins hit the Top Ten of the LP chart with *Seven Dreams* in January 1954.

Leaving Decca Records, Jenkins returned to NBC as a television producer in 1955. In November 1956 a revised and expanded version of his earlier work, *Gordon Jenkins Complete Manhattan Tower*, was released on Capitol Records in tandem with a TV broadcast. The LP spent several weeks in the charts, and there were singles chart entries for "Repeat after Me" (by Patti Page), "New York's My Home" (by Sammy Davis Jr.), and "Married I Can Always Get" (by Teddi King) from the score.

Starting in 1957, Jenkins primarily devoted himself to arranging and conducting for major popular singers. He conducted the orchestra behind Judy Garland for her appearance in London in 1957 and the same year he wrote the arrangements for Nat "King" Cole's chart-topping, million- selling LP *Love Is the Thing* and began a long association with Frank Sinatra by arranging his Top Ten *Where Are You?* album, followed at the end of the year by the million-selling *A Jolly Christmas with Frank Sinatra*. In contrast to the uptempo Sinatra albums arranged by Billy May, Jenkins's works were string-filled ballad albums with haunting charts. These included the Top Ten hit *No One Cares* (1959), *All Alone* (1962), and the gold-selling *September of My Years* (1965), featuring the Top 40 hit "It Was a Very Good Year" (music and lyrics by Ervin Drake), for which Jenkins won the 1965 Grammy Award for Best Arrangement Accompanying a Vocalist or Instrumentalist.

Jenkins continued to work in television in the late 1960s, notably writing *What It Was, Was Love*, an "original albumusical" released as an LP featuring Steve Lawrence and Eydie Gorme and broadcast as a TV special in 1969. In 1973 he conducted the orchestra for the chart album by Nilsson, *A Little Touch of Schmilsson in the Night* and for Frank Sinatra's gold- selling return-to-action *Ol' Blue Eyes Is Back*. In 1980 he wrote, arranged, and conducted the album-length biographical work "The Future," used as one of the three LPs in Sinatra's gold-selling *Trilogy* album. His final album with Sinatra was 1981's *She Shot Me Down*. He died at 73 in 1984 of amyotrophic lateral sclerosis (Lou Gehrig's disease).—WR

Jenkins, Graeme (James Ewers), English conductor; b. London, Dec. 31, 1958. He was a chorister at Dulwich Coll., attended the Univ. of Cambridge, where he conducted the British premiere of *Stiffelio*, and studied conducting with Del Mar and Willcocks at the Royal Coll. of Music in London, where he conducted student performances of *Albert Herring* and *The Turn of the Screw*. In 1982 he made his professional conducting debut with the Kent Opera with *The Beggar's Opera*. In 1986 he became music director of the Glyndebourne Touring Opera, a position he retained until 1991. He made his first appearance at the Glyndebourne Festival in 1987 conducting *Carmen*, the same year that he made his debut on the Continent in Geneva conducting *Hänsel und Gretel*. In 1988 he made his first appearance at the English National Opera in London conducting *Così fan tutte*. As a guest conductor, Jenkins has appeared with opera companies and orchs. at home and abroad. From 1992 he was music director of the Arundel Festival. In 1994 he became music director of the Dallas Opera. From 1997 he also was principal guest conductor of the Cologne Opera.—NS/LK/DM

Jenkins, John, eminent English composer; b. Maidstone, 1592; d. Kimberley, Norfolk, Oct. 27, 1678. He most likely was the son of the carpenter Henry Jenkins, who at his death (1617) bequeathed his son a bandora. Jenkins was active as a music teacher and as a performer on the lute and lyra viol in various households. He spent the Commonwealth years at country estates. After the Restoration, he was made theorbo player in the King's Musick (1660), and during his last years, lived in the home of Sir Philip Wodehouse in Kimberley, Norfolk. Jenkins was the foremost master of consort music in his day. Among his more than 800 known instrumental pieces are fantasias, fantasia- suites, airs, and solo works; he also composed sacred and secular vocal music. See H. Sleeper, ed., *John Jenkins: Fancies and Ayres*, Wellesley Edition, I (1950), A. Dolmetsch, ed., *John Jenkins: 7 Fantasien*, Hortus Musicus, CXLIX (1957), R. Warner, ed., *John Jenkins: Three-part Fancy and Ayre Divisions*, Wellesley Edition, X (1966), A. Ashbee, ed., *John Jenkins: Consort Music of Four Parts*, Musica Britannica, XXVI (1969; 2nd ed., rev., 1975), R. Nicholson, ed., *John Jenkins: Consort Music in Five Parts* (London, 1971), R. Nicholson and A. Ashbee, eds., *John Jenkins: Consort Music in Six Parts* (London, 1976), and D. Peart, ed., *John Jenkins: Consort Music of Six Parts*, Musica Britannica, XXXIX (1977).

BIBL.: R. Warner, *The Fantasia in the Work of J. J.* (diss., Univ. of Mich., 1951); A. Ashbee, *The Four-part Instrumental Compositions of J. J.* (diss., Univ. of London, 1967); A. Ashbee and P. Holman, eds., *J. J. and His Time: Studies in English Consort Music* (Oxford, 1996).—NS/LK/DM

Jenkins, Leroy, black American jazz violinist, bandleader, and composer; b. Chicago, March 11, 1932. He played violin in a local Baptist church and picking up the rudiments of theory while teaching in a local ghetto school; later he was a scholarship student of Bruce Hayden at Fla. A. & M. Univ. He played with members of the Assn. for the Advancement of Creative Musicians and founded The Creative Construction Co. in Chicago (1965–69). After helping to found The Revolutionary Ensemble in 1971, he led his own groups from

1978. In 1980 he appeared at N.Y.'s Carnegie Recital Hall and Town Hall. In addition to his tours of North America, he also performed in Europe. Jenkins is a master of improvisation, particularly of the atonal variety. Among his recordings are *Manhattan Cycles* (1972), *For Players Only* (1975), *Solo Concerto* (1977), *Legend of Ai Glatson* (1978), *Space Minds, New Worlds, Survival of America* (1978), and *Urban Blues* (1984).—NS/LK/DM

Jenkins, Newell (Owen), American conductor and musicologist; b. New Haven, Conn., Feb. 8, 1915. He studied at the Orchesterschule der Sachsischen Staatskapelle in Dresden, and later in Freiburg im Breisgau at the Städtische Musikseminar; also took courses with Wilibald Gurlitt in Freiburg im Breisgau and with Carl Orff in Munich. Upon his return to the U.S., he worked with Leon Barzin at the National Orch. Assn. in N.Y. Following army service in World War II, he received a Fulbright grant to study in Italy. In 1957 he founded the Clarion Music Soc. of N.Y., with which he presented a stimulating series of annual concerts of rarely performed works of the Baroque period. He also appeared as a guest conductor in London, Hilversum, Milan, Naples, Turin, Florence, Stuttgart, and Stockholm. In 1975 he founded the Festival of Venetian Music of the 17th and 18th Centuries at Castelfranco Veneto. From 1964 to 1974 he taught at N.Y.U.; from 1971 to 1979 he was a lecturer at the Univ. of Calif. at Irvine. He ed. (with B. Churgin) *Thematic Catalogue of the Works of G.B. Sammartini* (1976), and also ed. nine syms. of Brunetti (1979).—NS/LK/DM

Jenkins, Speight, American opera administrator; b. Dallas, Jan. 31, 1937. He was educated at the Univ. of Tex. at Austin (B.A., 1957) and at Columbia Univ. (LL.B., 1961). He was an ed. for *Opera News* (1967–73), music critic of the *N.Y. Post* (1973–81), and host for the "Live from the Met" telecasts on PBS (1981–83). In 1983 he became general director of the Seattle Opera. His tenure was highlighted with stagings of the *Ring* cycle (1986–87; 1991; 1995), Glass's *Satyagraha* (1988), Prokofiev's *War and Peace* (1990), *Pelléas et Mélisande* (1993), *Lohengrin* (1994), *Andrea Chénier* (1996), and *Tristan und Isolde* (1998).—NS/LK/DM

Jenko, Davorin, Slovenian conductor and composer; b. Dvorje, Nov. 9, 1835; d. Ljubljana, Nov. 25, 1914. He studied in Ljubljana and Trieste, and also studied law in Vienna, where he was conductor of the Slovene Choral Soc. (1858–62). He then was conductor of the Serbian Church Choral Soc. in Pancevo (1863–65). He was conductor of the Belgrade Choral Soc. (1865–77), and also a conductor and composer of the National Theater there (1871–1902). He was a leading figure in the development of Serbian music. His *Vračara* (The Fortune Teller; Belgrade, May 3, 1882), was the first Serbian operetta. Other works include four Singspiels, incidental music to about 90 plays, orch. pieces, choral works, and songs. The melody of the royal Serbian national anthem was taken from one of his choruses.

BIBL.: D. Cvetko, *D. J. i njeovo doba* (Belgrade, 1952); idem, *D. J.: Doba, življenje, delo* (Ljubljana, 1955).—NS/LK/DM

Jenks, Stephen, American composer and tunebook compiler; b. Glocester, R.I., March 17, 1772; d. Thompson, Ohio, June 5, 1856. He taught in New England and N.Y. State singing schools before settling in Ohio (1829), where he engaged in farming. A diligent advocate of American psalmody, he publ. 10 vols. of psalmody (1799–1818), which included 127 of his own works. Jenks was the leading composer of fuguing tunes of the 19th century.

BIBL.: D. Steel, *S. J. (1772–1856): American Composer and Tunebook Compiler* (diss., Univ. of Mich., 1982).—NS/LK/DM

Jennings, Waylon, baritone-voiced singer and leader of the 1970s outlaw movement in country music, b. Littlefield, Tex., June 15, 1937. Along with singer/songwriters Kris Kristofferson and Willie Nelson, Jennings expanded the subject matter of country music, while returning to a more primal, stripped-down recording sound that honored the roots of the great honky-tonk records of the 1950s.

Jennings came from a musical family, and was already performing over local radio when he was 12 years old. He got his first work as a deejay at the radio station in nearby Lubbock, Tex., where he met pop-rocker Buddy Holly. Holly produced his first single, a cover of Harry Choates's Cajun classic, "Jole Blon," and invited the young singer to be his bass player on what would turn out to be his last tour. Following Holly's death, Jenning's continued to work as a deejay and recorded rockabilly for the small Tex. label, Trend.

In the mid-1960s, Waylon hooked up with Chet Atkins at RCA records, where he was initially packaged as a folk singer. Although he had some minor country hits, he was unhappy with the way RCA was handling him, and began introducing different material into his recordings. In 1970, he recorded a couple of songs by a then-unknown writer named Kris Kristofferson including "Sunday Morning Coming Down," and a year later released an album titled *Ladies Love Outlaws*, featuring more contemporary songs by Hoyt Axton and Alex Harvey. In 1972, he renegotiated with RCA, gaining artistic freedom over his recordings. The first album made under this new contract was 1973's *Honky Tonk Heroes*, featuring Waylon's road band, The Waylors, on a set of hard-driving songs mostly written by Billy Joe Shaver. In 1976, RCA released an anthology album featuring Jennings and his wife, Jessi Colter, along with Willie Nelson and Tompall Glaser, called *The Outlaws*, which became the definitive collection for this new style of music. In 1978, he recorded the classic album of duets with Nelson called *Willie and Waylon*.

Although Jennings continued to produce hits well into the 1980s, he was starting to sound like a parody of himself. He recorded the theme song for TV's redneck comedy *The Dukes of Hazard* in the early 1980s, followed by a lackluster album of rock oldies. In the mid-1980s, he reunited with Kristofferson, Johnny Cash, and Nelson for the concept LP *The Highwaymen*, which showed how all four of these formally innovative performers had gotten awfully long-in-the-tooth. The group nonetheless toured and then reunited for a third album in 1995. Meanwhile Jennings left RCA for MCA in the late

1980s, but the quality of his recordings continued to drop.

At his best, Jennings embodied both physically and aurally the outlaw image. His accompaniment was tough, bass-driven, and reduced to the bare essentials, the perfect compliment to his rough baritone. In choosing to perform songs by then-innovative, younger Nashville songwriters, Jennings championed songs that went beyond the pop-schlock posturing that was then being produced by Nashville's establishment. And, in relocating to Austin, Tex., with his buddy Willie Nelson in the mid-1970s, he helped establish an alternative center for country music, paving the way for the new country revival of a decade later.

DISC.: *Only Daddy That'll Walk the Line* (rec. 1965–84; rel.1993). Glaser, Light, and Mansfield: *Honky Tonk Heroes* (1973). *Dreaming My Dreams* (1975). Nelson, Colter, and Tompall Glaser: *Wanted: The Outlaws* (1976). Willie Nelson: *Waylon & Willie* (1978); *Clean Shirt* (1991). *The Highwaymen* (1985); *Will the Wolf Survive* (1986); *Ol' Waylon* (1977); *Waylon* (1982); *Heroes* (with Johnny Cash; 1986); *A Man Called Hoss* (1988); *New Classic Waylon* (1989); *The Eagle* (1990); *The Highwayman: No. 2* (1990); *Too Dumb for New York City, Too Ugly for L.A.* (1992); *Thanks to Buddy* (1994); *Waymore's Blues* (1994); *The Road Goes on Forever* (1995); *Right for the Time* (1996).—RC

Jensen, Adolf, German composer, brother of **Gustav Jensen;** b. Königsberg, Jan. 12, 1837; d. Baden-Baden, Jan. 23, 1879. He began his studies with E. Sobolewski, the Königsberg Kapellmeister. He publ. a vol. of songs as his op.1 (1849; withdrawn and publ. as 6 songs, op.1, in 1859), and also continued his studies with Ehlert, Köhler, and F. Marpurg (1849–52). He went to Brest Litovsk as a music tutor (1856), then was a theater conductor in Posen, Bromberg, and Copenhagen (1857–58). He returned to Königsberg as asst. director of the Academy (1861), and subsequently taught at Tausig's school in Berlin (1866–68). He ultimately settled in Baden-Baden, where he died of consumption. A great admirer of Schumann, he closely imitated him in his songs, of which about 160 were publ. He also wrote an opera, *Die Erbin von Montfort* (1864–65; rev. by Kienzl, to a new libretto by Jensen's daughter, as *Turandot*). P. Kuczynski ed. his letters (Berlin, 1879).

BIBL.: A. Niggli, *A. J.* (Zürich, 1895); idem, *A. J.* (Berlin, 1900); G. Schweizer, *Das Liedschaffen A. J.s* (diss., Univ. of Giessen, 1932; publ. in Frankfurt am Main, 1933).—NS/LK/DM

Jensen, Gustav, German violinist and composer, brother of **Adolf Jensen;** b. Königsberg, Dec. 25, 1843; d. Cologne, Nov. 26, 1895. He studied with his brother, then with Dehn in Berlin (theory) and with Joachim (violin). In 1872 he became prof. of composition at the Cologne Cons., and held that position until his death. He wrote a Sym., String Quartet, Violin Sonata, Cello Sonata, *Ländliche Serenade* for String Orch., and various violin pieces. He publ. the series Klassische Violinmusik and also tr. into German Cherubini's *Manual of Counterpoint.*—NS/LK/DM

Jensen, Ludvig (Paul) Irgens
See **Irgens-Jensen, Ludvig (Paul)**

Jensen, Niels Peter, Danish organist and composer; b. Copenhagen, July 23, 1802; d. there, Oct. 19, 1846. He was blind from childhood, but learned to play the flute and organ. He was organist at St. Peter's Church in Copenhagen from 1828. His works include two sonatas and other pieces for the flute.—NS/LK/DM

Jensen, Thomas, admired Danish conductor; b. Copenhagen, Oct. 25, 1898; d. there, Nov. 13, 1963. He studied organ and cello at the Copenhagen Cons. He was a cellist in various Swedish and Danish orchs. (1917–27). After conducting studies in Paris and Dresden (1925–26), he went to Århus as conductor of the Phil. Soc. in 1927. He founded that city's first permanent sym. orch. in 1935, and also conducted the Tivoli summer concerts in Copenhagen (1936–48) and founded the Jutland Opera in Århus (1947). Subsequently he was conductor of the Danish Radio Sym. Orch. in Copenhagen (from 1957), with which he toured in Europe and the U.S. He was known especially as a champion of the music of Nielsen.—NS/LK/DM

Jenson, Dylana (Ruth), American violinist; b. Los Angeles, May 14, 1961. Her mother gave her early instruction in violin playing, and she also had lessons in childhood with Manuel Compinsky and, later, with Heifetz and Gingold. She made her formal debut as soloist in the Mendelssohn Concerto with Kostelanetz and the N.Y. Phil. at the age of 12; at 13, she made her European debut with Zürich's Tonhalle Orch. After further instruction in Milstein's master classes in Zürich (1973–76), she won second prize in the Tchaikovsky Competition in Moscow in 1978. Thereafter she appeared as a soloist with major orchs. and as a recitalist in North and South America, Europe, and the Far East. —NS/LK/DM

Jeppesen, Knud (Christian), eminent Danish musicologist and composer; b. Copenhagen, Aug. 15, 1892; d. Risskov, June 14, 1974. He began his career as an opera conductor, using the name Per Buch, in Elbing and Liegnitz (1912–14). He then studied organ at the Royal Danish Cons. of Music (diploma, 1916) and musicology with Angul Hammerich at the Univ. of Copenhagen (M.A., 1918), and also received instruction from Carl Nielsen and Thomas Laub. He prepared his Ph.D. diss., *Die Dissonanzbehandlung bei Palestrina*, at the Univ. of Copenhagen; however, the retirement of Hammerich made it necessary for the diss. to be approved by and completed under Guido Adler at the Univ. of Vienna (1922; publ., in an aug. ed., in Copenhagen in 1923 as *Palestrinastil med saerligt henblik paa dissonansbehandlingen*; Eng. tr. by M. Hamerik as *The Style of Palestrina and the Dissonance*, Copenhagen, 1927; 2nd ed., 1946). Jeppesen served as organist of Copenhagen's St. Stephen's (1917–32) and of the Holmens Church (1932–47), and also taught theory at the Royal Danish Cons. of Music (1920–46). He became the first prof. of musicology at the Univ. of Århus (1946), where he founded its musicological inst. in 1950, retiring in 1957. He was ed.-in-chief of *Acta Musicologica* (1931–54) and president of the International Musicological Soc.

(1949–52). Jeppesen was an authority on Palestrina and the music of the Italian Renaissance. As a composer, he demonstrated his erudition in his music: precise in its counterpoint, unfailingly lucid in its harmonic structure, and set in impeccable classical forms.

WRITINGS: *Kontrapunkt (vokalpolyfoni)* (Copenhagen, 1930; German tr., 1935; 5th ed., 1970; Eng. tr., 1939; new ed., 1992; 3rd Danish ed., 1962); *La frottola* (Copenhagen, 1968–70). **EDITIONS:** With V. Børndal, *Der Kopenhagener Chansonnier* (Copenhagen and Leipzig, 1927; 2nd ed., rev., 1965); *Vaerker af Mogens Pedersøn* (Copenhagen, 1933); with V. Brøndal, *Die mehrstimmige italienische Laude um 1500* (Copenhagen and Leipzig, 1935); *Die italienische Orgelmusik am Anfang des Cinquecento* (Copenhagen, 1943; 2nd ed., rev. and aug., 1960); *La flora, arie &c antiche italiane* (Copenhagen, 1949); *Antichi balli veneziani per cembalo* (Copenhagen, 1962); *Italia sacra musica: Musiche corali italiane sconosciute della prima metà del cinquecento* (Copenhagen, 1962).

WORKS: DRAMATIC: O p e r a : *Rosaura, eller Kaerlighed besejrer alt* (1946; Copenhagen, Sept. 20, 1950). **ORCH.:** *Sjaellandsfar*, sym. (1938–39); *Waldhorn Concerto* (1942). **VOCAL:** *Dronning Dagmar messe* (1945); *Te Deum danicum* for Soloists, 2 Choruses, Organ, and Orch. (1945); *Tvesang: Grundtvig- Kierkegaard* for Chorus and Orch. (1965; Danish Radio, Copenhagen, Jan. 12, 1967); cantatas; motets; songs. **OTHER:** Chamber music; organ pieces.

BIBL.: B. Hjelmborg and S. Sørenson, eds., *Natalicia musicologica K. J. septuagenario collegis oblata* (Copenhagen, 1962). **—NS/LK/DM**

Jepson, Helen, American soprano; b. Titusville, Pa., Nov. 28, 1904; d. Bradenton, Fla., Sept. 16, 1997. She studied in Philadelphia with Queena Mario at the Curtis Inst. of Music (B.Mus., 1934), and in 1936 went to Paris to study with Mary Garden. She sang with the Philadelphia Grand Opera (1928–30), then made her Metropolitan Opera debut in N.Y. as Helene in Seymour's *In the Pasha's Garden* on Jan. 24, 1935, remaining on its roster until 1943; also sang with the Chicago Opera (1935–42). Her roles of note included Eva in *Die Meistersinger von Nürnberg*, Marguerite in *Faust*, Desdemona in *Otello*, and Nedda in *Pagliacci*.**—NS/LK/DM**

Jeremiáš, Bohuslav, Czech conductor, composer, and teacher, father of **Jaroslav Jeremiáš** and **Otakar Jeremiáš**; b. Řestorky, Chrudim district, May 1, 1859; d. České Budějovice, Jan. 18, 1918. He studied with Skuherský at the Prague Organ School (1882–85), then was active as a conductor in Písek (1887–1906), where he promoted performances of works by Czech composers, including Smetana, Dvořák, Skuherský, and Foerster. He also organized a music school, and subsequently was founder-director of the Cons. in České Budějovice (1906–18). He composed a large output of sacred and secular music for choral forces, and also wrote several vocal manuals.**—NS/LK/DM**

Jeremiáš, Jaroslav, Czech pianist and composer, son of **Bohuslav Jeremiáš** and brother of **Otakar Jeremiáš**; b. Pisek, Aug. 14, 1889; d. České Budějovice, Jan. 16, 1919. He studied at his father's music school in Pisek, then studied piano with A. Miks at the Prague Cons. and privately with Novák (1909–10). Although he died at the age of 29, he left several significant works, including the opera *Starý král* (The Old King; 1911–12; Prague, April 13, 1919), the oratorio *Mistr Jan Hus* (1914–15; Prague, June 13, 1919), a Viola Sonata, and songs.

BIBL.: B. Bělohlávek, *J. J.* (Prague, 1935).**—NS/LK/DM**

Jeremiáš, Otakar, Czech conductor and composer, son of **Bohuslav Jeremiáš** and brother of **Jaroslav Jeremiáš**; b. Pisek, Oct. 17, 1892; d. Prague, March 5, 1962. He began his musical training with his parents, then studied composition at the Prague Cons. (1907) and privately with Novák (1909–10). He also took cello lessons with Jan Burian. He was a cellist in the Czech Phil. (1911–13), and in 1919 took over his father's music school. He then was conductor of the Prague Radio orch. (1929–45), and subsequently director of the Prague National Theater (1945–47). He was also the first chairman of the Union of Czech Composers. He was made a National Artist (1950) and received the Order of the Republic (1960). His music continues the traditions of the Czech national school, with a pronounced affinity to the style of Smetana, Foerster, and Ostrčil.

WORKS: DRAMATIC: *Romance o Karlu IV*, melodrama (1917); *Bratři Karamazovi* (The Brothers Karamazov), opera, after Dostoyevsky (1922–27; Prague, Oct. 8, 1928); *Enšpígl* (Til Eulenspiegel), opera (1940–44; Prague, May 13, 1949); film scores. **ORCH.:** *Písně jara* (Song of Spring; 1907–08); *Podzimní suita* (Autumn Suite; 1907–08); 2 syms. (1910–11; 1914–15). **CHAMBER:** Piano Trio (1909–10); String Quartet (1910); Piano Quartet (1911); String Quintet (1911); *Fantasie na staročeské choraly* (Fantasy on Old Czech Chorales) for Nonet (1938). **P i a n o :** 2 sonatas (1909, 1913). **VOCAL:** *Fantasie* for 2 Choruses and Orch. (1915; Prague Radio, Oct. 27, 1942); 2 cantatas: *Mohamedův zpěv* (1932) and *Písně o rodné zemi* (Song of the Native Land; 1940–41); songs.

BIBL.: J. Plavec, *O. J.* (Prague, 1943); idem, *Národni umělec: O. J.* (National Artist: O. J.; Prague, 1964; includes list of works). **—NS/LK/DM**

Jerger, Alfred, noted Austrian bass-baritone; b. Brünn, June 9, 1889; d. Vienna, Nov. 18, 1976. He studied at the Vienna Academy of Music, where his teachers included Fuchs, Grädener, and Gutheil, and then became an operetta conductor at the Zürich Opera (1913). He began his vocal career in 1915, appearing as Lothario in *Mignon* at the Zürich Opera in 1917, and then sang at the Bavarian State Opera in Munich (1919–21). He was a leading member of the Vienna State Opera (1921–53); also sang at the Salzburg Festivals, at London's Covent Garden, and other major music centers of Europe. In 1947 he joined the faculty of the Vienna Academy of Music; was also a producer at the Vienna Volksoper. He created the role of the Man in Schoenberg's *Die Glückliche Hand* (Vienna, Oct. 14, 1924) and the role of Mandryka in Strauss's *Arabella* (Dresden, July 1, 1933). His other outstanding Strauss roles included Baron Ochs, Orestes, John the Baptist, and Barak. He also was a fine Leporello, Don Giovanni, Pizzaro, Hans Sachs, Beckmesser, Grand Inquisitor, and King Philip. **—NS/LK/DM**

Jeritza (real name, **Jedlitzková**), **Maria,** celebrated Moravian-born American soprano; b. Brünn, Oct. 6, 1887; d. Orange, N.J., July 10, 1982. She studied in Brünn and sang in the Stadttheater chorus there. After completing her training in Prague, she made her formal operatic debut as Elsa in *Lohengrin* in Olomouc (1910), then became a member of the Vienna Volksoper. In 1912 Emperor Franz Josef heard her sing in Bad Ischl, after which he decreed that she should be engaged at the Vienna Court Opera, where she made her first appearance as Oberleitner's Aphrodite. Strauss then chose her to create the title role in his opera *Ariadne auf Naxos* (Stuttgart, Oct. 25, 1912), and also in its revised version (Vienna, Oct. 4, 1916); she likewise created the role of the Empress in his *Die Frau ohne Schatten* (Vienna, Oct. 10, 1919). On Nov. 19, 1921, she made her U.S. debut at the Metropolitan Opera in N.Y. in the first U.S. production of Korngold's opera *Die tote Stadt.* Her compelling portrayals of Tosca and Turandot quickly secured her place as the prima donna assoluta there, and she remained on its roster until 1932. She made her debut at London's Covent Garden as Tosca on June 16, 1926. Throughout the years, she remained a leading singer in Vienna as well, continuing to appear there until 1935. In 1943 she became a naturalized American citizen. She again sang in Vienna (1949–52); also appeared as Rosalinda in a Metropolitan Opera benefit performance of *Die Fledermaus* in N.Y. (Feb. 22, 1951). At the zenith of her career in the years between the two world wars, she won extraordinary acclaim in such roles as Sieglinde, Elisabeth, Santuzza, Fedora, Thaïs, Carmen, Salome, Octavian, Tosca, and Turandot. She led a colorful life, both on and off the operatic stage: she married three times, had many romantic affairs, and her spats with fellow artists became legendary. She publ. an autobiography, *Sunlight and Song* (N.Y., 1924).

BIBL.: E. Decsey, *M. J.* (Vienna, 1931); R. Werba, *M. J.: Primadonna des Verismo* (Vienna, 1981).—**NS/LK/DM**

Jersild, Jørgen, Danish composer and teacher; b. Copenhagen, Sept. 17, 1913. He received training in composition and theory from Schierbeck and in piano from Stoffregen in Copenhagen, and then continued his studies with Roussel in Paris (1936) and studied musicology at the Univ. of Copenhagen (M.A., 1940). After working in the music dept. of the Danish Radio in Copenhagen (1939–43), he became a teacher at the Copenhagen Cons. in 1943; later he was a prof. of theory there (1953–75). Among his pedagogical books were *Ear Training* (1966), *Advanced Rhythmical Studies* (1980), and *Analytisk Harmonilaere* (1989). He also publ. a study of Romantic harmony à la the music of César Franck (1970). His compositions are cast in a thoroughly cosmopolitan style while retaining essential Danish qualities.

WORKS: DRAMATIC: *Lunefulde Lucinda* (Capricious Lucinda), ballet (1954); *Alice in Wonderland,* musical fairy tale (1958); *Gertrude,* film music (1964); music for plays. **ORCH.:** *The Birthday Concert* (1945; rev. 1962); *Pastoral* for Strings (1946); *Little Suite* for Strings (1950); Harp Concerto (1971–72; Aldeburgh, June 9, 1972). **CHAMBER:** *Music Making in the Forest,* serenade for Wind Quintet (1947); *Pezzo Elegiaco* for Harp (1968); *Fantasia e Canto Affettuoso* for Harp, Flute, Clarinet, and Cello (1969); *Fantasia* for Harp (1977); String Quartet (1980); *Für Gefühlvolle Spieler* for 2 Harps (1982); *Lento* for 4 Cellos and Double Bass (1985); *10 Impromptus* for Violin and Guitar (1987). **KEYBOARD: Piano:** *Trois pieces en concert* (1945); Duo Concertante for Piano, 3- and 4-Hands (1956); *30 Polyrhythmic Études* (1976); *15 Piano Pieces for Julie* (1985); *Fantasia* (1989); *Jeu polyrythmique,* 3 études (1990); *2 Impromptus* (1993). **Organ:** *Fantasia* (1985). **VOCAL:** Numerous choruses, including *3 Madrigali* (1958), *3 Danish Love Songs* (1968), *3 Romantic Choral Songs* (1971), *3 Latin Madrigals* (1987), and *Il Cantico della Creature* (1991); pieces for Solo Voice and Piano.—**NS/LK/DM**

Jerusalem, Siegfried, prominent German tenor; b. Oberhausen, April 17, 1940. He received training in violin and piano at the Essen Folkwangschule, where he played principal bassoon in its orch. He began his career as an orchestral bassoonist in 1961, and was a member of the Stuttgart Radio Sym. Orch. (1972–77). He began serious vocal study in Stuttgart with Hertha Kalcher in 1972, appearing in minor roles at the Württemberg State Theater from 1975. He sang Lohengrin in Darmstadt and Aachen in 1976, and then at the Hamburg State Opera in 1977. That same year he made his debut at the Bayreuth Festival as Froh, returning in later seasons as Lohengrin, Walther, Parsifal, and Loge in the Solti-Hall mounting of the *Ring* cycle in 1983. After making his first appearance at the Berlin Deutsche Oper as Tamino in 1978, he became a leading member of the company. He made his U.S. debut with the Metropolitan Opera in N.Y. as Lohengrin on Jan. 10, 1980, his British debut at London's Coliseum as Parsifal on March 16, 1986, and his Covent Garden debut in London on March 18, 1986, singing Erik; he also appeared at the Vienna State Opera, Milan's La Scala, and the Paris Opéra. His later appearances at Bayreuth were highlighted by his portrayals of Siegfried (1990, 1992, 1995) and Tristan (1993). He also sang Siegfried at the Lyric Opera in Chicago in 1995 and in Berlin in 1996. His portrayal of Tristan at the Los Angeles Opera in 1997 was acclaimed, and he also won accolades for his Loge and Siegfried at the Metropolitan Opera that year.—**NS/LK/DM**

Jesinghaus, Walter, Swiss violinist and composer; b. Genoa, July 13, 1902; d. Ticino, Sept. 17, 1966. He studied violin in Milan and Lugano, and gave concerts as a child virtuoso. In 1918 he went to Zürich to study academic music subjects with Andreae and Jarnach, and later at the Basel Cons. After working as a theater conductor in Germany (1921–25), he settled in Lugano. He wrote several operas (*Tartuffe, Soeur Béatrice, Belinda e il mostro, La luna e la città*), as well as a *Symphonia choralis* and much chamber music, including a number of pieces for viola d'amore.

BIBL.: D. Poli, *W. J.*(Bologna, 1929).—**NS/LK/DM**

Jessel, Leon, German composer; b. Stettin, Jan. 22, 1871; d. Berlin, Jan. 4, 1942. At age 20, he began working as a theater conductor, appearing in Gelsenkirchen, Mülheim, Celle, Freiburg-im-Breisgau, Stettin, Chemnitz, and Lübeck. As a composer, he first attracted notice with his piano and instrumental pieces. His *Die Parade der Zinnsoldaten* (1905) became internationally celebrated. In 1911 he settled in Berlin, where he first won success as an operetta composer with his *Die beiden Husaren* (Feb. 6, 1913). He scored a signal triumph with his *Das Schwarzwaldmädel* (Aug. 25, 1917). Of his subsequent scores, the most successful were *Die närrische Liebe* Nov. 28, 1919), *Die Postmeisterin* (Feb. 3, 1921), *Das Detektivmädel* (Oct. 28, 1921), *Des Königs Nachbarin* (April 15, 1923), and the Viennese premiered *Meine Tochter Otto* (May 5, 1927). As a Jew, Jessel's works were banned after the Nazis came to power in 1933. His last operetta, *Die goldene Mühle*, received its premiere in Olten, Switzerland (Oct. 29, 1936). Jessel died as a result of manhandling by the Gestapo.—NS/LK/DM

Jethro Tull, prog-rock pioneers. **MEMBERSHIP:** Ian Anderson, flt., gtr., sax., lead voc. (b. Edinburgh, Scotland, Aug. 10, 1947); Mick Abrahams, gtr., voc. (b. Luton, Bedfordshire, England, April 7, 1943); Glenn Cornick, bs. (b. Barrow-in-Furness, Cumbria, England, April 24, 1947); and Clive Bunker, drm. (b. Blackpool, Lancashire, England, Dec. 12, 1946). Abrahams left in early 1969, to be replaced by Martin Barre (b. Nov. 17, 1946). Glenn Cornick left in 1971, to be replaced by Jeffrey Hammond-Hammond (b. Blackpool, England, July 30, 1946). John Evan, kybd. (b. Blackpool, England, March 28, 1948) joined in 1971. Clive Bunker left in late 1971, to be replaced by Barriemore Barlow (b. Blackpool, England, Sept. 10, 1949). Hammond-Hammond left in December 1975, to be replaced by John Glascock (b. London, England, 1952; d. there, Nov.17, 1979). Glascock was replaced by Dave Pegg (b. Birmingham, England, Nov. 2, 1947).

Ian Anderson moved to Blackpool, Lancashire, at the age of 12 and formed the Blades in 1963 with bassist Jeffrey Hammond-Hammond and keyboardist John Evan. Performing on the northern England club circuit, the group became the John Evan Band in 1965, with Glenn Cornick replacing Hammond-Hammond. In late 1967, the band moved to Bedfordshire to establish themselves on the nearby London club circuit, but the rest of the group soon left, leaving Anderson and Cornick to persevere. They quickly formed a new band with Mick Abrahams and Clive Bunker, with Abrahams and Anderson as the principal songwriters.

Adopting the name Jethro Tull, the group became an immediate success on the club circuit, gaining a residency at London's Marquee club in June 1968. Well received at August's Sunbury Jazz and Blues Festival, they signed with Island Records (Reprise in the U.S.). Their blues-oriented debut album *This Was* sold well in Great Britain but only modestly in the U.S. However, in late 1968, Abrahams departed to form Blodwyn Pig. Briefly replaced by future Black Sabbath guitarist Tommy Iommi and former Nice guitarist Davy O'List, Abrahams's permanent replacement was guitarist Martin Barre.

Ian Anderson effectively took over as Jethro Tull's leader, developing his songwriting talents for highly melodic folk and classically influenced songs often featuring wry, off-beat lyrics. "Living in the Past" became a smash British hit in the summer of 1969 and *Stand Up* was dominated by Anderson's songwriting,

containing group favorites such as the instrumental "Bouree," "Look into the Sun," and "We Used to Know." Jethro Tull soon scored smash British hits with "Sweet Dream" and "Witches Promise"/"Teacher."

By 1970, Jethro Tull was established as one of the top concert attractions in the U.S. through regular tours, perhaps to the detriment of their British popularity. Keyboardist John Evan joined Jethro Tull to record *Benefit*, their last blues-based album, and accompanied the others with Jeffrey Hammond- Hammond on their subsequent American tour. Glenn Cornick left the group in late 1970 to form Wild Turkey, later resurfacing in Bob Welch's power trio Paris in 1975. He was replaced on bass by Jeffrey Hammond-Hammond, formerly of The John Evan Band, and Evan himself joined the group on a permanent basis.

Jethro Tull convincingly broke through in the U.S. as an album band with *Aqualung*, their first "concept" album and certainly their best-known work. Although attacked by some critics as bombastic and pretentious, the album sold well in both Great Britain and the U.S. and included concert and FM radio favorites such as "Hymn 43" (a minor American hit), "Cross-Eyed Mary," "Locomotive Breath," and "Aqualung."

Clive Bunker departed Jethro Tull in mid-1971 to form Jude with Robin Trower, Frankie Miller, and Jim Dewar, later reemerging with the re-formed Blodwyn Pig. He was replaced on drums by Barriemore Barlow. Jethro Tull conducted extensive tours of the U.S. in 1971 and 1972, and *Thick as a Brick*, essentially an album-long ballad without individual cuts, sold spectacularly, staying on the American album charts for nearly a year. *Living in the Past* assembled live performances and early songs unreleased in the U.S. on Jethro Tull's new label Chrysalis, yielding the group's first major American hit, "Living in the Past," their British hit from 1969.

Jethro Tull's final concept album, *A Passion Play*, was critically lambasted by virtually every rock critic and sold poorly in Britain but massively in the U.S. The subsequent American tour featuring the theatrically oriented performance of the album was greeted by record-breaking, sellout crowds. However, the group, road weary and disillusioned by hostile press reviews, announced their "retirement" from live performance in August 1973. The group retreated to Switzerland, where they recorded the largely orchestral *War Child* as the soundtrack to a movie. The movie was eventually abandoned as too costly, but the album yielded the group's second (and last) major American hit with "Bungle in the Jungle."

Jethro Tull continued to record best-selling American albums through the 1970s, including *Minstrel in the Gallery* and *Songs from the Wood*, which revealed a decidedly folk-rock orientation. By early 1976, Jeffrey Hammond-Hammond had been replaced by John Glascock. The group conducted their first British tour in three years in February 1977 and added keyboardist David Palmer, the orchestrator of virtually all of Jethro Tull's albums, in May. Ian Anderson subsequently became involved in salmon farming. In the fall of 1979, Dave Pegg, a member of Fairport Convention, replaced ailing John Glascock on bass. On Nov. 17, 1979, Glascock died during open-heart surgery in a London hospital at the age of 27.

In 1980, Ian Anderson dismissed Barriemore Barlow, John Evan, and David Palmer. He then recorded *A*, perhaps his most fully realized folk-rock album, with Barre, Pegg, and violinist-keyboardist Eddie Jobson, who left after a single tour. With Anderson, Barre, and Pegg as mainstays, Jethro Tull continued to tour and record in the 1980s. In the meantime, Ian Anderson recorded the solo album *Walk into Light* and rerecorded a number of Jethro Tull classics with David Palmer conducting the London Symphony Orch., released as *A Classic Case*. In 1987, the group recorded their best-selling album in years, *The Crest of a Knave*, and toured for the first time in three years, with Fairport Convention as the opening act. Jethro Tull's 1992 world tour produced the acoustic album *A Little Light Music*. In 1995, Anderson recorded the solo instrumental album *Divinities* for Angel Records. The following year, Martin Barre recorded *The Meeting* for Imago Records.

DISC.: EARLY JETHRO TULL: *This Was* (1969); *Stand Up* (1969); *Benefit* (1970). **BLODWYN PIG (WITH MICK ABRAHAMS):** *Ahead Rings Out* (1969); *Getting to This* (1970). **MICK ABRAHAMS:** *Mick Abrahams* (1971). **WILD TURKEY (WITH GLENN CORNICK):** *Battle Hymn* (1972). **JETHRO TULL** *Aqualung* (1971); *Thick as a Brick* (1972); *A Passion Play* (1973); *War Child* (1974); *Minstrel in the Gallery* (1975); *Too Old to Rock 'n' Roll...Too Young to Die* (1976); *Songs from the Wood* (1977); *Heavy Horses* (1978); *Bursting Out* (1978); *Stormwatch* (1979); *"A"* (1980); *The Broadsword and the Beast* (1982); *Under Wraps* (1984); *The Crest of a Knave* (1987); *Rock Island* (1989); *Catfish Rising* (1991); *A Little Light Music* (1992); *Roots to Branches* (1995); *In Concert* (1995). **IAN ANDERSON:** *Walk into Light* (1983); *Divinities: Twelve Dances with God* (1995). **THE LONDON SYMPHONY ORCHESTRA:** *A Classic Case: The Music of Jethro Tull* (1986). **MARTIN BARRE:** *The Meeting* (1996).—BH

Jett (Larkin), Joan, rock and roll model for women; b. Philadelphia, Penn., Sept. 22, 1960. She grew up in the Baltimore area, learning guitar as a pre-teen. At 12, she recalled seeing the N.Y. Dolls and deciding that not only did she want to do that, but that she could. In her early teens, her family moved to L.A. By the time she was 15, she formed a band and encountered producer Kim Fowley. He renamed the group The Runaways and signed them to Mercury Records. Their 1975 debut had a proto-punk metal sound that sold dozens in the U.S. (outside of L.A., where they were very popular), but was very successful in England and Japan. They released three albums in the U.S. and a couple just for the Japanese and English markets before breaking up in 1979.

After the dissolution of The Runaways, Jett stayed in England for a while, afraid that the American music industry wouldn't take a former Runaway seriously. She worked with Sex Pistols Steve Cook and Paul Jones, recording three tracks. Two came out as a single in Holland. One, a cover of a song by English TV and recording stars Arrows called "I Love Rock and Roll," didn't get released at all until 1993. Moving back to the U.S., Jett first settled back in L.A., where she produced the debut album by the Germs and acted in a movie

loosely based on the Runaways called *We're All Crazy Now*. The movie never came out, but through it Jett met producer Kenny Laguna. She moved back to N.Y., sharing a house with Laguna and his wife. Together they made an album that included the Cook and Jones tracks. The rest of the album was made with the Blondie rhythm section of Clem Burke and Frank Infante, and Ducks Deluxe guitarist Sean Tyla. Laguna described the sound they were shooting for as a "hybrid of 'Yummy Yummy' meets the Germs." While they secured release in Europe, 23 U.S. labels passed on the project. Laguna and Jett decided to release it themselves on their own Blackheart label. Through non-stop touring with her new band, The Blackhearts, and word-of-mouth, the indie record sold well enough to get the attention of Neil Bogart. Having folded his tents at Casablanca, he was looking for new music for his new label, Board-walk. He signed Jett, re-releasing the album as *Bad Reputation*. It sold moderately well, but Jett fell between the formats at radio—too hard for soft rock, too female for AOR, too mainstream for alternative, too punk for Top 40.

For her next album, she recorded with her own band and redid the tune she had previously recorded with Cook and Jones. The centerpiece of her live show, "I Love Rock and Roll," started getting phone requests whereever Jett played. MTV started playing the video. The single climbed the charts and eventually topped the pop charts for seven weeks. The album rose to #2. Both went platinum. Her next single, a cover of Tommy James and the Shondell's "Crimson and Clover," went to #7. A final single, a cover of Gary Glitter's "Do You Wanna Touch Me (Oh Yeah)," rose to #20.

Bogart died shortly after the album peaked, and Boardwalk was dissolved. Laguna and Jett revived Blackheart records and secured distribution. *Album* had the Top 40 singles "Fake Friends" and a cover of Sly and the Family Stones' "Everyday People." The album hit #20 and went gold, but Jett had slipped noisily out of the mainstream. For *Glorious Results of a Misspent Youth*, Jett recut the closest thing the Runaways had to a U.S. hit, the song "Cherry Bomb," but it fared little better than the original and neither the album nor the single broke the Top 40. Her ambitious 1986 album, while featuring guest tracks with girl group star Darlene Love, The Beach Boys, and Scorpio from Grandmaster Flash and the Furious Five, didn't have a chart hit. Even her performance of Bruce Springsteen's "Light of Day," the title track from the movie she co-starred in with Michael J. Fox, didn't revive her pop career greatly, again just skimming the Top 40. It didn't help that the movie bombed at the box office.

For *Up Your Alley*, Jett took the 1990s approach to a hit, and asked Desmond Child for a power ballad. She brought far more to the by-rote "I Hate Myself for Loving You" than the song deserved, and it went to #8 in 1988, followed by "Little Liar," which broke the Top 20. The album went to #19 and sold platinum. While covers made up a large portion of her repertoire, her next album, *The Hit List*, was entirely composed of her versions of her favorite songs. She managed to bring AC/DC's "Dirty Deeds (Done Dirt Cheap)" into the Top

40. The album also included a duet with Ray Davies on The Kinks' "Celluloid Heroes" and charted respectably at #36. Her 1991 album, *Notorious*, featured "The Only Good Thing (You Ever Said Was Goodbye)" which was performed with Desmond Child and Dianne Warren, and also included the song "Backlash," with The Replacements' Paul Westerberg.

By the mid-1990s, Jett's pop credibility might have started to wane, but her influence on the burgeoning crop of women rockers, particularly the ones to the punkier end of the spectrum dubbed "riot grrrrls," was enormous. She produced an album for Bikini Kill and recorded a fundraising project with the group The Gits, called *Evil Stig*, to help raise funds to find the person who raped and murdered the group's lead singer, Mia Zapata. For Jett's own 1994 album, *Pure and Simple*, the band L7 recorded the track "Activity Grrrl" with her, and she co-wrote three other songs with Bikini Kill's Kathleen Hanna. "You Got a Problem" found Jett bridging the gap between the riot grrrls and contemporary pop, as she co-wrote it with Hanna and Child. Her most recent album, 1999's *Fetish*, found a more mature Jett working on a concept album about sex, fetishes, and other related topics. Even in a larger framework, Jett lost none of her rocking edge.

DISC.: *Joan Jett* (1980); *Bad Reputation* (1981); *I Love Rock and Roll* (1981); *I Love Playing with Fire* (1982); *Album* (1983); *Glorious Results of a Misspent Youth* (1984); *Good Music* (1986); *Up Your Alley* (1988); *The Hit List* (1990); *Notorious* (1991); *Pure and Simple* (1994); *Fetish* (1999).—**HB**

Ježek, Jaroslav, Czech composer; b. Prague, Sept. 25, 1906; d. N.Y., Jan. 1, 1942. He studied composition with Jirák and Suk, and also experimented with quarter-tone techniques under the direction of Alois Hába. In 1928 he became resident composer for the "Liberated Theater," a Prague satirical revue; produced the scenic music for 20 of its plays. In 1939, shortly before the occupation of Czechoslovakia by the Nazis, he emigrated to the U.S.

WORKS: DRAMATIC: Ballet: *Nerves* (1928). **ORCH.:** Piano Concerto (Prague, June 23, 1927); *Fantasy for Piano and Orch.* (Prague, June 24, 1930); Concerto for Violin and Wind Orch. (Prague, Sept. 26, 1930); *Symphonic Poem* (Prague, March 25, 1936). **CHAMBER:** Wind Quartet (1929); Wind Quintet (1931); 2 string quartets (1932, 1941); Violin Sonata (1933); Duo for 2 Violins (1934). **P i a n o :** Suite for Quarter Tone Piano (1927); *Capriccio* (1932); *Bagatelles* (1933); *Rhapsody* (1938); *Toccata* (1939); Sonata (1941).—**NS/LK/DM**

J. Geils Band, The, a hard-driving 1970s rock and blues band from the Boston region. **MEMBERSHIP:** Jerome "J." Geils, lead gtr. (b. N.Y.C., Feb. 20, 1946); Peter Wolf (real name, Blankfield), lead voc. (b. Bronx, N.Y., March 7, 1946); Seth Justman, kybd. (b. Washington, D.C., Jan. 27, 1951); Magic Dick (born Richard Salwitz), har. (b. New London, Conn., May 13, 1945); Danny Klein, bs. (b. Worcester, Mass., May 13, 1946); Stephen Bladd, drm. (b. Boston, Mass., July 31, 1942).

The J. Geils Band won a reputation as a performing band by touring almost constantly for more than a decade. Eventually breaking through as a recording band in the early 1980s, the J. Geils Band retained their original lineup for 15 years, until the departure of lead vocalist and front man Peter Wolf in 1983.

Formed in 1967 by the merger of two Boston bands, the J. Geils Blues Band and the Hallucinations, the J. Geils Band was completed with the addition of Seth Justman shortly after the group signed with Atlantic Records in 1968. Featuring blues and R&B covers, the J. Geils Band's overlooked debut album includes the underground favorite "First I Look at the Purse" (a hit for the Contours in 1965), whereas their second album, *The Morning After*, yielded their first moderate hit with "Looking for a Love" (a hit for the Valentinos in 1962). As the band continually crisscrossed the United States in search of a wider audience, they recorded the live *Full House* set. After the moderate hit "Give It to Me" from the best-selling *Bloodshot* album, the J. Geils Band scored their first near-smash hit with "Must of Got Lost" in late 1974. After three more albums and several minor hits for Atlantic, the band switched to EMI-America.

The J. Geils Band's debut for their new label, *Sanctuary*, sold quite well, yielding the moderate hit "One Last Kiss." The group added layered synthesizer parts to their sound for *Love Stinks*, which produced two moderate hits with "Come Back" and the title tune. They finally broke through in late 1981 with the top album *Freeze Frame*, for which Seth Justman wrote or cowrote with Peter Wolf all the songs. The album contained three hits: the top "Centerfold," the smash title song, and the moderately successful "Angel in Blue." However, tensions between Wolf and Justman led, in October 1983, to Wolf leaving the group. The J. Geils Band managed only minor hits through 1985, while Wolf scored major hits as a solo artist with "Lights Out" in 1984 and "Come as You Are" in 1987 on EMI-America. By 1990 he had switched to MCA Records for *Up to No Good!* In 1993 Wolf reunited with Magic Dick to form Bluestime to perform traditional blues and original numbers, releasing an album a year later on the specialty Rounder label.

DISC.: THE J. GEILS BAND: *The J. G. Band* (1971); *The Morning After* (1971); *Full House* (1972); *Bloodshot* (1973); *Ladies Invited* (1973); *Nightmares* (1974); *Hot Line* (1975); *Blow Your Face Out* (1976); *Monkey Island* (1977); *Best* (1979); *Best, Vol. 2* (1980); *Sanctuary* (1978); *Love Stinks* (1980); *Freeze Frame* (1981); *Showtime!* (1982); *You're Gettin' Even While I'm Gettin' Odd* (1984); *Flashback* (1987); *Anthology: Houseparty* (1993); *Must of Got Lost* (1995). **PETER WOLF:** *Lights Out* (1984); *Come as You Are* (1987); *Up to No Good* (1990). **BLUESTIME:** *Bluestime* (1994). —**BH**

Jílek, František, Czech conductor; b. Brünn, May 22, 1913; d. there (Brno), Sept. 16, 1993. He took courses with Balatka, Chalabala, and Kvapil at the Brno Cons. and with Novák at the Prague Cons., and then was répétiteur and conductor at the Brno Opera (1936–39). After serving as asst. conductor at the Ostrava Opera (1939–48), he returned to Brno as conductor (1948–52) and chief conductor (1952–78) at the Opera. He also taught at the Janáček Academy of Music there, and was chief conductor of the Brno State Phil. (1978–83). He acquired a fine reputation through his championship of the music of his homeland, most notably of works by Smetana and Janáček.—NS/LK/DM

Jiménez-Mabarak, Carlos, Mexican composer and pedagogue; b. Tacuba, Jan. 31, 1916; d. Cuautla, Morelos, June 21, 1994. He studied piano with Jesús Castillo in Guatemala (1923–27), and then continued his piano training at the Cons. in Santiago, Chile (1928–29), where he then attended the Liceo de Aplicación (1930–33). In 1933 he went to Brussels, where he received instruction in piano and harmony at the Inst. of Advanced Studies in Music and Drama, in harmony, counterpoint, and analysis with Wouters at the Cons., and in musicology with Van den Borren at the Univ. Returning to his homeland, he studied orchestration with Revueltas at the Cons. (1938), and still later (1953–56), he studied composition with Turchi at the Accademia di Santa Cecilia in Rome and dodecaphonic techniques with Leibowitz in Paris. From 1942 to 1965 he was prof. of music education, harmony, and composition at the National Cons. of Music in Mexico City. After serving as a prof. at the Villahermosa School of the Arts in Tabasco (1965–68), he was the cultural attaché of the Mexican Embassy in Vienna (1972–74). He first composed in a neo-Classical style but later became an accomplished dodecaphonist. He was one of the first Mexican composers to utilize electronics and to experiment with "musique concrète."

WORKS: DRAMATIC: O p e r a : *Misa de seis* (1960; Mexico City, June 21, 1962); *La guerra* (1980; Mexico City, Sept. 26, 1982). **B a l l e t :** *Perifonema* (Mexico City, March 9, 1940); *El amor del agua* (1945); *Balada del pájaro y las doncellas* (1947); *Balada del venado y la luna* (1948); *Danza fúnebre* (1949); *Recuerdo a zapata*, ballet-cantata (1950); *Balada mágico o danza de las cuatro estaciones* (1951); *Retablo de la annunciación* (1951); *El nanual herido* (1952); *La maestra rural* (1952); *Balada de los quetzales* (1953); *El paraíso de los Ahogados* (1960); *La llorona* (1961); *La portentosa vida de la muerte* (1964); *Pitágoras dijo...* (1966); *Balada de los rios de Tabasco* (1990). **O t h e r :** Incidental music to several plays, including Camus's *Caligula* (1947), and various film scores. **ORCH.:** 2 syms.: No. 1 (Mexico City, July 6, 1945) and No. 2, *Symphony in 1 Movement* (Mexico City, Aug. 1962); Concerto for Piano and Chamber Orch. (1945; Mexico City, Nov. 8, 1946); *Obertura para orquesta de arcos* (Mexico City, Sept. 2, 1963); Sinfonia concertante for Piano and Orch. (1968; Mexico City, March 11, 1977). **CHAMBER:** *Preludio y fuga* for Clarinet and Piano (1937); *Concierto del abuelo* for Piano and String Quartet (1938); Quartet (1947); *El retrato de lupe* for Violin and Piano (1953); Concerto for Piano, Timpani, Bells, Xylophone, and Percussion (1961); *5 Pieces* for Flute and Piano (1965); *La ronda junto a la fuente* for Flute, Oboe, Violin, Viola, and Cello (1965); *2 Pieces* for Cello and Piano (1966); *Invention* for Clarinet and Trumpet (1970); *Invention* for Oboe, Tenor Trombone, and Piano (1971). **P i a n o :** *Allegro romántico* (1935); *Pequeño preludio* (1935); *Danza española I* and *II* (1936); *Sonata del majo enamorado* (1936); *Retrato de Mariana Sánchez* (1952); *Variaciones sobre la alegría* for 2 Pianos (1952); *La fuente armoniosa* (1957). **VOCAL:** *Los niños heroes* for Chorus and Orch. (1947); *Traspié entre dos estrellas* for Reciter and 6 Instruments (1957); *Homenaje a Juarez* for Soloists, Chorus, and Orch. (1958); *Simón Bolívar* for Soloists, Chorus, and Orch. (1983); many choruses; songs. —NS/LK/DM

Jirák, K(arel) B(oleslav), distinguished Czech conductor and composer; b. Prague, Jan. 28, 1891; d. Chicago, Jan. 30, 1972. He received training in law and philosophy at the Univ. of Prague, and studied composition privately with Novák (1909–11) and J. B. Foerster (1911–12). He was a répétiteur and conductor at the Hamburg Opera (1916–19), and also conducted opera in Brno and Moravska Ostrava (1918–20). He then was conductor of Prague's Hlahol choir and second conductor of the Czech Phil. (1920–21), as well as prof. of composition at the Prague Cons. (1920–30). From 1930 to 1945 he was music director of the Czech Radio. From 1935 to 1946 he was married to **Marta Krásová**. In 1947 he went to the U.S., and in 1948 became chairman of the theory dept. at Roosevelt Coll. (later Univ.) in Chicago. He held the same position also at Chicago Cons. Coll. from 1967 to 1971. His music represents the finest traditions of Middle European 20th-century Romanticism. His 5th Sym. won the Edinburgh International Festival prize in 1951. He publ. a textbook on musical form (Prague, 1922; 5th ed., 1946); also biographies of Fibich (Ostrava, 1947), Mozart (Ostrava, 1948), and Dvořák (N.Y., 1961).

WORKS: DRAMATIC: O p e r a : *Žena a bůh* (The Woman and God; 1911–14; Brno, March 10, 1928). **ORCH.:** 6 syms.: No. 1 (1915–16), No. 2 (1924), No. 3 (1929–38; Prague, March 8, 1939), No. 4, *Episode from an Artist's Life* (1945; Prague, April 16, 1947), No. 5 (1949; Edinburgh, Aug. 26, 1951), and No. 6 (1957–70; Prague, Feb. 17, 1972); *Overture to a Shakespearean Comedy* (1917–21; Prague, Feb. 24, 1927); *Serenade* for Strings (1939); *Symphonic Variations* (Prague, March 26, 1941); *Overture "The Youth"* (1940–41); *Rhapsody* for Violin and Orch. (1942); *Symphonietta* for Small Orch. (1943–44); Piano Concerto (1946; Prague, Dec. 12, 1968); *Symphonic Scherzo* for Band or Orch. (1950; orch. version, Chicago, April 25, 1953); *Serenade* for Small Orch. (1952; Santa Barbara, Calif., March 24, 1965); *Legend* for Small Orch. (1954; Chicago, March 20, 1962); Concertino for Violin and Chamber Orch. (1957; Chicago, May 18, 1963). **CHAMBER:** 7 string quartets (1915; 1927; 1937–40; 1949; 1951; 1957–58; 1960); String Sextet, with Alto Voice (1916–17); Cello Sonata (1918); Violin Sonata (1919); Viola Sonata (1925); *Divertimento* for String Trio (1925); Flute Sonata (1927); Wind Quintet (1928); *Variations, Scherzo and Finale*, nonet (1943); *Serenade* for Winds (1944); Piano Quintet (1945); *Mourning Music* for Viola and Organ (1946; also for Orch.); Clarinet Sonata (1947); *Introduction and Rondo* for Horn and Piano (1951); *3 Pieces* for Cello and Piano (1952); Horn Sonata (1952); Oboe Sonata (1953); Trio for Oboe, Clarinet, and Bassoon (1956); Suite for Solo Violin (1964); Piano Trio (1966–67). **KEYBOARD: P i a n o :** *Summer Nights*, 4 pieces (1914); *Suite in Olden Style* (1920); *The Turning Point* (1923); 2 sonatas (1926, 1950); *Epigrams and Epitaphs* (1928–29); *4 Caprices in Polka Form* (1945); *5 Miniatures* (1954); *4 Pieces for the Right Hand* (1968–69). **O r g a n :** Suite (1958–64); Passacaglia and Fugue (1971). **VOCAL:** *Psalm 23* for Chorus and Orch. (1919); *Requiem* for Solo Quartet, Chorus, Organ, and Orch. (1952; Prague, Nov. 17, 1971); works for male chorus; song cycles (many with orch.), including *Lyric Intermezzo* (1913), *Tragicomedy*, 5 songs (1913), *Fugitive Happiness*, 7 songs (1915–16), *13 Simple Songs* (1917), *3 Songs of the Homeland* (1919), *Evening and Soul* (1921), *Awakening* (1925), *The Rainbow* (1925–26), *The Year* (1941), *7 Songs of Loneliness* (1945–46), *Pilgrim's Songs* (1962–63), and *The Spring* (1965).

BIBL.: M. Očadlík, *K.B. J.* (Prague, 1941); A. Tischler, *K.B. J.: A Catalog of his Works* (Detroit, 1975).—NS/LK/DM

Jirásek, Ivo, Czech composer; b. Prague, July 16, 1920. He studied composition with Šín in Prague and was a student at the Prague Cons. (1938–45) of Krejčí and A. Hába (composition) and Dědeček (conducting). After working as assistant to Kubelík and the Czech Phil. in Prague (1945–46), he conducted at the Zdeněk Nejedlý Theater in Opava (1946–53), where he then was director of its opera company (until 1956). From 1969 to 1978 he was active with the copyright union in Prague. In 1980 he was made a Merited Artist by the Czech government. His output was greatly influenced by French music, but it also owed much to Stravinsky and Berg.

WORKS: DRAMATIC: O p e r a : *Pan Johanes* (Mr. Johanes; 1951–52; Opava, March 24, 1956); *Svítání nad vodami* (Daybreak Over the Waters; 1960–61; Plzeň, Nov. 23, 1963); *Medvěd* (The Bear), after Chekhov (1962–64; Prague, Jan. 25, 1965); *Klíč* (The Key; 1967–68; Prague, March 15, 1971); *Danse macabre* (1970–71; Prague, Sept. 27, 1972); *Mistr Jeroným* (Master Jerome; 1979–80; Prague, March 26, 1992); *Zázrak* (Miracle; 1981). **B a l l e t :** *Faust* (1982–85). **ORCH.:** *Ciaconna* (1944); Concertante Sym. for Violin and Orch. (1958); *Small Suite* (1964); *Variations* (1965); *Festive Overture* (1971); *Mother Hope Symphony* (1973–74; Prague, March 16, 1974); *Mozartiana,* concertino for Chamber Orch. (1978); *4 Dramatic Studies* (1985); *Evening Music* for English Horn and Strings (1985); Concertino for Harpsichord and 11 Strings (1985); *Little Concert Music* for Synthesizer and Orch. (1988). **CHAMBER:** Violin Sonata (1946); 3 string quartets (*4 Studies,* 1963–66; *Ludi con tre toni,* 1977–78; *Meditation on a Theme by Bohuslav Martinů,* 1989); *Sonata da camera* for 13 Strings (1966); *Serenades* for Flute, Bass Clarinet, and Percussion (1967); *3 Pieces* for 4 Instruments (1971); *Partita for Winds* (1972); *Prague with Fingers of Rain,* suite for Dulcimer (1974); *Spectra* for Bass Clarinet and Piano (1975); Sonata for Viola and Percussion (1976); Trio for Violin, Cello, and Piano (1979); *Permutazione* for Flute, Cello, and Piano (1981); *Carnival in Rio* for Flute, Clarinet, Piano, Double Bass, and Percussion (1986); *Preludium, Fugue, and Chorale on a Theme by Domenico Scarlatti* for Flute, Clarinet, Piano, Double Bass, and Percussion (1987); *Oh, quels beaux jours!,* sonata for Solo Cello (1991); *Soirée dansante,* wind quintet (1993). **VOCAL:** *A Hospital Ballad,* cantata for Soloists, Chorus, and Orch. (1944; rev. 1957); *You, My Home,* song cycle for Baritone and Orch. (1960); *Love,* cantata for Bass, Women's Chorus, and Chamber Orch. (1960); *Year in a Rusty-Colored Forest,* 8 songs for Men's Chorus and Chamber Ensemble or Piano (1966); *Music for Soprano, Flute, and Harp* (1967); *Stabat Mater,* oratorio for Soloists, Chorus, Organ, and Wind Orch. (1968; Prague, March 3, 1969); *Song of the Planet Named Earth,* cantata for Soloists, Chorus, and Orch. (1975–76; Prague, April 2, 1977); *Portrait of a Woman* for Soprano, Flute, Bass Clarinet, Vibraphone, and Piano (1975–76); *4 Psalms* for Men's Chorus (1991); *Time,* 3 songs for Soprano and String Quartet (1992).—NS/LK/DM

Jirko, Ivan, Czech composer; b. Prague, Oct. 7, 1926; d. there, Aug. 20, 1978. He studied medicine at the Univ. of Prague (graduated, 1951), and also studied composition with K. Janeček (1944–49) and Bořkovec (1949–52) at the Prague Cons. He then pursued a dual career as a psychiatrist and a composer.

WORKS: DRAMATIC: O p e r a : *The Twelfth Night,* after Shakespeare (1963–64; Liberec, Feb. 25, 1967); *The Strange Story of Arthur Rowe,* after Graham Greene's novel *Ministry of Fear* (1967–68; Liberec, Oct. 25, 1969); *The Millionairess,* operatic divertimento (1969–71); *The Strumpet* (1970; Olomouc, June 23, 1974); *The Way Back* (1974). **ORCH.:** 4 piano concertos (1949, 1951, 1958, 1966); *Serenade* for Small Orch. (1951); Clarinet Concerto (1955); 3 syms.: No. 1 (1957), No. 2, *The Year 1945* (1962; withdrawn), and No. 3 (1977); *Macbeth,* symphonic fantasy (1962); *Elegy on the Death of a Friend* (1965); *Divertimento* for Horn and Orch. (1965); *Symphonic Variations* (1966); *Serenata giocosa* for Chamber String Orch. (1967; also for Violin and Guitar); Sonata for 14 Winds and Kettledrums (1967); *Capriccio all'antico* (1971); *Prague Seconds,* symphonic sketches (1972); Trumpet Concerto (1972); Flute Concerto (1973); *Prague Annals,* symphonic triptych (1973); *At the Turning Point,* symphonic fantasy (1972–73; uses material from the 2nd sym.); Double Concerto for Violin, Piano, and Orch. (Charleroi, Nov. 18, 1976). **CHAMBER:** Wind Quintet (1947); 6 string quartets (1954, 1962, 1966, 1969, 1972, 1974); Cello Sonata (1954–55); Suite for Wind Quintet (1956); Violin Sonata (1959); *Kaleidoscope* for Violin and Piano (1965); *Serenata in due tempi* for Nonet or Oboe Quartet (1970); *Guiocchi per tre* for String Trio (1972); *Partita* for Solo Violin (1974); Piano Quintet (1977–78). **P i a n o :** 2 sonatas (1956; *Elégie disharmonique,* 1970); *Preludio, Canzone e Toccata* (1977). **VOCAL:** *Requiem* (1971); *Štěsí* (Happiness), musical panorama for Narrator, Soprano, Baritone, and Orch. (1975–76); songs.—NS/LK/DM

Jírovec, Vojtěch Matyáš
See **Gyrowetz, Adalbert (Mathiás)**

Jo, Sumi, Korean soprano; b. Seoul, Nov. 22, 1962. She received her training in Seoul and at the Accademia di Santa Cecilia in Rome (1983–86). In 1986 she made her operatic debut as Gilda in Trieste. After engagements in Lyons, Nice, and Marseilles (1987–88), she won particular distinction as Barbarina at the Salzburg Festival in 1988, the year in which she also made her first appearance in Munich and her debut at Milan's La Scala as Thetis/Fortune in Jommelli's *Fetonte.* In 1989 she made her Metropolitan Opera debut in N.Y. as Gilda, and also sang in Vienna. She appeared at the Chicago Lyric Opera in 1990 as the Queen of the Night. In 1991 she made her debut at London's Covent Garden as Olympia in *Les Contes d'Hoffmann.* In 1992 she sang Matilde in Rossini's *Elisabetta regina d'Inghilterra* in Naples. In 1996 she was engaged as Zerbinetta in Lisbon. She portrayed Lucio Silla in N.Y. in 1997. Among her other roles are Fiorilla in *Il Turco in Italia,* Elvira in *I Puritani,* Adèle in *Le Comte Ory,* Zerlina in *Fra Diavolo,* and Oscar in *Un Ballo in Maschera.*—NS/LK/DM

Joachim, Amalie (née **Schneeweiss**), German soprano, later mezzo-soprano; b. Marburg, May 10, 1839; d. Berlin, Feb. 3, 1899. She began her career as a soprano, appearing in Vienna under the name Weiss (1854), and later became a mezzo-soprano. She married **Joseph Joachim** in 1863, but after a bitter lawsuit, in which he accused her of infidelity with the publisher Fritz Simrock, they were divorced (1884). She was a fine lieder artist, excelling particularly in songs by Schumann.

BIBL.: O. Plaschke, *A. J.* (Berlin, 1899).—NS/LK/DM

Joachim, Joseph, renowned Hungarian-born violinist, conductor, pedagogue, and composer; b. Kittsee, near Pressburg, June 28, 1831; d. Berlin, Aug. 15, 1907. His family moved to Pest in 1833 and he began to study violin with Szervaczinski in 1836, appearing with him in public at the age of 7. At the age of 10 he was sent to Vienna, where he studied with M. Hauser, G. Hellmesberger Sr., and his major influence, J. Bohm. He went to Leipzig when he was 12 and was befriended by Mendelssohn; studied composition at the Cons. with Hauptmann and David. He first played in Leipzig on Aug. 19, 1843, in a concert with Pauline Viardot, Clara Schumann, and Mendelssohn, then appeared as soloist with Mendelssohn and the Gewandhaus Orch. (Nov. 16, 1843). In 1844 he made his London debut. His fame was assured with his remarkable performance of the Beethoven Violin Concerto at a Phil. Soc. concert there under Mendelssohn (May 27, 1844). During his years in Leipzig, he played in the Gewandhaus Orch., becoming its assoc. concertmaster under David. He was concertmaster of the Weimar Court Orch. (1850–53), but did not gain the favor of Liszt, who reigned supreme there. In 1853 he became Royal Music Director in Hannover, where he was active as both concertmaster and conductor. It was there that he met Brahms, who, with A. Dietrich and Schumann, wrote a Violin Sonata, F-A-E, on Joachim's motto, "Frei aber einsam." His solitude ended in 1863 when he married the mezzo-soprano Amalie Weiss; they were divorced in 1884, following an acrimonious lawsuit brought by the overly jealous Joachim, charging her with infidelity with the publisher Fritz Simrock. A letter written by Brahms in support and defense of Mrs. Joachim was used in the trial, causing an estrangement between Joachim and Brahms, which was subsequently healed by the Double Concerto written by Brahms for Joachim, who gave its premiere (Cologne, Oct. 18, 1887). Joachim had previously assisted Brahms with the composition of the Violin Concerto, which they premiered (Leipzig, Jan. 1, 1879). In 1865 Joachim resigned from his Hannover duties in protest over anti-Jewish discrimination against J. Grun. He settled in Berlin in 1868 as director and prof. of violin at the Hochschule für Ausübende Tonkunst, where aspiring violinists flocked from all over Europe to study with him, including Auer, Hubay, and Huberman, who influenced subsequent generations of violinists in the Joachim tradition of excellence and faithful interpretation. From 1882 to 1887 he also was one of the principal conductors of the Berlin Phil. Joachim never abandoned his career as a virtuoso. He was particularly popular in England, which he visited annually from 1862. He received an honorary doctorate from the Univ. of Cambridge (1877), as well as from Oxford and Glasgow. He gave his farewell concert in Berlin on April 6, 1907.

Joachim's unswerving determination to interpret music in accordance with the intentions of the composer made him an outstanding exponent of the masterworks of the violin literature. Many composers, including Dvořák, Gade, Schumann, and Brahms, wrote large-scale concertos for him, consulting with him on the solo parts. As a player of chamber music, he was unexcelled in his day; in 1869 he organized the Joachim Quartet, which attained merited celebrity in Europe. His own compositions for the violin are virtuoso pieces that still attract performers, the most famous being the *Hungarian Concerto*. He also prepared cadenzas for violin concertos by Mozart (K. 218 and K. 219), Viotti (No. 22), Beethoven, and Brahms. With A. Moser, he publ. *Violinschule* (3 vols., Berlin, 1902–5; 2nd ed., rev., 1959 by M. Jacobsen).

WORKS: ORCH.: O v e r t u r e s : *Hamlet; Demetrius; Henry IV;* overture inspired by 2 plays of Gozzi; "To the Memory of Kleist"; *Scena der Marfa* for Contralto. **V i o l i n a n d O r c h . C o n c e r t o s :** No. 1 in G minor, op. 3, "in einem Satz" (c. 1855), No. 2 in D minor, op. 11, "in ungarischer Weise" (1857; Hannover, March 24, 1860), and No. 3 in G major (Hannover, Nov. 5, 1864; rev. 1889). **O t h e r :** *Andantino and Allegro scherzoso* (1850); *Notturno; Variations* in E minor (Berlin, Feb. 15, 1881). **V i o l i n a n d P i a n o :** 3 Stücke (*Romanze, Fantasiestück, Frühlingsfantasie*); 3 Stücke (*Lindenrauschen, Abendglocken, Ballade*); *Romance; Hebrew Melodies.* **OTHER:** *Variations on an Original Theme* for Viola and Piano; 2 songs.

BIBL.: A. Moser, *J. J., Ein Lebensbild* (Berlin, 1898; 5th ed., rev., 1910; Eng. tr. from 2nd Ger. ed., 1900); K. Storck, *J. J., Eine Studie* (Leipzig, 1902); J. Fuller Maitland, *J. J.* (London and N.Y., 1905); L. Brieger-Wasservogel, *J.- Gedenkbüchlein* (Dresden, 1907); Johannes Joachim and A. Moser, eds., *Briefe von und an J. J.* (3 vols., Berlin, 1911–13; abr. Eng. tr., 1913); G. Maas, *The Instrumental Music of J. J.* (diss., Univ. of N.C., 1973). —NS/LK/DM

Joachim, Otto, German-born Canadian composer, violinist, violist, and teacher; b. Düsseldorf, Oct. 13, 1910. He took violin lessons with his father, then studied at the Buths-Neitzel Konservatorium in Düsseldorf (1916–28) and at the Rheinische Musik Schule in Cologne (1928–31). He fled Germany in 1934 and spent the succeeding 15 years in the Far East, mainly in Singapore and Shanghai; constructed electronic string instruments of the entire violin family (1944–45). In 1949 he emigrated to Canada, becoming a naturalized citizen in 1957. He was a member (1952–57) and later principal violist (1961–65) of the Montreal Sym. Orch.; also was a co-founder-member of the Montreal String Quartet (1957–58) and was associated with Glenn Gould. In 1956 he organized his own electronic music studio; was founder-director of the Montreal Consort of Ancient Instruments (1958–68). He taught at McGill Univ. (1956–64) and at the Cons. de Musique de Montreal et Quebec (1956–76). His music is quaquaversal, but its favorite direction is asymptotic.

WORKS: ORCH.: *Asia,* symphonic poem (1928–39); Concertante No. 1 for Violin, String Orch., and Percussion (1955–57; Paris, Sept. 9, 1958) and No. 2 for String Quartet and String Orch. (1961; Montreal, March 12, 1962); *Contrastes* (Montreal, May 6, 1967). **C H A M B E R :** *Music* for Violin and Viola (1953); Cello Sonata (1954); String Quartet (1956); *Interlude,* saxophone quartet (1960); Nonet for Wind Quartet, String Quartet, and Piano (1960); *Divertimento* for Wind Quintet (1962); *Expansion* for Flute and Piano (1962); *Dialogue* for Viola and Piano (1964); *Illumination I* for Speaker, Chamber Ensemble, and Projectors (1965); *Kinderspiel* for Narrator, Violin, Cello, and Piano (1969); *12 12-Tone Pieces for the Young* for Violin and Piano (1970); 6 Pieces for Guitar (1971); *Requiem* for Violin or Viola or Cello (1977); 4 *Intermezzi* for Flute and Guitar (1978); *Night Music* for Flute and Guitar (1978); *Tribute to St. Romanus* for Organ, 4

Horns, and 4 Percussion (1981); *Paean* for Cello (1989). **KEY-BOARD: P i a n o :** *Bagatelles* (1939); *L'Eclosion* (1954). **O r - g a n :** *Fantasia* (1961). **ELECTROACOUSTIC AND MIXED MEDIA:** *Katimavik* for Tape (1967); *Illumination II* for Instruments, 4-track Tape, and Projectors (1969); *5.9* for 4-track Tape (1971); *6 1/2* for 4-track Tape (1971); *Mankind* for 4 Speakers, 4 Synthesizers, Organ, Timpani, Incense, Slides, and Projectors (1972); *Stimulus à Goad* for Guitar and Synthesizer (1973); *Uraufführung* for Guitar, 14 Instruments, and Electronics (1977); *7 Electronic Sketches* for Tape (1984); *Mobile für Johann Sebastian Bach* for 4 Woodwinds, Celesta, Organ, 4 Strings, and Tape (1985).—**NS/LK/DM**

João IV, King of Portugal; b. Villa-Vicosa, March 19, 1604; d. Lisbon, Nov. 6, 1656. As a prince he received a fine musical training at the court chapel. He began collecting church music, gradually accumulating a magnificent library, which was totally destroyed in the earthquake of 1755. However, a catalog of it was issued in Lisbon in 1649, and reprinted by Vasconcellos in 1873. João IV was a true music scholar, well acquainted with the flow of conflicting opinions regarding musical theory. He publ. (anonymously) the pamphlets *Defensa de la musica moderna contra la errada opinion del obispo Cyrillo Franco* (in Spanish; 1649) and *Respuesta a las dudas que se pusieron a la missa "Panis quem ego dabo" de Palestrina* (1654); Italian trs. were made of both. He composed a considerable quantity of church music. His motets *Crux fidelis* and *Adjuva nos* are reprinted in S. Luck's *Sammlung ausgezeichneter Kompositionen für die Kirche* (1884–85).

BIBL.: J. Freitas Branco, *D. J. IV, Músico* (Lisbon, 1956). —**NS/LK/DM**

Jobim, Antonio Carlos, Brazilian composer, guitarist, and pianist; b. Rio De Janeiro, Jan. 25, 1927; d. N.Y., Dec. 8, 1994. Jobim was the primary composer of bossa nova, which enjoyed international popularity in the early 1960s, especially because of his songs, such as "The Girl from Impanema" and "Desafinado."

Jobim studied piano as a child and eventually became music director of Odeon Records in Brazil. In 1958 he had João Gilberto record his composition "Chega de Saudade," which he described as *bossa nova*, a "new wave" of samba music. The record was a hit. In 1959 he scored the French-Brazilian film *Black Orpheus*. American jazz guitarist Charlie Byrd heard his music on a tour of Brazil in 1961 and adopted the style for his 1962 album with Stan Getz, *Jazz Samba*, which topped the pop charts in March 1963 and produced a Top 40 single in Jobim's "Desafinado." Byrd followed this success with the album *Bossa Nova Pelos Passaros* (1963) from which Jobim's "Meditation (Meditacao)" was a chart single; Pat Boone recorded a charting vocal version of the tune.

Stan Getz, meanwhile, utilized bossa nova on the 1964 album *Getz/Gilberto*, which he recorded with João Gilberto. The album hit the Top Ten and went gold, winning the Grammy for Album of the Year; Jobim's "The Girl from Ipanema" (Portuguese lyrics by Vinicuis De Moraes, English lyrics by Norman Gimbel), featuring Astrud Gilberto on vocals, became a Top Ten hit.

Jobim moved to L.A. in 1965. That December, Andy Williams reached the charts with his "Quiet Nights of Quiet Stars" (Portuguese title "Corcovado," English lyrics by Gene Lees). Jobim collaborated with Frank Sinatra on the album *Francis Albert Sinatra & Antonio Carlos Jobim* (1967), which spent more than six months on the charts. On Nov. 13, 1967, he appeared with Sinatra on the television special *Frank Sinatra: A Man and His Music*. He composed the music for the 1970 film *The Adventurers*. In 1971 he was featured on a second Sinatra album, *Sinatra & Company*. He also made several of his own albums.

Jobim died of heart failure in 1994 at the age of 67. —**WR**

Jochum, Eugen, eminent German conductor, brother of **Georg Ludwig Jochum** and **Otto Jochum,** and father of **(Maria) Veronica Jochum;** b. Babenhausen, Nov. 1, 1902; d. Munich, March 26, 1987. He began playing the piano at 4 and the organ at 7. After attending the Augsburg Cons. (1914–22), he studied composition with Waltershausen and conducting with Hausegger at the Munich Academy of Music (1922–25). He commenced his career as a répétiteur at the Bavarian State Opera in Munich and in Mönchengladbach, appearing as a guest conductor with the Munich Phil. in 1926. He then was a conductor at the Kiel Opera (1926–29) and conducted the Lübeck sym. concerts. After conducting at the Mannheim National Theater (1929–30), he served as Generalmusikdirektor in Duisburg (1930–32); then was music director of the Berlin Radio and a frequent guest conductor with the Berlin Phil. From 1934 to 1945 he was Generalmusikdirektor of the Hamburg State Opera. Although his tenure coincided with the Nazi era, Jochum successfully preserved his artistic independence; he avoided joining the Nazi party, assisted a number of his Jewish players, and programmed several works by officially unapproved composers. From 1934 to 1949 he also was Generalmusikdirektor of the Hamburg State Phil. In 1949 he was appointed chief conductor of the Bavarian Radio Sym. Orch. in Munich, a position he held with great distinction until 1960. He also appeared as a guest conductor throughout Europe. In 1953 he made his first appearance at the Bayreuth Festival, conducting *Tristan und Isolde*. He made his U.S. debut as a guest conductor with the Los Angeles Phil. in 1958. From 1961 to 1964 he was co-principal conductor of the Concertgebouw Orch. of Amsterdam, sharing his duties with Bernard Haitink. From 1969 to 1973 he was artistic director of the Bamberg Sym. Orch.; he also served as laureate conductor of the London Sym. Orch. (1977–79). His many honors included the Brahms Medal (1936), the Bruckner Medal (1954), the Bülow Medal of the Berlin Phil. (1978), and the Bruckner Ring of the Vienna Sym. Orch. (1980); he was also made an honorary prof. by the senate of the city of Hamburg (1949). Jochum became known as an outstanding interpreter of the music of Bruckner; he also gained renown for his performances of Bach, Haydn, Mozart, Beethoven, Schubert, Brahms, and Richard Strauss.—**NS/LK/DM**

Jochum, Georg Ludwig, German conductor, brother of **Eugen Jochum** and **Otto Jochum;** b. Babenhausen, Dec. 10, 1909; d. Mülheim an der Ruhr, Nov. 1, 1970. He studied at the Augsburg Cons. and then with Haas (composition) and Hausegger (conducting) at the Munich Academy of Music. He was music director in Münster (1932–34), and then a conductor at the Frankfurt am Main Opera and Museumgesellschaft concerts (1934–37). He subsequently was Generalmusikdirektor in Linz (1940–45) and Duisburg (1946–58), and also director of the Duisburg Cons. (1946–58). He appeared as a guest conductor in Europe, South America, and Japan.—NS/LK/DM

Jochum, (Maria) Veronica, gifted German pianist, daughter of **Eugen Jochum;** b. Berlin, Dec. 6, 1932. She studied piano with Eliza Hansen and then with Maria Landes-Hindemith at the Munich Staatliche Hochschule für Musik (M.A., 1955; concert diploma, 1957). After additional studies with Edwin Fischer in Lucerne (1958–59), she completed her training with Rudolf Serkin in Philadelphia (1959–61). She commenced her career in Germany in 1954; made tours of Europe from 1961. Following her successful N.Y. debut as soloist in Beethoven's 1st Piano Concerto with Gerard Schwarz and the Y Chamber Sym. (March 21, 1981), she made appearances throughout the U.S. She maintained an intriguing repertoire, ranging from Mozart and Beethoven to Bartók and Schoenberg; she also championed lesser-known scores by such diverse composers as Clara Schumann and Ernst Krenek; likewise performed new works, including the premiere of Gunther Schuller's 2nd Piano Concerto (1982).—NS/LK/DM

Jochum, Otto, German composer, brother of **Eugen Jochum** and **Georg Ludwig Jochum;** b. Babenhausen, March 18, 1898; d. Bad Reichenhall, Oct. 24, 1969. He studied at the Augsburg Cons. and at the Munich Academy of Music with Heinrich Kasper Schmid, Gustav Geierhaas, and Joseph Haas (1922–31). From 1932 to 1951 he served as director of the Augsburg Municipal Singing School.

WORKS: *Goethe-Sinfonie* (1941); *Florianer-Sinfonie* (1946); 2 oratorios: *Der jungste Tag* and *Ein Weihnachtssingen*; 12 masses; many choral works; arrangements of folk songs; songs. —NS/LK/DM

Jodál, Gábor, Romanian composer of Hungarian parentage; b. Odorhei, April 25, 1913. He received a doctorate in jurisprudence at the Univ. of Cluj (1937), then studied composition with Kodály, Kósa, and J. Adám at the Budapest Academy of Music (1939–42). He was a répétiteur at the Cluj National Theater (1942–44), then a lecturer at the Hungarian Inst. of Art (1948–50) and a lecturer (from 1950) and director (1965–73) of the Cons. As a composer, he continues an amiable but rhythmically incisive tradition of the ethnically variegated music of Transylvania.

WORKS: DRAMATIC: Ballet: *Meseorszag kapujaban* (At the Gate of the Land of Story; 1952). ORCH.: Sinfonietta (1957); *Divertimento* (1964); *Nocturne* for Chamber Orch. (1976); *Scherzo* for Chamber Orch. (1978); *Sinfonia brevis* (1981). CHAMBER: 2 violin sonatas (1946, 1953); 3 *Pieces* for Viola and Piano (1946); Suite for Flute and Piano (1955); String

Quartet (1955); 3 *Pieces* for Wind Quintet (1959); *Introduction and Scherzo* for Bassoon and Piano (1964); Suite for Wind Quintet (1966); 3 *Nocturnes* for Flute, Clarinet, Viola, Cello, and Piano (1967); Viola Sonata (1974); Piano Sonata (1977). VOCAL: 2 cantatas: *Revolutia* (1964) and *Treptele implinirii* (1977); choruses; songs.—NS/LK/DM

Jöde, (Wilhelm August Ferdinand) Fritz, prominent German music educator; b. Hamburg, Aug. 2, 1887; d. there, Oct. 19, 1970. He studied at the Hamburg teachers's training college and then began his career as a provincial school teacher. After service in the German army during World War I, he studied musicology with Abert at the Univ. of Leipzig (1920–21). In 1923 he was made prof. of choral conducting and folk music education at Berlin's Staatliche Akademie für Kirchen- und Schulmusik. He organized societies for the propagation of folk music, and was very active in various youth movements in Germany until the Nazis removed him from his positions in 1935. He joined the faculty of the Salzburg Mozarteum in 1939, but was compelled to give up that position as well in 1943. After the fall of the Third Reich, he resumed his various activities; was made director of the youth music program of Hamburg's Hochschule für Musik (1947) and also director of the Internationales Institut für Jugend- und Volksmusik. He edited several periodicals and many song collections.

WRITINGS: Ed. *Musikalische Jugendkultur* (Hamburg, 1918); *Musik und Erziehung* (Wolfenbüttel, 1919); *Pädagogik deines Wesens* (Hamburg, 1920); *Musikmanifest* (Rudolstadt, 1921); *Die Lebensfragen der neuen Schule* (Hamburg, 1921); *Unser Musikleben* (Wolfenbüttel, 1923; 2nd ed., 1925); *Musikschulen für Jugend und Volk* (Wolfenbüttel, 1924; 2nd ed., 1928); *Das schaffende Kind in der Musik* (Wolfenbüttel, 1928; 2nd ed., 1962); ed. *Musik in der Volksschule* (Berlin, 1928); *Kind und Musik* (Berlin, 1930; reprint, 1966); *Vom Wesen und Werden der Jugendmusik* (Mainz, 1954); *Die Herzberger Bachwochen* (Trossingen and Wolfenbüttel, 1959).

BIBL.: R. Stapelberg, *F. J.: Leben und Werk* (Trossingen and Wolfenbüttel, 1957); G. Trautner, *Die Musikerziehung bei F. J.: Quellen und Grundlagen* (Wolfenbüttel, 1968).—NS/LK/DM

Joel, Billy, a classically trained pianist, persevered through several N.Y. rock bands and solo albums before emerging as a pop-style singer- songwriter with 1974's autobiographical "Piano Man."; b. Hicksville, Long Island, N.Y., May 9, 1949. Unable to sustain public interest in his career, Billy Joel continued to write and record highly melodic, imaginatively arranged ballads, eventually breaking through into mass popularity with 1977's The Stranger. Although favorably compared to the other surviving 1970s pop-rock singer-songwriter, Elton John, Billy Joel was also likened to Neil Diamond and Barry Manilow for his superficial, facile songs and cloying, haughty style. Still, he achieved great success on the pop charts through the 1980s despite being the bane of rock critics everywhere.

Billy Joel grew up in the working-class community of Hicksville, on N.Y.'s Long Island, initiating a dozen years of classical piano training at age four. Raised by his mother after his parents's divorce at age seven, Joel formed his first band, the Echoes, in 1964. The group evolved into the Lost Souls, which was superseded by the Hassles by 1968. Signed to United Artists Records, the group recorded two albums before disbanding. Joel subsequently formed the rock duo Attila with Hassles drummer Jon Small, recording one album for Epic Records.

Signed to Family Productions in 1971, Billy Joel recorded his first album of all-original material, *Cold Spring Harbor*, for Epic, but the poorly produced album failed to generate any interest despite six months of touring to promote it. A live broadcast by Joel and his band in Philadelphia nonetheless produced a regional favorite with "Captain Jack," which was played regularly on radio station WMMR-FM for months. Joel, embroiled in legal disputes with Family Productions, moved to Los Angeles, where he took up residence at the Executive Room piano bar, performing as "Bill Martin" (this experience inspired his first hit, "Piano Man").

On the strength of "Captain Jack," Billy Joel was signed to Columbia Records in spring 1973. The blatantly autobiographical title song to *Piano Man* became a major hit, but interest in Joel waned. After a moderate hit with "The Entertainer" from *Streetlife Serenade*, Joel switched management and moved to upstate N.Y., forming a new band with drummer Larry DeVitto. *Turnstiles*, issued in 1976, sold poorly, yet contained Joel's classic "New York State of Mind" (covered by Barbra Streisand on her 1977 album *Superman*) and the Phil Spector—style "Say Goodbye to Hollywood."

Subsequently touring for nearly a year, Billy Joel initiated a decade-long relationship with producer Phil Ramone, well known in the industry for his work with Paul Simon and Phoebe Snow. They first collaborated on 1978's *The Stranger*, which remained on the album charts for more than two years and established Joel as a contemporary singer-songwriter. It yielded four hits: the smash "Just the Way You Are," and the major "Movin' Out (Anthony's Song)," "Only the Good Die Young" (which raised the ire of the Catholic Church), and "She's Always a Woman." His next album, *52nd Street*, produced three hits, the smash personal anthem "My Life," "Big Shot," and "Honesty"; it is also included the Spector-style "Until the Night."

Projecting a tougher image, Billy Joel's *Glass Houses* yielded four hits, with the facile "It's Still Rock and Roll to Me" (a top hit), "You May Be Right" (a near-smash), "Don't Ask Me Why," and "Sometimes a Fantasy." Following *Songs in the Attic*, 1980 tour recordings of older material, *The Nylon Curtain* exhibited a sense of social consciousness, containing the seven-minute Vietnam portrait "Goodnight Saigon" and yielding major hits with "Pressure" and "Allentown."

Billy Joel reaffirmed his mass popularity with the diverse *An Innocent Man*. Purposely recreating different pop styles, including 1950s doo-wop and 1960s soft rock, the album was perhaps Joel's most popular and successful. It produced four top easy-listening crossover hits with "Tell Her About It" (a top pop hit), "An Innocent Man," "The Longest Time," and "Leave Me a Tender Moment Alone," the pop smash "Uptown Girl,"

and the major pop hit "Keeping the Faith." In 1985 Joel married supermodel Christie Brinkley and scored a near-smash with "You're Only Human (Second Wind)," the royalties to which he donated to the National Committee for Youth Suicide Prevention. The following year he toured for the first time in three years and issued *The Bridge*, which produced major hits with "Modern Woman," "A Matter of Trust," and "This Is the Time"; it also included a duet with Ray Charles, "Baby Grand." Joel's 1987 international tour included stops in Moscow and Leningrad that resulted in two films, the HBO concert movie *Live from Leningrad* and the documentary *A Matter of Trust*, and a live album.

Billy Joel coproduced 1989's *Storm Front* with Foreigner's Mick Jones. The album yielded five hits, including the top hit "We Didn't Start the Fire" and the smash "I Go to Extremes." Joel toured in 1989–1990 and again in 1993. His next album, *River of Dreams*, produced by guitarist Danny Kortchmar (who had previously worked with James Taylor and Don Henley), entered the charts at Number One, a first for the singer. It produced the pop smash title song and the major hit "All About Soul," recorded with Color Me Badd, while containing "The Great Wall of China" and "No Man's Land." Joel and Brinkley were divorced in 1994 and Joel began to pursue projects outside of rock.

DISC.: THE HASSLES: *The Hassles* (1968); *Hour of the Wolf* (1969). ATTILA: *Attila* (1970). BILLY JOEL: *Cold Spring Harbor* (1972); *Piano Man* (1973); *Streetlife Serenade* (1974); *Piano Man/Streetlife Serenade* (1986); *Turnstiles* (1976); *The Stranger* (1977); *52nd Street* (1978); *Glass Houses* (1980); *Songs in the Attic* (1981); *The Nylon Curtain* (1982); *An Innocent Man* (1983); *Greatest Hits, Vols. 1 and 2* (1985); *The Bridge* (1986); *In Concert: KOHUEPT* (1987); *Storm Front* (1989); *River of Dreams* (1993).

BIBL.: Peter Gambaccini, *B. J.: A Photo-Bio* (N.Y., 1979). —BH

Johann Ernst, Prince of Weimar, German violinist and composer; b. Weimar, 1696; d. Frankfurt am Main, Aug. 1, 1715. He showed much promise as a child and, at a very early age, was given violin lessons by the court musician G. Eilenstein. At 10 he began keyboard instruction with J.G. Walther, and after attending the Univ. of Utrecht, he returned to Weimar in 1713 to study composition with Walther. Telemann, Bach, and Mattheson held him in high esteem. Telemann publ. his 6 violin concertos, op.1, in 1718, and Bach prepared keyboard concerto arrangements utilizing four of his scores. —LK/DM

Johannes de Lymburgia, composer who flourished in the first half of the 15th century. He most likely was from Limbourg, near Verviers (now in Belgium). About 1400 he became chaplain at the collegiate church of St. Jean l' Evangéliste in Liège, being made succentor there in 1408. In 1431 he went to Vicenza as instructor to the young clerics. In 1436 he became canon of Notre Dame in Huy. Among his output were mass movements and pairs, as well as a cycle, Magnificat settings, hymns, and laude.

BIBL.: H. Rosen, *Die liturgischen Werke des J. von Limburgia* (diss., Univ. of Innsbruck, 1929).—LK/DM

Johannes de Quadris or **Quatris,** composer who flourished in the first half of the 15ᵗʰ century. He most likely was active in the Veneto from about 1430 to 1440. Among his extant works are Magnificat settings and Lamentations. His works were edited by G. Catting in *Monumenta veneta sacra,* II (1972).—**LK/DM**

Johannesen, Grant, eminent American pianist and pedagogue; b. Salt Lake City, July 30, 1921. He studied piano with Robert Casadesus at Princeton Univ. (1941–46) and with Egon Petri at Cornell Univ.; also took courses in composition with Sessions and Boulanger. He made his concert debut in N.Y. in 1944. In 1949 he won first prize at the Ostend Concours Internationale, which was the beginning of his international career. He toured Europe with Mitropoulos and the N.Y. Phil. in 1956 and 1957; made another European tour with Szell and the Cleveland Orch. in 1968. From 1960 to 1966 he taught at the Aspen (Colo.) Music School; in 1973 he became music consultant and adviser of the Cleveland Inst. of Music; subsequently was its music director (1974–77), and finally its president (1977–85). He also taught at the Mannes Coll. of Music in N.Y. and at the Salzburg Mozarteum. Johannesen acquired a reputation as a pianist of fine musicianly stature, subordinating his virtuoso technique to the higher considerations of intellectual fidelity to the composer's intentions; he was particularly esteemed for his performances of French and American music. He also composed some piano works. He was married to **Zara Nelsova** from 1963 to 1973.—**NS/LK/DM**

Jóhannesson, Einar, Icelandic clarinetist; b. Reykjavík, Aug. 16, 1950. He entered the Children's Music School in Reykjavík when he was 6, and while still attending elementary school, he took up the clarinet. After training at the Reykjavík Coll. of Music (1963–69), where he studied with Gunnar Egilsson, he went to London to pursue training at the Royal Coll. of Music (1969–74) under Bernard Walton and John McCaw. In 1979 he was awarded the Sonning Prize for young Nordic soloists, which enabled him to complete his study with Walter Boeykens in Nice. Returning to Reykjavík, he became first clarinetist in the Iceland Sym. Orch. He also pursued a career as a soloist, recitalist, and chamber music player, touring throughout Europe. He has won particular distinction for his performances of contemporary scores.—**NS/LK/DM**

Jóhannsson, Magnús Blöndal, Icelandic conductor and composer; b. Skalar, Sept. 8, 1925. He was taken to Reykjavík as an infant, and showed a precocious musical talent. At the age of 10, he was admitted to the Reykjavík School of Music, where he studied under F. Mixa and V. Urbantschitsch (1935–37; 1939–45). He then took courses at the Juilliard School of Music in N.Y. (1947–53). He returned to Iceland in 1954 and was a staff member of the Iceland State Broadcasting Service (1956–76) as well as a conductor at the National Theater in Reykjavík (1965–72). As a composer, he was attracted to the novel resources of electronic music. His *Study* for Magnetic Tape and Wind Quintet (1957) was the first

Icelandic work employing electronic sound. His other works include 4 *Abstractions* for Piano (1955), *Ionization* for Organ (1956), *Samstirni* for Tape (1960), *Punktar* (Points) for Tape and Small Orch. (1961), *15 Minigrams* for Flute, Oboe, Clarinet, and Double Bass (1961), *Dimensions* for Violin (1961), *Sonorities I–III* for Piano (1961–68), *Birth of an Island,* tape music for the film depicting the volcanic creation of an island near Iceland (1964), *Sequence,* ballet for Dancers, Instruments, and Lights (1968), *The Other Iceland,* music from the film (1973), *Adagio* for Percussion, Celesta, and Strings (1980), and *Solitude* for Flute (1983).—**NS/LK/DM**

Johanos, Donald, American conductor; b. Cedar Rapids, Iowa, Feb. 10, 1928. He studied violin and conducting at the Eastman School of Music in Rochester, N.Y. (Mus.B., 1950; Mus.M., 1952). He received grants from the American Sym. Orch. League and the Rockefeller Foundation for conducting studies with Ormandy, Szell, Beecham, Beinum, Karajan, and Klemperer (1955–58). He won the Netherlands Radio Union conducting competition in 1957. From 1953 to 1956 he was music director of the Altoona (Pa.) Sym. Orch., and also of the Johnstown (Pa.) Sym. Orch. in 1955–56. In 1957 he became assoc. conductor of the Dallas Sym. Orch., and then its resident conductor in 1961, and subsequently its music director in 1962, achieving estimable results. He was assoc. conductor of the Pittsburgh Sym. Orch. and director of its chamber orch. (1970–80); was music director of the Honolulu Sym. Orch. (1979–94) and artistic director of the Hawaii Opera Theatre (1979–83).—**NS/LK/DM**

Johansen, David Monrad, Norwegian pianist, music critic, and composer, father of **(David) Johan Kvandal (Johansen);** b. Vefsn, Nov. 8, 1888; d. Sandvika, Feb. 20, 1974. He studied piano with Winge and Johnson (1904–09), then theory with Elling and Holter, as well as piano with Nissen at the Christiania Cons. (1909–15). In 1915 he went to Berlin, where he took lessons with Humperdinck and Kahn. By this time in middle age, he continued his studies in composition in Paris (1927) and in Leipzig (1933, 1935), where he took a special course in counterpoint with Grabner. In the meantime, he pursued an active career as a concert pianist and composer; made his debut in Christiania in 1910. He was ed. of *Norsk musikerblad* (1917–18); was music critic of *Norske intelligenss edler* (1916–18) and of *Aftenposten* (1925–45). He wrote a monograph on Grieg (Oslo, 1934; 3ʳᵈ ed., 1956; Eng. tr., 1938). His music continued the national Norwegian tradition, in the lyric manner of Grieg; as time went by, Johansen experienced a mild influence of Russian and French music, gradually forming an innocuous modern style with sporadic audacious incursions into the domain of sharp dissonance.

WORKS: ORCH.: *Symphonic Fantasy* (1936); *Pan,* symphonic poem (1939); Piano Concerto (1955). **CHAMBER:** Violin Sonata (1912); Piano Quartet (1947); Quintet for Flute and String Quartet (1967); String Quartet (1969); piano pieces. **VOCAL:** *Voluspa,* oratorio (1926); *Sigvat Skald* for Baritone and Orch. (1928); several choruses; songs.

BIBL.: O. Sandvik and O. Gaukstad, *D.M. J. i skrift og tate* (Oslo, 1968).—**NS/LK/DM**

Johansen, Gunnar, remarkable Danish-American pianist, composer, and teacher; b. Copenhagen, Jan. 21, 1906; d. Blue Mounds, Wisc., May 25, 1991. He made his public debut at the age of 12 in Copenhagen, where he studied with Schioler, then went to Berlin when he was 14, becoming a member of the Busoni circle. After further piano studies with Lamond and Fischer, he completed his training with Petri at the Hochschule für Musik (1922–24). He toured Europe (1924–29) and then settled in the U.S., where he pursued an active concert career, gaining particular distinction for his series of 12 historical piano recitals encompassing works from Frescobaldi to Stravinsky, which he presented in San Francisco, Chicago, and N.Y. in the late 1930s; then held the specially created position of artist-in-residence at the Univ. of Wisc. at Madison (1939–76). Johansen produced a sensation when he substituted on short notice for a colleague as soloist in the piano version of Beethoven's Violin Concerto with Ormandy and the Philadelphia Orch. in N.Y. (Jan. 14, 1969). He excelled in works of transcendental difficulty; he played and recorded the complete solo piano works of Liszt and Busoni, including the latter's Bach transcriptions, as well as the complete solo clavier works of Bach. In 1986 he appeared at the Indianapolis Romantic Music Festival playing works of Liszt in commemoration of the composer's death a century before. He was a composer of fantastic fecundity; among his compositions are three piano concertos (1930, 1970, 1981), 31 piano sonatas (1941–51), and 515 piano sonatas improvised directly on the keyboard and recorded on tape (1952–82). **—NS/LK/DM**

Johanson, Sven-Eric (Emanuel), Swedish composer, organist, and pedagogue; b. Västervik, Dec. 10, 1919; d. Göteborg, Sept. 29, 1997. He studied at the Ingesund School of Music (1938), then obtained diplomas as a music teacher (1943) and organist and choirmaster (1946) at the Stockholm Musikhögskolan. He also studied composition with Melchers, and later with Valen (1951) and finally with Dallapiccola in Florence (1957). After serving as organist and choirmaster at the Uppsala Missionary Church (1944–50), he settled in Göteborg in 1952 and was organist at the Alvsborg Church (until 1977). He was also active as a teacher. In 1971 he was made a member of the Royal Swedish Academy of Music in Stockholm. His output ranged from electro-acoustic compositions to popular scores.

WORKS: DRAMATIC: O p e r a : *Bortbytingarna* (1954–55); *Kunskapens vin* (Göteborg, May 21, 1959); *Sagan om ringen* (1972); *Reliken* (1974; Borås, Jan. 18, 1975); *Skandal, Ers Majestät* (Umeå, May 8, 1978); *Du människa* (1980); *Pojken med flöjten* (Göteborg, Dec. 3, 1980); *Tjuvens pekfinger,* opera-buffa (1968–82; Göteborg, Jan. 14, 1983); *Denize* (1994–95). **O t h e r :** Radio operas; incidental music; *Rivalerna,* micro-drama (1967; Swedish Radio, March 16, 1969); *Kassandras omvändelse,* monodrama (1977); *Slottet,* ballet (1983). **ORCH.:** Syms.: No. 1, *Sinfonia ostinata* (1949–54), No. 2, *Duinoelegi,* for Tenor, Chorus, and Orch. (1954; also for String Orch. as *Sinfonia elegiaca,* 1954–55; Göteborg, Feb. 8, 1956), No. 3 (1956; Göteborg, Sept. 23, 1959), No. 5, *Elementsymfonin* (1965–68), No. 6, *Sinfonietta pastorella* (1972; Abo, April 5, 1973), No. 7, *Spelmanssymfoni,* for Strings (1974), No. 8, *En Frödingsymfoni* (1983–84; Swedish Radio,

March 11, 1984), No. 9, *Sinfonia d'estate* (Malmö, May 6, 1987), No. 10, *Chez nous* (1990; Göteborg, Feb. 7, 1991), No. 11, *Sinfonia d'autunno* (1991), and No. 12, *Sinfonia da camera: Arnold Schönberg in memoriam* (1992); Concerto for Organ and Strings (1946); *Sinfonietta concertante* for Violin, Balalaika, and Chamber Orch. (1951–81); *Concerto da camera* for Cello and Orch. (1958; Swedish Radio, June 25, 1959); *Maskarad-Divertissement* (1958); *Variations on a Värmland Folk Tune* (1963; Göteborg, March 8, 1964); *Vagues* (1965; Göteborg, Jan. 28, 1966); *Fotia* (Uppsala, Oct. 6, 1966); *Vientos* (1967; Swedish Radio, March 7, 1968); *Terra* for Orch. and Tape (Göteborg, Sept. 12, 1968); *Fantyr* (Göteborg, Aug. 31, 1969); *Concerto Götenburghese* for Piano and Orch. (1970; Göteborg, Aug. 19, 1971); Concerto for Nyckel Harp (keyed fiddle) and Strings (1971); *Astrofonia* for Strings (Uppsala, July 11, 1974); *Nalle Puh,* symphonic saga (1979; Göteborg, Jan. 3, 1980); *Festuvertyr Gränna-Brahe* (1993); Concerto for Accordion and Chamber Orch. (1996). **CHAMBER:** 8 string quartets (1947; 1948; 1950; 1961, *Séquences variables;* 1964; 1976; 1980; 1981); Sonata for Solo Violin (1948); 4 piano sonatas (1949; 1956; 1959; 1982–83, *Sonata flexa*); Wind Quintet (1964); Trio for Clarinet, Violin, and Cello (1974); *Slag i slag* for Percussion and Tape (1979); *Sonatina per Marika* for Violin and Piano (1982); *Sagan om ringen: Ringmotivet* for Clarinet and Piano (1989); *A la recherche* for Flute (1992). **VOCAL:** *Aff Sancto Christofforo,* chamber oratorio (1948); *Anadyomene* for Soprano and Orch. (1950); Sym. No. 4, *Sånger i Förvandlingens Natt,* for Chorus (1958; Stockholm, April 3, 1959); *The Hazetrees* for Soprano, Clarinet, Violin, Cello, Piano, and Tape (1961); *Ave crax, ave crux* for Baritone, Chorus, Organ, and Tape (1967); *Concerto de chiesa: Den förlorade sonen* for Narrator, Chorus, Wind Quintet, Percussion, and Organ (1980); *Det stora ljuset,* Advent cantata for Narrator, Soprano, Alto, Chorus, and Strings (1983); *Cantata concertante* for Chorus, Brass Quintet, and Organ (1984); various sacred works; choruses.

BIBL.: P.-G. Bergfors, *Mitt hjärtas melodi: En Bok om S.- E. J.* (1994).**—NS/LK/DM**

Johansson, Bengt (Viktor), Finnish composer; b. Helsinki, Oct. 2, 1914; d. Visuvesi, June 22, 1989. He studied composition with Sulho Ranta and Selim Palmgren, and also cello at the Sibelius Academy in Helsinki, graduating in 1947. After making study trips to Europe, Italy, and America, he returned to Finland, where he served as director of music broadcasting for the Finnish Radio (1952–74). He was a teacher (from 1960) and a lecturer in music history (from 1965) at the Sibelius Academy. His music makes use of a wide variety of resources, including electronic sound.

WORKS: DRAMATIC: O p e r a : *Linna* (1975). **ORCH.:** *Serenade* for Strings (1945); *Petite suite de ballet* (1948); *Aquarelles* (1948); Piano Concerto (1951); Suite for Violin, Strings, Piano, and Timpani (1952); *Festivo,* overture (1952); *Expressions* for Strings (1954); *Tema con 7 variazioni in modo antico* for Cello and Orch. (1954); *Dialogeja* for Cello and Orch. (1970). **CHAMBER:** *Sonata piccola* for Cello and Piano (1945); *Dialogues* for Cello and String Quintet (1970); violin pieces. **VOCAL:** *Stabat Mater* for Chorus (1951); *It's Perfectly True,* "musical fairy tale" for Narrator, Solo Voices, Women's Chorus, and Orch. (1957); *Missa Sacra* for Tenor, Chorus, and Orch. (1960); *12 Passages from the Bible* for Men's Chorus and Organ (1960); *The Tomb at Akr Çaar* for Baritone and Chamber Chorus, after Ezra Pound (1964); *Triptych* for Soprano, Baritone, and Chorus (1965); *Requiem* for Baritone, 2 Choruses, 2 String Orchs., and Timpani (1966); *3 Classic Madrigals* for Chorus (1967); *Cantata* *humana* for Baritone, 4 Narrators on Tape, Chorus, and Orch., after Dag Hammarskjöld (Helsinki, April 9, 1970); *The Song of the Bride* for Soprano and Orch. (1972); *Venus and Adonis I-V* for Chorus (1972–74); *Songs of the Psyche* for Soprano and Piano (1978). ELECTRONIC: *3 Études* (1960).—NS/LK/DM

John, Elton, (originally, Dwight, Reginald)

(b. Pinner, Middlesex, England, March 25, 1947), in collaboration with lyricist Bernie Taupin (b. Sleaford, Lincolnshire, England, May 22, 1950), composed some of the most popular songs of the 1970s, characterized by Taupin's vaguely romantic, nostalgic, and often esoteric words and John's highly melodic music and ever-present hook.

With Bernie Taupin and Elton John established as poignant songwriters by 1971, and with John established as a virtual rock institution by 1972, Elton John elicited perhaps the broadest appeal of any rock performer (rivaled only by Paul McCartney) with his penchant for showmanship and catchy melodies and his command of a variety of musical styles. Although critically reproached as lacking evocative emotional commitment or a defined musical character, and regarded as a consolidator rather than as an innovator of musical styles, Elton John nevertheless bridged the gap between pop and rock with enormous success, particularly in the U.S. Although suffering a decline in popularity in the early to mid-1980s, John has since returned to his former prominence on the charts and as a performer with a somewhat more subdued style. He has also become an active fundraiser in the war against AIDS.

Reginald Dwight began playing piano at age four, winning a scholarship to the Royal Academy of Music in London at age 11. He later performed in a succession of local bands before joining Bluesology as a teenager. Taken over by "Long" John Baldry as his backing group by 1967, Bluesology backed visiting American black acts such as Major Lance, Patti Labelle and the Bluebelles, and Billy Stewart. After the smash British 1967 hit "Let the Heartaches Begin" by Baldry, Bluesology disbanded and Reginald Dwight became Elton John.

Unsuccessfully auditioning for Liberty Records, Elton John was put in touch with lyricist Bernie Taupin, and the two were signed to a three-year songwriting contract with Dick James Music. As the team had little luck writing commercial material, John recorded an anonymous series of budget albums covering current hits. Urged by publicist Steve Brown to follow their own muse, Taupin and John assembled new material and recorded an album, *Empty Sky* (eventually released in the U.S. in 1975), but both the album and John's first single, "Lady Samantha," sold minimally in Great Britain. Subsequently employing arranger Paul Buckmaster and producer Gus Dudgeon, John recorded *Elton John*, but the album's first single, "Border Song," became only a minor hit in Britain and the United States. John soon recruited drummer Nigel Olsson and bassist Dee Murray, former members of the Spencer Davis Group, for a promotional tour of Britain's college circuit.

Undaunted by initial failures, Elton John's American record company Uni (later absorbed by the parent company, MCA) launched a massive publicity campaign to hype John's American debut at the Troubadour in Los Angeles in August 1970. The tactic worked exceedingly well, and shows there, in N.Y., and in Philadelphia were greeted by ecstatic reviews. By late 1970 the second single from *Elton John*, "Your Song" (one of the duo's finest compositions), had become a near-smash American hit, and the album, which also included "Take Me to the Pilot," remained on the charts for nearly a year.

Tumbleweed Connection, revealing Bernie Taupin's fascination with the American Old West, contained "Burn Down the Mission" and "Country Comfort," already covered by Rod Stewart, yet yielded no hit singles. During 1971 two Elton John albums were issued in rapid succession: the soundtrack to *Friends* (on Paramount) and the live *11–17–70* (on Uni). *Madman Across the Water*, recorded with Nigel Olsson, Dee Murray, and guitarist Davey Johnstone, produced the major hit "Levon" and the moderate hit "Tiny Dancer," but was greeted harshly by British critics.

Over the next two years, Elton John enjoyed what was generally regarded as the artistic high point of his career. In early 1972 he and his band (Olsson, Murray, and Johnstone) traveled to France to record *Honky Chateau*, eschewing elaborate string arrangements in favor of Johnstone's guitar. "Rocket Man" and "Honky Cat" became smash hits from the album. *Don't Shoot Me, I'm the Piano Player* yielded the derivative top hit "Crocodile Rock" and the poignant smash hit "Daniel," another of the duo's finest compositions. The double-record set *Goodbye Yellow Brick Road* remained on the album charts nearly two years, containing the Marilyn Monroe tribute "Candle in the Wind" and "Funeral for a Friend," and featuring three smash hit singles, "Saturday Night's Alright for Fighting," "Bennie and the Jets," and the title song. *Caribou*, recorded in the United States, contained two more smash hits, "Don't Let the Sun Go Down on Me" and "The Bitch Is Back," and was followed by two more smash hits, a cover of the Beatles' "Lucy in the Sky with Diamonds" and "Philadelphia Freedom."

John was (in)famous for his elaborate stage shows through this period. Exhibiting a flair for outrageous showmanship, wearing wild and often silly costumes, and performing in a flamboyant and flashy fashion, he was compared to Little Richard and Jerry Lee Lewis, and, perhaps more accurately, Liberace. Often identified with the so-called glitter-rock movement, John nonetheless retained an ironic sense of tastefulness that avoided the garish and disconcerting image attached to David Bowie and others of the genre.

In 1973 Elton John and manager John Reid formed Rocket Records. In late 1974 Kiki Dee and American singer-songwriter Neil Sedaka had huge hits on the label, Dee with "I've Got the Music in Me" and Sedaka with "Laughter in the Rain." Sedaka's revitalized career with Rocket lasted through late 1976 (with "Bad Blood" and a slow version of his 1962 hit "Breaking Up Is Hard to Do"), when he switched to Elektra Records. Dee had a smash hit in duet with John on "Don't Go Breakin' My Heart" in 1976. In June 1974 Elton John concluded negotiations on a new recording contract with MCA Records valued at $8 million, the largest such deal in rock history until Stevie Wonder's $13 million contract with Motown in August 1975. John appeared as the Pinball Wizard in Ken Russell's bizarre film version of the Who's *Tommy* in 1975. *Captain Fantastic and the Brown Dirt Cowboy*, which dealt with the early career of John and Taupin, featured the smash hit "Someone Saved My Life Tonight."

During spring 1975 bassist Dee Murray and drummer Nigel Olsson left the Elton John Band. Olsson later scored a major hit with "Dancin' Shoes" and a moderate hit with "Little Bit of Soap" in 1978–1979. With holdover guitarist Davey Johnstone, the band brought in drummer Roger Pope, debuting at Wembley Stadium in June. *Rock of the Westies* produced the two-sided hit "Grow Some Funk of Your Own"/"I Feel Like a Bullet (In the Gun of Robert Ford)," and was followed by the live album *Here and There*. In August 1976 John announced that he was disbanding his group and retiring from live performance. *Blue Moves*, John's final album with producer Gus Dudgeon and collaborator Bernie Taupin, yielded the smash hit "Sorry Seems to Be the Hardest Word" and the moderate hit "Bite Your Lip (Get Up and Dance!)."

Elton John's next album, 1978's critically attacked *A Single Man*, recorded with lyricist Gary Osborne, yielded only one major hit, "Part-Time Love." In February 1979 John returned to live performances, accompanied only by percussionist Ray Cooper, culminating in several appearances in Russia that May. During the year, John recorded with Philadelphia International producer Thom Bell, scoring a near-smash hit with "Mama Can't Buy You Love." He also recorded the inane disco-fied *Victim of Love* under songwriter-producer Pete Bellotte. Late that year John toured the United States for the first time in three years, playing remarkably subdued concerts in medium-size halls, accompanied by only percussionist Cooper. During 1980 John scored a smash hit with "Little Jeannie," toured again with Dee Murray and Nigel Olsson, and signed to the newly formed Geffen Records.

Under producer Chris Thomas, Elton John recorded four albums for Geffen. The first two yielded the major hits "Nobody Wins"; the John Lennon tribute "Empty Garden (Hey Hey Johnny)," with lyrics by Taupin; and "Blue Eyes," with lyrics by Gary Osborne. John again toured with Johnstone, Murray, and Olsson in 1982 and 1984, retaining Johnstone into the 1990s. Dee Murray died on Jan. 5, 1992, in Nashville after suffering a stroke while fighting cancer. The defiant "I'm Still Standing" announced John's return to form. John returned to collaborating solely with Bernie Taupin on *Too Low for Zero* (for the first time since *Blue Moves*), resulting in the major hit "Kiss the Bride" and the smash "I Guess That's Why They Call It the Blues." *Breaking Hearts* produced three hits, including the smash "Sad Songs (Say So Much)." Elton John's *Ice on Fire* yielded two hit duets with George Michael, "Wrap Her Up" and the smash "Nikita." John joined Dionne Warwick, Gladys Knight, and Stevie Wonder for the top pop and R&B hit "That's What Friends Are For" in 1985 in support of AMFAR (for AIDS research). *Leather Jackets* marked a low point for John in the 1980s, yet he toured from September 1985 to June 1987, undergoing throat surgery in January 1987. The tour wrapped up with successful appearances in China.

Elton John returned to MCA for *Live in Australia*, recorded with the Melbourne Symphony Orch., which produced a smash hit with a live version of "Candle in the Wind." By 1988 he had given up his elaborate stage costumes and flamboyant stage demeanor in concert, while for the first time employing electric piano. *Reg Strikes Back*, recorded in England under Chris Thomas, yielded the smash "I Don't Wanna Go On with You Like This" and the major hit "A Word in Spanish." After the major hit "Through the Storm," recorded with Aretha Franklin, John scored three hits from *Sleeping with the Past*, including "Healing Hands" and "Sacrifice."

In 1991 Elton John had a top hit with "Don't Let the Sun Go Down on Me," recorded live in London with George Michael, from the tribute album to John and Taupin, *Two Rooms*. The socially aware album *The One*, recorded under producer Chris Thomas, yielded three hits: the title song (a near-smash), the poignant "The Last Song," and "Simple Life." In November 1992 Elton John and Bernie Taupin signed a $39 million songwriting contract with Warner Chappell Music. At the same time, John established the Elton John AIDS Foundation in Atlanta.

In 1994 Elton John scored a smash pop and top easy-listening hit with "Can You Feel the Love Tonight," and a major pop and smash easy listening hit with "Circle of Life," from the popular animated movie *The Lion King*. He was also inducted into the Rock and Roll Hall of Fame. In early 1995 Polygram Records bought out Elton John's remaining MCA contract to revive his Rocket label for *Made in England*, featuring the hit single "Believe."

DISC.: **ELTON JOHN:** *Empty Sky* (rec. 1969; rel. 1975); *E. J.* (1970); *Tumbleweed Connection* (1971); *Friends* (soundtrack; 1971); *11–17–70* (1971); *Madman Across the Water* (1971); *Honky Chateau* (1972); *Don't Shoot Me, I'm Only the Piano Player* (1973); *Goodbye Yellow Brick Road* (1973); *Your Songs* (1970–1973) (1986); *Caribou* (1974); *Greatest Hits* (1974); *Here and There* (rec. 1974; rel. 1976); *Captain Fantastic and the Brown Dirt Cowboy* (1975); *Rock of the Westies* (1975); *Blue Moves* (1976); *Greatest Hits, Vol. 2* (1977); *Rare Masters* (1992); *The Thom Bell Sessions* (rec. 1977; rel. 1989); *A Single Man* (1978); *Victim of Love* (1979); *21 at 33* (1980); *The Fox* (1981); *Jump Up!* (1982); *Too Low for Zero* (1983); *Breaking Hearts* (1984); *Ice on Fire* (1985); *Leather Jackets* (1986); *Greatest Hits, Vol. 3 (1979–1987)* (1987); *Live in Australia* (1987); *Reg Strikes Back* (1988); *Sleeping with the Past* (1989); *To Be Continued* (1990); *The One* (1992); *Greatest Hits, 1976–1986* (1992); *Duets* (1993); *Made in England* (1995). **NIGEL OLSSON:** *Drum Orchestra and Chorus* (1971); *Nigel Olsson* (1975); *Nigel Olsson* (1978); *Nigel* (1979); *Changing Tides* (1980). **BERNIE TAUPIN:** *Bernie Taupin* (1972); *He Who Rides the Tiger* (1980); *Tribe* (1987). **DAVEY JOHNSTONE:** *Smiling Faces* (1973).

BIBL.: Paul Gambaccini, *A Conversation with E. J. and Bernie Taupin* (N.Y., 1975); Cathi Stein, *E. J.* (London 1975); Dick Tatham and Tony Jasper, *E. J.* (London, 1976); Gerald Newman, *E. J.* (N.Y., 1976); Greg Shaw, *E. J.: A Biography in Words and*

Pictures (N.Y., 1976); David Nutter, *E. J.: It's a Little Bit Funny* (N.Y., 1977); Alan Finch, *E. J.: The Illustrated Discography* (London, 1981); Chris Charlesworth, *E. J., "Only the Piano Player": The Illustrated E. J.* (London, 1984).—**BH**

John, Little Willie (actually, **William**), one of the most overlooked pioneers of rock 'n' roll and soul; b. Cullendale, Ark., Nov. 15, 1937; d. Walla Walla, Wash., May 26, 1968. Little Willie John moved with his family to Detroit in 1942, singing in the gospel quartet The United Four with his older sister Mable. In 1960 Mable John became the first solo female vocalist to record for Motown Records. She scored a R&B smash on Stax Records with "Your Good Thing (Is About to End)" in 1966 and joined Ray Charles's Raeletts in 1968. William John began performing regularly at a Detroit venue by the age of 11 and was spotted by Johnny Otis at a Paradise Theater talent contest in 1951. Otis recommended three of the show's acts—Little Willie John, Jackie Wilson, and The Royals—to Syd Nathan of King Records, but only The Royals (who became The Midnighters with the addition of Hank Ballard) were signed to the label. John subsequently toured with R&B bandleader Paul Williams ("The Hucklebuck") and recorded for Prize Records.

Eventually signing with King Records in 1955, Little Willie John recorded under producer Henry Glover and quickly scored a R&B smash with "All around the World" (also known as "Grits Ain't Groceries"). In 1956 he achieved two two-sided R&B smashes with "Need Your Love So Bad"/"Home at Last" and "Fever"/"Letter from My Darling." "Fever," written by Otis Blackwell and Eddie Cooley, became a top R&B / major pop hit for John, but Peggy Lee had a near-smash pop hit with the song in 1958. John had a major pop/smash R&B hit with "Talk to Me, Talk to Me" in 1958. Other successes for John through 1960 included the major R&B and minor pop hits "You're a Sweetheart," "Leave My Kitten Alone," "Let Them Talk," and "Heartbreak (It's Hurtin' Me)," the pop-only "A Cottage for Sale," and the standard "Sleep," a major crossover hit. Several of Little Willie John's hits were covered by other artists. In 1959 Johnny Preston managed a minor pop hit with "Leave My Kitten Alone"; in 1963 Sunny and The Sunglows had a major pop hit with "Talk to Me"; and in 1969 Little Milton achieved a major R&B hit with "Grits Ain't Groceries."

In 1961 Little Willie John scored major R&B hits with "Walk Slow," the two-sided "(I've Got) Spring Fever"/"Flamingo," and "Take My Love (I Want to Give It All to You)." However, he never achieved another hit and, by 1963, King had dropped him from its roster. In October 1964 John stabbed a man to death in a Seattle club and, in July 1966 he was convicted of manslaughter and sentenced to 8-to-20 years in prison. He died at the Wash. State Penitentiary in Walla Walla on May 27, 1968, at the age of 30. The cause was variously reported as a heart attack or pneumonia. James Brown soon recorded the tribute album *Thinking about Little Willie John* and *A Whole New Thing* and, in 1996, Little Willie John was inducted into the Rock and Roll Hall of Fame.

DISC.: *Fever* (1957); *Talk to Me* (1958); *Mister Little Willie John* (1958); *Action* (1960); *Sure Things* (1961); *The Sweet, the Hot, the Teenage Beat* (1961); *Come on and Join Little Willie John* (1962); *These Are My Favorite Songs* (1964); *Little Willie John Sings All Originals* (1966); *Free at Last* (1970).—**BH**

Johner, Dominicus (actually, **Franz-Xaver Karl**), distinguished German music scholar; b. Waldsee, Dec. 1, 1874; d. Beuron, Jan. 4, 1955. He studied theology and music at the Benedictine abbeys in Prague, Seckau, and Beuron, his teachers at the latter being the cantor Ambrosius Kienle and the organist Raphael Molitor. After taking his vows in 1894, he studied theology at the Cucujães Monastery in Portugal (1896–1900), being ordained in 1898. In 1900 he returned to Beuron, where he was cantor of the abbey (1905–49). He was also prior there (1913–33), and taught at the church music school of Gregoriushaus, near Beuron (1906–14). He was a lecturer at the Hochschule für Musik in Cologne (from 1925). He was a leading authority on ecclesiastical music. He composed a cycle, *Neue Marienlieder* for Chorus and Organ (two books, 1916, 1918), and *Neue Kommunionslieder* (1916).

WRITINGS: *Neue Schule des gregorianischen Choralgesanges* (Regensburg, 1906; 7th ed., 1937, as *Grosse Choralschule*; 8th ed., 1956, as *Choralschule*); *Der gregorianische Choral: Sein Wesen, Werden, Wert und Vortrag* (Stuttgart, 1924); *Die Sonn- und Festtagslieder des vatikanischen Graduale, nach Text und Melodie erklärt* (Regensburg, 1928; 2nd ed., 1933); *Erklärung des Kyriae nach Text und Melodie* (Regensburg, 1933); *Wort und Ton im Choral: Ein Beitrag zur Aesthetik des gregorianischen Gesanges* (Leipzig, 1940; 2nd ed., 1953).

BIBL.: F. Tack, ed., *Der kultische Gesang der abendländischen Kirche: In gregorianisches Werkheftaus Anlass des 75. Geburtstages von D. J.* (Cologne, 1950).—**NS/LK/DM**

John of Damascus, St., Green theologian and hymn writer, also known as **Johannes Damascenus** and **Johannes Chrysorrhoas**; b. Damascus, c.645; d. near Jerusalem, Dec. 4, 749. Around 730 he became a monk at the Mar Saba monastery near Jerusalem. He was honored as a theological doctor of both the Greek Orthodox and Roman Catholic churches. He was the author of various "canons," or hymns for Greek liturgical use, and prepared a revision of the *Octoēchos*, the hymnbook of the Greek Orthodox Church.—**NS/LK/DM**

Johns, Clayton, American pianist, teacher, and composer; b. New Castle, Del., Nov. 24, 1857; d. Boston, March 5, 1932. He studied composition with J.K. Paine (1879–81) and piano and W.H. Sherwood (1879–82) at Harvard Univ., then composition with Kiel at the Berlin Hochschule fur Musik (1882–83); also studied piano privately with Rummel in Berlin. He settled in Boston in 1884, where he taught at the New England Cons. of Music (1912–16). His most popular work was the *Introduction and Fugue* for Piano (1899), which was often performed by Josef Hofmann. He also wrote other instrumental works and about 100 songs. He publ. an autobiography, *Reminiscences of a Musician* (1929) and the didactic *The Essentials of Pianoforte Playing* (1909). He also ed. *From Bach to Chopin* (1911).—**NS/LK/DM**

Johns, Paul Emile, Polish-born American pianist, music publisher, and composer; b. Kraków, c. 1798; d.

Paris, Aug. 10, 1860. He settled in New Orleans by 1818, where he was active as a pianist until 1830 and had his own music store in New Orleans (1830–46). During a visit to Paris in 1832, he was befriended by Chopin, who dedicated his 5 mazurkas, op. 7, to him. With Pleyel, he publ. his *Album louisianais*, a vol. of piano pieces and songs. His other works, including a comic opera, *The Military Stay, A Warlike Symphony*, and *Grand Military March*, are not extant. In later years he was active as a cotton magnate. From 1848 to 1860 he was Russian consul in New Orleans.—NS/LK/DM

Johnsen, Hallvard Olav, Norwegian flutist and composer; b. Hamburg (of Norwegian parents), June 27, 1916. He studied flute with Stenseth and Wang, conducting with Fjeldstad, harmony and counterpoint with Steenberg, and composition with Brustad at the Oslo Cons. (1930–41), and then studied composition with Karl Andersen in Oslo (1942–45), and later with Holmboe in Copenhagen (1956). He was a flutist in the orch. of the National Theater in Oslo (1945–47) and played in military bands (1947–73). His style of composition evolved from late Romanticism to free tonal techniques.

WORKS: DRAMATIC: O p e r a : *The Legend of Svein and Maria* (1971; Oslo, Sept. 9, 1973); *Det Kjempende Menneske* (1982); *Nattergalen* (1991). O R C H.: 2 suites for Chamber Orch. (1939, 1947); *Fantasia (Serenade)* for Chamber Orch. (1947); 23 syms. (1949; *Pastorale*, 1954; 1957; 1959; 1960; 1961; 1962; 1964; 1968; 1973; 1975; 1976; 1983; 1985; 1987; 1989; 1991; 1993; *Oceano*, 1994; 1996; 1997; 1998; 1999); *Ouverture Festivo* (1954); Concerto for Flute and Strings (1955); Concerto for Violin and Chamber Orch. (1959); Trumpet Concerto (1966); Violin Concerto (1968); *Ouverture Festoso* (1971); Cello Concerto (1977); *Norvegese alla Marcia* for Symphonic Band (1986); *Pastorale e Coral* (1995). C H A M B E R : Trio for Flute, Violin, and Viola (1938); Quartet No. 1 for Flute and String Trio (1945); 3 string quartets (1962, 1966, 1972); *Serenade* for Wind Quintet (1962); Suite for Flute and Horn (1964); Wind Quintet with Vibraphone (1965); Sextet for Flute, Horn, Vibraphone, Violin, Viola, and Cello (1974); *Serenade* for Flute, Viola, and Cello (1974); Saxophone Quartet (1974); *Divertimento* for Brass Quintet (1974); 3 brass quintets (1978–86); Trio for Trumpet, Trombone, and Vibraphone (1980); *Pastorale* for Flute, Violin, and Vibraphone (1981); *Canzona* for Trombone and Organ (1988); Septet for 2 Flutes, 3 Clarinets, and 2 Bassoons (1998); piano pieces. VOCAL: *Norsk Natur* (Norwegian Nature) for Chorus and Orch. (1952); 2 motets for Chorus (1959, 1965); *Krosspåske*, cantata for Baritone, Chorus, and Orch. (1963); *Der Ligger et Land*, cantata for Tenor, Men's Chorus, and Orch. (1966); *Fra Salmenes Bok*, cantata for Chorus and Organ (1977); *Logos*, oratorio for 8 Solo Voices, Chorus, Organ, and Orch. (1979); *10 Psalms* for Man's Voice and Organ (1979); *Bergammen*, melodrama for Man's Voice and Orch. (1980); Cantata for Voice and Orch. (1984); *Såkornet* for Narrator, 2 Violins, Viola, and Cello (1993).—NS/LK/DM

Johnson, Anthony Rolfe
See **Rolfe Johnson, Anthony**

Johnson, A(rtemas) N(ixon), American organist, music educator, and composer; b. Middlebury, Vt., June 22, 1817; d. New Milford, Conn., Jan. 1, 1892. He studied with George Webb and Lowell Mason in Boston

and later received instruction in theory from Schnyder von Wartensee in Frankfurt am Main (1842–43). He was active as a teacher in Boston for the Musical Education Soc. (1837–39), in the public schools (1839–c. 1855), and at the Academy of Music (1840–49). He was also organist and later director of music at the Park Street Church (1840–58), and likewise engaged in editorial and publishing affairs. He adopted his own "Johnson's System" (as opposed to Mason's "Pestalozzian" system) for vocal instruction in 1849, declaring that the student should learn his art by doing. He later produced the first formal choral method as the *Chorus Choir Instruction Book* (1877). At the close of the Civil War, he organized various music schools and conservatories from N.Y. to Ind. He wrote 2 cantatas, 67 anthems and similar pieces, 279 hymn tunes, and 26 Sabbath school and gospel songs. He publ. 11 vols. of sacred music, 10 collections of choral music, 3 books of keyboard pieces, and 6 theory books.—NS/LK/DM

Johnson, Bengt-Emil, Swedish composer and poet; b. Ludvika, Dec. 12, 1936. He studied piano and composition with Knut Wiggen (1956–62), at the same time pursuing his abiding interest in modernistic poetry. In 1966 he joined the staff of the Swedish Radio in Stockholm, where he later was named director of the music dept. (1979) and program director (1984). He publ. 14 collections of poetry (1963–86). Many of his compositions take the form of text-sound scores.

WORKS: *Disappearances* for Piano and Tape (1974); *Alpha* for Chorus (1975); *Escaping (Memories 1961–1977)* for 5 or More Performers (Swedish Radio, April 6, 1978); *Night Chants I*, radio piece (Swedish Radio, Aug. 19, 1981) and *II* for Voice and Tape (1985); *Döden sopran*, radio opera (Swedish Radio, Sept. 7, 1986); various text-sound scores.—NS/LK/DM

Johnson, Bill (actually, **William**), jazz alto saxophonist, clarinetist, arranger; b. Jacksonville, Fla., Sept. 30, 1912; N.Y., July 5, 1960. Originally a pianist, he played alto sax when he was 16. He worked with Smiling Billy Steward's Celery City Serenaders and C. S. Belton's Band. Johnson studied at Wisc. Cons., Ill. Cons., and Marquette Univ. While in Milwaukee, he worked with Jimmy Dudley and Jabbo Smith, subsequently playing with Sam Marshall, Baron Lee, and Tiny Bradshaw; he also joined Erskine Hawkins from 1936–43. Johnson arranged many great numbers for Hawkins and was co- composer of "Tuxedo Junction." He later moved to Canada, eventually returning to N.Y. where he died of a lung ailment.—JC/LP

Johnson, Bill (actually, **William K.**), jazz banjo player, guitarist, singer; b. Lexington, Ky., Dec. 13, 1893; d. there, Oct. 1955. Johnson played with local bands in and around Louisville. He traveled to N.Y. with the Dixie Ramblers in late 1926, played with drummer George Howe's Band (1927), and subsequently with Luis Russell from 1927–32 (also recorded with King Oliver). Johnson was occasionally featured on vocals ("You Might Get Better," Henry Allen Orch., 1930). He worked with Fess Williams 1933–34, and continued to work on guitar throughout the 1930s. Johnson left full-time music in the 1940s and moved back to Lexington. He lost his life in a fire that destroyed his home.—JC/LP

Johnson, Bill (actually, William Manuel),

jazz bassist, guitarist, and banjo player; b. Talladega, Ala., Aug. 10, 1872; d. Comales, Tex., Dec. 3, 1972. William Manuel played guitar from the age of 15 and took up string bass in 1900. He played locally at Torr Anderson's Café and with the Peerless Orch., and Frankie Dusen's Eagle Band, among others; he doubled on tuba for parade work. Moving to Calif. in 1909, Johnson sent for Freddie Keppard in late 1911 (and several other New Orleans musicians) to bring the Original Creole Orch. to the West Coast. After working in Calif., the band toured from coast to coast on the Orpheum Circuit-theater residencies in cities including Chicago and in N.Y. The original band broke up in N.Y., and Johnson returned to Chicago to organize his own band (1918). Later that year he led the Seven Kings of Ragtime in N.Y. and again toured the Orpheum circuit. He left to join King Oliver and remained with him until 1923. While leading his own band in Chicago for many years, he also worked for several bandleaders, including Johnny Dodds, Freddie Keppard, Jimmy Wade, and Clifford "Klarinet" King. Johnson spent a some time in the Smizer Trio in the 1930s. He continued to play in Chicago until the 1950s, but gave up playing in the early 1960s and moved to Mexico. His sister, Anita Johnson-Gonzales-Ford, was a close friend of Jelly Roll Morton (his muse for "Sweet Anita Mine") and featured in Morton's will.

Disc.: Louis Armstrong: *Portrait of the Artist as a Young Man* (1923). Count Basie: *Basie's Basement* (1929); *Beaver Junction* (1944); *Brand New Wagon: Count Basie 1947* (1947). The Bobs: *My, I'm Large* (1987). The Bop Brothers: *Doing the Classics* (1988). Albert Collins: *Truckin' with Albert Collins* (1969). Contraband: *Contraband* (1974). Lou Donaldson: *Pretty Things* (1970). Marvin Gaye: *Master 1961–1984* (1995). Lightnin' Hopkins: *Texas Blues* (1990). George Howard: *Love Will Follow* (1991). Abbey Lincoln: *Talking to the Sun* (1983). Maze featuring Frankie Beverly: *We Are One/Can't Stop the Love* (1999); *Inspiration/Joy and Pain* (1999). The Temptations: *Emperors of Soul* (1994). Lester Young: *The Lester Young Story [Proper]* (2000).—JC/LP

Johnson, Budd (Albert J.), jazz tenor and so-

prano saxophonist, clarinetist, arranger; b. Dallas, Tex., Dec. 14, 1910; d. Kansas City, Mo., Oct. 20, 1984. Brother of **Keg Johnson**. A glorious, impassioned player capable of great lyricism, he was never properly acknowledged as one of the masters of his generation. He was remarkably open to new ideas and moved smoothly from Armstrong's band to Dizzy Gillespie's, and from the influence of Hawkins around 1930 to that of Lester Young in the late 1930s.

Given his first music lessons by his father, who played cornet and organ; he later studied with Booker Pittman's mother, Mrs. Portia Pittman (daughter of Booker T. Washington). He originally played piano, then gigged on drums and did a brief spell with a touring show. Changing to tenor sax, he then played

with local bands. From 1927–32, he played with a variety of bands locally, in Tex., and finally, in Kansas City (c. 1930). He moved to Chicago in 1932 where he did spells with various bands. He then played with Louis Armstrong until Armstrong disbanded in July 1933. Between 1934–42, he played off and on with Earl Hines, taking short breaks to work with other leaders. Eventually he became music director of Hines's band in 1938. He was briefly with Don Redman in spring 1943, and then made a U.S.O. tour with Al Sears's Band. In February 1944 he joined Dizzy Gillespie at the Onyx Club, N.Y. From the mid-1940s he did several spells with Dizzy Gillespie, and also led his own band in N.Y.

Johnson pioneered the early days of bop by organizing (and arranging for) several important small groups. He acted as musical director for Billy Eckstine's Orch., also arranging for Woody Herman, Buddy Rich, Boyd Raeburn, and others. From the late 1940s he was a prolific freelancer working with a number of bands as a musician or arranger. In the early 1950s he regularly led his own small groups, worked as musical director for Atlantic Records, organized his own publishing company, and continued freelance playing and arranging.

He became part of the rock revolution with his arrangment and production of several records. He also published songs and helped Alan Freed by putting together huge bands for his shows. From the mid-1950s through the mid-1960s he toured with a variety of bands, including Benny Goodman (1956–57; tour in Asia), Quincy Jones (1960), Count Basie (1961 to early 1962), and Earl Hines (1965; summer 1966; 1967–69; including various European tours).

He left Earl Hines in the summer of 1969 and formed JPJ Quartet (with Bill Pemberton, drummer Oliver Jackson, and pianist Dill Jones). JPJ presented educational concerts through the early 1970s. From the 1970s through his death, he remained active on the festival circuit and as an educator.

Disc.: *Rock 'n' Roll Stage Show* (1954); *Blues a La Mode* (1958); *And the Four Brass Giants* (1960); *Let's Swing* (1960); *French Cookin* (1963); *Off the Wall* (1964); *Ya Ya* (1964); *Mr. Bechet* (1974); *In Memory of a Very Dear Friend* (1978); *The Ole Dude and the Fundance Kid* (1984).—JC/LP

Johnson, Buddy (Woodrow Wilson), jazz

pianist, leader, arranger/composer, vocals; b. Darlington, S.C., Jan. 10, 1915; d. N.Y., Feb. 9, 1977. Brother of Ella Johnson. He toured Europe with the Cotton Club Revue before World War II, and returned to N.Y. in 1939 to begin his recording career. He led his own small band during the early 1940s, and then formed his own big band. This band had long residencies at the Savoy Ballroom, N.Y., and with regular touring, achieved wide success in the R&B market. In the 1960s he led a small band, and was active in church welfare work.

Disc.: *Rock 'n' Roll Stage Show* (1956); *Wails* (1957); *Swing Me* (1958); *Go Ahead and Rock and Roll* (1958); *Rockin' 'n' Rollin'* (1995).—JC/LP

Johnson, Bunk (William Geary), pioneering

jazz trumpeter; b. New Orleans, La., Dec. 27, 1889 (not

1879; confirmed by censuses); d. New Iberia, La., July 7, 1949. Bunk's father had known slavery, and his mother was an indian of the Black Creek tribe. Bunk married twice, he raised a very large family, his second wife, Maude, was the sister of George Baquet. Bunk began playing cornet during early childhood, later he studied with "Professor" Wallace Cutchey of New Orleans Univ. During the 1890s he worked with Adam Olivier's Orch., later played in bands led by Buddy Bolden and Bob Russell.

By 1900 he had begun touring and visited Mexico with P. G. Loral's Circus Band; he traveled extensively in the early 1900s with McCabe's Minstrels, Hagenback's and Wallace's Circus, visiting N.Y. in 1903 and San Francisco in 1905. (Bunk also claimed to have worked in England about this time.) In between trips he returned regularly to New Orleans. He is said to have worked regularly on liners sailing to the Orient, Australia, and Europe. He eventually settled in New Orleans in 1910, worked with Frankie Dusen's Eagle Band and Billy Marrero's Superior Band. He also resumed playing dates with the Old Excelsior, Allen's Brass Band, etc. Bunk worked in Alexandria, La., with Clarence Williams and played regular dates at cabarets in New Orleans including a spell at Pete Lala's. Bunk left New Orleans c. 1914, taught for a while in Mandeville, then worked with various bands in Baton Rouge, Bogalusa, and Lake Charles. He then left La. to resume touring with minstrel shows and circus bands. Johnson later played in theatre orchestras, and then toured with Dee Johnson's Band (c. 1927–29). He settled temporarily in Tex. (1930), then worked with Sam Price at the Yellow Front Cafe in Kansas City, Mo. (c. 1930). He moved back to La., worked with the Imperial Band in Lake Charles (pianist Nellie Lutcher was in the band), Gus Fortinet's Band in New Iberia, the Yelping Hound Band in Crowley, and with trumpeter Evan Thomas's Black Eagle Band in November 1931. Thomas was stabbed to death by John Guillory while playing at a dance in Rayne. Unconfirmed reports say that Johnson's trumpet was damaged in the skirmish. Johnson continued gigging and played a one-nighter with Paul Barnes in 1933.

Eventually, Johnson lost all his teeth to pyorrhea and had to stop playing. He settled in New Iberia and did various day-jobs, including caretaking and driving a truck-and-trailer for sugar and rice companies. He also undertook paid engagements as a whistler at local fairgrounds. In early 1939 he was contacted by William Russel and Frederic Ramsey Jr. after Louis Armstrong and Clarence Williams mentioned Johnson during research interviews for the book *Jazzmen*. From May 1940–July 1941, Johnson was employed as a music teacher by the Works Progress Administration; the teaching schedule (which involved 118 pupils) prevented his taking part in a 1940 recording session in New Orleans. A plan to record with Earl Hines and Sidney Bechet failed to materialize, so Rex Stewart did the session. Johnson began gigging with local bands, moved into New Orleans temporarily and played one date with Allen's Brass Band.

In June 1942, Johnson issued his first recordings. He returned to New Iberia to do haulage work before leaving for Calif. He played his first concert in San Francisco on April 12, 1943. Along with doing day-work in a drugstore, he also gigged with Baker Millian and played Sunday afternoon sessions at the C.I.O. Hall with Lu Watters's sidemen (July 1943–January 1944). Johnson played one date with Kid Ory, and recorded for World Transcription Service just before leaving Calif. (July 1944). He returned to La. where he did more recordings; also playing dates in Opelousas with a band led by pianist Tex Parker. Johnson played at the New Orleans Jazz Foundation Concert in January 1945. He then moved to N.Y. in March 1945, playing one date at Jimmy Ryan's prior to working with Sidney Bechet's Band at Savoy Cafe, Boston, from March 12, 1945. Johnson left the band in April (temporarily replaced by Pete Bocage, whose place was soon taken by Johnny Windhurst) to return to La. There he organized a band for residency at Stuyvesant Casino, N.Y. (Sept. 28, 1945–Jan. 12, 1946), and again led at Stuyvesant Casino (April 10–31–May 1946). The unit disbanded and Bunk returned to New Iberia, and played dates as a guest star, including two concerts in Chicago in the fall of 1946. He worked in and around Chicago from April until June 1947. Johnson played concerts at the N.Y. Town Hall in autumn 1947, played gigs at Caravan Ballroom, N.Y.C., then organized his own band (aided by Harold Drob, a former G.I.), using N.Y. musicians. He made his last recordings in December 1947, then returned to his home in New Iberia. In late 1948 he suffered a stroke which paralyzed his left arm; for the rest of his life he was a semi-invalid.

Disc.: *Bunk and Lu* (1941); *Bunk Johnson and His Superior Jazz Band* (1942); *Bunk Johnson in San Francisco* (1943); *Plays Popular Songs* (1944); *1944 (#2)* (1944); *Spicy Advice* (1944); *King of Blues* (1944); *1944 (#1)* (1944); *Bunks Brass Band and Dance Band 1945* (1945); *Bunk Johnson & Mutt Carey in New York* (1947); *Last Testament of a Great Jazzman* (1947); *Last Testament* (1947); *Bunk Plays the Blues: The Spirituals* (1951); *The Bunk Johnson Band* (1952); *Bunk Johnson and the Yerba Buena Jazz Band* (1954); *Jazz Nocturne, Vol. 1: In Boston* (1998).

Bibl.: C. Hillman, *B. J.: His Life & Times* (N.Y., 1988); A. Sonnier and W. Geary, *"Bunk" J.: The New Iberia Years* (N.Y., 1977).—JC/LP

Johnson, Charlie (actually, Charles Wright),

jazz pianist, leader; b. Philadelphia, Nov. 21, 1891; d. N.Y., Dec. 13, 1959. Raised in Lowell, Mass. Johnson began on trombone, and played with various bands in N.Y. c. 1914. Then he moved to Atlantic City and concentrated on piano. There, he led his own band from c. 1918, until Oct. 22, 1925, when he brought the band to N.Y. to open at Small's Paradise. For over a decade he led the resident band at Small's (including Jabbo Smith in 1929), occasionally returning to Atlantic City for summer seasons. Johnson toured in the late 1930s, but ceased full-time leading in 1938. Through the 1940s, he gigged in N.Y., but a long spell of ill health curtailed his activities in the 1950s. He died in the Harlem Hospital and was buried in the Frederic Douglass Cemetery. He should not to be confused with the one-time Duke Ellington trumpeter, Charlie Johnson, who died early in 1937.

Disc.: *The Complete Charlie Johnson Sessions* (1925); *Harlem in the Twenties, Vol. 2* (1955); *The Complete Sessions* (1996). —JC/LP

Johnson, Dink (Oliver), early jazz pianist, clarinetist, drummer; b. Biloxi, Miss., Oct. 28, 1892; d. Portland, Ore., Nov. 29, 1954. Johnson first played drums, then later began learning the piano, working on both during his early years. He played in Las Vegas c. 1913, then joined the Original Creole Orch. on drums. After touring with them, he left in Los Angeles and formed his own Louisiana Six. He worked for a while on drums with Jelly Roll Morton until he was replaced by Ben Borders; he then began to learn the clarinet. He played with Kid Ory on clarinet and piano c. 1920, and played clarinet on Ory's first recordings in 1922. During early 1920s, he led his own band, Five Hounds of Jazz, in Los Angeles; he renamed the band Los Angeles Six when he moved to Chicago in 1924. After returning to Calif., he was mainly active on piano. He finally retired from full-time music, and ran his own small restaurant in Los Angeles during the 1940s. Johnson played occasionally during last years of his life, including recording sessions in 1945.—JC/LP

Johnson, Edward, distinguished Canadian-born American tenor and operatic administrator; b. Guelph, Ontario, Aug. 22, 1878; d. there, April 20, 1959. He sang in concert and oratorio performances before going to N.Y. in 1899 to study with Mme. von Feilitsch. After appearing in the U.S. premiere of Oscar Straus's *A Waltz Dream* in 1907, he continued his studies with Richard Barthélemy in Paris (1908) and Vincenzo Lombardi in Florence (1909). He made his operatic debut as Andrea Chénier at the Teatro Verdi in Padua on Jan. 10, 1912, using the stage name of Edoardo Di Giovanni. He subsequently appeared in Milan at La Scala, where he sang the title role in *Parsifal* at its first complete stage production in Italy, on Jan. 4, 1914. He made his U.S. debut as Loris in *Fedora* at the Chicago Grand Opera on Nov. 20, 1919, remaining on its roster until 1922. He then made his Metropolitan Opera debut in N.Y. as Avito in *L'amore dei tre Re* on Nov. 16, 1922, continuing to sing there until 1935, when he became its general manager, guiding its fortunes through the difficult years of World War II and the postwar era. He retired in 1950. Although he became a naturalized American citizen in 1922, he maintained a close connection with Canada, returning there after his retirement. He was particularly esteemed for such roles as Romeo, Tannhäuser, Don José, Siegfried, Canio, and Pelléas. He also created leading roles in Deems Taylor's *The King's Henchman* (1927) and *Peter Ibbetson* (1931) at the Metropolitan.

Bibl.: R. Mercer, *The Tenor of His Time: E. J. of the Met* (Toronto, 1976).—NS/LK/DM

Johnson, Floyd "Candy," jazz/R&B tenor and baritone saxophonist; b. Madison Co., Ill., May 20, 1922; d. Lucas, Ohio, June 1, 1981. When he was 13, he began playing drums, but quickly switched to first alto then tenor saxophone. In college, he played in the student band; after graduation, his first major job was as lead saxophone player with Andy Kirk's band (1942–47). He then led his own Detroit-based band for a while, before joining Count Basie (1951–53). He is best-remembered for his tenor and baritone sax work with Bill Doggett's R&B band (1958–64), including the hit "High and Wide." He retired from music making from the mid-1960s through 1971, when he toured Europe with Milt Buckner. He led the student band at Bowling Green State Univ. in 1974, and also briefly worked with Duke Ellington that year.

Disc.: *Bikini Beach* (1964); *Candy Johnson Show* (1964); *Live: BGSU* (1974).—JC/LP

Johnson, (Francis) Hall, black American choral conductor, composer, and arranger; b. Athens, Ga., June 2, 1887; d. N.Y., April 30, 1970. He studied at the Univ. of Pa. (B.A., 1910), where he took a course in composition with Hugh A. Clark; later studied with Goetschius at the Inst. of Musical Art in N.Y. (1923–24). In 1925 he formed the Hall Johnson Choir, with which he gave numerous concerts; from 1938 to 1946 he conducted the Festival Choir of Los Angeles, and then settled in N.Y. as conductor of the Festival Negro Chorus, with which he toured Germany and Austria under the auspices of the U.S. State Dept. (1951). He composed a folk opera, *Run Littl' Chillun* (1933), a cantata, *Son of Man* (1946), choral music, songs, and arrangements for film and television. —NS/LK/DM

Johnson, Frank (Francis), black bandmaster and composer; b. probably on the island of Martinique, 1792; d. Philadelphia, April 6, 1844. He settled in Philadelphia (c. 1809), where he organized his own band and dance orch. After touring England with his band in 1837, he led promenade concerts with his band throughout the U.S., highlighting his own works. In Philadelphia, his concerts were often graced by the presence of prominent white artists, an unheard-of practice in his era. Selected modern eds. of his works have been publ. by A. LaBrew (Detroit, 1977) and C. Jones and L. Greenwich, II (N.Y., 1983).

Bibl.: A. LaBrew, *Francis J. (1792–1844)* (Detroit, 1977). —NS/LK/DM

Johnson, Freddy, jazz pianist; b. N.Y., March 12, 1904; d. there, March 24, 1961. Johnson worked as Florence Mills's accompanist c. 1922 before forming his own band in N.Y. (1924). During 1925, he worked with Elmer Snowden, then joined Billy Fowler in 1926. After briefly working with other bands, he joined Sam Wooding's group from 1928–29, and traveled to Europe with them in June 1928. He remained in Paris in 1929, working for a long time at Bricktop's famous club. In February 1934, he left France to work in Belgium and Holland. He played regularly at the Negro Palace in Amsterdam, including several long spells in a trio with Coleman Hawkins. In 1941, he opened his own club La Cubana in Amsterdam until arrested by the Nazis on Dec. 11, 1941. From January 1942 until February 1944, he was interned in Bavaria, then repatriated to the U.S. in March 1944. During the late 1940s and 1950s, he was mainly active as a piano teacher and vocal coach, but also played solo club dates in N.Y. He went to Europe in late 1959 with the "Free and Easy" show. By then he was very ill with cancer, but after leaving the show was able to play for several weeks in Holland (1960). That autumn, he was hospitalized in Copenhagen, but then returned to N.Y., where he was immediately hospitalized until his death.

DISC.: *Live at B.B. Joe's* (1984); *1933–1939* (1933).—JC/LP

Johnson, Graham (Rhodes), esteemed Rhodesian-born English pianist, teacher, and writer on music; b. Bulawayo, July 10, 1950. He studied at the Royal Academy of Music in London (1967–72), and then with Geoffrey Parsons (1972–76) and Gerald Moore (1975–78). In 1970 he became a British citizen. He made his debut at London's Wigmore Hall in 1972. In 1976 Johnson founded and became artistic director of the Songmakers' Almanac in London, with which he has presented a remarkable series of innovative vocal concerts with leading singers of the day. An offshoot of this endeavor is his Young Songmakers series in which he features the younger generation of gifted vocal artists in London. In 1977 he toured the U.S. with Victoria de Los Angeles, and in 1985 with Margaret Price. He has since made tours of the U.S. with Peter Schreier, Matthias Goerne, and Dame Felicity Lott. In 1986 Johnson became prof. of accompaniment at the Guildhall School of Music and Drama in London. His most expansive project was the recording of all of Schubert's songs in 37 vols. in which he was the sensitive accompanist to a host of venerable singers. This series served as a welcome complement to the celebrations in honor of the 200th anniversary of Schubert's birth in 1997. In addition to an extensive ongoing survey of the French song repertoire, he launched a major series in 1996 to record the complete songs of Schumann. Johnson's perceptive observations on music may be found in his program notes to all of his recordings. He has also contributed reviews and articles to various journals. He published the vols. *The Spanish Song Companion* (1992), *The Songmakers' Almanac: Twenty years of song recitals in London: Reflections and Commentaries* (1996), and *A French Song Companion* (2000). Johnson was made a Fellow of the Royal Academy of Music in 1984, and of the Guildhall School of Music and Drama in 1988. In 1994 he was made an Officer of the Order of the British Empire. He was honored as an Instrumentalist of the Year in the Royal Phil. Soc. Awards in 1999.—LK/DM

Johnson, Gus (Jr.), jazz drummer; b. Tyler, Tex., Nov. 15, 1913; d. Westminster, Colo., Feb. 6, 2000. Johnson began playing piano, then studied drums and bass. While still at school in Dallas, he was featured on drums at the age of 10 at the Lincoln Theatre, Houston. He played with McDavid's Blue Rhythm Boys c. 1925 and joined the Lloyd Hunter Band in Omaha, Nebr. (on drums); he later played bass with the band, then reverted to drums. He worked for two years in a band led by pianist Ernest "Speck" Redd, then joined Jay McShann in Kansas City (1938). There he remained until joining the army in 1943; after his release, he was with the Jesse Miller Band in Chicago from spring 1945 until

1947. He worked with Earl Hines and Cootie Williams before joining Count Basie from late 1949–December 1954 (he appeared on film with Basie's sextet in 1950). After an appendectomy, he began regular studio and session work. In 1957–early 1960s, he worked regularly with Ella Fitzgerald. He was featured on hundreds of recording sessions throughout the 1960s, and in 1969 appeared regularly with The World's Greatest Jazz Band in N.Y. During the 1970s, he moved to Denver, Colo. —JC/LP

Johnson, Henry, American guitarist; b. Chicago, Ill., Jan. 28, 1954. If there is a second coming of George Benson, he is probably it. Both are outstanding guitarists influenced by Wes Montgomery and Kenny Burrell; both played with Jack McDuff; both are excellent jazz players; both love to play R&B; both travel back and forth between mainstream and R&B, depending on the occasion. They both even sing (though Benson wins that category hands down). Raised in Chicago, Johnson was playing guitar for Isaac Hayes by the time he was 14. In 1979 he started long-standing associations with Ramsey Lewis and Joe Williams. A versatile sideman, he has also played with Angela Bofill, the Boston Pops, Count Basie Orch., Dizzy Gillespie, Freddie Hubbard, Jimmy Smith, the Spinners, Stanley Turrentine, and Nancy Wilson. His solo releases are a bit erratic, mixing straight-ahead and R&B–based jazz, usually favoring the later, but he is very strong in the former.

DISC.: *New Beginnings* (1993).—PMac

Johnson, Horace, American composer; b. Waltham, Mass., Oct. 5, 1893; d. Tucson, Ariz., May 30, 1964. He studied with Bainbridge Crist. He wrote several popular pieces for orch., among them *Astarte* (Richmond, Jan. 2, 1936) and *Streets of Florence* (Mexico, July 9, 1937), as well as songs ("The Pirate," "When Pierrot Sings," "The Three Cherry Trees," and "Thy Dark Hair").—NS/LK/DM

Johnson, Howard (Lewis), jazz tubist, baritone saxophonist (also trumpet, flugelhorn, four different clarinets, bass saxophone, electric bass, and pennywhistle); b. Montgomery, Ala., Aug. 7, 1941. His fluency, range, and skill on the tuba are astonishing. A self-taught musician, Johnson started on baritone sax at age 13 and moved to tuba at 14. After serving in the Navy in the late 1950s, he settled in Boston, living with the family of drummer Tony Williams. In 1962, he moved to N.Y.C. on the advice of Eric Dolphy, where he met Pharoah Sanders, another recent arrival. From 1964–66, he worked with Charlie Mingus's band. Four days after hearing Johnson at a gig in 1966, Gil Evans called to invite Howard to join him in Monterey. That relationship lasted on and off until Evans's passing in 1988. Johnson also formed Substructure in 1966, a band that at one point included four tubas and backed Taj Mahal. He wrote arrangements for Maria Muldaur, Paul Butterfield, and B. B. King while working with Mahal. Over the years, Howard has worked with Hank Crawford, Archie Shepp, Buddy Rich, Freddie Hubbard, McCoy Tyner, Marvin Gaye, Miles Davis, Quincy Jones, The

Band (with whom he appeared at Woodstock '94), and the *Saturday Night Live* band (which he founded in 1975 and led in 1979). In 1971, he formed a second tuba band Gravity. They performed on *SNL*, in N.Y., and toured Europe. Johnson recorded with Jack DeJohnette's Special Edition, Jimmy Heath, and Crawford again in the 1980s. Through the 1990s, he toured the world with George Gruntz, Dizzy Gillespie, Abdullah Ibrahim's Ekaya, and others. He was heard on film soundtracks for Spike Lee's *School Daze, Mo' Better Blues, Malcolm X,* and *Clockers*. After a four-year association (1990–94) with the NDR Big Band in Hamburg, Germany, he returned to N.Y. and continued doing sessions and heading bands into the 1990s.

DISC.: *Arrival* (1995); *Gravity!!!* (1995); *Right Now* (1998). **—LP**

Johnson, Hunter, American composer and teacher; b. Benson, N.C., April 14, 1906. He studied at the Univ. of N.C. (1924–26), and at the Eastman School of Music in Rochester, N.Y., graduating in 1929. In 1933 he received the Rome Prize. He taught at the Univ. of Mich. (1929–33), the Univ. of Manitoba (1944–47), Cornell Univ. (1948–53), the Univ. of Ill. (1959–65), and the Univ. of Tex. (1966–71). In 1941 and 1954 he held Guggenheim fellowships. His output follows in the tradition of Ives and Copland.

WORKS: DRAMATIC: B a l l e t : *In Time of Armament* (1939); *Letter to the World* (1940); *Deaths and Entrances* (1942); *The Scarlet Letter* (1975). **ORCH.:** *Prelude* (1930); Sym. (1931); Concerto for Piano and Chamber Orch. (1935); *Elegy* for Clarinet and Strings (1937); *Concerto for Orchestra* (1944); *Music for Strings* (1949–54); *North State,* to commemorate the tricentennial of the Carolina Charter (1963); *Past the Evening Sun* (1964). **CHAMBER:** Piano Sonata (1934; rev., 1936 and 1947–48); *Elegy for Hart Crane* for Clarinet Quintet (1936); *Serenade* for Flute and Clarinet (1937); Violin Sonatina (1937); Trio for Flute, Oboe, and Piano (1954). **VOCAL:** Songs.

BIBL.: R. Monaco, *The Music of H. J.* (diss., Cornell Univ., 1960).**—NS/LK/DM**

Johnson, James P(rice), influential and talented jazz pianist, composer; b. New Brunswick, N.J., Feb. 1, 1894; d. N.Y., Nov. 17, 1955. His grandfather had fought in the Civil War; his father, William, was born in New Brunswick and was a hardware store helper and mechanic for a man named Price for whom James received his middle name. His mother's father was half–African American, half–Native American, and had bought his freedom; his mother, Josephine Harrison, was born in Petersburg, Va., and worked as a maid. He had three older brothers and a sister, Belle (b. c. 1886).

Johnson was originally taught piano by his mother. The family moved to Jersey City, then to N.Y. He played at local rent parties during his early teens, and his first professional work was at Coney Island in summer of 1912. Subsequently, he played solo piano in various clubs in N.Y. and Atlantic City; after touring the southern vaudeville circuit, he returned to N.Y. Beginning in May 1917, he cut piano rolls (just a few months after the Original Dixieland Jazz Band made its first records; this made him one of the first jazz artists whose work was documented, and certainly the first black artist) and worked in N.Y. clubs through 1918. He again did a theater tour, then left to play a residency in Toledo, Ohio (1919). In 1921, he began his prolific recording career, and also worked as musical director for Dudley's "Black Sensations/Smart Set" revues. He led his own Harmony Seven in N.Y. in 1922. In March 1923, he went to England with the *Plantation Days* show. 1923 he scored his own "Runnin' Wild" revue, including the hits "The Charleston" and "Old Fashioned Love." During the 1920s, he did many recording sessions with bands and accompanied singers such as Bessie Smith and Ethel Waters. By then, he was firmly established as a successful composer, having also written "If I Could Be with You," "Carolina Shout," and other tunes.

For the rest of his life, he devoted a great deal of his time to composing. He worked in "Keep Shufflin'" with Fats Waller in 1928, and premiered his extended work "Yamekraw" at Carnegie Hall in July—W. C. Handy conducted and Fats Waller played the piano part while reportedly Johnson played that night at "Keep Shufflin'." In 1929, he directed the orchestra for Bessie Smith's film *St. Louis Blues* (but he is not seen on-screen). During the 1930s, he concentrated on composing, writing his "Symphony Harlem" in 1932 (of which only the second movement survives), his piano concerto "Jazz-A-Mine" in 1934 (of which only the piano version of the second movement was published and survives), another symphony (lost), and several works for the stage, including the one-act work *De Organizer* in collaboration with the famous poet Langston Hughes; unfortunately, the score has been lost. He did, however, regularly lead his own orchestra during the early 1930s, also played occasionally in other bands ("Fess" Williams, 1936–37, for one). In 1939, Johnson began playing again regularly: he did a solo spot at Cafe Society (August), played for *Swingin' the Dream* show (November), and led his own band at Cafe Society (December). In 1940 he led at Elks' Rendezvous and Cafe Society, N.Y., until taken ill in summer of 1940. He returned to music the following year as musical director for *Pinkard's Fantasies*. He was with Wild Bill Davison in Boston (early 1943), then led his own band and solos in N.Y. (1944). He took part in Eddie Condon's *New York Town Hall* concerts and was also was featured as solo artist-composer at Carnegie Hall, including a complete performance of the "Harlem Symphony" (1945). He led at the Pied Piper (1945), and played at Eddie Condon's Club (1946) until suffering a stroke in October of that year. He was active again in spring 1947; in 1949, he worked in a Calif. production of his revue "Sugar Hill," and also played occasionally with the Albert Nicholas Quartet. He then returned to N.Y. and continued working until suffering a severe stroke in 1951; he was an invalid for the rest of his life. A benefit was held for him at Town Hall on Sept. 28, 1953, featuring Ellington, Basie, Calloway, and Hampton. He remained at his home for three years, but spent his last days in Queens Hospital.

WORKS: *Yamecraw* for Soloists, Chorus, and Orch. (1928); *Harlem Symphony* (1932); *Jasmine (Jazz-O-Mine), Concerto for*

Piano and Orch. (1935); *De Organizer* (folk opera; n.d.). **MUSI-CAL COMEDIES:** *Runnin' Wild* (1923); *Sugar Hill* (1948). **PIANO PIECES:** *Caprice Rag* (1914); *Harlem Strut* (1917); *Carolina Shout* (1925); *Snowy Morning Blues* (1927); *You've Got to Be Modernistic* (1930); *Fascination* (1939). **SONGS:** "Old-Fashioned Love" (1923); "Charleston" (1923); "If I Could Be with You" (1926). Also operettas, ballets, and film music.

DISC.: "Carolina Shout" (1917); *Rare Piano Roll Solos, Vol. 1* (1917); *Rare Piano Roll Solos, Vol. 2* (1918); *James P. Johnson & Perry Bradford* (1921); *Watch Me Go* (1921); *"Yamekraw" and Other Selections* (1921); *Snowy Morning Blues* (1930); *Rent Party Piano* (1943); *The Original James P. Johnson 1942–1945* (1943); *Ain'tcha Got Music* (1944); *Jazz Band Ball* (1944); *James P. Johnson Plays Fats Waller Favorites* (1944); *The Daddy of the Piano* (1950); *Stomps, Rags and Blues* (1951); *Rent Party* (1953); *Early Harlem Piano, Vol. 2* (1954); *Backwater Blues* (1955); *Harlem Rent Party* (1955).

BIBL.: S. E. Brown, *A Case of Mistaken Identity: The Life and Music of J. P. J.* (Metuchen N.J., London; 1986); F. H. Trolle, *J. P. J.: Father of Stride Piano* (Netherlands; 1981).—JC/LP/NS

Johnson, James Weldon,

black American man of letters, brother of **J(ohn) Rosamond Johnson;** b. Jacksonville, Fla., June 17, 1871; d. in an automobile accident in Wiscasset, Maine, June 26, 1938. He studied literature at Atlanta Univ. (B.A., 1894; M.A., 1904), and also passed the Fla. bar examination to practice law (1897). As a poet, he began writing texts to his brother's compositions; their song *Lift Every Voice and Sing* (1900) proved popular, becoming known as "the Negro National Anthem." The brothers settled in N.Y. in 1902, where they joined Bob Cole in the enormously successful songwriting team of Cole and Johnson Bros. Among their hit songs, mostly in black dialect, were *Under the Bamboo Tree* (1902), which was parodied by T.S. Eliot in "Fragment of the Agon," and *Congo Love Song* (1903). Under the pseudonym Will Handy, they produced *Oh, Didn't He Ramble* (1902), which became a jazz standard; the team's success was such that they became known as "Those Ebony Offenbachs." Johnson was then active as a diplomat (1906–14), serving as consul to Venezuela and, later, to Nicaragua. His tr. of Granados's *Goyescas* was used for the Metropolitan Opera's first performance of this work. He publ. anonymously the novel *The Autobiography of an Ex-Colored Man* (Boston, 1912), which includes vivid descriptions of the ragtime era in N.Y. He collaborated with his brother in compiling 2 books of American Negro spirituals (N.Y., 1926 and 1927); wrote *Black Manhattan* (N.Y., 1930), a history of blacks in N.Y. which includes valuable information on black musical life; also publ. an autobiography, *Along This Way* (1931). His papers are on deposit at Yale Univ.

BIBL.: E. Levy, *J.W. J.* (Chicago, 1973).—NS/LK/DM

Johnson, J. J. (James Louis),

influential jazz trombonist, composer; b. Indianapolis, Ind., Jan. 22, 1924. His speed and facility were so surprising that from 1946 on he was suspected of playing a valve rather than a slide trombone. He influenced several generations of players, including Robin Eubanks and Conrad Herwig. His early solos are filled with impressive runs that often get repeated from take to take; by the late 1950s his solos were moving and structured organically (one idea leading to the next) rather than from pre-determined licks.

Johnson began to play the piano at the age of nine with a church organist and the trombone at 14. His original influences were Lester Young, Roy Eldridge, and Fred Beckett. He toured with Clarence Love and Isaac "Snookum" Russell (1941–42; the latter with Fats Navarro) before attracting attention and making his first recordings and broadcasts as a member of Benny Carter's Orch. (1942–45), and an appearance with the band in "As Thousands Cheer." He also soloed at length on the first Jazz at the Philharmonic concert in 1944. After working with Count Basie (1945–46), he settled in N.Y. and did stints with various artists, notably Charlie Parker, with whom he recorded in December 1947. During this time period Parker and Gillespie had a great influence on him; he also began using a felt hat as a mute. He toured and recorded with Illinois Jacquet (1947–49). He toured Korea, Japan, and the South Pacific with a group led by Oscar Pettiford for the USO (1951). He temporarily left performing due to problems with drugs and worked as a blueprint inspector from August 1952–May 1954. During this period he recorded important sessions with Miles Davis and Clifford Brown, and as a leader, but declined gigs with Davis so as to hold onto his job. In 1954, he resumed his career, recording a much admired solo on "Walkin'" with Davis and touring with Kai Winding in a group known as Jay and Kai; then formed his own quintet (1956–60), with which he toured Europe. In the later 1950s, he became a major witness in the case against the N.Y.C. practice of requiring cabaret cards for musicians. From September 1960 to March 1961, he worked on "Perceptions," a piece written for orchestra with Dizzy Gillespie. The six-part work was recorded in May 1961 under the direction of Gunther Schuller and was performed at Monterey in September 1961. After working with Miles Davis (1961–62), Johnson took a year off from playing to work on arrangements for his album *J. J.'s Broadway.* He then formed his own quartet to play clubs and concerts. In July 1964, he toured Japan with a sextet including Clark Terry and Sonny Stitt. He gave increasing attention to composition, moving to Los Angeles as a composer for film and television in 1970; he studied with Earle Hagen and wrote music for television shows, including *The Mod Squad, Mike Hammer, Harry-O, Starsky and Hutch, Six Million Dollar Man, The Rookies,* and *Barefoot in the Park,* and films including *Across 110th Street, Shaft,* and *Cleopatra Jones.* He returned to active touring in 1977. His wife Vivian became ill, prompting a move back to Indianapolis in 1988, at which time he was awarded an honorary doctorate by Ind. Univ. On Nov. 17, 1987, while he played at the Village Vanguard, Slide Hampton made his way on-stage and presented him with a scroll signed by 40 trombonists in gratitude for his contribution to jazz.

In April 1996 he was honored with a retrospective concert of his works played by the Harvard Univ. Jazz Band directed by Tom Everett, and a brief residency. He gave his last public concert at William Paterson Coll. on Nov. 10, 1996. In the June 1997 he announced that he was retiring from playing live performances.

DISC.: *Mad Bebop* (1946); *Jazz Quintet* (1946); *Afternoon at Birdland* (1947); *Jay and Kai* (1947); *Jay and Kai, Vol. 3* (1949); *Modern Jazz Trombone Series, Vol. 1* (1949); *Trombone by Three*

(1949); *Modern Jazz Trombone Series, Vol. 2* (1949); *The Eminent Jay Jay Johnson, Vol. 2* (1954); *J. J. Johnson, Kai Winding, Bennie Green with Strings* (1954); *Kai Winding & J. J. Johnson: East Coast Jazz Series, Vol. 7* (1955); *The Finest of J. J. Johnson Jazz Workshop, Vol. 2 Trombone Rapport* (1955); *The Eminent J. J. Johnson, Vol. 3* (1955); *East Coast Jazz 7* (1955); *Trombone for Two* (1955); *Jay and Kai Octet* (1956); *Dave Brubeck and Jay & Kai at Newport* (1956); *Kai + J. J.* (1956); *J Is for Jazz* (1956); *Live at the Cafe Bohemia* (1957); *First Place* (1957); *Blue Trombone* (1957); *Trombone Master* (1957); *Mr. Jay Jay Johnson: Live* (1957); *At the Opera House* (live; 1957); *J. J. in Person* (1958); *Dial J. J.* (1958); *Really Livin'* (1959); *Trombone and Voices* (1960); *J. J. Inc.* (1960); *The Great Kai & J. J.* (1960); *A Touch of Satin* (1960); *Perceptions* (1961); *Andre Previn and J. J. Johnson Play "Mack the Knife"* (1962); *J. J.'s Broadway* (1963); *Proof Positive* (1964); *Say When* (1964); *J. J. with Big Band* (1964); *Goodies* (1965); *Broadway Express* (1965); *The Total J. J. Johnson* (1966); *Israel* (1968); *Betwixt and Between* (1968); *Stonebone* (1969); *Man & Boy* (1971); *Yokohama Concert* (live; 1977); *Pinnacles* (1979); *Concepts in Blue* (1980); *Aurex Jazz Festival* (1982): *All Star Jam* (live; 1982); *We'll Be Together Again* (1983); *Things Are Getting Better All the Time* (1983); *Quintergy: Live* (1988); *Standards: Live at the Village* (1988); *Vivian* (1992); *Let's Hang Out* (1992); *Tangence* (1994); *J. J.!* (1995); *Jazz Quintets* (1996); *Brass Orchestra* (1996); *Heroes* (1999).

BIBL.: D. Baker, *J. J. J.* (N.Y., 1979); J. Berrett and L. Bourgois III, *The Musical World of J. J. J. Johnson* (Lanham, Md., 1999).—LP/JB

Johnson, John, distinguished English lutenist and composer, father of Robert Johnson; b. c. 1540; d. c. 1594. He was made one of the three lute musicians to Queen Elizabeth I in 1579. Johnson was one of the most significant composers of lute music of his time, and helped to develop the lute duet. Many of his works survive in various MS collections.—NS/LK/DM

Johnson, J(ohn) Rosamond, black American composer and bass, brother of **James Weldon Johnson;** b. Jacksonville, Fla., Aug. 11, 1873; d. N.Y., Nov. 11, 1954. He studied at Atlanta Univ. and at the New England Cons. of Music in Boston, and took voice lessons with David Bispham. He set his brother's poem *Lift Every Voice and Sing* (1900) to music, which later became known as "the Negro National Anthem." The brothers collaborated on many other songs, selling them to various musical reviews in N.Y.; in 1902 they formed, with Bob Cole, the songwriting team of Cole and Johnson Bros. Johnson also wrote some songs that were accepted on the concert stage, among them *Li'l Gal* and *Since You Went Away*. In 1911–12 he was music director of Hammerstein's Opera House in London; also sang in opera, and later toured the U.S. and Europe in programs of Negro spirituals. With his brother, he compiled two vols. of Negro spirituals (1926, 1927), adding piano accompaniments; wrote a ballet, *African Drum Dance*, and many vocal works; also *Rolling Along in Song* (a history of black music with 85 song arrangements). He sang the role of Lawyer Frazier in the early performances of Gershwin's *Porgy and Bess*.—NS/LK/DM

Johnson, Keg (Frederic H.), jazz trombonist; brother of **Budd Johnson;** b. Dallas, Tex., Nov. 19, 1908; d. Chicago, Nov. 8, 1967. Johnson's first lessons were from his father, a cornetist. He later studied with Booker Pittman's mother (Portia Pittman, daughter of Booker T. Washington). He did day work in a local Studebaker car factory and gigged on various instruments until specializing on trombone from 1927. From 1929–30, he worked with various local bands and on the road, until settling in Chicago. He worked in revues and bands in Chicago, including recording and touring with Louis Armstrong from early 1932–July 1933. He moved to N.Y., and worked with Fletcher Henderson for a year in 1934, and then joined Cab Calloway in January 1935 and remained wtih him until the summer of 1948 (except for brief absence early in 1940). From 1948–50, he worked with Lucky Millinder, and then moved to Calif. in late 1951. He worked with Benny Carter (1952) and briefly with Duke Ellington (1953), then left full-time music to work as a house decorator. He continued to do regular gigs (some on guitar), however, with various leaders. He moved back to N.Y. in late 1950s, working with various bands. In 1961, he joined vocalist Ray Charles's Orch., and remained in that band for six years, dying suddenly while on tour.—JC/LP

Johnson, Lem(uel Charles), jazz tenor saxophonist, clarinetist, singer; b. Oklahoma City, Okla., Aug. 6, 1909; d. N.Y., April 1, 1989. He attended Douglass H.S., started on clarinet, gigged with local bands, and played in Oklahoma City in The Jolly Harmony Boys led by Charlie Christian's brother, Edward. He switched to sax in 1928, and received instruction from Walter Page while working a summer season (1928) with The Blue Devils in Shawnee, Okla. In 1929, he did regular radio work in Okla. and then played with various bands in Milwaukee. During the mid-1930s, he spent three years with Eli Rice (mainly in Minneapolis). In April 1937, he moved to N.Y., working with various leaders until he formed his own trio in late 1939. He led his own sextet during the early 1940s, but also worked brief spells with others. After the war, he reformed his sextet and played local gigs. For many years, he worked during the day for the N.Y. post office, but through the 1950s and 1960s continued to lead own highly successful band, which regularly featured many well-known musicians. He retired in the 1970s.—JC/LP

Johnson, Lockrem, American pianist, music publisher, and composer; b. Davenport, Iowa, March 15, 1924; d. Seattle, March 5, 1977. He studied at the Cornish School of Music in Seattle (1931–38) and at the Univ. of Wash. (1938–42); subsequently was a member of its faculty (1947–49); concurrently served as music director of the Eleanor King Dance Co. (1947–50) and pianist in the Seattle Sym. Orch. (1948–51). In 1952 he held a Guggenheim fellowship; lived in N.Y., where he served as education director for Mercury Music (1951–54), head of the orch. dept. of C. F. Peters (1954–58), and president of Dow Publishers (1957–62); subsequently returned to Seattle as head of the music dept. at the Cornish School of Music (1962–69); also founded Puget Music Publications (1970), which was devoted to publishing works by composers of the Northwest. His works reveal a fine lyrical gift of expression.

WORKS: DRAMATIC: *She,* ballet (1948; rev. 1950); *A Letter to Emily,* chamber opera (1951; N.Y., Jan. 25, 1955). **ORCH.:** *Lyric Prelude* (1948; rev. 1949); Sym. (Seattle, Dec. 2, 1966). **CHAMBER:** 3 violin sonatas (1942; 1948, rev. 1949; 1953); 2 cello sonatas (1949, 1953); Trumpet Sonatina (1950). **Piano:** 3 sonatas (1947, rev. 1983; 1949; 1954); 24 Preludes; many other pieces. **VOCAL:** *Suite of Noels,* cantata for Chorus and Keyboard (1954); songs.—NS/LK/DM

Johnson, Lonnie (Alonzo), important early jazz and blues guitarist, singer; b. New Orleans, Feb. 8, 1889; d. Toronto, Canada, June 16, 1970. Brother of pianist James "Steady Roll" Johnson. Lonnie Johnson did local gigs with his brother, and also played violin and guitar in cafes and theaters in New Orleans. He sailed to Europe (c. 1917) to do revue work in London and theater tours. Whe he returned to New Orleans, he found that the 1918–19 flu epidemic had almost wiped out his entire family. He moved on to St. Louis (c. 1922), and worked with Charlie Creath, Fate Marable, Nat Robinson, and others (mainly on violin and piano). He worked in a steel foundry for two years, but continued gigging, mainly on violin and piano. Circa 1925, he entered and won a talent contest organized by the OKeh Record Co. Shortly afterwards, he began his prolific recording career, worked as an OKeh staff musician until 1932. From this period on, he specialized on guitar, but also did some recorded work on piano and violin. During his OKeh years, he recorded with countless artists including Louis Armstrong (1927), Duke Ellington (1927), and Eddie Lang (guitar duets, 1928). He soloed on one of the earliest versions of "Stardust." He was reportedly a major influence on Robert Johnson and also a young B. B. King. In 1932, he moved to Cleveland and played on and off for a few years with Putney Dandridge's Band, and on numerous local radio shows; he also did day work in a tire factory and in a steel mill.

He moved to Chicago in 1937 and worked with Johnny Dodds, then became house musician at the Three Deuces until 1939. In the early 1940s, he led his own quartet in local clubs. From the mid-1940s he began appearing as a solo vocalist, accompanying himself on amplified guitar. He recorded many singles and composed the best-seller "Tomorrow Night" (1948). He visited London for a concert appearance in June 1952, then returned to the U.S. and made Cincinnati his home base for several years until moving to Philadelphia, where he worked as a chef at the Benjamin Franklin Hotel until the early 1960s. During the blues revival of the early 1960s, he recorded several albums with acoustic guitar accompaniment, and toured Europe. From the mid-1960s, he worked regularly in Toronto, Canada, and also toured. In 1969, he was injured in an accident and then suffered a stroke; he subsequently spent many months in the Riversdale Hospital, Toronto. He sang at a Toronto blues concert in 1970 shortly before his death.

DISC.: *He's a Jelly Roll Baker* (1939); *Lonesome Road* (1958); *Blues by Lonnie Johnson* (1960); *Blues & Ballads* (1960); *Blues, Ballads & Jumpin' Jazz, Vol. 2* (1960); *Losing Game* (1960); *Idle Hours* (1961); *Another Night to Cry* (1962); *Stompin' at the Penny* (1965); *Complete Folkways Recordings* (1967); *Lonnie Johnson* (1974); *Tomorrow Night* (1976); *Bluebird No. 13* (1977); *The Origi-*nator of Modern Guitar Blues* (1980); *It Feels Good* (1981); *Blues Roots, Vol. 8* (Swingin' with Lonnie) (1983); *Steppin' on the Blues* (1990); *Blues Masters* (1991); *Me & My Crazy Self* (1991); *Blues in My Fingers* (1995).—JC/LP

Johnson, Manzie (Isham), jazz drummer; b. Putnam, Conn., Aug. 19, 1906; d. N.Y., April 9, 1971. Johnson was raised in N.Y. from infancy. He studied violin and piano as a child, then specialized on drums. From the mid-1920s, he worked with various bands, before joining Don Redman from 1931 until early 1937. During the 1930s, Johnson did many studio sessions with Henry Allen, Lil Armstrong, and others. He worked again with Redman in the early 1940s, until he joined the army in 1944. After the war, he more or less retired, although he continued to gig on occasion through his death.—JC/LP

Johnson, Marc, American bassist; b. Omaha, Neb., Oct. 21, 1953. One of the most tasteful bassists around, he has impeccable jazz credentials. Most notably, he was in pianist Bill Evans's final trio in 1978–80. He first played piano and cello, taking up bass at age 16. By the time he was 19, he was playing professionally with the Fort Worth Symphony. He attended the prestigious jazz college at North Tex. State Univ. and then paid his dues with Woody Herman, Evans, Stan Getz, and John Abercrombie, among others. His own bands use electric guitars, but he has stuck with the acoustic upright and has a big, rich tone and considerable dexterity without making a fetish of either. His mid-1980s band Bass Desires, with guitarists Bill Frisell and John Scofield and drummer Peter Erskine, did much for the reputations of all concerned, though it put out only two albums. His next documented group, Right Brain Patrol, with guitarist Ben Monder (later replaced by Wolfgang Muthspiel) and percussionist/vocalist Arto Tunçboyaciyan, didn't really contract the size of the group, as Monder sometimes overdubs guitars, but it did expand Johnson's musical concepts thanks to Tunçboyaciyan, whose vocal contributions and frequent use of nontrapset percussion recall Nana Vasconcelos's role on some Pat Metheny albums. And a Johnson quartet with Frisell, Metheny, and drummer Joey Baron recalls the Bass Desires format. The gaps in between his albums reflect his busy session schedule; he can be heard on over 100 albums.

DISC.: *Bass Desires* (1986); *Second Sight* (1987); *Two by Four* (1991); *Right Brain Patrol* (1992); *Magic Labyrinth* (1995); *The Sound of Summer Running* (1998).—SH

Johnson, Mary Jane, American soprano; b. Pampa, Tex., March 22, 1950. She studied at West Tex. A. & M. Univ. In 1981 she made her operatic debut in N.Y. singing Weber's Agathe. In 1982 she made her first appearance at the Santa Fe Opera as Rosalinde, and subsequently sang there with fine success in later seasons. In 1983 she appeared as Freia in *Das Rheingold* at the San Francisco Opera. She made regular appearances at the Washington (D.C.) Opera from 1984, and at the Cincinnati Opera from 1986. After singing Desdemona at the Pittsburgh Opera and Helen of Troy in *Mefistofele* at the Lyric Opera in Chicago in 1991, she was engaged as Shostakovich's Lady Macbeth at Milan's La Scala and at the Opéra de la Bastille in Paris in 1992. In 1996 she sang Janáček's Emilia Marty at the Vancouver Opera. Among her other roles of note were Mozart's Countess, Leonore, Senta, Alice in *Falstaff*, Salome, and Tosca. —NS/LK/DM

Johnson, Money (Harold), trumpeter; b. Tyler, Tex., Feb. 23, 1918; d. Long Island, N.Y., March 28, 1978. Johnson began on trumpet at age 15, taking lessons from a local teacher, Leonard Parker. Soon, he did his first professional work with Eddie and Sugar Lou's Hotel Tyler Orch., then played in Dallas for two years in a band led by his cousin, saxophonist Red Calhoun. Johnson played with local bands before joining Nat Towles in 1937. He remained with that band for seven years, then with the rest of Towles's sidemen, he joined Horace Henderson (1942–44). He spent a long spell in Rochester with Bob Dorsey's Band before rejoining Nat Towles at Rhumboogie in Chicago. During the mid-to-late 1940s, he alternated between Cootie's Band and Lucky Millinder bands. During the 1950s, he worked for many leaders, including Louis Jordan, Lucky Thompson, Panama Francis (in South America), Buddy Johnson, Cozy Cole, Mercer Ellington, and others. During the 1960s, he played regularly with Reuben Phillips's Band at the Apollo, N.Y.; he also did prolific studio work. He also toured Russia and Europe with Earl Hines (1966, 1968). From 1968–71, he played occasionally with Duke Ellington, and then resumed active freelancing until the night of his death.—JC/LP

Johnson, Pete(r), jazz pianist; b. Kansas City, Mo., March 25, 1904; d. Buffalo, N.Y., March 23, 1967. Johnson spent part of his childhood in an orphanage. He left school at age 12 and did a variety of jobs before learning to play the drums. He worked as a drummer from 1922–26 and then, after piano lessons from his uncle Charles "Smash" Johnson, he began to gig on piano at many Kansas City clubs from 1926–38. During this period, he began working regularly with vocalist Big Joe Turner. While backing Turner at the Sunset Cafe, he was heard by famed producer/promoter John Hammond, who brought him to N.Y. in 1938. He appeared that December at the famous Carnegie Hall *Spirituals to Swing* concert, which was produced by Hammond, followed by gigs with Albert Ammons and Meade Lux Lewis as the Boogie Woogie Trio. They worked at Cafe Society, N.Y. (from 1939–1940s); Johnson later worked in duo with Albert Ammons at the same venue and residencies in Calif. (1947–48). During the 1940s, he also occasionally toured with Meade Lux Lewis, and played long solo residencies. He lived in Buffalo from 1950, and did long spells of day work, but continued to play in local clubs. He was part of a national tour with the "Piano Parade" package in 1952, along with Lewis, Art Tatum, and Errol Garner; later that year he again briefly teamed with Lewis. In 1955 he briefly reunited with Joe Turner, and also worked as accompanist for Jimmy Rushing. In May 1958, he went to Europe in a JATP show (including Joe Turner); in July of that year also appeared at the Newport Jazz Festival. He returned to Buffalo and continued to work until he suffered a stroke that autumn. For the rest of his life he suffered from ill health (heart trouble and diabetes), and the stroke had left him partly paralyzed. He continued to work on occasion through the 1960s. He is not related to the Kansas City drummer Murl Johnson (b. March 22, 1903), who worked regularly with Pete during the 1920s and 1930s.

DISC.: *Boogie Woogie Trio* (1939); *Boogie Woogie Trio, Vol. 3* (1939); *Pete's Blues* (1946); *Central Avenue Boogie* (1947); *Boogie Woogie Method* (1953); *Jumpin' with Pete Johnson* (1955); *Master of Blues and Boogie Woogie* (1975).
BIBL.: H. J. Mauerer, ed., *The Pete Johnson Story* (N.Y.; 1965). —JC/LP

Johnson, Robert, Scottish composer; b. Duns, c. 1500; d. c. 1560. He was a priest, and after being accused of heresy, he fled to England. About 1530 he was in York. Following a sojourn in Scotland, he settled in England about 1535. His extant works include Latin and English vocal music, as well as instrumental consorts.—LK/DM

Johnson, Robert (Leroy), American blues singer, songwriter, and guitarist; b. Hazelhurst, Miss., May 8, 1911; d. Greenwood, Miss., Aug. 16, 1938. Johnson is revered as the preeminent exponent of folk blues music from the Mississippi River delta. Drawing on the work of such predecessors as Charley Patton and Son House, he created a repertoire of songs, 29 of which were recorded to make up the most influential body of blues recordings in history. Immediate followers such as Muddy Waters and Elmore James built their careers around his work. Later, a generation of blues-based rock 'n' roll musicians, notably Eric Clapton and The Rolling Stones, displayed his influence and performed his songs, which included "I Believe I'll Dust My Broom," "Ramblin' on My Mind," "Cross Road Blues" (or, "Crossroads"), "Love in Vain," "Stop Breakin' Down," "Come on in My Kitchen," "Sweet Home Chicago," and "Walkin' Blues."

Biographical information about Johnson is relatively sparse. He was the illegitimate son of Noah Johnson, a sharecropper, and Julia Ann Majors Dodds. His mother was married to Charles Dodds Jr., a farmer who had been forced to flee Miss. around 1907 due to a business dispute and lived in Memphis. Johnson spent his first two years in labor camps with his mother. In 1914 they went to live with Dodds in Memphis; his mother later left him there and moved to Robinsonville, Miss., where she married Willie "Dusty" Willis in October 1916. Around 1918, Johnson joined them. His first musical instrument was the Jew's harp; then he progressed to harmonica and guitar. By his teens he was following local blues musicians like Willie Brown and attempting to learn from them.

Johnson married Virginia Travis in February 1929. She died in childbirth in April 1930. Johnson left Robinsonville and settled in Hazelhurst, where he married Calletta Craft in May 1931. He later deserted her. During the early 1930s he began to display enormous talent as a performer. He is thought to have performed throughout the mid-South and Midwest and even to have traveled to N.Y. In the fall of 1936, Jackson, Miss., music store owner H. C. Speir alerted American Record Co. (ARC) salesman and talent scout Ernie Oertle to Johnson, and Oertle took him to San Antonio, where Johnson made his first series of recordings Nov. 23–27, 1936. These resulted in 16 tracks, 12 of which were released on six singles by the Vocalion label, the most successful of them being the first, "Terraplane Blues"/"Kindhearted Woman Blues." (The songs were not copyrighted; they contained music and lyrics from traditional sources as well as original writing by Johnson.)

The popularity of his records led ARC to engage Johnson for a second set of recordings, which were made June 19–20, 1937. These sessions resulted in another 13 tracks, ten of which were released on five singles. (A final Johnson single, "Love in Vain"/"Preachin' Blues [Up Jumped the Devil]," was released after his death in 1939.)

Johnson was performing at Three Forks, a roadhouse near Greenwood, Miss., in August 1938, when he was poisoned by a man who was jealous of his attentions to his wife. Weakened, Johnson died three days later of pneumonia at the age of 27. Shortly after, his recordings brought interest from people who would have furthered his career: A&R man John Hammond sought him out for his celebrated From Spirituals to Swing concert held in December in Carnegie Hall, and in 1939 musicologist Alan Lomax looked for him to make more recordings.

Lomax recorded Muddy Waters, who acknowledged Johnson's influence. Singer and slide guitarist Elmore James scored a Top Ten R&B hit in April 1952 with his version of Johnson's "Dust My Broom." In 1961, Columbia Records, which owned the ARC catalog, released *King of the Delta Blues Singers*, a 16-track LP containing three previously unreleased songs and several alternate takes, along with reissues of some of Johnson's 1930s singles. The album was profoundly influential on the blues revival in England that spread to the U.S. after the British Invasion of 1964. Eric Clapton was especially important in exposing Johnson's music to a new generation. As a member of John Mayall's Bluesbreakers, he recorded "Ramblin' on My Mind" on the *Blues Breakers* album released in July 1966, then as a member of Cream put "(From) Four until Late" on *Fresh Cream*, released in December 1966. "Crossroads," his adaptation of "Cross Road Blues" containing a verse from "Traveling Riverside Blues," appeared on the Cream album *Wheels of Fire*, released in June 1968; it became a Top 40 single in February 1969. Led Zeppelin borrowed a different verse from "Traveling Riverside Blues" for "The Lemon Song," released on *Led Zeppelin II* in October 1969, and The Rolling Stones covered "Love in Vain" on *Let It Bleed*, released in November 1969.

In 1970, spurred by this exposure, Columbia Records issued *King of the Delta Blues Singers, Vol. II*, bringing into print the two remaining Johnson songs not previously released, along with most of his 1930s singles. Covers of Johnson songs by rock acts became ubiquitous in the 1970s. A sampling of such recordings (all released on gold- or platinum-selling albums) includes: "Stop Breaking Down" on The Rolling Stones' *Exile on Main Street* (1972); "Come on in My Kitchen" on the Steve Miller Band's *The Joker* (1973); "Terraplane Blues" on Foghat's *Fool for the City* (1975); "Sweet Home Chicago" on Foghat's *Stone Blue* (1978); and "Dust My Broom" on ZZ Top's *Deguello* (1979).

The 41-track double-CD set *The Complete Recordings* finally compiled and reissued all of Johnson's known recordings (the 29 songs plus 12 alternate takes) in 1990; it was on the charts for more than seven months and went platinum, winning the Grammy Award for Best Historical Album. In the 1990s, Johnson's work continued to be performed and recorded by rock acts, notably The Grateful Dead and their version of "Walkin' Blues" on *Without a Net* (1990), The Red Hot Chili Peppers' version of "They're Red Hot" on the four-million-selling *Blood Sugar Sex Magik* (1991), and Eric Clapton's versions of "Walkin' Blues" and "Malted Milk" on the ten-million-selling *Unplugged* (1992).

BIBL.: B. Groom, *R. J.* (Knutsford, U.K., 1967; rev. ed., London, 1969); S. Charters, *R. J.* (N.Y., 1973); A. Greenberg, *Love in Vain: The Life and Legend of R. J.* (Garden City, N.Y., 1983); P. Guralnick, *Searching for R. J.* (N.Y., 1989).—**WR**

Johnson, Robert Sherlaw, English pianist and composer; b. Sunderland, May 21, 1932. He was educated at King's Coll., Univ. of Durham (1950–53), and at the Royal Academy of Music in London (1953–57), then studied piano with Fevrier and composition with Boulanger in Paris (1957–58), where he also attended Messiaen's classes at the Cons. Returning to England, he gave piano recitals in programs of 20th-century music. He lectured at the univs. of Leeds (1961–63) and York (1965–70). In 1970 he was appointed to the faculty of the Univ. of Oxford; was a visiting prof. at the Eastman School of Music in Rochester, N.Y. (1985). He wrote a study on Messiaen (1974). In his music, he re-creates Renaissance forms and mannerisms in a modern modal idiom. He composes mainly for chamber ensembles and vocal groups.

WORKS: DRAMATIC: Opera: *The Lambton Worm* (1976). **ORCH.:** Piano Concerto (1983). **CHAMBER:** 2 string quartets (1966, 1969); *Triptych* for Flute, Clarinet, Violin, Cello, Piano, and Percussion (1973); Quintet for Clarinet, Violin, Viola, Cello, and Piano (1974); Sonata for Alto Flute and Cello (1976). **Piano:** 3 sonatas (1963, 1967, 1976); *Asterogenesis* for 8-octave (Bösendorfer) Piano (1973); *Nymphaea ("Projections")* (1976). **VOCAL:** *The Praises of Heaven and Earth* for Soprano, Tape, and Piano (1969); *Incarnatio* for Chorus (1970); *Green Whispers of Gold* for Voice, Tape, and Piano (1971); *Carmina vernalia* for Soprano and Instruments (1972); *Christus resurgens* for Chorus (1972); *Festival Mass of the Resurrection* for Chorus and Chamber Orch. (1974); *Anglorum feriae* for Soprano, Tenor, Chorus, and Orch. (1976); *Veritas veritatus* for 6 Voices (1980). —**NS/LK/DM**

Johnson, Thor, American conductor; b. Wisconsin Rapids, Wisc., June 10, 1913; d. Nashville, Tenn., Jan. 16, 1975. He studied at the Univ. of N.C. and later at the Univ. of Mich. (M.A., 1935), where he was founder and conductor of its Little Sym. Orch. (1934–36; 1938–42). He also took courses in conducting with Malko, Abendroth, Weingartner, and Walter in Europe (1936–37), and with

Koussevitzky at the Berkshire Music Center in Tanglewood (summers, 1940–41). He was conductor of the Grand Rapids (Mich.) Sym. Orch. (1940–42); subsequently enlisted in the U.S. Army (1942), and conducted the First Army Sym. Orch. in Fort Myers, Va.; subsequently conducted the Juilliard School of Music orch. in N.Y. (1946–47). From 1947 to 1958 he was music director of the Cincinnati Sym. Orch., one of the first native-born Americans to hold such a position with a major U.S. orch. From 1958 to 1964 he was a prof. and director of orchestral activities at Northwestern Univ. in Chicago, and from 1964 to 1967 was director of the Interlochen Arts Academy. He was music director of the Nashville (Tenn.) Sym. Orch. from 1967 until his death. —NS/LK/DM

Johnson, Tom, American composer; b. Greeley, Colo., Nov. 18, 1939. He was educated at Yale Univ. (B.A., 1961; M.Mus., 1967) and studied with Morton Feldman in N.Y. After writing music criticism for N.Y.'s *Village Voice* newspaper (1972–82), he settled in Paris to pursue his career as a composer. An anthology of his articles from the *Village Voice* appeared as *The Voice of New Music* (1991). He published the theoretical volume *Self-Similar Melodies* (1996). In his music, Johnson has made use of minimalist resources while steering his own independent course made refreshing by his wit and penchant for ironical expression.

WORKS: DRAMATIC: Opera: *The 4-Note Opera* (1972); *Window* (1978); *Dryer* (1978); *Drawers* (1978); *Door* (1978); *Sopranos Only* (1984); *Riemannoper* (1988); *Deux cents ans* (1989); *Una opera Italiana* (1991); *Trigonometry* (1996; Hamburg, Nov. 1997). **ORCH.:** *The Secret of the River* (1966); *Dragons in A* (1979); *Loops* (Graz, Sept. 1999). **CHAMBER:** *Action Music IV* for Violist (1968); *Failing, a very difficult piece for solo string bass* (1975); *60-note Fanfares* for 4 Antiphonal Trumpets (1976); *Monologue* for Tuba (1978); *Eight Patterns for Eight Instruments* (1979); *Nine Bells* for Suspended Bells (1979); *Movements* for Wind Quintet (1980); *Doublings* for Double Bass (1980); *Rational Melodies* for Melodic Instrument (1982); *Harpiano* for Harp and Piano (1982); *Self-Portrait* for Box Mover/Composer and 2 to 10 Musicians (1983); *Predictables* for Violin, Cello, and Piano (1984); *Bedtime Stories* for Clarinet and Narrator (1985); *Infinite Melodies* for Any Melodic Instrument (1986); *Chord Catalogue* for Any Keyboard Instrument (1986); *Eggs and Baskets* for 2 Instruments and Narrator (1987); *Music and Questions* for Bells or Glockenspiel and Questions for the Audience (1988); *Alexandrins pour guitare* (1989); *Narayana's Cows* for Instruments and Narrator (1989); *Maximum Efficiency* for 3 Instruments (1991); *Einstimmiger Polyrhythmus* for Tenor Saxophone, Guitar, and Bass (1992); *Sequenza Minimalista* for Trombone (1992); *Composition with Descending Chromatic Scales in 8-voice Canon Played in 3 Ways, Separated by 2 Piano Interludes, Which Bring the Music Back Up to its Starting Position* (1993); *Music With Mistakes* for Flute or Clarinet (1993–99); *Formulas* for String Quartet (1994); *Descent* for Handbell Ensemble (1996); *Simultaneous Progressions* for Clarinet, Trombone, Piano, and Cello (1996); *Automatic Music* for 6 Percussionists (1997); *La vie est si courte* for 8 Instruments (1998). **KEYBOARD: Piano:** *Spaces* (1969); *Scene* for Piano and Tape (1969); *An Hour for Piano* (1971); *Septapede* (1973; rev. 1993); *Private Pieces* (1976); *Triple Threat* (1979); *Symmetries* for Piano, 4-Hands (1981–90); *Counting Keys* (1982); *Tango* (1984); *Voicings* for 4 Pianists (1984); *Music for 88* (1988); *Cosinus* (1994). **Player Piano:** *Full Rotation of 60 Notes Through*

36 *Positions* (1996); *Two Curves* (1998). **Organ:** *Melodie de six notes* (1986); *Organ and Silence* (1999). **VOCAL:** *Trinity* for 4 Choruses (1978); *Counting Duets* for 2 Speaking Voices (1982); *Bonhoeffer Oratorium* for 4 Soloists, 2 Choruses, and Orch. (1988–92); *Le choeur* for Children's Chorus (1994); *Recycled Ostinato* for Bass, Baritone Saxophone, and Guitar (1996). —NS/LK/DM

Johnson, Walter, jazz drummer; b. N.Y., Feb. 18, 1904; there, April 26, 1977. Walter Johnson worked with Freddie Johnson's Red Devils and Bobby Brown's Band before joining Elmer Snowden (1925–29, except for a brief break in 1926). Until autumn 1937, he worked with Fletcher Henderson (except for spells in 1930 and 1935). He then worked with a string of bands, including Lucky Millinder (1938–39), Claude Hopkins (1939, summer 1940), and Coleman Hawkins's Big Band (winter/spring 1940). From 1941–42, he rejoined Henderson, and then worked in the house band at the Elks' Rendezvous, N.Y. Johnson worked primarily with Tab Smith from 1944 until 1954. Shortly afterwards, he left full-time music to work as a bank guard, but continued to freelance. During the 1960s, he continued to gig in N.Y., and occasionally worked with pianist Orville Brown.—JC/LP

Johnston, Ben(jamin Burwell), American composer and pedagogue; b. Macon, Ga., March 15, 1926. He studied at the Coll. of William and Mary in Williamsburg, Va. (A.B., 1949), the Cincinnati Cons. of Music (M.Mus., 1950), and Mills Coll. in Oakland, Calif. (M.A., 1953). He held a Guggenheim fellowship (1959–60). He taught at the Univ. of Ill. in Urbana (1951–83).

WORKS: DRAMATIC: Opera: *Gertrude, or Would She Be Pleased to Receive It?* (1965); *Carmilla* (1970). **Ballet:** *St. Joan* (1955); *Gambit* for Dancers and Orch. (1959; also concert version entitled *Ludes* for 12 Instruments). **ORCH.:** Concerto for Brass (1951); *Passacaglia and Epilogue* (1955–60); Quintet for Groups (1966); Sym. (Rocky Mount, N.C., Oct. 29, 1988); also 2 pieces for Jazz Band: *Ivesberg Revisited* and *Newcastle Troppo* (both 1960). **CHAMBER:** Septet for Wind Quintet, Cello, and Bass (1956–58); *9 Variations* for String Quartet (1959); *Knocking Piece* for 2 Percussionists and Piano (1962); Duo for Flute and String Bass (1963); string quartets (beginning with No. 2: 1964, 1966–73, 1973, 1980, 1980, 1985, 1986, 1988); Trio for Clarinet, Violin, and Cello (1982); *The Demon Lover's Double* for Trumpet and Microtonal Piano (1985); piano pieces. **VOCAL:** *Night*, cantata (1955); choral music; songs.

BIBL.: H. Von Gunden, *The Music of B. J.* (Metuchen, N.J., and London, 1986).—NS/LK/DM

Johnston, Fergus, Irish composer; b. Dublin, May 21, 1959. He was educated in Dublin, where he took a music degree from Trinity Coll. (1982) and then studied composition with James Wilson at the Royal Irish Academy of Music. From 1989 to 1991 he was chairman of the Assn. of Irish Composers. In 1992 he was elected a member of Aosdána, Ireland's state-sponsored academy of creative artists. Johnston's music explores the sonic potentials of sound.

WORKS: DRAMATIC: *Signals!*, ballet music for Violin (1989); *Bitter Fruit*, chamber opera (Dublin, Nov. 17, 1992).

ORCH.: *Samsara* (Dublin, June 14, 1991); Flute Concerto (1996; rev. version, Dublin, Jan. 17, 1997); *Le goûte le jeu...* for Strings (1997); Wind Sym. (1998). CHAMBER: Brass Quintet (1985); *Prelude and Passacaglia* for Violin (1987); *Kaleidoscope* for String Quartet, Harp, and Percussion (1992); *Cusp* for Violin and Piano (1992); *Rashad's Words* for Percussion (1999). P i a n o : *Carn* for 2 Pianos (1993); 3 Pieces (1994–95). VOCAL: 3 Songs for Soprano, Flute, Clarinet, and Bassoon, after e. e. cummings (1981; rev. 1982).—**LK/DM**

Johnston, Randy, American guitarist; b. Detroit, Mich., 1956. He is a veteran sideman whose credentials include associations with Ira Sullivan, Della Griffin, Lou Donaldson, Etta Jones, Houston Person, Sonny Fortune, Wayne Marsh, Lionel Hampton, and Jack McDuff. He began playing guitar around 1970, studied jazz at the Univ. of Miami, and headed for N.Y. in 1981. There he played with a variety of musicians, even backing singers Irene Reid and Della Griffin and others at various venues in uptown Harlem, where he dazzled with his blues- inflected playing. Etta Jones spotted him and recruited him for her Muse album, *Sugar*, a session in which Johnston impressed producer Houston Person to the extent that he hired Johnston to play on his albums *Why Not!* and *The Party*, which also featured organist Joey DeFrancesco. He appeared on a series of Muse albums including Jack McDuff's *Another Real Good 'Un*, and albums by Lionel Hampton, Della Griffin, and Larry O'Neill, as well as his own albums. As a leader, he owes much to Grant Green, Kenny Burrell, and Wes Montgomery. He made a series of albums for Muse that are currently are out of print. A good, though not exceptional player, Johnston has taught at the Univ. of Hartford's Hart School of Music since 1987. He also taught jazz and theory at the Brooklyn Cons. from 1982–87.

DISC.: ; *Walk On* (1992); *Jubilation* (1992); *In A- Chord* (1994); *Somewhere in the Night* (1997).—**PMac/NAL**

Jokinen, Erkki, Finnish composer and teacher; b. Janakkala, Oct. 16, 1941. He entered the Sibelius Academy in Helsinki in 1960, where he was a composition student of Kokkonen (from 1965) and then of Bergman, taking his degree in 1970. After further training with Ton de Leeuw in Bilthoven, the Netherlands (1971), he returned to Helsinki and later taught theory and composition at the Sibelius Academy. In 1987 he served as the composer of the year at the Helsinki Festival. In his music, Jokinen places emphasis upon tonal effects and structure with a utilization of occasional pointillistic and minimalistic infusions.

WORKS: ORCH.: Cello Concerto (1969–70; Helsinki, Oct. 21, 1971); Concerto for Accordion and Chamber Orch. (Helsinki, July 16, 1987); *Voyage No. 1*, concerto for Violin and Chamber Orch. (Helsinki, Aug. 28, 1990) and *No. 2* for Chamber Orch. (Hämeenlinna, Aug. 29, 1991). CHAMBER: *Taksis* for Flute and Piano (Hämeenlinna, April 28, 1968); *Contrasts* for Flute, Clarinet, Violin, Cello, and Piano (Helsinki, May 17, 1968); *Music* for 4 Brass Instruments (1968; Hämeenlinna, May 25, 1969); *CeGeda* for Cello (1969); 4 string quartets: No. 1 (1971; Helsinki, Feb. 28, 1973), No. 2 (Hämeenlinna, Nov. 28, 1976), No. 3 (1988; Oulu, Feb. 16, 1989), and No. 4 (1994); *Do der Sumer komen was* for Clarinet, Horn, Flugelhorn, Piano, and Percussion

(Hämeenlinna, June 9, 1978); *Distances* for Clarinet and Piano (Hämeenlinna, Aug. 17, 1978); *Air* for Bass Clarinet (1979); *Alone* for Accordion (1979); *Songs* for Bass Clarinet, Trombone, Piano, Percussion, and Double Bass (Hämeenlinna, June 8, 1980); *Face* for Flute, Harp, Harpsichord, Violin, Viola, and Cello (Helsinki, March 24, 1983); *Pillars* for Cello and Double Bass (1983); *Reflections* for 2 Accordions (1983); *Frieze* for Oboe, Horn, Piano, Violin, and Double Bass (1984); *Hommage à Marc Chagall* for Organ (1985; Helsinki, April 9, 1986); *Rise No. 1* for 4 Pianists (1989; Hämeenlinna, Nov. 22, 1990), *No. 2* for Flute, Clarinet, and Percussion (1992), and *No. 3* for Percussionist (1992); *...pressentir...* for Accordion and Double Bass (1989; Helsinki, Aug. 10, 1990); *Aspis* for Alto Flute, Accordion, Guitar, and Percussion (Tampere, April 22, 1990); *Pros* for Clarinet and Cello (1990; Helsinki, March 16, 1991). VOCAL: *Psalmus* for Chorus (1971); *Tempora per omnia* for Men's Chorus (1980; Hämeenlinna, Nov. 6, 1982); *Floating Leaves* for Soprano and Piano (Hämeenlinna, July 29, 1982); *Oh, Let the Heart Be Filled* for Chorus (1985); *Do You Remember the Time* for Chorus (1986); *That Time of Year* for Women's Chorus (1988).—**NS/LK/DM**

Jokl, Georg, Austrian composer, brother of **Otto Jokl**; b. Vienna, July 31, 1896; d. N.Y., July 29, 1954. He studied with Schreker, and was active as an accompanist and teacher in Vienna. In 1938 he settled in N.Y. Among his works are a Sym., a symphonic poem, *Heldensang* (Königsberg, 1923), and *Burletta piccola* for Wind Instruments (1952).—**NS/LK/DM**

Jokl, Otto, Austrian composer, brother of **Georg Jokl**; b. Vienna, Jan. 18, 1891; d. N.Y., Nov. 13, 1963. He studied with Hermann Grädener and Alban Berg (1926–30). His Suite for Orch. (1934) won the Hertzka Prize in Vienna. Other works include *Sinfonietta seria* (1935) and two string quartets. In 1940 he settled in N.Y. —**NS/LK/DM**

Jolas, Betsy, distinguished French-American composer and teacher; b. Paris, Aug. 5, 1926. She was the daughter of the poet and journalist Eugène Jolas, the founder and editor of the literary journal *transition*, and of the journalist Maria Jolas, who also sang. In 1940 she was taken to the U.S. by her family and received training in composition from Paul Boepple, in piano from Helen Schnabel, and in organ from Carl Weinrich. Upon her graduation from Bennington (Vt.) Coll. (B.A., 1946), she returned to Paris and completed her studies with Milhaud, Simone Plé-Caussade, and Messiaen at the Cons. She then worked for the ORTF until 1971, when she took over Messiaen's class at the Cons., being subsequently appointed prof. of analysis in 1975 and prof. of composition in 1978. Jolas received an American Academy of Arts and Letters Award (1973), a Koussevitzky Foundation Grant (1974), the Grand Prix National de la Musique (1974), the Grand Prix de la Ville de Paris (1981), the Grand Prix de la SACEM (1982), the Maurice Ravel Prix International (1992), and the Prix SACEM (1994). In 1983 she was made a member of the American Academy of Arts and Letters, in 1985 a Commandeur des Arts et des Lettres, in 1995 a member of the American Academy of Arts and Sciences, and in 1997 a Chevalier de la Légion d'honneur. Jolas's literary heritage is reflected in her use of the voice as the central element in much of her creative output. Her works reflect a masterful command of melody, harmony, timbre, and form.

WORKS: DRAMATIC: *La Pavillon au bord de la rivière,* chamber opera after Kuan Han Chin (Avignon, July 25, 1975); *Schliemann,* opera (1982–83; Lyons, May 3, 1995); *Le Cyclope,* chamber opera after Euripides (Avignon, July 27, 1986). **ORCH.:** *Quatre Plages* for Strings (1967); *D'un opéra de voyage* for Chamber Orch. (Royan, April 1967); *Musique d'Hiver* for Organ and Small Orch. (1971); *Trois Rencontres* for String Trio and Orch. (1973; Strasbourg, June 1974); *Tales of a Summer Sea* (Tanglewood, Aug. 1977); *11 Lieder* for Trumpet and Chamber Orch. (Paris, Oct. 1977); *Stances* for Piano and Orch. (Radio France, Paris, April 1978); *Cinq Pièces pour Boulogne* for Small Orch. (1982; Boulogne, June 7, 1983); *Préludes-Fanfares-Interludes-Sonneries* for Wind and Percussion Orch. (1983; Paris, Jan. 28, 1984); *Frauenleben,* 9 Lieder for Viola and Orch. (1992; Paris, April 2, 1993); *Lumor,* 7 Lieder spirituels for Saxophone and Orch. (Paris, Nov. 28, 1996); *Quatre Psaumes d'Heinrich Schütz* (1996); *Petite Symphonie Concertante* for Violin and Orch. (Besançon, March 27, 1997). **CHAMBER:** *Episode 1* for Flute (1964), *2: Ohne worte* for Flute (1977), *3* for Trumpet (1982), *4* for Tenor Saxophone (Budapest, Dec. 1983), *5* for Cello (1983; Paris, Jan. 17, 1984), *6* for Viola (1984; Nice, Feb. 1985), *7* for Electric Guitar (1984), *8* for Double Bass (1984; Nice, Feb. 1985), and *9: Forte magnum coloratum* for Clarinet (1990); *Figures* for 9 Instruments (1956–65; Evreux, March 20, 1984); *J.D.E.* for 14 Instruments (La Chaux-de-Fonds, Feb. 1966); *Points d'Aube* for Viola and 13 Winds (Havre, Dec. 1968); *Etats* for Violin and 6 Percussion (Persépolis, Sept. 1969); *Lassus Ricercare* for 10 Instruments (1970; Paris, Feb. 1971); *Remember* for Viola or English Horn and Cello (Royan, April 1971); *How Now* for Clarinet, Horn, Bassoon, 2 Violins, Viola, Cello, and Double Bass (1973; Paris, June 1974); *Quatuor III,* 9 études for String Quartet (1973; Washington, D.C., Jan. 1974), *IV: Menus propos* for String Quartet (1973; Paris, June 1990), *V* for String Quartet (1994; Paris, Feb. 16, 1995), and *VI: Avec clarinette* for Clarinet and String Trio (Radio France, Paris, Nov. 22, 1997); *Well Met* for 12 Instruments (1973; Paris, May 1976); *O Wall* for Wind Quintet (N.Y., Nov. 5, 1976); *Quatre duos* for Viola and Piano (1979; Radio France, Paris, April 1980); *D'un opéra de poupée en sept musiques* for 11 Players (1982); *Points d'Or* for Saxophone and 15 Instruments (1982; Paris, Feb. 14, 1983); *Quatre Pièces en marge* for Cello and Piano (1983); *Trois duos* for Tuba and Piano (1983; Lugano, March 23, 1984); *Music for Joan* for Vibraphone and Piano (Buffalo, Sept. 18, 1988); Trio for Violin, Cello, and Piano (1988; N.Y., June 26, 1989); *Petites musiques de cheve* for Bass Clarinet and Piano (1989); *E.A.* for Trumpet and Vibraphone (1990; Paris, March 19, 1991); *Les heures,* trio for Violin, Viola, and Cello (1990; Paris, May 14, 1991); *Études aperçues* for Vibraphone and 5 Bells (Paris, Dec. 9, 1992); *Musique pour Delphine* for Violin and Cello (Paris, Dec. 9, 1992); *Musique pour Xavier* for Clarinet, Tenor Saxophone, and Violin (Paris, June 25, 1993); *Quoth the Raven* for Clarinet and Piano (1993; Chambéry, Jan. 7, 1994); *Music for Here* for Bassoon, Viola, and Cello (Norfolk, Va., Aug. 6, 1994); *Music to Go* for Viola and Cello (Paris, Feb. 5, 1995); *Petite sonnerie de juin* for Horn, Trumpet, and Trombone (1997); *Sonate à 8* for 8 Cellos (1998); *Trio sopra "et sola facta"* for Clarinet, Violin, and Piano (1998; Washington, D.C., March 28, 1999). **KEYBOARD: Piano:** *Chanson d'Approche* (1972; London, Jan. 1973); Sonata (1973; N.Y., Jan. 1974); *3 Études campanaires* (1980; also for Carillon); *Pièce pour St. Germain* (1981); *Petite suite sérieuse pour concert de famille* (1983); *Signets, hommage à Maurice Ravel* (Montpellier, July 19, 1987);

Pièce pour (1997). **Organ:** *Musique de jour* (Royan, March 1976). **VOCAL:** *Pluparts du temps I* for Mezzo-soprano and Piano (1949) and *II* for Tenor, Tenor Saxophone, and Cello (1989; Zagreb, Nov. 1990); *Chansons pour Paule* for Mezzo-soprano and Piano (1951); *Enfantillages* for Women's Chorus (1954); *5 Poèmes de Jacques Dupin* for Soprano and Piano (1959); *L'Oeil égaré,* radiophonic cantata for Soloists, Chorus, and Chamber Orch. (1961); *Dans la chaleur vacante,* radiophonic cantata for Soloists, Chorus, and Chamber Orch. (1963); *Mots* for Soprano, Mezzo-soprano, Contralto, Tenor, Bass, and 7 Players (1963; Geneva, March 1964); *Quatuor II* for Soprano, Violin, Viola, and Cello (1964; Paris, March 1966); *Motet II* for Chorus and Small Orch. (1965; Angers, Oct. 1986) and *III: Hunc igitur terrorem* for Soloists, Chorus, and Baroque Orch. (Luxembourg, Dec. 12, 1999); *Diurnes* for Chorus (1970; Aix-en-Provence, July 1979); *Sonate à 12* for 3 Sopranos, 3 Altos, 3 Tenors, and 3 Basses (1970; Royan, April 1971); *Caprice à une voix* for Voice (La Rochelle, July 1975); *Caprice à deux voix* for Soprano and Countertenor or Contralto (1978; Radio France, Paris, March 1979); *Liring Ballade* for Baritone and Orch. (Metz., Nov. 20, 1980); *Perriault le déluné,* comédie-madrigal for Chorus (1993; Paris, April 25, 1997); *Sigrancia-Ballade* for Baritone and Orch. (1995; London, May 21, 1996); *Für Celia affettuoso* for Chorus (Paris, Oct. 30, 1998). —NS/LK/DM

Jolivet, André, prominent French composer; b. Paris, Aug. 8, 1905; d. there, Dec. 20, 1974. A son of artistically inclined parents, he took an interest in the fine arts, wrote poetry, and improvised at the piano. He studied cello with Louis Feuillard and theory with Aimé Théodas at Notre Dame de Clignancourt. At the age of 15, he wrote a ballet and designed a set for it, and then undertook a prolonged study of musical techniques with Le Flem (1928–33). Of decisive importance to the maturation of his creative consciousness was his meeting in 1930 with Varèse, then living in Paris, who gave him a sense of direction in composition. In 1935 he organized in Paris the progressive group La Spirale. In 1936, in association with Baudrier, Messiaen, and Daniel-Lesur, he founded La Jeune France, dedicated to the promotion of new music in a national French style. He served as conductor and music director of the Comédie Française (1943–59); was technical adviser of the Direction Générale des Arts et des Lettres (1959–62), and president of the Concerts Lamoureux (1963–68); he also was prof. of composition at the Paris Cons. (1965–70). He toured throughout the world as a conductor of his own music. Jolivet injected an empiric spirit into his music, making free use of modernistic technical resources, including the electronic sounds of the Ondes Martenot. Despite these esoteric preoccupations, and even a peripheral deployment of serialism, his music was designed mainly to provide aural stimulation and aesthetic satisfaction.

WORKS: DRAMATIC: Opera-buffa: *Dolorès, Le Miracle de la femme laide* (1942; Paris Radio, May 4, 1947). **Ballet:** *Guignol et Pandore* (1943; Paris, April 29, 1944); *L'Inconnue* (Paris, April 19, 1950); *Ariadne* (1964; Paris, March 12, 1965). **Other:** Incidental music. **ORCH.:** *Andante* for Strings (1935); *Danse incantatoire* for Orch. and 2 Ondes Martenot (1936); *Cosmogonie* (1938; Paris, Nov. 17, 1947; also for Piano); *5 danses rituelles* (1939; Paris, June 15, 1942); *Symphonie de danses* (1940; Paris, Nov. 24, 1943); *Psyché* (1946; Paris, March 5, 1947); Ondes Martenot Concerto (1947; Vienna, April 23,

1948); 2 trumpet concertos (1948, 1954); 2 flute concertos (1949, 1965); Piano Concerto (1949–50; Strasbourg, June 19, 1951); Concerto for Harp and Chamber Orch. (1952); 3 numbered syms.: No. 1 (1953; Haifa, May 30, 1954), No. 2 (Berlin, Oct. 3, 1959), and No. 3 (Mexico City, Aug. 7, 1964, composer conducting); Concerto for Bassoon, Harp, Piano, and Strings (Paris Radio, Nov. 30, 1954); *Suite transocéane* (Louisville, Ky., Sept. 24, 1955); *Suite française* (1957); Percussion Concerto (1958; Paris, Feb. 17, 1959); *Adagio* for Strings (1960); *Les Amants magnifiques* (Lyons, April 24, 1961); Sym. for Strings (1961; Paris, Jan. 9, 1962); 2 cello concertos: No. 1 (Paris, Nov. 20, 1962) and No. 2 (1966; Moscow, Jan. 6, 1967); Violin Concerto (1972; Paris, Feb. 28, 1973); *La Flèche du temps* for 12 Solo Strings (1973); *Yin-Yang* for 11 Solo Strings (1974). **CHAMBER:** Suite for String Trio (1930); String Quartet (1934); *3 poèmes* for Ondes Martenot and Piano (1935); *5 incantations* for Flute (1936); *Ballet des étoiles* for 9 Instruments (1941); *Suite delphique* for Winds, Harp, Ondes Martenot, and Percussion (1943; Vienna, Oct. 22, 1948); *Nocturne* for Cello and Piano (1943); *Pastorales de Noël* for Flute or Violin, Bassoon or Viola, and Harp (1943); *Chant des Linos* for Flute and Piano, or Flute, Violin, Viola, Cello, and Harp (1944); *Sérénade* for Oboe and Piano, or Wind Quintet (1945); *Sérénade* for 2 Guitars (1956); *Rhapsodie à 7* for Clarinet, Bassoon, Trumpet, Trombone, Percussion, Violin, and Double Bass (1957); Flute Sonata (1958); Sonatina for Flute and Clarinet (1961); Sonatina for Oboe and Bassoon (1963); *Alla rustica* for Flute and Harp (1963); *Suite rhapsodique* for Violin (1965); *Suite en concert* for Cello (1965); *5 églogues* for Viola (1967); *Ascèses* for Flute or Clarinet (1967); *Cérémonial en hommage à Varèse* for 6 Percussionists (1968); *Controversia* for Oboe and Harp (1968); *Arioso barocco* for Trumpet and Organ (1969); *Heptade* for Trumpet and Percussion (1971–72). **KEYBOARD: P i a n o :** *3 Temps* (1930); *Mana* (1935); 2 sonatas (1945, 1957); *Hopi Snake Dance* for 2 Pianos (1948); *Patchinko* for 2 Pianos (1970). **O r g a n :** *Hymne à l'univers* (1961); *Mandala* (1969). **VOCAL:** *3 chants des hommes* for Baritone and Orch. (1937); *Poèmes pour l'enfant* for Voice and 11 Instruments (1937; Paris, May 12, 1938); *3 complaintes du soldat* for Voice and Orch. or Piano (1940); *Messe pour le jour de la paix* for Voice, Organ, and Tambourine (1940); *Suite liturgique* for Voice, Oboe, Cello, and Harp (1942); *Epithalame* for 12-part Vocal "Orch." (1953; Venice, Sept. 16, 1956); *Messe "Uxor tua"* for 5 Voices and 5 Instruments or Organ (1962); *Madrigal* for 4 Voices and 4 Instruments (1963); *Songe à nouveau rêvé* for Soprano and Orch. (1970).

BIBL.: V. Fédorov and P. Guinard, compilers, *A. J.: Catalogue des oeuvres* (Paris, 1969); H. Jolivet, *Avec A. J.* (Paris, 1978).—NS/LK/DM

Joll, Philip, Welsh baritone; b. Merthyr Tydfil, March 14, 1954. He was a student of Nicholas Powell and Frederick Cox at the Royal Northern Coll. of Music in Manchester (1975–78) and of Hotter and Goodall at the National Opera Studio (1978–79). In 1978 he made his formal operatic debut as the Bonze in *Madama Butterfly* with the English National Opera in London, and then sang Donner and the Dutchman there. He made his first appearance at the Welsh National Opera in Cardiff as Strauss's Orestes in 1979, where he returned as Wotan in its *Ring* cycle (1983–85). In 1982 he made his debut at London's Covent Garden as the Second Nazarene in *Salome*, and was engaged as Wotan in its *Ring* cycle in 1986. In 1983 he sang Amfortas in Frankfurt am Main. He made his Metropolitan Opera debut in N.Y. on Oct. 9, 1987, as Donner. His Australian

debut followed in 1988 in Queensland as Jochanaan, the same year he appeared as the Dutchman at the Bregenz Festival. In 1990 he was engaged as Jochanaan for a tour to Japan with the Welsh National Opera. In 1992 he sang Orestes and in 1993 Macbeth with the company in Cardiff. In the latter year, he also sang Verdi's Francesco Foscari at the Edinburgh Festival and the Sacristan in *Tosca* at the Scottish Opera in Glasgow. He portrayed Sharpless in Auckland in 1994, and then sang Wozzeck in Brussels in 1995. In 1996 he was engaged as Simon Boccanegra and as Falstaff in Stuttgart, and as Scarpia at the English National Opera. He returned to the Welsh National Opera in 1997 as Rigoletto. He married **Penelope Walker.**—NS/LK/DM

Jolson, Al (originally, **Yoelson, Asa**), extroverted Lithuanian-born American singer, actor, and comedian; b. Seredzius, May 26, 1886; d. San Francisco, Oct. 23, 1950. Unabashedly billed as the World's Greatest Entertainer, Jolson was the most successful musical comedy star on Broadway in the 1910s and 1920s. He was also a major radio star and the most popular solo recording artist of the 1920s, his biggest hits being "Sonny Boy," "April Showers," and "Swanee," though he popularized dozens of songs. He inaugurated sound motion pictures with *The Jazz Singer* and made a series of musical films. He enjoyed a spectacular career comeback in the years before his death, largely due to the film biographies *The Jolson Story* and *Jolson Sings Again*. Jolson's use of blackface, dating from his early years in minstrel shows, and his bravura style made him a controversial figure. But his ability to move a live audience was unmatched.

Jolson was the son of Moshe Reuben Yoelson, a cantor and rabbi, and Naomi Cantor Yoelson; the date and year of his birth are uncertain. His father immigrated to the U.S. and the family followed several years later, arriving in April 1894 and settling in Washington, D.C. His mother died in childbirth in February 1895, and his father remarried in March 1896.

Jolson displayed an early interest in music and theater; he and his older brother Harry were street entertainers as early as the summer of 1896, singing to politicians in front of the Raleigh Hotel in Washington, D.C. In 1898 he entertained the troops assembled to fight the Spanish-American War in camps around the city. He ran away from home several times, working in a circus and a carnival. His first stage appearance was in a minor role in the play *Children of the Ghetto* in September 1899. From October 1900 to March 1902 he was a member of the Victoria Burlesquers, after which he toured in vaudeville and burlesque, usually as part of a song-and-comedy duo or trio, sometimes including his brother. By June 1906 he was working solo and appearing in blackface.

In October 1906, Jolson met dancer Henrietta Keller in her hometown of Oakland, Calif. They were married on Sept. 20, 1907, and divorced on July 8, 1920. In August 1908, Jolson joined Lew Dockstader's Minstrels, the leading minstrel show of the day. He remained with the troupe until December 1909, then returned to solo work in vaudeville. He made his Broadway debut in *La*

Belle Paree (N.Y., March 20, 1911), which was part of the initial offering at the newly built Winter Garden Theater. Singing Jerome Kern and Edward Madden's "Paris Is a Paradise for Coons," he became the hit of the show, which ran for 104 performances in N.Y. and went on a six-week tour in the fall. A Sunday night concert series at the Winter Garden was inaugurated on March 26, and Jolson appeared frequently, adding to his growing fame.

Jolson returned to the Winter Garden in *Vera Violetta* (N.Y., Nov. 20, 1911), taking a more prominent role, and the show was a success, running 112 performances. Signing with the Victor Talking Machine Co., he made his first issued recordings on Dec. 22, 1911. Among them was George M. Cohan's "That Haunting Melody" from *Vera Violetta*, which became a major hit in May 1912. *Vera Violetta* was followed immediately by *The Whirl of Society* (N.Y., March 5, 1912), in which Jolson for the first time played the part of Gus, a comic African-American servant. It ran for 136 performances in N.Y., then toured from September to January 1913. His second major record hit came in July 1912 with the million-seller "Ragging the Baby to Sleep."

Jolson's fourth Broadway show was *The Honeymoon Express* (N.Y., Feb. 6, 1913), which ran for 156 performances at the Winter Garden and then toured the country from September to May 1914. Jolson had a second million- selling disc in May 1913 with "The Spaniard That Blighted My Life," which he sang in the show. He also interpolated James V. Monaco and Joseph McCarthy's "You Made Me Love You" into the show and scored a massive hit with it in October, inaugurating a ten-year stint with Columbia Records.

Jolson's next Winter Garden appearance came with *Dancing Around* (N.Y., Oct. 10, 1914), which ran for 145 performances in N.Y., then toured from February 1915 to December. *Robinson Crusoe Jr.* (N.Y., Feb. 17, 1916) ran for 139 performances in N.Y., then toured for the entire 1916–17 season and into the fall of 1917, not closing until Nov. 17. Jolson's biggest record hit during the period was the comic "I Sent My Wife to the Thousand Islands" in September 1916, though he also enjoyed hits with songs featured in the show, such as "Yaaka Hula Hickey Dula" and "Where Did Robinson Crusoe Go with Friday on Saturday Night?"

Jolson's seventh Winter Garden show was *Sinbad* (N.Y., Feb. 14, 1918), which ran for 164 performances in N.Y., then toured for three full seasons, not playing its final performance until June 25, 1921. As much as any of Jolson's shows, it served largely as a vehicle for his comic singing act, and at times he simply dismissed the rest of the cast and gave a concert performance. The long run of the show found him interpolating a series of songs, many of which became signature numbers for him, though he also enjoyed record hits not related to *Sinbad*.

"I'm All Bound Round with the Mason Dixie Line" became a big hit in April 1918, followed by the topical "Hello, Central, Give Me No Man's Land" in July. But Jolson's biggest hit of the year came with the *Sinbad* song "Rock-a-Bye Your Baby with a Dixie Melody," an important song for him since it marked his success with a sentimental ballad rather than the comic songs for

which he had been known. During the 1918–19 tour he interpolated the uptempo "I'll Say She Does" into the show, and it became his next big record hit in August 1919, followed by "I've Got My Captain Working for Me Now" in January 1920. That month he recorded George Gershwin and Irving Caesar's "Swanee" and began singing it in *Sinbad*. It became a giant record hit in May, his third million-seller and the most popular song of his career to that point. (It also helped to establish Gershwin as a major songwriter.)

In the fall season of 1920, Jolson introduced "Avalon" into the show and scored a hit with it in early 1921, though his biggest record hit of the period was "O-H-I-O (O-My! O!)," a best-seller in April. ("Avalon," credited to Jolson and Vincent Rose, was the subject of a successful plagiarism suit brought by the publishers of Puccini's opera *Tosca*, who claimed the melody was stolen from the aria "E lucevan le stelle.") Jolson first sang "My Mammy," the song perhaps most closely associated with him, on Jan. 13, 1921, in Providence, but strangely he did not record it at the time, allowing others to score hits with it.

Jolson returned to Broadway in *Bombo* (N.Y., Oct. 6, 1921), which opened in a theater named for him, Jolson's 59th Street Theatre. After 218 performances in N.Y., it went on tour in April 1922 and stayed on the road for two years, until May 1924. The show's initial hit, and the biggest record hit of 1922, was "April Showers," though Jolson also enjoyed a hit with "Angel Child" in May. In the fall of 1922 he interpolated "Toot Toot Tootsie! (Goo'bye)" into the show, and it became a best-selling record in January 1923. The biggest hit interpolated into the show in the 1923–24 season was "California, Here I Come," which became a record hit in May 1924, his first for his third record company, Brunswick. He also scored big hits with "I Wonder What's Become of Sally?" in November 1924 and "All Alone" in January 1925. On June 9, 1919, he had met show girl Ethel Delmar (real name Alma Osborne). They married on July 22, 1922, and were divorced in October 1926.

Jolson's ninth Broadway show was *Big Boy* (N.Y., Jan. 7, 1925). The singer was plagued by illness, and the show amassed only 48 N.Y. performances, though it toured during the 1925–26 and 1926–27 seasons. His biggest record hits during the period, not featured in the show, were "I'm Sitting on Top of the World" in April 1926 and "When the Red, Red Robin Comes Bob-Bob-Bobbin' Along" in October. That same month he was featured in a short film, *Al Jolson in a Plantation Act*, singing three songs with synchronized sound.

In the summer of 1927, Jolson filmed *The Jazz Singer*, the first full- length feature with sound, which opened on Oct. 6, 1927, and became a sensation, transforming the motion picture industry. His songs from the film, "Mother of Mine, I Still Have You," "My Mammy," and "Dirty Hands! Dirty Face!," became record hits as well. His second sound film, *The Singing Fool*, which opened in September 1928, was an even bigger box office success than the first and featured the biggest record hit of his career, "Sonny Boy," a best-seller starting in October that was the most popular recording of the year. Its flip side, "There's a Rainbow Round My

Shoulder," was another big hit. Also in 1928, Jolson met tap dancer Ruby (Ethel Hilda) Keeler (b. Aug. 25, 1909; d. Feb. 28, 1993). She became his third wife on Sept. 21. He made impromptu appearances in her starring vehicle, *Show Girl* (N.Y., July 2, 1929), singing to her from the audience during the show's 111-performance run. (His recording of "Liza," the song he sang, was a hit.)

Jolson's career began to decline in the late 1920s, though he continued to work steadily in a variety of media. His third feature film, *Say It with Songs*, which opened Aug. 6, 1929, was unsuccessful, though it brought him record hits in "Little Pal" and "I'm in Seventh Heaven." *Mammy* (March 26, 1930) and the film adaptation of *Big Boy* (Sept. 11, 1930) met the same fate.

Jolson returned to Broadway in *The Wonder Bar* (N.Y., March 17, 1931), which ran 86 performances in N.Y. and toured through the 1931–32 season. He launched the first of several radio shows, *Presenting Al Jolson*, on Nov. 14, 1932; it ran into February. The same month saw the release of *Hallelujah, I'm a Bum*, a movie musical with songs by Richard Rodgers and Lorenz Hart. Critically and commercially unsuccessful at the time, it has since been praised as one of Jolson's best films. He returned to radio in August 1933, taking over the *Kraft Music Hall* for the 1933–34 season. He also made a film version of *Wonder Bar* (Feb. 28, 1934). He then hosted the radio shows *Shell Chateau* (1935–36) and *Café Trocadero* (1936–39). Jolson's next film was *Go into Your Dance* (May 2, 1935), in which he costarred with his wife, who had become a film star in her own right. Within days of the film's opening, the couple adopted a son; they were divorced on Dec. 27, 1940.

Jolson made one more film as a leading actor, *The Singing Kid* (April 3, 1936), after which he was relegated to second billing in *Rose of Washington Square* (May 25, 1939), a thinly veiled film biography of Fanny Brice in which he played a character much like himself and sang some of his biggest hits; *Hollywood Cavalcade* (Oct. 13, 1939), in which he played himself re-creating a scene from *The Jazz Singer*; *Swanee River* (Dec. 26, 1939), a film biography of Stephen Foster, in which he played minstrel show leader E. P. Christy; and *Rhapsody in Blue* (June 27, 1945), a film biography of Gershwin in which he again played himself.

Jolson returned to Broadway for the last time in *Hold On to Your Hats* (N.Y., Sept. 11, 1940), a show with music by Burton Lane and lyrics by E. Y. Harburg. After 158 performances in N.Y., it toured in the fall of 1941. With the U.S. entry into World War II, Jolson became a peripatetic entertainer of troops, traveling from base to base with a piano accompanist. He undertook a new radio series, *Al Jolson*, in the 1942–43 season, but by the summer he was back to entertaining troops in South America, Africa, and the Near East. Upon his return in the fall he was found to be suffering from malaria and pneumonia, but after a temporary recovery he was back on the road. He met Erle Chennault Galbraith (b. Dec. 1, 1923) an x-ray technician, at a hospital in Ark., in June 1944. She became his fourth wife on May 24, 1945, and they eventually adopted a son and daughter. Before that, he suffered a relapse in late 1944 and had part of his left lung removed in early 1945.

Shortly after the release of *Rhapsody in Blue*, Jolson signed a contract with Decca Records and made his first recordings in nearly 13 years, starting with "Swanee," the song he sang in the film. *Al Jolson—Vol. 1* became a chart-topping album in 1946. By this time he was involved in preparations for *The Jolson Story* (Oct. 10, 1946), starring Larry Parks with Jolson's voice dubbed in, which became the sixth highest grossing film in U.S. history up to that point and set off a major Jolson comeback. His Decca recordings of "Anniversary Song" and "April Showers" became million-sellers in 1947. *Al Jolson—Vol. 2* became a #1 album in 1947, followed by *Vol. 3* in 1948.

He returned as host of the *Kraft Music Hall* for the 1947–48 and 1948–49 seasons. *Jolson Sings Again* (Aug. 17, 1949), again starring Parks with Jolson's singing, was a success at the box office, as was Decca's identically titled album in the record stores. Jolson entertained the troops in his fourth war when he went to Korea in September 1950. His death from a heart attack prevented him from fulfilling a contract to work in television.

Jolson is credited as cowriter of many of the songs he sang, including the hits "I'll Say She Does," "California, Here I Come," "Me and My Shadow," "Golden Gate," "Sonny Boy," "There's a Rainbow Round My Shoulder," and "Anniversary Song." It is generally assumed that his actual creative involvement was limited to the suggestion of an idea, a title, or a few words of the lyrics at best, and that his songwriting credit was assigned in payment for his willingness to popularize the songs.

Though the more relaxed crooning style of microphone singing that became popular in the 1930s was at odds with Jolson's demonstrative style, he became a major influence on the next generation of popular singers in the 1950s, including Frank Sinatra, Judy Garland, Frankie Laine, and Sammy Davis Jr., who took a more aggressive approach. He was also an influence on such rock 'n' roll singers as Jerry Lee Lewis, who adopted his swagger (if little of his humor), and on such expressive 1960s pop singers as Tom Jones and Barbra Streisand.

It has been suggested that Jolson could only really be appreciated as a live performer, but his recordings, tapes of his radio shows, and the performance segments of his films testify to his enormous talent as an entertainer. His reputation doubtless would be greater if he were not so closely identified with blackface minstrelsy, which became a defining style in his work. (He appears in blackface in most of his films, many of which have not yet been released on videotape.) Blackface was popular when Jolson started out, and though his use of it reflected sympathy with African-Americans and was relatively free of stereotyping, the practice necessarily fell into ridicule in the wake of the civil rights advances of the post–World War II era, and Jolson's standing as a popular singer suffered. Still, many of the songs he popularized have become standards, and his enthusiastic and informal approach to performing has set high standards for his successors.

BIBL.: P. Sieben, *The Immortal J.: His Life and Times* (N.Y., 1962); M. Freedland, *J.* (London, 1972; rev. ed., *Jolie—The Story of*

A. J., 1985; reprinted as J.: The Story of A. J., 1995); B. Anderton, *Sonny Boy! The World of A. J.* (London, 1975); R. Oberfirst, *A. J., You Ain't Heard Nothin' Yet* (San Diego, 1980); L. Kiner, *The A. J. Discography* (Westport, Conn., 1983); D. McClelland, *Blackface to Blacklist: A. J., Larry Parks and the Jolson Story* (Metuchen, N.J., 1987); H. Goldman, *J.: The Legend Comes to Life* (N.Y., 1988); L. Kiner and P. Evans, *A. J.: A Bio-Discography* (Metuchen, N.J., 1992); J. Fisher, *A. J.: A Bio-Bibliography* (Westport, Conn., 1994).
—WR

Jommelli, Niccolò, greatly significant Italian composer; b. Aversa, near Naples, Sept. 10, 1714; d. Naples, Aug. 25, 1774. He began his musical studies with Canon Muzzillo, the director of the Cathedral choir in Aversa. In 1725 he entered the Cons. S. Onofrio in Naples, where he studied with Prota and Feo; in 1728 he enrolled in the Cons. Pietà dei Turchini in Naples, where he continued his studies with Fago, Sarcuni, and Basso. In 1737 he composed a comic opera, *L'errore amoroso*, for Naples; this was followed by a 2nd comic opera, *Odoardo* (Naples, 1738). On Jan. 16, 1740, his first serious opera, *Ricimero rè de' Goti*, was produced in Rome. After composing *Astianatte* (Rome, Feb. 4, 1741), he went to Bologna for the premiere of his *Ezio* (April 29, 1741). There he studied with Padre Martini, and was also elected to membership in the Accademia Filarmonica. He then proceeded to Venice, where his opera *Merope* was given on Dec. 26, 1741. In 1743 he became music director of the Ospedale degli Incurabili there; during this time he composed several notable sacred works, including the oratorios *Isacco figura del Redentore* and *La Betulia liberata*. In 1747 he left Venice for Rome, and in 1749 he went to Vienna, where his opera *Achille in Sciro* was successfully staged on Aug. 30, 1749. Several of his operas had been performed in Stuttgart, resulting in a commission for a new opera from Karl Eugen, the Duke of Württemberg. *Fetonte* was premiered in Stuttgart on the duke's birthday on Feb. 11, 1753. On Jan. 1, 1754, Jommelli became Ober-Kapellmeister in Stuttgart. Among the operas he composed for Stuttgart were *Pelope* (Feb. 11, 1755), *La Nitteti* (Feb. 11, 1759), and *L'Olimpiade* (Feb. 11, 1761); he also composed sacred music, including a *Miserere* and a *Te Deum*, both of which were widely performed. In 1768 Jommelli accepted an offer from King José of Portugal to compose operas and sacred music for the court of Lisbon. He left Stuttgart in 1769 and returned to Italy; for Naples he composed the operas *Armida abbandonata* (May 30, 1770) and *Ifigenia in Tauride* (May 30, 1771). His opera *Il trionfo di Clelia* was produced in Lisbon with great success on June 6, 1774.

The historical significance of Jommelli lies in his being a mediator between the German and Italian styles of composition, especially in opera. He introduced into Italian opera the German solidity of harmonic texture and also the expressive dynamics associated with the "Mannheim" school of composition; he also abandoned the formal Neapolitan convention of the da capo aria, thus contributing to a more progressive and realistic operatic form. This earned him the sobriquet "the Italian Gluck." On the other hand, he influenced the development, during his long stay in Stuttgart, of German opera in the direction of simple melodiousness and natural rhythmic flow without dependence on contrapuntal techniques. Thus his influence was beneficial both for his native art and for the most austere German operatic traditions.

WORKS: DRAMATIC: Opera: *L'errore amoroso*, comic opera (Naples, 1737; not extant); *Odoardo*, comic opera (Naples, 1738; not extant); *Ricimero rè de' Goti* (Rome, Jan. 16, 1740); *Astianatte* (Rome, Feb. 4, 1741; also known as *Andromaca*); *Ezio* (Bologna, April 29, 1741; 2nd ver., Naples, Nov. 4, 1748; 3rd ver., Stuttgart, Feb. 11, 1758, not extant; 4th ver., 1771; rev. by da Silva, Lisbon, April 20, 1772); *Merope* (Venice, Dec. 26, 1741); *Semiramide riconosiuta* (Turin, Dec. 26, 1741; 2nd ver., Piacenza, 1753; 3rd ver., Stuttgart, Feb. 11, 1762; *Don Chichibio*, intermezzi (Rome, 1742); *Eumene* (Bologna, May 5, 1742; 2nd ver., as *Artemisia*, Naples, May 30, 1747); *Semiramide* (Venice, Dec. 26, 1742); *Tito Manlio* (Turin, 1743; 2nd ver., Venice, 1746, not extant; 3rd ver., Stuttgart, Jan. 6, 1758, not extant); *Demofoonte* (Padua, June 13, 1743; 2nd ver., Milan, 1753; 3rd ver., Stuttgart, Feb. 11, 1764; rev., Ludwigsburg, Feb. 11, 1765; rev. by da Silva, Lisbon, June 6, 1775; 4th ver., Naples, Nov. 4, 1770); *Alessandro nell'Indie* (Ferrara, 1744, not extant; 2nd ver., Stuttgart, Feb. 11, 1760, not extant; rev. by da Silva, Lisbon, June 6, 1776); *Ciro riconosciuto* (Bologna, May 4, 1744; 2nd ver., 1747?; 3rd ver., Venice, 1749; completely new ver., 1751 or 1758); *Sofonisba* (Venice, 1746; not extant); *Cajo Mario* (Rome, Feb. 6, 1746; 2nd ver., Bologna, 1751); *Antigono* (Lucca, Aug. 24, 1746); *Didone abbandonata* (Rome, Jan. 28, 1747; 2nd ver., Vienna, Dec. 8, 1749; 3rd ver., Stuttgart, Feb. 11, 1763); *L'amore in maschera*, comic opera (Naples, 1748; not extant); *La cantata e disfida di Don Trastullo*, intermezzi (Rome, 1749; 2nd ver., Lucca, 1762); *Artaserse* (Rome, Feb. 4, 1749; 2nd ver., Stuttgart, Aug. 30, 1756); *Demetrio* (Parma, 1749); *Achille in Sciro* (Vienna, Aug. 30, 1749; 2nd ver., Rome, Jan. 26, 1771); *Cesare in Egitto* (Rome, 1751; not extant); *La Villana nobile*, comic opera (Palermo, 1751; not extant); *Ifigenia in Aulide* (Rome, Feb. 9, 1751; rev. with arias by Traetta, Naples, Dec. 18, 1753); *L'Uccellatrice*, intermezzi (Venice, May 6, 1751; 2nd ver. as *Il paratajo [ovvero] La Pipée*, Paris, Sept. 25, 1753); *Ipermestra* (Spoleto, Oct. 1751); *Talestri* (Rome, Dec. 28, 1751); *I Rivali delusi*, intermezzi (Rome, 1752); *Attilio Regolo* (Rome, Jan. 8, 1753); *Fetonte* (Stuttgart, Feb. 11, 1753, not extant; 2nd ver., Ludwigsburg, Feb. 11, 1768); *La clemenza di Tito* (Stuttgart, Aug. 30, 1753, not extant; 2nd ver., Ludwigsburg, Jan. 6, 1765, not extant; rev. by da Silva, Lisbon, June 6, 1771); *Bajazette* (Turin, Dec. 26, 1753); *Don Falcone*, intermezzi (Bologna, Jan. 22, 1754); *Lucio Vero* (Milan, 1754); *Catone in Utica* (Stuttgart, Aug. 30, 1754; not extant); *Pelope* (Stuttgart, Feb. 11, 1755; rev. by da Silva, Salvaterra, 1768); *Enea nel Lazio* (Stuttgart, Aug. 30, 1755, not extant; rev. by da Silva, Salvaterra, 1767); *Creso* (Rome, Feb. 5, 1757); *Temistocle* (Naples, Dec. 18, 1757; 2nd ver., Ludwigsburg, Nov. 4, 1765); *La Nitteti* (Stuttgart, Feb. 11, 1759, not extant; rev. by da Silva, Lisbon, June 6, 1770); *Endimione ovvero Il trionfo d'amore*, pastorale (Stuttgart, 1759, not extant; 2nd ver., Queluz, June 29, 1780); *Cajo Fabrizio* (Mannheim, Nov. 4, 1760; includes arias by G. Cola); *L'Olimpiade* (Stuttgart, Feb. 11, 1761; rev. by da Silva, Lisbon, March 31, 1774); *L'isola disabitata*, pastorale (Ludwigsburg, Nov. 4, 1761, not extant; 2nd ver., Queluz, March 31, 1780); *Il trionfo d'amore*, pastorale (Ludwigsburg, Feb. 16, 1763; not extant); *La pastorella illustre*, pastorale (Stuttgart, Nov. 4, 1763, not extant; rev. by da Silva, Salvaterra, 1773); *Il Re pastore* (Ludwigsburg, Nov. 4, 1764, not extant; rev. by da Silva, Salvaterra, 1770); *Imeneo in Atene*, pastorale (Ludwigsburg, Nov. 4, 1765; rev. by da Silva, Lisbon, March 19, 1773); *La Critica*, comic opera (Ludwigsburg, 1766; rev. as *Il giuoco di picchetto*, Koblenz, 1772; rev. as *La conversazione [e] L'accademia di musica*,

Salvaterra, 1775); *Vologeso* (Ludwigsburg, Feb. 11, 1766; rev. by da Silva, Salvaterra, 1769); *Il matrimonio per concorso*, comic opera (Ludwigsburg, Nov. 4, 1766, not extant; rev. by da Silva, Salvaterra, 1770); *Il Cacciatore deluso [ovvero] La Semiramide in bernesco*, serious-comic opera (Tübingen, Nov. 4, 1767; rev. by da Silva, Salvaterra, 1771); *La Schiava liberata*, serious-comic opera (Ludwigsburg, Dec. 18, 1768; rev. by da Silva, Lisbon, March 31, 1770); *Armida abbandonata* (Naples, May 30, 1770; rev. by da Silva, Lisbon, March 31, 1773); *L'amante cacciatore*, intermezzi (Rome, 1771; not extant); *Le avventure di Cleomede*, serious-comic opera (Naples, 1771?; rev. by da Silva, Lisbon, June 6, 1772); *Ifigenia in Tauride* (Naples, May 30, 1771; rev. by da Silva, Salvaterra, 1776); *Il trionfo di Clelia* (Naples, 1774?; rev. by da Silva, Lisbon, June 6, 1774); etc. O t h e r : *Componimento drammatico* (Rome, Feb. 9, 1747; not extant); *Componimento drammatico* (Ronciglione, Feb. 28, 1751; not extant); *La reggia de' Fati* (with G.B. Sammartini; Milan, March 13, 1753); *La pastorale offerta* (with G.B. Sammartini; Milan, March 19, 1753); *Il giardino incanto* (Stuttgart, 1755; not extant); *L'asilo d'amore* (Stuttgart, Feb. 11, 1758; not extant); *Le Cinesi* (Ludwigsburg, 1765; not extant); *L'unione coronata* (Solitude, Sept. 22, 1768; not extant); *Cerere placata* (Naples, Sept. 14, 1772). Also contributions to a number of pasticcios. **ORATORIOS, PASSIONS, AND SACRED CANTATAS:** *Che impetuoso è questo torrente* for 2 Sopranos, Tenor, and Orch. (Naples, 1740); *Isacco figura del Redentore* for 2 Sopranos, Alto, Tenor, Bass, Chorus, and Orch. (Venice, 1742); *La Betulia liberata* for Soprano, Alto, Tenor, Bass, Chorus, and Orch. (Venice, 1743); *Gioas* for 3 Sopranos, 3 Altos, Chorus, and Strings (Venice, 1745); *Juda proditor* for 3 Sopranos, 3 Altos, and Chorus (Venice, 1746?; not extant); *Ove son? Chi mi guida?* for Soprano, Alto, Tenor, and Orch. (Naples, 1747); *La passione di Gesù Cristo* for Soprano, Alto, Tenor, Bass, Chorus, and Orch. (Rome, 1749); *Giuseppe glorificato in Egitto* for 2 Sopranos, Tenor, and Orch. (Rome, 1749); *Le Spose di Elcana* for Chorus (Palermo, 1750; not extant); *In questa incolte riva* for 2 Sopranos and Orch. (Rome, May 20, 1751); *Non più: L'atteso istante* for Soprano, Alto, Tenor, and Orch. (Rome, 1752); *Il sacrifizio di Gefte* for Chorus and Strings (Palermo, 1753; not extant); *La reconciliazione della Virtù e della Gloria* for 2-part Chorus (Pistoia, 1754; not extant); *Gerusalemme convertita* (Palermo, 1755; not extant); *Il sogno di Nabucco* (Palermo, 1755; not extant); etc. **OTHER:** Additional sacred works include many masses, as well as graduals, offertories, antiphones, Psalms, motets, hymns, etc. His instrumental works include harpsichord concertos, quartets, divertimenti, and sonatas.

BIBL.: S. Mattei, *Elogio del J.* (Colle, 1785); P. Alfieri, *Notizie biografiche di N. J.* (Rome, 1845); H. Abert, *N. J. als Opernkomponist* (Halle, 1908); R. Pattengale, *The Cantatas of N. J.* (diss., Univ. of Mich., 1973); J. Carlson, *Selected Masses of N. J.* (diss., Univ. of Ill., 1974); L. Tolkoff, *The Stuttgart Operas of N. J.* (diss., Yale Univ., 1974); M. McClymonds, *N. J.: The Last Years, 1769–1774* (Ann Arbor, Mich., 1980); W. Hochstein, *Die Kirchenmusik von N. J. (1714–1774): Unter besonderer Berücksichtigung der liturgisch gebundenen Kompositionen* (2 vols., Hildesheim, 1984).—**NS/LK/DM**

Jonák, Zdeněk, Czech composer; b. Prague, Feb. 25, 1917. He studied composition with Řídký at the Prague Cons. (graduated, 1941), continuing his study with Řídký and Křička at its master school (graduated, 1947). He subsequently devoted himself mainly to pragmatic musical tasks, such as making arrangements of folk songs and writing music for the theater.

WORKS: O R C H .: *Prelude* (1939); *Passacaglia* (1940); *Suite* (1951); Chamber Sym. (1964); Trumpet Concerto (1972). **C H A M B E R :** 3 string quartets (1941, 1947, 1980); Cello Sonata (1955). **VOCAL:** *Epigrams*, song cycle for Chorus (1975).—**NS/LK/DM**

Jonás, Alberto, Spanish-American pianist, teacher, and composer; b. Madrid, June 8, 1868; d. Philadelphia, Nov. 9, 1943. He received primary music training in Madrid, then studied piano and theory of composition at the Brussels Cons. In 1890 he went to St. Petersburg, where he had some lessons with A. Rubinstein. After a brief concert career in Europe, he went to the U.S., where he taught piano at the Univ. of Mich. (1894–98) and the Detroit Cons. (1898–1904). From 1904 to 1914 he taught in Berlin. After the outbreak of World War I, he settled in N.Y., where he established a fine reputation as a piano pedagogue. In collaboration with 16 pianists, he publ. *Master School of Modern Piano Playing and Virtuosity* (N.Y., 1922), which went through five editions, and he also brought out several books of piano exercises for beginners. He wrote a number of attractive piano pieces in a salon manner, among them *Northern Dances, Humoresque, Nocturne,* and *Evening Song*.—**NS/LK/DM**

Jonas, Émile, French composer; b. Paris, March 5, 1827; d. St.-Germain-en-Laye, May 21, 1905. He studied at the Paris Cons. (1841–49), graduating with the Second Grand Prix de Rome for his cantata *Antonio*. He was an instructor there (1847–66), and also music director at the Portuguese Synagogue, for which he publ. *Receuil de chants hébraïques* (1854).

WORKS: DRAMATIC: L i g h t O p e r a (all 1st perf. in Paris): *Le Duel de Benjamin* (1855); *La Parade* (Aug. 2, 1856); *Le Roi boit* (April 1857); *Les Petits Prodiges* (Nov. 19, 1857); *Job et son chien* (Feb. 6, 1863); *Le Manoir de La Renardière* (Sept. 29, 1864); *Avant la noce* (March 24, 1865); *Les Deux Arlequins* (Dec. 29, 1865); *Le Canard à trois becs* (Feb. 6, 1869); *Désiré, sire de Champigny* (April 11, 1869). O t h e r : Also an operetta to an Eng. libretto, *Cinderella the Younger* (London, Sept. 25, 1871; in French as *Javotte*, Paris, Dec. 22, 1871).—**NS/LK/DM**

Jonas, Maryla, Polish pianist; b. Warsaw, May 31, 1911; d. N.Y., July 3, 1959. She was a precocious child pianist, and appeared in public at the age of 8. She took lessons with Turczynski and was commended by Paderewski. She began her professional career as a concert pianist at the age of 15. After the invasion of Poland in 1939, she made her way to Rio de Janeiro, and gave a series of concerts in South America. She then went to N.Y., where she made an exceptionally successful debut in Carnegie Hall (Feb. 25, 1946). Her auspicious career was thwarted by an irremediable illness.—**NS/LK/DM**

Jonas, Oswald, Austrian-American musicologist; b. Vienna, Jan. 10, 1897; d. Riverside, Calif., March 19, 1978. He studied musicology with Schenker (1915–22), and also studied law at the Univ. of Vienna (Ph.D., 1921). He taught at Berlin's Stern Cons. (1930–34), then worked at the Schenker Inst. at the New Vienna Cons. (1935–38). After the annexation of Austria by the Nazis in 1938, he went to the U.S., where he taught at Roosevelt Univ. in Chicago and associated schools

(1941–64). Following a sojourn as a teacher at the Vienna Academy of Music (1964–65), he became a prof. at the Univ. of Calif. at Riverside (1966). He publ. *Das Wesen des musikalischen Kunstwerks* (Vienna, 1934; 2nd ed., rev., 1973 as *Einführung in die Lehre Heinrich Schenkers*); also wrote numerous articles on Schenker's theories and ed. several of his works.—NS/LK/DM

Jonas, Peter, English opera administrator; b. London, Oct. 14, 1946. He was educated at the Univ. of Sussex (B.A., 1968), the Northern Coll. of Music, the Royal Coll. of Music in London, and the Eastman School of Music in Rochester, N.Y. From 1974 to 1976 he was assistant to the music director of the Chicago Sym. Orch., and then served as artistic administrator of that orch. from 1976 to 1985. He also was director of artistic administration of the Orchestral Assn. of Chicago from 1977 to 1985. He was managing director (later general director) of the English National Opera in London from 1985 to 1993. In 1993 he became Staatsintendant of the Bavarian State Opera in Munich and was made a Commander of the Order of the British Empire. Jonas's tenures in London and Munich were marked by his encouragement of contemporary opera performances. —NS/LK/DM

Joncières, Victorin de (real name, **Felix Ludger Rossignol**), French composer; b. Paris, April 12, 1839; d. there, Oct. 26, 1903. He was first a student of painting; music was his avocation. At the age of 20 he produced a light opera for a student performance. Encouraged by its success with the critics, he began to study music seriously, first with Elwart, then with Leborne at the Paris Cons. He was a great admirer of Wagner, and when Leborne expressed his opposition to Wagner, Joncières impulsively left his class.

WORKS: DRAMATIC: O p e r a (all 1st perf. in Paris): *Sardanapale* (Feb. 8, 1867); *Le Dernier Jour de Pompei* (Sept. 21, 1869); *Dimitri* (May 5, 1876; his most successful work); *La Reine Berthe* (Dec. 27, 1878); *Le Chevalier Jean* (March 11, 1885; successful in Germany under the title *Johann von Lothringen*); *Lancelot du lac* (Feb. 7, 1900). O t h e r : Music to *Hamlet* (Nantes, Sept. 21, 1867). ORCH.: *Symphonie romantique* (Paris, March 9, 1873); Violin Concerto (Paris, Dec. 12, 1869); symphonic ode, *La Mer*; etc.—NS/LK/DM

Jones, Ada, dominant female recording star of the early 20th century and comedienne; b. Manchester, England, June 1, 1873; d. Rocky Mount, N.C., May 2, 1922. A powerful contralto with a versatile style that allowed her to handle both serious and humorous material, Jones was the most popular female recording artist of the 1900s and 1910s. In fact, she was the first woman whose voice was recorded successfully. She immigrated to the U.S. when she was young and began her career as a musical comedy performer. Turning to recording in 1904, she sang such major hits as "I Just Can't Make My Eyes Behave" (1907), "The Yama Yama Man" (with the Victor Light Opera Co.; 1909), "I've Got Rings on My Fingers" (1909), "Call Me Up Some Rainy Day" (with the American Quartet), "Row! Row! Row!" (1913), and "By the Beautiful Sea" (with Billy Watkins).

Ada and Billy, the duet team of Jones and Billy Murray, was almost equally successful, with hits including "Let's Take an Old-Fashioned Walk" (1907), "Wouldn't You Like to Have Me for a Sweetheart?" (1908), "When We Are M-A-Double-R-I-E-D" (1908), "Cuddle Up a Little Closer, Lovey Mine" (1908), "Shine On, Harvest Moon" (1909), "Come, Josephine, in My Flying Machine" (with the American Quartet; 1911), and "Be My Little Baby Bumble Bee" (1912). She also maintained a successful partnership with Len Spencer that resulted in 20 hit comedy records between 1905 and 1910.

Jones was married to dancer Hughie Flaherty, and the couple had a daughter. She died suddenly of acute uremia while on a concert tour.—WR

Jones, Alton, American pianist and teacher; b. Fairfield, Nebr., Aug. 3, 1899; d. N.Y., Jan. 2, 1971. He studied at Drake Univ. (B.M., 1919) and at the Inst. of Musical Art in N.Y., where his teachers were Edwin Hughes and Richard Buhlig; he graduated in 1921. He made his concert debut in N.Y. in 1924, and then was a soloist with the N.Y. Phil. in 1949. He gave his last N.Y. recital in 1955. He taught at the Juilliard School of Music in N.Y. from 1921 until his death. His reputation as a pedagogue was high, and many American pianists were his pupils.—NS/LK/DM

Jones, Charles, Canadian-born American composer and teacher; b. Tamworth, June 21, 1910. He settled in the U.S. in 1928, where he studied violin at the Inst. of Musical Art (diploma, 1932) and composition with Wagenaar at the Juilliard School of Music (diploma, 1939) in N.Y. He taught at Mills Coll. in Oakland, Calif. (1939–44), then at the Juilliard School of Music (1954–60; 1973), and at the Mannes Coll. of Music (from 1972); also taught at the Aspen (Colo.) School of Music. After composing in a neo-Classical style, he developed a complex mode of expression notable for its chromaticism.

WORKS: DRAMATIC: B a l l e t : *Down with Drink* for Women's Voices, Piano, and Percussion (1943). ORCH.: Suite for Strings (1937); 4 syms.: No. 1 (1939), No. 2 (1957), No. 3 (1962), and No. 4 (1965); *Little Symphony for the New Year* (1953); *Galop* (1940); *Pastorale* for Chamber Orch. (1940); *Cowboy Song* for Oboe and Strings (1941); *Overture* (1942); *5 Melodies* (1945); *Cassation* (1948); *Introduction and Rondo* for Strings (1957); *Suite after a Notebook of 1762* for Chamber Orch. (1957); Concerto for 4 Violins and Orch. (1963); *Allegory* (1970). CHAMBER: 10 string quartets (1936–94); Sonatina for Solo Violin (1938); Violin Sonatina (1942); Suite for Violin and Piano (1945); Duo for Violin and Piano (1947); *Threnody for Viola* (1947); *Lyric Waltz Suite* for Wind Quartet (1948); *Sonata a tre* for Piano Trio (1952); Duo for Violin and Viola (1956); Violin Sonata (1958); *Sonata piccola* for Piccolo and Harpsichord (1961); Sonata for Oboe and Harpsichord (1965); *Music for 2 Violinists* (1966); String Trio (1968); *In Nomine* for Violin and Piano (1972); *Serenade* for Flute, Violin, Cello, and Harpsichord (1973); *Triptychon I* for Violin, Viola, and Piano (1975) and *II* for Violin and Piano (1981); Trio for Violin, Cello, and Piano (1982); *Meditation* for Bass Clarinet and Piano (1982); *Capriccio* for Cello and Piano (1983); *Ballade* for Violin and Piano (1986); *Serena* for 9 Instruments (1986). KEYBOARD: P i a n o : 2 sonatas (1946, 1950); Sonata for 2 Pianos (1947); *Toccata* (1955); *Psalm* (1976); *Book of the Hours*

(1979–81); Sonata for Piano, 4-Hands (1983). **H a r p s i - c h o r d** : *Keyboard Book* (1953); Suite (1993). **O r g a n** : *Noël* (1983); *Emblemata* (1994). **V O C A L** : *The Seasons*, cantata (1959); *I Am a Mynstrel* for Tenor, Violin, Harpsichord, Piano, and Percussion (1967); *Masque* for Speaker and 12 Players, after Pope's *Rape of the Lock* (1968); 4 scenes for Voice and Piano, after Pope (1982); *Poemata* for Voice, Violin, and Cello (1987); songs. **—NS/LK/DM**

Jones, Claude B., jazz trombone, vocals;

b. Boley, Okla., Feb. 11, 1901; d. Jan. 17, 1962. Brother-in-law of Quentin Jackson. He started trombone at age 13 and played in the town band, then at Langston H.S. where he also doubled on trumpet and drums. He attended Wilberforce Coll., and also served as a musician in the Students' Army Training Corps. He quit law studies at Wilberforce and subsequently joined the Synco Jazz Band in Springfield, Ohio (1922). This band later became McKinney's Cotton Pickers, and he played with them until spring 1929. In May 1929, he joined Fletcher Henderson, originally to play in the show *Great Day*. He remained with Henderson until September 1934, except for two years with Don Redman (1931–33). After leaving Henderson, he played briefly in Chick Webb's Band and then joined Cab Calloway in late 1934 (occasional vocal features with Cab's Band including "Jes Naturally Lazy"). He left Calloway in January 1940 and after working with a number of N.Y. bands left full-time music in 1941 to manage his own sausage-manufacturing company. Nonetheless, he continued to gig on the side, and returned to full-time playing to join Duke Ellington (on valve trombone) in spring 1944. He left Duke in October 1948, then worked with Machito, and briefly with Henderson and Ellington (January–March 1951), before leaving music again to become an Officers' Mess Steward on the S.S. *United States*; he died aboard the liner a decade later.—JC/LP

Jones, Dame Gwyneth, prominent Welsh so-

prano; b. Pontnewyndd, Nov. 7, 1936. She studied at the Royal Coll. of Music in London, and in Siena, Geneva, and Zürich, where she made her operatic debut as Gluck's Orfeo (1962). In 1963 she first appeared at the Welsh National Opera in Cardiff and at London's Covent Garden; she also sang at the Vienna State Opera and at the Bayreuth Festivals from 1966. In 1966 she made her U.S. debut in N.Y. in a concert version of Cherubini's *Médée*; her Metropolitan Opera debut followed there as Sieglinde in *Die Walküre* on Nov. 24, 1972. She also sang at the San Francisco Opera, Milan's La Scala, Munich's Bavarian State Opera, and the Rome Opera; appeared as Brünnhilde in the centenary performances of the *Ring* cycle at Bayreuth in 1976. In 1976 she was made a Commander of the Order of the British Empire and in 1986 a Dame Commander of the Order of the British Empire. On Sept. 12, 1988, she celebrated the 25th anniversary of her Covent Garden debut by opening its season as Turandot. In 1997 she celebrated the 35th anniversary of her operatic debut and was engaged to sing Ortrud at Covent Garden. In addition to Wagner and Verdi roles, she also won praise for her portrayals of Donna Anna, Medea, Leonore, the Marschallin, Tosca, and Salome.

BIBL.: T. Haberfeld, *G. J.: Pictures of Her Life and Career* (Zürich, 1991).—NS/LK/DM

Jones, Daniel (Jenkyn), remarkable Welsh com-

poser; b. Pembroke, Dec. 7, 1912; d. Swansea, April 23, 1993. Both his parents were musicians, and he absorbed the natural rudiments of music instinctively at home. He studied English literature at Univ. Coll. of Wales, Swansea (B.A., 1934; M.A., 1939), and also attended the Royal Academy of Music in London (1935–38), where he studied composition with Farjeon, conducting with Wood, viola with Lockyear, and horn with Aubrey Brain. He later completed his education at Univ. Coll. of Wales (D.Mus., 1951). He retained interest in literature, and was editor of the collected poems of Dylan Thomas (1971) and the author of *My Friend Dylan Thomas* (1973). He was made an Officer of the Order of the British Empire (1968). In 1936 he promulgated a system of "complex metres," in which the numerator in the time signature indicates the succession of changing meters in a clear numerical progression, e.g. 32–322–3222–322–32, followed by 332–3332–332, etc. His other innovation is a category of "continuous modes," with the final note of the mode (non-octaval) serving as the initial note of a transposed mode. He authored numerous articles expounding his philosophy of music, some of which were incorporated in the book *Music and Esthetic* (1954).

WORKS: D R A M A T I C : O p e r a : *The Knife* (1961; London, Dec. 2, 1963); *Orestes* (1967). **ORCH.:** *The Flute Player* (1942); *Comedy Overture* (1942); 12 syms.: No. 1 (1944; Liverpool, Aug. 6, 1948), No. 2 (1950), No. 3 (1951), No. 4, *In memoriam Dylan Thomas* (1954), No. 5 (1958), No. 6 (1964), No. 7 (1971), No. 8 (1972), No. 9 (1974), No. 10 (1981), No. 11 (1983), and No. 12 (1985); *Cloud Messenger* (1945); *Miscellany* (1946); *Dobra Niva*, suite (1956); *Ieuenctid* (Youth), overture (1956); *Salute to Dylan Thomas* (1956); *Capriccio* for Flute, Harp, and Strings (1965); Violin Concerto (1966); *Investiture Processional Music* for the Prince of Wales (1969); 2 sinfoniettas (1972, 1991); Oboe Concerto (1982); Cello Concerto (Swansea, Oct. 4, 1986); *Orpheus and Bacchus*, overture (Guildford, Surrey, Sept. 24, 1989). **C H A M - B E R :** 2 string trios (1946, 1970); 7 string quartets (1948, 1957, 1975, 1978, 1980, 1982, 1988); Cello Sonata (1973); Suite for Flute and Harpsichord (1979); Divertimento for Wind Quintet (1990). **V O C A L :** *Kyrie* for Chorus (1949); *The 3 Hermits* for Chorus and Piano or Organ (1969); *Triptych* for Chorus and Piano (1969); *The Witnesses* for Men's Chorus and Orch. (1971); *Hear the Voice of the Ancient Bard* for Chorus and Orch. (1977); *To Night* for Chorus and Piano (1978); *Come My Way, My Truth, My Life* for Tenor, Chorus, and Orch. (1987); songs.—NS/LK/DM

Jones, Della, Welsh mezzo-soprano;

b. Neath, April 13, 1946. She studied at the Royal Coll. of Music in London (1964–68), in Geneva (1968–70), and with Denis Dowling. After winning the Kathleen Ferrier Memorial Scholarship in 1969, she made her operatic debut as Fyodor in *Boris Godunov* in Geneva in 1970. She made her first appearance at the Sadler's Wells Opera in London in 1973 as Ninon in the British premiere of Penderecki's *The Devils of Loudon*. In 1977 she made her debut at the Welsh National Opera in Cardiff as Rosina. From 1977 she also made frequent appearances at the English National Opera in London, where she sang Rossini's Isabella in 1987. She made her debut at London's Covent Garden in 1983 as the Female Cat in *L'Enfant et les sortilèges*. Her U.S. debut came in 1986 when she sang Ruggiero in *Alcina* in Los Angeles. In 1990 she was engaged as Preziosilla at the Scottish Opera in Glasgow. After returning to the Welsh National Opera as Brangäne in 1993, she portrayed Clytemnestra at Opera North in Leeds in 1996. She appeared as a soloist with orchs. and as a recitalist in Europe, North America, and the Far East.—NS/LK/DM

Jones, Edward, Welsh harper, historian, and composer, known as **Barrd y Brenin**; b. Llandderfel, Merionethshire (baptized), March 29, 1752; d. London, April 18, 1824. He was taught by his father; the family organized an ensemble consisting of harps and string instruments. In 1774 he went to London; described himself as Harper or Bard to the Prince of Wales from about 1788; was known as the King's Bard from 1820. He composed a number of songs, as well as pieces for harp and harpsichord, and also publ. several anthologies of Welsh music, the most important being *Musical and Poetical Relicks of the Welsh Bards...* (1784; 2nd ed., rev. and aug., 1794), *The Bardic Museum...* (1802; 2nd ed., 1825), and *Hen Ganiadau Cymru: Cambro-British Melodies, or the National Songs and Airs of Wales* (1820), collectively containing over 200 Welsh melodies. Jones also publ. collections of melodies from other nations.

BIBL.: T. Ellis, *E. J., Barrd y Brenin* (Cardiff, 1957). —NS/LK/DM

Jones, Edwin Arthur, American violinist, organist, teacher, and composer; b. Stoughton, Mass., June 28, 1853; d. there, Jan. 9, 1911. He received training in violin, organ, and harmony at the New England Cons. of Music in Boston. Following additional studies at Dartmouth Coll., where he was organist of the Handel Soc., concertmaster of the orch., and director of the glee club, he returned to Stoughton to pursue his career. He composed several overtures and marches, the cantata *Song of Our Savior* (1881), the oratorio *Easter Concert* (1890), two trios for Piano, Violin, and Double Bass (1871), two string trios (1878), two string quartets (1880, 1887), and songs.

BIBL.: R. Hall, *E.A. J.: His Life and Music* (Stoughton, Mass., 1984).—LK/DM

Jones, Elvin (Ray), jazz drummer, band leader; younger brother of **Hank Jones** and **Thad Jones;** b. Pontiac, Mich., Sept. 9, 1927. He became a legend during his years with Coltrane (1960–66). His playing dances around the beat with unprecendented freedom, and creates an exceptionally hard-driving swing. He plays loudly, yet he is able to pick up on rhythmic nuances of other soloists with uncanny telepathy. He will solo at great length; his play with the pitches of the drums creates a musical composition that is spellbinding.

Jones joined the school band at age 13 and considered classical tympani as a career. He performed with local groups in Pontiac and Detroit before playing in military bands during his service in the U.S. Army (1946–49); there he played bass drum in the same group

as Willie Ruff. At this time, he first heard Charlie Parker recordings with Max Roach and decided to emulate them. After service, he performed in Mich., including groups led by Thad Jones and Billy Mitchell, and then came to N.Y. in mid-1955, where he played for about 18 months with J. J. Johnson's quintet (including a 1957 tour of Germany, France, Switzerland, and two months in Scandinavia). He also played in Donald Byrd's quintet, as well as working with Bud Powell, Sonny Rollins (sitting in for Pete LaRoca, the regular drummer, at a live Village Vanguard recording), Tyree Glenn, and Stan Getz. He first played with Coltrane in Philadelphia, probably in 1958 or 1959, replacing Philly Joe Jones in a group led by Coltrane while Miles Davis was between tours. Jones was touring and recording with veteran trumpeter Harry Edison at least through February 1960, and then is said to have been arrested for drug possession and served time at Riker's Island in N.Y.

Meanwhile, Coltrane had made it clear that Jones was his top choice to play in his quartet which began performing May 2, 1960, with Pete LaRoca. At the end of September 1960 Jones became available and Coltrane flew him to a gig at Sonny's Lounge in Denver, where he alternated with the drummer hired for the gig, Billy Higgins. Though Jones was the regular drummer for the quartet, he was notoriously unreliable, a heroin addict (and alcoholic, who chased women) and there are many drummers around the U.S. and in Canada who sat in for a set or more until Jones arrived. The longest absence occurred when Jones was incarcerated in Lexington, Ky., for drug possession from May through early August 1963; this was the delayed result of his having been busted in Boston returning from a European tour in early December 1962. During this period Coltrane's main drummer was Roy Haynes. When Coltrane hired Rashied Ali as second drummer in the fall of 1965, Jones became dissatisfied for two reasons: the emphasis was no longer on swinging but on free time, and he and Ali competed personally and in volume. Finally, on Jan. 26, 1966, Jones took off without notice from a Coltrane gig at San Francisco's Jazz Workshop and flew to Frankfurt, Germany, to accept an offer to join the Ellington band. However, to his dismay he found that Ellington intended to keep his other drummer, putting Jones back in a two-drum team. He played four concerts, then left, stopping off in Paris and finally returning to N.Y., where he announced plans to freelance. However he did return to Coltrane's group for a concert in early March 1967 at Stanford Univ. followed by a week at San Francisco's Jazz Workshop. His final performance with Coltrane appears to have been two shows on April 24 in Brooklyn at St. Gregory's Rectory.

He subsequently led his own groups, touring widely in the U.S., Europe, South America, and the Orient. His first trio with Joe Farrell was filmed (for BBC TV). Later versions of his groups included Frank Foster, Dave Liebman, Steve Grossman, Pat LaBarbera, Ravi Coltrane, and in 1997 Sonny Fortune (on tenor). Since the mid-1980s, his group was called the Elvin Jones Jazz Machine. He regularly tours Europe and Japan. In the late 1990s, he played in Europe with Sonny Sharrock and Charnett Moffett and Pharoah Sanders. He uses three 20-inch crash cymbals, high-hat cymbals of 14 inches (Istanbul), and Yamaha drums—two floor tom toms, respectively 18 x 18 and 16 x 16, mounted tom toms on the bass drum (8 x 12 and 9 x 13), and a custom-made snare drum, 8 x 14. This drum set gives him a pitch range of practically two octaves.

Disc.: *Elvin!* (1961); *Elvin Jones and Company* (1961); *Together* (1961); *Illumination* (1963); *Dear John C* (1965); *And Then Again* (1965); *Midnight Walk* (1966); *Heavy Sounds* (1968); *Ultimate Elvin Jones* (1968); *Puttin' It Together* (1968); *Live at the Village Vanguard* (1968); *Heavy Sounds* (1968); *Prime Element* (1969); *Poly-Currents* (1969); *Mr. Jones* (1969); *Coalition* (1970); *Merry-Go-Round* (1971); *Genesis* (1971); *Live at the Lighthouse, Vol. 1, 2* (1972); *New Agenda* (1975); *Impulse Years* (1975); *Elvin Jones Is on the Mountain* (1975); *Summit Meeting* (1976); *Elvin Jones Live at the Town Hall* (1976); *Time Capsule* (1977); *Very R.A.R.E.* (1978); *Remembrance* (1978); *Love & Peace* (1978); *Live in Japan 1978* (1978); *Different Drummer* (video; 1979); *Heart to Heart* (1980); *Reunited* (1982); *For John* (1982); *Earth Jones* (1982); *Brother John* (1982); *Love Me with All Your Heart* (1983); *Live at the Village Vanguard, V* (1984); *In Europe* (1991); *Elvin Jones Jazz Machine in Europe* (1991); *Youngblood* (1992); *It Don't Mean a Thing* (1993). **JONES BROTHERS:** *Jones Boys* (1957); *Keepin' up with the Joneses* (1958).—**LP**

Jones, Etta,

American jazz and blues singer; b. Aiken, S.C., Nov. 25, 1928. She has developed a highly inviting approach that has given her popular appeal since she first appeared with the Buddy Johnson band at the age of 16. She gained further experience in front of the groups of J. C. Heard and Earl Hines in the 1950s, before launching on her solo career. With her 1960 hit recording, *Don't Go to Strangers*, she began a productive association with Prestige Records that lasted five years and produced seven albums. For much of the 1970s she was relatively inactive until she entered her next great phase of recording activity. From 1976, she made albums for Muse and other labels, often in the company of Houston Person. Any one of her classic dates reveals her singular way with a song. Much like her inspirations, Billie Holiday and Dinah Washington, she clearly enunciates each syllable of a word, milking it for all its potential, and often ends a phrase with a melodic upturn. Although not a technically flashy vocalist, she inflects each performance with an emotional attachment that is always quite direct and inviting.

Disc.: *Don't Go to Strangers* (1960); *Something Nice* (1961); *So Warm* (1961); *From the Heart* (1962); *Lonely and Blue* (1962); *Love Shout* (1963); *Etta Jones Sings* (1965); *Ms. Jones to You* (1976); *My Mother's Eyes* (1977); *I'll Be Seeing You* (1987); *Fine and Mellow* (1987); *Sugar* (1989); *Reverse the Charges* (1991); *At Last* (1993); *My Gentleman Friend* (1994); *Melody Lingers On* (1997); *My Buddy: Songs of Buddy Johnson* (1998); *Doin' What She Does Best* (1998); *All the Way* (1999); *Easy Living* (2000).—**CH**

Jones, George,

the ultimate honky-tonk singer; b. Saratoga, Tex., Sept. 12, 1931. Jones is the one artist that new country male vocalists of the 1980s and 1990s consistently cite as a key influence on their vocal style. Indeed, his distinctive singing style, often jumping from a grumbling bass to a falsetto hiccup within the same measure, is immediately recognizable. Jones is also one of those artists whose legend (as a rabble-rousing, hard-drinking, hard-living performer) has more than once threatened to engulf him, yet somehow he survives and maintains his popularity.

Jones began performing honky-tonk material after his discharge from the Marines in the early 1950s. In 1954, he hooked up with Harold "Pappy" Daily, who served as his manager and also ran Starday records, which issued his first recordings. His early records showed the deep influence of Hank Williams, although he also briefly jumped on the rockabilly bandwagon, recording under the names "Thumper Jones" and "Hank Smith and The Nashville Playboys." His first big hits came at United Artists in the early 1960s with songs drenched in honky-tonk heartache, including 1962's "She Thinks I Still Care." He also recorded his first duets with Melba Montgomery at this time.

In the mid-1960s, Jones's recordings suffered from the typical girly chorus and mushy strings that were among the worst excesses of the Nashville Sound. He married Tammy Wynette in 1969, and moved to her label, Epic, in 1971, hooking up with producer Billy Sherrill. There he recorded a series of hugely successful duets with his then-wife, beginning with 1973's "We're Gonna Hold On," and continuing even after their divorce through the 1970s. He also recorded a number of solo hits, all custom-tailored to his legendary status as a heartbroken, heavy drinker: most notably 1981's "If Drinking Don't Kill Me (Her Memory Will)" and 1986's "The One I Loved Back Then." In the late 1980s, Jones branched out to cut a series of duets with unlikely younger partners, from Linda Ronstadt to Elvis Costello and James Taylor. Through the 1980s, Jones had a tendency to coast along on his reputation, both in the choice of his material and in often lack-luster (or missed) performances. Of late, he has made yet another comeback (although he's never really gone away) with "I Don't Need Your Rockin' Chair," a good-natured but defiant statement of where this old fella's coming from!

The revival of the honky-tonk sound among today's "New Nashville" vocalists is largely credited to the influence of Jones. Every time Randy Travis dramatically drops his voice to a low bass note, he's emulating the style pioneered by Jones. Although none of the new singers can match his unique vocal style, many try to emulate his image.

In 1992, Jones was elected to the Country Music Hall of Fame. Four years later, he published his much-sanitized autobiography. Jones has had trouble getting his more recent recordings played on country radio, despite the plaudits of many of today's country stars. He was so dismayed when he was told that he could only perform part of his most recent release on the 1999 CMA awards show that he refused to attend, a symbolic gesture of old Nashville's rejection of the more pop-oriented younger acts.

Disc.: *Sings* (1960); *Church Time* (1960); *Sings the Hits of His Country Cousins* (1962); *New Favorites* (1962); *Homecoming in Heaven* (1962); *Sings Bob Wills* (1963); *Sings Like the Dickens* (1963); *My Favorites of Hank Williams* (1963); *George Jones and Gene Pitney* (1965); *The Race Is On* (1965); *Live at Dancetown U.S.A.* (live; 1965); *At His Best* (1967); *I'll Share My World with You* (1969); *Sings the Songs of Leon Payne* (1973); *The Grand Tour* (1973); *Bartender's Blues* (1978); *My Very Special Guests* (1979); *I*

Am What I Am (1980); *Double Trouble* (with Johnny Paycheck; 1980); *Still the Same Old Me* (1981); *A Taste of Yesterday's Wine* (with Merle Haggard; 1982); *Who's Gonna Fill Their Shoes* (1984); *By Request* (1984); *Wine-Colored Roses* (1987); *I'm a One-Woman Man* (1988); *First Time Live* (1989); *You Oughta Be Here* (1990); *Halleluja Weekend* (1990); *And Along Came Jones* (1991); *Friends in High Places* (1991); *Walls Can Fall* (1992); *High Tech Red Neck* (1993); *Bradley Barn Sessions* (1994); *I Lived to Tell It All* (1996). **TAMMY WYNETTE:** *We Go Together* (1971); *We Love to Sing About Jesus* (1972); *Golden Ring* (1976); *Togetther Again* (1980); *Encore* (1981); *One* (1995).

BIBL.: G.J., *I Lived to Tell It All* (N.Y., 1996).—RC

Jones, Geraint (Iwan),

Welsh organist, harpsichordist, and conductor; b. Porth, May 16, 1917; d. May 3, 1998. He studied at the Royal Academy of Music in London. He made his debut as harpsichordist at the National Gallery in 1940; subsequently gave numerous recitals as an organist, often on historical instruments of Europe. In 1951 he founded the Geraint Jones Singers and Orch., which he led in many performances of Baroque music. He also was music director of the Lake District Festival (1960–78) and the Kirckman Concert Soc. (from 1963), and artistic director of the Salisbury Festival of the Arts (1972–77) and the Manchester International Organ Festival (from 1977).—NS/LK/DM

Jones, Hank (actually, Henry),

jazz pianist; brother of **Thad Jones** and **Elvin Jones**; b. Vicksburg, Miss., July 31, 1918. His sparkling, lyrical gift is evident in his earliest recordings. He was taken in early childhood to Pontiac, Mich, where he studied piano with Pauline Frisbee (later known as the actress Carlotta Franzell). He played gigs while in high school, prior to working in bands in Mich. and Ohio. In 1944 he went to N.Y., where he worked with Hot Lips Page, Andy Kirk, and John Kirby (1945). In 1947, he began long series of tours with "Jazz at the Philharmonic" (including European trips in the 1950s).

From 1948–53, he was Ella Fitzgerald's accompanist; at the same time, he recorded with various artists, including Charlie Parker in 1950. During the late 1950s, he worked on-and-off with Benny Goodman, including a tour of the Orient (1956–57). From 1959–76 he was a staff musician for CBS; during this period also did countless freelance recordings, and also worked in Thad Jones–Mel Lewis Big Band (1966) and did some touring. In 1976–77, he toured and recorded as part of the Great Jazz Trio. He was a pianist and conductor for the Broadway musical *Ain't Misbehavin'*, based on the music of Fats Waller. He has led his own trio and continues to do prolific freelance work. Through the 1990s, he has made innumerable recordings in countless settings (solo, trio, combo backup for vocalists, etc.). He won the Three Key Award from Int. Jazz Festival of Bern, Switzerland, in 1997.

DISC.: *Hank Jones Piano* (1950); *Trio* (1955); *Hank Jones Quartet/Quintet* (1955); *Bluebird* (1955); *Trio with Guests* (1956); *Relaxin' at Camarillo* (1956); *Have You Met Hank Jones?* (1956); *Hank Jones Quartet* (1956); *Talented Touch* (1958); *Hank Jones Swings "Gigi"* (1958); *Porgy and Bess* (1959); *Arrival Time* (1962); *Here's Love* (1963); *This Is Ragtime Now* (1964); *Happenings* (1966);

Hanky Panky (1975); *Solo Piano* (1976); *Satin Doll* (1976); *Hank* (1976); *Arigato* (1976); *Tiptoe Tapdance* (1977); *Just for Fun* (1977); *I Remember You* (1977); *Great Jazz Trio at the Village* (1977); *Bop Redux* (1977); *At the Village Vanguard* (1977); *Groovin' High* (1978); *Bluesette* (1978); *Ain't Misbehavin'* (1978); *In Japan* (1979); *Have You Met This Jones?* (1979); *Great Jazz Trio at the Village* (1980); *Hello, Hank Jones / Clifford Jordan* (1980); *Jones-Brown-Smith* (1983); *Duo* (1987); *Oracle* (1989); *Lazy Afternoon* (1989); *Live at Maybeck Recital Hall, V* (1991); *Hank Jones Trio* (1991); *Rockin' in Rhythm* (1992); *Handful of Keys: The Music of Hank Jones* (1993); *Upon Reflection—the Music of Thad Jones* (1994). —JC/LP/NS

Jones, (Herbert) Kelsey,

American-born Canadian composer, harpsichordist, and teacher; b. South Norwalk, Conn., June 17, 1922. He went to Canada in 1939, and became a naturalized Canadian citizen in 1956. He studied with Harold Hamer at Mount Allison Univ. (B.Mus., 1945), then with Sir Ernest MacMillan, Healey Willan, and Leo Smith at the Univ. of Toronto (B.Mus., 1946; D.Mus., 1951), and with Boulanger in Paris (1949–50). He was founder-conductor of the St. John (New Brunswick) Sym. Orch. (1950–54). From 1954 to 1984 he taught at McGill Univ. in Montreal. His output is traditional in nature but not without effective utilization of dissonant writing.

WORKS: CHAMBER O p e r a : *Sam Slick* (Halifax, Sept. 5, 1967). **ORCH.:** *Miramichi Ballad* (1954); *Suite for Flute and Strings* (1954); *Adagio, Presto, and Fugue* for String Quartet and String Orch. (1973); *Fantasy on a Theme* (1976). **J a z z B a n d :** *Jazzum Opus Unum* (1978). **CHAMBER:** *4 Pieces* for Recorder Quartet (1955); *Mosaic* for Flute, Viola, and Harp (1956); *Sonata da camera* for Flute, Oboe, and Harpsichord (1957); *Introduction and Fugue* for Violin and Piano (1959); *Rondo* for Flute (1963); *Sonata da chiesa* for Flute, Oboe, and Harpsichord (1967); *Wind Quintet* (1968); *Passacaglia and Fugue* for Brass Quintet (1978); *Musica d'Occasione* for Brass Quintet (1982). **VOCAL:** *Nonsense Songs* for Chorus (1955); *Songs of Time* for Chorus and Piano, 4-Hands (1955); *To Music,* song cycle for Alto and Piano (1957); *Songs of Experience* for Chorus (1958); *Prophecy of Micah* for Chorus and Instrumental Ensemble (1963); *Songs of Winter* for Soprano, Alto, and Piano (1973); *De Musica, con Amore* for Chorus and Brass Quintet (1977); *3 Preludes and a Fugue: A Little Offering* for Chorus and Saxophone (1982). —NS/LK/DM

Jones, Isham,

noted jazz band leader, composer; b. Coalton, Iowa, Jan. 31, 1894; d. Fla., Oct. 19, 1956. Raised in Saginaw, Mich. He led his own band at age 18, moved to Chicago in 1915, and concentrated on tenor saxophone. He then led his own trio at Mahoney's Club, and then later led an orchestra at Green Mill and Rainbow Gardens. Subsequently, his orchestra played a long residency at the Hotel Sherman from the early 1920s. He appeared in N.Y. before sailing to London in 1924.

Jones returned to the U.S. and established a national reputation. From 1926 until 1936, his orchestras enjoyed widespread popularity. His last band, Isham Jones's Juniors, contained the basic personnel for the orchestra formed by his sideperson Woody Herman. The Juniors broke up in 1936, and Jones decided to devote more time to composing. Until 1939, he assembled several temporary bands and occasionally fronted other bands.

Throughout the 1940s he ran his own general store in Colo., then moved to Fla. in 1955, where he died of cancer a year later. Jones was a prolific composer whose successes included: "Spain," "On the Alamo," "I'll See You in My Dreams," and "It Had to Be You."—JC/LP

Jones, Jack (John Allen), Grammy-winning saloon singer who brought rock to the casinos and swing to rock; b. Los Angeles, Jan. 14, 1938. The son of movie stars Allan Jones and Irene Hervey, Jack Jones was born on the day his father cut his only hit record, the 1938 #8 tune "Donkey Serenade." A high school friend of Nancy Sinatra, one of the high points of Jones's schooling was the afternoon her father sang for a school assembly. He began performing professionally in his father's nightclub act in his late teens, but went out on his own shortly thereafter, supporting his show business aspirations by pumping gas. He was signed to Capitol Records, but except for helping him land better gigs, his records did little. During a three-week run at a San Francisco club, Jones was signed to Kapp records. He continued to pump gas while recording for Kapp, and was surprised to hear one of his records coming from the radio of a customer as he washed their windshield.

While his 1962 single "Lollipops and Roses" didn't make the Top 40, it attracted enough attention to earn him a Best Male Pop Vocal Grammy. His first major hit was his 1963 version of "Wives and Lovers." The song went to #14 on the charts and also won him a Best Male Pop Vocal Grammy. Jones charted four more hits over the next three years, including "Dear Heart" (#30, 1964), "The Race Is On" (#15, 1965), "The Impossible Dream" (#35, 1966), and "Lady" (#39, 1967). He also became one of the first middle-of-the-road vocalists to record songs by rock bands like The Doors and The Beatles. His albums fared even better, with his 1966 *The Impossible Dream* hitting #9.

Jones became well-known on the musical theater touring circuit, playing in *Guys and Dolls*, *South Pacific*, and other productions. His voice reached a whole new generation of listeners with the theme to the TV show *The Love Boat*. Still actively recording into the 1990s, he cut swing versions of songs by The Police and Keb' Mo' for 1997's *New Jack Swing*. In 1998, Jones recorded a tribute to his friend Tony Bennett, just as Bennett was enjoying a revival among a new generation of young listeners.

DISC.: *Call Me Irresponsible* (1963); *Wives and Lovers* (1963); *Bewitched* (1964); *Where Love Has Gone* (1964); *My Kind of Town* (1965); *There's Love & There's Love & There's Love* (1965); *Dear Heart & Other Great Songs of Love* (1965); *For the In Crowd* (1966); *Jack Jones Sings* (1966); *The Impossible Dream* (1966); *Lady* (1967); *Our Song* (1967); *Without Her* (1967); *What I Did for Love* (1976); *With One More Look at You* (1977); *Jack Jones* (1982); *Here's to Love!* (1983); *The Jack Jones Christmas Album* (1987); *I Am a Singer* (1987); *White Christmas* (1989); *Jack Jones: The Gershwin Album* (1991); *The Mood Is Love* (1993); *Sings Michel Legrand* (1993); *Live at the Sands* (1993); *Christmas* (1994); *Music of the Night: Live at the London Palladium* (1995); *New Jack Swing* (1997); *Jack Jones Paints a Tribute to Tony Bennett* (1998).—HB

Jones, (James) Sidney, English composer and conductor; b. London, June 17, 1861; d. there, Jan. 29, 1946. He was the son of Sidney James, the conductor of the Leeds Grand Theatre and municipal band. He learned to play the clarinet and served as a musician under his father before setting out on his own as a touring theater conductor. In 1891 he toured the U.S. and Australia as conductor of London's Gaiety Theater company. Returning to England, he composed his first operetta, *Our Family Legend* (Brighton, Oct. 8, 1892). He made London the center of his activities, where he conducted at several theaters and had his first major success as a composer with *A Gaiety Girl* (Oct. 14, 1893). After bringing out *An Artist's Model* (Feb. 2, 1895), Jones scored a triumphant success with *The Geisha* (April 25, 1896). It subsequently was given around the globe and remained a staple in the repertoire of light theater works for decades. Following the premiere of *A Greek Slave* (June 8, 1898), he scored another outstanding success with *San Toy* (Oct. 21, 1899). Success also attended *My Lady Molly* (Brighton, Aug. 11, 1902). His London efforts resumed with the unsuccessful *The Medal and the Maid* (April 25, 1903), but he had better luck with *See See* (June 20, 1906). While his *King of Caledonia* (Sept. 3, 1908) met with public favor, *A Persian Princess* (April 27, 1909) did not. After an unsuccessful collaboration with Paul Rubens on *The Girl from Utah* (Oct. 18, 1913) and *The Happy Day* (May 13, 1916), Jones abandoned the musical theater.—NS/LK/DM

Jones, Jimmy (actually, James Henry), jazz pianist, arranger, composer; b. Memphis, Tenn., Dec. 30, 1918; d. Burbank, Calif., April 29, 1982. He was primarily an accompanist and chord player, of a high order. Originally a guitarist, he switched to piano, and worked in Chicago with Stuff Smith. He moved to N.Y. as part of that group. He worked with J. C. Heard (1946–47), then as an accompanist for singer Sarah Vaughan from October 1947 until April 1952. He had a period of inactivity while ill, then resumed working with Sarah from October 1954 until January 1958. During the 1960s, he did prolific freelance work as a player and arranger, and also led own trio. He worked as a musical director and accompanist for Ella Fitzgerald during the late 1960s; in 1969, he moved to Los Angeles, where he composed for television and movies as well as played gigs with jazz groups through the late 1970s.—JC/LP

Jones, Jo(nathan), noted swing-era drummer, long associated with Count Basie; b. Chicago, Oct. 7, 1911; d. N.Y., Sept. 3, 1985. Jones went to school in Ala., where he played trumpet, piano, and saxes from the age of 10. He left home to work in touring carnival shows, occasionally as a singer and dancer. He played drums in Ted Adams's Band in the late 1920s, then joined Harold Jones's Brownskin Syncopators in Lincoln, Nebr. (1931), where he remained working with various bands through 1933. He then moved to Kansas City, where he first worked with Count Basie in 1934, but did not become a permanent member of the band until early autumn of 1936, when the band was working at the Reno Club in Kansas City. (It was supposedly around this time that he threw his cymbal on the floor in disgust when Charlie Parker sat in at a jam session.) During early 1937, he was treated for syphilis but in those pre-penicillin times the treatment was not permanent. He remained with Count Basie until serving in the U.S. Army (October 1944); after his discharge, he worked mainly with Basie (April 1946–February 1948). He also did hundreds of freelance recordings with other leaders through his career. From the late 1940s, he primarily worked freelance. He made several tours with Norman Granz's Jazz at the Philharmonic (1947, 1951, 1957, with Ella Fitzgerald and Oscar Peterson), and worked with Illinois Jacquet (1948–50), Lester Young (1950), and the Joe Bushkin Quartet (1951–53). From the mid-1950s, he frequently led his own trio, while continuing to work with other leaders. In 1969 spent several months in Europe with Milt Buckner, then returned to N.Y. and resumed regular playing. He was featured at many jazz festivals during the 1970s. In later years, he was a strange figure with his raspy voice and strange intensity; perhaps the syphilis had progressed in his system. His final gig was at the Last Call Saloon, Providence, R.I., Nov. 10, 1984. He appeared in several films, including *Jammin' the Blues* (1944), *Born to Swing* (1973), and *Last of the Blue Devils* (1979). His son Jo is also a drummer.

Jones's swing attack on the ride cymbal was so powerful that one simply couldn't keep still. He was inventive, opening and closing his high-hat in unexpected places, not just on the second and fourth beats (hear Basie, "Time Out"). He generally accompanied trumpeters with lots of snare accents, while Lester Young got a swooshy ride cymbal (hear Basie, "Jumpin' at the Woodside," "After Theatre Jump").

DISC.: *Jo Jones Trio* (1950); *Jo Jones Special* (1955); *Jo Jones Plus Two* (1959); *Jo Jones Trio* (1959); *Jo Jones Sextet* (1960); *Percussion and Bass* (1960); *Vamp Till Ready* (1960); *Drums* (1973); *Main Man* (1976); *Our Man Papa Jo!* (1977).—**JC/LP**

Jones, Mason, American horn player, conductor, and teacher; b. Hamilton, N.Y., June 16, 1919. He was a pupil of Tabuteau and Reiner at the Curtis Inst. of Music in Philadelphia (1936–38). In 1938 he joined the Philadelphia Orch., where he was first horn (1940–78), personnel manager (1963–86), and conductor of the school concerts (1972–82); also was conductor of the Episcopal Academy Orch. (1958–60) and asst. conductor of the Philadelphia Chamber Orch. (1961–64). He was a founding member of the Philadelphia Woodwind Quintet (1950–80) and of the Philadelphia Brass Ensemble (from 1957). He taught at the Curtis Inst. of Music (from 1946) and at Temple Univ. Coll. of Music (1976–83), and in 1986–87 was president of the International Horn Soc. He ed. *Solos for the Horn Player* (1962) and *20th Century Orchestral Studies* (1971).—**NS/LK/DM**

Jones, Oliver, Canadian pianist; b. Montreal, Quebec, Canada, Sept. 11, 1934. Though internationally respected, he has been overlooked in the United States. The outstanding pianist performed his first public concert at the age of five, his first club date at nine. Though he studied with Oscar Peterson's sister, Daisy Peterson Sweeny, for 12 years—and the Peterson style is very evident in his playing and choice of sidemen Ray Brown and Ed Thigpen—he did not gain notoriety on the jazz

circuit until the 1980s. From 1962–80 he was the musical director and pianist for pop singer Ken Hamilton and worked in Puerto Rico as a music director for club shows. In 1980 he started his jazz career and has released some very good albums on the Canadian Justin Time label. Though currently in semi-retirement, Jones still tours every year and is a fixture at the International Montreal Jazz Festival.

DISC.: *Oliver Jones Trio Featuring Clark Terry* (1989); *A Class Act* (1991); *Just 88* (1993); *Yuletide Swing* (1994); *From Lush to Lively* (1995); *Have Fingers, Will Travel* (1997).—**PMac**

Jones, Parry, Welsh tenor; b. Blaina, Monmouthshire, Feb. 14, 1891; d. London, Dec. 26, 1963. He studied at the Royal Coll. of Music in London; also with Colli in Italy, Scheidemantel in Dresden, and John Coates in England. He made his debut in London in 1914; then sang in the U.S. He survived the German submarine attack on the *S.S. Lusitania* on his return trip to England in 1915, and then sang with the Beecham and D'Oyly Carte opera companies. He was a leading member of the Carl Rosa Opera Co. (1919–22) and the British National Opera Co. (1922–28); made his Covent Garden debut in London in 1921 as Turiddu; sang there again (1925–26; 1930–32; 1935; 1937), serving as a principal tenor there from 1949 to 1955, the 1953–54 season excepted. He then taught voice at the Guildhall School of Music in London. In 1962 he was made an Officer of the Order of the British Empire. He sang in the first British performances of *Wozzeck*, *Mathis der Maler*, and *Doktor Faust* in concert broadcasts by the BBC; was also active as an oratorio singer.—**NS/LK/DM**

Jones, Philip (Mark), outstanding English trumpeter; b. Bath, March 12, 1928; d. Jan. 17, 2000. He studied at the Royal Coll. of Music in London with Ernest Hall. He served as principal trumpet player in the Royal Phil. (1956–60), Philharmonia Orch. (1960–64), London Phil. (1964–65), New Philharmonia Orch. (1965–67), and BBC Sym. Orch. (1968–71). In 1951 he founded the Philip Jones Brass Ensemble, commissioning many composers to write works for his ensemble, remaining its director until 1986. He was head of the wind and percussion dept. at the Royal Northern Coll. of Music in Manchester (1975–77) and then at the Guildhall School of Music and Drama in London (1983–88). From 1989 to 1994 he was principal of Trinity Coll. of Music in London. He was made an Officer of the Order of the British Empire in 1977 and in 1986 a Commander of the Order of the British Empire.—**NS/LK/DM**

Jones, Richard, English opera and theater producer; b. London, June 7, 1953. He was educated at the Univ. of Hull and the Univ. of London. In 1982 he commenced his career as an opera producer with Argento's *A Water Bird Talk* at the Scottish Opera in Glasgow, where he returned to stage *Das Rheingold* in 1989 and *Die Walküre* in 1991. In 1984–85 he produced operas by Mozart, Salieri, and Paisiello at the Battignano Festival. After staging *Don Pasquale* at Opera Northern Ireland in Belfast (1985) and *Mignon* at the

Wexford Festival (1986), he produced *Manon* and *Carmen* at Opera North in Leeds (1987). His staging of Weir's *A Night at the Chinese Opera* was seen at the Kent Opera in 1988. In 1989 he produced the premiere of Blake's *The Plumber's Gift* at the English National Opera in London. After staging *Mazeppa* at the Bregenz Festival (1991), he oversaw the production of *Der fliegende Holländer* at the Netherlands Opera in Amsterdam (1993). In 1994 he staged *Giulio Cesare* at the Bavarian State Opera in Munich. Jones was responsible for the staging of the *Ring* cycle at London's Covent Garden in 1994–95. In 1998 he returned to Munich to produce *The Midsummer Marriage*.—**LK/DM**

Jones, Rickie Lee, hipster singer/songwriter; b. Chicago, Ill., Nov. 8, 1954. While her father, an actor and musician, taught her how to play guitar, Rickie Lee Jones's home life was not pacific. Her parents fought often and moved around a lot. Eventually, her father abandoned the family. Rickie became a teen-aged alcoholic and was thrown out of school in Washington. She migrated south and wound up waiting tables in L.A., playing at occasional open-mike nights, performing beat-like poetry and jazzy songs accompanied by her acoustic guitar. She met Tom Waits, and appeared on his *Blue Valentine* album; not in the grooves, but on the cover. She also performed one of his songs on the soundtrack to *The King of Comedy*.

Lowell George heard one of Jones's early songs, "Easy Money," and recorded it on his lone solo album, *Thanks, I'll Eat It Here*. This brought her to the attention of Warner Bros. (George's record company). A four-song demo clinched the deal, and Warner signed her. Her eponymous debut album became the surprise hit of 1979, with the #4 hit single "Chuck E.'s in Love" and the #40 follow-up "Youngblood." It marked the last time Jones hit the pop charts. The album went platinum and Jones earned Best New Artist honors at the Grammys. Her next effort, *Pirates*, was an even more fully realized project. Though it didn't generate any pop hits, it contained some of the most sophisticated music masquerading as pop. Tunes like "Woody and Dutch on the Slow Train to Peking" maintained the bebopping stance of the first album while expanding on it. Coupled with the heartwrenchingly beautiful ballad "We Belong Together," it made for an astounding album. Despite the lack of a hit, it rose to #5 on the album charts and went gold.

Jones didn't release her next album for two years, and when she did it was a curiosity. *Girl at Her Volcano* was a 10 inch vinyl EP, mostly of covers, including a ballad reading of "Under the Boardwalk" and her bohemian take on "My Funny Valentine." The collection hit #39 despite the odd configuration. Jones's 1984 release, *Magazine*, brought the twin urges of commercial constraint and jazzy freedom to a somewhat overproduced détente that ultimately satisfied no one. Five years later, *Flying Cowboys* remedied this. Sparely produced by Steely Dan's Walter Becker, the album featured several tracks with the Scottish band The Blue Nile. While you still couldn't hear Jones on the radio, she continued to sell better than the average cult artist.

The mixture of Jones and Becker breaking his long post–Steely Dan silence took this one to #39. With a reputation for reviving stalled careers, Don Was came in to produce Jones's next effort, 1991's *Pop Pop*. A sprawling album of covers, the songs ranged from Jimi Hendrix and The Jefferson Airplane to show tunes from *Peter Pan* and *Lili*. The album had guest musicians ranging from bandoneon virtuoso Dino Saluzzi to jazz greats Charlie Haden and Joe Henderson. It stalled without even cracking the Top 100. In between her own projects, Jones duetted with John Mellencamp and Dr. John, the latter earning the duo a Grammy for Best Jazz Vocal Performance. She also produced an album for 12-string guitar shaman Leo Kottke. Kottke performed on Jones's next album, *Traffic from Paradise* (1993), along with guests like Lyle Lovett, Brian Setzer, and David Hidalgo of Los Lobos. A cover of David Bowie's "Rebel Rebel" got some radio attention.

Jones came back with 1995's *Naked Songs*, an album consisting mostly of her acoustic guitar and vocals. A stint with the HORDE tour, however, put her in mind to record what she described as a "loud, electric, and very powerful" album. That record, 1997's *Ghostyhead*, took Jones's musical visions and translated it into trip-hop music with surprising success. Jones remains a remarkable artist who lives to surprise her audiences. Her 2000 release, *It's Like This*, is another unusual mix of cover songs.

DISC.: *Rickie Lee Jones* (1979); *Pirates* (1981); *Girl at Her Volcano* (1983); *Rickie Lee Jones/Pirates* (1983); *The Magazine* (1984); *Flying Cowboys* (1989); *Pop Pop* (1991); *Traffic from Paradise* (1993); *Naked Songs* (1995); *Ghostyhead* (1997); *It's Like This* (2000). Various Artists: *The King of Comedy* (1983).—**HB**

Jones, Robert, English lutenist and composer; b. c. 1570; d. c. 1615. He studied at the Univ. of Oxford (Mus.B., 1597). With several other musicians, he was granted a patent to form the "Children of the Revells of the Queene." He publ. 5 books of lute songs (1600, 1601, 1605, 1607, 1610; ed. by E.H. Fellowes in The English School of Lutenist Song Writers, 1920–32; rev., 1959, by T. Dart in The English Lute-Songs, 2nd series, IV) and a book of madrigals (1605; ed. by E.H. Fellowes in The English Madrigal School, 1913–24; rev., 1961, by T. Dart in The English Madrigalists).—**NS/LK/DM**

Jones, Sissieretta (born **Matilda Sissieretta Joyner**), noted black American soprano, known as the "Black Patti" (with reference to Adelina Patti); b. Portsmouth, Va., Jan. 5, 1868; d. Providence, R.I., June 24, 1933. She studied at the New England Cons. of Music in Boston, and with Louise Capianni and Mme. Scongia in London. She made her debut at a concert at N.Y.'s Steinway Hall on April 5, 1888, then began to tour from 1890, giving concerts in the West Indies, North America, and Europe. She gained prominence as a result of her appearances at the Grand Negro Jubilee at N.Y.'s Madison Square Garden and at the White House in a command performance for President Harrison (1892); then sang at the Pittsburgh Exposition and the Chicago World's Columbian Exposition (1893). N.Y.'s Metropolitan Opera considered her for African roles in

Aida and *L'Africaine*, but racial attitudes and conservative management policies precluded such appearances. She was the principal soprano of the vaudeville troupe known as Black Patti's Troubadours (1896–1915), with which she toured throughout the world; she starred in its operatic "kaleidoscope," in which she sang a medley of arias from operas in staged scenes; she also sang art songs and popular ballads.—NS/LK/DM

Jones, Slick (actually, **Wilmore**), jazz drummer; b. Roanoke, Va., April 13, 1907; d. N.Y., Nov. 2, 1969. His brother Gil led own band in Va. for many years; their father was also a musician. Jones worked with John Lockslayer's Band in 1925. He moved to N.Y. and began studying at the Damrosch Cons. He played with Fletcher Henderson from spring 1935 until February 1936, then joined Fats Waller (replacing Arnold "Scrippy" Boling); he worked on and off with Waller until 1942. Jones worked with various other leaders before a long spell with Gene Sedric's Band from late 1946. He was with Wilbur de Paris in 1954, and during the following year he worked in Boston with Wilbur de Paris, Doc Cheatham, and others. He played regularly in N.Y. after 1959, working a spell with Scoville Brown, then several years with the Eddie Durham Band. Jones was seriously ill in 1964, but temporarily recovered and resumed playing for a while.—JC/LP

Jones, Snags (actually, **Clifford**), jazz drummer; b. New Orleans, La., c. 1900; d. Chicago, Jan. 31, 1947. His irregularly placed teeth inspired his nickname. Jones went to school with Lee Collins and Buddie Petit, then played for a year in Petit's Band. He then joined Jack Carey's Band, and later played in Papa Celestin's Band and Armand Piron's Orch. In 1922, he moved to Chicago to join trumpeter Tig Chambers at Joyland Park; during the following year he worked with Al Simeon's Hot Six, then toured with King Oliver (1924). Jones spent several years based in Milwaukee with Art Simms and Bernie Young until 1931. He spent most of the 1930s working with various bands in the Chicago area. In the postwar Dixieland revival, he worked with Bunk Johnson in Chicago, playing club dates with him and other leaders until his death.—JC/LP

Jones, Spike (actually, **Lindley Armstrong Jones**), b. Long Beach, Calif., Dec. 14, 1911; d. Bel Air, Calif., May 1, 1965. Among Spike Jones's many musical accomplishments over his 30-plus-year career, perhaps his biggest was introducing such instruments as the latriophone (a toilet seat strung with wire) and the burpaphone (self-explanatory) to the lexicon of American popular music. Much more than a novelty act, Jones was a musical visionary. "I'm the dandruff in longhair music," Jones has said about his comical presence in the world of more serious bandleaders in the 1950s and 1960s. He began his career as a studio musician drummer, most notably playing on Bing Crosby's monster hit "White Christmas." Bored by conventional music, Jones began to add unusual instruments to his drum set and set out to form a band to fulfill his zany vision. In the early 1940s, he formed the City Slickers and Jones set out to turn the world of pop music on its ear with crazy parodies and bizarre musical collages. The band's unlikely first hit was 1942's Hitler spoof "Der Fuehrer's Face," on the basis of which the band successfully toured the country. By the late 1940s Jones had expanded the band's live shows to include midgets, jugglers, and other loony acts, while scoring on the charts with song interpretations like "Cocktails for Two"—replete with a hiccuping chorus. Jones and the band appeared in several films and brought their brand of musical folly to TV in the 1950s and early 1960s with four versions of *The Spike Jones Show*. Jones died of emphysema in 1965, but not before establishing himself as one of the true musical pioneers of the 20th century, and easily the most hilarious.

DISC: *The Nutcracker Suite* (1945); *Bottoms Up* (1952); *Spike Jones Presents a Christmas Spectacular* (1956); *Dinner Music for People Who Aren't Very Hungry* (1957); *Spike Jones in Hi- Fi* (1960); *Let's Sing a Song for Christmas* (1978); *Riot Squad* (1989); *Spiked! The Music of Spike Jones* (1994); *Musical Depreciation Review: The Spike Jones Anthology* (1994); *Louder & Funnier* (1994); *Corn's a-Poppin'* (1995); *Cocktails for Two* (1997); *Greatest Hits!!!* (1999).

Jones, Thad(deus Joseph), cornetist, flugelhornist, composer, leader, brother of **Hank Jones** and **Elvin Jones;** b. Pontiac, Mich., March 28, 1923; d. Copenhagen, Aug. 20, 1986. He was one of the most admired composers of his era, and a striking soloist. His writing featured a cocky wit, highly sophisticated voicings involving lots of subtle dissonance, and unusual pairings such as bass and muted trumpet. Most of his charts were published by Kendor music and they have been performed and analyzed at colleges everywhere. As a brass player he was clearly a disciple of Gillespie, one of the few who captured his oblique way with harmony and brash swagger. Some consider him to be one of the most brilliant brass soloists.

He taught himself to play trumpet when he was about 13, and subsequently appeared professionally with his brother Hank at age 16, along with Sonny Stitt. After working with various dance and show bands, he joined his brother Elvin as a member of Billy Mitchell's quintet in Detroit (1950–53). He worked with Charles Mingus (1954–55) and became well known as a featured soloist and arranger with Count Basie's Orch. (1954–63); also appeared with Thelonious Monk during this time in big band and quintet settings. Between 1963 and 1965 he appeared with Monk in a big band concert (1964) and Gerry Mulligan, worked with CBS TV, and co-led a quintet with Pepper Adams and Mel Lewis. In 1965, with Lewis he formed a big band, which played every Monday night at the Village Vanguard when not on tour. It continues to this day as the Vanguard Jazz Orch., and which established a tradition of Monday night big bands at other N.Y. venues. It subsequently gained fame through its tours of the U.S. and Europe, including a smashing visit to the former Soviet Union in 1972. He left the band in 1979 and settled in Denmark, where he organized his own big band, the Thad Jones Eclipse; he was also active as an arranger and composer with Danish Radio. In a bar fight his lips were damaged by broken glass. He returned to the U.S. to briefly take charge of Count Basie's Orch. in 1985. He worked until he was diagnosed with cancer around April 1986.

DISC.: *Thad Jones: Billy Mitchell Quintet* (1953); *Fabulous Thad Jones* (1954); *Lust for Life* (1954); *Thad Jones* (1955); *Detroit–N.Y. Junction* (1956); *Magnificent T. Jones, Vol. 3* (1956); *Magnificent Thad Jones* (1956); *After Hours* (1957); *Magnificent* (1957): *After Hours* (1958); *Motor City Scene* (1959); *Complete Solid State Recordings* (1966); *Mean What You Say* (1966); *Presenting Thad Jones: Mel Lewis* (1966); *Thad Jones Live at the Village* (1967); *Monday Night* (1968); *Central Park North* (1969); *Consummation* (1970); *Suite for Pops* (1972); *Potpourri* (1974); *New Life: Dedicated to Max Gordon* (1975); *Live in Munich* (1976); *Paris 1969* (1976); *Thad Jones with Mel Lewis* (1976); *Thad Jones and the Mel Lewis Quintet* (1977); *Live at Montmartre, Copenhagen* (1978); *Eclipse* (1979); *Thad Jones and Mel Lewis Quartet* (1979); *Three and One* (1984); *Mel Lewis and Friends* (1989).—**NS/LP**

Jones, Wallace (Leon), jazz trumpeter; b. Baltimore, Md., Nov. 16, 1906; d. March 23, 1983. Cousin of bandleader/drummer Chick Webb. Jones played in Ike Dixon's Harmony Birds (1928–29) and the Percy Glascoe Kit Kat Orch. (1930). He moved to N.Y. and played briefly with Chick Webb, then regularly with Willie Bryant in 1936–37. He was with Duke Ellington from March 1938 until March 1944. In September 1945, he played with Benny Carter in N.Y.; during the following year he worked in Snub Mosely's Band, with John Kirby (early 1947). Left full-time music to become a mortician. —**JC/LP**

Jones, William, English churchman, writer on music, and composer; b. Lowick, Northamptonshire (baptized), July 20, 1726; d. Nayland, Suffolk, Jan. 6, 1800. He studied at Oxford, and with James Oswald and Pepusch in London, and subsequently was a vicar and curate. He publ. *A Treatise on the Art of Music; in which the Elements of Harmony and Air are practically considered* (Colchester, 1784; 2nd ed., 1827) and *The Nature and Excellence of Music: a Sermon* (London, 1787).—**NS/LK/DM**

Jones, Willie (actually, William), jazz drummer; b. Brooklyn, N.Y., Oct. 20, 1929; d. there, April 9, 1989. He was self-taught on the drums. He became a prominent drummer in the mid-1950s N.Y. jazz scene. He worked with Thelonious Monk (1953), Charlie Mingus's Jazz Workshop (1955–56), and Lester Young (1958), among many others. He was a mainstay of the Brooklyn jazz community for many years, promoting jazz in the public schools.—**LP**

Jong, Marinus de, Dutch-born Belgian composer, pianist, and pedagogue; b. Osterhout, Aug. 14, 1891; d. Ekeren, June 13, 1984. He was a student of Bosquet (piano) and Mortelmans (composition) at the Antwerp Cons. After touring Europe and the U.S. as a pianist, he settled in Belgium in 1926 and was made a prof. of piano (1931) and of counterpoint and fugue (1948) at the Antwerp Cons. His works were in a neo-impressionistic style, with polytonal counterpoint as its mainstay.

WORKS: DRAMATIC: Opera: *Mitsanoboe* (1962); *Die häslichen Mädchen von Bagdad* (1966; Antwerp, Jan. 7, 1967); *Esmoreit* (Antwerp, Sept. 11, 1970). **Ballet:** *De vrouwen van Zalongo* (1951); *De kleine haven* (1952); *De kringloop* (1955);

Carrefour (1956); *De Reiskameraad* (1959). **ORCH.:** 3 piano concertos (1924; 1952; 1956–57); 3 syms. (1932; 1965–66; 1976); concertos for Trumpet (1937), Cello (1946; rev. 1969), Violin (1954), Viola (1958), Oboe (1966–67), Horn (1966–67), Bassoon (1967), Flute (1967), Clarinet (1967), and Organ (1974); *Heidestemmingen (Impressions de Bruyère)* (1937); *Hiawatha,* symphonic poem (1945); *Aphoristische tryptiek* (1952; also for Wind Quintet); *Flemish Rhapsody No. 1* (1955), *No. 2* (1971), and *No. 3* (1971); *Boublitschky Suite* (1956); *Ruimteraket, Atlas (Fusée interplanétaire),* symphonic poem (1964). **CHAMBER:** 6 string quartets (1923, 1926, 1947, 1956, 1956, 1962); *Pacis, Doloris et Amoris,* violin sonata (1927); Quartet for 4 Cellos (1936); Nonet (1939); 3 wind quintets (1952, 1965, 1971); Trio for Oboe, Clarinet, and Bassoon (1961); Wind Quartet (1968); Piano Quartet (1971); Sextet for Piano and Winds (1972). **KEYBOARD: Piano:** 3 sonatas (1926, 1933, 1934); *Fantaisie-Walsen* (1960); *12 Preludes* (1975). **Organ:** Various works. **VOCAL:** 4 oratorios: *Hiawatha's Lied* (1947), *Imitatio Christi* (1956), *Kerkhofblommen* (1957), and *Proverbia Bruegeliana* (1961); pieces for Soloists, Chorus, and Orch.; choruses; songs. —**NS/LK/DM**

Jongen, Léon (Marie-Victor-Justin), respected Belgian composer and pedagogue, brother of **(Marie-Alphonse-Nicolas-) Joseph Jongen;** b. Liège, March 2, 1884; d. Brussels, Nov. 18, 1969. He was trained at the Liège Cons. From 1898 to 1904 he was organist at St. Jacques in Liège. In 1913 he won the Belgian Grand Prix de Rome with his cantata *Les Fiancés de Noël* (1913). From 1927 to 1929 he was conductor of the Tonkin Opera in Hanoi. He was his brother's successor as director of the Brussels Cons. (1939–49). His Violin Concerto (1962) was the compulsory work for the 12 finalists of the 1963 Queen Elisabeth violin competition held in Brussels.

WORKS: DRAMATIC: *L'Ardennaise,* opera (1909); *Le Rêve d'une nuit de Noël,* musical fairy tale (1917; Paris, March 18, 1918); *Thomas l'Agnelet,* opera (1922–23; Brussels, Feb. 14, 1924); *Le Masque de la Mort rouge,* ballet, after Poe (1956). **ORCH.:** *Campéador* (1932); *Malaisie,* suite (1935); *In Memoriam Regis* (1935); *Prélude, Divertissement et Final* for Piano and Orch. (1937); *Rhapsodia belgica* for Violin and Orch. (1948); *Divertissement en forme de variations sur un thème de Haydn* (1956); Violin Concerto (1962). **CHAMBER:** String Quartet (1919); *Divertissement* for 4 Saxophones (1937); Trio for Oboe, Clarinet, and Bassoon (1937); Trio for Flute, Violin, and Viola (1937); Piano Quartet (1955); Quintet for Piano, Flute, Clarinet, Horn, and Bassoon (1958). **VOCAL:** *Geneviève de Brabant* for Chorus and Orch. (1907); *La Légende de St. Hubert* for Chorus and Orch. (1909; St. Hubert, July 21, 1968); *Les Fiancés de Noël,* cantata (1913); *Trilogie de Psaumes* for Chorus and Orch. (1937–39); songs.—**NS/LK/DM**

Jongen, (Marie-Alphonse-Nicolas-) Joseph, eminent Belgian composer and teacher, brother of **Léon (Marie-Victor-Justin) Jongen;** b. Liège, Dec. 14, 1873; d. Sart-lez-Spa, July 12, 1953. He studied at the Liège Cons., receiving a premier prix for each of the academic subjects and also for piano and organ. In 1891 he joined the faculty of the Liège Cons. as a teacher of harmony and counterpoint. In 1894 he gained attention as a composer when he won two national prizes; in 1897 he won the Belgian Prix de Rome. He then received advice from Strauss in Berlin and d'Indy in Paris. After returning to Brussels, he taught at a music academy. From 1898, he also held the position of professeur adjoint at the Liège Cons., where he became a prof. in 1911. After the outbreak of World War I in 1914, he went to London. He made appearances as a pianist and organist, and, with Defauw, Tertis, and Doehaerd, he organized a piano quartet, which became known as the Belgian Quartet. In 1919 he returned to Belgium. In 1920 he became a prof. of counterpoint and fugue at the Brussels Cons., and from 1925 to 1939 he was its director, being succeeded by his brother, Léon. During World War II, he lived in France. He then returned to his country estate at Sart-lez- Spa. While not pursuing extreme modern effects, Jongen succeeded in imparting an original touch to his harmonic style.

WORKS: ORCH.: Sym. (1899); Violin Concerto (1899); Cello Concerto (1900); *Fantasie sur deux Noëls populaires wallons* (1902); *Lalla-Roukh*, symphonic poem after Thomas Moore (1904); *Prélude et Danse* (1907); *2 Rondes wallones* (1912; also for Piano); Trumpet Concertino (1913); *Impressions d'Ardennes* (1913); Suite for Violin and Orch. (1915); *Épithalame et Scherzo* for 3 Violins and Orch. or Piano (1917); *Tableaux pittoresques* (1917); *Poème heroïque* for Violin and Orch. (1919); *Prélude élégiaque et Scherzo* (1920); *Fantasie rhapsodique* for Cello and Orch. (1924); *Hymne* for Organ and Strings (1924); *Symphonie concertante* for Organ and Orch. (1926); *Pièce symphonique* for Piano and Orch. (1928); *Passacaille et Gigue* (1929); *Suite No. 3, dans le style ancien* (1930); *10 Pièces* (1932); *Triptyque* (1935); *Ouverture Fanfare* (1939); *Alleluia* for Organ and Orch. (1940); *Ouverture de fête* (1941); Piano Concerto (1943); *Bourrée* (1944); Harp Concerto (1944); *In memoriam* (1947); *Ballade, Hommage à Chopin* (1949); *3 Mouvements symphoniques* (1951). CHAMBER: 3 string quartets (1893, 1916, 1921); Piano Trio (1897); Piano Quartet (1901); 2 violin sonatas (1902, 1909); Trio for Piano, Violin, and Viola (1907); Cello Sonata (1912); *2 Serenades* for String Quartet (1918); *2 Pièces* for Flute, Cello, and Harp (1924); *2 Pièces* for 4 Cellos (1929); *Sonata eroica* for Organ (1930); Wind Quintet (1933); Quintet for Harp, Flute, Violin, Viola, and Cello (1940); Concerto for Wind Quintet (1942); Quartet for 4 Saxophones (1942); String Trio (1948); a number of piano pieces, including 24 preludes in all keys (1941); solo pieces for various instruments with piano. VOCAL: *Mass* for Chorus, Organ, and Orch. (1946); choral pieces; songs. A catalog of his works was publ. by the Centre Belge de Documentation Musicale (Brussels, 1954).—NS/LK/DM

Jonsson, Josef Petrus, Swedish composer, music critic, and teacher; b. Enköping, June 21, 1887; d. Norrköping, May 9, 1969. He studied piano, and later received instruction in orchestration from Ivar Hellman in Norrköping. From 1922 to 1966 he was music critic of the newspaper *Östergötlands Folkblad*. His works reveal a fine command of classical forms in a late Romantic style. He wrote three syms. (*Nordland*, 1919–22; 1931; 1947), Chamber Symphony (1949), several orch. overtures and suites, Violin Concerto (Norrköping, April 10, 1960), *Festival Prelude* for Orch. (1961), *Korallrevet*, symphonic poem for Baritone, Chorus, and Orch. (1916), *Missa solemnis* for Chorus, Orch., and Organ (1934), Cantata for Speaking Chorus, Women's Chorus, Soloists, 2 Flutes, and Piano (Norrköping, May 5, 1962), chamber music, piano pieces, and songs.—NS/LK/DM

Joó, Arpád, Hungarian-born American conductor; b. Budapest, June 8, 1948. He pursued private musical instruction with Kodály (1954–65) and Ferencsik (1954–68). From 1958 to 1964 he was a piano student at the Béla Bartók Cons. in Budapest. He was also a private pupil of Carlo Zecchi (piano and conducting, 1963–65) and of Magaloff (piano, 1964–65), and studied piano with Joseph Gat and Kadosa at the Franz Liszt Academy of Music in Budapest (1964–68). After further piano lessons with Irwin Freundlich at the Juilliard School in N.Y. (1968–69), he concentrated on conducting studies with Rozsnyai in San Diego (1969), Wolfgang Vacano and Tibor Kozma at Ind. Univ. (1970–73), Markevitch (1972–73), and Giulini (1979). In 1975 he became a naturalized American citizen. He was music director of the Knoxville (Tenn.) Sym. Orch. (1973–78) and the Calgary (Alberta) Phil. (1978–81), subsequently serving as music adviser and principal conductor of the latter (1981–83). In 1985 he was principal guest conductor of the European Community Chamber Orch. in Eindhoven; from 1985 to 1987 he was music director of the Nyirbator Festival in Hungary. In 1986 he was appointed principal guest conductor of the Budapest Sym. Orch., and in 1987, music director of the sym. orch. and chorus of Spanish Radio and Television in Madrid, which position he held until 1991. He also was prof. of conducting at the master classes in Assisi (from 1987) and music adviser and principal guest conductor of the Brabant Orch. in Eindhoven (1989–91). He has won critical accolades for his idiomatic performances of Liszt, Bartók, and Kodály.—NS/LK/DM

Joplin, Janis, big-voiced rock/blues singer of the 1960s who revolutionized the role of women in rock; b. Port Arthur, Tex., Jan. 19, 1943; d. Hollywood, Calif., Oct. 4, 1970. BIG BROTHER AND THE HOLDING COMPANY: MEMBERSHIP: Janis Joplin, lead voc.; Sam Andrew, gtr., pno., sax., voc. (b. Taft, Calif., Dec. 18, 1941); James Gurley, gtr. (b. Detroit, Dec. 22, 1939); Peter Albin, bs., gtr., voc. (b. San Francisco, June 6, 1944); David Getz, drm. (b. Brooklyn, N.Y., Jan. 24, 1940).

Raised in Port Arthur, Tex., Janis Joplin had discovered the blues by the age of 17. She began singing locally in 1961, primarily at Ken Threadgill's Austin bar. She sojourned briefly to San Francisco in 1963 to perform at folk clubs and bars with Jorma Kaukonen or Roger Perkins before returning to Tex. to attend the Univ. of Tex. at Austin. During 1965, musicians Peter Albin, Sam Andrew, and James Gurley were playing at jam sessions hosted by Chet Helms at the Avalon Ballroom. With Helms's encouragement, they formed Big Brother and The Holding Company in September, replacing their original drummer with David Getz. Helms became the group's manager, and they debuted at the Trips Festival in January 1966. In June, Helms successfully recruited Tex. friend Janis Joplin as vocalist for the band, and the new lineup first took the stage at the Avalon Ballroom later that month.

Backed by screeching psychedelic guitars, Janis Joplin sang—virtually shouted—in the style of blues singers such as Bessie Smith, investing her performances with intense, agitated passion. Big Brother and The

Holding Company signed a recording contract with the small Chicago-based Mainstream label and were launched into international prominence with their celebrated appearance at the Monterey International Pop Festival in June 1967. The group's poorly produced debut album was released in September 1967 and featured Janis Joplin's stunning performances of "Women Is Losers" and "Down on Me," as well as the whole band's overlooked "Blindman." Signed to a management contract with Albert Grossman (then Bob Dylan's manager) in January 1968, the group switched to Columbia Records for their only other album with Joplin, *Cheap Thrills*. "Piece of My Heart" became a near-smash from the album, which included "Big Mama" Thornton's "Ball and Chain," Janis's own "Turtle Blues," and a moving rendition of George Gershwin's "Summertime." With Joplin garnering the bulk of the media attention, rumors of the group's breakup began to spread in November and were confirmed in December with Joplin's final appearance with the band at Chet Helms's Family Dog.

Retaining guitarist Sam Andrew, Janis Joplin formed a new band, alternately known as Squeeze and The Janis Joplin Revue, with organist Bill King, bassist Brad Campbell, and two horn players. Debuting equivocally at the Memphis Sound Party on Dec. 18, 1968, the group soon suffered a variety of personnel changes. After recording *Kozmic Blues* with the group, Joplin performed her final concert with this band on Dec. 29, 1969, at Madison Square Garden. In April 1970, she again appeared with Big Brother and The Holding Company, reconstituted by Sam Andrew and blues singer-songwriter Nick Gravenites, at Fillmore West. Big Brother (without Janis Joplin) subsequently recorded two albums for Columbia, the first featuring Gravenites's tongue-in-cheek ode to Merle Haggard, "I'll Change Your Flat Tire, Merle." Disbanding in 1972, the group re-formed in 1987 with vocalist Michelle Bastian.

Forming a new band, Full-Tilt Boogie, in May of 1970, Joplin debuted the group at Freedom Hall in Louisville, Ky., on June 12 of that year. The members included guitarist John Till (a later-day member of her prior band) and bassist Brad Campbell. By September, they had nearly finished recording their album, but on Oct. 4, 1970, Janis Joplin was found dead in her Hollywood hotel, the victim of a heroin overdose. Released posthumously, *Pearl* yielded a top hit with Kris Kristofferson's "Me and Bobby McGee." It also included "Cry Baby," the silly ditty "Mercedes Benz," and one of Joplin's theme songs, "Get It While You Can."

Columbia later released the live set *Joplin in Concert* (recorded with Big Brother and Full-Tilt Boogie), a soundtrack album to the 1975 film documentary *Janis*, and *Farewell Song*. The 1979 Bette Midler movie *The Rose* was inspired by the life of Janis Joplin. Joplin was inducted into the Rock and Roll Hall of Fame in 1995.

DISC.: BIG BROTHER AND THE HOLDING COMPANY: *Big Brother and The Holding Company* (1967); *Cheap Thrills* (1968); *Be a Brother* (with Kathy McDonald; 1970); *How Hard It Is* (1971); *Live at Winterland '68* (1998). **KATHY MCDONALD:** *Insane Asylum* (1974). **JANIS JOPLIN:** *I Got Dem Ol' Kozmic Blues Again Mama* (1969); *Pearl* (1971); *Joplin in Concert* (1972); *Janis* (soundtrack; 1975); *Farewell Song* (1982); *Janis Joplin* (1993).

BIBL.: D. Dalton, *Janis* (N.Y., 1971); D. Landau, *J. J.: Her Life and Times* (N.Y., 1971); P. Caserta, *Going Down with Janis* (Secaucus, N.J., 1973; N.Y., 1973); M. Friedman, *Buried Alive: The Biography of J. J.* (N.Y., 1973; N.Y., 1992); G. Carey, *Lenny, Janis, and Jimi* (N.Y., 1975); D. Dalton, *Piece of My Heart: The Life, Times and Legend of J. J.* (N.Y., 1986); E. Amburn, *Pearl: The Obsessions and Passions of J. J.: A Biography* (N.Y., 1992); L. Joplin, *Love, Janis* (N.Y., 1992).—**BH**

Joplin, Scott, preeminent American ragtime composer; b. in Texarkana, Tex., Nov. 24, 1868; d. N.Y., April 1, 1917. At a time when ragtime was at its popular peak, Joplin was its foremost practitioner. His piano rags, such as "Maple Leaf Rag" and "The Entertainer," were played throughout the U.S. and Europe. He aspired to a greater musical respectability, however, and worked for much of his life on more ambitious compositions, notably his opera, *Treemonisha*. His reputation was in eclipse during the decades immediately after his death, but by the 1970s his music had regained its currency.

Joplin's father, Giles Joplin, was a freed slave from N.C. who had moved to Tex. in his teens and become a farm laborer. His mother, Florence Givens, from Ky., was freeborn. By 1880 the family had moved to Texarkana, where his father found work on the railroad. After his parents separated in the early 1880s, his mother supported the family as a domestic. Both parents were musical: his father played the violin; his mother played the banjo and sang. Joplin was playing banjo by the age of seven, and he studied music with Mag Washington, J.C. Johnson, and, probably, a German named Julius Weiss who introduced him to European classical music. He also seems to have had some secondary schooling, though education for African-Americans was restricted at the time.

Joplin gained local renown as a musician. About 1885 he formed a vocal quartet, which sang professionally in the area for several years. He also played piano locally and taught guitar and mandolin. He then left Texarkana to make his living as a traveling pianist. Eventually he settled in St. Louis. In 1893 he traveled to Chicago for the World's Columbian Exposition, a world's fair remembered for quickening the emergence of ragtime as a popular genre, and he formed a band there in which he played cornet. He returned to St. Louis after the fair, and in 1894 moved to Sedalia, Mo., where he established, with his brothers Robert and Will, The Texas Medley Quartette (actually an octet), which toured as far as Syracuse, N.Y. He briefly joined The Queen City Cornet Band as first cornetist, then formed his own six-piece band to play dances while also continuing to play solo in clubs and brothels. He enrolled at the Smith Coll. of Music in Sedalia and studied composition.

After publishing a few works with other publishers, Joplin began a long association with a Sedalia-based music-store owner and music publisher, John Stark, who brought out "Maple Leaf Rag," for which Stark paid a royalty of one cent per copy of sheet music, an unusually generous arrangement at a time when most compositions by African-American artists were sold outright for small fees. Joplin agreed to a five-year exclusive contract with Stark, though he violated it by publishing works with others.

Though "Maple Leaf Rag," which became one of the most popular rags of the time, demonstrated his mastery of the form, Joplin always aspired to write more ambitious works. In 1899 he formed the Scott Joplin Drama Company and rented the Woods Opera House in Sedalia to stage a performance of his ballet (actually a work for singing narrator and dancers), *The Ragtime Dance*, apparently in an effort to convince Stark to publish it. But Stark initially declined. Joplin did find encouragement, however, when he met and began to study with German music teacher Alfred Ernst, who was the conductor of The St. Louis Choral Symphony Society, in late 1900 or early 1901.

Joplin moved back to St. Louis in the spring of 1901 with Belle (probably Belle Jones, the widow of his sometime collaborator Scott Hayden's brother Joe), who had become his wife, though it is not clear whether they were legally married. The couple separated in 1903, shortly after the death of an infant daughter. Joplin married Freddie Alexander in Little Rock, Ark., on June 14, 1904, but she died three months later. He seems to have entered into a common-law marriage with Lottie Stokes in N.Y. sometime between 1911 and 1913.

Joplin staged *The Ragtime Dance* a second time in late 1901, again without convincing Stark to publish it. But the increasing popularity of his rags eventually caused the publisher to relent, and the ballet finally was published the following year. While continuing to write notable rags such as "The Entertainer" and "Elite Syncopations," he set to work on an opera, *A Guest of Honor*, which seems to have been given a tryout in St. Louis in August 1903. He also took it on tour, but this was a failure, and his opera company devolved into a minstrel show before disbanding completely. (Although Joplin wrote to the Library of Congress to apply for a copyright for the opera on Feb. 16, 1903, no score has ever been found.)

For the next four years, Joplin lived variously in Chicago, St. Louis, and Sedalia, publishing his songs, rags, and other piano works, and traveling around the Midwest as a touring pianist. In the summer of 1907 he moved permanently to N.Y., where Stark, still his main publisher, had already relocated, and where the major music publishers were located. He published an instruction manual, *The School of Ragtime*, in 1908. While continuing to tour and to write popular rags, he worked on a second opera, *Treemonisha*, which he was forced to publish himself after established publishers rejected it. He managed to arrange a single informal performance in Harlem, probably in the fall of 1911, but this did not lead to a full-scale production.

As ragtime declined in popularity, Joplin found it more difficult to work as a composer and musician, and he turned increasingly to teaching music to support himself. By late 1915 he had begun to exhibit the symptoms of dementia paralytica, a late manifestation of terminal syphilis. His health declined over the next year-and-a-half until his death.

During Joplin's lifetime, the popularity of his work was reflected in the developing recording industry. In 1907 the U.S. Marine Band released a successful recording of "Maple Leaf Rag" on Victor, and Vess Ossman recorded a banjo version of it for Columbia. But as ragtime went out of fashion, Joplin lapsed into obscurity in the 1920s and 1930s. In the 1940s, articles about him began to appear, leading to the first significant biographical work about him and his contemporaries, *They All Played Ragtime*. A small but fervent following existed in the 1950s and 1960s, leading to the founding of *Rag Times* magazine in May 1966.

In December 1970, Elektra Nonesuch Records released *Piano Rags by Scott Joplin*, the first of three albums by Joshua Rifkin that began to bring Joplin back into public consciousness. In 1973 The New England Cons. Ragtime Ensemble, conducted by Gunther Schuller, reached the charts with *The Red Back Book*, an album of Joplin rags; it went on to win the Grammy Award for Best Chamber Music Performance. The same year, film director George Roy Hill decided to use Joplin's music in *The Sting* (even though the film was set in the 1930s), which opened in the fall of 1973 and became the second-biggest box office hit of the year. By now out of copyright, the rags were arranged by Marvin Hamlisch, who won an Academy Award for his adaptation. *The Sting* soundtrack album topped the charts and went gold, while "The Entertainer," released as a single, became a Top Ten gold-selling hit and won Hamlisch a Grammy Award for Best Pop Instrumental Performance. (When he also won the Best New Artist Grammy, Hamlisch accepted the award by noting that Joplin was "the real new artist of the year.")

Even before this success, *Treemonisha* had begun to attract notice, enjoying a world premiere performance at the Atlanta Memorial Arts Center and a second performance at Wolf Trap Farm outside Washington, D.C., in 1972. The Houston Grand Opera followed with a more elaborate production in May 1975 that moved to Broadway for a limited run five months later. In 1976, Joplin won a Pulitzer Prize, confirming the restoration of his place in American musical history.

WORKS: SONGS: "Please Say You Will" (copyright Feb. 20, 1895); "A Picture of Her Face" (July 3, 1895); "I Am Thinking of My Pickaninny Days" (April 9, 1902; lyrics by Henry Jackson); "Little Black Baby" (Oct. 7, 1903; lyrics by Louise Armstrong Bristol); "Sarah Dear" (Aug. 11, 1905; lyrics by Henry Jackson); "Snoring Sampson" (May 6, 1907; lyrics by Harry La Mertha); "When Your Hair Is Like the Snow" (May 18, 1907; lyrics by Owen Spendthrift). **PIANO:** "The Crush Collision March" (Oct. 15, 1896); "Harmony Club Waltz" (Nov. 16, 1896); "Combination March" (Nov. 16, 1896); "Original Rags" (March 15, 1899); "Maple Leaf Rag" (Sept. 18, 1899); "Swipesy Cake Walk" (July 21, 1900; with Arthur Marshall); "Sun Flower Slow Drag" (March 18, 1901; with Scott Hayden); "Peacherine Rag" (March 18, 1901); "Augustan Club Waltz" (March 25, 1901); "The Easy Winners" (Oct. 10, 1901); "Cleopha" (May 19, 1902); "March Majestic" (1902); "The Strenuous Life" (1902); "A Breeze from Alabama" (Dec. 29, 1902); "Elite Syncopations" (Dec. 29, 1902); "The Entertainer" (Dec. 29, 1902); "Something Doing" (Jan. 10, 1903; with Hayden); "Weeping Willow" (June 6, 1903); "Palm Leaf Rag" (Nov. 14, 1903); "The Favorite" (June 23, 1904); "The Sycamore" (July 18, 1904); "The Cascades"

(Aug. 22, 1904); "The Chrysanthemum" (Aug. 22, 1904); "The Rose-bud March" (1905); "Bethena" (March 6, 1905); "Binks' Waltz" (Aug. 11, 1905); "Leola" (Dec. 18, 1905); "Eugenia" (Feb. 26, 1906); "Antoinette" (Dec. 12, 1906); "Heliotrope Bouquet" (Dec. 23, 1907; with Louis Chauvin); "The Nonpareil" (April 1907); "Searchlight Rag" (Aug. 12, 1907); "Gladiolus Rag" (Sept. 4, 1907); "Lily Queen" (Nov. 7, 1907; with Marshall); "Rose Leaf Rag" (Nov. 15, 1907); "Fig Leaf Rag" (Feb. 24, 1908); "Sugar Cane" (April 21, 1908); "Pine Apple Rag" (Oct. 12, 1908); "Wall Street Rag" (Feb. 23, 1909); "Solace" (April 28, 1909); "Pleasant Moments" (May 11, 1909); "Country Club" (May 11, 1909); "Euphonic Sounds" (Oct. 28, 1909); "Paragon Rag" (Oct. 29, 1909); "Stoptime Rag" (Jan. 4, 1910); "Felicity Rag" (July 27, 1911; with Hayden); "Scott Joplin's New Rag" (May 1, 1912); "Kismet Rag" (Feb. 21, 1913; with Hayden); "Magnetic Rag" (July 21, 1914); "Reflection Rag (Syncopated Musings)" (Dec. 4, 1917). **BALLET**: *The Ragtime Dance* (Dec. 29, 1902). **OPERA**: *Treemonisha* (May 22, 1911).

DISC.: *The Entertainer: Classic Ragtime from Rare Piano Rolls* (1992); *Ragtime: Original Piano Rolls 1896–1917* (1995); *The Original Piano Rolls 1899–1916* (1995).

BIBL.: R. Blesh and H. Janis, *They All Played Ragtime* (N.Y., 1950, 4th ed., 1971); V. B. Lawrence, ed., *The Complete Works of S. J.* (N.Y., 1981); A. W. Reed, *The Life and Works of S. J.* (Ph.D. diss., Univ. of N.C., 1973); P. Gammond, *S. J. and the Ragtime Era* (N.Y., 1975); J. Haskins with K. Benson, *S. J.: The Man Who Made Ragtime* (N.Y., 1978); K. Preston, *S. J.* (N.Y., 1988); E. A. Berlin, *King of Ragtime: S. J. and His Era* (N.Y., 1994); S. Curtis, *Dancing to a Black Man's Tune: A Life of S. J.* (Columbia, Mo., 1994).—**WR**

Jora, Mihail, distinguished Romanian composer and pedagogue; b. Roman, Aug. 14, 1891; d. Bucharest, May 10, 1971. He received training in piano in Iaşi (1901–12), where he also studied theory at the Cons. (1909–11). After studies with Teichmüller (piano) and Krell and Reger (counterpoint and composition) at the Leipzig Cons. (1912–14), he completed his training with Schmitt in Paris (1919–20). Settling in Bucharest, he helped to organize the Soc. of Romanian Composers in 1920, serving as its vice-president. From 1939 to 1962 he was prof. of harmony, counterpoint, and composition at the Bucharest Cons. He was the author of *Momente muzicale* (Bucharest, 1968). Jora was notably influential as a teacher. In his compositions, he made effective use of Romanian folk music. He excelled as a composer of ballets and songs.

WORKS: DRAMATIC: B a l l e t : *La piaţă* (At the Market Place; 1928; Bucharest, March 17, 1932); *Demoazela Măriuţa* (1940; Bucharest, Oct. 5, 1942); *Curtea veche* (The Old Court; 1948); *Cînd strugurii se coc* (When the Grapes Ripen; 1953; Bucharest, 1954); *Întoarcerea din adîncuri* (Return to the Abyss; 1959; Bucharest, 1965); *Hanul Dulcinea* (The Inn Dulcinea; 1966; Bucharest, 1967). **ORCH.:** Suite (1914; Iaşi, Jan. 28, 1918); *Poveste indică* (Hindu Tale), symphonic poem (Bucharest, Dec. 15, 1920); *Privelişti moldoveneşti* (Moldavian Landscapes), suite (Bucharest, May 5, 1924); *Cortegiu* (1926; Bucharest, March 3, 1929; also for Piano, 1925); *Şase cîntece şio rumbă* (6 Songs and a Rumba; 1932); Sym. (Bucharest, Nov. 28, 1937); *Burlesca* (1949). **CHAMBER:** *Small Suite* for Violin and Piano (1917); 2 string quartets (1926, 1966); Viola Sonata (1951); Violin Sonata (1962). **P i a n o :** *Joujoux pour ma Dame* (1925); Sonata (1942); *Variations and Fugue on a Theme of Schumann* (1943); *Portraits and Jokes* (3 sets, 1948, 1959, 1963); *13 Preludes* (1960); Sonatina (1961).

VOCAL: *Baladă* for Baritone, Chorus, and Orch. (1955); choruses; numerous songs.—**NS/LK/DM**

Jordá, Enrique, Spanish-born American conductor and composer; b. San Sebastian, March 24, 1911. After training at the Colegio Católico Santa Maria in San Sebastian and at the Univ. of Madrid, he went to Paris to continue his education at the Sorbonne, and also was a student of Dupré (organ), Rühlmann (conducting), and Le Flem (composition). He conducted the Basque Ballet (1937–39), the Madrid Sym. Orch. (1940–45), and the Cape Town Sym. Orch. (1948–54). In 1952 he made his U.S. debut as a guest conductor with the San Francisco Sym. Orch., and then was its conductor from 1954 to 1963; later he was conductor of the Antwerp Phil. (1970–76) and the Euskadi Sym. Orch. in San Sebastian (1982–84). Among his compositions were ballets and choral pieces. He was the author of *El director de orquesta ante la partitura* (1969) and *De canciones, denzas y musicos del Pais Vasco* (1978).—**NS/LK/DM**

Jordan, Armin (Georg), Swiss conductor; b. Lucerne, April 9, 1932. He received his musical training in Lucerne and Geneva. After holding the post of first conductor at the Zürich Opera (1963–68), he was conductor in St. Gallen (1968–71) and at the Basel Opera (1968–89). From 1973 to 1985 he was music director of the Lausanne Chamber Orch., with which he toured the U.S. in 1983. From 1985 to 1997 he was chief conductor of l'Orchestre de la Suisse Romande in Geneva, while concurrently serving as principal guest conductor of the Ensemble Orchestral de Paris from 1986 to 1993. He conducted the soundtrack and also portrayed the role of Amfortas, with the vocal part dubbed in by Wolfgang Schöne, for the Syberberg film version of *Parsifal*. Jordan has appeared as a guest conductor with various opera houses and orchs., and has won particular distinction for his performances of the French repertoire. —**NS/LK/DM**

Jordan, Edward "Kidd", jazz saxophonist; b. Crowley, La., May 5, 1935. After graduating with a B.S. from Southern Univ., Baton Rouge, in 1955, he moved to New Orleans. He traveled frequently to Chicago, especially during summers, playing in blues and R&B bands. (He eventually earned an M.M. at Milliken Univ., Decatur, Ill., and did further study at Northwestern Univ., Evanston, Ill.) Jordan began teaching high school music in New Orleans in 1955 and at Southern Univ. in 1965. He has continued to be at the center of jazz education in New Orleans; he is an assistant professor of music and director of Bands and Jazz Studies at Southern Univ., and director of Heritage School, New Orleans Jazz & Heritage Foundation jazz education program. In 1970s, with Alvin Fielder, he co-founded the Improvisational Arts Quintet along with bassist London Branch, trumpeter Clyde Kerr, and saxophonist Alvin Thomas. In 1994, he formed a trio with Joel Futterman and Alvin Fielder, which is a current working unit. He has played with Ornette Coleman, Cannonball Adderley, Sun Ra, Muhal Richard Abrams, Edward Blackwell, Julius Hemphill, and David Murray. He has performed at many festivals including Sierra Leone, the Netherlands and Moers, Germany in 1982, France and Berlin in 1984, Rotterdam in 1988, the Chicago Jazz Festival in 1994, and others. He performed in the band for numerous touring Broadway musicals, and behind visiting artists such as Ray Charles, Lena Horne, Tony Bennett, Temptations, Aretha Franklin, Stevie Wonder, Four Tops, Liza Minnelli, and the O'Jays, sometimes as musical contractor for the band.

DISC.: IMPROVISATIONAL ARTS QUINTET: *No Compromise!* (1983); *The New New Orleans Music* (1988). JOEL FUTTERMAN—KIDD JORDAN QUARTET: *New Orleans Rising* (1997); *Nickelsdorf Konfrontation* (1996).—LP

Jordan, Irene, American soprano; b. Birmingham, Ala., April 25, 1919. She studied at Judson Coll. in Marion, Ala. (A.B., 1939) and with Clytie Mundy in N.Y. On Nov. 11, 1946, she made her Metropolitan Opera debut in N.Y. in the mezzo-soprano role of Mallika in *Lakmé*, and remained on its roster until 1948. After training as a soprano (1949–52), she sang opera in Chicago (1954), at the Metropolitan Opera (1957), and at the N.Y.C. Opera (1957); she also appeared as a soloist with various American orchs. Among his admired roles were Donna Elvira, the Queen of the Night, Leonore, Lady Macbeth, and Aida.—NS/LK/DM

Jordan, Louis (Thomas), American singer, saxophonist, and bandleader; b. Brinkley, Ark., July 8, 1908; d. Los Angeles, Feb. 4, 1975. Jordan was the most successful R&B musician of the 1940s and had a tremendous influence on subsequent R&B and rock 'n' roll performers, including Ray Charles, Chuck Berry, B.B. King, Fats Domino, Bill Haley, Bo Diddley, Little Richard, and James Brown. Himself influenced by Fats Waller and Cab Calloway, Jordan evolved a rhythmic small-group style with his Tympany Five that was initially dubbed "jump blues." Many of his songs were novelties, and his performances usually had a comic edge. His hits included "Is You Is or Is You Ain't (My Baby)," "Choo Choo Ch' Boogie," and "Ain't Nobody Here but Us Chickens."

Jordan's parents were James Aaron and Adell Jordan; his father was a music teacher, a bandleader, and a musician with touring minstrel shows. When Louis was seven, his father began to tutor him in music, and he joined the town brass band at nine. As a teenager he played clarinet and saxophone in minstrel shows. In 1927 he moved to Little Rock and began playing in local bands. He also married for the first time, to a woman named Julia. After playing around Ark. for a few years, he moved to the North in 1932 and played in bands in Philadelphia and N.Y. He married dancer Ida Fields before obtaining a divorce from his first wife.

Jordan joined Chick Webb's Orch. in the summer of 1936. He stayed with Webb two years, then launched his own band at the Elks Rendezvous club in N.Y. in August 1938. He was signed to Decca Records and made his first recordings under his own name on Dec. 29, 1938, resulting in the 1939 single "Honey in the Bee Ball" (music and lyrics by Jordan)/"Barnacle Bill the Sailor" (music and lyrics by Carson Robinson and Frank

Luther), credited to The Louie Jordan Elks Rendezvous Band. By the time of his second Decca release, he had adopted the billing Louis Jordan and His Tympany Five. Jordan spent four years building his name as a recording and touring attraction. He divorced his second wife and married Felice Ernestine "Fleecie" Moore on March 2, 1943. They divorced in 1951.

Jordan's first hit on what were then called the race charts (the term *rhythm and blues*, or R&B, was coined later in the decade) came with the novelty tune "What's the Use of Getting Sober (When You Gonna Get Drunk Again)" (music and lyrics by B. Meyers), which went to #1 in January 1943. But his breakthrough success came with "Ration Blues" (music and lyrics by Jordan, Anthonio Cosey, and Collenane Clark), which topped the R&B charts in January 1944 and the country charts in February 1944, and became his first entry on the pop charts. "G. I. Jive" (music and lyrics by Johnny Mercer) topped the R&B charts in July and the pop charts in August, while its flip side, "Is You Is or Is You Ain't (My Baby)" (music and lyrics by Billy Austin and Jordan) also reached the Top Ten of the R&B and pop charts and went to #1 on the country charts in July. Bing Crosby and the Andrews Sisters released a cover version that also became a Top Ten pop hit, and the song was featured in several films over the next year, including the all-star *Follow the Boys*, in which Jordan performed it. As his fame increased, he also appeared in several low-budget movies during the 1940s, among them *Meet Miss Bobby Socks* (1944); *Swing Parade of 1946* (1946); *Beware* (1946); *Reet Petite and Gone* (1947); and *Look Out Sister* (1949), as well as many shorts and "soundies," which served as precursors to music videos.

Jordan dominated the R&B charts during the second half of the 1940s, scoring a series of #1 hits: "Mop! Mop!" (music and lyrics by Claude Demetrius and J. Mayo Williams; April 1945); "Caldonia" (music and lyrics credited to Jordan's wife, Fleecie Moore, for contractual reasons, though, like other songs credited to her, he actually wrote it; June 1945), also a pop Top Ten; "Buzz Me" (music and lyrics by Danny Baxter, a pseudonym for Dave Dexter, and Fleecie Moore; January 1946), also a pop Top Ten; "Don't Worry 'Bout That Mule" (music and lyrics by Jordan and Bill Davis; March 1946); with Ella Fitzgerald, "Stone Cold Dead in the Market (He Had It Coming)" (music and lyrics by Frederick Wilmoth Hendricks under his stage name, Wilmouth Houdini; July 1946), also a pop Top Ten; the two-million-selling "Choo Choo Ch' Boogie" (music and lyrics by Denver Darling, Vaughan Horton, and Milt Gabler; August 1946), also a pop Top Ten; "Ain't That Just Like a Woman (They'll Do It Every Time)" (music and lyrics by Fleecie Moore and Claude Demetrius; November 1946; "Ain't Nobody Here but Us Chickens" (music and lyrics by Alex Kramer and Joan Whitney; January 1947), also a pop Top Ten; "Texas and Pacific" (music and lyrics by Jack Wolf Fine and Joseph E. Hirsch; April 1947); "Jack, You're Dead" (music and lyrics by Dick Miles and Walter Bishop; June 1947); "Boogie Woogie Blue Plate" (music by Joe Bushkin, lyrics by John De Vries; August 1947); "Run Joe" (music and lyrics by Dr. Walter Merrick, Joe Willoughby, and Jordan; July 1948); "Beans and Corn Bread" (music and lyrics by Freddie Clark and Fleecie Moore; October 1949); and "Saturday Night Fish Fry" (music and lyrics by Ellis Walsh and Jordan; October 1949). Jordan also peaked in the R&B and pop Top Ten with "Open the Door, Richard!" (music by Jack McVea and Don Howell, lyrics by Clinton "Dusty" Fletcher and John Mason; March 1947) and "Baby, It's Cold Outside" (music and lyrics by Frank Loesser; July 1949), a duet with Ella Fitzgerald.

After scoring a final R&B #1, "Blue Light Boogie" (music and lyrics by Jessie Mae Robinson and Jordan), in September 1950, Jordan declined rapidly as a record seller, last reaching the R&B charts in May 1951. In the summer of 1951 he organized a big band that played through the end of the year, after which he reverted to The Tympany Five. He married his long-time traveling companion Florence (Vicki) Hayes Johnson on Nov. 14.

Jordan left Decca in 1954 and recorded for several labels without commercial success. After 1957, he no longer maintained The Tympany Five as a permanent touring band, instead contracting musicians for specific tours or working as a solo artist. After divorcing his fourth wife, he married dancer and singer Martha Weaver on June 14, 1966; she often performed with him. He toured regularly until October 1974, when he suffered a heart attack. A second heart attack killed him at age 66 in 1975. A theatrical revue based on his hits, *Five Guys Named Moe*, was mounted in England in 1990, winning the Olivier Award for best musical; it opened on Broadway on April 8, 1992, where it played 445 performances.

DISC.: *Louis Jordan and His Tympany Five* (1944); *One Guy Named Louis* (1954); *Let the Good Times Roll* (1963); *Louis Jordan & His Orchestra* (1976); *The Best of Louis Jordan* (1977); *No Moe! Louis Jordan: The Greatest Hits* (1992); *Let The Good Times Roll: The Anthology 1938–1953* (1999); *Choo Choo Ch' Boogie* (1999); *Louis Jordan: 20th Century Masters: The Millennium Collection* (1999).

BIBL.: J. Lubin and D. Garçon, *L. J. Discographie* (Levallois-Perret, France, 1987); J. Chilton, *Let the Good Times Roll: The Story of L. J. and His Music* (London, 1992).—**WR**

Jordan, Marlon, American trumpeter; b. New Orleans, La., Aug. 21, 1970. He is the youngest of seven children of Edward "Kidd" and Edvidge Jordan, grew up in a musical household. His father, a saxophonist, is noted for his journeys into free-jazz, and three of Marlon's older siblings are music performers. Brother Kent plays flute, and introduced Marlon on his 1988 CBS album, *Essence*. Rachael plays violin with the New Orleans Symphony, and Stephanie is a vocalist. As a boy, he was accompanying his dad on the bandstand even before he really knew how to play. After experimenting with saxophone, violin, and drums, he finally settled on trumpet when he was in elementary school. Like the nearly decade-older Wynton Marsalis, he has performed classical concerts with orchestras from a young age. He spent two summers at Tanglewood performing in the Young Artists orchestra with Leonard Bernstein and Seiji Ozawa, and studied with Roger Voisin, principal trumpeter of the Boston Symphony, and with Ralph Smedzig, leader of the Empire Brass Quintet. He also studied with Marsalis in New Orleans,

with George Jansen (who also taught Marsalis) at Loyola School of Music in New Orleans, and with New Yorker trumpeter John Longo. He plays a Monette trumpet, the same horn Marsalis used to record *J-Mood*. Marsalis gave it to him as a Christmas gift and the younger trumpeter has used it to record all of his albums. Like many other New Orleans musicians of his generation, he has a mature, confident, easygoing interpersonal style that comes across in his music. He recorded three albums for Columbia. In the early 1990s, he switched recording labels from CBS to Arabesque, took six months to recover from a serious 1995 auto accident in New Orleans, had a second daughter, and moved his family from southern Ohio to hometown New Orleans, where he taught at a private school and performed festival and club dates.

DISC.: *For You Only* (1990); *Learson's Return* (1991); *The Undaunted* (1993); *Marlon's Mode* (1997).—**NAL**

Jordan, Steve (actually, **Stephen Philip**), jazz guitarist; b. N.Y., Jan.15, 1919; d. Alexandria, Va., Sept. 13, 1993. He studied with Allan Reuss. In 1939, he landed his first professional job with the Will Bradley–Ray McKinley Band for two years, then spent a year with Artie Shaw. From 1942–45, he was in the navy, serving in "Saxie" Dowell's Service Band. After WWII, he worked with a number of bands, including Glen Gray and the Casa Loma Band (1945–48), Stan Kenton (1948), and Boyd Raeburn (1949), and then worked on production staff at NBC for two years (1950–52). He played with Benny Goodman from summer 1954 until spring 1957. Jordan worked as tailor in N.Y. and Washington in late 1950s and early 1960s. In 1965, recommenced regular playing with group led by clarinettist/vibist Tom Gwaltney at the Blues Alley Club, in Washington, D.C. He worked in the club's house band in the 1970s. Late in life, he returned to the stage for a concert tour of Japan in 1992. He died of heart failure at his home.—**JC/LP**

Jordan, Sverre, Norwegian pianist, conductor, and composer; b. Bergen, May 25, 1889; d. there, Jan. 10, 1972. He studied piano in Bergen, then took courses in piano and composition with Da Motta, Ansorge, Klatte, and Gortatowski in Berlin (1907–14). He made his debut as a pianist in Bergen (1911). He was music critic of the *Morgenavisen* there (1917–31), and also conducted the Bergen Harmonien choir (1922–32) and was director of Den Nasjonale Scene, Bergen's major theater (1931–57). In his works, he made liberal use of national folk songs, which met the tastes of the general public. Typical of these nationally oriented works are *Suite in Old Style* for Small Orch. (1911), *Norvegiani* for Orch. (1921), *Smeden* (The Smith) for Baritone, Chorus, and Orch. (1924), *Norge i vare hjerter*, cantata for the opening of the Bergen Exhibition (1928), *Suite on Norwegian Folk Tunes* and Dances for Orch. (1936), *Holberg-silhuetter* for Orch. (1938), *Norwegian Rhapsody* for Orch. (1950), *Suite in Old Style on Holberg Themes* for Orch. (1954), *Concerto romantico* for Horn and Orch. (1956), and *Kongen* (The King), orch. melodrama with narration and choral finale (1957). Other works are a Piano Concerto (1945), Cello

Concerto (1947), *Concerto piccolo* for Piano and Orch. (1963), Violin Concerto (1966), two violin sonatas (1917, 1943), two piano trios (1958, 1963), Piano Sonata (1963), incidental music for plays, and over 200 songs, often with orch. accompaniment.—NS/LK/DM

Jørgensen, Erik, Danish composer and teacher; b. Copenhagen, May 10, 1912. He received lessons in theory from Jeppesen, in organ from Rung-Keller, and in piano from Anders Rachlew. Following training in composition with Høffding at the Copenhagen Cons. (from 1931), he took a course in conducting with Scherchen in Geneva (1936). From 1947 to 1982 he taught at the Copenhagen Inst. for the Blind. In his music, Jørgensen developed a personal style that utilized 12-tone procedures and aleatory.

WORKS: DRAMATIC: *Skyggen af en drøm* (Shadow of a Dream), chamber opera (1969); *Eventyret* (Fairytale), madrigal comedy (1973–74). ORCH.: Concerto grosso for Flute, Clarinet, Bassoon, and Strings (1933–34); Concerto for Violin, Strings, and Piano (1935); *Modello per archi* for Strings (1957); *Notturno* for 24 Solo Instruments (1965–66); *Confrontations* (1967–68); *A Piece of Life*, sym. (1981); *Dialogue* for Oboe, Horn, and Small Orch. (1984). CHAMBER: *Introduction and Theme with Variations* for Flute, Violin, Cello, and Piano (1937); Concertino for Flute, Clarinet, Violin, and Piano (1937); *Rhapsody* for Violin and Piano (1939–40); Sonatine for Clarinet and Bassoon (1942); *Figue in Tempo* for Cello and Percussion (1960–61); Quintet for 2 Pianos, 2 Percussionists, and Double Bass (1962); *Astrolabium* for 11 Instruments (1964); Piece for String Quartet (1964–65); *Improvisations* for Wind Quintet (1971); *Stemninger og tilstande* for Flute, Violin, Cello, and Horn (1973); Recorder Quartet (1975); Percussion Quintet (1982); *Symbiose* for Violin and Cello (1987); *Dobbeltspil* for Double Bass and Piano (1988); *Music* for Harp (1988); Concerto for Percussion Trio (1990); *Pastorale* for Oboe d'Amore and Chamber Ensemble (1990). VOCAL: *Tre vekselsange* for Soprano, Tenor, and Chamber Orch. (1934); *Havet* for Chorus (1936); *Modello 2* for Soli, Chorus, and Ensemble (1963); *Fragmenter af Hojsangen* for Soprano and 7 Instruments (1978); *Ode to a Grecian Urn* for Chorus (1979–80); *3 Gurresange* for Chorus (1990); other choral pieces and solo songs.—NS/LK/DM

Jørgensen, Poul, Danish conductor; b. Copenhagen, Oct. 26, 1934. He was educated at the Univ. of Copenhagen and the Royal Danish Cons. of Music in Copenhagen. In 1961 he became a conductor at the Royal Theater in Copenhagen, and in 1966 he was appointed Royal Conductor. He was also active in Sweden as a conductor of the Radio Sym. Orch. in Stockholm. In his concert programs, he steadfastly cultivated symphonic works by Danish, Norwegian, Swedish, and Finnish composers.—NS/LK/DM

Jörn, Karl, Latvian tenor of German descent; b. Riga, Jan. 5, 1873; d. Denver, Dec. 19, 1947. He studied with Schütte-Harmsen, Jacobs, and Ress in Berlin. He made his operatic debut as Lyonel in Martha in Freiburg im Breisgau (1896), then sang in Zürich (1898–99) and Hamburg (1899–1902). He was a member of Berlin's Royal Opera (1902–08). On Jan. 22, 1909, he made his Metropolitan Opera debut in N.Y. as Walther von Stolz-

ing, remaining on its roster until 1914. After further appearances in Berlin (1914), he returned to the U.S. He toured with Gadski's German opera company (1929–31) and then taught voice in N.Y. and later in Denver, where he settled. He was best known for his Wagnerian roles.
—NS/LK/DM

Joseffy, Rafael, eminent Hungarian-American pianist and teacher; b. Hunfalu, July 3, 1852; d. N.Y., June 25, 1915. At the age of eight he began to study piano with a local teacher at Miskolcz, and later at Budapest. In 1866 he entered the Leipzig Cons., where his principal teacher was E. Wenzel, although he also had some lessons with Moscheles. From 1868 to 1870 he studied with Tausig in Berlin, and the summers of 1870 and 1871 he spent with Liszt in Weimar. He made his debut at Berlin in 1870; his excellent technique and tonal variety elicited much praise; his career was then securely launched. He made his American debut in 1879, playing at a sym. concert of Leopold Damrosch in N.Y., where he settled; he taught at the National Cons. (1888–1906). He gained appreciation in the U.S. both as a virtuoso and as a musician of fine interpretative qualities; his programs featured many works of Brahms at a time when Brahms was not yet recognized in America as a great master. As a pedagogue, Joseffy was eminently successful; many American concert pianists were his pupils. He edited a major edition of Chopin's works in 15 vols., and also publ. a *School of Advanced Piano Playing* (1902). He composed a number of piano pieces and made arrangements of works by Schumann, Bach, Boccherini, Gluck, and Delibes.—NS/LK/DM

Joselson, Tedd, American pianist; b. Antwerp (of American parents), Oct. 4, 1954. He studied piano with Adele Marcus at the Juilliard School of Music in N.Y. In 1974 he was a soloist with the Philadelphia Orch., then made a coast-to-coast recital tour of the U.S. in 1976–77 and subsequently appeared as soloist with many of the major orchs. His forte is Russian music, but he also has a natural affinity with the masters of the Classical period.—NS/LK/DM

Josephs, Wilfred, esteemed English composer; b. Newcastle upon Tyne, July 24, 1927. He studied music with Arthur Milner (1947) and took a degree in dental surgery in 1951 from the Univ. of Durham Sutherland Dental School, and then was an orthodontist in the British army. In 1954 he entered the Guildhall School of Music in London, where he studied with Alfred Nieman until 1956. He then had private lessons with Max Deutsch in Paris (1958–59). In 1956 he won the Cobbett Prize, in 1957 the Harriett Cohen Medal, and in 1963 the first City of Milan and La Scala international composition competition for his *Requiem* set to the Hebrew Kaddish. He was a visiting prof. at the Univ. of Wisc. in Milwaukee (1970), Roosevelt Univ. in Chicago (1972), and Ohio State Univ. (1992). In 1988 he became a musical consultant to the London International Film School. He developed an individualistic style based on dodecaphony but not without exploiting his mastery of melodic invention.

WORKS: DRAMATIC: *The Magic Being*, ballet (1961; Newcastle upon Tyne, May 31, 1963); *The Nottingham Captain*, music theater (Wellingborough, Sept. 11, 1962); *The King of the Coast*, children's musical (1962–67); *Pathelin*, theater piece (1963); *La Répétition de Phèdre*, ballet (Newcastle upon Tyne, June 22, 1964); *The Appointment*, television opera (1968); *A Child of the Universe*, theater piece (1971); *Through the Looking Glass and What Alice Found There*, children's opera (1977–78; Harrogate, Aug. 3, 1978); *Equus*, ballet (Baltimore, March 21, 1980); *Rebecca*, opera (1981–83; Leeds, Oct. 15, 1983); *Alice in Wonderland*, children's opera (1985–88); *Cyrano de Bergerac*, ballet (1990–91); also numerous film and television scores. **ORCH.:** *The Ants*, comedy overture (1955; BBC, Feb. 6, 1961); 10 syms.: No. 1 (London, Dec. 17, 1955; rev. 1957–58 and 1974–75), No. 2 (1963–64; Cheltenham, July 5, 1965), No. 3, *Philadelphia*, for Small Orch. (1967; London, April 15, 1969), No. 4 (1967–70; BBC, May 26, 1983), No. 5, *Pastoral* (1970–71; Kingston- upon-Hull, Nov. 25, 1971), No. 6 for Soprano, Baritone, Chorus, and Orch. (1974), No. 7, *Winter*, for Small Orch. (1976; Bournemouth, Dec. 14, 1978), No. 8, *The 4 Elements*, for Wind Orch. or Symphonic Band (1975–77; Harrogate, Aug. 13, 1977), No. 9, *Sinfonia Concertante*, for Small Orch. (1979–80; Warrington, Feb. 11, 1981), and No. 10, *Circadian Rhythms* (Norwich, Oct. 19, 1985); *Elegy* for Strings (London, May 25, 1957); *Concerto a Dodici* (1959; BBC, March 18, 1967); *A Tyneside Overture* (1960); *Concerto da Camera* for Violin and Strings (1959–60; Maastricht, Dec. 20, 1961); *Meditatio de Boernmundo* for Viola and Strings (1960–61; Birmingham, May 7, 1961); *Aelian Dances* (1961; BBC, Dec. 1, 1962); *Monkchester Dances* (1961); *Cantus natalis*, cello concerto (1961–62; BBC, Jan. 16, 1971); *Canzonas on a Theme of Rameau* for Strings (1965; London, Feb. 13, 1966); 2 piano concertos: No. 1 (1965; London, March 5, 1967) and No. 2 (1971; Dudley, May 19, 1972); *Concerto for Light Orch.* (1966; Munich, Oct. 1, 1967); *Polemic* for Strings (Harrogate, Aug. 14, 1967); *Spirit of the Waltz* (1967); *Rail*, symphonic picture for Strings (Newcastle upon Tyne, June 15, 1967); Oboe Concerto (Hemel Hempstead, Sept. 25, 1967; rev. 1968); *Serenade* for Small Orch. (1968); *Variations on a Theme of Beethoven* (1969; N.Y., Jan. 23, 1970); Concerto for 2 Violins and String Orch. (London, Sept. 19, 1969); *The Last Last Post* (1971); *Saratoga Concerto* for Guitar, Harp, Harpsichord, and Chamber Orch. (1972; Manchester, April 16, 1978); Concerto for Brass Band (1972–73; Hanley, Aug. 9, 1974); *The 4 Horsemen of the Apocalypse*, overture (1973–74; Gloucester, Aug. 18, 1974); Clarinet Concerto (1975; Edinburgh, June 12, 1976); *Symphonic Poem Eve (d'après Rodin)* (1977–78); *Concerto d'Amore* for Violin(s) and Orch. (1979; 's-Hertogenbosch, Feb. 12, 1980); *Consort Music* (London, Dec. 21, 1980); Double Bass Concerto (1980; Chester, Aug. 1, 1981); *The Brontës*, overture (1981; Halifax, May 1, 1982); *High Spirits*, overture (1981–82; Sevenoaks, April 2, 1983); Percussion Concerto (1982; London, Jan. 15, 1983); Concerto for Viola and Small Orch. (1983; Adelaide, Feb. 21, 1987); *The Heaving Bagpipe*, overture (1984); *Feu de joie* (London, June 18, 1984); *Caen Wood*, "celebratrory" overture (London, June 8, 1985); *Disconcerto* for Piano and Orch. (1985; Freiburg im Breisgau, May 25, 1986); *Festival Overture (on Brabant Themes)* (1987); *In the North—Hommage à Sibelius* (1990); *Wordless Song* for Strings (1990). **CHAMBER:** 4 string quartets: No. 1 (1954; London, Dec. 17, 1955), No. 2 (1957–58; Belgian Radio, Sept. 1959; rev. 1960), No. 3 (1971; Milwaukee, March 3, 1974), and No. 4 (1981; London, Sept. 8, 1982); *Siesta* for Violin and Piano (1955); Sonata for Solo Violin (1957); *Wry Rumba* for Wind Quintet (1957–60); *An Old English Suite* for 5 Clarinets and Basset Horn (1961); *Requiescant pro defunctis fundaeis*, string quintet (1961; London, Sept. 24, 1965); *Chacony* (1962–63; N.Y.,

Oct. 23, 1963); Octet (1964; London, March 18, 1966); 3 violin sonatas: No. 1 (N.Y., Oct. 22, 1965), No. 2 (1975; BBC, Nov. 29, 1976), and No. 3 (1986–87); Trio for Flute, Violin, and Cello (1965–66; London, May 11, 1969); String Trio (1966; Birmingham, April 15, 1967); Sonata for Solo Cello (1970; BBC, Dec. 17, 1971); *Doubles* (1970–73); Trio for Horn, Violin, and Piano (Newport, Wales, Nov. 7, 1971); Piano Trio (1974; Newcastle upon Tyne, Feb. 21, 1979; rev. 1981); 2 sonatas for Brass Quintet: No. 1 (1974; Nottingham, Nov. 16, 1981) and No. 2 (1989); Piano Quintet (1974–76; Newcastle upon Tyne, Sept. 15, 1978); Flute Sonata (1976–77); Wind Quintet (London, March 5, 1978); Concerto for 4 Pianos and 6 Percussion (1978; Manchester, March 15, 1979); *Thoughts on a Spanish Guitar* (1979); Oboe Quartet (1979); Double Bass Sonata (1980); *8 Aphorisms* for Trombone Octet (1981; Bristol, July 26, 1982); *Arcadian Rhapsody* for Flute, String Trio, and Harp (Newcastle upon Tyne, Oct. 7, 1984); Clarinet Quinet (1984–85; Arundel, Sussex, Aug. 25, 1985); *Northumbrian Dances* for Soprano Saxophone and Piano (1986); *William's Fancye* for 5 Players (1986); Clarinet Sonata (1987–88); Oboe Sonata (1988); *Papageno Variations* for Wind Sextet (1989; Letchworth, Feb. 3, 1990). **KEYBOARD: Piano:** Sonata No. 2 (1963); *14 Studies* (1966); *29 Preludes* (1969); *Sonata Duo* for Piano Duet (1976); *Arabesques* (1985–88). **Organ:** *Fantasia on 3 Notes* (1978); *Tombeaux* (1980); *Testimony*, toccata (1981). **VOCAL:** *12 Letters*, "entertainment" for Narrator, Clarinet, String Trio, and Piano, after Belloc (1957; London, Jan. 19, 1964); Requiem for Bass, Baritone or Bass-Baritone, 2 Cellos, and Chorus (1962–63; Milan, Oct. 28, 1965); *Protégez-moi* for Children's or Women's Voices, Piano, Optional Recorders, Percussion, and School Orch. (1964; London, March 11, 1968); *Mortales* for Soloists and Choruses (1967–69; Cincinnati, May 23, 1970); *Adam and Eve*, "entertainment" for Narrator and Chamber Ensemble (1967–68; London, Feb. 4, 1968); *Nightmusic* for Voice and Orch. (1969–70; Liverpool, Oct. 23, 1974); *Aeroplanes and Angels* for Chorus and Piano Duet, after Günter Grass (1977–78; London, April 12, 1978); *Tenebrae* for Chorus, Piano Duet, Optional Flute, Optional Percussion, and Strings (1989); *William and the Bomb* for Narrator and Orch. (Cardiff, Sept. 25, 1993); choruses; song cycles; solo songs.—NS/LK/DM

Josephson, Jacob Axel, Swedish conductor, organist, teacher, and composer; b. Stockholm, March 27, 1818; d. Uppsala, March 29, 1880. He studied at the Univ. of Uppsala, and in 1844 he went to Germany, where he studied with Hauptmann and Gade in Leipzig. After further study in Rome (1845–46), he returned to Uppsala as conductor of the Univ. orch. He was founder-conductor of the Filharmoniska Sallskäpet (1849) and also conducted the noted men's chorus Orphei Dränger (from 1854). He was organist at the Cathedral (from 1864) and taught music history at the Univ. (from 1864). He composed a Sym., choral works, and songs, and also publ. two vols. of sacred songs (*Zion*, monthly issues, 1867–70; *Sånger i Zion*, 1880).

BIBL.: K. Nyblom, *J.A. J.* (Stockholm, 1926).—NS/LK/DM

Josif, Enriko, Serbian composer and teacher; b. Belgrade, May 1, 1924. He studied theory with Milenko Živkovič at the Belgrade Academy of Music (1947–54) and later was a student of Petrassi at the Accademia di Santa Cecilia in Rome (1961–62). He was a prof. of composition at the Belgrade Academy of Music from 1957.

WORKS: DRAMATIC: B a l l e t : *Ptico, ne sklapaj svoja krila* (Bird, Don't Break Your Wings; Belgrade, Oct. 7, 1970). **ORCH.:** Sinfonietta (1954); *Sonata antica* (1955); *Lyrical Symphony* (1956); Piano Concerto (1959); *Symphony in One Movement* (1964; Belgrade, Jan. 24, 1966); *Sinfonietta di tre re* (1968). **CHAMBER:** *Improvisations on a Folk Theme* for 14 Winds (1949); String Quartet (1953); *Dream Visions* for Flute, Harp, and Piano (1964); *Divertimento* for Wind Quintet (1964); *Epigram I* for Chamber Ensemble (1967) and *II* for Piano Trio (1967); *Chronicles* for Wind Quintet (1971); *Vatrenja* for Piano Trio (1972); piano pieces. **VOCAL:** *Oratorio profano da camera* for Narrator, Soprano, Celesta, Piano, and Percussion (1956); *The Death of Stefan of Decane*, chamber motets for Narrator, Soloists, Chorus, and 16 Instruments (1956; enl. and orchestrated as a dramatic epic, Belgrade, Oct. 7, 1970); *Rustikon*, cantata (1962). —NS/LK/DM

Josquin des Prez
See **Des Prez, Josquin**

Josten, Werner (Erich), German-born American conductor, teacher, and composer; b. Elberfeld, June 12, 1885; d. N.Y., Feb. 6, 1963. He studied with Siegel in Munich, then with Jaques-Dalcroze in Geneva. He later was made asst. conductor at the Bavarian State Opera in Munich (1918). In 1920 he went to the U.S., and became a naturalized American citizen in 1933. He taught at Smith Coll. in Northampton, Mass. (1923–49) and also conducted its orch. His compositions are couched in the lyrical manner of German Romantic music, with a strong undercurrent of euphonious counterpoint within the network of luscious harmonies. During his American period, he became interested in exotic art, and introduced impressionistic devices in his works.

WORKS: DRAMATIC: B a l l e t : *Batouala* (1930–31; symphonic suite as *Suite nègre*, Northampton, Mass., Nov. 10, 1963); *Joseph and His Brethren* (1932; N.Y., March 9, 1936; symphonic suite, Philadelphia, May 15, 1939); *Endymion* (1933; symphonic suite, N.Y., Oct. 28, 1936). **ORCH.:** *Concerto sacro I-II* (1925; N.Y., March 27, 1929); *Jungle*, symphonic movement inspired by Henri Rousseau's painting *Forêt exotique* (1928; Boston, Oct. 25, 1929); Serenade for Small Orch. (1934); 2 syms.: No. 1 for Strings (1935; Saratoga Springs, N.Y., Sept. 3, 1946) and No. 2 (Boston, Nov. 13, 1936); *Rhapsody* for Violin and Orch. (1959). **CHAMBER:** String Quartet (1934); Violin Sonata (1936); Sonata for Violin, Cello, and Piano (1938); Cello Sonata (1938); Concertante for 4 Bassoons (1939; also for 4 Cellos, 1941); Violin Sonatina (1940); Trio for Flute, Clarinet, and Bassoon (1941); Trio for Violin, Viola, and Cello (1942); Trio for Flute, Cello, and Piano (1943); Horn Sonata (1944); *Canzona seria* for Flute, Oboe, Clarinet, Bassoon, and Piano (N.Y., Nov. 23, 1957); piano pieces, including a sonata (1937). **VOCAL:** *Crucifixion* for Chorus (1915); *3 Songs* for Tenor and Orch. (1918–29); *Hymnus to the Quene of Paradys* for Chorus (1922); *Ode for St. Cecilia's Day* for Chorus (1925); *Fragments from the Brome Play "Abraham and Isaac"* for Solo Voices, Chorus, and Orch. (1926). **BIBL.:** W. J., *1885–1963. A Summary of His Compositions with Press Reviews* (N.Y., 1964).—NS/LK/DM

Joteyko, Tadeusz, Polish conductor and composer; b. Poczujki, near Kiev, April 1, 1872; d. Cieszyn, Silesia, Aug. 19, 1932. He studied at the Brussels Cons.

with Jacobs (cello) and Gevaert (composition) and with Noskowski (composition) and Cinke (cello) at the Warsaw Cons. He conducted the Warsaw Phil. (1914–18) and taught at the Warsaw Cons. He wrote the operas *Grajek* (The Player; Warsaw, Nov. 23, 1919), *Zygmunt August* (Warsaw, Aug. 29, 1925), and *Królowa Jadwiga* (Queen Jadwiga; Warsaw, Sept. 7, 1928), but is best remembered for his choral music. He also composed a Sym. (1895), chamber music, songs, and piano pieces. He publ. *Zasady muzyki* (Principles of Music; Warsaw, 1914) and *Historia muzyki polskiej i powszechnej w zarysie* (Warsaw, 1916).—NS/LK/DM

Joubert, John (Pierre Herman), distinguished South African- born English composer and teacher; b. Cape Town, March 20, 1927. He studied at the Diocesan Coll. in Rondebosch (1934–44) and at the South African Coll. of Music in Cape Town (graduated, 1944). He also received private instruction in composition from William Henry Bell in Cape Town. In 1945 he was awarded a Performing Right Soc. Scholarship from the Univ. of Cape Town Music Faculty to the Royal Academy of Music in London, where he was a student of Theodore Holland, Howard Ferguson, and Alan Bush (B.Mus., 1950). In 1949 he won the Royal Phil. Soc. Prize. In 1950 he became a lecturer at the Univ. of Hull, and in 1962 a senior lecturer at the Univ. of Birmingham, where he later served as a reader in music. He retired in 1986 but returned in 1997 as a senior research fellow. In 1991 he was awarded an honorary D.Mus. from the Univ. of Durham. Joubert's works, in whatever genre, are marked by a mastery of form, technique, melodic invention, and lyricism.

WORKS: DRAMATIC: *Legend of Princess Vlei*, ballet (Cape Town, Feb. 21, 1952); *Antigone*, radio opera (BBC, London, July 21, 1954); *In the Drought*, opera (1955; Johannesburg, Oct. 26, 1956); *Silas Marner*, opera after George Eliot (Cape Town, May 20, 1961); *The Quarry*, opera for young players (1964; London, March 25, 1965); *Under Western Eyes*, opera after Joseph Conrad (1968; London, May 20, 1969); *The Prisoner*, school opera (London, March 14, 1973); *The Wayfarers*, opera for young people (1983; Huntington, April 4, 1984); *Jane Eyre*, opera after Charlotte Brönte (1987–97). **ORCH.:** Overture (1951; Cheltenham, June 12, 1953); *Symphonic Prelude* (1953; Durban, May 15, 1954); Violin Concerto (York, June 17, 1954); 2 syms.: No. 1 (1955; Hull, April 12, 1956) and No. 2 (1970; London, March 24, 1971); Piano Concerto (1958; Manchester, Jan. 11, 1959); *A North Country Overture* (1958); *Sinfonietta* (Birmingham, April 1962); *In Memoriam 1820* (1962); Bassoon Concerto (1974; Carlisle, March 12, 1975); *Threnos* for Harpsichord and 12 Solo Strings (London, March 30, 1974); *Déploration* (Birmingham, Dec. 28, 1978); *Temps Perdu* for Strings (London, Oct. 1, 1984). **CHAMBER:** 4 string quartets: No. 1 (1950), No. 2 (1977; Birmingham, Feb. 18, 1978), No. 3 (1986; Birmingham, March 13, 1987), and No. 4, *Quartetto Classico* (1988; Birmingham, Oct. 19, 1989); Viola Sonata (1951); *Miniature String Quartet* (1953); Trio for Violin, Viola, and Cello (1958; Birmingham, Jan. 1960); Octet for Clarinet, Bassoon, Horn, String Quartet, and Double Bass (Hull, June 1961); *Sonata à cinque* for Recorder or Flute, 2 Violins, Harpsichord, and Cello (1963); Duo for Violin and Cello (London, Jan. 29, 1970); *Kontaktion* for Cello and Piano (Birmingham, Sept. 27, 1971); *Chamber Music* for Brass Quintet (Hereford, Aug. 22, 1985); Piano Trio (1986; Hereford, March 19, 1987); *Improvisation* for Treble Recorder and Piano (BBC, London, Oct. 21, 1988); *6 Miniatures after Kilvert* for Violin and Viola (Bleddfa, Powys, Aug. 23, 1997). **KEYBOARD: P i a n o:** *Divertimento* for Piano Duet (1950); *Dance Suite* (1956); 2 sonatas: No. 1 (1957) and No. 2 (1972; Birmingham, March 1, 1976). **O r g a n:** *Passacaglia and Fugue* (1961); *6 Short Preludes on English Hymn Tunes* (Peterborough, July 4, 1990); *Reflections on a Martyrdom* (Birmingham, Nov. 27, 1997). **VOCAL:** *Torches,* carol for Chorus and Organ or Orch. (1951); *The Burghers of Calais,* cantata for Soloists, Chorus, and Chamber Orch. (1953; Chelsea, March 1954); *Pro Pace,* 3 motets for Chorus (1955–59); *Urbs Beata,* cantata for Tenor, Baritone, Chorus, and Orch. (Cape Town, Nov. 1963); *The Choir Invisible,* choral sym. for Baritone, Chorus, and Orch. (Halifax, May 18, 1968); *The Martyrdom of St. Alban,* cantata for Speaker, Tenor, Bass, Chorus, and Chamber Orch. (1968; St. Alban's, June 1969); *6 Poems of Emily Brontë* for High Voice and Piano (1969); *Dialogue* for Soprano, Counter-tenor, Cello, and Harpsichord, after Andrew Marvell (1969; London, Jan. 1970); *African Sketchbook* for Chorus and Wind Quintet (London, April 1970); *The Raising of Lazarus,* oratorio for Mezzo-soprano, Tenor, Chorus, and Orch. (1970; Birmingham, Sept. 30, 1971); *3 Hymns to St. Oswald* for Chorus and Organ (Worcester, Aug. 29, 1972; rev. 1974); *5 Carols* for 5 Voices (London, Dec. 16, 1973); *Crabbed Age and Youth* for Counter-tenor, Recorder, Viola da Gamba, and Harpsichord (London, Nov. 9, 1974); *The Magus* for Tenor, 2 Baritones, Chorus, and Orch. (1976; Sheffield, Oct. 29, 1977); *Herefordshire Canticles* for Soprano, Baritone, Chorus, Boy's Chorus, and Orch. (Hereford, Aug. 23, 1979); *The Turning Wheel* for Soprano and Piano (1979; Dunedin, New Zealand, Oct. 1, 1980); *Gong-Tormented Sea,* choral sym. for Baritone, Chorus, and Orch. (1981; Birmingham, April 29, 1982); *The Phoenix and the Turtle* for 2 Sopranos, String Trio, and Harpsichord, after Shakespeare (Stratford-upon-Avon, Aug. 23, 1984); *The Hour Hand* for Soprano and Recorder (Birmingham, Sept. 1, 1984); *Magnificat and Nunc Dimittis* for Chorus and Organ (1984; Dundee, Oct. 20, 1985); *Rorate Coeli* for Chorus (Newcastle upon Tyne, Nov. 30, 1985); *South of the Line* for Soprano, Baritone, Chorus, Timpani, Percussion, and 2 Pianos (1985; Birmingham, March 1, 1986); *The Instant Moment* for Baritone and String Orch., after D.H. Lawrence (1986; Birmingham, March 21, 1987); *Tristia* for Soprano, Baritone, Clarinet, and Piano, after Mandelstam (1987; London, June 13, 1988); *Missa Brevis* for Soprano, Alto, Tenor, Bass, Chorus, and Chamber Orch. (Birmingham, Oct. 16, 1988); *For the Beauty of the Earth,* choral sym. for Soprano, Baritone, Chorus, and Orch. (Birmingham, Nov. 25, 1989); *Rochester Triptych* for Chorus and Organ, after John Wilmot, Earl of Rochester (1991–92; 1st complete perf., Prague, April 9, 1994; also for Chorus and Orch. 1996–97; Hereford, Aug. 19, 1997); *Landscapes,* song cycle for Soprano and Piano Trio (Cheltenham, Sept. 22, 1992); *The Secret Muse,* song cycle for Baritone, Flute, Clarinet, Harp, and String Quartet (Birmingham, Dec. 5, 1992); *3 Faces of Love,* chamber cantata for Soprano, Tenor, Baritone, Chamber Organ or Harpsichord, and Lute, after John Wilmot, Earl of Rochester (Oxford, April 25, 1997; also for Soprano, Tenor, Baritone, and Piano, Windsor, Sept. 24, 1997).—**NS/LK/DM**

Journet, Marcel, distinguished French bass; b. Grasse, Alpes Maritimes, July 25, 1867; d. Vittel, Sept. 5, 1933. He studied at the Paris Cons. with Obin and Seghettini. He made his operatic debut in *La Favorite* in Montpellier (1891), then sang at the Théâtre Royal de la Monnaie in Brussels (1894–1900). On July 10, 1897, he made his debut at London's Covent Garden as the Duke of Mendoza in d'Erlanger's *Inez Mendo.* He appeared

there regularly until 1907, and returned in 1927–28. He made his Metropolitan Opera debut in N.Y. on Dec. 22, 1900, as Ramfis, and remained on its roster until 1908. He then was a member of the Paris Opéra (1908–32), and also sang at the Chicago Grand Opera (1915–17; 1918–19) and at Milan's La Scala (1917; 1922–27), where he created the role of Simon Mago in Boito's *Nerone* (May 1, 1924). Among his finest roles were Hans Sachs, Gurnemanz, Wotan, Méphistophélès, Golaud, and Scarpia.—**NS/LK/DM**

Journey, the band that made "arena rock" a genre; f. 1973. **MEMBERSHIP:** Neal Schon, gtr. (b. San Mateo, Calif., Feb. 27, 1954); Ross Valory, bs. (b. San Francisco, 1950); Gregg Rolie, kybd. (b. June 17, 1947); Jonathan Cain, kybd.; Aynsley Dunbar, drm. (b. Liverpool, England, 1946); Steve Smith, drm. (b. Boston, Mass.); Steve Perry, voc. (b. Hanford, Calif., Jan. 22, 1953). Guitar prodigy Neal Schon had the mixed blessing of cutting his teeth as the second guitarist in Santana. This gave the teenaged musician a certain amount of credibility, but it didn't give him much opportunity to shine. Joined by former Steve Miller Band bassist Ross Valory and another former Santana sideman, Gregg Rolie (on keyboards), he put together a band with a fairly fluid lineup (Tubes drummer Prairie Prince passed through for a while, among others). The band was named Journey through a contest on KSAN, the San Francisco Bay Area progressive rock station. Signing with Santana's label, Columbia, the group recorded three albums of primarily instrumental rock with jazz overtones. As fusion lost favor with the progression of the 1970s, they took on vocalist Steve Perry for their fourth album, *Infinity.* The effect was immediate and direct. With rock radio singles "Lights" and "Wheel in the Sky," they captured a high gloss, radio ready sound that capitalized on Perry's overdubbed tenor (he often became a one man choir on record). The album rose to #21 and eventually sold three million copies. Their next album, *Evolution,* followed pretty consistently with *Infinity,* and gave the band the pop hit "Lovin', Touchin', Squeezin'." Once again, *Departure* followed neatly in the wake of the previous two albums, as the band developed both through radio and nearly constant touring. "Any Way You Want It" rose to #23 and the album became their third consecutive platinum success, rising to #8.

After *Departure,* Rolie made his departure from the band. The rest of the group had called him away from the restaurant he had started with his father to join the band, and he tired of the road and wanted to get back to a more settled life. Former Babys keyboard player Jonathan Cain joined the band, immediately making his mark by writing "Who's Crying Now" for the band's next album *Escape.* The song went to #4 and was followed by "Don't Stop Believing" at #9 and "Open Arms" at #2, kept out of the top slot for six weeks by Joan Jett's "I Love Rock and Roll." The #19 single "Still They Ride" finished the album at pop radio, but not before it rose to the top of the album charts. Eventually the album sold nine million copies. It even inspired a video game, *Journey-Escape.* Although that abum represented the peak of their career, they continued to be wildly successful. *Frontiers* went quintuple- platinum, spawning the #8 single "Separate Ways," the #12 hit "Faithfully," and two #23 charters, "After the Fall" and "Send Her My Love." Then the band took a recording hiatus, broken only by the #9 hit "Only the Young" from the soundtrack to the film *Vision Quest*. In the interim, Perry recorded his *Street Talk* album, which went to #12, bolstered by the #3 Journey-like hit "Oh Sherry." Schon, who had recorded a 1981 record with Jan Hammer, reunited with Hammer on *Here to Stay*. The band came back together for 1986's *Raised on Radio*. After the three-year break, they still managed to land a bunch of hit singles, including the #9 "Be Good to Yourself," two #17 songs, "Suzanne" and "Girl Can't Help It," and the #14 "I'll Be Alright without You." The album went double-platinum.

The group went on hiatus again, releasing a greatest-hits record that earned them a diamond record. Finally, the group petered out when Schon and Cain teamed up with the lead singer from Cain's old band The Babys to form Bad English, earning them something that eluded them with Journey: the #1 single "When I See You Smile." Valory managed to draw Rolie out of retirement again for a brief stay in the band Storm. Perry made another solo album, *For the Love of Strange Medicine*, which went to #15 on the strength of the #6 hit "You Better Wait." In 1996, the group came back together to record *Trial by Fire*. The album entered the charts at #3 and went platinum on the strength of the band's only gold single, the #1 adult contemporary hit "When You Love a Woman." However, friction soon arose because Perry, who had severe arthritis in his leg and hip, would no longer perform. Eventually Cain and Schon met with him and they agreed that he should leave the band. Steve Augeri took his place, and the group recorded a track for the soundtrack to the movie *Armageddon*.

DISC.: *Journey* (1975); *Look into the Future* (1976); *Next* (1977); *Infinity* (1978); *Evolution* (1979); *In the Beginning* (1979); *Departure* (1980); *Captured* (1981); *Escape* (1981); *Frontiers* (1983); *Dream after Dream* (1985); *Raised on Radio* (1986); *Trial by Fire* (1996). **STEVE PERRY:** *Street Talk* (1984); *For the Love of Strange Medicine* (1994). **NEAL SCHON:** *Late Nite* (1989); *Beyond the Thunder* (1995); *Electric World* (1997); *Piranha Blues* (1999); *Untold Passions* (with Jan Hammer; 1981); *Here to Stay* (with Jan Hammer; 1983). **JONATHAN CAIN:** *Back to Innocence* (1994); *Piano with a View* (1995); *Body Language* (1997); *For a Lifetime* (1998).—**HB**

Jovernardi, Bartolomé, Italian harpist and music theorist; b. Rome, c. 1600; d. Madrid, July 22, 1668. He studied mathematics, law, and music in Rome. In 1632 he went to Barcelona, and in 1633 he became harpist of the royal chapel and in 1642 a musician of the Cámara Real. In 1655 he returned to Italy. Jovernardi was the inventor of a cross-strung chromatic harp and reputedly of a harpsichord capable of producing a crescendo. His treatise *Tratado de la mussica* (1634) deals with the classification of instruments.—**LK/DM**

Joy, Geneviève, French pianist; b. Bernaville, Oct. 4, 1919. She studied at the Paris Cons. with Yves Nat (piano) and Jean and Noël Gallon (theory), and received the Premier Prix in piano in 1941. In 1945 she married Henri Dutilleux. She specialized in modern music; gave numerous first performances of piano works by French composers, some of them written especially for her. —**NS/LK/DM**

Joy Division, the band that bridged the gap between punk and new wave; f. 1976, Manchester England. **MEMBERSHIP:** Ian Curtis, voc. (b. Macclesfield, England, July 15, 1956; d. there, May 18, 1980); Bernard Albrecht (ne Bernard Sumner), gtr. (b. Bernard Dicken, Jan. 4, 1956); Peter Hook, bs. (b. Salford, England, Feb. 13, 1956); Steven Morris, drm. (b. Macclesfield, England, Oct. 28, 1957). Like so many other British bands of the late 1970s, Joy Division came together in the wake of a Sex Pistols concert. Peter Hook and Bernard Dicken, students at the time, saw a Pistols 1976 gig and decided they could do that. Dicken already played the guitar, Hook bought a bass, and a friend tried his hand at drums. Ian Curtis had also attended the show, and answered an advertisement when the trio sought a singer. It turned out he already knew them from the clubs. Through early 1977, the band practiced and played their first show as Stiff Kittens. By their second show, they called themselves Warsaw, after the song "Warszawa" from David Bowie's *Low* album. They went through several drummers before settling on Stephen Morris, again through a musician-wanted ad. The band developed a sound startlingly different from the punks, with Hook's echoed bass dominating the mix and Dicken's (who changed his name to Albrecht) guitar used largely to enhance the usually gloomy atmospherics, which reflected Curtis's baritone musings on death and disaster. Warsaw appeared on the compilation *Live at the Short Circuit* in the fall of 1977. Shortly afterwards, they released their own EP, *An Ideal for Living*. However, a London based band called Warsaw Pakt put out a major label album at the same time. To avoid confusion, the group changed its name to Joy Division, after the women kept in concentration camps during WWII for the "amusement" of Nazi soldiers. The group debuted under that name in January of 1978. By May, they were in the studio to cut an album, but one of the producers saw fit to add synthesizers to sweeten the music. The band refused to let them release it (it came out years later as *The Warsaw Album*).

The band frequently played at a venue called The Factory in Manchester. When the owners formed a label, they signed the band. By December, they had cut two songs for a sampler, "Digital" and "Glass." The sampler sold out in two months. During their first gig in London to promote the record, Curtis had a seizure on stage at the Hope and Anchor; he was diagnosed with epilepsy. The group released their debut album, *Unknown Pleasures*, which sold only as well as Factory could deliver the records—they were a very small independent label. The band became a critic's darling, but Factory didn't have the wherewithal to promote them properly. With his moody voice and demeanor, however, Curtis was beginning to attract both musical and popular attention. Women who followed the band became attached to Curtis, who was already married. Late in 1979, the band introduced the song "Love Will Tear Us Apart," a possible reaction to that situation.

While Curtis's health and marriage continued to deteriorate, the band recorded their sophomore effort, *Closer*. Even more dire than their debut, the album sounds like an extended suicide note, and is brilliant for it. Early in April of 1980, they played four shows in three days, which culminated in Curtis having a massive seizure. Several days later, he OD'd. The band took some time off, and canceled all their performances before they were set to make their American debut in May. The only date they had to keep was a date to film a video for their forthcoming single of "Love Will Tear Us Apart" and a show at Birmingham Univ. On May 18, Curtis hanged himself. The album came out and climbed into the U.K. Top Ten, while "Love Will Tear Us Apart" rose to #13.

Albrecht (now known as Bernard Sumner), Hook, Morris, and Morris's girlfriend, Gillian Gilbert, started playing shows that summer as New Order. With the rhythm section in charge, they built up the beat around Hook's bass and accentuated their dance rhythms, though their debut EP, *Movement*, sounds like a less charismatic version of Joy Division. Nonetheless, they scored the first in their string of dance hits with "Everything's Gone Green." They followed this in 1992 with "Temptation." In 1993 they released "Blue Monday," one of the best selling British singles ever, which went to #5 on the U.S. dance charts and is reputed to have sold three million copies worldwide, though the album *Power, Corruption and Lies* remained an underground hit in the U.S. Later that year, they teamed up with pioneering hip-hop producer Arthur Baker for "Confusion," which skimmed the bottom of the U.S. R&B charts. Their 1985 album, *Lowlife*, just broke the Top 100, while 1986's *Brotherhood* slipped a few notches below it, despite the underground hit "Bizarre Love Triangle." In 1987, however, they finally charted a single in the U.S: "True Faith" rose to #32, propelling the album *Substance* to #36 on the charts and platinum sales. Their follow-up album, *Technique*, charted even higher, rising to #32, but only went gold.

In 1988 the Joy Division compilation *Substance* came out, perhaps to remind people of New Order's roots. At that point, the band started looking for other projects. Sumner teamed with former Smiths guitarist Johnny Marr and Pet Shop Boys vocalist Neil Tennant in the band Electronic. Their album didn't quite crack the Top 100, but they did skim the Top 40 with the single "Getting Away with It." Hook released *Revenge*, which barely made the Top 200 album charts. Morris and Gilbert took another tack, writing themes for British television shows. New Order reunited in 1993, and the album *Republic* did surprisingly well, topping out at #11, with their highest charting U.S. single, "Regret," hitting #28. In 1995, Factory folded; London Records bought their assets and re-released "Love Will Tear Us Apart," which went to the U.K. Top 20. *Permanent*, a new Joy Division compilation, also came out, followed in 1997 by a four-disc "complete" Joy Division box set, *Heart and Soul*.

Never more than an underground success in the U.S., Joy Division nonetheless influenced much of the pop music that followed in their wake, from the Goth movement to the purveyors of synthpop. Not only did their sound influence Goth groups nearly as much as groups like The Cure, but more mainstream artists recognized the brilliance, if not necessarily the soul, of the band's songs. Grace Jones's cover of *She's Lost Control* is out of left field, while Paul Young treated "Love Will Tear Us Apart" as a confection rather than a confession. A 1995 tribute album, *Means to an End*, fared better.

DISC.: *Unknown Pleasures* (1979); *Closer* (1980); *Still* (1981); *Preston Warehouse 28 February 1980* (1999). **NEW ORDER:** *Movement* (1981); *1981–1982* (EP; 1982); *Power, Corruption and Lies* (1983); *Low-life* (1985); *Brotherhood* (1986); *BBC Live Windsong* (1987); *Substance: The Singles 1980–1987* (1987); *Technique* (1989); *The Peel Sessions* (1990); *Republic* (1993); *Republic—The Limited Run* (1993); *(The Best of) New Order* (1995). **ELECTRONIC:** *Electronic* (1991). **REVENGE:** *One True Passion* (1990).

BIBL.: D. Curtis, *Touching from a Distance* (London, 1995). —HB

Jozzi, Giuseppe, Italian castrato soprano, harpsichordist, and composer; b. probably in Rome, c. 1710; d. probably in Amsterdam, c. 1770. He sang in various theaters in Rome (1729–40). After appearances in Venice, Milan, and Bologna (1740–45), he sang in London at the Haymarket Theater. While in London, he appeared as a harpsichordist playing sonatas by Domenico Alberti, which he publ. under his own name. Walsh later publ. them under Alberti's name (1748). Jozzi sang in Stuttgart from 1750 to 1756. The Alberti sonatas were republ. in Amsterdam under Jozzi's name (1761, 1765). Jozzi's own sonatas are closely patterned after those of Alberti.—NS/LK/DM

Juanas, Antonio, composer who flourished in the late 18th and early 19th centuries. Although he spent much of his career in Mexico, he most likely was of Spanish birth. From about 1790 to 1816 he was maestro de capilla at the cathedral in Mexico City. In 1819 he settled in Spain. His notable output of Latin sacred works comprises over 200 compositions.—LK/DM

Juch, Emma (Antonia Joanna), noted American soprano; b. Vienna, July 4, 1863; d. N.Y., March 6, 1939. Born of Austrian-born American parents, she was taken at the age of four to the U.S., where she studied with her father and with Murio Celli in Detroit. She made her recital debut in N.Y.'s Chickering Hall (1881), then her stage debut as Philine in *Mignon* at London's Her Majesty's Theatre (1881); that same year she appeared at N.Y.'s Academy of Music. She was a leading member of the American (later National) Opera Co. (1884–89), subsequently touring the U.S., Canada, and Mexico with her own Emma Juch Grand Opera Co. (1889–91); she retired from the operatic stage upon her marriage (1894). She was a great advocate of opera in English. Her voice was admired for its extensive range, which enabled her to sing a wide repertoire. —NS/LK/DM

Juchelka, Miroslav, Czech composer; b. Velká Polom, March 29, 1922. He studied composition with

Řídký and Hlobil at the Prague Cons. (1939–43) and then with Albín Šíma at the Master School there (1943–47). He was music director of the Czech Radio in Prague (1953–78).

WORKS: ORCH.: *Symphonic Fantasy* (1952); Accordion Concerto (1954); *Burlesque* for Piano and Orch. (1958); Suite for Strings (1961); *Burlesque* for Clarinet and Promenade Orch. (1970); *From the Beskyds,* suite (1972); Clarinet Concerto (1974); Piano Concerto (1979); *Tarantela festiva* (1980). CHAMBER: *Miniatures* for Cello and Piano (1951); Suite for Nonet (1962); Clarinet Sonatina (1964); *5 Compositions for Due Boemi* for Bass Clarinet and Piano (1972); Violin Sonatina (1982).—NS/LK/DM

Judas Priest, the archetypal heavy metal band; f. 1969. MEMBERSHIP: Kenneth "KK" Downing, gtr. (b. West Midlands, England, Oct. 27, 1951); Ian Hill, bs. (b. West Midlands, England, Jan. 20, 1952); Rob Halford, voc. (b. Birmingham, England, Aug. 25, 1951); Glenn Tipton, gtr. (b. West Midlands, England, Oct. 25, 1949); John Hinch, Alan Moore, Simon Phillips, Les Binks, Dave Holland, Scott Travis, drms. Formed in Birmingham, England, Judas Priest took their name from the Bob Dylan song "The Ballad of Frankie Lee and Judas Priest." Beyond a cover of Joan Baez's musical recollection of her relationship with Dylan, "Diamonds and Rust," it was the closest they would come to the bard of Bleeker Street, or for that matter, ballads. By 1971, the band was gigging regularly through England with various vocalists and drummers. The group merged with another band called Hiroshima in 1973, taking on their drummer and singer, a theatrical lighting engineer named Rob Halford. In 1974, guitarist Glenn Tipton filled out the lineup. Together with Downing, Tipton created the pummeling dual guitar leads that, along with Halford's near castrato tenor, became the group's musical trademarks. They signed with a small U.K. company called Gull, releasing *Rocka Rolla* in 1974. Their road itinerary that year featured an appearance at the Reading Festival, which brought their music to a wider audience. They cut *Sad Wings of Destiny*, which earned good reviews, but didn't sell especially well. It did bring them to the attention of CBS Records, however, and the group signed with the worldwide major label in 1977. They went into the studio with former Deep Purple bassist Roger Glover, cutting *Sin after Sin*. The album captured the band's raw aggression, even in the aforementioned cover of "Diamonds and Rust." A year later, they put out *Stained Class*. When the band wasn't recording, they were on the road, though now their purview had expanded: they toured North America and Europe and were huge in Japan. Yet they had yet to have anything like a hit.

That began to change as the band celebrated its tenth anniversary with the release of *Hell Bent for Leather*. The single, "Take on the World," hit the British Top Ten, and the album scraped into the Top 100 in the U.S., selling three times as much as their previous work. They went on their first headlining tour, with all the bells and whistles and a Harley-Davidson motorcycle that Halford road onto the stage every night to thunderous applause. The album cracked the U.S. Top 50. This led to their breakthrough album, 1980's *British Steel*. A 30-city U.K. tour sold out three months in advance. The single

"Living after Midnight" became a U.K. Top Ten and a staple at U.S. album rock stations. The video for the next single, "Breaking the Law," fell into rotation at MTV. The album peaked at #34 in the U.S. and went platinum. This success continued with their next album, *Point of Entry*. This time, the video for "Heading out to the Highway" led radio and sent the album to #39 and gold status in the U.S. With *Screaming for Vengeance*, the band reached their popular and musical apex. The song "You've Got Another Thing Coming" remains their most popular on album rock. The tour sold out arenas, with a stage that included nearly 500 lights, many pyrotechnic effects, and hydraulic platforms that lifted the band. The album reached #17 and went platinum. The momentum continued with *Defenders of the Faith*, which reached #18 and went platinum. However, after 15 years of non-stop touring, the band took a year off to regroup and retool. What they came up with was *Turbo*, an album that reflected their heavy metal roots, but also paid tribute to the burgeoning new wave. The album featured guitar synthesizers. All but diehard fans saw this as a sell-out and the album tanked.

The band took little time making it up to the fans. Their live video and double live album, *Priest...Live!*, presented the band in all their leather and spectacle, with tunes from the heavy metal (as in gold and platinum) albums of the 1980s. The album went to #38. They continued the trend in 1988 with *Ram It Down*, which added a touch of thrash to the mix. It went to gold, topping out at #31. They continued the raw power approach with *Painkiller*. It also went gold and rose to #26. Before they could release another album, the band suffered two setbacks. Halford left the band to work on his own projects. Beyond that, the band found itself in court defending their music against charges that backwards masked messages had caused two fans to attempt suicide (one successfully). The case kept them in and out of court for three years, but they eventually won.

For their 20th anniversary with CBS, the band put out *Metal Works*, a collection of their favorite songs. In 1996, Tipton recorded his own solo album, assuring fans that it was just a side project. Then the group went about looking for a new singer to replace Halford. The singer was found in an unusual way. Tim Owens was brought to the band's attention when the band's current drummer's girlfriend caught him playing in a Judas Priest tribute band and videotaped the show. The group was suitably impressed and brought him over for an audition. Suddenly, the guy who was selling office supplies by day and singing in a Judas Priest tribute band by night was a member of the real thing! The group recorded *Jugulator* with Owens, nicknamed Ripper, and went on tour. After over 30 years, they may have slowed down the pace, but they haven't turned down the volume. As Tipton once put it, "We're all normal guys in Priest, but we become something special when we don the leather and go out there and play."

Judas Priest was arguably the first band to consciously play heavy metal. Though their leather and studs image might seem even quaint now, it was revolutionary and even shocking in its time. Their rotating drummer's throne and chauvinistic, band-centric personalities in interviews were the model for the mock-rock band Spinal Tap. However, over a quarter century in the trenches has earned Judas Priest a near rabid following.

DISC.: *Rocka Rolla* (1974); *Sad Wings of Destiny* (1976); *Sin after Sin* (1977); *Killing Machine* (1978); *Stained Class* (1978); *Unleashed in the East (Live in Japan)* (1979); *Hell Bent for Leather* (1979); *Hero, Hero* (1979); *British Steel* (1980); *Point of Entry* (1981); *Screaming for Vengeance* (1982); *Love Bites* (1984); *Sin after Sin/Stained Class* (1984); *Defenders of the Faith* (1984); *Judas Priest* (1986); *Turbo* (1986); *Priest...Live!* (1987); *Ram It Down* (1988); *Painkiller* (1990); *Beyond Metal* (1992); *Trouble Shooter* (1992); *Jugulator* (1997); *98 Live Meltdown* (1998).—**BH**

Judd, James, English conductor; b. Hertford, Oct. 30, 1949. He studied piano with Alfred Kitchin and conducting with Bernard Keefe at Trinity Coll. of Music in London (1967–71), then was active with the London Opera Centre. He subsequently was asst. conductor of the Cleveland Orch. (1973–75). He was co-founder and conductor of the Chamber Orch. of Europe in 1981, with which he toured in the U.S. in 1984–85. He also appeared widely as a guest conductor in England, on the Continent, and in the U.S. In 1987 he became music director of the Phil. Orch. of Fla. in Fort Lauderdale. He also was artistic director of the Greater Miami Opera (1993–98) and music director of the New Zealand Sym. Orch. in Wellington (from 1999).—**NS/LK/DM**

Judds, The, best-selling mother-daughter country duo of the 1980s; f. 1979. **MEMBERSHIP:** Wynonna Judd (Christina Claire Ciminella), gtr., voc. (b. Ashland, Ky., May 30, 1964); Naomi Judd (Diana Ellen Judd), voc. (b. Ashland, Ky., Jan. 11, 1946). The Judds were a popular mother-daughter duo in the 1980s. They came out of the new country movement, but became one of the most successful mainstream acts. Emulating the vocal harmonies of brother acts of the 1930s and 1940s, they scored many hits combining a repertoire of sexy uptempo numbers with ballads dripping with nostalgia for "the good old days." Oddly enough, Naomi hardly played the role of a country mother; her sex appeal was always much greater than her often dour-looking daughter, although Wynonna was musically the heart of the act.

Much has been made of the Judds's story, beginning with Wynonna's birth in rural Ky.; the family's move to Calif., where Naomi tried unsuccessfully to become a model; their return to Ky. and a "simple country life" in the mid-1970s, where Wynonna began to show her budding talent on the guitar; Wynonna's "wild teenage years" where only her music would soothe her; their discovery that they could relate to each other through their music; their relocation in 1979 to Nashville, where Naomi pursued a nursing degree while the duo recorded demo tapes on a $30.00 recorder purchased at K-Mart; and their final successful audition, performing The Blue Sky Boys's "The Sweetest Gift (A Mother's Smile)" for RCA executives, winning them a recording contract.

The first Judds recordings were very much in the mold of traditional country harmony singing, and the arrangements emphasized acoustic instruments without too much clutter. Their first #1 hit played off their mother-daughter relationship in "Mama He's Crazy." A string of hits came through the 1980s, including the sentimental "Grandpa (Tell Me 'Bout the Good Old Days)," the uptempo "Rockin' with the Rhythm of the Rain," through the anthemic "Love Can Build a Bridge," which showed the talents of Wynonna as a gutsy lead singer, tempered by her mother's sweet harmonies. As their career grew, their recordings became more heavily produced, and their act more elaborate, reflecting country music's tendencies to smother their best acts in glossy productions.

The Nashville music world was stunned by the announcement of Naomi's retirement from active performing, due to chronic hepatitis, in 1990; the duo undertook a year-long "farewell tour," culminating in a pay-per-view concert in the end of 1991. Wynonna came out from under her mother's shadow with her first solo LP, showing the influence of pop-rock singers, particularly Bonnie Raitt, on her style. However, without her mother on board to provide sex appeal, Wynonna has been put in the uncomfortable position of being gussied up by her handlers, who have even tried to give her a few dance steps, but she clearly remains most comfortable singing and playing the guitar without having to provide the "visual excitement" audiences seem to expect in this day of music videos. Wynonna has continued to release albums through the 1990s, although her later efforts have failed to garner much attention. Despite her "retirement," Naomi continues to show up at various Nashville events, looking none the worse for wear. She also gives inspirational talks (for a fee) to people facing illness. Mother and daughter reunited for a 1999 New Year's Eve concert, and also recorded four tracks together on a special "bonus EP" included with Wynonna's 2000 album, *New Day Dawning.*

DISC.: *The Judds* (1984); *Why Not Me* (1985); *Rockin' with the Rhythm* (1987); *Heart Land* (1988); *Christmas Time* (1988); *River of Time* (1990); *Love Can Build a Bridge* (1990); *In Concert* (1995); *The Judds Reunion Live* (2000). **WYNONNA JUDD:** *Wynonna* (1992); *Tell Me Why* (1993); *Revelations* (1996); *The Other Side* (1997); *New Day Dawning* (2000).

WRITINGS: N. Judd, *Love Can Build a Bridge* (N.Y., 1993).—**RC**

Judenkünig, Hans, German lutenist and composer; b. Schwäbisch Gmund, c. 1450; d. Vienna, 1526. He settled in Vienna, where he was associated with a fraternal order from 1518. Judenkünig was the foremost Viennese composer of lute music of his time. He publ. 2 valuable lutebooks with music in German tablature: *Utilis et compendiaria introductio* (Vienna, c. 1515–19) and *Ain schone kunstliche Underweisung...zu lernen auff der Lautten und Geygen* (Vienna, 1523; ed. by H. Mönkmeyer in *Die Tabulator,* X, 1970).

BIBL.: A. Koczirz, *Der Lautenist H. J.* (diss., Univ. of Vienna, 1903).—**LK/DM**

Judson, Arthur (Leon), influential American concert manager; b. Dayton, Ohio, Feb. 17, 1881; d. Rye,

N.Y., Jan. 28, 1975. He took violin lessons with Max Bendix and Leopold Lichtenberg in N.Y. He was dean of the music department at Denison Univ., Granville, Ohio (1900–1907), and subsequently was manager of the Philadelphia Orch. (1915–35) and the N.Y. Phil. (1922–56). He devoted much time to artist representation, organizing the Judson Radio Program Corp. (1926) in order to showcase his artists. He also organized Columbia Concerts Corp. (1932), which grew into one of the most powerful management agencies in the U.S.; it later became Columbia Artists Management, Inc. He later formed the Judson, O'Neill, Beall and Steinway (JOBS) Agency (1962), which was renamed Arthur Judson Management (1969). Upon his retirement in 1972, it became Harry Beall Management, Inc.—NS/LK/DM

Juhan, Alexander, American violinist, conductor, and composer, probably the son of **James Juhan;** b. Halifax, 1765; d. 1845. He was taken to Boston in 1768. He was a violinist in Philadelphia in 1783, and later went to Charleston, S.C., where he was active from 1790 to 1792, when he returned to Philadelphia. He composed six piano sonatas, of which 3 are accompanied by flute (or violin), as well as a book of 12 songs, with instrumental accompaniment.—NS/LK/DM

Juhan, James, French musician, probably the father of **Alexander Juhan.** He was active in Boston (1768–70), Charleston, S.C. (1771), and Philadelphia, where he exhibited the "great North American Forte Piano" (1786).—NS/LK/DM

Juilliard, Augustus D., American music patron; b. at sea during his parents' voyage from Burgundy to the U.S., April 19, 1836; d. N.Y., April 25, 1919. He was a prominent industrialist, and left the residue of his estate for the creation of the Juilliard Musical Foundation (1920). The Juilliard Graduate School was founded in 1924 and the Juilliard School of Music was organized in 1926. The latter's board then took control of the Juilliard Graduate School and the Inst. of Musical Art, which had been founded by Frank Damrosch and James Loeb in 1905. The two schools were merged as the Juilliard School of Music in 1946. After the expansion of its activities to include dance and drama, it was renamed the Juilliard School in 1968.—NS/LK/DM

Jullien, Gilles, French organist; b. c. 1650; d. Chartres, Sept. 14, 1703. He became organist at the Chartres Cathedral in 1667, and held this post until his death. His *Premier livre d'orgue* was publ. by Lesclop in Chartres (1680); a modern reprint, with annotations and an introduction by Norbert Dufourcq, was issued in Paris (1952).—NS/LK/DM

Jullien, (Jean-Lucien-) Adolphe, French writer on music; b. Paris, June 1, 1845; d. Chaintreauville, Seine-et-Marne, Aug. 30, 1932. He studied piano, violin, and voice, and then law in Paris, where he also studied harmony and counterpoint with Bienaime. He became a music journalist. He contributed to various magazines, and took a strong position in favor of the new music of Berlioz and Wagner.

WRITINGS: *L'Opéra en 1788* (1873); *La Musique et les philosophes au XVIIIe siècle* (1873); *La Comédie à la cour de Louis XVI, Le Théâtre de la reine à Trianon* (1873); *Histoire du théâtre de Mme. Pompadour, dit Théâtre des petits cabinets* (1874); *Les Spectateurs sur Le Théâtre* (1875); *Le Théâtre des demoiselles Verrières* (1875); *Les Grandes Nuits de Sceaux, Le Théâtre de la duchesse du Maine* (1876); *Un Potentat musical* (1876); *Weber à Paris* (1877); *Airs variés; Histoire, critique, biographie musicales et dramatiques* (1877); *La Cour et l'opéra sous Louis XVI; Marie-Antoinette et Sacchini; Salieri; Favart et Gluck* (1878); *Goethe et la musique* (1880); *L'Opéra secret au XVIIIe siècle* (1880); *Richard Wagner, sa vie et ses oeuvres* (1886; Eng. tr., Boston, 1892); *Hector Berlioz* (1888); *Musiciens d'Aujourd'hui* (1st series, 1891; 2nd series, 1894); *Musique* (1895); *Le Romantisme et l'éditeur Renduel* (1897); *Amours d'opéra au XVIIIe siècle* (1908); *Ernest Reyer* (1909).

BIBL.: F. Delhasse, *A. J.* (Paris, 1884).—NS/LK/DM

Jullien, Louis (George Maurice Adolphe Roch Albert Abel Antonio Alexandre Noé Jean Lucien Daniel Eugène Joseph-le-brun Joseph- Barême Thomas Thomas Thomas-Thomas Pierre Arbon Pierre-Maurel Barthélemi Artus Alphonse Bertrand Dieudonné Emanuel Josué Vincent Luc Michel Jules-de-la-plane Jules-Bazin Julio César), famous eccentric French conductor and composer; b. Sisteron, April 23, 1812; d. Paris, March 14, 1860. The son of a bandmaster, he went to Paris in 1833 and studied composition with Le Carpentier and Halévy, but could not maintain the discipline of learning music, and began to compose light dances instead; of these, the waltz *Rosita* attained enormous, though transitory, popularity in Paris. He left the Cons. in 1836 without taking a degree, and became engaged as conductor of dance music at the Jardin Turc. He also attempted to launch a musical journal, but an accumulation of carelessly contracted debts compelled him to leave France (1838). He went to London, where he conducted summer concerts at the Drury Lane Theatre (1840) and winter concerts with an enlarged ensemble of instrumentalists and singers (1841). He then opened a series of "society concerts," at which he presented large choral works, such as Rossini's *Stabat Mater,* as well as movements from Beethoven's syms. In 1847 he engaged Berlioz to conduct at the Drury Lane Theatre, which he had leased. He became insolvent in 1848, but attempted to recoup his fortune by organizing a "concert monstre" with 400 players, 3 choruses, and 3 military bands. He succeeded in giving 3 such concerts in London in 1849. He then essayed the composition of an opera, *Pietro il Grande,* which he produced at his own expense at Covent Garden, on Aug. 17, 1852. He used the pseudonym Roch Albert for his spectacular pieces, such as *Destruction of Pompeii;* publ. some dance music (*Royal Irish Quadrille,* etc.) under his own name. In 1853 he was engaged by P. T. Barnum for a series of concerts in the U.S. For his exhibition at the Crystal Palace in N.Y. (June 15, 1854), attended by a great crowd, he staged a simulated conflagration for his *Fireman's Quadrille.* Despite his eccentricities, however, Jullien possessed a true interest in musical progress. At his American concerts he made a point of including several works by American composers: *Santa Claus Symphony* by William Henry Fry and some chamber music by George Frederick Bristow. In 1854 he returned to London, where his managerial ventures resulted in another failure. In 1859 he went to Paris, but was promptly arrested for debt, and spent several weeks in prison. He died a few months later in an insane asylum to which he had been confined.

BIBL.: A. Carse, *The Life of J.: Adventurer, Showman-Conductor and Establisher of the Promenade Concerts in England* (Cambridge, 1951).—**NS/LK/DM**

Jumilhac, Dom Pierre-Benoit de, Benedictine monk and writer on Gregorian chant; b. Château St. Jean-de-Ligourre, near Limoges, 1611; d. St. Germain-des-Prés, March 21, 1682. He studied in Bordeaux. He became a novice of the Benedictine Order in the Congregation of St. Maur at St. Rémy in Rheims (1629); was professed there (1630). He was prior of St. Julien in Tours (1647–66), then retired to the Abbey in his birthplace. He publ. the erudite treatise *La Science et la pratique du plain-chant* (Paris, 1673; ed. by T. Nisard and A. Le Clerq, 1847).—**NS/LK/DM**

Junck, Benedetto, Italian composer; b. Turin, Aug. 21, 1852; d. San Vigilio, near Bergamo, Oct. 3, 1903. He studied harmony and counterpoint with Alberto Mazzucato and Antonio Bazzini at the Milan Cons. He was best known for his songs, including the cycle *La Simona* (1878) and the album *8 romanze* (1880). He also wrote a String Quartet (1886) and two violin sonatas (1884, 1885).—**NS/LK/DM**

Jung, Manfred, German tenor; b. Oberhausen, July 9, 1945. He studied with Hilde Wesselmann at the Essen Folkwangschule. After singing in the Bayreuth Festival chorus (1970–73), he made his operatic debut in Dortmund in 1974, and then sang in Kaiserslautern, Saarbrücken, and Karlsruhe. In 1977 he became a member of the Deutsche Oper am Rhein in Düsseldorf; made his debut at the Bayreuth Festival as Siegfried in *Götterdämmerung* (1977), and then appeared in the televised version of that role in the *Ring* cycle. He made his Metropolitan Opera debut in N.Y. in the title role of *Siegfried* on Sept. 24, 1981, and subsequently sang other Wagnerian roles there. He returned to the Bayreuth Festival in 1983 to sing Siegfried in the Solti-Hall production, commemorating the 100th anniversary of Wagner's death; also appeared in concert throughout Europe, North America, and the Far East.—**NS/LK/DM**

Junghänel, Konrad, distinguished German lutenist, conductor, and teacher; b. Gütersloh, Feb. 27, 1953. He studied at the Cologne Hochschule für Musik, where he became a member of its faculty in 1978. He soon established himself as a lute virtuoso via appearances as a recitalist, chamber player, and soloist with various leading early music ensembles. His engagements took him all over Europe, North and South America, Japan, and Africa. In 1987 he founded and became music director of the vocal ensemble Cantus Cölln, which has acquired notable distinction for its performances of music of the Italian and German Renaissance and Baroque eras. Junghänel was awarded the Deutscher Schallplattenpreis in 1985 for his recording of solo lute music of Sylvius Leopold Weiss. He has also won accolades for his performances of solo lute music of J. S. Bach. As a conductor, he has sought out works rarely performed and recorded.—**LK/DM**

Jungwirth, Manfred, Austrian bass; b. St. Pölten, June 4, 1919. He studied voice in St. Pölten, Vienna, Bucharest, Munich, and Berlin; entered the Univ. of Vienna to study medicine in 1937, but passed the examinations in voice, piano, and conducting instead (1940). He sang for German troops in Romania and Bulgaria (1941–45); made his operatic debut as Gounod's Méphistophélès at the Bucharest Opera (1942), and then sang at the Innsbruck Landestheater (1945–47). In 1948 he was awarded his Ph.D. in musicology in Vienna and also won first prize in the Geneva voice competition; then sang in Zürich, Berlin, Hamburg, Paris, and London; he made regular appearances at the Frankfurt am Main Opera (1960–67) and the Vienna State Opera (from 1967). On Feb. 16, 1974, he made his debut at the Metropolitan Opera in N.Y. as Baron Ochs, which became his most famous role.—**NS/LK/DM**

Junior Walker and The All Stars, Motown saxophonist. **MEMBERSHIP:** Junior Walker, sax., voc. (b. Autry DeWalt Jr., Blytheville, Ark., 1942; d. Battle Creek, Mich., Nov. 23, 1995); Willie Woods, gtr.; Vic Thomas, org.; James Graves, drm.

Autry DeWalt grew up in South Bend, Ind., where he took up saxophone in high school and played in local jazz and rhythm-and-blues clubs with bands such as The Jumping Jacks and The Stix Nix. Moving to Battle Creek, Mich., in the late 1950s, he formed Junior Walker and The All Stars in 1961 to play the local club circuit. The following year, the group was spotted by Johnny Bristol (half of the duo Johnny and Jack, who recorded the original version of "Someday We'll Be Together" in 1961). Bristol recommended the group to Harvey Fuqua, who signed them to his own Harvey label. Fuqua's labels Tri-Phi and Harvey were absorbed by Motown Records in 1963, and Junior Walker and The All Stars began recording for the subsidiary label Soul in 1964.

In early 1965, Junior Walker and The All Stars scored a top rhythm-and-blues and smash pop hit with Walker's classic "Shotgun." Following the uptempo "Do the Boomerang" and "Shake and Fingerpop" (moderate pop and major R&B hits), the group achieved hits with the instrumental "Cleo's Mood" and the Holland-Dozier-Holland classic "(I'm a) Roadrunner," a smash R&B and major pop hit. All these hits were contained on the group's debut album *Shotgun.* Subsequent hits included a cover of Marvin Gaye's smash 1965 pop and R&B hit "How Sweet It Is (To Be Loved by You)" and "Pucker Up Buttercup."

Home Cookin' yielded four hits with the title song, Holland-Dozier-Holland's "Come See about Me" (a top pop and smash rhythm-and-blues hit for The Supremes in 1965), "Hip City—Pt. 2," and "What Does It Take (To Win Your Love)," a smash pop and top R&B hit.

Subsequently working with Johnny Bristol as producer, Junior Walker and The All Stars scored smash rhythm-and-blues and major pop hits with a cover of The Guess Who's "These Eyes," "Gotta Hold on to This Feeling," and "Do You See My Love (For You Growing)."

Junior Walker and The All Stars continued to record for Soul Records with moderate success into the 1970s, scoring their last major rhythm-and-blues hit with the instrumental "Walk in the Night" in 1972. In 1976, Walker began recording solo for Soul Records, moving to Norman Whitfield's Whitfield Records in 1979. He provided the saxophone solo for Foreigner's 1981 smash pop hit "Urgent" and returned to Motown in 1983. Junior Walker and The All Stars toured into the 1990s. Junior Walker died in Battle Creek, Mich., of cancer on Nov. 23, 1995.

DISC.: JUNIOR WALKER AND THE ALL STARS: *Shotgun* (1965); *Soul Session* (1966); *Roadrunner* (1966); *Live!* (1967); *Home Cookin'* (1969); *What Does It Take to Win Your Love* (1970); *Live* (1970); *A Gasssss* (1970); *Rainbow Funk* (1971); *Moody Jr.* (1972); *Hot Shot* (1976); *Nothing but Soul: The Singles 1962–1983* (1994). **JUNIOR WALKER:** *Sax Appeal* (1976); *Whopper Bopper Show Stopper* (1976); *Smooth* (1978); *Back Street Boogie* (1979); *Blow the House Down* (1983); *Shake and Fingerpop* (1996).—**BH**

Juon, Paul (actually, **Pavel Fedorovich**), Russian composer of Swiss and German descent; b. Moscow, March 6, 1872; d. Vevey, Aug. 21, 1940. He was a pupil of Hřimaly (violin) and of Taneyev and Arensky (composition) at the Moscow Cons., then studied with Bargiel at the Berlin Hochschule für Musik (1894–95), where he won the Mendelssohn Prize; subsequently became a teacher (1906) and a prof. (1911) there. He was elected a member of the Prussian Academy of Arts in 1919; retired to Vevey in 1934. His works display pronounced Romantic inclinations.

WORKS: ORCH.: Sym. (1903); *Vaegtervise* (1906); *Aus einem Tagebuch*, suite (c. 1906); Chamber Sym. (1907); *Eine Serenadenmusik* (1909); 3 violin concertos (1909, 1913, 1931); *Episodes concertantes* for Piano Trio and Orch. (1912); *Mysterien*, symphonic poem for Cello and Orch. (1928); *Serenade* for Strings (1929); *Little Symphony* for Strings (1930); *Divertimento* for Strings (1933); *Anmut und Wurde*, suite (1937); *Rhapsodische Sinfonie* (1939); *Tanz-Capricen* (1941); *Burletta* for Violin and Orch. (1940); *Sinfonietta capricciosa* (1940). **CHAMBER:** 3 string quartets (1898, 1904, 1920); Piano Trios: No. 1 (1901), *Trio-Caprice* (1908), Trio (1915), *Litaniae* (1920; rev. 1929), *Legende* (1930), and *Suite* (1932); Sextet (1902); 2 piano quintets (1906, 1909); *Divertimento* for Wind Quintet and Piano (1913); Wind Quintet (1930); *Arabesken* for Oboe, Clarinet, and Bassoon (1941); various sonatas and piano pieces. **VOCAL:** *Psyche* for Tenor, Chorus, and Orch. (1906).—**NS/LK/DM**

Juozapaitis, Jurgis, Lithuanian composer; b. near Šiauliai, June 29, 1942. He studied with Juzeliunas at the Lithuanian State Cons. in Vilnius, graduating in 1968. His music is rooted in native folk modes, which are enhanced by a modernistic harmonic investiture and a rich employment of polyrhythmic percussion.

WORKS: DRAMATIC: Opera: *Sea Bird* (1976). **ORCH.:** Concerto for Organ, Strings, and Kettledrums (1970); *Vitrages*, symphonic poem (1971); *Rex*, sym. in memory of M.K.

Čiurlionis (1973); *Festive Poem* (1976); *Zodiacus*, sym. (1977). **CHAMBER:** Wind Quintet (1970); *Music* for Flute, Percussion, Piano, Viola, and Cello (1970); Concerto for 4 Percussionists (1971); Sonata for Solo Violin (1972); *Jūrate and Kastytis*, chamber sym. for Flute, Oboe, Viola, Cello, Piano, Percussion, and Electronic Tape (1974); *Diptych* for Wind Quintet (1977); 2 string quartets (1978, 1980); organ pieces. **VOCAL:** Songs; choruses.—**NS/LK/DM**

Jürgens, Fritz, German composer; b. Düsseldorf, April 22, 1888; killed in action in Champagne, Sept. 25, 1915. He studied music largely by himself, and wrote some fine lieder.—**NS/LK/DM**

Jürgens, Jürgen, German conductor and teacher; b. Frankfurt am Main, Oct. 5, 1925; d. Hamburg, Aug. 4, 1994. He studied with Kurt Thomas at the Frankfurt am Main Musisches Gymnasium and with Konrad Lechner at the Freiberg im Breisgau Staatliche Hochschule für Musik. In 1955 he became conductor of the Hamburg Monteverdi Choir, with which he toured throughout Europe, America, and the Far East. He became a lecturer (1960) and a prof. (1977) at the Univ. of Hamburg, and was made its music director in 1966. He edited works of Monteverdi and A. Scarlatti. As a conductor, he cultivated works of the Baroque period, while not neglecting modern music of a polyphonic nature.—**NS/LK/DM**

Jurgenson, Pyotr (Ivanovich), Russian music publisher; b. Reval, July 17, 1836; d. Moscow, Jan. 2, 1904. The youngest son of indigent parents, he learned the music trade with M. Bernard, owner of a music store in St. Petersburg. He served in three other music-selling houses there, before opening a business of his own in 1861, in Moscow. With a small investment, he gradually expanded his firm until it became one of the largest in Russia. Through N. Rubinstein he met the leading musicians of Russia, and had enough shrewdness of judgment to undertake the publication of works of Tchaikovsky, beginning with his op. 1. He became Tchaikovsky's close friend, and, while making a handsome profit out of his music, he demonstrated a generous regard for his welfare. He published full scores of Tchaikovsky's syms. and operas, as well as his songs and piano works. His voluminous correspondence with Tchaikovsky was published in a modern edition (2 vols., Moscow, 1938 and 1952). He also published many works by other Russian composers, and published the first Russian editions of the collected works of Chopin, Schumann, and Mendelssohn, and the scores of Wagner's operas. His catalog contained some 20,000 numbers. After his death, his sons Boris and Grigory Jurgenson succeeded to the business; it was nationalized after the Russian Revolution.—**NS/LK/DM**

Jurinac, Sena (actually, **Srebrenka**), famous Yugoslav soprano; b. Travnik, Oct. 24, 1921. She studied at the Zagreb Academy of Music, and also with Milka Kostrenńiń, making her operatic debut as the first Flower Maiden at the Zagreb Opera (1942); her first major role there was Mimi that same year. In 1945 she made her Vienna State Opera debut as Cherubino, and soon established herself as one of its outstanding members. She accompanied it on its visit to London's Covent Garden in 1947, where she sang Dorabella. That same year, she made her debut at the Salzburg Festival. She also appeared at the Glyndebourne Festivals (1949–56). She made her U.S. debut at the San Francisco Opera (1959); sang regularly at Covent Garden (1959–63; 1965; 1973). In 1953 she married **Sesto Bruscantini**. A distinguished interpreter of Mozart, she excelled as Fiordiligi, Cherubino, Pamina, and Donna Elvira, and later mastered the more demanding roles of Donna Anna and the Countess. She was also renowned for her portrayals of Octavian, the Composer, Elektra, and the Marschallin in the operas of Richard Strauss.

BIBL.: U. Tamussino, *S. J.* (Augsburg, 1971).—NS/LK/DM

Juris, Vic, American guitarist; b. Parsippany, N.J., 1953. Initially influenced by rock guitarist Chuck Berry, he first came to the notice of jazz fans by playing with saxophonist Eric Kloss. From there he went on to a stint with jazz-rock fusioneer Barry Miles before settling into an important role with saxophonist Richie Cole's fine late–1970s group. It was while playing for Cole that Juris got the chance to record under his own name, an opportunity that resulted in three albums for Muse Records (now out of print). Since his days with Cole, the guitarist has played a supporting role in organ groups led by Don Patterson, Wild Bill Davison, and Jimmy Smith in addition to working in Mel Tormé's backup band. His most recent long-term employer has been saxophonist Dave Liebman. He has also worked in tandem with some of the finest jazz guitarists of the 1980s and 1990s, including Larry Coryell and Birelli Lagrene. In the same vein, he took part in a 1997 concert with Coryell, David Fiuczynski, Russell Malone, and Jack Wilkins, called Five Guitars Play Mingus. In addition to his regular musicianly duties, Juris has worked the academic angle, teaching jazz improvisation and guitar at the New School (Mannes Coll.), Lehigh Univ., and William Patterson Univ.

DISC.: *Bireli Lagrene Ensemble Live featuring Vic Juris* (1986); *Night Tripper* (1995); *Music of Alec Wilder* (1996); *Pastels* (1996); *Moonscape* (1997).—GM

Jurjāns, Andrejs, Latvian composer; b. Erlaa, Sept. 30, 1856; d. Zehsis, Sept. 28, 1922. He studied organ with L. Homilius, horn with F. Homilius, and composition with Rimsky-Korsakov at the St. Petersburg Cons. (1875–82). He was a prof. at the Kharkov Cons. (1882–1916). He was active as a folklorist and publ. *Latvju tautas mūzikas materiāli* (Materials of Latvian Folk Music; Riga, 1894–1926). He composed a symphonic poem, a Cello Concerto, cantatas, choral songs, and chamber music; also made orch. arrangements of Latvian folk melodies, which he employed in his original works.

BIBL.: O. Grāvitis, *Jurgānu Andrejs* (Riga, 1953). —NS/LK/DM

Jurovský, Šimon, Slovak composer; b. Ulmanka, Feb. 8, 1912; d. Prague, Nov. 8, 1963. He attended the Bratislava Academy of Music (1931–36), then took courses in composition with Joseph Marx at the Vienna Academy of Music (1943–44). He was manager of the Bratislava Opera and director of the Slovak Folk Art Ensemble. In his music, he followed the broad tenets of national Romanticism, with frequent references to folk themes.

WORKS: DRAMATIC: O p e r a : *Dcery Abelovy* (The Daughters of Abel, 1961). **B a l l e t :** *Rytierska balada* (The Song of Chivalry; Bratislava, 1960). **O t h e r :** Much film music. **ORCH.:** 2 suites (1939, 1943); *Serenade* for Strings (1940); *Začatá cesta* (The Journey Begun), symphonic poem (1948); *Radostné súženie* (A Joyous Competition), symphonic scherzo (1949); 2 syms.: No. 1, *Mírová* (Peace), for Piano and Strings (1950), and No. 2, *Heroická* (Heroic), for Organ and Orch. (1960); Cello Concerto (1953); Concertino for Piano and Strings (1962). **CHAMBER:** Quartet for Winds (1936); *Melodies and Dialogues*, string quartet (1944); String Trio (1948); *Concert Dance* for Piano (1960). **VOCAL:** 3 *uspávanky* (Lullabies) for Soprano, Piano, Harp, and Strings (1947); choral pieces; folk song arrangements; songs.

BIBL.: Z. Bokesová, *Š. J.* (Bratislava, 1955).—NS/LK/DM

Just, Johann August, German keyboard player, violinist, and composer; b. Gröningen, c. 1750; d. probably in The Hague, Dec. 1791. He most likely was a student of Kirnberger in Berlin and of Schwindl in The Hague. In 1767 he became a court musician to William V, Prince of Orange and Nassau, in The Hague. He wrote three operas, a Violin Concerto, three harpsichord concertos, chamber music, and many keyboard pieces. —LK/DM

Juzeliūnas, Julius, Lithuanian composer; b. Čepole, Feb. 20, 1916. He studied with Gruodis at the Kaunas Cons. (graduated, 1948) and at the Leningrad Cons. with Voloshinov (graduated, 1952). Returning to Lithuania, he taught at the State Cons. in Vilnius (from 1952). His compositions follow the spirit of socialist realism, treating heroic themes in stage productions and romantic subjects in instrumental music; on occasion, he uses modern techniques, including dodecaphony.

WORKS: DRAMATIC: O p e r a : *Sukiléliai* (The Rebels; 1957; Vilnius, 1960); *Žaidimas* (The Game; 1968). **B a l l e t :** *Andromeda* (1982); *Lokis* (1997). **ORCH.:** 6 syms.: No. 1 (1948), No. 2 (1949), No. 3, *Žmogaus lyra* (Man's Lyre) for Baritone, Chorus, and Orch. (1965), No. 4, *Symphony for the Unknown Soldier* (1971–81), No. 5 (1974), and No. 6, *Hymn of the Plains*, for Women's Chorus and Strings (1982); *Heroic Poem* (1950); *African Sketches*, suite (1961); *Poem-Concerto* for Strings (1961); *Passacaglia-Poem* (1962); Concerto for Organ, Violin, and Strings (1963); *Concerto Grosso* for Strings, Wind Quintet, and Piano (1966); Concerto for Clarinet and Strings (1985; also for Clarinet and String Quartet); *Dionysia* (1992); *Wreath to Those Who've Left* (1992); *Contrast Music* for Violin and Orch. (1992); *Kaleidophony No. 3* for Strings (1995) and *No. 4* (1998). **CHAMBER:** 2 piano sonatas (1947, 1986); 4 string quartets (1962, 1966, 1969, 1980); Sonata for Oboe and Clarinet (1971); Violin Sonata (1972); Sonata for Solo Horn (1975); Sonata for Violin and Cello (1977); *Diptych* for Violin and Organ (1981); *Ragamalika* for Wind Quintet (1982); Sym. for Solo Organ (1984); *Flobo-Clavio*, quartet for Flute, Oboe, Harpsichord, and Cello (1987); *Kaleidophony No. 1* for Flute, Bass Clarinet, and Piano (1992). **P i a n o :** *Kaleidophony No. 2* (1994). **VOCAL:** Concerto for Tenor and Orch. (1955); *Pelenu lopšine* (Lullaby to the

Ashes), symphonic poem for Mezzo-soprano, Chorus, and Orch. (1963); *Melika*, sonata for Voice and Organ (1973); *Cantus magnificat*, sym.-oratorio for 2 Soloists, 2 Choruses, Organ, and Orch. (1979); *The Language of Flowers*, cantata for Soprano and String Orch. or Organ (1985).—**NS/LK/DM**

Jyrkiäinen, Reijo (Einari), Finnish composer; b. Suistamo, April 6, 1934. He studied composition with Fougstedt and Kokkonen at the Sibelius Academy in Helsinki (1956–63), theory at the Univ. of Helsinki (1958–63), and also attended modern music courses at Darmstadt (summers, 1962–63) and the electronic sessions at the Bilthoven Radio Studio in the Netherlands (1963). He was head of music programming for the Finnish Radio and TV in Helsinki (1967–71), then managing director of the Helsinki Phil. (1971–90). He also was vice-chairman of the Helsinki Concert Center (1980–87), later serving as its project chief for music (from 1990). In his works, he has pursued advanced experimentation, ranging from classical Schoenbergian dodecaphony to electronics.

WORKS: *5 Dodecaphonic Etudes* for Piano (1961); *Frammenti per il septetto d'archi* for 3 Violins, 2 Violas, Cello, and Double Bass (1962); *Sounds I, II,* and *III*, concrete music on Tape (1963–66); *Mesto* for Flute, Clarinet, Guitar, and Percussion (1963); *For 4* for Violin, Clarinet, Guitar, and Percussion (1963); *Contradictions* for Flute, Clarinet, Piano, Guitar, and String Quartet (1965); *5 Piano Pieces for Children* (1966); *Idiopostic I* and *II*, electronic music (1963, 1966); *Varianti* for Viola and Piano (1967).—**NS/LK/DM**

K

Kàan-Albest, Heinrich (originally, **Jindřich z Albestů Kàan**), Bohemian pianist and composer; b. Tarnopol, May 29, 1852; d. Roudná, March 7, 1926. He studied in Prague with Blodek and Skuherský. From 1889 he taught piano at the Prague Cons., serving as its director from 1907 to 1918. He wrote the operas *Escape* (1895) and *Germinal*, after Zola (1908), the ballets *Bajaja* and *Olim*, a symphonic poem, *Sakuntala*, *Frühlings-Eklogen* for Orch., and piano pieces.

BIBL.: Vrkoćová, *J. K.* (diss., Univ. of Prague, 1960). —NS/LK/DM

Kabaivanska, Raina (Yakimova), Bulgarian soprano; b. Burgas, Dec. 15, 1934. She studied at the Bulgarian State Cons. in Sofia. In 1957 she made her operatic debut at the National Opera as Tatiana. She studied with Zita Fumagalli-Riva in Milan and with Giulia Tess in Vercelli; then made her first appearance at La Scala as Agnese in *Beatrice di Tenda* (1961), and subsequently sang there regularly. In 1962 she made her debut at London's Covent Garden as Desdemona; made her American debut at the Metropolitan Opera in N.Y. as Nedda on Oct. 27, 1962; first sang at the Paris Opéra as Leonora in *La forza del destino* in 1975. She also made guest appearances in Chicago, San Francisco, Dallas, Vienna, and Buenos Aires. She was best known for her Verdi and Puccini roles.—NS/LK/DM

Kabalevsky, Dmitri (Borisovich), noted Russian composer and pedagogue; b. St. Petersburg, Dec. 30, 1904; d. Moscow, Feb. 14, 1987. When he was 14 years old, his family moved to Moscow, where he received his primary music education at the Scriabin Music School (1919–25). He also studied theory privately with Gregory Catoire, and in 1925 entered the Cons. as a student of Miaskovsky in composition and Goldenweiser in piano. In 1932 he was appointed instructor in composition there, becoming a full prof. in 1939. As a pedagogue, he developed effective methods of musical education. In 1962 he was elected head of the

Commission of Musical Esthetic Education of Children, and in 1969 he became president of the Scientific Council of Educational Aesthetics in the Academy of Pedagogical Sciences of the U.S.S.R. In 1972 he received the honorary degree of president of the International Soc. of Musical Education. As a pianist, composer, and conductor, he made guest appearances in Europe and the U.S. Kabalevsky's music represents a paradigm of the Russian school of composition in its Soviet period; his melodic writing is marked by broad diatonic lines invigorated by an energetic rhythmic pulse; while adhering to basic tonality, his harmony is apt to be rich in euphonious dissonances. In his operas, he successfully reflected both the lyrical and the dramatic aspects of the librettos, several of which are based on Soviet subjects faithful to the tenets of socialist realism. His instrumental writing was functional, taking into consideration the idiomatic capacities of the instruments.

WORKS: DRAMATIC: O p e r a : *Kola Bryunon: Master iz Klamsi* (Colas Breugnon: The Master of Klamsi), after Romain Rolland (1936–38; Leningrad, Feb. 22, 1938; rev. version, Leningrad, April 16, 1970); *Vogne: Pod Moskvoi* (Into the Fire: Near Moscow; 1942; Moscow, Sept. 19, 1943; rev. version, Moscow, Nov. 7, 1947); *Semya Tarasa* (The Family of Taras; Moscow, Nov. 2, 1947; rev. version, Leningrad, Nov. 7, 1950; 2nd rev. version, Moscow, Nov. 17, 1967); *Nikita Vershinin* (1954–55; Moscow, Nov. 26, 1955). **O p e r e t t a :** *Vesna poyot* (Spring Sings; Moscow, Nov. 4, 1957); *Syostrï* (The Sisters; 1967; Perm, May 31, 1969). Also incidental music for plays and film scores. **ORCH.:** 3 piano concertos: No. 1 (1928; Moscow, Dec. 11, 1931, composer soloist), No. 2 (1935; Moscow, May 12, 1936), and No. 3 (1952; Moscow, Feb. 1, 1953, Ashkenazy soloist, composer conducting); 4 syms.: No. 1 (Moscow, Nov. 9, 1932), No. 2 (Moscow, Dec. 25, 1934), No. 3, *Requiem for Lenin*, for Chorus and Orch. (1933; Moscow, Jan. 21, 1934), and No. 4 (1954; Moscow, Oct. 17, 1956); *The Comedians*, suite for Small Orch. (1940); Suite for Jazz Orch. (1940); Violin Concerto (Leningrad, Oct. 29, 1948); 2 cello concertos: No. 1 (1948–49; Moscow, March 15, 1949) and No. 2 (1964); *Pathétique Overture* (1960); *Spring*, symphonic poem (1960); *Rhapsody* for Piano and Orch. (1963); *In Memory of the*

Heroes of Gorlovka, symphonic poem (1965). **CHAMBER:** *2 Pieces* for Cello and Piano (1927); 2 string quartets (1928, 1945); *Improvisation* for Violin and Piano (1934); *Rondo* for Violin and Piano (1961); Cello Sonata (1962); *20 Simple Pieces* for Violin and Piano (1965). **P i a n o :** 3 sonatas (1927, 1945, 1946); 2 sonatinas (1930, 1933); *24 préludes* (1943–44); *6 Préludes and Fugues* (1958–59); many children's pieces. **VOCAL:** *Poem of Struggle* for Chorus and Orch. (1930); *The Mighty Homeland*, cantata for Voices and Orch. (1941–42); *The People's Avengers* for Chorus and Orch. (1942); *Song of Morning, Spring, and Peace*, cantata for Children's Chorus and Orch. (1957–58); *Leninists* for Youth and Adult Choruses (1959); *Requiem* for Voices and Orch. (1962; Moscow, Feb. 9, 1963); *Of the Homeland*, cantata for Voices and Orch. (1965); *Letter to the 30th Century*, oratorio for Voices and Orch. (1972); numerous choral pieces.

BIBL.: L. Danilevich, *D. K.* (Moscow, 1954); G. Abramovsky, *D. K.* (Moscow, 1960); R. Glezer, *K.* (Moscow, 1969); P. Nazarevsky, ed., *D.B. K.: Notograficheskiy i bibliografischeskiy spravochnik* (D.B. K.: Worklist and Bibliography; Moscow, 1969); Y. Korev, *K.* (Moscow, 1970).—**NS/LK/DM**

Kabasta, Oswald, prominent Austrian conductor; b. Mistelbach, Dec. 29, 1896; d. (suicide) Kufstein, Feb. 6, 1946. He studied at the Vienna Academy of Music. After conducting in Wiener-Neustadt and Baden bei Wien, he was Generalmusikdirektor in Graz (1926–31). He became music director of the Vienna Radio (1931), and took its orch. on tours of Europe; concurrently taught conducting at the Vienna Academy of Music. He was also conductor of the Gesellschaft der Musikfreunde and the Vienna Sym. Orch. (from 1935), and then Generalmusikdirektor of the Munich Phil. (1938–45). Having compromised himself by a close association with the Austrian Nazis, he committed suicide a few months after the conclusion of World War II. He championed the music of the late Austro-German Romantic school, becoming particularly known for his performances of the works of Bruckner.

BIBL.: E. Exl and M. Nagy, *"...mögen sie meiner still gedenken:" Die Beiträge zum O. K.-Symposium in Mistelbach von 23. bis 25. September 1994* (Vienna, 1995).—**NS/LK/DM**

Kabeláč, Miloslav, Czech conductor and composer; b. Prague, Aug. 1, 1908; d. there, Sept. 17, 1979. He studied composition with Jirák and conducting with Pavel Dědeček (1928–31) and piano with Kurz (1931–34) at the Prague Cons. He served as conductor and music director at the Czech Radio in Prague (1932–39; 1945–54); taught composition at the Prague Cons. (1958–62) and lectured on electronic music at the Czech Radio in Plzeň (1968–70). In his music, he followed a fairly advanced modern idiom, occasionally applying dodecaphonic devices, but hewing closely to the fundamentals of tonality.

WORKS: ORCH.: Sinfonietta (1931); *Fantasy* for Piano and Orch. (1934); 2 overtures (1939, 1947); 8 syms.: No. 1 for Strings and Percussion (1941–42), No. 2 (1942–46), No. 3 for Organ, Brass, and Timpani (1948–57), No. 4 for Chamber Orch. (1954–58), No. 5, *Dramatica*, for Soprano and Orch. (1959–60), No. 6, *Concertante*, for Clarinet and Orch. (1961–62), No. 7 for Narrator and Orch., on Old Testament texts (1967–68), and No. 8, *Antiphonies*, for Soprano, Chorus, Percussion, and Organ (1970); *Dětem* (For Children), suite (1955); *Mysterium času* (Mys-

tery of Time; Prague, Oct. 23, 1957); *Hamletovská improvizace* (Hamlet Improvisations), commemorating the Shakespeare quadricentennial (1962–63; Prague, May 26, 1964); *Zrcadlení* (Reflections), 9 miniatures (1963–64; Prague, Feb. 2, 1965); Variations on the chorale *Hospodine, pomiluj ny* (Our Lord, Forgive Us) *II* for Piano and Orch. (1978). **CHAMBER:** Wind Sextet (1940); *3 Pieces* for Cello and Piano (1941); *Ballade* for Violin and Piano (1956); *Suite* for Saxophone and Piano (1959); *8 Inventions* for Percussion (1963; as a ballet, Strasbourg, April 22, 1965); *8 Ricercari* for Percussion (1966–67; rev. 1971); *Laments and Smiles*, 8 bagatelles for Flute and Harp (1969; rev. 1976). **KEYBOARD: P i a n o :** *8 Préludes* (1955–56); *Motifs*, cycle (1959); *Small Suite* for Piano, 4-Hands (1960). **O r g a n :** *Fantasy* (1957); *4 Préludes* (1963). **VOCAL:** *Little Christmas Cantata* for Soprano, Men's Chorus, and Chamber Ensemble (1937); *Neustupujte* (Do Not Yield), resistance cantata (against the Nazi occpuation of Czechoslovakia) for Men's Chorus, Band, and Percussion (1939; Prague, Oct. 28, 1945); *Moravian Lullabies* for Soprano and Chamber Orch. (1951); 6 lullabies for Alto, Women's Chorus, and Orch. (1955); *3 Melodramas* for Narrators and Orch. (1957); *Tajemství ticha* (Euphemias Mysterion) for Soprano and Chamber Orch. (1964–65; Warsaw, Sept. 30, 1965); Variations on the chorale *Hospodine, pomiluj ny* (Our Lord, Forgive Us) *I* for Female Speaker, Baritone, Men's Chorus, and Mixed Chorus (1977).—**NS/LK/DM**

Kabos, Ilona, Hungarian pianist; b. Budapest, Dec. 7, 1893; d. London, May 28, 1973. She studied with Arpád Szendy, Kodály, and Leo Weiner at the Budapest Academy of Music, winning the Liszt Prize when she was 15. She then made her debut in Budapest at 16 and subsequently toured throughout Europe, eventually gaining a fine reputation as an interpreter of contemporary music. In later years, she made her home in London, where she was active as a teacher; also gave master classes in Europe and North America, numbering among her outstanding students Peter Frankl, John Ogdon, and Joseph Kalichstein. From 1931 to 1945 she was married to **Louis Kentner.**—**NS/LK/DM**

Kačinskas, Jerome, Lithuanian-born American conductor and composer; b. Viduklé, April 17, 1907. He studied with his father, a church organist; then at the State Music School in Klaipeda and at the Prague Cons. with Jaroslav Křička and Alois Hába. Returning to Lithuania, he was conductor of the Klaipeda Sym. Orch. (1932–38); in 1938, was appointed music director for the Lithuanian Radio in Kaunas; during World War II, conducted the Vilnius Phil. In 1944 he left Lithuania, and from 1945 to 1949 lived in a displaced-persons camp in Augsburg; in 1949 he settled in the U.S., and in 1954 became a naturalized American citizen. His music reflects the influences of Scriabin and French Impressionists. Among his works are a Trumpet Concerto, 2 string quartets, sacred choruses, and piano pieces. —**NS/LK/DM**

Kacsóh, Pongrác, Hungarian composer; b. Budapest, Dec. 15, 1873; d. there, Dec. 16, 1923. He received training in piano and flute in Kolozsvár, and also in theory with Ödön von Farkas. After studies in physics, he settled in Budapest as a secondary school teacher before devoting himself to composing and writing on music. He attracted notice as a composer with his songs. Following the success of the musical play *Csipkerózsa* (Wild Rose; 1904), he produced the most acclaimed Hungarian national operetta in his *János vitéz* (Hero John; Nov. 18, 1904). He continued to compose for the theater but without ever equaling this success. In later years, he was active as a chorus master and teacher.

WORKS: DRAMATIC: Music Theater (all 1st perf. in Budapest unless otherwise given): *Csipkerózsa* (Wild Rose; 1904); *János vitéz* (Hero John; Nov. 18, 1904); *Rákóczi* (Nov. 20, 1906); *A harang* (The Bell; Feb. 1, 1907; in collaboration with A. Buttykay); *Mary Ann* (Dec. 5, 1908); *Dorottya* (n.d.; Szeged, Jan. 9, 1929); also incidental music to F. Molnár's *Liliom* (1909) and *Fehér felhő* (1916). **OTHER:** Choral music; songs; piano pieces.

BIBL.: L. Koch, *K. P. János vitéze* (Budapest, 1942).—**LK/DM**

Kade, Otto,

eminent German music scholar; b. Dresden, May 6, 1819; d. Bad Doberan, near Rostock, July 19, 1900. He studied at the Dresden Kreuzschule, then took courses with Julius Otto and Moritz Hauptmann (harmony and counterpoint) and Johann Schneider (piano and organ); also studied choral conducting. In 1848 he founded in Dresden the Cecilian Soc. for the promotion of early sacred music. In 1860 he became music director of the court of the Grand Duke of Mecklenburg-Schwerin; also taught at the Gymnasium there (1866–93). His important writings include *Der neu aufgefundene Luthercodez vom Jahre 1530* (Dresden, 1871), *Die älteren Musikalien der Stadt Freiberg in Sachsen* (Leipzig, 1888), and *Die Musikalien-Sammlung des grossherzoglich Mecklenburg-Schweriner Füstenhauses aus den letzten zwei Jahrhunderten* (2 vols., Schwerin, 1893; suppl., *Der Musikalische Nachlass der Frau Erbgrossherzogin Auguste von Mecklenburg-Schwerin*, 1899). He also ed. the collections *Cantionale für die evangelisch-lutherischen Kirchen im Grossherzogtum Mecklenburg-Schwerin* (Schwerin, 1868–87) and *Vierstimmiges Choralbuch...zu dem ...Mecklenburgischen Gesangbuch* (Schwerin, 1869). —**NS/LK/DM**

Kadosa, Pál,

esteemed Hungarian composer and pedagogue; b. Léva, Sept. 6, 1903; d. Budapest, March 30, 1983. He studied piano with Arnold Székely and Kodály at the Budapest Academy of Music (1921–27). After a brief career as a concert pianist, he taught at Budapest's Fodor Music School (1927–43), Goldmark Music School (1943–44), and at the Academy of Music (from 1945). He won the Kossuth Prize (1950) and the Erkel Prize (1955, 1962), and was made a Merited Artist (1953) and an Honored Artist (1963) of the Hungarian People's Republic. In his music, he combined the elements of the cosmopolitan modern idiom with strong Hungarian rhythms and folklike melodies; in his treatment of these materials, and particularly in the energetic asymmetrical passages, he was closer to the idiom of Bartók than to that of Kodály. The lyrical element in modal interludes adds to the Hungarian charm of his music.

WORKS: DRAMATIC: Opera: *A huszti kaland* (The Adventure of Huszt; 1949–50; Budapest, Dec. 22, 1951). **ORCH.:** Chamber Sym. (1926); 4 piano concertos: No. 1 (1931; Amsterdam, June 9, 1933, composer soloist), No. 2 (1938), No. 3

(1953), and No. 4 (1966); 2 violin concertos (1932, rev. 1969–70; 1940–41, rev. 1956); 2 divertimentos (1933; 1933–34, rev. 1960); Concerto for String Quartet and Chamber Orch. (1936); Viola Concertino (1937); 8 syms.: No. 1 (1941–42; Budapest, 1965), No. 2, *Capriccio* (Budapest, 1948), No. 3 (1953–55; Budapest, 1957), No. 4 for Strings (1958–59; Budapest, 1961), No. 5 (1960–61; Hungarian Radio, 1962), No. 6 (Hungarian Radio, Aug. 19, 1966), No. 7 (1967; Budapest, 1968), and No. 8 (1968; Hungarian Radio, 1969); *Partita* (1943–44); *Morning Ode* (1945); *March*, overture (1945); *Honor and Glory*, suite (1951); Suite (1954); *Pian e forte*, sonata (1962); Suite for Small Orch. (1962); Sinfonietta (1974). **CHAMBER:** Solo sonatinas for Violin (1923) and Cello (1924); Sonatina for Violin and Cello (1923); 2 violin sonatas (1925, rev. 1969–70; 1963); Suite for Violin and Piano (1926; rev. 1970); 2 string trios (1929–30; 1955); *Partita* for Violin and Piano (1931); Suite for Violin (1931); 3 string quartets (1934–35; 1936; 1957); Wind Quintet (1954); Piano Trio (1956); *Improvisation* for Cello and Piano (1957); Flute Sonatina (1961); Violin Sonatina (1962); *Serenade* for 10 Instruments (1967). **Piano:** 3 suites (1921; 1921–23; 1923, rev. 1970); cycles: *7 Bagatelles* (1923), *8 Epigrams* (1923–24), *5 Sketches* (1931), *6 Hungarian Folksongs* (1934–35), *6 Little Preludes* (1944), *10 Bagatelles* (1956–57), *4 Caprichos* (1961), *Kaleidoscope* (8 pieces, 1966), and *Snapshots* (1971); 4 sonatas (1926, rev. 1970; 1926–27; 1930; 1959–60); Sonatina (1927); Sonata for 2 Pianos (1947); Suite for Piano Duet (1955); also albums for children. **VOCAL:** Cantatas; songs, including *3 Radnoti Songs* (1961) and *7 Attila Jozsef Songs* (1964); folk-song arrangements.

BIBL.: F. Bónis, *K. P.* (Budapest, 1965).—**NS/LK/DM**

Kaempfert, Bert,

German bandleader, composer, and arranger; b. Hamburg, Oct. 16, 1923; d. Majorca, June 21, 1980. Kaempfert achieved international success with his recording of "Wonderland by Night" in 1960, then went on to release a series of instrumental albums, reaching the U.S. charts with 22 of them through 1971. He also composed the music for several hits, including "Wooden Heart," "Danke Schoen," and "Strangers in the Night."

Kaempfert studied piano from the age of six and attended the Hamburg Hochschule für Musik, where he added clarinet, saxophone, and accordion. He served in the music division of the German army during World War II and conducted a band in a prisoner-of-war camp in Denmark in 1945. Returning to Hamburg after the war, he formed his own band in 1947 and in 1949 became director of North German Radio.

Kaempfert was signed to Polydor Records as a recording artist and as an A&R man; he achieved international recognition by arranging and producing "Morgen" (music and lyrics by Peter Mosser), recorded by Ivo Robic, which became a Top 40 hit in the U.S. in August 1959. His own instrumental recordings were picked up for American release by Decca Records, which issued the single "Wonderland by Night" (music by Klauss-Gunter Neuman, lyrics by Lincoln Chase) in the fall of 1960. It hit #1 in January 1961 and sold a million copies, and a *Wonderland by Night* LP also topped the charts and went gold.

Meanwhile, Kaempfert's adaptation of a German folk song, "Wooden Heart" (music and lyrics by Fred Wise, Benjamin Weisman, Kathleen G. Twomey, and Bert Kaempfert), had been used in the Elvis Presley film

G. I. Blues, which opened in October 1960, and was featured on the top-selling soundtrack LP. Released as a Presley single in the U.K., it hit #1 in March 1961. In the U.S. it was covered by Joe Dowell, whose recording topped the charts in August. That summer, Kaempfert signed the then-unknown Beatles to a one-year contract and recorded them as the backing group for British singer Tony Sheridan and on their own, resulting in the Sheridan/Beatles single "My Bonnie" (music and lyrics traditional), which made the U.K. charts in 1963 and the U.S. Top 40 in 1964, after The Beatles had become famous.

Kaempfert himself returned to the American Top 40 in April 1961 with an instrumental revival of the 1946 song "Tenderly" (music by Walter Gross, lyrics by Jack Lawrence) and scored a second chart album in November with *Dancing in Wonderland*. He had two more LPs in the charts in 1962, one of which was *Afrikaan Beat and Other Favorites*, and the single of his composition "Afrikaan Beat" reached the Top 40 in March. Billy Vaughn scored a Top 40 hit in August with Kaempfert's composition "A Swingin' Safari," later familiar to television viewers as the theme for *The Match Game*. Kaempfert charted with three new albums in 1963, but his greatest success for the year came as a songwriter when Wayne Newton scored a Top 40 hit in August with "Danke Schoen" (music by Bert Kaempfert, German lyrics by Kurt Schwabach, English lyrics by Milt Gabler).

In November 1964, Kaempfert released his second gold album, *Blue Midnight*, which hit the Top Ten in March 1965 due to the inclusion of the 1949 song "Red Roses for a Blue Lady" (music and lyrics by Sid Tepper and Roy Brodsky), which reached the Top 40 of the singles charts in February, and the 1921 song "Three O'Clock in the Morning" (music by Julian Robledo, lyrics by "Dorothy Terris," a pseudonym for Theodora Morse), which reached the Top 40 in May. A *Three O'Clock in the Morning* LP charted in July, followed in September by *The Magic Music of Far Away Places*, which featured "Moon over Naples" (music by Bert Kaempfert), a tune that had entered the singles charts in July. Charles Singleton and Eddie Snyder wrote a lyric to the melody, and it was recorded by Al Martino as "Spanish Eyes," reaching the Top 40 in December.

Kaempfert wrote and conducted the score for the film *A Man Could Get Killed*, which opened in May 1966. A theme from the score was adapted into a song with lyrics by Charles Singleton and Eddie Snyder under the title "Strangers in the Night." Recorded by Frank Sinatra, the song topped the charts in June and sold a million copies, also serving as the title song for a Sinatra album that hit #1 and went gold. It earned Kaempfert a Grammy nomination for Song of the Year. His own *Strangers in the Night* LP was one of three albums he placed in the charts in 1966, along with *Bye Bye Blues* (a Top Ten hit in the U.K.) and the gold-selling *Bert Kaempfert's Greatest Hits*.

Jack Jones had the next hit with a Kaempfert composition, "Lady" (music also by Herbert Rehbein, English lyrics by Larry Kusik and Charles Singleton), which reached the Top 40 and hit #1 on the easy-listening charts in March 1967. Sinatra recorded

Kaempfert's "The World We Knew (Over and Over)" (music also by Herbert Rehbein, English lyrics by Carl Singleton), reaching the Top 40 in August and the top of the easy-listening charts in September. Kaempfert himself charted with two LPs during the year, though his sales had begun to fall off. He continued to place albums in the charts until 1971 and occasionally wrote film scores, such as 1970's *You Can't Win 'Em All*. He died of a stroke at 56 in 1980.

DISC.: *Wonderland by Night* (1960); *Dancing in Wonderland* (1961); *Afrikaan Beat and Other Favorites* (1962); *Lights Out, Sweet Dreams* (1963); *Living It Up!* (1963); *Blue Midnight* (1965); *Three O'Clock in the Morning* (1965); *The Magic Music of Far Away Places* (1965); *Bye Bye Blues* (Decca; 1966); *Bye Bye Blues* (Taragon; 1966); *Strangers in the Night* (1966); *Hold Me* (1967); *The World We Knew* (1967); *My Way of Life* (1968); *Warm and Wonderful* (1969); *Traces of Love* (1969); *The Kaempfert Touch* (1970); *Orange Colored Sky* (1971); *Bert Kaempfert Now!* (1971); *Fabulous Fifties...and New Delights* (1973); *Christmas Wonderland* (1996); *That Happy Feeling* (1996); *Swingin' Safari* (1998); *Easy Loungin'* (1998); *Tropical Sunrise* (1998); *Swing* (1998); *Free & Easy* (1998); *Safari Swing Again* (1998); *Love that Bert Kaempfert* (1998); *Yesterday & Today* (1998); *Forever My Love* (1998); *A Man Could Get Killed/Strange* (1999); *April in Portugal & Wonderland by Night* (1999); *Wonderland of & Dancing in Wonderland* (1999); *Latin Feeling, Vol. 6* (1999); *One Lonely Night* (2000); *Live in London* (2000); *Spanish Eyes* (2000); *Bert Kaempfert's Greatest Hits* (1966); *Red Roses* (1993); *The Best of Bert Kaempfert* (1994); *The Very Best of Bert Kaempfert* (1995); *Instrumental Favorites* (1996); *That Latin Feeling/Blue Midnight* (1997); *Hold Me/World We Knew* (1999); *The Sound in My Heart & Afrikaan Beat* (1999); *Lights Out, Sweet Dreams & Living It Up* (1999); *Famous Swing Classics* (1999). The Beatles: *Anthology 1* (1995). Brenda Lee: *Wiedersehn Ist Wunderschon* (1994). Wayne Newton: *Best of Wayne Newton Now* (1985). Hank Snow: *Singing Ranger* (1959).—**WR**

Kafenda, Frico, significant Slovak pedagogue and composer; b. Mošovce, Nov. 2, 1883; d. Bratislava, Sept. 3, 1963. He studied conducting with Nikisch and composition with Jadassohn at the Leipzig Cons. (1901–05). In 1920 he became a piano instructor at the Bratislava Cons., where he served as its director from 1922 to 1949; then taught at the Bratislava Academy of Music and at the Univ. of Bratislava. As a teacher of composition, he had great influence upon Slovak music; among his students were R. Berger, M. Novák, and E. Suchoň. His wife, Anna Kafendová-Zochová, taught piano at the Cons. and the Academy in Bratislava. His compositions are permeated with the spirit of mid-European Romanticism, and include a Cello Sonata (1905), String Quartet (1916), Violin Sonata (1918), choral music, and songs. —**NS/LK/DM**

Kaffka (real name, **Engelmann**), **Johann Christoph,** German violinist, singer, and composer; b. Regensburg, 1754; d. Riga, Jan. 29, 1815. He studied violin with his father and theory with Riepel. He appeared on the stage as a singer and actor in various German cities (from 1777), and then settled in Riga as a bookseller (1803). He wrote Singspiels, ballets, oratorios, masses, and songs, most of which are lost. —**NS/LK/DM**

Kagan, Oleg, Russian violinist; b. Sakhalin, Nov. 22, 1946; d. Munich, July 15, 1990. He was a pupil at the Latvian State Cons. in Riga before going to Moscow, where he studied with Boris Kuznetsov and David Oistrakh at the Central Music School; then completed his training at the Cons. After taking prizes in the Enesco (Bucharest, 4th, 1964), Sibelius (Helsinki, 1st, 1965), Tchaikovsky (Moscow, 2nd, 1966), and Bach (Leipzig, 1st, 1968) competitions, he toured as a soloist with orchs., a recitalist, and a chamber music artist. Kagan often appeared in duo concerts with his wife, **Natlia Gutman.—NS/LK/DM**

Kagel, Mauricio (Raúl), notable Argentine composer and pedagogue; b. Buenos Aires, Dec. 24, 1931. He studied in Buenos Aires, taking courses in theory with Juan Carlos Paz and in piano, cello, organ, conducting, and voice with Alfredo Schiuma et al.; he also studed philosophy and literary history at the Univ. there. In 1949 he became active with the Agrupacion Nueva Musica and joined the staff of the Teatro Colón in Buenos Aires. In 1957 he went to Cologne on a stipend from the Deutscher Akademischer Austauschdienst. He taught at the courses for new music in Darmstadt from 1960, and was founder- director of the Cologne Ensemble for New Music from 1961. After serving as the Slee Prof. of Composition at the State Univ. of N.Y. in Buffalo (1964–65), he was director of the Inst. for New Music at the Rheinische Musikschule in Cologne (from 1969). In 1974 he became a prof. at the Cologne Hochscule für Musik. In 1989 he was composer-in-residence at the Cologne Philharmonie. In 1977 he became a member of the Akademie der Künste in Berlin. He was awarded the Mozart Medal of Frankfurt am Main in 1983 and was made a Commandeur de L'Ordre des Arts et des Lettres of France in 1985. He is the author of *Worte über Musik: Gespräche, Aufsätze, Reden, Hörspiele* (Munich, 1991). Kagel has developed an extremely complex system of composition in which a fantastically intricate and yet wholly rational serial organization of notes, intervals, and durations is supplemented by aleatory techniques. Some of these techniques are derived from linguistic permutations, random patterns of light and shadows on exposed photographic film, and other processes. In his hyper-serial constructions, he endeavors to unite all elements of human expression, ultimately aiming at the creation of a universe of theatrical arts in their aural, visual, and societal aspects.

WORKS: DRAMATIC: *Sur Scène,* chamber-music theater piece (1959–60); *Antithese* for 1 or 2 Performers and Electronics (1962); *Tremens,* scenic montage (1963–65); *Die Himmelsmechanik,* piece with theater scenery (1965); *Pas de cing,* variable scene for 5 Performers (1965); *Staatstheater,* scenic piece (1967–70); *Con voce* for 3 Mimes and Instruments ad libitum (1972); *Mare nostrum,* scenic piece (1973–75); *Présentation* for Speaker, Piano, and Tape (1976–77); *Variété,* concert spectacle for Artists and Musicians (1976–77); *Die Erschöpfung der Welt,* scenic illusion (1976–78); *Umzug* for Mime (1977); *Die Rhythmusmaschinen,* action for 10 Gymnasts and Instruments (1977–78); *Ex-Position,* action for Vocal Ensemble and Instruments (1977–78); *Aus Deutschland,* lieder opera (1977–80); *Der Tribun* for Political Orator, Marching Band, and Loudspeaker (1978–79); *Der mündliche Verrat* or *La Trahison orale,* musical epic

on the Devil for 1 Female Performer, 2 Male Singers, Tuba, Viola or Violin, Double Bass, Piano or Electric Organ, 3 Percussion, and Tape (1981–83); *...nach einer Lektüre von Orwell,* theater picture or scenic environment (1982–83); *Tantz-Schul,* ballet d'action (1985–87); *Zwei Akte* for 2 Actors, Saxophone, and Harp (1988–89). **ORCH.:** *Heterophonie* (1959–61); *Sonant* for Electric Guitar, Harp, Double Bass, and Small Orch. (1960); *Diaphonie II* for Orch. and 2 Slide Projectors (1964); *Music for Renaissance Instruments* for 23 Performers (1965–66); *Klangwehr I* for Military Marching Band (1969–70; *II* for Military Marching Band and Chorus); *Musi* for Strings (1971); *Variationen ohne Fuge* (1971–72); *10 Märsche, um den Sieg zu verfehlen* for Wind and Percussion Orch. (1978–79); *Finale* for Chamber Orch. (1980–81); *Rrrrrr...* (1980–82); *Szenario* for Strings and Tape (1981–82); *Musik* (1987–88); *Les idées fixes* (1988–89); *Die Stücke der Windrose* for Salon Orch. (1988–93); *Les idées fixes* (1988–89); *Opus 1.991* (1990); *Konzertstück* for Kettle Drum and Orch. (1990–92). **CHAMBER:** *Variationen* for Flute, Piano, Violin, and Cello (1951); String Sextet (1953; rev. 1957); *Transicion II* for Piano, Percussion, and 2 Tapes (1958–59); *Schlag auf Schlag* for 4 Music Saws and Percussion (1963–64); *Match* for 2 Cellos and Percussion (1964); 4 string quartets (1965, 1967, 1988, 1993); *Phantasie* for Organist, Assistants, and 2 Tapes (1967); *Der Schall* for 5 Performers (1968); *Acustica III* for 2 to 5 Instrumentalists or Tape (1968–70); *Unter Strom* for 3 Performers (1969); *Tactil* for Piano, 2 Guitars, and Electronics (1970); *Charakterstuck* for Zither Quartet (1971); *Exotica* for 6 Performers (1971–72); *Aus Zungen Stimmen* for Accordion Quintet (1972); *Dressur,* percussion trio (1976–77); *Blue's Blue* for 4 Performers (1978–79); *Klangwölfe* for Violin and Piano (1978–79); *Aus dem Nachlass* for Violin, Cello, and Double Bass (1981–86); Trio for Violin, Cello, and Piano (1984–85); *Pan* for Piccolo and String Quartet (1985); *For us: Happy birthday to you!* for 4 Cellos (1987), *Phantasiestück* for Flute and Piano (1987–88; also for Flute, Piano, Clarinet, Bass Clarinet, Violin, Viola, and Cello); *Zwei Akte* for Saxophone and Harp (1988–89). **VOCAL:** *Anagrama* for 4 Soloists, Speaking Chorus, and Chamber Ensemble (1957–58); *Diaphonie I* for Chorus, Orch., and Slide Projectors (1964) and *III* for Chorus and 2 or More Slide Projectors (1964); *Musik aus Diaphonie* for Voices and Instruments (1964); *Hallelujah* for Voices (1967–68); *Abend* for Double Vocal Quartet, Trombone Quintet, Electric Organ, and Piano (1972); *Kantrimiusik* for Voices and Instruments (1975); *Chorbuch* for Vocal Ensemble, Piano, and Harmonium or Electric Organ (1975–78); *Tango Alemán* for Voice, Violin, Bandoneon or Accordion, and Piano (1977–78); *Vox humana?,* cantata for Women's Voices, Orch., and Loudspeaker (1978–79); *Mitternachtsstük* for 4 Soloists, Speaking Chorus, and 9 Instruments (1980–81; 1986); *Sankt-Bach-Passion* for Mezzo-soprano, Tenor, Baritone, Speaker, Chorus, Speaking Chorus, Boy's Chorus, and Orch. (1981–85); *Fürst Igor, Strawinsky* for Bass and 6 Instruments (1982); *Intermezzo* for Speaker, Chorus, and Orch. (1983); *Ein Brief* for Mezzo-soprano and Orch. (1985–86); *Quodlibet* for Woman's Voice and Orch. (1986–88); *Fragende Ode* for Double Chorus, Winds, and Percussion (1988–89); *...den 24, XII. 31* for Baritone and Instruments (1988–91); *Liturgien* for Tenor, Baritone, Bass, Double Chorus, and Orch. (1989–90). **OTHER:** Film-collage; tape piece; electronic scores.**—NS/LK/DM**

Kagen, Sergius, Russian-born American pianist, teacher, and composer; b. St. Petersburg, Aug. 22, 1909; d. N.Y., March 1, 1964. He went to Berlin in 1921 and studied with Leonid Kreutzer and Paul Juon at the Hochschule für Musik; emigrated to the U.S. in 1925 and became a naturalized American citizen in 1930. He studied with Carl Friedberg, Rubin Goldmark, and Marcella Sembrich at the Juilliard School of Music in N.Y. (diploma, 1930). He later joined its faculty (1940), and also taught at the Union Theological Seminary (1957–64). He wrote the books *Music for the Voice* (N.Y., 1949; 2nd ed., rev., 1968) and *On Studying Singing* (N.Y., 1950). He composed an opera, *Hamlet* (Baltimore, Nov. 9, 1962), more than 70 songs, and various piano pieces.

BIBL.: B. Woods, *S. K.: His Life and Works* (diss., George Peabody Coll. for Teachers, 1969).—NS/LK/DM

Kahane, Jeffrey (Alan), American pianist and conductor; b. Los Angeles, Sept. 12, 1956. He began piano training with Howard Weisel and Jakob Gimpel, and completed his studies at the San Francisco Cons. of Music (graduated, 1977). In 1977 he took 2nd prize in the Clara Haskil Competition and in 1981 4th prize in the Van Cliburn Competition. He won the Arthur Rubinstein Competition in 1983, and that same year made his Carnegie Hall debut in N.Y. and was awarded an Avery Fisher Career Grant. His London debut followed in 1985, and in 1987 he received the first Andrew Wolf Chamber Music Award. In 1988 he made his conducting debut at the Ore. Bach Festival, and thereafter pursued a dual career as a pianist and conductor. He co-founded the Gardner Chamber Orch. in 1991, which he led as artistic director and conductor until 1995. In 1992 he became assoc. conductor of the San Luis Obispo Mozart Festival. He also became music director of the Santa Rosa (Calif.) Sym. Orch. in 1995 and of the Los Angeles Chamber Orch. in 1997.—NS/LK/DM

Kahl, Willi, German musicologist; b. Zabern, Alsace, July 18, 1893; d. Cologne, Oct. 3, 1962. He first studied in Freiburg im Breisgau and Munich, and then received his Ph.D. in 1919 from the Univ. of Bonn with the diss. *Das lyrische Klavierstück zu Beginn des 19. Jahrhunderts (1800 bis 1830) und seine Vorgeschichte im 17. und 18. Jahrhundert*; subsequently completed his Habilitation in 1923 at the Univ. of Cologne with his *Studien zur Geschichte der Klaviermusik des 18. Jahrhunderts*. In 1928 he became Bibliotheksrat of the Univ. of Cologne and of the city library; was also a reader at the Univ. from 1928; he retired in 1958. His writings include *Musik und Musikleben im Rheinland* (Cologne, 1923), *Herbart als Musiker* (Langensalza, 1936), and *Verzeichnis des Schrifttums über Franz Schubert, 1828–1928* (Regensburg, 1938). He also ed. various works and compiled the important documentary vol. *Selbstbiographien deutscher Musiker des XVIII. Jahrhunderts* (Cologne, 1948).—NS/LK/DM

Kahn, Erich Itor, German-American pianist and composer; b. Rimbach, July 23, 1905; d. N.Y., March 5, 1956. He studied at the Hoch Cons. in Frankfurt am Main. From 1928 to 1933 he was co-director of the Frankfurt am Main Radio. He went to France in 1933, and in 1938–39 toured as accompanist to Casals in France and North Africa. He emigrated in 1941 to the U.S., where he organized the Albeneri Trio in 1944 (the name being derived from assorted syllables of the first names of the participants: Alexander Schneider, violin;

Benar Heifetz, cello; and Erich Kahn, piano). He became the pianist of the Bach Aria Group in 1951. In 1948 he was awarded the Coolidge Medal for eminent service to chamber music. He was held in high esteem as a composer of inventive intellect.

WORKS: *Präludien zur Nacht*, suite for Chamber Orch. (1927); Suite for Violin and Piano (1937; rev. as Suite concertante for Violin and Orch., 1937; orchestration completed by R. Leibowitz, 1964); *3 chansons populaires* for Mezzo-soprano and Piano (1938); *3 caprices de Paganini* for Violin and Piano (1942); *Ciaccona dei tempi di guerra* for Piano (1943); *Actus tragicus* for 10 Instruments (1946; Baden-Baden, June 18, 1955); *4 Nocturnes* for Soprano and Piano (1954); String Quartet (1954); *Les symphonies bretonnes* for Orch. (1955).

BIBL.: R. Leibowitz and K. Wolff, *E.I. K., un grand représentant de la musique contemporaine* (Paris, 1958); H.-K. Metzger and R. Riehn, eds., *E.I. K.* (Munich, 1994).—NS/LK/DM

Kahn, Gus(tave), German-born American lyricist; b. Coblenz, Nov. 6, 1886; d. Beverly Hills, Oct. 8, 1941. Kahn was a prolific, consistently successful lyric writer in Tin Pan Alley, on Broadway, and in Hollywood for more than 30 years. His most memorable songs include "Pretty Baby," "I'll Say She Does," "Ain't We Got Fun?," "Carolina in the Morning," "My Buddy," "Toot, Toot, Tootsie! (Goo'bye)," "The One I Love Belongs to Somebody Else," "I'll See You in My Dreams," "It Had to Be You," "Yes Sir! That's My Baby," "Makin' Whoopee," "Dream a Little Dream of Me," and "You Stepped Out of a Dream." They were written with such collaborators as B.G. De Sylva and Walter Donaldson, and sung by such performers as Billy Murray, Al Jolson, Henry Burr, Gene Austin, and Eddie Cantor.

Kahn was the son of Isaac Kahn, a cattle dealer, who brought his family to the U.S. in 1891, settling in Chicago. Kahn began writing songs in high school and also wrote special material for vaudeville acts, though he supported himself at hotel, catering, and other jobs until the success of his first published song, "I Wish I Had a Girl," the music for which was written by his future wife, Grace LeBoy. (The couple eventually had a son and a daughter.) A series of recordings appeared in the spring of 1909, the most popular being the one by Murray.

The Kahns placed songs in two musicals, *The Isle of Love* (1910) and *Jumping Jupiter* (N.Y., March 6, 1911), but the lyricist's next hit came when he teamed up with composer Egbert Van Alstyne for "Sunshine and Roses," which "Edna Brown" (actually Elsie Baker) and James F. Harrison made into a popular recording in the summer of 1913. The Kahns' "Everybody Rag with Me" appears in the sheet music for the musical *Dancing Around* (N.Y., Oct. 10, 1914), which starred Jolson, but it may not have been performed in the show. Nevertheless, George O'Connor enjoyed a hit recording of it in the spring of 1915.

The team of Kahn and Van Alstyne became permanent with the hit "Memories." John Barnes Wells had the most popular recording in the spring of 1916. "Pretty Baby," which Van Alstyne co-composed with ragtime pianist Tony Jackson, was interpolated into *The Passing Show of 1916* (N.Y., June 22, 1916) and became a million-seller in sheet music, with a popular recording by Murray in the fall. Kahn's other notable lyrics for the year included "That Funny Jas Band from Dixieland" (music by Henry I. Marshall), a song about the Original Dixieland Jazz Band that was the first song to use a version of the word jazz in its title.

Kahn was brought in by Jolson to revise a song by De Sylva, "'N Everything." Jolson recorded the song for a big hit and interpolated it into *Sinbad* (N.Y., Feb. 14, 1918). Kahn once again collaborated with Jolson and De Sylva on "I'll Say She Does," which Jolson interpolated into the road tour of *Sinbad* and recorded for a giant hit in the summer of 1919. (There were also popular instrumental versions by the All- Star Trio and Wilbur Sweatman's Original Jazz Band.) Then came a third Kahn-Jolson-De Sylva song, "You Ain't Heard Nothin' Yet," interpolated into the road tour of *Sinbad* and recorded by Jolson for a hit in the spring. Later the same season, Kahn and Van Alstyne enjoyed success with John McCormack's recording of "Your Eyes Have Told Me So." The song had been featured in the show *Dere Mable*, which closed before reaching N.Y. A similar fate befell *Satires of 1920*, which featured Kahn, Whiting, and Egan's frothy comic song "Ain't We Got Fun?"; but the tune was picked up by the vaudeville team of Van and Schenck, who had a best-selling record with it in September 1921. The song's enduring appeal was suggested by its revival only a year later for a hit recording by Billy Jones.

Kahn's reluctance to move to N.Y. probably reduced his participation in Broadway shows, but it also led to fortunate local alliances. In 1922 he began writing lyrics to music by Chicago-based bandleader Isham Jones. Their first success came with "On the Alamo," a top hit in June 1922, in an instrumental recording by Jones. Kahn's first collaboration with Donaldson seems to have come with "Little Rover (Don't Forget to Come Back Home)," intended for the Eddie Cantor vehicle *Make It Snappy* (N.Y., April 13, 1922). But their first success as a team came with "Carolina in the Morning," used in *The Passing Show of 1922* (N.Y., Sept. 20, 1922). A million-seller in sheet music, the song enjoyed a best-selling record by Van and Schenck in March 1923, among many other recordings.

Kahn and Donaldson scored another sheet-music million-seller, "My Buddy," recorded for a best-selling record by Burr in December 1922, as well as in a popular instrumental version by Ben Bernie and His Orch. A third simultaneous hit for the team was "Dixie Highway," recorded by Aileen Stanley. Meanwhile, during the 1922–23 road tour of his show *Bombo*, Jolson introduced "Toot, Toot, Tootsie! (Goo'bye)" (music by Dan Russo and Ted Fiorito, lyrics also by Ernie Erdman).

The year 1924 brought a remarkable string of hits, including "When Lights Are Low" (music by Fiorito, lyrics also by Ted Koehler); "The One I Love Belongs to Somebody Else" (music by Isham Jones), with the most popular recording by Jolson; and the sheet-music million-seller "It Had to Be You" (music by Jones). Kahn's hit streak extended into 1925, starting with more sheet-music million-sellers, "I'll See You in My Dreams" (music by Jones) and "Yes Sir! That's My Baby" (music

by Donaldson). This song was written for and introduced by Cantor, but the record that hit in September was by Austin, with many competing vocal and instrumental versions. At the same time, Vaughn DeLeath was scoring a hit with "Ukelele Lady" (music by Whiting), and Georgie Price's recording of "Isn't She the Sweetest Thing? (Oh Maw, Oh Paw)" (music by Donaldson) was doing well.

Kahn finally took on a full Broadway musical score when he and Egan wrote the lyrics to Will Ortmann's music for *Holka-Polka* (N.Y., Oct. 14, 1925), an adaptation of the 1920 German light opera *Frühling im Herbst*. It ran only 21 performances and produced no hits. Kahn was the sole lyricist for *Kitty's Kisses* (N.Y., May 6, 1926), a show with music by Con Conrad that was more successful than *Holka-Polka*, running for 170 performances, but failed to produce any memorable songs.

Meanwhile, Kahn continued to produce sheet music and record hits. Abe Lyman and His California Orch. had a hit at the beginning of 1927 with "Just a Bird's Eye View of My Old Kentucky Home" (music by Donaldson), and "Whispering" Jack Smith hit with "There Ain't No Maybe in My Baby's Eyes" (music by Donaldson). "If You See Sally" (music by Donaldson) found success later in the year with Lewis and with Lou Gold and His Orch. In October, "Toot, Toot, Tootsie! (Goo'bye)" was sung by Jolson in the first sound film, *The Jazz Singer*.

Kahn continued to score hits in 1928, with both new compositions and revivals, including his first song written for Guy Lombardo and His Orch.; the band would enjoy a long and happy relationship with the composer. But Kahn's major creative effort for the year was his collaboration with Donaldson on the songs for the Cantor musical *Whoopee!* (N.Y., Dec. 4, 1928), a smash hit that ran for 407 performances and generated four hit songs: "My Blackbirds Are Bluebirds Now," "Love Me or Leave Me," and "I'm Bringing a Red, Red Rose," all recorded by Etting, who appeared in the show; and "Makin' Whoopee," its clever lyric about marriage and its consequences recorded by Cantor, with competing versions by Whiteman, using a vocal quartet including Bing Crosby, and Ben Bernie.

Fresh from *Whoopee!*, Kahn was brought in to help George and Ira Gershwin on the musical *Show Girl*. Its chief selling point was dancer Ruby Keeler, Jolson's wife. Though not cast in the show, Jolson took to singing one of the songs, "Liza (All the Clouds'll Roll Away)," to her from the audience, which helped *Show Girl* to a run of 111 performances and made his recording of the song a hit in September. By then Kahn had scored another hit, collaborating with Joe Sanders on "Little Orphan Annie," which was recorded by the Coon-Sanders Orch.

Though several of Kahn's songs had been used in Hollywood films since the dawn of sound, his first credit as lyricist for a movie came with the adaptation of *Whoopee!*, for which he and Donaldson contributed several new songs. When the movie opened in the fall of 1930, one of them, "My Baby Just Cares for Me," became a record hit for Ted Weems and His Orch. Nichols revived "It Had to Be You" for a hit in November, and college favorites Vallée and Ted Wallace and His Campus Boys had hits with "Sweetheart of My Student

Days" (music by Seymour Simons). In December, Kahn contributed lyrics to "The Waltz You Saved for Me" (music by Emil Flindt and Wayne King), which became a hit and the theme song for King, a Midwestern bandleader.

In January 1931, King followed with an instrumental version of "Goofus" (music by King and William Harold; it was a hit a year later when it was brought back by Russo's Oriole Orch.), and in April he released "Dream a Little Dream of Me" (music by Wilbur Schwandt and Fabian André), which became one of the biggest hits of the year. In July, Crosby had one of his earliest solo hits with "I'm Through with Love" (music by Matty Malneck and Fud Livingston). Kahn, Whiting and co- composer Harry Akst wrote "Guilty" for Etting; the flip side of Etting's record was "Now that You're Gone" (music by Fiorito), which also became a hit for her, though Guy Lombardo's recording was more popular. "Nobody's Sweetheart" was revived for a hit at the end of 1931 by the Mills Brothers, who put it on the flip side of their first record, "Tiger Rag."

Kahn, who had resisted the lure of Broadway, finally succumbed to the charms of Hollywood, moving west in 1933 to work in the movies. His first major credit came with *Peg o' My Heart* (1933), on which he shared lyric-writing duties with Arthur Freed for songs by Herbert Stothart and Nacio Herb Brown. "You've Got Everything" (music by Donaldson) was heard only instrumentally in the film *The Prize Fighter and the Lady* (1933), but Jan Garber and His Orch. recorded a vocal version for a hit in November. Kahn's biggest success during his first year in Hollywood came at the end of 1933 with *Flying Down to Rio*, for which he and Edward Eliscu wrote lyrics to the music of Vincent Youmans. The film generated four hits: "Orchids in the Moonlight"; the title song, recorded by Vallée and by Fred Astaire, who appeared in the film; the dance song "Carioca"; and "Music Makes Me," recorded by Astaire and by Emil Coleman and His Orch. "Carioca" earned Kahn his first Academy Award nomination.

Benny Goodman and His Orch. revived "Love Me or Leave Me" for an instrumental hit in February 1934. In March, Kahn enjoyed one of his few non- movie hits of the period with Vallée's recording of "Dancing in the Moonlight" (music by Donaldson). His next notable movie song was "Waitin' at the Gate for Katy" (music by Whiting) from *Bottoms Up*, which became a hit in May. His lyric for the title song of *Riptide* (music by Donaldson) was used only in the promotion of the film, but the song was picked up for record hits by Guy Lombardo and by Eddy Duchin and His Orch. in May. The flip side of the Duchin record, also a hit, was "I've Had My Moments" (music by Donaldson) from the film *Hollywood Party*.

The next film for which Kahn was the credited lyricist was *Operator 13* (1934), which featured "Sleepy Head" (music by Donaldson), a hit for The Mills Brothers and for Ben Pollack and His Orch. in June. Kahn also wrote songs for *Stingaree* (1934), including "Tonight Is Mine" (music by W. Franke Harling), which became a hit for Reisman in July. *One Night of Love* (1934) produced a hit in the title song (music by Victor Schertz-

inger) for its star, Grace Moore, whose recording was a best-seller in October. Kahn wrote lyrics but no hits for *Caravan* (1934) and a film adaptation of the Franz Lehar operetta *The Merry Widow* (1934), but his and Donaldson's score for *Kid Millions* (1934) brought record hits for the film's two stars, Ethel Merman, who scored with "An Earful of Music" in November, and Cantor, who had "Okay, Toots" in December.

Kahn's first hit of 1935 was another non-movie song, "Clouds" (music by Donaldson), recorded by the orchestras of Ray Noble and Goodman. He had another with "Footloose and Fancy Free" (music by Carmen Lombardo), which was in the hit parade in June and July. His first major film assignment for the year was to rewrite Rida Johnson Young's lyrics for an adaptation of Victor Herbert's 1910 operetta *Naughty Marietta*. He also wrote the title song for *Love Me Forever* (music by Schertzinger), which became a hit for Russ Morgan and His Orch. in July, and "You're All I Need" (music by Bronislaw Kaper and Walter Jurmann) for the film *Escapade*, a hit for Duchin the same month. In the fall, Kahn had two films out with music by Arthur Johnston: *The Girl Friend* and *Thanks a Million*, the latter producing hits in the title song and "I'm Sitting High on a Hilltop" (recorded by Guy Lombardo).

In early 1936, Kahn wrote new lyrics for a film adaptation of the 1924 Rudolf Friml operetta *Rose Marie* and collaborated with Jimmy McHugh on "With All My Heart," which was used in the film *Her Master's Voice*. In June, eight-year-old Bobby Breen, who appeared in *Let's Sing Again*, had a hit with the film's title song (music by McHugh), though the most popular record was by Fats Waller. In July, Garber had a hit with the title song from *Small Town Girl* (music by Stothart and Edward Ward), and that same month Kahn was the lyricist for the songs in *San Francisco* (music by Kaper and Jurmann), including the title song, a hit for Tommy Dorsey and His Orch. In the fall, Goodman again recorded an instrumental version of "Love Me or Leave Me," this time with his quartet, and scored an even bigger hit.

At the end of 1936, "Gone" (music by Franz Waxman) from the film *Love on the Run* was a hit for Guy Lombardo, and Kahn was the lyricist for songs by Kaper and Jurmann in *Three Smart Girls*, including "Someone to Care for Me," a hit for Morgan in January 1937. "Josephine" (music by King and Burke Bivens), a non-movie song, was the biggest hit of King's career in March; Dorsey had just as big a hit with it in October. Kahn wrote lyrics to Waxman's music for *Captains Courageous* (1937) and to Kaper and Jurmann's music for *A Day at the Races* (1937), the latter generating hits in Duke Ellington and Artie Shaw's recordings of "All God's Chillun Got Rhythm" and Fiorito's recording of "Tomorrow Is Another Day." Kahn was credited as lyricist for Friml's music in *Music for Madame* (1937) and again for Kaper and Jurmann's music in *Everybody Sing* (1938). The inclusion of "The One I Love Belongs to Somebody Else" inspired Dorsey to revive the song on record for another hit in February.

Kahn and Sigmund Romberg didn't get any hits out of their score for *The Girl of the Golden West* (1938), but Kahn had more success paired with Warren for *Honolulu*

(1939)—both Gray and Dorsey scored with "This Night Will Be My Souvenir," and Dorsey also had a hit with the title song. Stothart and Earl Brent adapted B. A. Prozorovsky's "Kak Strano," and Kahn added lyrics to create the song "How Strange?," used in *Idiot's Delight* (1939). The result was a hit for Fiorito in May. Kahn had no new hits in the fall, but Glenn Miller and His Orch. revived the 20-year-old "My Isle of Golden Dreams" in an instrumental recording, and Crosby followed with a vocal record to make the song a hit again.

Kahn's next newly written hit was "Blue Love Bird" (music by Kaper), which was used in the film *Lillian Russell* (1940) and inspired popular recordings by Kay Kyser and His Orch. and Mitchell Ayres and His Fashions in Music in the late spring and early summer of 1940. Goodman dug out "The Hour of Parting," a song Kahn had written in 1931 with Mischa Spoliansky, and had an instrumental hit with it in August, the same month that Dorsey issued a newly recorded revival of "The One I Love Belongs to Somebody Else," sung by Frank Sinatra and The Pied Pipers. Kahn didn't earn any hits from his collaboration with Robert Stolz and others on the songs for *Spring Parade* (1940), but he and Stolz did share an Academy Award nomination for "Waltzing in the Clouds." Kahn, Brent, and Kaper next contributed songs to *Go West* (1940). Kahn's last newly written hit was "You Stepped Out of a Dream" (music by Nacio Herb Brown), featured in *Ziegfeld Girl* (1941) and made into a popular record by Kyser in March 1941. His last published song was "Day Dreaming" (music by Jerome Kern), which was released on the flip side of Glenn Miller's January 1942 hit "A String of Pearls."

Kahn's song catalog had been mined extensively by the movies during his lifetime, a practice that only increased in the years immediately after his death. In 1943, six feature films used Kahn's songs; his lyrics were sung in another seven in 1944 and six more in 1945. The use of "It Had to Be You" in *Nobody's Darling* (1943) and *Show Business* (1944) revived the song to the extent that there were four chart records in the summer of 1944, the most successful of which was a duet by Dick Haymes and Helen Forrest, though the recordings by Betty Hutton, Shaw, and Earl Hines also did well. Hutton then performed the song in the film *Incendiary Blonde* (1945).

Comic musician Spike Jones sent up "Chloe" in *Bring On the Girls* (1945) and scored a Top Ten novelty hit with it, and Haymes and Forrest followed up "It Had to Be You" with a revival of "Some Sunday Morning" for another hit. Sam Donohue and His Orch. had the biggest hit of their career with a revival of "I Never Knew (that Roses Grew)" in the spring of 1947, and at the end of the year Margaret Whiting hit the Top Ten with "Guilty," which her father had written with Kahn, beating out competing versions by Ella Fitzgerald and Johnny Desmond. In 1948, Benny Strong and His Orch. had a Top Ten hit with "That Certain Party"; there was another version by Dean Martin and Jerry Lewis.

The appearance of "Toot, Toot, Tootsie! (Goo'bye)" in the film *Jolson Sings Again* (1949) led to a recording by Art Mooney and His Orch. as well as a parody record by Mel Blanc, both of which reached the charts. The summer of 1950 brought chart revivals of "Sometime" (by The Mariners, The Ink Spots, and Jo Stafford) and "Dream a Little Dream of Me" (by Jack Owens and Frankie Laine). In the fall Les Paul charted with "Goofus," the first of a series of instrumental versions of songs for which Kahn had provided lyrics that later included "Josephine" (1951) and "Carioca" (1952).

All of this attention helped to set up the Kahn film biography *I'll See You in My Dreams*, based on Grace LeBoy Kahn and Louis F. Edelman's book *The Gus Kahn Story*. The film starred Danny Thomas and Doris Day and opened at the end of 1951. Kahn songs continued to turn up in films throughout the 1950s and to come in for revival on the charts. The release of *Love Me or Leave Me*, the film biography of Ruth Etting, in 1955 led to new hit versions of the title song by Sammy Davis Jr. and Lena Horne. "Coquette" was revived by Fats Domino in 1958, and "I'll See You in My Dreams" by Pat Boone in 1962.

In 1968, Mama Cass with the Mamas and the Papas hit the Top Ten with "Dream a Little Dream of Me," and in 1985, nearly 100 years after Kahn's birth, Robert Palmer released the multiplatinum album *Riptide*, featuring his revival of the title song.—**WR**

Kahn, Otto Hermann, German-American music patron, brother of **Robert Kahn;** b. Mannheim, Feb. 21, 1867; d. N.Y., March 29, 1934. He was engaged in the banking profession in London (1888–93). He settled in N.Y. in 1893, and was a member of the firm Kahn, Loeb & Co. He became interested in the musical affairs of N.Y.C., and from 1907 to his death was on the board of the Metropolitan Opera; also was vice-president of the N.Y. Phil.

BIBL.: M. Matz, *The Many Lives of O. K.* (N.Y., 1963); J. Kobler, *O. the Magnificent: The Life of O. K.* (N.Y., 1989). —**NS/LK/DM**

Kahn, Robert, German pianist and composer, brother of **Otto Hermann Kahn;** b. Mannheim, July 21, 1865; d. Biddenden, Kent, May 29, 1951. He studied music with Lachner in Mannheim and with Rheinberger in Munich. In 1885 he went to Berlin, and in 1890 moved to Leipzig, where he organized a Ladies' Choral Union, which he conducted. In 1893 he was appointed instructor of piano at the Berlin Hochschule für Musik, retiring in 1931. After the advent of the Nazi government in Germany, he emigrated to England. He composed a considerable amount of respectable chamber music and choral works.

BIBL.: E. Radecke, *R. K.* (Leipzig, 1894); S. Fahl, *Tradition der Natürlichkeit: Zu Biographie, Lyrikvertonung und Kammermusik des spätromantischen Klassizisten R. K.* (Sinzig, 1998). —**NS/LK/DM**

Kahn, Tiny (Norman), jazz drummer, arranger; b. N.Y., May 1924; d. Martha's Vineyard, Mass., Aug.19, 1953. He played harmonica as a child, took up drums at age 15, working with the school band. He was admired by musicians for his sensitive playing and fine writing, but died young due to drug problems. He played with Georgie Auld (1947), Boyd Raeburn (1948), Charlie

Barnet (1949), Lester Young, and Stan Getz quintet (1951). He wrote arrangements for Barnet, Elliot Lawrence, and Woody Herman. He was a favorite in big bop bands of late 1940s–early 1950s.

DISC.: Red Rodney: *Early Bebob* (1947). Chubby Jackson: *The Bebop Era* (1949). Al Cohn: *Cohn's Tones* (1950). Stan Getz: *Getz at Storyville.*—**LP**

Kahowez, Günter, Austrian composer; b. Vöcklabruck, Dec. 4, 1940. He studied at the Bruckner Cons. in Linz and at the Vienna Academy of Music with Schiske. With neo-Classical precepts as points of departure, he rapidly progressed in the direction of modern serialism. Among his compositions were a Wind Quintet (1959), String Quartet (1960), *Klangrhythmen* for Piano (1962), *Flachengitter* for Flute (1962), *Megalyse* for Electronic Instruments (1962), *Duale* for Clarinet and Guitar (1963), *Schichtungen* for Orch. (1963), *Ouverture & Pantomime* for Orch. (1964), and *Elementalichemie* for Cello and Percussion (1975).—**NS/LK/DM**

Kaim, Franz, German literary historian and music patron; b. Kirchheim unter Tech, near Stuttgart, May 13, 1856; d. Munich, Nov. 17, 1935. After settling in Munich, he built a concert hall and organized the "Kaim-Konzerte" in 1891. Then in 1893 organized an orch., which had such notable permanent conductors as Löwe (1897–98) and Weingartner (1898–1905). With the end of the Kaim Orch. in 1908, the Konzertverein was formed with Löwe as conductor (1908–14); later conductors included Pfitzner (1919–20) and Hausegger (from 1920). When the Konzertverein orch. officially became the Munich Phil. in 1928, Hausegger continued as conductor until 1938, his eminent successors including Rosbaud (1945–48), Kempe (1967–76), Celibidache (1979–96), and Levine (from 1999).—**NS/LK/DM**

Kaipainen, Jouni (Ilari), Finnish composer; b. Helsinki, Nov. 24, 1956. He studied with Sallinen (1973–76) and Heininen (1976–82) at the Sibelius Academy in Helsinki. From 1991 to 1993 he was artistic director of the Helsinki Festival. His style of composition is typical of the modern school of Finnish music, drawing away from the nationalistic trends of Sibelius, creating a thoroughly individual style.

WORKS: DRAMATIC: Television Opera: *Konstanzin Ihme* (The Miracle of Konstanz; 1987). **ORCH.:** *Concerto grosso per orchestra di camera* (1974); *Apotheosis* for Chamber Orch. (1975); 3 syms. (1980–85; 1992–94; 1999); *Carpe diem!,* clarinet concerto (1990); Oboe Concerto (1994). **CHAMBER:** 4 string quartets (1973, 1974, 1984, 1994); *Aspetti* for Clarinet and Piano (1975); *"...la chimère de l'humidité de la nuit?"* for Alto Saxophone (1978); *Trois morceaux de l'aube* for Cello and Piano (1980–81); *Far from Home* for Flute, Alto Saxophone, Guitar, and Percussion (1981); *Altaforte* for Electric Trumpet and Tape (1982); *Trio No. 1* for Clarinet, Cello, and Piano (1983); *Elegia* for Cello and Piano (1983); *Parcours* for Flute and Harpsichord (1983); *Piping Down the Valleys Wild* for Bass Clarinet and Piano (1984); *Andamento: Trio No. 2* for Flute, Bassoon, and Piano (1986); *Trio No. 3* for Violin, Cello, and Piano (1986–87); *Gena* for Accordion (1987); *L'annello di Aurora* for Violin (1988). **Piano:** Sonatina (1976); *Ladders to Fire* for 2 Pianos (1979); *Je chante la chaleur désespérée* (1981); *Conte* (1985).

VOCAL: *Yölaujuja* (Nocturnal Songs) for Soprano and Chamber Ensemble (1978); *Cinq poèmes de René Char* for Soprano and Orch. (1978–80); *Pitkän kesän poikki iltaan* (Through the Long Summer to the Evening) for Soprano, Flute, Horn, Percussion, and Cello (1979); *Stjarnenatten* (Star Night) for Soprano and Ensemble (1989); *Lachrymosa* for Chorus (1989).—**NS/LK/DM**

Kaiser, Alfred, Belgian-born English composer; b. Brussels, Feb. 29, 1872; d. Bournemouth, Oct. 1, 1917. He studied composition with Bruckner in Vienna and with Foerster in Prague, and then went to London. During World War I, he changed his name to De Keyser to escape the odium attached to the Kaiser of Germany. Among his works are the operas *Le Billet de Josephine* (Paris, 1902), *Die schwarze Nina* (Elberfeld, 1905), and *Stella Maris* (Düsseldorf, 1910). He also wrote a Sym., a Piano Concerto, and chamber music.—**NS/LK/DM**

Kaiser, Henry, innovative American improvisational guitarist and keyboardist; b. Oakland, Calif., Sept. 19, 1952. He took up the guitar at 12, developing a unique and eclectic style that shows influences as varied as East Asian, classical North Indian, and Hawaiian music, free jazz and improvisation, and American steel-string guitar; he also draws freely from other abiding interests, which include information theory, experimental cinema and literature, mathematics, and scuba diving. He has performed extensively with such groups as Crazy-Backwards Alphabet, Invite the Spirit, The Henry Kaiser Band, The Obsequious Cheeselog, French-Frith-Kaiser-Thompson, and The Henry Kaiser Quartet. His list of collaborators is extensive; he also has assisted various composers and performers in their compositional and recording endeavors through his elaborate recording studio in Oakland, Calif. He is senior instructor in Underwater Scientific Research at the Univ. of Calif. at Berkeley. Among his solo recordings or recordings in which he is a featured artist are *Those Who Know History Are Doomed to Repeat It, Re-Marrying for Money,* and *Alternate Visions;* he also produced an instructional video, *Eclectric Electric, Exploring New Horizons of Guitar and Improvisation* (1990).—**NS/LK/DM**

Kajanus, Robert, outstanding Finnish conductor; b. Helsinki, Dec. 2, 1856; d. there, July 6, 1933. He studied with R. Faltin and G. Niemann at the Helsinki Cons., and later at the Leipzig Cons. with Reinecke, Richter, and Jadassohn (1877–79); then went to Paris, where he studied with Svendsen (1879–80). After returning to Helsinki in 1882, he founded an orch. society that sponsored concerts by the newly organized Helsinki Phil., which he led until his death; from 1897 to 1926 he was music director at the Univ. of Helsinki. He was an early champion of the music of Sibelius, and made the first recordings of the 1st and 2nd syms. with the London Sym. Orch. He composed the symphonic poems *Kullervo* (1881) and *Aino* (1885), 2 Finnish rhapsodies (1882, 1889), an orch. suite, *Sommarminnen* (Summer Memories; 1896), piano pieces, and songs.

BIBL.: Y. Suomalainen, *R. K.: Hänen elämänsä ja toimintansa* (R. K.: His Life and Work; Helsinki, 1952).—**NS/LK/DM**

Kakinuma, Toshie, significant Japanese musicologist and music critic; b. Shizuoka Prefecture, July 31,

1953. She was educated in Tokyo at the Kunitachi Coll. of Music (B.M., 1977) and Ochanomizu Univ. (M.A., 1981), and then took her Ph.D. at the Univ. of Calif., San Diego in 1989 with the diss. *The Musical Instruments of Harry Partch as an Apparatus of Production in Musical Theatre.* She taught at the Yoshiro Irino Music Inst. (from 1990), Nippon Electronics Coll. (from 1992), and Takushoku Univ. (from 1995); also was a guest lecturer at Nippon Univ. (1995). Kakinuma has been an important figure in the organization of new music festivals in Japan, including "Music History of Quotation" (1983) and "Sound Culture Festival" (1993); also was curator of Betty Freeman's photographic exhibitions at the B (NTT Shinuya) and Studio 200 in Tokyo. Her important writings, primarily on contemporary Japanese, American, and English composers, have appeared widely in publs. in both Japan and the U.S.; she is a regular writer/reviewer to *Ongakugeijutsu* (from 1980), *On-Stage* (from 1989), and *inTune* and the *Asahi Evening News* (from 1994); from 1981 to 1991 she was a regular contributor to *Philharmony,* the program guide for the NHK Sym. Orch. (1982–91). She also publ., with others, a number of music reference works (1982, 1983, 1993), and prepared a Japanese tr. of John Cage's *Silence* (Tokyo, 1995).—NS/LK/DM

Kalabis, Viktor, Czech composer; b. Červený Kostelec, Feb. 27, 1923. He studied with Hlobil at the Prague Cons. (1945–48) and with Řídký at the Prague Academy of Music (1948–52), and also took courses in philosophy and musicology at the Univ. of Prague. He was an ed. and music producer with the Czech Radio in Prague (1953–72), and then devoted himself totally to composition. In 1967 he received the Czech Music Critics' Prize and in 1969 the Klement Gottwald State Prize. In 1983 he was made an Artist of Merit by the Czech government. In 1952 he married **Zuzana Růžičková.** His early works adhered to traditional methods, but he later adopted modified serial procedures.

WORKS: ORCH.: Concerto for Chamber Orch., *Hommage à Stravinsky* (1948); Overture (1950); Cello Concerto (1951); *Strážnice Suite* (1953); 2 piano concertos (1954, 1985); 5 syms.: No. 1 (1957), No. 2, *Sinfonia Pacis* (1961), No. 3 (1971), No. 4 (1972), and No. 5 (1976); 2 violin concertos (1959, 1978); *Chamber Music* for Strings (1963); *Symphonic Variations* (1964); *Concerto for Orchestra* (1966); Trumpet Concerto (1973); Concerto for Harpsichord and Strings (1975); *Fable* for Chamber Orch. (1983); Concertino for Bassoon and Wind Instruments (1983); *Diptych* for Strings (1987); *Meantatioas* for 13 Wind Instruments (1988). **CHAMBER:** 6 string quartets (1949, 1962, 1977, 1984, 1984, 1987); *Divertimento* for Wind Quintet (1952); *Bagpiper,* suite for Oboe and Piano (1953); 2 nonets (*Classical,* 1956; *Homage to Nature,* 1975); Sonata for Violin and Harpsichord (1967); Small Chamber Music for Wind Quintet (1967); Cello Sonata (1968); Clarinet Sonata (1969); *Variations* for Horn and Piano (1969); Trombone Sonata (1970); Trio for Violin, Cello, and Piano (1974); *Spring Whistles,* Octet for Winds (1979); Suite for Clarinet and Piano (1981); 2 violin sonatas (1982, 1997); Duettino for Violin and Cello (1987); *Birdcall* for Flute (1995); *Ludus per quatro*

for Violin, Viola, Cello, and Piano (1996). **Piano:** 3 sonatas (1947, 1948, 1982). **VOCAL:** *The War,* chamber cantata for Chorus, Dulcimer, and Flute (1977); *Canticum Canticorum,* cantata for Contralto, Tenor, Chorus, and Chamber Orch. (1986); choruses; songs.—NS/LK/DM

Kalachevsky, Mikhail, Ukrainian composer; b. Polovka, near Elizavetgrad, Sept. 26, 1851; d. Kremenchug, c. 1910. He studied piano with C. Reinecke and theory with E.F.E. Richter at the Leipzig Cons. (1872–76). Returning to Russia, he occupied provincial government positions. His music reflects the modalities of Ukrainian folk songs; his *Ukrainian Symphony* (1876) has some historical value. He also composed a Requiem for Chorus, String Quartet, and Organ, a String Quartet in E-flat major, a Piano Trio in A minor, and several works for solo piano, including 19 romances.

BIBL.: N. Gordeichuk, *M.N. K.* (Kiev, 1954); ibid., *Ukrainskaya simfoniya M. K.* (The Ukrainian Symphony of M. K.; Kiev, 1963).—NS/LK/DM

Kalafati, Vasili (Pavlovich), Russian composer and pedagogue of Greek descent; b. Eupatoria, Feb. 10, 1869; d. Leningrad, Jan. 30, 1942. He studied at the St. Petersburg Cons. with Rimsky-Korsakov, graduating in 1899, and subsequently was on its teaching staff (1907–29). A musician of thorough knowledge, he was held in great esteem by his colleagues and students; Rimsky-Korsakov sent Stravinsky to him for additional training in harmony. As a composer, Kalafati faithfully continued the traditions of the Russian national school. His works include an opera, *Zygany* (The Gypsies; 1939–41), a Sym., a Piano Quintet, 2 piano sonatas, piano pieces, and a number of songs, all set in impeccably euphonious harmonies.—NS/LK/DM

Kalaš, Julius, Czech composer; b. Prague, Aug. 18, 1902; d. there, May 12, 1967. He studied composition with Foerster and Křička at the Prague Cons. (1921–24), then attended Suk's master classes there (1924–28). He was pianist and artistic director of the satirical male sextet the Teachers of Gotham (1925–53), for which he wrote numerous witty ballads and songs. He was a prof. in the film dept. of the Prague Academy of Musical Arts from 1948; was its dean (1949–50) and vice-dean (1955–57). He wrote 6 operas, the most notable being *Nepokoření* (The Proud Ones; 1960), 6 operettas, including the popular *Mlynárka z Granady* (The Miller's Wife of Granada; 1954), 2 ballets, Cello Concerto (1949), Viola Concerto (1950), cantatas, chamber music, and film scores.—NS/LK/DM

Kalbeck, Max, German writer on music; b. Breslau, Jan. 4, 1850; d. Vienna, May 4, 1921. He studied law and philosophy at the Univ. of Breslau, then music in Munich (1872–74). He returned to Breslau as music critic of the *Schlesische Zeitung* in 1875, and later wrote for the *Breslauer Zeitung;* then settled in Vienna in 1880, and wrote for the *Wiener Allgemeine Zeitung.* He was music critic for the *Neue Freie Presse* (1883–86), the *Neues Wiener Tageblatt* (1886–90), and the *Wiener Montags-Revue* (from

1890). In addition to his monumental biography of Brahms, he also ed. Brahms's correspondence (Vols. I-II, Berlin, 1907; VIII, Berlin, 1915; IX-XII, Berlin, 1917–19).

WRITINGS: *Richard Wagners Nibelungen* (Breslau, 1876; 2nd ed., 1883); *Das Bühnenfestspiel zu Bayreuth* (Breslau, 1877); *Richard Wagners Parsifal* (Breslau, 1883); *Gereimtes und Ungereimtes* (Berlin, 1885); *Wiener Opernabende* (Vienna, 1885); *Humoresken und Phantasien* (Berlin, 1896); *Opernabende* (2 vols., Berlin, 1898); *Johannes Brahms* (8 vols., Berlin, 1904–14).—NS/LK/DM

Kalenberg, Josef, German tenor; b. Cologne, Jan. 7, 1886; d. Vienna, Nov. 8, 1962. He received his training at the Cologne Cons. In 1911 he made his operatic debut as Turiddu at the Cologne Opera. After singing in Krefeld (1912–16), Barmen (1919–21), Düsseldorf (1921–25), and Cologne (1925–27), he made his first appearance at the Vienna State Opera as Parsifal in 1927, remaining on its roster until 1942. He also sang at the Salzburg Festivals (1928–36) and made guest appearances in France, Italy, and England before retiring in 1949.—NS/LK/DM

Kalichstein, Joseph, Israeli-American pianist; b. Tel Aviv, Jan. 15, 1946. He studied at the Juilliard School of Music in N.Y. with Kabos and Steuermann (M.S., 1969). He made his N.Y. recital debut and won the Young Concert Artists' Award (1967), then appeared as soloist in Beethoven's 4th Piano Concerto with Bernstein and the N.Y. Phil. on national television (1968). After winning 1st prize in the Leventritt Competition (1969), he pursued an active concert career; toured widely in a trio with the violinist Jaime Laredo and the cellist Sharon Robinson (from 1976).—NS/LK/DM

Kálik, Václav, Czech pianist, conductor, and composer; b. Opava, Oct. 18, 1891; d. Prague, Nov. 18, 1951. He studied with Novák at the Univ. of Prague (1911–13), and later attended Suk's master classes at the Prague Cons. (1924–26). He was mainly active as a pianist and conductor.

WORKS: DRAMATIC: O p e r a : *Jarní jitro* (A Spring Morning; 1933; Olomouc, 1943); *Lásky div* (Love's Miracle; 1942–43; Liberec, Nov. 20, 1950); *Posvěcení mládí* (Consecration of Youth; 1946–48). ORCH.: *Fantazie* (1915); *Moře* (The Sea), symphonic poem (1924); 2 syms.: No. 1, *Mírová* (Peace), for Soprano and Orch. (1927) and No. 2 (1941–43); *Prelude* (1931); *Venezia* for Strings (1932). OTHER: Chamber music; vocal pieces, including *Intermezzo* for Tenor, Violin, and Piano (1913), *Zlá láska* (Evil Love) for Soprano, Violin, and Piano (1919), and *Pražské obrazy* (Prague Pictures) for Men's Chorus (1949–50).

BIBL.: J. Vratislavský, *V. K.* (Ostrava, 1961).—NS/LK/DM

Kalinnikov, Vasili (Sergeievich), Russian composer; b. Voin, near Mtzensk, Jan. 13, 1866; d. Yalta, Jan. 11, 1901. He studied in Orel. In 1884 he enrolled at the Moscow Cons., but had to leave it a year later because of inability to pay; he then studied the bassoon at the Music School of the Moscow Phil. Soc. which provided free tuition. He earned his living by playing bassoon in theater orchs., and also studied composition with A. Ilyinsky and Blaramberg. While still a student,

he composed his first work, the symphonic poem *The Nymphs* (Moscow, Dec. 28, 1889). He later wrote another symphonic poem, *The Cedar and the Palm* (1897–98), incidental music for *Tsar Boris* (Moscow, Feb. 1, 1899), and the prelude to the unfinished opera *In the Year 1812* (1899–1900). In 1895 he completed his most successful work, the Sym. in G minor (Kiev, Feb. 20, 1897); a 2nd sym., in A major (Kiev, March 12, 1898), was not as successful. He also wrote a cantata, *John of Damascus* (1890; not extant), songs, and piano pieces.

BIBL.: V. Paskhalov, *V.S. K.: Life and Works* (Moscow and Leningrad, 1938; 2nd ed., aug., 1951); V. Kiselyo, ed., *V. K.: Letters, Documents, Materials* (2 vols., Moscow, 1959).—NS/LK/DM

Kalisch, Paul, German tenor; b. Berlin, Nov. 6, 1855; d. St. Lorenz am Mondsee, Austria, Jan. 27, 1946. He studied architecture, then went to Milan, where he took voice lessons with Leoni and Lamperti. He made his operatic debut under the name Paolo Alberti in Rome as Edgardo (1879), and subsequently sang in Milan's La Scala (1882) and other Italian opera houses. After appearing in Munich (1883), he was a member of Berlin's Royal Opera (1884–87). He made his first appearance in London at Her Majesty's Theatre (1887). In 1888 he married **Lilli Lehmann,** with whom he frequently appeared in operatic performances. On Jan. 30, 1889, he sang Tannhäuser in his Metropolitan Opera debut in N.Y.; sang there again in 1890 and 1891. He later separated from Lehmann, although they never legally divorced; after her death in 1929, he settled on her estate.—NS/LK/DM

Kalischer, Alfred, German writer on music; b. Thorn, March 4, 1842; d. Berlin, Oct. 8, 1909. After obtaining his Ph.D. at the Univ. of Leipzig, he took music courses with Burgel and Bohmer in Berlin. He ed. the *Neue Berliner Musikzeitung* (from 1873). He was best known for his writings on Beethoven. He ed. *Neue Beethovenbriefe* (1902) and *Beethovens sämtliche Briefe* (5 vols., 1906–8; Eng. tr., 1909).

WRITINGS: *Lessing als Musikästhetiker* (1889); *Die "Unsterbliche Geliebte" Beethovens* (1891); *Die Macht Beethovens* (1903); *Beethoven und seine Zeitgenossen* (4 vols., 1908: I, *Beethoven und Berlin*; II and III, *Beethovens Frauenkreis*; IV, *Beethoven und Wien*).—NS/LK/DM

Kalish, Gilbert, American pianist and teacher; b. N.Y., July 2, 1935. He studied at Columbia Coll. (B.A., 1956) and the Columbia Univ. Graduate School of Arts and Sciences (1956–58). In addition, he took piano lessons with Isabelle Vengerova, Leonard Shure, and Julius Herford. He made his N.Y. recital debut and his European debut in London in 1962; then made tours as a soloist in the U.S., Europe, and Australia; also was active with the Contemporary Chamber Ensemble and the Boston Sym. Chamber Players. He also was a regular accompanist to Jan DeGaetani. He was artist-in-residence at Rutgers, the State Univ. of N.J. (1965–67), and Swarthmore (Pa.) Coll. (1966–72). He was head of keyboard activities at the Berkshire Music Center in Tanglewood, and also taught at the State Univ. of N.Y. at Stony Brook (from 1970).—NS/LK/DM

Kalkbrenner, Christian, German composer and writer on music, father of **Frédéric (Friedrich Wilhelm Michael) Kalkbrenner;** b. Minden, Hannover, Sept. 22, 1755; d. Paris, Aug. 10, 1806. He studied piano with Becker and violin with Rodewald in Kassel. He was choirmaster at the court of the Queen in Berlin (1788) and at the court of Prince Heinrich in Rheinsberg (1790–96). In 1798 he became choirmaster at the Paris Opera, where he brought out the opera *Olimpie* (Dec. 18, 1798) as well as some pasticcios from music by Mozart and Haydn. He also wrote 2 syms., a Piano Concerto, and several piano sonatas. He publ. *Theorie der Tonkunst* (1789) and *Kurzer Abriss der Geschichte der Tonkunst* (1792).—NS/LK/DM

Kalkbrenner, Frédéric (Friedrich Wilhelm Michael), celebrated French pianist, pedagogue, and composer of German descent, son of **Christian Kalkbrenner;** b. near Kassel, between Nov. 2 and 8, 1785; d. Enghien-les-Bains, June 10, 1849. He most likely began his musical training with his father, then in 1799 entered the Paris Cons., where he studied with Louis Adam and Nicodami (piano) and Catel (harmony), taking 1st prizes in 1801. From 1803 to 1804 he was in Vienna, where he profited from the advice of Haydn. He then played in Munich, Stuttgart, and Frankfurt am Main on his return to Paris in 1805; was in great demand as a teacher in Paris. He went to Bath (1814–15), and then enjoyed considerable success as a pianist in London (1815–23). In 1818 he took up Logier's newly invented Chiroplast, simplified it, and applied it practically. He returned to Paris in 1824, becoming a partner in the Pleyel piano factory (the future Mme. Camilla Pleyel was one of his pupils). He continued to tour as a virtuoso, acquiring great renown until ill health compelled him to curtail his travels in 1835. During the last years of his life, he made only sporadic appearances as a pianist. Kalkbrenner was inordinately vain of the success of his method of teaching, which aimed at the independent development of the fingers and wrist; his practical method of octave playing became a standard of piano teaching. He also developed left-hand technique, and a proper management of the pedals. As for his playing, his technique was smooth and well-rounded, his fingers supple and of equal strength, and his tone full and rich; his style, while fluent and graceful, lacked emotional power. His numerous etudes (among them several for left hand alone) are interesting and valuable. Chopin took some advice from him in Paris, but did not become his pupil, despite Kalkbrenner's urging. His most distinguished students were Halle and Thalberg. He publ. the didactic works *Méthode pour apprendre le pianoforte à l'aide du guide-mains* (1830) and *Traité d'harmonie du pianiste* (1849).

WORKS: 4 piano concertos (1823, 1826, 1829, 1835); Concerto for 2 Pianos (1835); 13 piano sonatas (1807–45); many virtuoso pieces for Piano and Orch.; chamber music; numerous light pieces for Solo Piano.

BIBL.: L. Boivin, *K.* (Paris, 1840).—NS/LK/DM

Kallenberg, Siegfried Garibaldi, German composer; b. Bad Schachen, near Lindau, Nov. 3, 1867; d. Munich, Feb. 9, 1944. He studied with Faisst at the Stuttgart Cons. and at the Munich Academy of Music. He became director of the Stettin Cons. (1892), and later taught in Konigsberg, Hannover, and Munich (from 1910). He publ. *Musikalische Kompositionsformen* (Leipzig, 1913) and monographs on R. Strauss (Leipzig, 1926) and Reger (Leipzig, 1930). As a composer, he was inspired by neo-Romanticism; in some of his works there are touches of Impressionism; in others, his absorption in symbolic subjects brought him into a kinship with the Expressionist school in Germany. Apart from works on exotic subjects, he wrote music in a traditional style; he was particularly strong in choral polyphony.

WORKS: 3 operas: *Sun Liao, Das goldene Tor,* and *Die lustigen Musikanten;* 3 syms.; *Impressionen* for Orch.; *Konzertante Fantasie* for Piano and Orch.; about 10 chamber works; 3 piano sonatas; a set of *Miniaturen* for Piano; choral works: *90th Psalm, Germania an ihre Kinder, Requiem, Den Gefallenen, Eine kleine Passionmusik,* and *Eine Pfingstmusik;* some 300 songs. —NS/LK/DM

Kallir, Lilian, Czech-born American pianist and teacher; b. Prague, May 6, 1931. She was taken as a child to the U.S., where she studied with Isabelle Vengerova and Herman de Grab at the Mannes Coll. of Music in N.Y. (1946–49). She won the National Music League Award and the American Artists Award of the Brooklyn Inst. of Arts and Sciences at 16. She made her debut as soloist with the N.Y. Phil. at 17; her recital debut followed at N.Y.'s Town Hall at 18; thereafter she toured widely in the U.S., South America, Europe, and Israel, appearing as soloist with orchs. and as a recitalist. She married **Claude Frank** in 1959, and subsequently appeared in duo recitals with him. She has also given concerts with her daughter, **Pamela Frank.** In 1975 she joined the faculty of the Mannes Coll. of Music. —NS/LK/DM

Kalliwoda (Kalivoda), Johann Wenzel (Jan Křtitel Václav), Bohemian violinist, conductor, and composer, father of **Wilhelm Kalliwoda;** b. Prague, Feb. 21, 1801; d. Karlsruhe, Dec. 3, 1866. He studied at the Prague Cons. (1811–16) with Pixis (violin) and D. Weber (composition); played in the orch. of the Stavovské Theater in Prague (1816–21). In 1822 he became conductor of Prince Furstenberg's orch. in Donaueschingen, where he remained for some 30 years; his duties were minimal after the orch. was dissolved in the wake of the 1848 Revolution and the destruction of the theater by fire (1856). After giving a farewell concert as a violinist in Prague (1858), he retired to Karlsruhe. His early success as a composer was not sustained in the later years of his career; some of his music was praised by Schumann.

WORKS: DRAMATIC: O p e r a : *Blanda, die silberne Birke* (Prague, Nov. 29, 1827); *Prinzessin Christine von Wolfenburg* (Donaueschingen, 1828). **ORCH.:** 7 syms. (1826–41); 18 overtures; various works for Violin and Orch. **CHAMBER:** Various works; piano pieces. **VOCAL:** Songs.

BIBL.: K. Strunz, *J.W. K.* (Vienna, 1910).—NS/LK/DM

Kalliwoda, Wilhelm, German pianist, conductor, and composer, son of **Johann Wenzel (Jan Křtitel**

Václav) Kalliwoda (Kalivoda); b. Donaueschingen, July 19, 1827; d. Karlsruhe, Sept. 8, 1893. He studied with Hauptmann in Leipzig, and also took some lessons from Mendelssohn. He settled in Karlsruhe, where he was director of the Court Theater (from 1853). He wrote piano pieces and songs.—NS/LK/DM

Kallmann, Helmut (Max), esteemed German-born Canadian librarian, musicologist, and editor; b. Berlin, Aug. 7, 1922. He studied music with his father. He left Germany in 1939 for London, where he was interned as a German citizen in 1940, and then was interned in Canada (1940–43); after his release, he became a naturalized Canadian citizen (1946). He took music courses at the Univ. of Toronto (B.Mus., 1949), and then became a music librarian for the CBC in 1950. He was supervisor of its music collection from 1962. From 1970 to 1987 he served as chief of the music division of the National Library of Canada in Ottawa. In 1982 he co-founded and became chair of the Canadian Musical Heritage Soc. Its series of 25 vols., of which he ed. numbers 8 and 22, was completed in 1999. He publ. a number of useful books, including a *Catalogue of Canadian Composers* (Toronto, 1952) and *A History of Music in Canada 1534–1914* (Toronto, 1960); with G. Potvin and K. Winters, he ed. the authoritative *Encyclopedia of Music in Canada* (Toronto, 1981; 2nd ed., rev., 1992).

BIBL.: J. Beckwith and F. Hall, eds., *Musical Canada: Words and Music Honouring H. K.* (Toronto, 1988).—NS/LK/DM

Kallstenius, Edvin, Swedish composer; b. Filipstad, Aug. 29, 1881; d. Danderyd, Nov. 22, 1967. He studied science at the Univ. of Lund (1898–1903) and music at the Leipzig Cons. (1903–07), and then was active as a music critic in Stockholm. He also was a music librarian for the Swedish Radio (1928–46). In his early works, he followed the Romantic traditions of Scandinavian music; later turned to advanced modern techniques, including explicit application of dodeca-phonic configurations.

WORKS: ORCH.: *Scherzo fugato* for Small Orch. (1907; rev. 1923); *Sista Striden,* dramatic overture (1908); *En serenad i sommarnatten* (A Serenade in the Summer Night; 1918); *Sinfonia concertata* for Piano and Orch. (1922); 4 sinfoniettas (1923; 1946; *Dodicitonica,* 1956; *Semi-seriale,* 1958); 5 syms. (1926, rev. 1941; 1935; 1948; 1954; *Sinfonia su temi 12-tonici,* 1960); *Dalarapsodi* (1931); *Dalslandsrapsodi* (1936); *Romantico,* overture (1938); *Högtid och fest,* trilogy (1940); *Musica gioconda* for Strings (1942); *Cavatina* for Viola and Orch. (1943); *Passacaglia enarmonica* (1943); *Kraus-variationer* (1947); *Sonata concertate* for Cello and Orch. (1951); *Musica sinfonica* for Strings (1953; full orch. version, 1959); *Nytt vin i gamla läglar* (New Wine in Old Bottles) for Small Orch. (1954); *Choreographic Suite* (1957); *Prologo seriale* (1966). **CHAMBER:** 8 string quartets (1904; 1905; 1913; *Divertimento alla serenata,* 1925; 1945; 1953; *Dodecatonica,* 1957; 1961); Cello Sonata (1908); Violin Sonata (1909); Clarinet Quintet (1930); Suite for Winds and Percussion (1938); Wind Quintet (1943); *Trio divertente* for Flute, Violin, and Viola (1950); *Piccolo trio seriale* for Flute, English Horn, and Clarinet (1956); *Trio svagante* for Clarinet, Horn, and Cello (1959); solo sonatas for Cello (1961), Flute (1962), and Violin (1965); *Lyric Suite* for Flute, Saxophone, and Cello (1962); String Trio (1965). **VOCAL:** *När*

vi do (When Mankind Perishes), Requiem for Chorus and Orch. (1919); *Sångoffer* (Song Offering), cantata for Baritone and Orch. (1944); *Stjärntändningen* for Chorus and Orch. (1949); *Hymen, o, Hymenaios* for Soloists, Chorus, and Orch. (1955).—NS/LK/DM

Kálmán, Emmerich (actually, Imre), remarkable Hungarian composer; b. Siófolk, Oct. 24, 1882; d. Paris, Oct. 30, 1953. He went to Budapest, where he studied law at the Univ. and theory and composition with Koessler at the Royal Academy of Music. From 1904 to 1908 he was a répétiteur at the Vigszinhás, and also wrote music criticism. Although he attracted notice as a composer with his symphonic poem *Saturnalia* (1904) and a song cycle, which was awarded the Franz-Josef Prize (1907), he soon concentrated his activities on the musical theater. His first operetta, *Tatárjárás* (The Happy Hussars; Feb. 22, 1908), was so successful that it was subsequently performed throughout Europe and eventually made its way to N.Y. His next score, *Az obsitos* (March 16, 1910), assured his reputation when it was subsequently staged in Vienna as *Der gute Kamerad* (Oct. 10, 1911; rev. version as *Gold gab ich für Eisen*, Oct. 16, 1914). Its unqualified success led Kálmán to settle in Vienna, where he brought out the highly successful *Der Zigeunerprimás* (Oct. 11, 1912), which subsequently triumphed on various European stages and as *Sari* on Broadway. After producing *The Blue House* (London, Oct. 28, 1912), *Der kleine König* (Vienna, Nov. 27, 1912), and *Kivándorlók* (Budapest, Sept. 26, 1913), Kálmán had a notable success with *Zsuzsi kisasszony* (Budapest, Feb. 23, 1915), which later became a Broadway favorite as *Miss Springtime.* With Vienna again the center of his activities, he scored a triumph with his *Die Csárdás-fürstin* (Nov. 17, 1915), which ran for almost 600 performances and became a beloved repertoire piece. The success of *Die Faschingsfee* (Sept. 21, 1917) was followed by the popular *Das Hollandweibchen* (Jan. 31, 1920). Kálmán then composed 2 outstanding scores, *Die Bajadere* (Dec. 23, 1921) and *Gräfin Mariza* (Feb. 28, 1924), which were heard throughout Europe to great acclaim. The latter was so successful that it also became a repertoire work. After further success with *Die Zirkusprinzessin* (March 26, 1926), Kálmán attempted to transfer his golden touch to Broadway with *Golden Dawn* (Nov. 30, 1927) but without success. Back in Vienna, success was his again with *Die Herzogin von Chicago* (April 5, 1928), although *Das Veilchen vom Montmartre* (March 21, 1930) and *Der Teufelsreiter* (March 10, 1932) elicited little interest. He also wrote the film score for *Ronny* (1931). After composing *Kaiserin Josephine* (Zürich, Jan. 18, 1936), the ominous clouds of Nazism led Kálmán to go to Paris in 1939. In 1940 he emigrated to the U.S. and in 1942 became a naturalized American citizen. During his American sojourn, he had some success with the musical *Marinka* (N.Y., July 18, 1945). With World War II over, Kálmán returned to Europe. His last stage work, *Arizona Lady,* was premiered posthumously in Bern on Feb. 14, 1954.

BIBL.: J. Bistron, *E. K.* (Vienna, 1932); R. Oesterreicher, *E. K.: Der Weg eines Komponisten* (Vienna, 1954); V. Kálmán, *Gruss' mir die süssen, die reizenden Frauen: Mein Leben mit E. K.* (Bayreuth, 1966); R. Oesterreicher, *E. K.: Das Leben eines Operettenfürsten* (Vienna, 1988).—NS/LK/DM

Kálmán, Oszkár, Hungarian bass; b. Kis- Szent-Péter, June 18, 1887; d. Budapest, Sept. 18, 1971. He was a student at the Budapest Academy of Music of József Sík. In 1913 he made his debut as Sarastro at the Budapest Opera, where, in 1918, he created Bartók's Duke Bluebeard. After appearances in Hamburg (1926), at the Berlin Kroll Opera (1927), and in Vienna and Barcelona (1927–29), he again sang at the Budapest Opera (1929–54); also made appearances as a concert artist. Kálmán was particularly admired for his Wagnerian roles.—NS/LK/DM

Kalmár, László, Hungarian composer; b. Budapest, Oct. 19, 1931; d. there, May 27, 1995. He received training in composition from Major at the Bela Bartók Music School and later from Farkas privately. In 1957 he joined the staff of Editio Musica Budapest, where he became ed.-in-chief in 1970 and then head of music in 1987. In 1985 he was awarded the Erkel Prize.

WORKS: ORCH.: *Toccata concertante* for Piano and Strings (1968–70); *Cycles* for Strings (1971–74); *Notturno No. 1* for 15 Instruments (1973); *Horae* (1982); *Lectiones* for Chamber Ensemble (1982); *Hermes* (1983–84); Piano Concerto No. 2 (1984–85); *Ballet des fleurs blanches* for Strings (1984–85); *Ballet des amphores* (1985–86); Chamber Concerto (1986); *3 Symphonic Pictures* (1986–87); *At Janus's Gate* (1988). CHAMBER: *Divertimento* for 2 Violins and Cello (1961); Trio for Flute, Marimba, and Guitar (1968); *Monologo* for Guitar (1968), Violin (1973), Flute (1974), Cello (1975), Clarinet (1977), Saxophone (1978), and Horn (1983); Flute Sonata (1970–71); *Triangoli* for Clarinet, Horn, Harp, Violin, and Cello (1970–71); *Distichon* for Piano, Harp, and Percussion (1970–71); Quartet for English Horn, Viola, Vibraphone, and Harpsichord (1972); String Trio (1972); *Sotto voce* for Organ, Vibraphone, and Harp (1973); *La stanza quarta* for 3 Horns (1976); *Terzina* for Violin, Viola, and Harp (1976); *Morfeo* for String Quartet (1977); *Chorale* for 3 Clarinets (1979); *Serioso* for 2 Cimbaloms (1979); Trio Sonata for Clarinet, Horn, and Cello (1981); *Ad Blasium* for Brass Quintet (1984). VOCAL: Choral pieces; motets; songs.—NS/LK/DM

Kalninš, Alfreds, Latvian organist and composer, father of **Janis Kalninš;** b. Zehsis, Aug. 23, 1879; d. Riga, Dec. 23, 1951. He studied at the St. Petersburg Cons. (1897–1901) with Homilius (organ) and Liadov (composition), then was organist in various Lutheran churches in Dorpat, Libau, and Riga. He gave recitals in Russia, and was also active as a teacher in Riga. From 1927 to 1933 he lived in N.Y. He then returned to Riga, where he taught at the Latvian Cons. and was its rector (1944–48). He wrote the first national Latvian opera, *Banuta* (Riga, May 29, 1920), as well as the operas *Salinieki* (The Islanders; Riga, 1925) and *Dzimtenes atmoda* (The Nation's Awakening; Riga, Sept. 9, 1933). His other works include a symphonic poem, *Latvia,* some 100 choruses, piano pieces, about 200 songs, and arrangements of Latvian folk songs.

BIBL.: J. Vitolinš, *A. K.* (Riga, 1968).—NS/LK/DM

Kalninš, Imants, significant Latvian composer; b. Riga, May 26, 1941. He studied composition with A. Skulte at the Latvian Cons. in Riga, graduating in 1964. In 1959 he directed the choral organization Lachplesis in Lielvarde, then was pianist for a pantomime group in Riga (1962–64) and taught music in Liepaja and later at the Latvian Cons. (1973–80). About 1980 he turned his attention mostly to rock music. His output is innovative, fusing a diversity of styles; his 4th Sym. is scored for jazz ensemble and orch.

WORKS: DRAMATIC: Opera: *Is There Anyone Here?* (1971); *I Play, I Dance* (1977). Operetta: *Quo Vadis My Guitar?* (1971). ORCH.: Cello Concerto (1963); 4 syms. (1964, 1965, 1968, 1972); Concerto (1966). CHAMBER: *Toccata* for Cello and Piano (1962); Viola Sonata (1962); Piano Sonata (1962). VOCAL: Oratorios: *In October* (1967); *The Poet and the Mermaid* (1973); *Morning Drudgery* (1977).—NS/LK/DM

Kalninš, Janis, Latvian-born Canadian organist, conductor, pedagogue, and composer, son of **Alfreds Kalninš;** b. Pernu, Estonia (of Latvian parents), Nov. 3, 1904. He studied piano and organ with his father, then composition with Vitols at the Latvian State Cons. in Riga (1920–24). He also studied conducting with Kleiber in Salzburg, Abendroth in Leipzig, and Blech in Berlin. Returning to Riga, he served as music director of the Latvian National Theater (1923–33) and the Latvian National Opera (1933–44). In 1948 he emigrated to Canada, becoming a naturalized citizen in 1954. From 1948 to 1989 he was organist and choirmaster at St. Paul's United Church in Fredericton, New Brunswick; he served as prof. of music at the Fredericton Teachers' Coll. (1951–71), and was conductor of the Fredericton Civic Orch. (1951–58), the St. John Sym. Orch. (1958–61), and the New Brunswick Sym. Orch. (1961–67).

WORKS: DRAMATIC: Opera: *Lolita's Magic Bird* (1933); *Unguni* (1933); *In the Fire* (1934); *Hamlet* (1935; Riga, Feb. 17, 1936). Ballet: *Autumn* (1936); *The Nightingale and the Rose* (1936). ORCH.: *2 Latvian Peasant Dances* (1936); 5 syms.: No. 1 (1939–44), No. 2, *Symphony of the Beatitudes,* for Chorus and Orch. (1953), No. 3 (1972–73), No. 4 (1979), and No. 5 (1990); Violin Concerto (1945–46); *Marching Through Fredericton* (1963); *Theme and Variations* for Clarinet, Horn, and Orch. (1963); *Music for Strings* (1965); *New Brunswick Rhapsody* (1967); *Festival Overture* (1969); *Latvian Rhapsody* (1975); Concerto for Piano and Chamber Orch. (1985). CHAMBER: String Quartet (1948); Oboe Sonata (1963); Trio for Violin, Cello, and Piano (1966); *Klusa Stunda* for Violin and Piano (1968); Violin Sonata (1982); *Larghetto Serioso* for Violin and Organ or Piano (1975); Trio for Violin, Viola, and Cello (1979); Sonata for Solo Violin (1975); Piano Quartet (1987); piano pieces, including 2 piano sonatas; organ music. VOCAL: Cantata for Men's Chorus and Orch. (1965); *Spring Song,* cantata for Chorus and Orch. (1981); *Requiem* for Soprano, Baritone, Chorus, and Piano or Organ or Orch. (1988–89); choral pieces; songs.—NS/LK/DM

Kalomiris, Manolis, distinguished Greek composer and pedagogue; b. Smyrna, Dec. 26, 1883; d. Athens, April 3, 1962. He studied piano with Bauch and Sturm, theory and composition with Grädener, and music history with Mandyczewski at the cons. of the Gesellschaft der Musikfreunde in Vienna (1901–06), then went to Russia, where he taught piano at a private school in Kharkov. He settled in Athens, where he taught at the Cons. (1911–19). He was founder-director of the Hellenic Cons. (1919–26) and of the National Cons. (1926–48). He was greatly esteemed as a teacher, and also publ. several textbooks on harmony, counterpoint, and orchestration. Kalomiris was the protagonist of Greek nationalism in music. Almost all his works are based on Greek folk-song patterns, and many are inspired by Hellenic subjects. In his harmonies and instrumentation, he followed the Russian school of composition, with a considerable influx of lush Wagnerian sonorities.

WORKS: DRAMATIC: O p e r a : *O Protomastoras* (The Master-Builder), after Kazantzakis (Athens, March 24, 1916; rev. 1929 and 1940); *To dachtylidi tis manas* (The Mother's Ring; 1917; rev. 1939); *Anatoli* (Sunrise), musical fairy tale, to a libretto by the composer after Cambyssis (1945; rev. 1948); *Ta xotika nera* (The Shadowy Waters), after Yeats (1950; rev. 1952); *Constantinos o Palaeologus*, music legend after Kazantzakis (Athens, Aug. 12, 1962). **ORCH.:** *Greek Suite* (1907); *Iambs and Anapests*, suite (1914); *Greek Rhapsody* for Piano and Orch. (orchestrated by G. Pierné and conducted by him, Paris, April 3, 1926); *Island Pictures* for Violin and Orch. (1928); *3 Greek Dances* (1934); Piano Concerto (1935); *Triptych* (1940); *Minas the Rebel*, tone poem (1940); *The Death of the Courageous Woman*, tone poem (1945); Violin Concertino (1955). **CHAMBER:** Piano Quintet, with Soprano (1912); String Trio (1921); Quartet quasi fantasia for Harp, Flute, English Horn, and Viola (1921); Violin Sonata (1948). **P i a n o :** *Sunrise* (1902); *3 Ballads* (1906); *For Greek Children* (1910); *2 Rhapsodies* (1921); 5 preludes (1939). **VOCAL:** *The Olive Tree* for Women's Chorus and Orch. (1909); *Valor Symphony* for Chorus and Orch. (1920); *Symphony of the Kind People* for Mezzo-soprano, Chorus, and Orch. (1931); *At the Ossios Loukas Monastery* for Narrator and Orch. (1937); *Palamas Symphony* for Chorus and Orch., after Palamas (Athens, Jan. 22, 1956); choruses; songs.—**NS/LK/DM**

Kalter (real name, **Aufrichtig**), **Sabine,** noted Hungarian mezzo-soprano; b. Jaroslaw, March 28, 1889; d. London, Sept. 1, 1957. She studied at the Vienna Academy of Music, making her debut at the Vienna Volksoper in 1911. She then was a principal member of the Hamburg Opera (1915–35). After being compelled to leave Germany by the Nazis, she settled in London, where she sang at Covent Garden (1935–39). In later years she devoted herself to a concert career, making her last appearance with the Hamburg Radio in 1950. She was also active as a teacher. Her finest roles were Ortrud, Brangäne, and Fricka.—**NS/LK/DM**

Kamensky, Alexander, Russian pianist and teacher; b. Geneva (of Russian parents), Dec. 12, 1900; d. Leningrad, Nov. 7, 1952. He studied piano at the Petrograd Cons. (graduated, 1923), then developed an energetic career as a concert pianist. He did not interrupt his activities even during the siege of Leningrad in 1941–42, when he played almost 500 recitals under the most dangerous conditions. In 1934 he was appointed prof. of piano of the Leningrad Cons. In his programs, he featured many works by Soviet composers and also by modern Western music masters, including Schoenberg and Stravinsky.—**NS/LK/DM**

Kamieński, Lucian, Polish composer and pedagogue; b. Gniezno, Jan. 7, 1885; d. Thorn, July 27, 1964. He studied composition with Bruch and musicology with Kretzschmar and Wolf at the Univ. of Berlin (Ph.D., 1910, with the diss. *Die Oratorien von Johann Adolf Hasse;* publ. in Leipzig, 1912), then was a music critic in Königsberg (until 1919). He taught at the Poznań Academy of Music (1920–39), and also taught musicology at the Univ. of Poznań. After World War II, he taught privately.

WORKS: 2 comic operas: *Tabu* (Königsberg, April 9, 1917) and *Dami i huzary* (Poznan, Oct. 2, 1938); *Sinfonia paschalis* (1928); *Silesia Sings*, symphonic sketch (1929); Violin Sonata; several piano suites on Polish themes; an album of 60 workers' songs to his own words (Berlin, 1905–10), which he issued under the name Dolega- Kamieński.—**NS/LK/DM**

Kamieński, Maciej, significant Polish composer of Slovak descent; b. probably in Sopron or Magyar-Ovar, between Hungary and Slovakia, Oct. 13, 1734; d. Warsaw, Jan. 25, 1821. He studied composition in Vienna, then settled in Warsaw as a teacher, and brought out the first Polish opera to be premiered in a public theater, *Nędza uszczęśliwiona* (Poverty Made Happy; July 11, 1778). After its success, he wrote 7 more operas, only 2 of which are extant. He also composed a cantata for the unveiling of the Sobieski monument (Warsaw, Sept. 14, 1788). His other works include masses, offertories, and piano pieces.—**NS/LK/DM**

Kaminski, Heinrich, eminent German composer; b. Tiengen, Baden, July 4, 1886; d. Ried, Bavaria, June 21, 1946. He studied at the Univ. of Heidelberg with Wolfrum and in Berlin with Kaun, Klatte, and Juon. He settled in Ried (1914). After teaching a master class at the Prussian Academy of the Arts in Berlin (1930–33), he returned to Ried. His writing is strictly polyphonic and almost rigid in form. The religious and mystic character of his sacred music stems from his family origins (he was the son of a clergyman); the chief influences in his work were Bach and Bruckner. The Heinrich-Kaminski-Gesellschaft was organized in 1987.

WORKS: DRAMATIC: *Passionspiel* (1920); *Jürg Jenatsch*, opera (Dresden, April 27, 1929); *Das Spiel vom König Aphelius*, music drama (1946; Göttingen, Jan. 29, 1950). **ORCH.:** Concerto Grosso for 2 Orchs. (1922); *Dorische Musik* (1933); *Concerto for Orchestra* (1936); Piano Concerto (1937); *Tanzdrama* (1942). **CHAMBER:** Quartet for Clarinet, Viola, Cello, and Piano (1912); 2 string quartets (1913, 1916); Quintet for Clarinet, Horn, Violin, Viola, and Cello (1924); *Musik* for 2 Violins and Harpsichord (1931); *Hauskonzert* for Violin and Piano (1941); *Ballade* for Horn and Piano (1943). **KEYBOARD: P i a n o :** *Klavierbuch* (1934); *10 kleine Übungen für das polyphone Klavierspiel* (1935). **O r g a n :** *Wie schön leucht' uns der Morgenstern*, toccata (1923); *Chorale-Sonata* (1926); 3 chorale preludes (1928); *Toccata and Fugue* (1939). **VOCAL:** *O Herre Gott*, motet for Chorus and Organ (1918); *Magnificat* for Soprano, Viola, Chorus, and Orch. (1925); *Der Mensch*, motet for Alto, Chorus, and Orch. (1926); *Die Erde*, motet for Chorus (1928); *Triptychon* for Alto or Baritone and Organ (1926–29); *Die deutsch Messe* for Chorus (1934); *In memoriam Gabrielae* Alto, Violin, and Orch. (1940); other songs; folk-song arrangements.

BIBL.: K. Schleifer, *H. K.* (Kassel, 1945); K. Schleifer and R. Schwarz-Stilling, *H. K.: Werkverzeichnis* (Kassel, 1947); I. Samson, *Das Vokalschaffen von H. K., mit Ausnahme der Opern* (Frankfurt am Main, 1956); A. Suder, ed., *H. K.* (Tutzing, 1986); H. Hartog, *H. K.* (Tutzing, 1987).—**NS/LK/DM**

Kaminski, Joseph, Russian-born Israeli violinist and composer; b. Odessa, Nov. 17, 1903; d. Gedera, Oct. 14, 1972. He studied composition with Friedrich Koch in Berlin and Hans Gál in Vienna. He was concertmaster of the Warsaw Radio Orch., then emigrated to Tel Aviv, where he was concertmaster of the Palestine (later Israel Phil.) Orch. (1937–69).

WORKS: ORCH.: Trumpet Concertino (1940–41; Tel Aviv, May 5, 1941); *Ha'Alijah,* variations (1942); *Comedy Overture* (1944); *Ballade* for Harp and Chamber Orch. (Tel Aviv, Feb. 2, 1946); Violin Concerto (1947–49; Tel Aviv, 1954); *3 Israeli Sketches* (1955); *Variations* for English Horn and Strings (1958); *Symphonic Overture* (1960). CHAMBER: String Quartet (1945); *Triptych* for Piano (1958).—NS/LK/DM

Kaminsky, Max, jazz trumpeter; b. Brockton, Mass., Sept. 7, 1908; d. Castle Point, N.Y., Sept. 6, 1994. At 12, he led his own juvenile band in Boston, the Six Novelty Syncopators. During the early 1920s he worked with various bands in his home state, including a spell with Art Karle's Band in Cape Cod. He temporarily moved to Chicago in 1928 and played at the Cinderella Ballroom (with George Wettling and Frank Teschemacher). He returned to Boston before revisiting Chicago. He went to N.Y. in 1929, toured with Red Nichols, then returned to Boston. He played with Leo Reisman at the Bradlord Hotel (Boston), during the early 1930s and also gigged with various small bands. On his occasional trips to N.Y. he recorded with Mezz Mezzrow, Benny Goodman, and Eddie Condon. He worked with the Joe Venuti Orch. in N.Y. (early 1934), then with the Teddy Roy Band, Eddie Elkins, Jacques Renard, Jack Marshard, and Leo Reisman, before joining Tommy Dorsey (September–December 1936). He was in a small band with Pee Wee Russell before playing briefly with Ray Noble's Band (early 1937), and later that year worked in the short-lived Mezz Mezzrow's Disciples of Swing. He was with Artie Shaw from January–June 1938, then again with Pee Wee Russell before rejoining Tommy Dorsey in November 1938. He played with the Bud Freeman Summa Cum Laude Band 1939–40, then joined Tony Pastor Band for a few months until March 1941, when he rejoined Shaw, but left to join Alvino Rey (early 1942). He then played with Joe Marsala's Big Band until joining the U.S. Navy in summer of 1942. He served in Artie Shaw's Naval Band, including a tour of the Pacific area, during which he recorded with local jazzmen in Australia (1943). He returned to the U.S. in December 1943, gained an honorable discharge in March 1944. He participated in mid-1940s concerts at Carnegie Hall and Town Hall organized by Condon. He led his own band at Pied Piper, N.Y., until December 1944, played in Art Hodes's Band (1945), then from November 1945 until March 1946 he led his own band in Boston. He was with Eddie Condon until January 1947, then worked with Art Hodes and briefly with Jack Teagarden. He led his own band at the Village Vanguard from 1948. Through the 1950s, he combined small jazz-group work with regular stints in society orchs. In autumn 1957, he toured Europe with Jack Teagarden-Earl Hines All Stars, and in late 1958 began a tour of the Orient with Jack Teagarden's Band. From 1960 has he worked frequently in N.Y. jazz groups, occasionally leading his own small bands at various clubs including Eddie Condon's. He also made appearances at the Newport Jazz Festival and N.Y. World's Fair in the mid 1960s. During the late 1960s he was regularly featured at Jimmy Ryan's (N.Y.). He visited London in March 1970. During the 1940s, he played at many of Eddie Condon's N.Y. Town Hall Concerts. He had a prolific freelance recording career. He left Ryan's (1970), was active in N.Y. (1970–71), and toured Japan with George Wein (September 1971). He played regularly at Jimmy Ryan's Club (N.Y.) (1978–83).

DISC.: *The Eel* (1933); *Windy City Six* (1954); *Jazz on the Campus Ltd.* (1954); *Chicago Style* (1954); *Max Goes East* (1963); *Tea for Two* (1975).

WRITINGS: *My Life in Jazz* (N.Y., 1963).—JC/LP

Kamionsky, Oscar (Isaievich), Russian baritone; b. Kiev, 1869; d. Yalta, Aug. 15, 1917. He studied with Everard in St. Petersburg and Rossi in Naples, making his debut in Naples in 1891. He sang in Kharkov (1893–94; 1898–99), Kiev (1894–95), and Tiflis (1896–98; 1899–1901); also appeared in St. Petersburg, Moscow, and other cities as a guest artist. He later sang in Moscow at the Zimin Theater (1905–08; 1913–14), retiring from the stage in 1915. As a singer, he followed the precepts of the Italian school of bel canto. He was famous for his roles as Valentin in *Faust,* Rigoletto, Wolfram in *Tannhäuser,* and other lyrico-dramatic parts. —NS/LK/DM

Kammel, Antonín, Bohemian violinist and composer; b. Bělěc (baptized), April 21, 1730; d. probably in London, c. 1786. He received music training at the Patres Piares Coll. in Slaný (1746–51), and then studied at the Univ. of Prague (1751–54); he also was a student of Tartini in Padua. About 1764 he went to London, where he appeared in concerts with J.C. Bach and Abel from 1768 and where he also was active as a court musician. Kammel composed an extensive output of instrumental music, including sinfonias, divertimentos, violin concertos, string quartets, trios, duos, and violin sonatas. Many of his works were publ. in London and Paris between 1766 and 1790. A number of his compositions have been confused with those of Haydn and J.C. Bach, attesting to their intrinsic worth.—LK/DM

Kamu, Okko (Tapani), Finnish conductor; b. Helsinki, March 7, 1946. He studied violin at the Sibelius Academy in Helsinki under Onni Suhonen (graduated, 1967). He played in the Helsinki Youth Orch., and then was a member of the Helsinki Phil. (1965–66) and concertmaster of the orch. of the Finnish National Opera (1966–68) before holding the position of its 3rd conductor (1968–69). After winning 1st prize in the Karajan Competition for conductors (1969), he appeared as a guest conductor with the Royal Opera in Stockholm (1969–70). He then was a conductor with the Finnish Radio Sym. Orch. (1970–71), and subsequently its chief conductor (1971–77). He was chief conductor of the Oslo Phil. (1975–79) and of the Helsinki Phil. (1981–88). In 1988 he became principal conductor of the Sjaelland Sym. Orch. in Copenhagen. He also was chief conductor of the Helsingborg Sym. Orch. from 1991. From 1998 to 2001 he was the principal guest conductor of the Lausanne Chamber Orch.—NS/LK/DM

Kanai, Hideto, avant-garde Japanese jazz bassist; b. Tokyo, Japan, 1931. Along with guitarist Takayanagi Masayuki, he was a leader of the 1960s avant-garde in Japan. Like so many of his generation, his professional career began in American servicemen's clubs, but after meeting Duke Ellington he began a more formal study of music. Kanai and Masayuki founded the Jazz Academy (later New Century Music Workshop) in 1960, performing experimental jam sessions in coffee shops that incorporated their interest in contemporary classical music and the jazz of Sun Ra, Charles Mingus, and Ornette Coleman. He led the King's Roar orch. in the 1960s and 1970s, touring the U.S.S.R. and South America with jazz arrangements of Japanese children's songs. In the late 1990s he led the Yokohama Jazz Orch.

DISC.: *Ginparis Session: June 26, 1963* (1986); *Concierto de Aranjuez.*—ETA

Kancheli, Giya (Alexandrovich), notable Georgian composer; b. Tbilisi, Aug. 10, 1935. He received training in piano in childhood at the music school, and later was a student of I. Tuskiya at the Cons. (1959–63) in Tbilisi. In 1971 he became director of music at the Rustaveli Theater in Tbilisi, for which he composed much incidental music. From 1984 to 1989 he held the position of 1st secretary of the Union of Georgian Composers. In 1991 he emigrated to the West, and held a Deutscher Akademischer Austauschdienst grant in Berlin. He served as composer-in-residence of the Royal Flemish Phil. in Antwerp in 1995–96, and as co-composer-in-residence of the Lucerne Festival in 1999. Kancheli has created an electic compositional style that utilizes music from various eras.

WORKS: DRAMATIC: *Music for the Living,* opera (1982–84; Tbilisi, April 28, 1984); incidental music to numerous plays; many film scores. **ORCH.:** *Concerto for Orchestra* (1962; Tbilisi, Feb. 2, 1963); *Largo and Allegro* for Strings, Piano, and Timpani (Tbilisi, May 7, 1963); 7 syms.: No. 1 (1967; Tbilisi, May 12, 1968), No. 2, *Chants* (Tbilisi, Oct. 31, 1970), No. 3 (Tbilisi, Oct. 11, 1973), No. 4, *In Memoria di Michelangelo* (1974; Tbilisi, Jan. 13, 1975), No. 5 (1977; Tbilisi, Feb. 27, 1978), No. 6 (Tbilisi, April 7, 1980; rev. version, Leipzig, Oct. 22, 1981), and No. 7, *Epilogue* (Prague, Dec. 11, 1986; rev. version, Berlin, March 24, 1992); *Mourned by the Wind* for Viola and Orch. (1989; Berlin, Sept. 9, 1990; also for Cello and Orch., 1996); *Abii ne viderem* for Strings, Alto Flute, Piano, and Bass Guitar (Amsterdam, June 10, 1992; also for Strings, Viola, Piano, and Bass Guitar, 1993; New Haven, March 14, 1995); *Noch einen Schritt...* (1992; Donaueschingen, Oct. 15, 1993); *Wingless* (Saarbrücken, May 23, 1993); *Lament (Music of mourning in memory of Luigi Nono)* for Violin, Woman's Voice, and Orch. (1994; Hamburg, June 26, 1995); *V & V* for Violin, Strings, and Tape (1994; Gstaad, Aug. 8, 1995); *Trauerfarbenes Land* (Bonn, Dec. 9, 1994); *Simi* for Cello and Orch. (1995; Brussels, Feb. 14, 1996); *...à la Duduki* (1995; Mannheim, March 18, 1996); *Valse Boston* for Piano and Strings (Stuttgart, Dec. 20, 1996); *Diplipito* for Cello, Countertenor, and Chamber Orch. (Lisbon, May 11, 1997); Piece for Oboe and Strings (1998; Amsterdam, Feb. 6, 1999); Piece for Strings (Dresden, Dec. 22, 1998); *Rokwa* (1999). **CHAMBER:** *Magnum ignotum* for Flute/Alto Flute, 2 Oboes, 2 Clarinets, 2 Bassoons, 2 Horns, Double Bass, and Tape (Witten, April 23, 1994); *Having Wept* for Cello (Paris, Sept. 16, 1994); *Rag-Gidon-Time* for Violin and Piano (Morristown, N.J., Nov. 5, 1995); *Instead of a Tango* for Violin, Bandoneon, Piano, and Double Bass (Prague, April 1996); *Time...and Again* for Violin and Piano (London, April 7, 1997); Piano Quartet (1997; Seattle, June 1998). **VOCAL:** *Light Sorrow* for 2 Boy Sopranos, Boy's Chorus, and Orch. (Leipzig, May 9, 1985); *Exile* for Soprano and Chamber Ensemble (Ferrara, July 7, 1994); *Caris Mere* for Soprano and Viola (Ferrara, July 7, 1994); *And Farewell Goes Out Sighing...* for Countertenor, Violin, and Orch. (N.Y., Nov. 18, 1999); *Styx* for Chorus, Viola, and Orch. (1999). **OTHER:** *Life Without Christmas,* cycle of 4 pieces: *Morning Prayers* for Chamber Orch. and Tape (London, July 8, 1990), *Midday Prayers* for 19 Players, Boy Soprano, and Clarinet (Salzau, Aug. 8, 1991), *Evening Prayers* for Chamber Orch. and 8 Alto Voices (1991; Stuttgart, Jan. 31, 1992), and *Night Prayers* for String Quartet and Tape (Vienna, March 14, 1992; also for Soprano Saxophone, Strings, and Tape, 1994; Stuttgart, Sept. 28, 1995).—NS/LK/DM

Kander, John (Harold), and Fred Ebb, American songwriters of theater music. Composer Kander (b. Kansas City, Mo., March 18, 1927) and lyricist Ebb (b. N.Y., April 8, 1932) wrote the songs for 12 musicals that opened on Broadway between 1965 and 1997, among them *Cabaret, Chicago,* and *Kiss of the Spider Woman.* They specialized in period work, frequently writing musical pastiches reminiscent of the popular music of the 1920s to the 1940s, notably in their best-known songs, "Cabaret" and "New York, New York." They were closely associated with Liza Minnelli, who starred in four of their musicals and in three movie musicals for which they wrote songs, but their talent for composing strong material for female stars also benefitted Barbra Streisand, Gwen Verdon, Chita Rivera, and Lauren Bacall, among others.

Kander's parents were Harold Kander, who worked in the poultry business, and Bernice Aaron Kander. He began playing piano at age four, initially under the tutelage of an aunt, and began taking lessons at six. In his teens he studied with Wiktor Labunski. He began to compose early on, writing the school show in his senior year of high school. He attended Oberlin Coll., where he wrote two shows with his friend James Goldman. Graduating in 1951, he enrolled at Columbia Univ., where he studied with Jack Beeson, Otto Luening, and Douglas Moore and earned an M.A. in composition. He served in the army and the merchant marine, then began to work in the theater.

Kander was choral director and conductor at the Warwick Musical Theatre in R.I. during the summers of 1955 and 1957. In 1956 he played piano for the musical *The Amazing Adele,* which closed before reaching Broadway, and for a Fla. production of *An Evening with Beatrice Lillie.* He served as conductor for an Off-Broadway revival of Noël Coward's *Conversation Piece* in 1957. He earned his first Broadway credit arranging the dance music for Jule Styne's *Gypsy* (N.Y., May 21, 1959) and performed the same function for Marguerite Monnot's *Irma La Douce* (N.Y., Sept. 29, 1960). His first Broadway score came with the musical *A Family Affair* (N.Y., Jan. 27, 1962), with lyrics and book by James and William Goldman and directed by Harold Prince. It ran 65 performances. He then wrote incidental music for the Broadway play *Never Too Late* (N.Y., Nov. 27, 1962).

Kander was introduced to Ebb in 1962 by his publisher, Tommy Valando.

Ebb, the son of Harry and Anna Evelyn Gritz Ebb, graduated from N.Y.U. in 1955 and earned an M.A. in English literature from Columbia Univ. in 1957. In 1955, Jim Lowe recorded his novelty song "Close the Door," written with his first collaborator, composer Paul Klein. He and Klein wrote songs and special material for nightclub acts and then for revues such as *A to Z* (N.Y., April 20, 1960) and *Vintage '60* (N.Y., Sept. 12, 1960).

Kander and Ebb's first notable collaboration was "My Coloring Book," introduced by Kaye Ballard, then sung on *The Kraft Music Hall* television show by Sandy Stewart. Both Stewart and Kitty Kallen recorded it for chart singles by the end of 1962, and both enjoyed Top 40 hits with it. Ebb collaborated with Norman Martin on some songs for the Off-Broadway revue *Put It in Writing* (N.Y., May 13, 1963) and wrote both book and lyrics to Paul Klein's music for the Off-Broadway musical *Morning Sun* (N.Y., Oct. 6, 1963). But his work with Kander continued to gain recognition beyond the theater as another of their songs, "I Don't Care Much," was recorded by Barbra Streisand, who placed it on her gold-selling LP *The Second Barbra Streisand Album*, released in the summer of 1963.

Ebb wrote material for the television series *That Was the Week That Was*, a satirical look at the news, which ran from January 1964 to May 1965, but he also maintained his musical collaboration with Kander. The songwriters worked on a musical, *Golden Gate*, that was never produced but that led producer Harold Prince and co-librettist and director George Abbott to decide they should be hired to write the songs for *Flora, the Red Menace*. This musical satire on 1930s radicals based on the novel *Love Is Just around the Corner* by Lester Atwell was produced in the spring of 1965 and marked the Broadway debut of Liza Minnelli in the title role. It ran only 87 performances, but the cast album spent two months in the charts. The show established the long-running relationship between Kander and Ebb and Minnelli; they next wrote material for her nightclub debut at the Shoreham Hotel in Washington, D.C., on Sept. 14, 1965, a booking that helped establish her as a successful performer.

Harold Prince hired Kander and Ebb to write songs for his next effort, *Cabaret*, which he both produced and directed. The show was based on Joe Masteroff's 1951 play *I Am a Camera*, which in turn was based on Christopher Isherwood's novel *The Berlin Stories* concerning Weimar Germany. The songwriters' score, heavily influenced by Kurt Weill and Bertolt Brecht, helped the musical to a run of 1,166 performances, their greatest success. It won them Tony Awards for Best Musical and Best Composer and Lyricist. The cast album spent nine months in the charts and won the 1967 Grammy for Best Score from an Original Cast Show Album. The title song enjoyed a singles chart entry as an instrumental recording by Herb Alpert and The Tijuana Brass.

Kander and Ebb took on a more conventional subject for their next musical, *The Happy Time*, a romantic comedy set in French Canada and starring Robert

Goulet. Opening in January 1968, it ran 286 performances. Ten months later came *Zorbá*, librettist Joseph Stein's adaptation of Nikos Kazantzakis's novel, *Zorba, the Greek*; it ran 304 performances and the cast album reached the charts. In 1971, *70, Girls, 70*, for which Ebb co-wrote the libretto with Norman Martin, was the songwriters' least successful effort, running only 35 performances.

Liza Minnelli starred in the successful film version of *Cabaret*, directed by Bob Fosse, which was released in February 1972 with several new songs by Kander and Ebb. The soundtrack album went gold. Ebb and Fosse produced, and Kander and Ebb wrote songs for, Minnelli's television special, *Liza with a "Z,"* broadcast on Sept. 10, 1972, which won an Emmy for Outstanding Single Program—Variety and Popular Music, and produced a soundtrack album that spent more than five months in the charts. Kander and Ebb wrote songs for, and Fosse directed and choreographed, Minnelli's Broadway show *Liza*, which ran during January 1974 and resulted in her charting concert album *Live at the Winter Garden*.

Kander and Ebb wrote the new songs used in the film *Funny Lady*, a sequel to *Funny Girl*, continuing the story of Fanny Brice and starring Barbra Streisand. It was released in March 1975, accompanied by a soundtrack album that hit the Top Ten and went gold. The songwriters returned to Broadway three months later with *Chicago*, directed by Bob Fosse and starring Gwen Verdon and Chita Rivera. Ebb and Fosse wrote the libretto, based on a 1920s Broadway play by Maurine Dallas Watkins about a murder trial and its attendant publicity. The show ran 947 performances and the cast album reached the charts. Kander and Ebb next wrote the songs for the film *Lucky Lady*, starring Minnelli and released in December.

In 1976, Ebb and Cy Coleman produced Shirley MacLaine's television special *Gypsy in My Soul*, for which they won the Emmy for Outstanding Comedy-Variety or Music Special. Kander and Ebb wrote songs for Minnelli's next film, *A Matter of Time*, which was released in October 1976. That same month a revue featuring their songs, *2 by 5*, began a 57-performance run Off-Broadway. *New York, New York*, a film directed by Martin Scorsese and starring Minnelli and Robert De Niro, with songs by Kander and Ebb, opened in June 1977. The soundtrack album spent more than three months in the charts; Frank Sinatra recorded the title song three years later for a Top 40 hit, making it the songwriters' best-known composition.

Kander and Ebb again worked with Liza Minnelli on their next Broadway musical, *The Act*, which opened in October 1977 and ran 233 performances. The songwriters worked separately in the late 1970s and early 1980s, with Kander contributing music to the film *Kramer vs. Kramer* (1979), while Ebb continued to work with Liza Minnelli, producing two television specials in which she appeared, *Goldie and Liza Together* (with Goldie Hawn; 1979) and *Baryshnikov on Broadway* (1980). They reunited for *Woman of the Year*, based on the 1942 film originally starring Katharine Hepburn and Spencer Tracy and now starring Lauren Bacall. The musical opened in March

1981 and ran 771 performances; the cast album reached the charts. Kander wrote music for the 1982 film *Still of the Night*.

Kander and Ebb again worked with Liza Minnelli, who costarred with Chita Rivera, on their next musical, *The Rink*. Opening in February 1984, the show ran 204 performances. Their next show had an unusually long gestation period. It was *Kiss of the Spider Woman*, based on the novel by Manuel Puig that was also the source of a 1985 film by Hector Babenco, telling the story of two inmates in a South American prison and the film star one of them dreams about. The show was presented in a workshop production at the State Univ. of N.Y. in Purchase, N.Y., starting on May 1, 1990, then was revised for a version that ran in Toronto from June to August 1992. The show, starring Chita Rivera, opened in London in October 1992 and finally appeared on Broadway in May 1993, where it ran 906 performances and won the Tony for Best Musical. In the meantime, another anthology of Kander and Ebb's songs, *And the World Goes 'Round: The Songs of Kander and Ebb*, had opened Off-Broadway in March 1991, running 408 performances. The songwriters' most recent show, *Steel Pier*, concerning a 1930s dance marathon, opened on Broadway in April 1997 and ran 76 performances.

Kander and Ebb's shows were given frequent revivals on Broadway and elsewhere. In particular, a celebrated revival of *Chicago* was mounted on Broadway starting on Nov. 14, 1996. In the wake of the O. J. Simpson murder trial of 1994–95, the show's themes were deemed particularly relevant, and the revival became a major success, spawning a London production and a national touring company. An imaginative revival of *Cabaret* was mounted in a nightclub setting on Broadway starting on March 18, 1998, and won the Tony for Best Revival. Both shows were still running at the end of the 1998–99 season.

WORKS (only works for which Kander and Ebb, working together, were primary, credited songwriters are listed): **MUSICALS/REVUES** (dates refer to Broadway openings unless otherwise noted): *Flora, the Red Menace* (May 11, 1965); *Cabaret* (Nov. 20, 1966); *The Happy Time* (Jan. 18, 1968); *Zorbá* (Nov. 17, 1968); *70, Girls, 70* (April 15, 1971); *Liza* (Jan. 6, 1974); *Chicago* (June 3, 1975); *2 by 5* (Off-Broadway, Oct. 18, 1976); *The Act* (Oct. 29, 1977); *Woman of the Year* (March 28, 1981); *The Rink* (Feb. 9, 1984); *And the World Goes 'Round: The Songs of Kander and Ebb* (Off-Broadway, March 18, 1991); *Kiss of the Spiderwoman* (London, Oct. 20, 1992; N.Y., May 3, 1993); *Steel Pier* (April 24, 1997). **FILMS:** *Cabaret* (1972); *Funny Lady* (1975); *Lucky Lady* (1975); *New York, New York* (1977).—**WR**

Kang, Sukhi, Korean composer; b. Seoul, Oct. 22, 1934. He studied at the Coll. of Music at the Seoul National Univ. (graduated, 1960), the Hannover Hochschule für Musik (1970), and with Blacher and Yun at the Berlin Hochschule für Musik (1971–75). He subsequently taught at the Seoul National Univ. (1975–80; from 1982), and was named chairman of its composition dept. in 1987, which position he held until 1991. Kang has actively promoted contemporary music in South Korea; he served as founding director of the annual Pan-Music-Festival in Seoul in 1969. In 1972 he became president of the Korean section of the ISCM, and from 1984 to 1990 he was vice-president of the ISCM of UNESCO in Paris. His compositions have won various awards. He received the composer's prize of the Korean Ministry of Culture in 1978 and of the Korean president in 1979, and was named best musician of the year by the Assn. of Korean Musicians in 1989. Sukhi's compositions are meticulously crafted, utilizing densely stratified materials to create complex musical structures, including electronic sonorities. Many of these were presented in Berlin, securing for him international attention. His *The Feast of Id* (1966) was the first Korean composition to use electronically manipulated sounds.

WORKS: DRAMATIC: *Penthesilea*, music theater (1985; Berlin, March 2, 1986). **ORCH.:** *Generation '69* (Seoul, March 24, 1969); *Reflexionen* (Seoul, Sept. 9, 1975); *Catena* (Solingen, May 31, 1975); *Dal-ha* (Seoul, Sept. 14, 1978); *Mega-Melos* (Berlin, Sept. 14, 1980); *Man-pa* for Solo Flute and Flute Orch. (Berlin, March 31, 1982); *Symphonic Requiem* (Seoul, Nov. 7, 1983); *Successions* (Berlin, June 15, 1985); *Ch'uit'ahyang* for Traditional Korean Orch. (Seoul, June 23, 1987); *Prometheus kommt* (The Olympic Torch Music of the Seoul Olympiad; Seoul, Sept. 15, 1988). **CHAMBER:** *Nirmanakaya* for Cello, Piano, and Percussion (Seoul, Sept. 5, 1969); *Roundtone* for Flute, Oboe, Clarinet, Viola, Cello, Vibraphone, and Percussion (1969); *Parodie* for Flute and Organ (1972); *Nong* for Flute and Piano (1973); *Kleines Stück* for Oboe, Cello, and Harp (1973); *Strukturen* for 4 Cellos (1973); *Banya* for Flute, Oboe, Clarinet, Tuba, Violin, Cello, Piano, and Percussion (Berlin, March 6, 1974); *Metamorphosen* for Flute and String Quartet (Tokyo, July 17, 1974); *Dialog* for Viola and Piano (1976); *Myung* for 4 Huns, Taekum, Kayagm, and Tam-tam (1976); *Dala (Parodie Waltz)* for Clarinet, Trombone, Cello, Piano, and Tape (Warsaw, Sept. 22, 1980); *Bronzenzeit* for Percussion and Tape (Cologne, Aug. 5, 1980); *Manpa* for Flute Ensemble (Berlin, March 31, 1982); *Thal* for Contrabass Flute (1983); String Quartet (1983; Saarbrücken, May 29, 1986); *Aniri IV* for Harp (1987). **VOCAL:** *Lyebul* for Man's Voice, Men's Chorus, and 30 Percussionists (Seoul, Nov. 20, 1969); *Buro* for Woman's Voice, Flute, Clarinet, Piano, and 2 Percussionists (Berlin, Oct. 7, 1976); *Yong-Bi*, cantata for 3 Soloists, 2 Choruses, and Orch. (Seoul, April 21, 1978); *Vision* for Woman's Voice, Guitar, and Tape (1978); *Aniri II* for Woman's Voice and Tape (1983) and *III* for Woman's Voice (1984); *The Rite of Sun*, cantata for Soloists, Chorus, and Orch. (Seoul, Oct. 3, 1985). **ELECTRONIC:** *The Feast of Id* (Seoul, Dec. 9, 1966); *Mosaico* (Berlin, April 7, 1981); *Klanspuren* (Berlin, April 7, 1981). —**NS/LK/DM**

Kanitz, Ernest (actually, **Ernst**), Austrian-American composer and teacher; b. Vienna, April 9, 1894; d. Menlo Park, Calif., April 7, 1978. He changed his first name to Ernest in order to distinguish himself from a homonymous concert manager in Vienna. He studied with Heuberger (1912–14) and Schreker (1914–20) in Vienna, then taught at the Neues Konservatorium there (1922–38). After the Anschluss (1938), he emigrated to the U.S. He taught theory at various colleges, including the Univ. of Southern Calif. in Los Angeles (1945–59) and Marymount Coll. in Palos Verdes, Calif. (1960–64). He publ. *A Counterpoint Manual: Fundamental Techniques of Polyphonic Music Writing* (Boston, 1948).

WORKS: DRAMATIC: O p e r a : *Kumana* (1953); *Room No. 12* (1957; Los Angeles, Feb. 26, 1958); *Royal Auction* (1957; Los Angeles, Feb. 26, 1958); *The Lucky Dollar* (1959); *Perpetual*

(Los Angeles, April 26, 1961); *Visions at Midnight* (1963; Los Angeles, Feb. 26, 1964). ORCH.: *Heitere Ouvertüre* (1918); Theremin Concertino (1938); *Intermezzo concertante* for Saxophone and Orch. (1948); Concerto Grosso (1949); Bassoon Concerto (San Francisco, April 8, 1964); 2 syms.: No. 1, *Sinfonia seria* (St. Louis, Oct. 17, 1964) and No. 2 (1965; San Francisco, Dec. 11, 1968). CHAMBER: *Dance Sonata* for Flute, Clarinet, Trumpet, Bassoon, and Piano (1932); Quintettino for Piano and Winds (1945); Sonata for Violin and Cello (1947); *Divertimento* for Viola and Cello (1949); *Notturno* for Flute, Violin, and Viola (1950); String Trio (1951); *Sonata breve* for Violin, Cello, and Piano (1952); *Sonata Californiana* for Alto Saxophone and Piano (1952); Sonata for Solo Cello (1956); Viola Sonatina (1958); Suite for Brass Quintet (1960); *Little Concerto* for Saxophone (1970). VOCAL: *Das Hohelied*, oratorio (1921); *Zeitmusik*, radio cantata (1931); *Cantata 1961* for Chorus and 2 Pianos (1961). —NS/LK/DM

Kann, Hans, respected Austrian pianist, pedagogue, and composer; b. Vienna, Feb. 14, 1927. He studied piano with A. Bloch, A. Göllner, and F. Wührer, chamber music with O. Schulhoff, composition with J. Lechthaler, and analysis with J. Polnauer in Vienna, where he made his debut (1946). After winning the Silver Medal at the Geneva International Competition in 1948, he pursued an international career. Beginning in 1955, he made regular tours of Japan. He toured South America and Russia in 1966, gave concerts in China in 1980, 1982, and 1985, and played in the U.S. in 1981 and 1984. In 1987–88 he gave in Vienna the first complete performance of the Haydn sonatas; in 1988–89 he presented a "Biedermeier" cycle there, consisting of works by Beethoven and Schubert and their lesser-known contemporaries; in 1989–90 he performed the complete piano works of Mozart there, including Mozart's pieces for children and his didactic works. Among other places, Kann taught at the Vienna Academy of Music (1950–52), the Univ. of Arts in Tokyo (1955–58), and the Vienna Hochschule für Musik (from 1977). He also gave master classes at the Darmstadt Academy of Music (1961–67). He wrote a book on piano playing that was publ. in Japanese. His compositions include a ballet, theater and film scores, chamber music, lieder, works for synthesizer, and various pieces for solo piano, including a curious album entitled *10 Klavierstücke ohne Bassschlüssel*, and *12 Alt-Wiener Walzer*, as well as didactic pieces, exemplified by *33 Spezialstudien, Tägliche Fingerübungen*, and *Models*.—NS/LK/DM

Kannen, Günter von, German bass-baritone, b. Rheydt, March 22, 1940. He was a student of Paul Lohmann and Franziska Martienssen. After singing in Kaiserslautern, Bonn, and Karlsruhe, he was a principal member of the Zürich Opera from 1979 to 1990. He also was engaged as Alberich in the *Ring* cycles at the Bayreuth Festival from 1988 to 1992. In 1992 he joined the Berlin State Opera. He also sang in Hamburg, Dresden, Vienna, Salzburg, Paris, Lucerne, Amsterdam, Chicago, and Tokyo. In addition to Alberich, he was known for such roles as Osmin, the Commendatore, Pizarro, Hans Sachs, Klingsor, the Doctor in *Wozzeck*, Cardillac, and La Roche.—NS/LK/DM

Kanner-Rosenthal, Hedwig, Hungarian-American pianist and pedagogue; b. Budapest, June 3, 1882; d. Asheville, N.C., Sept. 5, 1959. She studied with Leschetizky and **Moriz Rosenthal**, whom she married and also appeared with him in duo recitals. She settled in N.Y. as a teacher (1939), numbering among her students Charles Rosen and Robert Goldsand. —NS/LK/DM

Kansas, America's premier progressive rock band (f. 1970). MEMBERSHIP: Kerry Livgren, gtr., kybd. (b. Kan., Sept. 18, 1949); Steve Walsh, kybd., voc. (b. St. Joseph, Mo., June 15, 1951); Robby Steinhardt, vln., voc. (b. Miss., May 25, 1951); Richard Williams, gtr. (b. Kans., Feb. 1, 1951); Phil Ehart, drm. (b. Kans., Feb. 4, 1951); Dave Hope, bs. (b. Kans., Oct. 7, 1949); John Elefante, kybd., voc. (b. Levittown, N.Y., 1958); Steve Morse, gtr. (b. Hamilton, Ohio, July 28, 1954).

Kerry Livgren, Dave Hope, and Phil Ehart started playing together in high school. The trio's sound took a turn for the bombastic when they added orchestral violinist Robbie Steinhardt to the lineup. With the addition of Steve Walsh and Richard Williams, the sextet started touring ceaselessly, building up a strong enough buzz and following that Kirshner records signed them in 1974. Their debut sold a respectable 100,000 copies, and after another more incessant touring, their next efforts, *Masque* and *Song for America* both sold around a quarter of a million copies each.

This all built up to their 1976 release, *Leftoverture*. The song "Carry On My Wayward Son" caught fire at album rock radio and crossed over to pop, eventually hitting #11 and going gold. The album hit #5 and sold triple platinum. Their follow-up, *Point of Know Return*, proved that this was not a flash in the pan, both from the musical point of view and the group's following. While the title track only hit #28, it was a huge song at album rock. However, "Dust in the Wind" became the group's second gold single, hitting #6. The album rose to #4 and, like its predecessor, also sold triple platinum. The group followed this success with the de rigueur live album, *Two for the Show*, which went platinum, hitting #32.

The band started producing themselves with *Monolith* in 1979. While the album produced the minor (#23) hit "People of the South Wind" and went to #10, it only went gold. The slip continued with *Audio-Visions*. The single "Hold On" just scratched the Top 40, and the album rose to #26, but did go gold.

Internal turmoil took hold of the band. Livgren and Hope became born-again Christians. About the same time, Walsh put out his solo album, *Schemer Dreamer*, and started sitting in with other groups. Livgren put out his own solo album, *Seeds of Change*. Walsh left the group and formed Streets. John Elefante replaced him, and the group's 1982 album, *Vinyl Confessions*, actually sold fairly well, reaching #16 on the charts, largely on the strength of the #17 single "Play the Game Tonight." However, 1983's *Drastic Measures* failed to generate any excitement and the group broke up. Livgren and Elefante started exploring contemporary Christian music.

By 1986, Streets was washed up. Walsh, Williams, and Ehart decided to go back to what they knew best.

As a master stroke, they added erstwhile Dixie Dregs guitarist Steve Morse and Streets bassist Billy Greer. They cut *Power*, the first Kansas album without violins. The album rose to #35 and the single, "All I Wanted" charted at #19. Their 1988 effort, *In the Spirit of Things* was less successful, and the band broke up again.

A German promoter offered the band a lot of money to play some shows in Germany in the early 1990s. The group as it broke up in 1986, did the tour, then toured the U.S. Livgren joined the band occasionally and Dave Ragsdale replaced Steinhardt. They put out an album of a show they did at L.A.'s Whiskey A Go-Go. A double disc retrospective followed with a new song co-written by Livgren. *Freaks of Nature* followed in 1995, their first new material in seven years. *Always Never the Same* was recorded at Abbey Road studios using members of the London Philharmonic. The group continues to tour continue to be a staple on classic rock radio—"Carry On My Wayward Son" was the top song in the format in 1997.

DISC.: *Kansas* (1974); *Masque* (1975); *Song for America* (1975); *Leftoverture* (1976); *Point of Know Return* (1977); *Two for the Show* (live; 1978); *Monolith* (1979); *Audio-Visions* (1980); *Vinyl Confessions* (1982); *Drastic Measures* (1983); *Power* (1986); *In the Spirit of Things* (1988); *Live at the Whiskey* (1992); *Freaks of Nature* (1995); *Always Never the Same* (1998); *At Tower Theater in Philadelphia* (1998).—**HB**

Kantorow, Jean-Jacques, French conductor and violinist; b. Cannes, Oct. 3, 1945. Following training at the Nice Cons., he pursued studies at the Paris Cons. (premier prix in violin, 1960, and in chamber music, 1963). In 1962 he won the medal of the Carl Flesch competition in London, and also prizes in the Genoa (Paganini), Brussels (Queen Elisabeth of Belgium), Helsinki (Sibelius), Montreal, and Geneva (1965) violin competitions. He began his career as an orch. player, but soon emerged as a solo artist and chamber music player. Eventually he gave increasing attention to a conducting career. In 1985 he became music director of l'Orchestre d'Auvergne in Clermont-Ferrand, and in 1993 of l'Ensemble Orchestral de Paris.—**NS/LK/DM**

Kapell, William, brilliant American pianist; b. N.Y., Sept. 20, 1922; d. in an airplane crash at King's Mountain, near San Francisco, Oct. 29, 1953. He studied with Dorothea La Follette in N.Y., and later with Olga Samaroff at the Philadelphia Cons. of Music and at the Juilliard School of Music in N.Y. After winning the Philadelphia Orch.'s youth competition and the Naumburg Award (1941), he made his N.Y. debut on Oct. 28, 1941; subsequently appeared as a soloist with the major American orchs. and in Europe. He died on a return flight from Australia, where he had been touring. Kapell was an outstanding technician who was also capable of the most refined playing.

BIBL.: T. Page, *W. K.: A Documentary Life History of the American Pianist* (College Park, Md., 1992).—**NS/LK/DM**

Kaplan, Mark, American violinist; b. Cambridge, Mass., Dec. 30, 1953. He was brought up in Syracuse, N.Y. and began violin lessons as a small child. At the age

of 8, he won a local violin competition, and enrolled as a student of Dorothy DeLay at the Juilliard School of Music in N.Y. He received its Fritz Kreisler Memorial Award. In 1973 he was awarded the prestigious Award of Special Distinction at the Leventritt Competition in N.Y., and subsequently was a soloist with many of the major orchs. of North America and Europe, meriting praise for his fine musicianship and virtuoso technique.
—**NS/LK/DM**

Kapp, Artur, significant Estonian composer, father of **Eugen (Arturovich) Kapp** and uncle of **Villem Kapp;** b. Suure-Jaani, Feb. 28, 1878; d. there, Jan. 14, 1952. He began his music training with his father, an organist and choral conductor; then continued his studies at the St. Petersburg Cons., where he received degrees in organ (1898) and composition (1900), studying the latter with Rimsky-Korsakov and Liadov. From 1903 to 1920 he was director of the Astrakhan Cons.; returning to Estonia, he was prof. of composition at the Tallinn Cons. (1924–43). He was the first Estonian composer to use native folk material, which he utilized in his first orch. suite (1906). His 4th Sym. was awarded the State Prize (1949) and the 1st Stalin Prize (1950).

WORKS: ORCH.: *Don Carlos*, symphonic poem (1900); 4 suites (1906, 1930, 1936, 1947); 5 syms. (1924–49); 5 concertos (1934–46). **CHAMBER:** Violin Sonata (1897); String Quintet (1918); Trio for Violin, Cello, and Organ (1936); String Sextet (1951). **VOCAL:** *Hiob*, oratorio (1929); 4 cantatas, including *For Peace* (1951); choral works; numerous songs.—**NS/LK/DM**

Kapp, Eugen (Arturovich), important Estonian composer and pedagogue, son of **Artur Kapp;** b. Astrakhan, May 26, 1908; d. Tallinn, Nov. 11, 1996. He graduated from his father's composition class at the Tallinn Cons. (1931), then became a teacher of composition there (1935). After serving as founder-director of the Estonian State Ensemble in Yaroslavl (1941–44), he became a prof. at the Estonian Cons. (1947) and was its director (1952–64). He received the Order of Lenin (1950) and was made a People's Artist of the Estonian S.S.R. (1950) and of the U.S.S.R. (1956). His operas *Tasuleegid* and *Vabaduse laulik* won Stalin Prizes in 1946 and 1950, respectively, as well as his ballet *Kalevipoeg* in 1952.

WORKS: DRAMATIC: Opera: *Tasuleegid* (Flames of Vengeance; Tallinn, July 21, 1945); *Vabaduse laulik* (Freedom's Singer; Tallinn, July 20, 1950); *Talvemuinasjutt* (Winter Fairy Tale; Tartu, Oct. 28, 1958); *Tabamatu* (Elusive Marta; 1960; Tartu, March 19, 1961); *Rembrandt* (March 30, 1975); *Enneolematu ime* (Unheard of Wonder), children's opera (Tallinn, May 8, 1983). **Operetta:** *Assol* (1965). **Ballet:** *Kalevipoeg* (1947); *Kullaketrajad* (Goldspinners; 1956). **ORCH.:** *The Avenger*, symphonic poem (1931); 6 suites (1933–57); 4 overtures (1938–69); 3 syms. (1942, 1954, 1964); Piano Concerto (1969); Flute Concerto (1975); Concerto-Fantasy for Violin and Chamber Orch. (1978; also for Violin and Orch., 1980); *Theme and Variations on Ukrainian Folk Music* for Strings (1982). **CHAMBER:** Piano Trio (1930); 2 string quartets (1935, 1956); 2 violin sonatas (1936, 1943); Cello Sonata (1948); *Meditations* for Cello (1969); 4 *Estonian Dances* for Violin and Piano (1973); 4 *Pieces* for Flute and Piano (1974); *Starling's Song to the Sun* for Violin (1983). **Piano:** Sonatina (1945); *Little Sonatina* (1975). **VOCAL:** Oratorios; cantatas; songs.

BIBL.: G. Polyanovsky, *E. K.* (Moscow, 1957).; H. Kyrvits, *E. K.* (Tallinn, 1964).—NS/LK/DM

Kapp, Julius, German writer on music; b. Seelbach, Baden, Oct. 1, 1883; d. Sonthofen, March 18, 1962. He studied in Marburg, Munich, and Berlin (Ph.D. in chemistry, 1907). From 1904 to 1907 he ed. Berlin's *Literarischer Anzeiger,* which he founded. He then was adviser on productions at the Berlin State Opera and ed. of its *Blätter der Staatsoper* (1921–45), and subsequently an adviser on productions at the Berlin Stadtische Oper (1948–54). He wrote significant biographies of Liszt and Wagner.

WRITINGS: *Richard Wagner und Franz Liszt: Eine Freundschaft* (Berlin and Leipzig, 1908); *Arthur Schnitzler* (Berlin, 1909); *Franz Liszt: Eine Biographie* (Berlin and Leipzig, 1909; 20th ed., 1924); *Franz Liszt: Gesammelte Schriften (allgemeine Inhaltsübersicht)* (Leipzig, 1910); *Franz Liszt und die Frauen* (Leipzig, 1910); *Liszt-Brevier* (Leipzig, 1910); *Richard Wagner: Eine Biographie* (Berlin, 1910; 32nd ed., 1929); ed. *Der junge Wagner: Dichtungen, Aufsätze, Entwürfe, 1832–1849* (Berlin, 1910); ed. *Franz Liszt: Gesammelte Schriften* (Leipzig, 1910); *Liszt- Brevier* (Leipzig, 1910); *Richard Wagner und die Frauen: Eine erotische Biographie* (Berlin, 1912; 16th ed., 1929; rev. 1951; Eng. tr., 1951, as *The Loves of Richard Wagner*); *Niccolò Paganini: Eine Biographie* (Berlin and Leipzig, 1913; 18th ed., 1954); ed. *Richard Wagner: Gesammelte Schriften und Dichtungen* (Leipzig, 1914); ed. *Richard Wagners gesammelte Briefe, I-II* (Leipzig, 1914–33); ed. *Richard Wagner an Mathilde und Otto Wesendonk* (Leipzig, 1915; 2nd ed., 1936); *Berlioz: Eine Biographie* (Berlin and Leipzig, 1917; 2nd ed., rev., 1922); *Das Dreigestirn: Berlioz, Liszt, Wagner* (Berlin, 1920); *Giacomo Meyerbeer: Eine Biographie* (Berlin, 1920; 8th ed., rev., 1932); *Franz Schreker: Der Mann und sein Werk* (Munich, 1921); *Das Opernbuch* (Leipzig, 1922; 18th ed., 1928; rev. 1939); *Die Oper der Gegenwart* (Berlin, 1922); *Carl Maria von Weber* (Stuttgart and Berlin, 1922; 15th ed., 1944); ed. *Ludwig van Beethovens sämtliche Briefe* (Leipzig, 1923; rev. ed. of Kastner); ed. *Richard Strauss und die Berliner Oper* (Berlin, 1934); *Geschichte der Staatsoper Berlin* (Berlin, 1937).—NS/LK/DM

Kapp, Richard, American conductor; b. Chicago, Oct. 9, 1936. He studied at Johns Hopkins Univ. (B.A., 1957), then took courses in conducting, composition, and piano at the Staatliche Hochschule für Musik in Stuttgart. Returning to the U.S., he studied jurisprudence at N.Y.U. (J.D., 1966) and had private lessons with Rosbaud and Halasz in conducting, Simon in piano, and Marlowe in harpsichord. He began his musical career as a répétiteur at the Basel Stadttheater (1960–62), and then was music director of the Opera Theater of the Manhattan School of Music in N.Y. (1963–65). In 1968 he led a concert in N.Y. with a specially assembled group billed as the Philharmonia Virtuosi, and later toured with it in programs of varied repertoire, from Baroque to jazz.—NS/LK/DM

Kapp, Villem, Estonian composer, nephew of **Artur Kapp;** b. Suure-Jaani, Sept. 7, 1913; d. Tallinn, March 24, 1964. He began his training with his uncle, then studied with Eller at the Tallinn Cons. (1939–44), where, from 1945 to 1964, he was a prof. of composition. He wrote in an expansive Romantic style rooted in folk song. His opera, *Lembitu* (Tallinn, Aug. 23, 1961), glorifies Estes Lembitu, the leader of the Estonian struggle against the invading Teutonic crusaders in 1217. He also wrote 2 syms. (1947, 1955), 4 cantatas (1949–63), Piano Sonata (1940), Piano Trio (1946), Wind Quintet (1957), and songs.

BIBL.: H. Tönson, *V. K.* (Tallinn, 1967).—NS/LK/DM

Kappel, Gertrude, noted German soprano; b. Halle, Sept. 1, 1884; d. Pullach, April 3, 1971. She studied with Nikisch and Noe at the Leipzig Cons. She made her debut in 1903 at the Hannover Opera, where she was a regular member (until 1924). She also sang at London's Covent Garden (1912–14; 1924–26) and the Vienna State Opera (1924–29). She was a principal member of the Bavarian State Opera in Munich (1927–31). She made her Metropolitan Opera debut in N.Y. as Isolde on Jan. 16, 1928, and remained a member until 1936; also sang with the San Francisco Opera. She returned to Germany, retiring in 1937. Her finest roles were Isolde and Brünnhilde, but she also was admired for her Senta, Sieglinde, Marschallin, and Elektra. —NS/LK/DM

Kapr, Jan, Czech composer; b. Prague, March 12, 1914; d. there, April 29, 1988. He studied with his father, a musician, then composition with Řídký and later with Křička in his master class at the Prague Cons. (1933–40). He was a music producer for the Czech Radio in Prague (1939–46), a music critic (1946–49), and an ed. in music publishing (1950–54); from 1961 to 1970 he taught at the Janáček Academy of Music and Dramatic Arts in Brno. His style of composition is derived from the Czech national school; in his later works, he audaciously introduced modernistic serial procedures. He publ. a vol. on contemporary music entitled *Konstanty* (The Constants; Prague, 1967).

WORKS: DRAMATIC: Opera: *Muzikantská pohádka* (Musicians' Fairy Tale; 1962). **ORCH.:** 3 piano concertos (1938, 1953, 1986); *Marathon,* symphonic scherzo (1939); Sinfonietta for Small Orch. (1940); 10 syms.: No. 1 (1943), No. 2 (1946), No. 3 for Small Orch. (1946), No. 4 (1957), No. 5, *Olympijská* (Olympic; 1959), No. 6 (1960; rev. 1964), No. 7, *Krajina dětstvi* (Country of Childhood), for Children's Chorus and Orch. (1968), No. 8, *Campanae Pragenses* (The Bells of Prague), for Chorus, Orch., and Bell Sounds on Tape (1970), No. 9 (1982), and No. 10, *Lanžhotská,* for 2 Vocal Soloists and Orch. (1985); *Harvested,* symphonic rhapsody (1950); *Zitra* (Tomorrow), symphonic picture (1953); *Léto* (Summer) for Chamber Orch. (1954); *Allegretto* for Violin and Orch. (1955); Violin Concerto (1955); *Variations for Flute and Strings* (1958); Concertino for Viola and Wind Orch. (1965); *Omaggio alla tromba* for 2 Solo Trumpets, Wind Orch., Piano, and Timpani (1967–68); *Anachron* for Chamber Orch. (1974); Concertino for Clarinet and Chamber Ensemble (1975). **CHAMBER:** 8 string quartets (1937; 1941; 1954; 1957; 1961; with Baritone, 1963; 1965; 1976); Nonet (1943); *Fantasy* for Violin and Piano (1958); *4 Moods* for Nonet (1959); *Šifry* (Ciphers) for Piano, Percussion, and Tape (1966); *Oscilace* (Oscillation) for Violin, Clarinet, Trumpet, Piano, Cello, and Percussion (1965); *Rotation 9* for Piano Quartet (1967); *Shadow Play and Dreambook* for Soprano, Flute, and Harp (1968); Sonata for Solo Cimbalom (1968); *Testimonies* for Cello, Bass Clarinet, Piano, and Light Source (1969); *Woodcuts* for 8 Brass (1973); *Colors of Silence* for 8 Instruments (1973); *Circuli* for Violin and Accordion

(1974); Sonata for Flute, Horn, and Piano (1976); *Claricello* for Clarinet and Cello (1981); *Miniatures* for Winds and Cello (1985). **P i a n o :** 4 sonatas (1945, 1947, 1958, 1980). **OTHER:** Cantatas; choruses; film music.—**NS/LK/DM**

Kaprál, Václav, Czech composer, father of **Ví-tězslava Kaprálová;** b. Určice u Prostějova, March 26, 1889; d. Brno, April 6, 1947. He studied with Janáček at the Brno Organ School (1908–10), Novák in Prague (1919–20), and Cortot in Paris (1923–24). He established his own music school in Brno in 1911, and also lectured at the Univ. of Brno (1927–36). He then taught at the Brno Cons. from 1936 until his 3-year internment in a concentration camp in Svatobořice during World War II. In 1946 he became a prof. at the Janáček Academy of Music in Brno. In his works, he shows a fine eclectic talent, enhanced by refulgent lyricism.

WORKS: CHAMBER: 2 string quartets (1925; 1927, with Baritone); *Ballad* for Cello and Piano (1946). **P i a n o :** 4 sonatas (1912, 1921, 1924, 1939); *Miniatury* (Miniatures; 1922); *Con duolo* for Piano, Left-hand (1926); 3 sonatinas (1930, 1936, 1943); *Fantasie* (1934). **VOCAL:** *Pro ni* (For Her) for Voice and Piano Quartet (1927); *Píseň podzimu* (Song of Autumn) for Voice and String Quartet (1929); *Uspavánsky* (Lullabies) for Voice and Chamber Orch. (1932; Barcelona, April 20, 1936).

BIBL.: E. Štaudová, *V. K., 1889–1947: Personální bibliografie* (Brno, 1989).—**NS/LK/DM**

Kaprálová, Vitězslava, Czech composer, daughter of **Václav Kaprál;** b. Brünn, Jan. 24, 1915; d. Montpellier, June 16, 1940. She received her early education from her father, then studied with Petrželka (composition) and Chalabala (conducting) at the Brno Cons. (1930–35); subsequently took master classes with Novák (composition) and Talich (conducting) at the Prague Cons. (1935–37). In 1937 she received a scholarship to Paris, where she took lessons in conducting with Munch and composition with Martinů. She appeared as a guest conductor with the BBC Sym. Orch. at the ISCM Festival in London in 1938. She returned to France in 1939, her promising career being cut tragically short by miliary tuberculosis.

WORKS: ORCH.: *Suite en miniature* (1932–35); Piano Concerto (Brno, June 17, 1935); *Military Sinfonietta* (Prague, Nov. 26, 1937); *Suita rustica* (Brno, April 16, 1939); *Partita* for Piano and Strings (Brno, Nov. 12, 1941); *Christmas Prelude* for Chamber Orch. (1939); Concertino for Violin, Clarinet, and Orch. (1940; unfinished). **CHAMBER:** *Legenda a Burleska* for Violin and Piano (1932); String Quartet (1936); *2 Ritournelles* for Cello and Piano (1940). **P i a n o :** *Sonata appassionata* (1933); *6 Variations on the Bells of the Church of Saint Etienne in Paris* (1938).

BIBL.: J. Macek, *V. K.* (Prague, 1958).—**NS/LK/DM**

Kapsberger, Johann Hieronymus, German instrumentalist and composer, known in Italy as **Giovanni Girolamo Tedesco della Tiorba** because of his virtuosity as a performer; b. Venice, c. 1580; d. Rome, 1651. He lived in Venice until settling in Rome about 1604, becoming celebrated as a player on the theorbo, chitarrone, lute, etc. He also organized his own academy, which gave concerts in his home. He enjoyed the favor of Pope Urban VIII. He was a notable composer of instrumental music.

WORKS (all publ. in Rome unless otherwise given): **VOCAL: S a c r e d :** *Libro I di* [20] *mottetti passeggiati* for Voice and Basso Continuo (1612); (21) *Cantiones sacrae* for 3 to 6 Voices and Basso Continuo (1628); *Modulatus sacri diminutis voculis concinnati* for Voice and Basso Continuo (1630); *I pastori di Bettelemme...dialogo recitativo* for 6 Voices and Basso Continuo (1630); (3) *Missae urbanae* for 4, 5, and 8 Voices and Basso Continuo (1631); (4) *Litaniae deiparae virginis* for 4, 6, and 8 Voices and Basso Continuo (1632). **S e c u l a r :** *Libro I de madrigali* for 5 Voices and Basso Continuo (1609); *Libro I di* [20] *villanelle* for 1 to 3 Voices and Basso Continuo (1610); *Libro I di* [22] *arie passeggiate* for Voice and Basso Continuo (1612); *Maggio,* cantata (Florence, 1612; not extant); *Libro II di* [21] *villanelle* for 1 to 3 Voices and Basso Continuo (1619); *Libro III di* [20] *villanelle* for 1 to 3 Voices and Basso Continuo (1619); *Libro IV di* [23] *villanelle* for 1 to 3 Voices and Basso Continuo (1623); *Libro II di* [30] *arie* for 1 and 2 Voices and Basso Continuo (1623); (10) *Poematia et carmina...liber I* for Voice and Basso Continuo (1624); *Coro musicale,* wedding cantata for 1 to 5 Voices, Instruments, and Basso Continuo (1627); *Epitalamio...recitativo a più voci* (1628; not extant); *Libro V di vallanelle* (1630; not extant); *Libro III d'arie passeggiate a una più voci* (1630; not extant); *Libro VI li firo di villanelle* (1632; not extant); *Poematia et carmina...liber II* (1633; not extant). **INSTRUMENTAL:** *Libro I d'intavolatura di chitarrone* (Venice, 1604); *Libro I d'intavolatura di lauto* (1611); *Libro I de* [8] *balli,* [6] *gagliarde et* [6] *correnti a 4* (1615); *Libro I di* [18] *sinfonie a 4* and Basso Continuo (1615); *Libro II d'intavolatura di chitarrone* (1616; not extant); *Capricci* for 2 Theorbos (1617; not extant); *Libro II d'intavolatura di lauto* (1623; not extant); *Libro III d'intavolatura di chitarrone* (1626); *Libro IV d'intavolatura di chitarrone* (1640).—**NS/LK/DM**

Karabtchewsky, Isaac, Brazilian conductor; b. São Paulo, Dec. 27, 1934. He studied in Brazil; then at the Hochschule für Musik in Freiburg im Breisgau. Upon his return to Brazil in 1969, he became music director of the Brazil Sym. Orch. in Rio de Janeiro; also was a guest conductor in the U.S. From 1987 to 1994 he was chief conductor of the Vienna Niederösterreichisches Tonkünstler Orch. His conducting is marked by an expansively Romantic quality, much in the vein of the old Russian school of interpretation.—**NS/LK/DM**

Karajan, Herbert (actually, **Heribert**) **von,** great Austrian conductor; b. Salzburg, April 5, 1908; d. Anif, near Salzburg, July 16, 1989. He was a scion of a cultured family of Greek-Macedonian extraction whose original name was Karajannis. His great-grandfather was Theodor Georg von Karajan (b. Vienna, Jan. 22, 1810; d. there, April 28, 1873), a writer on music; his father was a medical officer who played the clarinet and his brother was a professional organist. Karajan himself began his musical training as a pianist; he took lessons with Franz Ledwinka at the Salzburg Mozarteum. He further attended the conducting classes of the Mozarteum's director, Bernhard Paumgartner. Eventually he went to Vienna, where he pursued academic training at a technical college and took piano lessons from one J. Hofmann; then entered the Vienna Academy of Music as a conducting student in the classes of Clemens Krauss and Alexander Wunderer. On Dec. 17,

1928, he made his conducting debut with a student orch. at the Vienna Academy of Music; shortly afterward, on Jan. 23, 1929, he made his professional conducting debut with the Salzburg Orch. He then received an engagement as conductor of the Ulm Stadttheater (1929–34). From Ulm he went to Aachen, where he was made conductor of the Stadttheater; he subsequently served as the Generalmusikdirektor there (1935–42). On April 9, 1938, he conducted his first performance with the Berlin Phil., the orch. that became the chosen medium of his art. On Sept. 30, 1938, he conducted *Fidelio* at his debut with the Berlin State Opera. After his performance of *Tristan und Isolde* there on Oct. 21, 1938, he was hailed by the *Berliner Tageblatt* as "das Wunder Karajan." His capacity of absorbing and interpreting the music at hand and transmitting its essence to the audience became his most signal characteristic; he also conducted all of his scores from memory, including the entire *Ring des Nibelungen*. His burgeoning fame as a master of both opera and sym. led to engagements elsewhere in Europe. In 1938 he conducted opera at La Scala in Milan and also made guest appearances in Belgium, the Netherlands, and Scandinavia. In 1939 he became conductor of the sym. concerts of the Berlin State Opera Orch.

There was a dark side to Karajan's character, revealing his lack of human sensitivity and even a failure to act in his own interests. He became fascinated by the ruthless organizing solidity of the National Socialist party; shortly after Hitler became chancellor of Germany in 1933, Karajan was recruited to join the Austrian Nazi party in Salzburg, and then formally joined the German Nazi party in 1935 in anticipation of his Aachen appointment as Generalmusikdirektor. He lived to regret these actions after the collapse of the Nazi empire, but he managed to obtain various posts, and in 1947 he was officially denazified by the Allies' army of occupation. His personal affairs also began to interfere with his career. He married the operetta singer Elmy Holgerloef in 1938, but divorced her in 1942 to marry Anita Gütermann. Trouble came when the suspicious Nazi genealogists discovered that she was one-quarter Jewish and suggested that he divorce her. But World War II was soon to end, and so was Nazi hegemony. He finally divorced Gütermann in 1958 to marry the French fashion model Eliette Mouret.

Karajan was characteristically self-assertive and unflinching in his personal relationships and in his numerous conflicts with managers and players. Although he began a close relationship with the Vienna Sym. Orch. in 1948, he left it in 1958. His association as conductor of the Philharmonia Orch. of London from 1948 to 1954 did more than anything to re-establish his career after World War II, but in later years he disdained his relationship with that ensemble. When Wilhelm Furtwängler, the longtime conductor of the Berlin Phil., died in 1954, Karajan was chosen to lead the orch. on its first tour of the U.S. However, he insisted that he would lead the tour only on the condition that he be duly elected Furtwängler's successor. Protesters were in evidence for his appearance at N.Y.'s Carnegie Hall with the orch. on March 1, 1955, but his Nazi past did not prevent the musicians of the orch. from electing him

their conductor during their visit to Pittsburgh on March 3. After their return to Germany, the West Berlin Senate ratified the musicians' vote on April 5, 1955.

Karajan soon came to dominate the musical life of Europe as no other conductor had ever done. In addition to his prestigious Berlin post, he served as artistic director of the Vienna State Opera from 1956 until he resigned in a bitter dispute with its general manager in 1964. He concurrently was artistic director of the Salzburg Festival (1957–60), and thereafter remained closely associated with it. From 1969 to 1971 he held the title of artistic adviser of the Orchestre de Paris. In the meantime, he consolidated his positions in Berlin and Salzburg. On Oct. 15, 1963, he conducted the Berlin Phil. in a performance of Beethoven's 9th Sym. at the gala concert inaugurating the orch.'s magnificent new concert hall, the Philharmonie. In 1967 he organized his own Salzburg Easter Festival, which became one of the world's leading musical events. In 1967 he re-negotiated his contract and was named conductor-for-life of the Berlin Phil. He made a belated Metropolitan Opera debut in N.Y. on Nov. 21, 1967, conducting *Die Walküre*. He went on frequent tours of Europe and Japan with the Berlin Phil., and also took the orch. to the Soviet Union (1969) and China (1979).

In 1982 Karajan personally selected the 23-year-old clarinetist Sabine Meyer as a member of the Berlin Phil. (any romantic reasons for his insistence were not apparent). The musicians of the orch. rejected her because of their standing rule to exclude women, but also because the majority of the musicians had less appreciation of Meyer as an artist than Karajan himself did. A compromise was reached, however, and in 1983 she was allowed to join the orch. on probation. She resigned in 1984 after a year of uneasy co-existence.

In 1985 Karajan celebrated his 30th anniversary as conductor of the Berlin Phil., and in 1988 his 60th anniversary as a conductor. In 1987 he conducted the New Year's Day Concert of the Vienna Phil., which was televised to millions on both sides of the Atlantic. In Feb. 1989 he made his last appearance in the U.S., conducting the Vienna Phil. at N.Y.'s Carnegie Hall. In April 1989 he announced his retirement from his Berlin post, citing failing health. Shortly before his death, he dictated an autobiographical book to Franz Endler; it was publ. in an English tr. in 1989.

Through his superlative musical endowments, charismatic and glamorous personality, extraordinary capacity for systematic work, and phenomenal command of every aspect of the great masterworks of the symphonic and operatic repertoire fully committed to memory, Karajan attained legendary stature in his own time. A renowned orchestral technician, he molded the Berlin Phil. into the most glorious musical ensemble of its kind. His interpretations of Beethoven, Wagner, Brahms, Bruckner, Mahler, and Richard Strauss placed him among the foremost conductors in the history of his chosen profession.

BIBL.: E. Haeusserman, *H. v.K. Biographie* (Gütersloh, 1968; new ed., Vienna, 1978); C. Spiel, ed., *Anekdoten um H. v.K.* (Munich, 1968); P. Robinson, *K.* (Toronto, 1975); W. Stresemann, *The Berlin Philharmonic from Bülow to K.* (in Ger. and Eng.; Berlin,

1979); R. Bachmann, *K.: Anmerkungen zu einer Karriere* (Düsseldorf, 1983); H. Kröber, *H. v.K.: Der Magier mit dem Taktstock* (Munich, 1986); R. Vaughan, *H. v.K.: A Biographical Portrait* (N.Y. and London, 1986); H. Götze and W. Simon, eds., *Wo sprache aufhört...H. v.K. zum 5. April 1988* (Berlin, 1988); H. Grünewald, *H.v. K. zum Gedenken 1908–1989* (Berlin, 1989); R. Osborne, *Conversations with K.* (Oxford, 1989); R. Bachmann, *K.: Notes on a Career* (N.Y., 1991); W. Stresemann, *Ein seltsamer Mann: Erinnerungen am H. v.K.* (Frankfurt am Main, 1991); F. Endler, *K.: Eine Biographie* (Hamburg, 1992); K. Lang, *The K. Dossier* (London and Boston, 1992); G. Mortier, H. Landesmann, and H. Wiesmüller, eds., *H.v. K. und die Salzburger Festspiele: Dokumentation einer Partnerschaft, 1933, 1948–49, 1957–1989* (Salzburg, 1994); B. Wessling, *H. v.K.: Eine kritische Biographie* (Munich, 1994); F. Endler and K. Fritthum, *K. an der Wiener Oper: Dokumentation einer éra* (Vienna, 1997); R. Osborne, *H. v.K.: A Life in Music* (London, 1998).—**NS/LK/DM**

Karajan, Theodor Georg von, Austrian writer on music, great- grandfather of **Herbert von Karajan;** b. Vienna, Jan. 22, 1810; d. there, April 28, 1873. He studied history, philology, and law. After holding various minor posts, he was president of the Austrian Academy of Science (1866–69). His important monograph *J. Haydn in London, 1791 und 1792* (Vienna, 1861) contains Haydn's correspondence with Maria Anna von Genzinger. He also publ. *Aus Metastasios Hofleben* (Vienna, 1861). —**NS/LK/DM**

Karasowski, Moritz (actually, Maurycy), Polish cellist and writer on music; b. Warsaw, Sept. 22, 1823; d. Dresden, April 20, 1892. He studied in Warsaw, Berlin, Vienna, and Paris. He was a cellist in the opera orch. in Warsaw from 1851, and later settled in Dresden as a member of the opera orch. (1864), being named a court musician in 1868.

WRITINGS: *Rys historyczny opery polskiej* (Historical Outline of Polish Opera; Warsaw, 1859); *Zycie Mozarta* (Life of Mozart; Warsaw, 1868); *Friedrich Chopin: Sein Leben, seine Werke und Briefe* (2 vols., Dresden, 1877; 4th ed., 1914; Eng. tr., London, 1879; 3rd ed., 1938).—**NS/LK/DM**

Karastoyanov, Assen, Bulgarian composer; b. Samokov, June 3, 1893; d. Sofia, Sept. 8, 1976. He studied flute at the Sofia Music School (1914–18), and subsequently took courses with Juon (harmony) at the Berlin Hochschule für Musik (1921–22), Dukas (composition) at the École Normale de Musique in Paris (1930–31), and Raphael (composition) at the Leipzig Cons. (1931–32). He taught at the Sofia State Academy of Music (1933–44), where he was a prof. (1944–58).

WORKS: 7 operettas, including *Michel Strogoff*, after Jules Verne (1937–40); 7 patriotic cantatas; *A Balkan Suite* for Orch. (1928); 4 syms.: No. 1, *Miner's Symphony* (1940), No. 2, *Danubian*, for Brass Orch. (1960), No. 3, *Rhodopean* (1973), and No. 4, *Proto-Bulgarian* (1975); Flute Concerto (1959); *A Bogomil Legend* for String Orch. (1973); 2 string quartets (1937, 1970); 2 suites for Flute and Piano (1955, 1968); *Capriccio* for Violin and Piano (1970); *Scherzino* for Piano (1933); Piano Sonata (1938); songs. —**NS/LK/DM**

Karatygin, Viacheslav (Gavrilovich), Russian writer on music; b. Pavlovsk, Sept. 17, 1875; d.

Leningrad, Oct. 23, 1925. He learned to play the piano from his mother, who was a professional pianist, then took courses in physics and mathematics at the Univ. of St. Petersburg (graduated, 1897). He subsequently was a chemist in the naval dept. (until 1907), and also studied composition with Sokolov at the St. Petersburg Cons. (1897–1902). From 1907 to 1917 he was active as a music critic. He also taught aesthetics and music history at the Petrograd Cons. (from 1916), being made a prof. (1919). As a critic, he welcomed the music of Scriabin, Stravinsky, and Prokofiev at a time when most Russian critics regarded them as unacceptable, and he enunciated the idea of a "musical revolution." He publ. monographs on Mussorgsky, Chaliapin, and Scriabin, and also composed some piano pieces and songs.

BIBL.: A. Rimsky-Korsakov et al., eds., *V.G. K.:Zhizn, deyatelnost, stati i materiali* (V.G. K.: Life, Work, Articles, and Materials; Leningrad, 1927).—**NS/LK/DM**

Karayanis, Plato, American opera administrator; b. Pittsburgh, Dec. 26, 1928. He studied voice at Carnegie-Mellon Univ. in Pittsburgh, opera at the Curtis Inst. of Music in Philadelphia, and opera administration and production technology at the Hamburg State Opera. After singing baritone roles and working as a stage director in Europe, he was made head of the rehearsal dept. at the San Francisco Opera in 1964. From 1965 to 1967 he was asst. stage director and company administrator of the Metropolitan Opera National Co. In 1967 he joined Affiliate Artists, Inc., where he later was executive vice- president. In 1977 he became general director of the Dallas Opera, where his tenure saw the expansion of both the traditional and contemporary repertoires. From 1993 to 1997 he also was president of the board of directors of OPERA America, Inc.—**NS/LK/DM**

Karayev, Kara (Abulfazogli), Russian composer; b. Baku, Feb. 5, 1918; d. Moscow, May 13, 1982. He studied piano with Sharoyev at the Baku Music Technical School (1930–35) and then composition with Rudolf at the Azerbaijani Cons.; later took courses in composition with Alexandrov and Shostakovich and instrumentation with Vasilenko at the Moscow Cons. (graduated, 1946). He taught at the Azerbaijani Cons. (from 1946), serving as its director (1949–52). His music is derived mainly from his semi-oriental environment, comprising not only the native Tartar motifs, but also other Asian resources. Particularly effective are his theatrical spectacles featuring native dances and choral ensembles.

WORKS: DRAMATIC: O p e r a: *Fatherland* (1945). B a l l e t: *7 Beauties* (1952); *On the Track of Thunder* (1958). ORCH.: *Poem of Joy* for Piano and Orch. (1937); 3 syms. (1944, 1946, 1965); *Leyly and Medzhnun*, symphonic poem (1947); *Albanian Rhapsody* (1952); *Don Quixote*, symphonic sketches (1960); Violin Concerto (1967). OTHER: Chamber music; piano pieces; oratorio; cantatas; film scores.

BIBL.: L. Karagicheva, *K. K.* (Baku, 1956).—**NS/LK/DM**

Kardoš, Dezider, Slovak composer; b. Nadlice, Dec. 23, 1914; d. Bratislava, March 18, 1991. He studied composition with Moyzes at the Bratislava Academy of

Music (graduated, 1937) and with Novák at the Prague Cons. (1937–39). He worked for the Czech Radio in Prešov (1939–45) and Kosice (1945–51), and then became a teacher at the Bratislava Academy of Music (1963), being made a prof. in 1968. The thematic sources of his musical inspiration are found in eastern Slovak folklore.

WORKS: ORCH.: 7 syms.: No. 1 (1942), No. 2, *Of Native Land* (1955), No. 3 (1961), No. 4, *Piccola* (1962), No. 5 (1965), No. 6 (1974–75), and No. 7, *Ballade vom Traum*, for Baritone, Chorus, and Orch. (1983–84); 3 overtures: *My Home* (1946), *East Slovak* (1950), and *Res philharmonica* (1970); *Concerto for Orchestra* (1957); *Heroic Ballad* for Strings (1959); Concerto for Strings (1963); Piano Concerto (1969); *Partita* for 12 Strings (1972); *Slovakophonia*, variations on a folk theme (1975–76); Violin Concerto (1980); *Symphonietta* (1988). **CHAMBER:** 4 string quartets (1935, 1966, 1978, 1985); Wind Quintet (1938); *3 Compositions* for Violin and Piano (1966). **KEYBOARD: Piano:** 2 suites (both 1937); *Bagatelles* (1948). **Organ:** *Preludium quasi una fantasia* (1940); *Elevazioni* (1967). **VOCAL:** *Peace Cantata* (1951); *Songs about Life*, cycle of 4 microdramas for Soprano, Tenor, and Orch. (1973–74); choruses; songs. —NS/LK/DM

Kardos, István, Hungarian conductor and composer; b. Debrecen, June 6, 1891; d. Budapest, Dec. 22, 1975. He studied composition with Herzfeld at the Budapest Academy of Music, then was a theater conductor in Hungary, Germany, and Switzerland (1917–46). From 1948 to 1959 he taught at the Budapest Academy of Music.

WORKS: ORCH.: *Dance* (1918); 4 syms. (1919, 1958, 1967, 1968); *Hungarian Scherzo* (1936); Violin Concertino (1947); *Janus* (1950); 2 piano concertos (1956, 1963); Double Bass Concertino (1959); Double Concerto for Viola, Double Bass, and Orch. (1964); *Alliage* for Violin and Chamber Orch. (1966); *Intrada* (1968); *Visitation* (1969). **CHAMBER:** 6 string quartets (1917, 1925, 1951, 1960, 1967, 1971); Viola Sonata (1942); Double Bass Sonata (1949); Flute Sonata (1957); Wind Quintet (1959); String Trio (1960); *Bipartitum* for Bassoon and Piano (1963); Sonata for Solo Clarinet (1965); *Poem and Burlesque* for Double Bass and Piano (1969); 2 sextets for Clarinet, String Quartet, and Piano (1971); *Grotesque* for Octave Flute, Cello, and Double Bass (1971); *Notturno* for Horn, Flute, Violin, and Harp (1971). **Piano:** Sonata (1916); *Dickens Suite* (1957); *Toccata* (1960); *Variations and Fugue* (1969). **VOCAL:** *Áprilisi hajnal* (Dawn in April), cantata (1950); songs.—NS/LK/DM

Karel, Rudolf, Czech composer; b. Pilsen, Nov. 9, 1880; d. in the concentration camp in Terezín, March 6, 1945. He was the last student of Dvořáak, with whom he studied in Prague for 1 year during his term at the Prague Cons. (1901–04). In 1914 he went to Russia as a teacher. After the Revolution, he made his way to Irkutsk, Siberia; during the Russian civil war, he became a member of the Czechoslovak Legion and conducted an orch. organized by the legionnaires. He returned to Prague in 1920; from 1923 to 1941, taught at the Prague Cons. As a member of the Czech resistance in World War II, he was arrested by the Nazis in March 1943; was transferred to Terezín in Feb. 1945, and died there of dysentery shortly before liberation. His music reflects Romantic concepts. He had a predilection for program-

matic writing; the national element is manifested by his treatment of old modal progressions; his instrumental writing is rich in sonority and the polyphonic structure is equally strong.

WORKS: DRAMATIC: *Ilseino srdce* (Ilsea's Heart), lyric comedy (1906–09; Prague, Oct. 11, 1924); *Smrt Kmotřička* (Godmother Death), musical fairy tale (1928–33; Brno, Feb. 3, 1933); *Tři vlasy děda Vševěda* (3 Hairs of the Wise Old Man), musical fairy tale (1944–45; arranged by Z. Vostřak; Prague, Oct. 28, 1948); incidental music. **ORCH.:** Suite (1903–04); *Comedy Overture* (1904–05); *Fantasy* (1905); *The Ideals* (1906–09); 2 syms. (*Renaissance*, 1910–11; *Spring*, 1935–38); *4 Slavonic Dance Moods* (1912); *The Demon* (1918–20); *Capriccio* for Violin and Orch. (1924); *Revolutionary Overture* (1938–41). **CHAMBER:** 3 string quartets (1902–03; 1907–13; 1935–36); Piano Trio (1903–04); Violin Sonata (1912); Nonet for Wind Quintet and String Quartet (1945; completed by F. Hertl). **Piano:** *5 Pieces* (1902); *Notturno* (1906–07); Sonata (1910); *Thema con variazioni* (1910); *3 Waltzes* (1913); *Burlesques* (1913–14). **VOCAL:** *Vzkříšení* (Resurrection), sym. for Soloists, Chorus, and Orch. (1923–27; Prague, April 9, 1928); *Sladká balada dětská* (Sweet Ballad for a Child) for Soprano, Chorus, and Orch. (1928–30); *Černoch* (A Negro) for Baritone and Orch. or Piano (1934); choruses; songs.

BIBL.: O. Šourek, *R. K.* (Prague, 1947).—NS/LK/DM

Karetnikov, Nikolai, Russian composer; b. Moscow, June 28, 1930; d. there, Oct. 10, 1994. He was a student of Shebalin at the Moscow Cons. (1948–53). He embraced contemporary means of expression in his works, including 12-tone techniques. His advanced scores were not welcomed in official circles, although some of his music was performed abroad. His opera *Til Ulenshpigel* (Till Eulenspiegel; 1985) had to be recorded in secret, which prompted Gerard McBurney on BBC Radio 3 to dub it the first *samizdat* opera. It was finally performed in public in Bielefeld in 1993. He also composed the opera oratorio *Misteriya apostola Pavla* (The Mystery of St. Paul; 1972–87), ballet music, film scores, 4 syms., much chamber music, and piano pieces. —NS/LK/DM

Karg-Elert (real name, **Karg**), **Sigfrid,** distinguished German organist, pedagogue, and composer; b. Oberndorf am Neckar, Nov. 21, 1877; d. Leipzig, April 9, 1933. (His real name, which means "avaricious," sounded unattractive to his audiences, so he changed it to Karg-Elert.) He was a chorister at St. John in Leipzig, where he received instruction in music from the cantor Rothig. He studied with Homeyer, Jadassohn, Reinecke, and Teichmüller at the Leipzig Cons.; in 1919, joined its faculty. He gave organ recitals, becoming known as a great virtuoso; he also played the Kunstharmonium, for which he wrote many compositions. In 1931–32 he made a concert tour of the U.S. As a composer, he developed a brilliant style, inspired by the music of the Baroque, but he embellished this austere and ornamental idiom with impressionistic devices; the result was an ingratiating type of music with an aura of originality. He publ. *Akustische Ton-, Klang-, und Funktionsbestimmung* (1930) and *Polaristiche Klang- und Tonalitätslehre* (1931). In 1984 the Karg-Elert-Gesellschaft was organized in Heidelberg.

WORKS: KUNSTHARMONIUM: Sets of pieces: *Skiz-*

zen (1903); *Aquarellen* (1906); *Miniaturen* (1908); *Intarsien* (1911); *Impressions* (1914); *Idyllen* (1915); *Innere Stimmen* (1918). **FUNDAMENTAL TECHNICAL WORKS**: *Die Kunst des Registrierens; Die ersten grundlegenden Studien; Hohe Schule des Legatospiels; Die Harmoniumtechnik* (*Gradus ad Parnassum*); *Theoretische-praktische Elementarschule.* **ORGAN**: 66 chorale improvisations (1908–10); 20 chorale preludes and postludes (1912); *10 Poetic Tone Pictures; 3 Pastels, Cathedral Windows* (on Gregorian themes). **OTHER**: Wind Quintet; 2 clarinet sonatas; Sonata for Solo Flute; *Trio bucolico* for Violin, Flute, and Piano; lieder.

BIBL.: P. Schenk, *S. K.-E.* (Berlin, 1927); H. Avril, *S. K.- E.: Kompositions-verzeichnis mit einer monographischen Skizze* (Berlin, 1928); G. Sceats, *The Organ Works of K.-E.* (Orpington, 1940; rev. ed., London, 1950); W. Kwasnik, *S. K.-E.: Sein Leben und Werk in Heutiger Sicht* (Westerwald, 1971); S. Gerlach, *S. K.-E.: Verzeichnis sämtlicher Werke* (Frankfurt am Main, 1984); G. Hartmann, *Die Orgelwerke von S. K.-E.* (Bonn, 1985); A. Wollinger, *Die Flötenkompositionen von S. K.-E. (1877–1933)* (Frankfurt am Main, 1991).—**NS/LK/DM**

Karjalainen, Ahti,

Finnish conductor and composer; b. Oulu, March 20, 1907; d. Jyväskylä, Oct. 2, 1986. He studied composition at the Helsinki Cons., the Viipuri Inst., and the Sibelius Academy in Helsinki. After playing violin and trombone in various orchs., he conducted the Jyväskylä City Orch.

WORKS: ORCH.: *Polonaise* for Trombone and Orch. (1935); *Scherzo* for Trumpet, Trombone, and Orch. (1940); Trombone Concerto (1942); *Summer Scenes* for Oboe and Orch. (1944); *Winter Scenes* (1948); Sym. (1948); Concert Suite for Bassoon and Orch. (1949); Duo for 2 Trumpets and Orch. (1950); Violin Concerto (1952); *Ostinato* for Cello and Orch. (1954); 2 cello concertos (1956, 1966). **CHAMBER:** 6 partitas for Various Instrumental Combinations (1936, 1940, 1945, 1961, 1964, 1965); Wind Sextet (1945); solo pieces. **VOCAL:** *The Eagle's Way* for Chorus and Orch. (1965); *Setting Out* for Narrator, Baritone, Mixed Chorus, Men's Chorus, and Orch. (1968); *The Song of Wood*, cantata (1971).—**NS/LK/DM**

Karkoff, Maurice (Ingvar),

prominent Swedish composer and teacher; b. Stockholm, March 17, 1927. He began his training in theory with Blomdahl (1944–47), concurrently studying piano at the Stockholm Musikhögskolan (1945–51) and theory with Larsson (1948–53). He later pursued composition studies with Koch in Stockholm, Holmboe in Copenhagen, Jolivet in Paris, and Vogel in Switzerland. He was music critic of the Stockholm daily *Tidningen* (1962–66). In 1965 he became a teacher of theory and composition at the Stockholm Municipal Music Inst. In 1976 he was awarded the City of Stockholm Prize of Honor, and in 1977 was elected a member of the Royal Swedish Academy of Music in Stockholm. In his music, he absorbed many cultures; these are reflected in his compositions, many of which may be described as romantically modernistic and thematically sensitive to exotic resources and coloristic instrumental timbres.

WORKS: DRAMATIC: Chamber Opera: *Grandskibbutzen* (The Frontier Kibbutz; 1971–72). **ORCH.:** *Sinfonietta* (1954); *Saxophone Concertino* (1955); syms.: No. 1 (Bergen, Oct. 22, 1956), No. 2 (1957; Swedish Radio, Jan. 5, 1959), No. 3, *Sinfonia breve* (1958–59; Gavle, Jan. 10, 1960), No. 4

(1963; Stockholm, April 4, 1964), No. 5, *Sinfonia da camera* (Gavle, Nov. 11, 1965), No. 6 (1972–73; Stockholm, Oct. 12, 1974), No. 7, *Sinfonia da camera* (1975), No. 8 (1979–80), *Short Symphony* for Symphonic Band (1980–81; Stockholm, Sept. 27, 1982), *Dolorous Symphony* for Strings (1981–82); *Sinfonia piccola* (1982–83), No. 10 (1984–85); *Little Symphony* (1987), No. 11, *Sinfonia della vita* (1993–94), and No. 12, *Sinfonia semplice* (1994–96); Violin Concerto (1956); Piano Concerto (1957); Cello Concerto (1957–58); Trombone Concerto (1958); Horn Concerto (1959); *9 Aphoristic Variations* (1959); Clarinet Concerto (1959); *Variations* (1961); *Serenata* for Chamber Orch. (1961); *Suite* for Harpsichord and Strings (1962); *Concerto da camera* for Balalaika and Orch. (1962–63); *Concerto for Orchestra* (1963); *Oriental Pictures* (1965–66; also for Piano); *Transfigurate mutate* (1966); *Tripartita* (1966–67); *Textum* for Strings (1967); *Metamorphoses* (1967); *Sinfonietta grave* (1968–69); *Epitaphium* for Small Chamber Orch. (1968; also for Nonet); *5 Summer Scenes* (1969); *Triptyk* (1970); *Partes caracteris* (1971); *Symphonic Reflexions* (1971); *Passacaglia* for Strings (1971); Trumpet Concerto (1977); *Tre colori* for Strings (1978); *Textur* (1978); *Tre schizzi da Capri* for Small Orch. (1979–80); *Musica seria* for Flute, Harpsichord, and Strings (1980); *Fantasia* (1988); *4 Sketches* for Strings (1990); Concerto for Bassoon and Strings (1990); Concerto for Tuba and Strings (1991); *Concertino lirico* for Flute and Strings (1992). **CHAMBER:** Flute Sonata (1953); Cello Sonata (1954–55); Violin Sonata (1956); Wind Quintet (1956–57); 2 string quartets (1957, 1984); Quartet for 2 Trumpets, Horn, and Trombone (1958); Trio for Violin, Viola, and Cello (1960); *Chamber Concerto* for 14 Winds, Timpani, Percussion, and String Basses (1961); *Metamorphoses* for 4 Horns (1966); *Terzetto* for Flute, Cello, and Piano (1967); *Epitafium* for Flute, Oboe, Clarinet, Bassoon, Horn, and String Quartet (1968); *4 parte* for 13 Brasses and Percussion (1968); *Epitafium* for Accordion, Electric Guitar, and Percussion (1970); *Characters* for Wind Quintet, Trombone, Euphonium, and Percussion (1973–74); *Quasi una marcia* for 2 Wind Quintets and Percussion (1974); *Serenata* for Flute or Alto Flute and Piano (1975–76); *Ernst und Spass* for Saxophone Quartet (1984); *Profilen* for Alto and Baritone Saxophones (1984); *Sechs Albumblätter* for 11 Saxophones (1985–98); *Reflexionen* for Saxophone Quartet (1986); *Ballata quasi una fantasia* for Baritone Saxophone and Piano (1988); *Poem* for Clarinet, Viola, Alto Saxophone, and Piano (1988); *5 Poems* for English Horn and Piano (1991). **Piano:** Sonata (1956); *Partita piccola* (1958); *Capriccio on Football* (1961; a musical report on a football game); *Monopartita* (1969); *3 Expressions* for 2 Pianos (1971); *3 Nocturnes* (1974); *Femton albumblad* (1988–89); *Fantasia* for Piano, Left-Hand (1992). **VOCAL:** *6 Serious Songs* for Low Voice and Orch. (1955); *6 Allvarliga Songs* for High Voice and Orch. (1955); *Det Svenska Landet*, cantata for Baritone, Men's Chorus, and Orch. (1956); *Livet* (Life) for Alto and Orch. (1959); *10 Japanese Songs* for High Voice and Piano or Orch. (1959); *Gesang des Abgeschiedenen*, 5 romances for Baritone and Piano or Orch. (1959); *Himmel och Jord*, cantata (1960); *6 Nocturnes* for Soprano, Flute, Violin, Viola, and Guitar (1963); *Sju rosor senare* for Reciter, Speaking Chorus, Mixed Chorus, and Orch. (1964); *Jeremiah* for Reciter, Baritone, Speaking Chorus, Men's Chorus, and Orch. (1965); *Das ist sein Erlauten*, cantata (1965); *Landschaft aus Schreien* for Soprano, Reciter, Oboe or Oboe d'amore or English Horn, 2 Clarinets, Double Bass, and Harp, after Nelly Sachs (1967); *6 Chinese Impressions* for Soprano, Flute, Oboe, Clarinet, Cello, and Percussion (1973); *Varsel och aningar* for High Voice, Winds, and Percussion (1975); *Voices from the Past: Songs to 7 Korean Poems* for Contralto or Baritone and Small String Orch. (1981); *Karlak och var i japan* for 5 Women's Voices, Flute or Alto

Flute or Piccolo, Clarinet or Bass Clarinet, Guitar, and 2 Percussion (1986–87); *Ljus och mörker*, cantata (1991); *Herren är min herde*, cantata for Reciter, Soloists, Chorus, 4 Winds, and 3 Percussion (1992–93); *Främmande stad* for Voice and Orch. (1996); *Andlig musik* for Mezzo-soprano and Clarinet (1998); *Närvaro av Gud* for Soprano and Reciter (1998–99).
—NS/LK/DM

Karkoschka, Erhard, German composer, conductor, and pedagogue; b. Moravská Ostrava, Czechoslovakia, March 6, 1923. He studied composition with Marx at the Stuttgart Hochschule für Musik (1946–53) and musicology with Gerstenberg and Reichert at the Univ. of Tübingen (Ph.D., 1959, with a diss. on Webern's early compositional techniques). He was conductor of the orch. and choir at the Univ. of Hohenheim (1948–68), and in 1958 joined the faculty of the Stuttgart Hochschule für Musik, where he became a prof. in 1964 and director of its electronic music studio in 1973; he retired in 1987. He also founded its Ensemble for New Music (1962), which became an independent ensemble in 1976 under the name Contact-Ensemble. From 1974 to 1980 he was president of the Gesellschaft für Neue Musik. In 1987 he was elected a member of the Free Academy of the Arts in Mannheim. He adoped Webern's serial method of composition, often incorporating electronics and also occasionally resorting to graphic notation in order to achieve greater freedom of resulting sonorities; in his desire to unite the arts, he created various pieces of music sculpture.

WRITINGS: *Das Schriftbild der neuen Musik* (1965; Eng. tr., 1972, as *Notations of New Music*); *Analyse neuer Musik* (1976); *Neue Musik-Hören-Verstehen* (1978); with H. Haas, *Hörererziehung mit neuer Musik* (1982).

WORKS: CHAMBER Opera: *Orpheus? Oder Hadeshöhe* (1990–92). **ORCH.:** Concertino for Chamber Orch. (1952); *Symphonische Evolution aus zwei eigenen Themen* (1953); *Streichersonate* (1954); Little Concerto for Violin and Chamber Orch. (1955); *Polphone Studie* for Orch. and Piano obbligato (1956); *Symphonia choralis über "Veni Sancte Spiritus"* for Wind Orch. (1957); *Undarum continuum* (1960); *vier stufen* (1965); *Variationen zu keinem Originalthema und aus diesem heraus* (1974); *Teleologies* (1978); *Entfalten* for Clarinet, Cello, Percussion, Piano, and Orch. (1982–83); *Kammermusik* (1983–84). **CHAMBER:** String Quartet (1952); *Divertimento* for Wind Quintet (1952); *Festmusik* for 6 Winds (1954); *quattrologe* for String Quartet (1966); *antinomie* for Wind Quintet (1969); *tempora mutantur* for String Quartet (1971); *kammerkitsch* for Soprano, Tenor, Bass, 3 Instruments, and Tape (1974); *CHRONOS II: Komposition- Improvisation* for 4 Instruments (1975); *im dreieck* for 3 Flutes or Flute and Stereo Sound System (1975); *links und rechts*, march for Flute, 2 Microphones, Amplifier, and Loudspeaker (1976); *Spiralend I* and *II* for 15 Flutes or 3 Flutes and Tape (1980); *Aus einer Figur* for 3 Flutes or 3 Flutes and Tape (1982); *Bläsergedichte* for Woodwind Quintet (1987); *Nach Paul Celan* for Speaker, Guitar, Flute, Clarinet, Marimba, Viola, and Cello (1988); *Klangzeitspektakel* for String Quartet, Computer, and Projection (1988); *Zeitvariation* for Cello (1993); keyboard music. **ELECTRONIC:** *Drei Bilder aus der Offenbarung des Johannes* (1960); *LSD* (1973); *Improvisation* (1974); *CHRONOS I* (1975) and *V* (1976); *Gag-Montagen* (1977); *Meditationsmühle I* and *II* (both 1982); *Zeitmosaik I* (1985); *Skulpturmusik* (1985); multimedia creations; *Geburtztaxtextelein*, word-music score (1989); etc.
—NS/LK/DM

Karl, Tom, Irish tenor; b. Dublin, Jan. 19, 1846; d. Rochester, N.Y., March 19, 1916. He studied in England with Henry Phillips, and in Italy with Sangiovanni. He sang in Italy for many years, then settled in N.Y. His remarkable success as Ralph in Pinafore (1879) encouraged him to pursue a career in light opera. With H. Barnabee and W. MacDonald, he formed the light opera company The Bostonians, which had a repertoire of about 150 operas and operettas. After his retirement in 1896, he taught voice in N.Y. and Rochester.—NS/LK/DM

Karlins, M(artin) William, American composer and teacher; b. N.Y., Feb. 25, 1932. He studied in N.Y. with Frederick Piket (1954–57), Gianinni at the Manhattan School of Music (1958–61), and with Wolpe (1960–61) before completing his training with Bezanson and Hervig at the Univ. of Iowa (1963–65; Ph.D., 1965). From 1965 to 1967 he taught at Western Ill. Univ. in Macomb. In 1967 he became an assoc. prof., in 1973 a prof., and in 1998 the Harry N. and Ruth F. Wyatt Prof. of Music Theory at Northwestern Univ. in Evanston.

WORKS: ORCH.: *Concert Music I* (1959), *III* (1963–64), *IV* (1964), and *V* (1972–73); *Reflux*, concerto for Amplified Double Bass and Solo Wind Ensemble, Piano, and Percussion (1971–72); *Sym. No. 1* (1979–80); *Catena I* for Little Orch. and Clarinet Obbligato (1980–81) and *III*, horn concerto (1983); Alto Saxophone Concerto (1981–82); *Elegy* (1992). **Band:** *Passacaglia and Rounds* (1970). **CHAMBER:** *Concerto grosso I* for 9 Instruments (1959–60) and *II* for 7 Instruments (1961); String Quartet (1960); *Birthday Music I* for Flute, Bass Clarinet, and Double Bass (1962) and *II* for Flute and Double Bass (1963); String Trio (1962–63); *Little Pieces* for 4 Double Basses (1962); *4 Inventions and a Fugue* for Bassoon, Piano, and Optional Woman's Voice (1962); *Solo Piece with Passacaglia* for Clarinet (1964); *Variations on "Obiter dictum"* for Cello, Piano, and Percussion (1965); *Blues* for Saxophone Quartet (1965); *Music for Oboe, Bass Clarinet, and Piano* (1966); *Music for Cello Alone I* (1966) and *II* (1969); 3 saxophone quartets (1966–67; 1975; *Night Light*, 1992–93); *Lamentations: In Memoriam* for Speaker, Organ, Flutes, Brass, Harp, and Percussion (1968); *Music* for English Horn and Piano (1968); *Music for Alto Saxophone and Piano* (1968); *Music for Tenor Saxophone and Piano* (1969); *Graphic Mobile* for Any 3 or Multiples of 3 Instruments (1969); 2 woodwind quintets (1970; 1977–78); *Celebration* for Flute, Oboe, and Harpsichord (1970); Quintet for Alto Saxophone and String Quartet (1973–74); *Infinity* for Oboe d'Amore, Clarinet, Viola, and Woman's Voice (1978); *Fantasia* for Tenor Saxophone and Percussion (1978–79); *Fanfare with Fugato* for Cello, 2 Trumpets, and 2 Trombones (1981); *Catena II* for Soprano Saxophone and Brass Quintet (1982); *Impromptu* for Alto Saxophone and Organ or Electric Keyboard or Piano (1985–86); *Seasons* for Saxophone (1987); *Saxtuper* for Alto Doubling on Soprano Saxophone, Tuba, and Percussion (1989); *Introduction and Passacaglia* for 2 Saxophones and Piano (1990); *Nostalgie* for Saxophone Ensemble (1991); *Under and Over* for Flute Doubling Alto Flute and Contrabass (1994); *Kindred Spirits* for Mandolin, Guitar, and Harp (1997–98); *Yesterday's Memories* for Soprano Saxophone and Piano (1999). **KEYBOARD: Piano:** 3 sonatas (1959, 1962, 1965); *Outgrowths-Variations* (1961); *Suite of Preludes* (1988); *Humble Harvest* (1999–2000). **Organ:** *Obiter dictum* (1964). **Harpsichord:** *Chameleon* (1984); *Drei Kleine Cembalostücke* (1994). **VOCAL:** *Children's Bedtime Songs* for Chorus (1955); *3 Love Songs* for Men's Chorus (1957); *Concert Music II* for Chorus and Orch. (1960); Song for Soprano, Alto Flute, and

Cello (1963; rev. 2000); *3 Poems* for Chorus (1966); *3 Songs* for Soprano, Flute, and Piano (1967); *Returning the Scroll to the Arc* for Cantor and Organ (1985); *Looking Out My Window* for Treble Chorus and Viola (1990).—NS/LK/DM

Karlowicz, Mieczyslaw, Polish composer; b. Wiszniewe, Dec. 11, 1876; d. in an avalanche while mountain climbing in Zakopane, Feb. 8, 1909. He was the son of the music theorist Jan Karlowicz (b. Subortowicze, near Troki, May 28, 1836; d. Warsaw, June 14, 1903). He studied violin in Warsaw from 1887 with Jakowski and Barcewicz, and also composition with Noskowski, Roguski, and Maszynski; continued his studies in Berlin with Urban (1895–1901). He was director of the Warsaw Music Soc. (1904–06). After a sojourn in Germany (where he studied conducting with Nikisch in Leipzig), he settled in Zakopane (1907). Essentially a Romanticist, he succeeded in blending the national elements of Polish folk music with the general European genre of mild modernism; there is an influence of Richard Strauss in his expansive tone painting. The appreciation of his music in Poland rose after his death; some of his piano pieces and songs have been established in the Polish repertoire.

WORKS: ORCH.: S y m p h o n i c   P o e m s : *Powracajsce fale* (Returning Waves; 1904); *Odwieczne pieśni* (Eternal Songs; 1907); *Stanislaw i Anna Oświecimowie* (Stanislaw and Anna of Oświecim; 1908); *Smutna opowieść* (Sad Story; 1908); *Epizod na maskaradzie* (Episode at the Masquerade; 1908–09; unfinished; completed by G. Fitelberg). **OTHER:** *Serenade* for String Orch. (1898); Sym. in E minor, *Odrodzenie* (Renaissance; 1902); Violin Concerto (1902); *Rapsodia litewska* (1908).

BIBL.: F. Kęcki, *M. K.: Szkic monograficzny* (Warsaw, 1934); A. Chybiński, *M. K. (1876–1909): Kronika życia artysty i taternika* (M. K. [1876–1909]: Chronicle of the Life of an Artist; Kraków, 1949); E. Dziębowska, ed., *Z życia i twórczości M.a K.a* (From the Life and Works of M. K.; Kraków, 1970); A. Wightman, *H. K.: Portrait of a Twentieth-Century American Composer* (Lanham, Md., 1997).—NS/LK/DM

Karpath, Ludwig, Austrian singer and music critic; b. Budapest, April 27, 1866; d. Vienna, Sept. 8, 1936. He was a pupil at the Budapest Cons. and studied singing in Vienna. He was a member of the National Opera Co. in the U.S. (singing minor bass roles; 1886–88). Returning to Vienna, he became an influential music critic. He wrote for the *Neues Wiener Tageblatt* (1894–1921). He publ. *Siegfried Wagner als Mensch und Künstler* (1902), *R. Wagner, der Schuldenmacher* (1914), etc. —NS/LK/DM

Kárpáti, János, distinguished Hungarian musicologist; b. Budapest, July 11, 1932. He studied musicology with Kodály, Szabolcsi, and Bartha at the Franz Liszt Academy of Music in Budapest, then was an ed. with the music dept. of the Hungarian Radio (1957–59) and music producer with the Hungaroton Record Co. (1959–61). In 1961 he was named chief librarian of the Liszt Academy. He obtained his degree of Candidate of Sciences in 1968 and his Ph.D. in 1969 with the diss. *Bartók vonósnegyesi* (publ. in Budapest, 1967; rev. ed., 1976, as *Bartók' kamarazenéje*; Eng. tr., 1975, as *Bartók's*

String Quartets; rev. and aug. ed., 1993, as *Bartók's Chamber Music*). His books include *Domenico Scarlatti* (Budapest, 1959); *Arnold Schönberg* (Budapest, 1963); *Kelet zenéje* (Music of the Orient; Budapest, 1981). He compiled the 2nd and 4th vols. for an encyclopedic ed., *Muzsikáló zenetörténet* (History of Music). In 1981 he was guest lecturer at Harvard Univ. In 1982 he was a delegate at the Bartók Memorial Conference in Bloomington, Ind., and in 1983 was a guest lecturer at the Univ. of Calif. at Los Angeles, at North Tex. State Univ. in Denton, and at the Univ. of Tex. in Austin. —NS/LK/DM

Karpeles, Maud, English ethnomusicologist; b. London, Nov. 12, 1885; d. there, Oct. 1, 1976. She was educated in England and Germany. She was associated with Cecil Sharp in collecting and organizing English folk songs (from 1909). In 1914 she visited the U.S., where she assembled American songs of English origin. She founded the International Folk Music Council (1947), and ed. its journal (1949–63). She was made an Officer of the Order of the British Empire in 1961. With Sharp, she publ. the collections *English Folk Songs from the Southern Appalachians* (London, 1917; 3rd ed., 1960) and *The Country Dance Book*, V (London, 1918); her own collections included *The Lancashire Morris Dance Tunes* (London, 1930), *Folk Songs from Newfoundland* (London, 1934; 2nd ed., aug., 1971), and *Cecil Sharp's Collection of English Folk Songs* (London, 1973). She also publ. *Cecil Sharp* (with A.H. Fox Strangways; London, 1932; 2nd ed., 1955; rev. ed., 1967, as *Cecil Sharp: His Life and Work*), *Folk Songs of Europe* (London, 1956), and *An Introduction to English Folk Song* (London, 1973).—NS/LK/DM

Karpman, Laura, American composer; b. Los Angeles, March 1, 1959. She studied with Bolcom and Bassett at the Univ. of Mich. (B.M., 1983), Harbison at Tanglewood (1984), and Babbitt at the Juilliard School in N.Y. (M.M., 1983; D.M., 1985). She taught at the Manhattan School of Music (1985–87), the New School for Social Research (1986–87), and Whittier (Calif.) Coll. (from 1989). Her compositions are vaguely surrealistic, and include *Matisse and Jazz* for Soprano, Piano, Percussion, and Saxophone (1987), *Portrait of Jaco* for Violin, Viola, Cello, Double Bass, and Piano (1988), and *Caprices* for String Trio (1990).—NS/LK/DM

Karr, Gary (Michael), outstanding American double bass player; b. Los Angeles, Nov. 20, 1941. He was born into a family of double bass players, and at 8 began formal lessons with Uda Demonstein. He gained experience by playing in local synagogues; subsequently took cello lessons with Herman Reinshagen, Gabor Rejto at the Univ. of Southern Calif. in Los Angeles, and Stuart Sankey at the Juilliard School of Music in N.Y.; he also was a scholarship student at the Aspen (Colo.) Music School. In 1962 he made his N.Y. recital debut and in 1964 he toured Europe. He founded the International Inst. for the String Bass in 1967 and subsequently taught in the U.S. and Canada. His instrument, the 1611 Amati, was once owned by Koussevitzky and was given to Karr by Koussevitzky's widow. Karr's career was the subject of the BBC-TV documentary "Amazing Bass" (1985). In addition to performing the Classical repertoire, he has done much to enlarge the literature for his instrument by commissioning works from Henze, Schuller, Wilder, Arnold, and other composers; he also includes in his repertoire folk-inspired pieces, as well as modern rock and dance forms. —NS/LK/DM

Karrer, Paul (real name, **Paulos Karrerēs**), Greek composer; b. Zante, May 12, 1829; d. there, April 1, 1896. After studying in Liverpool (1843), he continued his training with Cricca and Maragoni in Zante and Mantzaros in Corfu. He then was active as a music teacher in Zante. With Xyandas, he helped to establish the national Greek opera. He wrote 2 operas on Greek subjects, *Marcos Botsaris* (1857; Patras, 1861; not extant) and *Kyra Frosyni* (Zante, 1869). Among his other works were choral pieces and songs.

BIBL.: N. Varvianis, *P. K., ho zakunthios mousourgos* (P. K., the Composer from Zante; Athens, 1951).—LK/DM

Kars, Jean-Rodolphe, Austrian pianist; b. Calcutta, March 15, 1947. He studied with Jeanne Manchon-Theist and Katchen at the Paris Cons. (1958–64). He made his London recital debut in 1967, and subsequently pursued an international career as a soloist. He champions the music of Messiaen, and excels as an interpreter of Mozart, Schubert, Liszt, Debussy, and Ravel.—NS/LK/DM

Kartsev, Alexander, Russian composer; b. Moscow, July 19, 1883; d. there, July 3, 1953. He was a pupil of Taneyev and Glière in Moscow, and later of Juon in Berlin. His works included an opera, *Undine*, Sym., Violin Concerto, and chamber music.—NS/LK/DM

Karyotakis, Theodore, Greek composer; b. Argos, July 21, 1903; d. Athens, June 14, 1978. He studied with Mitropoulos (composition) and Varvoglis (counterpoint and orchestration) in Athens, and concurrently was enrolled in the law dept. of the Univ. of Athens. He wrote music in a neo-Romantic vein, permeated with euphonious dissonances. Several of his works were inspired by Greek folk modes.

WORKS: DRAMATIC: O p e r a : *Tou fengariou louloudi* (Flower of the Moon; 1953–55). ORCH.: *Rhapsody* for Violin and Orch. (1940); *Epic Song* (1944); *Concerto for Orchestra* (1967); Sym. (1974). CHAMBER: 2 violin sonatas (1945, 1955); String Trio (1949); String Quartet, with Voice (1963); *11 Sketches* for Flute and Viola (1963); *9 Inventions* for Violin and Piano (1966); Trio for Clarinet, Viola, and Piano (1969); Duo for Flute and Clarinet (1969); *Music* for Flute, Clarinet, Horn, and Bassoon (1973); numerous piano pieces. VOCAL: *6 Erotic Songs* for Voice, Flute, and Harp (1948); *Serenities*, 10 songs for Voice, Clarinet, Celesta, Strings, and Percussion (1962); songs. —NS/LK/DM

Kasarova, Vesselina (Ivanova), admired Bulgarian-born Swiss mezzo-soprano; b. Stara Zagora, July 18, 1965. She was a student at the Christina Morfova music gymnasium in Stara Zagora (1979–84), and then pursued her musical education at the National Music Academy in Sofia, where her vocal mentor was Ressa Koleva (diploma, 1989). On April 17, 1988, she made her operatic debut as Rosina at the Bulgarian National Opera in Sofia. In 1989 she won 1st prize in the Neue Stimmen competition in Gütersloh. That same year she made her first appearance at the Zürich Opera as Stéphano in Gounod's *Roméo et Juliette*, and continued on its roster until 1991. After singing Annio in *La clemenza di Tito* at the Salzburg Festival in 1991, she returned there to critical acclaim in 1992 as Tancredi. She made her debut at the Vienna State Opera in 1991 as Rosina, and continued to sing there as a member of the company until 1993. In 1993 she made her first appearance at London's Covent Garden as Rosina, and as Cherubino at the Bavarian State Opera in Munich. From 1993 to 1996 she was a member of the Zürich Opera. She made her first appearance at the Deutsche Oper in Berlin in 1995 as Rossini's Isabella, which role she also portrayed that year at her debut at the Teatro Comunale in Florence. In 1996 she made her debut at the Opéra de la Bastille in Paris as Bellini's Romeo. Her U.S. debut followed in 1997 as Idamante at the Lyric Opera in Chicago. Following an engagement as Angelina in *La Cenerentola* in Pesaro in 1998, she sang Sesto in Munich in 1999. She appeared as a soloist with many leading orchs. and also toured widely as a recitalist.—NS/LK/DM

Kaschmann (Kašman), Giuseppe, Italian baritone; b. Lussimpiccolo, Istria, July 14, 1847; d. Rome, Feb. 7, 1925. He studied in Rome, making his operatic debut in Zagreb in 1869. He then sang the title role in Zajc's *Mislav* at the opening of the Zagreb Opera on Oct. 2, 1870; made his first appearance in Italy in Turin as Alfonso in *La Favorite* in 1876, and subsequently sang at Milan's La Scala in 1878. He made his Metropolitan Opera debut in N.Y. as Enrico in *Lucia di Lammermoor* on Oct. 24, 1883, returning for the 1895–96 season. He first appeared at the Bayreuth Festivals in 1892. In later years he took on buffo roles, making his farewell to the stage in Rome in 1921. His finest roles included Don Giovanni, Amfortas, Wotan, Telramund, Kurwenal, Dr. Bartolo, and Don Pasquale.—NS/LK/DM

Kasemets, Udo, Estonian-born Canadian conductor, composer, and teacher; b. Tallinn, Nov. 16, 1919. He studied at the Tallinn Cons., the Stuttgart Staatliche Hochschule für Musik, and the Darmstadt Kranichstein Institut; also took conducting courses with Scherchen. He emigrated to Canada in 1951, becoming a naturalized Canadian citizen in 1957. In addition to his work as a conductor and composer, he was music critic for the *Toronto Daily Star* (1959–63); was on the faculty of the dept. of experimental art at the Ontario Coll. of Art (1971–87). His early music is set in peaceful Romantic modalities with Estonian undertones, but soon he espoused serialism and the pantheatricalism of the most uninhibited avant-garde.

WORKS: *Estonian Suite* for Chamber Orch. (1950); *Sonata da camera* for Solo Cello (1955); Violin Concerto (1956); String Quartet (1957); *Logos* for Flute and Piano (1960); *Haiku* for Voice,

Flute, Cello, and Piano (1961); *Squares* for Piano, 4-Hands (1962); *5* for 2 Performers on 2 Pianos and Percussion (1962–63); *Trigon* for 1, 3, 9, or 27 Performers, a multidimensional score with thematic information provided by a deoxyribonucleic matrix (1963; 11 subsequent versions, 1964–66); *Communications*, noncomposition to words by e.e. cummings, a cybernetic manifestation for Singular or Plural Singers, Speakers, Instrumentalists, or Dancers, of an indeterminate duration (1963); *Cumulus* for Any Solo Instrument or Ensemble, and 2 Tape Recorders, the score consisting of 9 segments to be played in any order (1963–64; 2 later versions, 1966, 1968); *Calceolaria*, time/space variations on a floral theme, for Any Number of Performers (1966; version for 4-channel Tape, 1967); *Contactics*, choreography for Musicians and Audience (1966); *Variations on Variations on Variations* for Singers, Instrumentalists, and 4 Loudspeakers (1966); *Quartets of Quartets*, 4 separate works for varying ensembles of Readers, Tape, Calibrators, Wind-bells, Wind Generators, Opaque Projectors, and Any Other Sound-producing Media: *Music for Nothing, Music for Anything (Wordmusic), Music for Something (Windmusic)*, and *Music for Everything* (all 1971–72); *Music(s) for John Cage*, incorporating *Guitarmusic for John Cage* for Any Number of Guitars, Projections, and Dimmers, *Voicemusic for John Cage* for Any Number of Voices, *Saladmusic for John Cage* for Any Number of Salad Makers, and *Walking/Talking* for Any Number of Walkers/Talkers (all 1972); *Time-Space Interface* for Any Number of Participants and Any Media, in both indoor and outdoor versions (1971–73); *Quadraphony (Music of the Quarter of the Moon of the Lunar Year)*, an acoustical/architectural time/space exploration project (1972–73); *La Crasse du tympan* for Record/Tape Mix (1973); *WATEARTHUNDAIR: Music of the 10ᵗʰ Moon of the Year of the Dragon*, a nature-sound-mix with verbal and visual commentary (1976); *KANADANAK*, a "celebration of our land and its people..." for Readers, Drummers, and Audience participation (1976–77); *Counterbomb Renga*, spectacle by about 100 poets and musicians, protesting against the proliferation of nuclear weapons, conceived and coordinated by Kasemets (CBC, April 3, 1983); *Yi Jing Jitterbug: 50 Hz Octet* for 8 Winds and/or Bowed Strings (1984); *Duchampera*, music theater for Singers, Speakers, Actors, Glass Orch., Piano, Sound-playback, and Lighting Systems (1987); *Vertical Music: In Remembrance of Morton Feldman* for Any 7 Instruments (1987); a series entitled *Portrait: Music of the 12 Moons of the I Ching* for Various Instruments (1988).—**NS/LK/DM**

Kashin, Daniil Nikitich, Russian composer; b. Moscow, 1769; d. there, Dec. 22, 1841. He was a serf, the property of an aristocratic landowner, Gavril Bibikov, who engaged Sarti to teach him music. He demonstrated his ability by presenting a piano concerto and an overture of his composition in Moscow (March 17, 1790). Bibikov then sent him to Italy for further study, and, upon his return in 1798, he was given his liberty. On April 10, 1799, he gave in Moscow a monster concert with the participation of 200 executants, including an ensemble of Russian horns; he also presented several of his songs, which became popular. He wrote the operas *Natalya, boyarskaya doch* (Natalia, the Boyar's Daughter; Moscow, Oct. 21, 1801), *Selskiy prazdnik* (The Village Holiday; 1807), *Olga prekrasnaya* (Fair Olga; Moscow, Jan. 14, 1809), and *The 1-day Reign of Nourmahal*, after Thomas Moore's *Lalla Rookh* (1817; not perf.); also

collections of patriotic songs as well as Russian folk songs (3 vols., Moscow, 1833–34). He publ. *Zhurnal octechestvennoy muziki* (Journal of National Music; 1806–9).—**NS/LK/DM**

Kashkashian, Kim, lyrical American violist of Armenian descent; b. Detroit, Aug. 31, 1952. She studied with Trampler (1969–70) and Karen Tuttle (1970–75) at the Peabody Cons. of Music in Baltimore. After winning several competitions, she was a soloist with major American and European orchs. She taught at the New School of Music in Philadelphia (1981–86), the Mannes Coll. of Music in N.Y. (1983–86), the Ind. Univ. School of Music in Bloomington (1985–87), and the Freiburg im Breisgau Hochschule für Musik (from 1989). She has done much to promote contemporary music, commissioning many works for viola. Her recordings of works by the Greek composer Eleni Karaindrou, *The Suspended Step of the Stork* (1991) and *Ulysses' Gaze* (1995), are extraordinarily beautiful.—**NS/LK/DM**

Kashkin, Nikolai Dmitrievich, noted Russian music critic; b. Voronezh, Dec. 9, 1839; d. Kazan, March 15, 1920. After receiving rudimentary instruction in music from his father, an amateur, he went to Moscow (1860), where he studied piano with Dubuc. He commenced writing music criticism for the *Moskovskiye Vedomosti* (1862). That same year he became a teacher at the Moscow branch of the Russian Musical Soc., remaining there when it became the Moscow Cons. (1866), and serving as prof. until 1896. He was also music critic for the *Russkiye Vedomosti* (1877–78; 1886–97). As a music critic, his opinions exercised considerable influence in the musical life of Moscow in the last quarter of the 19ᵗʰ century. He publ. a textbook on elementary music theory (Moscow, 1875). A close friend of Tchaikovsky, he publ. a pamphlet entitled *Reminiscences of Tchaikovsky* (Moscow, 1896), which is valuable for its authentic biographical and psychological data. A selection of his articles was publ. in Moscow (1953).

BIBL.: V. Yakovlev, *N.D. K.* (Moscow and Leningrad, 1950); G. Glushchenko, *N.D. K.* (Moscow, 1974).—**NS/LK/DM**

Kashperov, Vladimir (Nikitich), Russian composer; b. Tchufarovo, Simbirsk region, Sept. 6, 1826; d. Romantsevo, near Mozhaisk, July 8, 1894. He studied with Voigt and Henselt in St. Petersburg and with Dehn in Berlin (1856), then went to Italy to study singing (1858), where he remained until 1864. He wrote several operas in the Italian style that were produced in Italy, including *Maria Tudor* (Milan, 1859), *Rienzi* (Florence, 1863), and *Consuelo* (Venice, 1865). In 1865 he returned to Russia and taught voice at the Moscow Cons. (1866–72), and in 1872 he opened his own school of singing. In Moscow he produced 2 operas with Russian librettos: *The Storm*, after Ostrovsky (1867), and *Taras Bulba*, after Gogol (1893). Even in his Russian works, Kashperov remained faithful to the Italian style of composition, taking Donizetti as a model.—**NS/LK/DM**

Kasianov, Alexander, Russian composer; b. Bolobonovo, near Nizhny-Novgorod, Aug. 29, 1891; d.

there (Gorky), Feb. 13, 1982. He studied composition with Sokolov at the Petrograd Cons. (graduated, 1917) and piano with Liapunov. In 1918 he went to Nizhny-Novgorod, where he organized radio broadcasts. In 1951 he joined the faculty of the Cons. In his compositions, he continued the tradition of early Russian music, his many choral works being quite effective.

WORKS: DRAMATIC: O p e r a : *Stepan Razin* (Gorky, Oct. 29, 1939; rev. version, Gorky, Nov. 14, 1953); *A Partisan Girl* (1941); *On Far North* (1947); *Ermak* (1957). **ORCH.:** *Overture on Russian Themes* (1943). **P i a n o :** 7 sonatas; 24 preludes. **VOCAL:** Numerous choruses and songs.

BIBL.: N. Ugrumov, *A. K.* (Moscow, 1957).—NS/LK/DM

Kašlík, Václav, Czech conductor, opera producer, and composer; b. Poličná, Sept. 28, 1917; d. Prague, June 4, 1989. He took courses in theory and aesthetics at the Charles Univ. in Prague (1936–39). He received training in composition with Karel and A. Hába and in conducting with Doležil and Dědeček at the Prague Cons. (1936–40), completing his studies in conducting in Talich's master classes there (1940–42). From 1941 to 1944 he was asst. director of the National Theater in Prague. He was principal conductor and opera producer in Brno (1944–45). Upon returning to Prague, he was director of the 5th of May Theater (1945–48); subsequently was an opera producer and conductor with the National Theater; also conducted at the Smetana Theater (1952–62). In addition to his long association with the National Theater, he was a guest producer in Leningrad, Moscow, Milan, Vienna, London, Geneva, Verona, and Houston. In 1956 he was awarded the Klement Gottwald State Prize and in 1958 was made an Honored Artist by the Czech government. His productions were noteworthy for their use of film, experimental lighting, stereophonic sound, and other modern innovations.

WORKS: DRAMATIC: O p e r a : *Zbojnická balada* (The Brigand's Ballad; 1939–42; Prague, June 17, 1948; rev. 1978; Prague, Oct. 2, 1986); *Křížova cesta* (The Way of the Cross; 1941–45; unfinished); *Krakatit* (Czech TV, March 5, 1961); *La strada* (1980; Prague, Jan. 13, 1982); *Krysar* (Pied Piper; 1983; Plzeň, Oct. 27, 1984). **B a l l e t :** *Don Juan* (1940); *Janošík* (1950); *Pražský karneval* (1954). Also film scores. **ORCH.:** *Vesnicka symfonie* (1955); *Slavnostic,* symphonic triptych (1981). **CHAMBER:** String Quartet (1938). **VOCAL:** *Dramatic Cantata* (1944).—NS/LK/DM

Kasparov, Yuri, Armenian composer; b. Moscow, June 8, 1955. He began his music training in childhood. He studied at the Moscow Power Inst. (1972–78), qualifying as an engineer. After further training at a music college (1978–80), he studied with Tchulaki at the Moscow Cons. (1980–84), where he later pursued postgraduate studies with Denisov (1989–91). In 1984 he joined the Central Studio of Documentary Films in Moscow, where he was ed.-in-chief from 1985 to 1989. He was also founder-artistic director of the Moscow Contemporary Music Ensemble from 1990, with which he presented many modern works. In 1985 his first Sym., *Guernica,* won 1st prize in the All-Union Composers Competition. In 1989 his *Ave Maria* for 12 Voices, Violin, Vibraphone, and Organ received 1st prize in the Guido d'Arezzo

International Composers Competition in Italy. In his works, Kasparov follows an advanced course reflective of contemporary trends.

WORKS: DRAMATIC: M o n o O p e r a : *Nevermore* (1991). **ORCH.:** 2 syms.: No. 1, *Guernica* (1984; Moscow, June 29, 1994) and No. 2, *Kreutzer* (Yaroslavl, Jan. 30, 1987); *Lincos* (1988; Norrköping, April 3, 1990); Oboe Concerto (1988; Moscow, Nov. 30, 1991); *Diffusion* (1988; Cheliabinsk, May 22, 1989); *Silencium,* chamber sym. (1989; Moscow, April 27, 1990); *Devil's Trills* for Chamber Orch. (Moscow, Dec. 14, 1990); *Over Eternal Peace,* chamber concerto for Bassoon and 14 Players (Zürich, Nov. 14, 1992); *Concerto for Orchestra* (1993). **CHAMBER:** *Epitaph in Memory of Alban Berg* for Oboe, Violin, Harp, and Percussion (1988); *Invention* for String Quartet (Moscow, Oct. 19, 1989); *Notturno* for Clarinet, Violin, and Piano (1989; Cologne, Sept. 15, 1991); *Sonata-Infernale* for Bassoon (1989; Frankfurt am Main, Aug. 14, 1992); *Sketch of Picture with Collage* for Violin, Trumpet, and Piano (1990); *Variations* for Clarinet and Piano (1990); *Cantus firmus* for Violin (1990); *Credo* for Organ (1990); *Postludio* for Harp (1990); *Landscape Fading into Infinity* for Clarinet, Violin, Cello, and Piano (1991; Frankfurt am Main, Sept. 24, 1992); *Goat's Song* for Bassoon, Double Bass, and Percussion (1991; Valencia, May 8, 1994); *Chaconne* for Bassoon, Cello, and Electronics (1992; Paris, Feb. 15, 1993); *Schoenberg's Space* for Violin, Cello, and Piano (Hamburg, Nov. 14, 1993); *Game of Gale* for Tenor Saxophone, Marimba, and Piano (1994); *Briefly About Serious Matters* for Trombone and Organ (1994). **VOCAL:** *Ave Maria* for 12 Soloists, Violin, Organ, and Vibraphone (1989; Moscow, Nov. 18, 1990); *Stabat Mater* for Soprano and String Quartet (1991); *Effet de Nuit* for Bass-Baritone, Clarinet, Horn, Piano, Vibraphone, and Cello (1996). —NS/LK/DM

Kaspszyk, Jacek, Polish conductor; b. Biala, Aug. 10, 1952. He received training in theory, composition, and conducting at the Warsaw Cons., graduating in 1975. In 1975 he made his debut at the Warsaw Opera. From 1976 to 1982 he was chief conductor of the Polish Radio National Sym. Orch. in Katowice. He then settled in England, where he made his first appearance at the London Promenade Concerts in 1984. Thereafter he appeared as a guest conductor with the principal British orchs., and also with many orchs. on the Continent. In 1992 he made his debut at the English National Opera in London with *Il Barbiere di Siviglia.* From 1998 he was artistic director of the Warsaw Opera.—NS/LK/DM

Kassern, Tadeusz (Zygfrid), Polish-born American composer; b. Lemberg, March 19, 1904; d. N.Y., May 2, 1957. He studied composition with Soltys and piano with Lalewicz at the Lwow Cons., and later with Opienski and Brzostowski at the Poznań Cons. (1922–26); also studied law. He went to Paris (1931), then was made cultural attaché at the Polish Consulate in N.Y. (1945). He broke with the Communist government in Poland, and remained in N.Y., becoming a naturalized American citizen in 1956. As a composer, he pursued a cosmopolitan trend. Although many of his works are inspired by Polish folk music, the idiom and the method are of a general European modern character.

WORKS: DRAMATIC: O p e r a : *The Anointed* (1949–51); *Sun-Up* (1952; N.Y., Nov. 10, 1954); *Comedy of the Dumb Wife* (1953); *Eros and Psyche* (1954; unfinished). **ORCH.:** Flute Concerto (1934); *Dies irae*, symphonic poem in memory of Marshal Pilsudski (1935; not extant); Concertino for Oboe and Strings (1936–37; rev. 1946); Double Bass Concerto (1937); Concerto for Strings (1944); Concertino for Flute, Strings, Xylophone, and Celesta (1948); *Teen-Age Concerto* for Piano and Orch. (1952; N.Y., May 1956). **OTHER**: Chamber music; piano pieces; choruses; songs.—NS/LK/DM

Kastalsky, Alexander (Dmitrievich), Russian choral conductor and composer; b. Moscow, Nov. 28, 1856; d. there, Dec. 17, 1926. He was a pupil of Tchaikovsky, Taneyev, and Hubert at the Moscow Cons. (1875–81). In 1887 he joined the faculty of Moscow's Synodal School; in 1910 he was appointed director of the school and principal conductor of the choir. In 1911 he took the choir on an extended European tour. In 1918 the Synodal School became a choral academy; in 1923 it merged with the Moscow Cons. Kastalsky was also a teacher of conducting at the Moscow Phil. Inst. (1912–22), and in 1923 he was appointed prof. of choral singing at the Moscow Cons. He wrote *Osobennosti narodno- russkoy muzïkalnoy sistemï* (Peculiarities of the Russian Folk Music System; Moscow and Petrograd, 1923; 2nd ed., 1961); V. Belaiev ed. his *Osnovï narodnovo mnogogolosiya* (Principles of Folk Polyphony; Moscow and Leningrad, 1948). He also wrote the article "My Musical Career and My Thoughts on Church Music," *Musical Quarterly* (April 1925). He was a notable composer of Russian sacred music, into which he introduced modern elements, combining them with the ancient church modes.

WORKS: DRAMATIC: *Clara Militch*, opera (1907); incidental music. **ORCH.**: *Pictures of Russian Festivities* (1912); *A Marketplace in Ancient Russia* (1924); *Rustic Symphony* (Moscow, Dec. 13, 1925). **VOCAL**: *Brotherly Prayer for the Dead* for Soloist, Chorus, and 17 Instruments (1916); *To Lenin: At His Graveside* for Reciter, Chorus, and Orch. (1924; perf. at Lenin's funeral); cantatas; numerous choral pieces. **OTHER**: Various editions and arrangements, folk- song collections, etc. —NS/LK/DM

Kastle, Leonard (Gregory), American composer and pianist; b. N.Y., Feb. 11, 1929. After attending the Juilliard School of Music in N.Y. (1938–40), he received training in piano from Sheridan and in composition from Szell at the Mannes Coll. of Music in N.Y. (1940–42). He then studied piano with Wittgenstein and Vengerova, and also held scholarships in composition with Scalero, Menotti, and Barber at the Curtis Inst. of Music in Philadelphia (1944–50; B.A., 1950). He further attended Columbia Univ. (1947–50), and was a student in conducting with Bamberger in N.Y. (1950–52). He was a visiting prof. of humanities and fine arts at the State Univ. of N.Y. at Albany (1978–88).

WORKS: DRAMATIC: Opera: *The Swing* (1954; NBC-TV, June 11, 1956); *Deseret* (1960; NBC-TV, Jan. 1, 1961; rev. for Voices, Piano, and Organ, 1978); *The Pariahs* (1962–66); *The Calling of Mother Ann* (Hancock Shaker Village, Mass., June 21, 1985); *The Journey of Mother Ann* (1986–87; Albany, N.Y., Jan. 22, 1987); *Professor Lookalike and the Children* (1988; Albany, N.Y., May 8, 1989); *The Countess Cathleen* (1995). **Play with Music:** *The Birdwatchers* (1980–81). **ORCH.**: Piano Concerto (Albany, N.Y., Feb. 14, 1981, composer soloist). **CHAM-**

BER: Piano Sonata (1950); Violin Sonata (1955; rev. version, Albany, N.Y., March 17, 1986); Piano Suite (1957). **VOCAL**: *From a Whitman Reader* for Voice and Orch. (1954); *3 Walt Whitman Songs* for Chorus (1956); *Acquainted with the Night*, song cycle, after Robert Frost (1957); *3 Songs from Moby Dick* for Chorus (1963); *Pontoosuc* for Baritone and Orch. (1974–75; Tanglewood, July 4, 1976); *Mass* for Chorus, Organ, and Piano (PBS, Dec. 25, 1977; rev. version, Albany, N.Y., May 30, 1978). —NS/LK/DM

Kastner, Alfred, Austrian harpist, composer, and teacher; b. Vienna, March 10, 1870; d. Los Angeles, May 24, 1948. He studied harp with Antonio Zamara at the Vienna Cons. (1882–88), then was 1st harp in the orchs. of the Warsaw Opera (1890) and the Budapest Opera (from 1893); was also active as a teacher. He was 1st harp in the Philadelphia Orch. (1901–02; 1903–04), and also toured Europe as a soloist. After playing in the Queen's Hall Orch. (1904–14) and teaching at the Royal Academy of Music (1909–13) in London, he joined the N.Y. Phil.; then was 1st harp in the Los Angeles Phil. (1919–36). He wrote several works for harp and made various arrangements.—NS/LK/DM

Kastner, Georges Frédéric Eugène (actually, **Georg Friedrich Eugen**), Alsatian acoustician, son of **Jean- Georges (Johann Georg) Kastner;** b. Strasbourg, Aug. 10, 1852; d. Bonn, April 6, 1882. He invented the Pyrophone, an organ whose sound was produced by gas jets. He publ. *Les flammes chantantes* (Paris, 1875).—NS/LK/DM

Kastner, Jean-Georges (Johann Georg), Alsatian music theorist and composer, father of **Georges Frédéric Eugène (Georg Friedrich Eugen) Kastner;** b. Strasbourg, March 9, 1810; d. Paris, Dec. 19, 1867. He studied organ as a child, and later entered the Strasbourg Lutheran Seminary. After abandoning theology, he was granted a stipend by the Strasbourg town council to continue his music studies in Paris with Reicha and H.-M. Berton. An industrious writer on music, he acquired enormous erudition in various arts and sciences. He pursued the study of acoustics and formulated a theory of the cosmic unity of the arts. His great project, *Encyclopédée de la musique*, was left unfinished at his death. Among the grandiose projects that he carried out were several vols. of "Livres-Partitions," that is, sym.-cantatas illustrating musico- historical subjects, preceded by essays upon them. Of these the following were publ.: *Musik der Zigeuner and Les Romnitschels, symphonie dramatique* with Orch. (1849–50), *Les Danses des morts; dissertations et recherches historiques, philosophiques, littéraires et musicales sur les divers monuments de ce genre qui existent tant en France qu'à l'étranger* and *La Danse macabre, grande ronde vocale et instrumentale* (1852), *Recherches historiques sur le chant en choeur pour voix d'hommes* and *Les Chants de la vie* for 28 Choruses for 4 to 6 and 8 Voices Unaccompanied (1854), *Essai historique sur les chants militaires des français* and *Les Chants de l'armée française* for 22 Choruses for 4 Voices Unaccompanied (1855), *La Harpe d'Eole, et la musique cosmique* and *Stéphen, ou La Harpe d'Eole, grand monologue avec* *choeurs* (1856), *Les Voix de Paris* and *Les Cris de Paris*, symphonie dramatique with Orch. (1857), *Les Sirènes* and *Le Rêve d'Oswald ou Les Sirènes, grande symphonie dramatique vocale et instrumentale* (1858), *Parémiologie musicale de la langue française* and *La Saint-Julien de ménétriers, symphonie-cantate à grand orchestre, avec solos et choeurs* (1866), and *Untersuchungen über die Beziehungen der Musik zum Mythus* and *La Fille d'Odin*, symphonie- cantate with Orch. (1866). He also composed the operas *Gustav Wasa* (1832), *Oskars Tod* (c. 1833), *Der Sarazene* (1834), *Die Königin der Sarmaten* (Strasbourg, June 13, 1835), *Beatrice, die Braut von Messina* (1839), *Juana* (1840), *La maschera* (Opéra-Comique, Paris, June 17, 1841), and *Le Dernier Roi de Juda* (concert perf., Paris, Dec. 1, 1844), as well as a Piano Concerto (1827), 10 serenades for Wind Band (1832–35), 3 syms. (1832–35), 5 overtures (1832–35), 2 festival overtures (1858–60), chamber music, piano pieces, and choruses.

WRITINGS (all publ. in Paris): *Traité général d'instrumentation* (1837; 2nd ed., aug., 1844); *Tableaux analytiques et résumé général des principes élémentaires de musique* (1838); *Cours d'instrumentation* (1839; 2nd ed., 1844); *Mémoire sur l'état de la musique en Allemagne* (1843); *Le Marseillaise et les autres chants nationaux de Rouget de Lisle* (1848).

BIBL.: H. Ludwig, *Jean Georges K.: Ein elsässischer Tondichter, Theoretiker und Musikforscher* (2 vols., Leipzig, 1886). —NS/LK/DM

Kastner, (Macario) Santiago, distinguished English pianist, harpsichordist, and musicologist; b. London, Oct. 15, 1908; d. Lisbon, May 12, 1992. He studied in London and Amsterdam, then took courses with Hans Beltz (piano), Ramin (harpsichord), Hans Prüfner (musicology), and Friedrich Högner (theory) in Leipzig. He completed his studies with Juan Gilbert Camins (harpsichord and clavichord) and Anglès (musicology) in Barcelona. He settled in Lisbon in 1933, and taught at the Cons. there (from 1947). He was an authority on Hispanic keyboard music. In addition to writing several important books, he ed. works by Portuguese and Spanish composers.

WRITINGS: *Música hispanica: O estilo do P.M. Rodrigues Coelho: A interpretação de música hispanica para tecla desde 1450 ate 1650* (Lisbon, 1936); *Contribución al estudio de la música española y portuguesa* (Lisbon, 1941); *Carlos Seixas* (Coimbra, 1947); *Federico Mompou* (Madrid, 1947); *Antonio und Hernando de Cabezón: Eine Chronik dargestellt am Leben zweier Generationen von Organisten* (Tutzing, 1977); *The Interpretation of 16th- and 17th-century Iberian Keyboard Music* (Stuyvesant, N.Y., 1987). —NS/LK/DM

Kastorsky, Vladimir (Ivanovich), Russian bass; b. Bolshive Soly, March 14, 1871; d. Leningrad, July 2, 1948. He studied with Cotogni and Gabel. He made his debut with Champagner's touring opera company (1894). He became a member of the Maryinsky Theater in St. Petersburg (1899) and later sang with Zimin's opera company in Moscow. He also appeared in Diaghilev's Russian Seasons in Paris and London (1907–08), and concurrently formed a vocal quartet specializing in Russian folk songs, with which he toured abroad. He

remained on the operatic stage for nearly 45 years, and appeared in concerts to the end of his life. In addition to his Russian operatic roles, he also was admired as King Marke, Hagen, and Wotan.—NS/LK/DM

Katchen, Julius, admired American pianist; b. Long Branch, N.J., Aug. 15, 1926; d. Paris, April 29, 1969. He studied in N.Y. with Saperton. When he was 11, he made his debut in a national radio broadcast and then was soloist in Mozart's D Minor Concerto with Ormandy and the Philadelphia Orch. on Oct. 21, 1937. He studied academic subjects at Haverford Coll. (graduated, 1945); after a period of study on a French scholarship, he settled in Paris. In subsequent years, he toured as a soloist with orchs., as a recitalist, and as a chamber music artist. His career was entering its most promising phase when he was fatally stricken with cancer. He maintained a broad repertoire extending from the Classical era to contemporary music.—NS/LK/DM

Kates, Stephen (Edward), American cellist and teacher; b. N.Y., May 7, 1943. He studied at the Meadowmount School of Music (1961–62), with Piatigorsky at the Univ. of Southern Calif. in Los Angeles (1964–67), and with Leonard Rose and Claus Adam at the Juilliard School of Music in N.Y. (diploma, 1969). He made his N.Y. debut in 1963. After winning 2nd prize in the Tchaikovsky Competition in Moscow (1966), he appeared as soloist with leading orchs. in the U.S.; also was active as a chamber music artist and recitalist. He taught at Ohio State Univ. in Columbus (1969–72), and then was a member of the cello and chamber music depts. of the Peabody Cons. in Baltimore (from 1974). He also conducted master classes, and was president of the Violoncello Soc. (1983–87). His repertoire extends from Bach to contemporary music. He commissioned and gave the first performance of Claus Adam's Cello Concerto (1973).—NS/LK/DM

Katims, Milton, American violist and conductor; b. N.Y., June 24, 1909. He attended Columbia Univ., studying violin with Herbert Dittler and conducting with Barzin (1931–35). From 1935 to 1943 he was solo violist and asst. conductor for WOR Radio in N.Y., and from 1943 to 1954 he was 1st violist in the NBC Sym. Orch. in N.Y., where he was asst. conductor under Toscanini from 1947. He also taught at the Juilliard School of Music in N.Y. (1947–54). From 1954 to 1976 he was music director of the Seattle Sym. Orch., from 1976 to 1984, artistic director of the Univ. of Houston School of Music, and from 1985 a prof. at the Shanghai Cons. of Music. He prepared various eds. of compositions for viola. In 1964 he received the Alice M. Ditson Award for conductors and in 1986 the Arturo Toscanini Artistic Achievement award.—NS/LK/DM

Katin, Peter (Roy), English-born Canadian pianist and teacher; b. London, Nov. 14, 1930. He studied with Harold Craxton at the Royal Academy of Music in London (1943–48), making his debut at London's Wigmore Hall in 1948. In subsequent years, he toured globally. He taught at the Royal Academy of Music

(1956–69) and at the Univ. of Western Ontario in Canada (1978–84); became a naturalized Canadian citizen. He is best known for his performances of works from the Romantic and Impressionist periods, most especially of Chopin.—NS/LK/DM

Katsaris, Cyprien, French pianist, teacher, and composer; b. Marseilles, May 5, 1951. He began piano lessons as a child, and later pursued studies with Aline von Barentzen, Monique de la Bruchollerie, and Jean Hubeau at the Paris Cons., where he won a premier prix for piano (1969) and for chamber music (1970). In 1970 he received the Albert Roussel Prize and in 1977 captured 1st prize in the Cziffra Competition. He subsequently appeared as a soloist with the world's major orchs., and also gave recitals and played in chamber music concerts. On May 23, 1986, he made his N.Y. recital debut at Alice Tully Hall with notable success. He also was active as a teacher and composer. His repertoire is catholic, ranging from works of Bach to those of Boulez; he won particular acclaim for his virtuoso performances of Liszt's piano transcriptions of the 9 Beethoven syms.—NS/LK/DM

Kats-Chernin, Elena, Uzbekistan-born Australian composer; b. Tashkent, Nov. 4, 1957. She emigrated with her family to Australia in 1975, where she studied piano and composition at the New South Wales State Conservatorium of Music in Sydney until 1980. In 1980 she went to Hannover to study with Helmut Lachenmann under the auspices of the Deutscher Akademischer Austauschdienst. After completing her studies in 1982, she remained in Germany and was active as an experimental theater performer. In 1994 she returned to Australia to concentrate on composition. Her music is an interesting eclectic mix of Western and Eastern European streams of the early to mid 20th century era.

WORKS: DRAMATIC: *Coco's Last Collection*, dance theater for 2 Pianists and Dancer (1994); *Iphis*, opera (Sydney, Dec. 3, 1997); *Matricide*, opera (Melbourne, Nov. 27, 1998). **ORCH.:** *Bienie* (1979); Piano Concerto (1979); *Stairs* (1983); *Transfer* (1990); *Retonica* (1993; Sydney, Nov. 11, 1994); *Zoom and Zip* for Strings (1997; Canberra, May 23, 1998). **CHAMBER:** *In Tension* for Violin, Cello, Flute, Clarinet, Percussion, and Piano (1982); *Duo I* for Violin and Piano (1984); *Tótschki: Dots* for Oboe and Clarinet (1992; rev. 1995); *Clocks* for Chamber Ensemble and Tape (1993); Concertino for Violin and Chamber Ensemble (1994); *Clip* for Percussion (1994; rev. 1995); *ProMotion* for 6 Amplified Instruments (1995); *Chamber of Horrors* for Harp (1995); *Cadences, Deviations, and Scarlatti* for 14 Instruments (1995); *Gypsy Ramble* for Piano, Viola, and Cello (1996); *Wild Rice* for Cello (1996); *Charleston Noir* for String Quartet or Double Bass (1996); *Russian Rag* for Chamber Ensemble or Piano (1996); *Hemispheres* for Chamber Ensemble (1997); *Umcha* for Percussion Ensemble (1998). **Piano:** Various pieces, including rags.—LK/DM

Kattnigg, Rudolf, Austrian composer and conductor; b. Oberdorf bei Treffen, April 9, 1895; d. Klagenfurt, Sept. 2, 1955. He went to Vienna and studied law at the Univ. before pursuing training in music at the Academy of Music with Mandyczewski, Löwe, J. Marx,

and Krauss (1918–22). From 1928 to 1934 he was director of the Innsbruck Music School. He also was active as a theater conductor, settling in Vienna in 1939. He became best known as an operetta composer, his finest score being *Balkanliebe* or *Die Gräfin von Durazzo* (1937).

WORKS: DRAMATIC: O p e r a : *Donna Miranda* (1953). **M u s i c   T h e a t e r :** *Der Prinz von Thule* (Basel, Dec. 13, 1936); *Kaiserin Katharina* (Berlin, Feb. 3, 1937); *Balkanliebe* or *Die Gräfin von Durazzo* (Leipzig, Dec. 22, 1937); *Mädels vom Rhein* (Bremen, 1938); *Die Mädel von St. Goar* (Bremen, Feb. 4, 1939); *Hansi fliegt zum Negerkral* (Vienna, Dec. 16, 1942); *Ben Ami* (Vienna, Jan. 18, 1949); *Rendezvouz um Mitternacht* (Vienna, May 20, 1956). **B a l l e t :** *Tarantella* (1942). Also film scores. **OTHER:** 2 syms. (1925, 1930); Piano Concerto (1934); chamber music.—NS/LK/DM

Katulskaya, Elena, Russian soprano; b. Odessa, June 2, 1888; d. Moscow, Nov. 20, 1966. She studied privately in Odessa (1904) and St. Petersburg (1905–07) before training with Natalia Iretskaya at the St. Petersburg Cons. (1907–09). She then made her operatic debut as Lakmé at the Maryinsky Theater in St. Petersburg, where she sang until 1911. From 1913 to 1945 she was a principal member of the Bolshoi Theater in Moscow. In 1948 she became a teacher at the Moscow Cons. In 1965 she was made a People's Artist of the U.S.S.R. While Katulskaya was particularly esteemed for her roles in Russian operas, she also had success in the Italian and French repertoires.—NS/LK/DM

Katwijk, Paul van, Dutch-American pianist, conductor, teacher, and composer; b. Delfshaters, Dec. 7, 1885; d. Dallas, Dec. 11, 1974. He studied at The Hague Cons., then in Berlin with Klatte and in Vienna with Godowsky. In 1912 he settled in the U.S., where he taught at Drake Univ. in Des Moines (1914–18) and also conducted the Des Moines Sym. Orch. In 1918 he was appointed dean of music at Southern Methodist Univ. in Dallas. He resigned in 1949, but continued to teach piano there until 1955. He was conductor of the Dallas Municipal Opera (1922–25) and the Dallas Sym. Orch. (1925–36). He composed several symphonic works, including the suite *Hollandia* (Dallas, March 15, 1931). —NS/LK/DM

Katz, Israel J(oseph), American ethnomusicologist; b. N.Y., July 21, 1930. He studied at the Univ. of Calif. at Los Angeles with Klaus Wachsmann and Boris Kremenliev (B.A., 1956; Ph.D., 1967, with the diss. *Judeo-Spanish Traditional Ballads from Jerusalem: An Ethnomusicological Study*; publ. in 2 vols., N.Y., 1972, 1975). He taught at McGill Univ. in Montreal (1968–69) and at Columbia Univ. (1969–75), then at York Coll. and the Graduate Center of the City Univ. of N.Y. (from 1977). He was ed. of *Ethnomusicology* (1971–72) and co-ed. of *Musica Judaica* (from 1975).—NS/LK/DM

Katz, Martin, American pianist and teacher; b. Los Angeles, Nov. 27, 1945. He began piano lessons at age 5, and later was a scholarship student at the Univ. of Southern Calif. in Los Angeles, where he received instruction in the art of accompaniment from Gwendolyn Koldofsky. While still a student there, he served as an accompanist in the master classes of Lehmann, Heifetz, Piatigorsky, and Bernac. After completing his education, Katz pursued a distinguished career as an accompanist, making tours throughout the world with many celebrated artists. He also taught at Westminster Choir Coll. in Princeton, N.J. (from 1976) and at the Univ. of Mich. in Ann Arbor (from 1983).—NS/LK/DM

Katz, Mindru, Romanian-born Israeli pianist and teacher; b. Bucharest, June 3, 1925; d. during a recital in Istanbul, Jan. 30, 1978. He studied with Floria Musicescu at the Royal Academy of Music in Bucharest. Katz made his debut with the Bucharest Phil. in 1947, and then played throughout Eastern Europe. He made his Western European debut in Paris in 1957, then settled in Israel (1959) but continued to make extensive tours. He joined the faculty of the Rubin Academy of Music in Tel Aviv in 1962, becoming a prof. of piano there in 1972.—NS/LK/DM

Katzer, Georg, German composer; b. Habelschwerdt, Silesia, Jan. 10, 1935. He studied with Wagner-Régeny and Zechlin at the Hochschule für Musik in East Berlin (1954–59), and then entered the classes of Eisler and Spies at the Akademie der Kunste there (1960–63), where he was elected to membership (1979) and became artistic director of its electronic music studio. He served as president of the national section of the International Soc. for Electroacoustic Music (from 1989). In 1981 he received the National Prize for Art of the German Democratic Republic. In his music, Katzer is a universalist, applying constructivist principles with lapidary precision. Under the influence of Eisler, he adopted a broad variety of methods, including 12-tone techniques, using his materials for specific purposes accessible to mass audiences.

WORKS: DRAMATIC: *Das Land Bum-Bum,* children's opera (1974); *Schwarze Vögel,* ballet (1974); *Ein neuer Sommernachtstraum,* ballet (1979–80); *Gastmahl oder über die Liebe,* opera (1987; Berlin, April 30, 1988); *Antigone oder die Stadt,* opera (1989); *De natura hominis,* radio piece (1997). ORCH.: 3 sonatas: No. 1 (1968), No. 2 (1969), and No. 3, *Homage à Jules Verne,* for Chamber Orch. (1970); *Baukasten* (1972); *Die D-Dur Musikmaschine* (1973); Concerto for Orchestra No. 1 (1973), No. 2 (1985), and No. 3 (1988; Berlin, Sept. 22, 1989); Concerto for Jazz Group and Orch. (1975); *Empfindsame Musik* for 58 Strings and 3 Percussionists (1976; Leipzig, June 2, 1977); *Dramatische Musik* (1977); *Sound-House* for Orch., 3 Orch. Groups, Organ, and Tape (1979); Piano Concerto (1980); Double Concerto for Cello, Harp, and Orch. (1980); Cello Concerto (1985; Karl-Marx-Stadt, Oct. 24, 1989); Flute Concerto (1985–86; Berlin, Feb. 25, 1986); Oboe Concerto (Leipzig, Sept. 21, 1989); *Offene Landschaft mit Obligatem Ton e* (1990); *Landschaft mit steigender Flut* for Orch. and Tape (1991); *Gloria* (1991–92; Berlin, Sept. 20, 1992); *Recit* for Chamber Orch. (1992); Triple Concerto for Saxophone, Percussion, Accordion, and Orch. (1994); *Geschlagene Zeit,* concerto for Percussion Sextet and Orch. (1996); *Gesang—Gegengesang—Abgesang* (1998); *Schrittweise Auflösung harmonischer Verhältnisse* for Chamber Orch. (1998); *Nänie für Johannes Bobrowski,* organ concerto (1998). CHAMBER: 3 string quartet (1966; with Soprano, 1967; 1987); *Streichmusik I* for 14 Solo Strings (1971) and *II* for 18 Solo Strings (1972); Piano Quintet (1972); *Scene* for Chamber Ensemble (1975); Concerto for Harpsichord and Wind Quintet (1977); Trio for Oboe, Cello, Piano, and Tape (1979); Concerto for Violin, 14 Strings, and Harpsichord (1980–81); *Ballade* for Clarinet and Percussion (1982); *Kommen und gehen* for Wind Quintet and Piano (1982); *La Mettrie I* (1985) and *II* (1987) for Wind Quintet and Piano; *Hex* for 6 Instruments (1988); *Zungen und Saiten* for String Trio and Accordion (1988); *Strahlung/Brechung* for String Quintet (1991); Saxophone Quartet (1992); String Trio (1992); *Odd and Even* for Flute, Percussion, and Piano (1993); *La Solidarietà* for Chamber Ensemble (1997); piano pieces. VOCAL: *Abgebrochene Sätze* for Contralto, Flute, Cello, Piano, and Percussion (1993); *Dialog imaginär 6* for Tenor, Saxophone, and Tape (1994); choruses; song cycles.—NS/LK/DM

Kauder, Hugo, Austrian-born American composer; b. Tobitschau, Moravia, June 9, 1888; d. Bussum, the Netherlands, July 22, 1972. He studied violin. He was a member of the Konzertverein Orch. in Vienna (1910–19), then went to the U.S. (1938), where he became a naturalized American citizen (1944). His music is contrapuntal, with canonic devices much used in free and often asymmetric rhythm, while the harmonies are conservative. He wrote 4 syms., a Cello Concerto, and a great number of works for chamber music combinations. He publ. *Entwurf einer neuen Melodie- und Harmonielehre* (Vienna, 1932) and *Counterpoint: An Introduction to Polyphonic Composition* (N.Y., 1960). —NS/LK/DM

Kauer, Ferdinand, Moravian-born Austrian conductor and composer; b. Klein-Tajax (baptized), Jan. 18, 1751; d. Vienna, April 13, 1831. As a boy he played organ in a local Jesuit church, then was organist at the Jesuit seminary in Tyrnau, Hungary, where he took courses in philosophy and medicine. He went to Vienna about 1777, where he studied composition with Heidenreich and Zimmermann. He then became a violinist in the orch. of the Theater in der Leopoldstadt about 1781. He was made director of the theater's music school (1789) and later 2nd Kapellmeister at the theater, scoring a success with his *Das Donauweibchen* (Jan. 11, 1798), which was subsequently performed all over Europe. After serving as Kapellmeister in Graz (1810–11), he returned to the Leopoldstadt theater. He then was Kapellmeister at the Theater in der Josefstadt (1814–18), and subsequently made a precarious living as a 2nd violinist in the Leopoldstadt theater orch. (1821–30). He lost almost all of his possessions, including his MSS, in the flood of 1830. He wrote about 200 works for the stage, as well as sacred music, syms., concertos, etc. He publ. *Singschule nach dem neuesten System der Tonkunst* (1790) and *Kurzgefasste Generalbass-Schule für Anfänger* (1800).

BIBL.: K. Manschinger, *F. K.: Ein Beitrag zur Geschichte des Wiener Singspiels um die Wende des 18. Jahrhunderts* (diss., Univ. of Vienna, 1929).—NS/LK/DM

Kauffmann, Emil, German composer and writer on music, son of **Ernst Friedrich Kauffmann;** b. Ludwigsburg, Nov. 23, 1836; d. Tübingen, June 17, 1909. He studied at the Stuttgart Cons. with Keller, Faiszt, Jung, and Singer, then joined the Court Orch. in 1863 as a violinist. He was a teacher in the music school at Basel (1868–77) and music director at the Univ. of Tübingen (Ph.D., 1885). He wrote Die Nacht, over 60 lieder, men's choruses, and sonatas and other piano pieces. He also publ. *Entwickelung der Tonkunst von der Mitte des 18. Jahrhunderts bis zur Gegenwart* (1884) and *Justinus Heinrich Knecht: Ein schwäbischer Tonsetzer* (1892) and contributed articles to the Leipzig *Musikalisches Wochenblatt*. —NS/LK/DM

Kauffmann, Ernst Friedrich, German composer, father of **Emil Kauffmann;** b. Ludwigsburg, Nov. 27, 1803; d. Stuttgart, Feb. 11, 1856. He studied at the Univ. of Tübingen (1825–27). He became principal of the Realschule at Ludwigsburg, but because of his connection with revolutionists he lost his position in 1835 and was imprisoned in Asperg (1838–42), where he wrote 6 sets of songs, which became popular.—NS/LK/DM

Kauffmann, Georg Friedrich, German organist and composer; b. Ostermondra, Thuringia, Feb. 14, 1679; d. Merseburg, Feb. 24, 1735. After keyboard training with J.H. Buttstett in Erfurt, he was a student of J.F. Alberti (keyboard and composition) in Merseburg. In 1698 he became Alberti's deputy organist, and in 1710 he succeeded his mentor as court and cathedral organist. Kauffmann later served as director of church music for the Duke of Saxe-Merseburg. In 1722 he went to Leipzig to compete for the post of Kantor at the Thomaskirche, a post eventually given to J.S. Bach. As a composer, Kauffmann's greatest legacy is found in his outstanding collection of 98 preludes on 63 chorales and 66 figured bass settings for organ that were publ. as the *Harmonische Seelenlust musikalischer Gönner und Freunde, das ist: Kurtze, jedoch nach besondern Genie und guter Grace elaborirte Praeludia von 2, 3 und 4 Stimmen über die bekanntesten Choral-Lieder* (Leipzig, 1733–36; ed. by P. Pidoux, 2 vols., Kassel, 1951). Among his other works are the oratorio *Die Himmelfahrt Christii* and several church cantatas.

BIBL.: P. Janson, *Explicatio textus or Dramma per musica? The Function of the Church Cantatas by G.F. K.* (diss., Univ. of Victoria, 1992).—LK/DM

Kauffmann, Leo Justinus, German composer; b. Dammerkirch, Sept. 20, 1901; d. in an air raid in Strasbourg, Sept. 25, 1944. He studied with Erb in Strasbourg and with Jarnach and Abendroth in Cologne. He taught at Cologne's Rheinische Musikschule (1929–32) and worked for the Cologne Radio (1932–33); later taught at the Strasbourg Cons., serving as its director until his death. He wrote the operas *Die Geschichte vom schönen Annerl* (Strasbourg, June 20, 1942) and *Das Perlenhem* (Strasbourg, 1944), as well as a Sym., Concertino for Double Bass and Chamber Orch., and Mass.—NS/LK/DM

Kaufman, Harry, American pianist and teacher; b. N.Y., Sept. 6, 1894; d. Beverly Hills, Aug. 22, 1961. He studied at the Inst. of Musical Art with Stojowski in N.Y.; later was a pupil of Josef Hofmann. In 1924 he was appointed teacher of the art of accompanying at the Curtis Inst. of Music in Philadelphia. Though principally known as an excellent accompanist, he also appeared as soloist with the N.Y. Phil., the Philadelphia Orch. et al. and as a member of several chamber music groups.—NS/LK/DM

Kaufman, Louis, distinguished American violinist; b. Portland, Ore., May 10, 1905; d. Los Angeles, Feb. 9, 1994. He studied with Kneisel. He won the Loeb Prize in 1927 and the Naumburg Award in 1928, and subsequently toured widely. He gave numerous first performances of works by contemporary composers, among them a violin concerto by Dag Wiren (Stockholm, Oct. 25, 1953), and first American performances of violin works by Milhaud, Knipper, Martinů, and others. He also played American works in Europe, and gave the first performance in England of Walter Piston's Violin Concerto (London, April 6, 1956). He ed. 6 sonatas for Violin by G.P. Telemann and *Sonata concertante* by L. Spohr; publ. *Warming Up Scales and Arpeggios* (1957). —NS/LK/DM

Kaufmann, Armin, Romanian-born Austrian composer; b. Itzkany, Bukovina, Oct. 30, 1902; d. Vienna, June 30, 1980. In 1914 his family settled in Vienna, where he enrolled at the Academy of Music, studying theory with Joseph Marx. From 1938 to 1966 he played the viola in the Vienna Sym. Orch.

WORKS: ORCH.: 4 syms. (1929, 1962, 1966, 1968); Tárogató Concerto (1967); Piano Concerto (1970). CHAMBER: 7 string quartets; Trio for Violin, Zither, and Guitar (1962); Quintet for Piano, Violin, Viola, Cello, and Double Bass (1965); Trio for Flute, Viola, and Harp (1967); *Rhapsody* for Guitar (1970).—NS/LK/DM

Kaufmann, Friedrich, German inventor; b. Dresden, Feb. 5, 1785; d. there, Dec. 1, 1866. He invented a trumpet automaton (1808), the Belloneon, the Klaviatur-Harmonichord, the Chordaulodion, and the Symphonion. In 1851 his son, Friedrich Theodor Kaufmann (b. Dresden, April 9, 1823; d. there, Feb. 5, 1872), made an Orchestrion from the Symphonion.—NS/LK/DM

Kaufmann, Julie, American soprano; b. Iowa, May 20, 1950. She studied at the Univ. of Iowa, the Zürich Opera School, and the Hamburg Hochschule für Musik. Following her operatic debut in Hagen, she sang in various German opera centers before joining the Bavarian State Opera in Munich in 1983. In 1984 she made her debut at London's Covent Garden as Zerlina. She chose Blondchen for her first appearance at the Salzburg Festival in 1987. In 1988 she toured Japan with the Bavarian State Opera, and then sang Woglinde in the staging of the *Ring* cycle in Munich in 1989. In 1991 she was made a Bavarian Kammersängerin. In 1992 she appeared at Milan's La Scala as Zdenka, and then sang Woglinde in Paris in 1994. At the Munich Festival in 1996 she portrayed Handel's Serse. As a concert artist, she sang with leading European orchs. and gave lieder recitals.—NS/LK/DM

Kaufmann, Walter, German-born American conductor, composer, and musicologist; b. Karlsbad, April 1, 1907; d. Bloomington, Ind., Sept. 9, 1984. He studied composition with Schreker in Berlin, and also studied musicology in Prague. In 1935 he traveled to India, where he remained for 10 years. He devoted much time to the study of the Hindu systems of composition, and also appeared as conductor, serving as music director of the Bombay Radio. In 1947 he moved to Nova Scotia and taught piano at the Halifax Cons.; from 1948 to 1957 he was music director of the Winnipeg Sym. Orch. In 1957 he settled in the U.S., where he joined the faculty of the Ind. Univ. School of Music in Bloomington. He became a naturalized American citizen in 1964. He wrote *Musical Notations of the Orient* (Bloomington, 1967), *The Ragas of North India* (Bloomington, 1968), *Tibetan Buddhist Chant* (tr. by T. Norbu; Bloomington, 1975), *Involvement with Music: The Music of India* (N.Y., 1976), *Musical References in the Chinese Classics* (Detroit, 1976), *The Ragas of South India* (Bloomington, 1976), and *Altinden* (Leipzig, 1981), and also valuable articles on Eastern music for American music journals.

WORKS: DRAMATIC: O p e r a : *Der grosse Dorin* (1932); *Der Hammel bringt es an den Tag* (1932); *Esther* (1931–32); *Die weisse Gottin* (1933); *Anasuya*, radio opera (Bombay, Oct. 1, 1938); *The Cloak*, after Gogol (1933–50); *A Parfait for Irene* (Bloomington, Feb. 21, 1952); *The Research* (1951); *The Golden Touch*, children's opera (1953); *Christmas Slippers*, television opera (1955); *Sganarelle* (1955); *George from Paradise* (1958); *Paracelsus* (1958); *The Scarlet Letter*, after Hawthorne (Bloomington, May 6, 1961); *A Hoosier Tale* (Bloomington, July 30, 1966); *Rip van Winkle*, children's opera (1966). B a l l e t : *Visages* (1950); *The Rose and the Ring* (1950); *Wang* (1956). ORCH.: 6 syms.:No. 1 for Strings (1931), No. 2 (1935), No. 3 (1936), No. 4 (1938), No. 5, *Sinfonietta No. 1* (1949), and No. 6 (1956); *Prag*, suite (1932); 2 piano concertos:(1934, 1949); 2 *Bohemian Dances* (1942); 2 violin concertos (1943, 1944); 6 *Indian Miniatures* (1943); *Navaratnam*, suite for Piano and Chamber Orch. (1945); *Phantasmagoria* (1946); Variations for Strings (1947); Concertino for Piano and Strings (1947); *Dirge* (1947); *Madras Express* (Boston Pops, June 23, 1948); *Fleet Street Overture* (1948); *Strange Town at Night* (1948); *Faces in the Dark* (1948); *Andhera* for Piano and Orch. (1942–49); Divertimento for Strings (1949); Cello Concerto (1950); *Chivaree Overture* (1950); *Main Street* for Strings (1950); *Kalif Storch*, fairy tale for Speaker and Orch. (1951); *Arabesques* for 2 Pianos and Orch. (1952); *Vaudeville Overture* (1952); *Sewanee River Variations* (1952); *Short Suite* for Small Orch. (1953); *Nocturne* (1953); *Pembina Highway* (1953); 4 *Skies* (1953); 3 *Dances to an Indian Play* (1956); 4 *Essays* for Small Orch. (1956); *Sinfonietta No. 2* (1959); Timpani Concerto (1963); *Festival Overture* (1968); Concertino for Violin and Orch. (1977). CHAMBER: 10 string quartets (1935–46); 3 piano trios (1942–46); 6 Pieces for Piano Trio (1957); String Quartet (1961); Partita for Woodwind Quintet (1963); *Arabesques* for Flute, Oboe, Harpsichord, and Bass (1963); 8 Pieces for 12 Instruments (1967); *Passacaglia and Capriccio* for Brass Sextet (1967); Sonatina for Piccolo or Flute Solo (1968). P i a n o : Concertino (1932); 2 sonatinas (1948, 1956); Sonata (1948–51); *Arabesques* for 2 Pianos (1952); Suite (1957). VOCAL: C a n t a t a s : *Galizische Baume* for Chorus and Orch. (1932); *Coronation Cantata* for Soloists, Chorus, and Orch. (1953); *Rubayyat* for Soloist and Orch. (1954). O t h e r : Songs.

BIBL.: T. Noblitt, ed., *Music East and West: Essays in Honor of W. K.* (N.Y., 1981).—NS/LK/DM

Kaul, Oskar, German musicologist; b. Heufeld, Oct. 11, 1885; d. Unterwössen, July 17, 1968. He studied at the Cologne Cons. (1905–08), then took courses in musicology with Sandberger and Kroyer at the Univ. of Munich (Ph.D., 1911, with the diss. *Anton Rosetti: Sein Leben und seine Werke*). He joined the faculty of the Würzburg Cons. (1913); was its deputy director (1924–45); was also a Privatdozent (1922–28) and reader (1928–45) at the Univ. of Würzburg. He ed. 5 syms. and chamber music of Rosetti for the Denkmäler der Tonkunst in Bayern, XXII, Jg. XII/1 (1912; 2nd ed., rev., 1968) and XXXIII, Jg. XXV (1925). His writings include *Die Vokalwerke Anton Rosettis* (Cologne, 1911), *Geschichte der Würzburger Hofmusik im 18. Jahrhundert* (Würzburg, 1924), and *Zur Musikgeschichte der ehemaligen Reichsstadt Schweinfurt* (Würzburg, 1935).—NS/LK/DM

Kaun, Hugo, German composer; b. Berlin, March 21, 1863; d. there, April 2, 1932. He studied at the Berlin Hochschule für Musik (1879–80), then with Oskar Raif (piano) and at the Prussian Academy of Arts with Friedrich Kiel (composition). He was active as a teacher and conductor of the Liederkranz in Milwaukee (1887–1901), then returned to Berlin, becoming a prof. at the Klindworth-Scharwenka Cons. (1922). He publ. *Harmonie- und Modulationslehre* (Leipzig, 1915; 2nd ed., 1921) as well as an autobiography, *Aus meinem Leben* (Berlin, 1932). A cultured composer, he incorporated in his well-crafted works elements of both Brahmsian and Wagnerian idioms.

WORKS: DRAMATIC: O p e r a : *Sappho* (Leipzig, Oct. 27, 1917); *Der Fremde* (Dresden, Feb. 23, 1920); *Menandra* (staged in Kiel and several other German opera houses simultaneously, Oct. 29, 1925). ORCH.: 3 syms.; 2 piano concertos; *Der Sternenbanner*, festival march on the *Star-Spangled Banner*; *Der Maler von Antwerpen*, overture (Chicago, Feb. 3, 1899); *Im Urwald*, 2 symphonic poems, after Longfellow's *Minnehaha* and *Hiawatha* (Chicago, Feb. 7, 1903). OTHER: Chamber music; many piano pieces; choral works; songs.

BIBL.: W. Altmann, *H. K.* (Leipzig, 1906); R. Schaal, *H. K., 1863–1932, Leben und Werk: Ein Beitrag zur Musik der Jahrhundertwende* (Regensburg, 1946).—NS/LK/DM

Kavafian, Ani, gifted Turkish-born American violinist of Armenian descent, sister of **Ida Kavafian;** b. Istanbul, May 10, 1948. In 1956 she went with her family to the U.S., where she took violin lessons with Ara Zerounian (1957–62) and Mischakoff (1962–66) in Detroit. She then entered the Juilliard School of Music in N.Y., where she received instruction in violin from Galamian and in chamber music performance from Galimir and members of the Juilliard Quartet (M.A., 1972). In 1969 she made her debut at Carnegie Recital Hall in N.Y.; her European debut followed in Paris in 1973. In 1976 she received the Avery Fisher Prize. She appeared as soloist with the leading orchs.; also played chamber music concerts, serving as an artist-member of the Chamber Music Soc. of Lincoln Center (from 1980); likewise gave duo performances with her sister. She taught at the Mannes Coll. of Music (from 1982), and at the Manhattan School of Music and Queens Coll. of the City Univ. of N.Y. (from 1983). On Sept. 24, 1993, she was soloist in the premiere of Machover's *Forever and Ever*, a concerto for Hyperviolin and Chamber Orch., with Hugh Wolff and the St. Paul (Minn.) Chamber Orch.—NS/LK/DM

Kavafian, Ida, talented Turkish-born American violinist of Armenian descent, sister of **Ani Kavafian;** b. Istanbul, Oct. 29, 1952. She went with her family to the U.S. (1956), where she took up violin studies with Ara Zerounian in Detroit at the age of 6, and later received instruction from Mischakoff there. She entered the Juilliard School in N.Y. (1969), where she continued her training with Shumsky and Galamian (M.A., 1975). She won the Vianna da Motta International Violin Competition in Lisbon (1973) and the silver medal at the International Violin Competition of Indianapolis (1982). She helped to found the chamber group Tashi (1973), and subsequently toured with it. She made her N.Y. recital debut (1978) and her European debut in London (1982), and also played in duo concerts with her sister. In 1988 she was awarded the Avery Fisher Career Grant. In 1993 she became a member of the Beaux Arts Trio. —NS/LK/DM

Kavrakos, Dimitri, Greek bass-baritone; b. Athens, Feb. 26, 1946. He studied at the Athens Cons. In 1970 he made his operatic debut as Zaccaria in *Nabucco* at the Athens Opera, of which he was a member until 1978. He then made his first appearance in the U.S. at N.Y.'s Carnegie Hall in Refice's *Cecilia*. On March 7, 1979, he made his Metropolitan Opera debut in N.Y. as the Grand Inquisitor in *Don Carlos*. He made his British debut at the Glyndebourne Festival in 1982 as Mozart's Commendatore, and then his first appearance at London's Covent Garden as Pimen in *Boris Godunov* in 1984. In 1987 he was engaged at the Paris Opéra as the Grand Inquisitor. He sang Silva in *Ernani* at the Rome Opera in 1989. During the 1992–93 season, he appeared as Timur in *Turandot* at the Lyric Opera in Chicago, as Banquo at the Cologne Opera, and as the Commendatore at the Aix-en-Provence Festival. He sang Banquo in Florence in 1995.—NS/LK/DM

Kawaguchi, George, Japanese jazz drummer, leader; b. Fukakusa, Kyoto, Japan, June 15, 1927. He leads a big band and is still very active with his New Big Four, playing crowd-pleasing hard-bop tunes, and taking 15-minute solos inspired by Gene Krupa on his theme song "Drum Boogie." He was a teen idol in his native country in the 1950s, appeared in numerous films aimed at teenagers and commanded top dollar in concerts.

DISC.: *Jazz at the Toris* (1957); *Yesterdays 1: The Original Big Four* (1959); *Original Big Four: Live* (1977); *Super Drums* (1979); *Killer Joe* (1981); *Big Two with Lionel Hampton* (1982); *Maiden Voyage* (1987); *Plays Herbie Hancock* (1987); *African Hot Dance* (1990); *The Legendary Japanese Jazz Scene Vol. 1: G.K. & The Big Four* (1995).—ETA

Kay, Hershy, American composer, arranger, and orchestrator; b. Philadelphia, Nov. 17, 1919; d. Danbury,

Conn., Dec. 2, 1981. He studied cello with Salmond and orchestration with Thompson at the Curtis Inst. of Music in Philadelphia (1936–40), then went to N.Y., and began a fruitful career as an arranger of Broadway musicals and ballets. He orchestrated a number of Leonard Bernstein's theater works: *On the Town* (1944), *Peter Pan* (incidental music; 1951), *Candide* (1956; revival, 1973), *Mass* (1971), and the Bicentennial pageant *1600 Pennsylvania Avenue* (1976). His last arrangement for Bernstein was *Olympic Hymn* (Baden-Baden, Sept. 23, 1981). His other orchestrations for Broadway include *A Flag Is Born* (1947), *The Golden Apple* (1954), *Once upon a Mattress* (1958), *Juno* (1958), *Sand Hog* (1958), *Livin' the Life* (1958), *Milk and Honey* (1961), *The Happiest Girl in the World* (1961), *110 in the Shade* (1963), *Coco* (1969), *A Chorus Line* (1975), *American Musical Jubilee* (1976), *Music Is* (1976), *On the Twentieth Century* (1977), *Evita* (1979), *Carmelina* (1979), and *Barnum* (1980). He made numerous arrangements for the N.Y.C. Ballet, among them *Cakewalk* (1951, after Gottschalk), *Western Symphony* (1954, after cowboy songs and fiddle tunes), *The Concert* (1956, after Chopin), *Stars and Stripes* (1958, after Sousa's marches), *Who Cares?* (1970, after Gershwin), and *Union Jack* (1976, after popular British music). His ballet arrangements for other companies include *The Thief Who Loved a Ghost* (1950, after Weber), *L'Inconnue* (1965), *The Clowns* (1968; a rare 12-tone arrangement), *Meadowlark and Cortège Burlesque* (1969), *Grand Tour* (1971, after Noel Coward), and *Winter's Court* (1972). He also orchestrated a Gottschalk piano piece, *Grand Tarantella*, for Piano and Orch. (1957) and completed the orchestration of Robert Kurka's opera *The Good Soldier Schweik* (N.Y., April 23, 1958).—NS/LK/DM

Kay, Ulysses Simpson, eminent black American composer and teacher; b. Tucson, Ariz., Jan. 7, 1917; d. Englewood, N.J., May 20, 1995. He received his early music training at home, and on the advice of his uncle "King" Oliver, a leading jazz cornetist and bandleader, he studied piano. In 1934 he enrolled at the Univ. of Ariz. at Tucson (Mus.B., 1938), and then went to study at the Eastman School of Music in Rochester, N.Y., where he was a student of Rogers and Hanson (M.M., 1940). Still later he attended the classes of Hindemith at the Berkshire Music Center in Tanglewood (1941–42). After serving in the U.S. Navy (1942–45), he studied composition with Luening at Columbia Univ. (1946–49). He went to Rome as winner of the American Rome Prize, and was attached there to the American Academy (1949–52). From 1953 to 1968 he was employed as a consultant by Broadcast Music Inc. in N.Y. He was on the faculty of Boston Univ. (1965) and of the Univ. of Calif., Los Angeles (1966–67), and, in 1968, he was appointed prof. of music at the Herbert H. Lehman Coll. in N.Y.; was made Distinguished Prof. there in 1972, retiring in 1988. He received honorary doctorates from several American univs. His music followed a distinctly American idiom, particularly in its rhythmic intensity, while avoiding ostentatious ethnic elements; in harmony and counterpoint, he pursued a moderately advanced idiom, marked by prudentially euphonious dissonances; his instrumentation was masterly.

WORKS: DRAMATIC: Opera: *The Boor*, after Chekhov (1955; Lexington, Ky., April 3, 1968); *The Juggler of Our Lady* (1956; New Orleans, Feb. 3, 1962); *The Capitoline Venus* (1970; Urbana, Ill., March 12, 1971); *Jubilee* (Jackson, Miss., April 12, 1976); *Frederick Douglass* (1980–85; Newark, April 14, 1991). B a l l e t : *Dance Calinda* (Rochester, N.Y., April 23, 1941). F i l m : *The Quiet One* (1988). O R C H .: Oboe Concerto (Rochester, N.Y., April 16, 1940); *5 Mosaics* for Chamber Orch. (Cleveland, Dec. 28, 1940); *Of New Horizons*, overture (N.Y., July 29, 1944); *Suite in 5 Movements* (1945; N.Y., May 21, 1950); *A Short Overture* (N.Y., March 31, 1947); *Portrait Suite* (1948; Erie, Pa., April 21, 1964); Suite for Strings (Baltimore, April 8, 1949); Sinfonia in E major (Rochester, N.Y., May 2, 1951); 6 Dances for Strings (1954); *Concerto for Orchestra* (N.Y., Feb. 1954); *Serenade* (Louisville, Sept. 18, 1954); *Fantasy Variations* (Portland, Maine, Nov. 19, 1963); *Umbrian Scene* (New Orleans, March 31, 1964); *Markings*, symphonic essay, dedicated to the memory of Dag Hammarskjöld (Rochester, Mich., Aug. 8, 1966); Sym. (1967; for the Ill. Sesquicentennial, Macomb, Ill., March 28, 1968); *Theater Set* (Atlanta, Sept. 26, 1968); *Scherzi musicali* for Chamber Orch. (Detroit, Feb. 13, 1969); *Aulos* for Flute and Chamber Orch. (Bloomington, Ind., Feb. 21, 1971); Quintet Concerto for 5 Brass Soloists and Orch. (N.Y., March 14, 1975); *Southern Harmony* (Raleigh, N.C., Feb. 10, 1976); *Chariots*, rhapsody (Saratoga, N.Y., Aug. 8, 1979, composer conducting); *String Triptych* (1987); band music. C H A M B E R : Quintet for Flute and Strings (1947); Piano Quintet (1949); 3 string quartets (1953, 1956, 1961); *5 Portraits* for Violin and Piano (1972); *Guitarra*, guitar suite (1973; rev. 1985); *Tromba* for Trumpet and Piano (1983); *5 Winds*, divertimento for Woodwind Quintet (1984); *Pantomime*, fantasy for Clarinet (1986); *Everett Suite* for Bass Trombone (1988). P i a n o : Sonata (1940); *2 Nocturnes* (1973); *2 Impromptus* (1986). V O C A L : *Song of Jeremiah*, cantata (Nashville, Tenn., April 23, 1954); *3 Pieces after Blake* for Soprano and Orch. (N.Y., March 27, 1955); *The Western Paradise* for Female Narrator and Orch. (Washington, D.C., Oct. 12, 1976); many choral pieces; songs.

BIBL.: L. Hayes, *The Music of U. K., 1939–1963* (diss., Univ. of Wisc., 1971); R. Hadley, *The Published Choral Music of U.S. K., 1943–1968* (diss., Univ. of Iowa, 1972); C. Hobson and D. Richardson, *U. K.: A Bio-Bibliography* (Westport, Conn., 1994).
—NS/LK/DM

Kaye, Sammy (actually, Samuel),

American bandleader and reed player; b. Rocky River, Ohio, March 13, 1910; d. Ridgeway, N. J., June 2, 1987. Kaye's orchestra, sometimes billed as Swing and Sway with Sammy Kaye, was one of the most popular bands of the Swing Era. Kaye's personal appearances and radio and television programs were sparked by such entertaining elements as his "so you want to lead a band" audience participation contests and his reciting of poetry submitted by his fans. He also made a long series of popular recordings, reaching the charts from 1937 to 1964, his biggest hits being "Daddy," "Chickery Chick," "The Old Lamp-Lighter," and "Harbor Lights."

The first-generation son of Czechoslovakian immigrants, Kaye organized his first band while studying civil engineering at Ohio Univ. After graduation he turned to bandleading professionally in 1933, first playing in Cleveland, then moving to Cincinnati and Pittsburgh. He made his recording debut for Vocalion Records on April 14, 1937. His first recording to reach the hit parade, "Rosalie" (music and lyrics by Cole Porter), went to #1 in January 1938. "Love Walked In"

(music by George Gershwin, lyrics by Ira Gershwin) followed, topping the hit parade in May. His third hit-parade entry, "When They Played the Polka" (music by Fabian André, lyrics by Lou Holzer), came in July. His fourth, "All Ashore" (music and lyrics by Billy Hill), coincided with his November debut at the Commodore Hotel in N.Y., where he maintained a residency for years, and was his first release through RCA Victor, the label with which he recorded until 1950.

Kaye returned to the hit parade for two weeks in February 1939 with "Hurry Home" (music and lyrics by Joseph Meyer, Buddy Bernier, and Bob Emmerich). On Jan. 1, 1940, he began a weekly half-hour radio series, *Sensation and Swing*, the first of many radio programs that would bolster his popularity during the 1940s and 1950s, notably *Sunday Serenade* and *So You Want to Lead a Band*. He returned to the hit parade in April 1940 with "Let There Be Love" (music by Lionel Rand, lyrics by Ian Grant).

Kaye scored occasional Top Ten hits during the early 1940s, including the self-penned "Until Tomorrow (Goodnight My Love)" in May 1941, his biggest all-time hit; the chart-topping "Daddy" (music and lyrics by Bobby Troup) in June 1941; "Remember Pearl Harbor" (music and lyrics by Don Reid and Kaye) in February 1942; and "I Left My Heart at the Stage Door Canteen" (music and lyrics by Irving Berlin) in September 1942. (During this period he was married to a woman named Ruth.) He also appeared in two films, *Iceland*, released in October 1942, and *Song of the Open Road*, released in June 1944.

But Kaye's greatest period of success on records came during the second half of the 1940s. In 1945 he reached the Top Ten 11 times, most successfully with the chart-topping "Chickery Chick" (music by Sidney Lippman, lyrics by Sylvia Dee) and "Don't Fence Me In" (music and lyrics by Cole Porter); he had another eight Top Ten hits in 1946, the most popular of which were "The Old Lamp-Lighter" (music by Nat Simon, lyrics by Charles Tobias) and "I'm a Big Girl Now" (music and lyrics by Al Hoffman, Milton Drake, and Jerry Livingston), each of which hit #1; the biggest of his three Top Ten hits in 1947 was "That's My Desire" (music by Helmy Kresa, lyrics by Carroll Loveday); among the three Top Ten hits he scored in 1948, the most popular was "Serenade of the Bells" (music and lyrics by Kay Twomey, Al Goodhart, and Al Urbano); and among his four Top Ten hits in 1949 was "Room Full of Roses" (music and lyrics by Tim Spencer). He also began to score with his albums, reaching the Top Ten in 1945 with *Stephen Foster* and in 1948 with *Dusty Manuscripts*.

Kaye enjoyed as much success at the beginning of the 1950s as he had in the previous several years. In March 1950 he hit the album charts with the Top Ten hit *Sammy Kaye Plays Irving Berlin*; in May, "It Isn't Fair" (music by Richard Himber, Frank Warshauer, and Sylvester Sprigato, lyrics by Himber) went to #1 and "Roses" (music and lyrics by Tim Spencer and Glenn Spencer) hit the Top Ten on the singles charts; and in June, "Wanderin'" (music and lyrics by Kaye, based on a folk song discovered by Carl Sandburg) hit the Top Ten. On June 11, Kaye premiered a television version of

So You Want to Lead a Band, the first of a series of television shows he would host off and on throughout the 1950s.

Kaye switched to Columbia Records and topped the charts with his first record for the label, "Harbor Lights" (music by Hugh Williams, a pseudonym for Will Grosz, lyrics by Jimmy Kennedy), in November 1950. This proved to be his last major hit, but he returned to the Top 40 with an instrumental version of "Charade" (music by Henry Mancini, lyrics by Johnny Mercer) in 1964, and he maintained his orchestra until his death from cancer in 1987 at the age of 77, after which it was led by Roger Thorpe.—WR

Kayser, Isfrid, German composer; b. Türkheim an der Wertach, near Augsburg, March 13, 1712; d. Marchtal, near Ulm, March 1, 1771. Following music studies with his father, the village organist and schoolmaster, he entered the Premonstratensian monastery in Marchtal in 1732, where he served as music director from about 1741 to 1750. Subsequently he was a parish priest until returning to Marchtal in 1761, where he was made sub-prior in 1763. Kayser was one of the principal Bavarian composers of sacred music in his day, publishing collections of cantatas, masses, Psalms, and other works. He also wrote keyboard suites.—LK/DM

Kayser, Leif, Danish composer, pianist, and organist; b. Copenhagen, June 13, 1919. He studied at the Copenhagen Cons., and later took courses with Rosenberg in Stockholm. He then went to Rome, where he studied theology (1942–49), and was ordained a Catholic priest; later studied with Boulanger in Paris (1955). He served as chaplain at St. Ansgar church in Copenhagen (1949–64); in 1964, was appointed to the faculty of the Royal Danish Cons. of Music in Copenhagen. He wrote 4 syms. (1939, 1940, 1956, 1963), *Christmas Oratorio* (1943), *Sinfonietta* for Amateur Orch. (1967), *Divertimento* for 4 Recorders (1968), Organ Sonata, sacred choruses, etc.—NS/LK/DM

Kayser, Philipp Christoph, German composer; b. Frankfurt am Main, March 10, 1755; d. Oberstrass, near Zürich, Dec. 23, 1823. In 1775 he settled in Zürich as a teacher. He wrote music for Goethe's Singspiel *Scherz, List und Rache* (1785–86) and incidental music for his drama *Egmont* (c. 1786–88; not extant). However, Kayser was best known for his songs, of which he wrote more than 100, a number of which were set to texts by Goethe.

BIBL.: C. Burkhardt, *Goethe und der Komponist P.C. K.* (Leipzig, 1879); E. Refardt, *Der Goethe-K.* (Zürich, 1950). —NS/LK/DM

Kazandjiev, Vasil, Bulgarian conductor and composer; b. Marten, near Ruse, Sept. 10, 1934. He studied composition privately with Iliev, then composition with Vladigerov and conducting with Simeonov at the Bulgarian State Cons. in Sofia, graduating in 1957; in 1964, was appointed to its faculty. In 1979 he became principal conductor of the Bulgarian Radio and Television Sym.

Orch. In his music, he applies modern techniques, including modified serialism, to modalities of Bulgarian folk music.

WORKS: ORCH.: Concerto for Strings (1951); *Sinfonietta* (1954); Trumpet Concerto (1955); Divertimento (1957); Concerto for Piano, Saxophone, and Orch. (1957–60); Violin Concerto (1961); *Complexi sonori* for Strings (1965); *Symphony of Timbres* (1968); *The Living Icons* for Chamber Orch. (1970); *Pictures from Bulgaria* for Strings and Percussion (1971); *Festive Music* (1972); *Capriccio* (1974); *Apocalypse* (1978); *Illuminations* (1980); Sym. No. 3 (1981). CHAMBER: Wind Quintet (1951); *Variations* for Oboe, Clarinet, Violin, Viola, Cello, and Piano (1954); Horn Sonata (1955); Clarinet Sonata (1956); Sonata for Solo Violin (1957); 2 string quartets (1965, 1970); *Concert Improvisations* for Flute, Viola, Harp, and Harpsichord (1974); *Poco a poco* for Percussion and Organ (1979); Piano Quintet (1981). P i a n o : Sonata (1957); *The Triumph of the Bells* (1974). VOCAL: Choruses; songs.—NS/LK/DM

Kazarnovskaya, Ljuba, admired Russian soprano; b. Moscow, July 18, 1960. She was 16 when she began vocal training with Nadezhda Malysheva in Moscow, and at 19 she enrolled at the Moscow Cons., where she continued her studies with Elena Shumilova. In 1982 she made her formal operatic debut as Tatiana at the Stanislavsky Theater in Moscow. She first sang at the Bolshoi Theater in Moscow in 1983. In 1986 she scored a fine success as Leonora in *La forza del destino* at the Kirov Theater in Leningrad, where she remained as a principal artist until 1989. She also toured with the company abroad, notably as Tatiana at the Paris Opéra and at London's Covent Garden in 1987. In 1989 she was engaged as a soloist in the Verdi *Requiem* at the Salzburg Festival, and subsequently she pursued a successful operatic and concert career in the West. In 1992 she made her North American debut as soloist in the Shostakovich 14th Sym. with the Boston Sym. Orch. Her Metropolitan Opera debut in N.Y. followed later that year, as Tatiana, to critical acclaim. After singing Desdemona there in 1993, she returned there to outstanding acclaim in 1994. In 1995 she sang Rimsky-Korsakov's Fevronia during the Kirov company's visit to the Brooklyn Academy of Music. Her engagements also took to her Milan's La Scala, the Vienna State Opera, the Bavarian State Opera in Munich, the Hamburg State Opera, the Teatro Colón in Buenos Aires, and Chicago's Lyric Opera. As a concert artist, she appeared with leading orchs. and at principal festivals. In addition to her esteemed Russian repertoire, she has won notable success as Donna Anna, Vitellia, Marguerite, Amelia, Violetta, Mimi, and Salome.—NS/LK/DM

Kazuro, Stanislaw, Polish composer; b. Teklinapol, near Vilnius, Aug. 1, 1881; d. Warsaw, Nov. 30, 1961. He studied in Warsaw, Paris, and Rome. He was active mainly in Warsaw as a pedagogue and choral conductor, and he also publ. several school manuals. His compositions, in an academic style, were chiefly designed for pedagogic purposes. Among them are 2 folk operas, orch. music, choral works, and piano pieces.—NS/LK/DM

Każyński, Wiktor, Polish pianist, conductor, and composer; b. Vilnius, Dec. 30, 1812; d. St. Petersburg,

March 18, 1867. He studied law at the Univ. of Vilnius, but was mostly self-taught in music. From 1836 to 1840 he was organist at Vilnius's Cathedral of St. John. He then went to Warsaw, where he took lessons with Chopin's teacher Elsner. In 1842 he settled in St. Petersburg, where he conducted the orch. of the Alexandrinsky Theater (1845–67). He was one of the first pianists to champion Chopin's works. His own compositions are of little importance, but they are of historical interest as early examples of Polish Romanticism. Among them are a melodrama to a Polish libretto, *Żyd wieczny tulacz* (The Wandering Jew; Vilnius, 1842), and a melodrama to a French libretto, *Mąż i żona* (Man and Wife; St. Petersburg, 1848), as well as 7 other works in that genre. He also wrote 3 comic operas, including *Antoni i Antosia* (Vilnius, 1840), 4 operettas, 4 ballets, orch. music, and songs. He publ. *History of Italian Opera* (St. Petersburg, 1851; in Polish and in a Russian tr.).—**NS/LK/DM**

KC and the Sunshine Band,

was, for a brief time, the hottest band in the world (f. 1973). **MEMBERSHIP:** Harry Wayne "KC" Casey, voc., kybd. (b. Hialeah, Fla., Jan. 31, 1951); Richard Finch, bs. (b. Indianapolis, Ind., Jan. 25, 1954); Jerome Smith, gtr. (b. Miami, Fla., June 18, 1953; d. West Palm Beach, Fla., Aug. 4, 2000); Robert Johnson, drm. (b. Miami, Fla., March 21, 1953); Fermin Coytisolo, congas (b. Havana, Cuba, Dec. 31, 1951); Ronnie Smith, trpt. (b. Hialeah, Fla., c. 1952); Denvil Liptrot, sax.; James Weaver, trpt.; Charles Williams, trmb. (b. Rockingham, S.C., Nov. 18, 1954).

From 1974 through 1979, Harry Wayne Casey and his partner Richard Finch were responsible for a dozen hits, half of which went to the top of the pop charts. The deceptively simple dance music they created helped spawn a dance genre that became known as the Miami Sound.

Casey worked in a record store, and through connections with the distributor started hanging out at TK records studio. He did various chores around the studio and learned how to use it. When the studio hired audio technician Finch a year later, the two became friends and started using down time to write and record their own material, a loose pop interpretation of Caribbean junkanoo music. One of their songs, "Rock Your Baby" became a chart topping hit for George McCrae in 1974, reportedly selling 11 million copies worldwide. On the strength of this success, TK put Casey and Finch to work on their own project, which they initially called KC and the Junkanoo Sunshine Band. Eventually the group lost the "Junkanoo."

The group's initial solo forays, "Blow Your Whistle" and "Sound Your Funky Horn" reached in the 20s on the R&B charts. "Queen of Clubs" and the debut *Do It Good* album didn't make ripples at home, but became big hits in England. The first release from their self-titled second album, "Get Down Tonight," with its simple lyric and double speed guitar, topped both the pop and R&B charts. The rhythmic, primal "That's the Way (I Like It)" followed suit. The group's debut album went to #4.

Casey and Finch went back into the studio and generated another set of dance tunes. Released in the summer of 1976, the first single "(Shake, Shake, Shake) Shake Your Booty" became their third consecutive record to top both the pop and R&B charts. The horn charts had developed a bit more depth, but the lyrics and rhythm were simple, classic dance music, the paradigm of disco. This perceived lack of complexity drew the lines between the "death to disco" rock fans and the ones who just wanted to dance. Their next single, "I Like to Do It," broke their streak, topping out at #37. However, the next single came back strong. "I'm Your Boogie Man" became the group's fourth chart topper in less than two years. "Keep It Coming Love" topped the R&B chart, but was kept out of the top pop slot by the Star Wars Cantina band and Debby Boone. Dance music was becoming a singles oriented sound, and the album *Part 3* that produced all four hits only rose to #13.

As one of the paradigms for contemporary dance music, it was only appropriate that they were featured in *Saturday Night Fever*. The song, "Boogie Shoes" only reached #35, as did their next single "It's the Same Old Song." After these two disappointing songs, though, they came back with a #8 R&B hit "Do You Wanna Go Party." In 1979, they topped the singles chart with the ballad "Please Don't Go." KC followed it off with another ballad, a duet with Teri DeSario "Yes, I'm Ready." The song topped the adult contemporary chart and went to #2 pop.

Casey was in a car accident in 1982 that left him paralyzed for a time. By the time he recovered, TK records had gone out of business. Signed to Epic, he couldn't buy a hit. One track, "Give It Up," topped the charts again in England, but Epic wouldn't release it. Casey formed his own label and put it out. It rose to #18. While it was the last hit under his own name, Casey and Finch continued to produce. In the 1990s, they reformed the band, started touring and even put out an album of new tunes.

DISC.: *Do It Good* (1974); *The Sound of Sunshine* (1975); *Part 3* (1976); *I Like to Do It* (1977); *Who Do Ya Love* (1978); *Do You Wanna Party* (1979); *Space Cadet* (1981); *The Painter* (1981); *KC Ten* (1984); *Oh Yeah!* (1993); *Get Down Live!* (1995); *New Best One* (1999).—**HB**

Keats, Donald (Howard),

significant American composer; b. N.Y., May 27, 1929. He received training in piano at the Manhattan School of Music in N.Y., and then studied composition with Porter and Hindemith and musicology with Einstein and Schrade at Yale Univ. (Mus.B., 1949). Following further training in composition with Luening, Moore, Beeson, and Cowell and in musicology with Lang at Columbia Univ. (M.A., 1953), he received a Fulbright grant in 1954 and studied with Jarnach at the Hamburg Hochschule für Musik. He completed his studies in composition with Fetler and Argento and in musicology with Riedel at the Univ. of Minn. (Ph.D., 1962). In 1948–49 he was a teaching fellow at the Yale Univ. School of Music. He then was called to military service and was an instructor at the U.S. Naval School of Music in Washington, D.C., in 1953–54. From 1957 to 1976 he taught at Antioch Coll. In 1969–70 he also was a visiting prof. of music at the Univ. of

Washington in Seattle. In 1976 he became prof. of music and composer-in-residence at the Univ. of Denver School of Music, retiring from both positions in 1999. He also gave performances of his own piano works in various parts of the world. In 1964–65 and in 1972–73 he held Guggenheim fellowships. He also received awards and prizes from the NEA, Yale Univ., the Rockefeller Foundation, ASCAP, and the Ford Foundation. In his compositions, Keats appears as a classical lyricist; his music is sparse in texture but opulent in sonorous substance, frugal in diction but expansive in elaborate developments; its expressive power is a musical equivalent of "Occam's razor," a medieval law of parsimony which proclaims the principle of multa paucis, multitude by paucity, abundance in concision. The titles of his works often indicate this economic precision of design: *Musica instrumentalis; Polarities; Diptych; Branchings.* In *An Elegiac Symphony*, he gives full expression to the lyric nature of his talent; it is an outgrowth of an orchestral *Elegy* inspired by the sadness upon the death of his infant son. His most performed work is his Piano Sonata.

WORKS: DRAMATIC: B a l l e t : *The New Work* (Dayton, Ohio, March 5, 1967). **ORCH.:** *Concert Piece* (1952; Columbus, Ohio, Feb. 3, 1968); 2 syms.: No. 1 (1955–57; Columbus, Ohio, April 1, 1959) and No. 2, *An Elegiac Symphony* (1962; Seattle, May 2, 1965); *Elegy* (1959; Cincinnati, Jan. 29, 1965); *Branchings* (1976; Boulder, Colo., July 5, 1980); Piano Concerto (1982–90; Denver, April 20, 1991). **CHAMBER:** Clarinet Sonata (1948); String Trio (1948); *Divertimento* for Winds and Strings (1949; Lake Placid, N.Y., Sept. 6, 1950); 3 string quartets: No. 1 (1951; Munich, April 6, 1956), No. 2 (1965; Yellow Springs, Ohio, May 22, 1966), and No. 3 (1997–99); *Polarities* for Violin and Piano (1968; Yellow Springs, Ohio, May 26, 1971); *Dialogue* for Piano and Winds (1973; Cincinnati, March 1, 1974); *Diptych* for Cello and Piano (1974; N.Y., May 30, 1975); *Musica Instrumentalis* for Chamber Ensemble (Boulder, Colo., July 8, 1980); *Revisitations* for Violin, Cello, and Piano (Los Angeles, Oct. 18, 1992). **P i a n o :** *Theme and Variations* (1954; Hamburg, July 13, 1956); Sonata (1960; Yellow Springs, Ohio, May 6, 1962). **VOCAL:** *The Naming of Cats* for Vocal Quartet and Piano, after T.S. Eliot (1951; N.Y., Dec. 19, 1961); *The Hollow Men* for Chorus, Clarinet, 3 Trombones, and Piano, after T.S. Eliot (1952; Hamburg, July 12, 1955); *anyone lived in a pretty town* for Chorus, after e.e. cummings (1965); *A Love Triptych*, song cycle for Soprano and Piano, after Yeats (1970; Kansas City, Mo., May 2, 1971); *Upon the Intimation of Love's Mortality* for Soprano and Piano, after Garrigue (1974; N.Y., May 30, 1975); *Tierras del Alma* for Soprano, Flute, and Guitar (1977; Denver, May 23, 1979).—NS/LK/DM

Kee, Cornelis, distinguished Dutch organist, pedagogue, and composer, father of **Piet(er Willem) Kee;** b. Zaandam, Nov. 24, 1900; d. there, Jan. 3, 1997. He studied organ and piano with de Pauw, composition with Dresden, and voice with Denijs at the Amsterdam Cons. He was active as a church and concert organist, becoming widely known as a master of improvisation. In 1951 he became a prof. at the Haarlem International Summer Academy. In 1976 he was made a Knight of the Order of Oranje-Nassau. He publ. 3 collections of Psalms for organ, which treat old Psalm tunes contrapuntally. In some of his own compositions (almost exclusively for organ), he applied polyphonic devices of the classical Flemish school in a modern way, including serial procedures.

WORKS: *Reeksveranderingen* (Serial Permutations; 1966); *Phases* for Organ (1966); *Phases* for Organ (1969); *Blijde incomste* (Joyful Entry), variations on a traditional song, for Brass, Percussion, and Piano (1969); *Sweelinck Variations* for Horn, 2 Trumpets, 2 Trombones, and Organ (1973); Suite for Harpsichord or Organ (1974); *Homopoly*, 4 pieces for Piano (1979); numerous teaching pieces for organ.—NS/LK/DM

Kee, Piet(er Willem), eminent Dutch organist, pedagogue, and composer, son of **Cornelius Kee;** b. Zaandam, Aug. 30, 1927. He received training in organ from his father, and then from Anthon van de Horst at the Amsterdam Cons. (graduated, 1948). In 1941 he made his debut as an organist in Zaandam. In 1953, 1954, and 1955 he won the International Organ Improvisation Competition. From 1952 to 1987 he served as organist at St. Laurens in Alkmar, and from 1956 to 1989 as municipal organist at St. Bavo in Haarlem. He was prof. of organ at the Sweelinck Cons. in Amsterdam from 1954 to 1987. In 1972 he was made a Knight of the Order of Oranje-Nassau, and in 1987 he was elected an honorary fellow of the Royal Coll. of Organists in London. Kee has composed many solo works for organ, including *Variations on a Carol* (1954), *Triptych on Psalm 86* (1960), *4 Manual Pieces* (1966), and *Bios* (1994), as well as *Confrontation* for 3 Street Organs and Church Organ (1979). Among his other works are *Music and Space* for 2 Organs, 3 Trumpets, and 3 Trombones (1969), *Integration* for Chorus, Flageolet, Mechanical Birds, Barrel Organs, and Church Organ (1980), *Flight* for Flute (1992), *Network* for 2 Organs, Recorder, Saxophone, and Synthesizer (1996), choral pieces, and arrangements of hymns and folk songs.—NS/LK/DM

Keene, Christopher, prominent American conductor and music administrator; b. Berkeley, Calif., Dec. 21, 1946; d. N.Y., Oct. 8, 1995. He studied piano as a child, and during his high school years conducted several groups; then attended the Univ. of Calif. at Berkeley (1963–67). In 1965 he made his public debut conducting Britten's *The Rape of Lucretia* in Berkeley; in 1966 he became an asst. conductor at the San Francisco Opera, and in 1967 at the San Diego Opera. In 1968 he made his European debut conducting Menotti's *The Saint of Bleecker Street* at the Spoleto (Italy) Festival. He was music director of the American Ballet Co. (1969–70). On Oct. 18, 1970, he made his N.Y.C. Opera debut conducting Ginastera's *Don Ridrigo*, and, on Sept. 24, 1971, his Metropolitan Opera debut in N.Y. conducting *Cavalleria rusticana*. He served as co-music director (1971–73), general manager (1973–75), and music director (1975–76) of the Spoleto Festival; was music director (from 1974) and president (1975–89) of Artpark, the Lewiston, N.Y., summer festival. From 1975 to 1984 he was music director of the Syracuse (N.Y.) Sym. Orch.; also held that title with the Spoleto Festival U.S.A. in Charleston, S.C. (1977–80), and with the Long Island (N.Y.) Phil. (1979–90). He was artistic supervisor (1982–83) and music director (1983–86) of the N.Y.C. Opera, returning there in 1989 as general director. Keene became well known for his championship of rarely heard operas during his years at the N.Y.C. Opera. His career was cut short by AIDS-induced lymphoma. —NS/LK/DM

Keene, Constance, American pianist and pedagogue; b. N.Y., Feb. 9, 1921. She studied with **Abram Chasins** (1938–49), whom she married in 1949 and with whom she subsequently performed. She was an early teacher of Arthur Rubinstein's children, and also taught at the Mannes School of Music in N.Y., numbering among her students Minoru Nojima, Peter Nero, and David Bar-Illan. Her 1964 recordings of the preludes of Rachmaninoff were critically acclaimed. As a soloist, she appeared with major orchs. in the U.S. and abroad. She also gave master classes.—NS/LK/DM

Keenlyside, Simon, English baritone; b. London, Aug. 3, 1959. He studied at St. John's Choir School in Cambridge, took a degree in zoology at the Univ. of Cambridge, and received vocal instruction from John Cameron at the Royal Northern Coll. of Music in Manchester, where he made his operatic debut as Lescaut in 1987. In 1986 he won the Richard Tauber Competition. Following a season with the Hamburg State Opera (1988–89), he joined the Scottish Opera in Glasgow, where he sang Rossini's Figaro in 1991 and Britten's Billy Budd in 1992. In 1989 he made his debut at London's Covent Garden as Silvio, and returned there as Guglielmo in 1995. He sang Gluck's Oreste at the Welsh National Opera in Cardiff in 1991. In 1993 he appeared as Don Giovanni with the Glyndebourne Touring Opera. In 1995 he portrayed Papageno at Milan's La Scala, and returned to Italy in 1997 to sing Don Giovanni. He appeared as Belcore at the Metropolitan Opera in N.Y. in 1996, the same year that he sang Thomas's Hamlet in Geneva. In 1997 he sang Pelléas at the San Francisco Opera. In 1998 he was engaged as Monteverdi's Orfeo in Brussels and in 1999 as Marcello at the Vienna State Opera. He also was active as a lieder artist.—NS/LK/DM

Kegel, Herbert, distinguished German conductor; b. Dresden, July 29, 1920; d. there, Nov. 20, 1990. He studied at the Dresden Staatskapelle's orch. school, where his mentors included Böhm and Blacher (1935–40). In 1946 he became conductor of the Rostock Opera; in 1949, was engaged as conductor of the Leipzig Radio Choir and Orch.; was made conductor (1953), Generalmusikdirektor (1958), and chief conductor (1960) of the Leipzig Radio Sym. Orch. From 1975 to 1978 he was a prof. at the Leipzig Hochschule für Musik, and in 1978 became a prof. at the Dresden Hochschule für Musik. From 1977 to 1985 he served as chief conductor of the Dresden Phil. He was regarded as one of the most competent conductors of East Germany, combining a thorough knowledge of his repertoire with a fine sense of effective presentation of the music. —NS/LK/DM

Kehr, Günter, German violinist and conductor; b. Darmstadt, March 16, 1920; d. Mainz, Sept. 22, 1989. He studied violin in Frankfurt am Main and Cologne, then took univ. courses in Berlin and Cologne, receiving a Ph.D. with the diss. *Untersuchungen zur Violintechnik um die Wende des 18. Jahrhunderts* (1941). As a violinist, he gave the first German performances of the concertos of Hindemith and Bartók; also played in a string trio. He then pursued a career as a conductor. In 1955 he founded the Mainz Chamber Orch., with which he made numerous tours. From 1953 to 1961 he was director of the Peter-Cornelius-Konservatorium in Mainz, and from 1959 he taught at the Hochschule für Musik in Cologne, becoming a prof. there in 1961 and remaining there until 1987. He ed. Urtext editions of the violin sonatas of Bach and Brahms and also supervised new editions of the orch. works of Albinoni, Rameau, Telemann, and other composers.—NS/LK/DM

Keil, Alfredo, Portuguese composer and painter of German descent; b. Lisbon, July 3, 1850; d. Hamburg, Oct. 4, 1907. He studied music with Antonio Soares, Oscar de la Cinna, and Ernesto Vieira in Lisbon, and then went to Nuremberg (1868), where he studied music with Kaulbach and painting with Kremling. Returning to Portugal (1870), he pursued a dual career as composer and painter; devoted his energies to the furtherance of national music. His comic opera, *Susana* (Lisbon, 1883), is generally considered the first substantial work of the Portuguese stage, and his song "A Portugueza" (1890) was adopted as the national anthem of Portugal in 1911. He also wrote the operas *Donna Bianca* (Lisbon, March 10, 1888), *Irene* (Turin, March 22, 1893), and *Serrana* (1st perf. in Italian at the Teatro San Carlos, Lisbon, March 13, 1899), as well as 3 symphonic suites, cantatas, piano pieces, and songs.—NS/LK/DM

Keilberth, Joseph, distinguished German conductor; b. Karlsruhe, April 19, 1908; d. while conducting a performance of *Tristan und Isolde* at the Nationaltheater in Munich, July 20, 1968. He studied in Karlsruhe, where he became a répétiteur (1925), then Generalmusikdirektor (1935–40) at the State Opera. He was chief conductor of the German Phil. Orch. of Prague (1940–45), and then Generalmusikdirektor of the Dresden Staatskapelle (1945–50). He was chief conductor of the Bamberg Sym. Orch. (1949–68), with which he toured Europe in 1951 and the U.S. and Latin America in 1954; was also a conductor at the Bayreuth Festivals (1952–56) and concurrently Generalmusikdirektor of the Hamburg State Phil. Orch. (1950–59); then of the Bavarian State Opera in Munich (1959–68). He was particularly esteemed for his performances of works from the Classical and Romantic Austro-German repertoire.

Bibl.: W.-E. von Lewinski, *J. K.* (Berlin, 1968). —NS/LK/DM

Keiser, Reinhard, important German opera composer; b. Teuchern, near Weissenfels, Jan. 9, 1674; d. Hamburg, Sept. 12, 1739. He received his early musical training from his father, Gottfried Keiser, an organist, and then was sent to Leipzig, where he studied at the renowned Thomasschule directed by Johann Schelle. In 1693 he was in Braunschweig, where he began his career as a composer for the stage. His first opera-pastorale, *Der königliche Schäfer oder Basilius in Arcadien*, was performed shortly after his arrival in Braunschweig; in 1694 he produced a Singspiel, *Procris und Cephalus*; there followed another pastorale, *Die wiedergefundenen Verliebten*, in 1695; it was revived in Hamburg in 1699 under the title *Die beständige und getreue Ismene*. In 1694 he was named Cammer-Componist in Braunschweig. In 1695 he went to Hamburg, which became his permanent residence. In 1696 he was engaged as Kapellmeister with the Hamburg Opera; in 1702 he became its co-director, retaining this position until 1707. Hamburg was then the main center of opera productions in Germany, and Keiser worked industriously producing not only his own operas there, but also the stage works of Handel and Mattheson. The number of Keiser's stage works was never calculated with credible precision; the best estimate is that he wrote in Hamburg at least 77 operas and 39 Singspiels and theatrical intermezzi. The subjects of his operas are still predominantly taken from Greek and Roman mythology, as was customary in the Baroque era, but he introduced a decisive innovation by using the German language in his dramatic works; he further made use of popular local themes; he made a concession, however, in resorting to the Italian language in arias. Thus his last opera, *Circe*, produced in Hamburg on March 1, 1734, contains 21 German arias and 23 Italian arias. Keiser also continued the common tradition of having other composers contribute to the music. In his ballets he followed the French *style galant* and effectively used Rococo devices. In so doing he formed a German Baroque idiom national in essence and cosmopolitan in treatment; this aspect of his work influenced his younger contemporaries Bach and Handel. In 1718 Keiser became a guest Kapellmeister to the Duke of Württemberg in Stuttgart. In 1721 he went to Copenhagen to supervise the productions of his operas *Die unvergleichliche Psyche*, *Ulysses*, and *Der Armenier*. In 1723 he returned to Hamburg, and in 1725 composed 2 operas on subjects connected with Hamburg history and society: *Der Hamburger Jahrmarkt* and *Die Hamburger Schlachtzeit*. In 1728 he became Canonicus minor and Cantor of the Katharinenkirche in Hamburg. Apart from operas, he wrote many sacred works (oratorios, cantatas, Psalms, Passions), of which several were publ. in the collections *R. Keisers Gemüths-Ergötzung bestehend in einigen Sing-Gedichten mit einer Stimme und unterschiedlichen Instrumenten* (1698), *Divertimenti serenissimi* (airs with harpsichord accompaniment, 1714), *Kaiserliche Friedenpost* (songs and duets with harpsichord, 1715), etc. Several excerpts from his operas were publ. in *Denkmäler Deutscher Tonkunst* and other collections.

WORKS: DRAMATIC: *Der königliche Schäfer oder Basilius in Arcadien* (Braunschweig, 1693); *Procris und Cephalus*, Singspiel (Braunschweig, 1694); *Die wiedergefundenen Verliebten*, Schäferspiel (Braunschweig, 1695; rev. as *Die beständige und getreue Ismene*, Hamburg, 1699); *Mahumet II*, Trauerspiel (Hamburg, 1696); *Der geliebte Adonis* (Hamburg, 1697); *Die durch Wilhelm den Grossen in Britannien wieder eingeführte Treue* (Hamburg, 1698); *Allerunterthäbigster Gehorsam*, Tantzspiel and Singspiel (Hamburg, Nov. 15, 1698); *Der aus Hyperboreen nach Cymbrien überbrachte güldene Apfel zu Ehren Friedrichs und Hedwig Sophiens zu Holstein* (Hamburg, 1698); *Der bey dem allge-*

meinen Welt-Friede und dem Grossen Augustus geschlossene Tempel des Janus (Hamburg, 1699); *Die wunderbahr-errettete Iphigenia* (Hamburg, 1699); *Die Verbindung des grossen Hercules mit der schönen Hebe*, Singspiel (Hamburg, 1699); *Die Wiederkehr der güldnen Zeit* (Hamburg, 1699); *La forza della virtù, oder Die Macht der Tugend* (Hamburg, 1700); *Das höchstpreissliche Crönungsfest Ihrer Kgl. Majestät zu Preussen*, ballet opera (Hamburg, 1701); *Störtebecker und Jödge Michaels* (2 versions; Hamburg, 1701); *Die wunderschöne Psyche*, Singspiel (Hamburg, Oct. 20, 1701); *Circe oder Des Ulisses erster Theil* (Hamburg, 1702); *Penelope oder Des Ulysses ander Theil* (Hamburg, 1702); *Sieg der fruchtbaren Pomona* (Hamburg, Oct. 18, 1702); *Die sterbende Eurydice oder Orpheus erster Theil* (Hamburg, 1702); *Orpheus ander Theil* (Hamburg, 1702); *Neues preussisches Ballet* (Hamburg, 1702); *Die verdammte Staat- Sucht, oder Der verführte Claudius* (Hamburg, 1703); *Die Geburt der Minerva* (Hamburg, 1703); *Die über die Liebe triumphierende Weissheit oder Salomon* (Hamburg, 1703); *Der gestürzte und wieder erhöhte Nebucadnezar, König zu Babylon* (Hamburg, 1704); *Die römische Unruhe oder Die edelmüthige Octavia* (Hamburg, Aug. 5, 1705); *Die kleinmüthige Selbstmörderinn Lucretia oder Die Staats-Thorheit des Brutus*, Trauerspiel (Hamburg, Nov. 29, 1705); *La fedeltià coronata oder Die gekrönte Treue* (Hamburg, 1706); *Masagniello furioso, oder Die Neapolitanische Fischer-Empörung* (Hamburg, June 1706); *La costanza sforzata, Die gezwungene Beständigkeit oder Die listige Rache des Sueno* (Hamburg, Oct. 11, 1706); *Il genio d'Holsatia* (Hamburg, 1706; used as prologue to succeeding work); *Der durchlauchtige Secretarius, oder Almira, Königin von Castilien* (Hamburg, 1706); *Der angenehme Betrug oder Der Carneval von Venedig* (Hamburg, 1707; includes arias by C. Graupner); *La forza dell'amore oder Die von Paris entführte Helena* (Hamburg, 1709); *Die blutdürstige Rache oder Heliates und Olympia* (Hamburg, 1709; with C. Graupner); *Desiderius, König der Langobarden* (Hamburg, July 26, 1709); *Die bis und nach dem Todt unerhörte Treue des Orpheus* (Hamburg, 1709; based on *Die sterbende Eurydice oder Orpheus erster Theil* and *Orpheus ander Theil*); *La grandezza d'animo oder Arsinoe* (Hamburg, 1710); *Le Bon Vivant oder Die Leipziger Messe* (Hamburg, 1710); *Der Morgen des europäischen Glückes oder Aurora*, Schäferspiel (Hamburg, July 26?, 1710); *Der durch den Fall des grossen Pompejus erhöhte Julius Caesar* (Hamburg, Nov. 1710); *Der hochmüthige, gestürtzte und wieder erhabene Croesus*, dramma musicale (Hamburg, 1710); *Die oesterreichische Grossmuth oder Carolus V* (Hamburg, June 1712); *Die entdeckte Verstellung oder Die geheime Liebe der Diana*, Schäferspiel (Hamburg, April 1712; rev. 1724); *Die wiederhergestellte Ruh oder Die gecrönte Tapferkeit des Heraclius* (Hamburg, June 1712); *L'inganno fedele oder Der getreue Betrug* (Hamburg, Oct. 1714); *Die gecrönte Tugend* (Hamburg, Nov. 15, 1714); *Triumph des Friedens*, serenata (Hamburg, March 1, 1715); *Fredegunda* (Hamburg, March 1715); *L'amore verso la patria oder Der sterbende Cato* (Hamburg, 1715); *Artemisia* (Hamburg, 1715); *Das römische Aprilfest*, Lust- und Tantz-spiel (Hamburg, June 1716); *Das verewigte und triumphirende Ertz-Haus Oesterreich*, serenata (Hamburg, 1716); *Das zerstörte Troja oder Der durch den Tod Helenen versöhnte Achilles* (Hamburg, Nov. 1716); *Die durch Verstellung und Grossmuth über die Grausamkeit siegende Liebe oder Julia* (Hamburg, Feb. 1717); *Die grossmüthige Tomyris* (Hamburg, Feb. 1717); *Der die Festung Siebenburgisch-Weissenburg erobernde und über Dacier triumphirende Kayser Trajanus* (Hamburg, Nov. 1717); *Das bey seiner Ruh und Gebuhrt eines Printzen frolockende Lycien unter der Regierung des Königs Jacobates und Bellerophon* (Hamburg, Dec. 28, 1717); *Die unvergleichliche Psyche* (Copenhagen, April 16, 1722); *Ulysses* (Copenhagen, Oct. 1722); *Der Armenier* (Copenhagen, Nov. 1722); *Die betrogene und nochmahls vergötterte Ariadne* (Hamburg, Nov. 25,

1722; based on the opera by Conradi of 1691); *Sancio oder Die siegende Grossmuth* (1723?); *Das wegen Verbannung der Laudplagen am Geburthstage Herrn Friedrich IV zu Dennemurk jauchzende Cimbrien*, serenata (Copenhagen, 1724); *Das frohlockende Gross Britannien*, serenata (Hamburg, June 8, 1724); *Der sich rächende Cupido*, Schäferspiel (Hamburg, 1724; based on *Die entdeckte Verstellung oder Die geheime Liebe der Diana*); *Bretislaus oder Die siegende Beständigkeit* (Hamburg, Jan. 27, 1725); *Der Hamburger Jahrmarkt oder Der glückliche Betrug* (Hamburg, June 27, 1725); *Die Hamburger Schlachtzeit oder Der misslungene Betrug* (Hamburg, Oct. 22, 1725); *Prologus beim Geburths Feste Friderici Ludovici von Hannover*, serenata (Hamburg, Jan. 31, 1726); *Mistevojus König der Obotriten oder Wenden* (Hamburg, 1726); *Der lächerliche Printz Jodelet* (Hamburg, 1726); *Buchhofer der stumme Printz Atis*, intermezzo (Hamburg, 1726); *Barbacola*, intermezzo (Hamburg, 1726; includes music by Lully); *Lucius Verus oder Die siegende Treue* (Hamburg, Oct. 18, 1728; based on *Berenice* by Bronner of 1702); *Der hochmuthige, gestürtzte und wieder erhabene Croesus*, Singspiel (Hamburg, 1730; based on the dramma musicale of 1710); *Jauchzen der Kunste* (1733); *Circe* (Hamburg, March 1, 1734; with arias by other composers). Of these, *Die römische Unruhe oder Die edelmüthige Octavia* was ed. by M. Schneider in the supplement to the Handel *Gesamtausgabe* (Leipzig, 1902); *Der lächerliche Printz Jodelet* was ed. by F. Zelle in the *Publikationen der Gesellschaft für Musikforschung* (1892); the 1730 version of *Der hochmüthige, gesturtzte und wieder erhabene Croesus* was ed. by M. Schneider in the Denkmäler Deutscher Tonkunst, vol. 37 (1912). **VOCAL: Secular:** *Gemuths-Ergotzung*, cantata (Hamburg, 1698); *Componimenti musicali, oder Teutsche und italienische Arien, nebst unterschiedlichen Recitativen aus Almira und Octavia* (Hamburg, 1706); *Divertimenti serenissima delle cantate, duette ed arie diverse senza stromenti oder Durchlauchtige Ergotzung* (Hamburg, 1713); *Musikalische Land-Lust, bestehend in verschiedenen moralischen Cantaten* (Hamburg, 1714); *Kayserliche Friedenspost, nebst verschiedenen moralischen Singgedichten und Arien* (Hamburg, 1715). **Sacred:** *Der blutige und sterbende Jesus* (Hamburg, Holy Week, 1704); *Der für die Sunde der Welt gemartete und sterbende Heiland Jesus* (Hamburg, 1712); *Der zum Tode verurtheilte und gecreutzigte Jesus* (Hamburg, 1715); *Passions Oratorium* (Hamburg, 1717?); *Die uber den Triumph ihres Heylandes Jesu jubilirende glaubige Seele* (Hamburg, Nov. 2, 1717; not extant); *Die durch Grossmuth und Glauben triumphirende Unschuld oder Der siegende David* (Hamburg, Aug. 9, 1721); etc. The *Passions Oratorium* has been publ. in a modern ed. in the *Geistliche Chormusik*, vol. X (Stuttgart, 1963).

BIBL.: H. Leichtentritt, *R. K. in seinen Opern* (diss., Univ. of Berlin, 1901); R. Petzold, *Die Kirchen-Kompositionen und weltliche Kantaten R. K.s* (Berlin, 1934); R. Brenner, *The Operas of R. K. in Their Relationship to the Affektenlehre* (diss., Brandeis Univ., 1968); D. Moe, *The St. Mark Passion of R. K.* (diss., Univ. of Iowa, 1968); K. Zelm, *Die Opern R. K.s* (Munich, 1975).—NS/LK/DM

Kelberine, Alexander, Russian-American pianist; b. Kiev, Feb. 22, 1903; d. (suicide) N.Y., Jan. 30, 1940. He studied at the Kiev Cons., then at the Univ. of Vienna. He took lessons from Busoni in Berlin, and in 1923 went to America and studied at the Juilliard Graduate School in N.Y. with Siloti (piano) and Goldmark (composition); later also studied with Toch. A victim of acute depression, he programmed his last recital for pieces in minor keys and of funereal connotations, concluding with Liszt's *Todtentanz*; he then went home and took an overdose of sleeping pills. He was married to **Jeanne Behrend**, but was estranged from her.—NS/LK/DM

Keldorfer, Robert, Austrian composer, son of **Viktor (Josef) Keldorfer;** b. Vienna, Aug. 10, 1901; d. Klagenfurt, Sept. 13, 1980. He received his early musical training from his father, then took courses at the Vienna Academy of Music with Prohaska, Springer, and Stöhr (1917–19). From 1930 to 1939 he was director of the Linz Cons., and from 1941 to 1966 director of the Klagenfurt Cons. Among his works are an opera, *Verena* (1951); Oboe Concerto (1965); *Sonata ritmica* for Alto Recorder and Piano (1964); Viola Sonata (1964); Sonata for Recorder and Guitar (1967); choral works; songs. —NS/LK/DM

Keldorfer, Viktor (Josef), Austrian conductor and composer, father of **Robert Keldorfer;** b. Salzburg, April 14, 1873; d. Vienna, Jan. 28, 1959. He was a student at the Salzburg Mozarteum. He was chief conductor of the Vienna Männergesang-Verein (1909–21). From 1922 to 1938, and again from 1945 to 1954, he was director of the Vienna Schubertbund; also conducted the Ostdeutscher Sängerbund, which became a model for many Austrian men's choruses. His works include a *Missa solemnis*, 2 vols. of *Lieder für grosse und kleine Kinder*, many men's choruses, and arrangements of Strauss waltzes for men's chorus and orch. He also ed. a complete collection of Schubert's men's choruses.

BIBL.: O. Dobrowolny, *V. K.: Leben und Wirken eines österreichischen Künstlers* (Vienna, 1947).—NS/LK/DM

Keldysh, Yuri (Vsevolodovich), eminent Russian musicologist; b. St. Petersburg, Aug. 29, 1907. He was a student in music history of Ivanov-Boretsky at the Moscow Cons. (graduated, 1930; candidate degree, 1940; Ph.D., 1947, with the diss. *Khudozhestvennoye mirovozzreniye V.V. Stasova* [The Artistic Views of V.V. Stasov]). From 1930 to 1950 he taught at the Moscow Cons., where he became a prof. in 1948. He again served on its faculty from 1957. From 1950 to 1956 he was a teacher at the Cons. and from 1955 to 1957 was director of the Inst. of Music and Theater in Leningrad. He was ed. of the journal *Sovetskaya muzika* (1957–60) and of the valuable *Muzikalnaya Entsiklopediya* (6 vols., 1973–82). Keldysh was one of the foremost Russian musicologists of the Soviet era, and was the author of numerous articles and books.

WRITINGS (all publ. in Moscow unless otherwise given): *Romansovaya lirika Musorgskovo* (Mussorgsky's Lyrical Songs; 1933); *Russkaya klassicheskaya muzika* (1945; 2nd ed., enl., 1960); *Istoriya russkoy muziki* (History of Russian Music; 3 vols., 1947–54); ed. with M. Druskin, *Ocherki po istoril russkoy muziki 1790–1825* (Essays on the History of Russian Music 1790–1825; Leningrad, 1956); *La musique russen en XIXe siècle* (Neuchâtel, 1958); *Russkaya sovetskaya muzika* (1958); ed. *Voprosi muzikoznaniya* (Questions of Musicology; 1960); *Kritika i zhurnalistika: Sbornik statey* (Criticism and Journalism: Collection of Articles; 1963); *Russkaya muzika XVIII veka* (Russian Music of the XVIII Century; 1965); *100 let Moskovskoy konservatorii* (100 Years of the Moscow Cons.; 1966); *Rakhmaninov i evo vremya* (Rachmaninoff and his Time; 1973).—NS/LK/DM

Kelemen, Milko, significant Croatian composer; b. Podrawska Slatina, March 30, 1924. He was taught to play piano by his grandmother, and in 1945 entered the Zagreb Academy of Music, where he studied theory with Šulek. He then went to Paris, where he took courses with Messiaen and Aubin at the Cons. (1954–55). He supplemented his studies at Freiburg im Breisgau with Fortner (1958–60), then worked on electronic music at the Siemens studio in Munich (1966–68). He taught composition at the Zagreb Cons. (1955–58; 1960–65), the Schumann Cons. in Düsseldorf (1969–73), and the Stuttgart Hochschule für Musik (1973–91). He publ. *Klanglabyrinthe: Reflexionen eines Komponisten über die Neue Musik* (Munich, 1981). As a composer, Kelemen began his career following the trend of European modernism well within academically acceptable lines, but changed his style radically about 1956 in the direction of the cosmopolitan avant-garde, adopting successively or concurrently the techniques of serialism, abstract expressionism, constructivism, and sonorism, making use of electronic sound; he also wrote alternatively valid versions for a single piece.

WORKS: DRAMATIC: *Der Spiegel,* ballet (Paris, Aug. 18, 1960); *Abbandonate,* ballet (Lübeck, Sept. 1, 1964); *Der neue Mieter,* musical scene, after Ionesco (Münster, Sept. 15, 1964); *Der Belagerungszustand,* opera, after Camus (1969–70; Hamburg, Jan. 13, 1970); *Yebell,* action for Soloists and Chamber Ensemble (Munich, Sept. 1, 1972); *Apocalyptica,* multimedia ballet-opera (concert perf., Graz, Oct. 10, 1979). **ORCH.:** *Preludio, Aria e Finale* for Strings (Zagreb, May 20, 1948); Sinfonietta for Chamber Orch. (Zagreb, May 4, 1950); Sym. (Zagreb, Feb. 18, 1952); Piano Concerto (Zagreb, Feb. 22, 1953); Violin Concerto (Zagreb, June 20, 1957); *Koncertantne improvizacije* for Strings (Zagreb, Oct. 10, 1955); *Adagio ed Allegro* for Strings (Zagreb, Feb. 16, 1956); Concerto for Bassoon and Strings (Zagreb, May 13, 1957); *Concerto giocoso* for Chamber Orch. (Zagreb, Jan. 10, 1957); Concertino for Double Bass or Cello and Strings (Zagreb, April 20, 1957); *Skolion* (Cologne, June 12, 1960); *Transfigurationen* for Piano and Orch. (Hamburg, April 6, 1962); *Équilibres* for 2 Orchs. (Bonn, March 19, 1962); *Sub Rosa* (Zagreb, May 12, 1965); *Surprise* for Strings (Zagreb, May 12, 1967); *Composé* for 2 Pianos and Orch. Groups (Donaueschingen, Oct. 23, 1967); *Changeant* for Cello and Orch. (Cologne, Nov. 8, 1968); *Floreal* (Washington, D.C., Oct. 30, 1970); *Olifant* for 5 Winds and 2 Orch. Groups (Royan, April 8, 1971); *Passionato* for Flute and 3 Orch. Groups (Berlin, Oct. 18, 1972); *Abecedarium* for Strings (Graz, Oct. 13, 1974); *Mirabilia* for Piano, Ring Modulator, and 2 Orch. Groups (Paris, April 21, 1975); *Mageia* (Augsburg, June 12, 1978); *Infinity* (Zagreb, May 18, 1979); *Grand Jeu Classique* for Violin and Orch. (Metz, Nov. 21, 1982); *Drammatico* for Cello and Orch. (Stuttgart, March 2, 1985); *Phantasmes* for Viola and Orch. (Stuttgart, Dec. 16, 1985); *Archetypon* (Hannover, Jan. 10, 1986); *Antiphony* for Organ and Orch. (1987). **CHAMBER:** *Musika* for Violin (Zagreb, April 4, 1958); *Études contrapuntiques* for Wind Quintet (Paris, Nov. 14, 1959); *Studie* for Flute (Darmstadt, Sept. 5, 1959); Oboe Sonata (Darmstadt, July 7, 1960); *Radiant* for Chamber Ensemble (Darmstadt, July 16, 1963); *Entrances* for Wind Quintet (Hanover, N.H., June 10, 1966); *Motion* for String Quartet (Madrid, March 4, 1969); *Fabliau I* for Flute (Stockholm, Oct. 20, 1972), *II* for Organ (Düsseldorf, May 10, 1972), and *III* for Flute and Harpsichord (Siena, Aug. 10, 1980); *Varia melodia* for String Quartet (Düsseldorf, Sept. 21, 1972); *Tantana,* improvisations for 10 to 20 Performers (Opatija,

Nov. 12, 1975); *Splintery* for String Quartet (Paris, Dec. 5, 1977); *Rontondo I* for Wind Trio (Cologne, April 27, 1977) and *II* for Harmonica and Wind Trio (Stuttgart, Oct. 3, 1980); *Love Song* for Saxophone Quartet (Stuttgart, Sept. 6, 1985); *Memories* for String Trio (1986; Zagreb, Jan. 30, 1987); *Sonette* for String Quartet (Bomberg, May 22, 1987). **VOCAL:** *Die Spiele,* song cycle for Baritone and Strings (Strasbourg, May 13, 1958); *Epitaph* for Mezzo-soprano, Viola, and Percussion (Darmstadt, Sept. 8, 1961); *Hommage à Heinrich Schütz* for Solo Voices and Chorus (Berlin, May 12, 1965); *O Primavera,* cantata for Tenor and Strings (Zagreb, May 19, 1965); *Die Wörter,* cantata for Mezzo-soprano and Orch. (Lübeck, May 9, 1966); *Musik für Heinssenbüttel* for Mezzo-soprano, Violin, Cello, and Clarinet (Rome, Feb. 24, 1968); *Gasho* for 4 Choral Groups (Tokyo, April 20, 1974); *Die sieben Plagen* for Mezzo- soprano (Vienna, Nov. 19, 1975); *Drei irische Volkslieder* (Cork, Ireland, May 10, 1980); *Landschaftbilder* for Mezzo-soprano and String Quartet (1985; Graz, Oct. 24, 1986).—**NS/LK/DM**

Kelemen, Zoltán, Hungarian bass; b. Budapest, March 12, 1926; d. Zürich, May 9, 1979. He was educated at the Budapest Academy of Music and at the Accademia di Santa Cecilia in Rome. He made his operatic debut in Augsburg (1959). After singing in Wuppertal, he joined the Cologne Opera (1961); also appeared at Bayreuth (from 1962) and Salzburg (from 1966). On Nov. 22, 1968, he made his Metropolitan Opera debut in N.Y. as Alberich in *Das Rheingold,* a role he repeated for his debut performance at London's Covent Garden (1970). Among his best roles were Osmin, Leporello, the Grand Inquisitor, Dulcamara, Falstaff, and Gianni Schicchi.—**NS/LK/DM**

Kéler-Béla (real name, **Adalbert Paul [Albrecht Pál] von Kéler**), noted Hungarian violinist, conductor, and composer; b. Bartfeld, Feb. 13, 1820; d. Wiesbaden, Nov. 20, 1882. He was a law student, and then became a farmer. He finally took up music in 1845, studying under Sechter and Schlesinger in Vienna, and playing the violin at the Theater-an-der-Wien. He went to Berlin to conduct the Gungl Orch. (1854–55) and to Vienna to conduct Janner's orch. (1855–56), then was bandmaster of the 10th Austrian Infantry Regiment (1856–63). From 1863 to 1873 he conducted the Wiesbaden Spa Orch. He wrote numerous dances and other light pieces, some of which attained enormous popularity, including the waltz *Hoffnungssterne,* the galop *Hurrah- Sturm,* and particularly the *Lustspiel Ouverture.*

BIBL.: Z. Sztehlo, *K. B.* (Budapest, 1930).—**NS/LK/DM**

Kell, Reginald (Clifford), noted English clarinetist and pedagogue; b. York, June 8, 1906; d. Frankfort, Ky., Aug. 5, 1981. He studied violin at an early age, but later took up the clarinet, and earned a living by playing in silent-movie houses. He received a scholarship to the Royal Academy of Music in London (1929–32), where he studied with Haydn Draper. From 1931 he played in various London orchs., serving as principal clarinet in the London Phil. (1932–36), the London Sym. Orch. (1936–39), and the Philharmonia Orch. (1945–48); also with the Liverpool Phil. (1942–45). He taught at the Royal Academy of Music (1935–39; 1958–59) and at the Aspen (Colo.) Music School (1951–57).—**NS/LK/DM**

Keller, Gottfried, German harpsichordist, teacher, and composer; b. place and date unknown; d. London, Nov. 1704. He settled in London at the close of the 17th century as a performer and harpsichord teacher, known as Godfrey or Godfrido Keller. He publ. *A Compleat Method for Attaining to Play a Thorough Bass upon either Organ, Harpsichord or Theorbo- lute* (London, 1705; 6th ed., 1717; also publ. as an appendix to the 1731 ed. of W. Holder's *A Treatise of the Natural Grounds, and Principles of Harmony*).

WORKS (all publ. in Amsterdam): *6 Sonates a 5* for 2 Recorders, 2 Oboes or 4 Violins, and Basso Continuo (1698; in collaboration with Finger); *8 sonates a trois instruments* for 2 Recorders or Violins, and Basso Continuo and Recorder or Violin, Oboe, and Basso Continuo (1699; 1 not by Keller); 6 Sonatas: 3 for Trumpet, Oboe or Violin, Bass, and Basso Continuo and 3 for 2 Recorders, Oboes or Violins, Bass, and Basso Continuo (1700); 6 Sonatas for 2 Recorders and Basso Continuo, op. posthumous (1706).—**NS/LK/DM**

Keller, Hans (Heinrich), Austrian-born English writer on music; b. Vienna, March 11, 1919; d. London, Nov. 6, 1985. He received training in violin in Vienna, and then settled in England in 1938 and became a naturalized British subject in 1948. He played in orchs. and string quartets. Keller mastered the English language to an extraordinary degree, and soon began pointing out solecisms and other infractions on the purity of the tongue to native journalists; wrote articles on film music, and boldly invaded the sports columns in British newspapers, flaunting his mastery of the lingo. In 1947 he founded (with D. Mitchell) the periodical *Music Survey* and was its co-ed. (1949–52); joined the music division of the BBC in 1959, retiring in 1979. He originated a system of functional analysis for radio, in which verbal communication was replaced solely by musical examples to demonstrate a composition's structure and thematic development. He publ. several articles expounding the virtues of his ratiocination, among them the fundamental essay "Functional Analysis: Its Pure Application," *Music Review*, XVIII (1957).

WRITINGS (all publ. in London): *Albert Herring* (1947); *Benjamin Britten: The Rape of Lucretia* (1947); *The Need for Competent Film Music Criticism* (1947); ed. with D. Mitchell, *Benjamin Britten: A Commentary on His Works from a Group of Specialists* (1952); *1975 (1984 minus nine)* (1977); *The Great Haydn Quartets: Their Interpretation* (1986); *Criticism* (1987).
—**NS/LK/DM**

Keller, Hermann, German organist and musicologist; b. Stuttgart, Nov. 20, 1885; d. in an automobile accident in Freiburg im Breisgau, Aug. 17, 1967. He studied with Reger (composition), Straube (organ), and Teichmüller (piano), then musicology at the Univ. of Tübingen (Ph.D., 1924, with the diss. *Die musikalische Artikulation insbesondere bei Joh. Seb. Bach*; publ. in Stuttgart, 1925). He held various posts as organist. From 1919 he taught at the Stuttgart Hochschule für Musik, serving as director of its church and school music dept. (from 1928) and then director (1946–52).

WRITINGS: *Reger und die Orgel* (Munich, 1923); *Schule des Klassichen Triospiels* (Kassel, 1928; 4th ed., 1955); *Schule des Generalbass-Spiels* (Kassel, 1931; 4th ed., rev., 1956; Eng. tr., 1965); *Schule der Choralimprovisation* (Leipzig, 1939); *Die Kunst des Orgelspiels* (Leipzig, 1941); *Die Orgelwerke Bachs* (Leipzig, 1948; Eng. tr., 1967); *Die Klavierwerke Bachs* (Leipzig, 1950); *Phrasierung und Artikulation* (Kassel, 1955; Eng. tr., 1965); *Domenico Scarlatti: Ein Meister des Klaviers* (Leipzig, 1957); *Das Wohltemperierte Klavier von Johann Sebastian Bach* (Kassel, 1965).
—**NS/LK/DM**

Keller, Homer, American composer; b. Oxnard, Calif., Feb. 17, 1915. He studied at the Eastman School of Music in Rochester, N.Y., with Hanson and Rogers (B.M., 1937; M.M., 1938), then in Paris, on a Fulbright grant, with Honegger and Boulanger (1950–51). He taught at the Univ. of Mich. (1947–54) and the Univ. of Ore. (1958–77).

WORKS: ORCH.: 3 syms.: No. 1 (N.Y. Nov. 2, 1940), No. 2 (Ann Arbor, Mich., April 1, 1948), and No. 3 (Honolulu, Dec. 9, 1950); Piano Concerto (Ojai, Calif., May 29, 1949); *Sonorities* (Eugene, Ore., Feb. 23, 1971). **OTHER:** Chamber music; vocal works.—**NS/LK/DM**

Kelley, Edgar Stillman, American composer and teacher; b. Sparta, Wisc., April 14, 1857; d. N.Y., Nov. 12, 1944. He studied with F. Merriam (1870–74), then with Clarence Eddy and N. Ledochowsky in Chicago (1874–76). Subsequently he took courses at the Stuttgart Cons. with Seifritz (composition), Krüger and Speidel (piano), and Friedrich Finck (organ). Returning to the U.S., he served as an organist in San Francisco. He taught piano and theory at various schools and at the N.Y. Coll. of Music (1891–92). He was music critic for the *San Francisco Examiner* (1893–95), lecturer on music for the Univ. Extension of N.Y.U. (1896–97), and then acting prof. at Yale Univ. (1901–02). In 1902 he went to Berlin, where he taught piano and theory. From 1910 to 1934 he was dean of the composition dept. of the Cincinnati Cons. He publ. *Chopin the Composer* (N.Y., 1913) and *Musical Instruments* (Boston, 1925). With his wife, Jessie (née Gregg) Stillman Kelley (b. Chippewa Falls, Wisc., 1865; d. Dallas, April 3, 1949), a pianist and teacher, he founded the Kelley Stillman Publishing Co., which brought out several of his scores. Although his stage and symphonic works were quite successful when first performed (some critics described him as a natural successor to MacDowell in American creative work), little of his music survived the test of time.

WORKS: DRAMATIC: *Music to Macbeth*, incidental music for Chorus and Orch. (1882–84; San Francisco, Feb. 12, 1885; rev. as the orch. suite *Gaelic March*); *Pompeiian Picnic*, operetta (1887); *Prometheus Bound*, incidental music (1891); *Puritania*, operetta (Boston, June 9, 1892); *Ben Hur*, incidental music for Solo Voices, Chorus, and Orch. (1899; N.Y., Oct. 1, 1900); *The Pilgrim's Progress*, musical miracle play (1917; Cincinnati May Festival, May 10, 1918). **ORCH.:** *Confluentia* for Strings (1882; arranged from No. 2 of the *3 Pieces* for Piano); *Aladdin: A Chinese Suite* (1887–93; San Francisco, April 1894); 2 syms.: No. 1, *Gulliver: His Voyage to Lilliput* (1900; Cincinnati, April 9, 1937) and No. 2, *New England* (Norfolk, Conn., June 3, 1913, composer conducting); *Alice in Wonderland*, suite (Norfolk, Conn., June 5, 1919, composer conducting); *The Pit and the Pendulum*, suite, after Poe (1925). **CHAMBER:** *Theme and Variations* for String Quartet (c. 1880); Piano Quintet (1898–1901). **Piano:** *3 Pieces*

(1891); *Lyric Opera Sketches* (1894). VOCAL: *A Wedding Ode* for Men's Chorus and Orch. (1882); *Phases of Love*, 6 songs for Soprano and Piano (1888); 2 songs (1901); *O Captain! My Captain!* for Chorus and Orch. (n.d.); *A California Idyll* for Soprano and Orch. (N.Y., Nov. 14, 1918); *America's Creed* for Chorus and Orch. (1919).

BIBL.: M. King, *E.S. K.: American Composer, Teacher, and Author* (diss., Fla. State Univ., 1970).—NS/LK/DM

Kelley, Jessie Stillman, American piano pedagogue; b. Chippewa Falls, Wisc., 1866; d. Dallas, April 3, 1949. She studied piano with William Mason and X. Scharwenka, and theory with **Edgar Stillman Kelley,** whom she later married. She received an L.H.D. from Western Coll. in Oxford, Ohio, and a Litt.D. from Miami Univ. She taught piano in San Francisco, N.Y., and Berlin, and from 1910 to 1934 was director of music at Western Coll.—NS/LK/DM

Kelley, Peck (John Dickson), jazz pianist, leader; b. Houston, 1898; d. Houston, Dec. 26, 1980. He was one of the unrecorded legends of jazz, ranked near Tatum by Jack Teagarden and others, until some private recordings from 1957 were issued after his death. They are quite impressive technically, though not like Tatum. He executes complex figures independently with each hand.

Kelly led own "Bad Boys" in and around Tex. from the early 1920s; many famous jazzmen worked in the band including: Jack Teagarden (1921–23, 1924), Pee Wee Russell (1924), Leon Roppolo (1924), Johnny Wiggs (1927), guitarist Snoozer Quinn (1927), Leon Prima, etc. During the 1920s and 1930s Kelly worked almost entirely in Tex., except for a brief spell in St. Louis (1925), Shreveport (1927), and a trip to New Orleans with Joe Gill's Band (ca. 1934). He steadfastly refused offers to join "name bands" and continued to play long residencies in Houston at Jerry's Inn, Rice Hotel Roof, and Southern Diners' Club. He served a brief spell in the U.S. Army until March 1943, then returned to Houston. Eyesight problems caused temporary retirement (1946–48), then he returned to play long residency at Dixie Bar (Houston), from December 1948. He retired from regular playing in the mid-1950s, and continued to reside in Houston until his death.

DISC.: *P.K. Jam* (1957).—JC/LP

Kellner, David, German organist, lutenist, music theorist, and composer; b. Leipzig, c. 1670; d. Stockholm, April 6, 1748. He settled in Stockholm, where he was active as a church organist and as a lute virtuoso from 1711. He publ. a collection of 17 lute pieces, *XVI* [sic] *Auserlesene Lauter-Stücke* (Hamburg, 1747), and a widely used manual, *Treulicher Unterricht im General-Bass* (Hamburg, 1732).—LK/DM

Kellner, Johann Christoph, German organist and composer, son of **Johann Peter Kellner;** b. Gräfenroda, Thuringia, Aug. 15, 1736; d. Kassel, 1803. He was a student of his father and in Gotha of Georg Benda. He served as court organist in Kassel, where he also was Kantor at the Lutheran Church. Among his works were the Singspiel *Die Schadenfreude* (Kassel, 1782), keyboard concertos, preludes, fugues, etc, chamber music, and cantatas. He also publ. the treatise *Grundriss des Generalbasses,* op.16, part 1 (Kassel, 1783; 7th ed., 1796).—LK/DM

Kellner, Johann Peter, German organist and composer, father of **Johann Christoph Kellner;** b. Gräfenroda, Thuringia, Sept. 28, 1705; d. there, April 19, 1772. He received training from Nagel, the Gräfenroda Kantor (1717–22), and from J. Schmidt in Zella and H.F. Kehl in Suhl (1722–23). Returning to Gräfenroda, he was made assistant to the Kantor in 1728; in 1732 he became Kantor. Among his students were Kirnberger and Rinck. His keyboard music, composed in an effective galant style, included organ preludes and fugues, suites, and variations.—LK/DM

Kellogg, Clara (Louise), noted American soprano and operatic impresario; b. Sumterville, S.C., July 9, 1842; d. New Hartford, Conn., May 13, 1916. She received her vocal training in N.Y. from Manzocchi, Errani, and Muzio, making her professional debut there at the Academy of Music as Gilda in *Rigoletto* (Feb. 27, 1861); then sang in Boston. She sang Marguerite in the N.Y. premiere of *Faust* (Nov. 25, 1863); made her London debut in the same role on Nov. 2, 1867. In 1872 she organized an opera company with Pauline Lucca, but their rivalry precluded its success. In 1873 she launched an opera enterprise of her own, the English Opera Co., for which she herself sang 125 performances (1874–75). In 1887 she married her manager, Karl Strakosch, nephew of Maurice and Max Strakosch, and retired from the stage. She wrote *Memoirs of an American Prima Donna* (N.Y., 1913).—NS/LK/DM

Kelly, Bryan, English composer; b. Oxford, Jan. 30, 1934. He studied with Jacob and Howells at the Royal Coll. of Music in London (1951–55), then with Boulanger in Paris. After teaching at the Royal Scottish Academy of Music in Glasgow, he was prof. of composition at his alma mater (1962–84).

WORKS: ORCH.: *Latin Quarter Overture* (1955); *Music for Ballet* (1957); *The Tempest Suite* for Strings (1964); *Cookham Concertino* (1969); *Oboe Concerto* (1972); *Guitar Concerto* (1978); 2 syms. (1983, 1986). BRASS BAND: *Divertimento* (1969); *Edinburgh Dances* (1973); *Andalucia* (1976); *Concertante Music* (1979). CHAMBER: *3 Pieces* for Violin and Piano (1959); *2 Concert Pieces* for Clarinet and Piano (1964); *Zodiac* for Clarinet and Piano (1978); *Suite parisienne* for Brass Quintet (1979); *Umbrian Variations* for 8 Cellos (1984). KEYBOARD: Piano: Sonata (1971). Organ: *Prelude and Fugue* (1960); *Pastorale and Paean* (1973). VOCAL: *Tenebrae Nocturnes* for Tenor, Chorus, and Orch. (1965); *The Shell of Achilles* for Tenor and Orch. (1966); *Stabat Mater* for Soprano, Bass, Chorus, and Orch. (1970); *At the Round Earth's Imagined Corners* for Tenor, Chorus, and Strings (1972); *Let There be Light* for Soprano, Narrator, Chorus, and Orch. (1972–73); *Latin Magnificat* for Chorus and Winds (1979); *St. Francis of Assisi,* cantata for Soloists, Chorus, and Orch. (1983); *Proud Music of the Storm* for Tenor, Chorus, and Orch. (1983).—NS/LK/DM

Kelly, (Edgar) Guy, early jazz trumpeter, singer; b. Scotlandville, La., Nov. 22, 1906; d. Chicago, Feb. 24, 1940. He played with the "Toots" Johnson Band in Baton Rouge, then toured Tex. before settling in New Orleans. He worked with Papa Celestin in 1927 and 1928 (including a residency in Mobile). In 1929 he began touring with Kid Howard's Band, then left to live in Chicago. Through the 1930s, he played with various leaders in Chicago including Erskine Tate (1931–32; again early 1938), Carroll Dickerson (1934; again 1937–38), and Albert Ammons (1935–36, and again in 1939 until his death).—**JC/LP**

Kelly, John (Joseph), gifted American experimental theater artist; b. Jersey City, N.J., Sept. 21, 1954. His education was varied and included ballet study at the James Waring Studio (1971), the American Ballet Theatre School (1972–74), and the Harkness House for Ballet Arts (1974–76), theater technique and repertoire classes at the Charles Weidman Expression of Two Arts Theatre (1972–74), drawing and printmaking study at the Parsons School of Design (1976–78), vocal training (with Peter Elkus) at the Accademia Musicale Ottorino Respighi in Assisi (1989), trapeze and tight- wire technique at the Pickle Family Circus in San Francisco (1992), and study of the Decroux Corporeal Mime technique at the Theatre d'Ange Fou in Paris. Kelly's career has been equally varied, and he functions, often simultaneously, as author, choreographer, director, and performer in works crossing a variety of genres, including solo and ensemble multi-media dance theater works which incorporate choreography, visual designs, film, and both solo and ensemble vocal work and song. Kelly has performed internationally, his U.S. appearances including three solo vocal recitals in N.Y. as well as in the San Francisco Sym.'s "Mavericks Series" (1998) in a particularly lyrical performance of John Cage's *Aria* with *Fontana Mix*. He was also a featured singer/actor in James Joyce's *The Dead* on Broadway in N.Y., a production that was subsequently mounted in Los Angeles. Other recent projects include a collaboration with David Del Tredici on *Gay Life Song Cycle*, in which he functions as both lyricist and composer. In the 2000–01 season John Kelly & Company, in collaboration with Dance Theatre Workshop, will give the first performance of *Find My Way Home*, a re-telling of the classic Greek myth of *Orpheus and Euridyce* for 10 Singers and Dancers that interpolates sections from Gluck's beloved opera. Particularly popular among audiences is his one-man show, *Joni's Jazz*, in which he emulates the vocal style of and performs works by the enduring American popular singer/songwriter, Joni Mitchell. Among his numerous honors are two Bessie Awards (1986, 1988), two Obie Awards (1987, 1991), the American Choreographer Award (1987), a Guggenheim fellowship (1989), the first Oscar Rubenhausen fellowship (1992), two fellowships from the N.Y. Foundation for the Arts (1991; 1997–98), five consecutive Choreographer fellowships from the NEA (1991–96), and a Rockefeller Foundation Grant (1999). He has also held various residencies, including repeat stays at both the Yaddo (1994, 1998, 2000) and MacDowell (1994, 1997) Colonies. In 1999 he began writing *Chronicles of a Performance Artist: A Comprehensive Visual Autobiography*.—**LK/DM**

Kelly, Michael, Irish tenor and composer; b. Dublin, Dec. 25, 1762; d. Margate, Oct. 9, 1826. He studied with Passerini and Rauzzini, then sang in Dublin. He then continued his studies with Fenarole and Aprile in Naples (1779). He sang in Palermo, Livorno, Florence, Bologna, and Venice. He was a member of the Vienna Court Opera (1783–87); a friend of Mozart, he created the roles of Don Curzio and Don Basilio in *Le nozze di Figaro* (May 1, 1786). In 1787 he appeared for the first time at Drury Lane in London, and sang there until his retirement some 30 years later; also was stage manager at the King's Theatre, Haymarket (1793–1824). He wrote music for 62 stage pieces and many songs. He also had a music shop (1802–11), and then was active in the wine trade. As to the quality of his compositions and wines, Sheridan quipped that he was "a composer of wines and an importer of music." T. Hook prepared his amusing and valuable autobiography and publ. it as *Reminiscences of Michael Kelly, of the King's Theatre, and Theatre Royal, Drury Lane* (London, 1826; ed. by R. Fiske, London, 1975).

BIBL.: S. Ellis, *The Life of M. K., Musician, Actor and Bon Viveur* (London, 1930).—**NS/LK/DM**

Kelly, R(obert), the sexy soul man of the 1990s (b. Chicago, Jan. 8, 1969). In the course of less than ten years, R. Kelly went from busking by the entrance to the "L" train in Chicago to Grammy awards and multi-platinum hits. He has worked with Michael Jackson and Michael Jordan, produced music both salacious and sacred.

Raised in a single parent home in the projects of Chicago's south side, Kelly saw basketball as his only way out. Even after muggers shot him during his early teens, he still pursued that dream—but stayed away from gangs. At the Kenwood Academy, one of his teachers heard him sing and started him on vocal training. Soon he was singing arias and developed a range from alto through baritone. By the time he finished school, he had also written hundreds of songs. With his band MGM, he won the *Big Break* television talent contest.

Out of school, Kelly went out with his piano and started playing by the entrance to the "L" train. Some days he claims he could clear $400. He would also sing at parties and audition for plays. At one of these events, a rep from Jive Records heard him and was floored. Within two years, he had released his debut, with the band Public Announcement, *Born in the '90s*. The singles "Slow Dance" and "Honey Love" topped the R&B chart, the latter scratching into the Top 40. The next song, "Dedicated," rose to #31. The album went platinum.

Kelly debuted without Public Announcement with the 1993 album *12 Play*. With the massive singles "Sex Me (Parts 1 & 2)" (gold and #20 pop), the platinum

"Bump and Grind," which topped the pop charts for four weeks and the R&B charts for 12, and the gold "Your Body Callin'" (#13 pop), Kelly became a major star.

Hoping to tap into this success, he was brought into the studio to work with bands ranging from teen sensation Aaliya, for whom he created two hit singles (and eventually married), to Michael Jackson. His own eponymous effort in 1995 featured the song "You Remind Me of Something." Women were of two minds about the performer. On the one hand, he sang melting romantic songs. On the other were lyrics like "You Remind Me of My Jeep/I Wanna Ride It." However, the song shipped gold, hit the charts at #1 on the R&B chart, #4 pop, and was certified platinum. His duet with Ronald Isley, "Down Low (Nobody Has to Know)," topped the R&B charts and went to #4 pop as well, going platinum. "I Can't Sleep Baby (If I)" rose to #5 and also went platinum. The album debuted at #1 on both the pop and R&B album charts, eventually going quintuple platinum.

However, that wasn't even his biggest triumph. Basketball star Michael Jordan asked Kelly to write a song for the film he had just finished acting in, *Space Jam*. The song topped both the R&B and pop charts, and went platinum. It won him three Grammy awards, Best Male R&B Vocal Performance, Best R&B Song, and Best Song Written Specifically for a Motion Picture or for Television.

His next album, the two-CD package *R* debuted on the chart at #2. It had already enjoyed lots of exposure, as the music video for Celine Dion's duet with Kelly, "I'm Your Angel," became the first to debut on a major television network outside of an entertainment special. The network gave the video its own four minute time slot. The single topped the adult contemporary and pop charts. Kelly described *R* as "50% ballads/30% R&B/20% hip-hop." In addition to Dion, rappers Jay Z, Nas, Noreaga, and Foxy Brown all did guest spots. Like his previous albums, *R* also went quintuple platinum.

DISC.: *Born into the 90's* (1992); *12 Play* (1993); *R. Kelly* (1995); *R* (1998).—**HB**

Kelly, Robert, American composer and teacher; b. Clarksburg, W.Va., Sept. 26, 1916. He studied violin with Gardner at the Juilliard School of Music in N.Y. (1935–36). After further violin training at the Cincinnati Coll. of Music (1937–38), he studied composition with Scalero at the Curtis Inst. of Music in Philadelphia (B.M., 1942) and with Elwell at the Eastman School of Music in Rochester, N.Y. (M.M., 1952). From 1946 to 1976 he taught at the Univ. of Ill. at Urbana. He wrote *The Evolution of an American Composer* (Urbana, Ill., 1998). His music, while experimental in nature, is skillfully written to utilize traditional forms and structures.

WORKS: DRAMATIC: *Paiyatuma*, ballet (1946); *Tod's Gal*, folk opera (1950; Norfolk, Va., Jan. 8, 1971); *The White Gods*, opera (Urbana, Ill., July 3, 1966). **ORCH.:** *Adirondack Suite* (Philadelphia, April 9, 1941); *Rounds* for Strings (1947; Urbana, Ill., Nov. 17, 1957); 3 syms.: No. 1, *A Miniature Symphony* (Austin, Tex., Oct. 15, 1950), No. 2 (1958), and No. 3, *Emancipation Symphony* (Washington, D.C., Feb. 5, 1963); Concerto for

Violin, Cello, and Orch. (Urbana, Ill., March 8, 1961); *An American Diptych* (Austin, Tex., April 26, 1963); *Colloquy* for Chamber Orch. (Chicago, April 17, 1965); Violin Concerto (Urbana, Ill., Oct. 17, 1968); Cello Concerto (1974; Urbana, Ill., March 2, 1975); Viola Concerto (1976; Urbana, Ill., Feb. 5, 1978); Concertino for Chamber Orch. (1977; Ft. Worth, Tex., Oct. 30, 1979); Concerto for Violin, Viola, and Orch. (Urbana, Ill., Feb. 5, 1978); *Garden of Peace: A Meditation* for Strings (1979; Aspen, July 24, 1980); *Tubulations*, concerto for Tuba, Winds, and Percussion (1979); *The Celestial Trumpet*, "trinity" for Trumpet, Symphonic Brass Ensemble, and Percussion (1982). **CHAMBER:** 4 string quartets (1944, 1952, 1963, 1982); Viola Sonata (1950); Violin Sonata (1952); Trombone Sonata (1952); Sonata for Oboe and Harp (1952); Quintet for Clarinet and Strings (1956); Cello Sonata (1958); *Triptych* for Cello and Piano (1962); *Variant* for Violin, Cello, and Piano (1967); *3 Expressions* for Violin and Cello or Viola (1971); *Fantasia* for Harp, Alto Flute, Oboe, and String Quartet (1984). **VOCAL:** *Patterns* for Soprano and Orch. (1953; Urbana, Ill., March 1954); *Walden Pond* for Narrator, Soprano, Chorus, Percussion Ensemble, Flute, and Piano (1975; Urbana, Ill., April 4, 1976); *Rural Songs* for Soprano and Orch. (1980; Urbana, Ill., Nov. 9, 1984); choruses.—**NS/LK/DM**

Kelterborn, Rudolf, prominent Swiss composer and pedagogue; b. Basel, Sept. 3, 1931. He studied at the Basel Academy of Music with Gustav Güldenstein and Walther Geiser (composition) and Alexander Krannhals (conducting). He subsequently took lessons in conducting with Markevitch and in composition with Burkhard in Zürich (1952), Blacher in Salzburg (1953), and Fortner and Bialas at the North-West German Music Academy in Detmold (1955). He taught at the Basel Academy of Music (1955–60) and at the North-West German Music Academy (1960–68); then was on the faculty of the Zürich Cons. and Musikhochschule (1968–75; 1980–83). He was ed.-in-chief of the *Schweizerische Musikzeitung* (1969–75) and director of the music division of the Radio D(eutschen und) R(ätoromanischen) S(schweiz) (1974–80). Kelterborn subsequently was a prof. at the Staatlichen Hochschule für Musik in Karlsruhe (1980–83) and director of the Basel Academy of Music from 1983. Kelterborn appeared as a guest conductor in performances of his own works, and also lectured in the U.S., England, and Japan. He was awarded the composer's prize of the Assn. of Swiss Musicians and the Kunstpreis of the City of Basel in 1984. He publ. *Zum Beispiel Mozart: Ein Beitrag zur musikalischen Analyse* (Basel, 1980; Japanese tr., Tokyo, 1986). In his music, he applies a precisely coordinated serial organization wherein quantitative values of duration form a recurrent series; changes of tempo are also subjected to serialization. Both melody and harmony are derived from a tone row in which the dissonant intervals of the major seventh and minor second are the mainstays.

WORKS: DRAMATIC: O p e r a : *Die Errettung Thebens* (1960–62; Zürich, June 23, 1963); *Kaiser Jovian* (1964–66; Karlsruhe, March 4, 1967); *Ein Engel kommt nach Babylon* (1975–76; Zürich, June 5, 1977); *Der Kirschgarten*, after Chekhov (1979–81; Zürich, Dec. 4, 1984); *Ophelia* (1982–83; Schwetzingen, May 2, 1984); *Die schwarze Spinne*, musical drama (1984); *Julia*, chamber opera (1989–90). **B a l l e t :** *Relations* (1973–74; Bern, Feb. 16, 1975). **ORCH.:** Suite for Brass, Percussion, and Strings (1954); Sonata for 16 Solo Strings (1955); *Mouvements* (1957; Winterthur, May 23, 1959); *Canto appassionato* (1958; Darmstadt,

July 6, 1960); Concertino for Piano, 2 Percussion, and Strings (1958–59; Lausanne, Sept. 3, 1960); *Kammersinfonie I* for Violin, 10 Winds, Percussion, Harp, and Strings (Kassel, Oct. 9, 1960) and *II* for Strings (Zürich, Aug. 21, 1964); *Variationen* for Oboe and Strings (1960; Lisbon, March 2, 1961); *Metamorphosen* (Basel, Nov. 7, 1960); *Lamentationes* for Strings (1961; Stuttgart, April 1, 1962); *Scènes fugitives* for Alto and Sopranino Recorders and Orch. (1961; Braunschweig, Nov. 9, 1962); *Vier Nachtstücke* for Chamber Orch. (Zürich, Dec. 11, 1963); *Musik* for Clarinet and Strings (1965–66; Lucerne, Aug. 28, 1966); *Phantasmen* (1965–66; Hannover, Jan. 28, 1967); *Sonata sacra* for Brass (1965–66; Basel, Jan. 18, 1968); 4 syms.: No. 1 (1966–67; Zürich, Jan. 5, 1968), No. 2 (1969–70; Munich, Oct. 22, 1970), No. 3, *Espansioni*, for Baritone, Orch. and Tape (1974–75; Basel, Sept. 29, 1976), and No. 4 (1985–86; Bamberg, Feb. 3, 1987); *Miroirs* (1966; Detmold, May 3, 1968); *Traummusik* for Small Orch. (1971; Zürich, Jan. 28, 1972); *Kommunikationen* for 6 Orch. Groups (1971–72; Lucerne, Aug. 15, 1973); *Changements* (1972–73; Montreux, Sept. 19, 1973); *Nuovi canti* for Flute and Chamber Orch. (1973; Munich, April 24, 1974); *Tableaux encadrés* for 13 Solo Strings (1974; Zürich, June 15, 1975); *Szene* for 12 Solo Cellos (1977; Lucerne, Aug. 30, 1980); *Erinnerungen an Orpheus* (1977–78; Bern, Jan. 18, 1979); *Visions sonorés* (1979; Basel, June 4, 1980); *Chiaroscuro: Canzoni* (1979–80; Salzburg, Aug. 29, 1980); *Musica luminosa* (1983–84; Locarno, Sept. 13, 1985); *Sonatas* for Winds (1986; Zürich, Feb. 24, 1987); *Musik* for Double Bass and Orch. (1986–87); *Rencontres* for Piano and Orch. (1991–92; Duisburg, Nov. 25, 1992); *Namelos*, 7 pieces for Large Ensemble and Electronic Sound (1996); *4 Movements* for Classical Orch. (1997); *Passions* for Strings (1998). **CHAMBER:** 5 string quartets: No. 1 (1954), No. 2 (1956; Munich, Oct. 27, 1959), No. 3 (1962; Hannover, Oct. 23, 1963), No. 4 (1968–70; Zagreb, May 12, 1971), and No. 5 (Basel, Oct. 25, 1989); *Kammermusik* for Flute, Violin, and Piano (1957), *Fünf Fantasien* for Transverse Flute, Cello, and Harpsichord (1958); *Sieben Bagatellen* for Wind Quintet (1958); *Lyrische Kammermusik* for Clarinet, Violin, and Viola (1959); *Varianti* for 6 Instruments (1959); Sonata for Oboe and Harpsichord (1960); *Esquisses* for Harpsichord and Percussion (1962); *Meditationen* for 6 Winds (1963); *Musik* for Violin and Guitar (1964); *Vier Miniaturen* for Oboe and Violin (1964); *Fantasia à tre* for Piano Trio (1967); *Moments musicaux* for Bassoon and Piano (1967); *Incontri brevi* for Flute and Clarinet (1967); Octet for Clarinet, Horn, Bassoon, 2 Violins, Viola, Cello, and Double Bass (1969; Zürich, Jan. 29, 1970); *Vier Stücke* for Clarinet and Piano (1969); *Inventionen und Intermezzi* for 2 Gambens and Harpsichord (1969); *Neuen Momente* for Viola and Piano (1973); *Reaktionen* for Violin and Piano (1973–74); *Kammermusik* for Flute or Piccolo, Oboe, Clarinet, Horn, and Bassoon (1974); *Consort-Music* for Flute or Piccolo or Alto Flute, Clarinet or Bass Clarinet, Trumpet, and String Quartet (1975; Hamburg, June 15, 1976); *7 Minute Play* for Flute and Piano (1976); *Monodie I* for Flute and Harp (1977); Trio for Flute, Oboe, and Bassoon (1980); *Notturni* for Cello and Double Bass (1981); *Musik* for 6 Percussionists (1983–84); *6 Short Pieces* for Flute, Viola, and Guitar (1984); Cello Sonata (1985); *Escursioni* for Flute, Cello, and Harpsichord (1988–89); String Trio (1995–96); *Ensemble-Buch III* for 10 Instruments (1997). **VOCAL:** *Elegie* for Alto, Oboe, Viola, Percussion, and Harpsichord (1955); *Missa* for Soprano, Tenor, Chorus, and Orch. (1958; Basel, Dec. 1, 1961); *Canta profana* for Baritone, Chorus, and 13 Instruments (1959–60); *Die Flut* for Speaker, Soprano, Alto, Tenor, Baritone, Chorus, and Orch. (1963–64; Basel, May 14, 1965); *Kana/Auferstehung* for Baritone, 2 Violins, and Organ (1964); *Der Traum meines Lebens verdämmert* for Mezzo-soprano, Flute, 2 Clarinets or Bass Clarinet, Harp, and String Quartet (1964); *Tres cantiones sacrae* for Chorus (1967; Kassel, April 12, 1969); *Fünf Madrigale* for Soprano, Tenor, and Orch. (1967–68; Lucerne, Aug. 20, 1969); *Dies unus* for Soprano, Men's Chorus, and Orch. (1971–72; Zürich, May 26, 1973); *Drei Fragmente* for Chorus (1973; Stuttgart, Feb. 10, 1974); *Gesänge zur Nacht* for Soprano and Chamber Orch. (1978; Zürich, March 2, 1979); *Fünf Gesänge* for Chorus, Clarinet, Horn, Trumpet, and Trombone (1980–81; Basel, Feb. 5, 1982); *Schlag an mit deiner Sichel* for 4 Voices and Renaissance Instruments (1981–82); *Lux et tenebrae* for Soprano, Baritone, Men's Chorus, and Orch. (1986–87); *Gesänge der Liebe* for Baritone and Orch. (1987–88); *Ensemble-Buch I* for Baritone and Chamber Ensemble (1990) and *II* for Mezzo-Soprano and Chamber Ensemble (1992–94).

BIBL.: D. Larese and F. Goebels, *R. K.* (Amriswiler, 1970); M. Weber, *Die Orchesterwerke R. K.s* (Regensburg, 1980); A. Briner, T. Gartmann, and F. Meyer, eds., *R. K.: Komponist, Musikdenker, Vermittler* (Bern, 1993).—**NS/LK/DM**

Kemble, Adelaide, English soprano; b. London, 1814; d. Warsash House, Hampshire, Aug. 4, 1879. She made her debut at a Concert of Ancient Music in London on May 13, 1835. After studies in Paris and Germany, she completed her vocal training with Pasta at Lake Como (1839). In 1839 she sang Norma in Venice, and then appeared in Trieste, Milan, Padua, Bologna, and Mantua with notable success in 1840. In 1841 she returned to London and sang in the English language productions of *Norma, Le nozze di Figaro, La sonnambula,* and *Semiramide* at Covent Garden. In 1843 she retired following her marriage. Her sister, the actress Fanny Kemble, recounted her life in *Record of a Girlhood* (London, 1878).—**NS/LK/DM**

Kemp, Barbara, German soprano; b. Kochem an der Mosel, Dec. 12, 1881; d. Berlin, April 17, 1959. She studied at the Strasbourg Cons. (1902–05). In 1903 she made her operatic debut as the Priestess in *Aida* in Strasbourg. She then sang in Rostock (1906–08) and Breslau (1908–13) before being engaged as a member of the Berlin Royal (later State) Opera (1913–31); made her first appearance at the Bayreuth Festival as Senta (1914), and returned there as Kundry (1924–27). She made her Metropolitan Opera debut in N.Y. as Mona Fiordalisa and the Wife in Max von Schilling's *Mona Lisa* (March 1, 1923), and married the composer that same year; sang there until 1924, and then continued her career in Europe. She later taught voice in Berlin.

BIBL.: O. Bie, *B. K.* (Berlin, 1921).—**NS/LK/DM**

Kemp, "Father" (Robert J.), American showman; b. Wellfleet, Mass., June 6, 1820; d. Boston, May 14, 1897. He was a shoe merchant but loved music. As a leading proponent of the old-folks concerts revival (an attempt to restore the music and performance practices of the 18th-century New England singing schools), he organized the Old Folks Concert Troupe in Boston (1855), which gave regular concerts in N.Y., Philadelphia, and Washington, D.C., as well as in Boston (until 1866); also took it on a tour of the West (1858–59) and of England (1861). He publ. a collection of New England psalmody, with some popular songs and patriotic numbers, as *Father Kemp's Old Folks' Concert Tunes* (Boston, 1860). He also wrote *Father Kemp and His Old Folks* (1868).—**NS/LK/DM**

Kemp, Hal (actually, **James Harold**), jazz-pop clarinetist, alto saxophonist, leader; b. Marion, Ala., March 27, 1905; d. Dec 21, 1940. He began playing piano, originally taught by his sister. During his early teens, he played in a movie theatre in Marion, then moved with his family to Charlotte, N.C. (1917). He played clarinet, led his own band (the Merry Makers) while at Alexander Graham H.S. He took up alto sax while studying at the Univ. of N.C., joined and eventually led the Carolina Club Orch,, composed of students from the university. He traveled with this band to London during the summer of 1924 for a residency at the Piccadilly Hotel. He returned to univ., during 1925, led another band, Hal Kemp and the Boys from the Hill, and returned again to univ. to graduate in the summer of 1926. The following year he launched his professional career, appearing at the N.Y. Strand Hoof in January 1927. He toured several states, had a long residency in Miami before visiting Europe from May until August 1930. During these early years Hal Kemp's Band also made many records using the name the Carolina Club Orch. Throughout the 1930s Kemp continued to lead his own commercially successful big band until his untimely death; he died of pneumonia after being very seriously injured in a car crash.

Kemp was among the most popular and commercially successful bandleaders of the 1930s, scoring a huge number of dance hits. Kemp's band was famous for a sentimental, "sweet" but substantial style; his arranger John Trotter did some innovative things for the era with instrumentation and contrast of brass and horn section parts. Lead vocalist Bob Allen was also an audience favorite on ballads. After Trotter left to join Bing Crosby, Art Mooney became the arranger, and the band continued to sparkle. They were boosted by assistance from a vocal trio called the Smoothies, and from appearances on radio and in film. Their last hit was a novelty-song version of "I'm Looking Over a Four Leaf Clover."

DISC.: *Got a Date with an Angel* (1992).—**JC/LP**

Kemp, Joseph, English organist, teacher, and composer; b. Exeter, 1778; d. London, May 22, 1824. He studied organ with William Jackson at Exeter Cathedral, and was organist of Bristol Cathedral (1802–07). He then taught in London, and later in Exeter (1814–18; from 1821). As one of the earliest promoters of music instruction by classes, he publ. *The New System of Musical Education, Being a Self-instructor and Serviceable Companion to Music Masters* (London, c. 1810–19). He composed *The Jubilee,* an entertainment (Haymarket, London, Oct. 25, 1809), *The Siege of Isca, or The Battles of the West,* a melodrama (London, May 10, 1810), *Musical Illustrations of The Lady of the Lake* (c. 1810), *Musical Illustrations of the Beauties of Shakespeare* (c. 1820), Psalms, anthems, songs, etc.—**NS/LK/DM**

Kempe, Rudolf, eminent German conductor; b. Niederpoyritz, near Dresden, June 14, 1910; d. Zürich, May 11, 1976. He studied oboe at the Orchestral School of the Dresden Staatskapelle. In 1929 he became 1st oboist of the Gewandhaus Orch. in Leipzig. He made his conducting debut at the Leipzig Opera in 1936. He served in the German army during World War II, then conducted in Chemnitz. He was director of the Opera there (1945–48) and at the Weimar National Theater (1948–49). From 1949 to 1953 he was Generalmusik-direktor of the Dresden Staatskapelle, and then served in an identical capacity with the Bavarian State Opera in Munich (1952–54). He also made appearances in opera in Vienna, in London (Covent Garden), and at the Metropolitan in N.Y. In 1960 Sir Thomas Beecham named him assoc. conductor of the Royal Phil. of London. Upon Beecham's death in 1961, he became its principal conductor, and from 1963 to 1975 he was artistic director as well. He was chief conductor of the Tonhalle Orch. in Zürich (1965–72) and of the Munich Phil. (from 1967); from 1975 he conducted the BBC Sym. Orch. in London. Kempe was a distinguished interpreter of Beethoven, Brahms, Wagner, Bruckner, and Richard Strauss; also conducted lighter scores with equal aplomb.

BIBL.: C. Kempe-Oettinger, *R. K.: Pictures of a Life* (Munich, 1977; Eng. tr., London, 1979).—**NS/LK/DM**

Kempen, Paul van, prominent Dutch-born German conductor; b. Zoeterwoude, near Leiden, May 16, 1893; d. Hilversum, Dec. 8, 1955. He studied violin in Amsterdam, then was a violinist in the Concertgebouw Orch. there (1913–15). In 1916 he went to Germany and served as concertmaster with several orchs. before embarking upon a conducting career, becoming music director in Oberhausen in 1932. He also became a naturalized German citizen. From 1934 to 1942 he was chief conductor of the Dresden Phil.; although he was obliged to conduct concerts for the German army, he refused to join the Nazi party. After serving as Generalmusikdirektor in Aachen (1942–43), he returned to the Netherlands. Following World War II, he made guest conducting appearances with the Rotterdam Phil. and the Residentie Orch. in The Hague; was chief conductor of the Radio Phil. in Hilversum (from 1949) and also taught conducting there and at the Accademia Chigiana in Siena. He proved himself a discriminating interpreter of the Austro-German repertoire.—**NS/LK/DM**

Kempers, Karel Philippus Bernet
See **Bernet Kempers, Karel Philippus**

Kempff, Wilhelm (Walter Friedrich), distinguished German pianist, pedagogue, and composer; b. Juterbog, Nov. 25, 1895; d. Positano, Italy, May 23, 1991. He studied piano with his father, also named Wilhelm Kempff; at the age of 9, he entered the Berlin Hochschule für Musik, where he studied composition with Robert Kahn and piano with Heinrich Barth; also attended the Univ. of Berlin. He began his concert career in 1916; in 1918 he made the first of many appearances with the Berlin Phil.; from that time he toured throughout Europe, South America, and Japan, featuring improvisation as part of his programs. From 1924 to 1929 he was director of the Stuttgart Hochschule für Musik; from 1957 he gave annual courses in Positano, Italy. He made his London debut in 1951 and his American debut in N.Y. in 1964. He continued to appear in concerts well past his octogenarian milestone; in 1979 he was a soloist with the Berlin Phil., after having had an association with it for more than 60 years. Kempff epitomized the classic tradition of German pianism; he eschewed flamboyance in his performances of Mozart, Beethoven, Schubert, and other masters. He publ. a book of memoirs, *Unter dem Zimbelstern* (Stuttgart, 1951).

WORKS: DRAMATIC: O p e r a : *König Midas* (Königsberg, 1930); *Familie Gozzi* (Stettin, 1934); *Die Fasnacht von Rottweil* (Hannover, 1937). **ORCH.:** 2 piano concertos (1915, 1931); 2 syms. (1923, 1926); Violin Concerto (1932); *Arkadische Suite* for Chamber Orch. (1939); *Epitaph* for Strings (1946); *Legende* for Piano and Orch. (1947). **CHAMBER:** 2 string quartets (1942); piano pieces. **OTHER:** *Von der Geburt des Herrn*, scenic mystery (1925); *Te Deum* (1926).

BIBL.: B. Gavoty and R. Hauert, *K.* (Monaco and Geneva, 1954).—**NS/LK/DM**

Kendrick, Rodney, jazz pianist, composer; b. Philadelphia, April 30, 1960. He is a hard swinging player and composer with a delightful Monkish wit and drive; he also notes the influence of Sun Ra and Randy Weston in his playing. He grew up in Miami with two sisters. Both sides of his family were musical, and also played or sang in church. His father, Jimmy Kay, played piano and accordion in church, as well as being keyboardist for Illinois Jacquet for seven years, and working with Sonny Stitt, Lou Donaldson, and Sam Rivers. Kendrick first played drums, then switched to piano. By the time he was out of high school he was working as a full-time professional, touring with James Brown, George Clinton, R&B harmony group Harold Melvin & the Blue Notes. When he turned 21, he moved to N.Y. to study with Barry Harris for a year. He served as sideman with such leaders as George Benson, Freddie Hubbard, Clark Terry, Frank Morgan, Terence Blanchard, J.J. Johnson, and Stanley Turrentine. A mutual friend brought him to Abbey Lincoln, with whom he worked for four years from 1993–97. At the same time, he formed his own trio and recorded beginning in 1993.

DISC.: *Dance, World, Dance* (1993); *Secrets of Rodney Kendrick* (1993); *Last Chance for Common Sense* (1996); *We Don't Die, We Multiply* (1997). Abbey Lincoln: *Who Used to Dance* (1996).—**LP**

Keneman, Feodor, Russian pianist and composer of German descent; b. Moscow, April 20, 1873; d. there, March 29, 1937. He studied with Safonov (piano; graduated, 1895) and Ippolitov-Ivanov (composition; graduated, 1897) at the Moscow Cons., and also with Taneyev (counterpoint) there. From 1899 to 1932 he taught theory at the Moscow Cons. He gave recitals and was the favorite accompanist of Chaliapin, for whom he composed the popular Russian ballad *As the King Went to War* and arranged the folk song *Ei ukhnem!* He toured the U.S. with Chaliapin (1923–24). He also composed military marches and band pieces.—**NS/LK/DM**

Kenessey, Jenö, Hungarian conductor and composer; b. Budapest, Sept. 23, 1905; d. there, Aug. 19, 1976. He studied with Lajtha (composition) and Sugár

(organ) at the Budapest Cons., Siklós (composition) at the Budapest Academy of Music, and Shalk (conducting) in Salzburg. He was a conductor at the Budapest Opera (1932–65), where he conducted his opera *Arany meg az asszony* (Gold and the Woman; 1942; May 8, 1943) and his ballet *May Festival* (Nov. 29, 1948). His other works included the ballets *Montmartre* (1930), *Johnny in Boots* (1935), *Mine Is the Bridegroom* (1938), *Perhaps Tomorrow* (1938), *Miraggio* (1938), *The Kerchief* (1951), and *Bihari's Song* (1954), *Dance Impressions* for Orch. (1933), *Divertimento* for Soprano and Orch. (1945), *Dances from Sarköz* for Orch. (1953), *Beams of Light*, cantata (1960), *Canzonetta* for Flute and Chamber Orch. (1970), *Dawn at Balaton*, symphonic poem, with Narrator and Women's Voices (1972), Piano Quartet (1928–29), Sonata for Flute and Harp (1940), 2 harp trios (1940, 1972), Sonata for Flute, Viola, and Piano (1940), *Divertimento* for Viola and Harp (1963), *Elegy and Scherzo* for Piano (1973), and songs and choruses.—**NS/LK/DM**

Kenins, Talivaldis, distinguished Latvian-born Canadian composer, teacher, pianist, organist, and choirmaster; b. Liepāja, April 23, 1919. He took up piano at 5 and composition at 8. While preparing for a diplomatic career at the Lycée Champollion (B.Litt., 1939) in Grenoble, he continued to pursue training in piano. He then was a student of piano and composition of Wihtol at the Latvian State Cons. in Riga (1940–44). With the Soviet occupation of his homeland, he went to Paris and studied at the Cons. (1945–51) with Plé-Caussade (counterpoint and fugue), Messiaen (analysis and aesthetics), and Aubin (composition; premier prix, 1950). In 1951 he emigrated to Canada and in 1956 became a naturalized Canadian citizen. He was organist and choirmaster at Toronto's St. Andrew's Lutheran Church from 1951, serving as founder-conductor of its noted St. Andrew's Latvian Choir (1951–58). From 1952 to 1984 he taught at the Univ. of Toronto. In 1973–74 he served as president of the Canadian League of Composers. In 1989 he was named an honorary prof. of the Latvian Academy of Music and in 1990 his life was the subject of a Latvian film documentary. In 1994 his 75th birthday was celebrated in Latvia by concerts of his music, where his music had been virtually forbidden during the 50-year Soviet occupation. Ottawa honored him with the naming of a street, only the 2nd living Canadian to receive such a distinction. In 1995 he was named an Officer of the National Three-Star Order of the Republic of Latvia. With G. Ridout, he ed. the vol. *Celebration* (Toronto, 1984). His French training proved crucial in his compositional development. While his music retains its adherence to formal design, he has effectively applied the resources of the cosmopolitan contemporary school to his extensive output.

WORKS: ORCH.: Piano Concerto (1946); Duo for Piano and Orch. (1951); *Scherzo Concertante* (1953); 8 syms.: No. 1 (1959), No. 2, *Sinfonia Concertante* (1967), No. 3 (1970), No. 4 (1972), No. 5 (1975), No. 6, *Sinfonia ad Fugam* (1978), No. 7 (1980), and No. 8, *Sinfonia Concertata*, for Organ and Orch. (1986); *Folk Dance and Fugue No. 1* (1964) and *No. 2* (1986); Concerto for Violin, Cello, and Strings (1964); *Nocturne and Dance* for Strings (1969); *Fantaisies Concertantes* for Piano and Orch. (1971); Violin Concerto (1974); *Naačnaača*, symphonic poem (1975); Sinfonietta (1976); *Beatae voces tenebrae* (1977); *Concerto da Camera No. 1* for Piano, Flute, Clarinet, and Strings (1981) and *No. 2* for Flute and Ensemble (1983); Concerto for 14 Instruments (1982); *Partita for Strings on Lutheran Chorales* (1983); Concerto for 5 Percussionists and Orch. (1983); *Aria per corde* for Strings (1984); Concerto for Flute, Guitar, Strings, and Percussion (1985); *Canzona- Sonate* for Viola and String Orch. (1986); Double Concerto for Violin, Piano, and Orch. (1987); Concerto for Piano, Strings, and Percussion (1990); *Honour and Freedom* (1991); Viola Concerto (1998). **CHAMBER:** String Quartet (1948); Septet for Clarinet, Horn, Bassoon, Violin, Viola, Cello, and Double Bass (1949); Cello Sonata (1950); Trio for Violin, Cello, and Piano (1952); Suite Concertante for Cello and Piano (1955); 2 violin sonatas (1955, 1979); 2 quartets for Piano and Strings (1958, 1979); *Diversions for Cello and Piano on a Gipsy Song* (1958); *Divertimento* for Clarinet and Piano (1960); Concertante for Flute and Piano (1966); *Fantasy-Variations* for Flute and Viola (1967); *Concertino a Cinque* for Flute, Oboe, Viola, Cello, and Piano (1968); *Serenade* for Oboe and Cello (1973); Sextet for Bassoon and Strings (1978); *Chaconne on a Latvian Folk Theme* for Violin (1978); Sonata for Solo Cello (1982); Quintet for Piano and Winds (1984); *Variations on a Theme by Schubert* for Woodwind Quintet (1984); *Adagio and Fugue* for Viola, Cello, and Organ (1985); *Concertino Barocco* for 2 Violins (1985); *Suite en Concert* for 2 Guitars and String Quartet (1987); Trio for Violin, Viola, and Cello (1989); *Die Zauberklarinette* for Clarinet (1991); Nonet, *L'Ultima Sinfonia*, for Oboe, Clarinet, Horn, String Quintet, and Piano (1993); Quintet for Piano and Strings (1994); Viola Sonata (1996); *Forgotten Pages*, trio for Clarinet, Cello, and Piano (1997); *Prelude, Chorale, and Fugue*, trio for Horn, Violin, and Piano (1999). **KEYBOARD: P i a n o :** Concertino for 2 Pianos (1956); 3 sonatas (1961–85); Sonata for 2 Pianos (1988); *Schumann Paraphrases and Fugue* (1995). **O r g a n :** Suite (1967); *Sinfonia Notturna* (1978); *Introduction, Pastorale, and Toccata* (1983); *Scherzo-Fantasy* (1989); *Ex Mari* (1992). **VOCAL:** *To a Soldier*, cantata for Soloists, Chorus, and Organ (1953); *Bonhomme, bonhomme* for Chorus (1964); *The Carrion Crow* for Men's Voices (1967); *Land of the Silver Birch* for Men's Voices (1967); *The Maiden's Lament* for Men's Voices (1967); *Chants of Glory and Mercy (Gloria)* for Soloists, Chorus, and Orch. (1970); *Cantata Baltica* for Chorus, 2 Trumpets, Timpani, and Organ (1974); *Songs to the Almighty* for Mezzo- soprano and Orch. (1986); *Cantata of Chorales on Themes by J.S. Bach* for Soprano, Chorus, Horn, Trumpet, and Organ (1992); *Agnus Dei* for Mezzo-soprano and String Orch. (1996); numerous other works, including original or folk songs on Latvian texts.

BIBL.: I. Zemzare, *T. K.: Starp Divām Pasaulēm* (T. K.: Between Two Worlds; Riga, 1994; with summaries in Eng. and Fr.).—**NS/LK/DM**

Kennan, Kent Wheeler, American composer and teacher; b. Milwaukee, April 18, 1913. He studied composition with Hunter Johnson at the Univ. of Mich. (1930–32), and then with Hanson and Rogers at the Eastman School of Music in Rochester, N.Y. (M.B., 1934; M.M., 1936). He won the American Prix de Rome, and took some lessons with Pizzetti in Rome. Returning to the U.S., he taught at Kent State Univ. (1939–40) and at the Univ. of Tex. in Austin (1940–42). During World War II, served as bandleader in the U.S. Army (1942–45), then taught again at the Univ. of Tex. (1945–46) and at Ohio State Univ. (1947–49). In 1949 he joined the staff of the Univ. of Tex. on a permanent basis, retiring in 1983. He publ. *The Technique of Orchestration* (N.Y., 1952; 5th

ed., rev., 1997 with D. Grantham); *Counterpoint Based on 18th-Century Practice* (N.Y., 1959; 4th ed., 1999); 2 workbooks on orchestration (1952, 1969); a counterpoint workbook (1959; 3rd ed., 1987).

WORKS: O R C H .: *Night Soliloquy* for Flute and Orch. (1936); *Il campo dei fiori* for Trumpet and Orch. (1937); *Nocturne* for Viola and Orch. (1937); *Dance Divertimento* (1938; also for 2 Pianos); *Promenade* (1938); Sym. (1938); *Andante* for Oboe and Orch. (1939); Piano Concertino (1946; also for Piano and Winds, 1963). **CHAMBER:** *Sea Sonata* for Violin and Piano (1939); *Scherzo, Aria, and Fugue* for Oboe and Piano (1948); Trumpet Sonata (1956). **P i a n o :** 3 *Preludes* (1939); Sonatina (1945); 2 *Preludes* (1951). **VOCAL:** *Blessed Are They That Mourn* for Chorus and Orch. (1939); *The Unknown Warrior Speaks* for Men's Chorus (1944); songs.—**NS/LK/DM**

Kennedy, (George) Michael (Sinclair), esteemed English music critic and writer on music; b. Manchester, Feb. 19, 1926. He was educated at the Berkhamsted School. In 1941 he joined the staff of the London *Daily Telegraph*, where he was its northern music critic (from 1950), northern ed. (1960–86), and joint chief music critic (1986–89). From 1989 he was music critic of the *Sunday Telegraph*. In 1981 he was made an Officer of the Order of the British Empire. In 1997 he became a Commander of the Order of the British Empire. In addition to his perceptive music criticism, he has published a number of valuable biographies and reference works.

WRITINGS: *The Hallé Tradition: A Century of Music* (Manchester, 1960); *The Works of Ralph Vaughan Williams* (London, 1964; rev. 1980; 2nd ed., 1996, as *A Catalogue of the Works of Ralph Vaughan Williams*); *Portrait of Elgar* (London, 1968; rev. 1982; 3rd ed., 1987); *Elgar: Orchestral Music* (London, 1969) *Portrait of Manchester* (Manchester, 1970); *A History of the Royal Manchester Coll. of Music* (Manchester, 1971); *Barbirolli: Conductor Laureate* (London, 1971); *Mahler* (London, 1974; rev. 1990); ed. *The Autobiography of Charles Hallé, with Correspondence and Diaries* (London, 1976); *Richard Strauss* (London, 1976; rev. 1983; rev. and aug., 1995); ed. *The Concise Oxford Dictionary of Music* (Oxford, 3rd ed., 1980; rev. 1995); *Britten* (London, 1981; rev. 1993); *The Hallé 1858–1983* (Manchester, 1983); *Strauss: Tone Poems* (London, 1984); *The Oxford Dictionary of Music* (Oxford, 1985; 2nd ed., rev., 1994); *Portrait of Walton* (London, 1989); *Music Enriches All: 21 Years of the Royal Northern Coll. of Music, Manchester* (Manchester, 1994); *Richard Strauss: Man, Musician, Enigma* (Cambridge, 1999).—**NS/LK/DM**

Kennedy, John, American composer, timpanist, and conductor; b. Albert Lea, Minn., April 7, 1959. After completing his formal education at the Oberlin (Ohio) Coll. Cons. of Music (B.M., 1982) and Northwestern Univ. (M.M., 1984), Kennedy's career has been almost equally divided between and among artistic direction, conducting, performing, and composition. From 1987 he was co-artistic director of N.Y.'s Essential Music, leading the acclaimed new music ensemble in over 80 world and 50 N.Y. premieres in nearly 100 concerts. From 1990 he served as artistic director at the Spoleto Festival USA, from 1990 to 1996 as artistic director of Twentieth Century Perspectives, and from 1997 as artistic director of "Music in Time," a significant concert series devoted to contemporary music. He has also made guest appearances as a percussionist with a variety of ensembles, including the St. Paul Chamber Orch. (1984–85), the Orch. of St. Luke's (1985–98), and the Sarasota Opera Orch. (1991–94; 1995–99). Appearances in commercial productions include the Broadway shows *Anything Goes* (1987–89), *Gypsy* (1990), and *Phantom of the Opera* (1991), as well as concert work with Natalie Cole, Judy Collins, Roberta Flack, James Taylor, Paul Winter, and others. Kennedy is the composer of over 30 works, ranging from solo instrumental, chamber, and chamber orch. pieces to opera and vocal scores; he has also composed music for the feature film *Bury the Evidence* (1998), as well as works for dance, theater, and the Internet and other new media formats.

WORKS: DRAMATIC: Music Drama: *Guadalupe* for Soloists, Women's Chorus, and Chamber Ensemble (2000). **CHAMBER:** *Chunt* for 3 Percussion (1988); *Collective Sentiments I* for Any Number of Strings, Winds, and Pitched Percussion (1988) and *II* for Piano, Drum, and Multiple Pitched Instruments (1991); *Grain* for Shakuhachi and 3 Percussion (1988); *Sacred Spaces* for 3 Percussion (1989); *Splendid Noises* for 3 or More Percussion with Text Recitation (1992); *The Big Hurt* for 4 Percussion (1995); *Nostalgic Patterns* for Piano, Drum, and Multiple Pitched Instruments (1995); *Exigencies of Inner Rhythm* for 4 Percussion (1997); *Full Measures of Devotion* for Piano, Marimbula, Steel Drum, Gamelan, and Percussion (1997); *The Winged Energy of Delight* for Toy Piano and Toy Percussion (1997); *Both* for Viola (1998); *Bury the Evidence*, soundtrack for Percussion and Computer- generated Sounds (1998); *Eagle Rounding Out* for Cello (1998); *The Current* for String Quartet (1998); *Five* for Flute, Cello, Piano, and 2 Percussion (1999); *King* for Horn (2000); *Transitional Songs*, quintet for Flute, Cello, Piano, and 2 Percussion (2000). **Piano:** *The Force of Its Spirit For Henry Cowell* (1997). **VOCAL:** *Summum Bonum* for Soprano and String Quartet, after Robert Browning (1994); *Sounds Heard* for Text Recitation, 4 Percussion, and Computer- generated Sounds (1995); *The Power Within* for Baritone, String Orch., and Percussion (1997); *All is Safe* for Mezzo-soprano and Piano, after Kenneth Patchen (1998); *Eagle Poem* for Mezzo-soprano and Piano, after Joy Harjo (1998); *On the Beach at Night Alone* for Mezzo-soprano and Piano, after Walt Whitman (1998); *One Body* for Baritone/Countertenor, String Quartet, and 2 Percussion, after Joy Harjo, John Kennedy, Kenneth Patchen, Gary Snyder, and Walt Whitman (1998); *Prayer for the Great Family* for Mezzo-soprano and Piano, after Gary Snyder (1998); *Someday* for Chorus (2000). **OTHER:** *Fanfare for the Common Gun* for Handguns (1994); *Animals in Distress* for 4 Players performing Animal Distress Calls (1995); *Hurrying Human Tides* for Digital Sounds (1999).—**LK/DM**

Kennedy, Nigel (Paul), versatile English violinist; b. Brighton, Dec. 28, 1956. He was born into a family of cellists; at 7, he won a piano scholarship to the Yehudi Menuhin School, but soon became a prize violin student there. In 1972 he became a student of Dorothy DeLay at the Juilliard School in N.Y. In 1977 he made his London debut as soloist with the Philharmonia Orch., and subsequently performed throughout his homeland and on the Continent; in 1985 he made his first tour of the U.S. His interests range over the field of serious, jazz, rock, and pop music. He has been closely associated with jazz notable Stephane Grappelli and has led his own rock group.—**NS/LK/DM**

Kennedy-Fraser, Marjorie (née Kennedy), Scottish singer, pianist, and folk-song collector, daughter of **David Kennedy;** b. Perth, Oct. 1, 1857; d. Edinburgh, Nov. 22, 1930. From the age of 12 she traveled with her father as his accompanist. She then studied voice with Mathilde Marchesi in Milan and Paris, and also took courses in piano with Matthay and in music history with Niecks. Inspired by the example of her father, she became a dedicated collector of folk songs. In 1905 she went to the Outer Hebrides, after which she made a specialty of research in Celtic music. She publ. the eds. *Songs of the Hebrides* (with K. Macleod; 3 vols., London, 1909, 1917, 1921), *From the Hebrides* (Glasgow and London, 1925), and *More Songs of the Hebrides* (London and N.Y., 1929), as well as the handbook *Hebridean Song and the Laws of Interpretation* (Glasgow, 1922). She wrote the libretto for and sang the title role in Bantock's opera *The Seal Woman* (1924). She also publ. the autobiography *A Life of Song* (London, 1928). —**NS/LK/DM**

Kenny, Yvonne, Australian soprano; b. Sydney, Nov. 25, 1950. She received her training at the New South Wales State Conservatorium of Music in Sydney and at the La Scala Opera School in Milan (1973–74). In 1975 she made her debut in London in a concert perf. as Donizetti's Rosamunda d'Inghilterra. On July 12, 1976, she made her first appearance at London's Covent Garden in the premiere of Henze's *We Come to the River*, and returned there in subsequent years to sing such roles as Mozart's Susanna, Pamina, and Ilia, Verdi's Oscar, Bizet's Micaëla, Handel's Semele, and Puccini's Liù. In 1977 she made her debut at London's English National Opera as Strauss' Sophie. In 1985 she made her first appearance at the Glyndebourne Festival as Ilia. In 1993 she sang Strauss' Madeleine at the Berlin State Opera. She appeared in Purcell's *The Fairy Queen* in London in 1995. In 1997 she portrayed the Marschallin at Covent Garden. She sang Poppea in Sydney in 1998, and returned there as Alice in *Falstaff* in 1999. Her guest engagements also took her to Paris, Vienna, Hamburg, Munich, Salzburg, Edinburgh, and other music centers. She was also very active as a concert artist. In 1989 she was made a Member of the Order of Australia. —**NS/LK/DM**

Kenny G, the single most successful instrumental pop artist of all time (b. Kenneth Gorelick, Seattle, Wash., June 5, 1956). Ken Gorelick comes from a black neighborhood in Seattle. He began playing the sax in the fourth grade, taking lessons in school. Before the year was out, he was first sax in the school band. At age 16, he saw Grover Washington perform circular breathing on stage; impressed, he began practicing the technique, and holds the world's record for the longest single unbroken note at 45 minutes and 47 seconds! He has been a professional sax player since high school, when a band teacher set him up with a gig as soloist for Barry White and the Love Unlimited Orchestra's stop on tour in Seattle. He continued backing touring musicians through his matriculation at the Univ. of Wash., backing artists ranging from the Spinners to Liberace.

He also worked with the fusion band Cold, Bold and Together, with who he recorded his first sides. Upon graduating Magna Cum Laude with a Phi Beta Kappa key and a degree in accounting (something to fall back on), Gorelick took the sax seat with fellow Pacific-Northwesterner Jeff Lorber and his fusion band. He cut several records with Lorber, and then, cut a deal with Lorber to make a solo album. Lorber cut a deal with his record company to put it out, and Kenny Gorelick became Kenny G and went solo.

His eponymous debut, an unintentional tribute to Grover Washington, sold well for a jazz-fusion record, moving some 100,000 pieces, as did the somewhat more pallid G-Force and Gravity. All of his early work had a certain lyrical charm, but largely lacked a sense of personality in the attempt to woo the R&B audience. His fourth album, Duotones broke him through on the strength of the monster instrumental hit "Songbird." Composed in his home studio, with Gorelick playing all the instruments, this lyrical piece of musical confection rose to #4 in the charts. Along with the #15 hit "Don't Make Me Wait for Love" (with vocals by Tower of Power's Lenny Williams), the album catapulted to #6. Within six months, the album went double platinum. It stands at quintuple platinum.

Where some artists find it tough to follow-up a hit like this, Gorelick did it with aplomb, with Silhouette. While the title track went to #13, the album rose to #8 and sold double platinum within months of release. Eventually it reached the quadruple platinum mark, as did the live album that followed it. The live album, recorded in Seattle, rose to #16 on the charts.

After cutting "Missing You Now," a duet with Michael Bolton that topped the adult contemporary chart, reaching #12 pop, Gorelick released his major pop statement, Breathless. With vocals by Peabo Bryson and Aaron Neville added to his already well-known soprano sax, the album would have reached his fans on word of mouth. He topped the adult contemporary charts with the #18 pop instrumental "Forever in Love," and topped it again with his collaboration with Bryson on "By the Time This Night Is Over," a #25 pop hit. Breathless shipped double platinum and by the end of the century had sold over 12 million copies. "Forever in Love" took home a Grammy in 1994 for Best Instrumental Composition.

Two years after releasing a holiday album that topped the pop album chart for three weeks in 1994, G released The Moment. The album debuted at #4 on the album charts and #1 Contemporary Jazz Chart, replacing Breathless, which stayed on that chart for nearly three years. The Moment held that place for the next year. The album shipped double platinum and eventually sold over four million copies.

His 1998 album, Classics in the Key of G, found him exploring the jazz standard repertoire with mixed results. An electronic duet with Louis Armstrong (a la Natalie Cole's "Unforgettable") on "What a Wonderful World" was a highlight of the album, with all proceeds from the single going to buy instruments for school music programs. The album sold a relatively modest one million, peaking at #17. He also released another holiday album, Faith, which included a version of "Auld Lang Syne" played over soundbites from the previous century. That album peaked at #6 and went double platinum.

Most jazz fans disparage Kenny G as a mere pop instrumentalist. Kenny G counters that he never claimed to be a jazz musician! As a pop instrumentalist, he is perhaps second only to Herb Alpert as a hitmaker. His playing has done much to popularize the soprano sax sound among listeners of all musical styles.

DISC.: Kenny G (1982); G Force (1983); Gravity (1985); Duotones (1986); Silhouette (1988); Kenny G Live (1989); Breathless (1992); Miracles: The Holiday Album (1994); The Moment (1996); Classics in the Key of G (1999); Faith: A Holiday Album (1999).—**HB**

Kent, James, English organist and composer; b. Winchester, March 13, 1700; d. there, May 6, 1776. He was a chorister at Winchester Cathedral and in the Chapel Royal. He was organist of Trinity Coll., Cambridge (1731–37), then of Winchester Cathedral and Coll. (1738–74). He publ. Twelve Anthems (1773). J. Corfe ed. A Morning and Evening Service with Eight Anthems (c. 1777).—**NS/LK/DM**

Kentner, Louis (actually, **Lajos Philip**), admired Hungarian-born English pianist; b. Karwin, July 19, 1905; d. London, Sept. 22, 1987. He studied piano with Székely and Weiner and composition with Koessler and Kodály at the Royal Academy of Music in Budapest. He made his formal debut in Budapest in 1920, then toured throughout Europe. In 1935 he settled in England, becoming a naturalized British subject in 1946. On Nov. 28, 1956, he made his U.S. debut in N.Y. In 1978 he was made a Commander of the Order of the British Empire. In 1931 he married **Ilona Kabos;** they divorced in 1945. He was praised for his interpretations of works by Mozart, Beethoven, Schubert, Chopin, and Liszt, as well as those by Bartók and various contemporary English composers.

BIBL.: H. Taylor, ed., K.: A Symposium (N.Y., 1987).—**NS/LK/DM**

Kenton (real name, **Kornstein**), **Egon,** Hungarian violinist, musicologist, and music librarian; b. Nagyszalonta, May 22, 1891; d. Paris, Dec. 3, 1987. He studied violin with Hubay at the Budapest Royal Academy of Music, graduating in 1911. He was violist in the Hungarian String Quartet (1911–23), and then emigrated to the U.S. In 1947 he received his M.A. in musicology from N.Y.U., and subsequently taught musicology at the Univ. of Conn. in Storrs (1950–61). From 1961 to 1971 he served as librarian of the Mannes Coll. of Music in N.Y. He wrote the first English-language study of the life and music of Giovanni Gabrieli (Rome, 1967).—**NS/LK/DM**

Kenton, Stan(ley Newcomb), highly influential jazz bandleader, composer, pianist; b. Wichita, Kans., Dec. 15, 1911; d. L.A., Aug. 25, 1979. Many musicians hated his band because it was so big and loud and brassy and bombastic; many audiences adored him and he inspired a kind of cultism. He was also criticized for rarely hiring black musicians; a letter he wrote to *Down Beat* protesting the paucity of awards to white musicians did not help his case. Yet it is undeniable that he encouraged and recorded innovative works by Bob Graettinger, Pete Rugolo, Bill Russo, and others that no one else might have dared to present, and that he was a key figure in the birth of modern jazz education in the 1960s.

Kenton's family moved to Calif. when he was six. He began on piano in his early teens, and at 14 took lessons from local pianist Frank Hurst. He played in a quartet at Bell H.S. (L.A.). He earned a living playing piano in local saloons and speakeasies. He did a six-week tour with the Flack Brothers' Sextet in 1930, then worked in Las Vegas prior to working with a territory band in Ariz. From 1933–39, he worked with a number of L.A.–based bands, beginning to take on leadership roles and also arranging for them. In 1940, he formed his own rehearsal band—Jimmie Lunceford's orch. was a prime influence—which obtained bookings a year later at Huntingdon Beach, quickly followed by a summer season at the Rendezvous Ballroom at Balboa Beach. In November 1941, the band played their first date at the Hollywood Palladium. Since then Kenton continued to lead highly successful big bands, despite several bouts of serious illness. He suffered nervous breakdowns, and at one time decided to abandon music and become a psychiatrist; he gave up the idea when he realized that he would have to learn Greek-derived words and unpronounceable German terms. He married frequently; one of his sons was indicted for conspiracy to commit murder (he put a snake in the mailbox of a bothersome attorney). When Pete Rugolo joined as staff arranger in 1945, the band began to dominate jazz popularity polls. Kenton's band in 1947 was a pioneer in Latin jazz, adding to the rhythm section Brazilian guitarist Laurindo Almeida; one Latin hit was an exciting arrangement of "The Peanut Vendor." His appearance at N.Y.'s Carnegie Hall with his Progressive Jazz orch. (1949) gave the name to that genre; after touring the country with his 40-piece Innovations in Modern Music Orch. (1950–51), he led various big bands. In 1954 he toured with guest soloist Charlie Parker. He made many recordings, garnering Grammy awards with his albums *West Side Story* and *Adventures in Jazz* (both 1961). He made many international tours, and in 1956 his became the first American big band to work unrestrictedly in Britain since 1937. From 1959 he devoted much time to music education, founding jazz clinics or Stage Band Camps at many institutions of higher learning. He founded his own publishing and recording company, Creative World, in 1970. His 1970s tours included Europe and Japan. During that decade he devoted a great deal of time and energy to taking his band to jazz clinics at various colls. and educational centres. Though inactive following a serious operation in 1977, Kenton sufficiently recovered to appear at the Newport Jazz Festival's Silver Jubilee concert at Saratoga, N.Y. in June 1978, but died just over a year later. The list of distinguished Kenton alumni include instrumentalists Stan Getz, Lucky Thompson, Lee Konitz,

Lennie Niehaus, Art Pepper, Kai Winding, singers June Christy, Anita O'Day, Chris Connor, composers Pete Rugolo, Bill Holman, and Bill Russo. The band made a film short, *Artistry in Rhythm*, in (1947). His personal papers are collected at the Univ. of North Tex., Denton.

Disc.: *Balboa/Summer 1941* (1941); *Uncollected S. K. & His Orch.* (1941); *Artistry in Rhythm* (1945); *Some Women I've Known* (1945); *Presents Claude Williamson* (1946); *Concert in Progressive Jazz* (1947); *Artistry in Jazz* (1950); *Innovations in Modern Music* (1950); *City of Glass* (1951); *Live in 1951 at the Hollywood Palladium* (1951); *Portraits on Standards* (1951); *Concert in Miniature* (1952); *New Concepts of Artistry in Rhythm* (1952); *Prologue: This Is an Orch.* (1952); *European Tour: 1953* (1953); *K. '53: Concert in Weisbaden* (1953); *Paris* (1953); *Sketches on Standards* (1953); *This Modern World* (1953); *S.K. Radio Transcriptions* (1953); *Music of Bill Russo and Bill Holman* (w. Parker, Gillespie; 1954); *Cuban Fire, Vol. 1, 2* (1956; arr. Johnny Richards); *In Concert* (1956); *In Stockholm* (1956); *Live at the Macumba Club: Pt. 1, 2* (1956); *Standards in Silhouette* (1959); *Viva K.* (1959); *Adventures in Blues* (1961); *Adventures in Jazz* (1961); *Adventures in Standards* (1961); *West Side Story* (1961; arr. Johnny Richards); *Adventures in Time* (1962); *Artistry in Bossa Nova* (1963); *K./Wagner* (1964); *7.5 on the Richter Scale* (1973); *Solo: S.K. without His Orch.* (1974); *50th Anniversary Celebration: Balboa* (1991; reunion groups and talks); *Back to Balboa* (1991).

Bibl.: Carol Easton, *Straight Ahead: The Story of S.K.* (1973); H. Dietzel and H. Lange, *S.K.* (Berlin, 1959); D. Schulz-K hn, *S. K.* (Wetzlar, Germany, 1961); W. Lee, *S.K.: Artistry in Rhythm* (L.A., 1980); L. Arganian, *S. K.: The Man and His Music* (East Lansing, Mich., 1989); C. Garrod, *S. K. and His Orch.* (Zepbyrhills, Fla.); M. Sparke, ed., *The Great K. Arrangers* (Whittier, Calif.); Anthony J. Agostinelli, *S.K.: The Many Musical Moods of His Orchs* (Providence R.I., 1986); Paul D. Bauer, *The Trombones in the Orchs. of S.K.* (Thesis, Music, North Tex. State Univ., 1980); Dick Bauman, *A Dissection of the History and Musical Product of S.K., Jazz Education in the Public School Program, and the Third Stream* (Thesis, Education, Northwest Mo. State Univ., 1970); Carol Easton, *Straight Ahead: The Story of Stan K.* (N.Y., 1973, 1981); Milton Lindskoog, *An Analysis of the Style of the S.K. Orch* (Thesis, Music, Eastman School, 1948); Christopher A. Pirie, with Siegfried Møller, *Artistry in K.: A Biodiscography of S.K. and His Music, Vol. I* (Vienna, 1969); Idem, *Artistry in K.: A Biodiscography of S.K. and His Music, Vol. II* (Vienna, 1973).—JC/NS/LP

Kepler, Johannes, illustrious German astronomer; b. Weil der Stadt, Württemberg, Dec. 27, 1571; d. Regensburg, Nov. 15, 1630. He explored Pythagorean concepts of harmony and relationships among music, mathematics, and physics in books 3 and 5 of his *Harmonices mundi* (Linz, 1619).

Bibl.: M. Dickreiter, *Der Musiktheoretiker J. K.* (Bern and Munich, 1973).—NS/LK/DM

Keppard, Freddie, influential early jazz cornetist; b. New Orleans, Feb. 15, 1889 (or Feb. 27, 1890); d. Chicago, July 15, 1933. He was known as "King" in New Orleans between Bolden and Oliver, among others. He was the brother of tuba-player and guitarist Louis Keppard (b. New Orleans, Feb. 2, 1888; d. New Orleans, Feb. 18, 1986). Both brothers began on fretted instruments: Freddie on mandolin, Louis on guitar. Freddie also played violin and accordion before switching exclusively to cornet. He was originally taught by Adolphe Alexander. After playing a few local gigs he organized the Olympia Orch. ca. 1906; during the period 1907–11 he also worked in Frankie Dusen's Eagle Band, and played regularly in various clubs and dance halls including Pete Lala's, Groshell's, George Fewclothes, Hanan's, etc. Early in 1912 (at bassist Bill Johnson's request) he and several colleagues traveled to L.A., Keppard became frontman and co-leader of the Original Creole Orch. The orch. toured the Orpheum Circuit for several years including visits to Chicago and N.Y. (1915). Keppard was offered a chance to record with Victor in 1916, but turned it down because he didn't want other bands to copy the group's style and take away potential work. Though this reasoning was sensible, in retrospect it was a mistake because the example of the ODJB, who became the first jazz band to record, showed that the potential gigs expanded enormously once recordings became available. The Original Creoles temporarily disbanded in 1917, but soon re-formed under Keppard's leadership. They played a residency at the Logan Square Theatre (Chicago), then briefly toured the Orpheum Circuit again. Keppard then settled in Chicago, played a residency at the Entertainers' Cafe, then toured with the Tan Town Topics. He returned to play at the Entertainers and at the De Lure. (Jasper Taylor once said that Keppard worked with Lt. Tim Brymn in N.Y.; this may have been in 1919). He was briefly with King Oliver at the Royal Gardens (ca. 1920), then worked at the Lorraine Club with Jimmie Noone, and doubled with Mae Brady's Band at Dreamland. He joined Doc Cooke at that venue in autumn 1922, remained for two years except for a brief spell with Erskine Tate in 1923. During this two-year period he also doubled in Ollie Powers's Band. From 1924 he was regularly employed at Bert Kelly's Stables; this arrangement continued for several years, but Keppard had long leaves of absence. He rejoined Doc Cooke in late 1925 until ca. early 1926, led his own band, and again worked at Bert Kelly's. He rejoined Doc Cooke from spring until September 1927, with Erskine Tate in early 1928, led his own band at LaRue's Dreamland (spring 1928), and later worked with Jerome Don Pasquall's Band at Harmon's Dreamland (late 1928). He toured Ill. and Ind. with his own band, then worked with Charlie Elgar at the Savoy Ballroom. He lived in musical obscurity for the last years of his life, and suffered from tuberculosis. After a long illness, he died in the Cook County Hospital in Chicago.—JC/LP

Kerckhoven, Abraham van den, Flemish organist and composer; b. probably in Malines, c. 1618; d. Brussels, late Dec. 1701. He settled in Brussels in his youth. In 1633 he became organist at Ste. Cathérine. In 1648 he was named organist in the domestic service of Archduke Leopold Wilhelm of Austria, Governor of the Low Countries. In 1656 he became a member of the royal chapel, where, from 1659, he held the position of 1st organist. His organ music, comprised of 8 fantasias, 4 fugues, and 2 pairs of preludes and fugues, reveal a gift for improvisation.—LK/DM

Kerle, Jacobus de, eminent South Netherlandish organist and composer; b. Ypres, 1531 or 1532; d.

Prague, Jan. 7, 1591. He is believed to have received his education at the monastery of St. Martin in Ypres. In 1555 was made magister capellae in Orvieto, where he most likely was active as a singer and master of the choristers; soon thereafter he became cathedral organist and town carillonist. After taking Holy Orders, he went to Venice in 1561 to prepare the publication of his *Liber psalmorum ad Vesperas.* The Bishop of Augsburg commissioned him to write his *Preces speciales pro salubri generalis Concilii successu* (1561–62) for the Council of Trent. He subsequently went to Rome in 1562 as director of the cardinal's private chapel. He accompanied the cardinal on his travels throughout northern Italy to Barcelona and back (1563–64), then was in Dillingen until the cardinal disbanded his chapel in 1565. He became director of music at Ypres Cathedral in 1565, but lost that post in 1567 and was excommunicated following legal proceedings and a dispute with the cathedral chapter. He then went to Rome, where Cardinal Otto made him a member of the chapter of Augsburg Cathedral in 1568. That same year he was made vicar-choral and organist as well, and he subsequently held a prebend in Cambrai (1575–87), and was made a member of the chapter of the Cathedral there (1579), but soon left owing to war. He served as Kapellmeister to Gebhard Truchess, the Archbishop and Elector of Cologne and Lord High Steward of Waldburg, in 1582. In Sept. 1582 he entered the Emperor's service in Augsburg, and in Oct. 1582 he became a member of the court chapel in Vienna. He settled in Prague in 1583, and was made honorary precentor of the Mons choir in 1587. He was also canon of the collegiate foundation of the Heilige Kreuz in Breslau (1587–88). Kerle was one of the last significant composers of the South Netherlandish tradition, excelling in sacred vocal music.

WORKS: VOCAL: Sacred : *Motetti* for 4 and 5 Voices (Rome, 1557); [23] *Hymni totius anni...et Magnificat* for 4 and 5 Voices (Rome, 1558; 2nd ed., 1560); [16] *Magnificat octo tonorum* for 4 Voices (Venice, 1561); *Liber* [20] *Psalmorum ad Vesperas* for 4 Voices (Venice, 1561); 6 *missae* for 4 and 5 Voices (Venice, 1562); *Preces speciales pro salubri generalis Concilii successu* for 4 Voices (Venice, 1562; ed. in Denkmäler der Tonkunst in Bayern, XXXIV, Jg. XVI, 1926; 2nd ed., rev., 1974); [15] *Selectae quaedam cantiones* for 5 and 6 Voices (Nuremberg, 1571); *Liber modulorum* for 4 to 6 Voices (Paris, 1572); *Liber* [11] *modulorum sacrorum* for 5 and 6 Voices, *quibus addita est recens cantio de sacro foedere contra Turcas* for 8 Voices (Munich, 1572); *Liber* [16] *modulorum sacrorum* for 4 to 6 Voices (Munich, 1573); *Liber* [16] *mottetorum* for 4 and 5 Voices, *adiuncto in fine Te Deum laudamus* for 6 Voices (Munich, 1573); [9] *Sacrae cantiones, quas vulgo moteta vocant...ecclesiastici hymni de resurrectione et ascensione* for 5 and 6 Voices (Munich, 1575); 4 *missae* for 4 and 5 Voices (Antwerp, 1582); 4 *missae...adiuncto in fine Te Deum laudamus* for 4 and 5 Voices (Antwerp, 1583); [9] *Selectiorum aliquot modulorum* for 4, 5, and 8 Voices (Prague, 1585). **Secular :** *Il primo libro capitolo del triumpho d'amore de Petrarca* for 5 Voices (Venice, 1570); *Madrigali, libro primo (Carmina italica musicis modulis ornata)* for 4 Voices (Venice, 1570); *Egregia cantio, in...honorem Melchioris Lincken Augustani* for 6 Voices (Nuremberg, 1574).

BIBL.: O. Ursprung, *J. d.K. (1531/32–1591): Sein Leben und seine Werke* (Munich, 1913).—NS/LK/DM

Kerll (also **Kerl, Kherl, Cherl, Gherl,** etc.), **Johann Kaspar,** renowned German organist and composer; b. Adorf, Saxony, April 9, 1627; d. Munich, Feb. 13, 1693. He most likely began his musical studies with his father, Kaspar Kerll, an organist, before being called to Vienna by Archduke Leopold Wilhelm to serve as a youthful court organist; he concurrently studied with the imperial court Kapellmeister, Giovanni Valentini. The archduke then sent him to Rome to complete his studies with Carissimi; he may have also studied with Frescobaldi. By 1650 he was in Brussels, where he was court organist to Archduke Leopold Wilhelm, who was serving as viceroy of the Spanish Netherlands. The Bavarian Elector Ferdinand Maria made him Vice-Kapellmeister of the Munich court on Feb. 27, 1656; he was promoted to Kapellmeister on Sept. 22, 1656. He wrote his first opera, *L'Oronte,* for the inauguration of Munich's opera house (Jan. 1657). For the coronation of Emperor Leopold I in Frankfurt am Main (July 22, 1658), he wrote a Mass and improvised on the organ with great success. He was ennobled in 1664. Although he was held in the highest regard at court, he found the Italian domination of the musical establishment not to his liking. He resigned his position in 1673 and went to Vienna, where he served as organist of St. Stephen's Cathedral (1674–77); he then (March 16, 1677) was appointed imperial court organist, a position he held until his death. He particularly distinguished himself as a composer of sacred music, and also wrote some fine keyboard pieces. For a selected edition of his works, see A. Sandberger, ed., Denkmäler der Tonkunst in Bayern, III, Jg. II/2 (1901).

WORKS: 18 extant masses, several of which were publ. in *Missae sex, cum instrumentis concertantibus, e vocibus in ripieno, adjuncta una pro defunctis cum seq. Dies irae* for 4 to 6 Voices, Strings, Bassoon, and Basso Continuo (Munich, 1689); *Delectus* [26] *sacrarum cantionum* for 2 to 5 Voices, 2 Violins, and Basso Continuo, op.1 (Munich, 1669); 16 Latin sacred works for 1, 3 to 6, 8, and 9 Voices, 3 Trombones, Strings, and Basso Continuo; 3 German sacred works for Voice, 2 Violins, and Basso Continuo; etc. His instrumental works include *Modulatio organica super Magnificat octo ecclesiasticis tonis respondens* for Keyboard (Munich, 1686; ed. by R. Walter, Altotting, 1956); 8 toccatas; 6 canzonas; many other keyboard pieces in MS; also a ricercata a 4 in A. Kircher, *Musurgia universalis* (Rome, 1650). Many other works are lost, including 11 operas.

BIBL.: A. Giebler, *The Masses of J.C. K.* (diss., Univ. of Mich., 1956); R. Schall, *Quellen zu J.K. K.* (Vienna, 1962).—**NS/LK/DM**

Kerman, Joseph (Wilfred), American musicologist and critic; b. London (of American parents), April 3, 1924. He studied at N.Y.U. (A.B., 1943), subsequently taking courses with Strunk, Thompson, and Weinrich at Princeton Univ. (Ph.D., 1950, with the diss. *The Elizabethan Madrigal: A Comparative Study*; publ. in N.Y., 1962). He also taught at Westminster Choir Coll. in Princeton, N.J. (1949–51). In 1951 he joined the faculty at the Univ. of Calif. at Berkeley, being made a prof. in 1960 and serving as chairman of its music dept. from 1960 to 1963 and again from 1991 to 1993. After serving as Heather Prof. of Music at the Univ. of Oxford (1971–74), he resumed his professorship at Berkeley. In 1977 he became a founding ed. of the journal *19th Century Music,* serving as its co-ed. until 1989. In 1997–98 he was the Charles Eliot Norton Prof. of Poetry at Harvard Univ. He is an Honorary Fellow of the Royal Academy of Music in London (1972) and a Fellow of the American Academy of Arts and Sciences (1973). A leading figure in the generation of American musicology directly following its mostly German or German-trained founders, Kerman has also been influential with general college students through the many editions of his "Introduction to Music" textbook *Listen* (1972), and with intellectuals at large through his writings in periodicals such as the *Hudson Review* and the *N.Y. Review of Books.* His first book, *Opera as Drama* (1956; rev. 1988), which has been called a minor classic, manifests along with evident shortcomings the level of critical insight developed further in Kerman's more sustained and scholarly work on Beethoven and Byrd. His tract *Contemplating Music* (1985) is credited with nudging the discipline of musicological from a more philological, positivist orientation toward criticism and cultural studies.

WRITINGS: *Opera as Drama* (N.Y., 1956; rev. 1988); *The Beethoven Quartets* (N.Y. and London, 1967); with H. Janson, *History of Art & Music* (N.Y. and Englewood Cliffs, N.J., 1968); ed. *L. van Beethoven: Autograph Miscellany ("Kafka Sketchbook")* (London, 1970); ed. *W.A. Mozart: Concerto in C, K. 503* (N.Y., 1970; Norton Critical Score); with V. Kerman, *Listen* (N.Y., 1972; 7th ed., 1999, with G. Tomlinson); *The Music of William Byrd: Vol. I, The Masses and Motets of William Byrd* (London, 1981); *Contemplating Music* (Cambridge, Mass., 1985; publ. in England as *Musicology,* London, 1985); ed. *Music at the Turn of the Century: A "19th-Century Music" Reader* (Berkeley and Oxford, 1990); *Write All These Down: Essays on Music* (Berkeley, 1994); *Concerto Conversations* (Cambridge, Mass., 1999).—**NS/LK/DM**

Kern, Adele, German soprano; b. Munich, Nov. 25, 1901; d. there, May 6, 1980. She received training in Munich. In 1924 she made her operatic debut there as Olympia in *Les Contes d'Hoffmann* at the Bavarian State Opera, singing there until 1926 when she became a member of the Frankfurt am Main Opera. In 1927–28 she toured South America. From 1927 to 1935 she appeared at the Salzburg Festivals. She also sang in Munich, as well as at the Vienna State Opera (1929–30) and the Berlin State Opera (1935–37). She subsequently sang at the Bavarian State Opera (1937–43; 1945–46). As a guest artist, she appeared at London's Covent Garden (1931, 1934), Milan's La Scala, the Rome Opera, and at other European operatic centers. She was especially admired for her Mozart and Richard Strauss roles, among them Despina, Susanna, Zerbinetta, Marzelline, and Sophie.—**NS/LK/DM**

Kern, Jerome (David), melodic American theatrical and film composer; b. N.Y., Jan. 27, 1885; d. there, Nov. 11, 1945. Kern was one of the most successful Broadway composers from 1915 through the mid-1930s. His stage works ranged from intimate shows at the Princess Theatre to the ambitious integrated musical *Show Boat.* In the last decade of his life he wrote primarily for musical films, among them such hits as *Swing Time.* Always highly melodic, his songs became increasingly complex structurally and harmonically without losing their popular appeal. Indeed, he consistently produced hits for 40 years, among them such standards as "Ol' Man River," "Smoke Gets in Your Eyes," and "The Way You Look Tonight."

Kern was the son of Henry Kern (b. April 26, 1842; d. Aug. 13, 1908), a German immigrant, and Fannie Kakeles Kern (b. May 27, 1852; d. Dec. 31, 1907), who was American-born, though her parents had emigrated from Bohemia. At the time of Kern's birth, his father ran a stable; later he became a successful merchant. Kern showed an early interest in music and initially was instructed in piano and organ by his mother, an accomplished player. The family moved to Newark in 1897. Kern wrote songs for a student show at Newark H.S. in 1901 and for an amateur musical adaptation of *Uncle Tom's Cabin* put on at the Newark Yacht Club in January 1902. Later that year he left high school without graduating and briefly studied in Germany. He also briefly worked with his father, who was by then executive vice president of Wolff & Co. department store (eventually he became president), but his business career ended within months when he purchased 200 pianos for the store after being sent to buy only two.

Kern found a job in the billing office at Lyceum, a music publisher, in the summer of 1902, and the firm gave him his first publication with the piano piece "At the Casino" in September. He resumed his schooling, enrolling for evening classes at the N.Y. Coll. of Music, where he studied counterpoint with Austin Pierce, piano with Albert von Doenhoff, and, possibly, harmony and composition with Paul Gallico and the school's director, Alexander Lambert. In 1903, after being promoted to song plugger at Lyceum, he moved to a similar job at another music publisher, T. B. Harms. (He later bought stock in the company and eventually became a vice president.) The association resulted in the first hearing of Kern's music on Broadway, when "To the End of the World Together," "Wine, Wine! (Champagne Song)" (both with lyrics by Edgar A. Smith), and possibly other songs were interpolated into the imported British musical *An English Daisy* (N.Y., Jan. 18, 1904).

Kern spent several months in 1903–04 in England attempting to place his songs in vaudeville and the legitimate theater; this began a lifelong love affair with Britain that led to many more trips and works created exclusively for the London stage. *Mr. Wix of Wickham*, an imported British show, marked the first time he wrote most of the songs for a Broadway show, though he was credited only with "additional musical numbers"; it ran for only 41 performances. He continued to contribute interpolations into shows primarily written by others extensively over the next decade, putting as many as 100 songs into as many as 30 shows in the U.S. and the U.K. between 1905 and 1912. The most successful of these—indeed, his only major hit of the period—was "How'd You Like to Spoon with Me?" (lyrics by Edward Laska), which was used in another British import, *The Earl and the Girl* (N.Y., Nov. 4, 1905). Connie Morgan, accompanied by The Haydn Quartet, made a record of the song that was a best-seller in January 1906. (While many of Kern's songs became hit records, he himself had little interest in having his work presented outside of the theater. He generally disapproved of recordings and radio broadcasts of his music, and on occasion he took action to prevent them.)

On another songwriting trip to England in late 1905 or early 1906, Kern met P.G. Wodehouse, with whom he began to collaborate. Several of their songs, including "Mr. Chamberlain," were used in *The Beauty of Bath* (London, March 19, 1906). In 1909, Kern met Eva Leale, daughter of the manager of the Swan hotel and pub in the village of Walton-on-Thames, England. They were married in 1910 and had a daughter in 1918. Kern shared composing credit with Frank Tours on *La Belle Paree*, which inaugurated the Winter Garden and marked the Broadway debut of its most illustrious inhabitant, Al Jolson, singing Kern's "Paris Is a Paradise for Coons" (lyrics by Edward Madden); it ran for 104 performances.

The first show for which Kern alone wrote a complete score was *The Red Petticoat*, which ran for only 61 performances. His first hit song in eight years came with the dance tune "You're Here and I'm Here," which was interpolated into *The Laughing Husband* (N.Y., Feb. 2, 1914) and subsequently added to other shows; the song was successfully recorded by the duo of Harry Macdonough and Olive Kline.

Kern contributed songs to the American version of the British show *The Girl from Utah* (N.Y., Aug. 24, 1914); among them was "They Didn't Believe Me" (lyrics by Michael Rourke under the pseudonym Herbert Reynolds), which was not immediately identified as the standard it later became. The first successful recording came with the version by Macdonough and Kline (under the pseudonym Alice Green), which became a big hit in November 1915; two more duos also scored hits with it: Walter Van Brunt and Gladys Rice in January 1916 and Grace Kerns and Reed Miller in July.

Though it failed, Kern's next show, *90 in the Shade*, served as his introduction to librettist Guy Bolton. He and Bolton immediately joined to begin writing the celebrated Princess Theatre shows, a series of small-scale musicals put on at the 299-seat N.Y. playhouse that proved highly influential as well as highly popular. The first of these was *Nobody Home*, which ran for 135 performances, becoming the first hit show credited to the 30-year-old composer, who had by now been contributing music to Broadway for 11 years. Its hit song was "The Magic Melody" (lyrics by Schuyler Greene), which became a successful record for Billy Murray in August.

Kern's first show of the 1915–16 season was *Miss Information*, a star vehicle for Elsie Janis, who herself wrote the lyrics to its most memorable song, "Some Sort of Somebody." Also featured in the next Princess Theatre show, *Very Good Eddie*, the song became a record hit for Murray and Elsie Baker (under the pseudonym Edna Brown) in June 1916. The other song to emerge from *Very Good Eddie* was "Babes in the Wood" (lyrics by Greene and Kern), which provided record hits for Van Brunt and Rice in August 1916, Prince's Orch. in September 1916, and the team of Macdonough and Lucy Isabelle Marsh (under the pseudonym Anna Howard) in January 1917. All this time the show continued to run, finally racking up 341 performances in N.Y., with touring versions that continued into the 1918–19 season.

Kern was asked to contribute to the *Ziegfeld Follies of 1916* (N.Y., June 12, 1916) and contributed four songs, among them "Have a Heart" (lyrics by Gene Buck), which inspired successful recordings by Conway's Band and by Kline and Lambert Murphy. Though Kern, Bolton, and Wodehouse were involved in *Miss Springtime* (Sept. 25, 1916), for which the music was written primarily by Emmerich Kalman, their first full-fledged collaboration as a team was *Have a Heart*, one of three musicals with Kern scores to open within six weeks at the start of 1917. It was only a moderate success, as was *Love o' Mike*, which followed within days. The biggest hit of the three was the next Princess Theatre show, *Oh, Boy!*, which ran 463 performances and spawned the hit song "Till the Clouds Roll By" (lyrics by Wodehouse). Anna Wheaton and James Harrold's recording was a best-seller in August, Prince's Orch. had an instrumental version that did almost as well, and Vernon Dalhart scored his first hit with his recording. *Leave It to Jane*, the fourth new Kern show of 1917, was also the third Kern-Bolton-Wodehouse collaboration of the year, and it was another hit, its most popular number being "The Siren's Song" (lyrics by Wodehouse), which enjoyed a hit recording by Helen Clark and Gladys Rice in May 1918. Kern, Bolton, and Wodehouse returned to the Princess Theatre a final time with *Oh, Lady! Lady!!*, another success.

Kern's first hit show of the 1920s came when the decade was barely a month old. *The Night Boat* (book and lyrics by Anne Caldwell) ran for more than 300 performances in N.Y. and for three seasons on tour, its notable songs including "Whose Baby Are You?" for a hit recording by Joseph C. Smith's Orch. and "Left All Alone Again Blues," a hit for Marion Harris. Kern had another successful show before the year was out with *Sally*, a Florenz Ziegfeld–produced vehicle for his *Follies* star Marilyn Miller with a book by Bolton. Running an amazing 570 performances (only the previous year's *Irene*, which had played in a much smaller theater, had had a longer run among Broadway musicals), it spun off several hit songs, including "Look for the Silver Lining" (lyrics by B.G. De Sylva), which was recorded by a host of recording artists, though Harris's version was the most successful, and "Whip-Poor-Will" (lyrics by De Sylva), a hit for Isham Jones and His Orch. The Vernon Country Club Band and Joseph C. Smith's Orch. each made popular recordings of instrumental medleys of the show's music.

Good Morning, Dearie, another teaming of Kern and Caldwell, was even more successful than *The Night Boat*, racking up 347 performances and producing a hit in the Hawaiian-styled "Ka-lu-a," which was successfully recorded by Elsie Baker (using the pseudonym Edna Brown) and Elliott Shaw. The song also was used in Kern's next show, the hit British musical *The Cabaret Girl*. His next American show was the flop *The Bunch and Judy*, which is worth mentioning because it marked the first time he worked with Fred Astaire. *Stepping Stones*, Kern's next American show, was a success, featuring "Raggedy Ann" (lyrics by Caldwell), an in-

strumental record hit for Paul Whiteman and His Orch. *Sitting Pretty* marked the reunion of the Princess Theatre team of Kern, Bolton, and Wodehouse, and the show's relative failure may have been due in part to Kern's refusal to allow its songs to be played on the radio, in cabarets, or to be recorded. His ire was directed specifically at jazz interpretations of his work.

In preparing *Sunny*, another vehicle for Miller, Kern worked for the first time with the book-and-lyric writers who would be his most frequent partners over the rest of his life: Otto Harbach and Oscar Hammerstein II. The result was a massive hit, running over 500 performances and featuring such compositions as the title song and "Who?," which made up the two sides of a gold record for George Olsen and His Orch., who appeared onstage in the show.

Kern initiated his most successful musical, *Show Boat*, after reading Edna Ferber's panoramic novel. He obtained the theatrical rights, interested Hammerstein in writing the book and lyrics, cast Helen Morgan in the role of Julie, and arranged for Ziegfeld to produce the show. It was a landmark production, acclaimed from the first out-of-town tryout as a masterpiece. *Show Boat* led to a startling maturation of the Broadway musical, introducing a serious, dramatic structure that integrated the songs with the plot and the characters, even putting onstage a consideration of civil rights decades before such a concern achieved national recognition. (Ironically, its very depiction of racial injustice would be mistakenly assailed as racist when a major revival was mounted in the 1990s.)

Aside from its importance in theater history and its political prescience, *Show Boat* was Kern's best and most successful score. Several of its songs became immediate hits and went on to become standards, most prominently among them "Ol' Man River," which was recorded by numerous performers, the most popular version coming from Whiteman with a vocal by Bing Crosby. (The other side of the Whiteman-Crosby record was "Make Believe," another hit from the show.) Whiteman rerecorded "Ol' Man River" with Paul Robeson singing and had a second hit with it. Robeson had been slated to play Joe and sing the song onstage, but the show's long gestation period found him unavailable at the opening. He played the role in London in 1928, in the first N.Y. revival in 1932, and in the second film version in 1936, and "Ol' Man River" became his signature song. Other hit versions were registered by Jolson and by The Revelers. Helen Morgan made a two-sided hit record of her songs from the show, "Bill" (lyrics by P.G. Wodehouse), which had been written much earlier and cut from previous Kern shows, and "Can't Help Lovin' Dat Man." Nat Shilkret and The Victor Orch. scored a hit with "Why Do I Love You?"; the score also boasted such memorable songs as "You Are Love" and "Life on the Wicked Stage." The original production ran 575 performances, the longest of any by Kern, and the show has been revived perennially since.

Kern eased his previously heavy composing schedule after *Show Boat*. His next production for Broadway was *Sweet Adeline*, a turn-of-the-century period piece written as a vehicle for Helen Morgan. A moderate hit, it was notable for the song "Why Was I Born?" (lyrics by Hammerstein), successfully recorded by Helen Morgan and by Libby Holman, whose tumultuous career would be the subject of the 1935 film *Reckless*, to which Kern would contribute music.

With the onset of talking motion pictures, Kern and his musicals became more attractive to Hollywood. He had scored the *Gloria's Romance* series of silent films in 1916, and an unsuccessful silent version of *Sally* had been made in 1925. In 1929 a second film version of *Sally* and a first one of *Show Boat* were attempted, and in 1930 Kern made his first trip to Hollywood to work on *Men of the Sky* (ultimately released without songs) and a film version of *Sunny*.

Returning to Broadway, Kern and Harbach produced *The Cat and the Fiddle*, which ran for 395 performances, a remarkable success during the Depression. Its best-remembered songs, "The Night Was Made for Love" and "She Didn't Say 'Yes,'" made up the two sides of a hit record by Leo Reisman and His Orch. Kern again teamed with Hammerstein for *Music in the Air*, another success; its two standout numbers, "I've Told Ev'ry Little Star" and "The Song Is You," appeared on a popular recording by Jack Denny and His Orch. before going on to become standards. *Roberta*, Kern's last Broadway musical for six years, also added several standards to his catalog, most prominent among them "Smoke Gets in Your Eyes," "Yesterdays," and "The Touch of Your Hand" (all lyrics by Harbach). Reisman recorded popular versions of all three, even using Tamara, who sang the song onstage, as vocalist on "Smoke Gets in Your Eyes." But the best-selling of many contemporary recordings of the song was the one by Whiteman. (Even though its popularity saved the show, which had been poorly reviewed, Kern expressed his displeasure with the recorded versions of "Smoke Gets in Your Eyes" and threatened to withdraw permission for radio broadcasts.) The rich score also boasted such songs as "You're Devastating" and "Let's Begin."

After the failure of *Three Sisters* in London, Kern turned to writing for the movies full-time. He and Hammerstein added songs to the film versions of *Music in the Air* and *Sweet Adeline*, while the score to *Roberta*, which became a vehicle for Astaire and Ginger Rogers, was largely replaced by new songs Kern wrote with lyrics by Dorothy Fields. Among these were "Lovely to Look At" and "I Won't Dance," the latter a revised version of a song from *Three Sisters*. The orchestras of Reisman and Eddy Duchin each made records pairing the two songs, with Duchin's the more successful. Both were among the country's most popular songs in April 1935. Before the end of the year, Kern and Fields teamed again for the Lily Pons vehicle *I Dream Too Much*, which produced modest hits in the title song (recorded by Reisman) and "I'm the Echo" (recorded by Whiteman).

Kern and Hammerstein wrote several new songs for the second film version of *Show Boat*, among them "It Still Suits Me," for Robeson. Kern and Fields next provided songs for the Astaire-Rogers film *Swing Time*, with successful recordings resulting from six of their contributions. Astaire recorded popular versions of five: "The Way You Look Tonight" (also recorded by Guy Lombardo and His Orch. and by Teddy Wilson and His Orch. with Billie Holiday on vocals); "A Fine Romance" (also recorded by Lombardo and by Holiday); "Never Gonna Dance"; "Pick Yourself Up"; and "Bojangles of Harlem." The instrumental "Waltz in Swing Time," recorded by Johnny Green and His Orch. and issued on the flip side of Astaire's version of "A Fine Romance," was also a modest hit. "The Way You Look Tonight" won the Academy Award for Best Song of 1936.

Kern gave up commuting between N.Y. and Calif. and settled in Beverly Hills in 1937. He and Hammerstein collaborated on *High, Wide and Handsome*, which produced hits in "Can I Forget You?," most successfully recorded by Crosby, and "The Folks Who Live on the Hill," a minor hit for Lombardo that went on to become a standard. Kern also composed the film's score. While working on songs for his next film he suffered a heart attack in March 1937 that incapacitated him for several months, delaying the completion of his next film with Fields, *Joy of Living*, until the following year. Of the four songs he contributed, the hit was "You Couldn't Be Cuter," which enjoyed its most popular recording by Tommy Dorsey and His Orch.

Kern made two more attempts at Broadway musicals during the next year, collaborating with Harbach and Hammerstein on *Gentlemen Unafraid* (St. Louis, June 3, 1938), which never made it to N.Y., and with Hammerstein on *Very Warm for May*, which ran a mere 59 performances despite a strong score that included the hit "All the Things You Are," successfully recorded by Dorsey and by the orchestra of Artie Shaw, who married Kern's daughter in 1941.

Kern wrote one of his few songs not inspired by a musical or film in 1940 when Hammerstein sent him the lyric for "The Last Time I Saw Paris," which he had been inspired to write by the recent Nazi occupation. Introduced by Kate Smith on radio and recorded by her, the song became a hit. It was interpolated into the film *Lady, Be Good!* (1941) and won the Academy Award for Best Song. Kern, however, felt that it should not have been eligible since it had not been written for the film and successfully petitioned to have the rules changed in the future.

Kern worked with a series of well-known but new collaborators on each of his last four films. Johnny Mercer wrote the lyrics to the songs in the Astaire movie musical *You Were Never Lovelier*. The major hit from the film was "Dearly Beloved," a Top Ten hit for Glenn Miller and His Orch. and for Dinah Shore; Astaire's recording of "I'm Old Fashioned" was also successful. Ira Gershwin joined Kern for *Cover Girl*, notable for the song "Long Ago (And Far Away)," which became a Top Ten hit for Crosby, for Jo Stafford, and for Perry Como, though the most successful recording was by Helen Forrest and Dick Haymes. E. Y. Harburg worked with Kern on *Can't Help Singing*, which featured "More and More," a Top Ten hit for Dorsey and also a hit for Como. And Leo Robin was the primary lyricist for *Centennial Summer*; he wrote "In Love in Vain," a hit for Haymes and Forrest and for Margaret Whiting, though the film's most successful song was the Kern-Hammerstein collaboration "All through the Day," taken into the Top Ten by Frank Sinatra and by Como. The song was also a hit for Whiting.

Kern's final songs thus continued to achieve widespread popularity up to the time of his death. When he died he was preparing for another revival of *Show Boat* (N.Y., Jan. 5, 1946) that would feature his last song, "Nobody Else But Me" (lyrics by Hammerstein). He had also planned to write a new Broadway musical, *Annie Oakley*, subsequently composed by Irving Berlin as *Annie Get Your Gun*.

Though largely fictional, the screen biography *Till the Clouds Roll By* featured a large number of Kern's best-known songs in renditions by such contemporary singers as Frank Sinatra and Judy Garland. This turned out to be a precursor for the extensive use of Kern's songs by the generation of post–World War II pop singers. His songs also occasionally returned to the hit parade, notably in the chart-topping gold record of "Smoke Gets in Your Eyes" by the Platters in 1958–59. Other notable films featuring Kern music include the Marilyn Miller screen biography *Look for the Silver Lining* (1949), the third version of *Show Boat*, the second version of *Roberta*, entitled *Lovely to Look At*, and *The Last Time I Saw Paris* (1954), based on F. Scott Fitzgerald's short story "Babylon Revisited." Kern's shows have been staged frequently on and Off- Broadway and regionally, including such major Broadway revivals as *Very Good Eddie* (Dec. 21, 1975) and *Show Boat* (Oct. 2, 1994), which won the Tony Award for Best Revival.

Though he was indifferent or antagonistic toward such popular genres of his time as ragtime, jazz, and swing, Kern readily adapted to changing trends in theater and film music and developed stylistically far more than such predecessors as Victor Herbert, such that his songs continued to become popular throughout his life. He was able to write in the light vaudeville and operetta styles of his youth, yet he helped foster the sophisticated song form developed further by George Gershwin and Cole Porter. He is credited with writing the first of the integrated musicals that, in the hands of Richard Rodgers and Frederick Loewe, would dominate Broadway after his death. But his greatest gift was an endless stream of melody that has served to make his songs timeless despite changes in musical fashion.

WORKS: MUSICALS/REVUES (only shows for which Kern was principal composer or co-composer are noted; all dates are for N.Y. opening unless otherwise noted): *Mr. Wix of Wickham* (Sept. 19, 1904); *La Belle Paree* (March 20, 1911); *The Red Petticoat* (Nov. 13, 1912); *Oh, I Say!* (Oct. 30, 1913); *90 in the Shade* (Jan. 25, 1915); *Nobody Home* (April 20, 1915); *Miss Information* (Oct. 5, 1915); *Very Good Eddie* (Dec. 23, 1915); *Have a Heart* (Jan. 11, 1917); *Love o' Mike* (Jan. 15, 1917); *Oh, Boy!* (Feb. 20, 1917); *Leave It to Jane* (Aug. 28, 1917); *Miss 1917* (Nov. 5, 1917); *Oh, Lady! Lady!!* (Feb. 1, 1918); *Toot-Toot!* (March 11, 1918); *Rock-a-bye Baby* (May 22, 1918); *Head over Heels* (Aug. 29, 1918); *She's a Good Fellow* (May 5, 1919); *The Night Boat* (Feb. 2, 1920); *Hitchy- Koo, 1920* (Oct. 19, 1920); *Sally* (Dec. 21, 1920); *Good Morning, Dearie* (Nov. 1, 1921); *The Cabaret Girl* (London, Sept. 19, 1922); *The Bunch and Judy* (Nov. 28, 1922); *The Beauty Prize* (London, Sept. 5, 1923); *Stepping Stones* (Nov. 6, 1923); *Sitting Pretty* (April 8, 1924); *Dear Sir* (Sept. 23, 1924); *Sunny* (Sept. 22, 1925); *The City Chap* (Oct. 26, 1925); *Criss Cross* (Oct. 12, 1926); *Show Boat* (Dec. 27, 1927); *Blue Eyes* (London, April 27, 1928); *Sweet Adeline* (Sept.

3, 1929); *The Cat and the Fiddle* (Oct. 15, 1931); *Music in the Air* (Nov. 8, 1932); *Roberta* (Nov. 18, 1933); *Three Sisters* (London, April 9, 1934); *Very Warm for May* (Nov. 17, 1939). FILMS (only films for which Kern was principal composer are noted): *Gloria's Romance* (1916); *Sally* (1925); *Show Boat* (1929); *Sally* (1929); *Sunny* (1930); *Men of the Sky* (1931); *The Cat and the Fiddle* (1934); *Music in the Air* (1934); *Sweet Adeline* (1935); *Roberta* (1935); *I Dream Too Much* (1935); *Show Boat* (1936); *Swing Time* (1936); *When You're in Love* (1937); *High, Wide and Handsome* (1937); *Joy of Living* (1938); *One Night in the Tropics* (1940); *Sunny* (1941); *You Were Never Lovelier* (1942); *Cover Girl* (1944); *Can't Help Singing* (1944); *Centennial Summer* (1946); *Till the Clouds Roll By* (1946); *Show Boat* (1951); *Lovely to Look At* (1952). OTHER WORKS: "Scenario for Orchestra on Themes from *Show Boat*" (Cleveland, Oct. 23, 1941; introduced by the Cleveland Symphony Orch., conducted by Artur Rodzinski); "Mark Twain (Portrait for Orchestra)" (Cincinnati, May 1942; introduced by the Cincinnati Symphony Orch., conducted by André Kostelanetz); "Montage for Orchestra" (1945).

BIBL.: D. Ewen, *The Story of J. K.* (N.Y., 1953); D. Ewen, *The World of J. K.* (N.Y., 1960); O. Hammerstein II, ed., *The J. K. Song Book* (N.Y., 1955); H. Fordin, *J. K.: The Man and His Music* (Santa Monica, 1975); A. Lamb, *J. K. in Edwardian London* (N.Y., 1981; 2nd ed., rev., 1985); M. Freedland, *J. K.: A Biography* (N.Y., 1978); G. Bordman, *J. K.: His Life and Music* (N.Y., 1980); L. Davis, *Bolton and Wodehouse and K.: The Men Who Made Musical Comedy* (N.Y., 1993).—WR

Kern, Patricia, Welsh mezzo-soprano; b. Swansea, July 4, 1927. She was a student at the Guildhall School of Music in London of Parry Jones (1949–52). In 1952 she made her operatic debut in *Cenerentola* with London's Opera for All group, remaining with it until 1955. In 1959 she made her first appearance with the Sadler's Wells Opera in London as Rusalka, singing there regularly for 10 seasons. In 1967 she made her debut at London's Covent Garden as Zerlina. She made her first appearance in the U.S. in 1969 in Washington, D.C. She also made guest appearances in Glyndebourne, Stockholm, Spoleto, N.Y., Chicago, Dallas, and other operatic centers. Among her esteemed roles were Cherubino, Marcellina, Dorabella, Rosina, Ottone, and Isabella. —NS/LK/DM

Kernis, Aaron Jay, American composer; b. Philadelphia, Jan. 15, 1960. He was a student of John Adams at the San Francisco Cons. of Music (1977–78), of Wuorinen and Elias Tanenbaum at the Manhattan School of Music in N.Y. (B.Mus., 1981), and of Druckman, Amy, Rands, and Subotnick at the Yale Univ. School of Music (1981–83). He won the Rome Prize and was in residence at the American Academy in Rome in 1984–85. In 1985 he received the Joseph N. Bearns Prize of Columbia Univ. In 1985–86 he held a Guggenheim fellowship. In 1988 he received the N.Y. Foundation for the Arts fellowship. In 1998 he won the Pulitzer Prize in Music for his 2nd String Quartet, *Musica Instrumentalis*. The early influence of traditional music, impressionism, and minimalism on his output eventually led to a more personal style, noted for its accessible but still modern means of expression.

WORKS: ORCH.: *Mirror of Heat and Light* (1985); *Invisible Mosaic III* (1988); 3 syms.: No. 1, *Symphony in Waves* (1989; 1st complete perf., N.Y., Nov. 9, 1991), No. 2 (1991; N.Y., Jan. 15, 1992), and No. 3, *Garden of Light*, for Soloists, Chorus, Boy's Chorus, and Orch. (N.Y., Oct. 8, 1999); *New Era Dances* (1992); *Colored Field*, English horn Concerto (San Francisco, April 21, 1994). **CHAMBER:** *Meditation*, in memory of John Lennon, for Cello and Piano (1981); *Music for Trio: Cycle IV* for Flute, Cello, and Piano (1982); *Suite in 3 Parts* for Guitar or Organ (1982); *Passacaglia-Variations* for Viola and Piano (1985); *Invisible Mosaic I* for Clarinet, Violin, Cello, and Piano (1986) and *II* for Chamber Ensemble (1988); *Phantom Polka* for Accordion (1987); *Delicate Songs* for Flute, Violin, and Cello (1988); 2 string quartets (*Musica Celestis*, 1990; *Musica Instrumentalis*, 1997); *Mozart en Route:"a little traveling music"* for Violin, Viola, and Cello (1991); *100 Greatest Dance Hits* for Guitar and String Quartet (1993); *Harlem River Reveille* for Brass Quintet (1993); *Still Movement with Hymn* for Piano Quartet (1993); *Hymn* for Accordion (1993); *Air* for Violin and Piano (1995). **P i a n o :** *Cycle II* for Piano Duo (1979); *Before Sleep and Dreams* (1987–90); *Superstar Etude No. 1* (1992). **VOCAL:** *Stein Times 7* for Chorus and Piano (1980); *Cycle III* for Soprano, Baritone, and Chamber Ensemble (1981); *Dream of the Morning Sky: Cycle V* for Soprano and Orch. (1982); *Morningsongs* for Baritone and Orch. (1982–83); *America(n) (Day) Dreams* for Mezzo-soprano and Chamber Ensemble (1984); *Love Scenes* for Soprano and Cello (1987); *Barbara Allen* for Soprano and Orch. (1988); *Songs of Innocents* for High Voice and Piano (2 books, 1989); *Brilliant Sky, Infinite Sky* for Baritone, Violin, Percussion, and Piano (1991); *La quattro stagioni dalla cucina futurismo* for Narrator, Violin, Cello, and Piano (1991); *Simple Songs* for Soprano or Tenor and Orch. (1991); *Goblin Market* for Narrator and Ensemble (1995). —NS/LK/DM

Kerr, Harrison, American composer; b. Cleveland, Oct. 13, 1897; d. Norman, Okla., Aug. 16, 1978. He studied composition with James H. Rogers and Claus Wolfram in Cleveland, and then continued his training in France with Boulanger (composition) and Philipp (piano) at the American Cons. in Fontainebleau, and with Vidal (composition) and Wolff (conducting). In 1927–28 he was director of music of Greenbriar Coll. in Lewisburg, W.Va., and then was director of music and art at the Chase School in N.Y. (1929–35). In subsequent years, he was active with the American Composers' Alliance and the American Music Center, serving as executive secretary for both organizations. From 1949 to 1960 he was dean of the Coll. of Fine Arts at the Univ. of Okla., where he continued on its faculty as composer-in-residence until 1968. He utilized traditional forms in his works, enfusing them with linear chromatic writing and judicious dissonances.

WORKS: DRAMATIC: O p e r a : *The Tower of Kel* (1958–60). **B a l l e t :** *Dance Sonata* (1938). **ORCH.:** 3 syms. (1927–29, rev. 1938; 1943–45; 1953–54); *Movement* for Strings (1936); *Dance Suite* (1939–40); Violin Concerto (1950–51; rev. 1956); *Variations on a Ground Bass* (1966); *Sinfonietta da Camera* (1967–68); *Episodes from The Tower of Kel* (1971–72). **CHAMBER:** 3 string quartets (1935, 1937, 1973); Trio for Clarinet, Cello, and Piano (1936); *Study* for Cello (1937); Piano Trio (1938); Suite for Flute and Piano (1940–41); *Overture, Arioso, and Finale* for Cello and Piano (1941–51; also for Cello and Orch., 1966–67); Sonata for Solo Violin (1954); Violin Sonata (1956); *Quasi Quodlibet* for 8 Trombones (1974); 3 Duos for 2 Flutes (1976). **P i a n o :** *Poem* (1929); 2 sonatas (1929, 1943); 4 *Preludes* (1943); *Frontier Day* (1956). **VOCAL:** 3 *Songs* for Voice and

Piano or Chamber Orch. (1924–28); *Notations on a Sensitized Plate* for High or Medium Voice, Clarinet, Piano, and String Quartet (1935); *Wink of Eternity* for Chorus and Orch. (1937); *In Cabin'd Ships at Sea* for Chorus and Orch. (1971); other songs.

BIBL.: R. Kohlenberg, *H. K.: Portrait of a Twentieth-century American Composer* (Lanham, Md., 1997).—NS/LK/DM

Kersjes, Anton (Frans Jan), Dutch conductor; b. Arnhem, Aug. 17, 1923. He studied conducting with Felix Hupka in Amsterdam and Eugene Bigot in Paris. In 1953 he became co-founder and conductor of the Kunstmaand Chamber Orch. in Amsterdam, which became the Kunstmaand Orch. in 1955 and the Amsterdam Phil. in 1969; was its principal conductor until 1983. He took this orch. to the Soviet Union in 1972, making it the first Dutch ensemble to give concerts there. From 1969 to 1979 he led the conducting class at the Sweelinck Cons. in Amsterdam.—NS/LK/DM

Kersters, Willem, Belgian composer and teacher; b. Antwerp, Feb. 9, 1929. He studied at the Royal Flemish Cons. of Music in Antwerp, and with Louël (counterpoint), Absil and Quinet (fugue), Poot (composition), and Defossez (conducting) at the Royal Cons. of Music in Brussels. From 1962 to 1994 he taught at the Royal Flemish Cons. of Music. He also taught at the Maastricht Cons. in the Netherlands from 1967 to 1994. In his music, Kersters has made imaginative use of both tonal and atonal resources.

WORKS: DRAMATIC: O p e r a : *Gansendonk* (1979–82; Antwerp, Sept. 29, 1984). **B a l l e t :** *Parwati* (1956); *Triomf van de Geest* (1959); *Halewyn* (1973; Brussels, Jan. 25, 1974); *Ulenspiegel de Geus* (1975–76). **ORCH.:** Concertino for Oboe and Strings (1953); Sinfonietta for Chamber Orch. (1955); Sinfonia concertante for Flute, Clarinet, Bassoon, and Strings (1957); *Sinfonia piccola* (1958); *Divertimento* for Strings (1958); 5 syms. (1962; 1963; 1967; *Gezelle*, 1979; 1987); *Plechtige Overture* (1963); Sinfonietta for Wind Orch. (1967); *Anaglyphos* for Percussion Orch. (1969); *Capriccio* (1972); *Serenade* for Chamber Orch. (1976); Piano Concerto (1977); *Valerius*, overture for Wind Orch. (1983); *Incantations* for Brass Band (1983); Violin Concerto (1989). **CHAMBER:** Wind Quintet (1954); Viola Sonata (1954); *Partita* for Violin and Piano (1956); 2 string quartets (1962, 1964); *Concert Music* for Strings, Piano, Percussion, and Timpani (1964); Suite for Clarinet and Strings (1964); Sonata for Solo Violin (1965); *De drie tamboers*, septet for 4 Clarinets, Percussion, Timpani, and Piano (1966); *Variations on a Theme of Giles Farnaby* for 4 Clarinets (1967); *Meditation on the Name of BACH* for Trumpet, Piano, and Strings (1968); *3 Rondos* for Brass Quintet (1969); *Contrasts* for Percussion and Piano (1969); Quartet for Violin, Viola, Cello, and Piano (1970); Quartet for Clarinet, Violin, Viola, and Cello (1971); *Laudes* for Brass and Percussion (1973); *Diagram* for Violin and Cello (1974); *Coincidences* for 9 Percussionists (1974); *Aveniana* for Oboe, Clarinet, and Bassoon (1984); Nonetto for 9 Instruments (1985); *Ballade* for Alto Saxophone and Strings (1987); Sextet for Piano and Strings (1990); *Idyll* for Harp and Strings (1992); Violin Sonata (1993). **KEYBOARD:** Piano pieces, including a sonata (1985); organ music. **VOCAL:** *De geestelikje bruiloft* for Soprano, English Horn, Clarinet, Piano, and String Quintet (1955); *La chanson d'Eve* for Soprano and String Quartet (1959); *Psalms* for Alto, Men's Chorus, Winds, Organ, and Timpani (1962); *A Gospel Song* for 4 Soloists, Chorus, and Orch. (1965); *A Hymn of Praise,* oratorio for Soloists, Chorus, and Orch. (1966); *Barbaarse dans* for Soloists, Chorus, and Instrumental Ensemble (1970); *Angst...een dans* for Tenor, Reciter, Chorus, Harp, Piano, and Percussion Orch. (1970); *Kinderwereld* for Choruses and Orch. (1988); *De Feesten van Angst en Pijn* for Tenor, Alto, Reciter, Chorus, Harp, Piano, Percussion, and Strings (1995).—**NS/LK/DM**

Kertész, István, noted Hungarian-born German conductor; b. Budapest, Aug. 28, 1929; d. (drowned while swimming in the Mediterranean) Kfar Saba, Israel, April 16, 1973. He studied violin and composition at the Franz Liszt Academy of Music in Budapest, where his principal teachers were Kodály and Weiner; also received instruction in conducting from Somogyi. He conducted in Györ (1953–55) and at the Hungarian State Opera in Budapest (1955–56); after the unsuccessful Hungarian revolution (1956), he settled in West Germany and became a naturalized citizen; he completed his conducting studies with Previtali at the Accademia di Santa Cecilia in Rome (1958). He was Generalmusikdirektor in Augsburg (1958–63); made his first appearances as a guest conductor in England in 1960 and in the U.S. in 1961. In 1964 he became Generalmusikdirektor of the Cologne Opera, a post he retained until his death; he was also principal conductor of the London Sym. Orch. (1965–68), which he led on a world tour (1965). His readings of the Romantic repertoire were especially admired for their warmth and lyricism.

BIBL.: K. Richter, *I. K.* (Augsburg, 1976).—**NS/LK/DM**

Kes, Willem, Dutch conductor and composer; b. Dordrecht, Feb. 16, 1856; d. Munich, Feb. 21, 1934. He studied violin with various teachers in the Netherlands, then with Ferdinand David at the Leipzig Cons. (1871), Wieniawski in Brussels (1873), and Joachim in Berlin (1875); also composition with Reinecke, Bargiel, and Kiel in Berlin. In 1876 he was made 1st concertmaster of Amsterdam's Park-Orkest; was its conductor in 1883 and also conductor of Dordrecht's orch., choir, and music school (1877–88). He became the first conductor of Amsterdam's Concertgebouw Orch., leading its inaugural concert on Nov. 3, 1888, and remaining with it until 1895. In 1895 he succeeded Henschel as conductor of the Scottish Orch. in Glasgow. In 1898 he went to Russia, where he conducted the Moscow Phil. Soc. (1901–05); subsequently was conductor of the Koblenz Orch. and director of the music school there (1905–26). Among his works are a Sym., overtures, Violin Concerto, Cello Concerto, *Der Taucher* for Chorus and Orch., chamber music, piano pieces, and songs.—**NS/LK/DM**

Kessler, Thomas, Swiss composer and teacher; b. Zürich, Sept. 25, 1937. He received training in German and Romance philology at the univs. of Zürich and Paris, and in composition with Hartig, Blacher, and Pepping at the Berlin Hochschule für Musik. In 1965 he organized his own electronic music studio in Berlin, and then served as director of the Electronic Beat Studio there and of the Centre Universitaire International de Formation et de Recherches Dramatiques in Nancy. In 1972 he beccame a teacher of theory and composition at the Basel Academy of Music. He also served as director of the Basel electronic music studio from 1987. Kessler has also made appearances as a synthesizer performer. In his works, he has pursued an advanced course which has prompted him to utilize electronics and tape.

WORKS: *Konstellationen I* for Flute, Trombone, Cello, and Piano (1965) and *II* for Flute, Piano, Violin, and Cello (1967); *4 Stücke* for String Quartet (1965); *Countdown for Orpheus* for Variable Performers (1966); *Musik* for Flute, Piano, and Tape (1966); *Musik* for Double Bass, Piano, and Tape (1966); *Revolutionsmusik* for Ensemble and Tape (1968); Trio for Violin, Viola, and Cello (1968); *Nationale Feiertage*, opera (1969); *Smog* for Trombone and Orch. (1970); *Portrait* for Ensemble (1971); *Aufbruch* for Instruments (1973); *Loop* for Tape and Instruments (1973); *Piano Control* for Piano and Synthesizer (1974); *Lost Paradise* for Harp, Piano, Alto Flute, English Horn, Viola, and 2 Synthesizers (1975); *Klangumkehr* for Orch. (1975); *Dialoge* for 4 Performers and Vocoder (1977); *Violin Control* for Violin and Synthesizer (1978); *Unisono* for 3 Clarinets (1978); *Schallarchiv*, radiophonic piece (1979); *Pujaparwata* for Gamelan Ensemble (1980); *Traumklang* for Ensemble and Live Electronics (1981); *Drumphony* for Percussion, Computer, and Orch. (1981); *Aufbruch* for Orch. and 5 Computers (1990).—**NS/LK/DM**

Kessner, Daniel (Aaron), American composer, conductor, flutist, and teacher; b. Los Angeles, June 3, 1946. He studied composition with Lazarof at the Univ. of Calif. in Los Angeles (B.A., 1967; M.A., 1968; Ph.D., 1971). In 1970 he joined the faculty of the Calif. State Univ. in Northridge, where became a prof. in 1980. He also serves as coordinator of composition/theory, and as director of its Discovery Players (formerly New Music Ensemble). In 1970 and 1971 he received BMI prizes. He won the Queen Marie-José International Composition Prize in Geneva in 1972. Kessner has received grants from the NEA (1974, 1977), American Music Center (1981), and Arts International (1996).

WORKS: DRAMATIC: *The Telltale Heart*, monodrama for Tenor and Chamber Orch. (1975–78); *The Masque of the Red Death*, tale in music, dance, and light for Dancer, Conductor, and 7 Players (1979); *Texts for Nothing*, musical-literary-theatrical stream for Soprano, Flute, Trombone, Viola, Cello, and Conductor (1980–82). **ORCH.:** *Strata* (1971); *Mobile* (1973); *Romance: Orchestral Prelude No. 1* (1979) and *Raging: Orchestral Prelude No. 2* (1981); Piano Concerto (1984–86); *Breath* for Cello and Orch. (1991); *Lyric Piece* for Piano and Orch. (1994); *Icoane Românesti* (Images of Romania) for Orch. and Narration (1996); *Celebrations* for Flute and Orch. (1998). **Symphonic Band:** *Wind Sculptures* (1973); *Variations* (1977); *Sky Caves* (1984–85); *Symphonic Mobile II* (1996); *Balkan Dance* (1999). **CHAMBER:** *Equali I* for 4 Flutes, Violin, Viola, Cello, and Double Bass (1968–69), *II* for Piano or Celesta and 3 Percussionists (1970), *III* (*Nebulae*) for String Trio, 2 Guitars, and Harpsichord (1972), *IV* for Brass Quintet (1977), *V* for 6 Horns (1977–82), and *VI* for Marimba Ensemble (1978); 7 chamber concertos: *No. 1* for Recorder, High Voice, Oboe, String Quartet, Piano, and Percussion (1972), *No. 2* for Marimba and Percussion Ensemble (1978), *No. 3* for Piano, Alto Flute, English Horn, Bass Clarinet, Bassoon, and String Quintet (1980; also for String Orch.), *No. 4* for Woodwind Quartet and String Quintet (1989), *No. 5* for Clarinet, Horn, Bassoon, and String Quintet (1992), *No. 6* for Flute/Alto Flute, English Horn, Violin, Viola, Cello, and Piano (1994–95; also for Percussion, Harp, and Piano), and *No. 7* for 2 Trumpets, 3 Horns, Trombone, Bass Trombone, Euphonium, and Tuba (1997); *Array*, pieces for 2, 3, and 4 Guitars

(1973); *6 Aphorisms* for Clarinet and Guitar (1975); Trio for Violin, Guitar, and Cello (1976); *The Bells of Poe* for Percussion Quartet (1978); *Ancient Song* for Alto Recorder, Viola, and Prepared Guitar (1980); *Continuum* for Marimba (1981–82); *Arabesque* for Alto Saxophone and Vibraphone (1983); *Incantations* for Trombone and Percussion (1984); *Circle Music I* for Piano and Solo Instrument (1985) and *II* for Flute and Guitar (1985); *Intersonata* for Guitar (1987); *2 Old English Songs* for Soprano, Flute, Viola, and Guitar (1988); *Droning* for Clarinet and Viola (1988); String Quartet (1990); *Studies in Melodic Expression* for Various Solo Instruments (1990–91); *2 Visions* for Flute, Clarinet, Violin, Cello, and Piano (1991); *Lament* for Clarinet and Tape (1991–92); *One Voice, Alone* for Flute, English Horn, Clarinet, Horn, and Bassoon (1993); *Shades of Pastel* for Alto Flute and Prepared Guitar (1993); *Simple Motion* for Alto Flute and Piano (1993); *Dueling* for Viola and Cello (1993); *Symphonic Mobile I* for 9 Flutes (1995); *Cantiones Duarum Vocum* for 2 Instruments of Similar Register (1996); *Divertimento* for Flute, Alto Flute, Vibes, and Piano (1997); *Tous les matins...* for Bass Flute (1997); *Dances* for Clarinet and Guitar (1997); Sonata for 4 Timpani (1999). **VOCAL:** *Madrigals* for Chorus and Organ (1970; also for Chorus, Winds, and Brass, 1972); *Ritual Music* for Chamber Chorus and Percussion (1974); *Alea-luia* for Chorus (1978); *Tre Solfeggi per Coro* for Chorus (1990). —NS/LK/DM

Kestenberg, Leo, eminent Hungarian-born Israeli music educator; b. Rosenberg, Nov. 27, 1882; d. Tel Aviv, Jan. 14, 1962. He studied piano with Franz Kullak and Busoni and composition with Draeseke in Berlin, and then taught at the Stern Cons. and at the Klindworth-Scharwenka Cons. He became music adviser to the Prussian Ministry of Science, Culture, and Education (1918). He was made director of the Central Inst. for Education and Training (1922), and subsequently devoted himself to reorganizing the system of music education in Prussia. After the Nazis came to power (1933), he went to Prague, where he was founder-director of the International Soc. for Music Education. He then settled in Tel Aviv, where he was general manager of the Palestine Sym. Orch. (1939–45) and subsequently founded Israel's first training college for music teachers there. He publ. his memoirs as *Bewegte Zeiten: Musisch-musikantische Lebenserinnerungen* (Zürich, 1961).

WRITINGS: *Musikerziehung und Musikpflege* (Leipzig, 1921; 2nd ed., 1927); *Schulmusikunterricht in Preussen* (Berlin, 1927); ed. *Musik im Volk, Schule und Kirche* (Leipzig, 1927); ed. with W. Günther, *Der Musiklehrer* (Berlin, 3rd ed., 1928); ed. *Musikpädagogische Gegenwartsfragen* (Leipzig, 1928); *Musikpflege im Kindergarten* (Leipzig, 1929); *Schulmusik und Chorgesang* (Leipzig, 1930); *Jahrbuch der deutschen Musikorganisation 1931* (Berlin, 1931); *Der Privatunterricht in der Musik* (Berlin, 5th ed., 1932).

BIBL.: G. Braun, *Die Schulmusikerziehung in Preussen von den Falkschen Bestimmungen bis zur K.-Reform* (Kassel, 1957); U. Günther, *Die Schulmusikerziehung von der K.-Reform bis zum Ende des Dritten Reiches* (Neuwied, 1967).—NS/LK/DM

Ketèlbey, Albert (William), English conductor and composer; b. Birmingham, Aug. 9, 1875; d. Cowes, Isle of Wight, Nov. 26, 1959. Precociously gifted in music, he wrote a piano sonata at the age of 11, and played it at the Worcester Town Hall; Elgar heard it and praised it. At the age of 13, he competed for a Trinity Coll. scholarship in London, and was installed as Queen Victoria Scholar; at 16, he obtained the post of organist at St. John's Church at Wimbledon; at 20, began tours as the conductor of a musical comedy troupe, then was a theater conductor in London. He became best known for such light orch. pieces as *In a Monastery Garden* (1915), *In a Persian Market* (1920), *In a Chinese Temple Garden* (1923), *Sanctuary of the Heart* (1924), and *In the Mystic Land of Egypt* (1931); also wrote many smaller pieces under various pseudonyms. His other works include the comic opera *The Wonder Worker* (1900) and chamber music.—NS/LK/DM

Ketting, Otto, Dutch composer, son of **Piet Ketting;** b. Amsterdam, Sept. 3, 1935. He studied composition at the Royal Cons. of Music at The Hague (1952–58). After teaching at the Rotterdam Cons. (1967–71) and the Royal Cons. of Music at The Hague (1971–74), he concentrated upon composition. In 1958 he received the Gaudeamus Composition Prize and in 1973 the Kees van Baaren Prize. He received 2nd prize in the UNESCO Rostrum of Composers and was awarded the Matthijs Vermeulen Prize in 1978. In 1992 he received the Barlow Prize of the U.S.

WORKS: DRAMATIC: Opera: *Dummies* (The Hague, Nov. 14, 1974); *O, Thou Rhinoceros* (Holland Festival, June 2, 1977); *Ithaka* (Amsterdam, Sept. 23, 1986). **Ballet:** *The Last Report* (1962); *Interior* (1963); *Collage No. 7* (1967). **ORCH.:** *Sinfonietta* (1954); *2 canzoni* (1957); *Passacaglia* (1957); 3 syms. (1957–59; 1978; 1990); Concertino for 2 Trumpets, Strings, 3 Horns, and Piano (1958); Concertino for Jazz Quintet and Orch. (1960); *Variations* for Wind Orch., Harp, and Percussion (1960); *Collage No. 9* (1965); *In memoriam Igor Stravinsky* (1971); *Time Machine* for Wind Ensemble (1972); *For Moonlight Nights* for Flute and Ensemble (1973); *Capriccio* for Violin and Ensemble (1987; rev. 1995); *Adagio* (1989); *Medusa* for Alto Saxophone and Orch. (1992; rev. 1996); *De aankomst* (1993); *Kom, over de zeeën* (1994); *Cheops* for Horn and Orch. (1995). **CHAMBER:** Sonata for Brass Quartet (1955); *Serenade* for Cello and Piano (1957); *A Set of Pieces* for Flute and Piano (1967; also for Wind Quintet, 1968); *Adagio* for 12 Players (1977); *Mars* for 4 Clarinets and 4 or 8 Saxophones (1979); *Quodlibet* for 2 Percussionists, Piano, Bass Clarinet, and String Quartet (1979); *Autumn* for Horn and Piano (1980); *Monumentum* for Brass Instruments, Piano, and 4 Percussionists (1983); *Summer* for Bass Clarinet, Flute, and Piano (1985); Trio for Violin, Cello, and Piano (1988; rev. 1995); *Winter* for Alto Flute, Harp, Violin, and Cello (1988); *Preludim* for 12 Saxophones (1989); *Windsor Hotel* for Alto Saxophone and Piano (1998). **Piano:** *Collage No. 5* (1976); *Palace Hotel* (1998). **VOCAL:** *Christmas Songs* for Chorus and Small Orch. (1953); *Song Without Words* for Soprano and Piano (1968); *The Light of the Sun* for Soprano and Orch. (1978; rev. 1983); *Summer Moon* for Soprano and Orch. (1992). —NS/LK/DM

Ketting, Piet, Dutch pianist, conductor, and composer, father of **Otto Ketting;** b. Haarlem, Nov. 29, 1904; d. Rotterdam, May 25, 1984. He studied with Averkamp in Utrecht, then took composition lessons with Pijper (1926–32). As a pianist, he formed a duo with the flutist Johan Feltkamp (1927), and a trio with Feltkamp and oboist Jaap Stotijn (1935). From 1930 to 1956 he taught at the Rotterdam Cons.; also served as director of the Amsterdam Music Lyceum (1946–49). He was founder-conductor of the Rotterdam Chamber Choir (1937–60) and Orch. (1949–60). From 1960 to 1974 he immersed himself in the numerical symbolism of J.S. Bach's works. In his own works, he pursued a modern Baroque system of composition, with a discreet application of euphonious dissonance.

WORKS: ORCH.: 2 syms. (1929, 1975); *Sinfonia* for Cello and Orch. (1963; radio perf., Dec. 1, 1965); Bassoon Concertino (1968); Clarinet Concertino (1973); *Tema con 6 variazioni, in modo cabalistico,* for Flute and Orch. (1976); *Concertone 1980* for Viola, Winds, and Percussion (1980). **CHAMBER:** String Trio (1925); 3 string quartets (1927–28); Cello Sonata (1928); Trio for Flute, Clarinet, and Bassoon (1929); Flute Sonata (1930); Sonata for Flute, Oboe, and Piano (1936); *Partita* for 2 Flutes (1936); *Fantasia No. 1* for Harpsichord, Descant, and Treble Recorders and Flute (1969) and *No. 2* for Harpsichord (1972); *Preludium e Fughetta* for Alto Flute and Piano (1969). **PIANO:** 4 sonatinas (1926, 1926, 1927, 1929); *Prelude, Interlude and Postlude* for 2 Pianos (1971). **VOCAL:** *De minnedeuntjes* (The Love Songs) for Chorus and Orch. (1966–67; Dutch Radio, May 9, 1968); *Jazon and Medea,* dramatic scene for Chorus, Piano, Flute, and Clarinet (1975).—**NS/LK/DM**

Keuris, Tristan,

Dutch composer and teacher; b. Amersfoort, Oct. 3, 1946; d. Amsterdam, Dec. 15, 1996. He was a student of Jan van Vlijmen at the Amersfoort Music School, and then of Ton de Leeuw at the Utrecht Cons. (1963–69; graduated with a composition prize, 1969). After teaching composition at the Utrecht Cons., he taught theory at the Hilversum Cons. In 1975 he was awarded the Matthijs Vermeulen Prize for his *Sinfonia.* His music evolved along postserial lines to embrace athematic writing with an assured command of technique, form, and structure.

WORKS: ORCH.: *Kwartet* (1967); *Choral Music* (1969); *Soundings* (1970); Alto Saxophone Concerto (1971); *Sinfonia* (1972–74; Amsterdam, Jan. 31, 1976); *Serenade* for Oboe and Orch. (1974–76); Piano Concerto (1979–80); *Movements* (1981); *7 Pieces* for Bass Clarinet and Orch. (1983); 2 violin concertos: No. 1 (1984) and No. 2 (Amsterdam, Oct. 1997); *Variations* for Strings (1985); Saxophone Quartet Concerto (1986; Amsterdam, June 21, 1987); *Aria* for Flute and Orch. (1987; Scheveningen, April 21, 1988); *Symphonic Transformations* (Houston, Sept. 18, 1987); *Catena: Refrains and Variations* for 31 Winds, Percussion, and Celesta (Amsterdam, Jan. 12, 1989); *3 Sonnets* for Alto Saxophone and Orch. (Amsterdam, Sept. 8, 1989); *Antologia* (Parma, June 22, 1991); Double Cello Concerto (Manchester, April 30, 1992); Organ Concerto (Amsterdam, March 18, 1993); *3 Preludes* (Amsterdam, Sept. 2, 1994); Sym. (The Hague, Sept. 29, 1995); *Arcade* (1995; Hilversum, Jan. 20, 1996). **CHAMBER:** *Play* for Clarinet and Piano (1967); Saxophone Quartet (1970); *Concertante Muziek* for 9 Instruments (1973); *Muziek* for Clarinet, Violin, and Piano (1973); *Fantasia* for Flute (1976); Concertino for Clarinet and String Quartet (1977; rev. 1979); Violin Sonata (1977); *Capriccio* for Chamber Ensemble (1978); *8 Miniatures* for 6 Instruments (1980); *Divertimento* for 8 Instruments (1982); 2 string quartets (1982, 1985); Clarinet Quartet (1983); Piano Trio (1984); *Music* for Saxophone Quartet (1986; London, March 3, 1987); *5 Pieces* for Brass Quintet (1988; Rotterdam, April 1, 1989); Clarinet Quintet (1988; Amsterdam, Jan. 20, 1989); *Intermezzi* for Chamber Ensemble (Manchester, Nov. 5, 1989); *Canzone* for Clarinet (1990); *Passeggiate* for 4 Recorder Players (1990; Am-

sterdam, Feb. 21, 1991); Chamber Concerto for Accordion and Ensemble (Amsterdam, April 16, 1995); String Sextet (1995). **PIANO:** Sonata (1970). **VOCAL:** *To Brooklyn Bridge* for 24 Voices and 15 Instruments (1988; Utrecht, Dec. 7, 1989); *3 Michelangelo Songs* for Mezzo-soprano and Orch. (1989; Arnhem, March 21, 1991); *L'Infinito* for Soprano, Mezzo-soprano, Alto, Tenor, Bass, and Chamber Ensemble (1990; Utrecht, Feb. 28, 1991); *Laudi* for Mezzo-soprano, Baritone, Chorus, and Orch. (1992–93; Utrecht, Dec. 17, 1993).—**NS/LK/DM**

Keussler, Gerhard von,

German conductor and composer; b. Schwanenburg, Livonia, July 5, 1874; d. Niederwartha bei Dresden, Aug. 21, 1949. He studied with Reinecke and Jadassohn at the Leipzig Cons., and musicology with Riemann and Kretzschmar at the Univ. of Leipzig (Ph.D., 1902, with the diss. *Die Grenzen der Aesthetik*). From 1906 to 1910 he was a choral conductor in Prague. He then went to Hamburg, where he conducted the Phil. concerts until 1920 and led the Singakademie. In 1931 he toured in Australia as a conductor; returning to Germany, he taught at the Prussian Academy of Arts in Berlin (1934–41). He publ. the books *Das deutsche Volkslied und Herder* (Prague, 1915), *Händels Kulturdienst und unsere Zeit* (Hamburg, 1919), *Die Berufsehre des Musikers* (Leipzig, 1927), and *Paul Bucaenus* (Riga, 1931). He composed several symphonic dramas, including *Wandlungen* (1903), *Gefängnisse* (Prague, April 22, 1914), and *Die Gesselfahrt* (Hamburg, 1923), as well as 2 syms. (1925, 1928), the symphonic fantasy *Australia* (1935), and many songs.—**NS/LK/DM**

Key, Francis Scott,

American lawyer and author of the words of the U.S. national anthem, *The Star-Spangled Banner*; b. Carroll County, Md., Aug. 1, 1779; d. Baltimore, Jan. 11, 1843. He wrote the text of the anthem aboard a British ship (where he was taken as a civilian emissary to intercede for release of a Md. physician) on the morning of Sept. 14, 1814, setting it to the tune of the popular British drinking song "To Anacreon in Heaven," written by John Stafford Smith. The text and the tune did not become the official national anthem until March 3, 1931, when the bill establishing it as such was passed by Congress and signed by President Herbert Hoover.

BIBL.: O. Sonneck, *Report on the Star Spangled Banner, Hail Columbia, Yankee Doodle* (1909); idem, *The Star Spangled Banner* (1914); J. Muller, *The Star Spangled Banner* (N.Y., 1935). —**NS/LK/DM**

Keyes, Joe,

jazz trumpeter; b. Houston, Tex., ca. 1907; d. N.Y., November 1950. From 1928 he played with various bands in Houston, including Johnson's Joymakers. He was with Eugene Coy (early 1930), then with Jap Allen (summer 1930), but left Allen to join Blanche Calloway in April 1931. He joined Bennie Moten (1932), was with Count Basie in Little Rock, Ark. (early 1934), then briefly was with Nat Towles before joining Rook Ganz in Minneapolis (1934). He rejoined Basie in Kansas City and traveled to N.Y. with him in late 1936. He left in 1937, gigged with various bands including Hot Lips Page's. He was with Claude Hopkins at Meadowbrook in 1939, briefly with Eddie Durham's Band (1940), and afterwards played for a short while with Fletcher Henderson and Fats Wailer (1941). In 1943 he worked in the Wildcats Band, organized by Claude Hopkins at the Eastern Aircraft Factory. Because of drinking problems, he did little regular playing in the last years of his life. Cab Calloway bought him a new trumpet and tried to get him to resume regular playing, but to no avail. On Nov. 6, 1950, his body was found floating in the Harlem River. A mystery surrounds the manner of his death; it was formally described as drowning from undetermined circumstances. Shortly before his disappearance he had been showing people a roll of money that his mother had sent him to join her in Dallas.—JC/LP

Khachaturian, Aram (Ilich), brilliant Russian composer of Armenian descent, uncle of **Karen (Surenovich) Khachaturian;** b. Tiflis, June 6, 1903; d. Moscow, May 1, 1978. He played tuba in the school band, and also studied biology. He then went to Moscow and entered the Gnessin Music School (1922–25); later studied composition with Gnessin (1925–29). In 1929 he became a student at the Moscow Cons., graduating in 1934 in the class of Miaskovsky; finished his postgraduate studies there (1937). He commenced composing at the age of 21, and soon progressed to the first rank of Soviet composers of his generation. His music was in the tradition of Russian Orientalism; he applied the characteristic scale progressions of Caucasian melos, without quoting actual folk songs. His *Sabre Dance* from his ballet *Gayane* became popular all over the world. In 1948 he was severely criticized by the Central Committee of the Communist party, along with Prokofiev, Shostakovich, and others, for modernistic tendencies; although he admitted his deviations in this respect, he continued to compose essentially in his typical manner, not shunning highly dissonant harmonic combinations. He was made a People's Artist of the U.S.S.R. in 1954. He appeared as a conductor of his own throughout Europe and in Japan. He made his American debut in Washington, D.C., on Jan. 23, 1968, conducting the National Sym. Orch. in a program of his works. A critical ed. of his works was publ. in Moscow (1982 et seq.). In 1933 he married **Nina Makarova.**

WORKS: DRAMATIC: B a l l e t : *Shchastye* (Happiness; Yerevan, 1939; Moscow, Oct. 24, 1939); *Gayane* (1940–42; Perm, Dec. 9, 1942; rev. 1952 and 1957; 3 symphonic suites, 1943; includes the immensely popular *Sabre Dance*); *Spartak* (Spartacus; 1950–56; Leningrad, Dec. 26, 1956; rev. 1957–58; 4 symphonic suites: Nos. 1–3, 1955, and No. 4, 1966). **I n c i d e n - t a l M u s i c :** *The Widow of Valencia* (1939–40; orch. suite, 1953); *Masquerade* (1940; orch. suite, 1944). **F i l m :** *The Battle of Stalingrad* (Moscow, Dec. 9, 1949). **ORCH.:** *Dance Suite* (1932–33); 3 syms.: No. 1 (1932–33; Moscow, April 23, 1935), No. 2 (Moscow, Dec. 30, 1943; rev., Moscow, March 6, 1944), and No. 3 for 15 Solo Trumpets, Orch., and Organ (Leningrad, Dec. 13, 1947); Piano Concerto (1936; Leningrad, July 5, 1937); Violin Concerto (Moscow, Nov. 16, 1940; transcribed for Flute by J.-P. Rampal, 1968); *2 Armenian Dances* for Cavalry Band (1943); *Solemn Overture* (1945); *Russian Fantasy* (1946); Cello Concerto (1945–46; Moscow, Oct. 30, 1946); *Ode in Memory of Lenin* (Moscow, Dec. 26, 1948); *Concerto-Rhapsody* for Piano and Orch. (1955–68); *Salutation,* overture (1958–59); *Concerto-Rhapsody* for Violin and Orch. (1961–62; Yaroslavl, Oct. 7, 1962; Moscow, Nov.

3, 1962); *Concerto-Rhapsody* for Cello and Orch. (1963; Gorky, Jan. 4, 1964). **CHAMBER:** *Song-Poem* for Violin and Piano (1929); Violin Sonata (1932); String Quartet (1932); Trio for Clarinet, Violin, and Piano (1932); *Jazz Composition* for Clarinet (1966; written for Benny Goodman); *Sonata-Monologue* for Solo Cello (1974); *Sonata-Fantasia* for Solo Violin (1975). **P i a n o : 2** albums of children's pieces (1926–47; 1965); *Poem* (1927); *7 Fugues with Recitatives* (1928–66); *Suite* (1932); *Toccata* (1932); *Suite,* 3 pieces for 2 Pianos (1945); Sonatina (1952); Sonata (1961). **VOCAL:** *Poem about Stalin* for Chorus and Orch. (Moscow, Nov. 29, 1938); *3 Concert Arias* for Soprano and Orch. (1946); *Ode to Joy* for Mezzo-soprano, Chorus, 10 Harps, Unison Violins, Band, and Orch. (1955); *Ballade about the Fatherland* for Bass and Orch. (1961); *In Memory of the Heroes,* cantata for Soprano, Men's Chorus, and Orch. (1976; a reworking of *The Battle of Stalingrad*); songs.

BIBL.: I. Martynov, *A. K.* (Moscow, 1956); G. Schneerson, *A. K.* (Moscow, 1960); G. Khubov, *A. K.* (Moscow, 1962; 2nd ed., 1966); V. Tigranov, *A.I. K.* (Leningrad, 1978; new ed., 1987); V. Iuzefovich, *A. K.* (N.Y., 1985; Russian tr., Moscow, 1990). —NS/LK/DM

Khachaturian, Karen (Surenovich), Russian composer, nephew of **Aram (Ilich) Khachaturian;** b. Moscow, Sept. 19, 1920. He studied at the Moscow Cons. with Litinsky. During World War II, he served in the entertainment division of the Red Army. He resumed studies in 1945 at the Moscow Cons. with Shebalin, Shostakovich, and Miaskovsky, graduating in 1949. He then joined its faculty in 1952. His music follows the general line of socialist realism, nationalist or ethnic in thematic resources and realistic in harmonic and contrapuntal treatment. He wrote a number of effective scores for films.

WORKS: DRAMATIC: *An Ordinary Girl,* operetta (1959); *Cipollino,* ballet (Kiev, Nov. 8, 1974). **ORCH.:** *Sinfonietta* (1949); *Youth Overture* (1949; Moscow, Dec. 10, 1951); *New-Year Tree,* suite (1951); *In Mongolia,* suite (1951); *Oriental Suite* (1952); *Sports Suite* (1954); 4 syms.: No. 1 (Moscow, March 12, 1955), No. 2 (Moscow, Nov. 27, 1968), No. 3 (Moscow, Oct. 15, 1982), and No. 4 (1991); *Friendship Overture* (1959); *At the Circus,* suite (1968); Concerto for Piano and Chamber Orch. (1974); Cello Concerto (1983); *Epitaph* for Strings and Percussion (1986). **CHAMBER:** Violin Sonata (1947); Cello Sonata (1966); String Quartet (1969); Trio for Horn, Violin, and Piano (1981); String Trio (1984). **VOCAL:** *Glory to Consomol* for Chorus and Orch. (Moscow, Oct. 29, 1948); *At the Lone Willow,* cantata (1950); *A Moment of History,* oratorio to documented texts of the Soviet Revolution of 1917 (Moscow, April 26, 1971); choruses; songs.

BIBL.: M. Uspenskaya, *K. K.* (Moscow, 1956); E. Dolinskaya, *K. K.* (Moscow, 1975).—NS/LK/DM

Khadzhiev, Parashkev, Bulgarian composer; b. Sofia, April 14, 1912. He studied composition with Vladigerov and piano with Stoyanov at the Sofia Cons., graduating in 1936. He then went to Vienna, where he studied composition with Marx (1937), and to Berlin, where he took a course in composition with Thiessen at the Hochschule für Musik (1938–40). Returning to Bulgaria, he occupied various teaching positions.

WORKS: DRAMATIC: O p e r a : *Imalo edno vreme* (Once upon a Time; Sofia, April 11, 1957); *Lud gidiya* (Madcap; Sofia, Nov. 15, 1959); *Albena* (Varna, Nov. 2, 1962); *Jukka nosht*

(July Night; 1964; Plovdiv, Feb. 16, 1965); *The Millionaire* (1964; Sofia, March 14, 1965); *Master Woodcarvers* (Sofia, Oct. 9, 1966); *The Knight* (Varna, 1969); *The 3 Brothers and the Golden Apple* (1970; Sofia, Jan. 28, 1971); *The Year 893* (1972; Ruse, March 26, 1973). O p e r e t t a : *Delyana* (1952); *Aika* (1955); *Madame Sans-Gêne* (1958); *King Midas Has Ass's Ears* (1976). M u s i - c a l : *Job Hunters* (1972). B a l l e t : *Srebarnite pantofki* (The Silver Slippers; 1961; Varna, March 20, 1962). ORCH.: *Skici* (Sketches; 1940); Violin Concertino (1941); Flute Concertino (1945); *Capriccio* (1951); *Small Dance Suite* (1952); *Rondino* (1969). CHAMBER: 2 violin sonatas (1940, 1946); *3 Pieces* for Wind Quintet (1942); 2 string quartets (1948, 1953); piano pieces. VOCAL: Choruses; folk-song arrangements.—NS/LK/DM

Khaikin, Boris (Emmanuilovich), prominent Russian conductor; b. Minsk, Oct. 26, 1904; d. Moscow, May 10, 1978. He studied piano with Goedicke and conducting with Saradzhev and Malko at the Moscow Cons. He was a conductor at the Stanislavsky Theater in Moscow (1928–35). From 1936 to 1943 he served as principal conductor of the Maly Theater in Leningrad; from 1943 to 1954, at the Kirov Theater in Moscow, and from 1954 to 1978, at Moscow's Bolshoi Theater. He taught at the Leningrad Cons. (1935–53); then was prof. of conducting at the Moscow Cons. (1954–78). His most famous student was Kirill Kondrashin. He was made a People's Artist of the U.S.S.R. in 1972. He conducted the premieres of a number of Soviet operas.—NS/LK/DM

Khan, Chaka (Yvette Marie Stevens), one of the great soul divas of the late 20th century (b. Great Lakes, Ill., March 23, 1953). By the time Yvette Marie Stevens was in the sixth grade, she was singing with a Motown-styled group, The Crystalettes. By the time she was 15, she was singing professionally, touring with Motown great Mary Wells as a part of the Afro-Arts Theater. She became involved with the Black Panthers, working with their breakfast program, and took on the African name Chaka (which means "woman of fire") Adunne Aduffe Ymoja Hodarhi Karifi. The name "Khan" came from a brief marriage during those late teen years.

After working with several unsuccessful bands, Khan hooked up with former American Breed (the gold 1967 single "Bend Me Shape Me") members Andre Fischer and Kevin Murphey, who were working in a band called Ask Rufus. They moved to Los Angeles and within two years they released their eponymous debut album, which didn't generate much excitement in the record stores. However, Stevie Wonder heard the band and wrote a song with Khan's voice in mind. That song, a slow soul groove called "Tell Me Something Good" rose to #3, went gold, and earned a best R&B Duo/Group with Vocal Grammy in 1974. The follow-up single "You Got the Love" topped the R&B charts and hit #11 pop. The album *Rags to Rufus* lived up to its name, going gold and rising to #4.

In less than a year, the group was on the stands again, this time with *Rufusized*. This record launched the funky dance tune "Once You Get Started" to #10 pop taking the album to #7 and gold. Less than a year after that, they released another album. Because Khan was up

front and the focal point of the group, it seemed appropriate calling the album *Rufus Featuring Chaka Khan*. That record also rose to gold and #7 on the charts, propelled by the gold #1 R&B hit "Sweet Thing" (#5 pop) and the #39 pop "Dance wit Me." In late 1976 they released *Ask Rufus* which hit #12 and went platinum with the #1 R&B hit "At Midnight (My Love Will Lift You)" (#30 pop) and the #32 pop hit "Hollywood." Almost exactly a year later, they put out *Street Player* which rose to gold and #14. It contained the #38 single "Stay."

Shortly after, Khan's first solo album, the Arif Mardin–produced *Chaka* was released in 1979. She took an infectious dance version of Ashford and Simpson's tune "I'm Every Woman" to the top of the R&B chart (#21 pop) and the album went gold. She spent the next five years splitting her time between Rufus and her solo career, including guest appearances on albums by artists ranging from David Bowie and Eric Clapton to Lenny White and Gladys Knight. Rufus's popularity was fading, although they continued to produce hits, including 1979's #1 R&B hit "Do You Love What You Feel" (#30 pop) and 1983's R&B top charter "Ain't Nobody" (#22 pop).

Khan, in the mean time, released 1980's *Naughty*, with the dance hit "Clouds," and followed a year later with the gold *What Cha Gonna Do for Me* which hit #17 powered by the R&B hit title track. She collaborated with members of Return to Forever, Freddy Hubbard, and Joe Henderson on the mainstream jazz record *Echoes of and Era*, an album that received critical praise but little sales or airplay. Her own 1982 outing, *Chaka Khan*, while not a major seller either, impressed her peers. The album moved easily from dance music to a bebop medley.

Breaking away from the band, Khan titled her next album, 1984's *I Feel for You* after a relatively obscure Prince track. Her version paired the original's spare electronic funk with a rap from Melle Mel of the Furious Five and a harmonica solo by Stevie Wonder. That song topped the R&B charts for three weeks, hitting #3 on the pop charts, going gold and winning a Best R&B Female Grammy for Khan and a Best R&B Song Grammy for Prince. The album went platinum.

Through the late 1980s and early 1990s, Khan's career had its share of ups and downs. Working with Quincy Jones on his 1988 *Back on the Block* album, she was paired with Ray Charles for "I'll Be Good to You," which topped the R&B charts, rising to #18 pop and winning a best R&B Duo/Group with vocal. Her own *CK*, produced by Prince, didn't fare as well. Her 1992 album *The Woman I Am* earned her another Best R&B Female Vocal Grammy. Ironically, after that victory, she spent the rest of the decade looking for a label until Prince signed her to his NPG records for *Come 2 My House*, which he co-produced and co-wrote in 1998. Khan currently is working as a deejay at a Los Angeles radio station. Her daughter heads the band Pretty in Pink, which recently was signed to record its first album.

DISC.: *Chaka* (1979); *Naughty* (1980); *What Cha' Gonna Do for Me* (1981); *Chaka Khan* (1982); *I Feel for You* (1984); *Destiny*

(1986); *C.K.* (1988); *Life Is a Dance* (1989); *Life Is a Dance (The Remix Project)* (1989); *The Woman I Am* (1992); *Come 2 My House* (1998). **RUFUS:** *Rufus* (1973); *Rags to Rufus* (1974); *Rufu-sized* (1974); *Rufus Featuring Chaka Khan* (1975); *Ask Rufus* (1977); *Street Player* (1978); *Numbers* (1979); *Masterjam* (1979); *Party 'Til You're Broke* (1981); *Camouflage* (1981); *Live Stompin' at the Savoy* (1983).—**HB**

Khandoshkin, Ivan (Yevstafievich), Russian violinist and composer; b. 1747; d. St. Petersburg, March 28, 1804. He was a liberated serf. He studied in St. Petersburg with an Italian musician, Tito Porta, then was sent to Italy, where he was a student at Tartini's school in Padua. Returning to Russia in 1765, he became a violinist at the St. Petersburg Imperial Chapel. He then concertmaster of the Court Orch. (1773), and also taught violin at the Academy of Arts there, and later in Moscow and Ekaterinoslav. His position in Russian musical life was highly unusual for a man of his origin. He was the first Russian violin virtuoso, and the first to write instrumental music on Russian folk themes. He publ. *6 sonates pour deux violons* (Amsterdam, 1781), *Chansons russes variées pour violon et basse* (Amsterdam, 1781), and *Nouvelles variations sur des chansons russes* for Violin (St. Petersburg, 1784).

BIBL.: A. Mischakoff, *K. and the Beginning of Russian String Music* (Ann Arbor, 1983).—**NS/LK/DM**

Kharitonov, Dimitri, Russian baritone; b. Kuibyshev, Oct. 18, 1958. He studied at the Rimsky-Korsakov Coll. of Music in Leningrad (from 1976), and received training in voice and piano at the Nezhdanova State Cons. in Odessa (1978–84). In 1984 he became principal baritone at the Odessa State Opera. After appearing at the Bolshoi Theater in Moscow (1985–88), he sang Strauss's Jochanaan at the Edinburgh Festival in 1989. His U.S. debut followed in 1990 when he portrayed Sonora in *La Fanciulla del West* at the Lyric Opera in Chicago. In 1991 he sang in San Francisco and Los Angeles. He made his first appearance at the Glyndebourne Festival in 1993 as Prince Yeletsky, and then sang Nabucco in Genoa in 1994.—**NS/LK/DM**

Khessin, Alexander (Borisovich), Russian conductor and pedagogue; b. St. Petersburg, Oct. 19, 1869; d. Moscow, April 3, 1955. After taking a law degree (1894), he studied composition with Soloviev at the St. Petersburg Cons. (1895–99) and conducting with Nikisch in Leipzig and Mottl in Karslruhe. He conducted the sym. concerts of the Russian Musical Soc. in St. Petersburg and the Moscow Phil. Soc. (1901–05), and also served as director of the latter's music school (1904–05). After protesting the dismissal of Rimsky-Korsakov from the St. Petersburg Cons. in 1905, he also was dismissed from his posts. He toured Western Europe and the Russian hinterlands (1907–10) before serving as director of the Count Sheremetiev Music School in St. Petersburg (1910–15). In 1921 he settled in Moscow as a teacher, becoming director of the opera studio in 1935 and a prof. in 1939 at the Cons. After teaching at the Sverdlovsk Cons. (1941–43), he was director of the

Soviet Opera Co. of the All-Russian Theater Soc. (1943–53). He introduced many operas to the public in concert form before they were staged. His memoirs were publ. in Moscow in 1959.—**LK/DM**

Khodzha-Einatov, Leon, Russian composer; b. Tiflis, March 23, 1904; d. Leningrad, Nov. 1, 1954. He studied with Spendiarov. In 1927 he went to Leningrad, where he wrote music for the stage. He wrote the opera *Rebellion* (Leningrad, May 16, 1938), as well as 3 Armenian operas: *Arshak* (1945), *David Bek* (1951), and *Namus* (1952). Also *Symphonic Dances* and a Sym. (1953). —**NS/LK/DM**

Khokhlov, Pavel (Akinfievich), noted Russian baritone; b. Spassky, Aug. 2, 1854; d. Moscow, Sept. 20, 1919. He studied in Moscow, making his debut with the Bolshoi Theater there as Valentin in *Faust* (March 3, 1879); remained on its roster until he retired in 1900, and also appeared at the Maryinsky Theater in St. Petersburg (1881; 1887–88). He sang the title role in *Eugene Onegin* at its first professional performance (Moscow, Jan. 23, 1881). His other outstanding roles included Rubinstein's Demon, Boris Godunov, Prince Igor, Don Giovanni, and Wolfram.

BIBL.: S. Durilin, *P.A. K. 1854–1919* (Moscow and Leningrad, 1947); B. Yakovlev, *P.A. K.* (Moscow and Leningrad, 1950). —**NS/LK/DM**

Khrennikov, Tikhon (Nikolaievich), important Russian music administrator and composer; b. Elets, June 10, 1913. He was the 10th child in the musical family of a provincial clerk; his parents and siblings played the Russian guitar and the mandolin and sang peasant songs. He took piano lessons with a local musician. In 1927 he went to Moscow, where he was introduced to Gnessin, who accepted him as a student in his newly founded musical Technicum; there he studied counterpoint with Litinsky and piano with Ephraim Hellman. After graduation, he entered the Moscow Cons., where he studied composition with Shebalin and piano with Neuhaus (1932–36). He later continued postgraduate work with Shebalin. He developed a mildly modernistic, and technically idiomatic, type of composition which remained his recognizable style throughout his career as a composer. In 1961 he joined the faculty of the Moscow Cons., and was named a prof. in 1966. In the meantime, he became engaged in the political life of the country. He was attached to the music corps of the Red Army and accompanied it during the last months of World War II. In 1947 he joined the Communist party, and also became a deputy of the Supreme Soviet. In 1948 he was named personally by Stalin as secretary-general of the Union of Soviet Composers, and in 1949 became president of the music section of the All- Union Soc. for Cultural Exchange with Europe and America. He further served as head of the organizing committee for the International Festivals and the Tchaikovsky Competitions in Moscow. He was named a Hero of Socialist Labor in 1973, and in 1974 received the Lenin Prize. Amid all this work, he never slackened the tempo of his main preoccupation, that of composition. During his entire career, he was a stout spokesman for Soviet musical policy along the lines of socialist realism. He compromised himself, however, by his vehement condemnation of "formalist" directions in modern music, specifically attacking Stravinsky, Prokofiev, Shostakovich, and, later, also Schnittke and Gubaidulina. But as Soviet aesthetical directions underwent a liberal change, Khrennikov himself became the target of sharp criticism. He defended himself by claiming that he had protected a number of young musicians from attacks by entrenched functionaries of the Soviet musical establishment, and he succeeded in retaining his position as secretary-general of the Union of Soviet Composers until 1991. His compositions express forcefully the desirable qualities of erstwhile Soviet music, a flowing melody suggesting the broad modalities of Russian folk songs, a vibrant and expressive lyricism, and effective instrumental formation.

WORKS: DRAMATIC: Opera: *V buryu* (Into the Storm; Moscow, May 31, 1939; rev. version, Moscow, Oct. 12, 1952); *Frol Skobeyev*, comic opera (Moscow, Feb. 24, 1950; rev. as *Bezrodniy zyat* [The Unrelated Son-in-Law], after Gorky, Novosibirsk, Dec. 29, 1966); *Mat* (Mother; Moscow, Oct. 26, 1957); *100 Chertey i odna devushka* (100 Devils and a Single Girl), operetta (Moscow, May 16, 1963); *Belaya noch* (White Night), operetta (Moscow, May 23, 1967); *Malchik- velikan* (Boy Giant), children's fairy-tale opera (Moscow, Dec. 19, 1969); *Mnogo shuma...iz-za serdets* (Much Ado about...Hearts), comic opera (Moscow, March 11, 1972); *Doroteya*, comic opera (Moscow, May 26, 1983); *Zolotoy telyonok* (The Golden Calf), comic opera (Moscow, March 9, 1985); *Goliy korol* (The Naked King), comic opera (Leningrad, May 1988). **Ballet:** *Much Ado About Nothing* (1976); *Napoleon Bonaparte* (1995); *The Captain's Daughter* (1999). **OTHER:** Incidental music to plays; film scores. **ORCH.:** 4 piano concertos (1933, 1970, 1982, 1992); 3 syms.: No. 1 (1935; Moscow, Oct. 10, 1955), No. 2, expressing "the irresistible will to defeat the Fascist foe" (1940–43; Moscow, Jan. 10, 1943), and No. 3 (1973); 2 violin concertos (1959, 1975); 2 cello concertos: No. 1 (Moscow, May 13, 1964) and No. 2 (1986). **OTHER:** Chamber music; piano pieces; choruses; many songs.

BIBL.: L. Kaltat, *T. K.* (Moscow, 1946); V. Kukharsky, *T. K.* (Moscow, 1957); Y. Kremlev, *T. K.* (Moscow, 1963); I. Martinov, *T.N. K.* (Moscow, 1987).—NS/LK/DM

Khristov, Dobri, Bulgarian choral conductor, pedagogue, and composer; b. Varna, Dec. 14, 1875; d. Sofia, Jan. 23, 1941. He began to teach himself music in his youth. While attending secondary school in Varna, he began to compose. He founded its choir and gained experience as a conductor before being invited to serve as conductor of the choir of Gusla, the town's music soc. After teaching school, he pursued training with Dvořák at the Prague Cons. (1900–1903). Following further work as a conductor and teacher in Varna, he settled in Sofia as a teacher in 1907. In 1908 he became chorus master of the Opera. In 1922 he became a teacher at the State Academy of Music, where he later was a prof. (1926–33) and director. In 1935 he was made choirmaster of the Alexander Nevsky Memorial Church. In 1928 Khristov was made a member of the Bulgarian Academy of Sciences, the first Bulgarian musician to be so honored. He was the author of *Tekhnicheskiyat stroezh na balgarskata narodna muzika* (The Technical Structure of Bulgarian Folk Music; Sofia, 1928; 2nd ed., 1956). His works were principally inspired by Bulgarian folk music. He was especially esteemed for his choral output.

WORKS: ORCH.: 2 Balkan suites (1903, 1914); *Ivailo*, festive overture (1907); *Tutrakan epopoeya* (1917). **VOCAL:** Numerous choral pieces; hundreds of songs; sacred music; many folk-song arrangements.

BIBL.: I. Kamburov, *D. K.* (Sofia, 1942); V. Krastev, *D. K.* (Sofia, 1954); idem, ed., *Muzikalno-teoretichno i publitsistichno nasledstvo na D. K.* (Sofia, 1971).—NS/LK/DM

Kiberg, Tina, Danish soprano; b. Copenhagen, Dec. 30, 1958. She received vocal training in Copenhagen. In 1983 she made her debut at the Royal Opera in Copenhagen as Leonora in Nielsen's *Maskarade*, and then returned there as Wagner's Elsa in 1984, Strauss's Marschallin in 1988, Mozart's Countess in 1990, Helene in *Les Vêpres siciliennes* in 1991, Strauss's Ariadne in 1992, and Wagner's Eva in 1996. As a guest artist, she appeared in various European music centers, among them as Elsa at the Vienna State Opera in 1990 and the Opéra de la Bastille in Paris in 1991, and as Elisabeth in *Tannhäuser* at the Bayreuth Festival in 1992, where she returned as Sieglinde in 1995. In 1993 she sang Sieglinde at the Lyric Opera in Chicago, returning there in 1996 in that role and as Freia. In 1998 she appeared as the Marschallin in Geneva. She also pursued an active career as a lieder artist and as a soloist with orchs. —NS/LK/DM

Kidson, Frank, English music scholar; b. Leeds, Nov. 15, 1855; d. there, Nov. 7, 1926. Originally a landscape painter, he became interested in historical studies and collected English, Scottish, and Irish folk songs and dance melodies. He subsequently became one of the founders of the Folk-Song Soc. (1898), and also studied the history of British music publishing. His most significant editions include *Old English Country Dances Gathered from Scarce Printed Collections and from Manuscripts* (London, 1890), *Songs of Britain* (London and N.Y., 1913), *A Garland of English Folk-songs* (London, 1926), and *English Peasant Songs with Their Traditional Airs* (London, 1929). His writings include *English Folk-song and Dance* (Cambridge, 1915) and *The Beggar's Opera: Its Predecessors and Successors* (Cambridge, 1922). —NS/LK/DM

Kiel, Friedrich, German composer and pedagogue; b. Puderbach, Oct. 7, 1821; d. Berlin, Sept. 13, 1885. He began to play the piano as a child, and attended the Soest teacher's training college where his musical talent was encouraged. After the family moved to Schwarzenau in 1827, the boy found a mentor in Prince Karl of the noble Sayn-Wittgenstein-Berleburg family, who taught him violin. He played in the Prince's court orch. before pursuing training in composition with Gaspar Kummer in Coburg. In 1840 he returned to his mentor's court orch. as concertmaster. In 1842 he returned to Berlin, where he studied piano, counterpoint, and composition on a royal grant with Wilhelm Dehn. After completing his studies in 1844, he devoted

1869

himself mainly to teaching piano. From 1866 to 1870 he taught at the Stern Cons., and then at the Hochschule für Musik. From 1882 he also gave a master class at the Akademie der Künste. In 1979 the Friedrich-Kiel-Gesellschaft was founded with the purpose of propagating his music.

WORKS: ORCH.: Overture (n.d.); Piano Concerto (n.d.). **CHAMBER:** 7 piano trios (1850–71); 2 piano quartets (1866, 1867); 2 string quartets (1868); 2 piano quintets (1874); piano pieces. **VOCAL:** 2 Requiems (1860, rev. 1878; 1881); *Missa solemnis* (1865); Te Deum (1866); 2 oratorios (*Christus*, 1872; *Der Stern von Bethlehem*, 1884).

BIBL.: E. Prieger, *F. K.* (Leipzig, 1904); E. Reinecke, *F. K.* (diss., Univ. of Cologne, 1937); H. Zimmermann, *Untersuchungen zum Kompositionsunterricht im Spannungsfeld von Traditionalismus und Neudeutscher Schule, dargestellet am Beispiel der Lehrtätigkeit F. K.s (1821–1885)* (diss., Univ. of Siegen, 1987); D. Jürgens, *Die Messkompositionen F. K.s* (Regensburg, 1993). **—NS/LK/DM**

Kielland, Olav, Norwegian conductor and composer; b. Trondheim, Aug. 16, 1901; d. B, Telemark, Aug. 5, 1985. He studied with Lhose (conducting) and Krehl (composition) at the Leipzig Cons. (1921–23) and took Weingartner's conducting class in Basel (1929). He was conductor of the Oslo Phil. (1931–45) and the Bergen Phil. (1952–55); also appeared as a guest conductor abroad. His music followed the tradition of Norwegian national trends.

WORKS: 4 sinfonias (1935, 1961, 1966, 1976); Violin Concerto (1939–40); *Overtura tragica* (1941); *Mot blåsnhgdom* (The White-capped Mountains), symphonic suite for High Voice and Orch. (1945–46); *Concerto grosso norvegese* for 2 Horns and Strings (1952); *Tvileikar* for 4 Instruments (1954); String Quartet (1964); *Marcia del Coraggio* for Orch. (1968); *Ouverture solenne* (1974); Piano Concerto (1977).**—NS/LK/DM**

Kienzl, Wilhelm, Austrian composer; b. Waizenkirchen, Jan. 17, 1857; d. Vienna, Oct. 3, 1941. He studied in Graz with Johann Buwart and Mortier de Fontaine (piano) and with Ignaz Uhl (violin); also with Mayer-Rémy (composition) at the Univ. there, and then with Krejči at the Univ. of Prague (1876), at the Univ. of Leipzig (1877), with Rheinberger in Munich, with Liszt in Weimar, and at the Univ. of Vienna (Ph.D., 1879, with the diss. *Die musikalische Deklamation*; publ. in Leipzig, 1880). He was director of Amsterdam's German Opera (1883); conducted in Krefeld before returning to Graz (1884); then was director of the Steiermärkischer Musikverein there until 1886. He held the post of 1st conductor of the Hamburg Opera (1890–92), then was court conductor in Munich (1892–94). His most successful work was the opera *Der Evangelimann* (Berlin, May 4, 1895). After World War I, he wrote the new national anthem of Austria (1918), replacing Haydn's; it was adopted on June 6, 1920, but was dropped on Dec. 13, 1929, in favor of Haydn's melody. He also completed Adolf Jensen's opera *Turandot*. He publ. several books, including an autobiography (1926).

WORKS: DRAMATIC: Opera: *Urvasi* (1884; Dresden, Feb. 20, 1886; rewritten 1909); *Heilmar, der Narr* (Munich, March 8, 1892); *Der Evangelimann* (Berlin, May 4, 1895); *Don Quichote*, "musical tragi-comedy" (Berlin, Nov. 18, 1898); *In Knecht Rupprechts Werkstatt*, Weihnachtsmärchenspiel (Graz, Dec. 25, 1907); *Der Kuhreigen (Ranz des Vaches)* (Vienna, Nov. 23, 1911); *Das Testament* (Vienna, Dec. 6, 1916); *Hassan der Schwarmer* (Chemnitz, Feb. 27, 1925); *Sanctissimum* (Vienna, Feb. 14, 1925). **Singspiel:** *Hans Kipfel* (Vienna, 1926). Also incidental music. **OTHER:** Chamber music; piano pieces; choral works; songs.

BIBL.: M. Morold, *W. K.* (Leipzig, 1909); H. Hagen, ed., *Festschrift zum 60. Geburtstag von W. K.* (Graz, 1917); *Festschrift zum 80. Geburtstag von W. K.* (Vienna, 1937); H. Sittner, *K.—Rosegger: Eine Künstlerfreundschaft* (Zürich, 1953); I. Samlick-Hagen, *Lehr- und Wanderjahre W. K.s (1874–1897)* (diss., Univ. of Vienna, 1979).**—NS/LK/DM**

Kiepura, Jan, Polish-American tenor; b. Sosnowiec, May 16, 1902; d. Rye, N.Y., Aug. 15, 1966. He studied in Warsaw and Milan. He made his operatic debut as Faust in Lwów (1924), then appeared in Vienna, Berlin, Milan, Paris, Buenos Aires, and other opera centers. He made his U.S. debut with the Chicago Opera in 1931. He first appeared with the Metropolitan Opera in N.Y. as Rodolfo (Feb. 10, 1938), singing there until 1939 and again in 1942. He was admired for such roles as Des Grieux and Faust, and was also successful as a film artist and as an operetta singer. He was married to **Martha Eggerth**. **—NS/LK/DM**

Kiesewetter, Raphael Georg, Edler von Wiesenbrunn, Austrian government official and writer on music; b. Holleschau, Moravia, Aug. 29, 1773; d. Baden, near Vienna, Jan. 1, 1850. He studied piano and voice in his youth, and later flute, bassoon, and guitar. He studied philosophy at the Univ. of Olmutz, took a course in counterpoint with Albrechtsberger, and studied law at the Univ. of Vienna before becoming an official in the chancellery of the Imperial Army in Schwetzingen. He was made a councillor in the War Office in Vienna (1807), where he served until his retirement (1845). In 1843 he was ennobled. **August Wilhelm Ambros** was his nephew.

WRITINGS: *Die Verdienste der Niederländer um die Tonkunst* (Vienna, 1828); *Geschichte der europäisch- abendländischen oder unserer heutigen Musik* (Leipzig, 1834; 2nd ed., 1846; Eng. tr., 1846); *Über die Musik der neuern Griechen, nebst freien Gedanken über altägyptische und altgriechische Musik* (Leipzig, 1838); *Guido von Arezzo: Sein Leben und Wirken* (Leipzig, 1840); *Schicksale und Beschaffenheit des weltlichen Gesangs vom frühen Mittelalter bis zur Erfindung des dramatischen Styles und den Anfängen der Oper* (Leipzig, 1841); *Die Musik der Araber nach Originalquellen* (Leipzig, 1842); *Der neuen Aristoxener zerstreute Aufsätze über das Irrige der musikalischen Arithmetik und das Eitle ihrer Temperaturrechnungen* (Leipzig, 1846; includes articles by Kiesewetter); *Catalog der Sammlung alter Musik des K. K. Hofrathes Raphael Georg Kiesewetter Edlen von Wiesenbrunn in Wien* (Vienna, 1847); *Gallerie der alten Contrapunctisten: Eine Auswahl aus ihren Werken in verständlichen Partituren* (Vienna, 1847); *Über die Octave des Pythagoras* (Vienna, 1848).

BIBL.: H. Kier, *R.G. K. (1773–1850): Wegbereiter des musikalischen Historismus* (Regensburg, 1968).**—NS/LK/DM**

Kiesewetter, Tomasz, Polish composer, conductor, and teacher; b. Sosnowiec, Sept. 8, 1911; d. Łódź,

Nov. 29, 1992. He was a student of Piotr Rytel (composition), Walerian Bierdiajew (conducting), and Margerita Trombini-Kazuro (piano) at the Warsaw Cons., where he took his degree in composition and conducting in 1936. In 1938 he attended the master classes in conducting at the Salzburg Mozarteum. In 1938–39 he conducted the Stanisław Moniuszko Choir. With the Nazi occupation of his homeland during World War II, he became active in the resistance. After the close of the War in 1945, he became a lecturer at the State Higher School of Music in Łódź, where he served as an assoc. prof. from 1959. He also was active as a conductor in Łódź from 1945 to 1970. In 1967 and 1974 he received the Minister of Culture and Arts Award, 1st Class.

WORKS: DRAMATIC: *Stańczyk (Królewski błazen)* (King's Jester), ballet (1954); *Bal samotnych* (The Lonely Ones), operetta (1963). **ORCH.:** *Menuetto* for Small Orch. (1933); Concerto grosso (1934); 2 suites: No. 1, *Tańce polskie* (Polish Dances; 1947; also for Large Wind Orch., 1952) and No. 2, *Suita taneczna* (Dance Suite; 1950); 3 syms. (1948, 1952, 1958); *Walc* (Waltz; 1949); *Krzesany w stylu góralskim* (Krzesany in Polish Highlander Style; 1949); Viola Concerto (1950); *Uwertura olimpijska* (Olympic Overture; 1952); 2 organ concertos: No. 1, *Koncert "w dawnym stylu"* (Concerto "In an Old Style") for Organ and Strings (1961) and No. 2 (1979). **CHAMBER:** 2 string quartets (1933, 1953); Wind Quintet (1951); Clarinet Sonatina (1968). **VOCAL:** *Stabat Mater*, oratorio for Soprano, Women's Chorus, and Organ (Rudka, March 1944); *Tryptyk* for Baritone or Medium Voice and Orch. or Piano (1948); *Siedem strof o słowikach* (Seven Stanzas on Nightingales) for Chorus (1968).—NS/LK/DM

Kijima, Kiyohiko, Japanese composer; b. Tokyo, Feb. 19, 1917; d. 1998. He studied composition with Ikenouchi at Nihon Univ., and later joined its faculty. He received 2 prizes given by the Tokyo newspaper *Mainichi* (1938, 1948).

WORKS: ORCH.: *Symphonic Overture* (1942); *Prelude and Fugue* (1948); *5 Meditations* (1956); *Divertimento* (1963). **CHAMBER:** 2 string quartets (1950, 1986); Violin Sonata (1951); Trio for Flute, Violin, and Piano (1958; rev. 1970); Piano Quintet (1965); *2 Legends* for Piano (1969); 2 cello sonatas (1980; 1991–92); Piano Trio (1990). **VOCAL:** *Satsukino*, poem for Soprano and Small Orch. (1940); *Mi-Chi-No-Ku* for Chorus, Flute, Piano, and Percussion (1963); *Unintentional Emotion in Autumn* for Voice, Flute, Cello, and Piano (1983); songs. —NS/LK/DM

Kiladze, Grigori, Russian composer; b. Batum, Oct. 25, 1902; d. Tbilisi, April 3, 1962. He studied at the Tiflis Cons. with Ippolitov-Ivanov (1924–27), then at the Leningrad Cons. with Shcherbachev (1927–29). He was an active proponent of ethnic Georgian music in a modern idiom derived thematically from folk melorhythms. He wrote 2 operas on subjects from Caucasian revolutionary history: *Bakhtrioni* (1936) and *Lado Ketzkhoveli* (1941); *Sinatle*, ballet (1947); *Poem about Stalin* for Chorus and Orch. (1935); *Heroic Symphony* (1944); *Childhood and Adolescence of the Leader*, oratorio (1951); *Triumph*, overture (1957).—NS/LK/DM

Kilar, Wojciech, Polish composer and pianist; b. Lwów, July 17, 1932. He received training in piano and composition from Bolesław Woytowicz at the State Higher School of Music in Katowice (degree, 1955), and then pursued postgraduate studies with that same mentor at the State Higher School of Music in Kraków (1955–58). He also attended the summer courses in new music in Darmstadt in 1957. A French government scholarship made it possible for him to study composition with Nadia Boulanger in Paris in 1959–60. He received the Minister of Culture and Arts Award in 1967 and 1975, the Polish Composers' Union Award in 1975, the Polish State Award, 1st Class, in 1980, the Alfred Jurzykowski Foundation Prize of N.Y. in 1984, an AS-CAP Award in 1992, and the Sonderpreis des Kulturpreis Schlesein des Landes Niedersachsen in 1996.

WORKS: DRAMATIC: 11 film scores (1965–99). **ORCH.:** 2 syms.: No. 1 for Strings (1955; Poznań, Feb. 8, 1957) and No. 2, Sinfonia concertante for Piano and Orch. (1956; Katowice, April 23, 1958); *Mała uwertura* (Little Overture; Katowice, June 25, 1955); Concerto for 2 Pianos and Percussion Orch. (Katowice, Dec. 16, 1958); *Riff 62* (Warsaw, Sept. 16, 1962); *Générique* (Warsaw, Sept. 24, 1963); *Springfield Sonnet* (Stockholm, Sept. 6, 1965); *Solenne* (1967; Warsaw, Sept. 22, 1968); *Przygrywka i kolęda* (Prelude and Christmas Carol) for 4 Oboes and Strings (Warsaw, Sept. 16, 1972); *Krzesany*, symphonic poem (Warsaw, Sept. 24, 1974); *Kościelec 1909*, symphonic poem (Warsaw, Nov. 5, 1976); *Orawa* for Chamber String Orch. (Zakopane, March 10, 1986); *Choralvorspiel* for Chamber String Orch. (1988; Stuttgart, Sept. 22, 1989); Piano Concerto (1996–97; Warsaw, Sept. 27, 1997). **CHAMBER:** Flute Sonatina (1951; Warsaw, Sept. 9, 1953); Wind Quintet (1952; Warsaw, Nov. 9, 1953); Horn Sonata (Warsaw, Nov. 22, 1954); *Oda Béla Bartók in memoriam* for Violin, Winds, and Percussion (1957; Katowice, Dec. 1958); *Training 68* for Clarinet, Trombone, Cello, and Piano (Warsaw, Sept. 25, 1968). **Piano:** 3 Preludes (1951). **VOCAL:** *Herbsttag* for Woman's Voice and String Quartet (1960; Warsaw, Sept. 24, 1961); *Diphthongos* for Chorus and Orch. (Venice, Sept. 13, 1964); *Upstairs Downstairs* for 2 Children's Choruses and Orch. (Warsaw, Sept. 25, 1971); *Bogurodzica* (Mother of God) for Chorus and Orch. (1975; Warsaw, Sept. 18, 1976); *Siwa mgła* (Hoary Fog) for Baritone and Orch. (Bydgoszcz, Sept. 14, 1979); *Exodus* for Chorus and Orch. (1979–81; Warsaw, Sept. 19, 1981); *Angelus* for Soprano, Chorus, and Orch. (1982–84; Katowice, Oct. 12, 1984); *Victoria* for Chorus and Orch. (Katowice, June 20, 1983).—NS/LK/DM

Kilenyi, Edward, Jr., American pianist and teacher, son of **Edward Kilenyi Sr.;** b. Philadelphia, May 7, 1910; d. Tallahassee, Jan. 6, 2000. He was 12 when he began private training with Dohnányi, and then continued to study under that mentor at the Budapest Academy of Music (1927–30; diploma, 1930). In 1929 he made his professional debut in Amsterdam, and then gave concerts throughout Europe. On Oct. 21, 1940, he made his N.Y. recital debut. From 1953 to 1983 he taught at Fla. State Univ. in Tallahassee, and then was adjunct prof. there. In addition to his championship of the works of Dohnányi, he performed the music of other Hungarian composers. His repertoire of the classics ranged from Bach to Debussy.—NS/LK/DM

Kilenyi, Edward, Sr., Hungarian-American composer, father of **Edward Kilenyi Jr.;** b. Békésszentrándrás, Jan. 25, 1884; d. Tallahassee, Fla., Aug. 15, 1968. He studied in Budapest, in Szarvas, with Mascagni at Rome's Scuola Nazionale Musicale, and at the Cologne Cons. He then settled in the U.S. (1908), where he completed his training at Columbia Univ. with Rybner and Daniel Gregory Mason (M.A., 1915). He was a teacher of George Gershwin (1919–21). In 1930 he went to Hollywood, where he wrote film scores. He also wrote an opera, *The Cry of the Wolf* (1916), a String Quartet (1912), and other chamber music.—NS/LK/DM

Kilgore, Rebecca, American vocalist and guitarist; b. Waltham, Mass., Sept. 24, 1949. She is a vocalist with a gentle, lilting natural swing who also plays rhythm guitar (and plays it very well). Her sound is soothing, often soft and willowy, and easy on the ears. Although she has her own style, at times she sounds as if she had listened at length to Anita O'Day, June Christy, and Ella Fitzgerald. Then again, there is a suggestion of Doris Day in the timbre or tonal quality of her warm delivery. Her material is somewhat eclectic because she is so comfortable with jazz, country, and western swing, and with her favorite composers Irving Berlin and Jerome Kern, and other writers of the American popular song.

She grew up with music and art in her home; her mother was a graphic artist, and her father had a music degree from Harvard as well as experience as a jazz pianist, a choir director, and writer of choral music. She began playing guitar while still in high school, attended the Univ. of Mass., became a computer programmer, and studied for a time with a music teacher who had taught at Berklee Coll. of Music. In 1979, she moved to Portland, Ore., and landed a secretarial job at Reed Coll. She befriended a girl singer and guitar player, Cyd Smith, who was then with a small swing band, Wholly Cats. She replaced Smith in the group in 1981, and began easing into a musician's career, learning lyrics, chord changes, and stage presence. She met versatile drummer Hal Smith and trumpeter Chris Tyle while in Wholly Cats, sang with guest artists such as tenor saxman Scott Hamilton, and appeared on the radio with the band in 1983. After Wholly Cats disbanded in 1985, she freelanced with a number of groups, including a Western swing band, Ranch Dressing; a small Django Reinhart–styled combo, Everything's Jake; and her own country-styled band, Beck-a-Roo.

In 1992, she began singing with noted pianist Dave Frishberg at Portland's Heathman Hotel, giving up her day job and turning full-time to music. Two 1994 record dates prompted national attention and subsequent invitations to jazz parties and festivals, with tours at home and abroad as guitarist-vocalist with Hal Smith's Roadrunners, and as member of another Smith-led group, The California Swing Cats. More record dates followed. In 1997, she appeared at the prestigious Jazz At Chautauqua, accompanied in various sets by pianists Dave McKenna and Keith Ingham, and bands fronted by Dan Barrett and Hal Smith. She continues to dazzle her audiences, making new fans wherever she appears.

DISC.: *I Saw Stars* (1994); *Looking at You* (1994); *Not a Care in the World* (1996); *Rhythm, Romance and Roadrunners!* (1996); *Hal Smith's Roadrunners, Vol. 2* (1996); *Swing, Brother, Swing* (1997); *Stealin' Apples* (1997).—JTB

Killebrew, Gwendolyn, black American mezzo-soprano; b. Philadelphia, Aug. 26, 1939. She studied at Temple Univ. in Philadelphia, and then in N.Y. at the Juilliard School of Music and at the Metropolitan Opera Studio. After winning 1ˢᵗ prize in the Belgian International Vocal Competition, she won a Metropolitan Opera audition and made her operatic debut with the company in N.Y. as Waltraute in *Die Walküre* on Nov. 21, 1967; made her first appearance at the N.Y.C. Opera as Ulrica in *Un ballo in maschera* (Sept. 11, 1971). She was a member of the Deutsche Oper am Rhein in Düsseldorf (from 1976); also appeared in Munich, Geneva, Salzburg, Bayreuth, and other European opera centers. She made numerous concert, oratorio, and lieder appearances on both sides of the Atlantic. Among her notable operatic roles are Gluck's Orfeo, Azucena, Mistress Quickly, Amneris, Fricka, and Baba the Turk in *The Rake's Progress*.—NS/LK/DM

Killmayer, Wilhelm, German composer and teacher; b. Munich, Aug. 21, 1927. He received training in composition and conducting from Waltershausen (1945–51), and also studied musicology at the Univ. of Munich (1949–52). Following private lessons with Orff (1951–53), he attended the master class given by Orff at the Staatliche Hochschule für Musik in Munich (1953–54). From 1955 to 1958 he taught at the Trapp Cons. in Munich. In 1958 and in 1965–66 he held the Villa Massimo scholarship in Rome. In 1970 he held a scholarship of the Cité des Arts in Paris. From 1973 to 1992 he was prof. of composition at the Staatliche Hochschule für Musik in Munich. In 1972 he was made a full member of the Bayerischen Akademie der Schönen Künste in Munich, in 1980 a member of the Akademie der Künste in Berlin, and in 1993 a member of the Bavarian Maximilian Order of Science and Art.

WORKS: DRAMATIC: O p e r a : *La Buffonata*, ballet-opera (1959–60; concert perf., South German Radio, Stuttgart, Oct. 21, 1960; stage perf., Heidelberg, April 30, 1961); *La Tragedia di Orfeo* (1960–61; Munich, June 9, 1961); *Yolimba oder Die Grenzen der Magie* (1962–63; Wiesbaden, March 15, 1964; rev. version, Munich, May 9, 1970); *Une leçon de français (Eine Französischstunde)* (concert perf., South German Radio, Stuttgart, Oct. 20, 1964; stage perf., Stuttgart, Oct. 19, 1966). **B a l l e t :** *Pas de deux classique* (1964; Munich, May 12, 1965); *Encore* (Munich, May 9, 1970); *Paradies* (1972–74). **ORCH.:** *Sechs leichte Stücke* for Strings (1952); Piano Concerto (1955; Munich, April 21, 1956); *Divertissement* (Stuttgart, Oct. 1957); 3 syms.: No. 1, *Fogli* (1968; Hannover, Feb. 9, 1971), No. 2, *Ricordanze* (1968–69; Berlin, May 14, 1969), and No. 3, *Menschen-Los* (1972–73; Nuremberg, April 19, 1974; rev. version, Munich, April 29, 1988); *Pezzi ed Intermezzi* for Piano, Cello, and Orch. (1968; Chicago, Feb. 21, 1971); *Fin al punto* for Strings (1970; Munich, Jan. 14, 1971); *Nachtgedanken* (Salzburg, Aug. 7, 1973); *The Broken Farewell* for Trumpet and Small Orch. (Braunschweig, Nov. 28, 1977); *Jugendzeit*, symphonic poem (1977; Freiburg im Breisgau, Jan. 16, 1978); *Verschüttete Zeichen*, symphonic essay (1977–78; Munich, March 20, 1981); *Überstehen und Hoffen*, symphonic poem (1977–78; Munich, May 6, 1978); *Im Freien*, symphonic poem (1980; Munich, March 20, 1981); *Grande Sarabande* for Strings (Zürich, May 2, 1980); *Zittern un Wagen* (Stuttgart, Oct. 4, 1980); *Sostenuto* for Cello and Strings (Deutschlandsberg, Oct. 4, 1984); *Le joie de vivre* for Small Orch. and

Oboe Obbligato (Berlin, March 5, 1996). **CHAMBER:** *Kammermusik* for Jazz Instruments (1957; Munich, Nov. 28, 1958); *Balletto* for Recorders and Rhythmic Instruments (1959); *Tre danze* for Oboe and Percussion (Munich, Dec. 1959); *Per nove strumenti* for 9 Instruments (1968; Munich, Jan. 21, 1969); *Tre pezzi* for Trumpet and Piano (1968); String Quartet (Munich, Oct. 7, 1969); *The woods so wilde: Kammermusik No. 1* for Flute, 3 Percussionists, Viola, and Guitar (1970; Munich, Jan. 26, 1971); *Schumann in Endenich: Kammermusik No. 2* for Piano, Electric Organ or Harmonium, and 5 Percussionists (Munich, May 8, 1972); *Kindertage: Kammermusik No. 3* for Flute, Viola, Electric Organ, Piano, Accordion, Zither, Guitar, and 5 Percussionists (Bonn, Nov. 6, 1973); *Führe mich, Alter, nur immer in Deinen geschnörkelten Frühlings-Garten! Noch duftet und taut frisch un würzig sein Flor* for Chamber Ensemble (1974; Nuremberg, May 1975); Quartet for 2 Violins, Cello, and Piano (1976; Munich, May 8, 1975); *Brahms Bildnis* for Violin, Cello, and Piano (1976; Munich, Feb. 19, 1978); Trio for 2 Violins and Cello (Hamburg, Dec. 7, 1984); *Fünf Romanzen* for Violin and Piano (Hall am Tirol, March 7, 1987); *Humoreske* for Violin and Piano (Hall am Tirol, March 7, 1987); *Fünf Romanzen* for Cello and Piano (Salzburg, Aug. 26, 1989); *Acht Bagatellen* for Cello and Piano (1990–91; Munich, Nov. 14, 1991); *Fantasie* for Violin and Piano (Cologne, Sept. 5, 1992); *Die Schönheit des Morgens* for Viola and Piano (Dresden, June 3, 1994). **Piano:** *Paradies* for Piano, 3-Hands or 2 Pianos (1972; Zürich, Nov. 6, 1974); *An John Field* (1975; Hamburg, March 14, 1978); *Drei Klavierstücke* (1982); *Fünf neue Klavierstücke* (1986–88; Witten, April 23, 1989); *Trois Etudes blancs* (1990–91; Munich, June 6, 1991); *Douze Etudes transcendentales* (1991–92; Frankfurt am Main, Sept. 24, 1994); *Rundgesänge und Morgenlieder* (Munich, Dec. 11, 1993). **VOCAL:** *Drei Lieder* for Tenor and Piano, after Heine (1947; Munich, Nov. 25, 1992); *Reveries* for Soprano, Piano, and Percussion (Bayreuth, July 30, 1953); *Canti amorosi* for Soprano, Tenor, and Chorus (1953–54); *Romanzen* for Soprano, Piano, and Percussion, after García Lorca (1954; Chicago, April 25, 1955); *Acht Shakespeare- Lieder* for Tenor, Violin, Clarinet, Bassoon, Piano, and Percussion (1955; Frankfurt am Main, May 26, 1956); *Le petit Savoyard* for Soprano and 7 Instrumentalists (Stuttgart, Oct. 22, 1956); *Sappho* for Soprano and Small Orch. (1959–60; Stuttgart, Feb. 8, 1961); *Lieder, Oden und Szenen* for Chorus, after Goethe (1962; South German Radio, Stuttgart, Aug. 16, 1963; concert perf., Munich, April 20, 1964); *Geistliche Hymnen und Gesange* for Chorus, after Racine (1964; Berlin, May 4, 1965); *Romantische Chorlieder* for Men's Chorus, after Tieck (1965); *Tre Canti di Leopardi* for Baritone and Orch. (1965; Munich, July 11, 1967); *Drei Gesänge* for Baritone and Piano, after Hölderlin (1965; Munich, April 23, 1968); *Antiphone* for Baritone, Orch., and Small Men's Chorus ad libitum (1967); *Lauda* for Double Chorus with or without Orch. (Stuttgart, June 27, 1968); *Blasons anatomiques du corps féminin I* for Soprano, Clarinet, Violin, Cello, and Piano (1968; Munich, July 6, 1969) and *II* for Soprano and Piano (1991); *Altissimu* for Soprano, Recorder, Bongo, 3 Tom-toms, and Timpani (Munich, July 7, 1969); *Preghiere* for Baritone and Orch. (1969; RIAS, Berlin, May 24, 1971); *Salvum me fac* for Baritone and Orch. (1969–71; Munich, Nov. 16, 1971); *Vier Chorstücke* for Chorus (1971–90; 1st complete perf., Munich, May 11, 1990); *Tamquam sponsus* for Soprano and Instruments (1974; Hamburg, Jan. 1975); *Französisches Liederbuch* for Soprano, Baritone, and Chamber Ensemble (1979–80; Schwetzingen, May 3, 1980); *Merlin-Liederbuch* for 4 Voices and Chamber Ensemble (1981–96; Munich, Jan. 11, 1996); *Hölderlin- Lieder I* for Tenor and Piano (1982–85; Frankfurt am Main, Aug. 23, 1989; also for Tenor and Orch., Munich, Feb. 3, 1986), *II* for Tenor and Piano (1983–87; Frankfurt am Main, Aug. 23, 1989; also for Tenor and Orch., Salzburg, Aug. 14, 1987), and *III* for Tenor and Piano (1983–91; Vienna, Nov. 22, 1991); *Aussicht* for Baritone and 9 Instruments, after Hölderlin (Frankfurt am Main, Sept. 8, 1989); *Drei Lieder* for Tenor and Piano, after Eichendorff (1991; Munich, Nov. 25, 1992); *Acht Lieder* for Tenor and Piano, after Trakl (1993); *Die Zufriedenheit* for Tenor and Piano, after Hölderlin (Munich, July 8, 1993); *Neun Lieder* for Mezzo-soprano and Piano (Stuttgart, Nov. 27, 1993); *Huit Poéses de Mallarmé* for Soprano and Piano (1993; also for Soprano and Small Orch., 1994–95; Munich, May 12, 1995); *Fünf Lieder der Sappho* for Soprano and Piano (1993–95; Munich, July 16, 1995); *Heine-Portrait* for Tenor and Piano, after Heine (1994–95; Stuttgart, Nov. 16, 1995); *...was dem kaum bewusst...* for Men's Chorus, after Eichendorff (1995).

BIBL.: S. Mauser, ed., *Der Komponist W. K.* (Mainz, 1992). —NS/LK/DM

Kilpatrick, Jack (Frederick), American composer; b. Stillwater, Okla., Sept. 23, 1915; d. Muskogee, Okla., Feb. 22, 1967. He studied at the Univ. of Redlands, Calif., and at the Catholic Univ. of America in Washington, D.C. Of Cherokee origin, he derived virtually all of his music from Indian folklore, with the pentatonic scale as its foundation. He wrote more than 200 works.

WORKS: DRAMATIC: Music Dramas: *Unto These Hills* (Cherokee, N.C., July 1, 1950); *The Golden Crucible* (Pittsburgh, 1959); *The Blessed Wilderness* (Dallas, April 18, 1959). **ORCH.:** 8 syms., including No. 4 for Voices and Orch. (Dallas, Jan. 17, 1951), No. 5 (Honolulu, Feb. 19, 1957), No. 6 (San Antonio, March 2, 1957), No. 7, *The Republic of Tex.* (San Antonio, March 2, 1957), and No. 8, *Oklahoma,* for Narrator, Dancers, and Orch. (Oklahoma City, Nov. 17, 1957); numerous other instrumental works.—NS/LK/DM

Kilpinen, Yrjö (Henrik), Finnish music critic and composer; b. Helsinki, Feb. 4, 1892; d. there, March 2, 1959. He studied with Furuhjelm at the Helsinki Music Inst. (1908–09; 1911–12; 1916–17), Hofmann and Heuberger in Vienna (1910–11), and Juon and Taubmann in Berlin (1913–14). He wrote music criticism in Helsinki (1919–31) and also taught at the Helsinki Cons.; he was elected a member of the Finnish Academy (1948). He was best known as a composer of songs, of which he wrote more than 750; many were popular in Germany as well as in Finland. He also wrote *Pastoral Suite* for Orch. (1944), *Totentanz* for Orch. (1945), more than 30 men's choruses, chamber music, 6 piano sonatas and other piano pieces.

BIBL.: W. Legge, *The Songs of Y. K.* (London, 1936); T. Karila, *Y. K.* (Borga, 1964); F. Pullano, *A Study of the Published German Songs of Y. K.* (diss., Univ. of Ill., 1970); M. Pulkinen, *Y. K.* (Helsinki, 1982).—NS/LK/DM

Kim, Byong-kon, prominent Korean-born American composer, conductor, and teacher; b. Taegu, May 28, 1929. He studied with Heiden, Tibor Kozma, Wolfgang Vacano, Apel, and Kaufmann at Ind. Univ. in Bloomington (M.M., 1964; D.M.A., 1968), then was on the faculty of Calif. State Univ., Los Angeles (from 1968). He was a guest conductor with the Seoul Phil. (1978–84), the Osaka Phil. (1980), the Korea Phil. (1984), and the Taegu

Sym. Orch. (1981, 1985). In 1986 he founded and became the first director of the Pacific Contemporary Music Center; also served as adviser to the Hong Kong-based Asian Youth Sym. Orch. He became a naturalized American citizen in 1974. His orch. compositions are boldly dramatic, making particularly effective use of brass and string instruments.

WORKS: ORCH.: *Nak-Dong-Kang*, symphonic poem (1964); Sym. (1967); *Sori* (1978); *Symphony of 3 Metaphors* (1983); *Festival Symphony* (1984); *Choyop* (1985). **Band:** *Essay* for Brass and Percussion (1962); *Seoul Fanfare* (1986). **CHAMBER:** *Theme and Variations* for Violin and Viola (1962); Suite for Clarinet, Flute, and Bassoon (1962); String Quartet (1964); Concertino for Percussion (1965); *Epitaph* for Flute, Cello, and Percussion (1985); *The 7 Last Words of Christ* for Organ and Percussion (1986); Sinfonietta for 15 Strings and Harpsichord (1987); also works for solo instruments. **VOCAL:** *Flower Seed*, song cycle for High Voice (1964); *A Sunday Hymn* for Chorus (1965); *i am a little church* for Chorus and Organ (1970). **—NS/LK/DM**

Kim, Earl (actually, **Eul**), American composer and pedagogue of Korean descent; b. Dinuba, Calif., Jan. 6, 1920. He commenced piano training at 9, and then studied with Homer Grun. He subsequently studied with Schoenberg (composition and theory) at the Univ. of Calif. at Los Angeles (1939), and then became a student of Bloch at the Univ. of Calif. at Berkeley (1940). His studies were interrupted by service in the U.S. Army Intelligence Service during World War II, after which he returned to Berkeley to study with Sessions (M.A., 1952). After serving as a prof. at Princeton Univ. (1952–67), he was James Edward Ditson Prof. of Music at Harvard Univ. (1967–90). In addition to his activities as a composer and teacher, he has made appearances as a pianist and conductor. Among his many honors are the Prix de Paris, a National Inst. of Arts and Letters award, the Brandeis Univ. Creative Arts Award, a Guggenheim fellowship, and an NEA fellowship.

WORKS: DRAMATIC: Opera: *Footfalls* (1981). **ORCH.:** *Dialogues* for Piano and Orch. (1959); Violin Concerto (N.Y., Oct. 25, 1979). **CHAMBER:** *2 Bagatelles* for Piano (1952); *12 Caprices* for Violin (1980); *Scenes from Childhood* for Brass Quintet (1984). **VOCAL:** *Letters Found near a Suicide*, song cycle (1954); *Exercises en Route* for Soprano, Flute, Oboe, Clarinet, Violin, Cello, and 2 Percussion (1961–71); *Narratives* for High Soprano, Woman's Voice, Actor, 2 Violins, Cello, 2 Trumpets, Trombone, Piano, Television, and Lights (1973–76); *Now and Then* for Soprano, Flute, Harp, and Viola (1981); *Where Grief Slumbers* for Soprano, Harp, and String Orch. (1982); *Cornet* for Narrator and Orch. (1983); *The 7th Dream* for Soprano, Baritone, Violin, Cello, and Piano (1986); *The 11th Dream* for Soprano, Baritone, Violin, Cello, and Piano (1988); *3 Poems in French* for Soprano and String Quartet (1989); *4 Lines from Mallarmé* for Voice, Flute, Vibraphone, and Percussion (1989); *Some Thoughts on Keats and Coleridge*, "in memoriam Roger Sessions," for Chorus (1990); *The 26th Dream* for Baritone, Chorus, and String Orch. (1991–92); *Dear Linda* for Woman's Voice, Flute or Piccolo, Piano, Marimba, Percussion, and Cello (1992).**—NS/LK/DM**

Kim, Jin Hi, talented South Korean composer and komungo player; b. Inchon, Feb. 6, 1958. She studied in Seoul at the National Univ. (1976–80), then went to the U.S., where she studied composition with Adams at the San Francisco Cons. of Music (1980–81) and electronic and ethnic music at Mills Coll. in Oakland, Calif. (M.F.A., 1985); she also had private lessons on the Indian bansun (bamboo flute) and the Chineze gu-chin (7-string zither), and studied gagaku noh kabuji (South Eastern Asian mask dance theater). Kim attemps to integrate the "living tones" concept of traditional Korean music within a contemporary perspective in her bi-cultural compositions, frequently combining native Korean and Western instruments; notable among these works are *Nong Rock* for Komungo (a 6-stringed Korean zither) and String Quartet (1992), *Piri Quartet* for 3 Piri (a Koream double reed instrument) and Oboe or English Horn (1993), *Tchong* for Daegum (a Korean membrane bamboo flute; 1993), and *Yoeum* for Korean Male Kagok Singer and Western Male Voice (1993); the precariously hovering and often luminous sonorities that emanate from her juxtaposed atonal and microtonal structures blend the best of the East and the New West. Kim has internationally pioneered in performance on the komungo; her solo and collaborative improvisations on the komungo are spare, gestural, and formal, ever respectful of the meditative origins of the instrument. Kim also co-built the first electric komungo and electric changgo, both interractive with computer systems. She has received awards and commissions from numerous organizations, including the NEA (1991), the N.Y. State Council on the Arts (1994), and the Rockefeller Foundation (1995), among many others. In 1995 she was composer-in-residence at the Djerassi Resident Artists program in Woodside, Calif. In 1995 she began work on her first multi-cultural music and dance theater piece, *Dragon Bond Rite*, based on Japanese noh theatre, which will feature Korean, Japanese, Indian, Indonesian, and Mongolain artists at its 1996 premiere at N.Y.'s Japan Society.

WORKS: *The Spider's Web* for Kayagum, Yangkum, Daegum, Ajang, Piri, and Percussion (1978); *Yopo* for Flute, Ajang, Yangkum, and 2 Daegums (1980); *Kee Maek No. 1* for Bamboo Flutes and Percussion (1980), *No. 2* for Violin (N.Y., April 22, 1986), *No. 3* for Violin and Cello (Los Angeles, Nov. 29, 1989), *No. 4* for Viola and Cello (N.Y., March 9, 1988), and *No. 5* for Cello (1995); *Woon* for Chamber Ensemble (1981); *Movement and Resonance* for Dancer with 10 Asian Gongs (Oakland, Calif., Feb. 22, 1985); *x4 for solo violin* (San Francisco, Sept. 18, 1985); *Jinyang Delay*, Kayagum improvisation with Electronics (N.Y., April 22, 1986); *Bamboo Permutations No. 1* for Prerecorded Bamboo Flutes and Digital Sampling Keyboard (San Francisco, Nov. 16, 1985); *Su Wol Yong Yul* for Computer-generated Tape, Harpsichord, and Cello (Oakland, Calif., Feb. 22, 1985; based on a 15th-century treatise about Korean music); *x5 for solo flute* for Alto and Soprano Flutes and Piccolos and Prerecorded Tape (N.Y., Oct. 7, 1986); *Tehjoo Goong* for Komungo and Alto Flute (N.Y., Nov. 18, 1986); *Linking* for String Quartet (1986); *Komungo Permutations No. 1* for Synthesizer (1988); *Tchong No. 1* for Komungo and Flute (N.Y., March 9, 1988), *No. 2* for Prepared Flute (Los Angeles, June 22, 1989), and *No. 3* for Korean Mabrain Bamboo Flute and Western Flutes (Los Angeles, April 11, 1995); *Dasrum* for Komungo, Clarinet, and Cello (N.Y., Oct. 17, 1988); *Liquid Migration* for Viola, Cello, and Piano (Middletown, Conn., March 28, 1990); *Refracted Confluence* for Komungo and Computer (San Francisco, Feb. 3, 1991); *Nong Rock* for

Komungo and String Quartet (N.Y., Feb. 15, 1992); *Piri Quartet* for 3 Piri and English Horn/Oboe (1993); *Electric Changgo Permutations* for MAX Computer System (N.Y., March 1994); *Yoeum* for Korean Male Kagok Singer and Western Male Voice (N.Y., April 1995); *Dragon Bond Rite*, multi-cultural music and mask dance theater piece (1995–96).—**NS/LK/DM**

Kim, Young-Uck, outstanding South Korean violinist; b. Seoul, Sept. 1, 1947. He began piano studies at 5 but turned to the violin at 6. While still a child, he performed with the Seoul Sym. Orch. At 11, he was sent to the U.S., where he continued his studies with Galamian at the Curtis Inst. of Music in Philadelphia; he also attended the Marlboro (Vt.) Music School. After making an auspicious appearance with Ormandy and the Philadelphia Orch. in a nationally televised concert on May 10, 1963, he toured with them in South America. In subsequent years, he appeared as a soloist with many of the principal North American, European, and Far Eastern orchs. On Feb. 13, 1976, he made his N.Y. recital debut at Alice Tully Hall. From 1979 he toured extensively in a trio with Emanuel Ax and Yo-Yo Ma. In addition to the standard repertoire, Kim has applied his brilliant virtuoso technique and interpretive insights to many contemporary works.—**NS/LK/DM**

Kimball, Jacob, Jr., American composer; b. Topsfield, Mass., Feb. 22, 1761; d. there, Feb. 6, 1826. In 1775 he was a drummer in the Mass. militia. He then entered Harvard Univ. (graduated, 1780). He subsequently studied law and was admitted to the bar, but soon gave up that profession for music, teaching in various New England towns. He died in an almshouse. He wrote hymns, Psalm tunes, and "fuguing pieces," in the style of Billings. He publ. 120 works, many of which appeared in the *Village Harmony* (Exeter, N.H., from 1800), as well as the collections *Rural Harmony* (Boston, 1793) and *Essex Harmony* (Exeter, N.H., 1800).

BIBL.: G. Wilcox, *J. K. Jr. (1761–1826): His Life and Works* (diss., Univ. of Southern Calif., 1957).—**NS/LK/DM**

Kimbrough, Frank, American pianist; b. Roxboro, N.C., Nov. 2, 1956. He started out his career as a protege of Shirley Horn and in 1985 won the Great American Jazz Piano Competition. Since then he has covered a lot of stylistic territory, working with bluesman B.B. King, World fusionist Paul Horn, and avant garde musician Anthony Braxton, as well as appearing on albums by Ted Nash and with the tonally adventurous Maria Schneider Jazz Orch. Although the first couple of recordings under his name (the solo *Star-Crossed Lovers* and piano/drums duet *Double Vision*, both on Mapleshade) were cassette-only affairs that have been discontinued, he has recorded some projects in the 1990s that should be around awhile. A founding member of the Jazz Composers Collective, he is a composer-in-residence with the collective and has received grants and fellowships from the National Endowment for the Arts and Meet the Composer. He also serves on the faculties of the Cannon Music Camp at Appalachia State Univ. and at N.Y.U.

DISC.: *Lonely Woman* (1990); *The Herbie Nichols Project: Love Is Proximity* (1997).—**GM/DPr**

Kincaid, Bradley, American folk-song collector and singer; b. Point Leavell, Ky., July 13, 1895; d. Springfield, Ohio, Sept. 23, 1989. He began to sing and play the guitar as a child, and after serving in the U.S. Army in World War I, he went to Chicago and studied at the YMCA Coll. He made his first appearances as a singer on the "National Barn Dance" radio program, and subsequently sang on the "Grand Ole Opry" in Nashville, Tenn. He also owned his own radio station in Springfield, Ohio (1949–53). As a folk-song collector, he publ. 13 songbooks containing material from traditional sources, as well as some compositions of his own.

BIBL.: L. Jones, *Radio's Kentucky Mountain Boy, B. K.* (Berea, Ky., 1980).—**NS/LK/DM**

Kincaid, William, outstanding American flutist and pedagogue; b. Minneapolis, April 26, 1895; d. Philadelphia, March 27, 1967. He studied flute with Georges Barrère at the Inst. of Musical Art in N.Y., then played in the N.Y. Sym. Orch. (1914–18). In 1921 Stokowski engaged him as 1st flutist of the Philadelphia Orch., a position he held with great distinction until his retirement in 1960; he also was a distinguished teacher at the Curtis Inst. of Music, where he taught a number of noted flutists. He maintained a valuable collection of historic flutes, his own instrument being a specially made platinum flute.

BIBL.: J. Krell, *K.iana: A Flute Player's Notebook* (Culver City, Calif., 1973).—**NS/LK/DM**

Kinder, Ralph, English-American organist and composer; b. Stalybridge, near Manchester, Jan. 27, 1876; d. Bala, suburb of Philadelphia, Nov. 14, 1952. He was taken to the U.S. at the age of 5, and was a chorister in Bristol, R.I. After studies in America, he then studied in London with E.H. Lemare. He held various posts as a church organist in Bristol (1890–98), Providence (1898), and Philadelphia (from 1899). He wrote numerous organ pieces of considerable charm, including *Arietta, Berceuse, Caprice, Festival March, Jour de printemps, Moonlight, Souvenir,* and *In Springtime.*—**NS/LK/DM**

Kindermann, August, German bass-baritone; b. Potsdam, Feb. 6, 1817; d. Munich, March 6, 1891. He sang in the chorus of the Berlin Royal Opera, then appeared at the Leipzig theater (1839–46). In 1846 he became a member of the Munich Court Opera, and remained on its roster until his death. He also sang at Bayreuth, where he created the role of Titurel in *Parsifal* (1882).—**NS/LK/DM**

Kindermann, Johann Erasmus, eminent German organist, pedagogue, and composer; b. Nuremberg, March 29, 1616; d. there, April 14, 1655. He began his training in Nuremberg with Johann Staden, and by the time he was 15 he was active as a bass singer and violinist in the concerts given by the Frauenkirche there. In 1634 he received assistance from the Nuremberg city council to pursue studies in Italy, where he studied in Venice and Rome. In 1636 he was recalled to Nuremberg as 2nd organist at the Frauenkirche. In 1640 he went to

Schwäbisch-Hall as organist, only to return later that year to Nuremberg as organist of the Egidienkirche, which position he retained for the rest of his life. Among Kindermann's notable students were Johann Agricola, Augustin Pfleger, Heinrich Schwemmer, and Georg Caspar Wecker. As a composer, he excelled in both vocal and instrumental music. His *Canzoni, sonatae* is one of the earliest collections to manifest scordatura in Germany. See F. Schreiber, ed., *Ausgewählte Werke*, Denkmäler der Tonkunst in Bayern, XXIV, Jg. XIII (1913) and XXXII, Jg. XXI-XXIV (1924).

WORKS (all publ. in Nuremberg unless otherwise given): **VOCAL:** *Cantiones [pathētikai], hoc est Ad memoriam passionis...Jesu Christi* for 3 and 4 Voices and Basso Continuo (motets; 1639); *Friedens Clag* for 3 Voices and Basso Continuo (3 motets; 1640); *Concentus Salomonis, das ist Geistliche Concerten auss dem Hohen Lied dess hebraïschen Königes Salominis* for 2 Voices, 2 Violins, and Basso Continuo (1642); *Dialogus, Mosis Plag, Sünders Klag, Christi Abtrag* for 1 to 6 Voices and Basso Continuo (1642); (8) *Musicalische Friedens Seufftzer* for 3 and 4 Voices and Basso Continuo (1642); *Opitianischer Orpheus, das ist* [13] *Musicalischer Ergetzligkeiten* for 1 and 2 Voices, 2 Violins, Violone or Bassoon, and Basso Continuo (1642); *Dess erlösers Christi, und sündligen Menschens heylsames Gesprach* for 7 Voices and Basso Continuo (1643); *Musica catechetica, das ist Musicalischer Catechismus* for 5 Voices and Basso Continuo (12 motets; 1643); *Lobgesang über den Frewdenreichen Geburtstag...Jesu Christi* for 4 Voices and *sampt 1 Sinfonia a 4* (1647); *Eines Christgleubigen Bekenners Hertzens Seuffzere* for 2 Violins, 3 Viols, and Basso Continuo (1648); *Musicalische Friedens Freud* for 1 and 2 Voices, 3 Viols, and Basso Continuo (14 strophic songs; 1650). **INSTRUMENTAL:** *Deliciae studiosorum* a 3 and 5 and Basso Continuo (4 parts, 1640–43); *Harmonia organica, in tabulaturam germanicam* (1645); (27) *Canzoni,* [9] *sonatae* for 1 to 3 Violins, Cello, and Basso Continuo (1653); 30 suite movements for Keyboard (ed. in Hortus Musicus, LXI, 1950).

BIBL.: F. Schreiber, *Der Nürnberger Organist J.E. K. (1616–1655)* (Leipzig, 1913).—NS/LK/DM

Kindler, Hans, Dutch-born American cellist and conductor; b. Rotterdam, Jan. 8, 1892; d. Watch Hill, R.I., Aug. 30, 1949. He studied at the Rotterdam Cons., receiving 1st prize for piano and cello in 1906, and also had lessons with Casals. In 1911 he was appointed prof. at Berlin's Klindworth-Scharwenka Cons., and 1st cellist of Berlin's Deutsches Opernhaus Orch. In 1912–13 he made a successful tour of Europe; from 1914 to 1920, was 1st cellist of the Philadelphia Orch. In 1927 he made his debut as a conductor in Philadelphia. Kindler organized the National Sym. Orch. in Washington, D.C., in 1931, and was permanent conductor until his resignation in 1948.—NS/LK/DM

King, Alec (actually, **Alexander**) **Hyatt,** esteemed English bibliographer and musicologist; b. Beckenham, Kent, July 18, 1911. He was educated at Dulwich Coll. and King's Coll., Cambridge (B.A., 1933). In 1934 he joined the Dept. of Printed Books of the British Museum; became superintendent of its music room in 1944, retiring in 1976. He publ. a number of valuable textual and bibliographical studies.

WRITINGS (all publ. in London unless otherwise given): *Chamber Music* (1948); *Handel's Messiah* (exhibition catalog of the British Museum; 1951); *Mozart in Retrospect: Studies in Criticism and Bibliography* (1955; 3rd ed., 1970); *Mozart in the British Museum* (1956; 2nd ed., 1966); *Henry Purcell 1659?–1695*; *George Frideric Handel 1685–1759* (exhibition catalog of the British Museum; 1959); *Some British Collectors of Music c. 1600–1960* (Cambridge, 1963); *Four Hundred Years of Music Printing* (1964; 2nd ed., 1968); *Handel and His Autographs* (1967); *Mozart Chamber Music* (1968; 2nd ed., 1969); *Mozart: A Biography, with a Survey of Books, Editions and Recordings* (1970); *Mozart Wind and String Concertos* (1978); *Printed Music in the British Museum: An Account of the Collections, the Catalogues, and Their Formation, up to 1920* (1979); *A Wealth of Music in the Collection of the British Library (Reference Section) and the British Museum* (1983); *A Mozart Legacy: Aspects of the British Library Collections* (1984); *Musical Pursuits: Selected Essays* (1987).

BIBL.: O. Neighbour, ed., *Music and Bibliography: Essays in Honour of A.H. K.* (London, 1980).—NS/LK/DM

King, B. B. (Riley B.), emphatic American blues guitarist, singer, and songwriter; b. near Itta Bena, Miss., Sept. 16, 1925. Widely regarded as the foremost blues guitarist of his time, King popularized blues music, placing 75 recordings on the R&B charts and 36 on the pop charts between 1951 and 1992, including his signature song, "The Thrill Is Gone." He was noted for his stinging, vibrato-laden, single-note guitar solos that distinguished his eclectic big band arrangements of blues songs, and for his spirited singing, in the hundreds of concerts he performed each year throughout the second half of the 20th century, at first exclusively for African-American audiences and then, as of the 1960s, for all audiences in the U.S. and abroad.

King's parents, Albert and Nora Ella Pully King, were tenant farmers who separated when he was four years old. He stayed with his mother until her death when he was nine, then worked on a plantation on his own until his father located him when he was 14 and took him back to the plantation where he had been born. He received instruction on the guitar from the brother of his stepmother and sang in a gospel group. He first moved to Memphis to work as an entertainer in 1946, returned to the plantation, then made a second, more successful trip in 1948.

King found work as a performer and disc jockey on a local radio station and made his first recordings for the Bullet label in 1949 before signing with Modern Records, which released his recordings on its RPM and later Kent subsidiaries. His single "3 O'Clock Blues" (music by Jules Taub, lyrics by B. B. King) was his first to reach the R&B charts; it hit #1 in February 1952, followed by a second chart-topper, "You Know I Love You" (music by Jules Taub, lyrics by B. B. King) in November. By the end of the year he had scored another R&B Top Ten hit with "Story from My Heart and Soul."

King went on to hit the R&B Top Ten 15 more times through the end of 1960, his most successful records being "Please Love Me" (music by Jules Taub, lyrics by B. B. King), "You Upset Me Baby" (music by Joe Josea, lyrics by Maxwell Davis)—both of which hit #1—and "Sweet Sixteen, Pt. 1" (music and lyrics by B. B. King and Joe Josea). During the 1950s he assembled his own touring band and spent most of the year traveling, playing in clubs and theaters in the African-American communities of the U.S. He moved to ABC–Paramount Records in the early 1960s, though Kent continued to release and chart with a backlog of his material for another decade. Kent's 1964 single of "Rock Me Baby" (music and lyrics by Joe Josea and B. B. King) became his first pop Top 40 hit in the spring of 1964.

King's popularity declined in the mid-1960s, as black audiences moved from his style of R&B to the more pop Motown Sound and the nascent soul style. But by 1968 he had been taken up by the rock audience, which turned to him in the wake of the success of blues-oriented performers such as Cream, with its King-influenced guitarist Eric Clapton. Increasingly, he was able to play in rock venues, and his records began to turn up more frequently in the pop charts: in May 1968 he had a second pop Top 40 hit with "Paying the Cost to Be the Boss" (music and lyrics by B. B. King), and in October his album *Lucille* (the name he gave his guitar) became his first to make the pop LP bestseller list. *Live & Well*, released in the spring of 1969, spent more than seven months in the pop charts, and *Completely Well*, released that fall while he was serving as an opening act for The Rolling Stones, spawned the biggest pop hit of his career, "The Thrill Is Gone" (music and lyrics by Ray Hawkins and Rick Darnell), which won him his first Grammy for Best Rhythm & Blues Vocal Performance, Male.

King was nominated for the same award in 1971 for the R&B and pop chart single "Ain't Nobody Home" (music and lyrics by Jerry Ragavoy), featured on his album *B. B. King in London*, on which he was backed by various British rock musicians. He continued to perform frequently and to record and release at least one chart album a year through 1983. Highlights of this period included a duet album with Bobby "Blue" Bland, *Together for the First Time...Live*, released in October 1974, which went gold, and several Grammy nominations and awards: he was nominated a third time for Best Rhythm & Blues Vocal Performance, Male, in 1977 for "It's Just a Matter of Time" from the album *King Size*; "When I'm Wrong" (music and lyrics by B. B. King) from *"Now Appearing" at Ole Miss* earned a 1980 nomination for Best Rhythm & Blues Instrumental Performance; *There Must Be a Better World Somewhere* won him his second Grammy for Best Ethnic or Traditional Recording in 1981; and he took home a third Grammy for Best Traditional Blues Recording in 1983 for *Blues 'n' Jazz*.

Though not as big a record seller after the mid-1980s, King continued to be revered and to perform and record extensively. In 1985 he made a cameo appearance in the film *Into the Night*, and his recording of the title song (music and lyrics by Ira Newborn) gave him his biggest R&B hit in over a decade. That same year, he won his fourth Grammy for Best Traditional Blues Recording for the track "My Guitar Sings the Blues" on *Six Silver Strings*. His performance of "Standing on the Edge of Love" was featured on the soundtrack of the 1986 film *The Color of Money* and earned a Grammy nomination for Best Contemporary Blues Recording. He joined U2 for the song "When Love Comes to Town" (music by

U2, lyrics by Bono) in their concert film *Rattle and Hum* (1988), and the song reached the Top Ten in the U.K., earning a 1989 Grammy nomination for Best Rock Performance by a Duo or Group with Vocal. He was also nominated for Best Contemporary Blues Recording for *King of the Blues: 1989*.

King continued to perform and record in the 1990s, alone and in collaboration with others. He won a Grammy in 1990 for Best Traditional Blues Recording for *Live at San Quentin* and was nominated the same year for "Waiting on the Light to Change," a duet with Randy Travis on Travis's album *Heroes and Friends*. *Live at the Apollo* won him his sixth Grammy in the Best Traditional Blues Album category in 1991, and he won his seventh in the same category for the 1993 album *Blues Summit*, on which he was joined by a host of other blues performers.

Though he announced in 1996 that his advancing age and delicate health condition—he suffered from diabetes among other troubles—would necessitate his cutting his annual concert schedule from 300 or so dates a year to a mere 200, King continued to record prolifically. In 1998 he released *Deuces Wild*, an album of duets that was nominated for the Grammy for Best Contemporary Blues Album.

King was married and divorced twice, and other liaisons with women brought him a total of 15 children.

WRITINGS: With D. Ritz, *Blues All Around Me: The Autobiography of B. B. K.* (N.Y., 1996).

DISC.: *Singin' the Blues* (1959); *The Blues* (1960); *B. B. King Wails* (1960); *B. B. King Sings Spirituals* (1960); *The Great B. B. King* (1961); *King of the Blues* (1961); *My Kind of Blues* (1961); *More* (1961); *Blues for Me* (1962); *Twist with B. B. King* (1962); *Easy Listening Blues* (1962); *Blues in My Heart* (1962); *Heart Full of Blues* (1962); *Mr. Blues* (1963); *Rock Me Baby* (1963); *Swing Low* (1963); *Let Me Love You* (1965); *B. B. King Live on Stage* (1965); *Live at the Regal* (1965); *Confessin' the Blues* (1965); *Boss of the Blues* (1965); *The Soul of B. B. King* (1966); *Pure Soul* (1966); *The Original Sweet Sixteen* (1966); *9 X 9.5* (1966); *Turn on to B. B. King* (1966); *The Jungle* (1967); *Blues Is King* (1967); *R&B Soul* (1967); *Blues on Top of Blues* (1968); *Lucille* (1968); *The Feeling They Call the Blues* (1969); *The Feeling They Call the Blues, Vol. 2* (1969); *From the Beginning* (1969); *Underground Blues* (1969); *Electric B. B.—His Best* (1969); *Live and Well* (1969); *Completely Well* (1969); *B. B. King* (1969); *Back in the Alley* (1970); *Take a Swing with Me* (1970); *The Incredible Soul of B. B. King* (1970); *Indianola Mississippi Seeds* (1970); *Better than Ever* (1971); *Doing My Thing, Lord* (1971); *Live at Cook County Jail* (1971); *In London* (1971); *Live* (1972); *L. A. Midnight* (1972); *Guess Who* (1972); *To Know You Is to Love You* (1973); *Friends* (1974); *Lucille Talks Back* (1975); *King of the Blues* (1976); *Original Folk Blues: B. B. King, 1949–1950* (1977); *King Size* (1977); *Midnight Believer* (1978); *Take It Home* (1979); *Live "Now Appearing" at Ole Miss* (1980); *Rarest B. B. King* (1980); *There Must Be a Better World Somewhere* (1981); *Love Me Tender* (1982); *King of the Blues Guitar* (instrumentals rec. 1960–61; rel. 1985); *Ambassador of the Blues* (1986); *Blues Is King* (1987); *Introducing B. B. King* (1987); *One Nighter Blues* (1987); *Blues 'n' Jazz/The Electric B. B.* (1987); *Six Silver Strings* (1988); *Doin' My Thing, Lord* (1988); *Across the Tracks* (1988); *The King of the Blues: 1989* (1989); *Lucille Had a Baby* (1989); *Live at San Quentin* (1990); *Live at the Apollo* (1990); *There Is Always One More Time* (1991); *Why I Sing the Blues* (1992); *The King of the Blues* (1992); *Blues Summit* (1993); *Better than Ever* (1993); *I Just Sing the*

Blues (1993); *You Done Lost Your Good Thing Now* (1993); *Mr. Blues* (1993); *B. B. King in London* (1994); *Catfish Blues* (1995); *B.B King and Friends* (1995); *Lucille and Friends* (1995); *How Blue Can You Get?* (1996); *Deuces Wild* (1997); *Paying the Cost to Be the Boss* (1997); *Blues on the Bayou* (1998); *Live in Japan* (1999); *Makin' Love Is Good for You* (2000); *All Over Again* (2000). **B. B. KING AND BOBBY "BLUE" BAND:** *Together for the First Time* (1974); *Live* (1982); *Together Again* (1976).

BIBL.: C. Sawyer, *The Arrival of B. B. K.: The Authorized Biography* (N.Y., 1980); D. Shirley, *Everyday I Sing the Blues: The Story of B. B. K.* (1995); J. Nazel, *B. B. K.: Jazz Musician* (1996); R. Kostelanetz and A. Pope, eds., *The B. B. K. Companion: Five Decades of Commentary* (N.Y., 1997); S. Danchin, *Blues Boy: The Life and Music of B. B. K.* (1998).—**WR**

King, Ben(jamin) E(arl Nelson),

the indestructible soul man (b. Henderson, N.C., Sept. 23, 1938). King's family migrated to N.Y. during the post WWII years and settled in Harlem where his father ran a restaurant. Although he started singing in the church, by his late teens, King was singing with the Four B's (for Ben, Billy, Bill, and Bobby—he married Billy and Bobby's sister, Betty). While working at the restaurant, he was scouted by the manager of The Five Crowns, a local vocal group that had been recording without much luck for about five years. Their luck changed when the manager of the Drifters spotted the Crowns doing an opening act at the Apollo. He had just hired the members of the Drifters, so he signed the Crowns on as the *new* Drifters. King cowrote and sang lead on the first Crowns/Drifters hit "There Goes My Baby." The song topped the R&B charts and went to #2 pop. Over the course of the next year or so, he sang lead on ten Drifters songs, five of which became substantial hits: "Dance with Me" (#15 pop/gold), "This Magic Moment" (#16 pop), "Lonely Winds" (Top Ten R&B), "I Count the Tears" (#17 pop), and "Save the Last Dance for Me" which topped by the R&B and pop charts, going gold. By the time that record came out, King had already started pursuing a solo career.

King's first two solo stabs, including a duet with LaVerne Baker, didn't do well. Soon, he and his wife were living on her earnings as a librarian. In 1961, he hooked up with songwriters Jerry Leiber and Mike Stoller, and famed "wall-of-sound" producer Phil Spector. Their first collaboration was on "Spanish Harlem." The song went to #10 pop, #15 R&B, and launched his solo career. His next single was a loose adaptation of the hymn "Lord Stand by Me." "Stand by Me" rose to #4 pop, topping the R&B charts for four weeks. Over the course of the next three years, King hit the Top 40 three more times: "Amor," a version of a hit from the 1940s, rose to #18 in 1961; "Don't Play That Song (You Lied)," a song he co-wrote (in his wife's name) with Ahmet Ertegun hit #11 in 1962; "I (Who Have Nothing)," a dramatic English version of an Italian hit, went to #23 in 1963.

After that, King fell out of favor with the Top 40, though he continued to record through the 1960s. He became a fixture on the lounge circuit. He was asked by Genesis to sing the chorus to the Drifter's "On Broadway" on their album *The Lamb Lies Down on Broadway*, despite the fact that he was long gone from the Drifters

when they had the hit. In the mid-1970s, Atlantic president Ahmet Ertegun saw his show, heard that he had lost none of his voice, and liked his harder soul sound that leavened the oldies. He resigned King to Atlantic where he topped the R&B charts and had a #5 hit with the proto-disco "Supernatural Thing." The album reached #39. A collaboration with the Average White Band produced the minor hit "Do It in the Name of Love" and the album *Benny and Us* rose to #33. However, after this short spurt of popularity, his career again fell on hard times and he and Atlantic parted company again in 1981.

Another King, author Stephen King, figures heavily in the next part of the story. His novella *The Body* was adapted into a motion picture in 1986. The film was retitled *Stand By Me* and used the Ben E. King song as its theme music. The single was revived and rose to #9, reviving interest in King's career as well. In England, the music was also used in a Levi's commercial, which sent the single to the top of the U.K. charts. King continued to record with lesser success, through the 1990s. He was inducted into the Rock and Roll Hall of Fame in 1988 as a member of the Drifters.

DISC.: *Spanish Harlem* (1961); *Don't Play That Song* (1962); *Sings for Soulful Lovers* (1962); *Young Boy Blues* (1964); *Seven Letters* (1965); *What Is Soul* (1967); *Rough Edges* (1970); *Beginning of It All* (1971); *Supernatural Thing* (1975); *I Had a Love* (1976); *Benny & Us* (1977); *Let Me Live in Your Life* (1978); *Music Trance* (1980); *Street Tough* (1981); *Here Comes the Night* (1984); *Save the Last Dance for Me* (1988); *Ben E. King/Percy Sledge* (1989); *Ben E. King & Percy Sledge* (1989); *What's Important to Me* (1992); *Drifters* (1996); *Shades of Blue* (1999).—**HB**

King, Carole (originally, Klein, Carol),

prolific songwriter in the 1960s, and then one of the first and most popular female singer-songwriters of the 1970s; b. Brooklyn, N.Y., Feb. 9, 1942; songwriting partner Gerry Goffin b. Queens, N.Y., Feb. 11, 1939. Carole King began singing and playing piano at the age of four. She formed the female vocal group The Co-Sines at age 14 and met songwriter Gerry Goffin in 1958 while attending Queens Coll. Signed as a staff songwriter to Al Nevins and Don Kirshner's Aldon Music at 17, she soon married Goffin and initiated their collaborative songwriting career at N.Y.'s Brill Building. She was first brought to the attention of the American record-buying public as the subject of Neil Sedaka's 1959 hit "Oh! Carol." King and Goffin scored their first songwriting hit, a top hit, in late 1960 with "Will You Love Me Tomorrow," recorded by The Shirelles.

In the first half of the 1960s, Gerry Goffin and Carole King wrote a series of hits recorded by a variety of artists. These included "Some Kind of Wonderful," "When My Little Girl Is Smiling," and the smash "Up on the Roof" for The Drifters; "Sharing You" and the top hit "Take Good Care of My Baby" for Bobby Vee; "Crying in the Rain" (with Howie Greenfield) for The Everly Brothers; "Her Royal Majesty" for James Darren; "Point of No Return" for Gene McDaniels; the smash "One Fine Day" for The Chiffons; "Hey Girl" for Freddie Scott; and "I Can't Stay Mad at You" for Skeeter Davis. In 1963, Goffin and King provided Steve Lawrence and Eydie Gorme with a number of hits, beginning with the top hit "Go Away, Little Girl" by Lawrence. The team also contributed hits to two British groups during the mid-1960s: "I'm for to Something Good" for Herman's Hermits in 1964 and "Don't Bring Me Down" for The Animals in 1966. The duo also collaborated with Phil Spector on "Just Once in My Life" for The Righteous Brothers in 1965.

In 1962, Don Kirshner formed Dimension Records, as Gerry Goffin learned production and Carole King arranging. Dimension's first release, "The Loco-Motion," written by Goffin and King and recorded by Little Eva, became a top hit. Carole King's version of "It Might as Well Rain until September," originally written for Bobby Vee, was Dimension's second hit, followed by Little Eva's "Keep Your Hands off My Baby," and two songs recorded by The Cookies, "Chains" and "Don't Say Nothin' (Bad about My Baby)," all written by Goffin and King.

During the mid-1960s, Goffin and King formed their own record label, Tomorrow, but singles by King and The Myddle Class failed to reach the charts. In 1967, they contributed hit songs to Kirshner's Monkees ("Pleasant Valley Sunday") and to Aretha Franklin ("A Natural Woman"), while providing The Byrds with "Goin' Back" and "Wasn't Born to Follow." Gerry Goffin and Carole King were inducted into the Rock and Roll Hall of Fame in 1990.

Carole King subsequently broke up the songwriting team, divorcing Goffin in 1968 and marrying the bass player from The Myddle Class, Charles Larkey. King moved to L. A., where she formed The City with Larkey and guitarist Danny Kortchmar and recorded one album, *Now That Everything's Been Said*, for Lou Adler's Ode Records. Although the album failed to sell, it did include "Wasn't Born to Follow" and Goffin and King's "Hi-De-Ho," a major hit for Blood, Sweat and Tears in 1970.

By 1970, Carole King had initiated a solo career, assisting James Taylor with *Sweet Baby James* and recording her debut solo album, *Writer*, with Larkey, Kortchmar, and Taylor. The album contained the Goffin-King songs "Up on the Roof," Goin' Back," and "No Easy Way Down," but sold only modestly. In 1971, King recorded the enormously successful *Tapestry* album. As James Taylor's version of King's "You've Got a Friend" was climbing the charts, so was her own double-sided top hit, "It's Too Late"/"I Feel the Earth Move." The album later yielded another major two-sided hit with "So Far Away"/"Smackwater Jack," while including "Way Over Yonder" and two Goffin-King compositions, "Will You Love Me Tomorrow" and "A Natural Woman." This collection of mature, sophisticated songs (in contrast to the prior teen melodramas) appealed to virtually every sector of the record-buying public, remaining on the album charts for nearly six years and eventually selling more than 15 million copies.

Carole King's next two albums, *Carole King Music* and *Rhymes and Reasons*, became best-sellers, each yielding a major hit single ("Sweet Seasons" and "Been to Canaan," respectively), but somehow lacking *Tapestry*'s magic. *Fantasy* was somewhat more socially conscious, producing moderate hits with "Believe in Humanity"

and "Corazón," but *Wrap around Joy*, with most lyrics supplied by David Palmer, was decidedly jazz-oriented. The album's smash hit "Jazzman" featured an exciting saxophone solo by Tom Scott and was followed by "Nightingale." After *Really Rosie*, an animated television show based on the children's books of Maurice Sendak and using Sendak's lyrics, King recorded *Thoroughbred* with the vocal assistance of Graham Nash, David Crosby, and James Taylor. The album included four Goffin-King songs and yielded a major hit with "Only Love Is Real."

At the end of 1976, Carole King severed relations with Lou Adler's Ode Records, switching to Capitol for the moderate hit "Hard Rock Café." By then separated from Charles Larkey, she collaborated with Rick Evers and the band Navarro for touring and recording. King later married Evers and moved to Idaho but, on March 21, 1978, he died from a cocaine overdose in L. A. Subsequent albums for Capitol sold only modestly and only *Pearls*, a collection of her versions of the Goffin-King classics of the 1960s, yielded a major hit, with "One Fine Day."

Settling into a less public lifestyle, Carole King recorded two albums for Atlantic and made a brief benefit tour for presidential hopeful Gary Hart in 1984. Working for protection of the wilderness since 1984, King provided the title song to *The Care Bears Movie*, acted in several movies and television shows, and starred in the play *Getting Out*. Following an album for Capitol in 1989, Carole King recorded *Colour of Your Dreams* for her own label in 1993, the year she performed at President Clinton's inaugural ball and made her Broadway acting debut in the musical *Blood Brothers*. Gerry Goffin and Carole King's daughter, Louise, started her modest recording career in the late 1970s.

DISC.: *Writer: Carole King* (1970); *Tapestry* (1971); *Carole King Music* (1971); *Rhymes and Reasons* (1972); *Fantasy* (1973); *Wrap around Joy* (1974); *Really Rosie* (TV soundtrack; 1975); *Thoroughbred* (1976); *Simple Things* (1977); *Welcome Home* (1977); *Touch the Sky* (1979); *Pearls—The Songs of Goffin and King* (1980); *One to One* (1982); *Speeding Time* (1983); *City Streets* (1989); *Colour of Your Dreams* (1993); *In Concert* (1994).

BIBL.: M. S. Cohen, *C. K.: A Biography in Words and Pictures* (N.Y., 1976).—**BH**

King, Harold Charles, Swiss-born Dutch composer; b. Winterthur, Dec. 30, 1895; d. Amsterdam, June 12, 1984. He went to the Netherlands to study engineering at the Delft Technical Univ. He served as a management consultant with a municipal corporation in Amsterdam, and while thus occupied took composition lessons with Dopper and Badings.

WORKS: ORCH.: *Serenade* for Strings (1934); *Per Ardua,* symphonic suite (1946–49); *Concerto da camera* for Flute and Strings (1962); *Triptyque symphonique* (1964); Sinfonietta (1965); Organ Concerto (1966). **CHAMBER:** Cello Sonata (1940); *Trio patetico* for Violin, Viola, and Cello (1942); *3 Impressions* for Cello (1948); Wind Quintet (1949); 2 string quartets (1953, 1962); *A fleur d'eau* for Flute, Violin, Spinet, and Viola da Gamba (1964); Sonata for Solo Cello (1966); Duo for 2 Cellos (1966); *Piccolo quartetto* for String Quartet (1976). **KEYBOARD:** *Little Laddie,* piano sonatina (1966); *King David's Dance* for 4-octave Carillon

(1975). **VOCAL:** *Cornet* for Chorus and Instruments (1977); *Missa 1978* for Chorus and Organ (1978); *3 chansons d'amour et une epigramme* for Voice and Instruments (1981); *Tres orationes* for Voice, Recorder, and Lute (1982); *O Leben, Leben, wunderliche Zeit* for Middle Voice and Orch. (1983).—**NS/LK/DM**

King, James, American tenor; b. Dodge City, Kans., May 22, 1925. He studied at the Univ. of Kansas City, and also received vocal training from Martial Singher and Max Lorenz. He then went to Europe and made his professional debut as Cavaradossi in Florence (1961). He subsequently sang at the San Francisco Opera (1961), the Berlin Deutsche Opera (1962), the Salzburg Festival (1962), the Bayreuth Festival (1965), the Metropolitan Opera in N.Y. (debut as Florestan, Jan. 8, 1966), London's Covent Garden (1966), and Milan's La Scala (1968). He taught voice at the Ind. Univ. School of Music in Bloomington (from 1984). Among his prominent roles were Lohengrin, Walther von Stolzing, Parsifal, Siegmund, Verdi's Otello, and Pfitzner's Palestrina. —**NS/LK/DM**

King, Karl L(awrence), American bandmaster and composer; b. Painterville, Ohio, Feb. 21, 1891; d. Fort Dodge, Iowa, March 31, 1971. After 8 grades of public schools in Cleveland and Canton, Ohio, during which he began to play brass instruments (primarily the baritone horn) under the tutelage of local musicians, he quit school to learn the printing trade, but soon began to play in and compose for local bands. In 1910 he initiated his short career as a circus bandsman, bandmaster, and composer, ending it in 1917–18 as bandmaster of the Barnum & Bailey Circus Band (for which he had already written what was to remain his most famous march, *Barnum & Bailey's Favorite*). In 1920 he conducted his first concert with the Fort Dodge Military Band, with which he was to be associated for half a century. In 1922 the band began to receive municipal tax support under the Iowa Band Law (for which one of King's marches is named), and its name was changed to the Fort Dodge Municipal Band, although it was known commonly as Karl L. King's Band. For 40 years it toured widely over its region. He was one of the founders, in 1930, of the American Bandmasters Assn.; he served as president of that group in 1939, and in 1967 was named honorary life president. Among his 260-odd works for band are concert works, novelties, waltzes, and all manner of dance forms; but marches predominate, from the circus marches of his early days to sophisticated marches for univ. bands (such as *Pride of the Illini* for Illinois and *Purple Pageant* for Northwestern) and especially to easy but tuneful and well-written marches for the less accomplished school bands. The musical *The Music Man* (1957) was inspired in part by King's music, according to its composer and fellow Iowan, Meredith Willson.

BIBL.: T. Hatton, *K.L. K., An American Bandmaster* (Evanston, Ill., 1975).—**NS/LK/DM**

King, Matthew Peter, English composer and music theorist; b. London, c. 1773; d. there, Jan. 1823. He received training from C.F. Horn. He wrote much stage music and publ. the treatises *Thorough Bass Made Clear to*

every Capacity (London, c. 1810) and *A General Treatise on Music, Particularly Harmony or Thoroughbass* (London, 1812).

WORKS: DRAMATIC (all 1st perf. in London): **C o m i c O p e r a :** *Matrimony* (Nov. 20, 1804); *The Weathercock* (Nov. 18, 1805); *False Alarms, or My Cousin* (Jan. 12, 1807; in collaboration with J. Braham); *Up All Night, or The Smuggler's Cave* (June 26, 1809); *Oh, This Love, or The Masqueraders* (June 12, 1810); *The Americans* (April 27, 1811; in collaboration with J. Braham). **M e l o d r a m a t i c O p e r a :** *Plots!, or The North Tower* (Sept. 3, 1810). **G r a n d R o m a n t i c O p e r a :** *One o'clock, or The Knight and the Wood Daemon* (Aug. 1, 1811; in collaboration with M. Kelly). **O t h e r D r a m a t i c :** Musical farces; melodramas. **OTHER:** *The Intercession*, oratorio (London, June 1, 1816); many glees and songs; numerous instrumental pieces.—**NS/LK/DM**

King, Robert (John Stephen), English conductor and harpsichordist; b. Wombourne, June 27, 1960. He received an M.A. degree from St. John's Coll., Cambridge. In 1979 he founded the King's Consort, with which he presented many enterprising programs. He became particularly well known for his championship of the music of Purcell. In 1986 he also served as music director of the European Baroque Orch., and from 1987 of the National Youth Music Theatre. As a guest conductor, he appeared with various European orchs. He publ. the valuable biography *Henry Purcell* (London, 1994).—**NS/LK/DM**

King, Thea, English clarinetist and teacher; b. Hitchin, Hertfordshire, Dec. 26, 1925. She studied clarinet at the Royal Coll. of Music in London (1943–47) with **Frederick Thurston**, whom she married in 1953. She played in the Sadler's Wells Orch. (1950–52), Portia Wind Ensemble (1955–68), London Mozart Players (1956–84), English Chamber Orch. (from 1964), Melos Ensemble (from 1974), and Robles Ensemble (from 1983); also made appearances as a soloist and recitalist. From 1961 to 1987 she was a prof. at the Royal Coll. of Music, and from 1988 at the Guildhall School of Music in London. In 1985 she was made an Officer of the Order of the British Empire. She has performed many works by contemporary British composers and has also resuscitated numerous scores of the past.—**NS/LK/DM**

King Crimson, seminal British progressive band of the late 1960s and 1970s. **MEMBERSHIP:** Robert Fripp, gtr. (b. Wimbourne, Dorset, England, May 16, 1946); Ian McDonald, rds., wdwnd., kybd., mellotron, vod. (b. London, England, June 25, 1946); Greg Lake, bs., lead voc. (b. Bournemouth, Dorset, England, Nov. 10, 1948); Mike Giles, drm., voc. (b. Bournemouth, Dorset, England, March 1, 1942); and lyricist Pete Sinfield. Giles and McDonald left at the end of 1969 and Lake departed in early 1970. Sinfield was dismissed at the end of 1971. Later members included Raymond "Boz" Burrell, bs., voc. (b. Lincoln, England, Aug. 1, 1946); Ian Wallace, drm. (b. Bury, England, Sept. 29, 1946); John Wetton, bs., voc. (b. Derby, England, June 12, 1950); Bill Bruford, drm. (b. Sevenoaks, Kent, England, May 17, 1949). King Crimson disbanded in 1974 and re-formed from 1981 to

1984 and 1993 to present with Fripp, Bruford, bassist Tony Levin, and guitarist Robert "Adrian" Belew.

Robert Fripp started playing the guitar at age 11 and worked with his first music group at 14. In Bournemouth, he helped form Giles, Giles and Fripp in 1967 with Giles brothers Mike and Peter on drums and bass, respectively. They never played in public, their sole album for Deram failed to attract any attention, and, by the fall of 1968, the group had disbanded.

Mike Giles and Robert Fripp began rehearsing a new band called King Crimson in January 1969 and debuted in London that April. With Pete Sinfield providing the lyrics, the other members were Greg Lake and Ian McDonald. The group's underground reputation was enhanced by a July appearance before 650,000 in Hyde Park at a free Rolling Stones concert. King Crimson's debut album, *In the Court of the Crimson King*, was greeted with near-unanimous critical acclaim and featured five extended pieces, including "Epitaph," "21st Century Schizoid Man," and the title song, a minor hit.

However, after King Crimson's first tour of the U.S., Giles and McDonald left the group in December 1969, later to record an album together for Cotillion. Reduced to a trio, King Crimson began recording their second album, only to see Greg Lake depart to join Emerson, Lake and Palmer during those sessions. *In the Wake of Poseidon* was completed with Gordon Haskell (bs., voc.), Mel Collins (flt., sax.), and the Giles brothers, with Fripp taking over on mellotron. Despite its remarkable resemblance to their debut, the album sold quite well.

By late 1970, Mel Collins and Gordon Haskell had become permanent members of King Crimson, as had drummer Andy McCulloch. Nonetheless, Haskell quit shortly before the final sessions for *Lizard*, later to record a solo album for Atco. Ian Wallace replaced McCulloch and Fripp recruited bassist Boz Burrell for *Islands*. Again, after a second American tour in early 1972, King Crimson disintegrated. Collins, Wallace, and Burrell left to join Alexis Korner, and Fripp dismissed lyricist Pete Sinfield. Sinfield later produced Roxy Music's debut album, recorded a solo album, and wrote songs for Emerson, Lake and Palmer.

After several months' layoff, Robert Fripp reconstituted King Crimson with avant-garde percussionist Jamie Muir, violin and mellotron player David Cross, lead vocalist–bassist John Wetton (from Family), and drummer Bill Bruford (from Yes). This aggregation recorded *Larks' Tongues in Aspic*, but Muir dropped out after the first tour. *Starless and Bible Black* was recorded by the remaining quartet, and *Red* was recorded without Cross, but with the assistance of Mel Collins and Ian McDonald. Fripp dissolved King Crimson in September 1974.

Boz Burrell joined in the formation of Bad Company in late 1973. Ian McDonald helped form Foreigner in early 1976. In the mid-1970s Robert Fripp recorded two esoteric albums with Roxy Music synthesizer player Brian Eno. They devised a system of music utilizing two tape recorders and solo guitar called "Frippertronics" that Fripp employed for his 1979 American "anti-tour." He launched his solo recording career that year with the amazing *Exposure* album, later recording with Daryl Hall, his own League of Gentlemen, and two instrumental albums with Andy Summers of The Police. He also played on David Bowie's *Scary Monsters* album, produced Peter Gabriel and The Roches, and served as sessions guitarist for Blondie and Talking Heads.

In 1981, Robert Fripp reconvened King Crimson with vocalist-guitarist Adrian Belew, bassist Tony Levin, and drummer Bill Bruford for three albums and two American tours through 1984. In the 1990s, Fripp assembled a large group of guitar players for recordings as The League of Crafty Guitarists. By 1994, King Crimson had reunited with Fripp, Belew, Levin, and Bruford and two others for the concept album *THRAK* and a 1995 tour.

DISC.: *In the Court of the Crimson King* (1969); *In the Wake of Poseidon* (1970); *Lizard* (1971); *Islands* (1972); *Larks' Tongues in Aspic* (1973); *Starless and Bible Black* (1974); *Red* (1974); *U.S. A.* (1975); *Discipline* (1981); *Beat* (1982); *Three of a Perfect Pair* (1984); *The Great Deceiver* (live, 1973–74; 1992).—**BH**

King (Ousley), Curtis,

the last great tenor saxophone soloist of the staccato, honking style; b. Fort Worth, Tex., Feb. 7, 1934; d. N.Y., Aug. 13, 1971.

Curtis Ousley grew up in Fort Worth, Tex., where he obtained his first saxophone at the age of 12. He played in his high school marching band and formed his first combo while still in high school, performing locally. He toured with Lionel Hampton's Band after graduation and moved to N.Y. in 1952. There he played engagements with a wide variety of groups, including a trio featuring pianist Horace Silver. Curtis replaced Arthur "Red" Prysock in Alan Freed's show band and joined Atlantic/Atco Records as a staff musician in 1958. He first received recognition for his clean, compelling tenor saxophone solos on The Coasters' "Yakety Yak" and subsequently backed virtually all of The Coasters' recordings for Atco.

King Curtis backed dozens of artists over the years, including Sam Cooke, Ray Charles, Bobby Darin, Sam and Dave, The Shirelles, Eric Clapton, The Allman Brothers, Delaney and Bonnie, and Aretha Franklin. He recorded two jazz albums with Wynton Kelly and Nat Adderley in 1960 and scored a top R&B / pop hit with his Noble Knights (later The Kingpins) in 1962 with the instrumental "Soul Twist" on Enjoy Records. He also toured with Sam Cooke in the early 1960s, most notably accompanying the vocalist on his *Feel It!—Live at the Harlem Square Club*, 1963. Curtis recorded for Capitol Records, with modest success, in 1963–64.

King Curtis returned to Atlantic Records in 1965, achieving near-smash R&B and moderate pop hits with "Memphis Soul Stew" and "Ode to Billie Joe" on Atco in 1967. He continued to record with The Kingpins on Atco with modest success until his death. Beginning in 1967, Curtis started taking a more active role in the studio, contracting sessions and later producing artists such as Sam Moore (of Sam and Dave), Roberta Flack, Delaney and Bonnie, Donny Hathaway, and Freddie King. In 1971 he was appointed to succeed Donald Towns as Aretha Franklin's permanent musical director. He performed with pianist "Champion" Jack Dupree at The Montreux Jazz Festival in June, but, on Aug. 13, 1971,

King Curtis was stabbed to death in front of his N.Y. apartment house. He was 37 years old.

DISC.: *Have Tenor Sax, Will Blow* (1959); *New Scene* (1960); *Azure* (1961); *Trouble in Mind* (1962); *Old Gold* (1962); *It's Party Time* (1962); *Country Soul* (1962); *Doing the Dixie Twist* (1963); *Soul Serenade* (1964); *Plays the Hits Made Famous by Sam* (1965); *That Lovin' Feeling* (1966); *"Live" at Small's Paradise* (1966); *Plays the Great Memphis Hits* (1967); *King Size Soul* (1967); *Sweet Soul* (1968); *Best* (1968); *Sax in Motion* (1968); *Instant Groove* (1969); *Get Ready* (1970); *Best—One More Time* (1970); *"Live" at the Fillmore West* (1971); *Everybody's Talkin'* (1972); *Watermelon Man* (1972); *Jazz Groove* (1973); *Soul Time* (1973); *Old Gold/Doing the Dixie Twist* (1995); *Night Train* (rec. 1961–62; rel. 1995). **KING CURTIS, WYNTON KELLY, AND NAT ADDERLEY:** *Soul Meeting* (1962); *King Soul* (1970). **KING CURTIS AND THE SHIRELLES:** *Eternally Soul* (1970); *Give a Twist Party* (1993). **KING CURTIS AND "CHAMPION" JACK DUPREE:** *Blues at Montreux* (1973).—**BH**

Kingsmen, The,

the ultimate garage band from the Pacific Northwest (f. 1958). **MEMBERSHIP:** Lynn Easton, voc.; Jack Ely, gtr., voc. (b. Portland, Ore., Sept. 11, 1943); Mike Mitchell, lead gtr.; Bob Nordby, gtr., bs.; Don Gallucci, kybd.; Garry Abbott, drm.; Norm Sundholm, bs.

One of the dozens of bands to rise out of the Pacific Northwest in the early 1960s, The Kingsmen created one of rock's most enduring records almost by accident. They started playing wherever they could get gigs in the competitive atmosphere fueled by peers like Paul Revere and the Raiders and The Wailers, among many others. Those two bands had already cut covers of Richard Berry's 1956 tune "Louie Louie." The Kingsmen cut it in hope of getting a job on a cruise ship. While the ship line rejected it, a local record company saw fit to press some up. While the Raider's version (released around the same time) eclipsed the Kingsmen's locally, a copy made its way to Boston where it started to break out throughout the East Coast. Because the recording was crude and the vocals were pretty garbled, controversy arose as to exactly what they were singing. The controversy begot record sales and the single climbed to #2, where it sat for six weeks. Millions of college-age males imagined that the song had something to do with sex, and even the FBI opened an investigation to see what—if anything—the song meant. Despite decades of listening, no one is quite sure, although Berry insists that *his* lyrics were just a simple romantic love song. On the strength of "Louie Louie," the album *The Kingsmen in Person* went to #20. A live version of "Money" hit #16. The album *Volume II* went to #15.

The band toured extensively, breaking attendance records at colleges and ballrooms. Their song "Jolly Green Giant" rose to #4 and the album *Volume III* rose to #22. That was their last hit. By 1968, they agreed to sign away their rights to "Louie Louie" for a percentage of future licensing fees and profits. Having never seen any of this money, they sued the company and won, recouping their back royalties. The song further became fodder for an entire book by critic and journalist Dave Marsh. The band continues to be a live attraction over 40 years after forming. Three of the members have been playing together since 1963.

DISC.: *The Kingsmen in Person* (1963); *The Kingsmen, Vol. 2* (1964); *How to Stuff a Wild Bikini* (original soundtrack; 1965); *The Kingsmen on Campus* (1965); *The Kingsmen, Vol. 3* (1965); *Up and Away* (1966); *Louie Louie* (1986); *Live & Unreleased* (1992); *Since We've Been Gone* (live; 1994); *Jolly Green Giant* (1996).—**HB**

Kingston Trio, The,

the most successful folk group to emerge in the late 1950s; **MEMBERSHIP:** Bob Shane, gtr., bjo., voc. (b. Hilo, Hawaii, Feb. 1, 1934); Dave Guard, gtr., bjo., voc. (b. Honolulu, Hawaii, Nov. 19, 1934; d. Rollinsford, N. H., March 22, 1991); Nick Reynolds, gtr., voc. (b. San Diego, Calif., July 27, 1933). Guard left in May 1961, to be replaced by John Stewart (b. San Diego, Calif., Sept. 5, 1939). The Kingston Trio disbanded in 1967, but Bob Shane reconstituted the group in 1972. Later members included Roger Gambill, George Grove, and Bob Haworth.

Collegians Bob Shane, Dave Guard, and Nick Reynolds formed The Kingston Trio in San Francisco, Calif., in 1957. All three played guitar and sang, with Guard and Shane doubling on banjo. Playing local coffeehouses and clubs, most notably the Hungry I and the Purple Onion, The Kingston Trio signed with Capitol Records in 1958. Their first and ultimately biggest success came with the top pop hit "Tom Dooley," which also became a near-smash R&B hit. By 1960, they had scored major hits with the silly "Tijuana Jail," "M.T.A.," and "Worried Man." Their early albums sold spectacularly, with their debut album, *The Kingston Trio*, staying on the charts nearly four years, and three of their next four remaining on the charts for more than two years.

Dave Guard left The Kingston Trio in May 1961 to form The Whiskeyhill Singers with Judy Henske. He later moved to Australia, where he hosted a television program, returning to the U.S. in 1968. He also authored two children's books and recorded *Up and In*, released in 2000. He died at his home in Rollinsford, N. H., on March 22, 1991, of lymphoma. He was replaced by John Stewart, the founder of the folk group The Cumberland Three. The Kingston Trio enjoyed hits through 1963, with Pete Seeger's "Where Have All the Flowers Gone," Dave Guard's "Scotch and Soda" (only a minor hit, but standard lounge fare today), Hoyt Axton's "Greenback Dollar," and Billy Edd Wheeler's "Reverend Mr. Black." Switching to Decca Records in 1964, they failed to achieve even a minor hit for the label. In 1967 The Kingston Trio disbanded.

In 1972 Bob Shane reconstituted the group with singer-guitarist Roger Gambill and banjoist George Grove, a Wake Forest Univ. music degree holder. They performed with symphony orchestras and persevered on the college and supper club circuits. All six members of The Kingston Trio—Shane, Reynolds, Guard, Stewart, Gambill and Grove—reunited for a concert at California's Magic Mountain Amusement Park that yielded a PBS television special hosted by Tom Smothers in 1982. Roger Gambill died in Atlanta, Ga., on March 20, 1985, at the age of 42 after suffering a heart attack and stroke. He was replaced by Bob Haworth of The Brothers Four until the late 1980s, when Nick Reynolds rejoined the group. In 1993 The Kingston Trio recorded *Live at the Crazy Horse* for the small Silverwolf label.

John Stewart subsequently pursued his own career, recording with Scott Engel, then Buffy Ford. In 1967 The Monkees had scored a top hit with Stewart's "Daydream Believer"; it was revived as a smash country hit by Anne Murray in 1980. Stewart's recordings for Capitol, including the critically acclaimed *California Bloodlines* (with "July, You're a Woman" and "Lonesome Picker") failed to sell, as did the overlooked *Lonesome Picker Rides Again* (with "All the Brave Horses" and "Touch of the Sun") for Warner Brothers and *Cannons in the Rain* (with "All Time Woman" and the minor hit "Armstrong") for RCA. John Stewart achieved his biggest success in 1979 with *Bombs Away Dream Babies* on RSO Records. The album featured the smash hit "Gold" and major hit "Midnight Wind," recorded with Stevie Nicks and Lindsey Buckingham of Fleetwood Mac, and the moderate hit "Lost Her in the Sun."

The follow-up to *Bombs Away Dream Babies* sold only modestly for John Stewart, leading him to form his own record company, Homecoming, in the 1980s. Albums for the label included *The Trio Years*, re-recordings of songs written for The Kingston Trio, and the poignant *The Last Campaign*, re-recordings of songs composed during and after Bobby Kennedy's 1968 presidential campaign. In 1987 Stewart recorded *Punch the Big Guy* for Cypress with Rosanne Cash, who scored a top country hit with his "Runaway Train" in 1988. In 1992 John Stewart recorded *Bullets in the Hour Glass* for the small but nationally distributed Shanachie label.

DISC.: *The Kingston Trio* (1958); *From the Hungry I* (1959); *Stereo Concert* (1959); *At Large* (1959); *Here We Go Again!* (1959); *Sold Out* (1960); *String Along* (1960); *The Last Month of the Year* (1960); *Make Way!* (1961); *Goin' Places* (1961); *Close-Up* (1961); *College Concert* (1962); *Something Special* (1962); *New Frontier* (1962); *#16* (1963); *Sunny Side!* (1963); *Sing a Song with the Kingston Trio* (1963); *Time to Think* (1964); *Back in Town* (1964); *Nick-Bob-John* (1965); *Stay Awhile* (1965); *Somethin' Else* (1965); *Children of the Morning* (1966); *Live at the Crazy Horse* (1993). —BH

Kinkeldey, Otto, eminent American musicologist; b. N.Y., Nov. 27, 1878; d. Orange, N.J., Sept. 19, 1966. He graduated from the Coll. of the City of N.Y. in 1898 (B.A.) and from N.Y.U. in 1900 (M.A.), and then took lessons with MacDowell at Columbia Univ. (until 1902). He went to Berlin (1902), where he undertook a course of study with Radecke, Egidi, and Thiel at the Königlisches Akademisches Institut für Kirchenmusik; then studied musicology at the Univ. of Berlin with Fleischer, Friedlaender, Kretzschmar, and Wolf (Ph.D., 1909, with the diss. *Orgel und Klavier in der Musik des 16. Jahrhunderts*; publ. in Leipzig, 1910). He taught at the Univ. of Breslau (1909–14). Returning to the U.S., he was chief of the music division of the N.Y. Public Library (1915–23; 1927–30). He was prof. of music at Cornell Univ. (1923–27), and subsequently prof. of musicology and a librarian there (1930–46). He was a guest prof. at various American univs., as well as president of the American Musicological Soc. (1934–36; 1940–42). He contributed numerous articles to scholarly journals and also publ. *What We Know about Music* (Ann Arbor, 1946). —NS/LK/DM

Kinks, The, one of the longest-lived groups of the 1960s British invasion (exceeded only by The Rolling Stones), The Kinks endured an erratic career of hit and flop singles, concept albums, and record company changes under leader Ray Davies and his brother Dave. **MEMBERSHIP:** Ray Davies, lead voc., rhythm gtr. (b. Muswell Hill, London, England, June 21, 1944); Dave Davies, lead and rhythm gtr., kybd., voc. (b. Muswell Hill, London, England, Feb. 3, 1947); Peter Quaife, bs., voc. (b. Tavistock, Devon, England, Dec. 27, 1943); Mick Avory, drm. (b. Hampton Court, Surrey, England, Feb. 15, 1944). Quaife left in March 1969, to be replaced by John Dalton (b. May 21, 1943). Keyboardist John Gosling was added in 1971, but Gosling and Dalton departed in 1978. Bassist Jim Rodford joined in 1978 and Bob Henrit replaced Avory in 1984.

Ray and Dave Davies received guitars from their parents as early teenagers. Dave played in The Bo Weevils with Peter Quaife before forming The Ravens to play the local debutante circuit in 1962, while brother Ray began playing with The Dave Hunt Band in 1963. Ray insinuated his way into The Ravens around December 1963, as the group was renamed The Kinks and "discovered" by American producer Shel Talmy, who secured them a recording contract with Pye Records (Reprise in the U.S.).

The Kinks' first two singles barely sold, but the third, "You Really Got Me," became a smash British and American hit. The like-sounding "All Day and All of the Night" was a smash hit in early 1965, followed by the slower-paced smash "Tired of Waiting" and "Set Me Free," a major hit. Other early recordings included "Everybody's Gonna Be Happy," "Something Better Beginning," and "See My Friend." They toured the U.S. in mid-1965, but, for missing a single engagement, they were banned from performing again until 1969 by the American Federation of Musicians.

The moderate hit "Who'll Be the Next in Line" echoed The Kinks' earlier raunchy sound, but "A Well Respected Man" marked the beginning of a new phase of astute satire in Ray Davies' songwriting. "Dedicated Follower of Fashion" poked fun at Carnaby Street fops, and the follow-up, "Sunny Afternoon," satirized the indolent upper class. Their 1967 album *Face to Face* included Ray's "Dandy," a smash hit for Herman's Hermits.

After *Something Else*, The Kinks' final album under producer Shel Talmy, Ray Davies produced their next two albums, including the neglected concept album *Village Green Preservation Society*, and scored the soundtracks to the movies *The Virgin Soldiers* and *Percy*. Dave Davies managed a smash British-only hit with "Death of a Clown" in 1967, and The Kinks scored smash British hits through 1968 with "Dead End Street," "Waterloo Sunset," "Autumn Almanac," and "Days." However, their albums and singles sold poorly in the U.S., in part due to the performance ban. In March 1969, Peter Quaife left the group, to be replaced on bass by John Dalton.

The Kinks' ambitious, critically acclaimed, historically conscious concept album *Arthur (Or the Decline and Fall of the British Empire)* sold modestly at best, despite the inclusion of "Shangri La" and "Victoria," a minor hit. The Kinks resumed touring the U.S. in late 1969 with their usual sloppy stage presentation, occasionally marred by open hostility between Ray and Dave Davies. Augmented by keyboardist John Gosling beginning in May 1971, The Kinks finally reestablished themselves in the U.S. in 1971 with *Lola Versus Powerman and The Moneygoround*, an acerbic look at the pop music industry and their situation in it. Songs included "Get Back in Line," "Top of the Pops," the moderate hit "Apeman," and the near-smash "Lola," apparently the first rock song to deal openly with transvetitism.

By 1971, The Kinks had switched to RCA Records. Their RCA debut, the decidedly countrified *Muswell Hillbillies*, sold only modestly, despite the inclusion of Kinks favorites such as "Alcohol," "Acute Schizophrenia Paranoid Blues," and "20th Century Man." The follow-up, *Everybody's in Show-Biz*, included "Sitting in My Hotel" and the excellent "Celluloid Heroes."

Ray Davies and The Kinks next embarked on a program of ambitious concept albums, complete with on-tour theatrical presentations. The character of Mr. Flash from *The Village Green Preservation Society* was resurrected, but *Preservation*, originally released in two separate *Acts*, sold poorly. During 1974, Ray and Dave Davies formed Konk Records as an outlet for productions outside the group, but recordings by Claire Hamill and Café Society proved unsuccessful. The Kinks' next two albums, *Soap Opera* and *Schoolboys in Disgrace*, sold rather well despite yielding no hit singles, but concurrent tours featuring theatrical performances of each album's material seemed to perplex rather than amuse American audiences.

During the late 1970s, personnel changes plagued The Kinks, with the Davies brothers and Mick Avory remaining as constants. By 1977, they had switched to Arista Records and abandoned the concept album format. *Sleepwalker*, their best-selling album in years, yielded the group's first, albeit minor, hit in six years with the title song. *Misfits* produced a major hit with "A Rock 'n' Roll Fantasy," and *Low Budget* included the underground favorite "A Gallon of Gas" and the moderate hit "(I Wish I Could Fly Like) Superman."

Following the minor hits "Destroyer" and "Better Things," The Kinks scored a smash hit with the nostalgic "Come Dancing" from *State of Confusion*. Subsequent hits included "Don't Forget to Dance" and "Do It Again." The 1985 made-for-British-TV movie *Return to Waterloo* marked the debut of Ray Davies as a film director/writer. He also appeared in the 1986 movie *Absolute Beginners* and wrote the music and lyrics for *80 Days*, a musical based on Jules Vernes's "Around the World in Eighty Days," performed at the La Jolla Playhouse in southern Calif. in 1988.

With Ray and Dave Davies as the only original members left, The Kinks switched to MCA Records in 1986. *Think Visual* featured Dave's "Rock 'n' Roll Cities," whereas 1989's *U.K. Jive* included the ballad "Now and Then" and "Aggravation." The Kinks were inducted into the Rock and Roll Hall of Fame in 1990. They conducted their first U.S. tour in more than three years in 1993. In 1996, the group issued a two-CD live retrospective *To the Bone*.

In 1994, Ray Davies published an account of his early life and career with The Kinks through 1973 titled *X-Ray*. He mounted a one-man show (accompanied by a second guitarist) performed in N.Y. and London that combined reminiscences, songs, and readings from his book, and presented an abbreviated form of the show as the inaugural edition of cable TV network VH1's *Storyteller* series. He later refined the presentation into *A Musical Evening with a 20th-Century Man* for tours in 1996 and 1997.

DISC.: *You Really Got Me* (1964); *Kinks-Size* (1965); *Kinda Kinks* (1965); *Kinks Kinkdom* (1965); *The Kinks Kontroversy* (1966); *Face to Face* (1966); *The "Live" Kinks* (1967); *Something Else by The Kinks* (1968); *Village Green Preservation Society* (1969); *Arthur (Or the Decline and Fall of the British Empire)* (1969); *Lola Versus Powerman and The Moneygoround* (1970); *The Great Lost Kinks Album* (1973); *Muswell Hillbillies* (1971); *Everybody's in Show-Biz* (1972); *Preservation, Act I* (1973); *Preservation, Act II* (1974); *Soap Opera* (1975); *Schoolboys in Disgrace* (1975); *Sleepwalker* (1977); *Misfits* (1978); *Low Budget* (1979); *One for the Road* (1980); *Give the People What They* (1981); *State of Confusion* (1983); *Word of Mouth* (1984); *Think Visual* (1986); *Live: The Road* (1988); *U.K. Jive* (1989); *Preservation: A Play in Two Acts* (1991); *To the Bone* (1996).

WRITINGS: R. Davies, *X-Ray* (N.Y., 1995); D. Davies, *Kink: An Autobiography* (N.Y., 1996).

BIBL.: J. Mendelsohn, *The Kink Kronikles* (N.Y., 1984); J. Savage, *The Kinks: The Official Biography* (London, 1984).—**BH**

Kinsella, John, Irish composer; b. Dublin, April 8, 1932. He began to study the violin, viola, and piano at an early age. He first was active as a chamber music player while pursuing a career as a computer programmer in the 1960s. In 1968 he went to work for the Radio Telefis Eireann, where he was head of music from 1983 until opting for early retirement in 1988 to concentrate on composing. He is a member of Aosdána, Ireland's state-sponsored academy of creative artists. Kinsella's early works were serial, but after 1980 his music became more intimate and expressive.

WORKS: ORCH.: *2 Pieces* for Strings (1965); *Rondo* (1969); *Music* for Cello and Chamber Orch. (1971); *The Wayfarer: Rhapsody on a Poem of P.H. Pearse* for Chamber Orch. (1979); 8 syms.: No. 1 (1980–84), No. 2 (1986–88), No. 3, *Joie de Vivre* (1989–90), No. 4, *The Four Provinces* (1990–91), No. 5, *The 1916 Poets*, for Male Speaker, Baritone, and Orch. (1991–92), No. 6 (1992–93), No. 7 (1997), and No. 8, *Into the New Millennium* (1998–99); 2 violin concertos (1981, 1989); *Sinfonietta: Pictures from The Odyssey* (1983); *Rhapsody on a Poem of Francis Ledwidge* (1986–87); *Nocturne* for Strings (1990); *Festive Overture* (1995). **CHAMBER:** 4 string quartets (1960; 1968; 1977; 1991–93); Chamber Concerto for Solo Violin, English Horn, 2 Horns, 4 Violins, and Percussion (1962); *Allegro Giocoso* for Harp (1966); *Dialogue* for Bassoon and Piano (1972); *Rhapsody on a Poem of Joseph Campbell* for Violin or Viola (1975); *Aberration* for Flute and Violin (1980); Piano Quartet (1984–85); *Synthesis* for String Quartet (1987); *The Splendid Years* for Traditional Whistle, String Quartet, and Speaker (1990); *Symphony for Five* (1996); Sonata for 2 Violins (1996). **P i a n o :** Sonata (1971); *Reflection I* (1995) and *II* (1996).—**LK/DM**

Kinsky, Georg Ludwig, distinguished German musicologist; b. Marienwerder, Sept. 29, 1882; d. Berlin, April 7, 1951. He was self-taught in music. After working under Klopfermann at the Prussian Royal Library in Berlin (1908–09), he was curator of the private museum of W. Heyer in Cologne from 1909 until it was closed in 1927. He also was a lecturer in musicology at the Univ. of Cologne (1921–32), where he received his Ph.D. in 1925 with the diss. *Doppelrohrblatt-Instrumente mit Windkapsel* (publ. in the *Archiv für Musikwissenschaft*, VII, 1925). In 1944 his home and his private library and collection were confiscated by the Nazi government; he then served a year at hard labor until the Allied victory in 1945. Although his health was shattered by this ordeal, he spent his last years in Berlin preparing a thematic catalog of Beethoven's works, a task completed by Hans Halm.

WRITINGS: *Musikhistorisches Museum von Wilhelm Heyer in Cöln: Katalog* (Cologne, Vol. I, 1910; Vol. II, 1912, and Vol. IV, 1916; Vol. III not publ.; greater portion of the MS not extant); ed. *Glucks Briefe an Franz Kruthoffer* (Vienna, 1927); with R. Haas and H. Schnoor, *Geschichte der Musik in Bildern* (Leipzig, 1929; Eng. tr., 1930; 2nd ed., 1951); *Erstlingsdrucke der deutschen Tonmeister der Klassik und Romantik* (Vienna, 1934); *Philobiblon*, VII (1934); *Die Originalausgaben der Werke Johann Sebastian Bachs* (Vienna, 1937); *Manuskripte, Briefe, Dokumente von Scarlatti bis Stravinsky, Katalog der Musik-autographen-Sammlung Louis Koch* (Stuttgart, 1951; ed. by M.-A. Souchay); *Das Werk Beethovens: Thematisch-Bibliographisches Verzeichnis siner sämtlichen vollendeten Kompositionen* (Munich and Duisburg, 1955; completed by H. Halm).—NS/LK/DM

Kipnis, Alexander, eminent Russian-born American bass, father of **Igor Kipnis;** b. Zhitomir, Feb. 13, 1891; d. Westport, Conn., May 14, 1978. He studied conducting at the Warsaw Cons. (graduated, 1912); later took voice lessons with Ernst Grenzebach at Berlin's Klindworth-Scharwenka Cons. In 1913 he sang at Monti's Operetten Theater and in 1914 at the Filmzauber operetta theater in Berlin. At the outbreak of World War I, he was interned as an enemy alien, but was soon released and made his operatic debut as the hermit in *Der Freischütz* at the Hamburg Opera in 1915; sang there until 1917, then was a member of the Wiesbaden Opera (1917–22). He made his U.S. debut as Pogner with the visiting German Opera Co. in Baltimore on Jan. 31, 1923; he then was a member of the Chicago Civic Opera (1923–32). He also sang regularly at the Berlin Städtische Oper (1922–30), the Berlin State Opera (1932–35), and the Vienna State Opera (1935–38). In 1927 he made his first appearance at London's Covent Garden as Marcel in *Les Huguenots*, and sang there again from 1929 to 1935. He became a naturalized American citizen in 1931. During these years, he made guest appearances at the Bayreuth, Salzburg, and Glyndebourne festivals, as well as at the Teatro Colón in Buenos Aires. On Jan. 5, 1940, he made his belated Metropolitan Opera debut in N.Y. as Gurnemanz, and continued to sing there until 1946; he then devoted himself mainly to teaching. Through the years he appeared as a distinguished concert artist. In addition to his remarkable portrayal of Gurnemanz, he was greatly esteemed for such roles as Sarastro, Rocco, King Marke, Hagen, and Boris Godunov.—NS/LK/DM

Kipnis, Igor, distinguished American harpsichordist, fortepianist, pianist, and music critic, son of **Alex-**

ander Kipnis; b. Berlin, Sept. 27, 1930. He was taken to the U.S. by his family in 1938, where he received training in piano from his maternal grandfather, **Heniot Lévy.** After attending the Westport (Conn.) School of Music, he studied with Randall Thompson and Thurston Dart at Harvard Univ. (B.A., 1952). He also studied harpsichord with Fernando Valenti. In 1955 he began writing music criticism and record reviews for various publications. He made his concert debut as a harpsichordist on WNYC radio in N.Y. in 1959. His formal concert debut followed at the N.Y.C. Historical Soc. in 1962, and thereafter he made frequent tours of the U.S. and Canada. In 1967 he made his first tour of Europe, and subsequently made regular tours there. He also appeared in South America, Israel, Australia, Russia, and the Far East. He taught at the Berkshire Music Center in Tanglewood (summers, 1964–67). Kipnis was assoc. prof. of fine arts (1971–75) and artist-in-residence (1975–77) at Fairfield (Conn.) Univ. He also played at the Festival Music Soc. in Indianapolis, where he served on the faculty of its Early Music Inst. (summers, 1974–84). In 1981 he made his debut as a fortepianist in Indianapolis. He was made a visiting tutor at the Royal Northern Coll. of Music in Manchester in 1982, and from 1993 to 1996 he was co-artistic director of the Conn. Early Music Festival. In 1992–93 he was host of the syndicated radio program "The Classical Organ." In 1995 he formed a modern piano, 4-hands duo with Karen Kushner, and subsequently toured widely with her. He became president of the Friends of Music of Fairfield County, Conn., a chamber music soc., in 1995, a position he held until 1999. Kipnis ed. the anthology *A First Harpsichord Book* (Oxford, 1970; 2nd ed., 1985). In 1969 he was awarded the Deutsche Schallplatten Preis and in 1993 he received an honorary doctorate from Ill. Wesleyan Univ. Kipnis's vast repertoire ranges from early music to contemporary scores. Among composers who have written works for him are Ned Rorem, George Rochberg, Richard Rodney Bennett, Barbara Kolb, and John McCabe.—NS/LK/DM

Király, Ernö, Hungarian composer and ethnomusicologist; b. Subotica, Yugoslavia, March 16, 1919. He studied trumpet at the Subotica School of Music (1939). In 1953 he became Hungarian folk music ed. for Novi Sad Broadcasting, and in 1958 head of the folk music dept. at the Vojvodina Museum in Novi Sad. He publ. several books and articles on Hungarian folk music and instruments. As a composer, he was interested in folk music and experimented with new intonational and interpretive structures. Among his works are a children's opera, *A kis torkos* (The Little Glutton; 1962), *Vocalizzazioni* for Chorus (1969), and *Indications* for 3 Performers and Tape (1973).—NS/LK/DM

Kirby, John, jazz bassist, leader, arranger; b. Baltimore, Dec. 31, 1908; d. L.A., June 14, 1952. He was orphaned at an early age. He learned to play the trombone and moved to N.Y. (ca. 1925). While scuffling to find gigs his instrument was stolen. He worked at a variety of day jobs (including a spell as a Pullman porter) before saving enough money to buy a tuba. He was with Bill Brown and his Brownies (1928–30), then joined Fletcher Henderson during 1930. He began doubling on string bass (with lessons from Wellman Braud and Pops Foster). After switching from an aluminum bass to a wooden one in 1933, he rarely played tuba. He was with Chick Webb from spring 1934, and led his own quartet at the President Hotel (N.Y., 1935). He rejoined Fletcher Henderson in late 1935, then rejoined Chick Webb in the summer of 1936, then worked with Lucky Millinder in autumn 1936. He was an original member of the small band that went into the Onyx Club (May 15, 1937); later Kirby was appointed leader, and during the sextet's initial 11-month residency, they gained a wide reputation. The group was known for "jazzin' the classics." The band's best-known personnel was Charlie Shavers, Buster Bailey, Russell Procope, Billy Kyle, and O'Neill Spencer, with vocals by Maxine Sullivan. Kirby occasionally doubled on trombone. From 1938 until 1941, Kirby was married to Sullivan. The sextet worked as John Kirby and His Onyx Club Boys at many N.Y. clubs, and at the N.Y. World's Fair Zombie Club (summer 1940), as well as residencies in Chicago, L. A., etc. They did dates at whites-only hotels and even were featured on a 1940 radio show, "Flow Gently, Sweet Rhythm." The band's personnel was virtually unchanged until 1942. Kirby struggled on through 1950 with new members, and the original sextet occasionally reunited for special concerts as well. Kirby led his own quartet (1950), then worked with Henry Allen at the Hickory Log, and with Buck Clayton at Terrasi's in the spring of 1951; later that year he moved to Calif. In early 1952 he played occasionally in Benny Carter's Band, then started to reorganize a new sextet (with arrangements by Gene Roland), but ill health forced him to abandon the project. He died in L.A. from complications from diabetes.

DISC.: *Peanut Vendor* (1978); *The Complete Charlie Shavers with Maxine Sullivan* (1953; re-creation).—**JC/LP**

Kirby, Percival Robson, Scottish-born South African musicologist, conductor, and composer; b. Aberdeen, April 17, 1887; d. Grahamstown, South Africa, Feb. 7, 1970. He studied with Terry at the Univ. of Aberdeen (degree, 1910) and with Stanford at the Royal Coll. of Music in London. In 1914 he emigrated to South Africa and became music organizer of the Natal Education Dept.; from 1921 to 1952 he was prof. of music at Univ. Coll. in Johannesburg (later the Univ. of the Witwatersrand). He founded and conducted the Johannesburg Sym. Orch. (1927) and the Univ. Orch. (1930). He is best known for his scholarly work on South African music, and much of his field research resulted in *The Musical Instruments of the Native Races of South Africa* (London, 1934). An expedition to the Kalahari Desert in 1936 led to important studies of Bushman music. He composed numerous songs.—**NS/LK/DM**

Kirbye, George, English composer; b. c. 1565; d. Bury St. Edmunds (buried), Oct. 6, 1634. He served as a domestic musician at Rushbrooke Hall, near Bury St. Edmunds. He was a gifted madrigalist, as revealed in his *The first set of English madrigalls, to 4. 5. & 6. voyces* (London, 1597; ed. by E. Fellowes and rev. by T. Dart in The English Madrigalists, London, 2nd ed., 1961). He was also a fine composer of sacred music, and contributed 19 pieces to East's *The Whole Booke of Psalmes* (London, 1592).—**NS/LK/DM**

Kircher, Athanasius, eminent German scholar; b. Geisa, near Fulda, May 2, 1601; d. Rome, Nov. 27, 1680. He attended a Jesuit school in Fulda (1612–18) and became a novice at the Jesuit college in Paderborn in 1618. He subsequently studied physical sciences and philosophy in Cologne (1622), languages in Koblenz (1623), and theology in Mainz (ordained 1628) before completing his training as a teacher in Speyer (1628–29). From 1629 to 1631 he taught mathematics, philosophy, and oriental languages at the Univ. of Würzburg. In 1631 he went to Avignon, and in 1633 to Vienna as court mathematician to Emperor Ferdinand II; that same year he went to Rome, where he taught at the Collegio Romano. His writings are a curious mixture of scientific speculation and puerile credulity. His principal work is the Latin compendium *Musurgia universalis, sive Ars magna consoni et dissoni* (Rome, 1650; ed. by W. Goldhan, Leipzig, 1988), one of the most significant treatises on music, most notably for its originality. He also wrote *Magnes, sive De arte magnetica* (Rome, 1641; 2nd ed., rev., 1643), *Ars magna lucis et umbrae* (Rome, 1646), *Oedipus aegiptiacus* (Rome, 1652–54), *Iter exstaticum coeleste* (Rome, 1656), *Organum mathematicum* (Würzburg, 1668; in collaboration with C. Schott), *Ars magna sciendi* (Amsterdam, 1669), *Phourgia nova, sive Conuigium mechanico-physicum artis et naturae* (Kenpten, 1673), *Tariffa Kircheriana* (Rome, 1679), and *Vita admodum reverendi P. Athanasii Kircheri SJ viri toto orbe celebratissimi* (MS).

BIBL.: U. Scharlau, *A. K. (1601–1680) als Musikschriftsteller* (Marburg, 1969).—**NS/LK/DM**

Kirchgässner, Marianne (Antonia), blind German glass harmonica player; b. Bruchsal, June 5, 1769; d. Schaffhausen, Dec. 9, 1808. Although stricken with blindness at the age of 4, she persevered in her determination to study music. After training with J.A. Schmittbauer, she made her first tour in 1791 and performed in Munich, Salzburg, Linz, and Vienna. Mozart heard her in /Vienna and was so taken by her talent that he composed his *Fantasie* for Glass Harmonica, Flute, Oboe, Viola, and Cello, K.Anh.92/616a, *Adagio and Rondo*, K.617, and *Adagio*, K.356/617a with her instrument in mind.—**LK/DM**

Kirchhoff, Walter, German tenor; b. Berlin, March 17, 1879; d. Wiesbaden, March 26, 1951. He studied in Berlin with Eugen Weiss and Lilli Lehmann. He made his operatic debut at the Berlin Royal Opera in 1906 as Faust; continued on its roster until 1920 after it became the Berlin State Opera in 1918; sang there again in 1923–24, 1928–29, and 1932; also appeared at the Bayreuth Festivals (1911–14) and at Covent Garden in London in 1913 and 1924. He made an acclaimed Metropolitan Opera debut in N.Y. as Loge in *Das Rheingold* on Jan. 28, 1927; remained on its roster until 1931. He was particularly successful in Wagnerian roles. —**NS/LK/DM**

Kirchner, Leon, distinguished American composer, pedagogue, conductor, and pianist; b. N.Y., Jan. 24, 1919. He began piano lessons when he was 4. In 1928 the family moved to Los Angeles, where he continued his piano training. While attending Los Angeles City Coll., he began to compose. He studied composition with Schoenberg at the Univ. of Calif. at Los Angeles (1938–39), and then theory with Albert Elkus and Edward Strickland at the Univ. of Calif. at Berkeley (B.A., 1940). In 1942 he had private lessons with Sessions in N.Y. Following service in the U.S. Army (1943–46), he pursued postgraduate studies with Bloch and Sessions at the Univ. of Calif. at Berkeley (1946; M.A., 1949). In 1946–47 he taught there. He also taught at the San Francisco Cons. of Music. From 1950 to 1954 he was on the faculty of the Univ. of Southern Calif. at Los Angeles. In 1954 he became the first Luther Brusie Marchant Prof. at Mills Coll. in Oakland, Calif. In 1961 he joined the faculty of Harvard Univ., where he served as the Walter Bigelow Rosen Prof. of Music from 1966 until his retirement in 1989. He also conducted the Harvard Chamber Players (from 1973) and the Harvard Chamber Orch. (from 1978), and was engaged as a guest conductor and as a pianist with orchs. in the U.S. and overseas. Kirchner received a Guggenheim fellowship in 1948–49, and again in 1949–50. He won the N.Y. Music Critics Circle Award for his 1st (1950) and 2nd (1960) string quartets, and the Pulitzer Prize in Music for his 3rd string quartet (1967). In 1962 he was made a member of both the National Inst. of Arts and Letters and the American Academy of Arts and Sciences. In 1994 he received a Kennedy Center Friedheim Award. Kirchner has followed a thoroughly contemporary but independent course as a composer. His finely crafted scores are notable for their linear chromaticism, asymmetric rhythms, and lyricism.

WORKS: DRAMATIC: O p e r a : *Lily* (1973–76; N.Y., April 14, 1977, composer conducting; also as *Lily* for Soprano, Chamber Orch., and Tape, N.Y., March 11, 1973). ORCH.: *Piece* for Piano and Orch. (1946); Sinfonia (1951; N.Y., Jan. 31, 1952); 2 piano concertos: No. 1 (1953; N.Y., Feb. 23, 1956, composer soloist) and No. 2 (Seattle, Oct. 28, 1963, composer conducting); *Toccata* for Strings, Solo Winds, and Percussion (1955; San Francisco, Feb. 16, 1956); Concerto for Violin, Cello, 10 Winds, and Percussion (Baltimore, Oct. 16, 1960, composer conducting); *Music* (N.Y., Oct. 16, 1969, composer conducting); *Music* for Flute and Orch. (Indianapolis, Oct. 20, 1978); *Music II* (1990); *Music* for Cello and Orch. (Philadelphia, Oct. 16, 1992). CHAMBER: Duo for Violin and Piano (1947); 3 string quartets: No. 1 (1949; N.Y., March 1950), No. 2 (1958), and No. 3, with Tape (1966; N.Y., Jan. 27, 1967); *Sonata Concertante* for Violin and Piano (N.Y., Nov. 30, 1952); 2 trios for Violin, Cello, and Piano: No. 1 (Pasadena, Calif., Nov. 30, 1954) and No. 2 (N.Y., Dec. 14, 1993); Fanfare for Brass Trio (1965; also for Flute and Optional Percussion, 1977, and as Fanfare II for 7 Instruments, 1985); *Flutings for Paula* for Flute and Optional Percussion (1973; rev. 1977); *Music for 12* for Chamber Ensemble (Boston, Feb. 17, 1985, composer conducting); *Illuminations*, fanfare for 9 Instruments for the 350th anniversary of Harvard Univ. (Cambridge, Mass., Sept. 4, 1986); *For Cello Solo* (1986; Charleston, S.C., May 28, 1988); 2 pieces for Violin: No. 1 (Indianapolis, Sept. 13, 1986) and No. 2 (1988; Washington, D.C., Jan. 22, 1989); *2 Duos* for Violin and Cello (1988); *Triptych* for Violin and Cello (Tanglewood, Aug. 17, 1988; comprised of *For Cello Solo* and *2 Duos* for Violin and Cello). P i a n o : Sonata (1948; N.Y., March 1949); *Litte Suite* (1949); *A Moment for Roger* (1978); *5 Pieces* (Boston, March 7, 1987); *Interlude* (N.Y., Nov. 11, 1989); *For the Left Hand* (N.Y., Dec. 6, 1995). VOCAL: *Dawn* for Chorus and Organ (1943–46; N.Y., Feb. 1946); *Words from Wordsworth* for Chorus (1966); *Lily* for Soprano, Chamber Orch., and Tape (N.Y., March 11, 1973; based on the opera); *The Twilight Stood*, song cycle for Soprano and Piano (Charleston, S.C., June 1, 1982); *Of Things Exactly As They Are* for Soprano, Baritone, Chorus, and Orch. (Boston, Sept. 26, 1997).
—NS/LK/DM

Kirchner, Theodor (Fürchtegott), German organist and composer; b. Neukirchen, near Chemnitz, Dec. 10, 1823; d. Hamburg, Sept. 18, 1903. On Mendelssohn's advice, he studied in Leipzig from 1838 to 1842 with C.F. Becker (theory) and J. Knorr (piano), and, in 1842–43, with Johann Schneider in Dresden. He was engaged as organist at Winterthur (1843–62), then went to Zürich, where he became director of the subscription concerts, choir conductor, and teacher at the music school. He was director of the Würzburg Cons. (1873–75), taught in Leipzig (1875), and gave courses in chamber music at the Dresden Cons. (1883–90). As a youth he also enjoyed the friendship of Schumann, who encouraged and aided him with advice. He wrote chamber music, about 90 piano works, some miniatures of very high quality, and numerous transcriptions for piano solo and piano duet.

BIBL.: A. Niggli, *T. K.* (Leipzig, 1880); O. Klauwell, *T. K.* (Langensalza, 1909); P. Schneider, ed., *T. K.: Briefe aus den Jahren 1860–1868* (Zürich, 1949).—NS/LK/DM

Kirchschlager, Angelika, admired Austrian mezzo-soprano; b. Salzburg, Nov. 24, 1965. She studied piano at the Salzburg Mozarteum before pursuing vocal training with Gerhard Kahry at the Vienna Academy of Music, from which she graduated with a diploma in 1992. She also studied the art of lieder and oratorio interpretation with Walter Berry. In 1993 she made her professional operatic debut as Octavian in Graz, a role she would make very much her own in subsequent years. In 1994 she sang Massenet's Chérubin at the Vienna Chamber Opera. She became a member of the Vienna State Opera in 1994, where she won notable distinction for her Mozart and Strauss roles. In 1995 she portrayed Octavian at the Berlin State Opera and sang in recital at N.Y.'s Town Hall. She portrayed Périchole at the Vienna Volksoper in 1996. In 1997 she made her U.S. operatic debut as Octavian at the Seattle Opera, and also sang Cherubino at the San Francisco Opera, Dorabella at the Vienna Festival, and Mozart's Annio in Paris, and appeared in recital at London's Wigmore Hall. She made her Metropolitan Opera debut in N.Y. as Annio on Nov. 26, 1997. On Dec. 31, 1998, she was a soloist with Masur and the N.Y. Phil. in a New Year's Eve Gala Concert that was televised live to the nation by PBS.
—LK/DM

Kirckman (also Kirchmann or Kirkman), Jacob, German-born English organist, composer, and harpsichord maker; b. Bischweiler, near Strasbourg,

March 4, 1710; d. Greenwich (buried), June 9, 1792. He settled about 1730 in London, where he was associated with a Flemish harpsichord maker, Hermann Tabel. After Tabel's death, he married his widow and acquired Tabel's tools. In 1755 he was naturalized as a British subject. About 1770 he formed a partnership with his nephew, Abraham Kirckman (1737–94), whose descendants continued the business until 1898, when the firm was merged with Collard; it was eventually absorbed by Chappell.—NS/LK/DM

Kiriac-Georgescu, Dumitru, Rumanian conductor, composer, and teacher; b. Bucharest, March 18, 1866; d. there, Jan. 8, 1928. He studied with Gheorghe Brătianu and Eduard Wachmann at the Bucharest Cons., then with Dubois, Widor, and Bourgault-Ducoudray at the Paris Cons. (1892–99), and with d'Indy at the Schola Cantorum. He became a prof. at the Bucharest Cons. (1900), and founded the Choral Soc. Carmen (1901). He was active as a folklorist. He composed a large output of sacred choruses.—NS/LK/DM

Kirigin, Ivo, Croatian conductor and composer; b. Zadar, Feb. 2, 1914; d. Zagreb, Oct. 21, 1964. He studied in Italy with Pizzetti. He was active as a theater conductor in Zagreb. Among his works were Concertino for Piano and Orch., Sym. (1950), *Pjesma o zemliji*, cantata (Song of the Land; 1952), *Kameni horizonti* (Stone Horizons; Zagreb, March 16, 1955), *5 Movements* for Strings (1958), and numerous songs.—NS/LK/DM

Kirk, Andy (actually, **Andrew Dewey**), seminal band leader, saxophonist, tuba player; b. Newport, Ky., May 28, 1898; d. N.Y., Dec. 11, 1992. During childhood he moved with his family to Denver. He made tentative efforts on piano, sang in the school choir, and later took up alto sax. He was tutored by Franz Roth, and also received harmony lessons from Walter Light. He did various day jobs before joining an 11-piece band led by violinist George Morrison (operating out of Denver) ca. 1918. Kirk was working mainly on tuba and bass-sax. After touring and recording with Morrison, Kirk worked temporarily as a postman, then in the mid-1920s joined the newly formed Terrence Holder Band in Dallas. This outfit was later known as the Dark Clouds of Joy. In January 1929, Holder left and Kirk was appointed the leader. The band was first fronted by vocalist Billy Massey, later by Pha Terrell. For one brief spell in 1931 the entire band worked under Blanche Calloway in Philadelphia. They immediately reverted to their former billing for a residency at Winwood Beach in Kansas City. Throughout the early 1930s, Andy Kirk and his Clouds of Joy steadily gained popularity, with much of their work in the Middle West, though as early as 1930 they had played dates in N.Y. The toured widely from 1936. The band enjoyed an international reputation from 1936 until 1948, when it disbanded. Pha Terrell's high note vocal on "Until the Real Thing Comes Along" was a hit. Mary Lou Williams was an important arranger in the late 1930s, and in the early 1940s Fats Navarro, Don Byas and Howard McGhee were other prominent members. They teamed with the Jubilaries

for hits in the 1940s. Kirk moved to the West Coast for a while, then returned to N.Y. to manage the Hotel Theresa. He continued to organize big bands for specific engagements during the 1960s. He visited Europe in the 1960s, then worked as a supervisor in stockroom of N.Y.'s Local 802, American Federation of Musicians. During the 1970s, he occasionally performed while working as a hotel manager in N.Y. He also preached as a newly converted Jehovah's Witness. He was the husband of pianist Mary Colston. Their son, Andy Kirk Jr. played tenor sax.

DISC.: *Lady Who Swings the Band* (1936); *Uncollected Andy Kirk and the Clouds of Joy* (1941); *Mellow Bit of Rhythm* (1956); *Moten Swing* (1992).—JC/LP

Kirkby, (Carolyn) Emma, admired English soprano; b. Camberley, Feb. 26, 1949. She studied classics at Oxford and received vocal training from Jessica Cash. She made her debut in London in 1974 and then specialized in early music. She was a member of the Academy of Ancient Music, the London Baroque, and the Consort of Musicke. In 1978 she toured the U.S.; then gave concerts in the Middle East with the lutenist Anthony Rooley (1980–83). She made her operatic debut as Mother Nature in Cupid and Death by Gibbons and Locke in Bruges in 1983. In 1989 she made her U.S. operatic debut when she sang Handel's Orlando. In subsequent years, she toured widely in England, appearing at the London Promenade Concerts in works by Charpentier and Monteverdi in 1993, and abroad. In 1996 she sang at the Purcell Celebration at the London Barbican. Her repertoire ranges from the Italian quattrocento to arias by Handel, Mozart, and Haydn. The careful attention she pays to the purity of intonation free from intrusive vibrato has been praised.—NS/LK/DM

Kirkby-Lunn, Louise, English mezzo-soprano; b. Manchester, Nov. 8, 1873; d. London, Feb. 17, 1930. She was a student of J.H. Greenwood in Manchester and of Albert Visetti at the Royal Coll. of Music in London. While still a student, she made her debut as Margaret in Schumann's *Genoveva* at London's Drury Lane Theatre in 1893. After singing minor roles at London's Covent Garden in 1896, she sang with the Carl Rosa Opera Co. until 1899. She then gave concerts until returning to Covent Garden in 1901, where she was a leading singer until 1914, winning particular success as Ortrud, Fricka, Brangäne, Carmen, Amneris, Dalila, and Hérodiade. On Dec. 26, 1902, she made her Metropolitan Opera debut in N.Y. as Ortrud, remaining on its roster for the season; she returned for the 1906–08 seasons, appearing principally as a Wagnerian. After appearing with the British National Opera Co. in London (1919–22), she pursued her concert career.—NS/LK/DM

Kirkeby, "Ed" Wallace Theodore, jazz band leader, manager; b. Brooklyn, N.Y., Oct. 10, 1891; d. June 12, 1978. His father was a part-time banjo player. Kirkeby played banjo, mandolin, and piano, but began work as a soap salesman before joining Columbia as a record promoter in 1916. He later became assistant director of popular recordings and managed the first dates for the Original Memphis Five. He also worked in music publishing. In 1920 he began managing The California Ramblers, who soon began a long residency at the Post Lodge in Westchester and subsequently commenced their prolific recordings. They also did sessions under a variety of pseudonyms (the Goofus Five, Univ. Six, Five Birmingham Babies, etc.). In 1926 Kirkeby led a band for a season at the Club Deauville (Miami), organized the McAlpineers for residency at the Hotel McAlpin (N.Y., 1928). During the 1920s and 1930s he organized bands for prolific recordings and extensive broadcasting (pseudonyms included Ted Wallace, Ed Loyd). He subsequently managed the Pickens Sisters and became an A&R man for RCA Victor. In 1938 he became Fats Waller's manager and travelled with Fats for the last five years of the pianist's life. He was with him on his last journey. He continued in management and for many years represented the Deep River Boys.

WRITINGS: With Duncan Schiedt and Sinclair Traill, *Ain't Misbehavin', The Story of Fats Waller* (1966).—**JC/LP**

Kirkendale, (John) Warren,

American musicologist; b. Toronto, Aug. 14, 1932. He was educated at the univs. of Toronto (B.A., 1955) and Vienna (Ph.D., 1961, with the diss. *Fuge und Fugato in der Kammermusik des Rokoko und der Klassik*; publ. in Tuzing, 1966; Eng. tr., 1979). After teaching at the Univ. of Southern Calif. in Los Angeles (1963–67), he was an assoc. prof. (1967–75) and a prof. (1975–83) at Duke Univ. From 1983 to 1992 he was prof. ordinarius of musicology at the Univ. of Regensburg. In 1986 he was made an honorary prof. of the Univ. of Bologna and a member of the Accademico filarmonico of Bologna in 1987. He publ. the books *L'Aria di Fiorenza, id est Il Ballo del Gran Duca* (Florence, 1972) and *The Court Musicians in Florence During the Principate of the Medici, With a Reconstruction of the Artistic Establishment* (Florence, 1993), and also contributed articles to various publications. In 1959 he married the German musicologist, Ursula (née Schottler) Kirkendale (b. Dortmund, Sept. 6, 1932). She was educated at the Univ. of Bonn (Ph.D., 1961). In addition to articles in journals and other publications, she publ. the study *Antonio Caldara: Sein Leben und seine venezianische-römischen Oratorien* (Graz, 1966).

BIBL.: S. Gmeinwieser, D. Hiley, and J. Riedlbauer, eds., *Musicologia Humana: Studies in Honor of W. and U. K.* (Florence, 1994).—**NS/LK/DM**

Kirkpatrick, Don(ald E.),

jazz pianist, arranger; b. Charlotte, N.C., June 17, 1905; d. N.Y., May 13, 1956. He married Johnny Hodges's sister. He came to N.Y. from Baltimore with drummer Johnny Ridgley's Band (summer 1926), and soon began working for Chick Webb. He worked mainly with Webb until late 1932, then spent a long spell with Don Redman from early 1933. During the late 1930s and 1940s, he was mainly active as an arranger, scoring for Webb, Don Redman, Benny Goodman, Alvino Rey, Cootie Williams, Count Basie, etc. He also gigged with various leaders including Zutty Singleton and Mezz Mezzrow. He left full-time music for a while, then did an overseas tour in 1943. He worked at Nick's, N.Y., from mid-1944 and

gigged with Bunk Johnson in N.Y. in November 1947. He was with Wilbur de Paris from 1952–55, then played in Boston with Doc Cheatham (late 1955). He played gigs at Stuyvesant Casino, Central Plaza, and Hotel Theresa (N.Y.), during the last few months of his life. He died of lobar pneumonia.—**JC/LP**

Kirkpatrick, John,

eminent American pianist and pedagogue; b. N.Y., March 18, 1905; d. Ithaca, N.Y., Nov. 8, 1991. He was educated at Princeton Univ. (graduated, 1926) and took courses with Boulanger in Fontainebleau (summers, 1925–28) and at the École Normale de Musique in Paris (1926–27); he also studied with I. Philipp and C. Decreus, completing his piano studies with Louta Nouneberg (1928–31). He specialized in the interpretation of 17th and 18th century chamber music, but gained extraordinary attention when he gave from memory the premiere of Ives' difficult *Concord Sonata* in N.Y. on Jan. 20, 1939. This premiere played an important role in the public recognition of Ives. Kirkpatrick gave many recitals and lecture-recitals in succeeding years. He served as chairman of the music dept. at Monticello Coll. (1942–43); he then taught at Mount Holyoke Coll. (1943–46), Cornell Univ. (1946–68), where he also was director of the Chapel Choir (1953–57), and Yale Univ. (1968–73), where he also was curator of the Charles Ives Collection. He ed. *A Temporary Mimeographed Catalogue of the Music Manuscripts and Related Materials of Charles Edward Ives* (1960), *Charles E. Ives: Memos* (1972), and various compositions by Ives.—**NS/LK/DM**

Kirkpatrick, Ralph (Leonard),

eminent American harpsichordist, clavichordist, pianist, music scholar, and pedagogue; b. Leominster, Mass., June 10, 1911; d. Guildford, Conn., April 13, 1984. He commenced piano studies when he was 6. He pursued his academic education at Harvard Univ. (A.B., 1931), where he received the Paine Traveling Scholarship. After making his public debut as a harpsichordist in Cambridge, Mass., in 1930, he went to Paris to pursue research at the Bibliothèque Nationale; he also had further instruction from Boulanger (theory) and Landowska (harpsichord) before continuing his training with Dolmetsch in Haslemere and with Ramin and Tiessen in Berlin.In 1933 he made his European debut as a harpsichordist. In 1933–34 he taught at the Salzburg Mozarteum. He was awarded a Guggenheim fellowship in 1937, which enabled him to study 17th and 18th century performing practices in chamber music in Europe. His findings in Spain were later utilized in his valuable biography *Domenico Scarlatti* (Princeton, N.J., and London, 1953; 3rd ed., rev., 1968). In 1940 he joined the faculty of Yale Univ., where he served as a prof. of music from 1965 to 1976. In 1964 he also served as the first Ernest Bloch Prof. of Music at the Univ. of Calif. at Berkeley. Kirkpatrick greatly distinguished himself as an interpreter of Baroque keyboard music, excelling particularly in the works of Bach and Domenico Scarlatti. He prepared a chronological catalogue of the latter's sonatas, and his "K." numbers became widely accepted. He also ed. 60 of the sonatas (N.Y., 1953) and a complete collection of the keyboard works in facsimile (N.Y., 1971 et seq.) of Scarlatti. Kirkpatrick was the author of *Interpreting Bach's "Well-tempered Clavier": A Performer's Discourse of Method* (New Haven and London, 1984) and of the memoir *Early Years* (N.Y., 1984).—NS/LK/DM

Kirkpatrick, William J(ames), American composer of hymns and compiler of Sunday school and gospel hymnbooks; b. Duncannon, Pa., Feb. 27, 1838; d. Germantown, Pa., Sept. 20, 1921. He received music training from Pasquale Rondinella, Leopold Meignen, T. Bishop, and David Wood. He taught music in Philadelphia and became active in the Methodist church. From 1878 he collaborated with John R. Sweeney in compiling some 50 songbooks and collections of sacred services. Millions of copies of their publications were issued. Among Kirkpatrick's most popular hymns were *Jesus Saves* (1882), *He Hideth My Soul* (1890), *Lord, I'm Coming Home* (1892), and *Lead Me to Calvary* (1921).—LK/DM

Kirnberger, Johann Philipp, German music theorist, pedagogue, and composer; b. Saalfeld (baptized), April 24, 1721; d. Berlin, July 26 or 27, 1783. He received training in violin and harpsichord at home. After studying organ with J.P. Kellner in Gräfenroada, he went to Sondershausen in 1738 to study violin with Meil and organ with H.N. Gerber before completing his musical training with Bach in Leipzig (1739–41). In 1741 he went to Poland, where he was in the service of various noblemen until going to Dresden in 1751 to complete his violin training. From 1751 to 1754 he was a violinist in the Prussian royal chapel in Berlin, and then a member of the chapel of Prince Heinrich of Prussia from 1754 to 1758. From 1758 until his death he was in the service of Princess Anna Amalia of Prussia. He also numbered J.F. Agricola, C.P.E. Bach, the Graun brothers, and J.A.P. Schulz among his students. Kirnberger was highly regarded as a theorist by his contemporaries, even though his presentations were often so disorganized that he had to call upon others to edit or even rewrite his publications. Among his most important treatises was *Die Kunst des reinen Satzes in der Musik* (2 vols., Berlin and Königsberg, 1771, 1776–79; 2nd ed., 1793). His compositions are of little interest.

WRITINGS (all publ. in Berlin unless otherwise given); *Der allezeit fertige Polonoisen- und Menuettencomponist* (1757); *Construction der gleichschwebenden Temperatur* (1760); *Die Kunst des reinen Satzes in der Musik, aus sicheren Grundsätzen hergeleitet und mit deutlichen Beyspielen erläutert* (2 vols., Berlin und Königsberg, 1771, 1776–79; 2nd ed., 1793); *Die wahren Grundsätze zum Gebrauch der Harmonie...als ein Zusatz zu der Kunst der reinen Satzes in der Musik* (Berlin und Königsberg, 1773; 2nd ed., 1793; written by J.A.P. Schulz under Kirnberger's supervision); *Grundsätze des Generalbasses als erste Linien zur Composition* (1781); *Gedanken über die verschiedenen Lehrarten in der Komposition, als Vorbereitung zur Fugenkenntniss* (1782; 2nd ed., 1793); *Anleitung zur Singcomposition mit Oden in verschiedenen Sylbenmassen begleitet* (1782); *Methode Sonaten aus'm Ermel zu schuddeln* (1783).

WORKS: *Allegro für das Clavier alleine, wie auch für die Violin mit dem Violoncell zur accompagniren...componirt und vertheidigt* (1759); *Clavierübungen mit der Bachischen Applicatur in einer Folge von den leichtesten bis zu den schwerstein Stücken* (1762–66); also various keyboard pieces, chamber music, cantatas, songs, etc.

BIBL.: A. Kirnberger, *Geschichte der Familie K.* (Mainz, 1922); S. Borris-Zuckermann, *K.s Leben und Werk und seine Bedeutung für den Berliner Musikkreis um 1750* (Kassel, 1930).—NS/LK/DM

Kirshbaum, Ralph (Henry), notable American cellist; b. Denton, Tex., March 4, 1946. He studied with Lev Aronson in Dallas. After making his formal debut with the Dallas Sym. Orch. in 1959, he studied with Parisot at Yale Univ. (B.A., 1968). He won the Cassadó Competition in Florence in 1969 and the Tchaikovsky Competition in Moscow in 1970. Thereafter he pursued a fine career as a soloist in the major music centers. He also joined the pianist Peter Frankl and the violinist György Pauk in organizing a trio in London in 1972, with which he appeared frequently. It celebrated its 25th anniversary in 1997. He was a soloist in the premiere of Tippett's Triple Concerto (London, Aug. 22, 1980). In 1987 he played Bach's 6 cello suites in London, repeating the feat there in 1993 as well as in Sydney and N.Y. with notable success. In 1988 he founded the Manchester International Cello Festival.—NS/LK/DM

Kirsten, Dorothy, noted American soprano; b. Montclair, N.J., July 6, 1910; d. Los Angeles, Nov. 18, 1992. She studied at the Juilliard School of Music in N.Y.; Grace Moore took an interest in her and enabled her to study with Astolfo Pescia in Rome. With the outbreak of World War II in 1939, she returned to the U.S. She became a member of the Chicago Opera Co. (debut as Pousette in *Manon*, Nov. 9, 1940). She made her first appearance in N.Y. as Mimi with the San Carlo Opera Co. (May 10, 1942), then appeared with the Metropolitan Opera in N.Y. in the same role on Dec. 1, 1945; sang there until 1952, from 1954 to 1957, and from 1960 until her official farewell performance as Tosca (Dec. 31, 1975). Among her finest roles were Manon Lescaut, Cio-Cio-San, Marguerite, Louise (coached by the composer), and Nedda in *Pagliacci*; also sang in several films, including *The Great Caruso*. She publ. an autobiography, *A Time to Sing* (Garden City, N.Y., 1982).—NS/LK/DM

Kishibe, Shigeo, Japanese ethnomusicologist; b. Tokyo, June 16, 1912. He studied at the Univ. of Tokyo (B.A. in oriental history, 1936; Ph.D. in literature, 1961), where he was a prof. (1949–73). He also lectured (from 1952) at the Tokyo National Univ. of Fine Arts and Music and at various American univs., including the Univ. of Calif. at Los Angeles, Harvard Univ., and Stanford Univ. He is a founding member of the Soc. for Research in Asiatic Music. His research has focused particularly on the music of China and Japan, but he has also done fieldwork in Korea, India, Iran, and the Philippines. Among his numerous publications is *The Traditional Music of Japan* (Tokyo, 1966).—NS/LK/DM

Kisielewski, Stefan, Polish composer, journalist, and novelist; b. Warsaw, March 7, 1911; d. there, Sept. 27, 1991. He received training in philology at the Univ. of Warsaw (1929–33) and pursued studies in piano with Lefeld (diploma, 1934) and in theory and composition with Sikorski (diplomas in both, 1937) at the Warsaw Cons., completing his training in Paris (1938–39). In 1935 he began writing on music and politics; during the Nazi occupation of Poland, he was an official of the cultural dept. of the Underground. After the liberation in 1945, he was a prof. at the Kraków Coll. of Music (until 1950); also served as ed.-in-chief of the music weekly *Puch Muzyczny* (1945–48) and was a columnist for the Catholic opposition weekly *Sygodnih Powysechny* (1945–83) in Kraków. In addition to his writings on music, he publ. novels and books on politics, some of which have appeared abroad in translations. For his musical efforts, he received awards from the City of Kraków (1956) and the Union of Polish Composers (1982). His compositions generally follow along neo-Classical lines.

WORKS: DRAMATIC: B a l l e t : *Diably polski* (Polish Devils; 1957; Warsaw, 1958); *System doktora Smoly i doktora Pierza* (The System of Dr. Pitch and Dr. Feathers; 1962); *Wesole miasteczzko* (Amusement Grounds; 1966; Gdansk, 1967). **OTHER:** Scores for theater and films. **ORCH.:** syms.: No. 1 (1939; not extant), No. 2 (1951), Chamber Sym. (1956), Sym. for 15 Performers (1961), and *Symphony in a Square* (1974–78); Concerto for Chamber Orch. (1948); *Rustic Rhapsody* (1950); *Perpetuum Mobile* (1953); *Little Overture* (1953); *Divertimento* for Flute and Chamber Orch. (1964); *Journey in Time* for Strings (1965); *Sport Signals*, overture (1966); *Cosmos I* (1970); *The Merry Kaleidoscope* (1970); *Voyage dans le temps* (1975); Piano Concerto (1980–91; Warsaw, Sept. 24, 1991). **CHAMBER:** Violin Sonata (1932); String Quartet (1935); Sonata for Solo Clarinet (1944); *Intermezzo* for Clarinet and Piano (1953); Suite for Oboe and Piano (1954); *Capriccio energico* for Violin and Piano (1956); Suite for Flute and Piano (1961); *Meetings in the Desert* for 10 Performers (1969); *Dialogues* for 14 Instruments (1970); Clarinet Sonata (1973); *Capricious Impressions* for Woodwinds (1982); *Scherzo* for Bassoon and Piano (1988). **P i a n o :** 2 sonatas (1936, not extant; 1945); *Toccata* (1944); *Fantasia* (1949); Suite (1955); *3 Stormy Scenes* (1983). **VOCAL:** Choral music; songs. —NS/LK/DM

Kiss, popular American touring and album band of the late 1970s, who combined elements of both glitter rock and heavy metal. **MEMBERSHIP:** Paul "Ace" Frehley, lead gtr. (b. Bronx, N.Y., April 27, 1951); Paul Stanley (real name, Paul Stanley Eisen), gtr. (b. Queens, N.Y., Jan. 20, 1952); Gene Simmons (real name, Klein), bs. (b. Haifa, Israel, Aug. 25, 1949); Peter Criss (real name, Crisscoula), drm. (b. N.Y., Dec. 20, 1947). Drummer Eric Carr (b. Brooklyn, N.Y., July 12, 1950; d. N.Y., Nov. 24, 1991) replaced Peter Criss in 1981, and Vinnie Vincent replaced Ace Frehley in 1982, leaving in 1984. Various others came and went through the 1980s.

Established through an extensive media campaign by their record company Casablanca and near-constant touring, Kiss wore garish costuming and makeup, utilized spectacular onstage special effects, and played barely competent, overloud guitar-based music. Universally attacked by critics, Kiss nonetheless endeared themselves to legions of prepubescent fans (much to the chagrin of their parents) with gimmicks such as blood-spitting, fire-breathing, explosions, dry-ice fogs, and rocket-firing guitars in performance.

The group was originally formed by Simmons and Stanley, who had previously worked together in a N.Y.—based rock band in 1970. Through advertisements in rock magazines, they enlisted drummer Criss and guitarist Frehley, while Bill Aucoin, a local TV producer, brought them to the attention of Casablanca Records. Their first three albums, released in 1974–1975, did little to endear them to critics or fans, but the band continued to tour and build an audience. Aucoin is purported to have underwritten their second major tour in 1975 on his American Express card; the gambit apparently paid off, because their first Top 20 hit, "Rock and Roll All Nite," came later that year. Criss wrote a ballad, "Beth," that hit for the normally ballsy rockers in 1976. Their fans, now known as the Kiss Army, took to emulating their stage costumery and makeup, and the group's popularity inspired two successful Marvel Comics publications and an animated TV special. In late 1978 Kiss became the first rock band whose members simultaneously issued solo albums, backed by the largest advertising-promotion budget in music history ($2.5 million). Their last major hit was 1979's "I Was Made for Loving You"; Criss left the group a year later to pursue a solo career. In 1981 the group, now with drummer Eric Carr, recorded a concept album, *The Elder*, featuring songs coauthored by Lou Reed, but it was a failure. A return to their usual style on *Creatures of the Night* failed to reignite their earlier success.

To support a mythology perpetrated by numerous fanzines, Kiss did not appear in public without their full-face greasepaint makeup until 1983, when they reverted to a mundane yet silly and vulgar hard-rock band. Nonetheless, all of their albums since then have gone gold or platinum, and it is said that the group had sold a mind-boggling 70 million albums by the early 1990s. A virtual rock industry unto themselves, Kiss merchandising includes T-shirts, comic books, jewelry, and films. In the mid-1980s second-generation member Vinnie Vincent assembled the Vinnie Vincent Invasion, while Ace Frehley formed Frehley's Comet. Carr died of cancer in 1991. In 1994 Mercury issued the tribute album *Kiss My Ass*, with recordings of Kiss songs by Garth Brooks, Lenny Kravitz, and Anthrax, among others.

DISC.: KISS: *K.* (1974); *Hotter Than Hell* (1974); *Dressed to Kill* (1975); *The Originals (reissue of above three)* (1976); *Alive!* (1975); *Destroyer* (1976); *Rock and Roll Over* (1976); *Love Gun* (1977); *Alive II* (1977); *Double Platinum* (1978); *Dynasty* (1979); *Unmasked* (1980); *Music from "The Elder"* (1982); *Creatures of the Night* (1982); *Lick It Up* (1983); *Animalize* (1984); *Asylum* (1985); *Crazy Nights* (1987); *Smashes, Thrashes and Hits* (1988); *Hot in the Shade* (1989); *Revenge* (1992); *Alive III* (1993). **TRIBUTE ALBUM:** *Kiss My Ass* (1994); *Kiss My A** (censored version)* (1994). **GENE SIMMONS:** *Gene Simmons* (1978). **PAUL STANLEY:** *Paul Stanley* (1978). **PETER CRISS:** *Peter Criss* (1978); *By Myself* (1980). **ACE FREHLEY:** *Ace Frehley* (1978); *Trouble Walkin'* (1989). **FREHLEY'S COMET:** *Frehley's Comet* (1987); *Live + 1* (1988); *Second Sighting* (1988). **VINNIE VINCENT INVASION:** *Vinnie Vincent Invasion* (1986); *All Systems Go* (1988).

BIBL.: John Swenson, *K.* (N.Y., 1978).—BH

Kiss, Janos, Hungarian-born American composer; b. Hosszupalyi, March 21, 1920. He studied at the

Budapest Academy of Music (teaching diploma, 1954). In the wake of the Soviet invasion of Hungary (1956), he emigrated to the U.S., becoming a naturalized American citizen in 1973. He took courses in music education at Case Western Reserve Univ. in Cleveland. He subsequently taught at the Cleveland Music School Settlement (1964–79), Western Reserve Academy in Hudson, Ohio (1967–72), Holy Family School in Parma, Ohio (1974–80), and other institutions. In 1982 he became choir director and composer-in-residence at Cleveland's West Side Hungarian Reformed Church. A prolific composer, he wrote numerous orch. and choral works which are distinguished by a facility of execution reflecting his experience as a teacher.

WORKS: ORCH.: Flute Concerto (1970); Trombone Concerto (1972); Cello Concerto (1975); *Divertimento* for Violin, Viola, Double Bass, Harp, and Chamber Ensemble (1977); *Suite in stilo antico* (1978); *Via Lactea*, symphonic fantasy (1978); *Sinfonia Atlantis* (1979); *Las Vegas* for Cimbalom and Orch. (1980); *Mount of Atlantis* for Clarinet, Synthesizer, and Orch. (1981); *Quo Vadis*, symphonic poem (1982); *Rainbow at the Sea* for Flute and Chamber Orch. (1982). **CHAMBER:** *Spring at Last!* for Harp Ensemble (1970); *Josepha* for 5 Alto Recorders, Violin, Viola, Cello, and Harp (1973); *Episode* for Horn, Oboe, Bassoon, and Harp (1978); *Benedictus Dominus* for Chorus and Orch. (1981).—**NS/LK/DM**

Kissin, Evgeny (Igorevich), phenomenal Russian pianist; b. Moscow, Oct. 10, 1971. His mother was a piano teacher who nurtured his amazing musical talent. When he was 6, he was enrolled at the Gnessin Music School for Gifted Children in Moscow, where his only teacher was Anna Pavlovna Kantor. She was to remain his mentor well into adulthood. At the age of 10, Kissin made his debut as a soloist playing Mozart's D Minor Concerto, K.466, with the Ulyanovska Orch. When he was 11, he made his recital debut in Moscow in May 1983. Following a recital at the House of Composers in Moscow and an engagement with the Leningrad Phil., Kissin made an extraordinary appearance as soloist in both Chopin concertos with the Moscow State Phil. under Kitaenko's direction in March 1984 at the age of 12. Engagements in Eastern Europe soon followed, and in 1986 he toured Japan with the Moscow Virtuosi under Spivakov's direction. In 1987 he made his debut in the West at the Berlin Festival. He then toured Europe with Spivakov and the Moscow Virtuosi in 1988. His appearance as soloist in the Tchaikovsky 1st Piano Concerto with Karajan and the Berlin Phil. at a New Year's Eve Concert in 1988 brought him international acclaim. On Sept. 20, 1990, he made his U.S. debut as soloist in Chopin's 1st Piano Concerto with the N.Y. Phil. under Mehta's direction. His U.S. recital debut followed at N.Y.'s Carnegie Hall on Sept. 30, 1990, which left both audience and critics alike astonished at his digital velocity and propulsive dexterity. In 1991 he made his first tour of the U.S. to enormous critical acclaim. In subsequent years, he appeared as a recitalist in many leading music centers and as a soloist with most of the foremost orchs. of the world. His appearance at Carnegie Hall in 1995 was recorded live and broadcast to millions by PBS. In 1997 he became the first musician ever invited to play a solo recital at the London Prom-enade Concerts. While Kissin is acknowledged as a master of the Romantic repertoire, he has also revealed a command for works from the Classical era.—**NS/LK/DM**

Kitaenko, Dmitri, Russian conductor; b. Leningrad, Aug. 18, 1940. He studied choral conducting at the Leningrad Cons. and the Moscow Cons. He then went to Vienna to study conducting at the Academy of Music (1966–67). Upon his return to Moscow, he became a conductor at the Nemirovich-Danchenko Music Theater; in 1970, became chief conductor there. He also appeared as a guest conductor in Western Europe, usually in programs of Russian music. In 1975 he served as asst. conductor during the U.S. tour of the Moscow Phil. (1975). In 1976 he was appointed its chief conductor. In 1990 he became music director of the Bergen Phil. He was concurrently chief conductor of the Frankfurt am Main Radio Sym. Orch. (1990–95) and the Bern Sym. Orch. (from 1991), and music director of the Bern City Theater (from 1994).—**NS/LK/DM**

Kitamura, Eiji, jazz clarinetist, band leader; b. Tokyo, Japan, April 8, 1929. He is a self-taught musician who first began to play jazz in college. He began working professionally in 1950 with Tetsuro Takahama's Esquire Cats, then worked for three years with Saburo Nambu (1951–53), before forming his first group, Cats Herd (1954–57). He then was a sideman again, working with Mitsuru Ono & his 6 Brothers Band, from 1957–60, before striking out on his own for good, leading a swing-styled sextet. He was influenced by Benny Goodman (who he met while Goodman was touring Japan in 1957) and Woody Herman (with whom he would record in the 1970s). Kitamura's group gained wide popularity in his native Japan and on the international jazz festival circuit. They continued to perform into the 1990s; in 1991, Kitamura co-founded the L.A.-based International Jazz Party with musician Bill Berry.

DISC.: *Because of You* (1976); *E.K. vs Suzuki Shoji* (1976); *My Monday Date* (1977); *Memories of You* (1978); *April Date* (1979); *Swing Eiji* (1980); *3 Degrees North* (1980); *Seven Stars* (1981).—**ETA**

Kittel, Bruno, German violinist and conductor; b. Entenbruch, near Posen, May 26, 1870; d. Wasserberg, near Cologne, March 10, 1948. He studied in Berlin and played in theater orchs. there. From 1901 until 1907 he was conductor of the Royal Theater Orch. in Brandenburg; also was director of the Brandenburg Cons. (until 1914). In 1902 he established the Kittelsche Chor., which quickly developed into one of the finest choral societies of Europe, and with which he made many tours. He was director of the Stern Cons. in Berlin (1935–45).—**NS/LK/DM**

Kittel, Caspar, German theorbist and composer; b. Lauenstein, 1603; d. Dresden, Oct. 9, 1639. He was a choirboy in the Dresden Hofkapelle, where he studied with Schütz, and in 1624 he was sent to Italy by the elector for further training. Upon returning to Dresden in 1629, he resumed his service in the Hofkapelle and was made court instrument inspector in 1632. In 1633–34 he took charge of the Hofkapelle in Schütz's absence. In his set of 30 songs publ. as *Arien und Cantaten* for 1 to 4 Voices and Continuo (1638), Kittel introduced to Germany the term "cantata," which he used for strophic variations. His son, Christoph Kittel (flourished from 1641 to 1680), was an organist who, in 1660, became organist of the Hofkapelle. His son, Johann Heinrich Kittel (b. Dresden, Oct. 31, 1652; d. there, July 17, 1682), was an organist and composer. In 1666 he became 2nd organist of the Hofkapelle, and in 1680 he succeeded his father as organist. He composed a set of 12 keyboard preludes, *Tabulatura Num: 12 Praeambulorum und einem Capriccio von eben 12 Variationen.* —LK/DM

Kittel, Hermine, Austrian contralto; b. Vienna, Dec. 2, 1879; d. there, April 7, 1948. She was an actress before making her operatic debut in Lemberg in 1897. Following vocal training with Materna in Vienna, she sang in Graz (1899–1900). In 1901 she returned to Vienna as a member of the Court (later State) Opera, where she sang until 1931 and again in 1936. She also appeared at the Bayreuth Festivals (1902, 1908), the Salzburg Festivals (1922, 1925), the Vienna Volksoper (1933–34), Paris, Budapest, Prague, and other European operatic centers. In later years, she devoted herself to teaching voice in Vienna. She was particularly known for her Mozart and Wagner roles.—NS/LK/DM

Kittel, Johann Christian, noted German organist and composer; b. Erfurt, Feb. 18, 1732; d. there, April 17, 1809. He studied at the Thomasschule in Leipzig, and was one of Bach's last students there. After Bach's death, he became organist at Langensalza (1751–56); then at Erfurt's Barfüsserkirche (1756–62) and Predigerkirche (from 1762). Despite his meager remuneration, he remained in Erfurt almost all his life. Although he seldom made extensive tours, he acquired a fine reputation as a virtuoso; gave a series of recitals in Hamburg (1803). His most outstanding pupil was J.C.H. Rinck. He ed. *Vierstimmige Choräle mit Vorspielen* (2 vols., Altona, 1803); other works include *Der angehende praktische Organist* (3 books; Erfurt, 1801–08; 3rd ed., 1831) and *Grosse Präludien, Hymne an das Jahrhundert* (2 vols., 1801). Among his compositions are 6 sonatas and a Fantasia for Clavichord, as well as smaller organ pieces.

BIBL.: A. Dreetz, *J.C. K., der letzte Bach-Schüler* (Leipzig, 1932).—NS/LK/DM

Kittl, Johann Friedrich (Jan Bedřich), prominent Bohemian composer; b. Castle Worlik, May 8, 1806; d. Lissa, German Poland, July 20, 1868. He studied law at the Univ. of Prague, and took private lessons in piano with Zavora and in composition with Tomaschek. His *Jagdsinfonie* was premiered by Spohr (Kassel, 1839), and subsequently performed widely in Germany. He was director of the Prague Cons. (1843–65). He was a friend of Liszt, Wagner, and Berlioz. As a symphonic composer, he pointed the way to Dvořák.

WORKS: DRAMATIC: O p e r a : *Daphnis' Grab* (Prague, 1825; not extant); *Die Franzosen vor Nizza* (Prague, Feb. 19,

1848; written to Wagner's libretto *Bianca und Giuseppe*); *Waldblume* (Prague, 1852); *Die Bilderstürmer* (Prague, 1854). **ORCH.:** 4 syms: No. 1 (1836), No. 2, *Jagdsinfonie* (1837; Kassel, 1839), No. 3 (1841–42), and No. 4 (1857; Prague, July 7, 1858); 3 concert overtures. **OTHER:** Choral works; chamber music; piano pieces; songs.

BIBL.: W. Neumann, *J.F. K.* (Kassel, 1857); E. Rychnovsky, *J.F. K.* (2 vols., Prague, 1904–05); M. Tarantová, *J.F. K.* (Prague, 1948).—NS/LK/DM

Kitzler, Otto, German conductor, teacher, and composer; b. Dresden, March 16, 1834; d. Graz, Sept. 6, 1915. He studied with Johann Schneider, J. Otto, and Kummer (cello), then at the Brussels Cons. with Servais and Fétis. He was cellist in the opera orchs. at Strasbourg and Lyons, and chorus master at theaters in Troyes, Linz, Königsberg, Temesvar, Hermannstadt, and Brünn. In 1868 he became director of the Brunn Music Soc. and Music School, and also conductor of the Männergesangverein, retiring in 1898. His reputation was very high; Bruckner, 10 years his senior, took orchestration lessons from him (1861–63). Kitzler wrote orch. music, piano pieces, songs, etc. He also publ. *Musikalische Erinnerungen* (1904; containing letters from Wagner, Brahms, and Bruckner).—NS/LK/DM

Kiurina, Berta, Austrian soprano; b. Linz, Feb. 19, 1882; d. Vienna, May 3, 1933. She studied voice with Geiringer at the Vienna Cons. She made her operatic debut in Linz in 1904, then sang at the Vienna Court (later State) Opera (1905–22; 1926–27). She also made guest appearances in Salzburg, Berlin, and Buenos Aires. A fine coloratura, she excelled in such roles as the Queen of the Night, Desdemona, Gilda, Eva, and the Empress in *Die Frau ohne Schatten.*—NS/LK/DM

Kiurkchiysky, Krasimir, Bulgarian composer; b. Troyan, June 22, 1936. He studied composition with Vladigerov at the Bulgarian State Cons. in Sofia (graduated, 1962), then went to Moscow and took some lessons with Shostakovich. His music reflects Shostakovich's influence in its rhapsodic compactness.

WORKS: DRAMATIC: *Yula*, opera (Zagora, 1969); incidental music. **ORCH.:** Piano Concerto (1958); *Adagio* for String Orch. (1959); Cello Sonata (1960); *Symphony Concertante* for Cello and Orch. (1960); *Symphony-Requiem* (1966); *Diaphonous Study* (1967); Concerto (1975). **CHAMBER:** Trio for Violin, Clarinet, and Piano (1959); String Quartet (1959); Violin Sonata (1961). **VOCAL:** Choruses.—NS/LK/DM

Kivy, Peter, American musical philosopher; b. N.Y., Oct. 22, 1934. He studied philosophy at the Univ. of Mich. (B.A., 1956; M.A., 1958), music history at Yale Univ. (M.A., 1960), and philosophy at Columbia Univ. (Ph.D., 1966). He joined the faculty of Rutgers Univ. in 1967. His importance to the field of music is in his writings on aesthetics, in which he has revitalized the complex and long-ignored problems of musical analysis as applied to external associations.

WRITINGS: *The Corded Shell: Reflections on Musical Expression* (Princeton, N.J., 1980); *Sound and Semblance: Reflections on*

Musical Representation (Princeton, N.J., 1984); *Osmin's Rage: Philosophical Reflections on Opera, Drama and Text* (Princeton, N.J., 1988); *Sound Sentiment: An Essay on the Musical Emotions* (Philadelphia, 1989); *Music Alone: Philosophical Reflections on the Purely Musical Experience* (Ithaca, N.Y., 1990); *The Fine Art of Repetition: Essays on the Philosophy of Music* (Cambridge, 1993); *Authenticities: Philosophical Reflections on Musical Performance* (Ithaca, N.Y., 1995).—NS/LK/DM

Kiyose, Yasuji, Japanese composer; b. Yokkaichi, Jan. 13, 1900; d. Tokyo, Sept. 14, 1981. He studied with Yamada, Komatsu, Pringsheim, and A. Tcherepnin. He was president of the Japanese section of the ISCM (1951–56).

WORKS: ORCH.: *Nihon sairei bukyoku* (Japanese Festival Dances; 1940); Piano Concerto (Tokyo, March 10, 1955); *Nihon no sobyo* (A Sketch of Japan; 1963). **CHAMBER:** 2 piano trios (1938, 1955); 3 violin sonatas (1941, 1948, 1950); String Trio (1949); String Quartet (1951); Quintet for Harp and Woodwinds (1957); *2 Movements* for Violin and Piano (1960); Quartet for 4 Recorders (1969); Duet for Flute and Clarinet (1970); *2 Movements* for Cello (1973). **VOCAL:** *Bokura wa umi ni yuku* (We Are Going on the Ocean, or Unknown Soldiers) for Soprano, Tenor, Chorus, and Orch. (1962).—NS/LK/DM

Kjellsby, Erling, Norwegian organist, choral conductor, and composer; b. Christiania, July 7, 1901; d. there (Oslo), Feb. 18, 1976. He studied composition with Brustad and Valen. He lectured on music at Oslo's Teacher's Coll. (1934–70) and was organist at Oslo's Uranienborg Church (1936–71). His early works, in a late Romantic style, eventually gave way to neo-Classical influences. He wrote *Norsk rapsodi* for Small Orch. (1937), choral works, 4 string quartets (1940–57), and piano pieces.—NS/LK/DM

Kjerulf, Halfdan, esteemed Norwegian composer; b. Christiania, Sept. 15, 1815; d. Grefsen, near Christiania, Aug. 11, 1868. He was a member of a family of artists and scholars. He studied piano as a child, then took up law, subsequently working as a journalist. In 1848–49 he took lessons with Carl Arnold and in 1849–50 with Gade in Copenhagen, then with E.F. Richter at the Leipzig Cons. (1850–51). He taught piano in his homeland from 1851, and in 1865 was elected a member of the Swedish Royal Academy of Music. A monument was erected to him in Christiania in 1874. He limited himself to composition in small forms; although he followed the German model, he injected melodic and rhythmic elements of a national Norwegian character into his songs. Grieg was deeply influenced by his example and expressed admiration for his music, and many celebrated singers (Jenny Lind, Christine Nilsson, and Henriette Sontag among them) included his songs in their programs. He wrote about 130 songs, utilizing Norwegian, Swedish, Danish, German, and French texts, some 40 works for men's chorus, as well as over 50 arrangements for chorus, and 10 albums of piano pieces and arrangements of Norwegian melodies for piano.

BIBL.: K. Nyblom, *H. K.* (1926); B. Qvamme, *H. K. og hans tid* (Oslo, 1998).—NS/LK/DM

Klafsky, Anton Maria, Austrian musicologist and composer, nephew of **Katharina (Katalin) Klafsky;** b. Winden, Burgenland, July 8, 1877; d. Baden, near Vienna, Jan. 1, 1965. He studied at the Univ. of Vienna, and took lessons in composition with Hermann Gradener. He composed much church music, 3 syms., piano pieces, and songs. He ed. sacred choral works of Michael Haydn for Denkmäler der Tonkunst in Österreich, vols. 44 and 62 (22 and 32.i).—NS/LK/DM

Klafsky, Katharina (Katalin), famous Hungarian soprano, aunt of **Anton Maria Klafsky;** b. St. Johann, Sept. 19, 1855; d. Hamburg, Sept. 22, 1896. She studied with Marchesi in Vienna and Hey in Berlin, then began her career as a chorus singer in various opera houses. She appeared in minor roles in Salzburg (1875), then was a member of the Leipzig Opera (1876–78); also studied with J. Sucher. In 1882 she attracted attention for her performance in the first London mounting of the *Ring* cycle; then toured with A. Neumann's Wagner company; was in Bremen (1884) and Vienna (1885). She was a leading member of the Hamburg Opera (1886–95), where she excelled as a Wagnerian; returned to London (1892, 1894). She married the conductor and composer Otto Lohse in 1893; they toured the U.S. with the Damrosch Opera Co. (1895–96), then were engaged for the 1896–97 season of the Metropolitan Opera in N.Y., but she died before her scheduled debut. As one of the outstanding sopranos of her day, she was widely mourned upon her early death.

BIBL.: L. Ordemann, *Aus dem Leben und Wirken von K. K.* (Hameln, 1903).—NS/LK/DM

Klami, Uuno (Kalervo), Finnish composer and music critic; b. Virolahti, Sept. 20, 1900; d. Helsinki, May 29, 1961. He left school when he was 15 and entered the Helsinki Coll. of Music. His studies were interrupted three times due to lack of funds, but he persevered until going to Paris in 1924 for further training. During his Paris sojourn, he met Ravel, Schmitt, and other composers who made a marked impression upon him. In 1925 he returned to Finland. The premiere of his *Karelian Rhapsody* for Orch. (Helsinki, Sept. 1928) earned him critical accolades. Following additional studies in Vienna (1928–29), Klami returned to Finland once again to pursue his career as a composer. He also served as music critic of the *Helsingin Sanomat* from 1932 to 1959. From 1938 to 1959 he held a Finnish state pension for artists, and in 1959 he was elected a member of the Finnish Academy. As a composer, Klami succeeded in developing a cosmopolitan style outside the orbit of Sibelius. While utilizing Finnish thematic materials, he deftly combined them with non-Finnish elements reflective of such masters as Ravel and Stravinsky. He was a master of orchestration, perhaps best revealed in his fine *Kalevala Suite* (1932; rev. 1943).

WORKS: DRAMATIC: Ballet: *Whirls* (1957–60; unfinished). **ORCH.:** 2 piano concertos (*Night in Montmartre*, 1924; 1950); *Sérénades espagnoles* (1924; rev. 1944); *Karelian Rhapsody* (1927; Helsinki, Sept. 1928); *Rhapsody* (1927); *Merikuvia* (Sea Pictures; 1928–30); 3 syms.: *Symphonie enfantine* (1928), No. 1 (1937) and No. 2 (1944); *Opernredoute* (1929); *Kuvia maalaiselämasta* (Rustic Scenes; 1930); *Helsinki March* (1930); *4 Folk Songs* for Piano and Strings (1930); *Cheremissian Fantasy* for Cello and

Orch. (1930); *Fantaisie tschérémisse* for Cello and Orch. (1931); *Kalevala Suite* (1932; rev. version, Helsinki, Oct. 1943); *Sérénades joyeuses* (1933); *Lemminkäinen* (1934); *Karelian Dances* (1935); *Suomenlinna* (Fortress of Finland; 1940; Stockholm, March 1941); Violin Concerto (1942; rev. 1954); *Revontulet* (Aurora Borealis; 1946); *Pyörailija* (The Cyclist), rondo (1946); *Karjalainen tori* (Karelian Market Place; 1947); *Theme and Variations* for Cello and Orch. (1950). **CHAMBER:** *Nain tragédie*, string quartet (1920); Piano Quartet (1921); Piano Quintet (1923). **VOCAL:** *Psalmus* for Soloists, Chorus, and Orch. (1935–36); *Vipusessa käynti* (In the Belly of Vipunen) for Baritone, Men's Chorus, and Orch. (1938); *Laulu Kuujärvestä* (The Song of Kuujarvi) for Baritone and Orch. (1956); *Kultasauvalliset* (The People with the Golden Staffs), festive cantata (1961).—**NS/LK/DM**

Klas, Eri, Estonian conductor; b. Tallinn, June 7, 1939. He was a student of Ernesaks at the Tallinn Cons., of Rabinovich at the Leningrad Cons., and of Khaikin at the Bolshoi Theater School in Moscow (1969–72). In 1964 he made his conducting debut with Bernstein's *West Side Story* at the Estonian Opera in Tallinn. From 1969 to 1971 he conducted at the Bolshoi Theater in Moscow, and led the company on tours abroad. In 1975 he became music director of the Estonian Opera. Afer serving as chief conductor of the Royal Opera in Stockholm from 1985 to 1990, he was music director of the Århus Sym. Orch. from 1990 to 1996. In 1991 he made his U.S. debut at the Hollywood Bowl. From 1994 he was a prof. at the Sibelius Academy in Helsinki. He served as chief conductor of the Netherlands Radio Sym. Orch. in Hilversum (from 1996) and as music director of the Tampere Phil. in Finland (from 1998). As a guest conductor, he appeared with major orchs. and operas companies throughout Europe, North America, and the Far East.—**NS/LK/DM**

Klatzow, Peter (James Leonard), South African composer and teacher; b. Springs, Transvaal, July 14, 1945. After training with Richard Cheery and Aïda Lovell, he obtained a scholarship that allowed him to pursue his training in London at the Royal Coll. of Music (1964–65), where he took courses in piano with Kathleen Long, Angus Morrison, and Frank Merrick, in composition with Bernard Stevens, in orchestration with Gordon Jacob, and in conducting with Sir Adrian Boult; he subsequently completed his studies in Paris with Nadia Boulanger (1965–66). He taught at the Rhodesian Coll. of Music in Salisbury (1966–68) and then was active with the music dept. of the South African Broadcasting Corp. (1968–72). In 1973 he became a prof. of composition at the Univ. of Cape Town. With Robert Grishkoff, he founded the music publishing concern Musications in 1981. He ed. the vol. *Composers in South Africa Today* (Cape Town, 1987). In his compositions, Klatzow generally follows the tonal path but he has not been adverse to utilizing serial and aleatoric procedures in some of his works.

WORKS: DRAMATIC: Opera: *The Begger's Opera* (1986). **Ballet:** *Drie Diere* (1980); *Vespers* (1986); *Hamlet* (1993). **ORCH.:** *Variations* (1964; London, Feb. 10, 1966); *Interactions* for Piano, Percussion, and Chamber Orch. (1971); *The Temptation of St. Anthony after Hieronymus Bosch* for Cello and Orch. (1972; Barcelona, May 14, 1977); *Symphony 1972, Phoenix*

(1972; 1st public perf., Cape Town, Oct. 21, 1975); *Time Structure II* (1974); *Still Life, with Moonbeams* (1975); Horn Concerto (Cape Town, June 16, 1978); Organ Concerto (1981); *Incantations* (1984); Concerto for Marimba and Strings (1985); *Figures in a Landscape* (1985); *Citiscape* (1986); *A Chrysalis in Flames* (1988); Concerto for Clarinet and Chamber Orch. (1991). **CHAMBER:** *The Garden of Memories and Discoveries* for 2 Pianos, 2 Guitars, 2 Percussion, Harpsichord, and Electric Organ (1975); *The World of Paul Klee* for Flute and Piano (1977); *Night Magic* for Violin, Horn, and Piano (1978); *Chamber Concerto for 7* for Flute, Clarinet, Horn, Guitar, Percussion, and Electric Organ (1979); *Cythera Among the Lynxes* for Flute and Harp (1982); *Figures in a Landscape I* for Flute and Marimba (1985); String Quartet (1987). **Piano:** *Moments of Night* (1969); *Piano Piece I* (1970); *Time Structure I* (1973); *3 Movements* (1980); *Murmurs of Tiger and Flame* (1982); *A Branch of Dreams* (1986). **VOCAL:** *In Memoriam N.P. van Wyk Louw* for Soprano and Strings (1970); *Charms and Incantations* for Soprano, Tenor, Horn, and Guitar (1979); *Mass* for Chorus, Horn, Marimba, and Strings (1988; rev. 1990); *Congregational Eucharist* for Chorus and Organ (1990); *Praise the Lord, O My Soul* for Chorus and Organ (1990).—**NS/LK/DM**

Klaus, Kenneth Blanchard, American composer; b. Earlville, Iowa, Nov. 11, 1923; d. Baton Rouge, La., Aug. 4, 1980. He studied violin with Burleigh and Krasner, and composition with Philip Greeley Clapp at the Univ. of Iowa (Ph.D., 1950), and also meteorology at the Univ. of Chicago, serving as a meteorologist in the Army Air Corps during World War II. In 1950 he joined the faculty at La. State Univ. In his works, he applied a sui generis synthesis of expanded tonality verging on serialism. In his vocal compositions, he modernized the medieval device of "sogetto cavato" by deriving a theme from the vowels of letter names. He publ. *The Romantic Period in Music* (Boston, 1970).

WORKS: DRAMATIC: Opera: *Tennis Anyone?* (1957); *Crimson Stones*. **Incidental Music To:** *Death of a Salesman* (1954). **ORCH.:** 6 syms.; several symphonic poems; 2 violin concertos; Flute Concerto; Cello Concerto; Clarinet Concerto; *Concerto brevis* for Percussion and Orch. (1955); Concerto for Piano, Right-hand, and Orch. **CHAMBER:** 4 string quartets (1947, 1951, 1957, 1963); Woodwind Quintet; Woodwind Sextet; sonatas.—**NS/LK/DM**

Klauwell, Otto (Adolf), German writer on music and composer; b. Langensalza, April 7, 1851; d. Cologne, May 11, 1917. He studied with Reinecke and Richter at the Leipzig Cons., also studied at the Univ. of Leipzig (Ph.D., 1874, with the diss. *Die historische Entwicklung des musikalische Canons*). He taught at the Cologne Cons. (from 1875), where he was made deputy director (1905). He wrote the operas *Das Mädchen vom See* (Cologne, 1889) and *Die heimlichen Richter* (Elberfeld, 1902) as well as overtures, chamber music, piano pieces, and songs.

WRITINGS: *Musikalische Gesichtspunkte* (Leipzig, 1882; 2nd ed., 1892, as *Musikalische Bekenntnisse*); *Der Vortrag in der Musik* (Berlin and Leipzig, 1883; Eng. tr., N.Y., 1890); *Die Formen der Instrumentalmusik* (Leipzig and N.Y., 1894; 2nd ed., rev. 1918 by W. Niemann); *Geschichte der Sonate* (Cologne and Leipzig, 1899); *L. von Beethoven und die Variationenform* (Langensalza, 1901); *Theodor Gouvy* (Berlin, 1902); *Studien und Erinnerungen* (Langensalza, 1906); *Geschichte der Programm-Musik* (Leipzig, 1910). —**NS/LK/DM**

Klebanov, Dmitri, outstanding Ukrainian composer; b. Kharkov, July 25, 1907; d. there, June 6, 1987. He studied with Bogatyrev at the Kharkov Inst. for Music and Drama, graduating in 1926. After playing viola in Leningrad (1927–28), he returned to Kharkov as director for several musical comedy theaters and as a teacher at the Cons. (1934–73; prof., 1960; emeritus, 1973). He wrote the Ukrainian State Hymn. Klebanov was president of the local Composer's Union (1945–49).

WORKS: DRAMATIC: O p e r a : *Aistenok*, children's opera (1934); *Single Life* (1947); *Vasily Gubanov* (1966; rev. as *Communist*, 1967); *Red Cossacks* (1971). B a l l e t : *Aistenok* (Moscow, 1936); *Svetlana* (Moscow, 1939); *Maïvka* (1980). O t h e r : Musical comedies; film scores. ORCH.: 8 syms. (1945, 1952, 1957, 1959, 1962, n.d., n.d., 1983); *Ukrainian Concertino* (1938); 2 violin concertos (1940, 1951); *Welcoming Overture* (1945); *Ukrainian Suite* (1946); 2 cello concertos (1950, 1973); Domra Concerto (1953; rev. for Orch. of Native Instruments, 1973); 4 *Preludes and Fugue* (1975). CHAMBER: 6 string quartets (1925, 1926, 1933, 1946, 1966, 1968); String Quintet (1953); Woodwind Quartet (1957); Piano Trio (1958); many piano works. VOCAL: Choruses; songs.

BIBL.: M. Cherkashina, *D. K.* (1968).—NS/LK/DM

Klebe, Giselher (Wolfgang), German composer and teacher; b. Mannheim, June 28, 1925. He went to Berlin and studied violin, viola, and composition with Kurt von Wolfurt at the Cons. (1940–43) before pursuing his composition studies with Rufer at the Internationales Musikinstitut (1946) and with Blacher (1946–51). He worked in the music division of the Berlin Radio (1946–49), and then taught composition and theory at the Nordwestdeutsche Musikakademie in Detmold from 1957. In 1962–63 he held a fellowship at the Deutsche Akademie in Rome. He was made a member of the Freie Akademie der Künste in Hamburg (1963), the Akademie der Künste in Berlin (1964; president, 1986–89), and the Bayerische Akademie der Schönen Künste in Munich (1978). Klebe has developed an expressive style of composition in which melody, harmony, timbre, and rhythm are complemented by a judicious handling of 12-tone writing.

WORKS: DRAMATIC: *Die Räuber*, opera (1951–56; Düsseldorf, June 3, 1957; rev. 1962); *Die tödlichen Wünsche*, opera (1957–59; Düsseldorf, June 14, 1959); *Die Ermordung Cäsars*, opera (1958–59; Essen, Sept. 20, 1959); *Alkmene*, opera (Berlin, Sept. 25, 1961); *Figaro lässt sich scheiden*, opera buffa (1962–63; Hamburg, June 28, 1963); *Jakobowsky und der Oberst*, comic opera (Hamburg, Nov. 2, 1965); *Das Märchen von der schönen Lilie*, opera (1967–68; Schwetzingen, May 15, 1969); *Das Testament*, ballet-sym. (1970–71; Wiesbaden, April 30, 1971; as Sym. No. 4, Bochum, Jan. 27, 1972); *Ein wahrer Held*, opera (1972–73; Zürich, Jan. 18, 1975); *Das Mädchen aus Domrémy*, opera (1975; Stuttgart, June 19, 1976); *Das Rendezvous*, opera (Hannover, Oct. 7, 1977); *Der jüngste Tag*, opera (1978–79; Mannheim, July 12, 1980); *Die Fastnachtsbeichte*, opera (Darmstadt, Dec. 20, 1983). ORCH.: *Con moto* (1948; Bremen, Feb. 23, 1953); *Divertissement joyeux* for Chamber Orch. (Darmstadt, July 8, 1949); *Die Zwitschermaschine* (Donaueschingen, Sept. 10, 1950); 2 *Nocturnes* (1951; Darmstadt, July 20, 1952); 6 syms.: No. 1 for 42 Strings (1951; Hamburg, Jan. 7, 1953), No. 2 (1953), No. 3 (1966; WDR, Cologne, Oct. 6, 1967), No. 4, *Das Testament*, ballet-sym. (1970–71; Bochum, Jan. 27, 1972; as a ballet, Wiesbaden, April

30, 1971), No. 5 (Duisburg, Sept. 13, 1977), and No. 6 (1995); *Rhapsody* (1953); Double Concerto for Violin, Cello, and Orch. (Frankfurt am Main, June 19, 1954); *Moments musicaux* (1955); Cello Concerto (1957); *Omaggio* (1960); *Adagio and Fugue* (1962); *Scene und Arie* (Detmold, May 8, 1968); *Herzschläge:Furcht, Bitte und Hoffnung* for Beat Band and Orch. (1969; Gelsenkirchen, June 1, 1970); Concerto for Electronically Altered Harpsichord and Small Orch. (1971; Schwetzingen, May 12, 1972); *Orpheus* (Zagreb, Oct. 22, 1976); *La Tomba di Igor Strawinsky* for Oboe, 14 Strings, and Piano (1978; Cologne, April 25, 1979); Organ Concerto (Duisburg, Nov. 19, 1980); *Begrussung* (Lüdenscheid, Nov. 6, 1981); *Boogie agitato* (Stuttgart, Oct. 24, 1981); Clarinet Concerto (1984; Marl, May 24, 1985); *Umbria verde* (1984); *Lied* (Ludwigshafen, Sept. 30, 1985); *Notturno* (1987; Salzburg, Jan. 30, 1988); Harp Concerto (1988; Münster, Oct. 25, 1989); Cello Concerto (1989; Berlin, May 19, 1990). CHAMBER: Wind Quintet (1948); 3 string quartets (1949, 1963, 1981); Viola Sonata (1949); 2 sonatas for Solo Violin (1952, 1955); 2 violin sonatas (1953, 1972); *Elegia appassionata*, piano trio (1955); *Dithyrambe* for String Quartet (1957); *Missa "Miserere nobis"* for 18 Winds (1965); *Concerto à cinque* for Piano, Harpsichord, Harp, Percussion, and Double Bass (1965); *Quasi una fantasia*, piano quintet (1966); *Variationen über ein Thema von Hector Berlioz* for Organ and 3 Percussionists (1970); Double Bass Sonata (1971); *Tennen No Bi* for Flute, Oboe, Clarinet, Harp, Piano, Cello, and Double Bass (1971–72); *Al Rovescio* for Flute, Harp, Piano, and Metallidiophone (1972); 6 Pieces for Double Bass (1973); *Nenia* for Cello (1974); *Alborada* for Harp (1977); *Cinq chants sans paroles* for Harpsichord and Percussionist (1978); *Der dunkle Gedanke* for Clarinet or Bassett Horn and Piano (1979); *Quattrofonia* for 2 Pianos and 2 Percussionists (1981–82); *Soirée* for Trombone and Chamber Ensemble (1987). KEYBOARD: P i a n o : *Nocturnes* (1949); Sonata for 2 Pianos (1949); 4 *Inventions* (1956); *Neun Klavierstücke für Sonja* (1973, 1974, and 1977); *Feuersturz* (1983); *Glockentürme* for Piano, 4-Hands (1990); *Widmungen*, 5 pieces (1993). O r g a n : *Passacaglia* (1968); *Fantasie und Lobpreisung* (1970); *Surge aquilo: et veni, auster* (1970); *Orgelfanfare* (1989). VOCAL: *Geschichte vom lustigen Musikanten* for Tenor, Chorus, and 5 Instruments (1946–47); 5 *Römische Elegien* for Narrator, Piano, Harpsichord, and Double Bass (1952); *Raskolnikows Traum* for Soprano, Clarinet, and Orch. (1956); 5 *Lieder* for Alto and Orch. (1962); *Stabat Mater* for Soprano, Mezzo- soprano, Alto, Chorus, and Orch. (1964); *Gebet einer armen Seele*, Mass for Chorus and Organ (Kassel, Oct. 8, 1966); *Beuge dich, du Menschenseele* for Medium Voices and Organ (1975–77); 3 *Lieder* for High Voice and Piano (1975–76); *Choral und Te Deum* for Soprano, Chorus, and Orch. (1977–78; Braunschweig, Sept. 24, 1978); *Weihnachtsoratorium* for Mezzo-soprano, Baritone, Speaker, Chorus, and Orch. (Bonn, Dec. 7, 1989).

BIBL.: M. Rentzsch, *G. K.: Werkverzeichnis und einführende Darstellung seines Opernschaffens* (diss., Univ. of Münster, 1990). —NS/LK/DM

Kleber, Leonhard, German organist; b. Göppingen, Württemberg, c. 1490; d. Pforzheim, March 4, 1556. He studied at the Univ. of Heidelberg. He was vicar-choral and organist in Horb (1516–17), and then organist in Esslingen (1517–21). From 1521 he was organist at the collegiate and parish church in Pforzheim. Between 1521 and 1524 he oversaw the compilation of a book of 112 pieces by Hofhaimer, Josquin, Obrecht, and others, arranged in keyboard tablature. Modern transcriptions of his books are to be found in: A. Ritter, *Zur Geschichte des Orgelspiels, vornehmlich des deutschen, im 14. bis zum*

Anfang des 18. Jahrhunderts, II (Leipzig, 1884), R. Eitner, *Monatshefte für Musikgeschichte*, XX (1888), H.J. Moser, *Paul Hofhaimer* (Stuttgart and Berlin, 1929), W. Apel, *Musik aus früher Zeit* (Mainz, 1934), and W. Apel and A. Davison, *Historical Anthology of Music*, vol. I (Cambridge, Mass., 1946).

BIBL.: H. Lowenfeld, *L. K. und sein Orgeltabulaturbuch als Beitrag zur Geschichte der Orgelmusik im beginnenden XVI. Jahrhundert* (Berlin, 1897; reprint, Hilversum, 1968); K. Kotterba, *Die Orgeltabulatur des L. K.* (diss., Univ. of Freiburg, 1958). —NS/LK/DM

Klee, Bernhard, esteemed German conductor and pianist; b. Schleiz, April 19, 1936. He studied piano and conducting at the Cologne Hochschule für Musik. He began his career as a répétiteur at the Cologne Opera in 1957, and then at the Bern City Theater in 1958 before serving as an assistant to Sawallisch and as a conductor at the Cologne Opera. He held the position of 1st conductor at the operas in Salzburg (1962–63), Oberhausen (1963–65), and Hannover (1965–66). From 1966 to 1977 he was Generalmusikdirektor in Lübeck. He was chief conductor of the Hannover Radio Orch. from 1976 to 1979. From 1977 to 1987 he was Generalmusikdirektor of the Düsseldorf Sym. Orch., and from 1985 to 1989 principal guest conductor of the BBC Phil. in Manchester. In 1991 he returned to the Hannover Radio Orch. as its chief conductor, where he was named honorary conductor in 1995. He became music director of the Rheinland-Pfalz State Phil. in Ludwigshafen in 1992. In 1998 he became music director of the Phil. State Orch. in Halle. Married to **Edith Mathis**, Klee served as her accompanist in orch. and recital settings. He is particularly admired for his insightful interpretations of the Austro-German repertoire.—NS/LK/DM

Klega, Miroslav, Slovak composer; b. Ostrava, March 6, 1929. He studied composition with Křička at the Prague Cons. (1942–44) and with Suchoň and Cikker at the Bratislava Cons. (1946–50). He taught at the Ostrava Cons. (1955–73) and was its director (1967–73). He then worked with the Czech Radio there.

WORKS: *Suite Bagatelle* for Piano (1948); *Černa země* (Black Soil), symphonic variations (1951); Sym. (1959); Concertino for 4 String Instruments (1961); *Pantomima*, suite for Orch. (1963); *Concerto-Partita* for Violin and Orch. (1965); *Výpověď osamělého pěšáka* (The Confession of a Lone Pedestrian) for Narrator and Orch. (1968); *Příběhy z zazraky*, sym.-ballet (1981).—NS/LK/DM

Kleiber, Carlos, outstanding German-born Austrian conductor, son of **Erich Kleiber**; b. Berlin, July 3, 1930. He left Nazi Germany with his parents in 1935, eventually settling in South America in 1940. He evinced an early interest in music, but his father opposed it as a career; after studying chemistry in Zürich (1949–50), he turned decisively to music and completed his training in Buenos Aires. In 1952 he became a répétiteur and stage assistant at the Theater am Gärtnerplatz in Munich, making his conducting debut in 1954 with Millöcker's *Gasparone* in Potsdam, where he was active until becoming a répétiteur (1956) and conductor (1958) at the Deutsche Oper am Rhein in Düsseldorf. After conducting at the Zürich Opera (1964–66), he served as 1st conductor at the Württemberg State Theater in Stuttgart (1966–68). From 1968 to 1978 he conducted at the Bavarian State Opera in Munich. In 1966 he made his British debut conducting *Wozzeck* at the Edinburgh Festival; he led performances of *Tristan und Isolde* for his first appearances at the Vienna State Opera in 1973 and at the Bayreuth Festival in 1974, the year in which he made his first appearances at London's Covent Garden and Milan's La Scala with *Der Rosenkavalier*. On Sept. 8, 1977, he made his U.S. debut conducting *Otello* at the San Francisco Opera. His first appearance with a U.S. orch. came in 1978, when he conducted the Chicago Sym. Orch. In 1979 he conducted the Vienna Phil. and in 1982 the Berlin Phil. On Jan. 22, 1988, he made his Metropolitan Opera debut in N.Y. conducting *La Bohème*. In 1989 and 1992 he conducted the New Year's Day Concert of the Vienna Phil. with noteworthy elan. He became a naturalized Austrian citizen in 1980. Kleiber has been accorded accolades from critics, audiences, and his fellow musicians. His brilliant performances reflect his unreserved commitment to the score at hand, his authority, and his mastery of technique. His infrequent appearances, combined with his passion for perfection, have made him a legendary figure among the world's contemporary podium celebrities.—NS/LK/DM

Kleiber, Erich, eminent Austrian conductor, father of **Carlos Kleiber**; b. Vienna, Aug. 5, 1890; d. Zürich, Jan. 27, 1956. He studied at the Prague Cons. and the Univ. of Prague. He made his debut at the Prague National Theater in 1911, then conducted opera in Darmstadt (1912–19), Barmen-Elberfeld (1919–21), Düsseldorf (1921–22), and Mannheim (1922–23). In 1923 he was appointed Generalmusikdirektor of the Berlin State Opera. His tenure was outstanding, both for the brilliant performances of the standard repertoire and for the exciting programming of contemporary works. He conducted the world premiere of Berg's *Wozzeck* (Dec. 14, 1925). In 1934, in protest against the Nazi government, he resigned his post and emigrated to South America. He conducted regularly at the Teatro Colón in Buenos Aires from 1936 to 1949. Having first conducted at London's Covent Garden in 1937, he returned there from 1950 to 1953. He then was appointed Generalmusikdirektor once more of the Berlin State Opera in 1954, but resigned in March 1955, before the opening of the season, because of difficulties with the Communist regime. He was renowned for his performances of the music of Mozart and Beethoven. He also composed, numbering among his works a Violin Concerto, Piano Concerto, orch. variations, *Capriccio* for Orch., numerous chamber music works, piano pieces, and songs.

BIBL.: J. Russell, *E. K.: A Memoir* (London, 1957); C. Dillon, *E. K.: A Discography* (Buenos Aires, 1990).—NS/LK/DM

Kleier, Roger (Wayne), adventurous American guitarist, composer, and improviser; b. Glendale, Calif., Oct. 2, 1958. He began playing the guitar at the age of 13, and later studied composition with Merrill Ellis at

North Tex. State Univ. and at the Univ. of Southern Calif. in Los Angeles, developing a strong interest in non-idiomatic improvisation and alternative techniques for the instrument. In 1981 he founded the Los Angeles Improvisers Collective, organizing and presenting numerous concert series in Calif. In 1992 he moved to N.Y. with his longtime partner, Annie Gosfield, with whom he often collaborates and performs. Kleier has been long dedicated to furthering the vocabulary of the electric guitar through the development of alternative techniques, preparations, and digital technology. He has worked in and composed pieces for a variety of new music ensembles, as well as in and for art installations. He has performed and/or recorded with such diverse artists as David Moss, Davey Williams, Elliott Sharp, Carl Stone, and Phill Niblock, among others, toured extensively throughout the U.S., Canada, Europe, and Australia, and also given composition and improvisation workshops in the U.S. (1995–99) and in Prague (1996). His funding sources have included the NEA, the Rockefeller Foundation, and Meet the Composer; he also held residencies at the Djerassi Foundation in Calif. (1998) and at Harvestworks in N.Y. (1998). His first solo CD, *KlangenBang*, appeared in 1999. Kleier's works reveal an eclectic hand, and incorporate a remarkably diverse array of sounds, including orchestral feedback. In addition to numerous works composed in collaboration with Gosfield, these include *Fanfare for the Cognitive Elite* for Digitally altered Guitars and Percussion (1996), *The Cheka's Cellar* for Digitally altered Guitars and Percussion (1996), *The Manufacture of Consent* for Multiple Electric Guitars (1996), *Sighted Sub, Sank Same* for Electric Guitar and Digital Delay (1997), *We Speak of Deep Autumn* for Multiple Electric Guitars (1998), *Brickyard* for Sampler (1998), *The Juan Cortina Suite* for Multiple Electric Guitars and Sampler (1998), *Lodi* for Electric Guitar and Sample Loops (1998), *We Speak of Deep Night* for Multiple Electric Guitars, Sampler, Prepared Piano, and Percussion (1998), and *Los Paseos* for Electric Guitar and Electronics (1999).—**LK/DM**

Klein, Bernhard (Joseph),

German composer; b. Cologne, March 6, 1793; d. Berlin, Sept. 9, 1832. He went to Paris in 1812 and received some advice from Choron, but he was mainly self-taught. Returning to Cologne, he was appointed music director of the Cathedral. In 1818 he settled in Berlin, and from 1820 he taught at the Royal Inst. for Church Music. He also taught singing at the Univ. of Berlin, retiring in 1830. He was greatly praised by his Berlin contemporaries for his contrapuntal craftsmanship in sacred works and as a composer of lieder. His stepbrother, Josef Klein (b. Cologne, 1802; d. there, Feb. 10, 1862), was his pupil; he was one of the first composers to set Heine's texts to music.

WORKS: DRAMATIC: Opera: *Dido* (Berlin, Oct. 15, 1823); *Ariadne* (Berlin, 1823). **VOCAL:** Several oratorios, including *Jephtha* (Cologne, 1828) and *David* (Halle, 1830); several cantatas, including *Worte des Glaubens* (1817) and *Hiob* (Leipzig, 1820); various other sacred vocal works; songs. **OTHER:** Piano Sonatas.

BIBL.: C. Koch, *B. K.* (diss., Univ. of Rostock, 1902).
—**NS/LK/DM**

Klein, Elisabeth,

Hungarian-born Danish pianist; b. Trencin, July 23, 1911. She studied at the Budapest Academy of Music (graduated, 1934), then had private lessons with Bartók. She settled in Denmark, becoming a naturalized Danish citizen. She made her debut in Copenhagen (1946). She toured extensively and was also active as a teacher. Klein championed the music of Bartók and contemporary Scandinavian composers.
—**NS/LK/DM**

Klein, Fritz Heinrich,

Austrian music theorist and composer; b. Budapest, Feb. 2, 1892; d. Linz, July 11, 1977. He took piano lessons with his father, then went to Vienna, where he studied composition with Schoenberg and Berg, and became their devoted disciple. From 1932 to 1957 he taught theory at the Bruckner Cons. in Linz. His most ingenious composition was *Die Maschine* (1921; N.Y., Nov. 24, 1924), subtitled "Eine extonale Selbstsatire" and publ. under the pseudonym "Heautontimorumenos" (i.e., self-tormentor); this work features instances of all kinds of tonal combinations, including a "Mutterakkord," which consists of all 12 different chromatic tones and all 11 different intervals, the first time such an arrangement was proposed. He also publ. an important essay bearing on serial techniques then still in the process of formulation, "Die Grenze der Halbtonwelt," in *Die Musik* (Jan. 1925). He made the vocal score of Berg's opera *Wozzeck*. His other works include *Partita* for 6 Instruments (1953), *Divertimento* for Strings (1954), *Ein musikalisches Fliessband* for Orch. (1960), *Musikalisches Tagebuch* for Orch. (1970), and several stage works, among them the opera *Nostradamus*.—**NS/LK/DM**

Klein, Gideon,

gifted Czech composer and pianist; b. Přerov, Dec. 6, 1919; d. in the concentration camp at Fürstengrube, Silesia, probably on Jan. 27, 1945. He was reared in a Jewish family of culture, and at age 11 began piano studies with Růžena Kurzová. In 1938 he entered the piano master class of Vilém Kurz at the Prague Cons., where he also received instruction in composition from Alois Hába; also pursued the study of theory at the Charles Univ. in Prague. His education was cut short by the Nazi occupation of his homeland in 1939; nonetheless, he persevered under the most daunting conditions, producing works under a pseudonym, which he presented in private concert settings. In 1941 he was deported to the concentration camp in Terezín, where he continued his activities as both composer and pianist. In late 1944 he was transported to the concentration camp in Auschwitz, and then on to the concentration camp in Fürstengrube, where he died a few months before the Allied victory. Although he perished at the age of 25, he succeeded in composing a significant number of works of enduring value. His early interest in Moravian folk modalities gave way to the influence of Janáček, Novák, and Schoenberg, which, in turn, prompted him to find his own compositional path, which included the use of microintervals and free tonality. All of his extant works were publ. in a collaborative ed. by the Czech Music Fund in Prague and by Bote & Bote in Berlin in 1993.

WORKS: *4 Movements* for String Quartet (1936–38); Duo for

Violin and Viola in Quarter Tones (1940); *Divertimento* for 8 Winds (1940); 3 songs for High Voice and Piano, after Klag, Hölderlin, and Goethe (1940); String Quartet (1941); Duo for Violin and Cello (1941; unfinished); 2 madrigals for 2 Sopranos, Alto, Tenor, and Bass (1942, 1943); *The First Sin* for Men's Chorus (1942); *Fantasy and Fugue* for String Quartet (1942–43); Piano Sonata (1943); Trio for Violin, Viola, and Cello (1944; arr. by V. Saudek as *Partita* for Chamber Orch.).

BIBL.: H.-G. Klein, ed., *G. K.: Materialien* (Hamburg, 1995); M. Slavický, *G. K.: Torzo života a díla* (Prague, 1996). —NS/LK/DM

Klein, John, American organist, pianist, and composer; b. Rahns, Pa., Feb. 21, 1915; d. there, April 30, 1981. He studied at the Philadelphia Musical Academy, then went to Salzburg, where he took courses at the Mozarteum, and later to Paris, where he had lessons with Boulanger in composition and with Dupré in organ. Returning to America, he was organist at the Presbyterian Church in Columbus, Ohio (1937–42). He then was engaged in radio shows as a pianist (1944–57). He played carillon in recitals and at carillon festivals in Cobb, Ireland, and at the World's Fair in Brussels. He publ. *The Art of Playing the Modern Carillon* and *The First 4 Centuries of Music.* Among his compositions were a Violin Concerto and a number of songs and marches, including the U.S. Army radio show theme, *Sound Off.* —NS/LK/DM

Klein, Kenneth, American conductor; b. Los Angeles, Sept. 5, 1939. He studied violin at the Univ. of Southern Calif. School of Music in Los Angeles with Eudice Shapiro, Vera Barstow, and Peter Meremblum, and took piano lessons with Gerhard Albersheim. He also studied conducting with Fritz Zweig in Los Angeles, Izler Solomon at the Aspen (Colo.) School of Music, and Richard Lert in Asilomar, Calif., and received instruction in theory from Boulanger in Paris. He was a violinist in the Pasadena Sym. Orch., then was founder-conductor of the Westside Sym. Orch. in Los Angeles (1963–68). He was music director of the Guadalajara Sym. Orch. (1969–78), the Nassau (L.I.) Sym. Orch. (from 1980), the Santa Cruz (Calif.) Sym. Orch. (1981–85), the N.Y. Virtuosi (from 1982), and the S.Dak. Sym. Orch. (1983–85). He also appeared widely as a guest conductor in Europe. He taught at the Univ. of Guadalajara (1968–69; 1973) and the Univ. of Calif. at Santa Cruz (1981–83).—NS/LK/DM

Klein, Lothar, German-born Canadian composer; b. Hannover, Jan. 27, 1932. He went to England in 1939 and to the U.S. in 1941, where he studied composition with Fetler at the Univ. of Minn. (B.A., 1954), and then composition with Petrassi at the Berkshire Music Center in Tanglewood (summer, 1956) and orchestration with Dorati in Minneapolis (1956–58). After winning a Fulbright fellowship, he went to Berlin to study composition with Rufer at the Free Univ. and with Blacher at the Hochschule für Musik (1958–60). He also studied with Nono in Darmstadt before completing his studies at the Univ. of Minn. (Ph.D., 1961), serving on its faculty (1962–64). He later taught at the Univ. of Tex. at Austin

(1964–68). In 1968 he joined the faculty of the Univ. of Toronto, where he was chairman of its graduate music dept. (1971–76). Klein has publ. extensively on various topics dealing with 20th century music. As a composer, he has devoted himself in the main to orch. pieces. His early music is essentially tonal, aesthetically derived from neo-Romantic procedures; he then experimented with various branches of serialism; also wrote collage pieces embodying elements of all historical periods through linkage of stylistic similarities.

WORKS: DRAMATIC: *Lost Love,* ballet (1950–56); *The Prodigal Son,* dance drama (1966); *Tale of a Father and Son,* opera (1983). **ORCH.:** *The Bluebird,* suite (1952); *Eclogues* for Horn and Strings (1954); 3 syms. (1955; 1966; *Symphonic Etudes,* 1972); Concerto for Winds, Timpani, and Strings (1956); *Appassionato* (1958); *Symmetries* (1958); *Trio concertante* for String Trio and Orch. (1961); *Epitaphs* (1963); *Rondo Giocoso* (1964); *Charivari: Music for an Imaginary Comedy* (1966); *Musique à Go-Go: A Symphonic Mêlée* (1966); *Paganini Collage* for Violin and Orch. (1967); *Le Trésor des dieux* for Guitar and Orch. (1969); *Janizary Music* for Military Orch. (1970); *Design* for Percussion and Orch. (1970); *Passacaglia of the Zodiac* for 14 Strings (1971); *Music* for Violin and Orch. (1972); *Slices of Time* for Trumpet and Orch. (1973; also for Trumpet and String Quartet); *Invention, Blues, and Chase* for Free Bass Accordion and Strings (1975); *Musica Antiqua* for Consort and Orch. (1975); *Boccherini Collage* for Cello and Orch. (1978); *Scenes* for Timpani and Strings (1979); *Concerto Sacro* for Viola and Orch. (1984); *Landscape with Pipers* for Chamber Orch. (1984); *Festival Partita* (1990); *Columbus Music* (1992); *Homage à Toulous-Latrec* (1994); *Danseries* (1994). **Band:** *Centre- Stage* (1992); *"Let the Kettle to the Trumpet Speak..."* (1998). **CHAMBER:** *Suite on 12th Night* for 7 Instruments (1951); Wind Quintet (1952); Piano Quintet (1954); *Partita I* for Flute, Clarinet, and Harp (1955) and *II* for Trumpet, Tuba, and Piano (1980); *3 Greek Rites* for 8 Percussion (1964); *Incantations* for 7 Percussion (1965); *Arias* for String Quartet (1966); Trio Sonata for Clarinet, Cello, Piano or Harpsichord, and Drum Set (1968); *Vaudeville,* "acrobatics" for Soprano Saxophone and Wind Quintet (1979); *Grand Duo Concertante* for Clarinet and Timpani (1979); *Cancioneros* for Violin and Piano (1980); *Meditation* "for John Lennon, Dec. 9, 1980" for Violin and Piano (1980); *Variations on 2 Well-known Airs* for 9 Instruments (1981); *Tombeau* for 2 Guitars (1981); *Choreagos* for Oboe, Percussion, and Optional Reciter (1982); *Virtuoso Music* for Viola, Cello, and Double Bass (1987); *Vice-Versa* for 2 Trombones (1991); 2 string quartets (*Quartets of the Sounds,* 1991; 1992); *Baroque Suite* for Oboe and English Horn (1992); *Scenes from Homer* for Horn and Harp (1994); *Trocadero* for Oboe, Clarinet, Bassoon, and Piano (1995); *Esprit* for Flute, Clarinet, and Piano (1997); *Paolo e Francesca* for Violin and Harp (1998); *Partita 2000* for Clarinet, Cello, Piano, and Harp (1999). **Piano:** Sonata (1968); *Canadiana* for 2 Pianos (1980). **VOCAL:** *The Masque of Orianna* for 2 Sopranos, Chorus, and Orch. (1973); *The Philosopher in the Kitchen,* "gastronomic meditations" for Contralto and Orch. (1974); *Orpheus* for Soprano, Tenor, Narrator, Chorus, and Instruments (1976); *Voices of Earth* for Soprano, Children's Chorus, and Orch. (1976); *Hachcava: Memorial Meditations* for Bass and 5 Instruments (1979); *The Jabberwock in Ogden Nash's Dining Room* for Women's Chorus and Percussion Ensemble (1991); *Symphonia armoniae celestium revelationem* for Soprano, Viola, 2 Harps, and Percussion Ensemble (1999); choruses; solo songs.—NS/LK/DM

Klein, Peter, German tenor; b. Zündorf, near Cologne, Jan. 25, 1907; d. Vienna, Oct. 4, 1992. He studied at the Cologne Cons. He made appearances in Düsseldorf, Kaiserslautern, and Zürich. He was a member of the Hamburg State Opera (1937–41), then at the Vienna State Opera, and also appeared at Bayreuth (from 1946). In 1947 he first appeared at London's Covent Garden as Jacquino with the visiting Vienna State Opera; he returned there regularly until 1960. He made his Metropolitan Opera debut in N.Y. on Nov. 21, 1949, as Valzacchi in *Der Rosenkavalier*, remaining on its roster until 1951. From 1956 to 1977 he was head of the opera dept. at the Vienna Cons. His other roles included Basilio, Mime in the *Ring* cycle, the Captain in *Wozzeck*, and Monsieur Taupe in *Capriccio.*—NS/LK/DM

Kleinheinz, Franz Xaver, German conductor and composer; b. Mindelheim (baptized), June 26, 1765; d. Budapest, Jan. 26, 1832. He played in the Munich Orch., and in 1803 went to Vienna to study with Albrechtsberger. He then was active in Brünn, and subsequently was a theater conductor in Budapest (1814–15; 1817–24). He wrote the operas *Harald* (Budapest, March 22, 1814) and *Der Kafig* (Budapest, 1816), as well as a Piano Concerto, chamber music, and sacred choral works. He also made transcriptions for string quartet of Beethoven's early piano sonatas.—NS/LK/DM

Kleinknecht, Jakob Friedrich, German flutist, violinist, and composer, brother of **Johann Stephan Kleinknecht** and **Johann Wolfgang Kleinknecht;** b. Ulm (baptized), April 8, 1722; d. Ansbach, Aug. 14, 1794. He studied with his father, then joined his brother Johann Wolfgang at the Bayreuth court. He turned to the violin in 1747, and was made asst. Kapellmeister in 1748, court composer in 1749, and Kapellmeister in 1761. He remained with the court when it moved to Ansbach in 1769. His extant works include a Sinfonia concertante for 2 Flutes, 2 Oboes, Strings, and Keyboard obbligato, a Violin Concerto, a Concerto for 2 Flutes and Orch. (publ. in Paris, 1776), 6 *sonate da camera* for Flute and Harpsichord or Cello (publ. in Nuremberg, 1748), and various keyboard sonatas.—NS/LK/DM

Kleinknecht, Johann Stephan, German flutist, brother of **Jakob Friedrich Kleinknecht** and **Johann Wolfgang Kleinknecht;** b. Ulm, Sept. 17, 1731; d. Ansbach, after 1791. He studied philosophy and languages at the Ulm Gymnasium, and later received training in flute. In 1750 he joined his brothers in Bayreuth. After serving the bishop of Breslau, he returned to Bayreuth in 1754 to enter the service of the court. He remained in its service after it moved to Ansbach in 1769. Kleinknecht gained a notable reputation via his tours as a soloist throughout Europe.—LK/DM

Kleinknecht, Johann Wolfgang, German violinist and composer, brother of **Jakob Friedrich Kleinknecht** and **Johann Stephan Kleinknecht;** b. Ulm, April 17, 1715; d. Ansbach, Feb. 20, 1786. He studied with his father and at the Ulm Gymnasium. In 1733 he became a member of the Stuttgart court chapel, where he had violin lessons with Brescianello. In subsequent years, he appeared as a soloist at various German courts until entering the service of the courts in Eisenach and Bayreuth. From 1738 to 1769 he was director of the music establishment at the Bayreuth court, continuing in its service when he moved to Ansbach in the latter year. Among his works were a number of sonatas. —LK/DM

Kleinmichel, Richard, German pianist, conductor, and composer; b. Posen, Dec. 31, 1846; d. Charlottenburg, Aug. 18, 1901. He studied with his father, Friedrich Kleinmichel (1827–94), a bandmaster; then at the Leipzig Cons. (1863–66). He was made music director of the Leipzig Theater (1882), and later held similar posts in Danzig and Magdeburg. He wrote the operas *Schloss de l'Orme,* after Prevost's *Manon Lescaut* (Hamburg, Oct. 8, 1883), and *Pfeifer von Dusenbach* (Hamburg, March 21, 1891) as well as 2 syms. and many piano pieces.—NS/LK/DM

Kleinsinger, George, American composer; b. San Bernardino, Calif., Feb. 13, 1914; d. N.Y., July 28, 1982. He studied with Bauer, Haubiel, and James at N.Y.U. (B.A., 1937) and with Jacobi and Wagenaar at the Juilliard Graduate School in N.Y. (1938–40). In 1942 he composed the first of a series of popular melodramas, *Tubby the Tuba.* Also notable was his chamber opera *Shinbone Alley* (N.Y., Dec. 6, 1954), which was based on Don Marquis' popular comic strip *Archy and Mehitabel.*

WORKS: DRAMATIC: Melodramas: *Farewell to a Hero* (1941); *Tubby the Tuba* (1942); *Peewee the Piccolo* (1945); *Pan the Piper* (1946); *The Story of Celeste* (1947); *The Tree that Found Christmas* (1955). **Chamber Opera:** *Shinbone Alley* (N.Y., Dec. 6, 1954). **Other:** Film scores and television music. **ORCH.:** Sym. (1942); Cello Concerto (1946); Harmonica Concerto (1947); Violin Concerto (1953). **CHAMBER:** String Quartet (1940); Clarinet Quintet (1949); Trio for Clarinet, Cello, and Piano (1955); piano pieces. **VOCAL:** *I Hear America Singing,* cantata (1940); *Brooklyn Baseball Cantata* (1942); songs. —NS/LK/DM

Klementyev, Lev (Mikhailovich), Russian tenor; b. St. Petersburg, April 1, 1868; d. Tiflis, Oct. 26, 1910. He appeared in operetta in Kharkov and St. Petersburg, then was a member of the Kiev Opera (1888–89), the Tiflis Opera (1889–90), and Moscow's Bolshoi Theater (from 1892). He was noted for his faithful rendition of Russian operatic roles.—NS/LK/DM

Klemetti, Heikki, Finnish composer and choral conductor; b. Kuortane, Feb. 14, 1876; d. Helsinki, Aug. 26, 1953. He studied philosophy, then music at the Stern Cons. in Berlin. In 1900 he founded the famous men's choir Suomen Laulu (became a mixed choir in 1907), with which he toured Scandinavia and Europe (1901–25) and the U.S. (1939). He led it until 1942. He publ. a history of music (several vols. from 1916), a textbook of choral singing (1917), and a textbook of voice production (1920); composed numerous choruses, masses, and antiphons (collected and officially approved as the hymnal of the State Church of Finland in 1924); also arranged songs for school and home (3 vols., 1927–28) and some early church music.—NS/LK/DM

Klemm, Johann Gottlob, German-American organ builder; b. near Dresden, May 12, 1690; d. near Bethlehem, Pa., May 5, 1762. He was trained in Dresden, most likely by G. Silbermann, and then was active with the Moravians in Herrnhut, Saxony. In 1733 he went to America, settling in Philadelphia in 1736. In 1741 he built the organ for N.Y.'s Trinity Church. After living in N.Y. (from c. 1745), he settled in Bethlehem, Pa., in 1757, where he took on David Tannenberg as his assistant. —NS/LK/DM

Klemmer, John, American saxophonist; b. Chicago, Ill., July 3, 1946. His descent is particularly disappointing in that he was once a barrier-melting innovator; his work was dominated by blandness after the mid-1970s, blacking out a talent that could have consistently explored new territory in the common ground between jazz, rock, and R&B. Growing up in the Chicago area, he studied with the charismatic jazz teacher and saxophonist Joe Daley and cut his teeth by playing professionally while still in his mid-teens. After an all-acoustic first date as a leader, he began to head into an exciting area where the rock of Hendrix met post-Coltrane soulful saxophone, sometimes beautifully mellow, sometimes incendiary, almost always amazingly agile. After moving to Los Angeles in the early 1970s, he produced work that became more commercially popular but artistically vapid. Sporadic dates in the 1980s gave way to silence in the 1990s.

DISC.: *Waterfalls* (1972); *Fresh Feathers* (1974); *Touch* (1975); *Barefoot Ballet* (1976); *Cry* (1978); *Arabesque* (1978); *Nexus for Duo and Trio* (1978); *Brazilia* (1979); *Mosaic: The Best of John Klemmer* (1979); *Blowin' Gold* (1982); *Music* (1989); *Simpatico* (1997). —**GB**

Klemperer, Otto, celebrated German conductor; b. Breslau, May 14, 1885; d. Zürich, July 6, 1973. After early musical training from his mother, he entered the Hoch Cons. in Frankfurt am Main (1901), where he studied piano with Kwast and theory with Knorr. He later received instruction in composition and conducting from Pfitzner in Berlin. He made his debut conducting Max Reinhardt's production of *Orpheus in the Underworld* in Berlin in 1906; on Mahler's recommendation, he then was appointed chorus master and subsequently conductor of the German Theater in Prague; he assisted Mahler in the latter's preparations for the Munich premiere of the *Symphony of a Thousand* in 1910. He became a conductor at the Hamburg Opera in 1910, but was obliged to leave in 1912 as the result of a scandalous liaison with the recently married soprano Elisabeth Schumann. After minor appointments at Barmen (1913–14) and Strasbourg (1914–17), where he was Pfitzner's deputy, he was appointed music director of the Cologne Opera in 1917. While in Cologne, he conducted the German premiere of Janáček's *Kát'a Kabanová*. In 1924 he was named music director of the Wiesbaden Opera. He made his U.S. debut as guest conductor with the N.Y. Sym. Orch. on Jan. 24, 1926. In 1927 he became music director of Berlin's Kroll Opera, where he was given a mandate to perform new works and present repertoire pieces in an enlightened manner. He conducted the world premiere of Hindemith's *Neues vom Tage* (June 8, 1929), as well as the furst Berlin performances of Hindemith's *Cardillac*, Stravinsky's *Oedipus Rex*, and Schoenberg's *Die glückliche Hand*; he also conducted the premiere performance of Schoenberg's *Begleitungsmusik* as part of the Kroll concerts. When political and economic pressures forced the Kroll Opera to close in 1931, Klemperer became a conductor at the Berlin State Opera. When the Nazis came to power in 1933, he was compelled to emigrate to the U.S. That same year, he became music director of the Los Angeles Phil.; he also appeared as a guest conductor in N.Y., Philadelphia, and Pittsburgh. His career was disrupted in 1939 when he underwent an operation for a brain tumor. In 1947 he was engaged as conductor at the Budapest State Opera, where he remained until 1950. He made his first appearance as a guest conductor with the Philharmonia Orch. of London in 1951; was appointed its principal conductor in 1959, and retained that position when the orch.'s manager, Walter Legge, unsuccessfully attempted to disband it in 1964.

Klemperer was accident-prone and a manic-depressive all his life. The two sides of his nature were reflected in his conducting styles on either side of World War II. He had earlier been noted for his energetic and hard-driven interpretations, but during his late London years he won great renown for his measured performances of the Viennese classics. He particularly distinguished himself by conducting a memorable series of the Beethoven syms. at the Royal Festival Hall. In the early 1960s he conducted new productions of *Fidelio*, *Die Zauberflöte*, and *Lohengrin* at Covent Garden. His serious and unsentimental readings of Mahler's syms. were largely responsible for the modern critical and popular interest shown in that composer's music. In 1970 he conducted in Jerusalem and accepted Israeli citizenship. He retired in 1972. He was also a composer. He studied with Schoenberg during the latter's American sojourn, but his compositional style had more in common with that of Pfitzner. He wrote an opera, *Das Ziel* (1915; rev. 1970), a *Missa sacra* (1916), 6 syms. (from 1960), 17 pieces for Voice and Orch. (1967–70), 9 string quartets (1968–70), and about 100 lieder. He publ. *Meine Erinnerungen an Gustav Mahler* (Zürich, 1960; Eng. tr., 1964, as *Minor Recollections*).

BIBL.: P. Heyworth, *Conversations with K.* (London, 1973); C. Osborne and K. Thomson, eds., *K. Stories: Anecdotes, Sayings and Impressions of O. K.* (London, 1980); P. Heyworth, *O. K.: His Life and Times*, vol. I, 1885–1933 (London, 1983), vol. II, 1933–1973 (Cambridge, 1996); M. Anderson, ed., *K. on Music: Shavings from a Musician's Workbench* (London, 1986). —NS/LK/DM

Klenau, Paul (August) von, Danish conductor and composer; b. Copenhagen, Feb. 11, 1883; d. there, Aug. 31, 1946. He studied violin with Hillmer and composition with Malling in Copenhagen, then took lessons in violin with Halíř and in composition with Bruch at the Berlin Hochschule für Musik (1902–04). In 1904 he went to Munich, where he studied composition privately with Thuille, and in 1908 he moved to Stuttgart, where he became a student of Schillings. He began his conducting career at the Freiburg im Breisgau Opera during the season of 1907–08. From 1909 to 1912 he was conductor at the Stuttgart Court Opera and in

1912 conductor of the Bach Soc. in Frankfurt am Main. He then returned to the Freiburg im Breisgau Opera (1913). After World War I, he studied with Schoenberg. From 1920 to 1926 he was conductor of the Danish Phil. Soc. in Copenhagen, concurrently conducting the Vienna Konzerthausgesellschaft (1922–30). He returned to Copenhagen in 1940.

WORKS: DRAMATIC: O p e r a : *Sulamith,* after the Song of Songs (Munich, Nov. 16, 1913); *Kjartan und Gudrun* (Mannheim, April 4, 1918; rev. version as *Gudrun auf Island,* Hagen, Nov. 27, 1924); *Die Lästerschule,* after Sheridan (Frankfurt am Main, Dec. 25, 1926); *Michael Kolhaas,* after Kleist (Stuttgart, Nov. 4, 1933; new version, Berlin, March 7, 1934); *Rembrandt van Rijn,* libretto by the composer (Berlin and Stuttgart, Jan. 23, 1937); *Elisabeth von England* (Kassel, March 29, 1939; title changed to *Die Königin* after the outbreak of World War II to avoid mentioning England). **B a l l e t :** *Kleine Idas Blumen,* after Hans Christian Andersen (Stuttgart, 1916); *Marion* (Copenhagen, 1920). **ORCH.:** 7 syms. (1908, 1911, 1913, 1913, 1939, 1940, 1941); *Inferno,* 3 fantasies. **OTHER:** Chamber music; piano pieces; songs.—NS/LK/DM

Klengel, August (Stephan) Alexander, esteemed German pianist, organist, pedagogue, and composer; b. Dresden, June 29, 1783; d. there, Nov. 22, 1852. He studied with Milchmayer, and from 1803, with Clementi, with whom he traveled in Germany and later to St. Petersburg (1805), where he remained as a private tutor to aristocratic families until 1811. He then lived in Paris. He visited London in 1815, returning to Dresden in 1816, where he was appointed organist at the Hofkapelle in 1817. He was a fine organist and pianist, and a champion of the music of Bach. As a composer, he was a master of contrapuntal forms; his canons were so ingenious that he was known under the sobriquet "Kanon-Klengel." His major achievement was an outstanding set of 48 canons and fugues (publ. 1854), inspired by Bach's *Das wohltemperierte Clavier.* He also wrote various other keyboard works, including a vol. of piano canons as *Les Avantcoureurs* (Dresden, 1841), chamber music, songs, etc.

BIBL.: R. Jager, *A.A. K., und seine Kanons und Fugen* (diss., Univ. of Leipzig, 1928).—NS/LK/DM

Klengel, Julius, German cellist, pedagogue, and composer, brother of **Paul Klengel;** b. Leipzig, Sept. 24, 1859; d. there, Oct. 27, 1933. Brought up in a musical atmosphere (virtually all members of his family were professional or amateur musicians), he developed rapidly, studying cello with Emil Hegar and theory with Jadassohn. He joined the Leipzig Gewandhaus Orch. when he was 15, and in 1881 became 1st cellist, remaining in that post until his resignation in 1924. He was Royal Prof. at the Leipzig Cons. (from 1881), numbering among his most distinguished students Suggia, Feuermann, and Piatigorsky. He composed 4 cello concertos and other works for cello, chamber music, etc. —NS/LK/DM

Klengel, Paul, German conductor and composer, brother of **Julius Klengel;** b. Leipzig, May 13, 1854; d. there, April 24, 1935. He studied at the Leipzig Cons.

and at the Univ. of Leipzig (Ph.D., 1876, with the diss. *Zur Ästhetik der Tonkunst*). From 1881 to 1886 he conducted the Leipzig Euterpe Concerts, and from 1888 to 1893 he was 2nd court conductor in Stuttgart. From 1898 to 1902 he conducted German choral societies in N.Y. He then returned to Leipzig, where he conducted the Arion Soc. (from 1902) and also taught at the Leipzig Cons. He wrote numerous works for violin, songs, and arrangements.—NS/LK/DM

Klenovsky, Nikolai (Semyonovich), Russian conductor and composer; b. Odessa, 1853; d. Petrograd, July 6, 1915. He studied violin with Hrimaly and harmony with Tchaikovsky at the Moscow Cons. (graduated, 1879), then conducted at Moscow's Bolshoi Theater (1883–93) and in Tiflis, where he also was made director of the Cons. (1893). He then was deputy director of the Imperial Chapel in St. Petersburg (1902–06). He wrote 3 ballets: *Prelesti gashisha* (The Delights of Hashish; Moscow, 1885), *Svetlana* (Moscow, 1886), *Salanga* (St. Petersburg, 1900), as well as orch. works, 4 cantatas, and songs.—NS/LK/DM

Klerk, Albert de, Dutch organist, choral conductor, pedagogue, and composer; b. Haarlem, Oct. 4, 1917; d. there, Dec. 1, 1998. He was a student of A. van der Horst (organ) and H. Andriessen (analysis) at the Amsterdam Cons. (1934–39; graduated, 1939), receiving the Prix d'Excellence in 1941. In 1934 he became organist at the St. Joseph Church in Haarlem, a post he retained for 60 years. He also served as conductor of the Catholic Choir (1946–91) and city organist (1956–83) in Haarlem. He was prof. of organ at the Inst. for Catholic Church Music in Utrecht (1946–64), and then at the Amsterdam Cons. (1965–85). As an organist, he toured as a recitalist, being particularly admired for his improvisational skills. His repertoire was an extensive one, and included the complete organ works of Franck and H. Andriessen.

WORKS: ORCH.: 2 organ concertos (1941, 1964); *Cantabile* (1952); *Suite Concertante* for Organ and Strings (1976); *Dans van de eeuwige bomen* (1986). **CHAMBER:** Sonatine for Violin and Cello (1937); *Fantasie* for Violin and Piano (1950); Concerto for Organ, 2 Horns, 2 Trumpets, and 2 Trombones (1967); *Fantasia* for Flute and Piano (1985); *Sequensen* for Flute and Piano (1989). **O r g a n :** Sonata (1940); Prelude and Fugue (1940); Inventions (1945); 10 Pieces (2 parts, 1946); Ricercare (1950); *Octo Fantasiae super themata Gregoriana* (1953); *12 Images* (1969); *Tres Meditationes Sacra* (1992–93). **VOCAL:** *Jam lucis orto sidere* for High Voice and Orch. (1942–43); *Stabat Mater* for Alto, Tenor, Chorus, and Chamber Orch. (1952); *Mater Sanctus Laelitiae* for Women's Chorus, Flute, English Horn, and Bassoon (1957); *Super omnia,* cantata for Alto, Chorus, and Organ (1960); *5 noëls français* for Alto and 10 Winds (1963); *Laudate Dominum (Psalm 150)* for Chorus and Organ (1968); *Te Deum* for Chorus and Orch. (1979); *In Honorem Sancti Bavonis* for Youth Chorus and Orch. (1983); 10 masses; many motets.—NS/LK/DM

Kletzki, Paul (originally, **Pawel Klecki**), distinguished Polish-born Swiss conductor; b. Łódź, March 21, 1900; d. while rehearsing the Royal Liverpool Phil. in Liverpool, March 5, 1973. He studied composition at the Warsaw Cons., where he also received instruction in violin from Mlynarski. After further studies at the Berlin Academy of Music, he played in the Łódź Phil. (1914–19). He was active as a conductor and composer in Berlin (1921–33), then taught composition at Milan's Scuola Superiora di Musica. At the outbreak of World War II (1939), he settled in Switzerland, becoming a naturalized Swiss citizen in 1947. After the war, he pursued a notable conducting career, appearing as a guest conductor with many of the major European orchs.; he also conducted in North and South America, and maintained a close association with the Israel Phil. He was music director of the Dallas Sym. Orch. (1958–62), the Bern Sym. Orch. (1964–66), and l'Orchestre de la Suisse Romande in Geneva (1968–70). He was a fine interpreter of the Romantic orch. repertoire, excelling in both the Austro-German and the Slavic schools. He composed 4 syms., a Piano Concerto, a Violin Concerto, chamber music, and songs, but most of his works were destroyed by the havoc wreaked during World War II.—NS/LK/DM

Kleven, Arvid, Norwegian composer; b. Drontheim, Nov. 29, 1899; d. Oslo, Nov. 23, 1929. He studied in Oslo, Paris, and Berlin. From 1919 he played flute in the National Theater Orch. in Christiania, and in the Phil. Orch. there. His early neo-Romantic style developed along expressionist lines. Among his works are *Sinfonia libera in due parte* (1927), *Symfonisk fantasi* for Orch., the symphonic poems *Lotusland* (1922) and *Skogens sovn* (The Sleeping Forest), songs with orch., Violin Sonata, Cello Sonata, and piano pieces.—NS/LK/DM

Klička, Josef, Bohemian organist, choral conductor, and composer, father of **Václav Klička;** b. Klattau, Dec. 15, 1855; d. there, March 28, 1937. He studied with Skuhersky in Prague, then conducted various choral societies there. From 1906 to 1920 he was inspector of music in Bohemia. He was appointed prof. of organ at the Prague Cons. in 1885 and taught until his retirement in 1924. He wrote an opera, *Spánila mylnářka* (Die Schöne Mullerin; Prague, 1886), 9 masses, 2 oratorios, chamber works, and many organ pieces.
Bibl.: K. Hoffmeister, *J. K.* (Prague, 1944).—NS/LK/DM

Klička, Václav, Czech harpist, teacher, and composer, son of **Josef Klička;** b. Prague, Aug. 1, 1882; d. there, May 22, 1953. He studied harp with Hanuš Trneček and theory and composition with Karel Knittl and Karel Stecker at the Prague Cons. After playing in the Pilsen theater orch. (1903–10), he made tours of Europe as a soloist with orchs. and as a recitalist. From 1922 until the Nazi occupation of his homeland he was a prof. of harp at the Prague Cons. Following the liberation of his country in 1945, he resumed his activities. He composed much harp music and also prepared various arrangements for the harp.—NS/LK/DM

Klien, Walter, admired Austrian pianist; b. Graz, Nov. 27, 1928; d. Vienna, Feb. 9, 1991. He studied in Frankfurt am Main (1939–45), Graz (1946–49), and with Josef Dichler at the Vienna Academy of Music (1950–53);

he also was a student of Michelangeli (piano) and Hindemith (composition). In 1951 and 1952 he took the Busoni prize in Bolzano, and in 1953 the Bösendorfer prize in Vienna. Subsequently he made extensive tours as a soloist with the leading orchs. and as a recitalist. He also toured in duo concerts with Wolfgang Schneiderhan from 1963. Klien displayed a special affinity for the music of Haydn, Mozart, Schubert, Schumann, and Brahms.—NS/LK/DM

Klima, Alois, Czech conductor; b. Klatovy, Dec. 21, 1905; d. Prague, June 11, 1980. He began his musical training with his father, and after taking courses in mathematics and physics at the Univ. of Prague, he studied with Dědeček and Doležil (conducting) and Křička and Řídký (composition) at the Prague Cons. He conducted the radio orchs. in Košice (1936) and Ostrava (1936–38), and then was chief conductor of the Prague Opera Studio (1939–46) and the Prague Radio Sym. Orch. (1950–70); he also was a teacher at the Prague Cons. and Academy of Music.—NS/LK/DM

Klimov, Valery (Alexandrovich), Russian violinist; b. Kiev, Oct. 16, 1931. His father was a professional conductor and a pedagogue. Klimov studied in Odessa and with D. Oistrakh at the Moscow Cons., graduating in 1956. He won 1st prize in the Prague and Paris competitions (1956) and then at the Tchaikovsky Competition in Moscow (1958), which opened for him great opportunities for world tours. He played with much success in Europe, the U.S., and Australia.—NS/LK/DM

Klindworth, Karl, eminent German pianist, conductor, pedagogue, and editor; b. Hannover, Sept. 25, 1830; d. Stolpe, near Potsdam, July 27, 1916. He learned to play violin and piano as a child, and obtained work as conductor of a traveling opera company when he was only 17. After travels in Germany as a concert pianist, he went to Weimar to study with Liszt (1852–53). In 1854 he went to London, where he remained until 1868, establishing himself as a popular piano teacher. When Wagner was in London in 1855, they became friends; as a result of his admiration for Wagner, Klindworth undertook the most important work of his life, the arrangement in vocal scores of Wagner's tetralogy *Der Ring des Nibelungen.* In 1868 he was engaged as a prof. at the newly founded Moscow Cons. at the invitation of its director, Nikolai Rubinstein. After Rubinstein's death in 1881, Klindworth returned to Germany, and from 1882 to 1987, was one of the principal conductors of the Berlin Phil. In 1884 he established in Berlin his own Klavierschule, which, in 1893, was merged with the Scharwenka Cons. in Berlin, as Konservatorium der Musik Klindworth-Scharwenka, which became one of the most famous music schools in Germany. Klindworth was an exceptionally competent arranger and music ed. Apart from his masterly transcriptions of Wagner's operas, he made an arrangement for 2 pianos of Schubert's C major Sym. He also wrote a number of virtuoso pieces for piano, of which the brilliant *Polonaise-Fantaisie* and 24 grand études in all keys enjoyed some vogue among pianists.

BIBL.: H. Leichtentritt, *Das Konservatorium der Musik K.-Scharwenka, 1881–1931* (Berlin, 1931).—**NS/LK/DM**

Klingenstein, Bernhard, German composer; b. probably in Peiting, near Schongau, Upper Bavaria, 1545 or 1546; d. Augsburg, March 1, 1614. He settled in Augsburg and began his training at its Cathedral choir school. In 1574 he was made Kapellmeister of the Cathedral. During his tenure there, he also studied composition with Johannes de Cleve. He later also served as Kapellmeister of the Jesuit church of St. Salvador. His collection of 34 Latin motets, *Liber primus s[acrum] symphoniarum* for 1 to 8 Voices (Munich, 1607), contains a setting of *Cantate Domino* for Bass Voice and Continuo, the earliest solo vocal concerto publ. in Germany. He also ed. 2 vols. of sacred music (Dillingen, 1604–05), in which 10 of his own works were included.

BIBL.: A. Singer, *Leben und Werke des Augsburger Domkapell-meisters B.us K. (1545–1614)* (diss., Univ. of Munich, 1921). —**LK/DM**

Klobučar, Berislav, Yugoslav conductor; b. Zagreb, Aug. 28, 1924. He was educated at the Zagreb Academy of Music, and studied conducting with Lovro von Matačić and Clemens Krauss. He was conductor at the Zagreb National Theater (1941–51). In 1953 he appeared at the Vienna State Opera, where he became a regular conductor. He was chief conductor of the Graz Phil. and Opera (1961–72). After serving as principal conductor at Stockholm's Royal Theater (1972–81), he was music director of the Orchestre Philharmonique de Nice (1982–88). He also appeared as a guest conductor with the major European and U.S. opera houses. —**NS/LK/DM**

Klöffler, Johann Friedrich, German conductor and composer; b. Kassel, April 20, 1725; d. Burgsteinfurt, Feb. 21, 1790. He became a musician and official at the court of the Counts of Bentheim and Steinfurt in 1750, organizing the court orch. in 1752, becoming Konzertmeister in 1753 and music director in 1754; in 1757 he also received a judicial appointment. He became well known as a conductor via tours of Europe, visiting Vienna, London, Moscow, and St. Petersburg (1781–87). In 1789 he retired from his court duties. He wrote numerous syms., many concertos, and much chamber music. His *Bataille Symphony* (1777) was written for 2 orchs., representing two opposing armies.

BIBL.: W. Götze, *J.F. K. (1725–1790)* (diss., Univ. of Münster, 1965).—**LK/DM**

Klose, Friedrich (Karl Wilhelm), Swiss composer; b. Karlsruhe (of Swiss parents), Nov. 29, 1862; d. Ruvigliana, near Lugano, Dec. 24, 1942. He studied with V. Lachner in Karlsruhe and Ruthardt in Geneva, then with Bruckner in Vienna (1886–91). He taught in Switzerland, Austria, and Germany before joining the faculty at Munich's Akademie der Tonkunst (1907–19). He publ. *Meine Lehrjahre bei Bruckner* (Regensburg, 1927) and *Bayreuth* (Regensburg, 1929).

WORKS: *Ilsebill,* dramatic sym. (Munich, Oct. 29, 1905); symphonic poems: *Elfenreigen* (1892), *Das Leben ein Traum* (1896), and *Festzug* (1913); Mass (1889); an oratorio, *Der Sonne-Geist* (Basel, 1918); String Quartet (1911); organ works; songs.

BIBL.: R. Louis, *F. K. und seine symphonische Dichtung "Das Leben ein Traum"* (Munich, 1905); H. Knappe, *F. K.: Eine Studie* (Munich, 1921); idem, ed., *F. K. zum 80. Geburtstag* (Lugano, 1942).—**NS/LK/DM**

Klosé, Hyacinthe-Eléonore, noted French clarinetist and pedagogue; b. Corfu, Oct. 11, 1808; d. Paris, Aug. 29, 1880. He studied with Frédéric Berr at the Paris Cons., where he then taught (1838–68). With the instrument maker Louis-Auguste Buffet, he developed a clarinet utilizing the ring-key system of the Boehm flute, which was first shown in 1839 and patented in 1844. He publ. *Grande méthode pour la clarinette à anneaux mobiles* (1844) based on that system. He also did much to promote the then-novel saxophone, and wrote some music both for it and for the clarinet. He was made a Chevalier de la Légion d'Honneur in 1864. —**NS/LK/DM**

Klose, Margarete, esteemed German contralto; b. Berlin, Aug. 6, 1902; d. there, Dec. 14, 1968. She studied at the Klindworth-Scharwenka Cons. in Berlin and received vocal training from Bültemann and Marschalk. She made her operatic debut in Ulm in 1927, then sang in Kassel (1928–29) and Mannheim (1929–31). She was a leading member of the Berlin State Opera (1931–49; 1955–61); also sang at the Bayreuth Festivals (1936–42) and London's Covent Garden (1935, 1937), and was a member of the Berlin Städtische Opera (1949–58). She was particularly praised for her Wagner and Verdi portrayals.—**NS/LK/DM**

Klotz (originally Kloz), family of outstanding German violin makers. Their instruments were brought into repute by Mathias Klotz (b. Mittenwald, June 11, 1653; d. there, Aug. 16, 1743), who served an apprenticeship with Giovanni Railich, a Paduan maker of lutes and other instruments. His violins date from late in his career, and are very rare. His son, Sebastian Klotz (b. Mittenwald, Jan. 18, 1696; d. there, Jan. 20, 1775), produced remarkable violins after Italian models. There followed, in the 18th century, several other violin makers named Klotz, but their relationship to the family cannot be established.—**NS/LK/DM**

Klucevsek, Guy, American composer and accordionist; b. N.Y., Feb. 26, 1947. He grew up in a Slovenian community in Pa., where he learned to play polkas. He studied theory and composition at the Ind. Univ. of Pa. (B.A., 1969) and with Subotnick at the Univ. of Pittsburgh (M.A., 1971) and the Calif. Inst. of the Arts (1971–72). In 1980 he discovered the polkas of Cajun and Texan/Mexican origin, and in 1986 he invited a number of composers to contribute to his recording *Polkas from the Fringe* (1987). He also encouraged and created virtuoso accordion music in other styles, and premiered various works by composers including Henry Cowell, Lois Vierk, and John Zorn. Among his compositions are *Sea Chandeliers* for Gamelan (1985), *Scenes from a Mirage* for Accordion (1986), and *Flying Vegetables of the Apocalypse* for Violin, Cello, and Accordion (1988). —**NS/LK/DM**

Klugh, Earl, American guitarist; b. Detroit, Mich., Sept. 16, 1954. He had studied piano and guitar as a child, opting for the guitar as his main instrument before hitting his teens. Influenced heavily by Chet Atkins and Lenny Breau, he also has a lifelong affection for show tunes and soundtrack music, all of which have shown up in his light, jazz-inflected playing and in many of the songs he chooses to cover on his albums. He was discovered while teaching guitar lessons in a Detroit music store by Yusef Lateef, who used the young guitarist on his 1970 *Suite 16.* Before he was out of his teens he was playing electric guitar with George Benson and with Chick Corea's Return to Forever. Upon returning to Detroit in the mid-1970s, he shifted his allegiance from electric to acoustic guitar and recorded his first album for Blue Note. Since that time he has led his own groups and recorded three albums with Bob James, including *One on One,* which won Klugh a Grammy. He has also received co-billing on an album he did with one of his old mentors, George Benson (*Collaboration*), and written music for the soundtracks *How to Beat the High Cost of Living* and *Marvin & Tige.* His later albums have found him experimenting more with Latino and Brazilian rhythms.

Disc.: *Love Songs* (1976); *Magic in Your Eyes* (1976); *Ballads* (1976); *Finger Painting* (1977); *Heart String* (1979); *One on One* (1979); *Crazy for You* (1981); *Two of a Kind* (1982); *Wishful Thinking* (1983); *Delta Lady* (1984); *Soda Fountain Shuffle* (1984); *Nightsongs* (1985); *Life Stories* (1986); *Journey* (1986); *Midnight in San Juan* (1989); *Solo Guitar* (1989); *Whispers and Promises* (1989); *The Earl Klugh Trio, Vol. 1* (1991); *The Best of Earl Klugh* (1991); *The Best of Earl Klugh, Vol. 2* (1992); *Cool* (1992); *Late Night Guitar* (1993); *Move* (1993); *Sudden Burst of Energy* (1995); *Peculiar Situationi* (1999).—**GM**

Klughardt, August (Friedrich Martin), German conductor and composer; b. Cothen, Nov. 30, 1847; d. Rosslau, near Dresden, Aug. 3, 1902. He was a pupil of Blassmann and Reichel in Dresden. From 1867 to 1868 he was a theater conductor in Posen, and then held similar posts in Neustrelitz (1868–69) and Lübeck (1869). He served as court music director in Weimar (1869–73), where he became a friend of Liszt. He then was music director in Neustrelitz (1873–82) and Dessau (from 1882).

Works: Dramatic: Opera: *Mirjam* (Weimar, 1871); *Iwein* (Neustrelitz, 1879); *Gudrun* (Neustrelitz, 1882); *Die Hochzeit Mönchs* (Dessau, Nov. 10, 1886). **Orch.:** 5 syms.; Cello Concerto (1894); Violin Concerto (1895). **Other:** Chamber music; piano pieces; songs.

Bibl.: L. Gerlach, *A. K.: Sein Leben und seine Werke* (Leipzig, 1902).—**NS/LK/DM**

Klusák, Jan, Czech composer; b. Prague, April 18, 1934. He studied theory with Řídký and Bořkovec at the Prague Academy of Music (1953–57).

Works: Dramatic: Opera: *Proces* (The Trial), after Kafka (1966); *Viola* (1984–85); *Zpráva pro akademii* (Report for the Academy), chamber opera after Kafka (1993–97). **Ballet:** *Stories from Tapestries* (1988). **Film:** *The Count of Monte Cristo* (1993; for H. Fescourt's silent film of 1928); *Erotikon* (1994). **Orch.:** Concertino for Flute and Strings (1955); *Partita* for Strings (1955); 3 syms. (1956, 1959, 1960); Concerto Grosso for Wind Quintet and Strings (1957); *Variations on a Theme of Mahler,* after the latter's 5th Sym. (1960–62); *Inventions I* (1961), *II* (1962), *III* (1962), *IV* (1964), *VII* (1973), and *VIII, Quadratura orbis* (Squaring of the Circle; 1973) for Chamber Orch.; *2 Czech Dances* for Wind Orch. (1964); *Lyric Fantasy, Hommage à Grieg* (1965); *Le Forgeron harmonieux,* after Handel's so-called *Harmonious Blacksmith* (1966); *Pasticcio olandese per orchestra, A Friesland Friday* (1969–70); *Hamburger Doppelinvention* (1974); *Kleine Farbenlehre, Hommage à Goethe* (1974–75); *6 Small Preludes* (1984); *Missing Mozart,* fantasy for Chamber Orch. (1991); Concertino for Oboe and Small Orch. (1991); *Tetragrammaton sive Nomina Eius* (1992). **Chamber:** *Music to the Fountain* for Wind Quintet (1954); 5 string quartets (1956; 1961–62; 1975; 1990; 1994); *Obrazy* (Pictures) for 12 Wind Instruments (1960); *Monoinvention* for Cello (1962); *Risposte* for Violin (1963); Sonata for Violin and Wind Instruments (1964–65); *Invention V, Hra v šachy* (Game of Chess) for Wind Quintet (1965); *1–4–3–2–5–6–7–10–9–8–11* (invertible all-interval 12-tone series) for Flute (1965); *Invention VI* for Wind Quintet and String Quartet (1969); *Contrapunto fiorito* for 8 Instruments (1966); *Short John* for Cimbalom (1971); *Jupiter-Duo* for Clarinet and Cello (1973); Percussion Sonata (1974); *Solo* for Trumpet (1975–76); *Die heilige Zahl,* duo for Violin and Percussion (1975–76); *Tango-Polka* for Clarinet, Trumpet, Cello, and Piano (1980); *Variations* for 2 Harps (1982); *Diario* for Cello (1982); *Once There Were 3 Goddesses* for Brass Quintet and Harp (1983); *Fantasia on Adam Michna of Otradovice* for Brass Quintet and Harp (1983); *Šmidří suita* for 4 Saxophones (1983); *Trigon* for Flute, Marimba, and Guitar (1983); *The Art of Harmony* for 13 Winds and Double Bass (1992); Tuba Sonatina (1997); piano pieces. **Vocal:** *Prislovi* (Proverbs) for Low Voice and Wind Instruments (1959); *4 Small Vocal Exercises* for Narrator and 11 Wind Instruments, after Kafka (1960); *Radix nativitatis I. S.* (memorial for Igor Stravinsky) for Voice, Flute, Clarinet, Viola, and Piano (1972); *Bridal Cantata 1979* for Men's Chorus and Orch. (1979); *The Moon in Zenith* for Mezzo-soprano, Clarinet, Viola, and Piano, after Anna Akhmatova (1981); solo songs. —**NS/LK/DM**

Kmentt, Waldemar, Austrian tenor; b. Vienna, Feb. 2, 1929. He was a student at the Vienna Academy of Music of Adolf Vogel, Elisabeth Rado, and Hans Duhan. While still a student, he toured the Netherlands and Belgium with a student ensemble of the Academy. In 1950 he made his formal debut as a soloist in Beethoven's 9th Sym. in Vienna, and then appeared as the Prince in *The Love for 3 Oranges* at the Vienna Volksoper in 1951. In the latter year, he became a member of the Vienna State Opera, where he appeared as Jaquino at the reopening of the opera house in 1955. He also sang regularly in Salzburg (from 1955) and Düsseldorf (from 1958), and made guest appearances in Milan, Paris, Rome, Bayreuth, Munich, and other operatic centers. As a concert artist, he sang widely in Europe as well. He acquired a fine reputation for his performances of works from the Austro-German repertoire.—**NS/LK/DM**

Knab, Armin, German composer; b. Neu-Schleichach, Feb. 19, 1881; d. Bad Wörishofen, June 23, 1951. He studied piano in Würzburg. From 1934 to 1943 he taught at the Hochschule für Musik-Erziehung in Berlin. He was particularly esteemed for his lieder. He followed the Romantic tradition, but tended toward a more severe modal style in his larger works.

WORKS: VOCAL: Sacred Cantatas: *Mariae Geburt* (1928); *Vanitas mundi* (1946); *Engelsgruss* (1950). **Musical Fairy Tale:** *Sneewittchen and Rumpelstilzchen.* **Folk-Song Cantatas:** *Singt und klingt* (1934); *Gruss Gott, du schöner Maien* (1935); *Glück auf, ihr Bergleute* (1946). **OTHER:** A great number of choral works; many instrumental pieces for school use.

BIBL.: O. Lang, *A. K., Ein Meister deutscher Liedkunst* (Munich, 1937; 2nd ed., rev., 1981).—NS/LK/DM

Knabe, William (actually, **Valentine Wilhelm Ludwig**), German-born American piano manufacturer; b. Kreuzberg, near Oppeln, Prussia, June 3, 1803; d. Baltimore, May 21, 1864. He settled in the U.S. in 1833. He formed a partnership to manufacture pianos with Henry Gaehle in Baltimore in 1839, which continued until the latter's death in 1855. The business was continued by Knabe's sons and grandsons until it was merged with the American Piano Co. in 1908. It became a part of the Aeolian American Corp. in 1932. —NS/LK/DM

Knack, The, 1970s-era pop sensations (f. 1978). **MEMBERSHIP:** Doug Fieger, voc., gtr. (b. Detroit, Aug. 20, 1952); Berton Averre, gtr. (b. Van Nuys, Calif., Dec. 13); Bruce Gary, drm. (b. Burbank, Calif., April 7, 1952); Prescott Niles, bs. (b. N.Y., May 2, 19); Billy Ward, drm.; Terry Bozzio, drm. (b. Dec. 27, 1950).

In the mid-1970s, Doug Fieger moved from Detroit to L.A. with his band Sky. They recorded two albums for RCA that stiffed. While in L.A., he met Berton Averre and they started writing songs together. When Sky dived, they put a band together and started playing the nascent late 1970s club scene in L.A. (most of the rock clubs had become discos). Their power pop band became a major attraction in Los Angeles, with their bouncy guitar licks and buoyant beat. Musicians like Bruce Springsteen, Ray Manzarek, and Tom Petty offered their stamp of approval by jamming on stage with them. By the end of 1978, nearly a dozen record companies were bidding for their services. Capitol won out and signed the band.

The band was so well-rehearsed, they went into the studio with producer Mike Chapman (Blondie, Pat Benetar) and turned out their debut album, *Get the Knack,* in 11 days for under $20,000. The first single, the infectious "My Sharona" had a simple, incredibly catchy guitar hook, Fieger's nervous vocals, and the group's powerful harmonies. It zoomed to the top of the charts where it stayed for six weeks. The song became epidemic and was virtually inescapable during the entire summer of 1979. The album also topped the chart for five weeks, going gold in less than two weeks, platinum in seven. Eventually it went double platinum; "Sharona" sold gold and the second single "Good Girls Don't" skirted the Top Ten, peaking at #11.

The group's success was so sudden that an inevitable backlash started. People began wearing "Knuke the Knack" T-shirts. Listeners became weary of their sound. Released less than a year after their debut, *...But the*

Little Girls Understand only went gold, hitting #15, and the single "Baby Talks Dirty" scraped into the Top 40 at #38. Taking on Jack Douglas (John Lennon, The Who) to produce their third album, *Round Trip* was an even bigger commercial failure, barely making the top 100 (#93) and not charting any singles at all. The tour was even more disappointing and the band broke up in disgust in 1981. Members of the band went into studio work and joined other bands. By 1987, Fieger, Averre, and Niles decided to give the Knack another shot and started playing together again with drummer Bill Ward, culminating in a Don Was produced album *Serious Fun* that was universally ignored. Again the band drifted apart, with Fieger taking on acting assignments on the TV series *Roseanne* and writing songs for other artists, including the Manhattan Transfer's Grammy-winning *Brazil* album. He recorded a Was-produced solo record that didn't see the light of day until Fieger released it himself in 1999.

While the Knack went their separate ways, "Sharona" was much more tenacious. The song became a pop culture touchstone for the summer of 1979 and was featured in several films, most notably *Reality Bites.* The group once again made tentative moves toward playing together again, first recording "No Matter What" for a Badfinger tribute and "Don't Look Back" for a Bruce Springsteen tribute. They played several shows, with Terry Bozzio now on the drummer's throne. Rhino Records signed them, and while their album *Zoom* met a similar fate to *Serious Fun*, the group continued to play together on occasion. Averre also had a musical he wrote produced, while Fieger became a pitchman for vintage guitars in Los Angeles.

DISC.: *Get the Knack* (1979); *...But the Little Girls Understand* (1979); *Round Trip* (1981); *Serious Fun* (1991); *Zoom* (1998).—HB

Knaifel, Alexander (Aronovich), Russian composer; b. Tashkent, Nov. 28, 1943. He began his training in the special music school at the Leningrad Cons. (1950–61). After attending the Moscow Cons. (1961–63), he studied composition with Arapov at the Leningrad Cons. (1963–67). In his works, Knaifel employs a variety of modern compositional techniques.

WORKS: DRAMATIC: *Kentervilskoe prividenie* (The Canterville Ghost), chamber opera (1965–66); ballets; film scores. **ORCH.:** *Burleska* for Trombone and Strings (1963); *Dream,* fantasia for Chamber Orch. (1963); *131* for Viola, Double Bass, Winds, and Percussion (1964); *Onrush,* ballet-sym. (1964); *Seekers of the Future City* for Strings, Percussion, and Organ (1965); *Magdalene Repentant,* choreographic scene (1967); *Medea,* choreographic sym. (1968); *Joan,* passion for 13 Instrumental Groups (1970–78); *Early Cranes* (1979); *Vera* for Strings (1980); *Madness* for Chamber Orch. (1987); *Litania* (1988). **CHAMBER:** *Dyad,* 2 pieces for Flute, Viola, Piano, and Percussion (1963); *Ostinati* for Violin and Cello (1964); *Disarmament,* choreographical striptease for Ensemble (1966); *Lamento* for Cello (1967); *Tournament Music* for Horn and Piano (1967); *A prima vista* for 4 Percussionists (1972); *Rafferti* for Jazz Ensemble (1980); *Yes* for Soloist and Ensemble (1980); *Nika* for 17 Players (1983–84); *Agnus Dei* for 4 Instrumentalists (1987). **VOCAL:** *Chuck it into My Garden* for Chorus and Orch. (1962); *Confession* for Reader and Percussion Ensemble (1963); *Petrograd Sparrows,* suite-phantasmagoria for Boy's Chorus and Chamber Orch. (1967);

150,000,000, dithyrambe for Chorus and Chamber Orch. (1968); *Monodia* for Woman's Voice (1968); *Lenin's Letter to the Members of the Central Committee* for Unison Bass Chorus (1969); *Anna Akhmatova: Midnight Poems* for 4 Performers (1972–73); *Status Nascendi* for 3 Performing Groups (1975); *Ainana* for Chamber Chorus, Percussion, and Tape (1978); *Stupid Horse*, 15 stories for Singer and Piano (1981); *Accidental* for Girl Soloist, Chorus, String Orch., and Organ (1982); *Pagan Rock* for Bass Chorus, Percussion, and Rock Group (1982); *Opposition* for Bass Chorus and Orch. (1984); *God* for 2 Choruses (1985); *The Wings of a Lackey*, vocal/choreographic fresco (1986); *Through the Rainbow of Unwilling Tears* for Singer and Cello (1988).—**NS/LK/DM**

Knap, Rolf, Dutch composer; b. Amsterdam, Oct. 17, 1937. He studied oboe at the Amsterdam Cons., took private composition lessons with Karel Mengelberg, and then studied electronic music at the Inst. of Sonology of the Univ. of Utrecht. He was an orch. oboist (1960–67), and then taught oboe.

WORKS: *(Sym)phonic Piece* for Orch. (1971); *Le Couple(t)* for Voice, Piano, and Electronics (1971); *Dilemmaniana for Marrie* for Narrator, Cello, and Live Electronics (1972); *Zelomanniana* for Oboe and Piano (1974); 2 song cycles: *Liederen van Doofstommen* (Songs of Deaf-Mutes; 1974, 1976); *Harmonische reflecties* for Piano (1976; rev. 1984); *De boetseerder* for Soprano and Piano (1978).—**NS/LK/DM**

Knape, Walter, German musicologist, conductor, and composer; b. Bernburg, Jan. 14, 1906. He studied at the Univ. of Leipzig, receiving his Ph.D. in 1934 with the diss. *Die Sinfonien von Karl Friedrich Abel.* He then joined its faculty. From 1948 to 1957 he was conductor of the Leipzig Sing-Akademie and the Phil. Choir; he also taught at the Berlin Hochschule für Musik (1954–57), and subsequently at the univs. of Hamburg, Hannover, and Cuxhaven. He devoted much time to the study of the life and works of Abel; ed. a complete edition of his works (16 vols., Cuxhaven, 1958–74) and a bibliographic-thematic catalog (Cuxhaven, 1971); also wrote *Karl Friedrich Abel: Leben und Werk eines frühklassischen Komponisten* (Bremen, 1973). He composed several symphonic and choral works, chamber music, and many piano pieces.—**NS/LK/DM**

Knapp, Phebe (Phoebe) Palmer, American philanthropist and composer of gospel songs; b. N.Y., March 8, 1839; d. Poland Springs, Maine, July 10, 1908. She and her husband, Joseph F. Knapp, the founder of the Metropolitan Life Insurance Co. of N.Y., were actively engaged in philanthropic endeavors as members of the Methodist Episcopal Church. She wrote over 500 gospel songs and publ. the collections *Notes of Joy* (1869) and *Bible School Songs* (1873). A friend and benefactor of the poet Fanny Crosby, she wrote the music to her *Assurance* ("Blessed Assurance, Jesus is Mine"). It was publ. in 1873 and became one of the most popular works of its kind.—**NS/LK/DM**

Knappertsbusch, Hans, eminent German conductor; b. Elberfeld, March 12, 1888; d. Munich, Oct. 25, 1965. He studied philosophy at the Univ. of Bonn before pursuing musical training with Steinbach and Lohse at the Cologne Cons. (1908–12). He was conductor in Mülheim and served as asst. conductor at the Bayreuth Festivals (1910–12), then conducted in Bochum (1912–13). He was director of opera in Elberfeld (1913–18); subsequently conducted opera in Leipzig (1918–19) and Dessau (1919–22). In 1922 he became Generalmusikdirektor of the Bavarian State Opera in Munich, a post he held with great distinction until resigning in the face of Nazi pressure in 1936; then conducted at the Vienna State Opera (1936–45); was also a conductor with the Vienna Phil. (1937–44). After World War II, he returned to Germany and made his home in Munich. He conducted at the Salzburg Festivals (1947–50; 1954–55); was a regular guest conductor with the Vienna Phil. (1947–64) and at the Bayreuth Festivals (from 1951). He was one of the great interpreters of the operas of Wagner and Richard Strauss. The authority and spontaneity he brought to such masterworks as *Götterdämmerung* and *Parsifal* were extraordinary.

BIBL.: R. Betz and W. Panofsky, *K.* (Ingolstadt, 1958). —**NS/LK/DM**

Knecht, Justin Heinrich, German organist, conductor, music theorist, and composer; b. Biberach, Sept. 30, 1752; d. there, Dec. 1, 1817. He was an organist and music director in Biberach from 1771 to the end of his life, traveling only briefly to Stuttgart, where he was court conductor from 1806 until 1808. Despite his provincial field of activity, he attained considerable repute in Germany through his compositions and theoretical writings. He was a follower of the Vogler system of harmony; taught chord building by thirds up to chords of the 11th on all degrees of the scale. He wrote 10 stage works, mostly Singspiels, sacred works, and the programmatic sym. *Le Portrait musical de la nature* (c. 1784), to which he supplied a programmatic description, seemingly anticipating Beethoven's *Pastoral Sym.*

WRITINGS: *Erklärung einiger...missverstandenen Grundsätze aus der Vogler's schen Theorie* (Ulm, 1785); *Gemeinnützliches Elementarwerk der Harmonie und des Generalbasses* (4 parts, 1792–98); *Kleines alphabetisches Wörterbuch der vornehmsten und interessantesten Artikel aus der musikalischen Theorie* (1795); *Vollständige Orgelschule für Anfänger und Geübtere* (3 parts, 1795–98); *Allgemeiner musikalischer Katechismus* (Biberach, 1803); *Luthers Verdienst um Musik und Poesie* (1817).

BIBL.: E. Kauffmann, *J.H. K.* (Tübingen, 1892); A. Bopp, *J.H. K.* (Biberach, 1917).—**NS/LK/DM**

Kneisel, Franz, German violinist and pedagogue; b. Bucharest (of German parents), Jan. 26, 1865; d. N.Y., March 26, 1926. He studied at the Bucharest Cons., graduating at the age of 14. In 1879 he went to Vienna, where he became a pupil of Grun and Hellmesberger at the Cons. He made his debut on Dec. 31, 1882, then was concertmaster of the Bilse Orch. in Berlin (1884–85). From 1885 to 1903 he was concertmaster of the Boston Sym. Orch. In 1886 he organized the celebrated Kneisel Quartet (with Emmanuel Fiedler as 2nd violin; Louis Svecenski, viola; Fritz Giese, cello), which gave performances of high quality in Boston, N.Y., and other American cities, and also in Europe, obtaining world fame before dissolving in 1917. He taught at N.Y.'s Inst. of Musical Art (from 1905). Kneisel was admirable in ensemble playing, and his service to the cause of chamber music in America was very great. He was made honorary Mus.Doc. by Yale Univ. (1911) and by Princeton Univ. (1915). He composed *Grand Concert Étude* for Violin, publ. *Advanced Exercises* for the violin (1900), and ed. a collection of violin pieces (3 vols., 1900).—NS/LK/DM

Knight, Joseph Philip, English clergyman, organist, and composer; b. Bradford-on-Avon, July 26, 1812; d. Great Yarmouth, June 2, 1887. He studied organ with Corfe in Bristol. During a stay in the U.S. (1839–41), he wrote his most celebrated song, "Rocked in the Cradle of the Deep." After 2 years as vicar and organist at St. Agnes in the Scilly Islands, he returned to England and continued to write songs. These included "Venice," "Say What Shall My Song Be Tonight?," "The Dream," "All on the Summer Sea," and "She Wore a Wreath of Roses."—NS/LK/DM

Knipper, Lev (Konstantinovich), important Russian composer; b. Tiflis, Dec. 3, 1898; d. Moscow, July 30, 1974. He studied piano with Gnesina and composition with Glière and Zhilyaev at Moscow's Gnessin School; also took private lessons with Jarnach in Berlin and Julius Weissmann in Freiburg im Breisgau. Under the influence of western European trends, he wrote music in a fairly advanced style of composition, but soon abandoned these experiments and devoted himself to the study of folk music of different nationalities of the Soviet Union.

WORKS: DRAMATIC: Opera: *Severniy veter* (The North Wind; 1929–30; Moscow, March 30, 1930); *Marya* (1936–38); *Aktrisa* (The Actress; 1942); *Na Baykale* (On the Baikal Lake; 1946–48); *Korenzhizni* (The Source of Life; 1948–49); also ballets. **ORCH.:** 14 syms. (1929–54); orch. suites on ethnic motifs; overtures; 3 violin concertos (1944, 1965, 1967); 2 cello concertos (1962, 1972); Clarinet Concerto (1966); Oboe Concerto (1967); Bassoon Concerto (1969). **CHAMBER:** 3 string quartets; other chamber music; piano pieces. **VOCAL:** Songs. —NS/LK/DM

Knittel, Krzysztof, Polish composer; b. Warsaw, May 1, 1947. He received training in composition from Tadeusz Baird, Andrzej Dobrowolski, and Włodzimierz Kotoński, and in computer music from Lejaren Hiller at the State Higher School of Music in Warsaw. After studying programming at the Mathematical Inst. of the Polish Academy of Sciences (1974–75), he was active at the Center for the Creative and Performing Arts at the State Univ. of N.Y. in Buffalo (1978). From 1973 he was associated with the Polish Radio Experimental Studio. In 1986 he founded the Freight Train Ensemble, with which he performed with various poets, artists, and jazz musicians. With Marek Chołoniewski, he founded the CH & K Studio in 1989, with which he made appearances throughout Europe and North America. In 1996 he co-founded the European Improvisation Orch. From 1995 to 1998 he was director of the Warsaw Autumn International Festival of Contemporary Music. He

served as vice president (1995–97) and president (from 1999) of the Polish Composers' Union. Knittel received the Solidarity Award in 1985 and the award of the Foundation for Contemporary Performance Arts in N.Y. in 1998.

WORKS: *à la Santé* for Clarinet, Trombone, Cello, and Piano (1974; Berlin, Dec. 6, 1975); *Lipps* for Jazz Trio and Sym. Orch. (1974–78; Poznań, April 19, 1990); *Robak Zdobywca* (The Conqueror Worm) for Tape (Poznań, April 4, 1976); *dorikos* for String Quartet and Tape (1976–77; Warsaw, Sept. 23, 1977); *resztki* (Odds and Ends) for Tape (Warsaw, Sept. 19, 1978); *5 Pieces* for Cello and Piano (1979–80); *Niskie dźwięki* (Low Sounds) for Instruments, Voices, and Tape (1980); *Norcet 1* and *2* for Computer (Warsaw, Sept. 24, 1980); *Głos kobiecy* (Woman's Voice), ballet for Percussion and Tape (Łódź, Dec. 6, 1980); *Dwadzieścia dziewięć pięciolinii* (Twenty-Nine Systems) for Chamber Orch. (1980–81; Munich, Aug. 9, 1986); *4 Preludes* for Piano (1984; N.Y., Nov. 21, 1991); *String Quartet '84-'85* (1984–85; Warsaw, Oct. 20, 1985); *Lapis* for Electronics (1985; Wrocław, Feb. 20, 1986); *Fourteen Variations by Piotr Bikont and Krzysztof Knittel on Fourteen Variations by Edwin Moran on Fourteen Words by John Cage* for Voices and Computers (1986–92; Wrocław, Feb. 28, 1992); *Histoire III* for Harpsichord and Tape (1989; Wrocäaw, Feb. 20, 1990); *Hommage to Charles Ives* for Flute, Oboe, Clarinet, Bassoon, Piano, Percussion, Viola, and Double Bass (1991–92; N.Y., April 25, 1992); *Szatan w Goraju* (Satan in Goray), ballet for Flute, Piano, Violin, Cello, and Tape (1993; Philadelphia, Feb. 3, 1994); *Sonatas da camera I-VII* for Instruments and Synthesizer (1994–99); *Wybraniec* (Der Erwählte), ballet for Chamber Ensemble (1995; Warsaw, April 14, 1996); *Surface en Rotation* for Tape (1997); *Przebudzenia* (Awakenings), ballet (Poznań, April 25, 1998); *The Heart Piece*, opera (Warsaw, Sept. 22, 1999; in collaboration with John King).—LK/DM

Knittl, Karel, Bohemian choral conductor and composer; b. Polna, Oct. 4, 1853; d. Prague, March 17, 1907. He was a pupil of Skuhersky at the Prague Organ School, and later of Pivoda (singing) and Smetana (conducting). From 1877 to 1890, and again from 1897 to 1901, he conducted the choral society Hlahol in Prague. He taught at the Prague Organ School (1882–89), and at the Prague Cons. (from 1889), serving as its administrative director (from 1901). He publ. a monograph on Skuhersky (Prague, 1894), and also composed orch. works, choruses, piano pieces, and songs.—NS/LK/DM

Knorr, Ernst-Lothar von, German conductor and composer; b. Eitorf, near Cologne, Jan. 2, 1896; d. Heidelberg, Oct. 30, 1973. He studied at the Cologne Cons. with Bram Eldering (violin), Franz Bölsche (composition), and Fritz Steinbach (conducting). After graduation, he played violin in various provincial orchs. In 1925 he moved to Berlin and taught violin at the Höchschule für Musik. He served as director of the Hannover Hochschule für Musik (1952–61) and the Heidelberg Hochschule für Musik (1961–69). Most of his MSS perished in an air raid on Frankfurt an Main in 1944. His extant works include Concerto for 2 Orchs., Chamber Concerto for Piano, Saxophone, Chorus, and Small Orch., cantatas, choral works, and chamber music.

BIBL.: O. Riemer, ed., *E.-L. v.K. zum 75. Geburtstag* (Cologne, 1971).—NS/LK/DM

Knorr, Iwan (Otto Armand), German composer and teacher; b. Mewe, Jan. 3, 1853; d. Frankfurt am Main, Jan. 22, 1916. His family went to Russia when he was 3 years old, returning to Germany in 1868. He entered the Leipzig Cons., where he studied piano with Moscheles, theory with Richter, and composition with Reinecke. In 1874 he went back to Russia, where he taught in Kharkov and was made head of theoretical studies of the Kharkov division of the Russian Imperial Musical Soc. (1878). He settled in Frankfurt am Main in 1883 as a teacher at the Hoch Cons., becoming its director in 1908. His most distinguished pupils were Cyril Scott, Pfitzner, and Ernst Toch. His works are conceived in a Romantic vein, several inspired by the Ukrainian folk songs which he had heard in Russia.

WRITINGS (all publ. in Leipzig): *Aufgaben für den Unterricht in der Harmonielehre* (1903); *Lehrbuch der Fugenkomposition* (1911); *Die Fugen des Wohltemperieten Klaviers in bildlicher Darstellung* (1912; 2nd ed., 1926).

WORKS: DRAMATIC: O p e r a : *Dunja* (Koblenz, March 23, 1904); *Die Hochzeit* (Prague, 1907); *Durchs Fenster* (Karlsruhe, Oct. 4, 1908). OTHER: *Ukrainische Liebeslieder* for Vocal Quartet and Piano, op.6 (1890); *Variationen* (on a Ukrainian folk song), op.7 (1891); Variations for Piano, Violin, and Cello, op.1; Piano Quartet, op.3; Variations for Piano and Cello, op.4; etc.

BIBL.: M. Bauer, *I. K.: Ein Gedenkblatt* (Frankfurt am Main, 1916).—NS/LK/DM

Knote, Heinrich, distinguished German tenor; b. Munich, Nov. 26, 1870; d. Garmisch, Jan. 12, 1953. He studied with Kirschner in Munich. On May 7, 1892, he made his operatic debut as Georg in Lortzing's *Der Waggenschmied* at the Munich Court Opera, where he soon became a principal singer, continuing on its roster when it became the Bavarian State Opera (1918); also sang at London's Covent Garden (1901; 1903; 1907–08; 1913). He made his Metropolitan Opera debut in N.Y. as Walther von Stolzing (Dec. 3, 1904), singing there until 1906 and again in 1907–08; later toured the U.S. with the German Opera Co. (1923–24). His remarkable Munich career spanned almost half a century; made his farewell appearance there as Siegfried (Dec. 15, 1931); subsequently taught voice. He was a greatly esteemed Heldentenor, excelling in such roles as Tannhäuser, Lohengrin, Tristan, and Siegfried.

BIBL.: J. Wagenmann, *Der sechzigjährige deutsche Meistersinger H. K. in seiner stimmbildnerischen Bedeutung und im Vergleich mit anderen Sängern* (Munich, 1930).—NS/LK/DM

Knüpfer, Paul, German bass; b. Halle, June 21, 1865; d. Berlin, Nov. 4, 1920. After attending the Sondershausen Cons., he received vocal lessons from Bernhard Gunzburger. In 1885 he made his operatic debut in Sondershausen, and then was a member of the Leipzig Opera (1887–98) and the Berlin Royal (later State) Opera (1898–1920). Following additional vocal studies with J. Kniese in Bayreuth (1900), he appeared at the Festivals there until 1912. He also sang at London's Covent Garden (1904; 1907–14). Among his finest portrayals were Osmin, Daland, Pogner, Gurnemanz, King Marke, and Baron Ochs.—NS/LK/DM

Knüpfer, Sebastian, eminent German composer; b. Asch, Bavaria, Sept. 6, 1633; d. Leipzig, Oct. 10, 1676. He studied with his father, a Kantor and organist in Asch. After private musical studies, he took courses in organ as well as academic subjects at the Regensburg Gymnasium Poeticum (1646–54). He then settled in Leipzig, where he taught and was a bass singer in church choirs. On July 17, 1657, he was appointed Kantor of the Thomaskirche and director of music for the city; during his tenure, Leipzig resumed its preeminence as a center for music-making of the highest order. He composed sacred vocal works to both Latin and German texts, and also wrote some secular madrigals and canzonettas. Although few of his works are extant, those that have survived reveal him as a gifted musician.

BIBL.: O. Kandmann, *Das Werk S. K.s im Überblick* (diss., Univ. of Leipzig, 1960).—NS/LK/DM

Knushevitsky, Sviatoslav (Nikolaievich), Russian cellist and teacher; b. Petrovsk, Jan. 6, 1908; d. Moscow, Feb. 19, 1963. He was a pupil at the Moscow Cons. of Kozolupov. From 1929 to 1943 he was first cellist in the orch. of the Bolshoi Theater in Moscow. After taking 1st prize in the All-Union competition in Moscow in 1933, he also pursued a solo career. From 1942 to 1963 he taught at the Moscow Cons., where he was head of the cello and double bass dept. (1954–59). Glière, Miaskovsky, and A. Khachaturian wrote concertos for him.—NS/LK/DM

Knussen, (Stuart) Oliver, English composer and conductor; b. Glasgow, June 12, 1952. Remarkably precocious, he began playing piano as a small boy and showed unusual diligence also in his composition studies, mostly with John Lambert (1963–69) while attending the Central Tutorial School for Young Musicians (1964–67). On April 7, 1968, he made musical headlines when, at the age of 15, he conducted the London Sym. Orch. in the premiere performance of his own 1st Sym., written in an eclectic, but astoundingly effective, modern style. He was awarded fellowships for advanced study with Schuller at the Berkshire Music Center in Tanglewood (1970–73). From 1977 to 1982 he taught composition at the Royal Coll. of Music in London. He served as an artistic director of the Aldeburgh Festivals (from 1983) and as coordinator of contemporary music activities at Tanglewood (1986–93). He served as composer- in-residence of the Philharmonia Orch. in London from 1984. With Steuart Bedford, he served as co-artistic director of the Aldeburgh Festival from 1989. In 1994 he was made a Commander of the Order of the British Empire. In his mature works, Knussen has revealed a penchant for experimentation with various styles and for revising scores without surcease, resulting in compositions of great refinement and lucidity.

WORKS: DRAMATIC: O p e r a : *Where the Wild Things Are* (1979–80; Bussels, Nov. 28, 1980; rev. 1980–83; London, Jan. 9, 1984); *Higglety Pigglety Pop!* (1983–85; Glyndebourne, Aug. 5, 1985). ORCH.: 3 syms.: No. 1 (1966–67; London, April 7, 1968), No. 2 for Soprano and Small Orch. (Windsor, Oct. 3, 1970; rev. 1970–71; Tanglewood, Aug. 18, 1971), and No. 3 (1973–79;

London, Sept. 6, 1979); *Concerto for Orchestra* (1968–69; London, Feb. 1, 1970; rev. 1974); *Choral* for Wind Orch. (1970–72; Boston, Nov. 8, 1973); *Music for a Puppet Court* for 2 Chamber Orchs., after John Lloyd (1972, 1983; London, Aug. 23, 1983); *Coursing* for Chamber Orch. (1979); *The Wild Rumpus* from the opera *Where the Wild Things Are* (1983; London, July 21, 1987); *Fanfares for Tanglewood* for Brass and Percussion (Tanglewood, Aug. 2, 1986); *Flourish with Fireworks*, overture (1988). CHAMBER: *Processionals* for Wind Quintet and String Quartet (1968, 1978; Bristol, Dec. 15, 1978); *Masks* for Flute (1969); *3 Little Fantasies* for Wind Quintet (1970; rev. version, Kingston-upon-Thames, June 1, 1983); *Turba* for Double Bass (1971); *Ophelia Dances, Book I*, for Flute, English Horn, Clairnet, Horn, Piano, Celesta, Violin, Viola, and Cello (N.Y., May 9, 1975); *Triptych: I, Autumnal*, for Violin and Piano (1976–77; London, July 10, 1980), *II, Sonya's Lullaby*, for Piano (1977–78; Amsterdam, Jan. 6, 1979), and *III, Cantata*, for Oboe and String Trio (1977; Athens, Sept. 17, 1979); Piano Variations (1989); *Secret Song* for Violin (1990); *Songs Without Voices* for 8 Instruments (N.Y., April 26, 1992). VOCAL: *Hums and Songs of Winnie-the-Pooh* for High Soprano, Flute, English Horn, Clarinet or Contrabass Clarinet, Percussion, and Cello (1970, 1983; Aldeburgh, June 14, 1983); *Rosary Songs* for Soprano, Clarinet, Viola, and Piano (London, Aug. 21, 1972); *Océan de terre* for Soprano, Flute or Alto Flute, Clarinet or Bass Clarinet, Percussion, Piano or Celesta, Violin, Cello, and Double Bass (1972–73; rev. version, London, July 29, 1976); *Trumpets* for Soprano and 3 Clarinets (London, Feb. 27, 1975); *Frammenti da "Chiara"* for 2 Women's Choruses (1975, 1986; London, June 23, 1986); *Songs and a Sea Interlude* for Soprano and Orch. from the opera *Where the Wild Things Are* (1979–81; BBC, Feb. 14, 1981); *4 Late Poems and an Epigram of Rainer Maria Rilke* for Soprano (1988); *Whitman Settings* for Soprano and Orch. or Piano (1991–92).—NS/LK/DM

Knyvett, Charles, Jr., English singer and organist, son of **Charles Knyvett Sr.**, and brother of **William Knyvett**; b. London, 1773; d. there, Nov. 2, 1859. He studied organ with Samuel Webbe. In 1801 he participated in the Vocal Concerts in London, and in 1802 he became organist at St. George's; also was active as a teacher. He publ. a *Selection of Psalm Tunes* (1823). —NS/LK/DM

Knyvett, Charles, Sr., English organist and tenor, father of **Charles Knyvett Jr.**, and **William Knyvett**; b. probably in London, Feb. 22, 1752; d. there, Jan. 19, 1822. He was a chorister at Westminster Abbey, and also studied at Westminster School. He became a member of the Royal Soc. of Musicians (1778). He was a Gentleman of the Chapel Royal (1786–1808), serving as its organist (1796–1822), and was also active with Samuel Harrison in various concert ventures (from 1789).—NS/LK/DM

Knyvett, William, English singer, conductor, and composer, son of **Charles Knyvett Sr.**, and brother of **Charles Knyvett Jr.**; b. London, April 21, 1779; d. Ryde, Isle of Wight, Nov. 17, 1856. He was a pupil of his father and of Samuel Webbe. He became a treble singer at the Concerts of Ancient Music (1788), and also sang alto there from 1795. He was its director (1832–40), and also of the Birmingham Festivals (1834–43). He became a Gentleman of the Chapel Royal (1797), and later was made a composer there (1802). He composed a number of glees, his *When the Fair Rose* winning a prize of the Harmonic Soc. in 1800.—NS/LK/DM

Kobayashi, Ken-Ichiro, Japanese conductor; b. Iwaki, April 13, 1940. He studied composition with Mareo Ishiketa and piano with Atsuko Ohhori, then took courses in composition and conducting at the Tokyo Univ. of Fine Arts and Music, where his principal mentors were Akeo Watanabe and Kazuo Yamada. In 1970 he became asst. conductor of the Tokyo Sym. Orch. After winning the Budapest conducting competition (1974), he appeared widely in Europe as well as in his homeland, and was a conductor with the Amsterdam Phil. (from 1976). He was chief conductor of the Kyoto Sym. Orch. (1985–90), and principal conductor of the Hungarian State Orch. in Budapest (1987–97). —NS/LK/DM

Kobbé, Gustav, American writer on music; b. N.Y., March 4, 1857; d. when his sailboat was struck by a Navy seaplane in the bay near Babylon, L.I., July 27, 1918. He studied piano and composition with Adolf Hagen in Wiesbaden (1867–72), and with Joseph Mosenthal in N.Y.; also attended Columbia Coll. (1877–79). His most successful book was his *Complete Opera Book* (N.Y., 1919; rev. and aug. ed. by the Earl of Harewood, 1954, as *Kobbé's Complete Opera Book*; rev. ed., 1987, as *The Definitive Kobbé's Opera Book*). He also wrote *Wagner's Life and Works* (1890), *The Ring of the Nibelung* (1899; part of the preceding, printed separately), *Opera Singers* (1901), *Loves of the Great Composers* (1905), *How to Appreciate Music* (1906), *Wagner and His Isolde* (1906), and *Famous American Songs* (1906). He also publ. a novel, *Signora, A Child of the Opera House* (1902).—NS/LK/DM

Kobelius, Johann Augustin, German organist and composer; b. Waehlitz, near Merseburg, Feb. 21, 1674; d. Weissenfels, Aug. 17, 1731. Following training with his grandfather, Nicolaus Brause, a Weissenfels organist, he studied organ with Christian Schieferdecker, the Weissenfels Kantor and organist; he may also have had composition lessons with J.P. Krieger. In 1702 he became organist of the Holy Trinity Church in Sangerhausen, and director of choruses there in 1703. In 1724 he also became choral director in Querfurt. In 1725 he was named Landrentmeister for the court of Saxe-Weissenfels. He wrote some 23 operas for the Weissenfels court between 1715 and 1729.—LK/DM

Koch, Caspar (Petrus), German-American organist, pedagogue, and composer; b. Karnap, Nov. 25, 1872; d. Pittsburgh, April 3, 1970. He was taken to the U.S. by his parents (1881). He graduated from St. Francis Coll. in Joliet, Ill., and later took courses with Heinrich Reimann and Franz Kullak in Berlin and at the Regensburg Kirchenmusikschule. He was Pittsburgh city organist (1904–54) and also organist at the Holy Trinity Catholic Church there; taught at the Carnegie Inst. of Technology (1914–41). He wrote the valuable *Book of Scales for the Organ* (1918) and the *Organ Student's Gradus ad Parnassum* (1945) and also composed organ music.—NS/LK/DM

Koch, Eduard Emil, German clergyman and music scholar; b. Schloss Solitude, near Stuttgart, Jan. 20,

1809; d. Stuttgart, April 27, 1871. He became pastor in Gross-Anspach (1837), then at Heilbronn (1847), where he was superintendent (1853–64). He was an authority on Lutheran church music and wrote *Geschichte des Kirchenliedes und Kirchengesanges, insbesondere der deutschen evangelischen Kirche* (1847; 3rd ed., 8 vols., 1866–77). —NS/LK/DM

Koch, Heinrich Christoph, German music theorist; b. Rudolstadt, Oct. 10, 1749; d. there, March 19, 1816. He studied with Gopfert in Weimar. He was made violinist in the Court Orch. in Rudolstadt (1768), then court musician (1772) and Konzertmeister (1777). He publ. the valuable *Versuch einer Anleitung zur Composition* (3 vols., Rudolstadt and Leipzig, 1782–93) and *Musikalisches Lexikon* (Frankfurt am Main, 1802; 2nd ed., 1817); also *Handbuch bei dem Studium der Harmonie* (Leipzig, 1811) and a manual of enharmonic modulation (Rudolstadt, 1812). He launched the unsuccessful *Journal der Tonkunst* (Erfurt, 1795). He composed a Choralbuch for Wind Band and various choral works. —NS/LK/DM

Koch, Helmut, German conductor; b. Wuppertal-Barmen, April 5, 1908; d. Berlin, Jan. 26, 1975. He studied conducting with Fiedler, Lehmann, and Scherchen. He led workers' choruses for many years. After World War II, he was active in East Germany as founder-conductor of the Berlin Chamber Orch. (1945), conductor of the Berlin Radio Choir (from 1948), and director of the Berlin Singakademie (from 1963); was also a guest conductor at the Berlin State Opera (from 1960). He was widely known in East Germany for his performances of the music of Handel. He made numerous arrangements of German folk songs.—NS/LK/DM

Koch, Karl, Austrian organist, choral conductor, and composer; b. Biberwier, Tyrol, Jan. 29, 1887; d. Innsbruck, Sept. 20, 1971. He studied religion and music at a Brixen seminary (1905–09) and also took courses in conducting with Max Springer and composition with Joseph Marx at the Vienna Academy of Music (1920–21). In 1924 he settled in Innsbruck as a choral conductor, retiring in 1967. He publ. *Harmonielehre* (Vienna, 1948) and *Erganzungsbuch zur Harmonielehre* (Vienna, 1957).

WORKS: *Jubilate Deo* for Chorus and Orch. (1916); *Festmesse zu Ehren der Geburt unseres Herren Jesu Christi* for Soloists, Chorus, and Orch. (1916; Bozen, Jan. 6, 1917); *Requiem* for Chorus and Organ (1916); *Missa "In medio vitae"* for Soloists, Chorus, and Orch. (1925); *Missa "Super flumina Babylonis"* for Soloists, Chorus, and Orch. (Innsbruck, Nov. 20, 1932); *Sinfonie "Aus den Bergen"* (1942; Innsbruck, Feb. 17, 1947); *Missa in honorem Papae Pii X* (2 versions, 1953); *Requiem* for Soloists, Chorus, and Orch. (1955–58; Innsbruck, Feb. 20, 1960); *Psalmkantate,* vocal sym. for Solo, Vocal Quartet, Women's Chorus, Mixed Chorus, and Orch. (Wattens, Austria, Oct. 26, 1958); *Brixner Dom Messe* for Soloists, Boy's Chorus, Mixed Chorus, Organ, and Orch. (Brixen, Sept. 10, 1958); *Hubertus- Messe* for Unison Chorus and Wind Septet or Organ (1967); also String Quartet (1948); 2 piano sonatas; sacred choruses; much organ music.

BIBL.: W. Isser, *K. K.: Das Bild eines zeitgenössischen Komponisten* (Innsbruck, 1969).—NS/LK/DM

Koch, (Richert) Sigurd (Valdemar) von, Swedish composer, father of **(Sigurd Christian) Erland von Koch;** b. Agno, near Stockholm, June 28, 1879; d. Stockholm, March 16, 1919. He studied piano at the Richard Andersson School and composition with Lindegren, and later piano in Berlin (1905, 1912) and Dresden (1905). He was active in Stockholm as an accompanist and music critic, as well as a painter and poet. He wrote orch. works, much chamber music, and numerous songs in a late Romantic idiom.—NS/LK/DM

Koch, (Sigurd Christian) Erland von, Swedish composer, son of **(Richert) Sigurd (Valdemar) von Koch;** b. Stockholm, April 26, 1910. He studied music with his father, then at the Stockholm Cons. (1931–35). He went to Germany, where he studied composition with Paul Höffer and conducting with Clemens Krauss and Gmeindl (1936–38), and also had piano lessons with Arrau. He subsequently taught at Wohlfart's Music School in Stockholm (1939–53), and also was a sound technician with the Swedish Radio (1943–45). In 1953 he joined the faculty of the Stockholm Musikhögskolan, becoming a prof. in 1968. In 1957 he became a member of the Royal Swedish Academy of Music in Stockholm.

WORKS: DRAMATIC: Children's Opera: *Pelle svanslös* (Tailless Peter; 1948; Göteborg, Jan. 7, 1949; rev. 1966). **Ballet:** *Askungen* (Cinderella; 1942; also an orch. suite); *Samson and Delila* (1963; orch. suite, 1964; rev. 1972). **Incidental Music:** For the radio play *Bjälbojarlen,* after Strindberg (Swedish Radio, Jan. 25, 1968). **ORCH.:** *Little Suite* for Chamber or String Orch. (1933); 3 piano concertos: No. 1 (1936), No. 2 (1962), and No. 3 for Wind Orch. (1970; for Full Orch., 1972); 2 violin concertos (1937; 1979–80); 6 syms.: No. 1 (1938), No. 2, *Sinfonia Dalecarlia* (1944), No. 3 (1948), No. 4, *Sinfonia seria* (1952–53; rev. 1962), No. 5, *Lapponia* (1976–77; Stockholm, Oct. 30, 1977), and No. 6, *Salvare la terra* (1991–92); *Nordic Capriccio* (1943); *Rural Suite* for Strings (1945); Viola Concerto (1945; rev. 1966); *Sinfonietta* (1949); *Triptychon* for Violin and Orch. (1949); *Arkipelag* (1950); *Musica intima* for Strings (1950; rev. 1965); Cello Concerto (1951); *Musica malinconica* for Strings (1952); *Concert Music* (1955); Concerto for Small Orch. (1955); the Oxberg trilogy: *Oxberg Variations* (1956), *Lapland Metamorphoses* (1957), and *Dance- Rhapsody* (1957); Concerto for Saxophone and Strings (1958); *Concerto lirico* for Strings (1959; rev. of 4th String Quartet); *Concerto piccolo* for Soprano and Alto Saxophones and Strings (1962); *Fantasia concertante* for Violin and Orch. (1964); the Impulsi trilogy: *Impulsi* (1964), *Echi* (1965), and *Ritmi* (1966); *Arioso e Furioso* for Strings (1967); *Polska svedese* (1968); *Musica concertante* for 8 Winds, Strings, and Percussion (1969); Double Concerto for Flute, Clarinet, and Strings (1971); *A Swede in New York* (1973); Concerto for Oboe and Strings (1978); Tuba Concerto (1978); *4 Symphonic Myths* (Stockholm, Oct. 9, 1982); Guitar Concerto (Göteborg, Feb. 3, 1983); *Svenska danser 1–6* (1982–83); *Trombonia* for Trombone and Strings (1983); *Romanza* for Violin and Orch. (1984); *Serenade* for Double Bass and Strings (1985); *Midvinterblot-Sommarsolstånd,* 2 Nordic frescoes (1986–87); *Presto* for Violin and Strings (1990); *Whirl Dance* (1991); *Dalarondo* (1993); *Lamentoso* (1994); Flute Concerto (1998); *Rondinato* (1998). **CHAMBER:** 7 string quartets: No. 1 (1934), No. 2 (1944), No. 3, *Musica intima* (1950), No. 4 (1956; rev. 1959), No. 5 (1961), No. 6, *Serenata espressiva* (1963), and No. 7, *Årstidspastoraler* (1997); *Larghetto* for Cello or Viola and Piano (1937; rev. 1965); *Berceuse* for Violin and Piano (1953); *Sonatina semplice* for

Violin and Piano (1960); *Varianti virtuosi II* for Violin and Piano (1968); *Quattro tempi* for Wind Quintet (1968); *Miniatures* for Saxophone Quartet (1970); *Canto e danza* for Flute and Guitar (1975); *Karaktarer* for Violin and Piano (1980: *Auda* for Brass Quintet (1981); *Polysaxo* for Saxophone Ensemble (1981); *Tubania* for Tuba and Piano (1983); Alto Saxophone Sonata (1985); *Fantasia melodica* for Guitar and Wind Quintet (1986–89); *Capricietto* for Flute and Piano (1992); *Suonata per tre* for Piano Trio (1993); piano pieces; organ music. **VOCAL:** *Midsommardalen* for Baritone, Chorus, and Orch. (1960–61); *Sängarkvall* for Baritone, Men's Chorus, and Wind Orch. (1972); *Te Deum* for Chorus and Orch. or Organ (1994–95); songs.—**NS/LK/DM**

Kochan, Günter, German composer and teacher; b. Luckau, Oct. 2, 1930. He studied composition with Blacher, Noetel, and Wunsch at the (West) Berlin Hochschule für Musik (1946–50), and then attended Eisler's master classes at the (East) Berlin Akademie der Künste of the German Democratic Republic (1950–53). From 1950 to 1991 he taught at the (East) Berlin Hochschule für Musik. In 1965 he was elected to the Akademie der Künste. His music is eminently functional, and there is a distinct affinity with the symphonic processes used by Eisler.

WORKS: DRAMATIC: *Karin Lenz*, opera (1968–70); *Luther*, melodrama (1981). **ORCH.:** 2 violin concertos (1951–52; 1980); *Kleine Suite* (1956); Piano Concerto (1958); Sinfonietta (1960); *Fröhliche Ouvertüre* for Chamber Orch. (1960); 2 concertos for orchestra (1961–62; 1988–90); 5 syms.: No. 1 for Chorus and Orch. (1963–64), No. 2 (1968), No. 3 for Soprano and Orch. (1972), No. 4 (1983–84), and No. 5 (1985–87); *Divertimento*, variations on a theme of C.M. von Weber (1964); *Variationen über eine venezianische Canzonetta* for Piano and Chamber Orch. (1966); 4 *Movements* for Strings (1966); 2 cello concertos (1967, 1976); *Mendelssohn-Variationen* for Piano and Orch. (1972); Viola Concerto (1974); Concerto for Wind Quintet and 2 String Groups (1975–77); 7 *Orchesterstücke* (1976–77); *Passacaglia und Hymne* (1979); *In memoriam* (1982); *Praludium* (1985); *Und ich lächle im Dunkeln dem Leben* (1987); *Herbstbilder*, metamorphosen for 28 Strings (1990–91); *Divertimento* for Recorder Ensemble (1998). **CHAMBER:** Piano Trio (1953–54); *Divertimento* for Flute, Clarinet, and Bassoon (1956); Cello Sonata (1960); 5 *Movements* for String Quartet (1961); *Short String Quartet* (1965); String Quartet (1973–74); 7 *Miniaturen* for 4 Tubas (1977); String Trio (1979–80); Violin Sonata (1984–85); 5 *Bagatelles* for 4 Trombones (1987); Piano Quintet (1992–93); 7 *Szenen* for Flute, Viola, and Guitar (1993); 7 *Deutsche Volkslieder* for 4 Trombones and Tuba (1993); Duo for Clarinet and Piano (1994–95); *Musik* for Recorder and Harpsichord (1996); *Miniaturen* for Double Bass (1999). **Piano:** Suite (1952); *Praludien, Intermezzi und Fugen* (1954); 11 *Short Pieces* for Piano, 4-Hands (1958); 5 *Piano Pieces* (1971); 7 *Short Piano Pieces* (1971); Sonata (1981). **VOCAL:** *Die Welt ist jung*, cantata (1952); *Ernst Thälmann*, cantata (1959); 3 *Shakespeare-Lieder* for Alto, Flute, and Strings (1964); *Asche von Birkenau*, cantata for Alto and Orch. (1965); *Aurora* for Women's Voices, Chorus, and Orch. (1966); *Wir, unaufhaltsam*, "symphonic demonstration" for Baritone, Speaker, Chorus, and Orch. (1970); *Das Testament von Ho Chi-Minh* for Speaker, Chamber Orch., and 9 Solo Instruments (1971); *Die Hände der Genössen*, cantata for Baritone and Orch. (1974); 3 *Epitaphe* for Baritone and Instruments (1975); *Das Friedensfest oder Die Teilhabe*, oratorio (1978); *Tryptichon* for Mezzo-soprano, Alto Flute, Bass Clarinet, Viola, and Cello (1991); choruses; songs.—**NS/LK/DM**

Kochánski, Paul (actually, **Pawel**), noted Polish violinist; b. Orel, Sept. 14, 1887; d. N.Y., Jan. 12, 1934. He studied with Mlynarski in Warsaw, and in 1901 became concertmaster of the Warsaw Phil. In 1903 he went to Brussels to study with César Thomson. In 1907 he was appointed prof. at the Warsaw Cons., and in 1913 at the St. Petersburg Cons. From 1917 to 1919 he taught at the Kiev Cons., then went to the U.S., making his debut with the N.Y. Sym. Orch. on Feb. 14, 1921. From 1924 he taught at the Juilliard School of Music in N.Y. He excelled in the performance of modern works. He did a great service in promoting the violin music of Szymanowski, inspiring him to write his *Mity* (Myths; 1915) and 1st Violin Concerto (1916) for him. He made many transcriptions for violin and piano.—**NS/LK/DM**

Köchel, Ludwig (Alois Ferdinand), Ritter von, Austrian botanist, mineralogist, and music bibliographer; b. Stein, near Krems, Jan. 14, 1800; d. Vienna, June 3, 1877. He studied law at the Univ. of Vienna (graduated, 1827), and attained distinction in botany and mineralogy; music was his hobby. His love for Mozart's art moved him to compile a Mozart catalog as methodically as he would a descriptive index of minerals. The result of this task of devotion was the monumental *Chronologisch-thematisches Verzeichnis samtlicher Tonwerke Wolfgang Amade Mozarts* (Leipzig, 1862; 2nd ed., by Waldersee, 1905; 3rd ed., extensively rev. by A. Einstein, who supplemented the "K numbers" used to identify Mozart's works by secondary numbers, 1937; reprinted, with further alterations and corrections and suppl., Ann Arbor, 1947; 6th ed., a major rev., by F. Giegling, A. Weinmann, and G. Sievers, Wiesbaden, 1964; further supplementary material in the *Mozart-Jahrbuch* 1971–72, pp. 342–401, as prepared by P. van Reijen). Köchel publ. some supplementary matter in the *Allgemeine Musikalische Zeitung* (1864). He also publ. *Über den Umfang der musikalischen Produktivität W.A. Mozarts* (Salzburg, 1862), *Drei und achtzig neuaufgefundene Original-Briefe Ludwig van Beethovens an den Erzherzog Rudolf* (Vienna, 1865), *Die Pflege der Musik am österreichischen Hofe vom Schlusse das XV. bis zur Mitte des XVIII. Jahrhunderts* (privately publ., 1866), *Die Kaiserliche Hof-Musikkapelle in Wien von 1543–1867* (Vienna, 1869), and *J.J. Fux Hofkompositor und Hofkapellmeister der Kaiser Leopold I, Joseph I, und Karl VI, von 1698–1740* (Vienna, 1872).

BIBL.: T. Konrad, *Weltberühmt, doch unbekannt: L.R. v. K.: Der Verfasser des Mozartregisters* (Vienna, 1998).—**NS/LK/DM**

Kocián, Jaroslav, noted Czech violinist and pedagogue; b. Ústí nad Orlicí, Feb. 22, 1883; d. Prague, March 9, 1950. He studied violin with Sevcik at the Prague Cons. (1896–1901), and also took lessons in composition with Dvořák. After his graduation, he traveled widely as a concert violinist, almost rivaling the success of his famous compatriot Jan Kubelik. He made 4 American tours; also appeared in Asia and Africa. He also served as a prof. at the Odessa Cons. (1907–09). In 1928 he abandoned his concert career. He was a prof. at the Master School of the Prague Cons. (1924–43), and also its rector (1939–40). He composed several effective violin pieces, as well as choruses and songs.

BIBL.: B. Urban, *Mistr J. K.* (Kolín, 1926); V. Polívka, *S K.em kolem světa* (With K. Round the World; Prague, 1945); C. Sychra, ed., *J. K.: Sborník statí a vzpomínek* (J. K.: Collections of Articles and Recollections; Prague, 1953); A. Šlajs, *J. K.* (Pardubice, 1958).—**NS/LK/DM**

Kocsár, Miklós, Hungarian composer; b. Debrecen, Dec. 21, 1933. He studied with Farkas at the Budapest Academy of Music (1954–59). He taught at the Béla Bartók Cons. in Budapest (from 1972), and was also on the staff of the music dept. of the Hungarian Radio (from 1974), serving as its deputy head (from 1983). He won the Erkel Prize in 1973 and again in 1980. In 1987 he was made a Merited Artist by the Hungarian government.

WORKS: ORCH.: Horn Concerto (1957); *Serenata per archi* (1959; rev. 1971); *Capriccio* (1961); *5 Movements* for Clarinet, Strings, and Harpsichord (1976); *Variations* (1977); *Capricorn Concerto* for Flute and Chamber Ensemble (1978); *Metamorphoses* (1979); *Sequenze per archi* (1980); *Dances from Pozsony* for Youth String Orch. (1980); *Episodi* for Oboe and Strings (1982); *Concerto—In Memoriam ZH* for Horn and Chamber Orch. (1983); *Elégia* for Bassoon and Chamber Orch. (1985); *Formazioni* (1986); Suite for Youth String Orch. (1986). **CHAMBER:** *Duo Serenade* for Violin and Viola (1955); *Divertimento* for Oboe, Clarinet, and Bassoon (1956); 3 wind quintets (1956, rev. 1959; 1968; 1984); *3 Duos* for Oboe and Clarinet (1956); Violin Sonata (1957); Trio for 2 Trombones and Trumpet (1958); *Dialoghi* for Bassoon and Piano (1964–65); *Ungaresca* for Oboe and Clarinet, or 2 Clarinets, or Flute and Clarinet (1968); *Saltus hungaricus* for Flute or Oboe or Violin and Piano (1970); *Repliche I* for Flute and Cimbalom or Harpsichord (1971), *II* for Horn and Cimbalom (1976), and *III* for Cimbalom (1983); *7 Variations* for Viola (1983); *Echos* for Horn (1984); *Quintetto d'ottoni* (1986). **VOCAL:** *Hegyi legények* (Mountain Lads), cantata for Men's Chorus, Brass, and Percussion (1957); *Magyanos enek* (Solitary Song) for Soprano and Chamber Ensemble (1969); *Az éjszaka képei* (Pictures of the Night), oratorio for Mezzo- soprano, Baritone, Chorus, and Orch. (1987); many choral pieces; songs.—**NS/LK/DM**

Kocsis, Zoltan (György), brilliant Hungarian pianist; b. Budapest, May 30, 1952. He began his studies at the Béla Bartók Cons. (1963–68), then trained with Pál Kadosa, Ferenc Rados, and György Kurtág at the Franz Liszt Academy of Music (graduated, 1973) in Budapest. In 1970 he won the Hungarian Radio Beethoven competition. After appearing as soloist with the Dresden Phil. in 1971, he made his first tour of the U.S. as soloist with the Hungarian Radio and Television Sym. Orch. In 1973 he won the Liszt Prize and soon launched an acclaimed international career. With the conductor Ivan Fischer, he founded in 1983 the Budapest Festival Orch., with which he frequently appeared as a soloist and for which he served as artistic director. In 1997 he became artistic director of the Hungarian National Phil. in Budapest. A performer of extraordinary versatility, he includes in his repertoire works ranging from Bach to the avant-garde. He has made numerous transcriptions for piano; has also composed orch. music, including the topical *Memento (Chernobyl '86)*. In 1978 he was awarded the Kossuth Prize, and in 1984 he was named a Merited Artist by the Hungarian government.—**NS/LK/DM**

Koczalski, Raoul (actually, **Raul Armand Georg**), Polish pianist and composer; b. Warsaw, Jan. 3, 1884; d. Poznań, Nov. 24, 1948. He was trained by his parents; at the age of 4, he played at a charity concert in Warsaw and was at once proclaimed an "infant phenomenon." He studied with Mikuli in Lemberg, and then with Anton Rubinstein. He performed in Vienna (1892), Russia, Paris, and London (1893), making nearly 1,000 public appearances before he was 12. His sensational success diminished to some extent as he grew out of the prodigy age, but he was appreciated as a mature pianist, and particularly for his sensitive playing of Chopin. He lived mostly in France, Germany, and Sweden; after World War II, he returned to Poland and taught in Poznań and Warsaw. He publ. *Frédéric Chopin: Betrachtungen, Skizzen, Analysen* (Cologne, 1936). His precocity extended to composition as well; he wrote some 50 works before he was 10; he later wrote the operas *Rymond* (Elberfeld, Oct. 14, 1902) and *Die Suhne* (Muhlhausen, 1909), as well as many piano pieces.

BIBL.: B. Vogel, *R. K.* (Leipzig and Warsaw, 1896); M. Paruszewska, *Biographical Sketch and the Artistic Career of R. K.* (Poznań, 1936).—**NS/LK/DM**

Koczirz, Adolf, Austrian musicologist; b. Wierowan, Moravia, April 2, 1870; d. Vienna, Feb. 22, 1941. He studied law, and also musicology with Adler, at the Univ. of Vienna (Ph.D., 1903, with the diss. *Der Lautenist Hans Judenkünig*). He was employed in the Ministry of Finance (1891–1935). He distinguished himself as an authority on the lute and guitar; ed. 2 vols. of 16th- and 17th-century lute music in Denkmäler der Tonkunst in Österreich, XXXVII, Jg. XVIII/2 (1911) and I, Jg. XXV/2 (1918).

BIBL.: R. Haas and J. Zuth, eds., *Festschrift A. K. zum 60. Geburtstag* (Vienna, 1930).—**NS/LK/DM**

Koczwara, František, Bohemian composer; b. probably in Prague, c. 1750; d. (by hanging) London, Sept. 2, 1791. He traveled in Europe, then settled in London toward the end of the 18th century. In 1790 he went to Dublin as a viola player in the orch. at the King's Theatre. Returning to London the same year, he played in the orch. at the Handel Commemoration in May. He is remembered solely for his horripilating piece *The Battle of Prague* for Piano or Harpsichord, Violin, Cello, and Drum ad libitum (publ. in Dublin, c. 1788), purporting to depict in appropriately loud banging chords the effect on the ear of the defeat inflicted by the Austrian armies upon the Prussians at the crucial encounter on May 6, 1757, during the 7 Years' War. A person of curious sexual diversions, he convinced a prostitute to enhance their encounter by strangling him through repeated hangings. This peculiar event became the subject of a court trial of the prostitute in question, held on Sept. 9, 1791, in which she was acquitted. An account of the legal proceedings was publ. in London on Sept. 16, 1791, under the title "The Trial of Susannah Hill for the Murder of F. Kotzwarra."—**NS/LK/DM**

Kodalli, Nevit, Turkish conductor and composer; b. Mersin, Jan. 12, 1924. He studied with Necil Kazim

Akses at the Ankara Cons., graduating in 1947. He then went to Paris, where he took lessons with Honegger and Boulanger (1948–53). After teaching at the Ankara Cons. (1953–55), he conducted at the Ankara Opera (from 1955). He was a composer at the Ankara State Theater (from 1962). His music preserves the traits of Turkish folk melos, but the harmonic and contrapuntal treatment is in the manner of the French modern school. Among his works are 2 operas (1955, 1963), a Sym. (Ankara, May 20, 1950), an oratorio, *Ataturk* (Ankara, Nov. 9, 1953), and 2 string quartets (1947, 1966).
—NS/LK/DM

Kodály, Zoltán, renowned Hungarian composer, ethnomusicologist, and music educator; b. Kecskemét, Dec. 16, 1882; d. Budapest, March 6, 1967. He was brought up in a musical family; received his general education at the Archiepiscopal Grammar School in Nagyszombat; at the same time, he took lessons in piano, violin, viola, and cello. He soon began to compose, producing an overture when he was 15; it was performed in Nagyszombat in 1898. He then went to Budapest (1900), where he entered the Univ. as a student of Hungarian and German; also studied composition with Koessler at the Royal Academy of Music (diplomas in composition, 1904, and teaching, 1905; Ph.D., 1906, with a diss. on the stanzaic structure of Hungarian folk song). He became associated with Bartók, collecting, organizing, and editing the vast wealth of national folk songs; he made use of these melodies in his own compositions. In 1906 he went to Berlin, and in 1907 proceeded to Paris, where he took some lessons with Widor, but it was the music of Debussy that most profoundly influenced him in his subsequent development as a composer. He was appointed a prof. at the Royal Academy of Music in Budapest in 1907. In collaboration with Bartók, he prepared the detailed paper "Az uj egyetemes népdalgyüjtemény tervezete" (A Project for a New Universal Collection of Folk Songs) in 1913. They continued their collecting expeditions until World War I intervened. Kodály wrote music criticism in Budapest (1917–19). In 1919 he was appointed deputy director of the Budapest Academy of Music, but lost his position that same year for political reasons; however, he resumed his teaching there in 1922. In 1923 he was commissioned to write a commemorative work in celebration of the half-century anniversary of the union of Buda, Pest, and Obuda into Budapest. The resulting work, the oratorio *Psalmus hungaricus* (1923), brought him wide recognition. The initial performance in Budapest was followed by numerous productions all over Europe, and also in America. Another major success was his opera *Háry János* (1926); an orch. suite from this work became highly popular in Hungary and throughout the world. His orch. works *Marosszéki táncok* (Dances of Marosszék; 1930; based on a piano work) and *Galántai táncok* (Dances of Galanta; for the 80th anniversary of the Budapest Phil. Soc., 1933) were also very successful. His reputation as one of the most significant national composers was firmly established with the repeated performances of these works. Among his most important subsequent works were the orch. pieces *Variations on a*

Hungarian Folk Song "Felszállott a páva," the *Peacock Variations* (for the 50th anniversary of the Amsterdam Concertgebouw Orch., 1939), and the *Concerto for Orchestra* (for the 50th anniversary of the Chicago Sym. Orch., 1941). His great interest in music education is reflected in his numerous choral works, which he wrote for both adults and children during the last 30 years of his life. He also pursued his ethnomusicological studies; from 1940 he was associated with the Hungarian Academy of Sciences, serving as its president (1946–49). He continued to teach at the Academy of Music until 1940, and then gave instruction in Hungarian folk music until 1942; even after his retirement, he taught the latter course there. He toured as a conductor of his own music in England, the U.S., and the Soviet Union (1946–47); then throughout Western Europe. In succeeding years, he held a foremost place in the musical life of his country, receiving many honors; was awarded 3 Kossuth Prizes (1948, 1952, 1957). He also received foreign honors, being made an honorary member of the Moscow Cons. (1963) and the American Academy of Arts and Sciences (1963); was also awarded the Gold Medal of the Royal Phil. Soc. of London (1967). An International Kodály Soc. was organized in Budapest in 1975.

As a composer, Kodály's musical style was not as radical as that of Bartók; he never departed from basic tonality, nor did his experiments in rhythm reach the primitivistic power of Bartók's percussive idiom. He preferred a Romantic treatment of his melodic and harmonic materials, with an infusion of Impressionistic elements. All the same, he succeeded in producing a substantial body of music of notable distinction. He was married twice; his first wife, Emma, whom he married in 1910, died in 1958; on Dec. 18, 1959, he married Sarolta Péczely, a student (b. 1940).

WRITINGS: With B. Bartók, *Erdelyi magyarsag: Nepdalok* (The Hungarians of Transylvania: Folk Songs; Budapest, 1923); *A magyar népzene* (Hungarian Folk Music; Budapest, 1937; 2nd ed., aug., 1943; 3rd ed., aug., 1952 by L. Vargyas; Eng. tr., 1960); with A. Gyulai, *Arany János népdalgyüjteménye* (The Folk Song Collection of János Arany; Budapest, 1953); A. Szöllöy, ed., *A zene mindenkie* (Budapest, 1954; 2nd ed., 1975); F. Bónis, ed., *Visszatekintés* (In Retrospect: Budapest, 1964; 2nd ed., aug., 1974); *The Selected Writings of Zoltán Kodály* (Budapest, 1974).

WORKS: DRAMATIC: *Notre Dame de Paris*, incidental music for a parody (Budapest, Feb. 1902); *Le Cid*, incidental music for a parody (Budapest, Feb. 1903); *A nagybácsi* (The Uncle), incidental music (Budapest, Feb. 1904); *Pacsirtaszó* (Lark Song), incidental music for Voice and Small Orch. (Budapest, Sept. 14, 1917); *Háry János*, Singspiel (Budapest, Oct. 16, 1926); *Székely fonó* (The Transylvanian Spinning Room), lyrical play (1924–32; Budapest, April 24, 1932); *Czinka Panna*, Singspiel (1946–48; Budapest, March 15, 1948). **ORCH.:** Overture in D minor (1897; Nagyszombat, Feb. 1898); *Nyári este* (Summer Evening; Budapest, Oct. 22, 1906; rev. 1929–30; N.Y., April 3, 1930); *Régi magyar katonadalok* (Old Hungarian Soldiers' Songs; 1917; Vienna, Jan. 12, 1918; also arranged for Cello and Piano as *Magyar Rondo*); *Ballet Music* (1925; Budapest, Oct. 16, 1926; originally for *Háry János*); *Háry János Suite* (version for Brass Band, not by Kodály, Barcelona, March 24, 1927; version for Orch., N.Y., Dec. 15, 1927); *Szinházi nyitány* (Theater Overture; 1927; Budapest, Jan. 10, 1928; originally for *Háry János*); *Marosszéki táncok* (Dances of Marosszék; Dresden, Nov. 28, 1930;

based on a piano work; also arranged as a ballet); *Galántai táncok* (Dances of Galanta; Budapest, Oct. 23, 1933); Sym. in C major (1930s–1961; Lucerne, Aug. 16, 1961); *Variations on a Hungarian Folk Song "Felszállott a páva," the Peacock Variations* (Amsterdam, Nov. 23, 1939); *Concerto for Orchestra* (1939–40; Chicago, Feb. 6, 1941); *Honvéd Parad March* for Brass Band (1948; from *Háry János*); *Minuetto serio* (1948–53; aug. from *Czinka Panna*). CHAMBER: *Romance lyrique* for Cello and Piano (1898); Trio in E-flat major for 2 Violins and Viola (1899); *Adagio* for Violin, Viola or Cello, and Piano (1905); 2 string quartets (1908–9; 1916–18); Cello Sonata (1909–10); *Duo* for Violin and Cello (1914); Sonata for Solo Cello (1915); *Capriccio* for Cello (1915); *Magyar Rondo* for Cello and Piano (1917); *Serenade* for 2 Violins and Viola (1919–20); Cello Sonatina (1921–22); *Hivogató tábortüzhöz* (Calling to Camp Fire) for Clarinet (1930); Exercise for Violin (1942); *Feigin* for Violin and Piano (1958; arrangement of *Kállai kettös*); Wind Quartet (c. 1960). PIANO: *Valsette* (1907); *Méditation sur un motif de Claude Debussy* (1907); *Zongoramuzsika* (Piano Music; 9 pieces; 1909); 7 pieces (1910–18); *Ballet Music* (1925; arrangement of orch. work); *Marosszéki táncok* (Dances of Marosszék; 1927; also arranged for orch. and as a ballet); *Gyermektancok* (Children's Dances; 1945). VOCAL: Chorus and Orch.: *Offertorium (Assumpta est)* for Baritone, Chorus, and Orch. (1901); *Psalmus hungaricus* for Tenor, Chorus, Organ, Orch., and Children's Chorus ad libitum (Budapest, Nov. 19, 1923); *Budavári Te Deum* for 4 Soloists, Chorus, Organ, and Orch. (Budapest Cathedral, Sept. 12, 1936); *Missa brevis* for Chorus and Organ or 3 Sopranos, Alto, Tenor, Bass, Chorus, Orch., and Organ ad libitum (1942–44; Budapest, Feb. 11, 1945); *Vértanúk sírjánál* (At the Martyr's Grave) for Chorus and Orch. (1945); *Kállai kettös* (Kallo Double Dance) for Chorus and Small Orch. (1950; Budapest, April 4, 1951); *The Music Makers: An Ode* for Chorus and Orch., after A. O'Shaughnessy (1964). Chorus and Instrument(s): *Mass* for Chorus and Organ (c. 1896; unfinished); *Ave Maria* for Chorus and Organ (c. 1899); 5 *Tantum ergo* for Children's Chorus and Organ (1928); *Pange lingua* for Chorus or Children's Chorus and Organ (1929); *Kuntonudul* (Soldier's Song) for Men's Chorus, Trumpet, and Side Drum (1934); *Karácsonyi pásztortánc* (Shepherds' Christmas Dance) for Children's Chorus and Recorder (1935); *Ének Szent István királyhoz* (Hymn to St. Stephen) for Chorus and Organ (1938); *Vejnemöjnen muzsikál* (Vejnemöjnen Makes Music) for High Voices and Harp or Piano (1944); *A 114. genfi zsoltár* (Geneva Psalm CXIV) for Chorus and Organ (1952); *Intermezzo* for Chorus and Piano (1956; from *Háry János*); *Magyar mise* (Hungarian Mass) for Unison Chorus and Organ (1966); *Laudes organi* for Chorus and Organ (1966). Also many choral works for mixed voices a cappella, children's choruses, and songs. OTHER: Organ music; numerous educational works; Bach arrangements.

BIBL.: A. Molnár, *K. Z.* (Budapest, 1936); B. Szabolcsi and D. Bartha, eds., *Emlékkönyv K. Z. 70. születésnapjára* (Budapest, 1953); L. Eősze, *K. Z. élete és munkassaga* (Z. K.'s Life and Work; Budapest, 1956; Eng. tr., 1962); idem, *K. Z. élete képekben* (Z. K.'s Life in Pictures; Budapest, 1957; 2nd ed., 1958; Eng. tr., 1971); P. Young, *Z. K.: A Hungarian Musician* (London, 1964); H. Szabó, *The K. Concept of Music Education* (London, 1969); E. Hegyi, *Solfege According to the K. Concept* (Kecskemet, 1975); L. Eősze, *K. Z. életének krónikája* (Z. K.: Chronicle of His Life; Budapest, 1977); J. Breuer, *K.-kalauz* (Budapest, 1982; Eng. tr., 1990, as *A Guide to K.*); E. Lendvai, *The Workshop of Bartók and K.* (Budapest, 1983); E. Szőnyi, *K. Z. nevelési eszméi* (Budapest, 1984); I. Kecskeméti, *K., the Composer: Brief Studies on the First Half of K.'s Oeuvre* (Kecskemét, 1986); G. Ránki, *Bartók and K. Revisited*

(Budapest, 1987); B. Reuer, *Z. K.s Bühnenwerk "Háry János": Beiträge zu seinen volksmusikalischen und literarischen Quellen* (Munich, 1991); M. Houlahan and P. Tacka, *Z. K.: A Guide to Research* (N.Y., 1998).—NS/LK/DM

Koeberg, Frits Ehrhardt Adriaan, Dutch composer; b. The Hague, July 15, 1876; d. there, Nov. 9, 1961. He studied with H. Viotta in the Netherlands and with Xaver Scharwenka in Berlin. Returning to The Hague in 1902, he taught at the Cons. and conducted the Musica orch.

WORKS: Opera, *Bloemenkind* (1917); 3 syms.; symphonic poems: *Zeelandia* (1920) and *Chimères* (1941); *Suite de Lage Landen* for Orch. (1946); *Dances in the Village* for Orch. (1948); *Hollandia* for Band (1933); chamber music; songs.—NS/LK/DM

Koechlin, Charles (Louis Eugène), noted French composer, pedagogue, and writer on music; b. Paris, Nov. 27, 1867; d. Le Canadel, Var, Dec. 31, 1950. He studied for a military career, but was compelled to change his plans when stricken with tuberculosis. While recuperating in Algeria, he took up serious music studies. He then entered the Paris Cons. (1890), where he studied with Gédalge, Massenet, Tadou, and Fauré, graduating in 1897. He lived mostly in Paris, where he was active as a composer, teacher, and lecturer. With Ravel and Schmitt, he organized the Société Musicale Indépendante (1909) to advance the cause of contemporary music, and with Satie, Roussel, Milhaud, and others, he was a member of the group Les Nouveaux Jeunes (1918–20), a precursor to Les Six. Although he composed prolifically in all genres, he became best known as a writer on music and as a lecturer. He made 3 lecture tours of the U.S. (1918, 1928, 1937). He became president of the Fédération Musicale Populaire (1937). His pro-Communist leanings caused him to promote music for the proletariat during the 1930s; he wrote a number of works "for the people" and also film scores. In spite of the fact that such works as his *Symphonie d'hymnes* (Prix Cressent, 1936) and Sym. No. 1 (Prix Halphan, 1937) won honors, his music made no real impact. Taking Fauré as his model, he strove to preserve the best elements in the French Classical tradition. A skillful craftsman, he produced works of clarity and taste, marked by advanced harmonic and polyphonic attributes.

WRITINGS: *Étude sur les notes de passage* (Paris, 1922); *Précis des règles du contrepoint* (Paris, 1926; Eng. tr., 1927); *Gabriel Fauré* (Paris, 1927; Eng. tr., 1946); *Claude Debussy* (Paris, 1927); *Traité de l'harmonie* (3 vols., Paris, 1927–30); *Étude sur le choral d'école* (Paris, 1929); *Théorie de la musique* (Paris, 1934); *Étude sur l'écriture de la fugue d'école* (Paris, 1934); *Pierre Maurice, musicien* (Geneva, 1938); *Les instruments à vent* (Paris, 1948); *Traité de l'orchestration* (4 vols., Paris, 1954–59).

WORKS (Koechlin orchestrated many of his works well after their original completion. Dates given are those of original, often unorchestrated, versions): DRAMATIC: Pastorale biblique: *Jacob chez Laban* for Soprano, Tenor, Chorus, and Orch. (1896–1908; Paris, May 19, 1925). Ballet: *La Forêt païenne* (1911–16; Paris, June 17, 1925); *La Divine Vesprée* (1917); *L'Âme heureuse* (1945–47); *Voyages: Film danse* (1947). ORCH.: Sym. (1895–1900; unfinished); *L'Automne,* symphonic suite (1896–1906); *La Forêt,* symphonic poem in 2 parts: No. 1, *Le*

Jour (1897–1904) and No. 2, La Nuit (1896–1907); 2 symphonic poems: Soleil et danses dans la forêt and Vers la plage lointaine (1898–1909); En mer, la nuit, symphonic poem, after Heine (1899–1904); Nuit de walpurgis classique (Ronde nocturne), symphonic poem, after Verlaine (1901–07; rev. 1915–16); 2 symphonic poems: (L'Été): Nuit de juin and Midi en août (1908–11); Suite légendaire (La Nuit féerique) (1901–15); Études antiques (Suite païenne; Poèmes antiques), symphonic suite (1908–14); La Course de printemps, symphonic poem, after Kipling (1908–25); 2 symphonic poems: Le Printemps and L'Hiver (1908–16); Ballade for Piano and Orch. (1911–15); 2 syms: No. 1 (1911–16; arranged from the String Quartet No. 2) and No. 2 (1943–44; arranged from several other works); Rapsodie sur des chansons françaises (1911–16); The Bride of a God, symphonic poem (1929; in collaboration with C. Urner); Symphonic Fugue (1932); Choral fugué (1933); Choral fugué du style modal for Organ and Orch. (1933); Sur les flots lointaines, symphonic poem (1933); Hymne à la jeunesse, after Gide (1934); Symphonie d'hymnes (1936; arranged from several other works); La Méditation de Purun Bhagat, symphonic poem, after Kipling (1936); La Cité nouvelle, rêve d'avenir, symphonic poem, after Wells (1938); Le Buisson ardent, symphonic poem, after Rolland (1938); La Loi de la jungle, symphonic poem, after Kipling (1939); Les Bandar- log, symphonic poem, after Kipling (1939); Le Docteur Fabricius, symphonic poem, after C. Dollfus (1941–44); Offrande musical sur le nom de BACH (1942); Silhouettes de comédie for Bassoon and Orch. (1942–43); Partita for Chamber Orch. (1945); Introduction et 4 interludes de style atonal-sériel (1947). CHAMBER: Viola Sonata (1902–15); Piano Quintet (1908; 1911; 1917–21); 3 string quartets (1911–13; 1911–16; 1917–21); Flute Sonata (1911–13); Suite en quatuor for Flute, Violin, Viola, and Piano (1911–15); Oboe Sonata (1911–16); Violin Sonata (1915–16); Cello Sonata (1917); Bassoon Sonata (1918–19; also for Horn and Piano); Sonata for 2 Flutes (1918–20); 2 clarinet sonatas (1923, 1923); Trio for Strings or Woodwinds (1924); Quintet Primavera for Flute, Harp, Violin, Viola, and Cello (1936); Wind Septet (1937); Trio for Oboe, Clarinet, and Bassoon (1945); Quintet for Flute, Harp, Violin, Viola, and Cello (1949); also many works for piano, including Paysages et marines (12 pieces; 1915–16), Les Heures persanes (16 pieces; 1916–19), and L'Ancienne Maison de campagne (12 pieces; 1932–33). OTHER: Choral works, music for band, film scores, organ music, and songs.

BIBL.: R. Orledge, A Study of the Composer C. K. (1867–1950) (diss., Univ. of Cambridge, 1973); J. Woodward, The Theoretical Writings of C. K. (diss., Univ. of Rochester, 1974); H. Sauget, ed., Oeuvres de C. K. (Paris, 1975; a catalog); E. Kirk, The Chamber Music of C. K. (diss., Catholic Univ. of America, Washington, D.C., 1977); R. Orledge, C. K. (1867–1950): His Life and Works (Vol. I, N.Y., 1989).—NS/LK/DM

Koehler, Ted, American lyricist; b. Washington, D.C., July 14, 1894; d. Santa Monica, Calif., Jan. 17, 1973. Koehler took an unusual route to prominence as a lyricist by writing songs and material for nightclub revues, primarily at Harlem's Cotton Club, in the 1930s. His most successful songs, including "Get Happy," "Stormy Weather," and "I've Got the World on a String," were written with composer Harold Arlen and introduced by such performers as Duke Ellington and Cab Calloway. Koehler went on to write primarily for motion pictures, earning three Academy Award nominations.

Growing up in Newark, Koehler had a public-school education and studied piano; he initially worked as a photoengraver in a N.Y. plant owned by his father. Then he played piano in clubs and for silent films. Soon he was writing lyrics and stage patter for vaudeville singers, eventually becoming a song plugger and staff writer with music publishers. His first published song was "Dreamy Melody" (music and lyrics by Koehler, Frank Magine, and C. Naset) in 1922; it became a million-selling instrumental record for Art Landry and His Orch. in June 1923. Koehler's next hit, in February 1924, was also recorded as an instrumental—it was "When Lights Are Low" (lyrics also by Gus Kahn, music by Ted Fiorito), performed by the Benson Orch. of Chicago. During this period, Koehler married Elvira Hagen; they had three children, two sons and a daughter.

In the summer of 1929, Koehler was introduced to singer Harold Arlen by Harry Warren, who suggested he put words to a tune of Arlen's. The result was "Get Happy," which the new songwriting team placed in the Nine-Fifteen Revue (N.Y., Feb. 11, 1930), where it was performed by Ruth Etting. The revue was a failure, running only seven performances, but the song became a hit for Nat Shilkret and The Victor Orch. in July. Koehler and Arlen were hired to write songs for another revue, Earl Carroll's Vanities of 1930 (N.Y., July 1, 1930), and their contributions included "Hittin' the Bottle," which became a hit for the Colonial Club Orch. in August. They also wrote two nightclub revues during the year, Biff-Boom-Bang and Brown Sugar, the latter playing at the Cotton Club. (Koehler's efforts at the club went beyond lyric-writing to include production as well as set design and construction.)

Koehler's next hit, "Wrap Your Troubles in Dreams," was cowritten with lyricist Billy Moll and composer Harry Barris. Barris had been one of Paul Whiteman's Rhythm Boys vocal trio with Al Rinker and Bing Crosby, and Crosby recorded the song for his first big solo hit in May 1931. Meanwhile, Koehler and Arlen had collaborated on another Cotton Club revue, Rhythmania, starring Cab Calloway and His Orch. It was the source of three hit songs: "Kickin' the Gong Around," for Calloway in November; "I Love a Parade," for The Arden-Ohman Orch. in February 1932; and "Between the Devil and the Deep Blue Sea," for Louis Armstrong in March 1932. "I Love a Parade" was interpolated into the 1932 Warner Bros. film Manhattan Parade along with another Koehler-Arlen song, marking the duo's first work for motion pictures.

Koehler and Arlen provided a series of hits for Calloway during 1932. "Minnie the Moocher's Wedding Day," later featured in the Cotton Club Parade revue and a follow-up to Calloway's signature song "Minnie the Moocher," was a popular record in June. "I've Got the World on a String," also in Cotton Club Parade, was a hit in November; and "I Gotta Right to Sing the Blues," one of several songs Koehler and Arlen contributed to Earl Carroll's Vanities of 1932 (N.Y., Sept. 27, 1932), was a hit for Calloway as well as others in January 1933.

Koehler and Arlen wrote "Stormy Weather" with Calloway in mind, but since he was not to be featured in the next edition of the Cotton Club Parade, it was given to Leo Reisman and His Orch., who recorded it with Arlen singing. The record became a massive hit in the spring of 1933, and the song was then sung by Ethel Waters in the *Cotton Club Parade*; her recording also became a best-seller, making "Stormy Weather" the most successful song of the year. Koehler initiated a new songwriting partnership with Rube Bloom in 1933, the two writing a song alternately called "Stay on the Right Side, Sister" and "Stay on the Right Side of the Road." Under the first title, it was introduced by Ruth Etting and later featured in her film biography, *Love Me or Leave Me* (1955), sung by Doris Day; under the second, it was recorded by Bing Crosby and also used in the MGM film *Penthouse*.

The success Koehler and Arlen had with their songs for the Cotton Club, combined with the upsurge in the production of movie musicals after the success of *42nd Street* in the spring of 1933, brought the team to Hollywood to write songs for Columbia Pictures' *Let's Fall in Love*. Only two of the five songs they wrote actually made it into the picture, which was released at the end of the year, but one of them was the title song, which became a best-seller for Eddy Duchin and His Orch. in February 1934. (Arlen's own recording was also a modest hit.) Koehler and Arlen were back in N.Y. by then to write the next *Cotton Club Parade*. (Koehler was also credited for conceiving and supervising the production.) "Ill Wind," its hit, was something of a follow-up to "Stormy Weather"; Duchin and Arlen teamed up to make it the most popular recording in April.

With Bloom, Koehler again scored with a weather-themed lyric when Glen Gray and the Casa Loma Orch. made a hit of "Out in the Cold Again" in September. By then, Koehler and Arlen had separated amicably to write book musicals with others. Arlen's was *Life Begins at 8:40*, with E.Y. Harburg and Ira Gershwin; Koehler teamed with Ray Henderson for *Say When*, which starred Harry Richman and Bob Hope and ran only 76 performances despite favorable reviews, generating no outside hits.

Nevertheless, Koehler and Henderson were engaged by the Fox studio for a Shirley Temple feature, *Curly Top*, and among their three songs was "Animal Crackers in My Soup" (lyrics also by Irving Caesar), which was forever associated with Temple. Koehler and Bloom wrote the 1935 edition of the *Cotton Club Parade* (the final revue staged at the club's Harlem location). Although the show's stars were Lena Horne and Jimmie Lunceford and His Orch., Fats Waller took its most popular song, "Truckin'," into the hit parade. Koehler moved permanently to Calif. and returned to the film studio now called 20th Century–Fox to write the songs for *King of Burlesque* with Jimmy McHugh. Their efforts yielded five compositions, two of which made the hit parade: "I'm Shootin' High" (for Jan Garber and His Orch.) and "Lovely Lady" (for Tommy Dorsey and His Orch.).

In 1936, Koehler worked on three films, contributing two songs with music by Sam Stept to Republic's *The Big Show*, four songs with music by McHugh to 20th Century–Fox's *Dimples*, another Shirley Temple vehicle, and four songs with music by M. K. Jerome to RKO's *Glory*. This freelance activity continued in 1937, as Koehler contributed lyrics to four films at four different studios, most notably a collaboration with Burton Lane at Paramount for *Artists and Models*, which produced the hit parade entry "Stop, You're Breaking My Heart" for Russ Morgan and His Orch. in August and marked a reunion with Arlen on "Public Melody Number One."

Reflecting the downturn in production of movie musicals in the late 1930s, Koehler was less active in 1938, working only on Columbia's *Start Cheering* with Johnny Green and contributing one song to RKO's March 1939 release *Love Affair*, "Sing, My Heart," with Arlen. He then accepted an assignment to conceive, write, and direct the World's Fair edition of the *Cotton Club Parade* with Bloom back in N.Y., and their songs included "Don't Worry 'bout Me," which was in the hit parade for two months starting in early May for Hal Kemp and His Orch. In September 1940, after working on it off and on for two years, Koehler and Arlen completed their six-song *Americanegro Suite*, a concert work; it was published in 1941 and recorded in 1942 by Decca Records under Arlen's supervision.

The early 1940s was an even less active time for Koehler, though he scored a minor hit with "Ev'ry Night about This Time" (music by James V. Monaco), recorded by Jimmy Dorsey and His Orch., in October 1942. He and Arlen contributed a song to the Trocadero Club revue *Symphony in Brown* in 1942. Koehler was reunited with many of the Cotton Club regulars for 20th Century–Fox's *Stormy Weather* in 1943. The film, a loosely based biography of dancer/singer Bill "Bojangles" Robinson, featured Lena Horne, who performed the title song, Cab Calloway, and Fats Waller. Koehler got a cowriting credit on the screenplay.

Koehler worked full-time during 1944, turning out songs for three films. RKO's *Up in Arms*, starring Danny Kaye and Dinah Shore, found him working for the last time with Arlen, notably on "Tess's Torch Song (I Had a Man)," which became a hit for Ella Mae Morse in May, and "Now I Know," which was nominated for an Academy Award. Koehler and Lane wrote four songs used in Paramount's *Rainbow Island*, and Koehler's three songs in the all-star *Hollywood Canteen* in December brought a second 1944 Oscar nomination to a man who had never been nominated before with "Sweet Dreams, Sweetheart" (music by M. K. Jerome). In November, Cab Calloway had scored a modest hit with Koehler's "The Moment I Laid Eyes on You." Koehler had three songs in three films in 1945, the most notable being "Some Sunday Morning" (music by Jerome and Ray Heindorf) in Warner Bros.' *San Antonio*—it became a Top Ten hit in the hands of Dick Haymes and Helen Forrest and earned Koehler his third Academy Award nomination.

Koehler probably was under contract to Warner Bros. between 1945 and 1947, when all of his efforts were released in the company's films. He had one song with Jerome in 1946's *Janie Gets Married*, then contributed to four features in 1947. The last of these was *My Wild Irish Rose*, a film biography of tenor Chauncey Olcott, for which Koehler and Jerome wrote six songs. Koehler then retired, though his catalog of songs turned up frequently in movies of the 1950s, one prominent example being the Judy Garland production number of "Get Happy" which was added to the 1950 MGM musical *Summer Stock* and remains one of Garland's most memorable performances. Major revivals of Koehler's work on record include Richard Hayes's recording of "Out in the Cold Again," which reached the Top Ten in 1951; Frank Sinatra's 1953 hit recording of "I've Got the World on a String" (subsequently one of his signature songs); and Peaches and Herb's cover of "Let's Fall in Love," a Top 40 hit in 1967.

WORKS (only works for which Koehler was the principal, credited lyricist are listed): **MUSICALS/REVUES:** *Biff-Boom-Bang* (N.Y., 1930); *Brown Sugar* (N.Y., 1930); *Earl Carroll's Vanities of 1930* (N.Y., July 1, 1930); *Rhythmania* (N.Y., March 1931); *Cotton Club Parade* (N.Y., Oct. 23, 1932) *Cotton Club Parade* (N.Y., April 6, 1933); *Cotton Club Parade* (1933); *Cotton Club Parade* (N.Y., March 23, 1934); *Say When* (N.Y., Nov. 8, 1934); *Cotton Club Parade* (1935); *Cotton Club Parade* (N.Y., March 24, 1939). **FILMS:** *Let's Fall in Love* (1933); *Curly Top* (1935); *King of Burlesque* (1935); *Dimples* (1936); *Glory* (1936); *The King and the Chorus Girl* (1937); *23 Hours Leave* (1937); *Artists and Models* (1937); *Start Cheering* (1938); *Up in Arms* (1944); *Rainbow Island* (1944); *Hollywood Canteen* (1944); *Cheyenne* (1947); *My Wild Irish Rose* (1947).—**WR**

Koellreutter, Hans Joachim,

German conductor, composer, and teacher; b. Freiburg im Breisgau, Sept. 2, 1915. He studied with Martienssen (piano), Scheck (flute), Thomas and Scherchen (conducting), Schunemann and Seifert (musicology), and Hindemith (composition) at the Berlin Academy of Music (1934–36), and then with Moyse (flute) at the Geneva Cons. (1937–38). He went to Rio de Janeiro, where he taught at the Brazilian Cons. (1937–52) and at the São Paulo Inst. of Music (1942–44). He was director of the São Paulo Free Academy of Music (1952–55) and the music dept. of Bahia Univ. (1952–62); was also chief conductor of the Bahia Sym. Orch. (1952–62). He then was in charge of the music programs of the Goethe Inst. in Munich (1963–65); was its regional representative in New Delhi (1965–69), where he also was head of the Delhi School of Music (1966–69). From 1970 to 1975 he was director of the Goethe Inst. in Tokyo, where he also was prof. at the Inst. of Christian Music and conductor of the Heinrich Schütz Chorale; then returned to Brazil (1975) and taught at the Goethe Inst. in Rio de Janeiro (until 1980). After serving as director of the Tatui Cons. (1983–84), he was a prof. at the Univ. in Minas Gerais (1984–88) and at the São Paulo Cons. (1988–90). His music follows Classical forms, while the thematic materials are modeled after the 12-tone method of composition; in several of his works, he makes use of exotic motifs of South America, India, and Japan.

WRITINGS: *Attitudes of Consciousness in Indian and Western Music* (New Delhi, 1966); *Three Lectures on Music* (Mysore, 1968); *Jazz Harmonia* (São Paulo, 1969); *Ten Lectures on Music* (New Delhi, 1969); *History of Western Music* (New Delhi, 1970).

WORKS: ORCH.: *4 Pieces* (1937); *Variations* (1945); *Música* (1947); *Sinfonia de camara* for 11 Instruments (1948); *Mutacoes* (1953); *Concretion* for Orch. or Chamber Orch. (1960); *Constructio ad synesin* for Chamber Orch. (1962); *Advaita* for Sitar and Orch. or Chamber Orch. (1968); *Sunyata* for Flute, Chamber Orch. of Western and Indian Instruments, and Tape (1968); *Acronon* (1978–79); *Wu-Li* (1988). **CHAMBER:** 2 flute sonatas (1937, 1939); Violin Sonata (1939); *Inventions* for Oboe, Clarinet,

and Bassoon (1940); *Variations* for Flute, English Horn, Clarinet, and Bassoon (1941); *Música 1947* for String Quartet (1947); *Diaton 8* for Flute, English Horn, Bassoon, Harp, and Xylophone (1955); *Tanka I-VII* for Voice and Instrument (1970–82). **VOCAL:** *Noturnos de Oneyda Alvarenga* for Mezzo-soprano and String Quartet (1945); *O cafe*, choral drama (1956); *8 Haikai de Pedro Xisto* for Baritone, Flute, Electric Guitar, Piano, and Percussion (1963); *Cantos de Kulka* for Soprano and Orch. (1964); *Indian Report*, cantata for Soprano, Speaker, Chamber Chorus, Speaking Chorus, and Chamber Orch. of Western and Indian Instruments (1967); *Yū* for Soprano and Japanese Instruments (1970); *Mu-dai* for Voice (1972); *O cafe* for Chorus (1975). —**NS/LK/DM**

Koenen, Tilly (actually, Mathilde Caroline),

Dutch mezzo-soprano; b. Salatiga, Java, Dec. 25, 1873; d. The Hague, Jan. 4, 1941. She studied piano, on which she became a proficient performer, then voice with Cornelia van Zanten. She toured Germany and Austria from 1900 with excellent success; visited the U.S. in 1909–10 and 1915–16. She was particularly impressive in her interpretations of German Romantic songs; also performed some songs by her compatriots. —**NS/LK/DM**

Koenig, Gottfried Michael,

German composer; b. Magdeburg, Oct. 5, 1926. He attended the Braunschweig Staatsmusikschule (1946–47), and then was a student of Bialas (composition) and Maler (analysis) at the North West German Music Academy in Detmold (1947–50); later he studied at the Cologne Hochschule für Musik (1953–54) and at the Univ. of Bonn (1963–64). After working in the electronic music studios of the West German Radio in Cologne (1954–64), he was artistic and scientific director of the Instituut voor Sonologie at the Univ. of Utrecht (1964–86). In 1987 he was awarded the Matthijs Vermeulen Prize of the City of Amsterdam. Koenig was one of the leading figures in the development of electronic music, being particularly influential in the application of the computer to the creation of musical works. As an important theorist on serial music, he has written extensively. Among his most significant works is the study on serial and aleatory music publ. as *Musik in ihrer technischen Rationalität* (Bilthoven, 1963).

WORKS: ORCH.: Harpsichord Concerto (1948–49); *Horae* (1951); *Beitrag* (1985–86). **CHAMBER:** Woodwind Quintet (1958–59); 2 string quartets (1959; 1987–88); *Project I* for 14 Instruments (1965–66; also 2 other versions); *Segmente 99–105* for Violin and Piano (1982); *Drei ASKO Stücke* for 14 Instruments (1982); *Segmente 92–98* for Violin and Cello (1983); *Segmente 85–91* for Flute or Piccolo, Bass Clarinet, and Cello (1984); *Intermezzo* for Flute or Piccolo or Bass Flute, Bass Clarinet or E-flat Clarinet, and Piano (1987). **Piano:** 2 Pieces (1957); *Übung* (1969–70); *Segmente 1–7* (1982). **ELECTRONIC:** *Klangfiguren I* (1955) and *II* (1955–56); *Essay* (1957–58); *Materialien zu einem Ballett* (1961); Suite (1961); *Terminus I* (1962), *2* (1966–67), and *10* (1967); *Funktion Grün* (1967); *Funktion Gelb* (1968); *Funktion Orange* (1968); *Funktion Rot* (1968); *Funktion Blau* (1969); *Funktion Indigo* (1969); *Funktion Violett* (1969); *Funktion Grau* (1969). **Computer:** *Output* (1979). —**NS/LK/DM**

Koering, René, French composer; b. Andlau, May 27, 1940. He studied piano and oboe in Strasbourg, worked with Boulez (1960), and attended the summer course in new music given by Maderna in Darmstadt. From 1974 he worked for France Musique. In 1990 he became general director of l'Orchestre Philharmonique de Montpellier Languedoc-Roussillon. He was made a Chevalier dans l'Ordre de la Légion d'honneur and a member de l'Ordre National du Mérite.

WORKS: DRAMATIC: O p e r a : *Elseneur* (1980); *La Lune Vague* (1981); *La Marche de Radetzky* (1988); *Marie de Montpellier* (1994). **ORCH.:** *Triple et Trajectoire* for Piano and 2 Orchs. (1965); *Quatre Extrêmes* (1969); 3 syms. (1973, n.d., 1999); *Trois Grands lieder* (1992); Violin Concerto (1992); *Fragments de songe* for Violin and Strings (1993); *Les Oiseaux dans la Tourmente* (1993); *Concert-Match* (1998). **CHAMBER:** *Suite Intemporelle* for Reciter and 8 Instruments (1961); 2 string quartets (1974, 1981); Piano Sonata (1976). **VOCAL:** *Le Cercle-Kleist* for Soprano and Orch. (1995).—NS/LK/DM

Koessler or **Kössler, Hans,** German pedagogue and composer; b. Waldeck, Jan. 1, 1853; d. Ansbach, May 23, 1926. After serving as organist in Neumarkt, Oberpfallz (1871–74), he studied with Rheinberger and Wüllner at the Munich Königliche Musikschule. He taught theory and choral singing at the Dresden Cons. (1877–81), and also conducted the Dresden Liedertafel (1879–82) and at the Cologne Theater (1880–82). In 1882 he settled in Budapest as a teacher of organ and choral music at the Royal Academy of Music; then taught composition there (1883–1908), subsequently heading its master classes (1920–25). Among his outstanding students were Bartók, Kodály, and Dohnányi. He himself was best known as a composer for his choral works.

WORKS: *Der Münzenfranz,* opera (Strasbourg, 1903); 2 syms.; Symphonic Variations (1909); Violin Concerto (1914); Cello Concerto; chamber music; *Triumph der Liebe,* oratorio (1897); choral pieces; songs.—NS/LK/DM

Koetsier, Jan, Dutch conductor and composer; b. Amsterdam, Aug. 14, 1911. He studied in Berlin at the Stern Cons. (1924–26) and at the Hochschule für Musik (1927–34). He was a conductor in Lübeck and Berlin, and then in The Hague (1941–42). After serving as 2nd conductor of the Concertgebouw Orch. in Amsterdam (1942–49), he again conducted in The Hague (1949–50). He was a conductor with the Bavarian Radio Sym. Orch. in Munich (1950–66), and then a prof. at the Munich Staatliche Hochschule für Musik (1966–76).

WORKS: DRAMATIC: *Demeter,* ballet (1943); *Frans Hals,* opera (1949). **ORCH.:** *Concerto capriccioso* for Piano and Orch. (1935; rev. 1975); *Adagietto e Scherzino* (1936; rev. 1952); *Barocksuite* (1936; rev. 1953); Oboe Concertino (1936; rev. 1953); *Serenata Serna* for Strings (1937; rev. 1953); *Duo concertante* for Flute, Violin, and Orch. (1937; rev. 1956); *Vision pastorale* for English Horn and Strings (1937; rev. 1954); *Symhonische Musik* (1939); *Valerius Overture* (1942; rev. 1966); *Music* for 2 String Orchs., 3 Trumpets, 3 Trombones, and Timpani (1943); Sinfonietta (1943; rev. 1960); *Divertimento* (1943); *Music* for 4 Orchs. (1944); 3 syms. (1945, rev. 1968; 1946; 1954); *Kreisleriana* for 2 Pianos and Orch. (1965); *Valerius-suite* (1966); Sinfonietta Concertante for Oboe, Clarinet, Horn, Bassoon, and Strings (1968); *Concertino lirico* for Violin, Cello, and Strings (1968); *Homage to*

Gershwin (1969); *Intrada classica* for Wind Instruments, Timpani, and Harp (1971); *Hymnus monaciensis* (1971); *Concertino drammatico* for Violin, Viola, and Strings (1981); Concertino for Trombone and Strings (1983); Concerto for 4 Horns and Orch. (1983); *Französisches Concerto,* suite for 2 Flutes and Strings (1984); *Dance Suite* (1985); *Burg-Serenade* (1987); *Konzertantes Rondo* for Piano and Strings (1991); Brass Quintet Concerto (1992; rev. 1994); *Sinfonische Fantasie: Metamorphosen über ein lyrisches Thema aus der "Neunten"* (1995). **CHAMBER:** Quintet for Flute, Oboe, Violin, Viola, and Cello (1932; rev. 1965); Septet (1932; rev. 1959); 2 divertimentos for Wind Quintet (1937, 1947); Trio for Flute, Oboe, and Piano (1938); English Horn Quintet (1955); String Quintet (1959); Octet for 2 Oboes, 2 Clarinets, 2 Horns, and 2 Bassoons (1968); Clarinet Quintet (1968); sonatinas for Trumpet, for Trombone, and for Tuba (all 1970); Trio for Alto Flute, Viola da Gamba, and Harpsichord (1971); Sonata for Cello and Harp (1972); Piano Trio (1975); *Serenade* for String Trio (1977); Trio for Flute, Bassoon, and Piano (1978); *Fantasie,* trio for Cello, Bassoon, and Piano (1981); Quartet for 4 Cellos (1981); Sonata for Horn and Harp (1984); String Quartet (1985); *Petit Concert pour Violin et Contrebasse* for Violin, Double Bass, Clarinet, Bassoon, Cornet, Trombone, and Percussion (1987); *Tänzerische Impressionen* for Marimba and Harp (1990); *Grosse Fantasie* for Trumpet, Trombone, and Organ (1990); *Cinque dialoghi* for Violin and Cello (1990); *Trois études* for Trombone (1990); 10 *Variationen und Fughetta über Themen von J.S. Bach* for 2 Oboes and English Horn (1991); *Dresdner Trio* for Oboe, Horn, and Piano (1992); *Introduktion und 12 Variationen über "Das Blümchen Wunderhold"* [by Beethoven] for Flute and Harp (1994); organ music; piano pieces. **VOCAL:** *Von Gottes und des Menschen Wesen,* 7 madrigals for Chorus and 7 Instruments (1940; rev. 1969); *Gesang der Geister über Wassern* for Chorus and 7 Instruments (1940; rev. 1973); *Der Mann Lot* for Baritone, Speaker, Men's Chorus, and Orch. (1940; rev. 1962); *Antonius Mass* (1984); songs.

BIBL.: H. Beermann et al., *J. K.* (Tutzing, 1988). —NS/LK/DM

Koffler, Józef, Polish composer; b. Stryj, Nov. 28, 1896; d. with his wife and child during a Nazi roundup of Jews in Wieliczka, near Kraków, 1943. He was a student in Vienna of Grädener (1914–16), Schoenberg (1920–24), and at the Univ. with Adler (Ph.D., 1925, with the diss. *Über orchestrale Koloristik in den symphonischen Werken von Mendelssohn-Bartholdy*). He went to wów, where he taught at the Cons. (1929–41) and ed. the periodicals *Orkiestra* (1930–38) and *Echo* (1936–37). Koffler was the first Polish composer to embrace Schoenberg's 12-tone system.

WORKS: ORCH.: *Hanifa,* overture (1925); *Suite orientale* (1925); *Sielanka: Capriccio pastorale* for Chamber Orch. (1925); *Variations sur une succession de douze tons* for Strings (1927; based on 15 *Variations d'après une suite de douze tons* for Piano); 4 syms.: No. 1 for Small Orch. (1931), No. 2 (1933), No. 3 for Winds (1935; London, June 17, 1938), and No. 4 (1940); Piano Concerto (1931); *Prelude and Fugue* (1936); *Polish Suite* for Small Orch. (1936); *Little Suite after J.S. Bach* (1937); *Joyful Overture* (1940); *Haendeliana,* 30 variations (1940). **CHAMBER:** String Trio (1928; Oxford, July 23, 1931); *Little Serenade* for Oboe, Clarinet, and Bassoon (1931); String Quartet (1934); *Capriccio* for Violin and Piano (1936); *Ukrainian Sketches* for String Quartet (1941). **P i a n o :** 40 *Polish Folk Songs* (1925); *Musique de ballet* (1926); *Musique quasi una sonata* (1927); 15 *Variations d'après une suite de douze tons* (1927; also as *Variations sur une succession de douze tons* for String Orch.); Sonatine (1930); Sonata (1935); *Variations sur une Valse de Johann Strauss* (1935). VOCAL: *Love*, cantata for Mezzo- soprano, Clarinet, Viola, and Cello (1931); songs.

BIBL.: M. Gołąb, *J. K.* (Kraków, 1995).—NS/LK/DM

Kogan, Leonid (Borisovich), outstanding Russian violinist and pedagogue, father of **Pavel Kogan;** b. Dnepropetrovsk, Nov. 14, 1924; d. on the train at the Mytishcha railroad station, Dec. 17, 1982. His father was a photographer who played the violin. When Kogan was 10 years old, the family moved to Moscow, where he became a pupil of Abram Yampolsky, first at the Central Music School and later at the Cons. (1943–48); subsequently pursued postgraduate studies with him (1948–51). In 1947 he was a co-winner of the 1st prize at the World Festival of Democratic Youth in Prague; then won 1st prize in the Queen Elisabeth of Belgium Competition in Brussels in 1951. His career was instantly assured; he played in Europe to unanimous acclaim. He made an auspicious American debut playing the Brahms Violin Concerto with Monteux and the Boston Sym. Orch. on Jan. 10, 1958. In 1952 he joined the faculty of the Moscow Cons.; was named prof. in 1963 and head of the violin dept. in 1969. In 1965 he received the Lenin Prize. His playing exemplified the finest qualities of the Russian School: an emotionally romantic elan and melodious filigree of technical detail. In addition to the standard repertoire, in which he excelled, he also played modern violin works, particularly those by Soviet composers. He was married to **Elizabeth Gilels.**

BIBL.: M. Zazovsky, *L. K.* (Moscow, 1956).—NS/LK/DM

Kogan, Pavel, Russian violinist and conductor, son of **Leonid (Borisovich) Kogan;** b. Moscow, June 6, 1952. He enrolled at Moscow's Central Music School when he was 6, and later pursued his training at the Moscow Cons. with Jankelevitch. After taking 1st prize in the Sibelius Competition in Helsinki in 1970, he toured extensively as a violin virtuoso. In later years, he took up a career as a conductor. In 1988 he became a conductor at the Bolshoi Theater in Moscow. He also conducted the Moscow State Sym. Orch. from 1989. —NS/LK/DM

Kogoj, Marij, Slovenian composer; b. Trieste, May 27, 1895; d. Ljubljana, Feb. 25, 1956. He was a student of Schreker and Schoenberg in Vienna (1914–18); then was active as a conductor at the Ljubljana Opera and as a music critic. Although Kogoj's promising career was thwarted in 1932 when he became mentally ill, he was one of the earliest Slovenian composers to experiment with expressionism, as evinced in his opera *Črne maske* (Black Masks; Ljubljana, May 7, 1929). Among his other works were choral pieces, chamber music, and piano pieces.

BIBL.: I. Klemenčič, ed., *M. K., 1892–1993* (Ljubljana, 1993). —NS/LK/DM

Kohaut, Karl, notable Austrian lutenist and composer; b. Vienna (baptized), Aug. 26, 1726; d. there, Aug. 6, 1784. He was a student of Gottfried von Swieten. In 1758 he entered the Austrian civil service, and eventually rose to the position of secretary of the imperial chancery. He also pursued a distinguished career as a lute virtuoso. His lute concertos are remarkable examples of effective writing for the instrument.—LK/DM

Köhler, Ernst, German organist, pianist, and composer; b. Langenbielau, May 28, 1799; d. Breslau, May 26, 1847. He was 1st organist of the Elisabethkirche in Breslau from 1827 until his death. He wrote 2 syms., 9 overtures, 12 church cantatas, 12 large vocal works with orch., organ works, and piano pieces.—NS/LK/DM

Köhler, Louis, German pianist, pedagogue, and composer; b. Braunschweig, Sept. 5, 1820; d. Königsberg, Feb. 16, 1886. He studied piano in Braunschweig with Sonnemann, then took courses in composition in Vienna (1839–43) with Sechter and Seyfried; also studied piano there with Bocklet. He settled in Königsberg (1847), where he established a successful piano school. In 1880 he was granted the title Royal Prof. He wrote 3 operas, a ballet, a Sym., overtures, cantatas, and other works, but is best remembered for his albums of piano studies, which were adopted in music schools all over the world; next to Czerny's, they were the most popular didactic piano works of their time. It must be observed that while his studies are of great instructive value, they are also worthwhile from a purely musical standpoint. His major work, in which he laid the foundation of methodical piano pedagogy, is *Systematische Lehrmethode für Klavierspiel und Musik: I, Die Mechanik als Grundlage der Technik* (1856; 3rd ed., rev. by Riemann, 1888), and II, *Tonschriftwesen, Harmonik, Metrik* (1858).—NS/LK/DM

Köhler, Siegfried, German composer, teacher, and administrator; b. Meissen, March 2, 1927; d. Berlin, July 14, 1984. He studied with MacGregor (piano), Hintze (conducting), and Finke (composition) at the Dresden Hochschule für Musik (1946–50) and with Serauky (musicology) and Jahn (art history) at the Univ. of Leipzig (Ph.D., 1955, with the diss. *Die Instrumentation als Mittel musikalischer Ausdrucksgestaltung*). In 1957 he became director of the Berlin International Music Library. After serving as artistic director of the Deutsche Schallplaten (1963–68), he was director of the Dresden Hochschule für Musik (1968–80), where he also was prof. of composition (from 1969). In 1982 he became president of the Assn. of Composers and Music Scholars of the German Democratic Republic. In 1983 he became Intendant of the Dresden State Opera.

WORKS: DRAMATIC: O p e r a : *Der Richter von Hohenburg* (1963). ORCH.: *Fröhliche Suite* (1956); 5 syms. (1965–84); Concertino for Clarinet and Strings (1968); Piano Concerto (1972). VOCAL: *Reich des Menschen*, oratorio (1962); cantatas; choruses; various songs.

BIBL.: G. Schonfelder, *S. K. für Sie porträtiert* (Leipzig, 1984).—NS/LK/DM

Kohlhase, Charlie, American saxophonist; b. Portsmouth, N.H., Nov. 28, 1956. He began playing alto saxophone in 1975 and added baritone a year later. He joined the Either/Orch. in 1987 and has appeared on all their albums except for the first. He also became a member of John Leahman's Mandala Octet in 1987 and has appeared on all their releases. In 1989 he formed a quintet with trombonist Curtis Hasselbring, saxophonist Matt Langley, bassist John Turner, and drummer Matt Wilson. In 1992 trumpeter John Carlson replaced Hasselbring. Besides three CDs of their own, the Charlie Kohlhase Quintet contributed a track to *Wavelength/Infinity (Rastascan)*, an anthology of Sun Ra compositions. In 1993 saxophonist John Tchicai appeared as a special guest with the quintet; trombonist John Rapson joined the band for a short New England tour in 1997. Kohlhase has also appeared in a quartet with saxophonist Michael Marcus. He is uncommonly skillful at using elements of the jazz tradition in witty compositions and arrangements that maintain a keen sense of swing as they blend structure and freedom. As a soloist, he is especially good at developing motives and longer linear elements into coherent statements that offer accompanists lots of room for interaction.

Disc.: *Research and Development* (1991); *Good Deeds* (1993); *Dart Night* (1996).—**EH/NAL**

Kohlman, (Louis) Freddie, early, long-careered jazz drummer, vocalist, leader; b. New Orleans, Aug. 25, 1918; d. New Orleans, Sept. 29, 1990. As a teenager, he began playing with numerous parade bands in his hometown, after receiving some basic lessons on the drums from Louis Cottrell Sr., and Manuel Marietta. When he was about 25, he moved to Chicago, where he worked in a more modern style with a quartet that featured boogie pianist Albert Ammons and violinist Stuff Smith. In the late 1930s, he briefly worked in Detroit before returning to his hometown in 1941. From 1944, he led his own New Orleans revival band, except for a brief six-month stint in the mid-1950s with Louis Armstrong's All Stars. In the late 1950s, he was back in Chicago working at clubs, but by the 1960s he was working again in New Orleans. In the last decades of his life, he made many European tours as a soloist and with revival bands. In the 1980s, he performed with the Milan, Italy-based Jambalaya Six on tours of Italy and Switzerland. He made two records; oddly, his earlier album, recorded in 1953, was the more modern of the two, with hints of bebop-meets-Dixieland in its arrangements. His second recording, 1980's *Take Me Back to New Orleans*, was a conscious attempt to recreate the old-style New Orleans parade bands, featuring British revivalist Chris Barber and American pianist Dr. John. Kohlmann died of cancer in his home.—**LP**

Kohn, Karl (Georg), Austrian-born American pianist, conductor, teacher, and composer; b. Vienna, Aug. 1, 1926. After the Anschluss in 1938, he emigrated with his family to the U.S., becoming a naturalized American citizen in 1945. He studied piano with C. Werschinger and conducting with Prüwer at the N.Y. Coll. of Music (graduated, 1944), then studied composition with Piston, Ballantine, Fine, and Thompson at Harvard Univ. (B.A., 1950; M.A., 1955), where he was a teaching fellow (1954–55). He also taught at the Berk-

shire Music Center in Tanglewood (summers, 1954, 1955, 1957). In 1950 he joined the music faculty at Pomona Coll. in Claremont, Calif., where he served as a prof. from 1965 to 1994. With his wife, Margaret, he performed the contemporary 2-piano repertoire in the U.S. and Europe. He also made appearances as a conductor. He held a Fulbright scholarship for study in Finland (1955–56), a Guggenheim fellowship (1961–62), and 4 grants from the NEA (1975, 1976, 1979, 1986). In his compositions, Kohn tends toward prudent serialism but also explores diatonic modalities, applying the power of pervicacious iteration of pandiatonic chordal complexes; he successfully adapts to contemporary usages medieval polyphonic devices such as the integration of precomposed thematic fragments, a technique anciently known as "centone" (literally, "patchwork quilt"). He makes use of topological rearrangements of Classical pieces, as in *Son of Prophet Bird*, dislocated and paraphrased from Schumann's *Bird as a Prophet*.

Works: ORCH.: *Sinfonia concertante* for Piano and Orch. (1951); *Overture* for Strings (1953); *Castles and Kings*, symphonic suite for children (1958); *Concerto mutabile* for Piano and Orch. (1962); *Episodes* for Piano and Orch. (1966); *Intermezzo I* for Flute and Strings (1969); *Centone per orchestra* (Claremont Music Festival, June 27, 1973); Concerto for Horn and Small Orch. (1974); *Innocent Psaltery*, "colonial music" (1976); *The Prophet Bird I* (metamorphosis of Schumann's *Bird as a Prophet*; 1976) and *II* for Piano and Chamber Orch. (Los Angeles, March 9, 1982); *Waldmusik*, clarinet concerto (1979; also for Clarinet, Piano, and Wind Ensemble, 1983); *Time Irretrievable* (1983); *An Amiable Piece* for 2 Pianos, Winds, and Percussion (1987); *Return*, symphonic essay for Brass, Percussion, and Strings (1990); *Ode* for Strings (1991); *Concert Music* for Strings (1993); *Memory and Hope: Essays* (Stockton, Calif., April 9, 1997). **Band:** *Serenade II* (1977); *Wind Chamber* (1981). **CHAMBER:** String Trio (1950); *Concert Music* for 12 Winds (1956); Violin Sonata (1956); *Capriccios I* for Flute, Clarinet, Cello, Harp, and Bassoon (1962) and *II* for Chamber Ensemble (1983); *Serenade* for Wind Quintet and Piano (1962); *Kaleidoscope* for String Quartet (1964); *Encounters I* for Flute, Piccolo, and Piano (1965), *II* for Horn and Piano (1967), *III* for Violin and Piano (1971), *IV* for Oboe and Piano (1972), *V* for Bassoon and Piano (1973), and *VI* for Cello and Piano (1977); *Introductions and Parodies* for Clarinet, Horn, Bassoon, String Quartet, and Piano (1967); *Rhapsodies* for Marimba, Vibraphone, and Percussion (1968); *Impromptus* for 8 Winds (1969); Trio for Violin, Horn, and Piano (1972); Brass Quintet (1976); *Son of Prophet Bird* for Harp (1977); *San Gabriel Set* for Clarinet, Violin, Viola, Cello, and Piano (1984); *Entr'acte* for String Quartet (1985); *Senza Sordino* for Horn and Viola (1985); *Choice Wood, Precious Metals* for Flute, Trumpet, Marimba, and Glockenspiel (1986); *Before Beethoven* for Clarinet, Cello, and Piano (1989); *Cassation* for Wind Quintet (1990); *Ternaries* for Flute and Piano (1993); *Set of Three: Start Piece* (1995), *Middle Piece* (1994), and *End Piece* (1993) for Flute, Viola, Cello, Marimba, Vibraphone, and Piano; *Reconnaissance* for 11 Players (1995); *SAX, for 4* for Saxophone Quartet (1996); *More Reflections* for Clarinet and Piano (1997); *Capriccio* for Violin, Alto and Soprano Saxophone, and Piano (1998); *Toccata and Virelais* for Accordion and Harp (1998); *Trio, 2 K* for Violin, Cello, and Piano (1999); a substantial body of pieces for 1 or 2 pianos; organ music. **VOCAL:** Choral works; songs. —**NS/LK/DM**

Kohoutek, Ctirad, prominent Czech composer, pedagogue, music theorist, and administrator; b. Zábřeh na Moravě, March 18, 1929. He studied at the Brno Cons. with Vilám Petrželka, and with Jaroslav Kvapil at the Janáček Academy of Music there (1949–53). He later attended Lutoslawski's lectures at the Dartington Summer School of Music (1963) and sessions given by Boulez and Ligeti at the Darmstadt summer courses in new music. He obtained his Ph.D. from Palacký Univ. in Olomouc (1973) and his C.Sc. from J.E. Purkyně Univ. in Brno (1980). In 1953 he joined the faculty of the Janáček Academy of Music in Brno (assoc. prof., 1965–80). In 1980 he became assoc. prof. of composition at the Prague Academy of Music, and later that year prof. of composition, which position he retained until 1990. He also served as artistic director of the Czech Phil. (1980–87). In 1988 he was made an Artist of Merit by the Czech government. His music follows the traditions of Central European modernism, well contained within Classical forms but diversified by serial procedures and glamorized by electronic sounds. He is the brother of the astronomer Luboš Kohoutek.

WORKS: DRAMATIC: O p e r a : *O Kohoutkovi a Slepičce* (About the Cock and Hen; 1988–89). **ORCH.:** *Mnichov* (Munich), symphonic poem (1952–53); *Festivalová předehra* (Festival Overture; 1955–56); Violin Concerto (1958); *Velký přelom* (Great Turning Point; 1960–62); *Symfonické tance* (Symphonic Dances; 1961); Symfonieta (1962–63); Concertino for Cello and Chamber Orch. (1964; also for Cello and Piano, 1966); *Preludia* for Chamber Orch. (1965); *Teatro del mondo*, symphonic rotation in 4 scenes (1968–69); *Panteon*, sound image (1970); *Slavonstní prolog* (Ceremonial Prologue; 1971); *Slavností světla* (Feast of Light), cycle of symphonic pictures (1975); *Symfonické aktuality* (Symphonic Newsreel), concert frescoes (1976–78); *Pocta životu* (Homage to Life; 1988–89; Brno, March 26, 1992). **CHAMBER:** *Sonatina semplice* for Oboe and Piano (1950); *Suita romantica* for Viola and Piano (1957); Suite for Wind Quintet (1958–59); String Quartet (1959); *Memento 1967*, concerto for Percussion and Winds (1966); *Panychida: Hudba o dvou zvukových vrstvách* (Prayer for the Dead: Music in 2 Sound Layers) for 2 Violas, 2 Pianos, Percussion, and Tape (1968); *Tkaniny doby* (Fabrics of Time), sound fantasies for Bass Clarinet or Cello, Piano, and Percussion (1977); *Minuty jara* (Minutes of Spring), impressions for Wind Quintet (1980); *3 Variations of Folk Dances* for 2 Accordions or Accordion Ensemble (1986); *Motivy léta* (Motifs of Summer) for Violin, Cello, and Piano (1990); *Žerty a úsměvy* (The Fun and the Smiles, or Funny Smiles) for Oboe, Clarinet, and Bassoon (1991); *V zahradách chrámu Kyota* (In the Gardens of Kyoto's Temples) for English Horn, Bass Clarinet, and Percussion (1992); *Zimní ticha* (Winter Silences) for Brass and Percussion (1992–93); *Oživené zátiší* (The Revived Still Life) for Horn (1994); *Podzimní zpěvy* (Autumn Songs) for String Quartet (1994–95); *Promeny vody* (Transformations of Water) for 4 Flutes (1996). **O r g a n :** *Dávno je tomu* (So Long Ago; 1998). **VOCAL:** *Za všechny děti: Ukolébavka černošské mamy* (For All Children: Black Mama's Lullaby), cantata for Contralto, Chorus, and Orch. (1951–52); *Balady z povstání* (Ballads from the Uprising), 2 cantatas (1960); *Pátý živel* (The 5th Element), melodrama for Reciter and Small Orch. (1964); *The Birth of Man*, monologues for Man's and Woman's Voice and Orch. or Piano (1981); *Broskvička* (The Little Peach) for Chorus, Piano, and Percussion (1993); choruses; songs.—**NS/LK/DM**

Kohs, Ellis (Bonoff), noted American composer and teacher; b. Chicago, May 12, 1916; d. Los Angeles, May 17, 2000. His mother was a good violinist, and when Kohs learned to play the piano he often accompanied her at home. In 1928 the family moved from San Francisco (following his early musical studies there at the Cons.) to N.Y., where he studied with Adelaide Belser at the Inst. of Musical Art. In 1933 he enrolled at the Univ. of Chicago as a student in composition with Carl Bricken (M.A., 1938). Upon graduation, he proceeded to N.Y., where he entered the Juilliard School of Music, studying composition with Wagenaar and musical pedagogy with Samaroff. He continued his musical studies at Harvard Univ., with Piston in composition and Leichtentritt and Apel in musicology (1939–41); also attended a seminar given by Stravinsky at Harvard Univ. in 1940–41. During the summer of 1940, he was a lecturer in music at the Univ. of Wisc. in Madison. From 1941 to 1946 he served in the U.S. Army as a chaplain's assistant and organist, and in the U.S. Air Force as a bandleader. After his discharge from service, he engaged in pedagogical work and in active composition; his teaching posts included Wesleyan Univ. (1946–48), the Kansas City Cons. of Music (1946–47), the Coll. of the Pacific in Stockton, Calif. (1948–50), Stanford Univ. (1950), and the Univ. of Southern Calif. in Los Angeles (1950–85). In his music, Kohs pursued the aim of classical clarity, being particularly adept in variation structures; the rhythmic patterns in his works are often asymmetrical, and the contrapuntal fabric highly dissonant; in some of his works, he made use of a unifying 12-tone row, subjecting it to ingenious metamorphoses, as revealed in his opera *Amerika*, after the novel by Kafka. A humorous streak is shown in his choral piece *The Automatic Pistol*, to words from the U.S. Army weapons manual, which he composed during his military service. He publ. the useful manuals *Music Theory, a Syllabus for Teacher and Student* (2 vols., N.Y., 1961), *Musical Form: Studies in Analysis and Synthesis* (Boston, 1976), and *Musical Composition: Projects in Ways and Means* (Metuchen, N.J., 1980).

WORKS: DRAMATIC: *Amerika*, opera, after Kafka (1969; abridged concert version, Los Angeles, May 19, 1970; 2 orch. suites, 1986, 1987); *Lohiau and Hiiaka*, Hawaiian legend for Narrators, Flute, Cello, Percussion, and Dancers (1987; also as a suite for Flute, Cello, and Percussion, 1988); incidental music. **ORCH.:** Concerto for Orch. (Berkeley, Calif., Aug. 9, 1942); *Passacaglia* for Organ and Strings (1946); *Legend* for Oboe and Strings (Columbus, Ohio, Feb. 27, 1947); Cello Concerto (1947); Chamber Concerto for Viola and String Nonet (1949); 2 syms.: No. 1 (1950) and No. 2 for Chorus and Orch. (Urbana, Ill., April 13, 1957); Violin Concerto (1980; Los Angeles, April 24, 1981). **CHAMBER:** 3 string quartets (1940–84); *Night Watch* for Flute, Horn, and Timpani (1943); Bassoon Sonatina (1944); *Short Concert* for String Quartet (1948); Clarinet Sonata (1951); *Variations* for Recorder (1956); Brass Trio (1957); *Studies in Variation* in 4 parts: for Woodwind Quintet, for Piano Quartet, for Piano, for Violin (1962); Snare Drum Sonata (1966); *Duo* for Violin and Cello, after Kafka's *Amerika* (1971); Concerto for Percussion Quartet (1979); Trio for Strings (1983); *Fantasies, Intermezzi, and Canonic Etudes on the Name EuDiCe SHApiro* for Violin (1985). **KEYBOARD: P i a n o :** *Étude in Memory of Bartók* (1946); *Variations* (1946); *Variations on L'Homme armé* (1947); *Toccata for* content.Harpsichord or Piano (1948); *Fantasy on La, Sol, Fa, Re, Mi* (1949); *10 Inventions* (1950). O r g a n : *Capriccio* (1948); *3 Chorale-Variations on Hebrew Hymns* (1952). VOCAL: *The Automatic Pistol* for Men's Voices (Washington, D.C., Sept. 5, 1943); *25th Psalm* (1947); *Fatal Interview*, song cycle, Edna St. Vincent Millay (1951); *Lord of the Ascendant* for Chorus, Soloists, Dancers, and Orch., after the Gilgamesh (1956); *3 Songs from the Navajo* for Chorus (1957); *3 Greek Choruses* for Women's Chorus (1957); *23rd Psalm* for Soloists and Chorus (1957); *Men* for Narrator and 3 Percussionists (1982; Los Angeles, March 15, 1984); *Subject Cases* for Narrator and Percussionist, after Gertrude Stein (Los Angeles, Feb. 14, 1983).—NS/LK/DM

Koizumi, Fumio, Japanese ethnomusicologist; b. Tokyo, April 4, 1927. He studied aesthetics at the Univ. of Tokyo (degree, 1951), and also took courses in music with Eishi Kikkawa. In 1960 he was appointed to the faculty of the Tokyo National Univ. of Fine Arts and Music. In 1969 and 1970 he lectured at Wesleyan Univ. in the U.S. His primary field of study is Japanese music, but he has also worked on the problems of national music in India, Iran, the Near East, Eastern Europe, and Spain. Among his publications is *Nihon dentō ongaku no kenkyū* (Study of Japanese Traditional Music; Tokyo, 1958).—NS/LK/DM

Koizumi, Kazuhiro, Japanese conductor; b. Kyoto, Oct. 16, 1949. He studied at the Tokyo Univ. of the Arts, and later at the Berlin Hochschule für Musik; also worked with Ozawa. In 1970 he won 1st prize in the Min-Ono conducting competition in Japan, and in 1972, 1st prize in the Karajan Competition in Berlin. After serving as asst. conductor of the Japan Phil. in Tokyo (1970–72), he was music director of the New Japan Phil. there (1975–80) and of the Winnipeg Sym. Orch. (1983–89); also was chief conductor of the Tokyo Metropolitan Sym. Orch. (1984–87). He was principal conductor of the Kyūshū Sym. Orch. in Fukuoka from 1988. —NS/LK/DM

Kojian, Varujan (Haig), Armenian-born American conductor; b. Beirut (of Armenian parents), March 12, 1935; d. Carpinteria, Calif., March 4, 1993. He studied violin at the Paris Cons. (1953–56), winning a premier prix, with Galamian at the Curtis Inst. of Music in Philadelphia, and with Heifetz in Los Angeles (1960). He became asst. concertmaster of the Los Angeles Phil. (1965); after conducting studies with Sasha Popov, he was made Mehta's assistant at the Los Angeles Phil. (1970); then went to Vienna for additional conducting studies with Swarowsky (1971), taking 1st prize in the Sorrento competition (1972). From 1973 to 1976 he was asst. conductor of the Seattle Sym. Orch., and from 1973 to 1980, principal guest conductor of the Royal Opera in Stockholm; then was music director of the Utah Sym. Orch. in Salt Lake City (1980–83), the Chautauqua (N.Y.) Sym. Orch. (1981–86), Ballet West in Salt Lake City (from 1984), and the Santa Barbara Sym. orch. (from 1985). In 1967 he became a naturalized American citizen. —NS/LK/DM

Kókai, Rezső, Hungarian composer and teacher; b. Budapest, Jan. 15, 1906; d. there, March 6, 1962. He was a student of Koessler (composition) and Emánuel Hegyi (piano) at the Budapest Academy of Music (1925–26), and of W. Gurlitt at the Univ. of Freiburg im Breisgau (Ph.D., 1933, with a diss. on Liszt's early piano music). He taught in Budapest at the National Cons. (1926–34) and at the Academy of Music (from 1929); he also was head of the music dept. of the Hungarian Radio (1945–48). In 1952, 1955, and 1956 he received the Erkel Prize.

WORKS: DRAMATIC: *István király* (King Stephen), scenic oratorio (1942); *A rossz feleség* (The Shrew), dance ballad (1942–45); *Lészen ágyú* (There Shall be Cannons), radio opera (1951); music for radio plays and films. ORCH.: *2 Rondos* for Small Orch. (1947); *Verbunkos szvit* (Recruiting Suite; 1950); Violin Concerto (1952); *Széki táncok* (Dances from Szék; 1952); *Rhapsody* for Clarinet and Folk Orch. (1952); *Kis magyar verbunk* (Little Hungarian Recruiting Dance) for Youth Orch. (1954); *Concerto all'ungherese* (1957); *Magyar táncok* (Hungarian Dances) for Youth Orch. (1960). CHAMBER: *Serenade* for String Trio (1949–50); *2 Dances* for Cello and Piano (1950); *4 Hungarian Dances* for Clarinet and Piano (1951); Quartettino for Clarinet and String Trio (1952); *Verbunkos rapszódia* (Recruiting Rhapsody) for Violin and Piano (1952); *Capriccio* for Violin and Piano (1952); *Aria seria: Burla ostinata* for Violin and Piano (1953). P i a n o : *Toccata* (1927); Sonata for 2 Pianos (1949); *Quattro improvvisazioni* (1949–50). VOCAL: Songs.—NS/LK/DM

Kokkonen, Joonas, prominent Finnish composer, pianist, pedagogue, and administrator; b. Iisalmi, Nov. 13, 1921. He was educated at the Univ. (M.A., 1948) and the Sibelius Academy (piano diploma, 1949) in Helsinki. In addition to appearances as a pianist, he was active as a music critic. He also was a teacher (1950–59) and a prof. (1959–63) of composition at the Sibelius Academy. He served as chairman of the Assn. of Finnish Composers (1965–71), the Nordic Composers Council (1968–71), and of TEOSTO, the Finnish copyright bureau (1968–88). In 1963 he became a member of the Academy of Finland, in 1968 he was awarded the Nordic Council Music Prize, and in 1973 he received the Sibelius Prize of the Wihuri Foundation. After composing in a highly personal dodecaphonic style, Kokkonen developed a compositional idiom marked by an intensive motivic technique and economy of expression tending toward the ascetic in his later works.

WORKS: DRAMATIC: O p e r a : *Viimeiset Kiusaukset* (The Last Temptations; 1973–75; Helsinki, Sept. 2, 1975). ORCH.: *Music for Strings* (Helsinki, March 5, 1957); 4 syms.: No. 1 (Helsinki, March 15, 1960), No. 2 (Helsinki, April 18, 1961), No. 3 (Helsinki, Sept. 12, 1967), and No. 4 (Helsinki, Nov. 16, 1971); *Sinfonia da camera* for 12 Strings (Lucerne, Aug. 31, 1962); *Opus sonorum* (1964; Helsinki, Feb. 16, 1965); *Symphonic Sketches* (Helsinki, May 16, 1968); Cello Concerto (Helsinki, Oct. 16, 1969); *Inauguratio* (Helsinki, Sept. 5, 1971); *Interludes From the Opera The Last Temptations* (Helsinki, Sept. 27, 1977); "*...durch einen Spiegel...*" for 12 Strings and Harpsichord (Lucerne, Aug. 25, 1977); *Il Paesaggio* for Chamber Orch. (1986–87; Järvenpää, Feb. 13, 1987). CHAMBER: Piano Trio (Oslo, Oct. 12, 1948); Piano Quintet (Helsinki, Oct. 26, 1953); Duo for Violin and Piano (Helsinki, Nov. 6, 1955); 3 string quartets: No. 1 (Helsinki, May 3, 1959), No. 2 (Helsinki, Oct. 17, 1966), and No. 3 (Helsinki, Aug. 24, 1976); Wind Quintet (1973; Oslo, April 15, 1975); Cello Sonata (1976; Basel, April 3, 1986); *Improvvisazione* for Violin and Piano (Indianapolis, Sept. 12, 1982). KEY-

BOARD: Piano: Sonatina (Helsinki, Oct. 26, 1953); *Religioso* (1956); *5 Bagatelles* (Göteburg, April 21, 1969). Organ: *Wedding March* (Tapiola, Aug. 17, 1968); *Funeral March* (Tuusula, June 14, 1969); *Lux aeterna* (Helsinki, Aug. 9, 1974); *Iuxta crucem* (Lahti, Aug. 5, 1979). VOCAL: *3 Songs of Einari* for High Voice and Piano (1941, 1947; Helsinki, Nov. 11, 1991); *The Evenings,* song cycle for Soprano and Piano (1955); *Christmas Songs* for Children for Medium Voice and Piano (1956, 1958, 1966); *The Hades of the Birds,* song cycle for Mezzo-soprano and Orch. (1958–59; Helsinki, April 7, 1959); *Psalm of the Frog in the Rain* for Men's Chorus (Helsinki, Nov. 30, 1963); *Missa a cappella* for Chorus (Helsinki, Aug. 7, 1963); *Laudatio domini* for Soprano and Chorus (1966; London, Feb. 1, 1967); *Erekhteion,* cantata for Soprano, Baritone, Chorus, and Orch. (1969; Turku, Feb. 28, 1970); *Sub rosa,* song cycle for Mezzo-soprano and Piano (Helsinki, March 25, 1973); *2 Monologues From the Opera The Last Temptations* for Bass and Orch. (1975; Helsinki, Aug. 26, 1977); *Requiem: In memoriam Maija Kokkonen,* the composer's wife, for Soprano, Baritone, Chorus, and Orch. (Helsinki, Sept. 17, 1981); *Väinämöinen Plucked the Strings* for Men's Chorus (1985; Helsinki, May 13, 1986).—NS/LK/DM

Kolar, Victor, Bohemian-American violinist, conductor, and composer; b. Budapest (of Bohemian parents), Feb. 12, 1888; d. Detroit, June 16, 1957. After initial violin training with Jan Kubelik, he studied violin with Ševčik and composition with Dvořák at the Prague Cons. (graduated, 1904). He then settled in the U.S. He was a violinist in the Chicago Sym. Orch. (1904–05), the Pittsburgh Sym. Orch. (1905–08), and the N.Y. Sym. Orch. (1908–20), serving the latter as asst. conductor as well (1914–20). He subsequently became a violinist in the Detroit Sym. Orch., and also held various conducting posts with it until 1942. After teaching at the Arthur Jordan Cons. of Music in Indianapolis, he returned to Detroit to conduct its Scandinavian Sym. Orch. (1950–53) and Women's Sym. Orch. (1950–57); also taught at the Inst. of Musical Arts (1950–56). He wrote a Sym. (N.Y., Jan. 28, 1916); *Hiawatha,* symphonic poem (Pittsburgh, Jan. 31, 1908); *Americana,* symphonic suite (1912); *Slovakia,* rhapsody for Orch. (1922); many songs.—NS/LK/DM

Kolb, Barbara, talented American composer; b. Hartford, Conn., Feb. 10, 1939. She received training in clarinet and composition at the Hartt School of Music in Hartford (1957–61; B.Mus., 1961), where she continued her composition studies with Arnold Franchetti (1961–64; M.Mus., 1965); she also taught there and played clarinet in the Hartford Sym. Orch. During the summer of 1964, she attended the composition courses of Schuller and Foss at the Berkshire Music Center at Tanglewood, and returned in the summer of 1968 to study again with Schuller. In 1966 she studied in Vienna on a Fulbright scholarship. In 1968 she held a MacDowell Colony fellowship, and returned there in 1969, 1971–72, 1980, 1983, and 1987–89. In 1969 she became the first American woman to receive the U.S. Prix de Rome, and was then active at the American Academy in Rome until 1971. In 1971–72 and 1976–77 she held Guggenheim fellowships. She was composer-in-residence at the Marlboro (Vt.) Music Festival in 1973 and at the American Academy in Rome in 1974–75.

After teaching at Brooklyn Coll. of the City Univ. of N.Y. (1973–75), she was artistic director of the "Music New to N.Y." series at the Third Street Music School Settlement (1979–82). In 1983–84 she was active at IRCAM in Paris. She was a visiting prof. at the Eastman School of Music in Rochester, N.Y., in 1984–85. In 1987 she received a Kennedy Center Friedheim Award for her *Millefoglie.* Her music is marked by a sui generis melodic, harmonic, and rhythmic environment in which atonal writing is occasionally complemented by elements à la American jazz and French impressionism.

WORKS: DRAMATIC: *Cantico,* tape collage score for J. Herbert's film on St. Francis of Assisi (N.Y., Dec. 5, 1982); dance score (N.Y., April 18, 1995). ORCH.: *Crosswinds* for Wind Ensemble and Percussion (1969; Rome, Sept. 24, 1970); *Trobar Clus* for Chamber Ensemble (Tanglewood, Aug. 17, 1970); *Soundings* for Chamber Ensemble and Tape (1971–72; N.Y., Oct. 27, 1972; rev. version for Orch., N.Y., Dec. 11, 1975; 2nd rev. version, Boston, Feb. 16, 1978); *Grisaille* (1978–79; Portland, Maine, Feb. 13, 1979); *Yet That Things Go Round* for Chamber Orch. (1986–87; N.Y., May 2, 1987; rev. 1988); *The Enchanted Loom* (1988–89; Atlanta, Feb. 15, 1990; rev. 1992); *Voyants* for Piano and Chamber Orch. (Paris, Feb. 22, 1991); *All in Good Time* (1993; N.Y., Feb. 24, 1994). CHAMBER: *Rebuttal* for 2 Clarinets (1964); *Figments* for Flute and Piano (1967; rev. 1969); *Solitaire* for Piano and Tape (1971; N.Y., Oct. 27, 1972); *Toccata* for Harpsichord and Tape (1971; San Marcos, Tex., Sept. 12, 1973); *Spring River Floers Moon Night* for 2 Pianos and Tape (1974–75; N.Y., Jan. 12, 1976); *Looking for Claudio* for Guitar and Tape (Belgian Radio and TV, Brussels, May 22, 1975); *Homage to Keith Jarrett and Gary Burton* for Flute and Vibraphone (Dallas, March 31, 1976; rev. 1977); *Appello* for Piano (Washington, D.C., Oct. 20, 1976); *3 Lullabies* for Guitar (Paris, March 27, 1980); *Related Characters* for Clarinet or Trumpet and Piano (1980; also for Viola and Piano, Los Angeles, Nov. 7, 1982, and for Alto Saxophone and Piano); *The Point That Divides the Wind* for Organ, Percussion, and 3 Men's Voices (1981–82; N.Y., March 7, 1983); *Cavatina* for Violin (Washington, D.C., May 21, 1983; rev. 1985); *Millefoglie* for 9 Instrumentalists and Computer-generated Tape (1984–85; Paris, June 5, 1985; rev. 1987); *Time-...and Again* for Oboe, String Quartet, and Computer Tape (Washington, D.C., Nov. 22, 1985); *Umbrian Colors* for Violin and Guitar (Marlboro, Vt., Aug. 13, 1986); *Introduction and Allegra* for Guitar (Washington, D.C., Feb. 19, 1992); *Extremes* for Flute and Cello (N.Y., March 15, 1989); *Cloudspin* for Organ and Tape (Cleveland, Oct. 23, 1991; also for Brass Quintet and Organ); *Monticello Trio* for Violin, Cello, and Piano (Charlottesville, Va., Oct. 11, 1992); *In Memory of David Huntley* for String Quartet (N.Y., Oct. 13, 1994); *Turnabout* for Flute and Piano (N.Y., March 16, 1994); *Sidebars* for Bassoon and Piano (Rotterdam, Sept. 1, 1995); *New York Moonglow* for Chamber Ensemble (N.Y., April 18, 1995). VOCAL: *Chansons bas* for Soprano, Harp, and 2 Percussionists (1966); *3 Place Settings* for Narrator, Clarinet, Violin, Double Bass, and Percussion (1968); *Songs Before an Adieu* for Soprano, Flute or Alto Flute, and Guitar (1976–79; WFMT-FM, Chicago, May 23, 1979); *Chromatic Fantasy* for Narrator and 6 Instruments (Minneapolis, Nov. 4, 1979); *The Sundays of My Life,* popular song (1982); *Virgin Mother Creatrix* for Chorus (Indiana, Pa., March 19, 1998).—NS/LK/DM

Kolb, Carlmann, German priest, organist, and composer; b. Kösslarn, Griesbach, Lower Bavaria (baptized), Jan. 29, 1703; d. Munich, Jan. 15, 1765. He was educated in Asbach and Landshut. In 1729 he became a priest at the Asbach Benedictine Abbey, where he also served as organist. He publ. a notable collection of organ music as *Certamen aonium* (Augsburg, 1733; ed. by R. Walter, Altötting, 1959). His Sinfonia for Harpsichord and Strings is also extant.—**LK/DM**

Kolberg, (Henryk) Oskar, Polish music scholar and composer; b. Przysucha, near Radom, Feb. 22, 1814; d. Kraków, June 3, 1890. He studied at the Warsaw Cons. with Elsner and Dobrzyski, then with Girschner and Rungenhagen in Berlin (1835–36). He devoted a major part of his life to traveling and collecting folk songs, his major achievement being the publication of a series of monographs on the various regions of his homeland (33 vols., 1861–90). His collected works began to appear under the auspices of the Polish Academy of Sciences in 1960. He composed a number of popular dances and songs as well as an entertainment, *Krol Pasterzy* (The Shepherd's King; Warsaw, March 2, 1859).

BIBL.: I. Kopernicki, *O. K.* (Kraków, 1889); S. Lam, *O. K.:Żywot i praca* (O. K.: Life and Works; Lemberg, 1914). —**NS/LK/DM**

Köler, David, German composer; b. Zwickau, c. 1532; d. there, July 13?, 1565. He was educated at the Univ. of Ingolstadt (1551). In 1556–57 he was Kantor in Joachimsthal, Bohemia, then town Kantor in Altenburg before taking up the post of Kapellmeister at the Mecklenburg court in Schwerin in 1563. In 1565 he returned to Zwickau as Kantor. His *Zehen Psalmen Davids* for 5 and 6 Voices (Leipzig, 1554) is a distinguished collection of Protestant motets.

BIBL.: G. Eismann, *D. K.: Ein protestantischer Komponist des 16. Jahrhunderts* (Berlin, 1956).—**LK/DM**

Kolessa, Filaret (Mikhailovich), significant Ukrainian ethnomusicologist; b. Chodowitschi, July 17, 1871; d. Lwów, March 3, 1947. He studied in Lemberg (Lwów); later took a course in musicology with Adler at the Univ. of Vienna (Ph.D., 1918). He taught at the state high school in Lemberg (from 1898); became a prof. at the Univ. of Lwów and director of the Ethnographic Museum there (1939). He laid the foundation for the comparative study of Slavonic and East European folk music.

WRITINGS: *Rytmika ukrayinskykh narodnykh pisen* (Rhythm in Ukrainian Folk Songs; Lemberg, 1906–07); "Pro muzychnu formu dum" (On the Musical Form of Historical Chants), *Melodiyi ukrayinskykh narodnykh dum* (Lemberg, 1910; 2nd ed., rev., 1969); *Varianty melodiy ukrainskykh narodnykh dum, ikh kharakterystyka i grupovannya* (Variations in Melody of Ukrainian Folk Historical Chants, Their Characteristics and Classification; Lemberg, 1913); *Pro genezu ukrayinskykh narodnykh dum (ukrainksi narodni dumy u vidnoshenni do pisen, virshiv i pokhoronnykh holosin)* (On the Origin of Ukrainian Folk Historical Chants in Relation to Songs, Religious Songs, and Folk Laments; Lwów, 1920–22). COLLECTIONS: *Melodii haivok, skhopleni na fonograf Y. Rozdolskym* (Easter Song Melodies Recorded by Rozdolsky; Lemberg, 1909); *Melodiyi ukrayinskykh narodnykh dum* (Tunes of Ukrainian Historical Chants; Lemberg, 1910–13; 2nd ed., rev., 1969); "Narodni pisni z pivdennoho Pidkarpattya" (Folk Songs from Southern Subcarpathia), *Naukoviy zbirnyk tovarystva "Prosvita" v Uzhhorodi* (1923); *Narodni pisni z halytskoyi Lemkivshchyny: Teksty i melodiyi* (Folk Songs from West Galicia, Lemky Country: Texts and Melodies; Lwów, 1929); "Narodni pisni z pidkarpatskoy Rusi, melodii i teksty" (Folk Songs from Subcarpathian Ruthenia, Melodies and Texts), *Naukovyy zbirnyk tovarystva "Prosvita" v Uzhhorodi*, XIII-XIV (1938).

BIBL.: S. Hrytsa, *F.M. K.* (Kiev, 1962); O. Palamarchuk, *M. K.* (Kiev, 1989).—**NS/LK/DM**

Kolinski, Mieczyslaw, Polish-born Canadian ethnomusicologist, music theorist, and composer; b. Warsaw, Sept. 5, 1901; d. Toronto, May 7, 1981. He began his musical training in Hamburg, and then studied piano and composition at the Berlin Hochschule für Musik; took courses in musicology, psychology, and anthropology at the Univ. of Berlin (Ph.D., 1930, with the diss. *Die Musik der Primitivstämme auf Malaka und ihre Beziehungen zur samoanischen Musik*; publ. in *Anthropos*, XXV, 1930). He assisted Hornbostel at the Berlin Staatliches Phonogramm-Archiv (1926–33); then moved to Prague, where he remained until 1938, when he went to Belgium to avoid the Nazis; during much of the German occupation, he was in hiding. He settled in N.Y. in 1951; was co-founder (1955) and president (1958–59) of the Soc. for Ethnomusicology; taught at the Univ. of Toronto (1966–76); became a naturalized Canadian citizen in 1974. He transcribed more than 2,000 works from all over the world; publ. *Konsonanz als Grundlage einer neuen Akkordlehre* (Prague, 1936).

WORKS: 2 piano sonatas (1919; 1946, rev. 1966); Violin Sonata (1924); Cello Sonata (1926); *Lyric Sextet* for Soprano, Flute, and String Quartet (1929); 4 piano suites (1929–46); String Quartet (1931); *Expresszug-Phantasie*, ballet (Salzburg, 1935); Concertino for Soprano, String Quartet, and Piano (1951); *Dahomey Suite* for Flute or Oboe and Piano or String Orch. (1951); *Hatikvah Variations* for String Quartet (1960); *Dance Fantasy* for Strings (1968); *Encounterpoint* for Organ and String Quartet (1973); Concertino for Soprano, Clarinet, and Piano (1974); music for recorder ensemble; songs; folk-song arrangements.—**NS/LK/DM**

Kolisch, Rudolf, Austrian-born American violinist; b. Klamm am Semmering, July 20, 1896; d. Watertown, Mass., Aug. 1, 1978. He began training in childhood. After sustaining an injury to his left hand, he learned to hold his violin with his right hand and the bow with his left. He continued his studies at the Vienna Academy of Music and the Univ. of Vienna (graduated, 1913), and took courses with Ševčik (violin) and Schreker and Schoenberg (theory and composition). In 1922 he organized the Kolisch Quartet, which systematically presented works by modern composers. It was the first string quartet to perform works from the standard repertoire from memory. In 1935 he went to the U.S.; after his quartet disbanded (1939), he became 1st violin of the Pro Arte Quartet (1942). He taught at the Univ. of Wisc. (1944–67), and served as artist-in-residence and head of the chamber music dept. of the New England Cons. of Music in Boston.—**NS/LK/DM**

Kollmann, Augustus Frederic Christopher (actually, August Friedrich Christoph), German-born English organist, music theorist, and composer; b. Engelbostel, March 21, 1756; d. London, April 19, 1829. He studied with Böttner, the Hannover organist. He was made organist and schoolmaster of Kloster Lüne, near Lüneburg (1781). Soon after, he went to London, where he served as organist and schoolmaster of the Royal German Chapel in St. James's (1782–1829); was also chapel-keeper (1784–1829). Among his practical works are 4 Sonatas for Harpsichord or Piano and Violin (1788), *The Shipwreck* for Piano, Violin, and Cello (1796), Piano Concerto (1804), and *The Praise of God*, oratorio (1817). He also composed a number of theoretico-practical works, including *A Symphony* [for Piano, Violin, and Cello] *with Analytical Explanations*, "Analyzed Sym." (1798), *The Melody of the Hundredth Psalm, with Examples and Directions for an Hundred Different Harmonies* for 4 Voices (1809), and *An Introduction to Extemporary Modulation, in Six General Lessons* for Piano, Harp, Violin, or Cello (1820).

WRITINGS: *An Essay on Musical Harmony* (1796; 2nd ed., 1817); *An Essay on Practical Musical Composition* (1799; 2nd ed., rev., 1812; reprint, 1973); *A Practical Guide to Thorough-Bass* (1801); *A New Theory of Musical Harmony* (1806; 2nd ed., rev., 1823); *A Second Practical Guide to Thorough- Bass* (1807).
—NS/LK/DM

Kollo (real name, **Kollodziejski**), **(Elimar) Walter,** noted German composer, grandfather of **René Kollo;** b. Neidenburg, Jan. 28, 1878; d. Berlin, Sept. 30, 1940. He studied at the Sondershausen Cons. He began his career writing songs and cabaret music, and also was active as a theater conductor. After working in Königsberg and Stettin, he settled in Berlin and composed several theater pieces before attaining notable success with his musical comedy, *Filmzauber* (Oct. 19, 1912). It soon was performed internationally with great success. Then followed another outstanding score, *Wie einst im Mail* (Oct. 4, 1913; in collaboration with W. Bredschneider). After composing *Der Juxbaron* (Hamburg, Nov. 14, 1913), Kollo produced a series of remarkably successful Berlin scores, including *Extrablätter* (Oct. 24, 1914; in collaboration with Bredschneider), *Immer feste druff!* or *Gloria Viktoria* (Oct. 1, 1914), *Wenn zwei Hochzeit machen* (Oct. 23, 1915; in collaboration with Bredschneider), *Auf Flügeln des Gesanges* (Sept. 9, 1916; in collaboration with Bredschneider), *Der selige Balduin* (March 31, 1916), *Die tolle Komtess* (Feb. 21, 1917), *Die Gulaschkanone* (Feb. 23, 1917), *Drei alte Schachteln* (Nov. 6, 1917), *Blitzblaues Blut* (Feb. 9, 1918), and *Sterne, die wieder leuchtet* (Nov. 6, 1918). Following the success of *Fräulein Puck* (Munich, June 25, 1919), Kollo resumed composing for the Berlin theaters, producing such successful scores as *Marietta* (Dec. 22, 1923) and *Drei arme kleine Mädels* (April 22, 1927). During this same period, he also composed the music for several highly popular revues, among them *Drunter und Drüber* (1923), which included the hit song *Solang noch Untern Linden*. While Kollo continued to compose until his death, he never succeeded in attaining the success of his earlier years.
—NS/LK/DM

Kolman, Peter, Slovak-born Austrian composer; b. Bratislava, May 29, 1937. In 1944 the Nazis imprisoned him at the Theresienstadt concentration camp, from which he was liberated in 1945. Returning to Bratislava, he pursued his composition studies at the Cons. (1951–56) and the Academy of Music (1956–60). In 1961 he became a music ed. in the division of serious music of the Czech Radio in Bratislava, where he was director of its experimental studio (studio for electronic music) from 1965 to 1977. After the Soviet-bloc invasion of his homeland in 1968, he was expelled from the Slovak Composers Soc. as a result of a performance ban on his music. In 1977 he emigrated to Austria and in 1979 became a naturalized Austrian citizen. He worked as an ed. at Universal Edition in Vienna. As a composer, Kolman followed in the paths of the 2nd Viennese School and the post-World War II avant-garde.

WORKS: ORCH.: *Funeral Music* (1958); *Violin Concerto* (1960); *4 Pieces* (1963; rev. 1996); *Monumento per 6,000,000* (1964–66; rev. 1996); *Concerto for Orch.* (1995). **CHAMBER:** *Partecipazioni* for 12 Instruments (1962); *Sonata canonica* for Clarinet and Bass Clarinet (1963); *Panegyrikos* for 4 Oboes, 4 Trumpets, 4 Percussion, and 4 Cellos (1964); *Molisation*, mobile for Flute and Vibraphone (1965); String Quartet (1970); *Movement for Winds and Percussion* (1971); *"...wie ein Hauch von Glückseligkeit"* for Violin and Piano (1978); *Music for 14 Strings* (1978). **KEYBOARD: Piano:** *3 Piano Pieces in Memory of Arnold Schönberg* (1960); *Note bene* (1978). **Organ:** *Laudatio* (1982); *Interludium* (1984); *Jeu de touches* (1986). **ELECTRONIC:** *Omaggio a Gesualdo* (1970); *Lentement mais pas trop* (1972); *Poliritmica* (1974); *E 15* (1974); *9* (1976).—NS/LK/DM

Kolneder, Walter, noted Austrian musicologist; b. Wels, July 1, 1910; d. Karlsruhe, Jan. 30, 1994. He studied composition privately with Johann Nepomuk David (1927–29); also studied with Paumgartner (conducting) and Strub (viola) at the Salzburg Mozarteum (1925–35); took courses in musicology at the Univ. of Vienna (1934–35) and with W. Fischer at the Univ. of Innsbruck (Ph.D., 1949, with the diss. *Die vokale Mehrstimmigkeit in der Volksmusik der österreichischen Alpenländer*); completed his Habilitation at the Univ. of Saarbrücken with his *Antonio Vivaldi: Neue Studien zur Biographie und Stilistik seiner Werke* (extracts in *Aufführungspraxis bei Vivaldi*, Leipzig, 1955; 2nd ed., 1973). He taught at the Graz Cons. (1936–39) and the Staatliche Hochschule für Musikerziehung in Graz-Eggenberg (1936–45); was director of the Luxembourg Cons. (1953–59); also was a Privatdozent at the Univ. of Saarbrücken (from 1956). He was director of the Darmstadt Academy from 1959 to 1965 and of the Karlsruhe Hochschule für Musik from 1966 to 1972; was made ausserplanmässiger prof. of musicology at the Univ. of Karlsruhe (1966). His writings included *Anton Webern: Einführung in Werk und Stil* (Rodenkirchen, 1961; Eng. tr., 1968, as *Anton Webern: An Introduction to His Works*); *Geschichte der Musik: Ein Studien- und Prüfungshelfer* (Heidelberg, 1961; 5th ed., 1973); *Musikinstrumentenkunde: Ein Studien- und Prüfungshelfer* (Heidelberg, 1963; 3rd ed., 1972); *Singen, Hören, Schreiben: Eine praktische Musiklehre in vier Lehr- und vier Übungsheften* (Mainz, 1963–67); *Antonio Vivaldi: Leben und Werk* (Wiesbaden, 1965; Eng. tr., 1970); *Das Buch der Violine* (Zürich, 1972); *Anton Webern: Genesis und Metamorphosen eines Stils* (Vienna, 1973); *Melodietypen bei Vivaldi* (Zürich, 1973); *Schule des General-*

bassspiels (2 vols., Wilhelmshaven, 1983–84); *Johann Sebastian Bach (1685–1750): Leben, Werk, und Nachwirken in zeitgenössischen Dokumenten* (Wilhelmshaven, 1991).
—**NS/LK/DM**

Kolodin, Irving, prominent American music critic and writer on music; b. N.Y., Feb. 22, 1908; d. there, April 29, 1988. He studied at the Inst. of Musical Art in N.Y. (1930–31). He was music critic for the *N.Y. Sun* (1932–50) and the *Saturday Review* (1947–82), and also served as program annotator for the N.Y. Phil. (1953–58). He also taught at N.Y.'s Juilliard School (from 1968).

WRITINGS (all publ. in N.Y. unless otherwise given): *The Metropolitan Opera...* (1936; 4th ed., rev., 1966); with Benny Goodman, *The Kingdom of Swing* (1939); ed. *The Critical Composer* (1940); *A Guide to Recorded Music* (Garden City, N.Y., 1941; 2nd ed., rev., 1946 as *New Guide to Recorded Music*; 3rd ed., rev., 1950); *Mozart on Records* (1942); with C. Burke and E. Canby, *The Saturday Review Home Book of Recorded Music and Sound Reproduction* (1952; 2nd ed., 1956); *Orchestral Music* (1955); *The Musical Life* (1958); ed. *The Composer as Listener: A Guide to Music* (1958); *The Continuity of Music: A History of Influence* (1969); *The Interior Beethoven: A Biography of the Music* (1975); *The Opera Omnibus: Four Centuries of Critical Give and Take* (1976); *In Quest of Music* (1980).—**NS/LK/DM**

Komitas (real name, **Sogomonian**), Armenian ethnomusicologist and composer; b. Kutina, Turkey, Oct. 8, 1869; d. Paris, Oct. 22, 1935. He studied at the Gevorkian Theological Seminary in Vagharshapat. He was made a vardapet (archimandrite) in 1894, taking the name Komitas, after a 7th-century Armenian hymn writer. In 1895 he went to Tiflis, where he studied theory. He then lived in Berlin (1896–99), where he took courses at Richard Schmidt's private cons. and with Bellermann, Fleischer, and Friedlaender at the Univ. He studiously collected materials on Armenian folk music, publishing articles on the subject and also composing works utilizing Armenian motifs. In 1910 he moved to Constantinople; the Armenian massacre of 1915 so affected him that he became incurably psychotic, and lived from 1919 in a Paris hospital. His body was reburied in the Pantheon of Armenian Artists in Yerevan in 1936. His collected compositions were ed. by R. Atayan (3 vols., Yerevan, 1960–69).

BIBL.: A. Shaverdian, *K. i armyanskaya musikalmaya kultura* (K. and Armenian Music; Yerevan, 1956); H. Begian, *Gomidas Vartabed: His Life and Importance to Armenian Music* (diss., Univ. of Mich., 1964); G. Geodakian, *K.* (Yerevan, 1969).—**NS/LK/DM**

Komjáti, Károly, Hungarian composer; Budapest, May 8, 1896; d. there, July 3, 1953. He received training at the Budapest Academy of Music. He then devoted himself to composing light theater works mainly for Budapest. After winning enormous success with his second operetta, *Pillangó főhadnagy* (Lieutenant Butterfly; June 7, 1918), he went on to write such successful works as *A harapós férj* (The Snappy Husband; March 22, 1931; rev. version, May 25, 1949), *Fizessen nagysád* (Jan. 23, 1932), and *Éjfeli tangó* (Feb. 27, 1932). After his *Ein Liebestraum* was premiered in Vienna (Oct. 27, 1933), he

resumed composing for the Budapest stage with such scores as *A szegény ördög* (The Poor Devil; Sept. 29, 1934), *Bécsi tavasz* (Nov. 15, 1935), *Antoinette* (Dec. 23, 1937), and *Csicsónénak három lánya* (Oct. 5, 1946).—**NS/LK/DM**

Komorous, Rudolf, Czech-born Canadian composer, bassoonist, and teacher; b. Prague, Dec. 8, 1931. He studied bassoon at the Prague Cons. (1946–52) before pursuing his training with Karel Pivoňka (bassoon) and Bořkovec (composition) at the Prague Academy of Music (1952–56); later he studied electronic music in Warsaw (1959). After teaching at the Beijing Cons. (1959–61), he returned to Prague as 1st bassoonist in the orch. of the National Theater. In 1961 he was co-founder of Musica Viva Pragensis. In 1969 he emigrated to Canada and in 1974 became a naturalized Canadian citizen. He was a visiting prof. at Macalester Coll. in St. Paul, Minn. (1969–71). In 1971 he joined the faculty of the Univ. of Victoria to teach composition and advanced theory, and also organized its electronic music studio; he then was acting chairman (1975–76) and director (from 1976) of its school of music. He was director of the School for the Contemporary Arts at Simon Fraser Univ. from 1989 to 1994, remaining on the Univ. faculty until his retirement in 1996. In his music, Komorous has explored various contemporary paths and byways. In some of his scores, he has made use of musical quotations by other composers. His *Sinfony No. 1, Stardust*, makes use of Hoagy Carmichael's famous song.

WORKS: DRAMATIC: Opera: *Lady Whiterose* (1966), *No no miyu*, chamber opera (Vancouver, Sept. 30, 1988). ORCH.: *Chamber Music* for Bassoon and Small Orch. (1959); *The Gloomy Grace* for Small Orch. (1968); *Bare and Dainty* (1970); *Rossi* for Chamber Orch. (1974; rev. 1975); *Sinfony No. 1, Stardust* (Toronto, Nov. 20, 1988), *No 2, Canadian* (1990; Vancouver, March 17, 1991), and *No. 3, Ex c*, for Strings (1994–95); *Demure Charm* for Bassoon, Flute, and Strings (Toronto, Oct. 17, 1990); Bassoon Concerto (1994–95; Rotterdam, Aug. 31, 1995). CHAMBER: *Duettino* for Clarinet and Bassoon (1954); *The Sweet Queen* for Mouth Harmonica, Bass Drum, and Piano (1962); *Olympia* for Flexatone, Mouth Harmonica, Nightingale, Acolyte Bells, Sleigh Bells, and Rattle (1964); *Mignon* for 4 String Bowed Instruments (1965); *Chanson* for Guitar, Clock Spiral, and Viola (1965); *York* for Flute, Oboe or Trumpet, Bassoon, Triangle, Piano, Mandolin, and Double Bass (1967); *Preludes* for 13 Early Instruments (1974); *The Midnight Narcissus* for Alto Flute, Piccolo, Horn, Oboe, Cello, Piano, and Triangle (1977); String Trio (1981; rev. as *Serenade* for String Orch., 1982); *Fumon Manga* for Flute, Oboe, Clarinet, Bassoon, and Horn (1981; rev. 1983); *Quartettino: Les Amours Jaunes* for Bassoon, Violin, Viola, and Cello (1983); *The Necklace of Clear Understanding* for Baroque Flute (1986); *Ritratto di Laura Battiferri* for 2 Violins, 2 Violas, and 2 Cellos (1989); *Aokigahara* for Bass Flute and Thing-spa (Tibetan Cymbals) (1989); *Dame's Rocket* for Clarinet, Cornet, Vibraphone, Marimba, Piano, and Contrabass (1991); *Hermione Dreaming* for Baroque Flute, Baroque Bassoon, Conga, Harpsichord, Baroque Viola, and Baroque Cello (1992). VOCAL: *23 Poems About Horses* for Narrator and 9 Instruments (1978; rev. 1985); *Vermilion Dust* for Baritone, Chorus, and Small Orch. (1980; rev. 1984); choral pieces; songs. ELECTRONIC: *The Tomb of Malevich* (1965); *Anatomy of Melancholy* (1974); *Listening to Rain* (1986).—**NS/LK/DM**

Komorzynski, Egon, Austrian musicologist; b. Vienna, May 7, 1878; d. there, March 16, 1963. He took courses at various univs., including those of Berlin, Leipzig, Munich, and Vienna (graduated, 1900). He was a prof. of German language studies and literature at Vienna's Handelsakademie (1904–34), and also music critic of the *Österreichische Volkszeitung* for 40 years.

WRITINGS: *Emanuel Schikaneder: Ein Beitrag zur Geschichte des deutschen Theaters* (Berlin, 1901; 2nd ed., rev., 1951); *Mozarts Kunst der Instrumentation* (Stuttgart, 1906); *Mozart: Sendung und Schicksal eines deutschen Künstlers* (Berlin, 1941; 2nd ed., rev., 1955); *Der Vater der Zauberflöte: Emanuel Schikaneders Leben* (Vienna, 1948).—**NS/LK/DM**

Komzák, Karel, Bohemian conductor and composer; b. Netěchovice, near České Budějovice, Nov. 4, 1823; d. there, March 19, 1893. After taking a teacher-training course at St. Henry's Coll. in Prague (1841–42), he began his career as a teacher and organist. In 1854 he founded his own orch. in Prague, which also served as the orch. of the Provisional Theater (1862–65); in 1865 it became the theater's official orch. In later years, Komzák pursued a career as a military bandmaster. He composed about 300 works, mainly marches and dances, some of which utilized Czech folk songs. His son, also named Karel Komzák (b. Prague, Nov. 8, 1850; d. Baden bei Wien, April 23, 1905), was a bandmaster and composer. He studied with his father and then at the Prague Cons. (1861–67), and subsequently was active as a bandmaster. He composed many dances in collaboration with his father, often utilizing Czech folk songs. Among his other works were an operetta, *Edelweis*, and some songs.

BIBL.: M. Schönherr and E. Brixel, *K. K.: Vater, Sohn, Enkel: Ein Beitrag zur Rezeptionsgeschichte der österreichischen Popularmusik* (Vienna, 1989).—**LK/DM**

Kondorossy, Leslie, Hungarian-American composer; b. Pressburg, June 25, 1915. He studied at the Academy of Music in Budapest. After World War II, he settled in Cleveland. He continued his studies at Western Reserve Univ., and later studied Japanese music and theater at Tokyo's Sophia Univ. He was active as a teacher, conductor, and composer. Kondorossy was especially proficient in producing short operas.

WORKS: DRAMATIC: Opera: *Night in the Puszta* (Cleveland, June 28, 1953); *The Voice* (Cleveland, May 15, 1954); *The Pumpkin* (Cleveland, May 15, 1954); *The Midnight Duel,* radio opera (Cleveland, March 20, 1955); *The String Quartet,* radio opera (Cleveland, May 8, 1955); *Unexpected Visitor* (Cleveland, Oct. 21, 1956); *The 2 Imposters* (Cleveland, Oct. 21, 1956); *The Fox* (Cleveland, Jan. 28, 1961); *The Baksis* (1964); *Nathan the Wise* (1964); *The Poorest Suitor,* children's opera (Cleveland, May 24, 1967); *Shizuka's Dance,* children's opera (Cleveland, April 22, 1969); *Kalamona and the 4 Winds,* children's opera (Cleveland, Sept. 12, 1971); *Ruth and Naomi,* church opera (Cleveland, April 28, 1974). **Ballet:** *Magic Dance* (1948); *The Ideal* (1950); *King Solomon* (1952). **ORCH.:** *Serenade* for English Horn and Chamber Orch. or Piano (Bavarian Radio, Munich, Feb. 2, 1948); Trombone Concerto (1958); Trumpet Concerto (1959); Harp Concerto (1961); *Prelude and Fugue* (1966); Harpsichord Concerto (1972); *Music* (1973). **CHAMBER:** 2 piano sonatas (No. 1, Cleveland, May 17, 1966; No. 2, 1955); Harpsichord Sonata

(1958); Trio for Violin, Viola, and Cello (1958); String Quartet No. 1 (Cleveland, Dec. 9, 1960); *Music* for Flute and Piano (1961); Suite for Violin and Piano (1964); Harpsichord Trio (Cleveland, Dec. 8, 1972); Suite for Brass Sextet (Cleveland, July 9, 1977); *Music* for Organ and Trumpet (1981). **VOCAL:** *Kossuth Cantata* (Cleveland, March 16, 1952); *New Dreams for Old,* cantata for Soloists, Chorus, and Chamber Orch. (Cleveland, Nov. 19, 1959); *David, a Son of Jesse,* oratorio (Cleveland, June 4, 1967); *Jazz Mass* for Voices and Jazz Band (1968); *Ode to the Loyalty of the First,* cantata for Soloists, Chorus, and Chamber Orch. (Cleveland, Sept. 19, 1971); *Sacred Fire,* oratorio (1979).
—**NS/LK/DM**

Kondrashin, Kirill (Petrovich), noted Russian conductor; b. Moscow, March 6, 1914; d. Amsterdam, March 7, 1981. He studied piano and theory at the Musical Technicum in Moscow, then took a course in conducting with Khaikin at the Moscow Cons. (1932–36). While still a student, he conducted light opera (1934–37), and then conducted at the Malyi Opera Theater in Leningrad (1937–41). In 1943 he received appointment to the staff of the Bolshoi Theater in Moscow, where he conducted a wide repertoire emphasizing Russian operas (until 1956). He received Stalin prizes in 1948 and 1949. In 1969 he was named People's Artist of the U.S.S.R. Kondrashin was the first Soviet conductor to appear in the U.S. (1958), and held numerous subsequent engagements in America, the last being a concert he conducted at the Hollywood Bowl in Feb. 1981. In 1960 he was appointed chief conductor of the Moscow Phil., with which he performed numerous new Soviet works, including Shostakovich's controversial 13th Sym. He also taught at the Moscow Cons. (1950–53; 1972–75). After 1975 he increased his guest engagements outside Russia, and in 1978 decided to emigrate; in 1979 he assumed the post of permanent conductor of the Concertgebouw Orch. in Amsterdam. His conducting style was marked by an effective blend of lyrical melodiousness and dramatic romanticism, without deviating from the prevalent Russian traditions. He publ. a book on the art of conducting (Leningrad, 1970).—**NS/LK/DM**

Konetzni, Anny, esteemed Austrian soprano, sister of **Hilde Konetzni;** b. Ungarisch-Weisskirchen, Feb. 12, 1902; d. Vienna, Sept. 6, 1968. She studied with Erik Schmedes at the Vienna Cons. and later in Berlin with Jacques Stückgold. She made her operatic debut as a contralto at the Vienna Volksoper in 1925; soon turned to soprano roles. She sang in Augsburg, Elberfeld, and Chemnitz; sang with the Berlin State Opera (1931–34) and also appeared with the Vienna State Opera, La Scala in Milan, the Paris Opéra, and London's Covent Garden. She made her Metropolitan Opera debut in N.Y. as Brünnhilde in *Die Walküre* on Dec. 26, 1934; remained on its roster until the close of the season. After her retirement in 1955, she taught voice in Vienna. She was particularly notable in Wagner and Strauss roles.
—**NS/LK/DM**

Konetzni, Hilde, famous Austrian soprano, sister of **Anny Konetzni;** b. Vienna, March 21, 1905; d. there, April 20, 1980. She studied at the Vienna Cons., and later in Prague with Prochaska-Neumann. She made her operatic debut as Sieglinde in *Die Walküre* in Chemnitz in 1929; then sang at the German Theater in Prague (1932–36). In 1936 she became a member of the Vienna State Opera; also appeared at Salzburg, La Scala in Milan, Covent Garden in London, South America, and the U.S. In 1954 she joined the faculty of the Vienna Academy of Music. She was an outstanding interpreter of Wagner and Strauss.—NS/LK/DM

König, Johann Balthasar, German composer; b. Waltershausen, near Gotha (baptized), Jan. 28, 1691; d. Frankfurt am Main (buried), April 2, 1758. About 1703 he became a chorister in the Frankfurt am Main municipal Kapelle. In 1721 he was made director of music at the Katharinenkirche but remained with the Kapelle, where in 1727 he was made Kapellmeister. König was esteemed for his cantatas for municipal and church occasions. He also prepared the important chorale book *Harmonischer Lieder Schatz* (Frankfurt am Main, 1738; 2nd ed., aug., c. 1750), which contains almost 2,000 melodies with basso continuo, 300 of which appear to be by him. It also includes all those for the Geneva Psalter.—LK/DM

König, Klaus, German tenor; b. Beuthen, May 26, 1934. He was a student in Dresden of Johannes Kemter. In 1970 he joined the Cottbus City Theater, and in 1973 became a member of the Dessau Landestheater. After singing with the Leipzig City Theater (1978–82), he was a member of the Dresden State Opera (from 1982). In 1984 he made debuts at Milan's La Scala and London's Covent Garden as Tannhäuser, one of his most striking roles. In 1985 he appeared as Tristan at the Théâtre Royal de la Monnaie in Brussels and as Weber's Max at the first performance of the restored Semper Opera House in Dresden. In 1988 he made his U.S. debut as Tannhäuser with the Houston Grand Opera. He also sang opera in Paris, Strasbourg, Madrid, Barcelona, Cologne, Munich, Vienna, and elsewhere in Europe. Among his other roles are Parsifal, Walther von Stolzing, Lohengrin, Don Alvaro, Florestan, Don José, Radames, and Don Carlos. He also appeared throughout Europe as a concert and oratorio artist.—NS/LK/DM

Königslöw, Johann Wilhelm Cornelius von, German organist and composer; b. Hamburg, March 16, 1745; d. Lubeck, May 14, 1833. He studied piano and voice with his father, and at 13 became a boy soprano in Lübeck's Abendmusiken under A. Kenzen at the Marienkirche. Kenzen taught him organ, violin, and composition. Königslöw became his assistant (1772) and successor (1781), and also took over the direction of his Abendmusiken (1773), quickly establishing himself as a leading figure in the musical life of Hamburg. He wrote a number of oratorios, most of which are lost, as well as cantatas, orch. works, and keyboard music.—NS/LK/DM

Königsperger, Marianus (actually, **Johann Erhard**), German organist and composer; b. Roding, near Regensburg, Dec. 4, 1708; d. Prüfening, near Regensburg, Oct. 9, 1769. He was a choirboy at the Benedictine abbey in Prüfening. Following theological studies, he entered the Benedictine order, serving as organist and choirmaster in Prüfening (1734–69). His prolific and esteemed output of Latin sacred music was publ. in 29 vols. (1733–60), which includes masses, Psalms, and offertories. He also wrote numerous Singspiels, chamber music, and keyboard pieces.

BIBL.: F. Zwickler, *Frater M. K. OSB (1708–1769): Ein Beitrag zur süddeutschen Kirchenmusik des 18. Jahrhunderts* (diss., Univ. of Mainz, 1964).—LK/DM

Konink, Servaas de, Netherlands composer; b. place and date unknown; d. Amsterdam, between Dec. 9, 1717 and Feb. 28, 1718. He was a musician in the Amsterdam theater orch., and also active as a teacher. He was a principal figure in the development of opera in the Dutch language, his *De vrijadje van Cloris en Rossje* (Amsterdam, 1688) being a pioneering work. Among his other works were incidental music to Racine's play *Athalie* (Amsterdam, 1697) and duo and trio sonatas.—LK/DM

Konitz, Lee, legendary jazz alto saxophonist; b. Chicago, Oct. 13, 1927. One of the true originals, his initial recorded solos were brilliantly virtuosic and intricately structured. Over the years he has gradually refined his style to play fewer and fewer notes, and his tone, always distinctive, has softened and spread.

He took up the clarinet at 11, but eventually made the saxophone his chosen instrument. He gained early experience with the Gay Claridge band in Chicago and there became a disciple of pianist Lennie Tristano. He appeared with Claude Thornhill (1947–48), Charlie Parker, and Tristano. In 1948, he performed with Miles Davis at the Royal Roost (broadcasts in quintet and nonet), and recorded with the Davis nonet (1949–51; including the famed *Birth of the Cool* sessions). During this time period he primarily performed with Tristano and his associates. After working with Stan Kenton (1952–54), he was involved mainly with his own combos, also working with Gerry Mulligan and Gil Evans. Always shy of publicity and exposure, he withdrew from music in the early 1960s. He returned to active performing in the mid-1960s with a major tour of Europe (1965–66). From the 1960s on, Konitz spent much time in Europe, also in Japan, and made many records in a wide variety of playing situations, from duets to his own nonet (active ca. 1975–80). He appeared at N.Y.'s Carnegie Hall (1980). In the 1990s, he has led a Brazilian-flavored quartet featuring pianist Peggy Stern. In 1992 he was awarded the prestigious Danish Jazzpar prize, and six years later the Order of Arts and Letters from the French government. A longtime resident of Manhattan's upper west side, in the 1990s he married a woman from Cologne, Germany and established a second residence there. He is the subject of *Konitz: Portrait of the Artist as Saxophonist* filmed at Montreal's Concordia Univ., 1988. He played with Ornette Coleman in Italy in July 1998.

DISC.: *Subconscious-Lee* (1949); *Ezz-Thetic* (1951); *K. Meets Mulligan* (1953); *With Gerry Mulligan Quartet* (1953); *Jazz at Storyville* (1954); *L.K. at Harvard Square* (1955); *With Warne Marsh*

(1955); *Real L.K.* (1957); *Tranquility* (1957); *An Image: L.K. with Strings* (1958); *Very Cool* (1958); *L.K. Meets Jimmy Giuffre* (1959); *Live at the Half Note* (1959); *You and Lee* (1960); *Motion* (1961); *Duets* (1967); *Alto Summit* (1968); *Zo-Ko-Ma* (1968); *L.K. Sax Duets* (1970); *Spirits* (1971); *I Concentrate on You* (1974); *Lone-Lee* (1974); *Satori* (1974); *Jazz Exchange (Vols. 1–3)* (1975); *Oleo* (1975); *Windows* (1975); *Figure and Spirit* (1976); *L.K. Meets Warne Marsh Again* (1976); *L.K. Nonet* (1977); *L.K. Quintet* (1977); *Pyramid* (1977); *Tenorlee* (1977); *Yes, Yes, Nonet* (1979); *Live at the Berlin Jazz Days* (1980); *Art of the Duo* (1983); *N.Y. Album* (1987); *Round and Round* (1988); *Zounds* (1990); *Friends* (1991); *And the Jazzpar All Star Nonet* (1992); *Lunasea* (1992); *Rhapsody* (1993); *Lullaby of Birdland* (1995).

BIBL.: M. Frohne, *Subconscious L.: 35 Years of Records and Tapes: The L. K. Discography 1947–82* (Freiburg, 1983); B. Washut, *L.K.'s Transcribed Solos for Alto Sax* (Houston, 1994).—**LP/NS**

Konjović, Petar,
Serbian composer; b. Sombor, May 6, 1882; d. Belgrade, Oct. 1, 1970. He studied at the Prague Cons. with Novák and Stecker. He was director of the Zagreb Opera (1921–26), the national theaters in Osijek, Split, and Novi Sad (1927–33), and again at the Zagreb Opera (1933–39). He then was prof. at the Belgrade Academy of Music (1939–50), where he also served twice as rector.

WORKS: DRAMATIC: Opera: *Vilin Veo* or *Ženidba Miloševa* (The Wedding of Milos; Zagreb, April 25, 1917); *Knez od Zete* (The Duke of Zeta; Belgrade, May 25, 1929); *Koštana* (Zagreb, April 16, 1931); *Sel jaci* (The Peasants; Belgrade, March 3, 1952); *Otadžbina* (Homeland; 1960). **ORCH.:** *Serbia liberata*, symphonic poem (1906); Sym. (1907; rev. by D. Jakšič, 1955); *Na selu* (In the Country), symphonic variations (1915; rev. 1935); *Jadranski capriccio* (Adriatic Capriccio) for Violin and Orch. (1920); *Makar Čudra*, symphonic poem (1944). **CHAMBER:** 3 string quartets; solo pieces for violin, cello, and piano. **VOCAL:** *Moja zemlja* (My Country), 100 folk songs, of which 25 are arranged for Voice and Small Orch.; songs.—**NS/LK/DM**

Kono, Kristo,
Albanian composer; b. Korçë, July 17, 1907; d. Tirana, Jan. 22, 1991. After training at the Milan Cons., he returned to Albania and became a prominent figure in the development of a national music. He eventually championed the cause of socialist realism. Kono composed the first Albanian operetta *Agimi* (The Dawn; Korçë, Nov. 22, 1954). Among his other works were the opera *Lulja e kujtimit* (The Flowers of Remembrance; Tirana, Nov. 5, 1961), orch. pieces, and choral works.—**NS/LK/DM**

Konoye, Hidemarō,
Japanese conductor and composer; b. Tokyo, Nov. 18, 1898; d. there, June 2, 1973. A member of an aristocratic Japanese family, he received his education in Japan and in Europe. After attending classes in composition of d'Indy at the Schola Cantorum in Paris, he took courses with Franz Schreker and Georg Schumann at the Berlin Cons. He made his European debut as a conductor with the Berlin Phil. on Jan. 18, 1924. Returning to Japan, he was principal conductor of the New Sym. Orch. in Tokyo (1926–34), specializing in new works of Japanese, European, and American composers. He conducted in the U.S. in 1937 and 1957. He was the composer of several orch. pieces based on

Japanese subjects; also orchestrated early Japanese court music for the modern Western orch.; arranged the music of *Madama Butterfly* for the films (inserting many Japanese folk melodies).—**NS/LK/DM**

Kont, Paul,
Austrian composer and teacher; b. Vienna, Aug. 19, 1920. He studied violin with Vittorio Borri and piano with Hans Nast at the Vienna Cons. (1939–40), then took a course in conducting with Josef Krips and Swarowsky (diploma, 1947) and in composition with Josef Lechthaler (diploma, 1948) at the Vienna Academy of Music; also studied analysis with Josef Polnauer. After attending Fortner's class in Darmstadt (1951), he completed his training with Messiaen, Milhaud, and Honegger in Paris (1952). In 1969 he joined the faculty of the Vienna Academy of Music, where he was a prof. of composition (1980–86). His honors included the Austrian State Prize (1964), the prize of the City of Vienna (1975), the Gold Medal of the City of Vienna (1986), and the Great Honorary Citation of the Austrian Republic (1987). He adopted a serial method applying the statistical principles of valid recurrences of all musical parameters, including pitch, rhythm, and dynamics. He publ. *Antianorganikum* (Vienna, 1967).

WORKS: DRAMATIC: Opera: *Indische Legende* (1950); *Peter und Susanne* (Vienna, June 26, 1959); *Inzwischen* (1953–66; Vienna, Jan. 5, 1967); *Lysistrate* (1957–60); *Plutos* (1975–76; Klagenfurt, Feb. 7, 1977); *Die Paare* (1985–86). **Ballet:** *Italia passata* (1967); *Komodie der Unart* (Vienna, Dec. 12, 1978); *Il ballo del mondo* (1980–82); *Arkadien* (1984); *K* (1984; Klagenfurt, Feb. 2, 1985); *Und der Engel sprach...* (1991; Vienna, July 9, 1992); *Daphnis und Chloe* (1993; Dresden, Dec. 11, 1994). **OTHER:** *Traumleben*, musical fairy tale (1958; Salzburg, Dec. 22, 1963); *Celestina*, musical play (1966); other works. **ORCH.:** *Drei Tanzskizzen* (1946–51); *Konzertantes Triptychon* (1950–69); *Komplex E* (1956; Vienna, Sept. 12, 1957); *Concerto des Infants* for Piano and Small Orch. (1956); *Streichersymphonie mit Quodlibet* (1956–65); Cello Concerto (1960; Vienna, May 2, 1966); Concerto for Winds and Strings (1964; Vienna, Nov. 27, 1970); *Divertimento* for Trumpet and Small Orch. (1966–73; Vienna, Feb. 1, 1976); Suite (1971; Vienna, Aug. 14, 1980); *Partita* for Strings (1971–72; Vienna, April 8, 1973); *Kurzkonzert* for Clarinet and Orch. (1973; Vienna, Jan. 25, 1974); *Der Raucher* for Cello and Strings (1973; Vienna, Jan. 22, 1975); *La Symphonie* (1974–80); *Mediterrane Harmonien* for Double Bass and Orch. (1976–77; Vienna, Feb. 28, 1983); *Konzert 1977* for Piano and Orch. (1977; Bregenz, Aug. 13, 1979); *Vivaldi-Monument* (1978; Vienna, Feb. 10, 1980); 5 syms.: No. 1 (1979), No. 2, *Der Toten*, for Soprano, Chorus, and Orch. (1983), No. 3 (1981), No. 4, *Den Liebenden*, for Tenor, Women's Chorus, and Orch. (1983), and No. 5 (1980; Vienna, March 11, 1982); *Sinfonia und Sinfonina* (1979; Vienna, Oct. 4, 1989); Percussion Concerto (1983; Vienna, May 11, 1986); Concerto (1984); *Sache für Musikanten* (1985); *Regeriana* (1987); *Miss Lyss Nausick* (1988); *Serenade* for Strings (1989); *Sequenzen* (1991); *Konzertante Symphonie* for Baritone Saxophone and Strings (Linz, April 30, 1991); *Barock Suite* (1992); *Der grosse Marsch* (1992). **CHAMBER:** *Sonate und Sonatine* for String Quartet (1944–81); Quartet for Oboe, Clarinet, Bass Clarinet, and Bassoon (1947); Quartet for Oboe, Clarinet, Horn, and Bassoon (1956); *Meditationes Beatae Virginis Mariae* for 7 Instruments (1956–61); *Holzmusik I* for Oboe, Clarinet, Bassoon, and Flute (1956–82) and *II* for 6 Instruments (1980–82); Piano Trio (1964); *Triptychon in progressiver Besetzung: I, Serenata a tre* for Flute, Violin, and Viola (1965), *II, Concerto lirico* for Flute,

Clarinet, Violin, Viola, and Cello (1963), and *III, Septett* for Flute, Clarinet, Bassoon, Violin, Viola, Cello, and Double Bass (1961); *Blechmusik I:* 1, Trio for Trumpet, Horn, and Trombone (1966), 2, Quartettino for Trumpet, 2 Horns, and Trombone (1966), and 3, Quartet for Trumpet, Horn, Trombone, and Tuba (1968) and *II:* 1, *Blechmusik* for 2 Trumpets, Horn, Trombone, and Tuba (1971), and 2, Harmonien for 2 Trumpets, 2 Horns, 2 Trombones, and Tuba (1973); *Finis austriae* for String Quartet (1973–76); *Musica marina* for 2 Violins, Viola, and Cello (1978); Viola Sonata (1979); *Kammertanz Suite* for Saxophone Quartet (1988); *5 Sketches* for Saxophone Quartet (1989); *En rose et noir* for Piano Trio (1989); *Quadrum I* and *III* for Piano (1992), *II* for Viola (1992), and *IV* for String Quartet (1992); *4 and Half Very Old Dances* for Bassoon Quartet (1992); *Eine Sinfonie* for 4 Harpsichords (1994); *Stuck-Werk*, 19 pieces for Alto Saxophone and Accordion (1994); *Toccata-Cantata-Sonata* for Violin and Piano (1994). **VOCAL:** *Bruchstücke zu Franz Grillparzers Trauerspiel "Sappho"* for Alto and Orch. (1993); choral works; songs.—**NS/LK/DM**

Kontarsky, Alfons, German pianist and teacher, brother of **Aloys Kontarsky** and **Bernhard Kontarsky;** b. Iserlohn, Westphalia, Oct. 9, 1932. He studied piano with Else Schmitz-Gohr and Maurits Frank at the Cologne Hochschule für Musik (1953–55) and with Eduard Erdmann in Hamburg (1955–57). With his brother Aloys, he won 1st prize for duo-piano playing in the Bavarian Radio Competition in Munich (1955); they subsequently toured throughout the world, giving performances of many modern scores. He taught at the Cologne Hochschule für Musik (from 1967). He publ. *Pro musica nova: Studien zum Spielen neuer Musik für Klavier* (Cologne, 1973).—**NS/LK/DM**

Kontarsky, Aloys, German pianist and pedagogue, brother of **Alfons Kontarsky** and **Bernhard Kontarsky;** b. Iserlohn, Westphalia, May 14, 1931. He studied piano with Else Schmitz-Gohr and Maurits Frank at the Cologne Hochschule für Musik (1952–55) and with Eduard Erdmann in Hamburg (1955–57). With his brother Alfons, he won 1st prize for duo-piano playing at the Bavarian Radio Competition in Munich (1955); thereafter they made tours throughout the world, specializing in contemporary music. He taught master classes at the Cologne Hochschule für Musik (from 1969).—**NS/LK/DM**

Kontarsky, Bernhard, German pianist and conductor, brother of **Alfons Kontarsky** and **Aloys Kontarsky;** b. Iserlohn, Westphalia, April 26, 1937. He studied at the Cologne Hochschule für Musik and at the Univ. of Cologne. In 1964 he received the Mendelssohn Prize in Chamber Music. He was a conductor at the Wurttemberg State Theater in Stuttgart; also appeared as a pianist, both as a soloist and in ensemble with his brothers.—**NS/LK/DM**

Konti, József, Polish-born Hungarian conductor and composer; b. Warsaw, Oct. 24, 1852; d. Budapest, Oct. 23, 1905. He studied at the Warsaw Cons. and in Vienna, where he began his career as asst. conductor at the Theater in der Leopoldstadt. After conducting in Salzburg, he held conducting appointments at theaters in Debrecen (1876) and in Kolozsvár (1878). In 1878 he composed his first stage piece for Budapest, where he settled. His first major work was the comic opera *Az eleven ördög* (The Living Devil; Aug. 8, 1884), which proved a significant score in the development of lighter works for the Hungarian stage. Its success was so great that Konti was made chief conductor of the Népszinház in 1886, a post he held until 1903. During these years, he also composed the operettas *Királyfogás* (The King's Capture; Oct. 29, 1886), *A suhanc* (The Good-for-Nothing; Jan. 12, 1888), *A kópé* (The Crafty One; Feb. 7, 1890), *A citerás* (The Zither Player; Feb. 23, 1894), and *Talmi hercegnő* (The Counterfeit Countess; Feb. 4, 1898). He also composed incidental scores for plays. In 1903 Konti became chief conductor of the Király Színház, where his last operetta, *A fecskék* (The Damsels; Jan. 20, 1904), was first heard.—**LK/DM**

Kontski, Antoine de, famous Polish pianist, brother of **Apollinaire Kontski** and **Charles de Kontski;** b. Kraków, Oct. 27, 1817; d. Ivanichi, near Okulova, Russia, Dec. 7, 1899. He studied with John Field in Moscow (1830), then toured widely, and also taught in Paris (1851–53), Berlin (1853–54), St. Petersburg (1854–67), and subsequently in London. He toured the U.S. (1883, 1885), and made a world tour when he was nearly 80 (1896–98). He composed 2 piano concertos and various virtuoso and salon pieces for piano. His picturesque *Réveil du lion* was enormously successful for many years; it was an epitome of Romantic exuberance to the point of being ludicrous. He also composed the light operas *Les Deux Distraits* (London, 1872) and *Le Sultan de Zanzibar* (N.Y., May 8, 1886).—**NS/LK/DM**

Kontski, Apollinaire de, Polish violinist and pedagogue, brother of **Antoine Kontski** and **Charles de Kontski;** b. Kraków, Oct. 23, 1825; d. Warsaw, June 29, 1879. He studied with his elder brother Charles, and appeared with his brothers as a small child in Russia and later in Germany, frankly exploited by his family for sensational publicity and gain. In 1837 he played for Paganini in Paris. In 1861 he became director of the Warsaw Cons., of which he was a founder, and remained in that post until his death. He publ. some violin music.—**NS/LK/DM**

Kontski, Charles de, Polish pianist and teacher, brother of **Antoine Kontski** and **Apollinaire de Kontski;** b. Kraków, Sept. 6, 1815; d. Paris, Aug. 27, 1867. Like his brothers, he was a child prodigy, and made appearances with them at various public exhibitions and concerts. He studied in Warsaw and in Paris, eventually settling in Paris as a private piano teacher, enjoying considerable success in society.—**NS/LK/DM**

Konwitschny, Franz, esteemed German conductor; b. Fulnek, northern Moravia, Aug. 14, 1901; d. Belgrade, July 28, 1962. He studied violin at the German Musikverein School in Brünn and at the Leipzig Cons. (1923–25) and while a student played viola and violin in the theater orch. and the Gewandhaus Orch. in Leipzig. He subsequently became a violist in the Fitzner Quartet in Vienna (1925), and also a teacher at the Volkskonservatorium there. He became répétiteur at the Stuttgart Opera in 1927, rising to chief conductor in 1930. After serving as Generalmusikdirektor in Freiburg im Breisgau (1933–38), he assumed that position with the Frankfurt am Main Opera and Museumgesellschaft concerts in 1938, and then with the Hannover Opera in 1945. He was appointed chief conductor of the Gewandhaus Orch. in 1949; was also Generalmusikdirektor of the Dresden State Opera (1953–55) and the (East) Berlin State Opera (1955–62). Although he held posts under both the Nazi and Communist regimes, he successfully avoided political encounters. He died while on tour and was given a state funeral by the German Democratic Republic; his request for a Requiem Mass was honored, much to the chagrin of the authorities.

BIBL.: H. Sanders, ed., *Vermächtnis und Verpflichtung: Festschrift für F. K.* (Leipzig, 1961).—NS/LK/DM

Konya, Sándor, Hungarian tenor; b. Sarkad, Sept. 23, 1923. He was educated at the Budapest Academy of Music, and also studied in Detmold, Rome, and Milan. He made his first professional appearance as Turiddu in Bielefeld in 1951, singing there until 1954. After appearing in Darmstadt (1954–55), he joined the Berlin Städtische Oper in 1955. In 1958 he sang for the first time at the Bayreuth Festival as Lohengrin; also sang at Milan's La Scala (1960) and the San Francisco Opera (1960–65). On Oct. 28, 1961, he made his Metropolitan Opera debut in N.Y. as Lohengrin; sang there regularly until 1973. He first appeared at London's Covent Garden in the same role (1963). His most notable roles included Walther von Stolzing, Parsifal, Max, and Don Carlos.—NS/LK/DM

Kool and the Gang, starting out in the mid-1960s as the jazz-oriented Jazziacs, evolved into a popular early–1970s funk band. **MEMBERSHIP:** Robert "Kool" Bell, bs. (b. Youngstown, Ohio, Oct. 8, 1950); Ronald Bell, ten. sax. (b. Youngstown, Ohio, Nov. 1, 1951); Robert "Spike" Mickens, trpt. (b. Jersey City, N.J.); Dennis "Dee Tee" Thomas, sax., flt. (b. Jersey City, N.J., Feb. 9, 1951); Charles "Claydes" Smith, lead gtr. (b. Jersey City, N.J., Sept. 6, 1948); Ricky West, kybd.; George "Funky" Brown, drm. (b. Jersey City, N.J., Jan. 5, 1949). Vocalist James "J.T." Taylor (b. Laurens, S.C., Aug. 16, 1953) was added in 1979.

Kool and the Gang gained popularity in the 1970s with crossover hits such as "Jungle Boogie" and "Hollywood Swinging," only to be swept aside by the disco craze of the later 1970s. Employing disco producer Eumir Deodato in the early 1980s, Kool and the Gang established themselves as purveyors of both dance and ballad hits with the addition of vocalist James "J.T." Taylor. Thereby expanding their audience to the easy-listening crowd, Kool and the Gang and vocalist Taylor fared far less well after Taylor's departure in 1988.

Bassist Robert "Kool" Bell formed the jazz quartet the Jazziacs in 1964 in Jersey City, N.J., for engagements around Greenwich Village, playing with artists such as Richie Havens and Pharoah Sanders at the Cafe Wha. The other members were tenor saxophonist and brother

Ronald Bell, trumpeter Robert Mickens, and saxophonist-flutist Dennis Thomas. Playing sessions in N.Y. from 1964 to 1968, the band was joined by lead guitarist Charles "Claydes" Smith, keyboardist Ricky West, and drummer George Brown. Moving toward soul and funk as the Soul Town Revue and the New Dimensions, the band changed their name to Kool and the Gang around 1968. Signed to De-Lite Records, the band soon achieved modest instrumental hits with "Kool and the Gang" and "The Gangs Back Again." They broke through with 1973's *Wild and Peaceful*, which yielded their first major pop (and smash R&B) hit with "Funky Stuff" and the crossover smashes "Jungle Boogie" and "Hollywood Swinging." Subsequently Kool and the Gang were largely relegated to the R&B field, where they scored smash hits with "Higher Plane," "Rhyme Tyme People," "Spirit of the Boogie," the instrumental "Caribbean Festival," and "Love and Understanding (Come Together)." Seemingly overwhelmed by the tamer and stylized sound of disco music, Kool and the Gang managed a minor pop and smash R&B hit with "Open Sesame" in 1976, and the song was later included on the soundtrack to *Saturday Night Fever*.

Languishing for several years and enduring the departure of Ricky West, Kool and the Gang added vocalist James "J.T." Taylor, whose smooth tenor voice could effectively handle ballads, thus allowing the group to expand its repertoire beyond dance hits. On *Ladies's Night*, the group employed, for the first time, an outside producer, Eumir Deodato, and the album yielded smash R&B, pop, and easy-listening hits with the title cut and "Too Hot." Retaining Deodato as their producer through 1982, Kool and the Gang scored a top pop, R&B, and easy-listening hit with "Celebration," adopted as the theme of hostages returning from Iran and featured as the theme song for the television broadcast of Superbowl XV (and since played to death at weddings and bar mitzvahs across the land). For the attendant album *Celebrate!*, the group was augmented by keyboardist Curtis Williams, trombonist Clifford Adams, and trumpeter Michael Ray.

Kool and the Gang's next album, *Something Special*, remained on the album charts for more than a year, producing a top R&B and easy-listening (and major pop) hit with the ballad "Take My Heart" and the pop and R&B smash "Get Down On It." The group had hits with "Big Fun" and "Let's Go Dancin' (Ooh La, La, La)" in 1982 and were soon established on the lucrative casino circuit. Robert and Ronald Bell returned to producing the group's albums with *In the Heart*, which yielded the crossover smashes "Joanna" and "Tonight." Their next album, *Emergency*, provided four hits: "Misled," "Fresh," "Cherish," and the title track. *Forever*, on Mercury Records, also produced four hits, including the crossover smashes "Victory" and "Stone Love."

By 1987 Ronald Bell had quit touring with Kool and the Gang and brother Robert had invested in a resort on the island of Boulay, off the west coast of Africa. In 1988 James "J.T." Taylor left the group, to be replaced by three singers. Neither Taylor nor Kool and the Gang have experienced much success since.

DISC.: KOOL AND THE GANG: *Live at the Sex Machine* (1971); *Best* (1971); *Live at P.J.'s* (1972); *Good Times* (1973); *Wild and Peaceful* (1973); *Kool Jazz* (1974); *Light of Worlds* (1974); *Greatest Hits!* (1975); *Spirit of the Boogie* (1975); *Love and Understanding* (1976); *Open Sesame* (1976); *The Force* (1978); *Spin Their Top Hits* (1978); *Everybody's Dancin'* (1978); *Ladies's Night* (1979); *Celebrate* (1980); *Something Special* (1981); *As One* (1982); *In the Heart* (1983); *Emergency* (1984); *Forever* (1986); *Everything's K. and the G.: Greatest Hits and More* (1988); *Sweat* (1989); *Best (1969–1976)* (1993); *Celebration: Best, 1979–1987* (1994). **JAMES "J.T." TAYLOR:** *Master of the Game* (1990); *Feel the Need* (1991); *Baby I'm Back* (1993).—**BH**

Koole, Arend (Johannes Christiaan), Dutch musicologist; b. Amsterdam, April 22, 1908. He studied at the Amsterdam Cons. (1925–30) and with Smijers (musicology; 1933–37) at the Univ. of Utrecht (Ph.D., 1949, with the diss. *Leven en werken van Pietro Antonio Locatelli da Bergamo*; publ. in Amsterdam, 1949; 2nd ed., rev., 1970). He taught at the Cons. in Rotterdam (1938–41), Utrecht (1933–37; 1941–44), and Amsterdam (1946–49); also made appearances as a pianist and conductor. In 1949 he went to South Africa, where he served as senior lecturer in musicology at the Univ. of Bloemfontein; from 1964 to 1973 he was a prof. of music history at the Univ. of Southern Calif. in Los Angeles; in 1974 he returned to South Africa. He publ. a monograph on Mendelssohn (Haarlem, 1953; 2nd ed., 1958). —**NS/LK/DM**

Kooper, Al, rock producer/keyboardist/songwriter/session musician/band leader with a checkered career; b. Brooklyn, N.Y., Feb. 5, 1944. An accomplished guitarist by age 13, Al Kooper turned professional when he joined The Royal Teens at 15, a year after the group scored a novelty smash with "Short Shorts." Kooper subsequently worked as a sessions guitarist for the likes of Connie Francis and Dion. Also, he coauthored Gary Lewis and The Playboy's first hit (a smash), "This Diamond Ring," from 1965.

In the mid-1960s, Al Kooper played folk clubs as Al Casey and met Bob Dylan through producer Tom Wilson. He accompanied Dylan on keyboards at his controversial Newport Folk Festival appearance in June 1965 and assisted in the recording of Dylan's *Highway 61 Revisited* album and its classic single, "Like a Rolling Stone." Later, Kooper helped record Dylan's monumental *Blonde on Blonde* album. In 1966 Kooper joined The Blues Project, one of the earliest white electric blues and folk bands. With member Steve Katz, for 1968 Kooper formed Blood, Sweat and Tears, probably the first jazz-rock band, with fellow Blues Project member Steve Katz.

After Blood, Sweat and Tears' debut album, Kooper left the group to accept a lucrative offer from Columbia Records to become a producer, although none of his projects proved successful. In 1968, he played sessions for Moby Grape (*Wow/Grape Jam*) and adopted the format for one of the first successful "jam" albums, *Super Session*, recorded with guitarists Stephen Stills and Mike Bloomfield. He also played sessions for The Nitty Gritty Dirt Band, Paul Butterfield, Jimi Hendrix, Taj Mahal, and The Rolling Stones. He also recorded a live album with Bloomfield. Initiating his own recording career by 1969, Kooper introduced Johnny Otis's guitar-playing son Shuggie in 1970.

In 1972, Al Kooper "discovered" and signed Lynyrd Skynyrd to MCA's newly formed Sound of the South label, producing their first three albums. He organized a reunion of The Blues Project in 1973 and later produced The Tubes' debut album and Nils Lofgren's *Cry Tough*. Releasing his final solo album in more than a decade in 1982, Kooper moved to Nashville in 1990 and subsequently became music director of The Rock Bottom Remainders, a band comprised of authors Steven King, Dave Barry, and Amy Tan, among others. He returned to recording with 1994's largely instrumental *Rekooperation* and 1995's *Soul of a Man*.

DISC.: KOOPER, BLOOMFIELD AND STILLS: *Super Session* (1968). **AL KOOPER AND MIKE BLOOMFIELD:** *Don't Say that I Ain't Your Man* (1964); *Live Adventures of Mike Bloomfield and Al Kooper* (1969); *Bloomfield: A Retrospective* (1984). **AL KOOPER:** *I Stand Alone* (1969); *You Never Know Who Your Friends Are* (1969); *Live Adventures* (1969); *Kooper Session: Al Kooper Introduces Shuggie Otis* (1970); *Landlord* (soundtrack; 1970); *Easy Does It* (1970); *New York City (You're a Woman)* (1971); *A Possible Projection of the Future/Childhood's End* (1972); *Naked Songs* (1973); *Al's Big Deal (Unclaimed Freight)* (1975); *Act Like Nothing's Wrong* (1976); *Four on the Floor* (1979); *Championship Wrestling* (1982); *Rekooperation* (1994); *Soul of a Man: Al Kooper Live* (1995); *Kooper Sessions, Vol. 2* (1999). **THE BLUES PROJECT:** *Live at Cafe Au-Go-Go* (1966); *Projections* (1966); *Best of the Blues Project* (1966); *Live at Town Hall* (1967); *Original Blues Project Reunion in Central Park* (1973). **BLOOD, SWEAT & TEARS:** *Child Is Father to the Mother* (1968); *Blood, Sweat & Tears* (1969); *Blood Sweat & Tears 4* (1971); *Classic BST* (1980); *Live and Improvised* (1991); *What Goes Up: The Best of Blood, Sweat & Tears* (1995). **AL KOOPER AND STEVE KATZ:** *Al Kooper & Steve Katz* (1969). **APPALOOSA:** *Appaloosa* (1971).

WRITINGS: With B. Edmonds., *Backstage Passes: Rock 'n' Roll Life in the Sixties* (N.Y., 1977; rev. as *Backstage Passes and Back-Stabbing Bastards*, N.Y., 1999).—**BH**

Koopman, Ton (actually, Antonius Gerhardus Michael), eminent Dutch organist, harpsichordist, conductor, musicologist, and pedagogue; b. Zwolle, Oct. 2, 1944. He studied musicology at the Univ. of Amsterdam (B.A., 1968) and took 1st prize in basso continuo playing at the Brugge Harpsichord Competition (1968). He studied organ with Simon Jansen (solo examination with distinction, 1969; Prix d'Excellence, 1972) and harpsichord with Gustav Leonhardt (solo examination with distinction, 1970; Prix d'Excellence, 1974) at the Amsterdam Cons. In 1968 he organized the chamber music ensemble Musica da Camera. In 1979 Koopman founded the Amsterdam Baroque Orch., which he led as music director and which he developed into one of the world's outstanding early music ensembles utilizing period instruments in performances notable for their expressive musicality and informed scholarship. He also founded the Amsterdam Baroque Choir in 1992, which he led as music director. In addition to his conducting positions in Amsterdam, he also became co-chief conductor of the Netherlands

Radio Chamber Orch. in Hilversum in 1994. He likewise served as prof. of harpsichord at the Royal Cons. of Music in The Hague. As a guest conductor, he has appeared with the Royal Concertgebouw Orch. in Amsterdam, the Gewandhaus Orch. in Leipzig, the North German Radio Sym. Orch. in Hamburg, the Mozarteum Orch. in Salzburg, and the Vienna Sym. Orch. As a scholar, he has contributed to various publications. Among his outstanding recordings are the complete organ works and cantatas of J.S. Bach. In 1994 he won the Prix de l'Académie du Disque Lyrique, in 1995 the Premio Internationale Del Disco "Antonio Vivaldi," and in 1997 the Deutsche Schallplattenpreis.—NS/LK/DM

Kopecký, Pavel, Czech composer; b. Prague, April 5, 1949. He studied with Dobiáš at the Prague Academy of Arts and Music (1972–77) and with Donatoni in Siena (1976). After pursuing postgraduate studies with Sidelnikov at the Moscow Cons. (1977–79), he joined the faculty of the film academy at the Prague Academy of Arts. His music explores the dynamics of modern compositional trends.

WORKS: 3 *Studies* for 2 Cellos (1974); 2 piano sonatas (1975, 1979); *Cesty* (The Roads), variations for String Orch. (1976); *Syntéza* for Piano and Tape (1976); Piano Concerto (1977); Quartet for Flute and Strings (1978); 4 *Symphonic Preludes—Moscow* (1979); *Bláznovy zápisky* (Madman's Diary), piano suite, after Gogol (1980); Piano Trio (1981); *On a oni* (He and They), concerto for Clarinet and Strings (1982). —NS/LK/DM

Kopelent, Marek, Czech composer; b. Prague, April 28, 1932. He was a student of Řídký at the Prague Academy of Music (1951–55). From 1956 to 1971 he worked as a music ed. for Supraphon, and from 1965 to 1973 he served as artistic director of the Musica viva Pragensis ensemble. In 1969–70 he was active in Berlin on a Deutscher Akademischer Austauschdienst scholarship. In 1991 he became a prof. of composition at the Prague Academy of Music. In his works, Kopelent has made use of the resources of the multimedia avant-garde.

WORKS: DRAMATIC: *Bludný hlas* (The Wandering Voice) for Actress, Chamber Ensemble, and Film and Light Projection ad libitum (1969–70); *Musica,* comic opera for Soprano, 2 Actors, Flute, Oboe, and Harpsichord (1979); *Lament of Women,* melodrama-monologue for Actress, 7 Brass, 4 Women's Voices, and Children's Chorus (1980). **ORCH.:** 3 *Movements* for Strings (1958); *Contemplation* for Chamber Orch. (1966); *Quarrels* for 12 Solo Instruments and Orch. (1967–68; Prague, March 7, 1969); *Seclusion* for Viola and Chamber Orch. (1968); *Appassionato* for Piano and Orch. (1970–71); *A Few Minutes with an Oboist* for Oboe and Chamber Orch. (1972); *Veronika's Veil* for 11 Strings (1972–73); *A Cozy Chat* for Saxophone and Orch. (1974–75); Sym. (1982–83; Basel, Feb. 17, 1983); Concertino for English Horn and Small Orch. (1984); *Musique concertante* for Solo Cello, 12 Cellos, and Orch. (1991–92); *ARRIÍJAh* (1996). **CHAMBER:** 5 string quartets (1954, 1955, 1963, 1967, 1980); Trio for Flute, Clarinet, and Bassoon (1962); Trio for Flute, Bass Clarinet, and Piano (1962); *Reflexe* for Flute, Violin, Viola, and Cello (1962); *Music for 5* for Oboe, Clarinet, Bassoon, Viola, and Piano (1964); *Intimissimo* for Chamber Group (1972); *Musique piquante* for Violin and Cimbalom (1971); Wind Quintet (1972);

Rondo for 5 Percussionists (1973); *Taps* for Harp, Harpsichord, Cimbalom, and Guitar (1974); *Capriccio* for Trumpet (1976); *Etres fins en mouvement* for 6 Percussionists (1989). **VOCAL:** *Bread and Birds,* oratorio (1957–62); *Nenie with Flute* for 9 Women's Voices, Flute, and Chamber Ensemble (1961); *Prayer of Stones* for Narrator, 2 Small Choruses, 3 Gongs, and Tam-tam (1965); *Love* for Soprano and Chamber Ensemble (1967); *Complaints* for 2 Choruses, Trumpet, Percussion, and Tape ad libitum (1969); *Il Canto degli Augei* for Soprano and Orch. (1978); *The Legend,* oratorio (1981); *Agnus Dei* for Soprano and Chamber Ensemble (1982–83); *Messaggio della povertà* for Soprano, Baritone, Children's Chorus, Chorus, and Orch. (1988); *Holanesque Reminiscences* for Mezzo-soprano, 2 Reciters, Clarinet, Trombone, and Piano (1995); *Cantus de dilectione filiarum Dei* for 5 Sopranos, Baritone, and 3 Trombones (1998).—NS/LK/DM

Koppel, Herman D(avid), Danish pianist, teacher, and composer of Polish parentage, father of **Thomas Herman Koppel;** b. Copenhagen, Oct. 1, 1908; d. there, July 14, 1998. He was a student of Simonson (piano), Bangert (theory), and Hansen (orchestrtion) at the Copenhagen Cons. (1926–29). He made his debut in 1930 as a concert pianist, and toured widely in Europe. He taught at the Royal Inst. of Music for the Blind in Copenhagen (1940–43; 1945–49), and lived in Örebro, Sweden (1943–45), to avoid the Nazi occupation. In 1949 he joined the faculty of the Royal Danish Cons. of Music in Copenhagen, and was a prof. there from 1955 to 1979. As a pianist, he performed the music of Nielsen and other 20th century Danish composers. His early compositions were influenced by Nielsen, Stravinsky, and Bartók, but he eventually developed an individualistic style, marked by rhythmic intensity and melodic expressivity.

WORKS: DRAMATIC: *Macbeth,* opera (1968; Copenhagen, 1970); also incidental music; music to 29 films. **ORCH.:** Violin Concerto (1929); 7 syms.: No. 1 (1930), No. 2 (1943), No. 3 (1944–45), No. 4 (1946), No. 5 (1955), No. 6, *Sinfonia breve* (1957), and No. 7 (1960–61; Copenhagen, May 16, 1961); *Music for Strings* (1930); 4 piano concertos (1931–32; 1936–37; 1948; 1960–63); *Music* for Jazz Orchestra (1932); *Capriccio* for Violin and Orch. (1934); *Variations* for Small Orch. (1935); 2 concertinos for Strings (1937–38; 1957); Clarinet Concerto (1941); Sinfonietta (1945); Concerto for Violin, Viola, and Orch. (1947); Cello Concerto (1952); Oboe Concerto (1970); Chamber Concerto for Violin and Strings (1970); Flute Concerto (1971); *Concerto for Orchestra* (1977–78); *Intrada* (1979); Concerto for Violin, Viola, Cello, and Small Orch. (1984); Bassoon Concerto (1989); *Memory* for the 50th anniversary of the liberation of Denmark (Århus, May 5, 1995). **CHAMBER:** 6 string quartets (1928–29; 1939; 1944–45; 1964; 1975; 1979); Trio for Clarinet, Violin, and Piano (1931); Sextet for Winds and Piano (1942); *Fantasy* for Clarinet (1947); Piano Sonata (1950); *Ternio I* for Cello or Violin and Piano (1951) and *II* for Saxophone (1973); Piano Quintet (1953); Cello Sonata (1956); *Variations* for Clarinet and Piano (1961); 9 *Variations* for Piano Trio (1969); Suite for Cello (1971); Piano Trio (1971); 8 *Variations and Epilogue* for Piano and 13 Players (1972); *Divertimento* for String Trio (1972); *Pastorale Variations* for Flute, Violin, Viola, and Cello (1975); Piano Quartet (1985); Trio for Clarinet, Cello, and Piano (1986); *Cantilena* for Violin and Cello (1988); *Music* for Wind Octet (1991); *Music* for Violin and Piano (1991). **VOCAL:** 3 *Psalms of David* for Tenor, Chorus, and Orch. (1949); *Immortalis mortalium* for Baritone, Boy's Chorus, and Orch. (1954); 2 *Biblical Songs* for Soprano and Orch. or

Piano (1955); *The Song of the Sun* for Children's Chorus, Strings, and Piano (1958); *Moses*, oratorio (1963–64; Copenhagen, Oct. 21, 1965); *Requiem* (1965–66); *Hymns of Thanksgiving* for Soloists, Chorus, and Orch. (1974).—NS/LK/DM

Koppel, Thomas Herman, Danish composer, son of **Herman D(avid) Koppel;** b. Örebro, Sweden, April 27, 1944. He studied piano and theory with his father at the Royal Danish Cons. of Music in Copenhagen (1963–67). In 1968 he organized in Copenhagen the pop group Savage Rose, and joined the Danish avant-garde in other venturesome activities.

WORKS: DRAMATIC: O p e r a : *Historien om en moder* (The Story of a Mother), after H.C. Andersen (Copenhagen, Oct. 17, 1965); *Bérénice* (1968). **B a l l e t :** *Triumph of Death* (1971); *The Emperor's New Clothes*, music for ice ballet (1985–86). **ORCH.:** *Visions fugitives* for Piano and Orch. (1965); *Overture solennelle* (1967); Recorder Concerto (1991). **CHAMBER:** 3 string quartets (1963, 1964, 1966); *Impressions lyriques* for Percussion (1968); *Skipper Klement* for 2 Violins, Viola, Guitar, and Double Bass (1984). **VOCAL:** *Cloches* for Voice and 6 Players (1964); *Phrases*, cantata for 2 Sopranos, 12 Mezzo-sopranos, 4 Solo Instruments, and Orch. (1966; Danish Radio, April 6, 1967); *Concert heroïque* for 3 Pianos, Orch., Chorus, and Wind Machine (Copenhagen, Jan. 9, 1967); *Petit air* for Soprano and 4 Instruments (1966); *Nocturne from a Long Gray Street* for Mezzo-soprano and String Trio (1983); *Carmen* for Voices, Piano, and Drums (1989); *Bella Vita* for Voice and Small Orch. (1993). —NS/LK/DM

Kopylov, Alexander (Alexandrovich), Russian composer; b. St. Petersburg, July 14, 1854; d. Strelna, near St. Petersburg, March 5, 1911. He studied violin and piano at the court chapel (1862–72), and upon graduation, took lessons in composition with Rimsky-Korsakov and Liadov. From 1872 to 1896 he taught singing to the court chapel choir. He was an epigone of the Romantic school of minor Russian composers. He wrote a Sym., an overture, 5 string quartets, and many piano pieces.—NS/LK/DM

Kopytman, Mark, Russian-born Israeli composer and pedagogue; b. Kamenets-Podolski, Dec. 6, 1929. He began his musical training at the music college (graduated, 1950) and pursued medical studies in Chernovtsy (M.D., 1952). He then studied with Simovitz at the Lwów Academy of Music (M.A., 1955) and with S. Bogatyrev at the Moscow Cons. (Ph.D., 1958). He taught in various Russian music institutes (1955–72), then emigrated to Israel, where he joined the faculty of the Rubin Academy of Music in Jerusalem in 1974, serving as its deputy director (from 1985). He also was a guest prof. at the Hebrew Univ. in Jerusalem (from 1979). In 1985 he was a visiting prof. at the Univ. of Pa. and composer-in-residence at the Canberra School of Music. In 1989 he again was at the Univ. of Pa.

WORKS: DRAMATIC: O p e r a : *Casa mare* (1966); *Chamber Scenes from the Life of Susskind von Trinberg* (1983). **ORCH.:** Sym. (1955); Violin Concertino (1963); *6 Moldavian Tunes* (1965); Piano Concerto (1971); Concerto (1976); *Rotations for Vocalise* (1979); *Kaddish* for Cello and Strings (1982); *Cantus III* for Bass Clarinet and Orch. (1984), *V* for Viola and Orch.

(1990), and *VI* for Oboe and Chamber Orch. (1995); *Ornaments* for Harpsichord and Orch. (1987); *Beyond All This* for Strings (1997). **CHAMBER:** *2 Miniatures on Kazakh Folk Tunes* for String Quartet (1961); String Quartet No. 2 (1965), No. 3 (1969), and No. 4 (1996); *For Percussion* (1975); *Monodrama* for Sextet (1975); *For Harp* (1976); *For Harpsichord* (1976); *About an Old Tune* for Piano Quartet (1977); *For Organ* (1978); *2 Poems* for Flute, Violin, and Viola (1978); *And a Time for Every Purpose* for Flute, Trumpet, Trombone, and Percussion (1979); *Cantus II* for String Trio (1980) and *IV: Dedication* for Violin (1987); *Discourse I* and *II* for Oboe and String Quartet (1994); *Tenero* for Cello (1994); *Strain* for String Quartet (1996); *Circles* for Violin, Clarinet, Cello, and Piano (1996–99); *Bassalargo* for Guitar (1999). **P i a n o :** Pieces (1963–83); *2 Preludes and Fugues* (1965); *For Piano I* (1973) and *II* (1974); *Basso Recitative* for 2 Pianos (1977); *Variable Structures* (1986); *Alliterations* (1993). **VOCAL:** *Songs of Kodr*, oratorio (1966); *Unfinished Lines* for Baritone and Orch. (1970); *October Sun* for Mezzo-soprano, Flute, Violin, Cello, Piano, and Percussion (1974); *Voices* for Voice, Flute, Trombones, Percussion, and Strings (1975); *Day and Night Will Rise to Heaven for* Soprano, Mime, Flute, Trumpet, Trombone, and Percussion (1977); *Memory* for Voice and Orch. (1981); *Life of the World to Come* for Voice and Chamber Orch. (1986); *Letters of Creation* for Voice and Strings (1986); *Circles* for Voice, Clarinet, Cello, and Piano (1987); *Scattered Rhymes* for Chorus and Orch. (1988); *A Poem for the Numbers of the Dead* for Baritone and Chamber Ensemble (1988); *Love Remembered* for Chorus and Orch. (1989); *Three Nights* for Voice and Chamber Ensemble (1996). —NS/LK/DM

Korchinska, Maria, Russian-born English harpist; b. Moscow, Feb. 16, 1895; d. London, April 17, 1979. She studied at the Moscow Cons., where she was the first harp student to graduate with the gold medal. She then was principal harpist in the orch. of the Moscow Opera (1918–24) and also taught at the Moscow Cons. In 1926 she settled in London, where she pursued a career as a soloist with orchs. and as a recitalist. She was particularly active in promoting the composition of new works for the harp.—NS/LK/DM

Korchmarev, Klimenti (Arkadievich), Russian composer; b. Verkhnedneprovsk, July 3, 1899; d. Moscow, April 7, 1958. He studied at the Odessa Cons. with Maliszewski and Biber (graduated with the gold medal, 1919), then went to Moscow (1923), where he became one of the first Soviet composers to embrace revolutionary themes. He wrote *Leviy marsh* (March on the Left; to words by Mayakovsky) for Chorus and Piano (1923), then composed the operas *Ivan-Soldat* (Ivan the Soldier; 1925–27; Moscow, April 3, 1927) and *Desyat dney, kotoriye potryasili mir* (10 Days That Shook the World; 1929–31) and the ballet *Krepostnaya balerina* (The Serf Ballerina; Leningrad, Dec. 11, 1927). His other works in this vein included the choral syms. *Oktyabr* (October; 1931) and *Narodi sovetskoy strani* (The Peoples of the Soviet Land; 1935). From 1939 to 1947 he was in Turkmenistan, where he collected native songs. He also composed the first native ballet, *Vesyoliy obmanschchik* (The Merry Deceiver). In 1950 he wrote a cantata, *Svobodniy Kitay* (Free China), for which he received a Stalin Prize.—NS/LK/DM

Kord, Kazimierz, Polish conductor; b. Pogórze, Nov. 18, 1930. He studied piano at the Leningrad Cons., then took courses in composition and conducting at the Kraków Academy of Music. He conducted at the Warsaw Opera (1960–62), and from 1962 to 1970 was artistic director of the Kraków Opera. From 1968 to 1973 he was chief conductor of the Polish Radio and Television Sym. Orch. in Katowice. He was chief conductor with the National Phil. in Warsaw (from 1977) as well as principal guest conductor of the Cincinnati Sym. Orch. (1980–82), chief conductor of the South-West Radio Sym. Orch. in Baden-Baden (1980–86), and principal guest conductor and music adviser of the Pacific Sym. Orch. in Santa Ana, Calif. (1989–91).—NS/LK/DM

Koréh, Endre, Hungarian bass; b. Sepsiszentgyörgy, April 13, 1906; d. Vienna, Sept. 20, 1960. He was a student of Arpad Palotay in Budapest. In 1930 he made his operatic debut at the Budapest Opera as Sparafucile, and then sang there regularly. In 1948 he became a member of the Vienna State Opera. He also appeared in Salzburg, Glyndebourne, Florence, Paris, Rome, and other European opera centers. On Jan. 22, 1953, he made his Metropolitan Opera debut in N.Y. as Baron Ochs, remaining on its roster until the close of the season. He was best known for his buffo roles, excelling especially in operas by Mozart, Verdi, and Wagner. He also created the role of Caliban in Frank Martin's opera *Der Sturm*, after Shakespeare's *The Tempest* (Vienna, June 17, 1956).—NS/LK/DM

Kořínek, Miloslav, Slovak composer and teacher; b. Brno, Jan. 29, 1925; d. Bratislava, July 8, 1998. He went to Bratislava, where he studied with Alexander Moyzes (composition) and Kornel Schimpl (conducting) at the State Cons. (1943–49). After teaching composition at the Academy of Music and Drama (1949–51), he taught theory and composition at the State Cons. (1949–85), where he also served as asst. director (from 1962).

WORKS: DRAMATIC: *The Adventures of the Travelling Egg*, children's opera (1959); *Atlantis*, stage cantata for Soloists, Chorus, and Orch. (1972). **ORCH.:** Viola Concertino (1951); *Funeral Music* (1953); 2 Pieces for Oboe and Orch. (1953); Accordion Concerto (1956); *Festive Overture* (1958); *Divertimento concertante* for Strings (1962); Flute Concerto (1964); *Song of Praise*, overture (1966); Chamber Concerto for Clarinet and Orch. (1966); Horn Concerto (1968); *Allegro brillante* (1976); Sym. (1983); Oboe Concerto (1987); *Bratislava, the City of Our Life* (1989); Bassoon Concerto (1991). **CHAMBER:** (10) *Sonatinas of Joyful Youth* for Various Instruments (1960); 4 Pieces for Cello and Piano (1960); Trio for 2 Oboes and English Horn (1961); *Music* for String Quartet (1963); Piano Quintet (1967); Sonatina for Double Bass and Piano (1970); Wind Quintet (1970); 2 *Capriccios* for Trombone and Piano (1973); *Grand Fantasy* for Flute and Guitar (1974); 5 *Grotesque Pieces* for 2 Oboes, 2 Clarinets, 2 Horns, and 2 Bassoons (1977); 3 Pieces for Horn and Piano (1981); *Metamorphoses d'Idea* for Accordion (1983); *Humoresques* for Flute, Cello, and Harpsichord (1985); Violin Sonata (1986); *Suite-Variations* for Harp (1987); *Music* for Cello (1987); *Studies I-II* for Guitar (1988); 3 *Bagatelles* for Oboe, Clarinet, and Bassoon (1988); *Variations* for Piano Trio (1989). **KEYBOARD: Piano:** *On Human Happiness* (1955–61); *Ferencko's Summer* (1956); *Apocrypha* (1969). **Organ:** *Cantus ad laudationem*

(1985). **Harpsichord:** Sonata Toccata (1989). **VOCAL:** Choruses; song cycles.—NS/LK/DM

Korn, Peter Jona, German composer, conductor, and pedagogue; b. Berlin, March 30, 1922; d. Munich, Jan. 14, 1998. He studied at the Berlin Hochschule für Musik (1932–33), with Rubbra in London (1934–36), Wolpe at the Jerusalem Cons. (1936–38), Schoenberg at the Univ. of Calif. at Los Angeles (1941–42), and Eisler and Toch at the Univ. of Southern Calif. in Los Angeles (1946–47); also studied film composition with Dahl and Rozsa. He was founder-conductor of the New Orch. of Los Angeles (1948–56), and then taught at the Univ. of Calif. at Los Angeles (1964–65). Returning to Germany, he was director of Munich's Richard Strauss Konservatorium from 1967 to 1987. He publ. a book of essays, *Musikalische Unwelt Verschmutzung* (Wiesbaden, 1975). His compositional style was a pragmatic Romanticism marked by polycentric tonality in the framework of strong rhythmic counterpoint.

WORKS: DRAMATIC: Opera: *Heidi in Frankfurt (Das fremde Haus)*, after Johanna Spyri (1961–63; Saarbrücken, Nov. 28, 1978). **ORCH.:** 4 syms.: No. 1 (1941–46; rev. 1956 and 1977), No. 2 (1950–51), No. 3 (1956; rev. 1969), and No. 4, *Ahasver* (1989–90); *Idyllwild*, overture (1947; rev. 1957); *Tom Paine Overture* (1949–50); *Rhapsody* for Oboe and Strings (1951); Concertino for Horn and Double String Orch. (1952); *In medias res*, overture (1953); *Variations on a Theme from The Beggar's Opera* (1954–55; Louisville, Oct. 1, 1955); Saxophone Concerto (1956; rev. 1982); Violin Concerto (1964–65); *Toccata* (1966); *Exorcism of a Liszt Fragment* (1966–68); *Serenade* for 12 Strings (1968); 4 *Pieces* for Strings (1970); *Eine Kleine Popmusik* (1972); *Morgenmusik* for Trumpet and Strings (1973); Overture for Strings (1976); *Beckmesser Variations* (1977); Trumpet Concerto (1979); *Romanza concertante* for Oboe and Small Orch. (1987); *Concerto classico* for Harpsichord and Orch. (1988). **Concert Band:** *Salute to the Lone Wolves*, sym. (1980). **CHAMBER:** Cello Sonata (1948–49); Oboe Sonata (1949); 2 string quartets (1949–50; 1963); *Passacaglia and Fugue* for 8 Horns (1952); Horn Sonata (1952); *Aloysia Serenade* for Flute, Viola, and Cello (1953); *Prelude and Scherzo* for Brass Quintet (1953); *Phantasy* for Horn, Violin, Cello, and Piano (1955); *Serenade* for 4 Horns (1957); *Quintettino* for Flute, Clarinet, Bassoon, Cello, and Piano (1964); Wind Quintet (1966); Trio for Violin, Cello, and Piano (1975); Wind Octet (1976); Duo for Viola and Piano (1978); *Fantasia* for Oboe and Organ (1981); piano pieces; organ works. **VOCAL:** *Eine Kleine Deutsche Stadt*, cantata for Tenor, Harpsichord, and Orch. (1980–81); *Psalm of Courage*, cantata for Baritone, Chorus, and Orch. (1983); songs.

BIBL.: N. Düchtel et al., *P. J. K.* (Tutzing, 1989). —NS/LK/DM

Kornauth, Egon, Austrian pianist and composer; b. Olmütz, May 14, 1891; d. Vienna, Oct. 28, 1959. He began piano training as a child and made his debut at age 15, and took a course in theory with Fuchs at the Vienna Academy of Music, winning the Austrian State Prize for his Viola Sonata (1912). He then studied musicology with Adler at the Univ. of Vienna (Ph.D., 1915, with the diss. *Die thematische Arbeit in Josef Haydns Streichquartetten seit 1780*). He toured widely with his Vienna Trio (1928–29); then received Vienna's Music Prize (1930). He became a teacher of theory at the

Vienna Hochschule für Musik (1940) and a prof. at the Salzburg Mozarteum (1945). His music generally followed along Romantic lines, demonstrating considerable contrapuntal skill.

WORKS: ORCH.: 4 symphonic suites (1913–39); Symphonic Overture (1914; rev. 1925); *Ballade* for Cello and Orch. (Vienna, Feb. 20, 1919); *Romantische Suite* (1932–36; rev. 1940); Suite (1937–38). **CHAMBER:** Viola Sonata (1912); Clarinet Sonata (1912–13); Violin Sonata (1913–14); Piano Sextet (1917); String Sextet (1918–19); 2 string quartets (1920, 1920); Piano Trio (1921); Cello Sonata (1922); 2 string quintets (1923; 1938, rev. 1947); Piano Quintet (1931); Clarinet Quintet (1931); piano pieces. **VOCAL:** Choral works; song cycles.

BIBL.: E. Müller von Asow, *E. K.* (Vienna, 1941); T. Leibnitz, *Österreichische Spätromantiker: Studien zu Emil Nikolaus von Reznicek, Joseph Marx, Franz Schmidt, und E. K.* (Tutzing, 1986). —NS/LK/DM

Korndorf, Nikolai, Russian composer, conductor, and teacher; b. Moscow, Jan. 23, 1947. He studied composition (M.M., 1970; D.M.A., 1973) and conducting (M.M., 1979) at the Moscow Cons., where he served on the faculty from 1972 until emigrating to Canada in 1991.

WORKS: DRAMATIC: *MR (Marina and Rainer)*, chamber opera (1989; Munich, May 20, 1994); *...si muove!*, music theater (1993). **ORCH.:** 4 syms.: No. 1 (1975; Moscow, Dec. 16, 1977), No. 2 (1980; Moscow, Oct. 25, 1982), No. 3 for Narrator, Boy's Chorus, Men's Chorus, Piano, and Orch. (1989; Frankfurt am Main, Sept. 8, 1992), and No. 4, *Underground Music* (1996; St. Petersburg, Dec. 19, 1997); *Con sordino* for Harpsichord and 16 Strings (Kraków, Sept. 10, 1984); *Concerto capriccioso* for Cello, Strings, and Percussion (1986); *Hymn I (Sempre tutti)* (1987; Munich, May 27, 1988), *II* (1987; Moscow, March 18, 1989), and *III (In Honor of Gustav Mahler)* (1990; Duisburg, May 8, 1991); *Prologue* (1992); *Epilogue* (1993; Montreal, Dec. 7, 1994); *Victor (The Victor)* (1995); *A Smile of Maud Lewis* (1998). **CHAMBER:** *Confessiones* for 14 Players and Tape (Moscow, Dec. 15, 1979); *Movements* for Percussion Ensemble (Moscow, Nov. 30, 1981); *Primitive Music* for 12 Saxophones (1981; Moscow, April 25, 1984); *Yarilo* for Piano and Tape (Moscow, June 8, 1981); Brass Quintet (1985); *Amoroso* for 11 Players (1986; Witten, April 25, 1987); *In Honor of Alfred Schnittke*, trio for Violin, Viola, and Cello (1986); *The Dance in Metal in Honor of John Cage* for Percussionist (1986); *Mozart- variationen* for String Sextet (1990; Berlin, May 11, 1991); *Continuum* for Organ and Tape (1991; Moscow, May 19, 1999); *Let the Earth Bring Forth* for Chamber Ensemble (Amsterdam, Sept. 29, 1992); String Quartet (1992; Moscow, May 19, 1999); *Get out!!* for Any 4 or More Instruments (1995; Munich, Jan. 31, 1996); *"Are You Ready, Brother?"* for Piano Trio (Amsterdam, July 2, 1996); *Music for Owen Underhill and his Magnificent Eight* for Chamber Ensemble (1997; Vancouver, May 31, 1998); *Passacaglia* for Cello (1997; Amsterdam, Oct. 9, 1999); *Canzone triste* for Harp (1998; Vancouver, Feb. 12, 1999). **Piano:** *Lullaby* for 2 Pianos (Moscow, Oct. 8, 1984); *A Letter to V. Martynov and G. Pelecis* (1999). **VOCAL:** *Yes!!* for 3 Singers, Chamber Ensemble, and Tape (1982; Moscow, Dec. 17, 1984); *Singing* for Mezzo-soprano and Tape (1982; Moscow, March 14, 1983); *Tristful Songs* for Chamber Chorus and Percussionist (1983); *Welcome!* for Women's Chorus and Instruments Played by a Singer (1995; also for 6 Women's Voices and Instruments Played by a Singer, 1995); *Echo* for Chorus and Ensemble (1999).—NS/LK/DM

Körner, Christian Gottfried, German music theorist; b. Leipzig, July 2, 1756; d. Berlin, May 13, 1831. He was the father of Theodor Körner, the poet. He publ. an essay, "Über den Charakter der Töne oder uber Charakterdarstellung in der Musik," in the *Horen* (1775). He also composed songs, etc.

BIBL.: W. Seifert, *C.G. K.: Ein Musikästhetiker der deutschen Klassik* (Regensburg, 1960).—NS/LK/DM

Korngold, Erich Wolfgang, remarkable Austrian-born American composer, son of **Julius Korngold**; b. Brünn, May 29, 1897; d. Los Angeles, Nov. 29, 1957. He received his first piano and theory lessons in his 6th year, and at the age of 9 he played his fairy tale cantata *Gold* for Mahler, who was so impressed with his precocity that he recommended the boy to Zemlinsky for further training. In 1908 he began work on the pantomime *Der Schneemann*, which he completed in 1910. The premiere of the version for 2 pianos took place in Vienna on April 14, 1910. Zemlinsky orchestrated the score, which was first performed at the Vienna Court Opera under Schalk's direction on Oct. 4, 1910, to acclaim. In 1909–10 he also composed a Piano Trio, which was publ. by Universal Edition as his Op.1 in 1910. His *Schauspiel-Ouvertüre* was premiered by the Gewandhus Orch. in Leipzig on Dec. 14, 1911, with Nikisch conducting. With his *Sinfonietta* (1911–12), Korngold revealed an astonishing mastery of the late Romantic style. Weingartner conducted its premiere with the Vienna Phil. on Nov. 13, 1913, an auspicious event for a composer of only 16 years of age. Korngold was not quite 19 when his 2 short operas *Der Ring des Polykrates* and *Violanta* were first performed under Walter's direction in Munich on March 28, 1916. The simultaneous premiere of his opera *Die tote Stadt* in Hamburg and Cologne on Dec. 4, 1920, was an extraordinary success, and the score was subsequently performed throughout Europe to great acclaim. In 1927 Korngold became a prof. at the Vienna Academy of Music. In 1929 he began a fruitful collaboration with the director Max Reinhardt. He went to Hollywood in 1934 to arrange Mendelssohn's music for Reinhardt's film version of *A Midsummer Night's Dream*. In 1936 Korngold won an Oscar for his score to the film *Anthony Adverse*. With the Anschluss in 1938, Korngold decided to settle in the U.S., becoming a naturalized American citizen in 1943. His success as a film composer was rewarded with another Oscar in 1938 for his score to *The Adventures of Robin Hood*. In subsequent years, he wrote many fine film scores, but he never abandoned his work as a composer of concert music. While he never attained the success of his early years in this genre, he persevered in composing major scores in a well crafted and late Romantic vein. In recent years, Korngold's concert works have been revived and recorded.

WORKS: DRAMATIC: Opera: *Der Ring des Polykrates* (1913–14; Munich, March 28, 1916); *Violanta* (1914–15; Munich, March 28, 1916); *Die tote Stadt* (1916–19; Hamburg and Cologne, Dec. 4, 1920); *Das Wunder der Heliane* (1923–26; Hamburg, Oct. 7, 1927); *Die Kathrin* (1932–37; Stockholm, Oct. 7, 1939). **Musical Comedy:** *Die stumme Serenade* (1946–50; Vienna Radio, March 26, 1951; stage perf., Dortmund, Nov. 10, 1954). **Pantomime:** *Der Schneemann* for 2 Pianos

(1908–10; Vienna, Oct. 4, 1910; orchestrated by Zemlinsky, Vienna, Oct. 4, 1910). I n c i d e n t a l M u s i c : *Viel Lärmen um nichts*, after Shakespeare (1918–19; Vienna, May 6, 1920). F i l m : *A Midsummer Night's Dream* (1934–35); *Give us this Night* (1935–36); *Captain Blood* (1935); *Anthony Adverse* (1936); *Another Dawn* (1936–37); *The Prince and the Pauper* (1937); *The Adventures of Robin Hood* (1938); *Juarez* (1938–39); *The Private Lives of Elizabeth and Essex* (1939); *The Sea Hawk* (1940); *The Sea Wolf* (1941); *Kings Row* (1941); *The Constant Nymph* (1942); *Devotion* (1943); *Between Two Worlds* (1944); *Of Human Bondage* (1944–45); *Deception* (1946); *Escape me Never* (1946); *Magic Fire* (1954–55). O R C H . : *Schauspiel-Ouvertüre* (Leipzig, Dec. 14, 1911); *Sinfonietta* (1911–12; Vienna, Nov. 30, 1913); *Militär-Marsch* (1917); Suite after the music to Shakespeare's *Viel Lärmen um nichts* for Chamber Orch. (1918–20; Vienna, Jan. 24, 1920); *Sinfonische Ouvertüre (Sursum corda!)* (1919; Vienna, Jan. 24, 1920); Concerto for Piano, Left-Hand and Orch. (1922–23; Vienna, Jan. 24, 1920); *Baby-Serenade* (1928–29; Vienna, Dec. 5, 1932); Violin Concerto (1937–39; 1945; St. Louis, Feb. 15, 1947); Cello Concerto (Los Angeles, Dec. 29, 1946); *Sinfonische Serenade* for Strings (1947–48; Vienna, Jan. 15, 1950); Sym. (1947–52; Vienna, Oct. 17, 1954); *Theme and Variations* (Inglewood, Calif., Nov. 22, 1953); *Straussiana*, after Johann Strauss (Inglewood, Calif., Nov. 22, 1953). C H A M B E R : Piano Trio (1909–10; Munich, Nov. 4, 1910); Violin Sonata (1912–13; Berlin, Oct. 21, 1913); String Sextet (1914–16; Vienna, May 2, 1917); *Vier Stücke* after the music to Shakespeare's *Viel Lärmen um nichts* for Violin and Piano (1918–19; Vienna, May 21, 1920); Piano Quintet (1921–22; Hamburg, Feb. 16, 1923); 3 string quartets: No. 1 (1920–23; Vienna, Jan. 8, 1924), No. 2 (1933; Vienna, March 16, 1934), and No. 3 (1944–45); Suite for 2 Violins, Cello, and Piano, Left-Hand (Vienna, Oct. 21, 1930). P i a n o : *Don Quixote*, 6 character studies (1907–09); 3 sonatas: No. 1 (1908–09), No. 2 (1910; Berlin, Oct. 13, 1911), and No. 3 (1931; Vienna, March 3, 1932); *Märchenbilder*, 7 pieces (1910; Berlin, March 30, 1912); *Vier Walzer* (1912); *Schach Brüggel!* after the opera *Die tote Stadt* (1916–19); *Tanzlied des Pierrot* after the opera *Die tote Stadt* (1916–19); *Drei Stücke* after the music to Shakespeare's *Viel Lärmen um nichts* (1918–19); *Zwischenspiel* after the opera *Das Wunder der Heliane* (1923–26); *Vier kleine Karikaturen für Kinder* (1926); *Geschichten von Strauss* after Johann Strauss (1927). V O C A L : *Einfache Lieder* for Voice and Piano (1911–16; Nos. 1–3, Frankfurt am Main, Feb. 15, 1912; also for Voice and Orch.); *Lieder des Abschieds* for Alto and Piano (1920–21; Vienna, Nov. 5, 1921; also for Alto and Orch., Vienna, Jan. 14, 1923); *Drei Gesänge* for Middle Voice and Piano (1924; Vienna, March 11, 1926); *Drei Lieder* for High Voice and Piano (1928–29; No. 1, Vienna, Dec. 9, 1928; No. 3, Vienna, Jan. 1, 1930); *Unvergänglichkeit* for High Voice and Piano (1933; Vienna, Oct. 27, 1937); *Songs of the Clown*, 5 songs for High Voice and Piano, after Shakespeare (1937; Los Angeles, June 28, 1941); *Vier Shakespeare-Lieder* for High Voice and Piano (1937; Los Angeles, June 28, 1941); *Fünf Lieder* for Middle Voice and Piano (1940–47; Vienna, Feb. 19, 1950); *Passover Psalm* for Soprano, Chorus, and Orch. (Los Angeles, April 12, 1941); *Prayer* for Tenor, Women's Voices, Organ, and Harp (Los Angeles, Oct. 1, 1941); *Tomorrow* for Mezzo-soprano, Women's Chorus, and Orch., after the film score *The Constant Nymph* (1941–42; N.Y., May 10, 1944); *Sonett für Wien* for Mezzo-soprano and Piano (1953; Vienna, Oct. 17, 1954).

BIBL.: R. Hoffmann, *E. W. K.* (Vienna, 1923); L. Korngold, *E. W. K.: Ein Lebensbild* (Vienna, 1967); B. Carroll, *E. W. K. 1897–1957: His Life and Works* (Paisley, 1984); J. Korngold, *Die K.s in Wien: Der Musikkritiker und das Wunderkind: Aufzeichnungen* (Zürich, 1991); B. Carroll, *The Last Prodigy: A Biography of E. W. K.* (Portland, Ore., 1997); M. Tedeschi Turco, *E. W. K.* (Verona, 1997); H. Pöllmann, *E. W. K.: Aspekte seines Schaffens* (Mainz, 1998).—NS/LK/DM

Korngold, Julius, noted Austrian music critic, father of **Erich Wolfgang Korngold;** b. Brünn, Dec. 24, 1860; d. Los Angeles, Sept. 25, 1945. He was a law student, and at the same time he studied music with Franz Krenn at the Vienna Cons. In 1902 he became music critic of the influential *Neue Freie Presse*, which position he retained until 1934. He was much in the limelight when his son began his spectacular career at the age of 13 as a child composer, and an unfounded suspicion was voiced that Korngold was using his position to further his son's career. He publ. a book on contemporary German opera, *Deutsches Opernschaffen der Gegenwart* (1922). In 1938 he joined his son in the U.S., settling in Hollywood.—NS/LK/DM

Kórodi, Andras, Hungarian conductor; b. Budapest, May 24, 1922; d. Treviso, Sept. 17, 1986. He studied with Ferencsik (conducting) and Lajtha (composition) at the Budapest Academy of Music, where he later taught conducting (1957–82). He was a conductor (1946–63) and principal conductor (1963–86) of the Hungarian State Opera in Budapest, where he led the premieres of many contemporary scores; was also conductor of the Budapest Phil. (1967–86).—NS/LK/DM

Korte, Karl (Richard), American composer; b. Ossining, N.Y., Aug. 25, 1928. He studied at Ill. Wesleyan Univ. (1948–49), and then took composition courses with Mennin and Bergsma at the Juilliard School of Music in N.Y. (B.S., 1953). In 1953 he went to Italy on a Fulbright grant and studied with Petrassi at the Accademia di Santa Cecilia in Rome. From 1954 to 1956 he was again a student at Juilliard, in the composition class of Persichetti (M.S., 1956), and then took private lessons with Luening (1956–59), and also attended seminars given by Copland at the Berkshire Music Center in Tanglewood (1960, 1961). He was awarded Guggenheim fellowships (1960, 1970). He taught at Ariz. State Univ. (1963–64), the State Univ. of N.Y. at Binghamton (1964–71), and the Univ. of Tex. in Austin (from 1971), where he was co-director of its electronic music studio (from 1984). After retiring in 1996, he served as a visiting prof. at Williams Coll. In 1985 he was a Fulbright lecturer on music in New Zealand. His music is quaquaversal in an attractively scientific manner, with the stylistic spectrum ranging from infrared, so to speak, in his archaically impressed works through the mandatory neo-Baroque essays to the ultra-violet rarefaction of mathematical conceits, abstractions, serialism, and electronics.

WORKS: O R C H . : *Concertato on a Choral Theme* (1955); *For a Young Audience* (1959); Sym. No. 2 (1961); *Southwest*, dance overture (1963); Sym. No. 3 (1968); Concerto for Piano and Wind Instruments (1976). B a n d : *Ceremonial Prelude and Passacaglia* (1962); *Nocturne and March* (1962); *Prairie Song* for Trumpet and Band (1963); *Gestures* for Wind Ensemble, Amplified Double Bass, Percussion, and Piano (1970); *I Think You*

Would Have Understood for Trumpet, Tape, and Band (1971); *Fibers* (1977); *Texarcana*, variations on a Tex. Folk Song for Large Wind Ensemble (1992). **CHAMBER:** 2 string quartets (1948, 1965); *Fantasy* for Violin and Piano (1959); Quintet for Oboe and Strings (1960); *Matrix* (1968); *Facets* (1969); *Remembrances* for Flute and Tape (1971); *Symmetrics* (1974); Trio for Piano, Violin, and Cello (1977; rev. 1982); Concertino for Trombone, Winds, and Percussion (1981); Double Concerto for Flute, Double Bass, and Tape (1984); *Vochi*, trio for Clarinet, Violin, and Piano (1984); *Colloquy* for Flute and Tape (1987); *Evocation and Dance* for Trombone and Tape (1988); *Extensions* for Percussion and Tape (1994). **P i a n o :** *Epigrams* (2 books, 1993–94). **VOCAL:** *Mass for Youth* for Women's Voices and Orch. (1963); *Aspects of Love* for Chorus (1968); *May the Sun Bless Us* for Men's Voices, Brass, and Percussion (1968); *Psalm XIII* for Chorus and Tape (1970); *Pale Is This Good Prince*, oratorio for Solo Voices, Chorus, 2 Pianos, and 4 Percussion (1973); *Of Time and Season* for Solo Voices, Chorus, Piano, and Marimba (1975); *Sappho Says* for Women's Voices, Solo Voice, Flute, and Piano (1980); *The Whistling Wind* for Mezzo-soprano and Tape (1983); *5 New Zealand Songs* for Voice and Piano (1989); *3 Psalm Settings* for Chorus (1991). **COMPUTER:** *Birds of Aotearoa* (1986); *Meeting the Enemy* (1994–95).—**NS/LK/DM**

Korte, Oldřich František, Czech composer; b. Šala, Slovakia, April 26, 1926. During World War II, he was held in a concentration camp. After his release, he studied with Pícha, and later at the Prague Cons. He toured as a pianist and actor with the modernistic group Laterna Magica; he also worked as a photographer. His music is similarly quaquaversal and quite uninhibited in its methods and resources.

WORKS: DRAMATIC: M u s i c a l : *The Pirates of the Fortune* (Vienna, April 15, 1974). **ORCH.:** *Sinfonietta* (1945–47); *Příběh fléten* (The Story of the Flutes; 1949–51; Prague Radio, Oct. 23, 1953); *Concerto grosso* for Strings, Trumpets, and Piano (1954 62; rev. 1968); *Kouzelný cirkus*, suite (1977); *Canzona a Ritornel* (1979); *Zrcadlení* (1981–82). **CHAMBER:** *Iniuria* for Piano (1942–44); *The Drinker's Transformations*, variations for Piano (1945); *In Praise of Death* for Piccolo and Glockenspiel (1948); *Philosophical Dialogues* for Violin and Piano (1964–68).—**NS/LK/DM**

Korte, Werner, German musicologist; b. Münster, May 29, 1906; d. there, Nov. 26, 1982. He studied mathematics, natural sciences, and musicology at the univs. of Freiburg im Breisgau and Münster (1924–26), then took courses in musicology, art history, and philosophy at the Univ. of Berlin (1926–28), where his principal mentor was Wolf (Ph.D., 1928, with the diss. *Die Harmonik des fruhen 15. Jahrhunderts in ihrem Zusammenhang mit der Formtechnik*; publ. in Münster, 1929). He completed his Habilitation in 1932 at the Univ. of Munster with his *Studien zur Geschichte der Musik in Italien im ersten Viertel des 15. Jahrhunderts* (publ. in Kassel, 1933). He was an asst. lecturer in musicology at the Univ. of Heidelberg (1928–31), then became director of the musicology dept. at the Univ. of Münster (1932), where he was made reader (1937) and prof. (1946).

WRITINGS: *Deutsche Musikerziehung in Vergangenheit und Gegenwart* (Danzig, 1932); *J.S. Bach* (Berlin, 1935); *Ludwig van Beethoven* (Berlin, 1936); *Robert Schumann* (Potsdam, 1937);

Musik und Weltbild (Leipzig, 1940); *Händel und der deutsche Geist* (Leipzig, 1942); *Bruckner und Brahms: Die spätromantische Lösung der autonomen Konzeption* (Tutzing, 1963); *De musica: Monolog über die heutige Situation der Musik* (Tutzing, 1966).—**NS/LK/DM**

Kortekangas, Olli, Finnish composer and teacher; b. Turku, May 16, 1955. He was a student of theory and composition of Rautavaara and Hämeeniemi at the Sibelius Academy in Helsinki (1974–81). In 1977 he was a founding member of the contemporary music society Korvat Auki (Ears Open). Following further training with Schnebel in Berlin (1981–82), he returned to Helsinki and taught at the National Theater Academy (1983–86) and then at the Sibelius Academy. As a composer, Kortekangas has followed an independent course in which he confronts and incorporates various styles and techniques in a stimulating fashion.

WORKS: DRAMATIC: *Short Story*, opera (1979–80; Helsinki, Oct. 15, 1980); *Grand Hotel*, opera (1984–85; Helsinki, Sept. 12, 1987); *Memoria*, radiophonic piece (1989); incidental music. **ORCH.:** *Arr* for Strings (1980); *Fanfares* for 3 Instrumental Groups (1980); *Ökologie 1: Vorspiel* (1983; Helsinki, Jan. 25, 1984) and *2: Konzert* (1986–87; Helsinki, March 11, 1987); *Alba* (1988; Espoo, March 19, 1989); *Fanfare* (Porvoo, June 28, 1991); *Concert Piece* for Clarinet, Cello, and Orch. (1993–94). **CHAMBER:** *Threnody* for Horn and Piano (1977; Helsinki, Dec. 13, 1978); *Konsequenz* for Violin and Piano (1982–83); *Sehr schnell* for Violin (1984); *Koraali "Punavuoren nuottikirjasta"* for Harmonium (1986); *Emotion* for Variable Ensemble and Electronics (Helsinki, Aug. 27, 1988); *Omaggio a M.C. Escher* for Alto Flute and Guitar (Viitasaari, July 22, 1990); *Iscrizione* for Clarinet and Cello (Warsaw, Sept. 12, 1990); *Mi* for Violin and Piano (1991). **KEYBOARD: P i a n o :** *Cereal Sweet* for Piano, 4-Hands (1978); *Fingerprints* (1980). **O r g a n :** Sonata (Helsinki, Sept. 25, 1979). **VOCAL:** *Vihreä madonna* (The Green Madonna) for Chorus (Espoo, Dec. 7, 1975); *3 Early Songs* for Voice and Piano (1975; rev. 1980); *Tuutulaulu* (Lullaby) for Soprano and Alto Voices (Nilsiä, June 1980); *Memoarer* (Memoirs) for Voice and Piano (1982; Jyväskylä, June 28, 1983); *Paraabeli* (Parable) for 5 Men's Voices (1983; Helsinki, March 1, 1985); *Metamatiikkaa* for Soprano and Alto Voices and Instruments Obbligato (1983); *Madrigaali* for Women's Chorus (Turku, May 12, 1984); *Lumen valo* (The Glow of Snow) for Men's Chorus and Percussion (1984; Helsinki, Dec. 8, 1985); *MAA* (Earth) for Children's Chorus and Instruments (1984–85; Joensuu, June 19, 1985); *3 Texts by Waltari* for Chorus (1985; Helsinki, March 15, 1986); *Istuin meren rannalla* (I Was Sitting by the Sea) for Voice (1987; Helsinki, Jan. 9, 1988); *Verbum* for Double Chorus (1987); *A* for Children's Chorus, Percussion, and Electronics (1987–88; Tampere, Feb. 20, 1988); *Amores*, 3 songs for Mezzo-soprano and Orch. (Oulu, Nov. 30, 1989). **ELECTRONIC:** *Memoria* (1988–89).—**NS/LK/DM**

Kósa, György, Hungarian pianist, teacher, and composer; b. Budapest, April 24, 1897; d. there, Aug. 16, 1984. He exhibited a precocious talent for music, and when he was 10 years old studied piano privately with Bartók and then later with him at the Royal Academy of Music in Budapest (1908–15). He also studied composition with Herzfeld and Kodály (1908–12) and piano with Dohnányi (1915–16) there. He was co-répétiteur at the Royal Opera House in Budapest (1916–17), then toured Europe and North Africa as a pianist (1917–20).

He subsequently was a theater conductor in Tripoli (1920–21). He then returned to Budapest as an accompanist (1921), and from 1927 to 1960 was prof. of piano at the Budapest Academy of Music, with the exception of a period during World War II when he was compelled to work as a manual laborer in a war camp. He was actively engaged in the promotion of modern Hungarian music; played both traditional and contemporary scores. He was awarded the Erkel Prize (1955); was made a Merited Artist (1963) and an Honored Artist (1972) of his homeland. As a composer, he was initially influenced by Bartók, but he later developed an individualistic style of expressionism.

WORKS: DRAMATIC: O p e r a : *A király palástja* (The King's Robe; 1926); *Az két lovagok* (2 Knights), comic opera (1934; Budapest, 1937); *Cenodoxus*, mystery opera (1942); *Anselmus diák* (Student Anselmus; 1945); *A méhek* (The Bees; 1946); *Tartuffe*, comic opera (1951); *Pázmán lovag* (Knight Pázmán), comic opera (1962–63); *Kocsonya Mihály házassága* (The Marriage of Mihály Kocsonya), comic opera (1971); *Kiálts város* (City, Shout!; 1980–81). **B a l l e t :** *Fehér Pierrot* (White Pierrot; 1916; Budapest, 1920); *Phaedra* (1918); *Dávid király* (King David; 1936); *Ének az örök bánatról* (Song about the Everlasting Sorrow; 1955). **P a n t o m i m e s :** *Mese a királykisasszonyról* (A Tale of a Princess; 1919); *Laterna Magica* (1922; Budapest, Feb. 23, 1927); *Árva Józsi három csodája* (The 3 Miracles of Józsi Arva; 1932; Budapest, Feb. 26, 1933). **ORCH.:** Suite (1915); 6 Pieces (1919); 9 syms. (1920, 1927, 1933, 1936, 1937, 1946, 1957, 1959, 1969); Suite, *Ironic Portraits* (1924); *Fantasy on 3 Folksongs* (1948); *Dance Suite* (1951); Concerto for Piano, Violin, Cymbals, Percussion, and Orch. (1973). **CHAMBER:** 8 string quartets (1920, 1929, 1933, 1936, 1956, 1959, 1963, 1965); *Chamber Music* for 17 Instruments (1928); *6 Portraits* for 6 Horns and Harp (1938); *Divertimento* for String Quartet and Cymbals (1938); Quintet for Flute, Clarinet, Bassoon, Horn, and Harp (1938); Trio for Flute, Viola, and Cello (1946); Trio for Soprano, Clarinet, and Violin (1947); Wind Quintet (1960); Piano Trio (1962); *Duo* for Violin and Cello (1964); Cello Sonata (1965); *6 Intermezzos* for String Trio (1969); *Dialogus* for Bass Tuba and Marimba (1975). **P i a n o :** 3 sonatas (1941, 1947, 1956); other works. **VOCAL: O r a t o r i o s :** *Jonah* (1931); *Easter Oratorio* (1932); *Saulus* (1935); *Joseph*, chamber oratorio (1939); *Elijah*, chamber oratorio (1940); *Christus*, chamber oratorio (1943); *Hajnóczy* (1954); *Villon* (1960). **C a n t a t a s :** *Laodomeia* (1924); *Job* (1933); *Küldetés* (Mission; 1948); *Szól az úr* (The Lord Is Saying; 1957); *Amor sanctus* (1958); 2 cantatas (1964); *Bárányka* (Lambkin; 1965); *Balázsolás* (St. Blaise Play; 1967); *Cantata humana* (1967); *Orpheus, Eurydike, Hermes* (1967); *Őszikék* (Autumn Songs; 1970); *Johannes* (1972); *Szalkak* (Splints; 1972); *Perlekedő prófécia* (A Quarrelling Prophecy; 1972); 2 cantatas (1973–74); *Cantata* (1974); *Bikasirato* (Dirge for a Bull; 1975); *Kakasszó* (Crowing of the Cock; 1975). **O t h e r :** *Dies irae* (1937); 2 masses (1946, 1949); 2 requiems (1949, 1966); *Te Deum* (1949); *Biblical Mass* (1951); *De profundis* (1970); some 500 songs.

BIBL.: M. Pándi, *K. G.* (Budapest, 1966).—**NS/LK/DM**

Kosakoff, Reuven, American pianist and composer; b. New Haven, Conn., Jan. 8, 1898; d. N.Y., May 6, 1987. He studied at Yale Univ. and at the Juilliard School of Music in N.Y., then went to Berlin as a private piano student of Artur Schnabel. He wrote several biblical cantatas; 2 Sabbath services, Piano Concerto on Hebrew themes (Pittsburgh, March 24, 1941), and *Jack and the Beanstalk* for Narrator and Orch. (New Haven, April 22, 1944).—**NS/LK/DM**

Koschat, Thomas, Austrian bass and composer; b. Viktring, near Klagenfurt, Aug. 8, 1845; d. Vienna, May 19, 1914. He sang in church choirs. He publ. his first vocal quartets in the Carinthian dialect in 1871, which became so successful that he publ. some 100 more. In 1875 he organized the famous Kärnthner Quintett with 4 other singers; their performances were exceedingly popular. His "Liederspiel" *Am Wörthersee* (Vienna, March 22, 1880), containing many of his favorite vocal numbers, had great vogue. He also produced a 4-act "Volksstück mit Gesang," *Die Rosenthaler Nachtigall*, and the Singspiel *Der Bürgermeister von St. Anna* (Vienna, May 1, 1884; given in Italian as *Un colpo di fuoco*).

BIBL.: K. Krobath, *T. K., der Sänger Kärnthners* (Leipzig, 1912).—**NS/LK/DM**

Köselitz, Johann Heinrich, German writer and composer; b. Annaberg, Jan. 10, 1854; d. there, Aug. 15, 1918. He studied with Richter at the Leipzig Cons. While in Basel, he formed a close friendship with Nietzsche, from whom he also took lessons in composition. After Nietzsche's death, Koselitz became his literary executor and also ed. Nietzsche's letters. As a composer, he elaborated the Wagnerian system of *Leitmotive*, using the pen name of Peter Gast for his musical productions, among them the operas *Wilbraum und Siegeheer* (1879), *Scherz, List und Rache* (1881), *Die heimliche Ehe* (Danzig, 1891; publ. in 1901 as *Der Löwe von Venedig*), *König Wenzel* (not produced), and *Orpheus und Dionysos* (not produced). He also composed a festival play, *Walpurgisnacht* (1903), a symphonic poem, *Helle Nächte*, choruses, and songs.

BIBL.: L. Brieger-Wasservogel, *Peter Gast* (Leipzig, 1906); F. Götz, *Peter Gast* (Annaberg, 1934).—**NS/LK/DM**

Koshetz, Nina (Pavlovna), Russian-American soprano; b. Kiev, Dec. 30, 1894; d. Santa Ana, Calif., May 14, 1965. Her father, Paul Koshetz, was a tenor. She began piano study when she was 4 and gave her first recital at 9, then enrolled at the Moscow Cons. at 11, studying piano with Igumnov and Safonov and voice with Enzo Masetti; later studied with Félia Litvinne. She toured Russia with Rachmaninoff, of whose songs she was a congenial interpreter. She also toured with Koussevitzky and his orch. She made her operatic debut as Donna Anna at the Imperial Opera in St. Petersburg (1913), and toured the U.S. with the Ukrainian National Chorus, under the conductorship of her brother (1920), where she settled. She sang the role of Fata Morgana in the first performance of Prokofiev's *The Love for 3 Oranges* (Chicago, Dec. 30, 1921). She subsequently devoted herself mainly to concert appearances, and still later taught voice.—**NS/LK/DM**

Kosleck, Julius, German trumpeter, cornetist, and pedagogue; b. Neugard, Dec. 3, 1825; d. Berlin, Nov. 5,

1904. He was a trumpeter in the Berlin Königliche Kapelle (1853–93), and also taught trumpet and trombone at the Berlin Hochschule für Musik (1872–1903). He was founder of the Kaiser-Kornettquartett (c. 1885), which became the Kosleck'sche Bläserbund (1890). He promoted the so-called Bach Trumpet, and played it in a performance of the Bach Mass in B minor in London (1885). He publ. the method *Grosse Schule für Cornet à piston und Trompete* (Leipzig, 1872; Eng. tr., c. 1907, by W. Morrow).—**NS/LK/DM**

Košler, Zdeněk, Czech conductor; b. Prague, March 25, 1928; d. there, July 2, 1995. He studied in Prague with Grünfeldová (piano), Jeremiáš and Řídký (theory and composition), and Dědeček (conducting), and then took conducting courses with Ančerl, Brock, and Doležil at the Academy of Music (1948–52). He made his conducting debut at the National Theater of Prague with *Il barbiere di Siviglia* (1951), and conducted there until 1958. He then conducted the Olomouc (1958–62) and Ostrava (1962–66) operas. In 1956 he won 1st prize in the Besançon competition, and in 1963 1st prize in the Mitropoulos competition. He was chief conductor of the Prague Sym. Orch. (1966–67). He also served as Generalmusikdirektor of the Komische Oper in East Berlin (1966–68), and as chief conductor of the Slovak National Theater in Bratislava (1971–79). He was chief conductor of the Prague National Theater from 1980 to 1985, and again from 1989 to 1991. In 1974 he was made an Artist of Merit and in 1984 a National Artist by the Czech government.—**NS/LK/DM**

Kosma, Joseph, Hungarian-French composer; b. Budapest, Oct. 22, 1905; d. La Roche-Guyon, near Paris, Aug. 7, 1969. He studied at the Budapest Academy of Music, then with Eisler in Berlin (1929). He settled in Paris (1933).

WORKS: DRAMATIC: Comic Opera: *Les Chansons de Bilitis* (1954); *Un Amour électronique* (Paris, 1962); *La Revolté des canuts* (Lyons, 1964); *Les Hussards* (Lyons, Oct. 21, 1969). Ballet: *Le Rendez-vous* (Paris, June 15, 1945); *Baptiste* (1946); *L'Ecuyère* (1948); *Le Pierrot de Montmartre* (1952). Also film scores to *La Grande Illusion, Les Enfants du paradis*, etc. OTHER: *Les Ponts de Paris*, oratorio (1947); piano pieces; songs.

BIBL.: M. Fleuret, ed., *J. K., 1905–1969: Un homme, un musicien* (Paris, 1969).—**NS/LK/DM**

Kospoth, Otto Carl Erdmann, Freiherr von, German composer; b. Muhltroff, Vogtland, Nov. 25, 1753; d. there (in a fire), June 23, 1817. He was trained at the Leignitz Ritterakademie. In 1776 he was made chamberlain and maître des plaisirs at the court of Friedrich II the Great in Potsdam, where he continued in the service of Friedrich Wilhelm II and where he brought out the successful Singspiels *Der Freund deutscher Sitten* (Sept. 25, 1778), *Adrast und Isidore, oder Die Serenate* (Oct. 16, 1779), *Der Irrwisch, oder Endlich fand er sie* (Oct. 2, 1780), *Das Fest der Schäfer* (Oct. 18, 1787), and *Der kluge Jakob* (Feb. 26, 1788). He also composed orch. works, chamber pieces, oratorios, and cantatas. In 1789 he retired to his estates in Muhltroff and pursued an eccentric life, dabbling in necromancy, spiritualism, and other byways. In the end, he lost his estates but was given a room in the castle. He lost his life in a fire there when he refused to leave, believing that he was impervious to the threat.—**LK/DM**

Kössler, Hans
See **Koessler, Hans**

Kostelanetz, André, highly successful Russianborn American conductor, uncle of **Richard Kostelanetz;** b. St. Petersburg, Dec. 22, 1901; d. Port-au-Prince, Haiti, Jan. 13, 1980. He studied at the St. Petersburg Cons. In 1922 he went to the U.S., becoming a naturalized American citizen (1928). He came to prominence as a conductor on the radio; appeared regularly with the CBS Sym. Orch. (from 1930); later enjoyed tremendous success with his own orch. on radio and recordings, making the lush "Kostelanetz sound" and arrangements his trademark. He married **Lily Pons** in 1938, but they subsequently were divorced. During World War II, he conducted many concerts for the U.S. armed forces. He later appeared as a guest conductor with leading orchs. in North America, Europe, Israel, and Japan. He also conducted popular concerts in America and in Europe; made successful arrangements of light music, his technique of massive concentration of instrumental sonorities and of harmonic saturation by means of filling in harmonies with inner thirds and sixths having influence upon film music. An intelligent musician, he commissioned special works from American composers, of which the most successful was Copland's *Lincoln Portrait*. With G. Hammond, he wrote *Echoes: Memoirs of André Kostelanetz* (N.Y., 1981).—**NS/LK/DM**

Kostelanetz, Richard, versatile American music critic, writer on contemporary music and the arts, and composer, nephew of **André Kostelanetz;** b. N.Y., May 14, 1940. He studied American civilization and history at Brown Univ. (A.B., 1962) and Columbia Univ. (M.A., 1966). He was a Fulbright scholar at King's Coll., Univ. of London (1964–65), and also attended classes at London's Morley Coll. and the New School in N.Y. He lectured at Harvard Univ., Wellesley Coll., Carnegie-Mellon Univ., and the Univ. of Calif. at Santa Cruz, among other institutions. His extensive list of publications includes articles, books, poetry, fiction, plays, and experimental prose; among his numerous anthologies on contemporary American arts are several with emphasis on music, including *The Theatre of Mixed Means* (N.Y., 1968), *Master Minds* (N.Y., 1969), *Conversing with Cage* (N.Y., 1988), *On Innovative Musicians* (N.Y., 1989), *On Innovative Art(ist)s* (Jefferson, N.C., 1992), *On Innovative Performance(s)* (Jefferson, N.C., 1994), and *Cage Ex(Plain)ed* (N.Y., 1995). Included in his compositional output are audiotapes and videotapes as well as a number of films and holograms, many of which have been exhibited and broadcast around the world. He was a visiting artist at Syracuse Univ. (1975), the Electronic Music Studio of Stockholm (1981–88), and the Experimental Television Center in Oswego, N.Y. (1985–90). He wrote numerous theatrical (*Epiphanies*, 1980) and performance (*Central Park*, 1980) texts; also composed choreographic works (*Invocations*, 1985). He prepared extended features for radio, and his work has appeared in both solo and group exhibitions. Among his awards are a Pulitzer fellowship for critical writing (1965), a Guggenheim fellowship (1967), and annual ASCAP stipends (from 1983). His compositions include audiocassette eds. (*The 8 Nights of Hanukah/Praying to the Lord*, 1983; *Onomatopoeia*, 1988; *Carnival of the Animals/Karneval der Tiere*, 1988) and hörspiels (*Die Evangelien*, 1982; *Invocations*, 1983; *New York City*, 1984; *The Gospels Abridged*, 1986; *Kaddish*, 1990), many of which were commissioned by the West German Radio; also *Lovings* (1990). His videotapes, for which he customarily provides the visuals, include *3 Prose Pieces* (1975), *Epiphanies* (1980), *Seductions/Relationships* (1987), and *Kinetic Writings* (1989). He describes his critical writings and his art as both "avant-garde" and "anarchist libertarian." —NS/LK/DM

Kostić, Dušan, Croatian composer; b. Zagreb, Jan. 23, 1925. He studied at the Belgrade Academy of Music (1947–55), and later took a course in conducting with Scherchen in Bayreuth (1955). He was music ed. for Radio Belgrade (1957–59), then taught at his alma mater (from 1964). He incorporated neo-Classical, impressionistic, and serial techniques in his music; also wrote occasional pieces on national folk themes.

WORKS: DRAMATIC: O p e r a B u f f a : *Majstori su prvi ljudi* (Belgrade, April 23, 1962). **ORCH.:** *Contrasts*, symphonic poem (1954); 2 syms. (1957, 1961); *Crnogorska suita* (1957); *Kragujevac*, symphonic poem for Voices and Orch., commemorating the execution of the schoolboys at Kragujevac in 1941 by the Nazi occupation forces (Belgrade, Feb. 5, 1962). **OTHER:** Chamber works, including *Sonata amorosa* for Violin and Piano (1957); piano pieces; choruses; songs.—NS/LK/DM

Kostič, Vojislav , Serbian composer; b. Belgrade, Sept. 21, 1931. He studied in his native city; adopted a sophisticated style of utilitarian music. His *Karakteri* for Clarinet, Piano, and 18 Percussion Instruments (1958) had numerous performances in Yugoslavia. He also wrote a *Divertimento* for Wind Quintet; Suite for Bassoon and Piano; *Ciganska pri-ča* (Gypsy Tale) for Men's Chorus and Chamber Orch., to Gypsy texts (1964). —NS/LK/DM

Kostov, Georgi, Bulgarian composer; b. Sofia, Jan. 21, 1941. He studied composition with Vladigerov and Stoyanov at the Bulgarian State Cons. in Sofia, graduating in 1966, and pursued his studies at the Moscow Cons. (1972). He then taught at his alma mater.

WORKS: DRAMATIC: B a l l e t : *The Broadside of "Avrora"* (1967). **ORCH.:** Clarinet Concerto (1958); Viola Concertino (1965); Concerto for Horn, Strings, and Timpani (1966); *Youth Overture* (1967); *3 Diaphonous Dances* (1972); *Poem for Trumpet, Percussion, and Strings* (1973); *Prelude, Chorale, and Fugue* (1974); *Rhythmic Movements* (1974); *Antiphonous Dialogues* (1974); *September Ballad* (1974). **OTHER:** 2 cantatas: *The Communist Man* (1964) and *We Are Proud of You, Our Party* (1975); 2 oratorios: *Glorious Days* (1969) and *Alive He Is* (1976); chamber music; choral songs; popular music.—NS/LK/DM

Kosugi, Takehisa, inventive Japanese composer and violinist; b. Tokyo, March 24, 1938. He studied at the Tokyo Univ. of Fine Arts and Music, then founded the group Ongaku, which introduced mixed-media improvisational performance in Japan. In 1969 he founded the Taj Mahal Travelers ("TMT"), with which he toured in India, the Near East, and Europe; upon returning to Japan, the group frequently participated in rock and jazz festivals. In 1976 Kosugi was invited to compose for the Merce Cunningham Dance Co., and, after moving to the U.S. in 1977, appeared in performances with John Cage and David Tudor. Kosugi regularly creates installations in which he employs acoustic and self-designed electronic instruments; his aesthetic premise is that a performance must make the invisible aspects of a given situation perceptible, audible, and tangible, revealing what is hidden and enabling sounds to be seen as well as heard. In this original capacity he has performed since 1978 in Paris, Rome, Berlin, Bremen, Cologne, and London. Among his commissioned works for the Merce Cunningham Dance Co. are *S.E. Wave/E.W. Song* (1976), *Interspersion* (1979), *Cycles* (1981), *Spacings* (1984), *Assemblage* (1986), *Rhapsody* (1987), and *Spectra* (1989). His major installations include *Interspersions for 54 Sounds* (1980), *Spacings* (audiovisual version; 1985), and *Loops* (1988). As a violinist, he made a remarkable recording, entitled simply *Violin Improvisations* (1990). In 1995 he succeeded David Tudor as music director of the Cunningham Dance Co.—NS/LK/DM

Kotek, (Eduard) Joseph (actually, **Yosif Yosifovich**), Russian violinist and composer; b. Kamenets-Podolsk, Nov. 11, 1855; d. Davos, Switzerland, Jan. 4, 1885. He studied violin with Ferdinand Laub and composition with Tchaikovsky at the Moscow Cons., and later took violin lessons with Joachim in Berlin. He was a close friend of Tchaikovsky, and often served as mediator in financial matters between him and Nadezhda von Meck. He also worked over the solo part of Tchaikovsky's Violin Concerto, and played it with the composer at the piano, privately, in Clarens, Switzerland (April 3, 1878); however, he was reluctant to try it out in public performance despite Tchaikovsky's urgings. He taught violin at the Berlin Hochschule für Musik (1878–82). He was stricken with tuberculosis at the age of 29, and Tchaikovsky made a special trip to Davos to visit before Kotek's death.—NS/LK/DM

Köth, Erika, German soprano; b. Darmstadt, Sept. 15, 1925; d. Speyer, Feb. 20, 1989. She was a student in Darmstadt of Elsa Bank. In 1947 she won 1st prize in a Hessian Radio competition, and then made her debut as Adele in a Darmstadt radio broadcast. In 1948 she made her stage debut as Philine in *Mignon* in Kaiserslautern. After singing in Karlsruhe (1950–53), she appeared with the Bavarian State Opera in Munich (from 1953), the Vienna State Opera (from 1953), and in Berlin (from 1961); she also made appearances at the Salzburg (1955–64) and Bayreuth (1965–68) festivals. In 1956 she was named a Bavarian and in 1970 a Berlin Kammersängerin. She taught at the Cologne Hochschule für Musik (from 1973), and then at the Heidelberg-Mannheim Hochschule für Musik (from 1980). Among her esteemed portrayals were Zerbinetta, the Queen of the Night, Susanna, Constanze, Donna Elvira, Lucia, and Sophie.

BIBL.: K. Adam, *Herzlichst! E. K.* (Darmstadt, 1969). —NS/LK/DM

Kotik, Petr, Czech-born American flutist and composer; b. Prague, Jan. 27, 1942. He studied flute with Frantisek Cech at the Prague Cons. (B.A., 1962) and at the Prague Academy of Music (M.A., 1969), and had lessons in composition with Rychlik in Prague, and in flute with Hans Resnicek (M.A., 1966) at the Vienna Academy of Music. He also studied composition at the Vienna Academy of Music with Schiske, Jelinek, and Cerha (B.A., 1966). In 1961 he founded Musica Viva Pragensis, and in 1966 the Prague experimental music ensemble QUAX. He went to the U.S. in 1969; became a naturalized American citizen in 1977. From 1969 to 1974 he was a member of the Center of the Creative and Performing Arts at the State Univ. of N.Y. in Buffalo. In 1970 he founded the S.E.M. Ensemble, with which he toured in the U.S. and abroad; also toured as a solo flutist. He taught flute (1971–77) and composition (1976–77) at the State Univ. of N.Y. in Buffalo; also taught composition at York Univ. in Toronto (1975–76). In 1983 he settled in N.Y.; continued to tour with the S.E.M. Ensemble and as a soloist.

WORKS: *Congo* for Flute, Oboe, Clarinet, Bassoon, Viola, Cello, and Double Bass (1962; Prague, Jan. 18, 1963); *Kontrapunkt II* for Alto Flute, English Horn, Clarinet, Bassoon, Viola, and Cello (1962–63; Vienna, Oct. 8, 1963); *Spontano* for Piano and 10 Wind Instruments (1964; Buffalo, May 22, 1973); *6 Plums* for Orch. (1965–68); *Contraband* for Live Electronics and 2 to 6 Performers (Cologne, April 28, 1967); *Aria*, tape or theater piece (1969; Buffalo, May 27, 1971); *Alley* for Instrumental Ensemble (1969–70; N.Y., March 18, 1971); *There Is Singularly Nothing*, 21 solos for Ensemble (1972; rev. version as *There Is Singularly Nothing II* for Voices and Instruments, N.Y., Dec. 19, 1995); *John Mary* for 2 Voices, 3 Melodic Instruments, and Percussionist (1973–74; Witten, April 27, 1974); *Many Many Women* for 2, 4, or 6 Singers and 2, 4, or 6 Instruments (1975–78); *Drums* for Percussion Ensemble (1977–81); *Explorations in the Geometry of Thinking* for Vocal Ensemble (1978–82); *August/October* for Viola or Cello and Ensemble (1981; rev. as *Apparent Orbit*, 1981–85); *Music for Winds* (1981–82); *Solos and Incidental Harmonies* for Flute, Violin, and 2 Percussion (1983–84); *Integrated Solo* for Flute, Tambourine, Trumpet, and Keyboard (1986–88); *Wilsie Bridge* for Winds, Keyboards, and Percussion (1986–87; N.Y., Jan. 13, 1987); *Letters to Olga* for 5 Voices, Flute, Trumpet, and 3 Guitars (1989–91; N.Y., May 7, 1991).—NS/LK/DM

Kotoński, Włodzimierz, Polish composer and pedagogue; b. Warsaw, Aug. 23, 1925. He studied composition with Piotr Rytel at the State Higher School of Music in Warsaw (1945–51), and also received private training in composition from Tadeusz Szeligowski (1950–51) and in piano from K. Klimont-Jacynowa. He later attended the summer courses in new music in Darmstadt (1957–61). From 1958 he was active with the Polish Radio Experimental Studio. In 1959 he composed the first electronic score in Poland, *Etiuda na jedno uderzenie w talerz* (Study on one cymbal stroke). In 1967 he became a lecturer in composition at his alma mater, becoming an assoc. prof. in 1972. In 1983 he was honored with the state title of prof. From 1983 to 1989 he was president of the Polish section of the ISCM. He received the Minister of Culture and Arts Award in 1973 and the Polish Composers' Union Award in 1976. Among his books are *Instrumenty perkusyjne we wspólczesnejorkiestrze* (Percussion instruments in the modern orchestra; Kraków, 1963; 2nd ed., 1981), *Muzyka elektroniczna* (Electronic music; Kraków, 1989), and *Leksykon współczesnej perkusji* (Lexicon of modern percussion; Kraków, 1999).

WORKS: *Poemat* (Poem) for Orch. (Poznań, Oct. 1949); *Tańce góralskie* (Danses montagnardes) for Orch. (1950); *Preludium i passacaglia* for Orch. (1953; Warsaw, March 5, 1954); 6 Miniatures for Clarinet and Piano (1957; Warsaw, Feb. 28, 1958); *Chamber Music* for 21 Instruments and Percussion (Warsaw, Oct. 3, 1958); *Musique en relief*, 5 miniatures for 6 Orch. Groups (Frankfurt am Main, Sept. 5, 1959); *Etiuda na jedno uderzenie w talerz* (Study on one cymbal stroke), musique concrète (1959; Warsaw, Sept. 21, 1960); Trio for Flute, Guitar, and Percussion (1960; Palermo, May 22, 1961); *Concerto per quattro* for Harp, Harpsichord, Guitar, Piano, and Chamber Orch. (1960; Venice, April 1961; also for Harp, Harpsichord, Guitar, Piano, and Chamber Orch., Lübeck, March 8, 1965); *Canto* for Chamber Group (Darmstadt, Sept. 4, 1961); *Selection I* for 4 Jazz Players (Warsaw, Oct. 17, 1962); *Pezzo* for Flute and Piano (Venice, April 23, 1962); *Musica* for Winds and Timpani (Cologne, May 20, 1963); *Mikrostruktury* (Microstructures) for Tape (Warsaw, Sept. 26, 1963); *Monochromia* for Oboe (1964); Wind Quintet (1964; Warsaw, Sept. 26, 1965); *A battere* for Guitar, Viola, Cello, Harpsichord, and Percussion (Warsaw, Sept. 20, 1966); *Pour quatre* for Clarinet, Trombone, Cello, and Piano (London, Feb. 22, 1968); *Muzyka* for 16 Cymbals and Strings (Warsaw, Sept. 20, 1969); *AELA czyli gra struktur aleatorycznych na jednym dźięku harmonicznym* (AELA or the interplay of aleatory structures on one harmonic tone), electronic piece (Warsaw, Sept. 21, 1970); *Multiplay*, instrumental theater for 6 Brass Instruments (Umeå, Feb. 12, 1971); *Concerto per oboe* for Oboe, Oboe d'amore, 6 Winds, and Orch. (Berlin, April 6, 1972); *Promenada I*, instrumental theater for 4 Players (Warsaw, Nov. 12, 1973) and *II*, instrumental theater for Clarinet, Trombone, Cello, and 3 Synthesizers (Warsaw, Nov. 12, 1973); *Harfa Eola* (Aeolian Harp) for Soprano and 4 Players (1973; Bonn, Dec. 1, 1974); *Musical Games* for Wind Quintet (1973; Oslo, May 21, 1974); *Róża wiatrów* (Wind Rose) for Orch. (Graz, Oct. 14, 1976); *Muzyka wiosenna* (Spring Music) for Flute, Oboe, Violin, and Synthesizer (Buffalo, May 7, 1978); *Pełnia lata* (Midsummer) for Clarinet, Piano, Cello, and Electronics (Stuttgart, Nov. 9, 1979); *Bora* for Orch. (Poznań, March 31, 1979); *Sirocco* for Orch. (1980; Dallas, April 4, 1981); *Pieśń jesienna* (Autumn Song) for Harpsichord and Tape (Dortmund, April 18, 1981); *Terra incognita* for Orch. (Warsaw, Sept. 30, 1984); *Textures* for Tape (1984); *Sceny liryczne* (Lyric Scenes) for 9 Instruments (Nuremberg, Nov. 16, 1986); *Tlaloc* for Harpsichord and Percussion (1986; Lisbon, May 8, 1987); *Ptaki* (Birds) for Clarinet, Cello, and Piano (1988; Copenhagen, April 18, 1989); *Cadenze e arie* for Guitar (1988; Warsaw, May 16, 1989); *Antiphonae* for Tape (Koriyama, Aug. 23, 1989); *Bucolica (Morton Feldman in memoriam)* for Flute (1989; Warsaw, June 5, 1990); *Trzy etiudy rytmiczne* (Three rhythmic studies) for Piano (1990; Warsaw, Sept. 21, 1995); *La gioia* for 9 Strings (Poznań, April 6, 1991; also for String Orch.); *Tierra caliente* for Tape (1992); *Motu proprio* for Bassoon and Piano (Amsterdam,

May 9, 1992); *7 Haiku* for Woman's Voice and 5 Instruments (1993; Warsaw, Sept. 17, 1994); Concerto for Electric Guitar and Instrumental Ensemble (1993; Apeldoorn, Sept. 30, 1994); *Podróż zimowa* (Winterreise) for Flute, Oboe, Clarinet, Violin, Cello, Harpsichord, and Tape (Warsaw, May 12, 1995); Sym. No. 1 (Warsaw, Sept. 18, 1995); *Mijikayo* for Japanese Instruments (1996; Tokyo, July 10, 1997); *Speculum* for Tape and Orch. (1996). —NS/LK/DM

Kotter, Hans (Johannes), Alsatian organist and composer; b. Strasbourg, c. 1485; d. Bern, 1541. He studied organ with Paul Hofhaimer. He was organist at the electoral court in Torgau, and then of the collegiate church of St. Nikolaus in Fribourg from 1514 until being banished in 1530 for espousing the doctrines of Zwingli. In 1534 Kotter was able to return to Switzerland, where he became a Bern schoolmaster. He compiled a collection of keyboard pieces in tablature (1513), including preambles, fantasies, dances, transcriptions of vocal music, and settings of plainchant. His setting of a *Nobis post hoc* was interpolated in a *Salve Regina* by Hofhaimer. See H. Marx, ed., *Tabulaturen des XVI. Jahrhunderts, I: Die Tabulaturen aus dem Besitz des Basler Humanisten Bonifacius Amerbach*, Schweizerische Musikdenkmäler, VI (1967).

BIBL.: W. Merian, *Die Tabulaturen des Organisten H. K.* (Leipzig, 1916).—NS/LK/DM

Kouguell, Arkadie, Russian-American pianist and composer; b. Simferopol, Dec. 25, 1898; d. Glen Head, L.I., N.Y., Nov. 20, 1985. He studied at the St. Petersburg Cons. After living in Beirut (1928–48) and Paris (1948–52), he settled in N.Y. as a piano teacher.

WORKS: *Impressions of Damascus* for Orch. (1930); Piano Concerto (1930); *Bédouin Dance* for 60 Cellos (1932); Piano Concerto for Left Hand (1934); *Rapsodi tartare* for Orch. (1947); Cello Concerto (1950); *Concertino* for Trombone and Piano (1956); suites for various chamber groups; chamber music; etc. —NS/LK/DM

Koukouzeles, Joannes, famous singer and composer of Byzantine chant; b. Dyrrachium, c. 1280; d. probably in Great Laura, Mount Athos, between 1360 and 1375. Although his surname has been given as Papadopoulos in some sources, there is no reason to believe that he was of Greek origin; he most likely was of Slavonic descent. While still a boy, he was sent to the imperial school in Constantinople by the Byzantine emperor. Following his studies, he established himself as a celebrated singer at the Constantinople court, becoming renowned as the angelophonos (angel voice) of the age. He eventually turned his back on the secular world to pursue a monastic life in the Great Laura, on the southern slopes of Mount Athos. In his epoch he was the foremost composer of chants, many of which appeared in various anthologies from the middle of the 14th century on.

BIBL.: E. Williams, *John K.'s Reform of Byzantine Chanting for Great Vespers in the Fourteenth Century* (diss., Yale Univ., 1968). —NS/LK/DM

Kounadis, Arghyris, Greek composer; b. Constantinople, Feb. 14, 1924. He was taken to Athens in his infancy. He studied piano at home and then with S. Farandatos at the Athens Cons. (graduated, 1952), and also studied law at the Univ. of Athens. After studying composition with Papaioannou at Athens's Hellenic Cons. (graduated, 1956), he continued his studies with Fortner in Freiburg im Breisgau (1958–61). In 1963 he joined the faculty of the Freiburg im Breisgau Hochschule für Musik, becoming a prof. there in 1972.

WORKS: DRAMATIC: *Der Gummisarg* (1968); *Die verhexten Notenstander* (1971); *Der Ausbruch* (1975); *Die Bassgeige* (1979; rev. 1987); *Lysistrata*, after Aristophanes (1983); *Der Sandmann* (1986). **ORCH:** *Chorikon I* (1958) and *II* (1960); *Triptychon* (1964); *Heterophonika Idiomela* (1967). **VOCAL:** *Quattro pezzi per trio et soprano* (1968); *Die Nachtigall* for Soprano and 10 or More Double Basses (1975); *9 Gedichte des M. Sochtouris* for Bass, Chorus, and Instrumental Ensemble (1980).—NS/LK/DM

Koussevitzky, Serge (Alexandrovich), celebrated Russian-born American conductor; b. Vishny-Volochok, July 26, 1874; d. Boston, June 4, 1951. His father and his 3 brothers were all amateur musicians. Koussevitzky learned to play the trumpet and took part, with his brothers, in a small wind ensemble, numbering 8 members in all; they earned their living by playing at balls and weddings and occasionally at village fairs. At the age of 14, he went to Moscow; since Jews were not allowed to live there, he became baptized. He then received a fellowship with free tuition at the Musico-Dramatic Inst. of the Moscow Phil. Soc., where he studied double bass with Rambousek; he also studied theory with Blaramberg and Kruglikov. In 1894 he joined the orch. of the Bolshoi Theater, succeeding Rambousek as principal double bass player in 1901, retaining that post until 1905. In the meantime, he became known as a soloist of the first magnitude; made his public debut in Moscow on March 25, 1901. He garnered great attention with a double bass recital in Berlin on March 27, 1903. To supplement the meager repertoire for his instrument, he arranged various works; also wrote several pieces. With some aid from Glière, he wrote a Double Bass Concerto, which he performed for the first time in Moscow on Feb. 25, 1905. On Sept. 8, 1905, he married Natalie Ushkov, daughter of a wealthy tea-merchant family. He soon resigned from the orch. of the Bolshoi Theater; in an open letter to the Russian publication Musical Gazette, he explained the reason for his resignation as the economic and artistic difficulties in the orch. He then went to Germany, where he continued to give double-bass recitals; played the 1st Cello Concerto by Saint-Saëns on the double bass. In 1907 he conducted a student orch. at the Berlin Hochschule für Musik; his first public appearance as a conductor took place on Jan. 23, 1908, with the Berlin Phil. In 1909 he established a publishing house, Editions Russes de Musique; in 1915 he purchased the catalog of the Gutheil Co.; among composers with whom he signed contracts were Scriabin, Stravinsky, Prokofiev, Medtner, and Rachmaninoff; the association with Scriabin was particularly fruitful, and in subsequent years Koussevitzky became the greatest champion of Scriabin's music. In 1909 he organized his own sym. orch. in Moscow, featuring works by Russian composers, but also including classical masterpieces; played many Russian works for the first time, among them Scriabin's *Prometheus*. In the summer of 1910 he took his orch. to the towns along the Volga River in a specially chartered steamboat. He repeated the Volga tour in 1912 and 1914. The outbreak of World War I in 1914 made it necessary to curtail his activities; however, he continued to give his concerts in Moscow; in 1915 he presented a memorial Scriabin program. After the Revolution of 1917, he was offered the directorship of the State Sym. Orch. (former Court Orch.) in Petrograd; he conducted it until 1920; also presented concerts in Moscow, despite the hardships of the revolutionary times. In 1920 he left Russia; went first to Berlin, then to Rome, and finally to Paris, where he organized the Concerts Koussevitzky with a specially assembled orch.; presented many new scores by French and Russian composers, among them Ravel's orchestration of Mussorgsky's *Pictures at an Exhibition*, Honegger's *Pacific 231*, and several works by Prokofiev and Stravinsky. In 1924 Koussevitzky was appointed the conductor of the Boston Sym. Orch., a position he held with great eminence until 1949. Just as in Russia he championed Russian composers, in France the French, so in the U.S. he encouraged American composers to write works for him. Symphonic compositions by Copland, Harris, Piston, Barber, Hanson, Schuman, and others were performed by Koussevitzky for the first time. For the 50th anniversary of the Boston Sym. Orch. (1931), he commissioned works from Stravinsky (Symphony of Psalms), Hindemith, Honegger, Prokofiev, Roussel, Ravel (piano concerto), Copland, Gershwin, and others. A highly important development in Koussevitzky's American career was the establishment of the Berkshire Music Center at Tanglewood, Mass. This was an outgrowth of the Berkshire Sym. Festival, organized in 1934 by Henry Hadley; Koussevitzky and the Boston Sym. Orch. presented summer concerts at the Berkshire Festival in 1935 for the first time; since then, the concerts have become an annual institution. The Berkshire Music Center was opened on July 8, 1940, with Koussevitzky as director and Copland as asst. director; among the distinguished guest instructors were Hindemith, Honegger, and Messiaen; Koussevitzky himself taught conducting; he was succeeded after his death by his former student Leonard Bernstein.

Koussevitzky held many honorary degrees: Mus. Doc. from Brown Univ. (1926), Rutgers Univ. (1937), Yale Univ. (1938), Univ. of Rochester (1940), Williams Coll. (1943), and Boston Univ. (1945); LL.D. from Harvard Univ. (1929) and Princeton Univ. (1947). He was a member of the French Legion of Honor and held the Cross of Commander of the Finnish Order of the White Rose. He became a naturalized American citizen on April 16, 1941. His wife died in 1942; he established the Koussevitzky Foundation as a memorial to her, the funds to be used for commissioning works by composers of all nationalities. He married Olga Naoumoff (1901–78), a niece of Natalie Koussevitzky, on Aug. 15, 1947.

As a conductor, Koussevitzky possessed an extraordinary emotional power; in Russian music, and particularly in Tchaikovsky's syms., he was unexcelled; he was capable of achieving the subtlest nuances in the works of the French school; his interpretations of Debussy were notable. As a champion of modern music, he had few equals in his time; his ardor in projecting unfamiliar music before new audiences in different countries served to carry conviction among the listeners and the professional music critics. He was often criticized for the liberties he allowed himself in the treatment of classical masterpieces; undoubtedly his performances of Haydn, Mozart, Beethoven, and other giants of the Austro-German repertoire were untraditional; but they were nonetheless musicianly in the sincere artistry that animated his interpretations.

BIBL.: A. Lourie, *S.A. K. and His Epoch* (N.Y., 1931); H. Leichtentritt, *S. K., The Boston Symphony Orchestra and the New American Music* (Cambridge, Mass., 1946); M. Smith, *K.* (N.Y., 1947; a controversial biography).—NS/LK/DM

Kout, Jiří, Czech conductor; b. Novedvory, Dec. 26, 1937. He received training in organ and conducting at the Cons. and the Academy of Music in Prague. In 1964 he became a conductor at the Plzeň Opera. His protest of the Warsaw Pact invasion of his homeland in 1968 led the Czech authorities to ban him from conducting. However, in 1973, he was allowed to resume his career with an engagement at the Prague National Theater. In 1976 he emigrated to West Germany and became a conductor at the Deutsche Oper am Rhein in Düsseldorf. From 1985 to 1991 he was Generalmusikdirektor of the Saarländisches Staatstheater in Saarbrücken; also appeared as a guest conductor of opera houses in Munich, Berlin, Vienna, Venice, Florence, Paris, Cincinnati, and Los Angeles. From 1991 he was a regular conductor at the Deutsche Oper in Berlin; that same year, he made his Metropolitan Opera debut in N.Y. conducting *Der Rosenkavalier*. In 1993 he conducted *Jenůfa* at London's Covent Garden. In 1993 he became music director of the Leipzig Opera and in 1996 of the St. Gallen Orch. He conducted a *Ring* cycle at the Deutsche Oper in Berlin in 1997. In addition to his idiomatic interpretations of the operas of Smetana, Dvořák, and Janáček, Kout has acquired a distinguished reputation for his performances of operas by Wagner and Strauss.—NS/LK/DM

Koutzen, Boris, Russian-American violinist, teacher, and composer; b. Uman, near Kiev, April 1, 1901; d. Mount Kisco, N.Y., Dec. 10, 1966. He studied violin with Leo Zetlin and composition with Glière at the Moscow Cons. (1918–22). In 1922 he went to the U.S. and joined the violin section of the Philadelphia Orch. (until 1927); later played in the NBC Sym. Orch. in N.Y. (1937–45). He was head of the violin dept. at the Philadelphia Cons. (1925–62) and a teacher at Vassar Coll. in Poughkeepsie, N.Y. (1944–66). His music possesses an attractive Romantic flavor in an old Russian manner. He composed a number of orch. pieces, among them *Solitude* (Philadelphia, April 1, 1927, composer conducting), *Valley Forge*, symphonic poem (N.Y., Feb. 19, 1940), Concerto for 5 Solo Instruments (Boston, Feb. 23, 1940),

Violin Concerto (Philadelphia, Feb. 22, 1952, Nadia Koutzen, composer's daughter, soloist), and *Concertante for 2 Flutes and Orch.* (1965), as well as an opera, *You Never Know* (1962).—NS/LK/DM

Kovačević, Krešimir, significant Croatian musicologist; b. Zagreb, Sept. 16, 1913. He studied at the Univ. of Leipzig (Ph.D., 1943, with a diss. on folk music from the Meotimurje region of Croatia). He taught music in Osijek and Dubrovnik (1940–50) and then at the Zagreb Academy of Music (prof., 1950; vice-dean, 1961–71; dean, from 1971). He was also a repetiteur in Zagreb and Belgrade (1936–39), conductor of the Dubrovnik Orch. (1946–50), and a music critic for several publications. He wrote primarily on Croatian contemporary music; publ. the valuable *Hrvatski kompozitori i njihova djela* (Croatian Composers and Their Works; Zagreb, 1960) and *The History of Croatian Music of the Twentieth Century* (in Eng.; Zagreb, 1967). He also edited the 2nd ed. of the *Muzička enciklopedija* (3 vols., 1971–77) and contributed the Croatian entries to the Slovene reference work *Jugoslovanska glasbena dela* (1980). —NS/LK/DM

Kovacevich, Stephen, distinguished American pianist and conductor; b. Los Angeles, Oct. 17, 1940. He began his piano studies with Lev Schorr in 1948, and in 1951 made his public debut in San Francisco under the name Stephen Bishop. In 1959 he went to London to pursue his piano training with Dame Myra Hess. After making his London recital debut in 1961, he appeared as a soloist with many of the major European and North American orchs., as a recitalist, and as a chamber music artist. In 1975 he began to use the name Stephen Bishop-Kovacevich, and finally assumed his original name Stephen Kovacevich in 1991. In 1984 he made his conducting debut with the Houston Sym. Orch., and thereafter pursued a dual career as a pianist and conductor. In 1986 he was appointed to an international chair at the Royal Academy of Music in London. From 1990 to 1993 he was music director of the Irish Chamber Orch. in Dublin. His wife is **Martha Argerich.** As a pianist, Kovacevich has demonstrated an extraordinary command of an expansive repertoire, ranging from the classics to contemporary scores. As a conductor, he has concentrated on works from the 18th and 19th centuries to good effect.—NS/LK/DM

Koval, Marian (Viktorovich), Russian composer; b. Pristan Voznesenya, Olonets district, Aug. 17, 1907; d. Moscow, Feb. 15, 1971. Following training in Nizhny-Novgorod and Petrograd, he studied composition with Gnessin and Miaskovsky at the Moscow Cons. (1925–30). Inspired by the revolutionary ideas of a new collective society, he organized with others a group named Procoll ("Productive Collective"), dedicated to the propaganda of music in its sociological aspects; was also a member of the Russian Assn. of Proletarian Musicians from 1929 until it was disbanded by the Soviet government in 1931 as being counterproductive. He became known mainly through his choruses and songs on socialist subjects; all of his music is derived from modalities of Russian folk songs and those of the ethnic group of the Urals, to which he belonged. He wrote the operas *Emelian Pugatchev* (Moscow, Nov. 25, 1939) and *Sevastopoltzy* (Perm, Nov. 28, 1946), the cantatas: *The People's Sacred War* (1941), *Valery Tchkalov* (1942), and *The Kremlin Stars* (1947), *The Wolf and 7 Little Goats*, children's opera (1939), 2 cycles of songs about Lenin, etc.

BIBL.: G. Polyanovsky, *M. K.* (Moscow, 1968). —NS/LK/DM

Kovalev, Pavel, Russian composer; b. Nikolayev, Jan. 6, 1890; d. Paris, Nov. 16, 1951. He studied at the Odessa Cons. and with Teichmuller and Reger at the Leipzig Cons., then taught at the Odessa Cons. (1919–22). In 1927 he left Russia via China and Japan and settled in Paris. He wrote an opera, *Ariane et Barbe-bleue,* ballet scores, chamber music, and songs. —NS/LK/DM

Kovařiček, František, Czech composer; b. Liteniny, May 17, 1924. He studied with Hlobil at the Prague Cons. and with Řídký at the Prague Academy of Music, graduating in 1952. He was music director of the Czech Radio in Prague (1953–58). From 1966 to 1985 he taught at the Prague Cons., and from 1990 to 1991 was its director.

WORKS: Cello Sonata (1958); *Serenade* for 9 Instruments (1958); *Divertimento* for Strings (1960); *Larghetto* for Clarinet and Piano (1963); Clarinet Concerto (1964); *Ukradený mesič* (The Stolen Moon), comic opera (1966; Czech Radio, July 1, 1970); *Capriccio* for Chamber Orch. (1970–71); *Music* for Chamber Orch. (1982; Prague, March 23, 1984); 2 piano sonatas; choral pieces; songs.—NS/LK/DM

Kovařovic, Karel, noted Czech conductor and composer; b. Prague, Dec. 9, 1862; d. there, Dec. 6, 1920. He studied clarinet, harp, and piano at the Prague Cons. (1873–79), and also composition privately with Fibich (1878–80). He was harpist in the orch. of Prague's National Theater (1879–85), and also was director of Pivoda's Vocal School (1880–1900). In 1900 he was appointed opera director of the National Theater in Prague, a position he held until his death; he also led sym. concerts in Prague. As a conductor, he demonstrated great craftsmanship and established a high standard of excellence in his operatic productions; his interpretations of Dvořák and Smetana were particularly notable; an ardent believer in the cause of Czech music, he promoted national compositions. In his own music, he also made use of national materials, but his treatment was mostly imitative of the French models; the influences of Gounod and Massenet are particularly noticeable. He publ. some of his lighter works under a series of humorously misspelled names of French composers (C. Biset, J. Héral, etc.).

WORKS: DRAMATIC: O p e r a (all 1st perf. in Prague): *Ženichové* (The Bridegrooms; May 13, 1884); *Cesta oknem* (Through the Window; Feb. 11, 1886); *Noc Šimona a Judy* (The Night of Simon and Jude; original title, *Frasquita;* Nov. 5, 1892); *Psohlavci* (The Dog-Heads; April 24, 1898); *Na starém bélidle* (At the Old Bleaching-House; Nov. 22, 1901). **B a l l e t :** *Hashish* (June 19, 1884); *Pohádka o nalezeném štěstí* (A Tale of Found

Happiness; Dec. 21, 1886); *Na zaletech* (Flirtation; Oct. 24, 1909). **OTHER:** Symphonic works, including Piano Concerto (1887); chamber pieces, including 3 string quartets (1878, 1887, 1894).

BIBL.: J. Němeček, *Opera Národního divadla za Karla Kovařovice* (Prague, 1968–69).—NS/LK/DM

Koven, (Henry Louis) Reginald de
See De Koven, (Henry Louis) Reginald

Kowalski, Jochen, German countertenor; b. Wachow, Jan. 30, 1954. He studied with Heinz Reeh at the Berlin Hochschule für Musik and with Marianne Fischer-Kupfer. In 1982 he made his debut at the Handel Festival in Halle in Handel's *Mucio Scevola.* He made his first appearance at the Komische Oper in Berlin as Fyodor in *Boris Godunov* in 1983, and subsequently served as a member of the company. In 1987 he sang Ptolomeo in *Giulio Cesare* at the Paris Opéra and Prince Orlovsky at the Vienna State Opera. He appeared as Gluck's Orfeo with the Komische Oper during its visit to London's Covent Garden in 1989. He returned to Covent Garden to sing Prince Orlovsky in 1990 and Farnace in *Mitridate* in 1991. In 1993 he appeared as Ottone in *L'incoronazione di Poppea* at the Salzburg Festival. He was engaged as Britten's Oberon at the Metropolitan Opera in N.Y. in 1996, and returned there as Prince Orlovsky in 1998. Kowalski also sang widely as a concert artist.—NS/LK/DM

Kowalski, Július, Slovak composer; b. Ostrava, Feb. 24, 1912. He went to Prague and studied at the Cons. (1929–33) with Karel (composition) and Dědeček (conducting), and then continued his training at its Master School (1933–34) with Dědeček and Talich (conducting) and Suk (composition). In 1935–36 he pursued studies in quarter-tone and sixth-tone music with A. Hába. He served as director of the music schools in Skalica (1954–56) and Pezinok (1956–57), and then of the art school in Bratislava (1957–59).

WORKS: DRAMATIC: O p e r a : *The Spinning-Wheel Tale,* children's opera (1954); *The Festival of Chinese Lanterns* (1961). **ORCH.:** *Russian Rhapsody* (1934); 7 syms. (1954, 1957, 1958, 1971, 1973, 1980, 1980); *Elegiac Poem* for Cello and Orch. (1959); *Impressions from Eisenach* (1967); *Symfonietta Concertante* for Wind Quintet and Orch. (1975); Concerto for String Quartet and Orch. (1976); Concerto for Violin and Chamber Orch. (1978); *Elegy* for Cello and Orch. (1978); *Epitaph* (1983); *Frescos* (1986); *4 Inventions* (1988). **CHAMBER:** 7 string quartets (1932, 1953, 1965, 1974, 1977, 1979, 1982); 2 trios for 2 Violins and Piano (1967, 1968); *Grimaces* for Wind Quartet (1971); 3 trios for Violin, Cello, and Piano (1969, 1975, 1988); Quartet for 3 Cellos and Piano (1979); Trio for Recorder, Violin, and Cello (1982); Piano Quintet (1985); Trio for 2 Oboes and Piano (1985); Piano Quartet (1990); Suite for Violin and Piano (1993); *Miniatures* for Flute, Cello, and Piano (1995). **VOCAL:** *Stabat mater* for Soloists, Chorus, and Orch. (1945); *Antithesis,* song cycle for High Voice and Piano (1957); 2 Songs for High Voice and String Quartet (1989); 2 Songs for Middle Voice and Piano (1992). —NS/LK/DM

Kowalski, Max, Polish-born German composer; b. Kowal, Aug. 10, 1882; d. London, June 4, 1956. He was taken to Frankfurt am Main as an infant, and received his primary education there. He also studied voice with Heinemann in Berlin and composition with Sekles in Frankfurt am Main, and obtained a law degree from the Univ. of Marburg. He wrote a song cycle to Guiraud's *Pierrot Lunaire* (1912), and during the following 20 years composed a number of lieder, which found favor in Germany. After the Nazis came to power (1933), he was sent to the Buchenwald concentration camp; after his release (1939), he settled in London and eked out a living as a teacher, synagogal cantor, and piano tuner. —NS/LK/DM

Kox, Hans, Dutch composer and teacher; b. Arnhem, May 19, 1930. He studied at the Utrecht Cons. and with Badings. After teaching at the Doetinchem Music School (1956–70), he served as a prof. of composition at the Utrecht Cons. In some of his works, he applied a scale of 31 equal intervals, invented by the Dutch physicist Adriaan Fokker. In his series of *Cyclophonies,* he experimented with open-end forms.

WORKS: DRAMATIC: O p e r a : *Dorian Gray* (1972–73; Scheveningen, March 30, 1974; rev. 1976); *Lord Rochester* (1978); *Das grüne Gesicht* (1991). **ORCH.:** *Little Lethe Symphony* (1956; rev. 1959); *Concertante Music* for Horn, Trumpet, Trombone, and Orch. (1956); Flute Concerto (1957); *Macbeth,* overture (1958); 3 syms.: No. 1 for Strings (1959), No. 2 (1960–66), and No. 3 (1985); *Concerto for Orchestra* (1959); Piano Concerto (1961); 2 violin concertos (1963; 1978, rev. 1981); Concerto for 2 Violins and Orch. (1964); *Cyclophony I* for Cello and Small Orch. (1964), *II* for 3 Orch. Groups (1964), *V* for Oboe, Clarinet, Bassoon, and 19 Strings (1966), *VI* for Violin, Trumpet, Piano, Vibraphone, and 16 Strings (1967), *IX* for Solo Percussion and Small Orch. (1974), and *XI* for Big Band (1978); *Music for Status Seekers* (1966); 2 cello concertos (1969, 1997); *Phobos* (1970); *Concerto bandistico* (1973); *Gothic Concerto* for Harp and Chamber Orch. (1975); *Sinfonia Concertante* for Violin, Cello, and Orch. (1976); *Vangoghiana* for Brass Band, Strings, and Percussion (1977); Alto Saxophone Concerto (1978); *Concertino chitarristico* for 3 Guitars and Small Orch. (1981); *Irold's Youth* (1983); *Notturno e danza* for Violin, Viola or Clarinet, Cello, Piano, and Strings (1983); *Le songe du vergier, dispute rêvée* for Cello and Orch. (1986); *Musica reservata* for Symphonic Band and Orch. (1986; rev. 1987); *Sinfonia Concertante* for Saxophone Quartet and Strings (1988); *Ruach* (1990); *Face to face,* concerto for Alto Saxophone and Strings (1992; rev. 1993); *Das grüne Gesischt,* suite after the opera (1994); *Symphonie de Zampillon* for Wind Ensemble (1995). **CHAMBER:** 4 violin sonatas (1952, 1955, 1961, 1966); 2 trios for 2 Violins and Viola (1952, 1954); 2 string quartets (1955, 1996); 4 sextets (1957, 1957, 1959, 1961); String Quintet (1957); *3 Pieces* for Violin, in the 31-tone system (1958); 2 piano quartets (1959, 1968); Sonata for Solo Cello (1959; rev. 1985); *4 Pieces* for String Quartet, in the 31-tone system (1961); *4 Pieces* for 2 Trumpets and Trombone, in the 31-tone system (1964); *Cyclophony IV* for Treble Recorder and 9 Strings (1965), *VII* for Violin, Piano, and 6 Percussionists (1971), *VIII* for Wind Quintet, Violin, Viola, Cello, and Double Bass (1971; rev. 1982), and *XII* for 8 Cellos (1979); Piano Trio (1976); Suite for Guitar Trio (1977); *Sweerts de Landas,* suite for Violin and Piano (1981); Tenor Saxophone Sonata (1983); 2 saxophone quartets (1985; 1987, rev. 1988); Alto Saxophone Sonata (1985); Cello Sonata (1987); 4 études for Double Bass (1988); *The 3 Chairs* for 3 Saxophones (1989); *Through a Glass Darkly* for Alto Saxophone and Piano (1989); *Asklepios* for 2 Oboes, 2 Clarinets, 2 Bassoons, and 2 Horns (1990); *Galgentrio* for Alto Saxophone, Cello, and Piano (1997). **KEYBOARD: P i a n o :** 2 sonatas (1954, 1955); 3 études (1961); *Cyclophony III* for Piano and Tape (1964); *Melancholies* (1975); *Looks and Smiles for the Orgellas* for 4 Pianists Playing 2 Pianos (1988). **O r g a n :** *Prelude and Fugue* (1954); *Passacaglia and Chorale,* in the 31-tone system (1960). **VOCAL: C h o r u s a n d O r c h .:** *Stichtse kantate* (1958); *Zoo,* cantata (1964); *In those days* (1969); *Requiem for Europe* (1971); *Cyclophony X* (1975); *Anne Frank Cantata: A Child of Light* (1984); *Amsterdam cantate* (1985); *Sjoah,* oratorio (1989); *Das Credo quia absurdum* (1995). **O t h e r :** *Cyclofonie XV* for Mezzo-soprano and Ensemble (1998).—**NS/LK/DM**

Koyama, Kiyoshige,
Japanese composer; b. Nagano, Jan. 15, 1914. He studied composition with Komei Abe. He wrote a number of works in a Japanese national style, among them *Shina no Bayashi* for Orch. (Tokyo, June 3, 1946), *Kobiki-Uta* for Orch. (Tokyo, Oct. 3, 1957), *Nomen,* symphonic suite, for a Noh play (Tokyo, Dec. 5, 1959), *Ubusuna* for Koto and other Japanese Instruments (1962), *Ainu no Uta* for Strings (Tokyo, May 23, 1964), *Sansho Dayu,* opera (Tokyo, March 29, 1972), and several pieces for Japanese instruments.—**NS/LK/DM**

Koželuh (Kozeluch, Koscheluch), Johann Antonin (Jan Evangelista Antonin Tomáš),
Bohemian composer, cousin of **Leopold (Jan Antonín) Koželuh (Kozeluch, Kotzeluch);** b. Welwarn, Dec. 14, 1738; d. Prague, Feb. 3, 1814. He began music studies at school in Welwarn, and was then a chorister at the Jesuit Coll. in Breznice. Subsequently he studied with J.F.N. Seger in Prague, then went to Vienna, where he had instruction from Gluck, Gassmann, and Hasse. Upon his return to Prague, he became Kapellmeister at St. Vitus's Metropolitan Cathedral (1784–1814). His cousin was one of his pupils. He composed the operas *Alessandro nell'Indie* (Prague, 1769) and *Il Demofoonte* (Prague, 1771), much sacred music, including 2 oratorios, about 45 masses, and 5 Requiems, etc., 4 syms., an Oboe Concerto, 2 bassoon concertos, and many other instrumental works.

BIBL.: R. Fikrle, *Jan Evangelista Antonin K.: Život, dilo a osobnost svatovitsheho kapelnika* (a study of his life and music with a list of works; Prague, 1946).—**NS/LK/DM**

Koželuh (Kozeluch, Kotzeluch), Leopold (Jan Antonín),
Bohemian pianist, teacher, and composer, cousin of **Johann Antonín (Jan Evangelista Antonín Tomáš) Koželuh (Kozeluch, Koscheluch);** b. Welwarn, June 26, 1747; d. Vienna, May 7, 1818. He began his musical studies in Welwarn, then had instruction with his cousin and with F.X. Dusek in Prague. He also studied law but turned to a career in music after the success he attained with his ballets and pantomimes. In 1778 he went to Vienna, where he established himself as a pianist, teacher, and composer; also was active as a music publisher. In 1792 he was appointed Kammer Kapellmeister and Hofmusik Compositor, succeeding Mozart, holding this position until his death. Although Beethoven referred to him contemptuously in a letter of 1812 as "miserabilis," Koželuh was an excellent pianist. He composed about 50 solo sonatas, 22 piano concertos,

28 syms., about 80 piano trios, and other pieces of chamber music. His stage works included operas, ballets, and pantomimes, but little of this music is extant; his only extant opera is *Gustav Wasa* (c. 1792).

BIBL.: G. Löbl, *Die Klaviersonate bei L. Kozeluch* (diss., Univ. of Vienna, 1937); M. Poštolka, *Leopold Koželuh:Život a dilo* (a study of his life and music with summary in Eng. and Ger.; Prague, 1964); C. Flamm, *L. Koželuch: Biographie und stilkritische Untersuchung der Sonaten für Klavier, Violine und Violoncello* (diss., Univ. of Vienna, 1968).—**NS/LK/DM**

Kozina, Marjan,
Slovenian composer and teacher; b. Novo Mesto, June 4, 1907; d. there, June 19, 1966. He studied mathematics at the Univ. and music at the Cons. (1925–27) in Ljubljana, and then was a student of Marx at the Vienna Academy of Music (1927–30) and of Suk at the Prague Cons. (1930–32); he also studied conducting with Malko. He was conductor and director of the music school Maribor Glasbena Matica (1934–39), and then taught at the Belgrade Academy of Music (1939–43). During the Nazi occupation, he took part in the armed resistance movement. After the liberation, he served as director of the Slovene Phil. (1947–50) before teaching composition at the Ljubljana Academy of Music (1950–60). His finely executed scores made circumspect use of modern harmonies, while deriving their melorhythmic essence from native Slovenian folk song patterns. Among his works were the opera *Ekvinokcij* (Equinox; Ljubljana, May 2, 1946); ballets; orch. music; choral pieces; songs.—**NS/LK/DM**

Kozlovsky, Ivan (Semyonovich),
Russian tenor; b. Maryanovka, near Kiev, March 24, 1900; d. Moscow, Dec. 21, 1993. He studied at the Kiev Cons. with Lysenko and Muravyova. He made his operatic debut as Faust in Poltava in 1918, then sang in Kharkov (1924) and Sverdlovsk (1925). In 1926 he joined the Bolshoi Theater in Moscow, where he was one of the leading singers until 1954. An artist of imaginative power, Kozlovsky expanded his activities into stage direction, striving to synthesize dramatic action with its musical realization. Apart from operatic performances, he gave recitals in programs of the classical repertoire as well as Russian and Ukrainian songs.

BIBL.: G. Polinovsky, *I. K.* (Moscow, 1945); V. Sletov, *I. K.* (Moscow, 1951); A. Kuznetzova, *I. K.* (Moscow, 1964).—**NS/LK/DM**

Kozma, Matei,
Romanian organist and composer; b. Tîrgu-Mureş, July 23, 1929. He acquired the rudiments of music from his father, Géza Kozma, a composer and cellist, then studied at the Cluj Cons. (1947–54), where his teachers were Jodal and Demian. He was organist (1955–57) and director (1959–66) of the Tîrgu-Mureş Phil.; then taught at the Music Inst. there.

WORKS: DRAMATIC: B a l l e t : *Baladă lacului Sf. Ana* (1957); *Baladă celui care cînta in cătuşe* (1963). **ORCH.:** Organ Concerto (1961; rev. 1965); *Omagiu eroilor,* overture (1967). **CHAMBER:** *Rondo* for Piano (1954); *Theme and Variations* for Organ (1963); Trio for Clarinet (1965); *Toccata, Trio, and Ricercari* for Organ (1968). **VOCAL:** *Trandafirii roşii,* poem for Chorus and Orch. (1962); choruses; songs.—**NS/LK/DM**

Kozolupov, Semyon Matveievich, Russian cellist and pedagogue; b. Krasnokholmskaya, April 22, 1884; d. Moscow, April 18, 1961. He was a pupil of Wierzbillowicz and Seifert at the St. Petersburg Cons. In 1911 he won the Moscow cello competition. He was principal cellist in the orch. of the Bolshoi Theater in Moscow (1908–12; 1924–31), and also a member of the Moscow Quartet. He taught at the Saratov Cons. (1912–16; 1921–22), the Kiev Cons. (1916–20), and the Moscow Cons. (from 1922), where he was also head of the cello dept. (1936–54). Among his outstanding students were Knushevitzky and Rostropovich. —NS/LK/DM

Krader, Barbara (née **Lattimer),** American ethnomusicologist; b. Columbus, Ohio, Jan. 15, 1922. She studied music with Krenek at Vassar Coll. (A.B., 1942), and later took courses in Russian and Slavonic languages, and in literature with Roman Jakobson at Columbia Univ. (A.M., 1948). After a brief period at the Univ. of Prague (1948–49), she completed her education with Jakobson at Radcliffe Coll. (Ph.D., 1955, with the diss. *Serbian Peasant Wedding Ritual Songs: A Formal, Semantic and Functional Analysis*). She worked as a reference librarian in the Slavonic division of the Library of Congress in Washington, D.C. (1959–63) and as a lecturer in Slavonic at Ohio State Univ. (1963–64); in 1965–66 she was executive secretary of the International Folk Music Council in London. On returning to the U.S., she taught at Columbia Univ. (1969) and also served as president of the Soc. for Ethnomusicology (1972–73). She made valuable field recordings in Czechoslovakia, Yugoslavia, Greece, and Romania.—NS/LK/DM

Kraemer, (Thomas Wilhelm) Nicholas, Scottish conductor; b. Edinburgh, March 7, 1945. He was educated at the Dartington Coll. of Arts and at the Univ. of Nottingham (B.Mus., 1967). He was active as a harpsichordist with the Monteverdi Choir and Orch. (1970–80) and the Academy of St. Martin in the Fields (1972–80). In 1978 he founded the Raglan Baroque Players, which ensemble he conducted for over 20 years. From 1980 to 1982 he conducted at Glyndebourne, and from 1980 to 1983 he was music director of Opera 80. He was associate conductor of the BBC Scottish Sym. Orch. in Glasgow from 1983 to 1985. From 1985 to 1990 he was artistic director of the Irish Chamber Orch. in Dublin. In 1985 he became artistic director of the London Bach Orch. He made his first appearance at the English National Opera in London in 1992 conducting *Die Zauberflöte*. His guest appearances as an opera conductor took him to Marseilles, Paris, Geneva, Amsterdam, and other European cities. He was principal conductor (1992–95) and then principal guest conductor (from 1995) of the Manchester Camerata. —NS/LK/DM

Kraft, Anton, Austrian cellist and composer, father of **Nikolaus Kraft;** b. Rokitzan, near Plzen, Dec. 30, 1749; d. Vienna, Aug. 28, 1820. He began to study at an early age with his father, an amateur cellist, and then went to Prague, where he studied with one Werner,

cellist of the Kreuzherren Church; also studied law and philosophy at the Univ. of Prague. He then was a cellist in the chapel of Prince Esterházy (1778–90), and also studied composition with Haydn (c. 1780). He subsequently was a cellist in the orch. of Prince Grassalkowicz de Gyarak in Pressburg (1790–96), and then of Prince Joseph Lobkowitz in Vienna. He toured widely as a virtuoso with his son (from 1789); became a teacher of cello at the Cons. of the Gesellschaft der Musikfreunde in Vienna (1820). Haydn wrote his Cello Concerto in D major, H VIIb: 2, for him, and Beethoven wrote his Triple Concerto with Kraft in mind. Kraft's own works include a Cello Concerto (publ. in Leipzig, 1792?; ed. in Musica Viva Historica, II, 1961), 6 sonatas for Cello (3 as op.2, Amsterdam and Berlin, 1790; 3 as op.2, Offenbach, 1790?), and 3 grands duos concertantes for Violin and Cello, op.3 (Leipzig, 1792?).—NS/LK/DM

Kraft, Leo (Abraham), American composer and pedagogue; b. N.Y., July 24, 1922. He studied composition with Rathaus at Queens Coll. of the City Univ. of N.Y. (B.A., 1945), Thompson at Princeton Univ. (M.F.A., 1947), and Boulanger in Paris on a Fulbright fellowship (1954–55). He taught at Queens Coll. (1947–89); was Distinguished Composer-in-Residence at N.Y.U. (1988–92). From 1976 to 1980 he was president of the American Music Center. He received various ASCAP awards (from 1961); in 1975 and 1978 he held NEA fellowships. Kraft's principal works have developed along atonal lines.

WRITINGS: With S. Berkowitz and G. Frontrier, *A New Approach to Sight Singing* (N.Y., 1960; 3rd ed., 1986); *Gradus: An Integrated Approach to Harmony, Counterpoint, and Analysis* (N.Y., 1976; 2nd ed., 1987); *A New Approach to Ear Training* (Melody) (N.Y., 1967); with others, *A New Approach to Keyboard Harmony* (N.Y., 1978).

WORKS: ORCH.: 6 concertos: No. 1 for Flute, Clarinet, Trumpet, and Strings (1951), No. 2 for 12 Instruments (1966; rev. 1972), No. 3 for Cello, Wind Quintet, and Percussion (1968), No. 4 for Piano and 14 Instruments (1978; rev. 1982), No. 5 for Oboe and Strings (1986), and No. 6 for Clarinet and Orch. (1986); *Larghetto in Memory of Karol Rathaus* for Strings and Timpani (1955); *Variations* (1958); *3 Pieces* (1963); *Music* (1975); Chamber Sym. (1980); *Symphony in 1 Movement* (1985); *A New Ricercar* for Strings (1985); *Pacific Bridges* for Strings and Clarinet obbligato (1989); *Tableaux* for 10 Winds and Piano (1989); *Symphonic Prelude* (1993). **CHAMBER:** Suite for Brass (1947); 4 string quartets (1951, 1959, 1966, 1994); *Short Suite* for Flute, Clarinet, and Bassoon (1951); Sextet for Clarinet, Piano, and String Quartet (1952); Cello Sonata (1954); Violin Sonata (1956); Wind Quintet (1956); Partita *No. 2* for Violin and Viola (1961), *No. 3* for Wind Quintet (1964); *No. 4* for Flute, Clarinet, Violin, Double Bass, and Piano (1975), and *No. 5* for Flute and Guitar (1987); *5 Pieces* for Clarinet and Piano (1962); *Fantasy No. 1* (1963) and *No. 2* (1980) for Flute and Piano; *Trios and Interludes* for Flute, Viola, and Piano (1965); *Dialogues* for Flute and Tape (1968); *Dualities* for 2 Trumpets (1971); *Line Drawings* for Flute and Percussion (1972); *Diaphonies* for Oboe and Piano (1975); *Dialectica* for Flute, Clarinet, Violin, Cello, and Tape (1976); *Conductus Novus* for Trombones (1979); *Strata* for 8 Instruments (1979; rev. 1984); *Interplay* for Trumpet and Percussion (1983); *O Primavera* for Flute, Oboe, and Clarinet (1984); *Inventions and Airs* for Clarinet, Violin, and Piano (1984); *Statements and*

Commentaries No. 2 for 2 Cellos (1988); *Tableau* for Double Wind Septet and Piano (1989); *Cloud Studies* for 12 Flutes (1989); *Washington Square* for Flute, Clarinet, Trombone, Cello, Double Bass, Piano, and Percussion (1990); *Green Mountain Notes* for Oboe, Clarinet, Bassoon, Horn, Violin, and Piano (1991); *Omaggio* for Flute, Clarinet, Violin, Viola, and Cello (1992); *No Time Like This Time* for Clarinet and Piano (1993); *7 Bagatelles* for Cello (1994). **P i a n o :** *Scherzo* (1949); *Variations* (1951); Sonata (1956); *Partita No. 1* (1958); *Allegro Giocoso* (1958); *Statements and Commentaries No. 1* (1965); *Easy Animal Pieces* (1968); *Antiphonies* for Piano, 4- Hands, and Tape (1971); *Sestina* (1971); *10 Short Pieces* (1976); *5 Short Pieces and a Reprise* (1981); *Venetian Reflections* (1989). **VOCAL:** *Festival Song* for Chorus (1948); *Let Me Laugh* for Chorus and Piano (1953); *A Proverb of Solomon* for Chorus and Chamber Orch. (1953); *Thanksgiving* for Chorus (1955); *When Israel Came Forth* for Chorus (1961); *I Waited Patiently* for Men's Voices (1963); *A New Song* for Men's Voices (1964); *Spring in the Harbor* for Soprano, Flute, Cello, and Piano (1969); *3 3-Part Songs* for Women's or Men's Voices (1975); *8 Choral Songs* for Chorus (1975); *4 Songs from the Chinese* for Soprano, Flute, and Percussion (1990).—**NS/LK/DM**

Kraft, Nikolaus, renowned Hungarian cellist, son of **Anton Kraft;** b. Esterhaz, Dec. 14, 1778; d. Eger, May 18, 1853. He studied with his father, and toured with him while quite young. During a visit to the Dresden court, they performed with Mozart (April 14, 1789). He joined the orch. of Prince Joseph Lobkowitz in Vienna (1796), and also was a member of the Schuppanzigh Quartet. After further study with Jean-Pierre Duport in Berlin (1801–02), he toured widely. He returned to Vienna as principal cellist of the orch. of the Kärnthnertortheater (1809), and also continued to serve Prince Lobkowitz as a chamber virtuoso. He subsequently was a chamber musician in Stuttgart from 1814 until an accident to his hand compelled him to retire in 1834. He wrote 4 cello concertos (1810?, 1813, 1819, 1820) and various salon pieces for the instrument. His son, Friedrich Anton Kraft (b. Vienna, Feb. 13, 1807; d. Stuttgart, Dec. 4, 1874), was a cellist in the Stuttgart Court Orch. from 1824.—**NS/LK/DM**

Kraft, Walter, German organist, pedagogue, and composer; b. Cologne, June 9, 1905; d. in a hotel fire in Antwerp, May 9, 1977. He studied piano with Rebbert and organ with Hannemann in Hamburg, and composition with Hindemith in Berlin. From 1924 to 1927 he was organist of the Markuskirche in Hamburg, and from 1927 to 1929 of the Lutherkirche in Altona-Bahrenfeld. From 1929 he was organist of the Marienkirche in Lübeck; the church was destroyed in 1942, but he resumed his post there after it was restored. He was also a prof. of organ at the Freiburg music college (from 1947); in addition, served as director of the Schleswig-Holstein Academy of Music (1950–55). He composed the oratorios *Christus* (1942–43), *Die Bürger von Calais* (1953–54), *Lübecker Totentanz* (1954), and *Die Gemeinschaft der Heiligen* (1956–57); Mass (1966); *Laudatio 71* for Speaker, Chorus, 5 Wind Groups, Bells, Percussion, and Organ (1971); organ music. As an organist, he gained wide distinction as an interpreter of Baroque music and as an improviser.—**NS/LK/DM**

Kraft, William, American percussionist, composer, and conductor; b. Chicago, Sept. 6, 1923. His parental name was Kashareftsky, which his parents Americanized to Kraft. The family moved to Calif. and Kraft began to study piano. He took music courses at San Diego State Coll. and at the Univ. of Calif. at Los Angeles, where he also had professional percussion instruction with Murray Spivack. In 1943 he was called to arms, and served in the U.S. forces as pianist, arranger, and drummer in military bands; while in Europe with the army, he attended music courses at the Univ. of Cambridge. Returning to the U.S. after discharge from military duty, he earned a living as percussionist in jazz bands. In the summer of 1948 he enrolled in the Berkshire Music Center in Tanglewood, where he studied composition with Fine and conducting with Bernstein. In 1949 he entered Columbia Univ., where his instructors in composition were Beeson, Luening, Bingham, Ussachevsky, and Cowell; he also attended classes in musicology with Hertzmann and Lang (B.S., 1951; M.A., 1954). He continued to perfect his technique as a percussionist, and took lessons with Morris Goldenberg and Saul Goodman; he attained a high degree of virtuosity as a percussion player, both in the classical tradition and in jazz. In 1955 he became a percussionist with the Los Angeles Phil., retaining this position until 1981. In the meantime he developed his natural gift for conducting; from 1969 to 1972 he served as asst. conductor of the Los Angeles Phil.; in a parallel development, he composed assiduously and successfully. From 1981 to 1985 he was composer-in-residence of the Los Angeles Phil.; also founded the Los Angeles Phil. New Music Group, presenting programs of modern works for chamber orch. combinations. From 1988 to 1990 he was a visiting prof. at the Univ. of Calif. at Los Angeles. He held 2 Guggenheim fellowships (1967, 1972). As a composer, he explores without prejudice a variety of quaquaversal techniques, including serial procedures; naturally, his music coruscates with a rainbow spectrum of asymmetrical rhythms. There is a tendency in the very titles of his works toward textured constructivism, e.g., *Momentum, Configurations, Collage, Encounters, Translucences, Triangles,* and *Mobiles;* but there are also concrete representations of contemporary events, as in *Contextures: Riots-Decade '60.*

WORKS: DRAMATIC: Music for Samuel Beckett's radio drama *Cascando* (1988); film scores. **ORCH.:** *A Simple Introduction to the Orchestra* (1958); *Variations on a Folksong* (Los Angeles, March 26, 1960); Sym. for Strings and Percussion (N.Y., Aug. 21, 1961); *Concerto grosso* for Violin, Flute, Cello, Bassoon, and Orch. (1961; San Diego, March 22, 1963); *American Carnival Overture* (1962); Concerto for 4 Percussionists and Orch. (Los Angeles, March 10, 1966); *Configurations,* Concerto for 4 Percussionists and Jazz Orch. (Los Angeles, Nov. 13, 1966); *Contextures: Riots-Decade '60* (1967; Los Angeles, April 4, 1968); Piano Concerto (1972–73; Los Angeles, Nov. 21, 1973); *Tintinnabulations: Collage No. 3* (Anaheim, March 22, 1974); *Dream Tunnel* for Narrator and Orch. (Los Angeles, May 12, 1976); *Andirivieni* for Tuba and Orch. (1977; Los Angeles, Jan. 26, 1978; rev. as Concerto for Tuba, 3 Chamber Groups, and Orch., 1979); *Settlers Suite* (Merced, Calif., March 10, 1981); *Double Play* for Violin, Piano, and Chamber Orch. (1982; St. Paul, Minn., Jan. 7, 1983); Timpani Concerto (1983; Indianapolis, March 9, 1984); *Contex-*

tures II: The Final Beast for Soprano, Tenor, and Chamber Orch. (Los Angeles, April 2, 1984; also for Soprano, Tenor, Boy's Chorus, and Orch., 1986; Los Angeles, April 2, 1987); *Interplay* (Los Angeles, Nov. 1, 1984); *Of Ceremonies, Pageants, and Celebrations* (Costa Mesa, Calif., Sept. 19, 1986; rev. 1987); *A Kennedy Portrait* for Narrator and Orch., in commemoration of the 25th anniversary of the assassination of President John F. Kennedy (Boston, Nov. 19, 1988); *Veils and Variations* for Horn and Orch. (1988; Berkeley, Calif., Jan. 27, 1989); *Vintage Renaissance* (Boston, June 10, 1989); *Vintage 1990–91* (Costa Mesa, Calif., Oct. 9, 1990). **WIND ENSEMBLE:** *Games: Collage I* (Los Angeles, Nov. 21, 1969); *Dialogues and Entertainments* (1980; Ann Arbor, Feb. 13, 1981); *Quintessence*, concerto for 5 Percussionists and Concert Band (1985; Washington, D.C., Nov. 5, 1986). **CHAMBER:** Nonet for 2 Trumpets, Horn, Trombone, Tuba, and 4 Percussion (Los Angeles, Oct. 13, 1958); *Triangles*, concerto for Percussion and 10 Instruments (1965–68; Los Angeles, Dec. 8, 1969); Double Trio for Piano, Prepared Piano, Amplified Guitar, Tuba, and 2 Percussion (Los Angeles, Oct. 31, 1966); *Mobiles* for 3 Instrumental Groups (1970); *Cadenze* for Flute, Oboe, Clarinet, Bassoon, Horn, Violin, and Viola (1971; Los Angeles, March 20, 1972); *In Memoriam Igor Stravinsky* for Violin and Piano (1972–74); *Des Imagistes* for 6 Percussion and Reciter(s) (Los Angeles, March 12, 1974); *Encounters V: In the Morning of the Winter Sea* for Cello and Percussion (1975; N.Y., Jan. 6, 1976); *Encounters IX* for Saxophone and Percussion (Nuremberg, July 9, 1982); *Melange* for Flute, Clarinet, Violin, Cello, Piano, and Percussion (1985; Dallas, March 10, 1986); *Quartet for the Love of Time* for Clarinet, Violin, Cello, and Piano (Portland, Ore., July 6, 1987); Quartet for Percussion (Sacramento, Calif., Nov. 7, 1988). **PERCUSSION:** *Theme and Variations* for Percussion Quartet (1956); *Suite* for 4 Percussion (1958; Los Angeles, Nov. 6, 1961); *French Suite* (1962); *English Suite* (1973); *Soliloquy: Encounters I* for Percussion and Tape (1975), *VI*, concertino for Roto-toms and Percussion Quartet (Atlantic City, N.J., March 10, 1976), *VII* for 2 Percussion (1977; Boston, Jan. 22, 1978), and *VIII* (1978); *Images* for Timpani (Los Angeles, Nov. 9, 1978); *Variations for King George* for Timpani (1980); *Weavings* for String Quartet and Percussion (San Francisco, Nov. 30, 1984). **VOCAL:** *Silent Boughs* for Soprano and String Orch. (Stockholm, Nov. 15, 1963); *The Sublime and the Beautiful* for Tenor, Flute, Clarinet, Percussion, Piano, Violin, and Cello (1979); *Feerie* for Mezzo-soprano, Flute, Clarinet, Viola, Cello, and Piano (1987; Los Angeles, Feb. 1, 1988); *Mein Bruder* for Soprano, Flute, Clarinet, Violin, Cello, and Piano (1988; Los Angeles, Jan. 25, 1989).—**NS/LK/DM**

Kraftwerk, pioneering electronic band credited with helping spur disco, new romantic, goth, hip-hop, techno, and ambient musics (f. 1970, Dusseldorf, Germany). **MEMBERSHIP:** Ralf Hutter, voc. elec. (b. Krefeld, Germany, Aug. 20, 1946); Florian Schneider, voc., elect. (b. Dusseldorf, Germany, April 7, 1947).

Although dozens of musicians have been through the band, the heart of Kraftwerk (German for "power plant") is Ralf Hutter and Florian Schneider. They pair met during the late 1960s at the Kunstakademie in Remschied. Both were classically trained musicians (Hutter on piano, Schneider on woodwinds and violin), and went on to the Dusseldorf conservatory, where they formed a free-form improvised noise group called Organisation. The group released on album in 1970 and disbanded. Hutter and Schneider started their own studio, Kling Klang and formed Kraftwerk. Their first

two albums, while successful in Germany, did not find their way out of the country at the time. With few synthesizers available at the time, the group made many of their own instruments using home-made oscillators and parts from other keyboards, as well as tape effects. The music was compared to avant-garde, "serious" composers like Karlheinze Stockhausen and Terry Riley: long on electronic texture, short on rhythm. By the time they recorded *Ralf und Florian*, they had added a drum machine to their arsenal. They were exploring new territory at the time, creating music that totally relied on technology.

By 1973, Moog synthesizers became generally available and were quickly added to Kraftwerk's arsenal. Using their new firepower, they created the musical equivalent of a drive on the highway, a 22-minute composition called "Autobahn," which became the title track of their fourth album. A shorter excursion, in the form of a three-minute edit, became a massive hit in Europe and a curiosity hit in the U.S., where it reached #25. The album went to #5 in the U.S. as well, and became one of the first hit records to use only electronic instruments. Their next album, *Radio-Activity*, also worked around a theme, this time broadcast communications. Acknowledging their new international status, they recorded the songs in both German and English. Similar in concept to *Autobahn*, though more rhythmic, 1977's *Trans-Europe Express* dealt with train travel in the group's increasingly mechanical sound, which they dubbed "robot pop." *Man Machine* solidified the robot pop gestalt with tunes like "Showroom Dummies" and "We Are the Robots." "The Model" topped the charts in England in 1978.

The band dropped out of site for three years, but they were hardly forgotten. Their recordings were extensively sampled by hip hop artists including Arthur Baker and Afrika Bambaataa. Artists ranging from the Human League to David Bowie cited their influence. The group returned to the scene in 1981 with their paean to technology, *Computer World*, and enjoyed minor dance hits with songs like "Numbers" and "Pocket Calculator." However, by the time they released *Electric Café* in 1986, the novelty of their sound had worn off and the synthetic textures they had introduced to popular music were commonplace. They continued to create and perform on occasion, headlining a European festival in 1997, but they seem to be biding their time in terms of releasing new music, though they did release a single "Expo 2000" in time for the turn of the century.

DISC.: *Kraftwerk 1* (1971); *Kraftwerk 2* (1972); *Ralf und Florian* (1973); *Autobahn* (1974); *Radio-Activity* (1975); *Trans-Europe Express* (1977); *The Man Machine* (1978); *Computer World* (1981); *Electric Cafe* (1986).—**HB**

Krainev, Vladimir (Vsevolodovich), Russian pianist; b. Krasnoyarsk, April 1, 1944. He studied with Anaida Sumbatian at Moscow's Central Music School (graduated, 1962), then with Heinrich Neuhaus (1962–64) and Stanislav Neuhaus (1964–67) at the Moscow Cons., where he completed his postgraduate studies (1969). He won 2nd prize in the Leeds Competition

(1963); then 1st prize in the Vianna da Motta Competition in Lisbon (1964) and the Tchaikovsky Competition in Moscow (1970). He subsequently made tours of Europe and the U.S.—NS/LK/DM

Krainik, Ardis (Joan), distinguished American opera administrator; b. Manitowoc, Wisc., March 8, 1929; d. Chicago, Jan. 18, 1997. She was educated at Northwestern Univ. (B.S., 1951; postgraduate studies, 1953–54). In 1954 she joined the staff of the Lyric Theater in Chicago, and remained with it after it became the Lyric Opera in 1956. She sang minor roles there until becoming asst. manager in 1960. From 1975 to 1981 she was its artistic administrator. In 1981 she became general director, and proceeded to mold the Lyric Opera into one of the most prestigious opera companies in the world. During her tenure, the Civic Opera House was renovated, new scores were commissioned, and a composer-in-residence program was established. In 1996 she oversaw the first complete staging of the *Ring* cycle by the company, but ill health forced her to retire that same year.—NS/LK/DM

Krall, Diana (Jean), jazz-pop vocalist/pianist; b. Nanaimo, British Columbia, Canada, Nov. 16, 1964. Krall comes from a long line of singers and pianists; she began her own piano training at age four. She formed her first trio in her high school years, and also worked as an accompanist in local restaurants. She won a scholarship to the Berklee Coll. of Music, which she attended from 1982–83. She moved to L.A. to study with Ray Brown and Alan Broadbent, and continued her training with pianist Jimmy Rowles from 1985–87. Krall was back home in 1988, and then spent about a year touring Europe, playing piano but not singing. In 1990, she moved to N.Y., and began to gain attention as both a vocalist and pianist. Her third album, 1996's *All for You*, a loving tribute to The Nat King Cole trio, jettisoned the young Canadian toward the top of the jazz charts. She has since toured with a Cole-styled trio of her own. Her bluesy, smoky contralto has developed into one of jazz's most inviting, invigorating vehicles.

DISC.: *Steppin' Out* (1993); *Only Trust Your Heart* (1994); *All for You: A Dedication to the Nat King Cole Trio* (1995); *Love Scenes* (1997); *Have Yourself a Merry Little Christmas* (EP; 1998); *When I Look in Your Eyes* (1998).—LP

Kramer, A(rthur) Walter, American music critic, publishing executive, and composer; b. N.Y., Sept. 23, 1890; d. there, April 8, 1969. He studied music with his father, and took violin lessons with Carl Hauser and Richard Arnold. After graduating from the Coll. of the City of N.Y. in 1910, he was on the staff of *Musical America* (1910–22) and served as its ed.-in-chief (1929–36). He then was managing director of the Galaxy Music Corp. (1936–56). He publ. over 300 compositions, including orch. pieces, choral works, chamber music, piano pieces, and songs.

BIBL.: J. Howard, *A.W. K.* (N.Y., 1926).—NS/LK/DM

Kramer, Jonathan, American composer, music theorist, teacher, and writer on music; b. Hartford,

Conn., Dec. 7, 1942. He studied at Harvard Univ. (A.B., 1965) and the Univ. of Calif. at Berkeley (M.A., 1967; Ph.D., 1969). He also received training in computer music at Stanford Univ. (1967–68) and was a postdoctoral fellow in criticism and theory at the Univ. of Calif. at Irvine (1976). He taught at the Univ. of Calif. at Berkeley (1969–70), the Oberlin Cons. (1970–71), and Yale Univ. (1971–78). In 1978 he joined the faculty of the Univ. of Cincinnati Coll.-Cons. of Music, where he later was prof. of composition and theory (1983–90). From 1988 he was a prof. of music at Columbia Univ. In 1980 he became program annotator of the Cincinnati Sym. Orch., and also was its composer-in-residence and new music advisor (1984–92). He publ. *The Time of Music* (N.Y., 1988) and *Listen to the Music* (N.Y., 1988).

WORKS: DRAMATIC AND MULTIMEDIA: *For Broken Piano, Truck, Shaving Cream, Fruit Salad, Toilet, Wife, San Francisco, Color TV, Tape, and Slide Projections* (1969–70; Santa Cruz, Calif., April 3, 1970); *Blue Music* for Tape and Actor (1970–72); *An Imaginary Dance* for Tape and Slide Projections (1970–73); *Fanfare* for Actors and Tape (1973–76); *En noir et blanc* for 2 Actor-Pianists and Actor-Dancer (1988). **ORCH.:** *Funeral March* (1957–61); *Rhapsody* (1958); *Prelude and Fugue* (1964); *Sinfonia* (1965); Clarinet Concerto (1965; Sacramento, March 30, 1967); *Requiem for the Innocent* (1970); *Moments in and out of Time* (1981–83; Cincinnati, Feb. 10, 1984); *Musica pro musica* (1986–87; Columbus, Ohio, Nov. 14, 1987); *About Face* (1988–89; Cincinnati, Nov. 10, 1989); *Cincy in C* (1994); also band music. **CHAMBER:** Suite for 10 Instruments (1958); *3 Inventions* for 2 Clarinets and Cello (1960); Trio for Violin, Viola, and Cello (1962–65); *Random Suite* for Clarinet and Piano (1965); *3 Pieces* for Clarinet (1965–66); *Obstacles* for Trumpet, Trombone, and Piano (1967); Septet (1968); *Renaissance Motet* for 2 Flutes and Bassoon (1970); *1 for 5 in 7, Mostly* for Woodwind Quintet (1971); *1 More Piece* for Clarinet (1972); *The Canons of Blackearth* for Percussion Quartet and Tape (1972–73); *Renascence* for Clarinet and Electronics (1974; rev. 1977, 1985, 1998); *Moving Music* for Solo Clarinet and 12 Clarinets (1975–76); *5 Studies on 6 Notes* for Percussion Trio or Harpsichord or Guitar (1976–80); *Licks* for 3 String Basses (1980–81); *Atlanta Licks* for Flute, Clarinet, Violin, Viola, Cello, and Piano (1984); *A Game* for Cello and Piano (1988–92); *Another Anniversary* for Clarinet (1989); *Another Sunrise* for 7 Instrumentalists (1990); *Notta Sonata* for 2 Pianos and 2 or 3 Percussionists (1992–93); *Serbelloni Serenade* for Clarinet, Violin, and Piano (1995); *Remembrance of a People* for Piano, String Quintet, and Optional Narrator (1996; also for Piano, String Orch., and Optional Narrator); *Surreality Check* for Violin, Cello, and Piano (1998); *Klangs Klang* for Clarinet, Violin, and Cello (1999); keyboard pieces. **VOCAL:** *No Beginning, No End* for Chorus and Orch. (1982–83; Cincinnati, Oct. 30, 1983). **OTHER:** Tape pieces.—NS/LK/DM

Krapf, Gerhard, German-American organist and composer; b. Meissenheim-bei-Lahr, Dec. 12, 1924. He studied piano and organ in Karlsruhe, then was church organist in Offenburg (1939–42). He was drafted into the German army and taken prisoner of war in Russia. Upon his release, he returned to Karlsruhe, where he studied organ, choral conducting, and composition (1950). In 1951 he went to the U.S., where he studied organ at the Univ. of Redlands in Calif., and took a course in composition with Paul Pisk. He then taught music at Albion, Mich. (1953–54), at the Northwest Mo. State Coll. in Maryville (1954–58), and at the univs. of

Wyo. (1958–61) and Iowa (1961–77). He joined the faculty of the Univ. of Alberta in Edmonton (1977), where he became chairman of the division of keyboard studies. He composed a great number of organ pieces and sacred choral works. He publ. *Liturgical Organ Playing* (Minneapolis, 1964), *Organ Improvisation: A Practical Approach to Chorale Elaborations for the Service* (Minneapolis, 1967), and *Bach: Improvised Ornamentation and Keyboard Cadenzas: An Approach to Creative Performance* (Dayton, Ohio, 1983). He also tr. H. Klotz's *The Organ Handbook* (St. Louis, 1969) and Werckmeister's 1698 *Orgelprobe* (Raleigh, N.C., 1976).—NS/LK/DM

Krapp, Edgar, distinguished German organist and pedagogue; b. Bamberg, June 3, 1947. He studied the organ at the Hochschule für Musik in Munich (1966–71), where he was a pupil of Franz Lehrndorfer, and subsequently took organ lessons with Marie-Claire Alain in Paris (1971–72). In 1970 he won 1st prize in the Competition of the German Academies in Munich, and in 1971 the prize of the Mendelssohn Competition in Berlin. In 1974 he was named successor to Helmut Walcha as prof. of organ at the Hochschule für Musik in Frankfurt am Main; from 1982 to 1991 he was a visiting prof. at the Salzburg Mozarteum. In 1993 he became prof. of organ at the Hochschule für Musik in Munich. He is particularly noted for his performances of the organ music of Bach.—NS/LK/DM

Krása, Hans (actually, **Johann**), Czech composer; b. Prague, Nov. 30, 1899; d. probably in the concentration camp in Auschwitz, Oct. 16(?), 1944. He began playing piano and composing as a child. He later studied with Zemlinsky at the Cons. and at the Deutsche Akademie für Musik und darstellende Kunst in Prague. After working at the Kroll Opera in Berlin (1927), he returned to Prague as répétiteur at the New German Theater. He subsequently became involved in avant-garde artistic circles and devoted much time to composition. Following the German occupation of his homeland, Krása was active at the Prague Jewish orphanage until the Nazis deported him to the Jewish ghetto camp in Theresienstadt in 1942. He continued to compose and to have works performed there. On the night of Oct. 16, 1942, Krása was herded into a railway car by the Nazis and never seen again. It is presumed that he was put to death in the concentration camp in Auschwitz. Krása adopted a neo-Classical style of composition enlivened by comedic and grotesque elements.

WORKS: DRAMATIC: *Die Verlobung in Traum*, opera (Prague, May 18, 1933); *Mládí ve hre*, incidental music to A. Hoffmeister's play (1935); *Brundibár* (The Bumble Bee), children's opera (1938; rev. version, Theresienstadt camp, Sept. 23, 1943). **ORCH.:** Sym. for Small Orch. (1923); Overture for Small Orch. (n.d.). **CHAMBER:** 2 string quartets (1923; *Theme and Variations*, 1943–44); *Chamber Music* for Harpsichord and 7 Instruments (1936); *Passacaglia and Fugue* for String Trio (1943); *Dance* for String Trio (1944). **VOCAL:** *Vier Orchesterlieder nach Gedichten von Christian Morgenstern* (1921); *Fünf Lieder* for Voice and Piano (1926); *Die Erde ist des Herrn* for Soloists, Chorus, and Orch. (1932); *Tři písně* (3 songs) for High Voice, Clarinet, Viola, and Cello, after Rimbaud (1943).—NS/LK/DM

Krasner, Louis, Russian-born American violinist; b. Cherkassy, June 21, 1903; d. Brookline, Mass., May 4, 1995. He was taken to the U.S. as a small child. He studied violin with Eugene Gruenberg and composition with Converse at the New England Cons. of Music in Boston, graduating in 1923, and then went abroad, where he studied violin with Flesch, Capet, and Ševčik. From 1944 to 1949 he was concertmaster of the Minneapolis Sym. Orch. He then was prof. of violin and chamber music at Syracuse Univ. (1949–71), and subsequently taught at the New England Cons. of Music (from 1974). He commissioned and gave the first performance of Berg's Violin Concerto (Barcelona, April 19, 1936); also gave the premiere of Schoenberg's Violin Concerto (Philadelphia, Dec. 6, 1940, Stokowski conducting).—NS/LK/DM

Krásová, Marta, prominent Czech mezzo-soprano; b. Protivín, March 16, 1901; d. Vráž u Berouna, Feb. 20, 1970. She studied with Olga Borová-Valoušková and Růžena Maturová in Prague; then with Ullanovsky in Vienna. She began her career as a soprano at the Slovak National Theater in Bratislava (1922), but soon turned to mezzo-soprano roles. She made her debut at the Prague National Theater as Azucena (1926), then was one of its principal singers (1928–66); also made successful guest appearances in Hamburg, Dresden, Madrid, Paris, Moscow, and Warsaw; toured the U.S. in 1937. In 1935 she married **Karel Boleslav Jirák**; they divorced in 1946. In 1958 she was made a National Artist. She achieved distinction for her roles in Czech operas; was also noted as a Wagnerian singer.

BIBL.: V. Šolín, *M. K.* (Prague, 1960).—NS/LK/DM

Kraus, Detlef, distinguished German pianist; b. Hamburg, Nov. 30, 1919. He made a notable debut at the age of 16, performing the complete *Well-tempered Clavier* in 2 successive recitals in Hamburg, and then continued his studies with Edwin Fischer and later with Wilhelm Kempff in Berlin and Potsdam. In 1958 he performed a cycle of Beethoven piano sonatas in London, in 1970 he gave Beethoven cycles in Tokyo, Valencia, and Pittsburgh, and in 1980 he played all of the solo piano works of Brahms in N.Y. He also taught classes at the Folkwang Hochschule für Musik in Essen. His playing is remarkable for its freedom from pedantry; his interpretations are notable for their spontaneity. He publ. *Johannes Brahms als Klavierkomponist: Wege und Hinweise zu seiner Klaviermusik* (Wilhelmshaven, 1986; Eng. tr., 1988). —NS/LK/DM

Kraus, Ernst, outstanding German tenor, father of **(Wolfgang Ernst) Richard Kraus**; b. Erlangen, June 8, 1863; d. Wörthsee, Sept. 6, 1941. He studied in Munich with Schimon-Regan and then in Milan with Cesare Galliera. He made his concert debut at a Kaim Concert in Munich (Jan. 18, 1893), and then his operatic debut in Mannheim on March 26, 1893, as Tamino; remained on its roster until 1896, and thereafter was a leading member of the Berlin Royal (later State) Opera until 1924. He also was a leading singer with the Damrosch Opera Co. in N.Y. (1896–99) and at the Bayreuth Festivals (1899–1909); appeared at London's Covent Garden (1900, 1907, 1910). He made his Metropolitan Opera debut in N.Y. on Nov. 25, 1903, as Siegmund in *Die Walküre*, remaining on its roster for a season. After retiring from the Berlin State Opera in 1924, he returned to Munich as a singing teacher. He was one of the foremost Wagnerians of his day, excelling in such roles as Siegfried, Siegmund, and Walther von Stolzing. —NS/LK/DM

Kraus, Felix von, noted Austrian bass; b. Vienna, Oct. 3, 1870; d. Munich, Oct. 30, 1937. He studied philology and music history, took a course in harmony with Bruckner in Vienna, and received training in theory from Mandyczewski at the Univ. of Vienna (Ph.D., 1894, with a diss. on Caldara); also received vocal instruction from C. Van Zanten in Amsterdam and from Stockhausen in Frankfurt am Main. He made his debut in a Vienna concert (1896); made his operatic debut as Hagen at the Bayreuth Festival (1899), and continued to appear there until 1909, excelling as Gurnemanz, the Landgrave, and King Marke; sang at London's Covent Garden (1907). In 1908 he became a prof. at the Munich Academy of Music. He married **Adrienne Osborne** (1899).—NS/LK/DM

Kraus, Joseph Martin, important German-born Swedish composer; b. Miltenberg-am-Main, June 20, 1756; d. Stockholm, Dec. 15, 1792. He attended the Jesuit School in Mannheim; subsequently studied law at the univs. of Mainz (1773–74), Erfurt (1775–76), and Göttingen (1777–78). In 1778 he went to Sweden, making his home in Stockholm; in 1780 he was elected a member of the Swedish Academy of Music, and in 1781 he was appointed deputy conductor of the Court Orch. His great interest in Swedish culture prompted King Gustavus III to send him to Germany, Austria, Italy, France, and England for study purposes between the years 1782 and 1787. During his travels, he met Gluck and Haydn, both of whom warmly praised his music. In 1788 he was appointed Hovkapellmästare in Stockholm, holding this position until his untimely death from tuberculosis. During his short life (he was almost an exact contemporary of Mozart), he composed several distinguished works for the stage; his operas (to Swedish texts) are estimable achievements, especially *Aeneas i Carthago (Dido och Aeneas)*, which was premiered posthumously in Stockholm on Nov. 18, 1799. He also composed a *Symphonie funèbre* and *Begravingskantata* for the assassinated Gustavus III. After Kraus's death, his MSS and letters were deposited in the library of the Univ. of Uppsala. In 1982 the Internationale Joseph-Martin-Kraus-Gesellschaft was organized in Buchen. His writings include *Versuch von Schäfergedichten* (Mainz, 1773) and *Etwas von und über Musik fürs Jahr 1777* (Frankfurt am Main, 1778).

WORKS: DRAMATIC: *Azire*, opera (1778; only fragments extant); *Proserpina*, opera (Ulriksdal Castle, June 1781); *Fintbergs Bröllop* (Fintberg's Wedding), comic play with music (Stockholm, Jan. 1788); *Soliman II, eller De tre sultaninnorna*, comic opera (Stockholm, Sept. 22, 1789); *Afventyraren* (The Adventurer), comic play with music (Stockholm, Jan. 30, 1791); *Aeneas i Carthago (Dido och Aeneas)*, opera (Stockholm, Nov. 18,

1799); etc. **ORCH.:** *Wiener Sinfonie* (1783); *Pariser Sinfonie* (1784); *Symphonie funèbre* (1792); Violin Concerto (1777); Sinfonia Concertante (1780); overtures, etc. **CHAMBER:** 9 string quartets, 4 violin sonatas, pieces for solo piano. **VOCAL:** *Cantata for the King's Birthday* (1782–83); *Begravingskantata* (1792); songs; sacred music.

BIBL.: F. Silverstolpe, *Biographie af K.* (Stockholm, 1833); K. Schreiber, *Biographie über den Odenwälder Komponisten J. M. K.* (Buchen, 1928); R. Engländer, *J. M. K. und die Gustavianische Oper* (Uppsala and Leipzig, 1943); V. Bungardt, *J. M. K....ein Meister des klassischen Klavierliedes* (Regensburg, 1973); I. Leux-Henschen, *J. M. K. in seinen Briefen* (Stockholm, 1978); F. Riedel, ed., *J. M. K. und Italien: Beiträge zur Rezeption italienischer Kultur, Kunst und Musik im späten 18. Jahrhundert* (Munich, 1987); B. Van Boer, *Die Werke von J. M. K.: Systematisch-thematisches Werkverzeichnis* (Stockholm, 1988); idem, *Dramatic Cohesion in the Music of J. M. K.: From Sacred Music to Symphonic Form* (Lewiston, N.Y., 1989); F. Riedel, *Das Himmlische lebt in seinen Tönen: J. M. K., ein Meister der Klassik* (Mannheim, 1992); B. Van Boer, *J. M. K. (1756–1792): A Systematic-Thematic Catalogue of His Musical Works and Source Study* (Stuyvesant, N.Y., 1998).—NS/LK/DM

Kraus, Lili, noted Hungarian-born English pianist; b. Budapest, March 4, 1903; d. Asheville, N.C., Nov. 6, 1986. She entered the Royal Academy of Music in Budapest while still a child, becoming a pupil of Bartók and Kodály; after graduating (1922), she studied with Steuermann at the Vienna Cons. before attending Schnabel's master classes in Berlin (1930–34). From 1935 to 1940 she toured with the violinist Szymon Goldberg. In 1942 she embarked on a major tour, only to be interned by the Japanese when they captured the island of Java during World War II. After the War, she resumed her career and appeared in many of the principal music centers of the world. During the 1966–67 season, she played all the Mozart piano concertos in N.Y. From 1967 to 1983 she served as artist-in-residence at Tex. Christian Univ. in Fort Worth. In 1948 she became a naturalized British subject. Kraus was especially esteemed for her interpretations of Mozart and Schubert.—NS/LK/DM

Kraus, Otakar, Czech-born English baritone; b. Prague, Dec. 10, 1909; d. London, July 28, 1980. He was a student of Konrad Wallerstein in Prague and of Fernando Carpi in Milan. He made his operatic debut as Amonasro in Brno (1935); then sang in Bratislava. At the outbreak of World War II, he went to England, where he sang with the Carl Rosa Opera Co. (1940); then joined the English Opera Group (1946), creating Tarquinius in Britten's *The Rape of Lucretia*. He sang with the Netherlands Opera (1950–51); created Nick Shadow in Stravinsky's *The Rake's Progress* (Venice, 1951); subsequently appeared at London's Covent Garden (1951–73), where he created Diomede in Walton's *Troilus and Cressida* (1954) and King Fisher in Tippett's *The Midsummer Marriage* (1955); also appeared as Alberich at the Bayreuth Festivals (1960–62). After his retirement, he devoted himself to teaching. He was made an Officer of the Order of the British Empire (1973).—NS/LK/DM

Kraus, (Wolfgang Ernst) Richard, German conductor, son of **Ernst Kraus;** b. Berlin, Nov. 16, 1902;

d. Walchstadt, April 11, 1978. He studied at the Berlin Hochschule für Musik. After working as a répétiteur at the Berlin State Opera (1923–27), he conducted opera in Kassel (1927–28), Hannover (1928–33), and Stuttgart (1933–37). He served as Generalmusikdirektor of the operas in Halle an der Sale (1937–44) and Cologne (1948–53), and then of the Nordwestdeutsche Phil. in Herford (1963–69). He was particularly admired for his performances of Wagner, Mahler, and R. Strauss.
—NS/LK/DM

Krause, Christian Gottfried, German writer on music and composer; b. Winzig, Silesia (baptized), April 17, 1719; d. Berlin, May 4, 1770. He studied violin, keyboard playing, and timpani with his father, and pursued the study of law at the Univ. of Frankfurt an der Oder (1740–45). In 1753 he was made a lawyer to the Berlin city council, and later served as a Justizrat of the High Prussian Court. His Berlin home became a center for the arts. His treatise, *Von der musikalischen Poesie* (Berlin, 1752; 2nd ed., 1753), which advocated a simple song style, served as the foundation of the first Berlin Lied style. With the poet Karl Ramler, he compiled several vols. of lieder (Berlin, 1753–68). He composed the Singspiel *Der lustige Schulmeister* (Berlin, 1766), 4 syms., chamber music, cantatas, and songs.

BIBL.: J. Beaujean, *C. G. K.: Sein Leben und seine Persönlichkeit im Verhältnis zu den musikalischen Problemen des 18. Jahrhunderts als Ästhetiker und Musiker* (Dillingen an der Donau, 1930).
—LK/DM

Krause, Tom, Finnish baritone; b. Helsinki, July 5, 1934. He received his training in Helsinki, Vienna, and Berlin. In 1957 he made his debut as a lieder artist in Helsinki, followed by his operatic debut at the Berlin Städtische Oper as Escamillo in 1959. In 1962 he made his first appearance at the Bayreuth Festival as the Herald in *Lohengrin*, and that same year he became a member of the Hamburg State Opera, where he established a reputation as an interpreter of Mozart, Wagner, and Verdi; he also sang in the premieres there of Krenek's *Der goldene Bock* (June 16, 1964) and Searle's *Hamlet* (title role, March 5, 1968). In 1962 he made his British debut as the Count in *Capriccio* at the Glyndebourne Festival. On Oct. 11, 1967, he made his Metropolitan Opera debut in N.Y. as Count Almaviva, remaining on its roster until 1973. He also sang opera in Chicago, San Francisco, and Houston. He also pursued an extensive concert career which took him to most of the leading music centers of the world. Among his prominent roles were Don Alfonso, Guglielmo, Pizarro, Amonasro, Amfortas, Kurwenal, King Philip II, and Golaud.—NS/LK/DM

Krauss, Clemens (Heinrich), eminent Austrian conductor, great- nephew of **(Marie) Gabrielle Krauss;** b. Vienna, March 31, 1893; d. Mexico City, May 16, 1954. His father was a court figure, and his mother a dancer; of illegitimate birth, he took his mother's maiden name. He was a chorister in the Imperial Choir; then studied piano with Reinhold, composition with Grädener, and theory with Heuberger at the Vienna Cons. (graduated, 1912). He was a chorus master at the Brünn Theater (1912–13), making his conducting debut there with a performance of *Zar und Zimmermann* (Jan. 13, 1913); then was 2nd conductor at Riga's German Theater (1913–14) and in Nuremberg (1915–16); after serving as 1st conductor in Stettin (1916–21), he conducted in Graz (1921–22). In 1922 he became Schalk's assistant at the Vienna State Opera; he also taught conducting at the Vienna Academy of Music (1922–24) and was conductor of the Vienna Tonkünstlerkonzerte (1923–27). He was director of the Frankfurt am Main Opera and its Museumgesellschaft concerts (1924–29), and then of the Vienna State Opera (1929–34); was also conductor of the Vienna Phil. (1930–33). In 1926 he made his first appearance at the Salzburg Festivals, and returned there regularly (1929–34); he also conducted in South America (1927) and was a guest conductor with the N.Y. Phil. and the Philadelphia Orch. (1929); he made his debut at London's Covent Garden in 1934. He was director of the Berlin State Opera (1934–37) and Generalmusikdirektor of the Bavarian State Opera in Munich (1937–44); also conducted at the Salzburg Mozarteum (1939–45) and appeared with the Vienna Phil. (1944–45). Having been a friend of Hitler and Göring, and a prominent figure in the musical life of the Third Reich, Krauss was held accountable for his actions by the Allied authorities after the end of World War II. There was a strain of humanity in Krauss, however, for he had assisted Jews to escape the clutches of the barbarous Führer's fury. In 1947 he was permitted to resume his career with appearances at the Vienna State Opera; he took it to London that same year. He was a conductor with the Vienna Phil. from 1947, and also served as conductor of its famous New Year's Day Concerts. From 1951 to 1953 he conducted at London's Covent Garden, and in 1953–54 at the Bayreuth Festivals. He died during a visit to Mexico. He was married to **Viorica Ursuleac,** who often appeared in operas under his direction; he also accompanied her in recitals. He was a close friend and collaborator of Richard Strauss, who considered him one of the finest interpreters of his works; he conducted the premieres of *Arabella, Friedenstag, Capriccio* (for which he wrote the libretto), and *Die Liebe der Danae.* Krauss was renowned as a conductor of works by Mozart, Wagner, and Verdi, as well as those by the Viennese waltz composers.

BIBL.: A. Berger, *C. K.* (Graz, 1924; 3rd ed., 1929); J. Gregor, *C. K.: Eine musikalische Sendung* (Vienna, 1953); O. van Pander, *C. K. in München* (Munich, 1955); G. Kende and S. Scanzoni, *Der Prinzipal. C. K.: Fakten, Vergleiche, Rückschlüsse* (Tutzing, 1988); G. Brosche, ed., *Richard Strauss, C. K. Briefwechsel: Gesamtausgabe* (Tutzing, 1997).—NS/LK/DM

Krauss, (Marie) Gabrielle, esteemed Austrian soprano, great- aunt of **Clemens (Heinrich) Krauss;** b. Vienna, March 24, 1842; d. Paris, Jan. 6, 1906. She studied with Mathilde Marchesi at the Vienna Cons., making her concert debut in Schumann's *Das Paradies und die Peri in Berlin* (1858). She then joined the Vienna Court Opera, where she made her first important appearance as Mathilde in *Wilhelm Tell* (July 20, 1860); remained on its roster until 1867. She made her debut at the Théâtre-Italien in Paris as Leonora in *Il Trovatore*

(April 6, 1867), becoming a great favorite. The Franco-Prussian War of 1870 compelled her to leave France; she sang in Italy and in Russia. When the new building of the Paris Grand Opéra was opened, she sang Rachel in *La Juive* (Jan. 5, 1875); remained with the Opéra until 1888, with the exception of the 1885–86 season. She subsequently gave concerts and was active as a teacher. She was greatly admired for her Donna Anna, Leonora, Aida, and roles in Meyerbeer's operas; she also created Catharine of Aragon in Saint-Saëns's *Henry VIII* (1883).
—NS/LK/DM

Kraus (Trujillo), Alfredo, distinguished Spanish tenor of Austrian descent; b. Las Palmas, Canary Islands, Sept. 24, 1927; d. Madrid, Sept. 10, 1999. He had vocal training with Gali Markoff in Barcelona and Francisco Andrés in Valencia, then completed his studies with Mercedes Llopart in Milan (1955). In 1956 he won the Silver Medal in the Geneva Competition and made his operatic debut as the Duke of Mantua in Cairo. That same year, he made his European debut in Venice as Alfredo Germont, a role he repeated for his British debut at London's Stoll Theatre in 1957. After he scored a remarkable success in the same role at Lisbon's Teatro São Carlo on March 27, 1958, an international career beckoned. On July 10, 1959, he appeared at London's Covent Garden for the first time as Edgardo. His U.S. debut followed at the Chicago Lyric Opera as Nemorino on Oct. 31, 1962. He made his Metropolitan Opera debut in N.Y. as the Duke of Mantua on Feb. 16, 1966. Thereafter his career took him to most of the major European and North American opera houses. He also toured as a recitalist. The Alfredo Kraus biennial vocal competition was inaugurated in Las Palmas in 1990. In 1996 he celebrated his 40th anniversary on the operatic stage. A consummate artist with a voice of remarkable beauty, he was particularly noted for his portrayals of Rossini's Count Almaviva, Don Ottavio, Ernesto in *Don Pasquale*, Des Grieux, Nadir in *Les Pêcheurs de perles*, and Massenet's Werther.

BIBL.: N. Dentici Bourgoa, *A. K.: Treinta y cinco años de arte en el País Vasco* (Bilbao, 1992).—NS/LK/DM

Krauze, Zygmunt, Polish composer and pianist; b. Warsaw, Sept. 19, 1938. He was a student in piano of Maria Wiłkomirska (graduated, 1962) and in composition of Kazimierz Sikorski (degree, 1964) at the State Higher School of Music in Warsaw, and then completed his training in composition with Nadia Boulanger in Paris on a French government scholarship (1966–67). In 1957 he won 1st prize in the Polish National Competition for performers of contemporary piano music, and in 1966 he took 1st prize in the Gaudeamus Competition in Utrecht for interpreters of contemporary music. From 1963 he made tours of Europe and the U.S., mainly as an exponent of contemporary scores. In 1967 he founded the Warsaw Music Workshop, a new music ensemble that gave over 100 premieres of contemporary works until disbanding in 1988. In 1973–74 he was in Berlin under the auspices of the Deutscher Akademischer Austauschdienst. He became artistic advisor to IRCAM in Paris in 1982. From 1987 to 1990 he was president of

the ISCM, and from 1989 he was president of the Polish section of the ISCM. He lectured extensively on contemporary music in Europe, the U.S., Israel, and Japan. In 1975 he was honored with the Silver Cross of Merit of the Polish government, in 1988 he was made a Chevalier dans l'Ordre des Arts et des Lettres of France, in 1988 he received the Polish Composers' Union Award, in 1989 he won the Minister of Culture and Arts Award, and in 1994 he was given the Gold Chopin Medal of the Chopin Soc. of Warsaw.

WORKS: DRAMATIC: *Gwiazda* (The Star), chamber opera (1981; Mannheim, April 7, 1982; rev. as a 1-act opera, Wrocław, June 12, 1994). **ORCH.:** *Piece No. 1* (1969; Wrocław, Feb. 19, 1970), *No. 2* (1970; Berlin, March 21, 1974), and *No. 3* (Metz, Nov. 21, 1982); *Folk Music* (Warsaw, Sept. 17, 1972); *Fête galante et pastorale* for 6 Instrumental Groups and 13 Tapes (Graz, Oct. 12, 1974; also for 4 Soloists and Orch., Warsaw, Sept. 25, 1975, and for 13 Instrumental Groups, 5 Voices, and 13 Tapes, Strasbourg, Sept. 23, 1984); 2 piano concertos: No. 1 (Donaueschingen, Oct. 23, 1976) and No. 2 (Tokyo, Oct. 30, 1996); *Suite de danses et de chansons* for Harpsichord and Orch. (Bonn, Dec. 12, 1977); Violin Concerto (Lisbon, June 7, 1980); *Tableau vivant* for Chamber Orch. (Vienna, Nov. 29, 1982); *Arabesque* for Piano and Orch. (1983; Paris, Jan. 7, 1984); *Blanc-rouge (Paysage d'un pays)* for 2 Orch. Groups of Winds, Mandolin Orch., Accordion Orch., and 6 Percussion (Strasbourg, Sept. 29, 1985); Double Concerto for Violin, Piano, and Orch. (1985; Paris, Oct. 1988); *Symfonia paryska* (Symphonie Parisienne) for Chamber Orch. (Paris, Nov. 17, 1986); *Rhapsod* for Strings (Warsaw, Nov. 22, 1995). **CHAMBER:** Reed Trio for Oboe, Clarinet, and Bassoon (1958); *Liczby pierwsze* (Prime Numbers) for 2 Violins (Warsaw, Oct. 30, 1961); *Pantuny Malajskie* (Malay Pantuns) for 3 Flutes and Mezzo-soprano (Warsaw, Oct. 25, 1961); 3 string quartets: No. 1 (Warsaw, Sept. 26, 1965), No. 2 (1970; Warsaw, Sept. 15, 1979), and No. 3 (1982; Paris, Jan. 24, 1983); *Entrée* for Clarinet, Trombone, Cello, and Piano (1968); *Polichromia* for Clarinet, Trombone, Cello, and Piano (London, Feb. 22, 1968); *Voices* for 15 Optional Instruments (1972; Berlin, March 6, 1974); *Aus aller Welt stammende* for 5 Violins, 3 Violas, and 2 Cellos (Innsbruck, March 7, 1973); *Song* for 4 to 6 Optional Melodic Instruments (Baden-Baden, Feb. 28, 1974); *Idyll* for 4 Folk Instrumentalists and Tape (Graz, Nov. 30, 1974); *Soundscape* for 4 Instrumental Soloists and Tape (1975; Graz, Oct. 17, 1976); *Quatuor pour la naissance* for Clarinet, Violin, Cello, and Piano (1984; Paris, Nov. 19, 1985); *Je prefère qu'il chante* for Bassoon (1984; Nice, Feb. 3, 1985); *Rivière Souterraine* for Clarinet, Trombone, Cello, Piano, Percussion, Guitar, Accordion, and 7 Tapes (Metz, Nov. 19, 1987; also for 7 Tapes, Metz, Nov. 19, 1987); *Siegfried und Siegmund* for Cello and Piano (1988); *For Alfred Schlee with Admiration* for String Quartet (Vienna, Nov. 18, 1991); Piano Quintet (Łódź, Nov. 25, 1993); *Terra incognita* for 10 Strings and Piano (Bonn, May 16, 1994); *Pastorale* for Flute, Oboe, Clarinet, Bassoon, and Horn (Budapest, Oct. 1, 1995). **KEYBOARD: P i a n o :** 3 Preludes (1956); 5 Pieces (1958); *Praeludium, intermezzo, postludium* (1958); 2 Inventions (1958); 6 Folk Melodies (1958); 7 Interludes (1958); Sonatina (1958); 3 Studies (1958); *Theme With Variations* (1958); *Monodia i fuga* (1959); 4 Dances (1959); *Ohne Kontraste* (1960); *5 Unistic Pieces* (Kraków, May 8, 1963); *Tryptyk* (Warsaw, June 22, 1964); *Esquisse* (1966–67; Warsaw, Sept. 20, 1967); *Fallingwater* (Malmo, Oct. 15, 1971); *Stone Music* (1972); *Gloves Music* (1972); *One Piano Eight Hands* for 4 Pianists at One Upright Piano Out of Tune (Witten, April 28, 1973); *Music Box Waltz* (Chicago, March 1978); *Ballade* (Cologne, June 19, 1978); *From Keyboard to*

Score (Zagreb, March 29, 1987); *Nightmare Tango* (1987; Amsterdam, Aug. 31, 1991); *La chanson de mal-aimé* (1990; Geneva, Sept. 15, 1991); *Blue Jay Way* (1990; Warsaw, Sept. 28, 1991); *Refren* (Refrain; Schleswig-Holstein, Aug. 2, 1993). **O r g a n :** *Diptychos* (Vienna, July 10, 1981). **H a r p s i c h o r d :** *Commencement* (Paris, March 5, 1982). **V O C A L :** *Pocztówka z gór* (Postcard from the Mountains) for Soprano and 8 Instruments (Bolzano, Nov. 14, 1988); *La Terre* for Soprano, Piano, and Orch. (1995; Paris, Feb. 24, 1996); *Trois chansons* for 16 Voices (Warsaw, May 10, 1997). **O T H E R :** *Spatial Music Composition No. 1* for 6 Tapes (Warsaw, Oct. 1968) and *No. 2* for 2 Tapes (Warsaw, Oct. 1970); *Automatophone* for 15 Mechanical Instruments and 15 Plucked Instruments (Berlin, Oct. 6, 1974; also for 3 or More Mandolins, 3 or More Guitars, and 3 or More Music Boxes, Warsaw, Sept. 18, 1976).—NS/LK/DM

Krebs (real name, Miedcke), Carl August,

German conductor and composer; b. Nuremberg, Jan. 16, 1804; d. Dresden, May 16, 1880. He studied with the tenor and composer Johann Baptist Krebs (1774–1851), who legally adopted him. He made his debut as a pianist at 6, and then commenced composing at 7. After studies with Schelble, he continued his training with Seyfried in Vienna (1825); then was 3rd Kapellmeister at the Karnthnertortheater there. He subsequently was Kapellmeister in Hamburg (1827–50), where he brought out the operas *Sylvia* (Feb. 4, 1830) and *Agnes* (Oct. 8, 1833; rev. as *Agnes Bernauer*, Dresden, 1858). He succeeded Wagner as Kapellmeister of the Dresden Court Opera (1850), where he remained until 1872; then was director of music of the city's Roman Catholic church. Krebs championed the works of Spontini, Meyerbeer, and the young Wagner. He wrote sacred music, piano pieces, and numerous songs, several of which became well known in his day. He married the mezzo-soprano Aloysia Michalesi (b. Prague, Aug. 29, 1826; d. Dresden, Aug. 5, 1904) in 1850; she made her debut in Brünn in 1843, then sang in Hamburg and Dresden. She retired from opera (1870) and subsequently appeared in concerts and taught. Their daughter Marie Krebs (b. Dresden, Dec. 5, 1851; d. there, June 27, 1900) was a talented pianist; made her debut in Meissen when she was 11. She later toured throughout Europe, becoming quite popular in England. She accompanied Vieuxtemps on a concert tour of the U.S. in 1870.—NS/LK/DM

Krebs, family of German musicians:

(1) Johann Tobias Krebs, organist and composer; b. Heichelheim, Weimar, July 7, 1690; d. Buttstädt, Weimar, Feb. 11, 1762. He became organist in Buttstädt (1710), and concurrently studied with J.G. Walther and later with Bach in Weimar. He was made organist of the Michaeliskirche in Buttstädt (1721). His sacred music is not extant; several chorale settings for organ have survived.

(2) Johann Ludwig Krebs, organist and composer, son of the preceding; b. Buttstädt, Weimar (baptized), Oct. 12, 1713; d. Altenburg, Jan. 1, 1780. He received methodical training in music from his father, and subsequently studied keyboard playing, lute, and violin at the Leipzig Thomasschule (1726–35), receiving valuable training from Bach. He then studied at the Univ. of Leipzig (1735–37), but continued to be active at the Thomaskirche and also performed as a harpsichordist in Bach's Collegium Musicum. Later he was organist at Zwickau's Marienkirche (1737–43), at the Zeitz castle (1744–55), and at the court of Prince Friedrich of Gotha Altenburg (from 1755). He was a talented composer whose works reveal the combined influences of Bach and the galant style. See C. Geissler, ed., *J.L. Krebs: Gesamt-Ausgabe der Tonstücke für die Orgel* (Magdeburg, 1847–49), K. Tittel, ed., *J.L. Krebs: Ausgewählte Orgelwerke*, Die Orgel, 2nd series, XVIII, XX, XXI, XXVI (Lippstadt, 1963–75), and G. Weinberger, ed., *J.L. Krebs: Sämtliche Orgelwerke* (1985–86).

WORKS: KEYBOARD: O r g a n : 8 preludes and fugues; 2 toccatas and fugues; 2 fantasias and fugues; 10 free preludes or fantasias; 16 fugues, including 1 on the name of B-A-C-H; 14 trios; many chorale settings; also a number of works for organ and other instruments. **O t h e r K e y b o a r d :** *Erste Piece, bestehend in 6 leichten...Praembulis* (Nuremberg, 1740); *Andere Piece, bestehend in einer leichten...Suite* (Nuremberg, 1741); *Dritte Piece, bestehend in einer...Ouverture* (Nuremberg, 1741); *Vierte Piece, bestehend in einem...Concerto* (Nuremberg, 1743); *Clavier- Übung, bestehend in verschiedenen Vorspielen und Veranderungen einiger Kirchen Gesange* (Nuremberg, n.d.); *Clavier-Übung bestehend in einer...Suite...zweyter Theil* (Nuremberg, n.d.); *Clavier-Übung bestehend in sechs Sonatinen ...IIIer Theil* (Nuremberg, n.d.); *Exercice sur le clavessin consistant en VI suites*, op.4 (Nuremberg, n.d.); Concerto for 2 Harpsichords (ed. by B. Klein, Leipzig, 1966). **INSTRUMENTAL:** 2 sinfonias for 2 Violins, Viola, and Basso Continuo; 2 concertos for Lute and Strings (ed. by R. Chiesa, Milan, 1970–71); Concerto for Harpsichord, Oboe, and Strings (ed. by K. Jametzky, Heidelberg, 1976); 6 trios for 2 Flutes or Violins and Basso Continuo (Nuremberg, n.d.); 6 *Sonata da camera* for Harpsichord and Flute or Violin (Leipzig, 1762; ed. by B. Klein as *Sechs Kammersonaten*, Leipzig, 1963); *Musikalischer und angenehmer Zeitvertreib bestehet in 2 Sonaten* for Harpsichord and Flute or Violin (Nuremberg, n.d.). **VOCAL:** A number of sacred works.

BIBL.: J. Horstman, *The Instrumental Music of J.L. K.* (diss., Boston Univ., 1959; with thematic catalog).

(3) Johann Gottfried Krebs, organist and composer, son of the preceding; b. Zwickau (baptized), May 29, 1741; d. Altenburg, Jan. 5, 1814. He served as Mittelorganist in Altenburg (1758–81), then was Stadtkantor there until his death. He wrote much sacred music, including some 70 cantatas and an oratorio, as well as a musical drama and keyboard pieces. His 2 brothers were also musicians: Carl Heinrich Gottlieb Krebs (1747–93) was court organist in Esenberg from 1774. Ehrenfried Christian Traugott Krebs (1753–1804) was his father's successor as Altenburg court organist (1780). He publ. 6 organ chorale-preludes (Leipzig, 1787).—NS/LK/DM

Krebs, Helmut,

German tenor; b. Dortmund, Oct. 8, 1913. He studied at the Berlin Hochschule für Musik. He made his debut at the Berlin Städtische Oper (1938); then sang with the Düsseldorf Opera (1945–47) and again with the Berlin Städtische Oper. He also sang opera in Hamburg, Munich, Milan, London, Glyndebourne, Edinburgh, and Salzburg; likewise appeared as an oratorio and concert artist. In 1963 he was made a Berlin Kammersänger. He taught at the Frankfurt am Main Hochschule für Musik (1963–75).—NS/LK/DM

Krehbiel, Henry (Edward),
noted American music critic; b. Ann Arbor, Mich., March 10, 1854; d. N.Y., March 20, 1923. He was music critic of the *Cincinnati Gazette* (1874–80), and subsequently of the *N.Y. Tribune* until his death. He also wrote the program notes for the N.Y. Phil., was American ed. of the 2nd edition of *Grove's Dictionary of Music and Musicians* (1904–10), and brought out the rev. and completed ed. of the Eng. version of Thayer's *Life of Beethoven* (3 vols., 1921). He was a brilliant writer of music criticism, able to project his opinions (and prejudices) in vivid prose. He was an ardent champion of Wagner, and also wrote with warm admiration for the late Romantic composers; however, he deprecated the modern school of composition, hurling invectives on Stravinsky, Prokofiev, and Schoenberg (whose music he described as excrement).

WRITINGS (all publ. in N.Y.): *Notes on the Cultivation of Choral Music, and the Oratorio Society of New York* (1884); *Review of the New York Musical Season* (5 vols., 1886–90); *Studies in the Wagnerian Drama* (1891); *The Philharmonic Society of New York: A Memorial Published on the Occasion of the Fiftieth Anniversary of the Founding of the Philharmonic Society* (1892); *How to Listen to Music* (1896); *Annotated Biography of Fine Art* (with R. Sturgis; 1897); *Music and Manners in the Classical Period* (1898); *Chapters of Opera* (1908; 2nd ed., 1911); *A Book of Operas* (1909); *The Pianoforte, and Its Music* (1911); *Afro-American Folksongs* (1914); *A Second Book of Operas* (1917); *More Chapters of Opera* (1919).—NS/LK/DM

Krein, Alexander (Abramovich),
Russian composer, brother of **Grigori (Abramovich) Krein** and uncle of **Julian (Grigorievich) Krein;** b. Nizhny-Novgorod, Oct. 20, 1883; d. Staraya Ruza, near Moscow, April 21, 1951. At the age of 13, he entered the Moscow Cons. and studied cello. He also studied composition privately with Nikolayev and Yavorsky. He taught at the People's Cons. in Moscow (1912–17). After the Revolution, he worked in the music division of the Commissariat of Education and in the Ethnographic Dept. From 1923 he was associated with the productions of the Jewish Drama Theater in Moscow, and wrote music for many Jewish plays. Together with Gnessin, he was a leader of the National Jewish movement in Russia. In general, his style was influenced by Scriabin and Debussy, but he made considerable use of authentic Hebrew material.

WORKS: DRAMATIC: O p e r a : *Zagmuk*, on a revolutionary subject based on an ancient Babylonian tale (Moscow, May 29, 1930); *Daughter of the People* (1946). B a l l e t : *Laurencie*, after Lope de Vega (1938). Incidental music to plays, including *The Eternal One* (1923), *Sabbati Zewi* (1924), *Ghetto* (1924), *The People* (1925), and *The Doctor* (1925). ORCH.: *Elegy* (1914); *The Rose and the Cross* (1917–21); 2 syms. (1922–25; 1946); *Salome* (1923); suites. CHAMBER: String Quartet; *Jewish Sketches* for Clarinet and String Quartet; *Elegiac Trio* for Violin, Cello, and Piano; Piano Sonata. VOCAL: *Kaddish* for Tenor, Chorus, and Orch. (1921); *U.S.S.R., Shock Brigade of the World Proletariat* for Narrator, Chorus, and Orch. (1925); *Threnody in Memory of Lenin* for Chorus and Orch. (1925); vocalises; songs.

BIBL.: L. Sabaneyev, *A. K.* (Moscow, 1928; in Russian and German); J. Krein and N. Rogozhina, *A. K.* (Moscow, 1964). —NS/LK/DM

Krein, Grigori (Abramovich),
Russian composer, brother of **Alexander (Abramovich) Krein** and father of **Julian (Grigorievich) Krein;** b. Nizhny-Novgorod, March 18, 1879; d. Komarovo, near Leningrad, Jan. 6, 1955. He studied with Juon and Glière. His music underwent the influence of Jewish culture, and he wrote many works on Jewish themes; however, he also cultivated strict classical forms, adapting them to his needs. He wrote a descriptive symphonic cycle on Lenin's life (1937), Violin Concerto, *Hebrew Rhapsody* for Clarinet and Orch., String Quartet, and piano pieces. —NS/LK/DM

Krein, Julian (Grigorievich),
Russian composer and musicologist, son of **Grigori (Abramovich) Krein;** b. Moscow, March 5, 1913; d. there, May 28, 1996. He studied with his father, and wrote his first compositions at the age of 13. In 1927 he went to Paris, where he completed his studies with Dukas at the École Normale de Musique (graduated, 1932). In 1934 he returned to Moscow. He publ. several monographs (all in Moscow), including ones on Falla (1960), Debussy (1962), Ravel (1962), and his uncle **Alexander (Abramovich) Krein** (with N. Rogozhina; 1964). His music was inspired by both Russian and French models, resulting in works of notable lyricism and harmonic inventiveness.

WORKS: ORCH.: *Razrusheniye* (Destruction), symphonic prelude (1929); Cello Concerto (1929); 3 piano concertos (1929, 1942, 1943); *Vesennyaya simfoniya* (Spring Symphony; 1935–59); *Serenade* (1943); *Arkticheskaya poema*, sym. (1943); *Poemasimfoniya* (1954); *Poema* for Violin and Orch. (1956); Violin Concerto (1959); *Rembrandt*, vocal-symphonic picture (1962–69). CHAMBER: 4 string quartets (1925, 1927, 1936, 1943); 2 violin sonatas (1948, 1971); Flute Sonata (1957); Piano Trio (1958); Clarinet Sonata (1961); *Sonata-Poema* for Cello and Piano (1972). P i a n o : 2 sonatas (1924, 1955); other pieces. VOCAL: Songs.

BIBL.: Y. Tyulin, *J. K.: Ocherk zhizni i tvorchestva* (J. K.: Sketch of His Life and Work; Moscow, 1971).—NS/LK/DM

Kreisler, Fritz (actually, Friedrich),
great Austrian-born American violinist; b. Vienna, Feb. 2, 1875; d. N.Y., Jan. 29, 1962. His extraordinary talent manifested itself when he was only 4, and it was carefully fostered by his father, under whose instruction he made such progress that at age 6 he was accepted as a pupil of Jacob Dont. He also studied with Jacques Auber until, at 7, he entered the Vienna Cons., where his principal teachers were Hellmesberger Jr. (violin), and Bruckner (theory). He gave his first performance there when he was 9 and was awarded its gold medal at 10. He subsequently studied with Massart (violin) and Delibes (composition) at the Paris Cons., sharing the premier prix in violin with 4 other students (1887). He made his U.S. debut in Boston on Nov. 9, 1888; then toured the country during the 1889–90 season with the pianist Moriz Rosenthal, but had only moderate success. Returning to Europe, he abandoned music to study

medicine in Vienna and art in Rome and Paris; then served as an officer in the Austrian army (1895–96). Resuming his concert career, he appeared as a soloist with Richter and the Vienna Phil. on Jan. 23, 1898. His subsequent appearance as a soloist with Nikisch and the Berlin Phil. on Dec. 1, 1899, launched his international career. Not only had he regained his virtuosity during his respite, but he had also developed into a master interpreter. On his 2nd tour of the U.S. (1900–1901), both as a soloist and as a recitalist with Hofmann and Gerardy, he carried his audiences by storm. On May 12, 1902, he made his London debut as a soloist with Richter and the Phil. Soc. orch.; was awarded its Gold Medal in 1904. Elgar composed his Violin Concerto for him, and Kreisler gave its premiere under the composer's direction in London on Nov. 10, 1910. At the outbreak of World War I in 1914, Kreisler joined his former regiment, but upon being quickly wounded he was discharged. He then returned to the U.S. to pursue his career; after the U.S. entered the war in 1917, he withdrew from public appearances. With the war over, he reappeared in N.Y. on Oct. 27, 1919, and once again resumed his tours. From 1924 to 1934 he made his home in Berlin, but in 1938 he went to France, and became a naturalized French citizen. In 1939 he settled in the U.S., becoming a naturalized American citizen (1943). In 1941 he suffered a near-fatal accident when he was struck by a truck in N.Y.; however, he recovered and continued to give concerts until 1950.

Kreisler was one of the greatest masters of the violin. His brilliant technique was ably matched by his remarkable tone, both of which he always placed in the service of the composer. He was the owner of the great Guarneri "del Gesu" violin of 1733 and of instruments by other masters. He gathered a rich collection of invaluable MSS; in 1949 he donated the original scores of Brahms's Violin Concerto and Chausson's *Poème* for Violin and Orch. to the Library of Congress in Washington, D.C. He wrote some of the most popular violin pieces in the world, among them *Caprice viennois, Tambourin chinois, Schön Rosmarin,* and *Liebesfreud.* He also publ. a number of pieces in the classical vein, which he ascribed to various composers (Vivaldi, Pugnani, Couperin, Padre Martini, Dittersdorf, Francoeur, Stamitz, and others). In 1935 he reluctantly admitted that these pieces were his own, with the exception of the first 8 bars from the "Couperin" *Chanson Louis XIII,* taken from a traditional melody; he explained his motive in doing so as the necessity of building up well-rounded programs for his concerts that would contain virtuoso pieces by established composers, rather than a series of compositions under his own, as yet unknown name. He also wrote the operettas *Apple Blossoms* (N.Y., Oct. 7, 1919) and *Sissy* (Vienna, Dec. 23, 1932), publ. numerous arrangements of early and modern music (Corelli's *La Folia,* Tartini's *The Devil's Trill,* Dvořák's *Slavonic Dances,* Granados's *Spanish Dance,* Albéniz's *Tango* et al.), and prepared cadenzas for the Beethoven and Brahms violin concertos. He publ. a book of reminiscences of World War I, *Four Weeks in the Trenches: The War Story of a Violinist* (Boston, 1915).

BIBL.: L. Lochner, *F. K.* (N.Y., 1950; 3rd ed., rev., 1981); A. Bell, *F. K. Remembered: A Tribute* (Braunton, Devon, 1992); A. Biancolli, *F. K.: Love's Sorrow, Love's Joy* (Portland, Ore., 1998). —NS/LK/DM

Kreissle von Hellborn, Heinrich, Austrian writer on music; b. Vienna, Jan. 19, 1822; d. there, April 6, 1869. He studied law; was a Dr.Juris, and secretary in the Ministry of Finance in Vienna. A passionate admirer of Schubert, he publ. *Franz Schubert, Eine biographische Skizze* (1861), followed in 1865 by the exhaustive biography *Franz Schubert* (condensed Eng. tr. by Wilberforce, 1866; full tr. by A.D. Coleridge, 1869).—NS/LK/DM

Kreizberg, Yakov, Russian conductor; b. Leningrad, Oct. 24, 1959. He was the brother of **Semyon Bychkov.** For personal and professional reasons, he assumed the surname of his maternal great-grandfather. Following private training from Musin in Leningrad, he went to the U.S. in 1976 and studied with Bernstein, Ozawa, and Leinsdorf at the Berkshire Music Center in Tanglewood. He was an assistant to Michael Tilson Thomas at the Los Angeles Phil. Inst. From 1985 to 1988 he was music director of the Mannes Coll. of Music Orch. in N.Y. In 1986 he won the Stokowski conducting competition in N.Y. In 1988 he became Generalmusikdirektor of the Niederrheinsichen Sym. Orch. and the Krefeld-Mönchengladbach Opera. He made his debut at the Glyndebourne Festival conducting *Jenůfa* in 1992. In 1994 he conducted *Der Rosenkavalier* at his first appearance at London's Covent Garden. During this period, he also made guest conducting appearances with major European and North American orchs. He was chief conductor of the Komische Oper in Berlin from 1994 to 2000, and principal conductor of the Bournemouth Sym. Orch. from 1995.—NS/LK/DM

Krejčí, Iša (František), prominent Czech composer and conductor; b. Prague, July 10, 1904; d. there, March 6, 1968. He studied composition with Jirák and Novák and conducting with Talich at the Prague Cons. (graduated, 1929). He conducted at the Bratislava Opera (1928–32), then at the Prague National Theater (1933–34) and at the Prague Radio (1934–45). From 1945 to 1958 he was chief conductor of the Olomouc Opera, then artistic director of the Prague National Theater (1958–68). His music, in a neo-Classical idiom, is distinguished by vivacious rhythms and freely flowing melody. While the national Czech element is not ostentatious, its presence is well marked.

WORKS: DRAMATIC: O p e r a : *Antigone* (1934); *Pozdviženi v Efesu* (The Revolt at Ephesus), after Shakespeare's *Comedy of Errors* (1939–43; Prague, Sept. 8, 1946). ORCH.: *Maly balet* (Small Ballet) for Chamber Orch. (1927–30); *Sinfonietta* (1929); Concertino for Piano and Wind Instruments (1935); Concertino for Violin and Wind Instruments (1936); Suite (1939); *Sinfonietta- Divertimento* (1939); Cello Concertino (1939–40); *20 Variations on an Original Theme* (1946–47); *Serenade* (1947–50); *14 Variations on the folk song Goodnight, My Beloved* (1951–52); 4 syms. (1954–55; 1956–57; 1961–63; 1961–66); *Vivat Rossini,* overture (1967). CHAMBER: *Divertimento-Cassation* for Flute, Clarinet, Bassoon, and Trumpet (1925); 5 string quartets (1928, rev. 1935; 1953; 1960; 1962; 1965); Viola Sonatina (1928–29); Clarinet Sonatina (1929–30); Trio for Oboe, Clarinet, and Bassoon (1935); Trio for Clarinet, Double Bass, and Piano (1936); Nonet (1937); *Sonatina concertante* for Cello and Piano (1939); Wind Quintet (1964); Piano Trio, with Woman's Voice (1967); *4 Pieces* for Violin and Piano (1967). **P i a n o :** Sonatina (1934); *3 Scherzinos* (1945). **VOCAL:** *A Little Mourning Music* for Alto, Violin, Cello, Double Bass, and Piano (1936); *Anticke motivy* (Antique Motifs) for Low Man's Voice and Orch. or Piano (1936); *Ohlasy* (Night Sounds) for Voice and Wind Quintet (1936); songs.—**NS/LK/DM**

Krejči, Josef, Bohemian organist and composer; b. Milostin, Dec. 17, 1821; d. Prague, Oct. 19, 1881. He studied with Josef Proksch in Prague, and was active as a church organist. In 1858 he became director of the Organ School in Prague, and in 1865 of the Prague Cons. He wrote mainly sacred choruses and organ pieces. —**NS/LK/DM**

Krejčí, Miroslav, Czech composer and teacher; b. Rychnov nad Kněžnou, Nov. 4, 1891; d. Prague, Dec. 29, 1964. He studied piano, organ, and theory at home, and subsequently took courses in natural history, geography, and music at the Univ. of Prague (1910–14). He also studied composition privately with Novák (1911–13). He then taught in Prague and Litoměřice (1915–53), and was a prof. at the Prague Cons. (1943–53).

WORKS: DRAMATIC: O p e r a : *Léto* (Summer; 1937; Prague, Dec. 4, 1940); *Poslední Hejtman* (The Last Captain; 1944; Prague, March 18, 1948). **ORCH.:** *King Lávra,* symphonic poem (1917); *Life and Time* for Horn and Strings (1927); *Vocal Sym.* (1930); 3 numbered syms.: No. 1 (1944–46), No. 2 (1952–54), and No. 3 (1955); Viola Concerto (1947); Clarinet Concerto (1949); *Capriccio* for Viola, Winds, and Percussion (1950); *Dance Suite* (1950); Violin Concerto (1953); *Funeral Music* for Wind Orch. (1960). **CHAMBER:** 7 string quartets (1913, 1918, 1926, 1941, 1943, 1953, 1955); Clarinet Quintet (1920); 3 string quintets (1926, 1952, 1957); *Divertimento* for Flute, Clarinet, Horn, and Bassoon (1926); 2 violin sonatas (1926, 1952); Viola Sonata (1942); Cello Sonata (1943); Sonatina for Bassoon or Oboe or Horn and Piano (1950); Septet (1950); Nonet (1953); Organ Sonata (1954); Quartet for Oboe, Clarinet, Bassoon, and Piano (1955); Wind Octet (1956); Suite for Horn (1956); *3 Pieces* for 3 Violas and Piano (1957); Flute Sonata (1958); *Divertimento* for 10 Winds (1958); Horn Sonata (1959). **VOCAL:** Cantatas; choruses; songs.—**NS/LK/DM**

Krek, Uroš, Slovenian composer; b. Ljubljana, May 21, 1922. He studied composition with Škerjanc at the Ljubljana Academy of Music, graduating in 1947. He worked for the Ljubljana Radio (1950–58), then did research for the Ljubljana Ethnomusicological Inst. (1958–67), and subsequently taught at his alma mater (1967–86). He was made a member of the Yugoslav Academy of Science and Art (1977) and the Slovene Academy of Science and Art (1979). His style of composition is classical in form, but contains some elements of folk modalities.

WORKS: ORCH.: Violin Concerto (1949); Bassoon Concerto (1954); *Mouvements concertants* for Strings (1956); Horn Concerto (1960); *Inventiones ferales* for Violin and Orch. (1962);

Piccolo Concerto (1966); Sinfonia for Strings (1973); Cello Concerto (1984). **CHAMBER:** Violin Sonata (1946); *Capriccio* for Viola and 10 Instruments (1971); Sonata for 2 Violins (1971); *La Journée d'un bouffon* for Brass Quintet (1973); Clarinet Sonata (1976); Trio for Violin, Viola, and Cello (1977); String Quartet (1979); Cello Sonata (1984); *Espressivo* for Flute and Piano (1985); *Jeux pour quatre* (1986). **VOCAL:** *Old Egyptian Stanzas* for Tenor and Orch. (1967); choral pieces. **OTHER:** Film scores.—**NS/LK/DM**

Kremenliev, Boris, Bulgarian-American musicologist and composer; b. Razlog, May 23, 1911; d. Los Angeles, April 25, 1988. He went to the U.S. in 1929, where he studied composition with La Violette at De Paul Univ. in Chicago (B.M., 1936; M.M., 1938) and with Hanson at the Eastman School of Music in Rochester, N.Y. (Ph.D., 1942). He was a member of the Psychological Warfare Branch of the U.S. Army in Europe during World War II. In 1947 he was appointed to the faculty of the Univ. of Calif. at Los Angeles. He publ. *Bulgarian-Macedonian Folk Music* (Los Angeles, 1952). Several of his compositions were imbued with Bulgarian melorhythms; of these, the most interesting are *Pravo Horo* for Orch. (Rochester, N.Y., April 18, 1940) and *Bulgarian Rhapsody* for Orch. (1952); he also composed various other orch. works, including *Crucifixion* (1952), *Elegy: June 5, 1968* (1968–69), and *Peasant Dance* (1984); among his chamber works are 2 string quartets (1954, 1965), 2 piano sonatas (1954, 1959), Double Bass Sonata (1966–67), and *Overtones* for Brass (1983–84); his vocal music included choral pieces and songs.—**NS/LK/DM**

Kremer, Gidon, brilliant Latvian violinist; b. Riga, Feb. 27, 1947. His parents were violinists in the Riga Sym. Orch. He obtained the elements of violin study from his father and grandfather. When he was 16, he won the 1st prize of the Latvian Republic, and then continued professional studies with David Oistrakh at the Moscow Cons. He took part in several competitions, culminating in 1st prizes at the Paganini Competition in Genoa in 1968 and the Tchaikovsky Competition in Moscow in 1970. Subsequently he appeared in Western Europe to notable acclaim. He made an auspicious N.Y. debut at Avery Fisher Hall on Jan. 14, 1977. In subsequent years, he appeared as a soloist with many of the major orchs. of the world, gave recitals, and performed in chamber music settings. He has won special commendation for his efforts to broaden the repertoire for his instrument; his great contribution to modern music has been the consistent presentation of new violin works, particularly those of Soviet composers, among them Alfred Schnittke and Sofia Gubaidulina. He has also given notable performances of the works of the Estonian composer Arvo Pärt.—**NS/LK/DM**

Kremlev, Yuli (Anatolyevich), Russian musicologist and composer; b. Essentuki, June 19, 1908; d. Leningrad, Feb. 19, 1971. He studied piano at the Leningrad Cons. (1925–28), where he pursued his general musical education (1929–33); later he was granted his Candidate (1944) and Ph.D. (1963) degrees. From 1957 he was head of the music dept. of the Leningrad

Inst. of the Theater, Music, and Cinematography. His most significant monographs (all publ. in Moscow) were those on Chopin (1949; 3rd ed., 1971), Grieg (1958), Debussy (1964), Massenet (1969), and Saint-Saëns (1970). He wrote a Sym., 14 piano sonatas, and songs. —NS/LK/DM

Krenek (originally, **Křenek**), **Ernst,** remarkable Austrian-born American composer, whose intellect responded equally to his musical philosophy and his imaginative compositional style; b. Vienna, Aug. 23, 1900; d. Palm Springs, Calif., Dec. 23, 1991. He studied with Schreker at the Vienna Academy of Music (1916–18). Following miltary service (1918), he enrolled at the Univ. of Vienna in 1919 to study philosophy. In 1920 he went to Berlin to continue his studies with Schreker at the Hochschule für Musik. The premiere of Krenek's atonally conceived 2nd Sym. (Kassel, June 14, 1923) brought him considerable notoriety. With his so-called "jazz" opera *Jonny spielt auf* (Leipzig, Feb. 10, 1927), Krenek became internationally known via performances of the score around the world. A commission from the Vienna State Opera led to his composing the 12-tone opera *Karl V* (1932–33). After the Nazis assumed control of Germany in 1933, Krenek was declared a degenerate artist and his works were banned. Pressure was brought to bear on the Austrian authorities and the scheduled premiere of *Karl V* in 1934 at the Vienna State Opera was cancelled. The opera finally received its premiere in Prague on June 22, 1938. Following the Anschluss of 1938, Krenek emigrated to the U.S. In 1945 he became a naturalized American citizen. After teaching at the Malkin Cons. in Boston (1938–39), he taught at Vassar Coll. (1939–42). From 1942 to 1947 he was head of the music dept. at Hamline Univ. in St. Paul, Minn. In 1947 Krenek went to Los Angeles, where he continued to teach. In 1966 he settled in Palm Springs and devoted himself mainly to composing and writing. As a composer, Krenek pursued a modified serial path. After coming into contact with the avant-garde in Darmstadt, he was moved to expand his horizons. In 1957 he embraced total serial writing. In 1970 he adopted the use of rows and serial techniques in a manner that led to a much greater freedom of expression and mastery. Although Krenek was elected to membership in the National Inst. of Arts and Letters (1960) and was awarded honorary titles and degrees from various American institutions, his importance as a composer was most fully realized in Europe. In 1959 he was made an extraordinary member of the Berlin Akademie der Künste. In 1960 he received the Gold Medal of the City of Vienna. He was awarded the Grand Austrian State Prize in 1963. In 1970 he received the Ring of Honor of Vienna, and in 1982 was accorded honorary citizenship of Vienna. In 1986 a composition prize was established in Vienna in his name. His 90th birthday was celebrated by special performances of a number of his scores. Krenek deposited the MS of his autobiography in the Library of Congress in Washington, D.C., in 1950, with the stipulation that it should not be made public until 15 years after his death.

WRITINGS: *Über neue Musik: Sechs Vorlesungen zur Einführung in die theoretischen Grundlagen* (Vienna, 1937; rev. ed., N.Y., 1939, as *Music Here and Now*); *Studies in Counterpoint, Based on the Twelvetone Technique* (N.Y., 1940; Ger. tr., Mainz, 1952, as *Zwölfton-Kontrapunkt Studien*); ed. *Hamline Studies in Musicology* (St. Paul, Minn., 1945, 1947); *Selbstdarstellung* (Zürich, 1948; rev. and enl. as "Self-Analysis," *University of New Mexico Quarterly,* XXIII, 1953); *Musik im goldenen Westen* (Vienna, 1949); autobiography (MS, 1950); *Johannes Okeghem* (N.Y., 1953); *De rebus prius factis* (Frankfurt am Main, 1956); *Zur Sprache gebracht* (Munich, 1958); *Tonal Counterpoint in the Style of the 18th Century* (N.Y., 1958); *Gedanken unterwegs: Dokumente einer Reise* (Munich, 1959); *Modal Counterpoint in the Style of the 16th Century* (N.Y., 1959); *Komponist und Hörer* (Kassel, 1964); *Prosa, Drama, Verse* (Munich, 1965); *Exploring Music* (London, 1966); *Horizons Circled: Reflections on My Music* (Berkeley, 1974); *Das musikdramatische Werk* (Vienna, 1974–82); *Im Zweifelsfalle: Aufsätze über Musik* (Vienna, 1984); *Franz Schubert: Ein Porträt* (Tutzing, 1990); C. Zenck, ed., *Ernst Krenek: Die Amerikanischen Tagebücher, 1937–1942: Dokumente aus dem Exil* (Vienna, 1992).

WORKS: DRAMATIC: *Cyrano de Bergerac,* incidental music (1917); *Die Zwingburg,* scenic cantata (1922; Berlin, Oct. 20, 1924); *Napoleon,* incidental music for G. Dietrich's play (1922); *Fiesco,* incidental music for S. Friedrich's play (1922); *Der sprung über den Schatten,* comic opera (1923; Frankfurt am Main, June 9, 1924); *Orpheus und Eurydike,* opera (1923; Kassel, Nov. 27, 1926); *Bluff,* operetta (1924–25; withdrawn); *Mammon,* ballet (1925; Munich, Oct. 1, 1927); *Der vertauschte Cupido,* ballet (Kassel, Oct. 25, 1925); *Das Leben ein Traum,* incidental music for Grillparzer's *La vida es sueño* (Kassel, 1925); *Vom lieben Augustin,* incidental music for Dietzenschmidt's folk play (Kassel, Nov. 28, 1925); *Die Rache des verhöhnten Liebhabers,* incidental music for E. Toller's puppet play (1925; Zürich, 1926); *Das Gotteskind,* incidental music for a radio play (Kassel Radio, 1925); *Der Triumph der Empfindsamkeit,* incidental music for Goethe's play (1925; Kassel, May 9, 1926; suite, 1926–27; Hamburg, Nov. 28, 1927); *Jonny spielt auf,* opera (1926; Leipzig, Feb. 10, 1927); *Ein Sommernachtstraum,* incidental music for Shakespeare's *A Midsummer Night's Dream* (Heidelberg, July 1926); *Der Diktator,* opera (1926; Wiesbaden, May 6, 1928); *Das geheime Königreich,* fairy tale opera (1926–27; Wiesbaden, May 6, 1928); *Marlborough s'en va-t-en guerre,* incidental music for a puppet play after a comedy by M. Archard (Kassel, May 11, 1927); *Schwergewicht, oder Die Ehre der Nation,* operetta (1927; Wiesbaden, May 6, 1928); *Die Kaiserin von Neufundlung,* incidental music for F. Wedekind's play (1927); *Leben des Orest,* opera (1928–29; Leipzig, Jan. 19, 1930); *Kehraus um St. Stephan,* opera (1930); *Herr Reinecke Fuchs,* incidental music for H. Anton's play (1931); *Karl V,* opera (1932–33; Prague, June 22, 1938; rev. 1954; Düsseldorf, May 11, 1958); *Cefalo e Procri,* opera (1933–34; Venice, Sept. 15, 1934); *L'incoronazione di Poppea,* orchestration of Monteverdi's opera (1936; Vienna, Sept. 25, 1937; suite, 1936); *8 Column Line,* ballet (Hartford, Conn., May 19, 1939); *Tarquin,* chamber opera (1940; Poughkeepsie, N.Y., May 13, 1941); *What Price Confidence?,* chamber opera (1945; Saarbrücken, May 22, 1946); *Sargasso,* ballet (1946; N.Y., March 24, 1965; based on the *Symphonic Elegy*); *Dark Waters,* opera (1950–51; Los Angeles, May 2, 1951); *Pallas Athene weint,* opera (1952–53; rev. version, Hamburg, Oct. 17, 1955; also as the *Symphony Pallas Athene*); *The Belltower,* opera (1955–56; Urbana, Ill., March 17, 1957); *Jedermann,* incidental music for Hofmannsthal's play (1960; Salzburg, July 30, 1962; film score, 1961); *Ausgerechnet und verspielt,* television opera (1960–62; Austrian TV, Vienna, July 25, 1962; with entr'acte *Roulette Sestina,* Mannheim, Oct. 15, 1964); *Jest of Cards,* ballet (San Francisco, April 17, 1962; based on *Marginal Sounds* for Chamber Ensemble, 1957); *Alpbach*

Quintet, ballet (Alpbach, Austria, Aug. 25, 1962); *Der goldene Bock*, opera (1962–63; Hamburg, June 16, 1964); *Der Zauberspiegel*, television opera (1963; 1965–66; Bavarian TV, Munich, Sept. 6, 1967); *König Oedipus*, incidental music for Sophocles' play (1964; Salzburg, July 27, 1965); *Sardakai, oder Das kommt davon*, opera (1968–69; Hamburg, June 27, 1970); *Flaschenpost vom Paradies, oder Der englische Ausflug*, television play (1972–73; Vienna, March 8, 1974). O R C H .: Suite for Piano and Orch. (1915–16); *Leonce und Lena*, overture (c. 1919); 4 unnumbered syms. (1920; 1924–25, Leipzig, 1926; *Kleine Symphonie* for Chamber Orch., Berlin, Nov. 3, 1928; *Symphony Pallas Athene*, Hamburg, Oct. 11, 1954, based on the opera *Pallas Athene weint*); 5 numbered syms.: No. 1 (1921; Berlin, March 17, 1922), No. 2 (1922; Kassel, June 11, 1923), No. 3 (1922; Berlin, 1923), No. 4 (N.Y., Nov. 27, 1947), and No. 5 (1947–49; Albuquerque, March 16, 1950); 2 concerti grossi: No. 1 (1921–22; Weimar, Aug. 19, 1922; withdrawn) and No. 2 (Zürich, Oct. 14, 1924); *Symphonische Musik* (Donaueschingen, July 30, 1922) and *Symphonische Musik No. 2* for Chamber Orch. (1923; Berlin, Feb. 1, 1924); 4 piano concertos: No. 1 (Winterthur, Dec. 19, 1923), No. 2 (1937; Amsterdam, March 17, 1938), No. 3 (Minneapolis, Nov. 22, 1946), and No. 4 (1950; Cologne, Oct. 22, 1951); Concertino for Flute, Violin, Harpsichord, and Strings (1924; Winterthur, Feb. 18, 1925); 2 violin concertos: No. 1 (1924; Dessau, Jan. 5, 1925) and No. 2 (1953–54; Cologne, Feb. 18, 1955); *Stücke* (1924; Winterthur, Nov. 4, 1926); (3) *Lustige Märsche* for Band (Donaueschingen, 1926); *Potpourri* (Cologne, Nov. 5, 1927; rev. 1954; Stuttgart, Oct. 22, 1957); *Theme and 13 Variations* (N.Y., Oct. 29, 1931); *Campo Marzio*, overture (1937); *Symphonic Piece* for Strings (1939; Basel, June 11, 1940); *Little Concerto* for Piano, Organ, and Chamber Orch. (1939–40; Poughkeepsie, N.Y., May 23, 1940; also for 2 Pianos and Chamber Orch.); *A Contrapuntal Excursion Through the Centuries* for Student String Orch. (1941); *I Wonder as I Wander*, variations on a N.C. folk tune (Minneapolis, Dec. 11, 1942); *Tricks and Trifles* (1945; Minneapolis, March 22, 1946; based on *Hurricane Variations* for Piano, 1944); *Symphonic Elegy* for Strings (Saratoga Springs, N.Y., Sept. 3, 1946; also as the ballet *Sargasso*); *Short Pieces* for Strings (1948; Basel, Jan. 17, 1955; also for String Quartet); Double Concerto for Violin, Piano, and Orch. (1950; Donaueschingen, Oct. 6, 1951); Concerto for Harp and Chamber Orch. (1951; Philadelphia, Dec. 12, 1952); Concerto for 2 Pianos and Orch. (1951; N.Y., Oct. 24, 1953); *Sinfonietta a Brasileira* for Strings (1952; Besançon, Sept. 6, 1953); 2 cello concertos: No. 1 (1952–53; Los Angeles, March 4, 1954) and No. 2 (1982; Salzburg, Aug. 9, 1983); *Scenes from the West* for School Orch. (1952–53); *11 Transparencies* (1954; Louisville, Feb. 12, 1955); Suite for Flute and Strings (1954; also for Flute and Piano); *Capriccio* for Cello and Orch. (Darmstadt, May 31, 1955); *Sieben leichte Stücke* for Strings (Mainz, 1955); Suite for Clarinet and Strings (1955; also for Clarinet and Piano); *Divertimento* (1956; Ossiach, Austria, Aug. 23, 1986); *Kette, Kreis und Spiegel, sinfonische Zeichnung* (1956–57; Basel, Jan. 23, 1958); *Hexahedron* for Chamber Orch. (Darmstadt, Sept. 7, 1958); *Quaestio temporis* (1959; Hamburg, Sept. 30, 1960); *From 3 Make 7* (1960–61; Berlin, March 3, 1965; rev. version, Baden-Baden, Feb. 16, 1968); *6 Profiles* (1965–68; Fargo, N.Dak., March 14, 1970); *Horizon Circled* (Rochester, Mich., Aug. 12, 1967); *Perspektiven* (1967; Chicago, July 6, 1968); *Exercises of a Late Hour* (1967; San Diego, Jan. 19, 1968; rev. 1969); *Fivefold Enfoldment* (1969; Bonn, Jan. 5, 1970); *Kitharaulos* (1971; The Hague, June 20, 1972; also as *Aulokithara* for Oboe, Harp, and Tape); *Statisch und Ekstatisch* (1971–72; Zürich, March 23, 1973); *Von vorn herein* for Chamber Orch. (Salzburg, Aug. 21, 1974); *Auf- und Ablehnung* (1974; Nuremburg, June 13, 1975); *Dream Sequence* for Sym-

phonic Band (1975–76; College Park, Md., March 11, 1977); Concerto for Organ and Strings (1978–79; Ossiach, Austria, July 22, 1979); *Im Tal der Zeit* (1979; Graz, Oct. 26, 1980); *Arc of Life* for Chamber Orch. (1981; Palm Springs, Calif., Feb. 24, 1982); Organ Concerto (1982; Melbourne, May 17, 1983). C H A M - B E R : *Variationen über ein lustiges Thema* for Violin, Cello, and Piano (1916); Cello Sonata (1917); *Serenade* for Clarinet, Viola, and Cello (1919; Berlin, Feb. 8, 1921); 2 unnumbered violin sonatas (1919–20, Berlin, June 21, 1921; 1944–45, Minneapolis, Oct. 21, 1945); *Albumblatt* for Violin and Piano (1920); 1 unnumbered string quartet (1920); 8 numbered string quartets: No. 1 (Nuremberg, June 16, 1921), No. 2 (1921; Berlin, April 24, 1922), No. 3 (Salzburg, Aug. 3, 1923), No. 4 (1923–24; Salzburg, Aug. 5, 1924), No. 5 (Copenhagen, Sept. 29, 1930), No. 6 (1936; Darmstadt, Jan. 16, 1953), No. 7 (1943–44; Indianapolis, Nov. 15, 1944), and No. 8 (1980–81; N.Y., June 7, 1981); *Kleine Suite* for Clarinet and Piano (1924; Bamberg, Jan. 7, 1967); 2 sonatas for Solo Violin: No. 1 (1924; Darmstadt, Nov. 28, 1960) and No. 2 (Washington, D.C., Dec. 19, 1948); *Intrada* for Clarinet, Bassoon, Trumpet, 2 Horns, Trombone, and Timpani (Kassel, June 1, 1927); *Triophantasie* for Violin, Cello, and Piano (1929; Berlin, May 15, 1930); *School Music* for Various Instruments (1938–39; Ann Arbor, July 27, 1939); Suite for Cello (Poughkeepsie, N.Y., Nov. 16, 1939); *Deep Sea* for Tuba and Piano (c. 1939); Sonatina for Flute and Viola (1942; Buenos Aires, Oct. 22, 1945; also for Flute and Clarinet, Buenos Aires, Oct. 30, 1944); Sonata for Solo Viola (1942; Chicago, April 11, 1947); Trio for Violin, Clarinet, and Piano (Minneapolis, Nov. 27, 1946); *Short Pieces* for String Quartet (1948; also for String Orch.); Viola Sonata (1948; San Francisco, March 1949); String Trio (1948–49; Los Angeles, April 4, 1949); *Parvula corona musicalis* for String Trio (1950; RAI, Rome, Jan. 15, 1951); *Invention* for Flute and Clarinet (1951; Bamberg, Jan. 7, 1967); Quintet for Flute, Clarinet, Oboe, Bassoon, and Horn (1952; rewritten 1957 as *Pentagramm*; Los Angeles, March 31, 1958); *Fantasy* for Cello and Piano (1953; Lucerne, April 6, 1954); Suite for Flute and Piano (1954; Santiago, Chile, July 5, 1956; also for Flute and String Orch.); Suite for Clarinet and Piano (1955; Miami, Nov. 29, 1962; also for Clarinet and String Orch.); Sonata for Solo Harp (1955; N.Y., Jan. 27, 1958); Oboe Sonatina (1956; N.Y., May 9, 1960); *Monologue* for Clarinet (1956; N.Y., May 9, 1960); *Marginal Sounds* for Violin, Piano, Celesta, Vibraphone, Xylophone, and Percussion (1957; N.Y., Feb. 22, 1960; also as the ballet *Jest of Cards*); Suite for Guitar (1957; Los Angeles, Feb. 16, 1959); *Flötenstück neunphasig* for Flute and Piano (1959; Venice, Sept. 22, 1960); *Hausmusik* for Various Instruments (Berlin, Nov. 22, 1959); *Toccata* for Accordion (1962); *Cello Studien* for 1 to 4 Cellos (1963; Riehen, Switzerland, April 23, 1968); *Fibonacci Mobile* for String Quartet and Piano, 4-Hands (1964; Hanover, N.H., July 7, 1965); *Stücke* for Oboe and Piano (1966; Zagreb, May 21, 1967); *Pieces* for Trombone and Piano (Buffalo, Nov. 5, 1967); Duo for Flute, Double Bass, and Tape (1970; Palm Desert, Calif., Jan. 24, 1971); *Aulokithara* for Oboe, Harp, and Tape (1971; Mainz, Oct. 11, 1972; based on *Kitharaulos* for Orch., 1971); *Acco-music* for Accordion (1976); *Opus 231* for Violin and Organ (1979; Vienna, March 10, 1980); *Streichtrio in zwölf Stationen* (1985; Ossiach, Austria, Aug. 23, 1987). K E Y B O A R D : P i a n o : 1 unnumbered sonata (1913); 6 numbered sonatas: No. 1 (1919; Salzburg, May 3, 1920), No. 2 (1928; Berlin, March 27, 1929), No. 3 (1942–43; St. Paul, Minn., Dec. 1, 1943), No. 4 (San Francisco, Nov. 5, 1948), No. 5 (1950), and No. 6 (Donaueschingen, Oct. 1951); 1 unnumbered suite (c. 1916); 2 numbered suites (Berlin, Dec. 12, 1924); 3 double fugues (1917, Vienna, May 14, 1918; for Piano, 4-Hands, 1917; for 2 Pianos, 1918); 5 sonatinas (1–4, 1920;

5, 1928–29); *Tanzstudie* (1920); *Toccata und Chaconne über den Choral Ja ich glaub an Jesum Christum* (Berlin, Oct. 16, 1922); *Eine kleine Suite von Stücken über denselbigen Choral, verschiedenen Charakters* (Berlin, Oct. 16, 1922); *Klavierstücke* (Kassel, Nov. 18, 1925); *Vier Bagatellen* for Piano, 4-Hands (1931; Vienna, April 25, 1937); *Zwölf Variationen in drei Sätzen* (Los Angeles, Dec. 16, 1937); 12 *Short Piano Pieces Written in the 12-tone Technique* (1938; NBC, Washington, D.C., Jan. 3, 1939); *Hurricane Variations* (1944; also as *Tricks and Trifles* for Orch.); *Piano Pieces* (1946; St. Paul, Minn., Feb. 9, 1947); *George Washington Variations* (Los Angeles, Sept. 24, 1950); *Miniature* (1953); 20 *Miniatures* (1953–54; St. Gallen, Sept. 21, 1954); *Sechs Vermessene* (1958; Kassel, Oct. 9, 1960); *Basler Massarbeit* for 2 Pianos (1960; Basel, Jan. 19, 1961); *Piano Piece in 11 Parts* (1967; Chicago, Dec. 4, 1970); *Doppelt beflügeltes Band* for 2 Pianos and Tape (1969–70; Graz, Oct. 26, 1970). **O r g a n :** Sonata (1941; Poughkeepsie, N.Y., May 3, 1942); *Organologia* (1962; Mülheim, Nov. 24, 1968); 10 *Choralvorspiele* (1971); *Orga nastro* for Organ and Tape (Ann Arbor, Oct. 18, 1971); 4 *Winds Suite* (1975; Düsseldorf, March 13, 1977). **VOCAL:** *Missa in Festo SS. Trinitatis* for Chorus and Organ (1913); *Grosse Ostersonate* for Chorus and Organ (c. 1914); *Missa symphonica prima* for Soloists, Chorus, Orch., and Organ (c. 1915); *Zwischen Erd und Himmel* for Soloists, Chorus, Violin, and Orch. (1916); *Um Mitternacht* for Soloists, Chorus, and Orch. (1916); *Über einem Grabe* for Soloists, Chorus, and Orch. (1916); *Bühnenmusik zu?* for Chorus and Orch. (c. 1917); *Gott gib dein Gericht dem König*, motets for Chorus (c. 1918); *O meine armen Füsse* for Voice and Small Orch. (c. 1921); (7) *Lieder* for Voice and Piano (1921–22); (2) *Lieder* for Voice and Piano (1922); (5) *Lieder* for Voice and Piano (1922); (5) *Lieder* for Voice and Piano (1923; Berlin, March 26, 1926); *Gemischte a cappella Chöre* (1923); (13) *Lieder* for Voice and Piano (1924); (3) *Lieder* for Mezzo-soprano, Clarinet, and String Quartet (1924); *Vier kleine Männerchöre* (1924; Vienna, March 25, 1935); *Die Jahreszeiten* for Chorus (Donaueschingen, July 1925); *Wechsellied zum Tanz* for Soprano and Piano or Orch. (1926); *Vier a cappella Chöre* (1926; Vienna, Dec. 7, 1927); *O Lacrymosa*, 3 songs for High or Medium Voice and Piano or 7 Instruments (1926; Cologne, Jan. 29, 1927); *Gedicht* for Baritone and 5 Instruments (1926); *Kleine Kantate* for Chorus (1927); (4) *Gesänge nach alten Gedichten* for Mezzo-soprano and Piano (1927; Berlin, Nov. 21, 1929; also for Mezzo-soprano and Winds, Munich, Oct. 1927); (3) *Gesänge* for Baritone and Piano (1927; Dresden, Nov. 5, 1928); *Konzert-Arie* for Soprano and Piano (Berlin, June 1928; as *Monolog der Stella* for Soprano and Orch., Hannover, Aug. 1928); (3) *Gemischte Chöre* (1929; Vienna, Nov. 27, 1932); *Reisebuch aus den österreichischen Alpen*, 20 songs for Voice and Piano or Orch. (1929; Leipzig, Jan. 17, 1930); *Kalendar* for 4 Men's Voices (1929–30); (7) *Fiedellieder* for Medium Voice and Piano (Dresden, April 11, 1930); *Wach auf mein Hort* for Chorus (Berlin, June 23, 1930); *Durch die Nacht* for Soprano and Piano (1930–31; Dresden, April 10, 1931; also for Soprano and Orch., Vienna, June 19, 1932); *Die Nachtigall* for Soprano and Piano (Frankfurt am Main, Nov. 26, 1931; also for Soprano and Orch., Bern, Oct. 27, 1931); (11) *Gesänge des späten Jahres* for Voice and Piano (1931; Dresden, March 25, 1932); *Kantate von den Lieden des Menschen* for Chorus and Orch. (1932); *Kantate von der Vergänglichkeit des Irdischen* for Soprano, Chorus, and Piano (1932; Zürich, Oct. 9, 1933); *Fragmente aus dem Bühnenwerk Karl V* for Soprano and Orch. (1932–33; Barcelona, April 19, 1936); *Jagd im Winter* for Men's Chorus, 4 Horns, and Timpani (1933); *Das Schweigen* for Bass and Piano (1933; Winterthur, Jan. 24, 1934); *Während der Trennung* for Mezzo-soprano, Baritone, and Piano (1933; Winterthur, Jan. 24, 1934); *Vocalise* for Voice and Piano (1934); (4) *Austrian Folk Songs* for Chorus (1934;

Vienna, Feb. 25, 1935); *Italian Ballads* for Voice and Piano (1934); *Symeon der Stylit*, oratorio for Soprano, Mezzo-soprano, Tenor, Baritone, Chorus, and Orch. (1935–37; 1987; Salzburg, July 27, 1988); (5) *Lieder nach Worten von Franz Kafka* for Voice and Piano (1937–38; Poughkeepsie, N.Y., March 1, 1942); *The Night is Far Spent* for Voice and Piano (1938); 2 *Choruses on Jacobean Poems* (1939; Poughkeepsie, N.Y., Dec. 7, 1940); *Proprium missae in festo SS. Innocentium martyrum (die 28 Decembris)* for Women's Chorus (Poughkeepsie, N.Y., Dec. 15, 1940); *La corona*, cantata for Mezzo-soprano, Baritone, Organ, and Percussion (1941; Copenhagen, 1958); *The Holy Ghost's Ark* for Mezzo-soprano, Oboe, Clarinet, Viola, and Cello (Madison, Wisc., July 24, 1941); *Lamentatio Jeremiae prophetae* for Chorus (1941–42; Kassel, Oct. 5, 1958); *Cantata for Wartime* for Women's Chorus and Orch. (1943; Minneapolis, March 24, 1944); 5 *Prayers for Women's Voices Over the Pater noster as Cantus Firmus* (1944; St. Paul, Minn., June 3, 1945); *The Ballad of the Railroads* for Medium Voice and Piano (1944; N.Y., April 5, 1950); *Santa Fe Time Table* for Chorus (1945; Los Angeles, Feb. 20, 1961); *Aegrotavit Ezechias*, motet for Women's Chorus and Piano (1945; St. Paul, Minn., March 12, 1947); *Etude* for Coloratura Soprano and Contralto (1945; St. Paul, Minn., 1946); *In paradisum*, motet for Women's Chorus (St. Paul, Minn., May 10, 1946); *O Would I Were*, canon for Chorus (1946); (4) *Songs on Poems by Gerard Manley Hopkins* for Tenor and Piano (1946–47; Waco, Tex., April 25, 1947); *Remember Now*, motet for Women's Voices and Piano (St. Paul, Minn., 1947); *Medea*, monologue for Mezzo-soprano and Orch. (1951; rev. 1952; Philadelphia, March 13, 1953); (2) *Sacred Songs* for Medium Voice and Piano (1952; N.Y., Jan. 4, 1953); (4) *Choruses* with Organ or Piano (1953); *Motette zur Opferung für das ganze Kirchenjahr* for Chorus (1954; Basel, March 27, 1955); *Proprium missae in domenica tertia in quadragesima* for Chorus (1955); *Psalmenverse zur Kommunion für das ganze Kirchenjahr* for Chorus (1955); *Ich singe wieder, wenn es tagt* for Chorus and String Orch. or String Quintet (1955–56; Linz, May 14, 1956); *Spiritus intelligentiae, Sanctus*, oratorio for Pentecost for 2 Singers, Speaker, and Electronics (1955–56; WDR, Cologne, May 30, 1956); *Egregii, carissimi*, 2 voice canon (1956); *Guten Morgen, Amerika* for Chorus (1956); *Psalmverse* for Chorus (1956); *Sestina* for Soprano and 8 Instruments (1957; N.Y., March 9, 1958); *Missa duodecim tonorum* for Women's or Men's Chorus and Organ (1957); 6 *Motetten nach Worten von Franz Kafka* for Chorus (Berlin, Sept. 29, 1959); (5) *Holiday Motets* for Chorus (1959–66); *Children's Song: 3 Madrigals* for Women's Chorus (1960); *Children's Songs: 3 Motets* for Women's Chorus (1960); *The Flea* for Tenor or Soprano and Piano (1960; Raleigh, N.C., 1968); *Like Dew* for 3 Voices (1962); *Kanon Igor Strawinsky zum 80. Geburtstag* for 2-voice Chorus (1962); *O Holy Ghost*, motet for Chorus (1964; Berlin, May 3, 1965); *Wechselrahmen* for Soprano and Piano (1964–65; Düsseldorf, Sept. 9, 1965); *Quintina über die fünf Vokale* for Soprano, 6 Instruments, and Tape (Danish Radio, Copenhagen, Oct. 3, 1965); *Glauben und Wissen* for 4 Speakers, Chorus, and Orch. (North German Radio, Hamburg, Dec. 21, 1966); *Proprium für das Dreifaltigkeitsfest* for Soprano, Chorus, 2 Trumpets, Timpani, and Organ (1966–67; Basel, July 2, 1967); *Instant Remembered* for Soprano and Orch. (Hanover, N.H., Aug. 1, 1968); *Proprium Missae per a le festa de la nativitat de la mare de Due (8 de setembre)* for Chorus, Instruments, and Tape (Montserrat, Abadia, Aug. 22, 1968); *Deutsche Messe (Ordinarium)* for Chorus, Clarinet, Trumpet, 2 Trombones, Timpani, and Percussion (1968; Lucerne, Oct. 1969); *Messe Gib uns den Frieden* for Chorus and Orch. (1970; Hamburg, Oct. 17, 1971); 3 *Sacred Pieces* for Chorus (Ann Arbor, Oct. 18, 1971); 3 *Lessons* for Chorus (Ann Arbor, Oct. 18, 1971); *Zeitlieder* for Mezzo-soprano and

String Quartet (1972; Augsburg, May 15, 1974); (3) *Lieder* for Soprano and Piano (1972; Vienna, Sept. 22, 1975); *Spätlese*, 6 songs for Baritone and Piano (1972; Munich, July 22, 1974); *Feiertags-Kantate* for Speaker, Mezzo-soprano, Baritone, Chorus, and Orch. (1974–75; Berlin, Sept. 12, 1975); 2 *Silent Watchers* for Voice and Piano (1975; Palm Springs, Calif., 1976); 2 *Kanons für Paul Sacher* for Voices (1975–76); (2) *Settings of Poems by William Blake* for Chorus (1976; Honolulu, May 1977); *They Knew What They Wanted* for Narrator, Oboe, Piano, Percussion, and Tape (1976–77; N.Y., Nov. 6, 1978); *Albumblatt* for Voice and Piano (1977); *The Dissembler*, monologue for Baritone and Ensemble (1978; Baltimore, March 11, 1979; *Deutsche Messgesänge zum 29. Sonntag im Jahreskreis* for Narrator, Chorus, and Organ (Graz, Oct. 19, 1980); *Opus sine nomine*, oratorio for Soprano, Mezzo-soprano, 2 Tenors, Baritone, Narrator, Chorus, and Orch. (1980–88); *For Myself, at Eighty-five*, 4-voice canon (1985). **TAPE:** *San Fernando Sequence* (San Francisco, March 15, 1963); *Quintona* (1965).

BIBL.: W. Grandi, *Il sistema tonale ed il contrappunto dodecafonico di E. K.* (Rome, 1954); F. Saathen, *E. K.* (Munich, 1959); L. Knessl, *E. K.* (Vienna, 1967); E. Marckhl, *Rede für E. K.* (Graz, 1969); W. Rogge, *E. K.s Opern: Spiegel der zwanziger Jahre* (Wolfenbüttel, 1970); C. Maurer-Zenck, *E. K.: Ein Komponist in Exil* (Vienna, 1980); O. Kolleritsch, ed., *E. K.: Studien zur Wertungsforschung* (Vienna, 1982); S. Cook, *Opera During the Weimar Republic: The Zeitopern of E. K., Kurt Weill, and Paul Hindemith* (Ann Arbor, 1987); G. Bowles, *E. K.: A Bio-Bibliography* (London, 1989); J. Stewart, *E. K.: The Man and His Music* (Berkeley, 1991).—NS/LK/DM

Krenn, Franz, Austrian organist, composer, and pedagogue; b. Dross, Feb. 26, 1816; d. St. Andrä, June 18, 1897. He studied music with his father, and was a church organist in Vienna. From 1869 to 1893 he was a prof. of harmony and counterpoint at the Vienna Cons. Gustav Mahler was his pupil. He wrote 29 masses, a Sym., chamber music, and a manual, *Musik-und Harmonielehre* (1890).—NS/LK/DM

Krenn, Fritz, Austrian bass; b. Vienna, Dec. 11, 1897; d. there, July 17, 1964. He studied at the Vienna Academy of Music. He made his operatic debut as the Herald in *Lohengrin* in Trieste in 1917, and then sang in Vienna at the Volksoper (1917–18) and in Bratislava (1918–19). He subsequently was at the Vienna State Opera (1919–25; 1934–42; 1946–59), and also sang with the Berlin State Opera (1927–43), and with Covent Garden in London (1935). He made his Metropolitan Opera debut in N.Y. on Jan. 5, 1951, as Baron Ochs; then continued his career in Europe. He was highly successful in buffo roles.—NS/LK/DM

Krenn, Werner, Austrian tenor; b. Vienna, Sept. 21, 1943. He sang in the Vienna Boys' Choir; then studied bassoon, and played in the Vienna Sym. Orch. (1962–66); took voice lessons with Elisabeth Rado in Vienna. In 1966 he made his operatic debut in Purcell's *The Fairy Queen* at the Berlin Deutsche Oper; then sang regularly at the Vienna State Opera. He made his English debut as Jaquino with the Scottish Opera (1970). He also appeared frequently as a concert and oratorio singer. He was married to **Helga Dernesch.**—NS/LK/DM

Krenz, Jan, Polish conductor and composer; b. Włocławek, July 14, 1926. During the German occupation, he managed to take lessons with Drzewiecki (piano) and Sikorski (composition). After the liberation, he studied at the State Higher School of Music in Łódź (1945–47) with Wiłkomirski (conducting) and Sikorski (composition). In 1946 he made his condcuting debut in Łódź, and then was a conductor with the Poznań Phil. (1947–49). From 1949 he was a conductor of the Polish Radio Grand Sym. Orch. in Katowice, where he was its principal conductor from 1953 to 1968. He was artistic director of the Warsaw Opera from 1968 to 1973. From 1979 to 1982 he was Generalmusikdirektor in Bonn. He was a conductor with the Dutch Radio in Hilversum from 1983 to 1985. He also appeared as a guest conductor throughout Europe. In 1968 and 1996 he was honored with the Award of the Polish Composers' Union.

WORKS: ORCH.: 2 syms.: No. 1 (1947–49; Warsaw, Jan. 13, 1950) and No. 2, *quasi una fantasia* (1989–92; Bonn, Feb. 11, 1993); *Serenada klasyczna* (Classical Serenade) for Small Orch. (1950); *Taniec symfoniczny* (Symphonic Dance; 1951); *Serenade wiejska* (A Country Serenade) for Small Orch. (1951); *Rapsodia* for Strings, Xylophone, Tam-tam, Timpani, and Celesta (Warsaw, May 30, 1952); Concertino for Piano and Small Orch. (Kraków, Oct. 30, 1952); *Capriccio* for 24 Instruments (1961–62; Warsaw, Sept. 20, 1962); *Epitaphion* (1989–90); *Sinfonietta* (1994–95; Zürich, March 20, 1996). **CHAMBER:** Quartet for Flute, Oboe, Clarinet, and Bassoon (1950); *Musica* for Clarinet (1958; Warsaw, Sept. 15, 1959); *Musica da camera* for String Quartet (1983; Wrocław, Feb. 21, 1986); *Sonatine per due* for Violin (1986; Warsaw, Jan. 1987). **VOCAL:** *Tryptyk* for Voice and Piano (1946); *Messa breve* for Chorus (1982; Warsaw, Jan. 1984).—NS/LK/DM

Kresánek, Jozef, Slovak musicologist and composer; b. Čičmany, Dec. 20, 1913; d. Bratislava, March 14, 1986. He studied composition with Karel at the Prague Cons. (1932–37) and with Novák at the Master School there (1937–39). He taught in Prešov, and in 1944 was appointed a lecturer at the Univ. of Bratislava, becoming a full prof. of musical science in 1963. As a music scholar, he dedicated himself mainly to the stylistic analysis and codification of Slovak folk songs, and publ. numerous treatises on the subject. He also publ. a monograph on Eugen Suchoň (Bratislava, 1961), as well as other musical studies. His compositions include a String Quartet (1935), Piano Trio (1939), 2 suites for Violin and Piano (1947, 1951), 2 suites for Orch. (1951, rev. 1961; 1953), *Prelude and Toccata* for Orch. (1957), and a Piano Quintet (1975).—NS/LK/DM

Kretschmer, Edmund, German organist and composer; b. Ostritz, Aug. 31, 1830; d. Dresden, Sept. 13, 1908. He studied with Julius Otto (composition) and Johann Schneider (organ) in Dresden, where he was its court organist (1863–1901). He was a successful composer. His choral work *Geisterschlacht* won a prize at the Dresden singing festival (1865), and his 3-part Mass for Men's Chorus won the Brussels Academy's prize in 1868. He wrote several operas to his own librettos in a Wagnerian manner, at least 2 of which were successful: *Die Folkunger* (Dresden, March 21, 1874) and *Heinrich der Löwe* (Leipzig, Dec. 8, 1877). He also produced 2 light operas: *Der Flüchtling* (Ulm, 1881) and *Schön Rotraut* (Dresden, 1887), several choral works for festive occasions, church music, etc.

BIBL.: O. Schmid, *E. K.* (Dresden, 1890).—**NS/LK/DM**

Kretzschmar, (August Ferdinand) Hermann,

eminent German musicologist; b. Olbernhau, Jan. 19, 1848; d. Nikolassee, near Berlin, May 10, 1924. He was a chorister and a pupil of Julius Otto at the Dresden Kreuzschule (1862–67), then studied with Paul, Ritschl, and Voigt at the Univ. of Leipzig (Ph.D., 1871, with the diss. *De signis musicis*; publ. in Leipzig, 1871). He also took courses with Paul, E.F. Richter, and Reinecke at the Leipzig Cons. (1869–70), where he then taught organ and harmony (1871–76). He was also active as a choral conductor. In 1876 he was a theater conductor in Metz, and in 1877 he was made music director at the Univ. of Rostock, becoming municipal music director there in 1880. He returned to Leipzig as music director of the Univ. (1887). He was conductor of the Riedelverein (1888–97) and founder-conductor of the Akademische Orchesterkonzerte (1890–95), and also a founder of the Neue Bach-Gesellschaft (1900). In 1904 he went to Berlin as a prof. at the Univ., and from 1909 to 1920 he was director of the Berlin Hochschule für Musik. Kretzschmar served as general ed. of the Denkmäler Deutscher Tonkunst (1911–19). He was a thoroughly educated musician, a good organist as well as choral conductor, and composer of some secular and sacred vocal music, but his importance in musicology lies in his establishment of certain musical and esthetic concepts that elucidate the historical process. He introduced the term "Hermeneutik" (taken from theology), applying it to the explanation of musical melodies and intervallic progressions as expressive of human emotions.

WRITINGS (all publ. in Leipzig): *Peter Cornelius* (1880); *Führer durch den Konzertsaal* (3 vols.; I, 1887, 7th ed., 1932; II, 1888, 5th ed., 1921; III, 1890, 5th ed., 1939); *Musikalische Zeitfragen* (1903); *Gesammelte Aufsätze über Musik und anderes aus den Grenzboten* (1910); *Aus den Jahrbüchern der Musikbibliothek Peters* (1911); *Geschichte des neuen deutschen Liedes* (1912); *Geschichte der Oper* (1919); *Einführung in die Musikgeschichte* (1920); *Bach-Kolleg* (1922).

BIBL.: *Festschrift zu K.s 70. Geburtstag* (Leipzig, 1918).
—**NS/LK/DM**

Kreubé, Charles Frédéric,

French conductor and composer; b. Luneville, Nov. 5, 1777; d. near St.-Denis, 1846. He studied violin in Paris with R. Kreutzer (1800). He joined the orch. of the Paris Opéra-Comique as a violinist, and from 1816 to 1828 was 1st conductor. He wrote 16 operas as well as violin pieces.
—**NS/LK/DM**

Kreuder, Peter Paul,

German composer; b. Aachen, Aug. 18, 1905; d. Salzburg, June 28, 1981. He studied in Munich and in Hamburg. He was active as music director of the Reinhardt theaters in Berlin (1928–30) and at the drama theater in Munich (1930–33). In 1936 he was appointed state music director in Munich. In 1945 he went to Argentina, where he occupied educational posts under the regime of Juan Perón. He wrote an opera, *Der Zerrissene* (Stockholm, 1940), and several operettas. His song *Schön war die Zeit* became extremely popular in Germany. It also served as the title of his autobiography (Munich, 1955).—**NS/LK/DM**

Kreusser, Georg Anton,

German composer; b. Heidingsfeld, near Würzburg, Oct. 27, 1746; d. Aschaffenburg, Nov. 1, 1810. After training in Heidingsfeld, he went to Amsterdam to study with his brother Adam Kreusser (b. Heidingsfeld [baptized], Nov. 28, 1732; d. Amsterdam, 1792), the concertmaster of the theater orch. there from 1752. He subsequently completed his training in Italy and France (1770–71). In 1773 he became deputy Konzertmeister and in 1774 Konzertmeister at the Mainz electoral chapel, where he was held in great esteem. He distinguished himself as a composer of both instrumental and vocal works, winning the admiration of Haydn. His best known work is the oratorio *Der Tod Jesu* (1783), but he also wrote many syms., a large output of chamber music, and several masses.

BIBL.: E. Peters, *G.A. K.: Ein Mainzer Instrumentalkomponist der Klassik* (Munich and Salzburg, 1975).—**LK/DM**

Kreutz, Arthur,

American composer, conductor, violinist, and teacher; b. La Crosse, Wisc., July 25, 1906; d. Oxford, Miss., March 11, 1991. He studied at the Univ. of Wisc. and Columbia Univ. After teaching at Columbia Univ. (1946–52), he was on the faculty of the Univ. of Miss. (1952–64). In 1940 he won the Prix de Rome, and later held a Guggenheim fellowship (1944–46).

WORKS: DRAMATIC: O p e r a : *Acres of Sky* (1949–50; Fayettville, Ark., Nov. 16, 1951); *The University Greys* (1953; Clinton, Miss., March 15, 1954); *Sourwood Mountain* (1958; Clinton, Miss., Jan. 8, 1959). **ORCH.:** *Paul Bunyan* (1939); 4 syms. (1940, 1943, n.d., n.d.); *American Dances* (1941); 2 violin concertos (1944, 1965); *Symphonic Blues* (c. 1946); *Mosquito Serenade* for Strings (1947); Clarinet Concerto (c. 1947); *Dixieland Concerto* (1949); *Dance Concerto* for Clarinet and Orch. (1950); *Concertino in Blue* for Violin and Orch. (1963); Saxophone Concerto (c. 1963); Piano Concerto (1970); *Concert Jazz* (1988). **CHAMBER:** Concertino for Oboe, Horn, and String Quartet (1944–45); String Quartet (1945); *Quartet Venuti* for String Quartet (1953); 3 *Jazzsonatas* for Violin and Piano (1961, 1968, c. 1984); *Song and Dance* for Oboe, 2 Violins, Viola, and Cello (1977); *Jam Session* for Soprano, Alto, Tenor, and Baritone Saxophones (1978); *Saxonata* for Tenor Saxophone and Piano (1979–80); *Fantasy* for Alto Saxophone and Piano (1983); several piano pieces. **VOCAL:** 3 *Shakespearean Love Lyrics* for High Voice and Chamber Orch. (1943); 4 *Poems by Robert Burns* for High Voice and Chamber Orch. (1944); *New England Folksing* for Chorus and Orch. (1946).—**NS/LK/DM**

Kreutzer, Conradin (originally, Conrad),

German conductor and composer; b. Messkirch, Baden, Nov. 22, 1780; d. Riga, Dec. 14, 1849. He was a pupil of Johann Baptist Rieger, the Messkirch choirmaster, and then entered the Zwiefalten monastery (1789), where he studied organ and theory with Ernst Weinrauch (1792–97). He then studied law at the Univ. of Freiburg im Breisgau (1799–1800) before devoting himself to music. He changed his first name to Conradin in 1799. About 1800 he brought out his first operetta, *Die lächerliche Werbung*, in Freiburg. After a sojourn in Switzerland, he went to Vienna (1804), where met Haydn and most likely studied with Albrechtsberger. His Singspiel *Jery und Bätely*, after Goethe (May 19, 1810), met with considerable success there. He then scored major successes in Stuttgart with the premieres of his operas *Konradin von Schwaben* (March 30, 1812) and *Feodora* (1812). He subsequently served as Hofkapellmeister there (1812–16), and then held that title in the service of Prince Carl Egon of Furstenberg in Donaueschingen (1818–22). After the success of his opera *Libussa* at Vienna's Kärnthnertortheater (Dec. 4, 1822), he served as its Kapellmeister (1822–27, 1829–32); was also active in Paris (1827–29). He was Kapellmeister of Vienna's Theater in der Josefstadt (1833–35), where he achieved his greatest success with *Das Nachtlager von Granada* (Jan. 13, 1834) and *Der Verschwender* (Feb. 20, 1834). After another period as Kapellmeister at the Kärnthnertortheater (1835–40), he served as municipal music director in Cologne (1840–42). He spent much time touring with his daughters Cäcilie and Marie, both of whom were singers. He accompanied the latter to Riga (1848). In all, he composed over 40 stage works. The success Kreutzer achieved during his lifetime was not sustained after his death. Only *Der Verschwender* is retained in the Austrian repertoire. He was also an effective composer of songs, several of which are still sung in Austria and Germany. He also composed several oratorios, masses, cantatas, 2 ballets, 3 piano concertos (1819?, 1822?, 1825?), much chamber music, and numerous piano pieces.

BIBL.: R. Rossmayer, *Konradin K. als dramatischer Komponist* (diss., Univ. of Vienna, 1928); A. Landau, *Das einstimmige Kunstlied C. K.s und seine Stellung zum zeitgenossischen Lied in Schwaben* (Leipzig, 1930); H. Leister, *C. K.s Lieder für Männerchor* (diss., Univ. of Mainz, 1963).—NS/LK/DM

Kreutzer, Jean Nicolas Auguste, French violinist and composer, brother of **Rodolphe Kreutzer** and father of **Léon Charles François Kreutzer;** b. Versailles, Sept. 3, 1778; d. Paris, Aug. 31, 1832. He studied with his brother at the Paris Cons. (premier prix, 1801). He played in the orch. of the Théâtre Favart (from 1798) and of the Opéra (from 1800), and also in the imperial chapel orch. (1804–30). He taught at the Paris Cons., later taking over his brother's class there (1826). He publ. a number of works for violin, including 2 concertos, 3 sonatas, duos, etc.—NS/LK/DM

Kreutzer, Léon Charles François, French music critic and composer, son of **Jean Nicolas Auguste Kreutzer;** b. Paris, Sept. 23, 1817; d. Vichy, Oct. 6, 1868. He studied piano with Fleche and composition with Benoist. He wrote for the *Revue et Gazette Musicale, Revue Contemporaine, La Quotidienne, L'Union,* etc. Among his compositions were 2 operas, 2 syms., 4 string quartets, a Piano Trio, 3 piano sonatas and other works for piano, some 50 songs, and organ pieces. —NS/LK/DM

Kreutzer, Rodolphe, famous French violinist, pedagogue, and composer, brother of **Jean Nicolas**

Auguste Kreutzer; b. Versailles, Nov. 16, 1766; d. Geneva, Jan. 6, 1831. His father, a wind player, gave him early instruction in music; he began studying violin and composition with Anton Stamitz in 1778. On May 25, 1780, he played a Stamitz violin concerto at the Paris Concert Spirituel, and returned there in May 1784 to play his own 1st Violin Concerto. In 1785 he became a member of the king's music, and soon established a notable reputation as a virtuoso. In 1789 he settled in Paris, where he first gained success as a composer for the theater with his opéra-comique *Paul et Virginie* (Jan. 15, 1791). His opéra-comique *Lodoiska* (Aug. 1, 1791) was also a success, being accorded an even warmer reception than Cherubini's score of the same name. In 1793 Kreutzer became a prof. at the Inst. National de Musique; when it became the Paris Cons. in 1795, he remained on its faculty, retiring in 1826. Beginning in 1798 he made a number of outstanding concert appearances at the Théâtre Feydeau and the Opéra in Paris, being made solo violin at the latter in 1801; he also became a member of Napoleon's chapel orch. (1802) and of his private orch. (1806). His ballet-pantomime *Paul et Virginie* (June 12, 1806) found favor with Paris audiences, as did his ballet *Les Amours d'Antoine et Cléopatre* (March 8, 1808) and his comédie lyrique *Aristippe* (May 24, 1808). In 1810 Kreutzer suffered a broken arm in a carriage accident, which effectively put an end to his career. However, he continued to hold his various positions as a violinist. In 1815 he was made maître de la chapelle du roi. In 1816 he was appointed 2nd conductor, and in 1817 1st conductor at the Opéra, retaining this post until 1824, at which time he became director (1824–26). His last opera, *Matilde* (c. 1826–27), was refused by the Opéra management. By then in declining health, he spent his remaining years in retirement. Kreutzer was one of the foremost violinists of his era. With Baillot and Rode, he stands as one of the founders of the French violin school. Beethoven greatly admired his playing, and was moved to dedicate his Violin Sonata, op.47 (the *Kreutzer*), to him. Kreutzer's most celebrated publication remains the brilliant 42 *études ou caprices* (originally 40) for Unaccompanied Violin. He also composed a number of fine violin concertos. His renown as a teacher brought him many students, including his brother, C. Lafont, and Massart. With Rode and Baillot, he publ. *Méthode de violon* (Paris, 1803).

WORKS: DRAMATIC (all 1st perf. in Paris unless otherwise given): *Jeanne d'Arc,* drame historique mêlée d'ariettes (May 10, 1790); *Paul et Virginie,* opéra-comique (Jan. 15, 1791); *Le franc breton,* opéra-comique (Feb. 15, 1791; in collaboration with Solié); *Lodoiska,* opéra-comique (Aug. 1, 1791); *Charlotte et Werther,* opéra-comique (Feb. 1, 1792); *Le siège de Lille,* opéra-comique (Nov. 14, 1792); *Le déserteur ou La montagne de Ham,* opera (Feb. 6, 1793); *Le congrès des rois,* opéra-comique (Feb. 26, 1793; in collaboration with 11 other composers); *On respire,* comédie mêlée d'ariettes (March 9, 1795); *Le brigand,* drame mêlée d'ariettes (July 25, 1795); *La journée du 10 août 1792,* opera (Aug. 10, 1795); *Imogène ou La gageure indiscrète,* comedie mêlée d'ariettes (April 27, 1796); *Le petit page,* comédie mêlée d'ariettes (Feb. 15, 1800; in collaboration with N. Isouard); *Flaminius à Corinthe,* opera (Feb. 27, 1801; in collaboration with N. Isouard); *Astyanax,* opera (April 12, 1801); *Le baiser et la quittance,* opéra-comique (June 18, 1803; in collaboration with Boieldieu, Isouard, and Méhul); *Les surprises ou L'étourdi en voyage*, opera (Jan. 2, 1806); *Paul et Virginie*, ballet-pantomime (St. Cloud, June 12, 1806); *François I ou La fête mystérieuse*, comédie mêlée d'ariettes (March 14, 1807); *Les amours d'Antoine et Cléopatre*, ballet (March 8, 1808); *Aristippe*, comédie lyrique (May 24, 1808); *Jadis et aujourd'hui*, opéra-comique (Oct. 29, 1808); *La fête de Mars*, divertissement-pantomime (Dec. 26, 1809); *Abel*, tragédie lyrique (March 23, 1810; rev. as *La Mort d'Abel*, March 17, 1823); *Le triomphe du mois de Mars*, ceremonial drama for the King of Rome's birth (March 27, 1811); *L'homme sans façon*, opéra-comique (Jan. 7, 1812); *Le camp de Sobieski*, opéra-comique (April 21, 1813); *Constance et Théodore*, opéra-comique (Nov. 22, 1813); *L'oriflamme*, opera (Jan. 31, 1814; in collaboration with Berton, Méhul, and Paër); *Les béarnais ou Henri IV en voyage*, opéra-comique (May 21, 1814; in collaboration with Boieldieu); *La perruque et la redingote*, opéra-comique (Jan. 25, 1815; in collaboration with Kreubé); *La princesse de Babylone*, opera (May 30, 1815); *L'heureux retour*, ballet (July 25, 1815; in collaboration with Berton and Persuis); *Le carnaval de Venise*, ballet (Feb. 22, 1816; in collaboration with Persuis); *Les dieux rivaux*, opera-ballet (June 21, 1816; in collaboration with Berton, Persuis, and Spontini); *Le maître et le valet*, opéra-comique (1816); *La servante justifiée ou La fête de Mathurine*, ballet villageois (Sept. 30, 1818); *Clari ou La promesse de mariage*, ballet-pantomime (June 19, 1820); *Blanche de Provence ou La cour des fées*, opera (May 3, 1821; in collaboration with Berton, Boieldieu, Cherubini, and Paër); *Le négociant de Hambourg*, opéra-comique (Oct. 15, 1821); *Le paradis de Mahomet*, opéra-comique (March 23, 1822; in collaboration with Kreubé); *Ipsiboe*, opera (March 31, 1824); *Pharamond*, opera (June 10, 1825; in collaboration with Berton and Boieldieu); *Matilde*, opera (c. 1826–27; not perf.). **ORCH.:** Violin Concertos: No. 1, op.1 (1783–84); No. 2, op.2 (1784–85); No. 3, op.3 (1785); No. 4, op.4 (1786); No. 5, op.5 (1787); No. 6, op.6 (c. 1788); No. 7, op.7 (c. 1790); No. 8, op.8 (c. 1795); No. 9, op.9 (c. 1802); No. 10, op.10 (c. 1802); No. 11, op.11 (c. 1802); No. 12, op.12 (1802–3); No. 13, op.A (1803); No. 14, op.B (1803–4); No. 15, op.C (1804); No. 16, op.D (1804); No. 17, op.E (1805); No. 18, op.F (1805–9); No. 19, op.G (1805–10). **S i n f o n i a s C o n c e r t a n t e s :** No. 1 for 2 Violins (c. 1793); No. 2 for 2 Violins and Cello (c. 1794); No. 3 for 2 Violins (1803); No. 4 for 2 Violins (n.d.); *Ouverture de la journée de marathon* for Woodwind and Brass (1794). **CHAMBER:** Quintet for Oboe or Clarinet and String Quartet (c. 1795). **S t r i n g Q u a r t e t s :** *6 quatuors concertans* (c. 1790); 3 quartets, op.2 (c. 1795); 2 quartets (c. 1795); *6 nouveaux quatuors*, op.2, part 1 (c. 1798). **T r i o s :** *Premier pot-pourri* for Violin Solo, Violin, and Bass (c. 1800); Trio for Oboe or Clarinet, Bassoon, and Viola (c. 1803); *3 trios brillans* for 2 Violins and Bass (c. 1803). **D u e t s :** Duos for Violin and Viola (1783); 3 violin duos, op.11, part 2 (c. 1800); 3 violin duos, op.3 (c. 1805); 3 duos concertans for 2 Violins, op.B (c. 1820); *6 nocturnes concertans* for Harp and Violin (c. 1822; in collaboration with C. Bochsa). **S o n a t a s :** 3 sonatas for Violin and Bass, op.1 (c. 1795); 3 sonatas for Violin and Bass, op.B (c. 1795); *Grande sonate* for Violin and Piano (1799); *3 sonates faciles* for Violin and Bass (c. 1803); 3 sonatas for Violin and Bass, op.2 (c. 1805). **O t h e r :** *42 études ou caprices* for Unaccompanied Violin (originally 40; 1796; 1st extant ed., c. 1807); *18 nouveaux caprices ou études* for Unaccompanied Violin (c. 1815).

BIBL.: J. Massart, *L'Art de travailler les études de K.* (Paris, n.d.; Eng. tr., 1926); H. Kling, *R. K.* (Brussels, 1898); J. Hardy, *R. K.* (Paris, 1910); M. Williams, *The Violin Concertos of R. K.* (diss., Ind. Univ., 1973).—**NS/LK/DM**

Křička, Jaroslav, eminent Czech composer and pedagogue; b. Kelc, Moravia, Aug. 27, 1882; d. Prague, Jan. 23, 1969. He studied law in Prague (1900–02), then music at the Prague Cons. (1902–05) and in Berlin (1905–06). He was in Ekaterinoslav (1906–09), where he was active as a teacher and conductor. He then returned to Prague as a choirmaster, and later was prof. of composition at the Prague Cons. (1918–45), where he also served as rector. His music was influenced by Dvořák and native folk songs.

WORKS: DRAMATIC: O p e r a : *Hypolita* (1910–16; Prague, Oct. 10, 1917); *Bílý pán* (The White Gentleman), after Oscar Wilde's *The Canterville Ghost* (1927–29; Brno, 1929; rev. 1930; Breslau, Nov. 14, 1931); *Kral Lavra* (King Lawrence; 1936–37; rev. 1938–39; Prague, June 7, 1940); *České jesličky* (The Czech Christmas Manger; 1936–37; rev. 1948; Prague, Jan. 15, 1949); *Jáchym a Juliána* (Joachim and Julia; 1945–48; Opavá, 1951); *Serenáda*, opera buffa (Plzen, 1950); *Kolébka* (The Cradle), musical comedy (1950; Opavá, 1951); *Zahořanský hon* (The Zahorany Hunt; Opavá, 1955). **C h i l d r e n ' s O p e r a :** *Ogaři* (Country Lads; 1918; Nové Město, Sept. 7, 1919); *Dobře to dopadlo or Tlustý pradědeček* (It Turned Out Well or The Fat Great-Grandfather; 1932); *Lupici a detekotyvove* (Robbers and Detectives; 1932; both operas, Prague, Dec. 29, 1932). **OTHER:** Several small operas for children's theater; television opera, *Kalhoty* (A Pair of Trousers; Czech TV, 1962). **ORCH.:** Sym., *Jarná* (Spring; 1905–06; rev. 1942); *Nostalgie* for Strings and Harp (1905); *Faith*, symphonic poem (1907); *A Children's Suite* (1907); *Scherzo Idyllic* (1908; Prague, Nov. 13, 1910; 3rd movement of an uncompleted Sym. No. 2); *Modrý pták* (A Blue Bird), overture, after a Maeterlinck fairy tale (1911; Prague, March 3, 1912, composer conducting); *Adventus*, symphonic poem (1920–21; Prague, Nov. 6, 1921); *Matěj Kopecký*, overture (1928); *Horácká suita* (Suite montagnarde; Prague, Sept. 8, 1935); Sinfonietta for Strings and Timpani (1940–41); *Majales*, overture (1942); Violin Concerto (1944); Concertino for Horn and String Quartet or String Orch. (1951); *Variations on a Theme of Boccherini* for Bassoon and String Quartet or String Orch. (1952); *Sinfonietta semplice* (1962). **CHAMBER:** *Small Suite in Old Style* for 2 Violins and Piano (1907); 3 string quartets (1907; 1938–39; *Wallachian*, 1949); *Doma* (At Home), piano trio (1924–25); Violin Sonata (1925); Sonatina for 2 Violins (1926–27; rev. for Violin and Viola); Concertino (septet) for Violin, Wind Quintet, and Piano (1940); *Partita* for Violin (1941); *Divertimento* for Wind Quintet (1950); Flute Sonatina (1951); *Variations* for Violin (1956); Violin Sonatina (1962); several albums of piano pieces. **VOCAL: C a n t a t a s :** *Pokušeni na poušti* (Temptation in the Desert; 1921–22); *Jenny, the Thief* (1927–28); *Tyrolese Elegies* (1930–31); *A Eulogy to a Woman* (1933); *Recollections of Student Years* (1934); *Moravian Cantata* (1935–36); *The Golden Spinning Wheel* (1943); *To Prague* (1960). **OTHER:** Songs; folk song arrangements.

BIBL.: J. Dostál, *J. K.* (Prague, 1944).—**NS/LK/DM**

Krieger, Adam, esteemed German organist and composer; b. Driesen, Neumark, Jan. 7, 1634; d. Dresden, June 30, 1666. He studied organ with Samuel Scheidt in Halle. From 1655 to 1657 he was organist at the Nikolaikirche in Leipzig. He then went to Dresden (1657), where he was made keyboard teacher to the Elector of Saxony's daughter and in 1658 chamber and court organist. He was one of the most important of the early composers of German lieder, which he called his

"Arien," ranging from the risque to the sublime. For most of them he wrote the words as well as the music.

WORKS: (50) *Arien* for 1 to 3 Voices, 2 Violins, Violone, and Basso Continuo (Leipzig, 1657; excerpts ed. by H. Osthoff and N. Schiørring in *Det 16. og 17. Arhundredes Verdslige Danske Visesang*, Copenhagen, 1950); (50) *Neue Arien in 6 Zehen eingetheilet* for 2, 3, and 5 Voices, 2 Violins, 2 Violas, and Basso Continuo (Dresden, 1667; 2nd ed., aug., 1676, with 10 more songs, and with ritornellos by J. Furchheim; selections in Denkmäler Deutscher Tonkunst, XIX, 1905). He also composed 5 sacred cantatas and 4 funeral songs, as well as an aria.

BIBL.: H. Osthoff, *A. K.* (Leipzig, 1929).—NS/LK/DM

Krieger, Armando,

Argentine pianist, conductor, and composer; b. Buenos Aires, May 7, 1940. He studied piano with John Montes and Robert Kinsky and composition with Ginastera, later with Copland, Dallapiccola, Maderna, R. Malipiero, and Messiaen at the Di Tella Inst. (1963–64); continued his piano training with Loriod at the Mozarteum Argentino (1964). He became widely known in his native country as a pianist and conductor, often giving performances of avant-garde music; also conducted his own chamber orch. and was active as a teacher. In his works, he adopted a serial technique in which rhythmic, melodic, and harmonic elements follow a predetermined formula of contrasts.

WORKS: Sym. for Strings (1959); Concerto for 2 Pianos and Orch. (1963); *Métamorfosis d'après une lecture de Kafka* for Piano and 15 Instruments (1968); *Angst* for Orch. (1970); several cantatas and various solo vocal works; 2 string quartets (1960, 1961); other chamber music; keyboard pieces.—NS/LK/DM

Krieger, Edino,

Brazilian composer; b. Brusque, Santa Catarina, March 17, 1928. He studied music with his father, a conductor, composer, and founder of the local Cons., and later studied violin with Edith Reis (1943) and composition with Koellreutter (1944–48) at the Rio de Janeiro Cons. He subsequently had lessons with Copland at the Berkshire Music Center in Tanglewood (summer, 1948) and with Mennin at the Juilliard School of Music in N.Y. (1948–49), and also studied violin with Nowinsky at N.Y.'s Henry Street Settlement School. He completed his studies with Krenek in Brazil (1952) and Berkeley at London's Royal Academy of Music (1955). Krieger was active as a broadcaster, music critic, conductor, and teacher in his homeland. He was director of the art and music dept. of the Radio Jornal do Brasil in Rio de Janeiro (1963–73), and also president of the Brazilian Soc. of Contemporary Music (1971–73). His early works were in a late Romantic and Impressionist style. After a brief dodecaphonic period (1947–53), he turned toward neo- Classicism with national allusions. He fused the latter 2 styles from 1966.

WORKS: ORCH.: *Movimento misto* (1947); *Contrastes* (1949); *Música 1952* for Strings (1952); *Chôro* for Flute and Strings (1952); *Suite* for Strings (1954); *Abertura sinfônica* (1955); *Concertante* for Piano and Orch. (1955); *Andante* for Strings (1956); *Divertimento* for Strings (1959); *Brasiliana* for Viola or Alto Saxophone and Strings (1960); *Variações elementares* for Strings (1964); *Ludus symphonicus* (1966); *Toccata* for Piano and Orch. (1967); *Canticum naturale* (1972). **CHAMBER:** Trio for Oboe, Clarinet, and Bassoon (1945); *Peça lenta* for Flute and

String Trio (1946); *Música 1947* for String Quartet (1947); *Música de câmara* for Flute, Trumpet, Timpani, and Violin (1948); String Quartet No. 1 (1955); piano pieces. **VOCAL:** *Melopéia* for Soprano, Tenor Saxophone, Trombone, and Viola (1949); choral pieces; songs.—NS/LK/DM

Krieger, Johann Philipp,

eminent German organist, keyboard player, and composer, brother of **Johann Krieger;** b. Nuremberg, Feb. 25, 1649; d. Weissenfels, Feb. 6, 1725. He was a pupil of Johann Dretzel and Gabriel Schütz in Nuremberg; went to Copenhagen, where he studied organ with the royal organist Johann Schröder and composition with Kaspar Förster. By 1672 he was court organist in Bayreuth. He went to Italy in 1673, continuing his studies in Venice with Rosenmüller (composition) and G. Volpe (clavier) and in Rome with A. Abbatini (composition) and B. Pasquini (composition and clavier). After playing before the Emperor Leopold I in Vienna, he was ennobled by the monarch in 1675. Krieger was subsequently court organist in Halle (from 1677). When the court moved to Weissenfels in 1680, he went with it as Kapellmeister, retaining that post for the rest of his life. He was particularly important as a composer of sacred cantatas; by introducing madrigal verse for his texts, he came to be regarded as the "father of the new cantata." He wrote more than 2,000 such works, only 74 of which are extant. He also composed some 18 operas, but only arias are extant, along with several librettos. His extant publ. instrumental works are *Lustige Feld- Music* (Nuremberg, 1704; 6 suites for Wind Instruments), *12 suonate* for 2 Violins (Nuremberg, 1688), and *12 suonate* for Violin and Viola da Gamba (Nuremberg, 1693). For eds. of his extant works, see the following: M. Seiffert, ed., *J.P. Krieger: 21 ausgewählte Kirchencomposition*, Denkmäler Deutscher Tonkunst, LIII-LIV (1916), idem, ed., *J.P. Krieger: Gesammelte Werke für Orgel und Klavier*, Denkmäler der Tonkunst in Bayern, XXX, Jg. XVIII (1917), idem, ed., *J.P. Krieger: Partie, Sonate*, Organum, III/9, 11 (Leipzig, 1925–26; 2nd ed., 1951–52), H.J. Moser, ed., *J.P. Krieger: 24 Lieder und Arien*, Nagels Musikarchiv, CLXXXIV-CLXXV (1930), H. Osthoff, ed., *J.P. Krieger: Triosonate*, ibid., CXXXV (1937), and C. Crussard, ed., *J.P. Krieger: Sonate a trois*, Flores Musicae, VII (1958).

BIBL.: D. Stout, *Four Cantatas by J.P. K.* (diss., Ind. Univ., 1966).—NS/LK/DM

Krieger, Johann,

distinguished German organist and composer, brother of **Johann Philipp Krieger;** b. Nuremberg, Dec. 28, 1651; d. Zittau, July 18, 1735. He received keyboard training from G.C. Wecker (1661–68) and then studied composition with his brother in Zeitz (1671), becoming his successor as court organist at Bayreuth (1673–77). He was subsequently Kapellmeister to Count Heinrich I in Greiz (1678–80), then held that post at the court of Duke Christian in Eisenberg (1680–82). He then went to Zittau, where he was active as organist of St. Johannis and director choris musici, a position he held for 53 years, playing for the last time on the day before he died. His music was appreciated by Handel. Some of his organ compositions are regarded as presaging the grand style of Bach.

WORKS: INSTRUMENTAL: *6 musicalische Partien*

(Nuremberg, 1697); *Anmuthige Clavier-Ubung* (Nuremberg, 1698); *Allein Gott in der Höh sei Ehr, a 4*; other pieces in MS. **ARIAS AND LIEDER:** *Neue musicalische Ergetzligkeit, das ist Unterschiedene Erfindungen welche Herr Christian Weise, in Zittau von geistlichen Andachten, Politischen Tugend-Liedern und Theatralischen Sachen bishero gesetzet hat* (Frankfurt and Leipzig, 1684); 19 occasional songs for weddings or funerals (publ. separately, 1684–97). Of some 235 known sacred vocal works, only 33 are extant: 12 German cantatas, 2 Latin cantatas, 5 settings of the Sanctus, 2 settings of the Magnificat, motets, and solo and choral concertos. He also wrote 10 operas, but only a few arias are extant. Some of his works are found in the following: M. Seiffert, ed., *Nuremberger Meister der zweiten Hälfte des 17. Jahrhunderts*, Denkmäler der Tonkunst in Bayern, X, Jg. VI/I (1906), idem, ed., *J. Krieger: Gesammelte Werke für Klavier und Orgel*, ibid., XXX, Jg. XVIII (1917), and F. Riedel, ed., *Johann Krieger: Präludiem und Fugen, Die Orgel*, II/3 (Leipzig, 1957). —NS/LK/DM

Krips, Henry (Joseph), Austrian-born Australian conductor, brother of **Josef Krips;** b. Vienna, Feb. 10, 1912; d. Adelaide, Jan. 25, 1987. He studied in Vienna at the Cons. and the Univ. He made his conducting debut at Vienna's Burgtheater in 1932, and subsequently was conductor in Innsbruck (1933–34), Salzburg (1934–35), and Vienna (1935–38). In 1938 he emigrated to Australia and became a naturalized Australian citizen in 1944. He conducted ballet and opera. He was principal conductor of the West Australia Sym. Orch. in Perth (1948–72) and the South Australia Sym. Orch. in Adelaide (1949–72); also made guest appearances in Europe. He was best known for his performances of light Viennese music.—NS/LK/DM

Krips, Josef, eminent Austrian conductor, brother of **Henry (Joseph) Krips;** b. Vienna, April 8, 1902; d. Geneva, Oct. 13, 1974. He studied at the Vienna Academy of Music, and also was a student of Weingartner and Mandyczewski. He was 1st violinist in the Volksoper orch. in Vienna (1918–21), then became répétiteur and chorus master there, making his conducting debut with *Un ballo in maschera* (1921). In 1924–25 he conducted opera in Aussig an der Elbe, in 1925–26, in Dortmund, and from 1926 to 1933 he was was Generalmusikdirektor in Karlsruhe. In 1933 he became a conductor at the Vienna State Opera. He also was made a prof. at the Vienna Academy of Music. In 1938 he lost these positions, after the annexation of Austria to Germany. He then conducted in Belgrade (1938–39). In 1945 he rejoined the Vienna State Opera as principal conductor, later that year conducting the first post-war subscription concert of the Vienna Phil., and quickly moving to reestablish the musical life of his native city. In 1947 he appeared with the Vienna State Opera at London's Covent Garden. After leaving the Vienna State Opera in 1950, he served as principal conductor of the London Sym. Orch. until 1954. In 1953 he made his U.S. debut as a guest conductor with the Buffalo Phil., and subsequently was its music director (1954–63); from 1963 to 1970 he was music director of the San Francisco Sym. Orch. He also was a guest conductor of the major opera houses and orchs. of Europe and the U.S.; he conducted at Chicago's Lyric Opera (1960, 1964), at Covent Garden (1963; 1971–74), and at N.Y.'s Metropolitan Opera (1966–67; 1969–70). He excelled in works of the Austro-German repertoire, his interpretations being notable for their authority, insight, warmth, and lyricism. Harrietta Krips ed. and publ. his autobiography (Vienna, 1994).—NS/LK/DM

Kristofferson, Kris, reinvigorated a staid Nashville country-and-western music scene in the early 1970s with his potent songwriting; b. Brownsville, Tex., June 22, 1936. Kris Kristofferson helped broaden the appeal of country music. In drawing critical attention from folk and rock critics and fans, he helped open the way for a new generation of country songwriters such as Billy Joe Shaver, Jerry Jeff Walker, Guy Clark, and Rodney Crowell. Composing the classics "Sunday Mornin' Comin' Down," "Help Me Make It Through the Night," and "Me and Bobby McGee," Kristofferson also enjoyed considerable success in the 1970s with then-wife Rita Coolidge. However, his subsequent musical career suffered as he sought to establish himself as an actor and, more recently, became committed to the cause of human rights. Nonetheless, Kristofferson enjoyed considerable success in the 1980s and 1990s as a member of the Highwaymen, with Johnny Cash, Willie Nelson, and Waylon Jennings.

Kris Kristofferson moved frequently with his military family before eventually settling in Calif. A creative-writing major at Pomona Coll., he won a Rhodes scholarship to Oxford Univ. in England upon graduation in 1958. A successful short-story writer, Kristofferson began pursuing songwriting as a sideline under the name Kris Carson while in England. Remaining at Oxford for less than two years, he then joined the Army and served as a helicopter pilot in Germany, where he played service clubs. Turning down an offer to teach literature at West Point, he was discharged after four and a half years and moved to Nashville in 1965. There he worked as a bartender and as a janitor at Columbia Records, where he met Johnny Cash. He eventually signed a songwriting contract with Fred Foster, providing Roger Miller with the major country hit "Me and Bobby McGee" and Ray Stevens with the minor country hit "Sunday Mornin' Comin' Down" in 1969.

Kristofferson recorded his debut album on Foster's Monument label in 1970, but it was overlooked by the record-buying public, despite the inclusion of "Me and Bobby McGee," "Sunday Mornin' Comin' Down," "For the Good Times," "Help Me Make It Through the Night," the satirical "Best of All Possible Worlds," and "To Beat the Devil," dedicated to Johnny Cash and his wife, June Carter. However, a number of country-and-western artists took notice, recording his songs. Veteran Ray Price scored a top country and major pop hit with "For the Good Times" in 1970, followed by the country smash "I'd Rather Be Sorry" in 1971. Mentor Johnny Cash had a top country hit with "Sunday Mornin' Comin' Down" and Sammi Smith had a top country and near-smash pop hit with "Help Me Make It Through the Night."

Making his first major club appearance at the Troubadour in Los Angeles in June 1970, Kris Kristofferson performed on Johnny Cash's ABC television show a number of times during the year. His popularity was soon broadened when Janis Joplin achieved a top pop hit with "Me and Bobby McGee" in early 1971. *The Silver-Tongued Devil and I* yielded Kristofferson's first major pop hit with "Loving Her Was Easier (Than Anything I'll Ever Do Again)," and included "The Taker," "The Pilgrim—Chapter 33," and the tender "When I Loved Her." *Jesus Was a Capricorn* contained the wry title song (dedicated to John Prine) as well as "Nobody Wins" and the major pop and top country hit "Why Me."

Kris Kristofferson initiated his acting career in 1972's *Cisco Pike*. In 1973 he costarred in *Pat Garrett and Billy the Kid* with veteran James Coburn (and Bob Dylan), and in August he married Rita Coolidge. The couple scored a minor pop and country hit with Tom Jans's "Loving Arms" for A&M, and later recorded an album for Monument Records. Kristofferson's own albums fared progressively less well as he worked on movies such as the highly acclaimed *Alice Doesn't Live Here Anymore* and *The Sailor That Fell from Grace with the Sea*. In 1976 he costarred with Barbra Streisand in an updated remake of the 1937 classic *A Star Is Born*, and the soundtrack album became a best-seller, featuring three solo songs by Kristofferson, including the minor pop hit "Watch Closely Now," two duets, and Streisand's top pop and easy-listening hit "Love Theme from *A Star Is Born* (Evergreen)." Other film roles of the 1970s include *Semi-Tough* (with Burt Reynolds and Jill Clayburgh), the made-for-TV movie *Freedom Road* (with Muhammad Ali), and the western (and infamous failure) *Heaven's Gate*. Kristofferson and Rita Coolidge divorced in 1980.

Kris Kristofferson switched to Columbia Records in 1977, managing minor country hits in the early 1980s with "Prove It to You One More Time Again" and "Nobody Loves Anybody Anymore." During the first half of the 1980s, Kristofferson starred in a series of largely forgettable movies, with the exception of *Songwriter* with Willie Nelson, acclaimed as one of the most astute movies about the country-music business since *Nashville*. In 1985 he teamed with Nelson, Johnny Cash, and Waylon Jennings for *Highwayman*, its top country hit "Highwayman" (written by Jimmy Webb), and its major country hit "Desperadoes Waiting for a Train" (written by Guy Clark). The following year he starred in the popular *Blood and Orchids* miniseries on CBS-TV and acted in the controversial miniseries *Amerika*. The show produced protests from the Soviet Union and the United Nations before its airing in early 1987. Although it proved to be a failure, the show stirred Kristofferson's growing interest in international human rights, as evidenced by the material on *Repossessed*, his first album in more than five years. It produced a minor country hit, "They Killed Him"—a tribute to Jesus Christ, Gandhi, and Martin Luther King—and contained other politically oriented songs such as "Shipwrecked in the Eighties." He subsequently visited the Soviet Union and Nicaragua, denounced American policy in Central America, and campaigned for Jesse Jackson.

In 1990 Kris Kristofferson reunited with Willie Nelson, Waylon Jennings, and Johnny Cash for an album and tour as the Highwaymen. *Singer/Songwriter*, from 1991, contained a disc of his recordings and a disc of his songs recorded by others. In 1992 Kristofferson returned to Monument for *Live at the Philharmonic*, recorded with Willie Nelson and Rita Coolidge. By 1995 Kris Kristofferson had reunited with the other Highwaymen to tour in support of *The Road Goes On Forever* on their new label, Liberty.

DISC.: KRIS KRISTOFFERSON: *Kristofferson* (1970); *(reissued as) Me and Bobby McGee* (1971); *The Silver-Tongued Devil and I* (1971); *Border Lord* (1972); *Jesus Was a Capricorn* (1972); *Spooky Lady's Sideshow* (1974); *Who's to Bless and Who's to Blame* (1975); *Surreal Thing* (1976); *Songs of Kristofferson (All-Time Greatest Hits)* (1977); *Easter Island* (1978); *Shake Hands with the Devil* (1979); *To the Bone* (1981); *My Songs* (1986); *Repossessed* (1986); *Third World Warrior* (1989); *Singer/Songwriter* (1991); *Live at the Philharmonic* (1992). **KRIS KRISTOFFERSON AND RITA COOLIDGE:** *Full Moon* (1973); *Breakaway* (1974); *Natural Act* (1979). **KRIS KRISTOFFERSON AND BARBRA STREISAND:** *A Star Is Born* (soundtrack; 1976). **KRIS KRISTOFFERSON, WILLIE NELSON, DOLLY PARTON, AND BRENDA LEE:** *The Winning Hand* (1983). **KRIS KRISTOFFERSON AND WILLIE NELSON:** *Music from Songwriter* (1984). **THE HIGHWAYMEN:** *Highwayman* (1985); *Highwayman 2* (1990); *The Road Goes On Forever* (1995).

BIBL.: Beth Kalet, *K. K.* (N.Y., 1979).—**BH**

Krivine, Emmanuel, French conductor; b. Grenoble, May 7, 1947. He studied violin at the Paris Cons., winning a premier prix at age 16. After further studies at Brussel's Chapelle Musicale Reine Elisabeth, he completed his training with Szeryng and Menuhin. While pursuing his career as a violinist, he also launched a 2nd career as a conductor in 1976, and received instruction in conducting from Bohm. Following an automobile accident in 1981, he was compelled to give up violin playing and devote himself to conducting. Having conducted regularly for the ORTF in Paris, he then was principal conductor of the Orchestre Philharmonique in Lorraine (1981–83). On Jan. 30, 1987, he made his U.S. debut as a guest conductor with the Indianapolis Sym. Orch. He was music director of the Orchestre de Lyon from 1987 to 2000. In addition to appearances with leading French orchs., he appeared widely in Europe and North America.—**NS/LK/DM**

Křivinka, Gustav, Czech composer; b. Doubravice nad Svitavou, April 24, 1928. He studied with Kapral and Petrželka at the Brno Cons. (1946–50), then with Kvapil at the Brno Academy of Music (graduated, 1954). He wrote 2 syms. (1951, 1955), 2 violin concertos (1950, 1952), 2 piano concertos, song cycles, and chamber music.—**NS/LK/DM**

Křížkovský, Pavel (baptized **Karel**), Bohemian choral conductor and composer; b. Kreuzendorf, Jan. 9, 1820; d. Brünn, May 8, 1885. He was a chorister at the Troppau monastery church, and was a student at the German Gymnasium there. In 1845 he joined the Old Brno Augustinian monastery, taking the name Pavel; was a theology student (1846–50), and also took holy orders (1848). He was greatly interested in Moravian folk songs and collected many of them in the field. At the same time, he began to compose choruses in the national manner. One of his earliest works, *Utonulá* (The Girl Who Drowned), became popular; other favorites were *Žaloba* (The Plaint) and *Odvedeného prosba* (The Recruit's Prayer). He also wrote much sacred music (Roman Catholic) for the Olmütz Cathedral, where he was music director from 1873. Among his pupils was Janáček. A complete ed. of his works was prepared by V. Steinman and J. Racek (Prague, 1949).

BIBL.: J. Geisler, *P. K.* (Prague, 1886); E. Eichler, *P. K.* (Brünn, 1904); J. Racek, *P. K.: Prameny, literatura a ikonografie* (P. K.: Sources, Bibliography, and Iconography; Olomouc, 1946).
—NS/LK/DM

Kroeger, Karl, American musicologist, teacher, and composer; b. Louisville, Ky., April 13, 1932. He studied with Claude Almand and George Perle (composition) at the Univ. of Louisville (B.M., 1954; M.M., 1959) and with Binkerd (composition) and Plamenac (musicology) at the Univ. of Ill. (M.S., 1961), before completing his education with Janet Knapp (musicology) at Brown Univ. (Ph.D., 1976). He was curator of the Americana Collection in the Music Division of the N.Y. Public Library (1962–64). Kroeger was composer-in- residence of the Eugene (Ore.) public schools (1964–67). He taught at Ohio Univ. (1967–68) and Moorhead (Minn.) State Coll. (1971–72), and then at Wake Forest Univ. in Winston-Salem, N.C., where he was also director of the Moravian Music Foundation (1972–80). In 1980–81 he taught at the Univ. of Keele in England. From 1982 to 1994 he was a prof. at the Univ. of Colo. in Boulder, where he was made prof. emeritus.

WRITINGS: Ed. with H. Nathan, *The Complete Works of William Billings* (4 vols., Charlottesville, Va., 1977–90); ed. *Catalog of the Musical Works of William Billings* (Westport, Conn., 1991); ed. *American Fuging Tunes, 1770–1820: A Descriptive Catalog* (Westport, Conn., 1994); ed. *The Collected Works of Daniel Read* (Music of the United States of America, Vol. 4, Madison, Wisc., 1995); general ed., *Music of the New American Nation* (15 vols., N.Y., 1995–99); ed. *Early American Anthems* (2 vols., Madison, Wisc., 2000).

WORKS: ORCH.: 2 sinfoniettas (1958, 1965); 2 chamber concertos: No. 1 for Oboe and Strings (1961; rev. 1990) and No. 2 for Clarinet and Strings (1996); *Dramatic Overture* (1964); 4 suites (1965, 1966, 1967, 1968); Concerto for Alto Saxophone and Winds (1982); band music. **CHAMBER:** 3 string quartets (1960, 1966, 1998); 4 canzonas for Brass Sextet (1961, 1966, 1967, 1988); *Partita* for Brass Quintet (1963); *Toccata* for Clarinet, Trombone, and Percussion (1968); *Fantasy* for Brass Quartet (1969); Sonata for Trombone Quartet (1978); Suite for Oboe and Harp (1979); *Parataxis* for Flute and Percussion (1989); *Banchetto Musicale* for Saxophone Ensemble (1993); Cello Sonata (1996); Brass Quintet (1998); Woodwind Quintet (1998); Woodwind Trio (1999); piano pieces; organ music. **VOCAL:** Choral works; anthems; songs.—NS/LK/DM

Krohn, Felix (Julius Theofil), Finnish conductor, teacher, and composer; b. Tampere, May 20, 1898; d. Lahti, Nov. 11, 1963. He studied with his father, and later at the Helsinki School of Music and the Hochschule für Musik in Berlin. Returning to Finland in 1922,

he was active as a conductor and teacher.

WORKS: *Sotarukous* (War Prayer) for Orch. (1918); *Vuodenajat* (The Seasons), sinfonia brevis (1921); *Kyllikki*, cantata (1923); *Odalisque* for Orch. (1924); 4 suites for Orch.: *Sysmäläinen* (The Man from Sysma; 1938), *Vihreä kulta* (Green Gold; 1939), *Anu and Mikko* (1940), and *Linnaisten kartanon vihreä kamari* (The Green Room at Linnainen Manor; 1944); *Uskollinen sisar* (The Faithful Sister), children's opera (1945); chamber music.
—NS/LK/DM

Krohn, Ilmari (Henrik Reinhold), eminent Finnish musicologist; b. Helsinki, Nov. 8, 1867; d. there, April 25, 1960. After studying with Richard Faltin in Helsinki (1885–86), he took courses at the Leipzig Cons. with Papperitz and Reinecke (1886–90); obtained his M.A. in 1894 and his Ph.D. in 1900 from the Univ. of Helsinki with the diss. *Über die Art und Enstehung der geistlichen Volksmelodien in Finnland* (publ. in Helsinki, 1899); later studied with Bausznern in Weimar (1909). He lectured at the Helsinki Music Inst. (1900–1901; 1905; 1907; 1914–16), the Phil. Orch. School (1900–1901; 1904–14), and the Univ. of Helsinki (1900–18); then was its first prof. of musicology (1918–35); also taught at the Church Music Inst. (1923–30; 1933–44). He was active in folk music research from 1886, resulting in his valuable compilation of some 7,000 Finnish folk songs in *Suomen kansan sävelmiä* (1898–1933). He founded the Finnish section of the IMS (1910); was founder (1916) and chairman (1917–39) of the Finnish Musicological Soc. Krohn was also a composer, numbering among his works an opera, *Tuhotulva* (Deluge; 1918; Helsinki, Oct. 25, 1928), 2 oratorios: *Ikiaartehet* (Eternal Treasures; 1912) and *Voittajat* (Victors; 1935), *St. John Passion* (1940), cantatas, Psalms, and songs.

WRITINGS: *Musiikin teorian oppijakso* (Principles of Music Theory; 5 vols., Porvoo: I, *Rytmioppi* [Rhythm; 1911–14; rev. ed., 1958]; II, *Säveloppi* [Melody; 1917]; III, *Harmoniaoppi* [Harmony; 1923]; IV, *Polyfoniaoppi* [Polyphony; 1929]; V, *Muoto-oppi* [Form; 1937]); *Puhdasvireisen säveltapailun opas* (Guide to Solfège in Natural Tuning; Helsinki, 1911); *Die Sammlung und Erforschung der Volksmusik in Finnland* (Helsinki, 1933); *Die finnische Volksmusik* (Griefswald, 1935); *Liturgisen sävellystyylin opas* (The Liturgical Style of Composition; Porvoo, 1940); *Der Formenbau in den Symphonien von Jean Sibelius* (Helsinki, 1942); *Der lutherische Choral in Finnland* (Åbo, 1944); *Der Stimmungsgehalt in den Symphonien von Jean Sibelius* (2 vols., Helsinki, 1945–46); *Sävelmuistoja elämäni varrelta* (Porvoo, 1951; memoirs); *Anton Bruckners Symphonien: Untersuchung über Formenbau und Stimmungsgehalt* (3 vols., Helsinki, 1955–57).—NS/LK/DM

Kroll, William, American violinist, teacher, and composer; b. N.Y., Jan. 30, 1901; d. Boston, March 10, 1980. He studied with Marteau (violin) at the Berlin Hochschule für Musik (1911–14). After making his debut in N.Y. in 1915, he continued his studies with Kneisel (violin) and Goetschius (theory) at the Inst. of Musical Art there (1917–22). He played in the Elshuco Trio (1922–29), then was 1st violinist of the Coolidge Quartet (1936–44) and subsequently of his own Kroll Quartet (1944–69); toured with these ensembles, and also made solo appearances. He taught at the Inst. of Musical Art (1922–38), the Mannes Coll. of Music in N.Y. (from 1943), the Peabody Cons. of Music in Baltimore

(1947–65), and the Cleveland Inst. of Music (1964–67); was made prof. of violin at Queens Coll. of the City Univ. of N.Y. (1969). He composed some chamber orch. works, chamber music, and violin pieces.—NS/LK/DM

Krombholc, Jaroslav, esteemed Czech conductor; b. Prague, Jan. 30, 1918; d. there, July 16, 1983. He studied composition with Novák (1937–40) and conducting with Dĕdeček, Ostrčil, and Talich (1940–41) at the Prague Cons. and its Master School; also studied quarter tone music with A. Hába and attended V. Nejedlý's classes at the Univ. of Prague. He first gained attention as a composer, winning 1st prize in a Czech Phil. competition with his Suite for Piano and Orch. (1939). He then made his conducting debut at the Prague National Theater (1940); after serving as chief conductor of the Ostrava Opera (1944–45), he rejoined the roster of the Prague National Theater; later was its chief conductor (1968–75), and chief conductor of the Prague Radio Sym. Orch. (1973–78). He also appeared as a guest conductor with leading European opera houses. He was especially renowned for his idiomatic performances of works by Smetana, Dvořák, Janáček, Martinů, and other Czech composers, as well as for his distinguished interpretations of the music of Prokofiev and Shostakovich.—NS/LK/DM

Krommer (Kramář), Franz Vincez (František Vincenc), Moravian violinist, conductor, and composer; b. Kamenitz, Nov. 27, 1759; d. Vienna, Jan. 8, 1831. He studied with his uncle, Anton Matthias Krommer, a choirmaster and composer in Tuřan (1773–76), but was self- taught in composition. He became a violinist in the orch. of the Duke of Styrum in Simontornya (1786), becoming its music director (1788). He was made Kapellmeister of Pecs Cathedral (1790), then Kapellmeister and composer to Duke Karólyi (1793) and Prince Grassalkovich de Gyarak; became Kapellmeister to Duke Ignaz Fuchs (1798). He returned to Vienna, and was made Ballett- Kapellmeister at the Hofkapelle (1810). He then was Kammertürhüter to the Emperor (1815). He was the last official director of chamber music and court composer to the Habsburg monarchy (from 1818). He wrote a number of accomplished solo concertos for wind instruments, as well as syms., sacred works, much chamber music, and piano pieces.

BIBL.: K. Padrta, *František K. a jeho orchestrální skladby* (F. K. and His Orchestral Compositions; diss., Univ. of Brno, 1949); idem, *František Vincenc Kramář-Krommer: Studie k životopismým a slohovým otázkám* (F.V. K.-K.: Bibliographical and Stylistic Questions; Brno, 1966).—NS/LK/DM

Kromolicki, Joseph, Polish-born German choral conductor, musicologist, and composer; b. Posen, Jan. 16, 1882; d. Berlin, Oct. 11, 1961. He studied with Haberl and Haller in Regensburg and with Pfitzner, Kretzschmar, and Wolf in Berlin, where he took his Ph.D. at the Univ. in 1909 with the diss. *Die Practica artis musicae des Amerus.* He was active as a choral conductor in Berlin. He ed. *Musica Sacra* from 1908 and vols. 45, 48, and 57 of Denkmäler Deutscher Tonkunst. Among his compositions were 5 masses, a Te Deum, organ preludes, and sacred songs.—NS/LK/DM

Kronold, Hans, Polish-American cellist and composer, brother of **Selma Kronold;** b. Kraków, July 3, 1872; d. N.Y., Jan. 10, 1922. He studied in Leipzig and Berlin, then went to the U.S. at the age of 14, where he joined the orch. of the Metropolitan Opera. He then played in the N.Y. Sym. Orch. and also taught at the N.Y. Coll. of Music. He publ. cello pieces and songs.—NS/LK/DM

Kronold, Selma, Polish-American soprano, sister of **Hans Kronold;** b. Kraków, Aug. 18, 1861; d. N.Y., Oct. 9, 1920. She made her debut as Agathe in *Der Freischütz* in Leipzig when she was 16, and then was engaged to sing Wagnerian roles in various European cities. In 1888 she went to the U.S., where she sang leading roles in the American premieres of *Cavalleria rusticana* (Philadelphia, Sept. 9, 1891) and *Pagliacci* (N.Y., June 15, 1893). She first appeared at the Metropolitan Opera in N.Y. as Helmwige in *Die Walküre* (Feb. 6, 1891). She was again on its roster (1898–99; 1903–04), and then founded the Catholic Oratorio Soc.—NS/LK/DM

Kroó, György, Hungarian musicologist; b. Budapest, Aug. 26, 1926. He studied violin at the National Cons. and at the Academy of Music in Budapest, and also attended classes in musicology there with Szabolcsi and Bartha. In 1957 he was named head of music education of the Hungarian Radio. In 1960 he became a guest lecturer at the Academy of Music, joining its permanent faculty in 1967, serving as chairman of its musicology dept. from 1973, and serving as a prof. of musicology (from 1975). His writings include *Robert Schumann* (Budapest, 1958), *Hector Berlioz* (Budapest, 1960), *Bartók Béla szinpadi müvei* (Béla Bartók's Stage Works; Budapest, 1962), *Wenn Schumann ein Tagebuch geführt hätte* (Budapest, 1962), *A "szabadito" opera* (The "Rescue" Opera; Budapest, 1966), *Richard Wagner* (Budapest, 1968), *Bartók kalauz* (A Guide to Bartók; Budapest, 1971; Eng. tr., 1974), *A magyar zeneszerzés harminc éve* (30 Years of Hungarian Composition; Budapest, 1975), *Rácz Aladár* (Budapest, 1979), *Heilawâc. Négy tanulmány Wagner a Nibelung gyürüjéről* (4 Studies on Wagner's *Ring des Nibelungen*; Budapest, 1983), and *Az albumtól a szvitig* (From the Album to the Suite; Budapest, 1986).—NS/LK/DM

Krow, Josef Theodor, Bohemian singer and composer; b. Nové Strašeci, Dec. 19, 1797; d. Draguignan, near Nice, March 1, 1859. He studied at the Piarist Gymnasium in Prague. He sang minor operatic roles in Hungary, Poland, and the Netherlands. After serving as a singing teacher in London (1835–40), he went to Nice (1858). His claim to a small niche in music history rests upon his publication of a drinking song to the words "Tĕšme se blahou nadĕjí" (Blissfully Hoping We Will Enjoy) in 1825, claiming it to be an authentic melody of the Bohemian religious reformer, martyr, and saint Jan Hus. His claim was widely believed; Liszt wrote a piano paraphrase of the song as *Hussittenlied aus dem 15. Jahrhundert,* Balfe made use of it in his opera *The Bohemian Girl,* and Angelo Tessaro in his opera *Giovanni Huss.* Even more spectacular was Krow's success in setting the same tune to his own German words, "Polen wird für ewig Polen," publ. under the pseudo- Polish pseudonym Workinski ("Work" is the crab form of "Krow") in 1831. Caught in the wave of universal sympathy for Poland after the unsuccessful rebellion, the song achieved tremendous popularity all over Europe.—NS/LK/DM

Kroyer, Theodor, eminent German musicologist; b. Munich, Sept. 9, 1873; d. Wiesbaden, Jan. 12, 1945. He studied piano with Lang, counterpoint with Rheinberger, and musicology with Sandberger, taking his Ph.D. from the Univ. of Munich with the diss. *Die Anfänge der Chromatik im italienischen Madrigal des XVI. Jahrhunderts* (publ. in Leipzig, 1902). He completed his Habilitation there in 1902 with his *Ludwig Senfl und sein Motettenstil* (publ. in Munich, 1902). He was music critic of the *Münchener Allgemeine Zeitung* (1897–1910). He taught at the univs. of Munich (1902–20), Heidelberg (1920–23), Leipzig (1923–33), and Cologne (1932–38). In 1925 he purchased for the Univ. of Leipzig the rich collection of instruments, MSS, and portraits from the famous Heyer Museum in Cologne; also in 1925 he began issuing the valuable series Publikationen Älterer Musik. He publ. the studies *Joseph Rheinberger* (Regensburg and Rome, 1916) and *Walter Courvoisier* (Munich and Berlin, 1929). He ed. a vol. (motets and Magnificat) of the complete works of Senfl in Denkmäler der Tonkunst in Bayern, V, Jg. III/2 (1903); also ed. a selection from the works of G. Aichinger for the same series (XVIII, Jg. X/I, 1909).

BIBL.: H. Zenck et al., eds., *T. K.: Festschrift zum 60. Geburtstage am 9. September 1933 überreicht von Freunden und Schülern* (Regensburg, 1933).—**NS/LK/DM**

KRS-One, hip-hop's most eminent teacher, philosopher, edutainer, and maker of hit records (b. Lawrence Krisna "Kris" Parker, Brooklyn, N.Y., Aug. 20, 1965). Kris Parker came of age as rap exploded through the streets of N.Y. in the mid-1970s. His mother brought home singles by groups like the Sugarhill Gang and others. By the time he was 13, however, Parker was homeless and living on the streets. For four years he spent his nights in shelters and his days at the library, where he educated himself in philosophy and theology, among other things. At one Bronx shelter he met a social worker named Scott Sterling, who worked weekends as a DJ, calling himself Scott La Rock. He and Parker started working together under the name Boogie Down Productions; Parker adopted the moniker KRS-One (which he says stands for "knowledge reigns supreme over every one"). They launched a series of records starting with the single "South Bronx." In the rap tradition, the song inspired a verbal battle; MC Shan answered their record with "South Bronx Chill That Noise." They replied with "The Bridge Is Over," followed by their groundbreaking debut album, *Criminal Minded*, released in 1987 by a small N.Y. independent. The record, a prototype for the gansta rap to follow, full of bold beats and solid rhymes about life on the street, sold well. The group was about to sign to Warner Brothers when Sterling was killed trying to break up a streetfight in the Bronx. He was 25 years old.

The loss of his partner only steeled Parker's persistence. Regrouping with his brother Kenny and Derrick "D-Nice" Jones, BDP signed with Jive records. They put out *By All Means Necessary* in 1988. The title is a quote from Malcolm X, whose philosophy inspired the record. The group broke away from violent imagery in favor of lyrics promoting an end to black-on-black crime, and encouraging education. The group also drew on a more varied palette of musical styles in creating their accompaniments, including snippets of reggae and other elements of African-American musical culture. KRS-One took on the sub- sobriquet of "The Teacher" and was even asked to lecture at such august institutions as Yale and Harvard. The album went gold. BDP's next album, 1989's *Ghetto Music: The Blueprint of Hip-Hop*, continued this trend, reaching an even broader audience. The album went to #36 on the pop chart and sold gold. By 1990, with the release of *Edutainment*, Parker had become downright preachy, but the album reached #32 on the charts and also went gold. *Man and his Music* did not fare as well, nor did the *Live Hardcore Worldwide*. 1992's *Sex and Violence* was a stronger, more dangerous album, but suffered from the preachy rep BDP had earned, so Parker started working under his own nom-de-rap, KRS-One.

The first KRS-One album, 1993's *Return of the Boom Bap*, was really a continunation of the BDP style, to the point that it reprised beats from *Criminal Minded* and updated an early track. The album went to #37 pop. Partnering with Marvel Comics, that same year he released a comic book and tape package called *Break the Chain*. Kris's eponymous second solo album didn't fare nearly as well in terms of sales, but it helped resuscitate his reputation among hard-core rappers. This set up the success of 1997's *I Got Next*. Featuring Redman and Rich Nice, the album typified the kind of visceral, socially conscious rap Parker had been putting out for a dozen years. It put him solidly into the Top Ten and sold gold.

KRS-One has become an icon of hip-hop and a bridge between old school and the current crop of rappers. There were cries of sellout when he did commercials for Sprite and Nike, the latter one rapping Gil-Scott Heron's "The Revolution Will Not Be Televised."

DISC.: KRS-ONE: *Return of the Boom Bap* (1993); *KRS-One* (1995); *I Got Next* (1997). **BOOGIE DOWN PRODUCTIONS:** *Criminal Minded* (1987); *By All Means Necessary* (1988); *Ghetto Music: The Blueprint of Hip Hop* (1989); *Edutainment* (1990); *Man and His Music* (1991); *Live Hardcore Worldwide* (1991); *Sex and Violence* (1992).—**HB**

Krstič, Petar, Serbian composer; b. Belgrade, March 2, 1877; d. there, Jan. 21, 1957. He studied with R. Fuchs at the Vienna Cons. He conducted opera at Belgrade's National Theater, and in 1930 became inspector of music schools. His works, based on Serbian national tunes, included the opera *Zulumćar* (Belgrade, Nov. 23, 1927), the cantata, *Jutro Slobode* (1919); several orch. suites of national dances, choruses, and songs. He ed. a Serbian music dictionary.—**NS/LK/DM**

Krückl, Franz, Moravian baritone; b. Edlspitz, Nov. 10, 1841; d. Strasbourg, Jan. 13, 1899. He studied with Dessoff. After making his debut in 1868 in Brünn, he sang in Kassel, Augsburg, Hamburg, and Cologne (1874–86). He taught at the Hoch Cons. in Frankfurt am Main, and in 1892 became director of the Strasbourg Municipal Theater. He publ. *Der Vertrag zwischen Direktor und Mitglied der deutschen Bühne* (1899).—NS/LK/DM

Krueger, Karl (Adalbert), American conductor; b. Atchison, Kans., Jan. 19, 1894; d. Elgin, Ill., July 21, 1979. He learned to play the cello and organ in his early youth, then studied at Midland Coll. in his hometown (B.A. 1913), with Chadwick (composition) and Goodrich (organ) at the New England Cons. of Music in Boston (1914–15), and at the Univ. of Kans. (M.A., 1916). He was an organist at St. Ann's Episcopal Church in N.Y. (1916–20). In 1920 he made a concert tour of Brazil as an organist; then went to Vienna, where he studied theory with Robert Fuchs and conducting with Franz Schalk. He also attended classes in economics at the univs. of Vienna and Heidelberg. He was conductor of the Seattle Sym. Orch. (1926–32), the Kans. City Phil. (1933–43), and the Detroit Sym. Orch. (1943–49). In 1958 he founded the Soc. for the Preservation of the American Musical Heritage and made numerous recordings of American works. He wrote *The Way of the Conductor: His Origins, Purpose and Procedures* (N.Y., 1958).—NS/LK/DM

Krug, (Wenzel) Joseph, German composer and conductor, known as **Krug-Waldsee**; b. Waldsee, Nov. 8, 1858; d. Magdeburg, Oct. 8, 1915. He developed precociously, entering the Stuttgart Cons. at 14 where he studied violin, piano, singing, and theory. After graduating in 1880, he went to Switzerland, where he was active as a teacher in Hofwyl. He then conducted a choral society in Stuttgart (1882–89) and then was chorus master in Hamburg (1889–92) and in Nuremberg and Augsburg (from 1894). He then lived in Magdeburg. He wrote several cantatas in a grand manner, 4 operas, chamber music, and songs.—NS/LK/DM

Krüger, Wilhelm, German pianist, teacher, and composer; b. Stuttgart, Aug. 5, 1820; d. there, June 16, 1883. He studied piano with Ziegele and composition with Lindpaintner. In 1845 he settled in Paris, where he enjoyed an excellent reputation as a pianist and teacher. In 1870 the outbreak of the Franco-Prussian War compelled him to return to Germany, where he was active as a pedagogue. He publ. a number of brilliant salon pieces for piano (168 opus numbers in all), which included caprices, nocturnes, genre pieces (*Harpe éolienne, Guitare*), a *Polonaise-Boléro*, études (*Les Six Jours de la semaine*, etc.), and transcriptions, fantasias, etc., of and on operatic airs.—NS/LK/DM

Krull, Annie (actually, **Marie Anna**), German soprano; b. Rostock, Jan. 12, 1876; d. Schwerin, June 14, 1947. She was a student in Berlin of Hertha Brämer. In 1898 she made her operatic debut in Plauen. From 1901 to 1910 she was a member of the Dresden Court Opera, where she was chosen to create Ulana in Paderewski's *Manru* (May 29, 1901), and Strauss's Di-

emut in *Feuersnot* (Nov. 21, 1901) and Elektra (Jan. 25, 1909). In 1910 she appeared as Elektra at London's Covent Garden, and then sang in Mannheim (1910–12), Weimar (1912–14), and Schwerin (1914–15).—NS/LK/DM

Krummacher, Friedhelm (Gustav-Adolf Hugo Robert), German musicologist; b. Berlin, Jan. 22, 1936. He studied musicology and philosophy in Berlin, Marburg, and Uppsala before completing his education at the univs. of Berlin (Ph.D., 1964) and Erlangen-Nuremberg (Habilitation, 1972). In 1975 he became a prof. at the Detmold Hochschule für Musik. He was a prof. at the Christian-Albrechts-Univ. in Kiel from 1976. From 1980 to 1986 he was vice- president of the Gesellschaft für Musikforschung. He served as chairman of the new Brahms Gesamtausgabe from 1983. In addition to his articles in various series and journals, he publ. the studies *Mendelssohn—der Komponist: Studien zur Kammermusik für Streicher* (Munich, 1978) and *Mahlers III. Symphonie* (Kassel, 1991).—NS/LK/DM

Krumpholtz, Anne-Marie (née **Steckler**), celebrated German harpist; b. Metz, c. 1755; d. London, after 1824. She studied with **Jean-Baptiste Krumpholtz** in Metz, becoming his second wife about 1778. She appeared at a Paris Concert Spirituel in 1779, and subsequently performed many of her husband's compositions there. After having taken a lover by 1788, she went to London. She made her first London appearance on June 2 of that year, and thereafter gave many concerts; also appeared under Salomon's auspices (1791–93). She retired in 1803. Krumpholtz was greatly renowned as a master of her instrument, being considered the equal and often the superior of her husband as a virtuoso.

BIBL.: H. Tribout de Morembert, *A.-M. Steckler: Une Virtuose de la harpe au XVIII° siècle* (Metz, 1962).—NS/LK/DM

Krumpholtz, Jean-Baptiste (Johann Baptist or Jan Křtitel), famous Bohemian harpist and composer; b. Budenice, near Zlonice, May 3, 1742; d. (suicide) Paris, Feb. 19, 1790. He received his first instruction from his father, a bandmaster in the service of Count Kinsky, and later studied and gave concerts in Vienna (1773). He also studied composition with Haydn and was harp soloist in the service of Count Esterházy. He made an extensive tour of Europe in 1776. During his stay in Metz, **Anne-Marie (née Steckler) Krumpholtz** became his pupil and then his second wife (c. 1778). However, she took a lover by 1788 and eloped to England. Krumpholtz, in despair, drowned himself in the Seine. Krumpholtz added to his fame as a harpist by inventing a harp with 2 pedals, loud and soft. He also stimulated Erard to make experiments that led to the invention of the modern pedal mechanism. He was a distinguished composer for the instrument as well, producing several concertos, many sonatas, and various other works. His brother, Wenzel (Václav) Krumpholtz (b. probably in Budenice, c. 1750; d. Vienna, May 2, 1817), was a violinist and composer; he was a member of Prince Esterházy's orch. before joining the orch. of the Vienna Hofoper (1796). He is best remembered as a close friend of Beethoven, and as one of his early champions; upon his death, Beethoven wrote the *Gesang der Mönche* for 3 Men's Voices after Schiller, Wo 0104. Krumpholtz himself wrote several violin pieces. —NS/LK/DM

Krupa, Gene, famed and flamboyant swing-era drummer, leader; b. Chicago, Jan. 15, 1909; d. Yonkers, N.Y., Oct. 16, 1973. He attended Bowen H.S., and later studied at St. Joseph's Coll. in Ind.; during summer vacations he played a season with the Frivolians in Madison, Wisc. In 1925 he began studying percussion with teachers Al Silverman, Ed Straight, and Roy Knapp. He made his first records with the McKenzie-Condon Chicagoans in 1927. Condon and others later claimed this was the first use of a full drum set with a bass drum, which is not true; even the ODJB's 1917 recordings have a quite audible bass drum. Krupa moved to N.Y. in 1929 and began working for Red Nichols. During the next two years he worked mainly in theatre bands directed by Nichols. During the early 1930s he played in various commercial bands. He starred with Benny Goodman from December 1934 until February 1938, then formed his own big band for his debut at Steel Pier, Atlantic City, in April 1938. In the early 1940s, his band featured both Roy Eldridge (in one of the early attempts at interracial performances) and Anita O'Day. He continued to lead his own successful band until May 1943 when circumstances outside of music forced him to disband. He was charged with hiring an underage band boy and was briefly arrested. In San Francisco for a short while, he returned to N.Y. and studied harmony and composition. He rejoined Benny Goodman in September 1943 until mid-December 1943, then joined Tommy Dorsey in N.Y, remaining with that band until the following July. He left to organize his own big band, which got under way late in 1944. Initially it proved to be an enormous band hovering between the 30- and 40-piece mark; it settled down to a more usual format and enjoyed wide success until 1951. From September 1951 he began to tour regularly in "Jazz at the Philharmonic" shows, usually featured with his own trio. He toured with his own trio/quartet in the 1950s (including trips overseas to Europe and Asia), and also appeared regularly at the Metropole (N.Y.). He was temporarily inactive in late 1960 due to heart strain, then resumed leading. In June 1963 led specially formed a big band in Hollywood, and a year later made second visit to Japan with own quartet. From 1954 Krupa and Cozy Cole ran a drum school in N.Y. He was in semi-retirement from October 1967 until leading own quartet at Hotel Plaza (N.Y.), 1970. He resumed regular playing, occasionally touring, and continued playing until shortly before his death from leukemia.

He appeared in many films, among them *George White's Scandals, Some Like It Hot* (1941, not the later film with Marilyn Monroe), *Beat the Band,* and *The Benny Goodman Story.* A supposedly biographical film, *The Gene Krupa Story* (retitled *Drum Crazy* in some countries) was released in 1959, the role of Krupa played by Sal Mineo; Krupa recorded the soundtrack.

Krupa was an exciting, effective, and highly interactive drummer. He is said to have "popularized" the drums with his extended, virtuosic solos. He got stereotyped by critics and some musicians for his tom-tom beat on "Sing, Sing, Sing," and has been often called loud and exhibitionistic. But in fact he was the lifeblood of the Goodman band, and his work with the small groups was sensational. Like other loud drummers such as Elvin Jones and Max Roach, he amazes by being able to respond to what he hears around him with great intuition. This is perhaps easiest to hear on the beautifully recorded reunion of the quartet for RCA in 1963, *Together Again.* As early as the mid-1930s, in a trio with Jess Stacy, his offbeat rimshots and snare accents create a counterpoint that was quite rare for the time. Yet he had little direct influence on the next generation, probably because his time feel was an older style—many forgot he had first recorded in 1927—which was probably, deep down, also the source for much of the criticism. That is, by the time he reached his height of fame with Goodman, his time feel was already outmoded by Jo Jones, Kenny Clarke and others.

DISC.: *Drummin' Man* (1938); *Drum Boogie* (1940); *Town Hall Concert* (1945); *Trio at JATP* (1946); *Let Me Off Uptown* (1949); *Sing Sing Sing* (1954); *Jazz Rhythms of G.K.* (1955); *G.K. Quartet* (1955); *Drummer Man* (1956); *Hey...Here's G.K.* (1957); *G.K. Plays Gerry Mulligan* (1958); *G.K. Story* (soundtrack; 1959); *Percussion King* (1961); *Great New G.K. Quartet* (1964); *Radio Years, 1940* (1995); *1946 Live!* (1995); *Disc Jockey Jump; Dark Eyes.* B. Goodman: *Together Again* (1963).

BIBL.: C. Garrod, B. Korst, *G.K. and His Orch.* (Zephyrhills, Fla.); Arnold Shaw, *G.K., Complete Life Story*; G. Hall and S. Kramer, *G. K. and His Orch.* (Laurel, Md., 1975); K. Stratemann, *Buddy Rich and G. K.: A Filmodiscography* (Lubeck, Germany, 1980); B. Crowther, *G. K.: His Life and Times* (Tunbridge Wells and N.Y., 1987); Bruce Klauber, *World of G.K.: That Legendary Drummin' Man* (Ventura, Calif. 1990).—JC/LP

Krushelnitskaya, Salomea (Ambrosivna), noted Russian soprano; b. Belavyntsy, near Tarnopol, Sept. 23, 1872; d. Lwów, Nov. 16, 1952. As a child she sang in a village choir. After studying voice with Wysocki in Lemberg, she made her debut there in *La Favorite* in 1892. She then went to Milan, where she took lessons with Crespi (1893–96. From 1898 to 1902 she was a member of the Warsaw Opera. She then scored a remarkable success as Cio-Cio-San in Brescia (1904). After singing at La Scala in Milan (from 1906) and in Buenos Aires (1906–13), she made her operatic farewell in Naples in 1920; subsequently devoted herself to concert appearances. She taught at the Lwów Cons. (from 1939). Her voice was of particular beauty, spanning fully 3 octaves. Among her most notable roles were Brünnhilde, Isolde, Elisabeth in *Tannhäuser,* Elsa in *Lohengrin,* Aida, Desdemona, and Elektra. In her concert programs she promoted songs by Ukrainian composers. A collection of articles about her career was publ. in Ukrainian (Lwów, 1956).—NS/LK/DM

Kruyf, Ton de, Dutch composer; b. Leerdam, Oct. 3, 1937. He attended the courses in new music in Darmstadt and studied with Fortner in Heidelberg. His works utilize various contemporary procedures, including serialism.

WORKS: DRAMATIC: Opera: *Spinoza* (Amsterdam, June 15, 1971); *Quauhquauhtinchan in den vreemde* (Quauhquauhtinchan in Foreign Parts), radio opera (1971; Hilversum, June 3, 1972). **Ballet:** *Chronologie II* (1967); *Himalaya* (1995); *Je maintiendrai...* (1999). **ORCH.:** *Mouvements symphoniques* (1956); *Sinfonietta* for Strings (1956; rev. 1965); *5 Impromptus* (1958); *Sinfonia II* (1969); *Quatre pas de deux* for Flute and Orch. (1972); *Echoi* for Oboe and Strings (1973); *Spring-time fantasietta* for Strings (1978); *Canti e capricci* for Cello and Orch. (1984; rev. 1989); *Adagio, in memoriam Wolfgang Fortner* (1987); *Intrada* for Wind Orch. (1989); *Partita* (1994); *Canto di speranza* (1998). **CHAMBER:** *Aubade* for Horn, 2 Trumpets, Trombone, and Tuba (1957; rev. 1967); Quartet for Flute, Bassoon, Viola, and Cello (1959); Flute Sonatina (1960); *Music* for String Quartet (1962); *Partita* for String Quartet (1962); Sonata for Solo Cello (1964); *Pas de deux* for Flute and Piano (1968); *Serenata per complesso da camera* for Flute, Clarinet, Harp, and String Quintet (1968); *Mosaico* for Oboe and String Trio (1969); *Séance* for Harp, Piano, 4 Horns, and 5 Percussion (1969); *Musica portuensis* for 4 Saxophones (1983); *7 Preludes* for Vibraphone and Xylorimba (1996). **Piano:** *Sgrafitti* (1960); *Arioso* for Piano, 4-Hands (1975); *Arcadia* (1996). **VOCAL:** *Einst dem Grau der Nacht enttaucht...* for Mezzo-soprano and Chamber Orch. (1964); *Pour faire le portrait d'un oiseau* for Mezzo-soprano and Chamber Orch. (1965); *Fragment No. IV from Shakespeare Sonnets* for Low Voice, Flute, and Cello (1965); *De blinde zwemmers* for Youth Chorus and Chamber Orch. (1966); *Töne aus der Ferne* for Alto and Chamber Orch. (1967); *Twee uur* for Speaker and Orch. (1973); *Meditations* for Baritone and Chamber Orch. (1976); *Cantate* for Tenor, Chorus, and Chamber Orch. (1978); *Ode to the West Wind* for Chorus and Orch. (1978).—NS/LK/DM

Kubelík, Jan, famous Czech-born Hungarian violinist, father of **(Jeroným) Rafael Kubelík;** b. Michle, near Prague, July 5, 1880; d. Prague, Dec. 5, 1940. He began violin training with his father, then studied with Ševčik (violin) and Foerster (composition) at the Prague Cons. (1892–98). After making his Prague debut in 1898, he continued his studies in Vienna, where he performed for the first time on Nov. 26, 1898. In 1900 he made his London debut, and thereafter made a series of triumphant tours of Europe and the U.S. He was awarded the Gold Medal of the Phil. Soc. of London in 1902. In 1903 he married a Hungarian countess and became a naturalized Hungarian citizen. He continued his active career for over 4 decades, giving a series of farewell concerts in 1939–40. On May 8, 1940, he gave his last concert in Prague, after his beloved homeland had been dismembered by the Nazis. Kubelík was one of the foremost virtuosos of his day. He also composed; wrote 6 violin concertos, as well as a Sym. and some chamber music; likewise prepared cadenzas for the Beethoven, Brahms, and Tchaikovsky violin concertos.

BIBL.: J. Celeda, *J. K.* (Prague, 1930); B. Voldan, *Skladby J.a K.a* (J. K.'s Compositions; Prague, 1933); H. Doležil, *Mistr housli J. K.* (The Master of the Violin J. K.; Prague, 1941); K. Hoffmeister, *J. K.* (Prague, 1941); J. Dostal, ed., *J. K.* (Prague, 1942).—NS/LK/DM

Kubelík, (Jeroným) Rafael, eminent Czech-born Swiss conductor, son of **Jan Kubelík;** b. Býchory,

near Kolín, June 29, 1914. He studied violin with his father, and then continued his musical training at the Prague Cons. He made his conducting debut with the Czech Phil. in Prague on Jan. 24, 1934, then was conductor at the National Theater in Brno (1939–41). He was chief conductor of the Czech Phil. from 1942 to 1948, one of the most difficult periods in the history of the orch. and the Czech nation. He refused to collaborate with the Nazi occupation authorities; when the Communists took control of the government in 1948, he left the country for the West, vowing not to return until the political situation changed. He appeared as a guest conductor in England and Western Europe, then made his U.S. debut with the Chicago Sym. Orch. on Nov. 17, 1949; his success led to his appointment as the orch.'s music director in 1950; however, his inclusion of many contemporary works in his programs and his insistence on painstaking rehearsals antagonized some of his auditors, including members of the Chicago press, causing him to resign his post in 1953. He subsequently was music director at the Royal Opera House at Covent Garden in London (1955–58); his tenure was notable for important productions of *Les Troyens*, *Boris Godunov* (in the original version), and *Jenůfa*. He then was chief conductor of the Bavarian Radio Sym. Orch. in Munich (1961–79). He made his Metropolitan Opera debut in N.Y. as its first music director on Oct. 22, 1973, conducting *Les Troyens*; however, he again became an epicenter of controversy, and soon submitted his resignation. In spite of the contretemps, his artistic integrity remained intact; he continued to appear widely as a guest conductor in Western Europe and the U.S. In light of his controversial tenure in Chicago, it was ironic that he became an honored guest conductor with that orch. in later years. He retired in 1985. Following the "velvet" revolution which toppled the hard-line Communist regime in Czechoslovakia in 1989, Kubelík was invited to return to his free homeland to conduct Smetana's *Má Vlast* at the Prague Spring Festival in 1990. Kubelík was the foremost Czech conductor of his generation; in addition to his idiomatic and authoritative performances of the music of his native country, he was greatly esteemed for his distinguished interpretations of the standard repertoire, which were marked by a pristine musicianship, unfettered by self-indulgence. Kubelík became a naturalized Swiss citizen in 1966. His 2nd wife was **Elsie Morison**. He also composed several operas, including *Veronika* (Brno, April 19, 1947) and *Cornelia Faroli* (Augsburg, 1972), a Sym. for Chorus and Orch. (1941), Sym. in 1 Movement (WDR, Cologne, 1974), *Sequences* for Orch. (Lucerne Festival, 1976), Sym., *Orphikon* (N.Y., April 2, 1981), *Symphonic Peripeteia* for Organ and Orch. (Chicago Sym. Orch., March 14, 1985), a number of choral works, 6 string quartets and other chamber music works, and songs.—NS/LK/DM

Kubiak, Teresa (originally, **Tersa Wojtaszek**), Polish soprano; b. Ldzan, Dec. 26, 1937. She studied with Olga Olgina at the ód Academy of Music. In 1965 she made her debut as Halk in Monziuszko's opera in ód, and then appeared with the Warsaw Opera. She made her U.S. debut in a concert performance of Goldmark's *Die Königen von Saba* in N.Y. (1970); then appeared with the San Francisco Opera, with the Chicago Lyric Opera, and at the Glyndebourne Festival (1971). In 1972 she made her first appearance at London's Covent Garden as Cio-Cio-San. She made her Metropolitan Opera debut in N.Y. as Liza in *The Queen of Spades* on Jan. 18, 1973; that same year, she appeared at the Vienna State Opera as Elsa. She continued to make occasional appearances at the Metropolitan Opera until her final appearance there as Elisabeth in *Tannhäuser* on Jan. 31, 1987. In 1990 she joined the faculty of the Ind. Univ. School of Music in Bloomington. Among her other roles were Senta, Aida, Tosca, Jenůfa, and many from the 20th-century repertoire.—**NS/LK/DM**

Kubik, Gail (Thompson), American composer; b. South Coffeyville, Okla., Sept. 5, 1914; d. Covina, Calif., July 20, 1984. He was a student of Samuel Belov (violin), Rogers (composition), and McHose (theory) at the Eastman School of Music in Rochester, N.Y. (B.M., 1934), Scott Willits (violin) and Sowerby (composition) at the American Cons. of Music in Chicago (M.M., 1936), and Piston (composition) at Harvard Univ. (1937–38); he also worked with Boulanger. After teaching at Monmouth (Ill.) Coll. (1934), Dakota Wesleyan Univ. in Mitchell, S.Dak. (1936–37), and at Teachers Coll. at Columbia Univ. (1938–40), he was a staff composer and adviser for NBC in N.Y. (1940–42). In 1942–43 he was director of music for the film bureau of the Office of War Information, and then was a composer-conductor for the U.S. Army Air Force Motion Picture Unit (1943–46). He later was composer-in-residence at Kans. State Univ. (1969), Gettysburg Coll. (1970), and Scripps Coll. in Claremont, Calif. (1970 80). In 1944 and 1965 he held Guggenheim fellowships. He held the American Prix de Rome in 1950–51. In 1952 he received the Pulitzer Prize in Music for his *Symphonie concertante*. He composed much music for films, radio, and television which exerted a liberating force on his serious scores. The latter were notable for their neo-Classical bent in which rhythmic patterns were apt to be stimulatingly asymmetric.

WORKS: DRAMATIC: *A Mirror for the Sky*, folk opera (Eugene, Ore., May 23, 1939); *Boston Baked Beans*, opera piccola (1950; N.Y., March 9, 1952); film scores: *Thunderbolt* (1943–45); *C-Man* (1949); *The Miner's Daughter* (1950); *Gerald McBoing-Boing* (1950; concert version for Narrator, 9 Instruments, and Percussion, 1950); *The Desperate Hours* (1955); radio and television scores. **ORCH.:** *American Caprice* for Piano and Orch. (1933); 2 violin concertos: No. 1 (1934; rev. 1936; Chicago, Jan. 2, 1938) and No. 2 (1940; rev. 1941); Suite (1935); *Scherzo* (1940); *Music for Dancing* (1940–46); *Folk Song Suite* (1941–46); *Bachata* (1947); *Spring Valley Overture* (1947); 3 syms.: No. 1 (1947–49), No. 2 (1955; Louisville, April 7, 1956), and No. 3 (1956; N.Y., Feb. 28, 1957); *Symphonie concertante* for Piano, Viola, Trumpet, and Orch. (1951; N.Y., Jan. 27, 1952; rev. 1953); *Thunderbolt Overture* (1953); *Scenario* (1957); *Scenes* (1964); *Prayer and Toccata* for Organ and Chamber Orch. (1968); Piano Concerto (1982–83). **CHAMBER:** *2 Sketches* for String Quartet (1932); *Trivialities* for Flute, Horn, and String Quartet (1934); Piano Trio (1934); Wind Quintet (1937); Suite for 3 Recorders (1941); Violin Sonatina (1941); *Little Suite* for Flute and 2 Clarinets (1947); *Soliloquy and Dance* for Violin and Piano (1948); *Divertimento No. 1* for 13 Players (1959), *No. 2* for 8 Players (1959), and *No. 3* for

Piano Trio (1970–71); *Music for Bells* for Handbells (1975). **P i a n o :** *Celebrations and Epilogue* (1938–50); *Song and Scherzo* for 2 Pianos (1940; rev. 1962); Sonatina (1941); Sonata (1947); *Intermezzo: Music for Cleveland* (1967); Sym. for 2 Pianos (1980; based on Sym. No. 1, 1947–49). **VOCAL:** *In Praise of Johnny Appleseed* for Bass- baritone, Chorus, and Orch. (1938; rev. 1961); *Choral Profiles, Folk Song Sketches* for Chorus (1938); *Litany and Prayer* for Men's Chorus, Brass, and Percussion (1943–45); *Memphis Belle* for Speaker and Orch. (1944); *Fables in Song* for Mezzo-soprano or Baritone and Piano (1950–60); *A Christmas Set* for Chamber Chorus and Chamber Orch. (1968); *A Record of Our Time*, cantata for Narrator, Soloist, Chorus, and Orch. (Manhattan, Kans., Nov. 11, 1970); *Scholastica* for Chorus (1972); *Magic, Magic, Magic!* for Alto, Chamber Chorus, and Chamber Orch. (San Antonio, April 25, 1976).—**NS/LK/DM**

Kubín, Rudolf, Czech composer and pedagogue; b. Ostrava, Jan. 10, 1909; d. there, Jan. 11, 1973. He was a student at the Prague Cons. (1924–29) of Junek (cello) and A. Hába (composition). In 1929 he became a cellist in the Prague Radio Sym. Orch., and beginning in 1935 he alternated as music director of the Ostrava and Brno sections of the Czech Radio. After World War II, he helped to organize the Ostrava Higher Music Teaching Coll., of which he served as director in 1953–54; when it became a cons., he was its director also (1958–60). In 1959 the Czech government honored him with the Order of Work. His studies with Hába prompted him to compose several quarter tone pieces early in his career. After pursuing expressionist paths, he took up the cause of socialist realism.

WORKS: DRAMATIC: *Žena, která zdělila muže* (The Woman Who Did Down Men) or *Ženich z prérie* (The Bridegroom from the Prairie), operetta (Prague, March 29, 1930); *Tři mušketýří* (The 3 Musketeers) or *Královnin náhrdelník* (The Queen's Necklace), musical comedy (Prague, April 19, 1931); *Letní noc* (Summer Night), radio opera (Czech Radio, Sept. 26, 1931); *Kavalír* (The Cavalier), operetta (1932); *Cirkus života* (Circus of Life), operetta (Prague, May 15, 1933); *Ta česká muzika, ta srdce pronika* (That Czech Music, it Speaks Straight to the Heart), folk play (1933); *Zasnoubení na paloučku* (A Greenwood Betrothal), folk play (1933); *Zpěv uhlí* (Song of Coal; unfinished; overture, 1936); *Děvčátko z kolonie* (The Girl From the Mining Settlement), operetta (Ostrava, March 22, 1942; rev. version, Ostrava, Sept. 10, 1955); *Naši furianti* (Our Defiant Ones), comic opera (1942–43; rev. version, Ostrava, Sept. 18, 1949); *Selský kníže* (The Village Prince), operetta-burlesque (Prague, April 10, 1947); *Koleje mládí* (The Ways of Youth), play (Brno, Sept. 15, 1949); *Pasekáří* (People of the Glades), operetta (1950–51; rev. version, Ostrava, April 30, 1954); *Jiříkovo vidění* (Jiřík's Vision), folk opera (1952; unfinished); *Heva*, folk operetta (1955–64). **ORCH.:** *Prologue* (1929); *Czech Overture* (1932); Sinfonietta (1935–36); Trombone Concerto (1936); *Symphony Concertante* No. 1 for 4 Horns and Strings (1937) and No. 2 for Cello and Orch. (1969); Clarinet Concerto (1939); 2 violin concertos (1940, 1960); *Moravian Rhapsody* (1942); *May*, overture (1945); Accordion Concerto (1950); *Ostrava*, symphonic cycle (1950–51); *Geroj, in memoriam Klement Gottwald* (1953); *Julius Fučík*, overture (1954); Cello Concerto (1960); Tuba Concertino (1962); *Salutation to Frenštát* (1968); *Reminiscence*, sym. (1968); *Ostrava Variations* (1971). **CHAMBER:** String Quartet (1925–26); *Scherzo* for 2 Clarinets and Piano (1933) and for Violin and Piano (1942); *Ballade* for 4 Cellos (1942); Nonet (1944); Suite for Cello (1970). **Q u a r t e r T o n e P i a n o :** 2 suites (1925,

1927); 2 fantasies (1926, 1927); *Piano Pieces* (1927). **VOCAL:** Cantatas; song cycles; solo songs.

BIBL.: V. Grebor, *R. K.: Obraz života a díla* (Ostrava, 1975). —NS/LK/DM

Kučera, Václav, Czech composer and musicologist; b. Prague, April 29, 1929. He studied musicology and aesthetics at the Charles Univ. in Prague (1948–51), and then composition (with Shebalin) and musicology at the Moscow Cons. (1951–56). Returning to Prague, he worked at the Czech Radio (1956–59). After serving as head of contemporary musical studies for the Union of Czech Composers (1959–62), he was head of studies in music aesthetics for the Inst. of Musicology (1962–69). From 1969 to 1983 he served as general secretary of the Union of Czech Composers and Concert Artists. In 1972 he joined the faculty of the Academy of Music and Dramatic Arts as a teacher of contemporary composition, and later was prof. of composition there from 1988. From 1988 to 1990 he was president of the "Prague Spring" International Music Festival. In 1972 he received the Prix d'Italia for his *Lidice* and in 1983 received the prize of the Union of Czech Composers and Concert Artists for his String Quartet, *Consciousness of Continuities*. In 1986 he was made a Merited Artist by the Czech government. After following the precepts of socialist realism in his scores, he developed an advanced compositional style in which he sometimes utilized electronics. Among his books are a study of Mussorgsky (1959) and a theoretical vol. on creative experiments in music (1973).

WORKS: DRAMATIC: *Zbojnický oheň* (Brigand's Fire), dance drama (1958); *Festivalová pohádka* (Festival Fairy Tale), ballet (1959); *Sdrce a sen* (Heart and Dream), ballet (1973); *Život bez chyby* (Life without Fault), ballet (1979). **ORCH.:** Sym. (1962); *Krysař* (The Pied Piper), stereophonic concertino for Flute and 2 Chamber Orchs. (1964); *Obraz* (Tableau) for Piano and Orch. (1966–70); *Salut*, symphonic mosaic (1975); *Operand* for Chamber Orch. (1979); *Fortunata, Omaggio à Vivaldi* for Chamber Orch. (1979); *Avanti* (1981); *Balada a romance* for Chamber Orch. (1984); *Sapporo*, symphonic poem with chorus (1991); *Imaginative Concerto: A Tribute to Salvador Dali* for Guitar and Strings (1994); *Vzývání radosti* (Invocation for Joy) for Guitar Orch. (1997; also for Guitar Quartet); *Hovory důvěrné* (Intimate Conversations), double concertino for Bass Clarinet, Piano, and Strings (1998). **CHAMBER:** *Dramas* for 9 Instruments (1961); *Protests* for Violin, Piano, and Timpani (1963); *Genesis* for Flute and Harp (1965); *Hic sunt homines* for Piano Quartet (1965); *Spectra* for Dulcimer (1965); *Diptchon* for Flute, Bass Clarinet, Piano, and Percussion (1966); *Duodrama* for Bass Clarinet and Piano (1967); *To be* for Percussion Quartet (1968); *Panta rhei* for Flute, Vibraphone, and Percussion (1969); *Invariant* for Bass Clarinet, Piano, and Tape (1969); *Scenario* for Flute, Violin, and Cello (1970); *Argot* for Brass Quintet (1970); *Diario* for Guitar (1971); *Taboo a Due Boemi* for Bass Clarinet, Piano, and Percussion (1972); *Spring Manifesto: In Memory of Prague, May 1945* for 4 Players (1974); *Consciousness of Continuities*, string quartet (1976); *Horizons* for 5 Players (1978); *Aphorisms* for Violin and Piano (1978); *Epigrams* for Violin and Cello (1978); *Science Fiction* for Jazz Ensemble (1980); *Rosen für Rosa* for Harpsichord (1980); *Aquarelles* for Flute and Guitar (1981); *Stenograms* for Flute, Cello, and Piano (1981); *Wagnerian Inventions* for Flute (1982); *Capriccios* for Violin and Guitar (1982); *Nouvelles* for Guitar (1984); *Eruptions* for 5 Cellos (1984); *Gogh's*

Self-Portrait for Bass Clarinet and Tape (1985); *Prague Ritornelles* for Bass Clarinet and Piano (1986); *Prefigurations, Hommage à Hans Arp* for Guitar (1986); *Ex abrupto* for 2 Percussionists (1987); *Elegy* for Viola (1988); *Duettinos* for Oboe and Bassoon (1988); *Pieter Brueghel Inspirations* for Flute, Bass Clarinet, and Piano (1988); *Pastoralissimo* for Horn (1990); *Consonanza*, trio for 2 Oboes and English Horn (1990); *Celebrations of Phantasy, Hommage à Max Ernst* for 2 Guitars (1991); *Vivaldiana* for 12 Instruments (1991); *Oraculum* for Bass Clarinet and Harp (1992); *Arcades* for Trombone and Piano (1993). **P i a n o :** *Cardiograms* (1983); *Tuning* (1990–94). **VOCAL:** *The Time Has Set In*, cantata for Men's Chorus and Orch. (1961); *The Blue Planet* for Men's Chorus (1964); *Orbis pictus* for Chorus and Ancient Instruments (1975); *Amoroso*, song cycle for Mezzo-soprano, Flute, and Harp (1975); *Catharsis* for Soprano and Chamber Ensemble (1979); *Ecce homo* for Bass, Violin, Viola, Cello, Harp, and Percussion (1980); *Listening to Time* for Voice and Percussion (1981); *Bird*, melodrama for Reciter, 2 Violins, Viola, Cello, and Marimba (1983); *The Painter is Painting* for Children's Chorus (1984); *Bitter and Other Songs* for Soprano and Piano (1985); *A Serious Hour*, song cycle for High Voice and Guitar (1986); *The Decisive Time*, cantata for Chorus and Orch. (1988); *Freedom* for Men's Chorus (1991). **ELECTRONIC:** *A Kinetic Ballet* (1968); *Kinechromie* (1969). **OTHER:** *Lidice*, radio musical-dramatic fresco (1972); *Spartacus*, quadrophonic musical score (1976). —NS/LK/DM

Kucharz, Johann Baptist (real name, **Jan Křtitel Kuchař**), Bohemian organist and composer; b. Chotec, March 5, 1751; d. Prague, Feb. 18, 1829. He began his music training with the Vrchlabí cantor and organist A. Tham. After organ studies at the Jesuit colleges in Königgratz and Gitschin, he completed his training in Prague with J.N. Seger. From 1772 to 1790 he was organist of Prague's Heinrichskirche, and then at the monastic church of the Premonstratensian Abbey from 1790 until his death. From 1791 to 1797 he also was maestro di cappella of Prague's Italian Opera. Kucharz was highly regarded as an organist. In addition to much organ music, he also composed some sacred works. He was the first to arrange vocal scores of works by Mozart. —NS/LK/DM

Kücken, Friedrich Wilhelm, German conductor and composer; b. Bleckede, Nov. 16, 1810; d. Schwerin, April 3, 1882. He studied thoroughbass with his brother-in-law, the organist Friedrich Lührss, and piano with Aron and Rettberg in Schwerin; in 1832, went to Berlin, where he studied counterpoint with Birnbach; from 1841 to 1843, studied with Sechter in Vienna, and later took courses in orchestration with Halévy and composition with Bordogni. He was Kapellmeister in Stuttgart (1851–61). He wrote the operas *Die Flucht nach der Schweiz* (Berlin, Feb. 26, 1839) and *Der Prätendent* (Stuttgart, April 21, 1847) as well as sonatas for violin and for cello, etc. However, he is most noted for his songs, which include *Ach, wie wär's möglich dann, Das Sternelein, O weine nicht, Trab, trab, Das Mädchen von Juda*, and *The Swallows*.—NS/LK/DM

Kuckertz, Josef, German ethnomusicologist; b. Würseln, near Aachen, Nov. 24, 1930. After initial schooling at the Rheinische Musikschule in Cologne, he studied musicology with Marius Schneider at the Univ. of Cologne (Ph.D., 1962, with the diss. *Gestaltvariation in den von Bartók gesammelten rumänischen Colinden*). He then taught at the Univ. of Cologne, completing his Habilitation with a study of South Indian music (1967). His research focuses on the music and theory of the more developed oriental cultures and the relationship between oriental and European music, with particular emphasis on South India.—NS/LK/DM

Kuebler, David, American tenor; b. Detroit, July 23, 1947. He was a student of Thomas Peck in Chicago and of Audrey Field in London. In 1972 he joined the Santa Fe Opera. Following his European debut at the Bern Opera in 1974 as Tamino, he sang for the first time at the Glyndebourne Festival in 1976 as Ferrando. In 1980 he appeared as the Steersman in *Der fliegende Holländer* at the Bayreuth Festival. He made his Metropolitan Opera debut in N.Y. on Feb. 4, 1981, as Tamino. From 1987 to 1990 he again sang at the Glyndebourne Festival. After appearing as Don Ottavio in Rome and Madrid in 1989, he sang at the London Promenade Concerts in 1991 in Dvořák's *The Spectre's Bride*. In 1992 he sang Berlioz's Faust at the Bregenz Festival. He returned to Rome in 1997 to sing Henry in *Les Vêpres siciliennes*. Among his other roles were Idamante, Nemorino, Jacquino, Pinkerton, Rodolfo, and Flamand.—NS/LK/DM

Kuerti, Anton (Emil), esteemed Austrian-born pianist; b. Vienna, July 21, 1938. He was taken by his parents to the U.S. as a child and was naturalized in 1944. He began piano studies with Edward Goldman in Boston and made his debut as soloist in the Grieg Piano Concerto with the Boston Pops Orch. at age 9. He also received training in piano from Bodky and Gregory Tucker and in composition from Arthur Shepherd at the Longy School in Cambridge, Mass. (1948–52), in piano from Balogh and in composition from Cowell at the Peabody Inst. in Baltimore (1952–53), in piano from Arthur Loesser and Beryl Rubinstein and in composition from Marcel Dick at the Cleveland Inst. of Music (B.Mus., 1955), and in piano from Rudolf Serkin and Horszowski at the Curtis Inst. of Music in Philadelphia (diploma, 1959). After winning the Levintritt Competition in N.Y. in 1957, he toured widely, settling in 1965 in Toronto, and later became a naturalized Canadian citizen (1984). He was pianist-in-residence (1965–68) and an assoc. prof. (1968–72) at the Univ. of Toronto; in later years, he gave occasional master classes, but he devoted himself mainly to concertizing. In 1988 he exercised his Canadian citizenship by running as a candidate for Parliament. He was awarded honorary doctorates in 1987 by York Univ. in Toronto and Laurentian Univ. in Sudbury. In 1998 he was made an Officer of the Order of Canada. While Kuerti has won accolades for his fine performances of the Viennese classics, he has also played various works by contemporary composers. Among his compositions are 2 string quartets (1954, 1972), *Linden Suite* for Piano (1970), *Magog* for Cello and Piano (1972), *Symphony "Epomeo"* (1973), Violin Sonata (1973), *6 Arrows* for Piano (1973), *Piano Man Suite* (1985), Piano Concerto (1985), and a Trio for Clarinet, Cello, and Piano (1989).—NS/LK/DM

Kufferath, Hubert Ferdinand, German violinist, pianist, conductor, and composer, brother of **Johann Hermann Kufferath** and **Louis Kufferath,** and father of **Maurice Kufferath;** b. Mülheim an der Ruhr, June 11, 1818; d. St. Josse-ten-Noode, near Brussels, June 23, 1896. He studied first with his brothers, then with Hartmann (violin) in Cologne and Schneider in Dessau (1833–36). He subsequently studied violin with David at the Leipzig Cons., where he also took courses with Mendelssohn and Hauptmann. He conducted the Cologne Männergesangverein (1841), then settled in Brussels (1844), where he ultimately served as prof. of counterpoint and fugue at the Cons. (1872–96). He wrote syms., piano concertos, and piano pieces.—NS/LK/DM

Kufferath, Johann Hermann, German violinist, conductor, and composer, brother of **Hubert Ferdinand Kufferath** and **Louis Kufferath;** b. Mülheim an der Ruhr, May 12, 1797; d. Wiesbaden, July 28, 1864. He studied with his father, then violin with Spohr and composition with Hauptmann. In 1823 he became music director in Bielefeld, and, in 1830, in Utrecht, of the Collegium Musicum and Gesangverein (until 1862). His works include overtures, cantatas, and motets.—NS/LK/DM

Kufferath, Louis, German pianist, conductor, and composer, brother of **Hubert Ferdinand Kufferath** and **Johann Hermann Kufferath;** b. Mülheim an der Ruhr, Nov. 10, 1811; d. St. Josse-ten-Noode, near Brussels, March 2, 1882. He studied with his brother Johann Hermann, and with Schneider in Dessau. He toured as a pianist in Holland and Germany. He was director of the Leeuwarden Cons. (1836–50), after which he was in Ghent, and later in Brussels. He wrote a Mass, a cantata, 250 canons, many piano pieces in salon style, and songs.—NS/LK/DM

Kufferath, Maurice, Belgian cellist, conductor, and writer on music of German descent, son of **Hubert Ferdinand Kufferath;** b. St. Josse-ten-Noode, near Brussels, Jan. 8, 1852; d. Uccle, near Brussels, Dec. 8, 1919. He studied with his father, then cello with the Servais (père and fils); also studied law and art history in Brussels and Leipzig. He wrote on politics for *L'Indépendance Belge,* and, from 1874, was ed. of *Le Guide Musical* (1875–90), subsequently being its main proprietor (until 1914). With G. Guidé, he was co-director of the Théâtre Royal de la Monnaie (1900–14). An ardent Wagnerian, he publ. *Le Théâtre de Wagner de Tannhäuser à Parsifal* (6 vols., Brussels, 1891–98). Under the pen name Maurice Reymont, he tr. Wagner's librettos and texts of songs by Brahms into French.

BIBL.: L. Solvay, *Notice sur M. K.* (Brussels, 1923).—NS/LK/DM

Küffner, Joseph, German composer; b. Würzburg, March 31, 1776; d. there, Sept. 8, 1856. He wrote 2 operas: *Sporn und Schärpe* and *Der Cornett*, 7 syms., 10 overtures, music for military band and wind instruments, Fantasy for Violin and Orch., Quintet for Flute and Strings, string quartets, trios and duets for flutes, duets for clarinet, violin sonatas, guitar music, etc.

BIBL.: M. Henke, *J. K.: Leben und Werk des Würzburger Musikers im Spiegel der Geschichte* (Tutzing, 1985).—NS/LK/DM

Kuhač, Franz Xaver (Franjo Zaver), Croatian music theorist; b. Osijek, Nov. 20, 1834; d. Agram, June 18, 1911. He studied with Thern in Leipzig and Liszt in Weimar (1856), then with Czerny and Hanslick in Vienna. He taught piano in Osijek (1858–71), and then was a music critic in Zagreb (1871–74). He subsequently taught at the Croatian Music Inst. (1872–76). He publ. 4 books of folk songs (1878–81; remaining songs publ. in 1941).

WRITINGS: *Katekizam glazbe: Prva hrvatska glazena teorija po J. Ch. Lobeu* (A Musical Catechism: The First Croatian Music Theory after Lobe; Zagreb, 1875; 2nd ed., enl., 1890); *Vatroslav Lisinski i njegovo doba* (V. L. and His Time; Zagreb, 1887; 2nd ed., enl., 1904); *Ilirski glazenici* (The Musicians of the Illyrian Movement; Zagreb, 1893); *Prva hrvatska uputa u glasoviranje* (The First Croatian School of Piano Playing; Zagreb, 1896–97); *Moj rad* (My Work; Zagreb, 1904).—NS/LK/DM

Kuhlau, (Daniel) Friedrich (Rudolph), German-born Danish pianist and composer; b. Ülzen, near Hannover, Sept. 11, 1786; d. Copenhagen, March 12, 1832. He lost an eye in a childhood accident, and studied piano during his recovery; later studied theory and composition with C.F.G. Schwenke, Kantor of Hamburg's Catherinenkirche. He went to Copenhagen in 1810 to avoid conscription into Napoleon's army. He prospered there, being made court chamber musician (1813). He appeared often in concerts, championing the music of Beethoven. D. Fog ed. a thematic and bibliographic catalog (Copenhagen, 1977).

WORKS: DRAMATIC (all 1st perf. in Copenhagen): *Røverborgen* (The Robber's Castle), Singspiel (May 26, 1814); *Trylleharpen* (The Magic Harp), opera (Jan. 30, 1817); *Elisa*, opera (April 17, 1820); *Lulu*, opera (Oct. 29, 1824); *William Shakespeare*, drama (March 28, 1826); *Hugo og Adelheid*, opera (Oct. 29, 1827); *Elverhøj* (The Fairies' Mound), incidental music (Nov. 6, 1828); *Trillingbrødrene, fra Damask* (The Triplet Brothers from Damascus), incidental music (Sept. 1, 1830). **OTHER:** Piano Concerto (1810); Concertino for 2 Horns and Orch. (1821); numerous chamber music pieces with flute; keyboard works, including pieces for piano 2- and 4-Hands; songs; etc.

BIBL.: C. Thrane, *F. K.: Zur 100-jährigen Wiederkehr seines Geburtstages* (Leipzig, 1886); K. Graupner, *F. K.* (Leipzig, 1930).
—NS/LK/DM

Kuhlmann, Kathleen, American mezzo-soprano; b. San Francisco, Dec. 7, 1950. She studied in San Francisco and at the Chicago Lyric Opera School, making her debut as Maddalena in *Rigoletto* with that company in 1979. She made her European debut in 1980 as Preziosilla in *La forza del destino* at the Cologne Opera; subsequently appeared at Milan's La Scala (as Meg Page in *Falstaff*; Dec. 7, 1980) and at London's Covent Garden (as Ino and Juno in Handel's *Semele*; Nov. 25, 1982). She sang the leading role in *La Cenerentola* at the Glyndebourne Festival in 1983. In 1987 she scored a major success as Falliero in Rossini's *Bianca e Falliero* in its U.S. premiere at the Greater Miami Opera. She made her Metropolitan Opera debut in N.Y. as Charlotte in *Werther* on March 2, 1989. In 1991 she was a soloist in Beethoven's 9th Sym. at the London Promenade Concerts. In 1992 she appeared as Cenerentola at Dresden's Semper Opera. She sang Cornelia in *Giulio Cesare* at the Munich Festival and at the Opéra de la Bastille in Paris in 1997. In 1999 she returned to Paris as Bradamante in *Alcina*. Among her other notable roles are Isabella in *L'Italiana in Algeri*, Dorabella, Rosina, Arsace in *Semiramide*, and Carmen.—NS/LK/DM

Kuhn, Gustav, Austrian conductor; b. Turrach, Aug. 28, 1947. He studied conducting at the Salzburg Mozarteum and with Swarowsky at the Vienna Hochschule für Musik; later had instruction from Maderna and Karajan, completing his education at the Univ. of Salzburg (Ph.D., 1970). He then served as conductor at the Istanbul Opera (1970–73) and 1st conductor at the Dortmund Stadttheater (1975–77). In 1978 he was named a conductor at the Vienna State Opera; also was chief conductor of the Bern Sym. Orch. and Opera (1979–81); conducted at the Glyndebourne and Salzburg festivals (1980) and made his U.S. debut at the Chicago Lyric Opera (1981). In 1983 he became Generalmusikdirektor of Bonn, a post he held until being dismissed in 1985 after he physically assaulted the director of the Stadttheater during a dispute. He then served as chief conductor of the Rome Opera (from 1987).—NS/LK/DM

Kuhn, Laura (Diane née **Shipcott),** spirited American musicologist, editor, teacher, arts administrator, writer on music, and singer; b. San Francisco, Jan. 19, 1953. She studied at Dominican Coll. in San Rafael, Calif. (B.A., 1981) and the Univ. of Calif. at Los Angeles (M.A., 1986; Ph.D., 1992, with the diss. *John Cage's Europeras 1 & 2: The Musical Means of Revolution*); also had private instruction in San Francisco (1975–82) with John Hudnall (voice) and Robert Hagopian (piano). She was a member of the San Francisco (1980) and Oakland (1980–82) Sym. Choruses, and also appeared as a vocalist in the Daniel Lentz Group (1983–85) and as a singing talk show guest in Mikel Rouse's *Dennis Cleveland* (1999). She was music critic of Marin County's *Independent Journal* from 1980 to 1982, and also wrote book and record reviews for the *Los Angeles* (1982–87) and *N.Y.* (1986–89) *Times*. From 1986 to 1992 she worked extensively with John Cage on various large-scale works, including his *Europeras 1 & 2* for the Frankfurt am Main Oper and his Harvard lectures as holder of the Charles Eliot Norton Chair in Poetry (publ in 1990 as *I-VI*). Shortly after Cage's death in 1992, she instituted, with long-time Cage associate Merce Cunningham, the John Cage Trust in N.Y., which she subsequently directed. Kuhn also worked extensively with the seeded Russian-born American lexicographer Nicolas Slonimsky, giving strong editorial assistance to the 7th and 8th editions of his *Baker's Biographical Dictionary of Musicians* (N.Y.,

1984, 1992) and to the 4th and 5th (rev.) eds. of his *Music since 1900* (N.Y., 1986, 1994). In 1995 she inherited the editorship of the present 9th ed. of *Baker's Biographical Dictionary of Musicians*. She also served as ed. of *A Pronouncing Pocket Manual of Musical Terms* (5th ed., N.Y., 1995), *Baker's Biographical Dictionary of 20th Century Classical Musicians* (N.Y., 1997), *Baker's Student Encyclopedia of Music* (3 vols., N.Y., 1999), and *Baker's Dictionary of Opera* (N.Y., 2000). She also contributed articles to various scholarly publications. From 1991 to 1997 she served as an asst. prof. at Ariz. State Univ. West in Phoenix; also lectured widely in the U.S., South America, and Europe. In 1995 she joined the board of the American Music Center, serving as its secretary until 2000.—**NS/LK/DM**

Kühn, Rolf, wide-ranging jazz clarinetist, leader; b. Cologne, Germany, Sept. 29, 1929. Kühn was classically trained in theory, harmony, and arranging. At age eight he took up the accordion, and at 12 the clarinet. As a teenager he discovered jazz while living in Leipzig. In 1946 he joined The Kurt Henkels Band, a group which emulated American swing bands, and over the next 10 years he became one of the top jazz musicians in Germany, regularly winning polls in the music magazines and playing in major festivals. In 1954, he caught the ear of jazz critic/author Leonard Feather, who encouraged him to move to N.Y., which he did in 1956. After arriving there, he attracted the interest of producer John Hammond, who arranged for some recording dates on the Vanguard label. In 1957 and 1958 he joined Benny Goodman's band, subbing for Goodman during an extended illness, and he also did time with Tommy Dorsey and Urbie Green's big band. During this time he also did small group work and recordings with both modern groups (in sessions with Art Farmer, Oscar Pettiford, and Toshiko Akiyoshi) and more traditional outfits (he played the Newport festival with Dick Johnson). He returned to Germany in 1962 to lead a jazz orch. in Hamburg, and his career has been based there ever since. During the early 1960s, he began experimenting with bringing free jazz to the clarinet. Through the 1960s he continued to perform and record in a variety of settings, including a co-operative group with his brother, a sextet, and various projects in the late 1960s and early 1970s featuring players such as John Surman, Barre Phillips, Chick Corea, Eberhard Weber, Tony Oxley and Randy Brecker. He continues to be active in both traditional and more experimental environments.

DISC.: *Streamline* (1957); *Be My Guest* (1961); *Solarius* (1964); *Impressions of N.Y.* (1967); *Transfiguration* (1967); *Mad Rockers* (1968); *The Day After* (1972; with Phil Woods); *Cinemascope* (1974); *Total Space* (1975); *R.K.* (1978); *Symphonic Swampfire* (1978); *Don't Split* (1982); *As Time Goes By* (1989); *Big Band Connection* (1993).—**LP/MS**

Kuhn, Steve (actually, **Stephen Lewis**), jazz pianist, composer; b. Brooklyn, N.Y., March 24, 1938. He is a unique talent who plays a truly two-handed piano where the left hand may join in with the right or produce a thunderous roll. He was a child prodigy and an article was written about his ability to identify his father's 78s by the labels at age two-and-a-half, before he could read. He studied in Boston with legendary classical teacher Margaret Chaloff, mother of Serge. He began taking lessons at five, and by 1959 he went to the Lenox School of Jazz. A demo from around that time has never been released. He was accomplished enough to earn stints with Kenny Dorham (fall 1959), who he'd studied with at Lenox, then Coltrane's first quartet (May 1960), then Stan Getz. He was a member of the Art Farmer Quartet from 1964–66. Kuhn moved to Sweden in 1967, living there until 1971 and heading his trio throughout Europe from his Stockhom base. He returned to N.Y. that year, heading a quartet and since then recording and touring frequently, appearing at festivals throughout America and Europe, usually in trio or solo. In the 1970s he experimented with strange and effective poetry readings/chanting over his playing. In the 1990s he appeared several times a year at Knickerbocker's in Manhattan.

DISC.: *Country and Western Sound of Jazz* (1963); *Three Waves* (1966); *October Suite: Three Compositions of Gary McFarland* (1966); *Watch What Happens* (1968); *Childhood Is Forever* (1969); *Steve Kuhn* (1972); *Raindrops (Steve Kuhn Live in N.Y.)* (1972); *Trance* (1974); *Ecstasy* (1974); *Motility* (1977); *Non- Fiction* (1978); *Playground* (1979); *Last Year's Waltz* (1981); *Mostly Ballads* (1984); *Life's Magic* (1986); *Porgy* (1988); *Oceans in the Sky* (1989); *Looking Back* (1990); *Live at Maybeck Recital Hall, V* (1990); *Years Later* (1992); *Seasons of Romance* (1995).—**LP**

Kuhnau (real name, **Kuhn**), **Johann,** erudite German organist, writer on music, and composer; b. Geising, April 6, 1660; d. Leipzig, June 5, 1722. He studied at the Kreuzschule in Dresden with Krügner and Kittel, then became a chorister at the Kreuzkirche (1671), where he studied organ with Heringk. He also received instruction from Albrici, and then from Edelmann at the Zittau Gymnasium (1680–82), where he was acting Kantor (1681–82). He attended the Univ. of Leipzig from 1682 to 1688, studying law; meanwhile, in 1684, he succeeded Kühnel as organist at the Thomaskirche. In 1688 he organized a Collegium Musicum and also began to practice law. He was appointed Thomaskantor (1701), and was also active as a teacher at the Thomasschule, a conductor of church music at the Thomaskirche and Nikolaikirche, and later as music director at the Peterskirche (1711). He likewise served as music director of the Univ. His last years became increasingly difficult owing to poor health. He also had to contend with the efforts of others to encroach upon his duties. For example, Telemann organized his own Collegium Musicum (1701), and was also successful in obtaining the right to compose for the Thomaskirche. Kuhnau remains best known for his keyboard music, especially the 6 program sonatas found in his *Musicalische Vorstellung einiger biblischer Historien* (Leipzig, 1700). His Sonata in B-flat major from the *Neue Clavier-Übung* (Leipzig, 1692) is of historical significance as the earliest known example of the genre in Germany. He also composed many sacred cantatas. His secular vocal music is not extant.

WRITINGS: *Divini numinis assistentia, illustrisque jure consultorum in florentissima academia Lipsiensi* (Leipzig, 1688); *Fundamenta compositionis* (MS, 1703); 2 other works not extant.

WORKS: *Neue Clavier-Übung, erster Theil* (Leipzig, 1689; 7 suites; ed. in Denkmäler Deutscher Tonkunst, IV, 1901); *Neue Clavier-Übung, anderer Theil* (Leipzig, 1692; 7 suites and 1 sonata; ed. in ibid.); *Frische Clavier Früchte* (Leipzig; 1696; 7 sonatas; ed. in ibid.); *Musicalische Vorstellung eininger biblischer Historien* (Leipzig, 1700; reprint, 1973; 6 program sonatas; ed. in ibid.).

BIBL.: J. Martin, *Die Kirchenkantaten J. K.s* (Leipzig, 1928); E. Rimbach, *The Church Cantatas of J. K.* (diss., Univ. of Rochester, 1966); J. Arbogast, *Stilkritische Untersuchungen zum Klavierwerk des Thomaskantors J. K. (1660–1722)* (Regensburg, 1983). —NS/LK/DM

Kühnau, Johann Christoph, German conductor and composer; b. Volkstadt, near Eisleben, Feb. 10, 1735; d. Berlin, Oct. 13, 1805. He studied piano and organ with Martin Grosse in Klosterbergen, then became a schoolteacher at Berlin's Realschule in 1763. He was founder-director of a choir there, which he led until his death, and a teacher (from 1783) and Kantor and music director (from 1788) of Berlin's Dreifaltigkeitskirche. He compiled several collections of vocal and instrumental works by his eminent contemporaries, the best known being the *Vierstimmige alte, und neue Choralgesange* (2 vols., Berlin, 1786–90; 10th ed., 1885). His son, Johann Friedrich Wilhelm Kühnau (b. Berlin, June 29, 1780; d. there, Jan. 1, 1848), was an organist at the Dreifaltigkeitskirche from 1814.—**NS/LK/DM**

Kühnel, August, German viola da gambist and composer; b. Delmenhorst, Aug. 3, 1645; d. c. 1700. He joined the Zeitz court chapel in 1661. After studies in Paris, he continued his service in Zeitz from 1665 but also acquired a notable reputation as a virtuoso on the viola da gamba via tours of Germany. His appearances in Dresden, Frankfurt am Main (1669), Munich (1680–81), and London (1682, 1686) were particularly notable. From 1686 to 1688 he was a musician and director of the instrumentalists of Landgravine Elisabeth Dorothea's musical establishment in Darmstadt. After a sojourn in a similar capacity at the Weimar court, he was Kapellmeister at the Kassel court from 1695 to 1699. He publ. a collection of 14 *Sonate ô partite* (Kassel, 1698), which contains 6 sonatas for 2 Gambas and 8 sonatas for 1 Gamba, all with basso continuo.—**LK/DM**

Kuhse, Hanne-Lore, German soprano; b. Schwaan, March 28, 1925. She was educated at the Rostock Cons. and the Stern Cons. in Berlin, and later studied in Potsdam. She made her debut in Gera in 1951 as Leonore in *Fidelio*. From 1952 to 1959 she was a member of the Schwerin Opera, and from 1959 to 1964 she sang at the Leipzig Opera. In 1964 she joined the East Berlin State Opera. In 1974 she was appointed prof. at the Hochschule für Musik in East Berlin. In 1954 she was named a Kammersängerin. A versatile artist, she was as stylistically faithful to her roles in Mozart's operas as to the heroic and lyric Wagnerian parts. —**NS/LK/DM**

Kuijken, prominent family of Belgian musicians, all brothers:

(1) Wieland Kuijken, cellist and viola da gambist; b. Dilbeek, near Brussels, Aug. 31, 1938. He studied piano and cello at the Bruges Cons. and the Brussels Cons. (1957), graduating with the prix d'excellence in 1962; was self-taught as a violist. He played in the Baroque group known as the Alarius Ensemble (1959–72) and in the avant-garde Musiques Nouvelles from 1962. He later appeared in concerts with his brothers, and also toured extensively as a soloist; likewise taught master classes.

(2) Sigiswald Kuijken, violinist, violist, and conductor; b. Dilbeek, near Brussels, Feb. 16, 1944. He enrolled at the Bruges Cons. at age 8 as a student of violin, then entered the Brussels Cons. in 1960, winning the premier prix in 1964. He was autodidact as a Baroque violinist, beginning his career on the instrument in 1970. He played in the Alarius Ensemble and the Musiques Nouvelles before gaining wide recognition with his own Baroque orch., La Petite Bande (founded 1972), which he subsequently led on many tours and in numerous recordings. He was also active as a teacher, serving on the faculties of the Royal Cons. of Music at The Hague (from 1971) and the Brussels Cons. (from 1994).

(3) Barthold Kuijken, flutist and recorder player; b. Dilbeek, near Brussels, March 8, 1949. He studied at the conservatories in Bruges, Brussels, and The Hague, his principal teachers being Franz Vester (flute) and Frans Brüggen (recorder); he was self-taught as a Baroque flutist. He performed in concerts with his brothers and with others, and also toured widely and was active as a teacher.—**NS/LK/DM**

Kuivila, Ron, American composer, instrument designer and programmer, and teacher; b. Boston, Dec. 19, 1955. He studied music and mathematics at Wesleyan Univ. (B.A., 1977) and electronic music and studio recording techniques at Mills Coll. in Oakland, Calif. (M.F.A., 1979), and then was artist-in-residence at Media Study in Buffalo (1979–80) and at Wesleyan Univ. (from 1981). Kuivila pioneered ultrasound (*In Appreciation*, 1979) and sound sampling (*Alphabet*, 1982) in live performance, and much of his music, the bulk of which is for live electronics, involves complex, often unpitched, electronic timbres; some of his compositions utilize existing recordings as source material. Throughout the 1980s he composed pieces based on high voltage phenomena, speech synthesis, and compositional algorithms, and his recorded works of the period seem to capture extremely complex improvisations utilizing complex musical rhetoric. Much of his work in the 1990s has taken the form of site-specific interactive multimedia installations, which have appeared throughout the U.S. and Europe. He has also designed commercial music software and exhibited at visual art galleries. Kuivila became active with one of America's masters in live electronic composition and performance, David Tudor, and in 1995–96 he programmed and developed Tudor's *Neural Synthesis*. In 1997, with John D.S. Adams and Matt Rogalsky, he made historically significant realizations of Tudor's *Rainforest II, Neural Synthesis, Dialects,* and *Anima Pepsi*. He is currently on the faculty of Wesleyan Univ., and also guest lectures widely.

WORKS: CONCERT: *In Appreciation* (1979); *Sketch* (1979); *Fast Feet, Slow Smoke* (1982); *Alphabet* (1982); *TI intends...*

(1983); *Household Object* (1982); *Canon Y* (1985); *A Keyboard Study* (1984); *Minute Differences/Closely Observed* (1985); *Water Surface* (1985); *Loose Canons* (1986); *Chronotopes* (1987); *The Linear Predictive Zoo* (1988); *Pythagorean Puppet Theatre* (1989), *Fine Muck and His Good Fellows* (1989); *Canon III* (1990); *Jocular State* (1991); *Distemper* (1991); *i am virtual (yellow)* (1991); *Athabasca* (1993); *Civil Defenses* (1993); *Parsable* (1995); *Fugue States* (1997); *Electric Wind (for BH)* (1996; rev. 1999); *A Question of Placement* (1998); *Windy States* (1999). INSTALLATIONS: *Comparing Habits* (1979); *Musical Chameleon* (1979); *Arrows* (1983); *Sailing Ship/Flying Machine* (1983); *Untitled* (1984); *Parallel Lines* (1985); *Unauthorized Prototype* (1984); *Aqua Vitae* (1986); *Second Wind* (1986; rev. 1996); *Conjugal Pairs* (1987); *Light Voices* (1987); *Spark Harp* (1989); *Radical Arc* (1988); *Dolci Mura* (1989); *Il Giardino de Babele* (1990); *Spark Armonica* (1990; rev. 1996); *Der Schnufflestaat* (1991); *Dolci Mura (Athabasca)* (1993); *The Factory of Light* (1993); *Ridge Walk* (1993); *Singing Shadows* (1993); *VR on $5 a Day* (1994); *Miracle on 42nd Street* (1994); *Killeroke* (1994); *Locus of Focus* (1995; rev. 1999); *ShadowPlay* (1996); *Hothouse* (1997); *Broken Lines* (1997); *Making the World Safe for Piezoelectricity* (1997); *Building 12* (1998); *Visitations* (1999); *Tall Stalks, sharing* (1999); *Tall Shadows* (1999). DANCE: *Hatchmarks* (1984); *Future Antiquities* (1984); *A Lover's Discourse* (1984); *Parodicals* (1985); *The Smell of Fact* (1985); *Blurred Genres* (1986); *Corpus Delecti* (1987); *Engrams* (1988); *Tune In/Spin Out* (1996).—NS/LK/DM

Kulenkampff, Georg, eminent German violinist and pedagogue; b. Bremen, Jan. 23, 1898; d. Schaffhausen, Oct. 4, 1948. He studied violin with Willy Hess in Berlin. In 1916 he became concertmaster of the Bremen Phil. From 1923 to 1926 he taught at the Berlin Hochschule für Musik; then toured throughout Europe as a soloist; from 1943 he taught at the Lucerne Cons. He was regarded as one of the most brilliant German violinists of his generation; his book *Geigerische Betrachtungen,* partly didactic, partly autobiographical in content, was ed. by G. Meyer-Stichtung (Regensburg, 1952). —NS/LK/DM

Kulenty, Hanna, Polish composer; b. Białystok, March 18, 1961. She studied composition with Włodzimierz Kotoński at the Warsaw Academy of Music (1980–86) and with Louis Andriessen at the Royal Cons. of Music in The Hague (1986–88). In 1990–91 she was in Berlin under the auspices of the Deutscher Akademischer Austauschdienst. Her music makes use of various advanced techniques, including an extensive employment of glissandos, toward a personal style she describes as "polyphony of the arcs."

WORKS: DRAMATIC: *Przypowieść o ziarnie* (Parable on Grain), monodrama (Toruń, March 18, 1985); *The Mother of Black-Winged Dreams,* opera (1995; Munich, Dec. 9, 1996). ORCH.: *Muzyka podwodna* (Underwater Music; 1984); *Ad Unum* (Groningen, Sept. 27, 1985); *Quatro* for Chamber Orch. (1986); 3 syms.: No. 1 (1986; Warsaw, Sept. 22, 1989), No. 2 for Chorus and Orch. (1987; Berlin, May 26, 1989), and No. 3 (1998); *Breathe* (1987); *Perpetuus* for Chamber Orch. (Arnhem, Oct. 20, 1989); *Trigon* for Chamber Orch. (Rotterdam, Nov. 29, 1989); 2 piano concertos: No. 1 for Piano and Chamber Orch. (Arnhem, Oct. 13, 1990) and No. 2 for 2 Pianos and Orch. (1991); *Air* for Chamber Orch. (1991); 2 violin concertos: No. 1 for Violin and Chamber Orch. (1992; also for Violin with Delay and Orch., 1993; Warsaw, Sept. 18, 1994) and No. 2 (1996); *Passacaglia* for

Chamber Orch. (1992); *Sinequan forte B* for Cello (Amplified and Delay) and Chamber Orch. (1994; Hilversum, May 1996); *Sinequan forte A* for Cello (Amplified and Delay) and Orch. (1994); *Going Up 2* for Chamber Orch. (Warsaw, Sept. 19, 1995); *Certus* (Amsterdam, Dec. 9, 1997); *Elfen* for Chamber Orch. (1997). CHAMBER: *Trzy minuty* (Three Minutes) for Double Bass (1983; Warsaw, April 7, 1984); 2 string quartets: No. 1, *Pieśń* (Song; 1983–84) and No. 2 (Huddersfield, Dec. 1, 1990); *Martwa natura ze skrzypcami* (Still Life with a Violin) for Violin (Warsaw, May 20, 1985); *Arci* for Percussion (1986; Zürich, Nov. 20, 1987); *Ride* for 6 Percussionists (Warsaw, June 21, 1987); *One by One* for Marimba (1988; Warsaw, May 17, 1990); *Arcus* for 3 Percussionists (1988; Munich, Feb. 24, 1989); *Cannon* for Violin and Piano (1988); *aaa Tre* for Viola, Cello, and Double Bass (1988; Kraków, Nov. 6, 1989); *Cadenza* for Violin and Delay (1992); *Still Life with a Cello* for Cello (Schleswig- Holstein, Aug. 6, 1993); *Sinequan* for Cello (Warsaw, Nov. 1993); *A Cradle Song* for Violin, Cello, and Piano (1993; Munich, May 1994); *A Fifth Circle* for Alto Flute and Delay (Dresden, Oct. 1994); *A Fourth Circle* for Violin or Viola or Cello and Piano (Odense, Nov. 1994); *Going Up 1* for Violin and Double Bass (Munich, May 7, 1995); *A Sixth Circle* for Trumpet and Piano (1995; Los Angeles, April 4, 1998); *Sierra* for Violin and Cello (Munich, Dec. 1996); *Blattinus* for Saxophone Quartet (1996; Amsterdam, Feb. 8, 1997); *Stretto* for Flute, Clarinet, Cello, and Guitar (Warsaw, Sept. 21, 1998); *Rapidus* for Saxophone Quartet (1998); *Harmonium* for Harmonium (1999); *MM-blues* for 2 Pianos and 2 Percussion (1999). KEYBOARD: Piano: *Sesto* (1985); *Quinto* for 2 Pianos (1986; Warsaw, Sept. 23, 1987); *A Third Circle* (1996). Harpsichord: *E for E* (1991; Warsaw, Sept. 26, 1992). OTHER: *Prośba o słońce* (Request for the Sun) for Tape (1984); *Lysanxia* for Gamelan Ensemble and Tape (Amsterdam, Oct. 1994); *Waiting for...* for Piano and Human Voice (1997).—NS/LK/DM

Kulesha, Gary, Canadian composer, conductor, and pianist; b. Toronto, Aug. 22, 1954. He studied composition with Samuel Dolin and piano at the Royal Cons. of Music of Toronto, receiving degrees in piano performance (1973) and composition (1978). He continued private studies in England with John McCabe and in N.Y. with John Corigliano. He returned to Canada in 1982, and from 1983 to 1985 was principal conductor of the Stratford Shakespearean Festival Theatre (Ontario), for which he provided incidental music. He was co-principal conductor of the Composer's Orch. of the Canadian Contemporary Music Workshops, where he served as artistic director (from 1987). From 1989 to 1992 he was composer-in-residence of the Kitchener-Waterloo Sym. Orch., and then of the Canadian Opera Co. from 1993 to 1995. His music makes eclectic use of influences as diverse as Prokofiev, Messiaen, musique concrete, jazz, and rock.

WORKS: ORCH.: *Variations* for Winds (1975); *Divertimento* for Strings (1975); *Essay No. 1* (1977), *No. 2* (1984; Kitchener, Jan. 18, 1985), and *No. 3* (1992); Concerto for Tuba and Orch. or Winds (1978–81); *Ensembles* for Winds (1979); *Chamber Concerto No. 1* for Winds and Percussion (Kitchener, Ontario, Nov. 28, 1981), *No. 2* for Trumpet, Piano, and Winds (Toronto, March 28, 1982), *No. 3* for Bass Clarinet and Winds (1982–83; Toronto, Jan. 31, 1984), and *No. 4* for 10 Winds, String Quintet, and Percussion (Kitchener, April 13, 1988); *Celebration Overture* (1985); *Nocturne* for Chamber Orch. (1985); *The Gates of Time* (Kitchener, Oct. 5, 1991); Recorder Concerto (1992); Viola Concerto (1992). CHAMBER: String Trio (1971); Sonata for

Horn, Tuba, and Piano (1975); Sonata for Tuba and Organ (1976); Duo for Bass Clarinet and Piano (1977); Sonata for Trumpet, Tuba, and Piano (1978); Trio for Flute, Cello, and Piano (1979; rev. 1985); *Concertante Music* for Soprano Saxophone and Wind Quintet (1979); 2 suites for 2 Trumpets (*The Grand Canyon*, 1979; *Pike's Peak*, 1981); Suite for Percussion Quartet (1981); *Passacaglia, Cadenzas, and Finale* for Trumpet, Tuba, and Piano (1981); *Nocturne and Toccata* for Piano and 3 Percussionists (1981); *Mysterium Coniunctionis* for Clarinet, Bass Clarinet, and Piano (1980); *Secrets* for Flute and Piano (1980); *Attitudes* for Clarinet and Piano (1980); *Canticles* for Brass Quintet and Organ (1982); *Pentagram* for 5 Trumpets (1982); *Angels* for Marimba and Tape (1983); *Jazz Music* for Brass Quintet, Marimba, and Piano (1985); *Complex* for Electric Bass Guitar and Tape (1986); Cello Sonata (1986–87); *Demons* for Tuba and Tape (1988); *Political Implications* for Clarinet Quartet (1988). P i a n o : 3 sonatinas (1969–71); 3 sonatas (1970; 1980, rev. 1984; 1986); Sonata for 2 Pianos (1970–72); *Aphorisms* (1978); *Monument* for Piano, 4-Hands (1978); *Mythologies* for 2 Pianos (1987). O T H E R : Incidental music; *Lifesongs* for Contralto and Strings (Markham, Ontario, Nov. 18, 1985); songs.—NS/LK/DM

Kulka, János, Hungarian conductor; b. Budapest, Dec. 11, 1929. He studied conducting with Ferencsik and Somogyi, and composition with Kodály at the Budapest Academy of Music. He became a répétiteur and choirmaster at the Budapest State Opera (1950), where he later was a conductor (1953–57). He conducted at the Bavarian State Opera in Munich (1957–59), then was 1st conductor at the Württemberg State Theater in Stuttgart (1959–61) and the Hamburg State Opera (1961–64). He subsequently was Generalmusikdirektor in Wuppertal (1964–76) and of the North-West German Phil. in Herford (1975–87).—NS/LK/DM

Kullak, Adolf, German music theorist, critic, and composer, brother of **Theodor Kullak;** b. Meseritz, Feb. 23, 1823; d. Berlin, Dec. 25, 1862. He studied at the Univ. of Berlin, then music with A.B. Marx in Berlin. He subsequently taught at his brother's academy there and wrote music criticism for various periodicals. He publ. *Das Musikalisch- Schöne* (Leipzig, 1858) and *Die Ästhetik des Klavierspiels* (Berlin, 1861; 4th ed., 1906, by W. Niemann; 5th ed., 1916; Eng. tr., N.Y., 1892), and also composed piano pieces and songs. His son, Ernst Kullak (b. Berlin, Jan. 22, 1855; d. there, 1914), was a pianist and composer.—NS/LK/DM

Kullak, Franz, German pianist, teacher, and composer, son of **Theodor Kullak;** b. Berlin, April 12, 1844; d. there, Dec. 9, 1913. He studied with his father and briefly with Liszt, and later with Wehle and Litolff in Paris. He was a piano teacher at his father's academy in Berlin (1867–82), serving as director (1882–90). He then was director of his own Akademie für Höheres Klavierspiel (1891–1900). He prepared a valuable ed. of the Beethoven piano concertos, and also publ. several piano methods. He composed an opera, *Ines de Castro* (Berlin, 1877), orch. works, piano pieces, and songs.—NS/LK/DM

Kullak, Theodor, famous German pianist and pedagogue, brother of **Adolf Kullak** and father of **Franz**

Kullak; b. Krotoschin, Sept. 12, 1818; d. Berlin, March 1, 1882. He studied piano with local teachers, and in 1837 went to Berlin at his father's behest to study medicine. He also studied there with Dehn (theory). He then went to Vienna, where he took lessons with Czerny, Sechter, and Nicolai (1842–43). Returning to Berlin in 1846, he became court pianist to the King of Prussia. In 1850 he founded a cons. in Berlin in partnership with Julius Stern and A.B. Marx; however, dissension soon arose among them, and in 1855 Kullak established his own school, the Neue Akademie der Tonkunst, which greatly prospered and became famous as Kullak's Academy, turning out such students as Moszkowski, N. Rubinstein, and the Scharwenka brothers. He publ. the methods *Schule des Oktavenspiel*, op.48 (Berlin, 1848; 3rd ed., 1877), *Schule der Fingerübungen*, op.61 (Berlin, c. 1850), *Ratschläge und Studien*, op.74 (Berlin, c. 1852), and *Materialien für den Elementar- Klavierunterricht* (Berlin, c. 1859). He also composed pieces for piano.

BIBL.: O. Reinsdorf, *T. K. und seine Neue Akademie der Tonkunst in Berlin* (Neusalz, 1870); H. Bischoff, *Zur Erinnerung an T. K.* (Berlin, 1883).—NS/LK/DM

Kullman, Charles, American tenor; b. New Haven, Conn., Jan. 13, 1903; d. there, Feb. 8, 1983. He entered Yale Univ., and sang at the Yale Glee Club, and then took courses at the Juilliard School of Music in N.Y. After singing with the American Opera Co. in Rochester, N.Y., he went to Berlin, where he made his European debut on Feb. 24, 1931, as Pinkerton in *Madama Butterfly* at the Kroll Opera. He sang at the Berlin State Opera (1932–35); also appeared at the Vienna State Opera, at the Salzburg Festivals, and at Covent Garden in London (1934–36). On Dec. 19, 1935, he made his debut at the Metropolitan Opera in N.Y. as Gounod's Faust. He remained on the roster of the Metropolitan until 1960. His repertoire comprised over 30 roles. He scored a signal success in the role of Eisenstein in *Die Fledermaus*. From 1956 to 1971 he taught at the Ind. School of Music in Bloomington.—NS/LK/DM

Kumer, Zmaga, Yugoslav ethnomusicologist; b. Ribnica, April 24, 1924. She studied Slovene literature at the Univ. of Ljubljana (degree, 1948) and musicology at the Ljubljana Academy of Music (degree, 1952). She then returned to the Univ., where she received her Ph.D. (1955, with a diss. on Slovene variants of the song *Puer natus in Bethlehem*) and subsequently taught (from 1966). Her studies focus on the texts of Slovene folk songs as well as on the migration and transformation of these songs among other Alpine cultures.—NS/LK/DM

Kummer, Friedrich August, noted German cellist, oboist, teacher, and composer; b. Meiningen, Aug. 5, 1797; d. Dresden, Aug. 22, 1879. His father, also named Friedrich August Kummer (1770–1849), was oboist at the courts in Meiningen and then Dresden (from 1805). The young Kummer went with his family to Dresden, where he studied cello with Dotzauer. He also studied oboe, and joined the electoral Court Orch. as an oboist (1814). After further cello studies, he became a cellist there, eventually succeeding Dotzauer as principal (1852–64). He made tours as a virtuoso in Germany and Italy, but was content to remain at his Dresden post. He taught at the Dresden Cons. and privately. He composed over 400 works, about half of which were publ. His output included virtuoso pieces for cello and orch., as well as chamber music, many didactic pieces, and some 200 entr'actes for the Dresden Court Theater. He publ. the *Violoncello-Schule*, op.60 (Leipzig, 1839).—NS/LK/DM

Kümmerle, Salomon, German organist, teacher, and editor; b. Malmsheim, near Stuttgart, Feb. 8, 1838; d. Samaden, Aug. 28, 1896. He was an organist and teacher in various German towns before taking positions in Nice (1861–66) and Samaden (1874–90). He ed. the valuable *Encyklopädie der evangelischen Kirchenmusik* (4 vols., 1888–95), and also ed. the vocal collections *Grabgesänge* (1869), *Musica sacra* (1869–70), *Zionsharfe* (1870–71), and *Choralbuch für evangelische Kirchenchore* (1887–89).—NS/LK/DM

Kunad, Rainer, German composer; b. Chemnitz, Oct. 24, 1936; d. Tübingen, July 17, 1995. He studied with Kurzbach and Hübschmann in Chemnitz, at the Dresden Cons. (1955–56), and with Finke, Gerster, and Schenk at the Leipzig Hochschule für Musik. He worked at the Dresden State Opera (1960–75). After serving as a prof. of composition at the Dresden Hochschule für Musik (1978–84), he settled in West Germany. Kunad was principally influenced by Lutosawski, with some indirect inspiration from Penderecki and Henze. He found his métier as a composer for the theater.

WORKS: DRAMATIC: *Bill Brook,* music theater (Dresden, March 14, 1965); *Old Fritz,* music theater (Dresden, March 14, 1965); *Maître Pathelin, oder Die Hammelkomodie,* opera (Dresden, April 30, 1969); *Sabellicus,* opera (Berlin, Dec. 20, 1974); *Der Eiertanz,* mini-opera (DDR-TV, 1975; 1st stage perf., Tübingen, June 7, 1986); *Litauische Claviere,* opera (Dresden, Nov. 4, 1976); *Vincent,* opera (Dresden, Feb. 22, 1979); *Amphytrion,* musical comedy (Berlin, May 26, 1984); *Der Meister und Margarita,* opera (Karlsruhe, March 9, 1986); *Die Menschen von Babel,* scenic mystery play (1986); *Der verborgene Name,* opera (1990); *Kosmischer Advent,* opera (1991). **ORCH.:** *Aphorismen* (1956); *Sinfonia variatione* (1959); 2 syms. (1964, 1967); *Concerto per archi* (1967); *Sinfonietta* (1969); Piano Concerto (1969); *Quadrophonie* for Strings, Winds, and Timpani (1973); *Die sieben Siegel,* choral sym. (1993). **OTHER:** Choral pieces; chamber music; piano works.

BIBL.: S. Kreter, *Alles auf Hoffnung: Bobrowski-Vertonungen von R. K.* (Münster and N.Y., 1994).—NS/LK/DM

Kunc, Božidar, Croatian-American pianist and composer, brother of **Zinka Milanov;** b. Zagreb, July 18, 1903; d. Detroit, April 1, 1964. He was a student of Stančíc (piano) and Bersa (composition) at the Zagreb Academy of Music, graduating in 1927. He taught there from 1929 to 1951, when he emigrated to the U.S. His music is impressionistic in its harmonic palette.

WORKS: ORCH.: 2 violin concertos (1928, 1955); *Dramatic Prologue* (1929); *Symphonic Intermezzo* (1934); 2 piano concertos: No. 1 (Zagreb, April 27, 1934, composer soloist) and No. 2 (1962); *Marcia funebre* (1936); *Triptihon* for Cello and Orch.

(1940); *3 Episodes* for Piano and Strings (1955); syms. **CHAMBER:** Cello Sonata (1927); *Cycle* for Piano and Percussion (1956); *Pieces* for Double Bass (1959). **Piano:** 4 sonatas (1930–43). **VOCAL:** Songs.—NS/LK/DM

Kunc, Jan, Czech composer; b. Doubravice, Moravia, March 27, 1883; d. Brno, Sept. 11, 1976. He studied at the Brno Teachers' Training Coll., with Janáček at the Brno Organ School (graduated, 1903), and with Novák in Prague (1905–06). He wrote music criticism in Brno (1909–18), then became an instructor at the Brno Cons. (1919); from 1923 to 1945, was its director. He lectured at the Masaryk Univ. in Brno (1947–52). He was best known as a composer of choral music and songs.

WORKS: DRAMATIC: Opera: *The Lady from the Seashore* (1919; unfinished). **ORCH.:** *Píseň mládí* (Song of Youth), symphonic poem (1915–16). **CHAMBER:** Piano Trio (1905); String Quartet (1909); Violin Sonata (1931); *Serenade* for Violin and Piano (1952). **Piano:** Sonata (1903); *4 Compositions* (1917); *Chronicle,* 20 variations on a Slovak folk song (1926); *Miniatures* (1954–57; also for Wind Quintet, 1958). **VOCAL:** *Sedmdesát tisíc* (70,000) for Chorus (1907); *Ostrava* for Men's Chorus (1912); *Stála Kačenka u Dunaja* (Catherine Stood by the Danube), ballad for Alto and Orch. (1918–19); *35 Folk Songs of Moravian Slovakia* for Women's Chorus (1960); many folk-song arrangements.—NS/LK/DM

Kundera, Ludvík, Czech pianist and musicologist; b. Brünn, Aug. 17, 1891; d. there (Brno), May 12, 1971. He studied voice and piano in Vienna and also took courses at the Univ. of Prague. He made his debut in a Prague recital in 1912; later attended Cortot's master classes in piano in Paris (1925) and studied musicology at the Univ. of Brno (Ph.D., 1925). He toured widely in Europe as a soloist and chamber music player, doing much to promote the music of Czech composers. He was prof. of piano and aesthetics at the Brno Cons. from 1922 until his removal by the Nazi occupation authorities in 1941. After the liberation of his homeland, he was director of the Brno Cons. (1945–46), prof. of piano and deputy dean of the Brno branch of the Prague Academy of Music (1946–47), and prof. of piano at the Brno Academy, serving as dean of its music faculty (1948–50) and as rector (1949–62).

WRITINGS: *O muzike chekhoslovatskovo naroda* (Music of the Czechoslovak Nation; Ekaterinburg, 1919); *Jaroslav Kvapil* (Prague, 1944); *Jak organizovati hudební výchovu v obnoveném státě* (How to Organize Music Education in the Renewed State; Brno, 1945); *Janáček a Klub přátel umění* (Janáček and the Club of the Friends of Art; Olomouc, 1948); *Janáčkova varhanická škola* (Janáček's Organ School; Olomouc, 1948); *Ludvík van Beethoven* (Prague, 1952); *Beethovenovy klavírní sonáty,* I (Prague, 1964); *Václav Kaprál: Kapitola z historie české meziválečné hudby* (Václav Kaprál: A Chapter in the History of Czech Music between the Wars; Brno, 1968).

BIBL.: J. Vysloužil, *L. K.* (Brno, 1962).—NS/LK/DM

Kunits, Luigi von (actually, **Ludwig Paul Maria**), Austrian violinist, conductor, pedagogue, and composer; b. Vienna, July 20, 1870; d. Toronto, Oct. 8, 1931. He studied composition with Bruckner, music history with Hanslick, and violin with Grün and Ševčik in Vienna. In 1893 he went to the U.S., where he played at the Chicago World's Columbian Exposition with an Austrian orch.; taught violin in Chicago (1893–96), and then at the Pittsburgh Cons. (1896–1910). He was also concertmaster of the Pittsburgh Sym. Orch. (1897–1910). He toured widely as a soloist in Europe (1910–12) before settling in Toronto; was a teacher at the Canadian Academy of Music, where he was a founder-member of the Academy String Quartet (1912–23); also founded the *Canadian Journal of Music* (1915–19). He was founder-conductor of the New Sym. Orch. (1922), which became the Toronto Sym. Orch. (1927); he remained with the orch. until his death. He wrote an unpubl. book on Beethoven, *The Hero as Musician* (1913). His compositions include 2 violin concertos, *Lullaby* for Violin and Orch. (1916), String Quartet (1890), Viola Sonata (1917), pieces for Violin and Piano, and songs.

BIBL.: A. Bridle, *L. v.K.* (Toronto, 1931).—NS/LK/DM

Kunkel, Charles, German-American pianist, teacher, music publisher, and composer, brother of **Jacob Kunkel;** b. Sipperfeld, Rheinpfalz, July 22, 1840; d. St. Louis, Dec. 3, 1923. He was taken to America in 1848 by his father, who gave him elementary musical training. In 1868 he and his brother went to St. Louis, where he established a music publishing business and started a music periodical, *Kunkel's Musical Review,* which included sheet music and articles. With his brother he also opened a music store selling pianos and other instruments. In 1872 he founded the St. Louis Cons. of Music, which continued in business for several years. Furthermore, he presented an annual series of concerts in St. Louis known as Kunkel's Popular Concerts (1884–1900). He taught piano to the last years of his life, and also publ. a method of piano playing, which was commended favorably by Liszt. Anton Rubinstein praised him as a pianist during his visit to St. Louis in 1873. Kunkel was reputed to be quite formidable as a sight reader. Altogether, he was certainly a shining light in the German musical colony in middle America in the 2nd half of the 19th century. With his brother he gave, to tumultuous applause, a series of concerts playing piano duets. His publishing business put out a cornucopia of his own piano solos with such titles as *Nonpareil, Galop Brilliant, Philomel Polka, Snowdrops Waltz,* and *Southern Jollification,* most of these highly perishable. However, one piece, *Alpine Storm,* deserves retrieval, if for no other reason than its dedication: "To my son, Ludwig van Beethoven Kunkel." (This piece also contains "tone clusters" played with the palm of the hand in the bass to imitate thunder.)—NS/LK/DM

Kunkel, Jacob, German-American pianist, teacher, music publisher, and composer, brother of **Charles Kunkel;** b. Kleiniedesheim, Oct. 22, 1846; d. St. Louis, Oct. 16, 1882. He studied with his brother, and was also a nominal pupil of Tausig, who, according to the Kunkel family report, refused to teach him because he thought that the younger man was equal to the master. He was taken to America with his brother, and participated in most of the latter's enterprises. He composed piano pieces in a salon manner.—NS/LK/DM

Künneke, Eduard, noted German composer; b. Emmerich-am-Rhein, Jan. 27, 1885; d. Berlin, Oct. 27, 1953. He was a student of Bruch at the Berlin Hochschule für Musik. After composing the operas *Robins Ende* (Mannheim, May 5, 1909) and *Coeur-As* (Dresden, Nov. 1913), he found his métier as a composer of light theater works in Berlin. He attracted favorable notice with his Singspiel *Das Dorf ohne Glocke* (April 5, 1919). The success of his operettas *Der Vielgeliebte* (Oct. 17, 1919) and *Wenn Liebe erwacht* (Sept. 3, 1920) was followed by the outstanding reception accorded his *Der Vetter aus Dingsda* (April 15, 1921). It quickly entered the repertoire as a favorite of the German operetta stage, and was heard all over the globe. After bringing out *Die Ehe im Kreise* (Nov. 2, 1921), *Verliebte Leute* (April 15, 1922), and *Casino-Girl* (Sept. 15, 1923), he failed to find success in N.Y. with the pasticcio *The Love Song* (Jan. 13, 1925) and *Mayflowers* (Nov. 24, 1925). In the interim, he brought out *Die hellblauen Schwestern* (Berlin, Aug. 22, 1925) with considerable success. After the failure in London of *Riki-Tiki* (April 16, 1926), he again found success with *Lady Hamilton* (Breslau, Feb. 25, 1926). His *Die blonde Liselott* (Altenburg, Dec. 25, 1927) became better known in its revised version as *Liselott* (Berlin, Feb. 17, 1932). After bringing out *Die singende Venus* (Breslau, June 9, 1928) and *Der Tenor der Herzogin* (Prague, Feb. 8, 1931), Künneke composed the opera *Nadja* (Kassel, 1931). Returning to the operetta, he then scored the 2nd triumph of his career when he composed *Glückliche Reise* (Berlin, Nov. 23, 1932). It too became a repertoire score of the German operetta stage. Although he never equalled this 2nd success, he went on to compose a number of well-crafted scores, including *Die Fahrt in die Jugend* (Zürich, March 26, 1933), *Die lockende Flamme* (Berlin, Dec. 25, 1933), *Klein Dorrit* (Stettin, Oct. 28, 1933), *Liebe ohne Grenzen* (Vienna, March 29, 1934), *Herz über Bord* (Zürich, March 30, 1935), *Die grosse Sünderin* (Berlin, Dec. 31, 1935), *Zauberin Lola* (Dortmund, April 24, 1937), *Hochzeit in Samarkand* (Berlin, Feb. 14, 1938), *Der grosse Name* (Düsseldorf, May 14, 1938), *Die Wunderbare* (Fürth, Jan. 25, 1941), *Traumland* (Dresden, Nov. 15, 1941), and *Hochzeiet mit Erika* (Düsseldorf, Aug. 31, 1949). Künneke also composed film scores, orch. works, and piano pieces.

BIBL.: O. Schneidereit, *E. K. der Komponist aus Dingsda* (Berlin, 1978); V. Karl, *E. K. (1885–1953): Komponistenportrait und Werkverzeichnis* (Berlin, 1995).—NS/LK/DM

Kunst, Jaap (Jakob), noted Dutch ethnomusicologist; b. Groningen, Aug. 12, 1891; d. Amsterdam, Dec. 7, 1960. He began playing the violin at an early age, and soon became interested in Dutch folk songs. He received a degree in law at the Univ. of Groningen (1917), then toured with a string trio in the Dutch East Indies (1919). He remained in Java, where he worked in a government post in Bandung while pursuing his interest in indigenous Javanese music. He subsequently founded an archive there for folk instruments, field recordings, books, and photographs for the Batavia museum. He returned to the Netherlands in 1934, and in 1936 became curator of the Royal Tropical Inst. in Amsterdam, which developed into one of the most important organizations of its kind in Europe. He gave lectures at the Univ. of Amsterdam (1953), becoming a member of its faculty (1958). Kunst is credited with having coined the word "ethnomusicology" as a more accurate term than "comparative musicology."

WRITINGS: With C. Kunst Van-Wely, *De toonkunst van Bali* (Weltevreden, 1924; part 2 in *Tijdschrift voor Indische taal-, land-en volkenkunde, LXV, Batavia, 1925); with R. Goris, Hindoe-Javaansche muziekinstrumenten* (Batavia, 1927; 2nd ed., rev., 1968, as *Hindu-Javanese Musical Instruments); A Study on Papuan Music* (Weltevreden, 1931); *Musicologisch onderzoek 1930* (Batavia, 1931); *Over zeldzame fluiten en veelstemmige muziek in het Ngada-en Nagehgebied, West-Flores* (Batavia, 1931); *De toonkunst van Java* (The Hague, 1934; Eng. tr., 1949, as *Music in Java*; 3rd ed., aug., 1973); *Verslagen van den ambtenaar voor het systematisch musicologisch onderzoek in den Indischen archipel omtrent de door hem verrichte werkzaamheden* (Bandung, 1934); *Een en ander over den Javaanschen gamelan* (Amsterdam, 1940; 4th ed., 1945); *De waardering van exotische muziek in den loop der eeuwen* (The Hague, 1942); *Music in Flores: A Study of the Vocal and Instrumental Music among the Tribes Living in Flores* (Leiden, 1942); *Music in Nias* (Leiden, 1942); *Een en ander over de muziek en den dans op de Kei-eilanden* (Amsterdam, 1945); *Muziek en dans in de buitengewesten* (Amsterdam, 1946); *De inheemsche muziek en de zending* (Amsterdam, 1947); *Around von Hornbostel's Theory of the Cycle of Blown Fifths* (Amsterdam, 1948); *The Cultural Background of Indonesian Music* (Amsterdam, 1949); *Begdja, het gamelan-jongetje* (Amsterdam, 1950); *De inheemsche muziek in Westelijk Nieuw-Guinea* (Amsterdam, 1950); *Metre, Rhythm and Multipart Music* (Leiden, 1950); *Musicologica: A Study of the Nature of Ethno-musicology, Its Problems, Methods and Representative Personalities* (Amsterdam, 1950; 2nd ed., aug., 1955, as *Ethnomusicology*; 3rd ed., 1959; suppl., 1960); *Kulturhistorische Beziehungen zwischen dem Balkan und Indonesien* (Amsterdam, 1953; Eng. tr., 1954); *Sociologische bindingen in der muziek* (The Hague, 1953). **FOLK SONG EDITIONS:** *Terschellinger volksleven* (Uithuizen, 1916; 3rd ed., 1951); *Noord-Nederlandsche volksliederen en -dansern* (Groningen, 1916–18; 2nd ed., 1918–19); *Het levende lied van Nederland* (Amsterdam, 1918–19; 4th ed., 1947); *Songs of North New Guinea* (Weltevreden, 1931); *Oude westersche liederen uit oostestersche landen* (Bandung, 1934).—**NS/LK/DM**

Kunst, Jos, Dutch composer and teacher; b. Roermond, Jan. 3, 1936; d. Jan. 18, 1996. He studied with Joep Straesser in Utrecht (1963–66) and with Ton de Leeuw at the Amsterdam Cons. (1965–70), where he subsequently taught. His works, which utilized a variety of modernistic techniques, included orch. music, chamber pieces, and tape scores.

WORKS: ORCH.: *Marine* (1963); *Insecten* for 13 Strings (1966); *Arboreal* (1968; Rotterdam, Sept. 11, 1969); *XVII One Way* for Small Orch. (Amsterdam, March 13, 1971); *Elements of Logic* for Wind Orch. (1972; in collaboration with J. Vriend). **CHAMBER:** *Ijzer* (Iron) for Violin and Piano (1965); *XVIII Outward Bound* for Harp (1971); *Solo Identity I* for Bass Clarinet (1972); *No Time at All* for Bass Clarinet and Piano (1973; fusion of *Solo Identity I and II); No Time* for 3 Clarinets, Bass Clarinet, Piano, and 3 Percussionists (1974; amplified version of *No Time at All); XXII: Any 2* for Woodwinds (1975); *Rafale* for 15 Flutes (1975–78); *Streams and Chorals* for Chamber Ensemble (1989–91); *Topos teleios* for String Quartet (1993–94); *Exchange for Fire* for Flute (1994); Concertino for Piano, Winds, and Percussion (1994–95). **PIANO:** *Stenen eten* (The Stone Eaters) for 2 Pianos (1965); *Glass Music* (1966); *Solo Identity II* (1973); *Flying Garundu* (1992); *6 Etudes* (1995). **VOCAL:** *Trajectoire* for 16 Voices and 11 Instruments (1970). **2-TRACK TAPE:** *Exterieur* (1967); *Expulsion* (1969).—**NS/LK/DM**

Kunwald, Ernst, Austrian conductor; b. Vienna, April 14, 1868; d. there, Dec. 12, 1939. He studied law at the Univ. of Vienna (Dr.Juris, 1891), and at the same time studied piano with Leschetizky and J. Epstein and composition with H. Grädener. He also studied at the Leipzig Cons. with Jadassohn. He conducted opera in Rostock (1895–97), Sondershausen (1897–98), Essen (1898–1900), Halle (1900–01), Madrid (1901–02), and Frankfurt am Main (1902–05), and at Kroll's Theater in Berlin (1905–06), and then served as 2nd conductor of the Berlin Phil. (1907–12). In 1906 he was guest conductor of the N.Y. Phil. In 1912 he became conductor of the Cincinnati Sym. Orch., and, from 1914, also of the May Festival. He was arrested as an enemy alien on Dec. 8, 1917, but was released on bail and allowed to continue to conduct until his internment. After his release, he conducted in Königsberg (1920–27). He then conducted the Berlin Sym. Orch. (1928–31).—**NS/LK/DM**

Kunz, Alfred (Leopold), Canadian organist, conductor, and composer; b. Neudorf, Saskatchewan, May 26, 1929. After training in composition and conducting at the Royal Cons. of Music of Toronto (1949–55), he pursued his composition studies in Europe, taking his diploma in choral conducting at the Mainz Hochschule für Musik in 1965. He settled in Kitchener, Ontario, where he founded the Kitchener-Waterloo Chamber Music Orch. and Choir in 1959. After serving as organist and choirmaster at Mount Zion Evangelical Lutheran Church (1959–64), he was principal of the Canadian Music Teachers' Coll. in Burlington, Ontario (1965–67) and director of musical activities of the Univ. of Waterloo (1965–79). He also conducted various choral groups, including the German-Canadian Choir from 1965. His extensive output included many choral pieces, piano music, and accordion works. Kunz's style ranged from tonal writing to advanced contemporary usages.

WORKS: DRAMATIC: *The Damask Drum,* chamber opera (1961); *The Watchful Gods,* operetta (1962); *Moses,* ballet (1965); *Let's Make a Carol,* play with music (1965); *Ceyx and Alcyone,* opera (1979). **ORCH.:** 2 sinfoniettas (1957, 1961); *Excursion* (1964); *5 Night Scenes* (1971); Percussion Concerto (1973); Piano Concerto (1975); Chamber Sym. (1976); *3 Pieces* for Clarinet and Strings (1977); *Overture for Fun* (1978; rev. 1986); *Classical Arcade* (1984); *Spring into Summer* (1984); *Winterlude* (1984; rev. 1986); *Saturday Night Barn Dance: Boy's Night Out* (1988; rev. 1989). Also band music. **CHAMBER:** Violin Sonata (1958); *Emanation No. 1* for Violin, Horn, and Piano (1962) and *No. 2* for Flute, Clarinet, Horn, and Bassoon (1964); *Fun for 2* for 2 Bassoons or 2 Bass Clarinets (1964); Wind Quintet (1964); many pieces for accordion; piano music. **VOCAL:** 2 oratorios: *The Big Land* (1967) and *The Creation* (1972); numerous choral works; many songs.—**NS/LK/DM**

Kunz, Erich, Austrian bass-baritone; b. Vienna, May 20, 1909; d. there, Sept. 8, 1995. He was a student of Theo Lierhammer and Hans Duhan at the Vienna Academy of Music. In 1933 he made his operatic debut as Osmin in Opava, and then sang in Plauen (1936–37) and Breslau (1937–41). In 1940 he became a member of the Vienna State Opera, and sang with the company during its visit to London's Covent Garden in 1947. He appeared as Beckmesser at the Bayreuth Festivals (1943–44; 1951) and as Guglielmo at the Glyndebourne Festivals (1948, 1950). On Nov. 26, 1952, he made his Metropolitan Opera debut in N.Y. as Leporello, and remained on its roster until 1954. Kunz was greatly esteemed in buffo roles, as an operetta singer, and as an interpreter of popular Viennese songs. His most successful operatic roles were Papageno, Leporello, Figaro, and Beckmesser.—NS/LK/DM

Kunz, Ernst, Swiss conductor and composer; b. Bern, June 2, 1891; d. Olten, Feb. 7, 1980. He went to Munich to study at the Univ. and with Klose and Kellermann at the Academy of Music. After conducting at the Bavarian Court Opera (1916–18), he pursued his career in his homeland. He wrote in a neo-Romantic style principally influenced by Richard Strauss and Pfitzner.

WORKS: DRAMATIC: Opera: *Der Fächer* (1924; Zürich, 1929); *Vreneli ab em Guggisberg* (1935); *Die Bremer Stadtmusikanten* (1937); *Der Traum ein Leben* (1968). Singspiel: *Die Hochzeitsreise* (1960). ORCH.: 5 syms.: (1917, 1921, 1942, 1965, 1966); Viola Concerto (1952); *Drei Lebensalter* (1964); *Serenata strana* (1971); Chamber Concerto for Flute, Piano, and Strings (1971). CHAMBER: 3 string quartets; Piano Quartet; piano pieces. VOCAL: Oratorios: *Vom irdischen Leben* (1931–49); *Weihnachts Oratorium* (1936); *Weisheit des Herzens* (1946); *Einkehr* (1951); *Psalter und Harfe* (1956). OTHER: Over 500 choruses; song cycles.—NS/LK/DM

Kunzel, Erich, American conductor; b. N.Y., March 21, 1935. He was educated at Dartmouth Coll. (B.Mus., 1957), and took postgraduate courses at Harvard Univ. and Brown Univ., teaching at the latter (1958–65). He also studied conducting with Monteux, serving as his assistant (1963–64); likewise was asst. conductor of the R.I. Phil. (1960–65). He was asst. conductor (1965–67), assoc. conductor (1967–69), and resident conductor (1969–74) of the Cincinnati Sym. Orch., and also taught at the Univ. of Cincinnati Coll.- Cons. of Music (1965–71). He was music director of the New Haven (Conn.) Sym. Orch. (1974–77), and subsequently conducted his own Cincinnati Pops Orch. (from 1977). He also toured widely as a guest conductor, leading the pops series of many U.S. orchs.—NS/LK/DM

Kunzen, family of German musicians:

(1) **Johann Paul Kunzen,** organist and composer; b. Leisnig, Saxony, Aug. 31, 1696; d. Lübeck, March 20, 1757. He studied organ at an early age, and was deputized for the Leisnig organist by the age of 9. He later studied various keyboard instruments and violin, and subsequently studied with Kuhnau in Leipzig (1716–18). He played and sang at the Leipzig Opera, and also was deputized as organist at the Nikolaikirche. He then was made Kapellmeister in Zerbst (1718). He served as director of the Hamburg Opera from 1723 to 1725, and became organist of Lübeck's Marienkirche in

1732. He achieved distinction as a composer and conductor, presenting a noteworthy series of Abendmusiken. Only a few of his compositions are extant.

(2) **Adolph Carl Kunzen,** organist and composer, son of the preceding; b. Wittenberg, Sept. 22, 1720; d. Lübeck (buried), July 11, 1781. He studied with his father and with W. Lustig in Hamburg, and toured in England with his father (1728–29). He was made Konzertmeister at the Mecklenburg-Schwerin court in 1749, and was its Kapellmeister (1752–53). In 1757 he settled in Lübeck as his father's successor as organist of the Marienkirche. He was also active as a composer and conductor, following in his father's footsteps with a distinguished series of Abendmusiken. He wrote 21 oratorios, but only 2 are extant; however, many of his fine songs exist. He also wrote syms., several concertos, and chamber music.

(3) **Friedrich Ludwig Aemilius Kunzen,** composer, son of the preceding; b. Lübeck, Sept. 24, 1761; d. Copenhagen, Jan. 28, 1817. He studied music with his father, then law at the Univ. of Kiel (1781–84). He was active as a keyboard player, concert organizer, and composer in Copenhagen (1784–89), then went to Berlin, where he set up a music shop with Reichert and ed. the journal *Musikalisches Wochenblatt* (1791). Subsequently he was made Kapellmeister at the theaters in Frankfurt am Main (1792) and Prague (1794), and finally settled in Copenhagen as Royal Kapellmeister (1795). He also served as director of the oratorio society Det Harmoniske Selskab. He composed a number of fine stage works, as well as cantatas and oratorios.

WORKS: DRAMATIC (all 1st perf. in Copenhagen unless otherwise given): *Holger Danske*, opera (March 31, 1789); *Das Fest der Winzer, oder Die Weinlese*, Singspiel (Frankfurt am Main, May 3, 1793; as *Viinhøsten*, Copenhagen, Dec. 1796); *Festen i Valhal*, prologue (Festival in Valhalla; 1796); *Hemmeligheden*, Singspiel (The Secret; Nov. 22, 1796); *Dragedukken*, Singspiel (The Dragon Doll; March 14, 1797); *Erik Ejegod*, opera (Jan. 30, 1798); *Naturens røst*, Singspiel (The Cry of Nature; Nov. 22, 1799); *Min bedste moder* (My Grandmother; May 15, 1800); *Hjemkomsten*, Singspiel (The Homecoming; 1802); *Gyrithe* (1807); *Kaerlighed paa landet* (Love in the Country; March 23, 1810); incidental music. OTHER: Various choral works; Sym.; several overtures; songs; keyboard music.

BIBL.: B. Friis, *F. A. K.: Sein Leben und Werk I. Bis zur Oper "Holger Danske" (1761–1789)* (diss., Univ. of Berlin, 1943).

(4) **Louise Friederica Ulrica Kunzen,** singer, daughter of **Adolph Carl Kunzen;** b. Lübeck, Feb. 15, 1765; d. Ludwigslust, May 4, 1839. She began singing in private concerts in Lübeck when she was 16. She joined the Ludwigslust Court Theater in 1787, where she enjoyed a remarkable career until her retirement in 1837. —NS/LK/DM

Kupfer, Harry, German opera director and administrator; b. Berlin, Aug. 12, 1935. He was trained at the Hans Otto Theaterhochschule in Leipzig. In 1958 he launched his career as an opera director with his staging of *Rusalka* at the Halle Landestheater. After holding the position of Oberspielleiter at the Stralsund Theater der Werfstadt (1958–62), he was senior resident producer at the Karl-Marx-Stadt Städtische Theater (1962–66). From

1966 to 1972 he was opera director at the Weimar Nationaltheater, and from 1967 to 1972 he was on the faculty of the Franz Liszt Hochschule für Musik in Weimar. He was opera director and chief producer at the Dresden State Opera from 1972 to 1981, where he established himself as one of the leading opera directors of his day through the staging of notable productions of both traditional and contemporary works. In 1978 he garnered acclaim with his thought-provoking staging of *Der fliegender Holländer* at the Bayreuth Festival. He was the chief producer at the Berlin Komische Oper from 1981 to 1994. In 1994 he became opera director at the Komische Oper and also artistic advisor to the Intendant of the Berlin State Opera. He collaborated with Penderecki in preparing the libretto for *Die schwarze Maske* (Salzburg Festival, Aug. 15, 1986). In 1988 he staged a compelling *Ring* cycle at the Bayreuth Festival and at the Berlin State Opera in 1995. His productions have also been mounted at the Hamburg State Opera, the Vienna State Opera, and at London's Covent Garden. In his most inspired productions, Kupfer fuses the finest elements of the traditional music theater experience with all that is best in contemporary stage direction.

BIBL.: D. Kranz, *'Ich muss Oper machen': Der Regisseur H. K.* (Berlin, 1988); M. Lewin, *H. K.* (Vienna and Zürich, 1988); R. Lummer, *Regie im Theater: H. K.* (Frankfurt am Main, 1989). —NS/LK/DM

Kupferberg, Herbert, American journalist and music critic; b. N.Y., Jan. 20, 1918. He was educated at Cornell Univ. (B.A., 1939) and Columbia Univ. (M.A., 1940; M.S., 1941). From 1942 to 1966 he was on the staff of the *N.Y. Herald Tribune*; was also music critic of the *Atlantic Monthly* (1962–69) and of the *National Observer* (1967–77). He served as rapporteur for the Twentieth Century Fund's N.Y. task force on cultural exchange with the Soviet Union, which led to the publication of the report *The Raised Curtain* in 1977.

WRITINGS: *Those Fabulous Philadelphians: The Life and Times of a Great Orchestra* (N.Y., 1969); *The Mendelssohns: Three Generations of Genius* (N.Y., 1972); *Opera* (N.Y., 1975); *Tanglewood* (N.Y., 1976); *The Book of Classical Music Lists* (N.Y., 1985); *Basically Bach* (N.Y., 1986); *Amadeus: A Mozart Mosaic* (N.Y., 1986); also 2 books for young readers, *Felix Mendelssohn: His Life, His Family, His Music* (N.Y., 1972) and *A Rainbow of Sound: The Instruments of the Orchestra and Their Music* (N.Y., 1973).—NS/LK/DM

Kupferman, Meyer, American composer, clarinetist, and teacher; b. N.Y., July 3, 1926. He attended N.Y.'s H.S. of Music and Art and then Queens Coll. of the City Univ. of N.Y. (1943–45). He was active as a clarinetist and taught at Sarah Lawrence Coll. (from 1951); was also composer-in-residence at the Calif. Music Center in Palo Alto (from 1977). With John Yannelli, he founded the recording and publishing company Soundspells Productions in 1986. He publ. the book *Atonal Jazz* (1993). In 1975 he received a Guggenheim fellowship and in 1981 an award from the American Academy and Inst. of Arts and Letters. While he has principally applied serial procedures in his music since 1948, his vast catalog of works is nevertheless highly eclectic, displaying significant examples of neo-Classicism, electronic music, and jazz.

WORKS: DRAMATIC: O p e r a : *In a Garden*, after Gertrude Stein (N.Y., Dec. 29, 1949); *Doctor Faustus Lights the Lights*, after Gertrude Stein (1952; rev. 1963); *The Curious Fern* and *Voices for a Mirror* (both perf. in N.Y., June 5, 1957); *Draagenfut Girl*, children's opera (N.Y., May 8, 1958); *The Judgement* (*Infinities No. 18a*) (1966–67); *Prometheus* (1975–77); *The Proscenium* (1991); *The Waxing Moon* (1993). **B a l l e t :** *Persephone* (1968); *The Possessed* (1974); *O Thou Desire Who Art About to Sing* (1977); *Icarus* (1980). **ORCH.:** 3 piano concertos (1948, 1978, 1993); *Divertimento* (1948); 11 numbered syms.: No. 1 (1950), No. 2, *Chamber Symphony* (1950), No. 3, *Little Symphony* (1952; rev. 1983), No. 4 (1955; Louisville, Jan. 28, 1956), No. 5, *Lyric Symphony* (1956), No. 6, *Symphony of the Yin-Yang* (1972), No. 7 (1974), No. 8, *Steps* (1975), No. 9 (1979), No. 10, *F.D.R.* (1981; for the 100th anniversary of the birth of President Franklin D. Roosevelt), and No. 11 (1983); *Jazz Symphony* for Mezzo-soprano, Jazz Saxophonist, and Orch. (Middletown, N.Y., Oct. 14, 1988); *Ostinato Burlesque* (1954; orchestration of a 1948 piano piece); *Variations* (1958); Concerto for Cello and Jazz Band (*Infinities No. 5*; 1962; rev. 1982); *Infinities No. 14* for Trumpet and Chamber Orch. (1965); *Schemata* (*Infinities No. 20*; 1967); *Infinities No. 24* for Strings (1968); Concerto for Cello, Tape, and Orch. (1974); *Sculptures* (1974); *Symphonia Breve* (1975); *Passage* for Strings (1976); Violin Concerto (1976); *Atto* (1977); Concerto for 6 Solo Instruments and Orch. (1978); *Sound Objects No. 10* for Small Orch. (1979); *Phantom Rhapsody* for Guitar and Small Orch. (1980); *Sound Phantoms No. 8* (1980); Tuba Concerto (1983); *Challenger* (1983); Clarinet Concerto (1984); *Quasar Infinities* (1984); *Wings of the Highest Tower* (1988); *Overture for Double Orch.* (1988); *Savage Landscape* (1989); *Symphonic Odyssey* (1990); Double Concerto for 2 Clarinets and Orch. (1991); *Ice Cream Concerto*, concerto grosso for 11 Instruments (1992); *Hot Hors D'Oeuvres* for Small Orch. (1993); Concerto for Amplified Guitar and Small Orch. (1993); *Hexagon Skies*, concerto for Amplified Guitar and Small Orch. (1994); *Banners* for Small Orch. (1995). **CHAMBER:** 5 numbered string quartets, including Nos. 4 (1958) and 5 (1959); Concerto for 11 Brass (1948); Wind Quintet (1958); *Infinities*, cycle of 34 pieces on the same tone row, mostly for Chamber Groupings (1961–83); *Moonchild and the Doomsday Trombone* for Oboe, Voice, and Jazz Band (1968); *Fantasy Concerto* for Cello, Piano, and Tape (1974); *Abracadabra Quartet* for Piano and String Trio (1976); *The Red King's Throw* for Clarinet, Cello, Piano, and Percussion (1977); *Masada*, chamber sym. for Flute, Clarinet, Cello, Double Bass, Piano, and Violin (1977); *Sound Objects*, cycle of 10 pieces, mostly for Chamber Groupings (1978–79); *Sound Phantoms*, cycle of 10 pieces, mostly for Chamber Groupings (1979–81); *Jazz Essay* for Saxophone Quartet (1982); *Symphony for 6* for Clarinet, Bassoon, Horn, Violin, Cello, and Bass (1984); Quintet for Piano and Strings (1985); *And 5 Quartets* for 5 String Quartets (1986); Quintet for Clarinet and Strings (1986); *Rock Shadows* for Brass Quintet (1986); *Summer Music* for 2 Guitars, Flute, and Cello (1987); *Top Brass 5* for 5 Trumpets (1989); *Moontrek Fantasy* for Trumpet, Flute, Cello, and Piano (1989); *Triple Suite* for 3 Flutes Doubling Piccolo (1989); *Currents* for Violin and Piano (1992); *Chaconne Sonata* for Flute and Piano (1993); *Going Home* for Guitar Quartet (1994); *Pipe Dream Sonata* for Guitar (1994). piano pieces. **VOCAL:** *Prometheus profundis* for Chorus, Brass, and Percussion (1975); *Ode to Shreveport*, cantata for 4 Soloists, Chorus, and Orch. (1985); *A Crucible for the*

Moon for Soprano, Alto Saxophone, and Percussion Orch. (1986); *Wicked Combinations*, song cycle for Mezzo- soprano and Piano (1989); *The Shadows of Jerusalem* for Mezzo-soprano, Clarinet, Cello, and Piano (1992).—NS/LK/DM

Kupkovič, Ladislav, Slovak conductor, teacher, and composer; b. Bratislava, March 17, 1936. He studied violin and conducting in Bratislava at the Cons. (1950–55) and at the Academy of Music (1955–61). In 1959–60 he was conductor of the Hungarian Folk Ensemble of Bratislava and then played violin in the Slovak Phil. there (1960–63). In 1963 he organized the chamber ensemble Hudba Dneska (Music of Today). He left Czechoslovakia after the Soviet invasion in 1968 and went to Germany; was a stipendiary at Berlin's Deutscher Akademischer Austauschdienst (1969–71); was made a lecturer (1973) and a prof. (1976) of composition at the Hannover Hochschule für Musik. His music utilizes the cosmopolitan resources of ultramodern music. He initiated "walking concerts," in which a group of musicians walk in the streets playing segments of familiar pieces.

WORKS: DRAMATIC: Singspiel: *Die Maske* (1986). **ORCH.:** *Dioe* for Orch., with Conductor (1968); *Notausgang* for Orch. and Microphones (1970); *Erinnerungen* for Orch. and Tape (1970); *Monolith* for 48 Strings (1971); *Ein Gespräch mit Gott* (1972); *Das Gebet* for Strings and Percussion (1972–73); *Concours* for the "orchestra of the future" (1973); *Čarovné sláčiky* (Magic Bows) for 30 Violins and Low Strings (1974); *Serenata* (1976); *Postillon-Cornet* for Trumpet and Orch. (1977); *K.-u. K. Musik* (1978); *Cassation* (1979); 3 violin concertos (1980, 1981, 1985); Cello Concerto (1980); Accordion Concerto (1980); Piano Concerto (1980); 2 syms. (1981, 1987); *2 Rococo Symphonies* (1982, 1982); *Little Rococo Symphony* for Strings (1981); Concertante for Violin, Cello, Piano, and Orch. (1982); *B-A-C-H Variations* (1989); *Katinkas Geheimnis*, children's fairy tale for Speaker and Small Orch. (1992). **CHAMBER:** *Maso kríža* (Flesh of the Cross) for Trombone and 10 Percussion Players (1961–62); *Psalm* for 4 Horns (1962); *Výkřiky* (Exclamations) for Flute, Bass Clarinet, Piano, and Percussion (1964); *Rozhovor času s hmotou* (A Conversation between Time and Matter) for Bassoon and 3 Percussion Players (1965); *Ozveny* (Echoes) for 31 Players (1966); *Pred s za* (Before and After) for Chamber Ensemble (1967); *Oktoedr* (Octohedron) for Chamber Ensemble (1968); *Ad libitum*, "happening" for a random group of Performers (1969); *312-SL/723* for 2 Accordions (1975); 3 string quartets (1978, 1978, 1984); String Quintet for 2 Violins, Viola, and 2 Cellos (1978); 2 violin sonatas (1979, 1980); Quartet for Flute, Violin, Viola, and Cello (1980); Wind Serenade (1981); 2 piano sonatas (1981, 1981); Cello Sonata (1984); Trio for Violin, Cello, and Piano (1985); Octet for Clarinet, Bassoon, Horn, 2 Violins, Viola, Cello, and Double Bass (1986); Quintet for 2 Violins, Viola, Cello, and Piano (1984); 2 quartets for Violin, Viola, Cello, and Piano (1986, 1986); Octet for 2 Oboes, 2 Clarinets, 2 Horns, and 2 Bassoons (1988); *24 Caprices* for Violin (1990); piano pieces. **VOCAL:** *Missa Papae Ioannis Pauli Secundi* for Chorus and Orch. (1979). **OTHER:** *Klanginvasion auf Bonn*, spectacle of indeterminate duration, representing the invasion of noise on the population of Bonn (1970).—NS/LK/DM

Kupper, Annelies (Gabriele), German soprano; b. Glatz, July 21, 1906; d. Haar, near Munich, Dec. 8, 1987. She studied at the Univ. of Breslau, and then taught in that city (1929–35). She made her debut at the Breslau Opera (1935), remaining there until 1937. She then sang in Schwerin (1937–38) and Weimar (1938–39). She was a principal member of the Hamburg State Opera (1940–46) and the Bavarian State Opera in Munich (1946–61); also sang at Bayreuth, Salzburg, and London's Covent Garden (Chrysothemis, 1953) and appeared as Danae in the first public performance of Richard Strauss's *Die Liebe der Danae* (Salzburg, 1952). She became a teacher at the Munich Academy of Music (1956). In addition to her Mozart and Strauss roles, she became known for her performances of works by contemporary German composers.—NS/LK/DM

Kurath, Gertrude Prokosch (Tula), American ethnomusicologist; b. Chicago, Aug. 19, 1903. She studied at Bryn Mawr Coll. (B.A., 1922; M.A. in art history, 1928), concurrently studying music and dance in Berlin, Philadelphia, N.Y., and Providence, R.I., and then attended the Yale School of Drama (1929–30). She conducted field research for the Wenner-Gren Foundation (1949–73), the American Philosophical Soc. (1951–65), and the National Museum of Canada (1962–65; 1969–70); also taught dance, lectured on dance history, and was dance ed. for *Ethnomusicology* (1958–72). Kurath made substantial contributions to the study of American Indian dance and to dance theory and notation.

WRITINGS: *Songs of the Wigwam* (Delaware, Ohio, 1955); *Iroquois Music and Dance: Ceremonial Arts of Two Seneca Longhouses* (Washington, D.C., 1964); *Michigan Indian Festivals* (Ann Arbor, 1966); *Dance and Song Rituals of Six Nations Reserve, Ontario* (Ottawa, 1968); with A. Garcia, *Music and Dance of the Tewa Pueblos, New Mexico* (Santa Fe, 1970: *Radiant Call* (Ann Arbor, 1971); with R. Miller, *With Magnetic Fields Disrupted* (Ann Arbor, 1972); *Tutelo Rituals on Six Nations Reserve, Ontario* (Ann Arbor, 1981); *Dance Memoires* (Cambridge, Mass., 1983). —NS/LK/DM

Kuri-Aldana, Mario, Mexican composer and teacher; b. Tampico, Aug. 15, 1931. He studied piano with Carlos del Castillo at the Academia Juan Sebastián Bach in Mexico City (1948–51) and composition with Tercero, Vazquez, and Michaca at the Escuela Nacional de Música of the Autonomous Univ. of Mexico (1952–60); took conducting courses from Markevitch and Giardino at the National Inst. of Fine Arts (1957–58); then privately studied advanced techniques of composition with Rodolfo Halffter and Luis Herrera de la Fuente (1961–62); took lessons with Ginastera, R. Malipiero, Messiaen, Maderna, Dallapiccola, Copland, and Chase in various venues (1963–64), and with Stockhausen at the Mexico City Cons. (1965). He was active as a teacher from 1955.

WORKS: ORCH.: 3 syms.: No. 1, *Sacrificio* (1959), No. 2 for Strings (1966), and No. 3, *Ce Actal–1521* (1976); *Los cuatro Bacabs*, suite for Double Wind Orch. and optional Narrator (1960); *Máscaras*, concerto for Marimba and Wind Orch. (1962); *Pasos* for Piano and Orch. (1963); *Bacab de las plegarias* for 2 Flutes, 2 Clarinets, Trumpet, Harp, and Strings (1966); *Formas de otros tiempos* for Strings and Harp (1971); *Concierto de Santiago* for Flute, Strings, and 2 Percussion Players (1973); *Concertino mexicano* for Violin and String Orch. (1974). **CHAMBER:**

Canto de 5-Flor for Cello and Piano (1957); *Sonatina mexicana* for Violin and Piano (1959); *Xilofonías* for Piccolo, Oboe, Bass Clarinet, Double Bassoon, and Percussion (1963); *Puentes* for String Quartet (1965; rev. 1977); *Candelaria*, suite for Wind Quintet (1965); *3-Silvestre*, concerto for 9 Instruments (1966); *Fuga para metales* (1968). **P i a n o** : *Suite ingenua* (1953); *Villancico, Canción y Jarabe* (1965); Sonata (1972). **VOCAL:** *Cantares para una niña muerta* for Mezzo-soprano, Flute, and Guitar (1961); *Este, ese y aquel* for Mezzo- soprano, Flute, Violin, Viola, Cello, and Vibraphone (1964); *Amarillo era el color de la Esperanza*, secular cantata for Narrator, Mezzo-soprano, and Jazz Band (1966); *Noche de verano* for Narrator, Soprano, and Small Orch (1975); *A mi hermano* for Baritone, Chorus, and Orch. (1977).—**NS/LK/DM**

Kurka, Robert (Frank), American composer; b. Cicero, Ill., Dec. 22, 1921; d. N.Y., Dec. 12, 1957. He studied violin with Kathleen Parlow and Hans Letz, and composition with Luening and Milhaud, but considered himself autodidact. He received a Guggenheim fellowship (1951–52), and taught at the City Coll. of N.Y., Queens Coll., and Dartmouth Coll. His satirical opera, *The Good Soldier Schweik*, the composition of which was delayed for years due to problems in clearing rights for the libretto and which existed only as an orchestral suite until 1956, was completed shortly before his untimely death from leukemia and was orchestrated by Hershy Kay; it was premiered with extraordinary success at the N.Y.C. Center on April 23, 1958. Kurka's music, though quite melodic, makes use of harmonious dissonance, imbuing neo- Classical forms with a rhythmic and harmonic intuition reminiscent of Prokofiev and Shostakovich.

WORKS: DRAMATIC: O p e r a : *The Good Soldier Schweik*, after J. Hašek (1952–57; N.Y., April 23, 1958; as a chamber orch. suite, N.Y., Nov. 24, 1952). **ORCH.:** Chamber Sym. (1946; N.Y., March 7, 1948); Sym. for Brass and Strings (1948; N.Y., March 13, 1950); Violin Concerto (1948); *Music for Orchestra* (1949); *3 Pieces* (1951); 2 numbered syms.: No. 1 (1951) and No. 2 (1953; San Diego, July 8, 1958); *Serenade* for Small Orch. (La Jolla, Calif., June 13, 1954); *John Henry*, portrait (1954); *Julius Caesar*, symphonic epilogue after Shakespeare (San Diego, July 12, 1955); Concertino for 2 Pianos, Strings, and Trumpet (1955); Marimba Concerto (1956; N.Y., Nov. 11, 1959); *Ballad* for Horn and Strings (1956); *Chamber Sinfonietta* (1957). **CHAMBER:** 5 string quartets (1945, 1947, 1949, 1950, 1954); 4 violin sonatas (1946, 1949, 1953, 1955); Sonata for Solo Violin (1947); *Music for Violin, Trumpet, Clarinet, Horn, and Double Bass* (1951); Piano Trio (1951); *7 Moravian Folksongs* for Wind Quintet (1951); Cello Sonatina (1953). **P i a n o :** Sonatina (1947); *For the Piano*, suite (1951); Sonata (1952); *Dance Suite* for Piano, 4-Hands (1955); *Sonatina for Young Persons* (1957). **VOCAL:** *Who Shall Speak for the People* for Men's Chorus and Orch., after Sandburg (1956); *Song of the Broad-Axe* for Men's Chorus (1956); songs. —**NS/LK/DM**

Kurpiński, Karol (Kazimierz), prominent Polish conductor and composer; b. Wloszakowice, March 6, 1785; d. Warsaw, Sept. 18, 1857. He studied with his father, Marcian Kurpiński, an organist, and in 1797 became organist in Sarnów. He then was a violinist in the private orch. of Feliks Polanowski at his Moszków estate (1800–08), and subsequently music master to the Rastawiecki family in Lemberg (1808–10). He settled in Warsaw, where he became a theater violinist. He then was made deputy conductor of the Opera, and also Kapellmeister of the Polish royal court (1819); was principal conductor of the Opera (1824–40). He also taught music at the schools of drama (1812, 1817) and voice (1835–40), which he founded. He was founder-ed. of the first Polish music journal, *Tygodnik Muzyczny* (Music Weekly; 1820–21). As one of the leading Polish composers of his day, he helped to establish the national Polish school. He wrote 24 stage works, including the operas *Jadwiga królowa Polska* (Jadwiga, Queen of Poland; Warsaw, Dec. 23, 1814) and *Zamek na Czorsztynce, czyli Bojomic i Wanda* (The Castle of Czorsztyn, or Bojomic and Wanda; Warsaw, March 5, 1819). His other works include sacred pieces, polonaises for orch., chamber music, and piano pieces.

BIBL.: T. Przybylski, *K. K., 1785–1857* (Warsaw, 1975). —**NS/LK/DM**

Kurt, Melanie, Austrian soprano; b. Vienna, Jan. 8, 1880; d. N.Y., March 11, 1941. She studied piano with Leschetizky at the Vienna Cons. (1887–94), winning the gold medal and Liszt prize; then took vocal lessons from Fannie Mütter in Vienna (1896), but also toured as a pianist (1897–1900). She then made her operatic debut as Elisabeth in *Tannhäuser* (Lübeck, 1902); then sang in Leipzig (1903–04). She completed her vocal training with Lilli and Marie Lehmann in Berlin. From 1905 to 1908 she sang in Braunschweig; then (1908–12) at the Berlin Royal Opera. She became an outstanding Wagner interpreter and appeared in London (Covent Garden, 1910, 1914), Brussels, Milan, Budapest, etc. When the Deutsches Opernhaus in Charlottenburg was opened in 1912, she was engaged as chief soprano for heroic roles. On Feb. 1, 1915, she made her debut at the Metropolitan Opera in N.Y. as Isolde; remained on its roster until her contract was terminated with the U.S. entry into World War I in 1917. After returning to Germany, she appeared at the Berlin Volksoper (1920–25); also taught there, and later in Vienna. In 1938 she settled in N.Y. Her roles included Pamina, Beethoven's Leonore, Sieglinde, Brünnhilde, Kundry, and the Marschallin.—**NS/LK/DM**

Kurtág, György, eminent Hungarian composer and teacher; b. Logoj, Romania, Feb. 19, 1926. At 14, he began lessons in piano with Magda Kardos and in composition with Max Eisikovits in Timişoara. In 1946 he went to Budapest and in 1948 became a naturalized Hungarian citizen. He pursued his training at the Academy of Music with Kadosa (piano), Veress and Farkas (composition), and Weiner (chamber music), graduating with diplomas in piano and chamber music in 1951 and in composition in 1955. In 1957–58 he was in Paris to study with Marianne Stein, and also attended the courses at the Cons. of Milhaud and Messiaen. From 1967 to 1986 he was a prof. at the Budapest Academy of Music. In 1971 he was in Berlin under the sponsorship of the Deutscher Akademischer Austauschdienst. From 1993 to 1995 he was a guest at the Wissenschaftskolleg in Berlin. In 1954, 1956, and 1969 he received the Erkel Prize. He was awarded the Kossuth Prize in 1973. In

1980 he was made a Merited Artist and in 1984 an Outstanding Artist by the Hungarian government. In 1987 he became a member of the Bavarian Akademie der Schönen Künste in Munich. He was awarded the Herder Prize in Hamburg in 1992. In 1994 he was honored with the Austrian State Prize. Kurtág has built upon advanced compositional techniques to produce his own distinctive style. His music is notable for its distinguished craftsmanship, integrity, refinement, and lyricism.

WORKS: ORCH.: *Movement* for Viola and Orch. (1954; 1st movement of the Viola Concerto, 1954); Viola Concerto (1954; 1st movement as *Movement* for Viola and Orch., 1954); *Grabstein für Stephan* for Guitar and Spatially Dispersed Instrumental Groups (1978–79; rev. version, Szeged, Oct. 26, 1989); *...Quasi una Fantasia...* for Piano and Spatially Dispersed Instrumental Groups (1987–88; Berlin, Oct. 16, 1988); Double Concerto for Piano, Cello, and 2 Spatially Dispersed Chamber Ensembles (1989–90; Frankfurt am Main, Dec. 8, 1990); *Stele* (Berlin, Dec. 14, 1994). **CHAMBER:** String Quartet (1959; Budapest, April 24, 1961); Wind Quintet (1959; Budapest, Nov. 17, 1963); 8 Duos for Violin and Cimbalom (1961; Budapest, March 22, 1963); *Signs* for Viola (1961; Budapest, March 22, 1963); *Splinters* for Cimbalom (1973; Budapest, April 12, 1975; also for Piano, 1978); *In Memoriam György Zilcz* for 2 Trumpets, 2 Trombones, and Tuba (1975); *Hommage à András Milhály*, 12 microludes for String Quartet (1977; Witten, April 21, 1978); *The Little Predicament* for Piccolo, Trombone, and Guitar (1978; Budapest, April 27, 1979); *Herdecker Eurythmie* for Flute, Violin, Speaking Voice, and Tenor Lyre (1979); *János Pilinszky: Gérard de Nerval* for Cello (1986); *Officium Breve in Memoriam Andreae Szervánszky* for String Quartet (Witten, April 22, 1988); *Ligatura-Message to Frances-Marie (The Answered Unanswered Question)* for Cello with 2 Bows, 2 Violins, and Celesta (1989; also for 2 Cellos, 2 Violins, and Celesta, and for 2 Organs and Celesta or Upright Piano); *Hommage à R. Sch.* for Clarinet, Viola, and Piano (Budapest, Oct. 8, 1990); *Lebenslauf* for 2 Pianos and 2 Basset Horns (Witten, April 26, 1992). **KEYBOARD: Piano:** Suite for Piano Duet (1950–51); *8 Piano Pieces* (Darmstadt, July 10, 1960); *Games* (1st series, 4 books, 1973–76; 2nd series, 3 books, 1975–93); *Pre-Games* (1974–75); *3 In Memoriam* (1988–90). **Organ:** *Ligature e Versetti* (1990). **VOCAL:** *Beads* for Chorus (1949 or 1950); *The Sayings of Péter Bornemisza*, concerto for Soprano and Piano (1963–68; Darmstadt, Sept. 5, 1968; rev. 1969 and 1975); *3 Old Inscriptions* for Voice and Piano (1967–86; Berlin, Oct. 16, 1988); *In Memory of Winter Sunset* for Soprano, Violin, and Cimbalom (Debrecen, May 18, 1969); *4 Capriccios* for Soprano and Chamber Orch. (1970; Budapest, Oct. 13, 1971; rev. for Soprano and 14 Instruments, 1997); *4 Songs to Poems by János Pilinszky* for Bass or Bass-baritone and Chamber Ensemble (Budapest, Oct. 1, 1975); *S.K. Remembrance Noise*, 7 songs for Soprano and Violin (1975; Budapest, Dec. 28, 1976); *Omaggio a Luigi Nono* for Chorus (1979; London, Feb. 3, 1981); *Messages of the Late Miss R.V. Troussova* for Soprano and Chamber Ensemble (1976–80; Paris, Jan. 14, 1981); *Songs of Despondency and Grief* for Chorus and Instruments (1980–94; Amsterdam, June 21, 1995); *Attila József Fragments* for Soprano (1981; Budapest, Oct. 26, 1982); *7 Songs* for Soprano and Cimbalom or Piano (1981; Glasgow, Oct. 7, 1985); *Scenes from a Novel* for Soprano, Violin, Double Bass, and Cimbalom (1981–82; Budapest, Oct. 1, 1983); *8 Choruses* (1981–82; rev. version, London, June 1, 1984); *Requiem for the Beloved* for Soprano and Piano (1982–87; London, Oct. 13, 1989); *Kafka-Fragment* for Soprano and Violin (1985–87; Witten, April 25, 1987); *Hölderlin: An...* for Tenor and Piano (1988–89; Aachen,

June 6, 1989); *Samuel Beckett: What is the Word* for Voice and Piano (1990; Sermoneta, June 5, 1993; also for Alto, Voices, and Spatially Dispersed Chamber Ensembles, Vienna, Oct. 27, 1991); *Friedrich Hölderlin: Im Walde* for Voice (1993). **TAPE:** *Mémoire de Laïka* (1990; Budapest, Jan. 1, 1991; in collaboration with his son, G. Kurtág Jr.).

BIBL.: F. Spangemacher, ed., *G. K.* (Bonn, 1986). —NS/LK/DM

Kurth, Ernst, eminent Austrian-born Swiss musicologist; b. Vienna, June 1, 1886; d. Bern, Aug. 2, 1946. He studied with Adler at the Univ. of Vienna (Ph.D., 1908, with the diss. *Der Stil der opera seria von Gluck bis zum Orfeo*; publ. in *Studien zur Musikwissenschaft*, I, 1913), then completed his Habilitation at the Univ. of Bern in 1912 with his *Die Voraussetzungen der theoretischen Harmonik und der tonalen Darstellungssystems* (publ. in Bern, 1913). He was made a reader (1920) and a prof. of musicology (1927) there. His principal work, *Grundlagen des linearen Kontrapunkts: Bachs melodische Polyphonie* (Bern, 1917; 5th ed., 1956), profoundly influenced musicology and practical composition, and also introduced the term "linear counterpoint." A companion vol., *Romantische Harmonik und ihre Krise in Wagners Tristan* (Bern, 1920; 3rd ed., 1923), is a psychological analysis of Romantic music. His *Musikpsychologie* (Berlin, 1931; 2nd ed., 1947) represents a synthesis of his theoretical ideas on musical perception. He also publ. *Anton Bruckner* (2 vols., Berlin, 1925). Le Rothfarb ed. and tr. *Ernst Kurth: Selected Writings* (Cambridge and N.Y., 1991).

BIBL.: L. Rothfarb, *E. K. as Theorist and Analyst* (Philadelphia, 1988).—NS/LK/DM

Kurtz, Efrem, Russian-born American conductor; b. St. Petersburg, Nov. 7, 1900; d. London, June 27, 1995. He studied with N. Tcherepnin, Glazunov, and Wihtol at the St. Petersburg Cons., then at the Univ. of Riga (1918–20). He then took music courses at the Stern Cons. in Berlin, graduating in 1922. He made his conducting debut in Berlin in 1921, and then was a guest conductor with the Berlin Phil.; subsequently was conductor of the Stuttgart Phil. (1924–33). He was conductor of the Ballets Russes de Monte Carlo (1933–42), with which he toured throughout Europe and the U.S. He then went to the U.S., becoming a naturalized American citizen in 1944. He was conductor of the Kansas City Phil. (1943–48) and the Houston Sym. Orch. (1948–54); then was joint conductor of the Liverpool Phil. (1955–57). In subsequent years, he appeared as a guest conductor in Europe, the U.S., and Japan. He was married to the flutist Elaine Shaffer from 1955.—NS/LK/DM

Kurz, Selma, noted Austrian soprano; b. Bielitz, Silesia, Nov. 15, 1874; d. Vienna, May 10, 1933. She studied with Johannes Ress in Vienna and Mathilde Marchesi in Paris. She made her first appearance as a mezzo-soprano as Mignon at the Hamburg Opera (May 12, 1895); then sang in Frankfurt am Main (1896–99). She made her first appearance at the Vienna Court Opera as Mignon (Sept. 3, 1899); after singing lyric-dramatic soprano roles, she turned to coloratura roles; continued on its roster when it became the State Opera (1918), singing there until her retirement (1927). She made her London debut at Covent Garden as Gilda (June 7, 1904), creating a profound impression; sang there again in 1905, 1907, and 1924. She appeared as a concert singer in the U.S. She was esteemed for such roles as Elizabeth, Eva, Sieglinde, Lucia, and Mimi; also created Zerbinetta in the rev. version of Richard Strauss's *Ariadne auf Naxos* (1916). She married the Austrian gynecologist Josef Halban in 1910; their daughter was the soprano Desi Halban-Kurz (b. Vienna, April 10, 1912).

BIBL.: H. Goldmann, *S. K.* (Bielitz, 1933); D. Halbin and U. Ebbers, *S. K.: Die Sängerin und ihre Zeit* (Stuttgart and Zürich, 1983).—NS/LK/DM

Kurz, Siegfried, German conductor and composer; b. Dresden, July 18, 1930. He studied conducting with Ernst Hintze, composition with Fidelio Finke, and trumpet with Gerd Seifert at the Staatlichen Akademie für Musik und Theater in Dresden (1945–50). From 1949 to 1960 he was conductor of music for dramatic productions at the Dresden State Theater. In 1960 he became a conductor at the Dresden State Opera; in 1975 he was named its music director; in 1979 he also became a prof. of composition at the Dresden Hochschule für Musik. He toured with the Dresden State Orch. to Austria, Japan, and the U.S. As a conductor, he was honored with the titles of Staatskapellmeister (1965) and Generalmusikdirektor (1971); as a composer, he received the Kunstpreis and the Nationalpreis of the German Democratic Republic. His compositions combine the principles of Classical lucidity with the dissonant counterpoint of the modern era.

WORKS: ORCH.: *Sinfonia piccola* (1953); Trumpet Concerto (1953); 2 syms. (1958, 1959); Chamber Concerto for Wind Quintet and Strings (1962); Piano Concerto (Dresden, Oct. 2, 1964); *Variations* (1968); *Sonatine* (1969); *Music* for Winds, Percussion, and Strings (1969); Horn Concerto (Dresden, Dec. 20, 1973). **CHAMBER:** Wind Quintet (1950); *Sonatine* for 7 Brass Instruments (1952).—NS/LK/DM

Kurz, Vilém, Czech pianist and pedagogue; b. Německý Brod, Dec. 23, 1872; d. Prague, May 25, 1945. He studied piano with Julius Höger (1884–86) and Jakub Holfeld (1886–98), and also received training in organ and theory at the Prague Organ School (1886–87) before passing the state music examinations at the Prague Cons. (1892). He was active as a soloist and chamber music player, founding the Czech Trio and playing in the Czech Quartet. He was prof. of piano at the Lwów Cons. (1898–1919) and the Brno Cons. (1919–20). After teaching at the Brno branch of the Prague Cons. (1920–28), he settled in Prague and taught at the Cons. (1928–40), where he also was its rector (1936–37; 1938–39). Kurz was highly regarded as a pedagogue and publ. several piano methods. His most famous pupil was Rudolf Firkušný.

BIBL.: Z. Böhmová-Zahradnikova, *V. K.:Život, práce, methodika* (V. K.: Life, Work, and Methods; Prague, 1954). —NS/LK/DM

Kürzinger, Ignaz Franz Xaver, German composer; b. Rosenheim, Upper Bavaria, Jan. 30, 1724; d.

Würzburg, Aug. 12, 1797. He studied for the priesthood in Innsbruck, but became a trumpeter in a Hungarian cuirassier regiment. He was taken prisoner during the first Silesian War, and was sent to Berlin, where he studied composition with C.H. Graun. He was later taken to Italy by the Elector Clemens August of Cologne, who made him grand master of the Teutonic Knights. He was active at its chapel in Mergentheim, Württemberg, where he later served as Kapellmeister (1751–63). He then went to Wurzburg as a violinist in the Court Orch. of the Prince-Bishop, and subsequently became music director of the orphanage at the Julius Hospital. He wrote sacred and secular vocal music, orch. works, and piano pieces, but much of his work was destroyed during World War II. He publ. the useful manual *Getreuer Unterricht zum Singen mit Manieren, und die Violin zu spielen* (Augsburg, 1763; 5th ed., 1821). His son, Paul Ignaz Kürzinger (b. Mergentheim, Württemberg, April 28, 1750; d. Vienna, after 1820), was also a composer. After studying with his father, he played violin in the Munich electoral Court Orch. (1775–77), and then in the orch. of the Prince of Thurn and Taxis in Regensburg (1777–80), where he was director of the Court Theater (1780–83). He subsequently settled as a theater composer and director of a private school in Vienna. He wrote the operas La Contessina (Munich, 1775), Robert und Kalliste (Regensburg, 1780), Der Bergknappen (Regensburg, 1782), and Die Illumination (Vienna, 1787; not extant), as well as 4 ballets, a cantata, piano pieces, and songs.—NS/LK/DM

Kusche, Benno, German bass-baritone; b. Freiburg im Breisgau, Jan. 30, 1916. He studied in Karlsruhe with his mother and in Freiburg im Breisgau with Fritz Harlan. He made his operatic debut in Koblenz in 1938, then sang in Augsburg (1939–44) and subsequently became a leading member of the Bavarian State Opera in Munich (1946). He made his debut at London's Covent Garden as Beckmesser (1952); chose that same role for his Metropolitan Opera debut in N.Y. on Dec. 27, 1971. He was made a Bavarian Kammersänger in 1955. His notable roles included Papageno, Figaro, Leporello, Don Alfonso, and Alberich.—NS/LK/DM

Kusser (or **Cousser**), **Johann Sigismund,** noted German conductor and composer of Hungarian parentage; b. Pressburg (baptized), Feb. 13, 1660; d. Dublin, Nov. 1727. He received his early musical training from his father, Johann Kusser (1626–75), a minister and organist. He lived in Stuttgart as a boy, then spent 8 years in Paris (1674–82), where he became a pupil of Lully. He subsequently was a violin teacher at the Ansbach court (1682–83), becoming opera Kapellmeister in Braunschweig in 1690. In 1695 he became co-director of the Hamburg Opera, but left the next year and was active in Nuremberg and Augsburg as an opera composer. He was again in Stuttgart from 1700 to 1704 as Ober-Kapellmeister. In 1705 he appeared in London, and in 1709 settled in Dublin, where he was made Chappel-Master of Trinity Coll. in 1717 and Master of the Musick "attending his Majesty's State in Ireland" in 1717. He was greatly esteemed as an operatic conductor;

Mattheson, in his *Volkommener Capellmeister*, holds him up as a model of efficiency. Kusser is historically significant for being the mediator between the French and the German styles of composition, and the first to use Lully's methods and forms in German instrumental music. Lully's influence is shown in Kusser's set of 6 suites for Strings, *Composition de musique suivant la méthode française* (Stuttgart, 1682).

WORKS: DRAMATIC: O p e r a : *Julia* (Braunschweig, 1690); *Cleopatra* (Braunschweig, 1691); *La Grotta di Salzdahl*, divertimento (Braunschweig, 1691); *Ariadne* (Braunschweig, Feb. 15, 1692); *Andromeda* (Braunschweig, Feb. 20, 1692); *Jason* (Braunschweig, Sept. 1, 1692); *Narcissus* (Braunschweig, Oct. 14, 1692); *Porus* (Braunschweig, 1693); *Erindo, oder Dir unsträfliche Liebe*, pastorale play (Hamburg, 1694); *Der grossmüthige Scipio Africanus* (Hamburg, 1694); *Gensericus, als Rom und Karthagens Überwinder* (Hamburg, 1694?; may be by Conradi); *Pyramus und Thisbe getreu und festverbundene Liebe* (Hamburg, 1694?); *Der verliebte Wald* (Stuttgart, 1698); *Erminia* (Stuttgart, Oct. 11, 1698); *The Man of Mode* (London, Feb. 9, 1705). **OTHER:** 18 ouvertures or suites, 6 publ. as *Composition de musique suivant la méthode française* (Stuttgart, 1682), 6 as *Apollon enjoué* (Stuttgart, 1700), and 6 as *Festin des muses* (Stuttgart, 1700).—**NS/LK/DM**

Kutavičius, Bronislovas,

Lithuanian composer; b. Molainiai, near Panevėžys, Sept. 13, 1932. He studied composition with Antanas Račiunas at the Vilnius Cons., graduating in 1964. In 1975 he was appointed to the music faculty at the Arts School in Vilnius. In his music, he evolves a complex system of varied techniques, impressionistic pointillism, intervallic serialism, and aleatory sonorism, all this intertwined with Lithuanian melorhythms.

WORKS: DRAMATIC: *Doddering Old Man on Iron Mountain*, children's opera-ballet (1976); *The Green Bird*, opera-poem (1981). **ORCH.:** *Sinfonietta* (1964); *Divertimento* for Piano and Strings (1967); Sym. for Men's Chorus and Orch. (1973); *Dzukija Variations* for Strings and Tape (1975); *The Northern Gates* for Strings (1991). **CHAMBER:** Violin Sonata (1962); *Prelude and Fugue* for 4 Violins (1966); *Poem* for Cello, Piano, and Wind Quintet (1967); Viola Sonata (1968); *From Madrigal to Aleatory*, children's suite for Violin and Piano (1972); 2 string quartets: No. 1 (1972) and No. 2, *Anno cum tettigonia* (Year with a Cicada; 1980); *Prutiena* (Buried Village) for Violin, Organ, and Chimes (1977); String Quintet (1978); *Clocks of the Past I* for String Quartet and Guitar (1978) and *II* for 13 Instruments (1988); *Dances of the Cranes*, clarinet sonata (1989); *The Gates of Jerusalem*, 4 pieces for Different Ensembles (1992–95); *Far Away, Until Midnight* for 5 Saxophones and 5 Strings (1995); *Erotics* for Recorder, Horn, and Phonogram (1997). **P i a n o :** *3 Metamorphoses* (1966); *Collages* for 2 Pianos (1970); Sonata (1975); *A Disputation with a Stranger*, concerto for 2 Pianos and Tape (1982). **VOCAL:** *Pantheistic Oratorio* for Soprano, Narrator, 4 Men's Voices, and 12 Instruments (1970); *On the Shore* for High Voice and 4 Violas (1972); *Little Performance* for Actress, 2 Pianos, and 2 Violins (1975); *2 Birds in the Thick of the Woods*, cantata for Soprano, Oboe, Prepared Piano, and Electronic Tape (1978); *The Last Pagan Rites*, oratorio for Soprano, Girls' Chorus, Horns, and Organ (1978); *The Stone of the Sudovians*, oratorio for Vocal Ensemble and Ancient Folk Instruments (1983); *Tree of the World*, oratorio for Chorus, Vocal Ensemble, Wind Orch., Organ, Percussion, Piano, and Ancient Folk Instruments (1986); *The Magic Circle of Sanskrit* for Ensemble and Actor (1990); *Der Kampf der Baume* for Soprano, Flute, Oboe, Harpsichord, and

Organ (1996); *Pronounce a Word—Lips Turn into Ice* for Chamber Chorus, Trumpet, Trombone, and Piano (1996); *Epitaphium tempori pereunti* for Chorus and Orch. (Odense, Denmark, Nov. 5, 1998).—**NS/LK/DM**

Kutev, Filip,

Bulgarian bandmaster, choral conductor, and composer; b. Aytos, June 26, 1903; d. Sofia, Nov. 27, 1982. He studied at the Sofia Academy of Music (graduated, 1929). He was a bandmaster in Burgas, and then in Sofia. In 1951 he organized an ensemble of largely untutored folksingers, musicians, and dancers, which he brought to a high point of virtuosity and toured in Europe (1958) and the U.S. (1963), eliciting great praise. Virtually all of his compositions are derived from Bulgarian melorhythms. These include *Bulgarian Rhapsody* for Orch. (1937), *September the 9th*, cantata in honor of the entry of the Soviet army into Bulgaria in 1944, *Stalin Cantata* (1949), and Sym. (1950).

BIBL.: S. Stoyanov, *F. K.* (Sofia, 1962).—**NS/LK/DM**

Kuti, Fela (also Fela Ransome Kuti and Fela Anikulapo-Kuti),

African musician and political activist; b. Abeokuta, Nigeria, Oct. 15, 1938; d. Lagos, Nigeria, Aug. 2, 1997. In Africa, Fela Kuti is best known as a musician, political irritant, and supporter of Pan-Africanism. Afrobeat, the musical hybrid created by Kuti, combines elements of highlife (via Ghana), soul (a la James Brown), and jazz for a potent rhythmic force to which he adds lyrics decrying government corruption sung in either Yoruba or pidgin English. He got his performance baptism as a vocalist with trumpeter and highlife superstar Victor Olaiya. In 1958 Kuti went to London and studied at Trinity Coll. of Music. While in England he formed a highlife band known as Koola Lobitos. After studying trumpet and musical theory for four years, he returned to Nigeria, where he re-formed Koola Lobitos. Between 1963 and 1968 Kuti unveiled the first version of "Afrobeat," but it was his trip to the United States in 1969 that helped to crystallize his musical ideas. Kuti lived and recorded in Los Angeles for most of the year, absorbing lessons in black history and Black Power through an impressive reading regimen that helped develop his political consciousness. He also rethought his approach to music, as he said in an interview that he had been using jazz to play African music, when he should have been using African music to play jazz. The horn section work from James Brown's funk band also made an impression on Kuti at this time. 1970 found him back in Nigeria with a newly minted evolution of Afrobeat, a band (Africa 70), and a vision of social justice that endeared him to much of the African populace while marking him as a gadfly for the ruling establishment. Since then Kuti has released more than 40 albums, been harassed, beaten up, and imprisoned by Nigerian governments, renamed his band Egypt 80, and remained as popular with the African masses as ever.

After his release from prison in 1986 (he had been charged with money laundering by the ruling Nigerian military junta), Kuti reclaimed his band, enlarged it to 40 pieces, and jumped back into the musical fray. *O.D.O.O. (Overtake Don Overtake Overtake)* (1990) shows a strengthening of Kuti's composing, arranging, and playing skills. There are only two pieces on the album, each hovering around the half hour mark, and both contain fiery solos within the context of Kuti's rhythm and polemic. *Black Man's Cry* (1992) is probably the best single-volume Fela sampler now available, binding together six of his most popular performances from the mid- to late 1970s. The version of "Black Man's Cry" comes from a 1975 recording that Kuti made with rock drummer Ginger Baker, while "Zombie," with its constantly moving rhythm accents, post-Masekela trumpet, and Maceo Parker–inspired sax playing, is a true Afrobeat classic.

In the early days of Afrobeat, drummer Tony Allen defined the jazz-oriented rhythm that would drive Kuti's music. The songs on *Open & Close* (1971) were breaking the five-minute barrier that many of Kuti's pre-Africa 70 songs had hovered near, and Allen's flexible stick work and sophisticated cymbal splashing provided the constant push needed to enhance the leader's horn charts. "Gbagada Gbagada Gbogodo Gbogodo" provides ample evidence of Allen's importance to this edition of the band, while the title tune, purporting to provide instruction for a brand new dance, is one of the last apolitical works Kuti recorded. He died on Aug. 2, 1997.

DISC.: *Original Sufferhead* (1981); *Beasts of No Nation* (1989); *Volumes 1 & 2* (1996).

BIBL.: Carlos Moore, F.: *This Bitch of a Life* (Paris, 1982). —GM

Kuula, Toivo (Timoteus), Finnish conductor and composer; b. Vasa, July 7, 1883; d. (shot to death during a street fight in the aftermath of the Finnish Civil War) Viipuri, May 18, 1918. He studied at the Helsinki Music Inst. with Sibelius, Wegelius, Nováček, and Järnefelt (1900–08), then with Bossi in Bologna, in Leipzig, and with Labey in Paris (1908–10), and finally in Berlin (1911–12). He taught and conducted in Vasa (1903–05). He was conductor of the Oulu Orch. (1910–11), vice- conductor of the Native Orch. (1912–14), and asst. conductor of the Helsinki Municipal Orch. (1914–16), then conducted the orch. of the Viipuri Friends of Music (1916–18). His music, rooted in Finnish folk song, is occasionally touched with Impressionism.

WORKS: *Etelapohjälainen sarja* (South Ostrobothnians Suites) for Orch. (1906–09; 1912–14); *Prelude and Fugue* for Orch. (1909); *Prelude and Intermezzo* for Strings and Organ (1909); *Orjanpoika* (The Son of a Slave), symphonic legend (1910); *Kuolemattomuuden toivo* (Hope of Immortality) for Baritone, Chorus, and Orch. (1910); *Merenkylpijäneidot* (Maids on the Seashore) for Soprano and Orch. (1910); *Impi ja pajarinpoika* (The Maid and the Boyar's Son) for Soprano and Orch. (1911); *Bothnic Poem* for Orch. (Petrograd, Oct. 26, 1918); Violin Sonata; music for plays; piano pieces; songs. He left unfinished a *Jupiter Symphony*; also a *Stabat Mater* for Chorus, Organ, and Orch. (1914–18; completed by Madetoja).

BIBL.: T. Elmgreen-Heinonen and E. Roiha, *T. K.: A Finnish Composer of Genius* (Helsinki, 1952).—NS/LK/DM

Kuusisto, Ilkka Taneli, Finnish composer, conductor, and administrator, son of **Taneli Kuusisto;** b. Helsinki, April 26, 1933. He studied organ at the Sibelius Academy in Helsinki; also composition with Arre Merikanto and Fougstedt. In 1958 he went to N.Y. to study organ with Seth Bingham, and later continued his studies in Germany and Vienna. Returning to Helsinki, he was a conductor at the City Theater (1965–68; 1971–75) and also head of the Klemetti Inst. (1969–71). After serving as artistic director of Fazer Music (1981–84), he was general manager of the Finnish National Opera (1984–92).

WORKS: DRAMATIC: Opera: *Muumiooppera* (1974); *Miehen kylkiluu* (1977); *Sota valosta* (1980; Helsinki, April 2, 1981); *Jääkäri Stahl* (1981); *Pierrot tai yon salaisuudet* (1991). **Musicals:** *Lumikuningatar* (1979); *Robin Hood* (1987). Also music for plays and films. **CHAMBER:** *3 Introductions* for Brass, Percussion, and Organ (1956); Duo for Flute and Cello (1957); *Coelestis aulae nuntius* for Trombone and Organ (1959); *Cassazione* for 2 Clarinets and 2 Horns (1961); *Jazzationes* for Jazz Quartet and String Quartet (1965); *Ritornells* for Viola and Marimba (1970); organ pieces. **VOCAL:** *3 Chinese Songs* for Soprano, Flute, and Piano (1956); *Daybreak*, cantata for Soloists, Youth Chorus, and Organ (1957); *Crucifixus* for Baritone and String Quartet (1959); *The Pain* and *Alfhid*, 2 songs for Baritone, 2 Clarinets, and Strings (1972); other songs.—NS/LK/DM

Kuusisto, Taneli, Finnish organist and composer, father of **Ilkka Taneli Kuusisto;** b. Helsinki, June 19, 1905; d. there, March 30, 1988. He studied at the Helsinki Inst. of Church Music (graduated, 1931), in Paris, and in Leipzig with J.N. David. He centered his career on Helsinki. He was asst. conductor of the Finnish Radio (1936–42) and chorus director of the Finnish National Opera (1942–46), and also organist of Töölö (1942–63). He taught at the Sibelius Academy (1948–57), serving as head of its church music dept. (1955–57) as well as vice-director (1956–59) and director (1959–71). He was a member of the Swedish Royal Academy of Music.

WORKS: ORCH.: *Pastorale* (1934); *Nocturne* for Cello and Orch. (1936); *Laatokka* (Lake Ladoga), symphonic legend (1944); *Toccata* (1953). **CHAMBER:** Sonatina for String Quartet (1927); *Sonatina di Natale* for Flute, Cello, and Piano (1936); Trio for Flute, Viola, and Piano (1945); keyboard pieces. **VOCAL:** *Psalm 40* for Baritone, Chorus, Organ, and Strings (1939); *Jouluyö* (Christmas Night) for Chorus, Organ, and Orch. (1941); *Kangastuksia* (Mirages) for Mezzo-soprano and Orch. (1945); *Saimoon helmi* (The Pearl of Saimaa), cantata (1949); sacred music.—NS/LK/DM

Kuyper, Elisabeth, Dutch conductor and composer; b. Amsterdam, Sept. 13, 1877; d. Lugano, Feb. 26, 1953. She studied with Max Bruch in Berlin. From 1908 to 1920 she taught theory at the Hochschule für Musik there. She was founder (1908) and conductor of the Berlin Tonkunstlerinnen Orch. In 1922 she led concerts of the London Women's Sym. Orch., and in 1923 she conducted the N.Y. Women's Sym. Orch. She settled in Lago Maggiore in Brissago. Kuyper composed a Sym., Violin Concerto, several violin sonatas, Ballade for Cello and Piano, Piano Trio, and songs.—NS/LK/DM

Kuznetsova, Maria (Nikolaievna), prominent Russian soprano; b. Odessa, 1880; d. Paris, April 25,

1966. She studied in St. Petersburg with Tartakov. She made her debut in an operatic production at the Cons. there (1904), then was a member of the Maryinsky Theater (1905–13), where she distinguished herself in Russian roles and as Juliette, Elsa, Carmen, and Madama Butterfly. She made guest appearances in Berlin (1908), at the Opéra (1908, 1910, 1912, 1914) and Opéra-Comique (1910) in Paris, and at Covent Garden in London (debut as Marguerite in *Faust*, 1909; returned in 1910, 1920). In 1915–16 she sang in Petrograd and in 1916 in Chicago. After the Russian Revolution (1918), she fled to Sweden; made appearances in Stockholm and Copenhagen (1920), and then toured with her own opera company; later was artistic adviser of Barcelona's Teatro Liceo.—NS/LK/DM

Kvam, Oddvar S(chirmer), Norwegian composer; b. Oslo, Sept. 9, 1927. He studied at the Oslo Cons. (1943–52), where he took a degree in harmony and counterpoint (1950) and received training in piano and theory. He also obtained a law degree from the Univ. of Oslo (1949). He later studied conducting with Grüner-Hegge (1955–57) and composition with David Monrad Johansen (1964–66) in Oslo, completing his training in composition with Herman Koppel in Copenhagen (1969). He practiced law while devoting much time to composition; was the first composer to hold the influential post of chairman of the Norwegian Arts Council (1985–88). Two of his orch. works, Prologue (1967) and Opening (1974), received awards at the inauguration of the Oslo Concert Hall in 1977. Kvam's compositions tend to be free of tonally based strictures, yet they preserve a feeling of tonality.

WORKS: DRAMATIC: O p e r a : *The Dream of the 13ᵗʰ Hour* (1986); *The Cabinet*, chamber opera (1989). **ORCH.:** *Prologue* (1967); *Afterwards Everything Is Too Late* (1967; rev. version for Narrator and Orch., 1977); *Concert Overture* (1969); 2 syms.: No. 1, *3 Contrasts* (1972) and No. 2, *Communication* (1981); *Dialogues* for Oboe and Strings (1973; also for Oboe and Clarinet Quintet); *Opening* (1974); *Suffragette* for Piano and Orch. (1975); *Legend* for Strings (1975); *Trim* for School Orch. (1976); *Ostinato festoso* (1976); *Vibrations* (1976–82); *From the Young People's World* for Orch., Percussion, and Electric Guitar (1978); *Phoenix* for Cello and Orch. (1988); *Colors* for Harmonica and Strings (1989); *Towards the End* (1989); *Carpe Diem* (1990–92); *The Cycle of Life* (1991); *NORGEnuis* for Piano and Orch. (1997). **S y m - p h o n i c   B a n d :** *Concert March* (1977); *Flight 77* (1977); *Blow Out!* (1978); *Vacation* (1982); *Apollonia* (1983); *Homecoming* (1984); *Sightseeing* (1987); *Downwards and Upwards* (1987); *The Winner* (1995). **CHAMBER:** *Divertimento* for Flute, Viola, and Cello (1971); 3 string quartets (1973, 1976, 1985); *3 Centrifuges* for Wind Quintet (1975); *Theme with Variations* for Violin (1976); *Trembling Trumpets* for 4 Trumpets (1977); *Drops* for Flute and Harp (1977); *5 Monophonies*, 2 for Each of the Woodwind Quintet Instruments (1977); Trio for Piano, Violin, and Cello (1979); Sonata for Clarinet and Percussion (1979); *Ave Maria* for Violin or Cello and Piano or Guitar (1981); *Duo ostinato* for Violin and Guitar (1981); *Trio ostinato* for Flute, Viola, and Guitar (1982); *Prelude and Rondo* for Violin (1983); *Andando e tornando* for 2 Violins (1984); *Clarimpette* for Clarinet and Trumpet (1985); *Sunset* for Violin and Organ (1988); *Changes* for Violin, Viola, and Cello (1988); *3 Stages* for Flute, Oboe, Violin, and Cello (1992). **P i a n o :** *A Rather Ordinary Week* (1960–68); *3 Mini Pieces* for Piano, 4-Hands (1970–71); *Encyclopedia* (1976); 12 *Proverbs* (1976); *Plastic Arts* (1979); *Hommage à Prokofiev* (1983); *Growing Influence* (1983); *4 Hands across the Sea* for Piano, 4-Hands (1984); *Counterplay*, suite (1994). **VOCAL:** *Festival Cantata* for Men's Chorus and Orch. (1966); *Epinikion* for Chorus and Orch. (1971–75); *Clarina the Clarinet*, fairy tale for Narrator and Clarinet (1975); *The Great Language* for Chorus (1977); *Psalmus XVIII* for Chorus and Organ (1979); *Come!* for Chorus and Piano (1982); *Querela pacis* for 2 Choruses and Orch. (1983); *Born Anew* for Chorus (1988); *The Inauguration* for Chorus and 2 Trumpets (1993–94); other choruses and songs.—NS/LK/DM

Kvandal (real name, **Johansen**), **(David) Johan,** distinguished Norwegian composer and organist, son of **David Monrad Johansen**; b. Christiania, Sept. 8, 1919; d. there (Oslo), Feb. 16, 1999. He graduated as a student of organ (under Sandvold) and of conducting at the Oslo Cons., where he also took courses with Tveitt (composition) and Steenberg (counterpoint and composition). He then pursued his composition studies with Marx in Vienna, Boulanger in Paris (1952–54), and Blacher in Berlin (1970). From 1959 to 1974 he was organist of Oslo's Valerengen Church. Kvandal's works were written in a well-crafted neo-Classical style but with obeisance to Norway's national musical tradition.

WORKS: DRAMATIC: *Skipper Worse*, television score (1967); *Mysteries*, opera (1993; Oslo, Jan. 15, 1994). **ORCH.:** *Divertimento* for Strings (1945); *Norwegian Overture* (1950); *Variations and Fugue* (1954); Sym. (1959); *Symphonic Epos* (1961–62); Concerto for Flute and Strings (1963); *Sinfonia concertante* (1968); *Antagonia*, concerto for 2 String Orchs. and Percussion (1972–73); Concerto for Oboe and Strings (1977); Violin Concerto (1979); *Triptychon* (1979); Concerto for Chamber Orch. (1980); *Poem* for Strings (1985; also for Piano or Organ); *Visions Norvegiennes* (1985); Concerto for 2 Pianos and Orch. (1993–94); *Fantasia* for Hardanger Fiddle and Strings (1995); Piano Concerto (1998). **CHAMBER:** String Trio (1951); 3 string quartets (1954, 1966, 1983); Duo for Violin and Cello (1959); *Aria, Cadenza and Finale* for Violin and Piano (1964); *Introduction and Allegro* for Horn and Piano (1969); *Do lontano* for Flute and Piano (1970); Wind Quintet (1971); Sonata for Solo Violin (1973–74); Quartet for Flute, Violin, Viola, and Cello (1975); *Night Music*, nonet (1981); *Overture Fantasy* for 8 Winds and Double Bass (1982); Sonata for Solo Harp (1984); Sonata for Solo Guitar (1984); Sonata for Solo Accordion (1987); Horn Quartet (1988); Violin Sonata (1995). **KEYBOARD: P i a n o :** Sonata (1940); Sonatina (1942); *3 Fantasy Country Dances* (1969); *Duo concertante* for 2 Pianos (1974). **O r g a n :** *Partita* (1971). **VOCAL:** *Song of Stella* for Soprano and Strings (1952); 3 solo cantatas: No. 1 for Soprano or Tenor and Orch. (1953), No. 2, *O Domine Deus*, for Soprano and Organ (1966), and No. 3 for Baritone and Organ (1970); *Nature*, chamber cantata for Baritone, Violin, and Piano (1972); Cantata for the Ibsen celebration (1978); *Draumkvaede-melodiene* for Soprano, Chorus, and Chamber Ensemble (1997); choruses; songs.

BIBL.: *Festskrift til J. K. i anledning 70-årsdagen 8. september 1989* (Oslo, 1989).—NS/LK/DM

Kvapil, Jaroslav, significant Czech composer; b. Fryšták, April 21, 1892; d. Brno, Feb. 18, 1958. He studied with Nešvera in Olmütz (1902–06), Janáček at the Brno Organ School (1906–09), and Reger at the Leipzig Cons. (1911–13). He was in the Austrian army during World War I, then was conductor of the Brno

Beseda (1919–47). He then taught at the Janáček Academy of Music there (1947–57). Kvapil's works show the double influence of Janáček's national and rhapsodic style and Reger's strong polyphonic idiom.

WORKS: DRAMATIC: Opera: *Pohádka máje* (A Romance in May; 1940–43; Prague, May 12, 1950; rev., Brno, 1955). ORCH.: *Thema con variazioni e fuga* (1912); 4 syms.: No. 1 (1913–14), No. 2 (1921), No. 3 (1936–37), and No. 4, *Vitzna* (Victory; 1943); 2 violin concertos (1927–28; 1952); *Z těžkých dob* (From Anxious Times), symphonic variations (1939); *Slavonic* (Jubilee) Overture (1944); *Burlesque* for Flute and Orch. (1945); *Svitani* (Daybreak), symphonic poem (1948–49); Oboe Concerto (1951); Piano Concerto (1954). CHAMBER: 3 violin sonatas (1910, 1914, 1931); Piano Trio (1912); Cello Sonata (1913); 6 string quartets (1914, 1926, 1931, 1935, 1949, 1951); Piano Quintet (1914–15); Brass Quintet (1925); *Variations* for Trumpet and Piano (1929); *Suite* for Trombone and Piano (1930); *Intimate Pictures* for Violin and Piano (1934); Wind Quintet (1935); Violin Sonatina (1941); *Fantasy* for Cello and Piano (1942); Nonet (1944); Quartet for Flute, Violin, Viola, and Cello (1948); Duo for Violin and Viola (1949); *Suite* for Viola and Piano (1955). KEYBOARD: Piano: 3 sonatas (1912, 1925, 1946); *Variations* (1914); *Fantasy in the Form of Variations* (1952); *10 Pieces* (1957). Organ: *Fantasy* (1935). VOCAL: 2 cantatas: *A Song on Time That Is Passing* (1924) and *Small Italian Cantata* (1950); *Lví srdce* (The Lion's Heart), oratorio (1928–31; Brno, Dec. 7, 1931); song cycles.

BIBL.: L. Kundera, *J. K.* (Prague, 1944).—NS/LK/DM

Kvernadze, Bidzina (actually, **Alexander Alexandrovich**), Russian composer; b. Signahi, Georgia, July 29, 1928. He studied with Balanchivadze at the Tbilisi Cons. (graduated, 1953). Among his works were 2 piano concertos (1950, 1965), Violin Concerto (1956), *Dance-Fantasy* for Orch. (1959), Sym. (1961), violin pieces, and film music.—NS/LK/DM

Kwast, James, famous German pianist and teacher; b. Nijkerk, the Netherlands, Nov. 23, 1852; d. Berlin, Oct. 31, 1927. He studied with his father and Ferdinand Bohme, and later with Reinecke and Richter at the Leipzig Cons., Theodor Kullak and Wüerst in Berlin, and Brassin and Gevaert in Brussels. He taught at the Cologne Cons. (1874–83) and the Frankfurt Hoch Cons. (1883–1903). He then went to Berlin as a prof. at the Klindworth- Scharwenka Cons. (1903–6) and the Stern Cons. (from 1906). He was greatly esteemed by his colleagues and students; among the latter were Grainger and Pfitzner. He wrote a Piano Concerto and other piano music. His first wife, Antonia (d. Stuttgart, Feb. 10, 1931), was a daughter of Ferdinand Hiller. His second wife, Frieda Hodapp-Kwast (b. Bargen, Aug. 13, 1880; d. Bad Wiessee, Sept. 14, 1949), was a pianist.—NS/LK/DM

Kwella, Patrizia, English soprano; b. Mansfield, April 26, 1953. She received vocal training at the Royal Coll. of Music in London. Following her debut at the London Promenade Concerts in 1979, she sang in Aldeburgh, Bath, Edinburgh, Bologna, Warsaw, Salzburg, and other European music centers. In 1983 she made her U.S. debut with the San Diego Sym. Orch., and subse-

quently appeared with other major U.S. orchs. In 1985 she was engaged to sing for various Bach, Handel, and Scarlatti tercentenary concerts. That same year, she appeared in the premiere of Colin Matthews's *Night's Mask* at the Aldeburgh Festival. Her operatic repertoire includes roles by Monteverdi and Handel, and her concert repertoire ranges from Bach to Britten. —NS/LK/DM

Kwiatkowski, Ryszard, Polish composer; b. Jaranów, June 27, 1931; d. Bydoszcz, March 23, 1991. He was a student of Szeligowski and Rudziński at the Warsaw State Higher School of Music (1958–63) and of Petrassi in Rome. He taught at the Bydgoszcz State Higher School of Music. His music reflects contemporary trends, including some use of dodecaphony.

WORKS: ORCH.: *Serenade* for Trombone and Orch. (1957); 4 syms. (1958, 1964, 1969, 1969); *Baltic Impressions* (1966); *Pictures* for Chamber Orch. (1966); *Baltic Songs* (1966); *Polyphonic Music* (1967); *Pulsation* (1967–69); *Music* for Flutes, Clarinets, Percussion, and Strings (1969); *Music* for Winds, Percussion, and Piano (1969); Concerto for Oboe, 4 Trumpets, Piano, and Strings (1970); *4 Lyrics* (1970–72); Tuba Concerto (1977); *Lyrics of Toruń* for Chamber Orch. (1980); *Sea Stories* for Strings (1984). CHAMBER: Wind Quintet (1960); 3 string quartets (1962; 1966–78; 1971); *Musica in memoriam Johannis Ciconia* for 2 Violins, Viola, Cello, and Piano (1967); *Song of the Sea Wind* for Violin and Piano (1967); *Baltic Wave Song* for Clarinet and Piano (1967); Piano Quartet, with metronome (1968); 2 percussion quartets (1968, 1971); *Lyric Music* for Violin and Double Bass (1969); *Baltic Sonnets* for 9 Instruments and Metronome (1971); *Legend* for Viola and Piano (1975); *Pictures from the Seaside* for Violin, Cello, and Piano (1975); Violin Sonata (1976–77); Viola Sonata (1978); Sonata for Viola and 2 Pianos (1978); Sonata for Oboe, Clarinet, and Bassoon (1981); *5 Little Sonatas* for Flute, Oboe, Clarinet, Horn, and Bassoon (1983). KEYBOARD: Piano: *7 Moon Pictures* (1960–69); 2 sonatas (1975, 1983); *Fields Under Water* (1982). Organ: Sonata (1980). VOCAL: *Baltic Pictures* for Mezzo-soprano, 2 Violins, Cello, and Piano (1975).—NS/LK/DM

Kyllönen, Timo-Juhani, Finnish composer; b. Saloinen, Dec. 1, 1955. He was reared in Sweden, where he commenced playing the accordion when he was 9. In 1976 he entered the Gnessin Inst. in Moscow as an accordion student of Friedrich Lips, and also took courses in composition and conducting before graduating in 1982. He then studied composition, orchestration, and counterpoint with Alexei Nikolaiev, Yuri Fortunatov, and Georgi Tchugaiev at the Moscow Cons., graduating in 1986. He then taught theory and composition at the Sibelius Academy in Helsinki.

WORKS: DRAMATIC: Stage, film, and television scores. ORCH.: Sym. No. 1 (Novosibirsk, June 17, 1986). CHAMBER: 2 string quartets (1985, 1989); Trio No. 1 for Violin, Cello, and Accordion (1986) and No. 2 for Piano, Violin, and Cello (1988); *Elegia "quasi una sonata"* for Violin and Piano (1987); *Desolazione* for Organ and Oboe (1987); *Contrasts* for 5 Percussionists (1988); several pieces for solo instruments. VOCAL: *Passio secularis* for Soprano, Men's Chorus, and Orch. (1988–89; Helsinki, Dec. 8, 1989); choral pieces.—NS/LK/DM

Kyriakou, Rena, Greek pianist; b. Iraklion, Feb. 25, 1918; d. Athens, Aug. 1994. She made her public debut in Athens at 6, and later studied in Vienna with Paul Weingarten and Richard Stöhr. She then joined the piano class of Isidor Philipp at the Paris Cons., and also studied composition there with Henri Busser; received its premier prix at the age of 15. She then embarked on a concert career in programs of neglected piano pieces by 18th- and 19th-century composers.—NS/LK/DM

Kyser, Kay (actually, James King Kern),

American bandleader and actor; b. Rocky Mount, N.C., June 18, 1905; d. Chapel Hill, N.C., July 23, 1985. Kyser was among the more successful big band conductors of the Swing Era, especially in the 1940s. His radio program, *Kay Kyser's Kollege of Musical Knowledge*, employed a humorous quiz-show format, and his music was given over largely to novelty material. His major hits include "Jingle Jangle Jingle," "Woody Woodpecker," and "Ole Buttermilk Sky." He also starred in seven motion pictures between 1939 and 1944.

Kyser's parents were Paul Bynam and Emily Royster Howell Kyser; both were pharmacists. Kyser was expected to enter the same profession, and he also considered a law career, but while attending the Univ. of N.C. at Chapel Hill he formed a six-piece dance orchestra that found work at colleges around the South. After he graduated in 1928, he expanded the band and continued to perform. By 1929 he had a contract with Victor Records. His break came in September 1934, when he gained a residency at the Blackhawk Restaurant in Chicago and began broadcasting his comic music program, initially called *Kay Kyser's Kampus Klass*, on WGN. In July 1935 he had his first entry in the hit parade, the instrumental "Star Gazing" (music by Jerry Livingston, lyrics by Marty Symes and Al J. Neiburg), released on the Brunswick label.

In 1938, Kyser gained a sponsor, the American Tobacco Company, and launched *Kay Kyser's Kollege of Musical Knowledge* on the NBC radio network. His popularity grew quickly. He scored his first major hit with "The Umbrella Man" (music by Vincent Rose and Larry Stock, lyrics by James Cavanaugh) featuring vocalists Ginny Simms and Harry Babbitt. The tune spent 11 weeks in the hit parade. Another big hit, starting in May, was "Three Little Fishies" (music and lyrics by Horace Kirby [Saxie] Dowell), with a vocal by Merwyn Bogue, also known as Ish Kabibble; it was in the hit parade nine weeks. In November, Kyser and his band appeared in their first film, RKO's *That's Right—You're Wrong*. Other bandleaders of the period

had only cameo roles in the movies, but Kyser's films were star vehicles in which he displayed his engaging, comic persona and re-created his radio show decked out in cap and gown.

After switching to Columbia Records, Kyser scored his next big hit in July 1940 with "Playmates" (music and lyrics by Saxie Dowell). The title, though not the song, would be used for his third film, released in December 1941. His second film, released in November 1940, was *You'll Find Out*. After the United States entered World War II, Kyser tried to enlist, then performed exclusively on military bases for the duration. His next major hit came in April 1942 with the million-selling "Who Wouldn't Love You" (music by Carl Fischer, lyrics by Bill Carey). *My Favorite Spy*, his fourth film, was released in May 1942. His recording of "Jingle Jangle Jingle" (music by Joseph J. Lilley, lyrics by Frank Loesser) topped the charts in July and sold a million copies. "He Wears a Pair of Silver Wings" (music by Michael Carr, lyrics by Eric Maschwitz) was a big hit in September, while "Strip Polka" (music and lyrics by Johnny Mercer) and "Praise the Lord and Pass the Ammunition!" (music and lyrics by Frank Loesser) both hit in October and went on to become million- sellers.

Unable to record during the musicians union ban of 1942–44, Kyser appeared in the all-star films *Stage Door Canteen* (June 1943) and *Thousands Cheer* (September 1943), as well as his own films, *Around the World* (November 1943), *Swing Fever* (January 1944), and *Carolina Blues* (December 1944). His male vocalist of the mid-1940s was Michael Douglas, who as Mike Douglas later became a successful talk-show host; his female vocalist was Georgia Carroll, whom he married in 1944. They had three children.

Kyser's next major hit was "Ole Buttermilk Sky" (music and lyrics by Hoagy Carmichael and Jack Brooks), which topped the charts in December 1946. "Woody Woodpecker" (music and lyrics by George Tibbles and Ramez Idriss) went to #1 in July 1948 and sold a million copies. In the fall, Kyser scored his last hit, the million-selling "On a Slow Boat to China" (music and lyrics by Frank Loesser).

Kyser took his radio program to television when *Kay Kyser's Kollege of Musical Knowledge* premiered as a one-hour weekly show on NBC-TV on Dec. 1, 1949. It ran until Dec. 28, 1950, after which Kyser retired from the entertainment business and went to work for the Christian Science Church. He died of a heart attack in 1985.—WR

La Barbara, Joan (Linda née **Lotz),** American composer and experimental vocalist; b. Philadelphia, June 8, 1947. She learned piano from her grandfather, and later sang in church and school choirs and joined a folk music group. She studied voice with Helen Boatwright at the Syracuse Univ. School of Music (1965–68), music education at N.Y.U. (B.S., 1970), and voice with Phyllis Curtin at the Berkshire Music Center at Tanglewood (summers, 1967–68) and with Marion Szekely-Freschl at the Juilliard School in N.Y. In 1971 she made her debut as a vocalist at N.Y.'s Town Hall with Steve Reich and Musicians, with whom she continued to perform until 1974; also worked with Philip Glass (1973–76). She toured in the U.S. and Europe; in 1979 she was composer-in-residence in West Berlin under the aegis of the Deutscher Akademischer Austauschdienst; taught voice and composition at the Calif. Inst. of the Arts in Valencia (1981–86). In 1979 she married **Morton Subotnick.** A champion of contemporary music, she developed her performing talents to a high degree; her vocal techniques include multiphonics and circular breathing, with unique throat clicks and a high flutter to match. Her compositions, often incorporating electronics, effectively exploit her vocal abilities. Among her numerous awards and fellowships are NEA grants (1979, 1982, 1986, 1988, 1989, 1991) and ASCAP and ISCM commissions; also numerous radio commissions. La Barbara has collaborated on interdisciplinary projects with visual artists, including Lita Albuquerque, Judy Chicago, Kenneth Goldsmith et al.; she has also given numerous first performances of works written for her by American composers, including Robert Ashley, John Cage, Charles Dodge, Morton Feldman, Daniel Lentz et al. In 1993 she appeared in the N.Y. premiere of Subotnick's opera, *Jacob's Room,* and in 1994 in the N.Y. premiere of Robert Ashley's quartet of operas, *Now Eleanor's Idea.*

WORKS (all voices amplified unless otherwise noted): **LARGE ENSEMBLE:** *Chandra* for Solo Voice, 5 Men's Voices, Electronics, and Chamber Orch. (Bremen, May 6, 1978; rev. 1983); *The Solar Wind III* for Voice and Chamber Orch. (San Francisco, May 12, 1984). **AMPLIFIED VOICE(S) AND INSTRUMENTS:** *Ides of March Nos. 1–7* for Voice and Instruments (1974–78); *Thunder* for Voice, 6 Timpani, and Electronics (1975); *WARP-32375–1* for Voice and Percussion (1975); *An Exaltation of Larks* for Voice and Electronics (1976); *Chords and Gongs* for Voice, Chinese Cymbal, Large Gong, and Finger Cymbals (1976); *As Is/Layers* for Voice, Electronics, and Acoustic and Electronic Percussion (1977); *Loisaida* for Voice, Kalimba, Hi-Hat, and Steel Drum (N.Y., Feb. 17, 1978); *Silent Scroll* for Voice, Flute, Cello or Double-bass, Percussion, Gong, and Zoomoozophone (N.Y., April 25, 1982); *Vlissingen harbor* for Voice, Flute and Piccolo, Clarinet and Bass Clarinet, Trumpet, Harp, Piano and Celesta, Violin, and Percussion (Los Angeles, Dec. 6, 1982), *The Solar Wind I* for Voice, Chamber Ensemble, Tape, and Percussion (1982; Los Angeles, Feb. 7, 1983) and *II* for 16 Solo Voices, 2 Percussion, Flute, and Electronic Keyboard (Copenhagen, Nov. 14, 1983); *A Rothko Study* for Voice and Chamber Ensemble (Los Angeles, Nov. 3, 1985); *A Rothko Study No. 2* for Voice, Cello, and Computer (1986); *ROTHKO* for Solo Voice, 16 Voices on Tape, and 2 Bowed Pianos (Houston, April 5, 1986); *Helga's Lied* for Voice and Chamber Ensemble (Århus, Oct. 10, 1986); *Urban Tropics* for Voice, Percussion, and Taped Sounds (Miami, Dec. 12, 1988); *Klangbild Köln* for Voice, Percussion, and Taped Sounds (WDR Cologne, May 7, 1991); *"to hear the wind roar"* for Voice, Percussion, and Tape (1991; Santa Fe, Aug. 8, 1992; also versions for 8 Voices and Percussion, Pasadena, May 9, 1992, and for Chorus and Percussion, Adirondack, N.Y., July 18, 1992); *Face to Face* for Voices, Electronics, and Percussion (Houston, Feb. 1, 1992; in collab. with David Moss); *Awakenings II* for Voice and Chamber Ensemble (Tempe, Ariz., Jan. 28, 1992); *Shaman Song* for Voice, Percussion, and Tape (Athens, March 2, 1992); *"73 Poems"* for Voices and Electronics (first complete perf., Miami, Dec. 4, 1993; in collab. with Kenneth Goldsmith); *"in the shadow and act of the haunting place"* for Voice and Chamber Ensemble (1993; San Francisco, Jan. 17, 1995); *Calligraphy II/Shadows* for Voice and Chinese Instruments (N.Y., June 8, 1995); *de profundis: out of the depths, a sign//a different train* for 4 Voices, Percussion, Bowed Pianos, and Tape, after M. Sumner Carnahan (1996); *A Different Train* for 4 Voices, Bowed Pianos, and Tape, after M. Sumner Carnahan (1996); *de* *profundis: Out of the depths, a sign,* after M. Sumner Carnahan for 4 Voices, Percussion, and Tape (1996). **AMPLIFIED VOICE(S)** (all for Solo Voice unless otherwise noted): *Hear what I Feel* (1974); *Performance Piece* (1974; rev. 1979); *Voice Piece: One-note Internal Resonance Investigation* (1974); *An Exploration in Vocal Sound and Movements* for 2 Performers using Voice and Movement (1975; in collab. with D. Reitz); *Circular Song* (1975); *Vocal Extensions* for Voice and Live Electronics (1975); *Chords* (1976); *Des Accords pour Teeny* (1976); *Les oiseaux qui chantent dans ma tête* (1976); *Cathing* for Voice and Tape (1977); *Twelve-song,* for Voice and Tape (Bremen, May 6, 1978; also as a radio work, Radio Bremen, Nov. 1, 1977); *Autumn Signal* for Voice and Buchla Synthesizer (Berlin, Oct. 22, 1978); *California Chant* ("*Raicha Tria*") for Amplified for Unamplified Voice (1979); *Klee Alee* for Voice and Tape (1979); *Shadowsong* for Voice and Tape (1979); *Twelve for Five in Eight* for 5 or More Voices (1979); *Erin* for Voice and Tape (Paris, June 21, 1980); *October Music: Star Showers and Extraterrestrials* for Voice and Tape (Paris, June 21, 1980); *Winds of the Canyon* for Voice and Tape (San Francisco, Nov. 12, 1982; rev. staged version, with visual environment, Los Angeles, March 3, 1986); *Berliner Träume (Berlin Dreaming)* for Voice and 16-track Tape (1983; Minneapolis, Feb. 18, 1984); *After "Obervogelsang"* for Voice and Tape (N.Y., June 5, 1984); *Time(d) Trials and Unscheduled Events* for 8 Solo Voices and Tape (1984; rev. for 8 Solo Voices, 1987); *Loose Tongues* for 8 Solo Voices and Tape (1985); *Voice Windows* for Voice and Interactive Video Systems (Los Angeles, March 3, 1986; in collab. with Steina and W. Vasulka); *Conversations* (Rome, Aug. 4, 1988). **TAPE:** *The Executioner's Bracelet* (1979); "*quatre petites bêtes*" (1978–79; Cologne, May 9, 1979); *Responsive Resonance with Features* for Piano and Tape (1979); *Autumn Signal* (1982); *l'albero dalle foglie azzurre (the tree of the blue leaves)* for Oboe and Tape (St. Louis, March 20, 1989); also versions of other live performance works listed in other categories. **OTHER:** *Hunters* (video; 1975); *Vermont II* (video; 1975); *Space Testings* for Acoustic Voice (1976); *CYCLONE* for Amplified Voice, Tape, and Light- panning Activating Device (1977; rev. as *CYCLONE CON(S)T(R)AINED*, sound installation, for 16-track Tape, 1978); *She is Always Alone* (video; 1979); *3 Space Trio/A Lament for the Wizard* (video; 1982; in collab. with E. Emschwiller); *as lightning comes, in flashes* for 2 to 6 Amplified Voices, Dancers, and Video (1982); *Prologue to The Book of Knowing...(and) of Overthrowing*, solo performance aria for Voice, Projections, Costumes, and Movement (1987–88; N.Y., July 6, 1988; in collab. with J. Chicago); *Events in the Elsewhere* (opera; 1990); *In the Dreamtime* (sound collage; 1990; Cologne WDR, May 7, 1991); *Anima*, filmscore for Voice, Cello, Gamelan, Music Box, Percussion, Electronic Keyboards, and Computer (1991; N.Y., Sept. 25, 1992); *Awakenings* for Chamber Ensemble (1991); *The Misfortune of the Immortals*, interdisciplinary interactive media opera for Voices, Dancers, Actors, Video Projections, MIDI Instruments, and Interactive Computer Systems (1994–95; in collab. with M. Coniglio and M. Subotnik); "*a trail of indeterminate light*" for Singing Cellist (1997); *Snowbird's Dance, Into the Light* for Voice and Chamber Ensemble (N.Y., May 19, 2000).—**NS/LK/DM**

La Barre (original name probably **Chabanceau**), prominent family of French musicians:

(1) Pierre de la Barre, organist and composer; b. Paris (baptized), Jan. 27, 1592; d. there (buried), March 31, 1656. He was the son of the organist Pierre de la Barre (d. Jan. 12, 1600), who was active in Paris from 1567. His own career as an organist was fully established by 1611. By 1618 he was a member of the king's chamber, by 1627 organist of the royal chapel and maître joueur d'epinette to the king, and by 1630 organist to the queen as well. About 1650 he founded the first concerts of sacred music in Paris at his home, where leading musicians of his day participated. La Barre was highly esteemed not only as an organist, but as a performer on the harpsichord and spinet as well. Three of his children became widely known musicians:

(2) Anne de la Barre, singer; b. Paris (baptized), July 3, 1628; d. before March 7, 1688. She was a principal singer at the French court before serving at the Swedish court (1652?–54). After serving at the Danish court (1654–55), she was active again at the French court (1656–64). She also gave private performances for the king, serving as ordinaire of his chamber music (1661–86).

(3) Joseph de la Barre, organist and composer; b. Paris (baptized), May 21, 1633; d. before May 6, 1678. He became organist of the royal chapel upon his father's death in 1656. In 1674 he received a benefice, the Benedictine abbey of St. Hilaire in the Carcassonne diocese. Thereafter he was known as L'abbé de la Barre. He publ. *Airs à deux parties, avec les seconds couplets en diminution* (Paris, 1669). The *Mecure galant* (Aug. 1678) publ. his air *Dolorosi pensieri*, which was greatly admired by the king. A number of his dances are included in MS collections.

(4) Pierre de la Bare, instrumentalist and composer; b. Paris (baptized), Oct. 18, 1634; d. before April 18, 1710. He appears to have entered the service of the king as a lutenist when he was only 10 years of age. From 1663 to at least 1708 he played the theorbo and the grosse basse de violon in the royal chapel. He also was in the service of the queen and the Duchess of Burgundy. In 1697 he was ennobled.—**LK/DM**

La Barre, Michel de, significant French flutist and composer; b. c. 1675; d. 1743 or 1744. He became a musician at the Académie Royale de Musique about 1700, where he was active until 1721. He also played in the Musettes et Hautbois de Poitou (1704–30) and in the royal chamber music. La Barre was held in high esteem as both a flutist and composer. His first book of solo suites for transverse flute and basso continuo (Paris, 1702) was the earliest book ever publ. of solo pieces for the flute. He also introduced suites for 2 unaccompanied flutes to France (13 books, Paris, 1709–25). Among his other works were the ballet *Le triomphe des arts* (Paris, May 16, 1700), the comédie-ballet *La vénitiennes* (Paris, May 26, 1705), and songs.—**LK/DM**

Labarre, Théodore (-François-Joseph), French harpist, conductor, teacher, and composer; b. Paris, March 5, 1805; d. there, March 9, 1870. He was a foster-brother of Napoleon III. After private training with Bocha, Cosineau, and Nadermann, he studied with Dourlen (harmony), Eler and Fétis (counterpoint), and Boieldieu (composition) at the Paris Cons., where he won 2nd prize in the Prix de Rome with his cantata *Pyramus et Thisbé* (1823). Following tours of England, Italy, and Switzerland as a harpist, he returned to Paris in 1831 and devoted himself to composing. In 1837 he married the singer Lambert. From 1847 to 1849 he was a conductor at the Paris Opéra-Comique. In 1852 he was named director of the imperial chapel. In 1867 he became prof. of harp at the Paris Cons. In 1862 he received the Légion d'honneur. Labarre publ. a *Méthode complète pour la harpe* (Paris, 1844).

WORKS: DRAMATIC (all first perf. in Paris): **O p e r a :** *L'aspirant de marine*, opéra-comique (June 2, 1834); *Le ménétrier ou Les deux duchesses*, opera (Aug. 9, 1845); *Pantagruel*, opéra-comique (Dec. 24, 1855). **B a l l e t :** *La révolte des femmes* (Dec. 4, 1833); *Jovita ou Les boucaniers* (Nov. 11, 1853); *La Fonti* (Jan. 8, 1855); *Graziosa* (March 26, 1861); *Le roir d'Yvetot* (Dec. 28, 1865). **OTHER:** *Fantaisie* for Harp and Orch. (1841); trios for Harp, Horn, and Bassoon; duos for Harp and Horn; salon pieces for Harp and Piano; many solo harp pieces; *Pyramus et Thisbé*, cantata (1823).—**NS/LK/DM**

Labatt, Leonard, Swedish tenor; b. Stockholm, Dec. 4, 1838; d. there, March 7, 1897. He studied with J. Günther, then with Masset in Paris. He made his debut in Stockholm as Tamino in *Die Zauberflöte* (1866). In 1868–69 he was at the Dresden Court Opera, and from 1869 to 1883 at the Vienna Court Opera. He sang in London in 1881, and made an American tour in 1888–89. He was especially fine in Wagnerian roles.—**NS/LK/DM**

L'Abbé (real name, **Saint-Sévin**), family of French musicians:

(1) Pierre-Philippe Saint-Sévin, cellist, known as **L'Abbé l'aîné**; b. probably in Agen, c. 1700; d. Paris, May 15, 1768. He was maître de musique at the church of St. Caprais in Agen, where he took Holy Orders and the name L'Abbé. After settling in Paris, he became a cellist in the orch. of the Opéra (1727); he was soon made first cellist, a post he held until his retirement in 1767. He also played in the orch. of the Concert Spirituel from the 1740s to 1762, and likewise was a member of the musique de la chambre of the French court from about 1753 until his death. He was greatly esteemed as a virtuoso on his instrument.

(2) Pierre Saint-Sévin, cellist, brother of the preceding, known as **L'Abbé le cadet**; b. probably in Agen, c. 1710; d. Paris, March 1777. He took minor orders at the church of St. Caprais in Agen, then settled in Paris, where he became a cellist in the orch. of the Opéra (1730). He was a member of the basses du Petit Choeur there until 1767, and then leader of the basses du Grand Choeur until his retirement in 1776. He also played at the Sainte-Chapelle (1764–77).

(3) Joseph-Barnabé Saint-Sévin, violinist and composer, son of **L'Abbé l'aîné**, known as **L'Abbé le fils**; b. Agen, June 11, 1727; d. Paris, July 20, 1803. A precocious child, he began his musical training with his father. He secured a position in the orch. of the Paris Comédie-Française through winning a competition when he was only 11. He then continued his studies with Leclair (1740–42). He was a member of the orch. of the Opéra from 1742 until his retirement in 1762; however, he was denied a pension on the ground that he was too young, although he had served the requisite number of years. He also appeared as a soloist. He made his solo debut at the Concert Spirituel in 1741, and continued to appear

there until 1754. In later years he devoted himself mainly to teaching. With the coming of the Revolution, he was forced to eke out a living as a member of the orch. of the Théâtre de la République et des Arts. He eventually was granted a minuscule pension and lived out his last days in obscurity. He was one of the most important French musicians of his day. A distinguished performer, he publ. the valuable treatise *Principes du violon pour apprendre le doigté de cet instrument, et les differens agremens dont il est susceptible* (Paris, 1761; 2nd ed., 1772). He was also a fine composer, producing a number of notable syms. and sonatas. He was among the first composers to write out cadenzas in full in several of his sonatas.

WORKS: ORCH.: *Premier simphonie en concert* for Strings and Basso Continuo (c. 1751); *Second simphonie* (c. 1752); 6 Syms. for Strings and Basso Continuo, op.2 (1753); *Menuet[s] de MM. Exaudet et Granier, mis en grand symphonie avec des variations* for 2 Violins, Oboes or Flutes, Viola, 2 Horns, and Cello or Bassoon (1764). **CHAMBER:** 6 Sonates for Violin and Basso Continuo, op.1 (1748); Symphonie for 2 Horns (1750); *Suite d'airs* for 2 Oboes, Viola d'Amore, and Viola (1754); *Premier [-Troisième] recueil d'airs français et italiens avec des variations*, op.3 (1756), op.4 (1757), and op.5 (1758); *Recueil d'airs* for Violin, op.6 (c. 1759); *Jolis airs ajustés et variés* for Violin, op.7 (1763); 6 Sonates for Violin and Basso Continuo, op.8 (1763); *Recueil quatrième de duos d'Opéra-Comique* for 2 Violins (1772).—**NS/LK/DM**

Labbette, Dora, English soprano; b. Purley, March 4, 1898; d. there, Sept. 3, 1984. She received training at the Guildhall School of Music in London. From 1917 she was active as an oratorio singer and recitalist. After making her operatic debut as Telaire in Rameau's *Castor et Pollux* in Oxford (1934), she took Beecham's advice and adopted the professional name of Lisa Perli. In 1935 she made her debut at London's Covent Garden as Mimi. In 1937 she made guest appearances in Berlin, Munich, and Dresden, and then sang once more at Covent Garden until 1939. Her final London engagement was as Mimi at the Sadler's Wells Theatre in 1943. Among her other admired roles were Marguerite, Mignon, Desdemona, and Mélisande.—**NS/LK/DM**

Labelle, Philadelphia-based "girl group" singers of the 1960s. **MEMBERSHIP:** Patti Labelle (born Patricia Louise Holt) (b. Philadelphia, Pa., May 24, 1944); Nona Hendryx (b. Trenton, N.J., Aug. 18, 1945); Sarah Dash (b. Trenton, N.J., Aug. 18, 1943); Cindy Birdsong (b. Camden, N.J., Dec. 15, 1939).

Patti Labelle and the Bluebelles were formed by Labelle and Cindy Birdsong, who had sung previously with the Ordettes, and Nona Hendryx and Sarah Dash, who had previously worked with the Del Carpis. They were credited with scoring a major hit in 1962 with "I Sold My Heart to the Junkman," although the song was actually recorded by the Starlets. The group had two other minor hits in 1964, then were reduced to a trio in 1967 when Birdsong left to join the Supremes. In 1971, as a black female vocal trio comprised of Patti Labelle, Nona Hendryx, and Sarah Dash, they were transformed into Labelle under the auspices of British television producer Vicki Wickham. Probably the first and perhaps the only major black female glitter-rock group, Labelle wore outlandish space-age costumes and projected a blatant, kinky sense of sexuality, developing a cult following among homosexuals. The first rock group to perform at N.Y.'s Metropolitan Opera House (in 1974), Labelle finally broke through in 1975 with the top hit "Lady Marmalade," a sexually charged and controversial single banned by many radio stations. With the group's breakup in 1977, all three members launched solo careers, with Patti Labelle establishing herself as a powerful vocalist and engaging onstage personality in the 1980s. Among her pop hits of the 1980s were "New Attitude," "Oh, People," and the top hit duet with Michael McDonald "On My Own."

DISC.: PATTI LABELLE AND THE BLUEBELLES: *On Stage* (1964); *Over the Rainbow* (1966); *Dreamer* (1967); *Greatest Hits* (1971); *Superpak* (1976); *Very Best* (1976); *Over the Rainbow: The Atlantic Years* (1994); *At the Apollo* (1995). **LABELLE:** *L.* (1971); *Moonshadow* (1972); *Pressure Cookin'* (1973); *Nightbirds* (1974); *Phoenix* (1975); *Chameleon* (1976). **PATTI LABELLE:** *Patti Labelle* (1977); *Tasty* (1978); *It's Alright with Me* (1978); *Released* (1980); *Best* (1982); *The Spirit's In It* (1981); *I'm in Love Again* (1984); *Patti* (1985); *Winner in You* (1986); *Be Yourself* (1989); *Burnin'* (1991); *Live!* (1992); *Gems* (1994). **NONA HENDRYX:** *Nona Hendryx* (1977); *Nona* (1983); *The Art of Defense* (1984); *The Heat* (1985); *Female Trouble* (1987); *SkinDiver* (1989). **SARAH DASH:** *Sarah Dash* (1978); *Oo-La-La, Sarah Dash* (1980); *Close Enough* (1981); *You're All I Need* (1988).—**BH**

Labèque, Katia (b. Hendaye, March 3, 1950) and Marielle (b. Hendaye, March 6, 1952),

extraordinarily gifted French sisters, duo-pianists. They began to study piano in early childhood with their mother, a pupil of Marguerite Long, making their formal debut in Bayonne in 1961. After completing their studies with Jean-Bernard Pommier at the Paris Cons., they were awarded first prize at their graduation in 1968. They subsequently embarked upon a remarkable career as duo-pianists, touring widely in Europe, North America, the Middle East, and the Far East. In addition to giving numerous recitals, they also appeared with the leading orchs. of the world. Their repertoire is catholic, ranging from the masterworks of the past to contemporary scores by Messiaen, Boulez, Berio, and others. They play popular works as well, from Scott Joplin to Gershwin; they championed the latter's duo-piano versions of *Rhapsody in Blue*, Piano Concerto in F, and *An American in Paris*.—**NS/LK/DM**

Labey, Marcel,

French conductor and composer; b. Le Vésinet, Seine-et-Oise, Aug. 6, 1875; d. Nancy, Nov. 25, 1968. He studied law in Paris, receiving his degree in 1898, then turned his attention to music, studying piano with Delaborde, harmony with Lenormand, and composition with d'Indy at the Paris Schola Cantorum. He taught piano there, and at d'Indy's death (1931), became director; was also director of the Cesar Franck School (from 1935). He wrote music in a late Romantic style.

WORKS: DRAMATIC: O p e r a : *Bérengère* (1912; Le Havre, April 12, 1929). **ORCH.:** 3 syms. (1903, 1908, 1934); *Ouverture pour un drame* (Paris, Jan. 22, 1921); *Suite champêtre* (1923). **CHAMBER:** Piano Sonata; Viola Sonata; 2 violin sonatas; String Quartet; Piano Trio; Piano Quartet; Piano Quintet. **VOCAL:** Songs.—**NS/LK/DM**

Labia, Fausta,

Italian soprano, sister of **Maria Labia**; b. Verona, April 3, 1870; d. Rome, Oct. 6, 1935. She studied with her mother and with Aldighieri. After making her operatic debut as Alice in *Robert le diable* in Verona (1892), she sang in Stockholm (1893–95) and Lisbon (1895–96); then appeared in various Italian opera centers, including Milan's La Scala and Rome's Teatro Costanzi (1901). She sang in Barcelona (1904–05); made her last stage appearance in Buenos Aires (1912); subsequently taught in Rome. In 1907 she married the tenor Emilio Perea. She wrote the method *L'arte del respiro nella recitazione e nel canto* (1936).—**NS/LK/DM**

Labia, Maria,

noted Italian soprano, sister of **Fausta Labia**; b. Verona, Feb. 14, 1880; d. Malcesine del Garda, Feb. 10, 1953. She received her musical education from her mother. Following concert engagements in Milan, Verona, and Padua (1902), and in Russia and Sweden (1903–04), she made her operatic debut as Mimi in Stockholm on May 19, 1905. She scored a remarkable success as Tosca at Berlin's Komische Oper (1907), continuing to sing there until 1911. Among her other notable roles there were Carmen, Thaïs, and Salome. She appeared as Tosca in her debut with the Manhattan Opera on Nov. 9, 1908. After a season there, she continued her career in Europe with engagements in Paris, Vienna, and Milan. She was arrested as a German agent by the Italian authorities in 1916 and spent a year in prison in Ancona. After the close of World War I, she resumed her career in Rome (1919); subsequently became closely associated with the role of Felice in Wolf-Ferrari's *I quatro rusteghi*, which she sang many times from 1922 until 1936. After teaching at the Warsaw Cons. (1930–34), she gave instruction in Rome and Siena. She wrote *Guardare indietro: Che fatica* (1950). —**NS/LK/DM**

Labinsky, Andrei (Markovich),

Russian tenor; b. Kharkov, July 26, 1871; d. Moscow, Aug. 8, 1941. He went to St. Petersburg, where he joined the chorus of the Maryinsky Theater. Following studies with Gabel, he made his operatic debut at the Maryinsky Theater in 1897, where he sang regularly from 1899 to 1912. In 1907 he created the role of Vsevolod in Rimsky-Korsakov's *Kitezh* there. From 1912 to 1924 he was a member of the Bolshoi Theater in Moscow. He taught at the Moscow Cons. from 1920. His finest roles included Don José, Lohengrin, Berendey in *The Snow Maiden*, Sinodal in *The Demon*, and Sobinin in *A Life for the Czar*.—**NS/LK/DM**

Labitzky,

family of German musicians of Bohemian descent:

(1) Joseph Labitzky, violinist, conductor, and composer; Schönfeld, July 3, 1802; d. Karlsbad, Aug. 19, 1881. He studied with Karl Veit in Petschau, where he joined a traveling orch. when he was 14. In 1820 he became a member of the Marienbad spa orch., and also held other positions. In 1823–24 he was in Munich, where he received violin lessons from Winter. Following a concert tour of southern Germany, he founded his own orch. in 1825. In 1835 he became conductor of the Karlsbad spa orch. He also made tours of Europe as a conductor. In 1868 he retired from his Karlsbad post and was succeeded by his son **August**. He composed more than 300 dances, many of which enjoyed a great vogue until the rise of Gungl and Johann Strauss Jr. Labizky had two sons who were also musicians:

(2) **Wilhelm Labitzky**, violinist; b. Petschau, 1829; d. Toronto, 1871. He received training at the Prague Cons. (1843–49) and eventually settled in Toronto.

(3) **August Labitzky**, violinist, conductor, and composer; b. Petschau, Oct. 22, 1832; d. Reichenhall, Bavaria, Aug. 28, 1903. He was a student at the Prague Cons. (1845–49), and then of David (violin) and Hauptmann (theory) in Leipzig. In 1853 he became a violinist in his father's Karlsbad spa orch., and in 1868 succeeded him as its conductor. He composed some 50 dances.

BIBL.: M. Kaufmann, *J. L.* (Reichenberg, 1930). —NS/LK /DM

Lablache, Luigi, famous Italian bass of French and Irish descent; b. Naples, Dec. 6, 1794; d. there, Jan. 23, 1858. He was admitted at 12 to the Cons. della Pietà dei Turchini in Naples, where he studied with Valesi. He commenced his operatic career as a buffo napoletano in Fioravanti's *La Molinara* at the Teatro San Carlino there (1812), then studied in Messina, where he appeared as a buffo; was made primo basso cantante in Palermo (1813). He gained acclaim at his La Scala debut in Milan as Dandini in Rossini's *La Cenerentola* (1817), and continued to sing there until 1823; also sang in Rome, Turin, and Venice. He then became a principal member of Barbaja's Vienna opera enterprise (1824); Ferdinand I of Naples made him a member of the royal chapel and the Teatro San Carlo in Naples. He scored a triumphant London debut at the King's Theatre as Geronimo in Cimarosa's *Il matrimonio segreto* (March 30, 1830), and continued to appear there every year until 1852 (1833–34 excepted). He made his Paris debut as Geronimo at the Théâtre-Italien (Nov. 4, 1830), where he was a great favorite until 1851; created the roles of Sir George Walton in Bellini's *I Puritani* (Jan. 25, 1835), and Marino Faliero (March 12, 1835) and Don Pasquale (Jan. 3, 1843) in Donizetti's operas, ensuring his success with Paris audiences. During one of his stays in England (1836–37), he served as singing teacher to Princess Victoria. He was a principal singer of Gye's company at Covent Garden (1854) until his retirement from the stage owing to ill health (1856). Although he was best known for his buffo roles, he was capable of remarkable serious portrayals as well.

BIBL.: F. Castil-Blaze, *Biographie de L.* (Paris, 1850); G. Widén, *L. L.* (Göteborg, 1897).—NS/LK/DM

Labor, Josef, Austrian pianist, organist, and composer; b. Horowitz, June 29, 1842; d. Vienna, April 26, 1924. He lost his sight as a youth. He studied with Sechter at the Vienna Cons. In 1863 he was tutor to the princesses of Hannover, who were then living in exile with their family in Vienna. He played in London (1865), Paris, and Russia. In 1868 he returned to Vienna, where he settled as a teacher; among his students were Bittner and Schoenberg. He wrote a Konzertstück for

Piano and Orch., church music, chamber music, keyboard pieces, and songs.

BIBL.: P. Kundi, *J. L., Sein Leben und Wirken* (Vienna, 1963; contains a thematic catalogue).—NS/LK/DM

La Borde or **Laborde, Jean-Benjamin (-François) de,** French violinist, writer on music, and composer; b. Paris, Sept. 5, 1734; d. there (guillotined), July 22, 1794. He was born into an aristocratic family, and received training in violin from Dauvergne and in composition from Rameau. While still young, he became a member of the Compagnie des Fermiers-Généreaux. In 1762 he entered the service of Louis XV, becoming his close friend and a premier valet de chambre. Following the king's death in 1774, he fell in and out of favor at the court. With the coming of the Revolution, he settled in Rouen only to be tracked down, sent back to Paris, and executed. He composed many stage works, mostly opéras-comiques, and brought out collections of chansons. He also designed a clavecin chromatique with 21 notes to the octave. His interest in early music resulted in his most notable work, the extensive *Essai sur la musique ancienne et moderne* (4 vols., Paris, 1780). This work remains valuable for its entries on 17th and 18th century musicians. His other writings included *Mémoires historiques sur Raoul de Coucy* [with] *receuil de ses chansons en vieux langage, avec la traduction et l'ancienne musique* (Paris, 1781) and *Mémoires sur les proportions musicales, le genre énarmonique...avec une lettre de l'auteur de l'Essai à M. l'Abbé Roussier* (Paris, 1781).

BIBL.: C. Mellinet, *Notice sur J.-B.d. L.B.* (Nantes, 1839); J. Warmoes, *L'exemplaire de l' "Essai sur la musique ancienne et moderne" de J.-B.d. L. annoté part Grétry* (diss., Univ. of Louvain, 1956).—NS/LK/DM

Labroca, Mario, Italian composer; b. Rome, Nov. 22, 1896; d. there, July 1, 1973. He studied composition with Malipiero and Respighi, and graduated from the Parma Cons. in 1921. He was manager of the Teatro Comunale in Florence (1936–44), artistic director of La Scala in Milan (1947–49), director of the music dept. of the RAI (1949–58), and artistic director of the Teatro La Fenice in Venice (from 1959). He also lectured at the Univ. of Perugia (from 1960).

WORKS: DRAMATIC: Opera: *La Principessa di Perepepe* (Rome, Dec. 11, 1927); *Le tre figliole di Babbo Pallino* (Rome, Jan. 27, 1928). **Other:** Many theater and film scores. **ORCH.:** Sinfonia for Strings (1927); Sym. (1935). **VOCAL:** *Stabat Mater* for Soprano, Chorus, and Orch. (Rome, Dec. 15, 1935); *3 cantate sulla Passione di Cristo* for Baritone, Chorus, and Orch. (1950); *8 madrigali di Tomaso Campanella* for Baritone and Orch. (1958). **CHAMBER:** 3 string quartets (1923, 1932, 1939); Suite for Viola and Piano (1923); Piano Trio (1925). —NS/LK/DM

Labunski, Felix (actually, **Feliks Roderyk**), Polish-born American composer, pedagogue, pianist, and music critic, brother of **Wiktor Labunski**; b. Ksawerynów, Dec. 27, 1892; d. Cincinnati, April 28, 1979. Following piano lessons as a child, he was a pupil of Marczewski and Maliszewski at the Warsaw Cons.

(1922–24), and of Dukas and Boulanger (composition) and Migot (musicology) at the École Normale de Musique in Paris (1924–34). In 1927 he was a founder of the Assn. of Young Polish Composers in Paris. After serving as director of classical music for the Polish Radio in Warsaw (1934–36), he emigrated to the U.S. and in 1941 became a naturalized American citizen. In 1940–41 he was a prof. of counterpoint and composition at Marymount Coll. in Tarrytown, N.Y., and thereafter taught at the Cincinnati Coll. of Music (1945–55), and its successor the Univ. of Cincinnati Coll.-Cons. of Music (1955–64). As a pianist, he mainly performed his own works. He composed basically along Romantic lines with some infusions of neo-Classical elements.

WORKS: DRAMATIC: Ballet: *God's Man* (1937). **ORCH.:** *Danse fantastique* (1926); *Triptyque champêtre* (1931); 2 syms. (1937, 1954); Suite for Strings (1938); *In Memoriam*, symphonic poem in memory of Paderewski (1941); *Variations* (1947); *Elegy* (1955); *Xaveriana*, fantasy for 2 Pianos and Orch. (1956); *Symphonic Dialogues* (1961); *Canto di aspirazione* (1963; based on the slow movement of the Sym. No. 2); *Polish Renaissance Suite* (1967); *Salut à Paris*, ballet suite (1968); *Music for Piano and Orch.* (1968); *Primavera* (1974). **CHAMBER:** 2 string quartets (1935, 1962); *Divertimento* for Flute and Piano (1936); *3 Bagatelles* for Brass Quartet (1955); *Divertimento* for Flute, Oboe, Clarinet, and Bassoon (1956); *Diptych* for Oboe and Piano (1958); *Intrada festiva* for Brass Choir (1968); piano pieces; organ music. **VOCAL:** *Polish Cantata* (1932); *The Birds* for Soprano and Orch. (1934); *Songs without Words* for Soprano and Strings (1946); *There Is No Death*, cantata for Chorus and Orch. (1950); *Images of Youth*, cantata (1956); choruses; songs.—**NS/LK/DM**

Labunski, Wiktor, Polish-born American pianist, teacher, and composer, brother of **Felix Labunski;** b. St. Petersburg, April 14, 1895; d. Kansas City, Mo., Jan. 26, 1974. He was a student at the St. Petersburg Cons. of Nikolayev (piano) and Kalafati and Wihtol (composition). After further training with F. Blumenfeld and Safonov (piano), he studied conducting in Poland with Mlynarski. He was head of the piano dept. at the Kraków Cons. (1919–28). In 1928 he made his Carnegie Hall debut in N.Y. After teaching at the Nashville (Tenn.) Cons. (1928–31), he was a prof. and director of the Memphis (Tenn.) Coll. of Music (1931–37). He became a teacher at the Kansas City (Mo.) Cons. in 1937, serving as its director from 1941 to 1971. His compositions followed along traditional lines.

WORKS: Piano Concertino (1932); Sym. (1936); Piano Concerto (1937); *Variations* for Piano and Orch. (1945); Concerto for 2 Pianos and Orch. (1951); many piano pieces; songs.

BIBL.: J. Belanger, *W. L.: Polish-American Musician in Kansas City, 1937–1974* (diss., Columbia Univ., 1982).—**NS/LK/DM**

Laburda, Jiří, Czech composer; b. Soběslav, April 3, 1931. He received private training in composition from Karel Hába and Zdeněk Hůla and in musicology from Eduard Herzog, and took courses in music education and philology at the Charles Univ. in Prague (1952–55). After studies at the Prague Teacher Training Coll. (1957–61), he returned to the Charles Univ., where he took his Ph.D. (1970, with a diss. on Shostakovich's syms.) and subsequently served on its faculty. His

works follow along traditional paths with infusions of aleatory and dodecaphonic writing; his vocal and chamber pieces are particularly effective.

WORKS: DRAMATIC: Ballet: *Les Petits Riens* (1967; Liberec, March 15, 1986). **ORCH.:** *Burlesca* for Horn and Orch. (Košice, April 11, 1963); Piano Concerto (1969; Prague, Feb. 5, 1973); Sinfonia (1975); Concerto for Accordion and Strings (Kralupy, April 21, 1980); Concertino for Trumpet and Strings (Mariánské Lazné, July 17, 1981); *Pastorale* for Flute and Strings (1981; Joschkar-Ola, Russia, March 2, 1987); *Overture solenne* (1983; Prague, June 18, 1985); *Divertimento in RE* for Strings (1983; České Budějovice, March 22, 1984); *Concerto da camera* for Violin and Orch. (1986); Double Concerto for Violin, Cello, and Strings (1989); Concerto for Organ and Strings (1991); Concerto for Bassoon and Strings (1997). **CHAMBER:** *Kasace I* for Flute, Clarinet, Horn, Trumpet, and Trombone (1978), *II* for Violin, Clarinet or Oboe d'Amore, Percussion, and Piano (1979), and *III* for Bass Clarinet and Percussion (1979); Partita for Violin (1978); Trumpet Sonatina (1979); Brass Quintet No. 2 (1980); *6 Inventions* for 2 Trumpets and Trombone (1980); Trombone Sonata (1981); Duo for Guitar and Double Bass or Cello (1981); Sonata for Solo Marimba (1983); *Peter with Trumpet* for Trumpet and Piano (1983); *Rondo* for 3 Violins (1984); Bassoon Sonatina (1985); Sonata for 2 Marimbas (1986); Clarinet Sonata (1987); Tuba Sonata (1987); *Signal*, scherzo for Trumpet and Piano (1987); *Aphorismes* for Clarinet (1987); Trio for Oboe, Clarinet, and Bassoon (1989); *Sonata da chiesa* for 2 Trumpets, Horn, Trombone, Tuba, and Organ (1989); Sonata for Solo Accordion (1989); *Sonata da chiesa* for 2 Trumpets, 2 Trombones, and Organ (1990); *Serenata* for 4 Trombones (1991); *Canto pasquale* for Trumpet and Organ (1993); *Partita* for 6 Trumpets (1993); Trumpet Sonatina (1994); *Valse* for Marimba (1994); Suite for Saxophone Quartet (1995); *Solenne* for Trombone and Organ (1996); *Sonata da chiesa No. 3, Nativitas Christi* for Trumpet and Organ (1997); piano pieces. **Organ:** *Golgotha*, sonata (1992). **VOCAL:** *Glagolitica* for Soloists, Chorus, Organ, Brass, and Percussion (1964; Freiburg im Breisgau, Jan. 11, 1990); *Metamorphoses* for Soloists, Chorus, and Orch. (1966; Wolfsburg, May 18, 1969); *Marriage* for Soloists, Women's Chorus, and Piano (1980; Prague, Nov. 12, 1989); *Missa pastoralis* for Soprano, Bass, Chorus, and Organ (1990; Prague, Jan. 12, 1991); *Missa* for Chorus, Trumpet, and Organ (1992); *Missa Sistina* for Chorus (1993; also for Chorus and Organ); *Missa clara* for Voices and Organ (1993); *Haec dies* for Chorus, Organ, String Orch., and Timpani (1997); *Exaudi nos, Domine* for Baritone and Women's Chorus (1998).—**NS/LK/DM**

La Casinière, Yves de, French composer, music publisher, administrator, and teacher; b. Angers, Feb. 11, 1897; d. Paris, Oct. 28, 1971. He settled in Paris, where he studied with Boulanger (organ), Caussade (counterpoint and fugue), and d'Ollone (composition and harmony) at the École de Normale d Musique. In 1935 he became founder-president of the Editions du Musagète. He was also active as an administrator and teacher. Among his works were 2 syms. (1922, 1930), chamber music, piano pieces, and songs.—**NS/LK/DM**

Lacépède, Bernard Germaine Etiènne Médard de la Villesur-Illon, Count of, French naturalist, music theorist, and composer; b. Agen, Dec. 26, 1756; d. Epinay-sur-Seine, Oct. 6, 1825. He studied composition in Agen and Bordeaux while pursuing his interest in science; later he studied music with Gossec. He served as director of the Jardin des Plantes and became highly regarded as a naturalist. Among his compositions were 5 operas, incidental music to Fénelon's *Télémaque* (1785), 2 syms., a Requiem, and chamber music. His writings on music included *Réflexions sur les progrès que la musique a encore à faire* (MS; ed. by R. du Page in *Le Figaro*, Dec. 19, 1925) and *La poétique de la musique* (Paris, 1785; 3rd ed., 1797). His *Oeuvres complètes* appeared in Paris (1826).

BIBL.: Mahorault, *Notice sur la vie et les ouvrages de M. L.* (Paris, 1825).—LK/DM

Lacerda, Francisco (Inácio da Silveira de Sousa Pereira Forjaz) de, Portuguese conductor, musicologist, and composer; b. Ribeira Seca, S. Jorge, Azores, May 11, 1869; d. Lisbon, July 18, 1934. He studied at the Lisbon Cons., then received a government stipend for study in Paris, where he took a course with d'Indy at the Schola Cantorum. In Paris he associated himself with Bourgault-Ducoudray and worked with him in the International Folklore Assn. He also conducted concerts. At the outbreak of World War I (1914), he returned to Portugal, where he later founded the Orquesta Filarmonica in Lisbon (1923). He ed. the important *Cancioneiro musical português* (Lisbon, 1935–36), a collection of some 500 folk songs. Among his compositions are the symphonic poems *Adamastor* (1902) and *Almourol* 1926), several ballets, incidental music, and piano pieces.

BIBL.: F. de Sousa, *F. d.L.: Exposição commemorativa do primeiro centenario do nascimento* (Lisbon, 1969).—NS/LK/DM

Lach, Robert, eminent Austrian musicologist and composer; b. Vienna, Jan. 29, 1874; d. Salzburg, Sept. 11, 1958. He studied law at the Univ. of Vienna, but in 1894 he entered the Austrian civil administration without obtaining his degree. He was a composition pupil of R. Fuchs at the Cons. of the Gesellschaft der Musikfreunde in Vienna (1893–99), and also studied philosophy and musicology at the Univ. there with Wallaschek and Adler (1896–99). He completed his study of musicology with Rietsch at the German Univ. in Prague (Ph.D., 1902, with the diss. *Studien zur Entwicklungsgeschichte der ornamentalen Melopoie*; publ. in Leipzig, 1913). In 1903 he left his government post and in 1911 joined the staff of Vienna's Hofbibliothek; from 1913 to 1918 he was director of its music collection; remained in that post when it became the Staatsbibliothek (1918–20). From 1915 he lectured at the Univ. of Vienna. He was prof. of musicology and chairman of its Musicological Inst. (1927–39), and also prof. at the Vienna Academy of Music (from 1924). He recorded for the Phonogram Archives of Vienna the songs of Russian prisoners of World War I (with particular emphasis on Asian and Caucasian nationalities), and publ. numerous papers on these melodies. He was pensioned in 1939, and lived in Vienna in retirement, devoting his time to the compilation of oriental glossaries (Babylonian, Sumerian, Egyptian, etc.). In 1954 he became general ed. of the new Denkmäler der Tonkunst in Österreich. In addition to his books, he contributed articles to various music

journals; also wrote philosophical poems and mystical plays. Among his compositions are 10 syms., 25 string quartets, 14 string quintets, 8 string sextets, other chamber music, 8 masses, cantatas, etc.

WRITINGS (all publ. in Vienna): *Sebastian Sailers "Schöpfung" in der Musik* (1916); *W.A. Mozart als Theoretiker* (1918); *Zur Geschichte des Gesellschaftstanzes im 18. Jahrhundert* (1920); *Eine Tiroler Liederhandschrift aus dem 18. Jahrhundert* (1923); *Zur Geschichte des musikalischen Zunftwesens* (1923); *Die vergleichende Musikwissenschaft: Ihre Methoden und Probleme* (1924); *Das Konstruktionsprinzip der Wiederholung in Musik, Sprache und Literatur* (1925); *Vergleichende Kunst-und Musikwissenschaft* (1925); *Die Bruckner-Akten des Wiener Universitätsarchivs* (1926); ed. *Gesänge russischer Kriegsgefangener* (1926–52); *Geschichte der Staatsakademie und Hochschule für Musik und darstellende Kunst in Wien* (1927); *Das Ethos in der Musik Franz Schuberts* (1928).

BIBL.: W. Graf, ed., *R. L.: Persönlichkeit und Werk* (Vienna, 1954).—NS/LK/DM

Lachenmann, Helmut (Friedrich), German composer and pedagogue; b. Stuttgart, Nov. 27, 1935. He was a student of Jürgen Uhde (piano) and J.N. David (theory and counterpoint) at the Stuttgart Staatliche Hochschule für Musik (1955–58), and of Nono (composition) in Venice (1958–60); he then pursued research at the electronic studio at the Univ. of Ghent (1965). He taught theory at the Stuttgart Hochschule für Musik (1966–70), and then music at the Ludwigsburg Pädagogische Hochschule (1970–76). He also served as coordinator of the composition studio at the Darmstadt Internationale Ferienkurse (1972) and led a master class in composition at the Univ. of Basel (1972–73). In 1976 he became a teacher at the Hannover Hochschule für Musik. He also taught at the Ferienkurse in Darmstadt (from 1978). From 1981 he was prof. of composition at the Stuttgart Hochschule für Musik. Among his honors are the cultural prize for music of Munich (1965), the composition prize of Stuttgart (1968), the Bach prize of Hamburg (1972), and the prize of the Ernst von Siemens Foundation (1997). He is also a member of the Akademie der Künste in Berlin, the Akademie der Schönen Künste in Munich, and the Freie Akademie der Künste in Mannheim. J. Häusler ed. a vol. of his writings as *Helmut Lachenmann: Musik als existentielle Erfahrung: Schriften 1966–1995* (Wiesbaden, 1996). While producing works based upon structural techniques, he has made it his central aim as a composer to create scores free of societal expectations.

WORKS: DRAMATIC: Music Theater: *Das Mädchen mit den Schwefelhölzern* (1990–96; Hamburg, Jan. 26, 1997). ORCH.: *Souvenir* for 41 Instruments (1959; Stuttgart, Nov. 11, 1994); *Notturno (Musik für Julia)* for Cello and Small Orch. (1966–68; Brussels, April 25, 1969); *Air* for Percussionist and Orch. (1968–69; Frankfurt am Main, Sept. 1, 1969; new version, Graz, Oct. 8, 1994); *Kontrakadenz* (1970–71; Stuttgart, April 23, 1971); *Klangschatten- mein Saitenspiel* for 3 Grand Pianos and 48 Strings (Hamburg, Dec. 20, 1972); *Fassade* for Orch. and Tape (Bonn, Sept. 22, 1973); *Schwankungen am Rand* for Brass and Strings (1974–75; Donaueschingen, Oct. 17, 1975); *Accanto* for Clarinet and Orch. (1975–76; Saarbrücken, May 30, 1976); *Tanzsuite mit Deutschlandlied* for String Quartet and Orch. (1979–80; Donaueschingen, Oct. 18, 1980); *Harmonica* for Tuba and Orch. (1981–83; Saarbrücken, May 15, 1983); *Mouvement*

(-vor der Erstarrung) (1982–84; Paris, Nov. 12, 1984); *Ausklang* for Piano and Orch. (1984–85; Cologne, April 18, 1986); *Staub* (1985–87; Saarbrücken, Dec. 19, 1987); *Tableau* (1988–89; Hamburg, June 4, 1989); *"...Zwei Gefühle..."*, *Musik mit Leonardo* (Stuttgart, Oct. 9, 1992); *Nun* for Flute, Trombone, and Orch. (1998–99). **CHAMBER:** *5 Strophen* for 9 Instruments (1961; Venice, April 13, 1962; *Introversion I* for 6 Instruments (1963; Darmstadt, July 19, 1964) and *II* for 6 Instruments (1964; Munich, Feb. 22, 1965); String Trio (1965; Ghent, March 29, 1966); *Interieur I* for Percussionist (1966; Santa Fe, N.Mex., Aug. 14, 1967); *Trio fluido* for Clarinet, Viola, and Percussion (1966; Munich, March 5, 1968); *temA* for Flute, Mezzo-soprano, and Cello (1968; Stuttgart, Feb. 19, 1969); *Pression* for Cello (1969; Como, Sept. 30, 1970); *Dal niente (Interieur III)* for Clarinet (Nuremberg, June 4, 1970); *Gran Torso* for String Quartet (1971–72; Bremen, May 6, 1972; rev. 1972–76, 1988); *Salut für Caudwell* for 2 Guitars (Baden-Baden, Dec. 3, 1977); *Toccatina* for Violin (1986; Stuttgart, May 20, 1988); *Allegro Sostenuto* for Clarinet, Violin, and Piano (1986–88; Cologne, Dec. 3, 1989); String Quartet No. 2, *Reigen seliger Geister* (Geneva, Sept. 28, 1989). **P i a n o :** *5 Variationen über ein Thema von Franz Schubert* (1956); *Rondo* for 2 Pianos, 4-Hands (1957; Stuttgart, March 12, 1958); *Echo Andante* (Darmstadt, July 18, 1962); *Wiegenmusik* (1963; Darmstadt, April 1, 1964); *Guero* (Hamburg, Dec. 1, 1970; rev. 1988); *Ein Kinderspiel* (1980; Toronto, Feb. 17, 1982). **VO-CAL:** *Consolation I* for 12 Voices and 4 Percussion (1967; Bremen, May 3, 1968) and *II* for 16 Voices (1968; Basel, June 15, 1969); *Les Consolations* for 16 Voices and Orch. (1967–68, 1977–78; Darmstadt, Aug. 10, 1978); *Dritte Stimme zu J.S. Bachs zweistimmiger Invention d-moll BWV 775* for 3 Voices (1985). **ELECTRONIC:** *Szenario* (1965).—NS/LK/DM

Lachmann, Robert, noted German musicologist; b. Berlin, Nov. 28, 1892; d. Jerusalem, May 8, 1939. He studied English, French, and Arabic at the univs. of Berlin and London. He served in the German army during World War I, when he began to collect folk melodies from African and Indian war prisoners; later studied musicology with Stumpf and Johannes Wolf, and Semitic languages with Mittwoch at the Univ. of Berlin, where he received his Ph.D. (1922) with the diss. *Die Musik in den tunesischen Städten*, publ. in the *Archiv für Musikwissenschaft*, V (1923). He worked at the Berlin State Library (1924–26). After a period in Kiel, he resumed his work at the Berlin State Library (1927), serving under Wolf. However, he was ousted by the Nazis as a Jew in 1933. He went to Palestine (1935) and became a member of the faculty of the Univ. of Jerusalem.

WRITINGS: *Musik des Orients* (Breslau, 1929); *Die Musik der aussereuropäischen Natur-und Kulturvölker* (1929); with M. el-Hefni, *Ja'qūb Ikn Ishāq al-Kindī: Risāla fi hubr tā'lif al'alhān-über die Komposition der Melodien* (Leipzig, 1931); E. Gerson-Kiwi, ed., *Robert Lachmann: Posthumous Works*, I (Jerusalem, 1974). —NS/LK/DM

Lachner, family of German musicians, all brothers:

(1) Theodor Lachner, organist and composer; b. Rain-am-Lech, 1788; d. Munich, May 23, 1877. He served as Munich court organist throughout most of his career. He was known as a composer of choral music and lieder.

(2) Franz Paul Lachner, conductor and composer; b. Rain-am- Lech, April 2, 1803; d. Munich, Jan. 20, 1890. He studied piano and organ with his father, Anton Lachner, the town organist. He then went to Vienna, where he studied with Sechter and Stadler. He became a close friend of Schubert, and also came to know Beethoven. He was made organist of the Lutheran Church (1823), and then was asst. conductor (1827–29) and principal conductor (1829–34) of the Kärnthnertortheater. He was conductor of the Mannheim National Theater (1834–36), and then court conductor (1836–52) and Generalmusikdirektor (1852–65) in Munich.

WORKS: DRAMATIC: O p e r a : *Die Bürgschaft* (Pest, Oct. 30, 1828); *Alidia* (Munich, April 12, 1839); *Catarina Cornaro* (Munich, Dec. 3, 1841); *Benvenuto Cellini* (Munich, Oct. 7, 1849). **ORCH.:** 8 syms. (1828–51); 7 suites (1861–81); 2 harp concertos (1828, 1833); Flute Concerto (1832). **VOCAL:** *Die vier Menschenalter*, cantata (1829); *Moses*, oratorio (1833); 8 masses; *Stabat Mater*; other choral works; songs. **OTHER:** Much chamber music; piano pieces.

BIBL.: G. Wagner, *F. L. als Liederkomponist, nebst einem biographischen Teil und dem thematischen Verzeichnis sämtlicher Lieder* (diss., Univ. of Mainz, 1969).

(3) Ignaz Lachner, organist, conductor, and composer; b. Rain-am-Lech, Sept. 11, 1807; d. Hannover, Feb. 24, 1895. He studied with his father and then in Vienna (1824) with his brother Franz, whom he succeeded as organist of the Lutheran Church. He was asst. conductor of the Kärnthnertortheater (1825–28) and the Court Opera (1828–31) there. He was court conductor in Stuttgart (1831–36) and Munich (1836–53), conductor of the Hamburg Opera (1853–58), then court conductor in Stockholm (1858–61). From 1861 to 1875 he was principal conductor in Frankfurt am Main.

WORKS: DRAMATIC: O p e r a : *Der Geisterturm* (Stuttgart, 1837); *Die Regenbrüder* (Stuttgart, May 20, 1839); *Loreley* (Munich, 1846). **O t h e r :** Singspiels and other dramatic works; ballets. **OTHER:** Syms.; masses; chamber music; piano pieces.

BIBL.: H. Müller, *I. L.: Versuch einer Würdigung, mit Werkverzeichnis* (Celle, 1974).

(4) Vincenz Lachner, organist, conductor, and composer; b. Rain-am-Lech, July 19, 1811; d. Karlsruhe, Jan. 22, 1893. He studied with his father and then with his brothers in Vienna, succeeding Ignaz as organist of the Lutheran Church and Franz as conductor of the Kärnthnertortheater (1834) and at the Mannheim National Theater (1836). He conducted the German Opera in London (1842), then became conductor of the Frankfurt am Main Opera (1848); he was pensioned in 1872. From 1884 he taught at the Karlsruhe Cons. He wrote syms., overtures, chamber music, and numerous songs, but was best known for his 4-part men's choruses. —NS/LK/DM

Lachnith, Ludwig Wenzel, Bohemian horn player and composer; b. Prague, July 7, 1746; d. Paris, Oct. 3, 1820. He studied violin, harpsichord, and horn, then joined the orch. in Pfalz-Zweibrücken. About 1780 he went to Paris and studied with Rodolphe (horn) and F.A. Philidor (composition). He is known chiefly for his pasticcios; an instance is his oratorio *Saul* (April 6, 1803), with music taken from scores by Mozart, Haydn, Cimarosa, Paisiello, Gossec, and Philidor. He also arranged the music of Mozart's *Die Zauberflöte*, to a libretto reworked by Étienne Morel de Chefdeville, and produced it under the title *Les Mystères d'Isis* (Aug. 20, 1801), justly parodied as *Les Misères d'ici*. In several of his ventures he had the older Kalkbrenner as his collaborator. Among his original works were the operas *L'Heureuse Réconciliation* (June 25, 1785) and *Eugénie et Linval* (1798), syms., 6 concertos for Harpsichord or Piano, and chamber music.—**NS/LK/DM**

Lacombe, Louis (Trouillon), French pianist and composer; b. Bourges, Nov. 26, 1818; d. Saint-Vaast-la-Hougue, Sept. 30, 1884. He studied piano at the Paris Cons. with Zimmerman, winning the premier prix at the age of 13. After touring through France, Belgium, and Germany, he took courses with Czerny, Sechter, and Seyfried in Vienna. Following another concert tour, he settled in Paris (1839), concentrating on composition. His essay *Philosophie et musique* was publ. posth. (Paris, 1895).

WORKS: DRAMATIC: *L'Amour*, melodrama (Paris, Dec. 2, 1859); *La Madone*, opera (Paris, Jan. 16, 1861); *Le Tonnelier de Nuremberg*, comic opera (perf. as *Meister Martin und seine Gesellen*, Koblenz, March 7, 1897); *Winkelried*, opera (Geneva, Feb. 17, 1892); *La Reine des eaux*, opera (perf. as *Die Korrigane*, Sondershausen, March 12?, 1901); *Der Kreuzritter*, comic opera (Sondershausen, March 21, 1902). OTHER: 2 dramatic syms. with Soloists and Chorus: *Manfred* (1847) and *Arva ou Les Hongrois* (1850); *Lassan et Friss*, Hungarian fantasy for Orch. (1890); *Sapho*, cantata (1878); choruses; chamber music; piano pieces.

BIBL.: E. Bourdin, *La Musique et les musiciens: L. L.* (Paris, 1882); H. Boyer, *L. L. et son oeuvre* (Paris, 1888); L. Gallet, *Conférence sur L. L. et son oeuvre* (Paris, 1891); E. Jongleux, *Un Grand Musicien méconnu: L. L.* (Bourges, 1935).—**NS/LK/DM**

Lacombe, Paul, French composer; b. Carcassonne, Aude, July 11, 1837; d. there, June 5, 1927. He studied in Carcassonne with François Teysserre, an organist. He was a prolific composer; his works total more than 150, including *Ouverture symphonique* (1876), 3 syms. (No. 3 won the prize of the Société des Compositeurs de Musique, 1886), *Suite pastorale* for Orch., *Marche dernière* for Orch., *Scène au camp* for Orch., 3 violin sonatas, Cello Sonata, 3 trios, String Quartet, Mass, Requiem, songs, and characteristic piano pieces.

BIBL.: L. Moulin, *P. L. et son oeuvre* (Paris, 1924). —**NS/LK/DM**

Lacome (actually, **Lacôme d'Estaleaux**), **Paul (-Jean-Jacques),** French composer; b. Le Houga, Gers, March 4, 1838; d. there, Dec. 12, 1920. He was a student of José Puig y Absubide in Aire-sur-l'Ardour (1857–60). After winning a competition with his operetta *Le Dernier des paladins* (1860), he went to Pris and composed orch. works, chamber music, and songs. He had his first real success with the opera-bouffe *La Dot mal placée* (March 9, 1873), but his greatest success as a theater composer came with *Jeanne, Jeannette et Jeanneton* (Oct. 27, 1876), which was subsequently heard

abroad. Among his later scores were *Le Beau Nicolas* (Oct. 8, 1880), *La Nuit de Saint-Jean* (Nov. 13, 1882), *Madame Boniface* (Oct. 20, 1883), *La Gardeuse d'oies* (Oct. 26, 1888), *Ma mie Rosette* (Feb. 4, 1890), and *Les Quatre Filles d'Aymon* (Sept. 20, 1898).—**NS/LK/DM**

Lacroix, Antoine, French violinist and composer; b. Rambouillers, near Nancy, 1756; d. Lübeck, June 18, 1806. He was a student of violin and composition of Joseph-Antoine Lorenziti, maître de chapelle at Nancy Cathedral. From 1780 to 1792 he was active in Paris, where he gained distinction as both a violinist and composer. After the Revolution, he toured in Denmark and Germany before settling in Lübeck as a town musician in 1796. Among his works were sonatas, duos, and variations for violin.—**LK/DM**

Lacy, Steve (originally, **Lackritz, Steven Norman**), jazz soprano saxophonist, composer; b. N.Y., July 23, 1934. Lacy has been one of the few to exclusively play the soprano saxophone, perhaps the first in the modern era, and he inspired John Coltrane to take it up. Lacy studied with Cecil Scott and attended both the Schillinger School of Music (now Berklee) and the Manhattan School of Music. He gigged with Dixieland groups in 1952, and then began working and playing with Cecil Taylor (1955–57). He worked for a period in the late 1950s with Gil Evans, Mal Waldron, and Jimmy Giuffre, and also began studying the works of Monk. Rollins invited Lacy to join him on the Williamsburg Bridge in 1960. He spent four months in Monk's quartet in 1960, then formed his own group with trombonist Roswell Rudd and drummer Dennis Charles, playing almost exclusively Monk material. Lacy left the group in 1965, playing at the Montmartre in Copenhagen, where he joined with Don Cherry and toured Paris, Rome, Amsterdam, and London. In 1966, Lacy left for Buenos-Aires with Enrico Rava, Johnny Dyani, and Louis Moholo; they ended up staying for nine months, but it was extremely difficult to survive as an interracial, free-music group considering the country's dictatorial and repressive regime (at the time one could be arrested for listening to the Beatles). However, by the end of their stay, the group had a small following for private concerts that Lacy organized, and had appeared on television. He subsequently returned to N.Y. and started another group with Rava. In 1967, Lacy returned to Europe to live with his wife, Irène Aebi. He spent three years in Rome, extensively studying electronics and sound. He moved to Paris in 1970 and since that time has worked regularly with Aebi and Kent Carter; in 1975 they were joined by Steve Potts, Michael Smith, and Oliver Johnson. This sextet has experienced only a few changes in personnel, with Takashi Kako and then Bobby Few replacing Smith, Jean-Jacques Avenel replacing Carter, and John Betsch temporarily replacing Johnson for five years. Lacy also regularly performs solo and in other contexts. In 1996 he was invited for a year's residency in Berlin, where he met the Bengal poet Taslima Nasreen, whose works he had set to music in *The Cry*. Returning to Paris in 1997, he continued to work in a trio with Avenel and Betsch, to perform his song cycle *Treize Regards* based on the writings of Marina Tsvetaïeva, to make music for the Merce Cunningham Dance Company, and planning to work with Eddy Louis. In 1997 he was nominated to lead the L'Orchestre National de Jazz, a jazz band founded in 1986 by the Ministère de la Culture with rotating directors, but because of his own inexperience leading big bands, and the French national government's requirement that the leader be a French citizen, he did not assume the post. He performed duets with Danilo Perez during a summer 1998 tour of the U.S. He is the subject of the documentary *Lift the Bandstand*.

DISC.: *Complete S. L.* (1954); *Soprano Saxophone* (1957); *Reflections* (1958); *Straight Horn of Steve Lacy* (1960); *Evidence* (with Don Cherry, 1961); *School Days* (1963); *Disposability* (1965); *Forest and the Zoo* (1966); *Wordless* (1971); *Solo* (1972); *Saxophone Special* (1974); *Scraps* (1974); *Axieme* (1975); *Stabs* (1975); *Clinkers* (1977); *Raps* (1977); *Stamps* (1977); *Capers* (1979); *Prospectus* (1982); *Regeneration* (1982); *Blinks* (1983); *Solo* (1985); *Flim-Flam* (1986); *Live in Budapest* (1986); *Only Monk* (1986); *Super Quartet Live at Sweet Basil* (1987); *More Monk* (1989); *Hot House* (1990); *Rushes: 10 Songs from Russia* (1990); *Remains* (1991); *Spirit of Mingus* (1991); *We See* (1992); *Vespers* (1993); *Revenue* (1995).

BIBL.: Clifford Preiss, *S. L. Festival Handbook* (N.Y.); H. Lukes Lindenmaier, *The S. L. Discography* (Germany).—LP

Laderman, Ezra,

notable American composer and teacher; b. N.Y., June 29, 1924. He studied at the H.S. of Music and Art in N.Y., where he appeared as soloist in the premiere of his First Piano Concerto with the school orch. in 1939. He pursued his training in composition with Wolpe in N.Y. (1946–49) and with Gideon at Brooklyn Coll. of the City Univ. of N.Y. (B.A., 1949), and took courses with Leuning and Moore (composition) and Lang (musicology) at Columbia Univ. (M.A., 1952). In 1955, 1958, and 1964 he was awarded Guggenheim fellowships. In 1960–61 he taught at Sarah Lawrence Coll. After holding the American Prix de Rome (1963–64), he again taught at Sarah Lawrence Coll. (1965–66). From 1971 to 1982 he was composer-in-residence and prof. at the State Univ. of N.Y. in Binghamton. He was also president of the American Music Center (1973–76) and director of the music program of the NEA (1979–82). In 1982–83 he was active at the American Academy in Rome. From 1987 to 1989 he was president of the American Music Coucil. He was dean of the Yale Univ. School of Music from 1989. After composing in a tonal style, Laderman turned to atonal, and later serial writing. Later in his career he came full circle by again exploring the resources of tonality in a synthetic form, utilizing a vast array of techniques and styles.

WORKS: DRAMATIC: O p e r a : *Jacob and the Indians* (1954; Woodstock, N.Y., July 24, 1957); *Goodbye to the Clowns* (1956; N.Y., May 22, 1960); *The Hunting of the Snark*, opera-cantata (1958; concert premiere, N.Y., March 26, 1961; stage premiere, N.Y., April 13, 1978); *Sarah* (CBS-TV, Nov. 30, 1958); *Air Raid* (1965); *Shadows Among Us* (1967); *And David Wept*, opera-cantata (1970; CBS-TV, April 11, 1971); *The Questions of Abraham*, opera-cantata (CBS-TV, Sept. 30, 1973); *Galileo Galilei* (1978; Binghamton, N.Y., Feb. 3, 1979; based on the oratorio *The Trials of Galileo*); *Marilyn* (N.Y., Oct. 6, 1993). **M u s i c a l C o m e d y :** *Dominique* (1962). **D a n c e :** Duet for Flute and Dancer (1956); *Dance Quartet* for Flute, Clarinet, Cello, and Dancer (1957); *Esther* for Narrator, Oboe, and String Orch. (1960); *Song of Songs* for Soprano and Piano (1960); *Solos and Chorale* for 4 Mixed Voices (1960). **I n c i d e n t a l M u s i c :** *Machinal* (N.Y., April 7, 1960); *The Lincoln Mask* (N.Y., Oct. 30, 1972); numerous film and television scores. **ORCH.:** 2 unnumbered piano concertos (N.Y., June 1939; 1957); 2 numbered piano concertos: No. 1 (1978; Washington, D.C., May 12, 1979) and No. 2 (1989; N.Y., Oct. 13, 1991); 1 unnumbered sym. (*Leipzig Symphony*, Wiesbaden, May 1945); 7 numbered syms.: No. 1 (1963; Rome, July 2, 1964), No. 2, *Luther* (1969), No. 3, *Jerusalem* (1973; Jerusalem, Nov. 7, 1976), No. 4 (1980; Los Angeles, Oct. 22, 1981), No. 5, *Isaiah*, for Soprano and Orch. (1982; Washington, D.C., March 15, 1983), No. 6 (1983; rev. version, Houston, March 19, 1988), and No. 7 (1984; Dallas, Dec. 7, 1989); Concerto for Bassoon and Strings (1948); Concerto for Violin and Chamber Orch. (1951; rev. 1960; CBS-TV, Nov. 10, 1963); *Organization No. 1* (1952); Sinfonia (1956); *Identity* (1959); *Stanzas* for 21 Solo Instruments (1959); *Magic Prison* for 2 Narrators and Orch. (N.Y., June 12, 1967); *Concerto for Orchestra* (Minneapolis, Oct. 24, 1968); *Celestial Bodies*, concerto for Flute and Strings (1968); *Priorities* for Jazz Band, Rock Band, and String Quartet (1969); Concerto for Viola and Chamber Orch. (1977; St. Paul, Minn., April 13, 1978); Violin Concerto (1978; Philadelphia, Dec. 12, 1980); *Summer Solstice* (Saratoga, N.Y., Aug. 15, 1980); Concerto for String Quartet and Orch. (1980; Pittsburgh, Feb. 6, 1981); Concerto for Flute, Bassoon, and Orch. (1981; Philadelphia, Jan. 28, 1983); *Sonore* (Denver, Nov. 10, 1983); Cello Concerto (1984; Chicago, Feb. 23, 1990); Flute Concerto (1985; Detroit, Jan. 22, 1987); *Pentimento* (1985; Albany, N.Y., May 16, 1986); *Sanctuary: An Original Theme and Variations* (1986; Louisville, April 2, 1987); Concerto for Violin, Cello, and Orch. (1986; Binghamton, N.Y., Feb. 25, 1988); Sinfonia Concertante (1988; Washington, D.C., June 1, 1989); *A Play Within a Play*, concerto for Double Orch. (1989); Concerto for Chamber Orch. (Martinsville, N.J., May 11, 1989; based on the middle 3 movements of *A Play Within a Play*); *Citadel* (Louisville, May 30, 1990). **CHAMBER:** Cello Sonata (1948); 2 flute sonatas (1951, 1957); Piano Quintet (1951); 1 unnumbered string quartet (1953); 8 numbered string quartets: No. 1 (1959), No. 2 (1962), No. 3 (1966), No. 4 (1974), No. 5 (1976; N.Y., Nov. 24, 1980), No. 6, *The Audubon* (1980; N.Y., April 1981), No. 7 (1983; N.Y., May 2, 1984), and No. 8 (1985); Wind Quintet (1954); *Music for Winds, Strings, and Harpsichord* (1955); Piano Trio (1955; rev. 1959); Violin Sonata (1956); *Theme, Variations, and Finale* for 4 Winds and 4 Strings (1957); Wind Octet (1957); Clarinet Sonata (1958); Sextet for Wind Quintet and Double Bass (1959); Oboe Quartet (1960); *A Single Voice* for Oboe and String Quartet (1967); *Double Helix* for Flute, Oboe, and String Quartet (1968); Nonette for Piano, Strings, Winds, and Brass (1968); *5 Trios and Fantasy* for Wind Quintet (1972); *Partita: Meditations on Isaiah* for Cello (1972); *Elegy* for Viola (1973); *Concerto: Echoes in Anticipation* for Oboe and 7 Instruments (1975); *Cadence* for 2 Flutes and Strings (1978; N.Y., Oct. 23, 1979); *Remembrances* for Violin, Clarinet, Cello, and Piano (1982); Double String Quartet (1983; Washington, D.C., April 1986); Duo for Cello and Piano (N.Y., Dec. 18, 1984); *Fantasy* for Viola (1985); Quintet for Clarinet and Strings (N.Y., Nov. 24, 1987); *Introduction, Barcarolle, and Allegro* for Flute and Harp (1987; N.Y., Dec. 9, 1989); *June 29* for Flute (1987); *MBL Suite* for 2 Flutes and String Quartet (Woods Hole, Mass., Aug. 14, 1988); *A Moment in Time* for Flute (1989; N.Y., Jan. 20, 1990); *Talkin'-Lovin'-Leavin': Recitative, Aria, and Finale* for Alto Recorder and String Quartet (N.Y., March 9, 1990);

Partita for Violin (N.Y., Feb. 20, 1990). **KEYBOARD: P i - a n o :** *Prelude in the Form of a Passacaglia* (n.d.); 2 sonatas (1952, 1955); *3 Pieces* (1956); *Momenti* (1974). **O r g a n :** *25 Preludes for Organ in Different Forms* (1975). **VOCAL:** *The Eagle Stirred*, oratorio for Soloists, Chorus, and Orch. (1961); *Songs for Eve* for Soprano and Piano (1966); *The Trials of Galileo*, oratorio for Soloists, Chorus, and Orch. (1967; reworked into the opera *Galileo Galilei*); *Songs from Michelangelo* for Baritone and Piano (1968); *From the Psalms* for Soprano and Piano (1970); *Thrive Upon the Rock* for Chorus and Piano (1973); *A Handful of Souls*, cantata for Soloists, Chorus, and Organ (1975); *Visions* *Columbus*, cantata for Bass-baritone and Orch. (Columbus, Ohio, Oct. 10, 1975); *Worship* for Soprano, Tenor, and Piano (1976); *Song of Songs*, chamber cantata for Soprano, Flute, Viola, and Cello (1977; based on the dance score); *A Mass for Cain*, oratorio for Soloists, Chorus, and Orch. (1983).—**NS/LK/DM**

Ladmirault, Paul (-Émile), French composer and teacher; b. Nantes, Dec. 8, 1877; d. Kerbili en Kamoel, St. Nazaire, Oct. 30, 1944. As a child, he studied piano, organ, and violin. He entered the Nantes Cons. in 1892, winning first prize in 1893. He was only 15 when his opera *Gilles de Retz* was staged in Nantes (May 18, 1893). He entered the Paris Cons. in 1895, studying with Tardou (harmony), Fauré (composition), and Gédalge (counterpoint and fugue); subsequently returned to Nantes, where he taught at the Cons. His *Suite bretonne* (1902–03) and symphonic prelude *Brocéliande au matin* (Paris, Nov. 28, 1909) were extracts from a 2nd opera, *Myrdhin* (1902–09), which was never performed. The ballet *La Prêtresse de Koridwen* was premiered at the Paris Opéra (Dec. 17, 1926). Other works included the operetta *Glycère* (Paris, 1928), Sym. (1910), *La Brière* for Orch. (Paris, Nov. 20, 1926), *En forêt*, symphonic poem (1932), incidental music to *Tristan et Iseult* (1929), *Valse triste* for Piano and Orch., *Airs anciens* for Tenor, String Quartet, and Piano (1897), *Ballet bohémien* for Flute, Oboe, Double String Quartet, and Piano (1898), *Fantaisie* for Violin and Piano (1899), *Chanson grecque* for Flute and Piano (1900), Violin Sonata (1901), *De l'ombre à la clarté* for Violin and Piano (1936), piano pieces, songs, and many arrangements of Breton folk songs.—**NS/LK/DM**

Ladnier, Tommy (originally, **Ladner, Thomas**), early jazz trumpeter; b. Florenceville, La., May 28, 1900; d. N.Y., June 4, 1939. Ladnier had trumpet instruction from Bunk Johnson. He moved to Chicago c. 1917, working with various small bands through 1923 (except for a brief stint in St. Louis c. 1921), and then joined King Oliver in late 1924. In spring 1925, Sam Wooding brought Ladnier to N.Y., and he subsequently sailed to Europe to join the band that June. A year later, he left Wooding in Berlin and journeyed into Poland as a member of the Louis Douglas Revue. By early August 1926, he had arrived back in N.Y., working in saxophonist Billy Fowler's Orch. That October, he joined Fletcher Henderson, remaining with him throughout 1927. He rejoined Wooding in early 1928 and sailed to Europe again with the group in June. He left Wooding in Nice (early 1929), working primarily in Paris through 1930 with various bands. In summer 1930, he joined Noble Sissle, playing in Paris, London (late 1930), N.Y. (1931), and Paris again (spring 1931). He returned to the U.S., and worked accompanying the Berry Brothers' dancing act. In fall 1932, he joined with Sidney Bechet to form the New Orleans Feetwarmers, playing in the N.Y. area. After they disbanded in the spring of 1933, Ladnier and Bechet worked in their own "Southern Tailor" shop in N.Y.; Ladnier shined shoes. When Bechet rejoined Noble Sissle in 1934, Ladnier left N.Y. He gigged for a while with his own group in the greater N.Y. area. In late 1938, through the efforts of famous jazz critic Hugues Panassie, Lanier was rediscovered and subsequently recorded with Mezzrow, Bechet, and Rosetta Crawford. He appeared with Sidney Bechet at the famous "Spirituals to Swing" concert in N.Y. (December 1938). Soon after, while staying at Mezz Mezzrow's apartment, he suffered a fatal heart attack.—**JC/LP**

Ladurner, Ignace Antoine (François Xavier) (actually, **Ignaz Anton Franz Xaver Joseph**), Austrian pianist, teacher, and composer of Tirolean descent, brother of **Joseph Aloix Ladurner**; b. Aldein, near Bolzano, Aug. 1, 1766; d. Villain, near Massy, March 4, 1839. He studied with his uncle at the Benediktbeuren monastery, and succeeded his father as organist in Algund. After studies at the Lyceum Gregorianum in Munich, he became a pianist in the service of Countess Heimhausen in Longeville. In 1788 he settled in Paris, where he became active as a teacher. He taught piano at the Paris Cons. (1797–1802). In 1836 he settled in Villain. He wrote the operas *Wenzel, ou Le Magistrat du peuple* (Paris, April 10, 1793) and *Les Vieux Fous, ou Plus de peur que de mal* (Paris, Jan. 15 or 16, 1796), as well as 15 piano sonatas, 6 violin sonatas, variations, divertissements, etc.—**NS/LK/DM**

Ladurner, Josef Aloix, Austrian composer of Tirolean descent, brother of **Ignace Antoine (François Xavier) Ladurner**; b. Algund, near Merano, March 7, 1769; d. Brixen, Feb. 20, 1851. He studied with his uncle at the Benediktbeuren monastery. In 1784 he became organist in Algund, but also studied theology and philosophy at the Munich Lyceum Gregorianum and took lessons in piano, composition, and counterpoint with Josef Graetz. In 1799 he was made a priest and then served at the prince-bishop's consistory in Brixen, where he was active as a musician; he also was active in Salzburg and Innsbruck. He wrote much sacred music as well as piano pieces and pedagogical works.—**LK/DM**

La Fage, (Juste-) Adrien (-Lenoir) de, French writer on music and composer; b. Paris, March 28, 1801; d. Charenton, March 8, 1862. He studied in Paris with Perne and Choron, and in Rome with Baini. Returning to Paris, he devoted himself to scholarly analysis of music theory. He ended his life at the Charenton Insane Asylum. He was a prolific composer of sacred music, and also produced much chamber music.

WRITINGS: *Manuel complet de musique vocale et instrumentale* (6 vols., 1836–38; elaborated from Choron's sketches and notes); *Séméiologie musicale* (1837; an epitome was also publ. in 1837 as *Principes élémentaires de musique*); *De la chanson considérée sous le rapport musical* (1840); *Histoire générale de la musique et de*

la danse (2 vols., 1844; incomplete); *De l'unité tonique et de la fixation d'un diapason universel* (1859); *Essais de diphthérographie musicale* (1864); many works on plainsong: *De la réproduction des livres de plain-chant romain* (1853); *Cours complet de plain-chant* (2 vols., 1855–56); *Nouveau traité de plain-chant* (1859; suppl. to the former); *Routine pour accompagner le plain-chant*; etc.

BIBL.: R. Denne-Baron, *A. d.L.F.* (Paris, 1863). —NS/LK/DM

LaFaro, Scott, noted jazz bassist; b. Newark, N.J., April 3, 1936; d. near Geneva, N.Y., July 6, 1961. LaFaro took up bass to play with a local R&B band in 1953. He traveled to L.A. with the Buddy Morrow Orch. in 1955 and remained there, working with various local jazz musicians. After only four years of playing, he began recording with Stan Getz. He first met pianist Bill Evans at an audition for Chet Baker in 1956 or 1957. In late 1958, LaFaro returned to N.Y. to accompany a singer; Bill Evans was working at a nearby club, Basin Street East, and for a few days LaFaro and Paul Motian accompanied him. They then worked as a trio when they were able, but they did not have much work together until late in 1959, when they played at the Sutherland Lounge in Chicago and an extended engagement in Greenwich Village. In late October 1959, they made their first recording together (along with Tony Scott) but it was not issued until 1986. Through recordings and club dates, the trio became much admired in the jazz world. LaFaro raised the bass to an equal voice in the group, playing countermelodies in free time, walking bass lines, and vamps, freeing it from its traditional role of providing a harmonic/rhythmic foundation. Many believe that the Evans's trio set the standard for the modern piano three-member lineup. LaFaro's light, dancing style and highly interactive manner of accompaniment—though he could lay down a solid walking line when called for—has influenced many acoustic players and, through Stanley Clarke and Jaco Pastorius, many electric bassists as well. LaFaro continued to work with Evans, while also recording with Booker Little and Ornette Coleman; at the Newport Jazz Festival in June 1961, he played as a member of Stan Getz's group. On the night of July 5, 1961, LaFaro and a friend named Frank visited a woman friend in Warsaw, N.Y. In the early morning hours, Lafaro wanted to leave and return to his mother's place in Geneva. Since they had been drinking, Gap Mangione, who was also there, discouraged the two from driving. LaFaro insisted, though, and he and his friend died when their car ran into a tree and caught fire.

DISC.: ORNETTE COLEMAN: *The Art of Improvisers* (1959); *Beauty Is a Rare Thing: The Complete Atlantic Recordings* (1961); *Ornette!* (1961); *Free Jazz* (1999); *Harlem's Manhattan* (1999). **MILES DAVIS AND STAN GETZ:** *Tune Up* (1953). **BILL EVANS/BILL EVANS TRIO:** *Jazz Showcase* (1956); *Portrait in Jazz* (1959); *On Green Dolphin Street* (1959); *Sunday at the Village Vanguard* (1961); *Explorations* (1961); *Village Vanguard Sessions* (1961); *Waltz for Debby* (1961); *At the Village Vanguard* (1961); *Complete Fantasy Recordings* (1973); *Incontournables* (2000). **VICTOR FELDMAN:** *Arrival of Victor Feldman* (1958); *Latinsville* (1959). **STAN GETZ/STAN GETZ TRIO:** *Artistry of Stan Getz, Vol. 2* (1952); *Stan Getz with Cal Tjader* (1958). **HAMPTON HAWES:** *For Real!* (1958); *Blues*

the Most (1998). **BOOKER LITTLE:** *Booker Little and Max Roach* (1958); *Booker Little* (1960); *Legendary Quartet Album* (1977).—LP

L'Affilard, Michel, French singer, music theorist, and composer; b. c. 1656; d. probably in Versailles, 1708. He was made chantre clerc at the Sainte-Chapelle in Paris (1679), and later was a member of the Versailles royal chapel (1683–1708). His major work is a treatise on sight singing, *Principes très faciles pour bien apprendre la musique* (Paris, 1694; 11th ed., 1747), which is notable because the tempo of the airs is indicated according to a pendulum, thus anticipating the use of the metronome. —NS/LK/DM

Lafont, Charles-Philippe, noted French violinist; b. Paris, Dec. 1, 1781; d. in a carriage accident near Tarbes, Aug. 14, 1839. He received violin instruction first from his mother, and then with his uncle. He then studied in Paris with Kreutzer and Rode. From 1801 to 1808 he toured Europe, then became solo violinist at the Russian court in St. Petersburg (1808). He returned to Paris in 1815 as solo violinist to Louis XVIII. He engaged in a violin contest of skills with Paganini in Milan (1816). He made an extended tour with the pianist Henri Herz beginning in 1831, losing his life in southern France. He was also a composer, numbering among his works an opera, *La Rivalité villageoise* (1799), 7 violin concertos and many other violin pieces with various instrumental groups, and about 200 romances for voice. These works have no intrinsic value.—NS/LK/DM

La Forge, Frank, American pianist, vocal teacher, and composer; b. Rockford, Ill., Oct. 22, 1879; d. while playing the piano at a dinner given by the Musicians' Club in N.Y., May 5, 1953. He studied piano with Leschetizky in Vienna, and toured Germany, France, Russia, and the U.S. as accompanist to Marcella Sembrich (1908–18) and to Schumann-Heink (1919). In 1920 he settled in N.Y. as a voice teacher, numbering among his students Lawrence Tibbett, Marian Anderson, Lucrezia Bori, and Richard Crooks. He wrote many effective songs, including *To a Violet, Retreat, Come Unto These Yellow Sands, My Love and I, To a Messenger, I Came with a Song, Before the Crucifix*, and *Like a Rosebud*, and piano pieces.—NS/LK/DM

La Garde, Pierre de, French composer and baritone; b. near Crécy-en-Brie, Seine-et-Marne, Feb. 1717; d. c. 1792. He served as an ordinaire de la chambre du roi and was in charge of the musical education of the children of Louis XV. After serving as asst. conductor at the Paris Opéra (1750–55), he was made compositeur de la chambre du roi in 1756. He later was director of the concerts for the Count of Artois. His most successful stage work was the pastorale héroïque *Aeglé* (Versailles, Jan. 13, 1748). He also wrote the pastorale héroïque *Silvie* (Versailles, Feb. 26, 1749), the opéra-ballet *La journée galante* (Versailles, Feb. 25, 1750), the divertissement comique *L'impromptu de la cour de marbe* (Bellevue, Nov. 28, 1751), several notable cantatas and cantatilles, and airs of great popular vogue.—NS/LK/DM

Lagger, Peter, Swiss bass; b. Buchs, Sept. 7, 1930; d. Berlin, Sept. 17, 1979. He studied at the Zürich Cons. and with Hans Duhan in Vienna. In 1953 he made his operatic debut in Graz, and appeared there until 1955. He then sang in Zürich (1955–57), Wiesbaden (1957–59), and Frankfurt am Main (1959–63), and from 1963 was a leading member of the Berlin Deutsche Oper. He made appearances in Hamburg, Vienna, Paris, and Geneva, and also at the Salzburg, Aix-en-Provence, and Glyndebourne festivals. His extensive operatic, concert, and lieder repertoire extended from Bach to Henze. —NS/LK/DM

Lagoanère, Oscar de, French conductor and composer; b. Bordeaux, Aug. 25, 1853; d. Paris, May 23, 1918. He studied at the Paris Cons. with Marmontel, Duprato, and Savard. From 1876 to 1908 he conducted operettas at various theaters in Paris, and from 1908 to 1914 he was administrator and director of music at the Théâtre de la Gaîté. He was a prolific composer of operettas, the most successful of which were *Le Cadeau d'Alain* (Paris, Sept. 14, 1902), *L'Habit de César* (Paris, May 14, 1906), *Amour et sport* (Paris, July 28, 1907), and *Un Ménage au violon*. He also composed piano pieces and songs. —NS/LK/DM

Lagoya, Alexandre, Egyptian-born French guitarist and teacher of Greek and Italian descent; b. Alexandria, June 29, 1929; d. Paris, Aug. 24, 1999. He took up the guitar when he was 8. After making his debut in a recital at 13, he gave numerous concerts throughout the Middle East. In 1948 he went to Paris and pursued his studies with Jean Saudry (guitar) and Villa-Lobos (harmony and counterpoint). Following his marriage to **Ida Presti,** the couple formed a remarkable guitar duo in 1950 and made frequent tours. Presti died during the couple's tour of the U.S. in 1967. Lagoya then resumed his solo career and toured throughout the world. He also appeared in concerts with Jean-Pierre Rampal. From 1969 he taught at the Paris Cons. Lagoya and his wife prepared transcriptions of keyboard pieces by various composers of the past. They also commissioned a number of contemporary composers to write works especially for them, including Castelnuovo-Tedesco, Rodrígo, and Jolivet. Lagoya's solo repertoire extended from the Baroque masters to Claude Bolling.—LK/DM

La Grange, Henry-Louis de, eminent French writer on music; b. Paris, May 26, 1924. He was a scion of a distinguished family, his father being French and his mother an American. After studying belles lettres in Aix-en-Provence and at the Sorbonne in Paris, he took courses at the Yale Univ. School of Music (1945–53); then completed his musical training with Y. Lefébure (piano) and Boulanger (harmony, counterpoint, and analysis) in Paris. He wrote music criticism for various American and French periodicals. In 1960 he commenced exhaustive research on the life and works of Gustav Mahler, resulting in his monumental biography *Gustav Mahler: Chronique d'une vie* (3 vols., 1973–84; also in Eng.). He also publ. *Vienne, une histoire musicale* (Arles, 1991). He was a guest lecturer at Columbia Univ., N.Y.U., Stanford Univ., and Ind. Univ. (1974–81); in Geneva (1982), Brussels (1983–84), and Leipzig (1985); and at the Juilliard School, the Univ. of Southern Calif. in Los Angeles, and Johns Hopkins Univ. (1986). In Paris in 1986 he founded the Bibliothèque Musicale Gustav Mahler, a vast repository for researchers. He received many awards and honors, including his being made a Chevalier de la Légion d'honneur.—NS/LK/DM

La Guerre, Élisabeth Jacquet de, French composer, organist, and clavecinist; b. Paris, 1659; d. there, June 27, 1729. A member of a family of professional musicians, she evinced talent at an exceptionally early age. She was favored by the court of Louis XIV, completing her education under the patronage of Mme. de Montespan. She married Marin de La Guerre, organist of several Paris churches. Her works include an opera, *Céphale et Procris* (Paris, March 15, 1694), a ballet (1691), keyboard suites, a Violin Sonata, cantatas, mostly sacred, etc.

BIBL.: C. Cessac, *E.J. d. L.G.: Une femme compositeur sous le règne de Louis XIV* (Arles, 1995).—NS/LK/DM

La Guerre, Michel de, French organist and composer; b. Paris, 1605 or 1606; d. there (buried), Nov. 13, 1679. He became organist at St. Leu when he was about 14, then was organist at Sainte-Chapelle from 1633 until his death; also was active at the court. His historical importance rests upon his being the composer of the first French comédie en musique, the pastorale *Le Triomphe de l'Amour sur bergers et bergères* (Louvre, Paris, Jan. 22, 1655), to a libretto by the court poet Charles de Beys; only the text is extant.—NS/LK/DM

La Hèle, George de, Netherlandish composer; b. Antwerp, 1547; d. Madrid, Aug. 27, 1586. After early training as a chorister, he was sent to Madrid to join the royal chapel of Philip II in 1560, remaining in Spain for 10 years. In 1571 he entered the Univ. of Louvain. In 1572 he became choirmaster at the church of Saint-Rombaud in Malines, remaining there until 1574, when he accepted a similar post at the Tournai Cathedral. He returned to Madrid in 1582 to take charge of music in the royal chapel. In 1576 he won prizes in the competition at Évreux for his motet *Nonne Deo subjecta* and his chanson *Mais voyez mon cher esmoy*. His 8 masses (Antwerp, 1578), dedicated to Philip II, are all parody masses and are modeled on works by Josquin, Lassus, Rore, and Crecquillon; he also wrote other sacred works. L. Wagner ed. *Collected Works of George de la Hèle,* Corpus Mensurabilis Musicae, LVI (1972).

BIBL.: G. van Doorslaer, *G. d.l.H., Maître de chapelle- compositeur* (Antwerp, 1924).—NS/LK/DM

La Houssaye, Pierre (-Nicolas), French violinist, conductor, and composer; b. Paris, April 11, 1735; d. there, 1818. He studied violin with J.-A. Piffet, then with Pagin (from 1750), and finally with Tartini in Padua (1753). He was briefly a member of the court musical entourage of the infante Dom Philippe in Parma, where he studied composition with Traetta. After working as a violinist and conductor in various Italian music centers, he went to London about 1768. By 1776 he was back in Paris, where he served as concertmaster and conductor of the Concert Spirituel (1777–81) and of the orch. of the Comédie-Italienne (1781–90); subsequently he was co-concertmaster and conductor of the orch. of the Théâtre de Monsieur (later Théâtre Feydeau) from 1790, being sole retainer of those posts from 1792 to 1801. From 1795 to 1802 he also taught at the Cons., and then was a violinist in the orch. of the Opéra and a private teacher until 1813. His last years were marked by poverty. La Houssaye publ. an accomplished vol. of *Sei sonate* for Violin and Bass (Paris, c. 1774). Also extant is his comic opera *Les Amours de Courcy* (Paris, Aug. 22, 1790). —NS/LK/DM

Laidlaw, Anna Robena, English pianist; b. Bretton, Yorkshire, April 30, 1819; d. London, May 29, 1901. She studied in Edinburgh with Robert Müller, in Königsberg, and in London with Henry Herz. In 1837 she played with the Gewandhaus Orch. in Leipzig, then continued her successful career as a concert pianist until her marriage in 1855. She was an acquaintance of Schumann, whose *Fantasiestücke* are inscribed to her. —NS/LK/DM

Laine, Cleo (originally, **Campbell, Clementina Dinah**), jazz vocalist; b. Southall, Middlesex, England, Oct. 28, 1927. Her father was a Jamaican street entertainer; despite the family's poverty, her mother succeeded in finding the means to pay for her singing, dancing, and piano lessons. After performing locally, Cleo quit school at age 14 to help support her family. She sang with local bands, mainly around West London, before joining John Dankworth's Seven in the spring of 1951. From 1947 to 1957 she was married to George Langridge and initially performed as Clementina Landridge. In 1951 she began singing with John Dankworth's jazz group, making her mark under the name Cleo Laine; she and Dankworth married on March 18, 1958. She acted in *Flesh to the Tiger* (1958), *Valmouth* (1959), *Here is the News* (1960), among other films, and made her cabaret debut in June 1961. Laine has been on the British pop charts twice: "Let's Slip Away" peaked at #42 in December 1960 and "You'll Answer to Me," a cover version of Patti Page's minor U.S. hit, realized greater success, reaching the #5 position in the U.K. in 1961. She became popular as a singer in cabarets, concerts, and recordings, and on television; she also appeared in stage and film roles as both a singer and an actress. After starring in a British revival of *Showboat*, in 1971 and 1973, she resumed working regularly with Dankworth and soon developed a formidable international reputation, fortified by regular tours of the U.S., Europe, and Australia. She made her U.S. debut at N.Y.'s Alice Tully Hall in 1972, followed by a sensational appearance at Carnegie Hall in April 1973. Thereafter she toured throughout the U.S., appearing with her husband and his group and also with the major symphony orchs. She did concerts and television work in L.A. in January 1975, including her own TV show with Dankworth, and a New Zealand and Australia

tour later that year. She has made numerous TV appearances in Britain, the U.S., Australia, and other countries. In 1978, the *Best of Friends* album, a Laine collaboration with classical guitarist John Williams, reached No.18 and logged 22 listed weeks. Flutist James Galway was her partner on the 1980 recording "Sometimes When We Touch," which climbed to #15 and remained on the chart for 14 weeks. As a solo artist Laine reached #68 in December 1978 with an album entitled *Cleo*. Her album *The 10th Anniversary Concert* (marking her 10th annual concert a N.Y.'s Carnegie Hall) won a Grammy in 1983. She continued to do occasional work as an actress. In 1985 she appeared on Broadway in Rupert Holmes's musical *The Mystery of Edwin Drood*. She gave acclaimed performances in *Hedda Gabler* (1980) and *Into the Woods* (1989), among other films. She was made an Officer of the Order of the British Empire (OBE) in 1979, and in 1997 she was made a Dame of the British Empire. She was also given an honorary doctoral degree by the Berklee Coll. of Music. A 70th birthday concert was held at Town Hall in N.Y. as part of the JVC festival on Oct. 26, 1997.

DISC.: *She's the Tops* (1957); *Lover and His Lass* (1962); *Shakespeare and All That Jazz* (1964); *If We Lived on Top of a Mountain* (1968); *Feel the Warm Columbia* (1972); *C. L. Live! at Carnegie Hall* (1973); *Beautiful Thing* (1974); *Day by Day* (1974); *I Am a Song* (1974); *Best Friends* (1976); *Born on a Friday* (1976); *Return to Carnegie* (1976); *Gonna Get Through* (1978); *Wordsongs* (1978); *Sometimes When We Touch* (1980); *Smilin' Through* (1982); *Cleo at Carnegie: the 10th Anniversary* (1983); *Let the Music Take You* (1983); *C. L. Sings Sondheim* (1987); *That Old Feeling* (1987); *Cleo's Choice* (1988); *Woman to Woman* (1989); *Jazz* (1991); *One More Day* (1991); *Blue & Sentimental* (1992); *Solitude* (1994).

WRITINGS: *Cleo: the Autobiography of C. L.* (N.Y., 1997).

BIBL.: Graham Collier, *Cleo and John: A Biography of the Dankworths* (London, 1976).—NS/MM/LP

Laine, Frankie (originally, **Lo Vecchio, Francesco Paolo**), vibrant American singer; b. Chicago, March 30, 1913. Among the most popular singers of the late 1940s and early 1950s, Laine epitomized the transition from the jazz-tinged pop ballads of the Swing Era to the inventively produced novelty material of the post–World War II period. His powerful voice lent itself well to impassioned performances of melodramatic songs such as "Mule Train," "Jezebel," and "I Believe," each of which became a million-selling record for him. Among his 60 pop chart entries between 1947 and 1969, his other biggest hits were "That Lucky Old Sun," "The Cry of the Wild Goose," and "Moonlight Gambler."

Laine's parents, Giovanni (John) and Cresenzia (Anna) Concetta Salerno Lo Vecchio, were Italian immigrants; his father was a barber. He sang in the church choir as a child and made his first public appearance at 15 at the Merry Garden Ballroom in Chicago. But he had an unusually long wait for recognition as a singer, during which time he competed in dance marathons and sometimes held jobs outside of music. In 1943 he moved to the West Coast, where he worked in the defense industry. His break came in March 1946 when he sang Hoagy Carmichael's "Rockin' Chair" while sitting in at a Hollywood nightclub. Carmichael, who was in the audience, was impressed and arranged for him to be hired by the club. There he came to the attention of Mercury Records, which signed him.

Laine's revival of the 1931 ballad "That's My Desire" (music by Helmy Kresa, lyrics by Carroll Loveday) became his first hit, peaking in the Top Ten in October 1947 and selling a million copies. A revival of the 1924 song "Shine" (music by Ford Dabney, lyrics by Cecil Mack and Lew Brown) reached the Top Ten in April 1948 and was another million-seller.

Laine was signed to Columbia Pictures and made his first brief movie appearance in *Make Believe Ballroom*, released in April 1949. At Mercury he began to work with A&R director Mitch Miller; Miller mounted elaborate productions to showcase Laine's emphatic delivery. Their first hit record together, "That Lucky Old Sun" (music by Beasley Smith, lyrics by Haven Gillespie), topped the charts in October 1949 and sold a million copies, becoming the biggest song of Laine's career. The defining recording of their collaboration, however, was the Western-themed "Mule Train" (music and lyrics by Johnny Lange, Hy Heath, and Fred Glickman), which featured the sound effect of a whip being cracked; it reached #1 in November 1949 and sold a million copies.

Laine scored a fifth million-seller with "The Cry of the Wild Goose" (music and lyrics by Terry Gilkyson), which topped the charts in March 1950. On June 15 he married actress Nan Grey (real name Eschal Miller); they remained together until her death on July 25, 1993. In August he appeared in his second motion picture, *When You're Smiling*.

Mitch Miller moved to Columbia Records in 1950, and Laine followed him after his Mercury contract expired at the end of March 1951. His first hit for Columbia was the single "Jezebel" (music and lyrics by Wayne Shanklin)/"Rose, Rose, I Love You" (music based on a traditional Chinese melody arranged by Chris Langdon, lyrics by Wilfred Thomas) in May; both songs hit the Top Ten, and the disc became his sixth million-seller. He starred in his third motion picture, *Sunny Side of the Street*, released in August, and in October began a short-lived network radio series, *The Frankie Laine Show*. His next Top Ten hit was a duet with Jo Stafford on a pop arrangement of the country song "Hey, Good Lookin'" (music and lyrics by Hank Williams) in November; in December he was back in the Top Ten with a revival of the 1925 British song "Jealousy (Jalousie)" (music by Jacob Gade, lyrics by Vera Bloom).

Laine and Stafford had another Top Ten hit in April 1952 with "Hambone" (music and lyrics by Leon Washington and Red Saunders, based on a traditional children's song), and Laine paired with Doris Day for the Top Ten hit "Sugarbush" (music and lyrics by Josef Marais) in August. That month he starred in his fourth film, *Rainbow 'Round My Shoulder*, and made a memorable appearance at the London Palladium. In September he reached the Top Ten with his recording of the theme from the motion picture *High Noon*, "Do Not Forsake Me" (music by Dimitri Tiomkin, lyrics by Ned Washington); thereafter, he became a favorite singer for songs associated with Westerns.

Laine's recording of the inspirational song "I Believe" (music and lyrics by Ervin Drake, Irvin Graham, Jimmy Shirl, and Al Stillman) entered the U.S. charts in February 1953, went to #1, and sold a million copies; it also hit #1 in the U.K., where it became the biggest hit of the year. Laine next paired with child star Jimmy Boyd on the novelty "Tell Me a Story" (music and lyrics by Terry Gilkyson), which hit the Top Ten in April, followed by "Hey Joe!" (music and lyrics by Boudleaux Bryant) in October. "Hey Joe!" topped the U.K. charts, as did "Answer Me" (music by Gerhard Winkler and Fred Rauch, English lyrics by Carl Sigman) in November.

Laine began appearing on his own syndicated television show, *Frankie Laine Time*, earning a 1954 Emmy nomination for Best Male Singer. In June 1955 he starred in his fifth film, *Bring Your Smile Along*. In July he launched a network TV series, *The Frankie Laine Show*, as a summer replacement for *Arthur Godfrey and His Friends*; it ran until September. He scored his next Top Ten hit, "Humming Bird" (music and lyrics by Don Robertson), in August.

Laine appeared briefly in the film *Meet Me in Las Vegas* in March 1956 and made his final screen appearance starring in *He Laughed Last* in July. *The Frankie Laine Show* returned to network television for a second summer from Aug. 1 to Sept. 19, 1956. Laine's recording of "A Woman in Love" (music and lyrics by Frank Loesser) from Columbia's studio cast recording of the Broadway musical *Guys and Dolls* hit #1 in Great Britain in October. In the U.S. the singer scored his eighth million-seller with "Moonlight Gambler" (music by Philip Springer, lyrics by Bob Hilliard), which reached the Top Ten in January 1957. He hit the Top Ten for the last time with "Love Is a Golden Ring" (music and lyrics by Richard Dehr, Frank Miller, and Terry Gilkyson) in April. That same month he had his first charting LP, *Rockin'*.

Laine continued to sing title songs for Westerns, notably the themes for *Gunfight at the O.K. Corral* (music by Dimitri Tiomkin, lyrics by Ned Washington), released in May 1957, and *3:10 to Yuma* (music by George Duning, lyrics by Ned Washington), released in August. And he was the voice for the title song of the television series *Rawhide* (music by Dimitri Tiomkin, lyrics by Ned Washington), which ran for seven years, from January 1959 to January 1966. Columbia Records took advantage of his affinity for Western material on his second charting LP, *Hell Bent for Leather!*, released in October 1961, which featured many of his movie and television themes and stayed in the charts more than eight months.

Laine left Columbia in 1964 and moved to Capitol Records for two years, without success. In 1966 he joined ABC Records and, working with producer Bob Thiele, enjoyed a modest comeback, returning to the Top 40 with a revival of the 1927 song "I'll Take Care of Your Cares" (music by James V. Monaco, lyrics by Mort Dixon) in March 1967, followed by "Making Memories" (music and lyrics by Larry Kusik and Eddie Snyder) in May; his *I'll Take Care of Your Cares* LP, released in April, spent more than six months in the charts. He continued to score minor hits through 1969, returning to the pop Top 40 and hitting #1 on the easy listening charts with "You Gave Me a Mountain," specially written for him by Marty Robbins, in March 1969.

Laine continued to perform and to record occasionally after the 1960s. In 1974 he spoofed his movie themes (albeit unwittingly) by singing the title song to the comedy film *Blazing Saddles* (music by John Morris, lyrics by Mel Brooks) and, when the song was nominated for an Academy Award, performed it at the Oscar ceremony in 1975. The compilation LP *The Very Best of Frankie Laine* hit the U.K. Top Ten in 1977. He underwent quadruple-bypass heart surgery in 1985, but by 1987 had recovered sufficiently to appear with the Cincinnati Pops Orch., conducted by Erich Kunzel, on *Round-Up*, an album containing many of his Western movie themes, released by Telarc. He underwent triple-bypass heart surgery in April 1990. In February 1998, at age 84, he released *Wheels of a Dream*, his first all-new studio album in many years, on the After 9 label.

DISC.: *Songs from the Heart* (1950); *Frankie Laine* (1952); *Mr. Rhythm* (1954); *Lover's Laine* (1955); *Command Performance* (1956); *Rockin'* (1957); *Frankie Laine, Balladeer* (1961); *Hell Bent for Leather!* (1961); *Call of the Wild* (1962); *I Want Someone to Love* (1967); *I'll Take Care of Your Cares* (1967); *To Each His Own* (1968); *You Gave Me a Mountain* (1969); *16 Greatest Hits* (1978); *Memories* (1985); *Mule Train* (1989); *16 Most Requested Songs* (1989); *You Gave Me a Mountain* (1990); *On the Trail* (1990); *The Frankie Laine Collection: The Mercury Years* (1991); *On the Trail Again* (1992); *High Noon* (1992); *Best of Frankie Laine* (1993); *The Essence of Frankie Laine* (1993); *The Uncollected Frankie Laine—1947* (1994); *Duets: Frankie Laine/Jo Stafford* (with Joe Stafford; 1994); *Return of Mr. Rhythm: 1945–1948* (1995); *Greatest Hits* (1995); *The Very Best of Frankie Laine* (1996); *Dynamic* (1996); *Portrait of a Legend* (1997); *Lucky Old Sun* (2000); *The Legend at His Best* (2000); *Cocktail Hour: Frankie Laine* (2000).—WR

Laine, Papa Jack (actually, **George Vitelle**), New Orleans–style jazz drummer, alto horn player, leader; b. New Orleans, Sept. 21, 1873; d. New Orleans, June 1, 1966. He played drums, brass bass, and alto horn during childhood. He formed his own ragtime band in New Orleans c. 1890. The success of his Reliance Band enabled him to form several other units bearing that name. These Reliance Bands worked throughout the Gulf Coast States during the early 1900s. In 1904 Laine led for three months in St. Louis. He retired from music in 1917 and worked at his own blacksmith's business, and later managed a garage for many years. During the 1940s he often attended meetings of the New Orleans Jazz Club, and in the early 1960s did taped sessions with Johnny Wiggs.—JC/LP

Lajarte, Théodore (-Édouard Dufaure de), French writer on music and composer; b. Bordeaux, July 10, 1826; d. Paris, June 20, 1890. He studied at the Paris Cons. with Leborne, and was archivist of the Paris Grand Opéra (1873–90). He wrote some 10 opéras comiques, the most successful being *Le Secret de l'oncle Vincent* (1855). His other works include 2 ballets, choral works, and music for military band. However, he is best known for his writings. He also prepared *Airs à danser de*

Lully à Méhul (Paris, 1876), *Chefs-d'oeuvre classiques de l'opéra français* (Paris, 1880), and various vocal scores for the Michaelis collection (1880–82).

WRITINGS: *Bibliothèque musicale du théâtre de l'opéra: Catalogue historique, chronologique, anecdotique* (2 vols., Paris, 1876–78; reprint, Geneva, 1969); *Instruments Sax et fanfares civiles* (Paris, 1867); with A. Bisson, *Grammaire de la musique* (Paris, 1880; 3rd ed., 1913); idem, *Petit traité de composition musicale* (Paris, 1881); idem, *Petite encyclopédie musicale* (Paris, 1881–84); *Les Curiosités de l'Opéra* (Paris, 1883).—NS/LK/DM

Lajovic, Anton, Slovenian composer and jurist; b. Vače, Dec. 19, 1878; d. Ljubljana, Aug. 28, 1960. He studied at the Ljubljana Gasbena Music School before taking a course in composition with Fuchs at the Vienna Cons. (1897–1902); concurrently studied law at the Univ. of Vienna. In subsequent years, Lajovic served as a judge in Slovenia and Coratia while pursuing a second career as a composer. He was a prominent figure in Slovenian music circles. Among his works were a number of orch. scores, choral pieces, and songs.

BIBL.: L. Skerjanc, *A. L.* (Ljubljana, 1958).—NS/LK/DM

Lajtai, Lajos, Hungarian composer; b. Budapest, April 13, 1900; d. there, Jan. 12, 1966. After training in Budapest and Vienna, he began his career writing various light theater works for the Budapest stage. His first major success came with *A régi nyár* (Once Upon a Time in Summer; June 15, 1928). Among his finest subsequent scores were *Sisters* (March 2, 1929), *Az okos mama* (The Clever Mama; Nov. 26, 1930), *Őfelsége frakkja* (His Majesty's Overcoat; Sept. 19, 1931; rev. version as *Katinka*, Paris, Feb. 22, 1933), *A régi orfeum* (The Old Time Music Hall; March 12, 1932), and *A Rotschildok* (The Rothschilds; Nov. 25, 1932). After a sojourn in Paris, Lajtai made his home in Sweden to escpe the deprivations of World War II.—NS/LK/DM

Lajtha, László, eminent Hungarian ethnomusicologist and composer; b. Budapest, June 30, 1892; d. there, Feb. 16, 1963. He studied piano with Arpád Szendy and theory with Victor von Herzfeld at the Budapest Academy of Music. After travels in Leipzig, Geneva, and Paris, he returned to Budapest in 1913 to take a law degree at the Univ. and to become an assoc. of the Ethnographical Dept. of the Hungarian National Museum. From 1919 to 1949 he was a prof. of composition and chamber music at the National Cons., and from 1952 was a teacher of aesthetics and the theory of Magyar music at the Academy of Music. In 1951 he was awarded the Kossuth Prize for his work on Hungarian folk music. He was a brilliant symphonist; his instrumental music is distinguished by consummate mastery of contrapuntal writing.

WORKS: DRAMATIC: Ballet: *Lysistrata* (1933; Budapest, Feb. 25, 1937); *Le Bosquet des quatre dieux* (1943); *Capriccio* (1944). ORCH.: *Hortobágy Suite* (1935); 10 syms.: No. 1 (1936), No. 2 (1938), *Les Soli* for Harp, Percussion, and Strings (1941), No. 3 (1947–48), No. 4, *Le Printemps* (1951), No. 5 (1952; Paris, Oct. 23, 1954), No. 6 (1955; Brussels, Dec. 12, 1960), No. 7 (1957; Paris, April 26, 1958), No. 8 (1959; Budapest, May 21, 1960), and No. 9 (1961; Paris, May 2, 1963); 2 divertissements

(1936, 1939); *In Memoriam* (1941); 2 sinfoniettas for Strings (1946, 1956); *11 Variations* (1947). **CHAMBER:** *Dramma per musica*, piano quintet (1922); 10 string quartets (1923; 1926; 1929; 1930; *5 études*, 1934; *4 études*, 1942; 1950; 1951; 1953; *Suite Transylvaine*, 1953); Piano Quartet (1925); 3 string trios (1927, 1932, 1945); Piano Trio (1928); Violin Sonatina (1930); Cello Sonata (1932); 2 trios for Harp, Flute, and Cello (1935, 1949); 2 quintets for Flute, Violin, Viola, Cello, and Harp (*Marionettes*, 1937; 1948); *Sonata en concert* for Cello and Piano (1940); *Sonata en concert* for Flute and Piano (1958); *Sonata en concert* for Violin and Piano (1962). **Piano:** *Des esquisses d'un musicien* (1913); *Contes I* (1913); Sonata (1914); *Scherzo and Toccata* (1930). **VOCAL:** *3 Nocturnes* for Chorus and Orch. (1941); *Missa in tono phrygio* for Chorus and Orch. (1949–50); *Mass* for Chorus and Organ (1951–52).
BIBL.: *L. L.* (Paris, 1954); *L. L.: Quelques oeuvres* (Paris, 1961).—**NS/LK/DM**

Lakes, Gary, American tenor; b. Dallas, Sept. 26, 1950. He studied with Thomas Hayward at Southern Methodist Univ. in Dallas and sang in the Dallas Opera Chorus. He also attended the Music Academy of the West in Santa Barbara, Calif., and pursued extensive vocal training with William Eddy at the Seattle Opera, where he made his professional operatic debut as Froh in 1981. After winning the Heldentenor Foundation competition in N.Y., he appeared as Florestan in Mexico City (1983), Samson in Charlotte, N.C. (1984), and Siegmund in Act I of *Die Walküre* in Paris (1985) before making his Metropolitan Opera debut in N.Y. as the High Priest in *Idomeneo* (Feb. 4, 1986). In return visits to the Metropolitan Opera, he sang Siegmund, Bacchus, Don José, the Emperor in *Die Frau ohne Schatten*, Erik, Parsifal, and Florestan. In 1991 he sang at the London Promenade Concerts, and returned to London in 1994 to portray Berlioz's Faust. He appeared as Florestan at the Lincoln Center Festival in N.Y. in 1996. He also sang in concerts with major orchs. in the U.S. and Europe. —**NS/LK/DM**

Lakner, Yehoshua, Slovak-born Swiss composer; b. Bratislava, April 24, 1924. He went to Palestine in 1941 and studied with Boscovich, Partos, and Pellig. After further training with Copland at the Berkshire Music Center in Tanglewood (summer, 1952), he went to Cologne and worked under Kagel, Koenig, and Stockhausen at the WDR (1959–60) and also with Zimmermann. In 1963 he went to Switzerland and in 1980 became a naturalized Swiss citizen. From 1965 to 1971 he served as composer-in-residence at the Theater an der Winkelwiese, and then was a teacher at the Zürich Cons. from 1974 to 1987. Lakner has utilized the full panoply of elements available to the contemporary composer. He developed a personalized serial technique, sometimes with Middle Eastern infusions. His later use of computers led him to experiment further with audio-visual time-figures.
WORKS: DRAMATIC: *Dmujoth*, ballet (1962); incidental music; film scores. **ORCH.:** *Toccata* (1953); *Hexachords* for Winds, Brass, and Strings (1959–60). **CHAMBER:** Flute Sonata (1948); Sextet for Winds and Piano (1951); *Improvisation* for Viola (1952); *Dance* for Clarinet, Percussion, and Piano (1955); *Umläufe* for Flute, Bass Clarinet, Piano, and 2 Tapes (1976). **Piano:** *3 Klavierstücke* (1947); *Notturno* (1949); *Mouvement* (1950); *5 Birthdays* (1965); *Fermaten* (1977); *Kreise und Signale* for

2 Pianos (1985); *Alef-Beth-Gimel* (1991). **VOCAL:** *Ki hineh hastaw awar* for Chorus (1950); *Mohammed's Traum* for Chorus and Tape (1968); *Kaninchen* for Speaker, Percussion, and Tape (1973); songs. **OTHER:** Computer pieces; tape works; audio-visual time-figures.—**NS/LK/DM**

Laks, Simon (actually, Szymon), Polish-born French composer; b. Warsaw, Nov. 1, 1901; d. Paris, Dec. 11, 1983. He studied at the Warsaw Cons. (1921–24) with Melcer (conducting) and Statkowski (composition), then went to Paris in 1925, continuing his studies under Rabaud and Vidal at the Cons. He was interned by the Nazis in the Auschwitz and Dachau concentration camps (1941–44), where he was active as a performer and music director. After his liberation, he returned to Paris. He publ. his experiences of his internment as *La Musique d'un autre monde* (Paris, 1948; Eng. tr., 1989).
WORKS: DRAMATIC: Opera Buffa: *L'Hirondelle inattendue* (1965). **ORCH.:** *Farys*, symphonic poem (1924); *Symphonic Blues*, jazz fantasy (1928); *Suite polonaise* (1936); Sinfonietta for Strings (1936); *Suite on Silesian Tunes* for Small Orch. (1945); *Songs of the Polish Earth* (1946); *3 Warsaw Polonaises* for Chamber Orch. (1947); Sym. for Strings (1964). **CHAMBER:** 5 string quartets (1928–64); Piano Trio (1950); *Concerto da camera* for Piano, 9 Wind Instruments, and Percussion (1963); Concertino for Wind Trio (1965); Piano Quintet on Polish Themes (1967); piano pieces. **VOCAL:** Songs.—**NS/LK/DM**

Lalande, Michel-Richard
See **Delalande, Michel-Richard**

La Laurencie, (Marie Bertrand) Lionel (Jules), Comte de, important French musicologist; b. Nantes, July 24, 1861; d. Paris, Nov. 21, 1933. After studying law and science, he became a pupil of Léon Reynier (violin) and Alphonse Weingartner (harmony) and of Bougault-Ducoudray at the Paris Cons. In 1898 he became a lecturer at the École des Hautes Études Sociales. He contributed regularly to several music journals. In 1916 he became ed. of Lavignac's *Encyclopédie de la musique et dictionnaire du Conservatoire*, to which he contributed articles on French music of the 17th and 18th centuries. The *Catalogue des livres de musiciens de la bibliothèque de l'Arsénal à Paris*, ed. by L. Laurencie and A. Gastoué, was publ. in 1936.
WRITINGS: *La Légende de Parsifal et la drame musical de Richard Wagner* (1888–94); *España* (1890); *Le Goût musical en France* (1905); *L'Académie de musique et le concert de Nantes* (1908); *Rameau* (1908); *Lully* (1911); *Les Créatures de l'opéra français* (1920; 2nd ed., 1930); *L'École française de violon, de Lully à Viotti* (3 vols., 1922–24); *Les Luthistes* (1928); *La Chanson royale en France* (1928); *Inventaire critique du fonds Blancheton à la Bibliothèque du Conservatoire* (2 vols., 1920–31); with Thibault and Mairy, *Chansons du luth et airs du XVIᵉsiècle* (1931); *Orfée de Gluck* (1934).
BIBL.: *Mélanges de musicologie offerts à M. L. d.l.L.* (Paris, 1933).—**NS/LK/DM**

La Liberté, (Joseph-François) Alfred, Canadian pianist, teacher, and composer; b. St.-Jean, Quebec, Feb. 10, 1882; d. Montreal, May 7, 1952. After initial training in Canada, he studied at the Stern Cons. in

Berlin (1902–06) with Lutzenko (piano), Baeker (harmony), and Klatte (counterpoint and composition). Following a successful recital debut in Montreal in 1906, he met Scriabin in N.Y. in 1907 who suggested that he pursue his piano training with Carreño in Berlin. Subsequently he became Scriabin's student in Brussels. Upon returning to Montreal in 1911, he became active as a teacher and as a champion of Scriabin's music. He also became an advocate of the music of Madtner and Dupré. Among La Liberté's own works were the opera *Soeur Béatrice* (piano score only), *Passacaille et choeur final* for Piano, Organ, Orch., and Wordless Chorus (unfinished), *La Chanson d'Eve*, song cycle for Orch. or Piano, chamber music, and harmonizations of folk songs from several nations.—NS/LK/DM

Lalo, Charles, French aesthetician; b. Périgueux, Feb. 24, 1877; d. Paris, April 1, 1953. He studied aesthetics and philosophy in Bayonne, and then at the Univ. of Paris (Ph.D., 1908, with 2 dissertations: *Esquisse d'une esthétique musicale scientifique*; publ. in Paris, 1908; 2nd ed., aug., 1939 as *Éléments d'une esthétique*; and *L'Esthétique expérimentale contemporaine*; publ. in Paris, 1908). He lectured at the Univ. of Bordeaux, then taught aesthetics and art history at the Sorbonne in Paris (1933–53); was also president of the Société Française d'Esthétique.

WRITINGS (all publ. in Paris): *Les Sentiments esthétiques* (1910); *Introduction à l'esthétique* (1912; 4th ed., rev., 1952 as *Notions de philosophie, notions d'esthétique*); *L'Art et la vie sociale* (1921); *La Beauté et l'instinct sexuel* (1922); *L'Art et la morale* (1922); *L'Expression de la vie dans l'art* (1933); *L'Art loin de la vie* (1939); *L'Économie des passions* (1947); *Les Grandes Évasions esthétiques* (1947).—NS/LK/DM

Lalo, Édouard (-Victoire-Antoine), distinguished French composer of Spanish descent, father of **Pierre Lalo**; b. Lille, Jan. 27, 1823; d. Paris, April 22, 1892. He studied violin and cello at the Lille Cons. After his father objected to his pursuing a career as a professional musician, he left home at age 16 to study violin with Habeneck at the Paris Cons.; he also studied composition privately with Schulhoff and Crèvecoeur. He then made a precarious living as a violinist and teacher; also began to compose, producing some songs and chamber music between 1848 and 1860. In the meantime, he became a founding member of the Armingaud Quartet (1855), serving first as a violist and subsequently as 2nd violinist. Since his own works met with indifference, he was discouraged to the point of abandoning composition after 1860. However, his marriage to the contralto Bernier de Maligny (1865), who sang many of his songs, prompted him to resume composition. He wrote an opera, *Fiesque*, and sent it to a competition sponsored by the Théâtre-Lyrique in Paris in 1867. It was refused a production, a rebuke that left him deeply embittered. He was so convinced of the intrinsic worth of the score that he subsequently reworked parts of it into various other works, including the first *Aubade* for Small Orch., the *Divertissement*, and the Sym. in G minor. Indeed, the *Divertissement* proved a remarkable success when it was introduced at the Concert Populaire (Paris, Dec. 8, 1872). Sarasate then

gave the premiere performance of his Violin Concerto (Paris, Jan. 18, 1874), and subsequently of his *Symphonie espagnole* for Violin and Orch. (Paris, Feb. 7, 1875). The latter work, a brilliant virtuoso piece with vibrant Spanish rhythms, brought Lalo international fame. It remains his best-known composition outside his native country. While continuing to produce orch. works, he had not given up his intention to write for the stage. In 1875 he began work on the opera *Le Roi d'Ys*. The major portion of the score was finished by 1881, which allowed extracts to be performed in concerts. However, no theater was interested in mounting a production. While pursuing his work on several orch. pieces, he accepted a commission from the Opéra to write a ballet. Although the resulting work, *Namouna* (Paris, March 6, 1882), failed to make an impression, he drew a series of orch. suites from it, which became quite popular. He finally succeeded in persuading the Paris Opéra-Comique to produce *Le Roi d'Ys*. Its premiere on May 7, 1888, was an enormous success. Lalo was rewarded by being made an Officer of the Legion of Honor (1888). While *Le Roi d'Ys* is considered his masterpiece by his countrymen, his instrumental music is of particular importance in assessing his achievement as a composer. His craftsmanship, combined with his originality, places him among the most important French composers of his time.

WORKS: DRAMATIC: *Fiesque*, opera (1866–67; not perf.; parts of the score subsequently used in various other works); *Namouna*, ballet (1881–82; Opéra, Paris, March 6, 1882; also made into a series of orch. suites); *Le Roi d'Ys*, opera (1875–88; Opéra-Comique, Paris, May 7, 1888); *Néron*, pantomime with Chorus (1891; Hippodrome, Paris, March 28, 1891; based on *Fiesque* and other works); *La Jacquerie*, opera (1891–92; Monte Carlo, March 9, 1895; Act 1 only; finished by A. Coquard). ORCH.: 2 syms. (n.d.; destroyed by the composer); 2 *Aubades* for 10 Instruments or Small Orch. (1872; based on *Fiesque*); *Divertissement* (Paris, Dec. 8, 1872; ballet music from *Fiesque* with the 2 aubades); Violin Concerto in F major, op.20 (1873; Paris, Jan. 18, 1874); *Symphonie espagnole* for Violin and Orch., op.21 (1874; Paris, Feb. 7, 1875); Cello Concerto in D minor (Paris, Dec. 9, 1877); *Fantaisie norvégienne* for Violin and Orch. (1878); *Rapsodie norvégienne* (Paris, Oct. 26, 1879; partly based on the *Fantaisie norvégienne*); *Romance-serenade* for Violin and Orch. (1879); *Concerto russe* for Violin and Orch., op.29 (1879); *Fantaisie-ballet* for Violin and Orch. (1885; from *Namouna*); *Andantino* for Violin and Orch. (from *Namouna*); *Sérénade* for Strings (from *Namouna*); Sym. in G minor (1886; Paris, 1887); Piano Concerto in F minor (1888–89). CHAMBER: *Fantaisie originale* for Violin and Piano, op.1 (c. 1848); *Allegro maestoso* for Violin and Piano, op.2 (c. 1848); *Deux impromptus* for Violin and Piano, op.4: *Espérance* and *Insouciance* (c. 1848); *Arlequin, esquisse-caractéristique* for Violin and Piano (c. 1848; also orchestrated); Piano Trio No. 1, in C minor, op.7 (c. 1850); *Pastorale* and *Scherzo alla Pulcinella* for Violin and Piano, op.8 (c. 1850); Piano Trio No. 2, in B minor (c. 1852); Violin Sonata, op.12 (1853; orig. *Grand duo concertant*); *Chanson villageoise*, *Sérénade* for Violin or Cello and Piano, op.14 (1854); *Allegro* for Cello and Piano, op.16 (c. 1856; also for Cello and Orch., op.27, and as *Allegro symphonique*); *Soirées parisiennes* for Violin and Piano, op.18 (1856; in collaboration with C. Wehle); Cello Sonata (1856); String Quartet in E-flat major, op.19 (1859; rev. as op.45, 1880); Piano Trio No. 3, in A minor, op.26 (1880;

Scherzo orchestrated, 1884); *Guitare* for Violin and Piano, op.28 (1882); *Valse* for Cello and Piano (n.d.); Piano Quintet in A-flat major (n.d.); *Adagio*, 2nd fantaisie- quintette for Piano and String Quartet (n.d.). **P i a n o :** *Sérénade* (1864); *La Mère et l'enfant* for Piano, 4-Hands, op.32 (1873). **VOCAL: C o l l e c t i o n s :** *6 romances populaires* (1849); *6 mélodies*, op.17 (1856); *3 mélodies* (c. 1870); *5 Lieder* (1879); *3 mélodies* (1887). **S o n g s :** *Adieux au désert* (1848); *L'Ombre de Dieu* (c. 1848); *Le Novice*, op.5 (1849); *Ballade à la lune* (1860); *Humoresque* (c. 1867); *Aubade* (1872); *Chant breton* (1884); *Marine*, op.33 (1884); *Dansons*, op.35 (1884; from *Namouna*); *Au fond des halliers* (1887; from *Fiesque*); *Le Rouge-gorge* (1887); *Veni, Creator, d'après un thème bohème* (n.d.). **C h o r a l :** *Litanies de la sainte Vierge* (1876); *O salutaris* for Women's Voices, op.34 (1884).

BIBL.: M. Dufour, *É. L.* (Lille, 1908); H. Malherbe, *É. L., conférence prononcée … 23 décembre, 1920* (Paris, 1921). **—NS/LK/DM**

Lalo, Pierre, French music critic, son of **Édouard (-Victoire-Antoine) Lalo**; b. Puteaux, Sept. 6, 1866; d. Paris, June 9, 1943. He studied literature and philosophy, and also took courses in modern languages at the École de Chartes and the École Polytechnique. He began writing music criticism for the *Journal des débats* (1896), then was music critic of *Le Temps* (1898–1914). He became known as a caustic critic of Debussy.

WRITINGS: *La Musique* (Paris, 1898–99; a selection of his articles); *Richard Wagner ou le Nibelung* (Paris, 1933); *De Rameau à Ravel: Portraits et souvenirs* (Paris, 1947).**—NS/LK/DM**

Lalouette, Jean Francois, French composer; b. Paris, 1651; d. there, Aug. 31, 1728. He studied at the choir school of St. Eustache in Paris, and then with Guy Leclerc (violin) and Lully (composition). He became Lully's secretary and was charged with composing the inner parts of the scores to Lully's *tragédies lyriques*, including *Isis* (1677). Lalouette's vanity led him to claim that he had composed the finest portion of this work, but his plan to ill-gotten glory backfired: when the score was viewed as a slander upon the King's mistress, Lully made Lalouette the scapegoat and dismissed him from his entourage. After serving as composer and director of the band of violins at the Savoy court in Turin (1678–79), Lalouette returned to Paris to oppose Lully's monopoly on operatic productions by organizing his own operatic enterprise. The authorities closed his venture down forthwith, however, and he remained a figure in disgrace until serving as choirmaster of Rouen Cathedral (1693–95). Returning to Paris, he finally won recognition as choirmaster of Notre Dame (1700–16; 1718–27). Among his works were motets (1726), a *Miserere* (1726), and a Mass (publ. in Paris, 1744).**—LK/DM**

Laloy, Louis, French musicologist and music critic; b. Grey, Haute-Saône, Feb. 18, 1874; d. Dole, March 3, 1944. He settled in Paris, where he studied at the Ecole Normale Supérieure (1893; agrégé des lettres, 1896; docteur ès lettres, 1904, with the diss. *Aristoxène de Tarente et la musique de l'antiquité*); also studied with Bordes, Breéille, and d'Indy at the Schola Cantorum (1899–1905). He was co-founder (1901) of the *Revue d'Histoire et de Critique Musicale,* and in 1905 he founded,

with J. Marnold, the *Mercure Musical.* He also contributed articles to *Revue de Paris, Grande Revue, Mercure de France,* and *Gazette des Beaux-Arts.* He was prof. of music history at the Paris Cons. (1936–41).

WRITINGS: *Jean Philippe Rameau* (Paris, 1908; 3rd ed., 1919); *Claude Debussy* (Paris, 1909; 2nd ed., 1944); *La Musique chinoise* (Paris, 1910); *The Future of Music* (London, 1910); *La Musique retrouvée, 1902–1927* (Paris, 1928); *Une Heure de musique avec Beethoven* (Paris, 1930); *Comment écouter la musique* (Paris, 1942).

BIBL.: D. Priest, *L. L. (1874–1944) on Debussy, Ravel and Stravinsky* (Brookfield, Vt., 1999).**—NS/LK/DM**

La Mara
  See **Lipsius, Marie**

La Marre (Lamare), Jacques-Michel-Hurel de, French cellist; b. Paris, May 1, 1772; d. Caen, March 27, 1823. He toured Europe, including Russia, with great success, and Clementi called him "the Rode of the violoncello." Four cello concertos and an *air varié* publ. under La Marre's name are actually by Auber.
—NS/LK/DM

Lamb, Joseph F(rancis), remarkable American ragtime pianist and composer; b. Montclair, N.J., Dec. 6, 1887; d. N.Y., Sept. 3, 1960. Although he had no formal music training and spent most of his life in the textile import business, he was one of the most important composers of piano rags during the heyday of ragtime; also wrote a number of songs for Tin Pan Alley. After almost 30 years, he was rediscovered in 1949 and began composing rags again; also appeared as a ragtime pianist. His most notable piano rags were *Sensation* (1908), *Ethiopia Rag* (1909), *Excelsior Rag* (1909), *Champagne Rag* (1910), *American Beauty Rag* (1913), *Cleopatra Rag* (1915), *Contentment Rag* (1915), *The Ragtime Nightingale* (1915), *Reindeer* (1915), *Patricia Rag* (1916), *Top Liner Rag* (1916), and *Bohemia Rag* (1919). An anthology of his works appeared in N.Y. in 1964.

BIBL.: M. Den, *J.F. L., a Ragtime Composer Recalled* (thesis, Brooklyn Coll., City Univ. of N.Y., 1975); J. Scotti, *J. L.: A Study of Ragtime's Paradox* (diss., Univ. of Cincinnati, 1977; with list of works).**—NS/LK/DM**

Lambardi, Camillo, Italian tenor, organist, and composer, father of **Francesco Lambardi**; b. Naples, c. 1560; d. there, Nov. 1634. He sang at the Santa Casa dell'Annunziata at Naples as a treble (from 1569) and as a tenor (from 1579). He studied there with Gian Domenico da Nola, whom he succeeded as a maestro di cappella in 1592; retired in 1631. He publ. music for Holy Week for 2 Choirs (1592), 2 books of motets (1613, 1628), 2 books of madrigals (1600, 1609), etc.
—NS/LK/DM

Lambardi, Francesco, Italian tenor, organist, and composer, son of **Camillo Lambardi**; b. Naples, c. 1587; d. there, July 25, 1642. He became a treble (1599) and an alto (1600) at the Santa Casa dell'Annunziata in Naples. He was made a tenor at the royal chapel (1607), and then served as its organist (1615–42); was also maestro di cappella of the Pièta dei Turchini Cons. (1626–30) and S. Maria della Nova (1628). In 1623 he founded a singing school. He publ. 2 sets of *villanelle* for 3 to 5 Voices (Naples, 1607, 1614) and a book of canzonette for 1 and 3 to 5 Voices (Naples, 1616).—NS/LK/DM

Lambe, Walter, English composer; b. c. 1450; d. 1499. He became a clerk of the choir of St. George's Chapel (1479), serving as Informator there (1479–85?), and resumed his post as clerk (1492). He distinguished himself as a composer of polyphonic choral music, and contributed many works to *The Eton Choirbook* (ed. by F. Harrison, Musica Britannica, X-XII, 1956–61; 2nd ed., 1969–73).—NS/LK/DM

Lambert, Dave (Dave Alden), noted jazz singer, arranger; b. Boston, Mass., June 19, 1917; d. Westport, Conn., Oct. 3, 1966. The singing he did on his own (as on "Keynote," 1947) is little known, but as the founder of the Dave Lambert Singers, later known as Lambert, Hendricks and Ross, he introduced perhaps the most celebrated vocal group in jazz history, and one of the most celebrated singers and lyricists, Jon Hendricks. A Miles Davis early work, "Becky's Night Out," was reportedly recorded by Lambert but has never been found. The group first recorded, with Hendricks's lyrics, "Four Brothers" (several takes at different tempos) in 1954 for an obscure label as the Lambert Singers, then became L, H, and R in 1957. Their Roulette album, *Sing a Song of Basie* was a sensation in 1958 with its overdubbing of their three voices to make a full band sound. They continued to record and work together through the early 1960s. In 1962, Ross left and was replaced for a while by Yolande Bavan; the group disbanded in 1964. Lambert died soon after.

DISC.: *D. L. Sings and Swings* (1958). L,H,R: *Sing a Song of Basie* (1957); *Sing Along with Basie* (1958); *Swingers!* (1958); *Everybody's Boppin'* (1959); *Hottest New Group in Jazz* (1960); *Lambert, Hendricks and Ross* (1960); *Sings Ellington* (1960); *Lambert, Hendricks and Ross Sing* (1961); *High Flying* (1962); *Swingin' Til the Girls Come Home* (1962); *At Basin Street East* (1963); *At Newport '63* (1963).—LP

Lambert, (Leonard) Constant, remarkable English conductor, composer, and writer on music; b. London, Aug. 23, 1905; d. there, Aug. 21, 1951. He won a scholarship to the Royal Coll. of Music in London, where he studied with R.O. Morris and Vaughan Williams (1915–22). His first major score, the ballet *Romeo and Juliet* (Monte Carlo, May 4, 1926), was commissioned by Diaghilev. This early association with the dance proved decisive, for he spent most of his life as a conductor and composer of ballets. His interest in jazz resulted in such fine scores as *Elegiac Blues* for Orch. (1927), *The Rio Grande* for Piano, Chorus, and Orch. (1927; to a text by S. Sitwell), and the Concerto for Piano and 9 Performers (1930–31). Of his many ballets, the most striking in craftsmanship was his *Horoscope* (1937). In the meantime, he became conductor of the Camargo Soc. for the presentation of ballet productions (1930). He was made music director of the Vic-Wells Ballet (1931), and remained in that capacity after it became the Sadler's Wells Ballet and the Royal Ballet, until resigning in 1947; he then was made one of its artistic directors (1948), and subsequently conducted it on its first visit to the U.S. (1949). He also appeared at London's Covent Garden (1937; 1939; 1946–47). He was assoc. conductor of the London Promenade Concerts (1945–46), and then frequently conducted broadcast performances over the BBC. He contributed articles on music to the *Nation* and *Athenaeum* (from 1930) and to the *Sunday Referee* (from 1931). He also penned the provocative book *Music Ho! A Study of Music in Decline* (London, 1934). Lambert was one of the most gifted musicians of his generation. However, his demanding work as a conductor and his excessive consumption of alcohol prevented him from fully asserting himself as a composer in his later years.

WORKS: DRAMATIC: Ballet: *Romeo and Juliet* (1924–25; Monte Carlo, May 4, 1926); *Pomona* (1926; Teatro Colón, Buenos Aires, Sept. 9, 1927); *Horoscope* (1937; Sadler's Wells, London, Jan. 27, 1938, composer conducting); *Tiresias* (1950–51; Covent Garden, London, July 9, 1951, composer conducting); also various arrangements. **ORCH.:** *The Bird Actors*, overture (1925; reorchestrated, 1927; London, July 5, 1931, composer conducting; orig. for Piano, 4-Hands); *Champêtre* for Chamber Orch. (London, Oct. 27, 1926); *Elegiac Blues* (1927; also for Piano); *Music for Orchestra* (1927; BBC, June 4, 1929); *The Rio Grande* for Piano, Chorus, and Orch., after S. Sitwell (1927; BBC, Feb. 27, 1928, composer conducting); Concerto for Piano, Flute, 2 Clarinets, Bass Clarinet, Trumpet, Trombone, Percussion, Cello, and Double Bass (London, Dec. 18, 1931, composer conducting); *Summer's Last Will and Testament* for Baritone, Chorus, and Orch., after T. Nashe (1932–35; London, Jan. 29, 1936, composer conducting); *Dirge from Cymbeline* for Tenor, Baritone, Men's Chorus, and Strings or Piano, after Shakespeare (with Piano, Cambridge, Nov. 1940; with Strings, BBC, March 23, 1947, composer conducting); *Aubade héroïque* (1942; London, Feb. 21, 1943, composer conducting). **Piano:** *Pastorale* (1926); *Elegiac Blues* (1927; also for Orch.); Sonata (1928–29; London, Oct. 30, 1929); *Elegy* (1938); *Trois pièces nègres pour les touches blanches* for Piano, 4-Hands (1949). **SONGS:** *8 Poems of Li-Po* for Voice, and Piano or 8 Instruments (1926–29; with Instruments, London, Oct. 30, 1929). **OTHER:** Film scores, incidental music, and arrangements or eds. of works by Boyce, Handel, and Purcell.

BIBL.: R. Shead, *C. L.* (London, 1973; 2nd ed., rev., 1987). —NS/LK/DM

Lambert, Lucien, French composer and pianist; b. Paris, Jan. 5, 1858; d. Oporto, Portugal, Jan. 21, 1945. He studied first with his father, and after a tour of America and Europe, he returned to Paris to study at the Cons. with Dubois and Massenet, taking the Prix Rossini in 1885 with his cantata *Prométhée enchaîné*. He settled in Portugal in 1914, where he was later a prof. of composition at the Oporto Cons. (1922–37).

WORKS: DRAMATIC: Opera: *Brocéliande* (Rouen, Feb. 25, 1893); *Le Spahi* (Paris, Oct. 18, 1897); *La Marseillaise* (Paris, July 14, 1900); *La Flamenca* (Paris, Oct. 31, 1903); *Harald* (1937); *Penticosa*; *La Sorcière*. **Ballet:** *La Roussalka* (Paris, Dec. 8, 1911); *Les Cloches de Porto* (1937). **Lyric Comedy:** *Florette* (1921). **ORCH.:** *Légende roumaine*, symphonic poem; *Fantaisie monothématique*, on an oriental theme (Paris, March 19, 1933); *Tanger le soir*, Moorish rhapsody; *Esquisses créoles*, suite, on themes by Gottschalk; *Andante et fantaisie tzigane* for Piano and Orch. CHAMBER: String Quartet; String Sextet; piano pieces. VOCAL: Mass; songs.—NS/LK/DM

Lambert, Michel, eminent French composer; b. Champigny-sur-Veude, near Chinon, Indre-et-Loire, 1610; d. Paris, June 29, 1696. He was a page in the Paris chapel of Gaston of Orleans, brother of Louis XIII, then a singer, member, and subsequently director of Mlle. de Montpensier's 6 "violons." He also appeared as a singer and dancer in the court ballets. He was maître de musique de la chambre du Roi (1661–96). His daughter married Lully (1662). Lambert was greatly esteemed as a composer, and also renowned as a singing teacher. Only some 300 of his airs are extant.

WORKS: *Les Airs de Monsieur Lambert* (Paris, 1660); (60) *Airs à 1–4* and Basso Continuo (Paris, 1689); *Airs de Monsieur Lambert non imprimez* (c. 1710); also airs in various collections; other works include dialogues and recrits for the stage and a few pieces of sacred music.—NS/LK/DM

Lambillotte, Louis, French organist, composer, and writer on music; b. Charleroi, Hainaut, March 27, 1796; d. Vaugirard, Feb. 27, 1855. He was an organist at Charleroi, then at Dinant. In 1822 he became maître de chapelle at the Jesuit Seminary at St.-Acheul, joining the order in 1825. He subsequently settled in Vaugirard. He wrote 4 masses (one in the Lydian mode), other sacred music, organ pieces, fugues, etc.

WRITINGS: *Antiphonaire de Saint-Grégoire, Facsimile du manuscrit de Saint-Gall* (1851); *Clef des mélodies grégoriennes* (1851); *Quelques mots sur la restauration du chant liturgique* (1855); *Esthétique, théorie et pratique du chant grégorien* (1855); other essays.

BIBL.: J. Dufour, *Mémoire sur les chants liturgiques restaurés par L.* (Paris, 1857); T. Nisard, *Le Père L. et Dom A. Schubiger* (Paris, 1857); M. de Monter, *L. et ses frères* (Paris, 1871). —NS/LK/DM

Lambro, Phillip, American composer, conductor, and pianist; b. Wellesley Hills, Mass., Sept. 2, 1935. He began his training in Boston, where he made his debut as a pianist in 1952, and after further studies in Miami (1953–55), he received a scholarship in 1955 to complete his training at the Music Academy of the West in Santa Barbara with György Sandor (piano) and Donald Pond (composition). Lambro's works have been performed by various major American orchs., and have also been performed abroad. He has also composed and conducted music for several films, including the documentaries *Energy on the Move* and *Mineral King*. As a composer, Lambro is basically autodidact. He learned the art of composition mainly by analyzing the various periods and styles in music, from the Renaissance to the contemporary era. All the same, he developed his own individual means of expression to extend the pathway of valid and divergent statements. Lambro believes in the existence of Elohim Extraterrestrials "who created mankind in a laboratory." To maintain his health, he practices the Japanese Zen Macrobiotic diet and way of life.

WORKS: *Miraflores* for String Orch. (1955); *Dance Barbaro* for Percussion (1958–60); *Toccata* for Piano (1963–65); *2 Pictures* for Solo Percussionist and Orch. (1965–66); *4 Songs* for Soprano and Orch. (1966–67); *Music for Wind, Brass, and Percussion* (1969); *Toccata* for Guitar (1969); *Structures* for String Orch. (1969–70); *Parallelograms* for Flute Quartet and Jazz Ensemble (1969–75); *Obelisk* for Oboist and Percussionist (1970); *Fanfare and Tower Music* for Brass Quintet (1971); *Trumpet Voluntary* (1972); *Biospheres* for 6 Percussionists (1973); *Night Pieces* for Piano (1973); *3 Little Trigrams* for Piano (1979).—NS/LK/DM

Lammers, Gerda, esteemed German soprano; b. Berlin, Sept. 25, 1915. She studied with L. Mysz-Gmeiner and M. Schwedler-Lohmann at the Berlin Hochschule für Musik. After appearances as a concert and lieder artist (1940–55), she made her operatic debut as Ortlinde at the Bayreuth Festival (1955). That same year she made her first appearance at the Kassel State Theater as Marie in Berg's *Wozzeck*, remaining there for some 15 years. She made an acclaimed debut as Elektra at London's Covent Garden (1957), substituting on short notice for an indisposed Christel Goltz; she returned there as Kundry in 1959. She made her Metropolitan Opera debut in N.Y. as Elektra on March 16, 1962. Her other distinguished roles included Alceste, Medea, Senta, Isolde, and Brünnhilde.—NS/LK/DM

Lamond, Frederick (Archibald), distinguished Scottish pianist; b. Glasgow, Jan. 28, 1868; d. Stirling, Feb. 21, 1948. He played organ as a boy in a local church, and also studied oboe and violin. In 1882 he entered the Raff Cons. in Frankfurt am Main, studying with Heermann (violin), Max Schwarz (piano), and Urspruch (composition); then piano with Bülow, Clara Schumann, and Liszt. He made his debut in Berlin (Nov. 17, 1885), then appeared in Vienna and Glasgow, and later in London, N.Y., and Russia. He married the German actress Irene Triesch (1904), making Berlin his center of activities until the coming of World War II, when he went to England. While continuing to make tours, he also was engaged as a pedagogue. He became renowned for his performances of Beethoven and Liszt; publ. an ed. of the Beethoven piano sonatas and the book *Beethoven: Notes on the Sonatas* (Glasgow, 1944); his reminiscences appeared as *The Memoirs of Frederic Lamond* (Glasgow, 1949). He was also a composer, numbering among his works a Sym. (Glasgow, Dec. 23, 1889), some chamber music, and numerous piano pieces. —NS/LK/DM

La Montaine, John, American composer and pianist; b. Oak Park, Ill., March 17, 1920. He studied piano with Muriel Parker and Margaret Farr Wilson, then received training in theory in Chicago from Stella Roberts (1935–38). He subsequently took courses in piano with Max Landow and in composition with Hanson and Rogers at the Eastman School of Music in Rochester, N.Y. (B.Mus., 1942). After further training from Rudolph Ganz at the Chicago Musical Coll. (1945), he completed his studies in composition with Wagenaar at the Juilliard School of Music in N.Y. and with Boulanger at the American Cons. in Fontainebleau. From 1950 to 1954 he was the pianist and celesta player in the NBC Sym. Orch. in N.Y. As a pianist, he often performed his own works. He received a Guggenheim fellowship (1959–60); in 1961 he was a visiting prof. of composition at the Eastman School of Music; in 1962, served as composer-in-residence at the American Academy in Rome. He received the Pulitzer Prize in Music for his First Piano Concerto in 1959. In 1977 he was a Nixon Distinguished Scholar at Nixon's alma mater, Whittier Coll., in Calif. While La Montaine's works incorporate various usages ranging from serialism to jazz, his scores reflect his penchant for accessibility and lyricism.

WORKS: DRAMATIC: O p e r a : Christmas trilogy on medieval miracle plays: *Novellis, Novellis* (Washington, D.C., Dec. 24, 1961), *The Shephardes Playe* (Washington, D.C., Dec. 27, 1967), and *Erode the Greate* (Washington, D.C., Dec. 31, 1969); *Be Glad, Then, America: A Decent Entertainment from the 13 Colonies*, bicentennial opera (Univ. Park, Pa., Feb. 6, 1976). ORCH.: *Canons* (n.d.); *6 Sonnets* (n.d.); *Recitative, Aria, and Finale* for Strings (n.d.; Rochester, N.Y., April 28, 1965); *Jubilant Overture* (n.d.); *Colloquy* for Strings (n.d.); *Passacaglia and Fugue* for Strings (n.d.); 4 piano concertos: No. 1 (Washington, D.C., Nov. 25, 1958), No. 2, *Transformations* (1987), No. 3, *Children's Games* (1987), and No. 4 (1989); *From Sea to Shining Sea* (inaugural concert of President John F. Kennedy, Washington, D.C., Jan. 19, 1961); *A Summer's Day* (Washington, D.C., May 25, 1964); *Birds of Paradise* for Piano and Orch. (Rochester, N.Y., April 29, 1964, composer soloist; also as the ballet *Nightwings*, N.Y., Sept. 7, 1966); *Incantations* for Jazz Band (n.d.; first concert perf., Rochester, N.Y., April 13, 1976); *Overture: An Early American Sampler* (1976); Flute Concerto (Washington, D.C., April 12, 1981); 2 *Scenes from the Song of Solomon* for Flute and Orch. (Carson, Calif., March 8, 1981); Concerto for Strings (Vancouver Radio, March 17, 1981); *Symphonic Variations* for Piano and Orch. (Peninsula Music Festival, Wisc., Aug. 20, 1982, composer soloist); *Of Age, after Euripides: An Ode, Epode, and Fanfares* (1990). CHAMBER: Cello Sonata; String Quartet; Sonata for Solo Flute; Woodwind Quartet; piano pieces; organ works. VOCAL: *Songs of the Nativity* for Chorus (Washington, D.C., Dec. 24, 1954); *Songs of the Rose of Sharon*, biblical cycle for Soprano and Orch. (Washington, D.C., May 31, 1956); *Fragments from the Song of Songs*, biblical cycle for Soprano and Orch. (New Haven, Conn., April 14, 1959); *Wonder Tidings*, Christmas carols for Incidental Solos, Chorus, Harp, Percussion, and Organ (N.Y., Jan. 26, 1964); *Te Deum* for Chorus, Winds, and Percussion (Washington, D.C., May 7, 1964); *Wilderness Journal*, sym. for Bass-baritone, Organ, and Orch., after Thoreau (Washington, D.C., Oct. 10, 1972); *9 Lessons of Christmas* for Incidental Solos, Chorus, Harp, and Percussion (Minneapolis, Nov. 30, 1975); *Mass of Nature (Missa Naturae)* for Chorus and Orch. (Washington, D.C., May 26, 1976); *The Whittier Service*, 9 hymn-anthems for Incidental Solos, Chorus, Guitar, Brass Quintet, Strings, and Optional Organ and Timpani (Washington, D.C., May 20, 1979); *The Lessons of Advent* for Incidental Solos, Chorus, Narrator, Trumpet, Drums, Handbell Choir, Harp, Oboe, Guitar, and Organ (San Francisco, Dec. 4, 1983); *The Marshes of Glynn* for Bass, Chorus, and Orch. (Rochester, N.Y., Nov. 11, 1984); *The Birth of Freedom*, dramatic cantata for 2 Tenors, Bass-baritone, Folk Singer, Chorus, and Orch. (1988); *In Praise of Britain's Queen and Elgar's Enigma* for Chorus (1994).—NS/LK/DM

Lamote de Grignon, Juan, Catalan conductor and composer, father of **Ricardo Lamote de Grignon y Ribas**; b. Barcelona, July 7, 1872; d. there, March 11, 1949. He studied at the Barcelona Cons., and upon graduation, became prof. (1890) and director (1917) there. He made his debut as a conductor in Barcelona (April 26, 1902). In 1910 he founded the Orquesta Sinfónica of Barcelona, which carried on its activity until 1924; also was founder-conductor of the Valencia Municipal Orch. (1943–49). He publ. *Musique et musiciens français à Barcelone: Musique et musiciens catalans à Paris* (Barcelona, 1935). He wrote an opera, *Hesperia* (Barcelona, Jan. 25, 1907), orch. works, an oratorio, *La Nit de Nadal,* and numerous songs.—NS/LK/DM

Lamote de Grignon y Ribas, Ricardo, Catalan cellist, conductor, and composer, son of **Juan Lamote de Grignon**; b. Barcelona, Sept. 23, 1899; d. there, Feb. 5, 1962. He studied cello and composition at the Barcelona Cons. He played cello in the Orquesta Sinfónica of Barcelona, conducted by his father; then conducted provincial orchs.; became asst. conductor of the municipal band of Barcelona. He publ. a manual, *Síntesis de técnica musical* (Barcelona, 1948). His *Enigmas* for Orch. won the Barcelona Municipal Prize in 1951.

WORKS: DRAMATIC: O p e r a : *La caperucita verde; La flor,* children's opera. ORCH.: *Joan de Os,* symphonic legend (Barcelona, April 19, 1936, composer conducting); *Boires,* symphonic poem; *Triptico de Rabindranath Tagore* for Soprano and Orch.; *Enigmas.* CHAMBER: Piano Trio.—NS/LK/DM

Lamoureux, Charles, renowned French conductor; b. Bordeaux, Sept. 28, 1834; d. Paris, Dec. 21, 1899. He began violin training with Baudoin, and then was a student at the Paris Cons. of Girard (violin; premiers prix, 1852, 1854), Tolbecque (harmony), Leborne (counterpoint and fugue), and Chauvet (composition). He began his career playing violin in several Parisian orchs., including those of Pasdeloup, at the Opéra, and at the Société des Concerts du Conservatoire. In 1860 he was one of the founders of the Séances Populaires de Musique in Paris. After gaining success as a choral conductor, he was appointed asst. conductor of the Conservatoire concerts in 1872 and subsequently established himself as a prominent Parisian symphonic and operatic maestro. In 1874 he founded the Société Française de l'harmonie Sacrée. In 1876 he conducted at the Opéra-Comique and then at the Opéra (1877–79). He then founded the Société des Nouveaux-Concerts, which he conducted for the first time on Oct. 23, 1881. These Lamoreux Concerts, as they came to be known, quickly became celebrated events, and his orch. attained the status of France's premiere ensemble. In 1891–92 he also served as music director of the Opéra. After retiring as conductor of the Lamoureux Concert in 1897, he was succeeded by his son-in-law **Camille Chevillard**. In 1887 Lamoureux was made an Officier of the Légion d'honneur in appreciation for his services to French music. Although acknowledged as a highly competent conductor, he acquired a reputation as an abusive and dictatorial taskmaster. He was so loathed by some of his musicians that he is reported to have carried a pistol for protection.—NS/LK/DM

Lampadarios (real name, **Klada), Joannes,** significant composer of Byzantine chant who flourished in the first half of the 15th century. He was the leader of the singers in the left-hand choir of the imperial church of Hagia Sophia in Constantinople. Lampadarios was a prolific composer whose works have been preserved in various MSS.—LK/DM

Lampe, John Frederick (actually, **Johann Friedrich**), German-born English composer; b. Saxony, c. 1703; d. Edinburgh, July 25, 1751. After training in Helmstedt, he went to London about 1724 and played bassoon in theater orchs. He composed a number of English operas in the Italian manner without success, but his lighter stage scores proved successful, particularly his burlesque *The Dragon of Wantley* (London, May 10, 1737) and his mock opera *Pyramus and Thisbe* (London, Jan. 25, 1745). He also composed the *Cuckoo Concerto* for Flute and Strings (c. 1740), *Hymns on the Great Festivals* to texts by Charles Wesley (1746), an anthem, a cantata, ballads, and songs. His wife was **Isabella Young**.

BIBL.: D. Martin, *The Operas and Operatic Style of J.F. L.* (Detroit, 1985).—LK/DM

Lamperti, Francesco, eminent Italian singing teacher, father of **Giovanni Battista Lamperti**; b. Savona, March 11, 1811; d. Cernobbio, May 1, 1892. He studied at the Milan Cons. He was director at the Teatro Filodrammatico in Lodi. He tutored many distinguished singers, including Albani, Artot, both Cruvelis, Campanini, Collini, and Lagrange. He also taught at the Milan Cons. (1850–75). He publ. *Guida teorico-pratico-elementare per lo studi del canto, Studi di bravura per soprano, Esercizi giornalieri per soprano o mezzo-soprano, L'arte del canto, Osservazioni e consigli sul trillo, Solfeggi,* etc. Two of his methods and studies in voice production have also appeared in Eng. tr.: *Studies in Bravura Singing for the Soprano Voice* (N.Y., 1875) and *A Treatise on the Art of Singing* (London, 1877; rev. ed., N.Y., 1890). —NS/LK/DM

Lamperti, Giovanni Battista, Italian singing teacher, son of **Francesco Lamperti**; b. Milan, June 24, 1839; d. Berlin, March 18, 1910. At the age of 9 he was a choirboy at the Milan Cathedral. He studied piano and voice at the Milan Cons., where he served as accompanist in his father's class. He taught first in Milan, then subsequently in Dresden for 20 years and in Berlin. Among his pupils were Sembrich, Schumann-Heink, Bispham, and Stagno. He publ. *Die Technik des Bel Canto* (1905; Eng. tr. by T. Baker, N.Y., 1905), *Scuola di canto* (8 vols. of solfeggi and vocalises), and other technical exercises. His pupil W.E. Brown publ. *Vocal Wisdom: Maxims of G.B. Lamperti* (N.Y., 1931; new ed., 1957). —NS/LK/DM

Lampugnani, Giovanni Battista, Italian teacher and composer; b. Milan, 1706; d. probably there, after 1786. From 1743 to 1745 he was active at the King's Theatre in London, and later he was maestro al cembalo at La Scala in Milan. Over the period of 1732–69, he wrote 28 operas in the style of Hasse, which were presented in London, Venice, Milan, and other cities. He also publ. some trio sonatas and also wrote syms. and concertos.—NS/LK/DM

Lamy, Fernand, French composer and pedagogue; b. Chauvigny, Vienne, April 8, 1881; d. Paris, Sept. 18, 1966. After training at the Poitiers Cons., he studied with Bleuzet, Caussade, Dukas, and Ropartz in Paris, where he began his career as a conductor at the Théâtre des Champs Elysées. From 1914 to 1943 he was director of the Vallencienne Cons. In 1951 he was made inspector general for the arts and literature. He wrote mainly orch. works and choral music.—NS/LK/DM

Lancen, Serge (Jean Mathieu), French composer and pianist; b. Paris, Nov. 5, 1922. He received training in piano from Marguerite Long and Lazare-Lévy, and later was a composition student of Aubin, Büsser, and N. Gallon at the Paris Cons. (premier prix, 1949). In 1950 he won the Premier Grand Prix de Rome. In later years he was active with the World Assn. for Symphonic Band and Ensembles, serving on the committee of its French section (1985–91).

WORKS: DRAMATIC: *Les Prix*, ballet (Bordeaux, March 13, 1954); *La Mauvaise Conscience*, chamber opera (1962; Paris, Jan. 4, 1964); radio scores. ORCH.: Piano Concerto (1947–51); Harmonica Concerto (1954); Concerto for Double Bass and Strings (1960); Concerto for Flute and Strings (1962); *Instants* for Strings, Piano, and Percussion (1963); *Triptyque* (1965); *Fantasie créole* for Piano and Orch. (1967); *Concerto champêtre* for Harp and Small Orch. (1968); Sinfonietta (1970); *Concerto-rhapsodie* for Piano and Orch. (1974); Concerto for Harp and Strings (1988). BAND: *Manhattan Symphony* (1962); *Ouverture texane* (1971); *Symphonie de Paris* (1973); *Rhapsodie symphonique* (1976); *Symphonie de l'eau* (1985); Concerto for Trombone and Band (1987); *Symphonie ibérique* (1988); Concerto for Horn and Band (1990). CHAMBER: String Quartet (1959); *Concert à 6* for 6 Clarinets (1962); *Jeux pour musiciens* for 13 or 14 Instruments (1981); Double Bass Sonata (1982); *Concert* for Violin, Double Bass, and Piano (1985). VOCAL: *Narcisse*, secular oratorio (1957); *Poème aecuménique* for 9 Soloists, Chorus, Children's Chorus, Organ, and Orch. (1975); *Missa solemnis* (1986); *Te Deum* (1991). —NS/LK/DM

Lanchbery, John (Arthur), English conductor, composer, and arranger; b. London, May 15, 1923. He held a composition scholarship at the Royal Academy of Music in London (1942–43; 1945–48). He quickly developed a reputation as a ballet conductor in London, where he conducted the Metropolitan Ballet (1948–50), the Sadler's Wells Theatre Ballet (1951–59), and the Royal Ballet at Covent Garden (1960–72). After conducting the Australian Ballet in Melbourne (1972–77), he conducted the American Ballet in N.Y. (1978–80). He also was a guest conductor throughout Europe and the Americas. In addition to his film, radio, and television scores, he also prepared new performing eds. of a number of ballets. In 1990 he was made an Officer of the Order of the British Empire.—NS/LK/DM

Lancie, John (Sherwood) de
See **de Lancie, John (Sherwood)**

Landau, Siegfried, German-born American conductor and composer; b. Berlin, Sept. 4, 1921. He studied at the Stern Cons. and at the Klindworth-Scharwenka

Cons. in Berlin. He continued his studies at the Guildhall School of Music and Drama and at Trinity Coll. of Music in London (1939–40). He then pursued conducting studies at the Mannes Coll. of Music in N.Y. (diploma, 1942), and also received conducting lessons from Monteux. In 1946 he became a naturalized American citizen. In 1955 he organized the Brooklyn Philharmonia, which he conducted until 1971. Concurrently he was conductor of the Chattanooga Opera Assn. (1960–73) and of the Music for Westchester (later White Plains) Sym. Orch. (1961–81); likewise served as Generalmusikdirektor of the Westphalian Sym. Orch. (1973–75). He wrote an opera, *The Sons of Aaron* (Scarsdale, N.Y., Feb. 28, 1959), ballet music, orch. pieces, chamber music, and film scores.—NS/LK/DM

Landi, Stefano, significant Italian composer; b. Rome, 1586 or 1587; d. there, Oct. 28, 1639. He became a boy soprano at Rome's Collegio Germanico (1595), taking minor orders there (1599), and then studied rhetoric and philosophy at the Seminario Romano (1602–07). He subsequently was organist of S. Maria in Trastevere (1610) and a singer at the Oratorio del SS. Crocifisso (1611). He served as maestro di cappella to Marco Cornaro, Bishop of Padua (1618–20), then returned to Rome, where he was made a clericus beneficiatus of St. Peter's and maestro di cappella of the church of the Madonna ai Monti (1624); was also active as a teacher, and was in the service of Cardinal Maurizio of Savoy and the Barberini family. He became an alto in the papal choir (1629). His opera *Il Sant' Alessio* is important in the history of opera as the first such work to treat the inner life of a human subject and to include true overtures in the form of sinfonias. His sacred music ranges from the stile antico of his 2 masses to the new concertato style of his Vespers Psalms and his Magnificats.

WORKS: DRAMATIC: O p e r a : *La morte d'Orfeo,* tragicommedia pastorale (Rome?, 1619; publ. in Venice, 1619; libretto ed. by A. Solerti in *Gli albori del melodramma,* III, Milan, 1904); *Il Sant' Alessio,* dramma musicale (Rome, 1631?; publ. in Rome, 1634; libretto ed. by A. della Corte in *Drammi per musica dal Rinuccini allo Zeno,* I, Turin, 1958). VOCAL: S a c r e d : *Psalmi integri* for 4 Voices and Basso Continuo (Rome, 1624; ed. by S. Leopold, Hamburg, 1976); *Missa in benedictione nuptiarum* for 6 Voices (Rome, 1628; ed. by S. Leopold, Hamburg, 1976); *Messa* for 5 Voices and Basso Continuo (ed. by S. Leopold, Hamburg, 1976); motets. S e c u l a r : (18) *Madrigali...libro primo* for 5 Voices and Basso Continuo (Venice, 1619); *Arie* for Voice and Basso Continuo (Venice, 1620); *Il secondo libro d'arie musicali* for Voice and Basso Continuo (Rome, 1627); *Il quinto libro d'arie* for Voice and Basso Continuo (Venice, 1637); *Il sesto libro d'arie* for Voice and Basso Continuo (Venice, 1638); Dialogues for Soprano and Basso Continuo; Cantata for Tenor and Basso Continuo (ed. by S. Leopold, Hamburg, 1976); etc.

BIBL.: S. Carfagno, *The Life and Dramatic Music of S. L. with a Transliteration and Orchestration of the Opera Sant' Alessio* (diss., Univ. of Calif., Los Angeles, 1960); S. Leopold, *S. L.: Beiträge zur Biographie: Untersuchungen zur weltlichen und geistlichen Vokalmusik* (Hamburg, 1976).—NS/LK/DM

Landini, Francesco (also known as **Franciscus Landino, Francesco degli orghany,**

Magister Franciscus de Florentia, Magister Franciscus Cecus Horghanista de Florentia, and **Cechus de Florentia**), important Italian composer; b. probably in Florence, c. 1325; d. there, Sept. 2, 1397. His father was the painter Jacopo Del Casentino, co-founder of Florence's guild of painters (1339). After being blinded by smallpox as a child, Francesco turned to music; he learned to play the organ and other instruments and also sang. He became well known as an organist, organ builder, organ tuner, and instrument maker, and he was also active as a poet. He was organist at the monastery of S. Trinita (1361), and cappellanus at the church of S. Lorenzo from 1365 until his death. His output is particularly significant, for it represents about a quarter of extant Italian 14th-century music. Some 154 works have been identified as his, including 90 ballate for 2 Voices, 42 for 3 Voices, and 8 in both 2- and 3-part versions; 9 madrigals for 2 or 3 Voices; 1 French virelai; 1 caccia. See L. Ellinwood, ed., *The Works of Francesco Landini* (Cambridge, Mass., 1939; 2nd ed., 1945), J. Wolf, ed., *Der Squarcialupi-Codex Pal. 87 der Biblioteca medicea laurenziana zu Florenz* (Lippstadt, 1955), and L. Schrade, ed., *The Works of Francesco Landini,* Polyphonic Music of the Fourteenth Century, IV (1958).

BIBL.: G. Galletti, ed., *Philippi Villani liber de civitatis Florentiae famosis civibus* (c. 1400; Florence, 1847); H. Nolthenius, *Renaissance in Mei: Florentijns leven rond F. Landino* (Utrecht, 1956); D. Baumann, *Die dreistimmige Satztechnik bei F. L.* (Baden-Baden, 1978).—NS/LK/DM

Landon, H(oward) C(handler) Robbins, eminent American musicologist; b. Boston, March 6, 1926. He studied music history and theory with Alfred J. Swan at Swarthmore Coll., and composition there with Harl McDonald. He also took a course in English literature with W.H. Auden (1943–45) and then studied musicology with Geiringer at Boston Univ. (B.Mus., 1947). In 1949 he founded the Haydn Soc., with a view to preparing a complete ed. of Haydn's works. He also instituted an energetic campaign to locate music MSS that had disappeared or been removed; thus, he succeeded in finding the MS of Haydn's Mass No. 13; also found the MS of the so-called Jena Sym., erroneously ascribed to Beethoven, and proved that it had actually been composed by Friedrich Witt. In *The Symphonies of Joseph Haydn* (London, 1955; suppl., 1961), he analyzes each sym. and suggests solutions for numerous problems of authenticity; in his new ed. of the syms. (12 vols., Vienna, 1965–68), he carefully establishes the version nearest to the original authentic text. He subsequently publ. his massive study *Haydn: Chronicle and Works* in 5 vols. (Bloomington, Ind., and London): Vol. I, *Haydn: The Early Years, 1732–1765* (1980), Vol. II, *Haydn at Esterháza, 1766–1790* (1978), Vol. III, *Haydn in England, 1791–1795* (1976), Vol. IV, *Haydn: The Years of "The Creation," 1796–1800* (1977), and Vol. V, *Haydn: The Late Years, 1801–1809* (1977). In addition to numerous other Haydn studies, he also publ. *The Mozart Companion* (ed. with D. Mitchell; London, 1956; 2nd ed., rev., 1965), *Beethoven: A Documentary Study* (London, 1970; 2nd ed., rev., 1993 as *Beethoven: His Life, Work, and World*), *Essays on the Viennese Classical Style: Gluck, Haydn, Mozart, Beethoven* (London and N.Y., 1970), *Mozart and the*

Masons (London, 1983), *1791: Mozart's Last Year* (London, 1988), *Mozart: The Golden Years* (N.Y., 1989), ed. *The Mozart Compendium* (N.Y., 1990), *Mozart and Vienna, including Selections from Johann Pezzl's "Sketch of Vienna" 1786–90* (N.Y., 1991), *Vivaldi: Voice of the Baroque* (London, 1993), and *The Mozart Essays* (London, 1995). He was a lecturer of distinction at various American and British colleges and universities. His wife, Christa Landon (b. Berlin, Sept. 23, 1921; d. Funchal, Madeira, Nov. 19, 1977), joined him as a research partner in the search for rare MSS in libraries, churches, and monasteries. She publ. eds. of works by Haydn, Mozart, and Bach; her ed. of Haydn's piano sonatas (3 vols., Vienna, 1963–66) supersedes the one by Hoboken.

BIBL.: O. Biba and D. Jones, eds., *Studies in Music History: Presented to H.C.R. L. on his Seventieth Birthday* (London, 1996). **—NS/LK/DM**

Landormy, Paul (Charles-René), French musicologist, music critic, and composer; b. Issy-les-Moulineaux, Jan. 3, 1869; d. Paris, Nov. 17, 1943. He was an agrégé des lettres of the École Normale in Paris, and studied voice with Sbriglia and Plancon. With Rolland, he organized a series of lectures on music history at the École des Hautes Études Sociales (1902) and was founder-director of its acoustic laboratory (1904–07). He became music critic of *La Victoire* (1918), and contributed articles to other publications. Among his compositions were piano pieces and songs.

WRITINGS (all publ. in Paris): *Histoire de la musique* (1910; 3rd ed., 1923); *Brahms* (1920; rev. ed., 1948); *Bizet* (1924); *La Vie de Schubert* (1928); *Albert Roussel* (1938); *Gluck* (1941); *Gounod* (1942); *La Musique française* (3 vols., 1943–44).**—NS/LK/DM**

Landowska, Wanda (Alexandra), celebrated Polish-born French harpsichordist, pianist, and pedagogue; b. Warsaw, July 5, 1879; d. Lakeville, Conn., Aug. 16, 1959. She was only 4 when she began to play the piano. Following lessons with Kleczyński, she continued her piano studies at the Warsaw Cons. with Michalowski. In 1896 she went to Berlin and completed her formal training with Moszkowski (piano) and Urban (composition). In 1900 she went to Paris, where she married Henri Lew, an authority on Hebrew folklore. He encouraged her to pursue her interest in the study and performance of 17th-and 18th-century music. While she continued to appear as a pianist, from 1903 she gave increasing attention to playing the harpsichord in public and making it once again an accepted concert instrument. Her tours as a harpsichordist took her all over Europe. In 1913 she went to Berlin to teach harpsichord at the Hochschule für Musik. At the outbreak of World War I in 1914, she and her husband were declared as civil prisoners on parole on account of their French citizenship. After the Armistice in 1918, Landowska went to Basel to give master classes in harpsichord at the Cons. in 1919. She then returned to Paris to teach at the Sorbonne and at the École Normale de Musique. In 1923 she made her first appearances in the U.S. In 1925 she settled in St.-Leu-la-Forêt, near Paris, where she founded the École de Musique Ancienne for the study, teaching, and performance of early music. She also continued to tour abroad. With the Nazi occupation of Paris in 1940, Landowska fled France and eventually arrived in N.Y. in 1941. In 1947 she settled in Lakeville, Conn. She continued to be active as a performer and teacher during these years. In 1952 she celebrated her 75th birthday in a N.Y. recital. Landowska was the foremost champion of the 20th- century movement to restore the harpsichord to concert settings. Her performance style was an assertive one highlighted by legato playing and variety of articulation. While she was best known for her interpretations of Bach, she also commissioned works from Falla (Harpsichord Concerto, Barcelona, Nov. 5, 1926), Poulenc (*Concert champêtre* for Harpsichord and Small Orch., Paris, May 3, 1929), and other composers. D. Restout and R. Hawkins ed. a collection of her articles as *Landowska on Music* (Briarcliff Manor, N.Y., 1964).

BIBL.: B. Gavoty and R. Hauert, *W. L.* (Geneva, 1957); A. Cash, *W. L. and the Revival of the Harpsichord: A Reassessment* (diss., Univ. of Ky., 1990).**—NS/LK/DM**

Landowski, Marcel (François Paul), eminent French composer and administrator; b. Pont-L'Abbé, Finistère, Feb. 18, 1915; d. Paris, Dec. 22, 1999. He was the great-grandson of **Henri Vieuxtemps** and the son of the sculptor Paul Landowski. He received training in piano from Marguerite Long (1922) and in conducting from Monteux (1932), and was a student of Fauchet (harmony), N. Gallon (fugue), Büsser (composition), and Gaubert (conducting) at the Paris Cons. (1934–37). While rising to eminence as a composer, Landowski also became a prominent administrator. From 1960 to 1965 he was director of the Boulogne-Billancourt Cons., and from 1962 to 1966 he was director of music of the Comédie- Française in Paris. In 1964 he was named inspector-general of music for the Ministry of Cultural Affairs, later serving as its chief of the music service (1966–70) and as director of music, lyric art, and dance (1970–74). In 1974 he became inspector-general of music for the Ministry of Education. From 1977 to 1979 he was director of cultural affairs for the City of Paris. He was president of the Théâtre du Châtelet in Paris from 1980 to 1991. He served as president and director-general of the Editions Salabert in Paris from 1991. In 1950 he received the Grand Prix of the City of Paris for composition. The Société des Auteurs, Compositeurs et Editeurs de Musique awarded him its Grand Prix in 1968 and its Prix Maurice Ravel in 1973. In 1975 Landowski was elected a member of the Académie des Beaux-Arts of the Institut de France, serving as its permanent secretary from 1968 to 1994. In 1987 he was made a Commandeur of the Légion d'honneur. In 1994 he was named Chancelier of the Institut de France. He was the author of *L'orchestre* (with L. Aubert; Paris, 1951), *Honegger* (Paris, 1957), *Batailles pour la musique* (Paris, 1979), and *La Musique n'adoucit pas les moeurs* (Paris, 1990). Landowski's compositions reveal his penchant for eclecticism. While his works are always expertly crafted, his generally accessible style is occasionally made more adventuresome by his utilization of atonal, electronic, and electroacoustic diversions. Some of his piano works were written for his wife, Jacqueline Potier, whom he married in 1941.

WORKS: DRAMATIC: *Le Tour d'une aile de pigeon*, operetta (Paris, April 1, 1938; in collaboration with J.-J. Grünewald); *Les Fleurs de la petite Ida*, ballet (Paris, June 19, 1938); *Clairs-obscurs*, ballet (Paris, Nov. 1938); *Après-midi champêtre*, ballet (Versailles, March 30, 1941); *Les Travaux et les jours*, ballet (1943); *Les Djinns*, ballet (Paris, March 11, 1944); *La Rire de Nils Halerius*, lyric legend (1944–48; Mulhouse, Jan. 19, 1951); *Le Fou*, lyric drama (1948–55; Nancy, Feb. 1, 1956); *Rabelais, François de France*, opera-ballet (Tours, July 26, 1953); *Le Ventriloque*, lyric comedy (1954–55; Paris, Feb. 6, 1956); *L'Opéra de Poussière*, lyric drama (1958–62; Avignon, Oct. 25, 1962); *Abîmes*, ballet (Essen, Feb. 12, 1959); *Les Adieux*, lyric drama (Radio Luxembourg, Nov. 1959; first stage perf., Paris, Oct. 8, 1960); *Le Leçon d'Anatomie*, ballet (The Hague, 1964; based on the Sym. No. 1); *Le Fantôme de l'Opéra*, ballet (1979; Paris, Feb. 22, 1980); *Les Hauts de Hurlevent*, ballet (Paris, Dec. 28, 1982); *La Sorcière du placard à balais*, children's mini-opera (Sevres, May 2, 1983); *Montségur*, lyric drama (Toulouse, Feb. 1, 1985); *La Vieille Maison*, musical (1987; Nantes, Feb. 25, 1988); *P'tit Pierre et la Sorcière du placard à balais*, children's opera (1991; Colmar, May 7, 1992); *Galina*, opera (1995; Lyons, March 17, 1996); incidental music; film scores. **ORCH.:** 2 piano concertos: No. 1, *Poème* (1939–40; Paris, March 1, 1942) and No. 2 (1963; Paris, Feb. 28, 1964); *Brumes*, symphonic poem (1943; Paris, March 5, 1944); Cello Concerto (1944–45; Paris, Nov. 25, 1946); *Edina*, symphonic poem (Paris, Dec. 17, 1946); *Le Petit Poucet*, suite (1946; Cannes, Feb. 1947); *Ballet des Jeux du Monde* (1948); *Le Voyageur et la voyageuse*, suite (1948); 5 syms.: No. 1, *Jean de la Peur* (Paris, April 3, 1949), No. 2 (1964; Paris, Nov. 16, 1965), No. 3, *Les Espaces* (Strasbourg, June 24, 1965), No. 4 (Paris, Oct. 15, 1988), and No. 5, *Les lumières de la nuit* (Paris, Nov. 20, 1998); *Trois histoires de la prairie*, suite (1950); Ondes Martenot Concerto (1954; Vichy, Sept. 16, 1955; also as *Concerto en trio* for Ondes Martenot, Percussion, and Piano, 1975); Bassoon Concerto (1957; Paris, June 1958); *La Passante*, suite (1958); *Mouvement* for Strings (1960); *L'Orage*, symphonic poem (1960); 2 flute concertos: No. 1 for Flute and Strings (Bordeaux, May 27, 1968) and No. 2 (Sofia, May 28, 1998); *Au bout de chagrin, une fenêtre ouverte*, concerto for Trumpet, Orch., and Tape (1976; Paris, June 24, 1977); *L'Horloge*, symphonic poem (Paris, May 6, 1982); *Improvisation* for Trombone and Orch. (Toulon, May 20, 1983; also for Trombone and Piano); *Les Orchestrades* (St. Libéral, Aug. 31, 1985); *Quatre préludes pour l'Opéra des Bastilles* (Paris, Dec. 12, 1989); Concertino for Trombone and Strings (Metz, July 2, 1990); *Adagio Cantabile* for Oboe, English Horn, Percussion, and Strings (1991; Paris, Jan. 7, 1992); Symphonie concertante for Organ and Orch. (Cannes, Oct. 24, 1993); *Que ma joie demeure* for Violin and Strings (Athens, Sept. 1994); Violin Concerto (Paris, Nov. 30, 1995); *Un Chant* for Cello and Orch. (Budapest, Nov. 21, 1996); *À Sainte Dévote* (Monte Carlo, July 20, 1997); *Ouverture pour un opéra imaginaire* (Besaçon, Sept. 12, 1997). **CHAMBER:** Trio for Horn, Trumpet, and Piano (1954); *Quatre préludes* for Percussion and Piano (Paris, June 1963); *Étude de sonorité* for Violin and Piano (1973; Paris, June 10, 1974); *Concerto en trio* for Ondes Martenot, Percussion, and Piano (1975; Paris, Dec. 1, 1976; also as the Ondes Martenot Concerto, 1954); *Souvenir d'un jardin d'enfance* for Oboe and Piano (Paris, June 1, 1977); *Cahier pour quatre jours* for Trumpet and Organ (1977; Munich, Feb. 1978); *Improvisation* for Trombone and Piano (1983; also for Trombone and Orch.); *Sonate brève* for Solo Cello (1985); *Blanc et feu* for Horn, 2 Trumpets, Trombone, and Tuba (1985); *Petite chanson de l'amitié* for 4 Cellos (1987–91); *Étude de technique et de sonorité* for Violin and Piano (Paris, Nov. 22, 1996); *Velléda et le coeur de chêne* for Violin and Harp (Pont l'Abbé, July 15, 1998).

PIANO: Sonatine (1940; Paris, May 10, 1941); *Deux nocturnes* (1945); *Le Petit Poucet* (1945); *En trottinant sur le sentier* (1959). **VOCAL:** *Les Sept loups* and *Les Sorcières*, ballades for Women's Chorus and Orch. (Paris, Oct. 24, 1937); *Trois melodies* for Soprano and Orch. (1938; Cannes, Sept. 1942); *Rythmes du Monde*, oratorio (1939–41; Paris, April 26, 1941); *Desbat du cuer et du corps* for Soprano, Tenor, Violin, Cello, and Piano (1943; Paris, Jan. 20, 1944); *La Quête sans fin*, oratorio (1943–44; Paris, March 1945); *Cantique d'actions de Grâces* for Soloist, Chorus, and Piano or Organ (1945); *Trois révérences à la mort* for Soprano and Piano (1946); *Jésus, là es-tu?*, cantata for Alto, Women's Chorus, and Piano or Strings, and Percussion (Paris, April 1948); *Le Lac d'Undeneur* for Contralto (1948–49); *Quatre chants d'Innocence* for Women's Chorus (1952); *Espoir* for Chorus, Reciter, and Orch. (1959); *Chant de Solitude* for 4 Women's Voices and Orch. (Paris, Aug. 21, 1960); *Les Notes de Nuit* for Reciter and Orch. (1961); *Aux mendiants du Ciel*, cantata for Soprano and Orch. (Fontevrault Abbey, June 11, 1966); *Messe de l'Aurore* for Soprano, Tenor, Baritone, Chorus, and Orch. (Paris, Nov. 14, 1977); *Un enfant appelle* for Soprano, Cello, and Orch. (1978; Washington, D.C., Jan. 9, 1979); *Le Pont de l'espérance*, oratorio for Soprano, Baritone, Chorus, 2 Dancers, and Orch. (Vaison-la-Romaine, Aug. 8, 1980); *La Prison* for Soprano and Orch. (1981; Aix-en-Provence, July 18, 1983; also for Soprano and Chamber Ensemble); *Chant de Paix "Ecoute ma voix..."* for Soprano or Child's Voice, Baritone, Children's or Mixed Chorus, and Orch. or Organ (Paris, July 4, 1985); *Help-Help Vatelot* for Soprano, Cello, Chorus, and Small Instrumental Ensemble (Paris, Nov. 1985); *Les Deux soeurs* for Vocal Quartet (Rome, June 24, 1986); *La Symphonie de Montségur* for Soprano, Baritone, and Orch. (Paris, Oct. 18, 1987); *Les Leçons des ténèbres* for Soprano, Bass, Chorus, Organ, and Cello (1991; also for Soprano, Bass, Chorus, Organ, Cello, and Instrumental Ensemble, Paris, Nov. 26, 1991, or Orch.); *Les Rois Mages*, cantata for Voices, Flute, and Trumpet (Bayoux, June 18, 1994).

BIBL.: C. Baigneres, *M. L.* (Paris, 1959); A. Golea, *M. L.: L'homme et son oeuvre* (Paris, 1969); A. Livio, *Conversations avec M. L.* (Paris, 1998).—NS/LK/DM

Landré, Guillaume (Louis Frédéric),

important Dutch composer, son of **Willem (Guillaume Louis Frédéric) Landré**; b. The Hague, Feb. 24, 1905; d. Amsterdam, Nov. 6, 1968. He took music lessons from his father and from Zagwijn, and then from Pijper in Utrecht, where he also studied law at the Univ. (M.A., 1929). He subsequently was active as a teacher of commercial law and as a music critic in Amsterdam. He was chairman of the Dutch Music Copyright Soc. (1947–58) and president of the Soc. of Netherlands Composers (1950–62). As a composer, he endeavored to revive the spirit and the polyphonic technique of the national Flemish School of the Renaissance in a 20th-century guise, with euphonious dissonances and impressionistic dynamics creating a modern aura. In his later works, he experimented with serial devices.

WORKS: DRAMATIC: O p e r a: *De Snoek* (The Pike), comic opera (1934; Amsterdam, March 24, 1938); *Jean Lévecq*, after Maupassant (1962–63; Amsterdam, June 16, 1965); *La Symphonie pastorale*, after André Gide (1965–67; Rouen, March 31, 1968). **ORCH.:** 4 syms.: No. 1 (1932; Amsterdam, June 9, 1933), No. 2 (1942; The Hague, March 6, 1946), No. 3 (Amsterdam, June 16, 1951), and No. 4, *Symphonie concertante* (1954–55; Stockholm, June 5, 1956); *Suite* for Piano and Strings (1936); *4 Pieces* (1937); *Concert Piece* (1938); Cello Concerto (1940); *Sinfo-*

nietta for Violin and Orch. (1941); *Symphonic Music* for Flute and Orch. (1947–48); *Sinfonia sacra in memoriam patris* (1948; Rotterdam, Nov. 7, 1948; uses motifs from his father's *Requiem*); *4 mouvements symphoniques* (1948–49; The Hague, Jan. 17, 1950); Chamber Sym. for 13 Instruments (1952; Amsterdam, Feb. 24, 1953); *Sonata festiva* for Chamber Orch. (1953); *Kaleidoscope*, symphonic variations (1956); *Symphonic Permutations* (1957); Clarinet Concerto (1958; Amsterdam, June 25, 1959); *Concertante* for Contrabass Clarinet and Orch. (1959); *Anugrams* (1960); Sonata for Chamber Orch. (1961); *Variazioni senza tema* (Amsterdam, Dec. 11, 1968). **CHAMBER:** Violin Sonata (1927); 4 string quartets (1927; 1942–43; 1949; 1965); Piano Trio (1929); 2 wind quintets (1930, 1960); *4 Miniatures* for Clarinet and String Quartet or String Orch. (1950); Sextet for Flute, Clarinet, and String Quartet (1959); *Quartetto piccolo* for 2 Trumpets, Horn, and Trombone (1961). **VOCAL:** *Piae memoriae pro patria mortuorum* for Chorus and Orch. (1942); *Groet der martelaren* (Salute to the Martyrs) for Baritone and Orch. (1943–44); *Berceuse voor moede mensen* for Soloists, Chorus, and Orch. (1952). **—NS/LK/DM**

Landré, Willem (actually, **Guillaume Louis Frédéric**), Dutch writer on music and composer, father of **Guillaume (Louis Frédéric) Landré**; b. Amsterdam, June 12, 1874; d. Eindhoven, Jan. 1, 1948. He was a pupil of Zweers in Amsterdam. In 1901 he became music critic of the *Oprechte Haarlemsche Courant* in Haarlem. He was music ed. of the *Nieuwe Courant* in The Hague (1901–05), then of the *Nieuwe Rotterdamsche Courant* in Rotterdam (1905–37). He taught theory, composition, and music history at the Rotterdam Cons., and was also ed. of *Caecilia, Het Muziekcollege.*

WORKS: DRAMATIC: O p e r a : *De Roos van Dekama* (Haarlem, 1897); *Beatrijs* (The Hague, 1925). **O t h e r :** Incidental music. **ORCH.:** *Nocturne* for Small Orch. (1921); *In memoriam matris* (1923); *Romantisch Pianoconcert* (1935). **OTHER:** Chamber music; piano pieces; vocal works, including *Requiem in memoriam uxoris* for Chorus (1931; rev. by G. Landré, 1954); and songs.**—NS/LK/DM**

Lane, Burton (originally, **Levy, Burton**), American composer; b. N.Y., Feb. 2, 1912; d. there, Jan. 5, 1997. Though his career writing music for stage and movie musicals lasted nearly 50 years, Lane was selective in the projects he accepted; he contributed songs to at least 56 feature films released between 1933 and 1982 (most of them during the 1930s), but was the primary composer on only 19. And he wrote the music for only six Broadway shows between 1931 and 1979. Nevertheless, the quality of his writing attracted such major lyric collaborators as Harold Adamson, E. Y. Harburg, Ralph Freed, Ted Koehler, Frank Loesser, and Alan Jay Lerner; it brought him Academy, Tony, and Grammy award nominations; and it resulted in such successful films as *Babes on Broadway* and the stage musical *Finian's Rainbow*, as well as many song standards, notably "How About You?," "How Are Things in Glocca Morra?," and "On a Clear Day You Can See Forever."

Lane's father, Lazarus Levy, was a successful realtor; his mother, Frances Fink Levy, played the piano. A child prodigy, he studied piano from the age of 11 and played viola and cello in his school orchestra, writing two marches that were published. While still in his early teens, he was hired by the Shubert organization to write songs for an Off-Broadway revue; it was canceled when the leading man became ill. At 15 he got a job with a music publishing company and dropped out of school. At the suggestion of his friend George Gershwin he studied with pianist and composer Simon Bucharoff from 1930 to 1933.

Lane's work was first heard onstage when he and his first lyric partner, Samuel Lerner, placed two songs in the revue *Artists and Models* (N.Y., June 10, 1930). Howard Dietz accepted two more Lane-Lerner songs for the revue *Three's a Crowd* (N.Y., Oct. 15, 1930), rewriting some of the lyrics with Ted Pola. Acquiring a new lyric partner, Harold Adamson, the following year, Lane placed a song in the revue *The Third Little Show* (N.Y., June 1, 1931) and wrote most of the music for the ninth edition of the revue *Earl Carroll's Vanities* (N.Y., Aug. 27, 1931), which ran 300 performances, as well as a song used in the play *Singin' the Blues* (N.Y., Sept. 16, 1931).

Lane worked for the first time with E. Y. Harburg on a song for the revue *Americana* (N.Y., Oct. 5, 1932). In April 1933 he and Adamson enjoyed their first hit, "Tony's Wife," recorded by Gertrude Niesen. The song was interpolated into the MGM film *Turn Back the Clock*, released in August, and Lane and Adamson went to Hollywood for six weeks under the auspices of Irving Berlin's music company to write songs for the MGM movie musical *Dancing Lady*; Lane stayed for 21 years. Fred Astaire, in his motion picture debut, sang "Everything I Have Is Yours," one of four Lane-Adamson songs in *Dancing Lady*, released in December, and in January 1934 Rudy Vallée had a hit with it.

Freelancing, Lane and Adamson contributed songs to seven films released by four different studios during 1934. In June they scored a hit with "Swing It, Sister," recorded by The Mills Brothers and featured in the RKO release *Strictly Dynamite* in July. They had songs in another five films in 1935 but had split up by the end of the year. Lane married Marian Seaman on June 28, 1935; they had a daughter. Lane briefly teamed up with Herb Magidson in 1936; he then signed to Paramount where he was teamed with Ralph Freed. Their first work together was used in *College Holiday*, released in December.

Usually working with Freed, Lane contributed to ten Paramount features released in 1937, in most cases only one song. The notable exception was *Artists and Models*, released in August, for which he got screen credit and on which he collaborated with Ted Koehler. "Stop! You're Breaking My Heart" from the score was recorded by Russ Morgan and His Orch. and reached the hit parade. Lane had songs in four Paramount films in 1938, and on three of them his lyric partner was Frank Loesser. Two of those efforts brought him hits: "How'd Ja Like to Love Me?" from *College Swing* was recorded by Jimmy Dorsey and His Orch. for a hit parade entry in March, and the Red Norvo Orch., with Mildred Bailey on vocals, topped the hit parade in June with "Says My Heart." Lane and Loesser also combined for three of the five films for which Lane wrote songs in 1939. "The Lady's in Love with You," released in May and featured in *Some Like It Hot*, was recorded by Glenn Miller and His Orch. and spent nine weeks in the hit parade.

Lane teamed up with E. Y. Harburg in 1940 to write the music for his first book musical, *Hold On to Your Hats*. The show marked Al Jolson's return to the Broadway stage, and it ran 158 performances, closing only because the star decided not to continue. Lane returned to Hollywood, where he signed to MGM and worked with Ralph Freed and E. Y. Harburg on the Judy Garland–Mickey Rooney movie musical *Babes on Broadway*. Released in December 1941, the film included "How About You?" (lyrics by Freed), which became a chart record for Tommy Dorsey and His Orch., with Frank Sinatra on vocals, and earned an Academy Award nomination. His next assignment, *Ship Ahoy*, released in June 1942, featured Dorsey and Sinatra, who reached the charts with two of the three songs included, "The Last Call for Love" (music and lyrics by Harburg, Margery Cummings, and Lane), which featured The Pied Pipers, and "I'll Take Tallulah" (lyrics by Harburg).

Lane worked steadily in Hollywood during the war years, contributing to another three films in 1942, three in 1943, and three in 1944. At the end of 1944 he returned to Broadway, writing both music and lyrics to the songs in the comic revue *Laffing Room Only*, which ran 232 performances. "Feudin' and Fightin'" (lyrics by Lane and Loesser) from the score took nearly three years to become a Top Ten hit and then did so in recordings by Dorothy Shay, Jo Stafford, and Bing Crosby. Lane returned to Hollywood in 1945 but had only a couple of song credits in films during the year. In 1946 he and Harburg began work on a new book musical for Broadway. *Finian's Rainbow*, which opened in early 1947, effectively mixed fantasy with social consciousness, becoming Lane's only financial success on Broadway with a run of 725 performances. The score featured the ballad "How Are Things in Glocca Morra?," which was given Top Ten recordings by Buddy Clark, Martha Tilton, Tommy Dorsey, and Dick Haymes, and "Old Devil Moon," which Margaret Whiting recorded for a chart entry.

Lane again returned to Hollywood, still under contract to MGM, but he was less active. He contributed a song to the December 1947 feature *This Time for Keeps* and in 1950 worked on an unproduced film version of *Huckleberry Finn* with Harburg. But his next project to be completed was the Fred Astaire film *Royal Wedding*, released in March 1951, on which he collaborated with Alan Jay Lerner. A box office hit, the film produced a Top Ten soundtrack album, and the song "Too Late Now" earned an Academy Award nomination.

Admittedly selective, Lane rejected most projects and sometimes dropped out of those he accepted. Thus in 1951 he abandoned the stage musical *Flahooley* after writing several songs with Harburg (it was completed with Sammy Fain and flopped), and there was another unsuccessful attempt at a *Huckleberry Finn* movie, this time with Lerner. In 1952 he worked with Leo Robin on a movie musical version of *Papa's Delicate Condition*, but it too went unproduced. An animated version of *Finian's Rainbow* in 1954 got only as far as the recording of the voices.

Lane completed two film projects that were produced, however: on *Give a Girl a Break*, released in December 1953, he collaborated with Ira Gershwin, and on *Jupiter's Darling*, released in February 1955, he was reunited with Harold Adamson. By the time the latter was released Lane had moved back to N.Y., where a revival of *Finian's Rainbow* (N.Y., May 18, 1955) was mounted.

In 1957, Lane was elected president of the American Guild of Authors and Composers, a post he held for ten years. He also collaborated with Dorothy Fields on songs for a television musical, *Junior Miss*, broadcast on CBS. This was his last new work for some time. A second revival of *Finian's Rainbow* (N.Y., April 27, 1960) was well received, resulting in a cast album. Lane divorced, and shortly after, on March 5, 1961, he married Lynn Baroff Kaye.

In the early 1960s, Alan Jay Lerner and Richard Rodgers collaborated on a stage musical concerning ESP. They split up, however, and Lerner turned to Lane instead, resulting in the October 1965 opening of *On a Clear Day You Can See Forever*. The show ran 273 performances, the Grammy-winning cast album spent seven months on the charts, and the title song became a Top Ten hit on the easy-listening charts for Johnny Mathis.

Lane's two book musicals were made into films over the next few years. *Finian's Rainbow*, starring Fred Astaire and Petulia Clark, was released in October 1968. It was not a financial success, but the soundtrack album was in the charts for six months. The same was true of *On a Clear Day You Can See Forever*, starring Barbra Streisand, which was released in June 1970. Lane was elected director of the Songwriters Hall of Fame in 1973. In 1979 he reunited with Alan Jay Lerner for the musical *Carmelina*, which was unsuccessful. In 1982 he teamed with Sammy Cahn for the songs in the children's movie musical *Heidi's Song*. He joined the ASCAP board of directors in 1985, serving until 1996. In 1990 and 1992 he accompanied Michael Feinstein on two *Songbook* albums devoted to his songs. He died of a stroke in 1997 at age 84.

WORKS (only works for which Lane was a primary, credited composer are listed): **MUSICALS/REVUES** (dates refer to N.Y. openings): *Earl Carroll's Vanities of 1931* (Aug. 27, 1931); *Hold on to Your Hats* (Sept. 11, 1940); *Laffing Room Only* (Dec. 23, 1944); *Finian's Rainbow* (Jan. 10, 1947); *On a Clear Day You Can See Forever* (Oct. 17, 1965); *Carmelina* (April 8, 1979). **FILMS:** *Dancing Lady* (1933); *Bottoms Up* (1934); *A Wicked Woman* (1934); *Here Comes the Band* (1935); *Artists and Models* (1937); *Spawn of the North* (1938); *St. Louis Blues* (1939); *She Married a Cop* (1939); *Dancing on a Dime* (1940); *Las Vegas Nights* (1941); *Babes on Broadway* (1941); *Ship Ahoy* (1942); *Rainbow Island* (1944); *Royal Wedding* (1951); *Give a Girl a Break* (1953); *Jupiter's Darling* (1955); *Finian's Rainbow* (1968); *On a Clear Day You Can See Forever* (1970); *Heidi's Song* (1982). **TELEVISION:** *Junior Miss* (Dec. 20, 1957).—**WR**

Lane, Eastwood, American composer; b. Brewerton, N.Y., May 22, 1879; d. Central Square, N.Y., Jan. 22, 1951. He attended Syracuse Univ. (1898–1901), but left before graduating. He taught himself piano but did not learn to read music until late in his life. From 1910 to 1933 he was asst. director of N.Y.'s Wanamaker Concerts. He wrote mostly piano pieces in a light, descriptive vein: *In Sleepy Hollow*, 4 tone pictures (1913); *5 American Dances* (1919); *Adirondack Sketches* (1922); *Mongoliana*, suite (1922); *Eastern Seas*, suite (1925; includes *Sea Burial*, orchestrated by F. Grofé); *Persimmon Pucker* (1926; orchestrated by F. Grofé); *Sold Down the River*, ballet suite (1928); *Pantomimes* (c. 1933); *4th of July* (1935; orchestrated by F. Grofé); *Here Are Ladies*, 5 pieces (1944).—NS/LK/DM

Lane, Louis, American conductor; b. Eagle Pass, Tex., Dec. 25, 1923. He studied composition with Kennan at the Univ. of Tex. (B.Mus., 1943), Martinů at the Berkshire Music Center in Tanglewood (summer, 1946), and Rogers at the Eastman School of Music in Rochester, N.Y. (M.Mus., 1947). He also took a course in opera with Sarah Caldwell (1950). In 1947 he became apprentice conductor to George Szell and the Cleveland Orch., and subsequently was asst. conductor (1956–60), assoc. conductor (1960–70), and resident conductor (1970–73) there. He also was co-director of the Blossom Festival School (1969–73). He served as music director of the Akron (Ohio) Sym. Orch. (1959–83) and of the Lake Erie Opera Theatre (1964–72). In 1973 he became principal guest conductor of the Dallas Sym. Orch., and later held various positions with it until 1978. From 1977 to 1983 he was co-conductor of the Atlanta Sym. Orch., then was its principal guest conductor (1983–88). He also was principal guest conductor (1982–83) and principal conductor (1984–85) of the National Sym. Orch. of the South African Broadcasting Corp. in Johannesburg. As a guest conductor, he appeared with major orchs. on both sides of the Atlantic; Lane also was adjunct prof. at the Univ. of Akron (1969–83), visiting prof. at the Univ. of Cincinnati (1973–75), and artistic adviser and conductor at the Cleveland Inst. of Music (from 1982). In 1971 he received the Mahler Medal and in 1972 the Alice M. Ditson Award. In 1979 he was named a Chevalier of the Order of Arts and Letters of France.—NS/LK/DM

Lang, Benjamin (Johnson), American pianist, organist, conductor, teacher, and composer, father of **Margaret Ruthven Lang**; b. Salem, Mass., Dec. 28, 1837; d. Boston, April 3, 1909. He studied with his father and with Alfred Jaell. In 1855 he went to Berlin for advanced studies and, for a time, took piano lessons with Liszt. Returning to America, he was engaged as a church organist. He was also organist of the Handel and Haydn Soc. in Boston (1859–95), and then was its conductor (1895–97). He directed the Apollo Club and the Cecilia Soc. from their foundation (1868 and 1874, respectively), and also gave numerous concerts of orch., choral, and chamber music on his own account. As a pianist, teacher, conductor, and organizer, Lang was in the first rank of Boston musicians for a third of a century, and brought out a long list of important works by European and American composers. Among his pupils were Arthur Foote and Ethelbert Nevin. He wrote an oratorio, *David*, a great many sacred works, songs, and piano pieces.—NS/LK/DM

Lang, David, American composer; b. Los Angeles, Jan. 8, 1957. He studied with Lou Harrison, Martin Bresnick, and Leland Smith at Stanford Univ. (A.B., 1978), with Richard Hervig, Donald Jenni, and William Hibbard at the Univ. of Iowa (M.M., 1980), and with Bresnick, Druckman, Reynolds, and Subotnick at Yale Univ. (D.M.A., 1989); also trained at the Aspen (Colo.) Music Festival (summers, 1977–81) and the Berkshire Music Center in Tanglewood (summer, 1983). Among his awards were an NEA grant (1986) and the Rome Prize (1990); also BMI awards (1980, 1981). In 1987, with Michael Gordon and Julia Wolfe, he founded the international N.Y. festival BANG ON A CAN. His compositions are starkly dissonant.

WORKS: DRAMATIC: *Judith and Holofernes*, chamber opera (1989; Munich, April 27, 1990); *Modern Painters*, opera (1994); *The Carbon Copy Building*, comic-book opera (Turin, Sept. 9, 1999). **ORCH.:** *Hammer Amour* for Piano and Chamber Orch. (1979; rev. version, Sept. 25, 1989, Alan Feinberg soloist); *Eating Live Monkeys* (Cleveland, April 19, 1985, Henze conducting); *Spud* for Chamber Orch. (St. Paul, Minn., March 6, 1986); *Are You Experienced?* for Chamber Orch. (Pittsburgh, May 27, 1988); *Dance/Drop* for Chamber Orch. (Toronto, Feb. 10, 1989, composer conducting); *International Business Machine* (Boston, Aug. 25, 1990, Slatkin conducting); *Bonehead* (N.Y., 1990); *Fire and Forget* (1992); *Concerto on Orpheus* (1994); *The Passing Measures* (1998). **CHAMBER:** *Hammer Amour* for Piano, 2 Flutes, 2 Clarinets, 2 Horns, Trumpet, Trombone, and Percussion (1979; rev. 1989); *Illumination Rounds* for Violin and Piano (N.Y., April 23, 1982); *Frag* for Flute, Oboe, and Cello (Philadelphia, Oct. 1, 1985); *Spud* for Flute, Oboe, Clarinet, Horn, Timpani, Violin, Viola, Cello, and Double-bass (1986); *Burn Notice* for Flute, Cello, and Piano (N.Y., Nov. 7, 1988) *Dance/Drop* for Bassoon, Baritone Saxophone, Piano, Synthesizer, and Percussion (1988–89); *The Anvil Chorus* for Percussion (1990); *Vent* for Flute and Piano (1990); *Hunk of Burnin' Love* for 14 Instruments (1991); *Press Release* for Bass Clarinet or Bassoon (1991); *Bitter Herb* for Cello and Piano (1992); *My Evil Twin* for 12 Instruments (1992); *Cheating, Lying, Stealing* for Chamber Ensemble (1993); *Slow Movement* for Amplified Ensemble (1993); *Street* for 13 Instruments (1993); *Thorn* for Flute (1993); *I Fought the Law* for Piccolo, Oboe, Clarinet, Trumpet, Violin, Viola, Cello, Double-bass, and 2 Pieces of Junk Metal (1 or 2 Players) (1998); *Link* for 11 Instruments (1998; in collab. with Michael Gordon); *Scraping Song* for Percussion (1998); *My Very Empty Mouth* for Flute, Clarinet, Violin, Viola, Cello, and Piano (1999); *Sweet Air* for Flute, Clarinet, Violin, Cello, and Piano (1999). **Piano:** *While Nailing at Random* (1983); *Orpheus Over and Under* for 2 Pianos (N.Y., March 27, 1989); *Cage* (1992); *Face So Pale* for 6 Pianos (1992); *Spartan Arcs* (1992); *3 Memory Pieces* (1992–94); *Deep* (1994). **VOCAL:** *By Fire* for Chorus (1984; London, June 30, 1986); *Are You Experienced?* for Narrator and Chamber Ensemble (1987–88); *Music for Gracious Living* for Narrator and String Quartet (1993).—NS/LK/DM

Lang, Eddie (originally, Massaro, Salvatore), pioneering jazz guitarist; b. Philadelphia, Oct. 25, 1902; d. N.Y., March 26, 1933. His father was a fretted-instrument maker; Eddie's sister, Eadie, worked on guitar during the 1930s. Eddie began on violin at age seven, and studied with teachers in Philadelphia. While still at school, he befriended Joe Venuti, with whom he would work for much of his career. He first worked professionally on violin at L'Aiglon restaurant, Philadelphia, then worked on banjo with Chick Granese's Trio (c. 1918). He played banjo, guitar, and doubled on violin with Charlie Kerr's Band (1920–23). He then played with Bert Estlow in Atlantic City, and Vic D'Ippolito (1923), and played a brief variety tour with Frank Fay and Barbara Stanwyck. He spent six months with Billy Lustig's Scranton Sirens until summer 1924, then joined Mound City Blue Blowers, and visited London with them. He did prolific freelance radio and recording work on guitar from 1925. In 1926 he spent the summer season with Vic D'ippolito, and then September with Joe Venuti's Band in N.Y. Two months later Lang and Venuti joined Roger Wolfe Kahn's band; they also did a series of theatre shows for Don Voorhees, and played in Adrian Rollini's short-lived big band in October 1927. Lang did prolific innovative recordings with Red Nichols and His 5 Pennies (1926), and made recordings with Trumbauer and Beiderbecke in 1927. Venuti and Lang co-led at the Vanity Club, in N.Y. (autumn 1928); from May 1929 until May 1930 they both worked with Paul Whiteman, including appearing in the film *King of Jazz*. Among Lang's many recordings during this period, his duets with African-American guitarist Lonnie Johnson were particularly innovative; because of the controversy of black and white musicians recording together, Lang took the pseudonym of Willie Dunn for these recordings. Lang subsequently did extensive freelance work, and then worked again with Roger Wolfe Kahn (spring 1932). For the last year of his life Lang was mainly employed as accompanist to Bing Crosby. He died from complications following a tonsillectomy.

Lang's interactive finger picking accompaniment, sometimes recorded very prominently, helped to create a novel style of rhythm section that was an unacknowledged factor in the success of "Singin' the Blues" and other recordings. He introduced classical technique and counterpoint to jazz guitar. His single string soloing, however, was quite limited. The Lang-Venuti duet inspired Gypsy jazz guitarist Django Reinhardt and French violinist Stephane Grappelli to form their famous Quintet of the Hot Club of France in the 1930s. Lang is prominent on many recordings by Bing Crosby, the Boswell Sisters, Red Nichols, Jean Goldkette, Paul Whiteman, Joe Venuti, Frankie Trumbauer, and Bix Beiderbecke.

DISC.: "Stringing the Blues" (1926); "Handful of Riffs" (1927). **LOUIS ARMSTRONG:** *Hot Fives & Sevens, Vol. 3* (1928); *Louis Armstrong and His Orch. (1928–1929)* (1929); *Portrait of the Artist as a Young Man* (1934). **BIX BEIDERBECKE:** *Indispensable* (1924); *Bix Beiderbecke, Vol 1: Singin' the Blues* (1927); *Bix Beiderbecke, Vol. 2: At the Jazz Band Ball* (1927); *Felix the Cat* (1993); *Wa Da Da* (1994); *His Best Recordings* (1996). **THE BOSWELL SISTERS:** *L'Art Vocal, Vol. 13: La Selection* (1930); *Boswell Sisters Collection, Vol. 1: 1931–1932* (1932); *Airshots & Rarities 1930–1935* (1935); *Okay, America!: Alternate Takes and Rarities* (1935); *Boswell Sisters Collection, Vol. 2* (2000). **RAY CHARLES:** *Early Years* (1988); *Genius & Soul: The 50th Anniversary Collection* (1993). **BING CROSBY:** *Bing! His Legendary Years, 1931 to 1957* (1957); *16 Most Requested Songs* (1992); *Classic Crosby: 1931 to 1938* (1994). **LONNIE JOHNSON:** *Steppin' on the Blues* (1990); *Complete Recorded Works, Vol. 1–7 (1925–1932)* (1991); *Complete Recorded Works, Vol. 4 (1928–1929)* (1991);

Complete Recorded Works, Vol. 5 (1925–1932) (1992); *Blues in My Fingers* (1995); *Swing Out Rhythm* (2000). **THE MILLS BROTHERS:** *Four Boys and a Guitar* (1931); *Mills Brothers, Vol. 1: 1931–1934* (1998). **RED NICHOLS/RED NICHOLS AND HIS 5 PENNIES:** *Rhythm of the Day* (1925); *1923–1931* (1996); *Introduction: His Best Recordings 1927–1931* (1998). **BESSIE SMITH:** *Essential Bessie Smith* (1923); *Complete Recordings, Vol. 4* (1928); *Bessie Smith Story, Vol. 3* (1951); *1925–1933* (1987); *Do Your Duty: The Essential Recordings of Bessie Smith* (1995); *Blue Spirit Blues* (1995); *Bessie Smith Sings the Jazz* (1996); *1921–1933* (1998). **JOE VENUTI/JOE VENUTI & EDDIE LANG:** *Joe Venut and Eddie Lang (1926–1933)* (1933); *Violin Jazz 1927–1934* (1934); *Stringing the Blues* (2000).—JC/LP

Láng, István, Hungarian composer and teacher; b. Budapest, March 1, 1933. He studied with Viski (1951–56) and Szabó (1956–58) at the Budapest Academy of Music. He pursued his career in Budapest, where he first worked at the Academy of Dramatic and Film Arts (1957–60). From 1966 to 1984 he was municipal consultant to the State Puppet Theater. He taught at the Budapest Academy of Music from 1973. From 1978 to 1990 he also was general secretary of the Assn. of Hungarian Musicians. In 1968 and 1975 he received the Erkel Prize. In 1985 he was made a Merited Artist by the Hungarian government. His music is rooted in euphonious dissonance, without venturing into fashionable ugliness.

WORKS: DRAMATIC: Opera: *Bernada háza* (Bernarda's House; 1959); *Pathelin mester* (Master Pathelin; Budapest, 1958); *A nagy drámaíró* (The Great Dramatist), television opera (1960; rev. 1974; Budapest, Feb. 14, 1975); *A gyáva* (The Coward; Budapest, 1968); *Álom a színházról* (A Dream about the Theater), television opera (1979–81; Budapest, March 25, 1984). **Ballet:** *Mario és a varázsló* (Mario and the Magician), after Thomas Mann (1962); *Hiperbola* (1963; suite, 1968); *Lebukott* (Nabbed; 1968); *Csillagra-török* (Starfighters), ballet-cantata (1972; rev. 1977). **ORCH.:** Viola Concerto (1957); Concerto for Strings (1960); Xylophone Concertino (1961; rev. 1967); 4 syms.: No. 1 (1965; withdrawn and reworked as *Variazioni ed Allegro*), No. 2 (1972–74), No. 3 (1981–82; Szombathely, June 7, 1982), and No. 4 (1983; Budapest, Nov. 28, 1984); *Gyászzene* (Funeral Music; 1969); *Impulsioni* for Oboe and Instrumental Groups (1969); *3 Sentences from Romeo and Juliet* for Strings (1969–70); *Concerto bucolico* for Horn and Orch. (1970–71); *Tüzoszlop* (Firepillar; 1972); *Egloga* (1976); Violin Concerto (1976–77; Budapest, May 1, 1980); Double Concerto for Clarinet, Harp, and Orch. (1979–80; Budapest, April 7, 1981); *Pezzo lirico* for Oboe and Orch. (1985); Organ Concerto (1987). **CHAMBER:** Sonata for Solo Cello (1960); 3 string quartets (1961, 1966, 1978); 3 wind quintets (1964; *Transfigurazioni*, 1965; 1975); *Monodia* for Clarinet (1965); *Dramma breve* for Flute (1970); *Cassazione* for Brass Septet (1971); *Rhymes* for Flute, Clarinet, Viola, Cello, and Piano (1972); *Villanások* (Flashes) for Violin (1973); *Improvisazioni* for Cimbalom (1973); *Constellations* for Oboe, Violin, Viola, and Clarinet (1974–75); *Surface Metamorphosis* for Tape (1975); *Constellations* for Oboe and String Trio (1975–76); *Waves II* for Flute, Guitar, and Harpsichord (1976); *2 Preludes for a Postlude* for Bass and String Trio (1977); *Music 2–4–3* for Ensemble (1979); *Prelude, 3 Mobils and Postlude* for Brass Quintet (1980); *Chagall Flies Away over His Sleeping Vitebsk* for Percussion Quartet (1985; Budapest, May 18, 1986); *Interpolations* for Bassoon (1988); *Cimbiosis* for Cimbalom and Chamber Ensemble (1991). **VOCAL:** 2 chamber cantatas: No. 1 for Soprano, Clarinet, Piano, Percussion, and

Cello (1962) and No. 2, *Iocaste,* for Soprano, Flute, Clarinet, Harp, and String Trio (1979); *Pezzi* for Soprano, Flute, Clarinet, Percussion, and Viola (1964; rev. 1967); *Laudate hominem,* cantata for Chorus and Orch. (1968); *In Memoriam N. N.,* cantata for Chorus and Orch. (1971); *Fragments* for Alto, Oboe, Bassoon, and Harp (1971–72); *Waves I* for Soprano and Vibraphone (1975); *3 Songs* for Bass and Orch. (1985).—**NS/LK/DM**

Lang, Johann Georg, Bohemian-born German composer; b. Svojšín, 1722; d. Ehrenbreitstein, July 17, 1798. He received training in violin and keyboard playing. After playing in the orch. of the Prince-Bishop of Augsburg (1746–49), he studied counterpoint with Durante and Abos in Naples. About 1758 he was made Konzertmeister by his Augsburg patron, continuing in that post when the orch. was moved to Ehrenbreitstein in 1769. He retired in 1794. Lang composed 38 syms. and 29 harpsichord concertos. His expertise as an instrumental composer led to the misattribution of some of his works to Haydn, J. Stamitz, and J.C. Bach. Among his other works were masses, litanies, Te Deums, ensemble sonatas with keyboard obbligato, and quartets with flute obbligato.

BIBL.: S. Davis, *The Keyboard Concertos of J.G. L. (1722–1798)* (diss., N.Y.U., 1971).—**LK/DM**

Lang, Josephine (Caroline), German composer; b. Munich, March 14, 1815; d. Tübingen, Dec. 2, 1880. She was the granddaughter of the soprano Sabina (née Renk) Hitzelberger and the daughter of the soprano Regina Hitzelberger-Lang (b. Würzburg, Feb. 15, 1788; d. Munich, May 10, 1827) and the court music director Theobald Lang (1783–1839). She studied with her mother and also took lessons in theory with Mendelssohn. She composed and publ. a considerable number of competent lieder in an amiably songful, Germanically Romantic vein, in addition to some very playable piano pieces. She was married to the lawyer and music theorist Christian R. Koštlin (1813–56), who sometimes wrote under the nom de plume C. Reinhold. —**NS/LK/DM**

lang, k. d. (originally, **Lang, Kathryn Dawn**), Canadian country-pop singer; b. Consort, Alberta, Canada, Nov. 2, 1961. Before venturing into pop turf, k. d. lang was a true revolutionary in country music: claiming to be the reincarnation of Patsy Cline, she dug straight to the roots of country on a series of gutsy records. Nashville barely gave her the time of day—she got a similar cold-shoulder treatment from country radio—and in 1992 lang abandoned her country career and applied her gorgeous vocals to smooth torch songs and other more urbane pop styles. The wildly popular and Grammy Award–winning *Ingenue* (1992) kicked off this phase of her career, which coincided with lang's coming out and becoming a spokesperson for gay and animal rights.

DISC: *A Truly Western Experience* (1984); *Angel with a Lariat* (1987); *Shadowland* (1988); *Absolute Torch and Twang* (1989); *Ingenue* (1992); *Even Cowgirls Get the Blues* (soundtrack; 1994); *All You Can Eat* (1995); *Drag* (1997); *Invincible Summer* (2000).

Lang, Margaret Ruthven, American composer, daughter of **Benjamin J(ohnson) Lang;** b. Boston, Nov. 27, 1867; d. there, May 29, 1972, at the age of 104(!). She studied in Boston with her father and later in Munich, and also with Chadwick and MacDowell. She was the first woman composer in the U.S. to have a work performed by a major orch. when Nikisch conducted the premiere of her *Dramatic Overture* with the Boston Sym. Orch. (April 7, 1893). She stopped composing in 1917. She attended the Boston Sym. Orch. concerts from their inception in 1881, being present at a concert 3 days before her 100th birthday, at which Leinsdorf included in the program the psalm tune *Old Hundredth* in her honor.

WORKS: *Witichis,* overture (1893); *Dramatic Overture* (Boston, April 7, 1893); *Sappho's Prayer to Aphrodite* for Mezzo-soprano and Orch. (1895); *Phoebus' Denunciation of the Furies at the Delphian Shrine* for Bass and Orch.; *Totila,* overture; *Ballade* for Orch. (1901); *Te Deum* for Chorus (1899); *The Lonely Rose,* cantata (1906); *The Night of the Star,* cantata (1913); *The Heavenly Noel* (1916); etc.; about 150 songs, including the popular *An Irish Love Song* (1895); piano pieces.—**NS/LK/DM**

Lang, Paul Henry, eminent Hungarian-born American musicologist, editor, and teacher; b. Budapest, Aug. 28, 1901; d. Lakeville, Conn., Sept. 21, 1991. He studied bassoon with Wieschendorf, chamber music with L. Weiner, composition with Kodály, and counterpoint with Koessler at the Budapest Academy of Music (graduated, 1922), then studied musicology with Kroyer and comparative literature with Ernst Curtius and Friedrich Gundorff at the Univ. of Heidelberg (1924). He subsequently studied musicology with Pirro, art history with Henri Focillon, literature with Fernand Baldensperger and Félix Gaiffe, and aesthetics with Victor Basch at the Sorbonne in Paris (degree in literature, 1928). He settled in the U.S. in 1928, becoming a naturalized American citizen in 1934; studied musicology with Kinkeldey and French literature and philosophy with James Frederick Mason at Cornell Univ. (Ph.D., 1934, with the diss. *A Literary History of French Opera*). He was an asst. prof. at Vassar Coll. (1930–31); assoc. prof., Wells Coll. (1931–33); visiting lecturer, Wellesley Coll. (1934–35); assoc. prof. of musicology, Columbia Univ. (1933–39; full prof., 1939; prof. emeritus, 1970). He was vice-president of the American Musicological Soc. (1947–49) and president of the International Musicological Soc. (1955–58). From 1945 to 1973 he was ed. of the *Musical Quarterly;* from 1954 to 1963, music ed. of the *N.Y. Herald Tribune.* He publ. the valuable and very popular book *Music in Western Civilization* (N.Y., 1941; many subsequent reprints) and the important and comprehensive study *George Frideric Handel* (N.Y., 1966). He also ed. several vols. of articles reprinted from the *Musical Quarterly,* and the anthologies *The Concerto 1800–1900* (N.Y., 1969) and *The Symphony 1800–1900* (N.Y., 1969). A. Mann and G. Buelow ed. his *Musicology and Performance* (New Haven, 1997).

BIBL.: E. Strainchamps and M. Maniates, eds., *Music and Civilization: Essays in Honor of P.H. L.* (N.Y., 1984).—**NS/LK/DM**

Lang, Walter, Swiss pianist, conductor, teacher, and composer; b. Basel, Aug. 19, 1896; d. Baden, Aargau canton, March 17, 1966. He was a pupil of Jaques-

Dalcroze in Hellerau and Geneva. After teaching at the Jaques-Dalcroze Inst. in Geneva, he completed his studies with Klose in Munich and with Andreae and W. Frey in Zürich. He then was active as a pianist and conductor; he also taught in Basel and Bern, serving as well as prof. of piano at the Zürich Cons. (1922–41) and Academy of Music (1949–64). His wife was the soprano Mimi Lang-Seiber.

WORKS: ORCH.: *Scherzo fugato* for Strings (1929); *Sonata festiva* for Chamber Orch. (1935); Piano Concerto (1940); *Fantasie* for Violin, Cello, and Orch. (1941); Sym. (1946); *Jour de Fete*, overture (1947); Cello Concerto (1951); *Konzertante Suite* for 2 Pianos and Strings (1954); *Divertimento* for Strings (1957). CHAMBER: String Quartet (1919); 2 violin sonatas (1920, 1939); Piano Trio (1925); Flute Sonata (1956); many piano pieces. —NS/LK/DM

Langdon, Michael (real name, **Frank Birtles**), English bass; b. Wolverhampton, Nov. 12, 1920; d. Hove, Sussex, March 12, 1991. He studied at the Guildhall School of Music in London, and subsequently took voice lessons with Alfred Jerger in Vienna, Maria Carpi in Geneva, and Otakar Kraus in London. In 1948 he joined the chorus at the Royal Opera House, Covent Garden, London; made his operatic debut there in 1950. In subsequent years, he sang with many of the major opera houses of the world. On Nov. 2, 1964, he made his Metropolitan Opera debut in N.Y. as Baron Ochs. He created several bass roles in operas by Benjamin Britten; was also noted for his command of the standard operatic repertoire. After his retirement from the stage in 1977, he was director of the National Opera Studio (1978–86). In 1973 he was made a Commander of the Order of the British Empire. He publ. *Notes from a Low Singer* (with R. Fawkes; London, 1982).—NS/LK/DM

Langdon, Richard, English organist and composer; b. Exeter, c. 1729; d. there, Sept. 8, 1803. He was educated at Oxford (Mus.Bac., 1761). He was made lay vicar-choral and organist (1753) and Master of the Choristers (1762) at Exeter Cathedral, and then was organist at the cathedrals of Ely (1777–78), Bristol (1778–82), and Armagh (1782–94).

WORKS (all publ. in London): *10 Songs and a Cantata* (c. 1754); *A Collection of Songs* (c. 1755); *Cupid and Chloe*, cantata (c. 1755); 6 harpsichord sonatas (1765); *12 Songs and 2 Cantatas* (c. 1770); *Divine Harmony...by the most Eminent Masters* (1774; Psalms, anthems, etc.); *12 Glees* for 3 to 4 Voices (c. 1780). —NS/LK/DM

Lange, prominent family of Dutch musicians:

(1) Samuel de Lange, organist and composer; b. Rotterdam, June 9, 1811; d. there, May 15, 1884. He studied organ and piano with Pruys and van Bree. He was organist of the Lutherse Kerk (1827–33), the Waalse Kerk (1833–54), the Zuider-Kerk (1854–64), and the St. Laurenskerk (1864–84); established a famous recital series at the latter. He also taught at the school of the Rotterdam Maatschappij tot Bevordering der Toonkunst from 1844 and was municipal carillonist. He wrote many works for the organ, including sonatas, fantasias, and various transcriptions, as well as some chamber music and songs. His 2 sons were also distinguished musicians:

(2) Samuel de Lange, organist, conductor, and composer; b. Rotterdam, Feb. 22, 1840; d. Stuttgart, July 7, 1911. He studied with his father and with J.F. Dupont and Verhulst. While on a concert tour with his brother, he studied with Winterberger in Vienna (1859) and then with Mikuli in Lemberg. He became a teacher at the school of the Rotterdam Maatschappij tot Bevordering der Toonkunst in 1862. He was also made director of the society's choir and organist of the Waalse Kerk, and conducted concerts of Bach's orch. works. After a period in Basel (1874–76) and Paris (1876–77), he taught organ at the Cologne Cons. (1877–84); was also active as a choral conductor. He became director of the (Toonkunst) Maatschappij music school at The Hague in 1885, then joined the faculty of the Stuttgart Cons. in 1893, serving as its director (1900–1908). He wrote 3 syms., a Piano Concerto, an oratorio, *Mozes*, cantatas, choruses, chamber music, organ pieces, songs, and piano pieces.

(3) Daniël de Lange, cellist, conductor, and composer; b. Rotterdam, July 11, 1841; d. Point Loma, Calif., Jan. 31, 1918. He studied with his father and with J.F. Dupont and Verhulst, then studied cello with Ganz in Rotterdam and with Servais at the Brussels Cons., where he also had lessons in composition with Damcke. After concert tours with his brother, he taught cello at the school of the Rotterdam Maatschappij tot Bevordering der Toonkunst (1863–64). He was an organist and choral conductor in Paris (1864–70), and then taught at the (Toonkunst) Maatschappij music school in Amsterdam, later serving as director of the Cons. (1895–1913). He was also active as a conductor, gaining distinction through his performances of early music and contemporary compositions. He then went to the U.S., where he became director of the music dept. of the Isis Cons. of Art, Music, and Drama in Point Loma, Calif., in 1914. He wrote an opera, *De val van Kuilenberg*, 2 syms., a Cello Concerto, cantatas, chamber music, and piano pieces.

BIBL.: A. Averkamp, *Levensbericht van D. d.L.* (Leiden, 1918). —NS/LK/DM

Lange, Francisco Curt (actually, **Franz Curt**), German musicologist; b. Eilenburg, Dec. 12, 1903. He received training in architecture in Munich (diploma, 1927) and pursued his musical studies at the univs. of Leipzig, Berlin, Munich, and Bonn (Ph.D., 1929, with the diss. *Über die Mehrstimmigket der Niederländischen Motetten*). In 1930 he went to Uruguay, where he founded the Instituto Interamericano de Musicologicá in 1938, which publ. works via its Editorial Cooperativo Interamericano de Compositores (1941–56); he also ed. the *Boletín Latino-Americano de Música* (from 1935) and the *Revista de estudios musicales* (1949–56). In 1943 he was made a corresponding member of the American Musicological Soc.—NS/LK/DM

Lange, Gustav, German pianist and composer; b. Schwerstedt, near Erfurt, Aug. 13, 1830; d. Wernigerode,

July 19, 1889. He studied with A.W. Bach, Grell, and Löschhorn. He wrote more than 400 piano pieces, generally facile, elegant, and effective, many of which gained great vogue.—NS/LK/DM

Lange-Müller, Peter Erasmus, Danish composer; b. Frederiksberg, Dec. 1, 1850; d. Copenhagen, Feb. 26, 1926. He spent his entire life in Copenhagen. Following piano lessons from G. Matthison-Hansen, he pursued piano training at the Cons. with E. Neupert. He also studied political science at the Univ. In 1879 he became conductor of the Concert Soc., but ill health compelled him to withdraw from public life in 1883. Thereafter he devoted himself fully to composition. He developed a Romantic style à la Brahms and the French school, particularly excelling as a composer of songs.

WORKS: DRAMATIC: O p e r a (all first perf. in Copenhagen): *Tove* (Jan. 19, 1878); *Spanske studenter* (Oct. 21, 1883); *Fru Jeanna* (Feb. 4, 1891); *Vikingeblod* (April 29, 1900). OTHER: Incidental music. ORCH.: *Alhambra*, suite (1875); 2 syms. (1879–81; 1889, rev. 1915); *Weyerburg*, suite (1894); Violin Concerto (1904). CHAMBER: Trio for Violin, Cello, and Piano; piano pieces. VOCAL: Some 200 songs.

BIBL.: J. Clausen, *P.E. L.-M.* (Copenhagen, 1938); H. Bonnen, *P.E. L.-M.* (Copenhagen, 1946).—NS/LK/DM

Langendorff, Frieda, German contralto; b. Breslau, March 24, 1868; d. N.Y., June 11, 1947. She was a student of J. Meyer, M. Mallinger, and A. Iffert. In 1901 she made her operatic debut in Strasbourg. After appearing at Bayreuth (1904), she sang at the German Theatre in Prague (1905–07). On Dec. 7, 1907, she made her Metropolitan Opera debut in N.Y. as Ortrud, remaining on its roster until 1908, and returning in 1910–11. After singing at the Berlin Kroll Opera (1909–11), she gave concerts in the U.S. (1912–13). From 1914 to 1916 she was a member of the Dresden Court Opera. Among her best roles were Dalila, Azucena, Amneris, and Fricka.—NS/LK/DM

Langer, Suzanne K(atherina), important American philosopher of musical aesthetics; b. N.Y., Dec. 20, 1895; d. Old Lyme, Conn., July 17, 1985. She studied philosophy at Radcliffe Coll. (Ph.D., 1926) and at the Univ. of Vienna, her principal teachers being Whitehead and Cassirer. She held teaching positions at Radcliffe and Columbia Univ., then became a prof. at Conn. Coll. in 1954, retiring in 1962. Her publications center on a philosophy of art derived from a theory of musical meaning, which in turn exemplify a general philosophy of mind. According to her theory, modes of understanding are forms of symbolic transformation, i.e. one understands any phenomenon by constructing an object analogous to it or referring to it. She extended this theory to argue that the patterns of musical form are structurally similar to those of human feelings. She later expanded this into a general theory of the fine arts, her final work suggesting that art criticism might form the basis of a new structure for the behavioral sciences. Her lucid, strong-minded writings are widely considered crucial in understanding musical aesthetics.

WRITINGS: *The Practice of Philosophy* (N.Y., 1930); *Philosophy in a New Key* (Cambridge, Mass., 1942); *Feeling and Form* (N.Y., 1953); *Problems of Art* (N.Y., 1957); *Mind: An Essay in Human Feeling* (3 vols., Baltimore, 1967–72).—NS/LK/DM

Langer, Victor, Hungarian composer; b. Budapest, Oct. 14, 1842; d. there, March 19, 1902. He studied in Budapest with R. Volkmann, and later at the Leipzig Cons. Returning to Budapest, he was active as a teacher, theater conductor, and ed. of a Hungarian music journal. His songs, Hungarian dances, arrangements, etc., publ. under the pen name of **Aladar Tisza**, are in the genuine national vein; they enjoyed great popularity. —NS/LK/DM

Langgaard, Rued (Immanuel), distinguished Danish composer and organist; b. Copenhagen, July 28, 1893; d. Ribe, July 10, 1952. His father, Siegfried Langgaard (1852–1914), a student of Liszt, pursued a career as a pianist, composer, and teacher at the Royal Academy of Music in Copenhagen; his mother, Emma Foss, was a pianist. He began his musical training with his parents, then studied organ with G. Helsted, violin with C. Petersen, and theory with V. Rosenberg in Copenhagen. He made his debut as an organist at age 11. He subsequently was intermittently active as a church organist until becoming organist of Ribe Cathedral (1940). His early works were influenced by Liszt, Gade, Wagner, and Bruckner; following a period in which he was at times highly experimental (1916–24), he returned to his Romantic heritage; however, even in his last period of production, he produced some works with bizarre and polemical overtones. During his lifetime, he was almost totally neglected in official Danish music circles and failed to obtain an important post. A quarter century after he died, his unperformed works were heard for the first time.

WORKS: DRAMATIC: *Antikrist*, biblical opera (1921–39; Danish Radio, June 28, 1980; stage perf., Innsbruck, May 2, 1999). ORCH.: 16 numbered syms.: No. 1, *Klippepastoraler* (Rock Pastorals; 1908–11; Berlin, April 10, 1913), No. 2, *Vaarbrud* (Awakening of Spring), for Soprano and Orch. (1912–14; Copenhagen, Nov. 17, 1914; rev. 1926–33; Danish Radio, May 21, 1948), No. 3, *Ungdomsbrus* (Youthfulness), for Piano, Chorus ad libitum, and Orch. (1915–16; April 9, 1918; rev. 1925?–29; Danish Radio, May 4, 1934), No. 4, *Lvfald* (Falling Leaves; 1916; Copenhagen, Dec. 7, 1917), No. 5, *Steppenatur* (1917–18, 1920, 1931; first version, rev. 1926; Copenhagen, April 11, 1927; 2nd version, Copenhagen, July 8, 1937), No. 6, *Det Himmelrivende* (Tearing the Heavens; 1919–20; Karlsruhe, Jan. 15, 1923; rev. c. 1926–30; Danish Radio, May 29, 1935), No. 7, *Ved Tordenskjold i Holmens Kirke* (By Tordenskjold's Tomb in Holmen's Church; 1925–26; Copenhagen, March 8, 1926; rev. 1930–32; Danish Radio, Dec. 10, 1935), No. 8, *Minder om Amalienborg* (Memories at Amalienborg), for Tenor, Chorus, and Orch. (1926–28; rev. 1932–34; not perf.), No. 9, *Fra Dronning Dagmars By* (From the Town of Queen Dagmar; 1942; Copenhagen, May 31, 1943), No. 10, *Hin Tordenbolig* (Yon Dwelling of Thunder; 1944–45; Danish Radio, July 22, 1947), No. 11, *Ixion* (1944–45; Odense, July 29, 1968), No. 12, *Hélsingeborg* (1946; Danish Radio, July 22, 1977), No. 13, *Undertro* (Belief in Miracles; 1947; Danish Radio, Oct. 21, 1970), No. 14, *Morgenen* (The Morning), for Chorus and Orch. (1948; Copenhagen, May 24, 1979), No. 15, *Sstormen* (The Gale at Sea), for Baritone, Men's Chorus, and Orch. (1937–49; Danish Radio, Nov. 23, 1976), and No. 16, *Syndflod af sol* (Flood of Sun; 1950–51; Danish Radio, March 17, 1966); 1 unnumbered sym., *Sinfonia Interna* for Soloists, Chorus, and Orch. (1915–45); *Heltedd* (Death of a Hero; 1907); *Drapa* (1907); *Sfinx*, tone picture (1909–10); *Saga blot* (A Thing of the Past; 1917–18); Violin Concerto (1943–44; Danish Radio, July 29, 1968). **CHAMBER:** 8 string quartets (1914–31); 5 violin sonatas (1915–49); Septet for Wind Instruments (1915); *Humoreske* for 5 Wind Instruments and Drum (1923); *Dies irae* for Tuba and Piano (1948); Quartet for Brass Instruments (1949); about 50 works for piano, including 6 sonatas; organ music, including *Messis (Hstens tid)* (Messis [The Time of Harvest]), drama in 3 "evenings" (1932–39), and some 100 preludes. **VOCAL:** *Musae triumphantes*, cantata for Soloists, Men's Chorus, and Orch. (1906); *Drmmen* (The Dream) for Soloists, Chorus, and Orch. (1915–16; rev. 1945); *Angelus* (The Gold Legend) for Soloists, Chorus, and Orch. (1915–37); *Sfaerernes musik* (Music of the Spheres) for Soprano, Chorus, and Orch. (1916–18; Karlsruhe, Nov. 26, 1921); *Endens tid* (The Time of the End; 1921–44); *Fra Hjsangen* (From the Song of Solomon), 6 works for Solo Voice and Orch. or Ensemble (1949; Danish Radio, Feb. 24, 1969); *Fra Dybet* (From the Deep) for Chorus and Orch. (1950–52); about 25 motets and 150 songs.

BIBL.: B. Nielsen, *R. L.s Kompositioner: Annoteret vaerkfortegnelse* (Odense, 1991); idem, *R. L.: Biografi* (Copenhagen, 1993). —NS/LK/DM

Langhans, (Friedrich) Wilhelm,

German composer and violinist; b. Hamburg, Sept. 21, 1832; d. Berlin, June 9, 1892. He studied at the Leipzig Cons. with David (violin) and Hauptmann and Richter (composition), then in Paris with Alard (violin). From 1852 to 1856 he played violin in the Gewandhaus Orch. at Leipzig, and from 1857 to 1860 he was concertmaster at Düsseldorf. He then was a teacher and violinist in Hamburg, Paris, and Heidelberg. He received his Ph.D. at Heidelberg (1871). He taught music history at Kullak's Neue Akademie der Tonkunst in Berlin (1874–81), and in 1881 joined the faculty of the Scharwenka Cons. there. In 1858 he married the pianist Louise Japha (divorced in 1874). He wrote a Sym., String Quartet, Violin Sonata, and violin studies.

WRITINGS: *Das musikalische Urtheil und seine Ausbildung durch die Erziehung* (Berlin, 1872; 2nd ed., 1886); *Die königliche Hochschule für Musik in Berlin* (Leipzig, 1873); *Die Musikgeschichte in zwölf Vorlesungen* (Leipzig, 1878; 2nd ed., 1879; Eng. tr., 1886); *Die Geschichte der Musik des 17., 18. und 19. Jahrhunderts in chronologischem anschlusse an die Musikgeschichte von A.W. Ambros* (Leipzig, 1881–87).—NS/LK/DM

Langlais, Jean (François-Hyacinthe),

admired blind French organist, teacher, and composer; b. La Fontenelle, Feb. 15, 1907; d. Paris, May 8, 1991. He was blind from birth. His life was centered on Paris, where he first studied at the Institution des Jeunes Aveugles (1917–30), his principal mentor being Marchal for organ; he then pursued his training at the Cons. with Dupré (organ; premier prix, 1930), N. Gallon (counterpoint), Dukas (composition; 2nd prix, 1935), and Tournemire (improvisation). From 1930 to 1968 he was a prof. at the Institution des Jeunes Aveugles, and from 1961 to 1976 he was prof. of organ and composition at the Schola Cantorum. After serving as organist at Notre-Dame de la Croix and at St.-Pierre de Montrouge (1935–45), he held that position at Ste.-Clotilde (1945–77). He also made tours as a concert artist in Europe, and in 1952 he made his first visit to the U.S. In 1988 he gave his farewell recital at London's Royal Festival Hall. In his compositions, Langlais displayed an adroit use of polymodal harmonies, Gregorian themes, hymn tunes, and Breton folk melodies.

WORKS: ORCH.: *Cloches* (1935); *Essai sur L'évangile de Noël* (1935; Lyons, Feb. 1936); *Hymne d'action des grâces* (1935; Lyons, Feb. 1936); *Piece in Free Form* for Organ and Orch. (1935; Paris, Jan. 28, 1936; also for Organ and String Quartet); *Suite concertante* for Cello and Orch. (1936); *Pièce symphonique* (1937); *Theme, Variations, and Finale* (1937; Paris, June 1938; rev. as *Theme and Variations* for Organ, Brass, and Strings, N.Y., April 21, 1978); *Le Diable qui n'est à personne* for Ondes Martenot and Orch. (1946; Paris, Feb. 14, 1947); *Légende de St. Julien l'hospitalier* (1947; Paris, March 8, 1948); *Premier Concerto* for Organ or Harpsichord and Orch. (1949); *Le Soleil se leve sur Assise* (Paris, Dec. 30, 1950); *Deuxième Concerto* for Organ and Orch. (1961; Cleveland Heights, Ohio, May 11, 1962); *Troisième Concerto: Reaction* (1971; Potsdam, N.Y., March 2, 1978); *Réminiscences* (Quimper, Aug. 6, 1980). **CHAMBER:** *Ave Maria Stella* for Organ and Horn (1934); *Fantaisie: Pièce en forme libre* for Piano and String Quartet (1935); Trio for Flute, Violin, and Viola (Paris, Feb. 9, 1935); *Ligne* for Cello (1937); *Suite bretonne* for Strings (Paris, Dec. 21, 1938); Duo for Violin and Cello, *Suite concertante* (1943); *Pièces* for Violin and Piano (1951); *Sonnerie* for 4 Trumpets and 4 Trombones (1961); *Elégie* for Flute, Oboe, Clarinet, Horn, Bassoon, and String Quintet (1965; Rennes, March 21, 1966); *Pièce* for Trumpet and Organ (1971; Pittsburgh, April 26, 1972); *Sept Chorals* for Trumpet and Organ (1972); *Diptyque* for Piano and Organ (French Radio, Feb. 11, 1974); Sonatine for Trumpet and Organ (1976; Pittsburgh, April 25, 1978); *Pastorale et rondo* for 2 Trumpets and Organ (1982); *Petite Rapsodie* for Flute and Piano (1983); *Mouvement* for Flute or Oboe or Violin (Pittsburgh, Oct. 6, 1987); *Vitrail* for Clarinet and Piano (1987). **KEYBOARD: P i a n o :** Suite for Piano, 4-hands (1934; rev. 1947); *Prélude et Fugue* (1936); *Suite armoricaine* (Paris, May 3, 1938); *Petite Suite* (1986); *Noël breton* (1987). **O r g a n :** *Prélude et Fugue* (1927); *Trois Poèmes évangéliques* (Paris, May 29, 1932); 3 syms.: No. 1 (1941–42; Paris, June 1943), No. 2 (1959; rev. 1979; Paris, May 31, 1982), and No. 3 (Elsah, Ill., April 3, 1977); *Suite française* (1948; Lorraine Radio, May 8, 1949); *Hommage à Frescobaldi* (1951); *Suite folklorique* (1952); *Organ Book* (1956); *American Suite* (1959–60); *Mosaïque I* (1959, 1976; Pittsburgh, Oct. 21, 1976), *II* (1976; Pittsburgh, Sept. 15, 1977), and *III* (1977; Pittsburgh, April 25, 1978); *Homage to J.Ph. Rameau* (1962–64; N.Y., July 20, 1965); *Poem of Life* (1965); *Poem of Peace* (1965; Washington, D.C., Jan. 16, 1967); *Poem of Happiness* (1966; Paris, May 17, 1969); *Sonate en trio* (1967); *Offrande à Marie* (1971; Washington, D.C., Aug. 20, 1972); *Cinq Méditations sur l'Apocalypse* (1973; Paris, April 11, 1974); *Suite baroque* (Mulhouse, Dec. 2, 1973); *Trois Esquisses gothiques* for 2 Organs (1975; Washington, D.C., Oct. 29, 1976); *Triptych grégorien* (Pittsburgh, Sept. 14, 1978); *Prélude et Allegro* (1982; Cardiff, May 28, 1983); *Huit Préludes* (Pittsburgh, Sept. 9, 1984); *B.A.C.H.*, 6 pieces (Paris, Dec. 21, 1985); *Talitha Koum: Resurrection* (Paris, Nov. 18, 1985); *American Folk Hymn Settings* (St. Louis, June 8, 1986); *Fantasy on 2 Scottish Themes* (1986; Edinburgh, June 10, 1987); many other pieces. **VOCAL:** *Deux Psaumes* for 4 Mixed Voices and Orch. or Piano or Organ (1937; Paris, March 19, 1938); *Psaume solennel I* for Choruses, Organ, Brass, and Timpani (1937; Boys Town, Nebr., Aug. 30, 1963), *II* for Choruses, Organ, and Optional Brass (1963; Providence, R.I., March 7, 1965), and *III* for Choruses, Organ, and Optional Brass (1964; Hartford, Conn., March 7, 1965); *Mystère du vendredi saint* for Chorus, Orch., and Organ (Montrouge, April 23, 1943); *Pie Jésu* for Soprano or Tenor, 2 Violins, Cello, Organ, and Harpsichord (1943; also for Soloists and Orch.); *Trois Motets* for Voice and Orch. or Organ (1943); *La Ville d'Ys* for Soprano, Chorus, and Orch. (1945; Paris, Dec. 19, 1948); *Cantate à St. Vincent de Paul* for Chorus and String Orch. or Organ (1946); *Messe solennelle* for 4 Mixed Voices, Congregation, and 2 Organs or Brass and Organ (1949; Paris, Oct. 15, 1950); *Cantate de Noël* for Soloists, Choruses, and 12 Instruments (Paris, Dec. 25, 1951); *Missa Salve Regina* for Men's Chorus, Congregation, Trumpets, Trombones, and Organs (Paris, Dec. 25, 1954); *La Passion* for 8 Soloists, Narrator, Choruses, and Orch. (1957; Paris, March 27, 1958); *Le Mystère du Christ* for Narrator, Soloists, Chorus, and Orch. (1957); *Psalm 150: Praise Ye the Lord* for Men's Voices and Organ (1958; Boston, Jan. 10, 1959); *Canticle of the Sun* for 3 Treble Voices and Instruments (1965; Philadelphia, March 7, 1967); *Solemn Mass* for 4 Mixed Voices, Congregation, Organ, and Brass (Washington, D.C., Nov. 1, 1969); *Hymn of Praise: Te Deum Laudamus* for 4 Mixed Voices, Congregation, Organ, Trumpets, and Percussion (1973); *Psaume 111: Beatus Via Qui Timet Dominum* for 4 Mixed Voices and Organ (1977; Cambridge, Mass., April 21, 1978); *Hymne de soir* for Men's Voices (Paris, May 14, 1984); *A Morning Hymn* for 4 Mixed Voices and Organ or Piano (1985; San Francisco, Jan. 12, 1986); *Ubi caritas* for 4 Mixed Voices and Organ (Boston, Oct. 12, 1986); *Mort et résurrection: In memoriam Jehan Alain* (1990); numerous other sacred and secular pieces, including songs.

BIBL.: R. Nyquist, *The Use of Gregorian Chant in the Organ Music of J. L.* (diss., Ind. Univ., 1968); K. Thomerson, *J. L.: A Bio-Bibliography* (Westport, Conn., 1988); M.-L. Jaquet-Langlais, *J. L., 1907–1991: Ombre et lumière* (Paris, 1995).—**NS/LK/DM**

Langlé, Honoré (François Marie), French music theorist and composer; b. Monaco, 1741; d. Villiers-le-Bel, near Paris, Sept. 20, 1807. He studied in Naples at the Conservatorio della Pietà dei Turchini with Cafaro. In 1768 he went to Paris, becoming a singing teacher at the Ecole Royale de Chant et de Declamation in 1784. He then was a prof. of harmony and librarian at the Paris Cons. (1795–1802). He composed a number of operas, including *Antiochus et Stratonice* (Versailles, 1786) and *Corisandre, ou Les Fous par enchantement* (Paris, March 8, 1791), as well as other vocal works. He ed. Mengozzi's *Méthode de chant du Conservatoire* (1804; 2nd ed., c. 1815) and collaborated with Cherubini on his *Méthode de chant.*

WRITINGS (all publ. in Paris): *Traité d'harmonie et de modulation* (1793; 2nd ed., 1797); *Traité de la basse sous le chant précédé de toutes les règles de la composition* (c. 1798); *Nouvelle méthode pour chiffrer les accords* (1801); *Traité de la fugue* (1805).—**NS/LK/DM**

Langridge, Philip (Gordon), esteemed English tenor; b. Hawkhurst, Kent, Dec. 16, 1939. He studied violin at the Royal Academy of Music in London; took voice lessons with Bruce Boyce and Celia Bizony. He was active as a violinist but also began to make appearances as a singer from 1962. He first sang at the Glyndebourne Festival in 1964, and made regular appearances there from 1977; also sang at the Edinburgh Festivals from 1970. He appeared at Milan's La Scala in 1979; then sang for the first time at London's Covent Garden as the Fisherman in Stravinsky's *The Nightingale* in 1983. He made his Metropolitan Opera debut in N.Y. as Ferrando in *Così fan tutte* on Jan. 5, 1985. He was chosen to create the role of Orpheus in Birtwistle's opera *The Mask of Orpheus* at London's English National Opera in 1986. In 1992 he appeared as Stravinsky's Oedipus Rex at the inaugural operatic production at the Saito Kinen Festival in Matsumoto. He portrayed Jupiter in *Semele* at Covent Garden in 1996. After singing Captain Vere in *Billy Budd* at the Metropolitan Opera in 1997, he returned there as Schoenberg's Aron in 1999. He was made a Commander of the Order of the British Empire in 1994. Admired as both an operatic and a concert singer, Langridge maintains an extensive repertoire ranging from the Baroque masters to contemporary works. He is married to **Ann Murray.**—**NS/LK/DM**

Lanier, Nicholas, English lutenist, singer, composer, and painter; b. London (baptized), Sept. 10, 1588; d. there (buried), Feb. 24, 1666. He was made lutenist in the King's Musick (1616), then Master of the Musick to Prince Charles, and subsequently Master of the King's Musick upon the latter's accession (1625), although no formal appointment as such was made. A large portion of his music is not extant. He was a significant composer of songs. He may have introduced the stylo recitativo to England in his music to Ben Jonson's masque *Lovers Made Men* (London, Feb. 22, 1617; music not extant); he sang in the production, and also painted the scenery. His other stage works were *Marke...at the Marriage of...the Earle of Somerset,* to a text by T. Campion (London, 1613; in collaboration with G. Coprario), *The Vision of Delight,* to a text by B. Jonson (London, 1617), *The Gypsies Metamorphosed,* to a text by B. Jonson (London, 1621; in collaboration with R. Johnson), and *The Masque of Augurs* (London, 1622). He also set to music (1630) Herrick's poem on the birth of Prince Charles and wrote the extended recitative "Nor can'st thou yet" for *Hero and Leander.* His song MSS are found in various British libraries; many of them appeared in various collections of his time. See I. Spink, ed., *English Songs 1625–1660,* Musica Britannica, XXXIII (1971), and E. Huws Jones, ed., *Nicholas Lanier: Six Songs* (London, 1976).

BIBL.: M. Wilson, *The Life and Times of N. L. (1588–1666), Master of the King's Musick* (Brookfield, Vt., 1994).—**NS/LK/DM**

Lanier, Sidney (Clopton), American poet, writer, flutist, and composer; b. Macon, Ga., Feb. 3, 1842; d. Lynn, N.C., Sept. 7, 1881. He received training in piano, flute, guitar, violin, and organ in his youth. After graduating from Oglethorpe Coll. in 1860, he served in the Confederate Army from 1861 until his capture by the Union Army in 1863. In 1865 he gained his freedom. In 1873 he became first flutist of the Peabody Sym. Orch. in Baltimore. He also lectured on literature at the Peabody Inst. and was lecturer in English literature at Johns Hopkins Univ. (from 1879). He discussed aspects of music in such books as *The Science of English* Verse

(N.Y., 1880) and *Music and Poetry* (N.Y., 1899); see C. Anderson, ed., *The Centennial Edition of the Works of Sidney Lanier* (10 vols., Baltimore, 1945). He composed songs and flute pieces.—NS/LK/DM

Lankester, Michael (John), English conductor; b. London, Nov. 12, 1944. He studied at the Royal Coll. of Music in London (1962–67). After making his formal conducting debut with the English Chamber Orch. in London (1967), he was a conductor (1969–80) and head of the opera dept. (1975–80) at the Royal Coll. of Music. He also was founder-conductor of Contrapuncti (1967–79) and music director of the National Theatre of Great Britain (1969–74) and of the Surrey Phil. (1974–79). He was asst. conductor (1980–82), assoc. conductor (1982–84), and conductor-in-residence (1984–88) of the Pittsburgh Sym. Orch.; was also music director of the Hartford (Conn.) Sym. Orch. (from 1986).—NS/LK/DM

Lankow, Anna, noted German contralto and singing teacher; b. Bonn, Jan. 13, 1850; d. there, March 19, 1908. She studied singing in Cologne, Leipzig, and Dresden. She began her career as a concert singer, then was engaged as a contralto in the Weimar Opera. However, because she had been lame since childhood, she was forced to abandon the stage. In 1883 she married the sculptor Paul Pietsch of Berlin; after his death in 1885, she went to in N.Y. as a singing teacher, subsequently returning to Germany. She publ. a treatise, *Die Wissenschaft des Kunstgesangs* (1899; in Ger. and Eng.).—NS/LK/DM

Lanner, August (Joseph), Austrian violinist, conductor, and composer, son of **Joseph (Franz Karl) Lanner**; b. Vienna, Jan. 23, 1834; d. there, Sept. 27, 1855. A talented violinist, dance composer, and conductor, he died in his 22nd year.—NS/LK/DM

Lanner, Joseph (Franz Karl), historically significant Austrian violinist, conductor, and composer, father of **August (Joseph) Lanner**; b. Vienna, April 12, 1801; d. Oberdöbling, near Vienna, April 14, 1843. A self-taught violinist and composer, he joined Pamer's dance orch. when he was 12. In 1818 he formed a trio, which Johann Strauss Sr. joined in 1819, making it a quartet. The group grew in size, and by 1824 it was a full-sized classical orch. that became famous and performed in coffeehouses, taverns, at balls, etc. The orch. was subsequently divided into 2 ensembles, with Lanner leading one, and Strauss the other. Strauss went his own way in 1825. With Strauss, Lanner is acknowledged as the creator of the mid-19th-century Viennese waltz. Lanner's output totals 209 popular pieces, including 112 waltzes, 25 Ländler, 10 quadrilles, 3 polkas, 28 galops, and 6 marches; overture to *Der Preis einer Lebensstunde*; *Banquet- Polonaise*; *Tarantella*; and *Bolero*. His complete works in 8 vols., ed. by E. Kremser, were publ. between 1889 and 1891 (reprint, N.Y., 1971); selections were brought out by O. Bie (Munich, 1920) and A. Orel in Denkmäler der Tonkunst in Österreich, LXV, Jg. XXXIII/2 (1926).

BIBL.: H. Sachs, *J. L.* (Vienna, 1889); F. Rebay and O. Keller, *J. L.* (Vienna, 1901); F. Lange, *J. L. und Johann Strauss: Ihre Zeit, ihr Leben, und ihre Werke* (Vienna, 1904; 2nd ed., 1919); A. Weinmann, *Verzeichnis der im Druck erschienen Werke von J. L.* (Vienna, 1948); M. Schönherr, *L., Strauss, Zuhrer: Synoptic Handbook of the Dances and Marches* (1982).—NS/LK/DM

Lansky, Paul, American composer and teacher; b. N.Y., June 18, 1944. He was a student of Perle and Weisgall at Queens Coll. of the City Univ. of N.Y. (B.A., 1966) and of Babbitt, Cone, and Kim at Princeton Univ. (Ph.D., 1973, with the diss. *Affine Music*). In 1965–66 he played horn in the Dorian Wind Quintet. He taught at Princeton Univ. (from 1969), where he also served as dept. chair (1990–97). He received NEA fellowships (1981, 1988, 1992), an American Academy and Instute of Arts and Letters Award (1977), and commissions from the Koussevitzky Fdn. (1981) and the Fromm Fdn. (1985). He served on the boards of *Perspectives of New Music*, the Fromm Foundation, and the International Music Assn. In 1994, with Joel Chadabe and Neil Rolnick, he founded the Electronic Music Foundation in Albany, N.Y.

WORKS: CHAMBER: *Modal Fantasy* for Piano (1970); *Fanfare* for 2 Horns (1976); *Crossworks* for Piano, Flute, Clarinet, Violin, and Cello (1978); *Dance Suite* for Piano (1977); *Serenade* for Violin, Viola, and Piano (1978); *As If* for String Trio and Tape (1981–82); *Values of Time* for String Quartet, Wind Quartet, and Tape (1987); *Stroll* for Piano, Flute, Cello, Marimba, and Tape (1988); *Hop* for Marimba and Violin (1993); *Dancetracks, for an Improvising Guitarist* for Electric Guitar and Tape (1994). **COMPUTER:** *mild und leise* (1973); *Artifice (on Ferdinand's Reflection)* (1975–76); *Six Fantasies on a Poem by Thomas Campion* (1978–79); *Folk-Images* (1980–91); *As it grew dark* (1983); *Guy's Harp* (1984); *Idle Chatter* (1985); *Wasting* (1985; in collaboration with B. Garton and A. Milburn); *just_more_idle_chatter* (1987); *Notjustmoreidlechatter* (1988); *Smalltalk* (1988); *The Lesson* (1989); *Talkshow* (1989); *Not So Heavy Metal* (1989); *Late August* (1989); *QuakerBridge* (1990); *NightTraffic* (1990); *The Sound of Two Hands* (1990); *Table's Clear* (1990); *Now and Then* (1991); *Word Color* (1992); *Memory Pages* (1993); *Still Time* (1994). **VOCAL:** *Three Campion Choruses* for Chorus (1992).—NS/LK/DM

Lantins, Arnold de, Franco-Flemish composer; b. probably in Lantin, near Liège, c. 1400; d. place and date unknown. He may have been related to Hugo de Lantins. He was in Venice in 1428, and a singer in the Papal Chapel in Rome between Nov. 1431 and July 1432. He wrote several sacred works, as well as ballades and rondeaux. His employment of carefully connected chords suggesting purely harmonic procedures is of historical interest. For his works, see C. Van den Borren, *Polyphonia Sacra: A Continental Miscellany of the 15th Century* (Burnham Wood, 1932; second ed., rev., 1962) and *Pièces polyphoniques profanes de provenance liégeoise (XVe siècle)* (vol. I, Brussels, 1950).—NS/LK/DM

Lantins, Hugo de, Franco-Flemish composer; b. probably in Lantin, near Liège, c. 1399; d. place and date unknown. He may have been related to Arnold de Lantins. He spent his early career in Italy, where he wrote the ballata *Tra quante regione* (1421). In addition to other ballate, he composed rondeaux and sacred music. For his works, see C. Van den Borren, *Polyphonia Sacra: A Continental Miscellany of the 15th Century* (Burnham Wood, 1932; 2nd ed., rev., 1962) and *Pièces polyphoniques profanes de provenance liégeoise (XVe siècle)* (vol. I, Brussels, 1950).—NS/LK/DM

Lanza, Alcides (Emigdio), Argentine-born Canadian pianist, conductor, teacher, and composer; b. Rosario, June 2, 1929. He studied piano with Arminda Canteros in Rosario (1951–52) before going to Buenos Aires to pursue musical training with Ruwin Erlich (1952–59) and Julián Bautista (1960–63); then attended the Instituto Di Tella there (1963–64), where he had advanced training in composition with Copland, Ginastera, Maderna, Malipiero, and Messiaen, and in piano with Loriod. Upon being awarded a Guggenheim fellowship, he went to N.Y. and studied with Ussachevsky and Mimaroglu at the Columbia-Princeton Electronic Music Center (1965–67). After serving as an instructor there (1967–70), he was a prof. of composition at McGill Univ. in Montreal (1971–93) as well as director of its electronic music studio (1974–93). In 1972–73 he was composer-in-residence at the Deutscher Akademischer Austauschdienst in Berlin. In 1976 he became a naturalized Canadian citizen. As a pianist and conductor, he has energetically promoted the cause of contemporary music, especially avant-garde works. As a composer, he has explored the realms of electronics and multimedia in many of his scores.

WORKS: ORCH.: *Transformaciones* for Chamber Orch. (1959); *Eidesis Sinfónica I* (1963), *III* for 1 or 2 Orchs. and Tape (1971), *V* for Chamber Orch. (1981), and *VI* for Strings and Piano (1983); 2 piano concertos: No. 1 for Amplified Piano and Orch. (1964) and No. 2 for Piano and Chamber Orch. (1993); *Bour-drones* for Strings (1985); Concerto for Amplified or Electric Guitar and Orch. (1988). **CHAMBER:** *Concierto de Cámara* for Chamber Ensemble (1960); Trio-Concertante for Any 3 Instruments (1962); *Cuarteto IV* for 4 Horns (1964) and *V* for String Quartet (1967); *Interferences I* for 2 Groups of Winds and Tape (1966), *II* for Percussion Ensemble and Tape (1967), and *III* for Chamber Ensemble and Tape (1983); *Acúfenos I* for Trombone and 4 Instruments (1966), *II* for Chamber Ensemble and Electronics (1971), *III* for Flute, Piano, and Tape (1977), *IV* for Wind Quintet (1978), and *V* for Trumpet, Piano, and Tape (1980); *Eidesis II* for 13 Instruments (1967) and *IV* for Wind Ensemble and Electronics (1977); *Strobo I* for Double Bass, Percussion, and Tape (1967); *Ekphonesis I* for String and/or Keyboard Instrument and Tape (1968) and *III* for Wind, Keyboard, String Instruments, and Tape (1969); *Penetrations II* for Wind, String, Percussion and/or Keyboard Instruments, and Tape (1969); *Hip'nos I* for 1 or More Instruments (1973); *Sensors I* for Percussion Ensemble (1976), *II* for Multiple Trombones (1980), *III* for Organ and Percussion (1982), *V* for Solo Percussion and Percussion Ensemble (1985), and *VI* for Percussion Ensemble (1986); *Módulos III* for Guitar and Chamber Ensemble (1983) and *IV* for Amplified or Electric Guitar and Tape (1986); *Arghanum I* for Accordion, Clarinets, Percussion, and Synthesizer (1986), *II* for Flute, Contrabass, and Chamber Ensemble (1987), and *V* for Accordion or Piano and Tape (1990); *Quodlibet, stylus luxurians* for Organ and Chamber Ensemble (1991). **Piano:** *Toccata* (1957); *Plectros II* for Piano and Tape (1966), *III* for Piano, Synthesizer, and Tape (1971), and *IV* for 2 Pianists of the Opposite Sex and Tape (1974); *Preludio (Preludio)* (1989).

VOCAL: *3 Songs* for Soprano and Chamber Ensemble (1963); *Ekphonesis II* for Voice, Piano, and Tape (1968), *V* for Actress-Singer and Tape (1979), and *VI* for Actress-Singer and Tape (1988); *Penetrations VI* for Actress-Singer, Tape, and Chamber Ensemble (1972) and *VII* for Actress-Singer and Tape (1972); *Kron'ikelz 75* for 2 Solo Voices, Chamber Ensemble, and Tape (1975); *Ekphonesis VI* for Actress-Singer and Tape (1988); *Un mondo imaginario* for Chorus and Tape (1989); *The Freedom of Silence* for Voice, Piano, and Tape (1990); *Vôo* for Acting Voice and Tape (1992). **OTHER:** Electronic and tape pieces. —NS/LK/DM

Lanza, Francesco, Italian pianist, teacher, and composer; b. Naples, 1783; d. there, 1862. He was taken to London at an early age and studied with Field (piano) and Fenaroli (theory). After teaching piano, he returned to Naples in 1808 and taught privately before serving on the faculty of the Cons. (1827–60). As a composer for piano, Lanza's music followed the precepts of Clementi. —LK/DM

Lanza, Mario (real name, **Alfredo Arnold Cocozza**), popular American tenor and actor; b. Philadelphia, Jan. 31, 1921; d. Rome, Oct. 7, 1959. He studied voice in Philadelphia and then attended the Berkshire Music Center in Tanglewood (summer, 1942) on a scholarship. Subsequently he was drafted and served in the U.S. Army Air Force, during which time he sang in productions of Frank Loesser's *On the Beam* and was a cast member in the *Winged Victory* show. After his discharge in 1945, he went to N.Y. and pursued further vocal training with Rosati. In 1946 he made an impressive appearance as a concert singer at Chicago's Grant Park. In 1947 he scored a major success as a concert artist at the Hollywood Bowl, and that same year he toured the U.S. and Europe as a member of the Bel Canto Trio with Frances Yeend and George London. In 1948 he made his only professional appearances on the operatic stage when he appeared in *Madama Butterfly* at the New Orleans Opera. Lanza then went to Hollywood, where he won a starring role in the film *That Midnight Kiss* (1949). Its success led to his appearance in the film *The Toast of New Orleans* (1950), which included his version of the song *Be My Love*. His recording of the song sold a million copies and made Lanza a rising star. Then followed his starring role in *The Great Caruso* (1951), a film made memorable by his rendition of the song *The Loveliest Night of the Year*. His recording of the song also sold a million copies. Subsequently he starred in the film *Because You're Mine* (1952). His recording of the theme song of the same title likewise sold a million copies. By this time, Lanza's tempermental outbursts, heavy drinking, and overeating had taken a heavy toll. During his filming of *The Student Prince* in 1953, he walked out on the project and only avoided damaging litigation for breach of contract by waiving his rights to the soundtrack. Ironically, the recording of the soundtrack preserved some of his finest singing. After starring in one more Hollywood film, *Serenade* (1956), Lanza settled in Rome. He appeared in the film *The 7 Hills of Rome* (1958), which was made in the Eternal City and made memorable by his performance of the song *Arrivederci, Roma*. In 1958 he appeared at London's

Royal Albert Hall and at the Royal Variety Show, and then toured throughout Europe. His last film appearance was in *For the First Time* (1959). While Lanza's death at only 38 in a Rome hospital was initially attributed to a heart attack, rumors later cropped up that he was murdered on orders of the Mafia after refusing to appear at a mobster-organized concert sponsored by Lucky Luciano.

BIBL.: R. Strait and T. Robinson, *L.: His Tragic Life* (N.Y., 1980); R. Bessette, *M. L.: Tenor in Exile* (Portland, Maine, 1999). —NS/LK/DM

Lanzetti, Salvatore, noted Italian cellist and composer; b. Naples, c. 1710; d. Turin, 1780. He studied at the Cons. di S. Maria di Loreto in Naples. After playing in the Lucca court chapel, he entered the service of Vittorio Amedeo II of Turin in 1727. He also made tours as a virtuoso. He was in London (c. 1739–54), where he established the cello as a favorite solo instrument. Lanzetti then returned to Naples, and later joined the Turin royal chapel about 1760. He publ. a method, *Principes ou l'application de violoncelle par tous les tons* (Amsterdam, c. 1769). His works include 12 sonatas for Cello and Basso Continuo (Amsterdam, 1736), *6 Solos* for 2 Cellos and Basso Continuo (Harpsichord) (London, 1740), *6 solos* for 2 Cellos or Flutes, and Bass (London, c. 1745), and *6 Solos after an Early & Elegant Taste* for Cello and Basso Continuo (Harpsichord) (London, c. 1760).—NS/LK/DM

Laparra, Raoul, French composer and music critic; b. Bordeaux, May 13, 1876; d. in an air raid in Suresnes, near Paris, April 4, 1943. He studied at the Paris Cons. (1890–1903) with Diemer, Fauré, Gédalge, and Lavignac, winning the Grand Prix de Rome with his cantata *Ulysse* (June 27, 1903). He was music critic of *Le Matin*, resigning in 1937 to dedicate himself entirely to composition. He was at his best in music inspired by Spanish subjects.

WORKS: DRAMATIC: Opera: *Peau d'âne* (Bordeaux, Feb. 3, 1899); *La Habanera* (Paris, Feb. 26, 1908); *La Jota* (Paris, April 26, 1911); *Le Joueur de viole* (Paris, Dec. 24, 1925); *Las toreras* (Lille, Jan. 17, 1929); *L'Illustre Fregona* (Paris, Feb. 16, 1931). **Incidental Music To:** *El Conquistador*. **ORCH.:** *Un Dimanche basque*, suite for Piano and Orch. —NS/LK/DM

Lapicida, Erasmus, composer; b. c. 1445; d. Vienna, Nov. 19, 1547. After entering the priesthood, he was a singer in the Heidelberg Hofkapelle (1510–21). About 1521 he settled in Vienna, where he held a benefice at the Schottenklister. He was at least 102 at the time of his death. His polyphonic adaptations of German folk songs and Hofweisen were particularly notable.—LK/DM

Laplante, (Joseph) André (Roger), Canadian pianist; b. Rimouski, Quebec, Nov. 12, 1949. He commenced piano studies at 7, then continued his training with Nathalie Pépin and Yvonne Hubert at the École Vincent-d'Indy in Montreal (B.Mus., 1968; M.Mus., 1970). He then pursued further studies with Gorod-

nitzki at the Juilliard School in N.Y. (1970–71; 1976–78) and with Lefébure in Paris (1971–74). He won 3rd prizes in the Long-Thibaud (Paris, 1973) and Sydney (1977) competitions, and then shared 2nd prize at the Tchaikovsky Competition in Moscow (1978); made his N.Y. recital debut (Oct. 21, 1978), and subsequently toured throughout North America, Europe, and the Far East. In 1988 he organized his own trio with the violinist Ernö Sebestyén and the cellist Martin Ostertag. He won accolades for his performances of the Romantic repertoire.—NS/LK/DM

LaPorta, John (D.), jazz saxophonist, clarinetist, educator; b. Philadelphia, April 1, 1920. He began studying clarinet with a band teacher at age nine and later continued his education at the Mastbaum School in Philadelphia, where one of his classmates was Buddy DeFranco; he also studied classical music with Joseph Gigliotti of the Philadelphia Orch., and later with Leon Russianoff at the Manhattan School of Music. He learned jazz from the recordings of Basie, Ellington, Lester Young, and Herschel Evans. He picked up both alto and tenor sax (later he came to prefer the alto) and also learned to write for large ensembles. As a teenager he played with bands in Philadelphia. In the early 1940s he joined the Bob Chester band as lead alto; he also wrote for the band. After playing with Chester, LaPorta became a member of Woody Herman's First Herd on third alto and some lead clarinet, but was frustrated that he did not get to solo. He continued to write, though, and was lucky enough to study with Igor Stravinsky's assistant Alexis Aieff, who was touring with the band to conduct the *Ebony Concerto*. He also studied with Ernest Toch on the West coast. He then settled in N.Y. and began a significant period of study with Lennie Tristano, with whom he cut four sides in late 1947 on clarinet; he also made radio broadcasts with Gillespie and Parker. Around this time he began to focus on teaching, first at the Parkway music school and eventually in public schools on Long Island, Manhattan School of Music, and ultimately at Berklee (beginning in 1958). He maintained a rehearsal band during the late 1940s for his own compositions, was a member of the Metronome All-Star band in 1951, and was a founding member, with Charles Mingus and Teo Macero, of the Jazz Composer's Workshop in N.Y in 1953. His association with Mingus actually began in 1951, when he appeared on several recordings on Mingus's own Debut label. LaPorta gravitated more and more to teaching, but continued to play and record into the 1960s. He recorded for the first time in many years in 1985 for the Powerhouse label. Now retired from teaching, LaPorta lives in Fla.

DISC.: *Three Moods* (1954); *Conceptions* (1956); *South American Brothers* (1956); *Clarinet Artistry of John LaPorta* (1957); *Most Minor* (1958); *Eight Men in Search of a Drummer* (1961); *Alone Together* (1985); *Life Cycle* (1999). **WOODY HERMAN:** *Woodchopper's Ball, Vol. 1* (1944); *Northwest Passage, Vol. 2* (1945); *First Herd* (1945); *Thundering Herds 1945–1947* (1947); *Second Herd—1948* (1948). **HELEN MERRILL:** *Complete Helen Merrill on Mercury Records* (1954); *Dreaming of You* (1956). **CHARLES MINGUS:** *Complete Debut Recordings* (1951); *Jazz Experiments of Charles Mingus* (1954); *Moods of Mingus* (1954);

Jazz Composers Workshop (1954); *Jazzical Moods* (1954); *Mingus Revisited* (1960); *Pre-Bird* (1960). **CHARLIE PARKER:** *Bird: Complete on Verve* (1946); *Live Performances* (1948); *Essential Charlie Parker* (1949); *Charlie Parker with Strings: The Master Takes* (1953); *Confirmation: The Best of the Verve Years* (1954).—**LP**

Laporte, André, Belgian composer and teacher; b. Oplinter, July 12, 1931. He received training in musicology and philosophy at the Catholic Univ. in Louvain (graduated, 1956), and then was a student of Flor Peeters (organ) and Marinus de Jong (counterpoint) at the Lemmens Inst. in Mechelen (1956–58), where he received the Lemmens-Tinel Prize for organ, piano, and composition (1958); subsequently he attended the courses in new music in Darmstadt (1960–65). In 1963 he joined the staff of the Belgian Radio and Television in Brussels, where he later served as manager of its Phil. Orch. (from 1988). In 1968 he became a teacher of theory and analysis at the Brussels Cons., and then taught composition there from 1988. He also taught composition at the Chapelle Musicale Reine Elisabeth from 1990. In 1971 and 1976 he was awarded the Koopal Prize of the Belgian Ministry of Culture. His oratorio *La vita non è sogno* won the Italia Prize in 1976. In 1991 he was made a member of the Belgian Royal Academy.

WORKS: DRAMATIC: O p e r a : *Das Schloss* (1981–85). **ORCH.:** *Night Music* (1970); *Transit* for 48 Strings (1978–79); *Fantasia-Rondino con tema reale* for Violin and Orch. (1989). **CHAMBER:** *Introduction and Fughetta* for Guitar (1956); *Sequenza I* for Clarinet (1964) and *II* for Bass Clarinet and 3 Clarinets (1965); *Jubilius* for 12 Brasses and 3 Percussion (1966); *Ludus fragilis* for Oboe (1967); *Story* for 3 Viola da Gambas and Harpsichord (1967); *Inclinations* for Flute (1968); *Alliances* for Cello and Piano (1968); *Reflection* for Clarinet (1970); *Péripétie* for Brass Sextet (1973); *Harry's Wonderland* for Bass Clarinet and 2 Tapes (1976); *Incontro notturno* for 13 Winds and Percussion (1976); *Icarus's Flight* for Piano and 13 Strings (1977); *Variaties op een akkoord* for Recorder and Wind Quintet (1979); *A Flemish Round* for Clarinet, Trombone, Cello, and Piano (1980); *C-isme* for Cello (1984). **P i a n o :** Sonata (1954); *Ascension* (1967). **VOCAL:** *Psalm* for 6 Voices and Brass (1956); *De profundis* for Chorus (1968); *Le morte chitarre* for Tenor, Flute, and 14 Strings (1969); *La vita non è sogno*, oratorio for Narrator, Tenor, Baritone, Chorus, and Orch. (Ghent, Sept. 13, 1972); *Chamber Music* for Soprano, Flute, Clarinet, Violin, and Piano (1973).—**NS/LK/DM**

Laporte, Joseph de, French writer on the theater and music; b. Belfort, 1713; d. Paris, Dec. 19, 1779. He was a Jesuit abbé.

WRITINGS: *Almanach historique et chronologique de tous les spectacles de Paris*, I (1752); *Calendrier historique de théâtre de l'Opéra et des Comédies Française et Italienne et des Foires*, II (1753); *Les Spectacles de Paris, ou Suite du Calendrier historique et chronologique des théâtres*, III-XXVII (1754–78; continued by Duchesne and others); with J. Suard, *Nouveaux choix de pièces tirées des anciens Mercures et des autres journeaux*, LX-CVIII (Paris, 1762–64); *L'Esprit de l' "Encyclopédie" ou Choix des articles les plus curieux* (Geneva and Paris, 1768); with J. Clement, *Anecdotes dramatique contenant toutes les pièces de théâtres...jusqu'en 1775* (Paris, 1775); with S. Chamfort, *Dictionnaire dramatique contenant l'histoire des théâtres et les règles du genre dramatique* (Paris, 1776).
—**NS/LK/DM**

La Pouplinière, Alexandre-Jean-Joseph Le Riche de, French musical amateur; b. Chinon, July 26, 1693; d. there, Dec. 5, 1762. A wealthy member of the nobility and a statesman, he was a patron of music and a pupil of Rameau. The musical soirées he sponsored in his Paris home and Passy country estate became famous; his directors were Rameau, J. Stamitz, and Gossec. Upon Stamitz's advice, he added horns, clarinets, and a harp to his orch., instruments seldom heard in a concert orch. before that time. La Pouplinière wrote a number of arias, some of which Rameau incorporated into his own works.

BIBL.: G. Cucuel, *L. P. et la musique de chambre au XVIIIᵉ siècle* (Paris, 1913).—**NS/LK/DM**

La Presle, Jacques de, French composer; b. Versailles, July 5, 1888; d. Paris, May 6, 1969. He studied at the Paris Cons., and received the Grand Prix de Rome in 1921. In 1937 he was appointed prof. of harmony at the Paris Cons. His works include *Apocalypse de St.-Jean* (1928), *Album d'images*, suite for Orch. (1935), Piano Concerto (1949), chamber music, and songs.
—**NS/LK/DM**

Laquai, Reinhold, Swiss composer and teacher; b. Zürich, May 1, 1894; d. Oberrieden, Oct. 3, 1957. He studied at the Zürich Cons., and later with Busoni in Berlin. In 1920 he became a teacher at the Zürich Cons. Among his compositions were 2 operas *Der Schleier der Tanit* and *Die Revisionsreise*, many orch. works, including 3 syms., 5 overtures, 2 serenades, a concert piece for Piano and Orch., etc., chamber music, including trios, sonatas for violin, flute, cello, bassoon, horn, clarinet, etc., Piano Quintet, piano pieces, and more than 200 songs.—**NS/LK/DM**

Lara, Agustín, notably successful Mexican composer of popular songs; b. Mexico City, Oct. 30, 1897; d. there, Nov. 5, 1970. He was autodidact as a musician and never learned to read or write music. He was 13 when he began playing piano in bordellos and bars, eventually finding his métier as a composer of popular songs. After a stint on his own radio program (1930), he wrote the score for *Santa* (1931), one of the first Mexican talking pictures. He subsequently wrote songs for some 30 films. Between 1932 and 1934 he had enormous success with the songs *Granada*, *Señora tentación*, *La clave azul*, *Palmera*, *La cumbancha*, *Pregón de las rosas*, and *Noche criolla*. Several of his hits were translated into English and were taken up by Frank Sinatra (*Granada*), Bing Crosby (*You Belong to My Heart*), the Ames Brothers (*Be Mine Tonight*), and the Glenn Miller Orch. (*The Nearness of You*). Among his various wives was the film star María Félix, whom he married in 1945 and for whom he wrote the songs *María Bonita*, *Palabras de mujer*, and *Humo en los ojos*. *María Bonita* became an international favorite. Lara's career was the subject of Alejandro Galindo's film *La vida de Agustín Lara* (1958). Mexico granted him many honors, and in 1966 Generalissimo Franco of Spain accorded him honorary Spanish citizenship in recognition of the songs he wrote denoting such Spanish cities as Granada, Madrid, Valencia, and Toledo. By order of the president of Mexico, Lara was buried in the Rotondo de los Hombres Ilustres. In 1971 a Mexican postage stamp was issued to commemorate him. Lara wrote over 800 songs in a remarkably broad and adaptable style, including romantic ballads, pasodobles, rancheras, chotis, tangos, and marches.

BIBL.: D. Castañeda, *Balance de A. L.* (Mexico City, 1941); P. Taibo, *La música A. L. en el Cine* (Mexico City, 1984); idem, *A. L.* (Mexico City, 1985); G. Abaroa Martínez, *El Flaco de Oro* (Mexico City, 1993).—NS/LK/DM

Lara, Isidore de
See De Lara, Isidore

Larchet, John F(rancis), Irish composer and teacher; b. Dublin, July 13, 1884; d. there, Aug. 10, 1967. He studied in Dublin with Esposito at the Royal Irish Academy of Music before completing his training at the Univ. (B. Mus., 1915; D. Mus., 1917). From 1907 to 1934 he was music director of Dublin's Abbey Theatre. He also was prof. of composition at the Royal Irish Academy of Music (1920–55) and prof. of music at Univ. Coll., Dublin. He composed the orch. works *Lament for Youth* (1939), *Dirge of Oisin* for Strings (1940), and *By the Waters of Moyle* (1957), choral pieces, and songs.—NS/LK/DM

Laredo, Ruth (née Meckler), American pianist; b. Detroit, Nov. 20, 1937. She studied with Rudolf Serkin at the Curtis Inst. of Music in Philadelphia (B.M., 1960). In 1962 she made her debut with Stokowski and the American Sym. Orch. in N.Y. In 1965 she played in Europe with Rudolf and Peter Serkin; in 1977 she toured Japan. In 1960 she married **Jaime Laredo**, with whom she played numerous recitals; they were divorced in 1974. She is particularly fond of Russian music, and plays piano works of Rachmaninoff and Scriabin with passionate devotion.—NS/LK/DM

Laredo (y Unzueta), Jaime (Eduardo), Bolivian violinist, conductor, and teacher; b. Cochabamba, June 7, 1941. He was taken to the U.S. as a child, and studied violin with Antonio de Grassi and Frank Houser in San Francisco, where he made his formal debut as a soloist with the San Francisco Sym. at age 11. He continued his training with Gingold in Cleveland and Galamian at the Curtis Inst. of Music in Philadelphia. In 1959, a week before his 18th birthday, he won the Queen Elisabeth of Belgium Competition in Brussels, and subsequently appeared with great success in America and Europe as a soloist with leading orchs. The proud Bolivian government issued a series of airmail stamps with Laredo's picture and a musical example with the notes A, D, C in the treble clef, spelling his name in Latin notation (La- Re-Do). In 1960 he married **Ruth Laredo** (née **Meckler**) (divorced in 1974); his second wife was **Sharon Robinson**. With Robinson and the pianist Joseph Kalichstein, Laredo formed a trio in 1976, which toured extensively. He appeared regularly as a soloist and conductor with the Scottish Chamber Orch. in Glasgow from 1977, and led it on tours of the U.S. He taught at the St. Louis Cons. from 1983; was

appointed co-artistic director of the Philadelphia Chamber Orch. in 1985. In 1992–93 he held the title of Distinguished Artist of the St. Paul (Minn.) Chamber Orch. In 1994 he served as president of the jury of the International Violin Competition of Indianapolis. —NS/LK/DM

Larmore, Jennifer, highly regarded American mezzo- soprano; b. Atlanta, June 21, 1958. She was a student at Westminster Choir Coll. in Princeton, N.J. (1976–80), and later of John Bullock in Washington, D.C. In 1986 she made her European opera debut as Mozart's Sesto in France. From 1990 she pursued a major career, garnering critical accolades for her portrayal of Rossini's Rosina in Paris, London, and Rome. During the 1992–93 season, she sang that role in Berlin, as well as Bellini's Romeo at N.Y.'s Carnegie Hall, Rossini's Angelina in Florence, and Mozart's Dorabella at the Salzburg Festival. In 1993 she made her first appearance at London's Wigmore Hall as a recitalist. She won the Richard Tucker Award in 1994 and gave a recital at Lincoln Center's Walter Reade Theater in N.Y. On Feb. 6, 1995, she made her Metropolitan Opera debut in N.Y. as Rosina. She portrayed Rossini's Elvira at the Los Angeles Opera in 1996, and returned there as Carmen in 1998. In 1999 she sang Handel's Giulio Cesare at the Metropolitan Opera. As a soloist with orchs. and as a recitalist, she appeared widely in North America and Europe. Among other operatic roles of note are Monteverdi's Orfeo, Rossini's Arsace and Isabella, and Strauss's Octavian.—NS/LK/DM

LaRoca, Pete (Sims, Peter), jazz drummer; b. N.Y., April 7, 1938. He played timpani in the junior high symphonic band and continued at the H.S. of Music and Art in Manhattan; he then played timbales with Latin bands (where he adopted the name LaRoca, or "the rock"), and finally jazz drums in a Catskills show at age 17. He continued playing through two years at the City Coll. of N.Y., then from 1957 to 1959 worked intermittently with Sonny Rollins, including a European tour in February 1959. He also played with Jackie McLean (with whom he recorded what some consider the first free-time drum solo), Tony Scott, and Slide Hampton (ca. February–April 1960). John Coltrane hired him for his first quartet gigs with Steve Kuhn (May 2nd through Aug. 1960), probably on the recommendation of Miles Davis. In September of 1960, Coltrane chose to use Billy Higgins on the West coast to save the cost of transporting LaRoca. He continued to work with Kuhn in the bands of Stan Getz (1961–62), but was eventually replaced by Roy Haynes), and in a trio. He also worked with Paul Bley, Marian McPartland, and Charles Lloyd. He was house drummer at Boston's Jazz Workshop in 1963 and 1964, and also led his own groups. Around 1964–65 he did a quartet version of Ravel's short opera *L'Enfant et Les Sortileges*. In 1965 he and Kuhn played with Art Farmer. By 1967, he was back in N.Y., driving a taxicab and planning to study law at N.Y.U. LaRoca is now a practicing attorney, specializing in entertainment law and other areas, using his birthname, Pete Sims. For many years he was not heard from musically, but around 1990 he began leading a group one night a week at Birdland, displaying all of his old brilliance

Disc.: *Basra* (1965); *Pete LaRoca* (1965); *Bliss!* (1967); *Turkish Women at the Bath* (1967); *Swingtime* (1997). **SONNY CLARK:** *Sonny Clark Quintet* (1957); *Cool Struttin,' Vol. 1–2* (1958). **KENNY DORHAM:** *West 42nd Street* (1961); *Best of Kenny Dorham: Blue Note Years* (1964). **ART FARMER:** *To Sweden with Love* (1964); *Sing Me Softly of the Blues* (1965). **SLIDE HAMPTON:** *Sister Salvation* (1960); *Somethin' Sanctified* (1960). **JOE HENDERSON:** *Best of the Blue Note Years* (1963); *Our Thing* (1963); *Page One* (1963); *Blue Note Years* (1963); *Ballads & Blues* (1963). **JACKIE MCLEAN:** *New Soil* (1959); *Vertigo* (1959); *Bluesnik* (1961). **J.R. MONTROSE:** *Message* (1959); *Straight Ahead* (1959). **SONNY ROLLINS/SONNY ROLLINS TRIO:** *Complete Blue Note Recordings* (1956); *More from the Vanguard* (1957); *Night at the Village Vanguard, Vol. 1* (1957); *Night at the Village Vanguard, Vol. 2* (1957); *Night at the Village Vanguard* (1957); *St. Thomas 1959* (1993). **GEORGE RUSSELL:** *Outer Thoughts* (1960); *Outer View* (1962).—LP

La Rosa Parodi, Armando,

Italian conductor and composer; b. Genoa, March 14, 1904; d. Rome, Jan. 21, 1977. He studied in Genoa and Milan. He began his career as a conductor in 1929, and was active as a guest conductor in Genoa, Milan, Turin, and Rome. In 1963 he was named chief conductor of the RAI Orch. of Rome, a post he held until his death. He composed the operas *Il Mercante e l'avvocato* (1934) and *Cleopatra* (1938), and several symphonic works.—NS/LK/DM

La Rotella, Pasquale,

Italian composer and conductor; b. Bitonto, Feb. 26, 1880; d. Bari, March 20, 1963. He studied in Naples. He was choirmaster at Bari Cathedral (1902–13) and also taught at the Liceo Musicale there (1934–49); toured Italy as an opera conductor. His works included the operas *Ivan* (Bari, Jan. 20, 1900), *Dea* (Bari, April 11, 1903), *Fasma* (Milan, Nov. 28, 1908), *Corsaresca* (Rome, Nov. 13, 1933), and *Manuela* (Nice, March 4, 1948), and much sacred music.—NS/LK/DM

Larrivée, Henri,

French bass-baritone; b. Lyons, Jan. 9, 1737; d. Vincennes, Aug. 7, 1802. He sang in the chorus of the Paris Opéra, making his debut there in Rameau's *Castor et Pollux* in 1755. He subsequently distinguished himself in the operas of Gluck, creating the roles of Agamemnon in *Iphigénie en Aulide* (1774), Ubalde in *Armide* (1777), and Orestes in *Iphigénie en Tauride* (1779). Gossec wrote the title role of his opera *Sabinus* (1773) for him. His wife, Marie Jeanne (née Le Miere) Larrivée (b. Sedan, Nov. 29, 1733; d. Paris, Oct. 1786), was a soprano at the Paris Opéra (1750–77); she created the title role of Ernelinde in Philidor's opera of 1767, and also the role of Eponine in *Sabinus*.—NS/LK/DM

Larrocha (y de la Calle), Alicia de,

brilliant Spanish pianist; b. Barcelona, May 23, 1923. She studied piano with Frank Marshall and theory with Ricardo Lamote de Grignon. She made her first public appearance at the age of 5, and was soloist with the Orquesta Sinfónica of Madrid at the age of 11. In 1940 she launched her career in earnest. She began making major tours of Europe in 1947, making her first visit to the U.S. in 1955. Thereafter she toured throughout the world to great acclaim. She also served as director of the Marshall Academy in Barcelona from 1959. Her interpretations of Spanish music have evoked universal admiration for their authentic quality, but she has also been exuberantly praised by critics for her impeccable taste and exquisitely polished technique in classical works. —NS/LK/DM

Larsen, Jens Peter,

distinguished Danish musicologist; b. Copenhagen, June 14, 1902; d. there, Aug. 22, 1988. He studied mathematics and musicology at the Univ. of Copenhagen (M.A., 1928), then joined its staff and later obtained his Ph.D. there in 1939 with the diss. *Die Haydn-Überlieferung* (publ. in Copenhagen, 1939). He retired in 1970. A leading authority on the music of Haydn, he served as general ed. of the critical edition sponsored by the Joseph Haydn Inst. of Cologne from 1955 to 1960; his studies on the music of Handel are also of value. He was the son-in- law of **Mogens Wöldike**, with whom he ed. the hymnbook of the Danish Church (1954, 1973).

WRITINGS: *Drei Haydn-Kataloge in Faksimile: Mit Einleitung und erganzenden Themenverzeichnissen* (Copenhagen, 1941; 2nd ed., rev., 1979); *Weyses sange: Deres betydning for sangen i hjem, skole og kirke* (Copenhagen, 1942); *Handel's "Messiah": Origins, Composition, Sources* (Copenhagen, 1957; 2nd ed., rev., 1972); *Essays on Handel, Haydn, and the Viennese Classical Style* (tr. by U. Kramer; Ann Arbor, 1988).

BIBL.: N. Schirring, H. Glahn, and C. Hatting, eds., *Festskrift J.P. L.: Studier udgivet af Musikvidenskabeligt institut ved Kbenhavns universitet* (Copenhagen, 1972).—NS/LK/DM

Larsen, Libby (actually, Elizabeth Brown),

American composer; b. Wilmington, Del., Dec. 24, 1950. She was a pupil of Argento, Fetler, and Eric Stokes at the Univ. of Minn. (B.A., 1971; M.A., 1975; Ph.D., 1978). With Stephen Paulus, she founded the Minn. Composers Forum in Minneapolis in 1973, serving as its managing composer until 1985; she also was composer-in-residence of the Minn. Orch. (1983–87). Her works have been widely performed in the U.S. and abroad. One of her most impressive scores, the choral sym. *Coming Forth into Day* (1986), utilizes a text by Jehan Sadat, the widow of the slain leader of Egypt.

WORKS: DRAMATIC: Opera: *The Words upon the Windowpane* (1978); *The Silver Fox*, children's opera (1979); *Tumbledown Dick* (1980); *Clair de lune* (1984); *Frankenstein: The Modern Prometheus* (1989; St. Paul, Minn., May 25, 1990); *Mrs. Dalloway*, chamber opera (1992; Cleveland, July 22, 1993); *Eric Hermannson's Soul* (1997). **ORCH.:** *Tom Twist* for Narrator and Orch. (1975); *Weaver's Song and Jig* for String Band and Chamber Orch. (1978); *Pinions* for Violin and Chamber Orch. (1981); *Ringeltanze* for Men's Chorus, Handbells, and Orch. (1982; Grand Rapids, Mich., Dec. 3, 1983); *Deep Summer Music* (1983); *Parachute Dancing*, overture (1983); 5 syms.: No. 1, *Water Music* (1984), No. 2, *Coming Forth Into Light*, for Soprano, Baritone, Chorus, and Orch. (1985; St. Paul, Minn., April 14, 1986), No. 3, *Lyric* (1990–91; Albany, N.Y., May 3, 1991), No. 4 for Strings (1998), and No. 5 (Denver, Sept. 17, 1999); *Coriolis* (1986); *What the Monster Saw* (1987); Trumpet Concerto (1988); *Collage Boogie*

(1988); *3 Summer Scenes* (1989); *Cold, Silent Snow*, concerto for Chamber Orch. (1989); Piano Concerto, *Since Armstrong* (1989; Minneapolis, May 8, 1992); *Ghosts of an Old Ceremony* for Orch. and Dancers (Minneapolis, April 17, 1991); Marimba Concerto, *After Hampton* (1992); *Mary Cassatt* for Mezzo-soprano, Trombone, and Orch. (1993); *Ways of Spreading Light* for Orch. and Chorus (1994); *Overture for the End of a Century* (1994). **CHAMBER:** *4 on the Floor* for Violin, Cello, Double Bass, and Piano (1977); *Bronze Veils* for Trombone and Percussion (1979); *Ulloa's Ring* for Flute and Piano (1980); *Scudding* for Cello (1980); *Triage* for Harp (1981); *Aubade* for Flute (1982); *Jazz Variations* for Bassoon (1984); *North Star Fanfare* for Chamber Ensemble (1984); *The Astonishing Flight of Gump* for Chamber Ensemble (1986); *Juba* for Cello and Piano (1986); *Love and Hisses* for Double Wind Quintet (1986); *Black Birds, Red Hills* for Soprano, Clarinet, and Piano (1987); *Vive* for Flute Quartet (1988); *Xibalba* for Bassoon and 2 Percussionists (1989); *Aspects of Glory* for Organ (1990); *Schoenberg, Schenker, Schillinger* for String Quartet (1991); *Celebration of Light* for Chorus and Brass Quintet (1994). —NS/LK/DM

Larsén-Todsen, Nanny, Swedish soprano; b. Hagby, Aug. 2, 1884; d. Stockholm, May 26, 1982. She received her training at the Stockholm Cons., in Berlin, and in Milan. In 1906 she made her operatic debut at the Royal Theater in Stockholm as Agathe, where she then was a member from 1907 to 1922. After appearing at Milan's La Scala (1923–24), she made her Metropolitan Opera debut in N.Y. as Brünnhilde in *Götterdämmerung* on Jan. 31, 1925; she remained on its roster until 1927, singing such roles as Isolde, Rachel in *La Juive*, Fricka, Kundry, Elsa, La Gioconda, and Leonore. Returning to Europe, she sang in various opera centers, including London's Covent Garden (1927, 1930) and the Bayreuth Festivals (1927–28; 1930–31). Shortly before the outbreak of World War II in 1939, she became a voice teacher in Stockholm.—NS/LK/DM

Larson, Sophia, Austrian soprano; b. Linz, 1954. She studied at the Salzburg Mozarteum and with Ettore Campogalliani. In 1976 she made her operatic debut as Amelia Boccanegra in St. Gallen, and then sang in Ulm (1979–80) and Bremen (1980–83). She also appeared as a guest artist in Hamburg, Stuttgart, and Rome. In 1984 she made her first appearance at the Bayreuth Festival as Gutrune, and returned there to sing Venus in 1987 and Sieglinde in 1989. In 1985 she sang the Duchess of Parma in Busoni's *Doktor Faust* in Bologna. After appearing as Gutrune in Munich, Tosca in Turin, and Isolde in Toronto in 1987, she was a soloist in Britten's *War Requiem* at N.Y.'s Carnegie Hall in 1988. In the latter year, she also appeared as Senta in San Francisco. She sang Els in Schreker's *Der Schatzgräber* at the Holland Festival in 1992. In 1995 she made her British debut as Turandot in London.—NS/LK/DM

Larsson, Lars-Erik (Vilner), important Swedish composer and pedagogue; b. Åkarp, near Lund, May 15, 1908; d. Hälsingborg, Dec. 27, 1986. After passing the organist's examination in Växjö (1924), he studied with Ernst Ellberg (composition) and Olalla Morales (conducting) at the Stockholm Cons. (1924–29).

He then completed his training with Berg in Vienna (1929–30) and with Reuter in Leipzig (1930–31). Returning to Stockholm, he was a conductor, composer, and producer with the Swedish Radio (1937–43). Later he served as supervisor of its radio orch. (1945–47) and led its chamber orch. (until 1953). He was prof. of composition at the Stockholm Musikhögskolan (1947–59) and director of music at the Univ. of Uppsala (1961–65). His early compositions were in a classical spirit, but with time his idiom became increasingly complex; there are some instances of dodecaphonic procedures in his later compositions. The importance of his works lies in the freedom of application of various techniques without adhering to any current fashion.

WORKS: DRAMATIC: *Prinsessan av Cypern* (The Princess of Cyprus), opera (1930–36; Stockholm, April 29, 1937); *Arresten på Bohus* (The Arrest at Bohus), opera buffa (1938–39); *Linden*, ballet (1958). **ORCH.:** 3 syms. (1927–28; 1936–37; 1945); 3 concert overtures (1929, 1934, 1945); *Symphonic Sketch* (1930); *Sinfonietta* for Strings (1932); *Little Serenade* for Strings (1934); *Saxophone Concerto* (1934); *Divertimento* for Chamber Orch. (1935); *Little March* (1936); *Ostinato* (Stockholm, Nov. 24, 1937); *En vintersaga* (A Winter Tale), suite (1937); *Pastoral Suite* (1938); *The Earth Sings*, symphonic poem (1940); *The Land of Sweden*, suite (1941); *Gustavian Suite* for Flute, Harpsichord, and Strings (1943); *Cello Concerto* (1947); *Music for Orchestra* (1948–49); *Violin Concerto* (1952); 12 concertinos, with Strings, for solo instruments: Flute, Oboe, Clarinet, Bassoon, Horn, Trumpet, Trombone, Violin, Viola, Cello, Double Bass, and Piano (1953–57); *Adagio* for Strings (1960); *3 Pieces* (1960); *Orchestral Variations* (1962); *Lyric Fantasy* for Small Orch. (1967); *2 auguri* (1971); *Barococo*, suite (1973); *Musica permutatio* (1980; Swedish Radio, Feb. 27, 1982). **CHAMBER:** *Intimate Miniatures* for String Quartet (1938); 3 string quartets (1944, 1955, 1975); *4 tempi*, divertimento for Wind Quintet (1968); Cello Sonatina (1969); *Aubade* for Oboe, Violin, and Cello (1972). **Piano:** 3 sonatinas (1936, 1947, 1950); *Croquiser* (1947); *7 Little Preludes and Fugues* (1969). **VOCAL:** *Förklädd gud* (The Disguised God), lyric suite for Narrator, Soprano, Baritone, Chorus, and Orch. (1940); *Väktarsånger* (Watchman's Songs) for Narrator, Baritone, Men's Chorus, and Orch. (1940); *Missa brevis* for Chorus (1954); *Intrada Solemnis* for 2 Choruses, Boy's Chorus, Winds, and Organ (1964); *Soluret och urnan* (The Sundial and the Urn), cantata (1965–66).—NS/LK/DM

LaRue, (Adrian) Jan (Pieters), eminent American musicologist; b. Kisaran, Sumatra (of American parents), July 31, 1918. During this period in Sumatra, his father invented the budgrafting method now used on all rubber plantations. After attending Harvard Univ. (B.S., 1940), he pursued his studies in composition with Sessions and in musicology with Strunk at Princeton Univ. (M.F.A., 1942). He then saw military service (from 1943), and was active in the Okinawa Campaign. Following his discharge in 1946, he returned to Harvard Univ. to complete his education under Piston and Davison (Ph.D., 1952, with the diss. *The Okinawan Classical Songs: An Analytical and Comparative Study*). Having taught at Wellesley Coll. in 1942–43, he was again on its faculty from 1946 to 1957, and also served as chairman of its music dept. (1950–57). In 1957 he became prof. of music at N.Y.U. (dept. chairman, 1970–73; director of graduate studies, 1973–80), retiring in 1988 as prof. emeritus. In addition to a Fulbright

Research Followship (Austria, 1954–56), he received grants from the American Council of Learned Societies (1964), the Guggenheim Foundation (1965–66), and the National Endowment for the Humanities (1980–84). From 1966 to 1968 he was president of the American Musicological Soc., and in 1998 was made an honorary member. LaRue has written pioneering articles on style analysis, authenticity and style in 18th century music, harmonic rhythm in Beethoven's syms., the music of Okinawa, catalogues and bibliographical methods, watermarks, and computer aids to music. He served as ed. of the *Report of the Eighth Congress of the International Musicological Society* (2 vols., 1961–62), and as co-ed. of the *Festschrift Otto Erich Deutsch* (1963) and of *Aspects of Medieval and Renaissance Music: A Birthday Offering to Gustave Reese* (1966; 2nd. ed., 1978).

WRITINGS: *Guidelines for Style Analysis* (1970; 2nd ed., 1992); *A Catalogue of 18th-Century Symphonies* (1988); with M. Ohmiya, *Methods and Models for Comprehensive Style Analysis* (1988); *Writing on Music Style: Models for a Comprehensive Approach* (1994).

BIBL.: E. Wolf and E. Roesner, eds., *Studies in Musical Sources and Style: Essays in Honor of J. L.* (Madison, Wisc., 1990). —NS/LK/DM

La Rue, Pierre de (Petrus Platensis, Pierchon, Pierson, Pierzon, Perisone, Pierazon de la Ruellien), eminent Flemish composer; b. probably in Tournai, c. 1460; d. Courtrai, Nov. 20, 1518. The first record of his activities is as a tenor at Siena Cathedral (1482; 1483–85). He then was at 's-Hertogenbosch Cathedral (1489–92), and subsequently became a member of the Marian Brotherhood. He most likely was also a singer in Archduke Maximilian's Hofkapelle in Burgundy. He was canon at the court of Philippe le Beau in Mechelen (1501), prebend at Courtrai, Namur, and Termonde (from 1501), and cantor principis at Courtrai (1502). He returned to the Netherlands about 1508. He was a singer at the court of Margaret of Austria at Mechelen, and then served Archduke Karl (1514–16). He wrote 47 masses, several of which have been publ. in modern eds., as well as 7 Mass sections, 7 Magnificats, a Lamentation, motets, etc. For his works, see A. Tirabassi, ed., *Pierre de La Rue: Liber missarum* (Kassel, 1941), and M. Picker, *The Chanson Albums of Marguerite of Austria* (Berkeley and Los Angeles, 1965).

BIBL.: J. Robyns, *P. d.l.R. (circa 1460–1518): Een bio- bibliographische studie* (Brussels, 1954).—NS/LK/DM

Laruette, Jean-Louis, French tenor and composer; b. Paris, March 7, 1731; d. there, Jan. 10, 1792. He made his debut at the Opéra-Comique in Paris in 1752. In 1762 he became a member of the Comédie-Italienne when it merged with the Opéra-Comique, and sang there with notable success until 1779. Although he specialized in light tenor roles, he was heard in comic roles generally sung by basses. These roles are known to this day as laurettes. His importance as a composer rests upon his contribution to the development of the opéra-comique. His wife, Marie- Thérèse (née Villette) Laruette (b. Paris, March 6, 1744; d. there, June 16, 1837), was also a singer who appeared at the Paris Opéra and the Comédie-Italienne (1758–77).

WORKS: DRAMATIC: Opéras-comiques: (all first perf. in Paris): *Le docteur Sangrado* (Feb. 13, 1758; in collaboration with E. Duni); *L'heureux déguisement, ou La gouvernante supposée* (Aug. 17, 1758); *Le médecin de l'amour* (Sept. 22, 1758); *Cendrillon* (Feb. 21, 1759); *L'ivrogne corrigé, ou Le mariage du diable* (July 24, 1759); *Le depit genereux* (July 16, 1761); *Le guy de chesne, ou La fête des druides* (Jan. 26, 1763); *Les deux compères* (Aug. 4, 1772).—NS/LK/DM

Laschi, Luisa, Italian soprano; b. Florence, c. 1760; d. c. 1790. She made an acclaimed debut in Vienna on Sept. 24, 1784, in Cimarosa's *Giannina e Bernardone*. On May 1, 1786, she created the role of the Countess in Mozart's *Le nozze de Figaro* in Vienna. That same year, she married **Domenico Mombelli**, and thereafter sang with him frequently. She appeared in the first Viennese production of Mozart's *Don Giovanni* on May 7, 1788, but later that year she and her husband were dismissed from court service.—NS/LK/DM

Laserna, Blas de, Spanish conductor and composer; b. Corella, Navarre (baptized), Feb. 4, 1751; d. Madrid, Aug. 8, 1816. He was official composer for several theaters, and also conductor of the Teatro de la Cruz (1790–1818). He composed the music for Ramón de la Cruz's comedy *El café de Barcelona* (Barcelona, Nov. 4, 1788), as well as the operas *La gitanilla por amor* (Madrid, 1791; successful) and *Idomeneo* (Madrid, Dec. 9, 1792). His other works include incidental music to plays of Calderón, Lope de Vega, Moreto, etc., and many *tonadillas, sainetes,* etc.

BIBL.: J. Gómez, J. de Arrese, and E. Aunós, *El músico B. d.L.* (Corella, 1952).—NS/LK/DM

Las Infantas, Fernando de
See **Infantas, Fernando de las**

Láska, Gustav, Bohemian composer and double-bass player; b. Prague, Aug. 23, 1847; d. Schwerin, Oct. 16, 1928. He studied at the Prague Cons. with Hrabe, Kittl, and Krejči. Following a year of giving double-bass concerts, he joined the Court Orch. in Kassel (1868–72), then in Sondershausen (1872–75). He was a theater conductor in Göttingen, Eisleben, and Halberstadt. He played double bass in Berlin, and in 1878 he became double-bass player in the Court Orch. in Schwerin.

WORKS: *Der Kaisersoldat,* opera; *Deutsches Aufgebot,* cantata; 2 syms.; 2 overtures; Double-bass Concerto; 3 masses; several works for Double Bass and Piano *(3 Romanzen, Rhapsodie, Erotik, Ballade und Polonaise, Schlummerlied, Karneval von Venedig,* etc.); piano pieces; songs.—NS/LK/DM

Laskine, Lily, noted French harpist and teacher; b. Paris, Aug. 31, 1893; d. there, Jan. 4, 1988. She studied at the Paris Cons. with Alphonse Hasselmans and Georges Marty, winning a premier prix there in 1905. She was then a member of the orch. of the Paris Opéra (1909–26), and from 1934 made numerous tours as a soloist. She was a prof. of harp at the Paris Cons. (1948–58). In 1936 she was awarded the cross of the Légion d'honneur, and in 1958 she was made a chévalier.—NS/LK/DM

Laskovsky, Ivan Fyodorovich, Russian pianist and composer; b. St. Petersburg, 1799; d. there, 1855. After serving as a military officer, he was employed in the war office (1817–32). He studied with John Field and became an accomplished pianist. Among his stylish works for piano were mazurkas, waltzes, and variations. He also composed 3 string quartets.—**LK/DM**

Lasoń, Aleksander, Polish composer, conductor, and teacher; b. Siemianowice, Śląskie, Nov. 10, 1951. He studied jazz and popular music at the State Higher School of Music (later Academy of Music) in Katowice (1970–74), where he completed his training in composition with Józef Świder (honors degree, 1979). In 1980 he received the Beethoven Prize of the City of Bonn, and in 1987 and 1989 the Witold Lutosławski Scholarship Award. He became a prof. at the Cieszyn branch of the Silesian Univ. and at the Academy of Music in Katowice, where he was founder and conductor of the latter's new music orch. (from 1996). In 2000 he was honored with the title of prof. of musical arts.

WORKS: ORCH.: *Impresje* (Impressions) for Piano and Orch. (Katowice, June 26, 1974); 3 syms.: No. 2 for Wind Instruments, Percussion, and 2 Pianos (1975; Katowice, Dec. 18, 1976), No. 2, *Koncertujaca* (Concertante) for Piano and Orch. (1977–79; Poznań, April 11, 1986), and No. 3, 1999 for Chorus and Orch. (1996–97; Kraków, Oct. 26, 1997); *Góry* (Mountains; 1979–80; Warsaw, Sept. 17, 1983); *Concerto "Pablo Casals in memoriam"* for Cello and Orch. (1985; Poznań, April 14, 1988); *Katedra* (Cathedral; 1987–89; Warsaw, Sept. 20, 1990); *Hymn i aria* for Strings (Mikołow, June 16, 1993); *Concerto festivo* for Violin and Orch. (1993–95; Kraków, Dec. 8, 1995); *Credo* (Poznań, Sept. 20, 1997). CHAMBER: Violin Sonata (1970–71; Katowice, June 4, 1971); 2 sonatas for Solo Violin: No. 1 (1975; Warsaw, Feb. 28, 1978) and No. 2 (1983–84; Darmstadt, Oct. 3, 1985); *Muzyka kameralna* (Chamber Music) No. 1 for Piano and String Quartet (1974–78; Baranów Sandomierski, Sept. 8, 1979), No. 2 for Piano, 2 Horns, Trumpet, 2 Trombones, and Tuba (1976; Katowice, Jan. 17, 1977), No. 3 for Winds, Percussion, and Piano (Stalowa Wola, May 20, 1978), and No. 5 for Clarinet, Trombone, Piano, and Strings (1981; Poznań, April 1, 1989); Concerto for Piano and 3 Tapes (Stalowa Wola, May 18, 1976); *Music in 4 Movements* for Double Bass and Piano (Warsaw, Sept. 18, 1977); 3 string quartets: No. 1 (1979–80; Warsaw, Dec. 14, 1980), No. 2 (Warsaw, Sept. 21, 1987), and No. 3 (1992–93; Ontario, June 13, 1993); Wind Quintet, *Wioseny* (Spring; 1980–81; Poznań, April 5, 1981); *Relief dla Andrzeja* (Relief for Andrzej) for String Quartet (Katowice, Oct. 2, 1995); *"2 plus 2" dla Witolda* ("2 plus 2" for Witold) for Violin, Cello, and 2 Pianos (Katowice, March 3, 1997); *"20 dia 4"* ("20 for 4") for String Quartet (Rybna, Dec. 13, 1998); *Fanfary "50"* (Fanfares "50") for Chamber Ensemble (1999–2000; Warsaw, Jan. 21, 2000). VOCAL: Songs for Soprano and Piano (1973; Katowice, May 8, 1974); *Muzyka u Szekspira* (Music at Shakespeare's) for Baritone and Tape (Katowice, May 21, 1975); 3 Songs for Alto, Oboe, Violin, Cello, and Piano, after Kazimiera Iłłakowicz (Lusławice, Sept. 12, 1983); *Musica Sacra—Sanctus* for 4 Men's Voices, Organ, and String Orch. (Skoczów, May 24, 1998).—**LK/DM**

Lassalle, Jean (-Louis), French baritone; b. Lyons, Dec. 14, 1847; d. Paris, Sept. 7, 1909. After training in industrial design and painting, he entered the Paris Cons. to study voice. He also studied privately with Novelli, making his debut as St. Bris in *Les Huguenots* in Liège (1868). He then he sang in Lille, Toulouse, The Hague, and Brussels. He made his first appearance at the Paris Opéra in the title role of Rossini's *Guillaume Tell* (June 7, 1872), remaining there for more than 20 years, with extended leaves of absence, during which he toured throughout Europe, Russia, and the U.S. (debut, Metropolitan Opera, N.Y., Jan. 15, 1892, as Nelusko in *L'Africaine*). He was again on the Metropolitan Opera roster in 1893–94 and 1896–97. He returned to Paris in 1901 and settled there as a singing teacher, and in 1903 became a prof. at the Paris Cons. His repertoire comprised about 60 operas, ranging from Donizetti to Wagner.—**NS/LK/DM**

Lassen, Eduard, Danish conductor and composer; b. Copenhagen, April 13, 1830; d. Weimar, Jan. 15, 1904. His family moved to Brussels when he was a child. He entered the Brussels Cons., taking the Belgian Prix de Rome (1851). Following a tour through Germany and Italy, he went to Weimar, where Liszt fostered the presentation of his 5-act opera *Landgraf Ludwigs Brautfahrt* (1857). He was court music director in Weimar (1858–95), where he led the world premiere of Saint-Saëns's opera *Samson et Dalila* (Weimar, Dec. 2, 1877). He also wrote the operas *Frauenlob* (Weimar, 1860) and *Der Gefangene* (given in Brussels as *Le Captif*, April 24, 1865), the ballet, *Diana*, 2 syms., *Fest- Cantate*, two overtures, Te Deum, a set of *Biblische Bilder* for Chorus and Orch., songs, and incidental music.—**NS/LK/DM**

Lasso, Orlando di, great Franco-Flemish composer, also known in Latin as **Orlandus Lassus**, and in French as **Roland de Lassus**, father of **Ferdinand de Lassus** and **Rudolph de Lassus**; b. Mons, 1532; d. Munich, June 14, 1594. He entered the service of Ferrante Gonzaga when he was about 12 years old, and subsequently traveled with him. He then was placed in the service of Constantino Castrioto of Naples at the age of 18. He later proceeded to Rome and entered the service of Antonio Altoviti, the Archbishop of Florence. Lasso then was maestro di cappella at St. John Lateran (1553–54). He went to Antwerp (1555), where he enjoyed a fine reputation both socially and artistically; his first works were publ. that year in Venice, containing 22 madrigals set to poems of Petrarch; also that year he brought out a collection of madrigals and motets set to texts in Italian, French, and Latin in Antwerp. In 1556 he became a singer at the Munich court chapel of Duke Albrecht of Bavaria. He took Regina Wechinger (Wäckinger), an aristocratic woman, in marriage in 1558. In 1563 he was made maestro di cappella of the Munich court chapel, a position he held with great eminence until his death. He made occasional trips, including to Flanders to recruit singers (1560), to Frankfurt am Main for the coronation of Emperor Maximilian II (1562), to Italy (1567), to the French court (1571; 1573–74), again to Italy (1574–79), and to Regensburg (1593). On Dec. 7, 1570, he received from the Emperor Maximilian a hereditary rank of nobility. Lasso represents the culmination of the great era of Franco-Flemish polyphony; his superlative mastery in sacred as well as secular music renders him one of the most versatile composers of his time; he was equally capable of writing in the most elevated style and in the popular idiom; his art was supranational; he wrote Italian madrigals, German lieder, French chansons, and Latin motets. Musicians of his time described him variously as the "Belgian Orpheus" and the "Prince of Music." The sheer scope of his production is amazing: He left more than 2,000 works in various genres. The Patrocinium Musices (1573–98), a 12-vol. series publ. in Munich by Adam Berg, under ducal patronage, contains 7 vols. of Lasso's works: Vol. I, 21 motets; vol. II, 5 masses; vol. III, Offices; vol. IV, a Passion, vigils, etc.; vol. V, 10 Magnificats; vol. VI, 13 Magnificats; vol. VII, 6 masses. Lasso's sons publ. 516 of his motets under the title *Magnum opus musicum* (1604). Eitner publ. *Chronologisches Verzeichnis der Druckwerke des Orlando di Lassus* (Berlin, 1874). His collected works (21 vols., 1894–1926) were issued by Breitkopf & Härtel of Leipzig under the editorship of F. Haberl and A. Sandberger. The *Sämtlicher Werke, neue Reihe* began publication in Kassel in 1956. W. Boetticher publ. a complete catalogue of his works (Berlin, 1956).

BIBL.: H. Delmotte, *Notice biographique sur Roland Delattre connu sous le nom d'Orland de Lassus* (Valenciennes, 1836); A. Mathieu, *Biographie de Roland de Lattre* (Mons, 1851); W. Bäumker, *Orlandus de Lassus, der letzte grosse Meister der niederländischen Tonschule* (Freiburg, 1878); E. Destouches, *O. d.L.: Ein Lebensbild* (Munich, 1894); J. Declève, *Roland de Lassus: Sa vie et ses oeuvres* (Mons, 1894); E. Schmitz, *O. d.L.* (Leipzig, 1915); E. Closson, *Roland de Lassus* (Turnhout, 1919); R. Casimiri, *O. d.L., maestro di cappella al Laterano nel 1553* (Rome, 1920); C. Van den Borren, *Orlande de Lassus* (Paris, 1920); A. Sandberger, *O. d.L. und die geistigen Strömungen seiner Zeit* (Munich, 1926); C. Van den Borren, *En quelle année Roland de Lassus est-il né?* (The Hague, 1926); E. Lowinsky, *Der Motettenstil O. d.L.s* (Heidelberg, 1933); L. Behr, *Die deutschen Gesänge O. d.L.s* (Erlangen, 1935); E. Lowinsky, *Das Antwerpener Motettenbuch O. d.L.s und seine Beziehungen zum Motettenschaffen der niederländischen Zeitgenossen* (The Hague, 1937); L. Balmer, *O. d.L.s Motetten* (Berne, 1938); J. Huschke, *O. d.L.s Messen* (Leipzig, 1941); C. Van den Borren, *Roland de Lassus* (1944); W. Boetticher, *O. d.L. und seine Zeit, 1532–1594* (2 vols., Kassel and Basel, 1958; new ed. with suppl., 1998; Vol. III, index of works, 1999); H. Leuchtmann, *Die musikalischen Wortausdeutungen in den Motetten des Magnum opus musicum von O. d.L.* (Strasbourg, 1959); W. Boetticher, *Aus O. d.L.s Wirkungskreis, Neue archivalische Studien zur Münchener Musikgeschichte* (Kassel and Basel, 1963); H. Leuchtmann, *O. d.L.: Sein Leben; Briefe* (2 vols., Wiesbaden, 1976–77); F. Messmer, *O. d.L.: Ein Leben in der Renaissance* (Munich, 1982); J. Roche, *Lassus* (London, 1982); R. Orlich, *Die Parodiemessen von O. d.L.* (Munich, 1985); D. Zager, *The Polyphonic Latin Hymns of O. d.L.: A Liturgical and Repertorial Study* (diss., Univ. of Minn., 1985); R. Luoma, *Music, Mode, and Words in O. d.L.'s Last Works* (Lewiston, N.Y., 1989); J. Erb, *O. d.L.: A Guide to Research* (N.Y., 1990); D. Crook, *O. d.L.'s Imitation Magnificats for Counter-Reformation Munich* (Princeton, 1994); B. Schmid, ed., *O. d.L. in der Musikgeschichten: Bericht über das Symposium der Bayerischen Akademie der Wissenschaften, München, 4.-6. Juli 1994* (Munich, 1996).—**NS/LK/DM**

Lassus, Ferdinand de, German singer and composer, son of **Orlando di Lasso** and brother of **Rudolph de Lassus**; b. Munich, c. 1560; d. there, Aug. 27, 1609. He became a member of the Bavarian court chapel in Munich (1584), then entered the service of Friedrich von Hohenzollern-Sigmaringen (1585). He subsequently returned to Munich and Landshut (1590), becoming Kapellmeister (1602). With his brother, he prepared and publ. a comprehensive survey of his father's motets as the *Magnum opus musicum* (1604). His son, also named Ferdinand de Lassus (1592–1630), was also a musician. He studied in Rome and then was Kapellmeister in Munich (1616–29).

WORKS: *Cantiones sacrae* for 6 Voices (Graz, 1587); *Apparatus musicus* for 8 Voices and Basso Continuo (organ) (Munich, 1622); various other works in contemporary collections. —**NS/LK/DM**

Lassus, Rudolph de, German organist and composer, son of **Orlando di Lasso** and brother of **Ferdinand de Lassus**; b. Munich, c. 1563; d. there, 1625. He was made a member of the Bavarian court chapel (1585), and was its first organist (1589–1625); was also court composer to the Duke (from 1609). With his brother, he compiled and publ. the *Magnum opus musicum* (1604), a comprehensive survey of his father's motets. In some of his settings of the Magnificat, he parodied pieces by his father.

WORKS: *Teutsche Psalmen: Geistliche psalmen* for 3 Voices (Munich, 1588; ed. by W. Lipphardt, Kassel, 1928); *Cantiones sacrae* for 6 Voices (Munich, 1601); *Selectae aliquot cantiones* for 4 Voices (Munich, 1606); *Circus symphoniacus commissi in arenam Phonomachi* for 9, 11, and 12 Voices (Munich, 1607); *Triga musica qua missae odaeque Marianae triplice fugantur: In Viadanae modo* for 4 to 6 Voices (Munich, 1612); *Virginalia Eucharistica* for 2 to 8 Voices (Munich, 1615); *Ad sacrum convivium modi sacri* for 2 to 6 Voices (Munich, 1617); *Alphabetum Marianum triplici cantionum* for 2 to 4 Voices and Basso Continuo (organ) (Munich, 1621); *Cygnaeum melos* for 2 to 4 Voices, *una cum litaneis* for 4 Voices (Munich, 1626); *Missae* (Ingolstadt, n.d.; not extant); also works in *Pantheon musicum* (Paris, 1600).—**NS/LK/DM**

László, Alexander, Hungarian-American composer; b. Budapest, Nov. 22, 1895; d. Los Angeles, Nov. 17, 1970. He was a student of A. Szendy (piano) and Herzfeld (composition) at the Royal Academy of Music in Budapest. In 1915 he went to Berlin, where he was active as a pianist and worked in radio and films; he also taught in Munich. He constructed a "color piano" (Farblichtklavier) for the purpose of uniting tones with colors, which he demonstrated at the Kiel music festival (June 14, 1925). To establish a correspondence between the proportional wavelengths in both acoustic elements and light waves, he invented an instrument he called the Sonchromatoscope and a new system of notation he called Sonchromography. His book *Die Farblichtmusik* (1925) discusses his new technique. In 1938 he emigrated to the U.S. and in 1945 settled in Los Angeles, where he composed film and television scores. In addition to his many works for the Sonchromatoscope, he wrote stage music and orch. scores.—**NS/LK/DM**

László, Magda, Hungarian soprano; b. Marosvársárhely, 1919. She studied at the Budapest Academy of Music and with Irene Stowasser. In 1943 she made her operatic debut at the Budapest Opera, where she sang until 1946. She then became well known via her appearances on the Italian Radio. On Dec. 4, 1949, she created the role of the Mother in Dallapiccola's *Il Prigionero* in a Turin Radio broadcast, and then sang that role in its first stage performance on May 20, 1950, in Florence. Thereafter she sang in various Italian music centers, and also throughout Europe. In 1953 she appeared as Alceste at the Glyndebourne Festival, returning there in 1954 and again in 1962–63. On Dec. 3, 1954, she created the role of Cressida in Walton's *Troilus and Cressida* at London's Covent Garden. She also sang widely as a concert artist. In addition to roles in operas by such contemporary composers as Dallapiccola, Walton, Casella, Malipiero, and Ghedini, she was admired for her portrayals of Handel's Agrippina, Cherubino, Norma, Senta, Isolde, Busoni's Turandot, and Berg's Marie.—NS/LK/DM

Lateiner, Jacob, American pianist and teacher of Austrian-Polish descent; b. Havana, May 31, 1928. He studied piano with Jascha Fischermann in Havana (1934–40), with Isabelle Vengerova at the Curtis Inst. of Music in Philadelphia, where he also attended the chamber music classes given by Piatigorsky and Primrose. He likewise had lessons in compositions with Felix Greissle and Schoenberg. Having won the Philadelphia Youth Competition, he made his debut as soloist in Tchaikovsky's First Piano Concerto at a youth concert of the Philadelphia Orch. (Dec. 6, 1944); subsequently performed throughout America and in Europe. He appeared regularly in chamber music recitals with Heifetz and Piatigorsky. From 1963 to 1970 he taught at the Mannes Coll. of Music in N.Y., and in 1966 he was appointed to the faculty of the Juilliard School of Music in N.Y. In addition to the standard repertoire, he has played a number of contemporary scores. He was soloist in the premiere of Elliott Carter's Piano Concerto (1967).—NS/LK/DM

Lates, James, English violinist and composer; b. c. 1740; d. Oxford, Nov. 21, 1777. After studies in Italy, he was an orch. player in Oxford. He was also associated with the Duke of Marlborough's musical ventures in Blenheim. Lates was an accomplished composer of chamber music. Among his works, all publ. in London, were 6 Duets for 2 Violins (1761) and for 2 Flutes (1761), 6 Solos for Violin and Basso Continuo (c. 1765), and 6 Sonatas for 2 Violins and Basso Continuo (c. 1768), and for Violin, Cello, and Basso Continuo (c. 1775).—LK/DM

Latham, William P(eters), American composer and educator; b. Shreveport, La., Jan. 4, 1917. He studied trumpet at the Cincinnati Cons. of Music (1936–38). He received his B.S. degree in music education from the Univ. of Cincinnati (1938) and continued his studies at the Coll. of Music in Cincinnati (B.M., 1940; M.M., 1941). Subsequently he studied composition with Hanson and Elwell at the Eastman School of Music in Rochester, N.Y. (Ph.D., 1951). During World War II, he served in the U.S. Army as a cavalry bandsman and later as an infantry platoon leader in active combat in Germany in 1945. After the war, he taught at Iowa State Teacher's Coll. in Cedars Falls (1946–65), becoming a prof. at North Tex.

State Univ. in Denton in 1965, director of graduate studies in music in 1969, and Distinguished Prof. in 1978. He retired in 1984. He excelled as a composer of sacred choruses and band music; in the latter, he boldly experimented with modern techniques, as exemplified by his *Dodecaphonic Set* and, most spectacularly, in *Fusion*, in which he endeavored to translate the process of atomic fusion into musical terms through an ingenious application of asymmetrical rhythms.

WORKS: DRAMATIC: *A Modern Trilogy*, ballet (Cincinnati, April 2, 1941); *Orpheus in Pecan Springs*, opera (Denton, Tex., Dec. 4, 1980); *Orpheus in Cow Town*, scenic cantata for Soloists, Chorus, Orch., and Ballet (1997). **ORCH.:** *The Lady of Shalott* (1939; Cincinnati, March 7, 1941); *Fantasy Concerto* for Flute, Strings, and Harp (NBC, Cincinnati, May 5, 1941); *Fantasy* for Violin and Orch. (1946; Minneapolis, May 23, 1948); *And Thou America* (1947; Rochester, N.Y., Oct. 18, 1948); 2 syms.: No. 1 (Rochester, N.Y., April 25, 1950) and No. 2, *Sinfonietta* (1953; Fish Creek, Wisc., Aug. 20, 1955); Suite for Trumpet and Strings (Rochester, N.Y., May 4, 1951); *Concerto Grosso* for 2 Saxophones and Symphonic Wind Ensemble (Chicago, Dec. 16, 1960; rev. 1962 for 2 Saxophones and Chamber Orch.); Concertino for Saxophone and Symphonic Wind Ensemble (1968; rev. 1969 for Saxophone and Orch.); *American Youth Performs* (Fort Worth, Aug. 1, 1969); *Jubilee 13/50* (Sherman, Tex., Nov. 4, 1978); *Supernovae* (1983); *Excelsior K-2* for Piano and Chamber Orch. (Fort Worth, Tex., Sept. 13, 1994). **Band:** *Brighton Beach*, march (1954); *Proud Heritage*, march (1955); *3 Chorale Preludes* (1956); *Court Festival* (1957); *Passacaglia and Fugue* (1959); *Plymouth Variations* (1962); *Escapades* (1965); *Dionysian Festival* (1965); *Dodecaphonic Set* (Colorado Springs, Colo., March 11, 1966); *Prayers in Space* (1971); *The Music Makers*, with Chorus, Rock Group, Tape, and Guru (1972); *Dilemmae* (1973); *Prolegomena* (1974); *Revolution!* (1975); *Fusion* (1975; New Orleans, April 12, 1976); *March 6* (Dallas, Feb. 23, 1979); *Drones, Airs, and Games* (1983); *Suite Summertime* (Lake Texoma Band Camp, July 1, 1995); *Y2K-The "New Millennium March"* (1999). **CHAMBER:** 3 string quartets (1938–40); 3 string trios (1938–39); Oboe Sonata (1947); Violin Sonata (1949); *Suite in Baroque Style* for Flute and Piano (1954); Sonata for Recorder and Harpsichord (1959); *Sisyphus 1971* for Alto Saxophone and Piano (1971); *Preludes before Silence*, 9 pieces for Flute and Piccolo (1974); *Eidolons* for Euphonium and Piano (1977); *Ex Tempore* for Alto Saxophone (1978); *Ion, the Rhapsode* for Clarinet and Piano (1984). **VOCAL:** *River to the Sea* for Baritone and Orch. (Cincinnati, Dec. 11, 1942); *Peace* for Chorus and Orch., after Rupert Brook (1943); *Prayer after World War* for Chorus (1945); *Prophecy of Peace* for Chorus, Organ, Piano, and Cymbals (1951; also for Chorus and Orch., 1952, and Chorus and Small Wind Ensemble, 1961); *Music for 7 Poems* for Chorus and Orch., after James Hearst (1958); *Blind with Rainbows*, cantata for Chorus (1962); *Te Deum* for Chorus, Wind Ensemble, and Organ (1964); *A Lenten Letter* for Soprano, Strings, and Percussion, after Alexander Solzhenitsyn (Denton, Tex., Oct. 9, 1974); *St. David's Mass* for Chorus (1977); *Epigrammata* for Chorus (1978); *Gaudeamus Academe* for Chorus, Tenor, Announcer on Tape, Bass Drum, Cymbals, and Slapstick (1981; Denton, Tex., April 27, 1982); *Te Deum Tejas*, 8 songs for Soprano, Flute, and Percussion to texts by the composer (1981); *Bitter Land* for Chorus, Brass Quintet, and Piano (1985); *My Heart Sings*, anthem for Chorus and Organ (1987); *Missa Novella* for Young Choruses (1988); *Metaphors*, 3 songs for Soprano and Piano (1988); *A Green Voice*, cantata for Soprano, Tenor, and Piano (1989); *The Sacred Flame*, cantata for

Baritone and Orch. (Denton, Tex., June 9, 1990); *Only in Texas* for Chorus, Piano, and Percussion (Lewisville, Tex., April 10, 1994); *Requiem for My Love*, 3 songs for High Voice, after Mary Coleridge (1996).—NS/LK/DM

Latham-Koenig, Jan, English conductor and pianist; b. London, Dec. 15, 1953. He was a student of Norman del Mar, Kendall Taylor, and Lamar Crowson at the Royal Coll. of Music in London. In 1976 he founded the Koenig Ensemble, and also was active as a concert pianist until 1981. From 1981 to 1986 he was a member of the Cantiere Internazionale d'Artre in Montepulciano. In 1985 he conducted *Giulio Cesare* at the Royal Opera in Stockholm. He first conducted at the English National Opera in London with *Tosca* and at the Wesford Festival with *La straniera* in 1987. In 1988 he conducted the premiere of Bussotti's *L'ispirazione* in Florence. That same year he made his debut at the Vienna State Opera with *Macbeth*, and from 1991 he served as its principal guest conductor. He conducted Weill's *Aufsteig und Fall der Stadt Mahagonny* at the Maggio Musicale Fiorentino in 1990. In 1996 he conducted *Aida* at London's Covent Garden. In 1997 he became music director of the Opéra du Rhin and of the Orchestre Philharmonique in Strasbourg. As a guest conductor, he has appeared with many European and North American orchs. His repertoire is particularly noteworthy for its inclusion of rarely heard scores of the past and of various contemporary works.—NS/LK/DM

Latilla, Gaetano, Italian composer; b. Bari, Jan. 21, 1711; d. Naples, Jan. 15, 1788. As a child, he sang in the choir of the Cathedral in Bari, then studied at the Conservatorio di S. Onofrio in Naples. IIe was 2nd maestro di cappella at S. Maria Maggiore in Rome (1738–41), then was in Venice as maestro di coro at the Conservatorio della Pieta (1753–66) and as 2nd maestro di cappella at S. Marco (1762–70?). He subsequently returned to Naples about 1774. He wrote 46 operas, but the music to most is not extant. His works include *Li Mariti a forza* (Naples, 1732), *Angelica ed Orlando* (Naples, 1735), *Gismondo* (Naples, 1737; also known as *La finta giardiniera*; perf. as *Don Colascione*, London, 1749), *Madama Ciana* (Rome, 1738; perf. as *Gli Artigiani arrichiti*, London, 1750, Paris, 1753), and *I Sposi incogniti* (Naples, 1779), as well as the oratorio *L'onnipotenza e la misericordia divina*, 3 sinfonias, 6 string quartets, church music, etc.—NS/LK/DM

La Tombelle, (Antoine Louis Joseph Gueyrand) Fernand (Fouant) de, French organist and composer; b. Paris, Aug. 3, 1854; d. Château de Fayrac, Dordogne, Aug. 13, 1928. He first studied with his mother, and then at the Paris Cons. with Guilmant (organ) and Dubois (composition); also with Saint-Saëns. From 1885 to 1898 he was asst. organist at the Madeleine, and from 1896 to 1904 prof. of theory at the Schola Cantorum. He publ. the book *L'Oratorio et la cantate* (Paris, 1911). He wrote the operettas *Un Bon Numéro* (1892) and *Un Rêve au pays du bleu* (1892), as well as 2 ballets, orch. music, incidental music, oratorios, masses, motets, chamber music, organ works, and songs.—NS/LK/DM

Latrobe, Christian Ignatius, English composer; b. Fulneck, Leeds, Feb. 12, 1758; d. Fairfield, near Liverpool, May 6, 1836. After being educated by the United Brethren in Niesky, Upper Lusatia (1771–84), he became a minister in the Moravian Church. In 1795 he was made secretary of the Univ. of the Brethren in England, and was also active in the missionary field. Latrobe was a skillful composer and ed. of sacred music. He ed. the valuable collections *The Hymn-tunes of the Church of the Brethren* (London, 1790), *A Selection of Sacred Music from the Work of Some of the Most Eminent Composers of Germany and Italy* (6 vols., London, 1806–26), and *Anthems for One or More Voices Sung in the Church of the United Brethren* (London, 1811; includes 12 of his own anthems). He composed the cantatas *The Dawn of Glory* (1803) and *In Memory of a Beloved Sister* (1826), various anthems and hymn tunes, and 3 piano sonatas.

BIBL.: C. Stephens, *The Musical Works of C.I. L.* (diss., Univ. of N.C., 1971).—LK/DM

Lattuada, Felice, Italian composer; b. Caselle di Morimondo, near Milan, Feb. 5, 1882; d. Milan, Nov. 2, 1962. He studied at the Milan Cons. with Ferroni, graduating in 1911, and then was director of the Milan Civic School of Music (1935–62). He wrote an autobiography, *La passione dominate* (Bologna, 1951).

WORKS: DRAMATIC: O p e r a: *La tempesta* (Milan, Nov. 23, 1922); *Sandha* (Genoa, Feb. 21, 1924); *Le Preziose ridicole* (Milan, Feb. 9, 1929); *Don Giovanni* (Naples, May 18, 1929); *La caverna di Salamanca* (Genoa, March 1, 1938); *Caino* (Milan, Jan. 10, 1957). **OTHER:** Film scores. **ORCH.:** *Sinfonia romantica* (1911); *Cimitero di guerra*; *Il mistero della Passione di Cristo*; *Incanti della notte*; *Divertimento rustico*; *Prelude and Fugue.* **OTHER:** Chamber works; vocal pieces, including *Canto augurale per la Nazione Eletta* for Tenor, Chorus, and Orch.—NS/LK/DM

Laub, Ferdinand, eminent Czech violinist and composer; b. Prague, Jan. 19, 1832; d. Gries, near Bozen, Tirol, March 18, 1875. A child of great precocity, he studied violin with his father and made his first public appearance when he was 6. He then studied with Mořic Mildner at the Prague Cons. (1843–46). He toured Austria and Germany (from 1846), then studied counterpoint with Sechter in Vienna, where he was soloist in the orch. of the Theater an der Wien (1848–50). He subsequently performed in London, Berlin, Paris, and St. Petersburg before serving as Konzertmeister in Weimar (1853–55). He then was prof. of violin at Berlin's Stern Cons. (1855–57), and also chamber virtuoso to the Prussian court (1856–58). He founded a series of chamber music concerts in Berlin (1858–62) and Vienna (1862–66), then went to Russia, where he attained great distinction as a performer and teacher. He was made a prof. of violin at the Moscow Cons. (1866), but ill health compelled him to return in 1874 to his homeland, where he made his last appearance that same year. He was held in great esteem by his contemporaries; his repertoire extended from Bach to the masters of his own day. He composed several brilliant virtuoso pieces for his instrument, and also some vocal music. His son, Váša (Václav) Laub (b. Berlin, Dec. 31, 1857; d. Khabarovsk,

Nov. 23, 1911), was a choirmaster, piano teacher, and composer. He studied with his father in Moscow and later in Prague with Karel Bendl (1875), and wrote orch. music, choruses, piano pieces, and songs.

BIBL.: L. Ginzburg, *F. L.* (Moscow and Leningrad, 1951); B. Šich, *F. L.* (Prague, 1951).—**NS/LK/DM**

Laub, Thomas (Linnemann), significant Danish organist and composer; b. Langaa, Fyn, Dec. 5, 1852; d. Gentofte, near Copenhagen, Feb. 4, 1927. Following training in theology, he studied with Gebauer at the Copenhagen Cons. (1873–76). He subsequently was organist at Copenhagen's Hellingåndskirken (1884–91) and Holmens Kirke (1891–1925). He devoted his life to reforming ecclesiastical music in Denmark, restoring the melody, rhythm, and harmony of hymns to their primordial form and composing music reflecting that tradition. The Danish Hymn Soc. was organized in 1922 to propagate his ideas. He publ. the books *Vor musikundervisning og den musikalske dannelse* (Copenhagen, 1884), *Om kirkesangen* (Copenhagen, 1887), and *Musik og kirke* (Copenhagen, 1920; 2nd ed., 1938).

WORKS (all publ. in Copenhagen unless otherwise given): **VOCAL: S a c r e d :** *80 rytmiske koraler* (1888); *Kirkemelodier, firstemmig udsatte* (1888–90); *Salmemelodier i kirkestil* (1896–1902); *Forspil og melodier: Forsg i kirkestil* (1890); *Dansk kirkesang: Gamle og nye melodier* (1918; suppl., 1930); *Aandelige sange* (1925); *24 salmer og 12 folkeviser* (ed. by M. Wöldike; 1928); *Liturgisk musik* (ed. by Wöldike; 1937). **S e c u l a r :** *10 gamle danske folkeviser* (1890); *Danske folkeviser med gamle melodier* (1899–1904; 2nd ed., 1930); with C. Nielsen, *En snes danske viser* (1915–17); *Ti Aarestrupske ritorneller* (1920); *Tolv viser og sange af danske digtere* (Kolding, 1920; 2nd ed., 1938); with Nielsen, O. Ring, and T. Aagaard, *Folkehjskolens melodibog* (1922; suppl., 1927); *30 danske sange for 3 og 4 lige stemmer* (1922); *Faerske og danske folkevisemelodier udsatte for mandskor af Henrik Rung og Thomas Laub* (ed. by K. Clausen; 1942); *Danske folkeviser* (ed. by Wöldike and A. Arnholtz; 1948); *Sange med klaver* (ed. by H. Glahn and Wöldike; 1957).

BIBL.: P. Hamburger, *Bibliografisk fortegnelse over T. L.s litteraere og musikalske arbejder* (Copenhagen, 1932); idem, *T. L.: Hans liv og gerning* (Copenhagen, 1942).—**NS/LK/DM**

Laubenthal (real name, **Neumann), Horst (Rüdiger),** German tenor; b. Duderstadt, March 8, 1939. He began his studies in Munich and continued his training with **Rudolf Laubenthal,** whose surname he took as his own for his professional career. In 1967 he made his operatic debut as Don Ottavio at the Würzburg Festival, and then was a member of the Württemberg State Theater in Stuttgart from 1968 to 1973. In 1970 he appeared as the Steersman in *Der fliegende Holländer* at the Bayreuth Festival, and in 1972 sang Belmonte at the Glyndebourne Festival. In 1973 he became a member of the Deutsche Oper in Berlin. His guest engagements took him to the Vienna State Opera, the Bavarian State Opera in Munich, the Hamburg State Opera, the Paris Opéra, the Aix-en-Provence Festival, and other music centers. He was especially successful for his roles in Mozart's operas, and was particularly noted for his work as a concert artist.—**NS/LK/DM**

Laubenthal, Rudolf, German tenor; b. Düsseldorf, March 18, 1886; d. Pöcking, Starnberger See, Oct. 2,

1971. At first he studied medicine in Munich and Berlin; simultaneously took vocal lessons with Lilli Lehmann. In 1913 he made his debut in Berlin at the Deutsches Opernhaus, and sang there regularly; from 1919 to 1923 he also was engaged by the Bavarian State Opera in Munich. He made his Metropolitan Opera debut in N.Y. as Walther von Stolzing in *Die Meistersinger von Nürnberg* on Nov. 9, 1923; continued on the company's roster until 1933; he also sang with the Covent Garden Opera in London (1926–30) and made guest appearances in Chicago and San Francisco. In 1937 he retired from the operatic stage. He was primarily noted as a Wagnerian.—**NS/LK/DM**

Lauffensteiner, Wolff Jacob, Austrian lutenist and composer; b. Steyr (baptized), April 28, 1676; d. Munich, March 26, 1754. He went to Graz, where he was active as a lutenist by 1709. From 1712 to 1739 he was a valet and lutenist in the service of the Bavarian court in Munich. He was highly esteemed as both a lutenist and as a composer for the instrument.—**LK/DM**

Launis (real name, **Lindberg), Armas (Emanuel),** Finnish composer; b. Hameenlinna, April 22, 1884; d. Nice, Aug. 7, 1959. He studied cello and composition at the orch. school of the Helsinki Phil. Soc. (1901–07). After training with Klatte at the Berlin Stern Cons. (1907–08) and with Bauszern in Weimar (1909), he completed his studies with I. Krohn at the Univ. of Helsinki (Ph.D., 1913, with the diss. *Über Art, Entstehung und Verbreitung der Estnisch-Finnischen Runenmelodien;* publ. in Helsinki, 1913). In 1930 he settled in Nice.

WORKS: DRAMATIC: O p e r a : *Seitsemän veljestäf* (The 7 Brothers; Helsinki, April 11, 1913); *Kullervo* (Helsinki, Feb. 28, 1917); *Aslak Hetta* (Helsinki, 1922); *Noidan laulu* (The Sorcerer's Song; 1932); *Lumottu silkkihuivi* (The Magic Silk Kerchief; 1937); *Jehudith* (1940). **ORCH.:** *Andante religioso* for Violin and Orch. (1932); *Northern Suite* for Violin and Orch. (1950); *Karelian Suite* (1952). **CHAMBER:** Piano Quintet; piano pieces. **VOCAL:** 2 cantatas (1906, 1910); songs.—**NS/LK/DM**

Lauper, Cyndi (actually, **Cynthia Ann Stephanie),** MTV-ready chanteuse of the mid-1980s (b. Brooklyn, N.Y., June 22, 1953). After passing through several arts-oriented high school programs as a teenager, Lauper started playing in cover bands in clubs around N.Y.C., singing rock that ranged from Janis Joplin to Led Zeppelin. Eventually, she blew out her voice and spent a year recovering with vocal coach Katie Agestra developing a voice that crossed power and range with a Bettie Boop sensual vulnerability. Late in the 1970s she started working with John Turi in a project that eventually became Blue Angel. The band released a record in 1980 that passed virtually unnoticed. The band's failure drove her to bankruptcy and she took odd jobs like singing in a Japanese restaurant dressed as a geisha while her manager tried to find her a new deal.

That deal came in 1983, with Portrait records; Lauper's solo debut, *She's So Unusual* became one of the year's biggest records. Made with the aid of The Hooters and others, her first single was the catchy "Girls Just Wanna Have Fun." Propelled by a clever video that featured both Lauper's mother and professional wrestler Captain Lou Albano (who Lauper would later manage), the single went platinum and rose to #2. With her multi-colored hair and thrift-shop clothes, Cyndi Lauper was the perfect artist for the video age. She became an icon at MTV. She followed her first hit with the moody ballad "Time After Time," a song since covered by artists ranging from Miles Davis to Inoj. The tune topped both the pop and adult contemporary charts and went gold. She struck gold again with "She Bop," a bouncy pop confection that rose to #3. She then took Jules Shear's atmospheric ballad "All Through the Night" to #5 and the Brains "Money Changes Everything" to #27. The album got to #4, spent well over a year on the charts, earned Lauper a Best New Artist Grammy (and the art director a Best Album Package), and eventually went sextuple platinum. It was the first debut album and the first album by a solo artist ever to spawn five hit singles. In addition to playing nearly 300 concerts that year, Lauper also designed the T-shirts for the tour.

Striking while the iron was hot and capitalizing on the MTV demographic, Lauper sang the theme song to the film *The Goonies* taking "Goonies R Good Enough" to #10. She finally followed up with her sophomore album *True Colors* in 1986. With guest artists including Billy Joel and Chic's Nile Rodgers, the eclectic album did not veer too far from the pop mainstream. The title track, a well-drawn ballad, topped the charts and the follow-up, "Change of Heart"—featuring The Bangles on backing vocals—went to #3. Her cover of Marvin Gaye's "What's Going On" became the last pop hit off the record, hitting #12. The album also topped off at #4, going double platinum.

Lauper spent the next couple of years involved in various projects that did nothing to advance her career. She attempted acting in the movie *Vibes*, which got almost universally panned. She toured extensively, even visiting Russia. When she finally hit the record racks again with 1989's *Night to Remember*, she had lost momentum and the love of the critics. The album produced one hit, "I Drove All Night," which rose to #6, but the album stalled at #37 and didn't break a half a millions sales. In 1991, Lauper married actor David Thornton at a ceremony presided over by the Reverend (Little) Richard Penniman. That year also saw the release of her fourth album, *Hat Full of Stars*. Taking the reins of her own music, she coproduced the record and cowrote most of the songs, as well as directing all the videos. The critics were thrilled, but the fans still stayed away. No singles broke from the album and again it didn't break a half a million sales.

While Lauper remained popular overseas (particularly in Europe and Asia), she became somewhat of a curiosity in America. For this reason, her greatest hits collection, *Twelve Deadly Cyns...And Then Some*, was released worldwide (except in the U.S.) in 1994; when it finally was released here, it actually went gold. Similarly, her project with new collaborator Jan Pulsford,

Sisters of Avalon, came out in Japan a year before the rest of the world. As it came out, Lauper announced her pregnancy on national television, then went on a three-month tour with Tina Turner. Her son was born in November of 1997.

Lauper explored acting on the small screen, taking on an occasional role in the comedy *Mad About You*, for which she earned an Emmy nomination. In 1998, Lauper concluded her contract with Sony by releasing a holiday album, *Merry Christmas...Have a Nice Life!*. She recorded a version of the Trampps's *Saturday Night Fever* hit "Disco Inferno" for the *Night at the Roxbury* soundtrack, and in the summer of 1999, it became a club hit. The turn of the century found Lauper shopping for a new label and developing a situation comedy for NBC.

DISC.: *She's So Unusual* (1984); *True Colors* (1986); *A Night to Remember* (1989); *A Hat Full of Stars* (1992); *Twelve Deadly Cyns* (1995); *Girls Just Want to Have Fun* (1995); *Sisters of Avalon* (1997); *Merry Christmas...Have a Nice Life!* (1998).—**HB**

Laurence, Elizabeth, English mezzo-soprano; b. Harrogate, Nov. 22, 1949. She studied at the Trinity Coll. of Music in London, and then pursued a concert career in Europe. In 1986 she sang Stravinsky's Jocasta at the Madrid Opera. She appeared in the premiere of Osborne's *The Electrification of the Soviet Union* at the Glyndebourne Festival in 1987. In 1988 she sang in the rev. version of Boulez's *Le visage nuptial* at Milan's La Scala and appeared as Fricka in *Das Rheingold* in Paris. Her debut at London's Covent Garden followed in 1989 in the British premiere of Berio's *Un re in Ascolto*, where she returned in 1991 to sing in the premiere of Birtwistle's *Gawain*. In 1989 she also sang in the premiere of Höller's *Der Meister und Margarita* in Paris. She was engaged to sing in the premiere of Osborne's *Terrible Mouth* in London in 1992. In 1993 she sang at the Salzburg Festival, returning there in 1996. In 1998 she appeared in *Lulu* in Paris.—**NS/LK/DM**

Laurencie, Lionel de la
   See **La Laurencie, Lionel de**

Laurenti, Bartolomeo Girolamo, Italian violinist and composer; b. Bologna, c. 1644; d. there, Jan. 18, 1726. He spent his entire life in his native city. After studying violin with Gaibrara, he was a violinist at the Basilica San Petronio until 1706. He was one of the earliest members of the Accademia Filarmonica. He publ. *12 Suonata per camera a violino e violoncello* (Bologna, 1691) and *Sei concerti a tre, cioè violino, violoncello ed organo* (Bologna, 1720). One of his sonatas also was publ. in a collection by C. Buffagnotti (c. 1700).—**NS/LK/DM**

Laurenzi, Filiberto, Italian composer; b. Bertinoro, near Forlì, c. 1620; d. after 1651. He was in Rome by 1633, where he was a soprano at S. Luigi dei Francesi. In 1640 he settled in Venice. He wrote the operas *La finta savia* (Venice, Carnival 1643; in collaboration with others) and *L'esiglio d'Amore* (Ferrara, 1651; in collaboration with A. Mattioli). He also publ. *Concerti ed arie* for 1 to 3 Voices, *con una serenata* for 5 Voices, 2 Violins, and Chittarone (Venice, 1641) and *Spiritualiun cantionum, liber primus* for 1 Voice (Venice, 1644).—**LK/DM**

Lauri-Volpi, Giacomo, famous Italian tenor; b. Lanuvio, near Rome, Dec. 11, 1892; d. Valencia, March 17, 1979. He received training in law before turning to vocal studies with Antonio Cotogni at the Accademia di Santa Cecilia in Rome; he completed his vocal training with Enrico Rosati. In 1919 he made his operatic debut under the name Giacomo Rubini in Viterbo as Arturo in *I Puritani*. He sang for the first time under his real name in Rome in 1920 as Des Grieux in *Manon*. In 1922 he made his debut at Milan's La Scala as the Duke of Mantua, and continued to sing there as a great favorite until the outbreak of World War II in 1939. On Jan. 26, 1923, he made his Metropolitan Opera debut in N.Y. as the Duke of Mantua, and subsequently was one of the principal members on its roster until 1933. While at the Metropolitan, he sang Calaf in the U.S. premiere of *Turandot* on Nov. 16, 1926, and also had notable success in such roles as Cavaradossi, Radamès, Pollione, Alfredo, Canio, Faust, and Rodolfo. In 1925 and in 1936 he was a guest artist at London's Covent Garden. On Feb. 28, 1928, he appeared as Boito's Nerone at the opening of the new Teatro Reale dell'Opera in Rome. He sang Arnold in the centenary staging of Rossini's *Guillaume Tell* at La Scala in 1929, and also appeared at the Paris Opéra and Opéra-Comique that same year. He settled in Burjasot, near Valencia. After World War II ended, he resumed singing in Italy, as well as in Spain. In 1959 he retired from public performances. However, in 1972, when he was in his 80th year, he astounded an audience at a gala performance at Barcelona's Teatro Liceo when he sang *Nessun dorma* from *Turandot*. At the apex of his career, Lauri-Volpi was hailed as one of the foremost lyrico-dramatic tenors of his era. The range and flexibility of his voice, his command of declamation, and his glorious legato, were memorable. He publ. the books *L'equivoco* (Milan, 1938), *Cristalli viventi* (Rome, 1948), *A viso aperto* (Milan, 1953), *Voci parallele* (Milan, 1955), and *Misteri della voce umana* (Milan, 1957).

BIBL.: J. Menéndez, *G. L.-V.* (Madrid, 1990).—NS/LK/DM

Lauro, Antonio, Venezuelan guitarist and composer; b. Ciudad Bolívar, Aug. 3, 1909; d. Caracas, April 17, 1986. He studied in Caracas. He wrote much guitar music, including a Guitar Concerto (Caracas, July 25, 1956, composer soloist), a choral symphonic poem, *Cantacharo*, several symphonic suites, choruses, and songs.—NS/LK/DM

Lauska, Franz (Seraphinus Ignatius), Bohemian pianist, teacher, and composer; b. Brünn, Jan. 13, 1764; d. Berlin, April 18, 1825. He studied in Vienna with Albrechtsberger, and was a chamber musician in Munich. From 1794 to 1798 he taught in Copenhagen. He settled in Berlin in 1798, becoming a teacher at the court and numbering among his pupils Meyerbeer. He wrote 24 sonatas (*Grande sonate, Sonate pathétique*, etc.), Cello Sonata, pieces for Piano, 4-hands (*6 Easy and Agreeable Pieces, Polonaise*, etc.), variations for 2-hands, rondos, etc.—NS/LK/DM

Lautenbacher, Susanne, German violinist; b. Augsburg, April 19, 1932. She studied at the Munich Hochschule für Musik, and took private lessons with Szeryng. She then appeared in Europe as a soloist and chamber music player and also taught violin. She was praised for her sensitive performances of the classical violin repertoire.—NS/LK/DM

Lavagne, André, French composer; b. Paris, July 12, 1913. He studied at the Paris Cons., winning first prize in piano (1933) and Premier Second Grand Prix de Rome (1938). In 1941 he was appointed inspector of music in Paris schools.

WORKS: DRAMATIC: Opera: *Comme ils s'aiment* (Paris, 1941); *Corinne* (Enghiens-les-Bains, 1956). OTHER: Several ballets (*Le Pauvre Jongleur, Kermesse* et al.). ORCH.: *Concert dans un parc* for Piano and Orch., inspired by Watteau's painting (1941); *Concerto romantique* for Cello and Orch. (1941). VOCAL: *Nox*, symphonic poem for Voice and Orch.; *Spectacle rassurant* for Voice and Orch.—NS/LK/DM

Lavagnino, Angelo Francesco, Italian composer; b. Genoa, Feb. 22, 1909; d. Gavi, Aug. 21, 1987. He studied with Renzo Rossi and Vito Frazzi at the Milan Cons., graduating in 1933. From 1948 to 1962 he was a prof. of film music at the Accademia Musicale in Siena. Among his compositions were an opera, *Malafonte* (Antwerp, 1952), the orch. pieces *Volo d'api* (1932), *Tempo alto* (1938), Violin Concerto (1941), and *Pocket Symphony* (1949), Piano Quintet (1942), and Violin Sonata (1943). —NS/LK/DM

Lavallée, Calixa, Canadian composer, pianist, conductor, and teacher; b. Verchères, Lower Canada (Quebec), Dec. 28, 1842; d. Boston, Jan. 21, 1891. His father (Jean-Baptiste André) Augustin Paquet dit Lavallée (b. Verchères, 1816; d. Montreal, Feb. 15, 1903), was a luthier, bandmaster, teacher, and music dealer. After initial training with him, he displayed proficiency as a pianist, violinist, organist, and cornetist. He also attended college in St.-Hyacinthe before going to Montreal to pursue training in piano with Paul Letondal and Charles Sabatier. In 1857 he went to the U.S., and during the Civil War served as principal cornet in the 4th R.I. Regiment (1861–62). Following his discharge, he was active in Canada (1862–65). In 1865 he returned once again to the U.S., eventually going to N.Y. as music director of the Grand Opera House (c. 1870). After further studies in Paris (1873–75) with Marmontel (piano) and Bazin and Boieldieu fils (composition), he went to Quebec City as choirmaster at St. James church (until 1879). When a national convention of French Canadians was announced, Lavallée proceeded to compose the music to a national song, "O Canada," to a text by Judge A.-B. Routhier, which was first performed with great success in Quebec City on June 24, 1880. After serving as accompanist to Etelka Gerster in the U.S., he settled in Boston about 1882 and taught at the Carlyle Petersilea Music Academy and was choirmaster at the Roman Catholic Cathedral of the Holy Cross. He also became a prominent figure in the Music Teachers' National Assn. Under its auspices, he organized and participated in the first concert ever devoted exclusively to American composers at its gathering in Cleveland on

July 3, 1884. In 1886 he was elected its president, and represented the organization at the National Soc. of Professional Musicians in London in 1888. Returning to the U.S., he resumed his varied activities until ill health overtook him in 1890. Lavallée was a pioneering figure in Canadian music who also contributed much to American music. As a composer, he was adept at producing operettas, cantatas, ballads, and piano pieces. In addition to "O Canada," he remains best known for his brilliantly written piano pieces, the most celebrated of which is his *Le Papillon*.

BIBL.: E. Lapierre, *C. L.: Musicien national du Canada* (Montreal, 1936); L.-J.-N. Blanchet, *Une vie illustrée de C. L.* (Montreal, 1951).—NS/LK/DM

Lavalle-García, Armando,

Mexican composer; b. Ocotlán, Jalisco, Nov. 23, 1924. He studied violin at the National Cons. of Music in Mexico City and took courses in composition with Bernal Jiménez, Revueltas, and R. Halffter. He subsequently played viola with the National Sym. Orch. of Mexico City and conducted the Xalapa Sym. Orch. His music is permeated with the essence of Mexican folklore, even in pieces of ostensibly abstract connotations.

WORKS: DRAMATIC: B a l l e t : *La canción de los Buenos Principios* (1957); *3 tiempos de amor* (1958); *Corrido* (1959). **ORCH.:** *Mi viaje*, symphonic poem (1950); *Estructuras geométricas* for Strings and Percussion (1960); Concerto for Viola and Strings (1965); Concerto for Violin, Strings, and Percussion (1966). **CHAMBER:** *Divertimento* for Wind Quintet (1953); Violin Sonata (1966); Oboe Sonata (1967); *Potencial* for Guitar, Psaltery, Harp, and Percussion (1967); *Trigonos* for Flute, Clarinet, and Bassoon (1968); Trio for Oboe, Bassoon, Cello, and Percussion (1969).—NS/LK/DM

LaVere, Charlie (Johnson, Charles La-Vere),

jazz pianist, leader, singer, songwriter; b. Salina, Kans., July 18, 1910; d. April 28, 1983. LaVere began playing piano from the age of seven, and began his professional career with a cousin, Stan Weis, as "Dan and Stan." He moved to Okla. City to attend college, and played alto sax (with Charlie Teagarden) in Herb Cook's Oklahoma Joy Boys. He left Okla. with Frank Williams and his Oklahomans, and was stranded in N.Y. at the end of the tour, ca. 1931. He subsequently toured with various groups, ending up in Chicago in 1933 working with Wingy Manone; he also recorded with Jack Teagarden at this time. After touring Tex. with Eddie Neibauer, he led his own all-star recording group in Chicago in 1935, which featured Jabbo Smith, Zutty Singleton, Joe Marsala, and Boyce Brown. In 1937, he moved to N.Y. and joined Paul Whiteman's Orch. until early 1938, when he relocated to L.A. He began a long career of working on radio and in studios, including regularly accompanying Bing Crosby on broadcasts until 1947. He had a million-seller record as vocalist with Gordon Jenkins in 1947, "Maybe You'll Be There." Through the late 1940s and 1950s, he led a Dixieland sextet with various personnel. From 1955–59, he played for the Golden Horse Shoe Revue at Disneyland. After a brief stint in N.Y. towards the end of 1960, he moved to Las Vegas (1961–63), playing solo residencies, and also

worked with Bob Crosby (late 1961 to early 1962) and with Wingy Manone (spring 1963). He returned to Southern Calif. in June 1963, for solo spots, theatre work, and a spell with Jack Coon, and also played on two cruises to Australia. He arranged and played for Russ Morgan in Las Vegas (1967), and then returned to Southern Calif. where he continued to play regularly through the 1970s, and also ran a piano-repair and tuning service. His compositions include: "The Blues Have Got Me" and "Cuban Boogie Woogie," among other pop numbers.—JC/LP

Lavigna, Vincenzo,

Italian composer and teacher; b. Altamura, Feb. 21, 1776; d. Milan, Sept. 14, 1836. He studied at the Cons. di S. Maria di Loreto in Naples, subsequently going to Milan, where he was maestro al cembalo at La Scala (1802–32). He also was prof. of solfeggio at the Milan Cons. (from 1823); he was a teacher of Verdi. He wrote 10 operas, of which his first, *La muta per amore, ossia Il Medico per forza* (Milan, 1803), was his best. He also composed 2 ballets.

BIBL.: G. De Napoli, *La triade melodrammatica altamurana: Giacamo Tritto, V. L., Saverio Mercadante* (Milan, 1931). —NS/LK/DM

Lavignac, (Alexandre Jean) Albert,

eminent French musicologist and pedagogue; b. Paris, Jan. 21, 1846; d. there, May 28, 1916. He studied at the Paris Cons. with Marmontel (piano), Bazin and Benoist (harmony), and A. Thomas (composition), winning first prize for *solfège* in 1857, for piano in 1861, for harmony and accompaniment in 1863, and for counterpoint and fugue in 1864; he won second prize for organ in 1865. He was appointed asst. prof. of solfege (1871), prof. of *solfège* (1875), and then prof. of harmony (1891) there. His *Cours complet théorique et pratique de dictée musicale* (6 vols., Paris and Brussels, 1882) attracted considerable attention and led to the introduction of musical dictation as a regular subject in all the important European conservatories; it was followed by *Dictées musicales* (additional exercises) in 1900. His magnum opus was the famous *Encyclopédie de la musique et Dictionnaire du Conservatoire* (Paris, 3 vols., 1920–31), which he ed. from 1913 until his death. Other writings include *École de la pédale du piano* (Paris, 1889), *La Musique et les musiciens* (Paris, 1895; 8th ed., 1910; entirely rev., 1950; Eng. tr. by H. Krehbiel, 1899), *Le Voyage artistique à Bayreuth* (Paris, 1897; rev. ed. by H. Busser, 1951; Eng. tr. as *The Music Dramas of Richard Wagner*, 1898; second Eng. ed., 1904), *Les Gaîtés du Conservatoire* (Paris, 1900), *L'Éducation musicale* (Paris, 1902; 4th ed., 1908; Eng. tr., 1903), *Notions scolaires de musique* (Paris and Brussels, 1905), and *Théorie complète des principes fondamentaux de la musique moderne* (Paris and Brussels, 1909).—NS/LK/DM

La Violette, Wesley,

American composer and teacher; b. St. James, Minn., Jan. 4, 1894; d. Escondido, Calif., July 29, 1978. He studied at the Northwestern Univ. School of Music (graduated, 1917) and at the Chicago Musical Coll. (D.Mus., 1925), where he was a member of the faculty (1923–33). After teaching at De Paul Univ. in Chicago (1933–40), where he also was director of De Paul Univ. Press, he taught at the Los Angeles Cons. (from 1946). He also was active as a lecturer on philosophy, religion, and the arts. Among his books were *Music and its Makers* (1938) and *The Crown of Wisdom* (1949), the latter devoted to religious mysticism. His compositions followed generally along traditional pathways, although he was not adverse to atonal usages.

WORKS: DRAMATIC: *Shylock*, opera (1927); *Schubertiana*, ballet (1935); *The Enlightened One*, opera (1935). ORCH.: *Penetrella* for Strings (Chicago, Nov. 30, 1928); *Osiris* (1929); 2 violin concertos (1929, 1938); 3 syms.: No. 1 (1936; Rochester, N.Y., Oct. 19, 1938), No. 2 (1939; Chicago, May 25, 1942), and No. 3 (1952); *Chorale* (Chicago, July 31, 1936); Piano Concerto (1937); Concerto for String Quartet and Orch. (1939); *Music from the High Sierras* (San Francisco, March 4, 1941); Flute Concertino (1943). CHAMBER: 3 string quartets (1926, 1933, 1936); Piano Quintet (1927); Sonata for 2 Violins (1931); Octet (1934); 2 violin sonatas (1934, 1937); Sextet for Piano, Flute, Oboe, Clarinet, Bassoon, and Horn (1940); Flute Quintet (1943). VOCAL: Choral pieces; songs.—NS/LK/DM

Lavista, Mario, Mexican composer; b. Mexico City, April 3, 1943. He studied harmony with R. Halffter and composition with Quintanar, and then attended classes and seminars of Stockhausen, Pousseur, Xenakis, and Ligeti in Darmstadt and Cologne. Returning to Mexico in 1970, he founded Quanta, an improvisational music group. In his music, he explores all resources of sound, and all idiomatic textures, from deliberate homophony to horrendous explosions of ear-splitting dissonance.

WORKS: DRAMATIC: Opera: *Aura* (1988–89). ORCH.: *Lyhannh* (1976; the title is Swift's word for the "swallow" in Part 4 of *Gulliver's Travels*); *Ficciones* (1980); *Clepsidra* (1990); *Lacrymosa in Memory of Gerhart Muench* (1992); *Tropo for Sor Juana* (1995). CHAMBER: *5 Pieces* for String Quartet (1967); *Divertimento* for Wind Quintet, 5 Woodblocks, and 3 Shortwave Radios (1968); 6 string quartets: No. 1, *Diacronía* (1969), No. 2, *Reflections of the Night* (1984; also for String Orch., 1986), No. 3, *Music for My Neighbor* (1995), No. 4, *Sinfonias* (1996), No. 5, *7 Inventions* (1998), and No. 6, *Suite in 5 Parts* (1999); *Game* for Flute (1970); *Continuo* for Brass, Percussion, 2 Prepared Pianos, and Strings (1970); Trio for 2 String Instruments and Ring Modulator (1972); *Diafonia* for 1 Performer on 2 Pianos and Percussion (1973); *Antifonia* for Flute, 2 Bassoons, and Percussion (1974); *Dialogos* for Violin and Piano (1974); *Quotations* for Cello and Piano (1975); Piano Trio (1976); *Marsias* for Oboe and 8 Crystal Glasses (1982); *Madrigal* for Clarinet (1985); *Responsorio in Memoriam Rodolfo Halffter* for Bassoon, 2 Bass Drums, and 4 Tubular Chimes (1988); *El Pífano: Portrait of Manet* for Piccolo (1989); *Las Musicas Dormidas* for Clarinet, Bassoon, and Piano, after Tamyao's painting (1990); *Dance of Degas' Dancers* for Flute and Piano (1991); *Isorhythmic Dance* for 4 Percussionists (1996); Wind Octet (1997). Piano: *Piece* for 1 Pianist and 1 Piano (1970; also as *Piece* for 2 Pianists and 2 Pianos, in which a second pianist maintains an absolute silence that must be "communicated" to the listeners); *Cluster* (1973); *Espejos* for Piano, 4-hands (1975); *Jaula* for any number of Prepared Pianos and Pianists (1976); *Simurg* (1980). VOCAL: *Monologue* for Baritone, Flute, Vibraphone, and Double Bass, after Gogol's *Diary of a Madman* (1966); *Homage to Samuel Beckett* for 3 Amplified Choruses (1968); *3 Nocturnes* for Mezzo-soprano and Orch. (1985); *From the Beginning* for Mezzo-soprano and Orch. (1985); *Missa Brevis ad Consolationis Dominam Nostram*

for Chorus (1994–95). OTHER: *Kronos* for a minimum of 15 Alarm Clocks, and Loudspeakers and Tapes, with an indeterminate chronometric duration of 5 to 1,440 minutes (1969); *Antinomia* for Tape (1973).—NS/LK/DM

Lavotta, János, Hungarian violinist and composer; b. Pusztafödémes, July 5, 1764; d. Tállya, Aug. 11, 1820. After taking violin lessons with his father, he pursued the study of law in Bratislava and Pest; later he completed his music training in Bratislava and Vienna. He made tours as a violin virtuoso but his career was hampered by alcoholism. Lavotta was one of the creators of the Hungarian national style in the form of the classical verbunkos. Among his works were verbunko dances, German dances, polonaises, contredanses, and minuets.

BIBL.: G. Bernáth, *L. élete* (L.'s Life; Pest, 1857); S. Szilágy, *L. J.* (Budapest, 1930).—LK/DM

Lavrangas, Dionyssios, Greek conductor, composer, and pedagogue; b. Argostólion, Oct. 17, 1860?; d. Razata, Cephalonia, July 18, 1941. After studies with N. Serao (violin) and Olivieri and Metaxas-Tzanis (harmony) in Argostólion, he went to Naples to pursue his training with Scarano (harmony and counterpoint) and Ross (piano); he also was a student at the Cons. of San Pietro a Majella there of Rossi and P. Serao (composition). He then went to Paris and had lessons with Dubois (harmony), Anthiome (piano), and Franck (organ); he also took courses at the Cons. there with Delibes and Massenet. After working as a touring opera conductor, he settled in Athens as conductor of the Phil. Soc. (1894–96); he then was founder-conductor of the Elliniko Melodhrama (Greek Opera; 1900–1935). He also was active as a teacher, and served as director of the opera school of the Hellenic Cons. (1919–24). Lavrangas was an important figure in the development of the Ionian school of composition. His works are reflective of French and Italian models.

WORKS: DRAMATIC: Opera: *Elda di Vorn* (c. 1886; Naples, c. 1890); *La vita è un sogno* (1887; Act 4 rev. as *Mayissa* [The Sorceress], Athens, Oct. 8, 1901); *Galatea* (c. 1887); *Ta dyo adelfia* (The 2 Brothers; Athens, April 24, 1900); *O lytrotis* (The Redeemer; 1900–1903; Corfu, Feb. 24, 1934); *Dido* (1906–09; Athens, April 10, 1909); *Mavri petaloudha* (Black Butterfly; Athens, Jan. 25, 1929); *Aida* (c. 1928); *Ikaros* (c. 1930); *Ena paramythi*, comic opera (1930); *Fakanapas*, comic opera (1935; Athens, Dec. 2, 1950); *Frosso* (1938). Operetta: *I aspri tricha* (The White Hair; Athens, March 22, 1917); *Sporting Club* (Athens, Aug. 4, 1917); *Dhipli Fotia* (Double Flame; Athens, Jan. 10, 1918); *Satore* (n.d.); *O Tragoudistis tou Kazinou* (The Casino Singer; Athens, July 7, 1934; in collaboration with others). OTHER: Ballets; orch. works; piano pieces; choral music; songs.—NS/LK/DM

Lavrovskaya, Elizaveta Andreievna, Russian mezzo-soprano; b. Kashin, Tver district, Oct. 13, 1845; d. Petrograd, Nov. 4, 1919. She studied at the Elizabeth Inst. and the St. Petersburg Cons., making her debut in Gluck's *Orfeo* (1867), then studied with P. Viardot in Paris. She sang opera in St. Petersburg (1868–72; 1879–80) and at the Bolshoi Theater in Moscow (1890); also appeared as a recitalist. She taught at the Moscow Cons. (from 1888). Tchaikovsky admired her vocal abilities and wrote his 6 songs of op.27 for her. —NS/LK/DM

Lavry, Marc, Latvian-born Israeli conductor and composer; b. Riga, Dec. 22, 1903; d. Haifa, March 20, 1967. After attending the Riga Cons., he studied with Teichmüller at the Leipzig Cons. and also received private instruction from Glazunov. He began his career conducting opera and ballet in Latvia and Germany. In 1935 he went to Palestine, where he was conductor of the Palestine Folk Opera (1941–47) and then director of the music dept. of the short-wave radio station Kol Zion La Gola (1950–58). In 1952 he visited the U.S. His music is imbued with intense feeling for Jewish folk motifs. Among his works prior to his going to Palestine, the most notable is *Fantastische Suite* for Orch. (1932). He was the composer of the first Palestinian opera in Hebrew to receive a stage performance, *Dan Hashomer* (Dan the Guard; Tel Aviv, Feb. 17, 1945, composer conducting); he also wrote an opera in the form of a series of cantillations with homophonic instrumental accompaniment entitled *Tamar and Judah* (1958; concert perf., N.Y., March 22, 1970). Other works include 5 syms., among them the *Tragic* (1945), the *Liberation* (1951), and No. 4 (1957), the symphonic poems *Stalingrad* (c. 1943) and *Negev* (c. 1954), 2 piano concertos (1945, 1947), Flute Concerto (1965), Harp Concerto, Viola Concerto, the oratorio *Esther ha'malka* (Queen Esther; 1960), and many songs.—NS/LK/DM

Law, Andrew, American singing teacher and composer; b. Milford, Conn., March 21, 1749; d. Cheshire, Conn., July 13, 1821. He graduated from R.I. Coll., receiving his M.A. in 1778, then studied theology and was ordained in Hartford (1787). He subsequently he was active as a preacher in Philadelphia and Baltimore, later as a pioneer singing teacher in New England. He invented a new system of notation, patented in 1802, which employed 4 (later increased to 7) different shapes of notes without the staff; it was not successful and was used in only a few of his own books. A second innovation (at least as far as American usages were concerned) was his setting of the melody in the soprano instead of in the tenor. In 1786 he received an honorary M.A. degree from Yale Univ., and in 1821 an LL.D. from Allegheny Coll. in Meadville, Pa. He compiled *A Select Number of Plain Tunes Adapted to Congregational Worship* (1775), *Select Harmony* (Cheshire, 1778), *A Collection of Hymns for Social Worship* (Cheshire, 1782), *The Rudiments of Music* (Cheshire, 1783), *The Art of Singing,* in 3 parts, each separately paged: I. *The Musical Primer;* II. *The Christian Harmony;* III. *The Musical Magazine* (Cheshire, 1792–93; 4th ed., Windsor, Vt., 1803; part III contains 6 books of tunes), *Harmonic Companion, and Guide to Social Worship: Being a Choice Selection of Tunes Adapted to the Various Psalms and Hymns* (Philadelphia, 1807), *The Art of Playing the Organ and Pianoforte* (Philadelphia, 1809), and *Essays on Music* (Philadelphia, 1814). Only one of his hymn tunes, *Archdale,* acquired some popularity; but his teaching books, quaintly but clearly written, contributed considerably to early music education in America.

BIBL.: R. Crawford, *A. L., American Psalmodist* (Evanston, Ill., 1968).—NS/LK/DM

Lawes, Henry, English composer, brother of **William Lawes**; b. Dinton, Wiltshire, Jan. 5, 1596; d. London, Oct. 21, 1662. He studied in London. In 1626 he became "pistoler" and Gentleman of the Chapel Royal, then clerk. In 1631 he became one of the King's musicians for the lutes and voices. He also was music master to the Earl of Bridgewater. He lost these appointments during the Protectorate, but was reinstated in 1660. He is interred in the cloisters of Westminster Abbey. Lawes is historically important because his infinite care in setting texts with proper note and accent marked a step in the development of vocal composition that culminated in Purcell.

WORKS (all publ. in London unless otherwise given): **VOCAL: S a c r e d :** *A Paraphrase upon the Psalmes of David by G[eorge]S[andys]* set to New Tunes for Private Devotion for Voice and Basso Continuo (1638); *Choice Psalmes put into Musick* for 3 Voices and Basso Continuo (1648; includes 30 full anthems); 3 other full anthems; 6 verse anthems; 11 anthems (only text extant). **S e c u l a r :** *Ayres and Dialogues...* for 1 to 3 Voices (3 vols., 1653, 1655, 1658); in all, his songs number 434; also the masques *Comus* (Sept. 29, 1634) and *The Triumphs of Peace.*

BIBL.: W. McClung Evans, *H. L., Musician and Friend of Poets* (N.Y., 1941); P. Willett, *The H. L. Manuscript* (London, 1969).—NS/LK/DM

Lawes, William, important English composer, brother of **Henry Lawes**; b. Salisbury (baptized), May 1, 1602; d. in battle at the siege of Chester, Sept. 24, 1645. He most likely commenced his musical studies with his father, then found a patron in Edward Seymour, Earl of Hertford, who enabled him to study with Coperario in London. He became active at the court, being made "musician in ordinary for the lutes and voices" to Charles I in 1635; he joined his monarch's army in 1642, losing his life during the Civil War. He excelled as a composer of both vocal and instrumental music. Of historical significance is the music he wrote for the court masques, which owe much to his remarkable contributions to the genre. For modern editions of his works, see A. Sabol, ed., *Songs and Dances for the Stuart Masque* (Providence, R.I., 1959; second ed., rev. and aug., 1978), M. Lefkowitz, ed., *William Lawes: Select Consort Music,* Musica Britannica, XXI (1963; second ed., 1971), idem, ed., *Trois masques à la cour de Charles Ier d'Angleterre* (Paris, 1970), I. Spink, ed., *English Songs, 1625–1660,* Musica Britannica, XXXIII (1971), and D. Pinto, ed., *William Lawes: Consort Sets in Five and Six Parts* (London, 1979).

WORKS: Over 200 songs; also music to Jonson's *Entertainment at Welbeck* (1633); Fletcher's play *The Faithful Shepherdess* (1633); Shirley's masque *The Triumph of Peace* (1634; in collaboration with S. Ives); Davenant's play *Love and Honour* (1634); Davenant's masque *The Triumphs of the Prince d'Amour* (1636; in collaboration with H. Lawes); Jonson's play *Epicoene, or The Silent Woman* (1636); W. Cartwright's play *The Royal Slave* (1636; in collaboration with H. Lawes); Shirley's play *The Duke's Mistress* (1636); W. Berkeley's play *The Lost Lady* (1637); J. Mayne's play *The City Match* (1637); J. Suckling's play *Aglaura* (1637); Beaumont and Fletcher's play *Cupid's Revenge* (1637);

Davenant's masque *Britannia triumphans* (1638); Ford's play *The Lady's Trial* (1638); Davenant's play *The Unfortunate Lovers* (1638); Suckling's play *The Goblins* (1638); Suckling's play *The Tragedy of Brennoralt* (1639); H. Glapthorne's play *Argalus and Parthenia* (1639); Cavendish's play *The Country Captain* (1640); Shirley's play *The Cardinal* (1641); J. Denham's play *The Sophy* (1641); R. Brome's play *The Jovial Crew* (1641); etc.; sacred vocal music, including some 48 anthems and 10 canons; instrumental music, including consort suites; sonatas or fantasia-suites; numerous aires, almans, corants, sarabands, and other dances; various pieces for virginals or harpsichord; etc.

BIBL.: A. Ashbee, ed., *W. L.: Essays on His Life, Times, and Work* (Aldershot, 1998).—**NS/LK/DM**

Lawrence, Arnie (Finkelstein, Arnold Lawrence), jazz alto saxophonist, educator; b. N.Y., July 10, 1938. He was featured with Chico Hamilton. Lawrence's own work has always been an innovative mix of hard bop, free improvisation, and eclectic influences. Privately he has also pursued an interest in Jewish liturgical music and has frequently played in a synagogue. He was a founding faculty member and original director of the jazz B.A. program at the New School for Social Research, though by the late 1980s his administrative duties were taken over by Martin Mueller. His style of music teaching is notable for its emphasis on ear training rather than sight reading. He moved to Israel in 1997 with the intention of starting a jazz school there.

DISC.: *Look Toward a Dream* (1968); *Inside an Hour Glass* (1970); *And Treasure Island* (1979); *Renewal* (1981). Mark Weinstein and His Cosa Nueva Orch.: *Cuban Roots* (ca. 1974).—**LP**

Lawrence, Dorothea Dix, American soprano and folk-song collector; b. N.Y., Sept. 22, 1899; d. Plainfield, N.J., May 23, 1979. She studied with Cesare Stunai, Henry Russell, and Katherine Opdycke in N.Y. She made her debut as Gounod's Marguerite with the Quebec Opera in Montreal in 1929, then appeared in opera in N.Y., Philadelphia, and elsewhere. She became active as a folk-song collector, presenting recitals in which she sang American Indian songs in their original languages as well as other folk songs and art songs by established composers. She also toured Europe as a recitalist (1952–54). She publ. the book *Folklore Songs of the United States* (1959).—**NS/LK/DM**

Lawrence, Doug(las Marshal), jazz tenor saxophonist; b. Oct. 11, 1956, Lake Charles, La. The last of six siblings in a family of musicians, he began playing classical music on the clarinet at age eight. At age 13, he picked up his father's saxophone. At a high school jazz competition, he won a scholarship to North Tex. State Univ. After briefly attending the school, he began his first road work, joining various bands in Dallas, Albuquerque, and Las Vegas. In 1979, the Special Services Band at West Point auditioned over two hundred tenor players before receiving a tape from Lawrence. They invited him to the school, and following a brief audition, offered him a position in their jazz band. Within a few months, he started commuting to N.Y., where he began to gain recognition. In 1986, he moved to Man-

hattan, where he has performed and recorded with George Benson, George Cables, Buck Clayton, "Wild Bill" Davis, Billy Eckstine, Dizzy Gillespie, Benny Goodman, Scott Hamilton, Lionel Hampton, Barry Harris, Jay McShann, the Smithsonian Jazz Masterworks Orch., Sarah Vaughan, Frank Wess, and Nancy Wilson. He has appeared throughout the U.S., Japan, and Europe at virtually every major jazz festival, club, and concert hall. His 1997 bookings included national and international tours with the Count Basie Orch., the Doug Lawrence Band, and numerous bookings as a freelance artist.

DISC.: *Soul Carnival Featuring the D. L. Quintet* (1997); *High Heel Sneakers* (1999).—**LP**

Lawrence, Gertrude (real name, **Gertrud Alexandra Dagmar Lawrence Klasen**), English actress, singer, and dancer; b. London, July 4, 1898; d. N.Y., Sept. 6, 1952. She began her career with appearances in British revues (from 1910), and then starred in *André Charlot's Revue* in London, with which she made her N.Y. debut (1924). George and Ira Gershwin wrote for her the musicals *Oh, Kay!* (1926) and *Treasure Girl* (1928). After working mainly as an actress in England and the U.S., she won great critical acclaim as Liza Elliot in the Kurt Weill and Moss Hart musical play *Lady in the Dark* (1941). Her last role was as Anna in the Rodgers and Hammerstein musical *The King and I* (1951). She publ. her autobiography as *A Star Danced* (1945).

BIBL.: R. Aldrich, *G. L. as Mrs. A.* (N.Y., 1954). —**NS/LK/DM**

Lawrence, Lucile, American harpist and teacher; b. New Orleans, Feb. 7, 1907. She studied with Salzedo and was first harpist in his harp ensemble. She organized her own Lawrence Harp Quintet and appeared as a soloist with major orchs., a chamber music artist, and a recitalist. She taught at the Curtis Inst. of Music in Philadelphia (1927–30), then founded the harp dept. at the Philadelphia Musical Academy; also taught at the Mannes Coll. of Music in N.Y. (from 1945), Boston Univ. (from 1966), the Manhattan School of Music in N.Y. (from 1967), and the Berkshire Music Center in Tanglewood (from 1968).—**NS/LK/DM**

Lawrence, Marjorie (Florence), noted Australian soprano; b. Dean's Marsh, Victoria, Feb. 17, 1907; d. Little Rock, Ark., Jan. 13, 1979. She studied in Melbourne with Ivor Boustead, then in Paris with Cécile Gilly. She made her debut as Elisabeth in *Tannhäuser* in Monte Carlo (1932), then sang at the Paris Opéra (1933–36), gaining success as Donna Anna, Aida, Ortrud, Brangäne, and Brünnhilde. She made her American debut at the Metropolitan Opera in N.Y. on Dec. 18, 1935, as Brünnhilde in *Die Walküre*, where she quickly established herself as a leading Wagnerian on its roster; she also appeared as Alceste, Thaïs, and Salome. She also made guest appearances with the Chicago, San Francisco, St. Louis, and Cincinnati operas. An attack of polio during a performance of *Die Walküre* (1941) interrupted her career. While she never walked again unaided, her determination to return to the operatic stage led to the resumption of her career; her first appearance at the Metropolitan Opera following her illness came on Dec. 27, 1942, when she sang the Venusberg duet in a concert with Melchior, reclining upon a couch. Her last appearance there took place when she sang Venus on April 6, 1944. She continued to make occasional appearances until her retirement in 1952, then devoted herself to teaching. She was a prof. of voice at Tulane Univ. (1956–60) and prof. of voice and director of the opera workshop at Southern Ill. Univ. (from 1960). She publ. an autobiography, *Interrupted Melody, The Story of My Life* (N.Y., 1949), which was made into a film in 1955. —NS/LK/DM

Lawrence (real name, **Cohen**), **Robert,** American conductor; b. N.Y., March 18, 1912; d. there, Aug. 9, 1981. He was educated at Columbia Univ. (M.A., 1934) and the Inst. of Musical Art in N.Y. From 1939 to 1943 he was a music critic for the *N.Y. Herald Tribune.* During World War II, he served in the U.S. Army in Italy. After conducting opera in Rome (1944–45), he was conductor of the Phoenix (Ariz.) Sym. Orch. (1949–52) and the Ankara Sym. Orch. (1957–58). In 1961 he founded the Friends of French Opera in N.Y., with which he conducted performances of many rarely heard scores. He later conducted opera in Atlanta and served as head of the opera dept. at the Peabody Cons. of Music in Baltimore. He was the author of the books *The World of Opera* (1958) and *A Rage for Opera* (1971). —NS/LK/DM

Lawrence, Vera Brodsky, American pianist and music editor; b. Norfolk, Va., July 1, 1909. She studied piano with Josef and Rosina Lhévinne and theory with Goldmark and Wagenaar at the Juilliard School of Music in N.Y. (1929–32). She gave duo-piano concerts with Harold Triggs, and appeared as a soloist with American orchs. In a radical change of direction, she abandoned her concert career in 1965 to become a historian of American music. In 1967 she was appointed administrator of publications for the Contemporary Music Project, and supervised the publication of numerous works by American composers. She publ. the collected piano works of Gottschalk (5 vols., 1969); the complete works of Joplin (2 vols., 1970); *Music for Patriots, Politicians, and Presidents,* tracing American history as reflected in popular music, profusely illustrated with title pages and musical excerpts from publ. songs and dances celebrating historical events, and campaign ballads written during presidential elections (1975), which received the ASCAP-Deems Taylor Award (1976); *Strong on Music: The New York Music Scene in the Days of George Templeton Strong, 1836–1875: Vol. I: Resonances, 1836–1850* (1988) and *Vol. II: Reverberations, 1850–1856* (1995). —NS/LK/DM

Laws, Hubert, black American flutist; b. Houston, Nov. 10, 1939. He learned to play saxophone, piano, and guitar as well as flute, then played saxophone with the Jazz Crusaders (1954–60) while pursuing classical music studies. He then was a member of several popular orchs. before joining the Metropolitan Opera orch. in N.Y. as a flutist. He also appeared as a soloist with the N.Y. Phil. while continuing to appear in jazz settings. —NS/LK/DM

Lawson, Yank (actually, **John Rhea**), jazz trumpeter; b. Trenton, Mo., May 3, 1911; d. Feb. 18, 1995. He had a powerful and thrilling sound in the tradition of Louis Armstrong. His mother was a pianist. Yank originally played saxophone and piano, but during his teens switched to trumpet. After playing with bands at the Univ. of Mo., he gigged around Shreveport with Wingy Manone and then Ben Pollack (1933 to autumn 1934). He left Pollack's band after Pollack refused to spotlight Lawson's girlfriend. He worked with Will Osborne (early 1935), did freelance studio work in N.Y., then became a founding member of the Bob Crosby Band (1935). He worked with Crosby until August 1938, then joined Tommy Dorsey until November 1939. He worked briefly with Abe Lyman, and then spent a few months with Richard Himber (early 1940); from summer 1940 until May 1941, he played in the theatre orch. for the show *Louisiana Purchase.* In May 1941 he rejoined Bob Crosby, then worked briefly with Benny Goodman (December 1942). From the mid-1940s, he worked for many years in N.Y. studio bands, and did prolific freelance recording. In the 1950s Lawson and Bob Haggart led a recording band that made several LPs. He toured with his own band (spring 1962), worked with Peanuts Hucko at Eddie Condon's Club (1964–66), and took part in several Bob Crosby Band reunions, including a tour of the Orient (late 1964) and residencies in N.Y. in 1965 and 1966. He led at Condon's in late 1966. Lawson co-led the World's Greatest Jazz Band, an outgrowth of the Lawson-Haggart band, from 1968 through the late 1970s. When the band folded, Lawson and Haggart continued to play together into the early 1990s, until his death at age 83, in 1995. His real name is Lawson, and not, as is often printed, Lausen.

DISC.: *Y. L.'s Dixieland Jazz* (1943); *Best of Broadway, Dixieland Style* (1959); *Big Y. Is Here* (1965); *Ole Dixie* (1966); *World's Greatest Jazz Band* (1968); *Live* (1970); *Century Plaza* (1972); *Y. L. and Bob Haggart* (1987); *Jazz at Its Best* (1989). The L.-Haggart Jazz Band: *Blues on the River* (1952); *L.-Haggart Band* (1952); *L.-Haggart Band Play King Oliver* (1952); *Plays Jelly Roll's Jazz* (1952); *Ragtime Jamboree* (1953); *South of the Mason-Dixon Line* (1954); *Louis' Hot 5s and 7s* (1956). —JC/LP

Lawton, Jeffrey, English tenor; b. Oldham, 1939. He studied with Elsie Thurston at the Royal Manchester Coll. of Music (1954–58) and with Patrick McGuigan. In 1974 he sang Don Alvaro with the Manchester Opera Co. His professional operatic debut followed in 1981 as Florestan with the Welsh National Opera in Cardiff, where he sang Siegfried in its *Ring* cycle in 1985. His other roles included those by Berlioz, Strauss, and Janáček. In 1986 he made his first appearance at London's Covent Garden as Siegfried, and returned there as Tristan in 1993. Following engagements in Paris and Brussels as Otello in 1987, he sang Siegmund in Cologne in 1988, returning there as Siegfried in 1989. In the latter year, he portrayed Edmund in Reimann's *Lear* at the English National Opera in London. He sang Shuisky in

Boris Godunov at Opera North in Leeds and Strauss's Herod at the London Promenade Concerts in 1993. In 1996 he created the role of Pedro in the premiere of MacMillan's *Inés de Castro* in Edinburgh. He also sang widely as a concert artist in Europe.—**NS/LK/DM**

Layolle, Francesco de, notable Italian composer and organist; b. Florence, March 4, 1492; d. Lyons, c. 1540. He became a singer at the chapel of the church of the Ss. Annunziata in Florence in 1505, and also received private training from Bartolomeo deglia Organi. After leaving Florence in 1518, he finally settled in Lyons in 1521, where he became organist at the church of Notre Dame de Confort. He was also active as a collector and ed. of music for various Lyons printers, and later contributed to and ed. volumes for the publisher Jacques Moderne. Layolle's works are marked by a mastery of melodic, harmonic, and contrapuntal writing. His son, Alamanne de Layolle (b. probably in Lyons, c. 1521; d. Florence, Sept. 19, 1590), was also a composer and organist. He was organist at St. Nizier in Lyons before going to Florence in 1565, where he was organist at the Badia (1570–75). His skill as a composer is revealed in his *Intavolatura di M. Alammano Aiolli*, a collection of 16 arrangements of contemporary keyboard pieces. Also extant are the *Canticum Zachariae* for 5 Voices and 3 madrigals. See F. D'Accone, ed., *Music of the Florentine Renaissance: Francesco de Layolle, Collected Works*, Corpus Mensurabilis Musicae, XXXII/3–6 (1969–73).

WORKS: VOCAL : S a c r e d : *Missa "Adieu mes amours"* for 4 Voices on Mouton's chanson; *Missa "Ces fascheux sotz"* for 4 Voices on Gardane's chanson; *Missa "O Salutaris hostia"* for 4 Voices; 7 penitential Psalms for 4 Voices; 35 motets for 2 to 6 Voices. **S e c u l a r :** *Venticinque canzoni a cinque voci* (Lyons, 1540); *Cinquanta canzoni a quatro voci* (Lyons, 1540?); 3 madrigals; 9 chansons.

BIBL.: D. Sutherland, *F.d. L. (1492–1540): Life and Secular Works* (diss., Univ. of Mich., 1968).—**LK/DM**

Lays, François, French tenor; b. La Barthe de Nesthes, Feb. 14, 1758; d. Ingrande, near Angers, March 30, 1831. He studied theology and music at the Guaraison monastery. After settling in Paris, he joined the Opéra in 1780, where he appeared as one of its principal members until 1823. He also was engaged at court concerts and at the Concert Spirituel. From 1795 to 1799 he was prof. of voice at the Cons. He was the principal singer at Napoleon's court from 1801 to 1814. From 1819 to 1826 he taught at the École Royale de Chant et de Déclamation. He publ. *Lays, artiste du théâtre des arts, à ses concitoyens* (Paris, 1793).—**NS/LK/DM**

Layton, Billy Jim, American composer and teacher; b. Corsicana, Tex., Nov. 14, 1924. He studied at the New England Cons. of Music in Boston with Francis Judd Cook and Carl McKinley (B.Mus., 1948), at Yale Univ. with Quincy Porter (M.Mus., 1950), and at Harvard Univ. with Piston (composition) and Gombosi and Pirrotta (musicology). He obtained his Ph.D. at Harvard with the diss. *Italian Music for the Ordinary of the Mass* (1960), then was on its faculty (1960–66). In 1966 he was appointed a prof. of music at the State Univ. of N.Y. at Stony Brook. His small output is a finely crafted oeuvre that utilizes various contemporary techniques from free atonality to jazz improvisation.

WORKS: *An American Portrait*, symphonic overture (1953); *3 Dylan Thomas Poems* for Chorus and Brass Sextet (1954–56); *Dante Fantasy* for Orch. (1964); chamber music.—**NS/LK/DM**

Layton, Robert, noted English musicologist; b. London, May 2, 1930. He was educated under Rubbra and Wellesz at Worcester Coll., Oxford (B.A., 1953), then went to Sweden, where he learned the language and took courses at the univs. of Uppsala and Stockholm (1953–55). In 1959 he joined the staff of the BBC in London, where he prepared music seminars. He became an authority on Scandinavian music. He contributed the majority of the articles on Scandinavian composers to *The New Grove Dictionary of Music and Musicians* (1980), and in a spirit of mischievous fun also inserted a biography of a nonexistent Danish composer, making up his name from the stations of the Copenhagen subway. The editor was not amused, and the phony entry had to be painfully gouged in the galleys for the new printing. Layton also prepared the Eng. tr. of E. Tawaststjerna's *Jean Sibelius* (1976–).

WRITINGS: *Franz Berwald* (in Swedish, Stockholm, 1956; Eng. tr., London, 1959); *Sibelius* (London, 1965; 3rd ed., rev., 1983); *Sibelius and His World* (London, 1970); ed. *A Companion to the Concerto* (London, 1988).—**NS/LK/DM**

Lažar, Filip, Romanian composer and pianist; b. Craiova, May 18, 1894; d. Paris, Nov. 3, 1936. He was a student of Kiriac (theory), Castaldi (harmony and counterpoint), and Saegiu (piano) at the Bucharest Cons. (1907–12), and of Krehl (harmony and composition) and Teichmüller (piano) at the Leipzig Cons. (1913–14). In subsequent years, he made tours as a pianist in Europe and the U.S. as a champion of modern music. In 1920 he helped to found the Romanian Composers' Soc. In 1928 he founded and served as chairman of the modern music soc. Triton in Paris. He was active as a piano teacher in France and Switzerland from 1928. In 1924 he won the Enesco Prize and in 1931 the prize of the Romanian Radio. His compositions were infused with Romanian folk tunes until he adopted a more adventuresome style in 1928, in which he utilized serial and neo-Classical elements.

WORKS: DRAMATIC: *La bouteille de Panurge*, ballet (1918); *Les images de Béatrice*, opera-cantata (1928). **ORCH.:** *Prelude* (1919); *Suita română* (1921); *Divertisment* (1924; Bucharest, Feb. 9, 1925); *Tziganes*, scherzo (1925); *Suite valaque* for Small Orch. (1925); *Music for an Orchestra* (1927; Boston, March 23, 1928); *Concerto grosso* (1927; Boston, May 1928); *Le Ring*, symphonic suite (1928; Paris, Jan. 10, 1930); *Musique per Radio*, overture for Small Orch. (1930; Paris, Feb. 26, 1931); Concerto for Piano and Small Orch. (1931); Piano Concerto (Paris, Nov. 4, 1934); *Concerto da camera* for Percussion and 12 Instruments (1934; Paris, Dec. 11, 1935). **CHAMBER:** Violin Sonata (1919); *Bagatelle* for Cello and Piano (1925); *3 Dances* for Violin and Piano (1927); Trio for Oboe, Clarinet, and Bassoon (1934); String Trio (1935); *Petite suite* for Oboe, Clarinet, and Bassoon (1936).

Piano: 2 sonatas (1913, 1929); 3 suites (1924, 1925, 1926); *Bagatelle* (1927); (6) *Pièces minuscules* for Children (1929); *Dans românesc* (n.d.). OTHER: Choral pieces; songs.

BIBL.: V. Tomescu, *F. L.* (Bucharest, 1963).—NS/LK/DM

Lazarev, Alexander, Russian conductor; b. Moscow, July 5, 1945. He was trained in Moscow at the Central Music School and at the Cons., and at the Leningrad Cons. In 1971 he took first prize in the Moscow Young Conductors Competition, and then was a prizewinner at the Herbert von Karajan competition in Berlin in 1972. In 1973 he became a conductor at the Bolshoi Theater in Moscow, where he founded the Ensemble of Soloists in 1978 to further the performance of contemporary music. He appeared as both an opera and sym. conductor throughout Europe. From 1987 to 1995 he was chief conductor of the Bolshoi Theater. From 1988 to 1993 he was Generalmusikdirektor of the Duisburg Sym. Orch. From 1992 he was also principal guest conductor of the BBC Sym. Orch. in London. —NS/LK/DM

Lazaro, Hippolito, Spanish tenor; b. Barcelona, Aug. 13, 1887; d. Madrid, May 14, 1974. He studied in Milan, then sang operetta in Barcelona. He went to London in 1912, singing at the Coliseum under the name of Antonio Manuele. In 1913 he returned to Italy, where Mascagni chose him to create the role of Ugo in *Parisina* at La Scala in Milan. He made his Metropolitan Opera debut in N.Y. on Jan. 31, 1918, as the Duke of Mantua in *Rigoletto*; remained on its roster until 1920. In 1921 he created the role of Piccolo Marat in Mascagni's opera in Rome; also the role of Giannetto in *La cena delle beffe* by Giordano at La Scala in 1924. He made guest appearances with the Vienna State Opera, the Budapest Opera, and the Teatro Colón in Buenos Aires. He retired in 1950.—NS/LK/DM

Lazarof, Henri, Bulgarian-born American composer and pedagogue; b. Sofia, April 12, 1932. After initial studies in Sofia, he went to Palestine to pursue his training with Ben-Haim and at the New Cons. of Music in Jerusalem (1949–52). Following advanced studies with Petrassi at the Accademia di Santa Cecilia in Rome (1955–57), he completed his training with Berger and Shapiro at Brandeis Univ. (M.F.A., 1959). In 1959 he became a naturalized American citizen, and that same year he became a teacher of French language and literature at the Univ. of Calif. at Los Angeles; subsequently he was prof. of composition there (1962–87). His music is marked by inventive originality in its thematic structure and subtle "sonorism" in instrumentation, with instances of serial procedures.

WORKS: DRAMATIC: B a l l e t : *Events* (1973); *Canti* (1980); *Mirrors, Mirrors* (1981). ORCH.: Piano Concerto (1956); *Piccola serenata* (Boston, June 15, 1959); Viola Concerto (1959–60; Monaco, Feb. 20, 1962); Concerto for Piano and 20 Instruments (1960–61; RAI, Milan, May 28, 1963); *Odes* (1962–63); *Tempi concertati*, double concerto for Violin, Viola, and Chamber Orch. (1964); *Structures sonores* (1966); *Mutazione* (1967); Cello Concerto (1968; Oslo, Sept. 12, 1969); *Omaggio*, chamber concerto for 19 Players (1968); *Textures* for Piano and 5 Ensembles (1970);

Konkordia for Strings (1971); *Spectrum* for Trumpet, Orch., and Tape (1972–73; Salt Lake City, Jan. 17, 1975); Flute Concerto (1973); *Ritratto* (1973); *Chamber Concerto No. 3* (1974); *Volo* for Viola and 2 String Ensembles (1975); Chamber Sym. (1976); Concerto for Orchestra No. 1 (1977) and No. 2, *Icarus* (1984; Houston, April 12, 1986); Sym. (1978); Sinfonietta (1981); *Poema* (1985; Seattle, May 10, 1986); Violin Concerto (1985); *Tableaux* for Piano and Orch. (1987); Concertante I for 16 Strings and 2 Horns (1988); Clarinet Concerto (1989; N.Y., May 31, 1992). CHAMBER: 3 string quartets (1956; 1961–62; 1980); String Trio (1957); Sonata for Solo Violin (1958); *Concertino da camera* for Wind Quintet (1959); *Inventions* for Viola and Piano (1962); *Asymptotes* for Flute and Vibraphone (1963); *Tempi concertati* for 9 Instruments (1964); *Rhapsody* for Violin and Piano (1966); *Espaces* for 10 Instruments (1966); *Cadence I* for Cello (1969), *II* for Viola and Tape (1969), *III* for Violin and 2 Percussion (1970), *V* for Flute and Tape (1972), and *VI* for Tuba and Tape (1973); *Continuum* for String Trio (1970); *Partita* for Brass Quintet and Tape (1971); *Concertazioni* for 7 Instruments and Tape (1973); Duo for Cello and Piano (1973); *Adieu* for Clarinet and Piano (1974); *Fanfare* for 6 Trumpets (1980); Wind Trio (1981); *Lyric Suite* for Violin (1983); *Serenade* for String Sextet (1985); *La Laurenziana*, string octet (1987); Concertante II, octet for Flute, Oboe, Clarinet, Violin, Cello, Double Bass, Percussion, and Piano (1988); Piano Trio (1989). P i a n o : *Quantetti* for Piano and 3 Pianos on Tape (1964); *Cadence IV* (1970).—NS/LK/DM

Lazarus, Daniel, French conductor and composer; b. Paris, Dec. 13, 1898; d. there, June 27, 1964. He studied with Diemer, Leroux, and Vidal at the Paris Cons., taking the premier prix in composition (1915). He was conductor of the Théâtre du Vieux Colombier (1921–25), then artistic director of the Paris Opéra-Comique (1936–39); later was chorus master of the Paris Opéra (1946–56), then prof. at the Schola Cantorum in Paris (from 1956). He publ. *Accès à la musique* (Paris, 1960). His compositions include the operas *L'Illustre Magicien* (1924), *La Veéitable Histoire de Wilhelm Meister* (1927), *Trumpeldor* (1935), and *La Chambre bleue* (1938), 3 ballets, incidental music, Piano Concerto (1929), 2 syms. (1933, 1934), chamber music, piano pieces, and songs. —NS/LK/DM

Lazzari, (Joseph) Sylvio, Austrian-born French conductor and composer; b. Bozen, Dec. 30, 1857; d. Suresnes, near Paris, June 10, 1944. He was born into a wealthy Austro-Italian family. After extensive travels, he settled in Paris and in 1883 he entered the Cons., where he was a student of Gounod, Guiraud, and Franck. In 1896 he became a naturalized French citizen. He became active as a theater conductor, and also wrote operas and incidental music. His most distinguished work was the tragic opera *La lépreuse* or *L'ensorcelé* (Paris, Feb. 7, 1912). His opera *La tour de feu* (Paris, Jan. 28, 1928) was the first to utilize film as an integral part of the score.

WORKS: DRAMATIC: O p e r a : *Armor* (1897; Prague, Nov. 7, 1898); *La lépreuse* or *L'ensorcelé* (1900–1901; Paris, Feb. 7, 1912); *Melaenis* (1913; Mulhouse, March 25, 1927); *Le sauteriot* (1913–15; Chicago, Jan. 19, 1918); *La tour de feu* (1925; Paris, Jan. 28, 1928). OTHER: A pantomime, *Lulu* (Paris, May 1889), and incidental music. OTHER: Sym.; symphonic poems; other orch. pieces; chamber music; piano pieces; choral works; songs. —NS/LK/DM

Lazzari, Virgilio, Italian-born American bass; b. Assisi, April 20, 1887; d. Castel Gandolfo, Oct. 4, 1953. He made his stage debut as L'Incognito in Suppe's *Boccaccio* with the Vitale Operetta Co. in 1908, remaining with the company until 1911. After studies with Cotogni in Rome, he made his operatic debut at the Teatro Costanzi there in 1914; then sang in South America. In 1916 he made his U.S. debut as Ramfis in St. Louis. He settled in the U.S. and became a naturalized American citizen. From 1918 to 1933 he was a member of the Chicago Opera. On Dec. 28, 1933, he made his Metropolitan Opera debut in N.Y. as Pedro in *L'Africaine*; remained on the roster until 1940; then returned for the 1943–51 seasons. He also sang at the Salzburg Festivals (1934–39) and appeared as Leporello at London's Covent Garden (1939). He became celebrated for his portrayal of Archibaldo in Montemezzi's *L'amore dei tre re.* —NS/LK/DM

Leach, James, English composer; b. Wardle, near Rochdale, Lancashire, 1762; d. Blackley, near Manchester, Feb. 8, 1798. He was a handloom weaver but pursued an interest in the performance and writing of psalmody for Methodist worship. About 1789 he became a professional musician. He was active as a singer at the leading festivals and as a teacher. He publ. the highly successful collections *A New Sett of Hymns and Psalm Tunes* (London, 1789) and *A Second Sett of Hymns and Psalm Tunes* (London, 1794).—LK/DM

Lead Belly (originally, **Ledbetter, Huddie**), troubled American folk and blues singer, guitarist, and songwriter; b. near Mooringsport, La., Jan. 20, 1888; d. N.Y., Dec. 6, 1949. (Although initially spelled as two words, for many years, his nickname was spelled as "Leadbelly"; however, recently the original two-word spelling has come back into favor.)

Lead Belly led a tumultuous, often violent life, but he galvanized the folk music community of the 1930s and 1940s with his vibrant performances, and his repertoire of songs (which he collected, adapted, and wrote) proved popular and influential after his death, when such works as "Goodnight, Irene," "Rock Island Line," and "The Midnight Special" became popular with folk, pop, and rock audiences.

Lead Belly was the son of John Wesley Ledbetter, a farmer, and Sallie Pugh Ledbetter, who married Feb. 21, 1888. The day and date of his birth are uncertain. The family moved from Caddo Parish, La., to Harrison County, Tex., still adjacent to Caddo Lake on the eastern border of Tex., when he was five. He showed an early interest in music, learning to play the button accordion (or "windjammer"), and eventually mandolin, guitar, harmonica, Jew's harp, piano, and organ. His chief instructors were his two uncles, Bob and Terrell Ledbetter. Terrell taught him "Goodnight, Irene," apparently derived from "Irene, Goodnight" by Gussie Lord Davis, published in 1886, but much altered. Lead Belly would alter it further.

Lead Belly attended grammar school, probably from the ages of eight to 12 or 13, after which he worked as a farmer with his father. He seems to have been given his first guitar about 1903, the same year that he began playing in public. In 1904 he moved to Shreveport, La., where he spent two years playing in the city's red-light district. After a brief return home, he wandered through Tex. and La., working as a musician, but went home again when he became ill, probably from a venereal disease. He may have attended Bishops Coll. in Marshall, Tex., for a time. On July 20, 1908, he married Aletha Henderson, and they lived on his parents' farm until late 1910, when they moved to Dallas. They picked cotton during the summer, and Lead Belly worked as a musician in the winter.

Around 1912, Lead Belly met a young Blind Lemon Jefferson, and the two worked together intermittently for several years. Lead Belly and his wife returned to Henderson County in the spring of 1915. He was arrested in June 1915, apparently due to an alleged assault, but his parents signed away their farm to get a lawyer, and when he came to trial in September he was convicted only of carrying a pistol and sentenced to 30 days on a chain gang. Nevertheless, he escaped, and he and his wife moved to Bowie County, where they became tenant farmers as Mr. and Mrs. Walter Boyd. After an altercation in December 1917, Lead Belly was convicted of murdering his cousin's husband and assaulting another man with intent to murder, drawing a sentence of seven to 30 years.

Lead Belly's marriage ended during his incarceration, although he does not seem to have been legally divorced. In 1920 he was transferred to Central State Farm near Houston, a facility known as Sugarland due to its proximity to a sugar refinery. There he became an entertainer in addition to the usual prison work, and he acquired and adapted many of the songs he later performed and recorded, most prominent among them "The Midnight Special," which referred to a late-night train that passed near the prison. Tex. governor Patrick Neff occasionally visited the prison during 1924, and Lead Belly entertained him, even singing a specially written song in which he pleaded for a pardon. Neff granted the pardon on Jan. 16, 1925, shortly before he left office, shortening Lead Belly's minimum sentence by several months. After a short time in Houston, he moved back to Mooringsport, where he worked at least part- time as a musician. In February 1930 he was convicted of "assault with intent to murder" in Mooringsport, sentenced to six to ten years, and sent to the state penitentiary in Angola, La.

Folk song collector John A. Lomax, under the auspices of the Library of Congress, made field recordings of Lead Belly at Angola in July 1933. Lomax returned the following year. Lead Belly's sentence was commuted for good behavior, and he was released on Aug. 1, 1934. He went to Shreveport, where he stayed with Martha Promise, whom he had known before going to prison; they married on Jan. 20, 1935. In September 1934 he went to work for Lomax as his driver and assistant; at one of their stops in Ark. they discovered "Rock Island Line," a song about a railroad running between Little Rock and Memphis that Lead Belly later adapted (adding a spoken introduction) and recorded.

Lomax took Lead Belly to N.Y. in early 1935; they made personal appearances around the Northeast through March, and Lead Belly made his first commercial recordings for the American Record Corporation (ARC) label (later Columbia Records). Like the other recordings he made, these sold poorly during his lifetime. He and Lomax signed a management contract, though they quickly had a falling-out and Lead Belly returned to the South.

Lead Belly moved to N.Y. in February 1936 and began to perform in public again, often at left-wing political gatherings. He made commercial recordings for Musicraft in April 1939. In May he was convicted of third-degree assault in N.Y. and sentenced to eight months incarceration. In June 1940 he made commercial recordings for RCA Victor. He appeared in N.Y. nightclubs such as the Village Vanguard and performed on radio, notably on the network program *Back Where I Come From* in September 1940 and on his own show, *Folksongs of America*, on the local WNYC station in the fall of 1940.

Starting in May 1941, Lead Belly recorded frequently for the small record labels operated by Moses Asch, including Asch, Disc, Stinson, and Folkways. The recordings were made both alone and with such partners as Woody Guthrie and the team of Sonny Terry and Brownie McGhee. Between the summer of 1944 and the spring of 1946, Lead Belly lived in L.A., where he recorded for Capitol Records in October 1944 and appeared on local radio station KRE. He returned to N.Y. and continued to perform, notably at concerts sponsored by the left-wing folk music organization People's Songs. He played in Paris in May 1949, where he was diagnosed as suffering from amyotrophic lateral sclerosis, better known as Lou Gehrig's disease, a rare and incurable paralytic affliction, which killed him.

In August 1950, "Goodnight, Irene" became the biggest record hit of the year in a version by Gordon Jenkins and His Orch. and the Weavers that sold two million copies. The song also generated Top Ten pop hits for Frank Sinatra and Jo Stafford, a chart-topping country version by Ernest Tubb and Red Foley, and a Top Ten country hit for Moon Mullican. In August 1951 the Weavers scored a Top 40 hit with "Kisses Sweeter Than Wine," a song they had adapted from Lead Belly's "If It Wasn't for Dickey," and that he had adapted from the Irish folk song "Drimmer's Cow." The song became a gold-selling Top Ten hit for Jimmie Rodgers in December 1957. In January 1956 the Lonnie Donegan Skiffle Group scored a Top Ten hit in the U.K. with "Rock Island Line," setting off the British skiffle music fad; the recording made the U.S. Top Ten in the spring, and the song was also a Top 40 Country hit for Johnny Cash in February 1970.

"The Midnight Special," which had been a minor R&B hit for the Tiny Grimes Quintet in November 1948, became a Top 40 pop hit for Paul Evans in January 1960 and for Johnny Rivers in February 1965. "Cotton Fields" (or "Old Cotton Fields at Home"), another song introduced by Lead Belly, became a Top 40 hit for the Highwaymen in December 1961. *Leadbelly*, a 1976 film biography directed by Gordon Parks and starring Roger E. Mosley, focused on the singer's life up to 1933.

BIBL.: J. and A. Lomax, eds., *Negro Folk Songs of L. B.* (N.Y., 1936); M. Jones and A. McCarthy, eds., *A Tribute to Huddie Ledbetter* (London, 1946); A. Lomax, *L.: A Collection of World-Famous Songs* (N.Y., 1959); M. Asch and J. Lomax, eds., *The L. Songbook* (N.Y., 1962); P. Seeger and J. Lester, *The 12-String Guitar as Played by L.—An Instructional Manual* (N.Y., 1965); R. Garvin and E. Addeo, *The Midnight Special: The Legend of L.* (N.Y., 1971); J. Bell, ed., *L.* (1976); C. Wolfe and K. Lornell, *The Life and Legend of L.* (N.Y., 1992).—**WR**

Lear, Evelyn (née **Shulman**), outstanding American soprano; b. N.Y., Jan. 8, 1926. She learned to play the piano and the horn before pursuing vocal training with John Yard in Washington, D.C., and with Sergius Kagen at the Juilliard School of Music in N.Y. She also attended N.Y.U. and Hunter Coll. of the City Univ. of N.Y. In 1955 she made her N.Y. recital debut, the same year that she married her second husband, **Thomas Stewart.** For professional reasons, however, she retained her first husband's surname of Lear. After obtaining a Fulbright grant, she pursued her studies with Maria Ivogün at the Berlin Hochschule für Musik. On May 17, 1959, she made her operatic debut as Strauss's Composer at the Berlin Städtische Oper. She attracted wide notice when she essayed the role of Lulu in a concert performance in Vienna in 1960, returning there in 1962 to sing the role on stage. In 1961 she created the title role in Klebe's *Alkmene* in Berlin, and in 1963 the role of Jeanne in Egk's *Die Verlobung in San Domingo* in Munich. At the Salzburg Festivals, she appeared as Cherubino (1962–64) and as Fiordiligi (1965). In 1965 she made her first appearance at London's Covent Garden singing Donna Elvira. On March 17, 1967, she made her Metropolitan Opera debut in N.Y. creating the role of Lavinia in Levy's *Mourning Becomes Electra*. In subsequent seasons, she returned to sing Octavian and Berg's Marie (1969), Strauss's Composer (1970), Tosca and Dido (1973), Donna Elvira (1974), Alice Ford (1975), and Countess Geschwitz (1980). She also created the roles of Irma Arkadina in Pasatieri's *The Seagull* in Houston (1974) and Magda in Ward's *Minutes to Midnight* in Miami (1982). On Oct. 15, 1985, she made her farewell appearance at the Metropolitan Opera as the Marschallin. In 1987 she sang Countess Geschwitz in Chicago. Throughout her operatic career, she also pursued a notably successful concert career. She often appeared in both opera and concerts with her husband.—**NS/LK/DM**

Le Bé, Guillaume, French type founder; b. Troyes, 1525; d. Paris, 1598. He was an apprentice in Robert Esteinne's household, learning the cutting of punches from Claude Garamond. After a sojourn in Italy, he went to Paris to work with Garamond. From 1552 to 1592 he had his own business. Le Bé followed Petrucci's method, printing notes and staff lines separately, thus necessitating two impressions. He also made tablature type. His punches and other equipment were acquired by Ballard, and were used for two more centuries. —**NS/LK/DM**

Lebègue, Nicolas-Antoine, distinguished French organist, harpsichordist, pedagogue, and composer; b. Laon, c. 1631; d. Paris, July 6, 1702. He received training in Laon, and then settled in Paris, where he served as organist at St. Merry (from 1664) and organiste du Roi (from 1678). Lebègue was an outstanding composer of keyboard music. His organ works are of historical interest for his development of the recit en taille and the use of independent pedal parts. N. Dufourcq ed. his harpsichord music (Monaco, 1956).

WORKS (all publ. in Paris): **INSTRUMENTAL:** *Les pièces d'orgue* (1676); *Les pièces de clavessin* (1677); *Second livre d'orgue* (1678?); *Troisième livre d'orgue* (1685?); *Second livre de clavessin* (1687); etc. **VOCAL:** *Motets pour les principales festes de l'année* for Voice and Basso Continuo *& plusieurs petits ritournelles,* Organ or Viols (1687); etc.

BIBL.: J. Gillespie, *The Music for Harpsichord of N. L. B.* (diss., Univ. of Southern Calif., 1951); N. Dufourcq, *N. L., organiste de la Chapelle Royale* (Paris, 1954); R. Hough, *The Organ Works of N. L.* (diss., Univ. of Ill., 1969).—**NS/LK/DM**

Lebert (real name, **Levi**), **Sigmund,** German pianist and pedagogue; b. Ludwigsburg, near Stuttgart, Dec. 12, 1821; d. Stuttgart, Dec. 8, 1884. He was a pupil of Tomaschek in Prague. In 1856 he founded, with Faiszt, Stark, Brachmann, and Speidel, the Stuttgart Cons. His *Grosse Klavierschule* (which included numerous studies of his own composition), publ. in cooperation with Stark, ran through many eds. (rev. by M. Pauer, 1904), and appeared also in Eng., French, Italian, and Russian trs. He also publ. an *Instructive Edition* of classical piano works and ed. Clementi's *Gradus ad Parnassum.*—**NS/LK/DM**

Leborne, Aimé-Ambroise-Simon, French composer; b. Brussels, Dec. 29, 1797; d. Paris, April 2, 1866. He went to France as a child. He studied at the Paris Cons. with Berton and Cherubini, winning the second Prix de Rome (1818) and then the First Prix de Rome (1820). He subsequently was on its faculty, later serving as prof. of counterpoint and fugue (1836–40), then of composition (1840–66). He also was made librarian of the Paris Opéra (1829) and of the Royal Chapel (1834). In 1853 he became a chevalier of the Legion of Honor. He ed. a new edition of Catel's *Traité d'harmonie* (Paris, 1848; with numerous additions). He wrote the operas *Les Deux Figaro* (Paris, Aug. 22, 1827; in collaboration with Carafa), *Le Camp du drap d'or* (Paris, Feb. 23, 1828; in collaboration with Baton and Rifaut), and *Cinq ans d'entr'acte and Lequel* (Paris, March 21, 1838), as well as songs.—**NS/LK/DM**

Leborne, Fernand, French music critic and composer; b. Charleroi, March 10, 1862; d. Paris, Jan. 15, 1929. He was a pupil at the Paris Cons. of Massenet, Saint-Saëns, and Franck. He lived mostly in Paris, where he was music critic for *Le Monde Artiste,* and later for the *Petit Parisien.* As a composer, he won the Prix Chartier in 1901.

WORKS: DRAMATIC: Opera: *Daphnis et Chloé* (Brussels, May 10, 1885); *Hedda* (Milan, 1898); *Mudarra* (Berlin, April 19, 1899); *Les Girondins* (Lyons, March 25, 1905); *La Catalane* (Paris, May 24, 1907); *Cléopâtre* (Rouen, 1914); *Néréa* (Marseilles, Jan. 12, 1926). **Incidental Music To:** *L'Absent* (Paris, 1903). **ORCH.:** *Suite intime, Symphonie dramatique, Aquarelles, Temps de guerre, Fête bretonne, Marche solennelle,*

Ouverture guerrière, Ouverture symphonique; Symphonie-Concerto for Violin and Piano, with Orch. String Quartet. **CHAMBER:** Piano Trio; Violin Sonata; piano pieces. **VOCAL:** Mass; motets; songs.—**NS/LK/DM**

Lebrun, Franziska (Dorothea née **Danzi),** renowned German soprano; b. Mannheim (baptized), March 24, 1756; d. Berlin, May 14, 1791. She made her debut as Sandrina in Sacchini's *La Contadina in corte in Schwetzingen* (Aug. 9, 1772), then became a prominent member of the Mannheim Court Opera, where she created the countess in Holzbauer's *Günther von Schwarzburg* (Jan. 5, 1777). She made her first appearance in London at the King's Theatre as Ariene in Sacchini's *Creso* (Nov. 8, 1777), then was chosen to sing in Salieri's *Europa riconosciuta* at the opening of Milan's Teatro alla Scala (Aug. 3, 1778). She appeared at the Paris Concert Spirituel (1779) and again in London (1779–81); also continued to sing with the Court Opera in Mannheim, and later when the court went to Munich; likewise made guest appearances in Vienna and Verona, and later in Naples (1786–87) and Berlin (1789–90). She also composed; publ. 36 sonatas for Violin and Piano. She married the oboist and composer Ludwig August Lebrun (1778), with whom she appeared in concerts. —**NS/LK/DM**

Lebrun, Jean, famous French horn-player; b. Lyons, April 6, 1759; d. Paris, c. 1809. He went to Paris about 1780 to study with Punto, then made his debut at the Concert Spirituel in 1781. He was first horn in the Paris Opéra orch. (1786–92) and in the Berlin Prussian Court Orch. (from 1792) and also toured in a celebrated duo with Türschmidt until the latter's death in 1797. He wrote a number of concertos, but they are lost. —**NS/LK/DM**

Lebrun, Louis-Sébastien, French tenor and composer; b. Paris, Dec. 10, 1764; d. there, June 27, 1829. He received training in voice and composition at the maîtrise of Notre Dame in Paris (1771–83). He served as music director of the church of St. Germain- l'Aurerrois before making his operatic debut in 1787 at the Paris Opéra as Polynices in Sacchini's *Oedipe à Colone.* He also appeared at the Concert Spirituel. From 1791 to 1799 he sang at the Théâtre Feydeau before serving as an understudy at the Opéra. In 1803 he became a singing tutor there. In 1807 he was made a tenor and in 1810 chef du chant at Napoleon's chapelle. Lebrun wrote about 15 stage works, the most successful being his operas *Marcelin* (Paris, March 22, 1800) and *Le Rossignol* (Paris, April 23, 1816).—**NS/LK/DM**

Lebrun, Ludwig August (actually, **Ludwig Karl Maria**), celebrated German oboist and composer; b. Mannheim (baptized), May 2, 1752; d. Berlin, Dec. 16, 1790. He studied with his father, Jakob Alexander Lebrun, an oboist and répétiteur at the Mannheim court (1747–71). A precocious talent, he was admitted to the Mannheim Court Orch. as a scholar at the age of 12, and at 15 became a full member, a position he held until his death. He also toured as a virtuoso from about 1772, increasing his appearances after his marriage to the soprano **Franziska (Dorothea) Lebrun** (née **Danzi**) in 1778. He visited Milan (1778), Paris (1779), London (1779–81), Vienna (1785), Prague (1785), Naples (1786–87), and Berlin (1789–90). In addition to solo appearances, he often appeared with his wife. He composed several fine oboe concertos, and also wrote ballets, chamber music, and duos for flute.—NS/LK/DM

Leça, Armando Lopes, Portuguese choral conductor, folk-song collector, and composer; b. Leça da Palmeira, Aug. 9, 1893; d. Vila Nova de Gaia, Sept. 7, 1977. He studied with Oscar da Silva. He was active as a choral conductor and a collector of native folk songs, and publ. an authoritative ed. of popular Portuguese music (1922; expanded ed. in 2 vols., 1947). He wrote several dance suites for Orch., of which the *Dansa de Don Pedro* attained considerable popularity. Other works include 2 operettas: *Maio florido* (1918) and *Bruxa* (1919), many piano pieces of pictorial character, and songs.—NS/LK/DM

Le Caine, Hugh, Canadian physicist, acoustician, and innovative creator of prototypical electronic musical instruments; b. Port Arthur, Ontario, May 27, 1914; d. Ottawa, July 3, 1977. Although his childhood training combined music and science, he chose to emphasize science in his formal studies; he received a B.S. degree from Queen's Univ. in Kingston, Ontario, in 1938 and an M.S. in 1939, and obtained his Ph.D. in nuclear physics from the Univ. of Birmingham in England in 1952; he also studied piano briefly at the Royal Cons. of Music of Toronto and privately with Viggo Kihl. His childhood dream was to one day apply scientific techniques to the development and invention of new musical instruments, and he went on to develop ground-breaking electronic musical instruments that ultimately formed the basis of pioneering electronic music studios at the Univ. of Toronto (1959) and McGill Univ. in Montreal (1964). He exhibited electronic music instruments at Expo '67 in Montreal. He contributed numerous articles on his findings in various scholarly journals. While he saw himself as a designer of instruments that assisted others in creative work, he himself realized a number of striking electronic compositions in the course of his development, among them the now-classic *Dripsody* (1959), which used only the sound of a single drop of water falling; other compositions were *Alchemy* (1964) and *Perpetual Motion* for Data Systems Computer (1970). His instruments revolutionized musical composition; his Sackbut synthesizer (1945–48; 1954–60; 1969–73) is today recognized as the first voltage-controlled synthesizer; among his other instruments were the Spectrogram (1959–62; designed to facilitate the use of complex sine tones in composition), the Alleatone (c. 1962; "a controlled chance device selecting one of 16 channels with weighted probabilities"), Sonde (1968–70; which can generate 200 sine waves simultaneously), and Polyphone (1970; a polyphonic synthesizer operated by a keyboard with touch-sensitive keys).

BIBL.: G. Young, *The Sackbut Blues: H. L.C.: Pioneer in Electronic Music* (Ottawa, 1989).—NS/LK/DM

Lechner, Leonhard (also **Leonardus Lechner Atheses** or **Athesinus**), outstanding Austrian-born German composer; b. in the Adige valley, Tirol, c. 1550; d. Stuttgart, Sept. 9, 1606. He was a chorister under Orlando di Lasso at the Munich Hofkapelle (1564?-68) and under Ivo de Vento and Antonius Gosswin at the Landshut Hofkapelle (1570). After serving as an asst. teacher at the St. Lorenz school in Nuremberg (1575–84), he obtained the position of Kapellmeister to Count Eitelfriedrich IV von Hohenzollern-Hechingen. However, being an adherent to Lutheranism, he found his position untenable at the Catholic Hofkapelle. In 1585 he secretly made his way to Tübingen. The Count sent Lechner a letter in which he promised to release him without prejudice. Lechner's reply was one of uncompromising defiance, prompting the angry Count to order his bodily return forthwith. Lechner then took refuge in Stuttgart in 1585 at the court of Duke Ludwig of Württemberg, who successfully mediated his dispute with his former patron and the Nuremberg town council. Lechner began his service in Stuttgart as a tenor, but soon was named composer in 1586. He served as asst. Hofkapellmeister until 1594; was formally installed as Hofkapellmeister in 1595, and proceeded to upgrade the Kapelle to a high level. Lechner's innovative genius is most strikingly revealed in his lieder. He was the first composer to set a complete cycle of German poems to music. A complete ed. of his works commenced publication in Kassel in 1954 under the editorship of K. Ameln et al.

WORKS (all publ. in Nuremberg): **VOCAL: S a c r e d :** *Motectae sacrae* for 4 to 6 Voices; *...addita esta in fine motecta* for 8 Voices (2 Choirs) (1575); *Sanctissimae virginis Mariae canticum, quod vulgo Magnificat inscribitur, secundum octo vulgares tonos* for 4 Voices (1578); *Sacrarum cantionum, liber secundus* for 5 to 6 Voices (1581); *Liber missarum...adjunctis aliquot introitibus in praecipua festa, ab Adventu Domini usque ad festum Sanctissimae Trinitatis* for 5 to 6 Voices (1584); *Septum psalmi poenitentiales...additis aliis quibusdam piis cantionibus* for 6 and More Voices (1587); also *Historia der Passion und Leidens Christi* for 4 Voices (perf. in Stuttgart, 1593). **L i e d e r :** *Neu teutsche Lieder, nach art der welschen Villanellen gantz kurtzweilig zu singen, auch auff allerley Seytenspil zu gebrauchen* for 3 Voices (1576; 3rd ed., 1586); *Der ander Theyl neuer teutscher Lieder, nach art der welschen Villanellen* for 3 Voices (1577; second ed., 1586); *Neue teutsche Lieder* for 4 to 5 Voices (1577; includes sacred lieder); *Neue teutsche Lieder, erstlich durch...Jacobum Regnart...componirt mit drey Stimmen, nach art der welschen Villanellen, jetzund aber...mit funff Stimmen gesetzet...con alchuni madrigali in lingua Italiana* for 5 Voices (1579); *Neue teutsche Lieder* for 4 to 5 Voices (1582; includes sacred lieder); *Neue lustige teutsche Lieder nach art der welschen Canzonen* for 4 Voices (1586); *Neue geistliche und weltliche teutsche Lieder* for 4 to 5 Voices (1589); also several works for special occasions.

BIBL.: M. Schreiber, *L. L. A. 1553–1606: Sein Leben und seine Kirchenmusik* (Birkeneck, 1932); idem, *Die Kirchenmusik des Kapellmeisters L. L. A.* (Regensburg, 1935); K. Ameln, *L. L. (um 1553–1606): Leben und Werk eines deutschen Komponisten aus Etschtal* (Lüdenscheid, 1957); U. Martin, *Historische und stilkritische Studien zu L. L.s Strophenliedern* (diss., Univ. of Göttingen, 1957).—NS/LK/DM

Lechthaler, Josef, Austrian composer and pedagogue; b. Rattenberg, Dec. 31, 1891; d. Vienna, Aug. 21,

1948. He studied philology in Innsbruck and then settled in Vienna, where he was a student of Springer and Goller at the Academy of Music and of Adler at the Univ. (Ph.D., 1919, with the diss. *Die kirchenmus: Werke von Uttendal*). In 1924 he became a teacher of theory at the Academy of Music, where he later was director of its church and school music dept. (1933–38; 1945–48). He became best known as a composer of church music, principally of 7 masses (1914–37) and a Stabat mater for Soloists, Chorus, Organ, and Orch. (1928). He also wrote choruses, songs, chamber music, and organ pieces.

BIBL.: E. Tittel, *J. L.* (Vienna, 1966).—NS/LK/DM

Leclair, family of notable French musicians, which included the following four brothers:

(1) Jean-Marie Leclair (l'aîné), celebrated violinist and composer; b. Lyons, May 10, 1697; d. (murdered) Paris, Oct. 22, 1764. His father was the master lacemaker and cellist Antoine Leclair. Jean-Marie studied violin, dancing, and lacemaking in his youth, excelling in all three. He then began his career as a dancer at the Lyons Opera, where he met Marie-Rose Casthagnié; they were married in 1716. About 1722 he went to Turin, where he was active as a ballet master. During a visit to Paris in 1723 to arrange for the publication of his op.1, a distinguished set of sonatas, he acquired a wealthy patron in Joseph Bonnier. Returning to Turin, he wrote ballets for the Teatro Regio Ducale and also received instruction from Somis. He then made a series of appearances at the Concert Spirituel in Paris in 1728. He also visited London, and then made a great impression when he played at the Kassel court with Pietro Locatelli. He subsequently received additional instruction from André Chéron in Paris. After the death of his first wife, Leclair married Louise Roussel in 1730; she engraved all of his works from op.2 forward. From 1733 to 1737 he served as ordinaire de la musique du roi to Louis XV. He then entered the service of Princess Anne at the Orange court in the Netherlands in 1738, and was honored with the Croix Neerlandaise du Lion. He was active three months of the year at the court, and, from 1740, spent the remaining months as maestro di cappella to the commoner François du Liz at The Hague. He returned to Paris in 1743. With the exception of a brief period of service with the Spanish Prince Don Philippe in Chambéry in 1744, he remained in Paris for the rest of his life. From 1748 until his death, he was music director and composer to his former student, the Duke of Gramont, who maintained a private theater in the Parisian suburb of Puteaux. Leclair separated from his wife about 1758. He was murdered as he was entering his home. The Paris police report listed three suspects: His gardener (who discovered his body), his estranged wife, and his nephew, the violinist Guillaume-François Vial, with whom he was on poor terms. The evidence clearly pointed to the nephew, but he was never charged with the deed. Leclair was the founder of the French violin school. He was also a distinguished composer who successfully combined the finest elements of the Italian and French styles of his day.

WORKS (all publ. in Paris): *Premier livre de sonates* for Violin and Basso Continuo (1723; 12 sonatas; 2 also for Flute; ed. as op.3, 1905, by A. Guilmant and J. Debroux), *Second livre de sonates* for Violin and Basso Continuo (c. 1728; 12 sonatas; 5 also for Flute; ed. in Publikationen Älterer Praktischer und Theoretischer Musikwerke, XXVII, 1903), (6) *Sonates* for 2 Violins, op.3 (1730; ed. by M. Pincherle, Paris, 1924, S. Beck, N.Y., 1946, and Rost, Locarno, Wilhelmshaven, and Amsterdam, 1963); (6) *Sonates en trio* for 2 Violins and Basso Continuo, op.4 (c. 1731–33; ed. by M. Pincherle, Paris, 1922); *Troisième livre de sonates* for Violin and Basso Continuo, op.5 (1734; 12 sonatas; ed. in Recent Researches in the Music of the Baroque Era, IV-V, 1968–69), *Première récréation de musique d'une exécution facile* for 2 Violins and Basso Continuo, op.6 (1736; suite with overture; ed. by H. Ruf, Kassel, 1976); 6 concertos for Violin, Strings, and Basso Continuo, op.7 (1737; No. 3 for Flute or Oboe, Strings, and Basso Continuo); *Deuxième récréation de musique d'une exécution facile* for 2 Recorders or Violin and Basso Continuo, op.8 (c. 1737; suite with overture; ed. by H. Ruf, Kassel, 1967); *Quatrième livre de sonates* for Violin and Basso Continuo, op.9 (1743; 12 sonatas; 2 also for Flute; 6 publ. as op.1, London, c. 1755; ed. in Recent Researches in the Music of the Baroque Era, X-XI, 1969–72); 6 concertos for Violin, Strings, and Basso Continuo, op.10 (1745); *Scylla et Glaucus*, opéra tragédie, op.11 (first perf. in Paris, Oct. 4, 1746; rev. version, Lyons, c. 1755); *Second livre de sonates* for 2 Violins, op.12 (c. 1747–49; 6 sonatas; ed. by M. Pincherle, Paris, 1950); (3) *Ouvertures et [3] sonates en trio* for 2 Violins and Basso Continuo, op.13 (1753; most arranged from other works); *Trio* for 2 Violins and Basso Continuo (1766; suite with overture; arranged from other works); *Sonate* for Violin and Basso Continuo (1767; ed. in Recent Researches in the Music of the Baroque Era, XI, 1972); his ballets and other works for the theater are not extant.

BIBL.: M. Pincherle, *J.-M. L. l'aîné* (Paris, 1952); P. Schwarze, *L.'s Contribution to the Concerto in France* (diss., Univ. of N.C., 1983).

(2) Jean-Marie Leclair (le second or le cadet), violinist and composer; b. Lyons, Sept. 23, 1703; d. there, Nov. 30, 1777. After serving as director of Besançon's Académie de Musique (1732–33), he returned to his native town to serve as director of its Académie des Beaux-Arts. He also was active as a teacher, and became widely known as a violinist. His works include *Premier livre de sonates* for Violin and Basso Continuo, op.1 (Paris, 1739; 12 sonatas), Sonates for 2 Violins, op.2 (Paris, c. 1750; 6 sonatas), Sym. (1768), Cantata, Divertissement, and other works, all of which are lost.

(3) Pierre Leclair, violinist and composer; b. Lyons, Nov. 19, 1709; d. there, April 2, 1784. He was active mainly as a violinist in Lyons. He publ. *Six sonates de récréation à deux violons*, op.1 (Versailles, 1764). He also composed a set of violin duets, op.2 (MS).

(4) Jean-Benoît Leclair, violinist and composer; b. Lyons, Sept. 25, 1714; d. after 1759. He was director of the Moulins Académie de Musique (1736–37) and later director of his own touring company of actors, dancers, and musicians (from c. 1747). He wrote a ballet héroïque, *Le Retour de la paix dans les Pays-Bas* (Brussels, April 27, 1749; only libretto extant).—NS/LK/DM

Lecoq, (Alexandre) Charles, noted French composer; b. Paris, June 3, 1832; d. there, Oct. 24, 1918. He learned to play the flageolet and piano as a youth, and later studied harmony with Crévecoeur; then was admitted to the Paris Cons. (1849), where he took courses with Bazin, Halévy, and Benoist. He won second prize in counterpoint and was primus accessit in the organ class, but was compelled to leave the Cons. to assist his family (1854). He first gained notice as a composer when he shared a prize with Bizet sponsored by Offenbach for the Théâtre des Bouffes-Parisiens, for the operetta *Le docteur Miracle* (April 8, 1857). Although he brought out 7 more works for the stage during the next decade, it was only with his *Fleur-de-thé* (Paris, April 11, 1868) that he attained success. After going to Brussels (1870), he scored notable successes with his operettas *Les cent vierges* (March 16, 1872), *La fille de Madame Angot* (Dec. 4, 1872), and *Giroflé-Girofla* (March 24, 1874); they subsequently were performed in Paris with great success, making Lecoq the leading Parisian operetta composer of his day after Offenbach. After returning to Paris, he brought out such popular favorites as *La petite mariée* (Dec. 21, 1875), *Le petit duc* (Jan. 25, 1878), *Janot* (Jan. 21, 1881), *Le jour et la nuit* (Nov. 5, 1881), and *Le coeur et la main* (Oct. 19, 1882). In subsequent years he continued to write works for the stage, but he failed to equal his previous successes. He was made a Chevalier (1900) and an Officer (1910) of the Légion d'honneur. His music was distinguished by melodic grace, instrumental finish, and dramatic acumen.

WORKS: DRAMATIC (all are operettas and were first perf. in Paris unless otherwise given): *Le docteur Miracle* (April 8, 1957); *Huis-clos* (Jan. 28, 1859); *Le baiser à la porte* (March 26, 1864), *Liline et Valentin* (May 25, 1864); *Le myosotis* (May 2, 1866); *Ondines au champagne* (Sept. 5, 1866); *Le cabaret de Ramponneau* (Oct. 11, 1867); *L'amour et son carquois* (Jan. 30, 1868); *Fleur-de-thé* (April 11, 1868); *Les jumeaux de Bergame* (Nov. 20, 1868); *Gandolfo* (Jan. 16, 1869); *Deux portières pour un cordon* (March 15, 1869); *Le rajah de Mysore* (Sept. 21, 1869); *Le beau Dunois* (April 13, 1870); *Le testament de M. de Crac* (Oct. 23, 1871); *Le barbier de Trouville* (Nov. 19, 1871); *Sauvons la caisse* (Dec. 22, 1871); *Les cent vierges* (Brussels, March 16, 1872); *La fille de Madame Angot* (Brussels, Dec. 4, 1872); *Giroflé-Girofla* (Brussels, March 21, 1874); *Les prés Saint-Gervais* (Nov. 14, 1874); *Le pompon* (Nov. 10, 1875); *La petite mariée* (Dec. 21, 1875); *Kosiki* (Oct. 18, 1876); *La marjolaine* (Feb. 3, 1877); *La petit duc* (Jan. 25, 1878); *La Camargo* (Nov. 20, 1878); *Le grand Casimir* (Jan. 11, 1879); *La petite mademoiselle* (April 12, 1879); *La jolie persane* (Oct. 28, 1879); *Janot* (Jan. 21, 1881); *La rousotte* (Jan. 25, 1881; completed by Hervé); *Le jour et la nuit* (Nov. 5, 1881); *Le couer et la main* (Oct. 19, 1882); *La princesse des Canaries* (Feb. 9, 1883); *L'oiseau bleu* (Jan. 16, 1884); *La vie mondaine* (Feb. 13, 1885); *Plutus*, opéra-comique (March 31, 1886); *Les grenadiers de Mont-Cornette* (Jan. 4, 1887); *Ali-Baba* (Brussels, Nov. 11, 1887); *La volière* (Feb. 11, 1888); *L'egyptienne*, opéra-comique (Nov. 8, 1890); *Nos bons chasseurs*, vaudeville (April 10, 1894); *Ninette* (Feb. 28, 1896); *Barbe-Bleu*, ballet-pantomime (May 12, 1898); *Ruse d'amour*, comédie (Boulogne, June 26, 1898); *Le cygne*, ballet (April 20, 1899); *La belle au bois dormant* (Feb. 19, 1900); *Yetta*, opéra-comique (Brussels, March 7, 1903); *Rose Mousse*, comédie-musicale (Jan. 28, 1904); *La salutiste*, opéra monologue (Jan. 14, 1905); *Le trahison de Pan*, opéra-comique (Aix-les-Bains, Sept. 13, 1910). He also wrote several orch. works, more than 100 songs, dances, and piano pieces.

BIBL.: L. Schneider, *Les Maîtres de l'operette française: Hervé, C. L.* (Paris, 1924); idem, *Une Heure de musique avec C. L.* (Paris, 1930).—**NS/LK/DM**

Lecuna, Juan Vicente, Venezuelan composer; b. Valencia, Nov. 20, 1891; d. Rome, April 15, 1954. He studied at the Escuela Normal, graduating in 1906, then went to Caracas and studied theory with Juan Vicente and piano with Salvador Llamozas at the Cons. He later took a course in composition with Jaime Pahissa in Buenos Aires (1937–41), where he also received instruction from Falla; likewise studied orchestration with Strube in Baltimore (1941). In the meantime, he entered the diplomatic service. In 1936 he was appointed a civil employee at the Venezuelan embassy in Washington, D.C. In 1943 he was sent by the Venezuelan dept. of education to study musical education in Brazil, Uruguay, Argentina, and Chile. In 1947 he was named Secretary of the Legation of Venezuela in Rome, and later was appointed a member of the Venezuelan legation at the Vatican. He composed a Piano Concerto, *Suite venezolana* for 4 Guitars, String Quartet, Harp Sonata, songs, and a suite of 4 Venezuelan dances for Piano.—**NS/LK/DM**

Ledenev, Roman (Semyonovich), Russian composer; b. Moscow, Dec. 4, 1930. He studied composition at the Moscow Cons. with Rakov and Anatoly Alexandrov, and later was an instructor there. His music is marked by a typically Russian lyric quality touched with permissible dissonances in harmonic treatment. He composed an oratorio, *The Chronicle of the Campaign of Igor* (1954), *The Song of Freedom* for Chorus, after Asian and African poets (1961), Violin Concerto (1964), Viola Concerto (1964), Sonata in memory of Prokofiev (1956), and numerous songs.—**NS/LK/DM**

Ledger, Philip (Stevens), noted English conductor, organist, harpsichordist, pianist, editor, and arranger; b. Bexhill-on-Sea, Sussex, Dec. 12, 1937. He was educated at King's Coll., Cambridge, and at the Royal Coll. of Music, London. He served as Master of the Music at Chelmsford Cathedral (1962–65) and as director of music at the Univ. of East Anglia (1965–73), where he served as dean of the School of Fine Arts and Music (1968–71). In 1968 he was named an artistic director of the Aldeburgh Festival; subsequently was engaged as conductor of the Cambridge Univ. Musical Soc. (1973) and director of music and organist at King's Coll. (1974). In 1982 he was appointed principal of the Royal Scottish Academy of Music and Drama in Glasgow. He ed. *The Oxford Book of English Madrigals* (1978) and works of Byrd, Purcell, and Handel. A versatile musician, he is renowned as an elegant performer of early English music. In 1985 he was made a Commander of the Order of the British Empire.—**NS/LK/DM**

Leduc, Alphonse, French music publisher and composer; b. Nantes, March 9, 1804; d. Paris, June 17, 1868. He studied harmony with Reicha at the Paris Cons., and also mastered the bassoon, flute, and guitar. He composed over 1,000 works, mainly piano pieces. In 1841 he founded a music publishing business in Paris. After his death, his son Alphonse Leduc II (b. probably in Paris, May 29, 1844; d. there, June 4, 1892) inherited the business; at the death of the latter, his widow

LEDUC

directed the firm until 1904, when their son Émile-Alphonse Leduc III (b. Nov. 14, 1878; d. Paris, May 24, 1951) became its director; his sons Claude-Alphonse and Gilbert-Alphonse Leduc (partners with their father from 1938) continued the business. From 1860 to 1895 the firm publ. *L'Art Musical*, which was then assimilated with the *Guide Musical*.—NS/LK/DM

Leduc, Jacques, Belgian composer and teacher; b. Jette, near Brussels, March 1, 1932. He studied music at the Royal Cons. in Brussels and privately with Jean Absil. He was director of the Uccle Academy of Music (1962–83). He was made a prof. of harmony (1968), of counterpoint (1972), and of fugue (1979) at the Royal Cons. in Brussels; was also director of the Chapelle Musicale Reine Elisabeth (from 1976). He was made a member of the Royal Academy of Sciences, Letters, and Fine Arts of Belgium in 1983.

WORKS: DRAMATIC: *Nous attendons Sémiramis*, lyric comedy (Belgian TV, Feb. 6, 1973). ORCH.: *Antigone*, symphonic poem (1960); Concertino for Oboe and Strings (1962); *Divertissement* for Flute and Strings (1962); *Fantaisie sur le thème de "La Folia"* for Clarinet and Chamber Orch. or Piano (1964); *4 Études* for Chamber Orch. (1966); *Le Printemps*, symphonic sketch (1967); *Ouverture d'été* (1968); Sym. (1969); Piano Concerto (1970); *5 croquis* (1971); *Dialogue* for Clarinet and Chamber Orch. or Piano (1972); *Instantanés*, 5 pieces for String Ensemble (1972); *Suite de danses* (1976); *3 Esquisses concertantes* (1978). CHAMBER: Wind Quintet (1960); *3 petites pièces en quatuor* for 4 Flutes or Clarinets (1963); String Trio (1963); *Suite en quatuor* for 4 Saxophones (1964); Flute Sonata (1966); Violin Sonata (1967); *Capriccio* for Wind Quartet (1969); *Serenade* for Wind Quintet (1977); *Rhapsodie* for Saxophone and Piano (1978); *Trois pièces* for 5 Brass Instruments (1980); *Pièces en trio* for 2 Violins and Piano (1984); *Lamento* for Viola (1986). KEYBOARD: P i a n o : *4 pièces brèves* (1965); *Prelude, Variations, and Fugato* (1965); *Contrastes* (1967); *Apostrophes* (1971); *Pochades* (1977); *4 Miniatures* (1981); *Scherzetto* (1986). O r g a n : Various pieces. VOCAL: *L'Aventure*, cantata (1961); *Sortilèges africains*, sequence for Voice, Saxophone, Percussion, and Piano (1966); choruses; songs.—NS/LK/DM

Leduc, Pierre (le jeune), French violinist and music publisher, brother of **Simon (l'aîné) Leduc**; b. Paris, 1755; d. the Netherlands, Oct. 1816. He received training in violin from his brother. In 1770 he made his debut at the Concert Spirituel in Paris, and thereafter performed there regularly. In 1775 he founded his own music publishing firm, which brought out works by many French composers of his day. His son (Antoine-Pierre) Auguste Leduc (b. Paris, 1779; d. there, May 25, 1823), took control of the firm in 1803.—LK/DM

Leduc (Le Duc), Simon (l'aîné), French violinist and composer, brother of **Pierre (le jeune) Leduc**; b. Jan. 15, 1742; d. Paris, Jan. 20, 1777. He studied violin with Gaviniès. He was second violin in the Concert Spirituel (1759–63), making his solo debut there on Sept. 8, 1763. He then was first violin there, but also made appearances as a soloist. With Gaviniès and Gossec, he

became a director there (1773). He was a talented composer of orch. and chamber music, and also active as a publisher exclusively of his own works.—NS/LK/DM

Led Zeppelin, the prototypical British heavy-metal band of the late 1960s and 1970s; MEMBERSHIP: Robert Plant, lead voc. (b. West Bromwich, Staffordshire, England, Aug. 20, 1948); Jimmy Page, lead gtr., mdln., pedal steel gtr., bjo. (b. London, England, Jan. 9, 1944); John Paul Jones (real name, John Baldwin), bs., kybd. (b. Sidcup, Kent, England, Jan. 3, 1946); and John Bonham, drm. (b. Birmingham, England, May 31, 1947; d. Windsor, Berkshire, England, Sept. 25, 1980).

Jimmy Page took up guitar in his early teens, later playing with Neil Christian and The Crusaders before attending art college for two years. Upon returning to music, he quickly became a much sought-after sessions guitarist, allegedly playing on more than half of all the records released in Great Britain between 1963 and 1965. Early sessions credits included The Who's "I Can't Explain," Them's "Here Comes the Night," and unspecified recordings by the Kinks (disputed by Ray Davies), The Rolling Stones, and Herman's Hermits. He turned down an offer to join The Yardbirds as Eric Clapton's replacement in 1965, instead serving as house producer-arranger for Andrew Oldham's Immediate label.

In mid-1966, Jimmy Page did join The Yardbirds, replacing departed bass player Paul Samwell-Smith, later to play twin lead guitars with Jeff Beck after Chris Dreja switched to bass. Yardbirds recordings with Beck and Page apparently included "The Train Kept a-Rollin'" from *Rave Up*, "Stroll On" from the soundtrack to the movie *Blow-Up*, and "Happenings Ten Years Time Ago." Jeff Beck left The Yardbirds at the end of 1966 and Page continued as the group's lead guitarist for another 18 months. Finally, in July 1968, The Yardbirds broke up, and Page and Dreja unsuccessfully attempted to continue as The New Yardbirds with vocalist-guitarist Terry Reid. Reid, unavailable to join the group, suggested that Robert Plant from the Birmingham group The Band of Joy be recruited as lead vocalist. Plant, in turn, recommended former Band of Joy drummer John Bonham. Dreja later dropped out to pursue a career as a photographer, and sessions bassist-keyboardist John Paul Jones was brought in as his replacement. Essentially formed in October 1968, Led Zeppelin quickly recorded their debut album for Atlantic Records, soon fulfilling The Yardbirds' remaining concert obligations. In the meantime, Page played sessions with Jeff Beck ("Beck's Bolero"), Donovan (*Hurdy Gurdy Man*) and Joe Cocker (*With a Little Help from My Friends*).

Led Zeppelin's debut album became an instant bestseller, remaining on the album charts for nearly two years. The album featured their first American singles chart entry, "Good Times Bad Times" and the classics "Dazed and Confused" and "Communication Breakdown." In 1969, the group completed their first American tour in support of Vanilla Fudge, soon returning as a headline act. Shortly thereafter, a plethora of heavy-metal rock acts developed in the wake of Led Zeppelin. *Led Zeppelin II* included the smash hit classic "Whole Lotta Love," as well as "Living Loving Maid (She's Just a Woman)" and "Ramble On."

Concentrating their activities on the U.S. (they never released a single in Great Britain), Led Zeppelin was conducting their fifth American tour by March 1970. The transitional *Led Zeppelin III* yielded the major hit "Immigrant Song," yet revealed a more acoustic sound, as evidenced by "That's the Way" and "Tangerine." *Led Zeppelin IV* was the album that finally brought the group critical recognition. In addition to containing the hits "Black Dog" and "Rock and Roll," the album included one of the definitive production arrangements of the 1970s, "Stairway to Heaven," which built from a subtle acoustic guitar and vocal to a thundering climax, ending with a gentle acoustic guitar–vocal reprise. *Led Zeppelin IV* stayed on the album charts for nearly five years and sold more than 11 million copies.

During the summer of 1972, Led Zeppelin again toured America, outdrawing The Rolling Stones in a number of cities. *Houses of the Holy* was the first Led Zeppelin album to utilize string arrangements (by Page), yielding a major hit with "D'yer Mak'er." The group's 1973 American tour was an instant sellout, and they broke both the single-artist concert attendance and gross income records with their Tampa, Fla., show. With the rock press finally acknowledging their enormous popularity, Led Zeppelin formed Swan Song Records with manager Peter Grant in 1974 for their own recordings, as well as recordings by Bad Company, Dave Edmunds, and The Pretty Things.

Physical Graffiti contained the mystical "Kashmir" and yielded the moderate hit "Trampled under Foot," but lead vocalist Robert Plant was seriously injured in an automobile accident in Greece on Aug. 4, 1975, necessitating a layoff of more than a year. *Presence* sold quite well without the benefit of either a tour or a single. The film (and soundtrack album) *The Song Remains the Same*, taken primarily from a 1973 concert at Madison Square Garden, was released as the group's first live album and movie.

During 1977, Led Zeppelin again toured the U.S., playing marathon three-hour sets to sellout crowds, but an ugly incident between shows at the Oakland Coliseum (in which three members of promoter Bill Graham's support crew were allegedly beaten up) served to reinforce the notion that Led Zeppelin had become arrogant, insensitive, and smug. The group subsequently maintained a low profile and eventually re-emerged in 1979 with *In through the Out Door* and the major hit "Fool in the Rain." That fall, Led Zeppelin's first British appearance in four years at the Knebworth Festival was reviewed as perfunctory at best, obsolete at worst. On Sept. 25, 1980, drummer John Bonham was found dead in the Windsor home of Jimmy Page, the victim of inhalation of vomit after a drinking spree. On Dec. 4, Led Zeppelin announced that it was disbanding. Led Zeppelin was inducted into the Rock and Roll Hall of Fame in 1995.

By 1982, Robert Plant was collaborating with guitarist Robbie Blount, recording three solo albums with him through 1985. Plant toured with Blount and drummer Phil Collins (of Genesis) in 1983, scoring a major hit with the oddly titled love song "Big Log" and a moderate hit with "In the Mood" from *The Principle of Moments*, the first album released on Plant's own Es Paranza label. In 1984, Plant helped form the short-lived "supergroup" The Honeydrippers with guitarists Jimmy Page, Jeff Beck, and Nile Rodgers, recording rhythm-and-blues material on the mini-album *Volume One* on Es Paranza. The recording yielded a smash hit with "Sea of Love" and a major hit with "Rockin' at Midnight."

In 1982, Jimmy Page recorded the largely instrumental soundtrack to the movie *Death Wish II*. Following benefit performances for Ronnie Lane's Appeal for Action Research into Multiple Sclerosis in late 1983 with former Bad Company vocalist Paul Rodgers, Page and Rodgers formed The Firm, a rather crass commercial venture, in July 1984. The group remained together until 1986, touring, recording two albums, and scoring a major hit with "Radioactive" in 1985.

In 1988, Jimmy Page recorded *Outrider* and toured with vocalist John Miles and drummer Jason Bonham, John Bonham's son, whereas Robert Plant reconstituted his band and began collaborating with keyboardist Phil Johnstone. Plant's *Now and Zen* produced a major hit with "Tall Cool One" (which sampled several Led Zeppelin guitar riffs) and the minor hit "Ship of Fools." Following 1990's *Manic Nirvana*, Plant expanded his band for 1993's *Fate of Nations*, a remarkably mature and engaging album that finally established him as a solo artist of some import.

In the later half of the 1980s, Led Zeppelin reunited briefly twice, once in July 1985 with drummers Phil Collins and Tony Thompson for the Live Aid concert in Philadelphia, and again in May 1988 for Atlantic Records' 40th anniversary celebration, with Jason Bonham on drums. In 1989, Jason Bonham formed Bonham, recording two albums for WTG Records. Jimmy Page and one-time Deep Purple vocalist David Coverdale recorded *Coverdale/Page*, released in 1993. In August 1994, Plant and Page performed with Egyptian and Moroccan musicians for what became the MTV cable network special *Unledded* (broadcast in October) and *No Quarter* album. The two, accompanied by several other rock musicians and a Middle Eastern ensemble, toured in support of the album in 1995 and later recorded *Walking into Clarksdale*. That same year, Atlantic Records issued the Led Zeppelin tribute album *Encomium*, recorded by Sheryl Crow, Stone Temple Pilots, and Hootie and The Blowfish, among others.

DISC.: **LED ZEPPELIN:** *Led Zeppelin* (1969); *Led Zeppelin II* (1969); *Led Zeppelin III* (1970); *Led Zeppelin IV* (1971); *Houses of the Holy* (1973); *Physical Graffiti* (1975); *Presence* (1976); *The Song Remains the Same* (soundtrack; 1976); *In through the Out Door* (1979); *Coda* (1982); *BBC Sessions* (rec. 1969–71; rel. 1997). **ROBERT PLANT:** *Pictures at Eleven* (1982); *The Principle of Moments* (1983); *Shaken 'n' Stirred* (1985); *Little by Little* (1985);

Now and Zen (1988); *Manic Nirvana* (1990); *Fate of Nations* (1993). **THE HONEYDRIPPERS:** *Volume One* (1984/1985). **THE FIRM:** *The Firm* (1985); *Mean Business* (1986). **JIMMY PAGE:** *Special Early Works* (1972); *Death Wish II* (soundtrack; 1982); *Outrider* (1988); *The Early Years* (1992). **DAVID COVERDALE/JIMMY PAGE:** *Coverdale/Page* (1993). **JIMMY PAGE AND ROBERT PLANT:** *No Quarter* (1994); *Walking into Clarksdale* (1998). **BONHAM:** *The Disregard of Timekeeping* (1989); *Mad Hatter* (1992).

BIBL.: M. Gross, *Robert Plant* (N.Y., 1975); R. Yorke, *The L. Z. Biography* (Toronto, 1976; N.Y., 1976); H. Mylett and R. Bunton, *L. Z.: In the Light 1968–1980* (N.Y., 1981); P. Kendall, *L. Z.: A Visual Documentary* (N.Y., 1982; N.Y., 1986); S. Davis, *Hammer of the Gods: The L. Z. Saga* (N.Y., 1985); C. R. Cross, *L. Z.: Heaven and Hell, An Illustrated History* (N.Y., 1991); D. Lewis, *L. Z.: A Celebration* (London, 1991); E. McSquare, *L. Z.: Good Times, Bad Times* (N.Y., 1991); R. Cole, *Stairway to Heaven: L. Z. Uncensored* (N.Y., 1992); W. Ruhlmann, *Led Zeppelin* (Stamford, Conn., 1992); R. Yorke, *L. Z.: The Definitive Biography* (Lancaster, Pa., 1993).—**BH**

Lee, Bill (actually, **William James Edwards**), jazz bassist, composer; b. Snow Hill, Ala., July 23, 1928. He worked as a studio musician in the 1950s and 1960s in N.Y., including work with folk-pop artists such as Bob Dylan. In the late 1960s he ran a jazz program in the Bronx sponsored by the State of N.Y.; the faculty included McCoy Tyner. Today he is best known as the father of filmmaker Spike Lee, for whom he wrote the delightful jazz score to *She's Gotta Have It*.—**LP**

Lee, Brenda (originally, **Tarpley, Brenda May**) aka **"Little Miss Dyn-a-mite"**), one of the most popular female vocalists of the late 1950s and early 1960s in pop-music, who then became a country star in the 1970s; b. Lithonia, Ga., Dec. 11, 1944. Brenda Lee began singing at the age of four, winning an Atlanta television station's children's talent contest at age six. She became a regular on the local radio show *Starmaker's Revue* at seven and performed on the local television show *TV Ranch* from 1951 to 1954. Introduced to country music veteran Red Foley in 1955, she later appeared on his television show Ozark Jubilee (later Country Music Jubilee and Jubilee U.S.A.) and toured with his road show. Signed to Decca Records in 1956, Lee initially recorded rockabilly, scoring her first moderate pop hit in early 1957 with "One Step at a Time," followed by "Dynamite." Debuting in Las Vegas in late 1956, she soon became known as "Little Miss Dynamite" for her powerful voice and diminutive stature.

Brenda Lee scored her first smash pop hit in 1960 with the seductive "Sweet Nothin's." That song and the top hit "I'm Sorry" were written by rockabilly artist Ronnie Self. The flip side of "I'm Sorry," the rollicking "That's All You Gotta Do" (written by Jerry Reed), also became a smash hit. Her two 1960 albums became best-sellers as her success continued with the top hit ballad "I Want to Be Wanted," the Christmas classic "Rockin' around the Christmas Tree," and the smashes "Emotions," "You Can Depend on Me," "Dum Dum" (co-written by Jackie DeShannon and Eddie Cochran girlfriend Sharon Sheeley), and "Fool #1." In 1962 Lee

began concentrating on nightclub appearances, rather than concerts, and smash hits continued through 1963 with "Break It to Me Gently," "Everybody Loves Me but You" (also written by Ronnie Self), "All Alone Am I," and "Losing You." Subsequent major hits through 1966 included "My Whole World Is Falling Down," "As Usual," "Is It True," "Too Many Rivers," and "Coming on Strong."

For Brenda Lee, the 1969 moderate pop hit "Johnny One Time" marked her re-entry into the country field. She seldom performed during the 1970s, and by 1973 Decca had been absorbed by MCA Records, for whom, through 1975, she scored country smashes with Kris Kristofferson's "Nobody Wins," "Sunday Sunrise," "Wrong Ideas," "Big Four Poster Bed," "Rock on Baby," and "He's My Rock." She managed country near-smashes with "Tell Me What It's Like," "The Cowgirl and the Dandy" and "Broken Trust" in 1979–80 and helped record *The Winning Hand* with Willie Nelson, Dolly Parton, and Kris Kristofferson in 1983. Her last major country hit came in late 1984 with "Hallelujah, I Love Her So," in duet with George Jones. Re-established on the Nev. casino circuit in the 1980s, Brenda Lee joined Loretta Lynn and Kitty Wells for "Honky Tonk Angels' Medley" from k.d. lang's *Shadowland* album and moved to Warner Bros. Records for *Brenda Lee*.

DISC.: BRENDA LEE: *Grandma, What Great Songs You Sang* (1959); *Brenda Lee* (1960); *This Is ... Brenda Lee* (1960); *Emotions* (1961); *All the Way* (1961); *Sincerely* (1962); *That's All, Brenda* (1962); *All Alone Am I* (1963); *Let Me Sing* (1963); *By Request* (1964); *Merry Christmas from Brenda Lee* (1964); *Top Teen Hits* (1965); *Versatile* (1965); *Too Many Rivers* (1965); *Bye Bye, Blues* (1966); *Ten Golden Years* (1966); *Coming on Strong* (1966); *Reflections in Blue* (1967); *Here's Brenda Lee* (1967); *Johnny One Time* (1969); *Memphis Portrait* (1970); *Let It Be Me* (1970); *Brenda* (1973); *The Brenda Lee Story* (1973); *New Sunrise* (1974); *Now* (1975); *Sincerely, Brenda Lee* (1975); *The L. A. Sessions* (1976); *Even Better* (1980); *Take Me Back* (1980); *Only When I Laugh* (1981); *Greatest Country Hits* (1982); *Feels So Right* (1985); *Brenda Lee* (1991); *A Brenda Lee Christmas* (1991); *Greatest Hits Live* (1992). **BRENDA LEE AND PETE FOUNTAIN:** *For the First Time* (1968). **BRENDA LEE, KRIS KRISTOFFERSON, WILLIE NELSON, AND DOLLY PARTON:** *The Winning Hand* (1983).

BIBL.: S. VanHecke, "B. L.: Little Miss Dynamite." *Goldmine* (March 15, 1996).—**BH**

Lee, Dai-Keong, Hawaiian composer of Chinese descent; b. Honolulu, Sept. 2, 1915. Following pre-med training at the Univ. of Hawaii (1933–36), he pursued musical studies with Sessions and Jacobi at the Juilliard Graduate School in N.Y. (1938–41), with Copland at the Berkshire Music Center in Tanglewood (summer, 1941), and with Luening at Columbia Univ. (M.A., 1951). He held 2 Guggenheim fellowships (1945, 1951). Lee's works utilize various native elements for the most part, although he has embraced a neo-Classical approach in some of his more ambitious scores.

WORKS: DRAMATIC: Opera: *The Poet's Dilemma* (N.Y., April 12, 1940); *Open the Gates* (1951); *Phineas and the Nightingale* (1952); *Speakeasy* (N.Y., Feb. 8, 1957); *2 Knickerbocker Tales* (1957); *Ballad of Kitty the Barkeep* (1979; based on *Speakeasy*). **Musical Plays:** *Noa Noa* (1972); *Jenny Lind* (1981;

based on *Phineas and the Nightingale*). I n c i d e n t a l M u - s i c : *Teahouse of the August Moon* (1953; orch. suite, 1954). B a l l e t : *Waltzing Matilda* (1951). O t h e r : Film scores. ORCH.: *Prelude and Hula* (1939); *Hawaiian Festival Overture* (1940); *Golden Gate Overture* (1941); *Introduction and Scherzo* for Strings (1941); 2 syms.: No. 1 (1941–42; rev. 1946) and No. 2 (San Francisco, March 14, 1952); *Pacific Prayer* (1943; rev. as *Canticle of the Pacific* for Chorus and Orch., 1968); Violin Concerto (1947; rev. 1955); *Polynesian Suite* (1958); *Mele olili* (Joyful Songs) for Soloists, Chorus, and Orch. (1960); *Concerto Grosso* for Strings (1985). OTHER: Chamber music; songs.—NS/LK/DM

Lee, Peggy (originally, Egstrom, Norma Delores)

Lee, Peggy (originally, **Egstrom, Norma Delores**), American singer, songwriter, and actress; b. Jamestown, N.Dak., May 26, 1920. Lee's small, carefully employed voice and sometimes arch phrasing allowed her to bridge musical styles from the Swing Era to the Rock Era; she began scoring hits while singing with Benny Goodman, notably "Why Don't You Do Right," cowrote some of her own novelty hits during her commercial peak in the late 1940s, among them "Mañana (Is Soon Enough for Me)," and continued to perform successfully for the next 50 years, scoring occasional hits such as "Lover," "Fever," and "Is That All There Is."

Lee's father, Marvin Olaf Egstrom, was a station agent at a railroad depot; her mother, Selma Emele Anderson Egstrom, died when she was a child. By the age of 14 she was singing with a local band and on local radio, and after graduating from high school she continued performing on radio and with territory bands in the Upper Midwest and in Calif. In 1941 she had an engagement at a hotel in Chicago, where she was seen by Benny Goodman, who hired her in August.

Lee's first chart record came with Goodman's recording of "Blues in the Night" (music by Harold Arlen, lyrics by Johnny Mercer) in February 1942. She also sang on the Goodman revival of the 1937 song "Somebody Else Is Taking My Place" (music and lyrics by Dick Howard, Russ Morgan, and Bob Elsworth), which reached the charts in March 1942 and hit the Top Ten. Goodman's cover of "Why Don't You Do Right" (music and lyrics by Joe McCoy), with a Lee vocal, charted in January 1943, becoming a Top Ten hit. Lee appeared with Goodman in the films *The Powers Girl* (January 1943) and *Stage Door Canteen* (June 1943), but she left his band in March 1943 and married guitarist David Michael Barbour, temporarily retiring from show business. She bore a daughter, but was lured back to music by Capitol Records, which signed her to a contract in 1945.

Lee reached the charts for the first time as a solo artist with "Waitin' for the Train to Come In" (music and lyrics by Sunny Skylar and Martin Block); it peaked in the Top Ten in December 1945. In June 1946 she began to appear on the weekly network radio series *Rhapsody in Rhythm*, remaining with the show until September 1947; during this period she also appeared on the show *Meet Me at Parky's*. Her next hit came with a song she wrote with her husband, "I Don't Know Enough about You": it peaked in the Top Ten in July 1946. Her recording of "It's All Over Now" (music and lyrics by Sunny Skylar

and Don Marcotte) reached the Top Ten in November 1946, and she returned to the Top Ten with "Chi-Baba, Chi-Baba (My Bambino Go to Sleep)" (music and lyrics by Mack David, Jerry Livingston, and Al Hoffman) in July 1947. That month she began hosting the network radio show *The Electric Hour Summer Series*, remaining with it through the end of August, then becoming the featured singer on *The Jimmy Durante Show* during the 1947–48 season.

Lee's next hit, "Golden Earrings" (music by Victor Young, lyrics by Jay Livingston and Ray Evans), peaked in the Top Ten in January 1948. She scored five more chart hits during the year, making her second only to The Andrews Sisters as the year's most successful recording artist. In March she hit #1 with the million-seller "Mañana (Is Soon Enough for Me)," another song she had written with her husband. The same month Capitol released her first album, *Rendezvous with Peggy Lee*, which hit the Top Ten.

During 1948, Lee began substituting for Jo Stafford on one night of the five- nights-a-week musical variety radio series *Chesterfield Supper Club*. For the 1949–50 season the show broadcast once a week, with Lee as the hostess. She reached the singles charts four times in 1949, enjoying greatest success with her cover of "Riders in the Sky (A Cowboy Legend)" (music and lyrics by Stan Jones), which peaked in the Top Ten in June. She was back in the Top Ten in January 1950 with "The Old Master Painter" (music by Beasley Smith, lyrics by Haven Gillespie), a duet with Mel Tormé. She made her third film appearance in *Mr. Music* in December 1950.

Increasingly, Lee turned to nightclub work, making her N.Y. club debut at the Copacabana in March 1951. During the summer of 1951 she had her own weekly network radio series, *The Peggy Lee Show*, and she and Mel Tormé cohosted a three-times-a-week, 15-minute musical program on network television, *TV's Top Tunes*. She also spent a few months as a regular on the TV series *Songs for Sale* starting in December 1951. She and David Barbour divorced that year.

Lee left Capitol Records and signed to Decca in 1952. For the new label she recorded an unusual arrangement of the 1932 Richard Rodgers and Lorenz Hart song "Lover"; the record reached the Top Ten in July. In January 1953 she essayed her first screen acting role in a remake of *The Jazz Singer*, also singing a song she had written. This was the first of nine feature films that would use her compositions. That same month she married actor Brad Dexter, from whom she was divorced before the end of the year. She did not appear in the film *White Christmas*, released in October 1954, but since Rosemary Clooney, who did, was contracted to another record company, Lee accompanied Bing Crosby and Danny Kaye on an album of songs from the film that made the Top Ten in early 1955. Her voice and her songs, written with Sonny Burke, were used in the animated feature *Lady and the Tramp*, released in June 1955, and she appeared in the film *Pete Kelly's Blues*, released in August 1955, earning an Academy Award nomination for Best Supporting Actress and sharing the Top Ten album *Songs from Pete Kelly's Blues* with Ella Fitzgerald.

Lee scored her first Top 40 hit in four years with "Mr. Wonderful" (music and lyrics by Jerry Bock, Larry Holofcener, and George David Weiss) in March 1956; the record reached the Top Ten in the U.K. In April she married actor Dewey Martin; they divorced in June 1959. Lee returned to Capitol Records in 1957 and began focusing on the album market, reaching the charts with the Nelson Riddle–arranged LPs *The Man I Love* in July 1957 and *Jump for Joy* in July 1958. But she also enjoyed a surprise Top Ten hit, as her drastically rearranged version of John Davenport and Eddie Cooley's 1956 song "Fever," for which she wrote several new verses, reached the Top Ten in August 1958. It earned nominations for Record of the Year and Best Vocal Performance, Female, at the first Grammy ceremony.

Lee next reached the charts with her *Things Are Swingin'* LP in December 1958; it featured the chart single "Alright, Okay, You Win" (music and lyrics by Sid Wyche), and that song brought her another Grammy nomination for Best Vocal Performance, Female. Her last chart album of the 1950s was *Beauty and the Beat!*, a live LP on which she was accompanied by George Shearing and his quintet. During this period she appeared regularly in prestigious nightclubs in major cities as well as shows in Las Vegas, and made occasional television appearances in both singing and acting roles. Two of her 1960 albums, *Latin à la Lee!* (January) and *Pretty Eyes* (July), made it big, with the former staying in the charts more than a year and earning a Grammy nomination for Best Vocal Performance, Album, Female. "Heart" (music and lyrics by Richard Adler and Jerry Ross), a chart single drawn from *Latin à la Lee!*, earned a Grammy nomination for Best Vocal Performance by a Pop Single Artist, and Lee's single "I'm Gonna Go Fishin'" (music by Duke Ellington, lyrics by Lee), from the film *Anatomy of a Murder*, was a Grammy nominee for Best Vocal Performance, Single Record or Track, Female.

Lee began 1961 by recording a live album at Basin Street East, the club she played regularly in N.Y. The *Basin Street East* LP, released in May, spent five months in the charts and earned her seventh Grammy nomination for Best Solo Vocal Performance, Female. She made her first tour of Europe during the year. In 1962 she charted with both the compilation album *Bewitching-Lee!*, which contained recordings from the 1940s, and the newly recorded *Sugar 'n' Spice*. At the end of the year she released the single "I'm a Woman" (music and lyrics by Jerry Leiber and Mike Stoller), which reached the charts and earned another Grammy nomination for Best Solo Vocal Performance, Female. During 1963 she charted with an *I'm a Woman* album (also a Grammy nominee for Best Vocal Performance, Female) and with the LP *Mink Jazz*. In February 1964 she married percussionist Jack Del Rio, from whom she was divorced within months.

While she continued to perform in the mid-1960s, Lee saw her record sales fall off, though she charted with the LPs *In the Name of Love* (1964), *Pass Me By* (1965), and *Big Spender* (1966), reaching the Top Ten of the easy-listening charts with the title song (music by Cy Coleman, lyrics by Carolyn Leigh) from the last. She scored a considerable comeback on records with "Is That All There Is" (music and lyrics by Jerry Leiber and Mike Stoller), which topped the easy-listening charts in October 1969 and reached the pop Top Ten, winning her first Grammy for Best Contemporary Vocal Performance, Female. An album titled after the single reached the charts, as did her next two albums, *Bridge Over Troubled Water* and *Make It with You*, both released in 1970.

The concept album *Norma Deloris Egstrom from Jamestown, North Dakota*, released in June 1972, was Lee's final chart album and final recording for Capitol. She continued to tour extensively and to guest-star in singing and acting roles on television, notably costarring with Anthony Quinn in the TV movie *A Man and a Woman* in 1972. Her next two albums, *Let's Love* (October 1974), with a title song written for her by Paul McCartney, and *Mirrors* (November 1975), containing specially written songs by Jerry Leiber and Mike Stoller, were major-label releases, but neither charted. Thereafter, she occasionally made records for small labels.

In October 1976, Lee was injured in a fall while appearing at the Waldorf-Astoria Hotel in N.Y. and sidelined for a couple of years. In December 1983 she wrote the book and the lyrics for the autobiographical Broadway revue *Peg*, in which she starred; it ran only five performances. She underwent heart surgery in October 1985 and spent years recovering. In 1988 she released a new album, *Miss Peggy Lee Sings the Blues*, and earned a Grammy nomination for Best Jazz Vocal Performance, Female. Her 1990 album of her own songs, *The Peggy Lee Songbook: There'll Be Another Spring*, earned another Grammy nomination in the same category.

Lee continued to perform in the 1990s, frequently in a wheelchair. She recorded her last full-length album, *Moments Like This*, in September 1992, and it was released in 1993. In the summer of 1997 she appeared at Carnegie Hall in N.Y. as part of the JVC Jazz Festival. She suffered a stroke on Oct. 27, 1998.

WORKS (only works for which Lee was a credited, primary songwriter are listed): **FILM:** *Lady and the Tramp* (1955). **MUSICAL:** *Peg* (N.Y., Dec. 14, 1983).

WRITINGS: *Softly, with Feeling* (1953); *Miss P. L.: An Autobiography* (N.Y., 1989).

BIBL.: R. Towe, *Here's to You: The Complete Bio-Discography of Miss P. L.* (1986).—**WR**

Leech, Richard, American tenor; b. Binghamton, Calif., 1956. During his student years, he made appearances as a baritone and then as a tenor. His professional career began in earnest in 1980. In subsequent years, he sang in Cincinnati, Pittsburgh, Baltimore, Houston, and Chicago. In 1987 he made his European debut as Raoul in *Les Huguenots* at the Berlin Deutsche Oper. He made his first appearance at the N.Y.C. Opera as the Duke of Mantua in 1988. In 1990 he made his Metropolitan Opera debut in N.Y. as Gounod's Faust and also sang for the first time at Milan's La Scala as Pinkerton. In the 1991–92 season he made his debut at London's Covent Garden as Raoul. He returned to the Metropolitan Opera in 1994 as Rodolfo.—**NS/LK/DM**

Leedy, Douglas, American composer and conductor; b. Portland, Ore., March 3, 1938. He studied at Pomona Coll. (B.A., 1959) and at the Univ. of Calif. at Berkeley (M.A., 1962). He played the horn in the Oakland (Calif.) Sym. Orch. and in the San Francisco Opera and Ballet orchs. (1960–65). In 1965–66 he held a joint U.S.-Polish government grant for study in Poland. From 1967 to 1970 he was on the faculty of the Univ. of Calif., Los Angeles. From 1973 to 1978 he taught at Reed Coll. in Portland, Ore. He was conductor of the Oregon Telemann Ensemble, later known as the Harmonie Universelle. In 1984–85 he was music director of the Portland Baroque Orch. In 1985 he conducted the Portland Pro Musica in complete, period-instrument performances of Handel's *Jephtha* and *Theodora*. His early works cultivated avant-garde methods of electronic application to mixed media, but later he sought to overcome the restrictions of Western music and its equal temperament; for this purpose, he began in 1979 to work with the Carnatic vocalist K.V. Narayanaswamy in Madras, India. He wrote "A Question of Intonation" which appeared in the *Journal of the Conductor's Guild* (Fall 1987). He contributed the article "Tuning Systems" to *The New Grove Dictionary of American Music* (1986), and also was a contributor to *The New Grove Dictionary of Music and Musicians* (second ed., 2000). His investigation into the musical aspects of Classical epic and lyric poetry resulted in his article "Some Experiments in Singing Ancient Greek and Latin Verse," which appeared in M. Cole and J. Koegel, eds., *Music in Performance and Society: Essays in Honor of Rolana Jackson* (Warren, Mich., 1997).

WORKS: *Exhibition Music* (1965; continued indefinitely); *Decay*, theater piece for Piano, Wagner Tuba, and Tape (1965); *Antifonia* for Brass Quartet (1965); *Usable Music I* for Very Small Instruments with Holes (1966); *Teddy Bear's Picnic*, audio-tactile electronic theater piece (1968); *Ave Maris Stella* for Soprano, Instrumental Trio, Organ, and Electronic Sound (1968); *88 Is Great*, theater piece for Piano, 8-hands (1968); *The Electric Zodiac*, electronic music (1969); *Entropical Paradise: 6 Sonic Environments* for Electronic Recordings (1970); *Gloria* for Soprano, Chorus, and Instruments (1970); *The 24th Psalm* for 6 Solo Soprano Voices, Chorus, and Orch. (1972); *Sebastian*, chamber opera for Soprano, Baritone, Chamber Ensemble, and Tape, based on documents of J.S. Bach (1971–74); *Wie schön leuchtet der Morgenstern*, chorale fantasia for Organ and Unseen Soprano (1972); String Quartet, in just intonation (1965–75); *Canti: Music* for Contrabass and Chamber Ensemble (1975); *Symphoniae sacrae* for Soprano, Bass, Viola da Gamba, and Harpsichord (1976); *Sur la couche de miettes* for Flute, Oboe, Violin, Viola, Cello, Guitar, Piano, Equal-temperament Harpsichord, and Just-intonation Harpsichord (1981); *Harpsichord Book, Parts I-II*, in traditional mean-tone temperament (1974, 1982); *Toccata, Utremifasolla and Chorale* for Just-intonation Harpsichord (1982); *4 Hymns from the Rigveda* for Chorus and Javanese or American Gamelan (1982–83); *5 Organ Chorales* (1983); *Music for Meantone Organ* (1983–84); arrangement of J.S. Bach's *Goldberg Canons*, S.1087, for Strings and Continuo (1984); *Pastorale* for Solo Voices, Chorus, and Just-intonation Piano (1987); *Fantasy on "Wondrous Love"* for Organ and Optional Chorus (1990); *3 Symphonies for Unison Orch.* (1993); Piano Sonata (1994); *White Buffalo*, string quartet (1995).—**NS/LK/DM**

Leeman, Cliff(ord; aka **Mr. Time, the Sheriff),** big-band jazz drummer; b. Portland, Maine, Sept. 10, 1913; d. April 26, 1986. He played in local bands during his early teens, and also played percussion with the Portland Sym. His first professional work was as a xylophonist on a variety tour, but he returned to Portland to finish high school. After working with two Boston-based bands in the mid-1930s, he joined Artie Shaw, staying with him for about a year a half (April 1937–late 1938, except for a brief absence in summer 1938 due to illness). After a month-long stint with Glenn Miller (April 1939), Leeman worked with Tommy Dorsey from May until November 1939 before joining Charlie Barnet, with whom he remained until early 1943. He worked briefly in Chicago with Johnny Long's Band (spring 1943), then joined Woody Herman. Early in 1944, he spent a few months in the Army, and then returned to N.Y., working with various bands, on radio, and leading his own band through 1950 (except for a period during 1946 where he returned to his native Portland). He did regular studio work throughout the 1950s, played occasional dates with Billy Butterfield, and also played regularly at Nick's and Condon's with various leaders. Through the 1960s, he worked with various jazz revivalists, including Bob Crosby, Wild Bill Davison, Yank Lawson, Dukes of Dixieland, and in a group accompanying vocalist Dick Haymes (1963). He toured Japan, Australia, and New Zealand with Eddie Condon (spring 1964); on his return to N.Y. that summer, he began two years mainly with Peanuts Hucko. In 1969, he toured for a while with George Wein's Newport All Stars, then in late 1969 worked in N.Y. with Joe Venuti. He toured Europe with Kings of Jazz (1974), and with Wild Bill Davison (1976), and played a stint with the World's Greatest Jazz Band (1976–77). He continued to work through the 1970s nearly to the time of his death.—**JC/LP**

Lees, Benjamin, distinguished American composer and teacher; b. Harbin, Manchuria, Jan. 8, 1924. He was taken to the U.S. in infancy. At 5, he began piano studies with K. Rodetsky in San Francisco. At 15, he became a piano student of Marguerite Bitter in Los Angeles. He also pursued training in harmony and theory and began to compose. Following studies in theory with Stevens, Dahl, and Kanitz at the Univ. of Southern Calif. in Los Angeles (1945–49), he studied with Antheil (until 1954). In 1954 he held a Guggenheim fellowship and in 1956 a Fulbright fellowship, which enabled him to live in Europe until 1962. In 1966 he held another Guggenheim fellowship. He taught at the Peabody Cons. of Music in Baltimore (1962–64; 1966–68), Queens Coll. of the City Univ. of N.Y. (1964–65), the Manhattan School of Music (1970–72), and the Juilliard School (1973–74). Lees's music possesses an ingratiating quality, modern but not arrogantly so. His harmonies are lucid and are couched in euphonius dissonances. He favors rhythmic asymmetry while the formal design of his works is classical in its clarity.

WORKS: DRAMATIC: O p e r a : *The Oracle* (1956); *Medea in Corinth* (1970; London, Jan. 10, 1971); *The Gilded Cage* (1970–72). **B a l l e t :** *Scarlatti Portfolio* (1978; San Francisco, March 15, 1979). **ORCH.:** *Profile* (NBC Radio, 1952; first concert perf., N.Y., April 18, 1954); 5 syms.: No. 1 (1953), No. 2 (Louisville, Dec. 3, 1958), No. 3 (1968; Detroit, Jan. 16, 1969), No. 4, *Memorial Candles*, for Mezzo-soprano, Violin, and Orch. (Dallas, Oct. 10, 1985), and No. 5, *Kalmar Nyckel* (1986; Wilmington, Del., March 29, 1988); *Declamations* for Piano and Strings (1953; Oklahoma City, Feb. 15, 1956); 2 piano concertos: No. 1 (1955; Vienna, April 26, 1956) and No. 2 (1966; Boston, March 15, 1968); *Divertimento-Burlesca* for Chamber Orch. (Fish Creek, Wisc., Aug. 11, 1957); *Interlude* for Strings (Toronto, July 1957); Violin Concerto (1958; Boston, Feb. 8, 1963); *Concertante Breve* for Chamber Orch. (1959; Vancouver, British Columbia, Oct. 1960); *Prologue, Capriccio, and Epilogue* (Portland, Ore., April 9, 1959); *Concerto for Orchestra* (1959; Rochester, N.Y., Feb. 22, 1962); Oboe Concerto (1963; Philadelphia, Dec. 12, 1964); Concerto for String Quartet and Orch. (1964; Kansas City, Mo., Jan. 19, 1965); *Spectrum* (La Jolla, Calif., June 21, 1964); Concerto for Chamber Orch. (Philadelphia, Oct. 9, 1966); *Fanfare for a Centennial* for Brass and Percussion (Baltimore, Nov. 13, 1966); *Silhouettes* (NET-TV, Oct. 3, 1967); *Etudes* for Piano and Orch. (Houston, Oct. 28, 1974); *Passacaglia* (1975; Washington, D.C., April 13, 1976); *Labyrinths* for Symphonic Band (Bloomington, Ind., Nov. 18, 1975); *Variations* for Piano and Orch. (Dallas, March 31, 1976); Concerto for Woodwind Quintet and Orch. (Detroit, Oct. 7, 1976); *Mobiles* (N.Y., April 13, 1979); Double Concerto for Piano, Cello, and Orch. (N.Y., Nov. 7, 1982); Concerto for Brass Choir and Orch. (Dallas, March 18, 1983); *Portrait of Rodin* (1984; Portland, Ore., April 5, 1987); Horn Concerto (Pittsburgh, May 14, 1992); *Borealis* (Wichita, Oct. 8, 1993); *Celebration* (1995); *Constellations* (1996–97); Percussion Concerto (1999). **CHAMBER:** Horn Sonata (1951); 4 string quartets: No. 1 (N.Y., Nov. 8, 1952), No. 2 (1955; Scranton, Pa., Jan. 31, 1956), No. 3 (1980; N.Y., May 16, 1982), and No. 4 (1989; San Francisco, March 11, 1990); *Evocation* for Flute (1953); 3 violin sonatas: No. 1 (N.Y., Feb. 1953), No. 2 (1972; Washington, D.C., May 4, 1973), and No. 3 (San Francisco, Nov. 21, 1991); *Movemente da camera* for Flute, Clarinet, Piano, and Cello (1954); *3 Variables* for Oboe, Clarinet, Bassoon, Horn, and Piano (Vienna, Oct. 1955); *Invenzione* for Violin (1965; N.Y., Jan. 26, 1966); Duo for Flute and Clarinet (1967); *Study No. 1* for Cello (1969); *Collage* for String Quartet, Wind Quintet, and Percussion (Milwaukee, May 8, 1973); *Dialogue* for Cello and Piano (N.Y., March 2, 1977); Cello Sonata (Washington, D.C., Nov. 13, 1981); 2 piano trios: No. 1 (Williamstown, Mass., Sept. 8, 1983) and No. 2, *Silent Voices* (1998); *Contours* for Piano, Cello, Violin, Clarinet, and Horn (1994); *Night Spectres* for Cello (1999). **P i a n o :** 4 sonatas: No. 1 (1949), No. 2 (1950), No. 3 (1956), and No. 4 (1963; Oberlin, Ohio, Jan. 7, 1964); Sonata for 2 Pianos (1951); *Toccata* (1953); *Fantasia* (1954); *10 Pieces* (1954); *6 Ornamental Etudes* (1957; N.Y., Feb. 16, 1961); *Kaleidoscopes* (1958); *3 Preludes* (1962; N.Y., Jan. 14, 1963); *Odyssey I* (1970) and *II* (1986; N.Y., May 27, 1992); *Fantasy Variations* (1983; N.Y., Feb. 1, 1984); *Mirrors* (Chicago, May 17, 1992). **VOCAL:** (6) *Songs of the Night* for Soprano and Piano (Los Angeles, June 15, 1952; 4 orchestrated as *4 Songs of the Night* for Soprano and 13 Instruments, Genoa, April 19, 1955); *3 Songs* for Contralto and Piano (1959; N.Y., Feb. 2, 1968); *Cyprian Songs* for Baritone and Piano (1960); *Visions of Poets*, cantata for Soprano, Tenor, Chorus, and Orch. (1961; Seattle, May 15, 1962); *The Trumpet of the Swan* for Narrator and Orch. (Philadelphia, May 13, 1972); *Staves* for Soprano and Piano (1977; N.Y., Jan. 29, 1978); *Paumanok* for Mezzo-soprano and Piano (N.Y., Dec. 9, 1980); *Echoes of Normandy* for Tenor,

Tape, Organ, and Orch. (Dallas, June 15, 1994); *Echoes of Normandy* for Tenor, Organ, Tape, and Orch. (1994); *The Golden Net* for Soprano, Tenor, Countertenor, and Baritone (1997).—NS/LK/DM

Leeuw, Reinbert de, Dutch composer and conductor, brother of **Ton de Leeuw**; b. Amsterdam, Sept. 8, 1938. He studied at the Amsterdam Cons. In 1963 he was appointed to the faculty of the Royal Cons. of The Hague. A political activist, he collaborated with Louis Andriessen, Mischa Mengelberg, Peter Schat, and Jan van Vlijmen on the anti-American multimedia spectacle *Reconstructie*, produced during the Holland Festival in Amsterdam on June 29, 1969. He further wrote an opera, *Axel* (with Vlijmen; 1977), *Solo I* for Cello (1961), *3 Positions* for Violin (1963), String Quartet (1963), *Interplay* for Orch. (1965), *Hymns and Chorals* for 15 Winds, 2 Electric Guitars, and Electric Organ (Amsterdam, July 5, 1970), *Duets* for Recorder (1971), and *Abschied*, symphonic poem (1971–73; Rotterdam, May 11, 1974). In later years, he was active as a conductor of contemporary music. In 1994 he became director of the Tanglewood Festival of Contemporary Music. He publ. a book about Ives (with J. Bemlef; Amsterdam, 1969) and a collection of 17 articles, *Muzikale anarchie* (Amsterdam, 1973).—NS/LK/DM

Leeuw, Ton (actually, **Antonius Wilhelmus Adrianus) de,** prominent Dutch composer and teacher, brother of **Reinbert de Leeuw**; b. Rotterdam, Nov. 16, 1926. He received training in piano and theory with Toebosch in Breda, and in composition with Badings in Amsterdam (1947–49) and with Messiaen and Hartmann in Paris (1949–50); he studied ethnomusicology with Kunst in Amsterdam (1950–54) and made a study trip to India, Iran, Japan, and the Philippines (1961). After working as director of sound at the Dutch Radio in Hilversum (1954–59), he taught composition at the Amsterdam Cons. (from 1959), where he also was director. From 1962 to 1984 he likewise lectured at the Univ. of Amsterdam. He publ. the book *Muziek van de Twintigste Eeuw* (Music of the Twentieth Century; Utrecht, 1964; second ed., 1977). As a composer, he was honored with the Prix Italia (1956), the Prix des Jeunesses Musicales (1961), the Mathijs Vermeulen Prize (1982), and the Johan Wagenaar Prize (1983). In his varied output, Leeuw has ranged widely, utilizing both contemporary Western and non-Western means of expression. He developed a personal static style in which his modal writing became increasingly diatonic.

WORKS: DRAMATIC: O p e r a : *Alceste*, television opera (Dutch TV, March 13, 1963); *De droom* (The Dream; 1963; Amsterdam, June 16, 1965); *Antigone* (1991). **T e l e v i s i o n P l a y :** *Litany of Our Time* (1969–70; Dutch TV, Jan 1, 1971). **B a l l e t :** *De Bijen* (The Bees; 1964; Arnhem, Sept. 15, 1965); *Krishna en Radha* (1964). **ORCH.:** Concerto Grosso for Strings (1946); *Treurmuziek, in memoriam Willem Pijper* (1948); 3 syms. (Sym. for Strings and Percussion, 1950; Sym. for Strings, 1951; Sym. of Winds, 1964); *Plutos- Suite* (1952); 2 violin concertos (1953, 1961); Suite for Youth Orch. (1954); *Mouvements rétrogrades* (1957); *Nritta*, orch. dance (1961); *Ombres* (1961); *Syntaxis II* (1966); *Spatial Music I* for 32 to 48 Players (1966), *III* for

Chamber Orch. in 4 Groups (1967), and *IV: Homage to Igor Stravinsky* for Chamber Orch. (1968); *Music for Strings* (1970); *Gending, a Western homage to the musicians of the gamelan* for Gamelan Orch. (1975); *Alba*, concerto da camera (1982; rev. 1986); *Résonances* (1985); Concerto for 2 Guitars and Chamber String Orch. (1988); *Danses sacrées* for Piano and Orch. (1990). **CHAMBER:** Trio for Violin, Viola, and Cello (1948); Flute Sonata (1949); Violin Sonata (1951); Trio for Flute, Clarinet, and Piano (1952); *5 Sketches* for Oboe, Clarinet, Bassoon, Violin, Viola, and Cello (1952); *Andante en vivace* for Flute and Piano (1955); Violin Sonatina (1955); 2 string quartets (1958; with tape, 1964); *Antiphonie* for Wind Quintet and Electronics (1960); *Schelp* for Flute, Viola, and Guitar (1964); *The 4 Seasons* for Harp (1964); *Night Music* for Flute (1966); *Music for Violin* (1967); *Music for Oboe* (1969); *Music for Organ and Chamber Ensemble* (1970–71); *Reversed Night* for Flute (1971); *Spatial Music II* for Percussion (1971); *Midare* for Marimba (1972); *Music for Trombone* (1973–74); *Canzone* for 4 Horns, 3 Trumpets, and 3 Trombones (1973–74); *Rime* for Flute and Harp (1974); *Mo-do* for Amplified Clavichord or Harpsichord (1974); *Mountains* for Bass Clarinet and Tape (1977); *Modal Music* for Accordion (1978–79); *Interlude* for Guitar (1984); *Apparances I* for Cello (1987) and *II* for Clarinet Quartet (1987); *Hommage à Henri* for Clarinet and Piano (1989); *Music for Double Bass* (1989–91); Trio for Flute, Bass Clarinet, and Piano (1990); *Fauxbourdon* for Flute, Clarinet, Piano, Synthesizer, Marimba, Mandolin, Violin, and Viola (1991–92; rev. 1993); Saxophone Quartet (1993). **Piano:** *Scherzo* (1948); Sonatina (1949); Sonata for 2 Pianos (1950); *4 Préludes* (1950); *Variations on a French Popular Song* (1950); *5 études* (1951); *4 Rhythmic Études* (1952); *3 African Études* (1954); *Lydic Suite* (1954); *Zes dansen* (1955); *Men Go Their Ways* (1964); *Linkerhand en rechterhand* (1976); *Les Adieux* (1988). **VOCAL:** *Hiob* (Job) for Soloists, Chorus, Orch., and Tape (1956); *Brabant* for Medium Voice and Orch. (1959); *Psalm 118* for Chorus and 2 Trombones or Organ (1966); *Huiku II* for Soprano and Orch. (1968); *Lamento Pacis* for Chorus and Instruments (1969); *The Magic of Music* for Chorus (1970); *The Birth of Music I* for Chorus (1975) and *II* for Voices, Speaker, and Tape (1978); *And They Shall Reign Forever* for Mezzo-soprano, Clarinet, Piano, and Percussion (1981); *Car nos vignes sont de fleurs (Cantique des Cantiques)* for Chorus (1981); *Invocations* for Chorus and Instruments (1983); *Chimères* for Men's Voices (1984); *Les chants de Kabir* for Men's Voices (1985); *Transperance* for Chorus, 3 Trumpets, and 3 Trombones (1986); *Cinq hymnes* for Chorus, 2 Percussion, and 2 Pianos (1988); *A cette heure du jour* for Chorus (1991–92). **OTHER:** *Electronic Suite* for Tape (1958); *Syntaxis I* for Tape (1966); *Chronos* for 4 Sound Tracks (1980); *Clair-Obscur* for Electronics (1981–82).—**NS/LK/DM**

LeFanu, Nicola (Frances), English composer and teacher; b. Wickham Bishops, Essex, April 28, 1947. She was the daughter of the medical historian William LeFanu and the composer **Elizabeth Maconchy.** Her mother was a major influence on her in her formative years. After initial training in composition with Jeremy Dale Roberts, she pursued her studies at St. Hilda's Coll., Oxford (B.A., 1968; M.A., 1971) and at the Royal Coll. of Music in London (1968–69). In 1973–74 she held a Harkness fellowship and studied with Earl Kim at Harvard Univ. and Seymour Shifrin at Brandeis Univ. She was active in London as director of music at Francis Holland School (1969–72) and St. Paul's Girls School (1975–77). In 1977 she became a senior lecturer at King's Coll., Univ. of London. She became prof. of music and head of the music dept. at the Univ. of York in 1994. In 1979 she married **David Lumsdaine,** with whom she served as composer-in-residence at the New South Wales State Conservatorium of Music in Sydney that same year. As a composer, she has won several honors, including the Cobbett Prize (1969), the BBC Composers Prize (1972), and the Leverhulme Award (1989). In 1995 she received an honorary D.Mus. degree from the Univ. of Durham and was made a fellow of the Royal Coll. of Music. In her works, she has developed a well-crafted style in which serial techniques are relieved by a deft handling of dramatic and lyrical writing.

WORKS: DRAMATIC: *Anti-World*, music theater (London, June 1972); *The Last Laugh*, ballet (1972; London, April 1973); *Dawnpath*, chamber opera (London, Sept. 29, 1977); *The Story of Mary O'Neill*, radio opera (1986; BBC, London, Jan. 4, 1989); *The Green Children*, opera (King's Lynn, July 1990); *Blood Wedding*, opera (1991–92; London, Oct. 1992); *The Wildman*, opera (Aldeburgh, June 9, 1995). **ORCH.:** *Preludio I* for Strings (1967; London, March 1969; rev. as *Preludio II*, 1976; London, March 19, 1977); *The Hidden Landscape* (London, Aug. 7, 1973); *Columbia Falls* (Birmingham, Nov. 20, 1975); *Farne* (Bradford, March 28, 1980); *Variations* for Piano and Orch. (London, Dec. 31, 1982); Concerto for Alto Saxophone and Strings (1989; Kaustinen, Finland, Jan. 28, 1990); Concerto for Clarinet and Strings (1997); Duo Concertante for Violin, Viola, and Orch. (1999). **CHAMBER:** *Soliloquy* for Oboe (1966; Oxford, March 1967); *Variations* for Oboe Quartet (1968); *Abstracts and a Frame* for Violin and Piano (London, Oct. 1971); *Deva* for Cello and 7 Players (London, March 23, 1979); *Collana* for Percussionist and 5 Players (Boston, April 25, 1976); *Trio 1* for Flute, Percussion, and Cello (1980; London, June 15, 1981); *SPNM Birthday Fanfare* for 2 Trumpets (London, May 23, 1983); *Moon Over Western Ridge, Mootwingee*, saxophone quartet (Stuttgart, Nov. 6, 1985); *Invisible Places*, clarinet quintet (Southampton, June 4, 1986); *Lament 1988* for Oboe, Clarinet, Viola, and Cello (London, March 30, 1988); 2 string quartets: No. 1 (Bedford, Oct. 13, 1988) and No. 2 (1996; London, April 1997); *Lullaby* for Clarinet and Piano (London, Oct. 20, 1988); *Nocturne* for Cello and Piano (London, Oct. 20, 1988); *Ervallagh* for Alto Saxophone (1993; London, Jan. 12, 1994); Sextet (1997). **KEYBOARD: Piano:** *Chiaroscuro* (1969; London, Feb. 1970). **Organ:** *Omega* (1971; rev. 1984); *A Little Sketchbook* for Piano Duet (2000). **VOCAL:** *Il Cantico dei Cantici II* for Soprano (1968; London, March 1969); *But Stars Remaining* for Soprano (1970; London, Feb. 1971); *Christ Calls Man Home* for 2 Sopranos and 3 Choruses (Cheltenham, July 4, 1971); *Rondeaux* for Tenor and Horn (London, Nov. 1972); *Paysage* for Baritone (Aldeburgh, June 21, 1973); *The Valleys Shall Sing* for Chorus, 2 Bassoons, 2 Trumpets, and 3 Trombones (Norfolk and Norwich Festival, Oct. 1973); *The Same Day Dawns* for Soprano, Flute, Clarinet, Percussion, Violin, and Cello (Boston, Nov. 4, 1974); *The Little Valleys* for Women's Chorus (1975); *For We Are the Stars* for 16 Solo Voices (1978; BBC, London, Sept. 30, 1982); *Verses from Psalm 90* for Soprano and 2 Choruses (London, Dec. 5, 1978); *Like a Wave of the Sea* for Chorus and Early Instruments (Nottingham, March 1, 1981); *The Old Woman of Beare* for Amplified Soprano and Orch. (London, Nov. 3, 1981); *A Penny for a Song* for Soprano and Piano (1981; Dublin, Jan. 8, 1982); *Rory's Rounds* for Young Singers (1983); *Trio 2: Song for Peter* for Soprano, Clarinet, and Cello (London, March 3, 1983); *Stranded on My Heart* for Tenor, Chorus, and String Orch. (St. Alban's, June 16, 1984); *I am bread* for Soprano and Piano (Brighton, May 21, 1987); *Wind Among the Pines: 5 Images of Norfolk* for Soprano and Orch. (Aldeburgh, July 31, 1987); *The Spirit Moves* for Chorus (London, Oct. 18, 1992); *Sundari and the Secret Message* for Storyteller, Flute, Cello, Sitar, Tabla, and Electric Keyboard (King's Lynn, July 1993); *La Cancion de la Luna* for Countertenor and String Quartet (1993–94; Bristol, Feb. 1994).—**NS/LK/DM**

Lefébure, Yvonne, French pianist and teacher; b. Ermont, Seine-et-Oise, June 29, 1898; d. Paris, Jan. 23, 1986. She began piano studies at an early age and won the "prix de petits prodigés" of the Paris Cons., where she took courses with Emmanuel, Georges Caussade, and Widor and won 6 premiers prix in all. She also studied privately with Cortot. She taught at the École Normale de Musique in Paris (from 1924), and was on the faculty of the Paris Cons. (1952–67). She toured widely as a soloist and recitalist.—**NS/LK/DM**

Lefébure-Wély, Louis James Alfred, French organist and composer; b. Paris, Nov. 13, 1817; d. there, Dec. 31, 1869. A pupil of his father, he took, at the age of 8, the latter's place as organist of the church of St.-Roch, becoming its regular organist at 14. Entering the Paris Cons. in 1832, he was taught by Benoist (organ), Laurent and Zimmerman (piano), and Berton and Halévy (composition). From 1847 to 1858 he was organist at the Madeleine, then at St. Sulpice.

WORKS: *Les Recruteurs*, opera (1861); *Après la victoire*, cantata (1863); 3 masses; 3 syms.; String Quintet; String Quartet; much elegant salon music for piano (his most celebrated piece is *The Monastery Bells*); 50 piano études; harmonium music. —**NS/LK/DM**

Lefebvre, Charles Edouard, French composer and teacher; b. Paris, June 19, 1843; d. Aix-les-Bains, Sept. 8, 1917. He was a student at the Paris Cons., winning the Premier Grand Prix de Rome with his cantata *Le judgement de Dieu* (1870). After completing his studies in Rome, he returned to Paris in 1873. He won the Prix Chartier in 1884 and 1891. From 1895 he was on the faculty of the Paris Cons.

WORKS: DRAMATIC: O p e r a : *Le florentin* (1868); *Le voile de Saint Walburge* (1877–78); *Lucrèce* (1877–78); *Le trésor* (Angers, March 28, 1883); *Zaïre* (Lille, Dec. 3, 1887); *Djelma* (Paris, May 25, 1894). **ORCH.:** *Ouverture dramatique* (1875); *Dalila*, symphonic poem (1875); Sym. (1879); *Melka*, legend (1880); *Une sérénade* (1884); *Eloâ*, poème lyrique (1888); *La fille de Jephté*, poème lyrique (1879). **OTHER:** *Le judgment de Dieu*, cantata (1870); *Judith*, biblical drama (1879); *Sainte-Cécile* for Voice, Chorus, and Orch. (1896); chamber music; piano pieces; organ music.—**NS/LK/DM**

Lefeld, Jerzy Albert, Polish pianist, composer, and pedagogue; b. Warsaw, Jan. 17, 1898; d. there, Feb. 22, 1980. He studied piano with Michalowski and composition with Statkowski at the Warsaw Cons., and in 1918 joined its faculty. He became known principally as a fine piano accompanist. His own compositions include 2 syms., a String Sextet, piano pieces, and songs. —**NS/LK/DM**

Lefèvre, (Jean) Xavier, Swiss-born French clarinetist and composer; b. Lausanne, March 6, 1763; d. Paris, Nov. 9, 1829. He studied with Michel Yost in Paris, and first appeared as a soloist at the Concert Spirituel (1783). He played in the Paris Opéra orch. (1791–1817), and was also principal cellist in the imperial (later royal) chapel from 1807. He was a prof. at the Cons. (1795–1824). He wrote a clarinet method (1802). Among his works were 7 clarinet concertos, as well as trios, duos, sonatas, and other works for his instrument. He popularized the sixth key of the clarinet, although he did not invent it.

BIBL.: L. Youngs, *J.X. L., His Contributions to the Clarinet and Clarinet Playing* (diss., Catholic Univ. of America, 1970). —**NS/LK/DM**

Leffler-Burckhard, Martha, German soprano; b. Berlin, June 16, 1865; d. Wiesbaden, May 14, 1954. She was a student in Dresden of Anna von Meichsner and in Paris of Pauline Viardot-García. In 1888 she made her operatic debut in Strasbourg, and then sang in Breslau (1889–90) and Cologne (1891–92). After a tour of North America (1892–93), she appeared in Bremen (1893–97) and Weimar (1898–99). From 1900 to 1912 she sang in Wiesbaden, and also appeared at London's Covent Garden (1903, 1907) and at the Metropolitan Opera in N.Y. (debut as Brünnhilde in *Die Walküre*, March 4, 1908). She was a member of the Berlin Royal Opera from 1913 to 1918. After singing at the Berlin Deutsches Opernhaus (1918–19), she taught voice. Among her best-known roles were Leonore, Isolde, the 3 Brünnhildes, Kundry, Ortrud, and Sieglinde.—**NS/LK/DM**

Le Flem, Paul, French composer, choral conductor, music critic, and teacher; b. Lézardrieux, Côtes-du-Nord, March 18, 1881; d. Trégastel, Côtes-du-Nord, July 31, 1984. He settled in Paris and studied harmony with Lavignac at the Cons. (1899) before completing his training with d'Indy and Roussel at the Schola Cantorum (1904); he also studied philosophy at the Sorbonne. Le Flem wrote perceptive music criticism for *Comoedia* (1921–36), and also served as prof. of counterpoint at the Schola Cantorum (1923–39). In 1924 he became chorus master at the Opéra-Comique, and from 1925 to 1939 he distinguished himself as director of the St. Gervais Choir. In 1951 he was awarded the Grand Prix Musical of Paris. From his earliest compositional efforts, Le Flem was influenced by his native Brittany. His later works also owe much to Debussy and d'Indy, and are skillfully written.

WORKS: DRAMATIC: *Endrymion et Sélémé*, opera (Paris, 1903); *Aucassin et Nicolette*, chante-fable (1908; private perf., Paris, May 19, 1909); *La folie de Lady Macbeth*, ballet (1934); *Le rossignol de St. Malo*, opera (1938; Paris, May 5, 1942); *Les paralytiques volent*, radio score (1938); *La clairière des fées*, opera (1943); *Magicienne de la mer*, opera (1946; Paris, Oct. 29, 1954); *Macbeth*, radio score (1950); *Côte de granit rose*, film score (1954). **ORCH.:** *En mer* (1901); *Scherzo* (1906); 4 syms. (1907; 1956; 1967; 1977–78); *Les voix de large* (1911); *Fantaisie* for Piano and Orch. (1911); *Pour les morts* (1913); *Le village* (1942); *Le ronde des fées* (1943); *Konzertstück* for Violin and Orch. (1965). **CHAMBER:** *Rèverie grise* for Cello and Piano (1899); Violin Sonata (1905); Piano Quintet (1909); *Claire de lune sous bois* for Flute, Harp, and Strings (1911); *Danse désuète* for Flute, Harp, and Strings (1911); *Pièce* for Horn (1955). **P i a n o :** *Par landes*

(1907); *Par greves* (1907); *Le vieux calvaire* (1910); *Le chant des genêts* (1910); *Avril* (1912). VOCAL: *Invocation* for Voice and Orch. (1920); *Le vin* for Chorus and Wind Orch. (1924); *Le fête de printemps* for Women's Chorus and Orch. (1937); *La maudite* for Voices and Orch. (1967; rev. 1971); choruses; songs.

BIBL.: G. Bernard-Krauss, *Hundert Jahre französischer Musikgeschichte in Leben und Werk P. L.s* (Frankfurt am Main and N.Y., 1993).—NS/LK/DM

Le Fleming, Christopher (Kaye), English composer; b. Wimborne, Feb. 26, 1908; d. Woodbury, Devon, June 19, 1985. He studied at the Brighton School of Music and at the Royal School of Church Music in London, then held many teaching posts. He wrote several orch. works, incidental music to plays, choral music, piano pieces, and songs.—NS/LK/DM

Le Gallienne, Dorian (Leon Marlois), Australian composer and music critic; b. Melbourne, April 19, 1915; d. there, July 27, 1963. He studied at the Univ. of Melbourne Conservatorium (graduated, 1938) and with Benjamin and Howells at the Royal Coll. of Music in London (1938–39); later he took lessons with Jacob in England (1951). He served as music critic for Melbourne's *Argus* (from 1950) and for *The Age* (from 1957). His output reveals English and French traits, along with the bitonal writing of early Stravinsky and late Bartók.

WORKS: DRAMATIC: 2 ballets: *Contes heraldiques* (1947) and *Voyageur* (1954); incidental music; film scores. **ORCH.:** Sinfonietta (1951–56); Overture (1952); Sym. (1952–53); *Symphonic Study* (1962–63; first movement of the unfinished second Sym.). **CHAMBER:** Flute Sonata (1943); Violin Sonata (1945); Duo for Violin and Viola (1956); Trio for Oboe, Violin, and Viola (1957); *Piece No. 1* for Violin, Cello, Clarinet, Percussion, and Harp (1959) and *No. 2* for 2 Clarinets and String Quartet (1959); piano pieces. **VOCAL:** Songs; part songs.—NS/LK/DM

Legge, Walter, influential English recording executive, orchestral manager, and writer on music; b. London, June 1, 1906; d. St. Jean, Cap Ferrat, March 22, 1979. He was autodidact in music. In 1927 he joined the staff of the Gramophone Co. (His Master's Voice) of London. He became an ardent champion of first-class recording projects, and in 1931 founded a subscription soc. for the purpose of recording unrecorded works. From 1938 he was active with the British Columbia recording label. He also wrote music criticism for the *Manchester Guardian* (1934–38). In 1938–39 he was asst. artistic director of London's Covent Garden. From 1942 to 1945 he was director of music of the Entertainments National Service Assn. In 1945 he founded the Philharmonia Orch. of London, which he managed with notable results as both a recording and concert ensemble until he unsuccessfully attempted to disband it in 1964. In 1953 he married **Elisabeth Schwarzkopf.**

BIBL.: E. Schwarzkopf, ed., *On and Off the Record: A Memoir of W. L.* (London, 1982; second ed., 1988); A. Sanders, ed., *W. L.: A Discography* (London, 1985); idem, ed., *W. L.: Words and Music* (N.Y., 1998).—NS/LK/DM

Leginska (real name, Liggins), Ethel, English pianist, teacher, and composer; b. Hull, April 13, 1886; d. Los Angeles, Feb. 26, 1970. She showed a natural talent for music at an early age; the pseudonym Leginska was given to her by Lady Maud Warrender, under the illusion that a Polish-looking name might help her artistic career. She studied piano wih Kwast at the Hoch Cons. in Frankfurt am Main, and later in Vienna with Leschetizky. After making her London debut (1907), she toured Europe; on Jan. 20, 1913, she appeared for the first time in America at a recital in N.Y. Her playing was described as having masculine vigor, dashing brilliance, and great variety of tonal color; however, criticism was voiced against an individualistic treatment of classical works. In the midst of her career as a pianist, she developed a great interest in conducting; she organized the Boston Phil. Orch. (100 players), later the Women's Sym. Orch. of Boston; appeared as a guest conductor with various orchs. in America and in Europe. In this field of activity, she also elicited interest, leading to a discussion in the press of a woman's capability of conducting an orch. While in the U.S., she took courses in composition with Rubin Goldmark and Ernest Bloch; wrote music in various genres, distinguished by rhythmic display and a certain measure of modernism. She married **Emerson Whithorne** in 1907 (divorced in 1916). In 1939 she settled in Los Angeles as a piano teacher.

WORKS: DRAMATIC: O p e r a : *The Rose and the Ring* (1932; Los Angeles, Feb. 23, 1957, composer conducting); *Gale* (Chicago, Nov. 23, 1935, composer conducting). **ORCH.:** *Beyond the Fields We Know*, symphonic poem (N.Y., Feb. 12, 1922); *2 Short Pieces* (Boston, Feb. 29, 1924, Monteux conducting); *Quatre sujets barbares*, suite (Munich, Dec. 13, 1924, composer conducting); *Fantasy* for Piano and Orch. (N.Y., Jan. 3, 1926). **CHAMBER:** String Quartet, inspired by 4 poems by Tagore (Boston, April 25, 1921); *From a Life* for 13 Instruments (N.Y., Jan. 9, 1922); *Triptych* for 11 Instruments (Chicago, April 29, 1928); piano pieces. **VOCAL:** *6 Nursery Rhymes* for Soprano and Chamber Orch.; songs.—NS/LK/DM

Legley, Victor, outstanding Belgian composer; b. Hazebrouck, June 18, 1915; d. Ostend, Nov. 28, 1994. He studied viola, chamber music, counterpoint, and fugue at the Brussels Cons. (from 1934), then took private lessons in composition with Absil (1941), subsequently winning the Belgian Second Prix de Rome (1943). He was a violist in the Belgian Radio Sym. Orch. (1936–48); then was a music producer for the Flemish dept. of the Belgian Radio, and later was made head of its serious music broadcasts on its 3rd program (1962). He taught at the Brussels Cons. (1949–80). He became a member of the Belgian Royal Academy (1965); was its president (1972); was chairman of the Société Belge des Auteurs, Compositeurs, et Editeurs (from 1981). In his works, Legley adheres to the pragmatic tenets of modern music, structurally diversified and unconstricted by inhibitions against dissonance. His Second Violin Concerto was a mandatory work of the 1967 Queen Elisabeth violin competition finals.

WORKS: DRAMATIC: O p e r a : *La Farce des deux nus* (Antwerp, Dec. 10, 1966). **B a l l e t :** *Le Bal des halles* (1954). **ORCH.:** 6 syms. (1942, 1947, 1953, 1964, 1965, 1976); *Concert à 13*, chamber sym. (1944); Suite (1944); *Music for a Greek Tragedy* (1946); *Symphonie miniature* for Chamber Orch. (1946); 2 violin

concertos: No. 1 (1947) and No. 2 (1966; Brussels, May 22, 1967); *The Golden River*, symphonic sketch (1948); Piano Concerto (1952); *Serenade* for Strings (1957); *La Cathedrale d'acier*, symphonic sketch after a painting by Fernand Steven (1958); *Overture to a Comedy* by Goldoni (1958); 3 *Pieces* for Chamber Orch. (1960); *Dyptiek* (1964); Harp Concerto (1966); *Paradise Regained* (1967); *Prelude for a Ballet* (1969); 3 *Movements* for Brass and Percussion (1969); *Espaces* for Strings (1970); Viola Concerto (1971); *Before Endeavors Fade* for Strings (1977); *Festival Overture* for Sym. Orch. and Jazz Band (1978); Concertino for Oboe and Strings (1982); Cello Concerto (1984); *Concert d'automne* for Alto Saxophone and Orch. (1984); *Concerto Grosso* for Violin, Alto Saxophone, and Chamber Orch. (1985). **CHAMBER:** 5 string quartets (1941; 1947; 1956; 1963; *Esquisses*, 1970); Quartet for 4 Flutes (1943); Violin Sonata (1943); Viola Sonata (1943); Sextet for Piano and Wind Quintet (1945); Cello Sonata (1945); *Musique de midi*, nonet (1948); Clarinet Sonata (1952); Trumpet Sonata (1953); *Serenade* for Flute, Violin, and Cello (1957); 5 *Miniatures* for 4 Saxophones (1958); Trio for Flute, Viola, and Guitar (1959); Wind Quintet (1961); 4 *Pieces* for Guitar (1964); Piano Quartet (1973); Piano Trio (1973); String Trio (1973); *Parades I* for 4 Clarinets (1977), *II* for 6 Saxophones (1978), and *III* for 4 Horns (1981); Duo for Violin and Cello (1983); *Suite en re* for Harpsichord (1986); 2 *pieces* for Accordion (1986). **P i a n o :** 4 sonatas (1946–85); 4 *Portraits* (1954–55); *Music for 2 Pianos* (1966); 3 *Marches* (1968); *Brindilles* (1974). **VOCAL:** *Zeng* for Soprano and String Quartet or String Orch. (1965); songs.

BIBL.: R. Wangermée, *V. L.* (Brussels, 1953).—NS/LK/DM

Legnani, (Rinaldo) Luigi, outstanding Italian guitarist and instrument maker; b. Ferrara, Nov. 7, 1790; d. Ravenna, Aug. 5, 1877. After making appearances as a tenor, he launched a remarkable career as a guitar virtuoso, creating a minor sensation in Milan in 1819. He subsequently toured widely in Europe, including concert appearances with Paganini (1836–38). He later settled in Ravenna and established a workshop as a maker of guitars and violins. He also composed duos for violin or flute and guitar.—NS/LK/DM

Legrand, Michel (Jean), prolific French composer, pianist, and conductor; b. Paris, France, Feb. 24, 1932. Legrand wrote the scores for at least 142 feature films released between 1955 and 1998, earning Grammys and Academy Awards for his efforts. Lushly romantic, his music served as the basis for such songs as "The Windmills of Your Mind," "How Do You Keep the Music Playing?" and "The Way He Makes Me Feel." His best-known scores included *The Umbrellas of Cherbourg*, the *Thomas Crown Affair*, *Summer of '42*, and *Yentl*.

Legrand was the son of composer, pianist, and conductor Raymond Legrand. He entered the Conservatoire Nationale de Musique at the age of 11 or 12 and studied with Nadia Boulanger, remaining at the school until the early 1950s. He became an accompanist for various singers and also played jazz in nightclubs. He first gained international recognition for his album containing his arrangements of French songs, *I Love Paris*, which entered the U.S. charts in November 1954 and made the Top Ten, as did its 1955 follow-up, *Holiday in Rome*; *Vienna Holiday* (1955) also made the charts, and *Castles in Spain* (1956) was his third Top Ten album in the U.S.

Meanwhile, Legrand had turned his attention to film scoring, and in the late 1950s and early 1960s he worked with many French directors associated with the *nouvelle vague*, or New Wave: Jean-Luc Godard (*Une Femme est une Femme* [*A Woman Is a Woman*]; 1960); Jacques Demy (*Lola*; 1961); and Agnès Varda (*Cléo de 5 à 7* [*Cleo from 5 to 7*]; 1962). As of 1963's *Love Is a Ball*, he also began to find work in Hollywood. He first gained broad American recognition for the Jacques Demy–directed musical *Les Parapluies de Cherbourg*, released in the U.S. in December 1964 under the title *The Umbrellas of Cherbourg*. It earned him three 1965 Academy Award nominations, for Scoring of Music—Adaptation or Treatment, for Music Score—Substantially Original, and for Best Song, "I Will Wait for You," the last two shared with Demy. He also earned two 1965 Grammy nominations, for Song of the Year for "I Will Wait for You" (along with Demy and English lyricist Norman Gimbel) and for Best Original Score Written for a Motion Picture or TV Show (with Demy).

The recognition increased Legrand's opportunities to write for American films, and by the late 1960s he was working as frequently in Hollywood as in Paris. For the comedy *How to Save a Marriage (And Ruin Your Life)*, released in January 1968, he wrote the song "Winds of Change," which Ray Conniff and the Singers took into the Top Ten of the easy listening charts. April 1968 saw the American release of Jacques Demy's 1967 follow-up to *The Umbrellas of Cherbourg*, *Les Demoiselles de Rochefort* (*The Young Girls of Rochefort*). It earned Legrand and Demy another Oscar nomination for Score of a Musical Picture—(Original or Adaptation).

But Legrand's biggest success of 1968 came with the June release of Norman Jewison's stylish crime film *The Thomas Crown Affair*, starring Steve McQueen and Faye Dunaway. The soundtrack album made the charts for several weeks during the summer and earned Legrand a Grammy nomination for Best Instrumental Arrangement for the song "The Windmills of Your Mind" (lyrics by Alan and Marilyn Bergman). But his work on the film gained its greatest recognition at Oscar time in 1969, when the score was nominated for Original Score—for a Motion Picture (Not a Musical) and "Windmills of Your Mind" won the Academy Award for Best Song. In the wake of the award, Dusty Springfield's recording of the song became a hit, making the pop Top 40 and the Top Ten of the easy listening charts.

Legrand's film work brought more awards and more hits during the early 1970s. "What Are You Doing the Rest of Your Life?" (lyrics by Alan and Marilyn Bergman) from the November 1969 film *The Happy Ending* brought another Oscar nomination, leading to an easy-listening chart entry for Jaye P. Morgan. The May 1970 film *The Magic Garden of Stanley Sweetheart* contained "Sweet Gingerbread Man," an easy-listening chart entry for the Mike Curb Congregation. "Pieces of Dreams" (lyrics by Alan and Marilyn Bergman) from the August 1970 film of the same name, was a Top Ten easy-listening chart hit for Johnny Mathis, with an instrumental version by Ferrante and Teicher also in the easy-listening charts, before it brought Legrand a best song Oscar nomination for the third year in a row. April

1971 saw the release of *Summer of '42*, with a soundtrack album that spent more than seven months in the charts, resulting in two Grammy nominations for Legrand: "Theme from *Summer of '42*" for Best Pop Instrumental Composition and Best Pop Instrumental Performance. And the score brought him his second Academy Award, for Best Original Dramatic Score.

By that time Legrand had enjoyed his next major success, his score for the 1971 television film *Brian's Song*. His "Brian's Song" instrumental theme made the pop and easy-listening charts and won him a Grammy for Best Instrumental Composition, and he had his first chart LP in 16 years with *"Brian's Song" Themes & Variations*. He returned to the charts less than four months later with Sarah Vaughan/Michel Legrand, which brought him another Grammy for Best Arrangement Accompanying Vocalist(s) for "What Are You Doing the Rest of Your Life?" as well as two Grammy nominations for "The Summer Knows" (lyrics by Alan and Marilyn Bergman; a song featured in *Summer of '42*), for Song of the Year and for Best Arrangement Accompanying Vocalist(s). By the end of the year he was back in the charts with Bobby Darin's recording of his collaboration with Smokey Robinson, "Happy," the love theme from the film *Lady Sings the Blues*.

In addition to his extensive film work, Legrand also found occasion to write and perform jazz, and in 1975 he won two more Grammys, for Best Jazz Performance by a Big Band for the album *Images*, on which he led the orchestra backing Phil Woods, and for Best Instrumental Composition for "Images."

Legrand again began to pick up airplay and awards in the early 1980s. His score for the 1982 film *Best Friends* featured "How Do You Keep the Music Playing?" (lyrics by Alan and Marilyn Bergman), which earned an Academy Award nomination, leading to a recording by James Ingram and Patti Austin that made the pop charts and the adult contemporary Top Ten in the spring of 1983. That fall saw the release of Barbra Streisand's film musical *Yentl*, with a song score by Legrand and the Bergmans. Streisand topped the adult contemporary charts and made the pop Top 40 with "The Way He Makes Me Feel" from the score, and "Papa, Can You Hear Me?" also reached the adult contemporary charts. The soundtrack album reached the Top Ten and sold a million copies. Legrand and the Bergmans won the Academy Award for Original Song Score or Adaptation Score, and they were nominated for best song for both "The Way He Makes Me Feel" and "Papa, Can You Hear Me?" The soundtrack album was nominated for the Grammy for Best Album of Original Score Written for a Motion Picture or TV Special, and Legrand earned a nomination for Best Instrumental Arrangement Accompanying Vocal(s) for "Papa, Can You Hear Me?".

Legrand continued to work on several films a year through the 1980s and did not slow down until the mid-1990s. In 1989 he made his directorial and screenwriting debut with the autobiographical *Cinq Jours en Juin* (*Five Days in June*), which recalled his youth during World War II. He earned a 1991 Grammy nomination for Best Instrumental Arrangement Accompanying Vocal(s) for the track "Nature Boy" on Natalie Cole's album *Unforgettable*.

WORKS (only works for which Legrand was a primary, credited composer are listed): **FILM SCORES:** *Les Amants du Tage* (Lovers' Net; 1955); *Rafles sur la Ville* (Sinners of Paris; 1958); *L'Amérique Insolite* (1960); *La Chien de Pique* (1960); *Les Portes Claquent* (1960); *Terrain Vague* (1960); *Une Femme est une Femme* (A Woman Is a Woman; 1960); *Les Sept Péchés Capitaux* (Seven Capital Sins; 1961); *Le Cave se Rebiffe* (The Counterfeiters of Paris; 1961); *Lola* (1961); *Me Faire Ça à Moi...* (1961); *Cléo de 5 à 7* (Cleo from 5 to 7; 1962); *Comme un Poisson dans l'Eau* (1962); *L'Empire de la Nuit* (1962); *Le Gentleman d'Epsom* (1962); *Un Coeur Gros Comme Ça!* (1962); *Une Grosse Tête* (1962); *La Baie des Anges* (Bay of Angels; 1963); *Le Joli Mai* (1963); *Les Amoureux du "France"* (1963); *Love Is a Ball* (1963); *Maigret Voit Rouge* (1963); *Vivre Sa Vie* (My Life to Live; 1963); *Bande à Part* (Band of Outsiders; 1964); *Les Plus Belles Escroqueries du Monde* (The Beautiful Swindlers; 1964); *Fascinante Amazonie* (1964); *Les Pieds-Nickelés 1964* (1964); *Une Ravissante Idiote* (Ravishing Idiot; 1964); *Les Parapluies de Cherbourg* (The Umbrellas of Cherbourg; 1964); *Corrida pour un Espion* (1965); *Eva* (1965); *L'Or et le Plomb* (1965); *Quand Passent les Faisans* (Les Escrocs; 1965); *Monnaie de Singe* (1965); *Et la Femme Créa l'Amour* (1966); *La Vie de Château* (A Matter of Resistance; 1966); *The Plastic Dome of Norma Jean* (1966); *Tendre Voyou* (Tender Scoundrel; 1966); *Qui Êtes-Vous, Polly Maggoo?* (Who Are You, Polly Maggoo?; 1966); *L'Homme à La Buick* (1967); *Pretty Polly* (aka *A Matter of Innocence*; 1967); *Le Plus Vieux Métier du Monde* (The Oldest Profession; 1967); *Les Demoiselles de Rochefort* (The Young Girls of Rochefort; 1967); *How to Save a Marriage (And Ruin Your Life)* (1968); *Ice Station Zebra* (1968); *Play Dirty* (1968); *Sweet November* (1968); *The Thomas Crown Affair* (1968); *Castle Keep* (1969); *The Happy Ending* (1969); *The Picasso Summer* (1969); *La Piscine* (The Swimming Pool; 1969); *La Dame dans l'Auto avec des Lunettes et un Fusil* (The Lady in the Car with Glasses and a Gun; 1970); *Les Mariés de l'An Deux* (1970); *The Magic Garden of Stanley Sweetheart* (1970); *Pieces of Dreams* (1970); *Wuthering Heights* (1970); *Peau d'Ane* (Donkey Skin; 1971); *The Go-Between* (1971); *Le Mans* (1971); *La Vieille Fille* (1971); *Les Feux de la Chandeleur* (Hearth Fires; 1971); *Summer of '42* (1971); *A Time for Loving* (aka *Paris Was Made for Loving*; 1971); *La Poudre D'Escampette* (Touch and Go; 1971); *Un Peu de Soleil dans l'Eau Froide* (1971); *Le Gang des Otages* (The Hostage Gang; 1972); *Lady Sings the Blues* (1972); *One Is a Lonely Number* (1972); *Pas Folle la Guêpe* (1972); *Portnoy's Complaint* (1972); *40 Carats* (1973); *Breezy* (1973); *Cops and Robbers* (1973); *A Doll's House* (1973); *Vérités et Mensonges* (F for Fake) (1973); *A Bequest to the Nation* (aka *The Nelson Affair*; 1973); *Un Homme Est Mort* (The Outside Man; 1973); *L'Evènement le Plus Important depuis que l'Homme a Marché sur la Lune* (A Slightly Pregnant Man; 1973); *L'Impossible Object* (Impossible Object [aka *Story of a Love Story*]; 1973); *Our Time* (aka *Death of Her Innocence*; 1974); *The Three Musketeers* (1974); *La Ville Bidon* (1975); *Le Sauvage* (The Savage [aka *Lovers Like Us*]; 1975); *Sheila Levine Is Dead and Living in New York* (1975); *The Smurfs and the Magic Flute* (1975); *Section Spéciale* (1975); *Gable and Lombard* (1976); *Le Voyage de Noces* (1976); *Ode to Billy Joe* (1976); *Black Joy* (1977); *Gulliver's Travels* (1977); *The Other Side of Midnight* (1977); *Semi-Tough* (1977); *Ça Fait Tilt!* (1978); *La Belle Emmerdeuse* (1978); *Le Baratineur* (1978); *Mon Premier Amour* (1978); *On Peut le Dire sans Se Facher* (1978); *Les Routes du Sud* (The Roads to the South; 1978); *Je Vous Ferai Aimer la Vie* (1979); *Lady Oscar* (1979); *Les Fabuleuses Aventures du Légendaire Baron de Munchausen* (1979); *Atlantic City* (1980); *Falling in Love Again* (aka *In Love*; 1980); *The Hunter* (1980); *Melvin and Howard* (1980); *The Mountain Men* (1980); *Les Uns et les Autres* (Bolero; 1981); *Finishing Touch* (1981); *Hi No Tori* (The Phoenix) (1980); *Best Friends* (1982); *Le Cadeau* (The Gift; 1982); *Qu-Est-Ce Qui Fait Courir David?*

(*What Makes David Run?*; 1982); *La Revanche des Humanoides* (1983); *Never Say Never Again* (1983); *Yentl* (1983); *Eine Liebe in Deutschland* (*Love in Germany*; 1984); *Micki + Maude* (1984); *Palace* (1984); *Partir Revenir* (1984); *Slapstick* (*Of Another Kind*) (1984); *Train d'Enfer* (1984); *Parking* (1985); *Secret Places* (1985); *Paroles et Musique* (*Love Songs*; 1986); *Club de Rencontres* (1987); *Spirale* (1987); *Switching Channels* (1988); *Trois Places pour le 26* (1988); *Cinq Jours en Juin* (*Five Days in June*; 1989); *Eternity* (1990); *Dingo* (1991); *Fuga dal Paradiso* (*Escape from Paradise*; 1991); *The Pickle* (1991); *Wrestling Ernest Hemingway* (1993); *Ready to Wear* (1994); *Les Misérables* (1995); *Les Enfants de Lumière* (*The Children of Lumiere*; 1995); *Die Schelme von Schelm* (*Aaron's Magic Village*; 1995); *The Truth About Cats and Dogs* (1996); *Madeline* (1998). **TELEVISION FILM SCORES:** *Brian's Song* (1971); *It's Good to Be Alive* (1974); *A Woman Called Golda* (1982); *The Jesse Owens Story* (1984); *As Summers Die* (1986); *Casanova* (1987); *Not a Penny More, Not a Penny Less* (1990); *The Ring* (1996).—**WR**

Legrense, Johannes, French music theorist, known as **Gallicus**; b. Namur, c. 1415; d. Parma, 1473. He received training in voice in Namur, and then pursued academic studies with Vittorino da Feltre in Mantua, where he became a Carthusian monk. His most important treatise was *Libelli musicalis de ritu canendi vetustissimo et novo*. He also wrote the treatises *Praefationcula in tam admirabilem quam tacitam et quietissimam novorum concinetiam* and *Tacita nunch inchoatur stupendaque numerorum musica*.—**LK/DM**

Legrenzi, Giovanni, celebrated Italian composer; b. Clusone, near Bergamo (baptized), Aug. 12, 1626; d. Venice, May 27, 1690. He was the son of a violinist and composer named Giovanni Maria Legrenzi. In 1645 he became organist at S. Maria Maggiore in Bergamo, and in 1651 he was ordained and made resident chaplain there; in 1653 became first organist. In 1656 he was named maestro di cappella of the Accademia dello Spirito Santo in Ferrara. His first opera, *Nino il giusto*, was given in Ferrara in 1662. He left Ferrara in 1665, and in 1671 settled in Venice, where he served as an instructor at the Cons. dei Mendicanti; in 1683 was its maestro di coro. In 1677 he was maestro of the Oratorio at S. Maria della Fava. In 1681 he became vice-maestro of S. Marco; in 1685 was elected maestro there. Under his regimen the orch. was increased to 34 instrumental parts (8 violins, 11 violettas, 2 viole da braccio, 3 violones, 4 theorbos, 2 cornets, 1 bassoon, and 3 trombones). Legrenzi was a noted teacher; among his pupils were Gasparini, Lotti, and Caldara, as well as his own nephew, Giovanni Varischino. Legrenzi's sonatas are noteworthy, since they served as models of Baroque forms as later practiced by Vivaldi and Bach. His operas and oratorios were marked by a development of the da capo form in arias, and his carefully wrought orch. support of the vocal parts was of historic significance as presaging the development of opera.

WORKS: DRAMATIC: O p e r a : *Nino il giusto* (Ferrara, 1662; not extant); *L'Achille in Sciro* (Ferrara, 1663; not extant); *Zenobia e Radamisto* (Ferrara, 1665); *Tiridate* (based upon the preceding; Venice, 1668; not extant); *Eteocle e Polinice* (Venice, 1675); *La divisione del mondo* (Venice, 1675); *Adone in Cipro* (Venice, 1676; not extant); *Germanico sul Reno* (Venice,

1676); *Totila* (Venice, 1677); *Il Creso* (Venice, 1681); *Antioco il grande* (Venice, 1681); *Il Pausania* (Venice, 1682); *Lisimaco riamato* (Venice, 1682); *L'Ottaviano Cesare Augusto* (Mantua, 1682; not extant); *Giustino* (Venice, 1683); *I due Cesari* (Venice, 1683); *L'anarchia dell'imperio* (Venice, 1684; not extant); *Publio Elio Pertinace* (Venice, 1684; not extant); *Ifianassa e Melampo* (Pratolino, 1685; not extant). **O r a t o r i o s :** *Oratorio del giuditio* (Vienna, 1665; not extant); *Gli sponsali d'Ester* (Modena, 1676; not extant); *Il Sedicia* (Ferrara, 1676); *La vendita del core humano* (Ferrara, 1676); *Il Sisara* (Ferrara, 1678; not extant); *Decollatione di S. Giovanni* (Ferrara, 1678; not extant); *La morte del cor penitente* (Vienna, 1705). **VOCAL: S a c r e d :** *Concerti musicali per uso di chiesa* (Venice, 1654); *Harmonia d'affeti devoti* for 2–4 Voices (Venice, 1655); *13 Salmi a 5* (Venice, 1657); *Sentimenti devoti* for 2–3 Voices (Venice, 1660); *Compiete con le lettanie & antifone della BV a 5* (Venice, 1662); *Sacri e festivi concenti, messa e psalmi a due chori* (Venice, 1667); *Acclamationi divoti* for 1 Voice (Bologna, 1670); *Sacri musicali concerti* for 2–3 Voices (Venice, 1689); *Motetti sacri* for 1 Voice (G. Varischino, ed.; Venice, 1692); Psalms; motets; etc. **S e c u l a r :** *Cantate e canzonette* for 1 Voice (Bologna, 1676; modern ed. in *Recent Researches in the Music of the Baroque Era*, XIV-XV, 1972); *Idee armonische* for 2–3 Voices (Venice, 1678); *Echi di riverenza di cantate e canzoni* (Bologna, 1678); cantatas; etc. **I n s t r u m e n t a l :** *18 Sonate a 2–3* (Venice, 1655); *30 Sonate da chiesa e da camera...a 3* (Venice, 1656); *16 Sonate a 2, 3, 5, & 6* (Venice, 1663); *La cetra, sonate a 2–4* (Venice, 1673); *Balletti e correnti a 5* (G. Varischino, ed.; Venice, 1691); *Sonate, 2–7 insts. con trombe e senza, overo flauti* (Venice, c. 1695; not extant); several of the sonatas have been publ. in *Hortus Musicus*, XXXI (1949) and LXXXIII and LXXXIV (1951), and in *Le Pupitre*, IV (Paris, 1968).

BIBL.: H. Nüssle, *G. L. als Instrumentalkomponist* (diss., Univ. of Munich, 1917); P. Fogaccia, *G. L.* (Bergamo, 1954); S. Bonta, *The Church Sonatas of G. L.* (diss., Harvard Univ., 1964); J. Swale, *A Thematic Catalogue of the Music of G. L.* (diss., Univ. of Adelaide, 1983); F. Passadore and F. Rossi, eds., *G. L. e la Cappella ducale di San Marco* (It., Eng., and Ger.; Florence, 1994). —**NS/LK/DM**

Legros, Joseph, French tenor and composer; b. Monampteuil, Sept. 7, 1739; d. La Rochelle, Dec. 20, 1793. He was a choirboy in Laon, making made his debut at the Paris Opéra in 1764 as Titon in Mondonville's *Titon et l'Aurore*. He subsequently created several roles in operas by Gluck, including Achilles in *Iphigénie en Aulide* (1774) and Pylades in *Iphigénie en Tauride* (1779); also sang in operas by Piccinni, Grétry, and others. He retired from the stage in 1783. He served as director of the Concert Spirituel (1777–90). Legros wrote several operas and a number of songs.—**NS/LK/DM**

Lehár, Franz (actually, **Ferenc**), celebrated Austrian operetta composer of Hungarian descent; b. Komárom, Hungary, April 30, 1870; d. Bad Ischl, Oct. 24, 1948. He began his music training with his father, Franz Lehár (1838–98), a military bandmaster. He then entered the Prague Cons. at 12 and studied violin with A. Bennewitz and theory with J. Foerster. In 1885 he was brought to the attention of Fibich, who gave him lessons in composition independently from his studies at the Cons. In 1887 Lehár submitted 2 piano sonatas to Dvořák, who encouraged him in his musical career. In 1888 he became a violinist in a theater orch. in Elberfeld;

in 1889, entered his father's band (50th Infantry) in Vienna, and assisted him as conductor. From 1890 to 1902 Lehár led military bands in Pola, Trieste, Budapest, and Vienna. Although his early stage works were unsuccessful, he gained some success with his marches and waltzes. With *Der Rastelbinder* (Vienna, Dec. 20, 1902), he established himself as a composer for the theater. His most celebrated operetta, *Die lustige Witwe*, was first performed in Vienna on Dec. 30, 1905; it subsequently received innumerable performances throughout the world. From then on Vienna played host to most of his finest scores, including *Der Graf von Luxemburg* (Nov. 12, 1909), *Zigeunerliebe* (Jan. 8, 1910), and *Paganini* (Oct. 30, 1925). For Berlin, he wrote *Der Zarewitsch* (Feb. 21, 1927), *Friederike* (Oct. 4, 1928), and *Das Land des Lächelns* (Oct. 10, 1929; rev. version of *Die gelbe Jacke*). Lehár's last years were made difficult by his marriage to a Jewish woman, which made him suspect to the Nazis. Ironically, *Die lustige Witwe* was one of Hitler's favorite stage works. After World War II, Lehár went to Zürich (1946); then returned to Bad Ischl shortly before his death. Lehár's music exemplifies the spirit of gaiety and frivolity that was the mark of Vienna early in the 20th century; his superlative gift for facile melody and infectious rhythms is combined with genuine wit and irony; a blend of nostalgia and sophisticated humor, undiminished by the upheavals of wars and revolutions, made a lasting appeal to audiences. S. Rourke ed. a thematic index of his works (London, 1985).

WORKS: DRAMATIC (all first perf. in Vienna unless otherwise given): O p e r e t t a : *Fräulein Leutnant* (1901); *Arabella, die Kubamerin* (1901; unfinished); *Das Club-Baby* (1901; unfinished); *Wiener Frauen (Der Klavierstimmer)* (Nov. 21, 1902; rev. as *Der Schlüssel zum Paradies*, Leipzig, Oct. 1906); *Der Rastelbinder* (Dec. 20, 1902); *Der Göttergatte* (Jan. 20, 1904; rev. as *Die ideale Gattin*, Vienna, Oct. 11, 1913; rev. as *Die Tangokönigin*, Vienna, Sept. 9, 1921); *Die Juxheirat* (Dec. 22, 1904); *Die lustige Witwe* (Dec. 30, 1905); *Peter und Paul reisen im Schlaraffenland (Max und Moritz reisen ins Schlaraffenland)* (Dec. 1, 1906); *Mstislaw der Moderne* (Jan. 5, 1907); *Der Mann mit den drei Frauen* (Jan. 21, 1908); *Das Fürstenkind* (Oct. 7, 1909; rev. as *Der Fürst der Berge*, Berlin, Sept. 23, 1932); *Der Graf von Luxemburg* (Nov. 12, 1909); *Zigeunerliebe* (Jan. 8, 1910; rev. as the opera *Garabonciás diák*, Budapest, Feb. 20, 1943); *Die Spieluhr* (Jan. 7, 1911); *Eva* (Nov. 24, 1911); *Rosenstock und Edelweiss* (Dec. 1, 1912); *Endlich allein* (Jan. 30, 1914; rev. as *Schön ist die Welt*, Berlin, Dec. 3, 1930); *Komm, deutscher Bruder* (Oct. 4, 1914; in collaboration with E. Eysler); *Der Sterngucker* (Jan. 14, 1916; rev. as *La danza delle libellule*, Milan, May 3, 1922; rev. as *Gigolette*, Milan, Oct. 30, 1926); *A Pacsirta (Wo die Lerche singt)* (Budapest, Jan. 1, 1918); *Die blaue Mazur* (May 28, 1920); *Frühling* (Jan. 20, 1922); *Frasquita* (May 12, 1922); *Die gelbe Jacke* (Feb. 9, 1923; rev. as *Das Land des Lächelns*, Berlin, Oct. 10, 1929); *Cloclo* (March 8, 1924); *Paganini* (Oct. 30, 1925); *Der Zarewitsch* (Berlin, Feb. 21, 1927); *Friederike* (Berlin, Oct. 4, 1928); *Das Frühlingsmädel* (Berlin, May 29, 1930); *Giuditta* (Jan. 20, 1934). O p e r a : *Der Kurassier* (1891–92; unfinished); *Rodrigo* (1893; unfinished); *Kukuška* (Leipzig, Nov. 27, 1896; rev. as *Tatjana*, Brünn, Feb. 21, 1905). F i l m : *Die grosse Attraktion* (1931); *Es war einmal ein Walzer* (1932); *Grossfürstin Alexandra* (1934); *Die ganze Welt dreht sich um Liebe* (1936); *Une Nuit à Vienne* (1937). **OTHER:** Orch. pieces, including several symphonic poems; 2 violin concertos; about 65 waltzes, the most famous being *Gold und Silber* (1899); more

than 50 marches; various works for piano, including sonatas; over 90 songs; etc.

BIBL.: E. Decsey, *F. L.* (Munich, 1924; second ed., 1930); S. Czech, *F. L.: Sein Weg und sein Werk* (Berlin, 1940; new ed., 1957, as *Schon ist die Welt: F. L.s Leben und Werk*); M. von Peteani, *F. L.: Seine Musik, sein Leben* (Vienna, 1950); W. Macqueen-Pope and D. Murray, *Fortune's Favourite: The Life and Times of F. L.* (London, 1953); B. Grun, *Gold and Silver: The Life and Times of F. L.* (London, 1970); M. Schonherr, *F. L.: Bibliographie zu Leben und Werk* (Vienna, 1970); O. Schneidereit, *F. L.: Eine Biographie in Zitaten* (Innsbruck, 1984); C. Marten, *Die Operette als Spiegel der Gesellschaft: F. L.s "Die lustige Witwe": Versuch einer sozialen Theorie der Operette* (Frankfurt am Main and N.Y., 1988); S. Frey, *"Was sagt ihr zu diesem Erfolg:" F. L. und die Unterhaltungsmusik des 20. Jahrhunderts* (Frankfurt am Main, 1999).—**NS/LK/DM**

Lehel, György, Hungarian conductor; b. Budapest, Feb. 10, 1926; d. there, Sept. 26, 1989. He was a student in Budapest of Kadosa (composition) and Somogyi (conducting). From 1950 he was a conductor with the Hungarian Radio in Budapest, serving as chief conductor of its radio and television sym. orch. from 1962. As a guest conductor, he made appearances in Europe, the U.S., and Japan. He was honored with the Liszt (1955, 1962) and Kossuth (1973) prizes, and was made an Artist of Merit (1967) by the Hungarian government for his services to the music of his homeland.—**NS/LK/DM**

Le Heurteur, Guillaume, French composer who flourished from 1530 to 1545. He became a priest and in 1545 he served as a canon and preceptor of the choirboys at St. Martin in Tours. His extant works comprise 4 masses, 2 Magnificats, 21 motets, and 23 chansons (see A. Smijers and A. Merritt, eds., *Treize livres de motets parus chez Pierre Attaingnant en 1534 et 1535*, Paris and Monaco, 1934–64). His sacred works are notable for their command of contrapuntal writing. In his secular works, he followed the precepts of the Paris school. —**LK/DM**

Lehmann, Hans Ulrich, Swiss composer and teacher; b. Biel, May 4, 1937. After training in cello and theory at the Biel Cons. (teacher's diplomas), he pursued studies in the composition master classes of Boulez and Stockhausen in Basel (1960–63); he also studied musicology with Fischer at the Univ. of Zürich. From 1961 to 1972 he taught at the Basel Academy of Music, and from 1969 to 1990 he lectured on new music and theory at the Univ. of Zürich. He became a teacher of composition and theory at the Zürich Hochschule für Music in 1972, serving as director of the Hochschule and Cons. from 1976. He also was president of S U I S A, the Swiss copyright soc. for authors of musical works, from 1991. In 1988 he was awarded the composition prize of the Swiss Musician's Assn. In 1993 he received the music prize of the City of Zürich. He has developed an individual style of composition with major serial connotations.

WORKS: ORCH.: *Quanti* for Flute and Chamber Orch. (1962; Geneva, Feb. 14, 1963); *Komposition für 19* (1964–65; Darmstadt, July 25, 1965); *Instants* for Piano and Strings (Geneva, May 2, 1969); Concerto for Flute, Clarinet, and Strings

(Lucerne, Sept. 6, 1969); *Positionen* (1971; Zürich, Jan. 7, 1972); *Dis-cantus I* for Oboe and Strings (Zagreb, May 9, 1971); *zu blasen* (1975–76; Graz, Oct. 17, 1976); *Kammermusik I (Hommage à Mozart)* for Small Orch. (1978–79; Lugano Radio, March 29, 1979), *II* for Small Orch. (1979; Zürich, Jan. 4, 1980), and *III* for 12 Solo Strings (1983); *Fragmente* for Small Orch. (1986–87); *Nocturnes* (1990–91). **CHAMBER:** *Régions* for Flute (1963); *Episoden* for Wind Quintet (1963–64); *Mosaik* for Clarinet (1964); *Spiele* for Oboe and Harp (1965); *Regions III* for Clarinet, Trombone, and Cello (1970); *Monodie* for Wind Instrument (1970); *Sonata "da chiesa"* for Violin and Organ (1971); *Tractus* for Flute, Oboe, and Clarinet (1971); *Faces* for Harpsichord or Piano and 5 Instruments (1972); *gegen-(bei-)spiele* for 5 Winds (1973); *"...zu streichen"* for 2 Cellos, 2 Violins, and 2 Violas (1974); *Air* for Clarinet and Piano (1977); *Contr'aire* for Clarinet and Piano (1979); *flautando* for 3 Recorders (1981); *"stroking"* for Percussionist (1982); *"battuto a tre-tratto"* for 3 Percussion (1983); *Mirlitonnades* for Flute (1983); *Triplum* for 3 Basset Horns or Bass Clarinets (1984); *"sich fragend nach frühster erinnerung"* for Recorder Quartet (1985); *"-ludes"* for Cello and Piano (1985); *"in memoriam S. Nicolai de Flue"* for 2 Flutes, 2 Cellos, and Organ (1986–87); String Quartet (1987–88); *"de profundis"* for Cello, Clarinet, and Percussion (1988–89); *"etwas Klang von meiner Oberfläche"* for Guitar (1991). **KEYBOARD: P i a n o :** *Instants* (1968). **O r g a n :** *Noten* for 1 or 2 Organs (1964–66); *Monolog* (1976); *Fundamentum* (1980). **VOCAL:** *Rondo* for Soprano and Orch. (1967; Donaueschingen, Oct. 20, 1968); *dis-cantus II* for Soprano, Organ, and Chamber Orch. (Bern, Aug. 17, 1971); *a la recherche...* for Voices and 2 Organs (1973); *Streuungen* for Chorus and Orch. (1975–76); *Tantris* for Soprano, Flute, and Cello (1976–77); *Motetus Paraburi* for Soprano, Tenor, and Baritone (1977–78); *Duette* for Soprano, Flute, and Cello (1980); *"Lege mich wie ein Stegel auf dein Herz"* for Soprano, Flute, and Clarinet (1980); *Canticum I* and *II* for Soprano and Instrument (1981); *"gottes panarchische nacht"*, cantata for Soprano, Trumpet, Women's Chorus, and Orch. (1981–82); *"Mon amour"* for Mezzo-soprano and Cello (1983); *Alleluja I* for Soprano, Clarinet, Japanese Temple Bell, and Organ (1985); *"Osculetur me"* for Soprano and Basset Horn (1988–89); *"Wandloser Raum"* for Speaker, Flute, Clarinet, and Harp (1989); *"ad missam Prolationum"* for Tenor, Baritone, Bass Clarinet, and Percussion (1989–90).—**NS/LK/DM**

Lehmann, Lilli, celebrated German soprano, sister of **Marie Lehmann**; b. Würzburg, Nov. 24, 1848; d. Berlin, May 16, 1929. Her father, August Lehmann, was a singer. Her mother, Marie Loew (1807–83), who had sung leading soprano roles and had also appeared as a harpist at the Kassel Opera under Spohr, became harpist at the National Theater in Prague in 1853, and there Lehmann spent her girlhood. At the age of 6 she began to study piano with Cölestin Müller, and at 12 progressed so far that she was able to act as accompanist to her mother, who was her only singing teacher. She made her professional debut in Prague on Oct. 20, 1865, as the First Page in *Die Zauberflöte*; then sang in Danzig (1868) and Leipzig (1869–70). In the meantime, she made her first appearance at the Berlin Royal Opera as Marguerite de Valois in *Les Huguenots* (Aug. 31, 1869); then joined its roster (1870) and established herself as a brilliant coloratura. During the summer of 1875 she was in Bayreuth, and was coached by Wagner himself in the parts of Wöglinde (*Das Rheingold* and *Götterdämmerung*), Helmwige, and the Forest Bird; these roles she created

at the Bayreuth Festival the following summer. She then returned to Berlin under a life contract with the Royal Opera; she was given limited leaves of absence, which enabled her to appear in the principal German cities, in Stockholm (1878), in London (debut as Violetta, June 3, 1880), and in Vienna (1882). She made her American debut at the Metropolitan Opera in N.Y. on Nov. 25, 1885, as Carmen; 5 days later she sang Brünnhilde in *Die Walküre*; then sang virtually all the Wagner roles through subsequent seasons until 1890; her last season there was 1898–99; she also appeared as Norma, Aida, Donna Anna, Fidelio, etc. She sang Isolde at the American premiere of *Tristan und Isolde* (Dec. 1, 1886), and appeared in Italian opera with the De Reszkes and Lassalle during the season of 1891–92. In the meantime, her contract with the Berlin Royal Opera was canceled (1889), owing to her protracted absence, and it required the intervention of Kaiser Wilhelm II to reinstate her (1891). In 1896 she sang the 3 Brünnhildes at the Bayreuth Festival. Her great admiration for Mozart caused her to take an active part in the annual Festivals held at Salzburg (1901–10), where she was artistic director. Her operatic repertoire comprised 170 roles in 114 operas (German, Italian, and French). She possessed in the highest degree all the requisite qualities of a great interpreter; she had a boundless capacity for work, a glorious voice, and impeccable technique; she knew how to subordinate her fiery temperament to artistic taste; on the stage she had plasticity of pose, grace of movement, and regal presence; her ability to project her interpretation with conviction to audiences in different countries was not the least factor in her universal success. Although she was celebrated chiefly as an opera singer, she was equally fine as an interpreter of German lieder; she gave recitals concurrently with her operatic appearances, and continued them until her retirement in 1920; her repertoire of songs exceeded 600. She was also a successful teacher; among her pupils were Geraldine Farrar and Olive Fremstad. On Feb. 24, 1888, in N.Y. she married **Paul Kalisch**, with whom she often sang in opera in subsequent years. They later separated, but never divorced. After her death, Kalisch inherited her manor at Salzkammergut, and remained there until his death in 1946, at the age of 90. Lehmann authored *Meine Gesangskunst* (Berlin, 1902; Eng. tr., 1902, as *How to Sing*; 3rd ed., rev. and supplemented, 1924 by C. Willenbücher); *Studie zu Fidelio* (Leipzig, 1904); *Mein Weg*, autobiography (Leipzig, 1913; second ed., 1920; Eng. tr., 1914, as *My Path through Life*).

BIBL.: J. Wagenmann, *L. L.s Geheimnis der Stimmbänder* (Berlin, 1905; second ed., 1926); L. Andro, *L. L.* (Berlin, 1907). —**NS/LK/DM**

Lehmann, Liza (actually, **Elizabeth Nina Mary Frederica**), English soprano and composer; b. London, July 11, 1862; d. Pinner, Sept. 19, 1918. She was the daughter of the painter Rudolf Lehmann and the composer and teacher Amelia Lehmann. She received vocal training from Randegger and Lind in London, and studied composition with Raunkilde in Rome, Freudenberg in Wiesbaden, and MacCunn in London. On Nov. 23, 1885, she made her debut in a recital at a Monday Popular Concert in London, and then sang in concerts throughout Europe. On July 14, 1894, she made her farewell concert appearance at St. James' Hall in London, and later that year she married the painter and composer Herbert Bedford. In 1910 she made a tour of the U.S., accompanying herself at the piano in song recitals. In 1911–12 she served as the first president of the Soc. of Women Musicians. In later years, she was a prof. of voice at the Guildhall School of Music in London. Her autobiography appeared as *The Life of Liza Lehmann, by Herself* (London, 1919). As a composer, she became best known for her song cycle *In a Persian Garden* for Soprano, Alto, Tenor, Bass, and Piano (1896; London, Jan. 10, 1897), based on selections from Fitzgerald's tr. of the *Rubaiyāt of Omar Khayyām*. Lehmann was the grandmother of **David Bedford** and **Steuart Bedford**.

WORKS: DRAMATIC: *Sergeant Brue*, musical farce (London, June 14, 1904); *The Vicar of Wakefield*, romantic light opera (London, Nov. 12, 1906); *The Happy Prince* (1908); *Everyman*, opera (London, Dec. 28, 1915); incidental music. **—NS/LK/DM**

Lehmann, Lotte, celebrated German-born American soprano; b. Perleberg, Feb. 27, 1888; d. Santa Barbara, Calif., Aug. 26, 1976. She studied in Berlin with Erna Tiedka, Eva Reinhold, and Mathilde Mallinger. She made her operatic debut on Sept. 2, 1910, as the second Boy in *Die Zauberflöte* at the Hamburg Opera; her first major role came before that year was out, and she soon was given important parts in Wagner's operas, establishing herself as one of the finest Wagnerian singers. In 1914 she made her first appearance in London as Sophie at Drury Lane. In 1916 she was engaged at the Vienna Opera. Richard Strauss selected her to sing the Composer in the revised version of his *Ariadne auf Naxos* when it was first performed in Vienna (Oct. 4, 1916); then she appeared as Octavian in *Der Rosenkavalier*, and later as the Marschallin, which became one of her most famous roles. She also created the roles of Fäbcrin (the Dyer's wife) in his *Die Frau ohne Schatten* (Vienna, Oct. 10, 1919) and Christine in his *Intermezzo* (Dresden, Nov. 4, 1924). In 1922 she toured in South America. In 1924 she made her first appearance at London's Covent Garden as the Marschallin, and continued to sing there regularly with great success until 1935; appeared there again in 1938. On Oct. 28, 1930, she made her U.S. debut as Sieglinde with the Chicago Opera, and on Jan. 11, 1934, sang Sieglinde at her Metropolitan Opera debut in N.Y. She continued to appear at the Metropolitan, with mounting success, in the roles of Elisabeth in *Tannhäuser*, Tosca, and the Marschallin, until her farewell performance as the Marschallin on Feb. 23, 1945. In 1946 she appeared as the Marschallin for the last time in San Francisco. In 1945 she became a naturalized American citizen. She gave her last recital in Santa Barbara, Calif., on Aug. 7, 1951, and thereafter devoted herself to teaching. Lehmann was universally recognized as one of the greatest singers of the century. The beauty of her voice, combined with her rare musicianship, made her a compelling artist of the highest order. In addition to her unforgettable Strauss roles, she excelled as Mozart's Countess and Donna Elvira, Beethoven's Leonore, and Wagner's Elisabeth, Elsa, and Eva, among others. She

publ. a novel, *Orplid mein Land* (1937; Eng. tr., 1938, as *Eternal Flight*); an autobiography, *Anfang und Aufstieg* (Vienna, 1937; in London as *Wings of Song*, 1938; in N.Y. as *Midway in My Song*, 1938); *More Than Singing* (N.Y., 1945); *My Many Lives* (N.Y., 1948); *Five Operas and Richard Strauss* (N.Y., 1964; in London as *Singing with Richard Strauss*, 1964); *Eighteen Song Cycles* (London and N.Y., 1971).

BIBL.: B. Wessling, *L. L....mehr als eine Sängerin* (Salzburg, 1969); B. Glass, *L. L.: A Life in Opera & Song* (Santa Barbara, Calif., 1988); A. Jefferson, *L. L.:1888–1976: A Centenary Biography* (London, 1988); B. Wessling, *L. L.:"Sie sang, dass es Sterne rührte": Eine Biographie* (Cologne, 1995).**—NS/LK/DM**

Lehmann, (Ludwig) Fritz, esteemed German conductor; b. Mannheim, May 17, 1904; d. Munich, March 30, 1956. He studied at the Mannheim Cons. and the univs. of Heidelberg and Göttingen. He was a conductor in Göttingen (1923–27), Hildesheim (1927–38), and Hannover (1929–38). In 1934 he became conductor of the Handel Festival in Göttingen; was also Generalmusikdirektor in Bad Pyrmont (1934–38), Wuppertal (1938–47), and Göttingen (1946–50). He subsequently was a teacher at the Hochschule für Musik in Munich (from 1953). A consummate conductor, he led notable performances in both the operatic and symphonic literature, ranging from the Baroque period to the 20th century.

BIBL.: M. Wick, *Bessessen von Musik: Der Dirigent F. L.* (Berlin, 1990).**—NS/LK/DM**

Lehmann, Marie, esteemed German soprano, sister of **Lilli Lehmann**; b. Hamburg, May 15, 1851; d. Berlin, Dec. 9, 1931. She received her training from her mother and her sister. On May 1, 1867, she made her operatic debut as Aennchen in Leipzig, and then appeared in Breslau, Cologne, Hamburg, and Prague. She sang with her sister in the first mounting of Wagner's *Ring* cycle at the Bayreuth Festival in 1876, appearing as Wellgunde and Ortlinde. From 1882 to 1896 she was a leading member of the Vienna Court Opera. In later years, she taught voice in Berlin. Among her notable roles were Mozart's Donna Elvira and Donna Anna, Bellini's Adalgisa, and Meyerbeer's Marguerite de Valois.**—NS/LK/DM**

Lehnhoff, Nikolaus, German opera director; b. Hannover, May 20, 1939. He attended the univs. of Munich and Venice. After gaining experience as an asst. stage director at the Berlin Deutsche Oper, the Bayreuth Festival, and the Metropolitan Opera in N.Y., he staged his first opera, *Die Frau ohne Schatten*, at the Paris Opéra in 1972. In 1975 he produced *Elektra* at the Lyric Opera of Chicago. His mounting of the *Ring* cycle at the San Francisco Opera (1983–85) and at the Bavarian State Opera in Munich (1987) were notably successful. His stagings of *Kát'a Kabanová* (1988) and *Jenůfa* (1989) at the Glyndebourne Festival were outstanding. In 1989 he produced *Salome* at the Metropolitan Opera. He staged *Idomeneo* at the Salzburg Festival in 1990. In 1991 he produced *Elektra* in Leipzig. After staging *The Makropulos Affair* at the Glyndebourne Festival in 1995, he produced *Palestrina* at London's Covent Garden in 1997. Lehnhoff places great importance upon his collaborations with the finest designers. He is the author of *Es war einmal* (Munich, 1987).—NS/LK/DM

Lehrman, Leonard J(ordan), American composer, pianist, and conductor; b. Ft. Riley, Kans., Aug. 20, 1949. He received private composition lessons from Siegmeister (1960–70), and also studied with Kim, Del Tredici, Kirchner, and Foss at Harvard Univ. (B.A., 1971) and attended the American Cons. in Fontainebleau (1969). He continued his training at the École Normale de Musique in Paris (1971–72), the Salzburg Mozarteum (1972), with Husa and Palmer at Cornell Univ. (M.F.A., 1975; D.M.A., 1977), and at the Ind. Univ. School of Music in Bloomington (1975–76). Later he studied library and information science at Long Island Univ. (M.A., 1995). After making his debut as a pianist at N.Y.'s Carnegie Recital Hall in 1979, he conducted at the Bremerhaven City Theater (1981–83) before going to Berlin, where he was founder-president of the Jewish Music Theater (1983–86) and a conductor at the Theater des Westens (1983–85). Returning to N.Y., he became founder-conductor of the Metropolitan Phil. Chorus in 1988. In 1990 he joined the faculty of the Jewish Academy of Fine Arts, which became the Performing Arts Inst. of Long Island in 1993. He served as assoc. ed. of the magazine *Opera Monthly* from 1993. He ed. *The Marc Blitzstein Songbook* (N.Y., 1999).

WORKS: DRAMATIC: O p e r a : *Tales of Malamud*, 2 operas after Malamud: *Idiots First* (completion of Blitzstein's work, 1973; Bloomington, Ind., March 14, 1976) and *Karla* (1974; Bloomington, March 7, 1976); *Sima* (Ithaca, N.Y., Oct. 23, 1976); *Hannah* (Mannheim, May 24, 1980); *The Family Man* (concert perf., Berlin, Jan. 6, 1985; stage perf., N.Y., June 27, 1985); *The Birthday of the Bank* (1988); *New World: An Opera About What Columbus Did to the "Indians"* (1991; Huntington, N.Y., Aug. 11, 1992). **M u s i c a l s :** *Growing Up Woman*, chamber musical (1980; Berlin, April 30, 1984); *E.G.: A Musical Portrait of Emma Goldman* (1986; N.Y., May 3, 1987); *Superspy! The Secret Musical* (1988; Paris, July 7, 1989). Also incidental music; cabarets, including *A Blitztein Cabaret, Memories and Music of Leonard Bernstein, An Israel Cabaret, Jewish-American Cabaret,* and *The Jewish Woman in Song.* **ORCH.:** *Bloody Kansas* (1975); Violin Concerto (1975); Flute Concerto (1982). **CHAMBER:** Flute Sonata (1964–65); String Trio (1968); Sonata for Piano and Tape (1968); Piano Trio (1969–70); Sonatina for Solo Tuba (1980). **VOCAL:** *The Universal Declaration of Human Rights* for Chorus and Piano or Winds and Percussion (N.Y., Oct. 26, 1988); *We Are Innocent*, cantata on letters of Julius and Ethel Rosenberg, for Soloists, Optional Chorus, and Piano or Orch. (1988; N.Y., June 11, 1989); *A Requiem for Hiroshima* for Soloists, Chorus, and Orch. or Chamber Ensemble (N.Y., Aug. 5, 1990); song cycles; solo songs.—NS/LK/DM

Leiber, Jerry (actually, **Jerome), and Mike** (actually, **Michael Endore) Stoller,** American songwriters and record producers. Lyricist Leiber (b. Baltimore, Md., April 25, 1933) and composer Stoller (b. N.Y., March 13, 1933) wrote and produced a series of recordings in the 1950s and early 1960s that expanded the appeal of R&B into the pop market and strongly influenced the development of rock 'n' roll. Their story

songs, such as "Searchin'," "Yakety Yak," and "Charlie Brown," recorded by The Coasters, rivaled the wit of Chuck Berry's best compositions. Elvis Presley established such songs of theirs as "Hound Dog," "Love Me," and "Jailhouse Rock" as standards. And they created hits for nonrock figures such as Peggy Lee, notably "Is That All There Is?"

Leiber was the son of Polish immigrants. His father, a Hebrew teacher, died when he was five, and his mother opened a grocery store to support the family. He began to take piano lessons at nine, becoming most intrigued with boogie-woogie. In 1945 he and his mother moved to L. A. By his teens he was working in a record store and writing blues-influenced lyrics. He met Stoller in high school.

Stoller was the son of an engineer; his mother was a former model and dancer. He began taking piano lessons as a child from an aunt, but his interest in boogie-woogie led him to study with James P. Johnson at the age of 11. He also developed a great interest in jazz. The family moved to L. A. in 1949, and he began to study music formally and to play in bands.

Leiber and Stoller both graduated from high school in 1950 and enrolled at L. A. City Coll., where Stoller studied composition with Arthur Lange until 1952. (He also studied with Stefan Wolpe from 1958 to 1960.) Writing songs and placing them with R&B acts, Leiber and Stoller had their first hit with "Hard Times," recorded by Charles Brown, which entered the R&B charts in March 1952 and made the Top Ten. That year Little Willie Littlefield cut their song "K. C. Lovin'" for Federal and it was a local hit. Their first major national hit, which they also produced, was "Hound Dog" by Willie Mae "Big Mama" Thornton, which topped the R&B charts in April 1953. With that they formed their own label, Spark Records. In 1955 they scored hits with two songs they wrote and produced, "Black Denim Trousers" by The Cheers, on Capitol Records, which peaked in the pop Top Ten in October, and "Smokey Joe's Café" by The Robins, originally released on Spark and then picked up for national distribution by Atlantic Records, which was in the pop charts and the R&B Top Ten in December.

Leiber and Stoller signed an independent production deal with Atlantic and moved to N.Y., taking with them two members of the Robins, Carl Gardner and Bobby Nunn, who, with the addition of three others, became The Coasters. Over the next five years the writer-producers turned out a remarkable series of hits with The Coasters and other Atlantic Records acts. Notably, with the Coasters, there were: "Down in Mexico" (R&B Top Ten, 1956); both sides of the million-selling single "Searchin'"/"Young Blood" (pop Top Ten, R&B #1, 1957); the million-selling "Yakety Yak" (#1 pop and R&B, 1958); the million-selling "Charlie Brown" (pop and R&B Top Ten, 1959); "Along Came Jones" (pop Top Ten, 1959); and the million-selling "Poison Ivy" (R&B #1, pop Top Ten, 1959).

Other Atlantic Records artists who benefited from their work included Joe Turner ("The Chicken and the Hawk [Up, Up and Away]," R&B Top Ten, 1956) and Ruth Brown ("Lucky Lips," R&B Top Ten, 1957). But the only other act they worked with as extensively as The Coasters was The Drifters, for whom they fashioned more romantic and sophisticated material, notably: "Ruby Baby" (R&B Top Ten, 1956); "Fools Fall in Love" (R&B Top Ten, 1957); the million-selling "There Goes My Baby" (music and lyrics also by Benjamin Nelson, Lover Patterson, and George Treadwell; pop Top Ten, R&B #1, 1959); and "On Broadway" (music and lyrics also by Barry Mann and Cynthia Weil; pop and R&B Top Ten, 1963). They also produced many Drifters hits they did not write, such as the million-selling #1 "Save the Last Dance for Me" (music and lyrics by Doc Pomus and Mort Shuman). When Drifters lead singer Ben E. King left the group to go solo in 1960, they wrote and produced two major hits for him, the pop Top Ten "Spanish Harlem" (music and lyrics by Jerry Leiber and Phil Spector) and the pop Top Ten, #1 R&B song "Stand by Me" (music and lyrics also by Ben E. King).

Leiber and Stoller's deal with Atlantic also allowed them to write for other artists, and earlier songs of theirs were also covered for hits once they became well known. The most notable of their non-Atlantic associations was with Elvis Presley, who came to national prominence just as they were moving to N.Y. Presley's revival of "Hound Dog" topped the pop and R&B charts in the summer of 1956, selling six million copies. He recorded Leiber and Stoller's 1954 song "Love Me," peaking in the Top Ten in January 1957. In the wake of these successes, the songwriters were asked to write songs for Presley's second motion picture, *Loving You*, released in July 1957. Their title song became a Top 40 hit. They also wrote the title song for Presley's third film, *Jailhouse Rock*, released in October 1957; it topped the pop and R&B charts, selling four million copies. Its B-side, "Treat Me Nice," also by Leiber and Stoller, made the R&B Top Ten. They were responsible for Presley's next single, "Don't," which hit #1 in February 1958 and sold two million copies, and they wrote the title song for Presley's next film, *King Creole*, released in June 1958. By that time Presley was in the army, and they had less involvement with him after he returned in 1960, though they did write the Top Ten hits "She's Not You" (1962) and the million-selling "Bossa Nova Baby" (1963).

In addition to Presley, many other artists revived Leiber and Stoller songs for hits. Among the most successful of these, Wilbert Harrison topped the pop and R&B charts in May 1959 with a million-selling version of "K. C. Lovin'" retitled "Kansas City," and Dion made the pop Top Ten in 1963 with two songs originally recorded by the Drifters, "Ruby Baby" and "Drip Drop."

Leiber and Stoller again launched their own record company, comprising the labels Red Bird and Blue Cat, in 1964, and topped the charts with their first release, The Dixie Cups' "Chapel of Love" (music and lyrics by Phil Spector, Ellie Greenwich and Jeff Barry). They were much less involved with the company as songwriters, however, and by 1966 had sold out to a partner. They took the Coasters to Columbia Records without success, worked on a proposed Broadway musical, and turned their attention more to cabaret material such as the declamatory "Is That All There Is?" which peaked in the Top 40 for Peggy Lee in November 1969. In the early 1970s they devoted themselves to music publishing.

Meanwhile, Leiber and Stoller's catalogue of songs continued to flourish. In 1965 The Searchers had a Top Ten hit with their revival of "Love Potion No. 9," previously recorded by the Clovers in 1959. Spyder Turner reached the R&B Top Ten with a revival of "Stand by Me" in 1967, one of a series of chart revivals of the song that would culminate in Ben E. King's Top Ten rerecording in 1986 in connection with a film of the same name. Aretha Franklin topped the R&B charts and hit the Top Ten of the pop charts with "Spanish Harlem" in 1971. And George Benson took "On Broadway" into the pop and R&B Top Ten in 1978.

Leiber and Stoller did some writing and producing during the 1970s, especially in the U.K., gaining greatest success with their productions of the 1973 Top Ten hit "Stuck in the Middle with You" (music and lyrics by Joe Egan and Gerry Rafferty) by Stealers Wheel and the 1975 chart album *Procol's Ninth* by Procol Harum. By the 1980s they were involved in creating stage presentations of their songs, the first of which was the London revue *Only in America* in 1980. The culmination of these efforts came with the Broadway revue *Smokey Joe's Café: The Songs of Leiber and Stoller* (N.Y., March 2, 1995), which was still running four years after it opened, by which time it had spawned international productions and touring companies as well.

WRITINGS: J. Leiber, *Selected Lyrics, 1950–1980* (N.Y., 1980).

BIBL.: R. Palmer, *Baby, That Was Rock & Roll: The Legendary L. & S.* (N.Y., 1978).—**WR**

Leibowitz, René, noted Polish-born French conductor, composer, writer on music, music theorist, and pedagogue; b. Warsaw, Feb. 17, 1913; d. Paris, Aug. 28, 1972. His family settled in Paris in 1926; from 1930 to 1933 he studied in Berlin with Schoenberg and in Vienna with Webern; also studied orchestration with Ravel in Paris (1933). He was active as a conductor from 1937. As a composer, he adopted the 12-tone method of composition, becoming its foremost exponent in France; he had numerous private students, among them Boulez. He publ. the influential books *Schoenberg et son école* (Paris, 1946; Eng. tr., N.Y., 1949) and *Introduction à la musique de douze sons* (Paris, 1949). He also wrote *L'Artiste et sa conscience* (Paris, 1950); *L'Évolution de la musique, de Bach à Schönberg* (Paris, 1952); *Histoire de l'Opéra* (Paris, 1957); with J. Maguire, *Thinking for Orchestra* (N.Y., 1958); with K. Wolff, *Erich Itor Kahn, Un Grand Représentant de la musique contemporaine* (Paris, 1958; Eng. tr., N.Y., 1958); *Schönberg* (Paris, 1969); *Le Compositeur et son double* (Paris, 1971); *Les Fantômes de l'opéra* (Paris, 1973).

WORKS: DRAMATIC: Opera: *La Nuit close* (1949); *La Rumeur de l'espace* (1950); *Ricardo Gonfolano* (1953); *Les Espagnols à Venise,* opera buffa (1963; Grenoble, Jan. 27, 1970); *Labyrinthe,* after Baudelaire (1969); *Todos caerán* (1970–72). **ORCH.:** Sym. (1941); 2 chamber concertos (1942, 1944); Chamber Sym. (1948); Piano Concerto (1954); Viola Concerto (1954); *Fantaisie symphonique* (1956); Violin Concerto (1959); *3 Bagatelles* for Strings (1959); Trombone Concertino (1960); Cello Concerto

(1962); *Rapsodie symphonique* (1964–65). **CHAMBER:** 8 string quartets (1940, 1950, 1952, 1958, 1963, 1965, 1966, 1968); *Marijuana* for Violin, Trombone, Vibraphone, and Piano (1960); *Sinfonietta da camera* (1961); *Capriccio* for Flute and Strings (1967); *Suite* for 9 Instruments (1967); Saxophone Quartet (1969); *Petite suite* for Clarinet Sextet (1970). **VOCAL:** *Tourist Death* for Soprano and Chamber Orch. (1943); *L'Explication des métaphores* for Speaker, 2 Pianos, Harp, and Percussion (1947); *Chanson Dada* for Children's Chorus and Instruments (1968); *Laboratoire central* for Speaker and Chorus (1970); numerous songs.—NS/LK/DM

Leich, Roland (Jacobi), American composer; b. Evansville, Ind., March 6, 1911. He studied composition with Borowski and Sowerby in Chicago, Webern in Vienna (1933–34), Scalero at the Curtis Inst. of Music in Philadelphia (B.M., 1934), and Rogers at the Eastman School of Music in Rochester, N.Y. (M.M., 1942); also studied at Dartmouth Coll. (B.A., 1935), where he served on the faculty (1935–41). In 1946 he became a teacher at the Carnegie Inst. of Technology (later Carnegie-Mellon Univ.) in Pittsburgh, remaining on its faculty until 1976. He was particularly successful as a composer of songs, of which he wrote more than 150.

WORKS: ORCH.: *Rondo* (1942); *Concert Piece* for Oboe and Strings (1952); *Prelude and Fugue* (1954). **CHAMBER:** String Quartet (1936); Flute Sonata (1953); *A Musical Christmas Wreath* for Woodwind Quintet and Harp (1980); piano pieces; organ music. **VOCAL:** *Housman Songs* (1932); 5 songs, after Housman (1939–78); 40 songs, after Milne (1940); 47 songs, after Dickinson (1950–65); 17 songs, after S. Hay (1956–84); also cantatas and other choral works, hymn tunes, and arrangements of folk melodies and hymns.—NS/LK/DM

Leichtentritt, Hugo, eminent German-American music scholar; b. Pleschen, Posen, Jan. 1, 1874; d. Cambridge, Mass., Nov. 13, 1951. He studied with J. K. Paine at Harvard Univ. (B.A., 1894); continued his studies in Paris (1894–95) and at the Berlin Hochschule für Musik (1895–98); obtained his Ph.D. at the Univ. of Berlin in 1901 with the diss. *Reinhard Keiser in seinen Opern: Ein Beitrag zur Geschichte der frühen deutschen Oper* (publ. in Berlin, 1901); he subsequently taught at the Klindworth-Scharwenka Cons. in Berlin (1901–24) and wrote music criticism for German and American publications. In 1933 he left Germany and became a lecturer on music at Harvard Univ. (until 1940); then taught at Radcliffe Coll. and N.Y.U. (1940–44). Although known chiefly as a scholar, he also composed a comic opera, *Der Sizilianer* (Freiburg im Breisgau, May 28, 1920); Sym.; Violin Concerto; Cello Concerto; Piano Concerto; much chamber music; several song cycles; numerous piano pieces. His MSS are in the Library of Congress in Washington, D.C.

WRITINGS: *Frédéric Chopin* (Berlin, 1905; 3rd ed., 1949); *Geschichte der Musik* (Berlin, 1905; Eng. tr., N.Y., 1938, as *Everybody's Little History of Music*); *Geschichte der Motette* (Leipzig, 1908); *Musikalische Formenlehre* (Leipzig, 1911; 5th ed., 1952; Eng. tr., Cambridge, Mass., 1951 as *Musical Form*); *Erwin Lendvai* (Berlin, 1912); *Ferruccio Busoni* (Leipzig, 1916); *Analyse der Chopin'schen Klavierwerke* (2 vols., Berlin, 1921–22); *Ignatz Waghalter* (N.Y., 1924); *Händel* (Berlin and Stuttgart, 1924); *Music, History, and Ideas* (Cambridge, Mass., 1938); *Serge*

Koussevitzky, The Boston Symphony Orchestra and the New American Music (Cambridge, Mass., 1946); *Music of the Western Nations* (ed. and amplified by N. Slonimsky; Cambridge, Mass., 1956). —NS/LK/DM

Leider, Frida, outstanding German soprano; b. Berlin, April 18, 1888; d. there, June 4, 1975. She was a student of Otto Schwarz in Berlin before completing her training in Milan. She made her operatic debut in Halle in 1915 as Venus in *Tannhäuser*; then sang at Rostock (1916–18), Königsberg (1918–19), and Hamburg (1919–23). She was engaged by the Berlin State Opera in 1923, and remained on its roster until 1940; was also highly successful in Wagnerian roles at London's Covent Garden (1924–38) and at the Bayreuth Festivals (1928–38). In 1928 she made her American debut at the Chicago Civic Opera as Brünnhilde in Die *Walküre*, and continued to appear there until 1932; then made her debut at the Metropolitan Opera in N.Y. on Jan. 16, 1933, as Isolde. In 1934 she returned to Germany; she encountered difficulties because her husband, Rudolf Deman, concertmaster of the Berlin State Opera Orch., was Jewish. She was confronted by the Nazis with the demand to divorce him, but refused; he succeeded in going to Switzerland. After the collapse of the Nazi regime (1945), she maintained a vocal studio at the (East) Berlin State Opera until 1952; also taught at the (West) Berlin Hochschule für Musik from 1948 to 1958. She publ. a memoir, *Das war mein Teil, Erinnerungen einer Opernsängerin* (Berlin, 1959; Eng. tr., N.Y., 1966 as *Playing My Part*). In addition to her celebrated portrayals of Isolde and Brünnhilde, Leider also was acclaimed for her roles of Venus, Senta, Kundry, and the Marschallin. She also was greatly renowned as a concert artist. —NS/LK/DM

Leiferkus, Sergei (Petrovich), Russian baritone; b. Leningrad, April 4, 1946. He was a student of Barsov and Shaposhnikov at the Leningrad Cons. In 1972 he became a member of the Maly Theater in Leningrad, in which city he made his debut at the Kirov Theater in Leningrad as Prince Andrei in *War and Peace* (1977); subsequently sang there with success. In 1982 he appeared as the Marquis in Massenet's *Griselidis* at the Wexford Festival in England. In 1985 he sang for the first time at the Scottish Opera in Glasgow as Don Giovanni. In 1987 he made his debut at the English National Opera in London as Zurga in *Les Pêcheurs de perles*, the same year he appeared as Eugene Onegin and Tomsky with the Kirov Opera at Covent Garden in London. He also made his U.S. debut that year as soloist in Shostakovich's 13th Sym. with the Boston Sym. Orch. In 1989 he returned to London to make his Wigmore Hall recital debut and his first appearance at the Royal Opera at Covent Garden as Luna; also sang for the first time at the Glyndebourne Opera as Mandryka and made his U.S. operatic debut at the San Francisco Opera as Telramund. In 1991 he sang Ruprecht in *The Fiery Angel* at the London Promenade Concerts. He made his Metropolitan Opera debut in N.Y. as Iago in 1994, and sang Ruprecht at his first appearance at Milan's La Scala. Following an engagement as Prince Igor at the San

Francisco Opera in 1996, he portrayed Telramund and Simon Boccanegra at Covent Garden in 1997. Among his other notable roles are Germont, Amonasro, Prince Igor, Rangoni, Escamillo, and Scarpia.—NS/LK/DM

Leifs, Jón, eminent Icelandic composer, conductor, and administrator; b. Sólheimar, May 1, 1899; d. Reykjavík, July 30, 1968. He entered the Leipzig Cons. in 1916, where he was a student of Graener and Szendrei (composition), Krehl (theory), Paul (harmony and counterpoint), Teichmüller (piano; diploma, 1921), and Lohse and Scherchen (conducting). With the exception of his tenure as music director of the Icelandic National Broadcasting Service in Reykjavík (1935–37), he worked in Germany as a composer and conductor. In 1926 he appeared as a guest conductor of the Hamburg Phil. on a tour of Norway, the Faeroes, and Iceland. After marrying a woman of Jewish descent, the Nazi regime banned Leifs' music in 1937. He and his family were able to flee to Sweden in 1944. In 1945 they settled in Iceland. He became president of the newly organized Soc. of Icelandic Composers. He also was the founder of STEF, an association of composers and copyright owners (1948), and of Islandia Edition (1949), as well as president of the Nordic Council of Composers (1952–54; 1964–66). Leifs publ. the books *Tónlistarhaettir* (Musical Form; Leipzig, 1922) and *Islands künstlerische Anregung* (Reykjavík, 1951). In his compositions, he utilized various resources, ranging from the medieval Icelandic tvisöngur to folk melos.

WORKS: DRAMATIC: *Galdra-Loftr*, incidental music to the drama (1925; Copenhagen, Sept. 3, 1938; orch. suite, 1925; overture, 1928); *Baldr*, music drama without words for Chorus, Dancers, and Orch. (1948; Reykjavík, March 24, 1991). ORCH.: *Trilogia piccoa* (1919–24; Karlsbad, Nov. 28, 1925); *Icelandic Overture*, with optional chorus (1926); *Variazione pastorale*, on a theme of Beethoven (1927; also for String Quartet); Organ Concerto (1927–28; Wiesbaden, April 26, 1935); *Icelandic Dances* (1928; also for Piano); *Sögu-Sinfónia* (Saga Sym.; 1941–42; Helsinki, Sept. 18, 1950); *Reflections from the North* for Strings (1952); *Landsýn* (Landfall), overture with optional chorus (1955; Reykjavík, Feb. 22, 1962); *prjú óhlutraen málverk* (3 Abstract Pictures; 1955–60; Reykjavík, Dec. 7, 1961); *Geysir* (1961; Reykjavík, Nov. 1, 1984); *Hekla*, overture with optional chorus (1961; Helsinki, Oct. 2, 1964); *Hinzta kveoja* [Last Greeting]: *In memoriam 30. Sept. 1961: Elegie* for Strings (1961); *Víkingasvar* (Viking Answer; 1962); *Fine I* (1963) and *II* for Vibraphone and Strings (1963); *Hughreysting* (Consolation) for Strings (1968). CHAMBER: *Étude* for Violin (1924); *Nocturne* for Harp (1931–33); 3 string quartets: No. 1, *Mors et vita* (1939), No. 2, *Vita et mors* (1948–51), and No. 3, *El Greco* (1965); Quintet for Flute, Clarinet, Bassoon, Viola, and Cello (1959); *Scherzo concreto* for 8 Winds, Viola, and Cello (1964). KEYBOARD: Piano: *Intermezzo-Torrek* (1919); 4 Pieces (1922); *Icelandic Dances* (1929); *New Icelandic Dances* (1931); *Juvenile Song* (1960). Organ: *Praeludia organo* (1951). VOCAL: *The Lord's Prayer* for Soprano or Tenor and Organ (1929); *Iceland Cantata* for Chorus, Children's Chorus, and Orch. (1929–30); *Icelandic Dances* for Voice, Chorus, and Orch. (1932); 3 oratorios: *Edda I: The Creation of the World* for Tenor, Bass, Chorus, and Orch. (1936–39), *II: The Life of the Gods* for Mezzo- soprano, Tenor, Bass, Chorus, and Orch. (1951–56), and *III: The Twilight of the Gods* for Chorus and Orch. (1966–68; unfinished); *Lay of Gudrún* for Mezzo-soprano, Tenor, Bass, and Orch. (1940; Oslo, Sept. 29, 1948); *Requiem* for Chorus (1947);

Mountain Songs for Soloists, Men's Chorus, Percussion, and Double Bass (1948); *Vorvísa* (Spring Song) for Chorus and Orch. (1958); *In Memoriam J(ónas) H(allgrímsson)* for Mezzo-soprano or Baritone and Piano (1958; also for Chorus and Orch., 1961); *Hekla* for Chorus and Orch. (1961); *Battle Song* for Chorus and Orch. (1964); *Dettifoss* for Baritone, Chorus, and Orch. (1964); *Night* for Tenor, Bass, and Small Orch. (1964); *Of Helgi the Hunding Killer* for Alto, Bass, and Chamber Orch. (1964); *Hafis* (Drift Ice) for Chorus and Orch. (1965); mixed and men's choruses; solo songs; folk song arrangements.—NS/LK/DM

Leigh, Carolyn (originally, **Rosenthal, Carolyn Paula**), exuberant American lyricist; b. Bronx, N.Y., Aug. 21, 1926; d. N.Y., Nov. 19, 1983. Leigh wrote confident, knowing lyrics to both popular songs such as "Young-at-Heart" and "Witchcraft," recorded by Frank Sinatra, and to Broadway musicals such as *Peter Pan* ("I Gotta Crow") and *Wildcat* ("Hey, Look Me Over!"). Her primary collaborator was composer Cy Coleman.

The daughter of Henry and Sylvia Rosenthal, Leigh began writing verse as a child. She attended Queens Coll. and N.Y.U., then worked as a writer in radio and in an advertising agency. In 1951 she was signed as a lyricist to a publishing company. Her first successful song was "I'm Waiting Just for You" (music and lyrics also by Henry Glover and Lucky Millinder), recorded by Lucky Millinder and His Orch. for a Top Ten R&B hit and also a pop chart entry for both Millinder and Rosemary Clooney in 1951; Pat Boone revived it in 1957 for a Top 40 hit.

Leigh's biggest early success came when she set a lyric to Johnny Richards's 1939 melody "Moonbeam" to create "Young-at-Heart." Frank Sinatra's recording peaked in the Top Ten in May 1954 and sold a million copies. It was heard by Mary Martin, who was looking for songwriters for a new theatrical production of *Peter Pan*, and Martin hired Leigh to work with composer Mark (Moose) Charlap on a few songs for what was then intended as a play with music. Their contributions included "I Gotta Crow," "I'm Flying," and "I Won't Grow Up"; the show was a success on the West Coast. For a transfer to Broadway it was expanded into a full musical, with new songs by Jule Styne and Betty Comden and Adolph Green. Opening in October 1954, the show ran 154 performances; it was broadcast on television, and the cast album became a Top Ten hit. The following year Leigh wrote the lyrics to music by Clay Warnick for a television musical version of *Heidi*.

Working with composer Philip Springer, Leigh continued to write songs for stage productions and recording stars in 1955–57. She and Springer had songs in *The Shoestring Revue* (N.Y., Feb. 28, 1955), *Shoestring '57* (N.Y., Nov. 5, 1956), and *Ziegfeld Follies of 1957* (N.Y., March 1, 1957), and their biggest pop hit came in June 1956 when Frank Sinatra peaked in the Top 40 with "(How Little It Matters) How Little We Know." In 1957 she switched partners and began working with Cy Coleman, writing songs for nightclub revues and for pop singers. In February 1958, Sinatra peaked in the Top Ten with their song "Witchcraft," and Tony Bennett peaked in the Top 40 in October 1958 with "Firefly."

(Sinatra and Bennett recorded several other Coleman-Leigh compositions, notably "The Best Is Yet to Come," cut by Bennett in 1960 and Sinatra in 1964, which became a standard without ever being a hit.)

Leigh, whose first husband was Julius Levine, married David Wyn Cunningham Jr., an attorney, in 1959; they later divorced.

Leigh and Coleman were given their first opportunity to write songs for a book musical in 1960, when director and coproducer Michael Kidd and librettist and coproducer N. Richard Nash put together *Wildcat*, a star vehicle for Lucille Ball, famous for her long-running television series *I Love Lucy*. Their score, which featured "Hey, Look Me Over!," resulted in a Top Ten cast album, but the show ran only 171 performances, closing after Ball withdrew from it. Leigh and Coleman returned to Broadway in 1962 with *Little Me*, another vehicle for a TV star, in this case, Sid Caesar. This show ran 257 performances and produced a charting cast album.

Leigh and Coleman ended their exclusive partnership after *Little Me*. Leigh wrote the lyrics for "Stay with Me" to music by Jerome Moross for the October 1963 film *The Cardinal*; Frank Sinatra's recording of the song was in the charts in January 1964. With Coleman she wrote "Pass Me By" for the November 1964 film *Father Goose*; Peggy Lee had a chart recording in February 1965.

Leigh returned to Broadway in December 1967 with the musical *How Now, Dow Jones*, on which she collaborated with Elmer Bernstein; the show ran 220 performances. This was her last work to run on Broadway. In subsequent years she sometimes appeared as a performer in nightclubs. On Labor Day, 1976, *Something to Do—A Salute to the American Worker*, a cantata by Morton Gould with her lyrics, was presented at the Kennedy Center in Washington, D.C., in commemoration of the American Bicentennial. *Hellzapoppin*, a musical revue to which she contributed lyrics for music by Cy Coleman and Jule Styne, had out-of-town tryouts starting in November 1976, but closed before reaching Broadway. In 1980 she was reported to be working on a show called *Flyers*. She and Coleman wrote two new songs for a Broadway revival of *Little Me* (N.Y., Jan. 21, 1982), and she was working on songs for a musical adaptation of the film *Smile* with Marvin Hamlisch when she died of a heart attack in 1983 at 57.

WORKS: STAGE (dates refer to Broadway openings): *Peter Pan* (Oct. 20, 1954); *Wildcat* (Dec. 16, 1960); *Little Me* (Nov. 17, 1962); *How Now, Dow Jones* (Dec. 7, 1967). **TELEVISION:** *Heidi* (Oct. 1, 1955).—**WR**

Leigh, Walter, English composer; b. London, June 22, 1905; d. in battle near Tobruk, Libya, June 12, 1942. He was an organ scholar at Christ's Coll., Cambridge (1922–26), where he studied with Dent; also took lessons with Darke and later with Hindemith at the Hochschule für Musik in Berlin (1927–29). He was particularly adept in his writing for the theater.

WORKS: 2 light operas: *The Pride of the Regiment, or Cashiered for His Country* (Midhurst, Sept. 19, 1931) and *The Jolly Roger, or The Admiral's Daughter* (Manchester, Feb. 13, 1933); 9 *Sharp*, musical revue (London, 1938); incidental music; pieces for amateur orch.; Sonatina for Viola and Piano (Vienna, June 17, 1932); Trio for 3 Pianos (1934); Trio for Flute, Oboe, and Piano (1935); songs; piano pieces.—**NS/LK/DM**

Leighton, Kenneth, English composer and teacher; b. Wakefield, Yorkshire, Oct. 2, 1929; d. Edinburgh, Aug. 24, 1988. He studied classics (1947–50) and composition with Rose (B.Mus., 1951) at Queen's Coll., Oxford, where he later earned his doctorate in music; also won the Mendelssohn Scholarship (1951), which enabled him to study with Petrassi in Rome. He was a lecturer at the Univ. of Edinburgh (1956–68); after serving as a lecturer at Worcester Coll., Oxford (1968–70), he returned to the Univ. of Edinburgh as Reid Prof. of Music (from 1970). He utilized 12-tone procedures while basically adhering to a diatonic style.

WORKS: DRAMATIC: O p e r a : *Columba* (1980; Glasgow, June 16, 1981). **ORCH.:** *Veris gratia*, suite for Oboe, Cello, and Strings (1950); 3 piano concertos: No. 1 (1951; BBC, Glasgow, March 7, 1958; rev. 1959), No. 2 (1960; BBC, Manchester, Jan. 18, 1962), and No. 3 (1969; Birmingham, March 11, 1970); Violin Concerto (1952; BBC, London, May 5, 1953); Concerto for Viola, Harp, Timpani, and Strings (1952; BBC, London, Sept. 5, 1954); *Burlesque* (1956; London, May 3, 1959); Cello Concerto (Cheltenham, July 20, 1956); *Passacaglia, Chorale, and Fugue* (1957; BBC, London, May 23, 1959); Concerto for Strings (1961; London, June 19, 1962); *Festive Overture* (1962); 3 syms.: No. 1 (1964; Trieste, May 31, 1966), No. 2, *Sinfonia mistica*, for Soprano, Chorus, and Orch. (1974; Edinburgh, March 4, 1977), and No. 3, *Laudes musicae*, for Tenor and Orch. (1983; Glasgow, March 15, 1985); 3 dance suites: No. 1 (Glasgow, July 10, 1968), No. 2 (1970; Farnham, May 12, 1971), and No. 3, *Scottish Dances* (1983; Edinburgh, Feb. 25, 1984); Organ Concerto (1970; Cambridge, Aug. 4, 1971); Concerto for Harpsichord, Recorder, and Strings (1982; Warrington, Feb. 14, 1983). **CHAMBER:** 2 violin sonatas (1951, 1956); 2 string quartets (1956, 1957); Piano Quintet (1959); *Partita* for Cello and Piano (1959); *7 Variations* for String Quartet (1964); Trio for Violin, Cello, and Piano (1965); *Metamorphoses* for Violin and Piano (1966); Sonata for Solo Cello (1967); *Quartet in 1 Movement: Contrasts and Variants* (London, Oct. 13, 1972); *Fantasy on an American Hymn Tune: The Shining River* for Clarinet, Cello, and Piano (1974; Cheltenham, July 8, 1975); *Fantasy on a Chorale* for Violin and Organ (1979; Washington, D.C., May 4, 1980); *Alleluia Pascha Nostrum* for Cello and Piano (1981; Manchester, Feb. 25, 1982); *Fantasy- Octet: Homage to Percy Grainger* for 4 Violins, 2 Violas, and 2 Cellos (Edinburgh, Aug. 29, 1982). **KEYBOARD: P i a n o :** *5 Studies* (1953); *Variations* (1955); *Fantasia Contrappuntistica: Homage to Bach* (1956); *9 Variations* (1959); *Conflicts: Fantasy on 2 Themes* (1967); *6 Studies: Study-Variations* (1969); *Household Pets* (1981); Sonata for Piano, 4-hands (1985). **O r g a n :** *Prelude, Scherzo, and Passacaglia* (1963); *Ex Resurrexit: Theme, Fantasy, and Fugue* (1966); *Martyrs: Dialogues on a Scottish Psalm Tune* for Organ Duet (1976); *Missa de Gloria* (1980). **VOCAL:** *The Birds* for Soprano, Tenor, Chorus, and Orch. (1954); *The Light Invisible: Sinfonia Sacra* for Tenor, Chorus, and Orch. (Hereford, Sept. 9, 1958); *Laudes Montium* for Baritone, Semi-chorus, Chorus, and Orch. (1975); *Columbia Mea: The Song of Songs* for Tenor, Chorus, and Orch. (1977; Glasgow, Feb. 5, 1979); *Animal Heaven* for Soprano, Recorder, Cello, and Harpsichord (Manchester, July 24, 1980); many sacred works, including masses, cantatas, anthems, and motets.—**NS/LK/DM**

Leighton, Sir William, English poet and composer; b. probably in Plash, Shropshire, c. 1565; d. London (buried), July 31, 1622. He publ. *The Teares or Lamentacions of a Sorrowfull Soule Composed with Musicall Ayres and Songs both for Voyces and Divers Instruments* (1613), containing 18 consort songs for 4 Voices (the first 8 are by Leighton), 12 unaccompanied songs for 4 Voices, and 25 unaccompanied songs for 5 Voices. See C. Hill, ed., Early English Church Music, XI (London, 1970).—**NS/LK/DM**

Leimer, Kurt, German-born Austrian pianist, teacher, and composer; b. Wiesbaden, Sept. 7, 1920; d. Vaduz, Liechtenstein, Nov. 20, 1974. He studied piano with his great-uncle Karl Leimer (b. Biebrich, June 22, 1858; d. Wiesbaden, July 19, 1944), W. Horbowski, and Edwin Fischer, and composition with Kurt von Wolfurt. In addition to pursuing a career as a pianist, he taught a master class in piano at the Salzburg Mozarteum (from 1953). In 1956 he became a naturalized Austrian citizen. He composed several works for piano, including 4 concertos (No. 2 for left hand) and some sonatas. His works are in an effective late Romantic style. —**NS/LK/DM**

Leinsdorf (real name, **Landauer**), **Erich,** eminent Austrian-born American conductor; b. Vienna, Feb. 4, 1912; d. Zürich, Sept. 11, 1993. He entered a local music school when he was 5, and began piano studies with the wife of Paul Pisk at age 8. He then continued his piano studies with Paul Emerich (1923–28), and subsequently studied theory and composition with Pisk. In 1930 he took a master class in conducting at the Mozarteum in Salzburg, and then studied for a short time in the music dept. of the Univ. of Vienna. From 1931 to 1933 he took courses at the Vienna Academy of Music, making his debut as a conductor at the Musikvereinsaal upon his graduation. In 1933 he served as asst. conductor of the Workers' Chorus in Vienna. In 1934 he went to Salzburg, where he had a successful audition with Bruno Walter and Toscanini at the Salzburg Festivals, and was appointed their assistant. In 1937 he was engaged as a conductor of the Metropolitan Opera in N.Y. He made his U.S. debut there conducting *Die Walküre* on Jan. 21, 1938, with notable success; he then conducted other Wagnerian operas, ultimately succeeding Bodanzky as head of the German repertoire there in 1939. In 1942 he became a naturalized American citizen. In 1943 he was appointed music director of the Cleveland Orch.; however, his induction into the U.S. Army in Dec. 1943 interrupted his tenure there. After his discharge in 1944, he once again conducted at the Metropolitan in 1944–45; also conducted several concerts with the Cleveland Orch. in 1945 and 1946, and made appearances in Europe. From 1947 to 1955 he was music director of the Rochester (N.Y.) Phil. In the fall of 1956 he was briefly music director of the N.Y.C. Opera; then returned to the Metropolitan as a conductor and musical consultant in 1957. He also appeared as a guest conductor in the U.S. and Europe. In 1962 he received the prestigious appointment of music director of the Boston Sym. Orch., a post he retained until 1969.

Leinsdorf subsequently conducted opera and sym. concerts in many of the major music centers of America and in Europe. From 1978 to 1980 he held the post of principal conductor of the (West) Berlin Radio Sym. Orch. He publ. a semi-autobiographical and rather candid book of sharp comments, *Cadenza: A Musical Career* (Boston, 1976), as well as *The Composer's Advocate: A Radical Orthodoxy for Musicians* (New Haven, 1981). These were followed by the posthumous vol. *Erich Leinsdorf on Music* (Portland, Ore., 1997).—**NS/LK/DM**

Leisentrit, Johannes, important Moravian-born German theologian, hymnologist, and composer; b. Olomouc, May 1527; d. Bautzen, Nov. 24, 1586. He received his theological training in Kraków. After his ordination in 1549, he was active in Meissen until becoming canon of Bautzen Cathedral in 1551. In 1559 he was made dean and in 1560 official-general for the diocese of Lusatia. When the bishopric of Meissen became Protestant in 1661, he was appointed administrator and commissioner-general of the see of Meissen for Upper and Lower Lusatia by the Prague papal nuncio. He publ. the most important Counter-Reformation hymnbook, *Geistliche Lieder und Psalmen* (Bautzen, 1567; 3rd ed., 1584), which contained some 250 hymns and 180 melodies, some of which were his own. —**LK/DM**

Leisner, David, American guitarist, teacher, and composer; b. Los Angeles, Dec. 22, 1953. He was educated at Wesleyan Univ. (B.A., 1976), received instruction in guitar from John Duarte, David Starobin, and Angelo Gilardino, in interpretation from John Kirkpatrick and Karen Tuttle, and in composition from Richard Winslow; won second prize at the Toronto International Guitar Competition (1975) and a silver medal at the Geneva International Guitar Competition (1981). He made his N.Y. debut in 1979, then toured extensively. He taught guitar at Amherst Coll. (1976–78) and at the New England Cons. of Music in Boston (from 1980). From 1993 he taught at the Manhattan School of Music in N.Y. He became well known for his programming of contemporary American music at his concerts. His own compositions include pieces for solo guitar and duos for guitar and viola, cello, or voice.—**NS/LK/DM**

Leitch, Peter, hard-bop guitarist; b. Ottawa, Ontario, Canada Aug. 19, 1944. He was born while his parents were in the air force. Following World War II, the family settled in Montreal, where Peter saw Coltrane, Wes Montgomery, and Monk perform. He played with R&B groups, organ bands, and back-up groups for all kinds of entertainers, and traveled from one small town to another. In 1973–74 he moved to Quebec City to do a television show. In 1975, he returned to Montreal, then moved to Toronto in about 1976, and then to N.Y. in late 1982, where he has remained. Most of his recordings feature his long-time rhythm section of pianist John Hicks, Ray Drummond, and Smitty Smith. He has recorded or performed with Oscar Peterson, Milt Jackson, Al Grey and Jimmy Forrest, and Woody Shaw and Pepper Adams. In the mid-1990s, he led the group

Guitars Play Mingus. He has also been an artist-in-residence and led clinics at several university jazz programs. He plays a Zoller guitar, which is a big hollow-bodied instrument made by the Hoffner and designed by Atilla Zoller. It is one of only two such models in existence (the other is owned by Jimmy Raney).

Disc.: *Jump Street* (1981); *Exhilaration* (1984); *Red Zone* (1984); *On a Misty Night* (1986); *Mean What You Say* (1990); *Portraits and Dedications* (1990); *Trio/Quartet '91* (1991); *From Another Perspective* (1992); *A Special Rapport* (1993); *Duality* (1995); *Colours and Dimensions* (1996); *Up Front* (1997).—LP

Leitham, John, American bassist, b. Scott Air Force Base, Ill., Aug. 10, 1953. He is a savvy, left-handed bassist whose swinging high- energy performances and remarkable technique have placed him in the jazz forefront through appearances and recordings with luminaries such as Mel Tormé, George Shearing, Herb Geller, Spike Robinson, Bill Perkins, and the late Bob Cooper, his good friend and mentor. Leitham grew up in Reading, Pa., attended high school in the Philadelphia area and, upon graduation, sang and played electric bass in local groups. As his musical studies became increasingly serious, he switched to acoustic bass under the tutelage of Al Stauffer, who heavily influenced him after Leitham saw Stauffer perform with French jazz pianist Bernard Peiffer. Within a few years, he was playing in big bands and jazz groups, and accompanying well-known traveling performers throughout Eastern Pa. While working in a South Philadelphia house band, he was recruited for the Woody Herman Young Thundering Herd in 1981, which resulted in extensive touring and exposure to the jazz festival scene.

In 1983, he left Philadelphia for Calif., where he quickly formed long-term musical associations with Ed Shaughnessy, Bob Cooper, Tommy Tedesco, Bill Watrous, Tom Ranier, and others. While freelancing in the Los Angeles area, he came to the attention of pianist George Shearing, who contacted him in 1987 to play a live-recorded gig at the Paul Masson Winery with singer Mel Tormé he subsequently recorded nine Tormé CDs, is seen on two of the singer's videos, and was scheduled to tour and record as part of Tormé's rhythm section right up to the time of the singer's August 1996 stroke. He currently works club dates on the West Coast, often with his own trio, and appears throughout the U.S. at festivals, where he has become a crowd favorite for his considerable instrumental skills and his friendly presence.

Disc.: *A Vintage Year* (1988); *Leitham Up* (1992); *The Southpaw* (1993); *Lefty Leaps In* (1996); *Live* (1998).—**JTB**

Leitner, Ferdinand, noted German conductor; b. Berlin, March 4, 1912. He studied composition with Schreker and conducting with Pruwer at the Berlin Hochschule für Musik; also studied piano with Schnabel and conducting with Muck. He then was active as a pianist until making his debut as a theater conductor in Berlin in 1943. He became conductor of the Württemberg State Theater in Stuttgart in 1947; was its General-musikdirektor (1950–69). He subsequently was chief conductor of the Zürich Opera (1969–84); also of the Residentie Orch. at The Hague (1976–80). From 1986 to 1990 he served as principal conductor of the RAI Orch. in Turin. He was known for his musicianly readings of works by Mozart, Wagner, Bruckner, and Richard Strauss; also conducted a number of modern scores, including premieres of works by Orff and Egk. —NS/LK/DM

Leiviskä, Helvi (Lemmikki), Finnish composer; b. Helsinki, May 25, 1902; d. there, Aug. 12, 1982. She studied under Erkki Melartin at the Helsinki Music Inst. (graduated, 1927) and with Arthur Willner in Vienna; then studied privately with Funtek and Madetoja. She was a librarian at the Helsinki Academy of Music (1933–66).

Works: Orch.: *Folk Dance Suite* (1929; rev. 1971); 2 suites (1934, 1938); Piano Concerto (1935); *Triple Fugue* (1935); 4 syms. (1947; 1954; *Sinfonia brevis*, 1962, rev. 1972; 1971). **Chamber:** Piano Quartet (1926); String Quartet (1926); Violin Sonata (1945). **Vocal:** *Pimeän peikko* (Goblin of Darkness) for Chorus and Orch. (1942); *Mennyt manner* (The Lost Continent) for Soloists, Chorus, and Orch. (1957).—NS/LK/DM

Le Jeune, Claude or **Claudin,** important French composer; b. Valenciennes, c. 1528; d. Paris, Sept. 25, 1600. He most likely studied in or near Valenciennes; was in Paris by 1564. After Baif and Courville founded the Académie de Poésie et de Musique in 1570, he became a major figure in promoting the new style of composition known as "musique mesurée a l'antique," in which the music is made to follow the metrical rhythm of the text in conformity with the rules of classical prosody. The type of poetry set to music in this manner was called "vers mesurez," and 33 examples of such settings by Le Jeune are to be found in the work entitled *Le Printemps*, publ. posthumously in Paris in 1603 by his sister Cécile Le Jeune. The metrical scanning is given at the head of each song. In the preface to this work Le Jeune is given credit for having been the first to achieve the "mating of ancient rhythm and modern harmony"; if not the first, he was at least, together with his contemporary and friend Jacques Mauduit, one of the earliest and most notable cultivators of this new and significant style. Having espoused the Huguenot cause during the wars of the Catholic League, he was compelled to flee Paris during the siege of 1588; his MSS were saved by the intervention of his Catholic colleague Mauduit. After a period of refuge in La Rochelle, he eventually returned to Paris. He served as maistre compositeur ordinaire de la musique de nostre chambre to Henri IV in 1596. Le Jeune cultivated every variety of vocal music known in his time, such as French chansons in "vers rimez," Italian madrigals, Latin motets, etc. Special mention must be made of his settings of the Psalms, of which 8 collections appeared between 1564 and 1612. So great was his renown even during his lifetime that a wood engraving dated 1598 bore the legend:"Le Phénix des Musiciens." His best- known work is his setting of the Genevan Psalter *a* 4 and 5, publ. by Cécile Le Jeune in 1613. This simple contrapuntal setting of the Psalms was widely used in the Reformed churches of France and the Netherlands, and it was also publ. in a German tr. Some of these harmonizations even found their way into early New England psalmbooks, such as *The Ainsworth Psalter* (see C. Smith, ed., *Early Psalmody in America*, N.Y., 1939). A more elaborate setting of some Psalms, *12 psaumes de David*, in motet style for 2 to 7 voices, was contained in the work entitled *Dodecacorde*, publ. at La Rochelle in 1598. In all, Le Jeune composed 347 Psalms, 146 airs (143 are mesurés), 66 secular chansons, 43 Italian madrigals, 38 sacred chansons, 11 motets, a Mass, and 3 instrumental fantasias.

WORKS (all publ. in Paris unless otherwise given): **VO-CAL: P s a l m s :** *Dix pseaumes de David* for 4 Voices, *en forme de motets avec un dialogue* for 7 Voices (1564; dialogue ed. in Monuments de la musique française au temps de la renaissance, VIII, 1928); *Dodécacorde* (12 psalms) for 2 to 7 Voices (La Rochelle, 1598; 3 in Les maîtres musiciens de la renaissance française, XI/1, 1900); *Les 150 pseaumes* for 4 to 5 Voices (1601; second ed., La Rochelle, 1608; 3rd ed., Paris, 1613; 4th ed., Amsterdam, 1629; 5th ed., Leiden, 1635; 6th ed., Paris, 1650; 7th ed., Schiedam, 1664); *Premier livre, contenant 50 pseaumes de David mis en musique* for 3 Voices (1602); *Pseaumes en vers mesurez* (26 psalms and a Te Deum) for 2 to 8 Voices (1606; ed. in Les maîtres musiciens de la renaissance française, XX-XXII, 1905–06); *Second livre contenant 50 pseaumes de David* for 3 Voices (1608); *Troisième livre des pseaumes de David* for 3 Voices (1610); 2 psalms for 5 and 6 Voices in *Second livre des meslanges* (1612; ed. in Monuments de la musique française au temps de la renaissance, VIII, 1928). Additional sacred vocal music includes: *Octonaires de la vanité etet inconstance du monde* (36 pieces) for 3 to 4 Voices (1606; ed. in Monuments de la musique française au temps de la renaissance, I, 1924); *Missa ad placitum* for 4 to 7 Voices (1607; ed. by M. Sanvoisin in Le pupitre, II, Paris, 1967); *Second livre des meslanges* (Magnificat, 3 motets, and sacred chansons) for 3 to 7 and 10 Voices (1612; also includes Psalms and secular works. **S e c u l a r :** *Livre de meslanges* (36 madrigals, 26 chansons, 5 motets, and a Latin echo piece) for 4 to 8 and 10 Voices (Antwerp, 1585; 13 chansons ed. in Monuments de la musique française au temps de la renaissance, XVI, 1903); (33) *Airs mis en musique* for 4 to 5 Voices (1594); *Le printemps* (33 airs mesurés and 6 chansons) for 2 to 8 Voices (1603; ed. in Monuments de la musique française au temps de la renaissance, XII-XIV, 1900–01); (68) *Airs* for 3 to 6 Voices (1608); *Second livre des* [59] *airs* for 3 to 6 Voices (1608); *Second livre des meslanges* (30 chansons, 7 madrigals, 3 airs, and 2 airs mesurés) for 4 to 8 Voices (1612; also includes various other works, both sacred and instrumental). **INSTRUMENTAL:** 3 fantasias in *Second livre des meslanges* (1612); also a Canzonetta, sacred chanson for Lute (1592), and 7 other pieces for Lute (1601).

BIBL.: E. Bouton, *Esquisse biographique et bibliographique sur C. L.J.* (Valenciennes, 1845); K. Levy, *The Chansons of C. L.J.* (diss., Princeton Univ., 1955); J. Hamersma, *Les dix Pseaumes of C. L.J.: A Study in 16th Century French Psalmody* (diss., Union Theological Seminary, 1961); J. MacMillan, *The Calvinistic Psalmody of C. L.J. with Special Reference to the Dodécacorde of 1598* (diss., N.Y.U., 1966); I. His, *Les Meslanges de C. L.J.* (Anvers: Plantin, 1585): *Transcription et étude critique* (diss., Univ. of Tours, 1990).—NS/LK/DM

Lekeu, Guillaume (Jean Joseph Nicolas),

promising Belgian composer; b. Heusy, near Verviers, Jan. 20, 1870; d. Angers, Jan. 21, 1894. After initial training in Poitiers, he studied in Paris with Vallin, Franck, and d'Indy. He won second prize in the Belgian Prix de Rome with his cantata *Andromède* (1891), which led Ysaÿe to commission his most important score, the Violin Sonata (1892). Among Lekeu's other notable works were the *Adagio* for String Quartet and String Orch. (1891) and the *Fantaisie sur deux airs populaires angevins* for Orch. (1892). His career was cut short by typhoid fever. In his works, he was mainly influenced by Franck.

WORKS: DRAMATIC: *Barberine*, operatic fragments (1889). **ORCH.:** *Chant de triomphal délivrance* (1889); *Hamlet* (1890); *Adagio* for String Quartet and String Orch. (1891); *Fantaisie sur deux airs populairs angevins* (1892). **CHAMBER:** *Andante et variations* for Violin and Piano (1885); String Quartet (1887); *Meditation* and *Minuet* for String Quartet (1887); Cello Sonata (1888; completed by d'Indy); *Adagio* for 2 Violins and Piano (1888); Piano Quartet (1888; completed by d'Indy); *Fantaisie contrapunctique sur un cramignon liègeois* for Oboe, Clarinet, Bassoon, Horn, and Strings (1890); *Epithalame* for String Quintet, 3 Trombones, and Organ (1891); *Introduction et adagio* for Brass and Tuba Obbligato (1891); Piano Trio (1891); Violin Sonata (1892). **P i a n o :** Sonata (1891); other pieces. **VOCAL:** *Noël* for 2 Sopranos, String Quartet, and Piano (1888); *Andromède*, cantata (1891); *Chant lyrique* for Chorus and Orch. (1891); Suite for Voice and Orch. (1892); songs.

BIBL.: A. Tissier, *G. L.* (Verviers, 1906); M. Lorrain, *G. L.: Sa correspondance sa vie et son oeuvre* (Liège, 1923); R. Stengel, *L.* (Brussels, 1944); P. Prist, *G. L.* (Brussels, 1946); L. Verdebout, *G. L.: Correspondance: Introduction, chronologie et catalogue des oeuvres* (Liège, 1993).—NS/LK/DM

Lellis, Tom (actually, Thomas Richard),

pop-jazz singer, pianist; b. Cleveland, Ohio, April 8, 1946. He began singing professionally at age 15 in Cleveland. At the age of 20, he went on the road, and a year later he became house singer at the Three Rivers Inn (Syracuse, N.Y.), working with a big band on bills with Ray Charles, Gregory Hines, Buddy Greco, and the Four Freshmen. He also led small house bands in clubs across the U.S., including the Frontier Hotel in Las Vegas. He began intensive piano instruction in 1970, studying and performing with Bill Dobbins and theorist Phil Rizzo. Three years later he was opening for Dizzy Gillespie, Bill Evans, and Jimmy Smith. In 1973 he moved to N.Y. He has performed in a variety of venues in and around the U.S. and Europe. He has set lyrics to works by McCoy Tyner, Keith Jarrett, Wayne Shorter, and has been engaged as a lyricist by Chick Corea, Dave Brubeck, and others. His first album became a fixture in London's jazz discos in the early 1980s. He was voted to *Down Beat*'s "International Critics Poll" in 1994 and performed in 1995 and 1998 at the International Association of Jazz Educators Convention. He performed and recorded his works with the Netherlands Metropole Orch. in 1999.

DISC.: *T.L.* (1979); *And in This Corner* (1979; w. Eddie Gomez, Jack DeJohnette, Jeremy Steig); *Double Entendre* (1991; w. Gomez, DeJohnette); *Taken to Heart* (1992).—LP

Lemacher, Heinrich, German composer, pedagogue, and writer on music; b. Solingen, June 26, 1891; d. Munich, March 15, 1966. He received training in

piano, conducting, and composition at the Cologne Cons. (1911–16), and in musicology at the Univ. of Bonn (Ph.D., 1916, with the diss. *Zur Geschichte der Musik am Hofe zu Nassau-Weilburg*). In 1924 he founded the Seminar des Reichsverbandes deutscher Tonkünstler und Musiklehrer, of which he served as director until 1933. He was a teacher of composition, theory, and music history (1925–28) and a prof. (1928–56) at the Cologne Hochschule für Musik. He concurrently taught at the Rheinische Musikschule and the Univ. of Cologne, and then was director of the Cäcilienverband from 1956. He was the author or collaborator of several books, among them *Handbuch der Hausmusik* (Regensburg and Graz, 1948), *Handbuch der Katholischen Kirchenmusik* (Essen, 1949), *Lehrbuch des Kontrapunktes* (Mainz, 1950; 4th ed., 1962), *Generalbassübungen* (Düsseldorf, 1954; second ed., 1965), *Harmonielehre* (Cologne, 1958; 8th ed., 1974), and *Formenlehre der Musik* (Cologne, 1962; second ed., 1968; Eng. tr., 1967, as *Musical Form*). His compositions followed in the paths of Bruckner and Reger. He wrote orch. works, chamber music, and secular vocal pieces but is best remembered for his Catholic church music, including numerous masses, motets, and cantatas.

BIBL.: W. Hammerschlag and A. Schneider, *Musikalisches Brauschtum: Festschrift H. L.* (Cologne, 1956).—NS/LK/DM

Lemaire (or Le Maire), Jean, French musician; b. Chaumont-en-Bassigny, Haute-Marne, c. 1581; d. c. 1650. He is said to have proposed the adoption of a 7th solmisation syllable *si* (so asserted by Rousseau in his *Dictionnaire de musique*; *za*, according to Mersenne's *Harmonie universalle*). However, the designation *si* seems to have been proposed even earlier, so the question of priority remains moot. Lemaire constructed a lute that he called the "Almerie" (anagram of Lemaire).
—NS/LK/DM

Lemaire, Louis, French composer; b. 1693 or 1694; d. Tours, c. 1750. He was a chorister at Meaux Cathedral, where he was a student of the organist Sebastien de Brossard. After settling in Paris, he established himself as the foremost composer of cantatilles, which were regularly performed at the Concert Français and the Concert Spirituel (1728–36). In all, he publ. 66 such works (1728–50; 5 not extant). Among his other works were the cantata collection *Les quatre saisons* (1724), motets (2 vols., c. 1728), airs, and instrumental pieces.
—LK/DM

Le Maistre, Mattheus, Netherlands composer; b. probably in Rocclenge-sur-Greet, c. 1505; d. Dresden, c. April 1577. He served as Kapellmeister at the Dresden Kantorei from 1554 to 1568. As a convert to the Lutheran faith, he composed in the manner of J. Walther and G. Rhau. His most significant works are his German sacred and secular songs.

WORKS: *Catechesis musicis inclusa* for 3 Voices (Nuremberg, 1559); *Geistliche und weltliche teutsche Geseng* for 4 to 5 Voices (Wittenberg, 1566); *Liber primus* [15] *sacrarum cantionum* (Dresden, 1570); *Officia de nativitate et ascensione Christi* for 5 Voices (Dresden, 1574); *Schöne und auserlesene deudsche und lateinische geistliche Gesenge* (Dresden, 1577); *Magnificat octo tonorum* (Dresden, 1577); Masses; motets.

BIBL.: O. Kade, *M. l.M.* (Mainz, 1862); D. Gresch, *M. L.M.: A Netherlander at the Dresden Court Chapel* (diss., Univ. of Mich., 1970).—NS/LK/DM

Lemare, Edwin (Henry), English-American organist and composer; b. Ventnor, Isle of Wight, Sept. 9, 1865; d. Los Angeles, Sept. 24, 1934. He received his early training from his father, an organist; then studied at the Royal Academy of Music in London. At the age of 17, he played at the Inventions Exhibition in London; in 1892 he began a series of weekly organ recitals at Holy Trinity Church in London, and also became a prof. at the Royal Academy of Music; from 1897 to 1902 he was organist at St. Margaret's, Westminster. In 1900–1901 he made a concert tour through the U.S. and Canada; from 1902 to 1905 he was organist at the Carnegie Inst. in Pittsburgh; continued to tour extensively on both sides of the Atlantic, and also in the Far East; then held the post of municipal organist in San Francisco (1917–21), Portland, Maine (1921–23), and Chattanooga, Tenn. (1924–29). He wrote about 200 organ works, an Easter cantata, anthems, settings of sacred texts, and songs; his *Andantino* acquired wide popularity when it was used for the American ballad *Moonlight and Roses*; he also prepared innumerable transcriptions for the organ. His reminiscences appeared as *Organs I Have Met: The Autobiography of Edwin H. Lemare, 1866–1934, Together With Reminiscences by His Wife and Friends* (Los Angeles, 1956).—NS/LK/DM

Lemeshev, Sergei (Yakovlevich), prominent Russian tenor; b. Knyazevo, near Tver, July 10, 1902; d. Moscow, June 26, 1977. In his youth, he worked at a cobbler's shop in Petrograd; then went to Moscow, where he studied at the Cons. with Raysky, graduating in 1925. He made his operatic debut at Sverdlovsk in 1926; then was a member of the Kharbin Opera in Manchuria (1927–29) and at the Tiflis Opera (1929–31). In 1931 he joined the Bolshoi Theater in Moscow, and gradually created an enthusiastic following; he remained on its roster until 1961 and was particularly admired for his performance of the role of Lensky in *Eugene Onegin*; in 1972, on his 70th birthday, he sang it again at the Bolshoi Theater. Other roles in which he shone, apart from the Russian repertoire, included Faust, Romeo, Werther, Alfredo, and the Duke of Mantua. He also made numerous appearances in solo recitals; he was the first to present an entire cycle of Tchaikovsky's songs in 5 concerts. His autobiography was publ. in Moscow in 1968.

BIBL.: M. Lvov, *S. L.* (Moscow, 1947); E. Grosheva, *S. L.* (Moscow, 1960).—NS/LK/DM

Lemière de Corvey, Jean Frédéric Auguste, French composer; b. Rennes, 1770; d. Paris, April 19, 1832. After studies in Rennes, he received training in harmony from Berton in Paris. While pursuing a military career, he composed many works for the stage, the most successful being his opera *Andros et*

Almona, ou Le français à Bassora (Paris, Feb. 4?, 1794). He also wrote many opéras-comiques, military band pieces, chamber music, piano pieces, and romances.—LK/DM

Lemmens, Jacques Nicolas (Jaak Nikolaas), eminent Belgian organist, pedagogue, and composer; b. Zoerle-Parwijs, Antwerp, Jan. 3, 1823; d. Zemst, near Mechelen, Jan. 30, 1881. He was first trained in music by his father, an organist, then attended the Brussels Cons., where he studied piano, organ (with Christian Girschner), and composition (with Fétis). He subsequently studied with Adolf Hesse in Breslau (1846–47). He became prof. of organ at the Brussels Cons. in 1849. In 1857 he married **Helen Lemmens-Sherrington.** His distinguished students included Guilmant and Widor. He publ. *École d'orgue basée sur le plainchant romain* (Brussels, 1862). His *Du chant grégorien, sa mélodie, son rhythme, son harmonisation* was publ. posth. (Ghent, 1884). A collection of his masses, motets, organ music, and other works appeared as *OEuvres inédites* (4 vols., Leipzig, 1883–87).—NS/LK/DM

Lemmens-Sherrington (originally, **Sherrington**), **Helen,** noted English soprano; b. Preston, Oct. 4, 1834; d. Brussels, May 9, 1906. When she was 4 her family took her to Rotterdam, where she had vocal training with Verhulst; then entered the Brussels Cons. (1852). She made her London debut as a concert singer (April 7, 1856); later sang with the English Opera (1860–65) and at Covent Garden (1866), where she appeared as Donna Elvira, Adalgisa, Isabella in *Robert le diable*, and Elisabeth de Valois; however, it was as a concert and oratorio singer that she gained her greatest distinction. She married **Jacques Nicolas Lemmens** (actually, **Jaak Nikolaas Lemmens**) in 1857. After his death, she made her home in Brussels. She continued to make appearances as a singer until 1894, but devoted herself mainly to teaching at the Brussels Cons. She also taught at the Royal Manchester Coll. of Music (1893–97).—NS/LK/DM

Lemnitz, Tiana (Luise), remarkable German soprano; b. Metz, Oct. 26, 1897; d. Berlin, Feb. 5, 1994. She studied with Hoch in Metz and Kohmann in Frankfurt am Main. She made her operatic debut in Lortzing's *Undine* in Heilbronn (1920), then sang in Aachen (1922–28). Lemnitz subsequently pursued a distinguished career as a member of the Hannover Opera (1928–33), the Dresden State Opera (1933–34), and the Berlin State Opera (1934–57). She also made guest appearances in Vienna, Munich, London's Covent Garden (1936, 1938), and Buenos Aires's Teatro Colón (1936, 1950). Her repertoire included many leading roles in German, Italian, French, and Russian operas. Among her most celebrated portrayals were Pamina, Sieglinde, Desdemona, Micaëla, Octavian, and the Marschallin.—NS/LK/DM

Lemoyne, Jean-Baptiste, French conductor and composer; b. Eymet, Périgord, April 3, 1751; d. Paris, Dec. 30, 1796. He studied with J. G. Graun, Kirnberger, and J. A. P. Schulz at Berlin, and also held a minor post in the service of the Prussian Crown Prince. He then went to Warsaw, where he brought out his opera *Le Bouquet de Colette* (1775). Returning to Paris, he brought out an opera, *Electre* (July 2, 1782), pretending to be a pupil of Gluck, an imposture that Gluck did not see fit to expose until the failure of Lemoyne's piece. In his next operas, Lemoyne abandoned Gluck's ideas, copied the style of Piccinni and Sacchini, and produced several successful works, including *Phèdre* (Fontainebleau, Oct. 26, 1786), *Les Prétendus* (Paris, June 2, 1789), and *Nephté* (Paris, Dec. 15, 1789). His son, Gabriel Lemoyne (b. Berlin, Oct, 14, 1772; d. Paris, July 2, 1815), was a pianist and composer who studied piano with C.-F. Clement and J.F. Edelmann. He wrote 3 opéras comiques, 2 piano concertos, chamber music, vocal romances, and piano pieces.—NS/LK/DM

Lenaerts, René Bernard (Maria), distinguished Belgian musicologist; b. Bornem, Oct. 26, 1902; d. Leuven, Feb. 27, 1992. He studied at the Mechelen theological seminary and at the Lemmens Inst., being ordained a priest (1927), then continued his education at the Univ. of Louvain (Ph.D., 1929, with the diss. *Het Nederlands polifonies lied in de zestiende eeuw*; publ. in Mechelen and Amsterdam, 1933); after additional studies with Pirro in Paris (1931–32), he taught in secondary schools in Geel and Antwerp; then was a junior lecturer (1944–46), lecturer (1946–49), and full prof. (1949–73) in musicology at the Catholic Univ. of Louvain; was also a reader in Renaissance music history at the Univ. of Utrecht (1958–71). In 1955 he was made a canon. In 1959 he became ed. of Monumenta Musicae Belgicae. Lenaerts was made a corresponding member of the American Musicological Soc. in 1981. He publ. *Oude Nederlandse muziek* (Brussels, 1937), *Johann Sebastian Bach* (Diest, 1943), *Belangrijke verzamelingen Nederlandse muziek uit de zestiende eeuw in Spanje* (Brussels, 1957), and *De Nederlandse muziek uit de vijftiende eeuw* (Louvain, 1959).

BIBL.: J. Robijns, ed., *Renaissance-Muziek 1400–1600: Donum natalicium R.B. L.* (Louvain, 1969).—NS/LK/DM

Lendvai, Ernő, Hungarian musicologist; b. Kaposvár, Feb. 6, 1925; d. Budapest, Jan. 31, 1993. He studied at the Budapest Academy of Music (1945–49). He was made director of the Szombathely Music School (1949) and the Győr Cons. (1954); was also prof. at the Szeged Cons. (from 1957) and a teacher at the Budapest Academy of Music (1954–56; from 1973). He distinguished himself as a writer on the life and works of Bartók.

WRITINGS: *Bartók stilusa* (Bartók's Style; Budapest, 1955); *Bartók's Dramaturgy: Stage Works and Cantata Profana* (Budapest, 1964); *Toscanini és Beethoven* (Budapest, 1967; Eng. tr., 1966, in *Studia musicologica Academiae scientiarum hungaricae*, VIII); *Bartók költői vilaga* (The Poetic World of Bartók; Budapest, 1971); *Béla Bartók: An Analysis of His Music* (London, 1971); *Bartók és Kodály harmóniavilága* (The Harmonic World of Bartók and Kodály; Budapest, 1975); *The Workshop of Bartók and Kodály* (Budapest, 1983); *Verdi és a 20. század A Falstaff hangzásdramaturgiája* (Budapest, 1984).—NS/LK/DM

Lendvai, (Peter) Erwin, Hungarian composer; b. Budapest, June 4, 1882; d. Epsom, Surrey, March 31,

1949. He was a student of Koessler in Budapest and of Puccini in Milan. After teaching at the Jaques Dalcroze school in Hellerau (1913–14), the Hoch Cons. in Frankfurt am Main (1914–19), the Klindworth-Scharwenka Cons. in Berlin (1919–22), and the Volksmusikschule in Hamburg (1923–25), he was active as a choral conductor. He eventually settled in England. He publ. the method *Chorschule*. Among his works were the opera *Elga* (Mannheim, Dec. 6, 1916; rev. 1918); Sym. (1909) and other orch. scores; chamber music; vocal pieces.

BIBL.: H. Leichtentritt, *E. L.* (Berlin, 1912).—**NS/LK/DM**

Lendvay, Kamilló, Hungarian composer, conductor, and teacher; b. Budapest, Dec. 28, 1928. He was a student in composition of Viski at the Budapest Academy of Music (1949–57), and also received lessons in conducting from Somogyi (1953–55). After conducting at the Szeged Opera (1956–57), he returned to Budapest and was music director of the State Puppet Theater (1960–66) and the Hungarian Army Art Ensemble (1966–68); he then was a conductor (1970–72) and subsequently music director (1972–74) of the Municipal Operetta Theater. From 1962 he was active with the Hungarian Radio. In 1973 he joined the faculty of the Academy of Music, where he was head of its theory dept. from 1978. He also served as president of Artisjus, the Hungarian Copyright Office. In 1962, 1964, and 1978 he was awarded the Erkel Prize. He was made a Merited Artist by the Hungarian government in 1981. In 1989 he received the Bartók-Pásztory Award. In his compositions, serial procedures serve as the foundation of his avant-garde explorations.

WORKS: DRAMATIC: *A bűvös szék* (The Magic Chair), comic opera (1972); *A tisztességtudó utcalány* (The Respectful Prostitute), opera (1976–78); incidental music for plays; film scores. **ORCH.:** *Tragic Overture* (1958); *Mauthausen*, symphonic poem (1958); Concertino for Piano, Winds, Percussion, and Harp (1959; also for Chamber Orch., 1982); *The Indomitable Tin Soldier*, suite (1961); 2 violin concertos (1961–62; 1986); *Quattro invocazioni* (1966); *Expressions* for Strings (1974); *Pezzo concertato* for Cello and Orch. (1975); *The Harmony of Silence* (1980); *Concertino semplice* for Cimbalon and Strings (1986); *Chaconne* (1987–88); *Symphony-Retrograde* (1990); Concerto for Trumpet and Wind Orch. (1990); Double Concerto for Violin, Cimbalom, and Strings (1991); *Rondo* for 2 Trumpets and Orch. (1994); *A Last Message from Maestro Tchaikovsky* for Wind Orch. (1994); Concerto for Soprano Saxophone, 12 Women's Voices, and Orch. (1996); *Rhapsody* (1997). **Band:** *Story-telling Dance* (1952); 2 suites (1956, 1996); *3 Carnival Masks* (1960); *Scherzo* (1972; arranged by L. Hollós); *Festspiel Overture* (1984). **CHAMBER:** *Trio Serenade* for String Trio (1954); *Rhapsody* for Violin and Piano (1955); String Quartet (1962); *Quattro duetti* for Flute and Piano (1965); *Concerto da camera* for Chamber Ensemble (1969); *Disposizioni* for Cimbalom (1975); *Fifthmusic* for Cello (1978–79); *Metamorphosis of a Cimbalom Piece* for Chamber Ensemble (1979); *5 Arrogant Ideas* for 3 Trumpets, 2 Trombones, and Tuba (1979); *5 Movements in Quotation Marks* for Horn, Trombone, and Tuba (1980); *Senza sordina* for Trumpet and Piano (1983; also for Trumpet and Band, 1985); *As You Like It* for 2 Pianos (1984); 24 Duos for 2 Violins (1985); *8 More Arrogant Ideas* for 2 Trumpets, Horn, Trombone, and Tuba (1986); *Variazioni con tema* for Trumpet and Organ (1986); *Respectfully yours, Mr. Goodman* for Clarinet (1988); *The Cricket, the Ant, and the*

Others for 7 Instruments (1993). **VOCAL:** *Orogenesis* for Chorus and Orch. (1969–70); *A Ride at Night* for Contralto and 7 Players (1970); *Pro libertate* for Tenor, Baritone, Men's Chorus, and Orch. (1975); *Scenes* for Soprano, Bass-baritone, and Orch. (1978–81); *Via crucis* for Chorus and 10 Instruments (1988–89); *Stabat Mater* for Soloists, Chorus, Organ, and Chamber Orch. (1991).—**NS/LK/DM**

Lenepveu, Charles (Ferdinand), French composer and pedagogue; b. Rouen, Oct. 4, 1840; d. Paris, Aug. 16, 1910. While a law student, he took music lessons from Servais, winning first prize at Caen in 1861 for a cantata. He entered Ambroise Thomas's class at the Paris Cons. in 1863, and in 1865 took the Grand Prix de Rome with the cantata *Renaud dans les jardins d'Armide* (Paris, Jan. 3, 1866). His comic opera *Le Florentin* also won a prize, offered by the Ministry of Fine Arts (1867), and was performed at the Opéra-Comique (Feb. 26, 1874). The grand opera *Velléda* was produced at Covent Garden in London (July 4, 1882), with Adelina Patti in the title role. In 1891 Lenepveu succeeded Guiraud as prof. of harmony at the Cons., and in 1893 again succeeded him as prof. of composition, taking an advanced class in 1894. In 1896 he was elected to Ambroise Thomas's chair in the Académie des Beaux-Arts. He was a Chevalier of the Legion of Honor and an Officer of Public Instruction.

BIBL.: R. de Saint-Arroman, *C. L.* (Paris, 1898). —**NS/LK/DM**

Léner, Jenö, Hungarian violinist; b. Szabadka, April 7, 1894; d. N.Y., Nov. 4, 1948. He was a student at the Royal Academy of Music in Budapest. After playing in theater orchs., he founded the Léner Quartet, which made its debut in Budapest in 1919. From 1922 to 1939 it appeared regularly in London. It made its N.Y. debut in 1929, and thereffer performed in the U.S. until disbanding in 1942. In was reorganized in 1945 but was dissolved upon Léner's death. The Léner Quartet was one of the most celebrated quartets of its time, being especially renowned for its interpretations of Beethoven's quartets.

BIBL.: A. Molnár, *A L.-vonósnégyes* (The L. Quartet; Budapest, 1968).—**NS/LK/DM**

Leng, Afonso, Chilean composer; b. Santiago, Feb. 11, 1884; d. there, Nov. 7, 1974. He was a student of Enrique Soro at the Santiago Cons. (1905–06), and also studied dentistry at the Univ. of Chile. While pursuing a career as an odontologist, he also was active as a composer. In 1957 he was awarded the National Arts Prize. His works were in a Romantic vein.

WORKS: ORCH.: *5 dolores* (1920); *La muerte de Alsino*, symphonic poem (1920; Santiago, May 30, 1931); *Canto de Invierno* (1932); *Fantasia* for Piano and Orch. (Santiago, Aug. 28, 1936). **CHAMBER:** *Andante* for Piano and String Quartet (1922). **Piano:** *Fantasia quasi Sonata* (1909); 10 Preludes (1919–32); 2 sonatas (1927, 1950); *2 Otoñales* (1932). **VOCAL:** *Psalm 77* for Soloists, Chorus, and Orch. (1941); many songs. —**NS/LK/DM**

Lennon, John, the first Beatle to perform and record outside the group while it was still nominally intact; b. Woolton, Liverpool, England, Oct. 9, 1940; d. N.Y., Dec. 8, 1980. John Lennon was certainly the most charismatic, controversial, and unorthodox of the group's members. After leaving the Beatles Lennon often worked with his new wife, Yoko Ono (b. Tokyo, Japan, Feb. 18, 1933), a performance artist in her own right. The duo often recorded together, or released parallel albums that would comment on each other's work. Lennon retired from active music-making in 1975 to become a househusband to his son, Sean (b. N.Y.C., Oct. 9, 1975); he and Ono were just returning to active recording when he was assassinated in December 1980. Son Julian Lennon (b. Liverpool, England, April 8, 1963), from his first marriage, enjoyed brief success as a recording artist in 1985; son Sean Ono Lennon has recently emerged as Yoko Ono's newest collaborator.

During 1966, while the Beatles were still intact, John Lennon met Japanese avant-garde artist Yoko Ono, when she had a solo art show in London. In 1968 the couple recorded *Two Virgins*, an album of tape collages that they assembled at Lennon's home; the cover featured a photo of the nude couple, which sparked consternation among record retailers. In 1969 they recorded *Life with the Lions* (for the short-lived Zapple label) and, following their March 20 wedding, *Wedding Album*. After the wedding, John and Yoko continued their controversial ways with their bed-in for peace in Amsterdam. "Give Peace a Chance," recorded with the loosely aggregated Plastic Ono Band in a Montreal hotel suite, became a major hit in July and was soon adopted by the antiwar movement as one of its anthems. That September Lennon, Ono, and the Plastic Ono Band—Eric Clapton (gtr.), Klaus Voorman (bs.), and Alan White (drm.)—played a rock festival in Toronto, producing a live album and a moderate hit with the ominous "Cold Turkey."

In February 1970 "Instant Karma (We All Shine On)," recorded with George Harrison and Billy Preston under producer Phil Spector, became a smash hit for John Lennon. He and Yoko later underwent primal-scream therapy under radical psychologist Dr. Arthur Janov that produced, at least in part, the intense, raw emotionalism of *John Lennon/Plastic Ono Band*. The album included such highly personal songs as "Mother" and "Isolation," as well as the litany "God" and the caustic sociopolitical song "Working Class Hero," banned by some radio stations for its use of obscenity. In the meantime, Yoko Ono recorded the album *Plastic Ono Band*. She recorded three more albums for Apple in the early 1970s, plus 1974's unreleased *A Story*, which eventually surfaced on 1992's *Onobox*.

Moving to N.Y., John and Yoko achieved a major hit with "Power to the People" in spring 1971. Lennon next recorded the relatively gentle and accessible *Imagine* album, essentially his first solo album. An instant best-seller, the album yielded a smash hit with the idealistic title song and contained the poignant "Jealous Guy," the satirical "Crippled Inside," and the vitriolic attack on Paul McCartney, "How Do You Sleep." At Christmas-time John and Yoko scored a smash hit with "Happy Xmas (War Is Over)," recorded with the Plastic Ono Band and the Harlem Community Choir.

Subsequently embroiled in legal proceedings by the U.S. Immigration and Naturalization Service, which sought to deport him (ultimately resolved in Lennon's favor in 1976), John Lennon, Yoko Ono, and the Plastic Ono Band recorded a double-record set, *Sometime in New York City*, with the N.Y.—based band Elephant's Memory. The politically charged album—featuring songs concerning the Attica Prison riots and Northern Ireland—and the profeminist anthem "Woman Is the Nigger of the World" (a minor hit) were critically attacked and sold modestly at best. Between August 1973 and January 1975 Lennon and Ono were estranged, and Lennon was better known for his drunken escapades in Los Angeles than for his recorded works. His *Mind Games* album was not well-received critically but nonetheless became a best-seller, yielding a major hit with the title song. The follow-up, *Walls and Bridges*, fared better, producing the top hit "Whatever Gets You Through the Night" and the near-smash "#9 Dream." Lennon next recorded an album of remakes of early rock hits, *Rock 'n' Roll*, such as "Stand By Me" and "Peggy Sue," again working with producer Phil Spector. It was followed by the anthology set *Shaved Fish*. John Lennon and Yoko Ono subsequently reunited and retired from the music business, as Lennon served as househusband to his wife and newborn son Sean. Ono managed their business affairs.

During 1980 John Lennon began writing again, returning to the studio in August with Yoko Ono and a group of hand-picked session players to record *Double Fantasy*. Comprised of seven Lennon and seven Ono songs, the album and its first single, Lennon's "(Just Like) Starting Over," were instant top hits. The album also included the smash hit "Woman," Lennon's revealing "Watching the Wheels" (a near-smash), and the touching "Beautiful Boy." The couple continued to work in the studio, but on Dec. 8, 1980, Lennon was shot to death outside the luxury apartment building the Dakota in Manhattan after returning from recording one night. Covered by the media in a manner usually reserved for world statesmen, Lennon's death forever quelled rumors of a Beatles reunion and ended the career of one of this century's most respected and profound artists.

A number of recordings by John Lennon were issued after his death. *Milk and Honey*, recorded in 1980, contained six songs by Yoko Ono and six by Lennon, including the smash hit "Nobody Told Me," and "I'm Stepping Out," "I Don't Wanna Face It," and "Grow Old with Me." *Live in New York City* was comprised of Lennon's final performance, Aug. 30, 1972, at Madison Square Garden (also issued on video), and *Menlove Avenue* was assembled from outtakes from the *Rock 'n' Roll* and *Walls and Bridges* sessions. *Imagine* was taken from the 1988 film documentary of the same name.

Lennon's life continued to be honored and celebrated through the 1980s and 1990s. In 1984 a favorite section of Central Park was renamed Strawberry Fields in his honor. On Oct. 9, 1990, Lennon's life was celebrated in a brief ceremony at the United Nations in N.Y., after which his song "Imagine" was broadcast on more than a thousand radio stations in more than 130 countries to an estimated audience of one billion people.

In 1991 Yoko Ono, Sean Ono Lennon, and Lenny Kravitz assembled an all-star cast to record Lennon's "Give Peace a Chance," with new lyrics by Sean and Kravitz. The performers included Peter Gabriel, Bonnie Raitt, Steve Van Zandt, Iggy Pop, Randy Newman, Tom Petty, and Frank Zappa's three children. The recording, issued on Virgin as performed by the Peace Choir, became a minor hit. In 1994 Lennon was inducted individually into the Rock and Roll Hall of Fame (the Beatles were inducted as a group six years earlier).

Yoko Ono recorded several albums after John Lennon's death, including 1981's *Season of Glass* and 1982's *It's Alright (I See Rainbows)*. In 1984 Polydor Records issued *Every Man Has a Woman*, on which artists such as Elvis Costello, Rosanne Cash, and Harry Nilsson performed songs written by Ono. Following 1985's *Starpeace*, Yoko Ono toured in 1986. Rykodisc compiled selections of her recordings, from 1969's *Life with the Lions* to *Starpeace*, on the six-CD box set *Onobox* in 1992, followed by *Walking on Thin Ice*, which contained 19 songs from *Onobox*. In 1994 Capitol Records released the original cast recording of Yoko Ono's Off-Broadway play *New York Rock*, loosely based on her life with Lennon. A year later a new album, recorded with son Sean's band, was well-received critically if not commercially.

John Lennon's son by Cynthia Powell, Julian Lennon, launched his own musical career in 1984 with *Valotte*. Julian was largely raised by his mother after his parents' divorce in 1968. His father had given him a guitar at age 11, and he later formed his first rock group with guitarist Justin Clayton as a teenager. In 1983 he secluded himself in Valotte, France, to write and compose. Signed to Charisma Records (Atlantic in the United States) on the strength of demonstration tapes, Julian Lennon recorded *Valotte* under veteran producer Phil Ramone. The album yielded the near-smash "Valotte," the smash hit "Too Late for Goodbyes," the major hit "Say You're Wrong," and the minor hit "Jesse." He toured America in 1985 and launched a world tour in 1986 in support of *The Secret Value of Daydreaming*, which included the moderate hit "Stick Around." Subsequent recordings by Julian Lennon have fared progressively less well.

DISC.: JOHN LENNON AND YOKO ONO: *Unfinished Music #1: Two Virgins* (1968); *Unfinished Music #2: Life with the Lions* (1969); *Wedding Album* (1969); *Double Fantasy* (1980); *Milk and Honey* (1984); *The J. L. Collection (1969–1980)* (1982). **JOHN LENNON/PLASTIC ONO BAND:** *Live Peace in Toronto, 1969* (1969); *Plastic Ono Band* (1970); *Sometime in New York* (1972). **JOHN LENNON:** *Imagine* (1971); *Mind Games* (1973); *Walls and Bridges* (1974); *Rock 'n' Roll* (1975); *Menlove Avenue* (rec. 1974–1975; rel. 1986); *Shaved Fish* (1975); *Live in New York City* (1986); *Imagine—The Motion Picture* (soundtrack; 1988); *Lennon* (1990). **TRIBUTE ALBUM:** *A Tribute to J. L.* (1995). **YOKO ONO/PLASTIC ONO BAND:** *Plastic Ono Band* (1970); *Fly* (1971). **YOKO ONO:** *Approximately Infinite Universe* (1973); *Feeling the Space* (1973); *Season of Glass* (1981); *It's Alright (I See Rainbows)* (1982); *Starpeace* (1985); *Onobox* (1992); *Walking on Thin Ice (excerpts from Onobox)* (1992); *New York Rock*

(original score) (1994); *Rising* (1995). **YOKO ONO TRIBUTE ALBUM:** *Every Man Has a Woman* (1984). **JULIAN LENNON:** *Valotte* (1984); *The Secret Value of Daydreaming* (1986); *Mr. Jordan* (1989); *Help Yourself* (1991).

BIBL.: Paul Young, *The Lennon Factor* (N.Y., 1972); Anthony Fawcett, *J. L.: One Day at a Time; A Personal Biography of the Seventies* (N.Y., 1976); George Tremlett, *The J. L. Story* (London 1976); Cynthia Lennon, *A Twist of Lennon* (London, 1978); Vic Garbarini and Brian Cullman, with Barbara Graustark, *Strawberry Fields Forever: J. L. Remembered* (N.Y., 1980); Ray Connolly, *J. L., 1940–1980: A Biography* (London, 1981); Jonathan Cott and Christine Doudna, *The Ballad of John and Yoko* (Garden City, N.Y., 1982); John Green, *Dakota Days: The Untold Story of John Lennon's Final Years* (N.Y., 1983); Ray Coleman, *Lennon* (N.Y., 1985); Peter McCabe and Robert D. Schonfeld, *J. L.: For the Record* (N.Y., 1985); Jon Wiener, *Come Together: J. L. in His Own Time* (London, 1985); Albert Goldman, *The Lives of J. L.* (N.Y., 1988); Andrew Solt and Sam Egan, *Imagine: J. L.* (N.Y., 1988); Elizabeth Thomson and David Gutman (eds.), *The Lennon Companion: 25 Years of Comment* (N.Y., 1988).—**BH**

Lenormand, René, French composer; b. Elbeuf, Aug. 5, 1846; d. Paris, Dec. 3, 1932. He received music training from his mother, who was an excellent pianist, and in 1868 went to Paris, where he studied with Damcke. Lenormand's main interest was in the creation of an international type of the German lied, and for that purpose he organized in Paris a society that he called Le Lied en Tous Pays. Besides his songs, he wrote an opera, *Le Cachet rouge* (Le Havre, 1925), Piano Concerto, *Le Lahn de Mabed* (on an old Arabian theme) for Violin and Orch., *Le Voyage imaginaire*, symphonic tableaux after Loti, *2 esquisses sur des thèmes malais* for Orch., and piano pieces (*Une Journée à la campagne, Le Nuage vivant, Valses sérieuses, Pièces exotiques*, etc.; for 4-hands: *Divertissement américain, La Nouba Medjenneba*, etc.). He also publ. a valuable manual on harmony, *Étude sur l'harmonie moderne* (Paris, 1912; Eng. tr. as *A Study of Modern Harmony*, London, 1915).

BIBL.: H. Woollett, *Un Mélodiste français: R. L.* (Paris, 1930). —**NS/LK/DM**

Lentz, Daniel (Kirkland), American composer; b. Latrobe, Pa., March 10, 1941. He studied music and philosophy at St. Vincent Coll. (B.A., 1962), music history and composition at Ohio State Univ. (M.A., 1965), and composition with Berger, Lucier, and Shapero at Brandeis Univ. (1965–67) and with Sessions and Rochberg at the Berkshire Music Center at Tanglewood (summer, 1966). He went to Stockholm on a Fulbright grant to study electronic music and musicology (1967–68), then was a visiting lecturer at the Univ. of Calif. at Santa Barbara (1968–70) and at Antioch Coll. in Yellow Springs, Ohio (1973). He formed the performing groups California Time Machine (1969–73) and San Andreas Fault (1974, 1976); later was active with the Los Angeles-based ensemble LENTZ (from 1982), featuring the agile American vocalist Jessica (actually Lynn Mary) Karraker (b. St. Louis, Mo., Sept. 4, 1953), other vocalists, multiple keyboardists, and occasional percussion. He held grants from various organizations, including the NEA (1973, 1975, 1977, 1979, 1993, 1994), the Deutscher Akademischer Austauschdienst in Berlin (1979),

Meet the Composer 1992, 1997), and N.Y.'s Peter Reed Memorial Fund Prize (1998). Lentz is a proponent of the avant-garde; one of his most interesting early works was *Love and Conception* (1968–69), in which a male pianist and his female page-turner are ultimately directed to crawl under the lid of a grand piano and engage in sexual intercourse. Their performance, which is at first accompanied by 2 tandem AM radio broadcasts of fictional reviews of the piece, is finally replaced by a live, synchronous FM broadcast of the piece itself, which frees them to waltz about the stage, fall into each other's arms, and, overcome with passion, fall into the piano. It was performed at the Univ. of Calif. at Santa Barbara on Feb. 26, 1969; as a result of this and later performances, Lentz was dismissed from his lectureship position there. He then devoted himself to composing, with increasing reliance on computer and synthesizer technologies. In 1991 he became a founding faculty member of a newly formed interdisciplinary arts and performance degree program at Ariz. State Univ. West in Phoenix; in 1992 he was a visiting prof. at the Univ. of Calif., Los Angeles. Since his relocation to the Sonoran desert in 1991, Lentz has collaborated on numerous pieces with Harold Budd, many of which have resulted in recordings, e.g. *Music for Pianos* (1992) and *Walk Into My Voice* (1995). Many of his works, such as the orchestral *An American in L.A.* (1989), are pure sensuality, with less attention given to formal procedures than to rhythmic vibrancy and sonorous effect. His text settings can challenge the ear; frequently phonemes are introduced in the beginning of a piece, which, through a gradual interlocking of parts, form audible words (and occasional truncated sentences) only at the very finish. While retaining its freshness and, at times, almost exquisite beauty, Lentz's music throughout the 1980s was heavily equipment-reliant, demanding much not only from the vocalists and instrumentalists in his ensemble, but from Lentz himself, who has had to function as composer, producer, editor, sound mixer, and recording engineer during live performances. While some of his work dating from 1989 has tended toward acoustic media (his *b.e.comings* [a.k.a. *Orgas-Mass*, 1991] was his last piece utilizing multi-tracking), by the mid-1990s he began developing sophisticated techniques involving virtual ensembles. *The Insect* for Performers and Virtual Ensemble (2000) is a 30-year retrospective compilation of performance practices mingled with new techniques.

WORKS: DRAMATIC: Theater and Mixed Media: *A Piano: Piece* (1965); *Ecumenical Council* (1965); *Gospel Meeting* (1965); *Paul and Judy Meet the Time Tunnel* (1966); *Paul and Judy Meet Startrek* (1966); *Hi-yo Paint* (1968); *Air Meal Spatial Delivery* (1969); *Work of Crow* (1970); *Lamentations on the Legacy of Cortez* for Chorus, Strings, 2 MIDI-Keyboards, and 2 Percussion (1993–95). **PERFORMERS AND ECHO DELAY:** *Canon and Fugue (Canon and Fugle)* (1971); *King Speech Songs* (1972); *You Can't See the Forest... Music* (1972); *Missa umbrarum* (1973); *Song(s) of the Sirens (Les Sirènes)* (1973); *3 Pretty Madrigals* (1976); *Dancing on the Sun* (1980); *Music by Candlelight (Love and Death)* (1980); *Uitoto* (1980); *b.e comings* (a.k.a. *Orgas-Mass*) for Soprano, Baritone, and Chamber Ensemble (1991). **PERFORMERS WITH MULTI-TRACKING:** *Is It Love* (1983; Santa Barbara, Calif., Aug. 1984); *On the Leopard Altar* (1983; Santa Barbara, Calif., 1984); *Time Is a Trick* (Rouen, Dec. 1985); *Bacchus with Wineglasses* (Los Angeles, Nov. 1985); *Wild Turkeys* for 3 Keyboard Synthesizers (N.Y., Dec. 1985); *La Tache* with Wineglasses (Boston, June 5, 1987); *NightBreaker* for 4 Pianos (Los Angeles, March 30, 1990). **VOCAL:** *I (Senescence sonorum)*, double concerto for Amplified Body Sounds, Chorus, and Orch. (1970); *Fermentation Notebooks*:1, *Kissing Song*; 2, *Rising Song*; 3, *Drinking Song* for 28 to 48 Unaccompanied Voices, with Wineglasses in No. 3 (1972); *O-Ke-Wa (North American Eclipse)* for 12 Solo Voices, Bells, Rasps, and Drums (1974); *Sun Tropes* for 7 Solo Voices, Recorders, and Kalimbas (1975); *Composition in Contrary and Parallel Motion* for 16 Solo Voices, Percussion, and 4 Keyboards (1977); *The Elysian Nymph* for 8 Solo Voices and 8 Marimbas (1978); *Wolf Is Dead* for Solo Voices and Percussion (1979; rev. for 6 Solo Voices and 8 Keyboards, 1982); *Wail Song* for Vocal Soloist, 5 Voices, and 8 Keyboards (1983); *wolfMASS* for Vocalist, Keyboards, and Percussion (Rouen, June 1988); *Cathedral of Ecstasy* for Vocalists, Electric Keyboards, and Percussion (1990; Tokyo, Nov. 1991); *Pear Blossom Highway* (aka *Abalone*) for Baritone and Electronic Keyboards (1990); *Talk Radio* for Vocalist and Chamber Ensemble (1990–91; Pittsburgh, Nov. 1991, Joan La Barbara soloist); *White Bee* for Solo Voice (1992; Tempe, Ariz., April 1993). **INSTRUMENTAL:** *Piano Piece for Little Kids with Big Hands* (1962); *3 Episodes from Exodus* for Organ and Percussion (1962); *3 Haiku in 4 Movements* for String Quartet (1963); *8 Dialectics 8* for 18 Instruments (1964); *Funke* for Flute, Vibraphone, Drums, Double Bass, and Piano (1964); *Sermon: Saying Something with Music* for String Quartet and Electronics (1966); *The Last Concert*, in 3: *Love and Conception, Birth and Death*, and *Fate and Death* for Piano and Electronics (1968); *Pastime* for String Instruments and Electronics (1969); *10 Minus 30 Minutes* for Strings (1970); *Point Conception* for 9 Pianos (1981); *Lascaux (Chumash Tombs)* for Vocalists and Wine Glasses (1984); *Topanga Tango* for Chamber Ensemble (Pittsburgh, Oct. 1985); *A Crack in the Bell* for Vocal Soloist, 3 Keyboards, and Optional Chamber Orch. (Los Angeles, Nov. 10, 1986); *An American in L.A.* for Synthesizer and Orch. (Los Angeles, March 30, 1989); *A California Family (Group Portrait)*, trio for Violin, Piano, and Percussion (N.Y., Nov. 1989); *Apache Wine* for Chamber Orch. (1989; Tucson, Feb. 16, 1990); *Blues for Mary J.* for Small Chamber Ensemble (1996). **PERFORMER(S) WITH VIRTUAL ENSEMBLE:** *Apologetica* (1994–95); *Temple of Lament* (1996); *Zeitghosts* (1996); *Apparitions of JB* (1997); *Huit ou Neuf Pièces Dorées à Point* (1998); *A Tiger In The Garden* (1998); *The Insect* (2000). **TAPE:** *Montage Shift* (1963); *No Exit* (1963); *Eleison* (1965); *Medeighnia's* (1965). —NS/LK/DM

Lenya, Lotte (real name, **Karoline Wilhelmine Blamauer**), Austrian-American singer and actress; b. Vienna, Oct. 18, 1898; d. N.Y., Nov. 27, 1981. She received training in Classical dance and the Dalcroze method in Zürich (1914–20), where she also worked at the Stadttheater's opera-ballet and at the Schauspielhaus. In 1926 she married **Kurt Weill** and made her debut as a singer in the premiere of his "songspiel" *Mahagonny* (Baden-Baden, July 17, 1927). She later sang in the first performance of its operatic version as *Aufstieg und Fall der Stadt Mahagonny* (Leipzig, March 9, 1930). She also created the role of Jenny in his *Die Dreigroschenoper* (Berlin, Aug. 31, 1928). In 1933 Lenya and Weill fled Nazi Germany for Paris. During their stay there, she created the role of Anna in his *Die sieben Todsunden der Kleinburger* (June 7, 1933). In

1935 they emigrated to the U.S. She created the roles of Miriam in his *The Eternal Road* (N.Y., Jan 7, 1937) and the Duchess in his *The Firebrand of Florence* (N.Y., March 22, 1945). Following Weill's death in 1950, Lenya devoted herself to reviving many of his works for the American stage. She also was active as an actress on stage and in films. Although she was not a professionally trained singer, she adapted herself to the peculiar type of half-spoken, half-sung roles in Weill's works with total dedication.

BIBL.: H. Marx, ed., *Weill-L.* (N.Y., 1976); L. Symonette and K. Kowalke, eds. and trs., *Speak Low (When You Speak of Love): The Letters of Kurt Weill and L. L.* (Berkeley, 1996).—**NS/LK/DM**

Lenz, Wilhelm von, Russian government official and writer on music of German descent; b. Riga, June 1, 1809; d. St. Petersburg, Jan. 31, 1883. He studied in Riga, then with Liszt in Paris (1828) and Moscheles in London (1829). He became a government councillor in St. Petersburg (1842). Although Fétis first suggested the division of Beethoven's output into 3 stylistic periods, it was Lenz who fully explored the idea in his study *Beethoven et ses trois styles: Analyses des sonates de piano suivies de l'essai d'un catalogue critique chronologique et anecdotique de l'oeuvre de Beethoven* (2 vols., St. Petersburg, 1852; 3rd ed., 1855; new ed. by M.D. Calvocoressi, Paris, 1909). This arbitrary division held sway for many decades until it was tempered by modern critical analysis. He also wrote *Beethoven: Eine Kunststudie*, I-II (Kassel, 1855); III/1–2, IV-V: *Kritische Katalog sämtlicher Werke Ludwig van Beethovens mit Analysen derselben* (Hamburg, 1860; ed. by A. Kalischer, Berlin, 1908; 3rd ed., 1921); *Die grossen Pianoforte-Virtuosen unserer Zeit aus persönlicher Bekanntschaft: Liszt, Chopin, Tausig, Henselt* (Berlin, 1872; Eng. tr., N.Y., 1899).—**NS/LK/DM**

Leo, Leonardo (actually, **Lionardo Ortensio Salvatore de**), important Italian composer; b. San Vito degli Schiavi, near Brindisi, Aug. 5, 1694; d. Naples, Oct. 31, 1744. In 1709 he went to Naples, where he studied with Fago at the Cons. S. Maria della Pietà dei Turchini; his sacred drama *S. Chiara, o L'infedeltà abbattuta* was given there in 1712. In 1713 he was made supernumerary organist in the Viceroy's Chapel; also served as maestro di cappella to the Marchese Stella. His first opera, *Il Pisistrato*, was performed in Naples on May 13, 1714. His first comic opera, *La 'mpeca scoperta*, in the Neapolitan dialect, was given in Naples on Dec. 13, 1723. In all, he wrote some 50 operas, most of them for Naples. Following A. Scarlatti's death in 1725, he was elevated to the position of first organist at the viceregal chapel. In 1730 he became provicemaestro of the Royal Chapel; in 1737 vicemaestro. He taught as vicemaestro at the Cons. S. Maria della Pietà dei Turchini from 1734 to 1737; from 1741 was primo maestro in succession to his teacher, Fago; also was primo maestro at the Cons. S. Onofrio from 1739. In Jan. 1744 he became maestro di cappella of the Royal Chapel, but died that same year. Among his famous pupils were Piccinni and Jommelli. Leo's music for the theater (especially his comic operas) is noteworthy; of no less significance were his theoreti-

cal works, *Istituzioni o regole del contrappunto* and *Lezione di canto fermo*.

WORKS: DRAMATIC: Opera (all first perf. in Naples unless otherwise given): *Il Pisistrato* (May 13, 1714); *Sofonisba* (Jan. 22, 1718); *Caio Gracco* (April 19, 1720); *Arianna e Teseo* (Nov. 26, 1721); *Baiazete, imperator dei Turchi* (Aug. 28, 1722); *Timocrate* (Venice, 1723); *La 'mpeca scoperta*, comic opera (Dec. 13, 1723); *Il Turno Aricino* (with L. Vinci; 1724); *L'amore fedele*, comic opera (April 25, 1724); *Lo pazzo apposta*, comic opera (Aug. 26, 1724); *Zenobia in Palmira* (May 13, 1725); *Il trionfo di Camilla, regina dei Volsci* (Rome, Jan. 8, 1726); *Orismene, ovvero Dalli sdegni l'amore*, comic opera (Jan. 19, 1726); *La semmeglianza de chi l'ha fatta*, comic opera (Fall 1726); *Lo matrimonio annascuso*, comic opera (1727); *Il Cid* (Rome, Feb. 10, 1727); *La pastorella commattuta*, comic opera (Fall 1727); *Argene* (Venice, Jan. 17, 1728); *Catone in Utica* (Venice, 1729); *La schiava per amore*, comic opera (1729); *Semiramide* (Feb. 2, 1730); *Rosmene*, comic opera (Summer 1730); *Evergete* (Rome, 1731); *Demetrio* (Oct. 1, 1732); *Amor da' senno*, comic opera (1733); *Nitocri, regina d'Egitto* (Nov. 4, 1733); *Il castello d'Atlante* (July 4, 1734); *Demofoonte* (Jan. 20, 1735; Act 1 by D. Sarro, Act 2 by F. Mancini, Act 3 by Leo, and intermezzos by G. Sellitti); *La clemenza di Tito* (Venice, 1735); *Emira* (July 12, 1735; intermezzos by I. Prota); *Demetrio* (Dec. 10, 1735; different setting from earlier opera of 1732); *Onore vince amore*, comic opera (1736); *Farnace* (Dec. 19, 1736); *L'amico traditore*, comic opera (1737); *Siface* (Bologna, May 11, 1737; rev. version as *Viriate*, Pistoia, 1740); *La simpatia del sangue*, comic opera (Fall 1737); *Olimpiade* (Dec. 19, 1737); *Il conte*, comic opera (1738); *Il Ciro riconosciuto* (Turin, 1739); *Amor vuol sofferenze*, comic opera (Fall 1739; rev. version as *La finta frascatana*, Nov. 1744); *Achille in Sciro* (Turin, 1740); *Scipione nelle Spagne* (Milan, 1740); *L'Alidoro*, comic opera (Summer 1740); *Demetrio* (Dec. 19, 1741; different setting from the earlier operas of 1732 and 1735); *L'ambizione delusa*, comic opera (1742); *Andromaca* (Nov. 4, 1742); *Il fantastico, od Il nuovo Chisciotte*, comic opera (1743; rev. version, Fall 1748); *Vologeso, re dei Parti* (Turin, 1744); *La fedeltà odiata*, comic opera (1744); he also contributed to a pasticcio setting of Demetrio (June 30, 1738); he likewise composed prologues, arias, etc., to operas by other composers. A number of operas long attributed to Leo are now considered doubtful. Leo also composed serenatas, feste teatrali, chamber cantatas, etc. He wrote the following sacred dramas and oratorios: *S. Chiara, o L'infedeltà abbattuta* (Naples, 1712); *Il trionfo della castità di S. Alessio* (Naples, Jan. 4, 1713); *Dalla morte alla vita di S. Maria Maddalena* (Atrani, July 22, 1722); *Oratorio per la Ss. vergine del rosario* (Naples, Oct. 1, 1730); *S. Elena al Calvario* (Bologna, 1734); *La morte di Abele* (Bologna, 1738); *S. Francesco di Paola nel deserto* (Lecce, 1738); *Il verbo eterno e la religione* (Florence, 1741); he also composed 6 Neapolitan masses, various Mass movements, 2 Magnificats, offertories, antiphons, motets, etc.; most notable is his *Miserere* for Double Choir and Organ (1739), publ. in a modern ed. by H. Wiley Hitchcock (St. Louis, 1961). His instrumental works include 6 concerti for Cello, String Orch., and Basso Continuo (1737–38); of these, 1 in D major has been ed. by F. Cilea (Milan, 1934), 1 in A major by E. Rapp (Mainz, 1938), and 3 in the Series of Early Music, VII (1973); he also wrote Concerto in D major for 4 Violins and Basso Continuo (publ. in *Musikschatze der Vergangenheit*, XXIV, Berlin, 1952); works for harpsichord; etc.

BIBL.: C. Leo, *L. L. e sua epoca musicale* (Brindisi, 1894); G. Leo, *L. L.: Musicista del secola XVIII e le sue opere musicali* (Naples, 1905); F. Schlitzer, ed., *Tommaso Traetta, L. L., Vincenzo Bellini: Noti e documenti raccolti da F. Schlitzer* (Siena, 1952); G. Pastore,

L. L. (Galatina, 1957); R. Krause, *Die Kirchenmusik vom L. L. (1694–1744): Ein Beitrag zur Musikgeshichte Neapels im 18. Jahrhundert* (Regensburg, 1987); M. Summa, *Amor vuol sofferenza: Il teatro giocoso di L. L.* (Fasano, 1994).—**NS/LK/DM**

León, Tania (Justina), Cuban-born American composer, conductor, pianist, and teacher; b. Havana, May 14, 1943. She studied in Havana at the Carlos Alfredo Peyrellade Cons. (B.A., 1963; M.A. in music education, 1964). She went in 1967 to the U.S., where she studied at N.Y.U. (M.S., 1973) and had conducting lessons with Halasz and at the Berkshire Music Center at Tanglewood with Bernstein and Ozawa. In 1968 she joined the Dance Theatre of Harlem as its first music director, a position she held until 1980; also organized the Brooklyn Phil. Community Concert Series (1977). She was a guest conductor with several U.S. and European orchs.; in 1992 she conducted the Johannesburg Sym. during the Dance Theatre of Harlem's historic trip to South Africa, when the company became the first multi-racial arts troupe to perform and teach there in modern times. Among her many awards were the Young Composer's Prize from the National Council of the Arts, Havana (1966), the Alvin John Award from the Council for Emigrés in the Professions (1971), and the Cintas Award (1974–75). She also was an NEA Fellow (1975). In 1978 she was music director for Broadway's smash musical *The Wiz*, and in 1985 served as resident composer for the Lincoln Center Inst. in N.Y. León also joined the composition faculty of Brooklyn Coll., and later was artistic director of the Composers' Forum in N.Y. She has also held composer and/or conducting residencies in the U.S. (Cleveland, Seattle et al.) and in Europe (Italy, Germany et al.). Her compositions are written in an accessible style, rhythmically vibrant, with some novel piano and percussion effects. Her *Kabiosile* for Piano and Orch. (1988) brings together the rich and disparate elements of her own cultural heritage, combining Afro-Cuban, Hispanic, and Latin jazz elements within a classical Western concerto format. Her ballet *Dougl"a* (with Geoffrey Holder; 1974) was heard in the Soviet Union during the Dance Theatre of Harlem's 1988 tour.

WORKS: DRAMATIC: *Tones,* ballet (1970; in collaboration with A. Mitchell); *The Beloved,* ballet (1972); *Dougla,* ballet (1974; in collaboration with G. Holder); *Maggie Magalita,* theater piece (1980; in collaboration with W. Kesselman); *The Golden Windows,* theater piece (1982; in collaboration with R. Wilson); *A Scourge of Hyacinths,* chamber opera, after Wole Soyinka (1992; Geneva, Jan. 25, 1999). **ORCH.:** *Concerto criollo* for Piano, 8 Timpani, and Orch. (1980); *Batá* (1985); *Kabiosile* for Piano and Orch. (N.Y., Dec. 4, 1988); *Carabalí* (1991); *Para Viola y Orquesta* for Violin and Orch. (Chicago, July 29, 1994). **CHAMBER:** *Haiku* for Flute, Bassoon, and 5 Percussion (1973); *Pet's Suite* for Flute and Piano (1980); *Ascend* for 4 Horns, 4 Trumpets, 3 Trombones, Tuba, and Percussion (1983); *Permutation Seven* for Flute, Clarinet, Trumpet, Violin, Cello, and Percussion (1985); *A La Par* for Piano and Percussion (1986); *Parajota Delaté* for Flute, Clarinet, Violin, Cello, and Piano (1988; also for Flute, Oboe, Clarinet, Bassoon, and Piano, 1992); *Indigena* for Instrumental Ensemble (1991); *Crossings* for Brass Ensemble (1992); *Aernas d'un Tiempo* for Clarinet, Cello, and Piano (1992); *Son Sonora* for Flute and Guitar (1993); *sin normas,*

ajenas for Large Chamber Ensemble (1994); *Hechizos* for Large Chamber Ensemble (1995); various works for solo instruments. **VOCAL:** *De- Orishas* for 2 Sopranos, Countertenor, 2 Tenors, and Bass (1982); *Pueblo Mulato,* 3 songs for Soprano, Oboe, Guitar, Double Bass, Percussion, and Piano, after Nicolás Guillén (1987); *Heart of Ours—A Piece* for Men's Chorus, Flute, 4 Trumpets, and 2 Percussion (1988); *Batéy* for 2 Sopranos, Countertenor, 2 Tenors, and Bass (1989; in collaboration with M. Camilo); *To and Fro* for Medium Voice and Piano (1990); *Journey* for Soprano, Flute, and Harp (1990); *"Or like a..."* for Baritone, Cello, and Percussion (1994).—**NS/LK/DM**

Leonard, Harlan (Quentin), jazz (soprano, alto, tenor) saxophonist, leader; b. Kansas City, Mo., July 2, 1905; d. Los Angeles, Calif., Nov. 10, 1983. He played clarinet in the Lincoln H.S. Band, taught by Major N. Clark Smith, and later received instruction from George Wilkenson and Eric "Paul" Tremaine. After playing briefly with George E. Lee's Band in Kansas City (1923), he played with Bennie Moten from late 1923 until 1931. With trombonist Thamon Hayes, Leonard co-led the Kansas City Skyrockets. After working in and around Kansas City, the group moved to Chicago in 1934. Hayes returned to Kansas City shortly after, and Leonard became the group's sole leader. This unit disbanded in 1937. The following year Leonard reorganized his own band, using several members of Jimmy Keith's Band. Following residencies in Kansas City, the band went to N.Y. and in 1940 appeared at the Savoy Ballroom and the Golden Gate Ballroom, and then returned to the Midwest, later taking up residency at Fairyland Park, Kansas City. In the spring of 1943, Leonard led the band for a residency at the Hollywood Club (L.A.), during this engagement he began fronting the band for the first time. He continued playing regularly until the mid-1940s, then took a permanent managerial position with the L.A. Internal Revenue Bureau. His brother, Walter, was a professional tenor saxophonist.—**JC/LP**

Léonard, Hubert, Belgian violinist, pedagogue, and composer; b. Bellaire, near Liège, April 7, 1819; d. Paris, May 6, 1890. He studied violin with Rouma in Liège, where he made his debut (March 13, 1832), then studied with Prume at the Brussels Cons. (1832), and later with Habeneck at the Paris Cons. (1836–39). He toured Europe (1845–48). He was a teacher at the Brussels Cons. (1853–66), and then was active in Paris. He was especially esteemed as a chamber music artist and as a teacher. He publ. *Petite gymnastique du jeune violiniste, 24 études classiques, Études harmoniques,* a method for violin, *École Léonard, L'Ancienne École italienne,* a collection of special studies in double stopping, including examples from Corelli, Tartini, Geminiani, and Nardini, and *Le Violon au point de vue de l'orchestration,* as well as 5 violin concertos, 6 concert pieces, with Piano, Serenade for 3 Violins, Concert Duo for 2 Violins, and fantasias and character pieces.

BIBL.: G. Weiss, ed., *Der Lehrer und Wegbereiter von Henri Marteau, H. L.* (Tutzing, 1987).—**NS/LK/DM**

Leoncavallo, Ruggero, noted Italian composer; b. Naples, April 23, 1857; d. Montecatini, Aug. 9, 1919.

He attended the Naples Cons. (1866–76), where his teachers were B. Cesi (piano) and M. Ruta and L. Rossi (composition), and then took courses in literature at the Univ. of Bologna (1876–78). His first opera, *Tommaso Chatterton*, was about to be produced in Bologna (1878) when the manager disappeared, and the production was called off. Leoncavallo earned his living playing piano in cafes throughout Europe before going to Paris, where he composed chansonettes and other popular songs. He wrote an opera, *Songe d'une nuit d'été* (after Shakespeare's *Midsummer Night's Dream*), which was privately sung in a salon. He began to study Wagner's scores, and became an ardent Wagnerian; he resolved to emulate the master by producing a trilogy, *Crepusculum*, depicting in epical traits the Italian Renaissance; the separate parts were to be *I Medici*, *Girolamo Savonarola*, and *Cesare Borgia*. He spent 6 years on the basic historical research; having completed the first part, and with the scenario of the entire trilogy sketched, he returned in 1887 to Italy, where the publisher Ricordi became interested in the project, but kept delaying the publication and production of the work. Annoyed, Leoncavallo turned to Sonzogno, the publisher of Mascagni, whose opera *Cavalleria rusticana* had just obtained a tremendous vogue. Leoncavallo submitted a short opera in a similarly realistic vein; he wrote his own libretto based on a factual story of passion and murder in a Calabrian village, and named it *Pagliacci*. The opera was given with sensational success at the Teatro dal Verme in Milan under the direction of Toscanini (May 21, 1892), and rapidly took possession of operatic stages throughout the world; it is often played on the same evening with Mascagni's opera, both works being of brief duration. Historically, these 2 operas signalized the important development of Italian operatic *verismo*, which influenced composers of other countries as well.

The enormous success of *Pagliacci* did not deter Leoncavallo from carrying on his more ambitious projects. The first part of his unfinished trilogy, *I Medici*, was finally brought out at the Teatro dal Verme in Milan on Nov. 9, 1893, but the reception was so indifferent that he turned to other subjects; the same fate befell his youthful *Tommaso Chatterton* at its production in Rome (March 10, 1896). His next opera, *La Bohème* (Venice, May 6, 1897), won considerable success, but had the ill fortune of coming a year after Puccini's masterpiece on the same story, and was dwarfed by comparison. There followed a light opera, *Zazà* (Milan, Nov. 10, 1900), which was fairly successful, and was produced repeatedly on world stages. In 1894 he was commissioned by the German Emperor Wilhelm II to write an opera for Berlin; this was *Der Roland von Berlin*, on a German historic theme; it was produced in Berlin on Dec. 13, 1904, but despite the high patronage it proved a fiasco. In 1906 Leoncavallo made a tour of the U.S. and Canada, conducting his *Pagliacci* and a new operetta, *La Jeunesse de Figaro*, specially written for his American tour; it was so unsuccessful that he never attempted to stage it in Europe. Back in Italy he resumed his industrious production; the opera *Maia* (Rome, Jan. 15, 1910) and the operetta *Malbrouck* (Rome, Jan. 19, 1910) were produced within the same week; another operetta, *La Reginetta delle rose*, was staged simultaneously in Rome

and in Naples (June 24, 1912). In the autumn of that year, Leoncavallo visited London, where he presented the premiere of his *Gli Zingari* (Sept. 16, 1912); a year later, he revisited the U.S., conducting in San Francisco. He wrote several more operettas, but they made no impression; 3 of them were produced during his lifetime: *La Candidata* (Rome, Feb. 6, 1915), *Goffredo Mameli* (Genoa, April 27, 1916), and *Prestami tua moglie* (Montecatini, Sept. 2, 1916); posthumous premieres were accorded the operetta *A chi la giarettiera?* (Rome, Oct. 16, 1919), the opera *Edipo re* (Chicago, Dec. 13, 1920), and the operetta *Il primo bacio* (Montecatini, April 29, 1923). Another score, *Tormenta*, remained unfinished. Salvatore Allegra collected various sketches by Leoncavallo and arranged from them a 3-act operetta, *La maschera nuda*, which was produced in Naples on June 26, 1925.

BIBL.: R. de Rensis, *Per Umberto Giordano e R. L.* (Siena, 1949); L. Guiot and J. Machder, eds., *Convegno internazionale di studie su R. L.* (Milan, 1995).—NS/LK/DM

Leonhardt, Gustav (Maria), eminent Dutch organist, harpsichordist, conductor, and pedagogue; b. 's Graveland, May 30, 1928. He went to Basel and studied organ and harpsichord with Eduard Müller at the Schola Cantorum Basiliensis (1947–50). In 1950 he made his debut as a harpsichordist in Vienna playing Bach's *Die Kunst der Fuge*. After pursuing studies in musicology there, he was prof. of harpsichord at that city's Academy of Music (1952–55). In 1954 he joined the faculty of the Amsterdam Cons. He also served as organist at the Waalse Kerk (until 1981), and then at the Nieuwe Kerk in Amsterdam. His recital tours took him all over Europe and North America. In 1955 he founded the Leonhardt Consort, with which he also toured extensively. In 1999 he founded the N.Y. Collegium, which he conducted in historically informed performances on period instruments. He ed. Bach's *Die Kunst der Fuge* (1952), many of Sweelinck's keyboard works for the critical ed. of that composer's works, and various other pieces. Leonhardt is held in the highest regard as a keyboard player, conductor, and teacher. His keyboard repertoire includes works by Bach, Handel, Sweelinck, Couperin, Frescobaldi, Rameau, Froberger, and other masters. As a conductor, he has led many performances of choral works but has also ventured into opera. His recordings have won various prizes, and in 1980 he was honored with the Erasmus Prize of the Netherlands. —NS/LK/DM

Leoni, Franco, Italian composer; b. Milan, Oct. 24, 1864; d. London, Feb. 8, 1949. He studied at the Milan Cons. with Dominiceti and Ponchielli. In 1892 he went to London, where he remained until 1917. He then lived in France and Italy, eventually returning to England.

WORKS: DRAMATIC: O p e r a : *Raggio di luna* (Milan, June 5, 1890); *Rip van Winkle* (London, Sept. 4, 1897); *Ib and Little Christina*, "picture in 3 panels" (London, Nov. 14, 1901); *L'oracolo* (London, June 28, 1905); *Tzigana* (Genoa, Feb. 3, 1910); *Le baruffe chiozzotte* (Milan, Jan. 2, 1920); *La terra del sogno* (Milan, Jan. 10, 1920); *Falene* (Milan, 1920). **O r a t o r i o s :** *Sardanapalus* (London, 1891); *The Gate of Life* (London, 1891); *Golgotha* (London, 1909).—NS/LK/DM

Leoni, Leone, distinguished Italian composer; b. Verona, c. 1560; d. Vicenza, June 24, 1627. He studied at the "academy" maintained by Count Mario Bevilacqua in Verona, then was maestro di cappella in Vicenza from Oct. 4, 1588, until his death. He was a disciple of the Venetian school, and his works are characteristic for their application of chromatic devices in harmony and antiphonal choral usages. He wrote about 130 madrigals (41 not extant) and around 185 motets (about 40 not extant). He was an important composer of motets.

WORKS (all publ. in Venice): VOCAL: S a c r e d : *Penitenza: Primo libro de* [21] *madrigali spirituali* for 5 Voices (1596); *Sacri fiori:*[20] *motetti* [and 1 Magnificat] for 2 to 4 Voices and Organ, *libro primo* (1606); [20] *Sacrarum cantionum liber primus* for 8 Voices and 2 Organs (1608); *Sacri fiori: Secondo libro de* [31] *motetti* for 1 to 3 Voices and Organ... *con una messa* for 4 Voices (1612); *Omnium solemnitatum psalmodia* for 8 Voices (1613); *Aurea corona ingemmata d'armonici, concerto a 10* for 4 Voices and 6 Instruments (1615); *Sacri fiori: quarto libro de* [25] *motetti* for 1 to 4 Voices and Organ (1622). S e c u l a r : *Il primo libro de* [21] *madrigali* for 5 Voices (1588); *Bella Clori: Secondo libro de* [22] *madrigali* for 5 Voices (1591); *Il terzo libro de* [21] *madrigali* for 5 Voices (1595); *Il quarto libro de* [20] *madrigali* (1598; not extant); *Bell'Alba: Quinto libro de* [21] *madrigali* for 5 Voices (1602).

BIBL.: H. Wing, *The Polychoral Motets of L. L.* (diss., Boston Univ., 1966).—NS/LK/DM

Leoninus (Magister Leoninus, Magister Leonini, Magister Leo, Magister Leonis), celebrated French composer and poet; b. Paris, c. 1135; d. there, c. 1201. He most likely received his initial education at the Notre Dame Cathedral schools in Paris. He was active at the collegiate church of St. Benoit in Paris by the mid-1150s, eventually serving as a canon there for some 20 years. He was also a member of the clergy of Notre Dame by reason of his position at St. Benoit. He had earned the academic degree of master by 1179, probably in Paris. He later became a canon at Notre Dame, where he was a priest by 1192, and was also a member of the congregation of St. Victor by 1187. His great achievement was the creation of organa to augment the divine service; this has come down to us as the *Magnus liber organi de graduali et antiphonario pro servitio divino multiplicando.* It is also possible that he prepared many of the revisions and variant versions of the organi, preceding the work of revision by Pérotin. The original form of the work is not extant, but there are 3 extant later versions dating from the 13th and 14th centuries: Florence, Biblioteca Medicea-Laurenziana, MS Pluteus 29.1, Wolfenbüttel, Herzog August Bibliothek, Cod. Guelf. 628 Helmst., and Wolfenbüttel, Cod. Guelf. 1099 Helmst. As a poet, he wrote the extensive *Hystorie sacre gestas ab origine mundi.*—NS/LK/DM

Leonova, Darya (Mikhailovna), Russian contralto; b. Vyshny-Volochok, March 21, 1829; d. St. Petersburg, Feb. 6, 1896. She studied at the St. Petersburg Imperial opera school. In 1852 she sang the part of Vanya in Glinka's A *Life for the Czar,* and was greatly praised by Glinka himself; then sang regularly in St. Petersburg and Moscow (until 1874). Between 1875 and 1879 she made tours of Russia, the Far East, Europe, and the U.S. In 1879 she traveled in southern Russia and the Crimea with Mussorgsky as accompanist. In 1880 she opened a singing school in St. Petersburg, with Mussorgsky acting as coach. She also taught at the Moscow drama school (1888–92). Her memoirs were publ. in *Istorichesky vestnik,* nos. 1–4 (1891). She devoted much of her career to promoting Russian music; created the roles of the Princess in Dargomyzhsky's *Rusalka* (1856) and the Hostess in Mussorgsky's *Boris Godunov* (1874). Her non-Russian roles included Orfeo, Azucena, and Ortrud.

BIBL.: V. Yakovlev, *D.M. L.* (Moscow, 1950).—NS/LK/DM

Leontovich, Mikola (Dmitrovich), prominent Ukrainian composer and teacher; b. Monastíryok, Podolia, Dec. 13, 1877; d. Markovka, near Tulchin, Jan. 25, 1921. He was educated at the seminaries in Stargorod and Kamenets-Podolsky. Although he lacked formal training in music, he was active as a singing teacher in various schools and as a conductor of amateur choirs and orchs. After completing sessions as an external student of the St. Petersburg court chapel choir (1904), he worked with Yavorsky (1909–14); in 1918, became a teacher at the Lissenko Music and Drama Inst. He also was active with various Ukrainian musical organizations. Leontovich possessed a remarkable talent for arranging Ukrainian folk songs for unaccompanied choral groups. Among his own works were several major unaccompanied choral works, instrumental pieces, and an unfinished opera. A number of collections of his works were publ., as were a vol. of his writings (Kiev, 1947).

BIBL.: V. Diachenko, *M.D. L.* (Kharkov, 1941); M. Gordichuk, *M.D. L.* (Kiev, 197?) —NS/LK/DM

Leopold I, Holy Roman Emperor (1658–1705), patron of music, and composer; b. Vienna, June 9, 1640; d. there, May 5, 1705. In addition to his general education, he received instruction on various instruments and in composition. During his reign, Vienna's musical life flourished, with over 400 dramatic works produced, as well as much sacred and instrumental music. In addition to being an enlightened patron, he was also a diligent composer of sacred music, producing about 10 oratorios, masses, motets, etc. He likewise wrote some 12 stage works, although a number are not extant. See G. Brosche, "Die musikalischen Werke Kaiser Leopold I: Ein systematisch-thematisches Verzeichnis der erhaltenen Kompositionen," *Beiträge zur Musikdokumentation: Franz Grasberger zum 60. Geburtstag* (Tutzing, 1975). —NS/LK/DM

Leoz, Jesús García, Spanish composer; b. Olite, Navarre, Jan. 10, 1904; d. Madrid, Feb. 25, 1953. He was a cantor in Olite before pursuing his studies in Pamplona, and later received training from del Campo (composition) and Balsa (piano), and finally from Turina (composition), his most significant influence. Leoz's output included zarzuelas, a ballet, orch. pieces, chamber music, piano pieces, songs, and film scores.

BIBL.: A. Fernández Cid, *J. L.* (Madrid, 1953). —NS/LK/DM

L'Épine, (Francesca) Margherita de, famous Italian soprano; b. c. 1683; d. London, Aug. 8, 1746. She began her career at the court in Mantua, then appeared in Venice (1700). She sang in the works of the German composer Jakob Greber at Lincoln's Inn Fields in London; was also his mistress (from 1702). She joined London's Drury Lane Theatre in 1704, making her first appearance in opera there in Haym's pasticcio *Camillo* in 1706, replacing her archrival, the English soprano Catherine Tofts. When the opera company moved to the Queen's Theatre in 1708, she continued as a leading member with it until 1714. She sang in several works by Handel, creating the roles of Eurilla in his *Il Pastor fido* (Nov. 22, 1712) and Agilea in his *Teseo* (Jan. 10, 1713). She also became associated with the composer Pepusch. She appeared in his works at Drury Lane (1715–17) and at Lincoln's Inn Fields (1718–19), and married him about 1718. In later years she was active mainly as a teacher. She made her last appearance at Drury Lane in 1733. She was the most celebrated soprano on the London stage of her time. Contemporary accounts praise her musical gifts highly but describe her as physically unattractive; indeed, Pepusch dubbed her "Hecate."
—**NS/LK/DM**

Leppard, Raymond (John), eminent English conductor; b. London, Aug. 11, 1927. He studied harpsichord and viola at Trinity Coll., Cambridge (M.A., 1952), where he also was active as a choral conductor and served as music director of the Cambridge Phil. Soc. In 1952 he made his London debut as a conductor, and then conducted his own Leppard Ensemble. He became closely associated with the Goldsbrough Orch., which became the English Chamber Orch. in 1960. He also gave recitals as a harpsichordist, and was a Fellow of Trinity Coll. and a lecturer on music at his alma mater (1958–68). His interest in early music prompted him to prepare several realizations of scores from that period; while his eds. provoked controversy, they had great value in introducing early operatic masterpieces to the general public. His first realization, Monteverdi's *L'incoronazione di Poppea*, was presented at the Glyndebourne Festival under his direction in 1962. He subsequently prepared performing eds. of Monteverdi's *Orfeo* (1965) and *Il ritorno d'Ulisse in patria* (1972), and of Cavalli's *Messa concertata* (1966), *L'Ormindo* (1967), *La Calisto* (1969), *L'Egisto* (1974), and *L'Orione* (1980). During this period, he made appearances as a guest conductor with leading European opera houses, orchs., and festivals. On Nov. 4, 1969, he made his U.S. debut conducting the Westminster Choir and N.Y. Phil., at which occasion he also appeared as soloist in the Haydn D-major Harpsichord Concerto. In 1973 he became principal conductor of the BBC Northern Sym. Orch. in Manchester, a position he retained until 1980. He made his U.S. debut as an opera conductor leading a performance of his ed. of *L'Egisto* at the Santa Fe Opera in 1974. Settling in the U.S. in 1976, he subsequently appeared as a guest conductor with the major U.S. orchs. and opera houses. On Sept. 19, 1978, he made his Metropolitan Opera debut in N.Y. conducting *Billy Budd*. He was principal guest conductor of the St. Louis Sym. Orch. (1984–90). From 1987 to 2001 he was music director of the Indianapolis Sym. Orch., thereafter its first conductor laureate. At the invitation of the Prince of Wales, he conducted his ed. of Purcell's *Dido and Aeneas* at London's Buckingham Palace in 1988. He returned there in 1990 to conduct the 90th-birthday concert of the Queen Mother. On Jan. 27, 1991, he conducted a special concert of Mozart's works with members of the N.Y. Phil. and the Juilliard Orch. at N.Y.'s Avery Fisher Hall in Lincoln Center; telecast live to millions via PBS, it re-created a concert given by Mozart in Vienna on March 23, 1783, and celebrated his 235th birthday and the launching of Lincoln Center's commemoration of the 200th anniversary of his death. In 1993 he conducted the Indianapolis Sym. Orch. on a major tour of Europe, visiting London, Birmingham, Frankfurt am Main, Cologne, Düsseldorf, Vienna, Munich, Geneva, and Zürich. In 1994 he was named artist-in-residence at the Univ. of Indianapolis. Leppard was made a Commander of the Order of the British Empire in 1983. As a composer, he produced film scores for *Lord of the Flies* (1963), *Alfred the Great* (1969), *Laughter in the Dark* (1969), *Perfect Friday* (1970), and *Hotel New Hampshire* (1985). He also orchestrated Schubert's "Grand Duo" Sonata and conducted its first performance with the Indianapolis Sym. Orch. (Nov. 8, 1990). Although long associated with early music, Leppard has acquired mastery of a truly catholic repertoire, ranging from Mozart to Britten. His thoughtful views on performance practice are set forth in his book *The Real Authenticity* (London, 1988). T. Lewis ed. the vol. *Raymond Leppard on Music* (White Plains, N.Y., 1993), an anthology of critical and personal writings, with a biographical chronology and discography.—**NS/LK/DM**

Lerdahl, (Al)Fred (Whitford), American composer and music theorist; b. Madison, Wisc., March 10, 1943. He studied at Lawrence Univ. (B.M., 1965) and Princeton Univ. (M.F.A., 1968), where his teachers included Babbitt, Cone, and Kim. He then studied with Fortner at the Freiburg im Breisgau Hochschule für Musik on a Fulbright grant (1968–69), and was composer-in-residence at IRCAM (1981–82) and at the American Academy in Rome (1987). He held teaching appointments at the Univ. of Calif. at Berkeley (1969–71), Harvard Univ. (1970–79), Columbia Univ. (1979–85), and the Univ. of Mich. (from 1985). From 1974 he collaborated with linguist Ray Jackendoff on a theory of tonal music based on generative linguistics; several articles along these lines culminated in the innovative *A Generative Theory of Tonal Music* (Cambridge, Mass., 1983). Lerdahl's studies include music cognition and computer-assisted composition. As a composer, he features in his works the dismantling of texts and a technique of "expanding variation" wherein each variation is longer than the preceding by a predetermined ratio.

WORKS: ORCH.: *Chromorhythmos* (1972); *Chords* (1974; rev. 1983); *Crosscurrents* (1987); *Waves* for Chamber Orch. (1988). **CHAMBER:** *Piano Fantasy* (1964); *String Trio* (1965–66); *6 Études* for Flute, Viola, and Harp (1977); *2 string quartets* (1978, 1982); *Episodes and Refrains* for Wind Quintet (1982); *Fantasy Etudes* for Chamber Ensemble (1985); *Marches* for Clarinet, Violin, Cello, and Piano (1992). **VOCAL:** *Wake* for Mezzo-soprano, Violin, Viola, Cello, Harp, and Percussion Ensemble (1968); *Aftermath*, cantata for Soprano, Mezzo-soprano, Baritone, and Chamber Ensemble (1973); *Eros: Variations* for Mezzosoprano, Alto Flute, Viola, Harp, Piano, Electric Guitar, Electric Bass, and Percussion (1975); *Beyond the Realm of Bird* for Soprano and Chamber Orch. (1981–84).—**NS/LK/DM**

Lerman, Richard, innovative American composer and sound artist; b. San Francisco, Dec. 5, 1944. He studied composition with Lucier and Shapero at Brandeis Univ. (B.A. in music, 1966), where he also received an M.F.A. in theater and film (1970) and was technical director of its electronic music studio (1965–70). From 1965 to 1970 he was active with numerous film, theater, and media productions. From 1977 he toured throughout North America and Europe, and also performed in Australia, New Zealand, Japan, and China. Lerman has made extensive use of self-built transducers and electronics to explore and reveal small sounds inside of materials and objects, and conversely to activate these materials to behave as loudspeakers. His diverse works include real-time performance pieces and sound installations, as well as works on film and video. From 1989 he has produced several collaborations with the installation artist Mona Higuchi, including *Los Desaparecidos* (1989), *Takuhon* (1991), *Kristallnacht* (1992), and *Threading History: The Japanese American Experience* (1995). His *A Matter of Scale* (1986) was premiered in the Houston Astrodome.

WORKS: DRAMATIC: Film : *The Ring Masters* (1966); *3rd Book of Exercises* (1967); *Think Tank* (1971); *Sections for Screen, Performers & Audience* (1974); *Glass Shots with Flower* (1981); *Transducer Series Films (1–54)* (1983–87). **Videos :** *Four Places at South Point* (1988); *A Street Demonstration in Santiago, Chile* (1989); *Windharps at the Tokugawa Women's Grave* (1989); *Hesselt Corn* (1992); *Manzanar and Dachau* (1993); *Tule Lake* (1994); *Border Fences at Gringo Pass & Nacos* (1998). **Electroacoustic and Music Theater :** *End of the Line: some recent dealings with death* (1973); *Travelon Gamelon* (concert version, 1977; promenade version, 1978); *Accretion Disk, Event Horizon, Singularity* (1978); *Entrance Music* (1979); *Incident at 3 Miles Island, perhaps an elegy for Karen Silkwood* (1980); *Music for Plinky and Straw* (1984); *Transduction System* (1983; in collaboration with T. Plsek); *A Matter of Scale* (1986); *Changing States I–VI* (1985–93); *Kristallnacht Music* (1992); *A Matter of Scale 2* (1993); *Cold Storage* (1994); *Sonic Journeys with Pitch to Midi* (1995); *Border Fences* (1998); *Isms* (1999; in collaboration with Milan Kohout); *Reeds* (1200); *From Dark to Light* (2000). **Sound Installations :** *Hand-Built Microphones* (1983); *News Filters* (1984); *2 Wind Harps in the Rain & Amplified Dory at Sea* (1986); *Metal Mesh Pieces* (1987); *A Footnote from Chernobyl* (1987); *Pacific Transducer Series* (1988); *20 X 24* (1988); *Sado Island Rice* (1991); *Heselt Corn* (1993); *A Loudspeaker from the Fields of California* (1999); *Border Fences* (2000).—**NS/LK/DM**

Lerner, Alan Jay, American lyricist, librettist, and screenwriter; b. N.Y., Aug. 31, 1918; d. there, June 14, 1986. Lerner was noted for his witty, thoughtful lyrics for songs used in 13 Broadway musicals, seven of them written with Frederick Loewe, including *My Fair Lady*, *Camelot*, and *Brigadoon*; they also wrote the film musical *Gigi*. The most successful recordings of Lerner's songs were contained on cast and soundtrack albums, though he had individual hits with such songs as "Almost Like Being in Love," "On the Street Where You Live," and "I Could Have Danced All Night."

Lerner was the son of Joseph J. Lerner, who ran a chain of women's clothing shops, and Edith Adelson Lerner. He wrote a football song while attending the Choate preparatory school and contributed to shows put on by the Hasty Pudding Club at Harvard, from which he graduated in June 1940. On June 26 he married Ruth O'Day Boyd; they had one child and divorced in 1947.

Lerner wrote radio shows and advertising copy in N.Y. after graduating from college. He contributed to shows put on by the Lambs Club and in August 1942 was approached by fellow member Frederick Loewe, who had written a couple of musicals and was looking for a new lyricist/librettist to replace his partner Earle Crooker, who had been drafted. Lerner wrote the book, based on the play *The Patsy* by Barry Connors, and revised some of Crooker's lyrics for *Life of the Party*, which opened Oct. 8, 1942, in Detroit but closed before reaching Broadway. Lerner and Loewe then wrote the songs, and Lerner cowrote an original book, for the musical *What's Up?* The production reached Broadway in November 1943 but ran only 63 performances. Next, Lerner wrote the original book and lyrics and Loewe wrote the music for *The Day Before Spring*, which opened in November 1945 and ran 165 performances.

Lerner and Loewe finally achieved success with their fourth musical, *Brigadoon*, another original book by Lerner about a Scottish village that comes to life once a century. Opening in March 1947, it ran 581 performances, while the cast album reached the Top Ten. Having divorced his first wife, Lerner married *Brigadoon*'s star, actress Marion Bell, in 1947; they divorced in 1949.

Lerner next wrote *Love Life*, a musical that traced a family through different periods of history. Loewe declined to work on it, so Lerner teamed with Kurt Weill. The show opened in October 1948 and ran 252 performances. "Here I'll Stay" from the score was recorded for a chart entry by Jo Stafford.

Lerner signed a contract with MGM to write scripts and lyrics. He married actress Nancy Olson on March 19, 1950. They had two children and divorced in 1957. Lerner wrote the screenplay and lyrics to music by Burton Lane for *Royal Wedding*, which starred Fred Astaire and was released in March 1951. The film was a box office success, the soundtrack album hit the Top Ten, and the song "Too Late Now" was nominated for an Academy Award. Lerner next wrote the screenplay for *An American in Paris*, a film utilizing the music of George Gershwin. Released in November 1951, it earned Lerner an Academy Award for Best Screenplay.

Lerner and Loewe reunited for the musical *Paint Your Wagon*, an original book by Lerner about the Calif. Gold Rush. With a run of 289 performances beginning in November 1951, the show was a financial failure, but the cast album reached the Top Ten. Lerner returned to Hollywood and wrote the screenplay for a film adaptation of *Brigadoon*, starring Gene Kelly and released in

September 1954. The soundtrack album reached the charts.

Lerner and Loewe reached their creative and commercial peak with *My Fair Lady*, a musical adaptation of George Bernard Shaw's play *Pygmalion*, which opened in March 1956. Its 2,717 performances made it the longest running Broadway musical up to that time. The cast album, featuring stars Rex Harrison and Julie Andrews, topped the charts and sold millions of copies. Vic Damone recorded "On the Street Where You Live" for a Top Ten hit, Sylvia Sims reached the Top 40 with "I Could Have Danced All Night," and three other songs from the score also made the singles charts: "I've Grown Accustomed to Your Face" (by Rosemary Clooney); "With a Little Bit of Luck" (by Percy Faith and His Orch.); and "Get Me to the Church on Time" (by Julius LaRosa). Lerner married Micheline Muselli Pozzo di Borgo, a lawyer, on Nov. 29, 1957. They had one child and were divorced on June 25, 1965.

Lerner and Loewe next wrote a film musical, *Gigi*, for which Lerner adapted the screenplay from the novel by Colette. It was released in May 1958 and became a box-office hit, winning the Academy Award for Best Picture. The title song also won an Oscar, and the soundtrack album hit #1 and won the Grammy in its category.

Returning to Broadway, Lerner adapted T. H. White's novel about King Arthur and the Round Table, *The Once and Future King*, as a musical, writing the songs with Loewe. Titled *Camelot*, the show opened in December 1960, and after an uncertain start it ran 873 performances, with a chart-topping, million-selling cast album featuring Richard Burton, Julie Andrews, and Robert Goulet.

Lerner and Loewe again separated, and Lerner initially turned to Richard Rodgers to collaborate on his next musical, with an original book about extrasensory perception. But their partnership did not work out. Lerner wrote the screenplay for a film adaptation of *My Fair Lady*, which opened in October 1964. Despite being one of the top grossing films of the year and winning eight Academy Awards, including Best Picture, the film did not break even due to its cost. But the cast album was a million-selling Top Ten hit, and Andy Williams's revival of "On the Street Where You Live" reached the Top 40.

Lerner brought Burton Lane in to work on his ESP musical, which finally opened on Broadway as *On a Clear Day You Can See Forever* in October 1965. It ran an unprofitable 273 performances, but the cast album reached the charts and won a Grammy, while Johnny Mathis scored a Top Ten hit on the easy-listening charts with the title song. Lerner was married for the fifth time on Nov. 15, 1966, to reporter Karen Gundersen. They divorced Dec. 9, 1974. Lerner wrote the screenplay for an adaptation of *Camelot* that opened in October 1967. Another expensive film, it was financially unsuccessful despite a high gross; the soundtrack album was a million-seller. Lerner produced the October 1969 film adaptation of *Paint Your Wagon*, and he is credited with writing the screenplay, which was adapted by Paddy Chayefsky. He also wrote five new songs with André

Previn. Reportedly the most expensive film made up to that time, it was an enormous failure at the box office, though the soundtrack album went gold.

Lerner again collaborated with Previn on his next project, *Coco*, a stage musical about fashion designer Chanel, starring Katharine Hepburn. Opening in December 1969, it was helped to profitability by Hepburn's appearance and ran 332 performances. Lerner wrote the screenplay for a film adaptation of *On a Clear Day You Can See Forever*, which starred Barbra Streisand and opened in June 1970. It was another expensive failure, though the soundtrack album reached the charts.

Lerner teamed with John Barry for the songs in *Lolita, My Love*, a stage musical he adapted from Vladimir Nabokov's novel *Lolita*. The show opened in Philadelphia on Feb. 15, 1971, but closed in Boston on March 27 without reaching Broadway. Lerner then reunited with Loewe and they wrote five new songs for a stage adaptation of *Gigi* that opened on Broadway in November 1973. It ran an unsuccessful 103 performances but won the Tony Award for Best Score. Lerner and Loewe's last work together was a film musical version of Antoine de Saint-Exupery's story for children, *The Little Prince*. It was released in November 1974 and earned the songwriters Oscar nominations for the score and the title song.

Lerner married Sandra Payne, an actress, on Dec. 10, 1974, and they divorced in 1976. He married Nina Bushkin, a college administrator, on May 30, 1977, and they divorced in 1980. Meanwhile, he wrote two unsuccessful Broadway musicals, *1600 Pennsylvania Avenue*, with music by Leonard Bernstein, in 1976, and *Carmelina*, with music by Burton Lane, in 1979. Michael Johnson revived "Almost Like Being in Love" as a Top 40 hit in 1978.

Lerner met his eighth wife, actress and singer Elizabeth Robertson, when she was appearing in a revival of *My Fair Lady* in London. They married on Aug. 13, 1981, and he collaborated with Charles Strouse on the musical *Dance a Little Closer*, based on Robert E. Sherwood's play *Idiot's Delight*, for a starring vehicle for her. It ran for only one performance in May 1983. Lerner finished writing *The Musical Theatre*, a historical study, before his death from lung cancer at 67 in 1986.

WORKS (only works for which Lerner was a primary, credited lyricist are listed): **MUSICALS/REVUES** (dates refer to N.Y. openings): *What's Up?* (Nov. 11, 1943); *The Day Before Spring* (Nov. 22, 1945); *Brigadoon* (March 13, 1947); *Love Life* (N.Y., Oct. 7, 1948); *Paint Your Wagon* (Nov. 12, 1951); *My Fair Lady* (March 15, 1956); *Camelot* (Dec. 3, 1960); *On a Clear Day You Can See Forever* (Oct. 17, 1965); *Coco* (Dec. 18, 1969); *Gigi* (Nov. 13, 1973); *1600 Pennsylvania Avenue* (May 4, 1976); *Carmelina* (April 8, 1979); *Dance a Little Closer* (May 11, 1983). **FILMS:** *Royal Wedding* (1951); *Brigadoon* (1954); *Gigi* (1958); *My Fair Lady* (1964); *Camelot* (1967); *Paint Your Wagon* (1969); *On a Clear Day You Can See Forever* (1970); *The Little Prince* (1974).

WRITINGS: *The Street Where I Live* (N.Y., 1978); *The Musical Theatre: A Celebration* (N.Y., 1986); B. Green, ed., *A Hymn to Him: Lyrics of A. J. L.* (London, 1987).

BIBL.: A. Sirmay, ed., *The L. and Loewe Songbook* (N.Y., 1962); G. Lees, *Inventing Champagne: The Worlds of L. and Loewe*

(N.Y., 1990); D. Shapiro, *We Danced All Night: My Life Behind the Scenes with A. J. L.* (N.Y., 1990); S. Citron, *The Wordsmiths: Oscar Hammerstein 2nd & A. J. L.* (N.Y., 1995); E. Jablonski, *A. J. L.: A Biography* (N.Y., 1996).—**WR**

Lerner, Bennett, American pianist; b. Cambridge, Mass., March 21, 1944. He was a piano student of Claudio Arrau, Rafael de Silva, German Diez, Sascha Gorodnitski, and Robert Helps; attended Columbia Univ. and the Manhattan School of Music (B.Mus., 1973; M.Mus., 1975); also profited from a close association with Copland, Thomson, and Bowles, whose music he came to champion. He taught at the Manhattan School of Music (1972–82), the Greenwich House Music School (from 1979), Sarah Lawrence Coll. (1983–84), and Brooklyn Coll.'s Cons. of Music (from 1987). He appeared as a soloist with the Boston Pops Orch. (1966–68); in 1976 he made his Carnegie Recital Hall debut. On Nov. 14, 1985, he gained national recognition when he appeared as soloist in Copland's Piano Concerto with Mehta and the N.Y. Phil.; the concert, marking Copland's 85th birthday, was telecast live to the nation by PBS. In 1987 Lerner gave a 4-hour marathon recital at N.Y.'s 92nd St. Y in which he performed premieres of works by Thomson, Harris, Barber, Diamond et al. On Feb. 4, 1988, he was the featured performer at Vittorio Rieti's 90th-birthday concert in N.Y., where he was soloist in Rieti's *Enharmonic Variations* for Piano and Orch., a score written especially for him. While Lerner has played much contemporary music, he has also programmed a number of neglected works from the past.—**NS/LK/DM**

Le Rochois, Marthe, French soprano and teacher; b. Caen, c. 1658; d. Paris, Oct. 9, 1728. She was a principal member of the Paris Opéra from 1678 to 1698, and then devoted herself to teaching. She gained distinction for her appearances in Lully's operas, creating major roles in his *Proserpine* (1680), *Persée* (1682), *Amadis* (1684), *Roland* (1685), and *Armide* (1686).—**NS/LK/DM**

Le Roux, François, French baritone; b. Rennes, Oct. 30, 1955. He studied at the Paris Opéra Studio, his principal mentors being Vera Rosza and Elisabeth Grümmer. After appearing at the Lyons Opera (1980–85), he made his debut at the Paris Opéra as Pelléas. His great success as Pelléas was repeated when he reprised that role in Milan (1986), Vienna (1988), Helsinki (1989), and Cologne (1992). In 1987 he made his first appearance at the Glyndebourne Festival as Ramiro in *L'heure espagnole*. He sang Lescaut in *Manon* at London's Covent Garden in 1988, and returned there in 1991 to create the title role in Birtwistle's *Gawain* and in 1993 to sing Pelléas. In 1996 he appeared as Nick Shadow in Madrid. Among his other roles were Mozart's Count, Papageno, and Don Giovanni. —**NS/LK/DM**

Le Roux, Gaspard, eminent French harpsichordist and composer; b. c. 1660; d. probably in Paris, c. 1707. He won great distinction as a harpsichordist. He also publ. the important collection *Pièces de clavessin* (Paris, 1705; modern ed., N.Y., 1959). Also extant are 3 motets, as well as an air serieux (Paris, 1701; ed. in *La Revue Musicale*, V, 1924).—**LK/DM**

Le Roux, Maurice, French conductor, composer, and writer on music; b. Paris, Feb. 6, 1923; d. Avignon, Oct. 19, 1992. He was a student at the Paris Cons. (1944–52) of Philipp and Nat (piano), Fourestier (conducting), and Messiaen (analysis), and also had private instruction in dodecaphonic techniques with Leibowitz. From 1951 he was active with the French Radio and Television in Paris, where he later was music director of its l'Orchestre National de l'ORTF from 1960 to 1968. After serving as musical councillor of the Paris Opéra (1969–73), he was inspector general of music in the Ministry of Culture (1973–88). He utilized serial procedures in his compositions. Among his works were the ballets *Le Petit Prince* (1949) and *Sables* (1956), incidental music, film scores, the orch. scores *Le Cercle des métamorphoses* (1953) and *Un Koan* (1973), and piano pieces, including a Sonata (1946). He publ. in Paris *Introduction à la musique contemporaine* (1947), *Monteverdi* (1947), *La Musique* (1979), and *Boris Godounov* (1980).—**NS/LK/DM**

Leroux, Xavier (Henry Napoléon), French composer; b. Velletri, Papal States, Oct. 11, 1863; d. Paris, Feb. 2, 1919. He was a pupil of Dubois and Massenet at the Paris Cons., and won the First Grand Prix de Rome in 1885. In 1896 he was appointed a prof. at the Cons.

WORKS: DRAMATIC: *Evangeline* (Brussels, Dec. 18, 1885); *Astarté* (Paris, Feb. 15, 1901); *La Reine Fiammette* (Paris, Dec. 23, 1903); *Vénus et Adonis* (Paris, 1897); *William Ratcliff* (Nice, Jan. 26, 1906); *Théodora* (Monte Carlo, March 19, 1907); *Le Chemineau* (Paris, Nov. 6, 1907); *Le Carillonneur* (Paris, March 20, 1913); *La Fille de Figaro* (Paris, March 11, 1914); *Les Cadeaux de Noël* (Paris, Dec. 25, 1915); *1814* (Monte Carlo, April 6, 1918); *Nausithoé* (Nice, April 9, 1920); *La Plus Forte* (Paris, Jan. 11, 1924); *L'Ingénu* (Bordeaux, Feb. 13, 1931). **OTHER:** Songs; piano pieces.—**NS/LK/DM**

Le Roy, Adrien, eminent French music printer, lutenist, guitarist, citternist, and composer; b. Montreuil-sur-mer, c. 1520; d. Paris, 1598. He was born into a family of wealth. With his cousin, **Robert Ballard,** he founded the printing concern of Le Roy & Ballard. King Henri II granted them a privilege to print music on Aug. 14, 1551. On Feb. 16, 1553, they were made printers to the king, an honor retained by the firm until the middle of the 18th century. Upon Ballard's death in 1588, Le Roy ceased publishing until 1591 when Ballard's widow, Lucrèce, joined him as a partner. At Le Roy's death, the childless widower bequeathed his share of the firm to Lucrèce and the Ballard heirs. Le Roy was a distinguished instrumentalist and composer. His chansons and music for the lute, guitar, and cittern are notable. He also wrote some court odes. His instruction books on the lute, guitar, and cistre were influential for more than a century, and his firm also publ. his treatise on music theory in 1583.—**LK/DM**

Le Roy, René, French flutist and teacher; b. Maisons-Lafitte, near Paris, March 4, 1898; d. Paris, Jan. 3, 1985. He studied at the Paris Cons. with Hennebains, Lafleurance, and Gaubert, and in 1918 won the premier prix for flute. In 1919 he succeeded Gaubert as director of the Société des Instruments à Vent. In 1922 he founded the Quintette Instrumental de Paris, with which he gave numerous concerts in Europe and America. He subsequently occupied various teaching positions; was prof. of chamber music for wind instruments at the Paris Cons. (1955–64). He compiled (with C. Dorgeuille) the manual *Traité de la flûte, historique, technique et pédagogique* (Paris, 1966).—NS/LK/DM

Le Sage de Richée, Philipp Franz, French-born German lutenist and composer who flourished at the close of the 17th century. He publ. a notable collection of 98 pieces engraved in French lute tablature and arranged in 12 suites as *Cabinet der Lauten, in welchem zu finden 12 neue Partien, aus unterschiedenen Tonen und neuesten Manier so aniezo gebräuchlich'* (Breslau, 1695?).

BIBL.: T. Wortmann, *P.F. L. S. d. R. und sein Cabinet der Lauten* (diss., Univ. of Vienna, 1919).—LK/DM

Lésbio, António Marques, Portuguese writer and composer; b. Lisbon, 1639; d. there, Nov. 21, 1709. He spent his entire career in Lisbon. In addition to his literary pursuits, he was made master of the royal chamber musicians (1668) and of the boys in the royal chapel choirs school (1679), curator of the royal music library (1692), and royal choirmaster (1698). He was a distinguished composer of Spanish villancicos and Portuguese vilhancicos, of which 16 are extant with the music. His polyphonic Latin sacred works were destroyed in the Lisbon earthquake of 1755.—LK/DM

Leschetizky, Theodor (Teodor), renowned Polish pianist and pedagogue; b. Lancut, June 22, 1830; d. Dresden, Nov. 14, 1915. He first studied with his father, who took him to Vienna, where he became a pupil of Czerny (piano) and Sechter (composition). He acquired a mastery of the piano in an amazingly short time, and was only 14 when he himself began to teach. He also attended the Univ. of Vienna as a student of philosophy, until its closure in the wake of the 1848 revolution. In 1852 he went to Russia; his initial concerts in St. Petersburg were extremely successful, and gradually he attracted many pupils. He was also active as music director to the Grand Duchess Helen. In 1862 Anton Rubinstein, director of the newly opened St. Petersburg Cons., engaged him as a teacher. After 16 years in Russia, Leschetizky returned to Vienna, where he married his former pupil **Anna Essipoff** (1880), with whom he appeared in duo recitals. They were divorced in 1892, and Leschetizky subsequently contracted 2 more marriages. He continued to make occasional concert tours, but concentrated mainly on teaching; his fame grew, and pupils flocked from all over the world to his studio in Vienna. His most celebrated pupil was Paderewski. Other pupils were Gabrilowitsch, Schnabel, and Isabelle Vengerova, as well as his third and fourth wives, Dominirska Benislavska and Marie Rozborska. His method of playing with the "Kugelhand" (arched hand) was to secure fullness of tone and finger dexterity, with the flexible wrist reserved for octave playing and chord passages. A Leschetizky Soc. was organized after his death, with a branch established in the U.S. He was also a composer, numbering among his

works 2 operas, *Die Brüder von Marco* (not perf.) and *Die erste Falte* (Prague, Oct. 9, 1867), some chamber music, and 49 pieces for piano, a number of which proved quite effective.

BIBL.: M. Brée, *Die Grundlage der Methode L.* (Vienna, 1902; 4th ed., 1914; Eng. tr., 1902); Countess A. Potocka, *T. L.* (London, 1903); A. Hullah, *T. L.* (London, 1906); E. Newcomb, *L. as I Knew Him* (London, 1921).—NS/LK/DM

Leslie, Henry (David), English conductor and composer; b. London, June 18, 1822; d. Llansaintfraid, near Oswestry, Feb. 4, 1896. He was a student of Charles Lucas, and then began his career as a cellist in the Sacred Harmonic Soc. In 1847 he became active with the Amateur Musical Soc., and later was its conductor. With Heming, he founded an a cappella singing soc. in 1855, which eventually evolved into the Henry Leslie Choir. In 1878 his choir won the International Choral Competition at the Paris Exhibition. The choir was disbanded in 1887. From 1863 to 1889 Leslie was also conductor of the Herefordshire Phil. Soc., and from 1864 to 1866 principal of the National Coll. of Music. He wrote the operas *Romance, or Bold Dick Turpin* (1857) and *Ida* (1864), the oratorios *Immanuel* (1853) and *Judith* (1858), the cantatas *Holyrood* (1860) and *Daughter of the Isles* (1861), the biblical pastoral *The First Christian Morn* (1880), a Sym., and the overture *The Templar*.
—NS/LK/DM

Lessard, John (Ayres), American composer and teacher; b. San Francisco, July 3, 1920. He commenced piano lessons when he was 5 and trumpet lessons at 9, and became a member of the San Francisco Civic Sym. Orch. at age 11. He received instruction in piano and theory from Elsie Belenky. After brief studies with Cowell, he continued his training with Boulanger, Dandelot, Cortot, and Lévy at the École Normale de Musique in Paris (1937–40); completed his studies with Boulanger at the Longy School of Music in Cambridge, Mass. In 1946–47 and 1953–54 he held Guggenheim fellowships; received a National Inst. of Arts and Letters award in 1952 and an NEA grant in 1976. From 1962 to 1990 he taught at the State Univ. of N.Y. at Stony Brook. His works follow along neo-classical lines with occasional adherence to serial procedures.

WORKS: ORCH.: Violin Concerto (1942); *Box Hill Overture* (1946); *Cantilena* for Oboe and Strings (1947); *Little Concert* (1947); Wind Concerto (1949); Concerto for Flute, Clarinet, Bassoon, String Quartet, and String Orch. (1952); *Sinfonietta Concertante* (1961); Harp Concerto (1963–83); *Pastimes and an Alleluia* (1974). **CHAMBER:** *3 Movements* for Violin and Piano (1948); *Partita* for Woodwind Quintet (1952); Wind Octet (1952); Cello Sonata (1956); Trio for Flute, Violin, and Piano (1959); String Trio (1963); *Trio in sei parti* for Violin, Cello, and Piano (1966); *Quodlibets I-III* for 2 Trumpets and Trombone (1967); Woodwind Quintet No. 2 (1970); Brass Quintet (1971); *Trios of Consanguinity* for 8 Combinations of Winds and Strings (1973); *Movements: I* for Trumpet and Vibraphone (1976), *II* for Trumpet and Viola (1976), *III* for Trumpet and Violin (1976), *IV* for Trumpet and Percussion (1976), *V* for Trumpet, Violin, and Cello (1977), *VI* for Trumpet, Viola, Cello, and Percussion (1978), *VII* for Trumpet and Cello (1978), and *VIII* for Trumpet, Marimba, and Vibraphone (1984); *Divertimento* for Guitar

(1981–83); *Music for Guitar and Percussion: I* for Guitar and Xylophone (1982), *II* for Guitar and Xylophone (1983), and *III* for Guitar, Vibraphone, and Bongos (1983); *Duet for Piano and Percussion* (1984); *4 Pieces* for Viola and Percussion (1985); *Weatherscenes* for Violin, Guitar, and Cello (1987); *Drift, Follow, Persist* for Horn, Piano, and Percussion (1988); *An Assembled Sequence* for Percussionist (1989); Quintet for Flute, Clarinet, Violin, Cello, and Piano (1993); *Gather and Disperse* for Flute, Clarinet, Trumpet, Trombone, 2 Percussionists, Piano, 2 Violins, and 2 Cellos (1994). **KEYBOARD: P i a n o :** Sonata (1940); *Mask* (1946); *New Worlds* (2 vols., 1965); *Threads of Sound Recalled* (1980); *For Aaron* (1981); *4 bagatelles* (1986, 1988, 1990, 1991). **H a r p s i c h o r d :** *Toccata in 4 Movements* (1951); *Perpetual Motion* (1952). **VOCAL:** *Don Quixote and the Sheep* for Bass-baritone and Orch. (1955); *12 Songs from Mother Goose* for Voice and String Trio (1964); *Fragments from the Cantos of Ezra Pound* for Baritone and 9 Instruments (1969); *The Pond in a Bowl* for Soprano, Piano, Marimba, and Vibraphone (1984); *The Seasons* for Soprano, 2 Percussionists, and Piano (1992).—**NS/LK/DM**

Lessel, Franz (actually, Franciszek),
Polish pianist and composer; b. probably in Pulawy, c. 1780; d. Petrikow, Dec. 26, 1838. He went to Vienna in 1797 to study medicine, but became a pupil of Haydn and one of his few close friends. He returned to Poland upon Haydn's death, continuing to compose. He was a talented composer, numbering among his works 5 syms., a Piano Concerto, sacred music, 8 string quartets, a Piano Trio, 3 piano sonatas, various piano pieces, and songs.—**NS/LK/DM**

L'Estocart, Paschal de,
French composer; b. Noyon, Picardy, 1539?; d. after 1584. He visited Italy in his youth and then matriculated at the Univ. of Basel (1581). His works, notable for their masterful harmonic writing, were particularly influenced by Italian models.

WORKS: *Premier livre des octonaires de la vanité du monde* for 3 to 6 Voices (Geneva and Lyons, 1582; ed. in Monuments de la Musique Française au Temps de la Renaissance, X, Paris, 1929); *Second livre des octonaires de la vanité du monde* for 3 to 6 Voices (Geneva and Lyons, 1582; ed. in ibid., XI, Paris, 1958); *126 quatrains du sieur de Pibrac* for 2 to 6 Voices (Geneva and Lyons, 1582); *Sacrae cantiones* for 4 to 7 Voices (Lyons, 1582); *150 pseaumes de David mis en rime françoise par Clément Marot et Théodore de Besze* for 4 to 8 Voices, *avec la melodie huguenote* (Geneva and Lyons, 1583).—**LK/DM**

Le Sueur or Lesueur, Jean François,
eminent French composer and writer on music; b. Drucat-Plessiel, near Abbeville, Feb. 15, 1760; d. Paris, Oct. 6, 1837. At 7 he was a choirboy at Abbeville, and at 14, in Amiens, where he took a course of studies. Interrupting his academic education, he became maître de musique at the Cathedral of Séez, and then served as asst. choirmaster at the Church of the Holy Innocents in Paris. During this time, he studied harmony and composition with Abbé Roze. He subsequently was maître de musique at the cathedrals of Dijon (1781), Le Mans (1783), and Tours (1784). He then returned to Paris, serving (upon the recommendation of Grétry) as maître de chapelle at the Holy Innocents. When the competition for the post of maître de chapelle at Notre Dame was announced in 1786, Le Sueur entered it, and won.

He organized an orch. for the chief festive days, and brought out masses, motets, services, etc., using a full orch., thus completely transforming the character of the services. He was greatly successful with the congregation, but the conservative clergy strongly objected to his innovations; other critics called his type of musical productions "opéra des gueux" (beggars' opera). He expounded his ideas of effective and descriptive music in a pamphlet, *Essai de musique sacrée ou musique motivée et méthodique, pour la fête de Noël, à la messe de jour* (1787). This evoked an anonymous attack, to which he replied with another publication, *Exposé d'une musique unie, imitative, et particulière à chaque solennité* (1787), reasserting his aim of making church music dramatic and descriptive. He left Notre Dame in 1788. After a sojourn in the country, he returned to Paris and produced 3 successful operas at the Théâtre Feydeau: *La Caverne* (Feb. 16, 1793), which had a popular success, *Paul et Virginie* (Jan. 13, 1794), and *Télémaque* (May 11, 1796). He also composed 10 hymns, written for various revolutionary festivals, which proved popular. He joined the Inst. National de Musique in 1793, the predecessor of the Paris Cons., which was organized in 1795, subsequently serving there as an inspector and a member of the Committee on Instruction. With Méhul, Langlé, Gossec, and Catel, he wrote the *Principes élémentaires de la musique* and the *Solfèges du Conservatoire*. Le Sueur was dismissed in 1802 because of an altercation that occurred following the rejection, by the Opéra, of 2 of his operas in favor of Catel's *Sémiramis*. For 2 years he lived in poverty and suffering, until Napoleon, in 1804, raised him to the highest position attainable by a musician in Paris by appointing him as his maître de chapelle, succeeding Paisiello. His rejected opera, *Ossian ou Les Bardes*, was then produced (Paris, July 10, 1804) with great applause; his other rejected opera, *La Mort d'Adam* (Paris, March 21, 1809), was a failure. After the restoration of the monarchy, and despite Le Sueur's avowed veneration of Napoleon, the government of Louis XVIII appointed him superintendent and composer to the Chapelle du Roi. He retained his post until 1830, and was also prof. of composition at the Paris Cons. from 1818 until his death, his celebrated pupils numbering Berlioz, Gounod, and Ambroise Thomas. He was made a member of the Institut (1813). His last operas, *Tyrtee* (1794), *Artaxerse* (1797), and *Alexandre à Babylone* (1815), were accepted for performance, but were not produced. His other works include the intermede *L'Inauguration du temple de la Victoire* (Paris, Jan. 20, 1807; in collaboration with L. Loiseau de Persuis) and the opera *Le Triomphe de Trajan* (Paris, Oct. 23, 1807; in collaboration with Persuis), several sacred oratorios (*Debora, Rachel, Ruth et Noémi, Ruth et Booz*), Solemn Mass for 4 Voices, Chorus, and Orch., the cantata *L'Ombre de Sacchini*, 3 Te Deums, 2 Passions, and *Stabat Mater*. These, and some other works, were publ., but he left many more (over 30 masses, etc.) in MS. His major theoretical and historical work was his *Exposé d'une musique unie, imitative et particulière à chaque solennité* (4 vols., Paris, 1787). J. Mongrédien ed. *Jean-François Le Sueur: A Thematic Catalogue of His Complete Works* (N.Y., 1980).

BIBL.: C. Ducanel, *Mémoire pour J.F. Lesueur* (Paris, 1802);

Raoul-Rochette, *Notice historique sur la vie et les oeuvres de J.-F. L.S.* (Paris, 1837); S. de la Madeleine, *Biographie de J.-F. L.S.* (Paris, 1841); W. Buschkötter, *J.F. L.S.* (Halle, 1912); F. Lamy, *J.F. L.S. (1760–1837)* (Paris, 1912); M. Herman, *The Sacred Music of J.-F. L.S.: A Musical and Biographical Source Study* (diss., Univ. of Mich., 1964).—NS/LK/DM

Lesur, Daniel
See **Daniel-Lesur, Jean Yves**

Lesure, François (-Marie), distinguished French music librarian, musicologist, and writer; b. Paris, May 23, 1923. He studied at the École des Chartres, the École Pratique des Hautes Études, and the Sorbonne, and musicology at the Paris Cons. A member of the music dept. at the Bibliothèque Nationale (from 1950), he was its chief curator (1970–88). From 1953 to 1967 he headed the Paris office (responsible for Series B) of the Répertoire International des Sources Musicales (RISM), for which he himself ed. *Recueils imprimés: XVIᵉ-XVIIᵉ siècles* (Munich, 1960); *Recueils imprimés: XVIIIᵉ siècle* (Munich, 1964; suppl. in *Notes*, March 1972, vol. XXVIII, pp. 397–418, and the two vols. of *Écrits imprimés concernant la musique* (Munich, 1971). He also was a prof. at the Free Univ. of Brussels (1965–77), ed. of the early music series known as Le Pupitre (from 1967), president of the Société Française de Musicologie (1971–74; 1988–91), and prof. at the École Pratique des Hautes Études (from 1973). He ed. such non-serial works as *Anthologie de la chanson parisienne au XVIᵉ siècle* (Monaco, 1953); the report of the 1954 Arras Conference, *La Renaissance dans les provinces du Nord* (Paris, 1956); P. Trichet's *Traité des instruments de musique (vers 1640)* (Neuilly, 1957); six vols. of *Chansons polyphoniques* (with A.T. Merrit, Monaco, 1967–72; the first five vols. constitute the collected works of C. Janequin); a collected ed. of Debussy's writings on music, *Monsieur Croche et autres écrits* (Paris, 1971; Eng. tr., 1977); ed. a *Catalogue de l'oeuvre de Claude Debussy* (Geneva, 1977); ed. the letters of Debussy for the period 1884–1918 (Paris, 1980; rev. ed., 1993); was ed.-in-chief of the complete works of Debussy (from 1986). His own publications include a *Bibliographie des éditions d'Adrian Le Roy et Robert Ballard, 1551–1598* (with G. Thibault, Paris, 1955; suppl. in *Revue de Musicologie*, 1957); *Musicians and Poets of the French Renaissance* (N.Y., 1955); *Mozart en France* (Paris, 1956); *Collection musicale A. Meyer* (with N. Bridgman, Abbeville, 1961); *Musica e società* (Milan, 1966; Ger. tr., 1966, as *Musik und Gesellschaft im Bild: Zeugnisse der Malerei aus sechs Jahrhunderten*; Eng. tr., 1968, as *Music and Art in Society*); *Bibliographie des éditions musicales publiées par Estienne Roger et Michel-Charles Le Cene, Amsterdam, 1696–1743* (Paris, 1969); *Musique et musiciens français du XVIᵉ siècle* (Geneva, 1976, a reprinting in book form of 24 articles orig. publ. 1950–69); *Claude Debussy avant 'Pelléas' ou Les Années symbolistes* (Paris, 1992). He contributed *L'Opera classique français: 17ᵉ et 18ᵉ siècles* (Geneva, 1972) and *Claude Debussy* (Geneva, 1975) to the series Iconographie Musicale. For the Bibliothèque Nationale, he prepared a series of exhibition catalogs, most notably one on Berlioz (Paris, 1969).

BIBL.: J.-M. Fauquet, ed., *Musiques, Signes, Images: Liber amicorum F. L.* (Geneva, 1988).—NS/LK/DM

Letelier (-Llona), Alfonso, Chilean composer and teacher; b. Santiago, Oct. 4, 1912; d. there, Aug. 28, 1994. He studied with Allende at the Cons. Nacional de Música of the Univ. of Chile in Santiago (1930–35). In 1946 he joined its faculty as a prof. of harmony, where he also was dean of its dept. of fine arts (1951–62) and vice-rector (1958–62). In 1973 he was made prof. emeritus but continued to teach there until 1983. From 1986 to 1989 he was dean of the faculty of arts and physical education at the Univ. Metropolitan de Ciencias de la Educación, and then was a prof. in its dept. of music education from 1989 until his death. In 1967 he was made a member of the Chilean Academy of Fine Arts and in 1968 he was awarded the Chilean National Arts Prize. In 1996 the faculty of arts of the Univ. of Chile was renamed the Alfonso Letelier Llona Branch in his memory. Among his works were *La vida del campo*, symphonic poem for Piano and Orch. (1937), *Los sonetos de la muerte* for Woman's Voice and Orch. (1948), *Vitrales de la Anunciación* for Soprano, Women's Chorus, and Orch. (1949–50), *Aculeo*, suite for Orch. (Louisville, Jan. 30, 1957), Guitar Concerto (1961), Concerto for Strings (1972), *Tres Canciones* for Woman's Voice and 16 Instruments (1974), and *El Hombre ante la ciencia*, sym. for Mezzo-soprano and Orch. (1983–85).—NS/LK/DM

Lettermen, The, pop vocal act of the 1960s that matured into a successful lounge and touring act (f. 1958). **MEMBERSHIP:** Tony Butala, lead voc. (b. Sharon, Pa., Nov. 20, 1940); Bob Engemann, voc. (b. Highland Park, Mich., Nov. 6, 1938); Jim Pike, voc. (b. St. Louis, Mo., Feb. 19, 1938); and a cast of dozens, Butala being the one constant element.

Tony Butala was already singing professionally in his native Pittsburgh at an early age. When he was eight years old, he was invited to join the Mitchell Boys Choir in Calif., and appeared with them in films including *White Christmas, Peter Pan,* and *War of the Worlds.* Later in the 1950s, he formed the vocal trio Lettermen, and an early version of the group appeared in a revue at the Desert Inn in Las Vegas. In 1960, he hooked up with Jim Pike and Bob Engemann. All three had previously recorded with little success. After two unsuccessful singles released by Warner Bros., the group signed with Capitol in 1961. They recorded a close-harmony version of an old Fred Astaire hit "The Way You Look Tonight" which went to #13 on the pop charts that fall. Three months later, they took a similar version of "When I Fall in Love" to the top of the adult contemporary charts and #7 pop. Their album with these songs, *A Song for Young Love,* rose to #6, beginning a curious trend for the band: their albums almost always sold better than their singles. This was unusual for 1960s-era pop groups, but could be explained by the fact that they appealed to a more mature audience, who tended to buy albums rather than singles that were aimed at teenagers.

Through the 1960s the group charted over 20 hits on the adult contemporary charts, placing another four on the pop charts, including "Come Back Silly Girl" (#17, 1962), "Theme from 'A Summer Place'" (#16, 1965), "Goin' out of My Head/Can't Take My Eyes Off You" (#7, 1968), and "Hurt So Bad" (#12, 1969). These last two hits featured Gary Pike, Jim's brother, taking the role of Bob Engemann, who had left the group. The group also scored four gold albums, including a 1966 "best of" compilation, *The Lettermen!!!...and "Live"*. The Letterman continued to perform and record through the 1990s, mostly selling tickets and albums to fans from the 1960s, with rotating personnel surrounding Butala.

DISC.: *A Song for Young Love* (1962); *Once Upon a Time* (1962); *Jim, Tony and Bob* (1962); *College Standards* (1963); *The Lettermen in Concert* (live; 1963); *A Lettermen Kind of Love* (1964); *The Lettermen Look at Love* (1964); *She Cried* (1964); *Portrait of My Love* (1965); *You'll Never Walk Alone* (1965); *The Hit Sounds of the Lettermen* (1965); *More Hit Sounds of the Lettermen* (1966); *New Song for Young Love* (1966); *The Lettermen!!...And Live!* (1967); *Warm* (1967); *Spring!* (1967); *Goin' out of My Head* (1968); *Special Request* (1968); *Put Your Head on My Shoulder* (1968); *I Have Dreamed* (1969); *Hurt So Bad* (1969); *Lettermen at the Waldorf* (1969); *Traces/Memories* (1970); *Reflections* (1970); *Everything's Good About You* (1971); *Feelings* (1971); *Love Book* (1971); *Letter-men1* (1972); *Alive Again...Naturally* (1973); *For Christmas This Year* (1990); *Close to You* (1992); *Sing We Noel* (1992); *When I Fall in Love* (1992); *Why I Love Her* (1993); *Deck the Halls* (1995); *Christmas with the Lettermen* (1997); *Today* (1997).—**HB**

Lettvin, Theodore, American pianist and teacher; b. Chicago, Oct. 29, 1926. He studied with Howard Wells, making his first public appearance at the age of 5 in Chicago. He was invited to perform at a young people's concert with the Chicago Sym. Orch. when he was 13, and then continued his studies at the Curtis Inst. of Music in Philadelphia with Serkin and Horszowski (Mus.B., 1949); also took courses at the Univ. of Pa. (1947–48). He made his European debut in Paris in 1952, and subsequently appeared as a soloist with American and European orchs. and as a recitalist. He was a visiting lecturer at the Univ. of Colo. (1956–57), then head of the piano dept. at the Cleveland Music School Settlement (1956–68); subsequently was prof. of piano at the New England Cons. of Music in Boston (1968–77), the Univ. of Mich. (1977–87), and Rutgers, the State Univ. of N.J. (from 1987).—**NS/LK/DM**

Leutgeb, Joseph (Ignaz), Austrian horn player; b. probably in Salzburg, c. 1745; d. Vienna, Feb. 27, 1811. He became first horn in the orch. of the Salzburg archbishop in 1770, and also made appearances in Paris, Vienna, Milan, and other music centers. After settling in Vienna, he became a cheesemonger but continued to play the horn until 1792. He was a close friend of Mozart, who wrote a number of works for him, including the horn concertos K. 417, 447, and 495. Although Mozart's autographs of many of the horn parts make Leutgeb appear an incompetent from the humorous asides he made (e.g., "Thank Heaven, that's enough" and "You ass"), independent reports of Leutgeb's playing praise him highly.—**NS/LK/DM**

Lev, Ray, Russian-American pianist; b. Rostov na Donau, May 8, 1912; d. N.Y., May 20, 1968. Her father was a synagogue cantor, and her mother a singer. The family went to the U.S. in 1913, and she sang in her father's synagogue choirs in N.Y. She studied piano

with Walter Ruel Cowles in New Haven and with Gaston Déthier. After taking lessons with Tobias Matthay in London (1930–33), she returned to N.Y. and appeared in recitals.—**NS/LK/DM**

Levadé, Charles (Gaston), French composer; b. Paris, Jan. 3, 1869; d. there, Oct. 27, 1948. He was a pupil of Massenet at the Paris Cons., winning the Grand Prix de Rome in 1899.

WORKS: DRAMATIC: O p e r a : *Les Hérétiques* (Béziers, Aug. 27, 1905). **L y r i c C o m e d i e s :** *La Rôtisserie de la reine Pédauque*, after Anatole France (Paris, Jan. 12, 1920); *La Peau de chagrin*, after Balzac (Paris, April 24, 1929). **OTHER:** Orch. suites; chamber music; piano pieces; songs.—**NS/LK/DM**

Levant, Oscar, American pianist and composer; b. Pittsburgh, Dec. 27, 1906; d. Beverly Hills, Aug. 14, 1972. He studied piano with Stojowski, and also took a few composition lessons with Schoenberg and Schillinger. As a pianist, he established himself by his authentic performances of Gershwin's music; also emerged as a professional wit on the radio. He publ. a brilliant book, *A Smattering of Ignorance* (1940), and *The Memoirs of an Amnesiac* (1965). He wrote music of considerable complexity, in the modern vein, and was soloist in his Piano Concerto (NBC Sym. Orch., Feb. 17, 1942). Other works were *Nocturne* for Orch. (Los Angeles, April 14, 1937), String Quartet (1937), piano pieces, and film scores.

BIBL.: S. Kashner and N. Schoenberger, *A Talent for Genius: The Life and Times of O. L.* (N.Y., 1994).—**NS/LK/DM**

Levarie, Siegmund, Austrian-born American musicologist and conductor; b. Lemberg, Galicia, July 24, 1914. He studied conducting with Joseph Mertin at the New Vienna Cons. (diploma, 1935) and musicology with Robert Haas at the Univ. of Vienna (Ph.D., 1938), and concurrently took private lessons in composition with Hugo Kauder. He emigrated to the U.S. in 1938, becoming a naturalized American citizen in 1943. He was director of concerts at the Univ. of Chicago (1938–52), where he conducted the Collegium Musicum, mostly in programs of medieval and Renaissance music; he also taught there. He was dean of the Chicago Musical Coll. (1952–54). From 1954 to 1962 he served as prof. of music and head of the music dept. at Brooklyn Coll.

WRITINGS: *Fugue and Form* (Chicago, 1941); *Mozart's "Le Nozze di Figaro": A Critical Analysis* (Chicago, 1952); *Fundamentals of Harmony* (N.Y., 1954); *Guillaume de Machaut* (N.Y., 1954); *Musical Italy Revisited* (N.Y., 1963); with E. Levy, *Tone: A Study in Musical Acoustics* (Kent, Ohio, 1968; second ed., rev., 1980); with E. Levy, *Musical Morphology: A Discourse and a Dictionary* (Kent, Ohio, 1983).—**NS/LK/DM**

Levasseur, Jean-Henri, French cellist, pedagogue, and composer; b. Beaumont-sur-Oise, May 29, 1764; d. Paris, c. 1826. He received training from J. Cupis and J.L. Duport. In 1782 he became a cellist in the orch. of the Paris Opéra, where he served as first cellist from 1789 to 1820. He also was prof. of cello at the Paris Cons.

(1795–1826), and served as an imperial musician under Napoleon and as a royal chapel musician under Louis XVIII. With Baillot, Baudiot, and Catel, he ed. the *Méthode de violoncelle et de basse d'accompagnement* (Paris, 1804) for use at the Paris Cons. He publ. sonatas, études, and duets for cello.—NS/LK/DM

Levasseur, Nicolas (-Prosper), prominent French bass; b. Bresles, March 9, 1791; d. Paris, Dec. 6, 1871. In 1807 he entered the Paris Cons., where he studied in Garat's singing class in 1811. He made his debut as Osman Pacha in Grétry's *La Caravane du Caire* at the Paris Opéra (Oct. 14, 1813). He made his London debut in Mayr's *Adeasia ed Alderano* at the King's Theatre (Jan. 10, 1815), and then returned to the Paris Opéra as an understudy until he made his debut at the Théâtre-Italien as Almaviva (Oct. 5, 1819). He appeared in the premiere of Meyerbeer's *Margherita d'Anjou* at Milan's La Scala (Nov. 14, 1820), and then returned to the Théâtre-Italien. In 1828 he rejoined the Paris Opéra, establishing himself as its principal bass; among the roles he created there were Bertram in *Robert le diable* (1831), Brogni in *La Juive* (1835), Marcel in *Les Huguenots* (1836), and Balthazar in *La Favorite* (1840). He left the Opéra in 1845, but was recalled by Meyerbeer to sing the role of Zacharie in the premiere of *Le Prophète* (1849); he retired from the stage in 1853. He was a prof. at the Paris Cons. (1841–69). He was made a Chevalier de la Légion d'honneur in 1869.—NS/LK/DM

Levasseur, Rosalie (actually, **Marie-Rose-Claude-Josèphe**), esteemed French soprano; b. Valenciennes, Oct. 8, 1749; d. Neuwied am Rhein, May 6, 1826. She was the illegitimate daughter of Jean-Baptiste Levasseur and Marie-Catherine Tournay, who married when she was 11. She made her debut under the name Mlle. Rosalie in the role of Zaide in Campra's *L'Europe galante* at the Paris Opéra (1766), and continued to appear in minor roles there until 1776. Taking the name Levasseur, she took on major roles there, gaining success as Eurydice and Iphigenia. She then was chosen over her rival, Sophie Arnould, to create the title role in the first Paris staging of Gluck's *Alceste* (1776). She was greatly admired by Gluck, who chose her to create the title roles in his *Armide* (1777) and *Iphigénie en Tauride* (1779); she likewise created roles in works by Philidor, Piccinni, and Sacchini, remaining at the Opéra until 1788. She was the mistress of Count Mercy-Argentau, the Austrian ambassador in Paris, who used his influence to promote her career.—NS/LK/DM

Leventritt, Edgar M(ilton), American music patron; b. San Francisco, Oct. 18, 1873; d. N.Y., May 31, 1939. After training at the Univ. of Calif. (graduated, 1894), he went to N.Y. and studied law. In 1896 he was admitted to the bar. As an amateur pianist, he helped to found the Perolé Quartet in 1925. In his will, he made provision for the establishment of an annual competition for young musicians via the Edgar M. Leventritt Foundation. The first competition was held in 1940. —NS/LK/DM

Leveridge, Richard, noted English bass and composer; b. London, c. 1670; d. there, March 22, 1758. He first gained notice in London in 1695. After a sojourn in Dublin (1699–1702), he returned to London. He was a member of Handel's company (1712–13), appearing in the premieres of his *Il Pastor fido* and *Teseo*; then sang at Lincoln's Inn Fields (1714–20). He ran a coffeehouse from about 1716. He returned to the stage in 1723. He was principal bass at Lincoln's Inn Fields, and subsequently at Covent Garden; retired in 1751. He publ. 5 collections of songs (London, 1697–1730). His most popular and enduring song was *The Roast Beef of Old England*, which he introduced at his Covent Garden benefit on April 15, 1735. He also wrote works for the stage, including incidental music to *Macbeth* (London, Nov. 21, 1702) and a number of masques.—NS/LK/DM

Levey, Richard C., Irish violinist, son of **Richard Michael Levey** and brother of **William Charles Levey**; b. Dublin, 1833; d. c. 1904. He became known as a touring violinist via an act dubbed as Paganini Redivivus.—NS/LK/DM

Levey (real name, **O'Shaughnessy**), **Richard Michael,** Irish violinist, conductor, teacher, and composer, father of **Richard C. Levey** and **William Charles Levey**; b. Dublin, Oct. 25, 1811; d. there, June 28, 1899. He received a practical musical education playing in various orchs. in Dublin and writing incidental music for productions of plays. About 1835 he became a theater conductor. He wrote some 50 overtures and a number of ballad scores. He publ. a *Collection of the Dance Music of Ireland* (1858) and the *Annals of the Theatre Royal, Dublin* (with J. O'Rorke; 1880).—NS/LK/DM

Levey, William Charles, Irish conductor and composer, son of **Richard Michael Levey** and brother of **Richard C. Levey**; b. Dublin, April 25, 1837; d. London, Aug. 18, 1894. He studied with his father, and then with Auber, Thalberg, and Prudent in Paris. He then was a conductor at London's Drury Lane Theatre (1868–74), Covent Garden, and other theaters. He wrote the operettas *Fanchette* (London, Jan. 4, 1864), *Punchinello* (London, Dec. 28, 1864), and *The Girls of the Period* (London, Feb. 25, 1869), as well as incidental music, pantomimes, *The Man of War*, fantasia for Chorus, Military Band, and Orch. (1874), 3 cantatas, many songs, and piano pieces. —NS/LK/DM

Levi, Hermann, eminent German conductor; b. Giessen, Nov. 7, 1839; d. Munich, May 13, 1900. He was a pupil of Vincenz Lachner in Mannheim (1852–55) and of Hauptmann and Rietz at the Leipzig Cons. (1855–58). He was music director in Saarbrücken (1859–61). After serving as asst. Kapellmeister of the Mannheim National Theater (1861), he was Kapellmeister of the German Opera in Rotterdam (1861–64). He became Hofkapellmeister in Karlsruhe in 1864, and in 1872 was named Hofkapellmeister of the Bavarian Court Opera in Munich; was made Generalmusikdirektor of the city in 1894, but was compelled by ill health to give up his duties in 1896. He enjoyed great respect among German musicians, and was influential in spreading the Wagnerian gospel. He conducted the first performance of

Parsifal at Bayreuth (July 26, 1882), and his interpretation received complete approval from Wagner himself, who, for the nonce, repressed his opposition to Jews. Levi conducted the musical program at Wagner's funeral. He was also a friend of Brahms until his championship of Wagner led to an estrangement. He wrote *Gedanken aus Goethes Werken* (1901; 3rd ed., 1911).

BIBL.: E. von Possart, *Erinnerungen an H. L.* (Munich, 1901); F. Haas, *Zwischen Brahms und Wagner: Der Dirigent H. L.* (Zürich, 1995).—NS/LK/DM

Levi, Paul Alan, American composer, teacher, and pianist; b. N.Y., June 30, 1941. After training at Oberlin (Ohio) Coll. (B.A. in music, 1963), he was a composition student of Overton and Persichetti at the Juilliard School in N.Y. (M.M., 1972; D.M.A., 1978). He also attended the Munich Hochschule für Musik (1973–74), held a Deutscher Akademischer Austauschdienst study grant in Germany (1973–74), and took summer courses in new music in Darmstadt (1974). From 1963 he was active as a piano accompanist. He taught at Baruch (1972–73), Queens (1979), and Lehman (1981–82) colleges of the City Univ. of N.Y. In 1979 he joined the faculty of N.Y.U.; also taught at the Manhattan School of Music (from 1992). In 1976 he served as composer-in-residence at the Wolf Trap Farm Park in Vienna, Va. From 1979 to 1982 he was president of the League of Composers. In 1983–84 he held a Guggenheim fellowship. In 1985 he became a founding partner of Mountain Laurel Music, a production company. In his varied output, Levi has revealed an imaginative handling of instrumentation and setting of vocal texts.

WORKS: DRAMATIC: *Thanksgiving,* serio-comic opera (N.Y., Nov. 2, 1977); *In the Beginning...,* opera parable (1987–95); incidental music to plays; television and film music. **ORCH.:** *Symphonic Movement* (1972; N.Y., Jan. 30, 1975); *Stringolevio* for Strings and Percussion (1973); *Allegrenino* for Symphonic Band (1973); *Transformations of the Heart* (N.Y., March 7, 1987). **CHAMBER:** String Quartet (1969; Norfolk, Va., Feb. 27, 1971); *5 Progressions for 3 Instruments* for Flute, Clarinet, and Viola (N.Y., Dec. 7, 1971); *Billet Doux/Billiger Duo* for Violin and Viola (Portland, Ore., June 29, 1980); *Elegy and Recreations* for Oboe, Clarinet, Horn, Violin, Viola, Cello, and Piano (N.Y., Nov. 9, 1980); *Bow Jest* for Cello (1983). **Piano:** *Summer Elegy* (1982; N.Y., April 24, 1987); *Touchings* (1990; N.Y., May 31, 1992); *Suite for the Best of Times* (1991). **VOCAL:** *Jabberwocky* for Voice and Piano (N.Y., April 17, 1968); *The Truth* for Soprano, Cello, Flute, Clarinet, Bassoon, Piano, Harpsichord, and String Quartet (1975; Portland, Ore., July 31, 1985); *Spring Sestina* for Soprano and 10 Instruments (N.Y., Jan. 13, 1982); *This Much I Know* for Soprano and Piano (N.Y., April 13, 1983); *Mark Twain Suite* for Tenor, Chorus, and Orch. (N.Y., April 30, 1983); *Black Wings* for Soprano and Piano (Columbia, S.C., Oct. 3, 1986); *Songs for the Synagogue* for Cantor, Adult and Children's Choruses, and Quintet or Chamber Orch. (Norwalk, Conn., May 5, 1989; in collaboration with Mark Lipson); *Bow Down Thine Ear, O Lord* for 8 Voices or Double Chorus (N.Y., Dec. 8, 1991); *Holy Willie's Prayer* for Chorus and Chamber Orch. (N.Y., Jan. 27, 1992); *Journeys & Secrets* for Chorus and Chamber Orch. (N.Y., May 25, 1994).—NS/LK/DM

Levi, Yoel, Romanian-born American conductor; b. Sotmar, Aug. 16, 1950. He was taken in infancy to Israel, where he received instruction in violin, percussion, cello, and piano. He then pursued training in violin and percussion at the Univ. of Tel Aviv (M.A., 1975), and concurrently studied conducting with Rodan at the Jerusalem Academy of Music (graduate degree, 1976). Subsequently he took instruction in conducting with Ferrara in Siena, at the Accademia di Santa Cecilia in Rome, at the Guildhall School of Music and Drama in London (diploma, 1978), and with Kondrashin in Hilversum. In 1975 he became a percussionist in the Israel Phil.; after winning first prize in the Besancon conducting competition in 1978, he was made a conducting assistant with the Cleveland Orch.; was its resident conductor (1980–84). In 1979 he made his European debut as a guest conductor with the (West) Berlin Radio Sym. Orch. In subsequent years, he appeared as a guest conductor with various major North American and European orchs. He became a naturalized American citizen in 1987. In 1988 he assumed the position of music director of the Atlanta Sym. Orch. In 1991 he conducted it on a European tour. During the Olympic Games in Atlanta in 1996, Levi and his orch. gave a series of Cultural Olympiad concerts.—NS/LK/DM

Levidis, Dimitri, Greek-born French composer and teacher; b. Athens, April 8, 1885?; d. Palaeon Phaleron, near Athens, May 29, 1951. He studied at the Lottner Cons. in Athens, then with Boemer, Choisy, Lavrangas, and Mancini at the Athens Cons. (1898–1905). He subsequently studied with Dénéreaz at the Lausanne Cons. (1906–07) and with Klose (fugue), Mottl (orchestration), and Strauss (composition) at the Munich Academy of Music (1907–08). He went to France (1910). He served in the French Army during World War I, and became a naturalized French citizen in 1929. He returned to Greece about 1932, and was active as a teacher; in 1934 he founded the Phaleron Cons., which became a part of the Hellenic Cons. He was the first to write works for the Martenot Ondes Musicales, including *Poème symphonique pour solo d'Ondes Musicales et Orchestre* (Paris, Dec. 23, 1928) and *De profundis* for Voice and 2 Soloists of Ondes Musicales (Paris, Jan. 5, 1930). Other works included a ballet, *Le Pâtre et la nymphe* (Paris, April 24, 1924), *Divertissement* for English Horn, Harps, Strings, Celesta, and Percussion (Paris, April 9, 1927), an oratorio, *The Iliad, Poem* for Violin and Orch. (1927), *Chant payen* for Oboe and Strings, compositions for the "Dixtuor aeolien d'orchestre," pieces for chamber ensembles, song cycles, and piano pieces. —NS/LK/DM

Levin, Robert, distinguished American pianist, fortepianist, harpsichordist, and music scholar; b. N.Y., Oct. 13, 1947. He attended the Chatham Square Music School in N.Y. (1957–61), where he received training in composition from Wolpe. He was a student at the summer courses at the American Cons. in Fontainebleau (1960–64), where his mentors included Boulanger (analysis, counterpoint, fugue, harmony, composition, and organ), and Jean Casadesus (piano), and where he also attended master classes given by Curzon and Robert Casadesus. He pursued training in conducting with Carvalho at the Berkshire Music Center at Tanglewood (summer, 1965) and with Swarowsky and Österreicher in Nice (summers, 1966–67), and completed his academic studies at Harvard Univ. (A.B., 1968, with the thesis *The Unfinished Works of W.A. Mozart*). From 1968 to 1973 he was head of the theory dept. at the Curtis Inst. of Music in Philadelphia and was harpsichordist and pianist of the Boston Sym. Orch., positions he also held with the Cantata Singers in Boston from 1968 to 1974. In 1971 he became the pianist of the N.Y. Philomusica, a position he retained for some 30 years. He was an assoc. prof. (1972–75) and a prof. (1975–86) at the State Univ. of N.Y. at Purchase. From 1984 to 1991 he was the pianist of the Ensemble Sequenza in Germany, and from 1986 to 1993 he was prof. of piano at the Staatliche Hochschule für Musik in Freiburg im Breisgau. In 1993 he became prof. of music and in 1994 the Dwight P. Robinson Jr., Prof. of the Humanities at Harvard Univ. He was awarded an honorary doctorate by the Eastman School of Music in Rochester, N.Y., in 1996. Levin has made many appearances as a soloist with orchs. in the U.S. and abroad, has toured extensively as a recitalist in the U.S., Europe, and Asia, and has played much chamber music in the U.S. and Europe. He has won particular distinction for his insightful interpretations of concertos by Mozart and Beethoven on the fortepiano, and for his improvised cadenzas and embellishments. His repertoire ranges from Byrd and Bach to Harbison and Kurtág. He has completed or reconstructed several scores by Mozart, including the Requiem, K.626 (1966–67; 1982; 1990–93), the Symphonie concertante in E-flat major, K.297b/Anh. 9 (1981–83), and the Horn Concerto in E-flat major, K.370b/371 (1993–97). With C. Eisen, he oversaw the complete edition of Mozart's piano concertos for Breitkop & Härtel. In addition to his contributions to scholarly books and journals, he publ. *Sightsinging and Ear Training Through Literature* (with L. Martin; Englewood Cliffs, N.J., 1988) and *Who Wrote the Mozart Four-Wind Concertante?* (Stuyvesant, N.Y., 1988).—LK/DM

Levin, Tony, jazz drummer, percussionist; b. Much Wenlock, Shropshire, England, Jan. 30, 1940. He lived in Birmingham from the age of five and was based there at least into the 1970s. He played in Hedley Ward's Big Band as a teenager and gained valuable experience in Johnny Coffins's Quartet, then worked as accompanist for visiting musicians. He worked regularly with Tubby Hayes from 1965 until 1968 (with Pyne, Matthewson). He began a long musical association with Alan Skidmore in the late 1960s. He was briefly with Mike Westbrook (1968) and worked with Mick Pyne's Trio, John Taylor, Les Condon Quar, Humphrey Lyttelton and in the Lionel Grigson-Pete Burden Quintet. He again worked with Tubby Hayes in the early 1970s, with Stan Sulzmann's Quartet, and with Gordon Beck's Gyroscope from 1973. During the 1970s he also worked with Ian Carr's Nucleus, with Michael Garrick, Norma Winstone (the group Edge of Time), Malcolm Griffiths, John Surman, Mick Pyne, etc. From 1979 he was part of a German group called The Third Eye, and again worked with Alan Skidmore (including gigs with Tenor Tonic). He led his own Trio in the early 1980s (with Paul Duninall. and Tony Moore) and worked in Holland

with Dutch pianist Rob Van Den Broeck. He was with the Keith Tippett lineups, and also ran his own Jazz Club Friday in Birmingham from 1986 to 1990. During the 1990s he often worked with guitarist Philip Catherine, and with Mujician (with Paul Dunmall, Paul Rogers and Keith Tippett). During autumn 1994 he did a wide- ranging tour of the Middle East with Trio (Sophia Domaneich on piano and Paul Rogers on bass), and subsequently worked in Europe with Tony Oxley's Celebrations, then did further freelance work throughout Europe. He also worked with the European Jazz Quartet (1996).—JC-B/LP

Levine, Gilbert, American conductor; b. N.Y., Jan. 22, 1948. He attended Reed Coll. (1965–67) and the Juilliard School of Music in N.Y. (1967–68), then studied music history with Mendel and Lockwood, conducting with Monod, and theory with Babbitt and Randall at Princeton Univ. (A.B., 1971), completing his study of theory at Yale Univ. (M.A., 1972). He also received instruction in conducting from Ferrara in Siena. In 1973 he made his professional debut as a guest conductor with the Nouvel Orch. Philharmonique de Radio France in Paris; then toured widely as a guest conductor, appearing in Europe and North America. In 1987 he became music director of the Kraków Phil., the first American conductor to hold such a position with a major Eastern European orch. He left his Kraków post in 1991 and was named its conductor laureate-honored guest conductor. In 1993 he conducted it on a tour of the U.S. On April 7, 1994, Levine conducted the Royal Phil. of London and the choir of St. Peter's Basilica in a concert of reconciliation for the victims of the Holocaust in the presence of Pope John Paul II in Rome. On Dec. 19, 1994, Levine became only the 4th Jew in history to receive the papal Equestrian Order of St. Gregory the Great.—NS/LK/DM

Levine, James (Lawrence), brilliant American pianist and conductor; b. Cincinnati, June 23, 1943. His maternal grandfather was a cantor in a synagogue; his father was a violinist who led a dance band, and his mother was an actress. He began playing the piano as a small child. At the age of 10, he was soloist in Mendelssohn's Second Piano Concerto at a youth concert of the Cincinnati Sym. Orch. He then studied music with Walter Levin, first violinist in the La Salle Quartet, and in 1956 took piano lessons with Serkin at the Marlboro (Vt.) School of Music. In 1957 he began piano studies with Lhévinne at the Aspen (Colo.) Music School. In 1961 he entered the Juilliard School of Music in N.Y., and took courses in conducting with Jean Morel. He also had conducting sessions with Wolfgang Vacano in Aspen. In 1964 he graduated from the Juilliard School and joined the American Conductors Project connected with the Baltimore Sym. Orch., where he had occasion to practice conducting with Wallenstein, Rudolf, and Cleva. In 1964–65 he served as an apprentice to Szell with the Cleveland Orch., and then was an asst. conductor with it (1965–70). In 1966 he organized the Univ. Circle Orch. of the Cleveland Inst. of Music. He also led the student orch. of the summer music inst. of Oakland Univ. in Meadow Brook, Mich. (1967–69). In 1970 he made a successful appearance as guest conductor with the Philadelphia Orch. at its summer home at Robin Hood Dell. He subsequently appeared with other American orchs. In 1970 he also conducted the Welsh National Opera and the San Francisco Opera. He made his Metropolitan Opera debut in N.Y. on June 5, 1971, in a festival performance of *Tosca*; his success led to further appearances and to his appointment as its principal conductor in 1973; he then was its music director from 1975 until becoming its artistic director in 1986. From 1973 to 1993 he was music director of the Ravinia Festival, the summer home of the Chicago Sym. Orch., and served in that capacity with the Cincinnati May Festival (1974–78). In 1975 he began to conduct at the Salzburg Festivals. In 1982 he conducted at the Bayreuth Festival for the first time. He conducted his first *Ring* cycle at Bayreuth in 1995, and led another mounting of that tetralogy at the Metropolitan Opera in 1997. In 1997 he received the National Medal of Arts. From 1999 he was also music director of the Munich Phil. He continued to make appearances as a pianist, playing chamber music with impeccable technical precision. But it is as a conductor and an indefatigable planner of the seasons at the Metropolitan Opera that he inspired respect.

Unconcerned with egotistical projections of his own personality, he presided over the singers and the orch. with concentrated efficiency.

BIBL.: R. Marsh, *Dialogues and Discoveries: J. L., His Life and His Music* (N.Y., 1998).—**NS/LK/DM**

Levitzki, Mischa, outstanding American pianist; b. Kremenchug (of naturalized Russian-born American parents), May 25, 1898; d. Avon-by-the-Sea, N.J., Jan. 2, 1941. He began his studies with Michalowski in Warsaw at the age of 7, at which time his parents returned to their adopted country and he continued his training at the Inst. of Musical Art in N.Y. with Stojowski (1906–11). In 1911 he went to Germany, where he studied with Dohnányi at the Hochschule für Musik in Berlin and won the Mendelssohn Prize. Following tours of Germany (1914–15) and Europe (1915–16), he returned to the U.S. and made his N.Y. recital debut on Oct. 17, 1916; subsequently made numerous tours in the U.S. and in the Orient. Levitzki acquired a remarkable reputation as one of the leading keyboard virtuosos of his day. He wrote a number of attractive piano pieces, a Piano Concerto, and a cadenza for Beethoven's 3rd PianoConcerto.—**NS/LK/DM**

ISBN 0-02-865528-1

90000

9 780028 655284